tests. The tests are well named for our culture; the skills involved *are* basic skills.

Much more might be said concerning the tests, but space forbids. They are a superbly engineered set of tools for the elementary schools. By way of summary, the following commendable characteristics should be noted: (*a*) The excellent manuals and accessories, including a pupil report folder, "How Are Your Skills?," designed to motivate pupils as well as to enable parents to gain better insights concerning testing and instructional goals; (*b*) the low cost of testing per pupil; (*c*) the uniform timing arrangements such that groups of mixed grades can be tested in one room; (*d*) the functional nature of the content; and (*e*) the authors' extensive, explicit, and candid reporting in the Manual for Administrators, Supervisors, and Counselors.

A consummation devoutly to be wished for would be tools to measure values (the affective domain) which were as good as this battery appears to be in the cognitive domain.

J Counsel Psychol 4:252–3 fall '57. Laurence Siegel. * both attractive and exceedingly efficient * Several outstanding characteristics of the *Iowa Tests* recommend this battery to the attention of administrators responsible for elementary school testing programs. Aside from the very excellent statistical foundation underlying the development of the battery, the format and arrangement of the testing materials is designed to eliminate or simplify many problems inherent in large scale testing programs. In the latter regard, the *Iowa Tests of Basic Skills* are much more than mere revisions of the well known *Iowa Every-Pupil Tests*. One of the unique features of the battery is that it consists of separate subtests for each grade. * Another unique and valuable feature of the *Iowa Tests* is that all subtests and all grade batteries are contained in a single 96-page reuseable booklet. * When the *Iowa Tests* are considered with respect to statistical characteristics and thoroughness of the research leading up to the final publication, it is obvious that this battery was not published prematurely. The authors' thoughtful consideration of matters of format was matched by their careful attention to the details of test development. The split-half reliability coefficients for some of the *subtests* within the five basic skills seem a little low, dipping occasionally to 0.70. This is a reflection of the fact that

these subtests are relatively brief. The *composite* scores for each skill area are, however, quite reliable. The only weakness in standardization data now available is the absence of information about predictive validity. One must, however, concur with the authors' opinion that the *Iowa Tests of Basic Skills* should yield correlations with future academic success in the vicinity of those obtained for editions of the *Iowa Every-Pupil Tests*. * this is a battery measuring those *generalized* intellectual skills and abilities that may be assumed to be acceptable to virtually all school systems. The battery was thoughtfully conceived and beautifully executed. It deserves serious consideration for inclusion in any elementary school testing program.

[17]

*The Iowa Tests of Educational Development. Grades 9–13; 1942–58; 10 scores on 9 subtests: understanding of basic social concepts, general background in the natural sciences, correctness and appropriateness of expression, ability to do quantitative thinking, ability to interpret reading materials in the social studies, ability to interpret reading materials in the natural sciences, ability to interpret literary materials, general vocabulary, subtotal, use of sources of information; 2 forms, 2 editions; prepared under the direction of E. F. Lindquist; Science Research Associates. *
a) SRA-SCORED EDITION. Forms X-3S, Y-3S ('52); examiner's manual ('58); administrator's manual, sixth edition ('58); teachers' and counselors' manual, sixth revision ('58); college planning manual, second edition ('57); confidential summary report, second edition ('57); IBM pupil profile card (no date); pupil's profile leaflet, fourth edition ('58); no norms for grade 13; separate answer sheets must be used; tests rented only; $1.10 per student; examination fee includes scoring and reporting of scores; $3 per college planning manual; $3 per specimen set; postage extra; 459(570) minutes in two days for full length version; 329(392) minutes in two days for class period version.
b) SCHOOL-SCORED EDITION. IBM; Forms X-3S, Y-3S ('52); subtests available as separates; examiner's manual ('58); battery manual ('54); pupil's profile leaflet, fourth edition ('58); profile card (no date); separate answer sheets must be used; $2 per 20 copies of any one test; $5 per 100 IBM answer sheets; 50¢ per hand and machine scoring key; $3 per complete specimen set; postage extra; 55–65(60–75) minutes for most tests in full length version; 40(45) minutes for most tests in class period version.

REFERENCES

1–3. See 4:17.
4. EDBERG, GEORGE. *Summary of a Study of the Value of the High School General Educational Development Tests as Predictors of College Success.* Master's thesis, University of North Dakota (Grand Forks, N.D.), 1948.
5. McCRACKEN, NAOMI M. *Success of University of Kentucky Veterans Who Received High School Credit Through GED Tests.* Master's thesis, University of Kentucky (Lexington, Ky.), 1948.
6. OLSON, DONALD J. *A Study of the Iowa Tests of Educational Development and the SRA Primary Mental Abilities in the Montana State Wide Cooperative Testing Program.* Master's thesis, Montana State University (Missoula, Mont.), 1951.
7. BOWMAN, HOWARD A. "Techniques for Graphical Representation of Pupil Personnel Data to Indicate Individual Deviates and to Provide a Basis for More Adequate Guidance." *Ed & Psychol Meas* 12:490–502 au '52. * (PA 27:6137)

8. KACALEK, LAUDIE B. *Effectiveness of Iowa Tests of Educational Development in Predicting High School Achievement.* Master's thesis, Iowa State College (Ames, Iowa), 1955.

9. PREBLE, ELIZABETH. "Iowa Tests of Educational Development." *High Points* 38:58–62 N '56. *

10. SILVER, IDA O. "A School-Wide Testing Program." *High Points* 38:35–41 Ap '56. *

11. *Using the Iowa Tests of Educational Development for College Planning, Second Edition.* Chicago, Ill.: Science Research Associates, Inc., 1957. Pp. 64. *

12. TRACY, MYLES A. "A New Approach to Pre-Admission Counseling of Junior College Business Students." *Jun Col J* 28:435–40 Ap '58. *

J. MURRAY LEE, *Professor of Elementary Education and Chairman of the Department, Southern Illinois University, Carbondale, Illinois.*

The *Iowa Tests of Educational Development* are excellent. They measure some of the important objectives which all high schools are attempting to attain. The manuals are complete and very helpful. It is possible to have the publisher score the tests and furnish the school with a comprehensive analysis of the results. With this service available, it would be a foolish waste of time to have teachers use their time to score tests on the secondary level.

A major use of the tests is to reveal the pattern of the individual student's development and to show growth in this development from year to year. This information would provide a basis for adapting instruction and guidance to meet the measured needs of each individual. The tests also give a good prediction of probable college success. A second major use is to provide the faculty with a more dependable and objective basis for evaluating important phases of the total educational offering of the school. With increasing pressures on the high school, it is important that there be objective data available as to individual progress and the attainment of the total group.

Lindquist, his associates, and the publisher should be highly commended for the careful construction and standardization of the tests, the completeness of statistical data and reports of studies of the tests, the completeness of the analysis of results made available to the school and the individual pupil, and for providing a scoring and reporting service which relieves teachers of clerical work.

STEPHEN WISEMAN, *Director, School of Education, University of Manchester, Manchester, England.*

The reviewer was supplied with copies of Forms X-3, Y-3, Y-3S, and Y-2 together with large numbers of manuals, keys, pamphlets, leaflets, and cards. This would form admirable material for a test for test reviewers, were it not for a suspicion that the difficulty level is too high, and the required time allowance too long. (Either that, or the present reviewer is at about the 5th percentile level.) The task was not made easier by the discovery that norms in different manuals differed as did the layout of items in Forms Y-2 and Y-3 (perhaps reasonably?) and—more difficult to understand—the order of items in Forms Y-3 and Y-3S. The *form* of at least one item (Item 8, Test 3) was even altered from Y-3 to Y-3S. Some of these discrepancies became understandable when the reviewer realised that these tests have been established for a number of years, that a good deal of revision has occurred over that time, and that the procedure for using the various forms differs. Consequently there appeared to be at least three sets of percentile norms in the literature supplied. An indication of this in each specimen set would not come amiss.

With the declared aims of the tests one can have no quarrel. As means of keeping track of "educational development" through the upper grades they are likely to be very effective. The nine tests provide a coverage which, to English eyes, is at first sight unusual, and rather heavily loaded on verbal skills. The claim made in one or two places in the library of booklets and manuals that the tests measure what a student can *do* rather than what he *knows* is not easy to substantiate in such tests as Test 1, Understanding of Basic Social Concepts, or Test 2, General Background in the Natural Sciences. But the reviewer would consider this a virtue rather than a fault for such measures. The test which caused most doubts in the reviewer's mind was Test 3, Correctness and Appropriateness of Expression. "This test is designed to give the teacher a reliable indication of the student's mastery of some of the basic elements in correct and effective writing." But, like so many tests of this kind, it seems overloaded with items which, while not to be stigmatised as "trivial," nevertheless seem relatively unimportant when compared with the basic skill of writing a sentence that means what one intends to say. In this test, perhaps more than in any other, the cramping influence of the multiple choice item form seems evident. The tendency in England to move away from "recognition" items to "creative" items finds no echo from across the Atlantic. Is this mainly because of the prestige, as well as the convenience, of machine scoring? Some of us over here have discovered that the open-ended question, to be answered by a word, a phrase, or a sentence, can be almost as reliable and sometimes more valid and discriminating. In tests of English usage—and of reading comprehension—this technique provides the testmaker with at least one additional degree of freedom and permits him to test skills and understandings which are extremely difficult to cover by means of the multiple choice technique.

Nevertheless, it would be churlish—and unfair—to seize on the Iowa tests as exemplifying poor test content or item form. With Lindquist so closely associated with the tests, one would be surprised not to find sensible, informed, and skillful use of questioning technique. Some of the reading tests, in particular, can well bear comparison with any other similar tests known to the reviewer. Only occasionally does Homer nod. In Test 5, for example, an extract describing the opening of the new House of Commons contains the clause "When William II built Westminster Hall in 1099." Item 75 asks "When was Westminster built?" Certainly grade 12 students cannot be expected to appreciate the subtle distinction between "Westminster" and "Westminster Hall," but the item writer ought to, perhaps. Leaving out "Hall," no doubt to increase the difficulty of the question, makes it practically impossible!

The tests are available in six parallel forms, but one gathers that Forms X-1 and Y-1 have been superseded by later versions.[1] It is curious that no evidence is provided of parallelism. The already noted variation in item order (and item content) makes one wonder about the validity of some of the statistics on reliability, etc. Reliability is quoted only for undesignated Form X and Form Y. The reporting of separate coefficients for X and Y would seem to suggest that X-1 is "more parallel" with X-2 than with Y-1—and yet "all six editions were constructed as parallel forms." No intercorrelations among forms are given, although a table of correlations among the nine tests in the Y form (1, 2 or 3?) is presented. The range is from .40 (Test 2 versus Test 3) to .78 (Test 5 versus Test 7). Since these are "within-grades within-schools" correlations, one imagines that the percentage of common variance is pretty high. Reliabilities of from .86 to .94 seem fairly low to English eyes for those of the tests which are of 60 minutes' duration, but the reduction in hetero-

geneity caused by a within-grades treatment may well account for this. It seems curious that, with tests which have been in existence for some years, only split-half correlations are given. Does no one in the United States use test-retest coefficients any more?

There is a most impressive and useful report manual summarizing the follow-up studies that have been carried out on the tests. This evidence on predictive validity is valuable and heartening, and does something to make up for the lack of evidence on construct validity. A factor analysis of the test intercorrelations would be a welcome addition to (or substitution for part of) the mass of verbal material provided by the publishers.

As with the *Sequential Tests of Educational Progress,* the standardisation procedure in the Iowa tests consists of converting raw scores to standard scores and thence to percentiles. A rough comparison of the raw score-standard score conversion tables shows close agreement between Y-2 and Y-3 forms for Test 4, quite good agreement for Test 1, and a good deal of divergence for Test 3 (e.g., a standard score of 10 corresponds to a score of 37 on Y-2 and 47 on Y-3S). This divergence indicates a lack of parallelism as the term is usually understood by test constructors. The standard score scale runs from 0 to about 30, so that one unit is roughly equivalent to the probable error of score. The intention of such a scale is excellent; one wonders whether it will in fact restrain teachers from making unjustifiable deductions about raw score differences.

The sampling programme for the norms shows the expected sensitivity to the problems involved, and the manual for the school administrator gives detailed tables of the sample used. Distributions of pupils by region, grade, and community size are given. Grade norms as well as pupil norms are provided, based on results from over 400 schools at each grade level.

In summary, it is perhaps fair to say that the reviewer wishes that a similar set of tests were available in England. Now that the separate booklet edition is available and hand scoring is possible, the teacher can, if he wishes, select from the battery those tests which he particularly needs. There is no doubt that by using them he can obtain evidence on progress, standards, and general educational development that would be difficult to obtain in other ways. It is likely that the greater part of any "backwash"

---

[1] Since the review was written, the publisher has also withdrawn Forms X-2 and Y-2.

effect these tests may have on the curriculum will be, on the whole, favourable—much more so than that of many other tests the reviewer knows.

For a review by Eric F. Gardner of Forms X-2 and Y-2, see 4:17; for reviews by Henry Chauncey, Gustav J. Froehlich, and Lavone A. Hanna of Forms X-1 and Y-1, see 3:12.

[18]

Municipal Battery: National Achievement Tests. Grades 3–6, 6–8; 1938–55; 2 levels; 2 editions; tests except in spelling and health published as separates; 50¢ per specimen set of either level of either edition; postage extra; Robert K. Speer and Samuel Smith; Acorn Publishing Co. *

a) COMPLETE BATTERY. 1938–55; grades 3–6: Forms A ('55, identical with test copyrighted in 1938 except for minor changes), B ('51, identical with test copyrighted in 1939 except for minor changes); grades 6–8: Forms A ('50, identical with test copyrighted in 1938 except for minor changes), B ('50, identical with test copyrighted in 1939 except for minor changes); 10 tests; no norms for part scores; directions for administering ('38, English norms revised in 1950); $5.50 per 25 tests; 203(225), 202(225) minutes for grades 3–6, 6–8.

  1) *Reading Comprehension.* 4 scores: following directions, sentence meaning, paragraph meaning, total.
  2) *Reading Speed.*
  3) *Spelling.*
  4) *Arithmetic Fundamentals.* 3 scores: computation, number comparisons, total.
  5) *Arithmetic Reasoning.* 4 scores: comparisons, problem analysis, problems, total.
  6) *English.* 5 scores: language usage-words, language usage-sentences, punctuation and capitalization, expressing ideas, total.
  7) *Literature.* 3 scores: motives and moods, miscellaneous facts, total.
  8) *Geography.* 3 scores: geographical ideas and comparisons, miscellaneous facts, total.
  9) *History and Civics.* 3 scores: lessons of history, historical facts, total.
  10) *Health.*
b) PARTIAL BATTERY. 1938–39; 6 tests; Forms A ('38), B ('39); directions for administering ('38); $3.75 per 25 tests; 138(155), 137(155) minutes for grades 3–6, 6–8.

  1) Subtests same as 1–6 in Complete Battery.

J. MURRAY LEE, *Professor of Elementary Education and Chairman of the Department, Southern Illinois University, Carbondale, Illinois.*

The materials accompanying the *Municipal Battery* provide very little of the specific data which have become customary. It is impossible to tell when or where the tests were standardized. The statements concerning validity are most general. The reliability data were obtained by the split-half method rather than by correlating Form A with Form B. The lack of a comprehensive manual forces the user to be one of great faith.

A number of questions concerning content arise. The reading speed test probably contains too few scorable units. A score difference of one point usually means at least a full half year difference in grade equivalent. There are no part scores in the English, literature, geography, and history tests. Yet Part 4 of English, "Expressing Ideas," and Part 1, "Motives and Moods," of the literature test might well be considered reading tests. Due to the great diversity of material covered throughout the United States in literature, geography, history, and health, it is most difficult to construct tests of facts in these areas on a national basis. That these authors had this difficulty can be seen in the history test, which is almost exclusively devoted to early American history, particularly explorers. Any user should carefully examine the content of these tests to see whether the content covered has been part of the curriculum of his school.

The scoring keys and methods are inadequate. A spaced key is provided only in arithmetic. The user would have to construct his own keys for most of the tests. This also applies to the tests scored according to the letters of a code word. To avoid many scoring errors, the user should construct his own spaced keys.

The profiling of scores on the back of the test booklet should be useful, but the handling of the scores appears to be cumbersome. For instance, there are three parts to reading comprehension which are recorded in different places in the test booklet and have to be added together mentally to obtain the total. Norms are provided for three IQ levels. This interpretive procedure gives the teacher some help, but conclusions concerning some children may be greatly in error because their MA's are not considered in judging their performance.

It is the feeling of the reviewer that there are other achievement batteries which would be much more useful for elementary schools. This test has been adequately reviewed in previous editions of *The Mental Measurements Yearbook* (see 4:20, 40:1191, 38:875). There is no reason to repeat criticisms of other reviewers.

For a review by Howard R. Anderson of the history and civics test, see 790. For a review by Ralph C. Preston, see 4:20; for reviews by A. M. Jordan of the complete battery for grades 6–8 and Hugh B. Wood of the batteries for grades 6–8, see 40:1191.

[19]

★**National Achievement Tests.** Grades 4-6, 7-9;
1954-58; 4 scores: language, mathematics, social stud-
ies-science-health, total; IBM; 2 levels; 25¢ per set of
manual and key; 6¢ per IBM answer sheet; 6¢ per
special IBM answer sheet (Intermediate Form A
only); $1 per specimen set of either level; postage
extra; Lester D. Crow, Alice Crow, and William H.
Bristow (Advanced); Acorn Publishing Co. *
a) INTERMEDIATE BATTERY. Grades 4-6; 1957-58;
Forms A ('57), B ('58); manual ('57); directions
sheet ('57); no data on reliability of Form B; $4 per
25 tests; 100(115) minutes.
b) ADVANCED BATTERY. Grades 7-9; 1954-57; Form A
('55); manual ('57, identical with manual copyrighted
in 1955); directions sheet ('54); no norms for total
score; $5.50 per 25 tests; 105(120) minutes.

WILLIAM E. COFFMAN, *Director, Test Development Division, Educational Testing Service,
Princeton, New Jersey.*

These tests have been advertised as "NEW—
COMPREHENSIVE—MODERN....EASY
TO ADMINISTER, EASY TO SCORE....
EASY TO INTERPRET AND EASY TO
ANSWER. In fact, it has already been reported to us by several teachers that their pupils
have enjoyed taking these tests." An examination of the tests and accompanying manuals suggests that ease of scoring and interpretation
have been achieved at the expense of an unjustified oversimplification; that rather than being
new, comprehensive, and modern, the tests contain all of the limitations of tests produced in
the 1920's; and that insufficient effort has been
devoted to editing and proofreading. It is difficult to see how tests carrying copyright dates of
1955, 1957, and 1958 could violate so many of
the generally accepted principles of test construction.

For each battery there is a 4-page manual
which reports in telegraphic form a modicum of
information. The first page is a cover page. The
last page contains a table of grade norms and
one showing the scores corresponding to the
quartiles of distributions for midyear groups at
each of the appropriate grade levels. The middle
two pages provide statements about purpose,
validity, reliability, administration, scoring, and
interpretation. All statistical data reported in
the manual for the Intermediate Battery are
presumably for Form A, the manual predating
Form B. Although these are highly speeded
tests, the reliability coefficients reported are
split-half coefficients, which are known to be
spuriously high for speeded tests. The authors
report that care was taken in selecting the norms
groups, but no evidence to support this claim is

offered. In the section devoted to validity they
report that "the items of each test....represent
samplings of curricular materials generally included in syllabi and courses of study" and that
test questions after experimental tryout were
arranged in order of difficulty. The manual is
certainly easy to read, but the reader will find
no information which documents the claims to
quality for the tests.

Ease of scoring is achieved for Form A of
each battery by having each option preceded by
letters which are assumed to appear to the pupils
as being in random order but which are so arranged that the right answer is always preceded
by one of the letters in a selected key word.
Since the items are arranged in order of difficulty, it is not necessary for the pupil to discover the key word in order to mark right answers without bothering to read the questions;
all he has to do is mark the right answers to the
first column of easy questions and then mark
the same key letters whenever they appear
throughout the test. Is it possible that the discovery of this simple solution might account for
the fact that some pupils find the test easy to
answer? Apparently the device has not proved
entirely satisfactory; the authors have eliminated it from the new Form B of the Intermediate Battery.

Errors in editing and proofing are too frequent to be attributable to the ever-present
human error which remains after sincere effort.
There are several misspellings, and sometimes
the options do not logically complete the item
stems. Some items are miskeyed; other items
have more than one defensible answer; still
other items have no right answer.

In the absence of evidence on item validity,
it is difficult to estimate the effect of careless
editing and proofing on the effectiveness of a
test as a measuring instrument. Undoubtedly
errors reduce discrimination in some cases. A
more serious consequence is the effect of faulty
copy on pupils who know enough to spot the
errors. A test is not only a measuring device;
it is also a model of what are considered suitable goals of education. A majority of the items,
while free from editorial and proofing errors,
test only isolated factual recall or simple textbook arithmetic. A highly speeded test, consisting of items of these types, is likely to be a better indication of general intelligence or scholastic aptitude than of achievement of defensible
goals of instruction. And there are certainly

many better tests of general intelligence, supported by extensive research data, available to the teacher. It is not necessary to use 270 items, as in the Elementary Battery, or 420 items, as in the Advanced Battery, to obtain a reliable and valid measure of intelligence.

These tests appear to have little to recommend them. As illustrations of faults that can appear in a test or test manual, they might have some value. For any other use, they should be carefully avoided.

[20]

★National Merit Scholarship Qualifying Test. Second semester juniors and first semester seniors seeking college scholarships; 1955–58; tests administered annually in April by individual schools; 8 scores: English usage, mathematics usage, social studies reading, natural sciences reading, word usage, humanities total, science total, total; Form A ['58]; manual ('58) ; technical manual ['58]; college planning manual, second edition ('57) ; pupil self-interpreting profile ['58]; examination fee, $1; school may administer test free to 2 deserving students; postage extra; fee includes reporting of scores; 170(190) minutes; Science Research Associates. * [This entry and the reviews below refer only to the SRA edition of the test used in the National Merit Scholarship Program in 1958; prior to 1958 the program employed the *Scholarship Qualifying Test* of the College Entrance Examination Board administered by Educational Testing Service.]

BENNO G. FRICKE, *Assistant Chief, Evaluation and Examinations Division, and Assistant Professor of Psychology, University of Michigan, Ann Arbor, Michigan.*

The *National Merit Scholarship Qualifying Test* prepared by Science Research Associates (subsequently referred to as the SRA-NMSQT) and administered to 479,000 high school juniors and seniors on April 29, 1958, is claimed to be a test of educational development, not a test of scholastic aptitude. The constructors of the SRA-NMSQT appear to have been influenced and perhaps directed by E. F. Lindquist of the State University of Iowa who heads SRA's National Test Advisory Committee. According to the Interpretive Manual, "the sub-tests of the NMSQT were constructed to parallel sub-tests of the Iowa Tests of Educational Development." The ITED, it will be recalled, was prepared under Lindquist to assess the educational growth of high school students.

In a "fact folder" the author-publishers of the SRA-NMSQT state that with their test "more students across the nation will have a better opportunity to demonstrate their fitness for college study." They also maintain that "the new test will enable the student, parent, and counselor to learn much more about his individual strengths and weaknesses, and consequently to approach decisions about the senior year in high school and planning for post-high school education or training with a great deal more confidence." These and numerous other claims in the "fact folder" are not supported by data. Almost every item dealing with the SRA-NMSQT examined by the reviewer exhibited characteristics suggestive of too much emphasis on salesmanship. The literature concerning the *Scholarship Qualifying Test* prepared by Educational Testing Service is cited as a wholesome contrast.

A major criticism of the SRA-NMSQT is against the presumption that it is an excellent measure of achievement and not another aptitude test. An inspection of the items in the various subtests convinces the reviewer that in only the first two subtests is achievement being measured. The items in these subtests, English usage and mathematics usage, are such that a bright but uneducated person would be unable to answer correctly many of the questions. For example, a 17-year-old farmhand with an IQ of 130 who dropped out of school three years ago while in the seventh grade probably would not be able to identify the right answer for Item 35, a relatively easy item for most students who have had algebra. This item reads:

35. The expression $b^2 + 4b - 5$ when divided by $b - 1$ is equal to:
 A. $b - 5$
 B. $b + 5$
 C. $b - 4$
 D. $b + 4$
 E. Not given

Items like this one which tap something not normally learned through everyday living qualify as indicators of proficiency. In short, most of the English usage and mathematics items seem to measure general academic preparation, that which the test purports to measure. Many of the ability tests now in widespread use, including the ETS-SQT and the College Board's *Scholastic Aptitude Test* (SAT), consist mostly of items of this general achievement type; the familiar *ACE Psychological Examination* is a noteworthy exception since it yields aptitude scores through items which are not "school achievement" loaded.

Items in the next two SRA-NMSQT subtests, the Social Studies Reading Test and the Natural Science Reading Test, unlike the items in the first two subtests, do not require the student to have learned anything specifically in social studies or natural science. The bright 17-year-old farmhand probably would do very well on these subtests even though he might not have learned much in these areas. His general ability should permit him to answer the questions asked at the end of the reading passages. In a real sense these two subtests indicate not what the student has learned (or how he has grown educationally) over a period of time but rather what he is able to learn on the spot. A student with a below average IQ who has performed well in social and natural science courses in school does not have an opportunity to show what he knows (or how he has grown educationally). He, unlike the bright farmhand, would be unable to master the new material quickly and to "figure out" the answers. It is highly improbable that a teacher would give material and questions of this type to evaluate the extent to which students have mastered their courses.

However, it is quite probable that the material in these two subtests could be used to provide a measure of *general ability to read and understand*. In fact, the widely used *Cooperative English Test: Reading Comprehension* does just that. The ETS-SQT, the SAT, the *Ohio State University Psychological Test,* and other tests use this type of reading test material to get a measure of verbal aptitude. In short, the reviewer believes the SRA-NMSQT social studies and natural science subtests do not reflect achievement in these two areas, but measure almost entirely reading ability and general verbal aptitude. (More will be said later in the statistical section about the role of these two subtests and the need for them.)

The fifth subtest of the SRA-NMSQT, the Word Usage Test, is a measure of vocabulary pure and simple. Since almost everyone knows that vocabulary items provide one of the best indications of general intelligence and scholastic aptitude, further comment is unnecessary.

The claim that the SRA-NMSQT measures something different from what is measured by the ETS-SQT or other scholastic aptitude tests is rejected outright by the reviewer. The item types used in the five subtests of the SRA-NMSQT could be and are found in most of the other widely used scholastic aptitude tests. The reviewer finds nothing different in the content of the SRA-NMSQT. Along with the comparable subtests of its sister test, the *Iowa Tests of Educational Development,* it taps what is

tapped by tests normally called academic ability tests (or scholastic aptitude tests, or educational intelligence tests). It should be regarded as an ability test regardless of the claims made for it. Test takers should not be led to believe that they can appreciably change their scores on the subtests by taking certain courses or by becoming more studious. A possible exception might be the student who has not yet taken mathematics in high school. Such a student would learn some things which would be reflected in a higher score on the Mathematics Usage Test. However, a student with a low score on the Word Usage Test is almost certain to remain low relative to his age group. Suggesting that students can substantially improve their vocabulary test scores is like suggesting that they can raise their IQ's markedly. Particularly objectionable in this connection is the statement in the folder "Your National Merit Scores and What They Mean" which says: "If you are relatively low in a particular area, remember you have the school year ahead in which to overcome this weakness."

Whether the SRA-NMSQT total score will predict school and college grades as well as the total score from other academic ability tests remains to be seen. The reviewer would be surprised to find that its predictive validity is significantly higher or lower than other tests. However, one or two factors suggest that the 3-hour SRA-NMSQT might be somewhat inferior to the 2-hour ETS-SQT and the College Board's 3-hour SAT as a predictor of the grades of students who go on to college. The reasons for this expectation are considered in the more technical section below.

But before leaving the topic of test validity, the reviewer would like to criticize the Interpretive Manual for giving the impression that the validity and usefulness of the SRA-NMSQT are known. In commenting upon the total score, the manual states: "This composite gives an overall picture of development as measured by the five sub-tests and *has proved* [italics added by reviewer] to be an excellent predictor of college success." Impossible! The manual was prepared before any of the students who took the test even entered college; whether the composite score of the SRA-NMSQT is an "excellent predictor" will not be known until the students have established a college record and until a systematic study has been conducted. A more accurate statement would resemble the following one found in the Bulletin of Information for Candidates for the ETS-SQT administered October 24, 1956. "The Scholarship Qualifying Test is a test of certain verbal and quantitative abilities that experience has shown to be closely related to success in college." A similar kind of incorrect reporting is found in the pages of the manual where SRA-NMSQT subtest profiles are presented for students majoring in eight academic areas. In orienting the reader to the profiles, the following statement is made: "The data presented in the charts represent what college graduates *have done* [italics in original] and provide valuable guide lines for the realistic selection of a college major." Impossible, again. While the reviewer is confident that the profiles were not pulled out of a hat, their origin is not explained. Although no mention of the ITED is made in the earlier pages of the manual, it is probable that the profiles are really based on the ITED. If the profiles are ITED profiles, this should have been made explicit and the titles of the five SRA-NMSQT subtests should not have been used. The ninth profile chart "summarizes the findings of one study which numbered 3,441 cases and shows the relationship of all college entrants to all college graduates studied in terms of scores on the *Iowa Tests of Educational Development.*" This information supports, perhaps, the guess that the earlier charts were based upon five of the nine ITED subtests. This last chart, however, does not use the SRA-NMSQT or ITED subtest titles but refers to five subtests by number (e.g., Test 1).

Part 2 of the Interpretive Manual, the Technical Supplement, contains incomplete and poorly identified but interesting data. It is here that the statistical character of the test is described and some results from two studies presented. As mentioned earlier, it is in the Technical Supplement that the important disclosure is made that the five SRA-NMSQT subtests were designed to parallel five of the nine ITED subtests. Since the ITED was designed for use with typical high school students, it follows that the difficulty level of the SRA-NMSQT could not be appropriate for the population of superior students in which discriminations are to be made. It is important to realize that the primary purpose of the administration of the test was to identify about 10,000 able students from which about 1,000 who survived additional screening hurdles would be awarded college scholarships in 1959. Previous experience has shown that the number of seriously interested scholarship candidates is very large, possibly numbering 100,000 to 200,000 of the nearly 500,000 who took the SRA-NMSQT in 1958. A major weakness of the test is that it was not suited to its task of identifying potential scholarship recipients. One reason why the reviewer believes the test might not predict college success as well as the ETS-SQT lies in the difference in difficulty of the two tests.

Statistics in the manual show that the average student who took the SRA-NMSQT got 56 per cent of the items right. It appears that the test was fairly well suited to the total group who took it and that it was much too easy for the superior group for which it was (or at least should have been) primarily intended. Consequently, by chance, luck, and other factors, students of less than outstanding quality could obtain scores that would be indistinguishable from the scores of the truly able, and an unnecessarily large proportion of the former could be selected for membership in the group of 10,000 semifinalists. If it was essential to have the test serve multiple purposes (e.g., identification of superior students, and guidance and evaluation of nonsuperior students), perhaps different subsets of the item pool should have been scored.

It is difficult to believe that the authors of the test were unaware of the role of item difficulty in the assessment of individual differences. But certainly considerable psychometric naïveté is exhibited in several sections of the Technical Manual. The section on item difficulty is one of them. After noting that the average student answered correctly 71 per cent of the items in the English Usage Test, the authors state it is not surprising that the English test is easiest "because by the time they have progressed to the junior year, most of these higher level students should have become at least moderately facile in using the English language effectively." They seem not to realize that an English test could have been constructed such that the average student would get only 20 per cent (or almost any other percentage) of the items right. The section on item difficulty is concluded by noting that "the most difficult of the five tests is *Mathematics Usage,* with a difficulty index of .39. This finding is consistent with the observation that many high school students, even the better ones, claim to experience difficulty with general mathematics." How naïve!

Another factor contributing to the item difficulty indices is to be found in the number of response alternatives. In the English Usage Test, 3 of the 76 items have only 2 alternatives, 16 have only 3, and 57 have only 4. Thus by chance alone (e.g., by marking answers on the answer sheet without reading the paragraphs or questions) the number right could be about 21, or 28 per cent; this is not far below the average percentage right (39) actually obtained on the mathematics subtest. In the mathematics subtest, all 40 items have 5 alternatives so the number right by chance alone would on the average be 8, or 20 per cent. (Incidentally, a raw score of 8 on the mathematics subtest would be equivalent to an SRA-NMSQT standard score of about 14 according to Table 19, and a standard score of 14 is higher than that obtained by about 20 per cent of the scholarship candidates according to Table 18! Since so many students obtain mathematics scores lower than scores that they could obtain by answering randomly, it must mean either that the incorrect alternatives are very plausible for some students, or that many students do not answer all the items in the subtest.) Since the students are told that their scores will be the number of items right and since only 40, or 13 per cent, of the items in the test have as many as 5 alternatives, it is probable that many relatively weak students might obtain very high scores through the operation of good luck and chance. When almost half a million students are tested, the probability is high that a substantial *number* (though admittedly a small percentage of the total) would obtain scores which do not accurately describe them. It would seem desirable to have *at least* 5-choice items in tests designed to identify a relatively small number of superior students from among the nation's high school population.

Some items are poorly written. For instance, Item 16 in the Mathematics Usage Test states, "Two bisecting lines are drawn in a circle as shown below." The lines are intersecting, not bisecting. While much more could be said about the test *items,* some comments about the test *scores* are in order. Table 19 of the manual presents the intercorrelations of the subtests and shows that far from independent measures are

obtained; the median coefficient is .54. The relatively high subtest intercorrelations, along with the relatively low Kuder-Richardson formula 21 reliability coefficients (median is .80), raises further doubt about the necessity of the five subtest scores. Certainly the test profile uses that are recommended in the manual should not be taken seriously. Analysis of the social and natural science subtest statistics confirms what was feared from the analysis of item content referred to earlier. Since these two subtests correlate .64 with each other and have K-R reliabilities of only .71 and .77 respectively, grave doubt about the desirability of two separate scores is raised. In Table 15, which gives the correlations between equivalent subtests of the SRA-NMSQT and ITED, it is found that the correlations between the two are .70 and .75 respectively. In other words it is *apparent that the social studies subtest predicts the natural science subtest scores (r = .64) about as well as these parts predict themselves.* As might be expected, the correlations between these subtests and the Word Usage (vocabulary) Test are also very high, .61 and .66 respectively. Most of the correlations among the four verbal subtests are in the .60's, and most of the correlations between these verbal subtests and the mathematics subtest are in the .40's.

It would seem from the correlation coefficients presently available that two good reliable tests measuring verbal and mathematical ability would be satisfactory from the statistical and selection points of view. Two scores rather than five are even more important from the standpoint of a counselor faced with the problem of guiding high school students; he would not have to keep in his head five scores, most of which do not measure anything sufficiently different to make any practical difference. Unless the counselor is especially sophisticated, he is in danger of reading significance into differences in subtest scores which are unreliable. Obviously, students "guided" according to chance differences are not being helped to see themselves realistically.

In conclusion, the SRA-NMSQT and the literature distributed about it do not seem to be a step forward. The reviewer is concerned that assessment psychology has been retarded and may have lost ground through the production and use of this test. He is amazed and disturbed that such inferior work can be conducted and tolerated on such a large scale. It is hoped that it will not be repeated.[1]

ROGER T. LENNON, *Director, Division of Test Research and Service, World Book Company, Yonkers, New York.*

The National Merit Scholarship Program was established in 1955 to provide scholarship assistance to students exceptionally capable of benefiting from a college education. Sponsored by business and industrial organizations, foundations, professional groups, and individuals, the program in its first three years made available about $12 million in such assistance. A privately financed non-profit operation, the National Merit Scholarship Program is the largest private scholarship activity in the history of United States education. Recipients of scholarship awards are selected initially on the basis of a nationwide qualifying examination. Any high school wishing to do so may participate in the program and designate two students who will be admitted without charge to the test; other students pay a fee of one dollar.

In the first three years of the program's existence, the qualifying examination was one developed by the College Entrance Examination Board and was administered early in the senior year of high school. In 1958 a different type of qualifying examination, developed by Science Research Associates, was introduced, and its administration moved to the junior year of high school for most candidates. This review is concerned with the qualifying test (Form A) administered in April 1958 to some 479,000 high school students.

NATURE OF THE TEST. The 1958 *National Merit Scholarship Qualifying Test* (NMSQT) comprises the following five tests: English Usage (76 items), Mathematics Usage (40 items), Social Studies Reading (51 items), Natural Science Reading (51 items), Word Usage (88 items). Scores are reported for each of the five tests; additionally, three composite scores are derived: a total composite, a humanities composite, and a science composite. Most of the questions are of the 4-option multiple choice type, a fifth "not given" option being included in the questions of the Mathematics

Usage Test. Examinees record responses on an MRC answer sheet; scoring and processing is handled on the Iowa electronic test scoring equipment. Total testing time is 2 hours and 50 minutes, and the time limits for the separate tests are described as liberal so that the emphasis is on power rather than speed. Two forms, A and B, were prepared, the second form being used as a make-up examination. The forms are stated to be equivalent, but no data on this matter are furnished.

The English Usage Test covers mechanics of expression, with the examinee being required to judge the correctness or incorrectness of usage in running text and to indicate kinds of changes called for. The Mathematics Usage Test is basically a test of problem solving ability, making no demands on any formal mathematics training beyond a first-year algebra course. The social studies and natural science reading tests consist of a series of reading selections averaging several hundred words in length, each selection followed by approximately 10 questions designed to measure various aspects of reading comprehension. The Word Usage Test is a conventional vocabulary measure. The quality of the individual items impresses this reviewer as acceptable, though more editorial scrutiny would have improved certain items (e.g., Test 1, Items 5, 20, 67; Test 2, Items 12, 16, 23, 34). Item difficulty data presented in the interpretive manual suggest that the English usage and word usage tests are somewhat too easy for maximum effectiveness with the candidate population, and that the mathematics test is perhaps a little too hard. Directions for administering are clear and comprehensive, including both directions to the examinees and instructions to examiners and proctors.

RELIABILITY. Kuder-Richardson formula 21 estimates of reliability, based on a sample of 2,011 second-semester junior students are as follows: Test 1, .86; Test 2, .80; Test 3, .71; Test 4, .77; and Test 5, .91. Reliability of the total composite, which is presumably the basis for scholarship award qualification, is .95, for the science composite, .96, and for the humanities composite, .98. These reliability estimates for the composite scores compare favorably with those of other instruments used for scholarship candidate selection, and are as high as are likely to be achieved in any reasonable testing time. The reliability estimates for the

---

1 Since this review was set in type the reviewer has received a supplement to the Interpretive Manual for Counselors, School Administrators and College Admissions Officers dated February 1959. No special or extended comment seems necessary. While the supplement presents some additional information which may be helpful to some users, in no sense can it be regarded as a satisfactory answer to criticisms of SRA's 1958 scholarship test and related literature.

several parts of the test, however, should give one pause with respect to efforts to interpret profile differences, particularly any differences involving either or both of the two reading tests. Intercorrelations among all the subtests are substantial (from .47 to .67) lessening the possibility of differential interpretation or prediction. The manual, unfortunately, pays scant heed to such considerations in discussing the guidance uses of the results.

NORMATIVE INFORMATION. While normative information is not necessary for identification of scholarship qualifying candidates, a mere ranking of examinees being sufficient for this purpose, the other purposes which NMSQT is intended to serve are dependent upon the types of normative data available. Scores on NMSQT may be converted to equivalent standard scores on the *Iowa Tests of Educational Development* and interpreted by means of the percentile ranks for the ITED scores. These ITED-equivalent percentile ranks are furnished for second-semester junior students, first-semester senior students, and for a sample of the NMSQT population itself. The correlations between the composite scores on NMSQT and ITED (.89 to .91) are sufficiently high to warrant confidence in the adequacy of this norming-by-equivalence technique for the total scores; but it would have been well to alert the user to the possible inaccuracies in the subtest norms thus derived, in light of the smaller correlations (.70 to .87) found between corresponding subtests of NMSQT and ITED. These equating-based percentiles are taken at face value in all the discussions in the interpretative manual on use of results. A table of estimated *Scholastic Aptitude Test* scores corresponding to NMSQT scores is also provided, based on joint administration of SAT and NMSQT to 1,366 juniors.

VALIDITY. The discussion in the interpretive manual of the validity of NMSQT as a predictor of college success points out that "more rigid proof of the predictiveness of the NMSQT must be deferred for several years until examinees....complete several semesters of college work." Meanwhile, the predictive validity of NMSQT is to be inferred from its similarity to ITED, which has been found in numerous studies to predict college freshman grades to the extent of .50 to .60, and from its similarity to the College Board *Scholastic Aptitude Test,* also known to have appreciable predictive validity for college success.

Does NMSQT, which seeks to predict college success through an achievement test placing emphasis on "broad intellectual skills, on understanding of and ability to use what is learned," do a better job of identifying exceptional college-potential students than "aptitude" tests, such as the *Scholarship Qualifying Test* which it superseded? As of now, we can only speculate; the data are not available. This reviewer's speculation, considering the content of the two types of examination and the magnitude of the correlation between their total scores, is that NMSQT will be found about as good a predictor—neither much better nor much worse—than the "aptitude" type instruments currently most widely used. It is pertinent to report that not all secondary school administrators share the Merit Scholarship Corporation's preference for an achievement type examination; considerable protest was voiced by many of them at the time when the present type of examination was introduced.

If NMSQT should, in fact, prove to be no better a predictor of college success than the earlier used "aptitude" type instruments, are its other values nevertheless such that it would be preferable for use in the Merit Scholarship Program? The Merit Scholarship Corporation, in adopting the present type of examination, pointed to the guidance values of a test yielding a profile of student strengths and weaknesses, and moved the date of administration back to the junior year to permit earlier reporting of scores and thus more time for their effective utilization. The validity of NMSQT scores for purposes other than prediction of college success must be inferred from an examination of the content of the tests rather than from any objective data. The interpretive manual stresses the significance of information presented in the profile which the student or counselor is encouraged to prepare, but without adequate recognition, in this reviewer's judgment, of the unreliability of some of the suggested comparisons. While the profile does not provide for any recording of the science composite or humanities composite scores, it is, nevertheless, suggested that attention be paid to these as well as to the total composite, despite reported intercorrelations among the three composites all in excess of .90. Occasional extravagances creep into the discussion of the meaning of part scores, as in the assertion that Test 3, Social Studies Reading, "measures the student's ability to draw significant inferences and to evaluate subjective topics. The student who does well on this test has the ability to deal with intangibles." Adequacy of counseling facilities and adequacy of other test data available obviously condition the additional usefulness of NMSQT scores.

Some, like this reviewer, may find it curious that a test intended to identify students having high potential for college success, a group constituting a small fraction at the upper end of the ability distribution, should be so similar in design and content to a test like *Iowa Tests of Educational Development,* intended as a broadly, if not universally, appropriate measure of growth from grade 9 to grade 12. Whatever the considerations that argue for a high degree of similarity in instruments intended for such apparently diverse purposes, it would be unfortunate if schools, in their zeal to have students do well on the scholarship examination, were influenced by the similarity to use ITED as, in effect, a warm-up or coaching exercise for the NMSQT.

To sum up: NMSQT impresses this reviewer as a well designed and competently constructed instrument likely to do as good a job of identifying exceptional college talent as any instrument of comparable length, and capable of serving certain, if not all, of the guidance purposes suggested, if not so fully, as the manual might imply.

[21]

★SRA Achievement Series. Grades 2–4, 4–6, 6–9; 1954–57; tests in language perception, arithmetic, language arts, reading, work-study skills available as separates; IBM for grades 4–9; 3 levels; school progress report ('55); technical supplement, second edition ('57); separate answer folders must be used in grades 4–9; 90¢ per 20 pupil progress folders ('55); 50¢ per administrator's manual ('56); 50¢ per teacher's handbook ('55); $1 per technical supplement; $3 per specimen set; postage extra; Louis P. Thorpe, D. Welty Lefever, and Robert A. Naslund; Science Research Associates. *

a) GRADES 2–4. Forms A ('55), B ('57, except language perception); 4 tests: language perception, arithmetic, language arts, reading; examiner's manual, second edition ('57); 40¢ per 20 language perception tests; $1.70 per 20 copies of any one of the other 3 tests; $1 per hand scoring stencil; 50¢ per specimen set; 92(125) minutes.

b) GRADES 4–6. 11 scores: references, charts, reading comprehension, vocabulary, capitalization and punctuation, grammatical usage, spelling, arithmetic (reasoning, concepts, computation), total; IBM; Forms A ('55), B ('56); examiner's manual, second edition ('56); *SRA-Scored Single Booklet Edition:* test materials are loaned to schools and scored by the publisher; 80¢ per student; *School-Scored Single Booklet*

Edition: $10 per 20 tests; $1.60 per 20 IBM scorable answer folders; $2 per 20 pupil profiles ['55]; 90¢ per 20 pupil profile booklets ('57); $2 per set of hand scoring stencils; $4 per set of machine scoring stencils; $1.35 per specimen set; *Separate Booklet Edition:* see entries for separate tests; 352(445) minutes in 3 sessions 1 day apart.

c) GRADES 6–9. Same as for grades 4–6 except: examiner's manual ('56); $3 per set of machine scoring stencils; 305(370) minutes in 3 sessions 1 day apart.

WARREN G. FINDLEY, *Assistant Superintendent for Pupil Personnel Services, Atlanta Public Schools, Atlanta, Georgia.*

The *SRA Achievement Series* is a new offering which measures achievement in basic skills from grade 2 through grade 9. Although it possesses its own distinctive characteristics, it may be said to be patterned closely after the *Iowa Every-Pupil Tests of Basic Skills.* It therefore possesses the virtue of highly reliable part scores based on large numbers of questions and lengthened periods of testing. The extensive accessory materials are in keeping with a wholesome trend in this direction in all new and revised achievement test batteries. The developmental procedures, including the establishing of norms, are well described and appear generally sound. Both analytical and teaching procedures attuned to the test data are described in usable form. The scope and content of the tests are generally appropriate and the tests are essentially unspeeded measures of "power" or "level." A particularly commendable feature is inclusion of a test of "language perception" at the level of grades 2–4.

On the debit side, the mechanics of handling the test materials have been made unnecessarily difficult for the pupil, e.g., answer sheets require working from right to left at a level at which working from left to right has just been nicely established. Inclusion of a "language arts" test of capitalization and punctuation at the grades 2–4 level, especially with its difficult response format, is highly questionable. Both these criticisms, and others, lead to the impression that the test producer's convenience, or even habit of mind, have taken precedence over adaptation to the age of the child being tested. Placement of analytical procedures related to instruction in the administrator's manual rather than in the teacher's handbook, requiring the teacher to "borrow" his manual from the administrator, is unfortunate. Setting the difficulty level of questions in each battery to measure well only those children who are above average and recommending that those below average be given a form designated for a lower level is un-realistic to say the least.

The series has been published in stages. The battery for grades 4–6 was published first, then the batteries for grades 2–4 and 6–9 were linked to the first battery. In this process a "parts of speech" section has given way to one on spelling. The literature promises a fourth battery for grades 1–2 and extension of the series horizontally to include substantive areas like science and social studies. This has meant revisions in accessory materials as projected features have had to be added, dropped, or modified, forcing the prospective user to make sure all of his manuals and handbooks are of one piece with his test booklets and answer sheets. For example, the Teacher's Profiles still listed in the current Teacher's Handbook have been abandoned, and a number of references to tables in other manuals give incorrect table numbers.

No extension of the series beyond grade 9 is contemplated. This publisher's *Iowa Tests of Educational Development* are designed for these grades and the publisher takes his stand alongside E. F. Lindquist, author of the Iowa tests, in maintaining that it is better to regroup the functions to be measured in high school and junior college than to attempt a continuity of measurement in the same skill areas through these grades, as do the *California Achievement Tests* and the Cooperative *Sequential Tests of Educational Progress*. It is significant to note that each publisher now feels the necessity to provide wide-range coverage, if not continuity, in achievement offerings. In doing so, he would appear to be reflecting a trend among school administrators to wish largely continuous measurement of achievement by one publisher's tests, a trend we may hope stems in some measure from published recommendations of test specialists that (a) continuous measurement of growth in achievement is more broadly useful to teachers, administrators, and guidance workers than is "spot-checking" or "survey" testing, and that (b) use of one publisher's achievement series is the only practical way currently to render achievement results at different levels comparable, because of inevitable differences between standardization groups used by different publishers.

Comment on the specific test content is to be found in the sections at the end of this review, where the content is discussed level by level and subject by subject. The accessory materials are so basic and so extensive that they are discussed first.

The Technical Supplement presents a convincing account of the rationale and developmental procedures, as well as reasonably clear and detailed evidence regarding reliability, validity, standardization, and equating of forms. The national normative sample appears to have been controlled adequately for geographical region, urban-rural ratio, and father's occupation. It must be presumed that the proportions in the smaller samples at each grade level did not deviate seriously from the statistics for the total sample of 21,512. The reliability of most of the parts of the tests at all levels is satisfactory for interpreting individual as well as group achievement. Exceptions would appear to include the arithmetic concepts test at all levels; the sight vocabulary test for grade 2; the reading vocabulary and computation tests in the battery for grades 2–4; and the charts test in the battery for grades 4–6. For these tests the median Kuder-Richardson (formula 21) reliability for the separate grades is below .80. The procedure for linkage of Forms A and B is thoroughly described and appears to have been most carefully done. Continuity of scores from level to level remains to be established empirically; cross-sectional evidence from three school systems suggests that the correction is of the order of only 0.1 or 0.2 grades between norms for grades 4–6 and norms at other levels.

Three points merit special mention. First, the decision to present the test material generally in the form of story units is well explained and justified, as is the decision to depart from this style in the work-study skills test at the grades 6–9 level because pupils at the higher level reject the approach as too juvenile. This shows a feeling for pupil motivation and the importance of explaining it not often found in test manuals.

Second, the reader should note that "each battery has been so constructed that it does not contain easy items suitable for the seriously retarded pupil to answer correctly, and only a relatively few items simple enough for the low-average learner to handle successfully. * These pupils will be clearly *identified* but not fully *measured*. It is strongly recommended that these retarded pupils be given the battery designed for the next lower school level." This reviewer feels the warning is well and clearly given, but prefers the adaptation to different levels of ability in the same class by use of different levels of tests not readily identified by pupils as to grade level, as in the STEP series. Reexamination on an easier test after failure on a purposely difficult test is not merely time-consuming, but provocative of bad pupil morale about taking tests. Moreover, in any large city system, a test that is designed primarily to challenge the best pupils at that grade level will produce low undifferentiated scores for the great majority of pupils in the socio-economically poorer areas of the community. For the present, then, in using most series, but especially this one, we face a "trilemma": (a) mass retesting is undesirable, as noted; (b) examining large numbers of pupils originally by tests bearing grade designations lower than the pupils' grade placement will bring public resentment; or (c) in most school systems, giving the same test to all in a given grade will produce large numbers of undifferentiated, hence uninformative, scores at the lower extreme.

Third, the factor analysis data are extensive and consistent. However, both school people and technical specialists will question the character of the general factor found to dominate the tested achievement. The wordiness, or verbality, of the arithmetic material and of the questions asked about charts and references brings the reading factor to the fore in all parts, and this may well be as important as "general achievement" in affecting scores. Such excessive verbality in the tests tends to make them unnecessarily "schoolish" and renders profile analysis of scores less profitable than it might be if the scores were freer of this dependence on verbal facility. Beyond this, most school people will be more concerned with the content validity of achievement tests at these grade levels, i.e., what skills and understandings the questions require the examinee to demonstrate, than on any construct based on a theory more relevant to aptitude testing for guidance purposes.

The Manual for the School Administrator appears to assume that the administrator is the person chiefly concerned about pupil mastery of specific skills within subject areas. This may be true in many small systems or individual schools. In many instances, however, the administrator properly delegates almost complete responsibility for this concern to the individual classroom teacher. It would make more sense either to incorporate this analytical material, which now forms the bulk of the administrator's manual, in the Teacher's Handbook or to put it in a separate booklet to which the administrator and teacher might both be referred at their stages of concern. Each teacher will want this information, to which reference is made seven times in the Teacher's Handbook, so should have it either in the handbook or separately for ready reference. If it appears only in the Manual for the School Administrator, there will be only one to a school and that may have been "filed."

The Teacher's Handbook should prove highly useful. The brief introductory discussion of norms, profiles, and analysis of errors is the best short statement of these matters in this reviewer's memory and, as such, would make an excellent discussion piece in an introductory course in tests and measurements. The statement brings out particularly clearly that it is proper to analyze individual achievement on large blocks of items, but that it is improper to draw strong inferences regarding individual mastery on the strength of one or two questions although it is quite proper to evaluate the general class achievement item by item. Substantial specific suggestions for developing the skills measured by the various parts of the tests are given clearly and are linked closely to the test content. An alert teacher could make very effective use of the whole booklet. The one present limitation, previously noted, is the necessity to refer to the administrator's manual for the breakdown of skills measured by the several parts of the test.

The Examiner Manual for each level is clear and efficient; it contains, in this order, preliminary activities, directions for administering the tests, directions for scoring the tests, and norms. Scoring keys are well designed to help the teacher avoid clerical errors, although those for grades 2–4 are cumbersome. The profile materials are also well designed, and they provide useful interpretative statements. For the administrator there is the School Progress Report, a profile form for grade medians for all grades. This form might be used to follow progress of a class through the several grades as well as for recording the average achievement of the different pupils currently in the several grades. For use with the pupil there is the Pupil Progress Folder for recording in grade equivalents his profile of achievement test results at successive grade levels. Space is also provided for recording school marks, other test data, health history, family background data, and other items commonly included in a cumulative record folder. For discussion with parents and pupils, separately or jointly, there is a leaflet entitled "Your Achievement Scores and What They Mean" with provision for profiling an individual pupil's scores with respect to national percentiles. For use by the school staff there is a pupil profile card in quadruplicate. For use in analysis of class strengths and weaknesses in specific areas item count forms are in process of development. Taken as a whole, these materials make possible constructive communication about test results to all concerned through forms specifically designed to serve each person's need for information and understanding.

The tests are quite unspeeded. The time limits at all levels guarantee that the pupil will have given a substantial sample of his ability to cope with the materials of each part. The testing schedule recommended at all levels calls for separate sessions of from 40 to 90 minutes of working time during successive half days. At the grades 2–4 level, provision is made for 5-minute intermissions after 15-minute intervals of work on the test material, while at the successively higher grade levels the intermissions are after correspondingly longer intervals of work. As an indirect measure of speededness this reviewer has sometimes applied the criterion that a test may be assumed to be speeded "if median scores in the norms run below 50 per cent right—after allowing for average chance success—in the highest grade for which the test is offered." Application of this criterion would indicate that none of the tests in the battery for grades 2–4 are speeded, but that the reading vocabulary section of the battery for grades 4–6 and the charts, arithmetic reasoning, and arithmetic concepts sections of the battery for grades 6–9 are speeded. The low medians in the norms may, however, reflect chiefly the avowed intention to produce tests better adapted to superior than to below average pupils. In the case of the vocabulary section of the battery for grades 4–6, the low median score may be due to the fact that vocabulary is tested in context. When vocabulary in context is tested by synonyms and the words to be defined are relatively simple, the synonym to be chosen as the correct definition is often more difficult than the key word to be defined.

The ability to measure poor learners in a grade depends on whether chance scores achieved by random guessing yield grade equivalents far enough below the lowest grade for which the test is offered. The battery for grades 2–4 is entirely unsatisfactory from this viewpoint, only the arithmetic computation test of this battery yielding chance scores more than half a grade below 2.0. The grade equivalent of the likely chance score on the grammatical usage section of this battery is 2.6! In the battery for grades 4–6 all tests show for the chance score a grade equivalent of six months or more below 4.0, the lower limit of the lowest grade for which the battery is intended—with two exceptions, arithmetic computation and reading vocabulary. In the battery for grades 6–9, all tests except that in arithmetic reasoning provide at least six months' "clearance." However, several tests at both levels fail to allow a clearance of a full grade, an absolute essential if any but the top half of an average class are to be measured as individuals to any useful purpose. This is a serious fault not to be explained away by the necessity of presenting challenging tests to superior pupils.

The tests are eminently more satisfactory in providing "ceiling" for measurement of superior pupils. All parts of the battery for grades 2–4, except language perception, which is designed to be useful primarily in grade 2, provide a score margin of two or more grades above the upper grade limit of 4.0 for which the battery is offered. The same is true for all tests in the battery for grades 4–6, while for the tests of the battery for grades 6–9 the margin is three grades or more.

GRADES 2–4. The test authors have made a real contribution by including a language perception test in an achievement battery. The subtitle, printed large for the pupils, is "Are These the Same?" The separate sections are familiar to those acquainted with reading readiness and diagnostic reading tests. In most schools there are many pupils at grade 2 about whom more useful information can be obtained from these diagnostic measures of readiness than from reading comprehension tests. The first grade teacher can pass on the information that such pupils have not made a beginning of reading. In the absence of such a test in the regular achievement battery, however, the principal and the second grade teacher are apt not to consider repeating this readiness diagnosis but to put the pupil to the ego-searing task of proving conclusively that he cannot read at all on a second grade reading test.

The answer form for this test uses the letters S and D for same and different, when the words themselves would be clearer. Moreover, the space between items is not sufficiently greater than the space between the two response boxes for a single item to help the beginner to visualize clearly the material that forms a response unit and to distinguish it from other units. Horizontal separation lines like those on page 4 would help.

The reading test, subtitled "What Is This About?," contains appropriate content, as regards difficulty and interest level, for grades 2 and 3, but probably not for grade 4. Two faults of format are serious. First, the reading material and questions are printed in double columns without even a vertical dividing line to keep the eye from reading full lines. Pupils will not have encountered this reading problem as yet in their regular reading. Second, and far more serious, the publishers have used progressively smaller type until the final reading passage and questions are in 10-point type.

The vocabulary section of the reading test at this and higher levels has the great virtue of measuring vocabulary in context. Many formal vocabulary tests are criticized because, in measuring vocabulary out of context, no account is taken of the important skill of identifying which of several connotations of a many-meaninged word is conveyed in particular uses. An inevitable, but not serious, drawback of this type of vocabulary measurement is that the word allowed as the correct answer is sometimes a less common word than the word being defined. For example, "foolish" is defined as "unwise," "trouble" as "difficulty."

The arithmetic test, subtitled "Let's Figure This Out," offers three significant sections. The one on arithmetical concepts is presented orally and the one on computation is free of words, the operation being indicated in each problem by the conventional symbol. The section on arithmetic reasoning or problem solving is designed to be readable, but it remains as much a test of reading skill as of quantitative reasoning.

The language arts test is aptly subtitled "How Should We Say This?" This reviewer has criticized other test offerings at the primary level for (a) stressing mechanics of expression and (b) offering what amounts to several different measures of reading under different titles because group testing requires reading to such a considerable degree. There appears to be no reason to amend this criticism here. As a schoolman, this reviewer must recommend against this test as measuring too early mechanics of expression that teachers are not and should not be teaching systematically before grade 5. As a test specialist, he must reject the test as too largely a measure of reading to appraise anything else at this grade level for most pupils. The stress on punctuating correspondence is particularly out of place.

GRADES 4–6. The work-study skills test is given wholesome prominence. Separate units of 15–20 items cover use of a table of contents, use of an index, knowledge of reference sources, and ability to interpret charts, tables, and graphs. The basic materials are excellent and most of the questions are sound. The reviewer would challenge those questions on the index that require the examinee to proceed from the page numbers to what is on these pages. These are artificial; the index is approached to find the page where certain desired information is located. Elsewhere, in reading charts and tables, the examinee is asked trivial questions or questions composed of an assemblage of one true and three false statements loosely connected by a short stem that lends itself to different completions. Despite these technical flaws, this test is an excellent instrument for drawing systematic attention of teachers and pupils to work-study skills that sometimes fail to get attention in formal testing of the 3 R's.

The well balanced reading test presents substantial passages of interesting material in the manner of textbook reading. Fiction, science, travel, and biography are all represented. One may question whether passages on space science and on national heroes may not give unintended advantages to readers who have pursued these subjects in their independent reading and hence can answer questions out of previous knowledge rather than by reading skill. The reviewer found this possible. The measurement of vocabulary in context has the virtues previously cited and is efficiently built into the total reading required.

The language arts test is artfully built around continuous material of an interesting and readable sort. The reviewer feels that there is more emphasis on punctuation of spoken discourse than is important in the life of the typical pupil or adult. He also feels that spelling could be tested more efficiently out of context. Sets of four different words, of which one or none is incorrectly spelled, give more coverage than items composed of one correct and two wrong spellings of the same word, as here.

The arithmetic test contains well motivated exercises on quantitative concerns. If more of the arithmetic reasoning problems could be presented pictorially, one could feel that reading was being kept from exerting an extraneous influence on the resulting scores.

GRADES 6–9. What has been said of the battery for grades 4–6 applies here. An additional good feature of the work-study skills test is the inclusion in both forms of a map interpretation question based on a hypothetical map. A passage on poetry that will command the respect of teen-agers has been added to the repertoire of material in the reading test in both forms. The language arts test strikes a better balance between direct discourse and correspondence, in favor of the latter. The arithmetic test includes questions on equations and geometric figures to carry the emphasis thought desirable by most mathematics educators at the junior high school level.

SUMMARY. The *SRA Achievement Series* may be described as offering a balanced program of testing basic skills from grade 2 through grade 9. Because of the length of the parts it is better adapted to instructional purposes than are most survey batteries. As a total battery it can be better justified from grade 4 up, but the battery for grades 2–4 contains a uniquely fortunate readiness emphasis in the language perception test. This battery will become more useful in local situations when the developmental processes are more stabilized and materials are adapted to meet internal as well as external criticism, particularly with respect to the format of the answer sheets and measurement of below average pupils. Meanwhile, excellent interpretative materials have been developed and local norms based on experience with the tests should give them added value in systems that use them.

WORTH R. JONES, *Assistant Professor of Education, University of Cincinnati, Cincinnati, Ohio.*

The *SRA Achievement Series* provides an integrated testing program for measuring the educational development of pupils in grades 2–9 in the following broad curricular areas: read-ing, arithmetic, language arts, work-study skills (grades 4–9), and language perception (grades 2–4). Since "survey type" batteries are employed, each battery can of necessity include only a small sampling of the many kinds and levels of skills. In order to provide an adequate sample of items for each difficulty level covered, but at the same time to reduce the total range of difficulty, the authors decided upon a procedure which is rather unique for achievement tests. The lower end of the difficulty scale was "lopped off." This means that each battery contains no easy items suitable for the seriously retarded pupil and only a few items simple enough for the low-average learner. The upper level of each battery has been extended so that it overlaps the next higher battery to a considerable extent. As the authors indicate, this means, of course, that the slow learners will be identified but not measured. Measurement of these pupils will necessitate their taking the battery designed for the next lower school level. The idea underlying this procedure is sound. One possible disadvantage, however, is the fact that some pupils may experience undue frustration and strain because of the difficulty of the items. The procedure is particularly questionable at the primary level where undue pressure on young children may do more harm than good.

The total administration time is approximately seven hours for the grades 2–4 battery, approximately six hours for the grades 4–6 battery, and approximately six hours for the grades 6–9 battery. The series rightly emphasizes power rather than speed, and all time limits appear to be quite generous.

The authors are to be commended for including comprehensive data concerning standard errors of measurement along with means, standard deviations, and Kuder-Richardson reliabilities (coefficients of internal consistency). The Technical Supplement indicates that, because Kuder-Richardson (formula 21) reliabilities yield much lower coefficients than the split-half technique, it would appear that the split-half reliabilities for the test scores are in the high .80's and low .90's. As the authors state, split-half coefficients of this magnitude are generally viewed as being reasonably sufficient for individual evaluation. It should be noted, however, that the reliabilities obtained for the battery for grades 2–4 are, in general, lower than those obtained for the higher grade levels.

As stated in the Technical Supplement, this tendency is most likely a function of increased heterogeneity of test scores as growth occurs in the basic achievement skills. Four scores based on relatively few items (charts, 4–6; spelling, 6–9; and arithmetic concepts, 4–6 and 6–9) yielded reliability coefficients sufficient for group evaluation only.

The product-moment intercorrelations among the various subtests generally run in the .50's and .60's. This seems to indicate that, while the separate tests are measuring several achievements in common, each score is providing some unique information regarding educational achievement.

In the Technical Supplement the authors report a few studies which have been made concerning the predictive validity of the series and state that "on the basis of the studies reported above, it is quite evident that the *SRA Achievement Series* predicts high school achievement." The correlations obtained are comparatively high, but this matter will require further investigation.

Content validity and construct validity are adequately discussed in the supplementary material, and the detailed presentation of the foundations and rationale of the series is better than the average. The authors are also to be commended for their cognizance of the fact that such tests do not provide adequate individual diagnosis when they state, "Although the items dealing with a specific skill are often too few in number to provide a reliable diagnostic instrument for individual pupils, the strengths and weaknesses of a group can be determined with much greater accuracy."

The Teacher's Handbook is a well-written guide to the interpretation and follow-up of achievement scores. The interesting and informative ideas presented in the booklet should be of value to any teacher of the lower school grades. Cautions to be observed in interpreting norms and pupil profiles and excellent discussions of the development of various skills are examples of the topics covered. There are some errors, however, in the footnote references to tables, specifically in the footnotes on pages 19, 26, and 38 of the handbook.

As an aid in curriculum evaluation and curriculum planning the school administrator should find the Manual for the School Adminstrator quite helpful. This manual includes statements of the specific objectives which served as the basis for constructing test items, analyses of the skills operating in each item, and suggestions for the series' use as a basis for organizing instruction. Much of the material would be useful to the classroom teacher when making his analysis of class errors. Consequently, additional copies of the manual might be needed for individual teachers to use along with the Teacher's Handbook.

THE SEPARATE TESTS. The reading test is composed of complete stories rather than isolated and disconnected short paragraphs. The stories reportedly were constructed on the basis of surveys of children's interests at the various grade levels and on the types of reading matter that children are called upon to read. Fiction, science, biography, and the social studies are represented in the selections. Comprehension scores and vocabulary scores are obtained.

The three sections of the arithmetic test involve reasoning, concepts and usage, and computation. The reasoning section uses a "story" approach to word problems; the concepts and usage section is composed of many different types of items in which the pupil is asked to translate verbal forms into mathematical symbols, to demonstrate his knowledge of the vocabulary of arithmetic, and to indicate the degree of his understanding of mathematical ideas; and the third section of the test measures the pupil's ability to compute whole numbers, fractions, decimals, and denominate numbers. At the advanced levels, questions deal with such specialized concepts as interest, insurance premiums, areas, and volumes. An examination of the number problems on the test for grades 2–4 reveals that in many instances the answer blocks are not properly spaced. The line on the right side of the block is often directly beneath the column of numbers to be computed. It is felt that the blocks should be extended so that pupils can keep their answers directly in line with the columns in the problems.

Three broad areas are measured by the language arts test: correct use of capitalization and punctuation, language usage, and spelling. The test items are presented in the context of a story or other type of reading selection. The pupil must judge whether the items are correct as they appear in the selection. When he does find an error, he indicates the correct form from a list of alternatives.

Two subscores are obtained from the work-study skills test: a composite score based on competence in the use of tables of contents, indexes, and general reference materials, and a score based on achievement in interpreting various types of charts. This particular test does not measure a specific content area of the curriculum, but it attempts to include basic skills common to all curriculum areas.

As an adjunct to the reading test, the language perception test has been designed, for general use in grade 2 and more limited use in grades 3, 4, and 5, to provide information as to possible causes of retarded reading. The three subtests correspond to three major phases of beginning reading: auditory discrimination, visual discrimination, and sight vocabulary. In administering this test, the examiner must read words which certainly require proper pronunciation and enunciation. Although it can be assumed that the examiner will speak clearly and distinctly, the manual should emphasize this point.

STANDARDIZATION. A total of some 8,000 pupils were tested at the tryout stages of the various batteries and forms, and each revision of a test was administered to at least three classes at each grade level. A total of 21,512 pupils from more than 100 different school systems were retained in the final normative sample. The total sample was broken down into eight groups, each group being designated by major geographical region (East, Midwest, South, West), and size of the community (urban or rural). An attempt was made to match the number drawn in each group with the proportion of each group in the American school population. Statements made indicate that quotas of pupils and school districts were selected "at random," although the precise randomizing method employed is not explained. Pupil variables considered in an effort to obtain representativeness included educational level, sex, place of residence, intelligence level, and socio-economic level. The South is under-represented in the total normative sample because of "unexpected difficulty in obtaining a sufficient number of representative southern schools." No further explanation is given in the material. Although the total number of pupils included in the normative sample is comparatively small, particularly the number taking the 4–6 battery, it is quite probable that a more representative norm group was obtained through the selective process involved.

Subsequent to the original development and standardization of the series several modifications have been made. The most important of these were the extension of the range of grade equivalent norms and the addition of a spelling test of the recall type to the 2–4 battery at the time Form B was developed.

SUMMARY. The *SRA Achievement Series* attempts to measure the development of understandings and skills in applying learning rather than the acquisition of factual knowledge only. This is done through a "true-to-life" or holistic approach which emphasizes "the embedding of test items in a background or the arranging of groups of items so that each member of the group is functionally related to the others." Although the reviewer agrees with this approach, he is not convinced that all the situations presented adequately meet the "true-to-life" criterion. Each individual must decide that himself.

In general, the items are well constructed. The format is attractive, the instructions are adequate, and the supplementary materials are quite good. The careful analysis of test items in relation to specific educational objectives adds much to the validity of the series. Prospective test users should keep in mind that the batteries yield an adequate measure of achievement at the grade levels designated for all but the slow learners. Retarded pupils will have to be given the battery designed for the next lower level.

For reviews by Constance M. McCullough and Winifred L. Post of the language test, see 200. For reviews by Robert D. North and J. Fred Weaver of the arithmetic test, see 483. For reviews by Norman Dale Bryant and Clarence Derrick of the reading test, see 649. For reviews by Robert L. Ebel and Ruth M. Strang of the work-study skills test, see 696.

[22]

★SRA High School Placement Test. Grades 8.5–9.5; 1957–58; the 1957 intelligence subtest is the same as Form T of the *Purdue Non-Language Test*, other subtests are the same as the corresponding tests in Form A of the *SRA Achievement Series* for grades 6–9; 5 scores: intelligence, arithmetic, reading, vocabulary, total; IBM; 2 editions: 1957, 1958; new form published annually; separate answer sheets must be used; $1 per student; fee includes loan of tests and scoring service; postage extra; 130(150) minutes; Science Research Associates. *

CYRIL J. HOYT, *Associate Professor of Education*, and W. WESLEY TENNYSON, *Assistant Professor of Education, University of Minnesota, Minneapolis, Minnesota.*

The 1957 form of this battery included a duplication of Form A of the arithmetic computation, reading comprehension, and vocabulary tests from the *SRA Achievement Series,* level 6–9. In the 1958 form the reading and arithmetic portions are reproductions of the corresponding sections of the *SRA Achievement Series* only in the sense that the item specifications are the same.

The reviewers' letter from the publisher's editorial department dated June 20, 1958 states: "though several reliability and validity studies are being planned for this summer, I have no unpublished data on the validities of the HSPT. A new Technical Supplement will be published at the end of the year, containing reports of the studies we conduct this summer." In the interests of producing a new and "secure" form of HSPT the publishers have neglected, according to this correspondence, to make reliability and validity studies prior to widespread marketing. This practice is inexcusable. In test publication some reputable publishers have been inclined to rely on their reputation for previous work well done.

The remaining part of the 1957 HSPT consists of the *Purdue Non-Language Test.* (The corresponding part of the 1958 edition parallels the Purdue test in item type but does not duplicate it.) This is a pictorial reasoning test composed of 48 items in which the testee is directed to indicate the one of a group of five geometric figures that "does not belong." The technical manual for the Purdue test (which is sent to users only at their request) states that "no situational validity studies of the test are yet available." This manual does give adequate information on the reliability of the nonlanguage test, but information is lacking regarding its correlation with other group tests of intellectual ability. Norm data reported in this manual are inadequate.

Norms for the achievement tests in the 1957 edition are apparently those developed with the 1955 standardization of the *SRA Achievement Series* of which the three tests are subtests. These are based on scores from a national sample of 5,512 school children. Sufficient care was taken in sampling to assure adequacy of these norm data. However, no information is given concerning the norm group for the achievement tests in the 1958 form.

The pictorial reasoning test (since it is not part of the *SRA Achievement Series*) was not included in the 1955 norming study. Two series of equating studies using the equipercentile method of test equating were undertaken "to make the pictorial-reasoning scores directly comparable to those of the achievement tests." Underlying this method of equating is the assumption that factors measured by the two kinds of tests are perfectly correlated. Is there any justification for a test publisher to make this assumption when the factors dealt with are intelligence and achievement? A user of the pictorial reasoning test will find it difficult to know what the scores of his students on this test really mean.

A technical supplement to the HSPT manual for the 1957 form gives the user some useful information about the predictive power of the achievement sections, but corresponding information on the current (1958) form was not available sufficiently soon to give prospective users an adequate basis for choosing this test in the spring of 1958.

The reviewers arranged to have the 1958 form of the HSPT administered during April 1958 to 71 pupils in the eighth grade at the University of Minnesota High School. Directions in the manual were adhered to explicitly in administering the test to these pupils. The following conclusions are based on this administration.

Administration is complicated by the arrangement of the manual. Some sections of the directions to be read aloud to the pupils are interspersed with others not to be read. Though brackets and boldface type are used to distinguish these sections, the manual would be improved if uniform indentation were used to indicate sections to be read aloud.

The directions to pupils, "You should not hurry....You will have plenty of time to work carefully on all the test questions," are misleading. Twenty per cent of the group tested by the reviewers did not complete the pictorial test within the time limits and 83 per cent did not complete the arithmetic section. Only a small percentage of the group, however, were working when time was called for the reading test.

The format and organization of the tests could be improved. Typographical errors and omissions, although not numerous, do occur in the test booklet. Some students appeared confused by the right to left marking of the answer sheet. Such would not be the case if answer sheet items corresponded spacewise with questions in the test booklet, and if students were instructed to slip the unused part of the answer sheet under the test booklet. A more serious weakness in format resides in the arrangement of tests within the booklet. Although it would not appear practical to issue a battery of this kind in separate booklets, it would seem wise to arrange the tests in the booklet in such a way that distinct separation is maintained for each. For example, an admonition contained in the directions that students are to "Stop Here" at the end of the pictorial test is contraindicated by the fact that the directions and sample exercises for the second test, arithmetic, lie open before them. This weakness in format becomes even more apparent in the reading achievement test, where the first section ends and the second sections begins on the same page.

Appropriateness of the story content and questions in the sample directions of the reading achievement test may be seriously questioned in the opinion of these reviewers. The sample story entitled "A Dog Hero" obviously is designed to appeal to students of a lower grade level than that for which the test is intended. A humorous element in the first story, "Of Dogs and Men," would prove less unsettling to the group tested if this story were placed at a later position in the test.

Though the sample used by the reviewers was small, it did consist of a whole grade in one school. The following correlations were found between scores on corresponding parts of the *Iowa Every-Pupil Test of Basic Skills* and the *SRA High School Placement Test:* reading, .75; vocabulary, .77; and arithmetic, .66. A correlation of .44 was found between scores on the pictorial reasoning subtest and verbal scores on the *Lorge-Thorndike Intelligence Test.*

OVERALL EVALUATION. Among the stated purposes to be served by this test are: (a) to determine which pupils to admit to high schools with limited enrollments, and (b) to classify incoming ninth graders according to ability. Private schools which must be selective and other schools which receive large numbers of transfer students would certainly find this type of testing desirable. The reviewers, however, have misgivings about the wisdom of encouraging schools to use a test which they have not seen, and for which there is a lack of adequate statistical data.

Although the content of the *SRA High School Placement Test* was determined jointly by members of the publisher's professional staff and a group of 77 administrators of public, private, and parochial high schools, the decision to include a nonlanguage test of intelligence does not appear to be in keeping with the intended functions mentioned above. The type of prediction needed to serve such purposes could be achieved more effectively by measuring students' present functioning ability with a good, verbal test of intelligence.

WILLIAM W. TURNBULL, *Executive Vice President, Educational Testing Service, Princeton, New Jersey.*

The *SRA High School Placement Test* is designed for use with entering high school students (grade 9) for purposes of selective admission, ability grouping, and guidance and placement with respect to curricula, general or academic. The test is not sold to schools. Rather, the necessary materials are loaned to schools and returned to the publisher for scoring and reporting of scores. It is the intention of the publisher to bring out a new edition yearly to maintain the security of the materials. For the first edition (1957), the intelligence test consists of a reproduction in toto of Form T of the *Purdue Non-Language Test,* while the remaining sections (Arithmetic Computation, Reading Comprehension, General Vocabulary) are reproductions of tests from the *SRA Achievement Series* for grades 6–9.

The four separate scores yielded by the test (other than the total score) cannot, of course, provide an adequate basis for high school placement (for instance, such topics as grammar, social studies, and science are omitted) but together with the total score they will probably serve fairly well as a basis for general ability grouping.

The first section of the test (Pictorial Test of Intelligence) represents an attempt to provide a measure of general ability independent of reading and arithmetic. This is a worthy goal. The dilemma is that usually the more independent a test is made the less useful it becomes. No data are provided on the relations between scores on this part of the test and the other sections individually, but correlations with the average of the three other scores are reported as .45 and .56 in two studies. This relation is low enough to suggest that the pictorial test is indeed fairly independent of the other scores. Whether the score relates in a useful way to any facet of school work is not indicated by any data so far reported. The technical supplement to the test manual states, "In general, this score should be regarded as an aid to pupil understanding and guidance, but it will probably not prove to be highly predictive of actual achievement in school work." It is hard to see how a score can be useful in guidance if it is not predictive of achievement. In this reviewer's opinion, the time given to this part of the test might better be used to permit more scores related to progress in areas of the curriculum not now covered.

The test of arithmetic computation is a well constructed section that should provide a useful score on this important achievement area. The tests of reading comprehension and vocabulary are also well made. The comprehension questions cover important skills in the main and the vocabulary items, derived from the reading passages, seem well chosen. Data on the intercorrelations of the comprehension and vocabulary scores show the relation to be so high that the scores could be combined to good advantage. In fact, this has been done in the validity studies. It might well be carried over to the scores reported to using schools.

The reliabilities of all of the tests seem adequate for work with individual students. As previously noted, the validity of the pictorial test is not predicated on its relation with school work and is not supported by any evidence presented. Data are given showing a good correlation (.60 to .66) between the reading scores (comprehension and vocabulary combined) and total grade averages. So far the studies reported are skimpy, but it is noted that further work is planned and there is every reason to expect that reliable scores based on the well proven varieties of reading materials here included will provide useful predictions of the general magnitude shown to date.

The data given do not permit an evaluation of the difficulties of the various sections: no score distributions or averages are presented. One wonders if a test designed for general use in grades 6 to 9 will be difficult enough to do a good job in determining "which students to admit to high schools with limited enrollments." It is noted that norms for arithmetic, reading, and vocabulary were derived from a carefully stratified sample of over 2,000 students in each of grades 8 and 9, but norms are not supplied. (Presumably they are furnished when the scores are reported.) For the pictorial test, which was not given to the norming group,

comparability of the scores with those on the other sections is provided through a study based on students in eastern parochial schools. Insofar as these students are unrepresentative of the total sample, the relation established is suspect. After the tests have been used as a complete set, it is to be hoped that norms for all of them will be derived from the same student group.

In summary, the *SRA High School Placement Test* will probably prove to be a useful aid in ability grouping in the junior high school. Inclusion of the pictorial intelligence test is questioned, as is omission of such important topics as grammar and social or natural science, without which the usefulness of the test for placement will be limited.

[23]

★**Scholastic Achievement Series.** Grades 1.5–2.5, 2.5–3, 4–6, 7–9; 1953–55; various titles used by publisher; for Catholic schools; 11–13 scores: English (total and 2–4 subtests), spelling, arithmetic (total and 2 subtests), religion (total and 3 subtests); IBM for grades 4–9; 2 forms; 4 levels; subtests in English-spelling and arithmetic available as separates; manual ('55) for each level; separate answer sheets may be used in grades 4–9; $3.50 per 35 IBM scorable answer sheets; 50¢ per specimen set of any one level; postage extra; Oliver F. Anderhalter, R. Stephen Gawkoski, and John O'Brien; Scholastic Testing Service, Inc. *
a) PRE-PRIMARY BATTERY. Grades 1.5–2.5; 1955; Form A; $4.85 per 35 tests; (65–75) minutes.
b) PRIMARY BATTERY. Grades 2.5–3; 1953–55; Forms A ('53), B ('55); $4.85 per 35 tests; (85–95) minutes.
c) ELEMENTARY BATTERY. Grades 4–6; 1954–55; IBM; Forms A ('54), B ('55); $6 per 35 tests; $4.90 per 35 IBM scorable answer sheets; 60¢ per set of scoring stencils; (145) minutes.
d) ADVANCED BATTERY. Grades 7–9; 1954–55; IBM; Forms A, B ('54); $6 per 35 tests; $4.55 per 35 IBM scorable answer sheets; 48¢ per set of scoring stencils; (145) minutes.

WILLIAM E. COFFMAN, *Director, Test Development Division, Educational Testing Service, Princeton, New Jersey.*

This series of tests has been specifically designed to measure "readily identifiable objectives of the Catholic school curriculum." The authors point out that the primary impetus for the development of the tests was the need for tests in religion, a major area of instruction in Catholic schools. They indicate, however, that evidence of cultural differences between the Catholic school population and the population of public school pupils, and the desirability of having comparable norms for tests in religion and in other subjects "call for a distinct set of norms to serve as standards of achievement in Catholic schools." The norms, based as they are on a total of 119,978 individuals representing 448 different schools in 304 different cities spread geographically from coast to coast, are probably representative of Catholic schools which use tests. With such a sample, it is unfortunate that the test authors have not reported information about the variability among schools. Without this information, it is likely that some schools will be satisfied at having exceeded the norms and that other schools will be deeply concerned at being below the norms without justification in either case. The users should certainly exercise extreme caution in using the norms "as standards of achievement" in the absence of evidence that Catholic schools are, in fact, sufficiently homogeneous to justify common standards of achievement.

The several tests and their accompanying manuals are excellent examples of the printer's art. The directions for administering and scoring the tests are specific and clear; the descriptions of the test development procedures indicate a clearly conceived and rigorously followed rationale; the statistical data required for a comprehensive evaluation of the tests as measuring instruments are provided in easily understood form. Particularly noteworthy are (a) the selection of items of middle difficulty wherever possible within the requirements of the content specifications, (b) the provision of three different types of reliability coefficients for the Elementary and Advanced Batteries—split-half, Kuder-Richardson formula 20, and parallel-forms, (c) the use of tertile norms for interpreting scores on certain subtests with too few items to give reliable scores, (d) the encouragement of the user to refer to percentile norms as a supplement in interpreting grade scores, and (e) the reporting of data regarding the statistical validity of the Advanced Battery. In general, the statistical procedures employed by the authors and the suggestions given for interpreting the statistical data are appropriate.

Unfortunately, there are a few instances where the user without special training might be misled. Validity data based on the Advanced Battery are reported in the manuals for both the Elementary and Primary Batteries and might be interpreted as directly applicable to those batteries. Similarly, the table of reliabilities for the Elementary Battery is printed in the manual for the Primary Battery without a clear indication that the figures are not directly ap-

plicable to the tests in that battery. The standard errors of measurement are reported in raw score form while the percentile tables are in grade score form. If one wishes to estimate the degree of error associated with the percentiles, it is necessary first to refer to the tables of equivalent scores either in the test booklet or on the answer sheet. The tables of equivalent scores are themselves somewhat misleading since they contain equivalent grade scores for the full range of raw scores even though, for most of the tests, scores at the low end of the range might easily be obtained by marking answers at random. This is particularly true for certain of the subtests in English and religion where there are 2-choice or 3-choice items. The reviewer marked answers at random to Test 2 of the Elementary Battery and obtained a score of 5.2, a score which is equivalent to the 75th percentile for fourth graders during the first half of the year. While it is true that school children generally take tests at their face value, the teacher should be warned of the possibility of relatively high chance scores in exceptional cases. At the pre-primary level, the test in religion is administered by having the teacher read both questions and answers while the pupil follows in his booklet and marks his answers. This procedure is subject to variation depending on the skill and orientation of the person administering the test. It is almost impossible, without considerable training of administrators, to achieve standardized administration conditions. For this reason a split-half reliability coefficient (the only type available since there is only one form of the test at this level) is likely to be significantly higher than a parallel forms coefficient based on the administration of two forms by different administrators.

The test items, with few exceptions, reflect considerable care in construction. Distractors are generally attractive, the several areas have been sampled adequately, and the two forms at the three higher levels are parallel in content and difficulty. Perhaps the most serious defect in item construction is the use of the option "not given" with arithmetic computation problems without a clear indication of the degree of exactness intended. For example, for Item 17 of Test 6A in Form B of the Advanced Battery, the answer is 54.5405405+. Shall the student mark "54.54" or "not given" as the answer? In Test 9 of the same booklet, Item 4 and Item 18 ask essentially the same question, with the correct response common to the two items and the other distractors being clearly different. The punctuation subtest is presented in a form which is difficult to use, the several options being printed on a single line in the same type as the option letters with successive lines separated by insufficient leading.

The authors have been reasonably successful in developing some items in the religion tests, particularly at the higher levels, which require the pupil to apply what he has learned in a new situation. Pupils who score high on these tests demonstrate more than rote memory. The arithmetic computation and arithmetic problems tests require the pupil to demonstrate skill and understanding. The English tests, however, are essentially exercise book questions, requiring the pupil to "fill in the blank" with a correct punctuation mark, to indicate which of a number of underlined letters should be capitalized, to identify points of formal grammar and syntax, to choose correct forms, or to supply pat answers to procedural questions such as: "Sentences not related to the topic of a paragraph are called (a) ending sentences, (b) misfit sentences, (c) independent sentences." Since each subtest is concerned with only one or two types of error, the pupil is able to concentrate on limited aspects of English expression, a procedure quite unlike the one he must use when writing his own composition. One completes a detailed study of the tests with the impression that if pupils are required to have such detailed knowledge of the minutiae of English, both they and their teachers will be tempted to focus on the minutiae to the neglect of the main objective, which is assumed to be the ability to speak and write correctly and effectively. A similar impression develops from an examination of the tests in religion at the primary and pre-primary levels.

There is always danger that when a test battery is limited to "readily identifiable objectives," it may encourage schools to strive for higher scores on these to the neglect of less easily identifiable but often more fundamental objectives. Certainly a test manual should warn of this danger and suggest the nature of other objectives which should be evaluated in other ways—such objectives as understanding in the sciences and in the social studies; ability to write and speak effectively; awareness of the wealth of our literary heritage; ability to use such tools of learning as the dictionary, the

encyclopedia, maps, charts, and graphs; and personal health. The development of a set of diagnostic tests in English, spelling, arithmetic, and religion is a worthy project. At the same time, the very excellence of the tests from a technical standpoint may encourage users to overemphasize the specifics of the diagnostic test to the exclusion of broad integrative skills and understandings.

The authors have made available to Catholic schools a set of diagnostic tests covering certain very limited outcomes toward which teachers in these schools may direct their efforts. The normative data and the evidence of reliability and validity are reasonably adequate for newly published tests; however, the tests themselves should be carefully examined to determine whether the questions really cover what the user wishes to measure. It would be well for the authors to consider the possibility of providing the users with additional data as they become available—data on the validity of the tests at the pre-primary, the primary, and the elementary levels; data on the reliability of the Primary Battery; information about the variability of mean scores for different schools; information about growth over a period of time. At the same time, they might consider providing in a supplement to the manual a clear statement of the need for additional kinds of information about student achievement if one wishes to make a comprehensive evaluation of an elementary school program in the complex 20th century culture of which we are a part.

James R. Hayden, *Assistant Superintendent, New Bedford Public Schools, New Bedford, Massachusetts.*

The distinctive feature of the *Scholastic Achievement Series* is the inclusion of a test of religion in addition to tests of English, spelling, and arithmetic at all four levels. In the words of the authors, the battery was constructed because "Differences existing in the Catholic Schools were felt to be of such magnitude as to cast considerable doubt upon the validity of many existing tests when used in such schools." The manuals indicate neither the magnitude nor the nature of these differences. Public and private school norms have been published for several achievement tests in the past. Some textbook publishing companies do print Catholic geography and history books giving weight to the history of the Catholic Church. A different and earlier approach in Catholic schools to the content of arithmetic and grammar undoubtedly does affect the content validity of some of the published achievement batteries. Hence, it is regrettable that the authors missed the opportunity to measure these differences and thus demonstrate the validity of their instruments.

CONTENT VALIDITY. Content validity is based on the analysis of courses of study in schools representing 46 per cent of the dioceses in the country. The distribution is not described. Items were contributed by teachers in each subject matter field and more than 27,000 Catholic elementary school children participated in the experimental tryout. No item was retained, the authors report, unless an increase of at least 8 per cent correct response was shown between successive grades. Relationship of test item to total score was determined in terms of tetrachoric coefficients of correlation and no item was retained if the average coefficient obtained from the several grades taking each item fell below .25.

CONCURRENT VALIDITY. Concurrent validity is based on the correlations with scores on the *Scholastic Mental Ability Test* and the *Scholastic Diagnostic Reading Test,* and with letter grades. No reliability data are presented concerning these criteria. The correlations based on the letter grades of 70 eighth grade students are presented in the manual for the Advanced Battery. In lieu of descriptive data, one is forced to conclude that the letter grades represent the opinions of two or three teachers at the most. These same 70 students were graded "superior," "average," and "low" and their median grade equivalents attained on the test battery are also presented. While data based on such small numbers are of questionable interest, one is at a loss to understand why the same tables with the same data are presented in the manuals intended for the primary and elementary grades from upper 2 through 6.

RELIABILITY. Reliability data based on correlations obtained by the split-half method, Kuder-Richardson formula 20, and the alternate-forms method are presented in each manual. The primary and elementary level manuals present exactly the same data as evidence of reliability. These tables report the same standard deviations and the same standard errors for this entire spread from upper grade 2 through grade 6. The authors state that 100 individuals were chosen at random at each grade

level and that the coefficients reported represent the median of the single-year coefficients. While this may be a space saving device, it certainly conceals more than it reveals. Reliability data for the preprimary and advanced levels do differ, but even here only the median estimates are given. Is it too much to ask for a standard deviation and a standard error of measurement at each grade level?

ADMINISTRATION. While the time required to take the battery differs from level to level, no directions are given as to the desirable number of sittings, total testing time, or estimated administration time. No correction for guessing is used on any of the tests, nor are there any directions given to students concerning guessing. Directions for the use of machine scored answer sheets are limited to space-blackening instructions and the mention of special pencils. Many manuals on the market today save the test user time and money by setting up definite routines concerning the proper marking of answer sheets before and after the test.

FORMAT. The printing of both booklets and answer sheets leaves much to be desired. The scales on the answer sheets are in some cases so small and blurred as to be unintelligible. In some of the booklets, certain words appear to be in bold face type, due perhaps to poor inking. This directs the attention of the pupil to these words in a confusing manner. Individual profiles are provided with each booklet on which may be plotted the student's performance in terms of grade equivalents. No cautions are given the test user concerning the interpretation of the profile or the reliability of the differences revealed.

NORMS. The normative group was drawn from 304 cities with "adequate representation from East, South, Midwest, Far West and Southwest." How adequate the representation is the test user must take on faith. The manual sets forth no breakdown of the standardization population. While the user is cautioned against the use of grade equivalents above 10.0, a paragraph at this point concerning the value of local norms and how they might be compiled would be a commendable service. Since no sampling plan or breakdown of the standardization population is published, one must assume that data were collected on the basis of availability. Willingness to participate is a selective factor which affects all sampling procedures to some degree. For this reason, a carefully planned and obtained stratified sample is extremely important. In the absence of such normative data, one can speculate but not conclude as to whether or not regional norms would have been more appropriate than a single set. Percentiles are furnished in addition to grade equivalents, but it is disappointing to find no evidence of standard scores. It would seem that standard scores would be essential to a battery with a range from grades 1 through 9 which is evidently intended for use in conjunction with other measures published by the same company.

SUMMARY. This achievement battery represents a commendable attempt to provide a private school system with a series of tests which have curricular validity. The inclusion of a test of religion makes the battery unique. On the other hand, it is disappointing to find incomplete statistical evidence on some very important aspects of interpretation and standardization. Since so many test publishers are giving test users a technical supplement to the manual of directions, it is felt that the authors might well collect additional data from current users of their instruments and issue a supplementary booklet. In this manner, they would make available in more detailed fashion some information concerning the enormous amount of fine work they must have put into the construction of an achievement battery which deserves attention and use.

For reviews by Geraldine Spaulding and Ruth Strickland of the English-spelling test, see 201. For reviews by Joseph Justman and Charles S. Ross of the arithmetic test, see 484.

[24]

★Sequential Tests of Educational Progress. Grades 4–6, 7–9, 10–12, 13–14; IBM; 1956–58; also called STEP; 7 tests: Reading, Writing, Mathematics, Science, Social Studies, Listening, Essay Test; 4 levels; 40¢ per 20 profiles ('57); 60¢ per set of 20 student reports ('58) and directions ('58); 90¢ per 50 score distribution sheets ('57); $1 per manual ('57); $1 per battery technical report ('57); postage extra; Cooperative Test Division, Educational Testing Service. *

REFERENCE

1. TRAXLER, ARTHUR E. "Some Data on the Results of the Sequential Tests of Educational Progress (STEP), Level 3, Form A, for Small Groups of Pupils in Two Independent Schools for Girls." *Ed Rec B* 72:69–73 Jl '58. *

ROBERT W. B. JACKSON, *Professor of Educational Research and Director of the Department, University of Toronto, Toronto, Canada.*

The *Sequential Tests of Educational Progress* (STEP) are designed to measure the out-

comes of educational experiences, both formal and informal, from elementary school to college. On the assumption that certain critical understandings and abilities in the major academic areas are capable of definition and assessment, tests have been constructed for four of these: communication (with separate tests for reading, writing, essay writing, and listening), science, mathematics, and social studies. Although the need for specific knowledge in particular fields has been recognized in the construction of the items, it has been the intention of the authors to emphasize in particular the utilization of learned skills in solving new problems. The objectives of the tests are, therefore, sufficiently general to be considered attainable by a variety of teaching procedures and materials.

Except for the essay test, each of the sets consists of two equivalent forms at each of four levels; the essay test provides four alternative forms at each level. For each test at each level, raw scores are converted to 3-digit scaled scores, which are interpreted with reference to a continuous score scale covering all levels. The continuous scale is designed to make it possible, for example, to compare the performance of a student taking a Level 1 test in reading with that of another student taking a Level 2 test in the same area, or to compare the reading performance of the same student at various stages in his educational career as he proceeds from one level to another.

Each test in the entire STEP series, with the exception of the essay test, consists of two sections, which may be administered together in one 70-minute working period or separately in two 35-minute periods. The essay tests have only one 35-minute section. The time allowed is sufficiently great to ensure that nearly every student has time to finish the tests at the appropriate level. With the exception, again, of the essay test, all tests are of the objective multiple choice type, each item offering four possible responses. The answer sheets, which have been so designed that they are the same for all tests at all levels, may be scored by hand or machine.

The objectives of the tests in each area were defined by planning committees of educators chosen in consultation with national professional organizations, and working in conjunction with the staff of the Educational Testing Service. Members of the planning committees obtained assistance from other educators in devising suitable items. A workshop procedure was followed in the actual construction of the tests. Great advantages were seen in the pooling of ideas contributed by teachers from various geographical areas, types of schools, and fields of competence.

The literature accompanying the tests contains a detailed description of the standardization procedure. The pretesting program provided evidence concerning the difficulty and discriminating effectiveness of each item and the effectiveness of the distractors. Each test in the series required horizontal and vertical equating. The former involved matching the A and B forms of each test, while the latter made it possible to associate a single score reporting scale with all levels of each test. Samples of students for the equating program were carefully chosen.

Percentile norms are given for each of the objective tests. The norms groups for Reading, Writing, Social Studies, Science, and Mathematics consisted in each case of random fifths of entire grade groups from 4–12 in a minimum of 50 schools. The norms for Listening were obtained from a special sample of 1,000 students per grade. Norms for Level 1 were obtained by administering each of the six tests to a random sample of two students in each of grades 13 and 14 in 120 colleges. Much more than the usual care exhibited by test constructors was apparently taken in the selection of the norms groups.

The norms are presented in the form of percentile bands or confidence intervals in order to safeguard against exaggerating the precision of individual scores. The use of the norms tables is explained with illustrations. The construction of local norms is recommended, and the procedure is outlined.

No statistical evidence of validity was presented at the time the tests were released, unless correlations with SCAT are so classified. The importance of content validity is emphasized. In the Technical Report accompanying the tests, the publisher indicates that validity studies, relating test scores to suitable criterion measures, will be conducted in the future.

The tests were released with reliabilities estimated only from internal analyses of Form A based on single administrations. Standard errors of measurement are also reported. Kuder-Richardson formula 20 was employed in arriving at the estimates, which were made for each of grades 5, 8, 11, and 13. The reliability coefficients, varying from a median of .92 for Reading to one of .84 for Mathematics, are in some cases surprisingly low for internal consistency measures. Complete information on the preliminary analysis of reliability is provided, however, and recognition is given to the necessity for further work, including correlation of equivalent forms administered to a new sample of students.

The STEP series makes possible a departure from the only too common piecemeal approach to testing. For the first time, a student's development of skills and understanding in the set of major fields has been seen as a continuous process, and an attempt has been made to measure his progress on a consistent basis. The use of tests at different levels providing scores on a continuous scale overcomes the necessity of attempting to compare scores obtained on independently constructed tests designed for different purposes and different levels of attainment. The series deserves recognition, therefore, as a pioneering venture of major importance, even if no other virtues or advantages could be discovered.

The length of the tests indicates a recognition of the fact that reliable measures of educational progress cannot be obtained in snippets of time as short as or even shorter than the single class period. At the same time, the division of each test into two parts makes it possible to administer the tests without disruption of the conventional organization of the school day.

There is no doubt that the resources, time, and effort thrown into the development of the STEP series have produced tests that are in many respects of superior quality. The printing is clear and on a good grade of paper. The directions to the student and to the examiner are straightforward, unambiguous, and complete. The items are well constructed, although subject to occasional criticisms (reserved for the detailed discussion of each test which follows). The norms are accompanied by more than usual interpretation and explanation, in recognition of the fact that may intelligent and experienced test users are in need of some instruction and assistance. The amount of explanatory material provided is formidable. However, the prospective user of measuring instruments with such a comprehensive purpose can hardly begrudge the time it takes to familiarize himself with their background and characteristics. In any event, he need not read all the material, but may confine himself to certain essential sections.

The tests merit praise, also, for their attempt to measure the student's ability to apply his learning in problems of practical consequence. But, while this is a most commendable objective, there seems to be an unjustified tendency to offer understanding and application of knowledge as alternatives to the acquisition of factual information. While the learning of facts may at the worst do nothing more than tax the memory, it may also, as a part of good educational method, be an aid to understanding and the ability to deal with practical problems. The tests in mathematics, science, and social studies might well be improved by increasing the proportion of items requiring factual knowledge not obtainable by reading a supplied passage; reading with understanding is not, after all, the primary objective in these areas. Such a change need not conflict with the objective of keeping the items independent of specific courses or teaching materials.

There is a more serious question to be raised with respect to the STEP series. No matter what admirable qualities the tests possess, they can be justified ultimately only on the ground that they touch on some dimension not measured, or at least not measured as efficiently, by some other instrument. In this connection, the correlations between STEP scores and Verbal, Quantitative, and Total scores on SCAT reported by the publisher are worth careful attention. For particular grade groups, some of these correlations are in the high .80's. In fact, they often approach in value the internal consistency coefficients reported for the same tests.

While the publisher notes that the SCAT-STEP correlations are quite high, the conclusion reached on the basis of the differences between these and the reliability coefficients is that "this evidence indicates that the total score on SCAT measures something different from a total score on STEP." Actually, in terms of the so-called "attenuation" effect, a more reasonable interpretation of the figures is that, with the possible exception of the higher grades, the two instruments often come so close to measuring the same thing as to cast doubt on the value of administering both to the same students. In their desire to keep clear of specific subject matter, the authors have apparently tended to arrive at something not too far from

a *set* of measures of general intelligence. Further evidence in this connection, particularly in regard to intercorrelations among the tests of the different STEP series, will be awaited with interest. The basic similarity among certain reading, science, and social studies items, it should perhaps be pointed out, leads to the expectation that these may be uncomfortably high.

READING. The reading test calls for ability "to understand direct statements, to interpret and summarize passages, to see motives of authors, to observe organization of ideas, and to criticize passages with respect to ideas and purposes of presentation." The degree of emphasis on particular objectives in this list was decided by expert opinion.

The passages are intended to represent the major types of material which students are called upon to read. In the opinion of the present writer, however, these passages are too heavily weighted on the side of the mundane and the prosaic. Beauty of thought and expression are given a less important place than they deserve. A student's education should help him to rise to higher levels of intellectual and emotional experience than he will gain simply by handling everyday problems. If such an aim is to be achieved, measurement, as part of the educational process, should assume some of the responsibility. Teachers' ideas of what is worth teaching are bound to be influenced by what testmakers consider worth using in their tests.

Some of the conventional problems of item construction have not been solved too satisfactorily. In most places, the student is expected to recognize the single correct response. Sometimes, however, he is confronted with the necessity of selecting the most satisfactory response from among several having some element of truth. A clearer distinction between these types of items would help to avoid confusion.

Where three independent responses are offered, and the fourth reads "all of these," the student need only recognize the appropriateness of any two of the former in order to realize that the fourth is correct. This type of item does not conform to the theory that each distractor should perform a useful function.

WRITING. The so-called "writing" test is not very satisfactorily named, especially in view of the existence of the test called "essay." The former does not actually involve any writing, but consists rather of a critical evaluation of what others have written. It purports to measure "ability to think critically in writing, to organize materials, to write material appropriate for a given purpose, to write effectively, and to observe conventional usage in punctuation and grammar." Whether these comprehensive objectives can be achieved by pointing out defects and suggesting improvements in actual student writing under various circumstances is to be doubted. More modest claims for what the test can do are in order.

The set contains several examples of defective items. In one case, what seems to be an obviously grammatically incorrect answer is designated as correct in the answer key (Form 1A, Part 2, Item 8) and in another (Form 3B, Part 2, Item 15) the substitute designated is very poor. The introductory question in another item, "What about the word *so* in Sentence 5?" (Form 2B, Part 2, Item 4) is a classic example of the vague wording that teachers-in-training are warned against using in practice teaching. Occasionally a pair of items may be found with an element of interdependence (Form 2B, Part 1, Items 25 and 28; Form 3B, Part 2, Items 20 and 21).

In general, the correct response is too often a matter of opinion. Some items involving suggested improvements offer no really satisfactory response (Form 1B, Part 2, Item 16).

LISTENING. This test is intended to measure the ability "to comprehend main ideas and remember significant details, to understand the implications of the ideas and details, and to evaluate and apply the material presented." As is true of the reading test, the passages upon which the items are based consist of a wide variety of types of material. This material appears to be, on the whole, very well chosen. It might be better, however, to include a less familiar poem than the one in Form 3A, since, to the extent that it has been studied or memorized by students, it is invalid for the purpose of testing listening skills.

One suspects that a certain number of items could be answered by choosing the most sensible sounding response or by relying on previously obtained information, without reference to the passage at all (Form 2B, Part 1, Item 15; Form 3A, Part 1, Item 29; Form 4A, Part 1, Items 1, 8, and 33). It might be an interesting experiment to see whether a group of students could obtain a better-than-chance score by

marking the items without hearing the passages read.

A few of the items have defects noted in connection with the reading and writing tests. Where the correct response is a matter of opinion, there is sometimes room for disagreement (Form 1B, Part 1, Item 30). In spite of the research the publisher claims was done on the effectiveness of the distractors, one wonders whether certain ones would actually have much appeal (Form 2B, Part 1, Item 13, choice D; Form 4B, Part 2, Item 11, choice C). Sometimes the answer designated as correct does not make much sense, even though it is better than the alternatives (Form 4A, Part 2, Item 24).

On the whole, only a very small proportion of the items can be adversely criticized. The test appears to be one of the most satisfactory of the series. It should perform a useful function in helping to emphasize the importance of oral communication among school-learned skills.

ESSAY. The essay writing test varies considerably from the others in the series, as has already been indicated. The most fundamental difference is in the inevitably large element of subjectivity in scoring. It has been rightly recognized, however, that this subjective element should not be used as an excuse to eliminate free response tests of writing ability.

The test has been standardized to the extent that the student is given a topic area in each of the four forms at each level, there is a definite time limit of 35 minutes, and writing performance is scored in terms of comparison of each paper with those written by other students and rated by committees of experts. A handbook provides at each level a number of comparison essays, together with ratings and brief comments. There is room for disagreement with the experts on the relative emphasis to be placed on such aspects as quality of thought, style, and mechanics.

A serious difficulty, which the test authors cannot be criticized for failing to overcome, is that considerable skill is needed to score the test. In this respect, the test does not represent much improvement over teacher-assigned topics and teacher-scored examinations; in fact, an imaginative teacher might well improve on at least the selection of topics.

Perhaps one of the chief values in the set lies in the educational effect it will have on teachers of language who study the comparison essays. There is, as always under such circumstances, some danger that average or typical performance may be accepted as a goal. However, the poor quality of even the better essays should prove a safeguard against such an eventuality, especially if the teacher accepts the responsibility of maintaining constant contact with models of good writing.

SCIENCE. The purpose of this series is to measure "ability to identify and define scientific problems, to suggest or eliminate hypotheses, to interpret data and draw conclusions, to evaluate critically statements by others, and to reason quantitatively and symbolically." The questions emphasize applications of science in home, economic, cultural, and social situations, with approximately 40 per cent of the questions relating to biology alone. It seems to the present writer that this emphasis is somewhat misplaced. While the test may measure quite satisfactorily a student's ability to fit into society and handle the "scientific" problems that he will find in everyday living if he leaves school at any particular level, it does not appear to be designed to indicate whether he has a foundation for more advanced and specialized scientific studies (the college level forms have many more items from the fields of chemistry and physics). In this connection, in particular, it would be well to include more items demanding a knowledge of basic facts. The student who does not know the facts and does not know where to find the facts is not a satisfactory educational product, and it is doubtful if he is capable of demonstrating the abilities listed at the beginning of this paragraph in any high degree.

One might question the inclusion of items referring to traffic safety in a science test (Form 4A, Part 1, Item 15) unless they involve scientific principles. There appears to be an unjustified overlap here with the social studies test.

An occasional item is weak. For example, the correct answer to Item 25, Form 1A, Part 1, is supposed to be that "most organisms show individual differences," even though the graph upon which this conclusion is based shows the growth curves of rats, and no information is given about any other type of organism. There is occasionally room for disagreement over the correct answer to an item (Form 3B, Part 2, Item 16) but, on the whole, the items are unusually free from defects.

MATHEMATICS. The purpose of this test is to measure "mastery of the following broad mathematical concepts: number and operation, symbolism, measurement and geometry, function and relation, deduction and inference, and probability and statistics." Like the science test, the mathematics test places undue emphasis on the type of problem one is likely to encounter in a rather routine everyday existence (presumably what is referred to as "a strong pragmatic emphasis"), and too little on understanding and knowledge that might provide a foundation for more advanced work. Little is demanded in this test beyond the common arithmetic operations and simple algebra and geometry.

Comparatively few of the items provide grounds for criticism. In the writer's opinion, those involving nonquantitative reasoning only (Form 3A, Part 2, Item 18; Form 2A, Part 2, Item 18; Form 2B, Part 2, Item 22) do not belong in a mathematics test. One distractor for an item referring to the orbits of satellites (Form 1A, Part 2, Item 19) is rendered ineffective by a discussion of a parabola on the same page.

SOCIAL STUDIES. The social studies test is intended to measure "social studies understandings, abilities to read and interpret social studies material (maps, graphs, the printed word, etc.), skills in seeing relationships among basic facts, trends, and concepts, and ability to analyze such material critically." Again there seems to be too little emphasis on knowledge of subject matter, although all significant areas of social studies are included in the problems. Too much of the material is apparently intended to test only reading skill, although one cannot quarrel with this objective if it is kept in its proper place.

While all tests in the STEP series were designed for American students, that fact need not, for the most part, prevent their serving a useful purpose if used in other English-speaking countries. The social studies test is inevitably an exception, and is not suitable for use outside the United States.

The "correct" response to at least one item is questionable (Form 3B, Part 1, Item 35). Some items intended to test ability to read a graph could be answered from general knowledge (Form 2A, Part 2, Item 2). A certain item based on the reading of climatic charts reads as follows: "A traveller would see sheep grazing and irrigated fields in and around which of the following cities?" It is obviously an unjustifiable assumption that these sights would necessarily greet the traveller around a city identified only by temperature and rainfall. Occasionally the correct response to an item in a series can be selected automatically if the answers to the others are known (Form 1A, Part 2, Items 9–12). These defects are, as in the case of the other tests, relatively uncommon.

SUMMARY. In summary, it is the belief of the writer that, from the technical point of view, the STEP series is undoubtedly one of the best available. In some respects, such as range and comparability, the series is quite unsurpassed. Test users can safely adopt the series, if they so desire, secure in the knowledge that the various tests have been carefully and competently prepared and standardized.

On the other hand, it must be pointed out that information in regard to reliability and validity is far from complete, and is in fact sadly lacking in some respects. More serious, of course, is the situation where a test user cannot accept as adequate or satisfactory the aims and purposes set out as the basis for the development of the series. For such an individual, the series would be altogether unsuitable. And this is far from being a remote contingency, since for many school people the acquirement of knowledge of subject matter is still deemed to be a primary and even laudable aim of education. While the functions measured, and competently measured, by the STEP series are undoubtedly important, it could be that they represent the far reach of the pendulum swing. Any such radical departure from accepted procedures is of course fraught with peril—the player stands to win, or to lose, all. Despite the criticisms voiced above, the writer would wish for ETS the winner's cast.

WILBUR L. LAYTON, *Professor of Psychology, and Assistant Director, Student Counseling Bureau, University of Minnesota, Minneapolis, Minnesota.*

The objectives of the authors of the *Sequential Tests of Educational Progress* can be indicated by the following quotation contained in a note to the reader of the STEP specimen set:

The three principal characteristics of this new series are apparent in examination of the test booklets. The tests are built to measure the *central learnings* of students in six fields. They offer *continuous* measurement in these six fields from the fourth grade of elementary school through the second year of college. They provide useful *comparability* of achievement from field to field and level to level because all of them have been built and standardized as a unit.

The STEP battery properly should be evaluated through determining whether it measures central learnings in a continuous and comparable fashion from the fourth grade through the second year of college. The STEP authors have attempted a tremendous task in designing and developing the STEP materials. Actually, the development project has only just begun. Consequently, in the early stages of the project this review may be too critical. A reviewer several years hence may find many of the present criticisms not applicable. However, there are certain aspects of the present STEP materials which need to be studied critically. In the following discussion, content validity, the price paid for the sequential feature, the continuous score scale, norms, the standardization processes, and reliability are considered, and possible shortcomings which would interfere with continuous measurement identified.

MEASUREMENT OF CONTINUOUS CENTRAL LEARNINGS. Of course, one difficulty in developing a battery of tests providing continuous measurement from grades 4 through 14 is that the skills and understandings taught over that range may not receive the same weight from one end of the educational continuum to the other. For example, is the "writing" content in the elementary school curriculum drawn from the same population of content as that of "writing" taught at the college level? One has to conceive of a subject matter area as being continuous from the elementary grades through college and perhaps even graduate school if one uses the ETS approach in STEP. This assumption visualizes the development of the individual's knowledge and understanding as a continuous process and is reasonable if measurement techniques adequately reflect the process. For proper measurement, one must assume that this process can be subdivided into increments of development closely associated with the school grades through which a student progresses. The pattern of course offerings in typical curriculum guides indicates there is no generally accepted pattern of presentation of subject matter in any particular grade. In fact, as a summary of a recent survey of course content in social studies illustrates, there may not be general agreement upon the important concepts that should be taught.[1] This lack of agreement,

[1] BRUNS, RICHARD F., AND FRAZIER, ALEXANDER. "A Survey of Elementary School Social Studies Programs." *Social Ed* 21:202–4 My '57.

of course, poses an almost unsolvable problem for all achievement testmakers.

CONTENT VALIDITY. The Cooperative Test Division established committees of educators competent in the areas of subject matter to be tested and these committees determined the content of the tests. We can assume that the results of this committee deliberation reflect adequately what the committees considered important educational objectives. It then behooves the test user to determine whether or not the content of the tests is "central" and adequate to measure the skills and understandings of his students as he wants to evaluate them.

Obviously, content validity is of utmost importance in a battery measuring continuous central learnings. Each of the STEP manuals of interpretation lists broad areas of skills or understandings which are to be measured by the specific STEP test. Approximate distributions of items by these broad areas are given in the manuals. In several tests the variation in these distributions from level to level is not great, and thus the items may not reflect shifts in curricular content. Therefore, the potential test user should carefully scrutinize the test content to make sure the specifics he wants to measure are included and in the proper proportion at the various grade levels. Space limitations allow only the following specific comments about the content of the tests.

The reading test slights science and social studies content, and at no level does it include materials which measure reading comprehension in mathematics, certainly a neglected area in most tests and most curricula. The listening test also neglects mathematical or statistical material. The science test may not have enough items asking for specific content to satisfy most science teachers. Some science items are too simple; some are irrelevant to basic science principles; and some assume a peculiar science background. The mathematics test at the college level places too much emphasis on polling and sampling statistics. In Levels 1–3, there is too much emphasis on graphs and measurement and not enough on algebraic concepts. At all levels, there is not enough emphasis on computational skills.

Several of the social studies items are ambiguous, including Item 31, Part 2, Form 2A, which asks the student to infer attitudes from the facial expression of a woman in an illustration. Form 4A attempts to measure understanding of some important concepts in a contrived fashion, using Switzerland as the reference for items when a country more familiar to most pupils could have been used.

The limitations listed would not be serious enough to preclude use of STEP from the standpoint of content. However, as the following section implies, scores resulting from application of STEP may be difficult to interpret meaningfully.

THE PRICE PAID FOR THE SEQUENTIAL FEATURE. The idea of securing "continuity" of measurement by maintaining exactly the same organization of a test battery over a span of several grades is, of course, good within limits, granting that appropriate scales are supplied with the tests. Even over a limited grade span, however, the advantages of this idea are gained at some sacrifice of other desirable values, and if the grade span is too wide, the disadvantages far outweigh the advantages. This is true even when genuine continuity is provided through comparable continuous scales. In committing themselves to a single fixed battery organization usable at all grade levels from 4 to 14, the authors have been forced to forego the separate measurement of specific skills which occupy an important place in instruction at some levels, but not at all. In selecting categories *broad* enough to be usable at all levels, they have had to sacrifice meaningfulness, specificity, and even appropriateness in the test titles. "Science" and "Social Studies" are quite appropriate as the names of categories of subject matter, but not as the names of attributes of the individual pupil. In describing the pupil, it is more appropriate to use such terms as "Understanding of Social Concepts," or "Skill in Reading Social Studies Materials," or "Ability to Think Critically About Social Problems." Finally, in order to maintain the same test categories, necessarily broad, the authors have been forced at certain levels to "pool" or intermix in the same test several dissimilar aspects of achievement, aspects which should have been separately measured at those levels but could not usefully be differentiated at others.

In the area of writing, for example, almost all language test authors have found it advisable, especially at the lower grade levels, to provide separate measures of specific skills in language mechanics like punctuation, capitalization, usage, and spelling. In the early stages of language development, mastery of these separate skills represents an important goal of instruction. Practice materials at these levels usually concentrate on specific skills. At the college level, however, we are concerned primarily with such things as diction or style, ability to organize, lucidity of exposition, and ideational content. Thus, content and emphasis in language instruction change systematically from grade to grade. Differentiated measurement is instructionally desirable at the lower grade levels and unnecessary at the higher grade levels. With a single test organization at all levels, this important feature of a measurement program must be sacrificed.

Similarly, in the area of arithmetic, we may desire separate measures for arithmetic concepts, fundamental arithmetic processes, and arithmetic reasoning at the lower grade levels, but may be satisfied with a single undifferentiated test of mathematical reasoning at a higher level. This kind of change in differentiation is not permitted under the "frozen" plan of organization of the STEP battery.

One of the important steps forward in the construction of achievement test materials in recent years has been the provision of tests of specific study skills—such as ability to use basic reference materials, the ability to interpret charts, graphs, and statistical tables, and the ability to read maps. It is notable that these important descriptive instruments have been omitted from the STEP battery, although some such items have been included. The probable reason for the omission is that satisfactory measurement of these skills would necessarily require a *different* test organization at the different levels.

Organization in the area of reading is of a somewhat different character. At the lower grade levels, reading is comprised of such skills as recognition of word meaning, recognition of sentence meaning, and ability to note detail, and there is little differentiation of reading skills with reference to content areas. At these lower levels, a single reading comprehension test, plus possibly a reading rate test, may be all that is needed. At the senior high school and college levels, however, reading and thinking skills have become quite clearly differentiated with respect to major content areas. To comprehend typical reading passages about social problems —passages taken from newspapers, periodicals, pamphlets, and books addressed to the general reading public, as well as passages from school

textbooks—the reader employs quite a different complex of skills than are needed in reading typical passages concerned with scientific topics or problems. Scientific materials usually require closer attention to detail and to exact or precise meanings. They usually are more explicit and definite, demand closer reasoning or more rigorous mathematical logic, and are more straightforward in style and objective in character than materials concerned with social problems. The latter tend to be somewhat more ambiguous, inexact, and indefinite; to deal with ideas rather than with things, with matters of opinion rather than with matters of fact; to require more often the ability to grasp implied meanings; to be qualitative rather than quantitative; and to call for evaluation with references to subjective human values rather than for objective evaluation. The reader of materials concerned with social problems, furthermore, must be aware of the fact that the writer is often attempting to influence his opinion by appealing to his emotions and prejudices, as well as to his intelligence, and must be on guard against the tricks of the propagandist and the demagogue. Furthermore, ability to interpret reading materials in either the social studies or the natural sciences is strongly affected by the informational and experiential background of the reader. A specialist who can readily comprehend the contents of an article in *Psychometrika* may be completely unable to "read" an article in a *Law Review*. These differences, however, have certainly begun to develop at the senior high school and junior college levels, and different tests of ability to read these differing types of materials are clearly needed.

The authors of STEP have recognized the need for such differentiation in the measurement of reading skills by including a large proportion of reading exercises in the social studies and science tests at the higher levels, even though the battery already contains a separate reading test. However, they have "lumped" these specialized reading test items together with items testing the student's "understanding," i.e., the student's *knowledge,* and have provided only a single undifferentiated score for both aspects of achievement in each area. Because a differentiation between knowledge and skills in these content areas is not needed and would not be convincing at the lowest grade levels, such differentiation must, under the frozen STEP organization, be precluded at the higher grade levels. Incidentally, by excluding from the "general" reading test the types of reading exercises included in the science and social studies tests, the authors have made the reading test a specialized reading test also, but one to which it would be difficult to give a meaningful descriptive name.

Had comparable continuous scales been provided, this sacrifice in the meaningfulness and utility of the measures provided would have had some point. As it is, without such scales, the real purpose for a frozen test organization is directly defeated.

THE CONTINUOUS SCORE SCALE. None of the usual techniques employed to measure educational *progress* such as standard scores, grade equivalents, or age equivalents are utilized for the STEP battery.

A discussion in the first few pages of the manual leads one to assume that ETS would attempt to develop a converted score system permitting direct comparisons from test to test within the same level and from level to level. However, this has not been done and the discussion is misleading on this point. If the attempt had been successful, the results would have been praiseworthy. However, the attempt failed and it is difficult to determine what benefits are gained from the converted score system presented. The whole converted score system appears to have been an exercise in drawing smooth curves through points determined at various grade levels rather than one which equated the score system to the ability which was being measured. The user converts from raw scores to converted scores and then to percentile ranks, whereas it would be much simpler to go directly from raw scores to percentile ranks. The technical manual states specifically that if scores on two or more tests are to be compared, they first must be converted to percentile ranks. The only utility of the converted scores presumably is to allow the use of either of two levels of a test with a pupil in a grade bordering those in which a given level of test would ordinarily be used. For example, a pupil in grade 6 might be tested with either Level 3 or Level 4.

To emphasize the lack of comparability of these converted scores from test to test, we need only note that on the reading test the converted score corresponding to the 50th percentile for the *ninth* grade population is 280,

while that for the mathematics test for the *twelfth* grade population is 278.

The unequal units of increase in converted scores from grade to grade for a specific test illustrate the lack of longitudinal meaning of these derived scores. Table 1 presents increments expressed in converted score units for the median student from grades 4 through 14. These increments are approximate and were linearly interpolated from Tables D1 to D24 in the Technical Report.

Table 1
Increments in Converted Score Units
of Median Scores on STEP Tests

Test	Grade									
	5	6	7	8	9	10	11	12	13	14
Reading	9	4	10	5	9	6	6	4	12	0
Writing	10	8	0	6	9	2	6	4	10	5
Listening	7	3	3	5	3	3	4	1	2	3
Social Studies	8	5	4	5	4	4	6	2	4	4
Science	10	5	4	5	2	5	5	0	4	4
Mathematics	8	8	3	6	5	6	3	2	4	4

Thus, the typical or 50th percentile student on the reading test gains 10 converted scale units from grade 6 to grade 7 but gains no units from grade 13 to grade 14. On the writing test, the typical student gains 10 units from grade 4 to grade 5 but none from grade 6 to grade 7.

The authors have not claimed normative significance for the converted score scales, but some type of normative standards are essential for making comparisons of growth along the same scale. For the STEP battery, any comparison of *growth* or gains in scores from level to level, *even for the same test,* will be meaningless. There is no way of plotting successive annual profiles on the same cumulative chart, and of noting areas in which score gains are relatively large or small, as can be done with other achievement batteries.

Comparable scales are obviously needed for satisfactory measurement and portrayal of progress or growth in test achievement. Without such scales, there is little point in retaining the same battery organization over several levels. The inclusion of the present "Converted Score Scales" in the test manual, together with the sequential character of the tests, gives the *impression* of continuity of measurement, even though no real continuity exists. The inclusion of the scales and the sequential feature definitely *appear* to give substance to the attractive promise so easily inferred from the test title. The publishers of STEP have undoubtedly been unaware of the ethical implications of these facts, but this is something to which they should give serious consideration.

THE "TRYOUT" AND NORMS SAMPLES AND THE NORMS PRESENTED. The following recommendation is listed as essential in *Technical Recommendations for Achievement Tests:* [2] "Norms should be based on a well-planned sample rather than on data collected primarily on the basis of availability. Where data are used on an 'availability' basis of selection, information concerning their representativeness or possible bias should be reported."

The STEP authors apparently planned carefully the sample on which data were to be collected for tryout and normative purposes. It appears that they attempted to obtain a representative sampling of schools and colleges throughout the country. However, their final samples were based on those schools *willing to administer the tests.* This well planned sample then immediately becomes an "availability" sample and, although the schools tested in the norms sample are listed in the Technical Report, there has been no attempt made to assess possible biases resulting from the basis of selection. We should know just what types of schools were oversampled and undersampled in the normative group. There exist good weighting techniques which can be applied to data of these kind to correct for over- and under-representation. The test publishers might have used the techniques of opinion and questionnaire surveyors who assay their nonrespondents to determine how they differ from respondents and use this knowledge to correct the data obtained from the respondents.

It is not clear from the description in the Technical Report whether or not the normative samples were actually drawn from nine regions of the United States or from only the four represented in Table 9. Even so, the data in this table indicate that the sampling is far from representative with respect to the four regions.

The attempt to adjust the norms by weighting the data obtained from the colleges is laudatory. However, it would appear that the sample was severely under-representative of large colleges and universities. Therefore, the weighting procedure may still have resulted in an under-representation of larger institutions.

Another criticism is that the number of

schools represented in the sample is small. The test authors wisely point out that the unit of sampling for norming purposes is properly the school rather than the pupil, and they present a description of how they sampled from the schools indicating a willingness to test. Norms for school means are needed especially when the tests are used for evaluation of a school's educational program. Here it is the school rather than the individual pupil that is being compared with others, and the evaluation is properly based on the average achievement of all pupils at a given level in the school. However, it is quite evident that a sample of only 50 schools does not provide a stable basis for establishing a school norm. The score of an individual pupil must be interpreted in terms of its position in the distribution of scores of all pupils on the same test in the same grade. The mean score on a given test in a given grade for a given school must likewise be interpreted in terms of its relationship to the distribution of such means for all schools in the population. Norms for school means are, therefore, highly desirable. However, quite obviously one cannot distinguish reliably between the 98th and 99th percentiles in a sample of only 42 cases, nor can one secure stable estimates of population percentiles from samples of this size.

The absence of comparable scales for the STEP materials makes it particularly important that the within-grade percentile norms be highly stable and comparable from grade to grade, since it is only through the percentile norms that any kind of grade to grade comparisons of pupil achievement may be made. To insure highest comparability or to reduce to a minimum the sampling variance of grade to grade differences in percentiles, the same schools or school systems should have been used at all levels from grades 4 to 12. Instead, there are no two successive grades for which the STEP norms are based on exactly the same schools, while the samples for the different levels presumably do not overlap at all. The result, to take an extreme instance, is that on one test the 98th percentile for one grade level is lower than that for the preceding grade (science test, grades 11 and 12). In fact, on the science test the normative sample 11th graders rather consistently scored higher than the 12th graders.

The Technical Report states that when the norms program was completed, several ambiguous items were found in the designated Form

2 *Technical Recommendations for Achievement Tests.* Prepared by the Committees on Test Standards of the American Educational Research Association and the National Council on Measurements Used in Education. Washington, D.C.: National Education Research Association, 1955. Pp. 36. *

1B of the writing test, and it was decided to withhold publication of this form. As a consequence, the manual goes on, Form 1B could not be equated to Form 1A. However, the authors *judge* that the present norms are appropriate for Form 1A and for a revised Form 1B and state, "A possible unreliability attributable to item ambiguity should not greatly alter a norms distribution." The norms and revised Form 1B should be thoroughly studied before publication and resulting judgments based upon data.

Norms are reported for fall testing only; there are none for spring testing; and no indication is given of the distribution of the schools with reference to the time (month in school year) at which the tests were administered.

In presenting the norm tables in the manuals for interpreting scores, the authors give a pair of percentiles for each score interval instead of the usual single percentile. This pair of percentiles represents roughly one standard error of measurement above and below the midpoint of the interval in which it appears. The authors hope that this form of presentation will encourage more realistic interpretations of scores. A better procedure would give an exact percentile score but indicate the band of error associated with it. From the tables presented by the test publishers, the test user may do his own interpolation and select a score which may not be the best estimate of the individual's percentile rank. This will be most likely to happen if the scores are to be recorded on school cumulative records rather than on STEP profile sheets.

Incidentally, in the absence of comparable continuous scales, the STEP authors recommend the use of independent percentile scales at each grade level for the plotting of profiles of individual achievement. The use of percentiles in plotting profiles is a good idea, but not the use of percentile *scales*. Much better would have been the use of normalized equipercentile scales for the various tests, along which the percentiles are spaced as in the normal distribution. The use of percentile *scales* makes the difference between a 50th and a 51st percentile performance look as large or as important as a 98th–99th percentile difference, which is obviously misleading. The *Technical Recommendations for Achievement Tests* recommends as very desirable that such profiles be plotted on the normal probability scale.

THE STANDARDIZATION PROCESS. The test items for the STEP battery were written by educators with the help of the test technicians of the Educational Testing Service. After a pool of appropriate test items has been written, the process of standardizing a test becomes essentially statistical. The procedures followed by the test development experts of ETS leave much to be desired. It is to the credit of the ETS people that they have described in the Technical Report the procedures they used in standardizing the STEP battery. However, some examples of procedures not to their credit in addition to those already discussed are illustrated in the following: The pretesting of the items for reading, writing, listening, and science was carried out in October of 1955; the pretesting program for mathematics and social studies was conducted in January of 1956. For some unspecified reason, the tryout tests were not administered to students in a consistent pattern of grades. For example, Level 1 of the science test was administered in grades 11 and 13; Level 2, in grades 8, 11, and 12; Level 3, in grades 5, 8, and 11; and Level 4, in grades 5 and 8. For mathematics and social studies, the testing pattern was as follows: Level 1 in grades 10, 13, and 14; Level 2 in grades 7, 9, 12, and 13; Level 3 in grades 5, 7, 9, 11; and Level 4 in grades 4, 6, and 8. The reading, writing, and listening tests were administered according to a pattern of one level per grade as follows: Level 1 in grade 13; Level 2 in grade 11; Level 3 in grade 8; and Level 4 in grade 5. The purposes served by this pattern of testing are unclear. It would appear to complicate unnecessarily the problem of equating the tests.

Although there were many more students tested, the item analyses for the science, mathematics, and social studies tests were based on 100 case random samples for each pretest form and each grade in which they were administered. The item analyses for the reading, writing, and listening tests were based on 200 case samples. These samples were divided into high-scoring and low-scoring halves on the basis of total score on the test. Then the item's difficulty in the grades for which it was intended and its increase in difficulty both from grade to grade and from the low-scoring to the high-scoring sample within a grade was determined. In the light of the further statistical computation and the shifting of items to match forms, it appears that samples of 100 were probably not large enough to give stable estimates of item difficulty. The manual states that the items for each level of each test finally were chosen to conform as closely as possible to a desired distribution of item difficulties for the midgrade for which the level was designed, and alternate forms of the same level were constructed with similar distributions of item difficulties in order to minimize differences between them with respect to the ranges of ability measured. It would have been desirable to try out cross-validating samples with these alternate form items to determine whether or not the desired distributions had been obtained. This becomes particularly important when one considers the size of samples on which the item statistics were based. Another argument for cross validation of item difficulties is that difficulties may shift from try-out form to finished test. The position of an item in a test may affect its difficulty even though all students attempt all items. Items moved from context in an experimental form to a new context in a final form sometimes show changed difficulty values.

HORIZONTAL EQUATING. In the horizontal equating (equating of Forms A and B) of the reading, writing, listening, and science tests, linear conversions were derived by defining as equivalent equal standard scores on pairs of forms at the same level. The weakness of this procedure is the need to make the assumption that the true score distributions for the two tests have similar shapes and that there is a linear relationship between the two series of scores. If the reliabilities of the two tests differ, then the standard score method introduces error since the distribution of true scores will be different. In this case, the standard scores should be adjusted or weighted by the respective reliability coefficients. There was evidently no testing of the adequacy or of the degree to which the tests met these assumptions, and, in fact, the reliability coefficients of Form B have not yet been computed. As Flanagan points out in his chapter on "Units, Scores, and Norms" in Lindquist's *Educational Measurement*,[3] the equipercentile method is probably a more satisfactory procedure for this type of equating than is the standard score method.

VERTICAL EQUATING. The vertical equating procedure used with Form A appears to be adequate. However, the test authors state that although only the A forms were used for vertical

equating the B forms were vertically equated automatically because the B forms had been horizontally equated to the A forms. This is a risky assumption since the amount of error introduced in each of the equating procedures is considerable, and this error is very likely to be compounded as one moves through two or more equating procedures.

HORIZONTAL AND VERTICAL COMPARABILITY OF DIFFICULTY OF THE TESTS. Much emphasis in the STEP materials is placed on educational progress as measured by the battery. Presumably one wants to make test-retest comparisons as well as horizontal comparisons within the battery, and it is unfortunate that the necessary information to do this is not made available. For example, a discussion of equivalence of the forms on page 11 of the Technical Report points out and Table 2 on page 12 indicates that Form 1A of both the listening and the science tests are quite different from Form 1B with respect to the ceiling of ability measured by the alternate forms. The authors state that additional information about the equivalence of the forms will be provided by correlational analyses. *These analyses should have been done before the battery was published.* It would also have been desirable for the authors to present the actual distributions for the norms groups, so that one might evaluate the adequacy of the difficulty level of the tests for the various grades. From evidence presented, it would appear that perhaps all the tests are too difficult at the fourth grade level. In addition, the mathematics test at all levels may be too difficult, especially so in grades 4–10.

RELIABILITY. Reliabilities were determined on the basis of internal consistency analyses, and only for Form A. The fact that test-retest or alternate form correlations have not been obtained indicates the haste with which these materials were prepared for publication. Since each test, as published, consists of two 35-minute subtests, it would have been desirable to correlate these two halves as another estimate of reliability. The authors' statement that only the Form A tests were analyzed but that the results should characterize the Form B tests reasonably well since the A and B forms are very similar in content may illustrate one attempt to justify premature publication. The procedures used in computing Kuder-Richardson formula 20 also indicate the hurried way in which the standardization process was

3 FLANAGAN, JOHN C. Chap. 17, "Units, Scores, and Norms," pp. 695–763. In *Educational Measurement*. Edited by E. F. Lindquist. Washington, D.C.: American Council on Education, 1951. Pp. xix, 819. *

completed. In computing the formula 20, which is a function of total score and item statistics, the authors used total score statistics based on all students in the norms group for the grade, whereas the item statistics were based on 100 case samples drawn at random from the total group tested for the grade. Such estimation procedures are permissible in exploration of the characteristics of a test before publication but are somewhat contrived when presented as final in a published manual.

SUMMARY AND RECOMMENDATIONS. The advertising materials publicizing STEP emphasize its promise for continuous measurement of central learnings in six achievement areas from grades 4 through 14. However, the promise of continuous measurement cannot be fulfilled by the information presently provided by the STEP authors, since the continuous score system and norms are inadequate. If the attempt to develop a system of scores providing for comparability of measures from year to year had been successful, the "fixed" pattern of testing adopted throughout the STEP series would have been justifiable. But the failure of the conversion system defeats the purpose of the inflexible testing pattern which disallows measurement of specific skills that are an important part of instruction in some grades but not in others. As a result of these failures, STEP is not very satisfactory for use even where repeated measurement is not a requirement.

It is recommended that STEP be used only in large school systems and on an experimental basis. It might be adopted in such schools if the test content appears to sample that deemed appropriate by school personnel and if the school system is able and willing to standardize (determine reliability, establish norms, etc.) on the local level. Of course, in this situation adequate national norms will still be lacking.

The concept of comparable continuous measurement of educational development over a span of school grades is an excellent one. Unfortunately, the STEP publishers have been unable to produce a measurement system which adequately exploits the concept.

J Counsel Psychol 5:73–4 sp '58. Laurence Siegel. * The potential user of STEP may be dismayed by the substantial variety of materials he will be required to purchase and to manipulate. Consider an order for materials to satisfy the requirements of a high school testing pro-gram wherein 100 students are to be examined simultaneously. First, one would need 700 test booklets equally divided among the equivalent forms for each of the achievement areas at level 2. This amounts to 16 different kinds of booklets. Perhaps a single scoring stencil for each of the forms of the six objective subtests would suffice (12 more items). Add a handbook for scoring essays, answer sheets, a set of directions for administering and scoring the area subtests, and you have nine additional kinds of objects to manipulate. Throw in six manuals for interpreting area scores, pads of score distribution sheets and a technical manual for good measure and you have 47 different kinds of material. In spite of the fact that each of these is carefully planned and serves a useful purpose, the sheer number of items of testing materials is apt to be a trifle bewildering. The reliability coefficients thus far available for STEP are based upon internal analyses; i.e., they relate only to subtest homogeneity. Applications of Kuder-Richardson formula 20 yielded satisfactory coefficients for all subtests at all levels. In the absence of correlational data between test and retest scores, the manual offers no reassurance regarding the stability of STEP scores. A more serious omission, at the present time, however, is the lack of correlational data between the alternate forms of each subtest. Every set of alternate forms was designed with a view toward equivalence, insofar as possible within the limits imposed by the original pool of items. Thus, it is probably safe to assume that correlations between forms would be high. These data are, however, much needed and the Technical Report indicates that they will be forthcoming in a Supplement. Validity coefficients for STEP are not yet available. The series possesses obvious content validity resulting from the careful preliminary work involving the definition of objectives of the battery and the structure of items which preceded the actual item-writing process. Furthermore, all items included in STEP survived a discriminatory analysis against the criterion of total subtest score. There is little question but that the series will have demonstrated validity against appropriate external criteria when such studies are done. At present, however, one can only wonder about the comparative validity of a measure like STEP (unique in the measurement of *applications*) in comparison to other instruments measuring rote memory. * The care with which the normative samples were se-lected and resultant data are presented is im-pressive. Just one of the commendable features of the percentile norms provided for STEP is the listing of conversions from score interval to a "percentile band" rather than to the usual single percentile value. * an achievement bat-tery meriting a good deal more than superficial consideration by persons responsible for test-ing programs at all educational levels. STEP is not just another series of achievement tests. The battery focuses upon measurement of ap-plications of knowledge rather than upon mere possession of knowledge and to this extent gets at a basic objective of the educational process. Certain criticisms of STEP are all too obvious. The publication of the battery really should have been accompanied by data supporting the stability and validity of subtest scores. This comment is not to be construed as an expression of doubt concerning either the fact that these data will shortly be available or the likelihood that they will meet the usual requirements for reliability and validity. Until the data are avail-able, however, STEP is still a bit of an un-known. This temporary deficiency is quite minor in view of the over-all excellence of the battery. The careful preliminary groundwork laid by the many educators and members of the publisher's professional staff engaged in a co-operative endeavor yielded powerful dividends. STEP is a superior battery on all counts rang-ing from the technical aspects of construction to the matter of preparation of test booklets and readable manuals. The wealth of materials necessary to administer and interpret the bat-tery will frighten some people off, and will cause others to spend more than the usual amount of time in preliminary study of the se-ries before attempting to administer it. The lat-ter group will find that their additional efforts have been well rewarded.

For reviews by John S. Diekhoff, John M. Stalnaker, and Louis C. Zahner of the essay test, see 206. For reviews by Charlotte Croon Davis, John M. Stalnaker, and Louis C. Zahner of the writing test, see 207. For reviews by Paul L. Dressel, Gordon Fifer, and Tom A. Lamke of the mathematics test, see 438. For reviews by E. F. Lindquist and Irving Lorge of the listening test, see 578. For reviews by Eric F. Gardner, James R. Hobson, and Stephen Wise-man of the reading test, see 653. For reviews

by Palmer O. Johnson, Julian C. Stanley, and Robert M. W. Travers of the science test, see 716. For reviews by Richard E. Gross, S. A. Rayner, and Ralph W. Tyler of the social stud-ies test, see 792.

[25]
*Stanford Achievement Test [1953 Revision]. Grades 1.9–3.5, 3–4, 5–6, 7–9; 1923–56; tests in arith-metic, reading, science, study skills, and social studies available as separates; IBM for grades 5–9; Forms J ('53), K ('53), L ('54), M ('55), N ('56); IBM scored Forms JM ('53), KM ('53), LM ('54); 4 levels; directions booklet ('53) for each level; 2¢ per profile ('53); 4¢ per pupil record blank; postage extra (specimen sets postpaid); Truman L. Kelley, Richard Madden, Eric F. Gardner, Lewis M. Terman, and Giles M. Ruch; World Book Co. *

a) PRIMARY BATTERY. Grades 1.9–3.5; 1923–56; 6 scores: paragraph meaning, word meaning, spelling, arithmetic reasoning, arithmetic computation, total; 5 forms; $2.95 per 35 tests; 35¢ per specimen set; (110) minutes in 3 sessions.

b) ELEMENTARY BATTERY. Grades 3–4; 1953–56; 7 scores: same as for Primary Battery plus language; 5 forms; $3.50 per 35 tests; 35¢ per specimen set; (175) minutes in 5 sessions.

c) INTERMEDIATE BATTERY. Grades 5–6; 1923–56; 50¢ per specimen set of any one test.

1) *Complete Battery.* 10 scores: same as for Elemen-tary Battery plus social studies, science, study skills; 5 forms; $5.80 per 35 tests; 213(260) minutes in 6 sessions.

2) *Partial Battery.* 7 scores: same as for Elemen-tary Battery; 2 editions; *hand scored edition:* 5 forms; $4.75 per 35 tests; *IBM scored edition:* 3 forms; $6.25 per 35 tests; $4.25 per 35 sets of IBM answer sheets; 138(170) minutes in 4 sessions.

d) ADVANCED BATTERY. Grades 7–9; 1923–56; 50¢ per specimen set of any one test.

1) *Complete Battery.* 10 scores: same as for Com-plete Intermediate Battery; 5 forms; $5.80 per 35 tests; 213(260) minutes in 6 sessions.

2) *Partial Battery.* 7 scores: same as for Partial In-termediate Battery; 2 editions; *hand scored edition:* 5 forms; $4.75 per 35 tests; *IBM scored edition:* 3 forms; $6.25 per 35 tests; $3.75 per 35 sets of IBM answer sheets; 138(170) minutes in 4 sessions.

REFERENCES
1–34. See 3:18.
35–54. See 4:25.
55. SCHMIDT, MARY ANN. *An Evaluation of the Stanford Achievement Test in Spelling.* Master's thesis, University of Florida (Gainesville, Fla.), 1949.
56. DOYLE, ANDREW M. "A Study of Spelling Achievement." *Cath Ed R* 48:171–4 Mr '50. *
57. TOWNSEND, AGATHA. "Results of the New Revision of the Stanford Achievement Test in Several Independent Schools." *Ed Rec B* 59:65–76 Jl '52. * (*PA* 29:2995)
58. BAKER, RUTH Y. *A Study of a Standardized Test as a Measure of the Qualitative Aspects of Vocabulary Growth.* Master's thesis, Bowling Green State University (Bowling Green, Ohio), 1954.
59. COLEMAN, WILLIAM, AND CURETON, EDWARD E. "Intel-ligence and Achievement: The 'Jangle Fallacy' Again." *Ed & Psychol Meas* 14:347–51 su '54. * (*PA* 29:2208)
60. FEINBERG, HENRY. "Achievement of Children in Orphan Homes as Revealed by the Stanford Achievement Test." *J Ge-netic Psychol* 85:217–29 D '54. * (*PA* 29:6979)
61. JACOBS, ROBERT, AND SPAULDING, GERALDINE. "An Evalu-ation of the 1953 Revision of the Stanford Achievement Test Battery." *Ed Rec B* 62:48–66 F '54. * (*PA* 28:8080)
62. TOWNSEND, AGATHA. "The Stanford Achievement Test—Results of Two Forms of the Revised Edition Administered Five Months Apart." *Ed Rec B* 63:59–67 Jl '54. * (*PA* 29: 4696)
63. TRAXLER, ARTHUR E., AND SPAULDING, GERALDINE. "Sex Differences in Achievement of Independent School Pupils as

Measured by Stanford Acheivement Test, Form K." *Ed Rec B* 63:69–80 Jl '54. * (*PA* 29:4698)

64. CANTONI, LOUIS J. "High School Tests and Measurements as Predictors of Occupational Status." *J Appl Psychol* 39:253–5 Ag '55. * (*PA* 30:4722)

65. COBB, HERBERT. *An Investigation of the Increment in Learning of Seventh Graders as Shown by the Stanford Achievement Tests.* Master's thesis, Kansas State Teachers College (Emporia, Kan.), 1955.

66. HIGHTOWER, HOWARD W. "Individual Differences." *Ed Adm & Sup* 41:458–61 D '55. *

67. LUNTZ, LESTER. "A Comparison of Results Obtained With Dictation and Multiple-Choice Spelling Tests." *Ed Rec B* 65:76–84 F '55. * (*PA* 29:7866)

68. NORTH, ROBERT D. "Achievement Growth Trends of Independent School Pupils as Reflected by Fall and Spring Results on the Stanford Achievement Test." *Ed Rec B* 66:57–68 Jl '55. * (*PA* 30:5242)

69. TAIT, ARTHUR T. "A Comparative Study of Five Major Achievement Tests." *Calif J Ed Res* 6:99–106 My '55. * (*PA* 30:1633)

70. TRAXLER, ARTHUR E. "Relationship of Certain Predictive Measures to Achievement in First-Year French and Latin." *Ed Rec B* 66:73–7 Jl '55. * (*PA* 30:5181)

71. NORTH, ROBERT D. "Relationship of Kuhlmann-Anderson IQ's and Stanford Achievement Test Scores of Independent School Pupils." *Ed Rec B* 68:53–60 Jl '56. * (*PA* 31:8837)

72. SCOTT, HELEN E., AND WILSON, GUY M. "A Critical Examination of Spelling Words in One Speller in Relation to Four Standardized Tests in Spelling." *J Ed Res* 49:331–43 Ja '56. * (*PA* 31:3658)

73. NORTH, ROBERT D. "Academic Achievement of Independent School Pupils as Reflected by Stanford Achievement Test Results, 1953–57." *Ed Rec B* 70:55–63 Jl '57. *

N. L. GAGE, *Professor of Education, University of Illinois, Urbana, Illinois.*

The present edition of the *Stanford Achievement Test* has batteries at four levels: primary, elementary, intermediate, and advanced. Each battery contains from five to nine tests: two reading tests (paragraph meaning and word meaning), spelling, language, two arithmetic tests (reasoning and computation), social studies, science, and study skills. Each battery is published in five forms: J, K, L, M, and N.

If we multiply the number of tests in each battery by five and sum the products, we find 134 separate tests comprising the putative subject of this review. Since all these tests cannot be satisfactorily examined without sinking our review under the sheer bulk of material, some sampling is necessary. Accordingly, the reviewer has focussed primarily on Form J, which will probably be most widely used.

Another circumstance deserves mention in characterizing the task of reviewing any major present-day battery of general achievement tests for the elementary school. Developing, publishing, and marketing achievement batteries like the Stanford is a massive venture. Thousands of dollars and many years out of professional lives must be invested. We can be sure that school systems in their turn pay out correspondingly great sums of money for such tests. Merely on economic grounds, we are dealing with no mean undertaking. And in educational terms—the importance of such tests in the schooling of millions of children—we have a manifestly serious matter at hand.

Finally, we must realize that a full review requires that the present battery be compared with its chief rivals: the *California Achievement Tests,* the *Coordinated Scales of Attainment,* the *Iowa Tests of Basic Skills,* the *Metropolitan Achievement Tests,* the *Sequential Tests of Educational Progress,* and the *SRA Achievement Series.* To look at the Stanford by itself would be like evaluating the Ford apart from the Chevrolet or Plymouth. Yet each of the competing batteries also contains several tests, in several forms, at several levels. For example, the *Sequential Tests of Educational Progress* contain seven tests, in two forms, at four levels, for a total of 56 separate sets of material, disregarding the various subtests. Making such comparisons would balloon our task to proportions unmanageable by the present reviewer. This review will not achieve such ideal scope.

In this review, we assume that the most important basis for judging an achievement test is its content, including the form of the items. Insofar as the content is found wanting, the other virtues of the test cannot help. But good content justifies concern with the test's reliability, administrability, and interpretability. Let us look at the Stanford from each of these angles in turn.

CONTENT. The content "was selected on the basis of recent analysis of contemporary textbooks, courses of study, and professional literature in the various fields. Each item proposed for use in the preliminary editions was carefully checked for its currency in the schools today. All content has been subjected to rigorous pre-publication experimentation in scores of schools throughout the country. * Due consideration is given to recent trends in curricular emphases and teaching methods. In particular, the authors have recognized the trend toward the teaching of meanings or understandings, rather than mere factual knowledge." Does the content show that all this work paid off?

First, the paragraph meaning test. In all batteries, this test consists of short paragraphs with one, two, or three words or phrases missing near the end. The pupil chooses among four alternatives for each of the words omitted from the paragraph. This technique differs from another often used, namely, having separate multiple choice questions about the paragraph. The Stanford method seems superior in that it puts a problem more intrinsic to the paragraph, as against the somewhat after-the-fact flavor of questions posed after the paragraph has been completely read. The Stanford test's approach requires that the proper word be fitted into the paragraph itself; in the questions-asked-after-the-paragraph-approach, the questions may get at points which seem unimportant to the reader and require that he look back into the paragraph. The Stanford procedure seems more lifelike.

The second test is on word meaning. Here the pupil picks that one of four words which will complete the sentence best. Even at the primary level, the problems are entirely verbal and printed, rather than consisting partly of pictures or of orally stated problems. Each item takes the form of a sentence. The more frequently used technique is to present one word, or a phrase in which the word is embedded, and ask the pupil to choose which of four words has most nearly the same (or sometimes the opposite) meaning. The Stanford form again seems more palatable, logically a bit more complex, and probably also factorially more complex. In many of these vocabulary items, there is an element of problem solving which is absent from vocabulary tests in the more usual form. To the reviewer, the problem-posing complexion of these vocabulary items seems all to the good, i.e., closer to the way in which words are used outside of tests. But, do word meaning or vocabulary test materials properly belong in an achievement test? Do pupils in present-day elementary schools actually study vocabulary, or word meaning, as such? Or do they acquire their vocabulary indirectly in the course of other learning in and out of school? Vocabulary test items are almost universally used in tests of so-called intelligence. This fact implies that vocabulary is not explicitly taught, is not an objective at which instruction is directly aimed. Note that some recent tests of achievement, such as the *Sequential Tests of Educational Progress,* have no vocabulary section; such tests measure vocabulary, of course, but only as embedded in the kinds of knowledge and understanding which schools teach. If a pupil's performance in "word meaning" is low, we should not infer that he needs to be taught vocabulary directly. That would amount to attacking a symptom. A richer intake of reading and cultural stimulation would get at causes. And these are implied

by other reading exercises more cogently than by vocabulary tests.

Spelling is the third subtest at all levels. In the two lower levels, the teacher dictates the words; at the higher levels, multiple choice items are used. The former procedure impresses the reviewer as having greater validity. Certainly it comes closer to the way in which spelling is taught and informally tested in the classroom. The multiple choice technique of testing spelling ability is easier to score. And it probably yields scores that correlate as high as .7 or .8 with spelling measured by the dictation method. Neither of these facts should be allowed to counter its less realistic quality. We want pupils to be able to write their own words with correct spelling; we care somewhat less whether they can recognize correct spellings among incorrect ones of the same word. That is, we want them to spell correctly primarily when they write, and only secondarily when they proofread. Correlations as high as .9 still permit two variables to have considerably different correlations with a third variable. Suppose our hypothetical third variable were tendency to spell correctly in out of school writing. The reviewer's expectation is that the dictation method would have importantly higher validity against such a criterion, even if the multiple choice spelling test correlated .9 with the dictation test. Here is one respect in which the machine scorable answer sheet has had a regrettable influence. If it is worth the trouble to have nonmachine scorable spelling tests at the primary and elementary levels, the reviewer should argue that this is also worth doing at the intermediate and advanced levels.

The language test appears next in all batteries except the primary. This consists of 2-choice items on an apparently judicious choice of topics in capitalization, punctuation, grammar, and diction. Presumably because this is the only test that uses 2-choice items, the authors here introduce the correction-for-guessing formula, $2R + O - T$, an algebraic equivalent of the better known $R - W$ formula. Since there are no instructions against guessing in this test, all pupils may answer all items; if so, the formula is useless. That is, R and $R - W$ scores will correlate perfectly. If instructions against "wild guessing" were presented in this test, as they are in others, the authors would probably call forth a response set of willingness-to-guess-or-take-a-chance. This response set would probably result in reliable variance, but whether it would be relevant to what the test is intended to measure is questionable. Perhaps, in the next edition, the authors ought to instruct pupils to answer all questions, guessing if necessary. Such instructions would eliminate the response set and allow doing away with the $R - W$ formula. The scoring formula may impress school people favorably. But if pupils answer all items, since they are *not* told not to guess, the formula has no effect and becomes a spurious way to increase sales appeal. Will not teachers accept a 2-choice test without a scoring formula if its rationale is explained?

The next two tests, Arithmetic Reasoning and Arithmetic Computation, consist of brief, disconnected problems. At the primary level, the first few problems are presented pictorially; answers are indicated by X marks or by being written in. At the intermediate and advanced levels, the answers are chosen from four alternatives plus a "not given" alternative. The "reasoning" problems draw upon a variety of contexts meaningful to pupils at the respective grade levels. But it is doubtful that "reasoning" is elicited by some of these items; e.g., "A foot is how many inches?" "Which of these figures is a square?" Apart from such a fault, the tests appear to be well crafted exemplars of their kind.

Here, however, we confront a problem that besets any user of these arithmetic tests and, to a lesser degree, the subsequent tests on social studies, science, and study skills. Does the particular school, or classroom, attended by the pupils being tested teach the things included in these tests *in the particular grades* in which these tests have incorporated the material? Arithmetic achievement is particularly "culture-bound" in the special sense of being dependent on the curriculum of the specific classroom. Pupils learn much about reading, word meaning, spelling, and even language in their out of school activities—at the library, watching television, reading billboards, and conversing with their parents. But when it comes to arithmetic, they are stuck with what their school offers them. If their school, for one reason or another, does not teach how to add fractions or multiply decimals in the grades to which the Stanford assigns these topics, there is seldom any other source from which they will have learned such things. Hence, pupils' scores on these tests reflect the curriculum, especially

the schedule according to which various topics are introduced in various grades, as much as the pupils' learning ability. A pupil's achievement here must be interpreted in the light of what his class has taken up. To judge the validity of the content of the arithmetic tests, no outsider can help the teacher or curriculum coordinator. Only by taking these tests and meticulously comparing their content with what has been taught in one's classroom or school system can the staff of the school decide how "fair," valid, relevant, and appropriate these tests are for their pupils.

Each of the three "content" or subject matter tests—Social Studies (history, geography and civic education), Science, and Study Skills —consists of a pot pourri of items broadly sampling knowledge. It is hard to see how the first two of these tests reflect "the trend toward the teaching of meanings or understandings, rather than mere factual knowledge" to which the authors pay their respects in the manual. These tests are long enough to provide the samples of knowledge necessary to attain substantial reliability in the sense of equivalence. But to judge their validity would again require painstaking content analysis and comparisons with a school's own curriculum.

RELIABILITY. Each manual presents split-half reliability coefficients corrected by the Spearman-Brown formula for each subject and each grade level for which a given battery is intended. Each of these is based on about 240 pupils drawn at random from 34 school systems. Along with these are presented the means, standard deviations, and standard errors of measurement. The 52 reliability coefficients range from .66 (for the arithmetic reasoning test in grade 1) to .96 (for the paragraph meaning test in grade 2), with a median value of approximately .88; all but nine of the reliability coefficients are .85 or higher. As the authors point out, however, "pupils in a single class, school, or even school system would probably exhibit somewhat less variability in various tests than these samples of pupils from numerous systems, and hence might yield reliability coefficients slightly lower than those here reported." In these days of electronic computers, would it not be feasible to compute several dozen reliability coefficients, each based on an entire intact classroom, for each of those here presented, and then to report the medians of these distributions of reliability coefficients? It certainly looks in any case as if reliability is high enough in most grade levels in most subtests to insure that the tests sample adequately the domain of pupil achievement which they do sample. To put it another way, the subtests tap large enough samples of whatever they measure that we should not expect confusing fluctuations in pupils' scores from one form to another.

A more direct means of estimating the reliability of these tests in the sense of their adequacy as samples would have been to report the correlations between one form and another. It is difficult, however, to administer more than one form of these lengthy batteries to the same pupils. The inferences we can make from corrected split-half coefficients are probably safe enough to make such a burdensome procedure unnecessary.

ADMINISTRABILITY. The directions to the teacher for giving these tests and to the pupil for taking them seem to be quite clear and complete. Time limits seem ample to allow all pupils to attempt all items. Speed will be a factor in the performance of only the exceptionally slow pupil. The format of the test booklets, the scoring keys, and various accessory materials for making profiles of individual and group scores seem efficient and attractive without the gaudy, distracting, multicolor "fanciness" which seems to have appealed to some test publishers in recent years.

INTERPRETABILITY. The authors properly make much of the fact that they offer modal-age grade norms for each of the subtests at each of the four levels. Such norms indicate the grade level of the pupils who attain a given average raw score on the test, using only that 65 per cent or so of the pupils who are in the grade which is typical for their age. Pupils in grades higher or lower than is typical for their age are omitted from the modal-age grade norms. Such norms make possible comparisons of an individual pupil's achievement with the achievement of the other pupils with whom he should most properly be compared. Total-group grade norms are also furnished; these are based on the performance of all the pupils in a given grade, including the accelerated and retarded. Again with good justification, it is recommended that total-group grade norms be used to interpret average scores of a total class, school, or school system.

In addition, percentile norms based on modal-age grade groups are furnished. These make possible comparisons between the scores of a pupil and the scores of other pupils of the same grade status rather than those of pupils in other grades. Such percentile norms are given for several possible testing dates—e.g., for grades 3.2, 3.5, and 3.8. As the manual wisely points out, "use of percentile norms tends to avoid erroneous inferences as to the desirability of effecting changes in grade placement, such as are sometimes drawn when a pupil's grade equivalents differ greatly from his actual grade placement. Percentiles have the further advantage of being easy to explain to parents or other teachers. Although the advantages of percentile norms are most apparent in the upper grades, it is becoming increasingly common to utilize this system for interpretation of scores at all levels."

If this is so, why is the whole score interpretation system of the *Stanford Achievement Test* geared to the modal-age grade norm? At the end of each subtest in each battery, a table juxtaposes the modal-age grade equivalent next to each possible raw score. The "grade scores" can be then converted into total-group grade equivalents, percentile ranks, or age equivalents. If percentile norms are more meaningful to most of the test's users, could they not have been substituted in these tables, as determined for the modal-age grade level at which the given battery is most frequently used? Then these percentile norms could have been made convertible, by appropriate tables, into the percentile ranks for other modal-age grade groups, other grades, and other ages. This procedure would be especially feasible if there is a grade level at which the various batteries are most frequently administered, and this seems to be a reasonable supposition. In this way, the advantages of percentile norms could have been more readily obtained without sacrificing the advantages of the other types of norms and without continually suggesting to teachers and parents that about 40 per cent of their pupils are achieving one or more grade levels too high or too low.

The latter problem arises with special force at the upper limits of the advanced battery, intended for grades 7–9. Below the individual profile chart on the cover page of each test booklet appears the statement, "Grade equivalent values above 10.0 are extrapolated values and not to be interpreted as signifying the typical performance of pupils of the indicated grade placement." According to the table in the manual presenting "Grade Scores Corresponding to Selected Percentiles for Modal-Age Groups—Advanced Battery," nearly 50 per cent of all pupils tested in grade 9.8 will achieve grade scores of 10.0 or higher. For all these pupils, the grade scores represent a kind of mathematical fiction that becomes meaningful primarily in terms of percentile ranks. It is also likely that the grade scores become quite unreliable for any of the batteries when pupils reach levels of achievement far above the grade levels to which the batteries were administered in the standardization program. Thus, the reviewer found one pupil in grade 6.2 who achieved grade scores of 9.3, 10.3, and 10.9 on the first three subtests of the Intermediate Battery and the next week achieved grade scores of 12.7, 11.9, and 12.3 on the same subtests, respectively, of the Advanced Battery. Bright pupils who approach the ceiling of one battery may get considerably higher grade scores on the next higher battery. But the percentile ranks of the pupil on the two batteries will not vary nearly so much.

The reviewer wishes the publishers had furnished data on the intercorrelations among the subtests of the various batteries. Such intercorrelations would show the empirical relationships among achievements in various phases of the elementary school curriculum, apart from the logical or intellectual connections between them, and the ways in which the batteries might operate when used for predictive purposes in multiple regression equations. Reports on predictive studies, which have surely been made by now with so widely used a battery as this, would also have been welcome. In one sense, at least, achievement tests yield useful information only insofar as they have predictive value. For many purposes, that is, we are interested in achievement as a result of past experiences only insofar as it permits us to predict grades, success, test performances, graduation, and the like. How scores on the Stanford are related to rural versus urban status, social class status, and regional, ethnic, and personality variables should be most useful information to farseeing users of these tests. To what extent the reporting of such research should be a function of the test publisher, no one can say. But no one is in a more strategic position than the test's authors and publisher to furnish such educationally and socially consequential facts.

CONCLUSION. All in all, the *Stanford Achievement Test* impresses this reviewer as a useful, plodding, dependable workhorse that can serve the middle-of-the-road school system well. Its content represents no thought provoking or imaginative innovations, from the standpoint of what leaders in curriculum development might nowadays desire. The well made criticisms of the previous edition, to the effect that it embodied outmoded conceptions of objectives in social studies and science, have had only a little, if any, discernible effect on the present edition; these tests still deal with miscellaneous knowledge rather than with problem solving skills, critical understandings, and applications of learning. The authors have perhaps been too cautious about getting too far ahead of the schools, with the possible consequence that they may be holding many schools back from advances which might with more encouragement be made. Tests and curricula interact, of course, and the tests cannot carry the burden of curricular progress by themselves. But the Stanford is perhaps not taking its rightful share of the leadership role to which decades of use in American schools have made it heir.

For reviews by Paul R. Hanna (with Claude E. Norcross) and Virgil E. Herrick of the previous edition, see 4:25; for reviews by Walter W. Cook and Ralph C. Preston, see 3:18. For a review by Robert L. Burch of the previous edition of the arithmetic test, see 4:419. For a review by Helen M. Robinson of the reading test, see 657; for a review by James R. Hobson of the previous edition, see 4:555; for a review by Margaret G. McKim, see 3:503. For reviews by Robert Ebel and Ruth M. Strang of the study skills test, see 700. For reviews by Bertram Epstein and Paul E. Kambly of an earlier edition of the science test, see 4:593. For a review by Harry D. Berg of the social studies test, see 799; for a review by Ray G. Wood of an earlier edition, see 3:595.

[26]

*Test for High School Entrants: [National Achievement Tests].** High school entrants; 1945–57; 5 scores: English, reading comprehension, arithmetic, general information, total; Forms A ('54, identical with test copyrighted in 1947 except for Item 42, Part 4), B ('57, identical with test copyrighted in 1951 except for minor changes); manual ('53, identical with manual copyrighted in 1947); directions sheet (A, '47; B, '51); $3 per 25 tests; 25¢ per manual; 50¢ per specimen set; postage extra; 40(50) minutes; Lester D. Crow and Alice Crow; Acorn Publishing Co. *

JACOB S. ORLEANS, *Lecturer in Psychology, Nevada Southern Regional Division, University of Nevada, Las Vegas, Nevada.*

The 4-page manual lists the purposes of this test as follows: (*a*) "To predict probable success in high school." (*b*) "To assist in planning the program of the incoming high school pupil." (*c*) "To aid in the diagnosis of individual difficulties or weaknesses." The test is, then, clearly intended as a predictive and diagnostic instrument. The manual, however, while it contains paragraphs on curriculum validity and reliability, presents no evidence to the effect that the test has any predictive value. Despite such lack of evidence, the authors offer these suggestions under the heading "Using the Test Results":

For promotional purposes it is suggested that the percentile equivalents for the entire test be used. For example, any pupil whose total score falls below 58 (the lowest 10%) probably is unready for promotion to high school.

For the classification of pupils upon entrance to high school, it is suggested that those pupils whose scores in any part of the test fall in the lowest 25% should be scheduled for simple or remedial work in the respective subjects.

The high school entrants whose scores fall within the middle 50% probably are sufficiently alike in their learning power that they may be grouped together for teaching purposes.

Those pupils whose scores in the respective parts of the test or in the entire test are found to fall within the highest 25% probably are ready for an enriched curriculum or for special *honors* classes. Those schools in which various curriculums are offered to meet differing ability levels will find the test helpful as a means of assisting pupils in the selection of courses that appear to be best fitted to their demonstrated power to gain from instruction.

It is true that these statements contain such words and expressions as "probably" and "it is suggested that," but the best that can be said about them is that they represent wishful thinking. The latest copyright date on either of the two forms of the test is 1957. Certainly by that date school personnel had learned to expect data to support contentions about published tests. The authors and publisher ask the user to accept on faith values of this test (the determination of which is far from an impossible task) which have not been established. The earliest copyright date on either form is 1945. Over the period of at least 12 years there has been ample opportunity to ascertain the degree to which the test can accomplish what the authors maintain its purpose to be.

The test consists of four sections: English, reading comprehension, arithmetic reasoning and computation, and general information, with 50, 40, 24, and 50 questions, respectively. All questions are 4-choice items. The questions on English cover vocabulary, spelling, language usage, sentence organization, and punctuation and capitalization. The reading section includes nine paragraphs and a poem, each followed by four questions. While most of the questions test the student's ability to note facts in the passages read, some do call for interpretation and inference. Almost all the arithmetic items deal with fractions, decimals, and per cents. The manual describes this section as a test of *"arithmetic power* that the young person has developed, and a prognostic measure of the individual's readiness to pursue mathematics on the high school level." This is one more unsubstantiated claim made by the authors. The general information part is described as "based upon the content of the elementary school curriculum and upon the pupil's interest in and ability to comprehend current happenings in the world about him." No facts are presented to explain how the items were chosen to meet these criteria.

"Curriculum validity" is explained in terms of such general statements as, "this test is based upon elementary courses of study," "the reading material....follows the type of material that is used for reading in the elementary school," "the material for Part III was selected from arithmetic texts that are in common use on the elementary level," and "the questions of Part IV have been taken from social science on the elementary school level and include textbook material and significant current events." The authors do state that the spelling words were selected from the *Buckingham Extension of the Ayres Spelling Scale.* They have not, however, explained how the words were selected, just as they have not divulged the courses of study, textbooks, or other sources they used. Curricular validity may be important for the diagnostic uses to be made of the test, although how it can be so used is not clarified. The authors fail to mention that curricular significance is not of significance insofar as the predictive value of the test is concerned.

As further evidence of curricular validity the authors present data showing the correlation between the first two parts of the test and the *Nelson Silent Reading Test,* and between total score on the test and the *Henmon-Nelson Tests of Mental Ability,* high school form. The former correlation is reported as .94 and the latter as .84. Both have been corrected by the Spear-man-Brown formula! What the authors and publisher apparently do not know is that a co-efficient so derived indicates (somewhat spuri-ously) what the correlation would be between scores on tests twice as long as the tests actually are.

Reliability correlations are reported as .97 for Part 1, .91 for Part 2, .94 for Part 3, .95 for Part 4, and .94 for the entire test. These coefficients are based on odd and even scores in one form, corrected by the Spearman-Brown formula. Reliability coefficients based on scores of the two forms would certainly be more de-sirable, in view of the fact that the Spearman-Brown formula produces corrected correlations which are consistently higher than those ob-tained from two forms.

Since all the items are of the 4-choice type, it would be expected that approximately one fourth of the answers would be in each of the four choice positions, with perhaps some weighting in favor of the third and fourth posi-tions. Of the 50 questions in the first part of Form A, the first and last choices are keyed as correct for only 9 questions each. In the third part, the first choice is the correct one for only 2 of the 24 questions, and the fourth choice for only 5. In the last part, the first choice is correct for only 4 of the 50 questions.

Percentile norms are furnished for each of the four parts and for total score. These norms are based on "a trial of 5,733 tests in a selected sampling of elementary school graduates in the East including New York City, in the Central and Far West and in the South." There is no indication of how many cases were drawn from each area, the time of year, the size of schools, or any other pertinent data. The norms are ex-actly the same for both forms of the test, as in-ferred from the fact that the same manual is furnished for both forms. However, no ex-plicit statement is made to this effect. In fact, there is no mention made in the manual of the fact that there are two forms, or anything about their comparability.

The time allotment for each part is 10 min-utes. It is somewhat difficult to understand how even the brighter students can finish the major part, especially of the reading and arithmetic tests, in so short a time, and, even more so, that so large a percentage of the students get as high scores as the norms indicate.

The instructions for administering the test are simple and clear. A scoring key is furnished for Form A, which makes the mechanics of scoring simple. No key is furnished for Form B since the letters of the correct choices are iden-tified as being in a key word.

The general format of the test appears to be satisfactory, except perhaps for the fact that the size of the type is rather small for a 6-inch type line. This possible defect is somewhat off-set by the clarity of the type used and by the amount of white space which increases read-ability.

For a review by Benjamin S. Bloom, see 3:19.

[27]
*Tests of General Educational Development. High school, college; 1944–57; IBM; 2 levels; sep-arate answer sheets must be used; $2.50 per 25 copies of any one test of Form B, either level; $1 per 25 IBM answer sheets; 50¢ per 25 hand scoring answer sheets; postage extra; (120) minutes per test; prepared by Examination Staff of United States Armed Forces Institute; Veterans' Testing Service, American Coun-cil on Education. *
a) HIGH SCHOOL LEVEL. Form B ('44); revised manual ('56); $2 per specimen set of the battery, postage extra; Forms C ('46), D ('46), E ('50), F ('55), G ('57) available only on rental basis for use in author-ized testing agencies; annual rental fee, $2.50 per bat-tery.
  1) *Test 1, Correctness and Effectiveness of Expres-sion.*
  2) *Test 2, Interpretation of Reading Materials in the Social Studies.*
  3) *Test 3, Interpretation of Reading Materials in the Natural Sciences.*
  4) *Test 4, Interpretation of Literary Materials.*
  5) *Test 5, General Mathematical Ability.*
b) COLLEGE LEVEL. Tests 1–4 same as high school level; no Test 5 at college level; Form B ('43); revised manual ('54); $1.75 per specimen set of the battery; Form A ('44) available only on rental basis for use in authorized testing agencies; annual rental fee, $2 per battery.
c) ARMED FORCES TESTING PROGRAM. Tests restricted to armed forces use; high school forms: W ('52), S, T ['56]; college forms: Y, Z ('54).

REFERENCES
1–11. See 3:20.
12–38. See 4:26.
39. PUTNAM, PHIL H. "Scholastic Achievement of GED Stu-dents at the Vanport Extension Center." *Sch & Soc* 66:161–3 Ag 30 '47. *
40. JOHNSTON, WILLIAM C. *The Scholastic Achievement of Veterans Admitted to the Municipal University of Wichita Under the Provisions of the General Educational Development Testing Program.* Master's thesis, Municipal University of Wichita (Wichita, Kan.), 1948.
41. McCRACKEN, NAOMI M. *Success of University of Ken-tucky Veterans Who Received High School Credit Through GED Tests.* Master's thesis, University of Kentucky (Lexington, Ky.), 1948.
42. SHOEMAKER, H. A., AND ROHRER, J. H. "Relationship Between Success in the Study of Medicine and Certain Psycho-logical and Personal Data." *J Assn Am Med Col* 23:190–201 My '48. * (*PA* 23:951)
43. FINDLEY, WARREN G. "Statistical Critique of USAFI Tests of General Educational Development," pp. 24–30. In *The Fifth Yearbook of the National Council on Measurements Used in Education, 1947–48.* Fairmont, W.Va.: the Council, Fair-mont State College, 1949. Pp. v, 56, viii. *
44. BERDIE, RALPH F., AND SUTTER, NANCY A. "Predicting Success of Engineering Students." *J Ed Psychol* 41:184–90 Mr '50. * (*PA* 24:6056)

45. ANDREW, DEAN C. "A Comparative Study of the Academic Achievement of High-School Graduates and Non-Graduates." *Col & Univ* 27:50–5 O '51. *
46. GLASER, ROBERT. "Predicting Achievement in Medical School." *J Appl Psychol* 35:272–4 Ag '51. * *(PA* 26:3046)
47. ANDREW, DEAN C. "Predicting College Success of Non-High-School Graduates." *Sch R* 60:151–6 Mr '52. *
48. BLEDSOE, JOSEPH CULLIE. *An Evaluation of the General Educational Development Tests.* Doctor's thesis, George Peabody College for Teachers (Nashville, Tenn.), 1952.
49. CHAUSOW, HYMAN M. "The G.E.D. and the Social Studies." *Jun Col J* 22:450–6 Ap '52. *
50. MONAHAN, FRANCIS X. *The General Educational Development (G.E.D.) Tests and Their Use in Colleges and Universities.* Master's thesis, Trinity University (San Antonio, Tex.), 1952.
51. WARDLAW, H. PAT. "The Use and Value of G.E.D. Tests for College Entrance of Veterans of the Armed Forces." *N Central Assn Q* 26:295–301 Ja '52. *
52. BERNS, SYLVIA A. "The High School Equivalency Diploma." *Bus Ed World* 33:379 Ap '53. *
53. BLEDSOE, JOSEPH C. "Success of Non-High School Graduate G E D Students in Three Southern Colleges." *Col & Univ* 28:381–8 Ap '53. *
54. D'AMICO, LOUIS ANTHONY. *The Comparative Achievement of Veterans Admitted to Indiana University on the Basis of General Educational Development Tests and a Selected Group of Other Indiana University Students.* Doctor's thesis, Indiana University (Bloomington, Ind.), 1953. *(DA* 13:718)
55. KOVNAR, MURRAY R. *A Statistical Evaluation of the USAFI GED Tests as Instruments for Counseling Air Force Personnel.* Doctor's thesis, University of Denver (Denver, Colo.), 1953.
56. ANDREW, DEAN C. "Differences in G.E.D. Test Scores According to Amount of High School Completed." *Col & Univ* 29:439–41 Ap '54. *
57. BERNARD, JACK. *Selection of Technical School Students: An Investigation of the Relationship Between Certain Personality Characteristics, Interests and Abilities, and Success in a Radio and Television Curriculum.* Doctor's thesis, New York University (New York, N.Y.), 1954. *(DA* 15:631)
58. GLASER, ROBERT, AND JACOBS, OWEN. "Predicting Achievement in Medical School: A Comparison of Preclinical and Clinical Criteria." *J Appl Psychol* 38:245–7 Ag '54. * *(PA* 29:6271)
59. GRAHAM, WARREN R. "Identification and Prediction of Two Training Criterion Factors." *J Appl Psychol* 38:96–9 Ap '54. * *(PA* 29:1798)
60. JONES, R. STEWART. "Do Retesting and Coaching Influence GED Test Scores?" *Sch R* 62:333–40 S '54. *
61. KOVNAR, MURRAY R. "A Statistical Evaluation of the USAFI GED Tests as Instruments for Counseling Air Force Personnel." Abstract. *Am Psychol* 9:409 Ag '54. *
62. MOSEL, JAMES N. "The General Educational Development Tests (High School Level) as a Predictor of Educational Level and Mental Ability." *J Ed Res* 48:129–34 O '54. * *(PA* 29:6279)
63. OLSON, EDWIN H., JR. *The Prediction of Academic Success by the General Educational Development Tests.* Doctor's thesis, University of Denver (Denver, Colo.), 1954.
64. TYLER, RALPH W. *The Fact-Finding Study of the Testing Program of the United States Armed Forces Institute.* Washington, D.C.: Office of Armed Forces Information and Education, Department of Defense, 1954. Pp. v, 304, 35. *
65. BATMALE, LOUIS F. *Achievement in College of Students Graduated From High School on the Basis of Performance on the General Educational Development Tests.* Doctor's thesis, University of California (Berkeley, Calif.), 1955.
66. American Council on Education, Committee on the Evaluation of the Tyler Fact-Finding Study of the American Council on Education. *Conclusions and Recommendations on a Study of the General Educational Development Testing Program.* Washington, D.C.: the Council, 1956. Pp. xv, 72. *
67. BLOOM, B. S. "The 1955 Normative Study of the Tests of General Educational Development." *Sch R* 64:110–24 Mr '56. *
68. DITTRICK, ALVA R., AND TURNER, CORNELIUS P. "What Is the Present Practice of Issuing High School Equivalency Certificates?" *B Nat Assn Sec Sch Prin* 40:117–22 Ap '56. *
69. PETERS, FRANK R. "Measurement of Informal Educational Achievement by the GED Tests." *Sch R* 64:227–32 My '56. *
70. TYLER, HARRY E. "The GED Tests—Friends or Foes?" *Calif J Sec Ed* 31:66–71 F '56. *
71. VAN WINKLE, HOWARD G. *A Determination of the Relationships Between Scores Obtained on the High School Level G.E.D. Tests and the Age and Prior Secondary School Training of the Examinees.* Master's thesis, Sacramento State College (Sacramento, Calif.), 1956.
72. American Council on Education, Commission on Accreditation of Service Experiences. *Policies of State Departments of Education for the Accreditation of Educational Experiences of Military Personnel and of Results on the Tests of General Educational Development.* Washington, D.C.: the Council, 1957. Pp. iii, 70. *
73. BLOOM, BENJAMIN S., AND STATLER, CHARLES R. "Changes in the States on the Tests of General Educational Development From 1943 to 1955." *Sch R* 65:204–21 su '57. *
74. D'AMICO, LOUIS A. "The Scholastic Achievement of GED Students at Indiana University." *N Central Assn Q* 31:256–9 Ja '57. *
75. D'AMICO, LOUIS A., AND SCHMIDT, LOUIS G. "The Comparative Achievement of Veterans Admitted to College on the Basis of General Educational Development Tests and a Selected Group of Other College Students." *J Ed Res* 50:551–6 Mr '57. *
76. American Council on Education, Commission on Accreditation of Service Experiences. *Credit Recommendations for USAFI and MCI Courses and Tests.* Washington, D.C.: the Council, 1958. Pp. iii, 5. *
77. LAPINE, HARRY J. "Do the GED Tests Really Measure the Outcomes of General Educational Learning Experiences?" *Univ Kans B Ed* 12:72–80 F '58. *

ROBERT J. SOLOMON, *Assistant Director, Test Development Division, Educational Testing Service, Princeton, New Jersey.* [Review of High School Form G.]

The purpose of the *Tests of General Educational Development* is, as stated in the manual, "to measure as directly as possible the attainment of some of the major objectives of the secondary school program of general education." These major objectives have been identified by the authors of the test as "competence in using major generalizations, concepts, and ideas....and....the ability to comprehend exactly, evaluate critically, and to think clearly in terms of concepts and ideas." Intended primarily to appraise the achievement of adults who have not completed their formal secondary school education, the tests focus on what the authors believe to be the broad, lasting outcomes of education rather than the more conventional subject matter centered definitions of school achievement. By means of these tests individuals who have not formally completed their secondary school education may be certified as having the equivalent of a secondary school diploma.

The GED battery is composed of five tests. None of the tests have time limits, but it is suggested that most examinees can finish the battery in 10 hours.

Test 1, Correctiveness and Effectiveness of Expression, is in two parts. Part 1 contains questions in which the examinee is required to select the one of four words which is misspelled. Part 2 consists of themes containing common faults found in the writing of high school students. The examinee is required to select the best way of correcting each theme. The questions require him to make judgments on matters of punctuation, grammar, and diction.

Test 2, Interpretation of Reading Materials in the Social Studies, consists of several reading passages each followed by several questions intended to test whether the examinee comprehends the main point or points of the passage, and whether he is able to draw generalizations, make inferences, and exercise other of the abilities of critical thinking. The passages in Test 2 are drawn from social studies materials of the kind that a student is likely to encounter in his school work. Test 3, Interpretation of Reading Materials in the Natural Sciences, is similar in purpose and design to Test 2 except that the reading selections are, of course, drawn from the various areas of the natural sciences.

Test 4, Interpretation of Literary Materials, consists of both prose and verse passages taken from American and English literature. The intent here is to measure the examinee's ability to understand the meaning of words in context, to interpret mood and intent, and to judge the effects achieved by certain simple literary techniques.

Test 5, General Mathematical Ability, is intended to measure the examinee's ability to solve practical problems requiring the application of basic arithmetical, algebraic, and geometric concepts and techniques.

In examining the content of the tests, two questions need to be raised. How adequately does the GED battery measure those areas of school achievement which it intends to measure, and, more basically, how adequate is the GED battery as a measure of school achievement?

The answer to the latter question must ultimately depend on the outlook of the test reviewer. The philosophy of the test authors, which is clearly set forth in the manual, is certainly a respectable one in the field of educational measurement. It maintains that certain skills, essentially the three R's, are the most important outcomes of secondary education. Is this sufficient? In a battery which requires approximately 10 hours should other important skills be tested? Is it sufficient to measure achievement in social studies, science, and literature by measuring the ability to read and comprehend written passages in these areas? Should an individual having the equivalent of a secondary school education be expected to have learned certain concepts and to have developed certain understandings or appreciations in social studies, science, and literature, and should a knowledge of these be measured in the tests? In sum, is there more to a secondary school education or its equivalent than is covered in the GED? Any institution contemplating use of this battery will probably wish to examine the tests to satisfy itself on some or all of these points.

The answer to the former question is easier. Within the limitations established by the test authors, these tests represent a workmanlike job of test construction. The test items reflect a degree of experience and sophistication which is not yet found in many present-day published tests. One is impressed with the obvious care that went into preparing items—items which require careful judgment, and which will trip the untutored or unthinking. The items are remarkably free of ambiguities or tricks demanding that the examinee read the examiner's mind in order to answer a particular question correctly.

If any criticism of the test content need be made, it concerns the coverage of the reading selections in Tests 2, 3, and 4. Probably by design, the materials in each of the tests sample more heavily from certain fields than from others. In the social studies test, the selections are predominantly from the area of American history and government. In the science test there is heavy emphasis on biology. The literary materials in Test 4 give considerably more coverage to "classical" English literature than to American literature and slight the increasing attention being given to contemporary literature in school courses. In general, the tests reflect a relatively traditional definition of school course materials. The explanation for this probably lies in the attempt of the test authors to make the test content representative of the materials covered in secondary school courses, as well as comparable to the content of earlier GED forms. Although detailed specifications for each of the tests are not given in the manual, the tests themselves clearly reflect careful planning. The manual does state that all forms of the GED were constructed "with a common set of specifications as to types of materials to be included, form of questions, and level of difficulty."

An indication of the comparability of Form G with other GED forms is given by presenting correlations between each of the tests of Form G and Form X, which, since 1955, has served as the criterion form to which all new forms, including G, have been equated. For Tests 1, 2, 4, and 5 in Form G, these correlations are .80 or higher, but, for Test 3, the science reading test, the correlation is .71. This is lower than one would expect with presumably parallel forms. This may perhaps be accounted for in part by the relatively low reliability (Kuder-

Richardson formula 21) of Test 3 in Form X, .80. No single administration reliability coefficient is given for Form G. The corresponding Kuder-Richardson reliabilities of the other four parts of Form X range between .86 and .89.

Available for Form G and all other forms of the high school level GED is a new set of norms developed in 1955. These norms are intended to replace the earlier ones developed in 1943 and to reflect any changes in the characteristics of the school population over the course of the 12 intervening years. The standard score for each test can be translated into a percentile rank for graduating public high school seniors for the total United States. Unfortunately, although data were collected by size of school, state, and region, no other norms are provided.

Evidence of the validity of the GED for determining admission to college is not directly furnished in the manual. Reference is made instead to the Tyler study of the use of the tests (64) and to certain of the findings of the committee which evaluated the Tyler study (66). The manual does report the statement of the Evaluation Committee that, although the data are limited, "large numbers of students admitted to college on the basis of GED succeed reasonably well academically. The failure of other students admitted on the basis of GED tests does not necessarily reflect unfavorably on the validity of the tests." Those interested in the validity of the GED tests will, however, need to refer to one or both of the suggested references for sufficient information, although even there the data are not conclusive. The same is true as regards data indicating the validity of the GED tests for predicting the success of non-high school graduates in industrial employment.

However, despite any suggested shortcomings, high school level Form G represents relatively high standards of test construction. The body of literature concerning the use and interpretation of the *Tests of General Educational Development* is considerable and apparently still growing. Future manuals, it is hoped, will give the user more detailed information as to test specifications, reliability, and validity, and more extensive normative data. Nevertheless, Form G represents another superior form of a series which continues to serve an important function in American education.

For a review by Gustav J. Froehlich of Form B, see 4:26; for reviews by Herbert S. Conrad and Warren G. Findley, see 3:20. For a review by Charlotte W. Croon Davis of Test 1, College Level, see 3:122. For reviews by W. E. Hall and C. Robert Pace of Test 2, College Level, see 3:528.

CHARACTER AND PERSONALITY

REVIEWS BY C. J. Adcock, Dan L. Adler, Mary D. Ainsworth, Dwight L. Arnold, Andrew R. Baggaley, Benjamin Balinsky, Warren R. Baller, Frank Barron, Robert H. Bauernfeind, Brent Baxter, Kenneth L. Bean, Samuel J. Beck, John E. Bell, George K. Bennett, Åke Bjerstedt, John D. Black, Donald T. Campbell, Cherry Ann Clark, Dorothy M. Clendenen, Charles N. Cofer, Lee J. Cronbach, W. Grant Dahlstrom, Richard H. Dana, D. Russell Davis, Dorothy H. Eichorn, Albert Ellis, Leonard D. Eron, H. J. Eysenck, Donald W. Fiske, John P. Foley, Jr., John W. French, Benno G. Fricke, N. L. Gage, Eugene L. Gaier, Cecil A. Gibb, John W. Gittinger, Harrison G. Gough, Wilson H. Guertin, J. P. Guilford, John W. Gustad, Nelson G. Hanawalt, Philip L. Harriman, Dale B. Harris, J. Thomas Hastings, Alfred B. Heilbrun, Jr., William E. Henry, Wayne H. Holtzman, John E. Horrocks, Arthur R. Jensen, Richard Jessor, Cecil D. Johnson, Walter Kass, E. Lowell Kelly, Douglas T. Kenny, Morris Krugman, Edward Landy, Roy D. Lewis, Maurice Lorr, Raymond J. McCall, Arthur W. Meadows, T. R. Miles, Kenneth R. Newton, Warren T. Norman, Raymond C. Norris, C. Robert Pace. John Pierce-Jones, Albert I. Rabin, John A. Radcliffe, John W. M. Rothney, Bert R. Sappenfield, David R. Saunders, William Schofield, S. B. Sells, Laurance F. Shaffer, Edwin S. Shneidman, Verner M. Sims, William Stephenson, Naomi Stewart, L. Joseph Stone, C. R. Strother, J. P. Sutcliffe, Clifford H. Swensen, Jr., Percival M. Symonds, Florence M. Teagarden, Robert L. Thorndike, Herbert A. Tonne, Neil J. Van Steenberg, Wimburn L. Wallace, Harold Webster, George Westby and C. Gilbert Wrenn.

NONPROJECTIVE

[28]

A-S Reaction Study: A Scale for Measuring Ascendance-Submission in Personality. College and adults; 1928–39; Form for men ('28), Form for women ('39); manual, second edition ('39); $3.04 per 35 tests; 40¢ per complete specimen set; postage extra; (20) minutes; Gordon W. Allport and Floyd H. Allport; Houghton Mifflin Co. *

REFERENCES

1–19. See 40:1198.
20–30. See 3:23.
31. THOMPSON, CLAUDE EDWARD. "Selecting Executives by Psychological Tests." Ed & Psychol Meas 7:773–8 w '47. * (PA 23:321)
32. BROWER, DANIEL. "The Relations of Visuo-Motor Conflict to Personality Traits and Cardio-Vascular Activity." J General Psychol 38:69–99 Ja '48. * (PA 22:3383)
33. HARDY, VIRGINIA T. "Relation of Dominance to Non-Directiveness in Counseling." J Clin Psychol 4:300–3 Jl '48. * (PA 23:179)
34. BARNETTE, W. LESLIE, JR. Occupational Aptitude Patterns of Counseled Veterans. Doctor's thesis, New York University (New York, N.Y.), 1949. *
35. CARTER, LAUNOR, AND NIXON, MARY. "Ability, Perceptual, Personality, and Interest Factors Associated With Different Criteria of Leadership." J Psychol 27:377–88 Ap '49. * (PA 23:4183)
36. HORRALL, BERNICE MOODY. "Relationships Between College Aptitude and Discouragement-Buoyancy Among College Freshmen." J Genetic Psychol 74:185–243 Je '49. * (PA 24:2090–1)
37. UHRBROCK, RICHARD STEPHEN. "Construction of a Selection Test for College Graduates." J General Psychol 41:153–93 O '49. * (PA 24:4874)
38. BENDER, I. E., AND HASTORF, A. H. "The Perception of Persons: Forecasting Another Person's Responses on Three Personality Scales." J Abn & Social Psychol 45:556–61 Jl '50. * (PA 25:988)
39. HOLMES, FRANK J. "Validity of Tests for Insurance Office Personnel." Personnel Psychol 3:57–69 sp '50. * (PA 24:5490)
40. BARNETTE, W. LESLIE, JR. "Occupational Aptitude Patterns of Selected Groups of Counseled Veterans." Psychol Monogr 65(5):1–49 '51. * (PA 26:2794)
41. HOLZBERG, JULES D., AND POSNER, RITA. "The Relationship of Extrapunitiveness on the Rosenzweig Picture-Frustration Study to Aggression in Overt Behavior and Fantasy." Am J Orthopsychiatry 21:767–79 O '51. * (PA 26:5619)
42. MCKENNA, FRANK S. "An Analysis of Nine Personality Scales." Abstract. Proc Ind Acad Sci 62:294 '52. *
43. STARER, EMANUEL. "Aggressive Reactions and Sources

of Frustration in Anxiety Neurotics and Paranoid Schizophrenics." J Clin Psychol 8:307–9 Jl '52. * (PA 27:5979)
44. BEAVER, ALMA P. "Dominance in the Personality of the Student Nurse as Measured by the A-S Reaction Study." J Psychol 38:73–8 Jl '54. * (PA 29:4842)
45. REINDL, MARY OLIVIA. The Relationship Between Attitudes Toward Obedience and Personality Characteristics Measured by the A-S Reaction Study and the Gordon Personal Profile. Master's thesis, Fordham University (New York, N.Y.), 1957.

For a review by William U. Snyder, see 3:23; for a review by Doncaster G. Humm of the 1928 edition, see 40:1198.

[29]

*Activity Vector Analysis. Adults; 1948–58; title on test is *Placement Analysis*; 5 scores: aggressiveness, sociability, emotional adjustment, social adaptability, activity level; Form A ('54); administrator's manual ('56); technical supplement ('58); profile ('53); distribution restricted to persons who have completed a 3-week course offered by the publisher; course fee, $1500; test materials must be purchased separately; postage extra; (5–10) minutes; [Walter V. Clarke]; Walter V. Clarke Associates, Inc. *

REFERENCES

1. MOSEL, JAMES N. "Response Reliability of the Activity Vector Analysis." J Appl Psychol 38:157–8 Je '54. * (PA 29:4076)
2. CLARKE, WALTER V. "The Construction of an Industrial Selection Personality Test." J Psychol 41:379–94 Ap '56. * (PA 31:5185)
3. CLARKE, WALTER V. "The Personality Profiles of Life Insurance Agents." J Psychol 42:295–302 O '56. *
4. CLARKE, WALTER V. "The Personality Profiles of Loan Office Managers." J Psychol 41:405–12 Ap '56. * (PA 31:5186)
5. CLARKE, WALTER V. "Personality Profiles of Self-Made Company Presidents." J Psychol 41:413–8 Ap '56. * (PA 31:5172)
6. FITZPATRICK, EUGENE D., AND MCCARTY, JOHN J. "Validity Information Exchange, No. 9–47: D.O.T. Code 1–86.45, Salesman, Communication Equipment." Personnel Psychol 9:526–7 w '56. *
7. WALLACE, S. RAINS; CLARKE, WALTER V.; AND DRY, RAYMOND J. "The Activity Vector Analysis as a Selector of Life Insurance Salesmen." Personnel Psychol 9:337–45 au '56. * (PA 31:8979)
8. HARKER, JOHN B. "A Comparison of Personality and Interest Patterns." Abstract. Am Psychol 12:408 Jl '57. *

9. WHISLER, LAURENCE D. "A Study of the Descriptive Validity of Activity Vector Analysis." *J Psychol* 43:205–23 Ap '57. *

10. MERENDA, PETER F., AND CLARKE, WALTER V. "AVA as a Predictor of Occupational Hierarchy." *J Appl Psychol* 42:289–92 Ag '58. *

11. MUSIKER, HAROLD R., AND CLARKE, WALTER V. "Descriptive Reliability of Activity Vector Analysis." *Psychol Rep* 4:435–8 S '58. *

BRENT BAXTER, *Director of Agencies Research, Prudential Insurance Company, Newark, New Jersey.*

The *Activity Vector Analysis* (AVA) is more than a test; it has become part of a system of personality analysis, part of a theory of personality. The role of the AVA is hard to define since the descriptions of its function have been modified from time to time. Originally it was a comprehensive measure of all significant aspects of personality. Later it was expanded to "become a human relations philosophy based on the understanding obtained from the study of people by the analysis." It has also been described as a tool to be used along with other personality tests (largely projective) and biographical information as an aid in helping the analyst understand the person tested.

Such variation in claimed function makes evaluation difficult. The last description makes the AVA results so interrelated with other data as to make separate evaluation of the AVA practically impossible. Let us turn to the available approaches to validity.

Many data have been provided to show that the test responses of members of one occupation differ from those in other occupations. In other words, presidents describe themselves in ways different from the general population. Your reviewer does not regard this as a useful form of validity if it can be regarded as validity at all. In business and industry it is more important to know whether the test can tell which members of an occupation are successful or, better yet, tell the probable future success of a person about to enter that occupation.

Several studies have been made by the test author and publisher to see if the test can tell which persons on a given job are successful, but these usually fail to have any cross validation to support them. The publisher does not always point out the lack of cross validation and concludes incorrectly that the data show the test is valid. Moreover, the comparison of results between two occupations has been improperly presented as cross validation. A few studies made by independent research men have not

shown the test to be effective in sorting out the more and less successful men on a given job.

In the AVA's early history, claims were made that prediction of job success was a simple function of this instrument. The publisher has since pointed out that this type of prediction does not rest alone on a sound measure of personality even if available. For one thing, an understanding of the relationship between personality and job function is necessary. Thus, some early failures to predict job success, it would seem, led the publisher to develop a parallel method of measuring job personality requirements. Research is still needed to determine the value of this job analysis method. Similarly, more evidence is needed to show if the test can contribute to the prediction of job success under any conditions.

The publisher has emphasized from the outset the importance of the function of the test administrator and, especially, of the test analyst to the validity of the instrument. For this reason a special training course is required for those wishing to use the test. The AVA Administrator is authorized only to administer and score the test, a relatively easy job. The interpretation is the responsibility of an AVA Analyst and "cannot be done by anyone other than that person." It is claimed that lay persons can become effective analysts with three weeks of training. While fairly standard interpretations that lay people can learn readily have been developed for some score profiles, there is conflicting evidence as to whether or not people with such training are likely to make the same test interpretations. It seems doubtful that such brief training can produce effective personality analysts.

There is evidence of fairly high consistency of responses made within a given test administration. Test-retest correlations run lower. One cannot tell whether this reflects unreliability of the instrument or sensitiveness to real changes in personality. Concern about reliability should not deter further study of this instrument.

The test publisher has made and is making extensive intratest analyses. Factor analyses and intercorrelation of score patterns have been made at length. While these purport to disclose the organization of personality, it is probably more a contribution to revealing the semantic jungle in which our personality vocabulary is involved.

In summary: Because of claims and counter-claims over the validity of this test, its use has become controversial. After an extensive search for studies which have tried an impartial evaluation of the instrument, your reviewer has seen little evidence on which to recommend its use. The analyses and interpretations derived from this test seem much more extensive than the original self-descriptions of the examinee justify. It must be recognized, however, that many of the criticisms directed toward this test can similarly be directed toward other personality instruments.

GEORGE K. BENNETT, *President, The Psychological Corporation, New York, New York.*

The *Activity Vector Analysis* is not a test which can be purchased but is part of a system which involves a contractual relationship, the training of "analysts," and other complexities. Consequently, this review deals both with the questionnaire and with the system.

The instrument which is central to the system is a single-sided sheet, 8½ by 11 inches in dimension, entitled "Placement Analysis." It contains blanks for identifying data, instructions, and a box for scores, as well as the list of 81 adjectives which constitute the form. Each adjective is preceded by two blank spaces. The instructions preceding the list read: "Place an X in the Columns headed (1) before every word that has *ever* been used by *anyone* in describing you. Draw a line through any word you do not understand. Be honest with yourself—remember no one is perfect." At the foot of the list are these instructions: "Now go back and place an X in the Columns headed (2) before every word which you honestly believe is descriptive of you. When you have finished, turn in your paper."

The 81 descriptive terms deal generally with overt aspects of personality and include such words or phrases as "good-natured," "persistent," "harmonious," "aesthetic," and "argumentative." The author describes them as nonderogatory and in general the term seems appropriate, although one might question it as applied to "scairdy cat," "nervy," and "egotist." An oddity in the list is the word "inducive," categorized as "rare" in Webster's unabridged dictionary.

Responses are counted separately for the columns and then added to obtain a "resultant" or total score. The first, or "activity," score is merely the number of X's. The remaining scores, V-1 to V-5, are obtained from a series of mask keys. With few exceptions, the same words are scored in both columns.

It is perhaps best to let the author define the scores. Quoting Clarke, we learn,

The following postulate, therefore, results: An organism behaves in a positivistic or negativistic manner in terms of the attitudes resulting from its perception of the given situation at that time, resulting in four basic ways of acting:

1. Positivistic, or approach behavior in a favorable or favorably perceived situation.
2. Positivistic, or approach behavior in an unfavorable or unfavorably perceived situation.
3. Negativistic, or avoidant behavior in a favorable or favorably perceived situation.
4. Negativistic, or avoidant behavior in an unfavorable or unfavorably perceived situation.

These four possible ways of acting are described by many different words depending upon *a*) the situation, and *b*) the degree of energy output.

Since these four behavior elements are dynamic—have direction and magnitude—they are designated as vectors and are numbered to eliminate the confusion often resulting from the interpretation of verbalized labels. The four major aspects of behavior are as follows:

Vector 1—Aggressiveness. In a less scientific description, it might be called "Do-ability."
Vector 2—Sociability, or "Social-ability."
Vector 3—Emotional Stability or Emotional Control. A less scientific description is "Sit-ability."
Vector 4—Social Adaptability, or the less scientific label of "Flex-ability."

If the reader feels less than thoroughly informed regarding the significance of the "Activity" and "V-5" scores, the reviewer is equally at sea, in spite of a diligent attempt to discover their meaning.

The V-1 score is based on 16 adjectives in each of the two columns. These include such words as "persistent," "forceful," and "determined." V-2 results from the marking of 19 in each column; representative words are "attractive," "enthusiastic," and "impressive." For V-3 there are 10 words in the first column and 14 in the second. Samples are "mild," "kind," and "complacent." V-4 derives from 30 adjectives in each column; among these are "harmonious," "obliging," and "fatalistic." V-5 has 12 words in the first and 7 in the second column. Words scored in one column are usually scored for the same vector in the other. Except for V-5, there is little overlap among the keys.

The 12 numbers from the scoring and the 6 sums or "resultants" are transferred to a "Record Summary" card. Here the raw scores are plotted in terms of "T" score units so that three profiles emerge, one for each column and one for the total or "resultant." Although the standard units are referred to as T scale scores (which are defined as having a mean of 50 and a standard deviation of 10), the effective range on the summary card is from 28 to about 110 units. The V-1 scale extends from 40 to 105, a most remarkable degree of asymmetry. Furthermore, the profiles for presidents, accountants, salesmen, machine operators, and teachers, as reported by Clarke, have means clustering around 60, with no single point falling so low as the ostensible mean of 50.

Up to this point the AVA Administrator has been permitted to proceed. Quoting from the manual:

> The AVA Administrator is authorized only to administer and score the Activity Vector Analysis. The interpretation of an AVA is the responsibility of a Certified AVA Analyst and cannot be done by anyone other than that person. Any attempt on the part of the Administrator to interpret an AVA will result not only in withdrawal of endorsement of the Administrator concerned but, more important, may result in irreparable harm to the person concerned.

Interpretation of the profiles is the function of the AVA Analyst, a person trained by Walter V. Clarke Associates for a fee of $1,500.00 in an intensive three-week course. In the booklet entitled *Ethical Standards for Activity Vector Analysts* there appears a form of Hippocratic oath:

> I hereby agree, in view of the responsibility placed upon me by my company, and in view of having been accepted by Walter V. Clarke Associates for training in the Activity Vector Analysis Program for Effective Human Relations, to make use of the knowledge and information bestowed upon me for the welfare of my fellow man; to maintain the confidential nature of the information entrusted in me; to act in accord with the highest ethical standards consistent with the professional nature of my work; to maintain the dignity and stability essential to the great responsibility vested in me; and to carry on the established principles of Activity Vector Analysis to the best of my ability.

The process used by the analyst in interpreting the profiles is not described. However, some clues appear in three supplementary publications furnished to analysts. The first of these, the *Manual for Job Activity Rating*, describes a method of job analysis by which a particular job is rated on a 9-point scale for each of 25 factors. Weighted equivalents for each factor scale are given in a series of tables in this manual. In a "Job Activity Rating" form these weights are added and converted into what seems to be an ideal "AVA Pattern Shape." The rationale underlying this protracted exercise in arithmetic is not disclosed. The weights are so arranged that the four values of any pattern shape will add to 20.

The pattern shape is then translated into a "Universe Shape," apparently through arbitrary expansion of the deviations from the pattern mean. In the example shown in the manual, the profile values of 4.8, 3.5, 6.5, and 5.2 became respectively 4, 1, 9, and 6. These latter numbers define the job pattern shape.

The second publication contributing to our knowledge of the process is entitled *Preliminary Atlas of AVA Pattern Universe 258*. The face page describes the content:

> This Preliminary Atlas contains a projected map of the spherical universe of AVA pattern shapes.
> Included are duplicate sheets without the pattern shapes which can be used for three dimensional distributions.
> A complete Atlas including all pattern intercorrelations will be made available at a later date.

The number of the "Universe" seems to derive from the fact that 258 profiles are shown in a sort of Mercator projection. The sum of the four values in each pattern is 20 and each has one or more extreme values.

The third supplementary publication is entitled *Correlation Tables: AVA Pattern Universe*. It consists of over 165 large pages. The prefatory section indicates that the purpose is to substitute a numerical and spatial definition of profile shapes for the "word-pictures" used in the past. The first portion of this volume is devoted to a description of vector theory and its relationship to AVA patterns. The major portion consists of 258 tables, one for each pattern shape, giving the correlation coefficients between that pattern and the remaining 257 patterns of the "Pattern Universe." Finally, there are distribution charts and polar tabulation charts.

Space does not permit, nor does the content warrant, a detailed discussion of the fallacies involved in the erection of this questionable mathematical superstructure. It is of more concern to examine the dependability and utility of the *Activity Vector Analysis*.

There is a series of articles prepared by the staff of Walter V. Clarke Associates dealing with various characteristics of the AVA. There is also a smaller number of reports of studies conducted by persons not so affiliated. Some of Clarke's articles have been published in the *Journal of Psychology*, others are private publications of Walter V. Clarke Associates, Inc.; while only one, under the joint authorship of Wallace, Clarke, and Dry (7) appears in a journal which adheres to conventional professional editorial standards.

With the exception of the latter article, the Clarke publications fail to describe the procedures used or to report the basic data in such manner as to permit independent replication of any of these investigations. This reviewer has been forced to the conclusion that the purpose of these writings is not to inform but to overwhelm and impress the naive or casual reader. All sorts of complex statistical techniques are flashed before the eyes without a report of the basic data or even a reasonably complete description of the circumstances under which the study took place. Cases are dropped for such reasons as, "Examination of the forty-one AVA resultant profiles obtained from the analyses resulted in the elimination of five (5) cases on the basis of the pattern shape deviation standard established for this Study." Such selective elimination of cases is, of course, a notorious way of obtaining spurious indications of validity.

It is customary, when the claims made by the originator of a technique seem extravagant, to look for verification through investigations conducted by competent and unbiased persons. Consequently, the available independent reports deserve careful attention.

Mosel (1) reports estimated reliabilities of .74 and .73 for "other" and "self" choices. These values approximate those reported for test-retest coefficients in the manual but raise questions regarding the dependability of profiles based on these variables.

A General Electric Company report entitled "A Study to Determine How Well the Activity Vector Analysis Measures Personality Characteristics of Draftsmen," prepared by H. H. Meyer in 1954, concludes that the AVA showed little correlation with the ratings of supervisors or associates on some 11 personality traits and that two trained analysts rating some 50 draftsmen on "Over-all Suitability for Drafting Work" agreed with each other to the extent represented by a correlation coefficient of .19.

Another study conducted by D. J. Moffie of North Carolina State College with employees of the Hanes Hosiery Mills Company was concerned with the productivity of 47 hosiery inspectors and 100 hosiery loopers. Two AVA Analysts working independently classified the inspectors into three categories of productivity. No significant relationship with production was found for the ratings of either analyst. With the 100 loopers, three analysts working independently classified the subjects into three categories of productivity. In this instance, none of the three analysts produced results significantly superior to chance. Moffie also investigated the extent of agreement between pairs of analysts and found that one of the three pairs agreed to a slightly greater extent than could be attributed to chance, while the remaining pairs showed less agreement.

A second General Electric Company report entitled "A Research Study of the Use of Tests and the Interview for Evaluating Technical Personnel," conducted at the Fort Wayne Works and reported in 1954, included 164 engineers. A composite ranking procedure was used to divide the group into quarters for criterion purposes. The AVA was scored and interpreted by a representative of Walter V. Clarke Associates. Comparison was made between the top and bottom quarters with respect to the criterion. For each group 55 per cent were given "Average" or "High" AVA ratings. Quoting the report, "This test purports to measure the ability and personality characteristics which contribute to success in engineering work. The ratings made by the test analyst in this study, however, showed no relationship to the job performance ratings made by the supervisors."

The most thorough of the investigations of the validity of the AVA is the one reported by Wallace, Clarke, and Dry (7). The subjects were 899 "financed" life insurance agents employed by any of five insurance companies. Each of these men took the AVA at the time of employment, but the AVA scores were not used in the hiring decision. The AVA forms were sent to the Clarke home office for scoring. Each man also completed the LIAMA *Aptitude Index,* which scores were used in selection. The criterion of success was remaining with the company throughout the period and producing more than the median volume of business for current first year agents of that company. About 24 per cent met these requirements for the first year and 17 per cent for the second. Neither for the first nor for the second year did the AVA ratings show any significant relationship to success.

Over the past forty years a great number of self-descriptive inventories have been constructed and tried out. This reviewer is unable to recall a well established instance of useful validity for this class of questionnaire against a criterion of occupational success. The *Activity Vector Analysis* is simply another such inventory, and, from a technical standpoint, a poorly constructed one. The mumbo jumbo of allegedly sophisticated statistical procedures is no substitute for demonstrated validity. The awarding of titles to those trained in administration and interpretation, the gaudy names given the accessory materials, and the apparent reluctance to disclose basic data are scarcely representative of a conservative scientific approach.

Subsequent to the preparation of the paragraphs above, three additional dittoed reports by Merenda and Clarke were received by *The Mental Measurements Yearbook* office and transmitted to the reviewer. These have been read with care, and in the reviewer's opinion, conform to the pattern of incomplete, statistically pretentious, and misleading accounts previously described.

[30]

The Adjustment Inventory. Grades 9–16, adults; 1934–39; 1 form; 2 levels; 50¢ per specimen set, cash orders postpaid; (20–25) minutes; Hugh M. Bell; [Consulting Psychologists Press, Inc.] *
a) STUDENT FORM. Grades 9–16; 1934–39; 4 scores: home, health, social, emotional; 2 editions; manual ['34]; tentative norms.
   1) [*Regular Edition.*] 1934–39; 1 form ('34) ; $3 per 25 tests; separate answer sheets ('39) may be used; $1.75 per 50 IBM answer sheets; $2.50 per set of hand scoring stencils and manual; $1.75 per set of machine scoring stencils.
   2) [*IBM Test-Answer Sheet Edition.*] 1939; $3.75 per 50 tests; $2.50 per set of machine scoring stencils.
b) ADULT FORM. Adults; 1938–39; 5 scores: home, occupational, health, social, emotional; 1 form ('38) ; manual ['38]; prices same as for Regular Edition of Student Form; separate answer sheets ('39) may be used.

REFERENCES

1–15. See 40:1200.
16–119. See 4:28.
120. AARONS, WILLIAM B. *A Study of Intra-Family Personality Similarities and Differences as Measured by Test Performance on the Bell Adjustment Inventory.* Master's thesis, Temple University (Philadelphia, Pa.), 1942.
121. HAHN, MILTON EDWIN. *An Investigation of Measured Aspects of Social Intelligence in a Distributive Occupation.* Doctor's thesis, University of Minnesota (Minneapolis, Minn.), 1942.
122. SOLOMON, LEWIS E. *Some Relationships Between Reading Ability and Degree of Academic Success in College.* Doctor's thesis, University of Colorado (Boulder, Colo.), 1944.
123. CASNER, DANIEL. *Certain Factors Associated With Success and Failure in Personal-Adjustment Counseling.* Doctor's thesis, New York University (New York, N.Y.), 1950.
124. JOHNSON, RALPH H., AND BOND, GUY L. "Reading Ease of Commonly Used Tests." *J Appl Psychol* 34:319–24 O '50. * (*PA* 26:299)
125. GOULD, HENRY. *Relation of Certain Personality Components to Achievement in Secondary School Science.* Doctor's thesis, New York University (New York, N.Y.), 1951. (*DA* 12:160)
126. MARSHALL, MAX L. *A Comparison of the Effects of Two Response Sets on a Structured Personality Test.* Master's thesis, Vanderbilt University (Nashville, Tenn.), 1951.
127. PAULSON, STANLEY F. "Changes in Confidence During a Period of Speech Training: Transfer of Training and Comparison of Improved and Non-Improved Groups on the Bell Adjustment Inventory." *Speech Monogr* 18:260–5 N '51. *
128. NEWMAN, SIDNEY H.; FRENCH, JOHN W.; AND BOBBITT, JOSEPH M. "Analysis of Criteria for the Validation of Selection Measures at the United States Coast Guard Academy." *Ed & Psychol Meas* 12:394–407 au '52. * (*PA* 27:6159)
129. OSBORNE, R. TRAVIS; GREENE, JAMES E.; AND SANDERS, WILMA B. "Urban-Rural Differences in Personality of College Students as Measured by an Adjustment Inventory." *Rural Sociol* 17:61–2 Mr '52. *
130. PRATT, MARTHA A. *The Predictive Significance of Scores on Bell's School Inventory.* Master's thesis, University of Georgia (Athens, Ga.), 1952.
131. SHAMES, GEORGE HERBERT. *An Investigation of Prognosis and Evaluation in Speech Therapy.* Doctor's thesis, University of Pittsburgh (Pittsburgh, Pa.), 1952.
132. CANTONI, LOUIS J. *A Follow-Up Study of the Personal Adjustment of the Subjects Who Participated in the 1939–1943 Flint, Michigan, Guidance Demonstration.* Doctor's thesis, University of Michigan (Ann Arbor, Mich.), 1953.
133. O'CONNOR, WILLIAM F. *The Relationship Between Emotionality as Measured by a Verbal Discrimination Scale and the Bell Adjustment Inventory.* Master's thesis, Fordham University (New York, N.Y.), 1953.
134. ABERNETHY, ETHEL M. "The Effect of Sorority Pressures on the Results of a Self-Inventory." *J Social Psychol* 40:177–83 Ag '54. * (*PA* 29:6189)
135. MUNGER, PAUL F. "Factors Related to Persistence in College of Students Who Ranked in the Lower Third of Their High School Class." *J Counsel Psychol* 1:132–6 fall '54. * (*PA* 29:6258)
136. PIERCE-JONES, JOHN. "The Readability of Certain Standard Tests." *Calif J Ed Res* 5:80–2 Mr '54. * (*PA* 28:8729)
137. SANDRA, M. ELAINE. *A Comparative Study of the Scores Obtained by Institutional Adolescent Girls on the Bell Adjustment Inventory and the P-F Test.* Master's thesis, Fordham University (New York, N.Y.), 1954.
138. SIMS, VERNER M. "Relations Between the Social-Class Identification and Personality Adjustment of a Group of High School and College Students." *J Social Psychol* 40:323–7 N '54. * (*PA* 29:7190)
139. CANTONI, LOUIS J. "High School Tests and Measurements as Predictors of Occupational Status." *J Appl Psychol* 39:253–5 Ag '55. * (*PA* 30:4722)
140. CANTONI, LOUIS J. "A Study in Emotional Adjustment: The Correlation of Student and Adult Forms of the Bell Adjustment Inventory Over a Period of Thirteen Years." *Ed & Psychol Meas* 15:137–43 su '55. * (*PA* 30:2449)
141. CHANCE, JUNE ELIZABETH. "Prediction of Changes in a Personality Inventory on Retesting." *Psychol Rep* 1:383–7 D '55. * (*PA* 30:5979)
142. JESSEN, MARGARET S. "Factors in Parents' Prediction of Adolescent Responses to Selected Items on the Bell Adjustment Inventory." Abstract. *Am Psychol* 10:365 Ag '55. *
143. THOMAS, CHARLES W., JR. *An Evaluation of the Bell Adjustment Inventory as a Predictor of Successful Medical School Candidates at John Carroll University.* Master's thesis, John Carroll University (Cleveland, Ohio), 1955.
144. WILLIAMS, JOSEPH L. *An Evaluation of the Bell Adjustment as an Instrument for Predicting Academic Success at Texas Southern University.* Master's thesis, Texas Southern University (Houston, Tex.), 1956.
145. BOYKIN, LEANDER L. "The Adjustment of 2,078 Negro Students." *J Negro Ed* 26:75–9 w '57. * (*PA* 32:922)

For reviews by Nelson G. Hanawalt and Theodore R. Sarbin, see 4:28; for reviews by Raymond B. Cattell, John G. Darley, C. M. Louttit, and Percival M. Symonds of the Student Form, and reviews by S. J. Beck, J. P. Guilford, and Doncaster G. Humm of the Adult Form, see 40:1200 (1 excerpt); for a review by Austin H. Turney of the Student Form, see 38:912 (although three reviews are listed under 38:912, only the review by Austin H. Turney is a review of Bell's Adjustment Inventory; *the other two are reviews of Bell's* School Inventory).

[31]

★**Adjustment Questionnaire.** Ages 12–17; 1951; 11 scores: self-confidence, sense of personal worth, sense of personal freedom, recognition, social relationships, nervous symptoms, moral attitudes, family relationships, school relationships, emotionality, total; IBM;

1 form ['51]; mimeographed manual ['51]; separate answer sheets must be used; 16s. per 100 tests; 5s. per 100 IBM answer sheets; postage extra; specimen set not available; Afrikaans edition available; (25–30) minutes; National Bureau of Educational and Social Research. *

[32]

★Behavior Preference Record: *What Would You Do?* (A Study of Some Home and School Problems). Grades 4-6, 7-9, 9-12; 1953; 6 scores: cooperation, friendliness, integrity, leadership, responsibility, critical thinking; IBM; Forms A, B; 3 levels: Elementary, Intermediate, Advanced; separate answer sheets must be used; $2.80 per 35 tests; 7¢ per Scoreze answer sheet; 4¢ per IBM answer sheet; 60¢ per set of scoring stencils; postage extra; 50¢ per specimen set of any one level, postpaid; (30–45) minutes; Hugh B. Wood; California Test Bureau. *

J. Thomas Hastings, *University Examiner; Director of Unit on Evaluation in Bureau of Educational Research; Professor of Education, University of Illinois, Urbana, Illinois.*

Of the four purposes stated by the author for this instrument—to determine understanding of democratic ideals, to determine stated preferences for various types of behavior, to determine the rationalization (critical thinking) for preferred behaviors, and to stimulate discussion and decisions about desirable social behavior—the fourth is by far the most appropriate. The "record" grew out of a discussion in an eighth grade class of characteristics of democratic behavior and a subsequent search for a means for "measuring" the characteristics. As a teaching device directed at getting students to think systematically about their behavior in daily situations and its meaning for democratic ideals, this type of discussion project should be useful in the hands of a good teacher. It does not follow that the instrument with its scores and norms on behavioral traits is equally useful.

To the contrary, the good teacher who wishes to use the *method* probably would find that the categorization of democratic behavior into five "traits" and an ability is restrictive of meaningful thinking on the part of the students. Certainly the teacher who cannot on his own handle such a discussion project usefully would be apt to err seriously in using the device as a measure of the characteristics. In the latter case, serious harm could come from labeling pupils (or helping them label themselves) according to the score categories—very high, high, average, low, and very low—on the five characteristics: cooperation, friendliness, integrity, leadership, and responsibility. It should be made clearer in the manual that these "characteristics" are labels for constructs which *may* seem to explain or make clearer the expressed choice of action in a given situation. In many cases some other label may be of more use in explaining the choice of action for certain individuals. For example, "aggressiveness" may seem a more useful construct than does "leadership" when a pupil chooses to tell others "to be quiet." Or again, "shyness" may be a more useful label than "integrity" when a student waits to ask a question until a teacher finishes talking to another student.

The manual does suggest what would appear to be some useful activities in a classroom discussion of the answers recorded by pupils in the class. However, the suggestion that regular teachers do individual counseling with students whose test scores show "unusual anti-social tendencies" is very likely to be harmful. The reliability and validity of the scores, the basis for norms, and the concepts themselves warrant individual counseling only by a well trained counselor, and such a counselor would not need the test for this purpose. The caution that the teacher refer cases which he should not handle is meaningless, since untrained people cannot sense referral needs.

The scores on characteristics are computed by giving one point on the characteristic if a student chooses a certain action in a given problem and by subtracting a point on that characteristic for the choice of some other action. The instrument is keyed in such a fashion that a given choice of action may add a point (or subtract a point) on two or three characteristics. Although the manual states that, from a table of intercorrelations, "it may be assumed that fairly discrete characteristics are being measured," it should be noted that some of the traits seem to appear together rather frequently on the key. For example: On one form containing 20 problems there is an aggregate of 70 possible actions. Twenty-eight of these would give a point on cooperation, whereas 18 are keyed to give a point on friendliness. Actually, 10 of the actions are common for the two characteristics, i.e., give a point on each. Therefore, more than half of the "friendliness points" are also "cooperation points." By the same type of count, only three of the choices which take a point away from friendliness do not also take a point away from cooperation. The user should be aware of the fact that there is this type of "built in" relationship, especially when he is using the profile.

Following the set of three to five possible actions among which the examinee may choose for each problem situation, there are a number of "reasons for choosing the action" which he may mark. The form of the test necessarily restricts the student to choosing among those reasons given—he cannot write out his own. Although this fact should be taken into consideration by the test user, he should also recognize that these reasons were pulled from among those most frequently given when the test was first designed. The "critical thinking" score for a student is the percentage representing the number of "keyed" or right reasons which he has marked. Two questions should be kept in mind by the user: (a) Do these reasons for action actually represent the construct I have for "critical thinking"? (b) Is the percentage for a given student based upon many, several, or few marked reasons? A high percentage based upon few attempts certainly suggests a different behavior from the one suggested by the same percentage based upon many attempts.

The author states, "The scores of over eight thousand students were used in developing the norms." According to the table in the manual, the total number of students taking any form at any level of any of the five editions since 1938 is 8,275. A statement to the effect that some 1,700 students were utilized for the norms on the 1953 edition should be noted to mean *all* students taking *all* forms at *all* levels. Actually, the norms for any one form of the current edition are based upon approximately 300 cases.

In summary, the main function of this test should be to serve as an informal teaching device, and the average teacher would run less danger of doing harm if he were to use it for class discussion without scoring it at all. Trained counselors might find it useful for eliciting certain clues or for starting certain kinds of client discussions, but it should certainly not be used by regular teachers as a measure of the traits or ability named in the scores.

EDWARD LANDY, *Director, Division of Counseling Services, Newton Public Schools, Newton, Massachusetts.*

The *Behavior Preference Record* employs the device of briefly describing a situation to which a pupil might respond in a variety of ways. He is then asked to select from several alternatives a course of action and the reasons for his selection. The accompanying manual

states that the primary value of the BPR lies in the opportunities which it presents for teaching by providing a tool for informal, but directed, character education. Face examination of the materials would seem to indicate that this is a valid claim.

It is unfortunate that the publishers were not content to stop with this claim, which is a very important one in its own right. Elsewhere in the manual the publishers make these additional claims: "The *Behavior Preference Record* is designed to: (a) provide a systematic analysis of some behavior situations to determine the individual's understanding of democratic ideals, (b) to determine his stated preferences for various types of behavior, (c) to determine his rationalizations (critical thinking) for his preferred behavior, and (d) to stimulate discussions and decisions about desirable social behavior." It is very doubtful to what extent (a) and (c) are achieved, if at all. What stopping or not stopping at a red traffic light, or liking or not liking your mother's cooking (these are samples of situations) have to do with democratic ideals is unclear. Instead of obtaining (c), one might, and probably does in many instances, get the pupil's best guess as to what he thinks teacher would like to have him answer.

The manual seems to make still another claim for which it presents no substantial evidence. It states: "The *Behavior Preference Record* provides analytical evidence on the extent of development of certain behavioral characteristics of the individual. From this evidence it is possible to identify certain shortcomings and recommend remedial measures to correct them." This statement can be interpreted as saying much or saying little. In the hands of the clinically unsophisticated classroom teacher it may lead to harm rather than good.

The possible confusion as to the interpretation of results is illustrated by the sample profile given on page 5 of the manual. The boy's profile ranks are very low in cooperation and critical thinking, low in friendliness, average in responsibility, high in integrity, and very high in leadership. The accompanying interpretation reads as follows: "The boy whose profile appears below shows an unusual potential for Leadership but he has a very low score in Cooperation and Critical Thinking. *This suggests aggressive rather than real leadership* [reviewer's italics]. He should be given special assistance in clarifying the concepts and developing the skills related to Cooperation." One is left wondering just what the labeled characteristics do measure.

An elaborate system of scoring with tables of norms and profiles tends to give an appearance of rigorous quantitative measurement of "certain characteristics of democratic behavior" which is not substantiated, in this review's judgment, by any evidence presented in the manual.

If the BPR were presented simply as a device for stimulating discussion and self-examination, particularly with respect to rationalization tendencies, it could be recommended as a useful teaching tool. It cannot be recommended as an instrument for measuring clearly defined characteristics of democratic behavior upon which remedial measures can be based.

J Consult Psychol 17:401–2 O '53. *Laurance F. Shaffer.* * While the blank may evoke some useful thinking about the social characteristics of pupils, it suffers from numerous faults. The prestige values of the responses were not controlled. As in all such short questionnaires, radically different interpretations from "average" to "very high" may be drawn from scores which differ by as little as 3 points when the standard error of measurement is as great as 2.8 points.

[33]

★**Bonney-Fessenden Sociograph.** Grades 4–12; 1955; 1 form; 50¢ per set of sociograph, 40 answer slips, and manual; 15¢ per sociograph; 15¢ per 40 answer slips; 25¢ per manual; postage extra; administration time not reported; Merl E. Bonney and Seth A. Fessenden; California Test Bureau. *

ÅKE BJERSTEDT, *Department of Psychology, University of Lund, Lund, Sweden.*

For the recording of interpersonal relations, two groups of devices have been mainly used: sociograms and sociomatrices. The *Bonney-Fessenden Sociograph* might, perhaps, be most quickly described as a folded sociomatrix: the ordinary sociomatrix, in which each pair-relation is described by two cells, may be thought of as folded along the main diagonal so that the two cells common to two people coincide. More concretely, we deal with a tabulation form of triangular shape, where each cell has two compartments, one for outgoing choices and one for incoming choices. By this device, mutual choices between two individuals occur in *one* cell and are consequently much more readily revealed than in the nonfolded type of tabulation. This is, in fact, the unique contribution of the socio-

graph, which could, therefore, be recommended as a timesaving device when we are especially interested in two-way relations.

Having pointed out its valuable contribution, the reviewer now has to criticize the overly enthusiastic claims made for this new technique in the manual. It is stated there that the sociograph not only simplifies the recording of sociometric data, but also "retains all of the advantages of the sociogram and the matrix heretofore required for sociometric appraisal." This is certainly not the truth. For example, the sociograph does not retain the surveyability for several-people relations, which is the unique feature of a good sociogram: one cannot trace chains, triangles, and squares as easily as one can in such a diagram. Neither does the sociograph retain all the advantages of the conventional sociomatrix: for example, one is not so easily able to use the tabulation as a basis for various computational analyses (array totals, matrix multiplication for the determination of several-step relations, and the like). Certain specific sociographic devices such as the target diagram and the chessboard diagram have made it possible to compare in a surveyable manner total status with single choice relations or status at different time points in one diagram. None of these possibilities exists in the sociograph. This criticism is not directed against the sociograph as such, for one instrument cannot have every advantage at the same time. However, it is directed against the "wholesale" statements in the manual about its value and uniqueness, statements which could be very misleading to those who are not familiar with existing techniques.

Besides, it should be pointed out that the simplifying effect of the sociograph is mainly limited to the locating of pair relations. In several other respects it is more confusing than the ordinary sociomatrix. In the conventional matrix, for example, outgoing choices may simply be read from the row of an individual and incoming choices from his column. In the sociograph, on the other hand, outgoing choices have to be read from the left half of the cells in an individual's row *plus* the right half of the cells in his column, and incoming choices from the right half of the cells in his row *plus* the left half of the cells in his column. That this is much more complicated is admitted implicitly when it is recommended that outgoing choices should be tabulated from the answer sheets rather than from the sociograph.

From the tabulation we are often interested in getting individual sums not only for the six basic variables (positive and negative choices given, received, and reciprocated), but also for the corresponding socioperceptual variables (positive and negative choice-guesses), for different preference levels, and for different choice aspects (criteria). In the flexible and informal sociomatrix, which we line up for our specific purpose on squared paper, we may include all these variables without great difficulty. On the present printed form, however, we cannot include more than six variables in all since space is supplied only for six array totals.

As this instrument is primarily a recording device and not a test, ordinary questions as to administration, norms, reliability, and validity are not of immediate concern. The manual, however, does give a helpful discussion of administration, including some original suggestions; the use of answer slips, for example, is not usual in conventional sociometry, but may be an important timesaver among group members sufficiently careful not to introduce unnecessary errors during the number checking procedure. Further, the manual presents a discussion of reliability, validity, and utility as related to the sociometric method in general. This discussion is, of course, very brief, but the authors succeed all the same in outlining some of the most important features in a helpful and judicious manner, although they seem too optimistic in a few instances.

Summing up, the *Bonney-Fessenden Sociograph* is a specific form of sociometric tabulation which, for certain purposes, especially for the quick location of mutual preferences, may be very useful. Its manual, in addition, outlines certain more general methodological questions within the field of sociometry in a helpful way. However, the explicit claims that at the same time it retains all the advantages of other types of sociograms and matrices do *not* seem warranted.

C. ROBERT PACE, *Professor of Psychology and Chairman of the Department, Syracuse University, Syracuse, New York.*

This is not a test; it is a tabulation chart for recording sociometric data. Its virtue is to be judged by the convenience of its format and by the explanations and cautions which its authors

give prospective users. On all these matters the device appears to be useful.

The chart may be used for groups up to 40 in number. Students are provided with answer slips on which they record their choices by checking numbers corresponding to the names of the persons chosen. The slips are then laid on the tabulation chart, and the choices recorded. Summary columns provide space for noting the number of choices given and received, the mutual choices, the rejections, and other information typically looked for in the sociometric technique. Directions for using the device are specific and detailed.

The manual contains a general discussion of the reliability and validity of sociometric scores, based on a selective survey of related literature. The suggestions for using and interpreting sociometric data are helpful and well balanced. Classroom teachers should welcome this systematic method and convenient chart for simplifying what, under the best of circumstances, is still a rather complicated task.

[34]

★A Book About Me. Grades kgn-1; 1952; workbook for gathering data about children's background, maturity, interests, and attitudes; 1 form; norms for experimental form only; 10 or more copies, 39¢ each; 60¢ per 20 analysis sheets; 50¢ per specimen set; postage extra; Edith Sherman Jay; Science Research Associates. *

FLORENCE M. TEAGARDEN, *Emeritus Professor of Psychology, University of Pittsburgh, Pittsburgh, Pennsylvania.*

By her choice of materials and her suggestions for their use the author shows intimate knowledge of kindergarten and first grade children as well as a philosophy underlying good curricula for these ages. The material to be used by the children is a workbook consisting of 32 pages of pictures (several hundred in all) of people and things pertinent to the lives of kindergarten and first grade children. The nature and use of this material will be most easily understood if readers will first thumb through all the pictures to see their charm, realism, and practicality, and then read carefully pages 18–30 and 1–17 in the manual.

If this sequence is followed, the reader will see that the pictures may actually be used as a *test* of the contents of the child's mind at the time he enters school. This, of course, should be done before the children are given individual copies of *A Book About Me* to use as a workbook. Directions for so using the book and for scoring the test are given in the teacher's manual. Such a test would require one class period every day for a week. Analysis sheets provide for the recording of pertinent data from this test, the results of which can become a part of each child's cumulative school record.

Innumerable suggestions are given for the use of *A Book About Me* as a workbook in the usual classroom sense. Questions which may be asked about the pictures are given, as are examples of ways in which the pictures may be marked, cut out, and mounted by the children.

In addition to suggestions for the use of *A Book About Me* as a survey testing device and as a classroom workbook, the author gives several interesting accounts of the ways in which individual teachers with particular aims in mind have used the book, e.g., the teacher who wanted to improve her children's oral English; the teacher who wanted a concrete way of acquainting parents with what the child and the school were doing; the teacher of older dull children obliged to do very elementary work; the teacher of ungraded classes, and the like. Examples of the book's use in college classes in child development, in clinic interviews, and even in play therapy sessions are also given.

Because of the various ways in which *A Book About Me* can be and has been used, there is little that can or need be said about matters of reliability and validity. The author does, however, show some interesting age and sex differences on responses to three pages of pictures by 50 boys and 50 girls at each age from 4 through 7—400 responses in all.

The reviewer is quite impressed with the possible uses of this device. She is obliged to say, however, that she would have come to an understanding of the purposes and uses of the material more readily if the suggestions made above as to the order in which the teacher or clinician should read the manual had been come by a little sooner and with less trial and error. As a clinical psychologist working primarily with preschool children, the reviewer hopes that some day the author will use her demonstrated ability to give us more material of this kind that can be used, particularly as a projective device, with little children.

[35]

★Bristol Social-Adjustment Guides. Ages 5–15; 1956–58; 1 form ('56); 3 rating scales; 4s. per 12 diagnostic forms ('56) for each scale; 25s. per manual ('58); 3s. per specimen set; postage extra; (10–20)

minutes; D. H. Stott and E. G. Sykes (*a*, *b*); University of London Press Ltd. *

a) THE CHILD IN SCHOOL. Separate editions for boys and girls; 6s. per 12 scales; 6d. per single copy; 3s. per set of scoring keys.

b) THE CHILD IN RESIDENTIAL CARE. 6s. per 12 scales; 6d. per single copy; 4s. per set of scoring keys.

c) THE CHILD IN THE FAMILY. Life history chart ('56); 9s. per 12 scales; 9d. per single copy; 2s. 6d. per scoring key.

[36]

Brown Personality Inventory for Children. Grades 4–9; 1935–46; 1 form ['35]; manual ['46]; $2.15 per 25 tests; 35¢ per specimen set; postpaid; administration time not reported; Fred Brown; Public School Publishing Co. *

REFERENCES

1–8. See 40:1240.
9. BROWN, FRED. "A Comparative Study of Stability and Maturity of Non-Delinquent, Pre-Delinquent, and Delinquent Boys." Abstract. *Psychol B* 34:779–80 N '37. *
10. MORRIS, CHARLES M. "An Experimental Analysis of Certain Performance Tests." Abstract. *Psychol B* 34:716–7 N '37. *
11. KORAN, S. *A Study of Developmental Age, Brown Personality Inventory Scores, and Certain Traits in Elementary School Boys.* Master's thesis, Pennsylvania State College (State College, Pa.), 1938.
12. BROWN, FRED. "An Experimental Study of Parental Attitudes and Their Effects on Child Adjustment." *Am J Orthopsychiatry* 12:224–30 Ap '42. * (*PA* 16:3336)
13. BROWN, FRED. "An Experimental Study of the Validity and Reliability of the Brown Personality Inventory for Children." *J Psychol* 17:75–89 Ja '44. * (*PA* 18:1449)
14. GOOCH, PAUL H. *A Study of the Responses of Children Nine to Fourteen Years of Age to the Brown Personality Inventory.* Master's thesis, Kansas State Teacher's College (Emporia, Kan.), 1953.
15. NOWELL, ANN. "Peer Status as Related to Measures of Personality." *Calif J Ed Res* 4:37–41 Ja '53. * (*PA* 28:1514)
16. ABRAMS, JULES C. *A Study of Certain Personality Characteristics of Non-Readers and Achieving Readers.* Doctor's thesis, Temple University (Philadelphia, Pa.), 1955. (*DA* 16:377)
17. NEUHAUS, EDMUND C. "A Personality Study of Asthmatic and Cardiac Children." *Psychosom Med* 20:181–6 My–Je '58. *
18. SARASON, SEYMOUR B.; DAVIDSON, KENNETH; LIGHTHALL, FREDERICK; AND WAITE, RICHARD. "Rorschach Behavior and Performance of High and Low Anxious Children." *Child Develop* 29:277–85 Je '58. *

For reviews by S. J. Beck and Carl R. Rogers, see 40:1240.

[37]

★California Psychological Inventory. Ages 13 and over; 1956–57; 18 scores: dominance (Do), capacity for status (Cs), sociability (Sy), social presence (Sp), self-acceptance (Sa), sense of well-being (Wb), responsibility (Re), socialization (So), self-control (Sc), tolerance (To), good impression (Gi), communality (Cm), achievement via conformance (Ac), achievement via independence (Ai), intellectual efficiency (Ie), psychological-mindedness (Py), flexibility (Fx), femininity (Fe); IBM; 1 form ('56); administrator's guide ('57, reprinted from manual); separate answer sheets must be used; $6.25 per 25 tests; $3.75 per 100 profiles ['57] and either hand scored or IBM answer sheets; $3 per set of either hand scoring stencils or IBM scoring stencils; $3 per manual ('57); $1 per specimen set; postage extra; scoring service available; (45–60) minutes; Harrison G. Gough; Consulting Psychologists Press, Inc. *

REFERENCES

1. GOUGH, HARRISON G. "A New Dimension of Status: I, Development of a Personality Scale." *Am Sociol R* 13:401–9 Ag '48. * (*PA* 24:523)
2. GOUGH, HARRISON G. "A New Dimension of Status: II, Relationship of the St Scale to Other Variables." *Am Sociol R* 13:534–7 O '48. * (*PA* 24:524)

3. GOUGH, HARRISON G. "The Construction of a Personality Scale to Predict Academic Achievement in Introductory Psychology Courses." Abstract. *Am Psychol* 7:367–8 Jl '52. *

4. GOUGH, HARRISON G. "Identifying Psychological Femininity." *Ed & Psychol Meas* 12:427–39 au '52. * (*PA* 27:5873)

5. GOUGH, HARRISON G. "On Making a Good Impression." *J Ed Res* 46:33–42 S '52. *

6. GOUGH, HARRISON G. "Predicting Social Participation." *J Social Psychol* 35:227–33 My '52. * (*PA* 27:3455)

7. GOUGH, HARRISON G., AND PETERSON, DONALD R. "The Identification and Measurement of Predispositional Factors in Crime and Delinquency." *J Consult Psychol* 16:207–12 Je '52. * (*PA* 27:5279)

8. GOUGH, HARRISON G.; McCLOSKY, HERBERT; AND MEEHL, PAUL E. "A Personality Scale for Social Responsibility." *J Abn & Social Psychol* 47:73–80 Ja '52. * (*PA* 26:6270)

9. GILMAN, SAMUEL F. *An Experiment in Validation of the Gough and Peterson Delinquency Prediction Scale.* Master's thesis, Boston College (Chestnut Hill, Mass.), 1953.

10. GOUGH, HARRISON G. "The Construction of a Personality Scale to Predict Scholastic Achievement." *J Appl Psychol* 37: 361–6 O '53. * (*PA* 29:1565)

11. GOUGH, HARRISON G. "What Determines the Academic Achievement of High School Students." *J Ed Res* 46:321–31 Ja '53. * (*PA* 28:1563)

12. WEBSTER, HAROLD. "Derivation and Use of the Masculinity-Femininity Variable." *J Clin Psychol* 9:33–6 Ja '53. * (*PA* 27:7803)

13. GOUGH, HARRISON G. "Systematic Validation of a Test for Delinquency." Abstract. *Am Psychol* 9:381 Ag '54. *

14. GOWAN, J. C., AND GOWAN, MAY SEAGOE. "The Guilford-Zimmerman and the California Psychological Inventory in the Measurement of Teaching Candidates." *Calif J Ed Res* 6:35–7 Ja '55. * (*PA* 29:7990)

15. KLUGH, HENRY E., AND BENDIG, A. W. "The Manifest Anxiety and ACE Scales and College Achievement." Abstract. *J Consult Psychol* 19:487 D '55. *

16. OETTEL, ARNOLD M. "Leadership: A Psychological Study." Abstract. *Am Psychol* 10:342 Ag '55. *

17. BENDIG, A. W., AND KLUGH, HENRY E. "A Validation of Gough's Hr Scale in Predicting Academic Achievement." *Ed & Psychol Meas* 16:516–23 w '56. * (*PA* 32:934)

18. BROWN, DONALD R., AND BYSTRYN, DENISE. "College Environment, Personality, and Social Ideology of Three Ethnic Groups." *J Social Psychol* 44:279–88 N '56. *

19. DUNNETTE, MARVIN D., AND AYLWARD, MERRIAM S. "Validity Information Exchange, No. 9-21: D.O.T. Code, Design and Development Engineers." *Personnel Psychol* 9:245–7 su '56. *

20. GOUGH, HARRISON G. "Potential Use of Personality Scales in Schools and Colleges," pp. 3–20. In *Fifth Annual Western Regional Conference on Testing Problems, April 13, 1956.* Princeton, N.J.: Educational Testing Service, [1956]. Pp. iii, 78. * (*PA* 31:8486)

21. NIYEKAWA, AGNES M. "A Comparative Analysis of Foreign and American Female College Groups on Three Personality Variables: Anxiety, Level of Aspiration and Femininity." *Psychol Newsl* 7:72–91 My–Je '56. * (*PA* 31:3697)

22. BENDIG, A. W. "The Validity of Two Temperament Scales in Predicting Student Achievement in Introductory Psychology." *J Ed Res* 50:571–80 Ap '57. *

23. BENNETT, LAWRENCE A., AND RUDOFF, ALVIN. "Evaluation of Modified Administration of the California Psychological Inventory." *J Clin Psychol* 13:303–4 Jl '57. *

24. CUADRA, CARLOS A., AND REED, CHARLES F. "Prediction of Psychiatric Aide Performance." *J Appl Psychol* 41:195–7 Je '57. *

25. DINITZ, SIMON; KAY, BARBARA; AND RECKLESS, WALTER C. "Delinquency Proneness and School Achievement." *Ed Res B* 36:131–6 Ap 10 '57. *

26. JACKSON, DOUGLAS N. "Response Acquiescence in the California Psychological Inventory." Abstract. *Am Psychol* 12:412–3 Jl '57. *

27. MORRIS, ROBERT P. "An Exploratory Study of Some Personality Characteristics of Gamblers." *J Clin Psychol* 13:191–3 Ap '57. * (*PA* 32:3294)

28. BENDIG, A. W. "Comparative Validity of Empirical Temperament Test Keys in Predicting Student Achievement in Psychology." *J Ed Res* 51:341–8 Ja '58. *

29. BENDIG, A. W. "Comparison of the Validity of Two Temperament Scales in Predicting College Achievement." *J Ed Res* 51:605–9 Ap '58. *

30. DUNNETTE, MARVIN D., AND KIRCHNER, WAYNE K. "Validation of Psychological Tests in Industry." *Personnel Adm* 21:20–7 My–Je '58. *

31. DUNNETTE, MARVIN D.; KIRCHNER, WAYNE K.; AND DE-GIDEO, JoANNE. "Relations Among Scores on Edwards Personal Preference Schedule, California Psychological Inventory, and Strong Vocational Interest Blank for an Industrial Sample." *J Appl Psychol* 42:178–81 Je '58. *

32. GOWAN, J. C. "Intercorrelations and Factor Analysis of Tests Given to Teaching Candidates." *J Exp Ed* 27:1–22 S '58. *

33. LIDDLE, GORDON. "The California Psychological Inventory and Certain Social and Personal Factors." *J Ed Psychol* 49:144–9 Je '58. *

LEE J. CRONBACH, *Professor of Education and Psychology, University of Illinois, Urbana, Illinois.*

The CPI is designed on the principle that questionnaire items which correlate with socially significant criteria are important, whether or not they fit into available personality theories. In this it resembles the *Minnesota Multiphasic Personality Inventory,* but the psychiatric states which provided the armature for the MMPI are here replaced by such external reference variables as social class membership, grade in introductory psychology, and prominence as a leader. Each criterion locates extreme groups who presumably have some psychological similarity, and a scale is formed from items which discriminate these extremes. The scale is thought of as measuring that underlying psychological complex, not merely as predicting the erstwhile criterion. The psychological nature of the complex is then established by further inquiry. The capacity-for-status (Cs) score, for example, consists of items marked differently in different social strata, and is regarded as a measure of whatever attitudes and attributes "underlie and lead to status," including ambition, communication effectiveness, and versatility.

The instrument has 480 true-false items (12 of which are duplicates), some from MMPI and others written to tap social and personal attitudes and interests. The items range over an exceptional variety of manifest content. Scores on 18 scales offer a descriptive profile of the high school student or adult. Eleven scales were based on external criteria. Four more scales were formed from items judged homogeneous. Finally, there are three control keys: Wb, based on responses given by normals asked to "fake bad"; Gi, based on responses given by normals when "faking good"; and Cm, a count of highly popular responses. Marked deviation on a control score casts doubt on the validity of the individual profile.

The development and technical work on the scale are of a high order. The reliabilities were carefully determined by retesting. Validity of each scale was determined by comparing groups which the scale presumably ought to discriminate; dozens of cross validities on sizeable samples are reported. Norms for males and females are based on several thousand accumulated cases; it might be better to have truly representative samples, but this is no serious weakness. The manual gives plentiful correlations with other tests. With its scientific yet readable style, its illustrative case interpretations, and its extensive data, the manual is in some respects a model for personality inventories. It does not, however, indicate recommended uses and necessary cautions as adequately as does the manual for the *Minnesota Counseling Inventory*.

The manual fails to tell what criteria were used in scale development. Tracing these in the literature, one finds puzzling disparities between the scale designations and the original criteria; e.g., the sociability scale consists of items that correlate with the number of extracurricular activities engaged in.

The presentation of validities, based largely on differences between extreme groups, is seriously misleading. On dominance, for example, the mean for 89 female leaders in high school is 29; for 4,056 nonleaders, 24. The SD within each group is 6, and CR is 8. This result would look less impressive if the substantial overlap were pointed out. For the same scale a CR of 6.42 is reported between girls rated high and girls rated low in dominance; the manual also reports a biserial r of .67 and a point biserial r of .53. These are illegitimate figures, since they ignore the intermediate group. Assuming that the selected cases are the highest and lowest 3 per cent of the group and estimating the product-moment r for all cases, we may conclude that the true validity is only about .22. This validity is representative. The extreme groups chosen to validate other scales also have notable overlap; for example, female jail inmates average at the 30th percentile of all females on the socialization scale. Ratings by qualified assessment teams never correlate above .50 with the corresponding CPI score, and values are often as low as .25.

Some aspects of the validity report are puzzling. In at least one instance a validity coefficient is given, not for the CPI key, but for an earlier scale using more items. For another scale, the manual gives no data but says that low scorers tend to be seen as cautious, confused, and easygoing; the published article on this scale gives data showing that they are seen as cynical, headstrong, and impatient. It would have been wiser to report meticulously a small number of well-substantiated findings than to invite misinterpretation by reporting too much, too casually.

One is inclined to say that personality scores with validities in the .20's are worthless, but Gough makes the possibly valid point that we should not expect any one scale to correlate highly with any datum on observed personality. Interpretation ought to rest on configurations: high Cs plus high responsibility, he says, implies efficiency and poise, but high Cs with low Re implies aggressiveness and opportunism. No data are offered to support this interesting proposal to take advantage of the superior "bandwidth" of this instrument. Ultimately we should be told the precise probability that a description inferred from an entire profile will correspond to the person's actual behavior.

Although actuarial instruments sometimes permit indirect and subtle measurement, the CPI is not appreciably less direct than other questionnaires on adjustment and character. Twelve of the principal scales are much affected by a desire to fake good or bad. Among males, eleven keys correlate .48 or higher with Bernreuter Self-Confidence. Despite the complex manner in which keys were developed, the test must be regarded as no more than a tabulation of overt self-descriptions. The chief difference between CPI and the majority of other inventories for school use is that its profile is much more elaborate. It measures the same seven dimensions as the new *Minnesota Counseling Inventory* (with no worse validities) and adds seven others.

The variables describe character in value loaded terms. Teachers and principals very likely will approve this, but the inventory seems to encourage the idea that there is just one ideal personality. Such scale titles as Responsibility, Tolerance, and Socialization have a pronounced ethical overtone which suggests that low scores reflect faults, rather than symptoms of needs, skills, and cultural pressures. Because of this implicit conflict with modern views of personality, it would be deplorable if CPI profiles were interpreted by principals, teachers, parents, or students without guidance from a psychologically-trained person. For use by the well-qualified counselor, the reviewer regards the *Edwards Personal Preference Schedule* as more suitable, its profile being more descriptive and less evaluative. To identify students needing counseling and to aid in counseling by teachers, the simpler *Mooney Problem Checklist* seems preferable. Further research may prove that the CPI patterns are richly significant. The reviewer's prejudices, however, lead him to prefer profiles describing the individual in psychological terms to profiles defined around complex social resultants such as disciplinary problems, presence in numerous school activities, and high grades. Gough is to be commended for pursuing his own contrary view skillfully, but the usefulness of his instrument is still in question.

ROBERT L. THORNDIKE, *Professor of Education, Teachers College, Columbia University, New York, New York.*

This inventory has been described as the "sane man's MMPI." That is, it is an inventory the development of which proceeded essentially by (*a*) assembling a large stock of items of various types which looked as though they might relate to something of significance about personality, (*b*) identifying criterion groups that differed sharply in some attribute judged to be socially significant and psychologically meaningful, and (*c*) developing a scoring key which included those items that were found empirically to differentiate the criterion groups. The criterion groups were, in this case, groups from the general population which differed in some significant respect.

This procedure has both strength and weakness. The strength lies in the efficiency of the scoring key for discriminating with respect to the *specific* criterion dimension on the basis of which the items were selected. The weakness lies in the possibility that this criterion dimension may not have clear, distinctive, and unequivocal psychological meaning. Furthermore, there is no limit to the number of criterion dimensions with respect to which one may undertake to establish keys (note, for example, the more than 40 keys for the *Strong Vocational Interest Blank*).

In the case of the CPI, the evidence is not clear as to how many of the 18 dimensions for which keys are provided by the author have a unique practical value that would justify them on that basis. However, it *is* clear that the 18 provide a very redundant, inefficient, and (to the reviewer) confused picture of individual personalities. Correlations between many of the scales are high—in some cases apparently approaching the reliabilities of the individual scales. Of the 18 scales, there are only 4 that fail to correlate at least .50 with some other scale, and many have correlations of this size with several others. There is, of course, no limit to the number of scales that *can* be developed for an inventory such as this except that set by the endurance of the originator. The problem is how many and which ones provide an efficient, parsimonious, and understandable description of an individual. Eighteen highly overlapping scores, many of which appear redundant both in name and in statistics, hardly appear to accomplish this.

Evidence provided on the reliability of the scales is hardly adequate to permit an appraisal of the uniqueness, if any, of the separate scales. Since the items making up a particular scale can be thought of as a sample from a universe of items that might have been used, it seems reasonable to ask for evidence on the split-half reliability, or some other indication of stability over samples of items. No such evidence is provided, data being limited to retest reliability on the same items. Application of Kuder-Richardson formula 21 to some of the data reported in the manual suggests that split-half reliabilities would be likely to be in the .70's.

The author has shown commendable industry in obtaining data for his instrument from many criterion groups. Selections from this material are presented in the manual. Unfortunately, the presentation is marred by faulty statistical analysis. Repeatedly, biserial correlations are reported for extreme groups, leaving out a large middle group. The resulting coefficients are, of course, grossly inflated and provide an unrealistic picture of the accuracy with which the instrument would make discriminations in an intact group.

It is conceivable that there may be a role for a personality inventory developed by the procedures and following the rationale of the CPI. However, this reviewer feels that the role will not be that of providing a clear, efficient, and simple personality description.

J Consult Psychol 21:359 Ag '57. Laurance F. Shaffer. * bears considerable resemblance to the group MMPI, from which about 200 of its 468 items were adapted. But the purpose of the CPI is quite different. It is intended primarily for use with normal subjects, not patients, and strives to assess personality characteristics important for social living. * The manual contains a wealth of information on the validities of scales and on the interpretations of single scales, interactions, and profiles. * By both objective and subjective evaluation, the CPI appears to be a major achievement. It will surely receive wide use for research and for practical applications.

[38]

*California Test of Personality, 1953 Revision. Grades kgn–3, 4–8, 7–10, 9–16, adults; 1939–53; 15 scores: self-reliance, sense of personal worth, sense of personal freedom, feeling of belonging, withdrawing tendencies, nervous symptoms, total personal adjustment, social standards, social skills, anti-social tendencies, family relations, school relations or occupational relations, community relations, total social adjustment, total adjustment; IBM for grades 4 and over; Forms AA, BB ('53); 5 levels; manual ('53); profile ('53); $3.15 per 35 tests; separate answer sheets may be used; 4¢ per IBM answer sheet; 7¢ per Scoreze answer sheet; 20¢ per hand scoring stencil; 60¢ per machine scoring stencil; postage extra; 50¢ per specimen set of any one level, postpaid; (45–60) minutes; Louis P. Thorpe, Willis W. Clark, and Ernest W. Tiegs; California Test Bureau. *

a) PRIMARY. Grades kgn–3; 1942–53.
b) ELEMENTARY. Grades 4–8; 1939–53.
c) INTERMEDIATE. Grades 7–10; 1939–53.
d) SECONDARY. Grades 9–16; 1942–53.
e) ADULT. Adults; 1942–53.

REFERENCES

1–24. See 3:26.
25. WALKER, ELSIE MEINE. A Comparative Study of Personalities of Elementary and Secondary Education Majors. Master's thesis, North Texas State Teachers College (Denton, Tex.), 1941.
26. ADOLPHSON, GUDRUN. The Relation of General Motor Ability to Personality Adjustment. Master's thesis, University of Colorado (Boulder, Colo.), 1942.
27. MARY VERA, Sister. "A Critical Study of Certain Personality Factors as Determining Elements in a Remedial Reading Program." Cath Ed R 40:145–61 Mr '42. *
28. ANDERSON, WILLIAM E. A Study of the Personality Characteristics of 153 Negro Pupils, Dunbar High School, Okmulgee, Oklahoma. Doctor's thesis, Colorado State College of Education (Greeley, Colo.), 1944.
29. YOUNG, LYLE L., AND COOPER, DAN H. "Some Factors Associated With Popularity." J Ed Psychol 35:513–35 D '44. * (PA 19:1000)
30. BOWERS, SCOTT T. Some Aspects of Personality Development of Children in an Institution. Master's thesis, Ohio University (Athens, Ohio), 1945.
31. ENGLE, T. L. "Personality Adjustments of Children Belonging to Two Minority Groups." J Ed Psychol 36:543–60 D '45. * (PA 20:2136)
32. BUTTIMORE, DENNIS J. Some Aspects of the Personality of Male Juvenile Delinquents. Doctor's thesis, New York University (New York, N.Y.), 1946.
33. BURKE, HENRY R. Personality Traits of Successful Minor Seminarians. Washington, D.C.: Catholic University of America Press, 1947 Pp. viii, 65. * (PA 22:848)
34. EDMISTON, R. W.; HINTON, M. E.; AND RASOR, FLOYD. "Special Emphases to Improve Attendance." J Ed Res 41:35–40 S '47. * (PA 22:1856)
35. McFADDEN, JOHN HAROLD. Emotional and Personality Adjustment of Public School Children. Master's thesis, University of North Dakota (Grand Forks, N.D.), 1947.
36. PFLIEGER, ELMER F. "Pupil Adjustment Problems and a Study of Relationships Between Scores on the California Test of Personality and the Mooney Problem Check List." J Ed Res 41:265–78 D '47. * (PA 22:2746)
37. SEEMAN, MELVIN. Prejudice and Personality: A Study in the Social Psychology of Attitudes. Doctor's thesis, Ohio State University (Columbus, Ohio), 1947.
38. ALLEN, CHARLES L. The Development of a Battery of Psychological Tests for Determining Journalistic Interests and Aptitudes. Doctor's thesis, Northwestern University (Evanston, Ill.), 1948.
39. CALIFORNIA TEST BUREAU, EDITORIAL STAFF. California Test of Personality. Summary of Investigations, No. 1. Los Angeles, Calif.: California Test Bureau, 1948. Pp. 19. *
40. GROSSMAN, BEVERLY, AND WRIGHTER, JOYCE. "The Relationship Between Selection-Rejection and Intelligence, Social Status, and Personality Amongst Sixth Grade Children." Sociometry 11:346–55 N '48. * (PA 25:7667)
41. HORGAN, CORNELIUS M. A Comparative Study of Leaders and Non-Leaders Among Catholic Boy Scouts. Doctor's thesis, Fordham University (New York, N.Y.), 1948.
42. HUNTER, E. C. "A Summary of Mental Health Survey of Spartanburg County, Spartanburg, South Carolina." J Exp Ed 17:294–308 D '48. * (PA 23:4804)

43. PHILLIPS, E. LAKIN; BERMAN, ISABEL R.; AND HANSON, HAROLD B. Intelligence and Personality Factors Associated With Poliomyelitis Among School Age Children. Monographs of the Society for Research in Child Development, Vol. 12, No. 2, Serial No. 45. Evanston, Ill.: Child Development Publications, the Society, 1948. Pp. vii, 60. *
44. SEIDENFELD, MORTON A. "The Psychological Sequelae of Poliomyelitis in Children." Nerv Child 7:14–28 Ja '48. * (PA 22:4080)
45. SNYDER, WILLIAM U., AND SNYDER, BARBARA JUNE. "Implications for Therapy of Personality Changes Resulting From a Course in Mental Hygiene." Abstract. Am Psychol 3:286–7 Jl '48. *
46. BAIRD, FRANCES. The Adjustment of Orphanage Children. Master's thesis, Miami University (Oxford, Ohio), 1949.
47. CALIFORNIA TEST BUREAU, EDITORIAL STAFF. California Test of Personality, Revised Edition. Summary of Investigations, No. 1 (Revised Edition). Los Angeles, Calif.: California Test Bureau, 1949. Pp. 24. *
48. CHRISTY, WILLIAM J. A Study of Relationships Between Sociometric Scores and Personality Self-Ratings. Master's thesis, North Texas State College (Denton, Tex.), 1949.
49. DENT, RALPH W. Varied Reliability Coefficients for the California Test of Personality, Obtained by Different Methods. Master's thesis, University of Toronto (Toronto, Ont., Canada), 1949.
50. EAGER, MARY FLOY. A Comparative Study of the Personality Traits of Handicapped and Normal Children. Master's thesis, North Texas State College (Denton, Tex.), 1949.
51. EDMISTON, R. W., AND BAIRD, FRANCES. "The Adjustment of Orphanage Children." J Ed Psychol 40:482–8 D '49. * (PA 24:3103)
52. GLASER, ROBERT. "A Methodological Analysis of the Inconsistency of Response to Test Items." Ed & Psychol Meas 9:727–39 W '49. * (PA 26:2747)
53. JENSEN, GERALD LEROY. Relationship Between School Achievement and Scholastic Aptitude: Techniques for Ascertaining This Relationship, Their Application to Data From a Group of High School Pupils and Their Use in School Practice. Doctor's thesis, Stanford University (Stanford, Calif.), 1949.
54. KING, CLYDE D. Personality Traits of Teachers. Master's thesis, North Texas State College (Denton, Tex.), 1949.
55. LEHNER, GEORGE F. J. "Some Relationships Between Scores for Self and Projected 'Average' Scores on a Personality Test." Abstract. Am Psychol 4:390 S '49. *
56. PURVIS, LEO C. Relationship Between Intelligence as Determined by California Test of Mental Maturity and Achievement in the Seventh Grade. Master's thesis, North Texas State College (Denton, Tex.), 1949.
57. RICCIUTI, EDWARD A. A Study of Listeners and Non-Listeners to Various Types of Radio Programs in Terms of Selected Ability, Attitude and Behavior Measures. Doctor's thesis, Fordham University (New York, N.Y.), 1949.
58. ROBINSON, CLARE AVIS. The Relationship of Estimates of Personal and Social Adjustment to Attained Scores of the California Test of Personality. Master's thesis, Pennsylvania State College (State College, Pa.), 1949.
59. THOMPSON, BILLYE FAYE. The Relationship of Personality to Accident-Prone and Accident-Free Pupils in the North Dallas High School. Master's thesis, North Texas State College (Denton, Tex.), 1949.
60. VOLBERDING, ELEANOR. "Characteristics of Successful and Unsuccessful Eleven-Year-Old Pupils." El Sch J 49:405–10 Mr '49. * (PA 23:5003)
61. ZAKOLSKI, F. C. "Studies in Delinquency: I, Personality Structure of Delinquent Boys." J Genetic Psychol 74:109–17 Mr '49. * (PA 23:4925)
62. BEEBE, EMILY NOYES. A Study of Personality and Personality Deficiencies Among Intermediate Grade Pupils in Three New Orleans Public Schools. Master's thesis, Tulane University (New Orleans, La.), 1950.
63. BRYAN, J. R. A Study of Personality Adjustment Differences of Delinquent and Nondelinquent Groups as Measured by the Bell Adjustment Inventory and the California Test of Personality. Master's thesis, University of Toronto (Toronto, Canada), 1950.
64. BURNS, L. A Correlation of Scores on the Wechsler Intelligence Scale for Children and the California Test of Personality Obtained by a Group of 5th Graders. Master's thesis, Pennsylvania State College (State College, Pa.), 1950.
65. CASSEL, RUSSELL N. An Experimental Investigation of the "Reality-Strata" of Certain Objectively Defined Groups of Individuals by Use of the Level of Aspiration Technique. Doctor's thesis, University of Southern California (Los Angeles, Calif.), 1950.
66. CLARK, JERRY H. "Interest Variability on the California Test of Mental Maturity in Relation to the Minnesota Multiphasic Personality Inventory." J Consult Psychol 14:32–4 F '50. * (PA 24:4112)
67. CURRY, EDNA MAE. Relationship of Achievement and Personality in the Fourth, Fifth, and Sixth Grades of the Northwest Elementary School, Justin, Texas. Master's thesis, North Texas State College (Denton, Tex.), 1950.
68. GIBSON, NORMA LEE BODENHEIMER. The Influence of the Study of Biographies Upon the Personality Adjustment of the Junior High School Student as Measured by the California Test of Personality. Master's thesis, University of Southern California (Los Angeles, Calif.), 1950.

69. HAND, WILL M. *A Comparison and Analysis of Scores in Self and Social Adjustment Made on the California Test of Personality and the Bernreuter Personality Inventory.* Master's thesis, University of Florida (Gainesville, Fla.), 1950.

70. KING, F. J. *Item Analysis of the California Test of Personality.* Master's thesis, North Texas State College (Denton, Tex.), 1950.

71. SALYERS, MARTHA HOPKINS. *An Item Analysis of the California Test of Personality as Correlated With Intelligence.* Master's thesis, Illinois State Normal University (Normal, Ill.), 1950.

72. WOODWARD, RICHARD HUGH. *An Examination of the Internal Consistency of the California Test of Personality, Series 1, Form A.* Master's thesis, Miami University (Oxford, Ohio), 1950.

73. CARLIN, LESLIE ORVILLE. *A Comparison of the College Marks by Subject Made by 312 of the June, 1950 Graduating Seniors at Central Michigan College of Education With Their Battery of Guidance Tests and Inventory Percentile Scores.* Doctor's "Field Study No. 2," Colorado State College of Education (Greeley, Colo.), 1951.

74. COWEN, EMORY L., AND THOMPSON, GEORGE G. "Problem Solving Rigidity and Personality Structure." *J Abn & Social Psychol* 46:165–76 Ap '51. * *(PA 25:7940)*

75. ELIAS, JACK Z. *Non-Intellective Factors in Certain Intelligence and Achievement Tests: An Analysis of Factors in Addition to the Cognitive Entering Into the Intelligence and Achievement Scores of Children at the Sixth Grade Level.* Doctor's thesis, New York University (New York, N.Y.), 1951. *(Microfilm Abstr* 11:558)

76. ELLIOT, JANE. *Personality Traits of 199 School Children With Speech Deviations as Indicated by the California Test of Personality, Primary and Elementary Series, Form A.* Master's thesis, University of Michigan (Ann Arbor, Mich.), 1951.

77. FORLANO, GEORGE, AND WRIGHTSTONE, J. WAYNE. "Sociometric and Self-Descriptive Technics in Appraisal of Pupil Adjustment." *Sociometry* 14:340–50 D '51. * *(PA 28:6531)*

78. SINGER, ARTHUR. "Certain Aspects of Personality and Their Relation to Certain Group Modes, and Constancy of Friendship Choices." *J Ed Res* 45:33–42 S '51. * *(PA 26:2998)*

79. SKIDMORE, REX A., AND MCPHEE, WILLIAM M. "The Comparative Use of the California Test of Personality and the Burgess-Cottrell-Wallin Schedule in Predicting Marital Adjustment." *Marriage & Family Living* 13:121–6 Ag '51. * *(PA 26:2197)*

80. WEILAND, ELIZABETH JUNE. *The Use of the California Test of Personality as a Measure of the Personality Adjustment of a Seventh Grade Population in Relation to Achievement in School.* Master's thesis, Pennsylvania State College (State College, Pa.), 1951.

81. BROWN, LILLIAN PENN; GATES, HELEN D.; NOLDER, EVANGELINE L.; AND VAN FLEET, BARBARA. "Personality Characteristics of Exceptional Children and of Their Mothers." *El Sch J* 52:286–90 Ja '52. * *(PA 27:6444)*

82. LINDGREN, HENRY CLAY. "The Development of a Scale of Cultural Idealization Based on the California Test of Personality." *J Ed Psychol* 43:81–91 F '52. * *(PA 26:7004)*

83. MASTEN, FRANK D. *The Personality Development and Occupational Interests of the Sixth, Seventh, and Eighth Grade Pupils at Father Flanagan's Boys' Home, Boys Town, Nebraska.* Doctor's field study, Colorado State College of Education (Greeley, Colo.), 1952.

84. SEWELL, WILLIAM H. "Infant Training and the Personality of the Child." *Am J Sociol* 58:150–9 S '52. * *(PA 27:3388)*

85. TAYLOR, CHARLES, AND COMBS, ARTHUR W. "Self-Acceptance and Adjustment." *J Consult Psychol* 16:89–91 Ap '52. *

86. BURRALL, LUCILLE. *A Study of Internal or Trait Variability in Achievement of Pupils at the Fifth Grade Level.* Doctor's thesis, Pennsylvania State College (State College, Pa.), 1953.

87. CARILLO, EDITH MARIA. *Relationship of Certain Personality Characteristics to the School-Related Problems of Junior High School Pupils.* Doctor's thesis, University of Michigan (Ann Arbor, Mich.), 1953. *(DA* 13:331)

88. CARLIN, LESLIE C. "A Longitudinal Comparison of Freshman-Senior Standing." *J Ed Res* 47:285–90 D '53. * *(PA 28:6586)*

89. FEIVESON, PHILIP. "The Value of a Personality Inventory in a Self-Appraisal Course on the Secondary School Level." *Calif J Ed Res* 4:69–72 Mr '53. * *(PA 28:1472)*

90. HINKELMAN, EMMET ARTHUR. "A Comparative Investigation of Differences in Personality Adjustment of Delinquents and Non-Delinquents." *J Ed Res* 46:595–601 Ap '53. * *(PA 28:2971)*

91. LEIBMAN, OSCAR BERNARD. *The Relationship of Personal and Social Adjustment to Academic Achievement in the Elementary School.* Doctor's thesis, Columbia University (New York, N.Y.), 1953. *(DA* 14:67)

92. NOWELL, ANN. "Peer Status as Related to Measures of Personality." *Calif J Ed Res* 4:37–41 Ja '53. * *(PA 28:1514)*

93. ROS, PAZ DE MINGO MELITON. *Social Acceptance or Rejection as Related to Personality Adjustment and Participation in Group Task Roles.* Doctor's field study, Colorado State College of Education (Greeley, Colo.), 1953.

94. SCANDRETTE, ONAS C. "Classroom Choice Status Re-

lated to Scores on Components of the California Test of Personality." *J Ed Res* 47:291–6 D '53. * *(PA 28:6545)*

95. BURRALL, LUCILLE. "Variability in Achievement of Pupils at the Fifth Grade Level." *Calif J Ed Res* 5:68–73 Mr '54. * *(PA 28:9038)*

96. CURRAN, GRACE THERESE. "The Effect of Immediate Experiences Upon Responses on the California Personality Test." *J Ed Res* 48:289–95 D '54. * *(PA 29:7266)*

97. HANLON, THOMAS E.; HOFSTAETTER, PETER R.; AND O'CONNOR, JAMES P. "Congruence of Self and Ideal Self in Relation to Personality Adjustment." *J Consult Psychol* 18:215–8 Je '54. * *(PA 29:2229)*

98. LANGFORD, LOUISE M., AND ALM, O. W. "A Comparison of Parent Judgments and Child Feelings Concerning the Self Adjustment and Social Adjustment of Twelve-Year-Old Children." *J Genetic Psychol* 85:39–46 S '54. * *(PA 29:5381)*

99. LINDEMANN, SALLY J. *The Effect on Scores of Individual vs. Group Administration of the California Test of Personality.* Master's thesis, Pennsylvania State University (State College, Pa.), 1954.

100. ZELEN, SEYMOUR L. "Acceptance and Acceptability: An Examination of Social Reciprocity." Abstract. *J Consult Psychol* 18:316 O '54. *

101. BAKER, LAURENCE S. *The Relationship of Maternal Understanding of the Child and Attitudes Toward the Child to the Adjustment of the Child.* Doctor's thesis, New York University (New York, N.Y.), 1955. *(DA* 16:567)

102. CHANNELL, R. R. *Self Inventories, Teacher Ratings and Interviews as a Means of Determining Maladjustment.* Master's thesis, Utah State Agricultural College (Logan, Utah), 1955.

103. COWDEN, RICHARD C. "Empathy or Projection?" *J Clin Psychol* 11:188–90 Ap '55. * *(PA 30:905)*

104. KELLEY, ELVAN PRESSLOR. *An Investigation Into the Value of Selected Tests and Techniques for Guidance of Prospective Teachers Enrolled in Community Experiences Course.* Doctor's thesis, University of Houston (Houston, Tex.), 1955. *(DA* 15:1209)

105. PHILLIPS, BEEMAN N., AND DEVAULT, M. VERE. "Relation of Positive and Negative Sociometric Valuations to Social and Personal Adjustment of School Children." *J Appl Psychol* 39:409–12 D '55. * *(PA 30:7706)*

106. SHUTTLESWORTH, REBA HUDSON. *The Relationship of Socio-Economic Status to the Measured Adjustment of Seventh Grade Students in Johnston Junior High School, Houston, Texas, for the Year of 1951–1952.* Doctor's field study, Colorado State College of Education (Greeley, Colo.), 1955.

107. SMITH, LOUIS MILDE. *A Validity Study of Six Personality and Adjustment Tests for Children.* Doctor's thesis, University of Minnesota (Minneapolis, Minn.), 1955. *(DA* 16:791)

108. TINDALL, RALPH H. "Relationships Among Indices of Adjustment Status." *Ed & Psychol Meas* 15:152–62 su '55. * *(PA 30:2330)*

109. DAGER, EDWARD ZICCA. *Social Factors in Personality Change.* Doctor's thesis, Ohio State University (Columbus, Ohio), 1956. *(DA* 17:1619)

110. KEELER, HAROLD JAY. *Predicting Teacher Effectiveness of Graduates of the State University of New York Teachers Colleges.* Doctor's thesis, Cornell University (Ithaca, N.Y.), 1956. *(DA* 17:545)

111. LEHNER, GEORGE F. J. "Personal Adjustment Scores and Assigned 'Average' Scores." *J Psychol* 42:227–36 O '56. *

112. MELTON, WILLIAM R., JR. "An Investigation of the Relationship Between Personality and Vocational Interest." *J Ed Psychol* 47:163–74 Mr '56. * *(PA 31:8791)*

113. SPILKA, BERNARD, AND STRUENING, E. L. "A Questionnaire Study of Personality and Ethnocentrism." *J Social Psychol* 44:65–71 Ag '56. *

114. GUNNELL, DOROTHY C., AND NUTTING, RUTH E. "Prediction of Achievement in Schools of Nursing." *Calif J Ed Res* 8:184–91 S '57. *

115. MITCHELL, JAMES V., JR. "The Identification of Items in the California Test of Personality That Differentiate Between Subjects of High and Low Socio-Economic Status at the Fifth- and Seventh-Grade Levels." *J Ed Res* 51:241–250 D '57. *

116. CLEVENGER, THEODORE, JR. *An Analysis of Variance of the Relationship of Experienced Stage Fright to Selected Psychometric Inventories.* Doctor's thesis, Florida State University (Tallahassee, Fla.), 1958. *(DA* 19:598)

117. SMITH, LOUIS M. "The Concurrent Validity of Six Personality and Adjustment Tests for Children." *Psychol Monogr* 72(4):1–30 '58. *

VERNER M. SIMS, *Professor of Psychology, University of Alabama, University, Alabama.*

Rereading reviews of this test in earlier *Yearbooks* has impressed this reviewer with the fact that a review of a personality test reveals at least as much concerning the frame of reference within which the reviewer approaches the task as it does of the test itself. Let us start off, therefore, with a statement of this reviewer's own bias: He feels, first of all, that in spite of the fact that authors often have exaggerated ideas concerning the usefulness of self-inventories and that in the hands of unskilled persons they be harmful, there is a place for them in the scheme of psychological testing; and secondly, he takes the position that the worth of such inventories is to be measured in terms of the extent to which they meet the conventional criteria of good measurement.

Since the earlier edition was evaluated in the *Yearbook* by five competent persons, this review is limited chiefly to a consideration of changes that have been made in the current revision. According to its authors, "Among the reasons which led to the 1953 Revision....were: (1) the development of additional validity data, (2) the extension of suggestions for interpretation, (3) the development of additional data regarding reliability (particularly for the lower scores on the test instrument), (4) the reexamination of the comparability of the two forms for each level so that one set of norms could be utilized, and (5) the reorganization of items for each of the equivalent components so that one SCOREZE answer sheet could be used with either Form AA or BB on each level." Examination of the test and manual leaves one with the feeling that another reason may well have been the attempt to answer criticisms of the test made by previous reviewers. And, as a matter of fact, some of the criticisms of the early test are no longer valid. Other shortcomings pointed out are, however, defended, ignored, or brushed aside as not worthy of comment.

Evidence on the validity of personality inventories will, generally speaking, be indirect. The authors in this edition base their case mainly on the care taken in the construction of the revised test, and the reported usefulness of the first edition as a pre- and in-service training device for teachers, as an aid to counselors, clinical psychologists, and teachers in the study of problem cases, and as a tool useful in personality research. In support of their contention, they marshal a considerable amount of evidence, although one wishes at times that it all were reported with the exactitude contained in the statement that in some 90 publications of research the test has been found useful. Such expressions as "school officials in increasing number" or "many clinical psychologists" are, for example, not too easy to interpret.

In spite of limitations, however, the additional evidence on validity reported or referred to in the manual not only answers some of the earlier criticisms but convinces this reviewer that as a measure of self-concept in the, as of now, vaguely defined area called adjustment, this test is as valid as most such instruments.

An attempt has been made to word the questions so as to reduce to a minimum any suggestion that they should be answered a certain way. In spite of this effort, the "right" answer to many items is probably obvious to all except the very naive. Although this is a limitation of most personality inventories (all that the writer has seen), it means, nevertheless, that the validity of this test will vary with the degree of rapport established with the testee. This fact raises serious doubt concerning its usefulness in the selection and placement of employees, a use which the authors recommend.

Tests of internal consistency are reported for the revision in considerable detail. They indicate a fair degree of reliability for the total and the two main components, social and personal adjustment, particularly for the lower scores. They do not, however, convince this reviewer that use of the six subscores under each of these two components is justified for individual diagnosis. For example, let us look at Withdrawing Tendencies in the primary form. The chances are 1 in 3 that the true score is 1.08 points greater or less than the obtained score. From the table of norms it can be seen that this means that the chances are that the true score of 1 child in 3 with a score of 5 (40th percentile) is above the 60th percentile or below the 30th percentile, and that for 1 child in 20 the true score is below the 20th or above the 80th percentile. Expressed in such terms, it is hard to see that we have any very dependable information on how far he withdraws! And this is not an exaggerated example. Here is another from the secondary form: A student answering 8 of the 15 items correctly on Self-reliance is rated at the 30th percentile. The chances are 1 in 3 that his true score is below the 15th or above the 45th percentile, and 1 in 20 that it is below the 5th or above the 70th percentile. How self-reliant is he? Interestingly enough, subscores on the adult form appear to be the least reliable of all.

In a forced-choice test it is inevitable that some questions will be answered at random, and in a yes-no test it is obvious that their weight will also be at a maximum. In a self-inventory the number of such "guesses" would presumably vary with such things as reading ability, the amount of self-understanding, a willingness to introspect, and the desire to report things as they are. It would, therefore, seem highly desirable, particularly in a test recommended for use with groups relatively unskilled in reading and not too understanding, that chance responses move a person toward a neutral position. This might mean that we miss some cases who are maladjusted but it would prevent us from labeling as maladjusted poor readers, persons without self-understanding, and the like.

Spencer (3:26) called attention to the disproportionate number of "No's" among the correct answers in the first edition. In the current edition this ratio continues to be between 60 and 70 per cent instead of the expected 50 per cent. Add to this the fact that at all levels the median score of the group used to establish norms was well above the median number of questions in the test and it is inevitable that one who answers the questions on a basis of chance will show up as seriously maladjusted. In the primary test, for example, he would be at the 10th percentile in personal, social, and total adjustment; in the secondary test he would be at the 5th, 2nd, and 5th percentiles. The subscores tell an even worse story. The reviewer does not mean to imply that many of those tested will answer all questions on the basis of chance, but rather to point out that in this test any questions so answered increase the apparent maladjustment of the testee. The fact that many other personality inventories are subject to the same criticism is irrelevant.

The test itself is mechanically satisfactory and it and the manual are made up in a manner which makes for ease and accuracy in administering and scoring. The printing is excellent. In many schools, however, poor reading ability of the children will require that the elementary form be read to the children well beyond the recommended fourth grade. The profile which appeared on the front of the test booklet in the earlier editions has been moved to the back of the answer sheet. The manual still contains a section on the uses of test results which undertakes to classify personality problems and suggests ways of dealing with the various types of difficulties. This reviewer, like previous reviewers, is skeptical of the worth of this material. In the hands of untrained users it may actually be harmful, and persons with a minimum of training in counseling or clinical psychology would have no need for it.

The norms on this edition are considerably better than those for the earlier test. The samples are much larger and, if one can assume that the cases are fairly distributed among the states from which they were drawn, are geographically more representative. All in all, in spite of criticism, as personality inventories go, the California test would appear to be among the better ones available.

For reviews by Laurance F. Shaffer and Douglas Spencer of the original edition, see 3:26 (1 excerpt); for reviews by Raymond B. Cattell, Percival M. Symonds, and P. E. Vernon of the elementary and secondary levels, see 40:1213 (1 excerpt).

[39]
★The Cassel Group Level of Aspiration Test, 1957 Revision. Grades 5–16 and adults; 1952–57; 7 scores: clinical difference, Hausmann, aspiration difference, first goal, psychological response to failure, physiological response to failure, level of aspiration quotient; 1 form ('57); manual ('57); $4 per 25 tests, postpaid; specimen set not available; 247 seconds (40 minutes); Russell N. Cassel; Western Psychological Services. *

REFERENCES

1. CASSEL, RUSSELL N., AND SAUGSTAD, RANDOLF G. "Level of Aspiration and Sociometric Distance." *Sociometry* 15:319–25 Ag–N '52. * (PA 27:7386)
2. CASSEL, RUSSELL N. "The Relationship of Certain Factors to the Level of Aspiration and Social Distance for Forty Four Air Force Prisoners." *J Crim Law & Criminology* 44(5):604–10 Ja–F '54. *
3. CASSEL, RUSSELL N., AND VAN VORST, ROBERT. "Level of Aspiration as a Means for Discerning Between 'In-Prison' and 'Out-of-Prison' Groups of Individuals." *J Social Psychol* 40: 121–35 Ag '54. * (PA 29:5692)
4. CASSEL, RUSSELL N., AND VAN VORST, ROBERT. "Level of Aspiration Comparisons for Varying Stages of Penal Experience." *J Ed Res* 48:597–603 Ap '55. * (PA 30:1295)
5. NIYEKAWA, AGNES M. "A Comparative Analysis of Foreign and American Female College Groups on Three Personality Variables: Anxiety, Level of Aspiration and Femininity." *Psychol Newsl* 7:72–91 My–Je '56. * (PA 31:3697)

W. GRANT DAHLSTROM, *Associate Professor of Psychology, University of North Carolina, Chapel Hill, North Carolina.*

The revised form of this test is based upon eight repetitions of a simple motor task: drawing squares around small circles as rapidly as possible. For each trial the subject estimates the number of squares he will be able to complete in 30 seconds. Group administration requires that the subject record his aspiration in the form of a bid, tally his performance, and correct his score for any discrepancies with his bid. The next to the last trial is stopped three seconds short of the usual time in an effort to introduce failure, the effects of which are evaluated in the bid (psychological response) and in the performance (physiological response) on his last trial.

The test booklet is simple, neat, and well planned. The scoring blanks are labeled so explicitly, however, that some of the features of the test may be given away, e.g., "Psychological Response to Failure." The test instructions are very complicated, including five elaborate rules covering the level of aspiration bids, the performance, and the scoring. Little effort is made in these instructions to convey to the subject just why he should do well or why he should try to make his bids correspond to his subsequent performance. There is no reason why a subject should not pace his performance to fit his prior bid.

The manual contains several errors per page, some seriously interfering with the administration and the scoring of the test. Although in the revision of this test the basic psychomotor task has been changed from making small circles above and below an X to drawing squares around circles, the manual does not indicate this change or the degree of equivalence of the two forms. Most of the normative data in the manual are based upon the original form, precisely the same cutting scores being retained, although this is not indicated anywhere in the tables. In fact, no references to previous research on the test are included in the manual. Although normative data from general, Latin descent, and penal populations are listed, no description is provided of the sampling procedures used in collecting them, the background characteristics of the groups, the nature of any sex differences, or the representativeness of these data.

The directions for administration are poorly organized. The examiner and the subjects begin reading the directions together. Then, in the middle of a paragraph, the examiner has the subjects fill in the test headings and turn to the next page of the test booklet; finally he has them return to the first page for the remainder of the directions. The vocabulary level is uneven and the self-recording provisions are poorly written and confusing.

The scoring instructions are also lacking in organization. The sequence does not correspond to the order on the test profile. The examiner is asked to compute one score based upon another that is yet to be defined. This score (clinical difference score) is a qualitative series of categories but is treated like a 7-interval continuous scale; means, standard deviations, and T score

conversions are provided for it! The instructions for the psychological response to failure score involve the wrong trials. Computation of the level of aspiration quotient (LAQ), which the author considers to be the most valuable score in the test, is based in part on an intelligence quotient that cannot be obtained from this test itself. No specification of the test to be used to furnish the IQ is included in the LAQ instructions; any standard intelligence test is deemed acceptable. Reference to the *California Test of Mental Maturity* is made in some of the tables in the manual, but no recommendation is made to use this instrument. Apparently the assumption is made that IQ's from different tests are completely equivalent in their central tendencies, their dispersions, and in the abilities they sample. The conversion table for IQ's assumes a mean of 100 and a standard deviation of 16 points.

The LAQ is the ratio of two standard scores with means of 5.0 and standard deviations of 1.0, one for the IQ and the other for the Hausmann score which is the average weighted achievement score on trials three through six. Use of this ratio assumes that for subjects who are well adjusted in their level of aspiration the Hausmann score and intelligence are generally proportional. No evidence is submitted for this assumption; only the correlation of .39 between the Hausmann score and IQ (test unspecified) is given in the manual.

Intercorrelations among the component scores are provided based on two different populations, but the columnar headings for one table are so misleading as to make the data uninterpretable.

Correlations of odd and even trials (corrected for attenuation) and test-retest coefficients are reported for each score except the LAQ. The author says the reliabilities for the LAQ will be the same as the Hausmann score on which it is partly based. This latter point is in error since the LAQ is also a function of the IQ derived from some other recent test. The retest interval over which the temporal stability of these scores was determined is not specified for either group studied.

In spite of the numerous errors and limitations already listed, the question of validity is the most important one in evaluating this instrument. The manual mentions briefly and superficially four forms of validity: face, content, construct, and status. It is difficult to assess these validities from the descriptions and data provided by the author. Although he calls his test a measure of level of aspiration, Cassel seems to disclaim any intention to measure this attribute. However, many test users will turn to this device seeking a measure of an individual's general level of aspiration. Except for the trivial face validity of the goal-setting behavior on a simple psychomotor task, there is no evidence of construct validity of this sort implied in the title. There is very little evidence [1] that there is any trait of this sort with enough generality to be useful in describing individuals. The research on this problem has been based on many kinds of tasks from the dart-throwing problem of Hausmann to the pool-cue manipulations of the Rotter board. There seems to be a cavalier disregard for the particular task used to sample goal-setting behavior, as if an individual were equally confident or self-doubting in all situations. Cassel offers no evidence that guesses about one's accomplishments in drawing squares bear any relationship to professional striving or any other aspirations.

Cassel prefers to discuss the test implications in terms of an "irreality dimension" of personality. "The term irreality here refers to the presence of reality, rather than the non-existence of it, but implies a degree of absence of acceptable sensory phenomena for the generation of self-perceptions in relation to previous performance." The manual does not provide sufficient material elaborating this construct or its interpretative implications to judge the suitability of these scores for this personality characteristic. The previous writings of the author [2] help elaborate the concept of reality levels, but they are not definitive enough to be clinically useful.

The manual also implies that predictive validity for delinquent behavior (delinquency proneness) has been established, but the evidence offered applies only to status validity, since Cassel examined delinquent and penal samples after they had developed their propensities and had been apprehended and incarcerated (2, 3, 4).

Cassel implies these scores can evaluate an individual's popularity, as measured by socio-

metric preferences. While there was some tendency for the clinical discrepancy score and the LAQ from the first edition of the test to show a curvilinear relationship to sociometric distance (1), this separation did not stand up on a young prisoner group (2). There is mention made of the test's implications of neurotic tendencies, hypochondriacal and hysterical ailments, vulnerability to culture, or disorientation, but no data are provided on these attributes.

This test is poorly prepared and presented, inadequately standardized, and pretentious in its claims. It is unready for the test market and should be labeled FOR RESEARCH ONLY. A need exists for a simple, objective measure of tendencies either to overrate or underevaluate one's abilities and capacities; this test does not fill this need.

Harrison G. Gough, *Associate Professor of Psychology, University of California, Berkeley, California.*

This test has eight parts, each containing three rows of 20 small circles (60 circles per part). Within the time allotted for each part, the subject is asked to draw squares around as many of these circles as he can. Before beginning each part, he must predict how many squares he will draw. After time has been called, he counts the number actually drawn. His score for each part is based directly on his "bid" or estimate. If he bids 26 squares and draws 26 or more, his score is 26. If he fails to make his bid he is penalized two points for each missing square. This procedure is designed to encourage optimistic, but cautious, forecasts.

Based on various combinations and manipulations of the bids, actual performance figures, and these adjusted scores, five scores which comprise the "level of aspiration profile" are derived. The two additional scores which can be obtained (those for psychological response to failure and physiological response to failure) are computed only when "failure," as defined in the manual, has taken place. Part 7 has, unknown to the subject, a reduced time of 27 seconds. Presumably many subjects, therefore, will fail to make their bids on Part 7. These two scores are concerned with the effect of this failure on the subject's estimates and performance.

The above gives an idea of the mechanics of the test. The manual ties the tasks and the scored variables to a prolix and murky discussion of the "irreality scale of human personali-

1 Rotter, Julian B. "Level-of-Aspiration Techniques as Measures of Personality," pp. 313–26. In his *Social Learning and Clinical Psychology.* New York: Prentice-Hall, Inc., 1954. Pp. xiv, 466. *
2 Cassel, Russell N. "An Experimental Investigation of the 'Reality-Strata' of Certain Objectively Defined Groups of Individuals by Use of the Level of Aspiration Technique." Abstract. *Am Psychol* 5:471–2 Ag '50. *
Cassel, Russell N. "Psychological Aspects of Happiness." *Peabody J Ed* 32:73–82 S '54. *
Cassel, Russell N. "Motivation as a Synthesis of Contemporary Psychology." *J Ed Psychol* 43:157–66 Mr '52. *

ties," Lewin's "life space" notion, and Tolman's view (alleged) that all behavior is goal-directed. This theorizing, in the reviewer's judgment, is not only poorly done but is more or less gratuitous to the specific tasks assigned in the test and to the scorings made.

The manual, however, has more serious deficiencies. One of these is a distressing series of errors. Seventeen typographical, grammatical, and content errors were found in the text. In one of the tables two columns of correlation coefficients are erroneously identified.

Instructions for scoring the seven defined variables are not given in a clear, succinct fashion; most readers would find it very difficult to decide just what specific steps to take to score certain of the variables, especially the clinical "D" score.

The section of the manual on "validity and standardization" contains misleading and confused discussions of topics like "content validity" and "construct validity," and little evidence pertaining to what one would expect to be the key external criteria for this test: indices of ambition or "level of aspiration" in various life settings and (perhaps) on other "level of aspiration" tests. Most of the data which are presented have to do with school and educational achievement, or with differences between delinquent and nondelinquent populations.

It is with respect to this latter distinction that the test shows its greatest promise. The Hausmann score, for example, yielded mean 28.4 and SD 5.4 in a nondelinquent sample of 1,710 as compared to mean 21.5 and SD 5.3 in a sample of 775 delinquents. The difference is obviously highly significant. However, one is tempted to ascribe it more to the difficulty the delinquents had with the strict time requirements and the record-keeping than to basic differences in the "level of aspiration" aspect of personality.

To summarize, this test does seem to offer certain promises, for example in the study of "under-control" and problems of asocialization. The chief weakness is the manual, which is poorly organized, frequently in error, and written in an awkward, stilted manner. The reduction of the number of scored variables to those having greatest predictive significance for nontest behavior, preparation of clear and precise instructions for scoring, elimination of superfluous theorizing, and a thoroughgoing editorial review for matters of grammar, form, and clarity would do a lot for this device.

J. P. SUTCLIFFE, *Senior Lecturer in Psychology, University of Sydney, Sydney, Australia.*

The test was devised to measure "irreality" and face validity is claimed for it on the basis that one may consider discrepancies between the "real world" (performance) and the "perceived world" (aspiration). Scores from the test are reported to have medium or low correlations with age, intelligence, school achievement, and certain background and social insight factors of personality. Also reported are some small differences in the scores of "delinquent" and "normal" groups. Reliabilities range from .55 to .93 and vary with type of score and sample. Some norms are reported for "typical" individuals, "delinquent and in-prison" subjects, and "youth of Latin descent." No literature is cited; information in Cassel's other publications is scant.

A group test of "aspiration" could be a useful tool. The author of this test, however, appears not to have consulted the literature on level of aspiration concerning generality and validity. He gives no rationale for his choice of the particular task used, or for the manner of scoring recommended. As a consequence, the test has a major defect which completely invalidates it as a measure of aspiration or irreality.

All of the seven scores derived are functions, directly or indirectly, of performance on the square drawing task. To make the functions explicit, one must consider the relationship of aspiration to performance. Cassel does not report data which would specify this relationship, but, on other grounds,[1] one would expect high dependence of aspiration on performance on this task. This was confirmed by the following results using the CGAT with a sample of 20 subjects (clerical workers and university students, 10 men and 10 women aged 18–30). Inter- and intra-subject variance and covariance of aspiration and performance was analyzed, and split-half reliabilities of mean aspiration and performance per subject were determined from odd and even trials. When the variance of aspiration was adjusted for regression of aspiration on performance, subject variance dropped to 11 per cent of the original and trial variance dropped to 30 per cent of the original. Part, if not all, of this residual variance would be due to measurement error (unreliability), so that variance of "aspiration," independent of perform-

1 SUTCLIFFE, J. P. *Task Variability and the Level of Aspiration.* Australian Journal of Psychology Monograph Supplement No. 2. Melbourne, Australia: Melbourne University Press, October 1955. Pp. 86. *

ance and error, is negligible. It is doubtful, then, that a subject's "aspiration" or judgment of performance is anything but another measure of that performance, i.e., a measure of manual dexterity. This result is not surprising when it is seen that the test is a "low variability" task with a stable and predictable performance trend, and that the test instructions demand accurate estimation by the subject.

Taking this argument to the limit, one would substitute performance for aspiration in all of Cassel's scores to find that they are all concerned either with level of performance or with rate of change of performance. Cassel's reported results are explicable in these terms. The relatively high reliability of his scores follows from the high reliability of average performance. Dexterity with a pencil should have some correlation with age and school achievement. The group differences between delinquents, normals, and Latins would need to be reconsidered in terms of the elements involved—viz., average performance on the CGAT, mental age, and chronological age—since selection with respect to any one of these could be responsible for the differences reported.

While the sample upon which these contentions are based is small, the results are so clear cut that the same pattern may confidently be expected to occur with larger samples.

To conclude: Aspiration on the CGAT is primarily, if not wholly, a measure of dexterity with a pencil. If one wishes to measure "aspiration," one must seek a situation in which it is independent of performance. The necessary conditions are described elsewhere,[2] together with the mathematical rationale of level of aspiration scoring. A group level of aspiration test adequate in the latter sense to the measurement of "irreality" has yet to be devised.

B Menninger Clinic 17:115 My '53. Robert R. Holt. (Review of manual.) One of the familiar techniques of the psychological laboratory has been made into a group test, here reported in a brief manual that is exemplary for the confusion, and pretentiousness of the author's thinking and writing. The test's reliability is insufficient for use in counseling individuals, as the author recommends, and its validation is a muddle because of the author's evident misunderstanding of theoretical foundations.

2 *Ibid.*

J Consult Psychol 16:476 D '52. Laurance F. Shaffer. * The author may be commended for standardizing a useful but hitherto unstandardized technique, and for publishing such relatively full data about it. At the present time, however, our knowledge of the level-of-aspiration experiment by no means justifies all of the clinical implications that Cassel seems to draw from some of his scores. The test is a good instrument for further research, not a finished clinical tool.

[40]
★The Cassel Psychotherapy Progress Record. Mental patients; 1953; 3 ratings: emotional development, barrier vulnerability development, overall psychotherapy development; no data on reliability and validity; no norms; $6 per set of 25 record forms and manual, postpaid; specimen set not available; Russell N. Cassel; Western Psychological Services. *

[41]
★Child Personality Scale. Grades kgn–9; 1951; scale for ratings by classmates and teachers, and for self-ratings; 22 ratings: pep, intelligence, sociability, nervous-calmness, popularity, religiousness, punctuality, courtesy, cooperation, generosity, persistence, honesty, neatness, patience, interests, disposition, good sport, quietness, entertaining, thoughtfulness, sense of humor, dependability; 1 form; no data on reliability and validity; $2.50 per 25 scales; 50¢ per specimen set; postpaid; (20–40) minutes for rating 10 classmates; Mary Amatora;. C. A. Gregory Co. *

REFERENCES
1. TSCHECHTELIN, M. AMATORA. *An Investigation of Some Elements of Teachers' and Pupils' Personalities.* Purdue University, Studies in Higher Education, No. 48; Further Studies in Attitudes, Series 6. Lafayette, Ind.: the Division, January 1943. Pp. 87. *
2. TSCHECHTELIN, M. AMATORA. "Comparability of Child and Adult Personality Rating Scales." *J Ed Psychol* 35:309–13 My '44. * (*PA* 18:3780)
3. TSCHECHTELIN, M. AMATORA. "Factor Analysis of Children's Personality Rating Scale." *J Psychol* 18:197–200 O '44. * (*PA* 19:178)
4. TSCHECHTELIN, M. AMATORA. "A 22-Trait Personality Rating Scale." *J Psychol* 18:3–8 Jl '44. * (*PA* 19:177)
5. TSCHECHTELIN, M. AMATORA. "Self-Appraisal of Children." *J Ed Res* 39:25–32 S '45. * (*PA* 20:614)
6. TSCHECHTELIN, M. AMATORA. "Teachers Rate Their Pupils." *Ed Adm & Sup* 31:122–6 Ja '45. * (*PA* 19:1608)
7. TSCHECHTELIN, M. AMATORA. "Teacher Ratings of Pupil Personality." *Ed Adm & Sup* 34:412–20 N '48. *
8. AMATORA, MARY. "Studies in Personality: The Age Factor." *Cath Ed R* 48:223–30 Ap '50. *
9. TSCHECHTELIN, M. AMATORA. "Norms on a Child Personality Scale." *El Sch J* 51:209–13 D '50. *
10. TSCHECHTELIN, M. AMATORA. "A Study in Teacher Personality." *J Ed Res* 44:709–14 My '51. * (*PA* 26:1730)
11. AMATORA, MARY. "Boys' Personality Appraisals Differentiate Teacher Groups." *Sch & Soc* 76:184–7 S 20 '52. *
12. TSCHECHTELIN, M. AMATORA. "Reliability of a Personality Scale." *Ed & Psychol Meas* 12:132–6 sp '52. * (*PA* 27:5912)
13. AMATORA, MARY. "Pupil Evaluation or Teacher Evaluation in Personality?" *Prog Ed* 31:44–5+ N '53. *
14. AMATORA, MARY. "Contrasts in Boys' and Girls' Judgments in Personality." *Child Develop* 25:51–62 Mr '54. * (*PA* 29:5352)
15. AMATORA, MARY. "Similarity in Teacher and Pupil Personality." *J Psychol* 37:45–50 Ja '54. * (*PA* 28:8097)
16. AMATORA, MARY. "Comparisons in Personality Self-Evaluation." *J Social Psychol* 42:315–21 N '55. * (*PA* 31:601)
17. AMATORA, MARY. "Validity in Self Evaluation." *Ed & Psychol Meas* 16:119–26 sp '56. * (*PA* 31:6054)
18. AMATORA, MARY. "Developmental Trends in Pre-Adolescence and in Early Adolescence in Self-Evaluation." *J Genetic Psychol* 91:89–97 S '57. *

ROBERT H. BAUERNFEIND, *Director, Test De-partment, Science Research Associates, Chicago, Illinois.*

The *Child Personality Scale* provides a means for having each child rated on 22 traits by himself, by his classmates, and by his teacher. Each trait is rated on a 10-point scale.

In theory, this instrument presents a promising idea for sociometric research, for programs of child study, and for improving teachers' understanding of their own values and those of their pupils. Consensus ratings on the part of 10 children should show a high degree of reliability in most classroom situations. Another promising idea is the profile, which permits comparisons of ratings among the several traits for each child. Use of 10-point scales is another plus-value, such scales permitting and encouraging graded expressions of opinion on the part of each rater.

In its present form, however, this scale presents serious obstacles to the fulfillment of its own purposes. Some of these obstacles are:

a) The manual lacks a statement of rationale. Many readers will feel a need to know something of the history of the instrument and the author's reasons for suggesting ratings of these particular 22 traits.

b) The directions are awkward, wordy, and too rigid for use with all children in grades 3 to 9. The manual offers no encouragement to teachers who would prefer to ad-lib the directions at a level appropriate to their classes.

c) The published forms fail to give children help in interpreting each new item in terms of a 10-point scale. Many third, fourth, and fifth grade pupils will experience difficulty in making ratings appropriately in the absence of specific visual aids.

d) The instrument includes an explicitly religious item:

Does he like to pray and go to church?
not at all .... very much

This item per se, not to mention its interpretation, would cause difficulties in many public schools.

e) The instrument includes at least one ambiguous item:

Is he generally quiet, or loud and rude?
noisy, must be heard .... very quiet

This item covers two traits: "noisy—quiet," *and* "rude—sensitive." While interpretation of all 22 items will require searching value judgments, this item will present special difficulties. The

values of our Western civilization clearly prefer sensitivity to rudeness; however, our cultural values (and certainly the constructs of clinical psychology) do not necessarily prefer quietness to noisiness.

f) The manual suggests, without qualification, that children be shown their self-ratings, teacher ratings, and classmates' ratings for purposes of planning programs of self-improvement. Recalling that some children will have been rated by their teachers and classmates as "very dull," "very boring," or "has no sense of humor," most responsible readers will feel this broad suggestion to be extremely hazardous.

g) The manual includes no résumé of the author's research, although the bibliography shows that nine research studies have been reported in the professional literature.

h) The problem of assessing "growth," always elusive in measurement, would be even more difficult in the case of this instrument. While each child draws on his own background of experience in making ratings, his background for evaluating child behavior is largely drawn from experiences with his own classmates. On this type of rating scale, therefore, significant growth on the part of one or two pupils in a classroom would often result in lower ratings for the other pupils—even though the other pupils' qualities of behavior on the trait in question remained constant, or even improved slightly! There can be no "norms," elusive as they are, and there can be no absolutes to help in interpreting changes in ratings derived from this scale. Thus, the second section of the manual, dealing with improvement of character and personality, is oversimplified. Much research is needed on the problem of how this type of instrument can measure fairly changes in character and personality for all members of a class.

In summary, the *Child Personality Scale* in its present form is not recommended for general school use. The instrument may have occasional value as a fact-finding device for study of individual "problem" youngsters. Even in these cases, however, users are cautioned that the manual will be of very little help and that efforts at interpretation will often confront them with unexpected problems in basic personal philosophy as well as in measurement.

DALE B. HARRIS, *Professor of Psychology, and Director, Institute of Child Development and*

Welfare, University of Minnesota, Minneapolis, Minnesota.

The manual recommends that each child rate 10 preassigned children in his school class and himself. A child's "scores" on the several traits consist of the mean of 10 ratings assigned him on each trait. No data are offered in the manual to indicate the reliability of ratings based on such a small sample, or how 10 was selected as an adequate number of judges to rate one case. Although the principle of the graphic rating scale is followed, the form of such a scale is not used. The teacher places a model containing 10 steps on the blackboard. The child rater selects a digit which he enters on his answer sheet as his rating for that trait in the child under consideration. Working trait by trait, each child rates his 10 preassigned "subjects," entering their scores under the names which he has written at the top of 10 adjacent columns.

The author affirms that this method can be successfully used for peer ratings as low as the third grade. This reviewer has not had success with graphic methods with children in the intermediate grades, even when a graphic form is reproduced separately for each quality to be rated. Nor do these children successfully transfer their responses from a stimulus page to an answer sheet. The reviewer would, therefore, question the validity of peer judgments of children 8 or 9 years of age when recorded by this method. He does not question this method, however, for ratings by teachers, although the measurement literature suggests that an odd rather than an even number of ratings has certain advantages, and that 7 points rather than 10 may represent the discriminations which can be made optimally by many raters.

The nomination or "Guess Who" technique, because of the type of judgments required, appeals to this reviewer as having more validity with elementary school children than the rating scale technique. While the former technique is bound to the group wherein judgments are made, and the latter technique is theoretically more related to a general norm or "average," the reviewer questions the elementary school child's ability to conceptualize a range of differences along a trait dimension and to make accurate judgments with respect to particular children. The ability of children to make such judgments could well be a subject for study and experiment. With more adequate research on children's concepts and their judgmental processes concerning personality phenomena, we would be in a better position to formulate scales for use by children.

It is well to point out that the traits do not appear on the rating sheet as named in the entry above. For example, "punctuality" appears as "Is he usually on time?" with the extremes of the characteristic being designated as "usually late" and "never late." The careful grading of the language is a distinct advantage of these scales.

The author is to be commended for her diligent reporting in professional journals of much useful data concerning the scales; it is regrettable that her data on reliability and validity and grade differences do not appear in the manual. The norms that are supplied give means and standard errors of peer ratings and ratings by teachers for several thousand children of mixed ages. Means (but no measures of variance or of standard error) are also given for girls' ratings of peers of each sex, for boys' ratings of peers of each sex, for teachers' ratings of boys and girls, and for self ratings, by sex. The value to the ordinary teacher of such "norms," virtually all of which approximate the theoretical midpoint between 5 and 6 on a 10-point scale, is not at once apparent. If she follows instructions faithfully and relates her judgment to her experience, her mean can scarcely deviate from this theoretical value.

The principal value of these scales, as the manual suggests, is probably in identifying deviates in the classroom group, and in identifying children who consider themselves deviates. One may hold some philosophical reservations about the author's assertions that group and self-ratings of this type should be made the subject of concern and study by young children.

The instructions in the manual are adequate for the few classroom teachers who are thoroughly sophisticated in rating procedures, but hardly so for the many who have only the usual experiences with such evaluations. To use the scales most effectively, one should have knowledge of guidance and counseling theory and procedures as well as of measurement theory and practice.

[42]

★Community Improvement Scale. Adults; 1955; community morale; 1 form; hectographed manual; $3 per 50 tests; $1 per specimen set (must be purchased to obtain manual); postage extra; [5–10] minutes; Inez Fay Smith; Psychometric Affiliates. *

WIMBURN L. WALLACE, *Director, Professional Examinations Division, The Psychological Corporation, New York, New York.*

The 2-page hectographed manual states that the *"Community Improvement Scale* is a device for measuring neighborhood morale while at the same time obtaining a diagnostic analysis of principal areas of neighborhood morale maintenance. * It samples such attitudes as those relating to local business people, recreation, beauty, gossiping, public library facilities, transportation, school convenience, economic status, outlook, community services, friendliness." Only 13 items are used to obtain the single score. The items are multiple choice in form, with each set of alternatives arranged as a 5-point scale rating from bad to good a particular aspect of the respondent's neighborhood. Unfortunately, some of the sets of alternatives do not lie on a true continuum.

The printed questionnaire is bizarre. It comprises a peculiar collection of type faces and is bordered with baroque scrollwork and other symbols. The system of responding to the items calls for the tearing of arrowheads at the edge of the page next to the option; this is an awkward procedure with no apparent advantage over conventional marking with a pen or pencil.

Development of the scale involved tryout of a preliminary form on 100 respondents in the northwest Chicago area, and modification in the light of suggestions received. Since directions for administration prohibit telling the respondents that the purpose of the scale is to measure neighborhood morale, the suggestions of even sophisticated respondents could hardly have been pertinent.

All the data reported in the manual were gathered in the Chicago area. The corrected odd-even coefficient of reliability is given as .86 "for a random sample of 150 Chicago-area homes." One norms table shows percentile equivalents for raw scores for "218 individuals randomly sampled from the Chicago metropolitan area." How the score of an individual is to be interpreted in terms of "neighborhood morale" is not made clear. Along with the norms table, median scores are given for 19 suburban and postal zone areas of Chicago; the number of cases in each area is not shown. It is striking that the medians for 15 of these 19 areas exceed the median shown in the norms table; the undescribed sampling methods appear to yield results which need clarification.

The one validity study mentioned in the manual used postal zone numbers in Chicago as a criterion measure. Unidentified research is supposed to have shown that "residential conditions" are worst near the "business core of the city" and improve in direct proportion to the distance from that center. One has to infer that the magnitude of postal zone numbers in Chicago indicates distance from the center of the city. Cases were drawn from 31 postal zone areas and five suburbs. Number of respondents, sampling technique, mean scores, and standard deviations are not given. The coefficient of correlation between zone numbers and scores on the scale is reported as .67. The extent to which this statistic provides evidence that the scale measures neighborhood morale is patently questionable. Nothing is mentioned concerning the applicability of the scale elsewhere than in Chicago.

In summary, it may be said that the *Community Improvement Scale* is an unsophisticated attempt to measure neighborhood morale. In its present state it meets practically none of the criteria of worthiness for publication for sale. Almost any sociologist could quickly write a questionnaire that would immediately have at least as much value as this one.

[43]

Cornell Index. Adults; 1944–49; revision for civilian use of the *Cornell Selectee Index Form N* and the *Cornell Service Index;* title on test is C.I.—Form N2; psychosomatic and neuropsychiatric symptoms; Form N2 ['45]; revised manual ('49); $2.80 per 50 tests; 35¢ per specimen set; postpaid; (5–15) minutes; Arthur Weider, Harold G. Wolff, Keeve Brodman, Bela Mittelmann, and David Wechsler; Psychological Corporation. *

REFERENCES

1–41. See 4:37.
42. RICHARDS, T. W. "Personality of the Convulsive Patient in Military Service." *Psychol Monogr* 66(14):1–23 '52. * (PA 27:7364)
43. TAAFFE, GORDON. *The Discrimination of Alcoholics, Psychopaths, and Psychoneurotics by Means of the Manson Evaluation, the Pd Scale, MMPI, and the Cornell Index.* Master's thesis, University of Southern California (Los Angeles, Calif.), 1952.
44. WILLIAMS, MARIE E. *A Comparison of the Cornell Index, Form N2 With the Psycho-Somatic Experience Blank.* Master's thesis, Fordham University (New York, N.Y.), 1952.
45. LAUFER, LUDWIG G. "Cultural Problems Encountered in Use of the Cornell Index Among Okinawan Natives." *Am J Psychiatry* 109:861–4 My '53. * (PA 28:2483)
46. LYON, BLANCHARD; MOLISH, HERMAN B.; AND BRIGGS, DENNIE L. "The Cornell Index: A Comparison of a Matched Sample of Psychiatric 'Suspects' and Nonsuspects." *US Armed Forces Med J* 4:977–85 Jl '53. * (PA 29:2454)
47. BARNES, JAMES R. *A Critical Study of the Results of the Mooney Problem Check List and the Cornell Index as a Means of Identifying Possible Cases of Psychosomatic Illness Among 400 North Carolina College Students.* Master's thesis, North Carolina College (Durham, N.C.), 1954.
48. TUCKMAN, JACOB; LORGE, IRVING; AND ZEMAN, FREDERIC D. "Retesting Older People With the Cornell Medical Index and With the Supplementary Health Questionnaire." *J Gerontol* 9:306–8 Jl '54. * (PA 29:5436)

For reviews by Hans J. Eysenck, Nelson G. Hanawalt, and Laurance F. Shaffer, see 4:37.

[44]

★**Cornell Word Form 2.** Adults; 1946–55; civilian edition of *Cornell Word Form* designed for use in military psychiatric screening; title on test is *C.W.F.–2*; 1 form ['55]; manual ('55, reprint of *11* below); $5 per 100 tests; specimen set free; postage extra; [5–15] minutes; Arthur Weider, Bela Mittelmann, David Wechsler, and Harold Wolff; Cornell University Medical College (Room F-636, 1300 York Ave., New York, N.Y.). *

REFERENCES

1. MITTELMANN, BELA; WEIDER, ARTHUR; VONACHEN, HAROLD A.; KRONENBERG, MILTON; WEIDER, NORMA; BRODMAN, KEEVE; AND WOLFF, HAROLD G.; WITH THE TECHNICAL ASSISTANCE OF MARGARET D. MEIXNER. "Detection and Management of Personality and Psychosomatic Disorders Among Industrial Personnel." *Psychosom Med* 7:359–67 N '45. * (*PA* 20:1654)
2. MITTELMANN, BELA; AND BRODMAN, KEEVE. "The Cornell Indices and the Cornell Word Form: 1, Construction and Standardization." *Ann NY Acad Sci* 46:573–7, discussion 603–5 Jl 30 '46. * (*PA* 20:4674)
3. WEIDER, ARTHUR, AND WECHSLER, DAVID. "The Cornell Indices and the Cornell Word Form: 2, Results." *Ann NY Acad Sci* 46:579–87, discussion 603–5 Jl 30 '46. * (*PA* 20:4684)
4. WOLFF, HAROLD G. "The Cornell Indices and the Cornell Word Form: 3, Application." *Ann NY Acad Sci* 46:589–91, discussion 603–5 Jl 30 '46. * (*PA* 20:4688)
5. BROWER, DANIEL. "The Relations of Visuo-Motor Conflict to Personality Traits and Cardio-Vascular Activity." *J General Psychol* 38:69–99 Ja '48. * (*PA* 22:3383)
6. STACK, HERBERT J. *Personal Characteristics of Traffic-Accident Repeaters.* Saugatuck, Conn.: Eno Foundation for Highway Traffic Control, 1948. Pp. 64. *
7. SASLOW, GEORGE, AND SHOBE, FRANK O. "Evaluation of a Psychiatric Screening Test: Cornell Word Form-I." *Am J Psychiatry* 106:37–45 Jl '49. * (*PA* 24:1207)
8. DuBOIS, PHILIP H., AND WATSON, ROBERT I. "The Selection of Patrolmen." *J Appl Psychol* 34:90–5 Ap '50. * (*PA* 25:2076)
9. DuBOIS, PHILIP H., AND WATSON, ROBERT I. "Validity Information Exchange, No 7-075: D.O.T. Code 2-66.23, Policeman." *Personnel Psychol* 7:414–7 au '54. *
10. BARRY, JOHN R.; SELLS, SAUL B.; AND TRITES, DAVID K. "Psychiatric Screening of Flying Personnel With the Cornell Word Form." Abstract. *J Consult Psychol* 19:32 F '55. *
11. WEIDER, ARTHUR; MITTELMANN, BELA; WECHSLER, DAVID; AND WOLFF, HAROLD G. "Further Developments of the Cornell Word Form." *Psychiatric Q* 29:588–94 O '55. *

[45]

★**DF Opinion Survey.** Grades 12–16 and adults; 1954–56; IBM; 1 form ('54); 10 scores: need for attention, liking for thinking, adventure vs. security, self-reliance vs. dependence, aesthetic appreciation, cultural conformity, need for freedom, realistic thinking, need for precision, need for diversion; separate answer sheets must be used; $3.75 per 25 tests; 20¢ per single copy; 3¢ per IBM answer sheet; $2 per set of either hand or machine scoring stencils; 3¢ per profile ('55); 25¢ per manual ('56); postage extra; [45] minutes; J. P. Guilford, Paul R. Christensen, and Nicholas A. Bond, Jr.; Sheridan Supply Co. *

ANDREW R. BAGGALEY, *Associate Professor of Psychology, University of Wisconsin—Milwaukee, Milwaukee, Wisconsin.*

This inventory is based on an extensive factor analysis. It attempts to encompass dimensions of "motivation" as well as "vocation-interest." Thus it is a kind of combination of the approaches of the *Kuder Preference Record* and *Edwards Personal Preference Schedule,* although it differs from both in using the "yes-?-no" response form instead of forced choices.

Thirty items are scored for each of 10 scales. Most of the questions are of the form "You would like to...," which seems rather awkward. Also, many testees may wonder whether Parts 1 and 2 are separately timed.

Odd-even reliabilities are given for male and female college students separately and combined. The mean of the latter (by Fisher's *z* transformation) is .86. Also, scale intercorrelations are reported for both sexes. Most of these are below .30. Thus the reliability of intraindividual differences as measured by the scales is quite high. All in all, the construct validity of the survey is rather convincing, although it would be interesting to have correlations with similarly-named scales of inventories already in wide use. The authors claim nothing further about the validity of this inventory and recommend separate predictive validation in each practical application. In fact they call it an "experimental test" in the manual, though not on the test booklet. Nevertheless, if the survey is to be used for vocational guidance, as the authors suggest, it would obviously be useful to have available some predictive validities for *general* types of criterion activities, so that a counselor could judge in advance whether or not administration of the survey would be a complete waste of time for some of his problems. College norms are given for each sex separately on those scales showing significant sex differences. As the authors imply, this inventory should probably be used for guidance rather than selection, since it seems not too difficult for a testee to "fake" a desired impression on the scale scores.

In summary, this is a well designed inventory with certain limitations—limitations which are clearly stated in the manual. It should provide good competition for both temperament and interest inventories already on the market.

JOHN W. FRENCH, *Research Associate, Educational Testing Service, Princeton, New Jersey.*

The *DF Opinion Survey* is a well set up personality questionnaire based on the authors' long research experience. It is intended to fill a need for an "extensive, rational coverage of the many variables that should be included in an adequate assessment of personality." It can be said that nobody is sure yet exactly how best to describe personality, whether it should be in terms of traits, interests, attitudes, motivations, or some combination of things. This instrument concentrates on "dynamic factors" and yields 10 scores as listed in the above entry. The manual explains that these traits were selected as being non-vocational interest or motivational traits found by factor analysis. While this kind of selection seems reasonable, no specific reasons are given for including some traits rather than others. Why, for example, are interests in thinking and in aesthetics included, while interests in athletics and in people are not? Why are self-reliance and conformity included, while emotionality, persistence, and sociability are not? Why are the needs for attention, precision, diversion, and security included, while the need for affection is not? While answers to these questions are not provided, the reviewer has no specific reason for criticizing the selection that was made. Considering that the test requires less than one hour to administer, the areas of the personality domain represented seem to cover very well the important motivational factors.

As one takes the *DF Opinion Survey,* there appears a noticeable repetitiveness associated with certain columns on the answer sheet. This is a consequence of (*a*) simplifying the scoring keys by placing all items for a given scale in the same column, and (*b*) insuring high reliability by including many items of each type. This replication of similar items was done for subcategories within each of the 10 reportable scores rather than for the reportable scores themselves. In some cases the subcategories within a score do not seem, on an introspective basis, likely to be related to each other as well as they should be. For example, adventure vs. security consists of four homogeneous item subcategories: exploration, personal risk-taking, harm avoidance, and monotony. Each one of these is probably highly reliable for the number of items involved. Yet the reportable score would suffer if, for example, people who would like exploring do not usually enjoy taking needless personal risks. Another seemingly odd mixture of subcategories occurs in the cultural conformity score, where conscientious and competitive people are grouped with conventional conformists. Perhaps the manual could be improved by the inclusion of factor-analytic or other evidence justifying the subcategories that are listed for the 10 scores. Similar reliability, less repetitiveness, and greater validity might have been achieved by having the items more evenly cover the full scope of each reportable score rather than having them repetitively define subcategories. On the other hand, the homogenous subcategories of items make available some opportunities for research that would not have been available had the items been set up more ideally for operational measurement of the survey's 10 scores. For example, with a reasonably large population of subjects, a satisfactory validation could be made separately for each of more than 30 groups of items. The manual mentions the possible use of the item subcategories in factor analysis studies.

This inventory, as the authors suggest, should be regarded to some extent as a research instrument, because evidence for its validity is not yet available. Nevertheless, the general findings of the authors and others in the field of personality measurement make it seem likely that the factors being measured here will serve an important function when used as recommended in conjunction with vocational interest inventories for vocational guidance, for predicting happiness in an occupation, and for gathering information about personal adjustment.

ARTHUR W. MEADOWS, *Head, Psychology Department, University of Adelaide, Adelaide, Australia.*

This inventory of dynamic factors of interest is the result of a factor-analytic investigation. Each of the 10 traits it measures is contributed to by a number of categories of interest, e.g., "liking for thinking" is contributed to by items assessing interest in mathematics, logical processes, organising, and puzzle solving; "need for freedom," by items designed to reveal aversion to organising, nonconformity, independence, and disorderliness, and so on. The original variables selected were developed from a large number of human needs including those formulated by Murray in his *Explorations in Personality.* The survey is administered with a separate answer sheet and is hand or machine scored.

The authors selected items by item analysis from a pool and prepared new items after trial. The resulting items were analysed again on the basis of the factor scores. An attempt was made to make the items as unidimensional as possible. Interpretation of the scores is given in terms which generalise from the original items. For example, a high score on "need for attention" is said to imply a craving for recognition, the enjoyment of status, and exhibitionism. These terms are derived from the implications and sense of the items. Careful perusal of the items indicates that, with very slight rephrasing, the inventory could be used in English speaking countries other than America.

Reliabilities of the trait scores were computed separately for men and for women, and for men and women combined. The corrected odd-even coefficients range from .65 to .96. The intercorrelations of the scores on the traits indicate that 70 per cent of the coefficients are below .30. Thus, a fair proportion of the scores are relatively independent.

There are clear sex differences and differences due to educational level (probably due to age), but separate norms in terms of means and standard deviations of scores on each scale are provided for men and women and for high school and college groups.

This test should prove useful in conjunction with vocational interest inventories because certain occupations may sometimes be distinguished more clearly than others as including such interest factors as "liking for thinking," "need for precision," and "need for diversion." In addition, behaviour problems might be predictable on the basis of scores on such factors as, say, "need for freedom" and "cultural conformity."

There are no validity data with practical criteria and the survey must be designated as an experimental test for future use in vocational and counseling fields.

[46]
*Detroit Adjustment Inventory. Ages 5–8, grades 3–6, 7–12; 1942–54; title on test for Gamma and Alpha Forms is *Telling What I Do;* 3 levels; record blanks (no date); no data on reliability; no norms; $3.25 per 25 tests; 55¢ per specimen set; 95¢ per set of remedial leaflets; postage extra; Harry J. Baker; Public School Publishing Co. *
a) DELTA FORM. Ages 5–8; 1954.
b) GAMMA FORM. Grades 3–6; 1950–52; test ('52); manual ('52); (20–50) minutes.
c) ALPHA FORM. Grades 7–12; 1942; (20–40) minutes.

REFERENCE
1. BOUISE, LOUISE METOYER. "Emotional and Personality Problems of a Group of Retarded Readers." *El Engl* 32:544–8 D '55. *

LAURANCE F. SHAFFER, *Professor of Education, Teachers College, Columbia University, New York, New York.*

Although the three levels of the *Detroit Adjustment Inventory* were published from 1942 to 1954, they bear a marked resemblance to the primitive instruments for appraising personality that first appeared in the 1920's. Their characteristics have to be summed by a string of negatives—no evidence about item construction except reference to the author's subjective ex-

perience, no sign of item analysis against internal or external criteria, no data on reliability, no norms. The only evidence of validity, for Alpha and Gamma, is the ability of the total score to distinguish extremely maladjusted pupils in special classes from superior or average pupils. There is no evidence at all about Delta.

The items in all three forms of the test are arranged under 24 topics. The Alpha and Gamma forms are pupil-answered questionnaires of 120 five-choice and 128 three-choice items, respectively. Delta, completed by the teacher from observation and parent interviews, has 64 four-choice items.

The complete program for the use of the inventory does not stop with diagnosis, but goes on to treatment. Pupils who have taken Alpha may receive any of 24 remedial leaflets selected according to the areas of their maladjustment. For Gamma there are 16 pupil leaflets, and for Delta, 16 for the use of teachers and parents. These leaflets were not seen by the reviewer, but the manual for Alpha gives four samples. These are not at all impressive.

In spite of its shortcomings, the inventory may have some value when used by teachers or counselors whose skills and attitudes are optimal. The very absence of the trappings of psychometrics may make a wise teacher look beyond the ridiculously numerous "scores," and see the primary communication from the pupil. But even for this purpose, modern conceptions of test construction can surely produce a far sharper instrument.

For a review by Albert Ellis of the Alpha Form, see 3:31.

[47]
★Edwards Personal Preference Schedule. College and adults; 1953–57; 15 scores: achievement, deference, order, exhibition, autonomy, affiliation, intraception, succorance, dominance, abasement, nurturance, change, endurance, heterosexuality, aggression; 2 supplementary scores: test consistency, profile stability; IBM; 1 form ('53); revised manual ('57); college norms only; separate answer sheets must be used; $3 per 25 tests; $2.25 per 50 hand scoring answer sheets; $2.20 per 50 IBM answer sheets; $1.50 per set of either hand or machine scoring stencils; 60¢ per specimen set; postpaid; (40–55) minutes; Allen L. Edwards; Psychological Corporation.

REFERENCES
1. EDWARDS, ALLEN L. "The Relationship Between the Judged Desirability of a Trait and the Probability That the Trait Will Be Endorsed." *J Appl Psychol* 37:90–3 F '53. * (*PA* 28:551)
2. NAVRAN, LESLIE, AND STAUFFACHER, JAMES C. "Social Desirability as a Factor in Edwards' Personality Preference Schedule Performance." Abstract. *J Consult Psychol* 18:442 D '54. *
3. SCHLAG, MADELEINE. *The Relationship Between the Personality Preference Schedule and the Allport, Vernon and Lindzey Study of Values: A Personality Study of a Group of*

Medical Students. Master's thesis, University of Washington (Seattle, Wash.), 1954.

4. MERRILL, REED M. "Relation of the Edwards Personal Preference Schedule to the Clinical and Experimental Scales of the MMPI." Abstract. *Am Psychol* 10:366 Ag '55. *

5. PIROJNIKOFF, L. *The Achievement Motive and Other Personality Traits as Measured by Edwards Personal Preference Schedule and Their Relation to Learning, the Authoritarian Scale, and Speed of Performance.* Master's thesis, University of Washington (Seattle, Wash.), 1955.

6. STROTHER, CHARLES R., AND SCHAIE, K. WARNER. "Age Differences in Personality: A Comparison of Young and Old Groups of Superior Ability." Abstract. *Am Psychol* 10:339 Ag '55. *

7. BENDIG, A. W. "The Personality of Judges and Their Agreement With Experts in Judging Clinical Case Histories." Abstract. *J Consult Psychol* 20:422 D '56. *

8. FUJITA, BEN. *An Investigation of the Applicability of the Edwards Personal Preference Schedule to a Cultural Sub-Group, the Nisei.* Master's thesis, University of Washington (Seattle, Wash.), 1956.

9. HORN, J. B. *A Comparison of Robbers, Burglars, and Forgers on the Edwards PPS.* Master's thesis, University of Washington (Seattle, Wash.), 1956.

10. KLETT, C. J. *A Study of the Edwards Personal Preference Schedule in Relation to Socio-Economic Status.* Doctor's thesis, University of Washington (Seattle, Wash.), 1956.

11. MERRILL, REED M., AND HEATHERS, LOUISE B. "The Relation of the MMPI to the Edwards Personal Preference Schedule on a College Counseling Center Sample." *J Consult Psychol* 20:310–4 Ag '56. * (*PA* 31:7949)

12. SHEPHERD, JOHN R., AND SCHEIDEL, THOMAS M. "A Study of the Personality Configuration of Effective Oral Readers." *Speech Monogr* 23:298–304 N '56. * (*PA* 32:2128)

13. TOBIN, W. W. *Use of the Edwards Personal Preference Schedule in Establishing Personality Profiles for Teachers and Education Students.* Master's thesis, University of Washington (Seattle, Wash.), 1956.

14. ALLEN, ROBERT M. "Edwards Personal Preference Schedule Intercorrelations for Two Groups." *Psychol Rec* 7:87–91 Jl '57. *

15. ALLEN, ROBERT M. "The Relationship Between the Edwards Personal Preference Schedule Variables and the Minnesota Multiphasic Personality Inventory Scales." *J Appl Psychol* 41:307–11 O '57. *

16. ALLEN, ROBERT M., AND DALLEK, JEFFREY I. "A Normative Study of the Edwards' Personal Preference Schedule." *J Psychol* 43:151–4 Ja '57. *

17. ANDREWS, JOHN H. M. "Administrative Significance of Psychological Differences Between Secondary Teachers of Different Subject Matter Fields." *Alberta J Ed Res* 3:199–208 D '57. *

18. BERNARDIN, ALFRED C., AND JESSOR, RICHARD. "A Construct Validation of the Edwards Personal Preference Schedule With Respect to Dependency." *J Consult Psychol* 21:63–7 F '57. * (*PA* 32:485)

19. CROW, W. R. *Relationships Between Edwards PPS and the MMPI.* Master's thesis, University of Washington (Seattle, Wash.), 1957.

20. FISHER, SEYMOUR, AND MORTON, ROBERT B. "An Exploratory Study of Some Relationships Between Hospital Ward Atmospheres and Attitudes of Ward Personnel." *J Psychol* 44:155–64 Jl '57. *

21. FUJITA, BEN. "Applicability of the Edwards Personal Preference Schedule to Nisei." *Psychol Rep* 3:518–9 D '57. *

22. GRAINE, GEORGE N. "Measures of Conformity as Found in the Rosenzweig P-F Study and the Edwards Personal Preference Schedule." Abstract. *J Consult Psychol* 21:300 Ag '57. *

23. GROSSACK, MARTIN M. "Some Personality Characteristics of Southern Negro Students." *J Social Psychol* 46:125–31 Ag '57. *

24. JACKSON, PHILIP W., AND GUBA, EGON G. "The Need Structure of In-Service Teachers: An Occupational Analysis." *Sch R* 65:176–92 Je '57. *

25. KELLEHER, D. *The Social Desirability Factor in Edwards PPS.* Master's thesis, University of Washington (Seattle, Wash.), 1957.

26. KLETT, C. JAMES. "Performance of High School Students on the Edwards Personal Preference Schedule." *J Consult Psychol* 21:68–72 F '57. * (*PA* 32:949)

27. KLETT, C. JAMES. "The Social Desirability Stereotype in a Hospital Population." *J Consult Psychol* 21:419–21 O '57. *

28. KLETT, C. JAMES. "The Stability of the Social Desirability Scale Values in the Edwards Personal Preference Schedule." *J Consult Psychol* 21:183–5 Ap '57. *

29. KLETT, C. JAMES, AND TAMKIN, ARTHUR S. "The Social Desirability Stereotype and Some Measures of Psychopathology." Abstract. *J Consult Psychol* 21:450 D '57. *

30. KLETT, SHIRLEY LOUISE. *The Edwards Personal Preference Schedule and Academic Achievement.* Doctor's thesis, University of Washington (Seattle, Wash.), 1957. (*DA* 18:1490)

31. KOPONEN, ARTHUR. *The Influence of Demographic Factors on Responses to the Edwards Personal Preference Schedule.* Doctor's thesis, Columbia University (New York, N.Y.), 1957. (*DA* 17:2697)

32. SILVERMAN, ROBERT E. "The Edwards Personal Preference Schedule and Social Desirability." *J Consult Psychol* 21:402–4 O '57. *

33. VENING, GEORGE H., AND PEPINSKY, HAROLD B. "Normative Data Information Exchange, No. 10-16." *Personnel Psychol* 10:235 su '57. *

34. ALLEN, ROBERT M. "An Analysis of Edwards Personal Preference Schedule Intercorrelations for a Local College Population." *J Ed Res* 51:591–7 Ap '58. *

35. BENDIG, A. W. "Comparison of the Validity of Two Temperament Scales in Predicting College Achievement." *J Ed Res* 51:605–9 Ap '58. *

36. BORISLOW, BERNARD. "The Edwards Personal Preference Schedule (EPPS) and Fakability." *J Appl Psychol* 42:22–7 F '58. *

37. CORAH, NORMAN L.; FELDMAN, MARVIN J.; COHEN, IRA S.; GRUEN, WALTER; MEADOW, ARNOLD; AND RINGWALL, EGAN A. "Social Desirability as a Variable in the Edwards Personal Preference Schedule." *J Consult Psychol* 22:70–2 F '58. *

38. DUNNETTE, MARVIN D., AND KIRCHNER, WAYNE K. "Validation of Psychological Tests in Industry." *Personnel Adm* 21:20–7 My–Je '58. *

39. DUNNETTE, MARVIN D.; KIRCHNER, WAYNE K.; AND DeGIDIO, JoANNE. "Relations Among Scores on Edwards Personal Preference Schedule, California Psychological Inventory, and Strong Vocational Interest Blank for an Industrial Sample." *J Appl Psychol* 42:178–81 Je '58. *

40. FRENCH, ELIZABETH G. "A Note on the Edwards Personal Preference Schedule for Use With Basic Airmen." *Ed & Psychol Meas* 18:109–15 sp '58. *

41. GEBHART, G. GARY, AND HOYT, DONALD P. "Personality Needs of Under- and Overachieving Freshmen." *J Appl Psychol* 42:125–8 Ap '58. *

42. HEILBRUN, ALFRED B., JR. "Relationships Between the Adjective Check-List, Personal Preference Schedule and Desirability Factors Under Varying Defensiveness Conditions." *J Clin Psychol* 14:283–7 Jl '58. *

43. KELLEHER, DANIEL. "The Social Desirability Factor in Edwards' PPS." Abstract. *J Consult Psychol* 22:100 Ap '58. *

44. LÖVAAS, O. IVAR. "Social Desirability Ratings of Personality Variables by Norwegian and American College Students." *J Abn & Social Psychol* 57:124–5 Jl '58. *

45. MANN, JOHN H. "Self-Ratings and the EPPS." *J Appl Psychol* 42:267–8 Ag '58. *

46. MELIKIAN, LEVON H. "The Relationship Between Edwards' and McClelland's Measures of Achievement Motivation." *J Consult Psychol* 22:296–8 Ag '58. *

47. PETERSON, TED TANGWALL. *Selecting School Administrators: An Evaluation of Six Tests.* Doctor's thesis, Stanford University (Stanford, Calif.), 1958. (*DA* 19:262)

48. STOLTZ, ROBERT E. "Note on Intercorrelations of Edward's Personal Preference Schedule Variables." *Psychol Rep* 4:239–41 Je '58. *

49. SUMNER, EARL DAVID. *On the Relation of Manifest Needs to Personal Values: A Factor Analytic Study Involving R and Q Techniques.* Doctor's thesis, Wayne State University (Detroit, Mich.), 1958. (*DA* 18:2219)

50. ZUCKERMAN, MARVIN. "The Validity of the Edwards Personal Preference Schedule in the Measurement of Dependency-Rebelliousness." *J Clin Psychol* 14:379–82 O '58. *

FRANK BARRON, *Research Psychologist, Institute of Personality Assessment and Research, University of California, Berkeley, California.*

The freewheeling explorations in personality which were carried on in depth and breadth at the Harvard Psychological Clinic under the aegis of Henry A. Murray in the early 1930's have proved in the intervening two decades to be peculiarly resistant to compression into the sort of "objective" psychometric mapping which personality inventories seek to provide. Murray and his co-workers did in fact construct quite subtle and comprehensive inventory type scales (e.g., the *Psychological Insight Test*) to measure the variables in the need system which was the fundament of their research, but as time went on they became increasingly dissatisfied with those scales and finally abandoned them. Oddly enough, they did so in the face of evidence (which Murray reports in the section on questionnaires in *Explorations in Personality*) that the correlations between the scales and staff ratings of the same variables, given in ignorance of the scale scores, were steadily increasing with each study, to the final point of an average correlation of .57, which in that more sanguine climate of psychological truth seeking apparently was interpreted as rather discouraging.

The Murray need system did, of course, continue its psychometric life in a somewhat more complex but less rigorous embodiment, the scoring scheme for the *Thematic Apperception Test*. This or that "need" has also been taken into camp by individual investigators, so that scales bearing such names as "deference," "dominance," "abasement," "orderliness," and "achievement" have appeared in inventory type tests, both of the factor-analytically based sort and the empirically based kind. However, until the development of the *Edwards Personal Preference Schedule* no really thoroughgoing attempt had been made to measure most of the manifest needs in the Murray system by the inventory method.

Fifteen of the variables of the Murray need system were selected for inclusion in the Edwards schedule: achievement, deference, order exhibition, autonomy, affiliation, intraception, succorance, dominance, abasement, nurturance, change, endurance, heterosexuality, and aggression. The schedule consists of 210 pairs of items in a forced-choice format, with items from each of the 15 scales being paired off twice against items from the other 14. In addition, 15 items are repeated in order to obtain an estimate of the respondent's consistency. The pairing of variables against one another thus yields an assessment of the relative strength of competing needs within the person; however, the relative strength of such needs in persons representative of the general population remains the basic point of reference.

The first step in the construction of the schedule was to establish a pool of 140 items, 10 for each of 14 scales, which appeared face valid for measurement of the need variables when a true-false rather than paired comparison format was used. In an early study with the schedule in that form, however, Edwards found (*1*) that the frequency of endorsement of an item was closely related to the judged social desirability of the item. Using the method of successive intervals [1] for the scaling of the items (with 152 judges),

he discovered that social desirability correlated .87 with actual frequency of endorsement in a new sample when the items were responded to as a test.

This rather disconcerting finding led Edwards to adopt a forced paired comparison method, with the items in each pair being matched for scale values on the social desirability scale. However, when he fitted the items into pairs he did not take the further step of ascertaining whether the social desirability of the item changed as a result of the changed context in which it was presented. Nevertheless, he had succeeded in introducing a new wrinkle into personality test construction by his dramatization of the importance of social desirability as a determinant of response. In doing so, he continued to build upon the experience of the Harvard group; speaking of the *Psychological Insight Test*, Murray had commented in *Explorations in Personality*, "As might be expected, however, it was found that there was a general tendency for the subjects to give themselves relatively high marks on the more desirable traits and relatively low marks on the less desirable."

A series of studies by Klett (*26, 27, 28*) and an unpublished master's thesis by Fujita (*8*) have provided supporting evidence for the generality of the social desirability stereotype found in Edwards' original study. In a high school sample, Klett found a correlation of .94 between social desirability scale values (using the 140 items singly) and those obtained by Edwards. He also found high agreement concerning social desirability between normal subjects and individuals hospitalized with mental illness, both psychotic and nonpsychotic. Fujita established equally high agreement (*circa* .90) between the Edwards scale values and social desirability of the items as judged by nisei college students. Klett makes reference to a personal communication from Ivar Lövaas in Norway, who obtained similar results with Norwegian judges.

A fly has appeared in the ointment, however, with the publication of a study by Corah, Feldman, et al. (*37*) which took up the question of whether items in pairs retained the approximately equated social desirability values assigned to them singly. Using 30 item pairs which in the PPS provide comparisons between needs for achievement, order, succorance, abasement, heterosexuality, and aggression, they found highly significant differences in social desirabil-

1 Edwards, Allen L. "The Scaling of Stimuli by the Methods of Successive Intervals." *J Appl Psychol* 36:118–22 Ap '52. * (*PA* 27:21)

ity between paired items which presumably were matched for it. Indeed, they discovered that the correlation between social desirability scale values for the items in pairs and actual choice of alternatives A or B was .88, which wins by a nose over the correlation of .87 reported by Edwards in his disenchanting earlier report. It appears that the *Edwards Personal Preference Schedule* is a promising test, but that something needs to be done about its failure to control for social desirability!

This unusually ironic retaliation points up one of the major failures of work thus far with the PPS. On a number of counts it appears soundly based: (a) it is tied to a powerful theoretical formulation concerning motives in psychologically normal human beings; (b) by use of the forced-choice method and systematic comparisons of strengths of needs within the person it avoids some of the difficulties inherent in the simple true-false dichotomy employed by earlier inventories; (c) it has satisfactory reliability and it offers measures which are relatively independent of one another, although perhaps not so independent as was first thought (*15*). While thus well begun, the PPS nevertheless cannot be said to have demonstrated validity in measurement of the variables. Following the publication of the manual in 1954, which set forth trenchantly the virtues of the test but which had to be content with a promissory note on validity, a number of studies have been reported. However, a good deal of the energy of the interested University of Washington researchers seems to have been expended in tilting at the *Minnesota Multiphasic Personality Inventory* and in beating the drums for inventories which will be free of "social desirability variance," with consequent impoverishment of imagination and effort in the task of assessing the real world validity of the face valid scales incorporated into the schedule.

In their first enthusiasm over the discovery that social desirability of a trait affects the likelihood that an individual will attribute it to himself, such investigators as Klett and Tamkin (*29*) proceeded rapidly to the limit and argued that tests (particularly such a test as the MMPI) which did not control for social desirability could hardly be valid for the diagnostic categories which served as the empirical basis for the construction of scales. This argument ignores two facts: (a) that one may candidly ascribe to oneself with high accuracy some traits, particularly symptoms, which even to oneself appear quite undesirable; and (b) that among a set of traits of a high degree of social undesirability there may exist substantial communities of variance corresponding to covariances in the real world. In assessing the validity of a measure, one looks for direct evidence pro or con; one does not say that a measure cannot be valid because high scores on it are socially desirable and low scores are socially undesirable. And conversely, nothing may be promised concerning the validity of a test simply because social desirability is controlled.

These remarks should, in the face of the Corah, Feldman et al. results, give some comfort to users of the PPS, since it may yet prove to have validity in spite of the uncontrolled variance in social desirability. To date, however, the evidence for validity is rather scanty. Bernardin and Jessor (*18*) have shown, on the positive side, that "dependent" subjects (those who score at or above the 70th percentile on need: deference and at or below the 50th percentile on need: autonomy) perform less well on a maze learning task when they are subjected to critical comments from the experimenter, and that when confronted with difficult problems, they are more likely to ask for help. These same investigators, however, in a third experiment using the Asch technique of putting subjects under pressure to agree with an apparent group consensus which is false, found no difference in yielding tendencies between dependent and independent subjects (classified on the basis of PPS scores). Graine (*22*) found, contrary to expectations, that need: autonomy had a significant positive correlation with the group conformity rating derived from the *Rosenzweig Picture-Frustration Study*. Gebhart and Hoyt (*41*) studied academic overachievement and underachievement in first year college students, and established that overachievers score significantly higher on such needs as achievement, order, and intraception, and lower on such needs as nurturance, affiliation, and change. Interestingly enough, when ability level is considered independently of overachievement and underachievement, persons of high ability also score higher on need: achievement, which conceivably could reflect either motivation to do well on tests of ability as a result of high need: achievement, or, on the other hand, the development of strong achievement drive as a result of a history of positive reinforcement of good academic performance.

Apart from these few studies which do make some approach to assessing the construct validity of some of the PPS measures, the only validity evidence available in the literature at the time of this review consisted of correlations of PPS scales with scales of the MMPI (*11, 15*), the *California Psychological Inventory* (*39*), and the *Strong Vocational Interest Blank* (*39*). Allen (*15*) found 90 (of a possible 630) correlations between PPS and MMPI scales significant at the .05 level; he also, however, found that one third of the correlations among PPS scales themselves were statistically significant. Dunnette, Kirchner, and De Gidio (*39*) have shown that a number of the PPS scales correlate significantly with CPI variables, although the correlations are generally not over .40 and do not make any consistent sense. For example, need:heterosexuality correlates —.38 with the CPI good impression scale, —.29 with sense of well-being, and —.26 with responsibility; need: achievement correlates positively with sociability, but does not relate to the CPI achievement scales, which were developed by item analysis against the criterion of actual academic performance in high schools and colleges throughout the country. Need:order also produces some unexpected relationships, among them an *r* of —.37 with capacity for status. All in all, the yield from these tangential sorts of validity studies may be described not only as meagre but as rather spotty at best.

Judging from the literature on the PPS at this date, the verdict of caution would be that the test is not yet ready for use in counseling or personnel selection. A study by Borislow (*36*) indicates that the PPS is readily fakable, and that neither the consistency score nor an index of profile stability (designed to reveal uniformity of response) distinguishes faked profiles from profiles earned under ordinary self-appraisal conditions. This is a particularly fatal defect in the personnel selection situation, where the respondent is not so motivated to be candid as he would be in a counseling center. The crucial point, however, is not the susceptibility to faking, but the fact that there is no warrant in available research for considering the PPS to have met even minimum standards of evidence for validity.

ÅKE BJERSTEDT, *Department of Psychology, University of Lund, Lund, Sweden.*

It has been a definite drawback in many inventories that subjects tend to endorse desirable and reject undesirable items. One outstanding characteristic of the *Edwards Personal Preference Schedule* is the attempt to minimize this disturbing influence by means of a specific kind of forced choice. The subject is forced to choose in each pair of statements the one which is most characteristic of himself. The two statements in each pair represent different personality variables, but—and this is the important point— they have at the same time a comparable degree of social desirability, as operationally determined by a scaling procedure using the method of successive intervals. We may regret that the manual gives too few details about this prequestionnaire scaling research, as well as too little discussion of the possible disadvantages of the forced-choice technique in the case of experienced "equal preference." Nevertheless, it gives us sufficient information about the *effect* of this scaling: low correlations with specific "desirability" scales are evidently obtained for most of the present variables.

Although this equating for social desirability is an interesting and important step forward, it should be pointed out that the desirability values of questionnaire items cannot be stable entities, equally valid in all times and places. On the contrary, we must expect that different social norm groups will have very different value hierarchies. This does not mean, of course, that attempts to minimize the influence of social desirability are unimportant or useless; but it means that test users should be careful when applying the instrument to other groups of subjects. It might well be that the influence of social desirability is much stronger in other samples than in the one in which the primary scaling was carried through. The problem of social desirability as a disturbing factor should, therefore, not be thought to have been solved once and for all (a fact of which the test constructor is, of course, well aware) but should be the subject of continuous interest and research.

The questionnaire furnishes scores for 15 personality variables selected from the lists presented by Murray in his *Explorations in Personality.* The manual gives no information concerning the criteria of selection: we do not know why certain variables were chosen and others rejected. Neither do we know how the specific items, representing these different variables, were selected. Nevertheless, the items chosen in most instances give the impression of adequate face validity, and, what may be more important, internal-consistency coefficients reported are in most cases satisfactory, as is the fact of low intercorrelations between most of the variables.

The manual gives data from a normative sample of 749 college women and 760 college men, in which certain sex differences were found. The men, for instance, scored higher on achievement, autonomy, dominance, heterosexuality, and aggression. There is no discussion of whether these differences may be partly a function of age (the modal age interval among the men being 20–24; among the women, 15–19).

Very little information on validity is reported in the manual. Some correlations with two other questionnaires are given, but, as the variables of these two are only very slightly related to the present instrument, this information is not very helpful. A few studies of ratings are referred to, but no quantitative results are given. The kind of validity investigation which would seem to be the most natural and immediately interesting would be a comparison between TAT measures of the 15 variables and the PPS measures of the same variables. Unfortunately, no such investigation is mentioned. We have the general impression that the test constructor has been somewhat more interested in the technical aspects of his instrument than in its psychological rationale. However, the good work done in the technical phase will certainly give the test sufficient research appeal. This should, at the same time, be a definite guarantee that such problems of construct validity as are still unsolved will not remain unsolved for long.

Summing up, the *Edwards Personal Preference Schedule* is an instrument which has several unique and useful characteristics and which promises to be very helpful in general personality-oriented research. More information as to the variability of social desirability values in different social groups and more studies on validity are desirable, however, if we wish to use this instrument confidently for *other* than research purposes.

DONALD W. FISKE, *Associate Professor of Psychology, University of Chicago, Chicago, Illinois.*

This schedule represents a desirable departure from the classical personality inventory in several respects: intended function, item form and construction, and variables measured. It "was designed primarily as an instrument for research and counseling purposes" with college students. For a self-report procedure, these functions are more suitable than diagnosis or selection.

The items are in forced-choice form, with the alternatives rather closely matched on social desirability. This is a technically optimal practice which is still uncommon in test construction: it minimizes or eliminates several response sets which attenuate or confound much personality measurement.

The forced-choice format makes the resulting scores slightly interdependent. They tend to have small negative intercorrelations because the sum of the 15 scores is a fixed quantity. This is a slight disadvantage for persons wishing to use the several scales separately. However, the resulting profile for each subject is ipsative: the format requires the subject to order the several variables in terms of their applicability to him. In the reviewer's opinion, this is a theoretically desirable approach in self-administered personality assessment.

Another consequence of the forced-choice technique is the narrow range of content involved in the assessment of each variable. It would appear that nine statements are utilized for each variable, most of which are used three times.

The schedule has the advantage of being based on a more sophisticated theoretical formulation than most inventories: it assesses 15 of Murray's variables. In addition, it provides a measure of consistency of response within a single testing session and a measure of profile stability (consistency of relative standing on the 15 variables). The latter is a promising innovation. Unfortunately, the manual reports little data on these stability scores, probably because of the time required to compute a product-moment correlation for each case. Since the essential information is the ordering of the 15 variables, a rank correlation (rho or tau) would seem appropriate and convenient.

The manual reports test-retest coefficients between .74 and .88. The internal consistencies estimated from split-half correlations range from .60 to .87. In view of the intended research applicability of the schedule, it would seem advisable to report, in addition, the estimated homogeneity of each score. No internal consistency is given for the test consistency score and no reliability figure of any kind is reported for the measure of profile stability.

From the published table of consistency scores, the median proportion of consistent responses appears to be about .78. This is lower than that for some other inventories because the responses on this schedule are relatively free from the influence of social desirability, an effect which increases consistency of response.

The validation of scores for variables such as these requires extensive research. The manual reports studies comparing scores with subjects' rankings of the same variables described in essentially the same words, but no descriptive statistic is given. The sex differences in the normative group and the reported correlations with other inventories are supportive but insufficient. The evaluation of the validity of the schedule must be withheld until further studies are reported.

The order of the items was apparently based on convenience for hand scoring. As a result, half of the items for each variable occur in blocks of five, with the alternative for that variable being in the same position within each of the several items. Furthermore, the format of both the IBM and the hand scored answer sheet is determined by these considerations. Thus, position sets might enter, and subjects might detect the basis for the groupings. While these are probably minor weaknesses, it is possible that the unusual sequence of item positions on the answer sheets may produce some confusion or irritation in subjects.

The possibility of inverted factor analyses from the profiles of scores is mentioned, but the reader is not cautioned about the instability of correlations based on 15 pairs of observations. While the manual has an extensive bibliography, the text occasionally fails to indicate relevant citations from it. Only one trivial error was noted in the manual, in a page reference.

In general, the manual is highly satisfactory. It presents in detail the procedures for administration and scoring, and the background of the schedule. It is conservative and professional in tone. The inventory itself represents a distinct step forward in techniques for the measurement of personality. While it is admittedly based on self-report, it is theoretically oriented and technically sound.

J Consult Psychol 19:156 Ap '55. Laurance F. Shaffer. * An ingenious and novel instrument for personality assessment which will surely evoke wide comment, considerable clinical use, and much research. The *Schedule* is designed in terms of 15 of Murray's manifest needs—achievement, deference, order, exhibition, autonomy, etc.—each of which is paired twice with each of the others. The 225 forced-choice items each consist of a pair of alternatives carefully equated for social desirability. As a result of this unusual and valuable matching, only two of the need scores have correlations with social desirability significantly above zero and these two are low (.32). The *PPS* thereby sidesteps that pitfall of many questionnaires, ego involvement. Because the need scales are short, the modest reliabilities are not unexpected: internal consistencies range from .60 to .87, and retest correlations from .74 to .88. The subscore intercorrelations are low. The validity of such a schedule is not easily expressed in simple terms, but the manual contains interesting data on clinical observations, and on relationships with ratings and other questionnaires. It is a long time since this reviewer has seen a questionnaire that seems to possess such potentialities for use and research.

J Consult Psychol 20:322–4 Ag '56. John W. Gustad. * Either Edwards has based his claims for the validity of the PPS on construct validity or on some other kind. Since the manual contains nothing to support claims of any other kind of validity, we must consider his efforts in regard to construct validity. He has correlated his scales with four others, drawn from the Guilford-Martin and the Taylor. The significant correlations are not interpreted to bear on the construct validity of the PPS. That is to say, no reasons are given to support the notion that the PPS does in fact measure the manifest needs proposed by Murray. It would seem, therefore, that the only conclusion to be drawn is that no usable information is presented regarding the validity of the PPS. It is the responsibility of the test author and the test publisher to establish the validity of any instrument made available commercially for use in one or several practical situations. In the case of this instrument, both the author and the publisher seem to have fallen short of meeting their responsibilities in this respect. One single, simple step might have been—and still might be—taken to correct this. Across the front of each test and each manual, there should be stamped, in large, red letters (preferably letters which will glow in the stygian darkness of the personality measurement field) the word EXPERIMENTAL. It is experimental. It is an intriguing, promising, in many ways very carefully conducted experiment, but it is still an experiment. Until its validity has been established, it must remain an experiment, and it should not be released for any other purpose. [See original review for additional critical comments not excerpted.]

[48]

★The Ego Strength Q-Sort Test. Grades 9–16 and adults; 1956–58; 6 scores: ego-status, social status, goal setting and striving, good mental health, physical status, total; 1 form ('56, essentially the same as the form copyrighted in 1956); manual ('58); no data on reliability; $5 per examiner's kit of 25 tests, manual, stencils, sorting board; $3 per 25 tests; postage extra; (50–90) minutes; Russell N. Cassel; Psychometric Affiliates. *

[49]

★Embedded Figures Test. Ages 10 and over; 1950–57; 1 form ['57]; manual ('50, reprint of 1 below); college norms only; $5 per set of test materials, postage extra; (15–40) minutes; Herman A. Witkin; the Author. *

REFERENCES

1. WITKIN, H. A. "Individual Differences in Ease of Perception of Embedded Figures." *J Personality* 19:1–15 S '50. * (PA 25:5958)
2. WITKIN, H. A.; LEWIS, H. B.; HERTZMAN, M.; MACHOVER, K.; MEISSNER, P. BRETNALL; AND WAPNER, S. *Personality Through Perception: An Experimental and Clinical Study.* New York: Harper & Brothers, 1954. Pp. xxvi, 571. * (PA 28:8566)
3. BELL, ELAINE GRAHAM. *Inner Directed and Other Directed Attitudes.* Doctor's thesis, Yale University (New Haven, Conn.), 1955.
4. FLIEGEL, ZENIA ODWS. *Stability and Change in Perceptual Performance of a Late Adolescent Group in Relation to Personality Variables.* Doctor's thesis, New School for Social Research (New York, N.Y.), 1955.
5. GRUEN, ARNO. "The Relation of Dancing Experience and Personality to Perception." *Psychol Monogr* 69(14):1–16 '55. * (PA 31:218)
6. JACKSON, DOUGLAS N. "A Short Form of Witkin's Embedded-Figures Test." *J Abn & Social Psychol* 53:254–5 S '56. * (PA 32:2897)
7. LONGENECKER, E. D. *Form Perception as a Function of Anxiety, Motivation, and the Testing Situation.* Doctor's thesis, University of Texas (Austin, Tex.), 1956.
8. TAYLOR, JAMES N. *A Comparison of Delusional and Halluncinatory Individuals Using Field-Dependency as a Measure.* Doctor's thesis, Purdue University (Lafayette, Ind.), 1956.
9. BIERI, JAMES; BRADBURN, WENDY M.; AND GALINSKY, M. DAVID. "Sex Differences in Perceptual Behavior." *J Personality* 26:1–12 Mr '58. *

[50]

*The Empathy Test. Ages 13 and over; 1947–55; Forms A ('47), B ('51), C ('54, adaptation of Form A for Canadian use); manual ('55); $3 per 50 tests; $1 per specimen set (must be purchased to obtain manual); postage extra; (10–15) minutes; Willard A. Kerr and Boris J. Speroff; Psychometric Affiliates. *

REFERENCES

1. TOBOLSKI, FRANCIS P., AND KERR, WILLARD A. "Predictive Value of The Empathy Test in Automobile Salesmanship." *J Appl Psychol* 36:310–1 O '52. * (PA 27:5479)
2. VAN ZELST, RAYMOND H. "Empathy Test Scores of Union Leaders." *J Appl Psychol* 36:293–5 O '52. * (PA 27:5463)
3. HALL, HARRY S., AND KERR, GRAHAM B. "The Relationship Between Two Tests of Empathy: Dymond's and Kerr's." Abstract. *Am Psychol* 8:361–2 Ag '53. *

4. SPEROFF, B. J. "Empathic Ability and Accident Rate Among Steel Workers." *Personnel Psychol* 6:297–300 au '53. * (PA 28:5077)
5. VAN ZELST, RAYMOND H. "Validation Evidence on the Empathy Test." *Ed & Psychol Meas* 13:474–7 au '53. * (PA 28:4403)
6. ALDEN, PRISCILLA JEAN. *An Exploratory Study of Self-Rated Empathy.* Doctor's thesis, University of Michigan (Ann Arbor, Mich.), 1954.
7. BASS, BERNARD M.; KARSTENDIEK, BARBARA; McCULLOUGH, GERALD; AND PRUITT, RAY C. "Validity Information Exchange, No. 7-024: D.O.T. Code 2-66.01, 2-66.11, 2-66.12, 2-66.23, Policemen and Detectives, Public Service." *Personnel Psychol* 7:159–60 sp '54. *
8. BELL, GRAHAM B., AND HALL, HARRY E., JR. "The Relationship Between Leadership and Empathy." *J Abn & Social Psychol* 49:156–7 Ja '54. * (PA 28:7326)
9. KERR, WILLARD A., AND SPEROFF, BORIS J. "Validation and Evaluation of the Empathy Test." *J General Psychol* 50:269–76 Ap '54. * (PA 29:4067)
10. SIEGEL, ARTHUR I. "An Experimental Evaluation of the Sensitivity of the Empathy Test." *J Appl Psychol* 38:222–3 Ag '54. * (PA 29:5728)
11. SMITH, FRANK JOHN. *The Role of an Empathy Score in Predicting Supervisory Success.* Master's thesis, Illinois Institute of Technology (Chicago, Ill.), 1954.
12. SPEROFF, B. J. "Relationship Between Empathic Ability and Supervisory Knowledge." *J Personnel Adm & Ind Rel* 1:195–7 '54. * (PA 29:8103)
13. BELL, GRAHAM B., AND STOLPER, RHODA. "An Attempt at Validation of the Empathy Test." *J Appl Psychol* 39:442–3 D '55. * (PA 30:7186)
14. JARRARD, LEONARD E. "Empathy: The Concept and Industrial Applications." *Personnel Psychol* 9:157–67 su '56. * (PA 31:8993)
15. ROSE, GRACE; FRANKEL, NORMAN; AND KERR, WILLARD. "Empathic and Sociometric Status Among Young Teen-Agers." *J Genetic Psychol* 89:277–8 D '56. *
16. TOBOLSKI, FRANCIS P.; JULIANO, CHARLES V.; AND KERR, WILLARD A. "Conformity and Success in the Field of Dramatics." *J Social Psychol* 43:269–73 My '56. *
17. McCARTY, JOHN J. "Normative Data Information Exchange, No. 10-11." *Personnel Psychol* 10:227 su '57. *
18. McCARTY, JOHN J. "Normative Data Information Exchange, No. 10-25." *Personnel Psychol* 10:359 au '57. *
19. McCARTY, JOHN J. "Validity Information Exchange, No. 10-14: D.O.T. Code 1-33.01, Secretary." *Personnel Psychol* 10:202–3 su '57. *
20. McCARTY, JOHN J. "Validity Information Exchange, No. 10-15: D.O.T. Code 1-33.01, Secretary." *Personnel Psychol* 10:204–5 su '57. *

ROBERT L. THORNDIKE, *Professor of Education, Teachers College, Columbia University, New York, New York.*

In this so-called *Empathy Test,* the author attempts to measure the ability of examinees to predict the behavior of what we may call the "generalized other." This he does by calling for rankings of (a) the popularity of 15 types of music for a defined type of worker, (b) the circulation of 15 magazines, and (c) the prevalence of 10 types of annoyances. The key is based on certain empirical facts in each case.

The author's use of the term "empathy" is different from the usual usage in which it means ability to react in a differential way to the "specific other." The two abilities may be quite different. The reviewer is not aware of evidence to show that they are related.

There appears to be no inherent validity in the operations called for in this test, and so its validity must be established empirically through its ability to predict socially important criteria, or its relationships to other variables that would make it a meaningful construct. The manual reports several studies presenting evidence on the validity of the test, and certain of these appear quite impressive. However, the relatively few studies by persons not associated with the author have tended to yield predominantly negative results. Unless the positive results reported in the manual are verified in the findings of other workers, this test cannot be recommended as either a useful practical device or a contribution to the description and understanding of an individual.

[51]

★**Evaluation Modality Test.** Adults; 1956; 3 scores: realism, moralism, individualism; 1 form; no data on reliability; $1.95 per 20 tests; $1 per specimen set (must be purchased to obtain manual) including 10 tests, manual, and scoring key; postage extra; (25–35) minutes; Hugo O. Engelmann; Psychometric Affiliates. *

WILSON H. GUERTIN, *Supervisory Research Psychologist, Veterans Administration Hospital, Knoxville, Iowa.*

This test purports to measure the characteristic way an individual "valuates." "The test is restricted to those modes of valuation which are most significant in contemporary American society, *viz.,* the moralist, realist, and individualist one [sic]." A test item will illustrate the nature of the test:

> 3. If you were to consider joining an organization would you ask yourself whether:
> _____a) doing so would be likely to improve your economic opportunities or your standing in the community?
> _____b) joining this organization would make it easier or harder for you to do the things you want to do?
> _____c) it is the right thing to do and/or the organization stands for the right things?

The author claims that the first response would be selected by a realist, the second by an individualist, and the third by a moralist.

This very brief test with its minimal statistical buttressing provokes some interesting thought. Psychologists ordinarily do not concern themselves about an individual's mode of valuation; thus, the use of the test is restricted by the limited professional interest in the area evaluated. The author states, "Information on the mode in which an individual valuates most frequently should prove useful in general counseling and particularly in occupational placement."

The test has several apparent shortcomings: (*a*) Social desirability is not controlled. (*b*) No item analysis has been made. (*c*) Reliability is not reported. (*d*) The standardization sample is inadequately described. (*e*) There are no norms for college subjects. (*f*) There is no information about various variables and data that might be related to the test scores.

At present the test would seem to be primarily a research tool. At best, it might prove to be a preliminary form of a test that could be developed eventually into a usable instrument.

[52]

*Examining for Aphasia: A Manual for the Examination of Aphasia and Related Disturbances, Revised Edition.** Adolescents and adults; 1946–54; 1 form ('46); no data on reliability and validity; no norms; $6 per set of 25 record booklets and manual; $3.50 per 25 record booklets ('54); $3.50 per manual ('54); postpaid; (30–120) minutes; Jon Eisenson; Psychological Corporation. *

REFERENCES

1. BLATT, BENJAMIN. *The Problem of Language Localization Into Specific Brain Areas: Psychological Tests as a Means of Localizing Brain Lesions in Patients With Aphasia.* Doctor's thesis, New York University (New York, N.Y.), 1949. (*Microfilm Abstr* 10:145)
2. EISENSON, JON. "Examining for Aphasia and Related Disturbances," pp. 766–71. (*PA* 27:7766) In *Contributions Toward Medical Psychology: Theory and Psychodiagnostic Methods, Vol. II.* Edited by Arthur Weider. New York: Ronald Press Co., 1953. Pp. xi, 459–885. *
3. FELDMAN, LOUISE P. *An Investigation and Analysis of Scores Made by First to Sixth Grades on the Eisenson Test for Aphasia and Related Disturbances.* Master's thesis, University of Michigan (Ann Arbor, Mich.), 1953.

T. R. MILES, *Lecturer in Psychology, University College, Bangor, Wales.*

This seems to the reviewer an excellent manual, both on the theoretical and on the practical side. The opening sections contain a discussion of the different types of aphasic disability, and reference is made to earlier work on the subject, in particular that of Goldstein and Scheerer and that of Weisenburg and McBride. This is followed by a series of tests, suitable both for children and adults, based on the author's own theory of how aphasic disorders should be classified—tests of visual, auditory, and tactile recognition, tests of comprehension, naming, calculation, and so on. The problem of classification must inevitably remain for the moment a matter of controversy; broadly, what is required is that we should be able to recognise similarities between apparently different failures at the behavioural level, and at the same time produce a theory of cortical breakdown which accounts for all failures which have been classified as similar. The classification in this manual is at any rate suggestive and helpful, and this is all, in the reviewer's opinion, that the author would wish to claim.

Nowhere does Eisenson make the mistake of oversimplification. He is never content, for instance, with a straightforward summing of test scores in the hope that they will make a meaningful whole. Recognised tests, such as the Kohs block design, the Goddard and Seguin formboards, and the Goldstein-Scheerer battery, receive favourable mention, but the author clearly views with disfavour an overrigid administrative procedure. Nor does he make the mistake of supposing that the test situation involves purely cognitive factors; on the contrary, he recognizes that the patient's motivation is an all-important variable which may be different on different occasions. In effect, throughout the manual the user is encouraged to look for a general clinical picture rather than for a quantitative measure of the degree of aphasic impairment. In the present state of knowledge, this policy seems to the reviewer clearly right. At one point the author even warns that, in the case of paraphasic errors such as substitution of the wrong word, an explanation in psychodynamic terms should not be ruled out. In view of the widespread rivalry between those who offer explanations in terms of unconscious motivation and those who want to explain in terms of cortical failure, such a warning seems to the reviewer commendably broad-minded, though whether the two types of explanation are mutually exclusive, as Eisenson assumes, is perhaps open to question.

A further merit is that the style is always lucid; the more formidable varieties of technical jargon are avoided, and there is no waste of words.

There is a useful bibliography. A minor criticism here is that, of the British writers who have made contributions in this field, only Hughlings Jackson and Head are mentioned. Some reference to the pioneer work of Hinshelwood and the more recent work of Brain, Zangwill, and McMeeken might have been helpful. McMeeken's concept of *developmental aphasia,* introduced as a result of the finding that disabilities resembling standard aphasic ones can occur in children even when there is no independent evidence for brain injury, seems to the reviewer to be of considerable importance. Eisenson's dichotomy into *congenital* and *acquired* aphasia, according to whether the injury occurred before or after the time of speech development, does not allow for a third group of this kind.

In general, this manual seems to the reviewer to be both a useful instrument for practical purposes and a valuable contribution to the psychology of thinking.

Am J Mental Def 60:196–7 Jl '55. Louis M. DiCarlo. * The plates Eisenson presents for testing in the revised manual are more appropriate than his earlier plates, since the selection of these plates is based upon materials which would appear in present-day situations. The variations in the pictures are beneficial and provide important cues for the examiner. Color for testing color agnosia is somewhat sharper and the selection of his reading material would appear judicious. The theoretical and clinical material presented in the first section of the book (Chapters I to IV) may be confusing to an unsophisticated examiner. For one who has a great deal of experience with aphasia, the first few chapters offer an excellent review and also tend to emphasize the importance of not only observing the language disability that the aphasic individual presents, but also indicate the importance of arriving at adequate estimates of his perceptive impairments. Dr. Eisenson's discussion of aphasic children certainly may not bring about agreement since many individuals do not feel that aphasia occurs where language has not already been established. In his desire to sharpen some of the problems, he has introduced several controversial concepts, specifically "dis-inclination to assume and use the abstract attitude" as opposed to the definition of abstract-concrete by Goldstein. One wonders whether this material would be best presented in a text or article rather than in a manual. This revised manual is more than a manual but at the same time, less than a text. For the individual who is skillful in testing the aphasic individual, the book certainly provides him with a very efficient tool. If used judiciously and under supervision, the manual ought to become a very good instrument for the beginning examiner and can help him while he is crystallizing his methodology. Dr. Eisenson's new manual is consistent in terms of testing specific functions and higher order performance. This manual should be part of every psychologist's and hearing and speech therapist's clinical kit.

J Consult Psychol 18:309 Ag '54. Laurance F. Shaffer. * An examination for aphasia is necessarily qualitative, and the tests therefore cannot be judged by the usual standards for reliability and validity. Some approximate quantifications of these tests would be helpful, however, at least to give an examiner clues for judging whether the disability in a given area is "moderate" or "severe." The manual is more extensively revised than the test itself, the first 28 pages comprising a miniature textbook on nature, symptoms, and varieties of aphasia, and the examination of aphasic children. Perhaps because of its condensation, this introductory material tends to be arbitrary and uncritical. Still, it provides a useful check list of definitions and procedures for the use of experienced psychologists.

For a review by D. Russell Davis, see 4:42 (2 excerpts); for a review by C. R. Strother, see 3:39 (1 excerpt).

[53]

★**Family Adjustment Test.** Ages 12 and over; 1952–54; title on test is *Elias Family Opinion Survey;* 11 scores: attitudes toward mother, attitudes toward father, father-mother attitude quotient, oedipal, struggle for independence, parent-child friction-harmony, interparental friction-harmony, family inferiority-superiority, rejection of child, parental qualities, total; 1 form ('52); manual ('54); $2 per 20 tests; $1 per specimen set (must be purchased to obtain manual); postage extra; (35–45) minutes; Gabriel Elias; Psychometric Affiliates.*

REFERENCES

1. ELIAS, G. *Construction of a Test of Non-Homeyness and Related Variables.* Doctor's thesis, Purdue University (Lafayette, Ind.), 1949.
2. BLACKSHIRE, R. E., AND DILES, D. *Student Cheating.* Master's thesis, University of Arkansas (Fayetteville, Ark.), 1950.
3. RICHMOND, ELISE. *Relationship Between Selected Variables and Homelessness Test Scores, and Suggested Varying Standardizations.* Master's thesis, University of Arkansas (Fayetteville, Ark.), 1950.
4. GARDNER, R. *The Relationship Between Elias Family Opinion Survey Scores and Selected Indices of Undesirable Behavior.* Master's thesis, University of Arkansas (Fayetteville, Ark.), 1951.
5. ELIAS, GABRIEL. "A Measure of 'Homelessness.' " *J Abn & Social Psychol* 47:62–6 Ja '52. * (PA 26:6209)
6. STEVENSON, FRANK. *A Study of Objective Measurement of Family Feelings Among a High School Population.* Master's thesis, Alabama Polytechnic Institute (Auburn, Ala.), 1953.

ALBERT ELLIS, *Consulting Psychologist, 333 West 56th St., New York 19, New York.*

This relatively new instrument is of the "projective" questionnaire type. Its 114 questions are indirectly stated in the form: "Parents are _____ happy when they are together" and "Children _____ have to make excuses for their parents." The subject responds by inserting in the blank whichever one of the words "always, often, sometimes, rarely, never" will make the sentence most correct for him. The assumption is that the respondents will project their own attitudes and feelings into the answering of these questions, rather than give objective responses. The scoring of the subject's "homey" or "homeless" feelings in general, as well as the subtest categories listed at the head of this review, is based on this assumption.

The *Elias Family Opinion Survey* (or *Family Adjustment Test,* as it is called in its non-disguised form) has several advantages when used within a limited area. It measures several aspects of home life and attitudes which few other paper and pencil tests try to assess. When used with a "homey" and a "homeless" group of subjects, the test impressively showed virtually no overlap between the scores of the two groups. Its armchair validity has been checked and attested to by several groups of clinical psychologists.

On the other hand, the survey appears to have several possible shortcomings:

a) Some of the subtest scores, such as oedipal, struggle for independence, and parental qualities, are calculated on the basis of the subject's answers to very few questions.

b) Although group validity, as noted above, is impressively high, the manual contains no validity figures for the subtests.

c) No allowance seems to be made for individual respondents who do not project their own attitudes into the test, but who answer all or most of the questions with reasonable objectivity. Thus, the objective or "true" answer to most of the questions on the test quite obviously is "sometimes." But this answer is invariably given the fairly high or "negative" weight of 3 in the scoring key. If, therefore, any respondent consistently gives this answer to the questions, he will obtain a total score of 352 on the 114-item test. Such a score puts him at about the 99th percentile as far as his being "overtly homeless" is concerned. Quite a negative premium, apparently, for the subject's being objective and "truthful"!

d) The basic assumption of the test, that the average respondent *will* project his own attitudes into these paper and pencil test answers, is one that has never been clearly substantiated. There is much reason to believe that adults or very bright children might easily see through the "projective" aspects of the test; and there is some experimental evidence [1] that while *some* children actually do project themselves into this kind of test in the assumed manner, many definitely do not.

In conclusion: the *Elias Family Opinion Survey* is an interesting and somewhat unique "projective" paper and pencil test which may be useful for experimental purposes, but should be employed for clinical diagnosis only with extreme caution.

[1] ELLIS, ALBERT. "A Comparison of the Use of Direct and Indirect Phrasing in Personality Questionnaires." *Psychol Monogr* 61(3):1–41 '47. *

[54]

★**Fatigue Scales Kit.** Adults; 1944–54; 1 form; 3 scales; mimeographed manual ('54); $5 per set of test materials including 25 copies of each scale; $2 per 50 copies of any one scale; postage extra; specimen set not available; (10) minutes; [Willard A. Kerr]; Psychometric Affiliates. *

a) INDUSTRIAL SUBJECTIVE FATIGUE AND EUPHORIA SCALES. Adults; 1944–54; 1 form ('54, identical with scale published in 1944).

b) RETROSPECTIVE WORK CURVE FEELINGS FOR NATIONAL RESEARCH PROGRAM ON EMPLOYEE FEELINGS AT WORK. Adults; 1954.

c) STUDY OF DAY [MOTHER'S DAY FATIGUE SCALE]. Housewives; 1954; no data on validity.

[55]

★**The Freeman Anxiety Neurosis and Psychosomatic Test.** Mental patients; 1952–55; title on test is *The Freeman AN and PS Test;* 9 scores: anxiety neurosis, psychosomatic syndrome, and 7 subscores; 1 form ('52); no norms for subscores; revised manual ('55); revised profile ('55); $1.75 per 10 tests; $1.25 per manual; postage extra; specimen set not available; administration time not reported; M. J. Freeman; Grune & Stratton, Inc. *

REFERENCES

1. FREEMAN, M. J. "The Standardization of a Psychosomatic Test: Validation of a Psychosomatic Syndrome." *J Personality* 19:229–43 D '50. * (*PA* 25:6608)
2. FREEMAN, M. J. "The Development of a Test for the Measurement of Anxiety: A Study of Its Reliability and Validity." *Psychol Monogr* 67(3):1–19 '53. * (*PA* 28:2903)
3. ENDS, EARL J., AND PAGE, CURTIS W. "A Study of Functional Relationships Among Measures of Anxiety, Ego Strength and Adjustment." *J Clin Psychol* 13:148–50 Ap '57. *

[56]

★**Friend-Critic Statement.** Adults; 1948; subject's essays on himself as seen by a good friend and by a strong critic; 1 form ['48]; no manual; no data on reliability and validity; $1.50 per 25 forms; cash orders postpaid; free specimen set; [20–30] minutes; Aptitude Associates. *

[57]

*****Goldstein-Scheerer Tests of Abstract and Concrete Thinking.** Adults; 1941–51; individual; 1 form; 5 tests; manual ('41, see 9 below); supplementary manual ('47); no data on reliability; no norms; $58 per complete set of test materials; $2.25 per manual; postpaid; [30–60] minutes; Kurt Goldstein, Martin Scheerer, and Louis Rosenberg (*c*, record booklet); Psychological Corporation.

a) GOLDSTEIN-SCHEERER CUBE TEST. 1941–45; $3.40 per 50 record booklets ('45) for designs 1–6; $3.40 per 50 record booklets ('45) for designs 7–12.

b) GELB-GOLDSTEIN COLOR SORTING TEST. 1941–51; $2.70 per 50 record booklets ('51).

c) GOLDSTEIN-SCHEERER OBJECT SORTING TEST. 1941–51; $4.10 per 50 record booklets ('51); supplement sheet ('51) for experiment 3, $1 per 100 copies.

d) WEIGL-GOLDSTEIN-SCHEERER COLOR FORM SORTING TEST. 1941–45; $2.70 per 50 record booklets ('45).

e) GOLDSTEIN-SCHEERER STICK TEST. 1941–45; $2.70 per 50 record booklets ('45).

REFERENCES

1–28. See 3:41.
29. TOOTH, GEOFFREY. "On the Use of Mental Tests for the Measurement of Disability After Head Injury: With a Comparison Between the Results of These Tests in Patients After Head Injury and Psychoneurotics." *J Neurol Neurosurg & Psychiatry* 10:1–11 F '47. *
30. BOYD, FOSTER. "A Provisional Quantitative Scoring With Preliminary Norms for the Goldstein-Scheerer Cube Test." *J Clin Psychol* 5:148–53 Ap '49. * (*PA* 24:1880)
31. ROSENBERG, LOUIS M. *A Comparison of Concept Forma-*

tion in Poorly-Educated Normals, Non-Deteriorated Schizophrenics and Brain-Damaged Patients. Doctor's thesis, New York University (New York, N.Y.), 1951. (*Microfilm Abstr* 11:761)
32. SCHEERER, MARTIN. Sect. 11, "Measures of Impairment of Intellectual Function: The Goldstein-Scheerer Tests," pp. 116–50. In *Military Clinical Psychology.* Department of the Army Technical Manual TM 8–242; Department of the Air Force Manual AFM 160–45. Washington, D.C.: U.S. Government Printing Office, 1951. Pp. iv, 197. *
33. WATSON, ROBERT I. *The Clinical Method in Psychology,* pp. 366–89. New York: Harper & Brothers, 1951. Pp. xii, 779. * (*PA* 26:5577)
34. McFIE, J., AND PIERCY, M. F. "The Relation of Laterality of Lesion to Performance on Weigl's Sorting Test." *J Mental Sci* 98:299–305 Ap '52. * (*PA* 27:625)
35. BROWN, IRWIN. *Abstract and Concrete Behavior of Dysphasic Patients and Normal Subjects on the Goldstein-Scheerer Tests.* Doctor's thesis, University of Michigan (Ann Arbor, Mich.), 1953. (*DA* 13:908)
36. GOLDSTEIN, KURT, AND SCHEERER, MARTIN. "Tests of Abstract and Concrete Behavior," pp. 702–30. (*PA* 27:7768) In *Contributions Toward Medical Psychology: Theory and Psychodiagnostic Methods, Vol. II.* Edited by Arthur Weider. New York: Ronald Press Co., 1953. Pp. xi, 459–885. *
37. HEALD, JAMES E., AND MARZOLF, STANLEY S. "Abstract Behavior in Elementary School Children as Measured by the Goldstein-Scheerer Stick Test and The Weigl-Goldstein-Scheerer Color Form Sorting Test." *J Clin Psychol* 9:59–62 Ja '53. * (*PA* 27:7679)
38. RAPPAPORT, SHELDON R. "Intellectual Deficit in Organics and Schizophrenics." *J Consult Psychol* 17:389–95 O '53. * (*PA* 28:6365)
39. SCHULMAN, IRVING. "Concept Formation in the Schizophrenic Child: A Study of Ego Development." *J Clin Psychol* 9:11–5 Ja '53. * (*PA* 27:7942)
40. HALPIN, VIRGINIA G., AND PATTERSON, RUTH M. "The Performance of Brain-Injured Children on the Goldstein-Scheerer Tests." *Am J Mental Def* 59:91–9 Jl '54. * (*PA* 29:4551)
41. KORSTVEDT, ARNE; STACEY, CHALMERS L.; AND REYNOLDS, WILLIAM F. "Concept Formation of Normal and Subnormal Adolescents on a Modification of the Weigl-Goldstein-Scheerer Color Form Sorting Test." *J Clin Psychol* 10:88–90 Ja '54. * (*PA* 28:7694)
42. SATTER, GEORGE, AND McGEE, EUGENE. "Retarded Adults Who Have Developed Beyond Expectation: Part II, Non-Intellectual Functions." *Training Sch B* 51:67–81 Je '54. * (*PA* 29:2663)
43. HALPIN, VIRGINIA G. "Rotation Errors Made by Brain-Injured and Familial Children on Two Visual-Motor Tests." *Am J Mental Def* 59:485–9 Ja 55. * (*PA* 29:7487)
44. COONS, W. H. "Abstract Ability in Schizoprenia and the Organic Psychoses." *Can J Psychol* 10:43–50 Mr '56. * (*PA* 31:3452)
45. KRESS, ROY ALFRED, JR. *An Investigation of the Relationship Between Concept Formation and Achievement in Reading.* Doctor's thesis, Temple University (Philadephia, Pa.), 1956. (*DA* 16:573)
46. THALER, MARGARET. "Relationships Among Wechsler, Weigl, Rorschach, EEG Findings, and Abstract-Concrete Behavior in a Group of Normal Aged Subjects." *J Gerontol* 11:404–9 O '56. * (*PA* 31:5871)
47. McGAUGHRAN, LAURENCE S., AND MORAN, LOUIS J. "Differences Between Schizophrenic and Brain-Damaged Groups in Conceptual Aspects of Object Sorting." *J Abn & Social Psychol* 54:44–9 Ja '57. *
48. PARKER, JAMES W. "The Validity of Some Current Tests for Organicity." *J Consult Psychol* 21:425–8 O '57. *
49. SEMEONOFF, BORIS. "Projective Techniques in Selection for Counseling." *Human Relations* 11:113–22 no 2 '58. *

For reviews by Kate Levine Kogan, C. R. Strother (with Ludwig Immergluck), and O. L. Zangwill, see 3:41; for a related review, see 3:42.

[58]

★**Gordon Personal Inventory.** Grades 9–16 and adults; 1956, c1955–56; 4 scores: cautiousness, original thinking, personal relations, vigor; 1 form ('56); revised manual ('56); no adult norms; $2.75 per 35 tests, postage extra; 50¢ per specimen set including the complementary *Gordon Personal Profile* (see 59), postpaid; (15–20) minutes; Leonard V. Gordon; World Book Co. *

REFERENCE

1. BASS, BERNARD M. "Normative Data Information Exchange, No. 11–5." *Personnel Psychol* 11:269–70 su '58. *

BENNO G. FRICKE, *Assistant Chief, Evaluation and Examinations Division, and Assistant Professor of Psychology, University of Michigan, Ann Arbor, Michigan.*

The *Gordon Personal Inventory* has much in common with the *Gordon Personal Profile*. The writer's review of the profile contains additional material applicable to the inventory.

The major difference in the manuals for the two tests is to be found in the validity section. In the manual for the Personal Inventory not one bit of information is presented to support the presumed validity of the test. A footnote indicates, "A number of validation studies are presently under way, the results of which will be presented in a revised manual. The author will welcome reports of the results of any other studies that may be undertaken." Although it is about three years since the test was released for use, the reviewer has been unable to find a single study by the author or anyone else in which the inventory has been reported upon. Certainly it seems fair to conclude that if the test has any validity not many people know about it.

In the section on validity and elsewhere in the manual, the point is made that the forced-choice item used is effective in reducing faking. But a more important point is that if a test has no initial validity, then it is not possible to fake "good" or "poor" scores because there are none; high and low scale scores are no better or worse than average scores on an invalid test. Of course, if two reasonably valid tests have the same initial validity, the one which is least fakable is to be preferred.

Despite the lack of validity data, the manual for the inventory, as did the manual for the profile, presents many suggestions in the section on uses of the test. The author claims, for example, that the inventory "has certain attributes which give it unique potentialities for use in personnel activities, such as the selection of individuals for specific types of work, the placement of individuals in specific jobs, and the counseling or transferring of employees not performing well in their present job."

The inventory was constructed by essentially the same rational-factor analytic method used to construct the profile, but with a little more care in equating the social desirability of the four parts of each item. An inspection of the phrases in the items suggests that their preference value is not likely to be the same for ninth graders, college seniors, and employed adults, but the inventory is recommended as being suitable for them and, it would appear, for almost anyone able to take a group test. While the potential number to be tested is certainly increased by maintaining that a test is appropriate for a wide age or education range, such a claim should only be made after substantiating research data have been assembled. The entire testing business might profit from having test producers design their tests more specifically for a particular and relatively limited group.

The four scales of the inventory measure reliably (median of 15 coefficients is about .83) and independently (median of the intercorrelations is about .22) something that is not related to ACE aptitude scores (median of 15 intercorrelations is about .10) or profile scores (median of 16 intercorrelations is about .19).

The manual states that the inventory is a companion instrument to the *Gordon Personal Profile* and that "the two instruments may be used together to provide an economical coverage of eight important factors in the personality domain." Even if these instruments do in fact measure eight important dimensions of personality in college students, a user would still have difficulty in comparing accurately the performance of subjects on the two tests since different norm groups have been used. One wonders why Gordon did not attach the 20 items in the inventory at the end of the 18 items in the profile; while this would not solve his major problem (lack of external validity) it would have improved matters considerably for those who might wish to obtain the eight scores.

But frankly, and in summary, the reviewer at this time can see no good reason why a test user should want to obtain the *Gordon Personal Inventory* scores.

JOHN A. RADCLIFFE, *Lecturer in Psychology, University of Sydney, Sydney, Australia.*

This is a companion test to the *Gordon Personal Profile* and is intended to measure four additional "significant" aspects of personality. Test format, administrative instructions, marking procedure, and recommendations concerning score interpretation are almost identical between the two. For the inventory, however, both high school and college norms are provided. Split-half (.77–.89, n = 103, high school; .80–.88, n = 168, college) and Kuder-Richardson (.79–.88, n = 124, college) reliabilities are reported and are comparable with those reported for the profile. No retest coefficients are given, however.

The general development of the inventory has followed lines similar to those of the profile —choice of factors to be measured, construction of a questionnaire, factor analysis of the questionnaire, and construction of forced-choice items testing some of the factors obtained. But, in the case of the inventory, no external criterion was used. For this reason and because the test had been developed too recently for other validity data to be available, the only data on validity reported relate to internal consistency— illustrative factor loadings obtained from the questionnaire analysis, intercorrelations among the scales, and brief descriptions of a number of revisions, "each....improving the balance of preference values within the tetrads and the reliabilities of the scales." With the profile, it is noted that low scores have been found to indicate "poor personality adjustment." This has *not* been verified for the inventory. Again, Gordon has made no attempt to relate his factors to those of other investigators.

The author reports considerable data for the profile to support his contention that the factors are "significant" and "meaningful." No such data are reported for the inventory. The profile is a workmanlike job. The inventory has been rushed into print and spoils the author's record. Except as an exploratory device and a "companion test," there is little to justify its use.

J Consult Psychol 21:281 Je '57. Laurance F. Shaffer. * Like the earlier questionnaire, the *Inventory* is characterized by brevity, the use of tetrads of statements controlled for social desirability, and the identification of components by factor analysis. The method of construction shows a high degree of technical competence. * The two Gordon questionnaires commend themselves favorably for use when economy of time is essential. Few other instruments obtain as broad a picture of self-reported personality in less than 30 minutes.

J Counsel Psychol 4:76 sp '57. Laurence Siegel. * An outstanding weakness of the *Personal Inventory* from an operational standpoint, is that predictive validities are not reported in the manual. * Until such validation data become available, however, the *Personal Inventory* must be treated as an experimental instrument. This deficiency is not sufficiently emphasized in the manual. Furthermore a poor choice of wording

on the folder containing specimen sets of both the *Profile* and *Inventory* may lead to the erroneous conclusion that validation is not only accomplished, but that the resultant coefficients are high! A bold–face heading on the folder asserts: "Forced-choice responses make for high validity." While it is theoretically possible for a forced-choice format to improve the validity potential of an instrument, there is no evidence that this format has improved the validity of the *Inventory*. In fact, there is no evidence that the instrument is valid, *period*. A better choice of words for this heading might have been something like: "Forced-choice responses a feature." If, for research purposes, one wants to measure the four traits included in the *Gordon Personal Inventory,* this instrument will yield results with a minimum expenditure of subject testing time. The application of the *Inventory* in the counseling situations suggested by the manual should, however, be undertaken with extreme caution and with the realization that this is still an experimental form pending validation.

[59]

★**Gordon Personal Profile.** Grades 9–16 and adults; 1953–54; c1951–53; 5 scores: ascendancy, responsibility, emotional stability, sociability, total; 1 form ('53); manual ('53); supplementary mimeographed norms ['54]; $2.75 per 35 tests, postage extra; 50¢ per specimen set including the complementary *Gordon Personal Inventory* (see 58), postpaid; (15–20) minutes; Leonard V. Gordon; World Book Co. *

REFERENCES

1. GORDON, LEONARD V. "Validities of the Forced-Choice and Questionnaire Methods of Personality Measurement." *J Appl Psychol* 35:407–12 D '51. * (*PA* 27:424)
2. GORDON, LEONARD V. "The Effect of Position on the Preference Value of Personality Items." *Ed & Psychol Meas* 12:669–76 w '52. * (*PA* 27:6531)
3. GORDON, LEONARD V. "Personal Factors in Leadership." *J Social Psychol* 36:245–8 N '52. * (*PA* 27:7115)
4. GORDON, LEONARD V. "Some Interrelationships Among Personality Item Characteristics." *Ed & Psychol Meas* 13:264–72 su '53. * (*PA* 28:4037)
5. BASS, BERNARD M. "Validity Information Exchange, No. 7-045: ROTC Cadets." *Personnel Psychol* 7:279 su '54. *
6. BASS, BERNARD M.; KARSTENDIEK, BARBARA; McCULLOUGH, GERALD; AND PRUITT, RAY C. "Validity Information Exchange, No. 7-024: D.O.T. Code 2-66.01, 2-66.11, 2-66.12, 2-66.23, Policemen and Dectectives, Public Service." *Personnel Psychol* 7:159–60 sp '54.
7. FICK, DORCAS J. *A Comparison of Personality Traits of a Group of Sunday School Teachers and a Group of Non-Sunday School Teachers as Found on the Heston Personal Adjustment Inventory and the Gordon Personal Profile.* Master's thesis, Boston University (Boston, Mass.), 1955.
8. BRESEE, CLYDE WESLEY. *Affective Factors Associated With Academic Underachievement in High-School Students.* Doctor's thesis, Cornell University (Ithaca, N.Y.), 1956. (*DA* 17:90)
9. GORDON, LEONARD V., AND STAPLETON, ERNEST S. "Fakability of a Forced-Choice Personality Test Under Realistic High School Employment Conditions." *J Appl Psychol* 40:258–62 Ag '56. * (*PA* 31:6084)
10. PHILLIPS, RAYMOND V. *A Study of Attitude and Personality Variables Among In-Service Teachers.* Doctor's thesis, Temple University (Philadelphia, Pa.), 1956. (*DA* 16:2528)
11. RUSMORE, JAY T. "Fakability of the Gordon Personal Profile." *J Appl Psychol* 40:175–7 Je '56. * (*PA* 31:6661)
12. BASS, BERNARD M. "Faking by Sales Applicants of a Forced Choice Personality Inventory." *J Appl Psychol* 41:403–4 D '57. *
13. COOK, JOHN M., AND FARBRO, PATRICK C. "Normative

Data Information Exchange, No. 10–15." *Personnel Psychol* 10:233–4 su '57. *

14. REINDL, MARY OLIVIA. *The Relationship Between Attitudes Toward Obedience and Personality Characteristics Measured by the A-S Reaction Study and the Gordon Personal Profile.* Master's thesis, Fordham University (New York, N.Y.), 1957.

15. BARRETT, RICHARD S. "The Process of Predicting Job Performance." *Personnel Psychol* 11:39–57 sp '58. *

16. WILLINGHAM, WARREN W.; NELSON, PAUL; AND O'CONNOR, WILLIAM. "A Note on the Behavioral Validity of the Gordon Personal Profile." *J Consult Psychol* 22:378 O '58. *

BENNO G. FRICKE, *Assistant Chief, Evaluation and Examination Division, and Assistant Professor of Psychology, University of Michigan, Ann Arbor, Michigan.*

The method used to construct the *Gordon Personal Profile* will probably please those who favor the rationally and factor-analytically constructed personality tests and displease those who prefer the empirically constructed ones. Gordon has succeeded very well in obtaining four reliable and independent measures which he has called Ascendancy (A), Responsibility (R), Emotional Stability (E), and Sociability (S). Whether the test scores indicate aspects in the nontest behavior of subjects or merely aspects in their test behavior (i.e., tendency to mark responses they and the author believe indicate certain behavior) remains to be seen. It is readily apparent from the generally well written manual that the author believes that the four factor scores are "external validity indicators," that they tell something about the test takers nontest-taking behavior. He has shown himself to be much more sensitive than most nonempirical personality test constructors to the importance of relating test scores to real life behavior.

Unfortunately, and this is the major point of the review, while Gordon has given some validity data and makes many references to completed studies, the total impression is that adequate validity has not been demonstrated. Most of the studies involve very small validity-check samples (e.g., "17 applicants for jobs with a state highway patrol," "30 salespeople at a large department store," 27 clients rated by "the senior counselor at the Boston University counseling center," "54 clients at a counseling center to whom the *Personal Profile* had been administered"). In other studies, very little information is provided (e.g., "In one study, the average A score of administrators was found to be significantly higher (at the 1% level) than the average of college men"; "In one study of engineers, the average R score was found to be significantly higher than that of college men (at the 1% level)"; "In one study of external salesmen, the average S score was found to be significantly

higher (at the 1% level) than the average S score of college men"). The reviewer was inclined to wonder whether all pertinent data and studies were included in the manual. For instance, if more than one study of engineers and external salesmen was conducted, the results would be of interest, especially since the test is recommended for personnel purposes.

The reviewer's first but rapid reading of the manual, particularly the first seven pages dealing with general characteristics, directions for administering, directions for scoring, conversion to percentiles, meaning of scales, and interpretation of scores was favorable, but after serious study of the entire manual (particularly the last three pages dealing with validity and the development of the profile), the reviewer began to feel that the manual represents the author and publisher "with best foot forward." Used too rarely are phrases such as "the profile might be of value for such and such"; too frequently, too much is claimed (e.g., "Extensive evidence substantiates the conclusion that the *Profile* does measure these traits, as defined."). If there is extensive and convincing evidence it is not shared with the reader.

On the last page we learn that "From 657 applicants for college admission, the high school records of individuals with *T* [total] scores below the 5th percentile were examined. Summary statements made by the high school principals showed definite problem or personality maladjustment indications for a very large proportion of this group. No such indications were found in a sampling of cases selected at random." It would be helpful to know precisely the proportion of "personality maladjustment indications" found in the "below the 5th percentile" and "cases selected at random" groups. While sufficient detail is not given on this important aspect, complete information is given on the relationship of the profile scores to scores on two scholastic aptitude tests. Rather than presenting the 20 low intercorrelations it would have been quite satisfactory simply to have indicated the median value, about .10.

At times when an attempt seems to have been made to spell out a validity study the explanation is ambiguous. For example, in discussing research with the "first experimental form" Gordon states that "empirical scoring keys were developed on one group (n = 104) and cross-validated on the other two groups at the second college." If Gordon is familiar with the procedure for developing empirical scoring keys and if he did what he says, then he should have presented validity coefficients (correlations with ratings made by dormitory students) for eight scales (four rational-factor keys, and four empirical keys). But coefficients are given for only four scales. Are they for the rational-factor keys or for the special empirical keys? The coefficients certainly are high (median about .54), higher than most coefficients obtained with empirical keys and much higher than those obtained with rational-factor keys.

A few final comments need to be made concerning validity, the only really important consideration for this or any test. The acid test for any test is validity demonstrated by individuals other than the author or those linked intimately with the test's design and construction. The manual cites validity data from one such study. Although the manual presents the validity coefficients (.21, .50, .25, and .34 for A, R, E, and S respectively), it does not point out that for the 22 cases in the study only the .50 coefficient is statistically significant, and then at only the 5 per cent level. Since the profile became available commercially in 1953, it is perhaps significant that the reviewer was unable to locate one study in the literature bearing on the test's validity; not only have individuals other than the author not reported on its validity, but the author himself has not done so. If the claims the author makes for the test are even partially substantiated by other investigators, it would definitely be a test worth using.

Now for some relatively minor matters. Like almost all standardized tests, the profile has adequate reliability (median of 24 coefficients is about .85) ; the author is to be congratulated for devoting little space to reliability and for not claiming much for the test because of its adequate reliability. The directions to the test taker are very clear. The test takes little time to complete, "from 7 to 15 minutes." The forced-choice type of item consisting of two complimentary and two uncomplimentary phrases from which the test taker selects the one (of the four) which is "most like" him and the one which is "least like" him, seems like a good one. But no attention appears to have been given to the relative social desirability of the phrases after they were combined in the tetrad item format.

It is not clear whether any of the research results that are presented in the manual were obtained by use of the present form or by use of earlier forms. For example, after the intercorrelations of the scales for the "First Form (N = 118)" and the "Early Revision (N = 200)" are discussed and presented in table 9 (the next to last table on the next to last page of the manual), the following statement is found: "Revisions of the *Personal Profile* ensued, each designed to heighten the validity of the scales." Although the main point here is that it seems that none of the data in the manual pertains to the present form, it is worth noting that the nature and extent of the revisions which ensued are not mentioned.

Probably the inclusion of a scale to assess the extent to which test takers have given the most socially desirable response would be profitable. Similarly, a scale to identify those who give infrequently marked responses (similar to the F scale of the MMPI) would seem to be worthwhile. The existence of other response sets, such as the set to mark as "most like" the first of the four response alternatives, should be investigated and, if found, either controlled or used in arriving at the traits the test purports to measure. In short, if the profile's four scales (A, R, E, S) are shown to be useful in indicating something about the test taker's *nontest-taking* behavior (i.e., to function as external validity indicators), then some additional scales should be developed to indicate something about the test taker's *test-taking* behavior (i.e., to function as internal validity indicators). Internal validity indicators would permit test users to determine, at least better than at present, whether an individual's external validity indicators are correct or distorted. In this connection, the trait scores of a die are of interest. The reviewer obtained the following college norm percentile ranks on the first "take" by marking answers according to the dictates of a die: A 4, R 63, E 29, and S 13. Effective internal validity indicators would disclose to the test user that the owner of this profile of scores had not behaved appropriately in taking the test (i.e., did not read the items but marked a "most like" and a "least like" response for each item at random), and therefore would discourage him from concluding that the subject was about average in responsibility (R 63), very submissive (A 4), etc.

Gordon concludes his 16-page manual by expressing his belief that "the present form of the Personal Profile is sufficiently reliable and valid to warrant meaningful interpretation for the individual case." On the basis of the information available to the reviewer, he does not share Gordon's belief, nor does he recommend the profile for routine use with groups. He does recommend that a few investigators who are interested in researching upon "rational-factor" personality tests conduct satisfactory validity studies to determine how much, if any, validity the profile has, and that the results be communicated to prospective users.

JOHN A. RADCLIFFE, *Lecturer in Psychology, University of Sydney, Sydney, Australia.*

The *Gordon Personal Profile* is intended to measure five aspects [1] of personality considered to be "especially significant in the daily functioning of the normal person." Four of these aspects are said to be "relatively independent, psychologically meaningful factors" and the fifth (total or overall self-evaluation) to have been "found to have value in its own right." The main features of the profile are: (*a*) factorial derivation of the traits being measured; (*b*) use of both internal and external validating procedures; (*c*) frequent cross validations against external criteria; (*d*) use of forced-choice responses; and (*e*) the more-than-average validity data reported in the manual.

The test consists of 18 sets of four descriptive phrases (tetrads), all four factors being represented in each tetrad. This tetrad arrangement is preferable to forced-choice sets composed of only two or three items because the greater sense of freedom of choice is more acceptable to the respondent. The subject responds to each tetrad by choosing the phrase which is least like himself and that which is most like himself. A natural consequence is that a respondent may not score high or low simultaneously on all four factors, but this is believed not to constitute "a practical limitation" and the evidence seems to support this view.

The forced-choice technique is stated to be less subject to faking and more valid than the conventional questionnaire method, particularly for low criterion individuals. The validity data are certainly more impressive than that typical of questionnaires. On fakability, two studies are reported in which changes on some profile scores occurred between guidance and employment conditions, but these changes were smaller than those usually obtained with questionnaires under comparable conditions.

Illustrations of the profile's possible use for educational and personnel purposes are given, accompanied by sample profiles, but, especially for personnel work, the author insists that they are *illustrations only* and that, for the present, the user must establish his own critical scores. He does, however, consider that the data he reports (for example, on differences between occupational groups and on relationship with sales proficiency) indicate that the test is likely to prove useful. Validation data on the meaning of the scales is well reported and quite extensive.

In all, this is a carefully constructed test which is easily administered and scored. For a personality test, reliabilities are encouraging, especially those for the total score. Validity data are above average, yet the author commits no extravagances. The manual is clearly written and well organised and there are no significant omissions.

An improvement in future editions of the manual would be that the author indicate how his factors relate to those found by others, especially the dimensions reported by investigators such as Cattell, Eysenck, and Guilford. This is desirable for three reasons: (*a*) He began by choosing items to measure some of Cattell's and one of Mosier's factors, but does not relate his results to theirs.[2] (*b*) He uses the little known Wherry-Gaylord iterative procedure of factor analysis, a form of cluster analysis which does not require the calculation of a complete intercorrelation matrix. Comparison of his factors with those obtained with more traditional procedures would add to the scant data available on the use of this method. (*c*) Factor analyses have become so numerous that cross identifications among studies, preferably related to a standard list such as the Universal Index which has been proposed by Cattell, are becoming increasingly necessary.

J Consult Psychol 18:154 Ap '54. Laurance F. Shaffer. * Like many other recently developed inventories, and in marked contrast to the subjectivity of earlier ones, this questionnaire is issued with an impressive array of research evidence. * The tentative norms....are based only on college students from one geographical region * As in the case of other short questionnaires, the problem of interpreting score differences with due regard for standard errors is

---

1 Four additional "significant aspects" are measured by the *Gordon Personal Inventory* (see 58).

2 Profile factors are closely related to Cattell's E (dominance), G (super-ego strength), C (general emotionality), and A (cyclothymia-schizothymia).

bothersome. The suggestions for interpretation are, however, conservatively stated in terms of probabilities.

[60]
★The Grassi Block Substitution Test: For Measuring Organic Brain Pathology. Mental patients; 1947–53; formerly called *The Fairfield Block Substitution Test;* individual; 1 form ['47]; revised record booklet ('49); $12 per set of blocks; $4.50 per 25 record booklets; $3.50 per manual ('53, see 1 below); postpaid; (20) minutes; Joseph R. Grassi; Western Psychological Services. *

REFERENCES

1. GRASSI, JOSEPH R. "The Fairfield Block Substitution Test for Measuring Intellectual Impairment." *Psychiatric Q* 21:474–89 Jl '47. * *(PA* 22:5203)
2. GRASSI, JOSEPH R. *The Grassi Block Substitution Test for Measuring Organic Brain Pathology.* Springfield, Ill.: Charles C Thomas, 1953. Pp. ix, 75. * *(PA* 28:105)
3. PTACEK, JAMES E., AND YOUNG, FLORENCE M. "Comparison of the Grassi Block Substitution Test With the Wechsler-Bellevue in the Diagnosis of Organic Brain Damage." *J Clin Psychol* 10:375–8 O '54. * *(PA* 29:4082)
4. HARRIS, PEARL. "Validity of the Grassi-Fairfield Block Substitution Test in Differential Diagnosis." Abstract. *J Consult Psychol* 19:330 O '55. *
5. HIRT, MICHAEL. "An Evaluation of the Grassi Test for Organic Involvement." *J Clin Psychol* 14:48–50 Ja '58. *

Can J Psychol 8:240 D '54. J. G. McMurray. * This diagnostic device may prove to be a valuable addition to the growing field of neuropsychology.

J Clin Psychol 9:405 O '53. * The standardization data indicate that this test may be a sensitive indicator of organic brain pathology.

[61]
★The Grayson Perceptualization Test. Detection of cortical impairment; 1950–57; Forms A, B ('56); mimeographed manual ('57); no data on reliability; no norms; $4 per 25 tests, cash orders postpaid; specimen sets not available; 4(15) minutes; Harry M. Grayson; Western Psychological Services. *

D. RUSSELL DAVIS, *Reader in Clinical Psychology, University of Cambridge, Cambridge, England.*

The test involves reading letters in relatively small print and marking off words by vertical lines. The main score is one of speed of performance. The other score, which is based on the quality of performance and which would appear to be more useful, has not been standardised. Both scores are said to be affected by age, education, and intelligence. The author claims no more than that the test is a device for the rapid screening of "organics" from normals.

The limitations of the test are severe. It is not suitable for use with poorly educated or elderly patients or with those who suffer from visual or motor defects. Patients in poor health and those who are depressed or retarded are likely to obtain low scores, whether or not they also suffer from organic disease of the brain.

The test does not appear to have any use in the differential diagnosis of organic impairment, functional impairment, and mental deficiency, although it may help to distinguish the impaired, whatever the cause, from the normal.

WILLIAM SCHOFIELD, *Associate Professor of Psychology and Psychiatry, University of Minnesota, Minneapolis, Minnesota.*

This is an ingenious task which was devised in 1947 as part of a psychological test battery for use in screening hospital admissions. It has been used in a variety of settings; experience gained over 10 years has contributed to its present format and content. The rationale for this test is similar to that for the *Sherman Mental Impairment Test,* i.e., it is held that patients with brain pathology of a nonfocal type suffer a "relative inflexibility of mental processes" and that presence of such inflexibility will be reflected in tasks requiring a continual "shifting" in perception and cognition.

Two forms of the GPT are available, each consisting of two simple reading selections of 100 words, with equal spacing between letters of words and between words. The subject's task is to separate the letters with vertical pencil lines so as to create words which are both individually meaningful and fit a context.

Directions to the subject are printed on the test booklet, which also includes a practice exercise and 10 clinical "stop" questions such as, "I once had a serious head injury." The administrator's task is simple and consists primarily of indicating the two-minute time limit for each selection.

Two scores are derived, a speed score and a quality score. The speed score consists of the total number of words marked off, without regard to accuracy, and can be obtained quickly by use of a keyed guide. The quality score is determined by the relative presence of three types of error: omissions of separation marks, concrete errors (marking off words which are real but do not make contextual sense), and bizarre errors (marking off letters which do not form meaningful words).

The amount and nature of the standardization material reported is very inadequate. Both forms were administered to two samples of normals (n = 32, 35) and two samples of "organics" (n = 40, 43). No descriptive data such as age and sex are provided for the normals; the only description of the organics consists of the statement that they cover a "wide range of diagnoses and degrees of impairment" and the listing of the kinds of diagnoses represented. No cross-validational studies are reported. Use of optimal cutting scores on the original groups resulted in correct identification of approximately 82 per cent of organics and 85 per cent of normals. Numerous clinical observations are offered as to the significance of various kinds of performance on the GPT. The author states that it may be "expected" that schizophrenics will yield the same percentage of false positives as normals.

The GPT is an ingenious task and deserves study as one of a battery of measures of intellectual function. One would seriously question the justification for its being formally offered as a *test* of cortical impairment.

[62]

★Group Cohesiveness: A Study of Group Morale. Adults; 1958, c1957–58; title on test is *A Study of Group Morale;* 5 scores: satisfaction of individual motives, satisfaction of interpersonal relations, homogeneity of attitude, satisfaction with leadership, total; 1 form ('57); $3 per 30 tests; 50¢ per manual ('58); $1 per specimen set; postage extra; (10–15) minutes; Bernard Goldman; Psychometric Affiliates. *

[63]

The Guilford-Martin Inventory of Factors GAMIN, Abridged Edition. Grades 10–16 and adults; 1943–48; 5 scores: general activity, ascendance-submission, masculinity-femininity, inferiority feelings, nervousness; IBM; 1 form ('43); mimeographed supplement ('46); $2.50 per 25 tests; 10¢ per single copy; separate answer sheets may be used; 3¢ per IBM answer sheet; 25¢ per scoring key; $2.50 per set of either hand or machine scoring stencils; 15¢ per manual ['48]; postage extra; (30) minutes; [J. P. Guilford and H. G. Martin]; Sheridan Supply Co. *

REFERENCES

1–7. See 3:43.
8–25. See 4:47.
26. BRUECKEL, JOYCE E. *A Comparison of the Three Guilford-Martin Personality Inventories With Self-Ratings and Student-Ratings.* Master's thesis, University of Colorado (Boulder, Colo.), 1948.
27. GUILFORD, J. S. *The Relative Value of Fourteen Test Variables for Predicting Success in Executive and Supervisory Positions.* Master's thesis, University of Southern California (Los Angeles, Calif.), 1951.
28. MANZANO, ILUMINADO BILLARINIA. *The Relation of Personality Adjustment to Occupational Interests.* Doctor's thesis, University of Southern California (Los Angeles, Calif.), 1951.
29. BAEHR, MELANY E. "A Factorial Study of Temperament." *Psychometrika* 17:107–26 Mr '52. * (PA 27:1834)
30. BORG, WALTER R. "Personality Characteristics of a Group of College Art Students." *J Ed Psychol* 43:149–56 Mr '52. * (PA 27:3764)
31. COCKRUM, LOGAN V. "Personality Traits and Interests of Theological Students." *Relig Ed* 47:28–32 Ja–F '52. * (PA 26:4229)
32. GUILFORD, J. P. "When Not to Factor Analyze." *Psychol B* 49:26–37 Ja '52. * (PA 27:33)
33. GUILFORD, JOAN S. *Temperament Traits of Executives and Supervisors Measured by the Guilford Personality Inventories.*" *J Appl Psychol* 36:228–33 Ag '52. * (PA 27:3801)
34. MARQUIS, DOROTHY P.; SINNETT, E. ROBERT; AND WINTER, WILLIAM D. "A Psychological Study of Peptic Ulcer Patients." *J Clin Psychol* 8:266–72 Jl '52. * (PA 27:6672)
35. MOORE, JOSEPH E., AND STURM, NORMAN H. "Relation of Hand Strength to Personality Measures." *Am J Psychol* 65:111 Ja '52. * (PA 27:2749)

36. NEILEN, GORDON C. *A Study of the Cattell 16 PF Test by Comparison With the A. C. E. and Guilford-Martin Personality Battery.* Master's thesis, Kent State University (Kent, Ohio), 1952.
37. POE, WESLEY A., AND BERG, IRWIN A. "Psychological Test Performance of Steel Industry Production Supervisors." *J Appl Psychol* 36:234–7 Ag '52. *
38. TOMEDY, FRANCIS JOSEPH. *The Relationship of Personality Characteristics to Measured Interests of Women Teachers of English, Social Science, Mathematics, and Physical Science in Certain Senior High Schools.* Doctor's thesis, New York University (New York, N.Y.), 1952. (Abstracts: DA 12:540, Am Psychol 7:384)
39. KORNREICH, MELVIN. "Variations in the Consistency of the Behavioral Meaning of Personality Test Scores." *Genetic Psychol Monogr* 47:73–138 F '53. * (PA 27:6535)
40. ROSENBERG, NATHAN; IZARD, CARROLL E.; AND HOLLANDER, E. P. "Middle Category ("?") Response: Reliability and Relationship to Personality and Intelligence Variables." Abstract. *Am Psychol* 8:425 Ag '53. *
41. TRUMBELL, RICHARD. "A Study of Relationships Between Factors of Personality and Intelligence." *J Social Psychol* 38:161–73 N '53. * (PA 28:5589)
42. ABERNETHY, ETHEL M., AND WHITE, JAMES CLYDE, JR. "Correlation of a Self-Inventory of Personality Traits With Laboratory Measures of Vigor and Motility." *J Social Psychol* 40:185–8 Ag '54. * (PA 29:5295)
43. GOCHE, L. N. *Relationship of Interests and Temperament Traits to Attrition and Survival of Engineering Students.* Master's thesis, Iowa State College (Ames, Iowa), 1954.
44. GUILFORD, J. P. "The Validation of an 'Indecision' Score for Prediction of Proficiency of Foremen." *J Appl Psychol* 38:224–6 Ag '54. * (PA 29:6369)
45. HUEBER, JOANNE. "Validity Information Exchange, No. 7-089: D.O.T. Code 5-83.641, Maintenance Mechanic II." *Personnel Psychol* 7:565–6 w '54. *
46. NORMAN, RALPH D., AND AINSWORTH, PATRICIA. "The Relationships Among Projection, Empathy, Reality, and Adjustment, Operationally Defined." *J Consult Psychol* 18:53–8 F '54. * (PA 28:8700)
47. BORG, WALTER R. "The Effect of Personality and Contact Upon a Personality Stereotype." *J Ed Res* 49:289–94 D '55. * (PA 30:6911)
48. BROWN, VICTOR H. *Relationship of the Cureton Strength-Weight Index to the Guilford-Martin Inventory of Factors GAMIN.* Master's thesis, Iowa State College (Ames, Iowa), 1955.
49. COOPER, MATTHEW NATHANIEL. *To Determine the Nature and Significance, If Any, of Certain Differences in the Social and Personal Adjustment of Fifty-One Successful and Fifty-One Non-Successful College Students at Texas Southern University.* Doctor's thesis, New York University (New York, N.Y.), 1955. (DA 16:497)
50. JACOBS, ALFRED, AND LEVENTER, SEYMOUR. "Response to Personality Inventories With Situational Stress." *J Abn & Social Psychol* 51:449–51 N '55. * (PA 31:3041)
51. ROSENBERG, NATHAN; IZARD, CARROLL E.; AND HOLLANDER, E. P. "Middle Category Response: Reliability and Relationship to Personality and Intelligence Variables." *Ed & Psychol Meas* 15:281–90 au '55. * (PA 30:4592)
52. THURSTON, DONALD REID. *An Investigation of the Possibilities of Parole Prediction Through the Use of Five Personality Inventories.* Doctor's thesis, Michigan State University (East Lansing, Mich.), 1955. (DA 15:1206)
53. ZIMMERMAN, WAYNE S., AND GUILFORD, J. P. "The Guilford-Martin Inventories Reanalyzed." Abstract. *Am Psychol* 10:330 Ag '55. *
54. GUILFORD, J. P., AND ZIMMERMAN, WAYNE S. "Fourteen Dimensions of Temperament." *Psychol Monogr* 70(10):1–26 '56. * (PA 31:5789)
55. HINES, VYNCE A. "F Scale, GAMIN, and Public School Principal Behavior." *J Ed Psychol* 47:321–8 O '56. *
56. SPROTT, JUANITA. *Personality Correlates of Religious Attitudes.* Master's thesis, Vanderbilt University (Nashville, Tenn.), 1956.
57. COE, ROBERT STANFORD. *The Personality and Adjustment Characteristics of Females in Various Occupational Groups.* Doctor's thesis, University of Houston (Houston, Tex.), 1957. (DA 17:2309–10)
58. FARBRO, PATRICK C., AND COOK, JOHN M. "Normative Data Information Exchange, No. 10-12." *Personnel Psychol* 10:228 su '57. *

For a review by Hubert E. Brogden, see 4:47; for a review by H. J. Eysenck, see 3:43; for a related review, see 3:45.

[64]

The Guilford-Martin Personnel Inventory. Grades 10–16 and adults; 1943–46; 3 scores: objectivity, agreeableness, cooperativeness; IBM; 1 form ('43); mimeographed supplement ('46); $2.50 per 25 tests; 10¢ per single copy; separate answer sheets may be used; 3¢ per IBM answer sheet; 25¢ per scoring key; $2.50 per set of either hand or machine scoring stencils; 15¢ per manual ['43]; 3¢ per profile ['43]; postage extra; (30) minutes; [J. P. Guilford and H. G. Martin]; Sheridan Supply Co.

REFERENCES

1-7. See 3:44.

8-27. See 4:48.

28. BRUECKEL, JOYCE E. *A Comparison of the Three Guilford-Martin Personality Inventories With Self-Ratings and Student-Ratings.* Master's thesis, University of Colorado (Boulder, Colo.), 1948.

29. GUILFORD, J. S. *The Relative Value of Fourteen Test Variables for Predicting Success in Executive and Supervisory Positions.* Master's thesis, University of Southern California (Los Angeles, Calif.), 1951.

30. MANZANO, ILUMINADO BILLARINIA. *The Relation of Personality Adjustment to Occupational Interests.* Doctor's thesis, University of Southern California (Los Angeles, Calif.), 1951.

31. BAEHR, MELANY E. "A Factorial Study of Temperament." *Psychometrika* 17:107–26 Mr '52. * (PA 27:1834)

32. BORG, WALTER R. "Personality Characteristics of a Group of College Art Students." *J Ed Psychol* 43:149–56 Mr '52. * (PA 27:3764)

33. GUILFORD, JOAN S. "Temperament Traits of Executives and Supervisors Measured by the Guilford Personality Inventories." *J Appl Psychol* 36:228–33 Ag '52. * (PA 27:3801)

34. NEILEN, GORDON C. *A Study of the Cattell 16 PF Test by Comparison With the A. C. E. and Guilford-Martin Personality Battery.* Master's thesis, Kent State University (Kent, Ohio), 1952.

35. POE, WESLEY A., AND BERG, IRWIN A. "Psychological Test Performance of Steel Industry Production Supervisors." *J Appl Psychol* 36:234–7 Ag '52. * (PA 27:3794)

36. TOMEDY, FRANCIS JOSEPH. *The Relationship of Personality Characteristics to Measured Interests of Women Teachers of English, Social Science, Mathematics, and Physical Science in Certain Senior High Schools.* Doctor's thesis, New York University (New York, N. Y.), 1952. (Abstracts: *DA* 12:540, *Am Psychol* 7:384)

37. ROSENBERG, NATHAN; IZARD, CARROLL E.; AND HOLLANDER, E. P. "Middle Category ("?") Response: Reliability and Relationship to Personality and Intelligence Variables." Abstract. *Am Psychol* 8:425 Ag '53. *

38. STACEY, CHALMERS L., AND GOLDBERG, HERMAN D. "A Personality Study of Professional and Student Actors." *J Appl Psychol* 37:24–5 F '53. * (PA 28:1685)

39. GRANT, DONALD L. "Validity Information Exchange, No. 7-085: D.O.T. Code 1-01.05, Budget Clerk." *Personnel Psychol* 7:557–8 w '54.*

40. GRANT, DONALD L. "Validity Information Exchange, No. 7-086: D.O.T. Code 1-01.05, Budget Clerk." *Personnel Psychol* 7:559–60 w '54.*

41. GUILFORD, J. P. "The Validation of an 'Indecision' Score for Prediction of Proficiency of Foremen." *J Appl Psychol* 38:224–6 Ag '54. * (PA 29:6369)

42. McCARTY, JOHN J. "Validity Information Exchange, No. 7-077: D.O.T. Code 5-92.621, (Foreman II)." *Personnel Psychol* 7:420–1 au '54. *

43. McCARTHY, JOHN J.; WESTBERG, WILLIAM C.; AND FITZPATRICK, EUGENE D. "Validity Information Exchange, No. 7-001: D.O.T. Code 5-92.621, (Foreman II)." *Personnel Psychol* 7:568–9 w '54. *

44. WESTBERG, WILLIAM C.; FITZPATRICK, EUGENE D.; AND McCARTY, JOHN J. "Validity Information Exchange, No. 7-073: D.O.T. Code 1-37.32, Typist." *Personnel Psychol* 7:411–2 au '54. *

45. WESTBERG, WILLIAM C.; FITZPATRICK, EUGENE D.; AND McCARTY, JOHN J. "Validity Information Exchange, No. 7-087: D.O.T. Code 1-37.32, Typist." *Personnel Psychol* 7:561–2 w '54. *

46. BORG, WALTER R. "The Effect of Personality and Contact Upon a Personality Stereotype." *J Ed Res* 49:289–94 D '55. * (PA 30:6911)

47. COOPER, MATTHEW NATHANIEL. *To Determine the Nature and Significance, If Any, of Certain Differences in the Social and Personal Adjustment of Fifty-One Successful and Fifty-One Non-Successful College Students at Texas Southern University.* Doctor's thesis, New York University (New York, N.Y.), 1955. (DA 16:497)

48. KELLEY, ELVAN PRESSLOR. *An Investigation Into the Value of Selected Tests and Techniques for Guidance of Prospective Teachers Enrolled in Community Experiences Course.* Doctor's thesis, University of Houston (Houston, Tex.), 1955. (DA 15:1209)

49. ROSENBERG, NATHAN; IZARD, CARROLL E.; AND HOLLANDER, E. P. "Middle Category Response: Reliability and Relationship to Personality and Intelligence Variables." *Ed & Psychol Meas* 15:281–90 au '55. * (PA 30:4592)

50. ZIMMERMAN, WAYNE S., AND GUILFORD, J. P. "The Guilford-Martin Inventories Reanalyzed." Abstract. *Am Psychol* 10:330 Ag '55. *

51. GUILFORD, J. P., AND ZIMMERMAN, WAYNE S. "Fourteen Dimensions of Temperament." *Psychol Monogr* 70(10):1–26 '56. * (PA 31:5789)

52. McCARTY, JOHN J., AND FITZPATRICK, EUGENE D. "Validity Information Exchange, No. 9-26: D.O.T. Code 5-92.621, (Foreman II)." *Personnel Psychol* 9:253 su '56. *

53. COE, ROBERT STANFORD. *The Personality and Adjustment Characteristics of Females in Various Occupational Groups.* Doctor's thesis, University of Houston (Houston, Tex.), 1957. (DA 17:2309)

54. FARBRO, PATRICK C., AND COOK, JOHN M. "Normative Data Information Exchange, No. 10-1." *Personnel Psychol* 10:93 sp '57. *

For a review by Neil Van Steenberg, see 4:48; for a review by Benjamin Shimberg, see 3:44; for a related review, see 3:45.

[65]

*The Guilford-Zimmerman Temperament Survey. Grades 9–16 and adults; 1949–55; revision and condensation of *Inventory of Factors STDCR, Guilford-Martin Inventory of Factors GAMIN,* and *Guilford-Martin Personnel Inventory;* 10 scores: general activity, restraint, ascendance, sociability, emotional stability, objectivity, friendliness, thoughtfulness, personal relations, masculinity; IBM; 1 form ('49); norms ('55); separate answer sheets must be used; $3.75 per 25 tests; 20¢ per single copy; 3¢ per IBM answer sheet; $2 per set of either hand or machine scoring stencils; 2¢ per profile ('55); 25¢ per manual ('49); $3.25 per set of scoring stencils and manual for *Falsification Scales* ('55) by Alfred Jacobs and Allan Schlaff; 2¢ per copy of *G-Z Temperament Map* ('52) by Philip C. Perry; postage extra; (50) minutes; J. P. Guilford and Wayne S. Zimmerman; Sheridan Supply Co.

REFERENCES

1-5. See 4:49.

6. PINKSTON, JOHN RAY. *An Evaluation of Teaching Techniques as Evidenced by the Guilford-Martin Temperament Inventory.* Master's thesis, North Texas State College (Denton, Tex.), 1950.

7. VAUGHAN, GEORGE E., JR. *Interest and Personality Patterns of Experienced Teachers.* Master's thesis, North Texas State College (Denton, Tex.), 1950.

8. OLTMAN, RUTH M. *A Study of the Difference Between Art and Non-Art Students as Measured by the Guilford-Zimmerman Temperament Survey and a Biographical Questionnaire.* Master's thesis, Western Reserve University (Cleveland, Ohio), 1951.

9. BARNES, CHARLES A. "A Statistical Study of the Freudian Theory of Levels of Psychosexual Development." *Genetic Psychol Monogr* 45:105–75 My '52. * (PA 27:3112)

10. HOLLEY, JASPER W. *The Isolation of Personality Traits in the Domain of Military Leadership.* Doctor's thesis, University of Southern California (Los Angeles, Calif.), 1952.

11. ISAACSON, LEE E. "Predictors of Success for Cooperative Occupational Education Classes in Kansas City, Missouri, High Schools." Abstract. *Am Psychol* 7:379 Jl '52. *

12. ISAACSON, LEE E., AND COTTLE, WILLIAM C. "The Guilford-Zimmerman Temperament Survey: II, Urban High School Students." *Univ Kans B Ed* 6:46–50 F '52. *

13. JOHNSON, ANN, AND COTTLE, WILLIAM C. "The Guilford-Zimmerman Temperament Survey: III, With Urban Negro High School Students." *Univ Kans B Ed* 6:75–80 My '52. *

14. KRUMM, RICHARD L. *Inter-Relationships of Measured Interests and Personality Traits of Introductory Psychology Instructors and Their Students as Related to Student Achievement.* Doctor's thesis, University of Pittsburgh (Pittsburgh, Pa.), 1952.

15. SCHAPERO, MAX, AND HIRSCH, MONROE J. "The Relationship of Refractive Error and Guilford-Martin Temperament Test Scores." *Am J Optom* 29:32–6 Ja '52. * (PA 26:4569)

16. WRENN, C. GILBERT. "The Selection and Education of Student Personnel Workers." *Personnel & Guid J* 31:9–14 O '52. * (PA 27:4782)

17. SMITH, FLOYD RAY. *Changes in Some Personal Qualities of Student Teachers at the University of Missouri.* Doctor's thesis, University of Missouri (Columbia, Mo.), 1953.

18. BENDIG, A. W., AND SPRAGUE, J. L. "The Guilford Zimmerman Temperament Survey as a Predictor of Achievement Level and Achievement Fluctuation in Introductory Psychology." *J Appl Psychol* 38:409–13 D '54. * (PA 29:4990)

19. BERNBERG, RAYMOND E. "Personality Correlates of Social Conformity." *J Appl Psychol* 38:148–9 Je '54. * (PA 29:3664)

20. COTTLE, W. C., AND LEWIS, W. W., JR. "Personality Characteristics of Counselors: II, Male Counselor Responses to the MMPI and GZTS." *J Counsel Psychol* 1:27–30 F '54. * (PA 28:7476)

21. HERZBERG, FREDERICK. "Temperament Measures in Industrial Selection." *J Appl Psychol* 38:81–4 Ap '54. * (*PA* 29:3133)

22. MILLER, ROBERT S. *A Study of the Relationships Between MMPI Scales and GZTS Scales.* Master's thesis, University of Kansas (Lawrence, Kan.), 1954.

23. PIERCE, KYLE KARR. *The Personality Inventory Correlates of the Level of Aspiration.* Doctor's thesis, University of Arizona (Tucson, Ariz.), 1954. (*DA* 14:1102)

24. BEAVER, ALMA P. "Temperament and Nursing." *Psychol Rep* 1:339–44 D '55. * (*PA* 30:6431)

25. BENDIG, A. W. "Ability and Personality Characteristics of Introductory Psychology Instructors Rated Competent and Empathetic by Their Students." *J Ed Res* 48:705–9 My '55. * (*PA* 30:162)

26. FELZER, STANTON B. "A Statistical Study of Sex Differences on the Rorschach." *J Proj Tech* 19:382–6 D '55. * (*PA* 30:7194)

27. FITZPATRICK, EUGENE D., AND McCARTY, JOHN J. "Validity Information Exchange, No. 8-35: D.O.T. Code 9-00.91, Assembler VII (Electrical Equipment)." *Personnel Psychol* 8:501–4 w '55. *

28. GOWAN, J. C., AND GOWAN, MAY SEAGOE. "The Guilford-Zimmerman and the California Psychological Inventory in the Measurement of Teaching Candidates." *Calif J Ed Res* 6:35–7 Ja '55. * (*PA* 29:7990)

29. MILLER, ROBERT S., AND COTTLE, WILLIAM C. "Evidenced Relationships Between MMPI and GZTS Scales: An Adult Male Sample." *Univ Kans B* 9:91–4 My '55. *

30. WOEHR, HARRY JOSEPH. *The Relationship of Masculinity-Femininity Scores to Temperament and Interest Profiles.* Doctor's thesis, Temple University (Philadelphia, Pa.), 1955. (*DA* 16:388)

31. ASHCRAFT, K. B. "Normative Data Information Exchange, No. 14." *Personnel Psychol* 9:389 au '56. *

32. FINKLE, ROBERT B., AND McCABE, FRANK J. "Normative Data Information Exchange, No. 1." *Personnel Psychol* 9:263–4 su '56. *

33. GOODLING, RICHARD A. "Relationship Between the IM Scale of the SVIB and Scales of the Guilford-Zimmerman Temperament Survey." *J Counsel Psychol* 3:146+ su '56. *

34. JONES, MARGARET LOIS. "Analysis of Certain Aspects of Teaching Ability." *J Exp Ed* 25:153–80 D '56. *

35. KIRKPATRICK, JAMES J. "Validation of a Test Battery for the Selection and Placement of Engineers." *Personnel Psychol* 9:211–27 su '56. * (*PA* 31:8964)

36. LEEDS, CARROLL H. "Teacher Attitudes and Temperament as a Measure of Teacher-Pupil Rapport." *J Appl Psychol* 40:333–7 O '56. * (*PA* 31:8873)

37. PORTER, LOUIS G., AND STACEY, CHALMERS L. "A Study of the Relationships Between Self-Ratings and Parent-Ratings for a Group of College Students." *J Clin Psychol* 12:243–8 Jl '56. * (*PA* 31:6628)

38. REISNER, MARTIN. *A Comparative Investigation of Personality Factors Associated With Appropriate and Inappropriate Levels of Vocational Aspiration.* Doctor's thesis, New York University (New York, N.Y.), 1956. (*DA* 17:678)

39. VOAS, ROBERT B. "The Relationship Between Self-Descriptive and Socially Acceptable Responses to Two Personality Inventories." Abstract. *Am Psychol* 11:406 Ag '56. *

40. BRUCE, MARTIN M. "Normative Data Information Exchange, No. 10-36." *Personnel Psychol* 10:525–6 w '57. *

41. COOKE, TERENCE F. *Premature Responses in Simple Reaction Time as Related to Traits of General Activity and Restraint in the Guilford-Zimmerman Temperament Survey.* Master's thesis, Fordham University (New York, N.Y.), 1957.

42. HEDBERG, RAYMOND, AND BAXTER, BRENT. "A Second Look at Personality Test Validation." *Personnel Psychol* 10:157–60 su '57. *

43. KAESS, WALTER A., AND WITRYOL, SAM L. "Positive and Negative Faking on a Forced-Choice Authoritarian Scale." *J Appl Psychol* 41:333–9 O 57. *

44. McCARTY, JOHN J. "Normative Data Information Exchange, No. 10–13." *Personnel Psychol* 10:229–30 su '57. *

45. McCARTY, JOHN J. "Validity Information Exchange, No. 10–14: D.O.T. Code 1-33.01, Secretary." *Personnel Psychol* 10:202–3 su '57. *

46. McCARTY, JOHN J. "Validity Information Exchange, No. 10–15: D.O.T. Code 1-33.01, Secretary." *Personnel Psychol* 10:204–5 su '57. *

47. SHAH, SALEEM ALAM. *An Investigation of Predictive Ability in Hospital Personnel and University Students.* Doctor's thesis, Pennsylvania State University (State College, Pa.), 1957. (*DA* 18:288)

48. VOAS, ROBERT B. "Personality Correlates of Reading Speed and the Time Required to Complete Questionnaires." *Psychol Rep* 3:177–82 Je '57. *

49. VOAS, ROBERT B. "Validity of Personality Scales for the Prediction of Success in Naval Aviation Training." *Abstract. Am Psychol* 12:465 Jl '57. *

50. BARRETT, RICHARD S. "The Process of Predicting Job Performance." *Personnel Psychol* 11:39–57 sp '58. *

51. COROSO, JOAN. *Relationship Between the IPAT Music Preference Test of Personality and E, S, and T Scores on the Guilford-Zimmerman Temperament Survey.* Master's thesis, College of New Rochelle (New Rochelle, N.Y.), 1958.

52. GOWAN, J. C. "Intercorrelations and Factor Analysis of Tests Given to Teaching Candidates." *J Exp Ed* 27:1–22 S '58. *

53. VOAS, ROBERT B. "A Procedure for Reducing the Effects of Slanting Questionnaire Responses Toward Social Acceptability." *Ed & Psychol Meas* 18:337–45 su '58. *

DAVID R. SAUNDERS, *Research Associate, Educational Testing Service, Princeton, New Jersey.*

With the passage of time since the publication of this survey in 1949, it has become possible to apply fresh yardsticks to its evaluation. Because the instrument has appeared to merit relatively widespread use, substantial practical experience has been accumulated and begun to be reported. Thus, rather than reconsider how well the survey satisfies any idealized criteria for a factor-analytic personality inventory, we may examine the degree of its demonstrated utility for two classes of application representative of the interests of most users—in individual evaluation and in personality research.

The bottleneck in the use of any personality instrument for individual evaluation is the step whereby the information contained in the test scores is transmuted into a specific prediction of how an individual will perform. The relevant expectation if one listens to factorial theory is that, with a properly developed inventory, whatever validity exists for a particular criterion will be concentrated into one or just a few of the scales, rather than be present a little bit in most or all of them. In other words, one expects the parsimony that has been achieved for the factorial descriptions of the items to carry over into the realm of their correlations with as yet unstudied variables. The achievement of this result will depend primarily on the skill with which the underlying factor studies have been rotated. Several validity studies employing this survey have been reported, some yielding highly significant correlations and some yielding nothing. It is notable that the only studies in which a major proportion of these scales have been significant have employed relatively nonspecific criteria, i.e., criteria with only indirect significance for test interpretation in an individual case. Given a reasonably defined criterion, there appears to be about a fifty-fifty chance that one or perhaps two or three of the survey scales will be significantly related to it. All this is as it should be.

Now, if the validity of the survey is really effectively confined to just one or two scales in a particular application, this means that no one needs to get tangled up in the difficult and uncertain task of integrating—whether clinically or statistically—the clues from a number of individually almost insignificant sources. But this also puts a premium on the reliability of each of the individual scales in the survey. Reliabilities of the order of .8 are *not* generally considered to be sufficient to bear the burden of this kind of interpretation, at least not unless one is willing to hedge or to regard as uninterpretable a rather broad band of scores near the cutting level. These scales cannot suffice if one must always make a definite recommendation.

On the other hand, one almost never has to make a recommendation about the subjects used in personality research. (Certainly this is the most common application of this instrument if one may judge by the number of master's and doctoral studies in which it has been used.) The principal consideration in such use is the sheer efficiency of information collection, for the experimenter is typically trying to cram as much testing into a few hours as his harried subjects will permit. Three subjects who independently respond to 10 factorially homogeneous items will almost surely provide more information bearing on the basic objectives of such research than could any one of them by marking 30 items all belonging to the same scale. One can easily generate a statistically significant correlation for any relation of practical importance using scales with reliabilities of the order of .5, and one can even investigate nonlinear and interactive effects without much more than this. It is notable that a good many of the results reported using scales from this survey *do* involve these relatively complex forms of relationship.

In short, in the light of present knowledge it seems fair to say that studies using this survey have done much to demonstrate the potential advantages of the factor-analytic approach to personality measurement, but that the instrument itself is neither fish nor fowl so far as practical applications are concerned. Since other instruments which may better serve the researcher's purposes already exist, it would seem advisable to focus attention on changes in the survey that would improve the reliability of the individual scales, even at the expense of some increase in overall length.

For reviews by William Stephenson and Neil Van Steenberg, see 4:49.

[66]

Heston Personal Adjustment Inventory. Grades 9–16 and adults; 1949; 6 scores: analytical thinking,

sociability, emotional stability, confidence, personal relations, home satisfaction; IBM; 1 form; no non-college adult norms; $4.25 per 35 tests; separate answer sheets may be used; $1.80 per 35 IBM answer sheets; 40¢ per set of machine scoring stencils; postage extra; 50¢ per specimen set, postpaid; (40–55) minutes; Joseph C. Heston; World Book Co. *

REFERENCES

1–2. See 4:50.
3. FARBER, ROBERT HOLTON. *Guidance Implications of the Freshman Testing Program at DePauw University.* Doctor's thesis, Indiana University (Bloomington, Ind.), 1951.
4. McKENNA, FRANK S. "An Analysis of Nine Personality Scales." Abstract. *Proc Ind Acad Sci* 62:294 '52. *
5. TYLER, FRED T. *The Prediction of Student-Teaching Success From Personality Inventories.* University of California, Publications in Education, Vol. 11, No. 4. Berkeley, Calif.: University of California Press, 1954. Pp. 233–313. * (*PA* 29:4709)
6. FICK, DORCAS J. *A Comparison of Personality Traits of a Group of Sunday School Teachers and a Group of Non-Sunday School Teachers as Found on the Heston Personal Adjustment Inventory and the Gordon Personal Profile.* Master's thesis, Boston University (Boston, Mass.), 1955.
7. HOLMES, JACK A. "Personality and Spelling Ability." Abstract. *Am Psychol* 10:353–4 Ag '55. *
8. LODATO, FRANCIS JOSEPH. *The Relationship Between Interest and Personality as Measured by the Kuder and the Heston and Gordon Inventories.* Doctor's thesis, St. John's University (Brooklyn, N.Y.), 1955.
9. TINDALL, RALPH H. "Relationships Among Indices of Adjustment Status." *Ed & Psychol Meas* 15:152–62 su '55. * (*PA* 30:2330)
10. ARBUCKLE, DUGALD S. "Client Perception of Counselor Personality." *J Counsel Psychol* 3:93–6 su '56. * (*PA* 31:4639)
11. AUBLE, DONAVON. "Validity Indices for the Heston Personal Adjustment Inventory." *J Appl Psychol* 41:79–81 Ap '57. *
12. SCARBOROUGH, BARRON B., AND WRIGHT, JOHN C. "The Assessment of an Educational Guidance Clinic." *J Counsel Psychol* 4:283–6 w '57. *
13. GINGLES, RUBY HEATHER. "Personality Adjustment of College Students." *J Home Econ* 50:194–200 Mr '58. *

For reviews by Albert Ellis, Hans J. Eysenck, and E. Lowell Kelly, see 4:50. (1 excerpt).

[67]

★**Hospital Adjustment Scale.** Mental patients; 1951–53; 4 ratings: communication and interpersonal relations, self-care and social responsibility, work and recreation, total; 1 form ('53); $3 per 25 tests; 25¢ per set of scoring key and manual ('53); 50¢ per specimen set; cash orders postpaid; (10–20) minutes; James T. Ferguson, Paul McReynolds, and Egerton L. Ballachey (test); [Consulting Psychologists Press, Inc.]. *

REFERENCES

1. McREYNOLDS, PAUL; BALLACHEY, EDGERTON; AND FERGUSON, JAMES T. "Development and Evaluation of a Behavioral Scale for Appraising the Adjustment of Hospitalized Patients." Abstract. *Am Psychol* 7:340–1 Jl '52. *
2. DUTTON, CHARLES EDWIN. *An Investigation of the Internal Consistency and Validity of the Hospital Adjustment Scale.* Doctor's thesis, Stanford University (Stanford, Calif.), 1953. (*DA* 13:589)
3. LORR, MAURICE. "Rating Scales and Check Lists for the Evaluation of Psychopathology." *Psychol B* 51:119–27 Mr '54. *
4. GUERTIN, WILSON H. "A Factor Analysis of Schizophrenic Ratings on the Hospital Adjustment Scale." *J Clin Psychol* 11:70–3 Ja '55. * (*PA* 29:7648)
5. STILSON, DONALD W.; MASON, DONALD J.; SYNTHER, MALCOLM D.; AND GERTZ, BORIS. "An Evaluation of the Comparability and Reliabilities of Two Behavior Rating Scales for Mental Patients." *J Consult Psychol* 22:213–6 Je '58. *

MAURICE LORR, *Director, Neuropsychiatric Research Laboratory, Veterans Benefits Office, Washington, D.C.*

The *Hospital Adjustment Scale* (HAS) purports to provide an estimate of hospital adjustment for use with adult patients of either sex hospitalized in any type of psychiatric institution. The scale consists of 90 statements descriptive of the behavior of hospitalized psychiatric patients. Each statement is marked as "True" (T), "Not True" (NT), or, in some cases, "Doesn't Apply" (DA). The scale is designed to be completed by the psychiatric aide, psychiatric technician, or nurse familiar with the day-to-day behavior of the patient. The recommended observation period is from two weeks to three months.

The statements were derived from descriptions made by psychiatric aides and rated by 16 professional judges on a 9-point scale with respect to goodness of hospital adjustment measured. The final set was selected on the basis of percentage of T, NT, and DA, measures of internal consistency, item reliabilities, and weighted scale values. There are two scoring methods, one a rather cumbersome item weight scoring method, and the other a more straightforward system in which items are keyed as indicating "expanding" or "contracting" personality traits. Expansion (E) refers to increased ability in social functioning and work efficiency; contraction (C) refers to decreased ability in social functioning and work efficiency.

Norms are based on the records of 353 men and 165 women drawn from four hospitals and clinics. Each sample is described in terms of age range, types of psychiatric disorder represented, type of treatment extended, length of hospitalization, and minimum period of observation prior to rating.

Four scores, three group scores and a total score, are obtained from the HAS. One group score is based on 42 items relating to communication and interpersonal relations; a second, on 25 items relating to care of self and social responsibility; and a third on 23 items relating to work activities and recreation. The total score is based on all 90 items. A table of percentile values is provided for interpretation of the raw scores. Of the 180 possible T and NT choices, 79 are keyed E, 57 are keyed C, and 44 are not keyed. The correlations among the subscales are sufficiently high (.72, .70, and .71) to render questionable their independent value. Correlations of each of the subscores with the total scores are .93, .89, and .85, respectively.

The validity of the HAS is primarily based on the judgments of the expert experienced raters. Additional evidence is available in the form of a comparison of the scores of two groups of patients, one approaching release

from the hospital and one judged to be extremely disturbed or long term residents. These differed at the .01 level of confidence. Further, the HAS distinguished a group of schizophrenics in remission from a group not in remission. Item reliabilities are presented in the form of phi coefficients between pairs of raters rating the same patients. The reported reliability of the total scores (ratio of expansion score to expansion plus contraction score) is .84 for two different aides.

The HAS is probably the best developed of the commercially available checklists for use in describing hospital adjustment. The manual is clear, the scoring is simple and straightforward, and the norms are well described. However, a few lacks should be noted. The flexible observation period of two weeks to three months is likely to alter the score from a record of current behavior to a statement of history. Information is needed as to the minimum observation period required to note the behaviors listed. The internal consistency appears to be sufficiently high to suggest that a shorter scale could measure the same function with equal reliability. Finally, further evidence is needed that the expansion-contraction scoring is more than a duplicate of the sum of the weighted keyed items.

[68]

★Human Relations Inventory. Grades 9–16 and adults; 1954–55; social conformity; Form A ('54); mimeographed manual ['54]; additional norms ('55); $2 per 20 tests; $1 per specimen set (must be purchased to obtain manual); postage extra; (20) minutes; Raymond E. Bernberg; Psychometric Affiliates. *

REFERENCES

1. BERNBERG, RAYMOND E. "A Measure of Social Conformity." J Psychol 39:89–96 Ja '55. * (PA 29:8529)
2. BERNBERG, RAYMOND E. "Personality Correlates of Social Conformity: II." J Social Psychol 43:309–12 My '56. *

RAYMOND C. NORRIS, Associate Professor of Psychology, George Peabody College for Teachers, Nashville, Tennessee.

The test consists of 37 items aimed at six determinant areas of social conformity: moral values, positive goals, reality testing, ability to give affection, tension level, and impulsivity. Each item is presented as a 5-option multiple choice question concerning the percentage of some group who hold or exercise a certain belief in one of the determinant areas. Since there is presumably no foundation in fact for a choice among the possible answers, "the tendency of the subject to deviate toward one extreme or the other is presumed to express a direction of perception based on his need-value system." It speaks well for the realism of the test items that, with some clarification of terms, data could be obtained on the questions posed by most of the items. However, it also is apparent that under any customary definition of terms most of the responses which contribute toward the nonconformity score are the bizarre, unrealistic responses. Whether this instrument provides a measure of the direction rather than extent of social perception is a question on which the prospective user must satisfy himself before he accepts the inventory as a measure of social conformity.

The author states that conformity scores are not significantly influenced by the intelligence, socioeconomic level, cultural background, age, sex, or religious affiliation of the respondent. The studies on which these contentions are based are not described in sufficient detail to permit close evaluation. However, in accepting the author's evaluation of his evidence, the nature of the variable measured by the inventory is once again called into question. The relationships between conformity to essentially middle class standards and such variables as cultural background, age, etc. seem sufficiently well established to warrant general acceptance; failure to verify them with the inventory suggests the test may be lacking in either sensitivity or relevance as a measure of conformity. Since the test scores do successfully differentiate a heterogeneous general population group from such diverse groups as regular churchgoers, police officer trainees, male juvenile offenders, and both male and female prison inmates whose medians often differ only slightly, lack of sensitivity does not seem to be an issue.

With a format that would make reading the items, making a response, and obtaining a score simpler than it now is, the *Human Relations Inventory* would seem quite worthy of further research. However, uncertainty as to the phenomenon being measured, the inadequate norms, and the absence of predictive validity evidence would argue against its use as a screening or diagnostic instrument at this time.

JOHN A. RADCLIFFE, *Lecturer in Psychology, University of Sydney, Sydney, Australia.*

This is intended to be a measure of social conformity, defined by "the tendencies of members of a society to manifest communality of attitudes" in six arbitrarily defined "determinant areas": moral values, positive goals, reality testing, ability to give affection, tension level, and impulsivity. No bases for the selection of these determinant areas are given, nor is there any correlation data to show that they do represent separable areas. A factor analysis would have been relevant here. Actually, high scores represent *nonconformity* defined by choice of responses which are atypical of people in general (high school seniors), especially in so far as these atypical responses are characteristic of prison inmates. Item weights for 17 of the 37 items were derived from differences between the response distributions of high school seniors and prison inmates. It would be useful if the manual indicated which are these 17 items.

Norms consist of scores corresponding to the 25th, 50th, 75th, and 99th percentiles for seven samples—two for people in general (high school seniors and college students); two for "conformists" (churchgoers and police officers); and three for prison inmate samples. Validity consists in showing that the scores for these broad groupings differ in the expected way. When differences are stated to have $p > .001$ presumably this is intended to mean $p < .001$. Additional norms provide percentile ranks for 14-year-old male high school freshmen ($n = 159$) and male delinquents ($= 124$), but differences between these groups are too slight to suggest that the test can differentiate between delinquents and nondelinquents at this age level. Reliability is only fair—split-half, .77 with a youth prison group (sample size not stated but presumably 160).

The main feature of the test is its use of what the author calls the "direction of perception" technique, an outgrowth of the Hammond error-choice method to which acknowledgement might well have been made in the manual. The items are of the form: "Social studies reveal what percentage of young men feel women are inferior and dirty? a) 10% b) 20% c) 30% d) 40% e) 50%." Choice of alternative is presumed to express "direction of perception" based on the subject's "need-value system." This is a device similar to that used by Cattell as a measure of Autism, based upon the rationale that the subject will perceive others to be like himself. In this sense, the data show that prison inmates and nonprison inmates have different perceptions. It is interesting that typical high school responses are not necessarily "desirable" responses, for example: "It has been found that the following percentage of people who find lost articles return them to their owners: a) 27% b) 40% c) 53% d) 66% e) 79%." The conforming responses to this item are a) and b). Perhaps it may be argued that this shows how "realistic" the technique is, but one is surprised to find that in Item 5 ["According to a well-known report, what percentage of unmarried American males would attempt sexual intercourse if they were sure of not being caught? a) 15% b) 24% c) 33% d) 42% e) 51%"], a) is the *atypical* response of people in general, and presumably the *typical* response of prison inmates! This illustrates the need for an indication of which items were weighted by comparing high school and prison inmate responses and how, in their present form, the scores represent a mixture both of deviation from the conforming norm and similarity with the nonconforming norm.

Some of the items are strangely worded—for example, the item above on inferiority and dirtiness in women. This would seem more appropriate in a "neuroticism" questionnaire, but perhaps neuroticism is a form of social nonconformity. But, in all, the items are a heterogeneous lot and better evidence that they constitute a meaningful pool or set of subpools would be an improvement. All the items are worded to apply to men only, but, in the later stages of validation, the scale was also applied to women. While the author reports absence of sex differences in the test, it is unclear whether this refers to total scores or to item responses. It remains likely that item wording could lead to sex differences in responses to some items. There is no evidence on fakability.

The author suggests the scale be used "(1) as a research tool; (2) as a demonstration tool of a socio-psychological concept and indirect method of attitude measurement; and (3) for screening and diagnostic purposes where social conformity as defined is either desirable or undesirable." There is no evidence on screening or diagnostic value, or on conditions under which "social conformity as defined" might be relevant. In its present unpolished form, the test is unlikely to be useful for (1). This leaves (2) as its most likely area of use, and this is far too limited an area of application to have justified its publication as a psychological test.

[69]

*The Humm-Wadsworth Temperament Scale. Adults; 1935–56; 41 scores: normal (4 subscores),

hysteroid (6 subscores), manic (4 subscores), depressive (5 subscores), autistic (5 subscores), paranoid (3 subscores), epileptoid (4 subscores), response bias, self mastery (component control, integration index); 1 form ('34); revised manual ('54–55); work sheet ('54); nomograph ('54); distribution restricted; license fees for business organizations retaining publisher as consultant: $1,350 for first year, $120 a year thereafter; no license fees for psychologists; test materials are rented to licensees only; $25 for use of a set of test materials for first year, $5 a year thereafter; 25¢ per answer sheet; postage extra; (45–90) minutes; Doncaster G. Humm and Kathryn A. Humm; Humm Personnel Consultants. *

REFERENCES

1–13. See 40:1223.
14–44. See 3:48.
45. HATHAWAY, S. R. "The Personality Inventory as an Aid in the Diagnosis of Psychopathic Inferiors." *J Consult Psychol* 3:112–7 Jl–Ag '39. * (*PA* 13:5704)
46. CERF, ARTHUR Z. "The Humm-Wadsworth Temperament Scale, CE418A," pp. 581–5. In *Printed Classification Tests.* Edited by J. P. Guilford. Army Air Forces Aviation Psychology Program Research Reports, Report No. 5. Washington, D.C.: U.S. Government Printing Office, 1947. Pp. xi, 919. * (*PA* 22:4145)
47. MARSHALL, HELEN. *A Study of the Personality of Alcoholic Males.* Doctor's thesis, Stanford University (Stanford, Calif.), 1947.
48. HUMM, DONCASTER G. "Note Concerning 'The Validity of Standard and Custom-Built Personality Inventories in a Pilot Selection Program' by Donald E. Super." *Ed & Psychol Meas* 8:257–61 su '48. * (*PA* 23:4446)
49. JURGENSEN, C. E. "Note on Personality Questionnaires." Letter. *Mgmt Rec* 10:177 Mr '48. *
50. CAINE, THOMAS MacKENZIE. *An Investigation of the Relationship Between the Performance of Pilot Trainees on the Humm-Wadsworth Temperament Scale and Their Subsequent Success in Flying Training.* Master's thesis, University of Toronto (Toronto, Ont., Canada), 1949.
51. CONRAD, HERBERT S., AND ELLIS, ALBERT. "Reply to the Humms' 'Notes on "The Validity of Personality Inventories in Military Practice."'" *Psychol B* 46:307–8 Jl '49. * (*PA* 24:2598)
52. FORTUNE, DONALD McA. *An Investigation of the Validity of the Humm-Wadsworth Temperament Scale in Predicting Academic Achievement of Second Year Pass Arts University Students.* Master's thesis, University of Toronto (Toronto, Ont., Canada), 1949.
53. HARRELL, THOMAS W. "Humm-Wadsworth Temperament Scale and Ratings of Salesmen." *Personnel Psychol* 2:491–5 w '49. * (*PA* 24:4279)
54. HUMM, DONCASTER G. "Some Considerations Basic to the Interpretation of Measures of Temperament, With Special Reference to the Humm-Wadsworth Temperament Scale." *J Social Psychol* 30:293–304 N '49. * (*PA* 24:4117)
55. HUMM, DONCASTER G., AND HUMM, KATHRYN A. "Notes on 'The Validity of Personality Inventories in Military Practice,' by Ellis and Conrad." *Psychol B* 46:303–6 Jl '49. * (*PA* 24:2604)
56. CANNING, WILLIAM; HARLOW, GEORGE; AND REGELIN, CLINTON. "A Study of Two Personality Questionnaires." *J Consult Psychol* 14:414–5 O '50. * (*PA* 25:4561)
57. HUMM, DONCASTER G., AND HUMM, KATHRYN A. "Humm-Wadsworth Temperament Scale Appraisals Compared With Criteria of Job Success in the Los Angeles Police Department." *J Psychol* 30:63–75 Jl '50. * (*PA* 25:1311)
58. HUMM, DONCASTER G., AND HUMM, KATHRYN A. "Measure of Mental Health From the Humm-Wadsworth Temperament Scale." *Am J Psychiatry* 107:442–9 D '50. * (*PA* 25:6870)
59. GILLILAND, A. R. "The Humm-Wadsworth and the Minnesota Multiphasic." *J Consult Psychol* 15:457–9 D '51. * (*PA* 26:6998)
60. GREENBERG, PAUL, AND GILLILAND, A. R. "The Relationship Between Basal Metabolism and Personality." *J Social Psychol* 35:3–7 F '52. * (*PA* 27:3345)
61. GILLILAND, A. R., AND NEWMAN, S. E. "The Humm-Wadsworth Temperament Scale as an Indicator of the 'Problem' Employee." *J Appl Psychol* 37:176–7 Je '53.* (*PA* 28:3350)
62. HUMM, D. G., AND HUMM, KATHRYN A. "Discussion of Gilliland and Newman's 'The Humm-Wadsworth Temperament Scale as an Indicator of the "Problem" Employee.'" *J Appl Psychol* 38:131–2 Ap '54. * (*PA* 29:3135)
63. SMITH, GUDMUND, AND MARKE, SVEN. "The Influence on the Results of a Conventional Personality Inventory by Changes in the Test Situation: A Study on the Humm-Wadsworth Temperament Scale." *J Appl Psychol* 42:227–33 Ag '58. *
64. SMITH, GUDMUND, AND MARKE, SVEN. "The Internal Consistency of the Humm-Wadsworth Temperament Scale." *J Appl Psychol* 42:234–40 Ag '58. *

For reviews by H. J. Eysenck, H. Meltzer, and Lorenz Misbach of the 1940 edition, see 3:48; for reviews by Forrest A. Kingsbury and P. E. Vernon, see 40:1223; for a review by Daniel A. Prescott of an earlier edition, see 38:920.

[70]

★The IPAT Anxiety Scale. Ages 14 and over; 1957; title on test is *IPAT Self Analysis Form;* 6 scores: self sentiment development, ego strength, protension or paranoid trend, guilt proneness, ergic tension, total anxiety; 1 form; mimeographed manual; $3 per 25 tests; 40¢ per scoring key; $1 per manual; $2 per specimen set including 5 tests, scoring keys, and manual; cash orders postpaid; (5-10) minutes; Raymond B. Cattell; Institute for Personality and Ability Testing. *

REFERENCES

1. CATTELL, RAYMOND B. "The Conceptual and Test Distinction of Neuroticism and Anxiety." *J Clin Psychol* 13:221–33 Jl '57. *
2. RAWN, Moss L. "The Overt-Covert Anxiety Index and Hostility." *J Clin Psychol* 14:279–80 Jl '58. *

J. P. GUILFORD, *Professor of Psychology, University of Southern California, Los Angeles, California.*

The author claims for this 40-item questionnaire that it is "probably the most effective available brief questionnaire instrument for supplementary clinical diagnosis and giving an objective measure for research purposes." The instrument is based upon considerable background research.

The author defines his anxiety syndrome as comprising the qualities of tension, irritability, lack of self-confidence, unwillingness to take risks, tremor, and various psychosomatic signs. This definition suggests to the reviewer that the primary traits of composure-nervousness, confidence-inferiority, and liking for adventure versus security are involved. Examination of the items suggests that the first two of these traits are heavily represented, as are the primary traits of depression and emotional immaturity, but that there are no items on liking for adventure versus security, at least to casual inspection.

In addition to the scores mentioned in the entry preceding this review, two other scores can be obtained. One is said to indicate the "role of personality structures in contributing to anxiety," and the other, "overt, symptomatic anxiety" versus "covert anxiety, not consciously displayed." Little is said in the manual concerning interpretation or use of these scores.

Raw scores are converted to common-scale scores on the "sten" and decile scales. Before making conversions, the user is to apply minor corrections in raw scores for age of the subject.

Separate male and female norms are given, based upon fairly large samples, with no demographic information being supplied concerning the samples.

For the total score, split-half reliabilities of .84 in a normal population and .91 in a mixed normal and pathological population are reported. No estimates of reliability are given for the component trait scores which are based upon only 4 to 12 items each.

Validity studies were made against three kinds of external criteria—ratings of anxiety in pathological subjects given by psychiatrists, physiological and behavioral test scores, and performances of classified groups of normals, neurotics, and anxiety hysterics. A validity coefficient of .92 is mentioned in connection with the first criterion. This is evidently a loading in a factor that the ratings and scores have in common, and not their intercorrelation. Discrimination of anxiety hysterics from normals is reported as highly significant, as is the discrimination of neurotics from normals. It would seem that the anxiety score would correlate very highly with a score for neuroticism. No information of this kind is given.

The author recommends that in using the total score, sten scores of 7 and higher indicate that the person "could be" an anxiety neurotic and that scores of 8 and higher indicate that the person definitely needs help. In the former instance, the highest 31 per cent of the cases would be involved and, in the latter case, the highest 16 per cent.

It would seem that the instrument should have its best use as a quick screening device used with large groups. The use of the five part scores cannot be recommended except for suggestive leads calling for further analytical testing. For the sake of orientation of users, it would have been desirable for the author to report correlations between his score and scores from other recognized measures purported to assess anxiety, even though he could maintain that he has the best information concerning construct validity in terms of factor-analytical results.

A general comment would be that there is a danger that such an instrument indicates too much. The score discriminates neurotics from normals somewhat, which is reasonable, since anxiety cases are also in the general category of neurotic, but it is hinted by the author that the score also discriminates psychotics. Questions on lack of confidence, nervousness, and depression represent item types that any person who does not feel well for any reason is likely to answer similarly, particularly if he knows he is not well and is ready to admit it.

E. LOWELL KELLY, *Professor of Psychology, University of Michigan, Ann Arbor, Michigan.*

This 40-item inventory is a highly promising, brief assessment instrument. Although but recently published, it is a product of the author's very extensive program of research aimed at mapping the "personality sphere" and hence deserves more serious consideration than the typical newly offered inventory.

The inventory consists of a neatly printed 4-page folder. The first page provides a set of instructions sufficiently clear to make the instrument self-administering for most subjects. Page 2 contains 20 items judged by the author to be the more subtle or cryptic items; hence, responses to them are scored separately to provide an estimate of "cryptic anxiety." Page 3 contains the remaining 20 presumably less subtle items; these are scored to provide an estimate of "overt anxiety." The total score based on all 40 items is labeled "total anxiety." The author suggests that the ratio of "overt to cryptic" scores may prove to have clinical significance but provides no norms, reliability estimates, or evidence for the validity of this ratio score.

The author's decision to publish an inventory to assess "general anxiety" was based on a second order factor analysis [1] of the 75 most representative items from his earlier *Sixteen Personality Factor Questionnaire.* Of the four resulting second order factors, the one accounting for the largest amount of variance had loadings ranging from .53 to .66 for five of the 16 PF scores: $Q_3(-)$, "lack of will control"; $O(+)$ "insecurity or free floating anxiety"; $Q_4(+)$ "nervous tensions (somatic anxiety)"; $L(+)$ "paranoid trend"; and $C(-)$ "lack of ego strength." Other studies (1) showed that this second order factor correlated highly with other accepted indices of anxiety (e.g., judgments of psychiatrists, scores on the *Taylor Manifest Anxiety Scale,* and the author's Factor U.I. 24, based on objective performance and autonomic measures).

The 40 items included in the scale were selected to represent the above 16 PF dimensions in proportion to the loadings of each of the five on the second order factor: O(guilt proneness), 12 items; Q_4(ergic tension or id pressure), 10 items; Q_3- (lack of will control, relabeled "defective integration or binding by the organized self-sentiment"), 8 items; $C-$ (lack of ego strength), 6 items; and L,(protension or paranoid insecurity), 4 items. These items have been grouped in a manner which permits five separate scores thus providing a very crude estimate of the relative contribution of each of these five components to the total anxiety score. However, the manual emphasizes the low reliability of subscores based on so few items per scale and suggests that the user regard even extreme subscores "as evidence of a probable 'problem'....worthy of investigation in conjunction with other evidence" and more extended testing.

The reliability of the total score is reported to be .84 for a sample of 240 normal adults, and .91 for a mixed group of normals and hospitalized neurotics. These reliability estimates compare favorably with those for other available inventories, some containing many more items and hence being more time consuming. The reliabilities for the five component scores are reported as .46 for O, .55 for Q_4, .47 for Q_3, .44 for C, and .26 for L.

What about validity? The term anxiety appears to mean different things to different people; for example, the interjudge agreement of two psychiatrists who interviewed subjects is reported as only .29(1). Since scores on this instrument correlate higher with the pooled judgment of the two psychiatrists than with the ratings of either, the scale would appear to be measuring whatever was common to each of them when perceiving "anxiety." Furthermore, the relatively high reported correlation of this second order factor with scores on other "anxiety" scales suggests that the present scale is not mislabeled.

The author, however, defends the validity of the scale on two other grounds: the external or construct validity of the items used and its validation against external criteria. With respect to the former, he reminds us that the 40 items finally selected out of 2,000 tried out are the most highly correlated with the five oblique primary factors making up this second order factor of general anxiety, now replicated in six separate studies. As evidence for external valid-

1 CATTELL, RAYMOND B. "Second-Order Personality Factors in the Questionnaire Realm." *J Consult Psychol* 20:411–8 D '56. * (PA 32:1614)

ity, he emphasizes (a) the correlation of the scores with psychiatrists' estimates of anxiety level in 85 patients, (b) its correlations with behavioral, physiological and other laboratory tests of anxiety, and (c) the degree to which the scores differentiate between normals, neurotics, and anxiety hysterics, e.g., roughly three fourths of a sample of anxiety hysterics have a standard score (sten) above 7 and three fourths of a sample of normals score below this point. Separation of diagnosed neurotics and normals is less dramatic but still highly significant, CR = 10.67. This finding is in accord with Cattell's related research (1) pointing to a correlation but nonidentity of "anxiety" and "neuroticism."

Standard score and decile norms are provided. These are based on 795 men and women (proportions not specified). Since slight sex and age differences appear, appropriate corrections are suggested.

Judged by the criteria established by the APA Committee on Test Standards, the mimeographed manual is reasonably adequate, especially for a newly published instrument. It suffers somewhat from the author's use of his own specialized vocabulary and parts of it are probably more argumentative than necessary. Unfortunately, as is the case with most test manuals, the reader is not provided with correlations between the particular instrument and other widely used measures of the same variable. A limited amount of such information is provided in the references listed.

This is a highly promising brief scale for assessing a pervasive personality variable. It is likely to be widely used as a research instrument and probably should be in view of the substantial evidence for its construct validity. Clinicians who are willing to give the scale a trial (in spite of its being a by-product of factor analysis!) are likely to find it a useful diagnostic device for initial screening purposes.

J Consult Psychol 21:438 O '57. Laurance F. Shaffer. In view of the widespread current interest in the concept of anxiety, the publication of a new scale for its measurement is a noteworthy event. The *I.P.A.T. Anxiety Scale* is product of its author's extensive studies of the factorial structure of personality. A prominent second-order factor of his *Sixteen Personality Factor Questionnaire* has been identified as anxiety * The present questionnaire consists of 40 items which best represent the five scales

most heavily loaded in the anxiety factor * the *I.P.A.T. Anxiety Scale* has a sounder conceptual base than other current instruments of its type. Many of the functional properties of its scores remain to be established by future research, which will almost surely be forthcoming.

[71]
★IPAT Contact Personality Factor Test. Grades 8–16 and adults; 1954–56; title on test is C.P.F.; 2 scores: extroversion-introversion, distortion; Forms A, B ('54); mimeographed bits serving as manual ['56]; adult norms ('54) only; 20¢ per test (10¢ to educational institutions); $2 per complete specimen set (must be purchased to obtain manual); cash orders postpaid; (10) minutes; Raymond B. Cattell, Joseph E. King, and A. K. Schuettler; Institute for Personality and Ability Testing. * (Form A is also published by Industrial Psychology, Inc.)

REFERENCE
1. CATTELL, RAYMOND B. *Personality and Motivation Structure and Measurement.* Yonkers, N.Y.: World Book Co., 1957. Pp. xxv, 948. *

CECIL D. JOHNSON, *Task Leader, New Classification Techniques, Personnel Research Branch, The Adjutant General's Office, Department of the Army, Washington, D.C.*

The CPF is designed to measure a "contact personality factor," often referred to as extroversion-introversion, which is more or less the centroid of five more basic factors. The test purports to be basically designed for "sales and other contact job areas." However, no basis of item selection is given other than loadings on the particular primary factor each item represents. The basic factors and number of items representing each are as follows: cyclothymia versus schizothymia (10), dominance versus submission (6), surgency versus desurgency (6), adventurousness versus withdrawal (6), and group identification versus self-sufficiency (6). In addition to the keyed items, there are six additional items in each form from which a distortion (exaggeration of CPF tendencies) score can be obtained. Correlation of results on the two forms for 125 cases yielded a coefficient of .86.

The factor loadings of items are provided for one factor only. Loadings range in magnitude from .11 to .57. Mean loadings across the two forms range from .20 for items contributing to group identification versus self-sufficiency to .38 for items contributing to surgency versus desurgency. The table for converting CPF raw scores to 9-point ranks indicates that examinees in the standardization sample selected the non-keyed alternatives as often as the keyed responses. Such independence between direction of keying and examinee preference for alternatives would usually indicate a relatively low relationship between direction of keying and the social desirability of responses. Thus, the CPF may be relatively uncontaminated with this general factor which permeates most self-description tests used for personnel selection.

Each item is a self-descriptive statement which is either to be completed by the selection of one of two alternatives or an intermediate response, or, where the statement is already complete, to be answered with "yes," "no," or such intermediate responses as "rarely," "uncertain," or "partly." The keyed response is given a weight of 2 and is always at one end of the 3-point response scale; the intermediate and opposite responses are given weights of 1 and 0, respectively.

Approximately 300 companies are said to be cooperating to supply a minimum of 200 cases in each of 24 basic job areas. These studies will be used for converting raw scores to stanine scores, relating scores to merit ratings, and possibly (at some later date) developing job area scoring keys. Pending the completion of these studies, a table has been prepared, based "both on statistical evidence and on clinical judgment," which labels one or more stanine scores on the CPF as identifying, for each of the 24 job areas, the underqualified, minimum qualified, well qualified, and best qualified. Extreme CPF stanine scores (9, 1, and 2) are not credited with identifying the "best qualified" for any job. No one of the 24 basic job areas is recognized by the test authors as yielding less predictive validity than any other.

The optimal score on CPF for performance on each job is recommended, without sufficient indication as to the kind of evidence leading to the recommendation. Neither is the level of validity indicated for any of the jobs.

The present content of this test and the contemplated further development of it, as described in the accompanying literature, constitute a step in the direction of recognizing that pure factors identified in the absence of job performance measures are seldom of interest to personnel departments. It has been a short step, however, and those who value knowing what they are measuring factorwise over predicting job criteria are the most likely to be satisfied with the present test and norms.

S. B. SELLS, *Professor of Psychology, Texas Christian University, Fort Worth, Texas.*

This streamlined, 40-item, three-choice format, factored personality questionnaire is one of several special purpose tests for clinical and industrial application described by Cattell in his latest book summarizing a monumental research program on the structure and measurement of personality and motivation (1). The overall program has been summarized and analyzed critically by this reviewer elsewhere.[1]

The term "contact personality factor" is a nontechnical name for Cattell's second order questionnaire factor of extraversion-introversion which is assumed by the test authors to provide a basis for accurate measurement of the needs of people for contact with other people in their work. For example, the authors' confidential manual on interpretation of the CPF describes a person with the highest stanine score of 9 as follows:

This employee needs a job assignment which is completely contact. His duties should stress continuous association with people, and 95 per cent or more of his time should be spent in contact work. He has more contact personality than 19 out of every 20 adults. He is overly enthusiastic, talkative, expressive, participating, assertive, adventurous, uninhibited in emotional response. This employee would be definitely maladjusted in a non-contact job. Due to his very high extraversion, the 9-employee may lack emotional balance.

At the other extreme, the person with the lowest stanine score of 1 is described as showing:

extreme withdrawal and self-sufficiency. He is happy to work things and ideas, with no sense of deprivation if he has no contacts at all. Such an employee would show such characteristics as being inaccessible, hard to understand, and cantankerous. He will tend to be melancholic, cold, stiff, depressed, withdrawing, individualistic. He may be respected by other employees, if he maintains his emotional stability and character.

The confidential manual on the development of this test states that for some time there has been a need for "a shorter measure of personality to differentiate the contact versus the non-contact personality type in business and industry." The specific need for this test is attributed to the recognition, following the release of a personnel testing manual to 6,000 member associations by the United States Savings and Loan League in 1953, that "in savings associations the contact personality factor was of equal importance with aptitude in predicting

1 SELLS, S. B. "Review of *Personality and Motivation Structure and Measurement* by Raymond B. Cattell." *Am J Psychol* 71:620–8 S '58. *

SELLS, S. B. "Structured Measurement of Personality and Motivation: A Review of Contributions of Raymond B. Cattell." *J Clin Psychol* (in press)

job success." No evidence is presented or referenced in support of these sweeping assumptions or of the cookbook interpretations, norms, and job qualification standards presented for the using public. One wonders whether these were regarded as self-evident by the authors.

Each form of the test consists of 34 factored items from Cattell's pool of factor-analyzed personality test items, developed in conjunction with the 16 PF test, plus 6 "distortion" items which in combination provide a score representing the extent of favorable distortion of response by industrial examinees. All items are structured for response to variants of yes, inbetween, or no. The 34 factored items represent markers from each of the primary questionnaire factors comprising the second order factor in Cattell's broader taxonomic research. These are: A—cyclothymia versus schizothymia (10 items), and E—dominance versus submission, F—surgency versus desurgency, H—adventurousness versus withdrawal, and Q₂—group identification versus self-sufficiency (6 items each). Each item is scored for only one factor and the total C (contact factor) score is the linear sum of the 34 items; these are uniformly weighted 2, 1, 0 in the positively loaded direction of the primary on the second order factor. The test format is simple and easy to handle. The tests are printed clearly on green, eye-ease paper and a simple overlay stencil is used to score both forms of this and the companion *IPAT Neurotic Personality Factor Test.*

The standardization of this test is yet to be done. The only research data presented are the factor loadings of the personality items on their respective primary factors; these are incorporated in the present test as by-products of the 16 PF research. The factor loadings (for all five factors) range from .14 to .57 with a median of .34 for Form A, and from .11 to .53 with a median of .28 for Form B. The larger representation of Factor A in the test structure reflects its greater loading in the secondary factor. Internal validity is claimed on the basis of these data; however, no quantitative estimate of internal validity for the composite of the two samples of 34 items each is reported. The implication seems to be that since these items are taken from the 16 PF, a test made up from them must have internal validity.

A reliability estimate is given for a sample of 125 otherwise undescribed cases, for whom the correlation between Forms A and B was .86.

No information is available on predictive, external validity and the only statement concerning the basis for the norms presented is that they are based on "the employed adult population." Validity studies are reported in progress in 300 companies in the United States and Canada, with minimum samples of 200 cases in each of 24 job areas. However, although this test was published in 1954, no data in support of its validity have yet emerged, to this writer's knowledge.

No clear-cut statement is presented concerning the reliability and validity of the distortion scale and no attempt has apparently been made to incorporate it quantitatively into the personality measure as a "correction." Neither the small number of items nor the account of their development inspires confidence in the distortion index. Although the importance of test taking attitudes in selection and other employment testing is recognized by the authors, provision for them here appears more as a gesture than as a competent correction scale. The manual needs an adequate demonstration of the validity of the contact personality score, under the various employment conditions for which the test is designed, in which a correction for hypothesized distortion is included.

On the basis of information available it appears that the CPF test is a preliminary draft, implementing an idea about its possible use, which requires the full research treatment of any new test. Unfortunately, it is being made available to the public (personnel administrators and guidance counselors) with norms, interpretation and employment qualification guides, and a pretence of extensive research which cannot be defended. The relation of the second order factor of introversion-extraversion to various job requirements is an important and valid research problem. Whether the present streamlined (possibly too abbreviated) test measures this factor adequately and whether either the factor or this measure of it has any relevance to job success should have been determined before the test was offered for sale to users. Its use by research workers, in industry particularly, is presently of greater importance.

[72]

★**IPAT High School Personality Questionnaire.**
Ages 12-18; 1953-58; formerly called *The Junior Personality Quiz;* title on test is H.S.P.Q.; 14 scores: schizothymia vs. cyclothymia, mental defect vs. general intelligence, general neuroticism vs. ego strength, phlegmatic temperament vs. excitability, submissiveness vs.

dominance, desurgency vs. surgency, lack of rigid internal standards vs. super ego strength, threctia vs. parmia, harria vs. premsia, dynamic simplicity vs. neurasthenic self-critical tendency, confident adequacy vs. guilt proneness, group dependency vs. self-sufficiency, poor self sentiment formation vs. high strength of self sentiment, low ergic tension vs. high ergic tension; Forms A, B ('58); mimeographed supplement ['58]; separate answer sheets must be used; $4 per 25 tests; $1.90 per 50 answer sheets; 60¢ per set of scoring stencils; $2.20 per manual ('58); $3.10 per specimen set; postage extra; (40) minutes; R. B. Cattell, H. Beloff, and R. W. Coan; Institute for Personality and Ability Testing. *

REFERENCES

1. Cattell, Raymond B., and Beloff, Halla. "Research Origin and Construction of the I.P.A.T. Junior Personality Quiz." *J Consult Psychol* 17:436–42 D '53. * (*PA* 28:7514)
2. Cattell, Raymond B.; Blewett, Duncan B.; and Beloff, John R. "The Inheritance of Personality: A Multiple Variance Analysis Determination of Approximate Nature-Nurture Ratios for Primary Personality Factors in Q-Data." *Am J Human Genetics* 7:122–46 Je '55. * (*PA* 30:2451)
3. Cattell, Raymond B., and Gruen, Walter. "Primary Personality Factors in the Questionnaire Medium for Children Eleven to Fourteen Years Old." *Ed & Psychol Meas* 14:50–76 sp '54. *
4. Cattell, Raymond B. *Personality and Motivation Structure and Measurement.* Yonkers, N.Y.: World Book Co., 1957. Pp. xxv, 948. *

[73]

★**IPAT Music Preference Test of Personality.** Ages 6 and over; 1952–53; 11 scores of which the following 8 are profiled: adjustment vs. frustrated emotionality, hypomanic self-centeredness vs. self-distrust and doubt, tough sociability vs. tenderminded individuality, introspectiveness vs. social contact, anxiety and concern vs. paranoid imperiousness, complex eccentricity vs. stability normality, resilience vs. withdrawn schizothymia, schizothyme tenacity vs. relaxed cyclothymia; Forms A, B (on one record); adult norms only; $13.50 per LP microgroove 12-inch record (33⅓ rpm), 100 answer sheets ('53), scoring stencil, and manual ['52]; $1.80 per 50 answer sheets; $1.60 per specimen set without record; cash orders postpaid; (25–30), (30–35) minutes for Forms A, B; Raymond B. Cattell and Jean C. Anderson; Institute for Personality and Ability Testing. *

REFERENCES

1. Cattell, Raymond B., and Anderson, Jean C. "The Measurement of Personality and Behavior Disorders by the I.P.A.T. Music Preference Test." *J Appl Psychol* 37:446–54 D '53. * (*PA* 29:912)
2. Cattell, Raymond B., and Saunders, David R. "Musical Preferences and Personality Diagnosis: I, A Factorization of One Hundred and Twenty Themes." *J Social Psychol* 39:3–24 F '54. * (*PA* 28:8495)
3. Cattell, Raymond B. *Personality and Motivation Structure and Measurement.* Yonkers, N.Y.: World Book Co., 1957. Pp. xxv, 948. *
4. Coroso, Joan. *Relationship Between the IPAT Music Preference Test of Personality and E, S, and T Scores on the Guilford-Zimmerman Temperament Survey.* Master's thesis, College of New Rochelle (New Rochelle, N.Y.), 1958.

Neil J. Van Steenberg, *Research Psychologist, Personnel Research Branch, Personnel Research and Procedures Division, The Adjutant General's Office, Department of the Army, Washington, D.C.*

This test is designed to measure various personality traits by the scores obtained from recorded reactions ("like," "indifferent," or "dislike") of subjects to musical selection items presented on a gramophone record. There are,

in all, 100 such items, each consisting of a 15- to 20-second piano rendition of a musical composition, with 50 items on each side of the record. The test is suitable for group administration. All necessary instructions for the subjects, including those for marking the answer sheet, are given audibly on the A side of the record. (If the B side is not played directly after the A side, it is necessary to play the instructions and fore-exercise from the A side, then stop and reverse the record). Apart from the 3-minute time of instruction, Form A (i.e., the 50 items on the A side) takes about 24 minutes, Form B about 27 minutes.

Overlay keys are furnished with the test. With the use of these, scores are obtained on 11 factors. Maximum raw scores vary from 12 to 24 (combined score of A and B forms). Some items are negatively weighted and thereby purify the factor measured. The raw scores are changed to standardized ones by the use of tables furnished in the manual. Norms are given for Form A separately and for Forms A and B taken together. Separate norms are given for men and women; minor adjustments are made for age on some factors. These standardized scores are then interpreted in terms of seven or eight of the factors. The three or four additional factors are not considered reliable enough for interpretation.

Beyond the references cited above, no mention has been found in the literature on the use of this instrument; this review must therefore be based entirely on a priori judgment of the available references and the test material itself.

The power of music to influence the mood of listeners has, of course, been recognized for centuries. That certain personality types should prefer a definite type of music is a new hypothesis assumed in this study. It will be necessary here to differentiate between what Thurstone has called temperament, that is, the stable enduring aspects of personality, and the ephemeral aspects such as attitudes, opinion, and moods. If mood, then, is defined as that which is influenced by music, the assumption implies that a certain type of mood is a permanent aspect of a definite personality trait. This assumption may be questioned. The authors (2) suggest that "factors other than enduring personality traits which might be responsible for consistent patterns are: the mood of subjects through events prior to listening; the stimulus situation; a special pattern of musical or general cultural level" (social status, age). There is little evidence for assuming any permanence of such a mood. The authors state that correlation of test-retest data on the 120 (the number of items used in this study) choices ranged from .36 to .75 with a mean of .54 when retesting was done after a lapse of 24 hours, .38 to .58 with a mean of .48 after a lapse of two months, and .33–.39 with a mean of .36 after a lapse of one year. The latter measurement is for two persons! This is indeed scant evidence of any permanence of preference. One might well ask if the same type of music would be preferred by the average individual at the breakfast table and in an easy chair after the day's worries were put aside. The differential degrees of musical sophistication must also be a factor to be considered.

Tetrachoric correlation coefficients were computed between the expressed preferences, and these coefficients in turn were divided into two matrices, one of 62 and the other of 80 items (20 items of the first matrix were included in the second as controls). Both matrices were then factor analyzed and 9 factors were extracted from one, 11 from the other. Next the reference vectors for the configurations were rotated toward simple structure (but not positive manifold). The final positions are almost orthogonal. An examination of the factor loadings on the rotated vectors reveals about as many negative as positive factor loadings and both of about the same magnitude. The factor loadings on the overlapping items show that the two configurations are very close to identical. Factors are then identified by the dual loadings of 19 of the overlapping items. Many of these loadings are less than what is commonly acceptable for these purposes but they do occur in two independently derived matrices. The identification of 9 factors in terms of 19 variables used for this purpose is also somewhat unorthodox. Some items are used in identification of as many as three of four factors. Two additional factors are extracted from the 80-item matrix. It is also worth noting that the numbers of 62 and 80 must be accepted with the understanding that many items contribute little or nothing toward determination of the structure. The 142 communalities vary between .07 and .94 with a median of .44 (seven lie between .10 and .19 and fourteen between .20 and .29). It would therefore appear that either many of the tetrachorics were so small as to make questionable

their suitability for the total superstructure erected, or the factors account for only a relatively small proportion of the covariances.

With reference to the use of this test to discriminate between normal and abnormal subjects, and among various types of abnormalities, the authors seem to have established a valid procedure. This raises a point of whether in such cases the abnormal individuals may be said to suffer from a "frozen" mood enabling interpretation of the factor to be based, at least in part, on these extreme values.

The testing instrument could have been improved considerably by the use of a clean tape. Side A in particular suffers from leakage of incompletely erased sounds. A tape record might also serve better.

If further research in this field is to be undertaken, the following ideas might be suggested for consideration: (a) Some question might be raised about the medium. All selections are recorded from the piano playing of a single individual. It is too much to expect that such an individual will perform equally well on all kinds of music. In the present case, the rendition of classical music is uniformly good, sometimes even superb. The modern music items do not appear up to the same standards. If the music is to be confined to piano renditions (the authors state that this medium is chosen to control other factors), could not several pianists be employed? (b) The point of confining the music to that from a piano in order to control preference for a particular instrument does not appear to be well taken. If the items were played in the instrumentation for which they were originally intended, even more reliable results should be obtained. The music could be dubbed in from existing records. Some compositions do tend to "fall flat" when played on the piano (e.g., "Prelude to Tristan and Isolde"), and the listener, if he knows the original, might be puzzled over how to mark his answer. He might answer "I dislike this," meaning the rendition, or he might remember the strings and answer "I like this," meaning the composition as he remembers it. (c) There is, finally, a question whether the abrupt endings of the various selections lead to better results than would a gradual fade out.

In summary, it might be noted that this test (at least as one of the tests at a session) is of very high interest value to the listeners, that it is exploring a new field, and that it represents a good beginning. The test should serve as a basis for further critical research on personality and its anomalies, but, at its present stage of development, the results obtained from it should be interpreted with the utmost caution.

[74]

★IPAT Neurotic Personality Factor Test. Grades 8-16 and adults; 1955; title on test is N.P.F.; 2 scores: neuroticism, distortion; 1 form ('55); mimeographed manual ['55]; adult norms ['55] only; 20¢ per test (10¢ to educational institutions); $2 per specimen set (must be purchased to get manual); cash orders postpaid; (10-15) minutes; R. B. Cattell, J. E. King, and A. K. Schuettler; published jointly by Institute for Personality and Ability Testing and Industrial Psychology, Inc. *

S. B. SELLS, *Professor of Psychology, Texas Christian University, Fort Worth, Texas.*

This is a companion test to the *Contact Personality Factor Test* in Cattell's series of personality tests for clinical and industrial application. Its purpose is to provide business and industry with "a short, but scientifically sound, test of neurotic versus stable personality in employees." By sampling marked items representing six primary personality factors which Cattell has included in the 16 PF test and which his research has shown to be related to neuroticism, the validity of the present 34-item NPF scale is assumed to be demonstrated. The six factors are: C—mature versus emotional, G—conscientious versus changeable, I—tough-minded versus sensitive, N—realistic versus sentimental, O—confident versus insecure, and Q—steady and relaxed versus tense and overanxious.

The confidential bulletins which make up the manual for this test present even less information than those for the CPF; item factor loadings have been omitted and no reliability correlations are reported. All of the critical comments incorporated for the CPF apply equally to this test. It is brief; but whether this streamlined test is an adequate measure of the neurotic versus stability factor and whether either the factor or this measure of it has any relevance to job success is still a research problem which should have been investigated by the authors before the test was offered for sale to industrial users.

WILLIAM STEPHENSON, *Consulting Psychologist, 20 Brookside Drive, Greenwich, Connecticut.*

This questionnaire is an application of Cattell's factor system of personality evaluation. Its two pages (of a 4-page folder) contain 40 questions with "yes," "no," and middle answers. The language of the questions, we are told, is that of the daily newspaper. The test is given without a time limit, and purportedly takes about 5 minutes to complete—10 or 15 minutes would perhaps be a better guess.

Thirty-four of the 40 questions cover 6 of the 16 factors which Cattell relates to neurotic versus stable personality tendencies. The other six items are an innovation: they are called "distortion" questions, and are a built-in effort to determine whether the subject is distorting his responses to give a favorable impression. Maximum score for distortion suggests that high scores on the NPF should be "definitely questioned."

The questionnaire was designed to spot neurotic and maladjusted employees, as well as to select individuals of high stability and (sense of) responsibility. It is suggested in the confidential notes going with the instructions, that "even when neurotic employees do not actually make trouble, their presence considerably lowers the morale and productivity of the group." Nothing is said about what might be done with such unfortunates, but a number of companies in the United States and Canada are cooperating with Cattell and his associates in validating the questionnaire on samples of not less than 200 each for 24 job areas.

To this reviewer the questionnaire legitimately follows the factorial system of personality appraisal. For some practical purposes, if 10 minutes is about all the time that can be made available for personality assessment, it might be very difficult to find anything better than this, in principle, and granted everything works according to plan. Granted the premises, the questionnaire makes use of the best available knowledge and technology, and the "distortion" probe is particularly interesting.

Unhappily, though, the man who gains the highest score for stability also gains the highest for "distortion." Moreover, though the authors caution against the tentative nature of the "distortion" probe, there are reasons to suppose that it, rather than the NPF, is on the "right line." The reasons are as follows.

It is noted by the authors that a "goodly number of the relations between N.P.F. and job efficiency are curvilinear (middle score is most desirable), rather than linear (high score is most desirable)." This is what we should expect if the highest scorers on the NPF are indeed the biggest self-deceivers; or, at least, if their supposed stability is a pose of defensive conformity.

Again, one should consider the highest scoring person on the NPF, as interpreted by Cattell and his associates, in terms of the answers with which he gains his high score. According to the interpretation, he is "an employee of outstanding emotional stability, responsibility, and resistance to stress." He will "tend to view situations with great objectivity and realism, to be highly dependable, and to show great reserves against nervous exhaustion and stress." His answers to questions show him to be interested in baseball, wrestling, bullfights, and poker (a hard game of cards) rather than in dancing or art galleries. He never gets tense or anxious at train time, and hardly ever gets annoyed at unnecessary waiting for people. He takes the untidiness of people as "all in the day's work," and never gets irritated by rules and regulations which, in calmer moments, he knows are right. He practically never thinks that a lot of work around him is pretty poor; nor does he ever "get worked up" on hearing people say unpleasant things about him. Yet, of course, he insists on getting his way! At least, if he is responsible for a group project, he "insists on having his own way in any dispute in the group, or else he resigns." Mercifully (or else the scoring key is in error) he has several times "come near to fainting at a sudden pain or the sight of blood." It seems to this psychologist that any man acceding to the above list of virtues is either very dull or else of little discernment; and if these qualities add up to stability, then the less of this kind of stability there is in the leadership of men, or in responsible positions, the better for industry.

But facts will tell. The curvilinear relationships restore this reviewer's faith in the essential verities. It is easy enough, of course, for the questionnaire to pick up the grossly timid, the frightened, or the alarmed, at the neurotic end of the NPF scale.

Because of his known prejudices, this reviewer leans heavily backwards to do justice to a questionnaire of this kind. It is hard, however, in face of a contradiction of the above order, to believe that this particular test has achieved what it set out to do. Revision of norms and interpretation may bring about adjustment, but the necessity for this raises some question con-

cerning the soundness of a theory that lends itself so readily to distortions of this order.

[75]

★Institute of Child Study Security Test. Grades 4–8; 1957; title on test is *The Story of Jimmy;* 2 scores: consistency, security; Elementary Form; reliability data for grade 5 only; tentative norms; $3.75 per 25 tests; 90¢ per specimen set; postage extra; (20–25) minutes; Michael F. Grapko; distributed by Guidance Centre. *

LAURANCE F. SHAFFER, *Professor of Education, Teachers College, Columbia University, New York, New York.*

The *Institute of Child Study Security Test* is a verbal method, based on the assumption of projection, which seeks to disclose a child's degree of security, the levels of behavior by which he maintains it, and his consistency in the use of these levels. The child reads "The Story of Jimmy," which is interrupted 15 times by a need to make a decision. At each of these points, the child ranks five statements which are designed to illustrate "independent security," "mature dependent security," "immature dependent security," "deputy agent" (equivalent to the use of various defense mechanisms), and "insecurity."

The teacher or psychologist interprets the child's performance by means of a conveniently designed scoring form. The security score is a measure, ranging from 0 to 100, of the degree to which the child's ranking of the items agrees with an "ideal" order. The consistency score measures the degree of uniformity the child shows in giving the same rank to the 15 statements for each of the five security categories. The latter is calculated by means of Kendall's coefficient of concordance, W, but the ingenious worksheet removes all terrors of statistics. Any teacher who can enter grades in a classbook can score this test.

How good is the test? Its author tries to tell his readers candidly. Retest reliability after two months is satisfactory for grade 5 (.91 for security and .85 for consistency scores). There are no data for the other grades. Data relevant to validity are not strong, but some are given—a rare and praiseworthy exception among new projective methods. Judges show good agreement with the selection of the items as illustrative of the types of behavior specified. There is some increase in "independent security" and some decrease in inferior choices with increasing age. In grades 4 and 5, both the security and consistency scores show reasonable correlations (.20 to .50) with teacher ratings of pupil adjustment, but the correlations are mainly insignificant for grades 6 to 8. The author reasons that the younger child is more naive, while the older one "resists a spontaneous identification (or 'projection') with the child in the story, or attains a sophistication in understanding the intention of the test items." Probably so.

Percentile norms, properly called tentative, are given for boys and girls and for grades 4–5 and 6–8. Girls in grades 4–5 are more consistent than boys, but not more secure. The sexes differ significantly in both scores in the higher grades.

The data reveal some perplexities and some further problems. The security and consistency scores are logically quite separate, but they correlate .87, as high as the reliability of either. Why? The child in the story is a boy, and the projective hypothesis is thereby made hazardous for girl subjects. But the author does not discuss the validity of the method for boys and for girls separately.

In spite of these shortcomings, the *Institute of Child Study Security Test* clearly demands consideration, at least as an instrument for children 10 to 11 years old. It has more evident merit than many better known tests, and deserves further development.

[76]

*Interaction Chronograph. All ages; 1944–57; device for recording interaction between 2 individuals; used in a standardized interview to obtain ratings on 29 personality characteristics; 1 form ['47]; hectographed manual ('56); profile ['57]; no data on reliability; price information and sales arrangements for renting test materials available from publisher; no charge for manual; postage extra; [35–55] minutes; Eliot D. Chapple; E. D. Chapple Co., Inc. *

REFERENCES

1–5. See 3:688.
6. CHAPPLE, ELIOT D. "Quantitative Analysis of the Interaction of Individuals." *Proc Nat Acad Sci* 25:58–67 F '39. * (*PA* 13:3770)
7. CHAPPLE, ELIOT D. "'Personality' Differences as Described by Invariant Properties of Individuals in Interaction." *Proc Nat Acad Sci* 26:10–6 Ja '40. * (*PA* 14:2470)
8. CHAPPLE, ELIOT D.; with the collaboration of CONRAD M. ARENSBERG. "Measuring Human Relations: An Introduction to the Study of the Interaction of Individuals." *Genetic Psychol Monogr* 22:3–147 F '40. * (*PA* 14:3069)
9. CHAPPLE, ELIOT D. "Applied Problems in Industry." *Appl Anthrop* 1:2–9 O–D '41. *
10. CHAPPLE, E. D., AND LINDEMANN, ERICH. "Clinical Implications of Measurements of Interaction Rates in Psychiatric Interviews." *Appl Anthrop* 1:1–11 Ja–Mr '42. * (*PA* 17:1982)
11. FINESINGER, JACOB E.; LINDEMANN, ERICH; BRAZIER, MARY A. B.; AND CHAPPLE, ELIOT D. "The Effect of Anoxia as Measured by the Electroencephalogram and the Interaction Chronogram on Psychoneurotic Patients." *Am J Psychiatry* 103:738–47 My '47. * (*PA* 22:1813)
12. "Machine Helps Interview Job Applicants." *Ind Relations* 5:31 Mr '48. *
13. CHAPPLE, ELIOT D. "The Interaction Chronograph: Its Evolution and Present Application." *Personnel* 25:295–307 Ja '49. * (*PA* 24:177)
14. SHARP, L. HAROLD, AND HOUSTON, THOMAS J. "Relationship Between Check-List and Machine Recordings of the Interaction Chronograph Interview." Abstract. *Am Psychol* 5:332 Jl '50. *
15. GOLDMAN-EISLER, FRIEDA. "The Measurement of Time Sequences in Conversational Behaviour." *Brit J Psychol, Gen Sect* 42:355–62 N '51. * (*PA* 26:5548)
16. GOLDMAN-EISLER, FRIEDA. "Individual Differences Between Interviewers and Their Effect on Interviewees' Conversational Behavior." *J Mental Sci* 98:660–70 O '52. * (*PA* 27:5844)
17. CHAPPLE, ELIOT D. "The Standard Experimental (Stress) Interview as Used in Interaction Chronograph Investigations." *Human Org* 12:23–32 su '53. * (*PA* 29:5503)
18. GOLDMAN-EISLER, F. "A Study of Individual Differences and of Interaction in the Behaviour of Some Aspects of Language in Interviews." *J Mental Sci* 100:177–97 Ja '54. *
19. SASLOW, GEORGE; MATARAZZO, JOSEPH D.; AND GUZE, SAMUEL B. "The Stability of Interaction Chronograph Patterns in Psychiatric Interviews." *J Consult Psychol* 19:417–30 D '55. * (*PA* 30:7176)
20. MATARAZZO, JOSEPH D.; SASLOW, GEORGE; AND GUZE, SAMUEL B. "Stability of Interaction Patterns During Interviews: A Replication." *J Consult Psychol* 20:267–74 Ag '56. *
21. MATARAZZO, JOSEPH D.; SASLOW, GEORGE; AND MATARAZZO, RUTH G. "The Interaction Chronograph as an Instrument for Objective Measurement of Interaction Patterns During Interviews." *J Psychol* 41:347–67 Ap '56. * (*PA* 31:4662)
22. SASLOW, GEORGE; GOODRICH, D. W.; AND STEIN, MARVIN. "Study of Therapist Behavior in Diagnostic Interviews by Means of the Interaction Chronograph." *J Clin Psychol* 12:133–9 Ap '56. * (*PA* 31:4665)
23. PHILLIPS, JEANNE S.; MATARAZZO, JOSEPH D.; MATARAZZO, RUTH G.; AND SASLOW, GEORGE. "Observer Reliability of Interaction Patterns During Interviews." *J Consult Psychol* 21:269–75 Je '57. *
24. SASLOW, GEORGE; MATARAZZO, JOSEPH D.; PHILLIPS, JEANNE S.; AND MATARAZZO, RUTH G. "Test-Retest Stability of Interaction Patterns During Interviews Conducted One Week Apart." *J Abn & Social Psychol* 54:295–302 My '57. *
25. MATARAZZO, RUTH G.; MATARAZZO, JOSEPH D.; SASLOW, GEORGE; AND PHILLIPS, JEANNE S. "Psychological Test and Organismic Correlates of Interview Interaction Patterns." *J Abn & Social Psychol* 56:329–38 My '58. *

CECIL A. GIBB, *Professor of Psychology, Canberra University College, Canberra, Australia.*

Essentially the *Interaction Chronograph* is an ingenious computing device which permits an observer, operating two keys only to record, with 11 different clocks and counters, a great variety of data relating to time sequences in a conversation between two persons. Presumably it could be used for a larger group but operation would undoubtedly become very demanding. One key is depressed whenever individual A is acting, i.e., talking, nodding, gesturing or in other ways communicating with B, and the same is done for the other person.

The direct interaction chronograph variables in a conversation between A and B are: (*a*) A's units, a frequency count of the actions of A; (*b*) B's units, a frequency count of the actions of B; (*c*) Tempo, the duration of each action plus its following interaction; (*d*) Activity, a comparison measure of activity with silence; (*e*) A's adjustment, a count of the duration of A's interruptions of B minus the duration of A's failures to respond to B; (*f*) B's adjustment, a similar measure for B; (*g*) Initiative, a count, recorded only after a period of silence, added when A takes the initiative in breaking the silence and subtracted when B takes the initiative; (*h*) Dominance, a count of the frequency with which A outtalks or outacts B when there has been an interruption; (*i*) A's synchronization, a count of the number of times A interrupts B or fails to respond to B, i.e., fails to synchronize with B; and (*j*) B's synchronization, a similar count for B.

In a report on the reliability of these variables Saslow, Matarazzo, and Guze (*19*) say: "Some of these variables may seem unusually arbitrary, since they represent algebraic sums of two variables rather than individual measures of each of these variables. Apparently Chapple, in developing his interaction theory of personality, has found these derived variables more useful than the first order variables from which they were obtained." The "apparently" in this last sentence is a significant key to the state of validation data relating to this instrument. The 1956 manual does nothing to correct the deficiency. The manual is equally silent on the question of stability of interaction patterns or reliability. Goldman-Eisler (*15*) however, reports that she has "strong support for the hypothesis that certain relations of time sequences of action and silence in conversation tend to be constant within limits and characteristic of individuals independent of changing partners and topics." Saslow, Matarazzo, and Guze confirm the reliability of the variables, but find a flexibility of pattern in a standard psychiatric interview with different interviewers.

The *Interaction Chronograph,* as described in the 1956 manual, however, is much more than a research recording instrument. It is integrated with a standard stress interview (*17*) of the nondirective type to become a personality test. Under these conditions measures are derived from the record of variables printed out by the machine of nine "personality factors" and some twenty "temperament factors." Space forbids any detailed account of these factors. Since all follow the same pattern of very rash generalization and since none seem to have more than putative validity, a sample or two of the claims of the manual will suffice.

The initiative factor is measured directly by the initiative variable as described above. "This" says the manual, "is the 'drive' aspect of behavior for it is an indicator of the subject's willingness and ability to start action."

"The anxiety factor is determined by the drop in Activity and Tempo from the first period to very low values in the second [silence] period, and by the relative stability of the values of the periods thereafter." And of this factor it is said: "Although the presence of the Anxiety Factor is evidence of psychoneurosis, it occurs in many people who have various so-called neurotic symptoms associated with feelings of anxiety, who may not have overt anxiety attacks during the interview."

Apart from the extraordinary generality of these claims, with no validating evidence at all, sight seems to have been lost of the fact that this is action vis-à-vis an interviewer who is seen in the role of expert. If the action were between equals, the generalizations would be easier to accept, though they still would demand testing. As hypotheses these proposals would be reasonable in most instances, but as dogmatic assertions in a manual they must remain unacceptable. No indication is given even of correlation among the variables, though frequent assertions are made that imply that some might be taken together as cooperating factors.

The *Interaction Chronograph* seems to be a most ingenious device demanding research attention. A few isolated studies confirm the reliability of the measures. Very little is known of their validity for any purpose whatever. Publication of the manual in its present form is presumptuous.

[77]

Interaction Process Analysis. Groups of from 2–20 people (ages 4 and over); 1948–50; method of analyzing group character and processes; scoring form ['50]; manual ('50, see *2*) out of print; the *Interaction Recorder,* an optional instrument which facilitates the recording of observations in sequence, is described in *2*; Robert F. Bales; Addison-Wesley Publishing Co., Inc. *

REFERENCES

1–3. See 4:56.
4. BALES, ROBERT F. "A Set of Categories for the Analysis of Small Group Interaction." *Am Sociol R* 15:257–63 Ap '50. * (*PA* 26:4733)
5. BUTLER, WILLIAM R. *A Study of Interaction Process Analysis in Problem-Solving Situations as Revealed by Ohio University Students in Human Relations Classes.* Master's thesis, Ohio University (Athens, Ohio), 1951.
6. BORGATTA, EDGAR F., AND BALES, ROBERT F. "The Consistency of Subject Behavior and the Reliability of Scoring in Interaction Process Analysis." *Am Sociol R* 18:566–9 O '53. *
7. HEINICKE, CHRISTOPH, AND BALES, ROBERT F. "Developmental Trends in the Structure of Small Groups." *Sociometry* 16:7–38 F '53. * (*PA* 28:692)
8. PARSONS, TALCOTT; BALES, ROBERT F.; AND SHILS, EDWARD A. *Working Papers in the Theory of Action.* Glencoe, Ill.: Free Press, 1953. Pp. 269. *
9. BALES, ROBERT F. "How People Interact in Conferences." *Scientific Am* 192:31–5 Mr '55. *
10. BALES, ROBERT F., AND BORGATTA, EDGAR F. "Size of Group as a Factor in the Interaction Profile," pp. 396–413. In *Small Groups: Studies in Social Interaction.* Edited by A. Paul Hare, Edgar F. Borgatta, and Robert F. Bales. New York: Alfred A. Knopf, Inc., 1955. Pp. xv, 666. *
11. BORGATTA, EDGAR F., AND BALES, ROBERT F. "Sociometric Status Patterns and Characteristics of Interactions." *J Social Psychol* 43:289–97 My '56. *
12. FINE, HAROLD J., AND ZIMET, CARL N. "A Quantitative Method of Scaling Communication and Interaction Process." *J Clin Psychol* 12:268–71 Jl '56. * (*PA* 31:5917)
13. BORGATTA, EDGAR F.; COTTRELL, LEONARD S., JR.; AND MANN, JOHN H. "The Spectrum of Individual Interaction Characteristics: An Inter-Dimensional Analysis." *Psychol Rep* 4:279–319 Je '58. *

CECIL A. GIBB, *Professor of Psychology, Canberra University College, Canberra, Australia.*

The *Interaction Recorder* is a mechanical device to provide a continuously and constantly moving paper tape, some 12 inches wide, on which a sequential record of group behavior may be kept by an observer who indicates the "who-to-whom" action in a small group by categories. These categories are the crucial feature of the Bales instrument.

There are 12 Bales categories, developed over a period of research from a starting list of 89 categories which were "gradually refined by experience and theoretical criticism." [1] Unfortunately, this is probably the least empirical of all Bales' researches. The data relevant to the refinement from 89 to 12 categories have not been made available in published form. What criticism there is of the Bales method is largely centered about this categorization. In *The Fourth Mental Measurements Yearbook,* Carter indicated that he had found these categories to be "not entirely appropriate for groups engaged in work on tasks requiring manipulation of material." This reviewer has had a similar experience, but it must be added that it may well be that the categories could be made appropriate by slight extension of the definitions and by an extended training of observers with this kind of group situation. Another criticism has been directed to the high proportion of all actions which fall in two categories: "gives opinion, evaluation, analysis, expresses feeling, wish"; and "gives orientation, information, repeats, clarifies, confirms." In general, a little more than half of all actions recorded are in these two categories (*10*). On the basis of the very full definitions given by Bales (*2*) and in view of the fact that each of these categories has several subcategories, one wonders if more useful results would be given if these two categories were subdivided. Some of the neat formality of Bales' set might be lost, but formality for its own sake is of little value.

Bales has at all times revealed an acute awareness of the need to demonstrate both between-observer reliability and self-self observer reliability. In the former case, correlations ranging from .75 to .95 depending upon the category are reported by Heinicke and Bales (*7*). It is reasonable to expect that self-self reliability will be at least as high as this, though direct testing of the latter can be achieved only when complete reproductions of the situation—as in film—can be obtained. Borgatta and Bales (*6*), however, find self-self reliabilities for trained observers working from limited written protocols to range between .65 for Category 8 ("asks for opinion, evaluation, analysis, expression of feeling") and .98 for Category 1 ("shows solidarity, raises others status, gives help, reward"). With respect to reliability, the *Interaction Process Analysis,* used by trained observers, is quite adequate to its purposes.

As Carter pointed out in his earlier review, "the validity of the technique is self-evident since it allows the recording of immediately perceived behavior."

Finally, though this instrument has not been widely used outside the Harvard Laboratory, it has been used there by a number of people; and in judging it, one cannot overlook the valuable findings in group dynamics with which its use has been associated. Among these are Phase Movement in Groups (*8*), the effects of group size on the kind of social interaction among members (*10*), and consistency of subject behavior in groups (*6*).

Interaction Process Analysis presents a technique for recording and analyzing as much as possible of the social interaction among and between members of small groups. The wealth of data now obtained with the technique by Bales and his coworkers must recommend it to research workers in this area. The problems of extending the technique to larger "real life" groups are great and have not yet been faced, but they are by no means clearly insuperable.

For a review by Launor F. Carter, see 4:56; for related reviews, see 4:57.

[78]

An Inventory of Factors STDCR. Grades 9–16 and adults; 1934–46; 5 scores: social introversion-extraversion, thinking introversion-extraversion, depression, cycloid disposition, rhathymia; IBM; 1 form ('40); revised manual ['45]; mimeographed supplement ('46); $2.50 per 25 tests; 10¢ per single copy; separate answer sheets may be used; 3¢ per IBM answer sheet; 25¢ per scoring key; $2.50 per set of either hand or machine scoring stencils; 15¢ per manual; postage extra; (30) minutes; J. P. Guilford; Sheridan Supply Co. *

REFERENCES

1–10. See 3:55.
11–27. See 4:59.
28. BRUECKEL, JOYCE E. *A Comparison of the Three Guilford-Martin Personality Inventories With Self-Ratings and Student-Ratings.* Master's thesis, University of Colorado (Boulder, Colo.), 1948.
29. NEUMANN, THOMAS MICHAEL. *A Study of the Relation of Occupational Interests to Certain Aspects of Personality.*

1 BALES, ROBERT F. *Some Uniformities of Behavior in Small Groups.* Unpublished report, Laboratory of Social Relations, Harvard University (Cambridge, Mass.), 1952.

Master's thesis, Illinois State Normal University (Normal, Ill.), 1950.

30. GUILFORD, J. S. *The Relative Value of Fourteen Test Variables for Predicting Success in Executive and Supervisory Positions.* Master's thesis, University of Southern California (Los Angeles, Calif.), 1951.

31. MANZANO, ILUMINADO BILLARINIA. *The Relation of Personality Adjustment to Occupational Interests.* Doctor's thesis, University of Southern California (Los Angeles, Calif.), 1951.

32. BAEHR, MELANY E. "A Factorial Study of Temperament." *Psychometrika* 17:107–26 Mr '52. * (*PA* 27:1834)

33. BORG, WALTER R. "Personality Characteristics of a Group of College Art Students." *J Ed Psychol* 43:149–56 Mr '52. * (*PA* 27:3764)

34. CARROLL, JOHN B. "Ratings on Traits Measured by a Factored Personality Inventory." *J Abn & Social Psychol* 47:626–32 Jl '52. * (*PA* 27:3340)

35. COCKRUM, LOGAN V. "Personality Traits and Interests of Theological Students." *Relig Ed* 47:28–32 Ja–F '52. * (*PA* 26:4229)

36. GUILFORD, J. P. "When Not to Factor Analyze." *Psychol B* 49:26–37 Ja '52. * (*PA* 27:33)

37. GUILFORD, JOAN S. "Temperament Traits of Executives and Supervisors Measured by the Guilford Personality Inventories." *J Appl Psychol* 36:228–33 Ag '52. * (*PA* 27:3801)

38. McKENNA, FRANK S. "An Analysis of Nine Personality Scales." Abstract. *Proc Ind Acad Sci* 62:294 '52. *

39. NEILEN, GORDON C. *A Study of the Cattell 16 PF Test by Comparison With the A. C. E. and Guilford-Martin Personality Battery.* Master's thesis, Kent State University (Kent, Ohio), 1952.

40. SHAMES, GEORGE HERBERT. *An Investigation of Prognosis and Evaluation in Speech Therapy.* Doctor's thesis, University of Pittsburgh (Pittsburgh, Pa.), 1952.

41. TOMEDY, FRANCIS JOSEPH. *The Relationship of Personality Characteristics to Measured Interests of Women Teachers of English, Social Science, Mathematics, and Physical Science in Certain Senior High Schools.* Doctor's thesis, New York University (New York, N.Y.), 1952. (Abstracts: *DA* 12:540, *Am Psychol* 7:384)

42. KORNREICH, MELVIN. "Variations in the Consistency of the Behavioral Meaning of Personality Test Scores." *Genetic Psychol Monogr* 47:73–138 F '53. * (*PA* 27:6535)

43. ROSENBERG, NATHAN; IZARD, CARROLL E.; AND HOLLANDER, E. P. "Middle Category ("?") Response: Reliability and Relationship to Personality and Intelligence Variables." Abstract. *Am Psychol* 8:425 Ag '53. *

44. STACEY, CHALMERS L., AND GOLDBERG, HERMAN D. "A Personality Study of Professional and Student Actors." *J Appl Psychol* 37:245 F '53. * (*PA* 28:1685)

45. GOCHE, L. N. *Relationship of Interests and Temperament Traits to Attrition and Survival of Engineering Students.* Master's thesis, Iowa State College (Ames, Iowa), 1954.

46. GUILFORD, J. P. "The Validation of an 'Indecision' Score for Prediction of Proficiency of Foremen." *J Appl Psychol* 38:224–6 Ag '54. * (*PA* 29:6369)

47. BORG, WALTER R. "The Effect of Personality and Contact Upon a Personality Stereotype." *J Ed Res* 49:289–94 D '55. * (*PA* 30:6911)

48. COOPER, MATTHEW NATHANIEL. *To Determine the Nature and Significance, If Any, of Certain Differences in the Social and Personal Adjustment of Fifty-One Successful and Fifty-One Non-Successful College Students at Texas Southern University.* Doctor's thesis, New York University (New York, N.Y.), 1955. (*DA* 16:497).

49. ROSENBERG, NATHAN; IZARD, CARROLL E.; AND HOLLANDER, E. P. "Middle Category Response: Reliability and Relationship to Personality and Intelligence Variables." *Ed & Psychol Meas* 15:281–90 au '55. * (*PA* 30:4592)

50. THURSTON, DONALD REID. *An Investigation of the Possibilities of Parole Prediction Through the Use of Five Personality Inventories.* Doctor's thesis, Michigan State University (East Lansing, Mich.), 1955. (*DA* 15:1206)

51. ZIMMERMAN, WAYNE S., AND GUILFORD, J. P. "The Guilford-Martin Inventories Reanalyzed." Abstract. *Am Psychol* 10:330 Ag '55. *

52. GUILFORD, J. P., AND ZIMMERMAN, WAYNE S. "Fourteen Dimensions of Temperament." *Psychol Monogr* 70(10):1–26 '56. * (*PA* 31:5789)

53. NELSON, MARVEN O., AND SHEA, SALLY. "MMPI Correlates of the Inventory of Factors STDCR." *Psychol Rep* 2:433–5 D '56. * (*PA* 31:4704)

54. SPILKA, BERNARD, AND STRUENING, E. L. "A Questionnaire Study of Personality and Ethnocentrism." *J Social Psychol* 44:65–71 Ag '56. *

55. COE, ROBERT STANFORD. *The Personality and Adjustment Characteristics of Females in Various Occupational Groups.* Doctor's thesis, University of Houston (Houston, Tex.), 1957. (*DA* 17:2309)

For a review by Hubert E. Brogden, see 4:59; for a review by H. J. Eysenck, see 3:55; for a related review, see 3:45.

[79]

*KD Proneness Scale and Check List. Grades 7–12, ages 7 and over; 1950–56; 1 form; revised manual ('53) ; supplement ('56, reprinted from 6 below) ; $3.70 per set of 35 scales and check lists ; 75¢ per supplement ; postage extra ; 35¢ per specimen set, postpaid ; William C. Kvaraceus ; World Book Co. *

a) KD PRONENESS SCALE. Grades 7–12 ; also called *Delinquency Proneness Scale;* 1 form ('50) ; (15–25) minutes.

b) KD PRONENESS CHECK LIST. Ages 7 and over ; ratings made by teachers ; 1 form ('53) ; no data on reliability ; norms for grades 5–8 only ; [6–25] minutes.

REFERENCES

1. WRIGHT, MILDRED LACEY. *A Study of Juvenile Proneness Groups.* Master's thesis, Alabama Polytechnic Institute (Auburn, Ala.), 1952.

2. PATTERSON, CHARLES C. *The Relationship Between Pupil Citizenship as Rated by Teachers and Delinquent Tendencies as Shown by K.D. Proneness Scale and Check List Scores.* Master's thesis, Boston University (Boston, Mass.), 1953.

3. McDONELL, ISABELLE. *A Study of the Validity of the K.D. Proneness Scale.* Master's thesis, Catholic University of America (Washington, D.C.), 1954.

4. BALOGH, JOSEPH K., AND RUMAGE, CHARLES J. *Juvenile Delinquency Proneness: A Study of the Kvaraceus Scale.* Washington, D.C.: Public Affairs Press, 1956. Pp. iv, 35. * (*PA* 31:3398)

5. KOVALCHIK, ROBERT J. *A Study of the Use of the K.D. Proneness Scale in a Counseling Program.* Master's thesis, Catholic University of America (Washington, D.C.), 1956.

6. KVARACEUS, WILLIAM C. "Forecasting Juvenile Delinquency: Supplement to the Manual of Directions for KD Proneness Scale and Check List." *J Ed (Boston)* 138:1–43 Ap '56. *

JOHN W. M. ROTHNEY, *Professor of Education, University of Wisconsin, Madison, Wisconsin.*

The author suggests that various studies comparing delinquents and nondelinquents have identified specific traits or environmental features—such as truancy, immaturity, family mobility, school retardation, and family relationships—that tend to characterize boys and girls who are "exposed to the disease of delinquency." The *KD Proneness Scale* is said to use these predictive signs to identify the delinquent as early as possible. The *KD Proneness Check List* is provided as an aid in the process. Both instruments are said to be useful supplements for persons who find it necessary to identify youth who are especially vulnerable to the development of delinquent behavior.

The scale consists of 75 multiple choice items in the form of incomplete statements. Asserting that one can have more fun around midnight than in the morning or afternoon; that watching a prize fight is preferable to watching baseball, basketball and horse racing; and that going to college is a waste of time and money adds to one's plus score (delinquency proneness). A "minus score," reflecting the opposite, is obtained by indicating that failure usually results from lack of hard work; that going to high school is necessary for success; that going to a concert is preferable to going to a dance, movie, or bowling alley; and that most policemen try to help, rather than scare, boss, or get something on you. The total score is the difference between plus and minus scores. Separate keys for boys and girls are offered. A visual check shows that many items are scored similarly for both sexes, although there seem to be more responses by which boys can indicate delinquency proneness or lack of it.

Many studies have compared scores made by students of "high morale" (those who are doing well scholastically and are good citizens in school), "average morale," and "low morale" students, random groups of high school pupils, and institutionalized delinquents. The differences reported between the average scores of the groups are usually significant but there is so much overlap in the distributions that one could not possibly use the scale for individual prognosis. Although a supplement to the manual is entitled "Forecasting Juvenile Delinquency," *no evidence of predictive validity is presented*. The author promises to report on predictive studies now being made. The scores correlate negatively with intelligence test scores and it is said that this finding "is in accordance with the frequently reported observation that delinquents, as a group, tend to have average IQ's of approximately 90." No further interpretation or comment follows the statement.

Stability studies made by administering the scale to 53 institutionalized girls twice within a six-week period and to 37 boys in an industrial school with a two-day interval produced coefficients of .75 and .71. A Spearman rank correlation coefficient obtained from scores of 24 boys in a summer camp obtained on two successive days was .81. The authors states that on the basis of these three coefficients the scale is "sufficiently reliable for use in spot-checking and survey purposes in the process of identifying those children who may be susceptible to the development of delinquent patterns of behavior." Since the subjects used in the studies are insufficiently described and few in number, the generalization is questionable. Certainly the coefficients suggest that use of the scale with individuals cannot be recommended.

The checklist consists of 70 statements such as, " 'runs' with a 'gang,' " "attends movies at least twice a week," "drunkenness in family," and "mother is employed outside the home." These are to be answered by an observer who checks "yes," "no," or "?". Three studies involving 130 delinquent boys and 434 boys and girls in general school populations indicate that the delinquents are usually given more checks in the yes column. The results might have been anticipated in view of the fact that the delinquents had already been institutionalized. No evidence of use of the checklist with subjects whose delinquency records were not known to the rater is provided.

The author of this scale and checklist has written much and well on the subject of delinquency. The fact that he has produced two instruments which can be described only as crude survey devices of questionable stability and of unknown prognostic value attests to the difficulties involved in the use of instruments in which individuals are invited to indict themselves. The many problems in securing adequate uncontaminated information in the area of delinquency and dependable longitudinal data upon individuals who develop delinquent patterns of behavior have not been solved in the process of developing either the scale or the checklist. Persons who buy these instruments should be warned that there is little evidence that they indicate delinquency proneness of individuals who have not already been caught and sent to correctional institutions.

For reviews by Douglas Courtney and Dale B. Harris, see 4:64.

[80]

*Kuder Preference Record—Personal.** Grades 9–16 and adults; 1948–54; 6 scores: group activity, stable situations, working with ideas, avoiding conflict, directing others, verification; IBM; 1 form ('48); 2 editions; manual, fourth edition ('53); separate answer pads or answer sheets must be used; $9.80 per 20 tests; 60¢ per 20 profile sheets for adults ('52) or for children ('49); 90¢ per 20 profile leaflets for adults ('54) or for children ('53) for comparing vocational and personal scores; 75¢ per specimen set of either edition; postage extra; (40–45) minutes; G. Frederic Kuder; Science Research Associates. *
a) [HAND SCORING EDITION.] Form AH ('48); $2.35 per 20 answer pads.
b) [MACHINE SCORING EDITION.] IBM; Form AM ('48); $5 per 100 IBM answer sheets; $4 per set of scoring stencils.

REFERENCES

1–4. See 4:65.
5. FJELD, HARRIETT A. "A Comparison of Major Groups of College Women on the Kuder Preference Record—Personal." *Ed & Psychol Meas* 12:664–8 w '52. * (PA 27:6755)
6. WARDLOW, MARY E., AND GREENE, JAMES E. "An Exploratory Sociometric Study of Peer Status Among Adolescent Girls." *Sociometry* 15:311–8 Ag–N '52. * (PA 27:7097)
7. ISCOE, IRA, AND LUCIER, OMER. "A Comparison of the Revised Allport-Vernon Scale of Values (1951) and the Kuder Preference Record (Personal)." *J Appl Psychol* 37:195–6 Je '53. * (PA 28:3352)
8. MURRAY, L. E., AND BRUCE, MARTIN M. "Normative Data

Information Exchange, No. 10-2." *Personnel Psychol* 10:94–6 sp '57. *

9. SMITH, D. D. "Abilities and Interests: I, A Factorial Study." *Can J Psychol* 12:191–201 S '58. *

DWIGHT L. ARNOLD, *Professor of Education, Kent State University, Kent, Ohio.*

The Kuder-Personal deals with the important area between measurement of interests, which has proved valid and useful in vocational guidance, and measurement of personality, which has not yet proved valid in this field. Such an instrument would be useful if distinct differences in scores could be shown between different vocational groups and if the traits measured seemed to represent factors which could be identified and named.

Do the scales of the Kuder-Personal actually measure what the titles and explanations indicate? The method of developing the test is described in the manual. A survey of the literature on factorial analyses of personality and interest tests was made. From this survey a list of factors was assembled. Then seven scales, two of which were later abandoned, were selected, and items judged to be measures of pertinent factors were assembled for each scale. As far, then, as construction of the test is concerned, the validity of this instrument rests largely upon the judgment of the author that these items actually measure the interest patterns as named and explained.

The evidence presented in the manual does not support the belief that these five subtests measure traits or behavior patterns of sufficient stability and clarity to be very useful in individual counseling. Nor do these data support the assumption that the titles to these subtests are accurate and valid. This opinion is supported by the very low correlations reported between parts of the Kuder-Personal and similarly labeled parts of the *Thurstone Temperament Schedule.* The highest correlation, .57, is found between Part A, Preference for Being Active in Groups, and Part 4, Dominance, on the Thurstone schedule. The titles do not suggest a common factor. Likewise, Part E, Preference for Directing Others, correlates only .30 with Part 4 of the Thurstone test, a relationship which should be much higher if the titles really mean what they indicate.

Of 34 traits scored for Part A, 8 have to do with public speaking, 7 with prestige situations such as sitting next to an honored guest rather than with a well known friend, and 2 with enjoying being watched "while you work." It is

difficult to figure out what these items actually measure, but it is very doubtful that we can say to the student that his response to these items indicates that he likes "working with people."

On the profile sheet is this statement about Part E: "Preference for directing others. High interest indicates that you like situations in which you can influence the thoughts and activities of other people. You like to be in a position of authority." All this can be found out about an individual by the way he responds to 38 groups of three items each! Of the 38 traits used for Part E, 26 involve terms indicating distinct prestige positions such as being President of the United States, an executive, a manager, or a judge. For a student to mark these may mean that he likes the symbols of prestige, or that he likes to say that he wants to be president; but to say to such a student that he likes "to be in a position of authority" goes entirely too far.

There is real danger with instruments such as the Kuder-Personal that the title of a part will be taken as a defined, accurately measured factor in planning and counseling, when it is not. To the person taking this test the title of a part easily becomes an important characteristic of his personality. Especially is this likely to be true in the early years of high school when students have not yet developed mature patterns of judgment. It is very doubtful whether this instrument should be used at all below the 11th or the 12th grade until more data are secured which relate the scores to actual behavior or choices in the earlier age group.

The greatest value of the Kuder-Personal lies in the fact that for several occupational groups significantly different scores are found on parts of the test. For engineers, lawyers, physicians and surgeons, public school superintendents, administrators, insurance salesmen, and factory foremen, the cases on which the scores are based number more than one hundred. Thus a counselor can say, "You have a score on Part A which is similar to the average score made by a group of over a hundred insurance salesmen." This is helpful. For other occupational groups the number of cases is so small as to make the data of doubtful value in individual counseling.

In summary, because of the weaknesses discussed above, the reviewer is of the opinion that the *Kuder Preference Record—Personal* is of only limited value. Counselors using it should guard carefully against overinterpretation.

[81]

★Life Experience Inventory. Ages 13 and over; 1957; 4 scores: childhood, social, emotional, total; 1 form; $3.50 per 25 tests; 50¢ per manual; 65¢ per specimen set; postpaid; (50–60) minutes; Gilbert L. Betts and Russell N. Cassel; distributed by C. A. Gregory Co. *

REFERENCE

1. CASSEL, RUSSELL N., AND BETTS, GILBERT L. "The Development and Validation of a *Life Experience Inventory* for the Identification of 'Delinquency Prone' Youth." Abstract. *Am Psychol* 11:366 Ag '56. *

DAN L. ADLER, *Professor of Psychology, San Francisco State College, San Francisco, California.*

The *Life Experience Inventory* purports to assess the delinquency-proneness of "youth" by sampling life experiences under the categories of Childhood and Early Family Experiences; Social, Recreational and Educational Experiences; and Personal Feelings. Such, at any rate, is the tenor of the concluding remarks and the examples to be found in the manual. Unfortunately, the introduction to this same manual implies that, in addition, the inventory will measure on an individual basis, the *sources* of accident-proneness, alcoholism, narcotic addiction, suicide, and adult untrustworthiness. It will serve, it is claimed, as "either a supplement or as a substitute for the Case History of an individual." It may, finally, "be used to formulate a preventive program—one exactly suited to local needs."

Since achieving the first-stated objective alone would constitute a sufficient *raison d'être,* the reviewer was interested naturally in the validity of the inventory. No less than five kinds of validity are presented: face validity, content validity, status validity, prediction validity, and construct validity. One would expect from this array of "evidence" that the achievement of the objective would be amply and convincingly demonstrated. In truth, there is an indication of suggestive relationship between scores on the inventory and the status of delinquent and "typical" groups. However, there is no evidence (despite a 10-year period of "research and development") that the inventory actually pre-selects delinquency-prone youngsters. There is certainly no evidence presented which links inventory scores to other nonsocial behaviors.

The standardization information also leaves much to be desired. One has difficulty in finding appropriate normative tables amid the welter of criterion groups—each used for different "types" of validation and consisting in different sized or variously combined populations. One

should have misgivings about the (apparent) normative pooling of "in-prison airmen" with "delinquent youths" ranging upward from 13 years of age. One should also look askance at a group referred to only as "typical Latin youth" which contains a mixture (proportions unknown) of males and females, although sex-linked differences are clearly evident from other data and recognized specifically by the authors.

The usefulness of the inventory must surely lie within the frame of reference intended by the authors. Nevertheless, the manual gives no research definition of "delinquency," nor does it supply information about the nature of the delinquent acts represented in the populations used—either of which might give the potential user a referent for linking score values to behavior.

Finally, since the authors acknowledge the dangers of individual prediction from the inventory, it seems particularly inappropriate to emphasize the value of the device for "formulating preventive programs." No such program can be derived from the inventory, and one would not readily alter the environmental situation of an individual who *might* be delinquency-prone unless committed to the assumption that he is. This assumption cannot be justified by reference to the standardization data since, as the authors point out, cutting scores have not been shown to predict delinquency.

It does not appear reasonable, therefore, to put much faith in the inventory as a selector of delinquency-prone youth or untrustworthy adults unless one is interested in group investigations. In such cases, it might be worthwhile restandardizing the material on well defined populations with a view to eventually establishing pragmatic criteria of validity. In no case does it appear likely that the instrument will supplant the social case history.

DOUGLAS T. KENNY, *Associate Professor of Psychology, University of British Columbia, Vancouver, British Columbia, Canada.*

This inventory covers, in 150 four-choice items, what the authors believe to be the three areas of life experience which are causally related to delinquency. It is designed to identify adolescents who will became delinquents, to be used as either a supplement to or a substitute for the case history of an individual, and to be of value in screening out untrustworthy job applicants.

A critical incident study of the life experiences of 500 delinquents, drawn primarily from correctional institutions of three states, formed the basis for both the item content and the division of the scale into three parts. Fifteen hundred critical incidents were obtained and items were written "to incorporate proportionate numbers of items paralleling the number of critical incidents." The authors presume that such a procedure will produce a sampling of questions which are representative of those life experiences "which might conceivably be related to delinquency." Unless it may be assumed that delinquents from three states, supplemented by "smaller numbers" of military prisoners from 25 other states, have had life experiences similar to those of delinquents in other regions of the country and that few nondelinquents have had similar experiences, such a claim would be open to question.

The inventory is self-administering and has brief, clear instructions. However, the weighted scoring and the lack of a separate answer sheet makes it a time-consuming inventory to score. One wonders if the weighted scores could not have been validly replaced by unit weights.

Unfortunately, the four alternatives for every item are arranged so that alternative A is always the least socially desirable answer and D the most socially desirable, with alternative C more desirable than B. While such a sequence facilitates scoring, it probably means that most testees could spot the arrangement.

T scores and quality scores which indicate the degree of normality are provided for the three parts and the total. The T score norms are reported for typical individuals of mixed sex (n = 1,710), delinquent male youth and adults (n = 515), delinquent female youth (n = 260), and typical youth of Latin (sic) descent (150 of mixed sex). It is unfortunate that the manual does not provide descriptive information about these groups, such as geographic spread, age distribution, educational level, socioeconomic status, and nature of delinquencies. The combining of the sexes, the mixing of youths with adults, the failure to provide descriptive information mean that one cannot be sure that it would be meaningful to compare a given case with the normative groups.

The authors are to be commended for providing extensive data on reliability and the standard error of measurement for the part and total scores. While the reliability coefficients,

based on seven different groups, are not strikingly high, they are adequate. The odd-even reliability is of the order .82 for Part 1, .73 for Part 2, and .76 for both Part 3 and total score. In view of the size of the reliability coefficients and the substantial intercorrelations (ranging from .54 to .62) between the part scores, the manual might have cautioned users that most differences between part scores are not likely to be reliable.

Can this inventory pick out youths who will eventually become delinquents? While this would seem to be the crucial validity question for a delinquency scale, no data are presented to enable one to answer this question. Can this inventory discriminate between those in and out of correctional institutions? The manual presents quite a bit of data showing that it might be able to perform this function fairly well, having yielded an accuracy of correct classification of about 80 per cent for all cases. As the reviewer is convinced that the main purpose of a delinquency scale is to predict *who will become delinquent,* he is not overly impressed with data showing correlations between scores and the dichotomous criterion of in-out of prison.

While the manual states that the inventory can be used as a supplement or substitute for the case history and is useful in spotting adults who would be untrustworthy on a job, no data are presented to substantiate such ingenuous assertions. It is doubtful that this inventory would be useful in an employment situation because it is open to serious distortion.

While the inventory has face validity and much work has gone into its construction, it is not known whether it will identify a youth who will become a delinquent. Hence, the authors have not yet achieved what they set out to do, namely, to devise a predictive scale.

[82]

★The MACC Behavioral Adjustment Scale: An Objective Approach to the Evaluation of Behavioral Adjustment of Psychiatric Patients. Mental patients; 1957; 5 ratings: affect, cooperation, communication, total adjustment, motility; 1 form; mimeographed manual; $4 per 25 scales, postpaid; specimen set not available; [5–15] minutes; Robert B. Ellsworth; Western Psychological Services. *

MAURICE LORR, *Director, Neuropsychiatric Research Laboratory, Veterans Benefits Office, Washington, D.C.*

This scale purports to be a measure of levels of behavioral adjustment of hospitalized psychiatric patients. It consists of 14 five-point linear scales which yield four cluster scores—motility, affect, cooperation, and communication—and a total adjustment score. The total adjustment score is based on the last three cluster measures.

The scales included were selected by means of a comparison of drug-improved and drug-nonimproved groups. The selected items were submitted to two cluster analyses, which resulted in four relatively independent groups of scales. The number and types of patients compared are not stated in the manual. Only stability (test-retest) coefficients are offered as indices of reliability. The more important and essential inter-rater reliabilities for the clusters are not reported. It is reported that two raters correlate .86 on their total score ratings. Here, however, compensation for differences between raters on individual scales can increase the correlation.

The behavior clusters (except motility) and the total adjustment score are reported as discriminating significantly between closed and open ward patients. The amount of overlap and number of correct identifications are not reported.

The norms provided in the manual are based on all patients from one western hospital and a representative sample drawn from another. Unfortunately, such characteristics of the norms sample of 335 patients as age, sex, length of hospitalization, educational background, or severity of illness are left to the reader's imagination. The length of the observation period and the types of observers used are also left unspecified. The manual does indicate that the age range was wide and that a variety of diagnostic groups was sampled. The user is provided with a profile chart with centile ranks spaced to approximate an equal-interval sigma scale. However, since some of the distributions are positively skewed and others are negatively skewed, interpretation is clouded. Profile reliability is not reported.

The MACC scale is said to be unique in that nearly all personnel working with patients can complete the form. Further, it is contended that most other behavior scales do not measure clearly defined areas of behavior. Both of these assertions seem questionable. Nor is it demonstrated that different types of personnel can in fact apply the scale with equal reliability.

In summary, the MACC scale appears to be a promising device for the evaluation of behavioral adjustment in a limited number of areas. It compares favorably with the *Gardner Behavior Chart,* the Ward Section of the *Multidimensional Scales for Rating Psychiatric Patients,* and the *Northampton Activity Rating Scale.* Routine use of this scale is questionable in view of the limited normative data presented and the restricted validational information.

[83]

★McCleery Scale of Adolescent Development. Grades 9–12; 1955; 11 scores: peer relations, social role, physique acceptance, independence of adults, economic independence, occupational preference, family life, civic competence, social responsibility, ethical system, total maturity; IBM; 1 form ['55]; profile ['55]; separate answer sheets must be used; $3.50 per set of 25 tests; 50¢ per 25 IBM answer sheets; postage extra; specimen set not available; (30) minutes; Robert L. McCleery; University of Nebraska Press. *

REFERENCE

1. NELSON, SUZANNE. *Changes in the Solution of Adolescent Tasks by Eleventh Grade Boys During One Year and in Terms of Socio-Economic Status.* Doctor's thesis, University of Nebraska (Lincoln, Neb.), 1957. (*DA* 17:1952)

EUGENE L. GAIER, *Assistant Professor of Psychology, Louisiana State University, Baton Rouge, Louisiana.*

According to the author, this scale was constructed to enable comparison of the responses of the individual adolescent with those of mature and immature adolescents to items relating to the 10 developmental tasks described by Havighurst. In taking the scale, the subject checks 150 statements dealing with problems which "many young persons face" as being "important," "of little importance," or "of no importance" to him.

The norms supplied, based on responses of 316 high school boys, are limited both in number and meaning, though the manual indicates that "there is reason to believe that the norms.... presented will be representative of the responses of adolescents nationwide." This assumption is based on the fact that the performance of the mature group, drawn from a nationwide sampling of high school boys in attendance at the 1953 National Hi-Y Congress (n = 71), differed significantly from that of a randomly selected group of high school students in Nebraska (n = 235). From the limited discussion presented in the manual, one may conclude that the only thing "normative" about these data is the mean scores reported for each group. In selecting the two samples, the author apparently reasoned that leaders, as defined by election to office, are mature (ergo, have more successfully mastered the developmental tasks presented in the scale), and any other unselected group is immature. What, thus, emerges is that the norms indicate nothing more than the fact that the average leader is more "mature" as defined by the author than a more heterogeneous high school group.

The range of odd-even reliability coefficients for the parts varies from .60 to .99 (.75 to .99 when computed according to the Spearman-Brown formula). The author indicates that the reliability coefficients are "presumed adequate by criteria presently in wide acceptance." The presented coefficients have implied adequacy, and are offered as proof of the extent to which the scale "differentiates between mature....and immature boys." The odd-even and Spearman-Brown coefficients are apparently to be accepted as indicating the reliability of differences in scores. In the 1955 manual, the validity coefficients had not been completed, "since this is done by comparing a test with an established criterion. The lack of such standard is the primary reason for the origination of this scale." At best, one would have to be most skeptical to accept as justification for the lack of attempts at validation the author's implication that no other means exist for differentiating mature and immature adolescents than this scale.

The advantages of this scale are the ease of administration and scoring, but these features do not serve to offset the question of the real meaning of the scores after the profile has been constructed. The items are evidently also intended for use with adolescent girls (e.g., "Knowing what is expected of a husband or wife."), yet no norms have been established for women. Failure to take into account socioeconomic differences as well as area pressures for developmental skills further serves to depress the scale's usefulness.

After studying the scale, one can only ask the question, "So what?" If the subject, in making up his profile for the 10 task areas, falls below the presented standards for maturity, where do we go from there? The present reviewer feels that the test constructor, especially when constructing an instrument geared for an age range in which comparisons with age mates and differences in maturity rate are all-important, is under some obligation to tell how not to use the test and to indicate what implications and responsibilities hold for both the subject and the test administrator. Finally, the title appears misleading for the standardization procedure employed. The term *adolescence* is used in the title for a scale standardized with all levels of high school boys, yet adolescence may commence as early as age 11, which may be long before high school.

JOHN E. HORROCKS, *Professor of Psychology, The Ohio State University, Columbus, Ohio.*

This is a 150-item test yielding a whole score and 10 subscores. Each item requires the examinee to indicate whether, to him, the item represents a problem area of importance, of little importance, or of no importance. The test has been designed to provide a relative picture of a late teen-ager's "maturity" status based on his answers to items related to the "developmental tasks" discussed by Havighurst, Tryon, and others.

Persons who use the McCleery scale must be willing to accept the concept of "developmental tasks" as a useful means of describing a child's developmental status. They must further accept the premise that deviation from the "mature" criterion group selected by McCleery represents some kind of "immaturity." Many who work with adolescents would be unwilling to accept either the concept of "developmental tasks" or the premises provided by McCleery's criterion group of "mature" children. Even if one did accept the statement in the manual that "the person who may be called 'well-adjusted' is one who has attained a harmonious relationship between his own fundamental psychological needs and the cultural restrictions and requirements which impinge on him," it is difficult to see how the test items are able to provide an index to such a large picture. The 8-page manual does not tell how the items were arrived at, and, other than satisfactory subscore reliabilities and norms based on 316 high school boys, does not provide any statistical information. Norms are cited in terms of the mean scores of "mature" and "immature" boys on the whole test and on each of the 10 subscores. The profile sheet provided does not tell what deviation from the mean represents. It may be assumed from the profile that a high score represents deviation toward "immaturity," but it is not stated what deviation in the other direction represents. Such cursory citation of normative information is most unfortunate and represents a real defect of this scale. The normative group of 316 is inadequate and, in the opinion of this reviewer, can only provide a basis for meaningless information. No validity data are cited because, according to the author, of the lack of an established criterion. Criteria do exist and some attempt to provide various kinds of validity information should have been attempted.

Most unfortunate of all is the author's selection of a "mature" group. This consisted of 71 seventeen- and eighteen-year-olds who, as elected officers of a local Hi-Y or other organization, attended a 1953 National Hi-Y Congress. The members of such a group might possess interesting characteristics to distinguish them from other youth, but maturity might not be among those characteristics. It is not clear from the manual whether these youth were selected because they were at the convention or because they did well on the basis of a previously prepared "arm-chair" key to the test. The manual leaves nearly all the pertinent questions unanswered.

A number of the items are ambiguous to the point that a respondent might interpret an answer in either of two ways with a corresponding difference in his answer. Occasionally a loaded item appears, such as "getting *needed* experience" [reviewer's italics]. The test rephrases the same items from time to time and children may tend to grow uninterested in finishing it after they have completed about one third of the items.

The McCleery scale is an interesting attempt and the author might well continue to work on it, but it would appear that its publication was premature. In its present form, it yields information of dubious meaning and significance; a great deal of statistical information as well as adequate norms should be worked up. The title is misleading since the scale is presumably confined to boys. On the whole, the McCleery scale is representative of the too-numerous category of tests that find publication several years before they are ready. Under the circumstances, the unavailability of a sample set for the prospective user's examination before purchasing 25 sets is to be regretted.

[84]

★A Marriage Prediction Schedule. Adults; 1939–58; 1 form ['58]; reprinted from *Predicting Success or Failure in Marriage* (see *1* below); manual ['58]; no data on reliability and validity; $2.50 per 25 tests; 35¢ per specimen set; postage extra; (30–50) minutes; Ernest W. Burgess; Family Life Publications, Inc. *

REFERENCES
1. BURGESS, ERNEST W., AND COTTRELL, LEONARD S., JR. *Predicting Success or Failure in Marriage.* New York: Prentice-Hall, Inc., 1939. Pp. xxiii, 472. *
2. STROUP, ATTLEE L. *A Study of the Burgess-Cottrell System of Predicting Marital Success or Failure.* Doctor's thesis, Ohio State University (Columbus, Ohio), 1950.
3. FRUMKIN, R. M. *A Critical Analysis of the Kirkpatrick Scale of Family Interests as an Instrument for the Indirect Assessment of Marital Adjustment.* Master's thesis, Ohio State University (Columbus, Ohio), 1951.
4. KING, CHARLES E. *Factors Making for Success or Failure in Marriage Among 466 Negro Couples in a Southern City.* Doctor's thesis, University of Chicago (Chicago, Ill.), 1951.
5. SKIDMORE, REX A., AND McPHEE, WILLIAM M. "The Comparative Use of the California Test of Personality and the Burgess-Cottrell-Wallin Schedule in Predicting Marital Adjustment." *Marriage & Family Living* 13:121–6 Ag '51. * (*PA* 26:2197)
6. KING, CHARLES E. "The Burgess-Cottrell Method of Measuring Marital Adjustment Applied to a Non-White Southern Urban Population." *Marriage & Family Living* 14:280–5 N '52. * (*PA* 27:5820)
7. FRUMKIN, ROBERT M. "The Kirkpatrick Scale of Family Interests as an Instrument for the Indirect Assessment of Marital Adjustment." *Marriage & Family Living* 15:35–7 F '53. * (*PA* 28:725)
8. FRUMKIN, ROBERT M. *Measurement of Marriage Adjustment.* Washington, D.C.: Public Affairs Press, 1954. Pp. ii, 13. Paper. * (*PA* 29:2358)

[85]

★Minnesota Counseling Inventory. High school; 1953–57; 9 scores: family relationships, social relationships, emotional stability, conformity, adjustment to reality, mood, leadership, validity, questions; IBM; 1 form ('53); profile ('57); manual ('57); no data on reliability of question score; separate answer sheets must be used; $3.50 per 25 tests; $3.60 per 50 IBM answer sheets; $1.90 per 50 Hankes answer sheets; 60¢ per set of hand scoring stencils and manual ('57); 90¢ per set of machine scoring stencils and manual; 75¢ per specimen set; postpaid; scoring service available; (50) minutes; Ralph F. Berdie and Wilbur L. Layton; Psychological Corporation. *

J Consult Psychol 22:241 Je '58. Laurance F. Shaffer. * The extensive data given in the Manual reveal both favorable and unfavorable features of the development of the Inventory. Both split-half and retest reliabilities are mainly satisfactory. * Standard score norms....are based on adequate methods and numbers. The manual's suggestions for interpretation are explicit and appropriately modest. One weakness is revealed by the data on validities and intercorrelations. Validities of entire scales are reported in terms of the CRs of differences between the scores of random samples of pupils and of extreme cases nominated by teachers and school administrators. There is no indication of item analysis against a criterion. Some scales, such as *SR,* differentiate well, but others, such as *R* (*Sc*), fail to do so. The tables of intercorrelations show that most r's run from .35 to .60, but that the correlations between *SR* and *L,* and between *ES* and *R,* are as high as the scales' reliabilities. The authors might well have refined the scales further by item analysis, or at least might have warned users that the evidence points to five interpretable scores, not seven.

Even so, the Inventory is a serviceable instrument for counselors whose knowledge of test construction permits them to be aware of its limitations.

[86]
*Minnesota Multiphasic Personality Inventory, Revised Edition. Ages 16 and over; 1943–51; 14 scores: hypochondriasis (Hs, '43), depression (D, '43), hysteria (Hy, '43), psychopathic deviate (Pd, '43), masculinity and femininity (Mf, '43), paranoia (Pa, '43), psychathenia (Pt, '43), schizophrenia (Sc, '43), hypomania (Ma, '43), social (Si, '51), question (?, no key), lie (L, no key), validity (F, '43), test taking attitude (K, '46); IBM; 1 form; 2 editions (individual and group); $1.50 per manual ('51); postpaid; (30–90) minutes; Starke R. Hathaway and J. Charnley McKinley; Psychological Corporation. *
a) INDIVIDUAL FORM ("THE CARD SET"). 1943–51; $24 per set of testing materials ('43) including 50 record blanks ('43); $3 per 50 record blanks; $8.50 per set of manual and scoring stencils.
b) GROUP FORM ("THE BOOKLET FORM"). 1943–51; IBM; separate answer sheets must be used; $5.50 per 25 tests ('43); $3.60 per 50 sets of IBM answer sheet and case summary card ('43); $4.50 per set of manual and either hand or machine scoring stencils; $1.75 per specimen set without scoring stencils.

REFERENCES

1–72. See 3:60.
73–283. See 4:71.
284. BOLANDER, W. G. *A Study of the MMPI as an Indicator in the Prediction of College Success.* Master's thesis, University of Oregon (Eugene, Ore.), 1947.
285. ALBEE, GEORGE W. "Psychological Concomitants of Pulmonary Tuberculosis." *Am R Tuberc* 58:650–61 D '48. * (*PA* 25:492)
286. DALY, JULIETTE M. *Relationship of MMPI and Kuder Preference Record Scores.* Master's thesis, Catholic University of America (Washington, D.C.), 1948.
287. BENARICK, STANLEY JOHN, JR. *An Investigation of the Schizophrenia Scale of the Minnesota Multiphasic Personality Inventory.* Master's thesis, Pennsylvania State College (State College, Pa.), 1950.
288. CASNER, DANIEL. *Certain Factors Associated With Success and Failure in Personal-Adjustment Counseling.* Doctor's thesis, New York University (New York, N.Y.), 1950.
289. DE CILLIS, OLGA E., AND ORBISON, WILLIAM D. "A Comparison of the Terman-Miles M-F Test and the Mf Scale of the MMPI." *J Appl Psychol* 34:338–42 O '50. * (*PA* 26:294)
290. FASSETT, KATHERINE K. "Interest and Personality Measures of Veteran and Non-Veteran University Freshman Men." *Ed & Psychol Meas* 10:338–41 su '50. * (*PA* 25:6212)
291. HORLICK, REUBEN S. *The Relationships of Psychometric Test Scores to Personality Disorders.* Doctor's thesis, New York University (New York, N.Y.), 1950.
292. JOHNSON, RALPH H., AND BOND, GUY L. "Reading Ease of Commonly Used Tests." *J Appl Psychol* 34:319–24 O '50. * (*PA* 26:299)
293. MCALLISTER, CATHERINE ELIZABETH. *A Study of Item Behavior in the Depression Scale of the Minnesota Multiphasic Personality Inventory.* Master's thesis, Pennsylvania State College (State College, Pa.), 1950.
294. MITCHELL, WALTER M. *An Analysis of the Relationship Between Performance on the MF Scale of the Minnesota Multiphasic Personality Inventory and the Strong Vocational Interest Blank for Men.* Master's thesis, Montana State University (Missoula, Mont.), 1950.
295. MORGAN, CARL ELWOOD. *Selected Curricular Choices and Personality Tendencies as Measured by the Minnesota Multiphasic Personality Inventory.* Master's thesis, Kansas State College (Manhattan, Kan.), 1950.
296. PEMBERTON, W. H. *Test Characteristics of Student Teachers Rated at the Extremes of Teaching Ability.* Doctor's thesis, University of California (Berkeley, Calif.), 1950. (*PA* 26:4334)
297. ANDRULONIS, JEROME A. *Relation Between Machover's Drawing of the Human Figure Test and Certain Variables on the Minnesota Multiphasic Personality Inventory.* Master's thesis, Fordham University (New York, N.Y.), 1951.
298. BLAU, THEODORE H. *Effects of High Intensity Sound on Certain Psychological Variables.* Doctor's thesis, Pennsylvania State College (State College, Pa.), 1951.
299. BOTWINICK, JACK, AND MACHOVER, SOLOMON. "A Psychometric Examination of Latent Homosexuality in Alcoholism." *Q J Studies Alcohol* 12:268–72 Je '51. (*PA* 26:390)

300. CARPENTER, LEWIS G., JR.; FREEDMAN, MERVIN B.; HARRIS, ROBERT E.; AND SOKOLOW, MAURICE. "A Scale for the Measurement of Personality in Patients With Essential Hypertension." Abstract. *Am Psychol* 6:493 S '51. *
301. FELDMAN, MARVIN J. "A Prognostic Scale for Shock Therapy." *Psychol Monogr* 65(10):1–27 '51. * (*PA* 26:7028)
302. GALLAGHER, JAMES J. *An Investigation Into Factors Differentiating College Students Who Discontinue Non-Directive Counseling From College Students Who Continue Counseling.* Doctor's thesis, Pennsylvania State College (State College, Pa.), 1951.
303. GOINES, VALMORE R. *Personality Characteristics of a Certain Ethnic Group.* Doctor's thesis, Northwestern University (Evanston, Ill.), 1951.
304. GOULDING, CHARLES W. *A Study of the Distribution of MMPI Profiles in a College Population.* Master's thesis, University of Minnesota (Minneapolis, Minn.), 1951.
305. GROSSMAN, DONNA J. *A Study of the Parents of Stuttering and Nonstuttering Children Using the MMPI and Minnesota Scale of Parents Opinion.* Master's thesis, University of Wisconsin (Madison, Wis.), 1951.
306. HANSON, ANNA JEAN. *An Analysis of "Drop Out" Students at Montana State University.* Master's thesis, Montana State University (Missoula, Mont.), 1951.
307. HOLTZMAN, PAUL DOUGLAS. *An Experimental Study of Some Relationships Among Several Indices of Stage Fright and Personality.* Doctor's thesis, University of Southern California (Los Angeles, Calif.), 1951.
308. HUFFMAN, WARREN JUSTUS. *Personality Variations Among Men Preparing to Teach Physical Education.* Doctor's thesis, University of Illinois (Urbana, Ill.), 1951. (*DA* 12:28–9)
309. HUNT, FOLGER DEFOE. *A Study of the Relationship of Personality Scores to Level of Achievement.* Master's thesis, Ohio University (Athens, Ohio), 1951.
310. JOHN, WATKINS F. *A Study of the Relationship Between the Clinical Variables of the Minnesota Multiphasic Personality Inventory and Major Field of Study of Ohio University Students.* Master's thesis, Ohio University (Athens, Ohio), 1951.
311. MANZANO, ILUMINADO BILLARINIA. *The Relation of Personality Adjustment to Occupational Interests.* Doctor's thesis, University of Southern California (Los Angeles, Calif.), 1951.
312. MORGAN, HENRY HOLLINSHEAD. *An Analysis of Certain Structured and Unstructured Test Results of Achieving and Nonachieving High Ability College Students.* Doctor's thesis, University of Minnesota (Minneapolis, Minn.), 1951. (*DA* 12:335)
313. NAVRAN, L. A. *A Rationally Derived Minnesota Multiphasic Personality Inventory Scale to Measure Dependence.* Doctor's thesis, Stanford University (Stanford, Calif.), 1951.
314. REDLO, MIRIAM. *MMPI Personality Patterns for Several Academic Major Groups.* Master's thesis, University of New Mexico (Albuquerque, N.M.), 1951.
315. RUBIN, STANLEY B. *A Scale of Morale in the Minnesota Multiphasic Personality Inventory.* Master's thesis, University of California (Berkeley, Calif.), 1951.
316. TAFEJIAN, THOMAS T. "The E-F Scale, the MMPI and Gough's Pr Scale." Abstract. *Am Psychol* 6:501 S '51. *
317. WILLIAMS, HAROLD L. *Differential Effects of Focal Brain Damage on the Minnesota Multiphasic Personality Inventory.* Doctor's thesis, University of Minnesota (Minneapolis, Minn.), 1951. (*DA* 12:397)
318. WILLIAMS, JANET T. *A Study of the Parents of Cerebral Palsied and Noncerebral Palsied Children Using the MMPI.* Master's thesis, University of Wisconsin (Madison, Wis.), 1951.
319. ALTUS, WILLIAM D. "Personality Correlates of Q-L Variability on the ACE." *J Consult Psychol* 16:284–91 Ag '52. * (*PA* 27:4237)
320. BALIAN, LUCY J. *The Performance of 80 Normal Subjects on a German Translation of the MMPI.* Master's thesis, University of Minnesota (Minneapolis, Minn.), 1952.
321. BORKO, HAROLD. *A Factor-Analytic Study of the Minnesota Multiphasic Personality Inventory Using a Transpose Matrix (Q-Technique).* Doctor's thesis, University of Southern California (Los Angeles, Calif.), 1952. (Abstract: *Am Psychol* 7:342)
322. BROZEK, JOSEF. "Personality of Young and Middle-Aged Normal Men: Item Analysis of a Psychosomatic Inventory." *J Gerontol* 7:410–8 Jl '52. * (*PA* 27:3328)
323. BROZEK, JOSEF, AND KEYS, ANCEL. "Personality Differences Between Normal Young and Middle-Aged Men: Item Analysis of A Psychosomatic Inventory." Abstract. *Am Psychol* 7:402–3 Jl '52. *
324. BUECHLEY, ROBERT, AND BALL, HARRY. "A New Test of 'Validity' for the Group MMPI." *J Consult Psychol* 16:299–301 Ag '52. * (*PA* 27:4243)
325. BURSCH, CHARLES W., II. "Certain Relationships Between the Kuder Preference Record and the Minnesota Multiphasic Personality Inventory." *Calif J Ed Res* 3:224–7+ N '52. * (*PA* 27:5144)
326. CANTOR, JOEL MALCOLM. *Syndromes Found in Psychiatric Population Selected for Certain MMPI Code Endings.* Doctor's thesis, University of Minnesota (Minneapolis, Minn.), 1952. (*DA* 12:394)
327. CLARK, JERRY H. "The Relationship Between MMPI Scores and Psychiatric Classification of Army General Prisoners." *J Clin Psychol* 8:86–9 Ja '52. * (*PA* 27:2103)

328. DAHLSTROM, W. GRANT, AND CRAVEN, DOROTHY DRAKE-SMITH. "The Minnesota Multiphasic Personality Inventory and Stuttering Phenomena in Young Adults." Abstract. *Am Psychol* 7:341 Jl '52. *

329. DEVLIN, JOHN P. *A Study of Verbalized Self-Attitudes and Reactions to Social Frustration as Methods of Predicting Success in Brief Psychotherapy.* Doctor's thesis, Pennsylvania State College (State College, Pa.), 1952.

330. DREBUS, RICHARD W. *An Investigation of the Responses of Industrial Supervisors to the Minnesota Multi-Phasic Personality Inventory in Relationship to Their Performance Levels.* Doctor's thesis, University of Wisconsin (Madison, Wis.), 1952.

331. DRUCKER, MELVIN BRUCE. *An Underachiever-Overachiever Scale From the Minnesota Multiphasic Personality Inventory.* Master's thesis, Ohio University (Athens, Ohio), 1952.

332. ESTENSON, LYLE O. *An Investigation of the Relationship Between Personality as Measured by the Minnesota Multiphasic Personality Inventory and Occupational Interests as Measured by Strong's Vocational Interest Blanks.* Doctor's thesis, University of Minnesota (Minneapolis, Minn.), 1952.

333. FELDMAN, MARVIN J. "The Use of the MMPI Profile for Prognosis and Evaluation of Shock Therapy." *J Consult Psychol* 16:376–82 O '52. * (PA 27:5922)

334. FOUNTAIN, RALPH WARREN, JR. *Performance of College Students on the Mosaic Test and on the Minnesota Multiphasic Personality Inventory.* Master's thesis, University of Florida (Gainesville, Fla.), 1952.

335. FREEMAN, ROBERT A., AND MASON, HARRY M. "Construction of a Key to Determine Recidivists From Non-Recidivists Using the MMPI." *J Clin Psychol* 8:207–8 Ap '52. * (PA 27:1957)

336. FRY, FRANKLYN D. *A Normative Study of the Reactions Manifested by College Students, and by State Prison Inmates in Response to the Minnesota Multiphasic Personality Inventory, the Rosenzweig Picture Frustration Study, and the Thematic Apperception Test.* Doctor's thesis, Pennsylvania State College (State College, Pa.), 1952.

337. FRY, FRANKLYN D. "A Normative Study of the Reactions Manifested by College Students and by State Prison Inmates in Response to the Minnesota Multiphasic Personality Inventory, the Rosenzweig Picture-Frustration Study, and the Thematic Apperception Test." *J Psychol* 34:27–30 Jl '52. * (PA 27:2976)

338. GEIST, HAROLD. "A Comparison of Personality Test Scores and Medical Psychiatric Diagnosis by The Inverted Factor Technique." *J Clin Psychol* 8:184–8 Ap '52. * (PA 27:1958)

339. GILBERSTADT, HAROLD. *An Exploratory Investigation of the Hathaway-Meehl Method of Minnesota Multiphasic Personality Inventory Profile Analysis With Psychiatric Clinical Data.* Doctor's thesis, University of Minnesota (Minneapolis, Minn.), 1952. (DA 13:256–7)

340. GOUGH, HARRISON G., AND PEMBERTON, WILLIAM H. "Personality Characteristics Related to Success in Practice Teaching." *J Appl Psychol* 36:307–9 O '52. * (PA 27:5426)

341. GOUGH, HARRISON G.; MCCLOSKY, HERBERT; AND MEEHL, PAUL E. "A Personality Scale for Social Responsibility." *J Abn & Social Psychol* 47:73–80 Ja '52. * (PA 26:6270)

342. GREENBERG, PAUL, AND GILLILAND, A. R. "The Relationship Between Basal Metabolism and Personality." *J Social Psychol* 35:3–7 F '52. * (PA 27:3345)

343. GUILFORD, J. P. "When Not to Factor Analyze." *Psychol B* 49:26–37 Ja '52. * (PA 27:33)

344. GUTHRIE, GEORGE M. "Common Characteristics Associated With Frequent MMPI Profile Types." *J Clin Psychol* 8:141–5 Ap '52. * (PA 27:1963)

345. HARMON, LINDSEY RICHARD. *Inter-Relations of Patterns on the Kuder Preference Record and the Minnesota Multiphasic Personality Inventory.* Doctor's thesis, University of Minnesota (Minneapolis, Minn.), 1952. (DA 13:257–8)

346. HATHAWAY, STARKE R., AND MONACHESI, ELIO D. "The Minnesota Multiphasic Personality Inventory in the Study of Juvenile Delinquents." *Am Sociol R* 17:704–10 D '52. * (PA 28:1290)

347. HERZBERG, FREDERICK I. "A Study of the Psychological Factors in Primary Dysmenorrhea." *J Clin Psychol* 8:174–8 Ap '52. * (PA 27:2155)

348. HOLLAND, JOHN LEWIS. *A Study of Measured Personality Variables and Their Behavioral Correlates as Seen in Oil Painting.* Doctor's thesis, University of Minnesota (Minneapolis, Minn.), 1952. (DA 12:380)

349. JANDA, EARL JOSEPH. *On the Relationship Between Anxiety and Night Vision.* Doctor's thesis, University of Michigan (Ann Arbor, Mich.), 1952. (DA 12:219)

350. JENKINS, WILLIAM LORNE. *The Minnesota Multiphasic Personality Inventory Applied to the Problem of Prognosis in Schizophrenia.* Doctor's thesis, University of Minnesota (Minneapolis, Minn.), 1952. (DA 12:381)

351. KIRK, BARBARA. "Test Versus Academic Performance in Malfunctioning Students." *J Consult Psychol* 16:213–6 Je '52. * (PA 27:5417)

352. KLETTI, LEROY. *The Agreement in Anxiety Measurement Between the Rorschach Test and the Minnesota Multiphasic Personality Inventory.* Master's thesis, University of North Dakota (Grand Forks, N.D.), 1952.

353. LAYTON, WILBUR L. "The Variability of Individuals' Scores Upon Successive Testings on the Minnesota Multiphasic Personality Inventory." Abstract. *Am Psychol* 7:384 Jl '52. *

354. LEADINGHAM, ROBERT L. *A Validity Study of an Underachiever-Overachiever Scale From the Minnesota Multiphasic Personality Inventory.* Master's thesis, Ohio University (Athens, Ohio), 1952.

355. LINDGREN, HENRY CLAY. "The Development of A Scale of Cultural Idealization Based on The California Test of Personality." *J Ed Psychol* 43:81–91 F '52. * (PA 26:7004)

356. MACDONALD, GORDON L. "Effect of Test-Retest Interval and Item Arrangement on the Shortened Forms of the MMPI." *J Clin Psychol* 8:408–10 O '52. * (PA 27:5883)

357. MACDONALD, GORDON L. "A Study of the Shortened Group and Individual Forms of the MMPI." *J Clin Psychol* 8:309–11 Jl '52. * (PA 27:5884)

358. MACHOVER, SOLOMON, AND SCHWARTZ, ANITA. "A Homeostatic Effect of Mood on Associative Abstractness and Reaction Time." *J Personality* 21:59–67 S '52. * (PA 27:5697)

359. MCQUARY, JOHN P., AND TRUAX, WILLIAM E., JR. "A Comparison of The Group and Individual Forms of The Minnesota Multiphasic Personality Inventory." *J Ed Res* 45:609–14 Ap '52. * (PA 27:2742)

360. MALOS, HERBERT BERNARD. *Some Psychometric Evaluations of Epilepsy.* Doctor's thesis, University of Minnesota (Minneapolis, Minn.), 1952. (DA 12:396)

361. MEE, ELIZABETH ANN. *A Psychometric Study of Diffuse and Focal Cerebral Pathology Groups.* Doctor's thesis, University of Minnesota (Minneapolis, Minn.), 1952. (DA 12:338)

362. MELEIKA, LOUIS KAMEL. *Intra-Individual Variability in Relation to Achievement, Interest, and Personality.* Doctor's thesis, Stanford University (Stanford, Calif.), 1952.

363. MORGAN, HENRY H. "A Psychometric Comparison of Achieving and Nonachieving College Students of High Ability." *J Consult Psychol* 16:292–8 Ag '52. * (PA 27:4570)

364. MORTON, SHELDON IVAN. *Personality Differences in Preprofessional Groups.* Doctor's thesis, Stanford University (Stanford, Calif.), 1952.

365. MYATT, MARY FRANCES. *A Study of the Relationship Between Motivation and Test Performance of Patients in a Rehabilitation Ward.* Doctor's thesis, University of Minnesota (Minneapolis, Minn.), 1952. (DA 12:339)

366. NARCISO, JOHN C., JR. "Some Psychological Aspects of Dermatosis." *J Consult Psychol* 16:199–201 Je '52. * (PA 27:5335)

367. NAVRAN, LESLIE. "The Dependence Scale Scores of Graduate Students Classified by Major Subjects." Abstract. *Calif J Ed Res* 3:182 S '52. *

368. NAVRAN, LESLIE. *A Rationally Derived Minnesota Multiphasic Personality Inventory Scale to Measure Dependence.* Doctor's thesis, Stanford University (Stanford, Calif.), 1952.

369. NELSON, SHERMAN EDDIE. *The Development of an Indirect, Objective Measure of Social Status and Its Relationship to Certain Psychiatric Syndromes.* Doctor's thesis, University of Minnesota (Minneapolis, Minn.), 1952. (DA 12:782)

370. NORMAN, RALPH D., AND REDLO, MIRIAM. "MMPI Personality Patterns for Various College Major Groups." Abstract. *J Colo-Wyo Acad Sci* 4:80 O '52. *

371. NORMAN, RALPH D., AND REDLO, MIRIAM. "MMPI Personality Patterns for Various College Major Groups." *J Appl Psychol* 36:404–9 D '52. * (PA 27:6750)

372. PETERSON, DONALD ROBERT. *Predicting Hospitalization of Psychiatric Outpatients.* Doctor's thesis, University of Minnesota (Minneapolis, Minn.), 1952. (DA 12:783)

373. PURCELL, CLAIRE KEPLER. "The Relationship Between Altitude—I.Q. Discrepancy and Anxiety." *J Clin Psychol* 8:82–5 Ja '52. * (PA 27:1978)

374. RICHARDS, T. W. "Personality of the Convulsive Patient in Military Service." *Psychol Monogr* 66(14):1–23 '52. * (PA 27:7364)

375. RITTENHOUSE, CARL H. "Masculinity and Femininity in Relation to Preferences in Music." Abstract. *Am Psychol* 7:333 Jl '52. *

376. RITTENHOUSE, CARL H. *Masculinity and Femininity in Relation to Preferences in Music.* Doctor's thesis, Stanford University (Stanford, Calif.), 1952.

377. ROSEN, ALBERT. *Development of Some New Minnesota Multiphasic Personality Inventory Scales for Differentiation of Psychiatric Syndromes Within an Abnormal Population.* Doctor's thesis, University of Minnesota (Minneapolis, Minn.), 1952. (DA 12:785)

378. ROSEN, ALBERT. "Reliability of MMPI Scales." Abstract. *Am Psychol* 7:341 Jl '52. *

379. ROSEN, EPHRAIM. "MMPI and Rorschach Correlates of the Rorschach White Space Response." *J Clin Psychol* 8:283–8 Jl '52. * (PA 27:5899)

380. ROSEN, IRWIN C. *Parallel Researches in Sexual Psychopathology: I, A Comparison of a Group of Rapists and Controls on Certain Psychological Variables.* Doctor's thesis, University of Pittsburgh (Pittsburgh, Pa.), 1952.

381. SANDERSON, J. WESLEY. *An Evaluation of a Technique of Profile Classification for the Minnesota Multiphasic Personality Inventory.* Doctor's thesis, University of California (Los Angeles, Calif.), 1952.

382. SEEMAN, WILLIAM. "'Subtlety' in Structured Personality Tests." *J Consult Psychol* 16:278–83 Ag '52. * (PA 27:4270)

383. SHNEIDMAN, EDWIN S. "The Case of Jay: Psychological Test and Anamnestic Data." *J Proj Tech* 16:297–345 S '52. * (PA 28:2676)

384. SOPCHAK, ANDREW L. "College Student Norms for the

Minnesota Multiphasic Personality Inventory." *J Consult Psychol* 16:445–8 D '52. * (*PA* 28:969)

385. SOPCHAK, ANDREW L. "Parental 'Identification' and 'Tendency Toward Disorders' as Measured by the Minnesota Multiphasic Personality Inventory." *J Abn & Social Psychol* 47:159–65 Ap '52. * (*PA* 27:2825)

386. SULLIVAN, PATRICK L., AND WELSH, GEORGE S. "A Technique for Objective Configural Analysis of MMPI Profiles." *J Consult Psychol* 16:383–88 O '52. * (*PA* 27:5908)

387. SUNDBERG, NORMAN, DALE. *The Relationship of Psychotherapeutic Skill and Experience to Knowledge of Other People.* Doctor's thesis, University of Minnesota (Minneapolis, Minn.), 1952. (*DA* 12:390)

388. SUTTON, MARY LYON. *Profile Patterning and Descriptive Correlates of Patients Having Low Scores on Scale 9 of the MMPI.* Doctor's thesis, University of Minnesota (Minneapolis, Minn.), 1952. (*DA* 12:786)

389. TAAFFE, GORDON. *The Discrimination of Alcoholics, Psychopaths, and Psychoneurotics by Means of the Manson Evaluation, the Pd Scale, MMPI, and the Cornell Index.* Master's thesis, University of Southern California (Los Angeles, Calif.), 1952.

390. TAYLOR, KENNETH E. *Parallel Researches in Sexual Psychopathology: II, A Comparison of a Group of Pedophiliacs and Controls on Certain Psychological Variables.* Doctor's thesis, University of Pittsburgh (Pittsburgh, Pa.), 1952.

391. TREECE, RUSSELL RAY. *A Study of a Group of Imprisoned Homosexuals, Using the Minnesota Multiphasic Personality Inventory.* Master's thesis, University of Pittsburgh (Pittsburgh, Pa.), 1952.

392. WELSH, GEORGE S. "An Anxiety Index and an Internalization Ratio for the MMPI." *J Consult Psychol* 16:65–72 F '52. * (*PA* 27:1985)

393. WELSH, GEORGE S. "A Factor Study of the MMPI Using Scales With Item Overlap Eliminated." Abstract. *Am Psychol* 7:341–2 Jl '52. *

394. WEST, PHILIP M.; BLUMBERG, EUGENE M.; AND ELLIS, FRANK W. "An Observed Correlation Between Psychological Factors and Growth Rate of Cancer in Man." Abstract. *Cancer Res* 12:306–7 Ap '52. *

395. WHOOLEY, JOHN P. *The Application of the Minnesota Multiphasic Personality Inventory to Hospitalized Tuberculous Patients.* Master's thesis, Catholic University of America (Washington, D.C.), 1952.

396. WIENER, DANIEL N. "Personality Characteristics of Selected Disability Groups." *Genetic Psychol Monogr* 45:175–255 My '52. * (*PA* 27:3746)

397. WILLIAMS, HAROLD L. "The Development of a Caudality Scale for the MMPI." *J Clin Psychol* 8:293–7 Jl '52. * (*PA* 27:6088)

398. WILLIAMSON, E. G., AND HOYT, DONALD. "Measured Personality Characteristics of Student Leaders." *Ed & Psychol Meas* 12:65–78 sp '52. * (*PA* 27:6135)

399. WILLMOTT, ELIZABETH H. *An Experimental Study of the Relationship Between the Success of Group Counselors at a Therapeutic Camp and Their Personality Characteristics as Measured by the Minnesota Multiphasic Personality Inventory.* Master's thesis, University of Michigan (Ann Arbor, Mich.), 1952.

400. WINDLE, CHARLES. "Psychological Tests in Psychopathological Prognosis." *Psychol B* 49:451–82 S '52. * (*PA* 27:3567)

401. WINFIELD, DON L. "An Investigation of the Relationship Between Intelligence and the Statistical Reliability of the Minnesota Multiphasic Personality Inventory." *J Clin Psychol* 8:146–8 Ap '52. * (*PA* 27:1987)

402. WRENN, C. GILBERT. "The Selection and Education of Student Personnel Workers." *Personnel & Guid J* 31:9–14 O '52. * (*PA* 27:4782)

403. ALTUS, W. D., AND TAFEJIAN, T. T. "MMPI Correlates of the California *EF* Scale." *J Social Psychol* 38:145–9 Ag '53. * (*PA* 28:6011)

404. APPLEZWEIG, MORTIMER H. "Educational Levels and Minnesota Multiphasic Profiles." *J Clin Psychol* 9:340–4 O '53. * (*PA* 28:4327)

405. ASHBAUGH, JAMES H. Study 3, "Personality Patterns of Juvenile Delinquents in an Area of Small Population," pp. 54–60. In *Analyzing and Predicting Juvenile Delinquency With the MMPI.* Edited by Starke R. Hathaway and Elio D. Monachesi. Minneapolis, Minn.: University of Minnesota Press, 1953. Pp. viii, 153. * (*PA* 28:2970)

406. AUSUBEL, DAVID P.; SCHIFF, HERBERT M.; AND ZELENY, MARJORIE P. " 'Real-Life' Measures of Level of Academic and Vocational Aspiration in Adolescents: Relation to Laboratory Measures and to Adjustment." *Child Develop* 24:155–68 S–D '53. * (*PA* 29:3700)

407. BARRON, FRANK. "An Ego-Strength Scale Which Predicts Response to Psychotherapy." *J Consult Psychol* 17:327–33 O '53. * (*PA* 28:6072)

408. BARRON, FRANK. "Some Test Correlates of Response to Psychotherapy." *J Consult Psychol* 17:235–41 Ag '53. * (*PA* 28:4410)

409. BEAVER, ALMA PERRY. "Personality Factors in Choice of Nursing." *J Appl Psychol* 37:374–9 O '53. * (*PA* 29:1484)

410. BECHTOLDT, HAROLD P. "Response Defined Anxiety and MMPI Variables." *Proc Iowa Acad Sci* 60:495–9 '53. * (*PA* 29:2429)

411. BEIER, ERNST G., AND RATZEBURG, FRED. "The Parental

Identifications of Male and Female College Students." *J Abn & Social Psychol* 48:569–72 O '53. * (*PA* 28:6529)

412. BERGER, EMANUEL M. "Relationships Among Expressed Acceptance of Self, Expressed Acceptance of Others, and the MMPI." Abstract. *Am Psychol* 8:320–1 Ag '53. *

413. BITTERMAN, M. E., AND KNIFFIN, CALVIN W. "Manifest Anxiety and 'Perceptual Defense.' " *J Abn & Social Psychol* 48:248–52 Ap '53. * (*PA* 28:2266)

414. BLACK, JOHN DAVIES. *The Interpretation of MMPI Profiles of College Women.* Doctor's thesis, University of Minnesota (Minneapolis, Minn.), 1953. (*DA* 13:870)

415. BURGESS, ELVA. *Personality Factors in Over- and Under-Achievers in Engineering.* Doctor's thesis, Pennsylvania State College (State College, Pa.), 1953.

416. CALVIN, A. D., AND HOLTZMAN, WAYNE H. "Adjustment and the Discrepancy Between Self Concept and Inferred Self." *J Consult Psychol* 17:39–44 F '53. * (*PA* 28:932)

417. CALVIN, ALLEN, AND McCONNELL, JAMES. "Ellis on Personality Inventories." *J Consult Psychol* 17:462–4 D '53. * (*PA* 28:7513)

418. CAPWELL, DORA F. Study 1, "Personality Patterns of Adolescent Girls: Delinquents and Nondelinquents," pp. 29–37. In *Analyzing and Predicting Juvenile Delinquency With the MMPI.* Edited by Starke R. Hathaway and Elio D. Monachesi. Minneapolis, Minn.: University of Minnesota Press, 1953. Pp. viii, 153. * (*PA* 28:2970)

419. CLARK, J. H. "Grade Achievement of Female College Students in Relation to Non-Intellective Factors: MMPI Items." *J Social Psychol* 37:275–81 My '53. * (*PA* 28:3187)

420. CLARK, JERRY H. "Additional Applications of the AWOL Recidivist Scale." *J Clin Psychol* 9:62–4 Ja '53. * (*PA* 27:7914)

421. CLARK, JERRY H. "The Interpretation of the MMPI Profiles of College Students: A Comparison by College Major Subject." *J Clin Psychol* 9:382–4 O '53. * (*PA* 28:4915)

422. COHART, MARY S. *The Differential Value of the Group Rorschach and the MMPI in the Evaluation of Teacher Personality.* Doctor's thesis, Yale University (New Haven, Conn.), 1953.

423. COTTLE, WILLIAM C. *The MMPI: A Review.* Kansas Studies in Education, Vol. 3, No. 2. Lawrence, Kan.: University of Kansas Press, March 1953. Pp. vi, 82. *

424. DRAKE, L. E. "Differential Sex Responses to Items of the MMPI." *J Appl Psychol* 37:46 F '53. * (*PA* 28:937)

425. ELLIS, ALBERT. "Recent Research With Personality Inventories." *J Consult Psychol* 17:45–9 F '53. * (*PA* 28:939)

426. FELDMAN, MARVIN J. "The Effects of the Size of Criterion Groups and the Level of Significance in Selecting Test Items on the Validity of Tests." *Ed & Psychol Meas* 13:273–9 su '53. * (*PA* 28:3569)

427. FRICK, J. W. *The Prediction of Academic Achievement in a College Population From a Test of Aptitude and a Standardized Personality Inventory.* Master's thesis, University of Southern California (Los Angeles, Calif.), 1953.

428. GALLAGHER, JAMES J. "Manifest Anxiety Changes Concomitant With Client-Centered Therapy." *J Consult Psychol* 17:443–6 D '53. * (*PA* 28:7589)

429. GALLAGHER, JAMES J. "MMPI Changes Concomitant With Client-Centered Therapy." *J Consult Psychol* 17:334–8 O '53. * (*PA* 28:6100)

430. GANUNG, G. R. *A Study of Scholastic Achievement Related to Personality as Measured by the Minnesota Multiphasic Personality Inventory.* Master's thesis, Utah State Agricultural College (Logan, Utah), 1953.

431. GOUGH, HARRISON G. "Minnesota Multiphasic Personality Inventory," pp. 545–67. (*PA* 27:7769) In *Contributions Toward Medical Psychology: Theory and Psychodiagnostic Methods, Vol. II.* Edited by Arthur Weider. New York: Ronald Press Co., 1953. Pp. xi, 459–885. *

432. GRANICK, SAMUEL, AND SMITH, LEON J. "Sex Sequence in the Draw-a-Person Test and Its Relation to the MMPI Masculinity-Femininity Scale." *J Consult Psychol* 17:71–3 F '53. * (*PA* 28:950)

433. GULLION, MARY E. *An Elementary Teacher Attitude Study: Using an Inventory of Teacher Adjustment to Selected Problem Situations and the Minnesota Multiphasic Personality Inventory.* Master's thesis, University of Oregon (Eugene, Ore.), 1953.

434. HAMPTON, PETER JAN. "The Development of a Personality Questionnaire for Drinkers." *Genetic Psychol Monogr* 48:55–115 Ag '53. * (*PA* 28:4571)

435. HANES, BERNARD. *A Factor Analysis of MMPI, Aptitude Test Data and Personal Information Using a Population of Criminals.* Doctor's thesis, Ohio State University (Columbus, Ohio), 1953.

436. HANES, BERNARD. "Reading Ease and MMPI Results." *J Clin Psychol* 9:83–5 Ja '53. * (*PA* 27:7771)

437. HARDER, DONALD FREDERICK. *A Study of Item Responses on the Minnesota Multiphasic Personality Inventory of Male Senior Students in Business, Education, and Engineering Curricula.* Doctor's thesis, University of Kansas (Lawrence, Kan.), 1953.

438. HATHAWAY, STARKE R., AND MONACHESI, ELIO D., EDITORS. *Analyzing and Predicting Juvenile Delinquency With the MMPI.* Minneapolis, Minn.: University of Minnesota Press, 1953. Pp. viii, 153. * (*PA* 28:2970)

439. HATHAWAY, STARKE R.; HASTINGS, DONALD W.; CAPWELL, DORA F.; AND BELL, DOROTHY M. Study 5, "The Relationship Between MMPI Profiles and Later Careers of Juvenile

Delinquent Girls," pp. 70–86. In *Analyzing and Predicting Juvenile Delinquency With the MMPI*. Edited by Starke R. Hathaway and Elio D. Monachesi. Minneapolis, Minn.: University of Minnesota Press, 1953. Pp. viii, 153. * (PA 28:2970)

440. HATTON, ROBERT OLIVER. *Personality Patterns of Agricultural Extension Workers as Related to Selected Aspects of Work Adjustment*. Doctor's thesis, Michigan State College (East Lansing, Mich.), 1953. (DA 15:374)

441. HOLMES, W. O. *The Development of an Empirical MMPI Scale for Alcoholism*. Master's thesis, San Jose State College (San Jose, Calif.), 1953.

442. HOVEY, H. BIRNET. "MMPI Profiles and Personality Characteristics." *J Consult Psychol* 17:142–6 Ap '53. * (PA 28:2639)

443. HOVEY, H. BIRNET, AND STAUFFACHER, JAMES C. "Intuitive Versus Objective Prediction From a Test." *J Clin Psychol* 9:349–51 O '53. * (PA 28:4362)

444. LAUBER, MARGARET, AND DAHLSTROM, W. GRANT. Study 4, "MMPI Findings in the Rehabilitation of Delinquent Girls," pp. 61–9. In *Analyzing and Predicting Juvenile Delinquency With the MMPI*. Edited by Starke R. Hathaway and Elio D. Monachesi. Minneapolis, Minn.: University of Minnesota Press, 1953. Pp. viii, 153. * (PA 28:2970)

445. MACHOVER, SOLOMON, AND ANDERSON, HELEN J. "Validity of a Paper-and-Pencil Form of the MMPI Psychopathic Deviate Scale." *J Consult Psychol* 17:459–61 D '53. * (PA 28:7537)

446. MACLEAN, ANGUS G.; TAIT, ARTHUR T.; AND CATTERALL, CALVIN D. "The F Minus K Index on the MMPI." *J Appl Psychol* 37:315–6 Ag '53. * (PA 28:6044)

447. MILL, CYRIL R. "Personality Patterns of Sociometrically Selected and Sociometrically Rejected Male College Students." *Sociometry* 16:151–67 My '53. * (PA 28:4886)

448. REGAL, JACOB. *Pattern Analysis of the Minnesota Multiphasic Personality Inventory*. Doctor's thesis, University of California (Berkeley, Calif.), 1953.

449. RINNE, KONRAD WILLIAM. *A Differential Analysis of Various Group Responses to Characteristics of Personality as Measured by the Minnesota Multiphasic Personality Inventory*. Doctor's thesis, Indiana University (Bloomington, Ind.), 1953. (DA 13:1263)

450. RORABAUGH, MILDRED E., AND GUTHRIE, GEORGE. "The Personality Characteristics of Tuberculous Patients Who Leave the Tuberculosis Hospital Against Medical Advice." *Am R Tuberc* 67:432–9 Ap '53. * (DA 30:3275) *

451. ROSEN, ALBERT. "Test-Retest Stability of MMPI Scales for a Psychiatric Population." *J Consult Psychol* 17:217–21 Je '53. * (PA 27:2669)

452. SANDERSON, JAMES WESLEY. *An Evaluation of a Technique of Profile Classification for the Minnesota Multiphasic Personality Inventory*. Doctor's thesis, University of California (Berkeley, Calif.), 1953.

453. SCHMIDT, RICHARD H. H. *The Value of the Minnesota Multiphasic Personality Inventory in Assessing the Desirability of Dormitory Residences*. Doctor's thesis, Oklahoma Agricultural and Mechanical College (Stillwater, Okla.), 1953.

454. SCHOFIELD, WILLIAM. "A Further Study of the Effects of Therapies on MMPI Responses." *J Abn & Social Psychol* 48:67–77 Ja '53. * (PA 28:1075)

455. SCHOFIELD, WILLIAM. "A Study of Medical Students With the *MMPI*: I, Scale Norms and Profile Patterns." *J Psychol* 36:59–65 Jl '53. * (PA 28:3445)

456. SCHOFIELD, WILLIAM. "A Study of Medical Students With the *MMPI*: II, Group and Individual Changes After Two Years." *J Psychol* 36:137–41 Jl '53. * (PA 28:3446)

457. SCHOFIELD, WILLIAM. "A Study of Medical Students With the *MMPI*: III, Personality and Academic Success." *J Appl Psychol* 37:47–52 F '53. * (PA 28:1683)

458. SEEMAN, WILLIAM. "Concept of 'Subtlety' in Structured Psychiatric and Personality Tests: An Experimental Approach." *J Abn & Social Psychol* 48:239–47 Ap '53. * (PA 28:2674)

459. SKRINCOSKY, PETER C. *A Comparative Study of the Standard Form of the Minnesota Multiphasic Personality Inventory and a Modified Form of the Same Adapted for a Seminary Group*. Master's thesis, Fordham University (New York, N.Y.), 1953.

460. STERNBERG, CARL. "Differences in Measured Interest, Values, and Personality Among College Students Majoring in Nine Subject Areas." Abstract. *Am Psychol* 8:442–3 Ag '53. *

461. STERNBERG, CARL. *The Relation of Interests, Values and Personality to the Major Field of Study in College*. Doctor's thesis, New York University (New York, N.Y.), 1953. (DA 13:1095)

462. SWAN, ROBERT JUNIOR. *The Application of a Couple Analysis Approach to the Minnesota Multiphasic Personality Inventory in Marriage Counseling*. Doctor's thesis, University of Minnesota (Minneapolis, Minn.), 1953. (DA 13:1095)

463. SWEETLAND, ANDERS, AND QUAY, HERBERT. "A Note on the K Scale of the Minnesota Multiphasic Personality Inventory." *J Consult Psychol* 17:314–6 Ag '53. * (PA 28:4398)

464. SYDOW, DONALD WAYNE. *A Psychometric Differentiation Between Functional Psychotics and Non-Psychotics With Organic Brain Damage*. Doctor's thesis, University of Minnesota (Minneapolis, Minn.), 1953. (DA 13:1267)

465. TAYLOR, JANET A. "A Personality Scale of Manifest Anxiety." *J Abn & Social Psychol* 48:285–90 Ap '53. * (PA 28:2683)

466. TONNINGSEN, EDWARD L. *The Standardization of the Minnesota Multiphasic Personality Inventory on a Norm Group*

of High School Seniors. Master's thesis, University of California (Berkeley, Calif.), 1953.

467. TRUMBULL, RICHARD. "A Study of Relationships Between Factors of Personality and Intelligence." *J Social Psychol* 38:161–73 N '53. * (PA 28:5589)

468. TYDLASKA, MARY, AND MENGEL, ROBERT. "A Scale for Measuring Work Attitude for the MMPI." *J Appl Psychol* 37:474–7 D '53. * (PA 29:1662)

469. TYLER, FRED T., AND MICHAELIS, JOHN U. "A Comparison of Manual and College Norms for the MMPI." *J Appl Psychol* 37:273–5 Ag '53. * (PA 28:6057)

470. TYLER, FRED T., AND MICHAELIS, JOHN U. "K-Scores Applied to MMPI Scales for College Women." *Ed & Psychol Meas* 13:459–66 au '53. * (PA 28:4973)

471. WEST, LOUIS J. "Measurement of Changing Psychopathology With the Minnesota Multiphasic Personality Inventory." Discussion by Burtrum C. Schiele. *Am J Psychiatry* 109:922–8 Je '53. * (PA 28:2691)

472. WILLERMAN, BEN. "The Relation of Motivation and Skill to Active and Passive Participation in the Group." *J Appl Psychol* 37:387–90 O '53. * (PA 29:715)

473. WINFIELD, DON L. "The Relationship Between IQ Scores and Minnesota Multiphasic Personality Inventory Scores." *J Social Psychol* 38:299–300 N '53. * (PA 28:6063)

474. YOUNG, NORMAN, AND GAIER, EUGENE L. "A Preliminary Investigation Into the Prediction of Suggestibility From Selected Personality Variables." *J Social Psychol* 37:53–60 F '53. * (PA 28:571)

475. ZWETSCHKE, EARL THEODORE. *The Function of the MMPI in Determining Fitness for Student Teaching at the Nursery School, Kindergarten, and Primary School Level*. Doctor's thesis, University of Minnesota (Minneapolis, Minn.), 1953. (DA 14:500)

476. ABDEL-MEGUID, SAAD GALAL MOHAMED. *Delinquency Related to Personality, Intelligence, School Achievement, and Environmental Factors*. Doctor's thesis, Stanford University (Stanford, Calif.), 1954. (DA 14:1616)

477. ABRAMSON, HAROLD A., AND TIEGE, ERNA. "Minnesota Test as a Guide to Therapy in Multiple Sclerosis." *Ann NY Acad Sci* 58:648–55 Jl 28 '54. *

478. ARNDT, WILLIAM B. "Minnesota Multiphasic Personality Inventory: A Supplementary Method for Its Clinical Analysis." *Med Tech B* 5:267–8 N–D '54. *

479. AUMACK, LEWIS. "Misconceptions Concerning the Interpretation of Sub-Group Variations Within Normative Data." *J Psychol* 38:79–82 Jl '54. * (PA 29:3281)

480. AUSUBEL, DAVID P.; SCHIFF, HERBERT M.; AND ZELENY, MARJORIE P. "Validity of Teachers' Ratings of Adolescents' Adjustment and Aspirations." *J Ed Psychol* 45:394–406 N '54. * (PA 29:7981)

481. BRACKBILL, GLEN, AND LITTLE, KENNETH B. "MMPI Correlates of the Taylor Scale of Manifest Anxiety." *J Consult Psychol* 18:433–6 D '54. * (PA 29:7260)

482. BROIDA, DANIEL C. "An Investigation of Certain Psychodiagnostic Indications of Suicidal Tendencies and Depression in Mental Hospital Patients." *Psychiatric Q* 28:453–64 Jl '54. * (PA 29:6019)

483. BURDOCK, EUGENE I. *A Statistical Technique for the Isolation of Personality Types by Means of the Minnesota Multiphasic Personality Inventory*. Doctor's thesis, University of California (Los Angeles, Calif.), 1954.

484. CHAREN, SOL. "A Note on the Use of a Paper-and-Pencil Form of the MMPI *Hs* Scale for Hospital Use." Abstract. *J Consult Psychol* 18:344 O '54. *

485. CLARK, JERRY H. "The Interpretation of the *MMPI* Profiles of College Students: Mean Scores for Male and Female Groups." *J Social Psychol* 40:319–21 N '54. * (PA 20:7264)

486. CONNER, HAROLD THOMAS. *An Investigation of Certain Factors for the Selection and Guidance of Prospective Students Entering a School of Public Health*. Doctor's thesis, University of North Carolina (Chapel Hill, N.C.), 1954.

487. COOK, WALTER W., AND MEDLEY, DONALD M. "Proposed Hostility and Pharisaic-Virtue Scales for the MMPI." *J Appl Psychol* 38:414–8 D '54. * (PA 29:5694)

488. COTTLE, W. C., AND LEWIS, W. W., JR. "Personality Characteristics of Counselors: II, Male Counselor Responses to the MMPI and GZTS." *J Counsel Psychol* 1:27–30 F '54. * (PA 28:7476)

489. COTTLE, WILLIAM C. "Interest and Personality Inventories." *Personnel & Guid J* 33:162–7 N '54. * (PA 29:5695)

490. DAHLSTROM, W. GRANT. "Prediction of Adjustment After Neurosurgery." Abstract. *Am Psychol* 9:353–4 Ag '54. *

491. DOLEYS, E. J., JR. *The Validity of the Depression Scale of the MMPI*. Master's thesis, De Paul University (Chicago, Ill.), 1954.

492. DRAKE, L. E. "MMPI Profiles and Interview Behavior." *J Counsel Psychol* 1:92–5 su '54. * (PA 29:3012)

493. DYMOND, ROSALIND. "Interpersonal Perception and Marital Happiness." *Can J Psychol* 8:164–71 S '54. * (PA 29:3901)

494. ERIKSEN, CHARLES W. "Psychological Defenses and 'Ego Strength' in the Recall of Completed and Incompleted Tasks." *J Abn & Social Psychol* 49:45–50 Ja '54. * (PA 28:7217)

495. GALLAGHER, JAMES J. "Test Indicators for Therapy Prognosis." *J Consult Psychol* 18:409–13 D '54. * (PA 29:7356)

496. GLASSCOCK, EDWIN MOORE. *An Investigation of the Value of the Minnesota Multiphasic Personality Inventory as a*

Prognostic Instrument. Doctor's thesis, Washington University (St. Louis, Mo.), 1954. (*DA* 15:874)

497. GOLDBERG, SHEPHARD; HUNT, RAYMOND G.; COHEN, WALTER; AND MEADOW, ARNOLD. "Some Personality Correlates of Perceptual Distortion in the Direction of Group Conformity." Abstract. *Am Psychol* 9:378 Ag '54. *

498. GOODSTEIN, LEONARD D. "Regional Differences in MMPI Responses Among Male College Students." *J Consult Psychol* 18:437–41 D '54. * (*PA* 29:7279)

499. GOUGH, HARRISON G. "Some Common Misconceptions About Neuroticism." *J Consult Psychol* 18:287–92 Ag '54. * (*PA* 29:4468)

500. GREENE, EDWARD B. "Medical Reports and Selected MMPI Items Among Employed Adults." Abstract. *Am Psychol* 9:384 Ag '54. *

501. HANCOCK, JOHN W., AND CARTER, GERALD C. "Student Personality Traits and Curriculae of Enrollment." *J Ed Res* 48:225–7 N '54. * (*PA* 29:7909)

502. HATHAWAY, STARKE R., AND MONACHESI, ELIO D. "The Occurrence of Juvenile Delinquency With Patterns of Maladjustment as Exemplified in MMPI Profiles." Abstract. *Am Psychol* 9:391–2 Ag '54. *

503. HORGAN, JAMES FRANCIS. *A Comparison of the Relative Effectiveness of Prediction and Postdiction Methods in Assessing Ethnocentrism From Scores on the Minnesota Multiphasic Personality Inventory.* Doctor's thesis, University of Pittsburgh (Pittsburgh, Pa.), 1954. (*DA* 14:873)

504. HOVEY, H. BIRNET. "MMPI Aberration Potentials in a Nonclinical Group." *J Social Psychol* 40:299–307 N '54. * (*PA* 29:8156)

505. HOYT, DONALD P., AND NORMAN, WARREN T. "Adjustment and Academic Predictability." *J Counsel Psychol* 1:96–9 su '54. * (*PA* 29:3043)

506. KOSTLAN, ALBERT. "A Method for the Empirical Study of Psychodiagnosis." *J Consult Psychol* 18:83–8 Ap '54. * (*PA* 29:2415)

507. LAFORGE, ROLFE; LEARY, TIMOTHY F.; NABOISEK, HERBERT; COFFEY, HUBERT S.; AND FREEDMAN, MERVIN B. "The Interpersonal Dimension of Personality: II, An Objective Study of Repression." *J Personality* 23:129–53 D '54. * (*PA* 29:5313)

508. LA PLACE, JOHN P. "Personality and Its Relationship to Success in Professional Baseball." *Res Q* 25:313–9 S '54. *

509. LAYTON, WILBUR L. "The Variability of Individuals' Scores Upon Successive Testings on the Minnesota Multiphasic Personality Inventory." *Ed & Psychol Meas* 14:634–40 w '54. * (*PA* 29:7292)

510. LEVITT, EUGENE E. "A Note on the Welsh MMPI Anxiety Index." Abstract. *J Consult Psychol* 18:112 Ap '54. *

511. LITTLE, KENNETH B., AND SHNEIDMAN, EDWIN S. "The Validity of MMPI Interpretations." *J Consult Psychol* 18:425–8 D '54. * (*PA* 29:7295)

512. LOCKMAN, ROBERT F. "Some Relationships Between the MMPI and a Problem Checklist." *J Appl Psychol* 38:264–7 Ag '54. * (*PA* 29:5716)

513. McGEE, SHANNA. "Measurement of Hostility: A Pilot Study." *J Clin Psychol* 10:280–2 Jl '54. * (*PA* 29:2699)

514. MASTEJ, M. MARTINA. *A Study of the Influence of Religious Life on the Personality Adjustment of Religious Women as Measured by a Modified Form of the Minnesota Multiphasic Personality Inventory.* Doctor's thesis, Fordham University (New York, N.Y.), 1954.

515. MILLER, CHRISTINE. "Consistency of Cognitive Behavior as a Function of Personality Characteristics." *J Personality* 23:233–49 D '54. * (*PA* 29:5315)

516. MILLER, ROBERT S. *A Study of the Relationships Between MMPI Scales and GZTS Scales.* Master's thesis, University of Kansas (Lawrence, Kan.), 1954.

517. MILLS, WILLIAM WILLIS. *MMPI Profile Pattern and Scale Stability Throughout Four Years of College Attendance.* Doctor's thesis, University of Minnesota (Minneapolis, Minn.), 1954. (*DA* 14:1259)

518. NAVRAN, LESLIE. "A Rationally Derived MMPI Scale to Measure Dependence." Abstract. *J Consult Psychol* 18:192 Je '54. *

519. OLSON, GORDON W. "The Hastings Short Form of the Group MMPI." *J Clin Psychol* 10:386–8 O '54. * (*PA* 29:4078)

520. PEARSON, JOHN SUMNER. *Psychometric Correlates of Emotional Immaturity.* Doctor's thesis, University of Minnesota (Minneapolis, Minn.), 1954. (*DA* 14:2129)

521. PETERSON, DONALD R. "The Diagnosis of Subclinical Schizophrenia." *J Consult Psychol* 18:198–200 Je '54. * (*PA* 29:2821)

522. PETERSON, DONALD R. "Predicting Hospitalization of Psychiatric Outpatients." *J Abn & Social Psychol* 49:260–5 Ap '54. * (*PA* 29:1094)

523. PIERCE, KYLE KARR. *The Personality Inventory Correlates of the Level of Aspiration.* Doctor's thesis, University of Arizona (Tucson, Ariz.), 1954. (*DA* 14:1102)

524. PIERCE-JONES, JOHN. "The Readability of Certain Standard Tests." *Calif J Ed Res* 5:80–2 Mr '54. * (*PA* 28:8729)

525. QUAY, HERBERT, AND SWEETLAND, ANDERS. "The Relationship of the Rosenzweig PF Study to the MMPI." *J Clin Psychol* 10:296–7 Jl '54. * (*PA* 29:2464)

526. REGAL, JACOB M. *Pattern Analysis of the Minnesota Multiphasic Personality Inventory.* Doctor's thesis, University of California (Berkeley, Calif.), 1954.

527. ROESSEL, FRED PAUL. *Minnesota Multiphasic Personality Inventory Results for High School Drop-Outs and Gradu-*

ates. Doctor's thesis, University of Minnesota (Minneapolis, Minn.), 1954. (*DA* 14:942)

528. ROSEN, ALBERT; HALES, WILLIAM M.; AND SIMON, WERNER. "Classification of 'Suicidal' Patients." *J Consult Psychol* 18:359–62 O '54. * (*PA* 29:6040)

529. RUBIN, HAROLD. "Validity of a Critical-Item Scale for Schizophrenia on the MMPI." *J Consult Psychol* 18:219–20 Je '54. * (*PA* 29:2831)

530. SCHULTZ, STARLING DONALD. *A Differentiation of Several Forms of Hostility by Scales Empirically Constructed From Significant Items on the Minnesota Multiphasic Personality Inventory.* Doctor's thesis, Pennsylvania State University (University Park, Pa.), 1954.

531. SIMON, WERNER, AND GILBERSTADT, HAROLD. "Minnesota Multiphasic Personality Inventory Patterns Before and After Carbon Dioxide Inhalation Therapy." *J Nerv & Mental Dis* 119:523–9 Je '54. * (*PA* 29:4173)

532. SINGER, ARTHUR. "Social Competence and Success in Teaching." *J Exp Ed* 23:99–131 D '54. * (*PA* 29:8009)

533. TURBOVSKY, JOSEPH M. *Developing a Teaching Interest Scale from the Minnesota Multiphasic Personality Inventory.* Master's thesis, Fresno State College (Fresno, Calif.), 1954.

534. TYLER, FRED T. *The Prediction of Student-Teaching Success From Personality Inventories.* University of California, Publications in Education, Vol. 11, No. 4. Berkeley, Calif.: University of California Press, 1954. Pp. 233–313. * (*PA* 29:4709)

535. VAN DYKE, PAUL. *An Investigation of Self-Mutilation at the Texas Prison System in Terms of the Minnesota Multiphasic Personality Inventory and Other Measures.* Master's thesis, University of Texas (Austin, Tex.), 1954.

536. WALNUT, FRANCIS. "A Personality Inventory Item Analysis of Individuals Who Stutter and Individuals Who Have Other Handicaps." *J Speech & Hearing Dis* 19:220–7 Je '54. * (*PA* 29:4346)

537. WEISGERBER, CHARLES A. "Norms for the Minnesota Multiphasic Personality Inventory With Student Nurses." *J Clin Psychol* 10:192–4 Ap '54. * (*PA* 29:967)

538. WEXNER, LOIS B. "Relationship of Intelligence and the Nine Scales of the Minnesota Multiphasic Personality Inventory." *J Social Psychol* 40:173–6 Ag '54. * (*PA* 29:5734)

539. WILLIAMS, HAROLD L., AND LAWRENCE, JAMES F. "Comparison of the Rorschach and MMPI by Means of Factor Analysis." *J Consult Psychol* 18:193–7 Je '54. * (*PA* 29:2484)

540. WORSLEY, ROBERT. *An Investigation of the Minnesota Multiphasic Personality Inventory as a Device for Differentiating Parole Violators, Non-Violators, Burglars and Forgers.* Master's thesis, University of Texas (Austin, Tex.), 1954.

541. WRIGHT, STUART. "Some Personality Characteristics of Academic Underachievers." Abstract. *Am Psychol* 9:496 Ag '54. *

542. BARRON, FRANK, AND LEARY, TIMOTHY F. "Changes in Psychoneurotic Patients With and Without Psychotherapy." *J Consult Psychol* 19:239–45 Ag '55. * (*PA* 30:4616)

543. BARTELME, KENWOOD, AND RILEY, GORDON L. "A Study of Psychiatric Technicians on Selected Measures of Intelligence and Personality." Abstract. *Am Psychol* 10:321 Ag '55. *

544. BERGER, EMANUEL M. "Relationships Among Acceptance of Self, Acceptance of Others, and MMPI Scores." Comment by Victor Raimy. *J Counsel Psychol* 2:279–84 w '55. * (*PA* 31:1020)

545. BLOCK, JACK, AND THOMAS, HOBART. "Is Satisfaction With Self a Measure of Adjustment?" *J Abn & Social Psychol* 51:254–9 S '55. * (*PA* 30:4178)

546. BONK, EDWARD C. *Counseling Implications of the Minnesota Multiphasic Personality Inventory for Blind People in Selected Occupations.* Doctor's thesis, Indiana University (Bloomington, Ind.), 1955. (*DA* 15:2095)

547. BROTMAN, SANFORD. "An Investigation of Psychological and Physiological Factors Related to Rate or Recovery in Pulmonary Tuberculosis." Abstract. *Am Psychol* 10:362 Ag '55. *

548. BROZEK, JOSEF. "Personality Changes With Age: An Item Analysis of the Minnesota Multiphasic Personality Inventory." *J Gerontol* 10:194–206 Ap '55. * (*PA* 30:2587)

549. CALDEN, GEORGE; THURSTON, JOHN R.; STEWART, BARBARA M.; AND VINEBERG, SHALOM E. "The Use of the MMPI in Predicting Irregular Discharge Among Tuberculosis Patients." *J Clin Psychol* 11:374–7 O '55. * (*PA* 30:6203)

550. CANTOR, JOEL M. "A Brief Screening Scale for Psychopathological Patients Developed From MMPI Score-Patterning." *J Clin Psychol* 11:20–4 Ja '55. * (*PA* 29:7262)

551. CLARKE, S. C. T., AND McGREGOR, J. R. "Teachers' Adjustment and Teachers' Achievement in University Courses." *Can J Psychol* 9:55–8 Mr '55. * (*PA* 30:1641)

552. CONWELL, D. V.; KURTH, C. J.; AND MURPHY, PAUL G. "Use of Psychologic Tests in Determining Prognosis and Treatment in Geriatric Mental Illness." *J Am Geriatrics Soc* 3:232–8 Ap '55. *

553. COOK, WALTER W., AND MEDLEY, DONALD M. "The Relationship Between Minnesota Teacher Attitude Inventory Scores and Scores on Certain Scales of the Minnesota Multiphasic Personality Inventory." *J Appl Psychol* 39:123–9 Ap '55. * (*PA* 30:1642)

554. COOMBS, ROBERT WARREN. *The Appraisal of Personal Problems of High School Seniors.* Doctor's thesis, University of Southern California (Los Angeles, Calif.), 1955.

555. COOPER, MATTHEW NATHANIEL. *To Determine the Nature and Significance, If Any, of Certain Differences in the*

Social and Personal Adjustment of Fifty-One Successful and Fifty-One Non-Successful College Students at Texas Southern University. Doctor's thesis, New York University (New York, N.Y.), 1955. (DA 16:497)

556. CRADDICK, R. A. *MMPI Scores of Psychopathic and Non-Psychopathic Prisoners of a Provincial Gaol.* Master's thesis, University of Alberta (Edmonton, Alta., Canada), 1955.

557. DAHLSTROM, W. GRANT, AND WAHLER, H. J. "Application of Discriminant Function Techniques to Problems of Psychiatric Classification." Abstract. *Am Psychol* 10:478 Ag '55. *

558. ERIKSEN, CHARLES W., AND DAVIDS, ANTHONY. "The Meaning and Clinical Validity of the Taylor Anxiety Scale and the Hysteria-Psychasthenia Scales From the MMPI." *J Abn & Social Psychol* 50:135-7 Ja '55. * (PA 29:7273)

559. FREEDMAN, MERVIN B.; WEBSTER, HAROLD; AND SANFORD, NEVITT. "Some Psychodynamic Correlates of Authoritarianism in Women." Abstract. *Am Psychol* 10:341 Ag '55. *

560. FRICK, J. W. "Improving the Prediction of Academic Achievement by Use of the MMPI." *J Appl Psychol* 39:49-52 F '55. * (PA 30:1618)

561. GOWAN, J. C. "Relation of the 'K' Scale of the MMPI to the Teaching Personality." *Calif J Ed Res* 6:208-12 My '55. * (PA 30:6349)

562. GOWAN, J. C., AND GOWAN, MAY SEAGOE. "A Teacher Prognosis Scale for the MMPI." *J Ed Res* 49:1-12 S '55. * (PA 30:5261)

563. GRAYSON, HARRY M., AND OLINGER, LEONARD B. "Simulation of 'Normalcy' by Psychiatric Patients on Psychological Tests (MMPI)." Abstract. *Am Psychol* 10:332 Ag '55. *

564. HACKETT, HERBERT R. "Use of the MMPI to Predict College Achievement." *J Counsel Psychol* 2:68-9 sp '55. *

565. HALBOWER, CHARLES CARSON. *A Comparison of Actuarial Versus Clinical Prediction to Classes Descriminated by the Minnesota Multiphasic Personality Inventory.* Doctor's thesis, University of Minnesota (Minneapolis, Minn.), 1955. (DA 15:1115)

566. HANLEY, CHARLES. "Judged Social Desirability and Probability of Endorsement of Items on the MMPI Sc and D Scales." Abstract. *Am Psychol* 10:404-5 Ag '55. *

567. HECHT, SHIRLEY, AND KROEBER, THEODORE C. "A Study in Prediction of Attitudes of Patients Toward Brief Psychotherapy." Abstract. *Am Psychol* 10:370 Ag '55. *

568. HOLMES, JACK A. "Personality and Spelling Ability." Abstract. *Am Psychol* 10:353-4 Ag '55. *

569. HORLICK, REUBEN S. "The Discriminant Value of Minnesota Multiphasic Personality Inventory Items in Personality Disorders." *J Clin Psychol* 11:362-5 O '55. * (PA 30:5984)

570. JACOBS, ALFRED, AND LEVENTER, SEYMOUR. "Response to Personality Inventories With Situational Stress." *J Abn & Social Psychol* 51:449-51 N '55. * (PA 31:3041)

571. JOHNSTON, R. W. *Selection of Candidates for Adult Probation in Saskatchewan by the Use of a Biographical Questionnaire and the Minnesota Multiphasic Personality Inventory.* Master's thesis, University of Saskatchewan (Saskatoon, Sask., Canada), 1955.

572. KAMMAN, GORDON R., AND KRAM, CHARLES. "Value of Psychometric Examinations in Medical Diagnosis and Treatment." *J Am Med Assn* 158:556-60 Je 18 '55. * (PA 31:1044)

573. KAUFMAN, MELVIN. *The Formation of Learning Sets With Mentally Retarded Children.* Doctor's thesis, University of Pittsburgh (Pittsburgh, Pa.), 1955. (DA 16:156)

574. KOSTLAN, ALBERT. "A Reply to Patterson." *J Consult Psychol* 19:486 D '55. *

575. LABUE, ANTHONY C. "Personality Traits and Persistence of Interest in Teaching as a Vocational Choice." *J Appl Psychol* 39:362-5 O '55. * (PA 30:7783)

576. LAVER, A. B. *Item Analysis of the Minnesota Multiphasic Personality Inventory Against an Army Misconduct Criterion.* Master's thesis. Queen's University (Kingston, Ont., Canada), 1955.

577. LITTLE, KENNETH B., AND SHNEIDMAN, EDWIN S. "A Comparison of the Reliability of Interpretations of Four Psychological Tests." Abstract. *Am Psychol* 10:322 Ag '55. *

578. McQUARY, JOHN P., AND TRUAX, WILLIAM E., JR. "An Under-Achievement Scale." *J Ed Res* 48:393-9 Ja '55. * (PA 29:8997)

579. MAHLER, IRWIN. "Use of the MMPI With Student Nurses." *J Appl Psychol* 39:190-3 Je '55. * (PA 30:3657)

580. MARSH, JAMES T.; HILLIARD, JESSAMINE; AND LIECHTI, ROBERT. "A Sexual Deviation Scale for the MMPI." *J Consult Psychol* 19:55-9 F '55. * (PA 29:8644)

581. MATARAZZO, JOSEPH D. "MMPI Validity Scores as a Function of Increasing Levels of Anxiety." *J Consult Psychol* 19:213-7 Je '55. * (PA 30:2900)

582. MERRILL, REED M. "Relation of the Edwards Personal Preference Schedule to the Clinical and Experimental Scales of the MMPI." Abstract. *Am Psychol* 10:366 Ag '55. *

583. MILLER, ROBERT S., AND COTTLE, WILLIAM C. "Evidenced Relationships Between MMPI and GZTS Scales: An Adult Male Sample." *Univ Kans B Ed* 9:91-4 My '55. *

584. PAGE, HORACE; THURSTON, JOHN; NUTHMANN, CONRAD; CALDEN, GEORGE; AND LORENZ, THOMAS. "An Empirical Study of the Relationship of Four Classes of Body Habitus to Responses on the MMPI." *Psychol Rep* 1:159-65 S '55. * (PA 30:5770)

585. PATTERSON, C. H. "Diagnostic Accuracy or Diagnostic Stereotypy?" *J Consult Psychol* 19:483-5 D '55. * (PA 30:7171)

586. QUAY, HERBERT. "The Performance of Hospitalized Psychiatric Patients on the Ego-Strength Scale of the MMPI." *J Clin Psychol* 11:403-5 O '55. * (PA 30:6182)

587. QUAY, HERBERT, AND ROWELL, JOHN T. "The Validity of a Schizophrenic Screening Scale of the MMPI." *J Clin Psychol* 11:92-3 Ja '55. * (PA 29:7309)

588. REID, ALICE RUTH. *The Contribution of the Freshman Year of Physical Education in a Liberal Arts College for Women to Certain Personality Variables.* Doctor's thesis, State University of Iowa (Iowa City, Iowa), 1955. (DA 15:2091)

589. REITAN, RALPH M. "Affective Disturbances in Brain-Damaged Patients: Measurements With the Minnesota Multiphasic Personality Inventory." *A.M.A. Arch Neurol & Psychiatry* 73:530-2 My '55. * (PA 30:1436)

590. REMPEL, PETER. *The Use of Multivariate Statistical Analysis of Minnesota Multiphasic Personality Inventory Scores in the Classification of Delinquent and Nondelinquent High School Boys.* Doctor's thesis, University of Minnesota (Minneapolis, Minn.), 1955. (DA 15:1788)

591. ROSS, ALEXANDER T., AND REITAN, RALPH M. "Intellectual and Affective Functions in Multiple Sclerosis." *A.M.A. Arch Neurol & Psychiatry* 73:663-77 Je '55. * (PA 30:3319)

592. SHONTZ, FRANKLIN C. "MMPI Responses of Patients With Multiple Sclerosis." Abstract. *J Consult Psychol* 19:74 F '55. *

593. SMITH, ROBERT EDWARD. *Personality Configurations of Adult Male Penal Populations as Revealed by the Minnesota Multiphasic Personality Inventory.* Doctor's thesis, University of Minnesota (Minneapolis, Minn.), 1955. (DA 16:160)

594. SNYDER, WILLIAM U. "The Personality of Clinical Students." *J Counsel* 2:47-52 sp '52. * (PA 30:1182)

595. STANTON, JOHN M. *The Use of the Minnesota Multiphasic Personality Inventory to Determine the Group Personality Profile of State Prison Inmates and the Relation of Selected Aspects of Known Anti-Social Behavior to Profile Components.* Doctor's thesis, Fordham University (New York, N.Y.), 1955.

596. STATON, WESLEY M., AND RUTLEDGE, JOHN A. "Measurable Traits of Personality and Incidence of Somatic Illness Among College Students." *Res Q* 26:197-204 My '55. * (PA 30:1571)

597. STERNBERG, CARL. "Personality Trait Patterns of College Students Majoring in Different Fields." *Psychol Monogr* 69(18):1-21 '55. * (PA 31:1705)

598. STEWART, BARBARA M., AND VINEBERG, SHALOM E. "MMPI Characteristics of Hospitalized Tuberculosis Patients." Abstract. *Am Psychol* 10:361-2 Ag '55. *

599. THURSTON, DONALD REID. *An Investigation of the Possibilities of Parole Prediction Through the Use of Five Personality Inventories.* Doctor's thesis, Michigan State University (East Lansing, Mich.), 1955. (DA 15:1206)

600. WADSWORTH, HELEN MARY MAERTENS. *The Relationship Between Experimentally Induced Stress and the Characteristic Mode of Expression and Level of Anxiety.* Doctor's thesis, University of Michigan (Ann Arbor, Mich.), 1955. (DA 15:883)

601. WINDLE, CHARLES. "Further Studies of Test-Retest Effect on Personality Questionnaires." *Ed & Psychol Meas* 15:246-53 au '55. * (PA 30:4608)

602. WINDLE, CHARLES. "The Relationships Among Five MMPI 'Anxiety' Indices." *J Consult Psychol* 19:61-3 F '55. * (PA 29:8657)

603. WIRT, ROBERT D. "Further Validation of the Ego-Strength Scale." Abstract. *J Consult Psychol* 19:444 D '55. *

604. ANDERSON, WAYNE. "The MMPI: Low Pa Scores." *J Counsel Psychol* 3:226-8 fall '56. * (PA 31:7889)

605. ARBUCKLE, DUGALD S. "Client Perception of Counselor Personality." *J Counsel Psychol* 3:93-6 su '56. * (PA 31:4639)

606. BARNES, EUGENE H. "Factors, Response Bias, and the MMPI." *J Consult Psychol* 20:419-21 D '56. * (PA 32:1608)

607. BARNES, EUGENE H. "Response Bias and the MMPI." *J Consult Psychol* 20:371-4 O '56. * (PA 31:7892)

608. BARTHOL, RICHARD P., AND KIRK, BARBARA A. "The Selection of Graduate Students in Public Health Education." *J Appl Psychol* 40:159-63 Je '56. * (PA 31:6666)

609. BEALL, HERBERT S., AND PANTON, JAMES H. "Use of the Minnesota Multiphasic Personality Inventory as an Index to 'Escapism.'" *J Clin Psychol* 12:392-4 O '56. *

610. BEAVER, ALMA P. "Psychometric Data and Survival in a College of Nursing." *Psychol Rep* 2:223-6 Je '56. * (PA 31:1738)

611. BELLEVILLE, RICHARD E. "MMPI Score Changes Induced by Lysergic Acid Diethylamide (LSD-25)." *J Clin Psychol* 12:279-82 Jl '56. * (PA 31:6057)

612. BERNBERG, RAYMOND E. "Personality Correlates of Social Conformity: II." *J Social Psychol* 43:309-12 My '56. *

613. BORGHI, EUGENE. *A Study Comparing the Basic Personalities of the Mothers of Stuttering Sons with Mothers of Non-Stutterers as Measured by the MMPI.* Master's thesis, University of Redlands (Redlands, Calif.), 1956.

614. BURGESS, ELVA. "Personality Factors of Over- and Under-Achievers in Engineering." *J Ed Psychol* 47:89-99 F '56. * (PA 31:8811)

615. BUTTON, ALAN D. "A Study of Alcoholics With the Minnesota Multiphasic Personality Inventory." *Q J Studies Alcohol* 17:263-81 Je '56. (PA 31:6307)

616. CLARK, JERRY H., AND DANIELSON, JACK R. "A Shortened Schizophrenic Scale for Use in Rapid Screening." *J Social Psychol* 43:187-90 F '56. * (PA 31:3449)

617. COHN, THOMAS S. "The Relation of the F Scale to a Response Set to Answer Positively." *J Social Psychol* 44:129–33 Ag '56. *

618. COLE, DAVID L. "The Use of the MMPI and Biographical Data in Predicting Practice-Teaching Performance and Subsequent Attitudes Toward Teaching." Abstract. *Am Psychol* 11:367 Ag '56. *

619. DANSEREAU, RAYMOND A. *An Analysis of the Responses of Public and Private High School Students on the Minnesota Multiphasic Personality Inventory.* Doctor's thesis, Fordham University (New York, N.Y.), 1956.

620. DIDATO, S. VINCENT, AND KENNEDY, THOMAS M. "Masculinity-Femininity and Personal Values." *Psychol Rep* 2:231 Je '56. * (*PA* 31:608)

621. DRAKE, L. E. "Interpretation of MMPI Profiles in Counseling Male Clients." *J Counsel Psychol* 3:83–8 su '56. * (*PA* 31:4683)

622. EARLE, J. B. *The Development of a Quantitative Method for Differentiating Between Pathological Groups With the MMPI.* Doctor's thesis, University of Ottawa (Ottawa, Ont., Canada), 1956.

623. EVERSMEYER, GOLDA JOAN. *Personality, Stress, and Temporal Generalization.* Doctor's thesis, State University of Iowa (Iowa City, Iowa), 1956. (*DA* 16:1943)

624. FORDYCE, WILBERT E. "Social Desirability in the MMPI." *J Consult Psychol* 20:171–5 Je '56. * (*PA* 31:6076)

625. FREEDMAN, MERVIN; WEBSTER, HAROLD; AND SANFORD, NEVITT. "A Study of Authoritarianism and Psychopathology." *J Psychol* 41:315–22 Ap '56. * (*PA* 31:4688)

626. FRACK, J. W., AND KEENER, HELEN E. "A Validation Study of the Prediction of College Achievement." *J Appl Psychol* 40:251–2 Ag '56. * (*PA* 31:6674)

627. FRICKE, BENNO G. "Conversion Hysterics and the MMPI." *J Clin Psychol* 12:322–6 O '56. *

628. FRICKE, BENNO G. "Response Set as a Suppressor Variable in the OAIS and MMPI." *J Consult Psychol* 20:161–9 Je '56. * (*PA* 31:6080)

629. GASTON, CHARLES O.; TAULBEE, EARL S.; SEAQUIST, MAURICE R.; AND SELLS, SAUL B. "A Conversion Table for Relating the MMPI Group and Individual Form Items." *J Clin Psychol* 12:49–52 Ja '56. * (*PA* 30:4572)

630. GOODSTEIN, LEONARD D. "MMPI Profiles of Stutterers' Parents: A Follow-Up Study." *J Speech & Hearing Disorders* 21:430–5 D '56. * (*PA* 31:4903)

631. GOODSTEIN, LEONARD D., AND DAHLSTROM, W. GRANT. "MMPI Differences Between Parents of Stuttering and Nonstuttering Children." *J Consult Psychol* 20:365–70 O '56. * (*PA* 31:8387)

632. GOWAN, J. C. "Achievement and Personality Test Scores of Gifted College Students." *Calif J Ed Res* 7:105–9 My '56. * (*PA* 31:3783)

633. GREENFIELD, NORMAN S., AND FEY, WILLIAM F. "Factors Influencing Utilization of Psychotherapeutic Services in Male College Students." *J Clin Psychol* 12:276–9 Jl '56. * (*PA* 31:6653)

634. HAFNER, JAMES L. *Social Leadership as Related to the Minnesota Multiphasic Personality Inventory.* Doctor's thesis, Oklahoma Agricultural and Mechanical College (Stillwater, Okla.), 1956.

635. HANLEY, CHARLES. "Social Desirability and Responses to Items From Three MMPI Scales: D, Sc, and K." *J Appl Psychol* 40:323–8 O '56. * (*PA* 31:7920)

636. HARTSHORN, ELIZABETH. "A Comparison of Certain Aspects of Student Leadership and Non-Leadership; Significant Differences on Four Psychometric Tests." *J Ed Res* 49:515–22 Mr '56. * (*PA* 31:5098)

637. HEWER, VIVIAN H. "A Comparison of Successful and Unsuccessful Students in the Medical School at the University of Minnesota." *J Appl Psychol* 40:164–8 Je '56. * (*PA* 31:6675)

638. KANUM, CLARA. *Predicting Delinquency From the MMPI Using Items Instead of Clinical Scales.* Doctor's thesis, University of Minnesota (Minneapolis, Minn.), 1956. (*DA* 16:2547)

639. KARSON, SAMUEL, AND FREUD, SHELDON L. "Predicting Psychiatric Diagnoses With the MMPI." *J Clin Psychol* 12:376–9 O '56. *

640. KORNETSKY, CONAN, AND HUMPHRIES, OGRETTA. "The Relationship Between the Effects of a Number of Centrally Acting Drugs and Four MMPI Scales." Abstract. *Am Psychol* 11:366 Ag '56. *

641. LAVER, A. B. *Item Analysis of the Minnesota Multiphasic Personality Inventory.* Master's thesis, Queen's University (Kingston, Ont., Canada), 1956.

642. LEWINSOHN, PETER M. "Personality Correlates of Duodenal Ulcer and Other Psychosomatic Reactions." *J Clin Psychol* 12:296–8 Jl '56. * (*PA* 31:6484)

643. MEIER, MANFRED JOHN. *Interrelationships Among MMPI Variables, Kinesthetic Figural Aftereffect, and Reminiscence in Motor Learning.* Doctor's thesis, University of Wisconsin (Madison, Wis.), 1956. (*DA* 17:678)

644. MERRILL, REED M., AND HEATHERS, LOUISE B. "The Relation ot the MMPI to the Edwards Personal Preference Schedule on a College Counseling Center Sample." *J Consult Psychol* 20:310–4 Ag '56. * (*PA* 31:7949)

645. NELSON, MARVEN O., AND SHEA, SALLY. "MMPI Correlates of the Inventory of Factors STDCR." *Psychol Rep* 2:433–5 D '56. * (*PA* 31:4704)

646. OLMSTED, DONALD W., AND MONACHESI, ELIO D. "A

Validity Check on MMPI Scales of Responsibility and Dominance." *J Abn & Social Psychol* 53:140–2 Jl '56. * (*PA* 32:1638)

647. OSBORNE, R. T.; SANDERS, WILMA B.; AND YOUNG, FLORENE M. "MMPI Patterns of College Disciplinary Cases." *J Counsel Psychol* 3:52–6 sp '56. * (*PA* 31:3699)

648. PEEK, ROLAND M., AND STORMS, LOWELL H. "Validity of the Marsh-Hilliard-Liechti MMPI Sexual Deviation Scale in a State Hospital Population." *J Consult Psychol* 20:133–6 Ap '56. * (*PA* 31:6115)

649. POTHAST, MILES DALE. *A Personality Study of Two Types of Murderers.* Doctor's thesis, Michigan State University (East Lansing, Mich.), 1956. (*DA* 17:898)

650. PRAAG, JULES VAN. *A Rorschach and MMPI Study of a Fundamentalist Religious Sect.* Doctor's thesis, University of Denver (Denver, Colo.), 1956.

651. RAYMAKER, HENRY, JR. *Relationships Between the Self-Concept, Self-Ideal Concept and Maladjustment.* Doctor's thesis, Vanderbilt University (Nashville, Tenn.), 1956. (*DA* 17:409)

652. ROSEN, EPHRAIM. "Self-Appraisal and Perceived Desirability of MMPI Personality Traits." *J Counsel Psychol* 3:44–51 sp '56. * (*PA* 31:3070)

653. ROSEN, EPHRAIM. "Self-Appraisal, Personal Desirability, and Perceived Social Desirability of Personality Traits." *J Abn & Social Psychol* 52:151–8 Mr '56. * (*PA* 31:2568)

654. SARASON, IRWIN G. "The Relationship of Anxiety and 'Lack of Defensiveness' to Intellectual Performance." *J Consult Psychol* 20:220–2 Je '56. * (*PA* 31:5779)

655. SIEGEL, SAUL M. "The Relationship of Hostility to Authoritarianism." *J Abn & Social Psychol* 52:368–72 My '56. * (*PA* 31:4494)

656. SMITH, DAVID WAYNE. *The Relation Between Certain Physical Characteristics and Selected Scales of the Minnesota Multiphasic Personality Inventory.* Doctor's thesis, Indiana University (Bloomington, Ind.), 1956. (*DA* 16:1953)

657. SMITH, ROBERT E. "Personality Configurations of Adult Male Penal Populations as Revealed by the MMPI." Abstract. *Am Psychol* 11:382 Ag '56. *

658. SPILKA, BERNARD, AND STRUENING, E. L. "A Questionnaire Study of Personality and Ethnocentrism." *J Social Psychol* 44:65–71 Ag '56. *

659. STERNBERG, CARL. "Interests and Tendencies Toward Maladjustment in a Normal Population." *Personnel & Guid J* 35:94–9 O '56. * (*PA* 31:7975)

660. STONE, DAVID R., AND GANUNG, GEORGE R. "A Study of Scholastic Achievement Related to Personality as Measured by the Minnesota Multiphasic Personality Inventory." *J Ed Res* 50:155–6 O '56. * (*PA* 32:959)

661. STONE, DAVID R., AND WEST, LEROY L. " 'First Day' Orientation Testing With the Minnesota Multiphasic Personality Inventory Contrasted With a Re-Test." *J Ed Res* 49:621–4 Ap '56. * (*PA* 31:5152)

662. STRAIGHT, GLENN H. *Identifiable Personality Characteristics Resulting From Membership in a Conspicuous Religious Minority in Public High Schools.* Doctor's thesis, University of Nebraska (Lincoln, Neb.), 1956. (*DA* 17:810)

663. SUNDBERG, NORMAN D. "The Use of the MMPI for Cross-Cultural Personality Study: A Preliminary Report on the German Translation." *J Abn & Social Psychol* 52:281–3 Mr '56. * (*PA* 31:3083)

664. SUNDBERG, NORMAN D., AND BACHELIS, WARREN D. "The Fakability of Two Measures of Prejudice: The California F Scale and Gough's Pr Scale." *J Abn & Social Psychol* 52:140–2 Jl '56. * (*PA* 31:2757)

665. TESSENEER, RALPH, AND TYDLASKA, MARY. "A Cross-Validation of a Work Attitude Scale From the MMPI." *J Ed Psychol* 47:1–7 Ja '56. * (*PA* 31:6139)

666. THOMPSON, JORGEN SOGN. *A Study of the Relationships Between Certain Measured Psychological Variables and Achievement in the First Year of Theological Seminary Work.* Doctor's thesis, University of Minnesota (Minneapolis, Minn.), 1956. (*DA* 16:1846)

667. VOAS, ROBERT B. "Comparison of the Taylor Anxiety Scale Administered Separately and Within the MMPI." *Psychol Rep* 2:373–6 D '56. * (*PA* 31:4720)

668. WEINER, IRA W. "Psychological Factors Related to Results of Subtotal Gastrectomy." *Psychosom Med* 18:486–91 N–D '56. *

669. WELSH, GEORGE SCHLAGER, AND DAHLSTROM, W. GRANT, EDITORS. *Basic Readings on the MMPI in Psychology and Medicine.* Minneapolis, Minn.: University of Minnesota Press, 1956. Pp. xvii, 656. * (*PA* 31:1080)

670. WINTER, WILLIAM D., AND FREDERICKSON, WILBUR K. "The Short-Term Effect of Chlorpromazine on Psychiatric Patients." *J Consult Psychol* 20:431–4 D '56. * (*PA* 32:1876)

671. WIRT, ROBERT D. "Actuarial Prediction." *J Consult Psychol* 20:123–4 '56. * (*PA* 31:6037)

672. ZEAMAN, JEAN BURGDORF. *Some of the Personality Attributes Related to Achievement in College: A Comparison of Men and Women Students.* Doctor's thesis, Michigan State University (East Lansing, Mich.), 1956. (*DA* 18:290)

673. ZIMET, CARL N., AND BRACKBILL, GLEN A. "The Role of Anxiety in Psychodiagnosis." *J Clin Psychol* 12:173–7 Ap '56. * (*PA* 31:4722)

674. ADRIAN, ROBERT JOHN. *The Relationship of Parental Personality Structures to Child Adjustment and Adoption Selection.* Doctor's thesis, University of Minnesota (Minneapolis, Minn.), 1957. (*DA* 17:1386)

675. ALLEN, ROBERT M. "The Relationship Between the Ed-

wards Personal Preference Schedule Variables and the Minnesota Multiphasic Personality Inventory Scales." *J Appl Psychol* 41:307–11 O '57. *

676. BEIER, ERNST G.; GARFIELD, REED L.; AND ROSSI, ASCONIA M. "Projections of Personality Characteristics on Liked and Disliked Persons." Abstract. *Am Psychol* 12:372 Jl '57.

677. BRAMS, JEROME MARTIN. *The Relationship Between Personal Characteristics of Counseling Trainees and Effective Communication in Counseling.* Doctor's thesis, University of Missouri (Columbia, Mo.), 1957. (*DA* 17:1510)

678. BRAYFIELD, ARTHUR H., AND MARSH, MARY MARKLEY. "Aptitudes, Interests, and Personality Characteristics of Farmers." *J Appl Psychol* 41:98–103 Ap '57. *

679. BRUCE, MARTIN M. "Normative Data Information Exchange, No. 10-24." *Personnel Psychol* 10:357–8 au '57. *

680. CALVIN, ALLEN D., AND HANLEY, CHARLES. "An Investigation of Dissimulation on the MMPI by Means of the 'Lie Detector.'" *J Appl Psychol* 41:312–6 O '57. *

681. CHANSKY, NORMAN M., AND BREGMAN, MARTIN. "Improvement of Reading in College." *J Ed Res* 51:313–7 D '57. *

682. COMREY, ANDREW L. "A Factor Analysis of Items on the MMPI Depression Scale." *Ed & Psychol Meas* 17:578–85 w '57. *

683. COMREY, ANDREW L. "A Factor Analysis of Items on the MMPI Hypochondriasis Scale." *Ed & Psychol Meas* 17:568–77 w '57. *

684. COMREY, ANDREW L. "A Factor Analysis of Items on the MMPI Hysteria Scale." *Ed & Psychol Meas* 17:586–92 w '57. *

685. COMREY, ANDREW L. "Factors in the Items of the MMPI." Abstract. *Am Psychol* 12:437 Jl '57. *

686. CROW, W. R. *Relationships Between Edwards PPS and the MMPI.* Master's thesis, University of Washington (Seattle, Wash.), 1957.

687. DAHLSTROM, W. G., AND MEEHL, P. E. "Objective Configural Identification of Psychotic MMPI Profiles." Abstract. *Am Psychol* 12:367 Jl '57. *

688. DANA, RICHARD H. "MMPI Performance and Electroshock Treatment." *J Clin Psychol* 13:350–5 O '57. *

689. DEAN, SIDNEY I. "Adjustment Testing and Personality Factors of the Blind." *J Consult Psychol* 21:171–7 Ap '57. *

690. DRAKE, L. E., AND OETTING, EUGENE R. "An MMPI Pattern and a Suppressor Variable Predictive of Academic Achievement." *J Counsel Psychol* 4:245–7 fall '57. *

691. DRASGOW, JAMES, AND BARNETTE, W. LESLIE, JR. "F-K in a Motivated Group." *J Consult Psychol* 21:399–401 O '57. *

692. ENDS, EARL J., AND PAGE, CURTIS W. "A Study of Functional Relationships Among Measures of Anxiety, Ego Strength and Adjustment." *J Clin Psychol* 13:148–50 Ap '57. * (*PA* 32:3074)

693. FRICKE, BENNO G. "A Response Bias (B) Scale for the MMPI." *J Counsel Psychol* 4:149–53 su '57. *

694. FRICKE, BENNO G. "Subtle and Obvious Test Items and Response Set." *J Consult Psychol* 21:250–2 Je '57. *

695. GRAYSON, HARRY M., AND OLINGER, LEONARD B. "Simulation of 'Normalcy' by Psychiatric Patients on the MMPI." *J Consult Psychol* 21:73–7 F '57. * (*PA* 32:491)

696. HANLEY, CHARLES. "Deriving a Measure of Test-Taking Defensiveness." *J Consult Psychol* 21:391–7 O '57. *

697. HATHAWAY, STARKE R., AND BRIGGS, PETER F. "Some Normative Data on New MMPI Scales." *J Clin Psychol* 13:364–8 O '57. *

698. HOLZ, WILLIAM C.; HARDING, GEORGE F.; AND GLASSMAN, SIDNEY M. "A Note on the Clinical Validity of the Marsh-Hilliard-Liechti MMPI Sexual Deviation Scale." *J Consult Psychol* 21:326 Ag '57. *

699. JENSEN, ARTHUR R. "Authoritarian Attitudes and Personality Maladjustment." *J Abn & Social Psychol* 54:303–11 My '57. *

700. KARSON, SAMUEL, AND POOL, KENNETH BRYNER. "The Construct Validity of the Sixteen Personality Factors Test." *J Clin Psychol* 13:245–52 Jl '57. *

701. KIMBER, J. A. MORRIS. "An Alphabetical List of MMPI Items." *J Clin Psychol* 13:197–202 Ap '57. * (*PA* 32:2902)

702. LAIRD, JAMES T. "Emotional Disturbances Among the Physically Handicapped." *Personnel & Guid J* 36:190–1 N '57. *

703. LEARY, TIMOTHY. *Interpersonal Diagnosis of Personality: A Functional Theory and Methodology for Personality Evaluation.* New York: Ronald Press Co., 1957. Pp. xix, 518. (*PA* 31:2556)

704. LINGOES, JAMES C. "Minnesota Multiphasic Personality Inventory Test Correlates of Szondi Picture Preferences." *Szondi Newsl* 6:1–6 S '57. *

705. MAYO, GEORGE DOUGLAS, AND GUTTMAN, ISAIAH. "Faking in a Vocational Classification Situation." Abstract. *Am Psychol* 12:424 Jl '57. *

706. MILLER, ROBERT S., AND COTTLE, WILLIAM C. "Relationships Between MMPI Scales and GZTS Scales: An Adult Female Sample." *Univ Kans B Ed* 11:54–9 F '57. *

707. MOORE, CLARK H., AND COLE, DAVID. "The Relation of MMPI Scores to Practice Teaching Ratings." *J Ed Res* 50:711–6 My '57. *

708. MORRICE, J. K. W. "The Minnesota Multiphasic Personality Inventory in Recidivist Prisoners." *J Mental Sci* 103:632–5 Jl '57. *

709. MURPHY, DONAL GERALD. *Psychological Correlates of Alcohol Addictions.* Doctor's thesis, Columbia University (New York, N.Y.), 1957. (*DA* 18:1496)

710. NELSON, KENNETH G. "Use of the MMPI as a Predictor of High School Teacher Effectiveness." Abstract. *Am Psychol* 12:390 Jl '57. *

711. O'CONNOR, JAMES P.; STEFIC, EDWARD C.; AND GRESOCK, CLEMENT J. "Some Patterns of Depression." *J Clin Psychol* 13:122–5 Ap '57. * (*PA* 32:2914)

712. QUINN, STANLEY BRITTAIN. *Relationships of Certain Personality Characteristics to College Achievement.* Doctor's thesis, University of Wisconsin (Madison, Wis.), 1957. (*DA* 17:809)

713. REED, MAX R. "The Masculinity-Femininity Dimension in Normal and Psychotic Subjects." *J Abn & Social Psychol* 55:289–94 N '57. *

714. SCOTT, EDWARD M. "Personality and Movie Preference." *Psychol Rep* 3:17–8 Mr '57. *

715. SHELDON, M. STEPHEN. "The Fakability of Four MMPI Scales Used in Teacher Selection." Abstract. *Am Psychol* 12:390 Jl '57. *

716. SMITH, DAVID WAYNE. "The Relation Between Ratio Indices of Physique and Selected Scales of the Minnesota Multi-Phasic Personality Inventory." *J Psychol* 43:325–31 Ap '57. *

717. SOPCHAK, ANDREW L. "Relation Between MMPI Scores and Musical Projective Test Scores." *J Clin Psychol* 13:165–8 Ap '57. * (*PA* 32:2921)

718. SWAN, ROBERT J. "Using the MMPI in Marriage Counseling." *J Counsel Psychol* 4:239–44 fall '57. *

719. SYME, LEONARD. "Personality Characteristics and the Alcoholic: A Critique of Current Studies." *Q J Studies Alcohol* 18:288–302 Je '57. *

720. TAFT, RONALD. "A Cross-Cultural Comparison of the MMPI." *J Consult Psychol* 21:161–4 Ap '57. *

721. TAFT, RONALD. "The Validity of the Barron Ego-Strength Scale and the Welsh Anxiety Index." *J Consult Psychol* 21:247–9 Je '57. *

722. TAMKIN, ARTHUR S. "An Evaluation of the Construct Validity of Barron's Ego-Strength Scale." *J Clin Psychol* 21:156–8 Ap '57. * (*PA* 32:2923)

723. TAMKIN, ARTHUR S., AND SCHERER, ISIDOR W. "What Is Measured by the 'Cannot Say' Scale of the Group MMPI?" Abstract. *J Consult Psychol* 21:370 O '57. *

724. TAULBEE, EARL S., AND SISSON, BOYD D. "Configurational Analysis of MMPI Profiles of Psychiatric Groups." *J Consult Psychol* 21:413–7 O '57. *

725. TOPETZES, NICK JOHN. "A Program for the Selection of Trainees in Physical Medicine." *J Exp Ed* 25:263–311 Je '57. *

726. VOAS, ROBERT B. "Personality Correlates of Reading Speed and the Time Required to Complete Questionnaires." *Psychol Rep* 3:177–82 Je '57. *

727. VOAS, ROBERT B. "Validity of Personality Scales for the Prediction of Success in Naval Aviation Training." Abstract. *Am Psychol* 12:465 Jl '57. *

728. WATSON, GEORGE. "Vitamin Deficiencies in Mental Illness." *J Psychol* 43:47–63 Ja '57. *

729. YEOMANS, WILLIAM N., AND LUNDIN, ROBERT W. "The Relationship Between Personality Adjustment and Scholarship Achievement in Male College Students." *J General Psychol* 57:213–8 O '57. *

730. AARONSON, BERNARD S. "Age and Sex Influences on MMPI Profile Peak Distributions in an Abnormal Population." *J Consult Psychol* 22:203–6 Je '58. *

731. ALTUS, WILLIAM D. "Q-L Variability, MMPI Responses, and College Males." *J Consult Psychol* 22:367–71 O '58. *

732. BINDER, ARNOLD. "Personality Variables and Recognition Response Level." *J Abn & Social Psychol* 57:136–42 S '58. *

733. BOOTH, E. G., JR. "Personality Traits of Athletes as Measured by the MMPI." *Res Q* 29:127–38 My '58. *

734. BRIGGS, PETER F. "Prediction of Rehospitalization Using the MMPI." *J Clin Psychol* 14:83–4 Ja '58. *

735. COMREY, ANDREW L. "A Factor Analysis of Items on the F Scale of the MMPI." *Ed & Psychol Meas* 18:621–32 au '58. *

736. COMREY, ANDREW L. "A Factor Analysis of Items on the K Scale of the MMPI." *Ed & Psychol Meas* 18:633–9 au '58. *

737. COMREY, ANDREW L. "A Factor Analysis of Items on the MMPI Hypomania Scale." *Ed & Psychol Meas* 18:313–23 su '58. *

738. COMREY, ANDREW L. "A Factor Analysis of Items on the MMPI Paranoia Scale." *Ed & Psychol Meas* 18:99–107 sp '58. *

739. COMREY, ANDREW L. "A Factor Analysis of Items on the MMPI Psychasthenia Scale." *Ed & Psychol Meas* 18:293–300 su '58. *

740. COMREY, ANDREW L. "A Factor Analysis of Items on the MMPI Psychopathic Deviate Scale." *Ed & Psychol Meas* 18:91–8 sp '58. *

741. COMREY, ANDREW L., AND MARGGRAFF, WALTRAUD M. "A Factor Analysis of Items on the MMPI Schizophrenia Scale." *Ed & Psychol Meas* 18:301–11 su '58. *

742. DRASGOW, JAMES, AND MCKENZIE, JAMES. "College Transcripts, Graduation and the MMPI." *J Counsel Psychol* 5:196–9 fall '58. *

743. ERIKSEN, CHARLES W.; KUETHE, JAMES W.; AND SUL-

livan, Daniel F. "Some Personality Correlates of Learning Without Verbal Awareness." *J Personality* 26:216–28 Je '58. *

744. FELDMAN, MARVIN J. "An Evaluation Scale for Shock Therapy." *J Clin Psychol* 14:41–5 Ja '58. *

745. FINE, BERNARD J. "The Relationship Between Certain Scales of the Minnesota Multiphasic Personality Inventory and Susceptibility to Prestige Suggestion." *Psychol Newsl* 9:200–3 My–Je '58. *

746. GOWAN, J. C. "Intercorrelations and Factor Analysis of Tests Given to Teaching Candidates." *J Exp Ed* 27:1–22 S '58. *

747. GRAHAM, LEO R. "Personality Factors and Epileptic Seizures." *J Clin Psychol* 14:187–8 Ap '58. *

748. GREENFIELD, NORMAN S. "Personality Patterns of Patients Before and After Application for Psychotherapy." Abstract. *J Consult Psychol* 22:280 Ag '58. *

749. GRIFFITH, ALBERT V.; UPSHAW, HARRY S.; AND FOWLER, RAYMOND D. "The Psychasthenic and Hypomanic Scales of the MMPI and Uncertainty in Judgments." *J Clin Psychol* 14:385–6 O '58. *

750. HARDING, GEORGE F.; HOLZ, WILLIAM C.; AND KAWAKAMI, DANIEL. "The Differentiation of Schizophrenic and Superficially Similar Reactions." *J Clin Psychol* 14:147–9 Ap '58. *

751. HOYT, DONALD P., AND SEDLACEK, GORDON M. "Differentiating Alcoholics From Normals and Abnormals With the MMPI." *J Clin Psychol* 14:69–74 Ja '58. *

752. JACKSON, KARMA RAE, AND CLARK, SELBY G. "Thefts Among College Students." *Personnel & Guid J* 36:557–62 Ap '58. *

753. JENSEN, VERN H. "Influence of Personality Traits on Academic Success." *Personnel & Guid J* 36:497–500 Mr '58. *

754. KARSON, SAMUEL. "Second-Order Personality Factors and the MMPI." *J Clin Psychol* 14:313–5 Jl '58. *

755. LINDE, TOM, AND PATTERSON, C. H. "The MMPI in Cerebral Palsy." *J Consult Psychol* 22:210–2 Je '58. *

756. LITTLE, KENNETH B., AND FISHER, JEROME. "Two New Experimental Scales of the MMPI." *J Consult Psychol* 22:305–6 Ag '58. *

757. MCCALL, RAYMOND J. "Face Validity in the D Scale of the MMPI." *J Clin Psychol* 14:77–80 Ja '58. *

758. MEHLMAN, BENJAMIN, AND KAPLAN, JANICE E. "A Correction: A Comparison of Some Concepts of Psychological Health." *J Clin Psychol* 14:438 O '58. *

759. MELLO, NANCY K., AND GUTHRIE, GEORGE M. "MMPI Profiles and Behavior in Counseling." *J Counsel Psychol* 5:125–9 su '58. *

760. MOTTO, JOSEPH J. "The MMPI Performance of Veterans With Organic and Psychiatric Disabilities." Abstract. *J Consult Psychol* 22:304 Ag '58. *

761. PANTON, JAMES H. "MMPI Profile Characteristics of Physically Disabled Prison Inmates." *Psychol Rep* 4:529–30 S '58. *

762. PANTON, JAMES H. "MMPI Profile Configurations Among Crime Classification Groups." *J Clin Psychol* 14:305–8 Jl '58. *

763. PANTON, JAMES H. "Predicting Prison Adjustment With the Minnesota Multiphasic Personality Inventory." *J Clin Psychol* 14:308–12 Jl '58. *

764. PINNEAU, SAMUEL R., AND MILTON, ALEXANDER. "The Ecological Veracity of the Self-Report." *J Genetic Psychol* 93:249–76 D '58. *

765. PUMROY, DONALD K., AND KOGAN, WILLIAM S. "A Validation of Measures That Predict the Efficacy of Shock Therapy." *J Clin Psychol* 14:16–7 Ja '58. *

766. PUSTELL, THOMAS E. "A Note on Use of the MMPI in College Counseling." *J Counsel Psychol* 5:69–70 sp '58. *

767. REMPEL, PETER P. "The Use of Multivariate Statistical Analysis of Minnesota Multiphasic Personality Inventory Scores in the Classification of Delinquent and Nondelinquent High School Boys." *J Consult Psychol* 22:17–23 F '58. *

768. ROSEN, ALBERT; HALES, WILLIAM M.; AND PEEK, ROLAND M. "Comparability of MMPI Card and Booklet Forms for Psychiatric Patients." *J Clin Psychol* 14:387–8 O '58. *

769. SLOAN, THOMAS J., AND PIERCE-JONES, JOHN. "The Bordin-Peninsky Diagnostic Categories: Counselor Agreement and MMPI Comparisons." Comments by William A. Hunt. *J Counsel Psychol* 5:189–95 fall '58. *

770. SOPCHAK, ANDREW L. "Spearman Correlations Between MMPI Scores of College Students and Their Parents." *J Consult Psychol* 22:207–9 Je '58. *

771. SPILKA, B., AND KIMBLE, GLORIA. "Personality Correlates of Q-L Differentials on the ACE." Abstract. *J Consult Psychol* 22:142 Ap '58. *

772. SULLIVAN, PATRICK L.; MILLER, CHRISTINE; AND SMELSER, WILLIAM. "Factors in Length of Stay and Progress in Psychotherapy." *J Consult Psychol* 22:1–9 F '58. *

773. TARNAPOL, LESTER. "Personality Differences Between Leaders and Non-Leaders." *Personnel J* 37:57–60 Je '58. *

774. TAULBEE, EARL S. "Relationship Between Certain Personality Variables and Continuation in Psychotherapy." *J Consult Psychol* 22:83–9 Ap '58. *

775. TAULBEE, EARL S. "A Validation of MMPI Scale Pairs in Psychiatric Diagnosis." *J Clin Psychol* 14:316 Jl '58. *

776. VOAS, ROBERT B. "A Procedure for Reducing the Effects of Slanting Questionnaire Responses Toward Social Acceptability." *Ed & Psychol Meas* 18:337–45 su '58. *

777. WATTRON, JOHN B. "Validity of the Marsh-Hilliard-

Liechti MMPI Sexual Deviation Scale in a State Prison Population." Abstract. *J Consult Psychol* 22:16 F '58. *

778. WILCOX, GEORGE T. "Note on a Rapid Scoring Procedure for the Card Form MMPI." *J Clin Psychol* 14:85 Ja '58. *

779. WINTER, WILLIAM D., AND SALCINES, RAMON A. "The Validity of the Objective Rorschach and the MMPI." *J Consult Psychol* 22:199–202 Je '58. *

ALBERT ELLIS, *Consulting Psychologist, 333 West 56th St., New York 19, New York.*

Although there have been no significant changes in the format, administration, scoring, or interpretation of the MMPI itself since the revised manual and *Atlas* were issued in 1951, basic research with the instrument has continued apace, culminating in Hathaway and Monachesi's *Analyzing and Predicting Juvenile Delinquency with the MMPI* (438) and Welsh and Dahlstrom's *Basic Readings on the MMPI in Psychology and Medicine* (669). As a result of this continuing research, it can confidently be stated that in the whole history of modern psychology there has been no other personality inventory on which so much theoretical and practical work has been done.

In spite of all this research activity, the question of just how valid a clinical instrument the MMPI is has still not been finally settled. Calvin and McConnell (417), objecting vigorously to some general remarks on personality inventories made by the present reviewer (425), assayed 80 research studies in which the MMPI was used from 1940 to 1950 and reported that significant discriminations between different kinds of groups tested were found in 71 out of 80 studies. Calvin and McConnell's sample of research studies, however, is far from being complete. The reviewer found 160 studies employing the MMPI published between 1946 and 1951. Of these studies, 102 (64 per cent) showed significant discriminations. Of 339 research studies employing other personality inventories published during the same period, 188 (55 per cent) showed significant discriminations. Although it may be concluded, therefore, that the MMPI may be *more* valid for group discrimination than the average inventory, its *absolute* validity remains in doubt.

Assuming that the MMPI has some fair degree of validity for distinguishing one kind of group from another, the efficacy of its use for individual diagnosis still remains to be proved. As the manual attests, "a high score on a scale has been found to predict postively the corresponding final clinical diagnosis or estimate in more than 60 per cent of new psychiatric admissions." But the same manual also makes it

of a Group of Defective Delinquents." *Brit J Psychol, Gen Sect* 40:124–7 Mr '50. * *(PA* 24:5955)

5. RAVEN, J. C. "The Comparative Assessment of Personality." *Brit J Psychol, Gen Sect* 40:115–23 Mr '50. * *(PA* 24:5879)

6. KALDEGG, A. "A Study of German and English Teacher-Training Students by Means of Projective Techniques." *Brit J Psychol, Gen Sect* 42:56–113 Mr & My '51. * *(PA* 26:550)

7. MARTIN, A. W., AND WEIR, A. J. "A Comparative Study of the Drawings Made by Various Clinical Groups." *J Mental Sci* 97:532–44 Jl '51. * *(PA* 26:2189)

8. ANDERSON, J. W. " 'Controlled Projection' Responses of Delinquent Boys." *J Mental Sci* 100:643–56 Jl '54. * *(PA* 29:4349)

Brit J Ed Psychol 22:221 N '52. This is the second edition of the book first published in 1944. Since then the author has continued work on "Controlled Projection," and this edition takes account of that work and of recent investigations by other psychologists. The appendices contain a great mass of details (responses and reactions, etc.) by 150 school children and 80 children visiting Child Guidance Clinics. The author disclaims any pretence to give a comprehensive account of personality or of its measurement, but seeks chiefly to describe the technique and show its uses for genetic, social and clinical psychology.

Brit J Psychol 44:272 Ag '53. R. W. Pickford. * The test forms a useful method of research into the social attitudes, habits and personal relationships of children, and for examination of children for clinical purposes. It has been widely used and a number of interesting papers have been published about its application. The present edition is amplified in useful ways and contains some illustrations of children's drawings, beautifully reproduced, two of them in colour, tabulated responses of 150 children of ages 6½, 9½ and 12½ years, and a great amount of other valuable material obtained by the application of the test. *

Psychoanalytic Q 22:589–90 O '53. Geraldine Pederson-Krag. * Ideally the subject's responses are written down by a stenographer so as to allow the testing psychologist unimpeded opportunity to note the subject's behavior, but in practice it seems that the psychologist usually does his own recording. * All terms used are meticulously defined. The logic of the rules for scoring appears to be impeccable. The method seems to fulfil its goal which is to determine the extent to which each child tested resembles others in its group. It can also be used to show similarities and differences among various groups. It is perhaps irrelevant to criticize this book for its failure to reach objectives it does not seek. It may, however, be observed that the concepts and classifications upon which this technique is based are too loose and superficial to be useful to those

schooled in psychoanalysis. Though the material gathered by the spontaneous drawings and the answers to specific questions on intimate subjects is rich, the interpretation given according to the directions cited here is confused and meager.

For reviews by Arthur L. Benton and Percival M. Symonds of the original edition, see 3:29.

[128]

★**Curtis Completion Form.** Grades 11–16 and adults; 1950–53; emotional maturity and adjustment; Form A ('50); manual ('53); $2 per 20 tests; 25¢ per specimen set; postage extra; (45) minutes; James W. Curtis; Science Research Associates. *

REFERENCE

1. WATSON, WALTER S. "The Validity of the Curtis Completion Form as a Predictor of College Student Personality Deviates." *Yearb Nat Council Meas Used Ed* 12(pt 2):82–5 '55. *

ALFRED B. HEILBRUN, JR., *Assistant Professor of Psychology, State University of Iowa, Iowa City, Iowa.*

This 52-item sentence completion test combines features of both objective and projective personality measures. The first 50 items are in the form characteristic of the usual completion task: set-producing words followed by space for the free response. Items 51 and 52 are more highly structured but still allow the subject to formulate his own answer. Space is provided at the end of the form for remarks which the subject considers important.

Although the item format does not differ much from that of many other published sentence completion tests, the *Curtis Completion Form* retains some individuality in the manner in which the items were developed and the way in which they are scored. Evaluation of the responses is partially objective, making possible the derivation of a cumulative point score which serves as the primary basis for personality inferences. This contrasts with the usual method in which the examiner makes his appraisal of the responder through more intuitive clinical judgments of the free responses. Each item is given a score of 2, 1, or 0, with a higher score indicative of poorer emotional adjustment. Two points are assigned to responses characterized by antagonism, suspicion, jealousy, self-pity or pessimism, insecurity, social inadequacy, environmental deprivation, or severe conflict (Group A factors). Unclear, incomplete, or avoidant sentences (Group B factors) receive a score of 1, as do responses containing erasures, crossed-out content, or emphatic punctuation (Group C factors). The remarks section at the end is eval-

uated for Group A factors only, and a 4-point weight is assigned if any are judged to be present. Curtis reports rather high agreement when pairs of judges scored independently the same tests; interjudge correlations ranged from .89 to .95.

The only validation data which could be found are those reported in the manual. The following mean scores were obtained for three groups rated as showing substantial differences in adjustment by clinical personnel: normals, 22.6; neurotics, 37.0; and psychotics, 49.5. These results, if replicable, would lend a great deal of confidence to the use of the instrument in making this kind of gross discrimination.

Even though it is designed primarily for educational and industrial use, there is nothing about the test which precludes a wider range of application. The reported low correlation with intelligence, .09, is advantageous in this kind of measure. On the other hand, some caution is suggested by the split-half reliability coefficient of .83 which is not out of line with most personality measures but still leaves something to be desired. There is much in the development and limited validational data to recommend the clinical and research use of the *Curtis Completion Form,* but as with all new psychometric procedures reasonable caution should be maintained until further studies substantiate its effectiveness.

[129]

★**Draw-A-Person Quality Scale.** Ages 16–25; 1955; level of intellectual functioning; 1 form; $2 per manual, postpaid; [10–20] minutes; Mazie Earle Wagner and Herman J. P. Schubert; Herman J. P. Schubert, 500 Klein Road, Route 2, Buffalo 21, N.Y. *

REFERENCES

1. WAGNER, MAZIE EARLE, AND SCHUBERT, HERMAN J. P. "Figure Drawing Norms, Reliability, and Validity Indices for Normal Late-Adolescents: II, Development of a Pictorial Scale of DAP Quality." Abstract. *Am Psychol* 10:321 Ag '55. *
2. SCHUBERT, HERMAN J. P., AND WAGNER, MAZIE EARLE. "Deviant Perspective of DAP Figures Associated With Other Deviant Behavior." Abstract. *Am Psychol* 12:409–10 Jl '57. *
3. WAGNER, MAZIE EARLE, AND SCHUBERT, HERMAN J. P. "Atypical DAP Page Placement as an Indication of Atypical Behavior." Abstract. *Am Psychol* 12:389 Jl '57. *

PHILIP L. HARRIMAN, *Professor of Psychology, Bucknell University, Lewisburg, Pennsylvania.*

The authors evidently regard the Goodenough draw-a-man scale as meritorious but atomistic. It can be inferred that they also believe that the Machover technique does not fill the need for a "global test"—a drawing test in which the total final impression is rated. The Wagner-Schubert scale requires two drawings, one of each sex, which are rated in terms of a seven-point quality scale. Any production which emphasizes such details as toe nails, genitalia, or other representations indicating mental disturbances is arbitrarily relegated to Quality 8. Attention is concentrated upon qualities ranging from artistic, life-like human figures (Scale Value 1) to figures which are barely recognizable as human beings (Scale Value 7). Additional gradations at 0 and 8 are also described for productions as superior or inferior in quality that they are almost never found in "normal populations."

Guidance in estimating the quality of the productions is given by four series of rated pictorial specimens, front view and side view each for male and female. These typical drawings were chosen from 1,579 specimens collected from normal late adolescents and college students. In fact, this scale purports to deal only with gradations in the quality of drawings done by normal young persons. It also purports to furnish a basis for a quantification of the rater's impressionistic evaluation of each production. The authors imply that the numerical score on this test is a reasonably useful measure of academic aptitude for college work.

Obviously, the test has merit as a measure of aptitude for freehand drawing of the human figure. The authors, however, are most impressed with its use as a predictor of marks in a teachers college. Though they strive to maintain an austere point of view regarding clinical insights, they make one interesting comment of an intuitive nature. High-quality productions, they observe, may indicate conformity behavior, and college teachers—in some places, at least—regard it by assigning high marks. Caricatures of the human figure, as well as drawings of a figure with a glass in hand, are said to presage low marks at the end of the term. Steig and Adams, rated by this scale, would stand little chance for success in the elementary-education curriculum where this test was standardized.

Young adults who are facile in drawing the human figure are not dolts. Consequently, it occasions no surprise to find that many who achieve a high rating on this scale are also successful in a teachers college. This association between freehand-drawing quality and marks at the end of one term in a teachers college is to be expected. The fact, once admitted, does not obviate the need for the College Board or the American Council tests as the appropriate predictors. This initial and exploratory report on some in-

teresting research, however, is a rather important supplement to draw-a-person techniques. This reviewer wishes that the authors had not imposed upon themselves a rigid hostility towards clinical intuitions. It does seem a bit doubtful whether they have succeeded in "bringing back the drawing-of-a-person into the focus of attention of those who wish to predict human behavior."

A considerable amount of study would be required to develop a coherent and tenable theory for this test. Its publication at this time seems to be premature. In cases where human welfare is involved, the *Draw-A-Person Quality Scale* is contraindicated. The hackneyed phrase of many other reviewers of novel projective techniques is pertinent here: Much further research should be done.

[130]

★The Drawing-Completion Test: A Projective Technique for the Investigation of Personality. Ages 5 and over; 1952; based on *Wartegg Test Blank;* 1 form ['52]; manual (see *1* below); no data on reliability; $3 per 100 tests; $3 per 100 profiles ['52]; $7.50 per manual; postage extra; (15–40) minutes; G. Marian Kinget; Grune & Stratton, Inc. *

REFERENCES

1. KINGET, G. MARIAN. *The Drawing-Completion Test: A Projective Technique for the Investigation of Personality Based on the Wartegg Test Blank.* New York: Grune & Stratton, Inc., 1952. Pp. xv, 238. * (*PA* 27:430)
2. OLSON, JOHN T. *The Test-Retest Reliability of the Kinget Drawing-Completion Test.* Master's thesis, Fresno State College (Fresno, Calif.), 1956.
3. KINGET, G. MARIAN. Chap. 15, "The Drawing Completion Test," pp. 344–64. In *The Clinical Application of Projective Techniques.* Edited by Emanuel F. Hammer. Springfield, Ill.: Charles C Thomas, 1958. Pp. xxii, 663. *

Am J Psychol 66:669–70 O '53. John P. Foley, Jr. * No objective norms are reported. In discussing the interpretation of scores, Kinget reverts to the usual vague and subjective statements which have plagued most projective tests for many years. The validation sample is described as consisting of 383 adults, between the ages of 18 and 50; presumably, all were Europeans. The criterion data were obtained by: (1) a self-report inventory, (2) a forced-choice test, and (3) a rating scale filled out by friends and acquaintances of the *S*s. One searches in vain for an adequate report of the procedures employed in analyzing these data. Despite Symonds' statement, in the *Foreword,* that he is impressed by "the criterion against which she determined the significance of each element of the drawings" (p. v), no objective method is described whereby the criterion status of each *S* was determined. After pointing out (p. 21) that there was considerable lack of agreement among the three criterion measures,

Kinget rejected any attempt to arrive at a composite criterion in favor of a criterion based upon "the main trends manifested" in the three criterion measures. There is no indication of the degree of consistency necessary to constitute a "main trend." Here, then, we are confronted with a highly subjective instrument. Until such time as more objective scoring procedures are developed, and until the validity of the test has been more clearly established, it is virtually worthless as a measuring instrument. For these reasons, the unqualified and popularized account of this test in such a magazine as *Life* (June 9, 1952, p. 65 ff.) would seem to be premature and misleading.

B Menninger Clinic 17:114 My '53. Walter Kass. Similar to the Horn-Hellersberg method, this projective drawing completion technique is briefer (containing only 8 stimulus frames), easier therefore to administer, and also more readily interpretable according to the rationale supplied by the author. It is offered as a means of analyzing certain structural and functional aspects of personality. Since psychopathologic conditions were not included in its validation, it is not immediately applicable as a clinical test. But, as with other drawing products, diagnostic inferences are possible. The ingenuity of its small graphic stimulus elements, the brevity of its format, and the richness of the productions it elicits, presage a popularity for this test as a research instrument applicable to clinical populations.

J Ed Psychol 44:251–3 Ap '53. Goldine C. Gleser. * It is particularly gratifying to note that the scoring for the Drawing-completion test was established on the basis of an investigation of three hundred eighty-three "normal" subjects, divided about equally between the sexes, and ranging in age from eighteen to fifty years. A three-fold criterion was used, consisting of a questionnaire, a forced-choice test, and a rating scale, all designed expressly to measure the psychological functions represented in the personality schema. However, apparently the author has employed the questionable expedient of using the same data both for validation of the test and for subsequent changes and elaboration of the scoring system. Thus the diagnostic value of the final scoring variables as presented in this book cannot be considered to have been validated. Part two of the book, entitled "The Diagnostic Mechanism," presents the method of administration, the basis for interpretation, and

the scoring procedure for the test. This is the most extensive portion of the book. Each scoring category is defined and discussed in terms of the personality characteristics which it is claimed that it reveals or indicates. In these interpretations, the author appears to have allowed her enthusiasm to carry her far beyond the personality schema previously presented. * The author is to be congratulated for having designed a projective test which can be scored on objective criteria and for having attempted to establish the scoring on the basis of experimental evidence. However, as a test manual, this book leaves much to be desired. At least three major omissions make it impossible to evaluate the usefulness of the test, or to take advantage of the underlying experimental data in utilizing the test. In the first place, almost no statistical data are presented; in fact, the only results presented from the experimental study are the percentages of agreement between the three-fold criterion and the drawing test on three of the four functions measured. It appears from the text that the stated agreement was computed solely on the relative weight of the polar aspects of these functions; i.e., whether the person was more outgoing than seclusive, etc. However, it is impossible to ascertain the exact method by which the results were obtained, or their statistical significance. The only facts which are evident are that there was a greater amount of agreement among the tests for the females than for the males, and for both sexes the validity was lower for Emotion and Activity than for Intellect. Considering the enormous amount of work which has evidently gone into the investigation of relationships between personality and drawing characteristics, it is unfortunate that the author did not deem it practical to present a more complete summary of results in this manual, nor make it available in published form elsewhere. The second omission is that the author has made no attempt to provide any norms for the profile scores. She excuses this omission on the ground that "free drawings, like all products of creative activity, do not permit establishment of rigorous norms." However, in the case studies remarks such as the following are made: "The degree of Emotion and Imagination exhibited here is exceptional for a male, though admissible at the age level of A." It is evident that without some idea of what is "normal" for a given age and sex it would be difficult to draw such conclusions, and hence norms are implied

even though they are not presented. Lastly, no data are presented regarding the reliability of the external criteria used in developing the qualitative interpretations of the various scoring categories. This is particularly important, since these interpretations were derived from study of clusters of items and even differential responses to single items in the criterion tests (page 24). As a preliminary manual to aid in the attainment of standard administration and scoring procedures and some common basis of interpretation this book should be of service to those who may wish to do research on this test. However, it is hoped that other material in the form of norms and validity data will soon be made available to aid the clinician in his interpretation of the drawings and his evaluation of the usefulness of the test.

J Proj Tech 17:367–8 S '53. Fred Brown. * Much work and thought have gone into the construction and validation of this test, but the psychodynamically oriented and sophisticated clinician will be disappointed with a technique which follows an outmoded typology. The author states that it is not her intention to offer a depth exploring instrument, but the critical reader will then wonder why she uses the term "diagnosis" so often. Psychoanalytically trained clinicians, accustomed and attuned to the depth implications of other methods, will look in vain for the dynamic material which gives diagnosis as such its intrinsic significance. They will find, instead, diffuse categorizations, trait-name listings, and philosophically attenuated descriptions which possess only the remotest significance for an integrated diagnostic formulation. One would be inclined to take issue with the typological schema itself as a base of operations, especially when it is noted that the author herself seems to be committed to unconfirmed generalizations and stereotypes (e.g., "The remaining stimuli....have the round and supple character of the organic world which generally appeals more to the predominantly emotional-imaginative character of the feminine mind," p. 125). Such terms as "nature-relatedness," "life-relatedness," and "esthetic-emotional" would seem to have slight value for the clinician who maintains a psychologist-psychiatrist relationship and who is interested in delineating the personality and character structure in terms of psychosexual levels, areas of arrest and/or regression, predominant figures, defenses, conflicts, and diagnostic formulation. Study of the case illustrations makes

one doubt whether the results of a very detailed, highly refined, and time-consuming evaluative procedure are sufficiently rewarding. At the very least, the personality profiles impress one as markedly intellectualistic and over-abstract. The author is undoubtedly familiar with other projective methods and the current trend in American psychiatry and clinical psychology. Her orientation in this work does not reflect this knowledge. Apart from these criticisms, the psychologist who works with graphic projective and expressive techniques will find much that is thought-provoking in the author's detailed explanations of her variables. Shrewd insights, based upon the structural aspects of the drawings, may well be utilized in the interpretation of other drawing tests. But while the Drawing-Completion Test has heuristic and research potentialities, its immediate acceptance as a member of the practicing psychologist's test battery is contraindicated by its narrow and obsolete typological foundation.

[131]

★**The Eight Card Redrawing Test (8CRT).** Ages 7 and over; 1950–57; 1 form ('56); directions for administering ('56); no data on reliability; no norms; $6 per set of test materials; $4.50 per manual ('57, see 5 below); postpaid; (30–60) minutes; Leopold Caligor; 8CRT. *

REFERENCES

1. CALIGOR, LEOPOLD. *The Determination of the Individual's Unconscious Conception of His Own Masculinity-Femininity Identification.* Doctor's thesis, New York University (New York, N.Y.), 1950. (*Microfilm Abstr* 10:292)
2. CALIGOR, LEOPOLD. "The Determination of the Individual's Unconscious Conception of His Own Masculinity-Femininity Identification." *J Proj Tech* 15:494–509 D '51. * (*PA* 26:6228)
3. CALIGOR, LEOPOLD. "The Detection of Paranoid Trends by the Eight Card Redrawing Test." *J Clin Psychol* 8:397–401 O '52. * (*PA* 27:5861)
4. CALIGOR, LEOPOLD. "Quantification on the Eight Card Redrawing Test (8CRT)." *J Clin Psychol* 9:356–61 O '53. * (*PA* 28:4338)
5. CALIGOR, LEOPOLD. *A New Approach to Figure Drawing: Based Upon an Interrelated Series of Drawings.* Springfield, Ill.: Charles C Thomas, 1957. Pp. xii, 149. * (*PA* 31:7902)
6. HAMMER, EMANUEL F., EDITOR. *The Clinical Application of Projective Drawings,* pp. 418–34, 459–70, passim. Springfield, Ill.: Charles C Thomas, 1958. Pp. xxii, 663. *

CHERRY ANN CLARK, *The Meyers Clinic, Los Angeles, California.*

The *Eight Card Redrawing Test* (8 CRT) is another variation on the projective method of figure drawing. The test requires the subject to draw successively eight human figures, using a special drawing pad in which a blank cardboard is interleafed to block from the subject's view all but the immediately preceding drawing. *A New Approach to Figure Drawing* is not a formal test manual, but the author does refer to it as a manual in his development of the scoring rules. Caligor writes that the book is intended "(1) to describe each of the test's scoring di-

mensions in detail; (2) to formulate a tentative definition of each dimension's personality implications, and (3) to demonstrate to the experienced clinician how the integration of the presently delineated structural dimensions and cumulative, interrelated graphic content can yield a personality picture."

Over a period of about 10 years Caligor has evolved a rather complex scoring system to analyze the structural aspects of the series of eight interrelated figure drawings. He asserts that his method of analysis leads to more stable test-retest evaluation than does content analysis of drawings. The assertion seems plausible, but the available evidence is unconvincing.

Caligor attempted to demonstrate the interscorer reliability of three trained judges, using an inspection technique to diagnose paranoid schizophrenic characteristics in drawings done by hospitalized paranoid schizophrenics. Using but one drawing per subject, the judges found 25 per cent of them showing strong paranoid trends; using the 8 CRT, the same judges found 85 per cent showing paranoid trends. With no further support than this single inadequate instance, the author writes, "This study affirmed that the 8 CRT could prove valuable to the clinician, especially within the context of a battery of tests."

As a demonstration that the 8 CRT lends itself to objective quantification, Caligor cites two examples: drawings can be scored for sex of figure and its physical maturity, placing the subject on a 7-point scale ranging from adult identification with one's own sex through infantile undifferentiated sexual identification to adult identification with the opposite sex. On the basis of the evidence, the validity of these claims is unsupported.

Equally unconvincing is the evidence offered for the relevance of the scoring system. Using "clinical experience and pilot studies," the author devised deviation scores "from a statistical norm approximating the mode scores of normal subjects." The scoring system thus devised was found to differentiate satisfactorily college students (with scores ranging from 0 to 6) from hospitalized schizophrenic patients (with scores ranging from 6 to 66).

These three studies which allegedly demonstrate the psychodiagnostic merits of the techniques are unacceptable evidence beyond the level of clinical intuition.

Caligor describes in detail the scoring dimen-

sions. Dimensions are scored in three groups: along a graded scale, by placement within one of a group of categories, and for presence or absence. Among the dimensions scored are part-whole relations, height of figure, page placement, head and body direction, sex, physical maturity, erasures, line quality, symmetry, eyes, and omissions. Four masks for scoring body angle, figure placement and symmetry are included among the test materials.

The scoring system based upon the successive, interrelated sampling of performance on figure drawings is an ingenious one, but the reviewer questions the relevance and practicality of the procedure after repeated failures to maintain patients' cooperation for the complete administration of the test. In an informal study, no better planned than those reported by Caligor, the reviewer failed to gain agreement of even two out of five clinical psychologists in scoring the protocols of 11 willing subjects on two or more dimensions within any set of drawings.

As a diagnostic technique the 8 CRT has scarcely got off the drawing board. In the reviewer's mind it cannot be said to meet even minimal standards of test development for psychodiagnostic techniques. Only three studies of a decidedly clinical and intuitive nature are reported in the book. These studies are interesting as far as they go, but the adequacy of the experimental methodology employed in them is questionable. The clinical inferences Caligor makes from the three case presentations are probably as legitimate as other informal case study evaluations. Far more questions and issues are raised than are met in the book. One may philosophize that there is room for every effort of any kind in a clinician's armamentarium, but clinical procedures must not be confused with the goals of formal assessment and measurement of human behavior.

PHILIP L. HARRIMAN, *Professor of Psychology, Bucknell University, Lewisburg, Pennsylvania.*

The Caligor extension of the draw-a-person technique in psychodiagnostics has two original features.

The first feature is the ingenious method of obtaining an interrelated series of eight drawings of the human figure. The subject is instructed by the examiner to draw a whole person. After the drawing has been completed, the examiner rolls a sheet of thin paper over it, and instructs the subject again to draw a whole person. After the second drawing has been finished, a cardboard insert is placed over the first drawing and the instructions are repeated. The process is continued until eight drawings have been done, in each instance only the immediately preceding figure being exposed under the onionskin sheet added seriatim. Hence, Caligor's technique is appropriately labeled the 8CRT, or the *Eight Card Redrawing Test.*

The second feature is the elaborate attempt to develop an objective scoring plan. Explicit instructions are given for scoring in terms of 23 major dimensions. There being eight drawings, and provision having been made for some trend analysis, the score blank includes more than 200 cells. These symbolic data, properly entered on the blank, make an impressive appearance. A novice in the 8CRT recalls nostalgically the Klopfer-Davidson scoring blank for the Rorschach, which is rather similar in general plan. Though it is most commendable to objectify the scoring of a draw-a-person series, the reviewer is perplexed about Caligor's reasons for a choice of "dimensions." Further publications are to be expected, however, and this issue may be more fully discussed later on.

The interpretations of the dimensions, following Caligor's intuitive understandings and clinical experience, are quite interesting. They are expounded with assurance and made plausible by three sample records analyzed by the author. By this time, most students of psychology are familiar with the glib, winsome styles used by enthusiastic proponents of ingenuous, and ingenious, expressive drawing techniques. Here, through a minor lapse, Caligor interrupts the student's trance by alluding to "lowered critical and corrective faculties." Quite acceptable as a literary term, "faculties" may have been the result here of a purposive accident. The directions for interpreting the interrelated series of drawings may, indeed, be intended, not as an empirical-clinical exposition, but as literature. If so, a Titchener would genially but forcefully exclaim, "Verboten!" were a candidate for a degree to propose to write a term paper incorporating 8CRT results.

Even though the objective scores might lend themselves to impressive charts and tabular arrays of data, and even though the interpretations were couched in the style of a Walter Pater, it is doubtful whether any academic psy-

chologist would regard this test, and other diagnostic draw-a-person techniques, seriously.
Challenging, novel, fun to try out in a class,
helpful in keeping a pedagogue's intellectual
joints supple—yes, such techniques cannot be
disregarded as literary psychology. As for
tangible evidence to substantiate the admirable
enthusiasms of those who make them up, these
psychodiagnostic techniques are still in the ovum
stage of development. Caligor's technique is not
an exception. Yet he toiled valiantly for more
than a decade, and a reviewer feels chastened
not to be able to recommend this test as the royal
road to a valid diagnosis of personality.

*Brit J Psychol 48:319–20 N '57. H. C. Gunz-
burg.* * The new technique is intriguing—the
subject goes from one drawing to the next
whilst the preceding drawing is visible to him
through the transparent paper; he may trace it
and virtually repeat it, modify it or ignore it
completely. His handling of this situation, as
well as the various details of the drawing, the
placement and line quality are considered valid
diagnostic clues. Dr Caligor provides a scoring
system based on objectively scorable dimensions
and attains a high interscores agreement. The
scores are stated "in terms of a deviation from
a statistical norm approximately the mode
scores of normal subjects." Unfortunately the
book contains no statistical material and the
only relevant reference given by the author refers to a study of items differentiating between
21 college males and 21 hospitalized paranoid
schizophrenics—this could scarcely be called a
normative study serving as a basis for a complete test manual to be used in clinical practice.
Even more disappointing is the systematic list
of suggested interpretations for the various
scoring categories which are, no doubt, based on
wide clinical experience, but which would be
more convincing and valid if supported by some
evidence. Though Dr Caligor's technique shares
this fault with the systems devised by his predecessors, one feels that nowadays, having demonstrated the wealth of clinical material obtainable from drawings, investigators should approach this field more systematically and not
by-pass such important factors as sex, age, intelligence, cultural background, etc. In the
meantime, this new publication's main merit is
the presentation of a novel and promising projective technique and of a scoring method which

may well be used for testing experimentally the
validity of drawing interpretations.

[132]
★**Family Relations Test: An Objective Technique
for Exploring Emotional Attitudes in Children.**
Ages 3–7, 7–15; 1957; individual; 1 form ['57]; 2
levels; 132s. per set of test materials; 12s. 9d. per manual; postpaid within the United Kingdom; (20–25)
minutes; Eva Bene and James Anthony; distributed
by National Foundation for Educational Research in
England and Wales. *
a) YOUNGER CHILDREN. Ages 3–7; 40 item cards; 3s. 6d.
per 10 record booklets ['57].
b) OLDER CHILDREN. Ages 7–15; 86 item cards; 3s. 6d.
per 10 record booklets; 2s. 9d. per 10 scoring blanks.
REFERENCE
1. ANTHONY, E. J., AND BENE, EVA. "A Technique for the
Objective Assessment of the Child's Family Relationships."
J Mental Sci 103:541–55 Jl '57. *

JOHN E. BELL, *Acting Chief, Mental Health
Services, United States Public Health Service,
San Francisco, California.*

The test materials consists of 20 cardboard
figures representing people of various ages from
babyhood to old age. These are relatively ambiguous and permit a child to select figures to
represent each member of his family including
himself. In addition, a figure standing for "Nobody" is included in the materials. The figures
are attached to cardboard boxes with slots in
the top. In the form for children 8 years old
and above there are 86 cards containing statements reflecting feelings of like and dislike,
stronger feelings of love and hate, and attitudes
relating to parental overprotection and overindulgence. In the form for younger children
there are 40 similar cards.

After selecting figures to represent his own
family, the child places each card in a box behind the figure for which the statement is most
appropriate. If the statement applies to none,
it is deposited in the box attached to "Nobody."
The child's test performance is tallied on a scoring sheet; evaluation of the results and behavior
notes are entered on a separate record sheet.

The distinct advantage of the test is its relative objectivity. There are a limited number of
standardized responses that can be made in the
test situation. This permits a formal analysis
to be undertaken and facilitates the establishing
of norms and the conducting of statistical studies of the test performance with various subjects under different conditions. Little research
with the technique is presently available.

The test is subtitled "An Objective Technique for Exploring Emotional Attitudes in
Children." Its objectivity is, however, only par-

tial. The test involves a rather complex set of choices. Each card may apply to one family member other than the self, several family members other than the self, the self alone, the self along with one or more other family members, or nobody. Functionally, the child has to hold in mind all these possibilities and make appropriate choices for each item in terms of them. It may appear that the full range of possible responses is considered each time, but this demands that attention to the instructions has been of a high quality and that memory for them and a set for carrying them out are kept alive. Thus, while the actual manipulation of the cards engenders objectivity, the task itself is sufficiently complex that one may not be sure that the test conditions are comparable from one subject to another, or from one testing to another with the same subject. This has real importance, since the deductions about the performance are based on tallies of the responses without regard to the quality of the subject's attention and memory, his conceptual ability, and the processes by which he makes decisions.

An additional factor confounding the results grows out of the implicit assumption that the task of perceiving the self in the family situation is comparable to the task of perceiving the other. In practice, different processes are involved in evaluating the pertinence of the test items to the self than in assessing their relevance to others. The value of the test figures of other members of the family for symbolizing those individuals differs from the value of the self figure for personifying the self. In the former instances there is a closer parallel between the object nature of the test figure and the family member; in the latter instance there is a subject-object confusion in the approach to the figure and variability in the amount of distance of the self as embodied there. It might be constructive, then, to test the comparability of performances when the self-figure is included and excluded. The test items would not seem to lend themselves especially well to a test of reactions to the self where the simple choice of "applies" or "does not apply" would be required of the child, although this might be examined.

It is apparent that actualizing the family members by the pictures, concretizing the test task by placing items in the slots, and limiting the responses by standardized items represent a new combination of features in attitude testing. The clinical illustrations in the manual

demonstrate that the test has real merit for rapid assessment of latent and overt attitudes to the family. It does not permit discrimination between the felt and the expressed attitudes, but it reduces the range of observations required additionally to produce a realistic picture of family relations.

DALE B. HARRIS, *Professor of Psychology, and Director, Institute of Child Development and Welfare, University of Minnesota, Minneapolis, Minnesota.*

This is an ingenious projective "test" which records the subject's reactions through the sorting of cards on which stimulus items appear. Thus it has the virtue of presenting identical stimulus material to all subjects while preserving some of the flexibility considered essential to projective devices. The emphasis, however, is on the reaction to the items printed on cards. The schematic human figures are primarily vehicles to facilitate the child's reaction to the content of the printed items; they are not designed to elicit elaborate fantasy. The authors believe this technique appeals directly to the child's interest in manipulating materials and his tendencies to respond covertly, and to express emotion through play. The items are presented to the child after he has identified the members of his own family circle from among the role figures.

The items devised for older children are of this type: "This person in the family is sometimes a bit too fussy." Items are grouped into several categories as follows: mild positive (affectionate) feelings coming from the child, strong positive (sexualized) feelings coming the child, mild negative feelings coming from the child (the example above is taken from this category), and strong negative (hostile) feelings coming from the child. Four additional groups of items in the same patterns of affect represent feelings going *towards* the child. An example of the fourth type of feeling toward the child is "This person in the family hits me a lot." Three additional groups of items represent maternal over-protection, paternal over-indulgence, and maternal overindulgence.

The items for young children are expressed more simply and represent five classes only: positive and negative feelings coming from the child, positive and negative feelings going toward the child, and dependence. "N....[name of child subject] wants you to tuck him (her) into

bed at night. Who should tuck N....in at night?" represents this last category.

In theory the test helps the child express conscious attitudes, including those very private feelings which he would find difficult to state directly. The test admittedly does not investigate unconscious attitudes. The authors believe, however, that it is important to investigate the child's phenomenal world, or as they speak of it, his "psychic reality."

Scoring is accomplished by tallying the items assigned to particular role figures, excluding the items assigned to "Nobody." The balance among proportions of items in the several degrees and directions of affect assigned to the several family roles provides the basis for interpretation. The manual offers profiles for a number of briefly described examples in each of the following personality patterns: idealizing tendency, paranoid tendency, and egocentric states, both auto-aggressive and auto-erotic. Other dynamic mechanisms revealed by the use of items include reaction formation, projection, regression, displacement, idealization and denial. The authors attach considerable significance to the child's selection and treatment of significant figures, to his deviation from a theoretical frequency of items expected to be assigned to the usual family roles, to the balance he achieves between self love and self hate items (which indicates his egocentric state), to the relationship between positive and negative outgoing and positive and negative incoming affect items used by the child (which indicates his ambivalence, or lack of it, toward family figures).

The authors rest the case for the test's validity on the concept of construct validity, on comparison of test results with extensive case history material for several small groups of children (which showed considerable correspondence), on comparisons of results of mutual feelings reported in sets of siblings, where agreement of 64 per cent satisfied the 5 per cent level of confidence, and on the congruence of test findings with predictions made independently from psychiatric diagnoses in several small samples of cases. Some data are quoted to show that results are independent of the sex of the examiner. Split-half reliabilities for combinations of affect categories vary from .68 to .90, number of cases not reported.

As is frequently the case with tests of this type, no norms are given beyond a few illustrative cases and interpretations: The test is ingenious and simple, and the questions are phrased in children's language and represent common personal and family experiences; none are too threatening, on the surface at least. The device of sending "messages" should appeal to many children; the test certainly deserves further study.

ARTHUR R. JENSEN, *USPHS Research Fellow, Institute of Psychiatry, University of London, London, England.*

The *Family Relations Test* (FRT) is a semistandardized play situation which permits the child to express his emotional attitudes toward members of his family and the attitudes he believes that members of his family have toward him.

The test materials consist of 20 cardboard figures "representing people of various ages, shapes, and sizes, sufficiently stereotyped to stand for members of any child's family, yet ambiguous enough to become, under suggestion, a specific family." Each figure is attached to a red cardboard box into which can be inserted small cards which bear various expressions of attitudes: positive feelings, negative feelings, dependence, maternal overprotection, and paternal overindulgence, some expressed as emanating from the child toward family figures and some expressed as emanating from family figures toward the child. There are two sets of cards, 40 for use with younger children and 86 for use with older children.

The subject is asked to select from the 20 figures a figure to represent each member of his family, including himself. Another figure, Nobody, is introduced by the examiner to receive those attitudes which the child will not assign to any member of the family. The statement on each card is then read aloud by the examiner and the card given to the child, who is instructed to deposit it in the box attached to the family figure to whom it best applies. If the statement does not fit anybody, the card is put in Nobody. If the statement fits several people, the examiner makes a note of it. The cards are collected from the boxes and are tabulated on a special scoring form, the scoring consisting of counting the number of items of each kind of feeling assigned by the child to each member of his family. The test takes between 20 and 25 minutes to administer.

The test would seem to have possibilities, con-

sidering that there are few, if any, other objective techniques which serve the functions for which it is designed and that projective techniques are of doubtful validity. A good deal of clinical wisdom as well as an accumulation of experience with the FRT would, however, seem to be necessary for making judicious interpretations from the test material. Unfortunately neither the manual nor the one article (*I*) on the test presents any normative data. Apparently the test has never been given to normal children; at least, only clinical patients are described in the reports of the test's use. The evidence for the test's validity is too meagre and unsystematic to provide an adequate basis for evaluation. From a statistical point of view the reliability evidence is not impressive. Also some of the statistical procedures and computations in the manual and the article are both inappropriate and incorrect. For example, a 2×2 contingency table is presented in the manual (p. 48) as evidence of a significant relationship between an independent rating and the FRT regarding sibling conflicts. The "measure of agreement" is given as 64 per cent. When the appropriate test, chi square, is performed, however, it shows the results to be quite nonsignificant ($\chi^2 = .292$). In another instance (p. 46) the authors have slighted the actual significance of their data. Simply dividing the sum of the diagonal frequencies of the contingency table by the total frequencies, the authors report 64 per cent agreement and state that this result is significant at the 5 per cent level. The 5 per cent significance level was probably based on a chi square test (not given by the authors), but actually the chi square is significant at the 5 per cent level only if it is interpreted as a one-tailed test, a rather unusual procedure in the case of chi square. A more appropriate test of the significance of these data is by means of a test of trend,[1] a more refined and powerful test than chi square. When a test of trend was performed, the results show a relationship significant beyond the 0.1 per cent level.

The FRT may be a potentially useful test in the clinic, though this still remains to be demonstrated; at present it must be regarded as being in the trial stage. It can be recommended for use by those who are primarily interested in investigating the test itself. It is not a finished product about which there is sufficient informa-

tion to warrant its being recommended for routine clinical assessment of child-family relationships.

[133]

★The Five Task Test: A Performance and Projective Test of Emotionality, Motor Skill and Organic Brain Damage. Ages 8 and over; 1955; 1 form; mimeographed manual; no data on reliability; $15 per set of test materials; $3 per manual; postpaid; (15–20) minutes; Charlotte Buhler and Kathryn Mandeville; Western Psychological Services. *

DOROTHY H. EICHORN, *Assistant Research Psychologist, Institute of Child Welfare, University of California, Berkeley, California.*

Adequacy of standardization varies with the subtest, category of scoring, and age group. The first three tasks—cutting out a circle, heart, and star—are scored for "quality" ("edge-cutting," "form-cutting," and "symmetry") and "quantity" (number of scraps). "Quality" scores measure "manual dexterity," "artistic ability," and "level of aspiration." "Quantity" scores indicate "emotionality." These tasks have been administered to 327 Viennese girls aged 8–15 years, 233 parochial school children from one American city, 141 public school children from two cities, and 30 adults. However, the only statistical data reported for the "quality" scores are the means for 134 boys and 145 girls, aged 8–13 years, drawn from the American samples. Validation of the "quantity" scores as an indication of "emotionality" consists of one table listing the per cent of each of three "adjustmental" groups (good, average, and poor) producing 15 or more scraps. Adjustment was rated by teachers. The sample is some portion of the American groups, but the frequencies from which the percentages were derived are not given.

The fourth task, a projective cutout, has not been standardized.

The fifth task, Terman's ball and field problem, is used to assess "emotionality." Solutions are assigned to one of 10 categories (5 positive and 5 negative or "problematic"). Validation is based primarily on 165 solutions by 157 children, aged 7–15 years—65 by neurotic children and 100 by "emotionally stable" children (25 of high intelligence; 39, average; 24, low; and 12, mentally defective). The proportion of positive solutions was significantly lower for the neurotics than for any of the first three "normal" groups. Mystified that the percentage passing a subtest of the Stanford-Binet should be almost identical for these three groups, the re-

1 ARMITAGE, P. "Tests for Linear Trends in Proportions and Frequencies." *Biometrics* 11:375–86 S '55. *

viewer referred to Buhler's original article.[1] This study includes a table of the number of solutions in the various categories by normals, neurotics, and mental defectives at each of nine age levels. The frequencies within the table do not always sum to the marginal totals, and the marginal totals differ slightly between article and manual. Nevertheless, the reviewer computed tests of the goodness of fit of the age distributions of passes for normals and neurotics against the marginal proportions for the two groups combined. Chi square in each case had a probability of about .60. Further tests revealed that the higher total proportion of passes by normals was due to three age groups (9–10, 10–11, and 11–12 years) where the number of normals passing (33 out of 34) was much larger than at subsequent ages for this subgroup (46–80 per cent) or the same ages for the Stanford-Binet standardization sample (27–47 per cent). The difference between normals and neurotics may be attributable to biased sampling rather than "emotionality." Buhler's article describes the total sample as children tested in her clinics in London and the United States.

Diagnosis of organic brain damage apparently rests on the performance of the 12 mental defectives. Four failures among this group were by children under 10 years. Above 10 years, the proportion passing is higher than for the normals.

The subgroups are further differentiated on the basis of the type of negative solution, e.g., neurotics tend to give "Confused, Involved, and Formalistic" solutions. An incomprehensible table entitled "Independent Values with the Contingency Correlation by Groups" constitutes the evidence. After much experimentation the reviewer found these values to be $(o - e)/e$, not even $(o - e)^2/e$, where o is the observed frequency and e is the expected or theoretical frequency. Without Buhler's article, the bewildered reader cannot compute the contingency coefficient for himself. The contingency table of "problematic" solutions for normals versus neurotics, combining "Borderline" and "Gives Up" solutions to avoid small expected frequencies, yields a chi square with a probability between .20 and .10. The chi square for sex differences on the same categories has a probability between .10 and .05, although sex differences are not claimed to be significant.

1 BUHLER, CHARLOTTE. "The Ball and Field Test as a Help in the Diagnosis of Emotional Difficulties." Char & Pers 6:257–73 Je '38. *

The fifth task was also validated against ratings of adjustment. Neither the sample nor the raters are identified, but the proportions passing differ significantly among children rated as making a "good," "average," or "poor" adjustment (n's of 33, 74, and 18 respectively).

With no reliability data (test-retest or rater agreement on "quality" subscores or classification of ball and field solutions) and only meager validation data, this test must be regarded as exploratory. Such data as are available for "quantity" scores on the circle, heart, and star tasks and failure patterns on the ball and field problem are suggestive. These subtests may merit more adequate attempts at standardization. It is doubtful that the "quality" score constitutes a satisfactory measure of "motor skill," since intercorrelations among motor tests have almost uniformly been found to be low.

BERT R. SAPPENFIELD, *Professor of Psychology, Montana State University, Missoula, Montana.*

The subtitle of this test, "A Performance and Projective Test of Emotionality, Motor Skill and Organic Brain Damage," is reminiscent of the medicine show nostrum which promised a cure for every ill. As would be expected, the *Five Task Test* is found wanting when measured against the promise of its subtitle. There are better tests of emotionality, better tests of motor skills, and better tests of organic brain damage (if indeed this one may be regarded as a test of brain damage at all).

Many children, and some adults, will probably find the five tasks interesting to perform. It is to be hoped, however, that performance on them will not be the basis of decisions significantly affecting the futures of persons who take the test.

The *Five Task Test* was designed, it would appear, after accidental observations that performance on tests of "manual skill" (freehand scissors cutting of circle, heart, and star) and of "practical judgment" (Terman's ball-and-field test) was affected by non-intellectual variables. Systematic studies subsequently yielded evidence indicating (*a*) that the number of scraps produced in cutting the circle, heart, and star was related to rated adjustment level in children, but not related to age, sex, or intelligence level; and (*b*) that quality ratings of the cut-out circle, heart, and star were related to age of children up to 9 years, but not related to

either intelligence level or adjustment level. The fifth task (numbered fourth in sequence of administration), which involves asking the subject to cut out anything he wishes, was apparently added without prior experimental justification.

The test is represented to be applicable to both children and adults, although quality scoring of the circle-heart-star tasks shows no age differentiation after age 9. Interpretations involving the quality score are suggested, without restrictions as to age group or otherwise, on the basis of intuitive hypotheses for which no validity evidence is given in the manual.

Although some of the scores obtainable on the *Five Task Test* would lend themselves to reliability studies, the manual does not provide any evidence concerning reliability or objectivity of scores. Perhaps, in any case, such evidence would be of little value, in view of the fact that data relative to the test's validity are at variance with the authors' suggestion that the test be used, however tentatively, for individual diagnosis. While it is true that the tabular data presented in the manual suggest a positive relationship between number of scraps produced and level of adjustment, and between type of solutions to the ball-and-field task and level of adjustment, these data also indicate that, if cutting scores on these tasks were utilized to predict level of adjustment, the percentage of false diagnoses would be extremely high. It is also worth mentioning that, although cutting scores are prescribed in the manual for dividing subjects into three levels of adjustment, these cutting scores have not been cross validated.

Finally, there is not to be found in the manual any reference to data in support of the assumption that the *Five Task Test* may be used for interpretations concerning the possibility of organic brain damage, in spite of the fact that the subtitle of the test makes such a claim.

In summary, it may be concluded that, although the *Five Task Test* is interesting and somewhat ingenious in its conception, there appears to be little justification for its publication or use as a test.

J Consult Psychol 20:159–60 Ap '56. Laurance F. Shaffer. Buhler's "five tasks" are related performance tests, which are reported to have some relationships to emotionality and organic brain damage. The first three tasks are to cut a circle, a heart, and a star from four-inch

squares of paper. The qualities of the products are rated against scaled specimens, and the number of scraps is counted as a measure of "emotionality." The fourth task is cutting "anything you wish" and is given a projective interpretation. The fifth task, the Terman ball-and-field test, is rated as normal, borderline, or problematic with the aid of scoring specimens. Like many other behavior samples, performance on these tasks may give a sensitive and alert psychologist many clues about a child's typical responses to his world. The evidence supporting these particular tasks as clinical instruments is weak. No data on reliability are given; the very moderate reported validities were tested against inadequately defined criteria. Perhaps the test is worthy of further research; perhaps it will remain a subjective instrument of some value to clinicians who depend on observations and hunches rather than on scores.

[134]

★The Forer Structured Sentence Completion Test. Ages 10–18, adults; 1957; 1 form; separate editions for boys, girls, men, and women; mimeographed manual; no data on reliability; no norms; $4 per set of either 25 tests or 25 record booklets; 75¢ per manual; $8.50 per set of 25 tests, 25 record booklets, and manual; specimen set not available; [30–45] minutes; Bertram R. Forer; Western Psychological Services. *

REFERENCES

1. FORER, BERTRAM R. "A Structured Sentence Completion Test." *J Proj Tech* 14:15–30 Mr '50. * (*PA* 25:665)
2. SHNEIDMAN, EDWIN S. "The Case of Jay: Psychological Test and Anamnestic Data." *J Proj Tech* 16:297–345 S '52. * (*PA* 28:2676)
3. CARR, ARTHUR C. "Intra-Individual Consistency in Response to Tests of Varying Degrees of Ambiguity." *J Consult Psychol* 18:251–8 Ag '54. * (*PA* 29:4041)
4. MEYER, MORTIMER M., AND TOLMAN, RUTH S. "Parental Figures in Sentence Completion Test, in TAT, and in Therapeutic Interviews." Abstract. *J Consult Psychol* 19:170 Je '55. * (*PA* 30:2904)
5. CARR, ARTHUR C. "The Relation of Certain Rorschach Variables to Expression of Affect in the TAT and SCT." *J Proj Tech* 20:137–42 Je '56. * (*PA* 31:4674)

CHARLES N. COFER, *Professor of Psychology, University of Maryland, College Park, Maryland.*

This test consists of 100 incomplete sentences designed to yield diagnostic information of value for therapeutic planning. The forms for men and women are virtually identical except for personal pronouns; the forms for boys and girls differ from those for adults in a number of sentences but closely resemble each other. The sentence stems, supposedly, are sufficiently specific so that the kind of situation to which the completion is being made can be identified with some accuracy.

The 100 sentence stems are allocated to a number of categories. On the record form, for example, the several stems are indicated as per-

taining to six types of interpersonal figures (mother, males, females, groups, father, authority) ; to wishes ; to causes of one's own aggression, anxiety (fear), giving up, failure, guilt, and inferiority feelings ; and to reactions to aggression, rejection, failure, responsibility, and school. For each sentence a number of spaces are provided so that the particular completion may be evaluated by a check mark under the appropriate category. For causes of one's own aggression, for example, the examiner may check any one of the following categories as descriptive of a particular completion: unclear, denial, aggression (press), aggression (own), authority, criticism, economic, failure, family, father, females, future, health, inadequacy, males, mother, others' welfare, rejection, physical events, sex. A different but overlapping set of categories is provided for each of the other broad areas (interpersonal figures, wishes, reactions). The record form also provides space for summarizing predominant affective attitudes, for evaluating direction and amount of aggression, and for indicating the total number of items in which affective words are used.

The manual indicates the significance of a variety of reactions, such as omissions, denials, unclear responses, and variations in response length more or less along the lines of "complex" indicators in free word association. A number of other comments are made like the suggestion that "schizoids" and "compulsives" will show few affective responses, whereas many will be given by "hysterics" and "hypomanics."

Most of what is said in the manual is plausible, but there is not a shred of evidence that completions to these particular sentences applied to just anybody can or should be validly interpreted in the ways indicated. There are no norms, and neither the word reliability nor the word validity occurs in the manual. This test, if "test" can be appropriately used here, is an open invitation to free clinical speculation. One must take the completions, enter an evaluation in the appropriate space on the record blank, and then compare and contrast, following whatever speculative hunches one may have. We know nothing about what responses are common or unusual or what comparisons and contrasts have validity. Speculation is not objectionable, but it should, in a practical clinical situation, be subject, in the interest of the client, to the constraints provided by norms and the limits of known reliability and validity.

PERCIVAL M. SYMONDS, *Professor of Education, Teachers College, Columbia University, New York, New York.*

For this projective technique there is no evidence as to validity or reliability, and no norms are provided. However, in the judgment of this reviewer these data do not seem to be called for since the test is intended to be used essentially as a clinical or diagnostic instrument.

The author attributes the structured nature of the test to the item arrangement and item form employed. The items, designed to explore a number of predetermined categories, are scattered throughout the test in such a way that the subject is not called upon to respond to items in the same category in sequence ; however, the items that furnish evidence for each of the categories are indicated in the checklist and clinical evaluation sheet which accompanies the test. The author uses Item 5 to illustrate how structure is implemented by item form: "When she refused him, he...." The addition of the "he" in this sentence requires that the subject taking the test respond in some way to the refusal of the female in the first part of the sentence. The author calls this an "open-ended attitude test" because of the controls that are used.

There is an excellent manual which describes the test, the categories under which the results may be analyzed, and the uses of the checklist and clinical evaluation folder. Responses are evaluated in terms of interpersonal figures in the subject's life, dominant needs or drives, causes of various personality trends, reactions to interpersonal relationships, predominant emotional attitudes, direction and amount of aggressive tendencies, and total affective level. Special attention is given to those responses which are unclear, which indicate denial, or which have been omitted. The manual also provides a number of general and heuristic hypotheses which may be used as guides in interpreting the sentence completions. As is true with any projective technique, the meaning of the responses cannot be defined unequivocally in a manual ; much depends upon the judgment, sagacity, and experience of the test user. The author is quite aware that no response on a projective technique can be interpreted singly, but that it must be looked at in the light of other responses and interpreted in context of other facts known about the subject.

The *Forer Structured Sentence Completion Test* seems to have been constructed with con-

siderable thought and care. It should be service-able for clinical use within the somewhat nar-row limits of any test which yields responses in terms of isolated sentences.

[135]

★The Forer Vocational Survey. "Young adoles-cents"; 1957, vocational adjustment; 1 form; separate editions for men and for women; mimeographed man-ual; no data on reliability and validity; no norms; $13.50 per set of either 100 tests or 100 record blanks; $1.50 per manual; $8 per 25 sets of both editions and manual; postpaid; specimen set not available; [20–30] minutes; Bertram R. Forer; Western Psychological Services. *

BENJAMIN BALINSKY, *Associate Professor of Psychology, Bernard M. Baruch School of Bus-iness and Public Administration, The City Col-lege, New York, New York.*

This is a sentence completion test devised to explore nonintellectual processes related to job functioning. The forms for men and women are identical except for the use of she (he) and her (him). While this practice is apparently customary for sentence completion tests, there may be some question as to whether the same items are equally applicable in vocational situa-tions since differences in attitude between the sexes toward work and employment conditions have been found in various studies.

No studies of validity are reported. This is an oversight that requires remedy as soon as possible. Authors of other sentence completion tests, like Rotter (see 156) and Spache (see 142), have attempted studies of validity. The specific items could have been tested for dis-criminability if for no other reason than to de-termine which might be the strongest ones to include in the test. In a study of the sentence completion test of the Office of Strategic Serv-ices, Stein [1] included measures of an index of stereotypy and an index of individuality. Those responses that had high stereotypy, being an-swered similarly by 50 to 75 per cent of the sampling, were eliminated. We have no way of knowing without further research which of Forer's sentence completion items lend them-selves to stereotyped responses.

The test items are structured to a greater ex-tent than is usual in sentence completion tests. This was done deliberately in order to gain more specific information about the examinee's re-actions to different work conditions and to rela-tionships with others in the work setting. Al-though this may mean a gain in specific infor-mation, it may also mean a loss in free expres-sion. However, since the author expects the test to be used more as an interview aid than as a test by itself, the answer to any incomplete sen-tence can be explored more fully in the inter-view situation.

The selection of items was guided by a ra-tionale that includes three sectors: (*a*) reac-tions to authorities, co-workers, criticism, fail-ure, taking orders, and responsibility; (*b*) causes of feelings and actions of aggression, anxiety, failure, and job change; and (*c*) voca-tional goals and positive and negative factors that motivate job satisfaction and vocational choice. While these three sectors seem to in-clude much that is important in vocational func-tioning, there are other factors that might have proved even more significant.

The interpretation of the responses is qualita-tive, and the proper cautions are advised by the author. However, he supplies only one sample protocol and does not give the original re-sponses, only the comments about them. In it-self this is not enough. While more detailed in-terpretational material for this test is given in the manual for the *Forer Structured Sentence Completion Test* (see 134), additional samples are needed in the manual for this test.

As a research instrument or as an aid to the interview, the *Forer Vocational Survey* will serve a useful purpose. It does seem to stimu-late the expression of clues important to voca-tional adjustment; however, the counselor must follow these clues through with other tests and techniques and not accept them at face value.

CHARLES N. COFER, *Professor of Psychology, University of Maryland, College Park, Mary-land.*

This test consists of 80 incomplete sentences, designed to get at material relevant to facts con-cerning "work adjustment, attitudes, interests and conflicts of use to a vocational counselor or clinician." Many items explicitly refer to jobs, such as "Responsibility at work....," "The job looked impossible, so he (she)...." (the word "impossible" is misspelled on the form for men which the reviewer examined). The editions for men and women differ mainly in the pro-nouns used in the sentence stems. The sentence stems themselves are described as highly struc-tured, a feature designed to help the examiner discover to what the client's completion refers.

1 STEIN, MORRIS I. "The Use of a Sentence Completion Test for the Diagnosis of Personality." *J Clin Psychol* 3:47–56 Ja '47. * (*PA* 21:2337)

The 80 items are allocated to 11 areas of interest, and the record blank provides space for a summary of reactions to each of these areas (in one case the names of the areas do not correspond in the manual and the record blank). Six areas pertain to situations "representative of significant work problems" involving reactions to authorities, to co-workers, to criticism, to failure (or challenge), to taking orders, and to responsibility. Four other areas pertain to the client's beliefs about the causes of his own aggression, anxiety, failure, and job change, and the eleventh area deals with vocational goals.

The manual provides a "sample protocol and FVS record form data." However, the information provided includes what are apparently summaries of sentence completions given to the items which tap the 11 areas listed above; the sentence completions themselves are not given. The summary of impressions for this case is organized around headings such as Stability of Occupational Choice, Realism of Occupational Choice, and Capacity to Use Abilities in Chosen Occupational Setting. There is no discussion of how the summary evaluations on these points were derived from the 11 area summaries of the sentence completions.

The reliability and the validity of this test admittedly have not been determined. It is the counselor, rather than the test, which "is the crucial factor in determining test data validity." Since the counselor receives few guides in terms either of instructions or of data about experience with or use of the test (let alone norms), it will be impossible for him to know, without careful follow-up studies, how well his inferences hold up against criteria. Furthermore, there is no evidence to support the claim of validity for the content of the items as representative of the areas to which they are ordered. How does one know, for example, that "the items dealing with authorities and co-workers reveal habitual emotional attitudes and patterns of relationships which define the nature of the client's interpersonal feelings as manifested in the work situations"? While the author says the FVS is a "research instrument" (underlining in manual), almost everything the manual says suggests that it is to be used by the counselor or clinician in his daily work with clients.

What we have here is a set of 80 incomplete sentences which have unknown validity as indices to 11 areas important to vocational functioning and which are unevaluated so far as the reliability and validity of clients' responses to them are concerned. While the items may be quite useful as a sort of interview aid, it is inappropriate to call them a test, even a projective test, since none of the properties ordinarily associated with a test is indicated here.

J Counsel Psychol 5:74–5 sp '58. *Laurence Siegel.* * One is tempted to wonder....who does the major share of projecting when projective inventories are interpreted. To what extent does the interpretation made by the evaluator reveal his own personality rather than that of the client? As with anything else, some persons are probably much more insightful in extrapolating from the FVS than others. It is appropriate to inquire about the agreement in interpretation of FVS responses using a technique like that of "blind analysis" and several interpreters. This question is not approached in the manual. The matter of validity is also treated much too lightly. The absence of validity data is excused in the manual on the grounds that FVS is a projective instrument. One must agree with the assertion that "responses will most likely be interpreted qualitatively rather than in routine metric fashion." It is possible, however, to validate categories of qualitative interpretation against behavioral criteria. * The user is here cautioned against equating written responses on the record form with a client's behavior in the job setting. The FVS provides the counselor with another set of stimuli generated by his client. The old saw that *anything* a client does reveals something of himself may be invoked to justify the use of the instrument. To this may be added the potential values of FVS as an "icebreaker," source of interview material, and fertile spawning ground for clues about client behavior and hunches regarding the dynamics of a client's personality. There is always the danger, however, of looking to the datum that a client scratches his left ear (rather than his right) to serve the same ends. The manual asserts that interpretation of FVS responses is much dependent upon the experience, ingenuity and insight of the interpreter. This art of interpretation may nonetheless legitimately be subjected to certain logical requirements of verifiability and replicability. These further steps still need to be taken with the FVS, even if its use is to be restricted to research rather than operational applications.

[136]

★**Franck Drawing Completion Test.** Ages 6 and over; 1951–52; masculinity-femininity; 1 form ['51]; mimeographed; preliminary manual ['52]; no data on reliability and validity; 9s. per 10 tests; 3s. per 10 scoring sheets; 2s. 6d. per manual; 6s. 6d. per specimen set; postpaid within Australia; (15–60) minutes; Kate Franck; Australian Council for Educational Research. *

REFERENCES

1. FRANCK, KATE, AND ROSEN, EPHRAIM. "A Projective Test of Masculinity-Femininity." *J Consult Psychol* 13:247–56 Ag '49. * (PA 24:874)
2. ARONSON, MARVIN LUCIUS. *A Study of the Freudian Theory of Paranoia by Means of a Group of Psychological Tests.* Doctor's thesis, University of Michigan (Ann Arbor, Mich.), 1951. (*Microfilm Abstr* 11:443)
3. SHEPLER, BERNARD F. "A Comparison of Masculinity-Femininity Measures." *J Consult Psychol* 15:484–6 D '51. * (PA 26:7011)
4. KOOSER, EDWIN DeTURCK. *The Relationship of Masculinity-Femininity Orientation to Self-Report of Anxiety.* Master's thesis, University of North Carolina (Chapel Hill, N.C.), 1955.
5. REED, MAX R. "The Masculinity-Femininity Dimension in Normal and Psychotic Subjects." *J Abn & Social Psychol* 55:289–94 N '57. *

ARTHUR W. MEADOWS, *Head, Department of Psychology, University of Adelaide, Adelaide, Australia.*

This masculinity-femininity test requires the subject to complete a number of incomplete drawings. From the application of seven principles to the analysis of the finished drawings, a score is derived which is said to place the person on a masculinity-femininity continuum. The test has been released, to quote, "not as a finished product, but rather as a useful tool in a clinical battery of tests."

The instructions and scoring are simple and the manual is adequate. The test takes anything from 15 minutes to one hour to complete.

Cultural factors are less emphasized in this test than in the Miles-Terman masculinity-femininity test (see 3:24). The present 36 drawings are those of an original 60 which showed statistically significant differences between methods of completion by men and by women (n = 250) in an elementary psychology class. By comparing the performances of eight nationality groups (men and women separately) comprising anything from 10 to 70 subjects, it was shown that there were no significant differences between the mean scores of men of different nationalities and that, among women, only some non-English speaking groups differed significantly. Results from small groups of children, in age groups 6, 10, and 14, showed differences between boys and girls in the hypothesized direction.

After training, scoring differences between scorers is low, the reliability coefficients ranging from .84 to .90. Although reference is made to the reliability of scoring, there is no indication of the reliability, i.e., the repeatability, of the test.

In support of validity, evidence is presented to show that there is a significant difference between the mean scores of 265 men and 132 women. This difference does not establish the existence of a masculinity-femininity continuum. What is needed is a correlation between the test scores and some admitted criterion of masculinity-femininity characteristic or, say, evidence that certain deviant groups like homo-erotics are significantly placed on the scale.

The rationale of the test has some weaknesses. It is said that it is a projective-constructive test in which the subject both projects and represents his body image in the drawings.

This is an ingenious technique and merits consideration for inclusion in experimental batteries in which validation of the existence of the masculinity-femininity continuum could be obtained from criterion groups.

[137]

★**The Graphomotor Projection Technique.** Mental patients; 1948–54; individual; 1 form ['48]; $3.50 per set of test materials; $5.75 per 25 record blanks ('48); $3.75 per manual ('54, see 7 below); postage extra; (20–30) minutes; Samuel B. Kutash and Raymond H. Gehl; C. H. Stoelting Co. *

REFERENCES

1. GEHL, RAYMOND H., AND KUTASH, SAMUEL B. "Psychiatric Aspects of a Graphomotor Projection Technique." *Psychiatric Q* 23:539–47 Jl '49. * (PA 24:6351)
2. KUTASH, SAMUEL B., AND GEHL, RAYMOND H. "A Simple Scoring Device for Quantifying Graphic Productions." *J Clin Psychol* 5:424–5 O '49. *
3. GEHL, RAYMOND H., AND KUTASH, SAMUEL B. "A Reply to Elkisch's Critique of the Graphomotor Projection Technique." *J Proj Tech* 15:510–3 D '51. * ELKISCH, PAULA. "Comment to a Reply by Drs. Gehl and Kutash." *J Proj Tech* 15:514–5 D '51. * (PA 26:6264, 6269)
4. LEVINE, SOLOMON. *The Relationship Between Personality and Efficiency in Various Hospital Occupations.* Doctor's thesis, New York University (New York, N.Y.), 1951. (*Microfilm Abstr* 11:741)
5. KUTASH, SAMUEL B. "A New Personality Test: The Graphomotor Projection Technique." *Trans N Y Acad Sci*, Series II 15:44–6 D '52. * (PA 27:6874)
6. KEYES, EDWARD J., AND LAFFAL, JULIUS. "The Use of a Graphomotor Projective Technique to Discriminate Between Failure and Success Reactions in a Level of Aspiration Situation." *J Clin Psychol* 9:69–71 Ja '53. * (PA 27:7779)
7. KUTASH, SAMUEL B., AND GEHL, RAYMOND H. *The Graphomotor Projection Technique: Clinical Use and Standardization.* Springfield, Ill.: Charles C Thomas, 1954. Pp. xi, 133. * (PA 29:1768)

PHILIP L. HARRIMAN, *Professor of Psychology, Bucknell University, Lewisburg, Pennsylvania.*

The administration of the Kutash-Gehl technique is simple and inexpensive. S assumes a writing posture, listens to simple instructions, and then, blindfolded, is asked to move the pencil freely on the paper but to try not to make anything. E makes notes during the performance, which requires 5 minutes. Then S is directed to repeat the performance on a second

sheet of paper, after which, still blindfolded, he is asked to report what he wrote or drew on the first paper and on the second, and what thoughts ran through his mind while he was working. After the removal of the blindfold, S indicates on superimposed onionskin any meaningful or imaginary representations discernible in the originals. His free associations are carefully recorded. With college students who volunteered to serve as S's, the reviewer found that from 30 to 45 minutes were required for administration.

The scoring methodology is clearly expounded in the manual. The hints for clinical interpretations of the data, however, seem to be an admixture of intuitive opinions and the authors' own experience in the use of the technique on normal and schizophrenic individuals. Some of the interpretive comments are based upon statistical reports; others are based upon broad experience, particularly with psychotics. Rigidly following the vague counsel for interpreting some graphomotor projection records and notes, the reviewer found incipient or grave indices to mental ill health among his volunteer subjects.

Techniques of this pattern are customarily developed in mental hosptials, outpatient clinics, or other centers for diagnosis and rehabilitation of maladjusted persons. Naturally, "all looks yellow to the jaundic'd eye." Symptoms, latent or manifest, distribute the S's on a continuum of psychopathology. The Kutash-Gehl technique is no exception. Clinical write-ups become, willy-nilly, "sicklied o'er with the pale cast" of morbidity. To be sure, Case C described in the manual, is a norm of reference for understanding how to interpret a nonpsychotic's record; and Case A, which deals with a youth just emerging from adolescence, is discussed in some detail. But more reports are needed for normal young adults. It would be interesting, also, to have more data on young women. The single case presented in the manual suggests that these authors have a mild hostility (!) towards women.

The *Graphomotor Projection Technique* does not seem to be well enough standardized for use in cases where human welfare is involved. Recommendations for commitment to, or release from, an institution for treatment of mental disturbance should not be based on performance on this technique. Used by college deans and counselors, with but a layman's acquaintance with psychopathology, it would induce profound

dysphoria. It does, however, seem to be decidedly worthy of further research, particularly by those who are neither recognized nor "volunteer" psychiatrists. For a term paper by a first year graduate student in clinical psychology, the data collected through the use of the Kutash-Gehl technique, on, say, 50 candidates for the doctorate, might rate a "B." Perhaps, however, the time might be better devoted to mastering courses in experimental design, intermediate statistics, and administration of a Binet-type test.

Am J Psychiatry 111:877–8 My '55. Marion Font. * An interesting aspect of the technique is the use of a blindfold, which the authors believe enables a subject to confront himself and be receptive to prompting from within. * It would seem....that a psychodiagnostic tool of real merit has been added to the armamentarium of the clinical psychologist. Only application of the method over an extensive period, to a wide variety of cases, can determine its clinical value.

Brit J Psychol 46:73 F '55. H. Phillipson. * Some claim is made for this projective technique that it is an attempt to realize an aim, which arose out of the Allport and Vernon Studies in Expressive Movement, that it is important to study movements not in isolation nor as single traits but rather in respect to the basic motivation of the individual. Although the authors for the most part adopt a holistic and dynamic approach, this claim is not substantiated. In the reviewer's opinion a projective technique designed for clinical use should be capable of throwing light on the nature of personality dynamics, conflicts and their causation in terms of concepts directly relatable to therapeutic work. The rationale of the test and the results demonstrated are in far too general terms for this purpose. As an aside one would also express doubts as to whether the test, in the way it is given, represents a task which patients can readily and meaningfully accept. The book makes some thoughtful contributions to an interesting area of research; it may well be that it would have been more advisable at this stage to present the work as such, rather than as a clinical technique. As with all books from this publishing company the production is serviceable and pleasing.

[138]

Group Projection Sketches for the Study of Small Groups. Groups of 3-40 people (ages 16 and over); 1949; 1 form; mimeographed manual; no data on reli-

ability and validity; $2.50 per set of 5 pictures and manual, postpaid; (60) minutes; William E. Henry and Harold Guetzkow; Department of Psychology, University of Michigan. *

REFERENCE

1. HENRY, WILLIAM E., AND GUETZKOW, HAROLD. "Group Projection Sketches for the Study of Small Groups." *J Social Psychol* 33:77–102 F '51. (PA 26:917)

CECIL A. GIBB, *Professor of Psychology, Canberra University College, Canberra, Australia.*

It is difficult to decide whether this technique should be treated seriously in 1958. The manual was first published (in mimeograph form) in 1949 and a quick review of the literature since that date reveals only the commission of the mimeo to print in the *Journal of Social Psychology.* Two quite favorable reviews were presented in *The Fourth Mental Measurements Yearbook,* but no research worker seems to have been encouraged to produce the validation data which would, perhaps, recommend the method to investigators of small groups.

The *Group Projection Sketches* were developed by analogy with TAT, and on the assumption (now frequently made) that groups have properties analogous to the personality properties of individuals. There are five pictures, each 21 by 18 inches, attractively presented and quite easily seen by members of groups as large as 20. The group is asked to write a story about each picture, taking about 10 minutes for each story. (In groups as large as 20 this time limit is rather too short, even when one wishes to preserve a time pressure as is recommended.)

Analysis is focused upon the final written stories and, indeed, the procedure was developed to avoid the necessity for observation and recording of the group process itself. Two methods of analysis are suggested: (*a*) a clinical type interpretation, and (*b*) a type of quantitative analysis based on a number of rating scales expressing judgments of the analyst.

In most cases, however, one has the feeling that the clinical interpretation could be made at least as well by a person who observed the group process, while many of the judgments called for by the rating scales could be far better done by an observer of process. It may be cute to make such judgments from group stories, but more reliable data would almost certainly be obtained by the process observer. One of the reasons this technique has not won advocates, as TAT has, would seem to be that, whereas the TAT protocol gives quick access to personality material otherwise available only with depth interviewing, the *Group Projection*

Sketches offer very little, if anything, which is not openly available to the process observer.

Further restrictions upon the use of the technique are almost certainly the absence of reliability and validity data and the failure of the authors to fulfil their promise of producing these at a later date, and the highly tentative way in which the manual presents the analysis.

Criticism has also been leveled at the pictures themselves for their failure to meet the needs of female groups and of non-white-collar, non-urban male groups. These restrictions, however, hardly account for the assiduity with which the *Group Projection Sketches* have been ignored. A far more serious stricture is that this technique overlooks direct information about the relationships of individuals to the group and within the group.

It may still be true, as the authors hopefully observed in 1949, that "the instrument holds promise....in suggesting clues to insightful analysis of the structure and internal dynamics of groups."

For reviews by Robert R. Holt and N. W. Morton, see 4:106.

[139]

*H-T-P: House-Tree-Person Projective Technique. Ages 5 and over; 1946–56; 1 form; manual ('48, see 6 below); no norms for ages 5–14; $2 per 25 drawing forms ['46]; $3.50 per 25 interrogation folders: adult form ('50), children's form ('56); $3.50 per 25 scoring folders ('50); $3 per manual; postpaid; specimen set not available; (60–90) minutes; John N. Buck and Isaac Jolles (children's interrogation folder); Western Psychological Services. *

REFERENCES

1-5. See 3:47.
6-19. See 4:107.
20. DEMMING, J. A. *The H-T-P Test as an Aid in the Diagnosis of Psychopathic Personality.* Master's thesis, Kent State University (Kent, Ohio), 1949.
21. SIEGEL, J. H. *A Preliminary Study of the Validity of the House-Tree-Person Test With Children.* Master's thesis, Southern Methodist University (Dallas, Tex.), 1949.
22. GÜNZBURG, H. C.; LOND, B. A.; AND VIENNA, PHIL. "The Significance of Various Aspects in Drawings by Educationally Subnormal Children." *J Mental Sci* 96:951–75 O '50. * (PA 25:5413)
23. SINGER, R. H. *A Study of Drawings (H-T-P) Produced by a Group of College Students and a Group of Hospitalized Schizophrenics.* Master's thesis, Pennsylvania State College (State College, Pa.), 1950.
24. BROWN, FRED. Chap. 10, "House-Tree-Person and Human Figure Drawings," pp. 173–84. (PA 27:3546) In *Progress in Clinical Psychology, Vol. I, Sect. 1.* Edited by Daniel Brower and Lawrence E. Abt. New York: Grune & Stratton, Inc., 1952. Pp. xi, 328. *
25. JOLLES, ISAAC. *A Catalogue for the Qualitative Interpretation of the H-T-P.* Beverly Hills, Calif.: Western Psychological Services, 1952. Pp. 97. *
26. JOLLES, ISAAC. "A Study of the Validity of Some Hypotheses for the Qualitative Interpretation of the H-T-P for Children of Elementary School Age: I, Sexual Identification." *J Clin Psychol* 8:113–8 Ap '52. * (PA 27:1968)
27. JOLLES, ISAAC. "A Study of the Validity of Some Hypotheses for the Qualitative Interpretation of the H-T-P for Children of Elementary School Age: II, The 'Phallic Tree' as an Indicator of Psycho-Sexual Conflict." *J Clin Psychol* 8:245–55 Jl '52. * (PA 27:5879)

28. BUCK, JOHN N. "House-Tree-Person Drawing Technique," pp. 688–701. (*PA* 27:7758) In *Contributions Toward Medical Psychology: Theory and Psychodiagnostic Methods, Vol. II.* Edited by Arthur Weider. New York: Ronald Press Co., 1953. Pp. xi, 459–885. *

29. DUFFY, F. X. *The Development of Form Concepts in the Drawing of a Tree by Children: Kindergarten Through the Ninth Grade.* Master's thesis, Richmond Professional Institute (Richmond, Va.), 1953.

30. HAMMER, EMANUEL F. "Frustration-Aggression Hypothesis Extended to Socio-Racial Areas: Comparison of Negro and White Children's H-T-P's." *Psychiatric Q* 27:597–607 O '53. * (*PA* 28:5880)

31. HAMMER, EMANUEL F. "An Investigation of Sexual Symbolism: A Study of H-T-P's of Eugenically Sterilized Subjects." *J Proj Tech* 17:401–13 D '53. * (*PA* 28:6629)

32. HAMMER, EMANUEL F. "Negro and White Children's Personality Adjustment as Revealed by a Comparison of Their Drawings (H-T-P)." *J Clin Psychol* 9:7–10 Ja '53. * (*PA* 27:7715)

33. HAMMER, EMANUEL F. "The Role of the H-T-P in the Prognostic Battery." *J Clin Psychol* 9:371–4 O '53. * (*PA* 28:4437)

34. HAMMER, EMANUEL F., AND PIOTROWSKI, ZYGMUND A. "Hostility as a Factor in the Clinician's Personality as It Affects His Interpretation of Projective Drawings (H-T-P)." *J Proj Tech* 17:210–6 Je '53. * (*PA* 28:4359)

35. JOLLES, ISAAC, AND BECK, HARRY S. "A Study of the Validity of Some Hypotheses for the Qualitative Interpretation of the H-T-P for Children of Elementary School Age: III, Horizontal Placement." *J Clin Psychol* 9:161–4 Ap '53. * (*PA* 28:2640)

36. JOLLES, ISAAC, AND BECK, HARRY S. "A Study of the Validity of Some Hypotheses for the Qualitative Interpretation of the H-T-P for Children of Elementary School Age: IV, Vertical Placement." *J Clin Psychol* 9:164–7 Ap '53. * (*PA* 28:2641)

37. LANDISBERG, SELMA. "Relationship of the Rorschach to the H-T-P." *J Clin Psychol* 9:179–83 Ap '53. * (*PA* 28:2645)

38. LEVINE, MURRAY, AND GALANTER, EUGENE H. "A Note on the 'Tree and Trauma' Interpretation in the HTP." *J Consult Psychol* 17:74–5 F '53. * (*PA* 28:956)

39. MICHAL-SMITH, HAROLD. "The Identification of Pathological Cerebral Function Through the H-T-P Technique." *J Clin Psychol* 9:293–5 Jl '53. * (*PA* 28:3136)

40. RUBIN, HAROLD. "A Quantitative Study of the H-T-P and Its Relationship to the Wechsler-Bellevue Scale." Abstract. *Am Psychol* 8:426–7 Ag '53. *

41. DIAMOND, SOLOMON. "The House and Tree in Verbal Fantasy: I, Age and Sex Differences in Themes and Content." *J Proj Tech* 18:316–25 S '54. * (*PA* 29:4046)

42. DIAMOND, SOLOMON. "The House and Tree in Verbal Fantasy: II, Their Different Roles." *J Proj Tech* 18:414–7 D '54. * (*PA* 29:7270)

43. HAMMER, EMANUEL F. "A Comparison of H-T-P's of Rapists and Pedophiles." *J Proj Tech* 18:346–54 S '54. * (*PA* 29:4370)

44. HAMMER, EMANUEL F. "Guide for Qualitative Research With the H-T-P." *J General Psychol* 51:41–60 Jl '54. * (*PA* 30:2882)

45. HAMMER, EMANUEL F. "Relationship Between Diagnosis of Psychosexual Pathology and the Sex of the First Drawn Person." *J Clin Psychol* 10:168–70 Ap '54. * (*PA* 29:920)

46. JOHNSON, WARREN R.; HUTTON, DANIEL C.; AND JOHNSON, GRANVILLE B., JR. "Personality Traits of Some Champion Athletes as Measured by Two Projective Tests: Rorschach and H-T-P." *Res Q* 25:484–5 D '54. *

47. MARKHAM, SYLVIA. "An Item Analysis of Children's Drawings of a House." *J Clin Psychol* 10:185–7 Ap '54. * (*PA* 29:935)

48. PENNINGTON, L. W., JR. *Developmental Patterns in Drawings of a Person by Children From the Age 4½ to 15.* Master's thesis, Richmond Professional Institute (Richmond, Va.), 1954.

49. REPUCCI, L. C. *A Quantitative Scoring System for Children's Drawings of a House in the H-T-P.* Master's thesis, Richmond Professional Institute (Richmond, Va.), 1954.

50. RUBIN, HAROLD. "A Quantitative Study of the HTP and Its Relationship to the Wechsler-Bellevue Scale." *J Clin Psychol* 10:35–8 Ja '54. * (*PA* 28:7545)

51. SATTER, GEORGE, AND McGEE, EUGENE. "Retarded Adults Who Have Developed Beyond Expectation: Part II, Non-Intellectual Functions." *Training Sch B* 51:67–81 Je '54. * (*PA* 29:2663)

52. SLOAN, WILLIAM. "A Critical Review of H-T-P Validation Studies." *J Clin Psychol* 10:143–8 Ap '54. * (*PA* 29:957)

53. WOODS, WALTER A., AND COOK, WILLIAM E. "Proficiency in Drawing and Placement of Hands in Drawings of the Human Figure." *J Consult Psychol* 18:119–21 Ap '54. * (*PA* 29:2485)

54. BECK, HARRY S. "A Study of the Applicability of the H-T-P to Children With Respect to the Drawn House." *J Clin Psychol* 11:60–3 Ja '55. * (*PA* 29:7256)

55. COWDEN, RICHARD C.; DEABLER, HERDIS L.; AND FEAMSTER, J. HARRY. "The Prognostic Value of the Bender-Gestalt, H-T-P, TAT, and Sentence Completion Test." *J Clin Psychol* 11:271–5 Jl '55. * (*PA* 30:2864)

56. DIGIAMMO, J. J. *Relationship Between Performance on*

Visual-Form Perception Measures and Drawings on the H-T-P Technique. Master's thesis, Richmond Professional Institute (Richmond, Va.), 1955.

57. HAMMER, EMANUEL F. "A Comparison of H-T-P's of Rapists and Pedophiles: III, The 'Dead' Tree as an Index of Psychopathology." *J Clin Psychol* 11:67–9 Ja '55. * (*PA* 29:7530)

58. HAMMER, EMANUEL F. *The H-T-P Clinical Research Manual.* Beverly Hills, Calif.: Western Psychological Services, 1955. Pp. iii, 58. *

59. JOHNSON, WARREN R., AND HUTTON, C. DANIEL. "Effects of a Combative Sport Upon Personality Dynamics as Measured by a Projective Test." *Res Q* 26:49–53 Mr '55. * (*PA* 30:1559)

60. KLINE, MILTON V. "Hypnodiagnosis With a Visual-Imagery Induction Technique and Modification of the House-Tree-Person and Thematic Apperception Tests." *Psychiatric Q Sup* 29:267–71 pt 2 '55. * (*PA* 31:1122)

61. KORKES, LENORE, AND LEWIS, NOLAN D. C. "An Analysis of the Relationship Between Psychological Patterns and Outcome in Pulmonary Tuberculosis." *J Nerv & Mental Dis* 122:524–63 D '55. *

62. LYONS, JOSEPH. "The Scar on the H-T-P Tree." *J Clin Psychol* 11:267–70 Jl '55. * (*PA* 30:2897)

63. MEYER, BERNARD C.; BROWN, FRED; AND LEVINE, ABRAHAM. "Observations on the House-Tree-Person Drawing Test Before and After Surgery." *Psychosom Med* 17:428–54 N–D '55. * (*PA* 30:7215)

64. QUIRK, EVE-LYN. *The Reliability and Validity of the H-T-P as a Measure of Intelligence in Adolescents.* Master's thesis, University of Toronto (Toronto, Ont., Canada), 1955.

65. VERNIER, CLAIRE M.; WHITING, J. FRANK; AND MELTZER, MALCOLM L. "Differential Prediction of a Specific Behavior From Three Projective Techniques." *J Consult Psychol* 19:175–82 Je '55. * (*PA* 30:2932)

66. WAXENBERG, SHELDON E. "Psychosomatic Patients and Other Physically Ill Persons: A Comparative Study." *J Consult Psychol* 19:163–9 Je '55. * (*PA* 30:3281)

67. BAILEY, ROBERT BAIN. *A Study of Predicting Academic Success in Elementary School Reading From Projective Tests.* Doctor's thesis, University of Oklahoma (Norman, Okla.), 1956. (*DA* 16:1397)

68. BIELIAUSKAS, VYTAUTAS J. "Scorer's Reliability in the Quantitative Scoring of the H-T-P Technique." *J Clin Psychol* 12:366–9 O '56. *

69. BOLIN, B. J.; SCHNEPS, ANN; AND THORNE, W. E. "Further Examination of the Tree-Scar-Trauma Hypothesis." *J Clin Psychol* 12:395–7 O '56. *

70. KIRKHAM, SANDRA L. *The Identification of Organicity Using the House-Tree-Person Test on an Institutionalized Population.* Master's thesis, Richmond Professional Institute (Richmond, Va.), 1956.

71. NAZARIO-ORTIZ, I. *Quantitative Differences Between Puerto-Rican and Resident American College Students on H-T-P Drawings.* Master's thesis, Richmond Professional Institute (Richmond, Va.), 1956.

72. PERKINSON, PATRICIA R. *Shading on the H-T-P Drawings and Its Relationship With Anxiety and Intelligence.* Master's thesis, Richmond Professional Institute (Richmond, Va.), 1956.

73. BIELIAUSKAS, VYTAUTAS J. *The H-T-P Bibliography.* Los Angeles, Calif.: Western Psychological Services, July 1957. Pp. 10. *

74. HEIDGERD, EVERETT. *The Validity of the H-T-P as a Detector of Aggression in Boys 8 to 12.* Doctor's thesis, Columbia University (New York, N.Y.), 1957.

75. JOLLES, ISAAC. "Some Advances in Interpretation of the Chromatic Phase of the H-T-P." *J Clin Psychol* 13:81–3 Ja '57. *

76. ROYAL, E. ANN. *A Comparative Study of the Qualitative Aspects of the Achromatic and Chromatic H-T-P Test.* Master's thesis, Richmond Professional Institute (Richmond, Va.), 1957.

77. BIELIAUSKAS, VYTAUTAS J., AND KIRKHAM, SANDRA L. "An Evaluation of the 'Organic Signs' in the H-T-P Drawings." *J Clin Psychol* 14:50–4 Ja '58. *

78. CASSEL, ROBERT H.; JOHNSON, ANNA P.; AND BURNS, WILLIAM H. "Examiner, Ego Defense, and the H-T-P Test." *J Clin Psychol* 14:157–60 Ap '58. *

79. HAMMER, EMANUEL F., Editor. *The Clinical Application of Projective Drawings,* pp. 163–308, passim. Contributions by Emanuel F. Hammer, Isaac Jolles, Fred Brown, and John N. Buck. Springfield, Ill.: Charles C Thomas, 1958. Pp. xxii, 663. *

80. WAWRZASZEK, FRANK; JOHNSON, ORVAL G.; AND SCIERA, JOHN L. "A Comparison of H-T-P Responses of Handicapped and Non-Handicapped Children." *J Clin Psychol* 14:160–2 Ap '58. *

PHILIP L. HARRIMAN, *Professor of Psychology, Bucknell University, Lewisburg, Pennsylvania.*

Among the freehand drawing techniques in personality appraisal, the *H-T-P* technique cannot be cavalierly dismissed as just one more

contribution to projective methods. The literature on this technique already extends to more
than 100 titles. Rather complete and explicit
manuals are available for those who desire to
have a systematic exposition of the technique,
its rationale, and its use in clinical studies and
research. Interest in Buck's contribution is no
evanescent phenomenon. On the contrary, to
judge from accelerations in journal articles
since 1948, the *H-T-P* cannot be ignored by
students of personality theory or by clinical
psychologists. It is trite, though germane here,
to remark, *pari passu,* that many other projective drawing tests have had a brief heyday, and
then passed into well-deserved oblivion. No
such fate seems to await the *H-T-P* in the immediate future.

To administer this test is both absurdly easy
and unduly arduous. This paradox will be discovered by anyone who makes a serious effort
to learn what the ingenious Buck has done.
The subject is asked to draw first a house,
then a tree, and finally a person. What could
be easier for a teacher or a clinical psychologist
than to establish rapport and to obtain those
three drawings? The arduous task, however, is
to make copious notes on sequences of detail,
spontaneous comments, tempo, and general behavior. This reviewer, proceeding as a rank
amateur on the *H-T-P* periphery, wished that
he had learned W. S. Taylor's system of note-
taking. It was convincing, however, to attempt
to take notes and find out why they are considered indispensable and why Buck insists
upon their necessity.

In a second meeting the subject may be asked
to use an 8-color assortment of crayons in another set of freehand drawings of a house, a
tree, and a person. This extension of the Buck
technique, initiated by Payne (*15*), has been
adopted by Buck as a very helpful way of obtaining further data for exploring personality
dynamics. Both the achromatic and the chromatic drawings may be obtained from groups
as well as from individual testing sessions. A
group administration, it is evident, precludes
any clinical notes, though it may be a convenient screening device. This reviewer believes
that the author has a reserved opinion about
the *H-T-P* as a group technique. As in the case
of the Binet-Simon scale, administration of the
H-T-P technique requires a face-to-face situation for maximum usefulness. In the review-

er's opinion Buck should have held to his convictions about this matter.

An inquiry follows the administration of the
technique. This takes the form of a planned
interview, but the examiner is encouraged to
ask supplemental questions, especially about
deviant aspects of the productions. Again, a
user of the *H-T-P* will regret inability to record notes in an efficient manner. The free
associations are impeded if one must ask for a
repetition. Nevertheless, about six pages of
notes were collected by the reviewer on the
behavior of each of several congenial students
and a few children of faculty members. Thus,
a total of more than 120 pages of *H-T-P* data,
all from normal individuals, represents this reviewer's momentary enthusiasm for his task.
No doubt, a pedagogue's excursion into this
phase of *H-T-P* will be incorporated into many
a classroom discussion henceforth.

Quantitative scoring might be learned from
the manual. A helpful supplement is the mimeographed report (*14*) from the 1950 Veterans
Administration seminar on the *H-T-P*. Innumerable questions arise, and the self-taught examiner soon becomes frustrated. Mons, it is well
known, became an expert in Rorschach through
his self-directed mastery of the literature. Perhaps, with great patience and assiduity, a psychologist could achieve some competence in
quantitative scoring of the Buck technique. A
skilled textbook writer might clarify the ex-
positions. Meanwhile, the reviewer would
strongly advise a residence in one of the *H-T-P*
workshops.

Qualitative scoring, presumably an infinitely
more recondite problem, is not difficult. A thorough knowledge of neo-Freudian and psychoanalytic concepts, experience in the intuitive
judgments of a psychoclinician, and a complete
renunciation of all the objective-experimental
psychology one had to learn in graduate school
would facilitate the interpreter's work. A flair
for convincing expression of bold hypotheses,
an austere rejection of nomothetic studies of
personality, and a will to believe are further
assets in *H-T-P* qualitative appraisals. These
comments are not intended to be judgmental
or captious. The reviewer is second to none in
his admiration of the insights of Buck and
Jolles, based upon their own clinical use of the
H-T-P technique. An academic fuddyduddy
would be a lively instructor, indeed, if he or

she had similar clinical insights and eagerness to impart them.

Three conclusions are ventured. First, the *H-T-P* technique cannot be properly mastered from manuals and journal articles. Secondly, it seems 'to be one of the most thorough projective techniques of its type, and it must be taken with utmost seriousness. It is not yet beyond its early adolescence; it should be brought to a higher development. Buck and his enthusiastic colleagues should be afforded every encouragement. Thirdly, most of the *H-T-P* publications are from the pens, or the typewriters, of those who have *Sprachgefühl*. No matter what technique they might advocate, it would be plausible and lucid per se. The next morning wish, however, is for more empirical data. Perhaps, while still adhering to Windelband's ideographic method, members of the *H-T-P* group are going to become more self-critical and cautious about their qualitative interpretations.

For reviews by Albert Ellis and Ephraim Rosen, see 4:107 (1 excerpt); for reviews by Morris Krugman and Katherine W. Wilcox, see 3:47; for related reviews, see B234.

[140]
★The Holtzman Inkblot Test. Preschool children through adults; 1958; 24 provisional scoring categories: location, space, form definiteness, form appropriateness, color, shading, movement energy level, pathognomic verbalization, integration, human, animal, anatomy, sex, abstract, anxiety, hostility, barrier, penetration, balance, affect arousal, reaction time, card position, popularity-originality, number of rejections; individual; Forms A, B; no norms; present distribution restricted for research use; no charge for test booklets, provisional manual, manual supplements, or sets of the inkblots when used for research purposes during initial standardization and validation phase; (75) minutes; Wayne H. Holtzman; the Author, University of Texas, Austin, Texas. *

REFERENCE
1. HOLTZMAN, WAYNE H. "Development of an Experimental Inkblot Test, a New Departure From the Rorschach." Abstract. *Am Psychol* 11:400 Ag '56. *

[141]
★The Howard Ink Blot Test. Adults; 1953; individual; 1 form; no data on reliability; $12.50 per set of 12 cards; $2 per manual (reprint of *1* below); cash orders postpaid; (90–105) minutes; James W. Howard; *Journal of Clinical Psychology.* *

REFERENCES
1. HOWARD, JAMES W. "The Howard Ink Blot Test: A Descriptive Manual." *J Clin Psychol* 9:209–55 Jl '53. * (*PA* 28:1848)
2. SCOTT, EDWARD M., AND DOUGLAS, FREDERICK. "A Comparison of Rorschach and Howard Tests on a Schizophrenic Population." *J Clin Psychol* 13:79–81 Ja '57. *
3. SCOTT, EDWARD M. "A Comparison of Rorschach and Howard Ink Blot Tests on a Schizophrenic Population From a Content Point of View." *J Clin Psychol* 14:156–7 Ap '58. *

C. R. STROTHER, *Professor of Clinical Psychology, University of Washington, Seattle, Washington.*

This test consists of a series of 12 Rorschach-type plates, 6 of which are chromatic. They are slightly larger than the Rorschach blots and contain more variations in shading. Three principal criteria entered into the selection of blots: a reasonable degree of uniformity of responses, the use of a fair number and range of determinants other than form, and the exclusion of blots which tended to stimulate large numbers of responses.

Administration and scoring follow Beck's system. The manual is clear and explicit. Norms are provided for a population of 229 adult, English-speaking Canadians of average intelligence or above, with at least a high school education, and without "obviously disabling personality difficulties." No information is given as to the methods used in obtaining this sample.

The author maintains that this test produces more white space, shading, color, movement, and human content responses than the Rorschach blots. The limited amount of published data available tends to support this claim, at least with respect to use with a schizophrenic population.

A great deal of time, care, and ability has been invested in the development of this test. Scoring can be easily learned, particularly by an examiner familiar with Beck's system. For anyone seeking an ink blot test other than the Rorschach, the choice lies between the Howard and the Behn blots. Responses obtained with the Howard blots will probably differ from Rorschach protocols to a greater extent than will protocols obtained from the Behn series.

J Proj Tech 18:254–6 Je '54. Walter G. Klopfer. The advertising for the Howard Ink Blot Test, which is extensive, makes statements such as, "The test is derived experimentally;" "It has a wider range of stimulating features;" "There are statistical findings from a 'normal' group;" and "It has greater diagnostic sensitivity." Some of these statements will be examined in the review below. In regard to the question of experimental derivation Howard points out in the manual that he had a large number of ink blots from which the present series have been selected. The data presented in the manual are derived from 229 subjects. He makes the

statement, "It is believed that some of these differences (from the Rorschach) may indicate that the test is worthy of the research effort by clinicians or other interested psychologists." This is at some variance with the advertising claim that this research has already been done. Later on in the preface to the manual he states that it would not be possible at this time to give a full description of the administration and scoring of the test and that nothing at all would be said about the interpretation of findings since it was assumed that these could be done by anyone familiar with the Rorschach Test. This is stated in spite of the fact that the author continually emphasizes the point that this test is different from the Rorschach Test and that the cards have a considerably different stimulus value. Why he should, therefore, assume that the principles of interpretation empirically derived from the Rorschach Test should be applicable to this different test is difficult to determine. During the rest of this very brief manual the author makes a number of other statements which might be thrown into question by the clinical observer. Discussing the derivation of this test, he makes the statement that the Rorschach (when used as a group test) could not furnish sufficient data for appraising or describing the individual personality. He cites no evidence to support this contention. He makes the point that the Howard Ink Blot Test is a better test because it has more ink blots, more color, more movement, et cetera. These features he describes as greater "sensitivity" of the test. The reader is left at a loss to know why these features should make the test more sensitive to the assessment of personality, and it is not clear just exactly what the author means by "sensitivity." There is some reason to believe that the Rorschach Test has been found to be of some use in the assessment of personality. There is no evidence at all that the Howard Ink Blot Test has been able to be of any use in this regard. At least, if there is some evidence, it has not been presented in the material discussed here. Howard's "statistics" in regard to the "manner of approach" consist of giving the mean and standard deviation of the various location categories for his normal group. This is not very useful to the clinician since it is not expressed in such a way as to be applicable to a record with any number of responses. His subsequent discussion of the various determinants is the

practice of group averaging which the author himself admits distorts the individual patterns. If this is the case, what is the particular point in presenting this kind of data? He points out that there are more color and more human movement responses elicited by his blots. It seems to the present reviewer that if this is the case, an entirely new rationale and new method of interpreting these determinants must be found because the interpretative hypotheses derived from the Rorschach Test are quite closely bound up with the stimulus value of the particular blots used in that test. His "new" symbol IF, standing for interior form, bears a striking resemblance to a symbol, di, which was suggested by Klopfer eleven years ago. His list of plus and minus form responses presumably analogous to the list presented by Beck and Hertz are completely unjustifiable in view of the fact that the author has not done any extensive standardization in comparing normal and pathological groups. In conclusion it is the opinion of the present reviewer that the Howard Ink Blot Test does not appear upon the market place of clinical psychology with sufficient evidence to back up any of the contentions made. No adequate standardization data have been presented. No research concerning validity has been done, and no information has been presented whatsoever about the means that should be used in interpreting the responses to this kind of material. Indeed, under these circumstances, the question might be raised as to the appropriateness of publishing this test at this time for commercial distribution.

[142]

★An Incomplete Sentence Test for Industrial Use. Adults; 1949; Forms M (men), W (women); no data on reliability; no norms; 5¢ per test; 25¢ per manual ['49]; postage extra; (15–25) minutes; George Spache; the Author, Reading Laboratory and Clinic, University of Florida, Gainesville, Fla. *

BENJAMIN BALINSKY, *Associate Professor of Psychology, Bernard M. Baruch School of Business and Public Administration, The City College, New York, New York.*

The test was devised to obtain more useful information about an employee's personality trends than paper and pencil personality tests might give. It was considered that a more unstructured test would allow for fuller and truer expressions than the usual personality tests. The latter certainly have been shown to be fakable. The more unstructured tests are less obviously fakable, but it has not been demonstrated how

well the sentence completion technique forestalls the tendencies of people to try to show their most desirable points in a job situation. Spache is aware of the fact that some people will give evasive or noncommittal responses. It can be presumed that one will have to utilize other techniques to obtain information about personality and not leave it all to the sentence completion test.

Only 27 of the 84 items have been validated. There was a good attempt at standardizing, validating, and devising a scoring key for a larger group of items based upon the personality symptoms and attitudes sampled in an inventory used earlier by the author. However, only 50 people were included in this validation sampling and the scoring key did not function well. The 27 items which were found to have highest validity were used as the core of the present test. The manual does not indicate that the remaining items have been validated. It would have been much better to have tried out the test as it is published; as it stands now, one cannot be certain about its validity. However, incomplete sentence tests have been found to be useful in individual instances where they offered clues about the personality that fitted and bolstered clues obtained from other sources. It is in this respect that the test most likely offers valid information.

The personality categories to which items are assigned resemble those reported by Stein [1] on a sentence completion test developed in the Office of Strategic Services Assessment Program. Whether these are the best categories is not known and only much more understanding of the nature of personality will tell. The number of incomplete sentence items measuring each category varies and no reason is given for this variation. Presumably, some categories require more items than others because of differences in complexity, but this has not been spelled out. Following the suggestion of Stein, Spache employs the first person as well as the third person in his incomplete sentences. Since there is some evidence from other sources that the third person is more "projective" than the first person, it would have been a good idea to have experimented more upon this point.

Suitable cautions regarding the interpreting of the test are provided, along with an interpretation of one actual case. More criteria than the

1 STEIN, MORRIS I. "The Use of a Sentence Completion Test for the Diagnosis of Personality." *J Clin Psychol* 3:47–56 Ja '47. * (PA 21:2337)

manual presents could well have been supplied to aid in the interpretation of the incomplete sentences and of the test as a whole. However, in comparison with some other incomplete sentence tests, this one has had more than the average amount of standardization. It will be useful as an additional aid in the study of personality, but it cannot be relied upon as the sole source of information. It is particularly slanted toward employees and will probably supply worthwhile information about worker problems and attitudes.

[143]

★The Insight Test: A Verbal Projective Test for Personality Study. Adults; 1944–53; title on test is *Test of Insight Into Human Motives;* Forms 1, 2 ('53); separate editions for men and women; manual ('53, see 2 below); tentative norms; $2.50 per pad of 50 tests of either edition; $2.50 per pad of 50 scoring charts ('53); $7.50 per manual; postage extra; (60) minutes; Helen D. Sargent; Grune & Stratton, Inc. *

REFERENCES

1. FASSETT, KATHERINE K. "A Preliminary Investigation of the Sargent Test." *J Clin Psychol* 4:45–56 Ja '48. * (PA 22:5424)
2. SARGENT, HELEN D. *The Insight Test: A Verbal Projective Test for Personality Study.* The Menninger Clinic Monograph Series No. 10. New York: Grune & Stratton, Inc., 1953. Pp. xii, 276. * (PA 28:2672)
3. FASSETT, KATHERINE K. "Note on an Experimental Scoring System for the Insight Test." *J Clin Psychol* 10:393 O '54. * (PA 29:4051)
4. SARGENT, HELEN D. "Insight Test Prognosis in Successful and Unsuccessful Rehabilitation of the Blind." *J Proj Tech* 20:429–41 D '56. * (PA 32:1961)
5. DE VOS, GEORGE A. "Japanese Value-Attitudes Assessed by Application of Sargent's Insight Test Method." Abstract. *Am Psychol* 11:410 Ag '56. *
6. DEAN, SIDNEY I. "Adjustment Testing and Personality Factors of the Blind." *J Consult Psychol* 21:171–7 Ap '57. *
7. FISKE, DONALD W. "An Intensive Study of Variability Scores." *Ed & Psychol Meas* 17:453–65 w '57. *
8. ENGEL, MARY. "The Development and Applications of the Children's Insight Test." *J Proj Tech* 22:13–25 Mr '58. *

RICHARD JESSOR, *Associate Professor of Psychology, and Director, Clinical Training Program, University of Colorado, Boulder, Colorado.*

The *Insight Test* is a very interesting verbal projective technique consisting of 15 items, called armatures, in each of which a problem or conflict is described. The task of the subject is to write or state what the leading character in the situation did and why, and how he or she felt. Ambiguity of the stimulus items is sought by minimal description of the situations or the persons involved, and task- rather than self-orientation is emphasized in the instructions. The test, which is not a measure of insight despite its title, is assumed by its author to assess the characteristic affective and cognitive reactions and expressions of the subject across a variety of areas of conflict such as family, opposite sex, and vocation. There are eight forms of the test: two alternate forms for men and

two for women, and short (10-item) forms corresponding to each of these.

The present manual, an elaboration of an earlier monograph, is a model of clarity and comprehensiveness. The author skillfully describes the development of the test, its rationale, and its role in clinical diagnosis and personality appraisal, and judiciously calls attention to deficiencies, gaps, and unanswered questions. The reader is unlikely to be mislead as to the test's assets or liabilities.

As to the former, the *Insight Test* shares the virtues of techniques like story completion, sentence completion, and the TAT. It presents a socially meaningful situation to which the subject must react in a directed way. Unlike the more ambiguous tasks such as those presented by the Rorschach, there is coordination of the subject's behavior to a concrete interpersonal context. Unfortunately, this latter asset is not fully exploited by the author who, following psychoanalytic theory within which the test is interpreted, tends to consider content as relatively superficial and to stress, instead, analysis of formal structural aspects of the protocol. She does point out, however, that *Insight Test* protocols are amenable to analysis by any procedure for scoring or interpreting verbal productions, e.g., the various schemes employed in TAT content analyses. Another virtue of the test is its adaptability to particular problem areas for which specific armatures can be constructed. Sargent (4) reports, for example, on the special use of the test with blind subjects; it should be an interesting instrument also for studies of different culture groups, developmental levels (Engel (8) has developed a children's form), etc.

These latter points stress the potential value of the *Insight Test* protocol when used in much the same way as is the TAT. The author aspires, however, to a different goal—the achievement of a quasi-psychometric scoring scheme which will show the degree of balance between emotion and feeling (impulse) on the one hand, and coping or defense (impulse-control) on the other. The manual presents an elaborate scoring scheme with satisfactory definitions of variables and illustrative protocols from various diagnostic groups. There are three major scores: affect (A), defense (D), and malignancy (M), and various subscores within and in addition to these categories. When the *Insight Test* is considered from this viewpoint, however, it is an extremely dubious instrument.

The reasons for this conclusion are several: (*a*) Foremost is the fact that the standardization research is very limited and inadequate both in the number and variety of subjects tested and in the control of variables which very likely affect performance on the test. Thus, only 20 normal subjects were used in the reference or "control" group, and these were all university students. Further, the normals and the different groups of patients were not matched on such important variables as age, education, and intelligence. Conclusions about differences between groups are, therefore, difficult to ascribe to the particular pathology. For example, in a task where different categories of verbalization are scored, intelligence is very likely a contribution to variance. Yet no thorough attempt has been made to ascertain what relation exists between IQ and the various *Insight Test* scores. The recent study by Engel did show one statistically significant correlation between Stanford-Binet IQ and a subscore on the *Children's Insight Test*. Given a more heterogeneous population, it seems probable that other such correlations might be found. Research, therefore, is needed to show just how much of what the test is measuring is simply verbal fluency. (*b*) Reliability, both test-retest and interscorer, is unimpressive. The former has not been adequately assessed experimentally, and it is simply not clear what degree of consistency of performance can be expected over given time intervals. The main problem with interscorer reliability is getting agreement on what constitutes a scorable unit in a protocol. With further training, however, it should be possible to achieve satisfactory agreement among scorers. (*c*) Validity of the major scoring variables, especially the ratio of affect to defense scores, A/D, on which the author places so much importance, has not been demonstrated. In fact, two recent researches—Sargent's (4) with blind subjects and Engel's with children—showed no relation between A/D and level of psychological adjustment. Part of the validity problem seems to this reviewer to revolve around the theoretical framework within which the test was developed. There is a tendency to speak of entities like *amounts* of affect or *amounts* of cognition, and there is an undue reliance on traditional psychiatric nosology as a validity criterion.

Thus far, then, the value of the *Insight Test* as a psychometric instrument remains dubious or at least unproven. As a clinical instrument, like the TAT or incomplete sentences, it is highly provocative, seems to provide a valuable sample of verbal behavior, and strongly merits further research and development. Such research should involve rigorous experimental tests of the theoretical properties of the concepts employed, as well as adequate standardization and the accumulation of norms. Given such research, the *Insight Test* seems to this reviewer to have promise.

For related reviews, see B370.

[144]

★**Interpersonal Diagnosis of Personality.** Adults; 1955–58; a combination of assessment procedures consisting of the *Minnesota Multiphasic Personality Inventory*, the *Interpersonal Check List*, and the *Thematic Apperception Test* or the *Interpersonal Fantasy Test* (see *e* below); $12.50 per manual ('56); free specimen sets of booklets listed below; cash orders postpaid; Timothy Leary; Rolfe LaForge and Robert Suczek (*a*); Psychological Consultation Service. *
a) INTERPERSONAL CHECK LIST. [1955]; 1 form; $4 per 20 tests; $3 per scoring template, Form 4 ['54]; (15–45) minutes, depending on number of persons rated.
b) RECORD BOOKLET FOR INTERPERSONAL DIAGNOSIS OF PERSONALITY. [1955]; $5 per 20 booklets.
c) RECORD BOOKLET FOR INTERPERSONAL ANALYSIS OF GROUP DYNAMICS. [1956]; $5 per 20 booklets.
d) RECORD BOOKLET FOR INTERPERSONAL DIAGNOSIS OF FAMILY DYNAMICS. [1956]; $5 per 20 booklets.
e) INTERPERSONAL FANTASY TEST. 1957–58; 1 form ('57); no data on reliability and validity; manual ('58), free; $15 per set of 26 cards.

REFERENCES
1. FREEDMAN, MERVIN B.; LEARY, TIMOTHY F.; OSSORIO, ABEL G.; AND COFFEY, HUBERT S. "The Interpersonal Dimensions of Personality." *J Personality* 20:142–61 D '51. *
2. LAFORGE, ROLFE; LEARY, TIMOTHY F.; NABOISEK, HERBERT; COFFEY, HUBERT S.; AND FREEDMAN, MERVIN B. "The Interpersonal Dimension of Personality: II, An Objective Study of Repression." *J Personality* 23:129–53 S '54. *
3. LEARY, TIMOTHY, AND COFFEY, HUBERT S. "The Prediction of Interpersonal Behavior in Group Psychotherapy." *Group Psychother* 7:7–51 My '54. * (*PA* 29:4144)
4. LAFORGE, ROLFE, AND SUCZEK, ROBERT F. "The Interpersonal Dimension of Personality: III, An Interpersonal Check List." *J Personality* 24:94–112 S '55. * (*PA* 30:5990)
5. LEARY, TIMOTHY. "The Theory and Measurement Methodology of Interpersonal Communication." *Psychiatry* 18:147–61 My '55. * (*PA* 30:2694)
6. LEARY, TIMOTHY, AND COFFEY, HUBERT S. "Interpersonal Diagnosis: Some Problems of Methodology and Validation." *J Abn & Social Psychol* 50:110–24 Ja '55. * (*PA* 29:7241)
7. LEARY, TIMOTHY. "A Theory and Methodology for Measuring Fantasy and Imaginative Expression." *J Personality* 25:159–75 D '56. *
8. LEARY, TIMOTHY, AND HARVEY, JOAN S. "A Methodology for Measuring Personality Changes in Psychotherapy." *J Clin Psychol* 12:123–32 Ap '56. *
9. EDWARDS, ALLEN L. "Social Desirability and Probability of Endorsement of Items in the Interpersonal Check List." *J Abn & Social Psychol* 55:394–6 N '57. * (Abstract: *Am Psychol* 11:378)
10. LEARY, TIMOTHY. *Interpersonal Diagnosis of Personality: A Functional Theory and Methodology for Personality Evaluation.* New York: Ronald Press Co., 1957. Pp. xix, 518. * (*PA* 31:2556)
11. ARMSTRONG, RENATE GERBOTH. "The Leary Interpersonal Check List: A Reliability Study." *J Clin Psychol* 14:393–4 O '58. *

For related reviews, see B261.

[145]

★**Kahn Test of Symbol Arrangement.** Ages 6 and over; 1949–57; 1 form; record blank ('56); worksheet ('56); summary card ['57]; administrative manual ('56, see *11* below); clinical manual ('57, see *14* below); $25 per set of test materials; $7.50 per 50 record blanks; $2 per administrative manual; $3 per clinical manual; postage extra; (15–30) minutes; Theodore C. Kahn; Psychological Test Specialists. *

REFERENCES
1–2. See 4:110.
3. FILS, DAVID H. "Comparative Performance of Schizophrenics and Normals on a New Projective Test of Object-Symbol Arrangement." Abstract. *Am Psychol* 6:501 S '51. *
4. KAHN, THEODORE C. "Comparative Performance of Psychotics With Brain Damage and Non-Psychotics on an Original Test of Symbol Arrangement." Abstract. *Am Psychol* 6:501 S '51. *
5. KAHN, THEODORE CHARLES. *Comparative Performance of Psychotics With Brain Damage and Nonpsychotics on an Original Test of Symbol Arrangement.* Doctor's thesis, University of Southern California (Los Angeles, Calif.), 1951.
6. BRODSLY, WILLIAM J. *Comparison of Epileptic and Non-Epileptic Children on a Projective Symbol Arrangement Test.* Master's thesis, University of Southern California (Los Angeles, Calif.), 1952.
7. ESTERLY, G. R. *Comparison of Chronic Undifferentiated Schizophrenics With Brain Damaged Psychotics Using the Kahn Test of Symbol Arrangement.* Master's thesis, Trinity University (San Antonio, Tex.), 1954.
8. SZENAS, J. J. *Comparative Performance of Paranoid Schizophrenics and Brain Damaged Psychotics on a Projective Symbol Arrangement Test.* Master's thesis, Trinity University (San Antonio, Tex.), 1954.
9. KAHN, THEODORE C. "Cross Validation of the Organic Brain Pathology Scale for a Test of Symbol Arrangement." Abstract. *J Consult Psychol* 19:130 Ap '55. *
10. KAHN, THEODORE C. "Personality Projection on Culturally Structured Symbols." *J Proj Tech* 19:431–42 D '55. * (*PA* 30:7169)
11. KAHN, THEODORE C. "Kahn Test of Symbol Arrangement: Administration and Scoring." *Percept & Motor Skills* 6:299–334 D '56. * (*PA* 31:6092)
12. FINK, HOWARD H., AND KAHN, THEODORE C. "A Comparison Between Normal and Emotionally Ill Children on the Kahn Test of Symbol Arrangement." Abstract. *Am Psychol* 12:373 Jl '57. *
13. GOULDING, A. V. *Overt Acceptance of the Regulations of the Parole Board of Parolees From a Maximum Security Prison as Measured by the Kahn Test of Symbol Arrangement.* Doctor's thesis, New York University (New York, N.Y.), 1957.
14. KAHN, THEODORE C. "Kahn Test of Symbol Arrangement: Clinical Manual." *Percept & Motor Skills* 7:97–168 Je '57. * (*PA* 32:2899)
15. MURPHY, PAUL D.; FERRIMAN, M. RICHARD; AND BOLINGER, RUSSELL W. "The Kahn Test of Symbol Arrangement as an Aid to Psychodiagnosis." *J Consult Psychol* 21:503–5 D '57. *
16. KAHN, THEODORE C. "Performance of Two Types of Depressives on a Test of Symbol Arrangement." *J Clin Psychol* 14:197–9 Ap '58. *
17. KAHN, THEODORE C., AND MURPHY, PAUL D. "A New Symbol Approach to Personality Assessment." *Am J Psychiatry* 114:741–3 F '58. *
18. MURPHY, PAUL D.; BOLINGER, RUSSELL W.; AND FERRIMAN, M. RICHARD. "Screening Neuropsychiatric Patients by Means of the Kahn Test of Symbol Arrangement." *Behavioral Sci* 3:344–6 O '58. *

CHERRY ANN CLARK, *The Meyers Clinic, Los Angeles, California.*

In preparing his 1956–57 test manuals, the author obviously has given serious consideration to the *Technical Recommendations for Psychological Tests and Diagnostic Techniques,* as well as to Shoben's critique of the test in *The Fourth Mental Measurements Yearbook.* Compared with other manuals for projective techniques, Kahn's work appears to be a singularly praiseworthy effort.

The Kahn test has made notable advances in its psychometric development, but it still requires a great deal of work to establish its re-

liability and validity, with larger, more heterogeneous samples and nonparametric methods,
and more rigorous experimental designs to overcome the possible distorting effects of irregu-
larities in the distribution of samples. Investigation of specific sources of variance in relation
to criterion validation seems to be desirable and
feasible. To the reviewer, this would seem to be
one projective technique whose underlying assumptions, such as the variations in cultural determination of symbol meaning, would be relatively amenable to experimental investigation.
A parallel test would be a very valuable adjunct
to the continuing psychometric and construct
validation of the test. As a technique useful for
theoretical and empirical investigation of relatively complex personality functions, the *Kahn
Test of Symbol Arrangement* appears to warrant further carefully planned experimentation.
Before the larger theoretical problems can be
effectively handled, a concerted effort to collect
normative data remains an urgent need if the
test is to attain status as a psychometric instrument.

RICHARD JESSOR, *Associate Professor of Psychology, and Director, Clinical Training Program, University of Colorado, Boulder, Colorado.*

The *Kahn Test of Symbol Arrangement*
(KTSA) employs a set of 16 small plastic objects, such as dogs, hearts, stars, butterflies, an
anchor, a circle, and a cross, which are arranged
by a subject along a narrow felt strip marked off
into 15 equal segments numbered consecutively
from 1 to 15. Five arrangements are required—
the first two are made any way the subject
wishes; the third is made exactly like the second
(from memory); the fourth is ordered according to the subject's liking for the objects; and
the fifth is again made any way the subject
wishes. During the various trials, the subject is
asked to name the objects, to give reasons for his
arrangements and for his likings and dislikings,
and to state what each object symbolizes. These
verbalizations are categorized as to level of symbolization or abstraction and are the basis for
the major score—the symbol pattern—provided
by the test. When the various arrangements
have been concluded, the subject is required to
sort the objects into eight categories: Love,
Hate, Bad, Good, Living, Dead, Small, Large.
The administration and scoring of the test is
simple and the manual provides adequate in-

structions for both. Interscorer reliability has
been shown to be very high (above .95 in several
studies), but test-retest correlations of .95 in
two studies and .66 in one study leave this aspect
of reliability still in some doubt. The test would
seem to be of interest to a wide variety of subjects, although the required repetition of arrangements and the apparent arbitrariness of
certain instructions, e.g., the placing of some of
the objects over other objects, may irritate some
adults.

No satisfactory rationale is provided for the
test either in its construction or its validation.
The rationale section of the clinical manual is
not well thought out and is sometimes confusing, as in its discussion of the problem of behavior sampling in testing. While the author of
the test asserts the need to utilize stimuli which
are representative of life situations, there is no
demonstration of the representativeness of the
plastic objects employed. The most obvious
omissions are human objects, and their exclusion is difficult to understand. Inclusion of human figures would seem to provide a more direct basis for eliciting and inferring interpersonal reactions and attitudes than any of the
present set of objects.

The empiricism of the development of this
test is best seen in the attempts at validation.
These have been oriented almost exclusively toward the prediction of psychiatrists' decisions.
Beginning with the original study by the author
of the test, several attempts using various empirically derived formulas have been made to
demonstrate differential diagnosis of normals,
psychotics, brain damaged psychotics, character disorders, neurotics, etc. The research evidence does show some success in differential
diagnosis based primarily on the symbol pattern
score. Nevertheless, this is not sufficient evidence to justify adoption of the test for screening purposes. What remains to be shown is that
the test improves classification significantly beyond the efficiency of simple reliance on population base rates, or that it predicts diagnosis by
the psychiatrist more successfully than, say, a
15-minute interview. Claims for the utility of
the test in a remarkable array of activities from
determining vocational interests to indicating
prognosis in psychotherapy are extravagant and
unwarranted at this stage of development.
While the author is commendably cautious in
qualifying his interpretation and conclusions,
the overall impression given the reader by the

clinical manual and the publisher's descriptive sheet is, unfortunately, an inflated one.

While the KTSA seems to yield a potentially interesting sample of symbolizing behavior, the meaning of such behavior and its relation to other classes of behavior is still unclear. A thoroughgoing construct validation research program oriented toward specifying the conceptual properties of the KTSA variables would seem highly desirable if the test is to be employed in any way beyond differential diagnosis. The latter function, its main claim to fame thus far, seems of little importance to this reviewer, given the well known unreliability of disease-entity language. Where the test is used for personality evaluation rather than clinical diagnosis, its interpretation relies, according to the clinical manual, on a great deal of arbitrary analogy and undemonstrated psychoanalytic symbolism rather than on any systematic theory coordinating the test with behavior prediction. Other tests, such as the *Thematic Apperception Test,* would seem more useful than the Kahn test for such personality or motivational appraisal.

At one point in the clinical manual, the author cautions the reader that "the work presented here represents only the beginning of the long and difficult process of establishing validity." The need for further and more thoughtful research is clear. Considering the variety of already available tests, there is some question in this reviewer's mind as to whether the KTSA, as developed thus far, has shown itself worthy of such additional labor.

J Consult Psychol 21:506–7 D '57. Laurance F. Shaffer. * an intriguingly novel method for clinical appraisal which combines some features of an objective test with some of a projective technique * The *General Manual* gives clear and orderly instructions for administering and scoring the test. * The 15 research studies, several of them not previously published, give considerable information about the validity of the KTSA but have a number of shortcomings. Two studies show clear success in differentiating brain damaged cases from normals. In one study, schizophrenics were not satisfactorily separated from either normals or the brain damaged; in another all psychotics including organics were thrown together in unspecified proportions. Studies seem to give conflicting evidence as to whether neurotics are differentiated to a clinically useful degree. In no study

was attention given to the troublesome problem of the base rate. If the base rate for psychosis is 1%, the test probably yields more false positives than true positives. The projective interpretations of the instrument are stated with becoming modesty, e.g., "slanting hearts *may* indicate hostility to the opposite sex." As with many other projective methods, such interpretations spring from clinical sense and may well lead to useful idiographic hypotheses. They are supported by no evidence. Although the KTSA has been under development for about ten years, it shows many signs of still being in a process of evolution. For example, the rules for interpretation given in the manual are not those used in any reported research study. The symbol pattern interpretations stated on a reference card supplied with the set even differ a little from those in the manual. The test is clearly an interesting device for further research, but it is not yet ready for unqualified use.

For a review by Edward Joseph Shoben, Jr., see 4:110.

[146]

★**The Lowenfeld Kaleidoblocs.** Ages 2.5 and over; 1958; individual; 1 form ['58]; 2 mimeographed manuals ['58]; no data on reliability and validity; no norms; 52s. 6d. per set of test materials, postage extra; adults: 46[60] minutes; children: [30–60] minutes; Margaret Lowenfeld; Badger Tests Co., Ltd. *

REFERENCES

1. AMES, LOUISE BATES, AND LEARNED, JANET. "Developmental Trends in Child Kaleidoblock Responses." *J Genetic Psychol* 84:237–70 Je '54. * (PA 29:4023)
2. AMES, LOUISE BATES, AND LEARNED, JANET. "Individual Differences in Child Kaleidoblock Responses." *J Genetic Psychol* 85:3–38 S '54. * (PA 29:5686)

[147]

Lowenfeld Mosaic Test. Ages 2 and over; 1930–58; 1 form ['30]; 2 sets: standard (456 pieces), minor (228 pieces); directions for administering ['58]; no data on reliability; 205s. per standard set; 110s. per minor set; 10s. 6d. per tray; 21s. per 25 record booklets ('51); 50s. per manual ('54, see 25 below); postage extra; directions for administering available in French, German, and Spanish; (20–40) minutes; Margaret Lowenfeld; Badger Tests Co., Ltd. *

REFERENCES

1–13. See 4:115.
14. LOWENFELD, MARGARET. "The Mosaic Test." *Am J Orthopsychiatry* 19:537–50 Jl '49. * (PA 24:1891)
15. BLISS, WILLIAM. *The Effect of Set on Performance on the Mosaic Test.* Master's thesis, University of Florida (Gainesville, Fla.), 1950.
16. WRONG, ELIZABETH. *Comparison of the Mosaic Constructions of Children and Adults With Mental Ages Held Constant.* Master's thesis, George Washington University (Washington, D.C.), 1950.
17. BOWEN, BARBARA. *Experimentally Induced Variations in Lowenfeld Mosaic Design Types.* Master's thesis, College of the City of New York (New York, N.Y.), 1951.
18. BOWEN, BARBARA. "An Extension of the Mosaic Test, Designed to Increase Its Prognostic Value." Abstract. *J Proj Tech* 16:388–9 S '52. *
19. DÖRKEN, HERBERT, JR. "The Mosaic Test: Review." *J Proj Tech* 16:287–96 S '52. * (PA 28:2626)
20. FOUNTAIN, RALPH WARREN, JR. *Performance of College Students on the Mosaic Test and on the Minnesota Multiphasic*

Personality Inventory. Master's thesis, University of Florida (Gainesville, Fla.), 1952.

21. GELBMANN, FREDERICK. *A Study of Sex Differences in Personality Characteristics of the Deaf as Determined by the Mosaic Test.* Master's thesis, Catholic University of America (Washington, D.C.), 1952.

22. GOLDSTEIN, SEDELL. *An Exploratory Investigation of Mosaic Patterns Made by Dysphasic Clients.* Master's thesis, University of Michigan (Ann Arbor, Mich.), 1952.

23. HEALEY, ROBERT E. *A Study of Personality Differences Between Hearing and Non-Hearing Girls as Determined by the Mosaic Test.* Master's thesis, Catholic University of America (Washington, D.C.), 1952.

24. LOWENFELD, MARGARET. "The Lowenfeld Mosaic Test." *J Proj Tech* 16:200–2 Je '52. * (*PA* 28:2651)

25. LOWENFELD, MARGARET. *The Lowenfeld Mosaic Test.* New York: Grune & Stratton, Inc., 1952. Pp. 4. *

26. PASCAL, GERALD R. Chap. 11, "Gestalt Functions: The Bender-Gestalt, Mosaic and World Tests," pp. 185–90. (*PA* 27:3559) In *Progress in Clinical Psychology, Vol. I, Sect. 1.* Edited by Daniel Brower and Lawrence E. Abt. New York: Grune & Stratton, Inc., 1952. Pp. xi, 328. *

27. SCHANBERGER, WILLIAM J. *A Study of the Personality Characteristics of the Deaf and Non-Deaf as Determined by the Mosaic Test.* Master's thesis, Catholic University of America (Washington, D.C.), 1952.

28. SHNEIDMAN, EDWIN S. "The Case of Jay: Psychological Test and Anamnestic Data." *J Proj Tech* 16:297–345 S '52. * (*PA* 28:2676)

29. STEWART, URSULA G., AND LELAND, LORRAINE A. "American Versus English Mosaics." *J Proj Tech* 16:246–8 Ja '52. * (*PA* 28:2505)

30. BOVA, LOUIS WILLIAM, JR. *The Effect of Restrictions on Pattern Stability in Mosaic Productions.* Master's thesis, University of Florida (Gainesville, Fla.), 1953.

31. FORTIER, ROBERT H. "The Response to Color and Ego Functions." *Psychol B* 50:41–63 Ja '53. * (*PA* 27:7046)

32. LANE, WILLIAM PERRY. *A Replication of the Mosaic Test at Different Time Intervals.* Master's thesis, University of Florida (Gainesville, Fla.), 1953.

33. PEAK, HORACE M. *A Quantitative Approach to the Lowenfeld Mosaic Test.* Doctor's thesis, University of Southern California (Los Angeles, Calif.), 1953.

34. WIDEMAN, HARLEY R. "The Application of Quantitative Procedures to the Scoring and Validation of the Lowenfeld Mosaic Test." Abstract. *Am Psychol* 8:455 Ag '53. *

35. WIDEMAN, HARLEY R. *Development and Initial Validation of an Objective Scoring Method for the Lowenfeld Mosaic Test.* Doctor's thesis, University of Toronto (Toronto, Ont., Canada), 1953.

36. WOOLF, HENRIETTE, AND GERSON, ELAINE. "Some Approaches to the Problem of Evaluation of Mental Ability With the Mosaic Test." Discussion by M. Gertrude Reiman. *Am J Orthopsychiatry* 23:732–9 O '53. * (*PA* 28:6065)

37. BOWEN, BARBARA. "An Extension of the Mosaic Test Designed to Increase Its Prognostic Value." *J Proj Tech* 18:5–10 Mr '54. * (*PA* 29:910)

38. LALONDE, GISELE. *The Use of Twenty Characteristics in the Discrimination of Masculinity and Femininity With the Mosaic Test.* Master's thesis, University of Ottawa (Ottawa, Ont., Canada), 1954.

39. LOWENFELD, MARGARET. *The Lowenfeld Mosaic Test.* London: Newman Neame Ltd., 1954. Pp. 360. *

40 MAHER, BRENDAN A., AND MARTIN, ANTHONY W. "Mosaic Productions in Cerebro-arteriosclerosis." *J Consult Psychol* 18:40–2 F '54. * (*PA* 28:8939)

41. MARTIN, ANTHONY WILLIAM. *A Correlation of Affective States With the Use of Color on the Mosaic Test.* Doctor's thesis, Purdue University (Lafayette, Ind.), 1954. (*DA* 14:2129)

42. MORAN, MAURICE J. *An Experimental Study of Certain Aspects of Paranoid Schizophrenic Mosaic Field Organization and Their Interrelationships.* Washington, D.C.: Catholic University of America Press, 1954. Pp. 55. * (*PA* 29:2814)

43. RIOCH, MARGARET J. "The Mosaic Test as a Diagnostic Instrument and as a Technique for Illustrating Intellectual Disorganization." *J Proj Tech* 18:89–94 Mr '54. * (*PA* 29:948)

44. BRODY, CLAIRE M. H. *A Study of the Personality of Normal and Schizophrenic Adolescents Using Two Projective Tests: A Differentiation on the Basis of Structural and Behavioral Rigidity Using the Lowenfeld Mosaic and Rorschach Tests.* Doctor's thesis, New York University (New York, N.Y.), 1955. (*DA* 16:381)

45. HORNE, E. PORTER, AND BLISS, WILLIAM. "The Effect of Set on Mosaic Test Performance." *J General Psychol* 53:329–33 O '55. * (*PA* 31:7924)

46. STEWART, URSULA G., AND LELAND, LORRAINE A. "Lowenfeld Mosaics Made by First Grade Children." *J Proj Tech* 19:62–6 Mr '55. * (*PA* 30:1063)

47. WIDEMAN, HARLEY R. "Development and Initial Validation of an Objective Scoring Method for the Lowenfeld Mosaic Test." *J Proj Tech* 19:177–91 Je '55. * (*PA* 30:2936)

48. WOLFF, FRANCES. *An Exploratory Study of the Relationship of Certain Aspects of the Mosaic Test to Self-Esteem.* Master's thesis, Cornell University (Ithaca, N.Y.), 1955.

49. DÖRKEN, HERBERT, JR. "The Mosaic Test: A Second Review." *J Proj Tech* 20:164–71 Je '56. * (*PA* 31:4681)

50. LEVIN, MONROE L. "Validation of the Lowenfeld Mosaic Test." *J Consult Psychol* 20:239–48 Ag '56. * (*PA* 31:7941)

51. MILBURN, BRAXTON. *Performance of the Deaf on the Lowenfeld Mosaic and the Mooney Closure Tests.* Master's thesis, University of Texas (Austin, Tex.), 1956.

52. JOHNSON, THOMAS F. "The Function of the Mosaic Test in Clinical Practice." *J General Psychol* 56:51–8 Ja '57. *

53. ROBERTSON, MALCOLM H. "Scoring Intelligence on the Lowenfeld Mosaic Test." Abstract. *J Consult Psychol* 21:418 O '57. *

54. STEWART, URSULA; LELAND, LORRAINE; AND STRIETER, EDITH. "Mosaic Patterns of Eighth Grade Children." *J Proj Tech* 21:73–9 Mr '57. * (*PA* 32:2922)

55. WALKER, RICHARD NORRIS. *Children's Mosaic Designs: A Normative and Validating Study of the Lowenfeld Mosaic Test.* Doctor's thesis, University of Minnesota (Minneapolis, Minn.), 1957. (*DA* 19:367)

56. CARR, GWEN L. "Mosaic Differences in Non-Institutionalized Retarded Children." *Am J Mental Def* 62:908–11 Mr '58. *

C. J. ADCOCK, *Senior Lecturer in Psychology, Victoria Univesrity of Wellington, Wellington, New Zealand.*

This test invites a very ambivalent attitude. On the one hand, one observes a vast range of responses to the invitation to "make anything you want" with the delightful collection of brightly coloured squares, triangles, and diamonds provided. An examination of several such efforts convinces one that it should be possible to discover fundamental principles underlying the variety. On the other hand, when one attempts to interpret the results in the light of the 300-odd pages of text now available, one is impressed by how little in the way of systematic principles is at one's disposal. Patterns can be classified as representational, conceptual, or abstract; as edge, frame, corner, or pendant; as compact, intermediate, or spaced. But when all this has been learned, one has merely acquired a few useful descriptive terms and must wrestle with new subtleties—some very difficult to convey and all very difficult to assess.

Most projective tests depend upon skill rather than any simple set of rules, but this applies with special force to the mosaic test. Long training under an expert and much experience are necessary for the would-be user. The need for such extensive training may be simply a reflection of the fact that this test is responsive to so many influences, cognitive, affective, and environmental, and that there are no simple factors of a psychological nature underlying it. It appears never to be safe to make a blind diagnosis, even with regard to the most obvious matters. Nevertheless, the testee does appear to reveal in his designs important aspects of his way of life. The test invites a useful slice of behaviour and sometimes, e.g., with schizophrenics, obtains this sample when most other methods fail. As a clinical tool it has very important possibilities. Used in conjunction with

interview and analytic techniques, it might be very fruitful, but it might be a very dangerous instrument in the hands of the unskilled and without the insight of the trained analyst.

This reviewer cannot help feeling that some of the difficulty in the application of this test arises from the fact that it has been developed largely in a clinical setting with little opportunity or incentive to carry out careful statistical investigations. Systematic experimentation might reveal some useful information with regard to personality variables involved or, at least, throw some light on factors of a nonpersonality type which influence the test and which need to be allowed for interpretation. In the meantime, it is safe to say that the mosaic test is not for the dabbler.

For related reviews, see B274.

[148]

Machover Draw-A-Person Test. Ages 2 and over; 1949; also called *Machover Figure Drawing Test*; individual; $4.25 (30s.) per manual (see 5 below); cash orders postpaid; (5–60) minutes without associations, (20–90) minutes with associations; Karen Machover; Charles C Thomas, Publisher. * (English publisher: Blackwell Scientific Publications, Ltd.)

REFERENCES

1–13. See 4:111.
14. ANDRULONIS, JEROME A. *Relation Between Machover's Drawing of the Human Figure Test and Certain Variables on the Minnesota Multiphasic Personality Inventory.* Master's thesis, Fordham University (New York, N.Y.), 1951.
15. FINNEGAN, SHIRLEY DEWITT. *Comparison of Responses of a Matched Group of Normal and Mentally Retarded Children on the Children's Apperception Test and the Machover Draw-a-Person Test.* Master's thesis, San Francisco State College (San Francisco, Calif.), 1951.
16. MARLENS, HANNA STEINER. *Graphic Syndromes of Reading Disabilities in the Machover Human Figure Drawing Test.* Master's thesis, College of the City of New York (New York, N.Y.), 1951.
17. BROWN, FRED. Chap. 10, "House-Tree-Person and Human Figure Drawings," pp. 173–84. (PA 27:3546) In *Progress in Clinical Psychology, Vol. I, Sect. i.* Edited by Daniel Brower and Lawrence E. Abt. New York: Grune & Stratton, Inc., 1952. Pp. xi, 328. *
18. HOLTZMAN, WAYNE H. "The Examiner as a Variable in the Draw-A-Person Test." *J Consult Psychol* 16:145–8 Ap '52. *
19. SHNEIDMAN, EDWIN S. "The Case of Jay: Psychological Test and Anamnestic Data." *J Proj Tech* 16:297–345 S '52. * (PA 28:2676)
20. BARKER, ALMAN J.; MATHIS, JERRY K.; AND POWERS, CLAIR A. "Drawing Characteristics of Male Homosexuals." *J Clin Psychol* 9:185–8 Ap '53. * (PA 28:2885)
21. GRANICK, SAMUEL, AND SMITH, LEON J. "Sex Sequence in the Draw-a-Person Test and Its Relation to the MMPI Masculinity-Femininity Scale." *J Consult Psychol* 17:71–3 F '53. * (PA 28:950)
22. MAINORD, FLORENCE R. "A Note on the Use of Figure Drawings in the Diagnosis of Sexual Inversion." *J Clin Psychol* 9:188–9 Ap '53. * (PA 28:2654)
23. MACHOVER, KAREN. "Drawings of the Human Figure." *Monogr Soc Res Child Develop* 16(53):89–137, 214–316 '53. * (PA 28:4077)
24. WHARTON, LYLE HARRISON. *Effect of Stress-Produced Anxiety on Rorschach, Draw-A-Person, and Visual Performance.* Doctor's thesis, State University of Iowa (Iowa City, Iowa), 1953. (DA 13:1268)
25. BLISS, MONTE, AND BERGER, ANDREW. "Measurement of Mental Age as Indicated by the Male Figure Drawings of the Mentally Subnormal Using Goodenough and Machover Instructions." *Am J Mental Def* 59:73–9 Jl '54. * (PA 29:4253)
26. BLUM, RICHARD H. "The Validity of the Machover DAP Technique: A Study in Clinical Agreement." *J Clin Psychol* 10:120–5 Ap '54. * (PA 29:906)
27. GALLESE, ARTHUR J., JR., AND SPOERL, DOROTHY TILDEN. "A Comparison of Machover and Thematic Apperception Test Interpretation." *J Social Psychol* 40:73–7 Ag '54. * (PA 29:5703)
28. MACHOVER, K. Chap. 12, "The Figure-Drawing Test," pp. 235–54, passim. In *Personality Through Perception: An Experimental and Clinical Study.* By H. A. Witkin and others. New York: Harper & Brothers, 1954. Pp. xxvii, 571. * (PA 28:8566)
29. WILLE, WARREN S. "Figure Drawings in Amputees." *Psychiatric Q Sup* 28:192–8 pt 2 '54. * (PA 29:7814)
30. WITKIN, H. A.; LEWIS, H. B.; HERTZMAN, M.; MACHOVER, K.; MEISSNER, P. BRETNALL; AND WAPNER, S. *Personality Through Perception: An Experimental and Clinical Study.* New York: Harper & Brothers, 1954. Pp. xxvi, 571. * (PA 28:8566)
31. FRANK, GEORGE H. "A Test of the Use of a Figure Drawing Test as an Indicator of Sexual Inversion." *Psychol Rep* 1:137–8 S '55. * (PA 30:6111)
32. HAWARD, L. R. C., AND ROLAND, W. A. "Some Inter-Cultural Differences on the Draw-a-Man Test: Part II, Machover Scores." *Man* 55:27–9 F '55. *
33. HAWARD, L. R. C., AND ROLAND, W. A. "Some Inter-Cultural Differences on the Draw-a-Man Test: Part III, Conclusion." *Man* 55:40–2 Mr '55. *
34. SWENSEN, CLIFFORD H., AND NEWTON, KENNETH R. "The Development of Sexual Differentiation on the Draw-A-Person Test." *J Clin Psychol* 11:417–9 O '55. * (PA 30:6006)
35. BAILEY, ROBERT BAIN. *A Study of Predicting Academic Success in Elementary School Reading From Projective Tests.* Doctor's thesis, University of Oklahoma (Norman, Okla.), 1956. (DA 16:1397)
36. CRAMER-AZIMA, FERN J. "Personality Changes and Figure Drawings: A Case Treated with ACTH." *J Proj Tech* 20:143–9 Je '56. * (PA 31:4678)
37. EVERETT, EVALYN G. *A Comparative Study of Paretics, Hebephrenics, and Paranoid Schizophrenics on a Battery of Psychological Tests.* Doctor's thesis, New York University (New York, N.Y.), 1956. (DA 16:1502)
38. LAKIN, MARTIN. "Certain Formal Characteristics of Human Figure Drawings by Institutionalized Aged and by Normal Children." *J Consult Psychol* 20:471–4 D '56. * (PA 32:1629)
39. MACHOVER, KAREN, AND ZADEK, MILDRED. "Human Figure Drawings of Hospitalized Involutionals." *Psychiatric Q Sup* 30:222–40 pt 2 '56. *
40. MARCUS, MURRAY. *Behavioral Differences on the Machover Draw-A-Person Test Between Slow and Fast College Readers.* Doctor's thesis, University of Denver (Denver, Colo.), 1956.
41. REZNIKOFF, MARVIN, AND TOMBLEN, DONALD. "The Use of Human Figure Drawings in the Diagnosis of Organic Pathology." *J Consult Psychol* 20:467–70 D '56. * (PA 32:1642)
42. SIPPRELLE, CARL N., AND SWENSEN, CLIFFORD H. "Relationship of Sexual Adjustment to Certain Sexual Characteristics of Human Figure Drawings." *J Consult Psychol* 20:197–8 Je '56. * (PA 31:6133)
43. SWENSEN, CLIFFORD H., AND SIPPRELLE, CARL N. "Some Relationships Among Sexual Characteristics of Human Figure Drawings." *J Proj Tech* 20:224–6 Je '56. * (PA 31:4717)
44. WANNER, PAUL W. *A Partial Test of Validity of the Machover Drawing-of-a-Human-Figure Technique.* Master's thesis, Sacramento State College (Sacramento, Calif.), 1956.
45. MURPHY, MARY MARTHA. "Sexual Differentiation of Male and Female Job Applicants on the Draw-A-Person Test." *J Clin Psychol* 13:87–8 Ja '57. *
46. REED, MAX R. "The Masculinity-Femininity Dimension in Normal and Psychotic Subjects." *J Abn & Social Psychol* 55:289–94 N '57. *
47. SOHLER, DOROTHY TERRY; HOLZBERG, JULES D.; FLECK, STEPHEN; CORNELISON, ALICE R.; KAY, ELEANOR; AND LIDZ, THEODORE. "The Prediction of Family Interaction From a Battery of Projective Techniques." *J Proj Tech* 21:199–208 Je '57. *
48. FELDMAN, MARVIN J., AND HUNT, RAYMOND G. "The Relation of Difficulty in Drawing to Ratings of Adjustment Based on Human Figure Drawings." *J Consult Psychol* 22:217–9 Je '58. *
49. GRAMS, ARMIN, AND RINDER, LAWRENCE. "Signs of Homosexuality in Human-Figure Drawings." Abstract. *J Consult Psychol* 22:394 O '58. *
50. REZNIKOFF, MARVIN, AND NICHOLAS, ALMA L. "An Evaluation of Human-Figure Drawing Indicators of Paranoid Pathology." *J Consult Psychol* 22:395–7 O '58. *
51. SHERMAN, LEWIS J. "Sexual Differentiation or Artistic Ability?" *J Clin Psychol* 14:170–1 Ap '58. *
52. VILHOTTI, ANTHONY J. "An Investigation of the Use of the D.A.P. in the Diagnosis of Homosexuality in Mentally Deficient Males." *Am J Mental Def* 62:708–11 Ja '58. *

For reviews by Philip L. Harriman and Naomi Stewart, see 4:111; for related reviews, see 4:112.

[149]

*Make A Picture Story. Ages 6 and over; 1947–52; individual; 1 form ('47); manual ('52, see 27 below); no data on reliability and validity; $16 per set of test materials, 25 figure location sheets, and manual; $1.60 per 25 figure location sheets ('48); $2.50 per manual; postpaid; (45–90) minutes; Edwin S. Shneidman; Psychological Corporation. *

REFERENCES

1–19. See 4:113.
20. FRAIMOW, IDA SYLVIA. *The Use of the Make-A-Picture-Story Tests (MAPS) With Mentally Retarded Children and Children of Normal Intellectual Development.* Master's thesis, Pennsylvania State College (State College, Pa.), 1950.
21. CONANT, JAMES C. *A Comparison of Thematic Fantasy Among Normals, Neurotics, and Schizophrenics.* Doctor's thesis, University of Southern California (Los Angeles, Calif.), 1951.
22. SHNEIDMAN, EDWIN S.; JOEL, WALTHER; AND LITTLE, KENNETH B. "An Empirical Categorization of Psychological Test Report Items." Abstract. *Am Psychol* 6:492 S '51. *
23. FINE, REUBEN. "Interpretation of Jay's Make-A-Picture-Story Method: The Case of Jay: Interpretations and Discussion." *J Proj Tech* 16:449–53, discussion 444–5, 462–73 D '52. * (*PA* 28:2678)
24–5. MCDONALD, FRANKLIN RANDOLPH. *The Effect of Differential Cultural Pressures on Projective Test Performances of Negroes.* Doctor's thesis, University of Southern California (Los Angeles, Calif.), 1952.
26. SHNEIDMAN, EDWIN S. "The Case of Jay: Psychological Test and Anamnestic Data." *J Proj Tech* 16:297–345 S '52. * (*PA* 28:2676)
27. SHNEIDMAN, EDWIN S. *Manual for the Make A Picture Story Method.* Projective Techniques Monograph No. 2. New York: Society for Projective Techniques and Rorschach Institute, Inc., July 1952. Pp. iv, 92. * (*PA* 27:6542)
28. CHAREN, SOL. "The Interaction of Background and Characters in Picture Test Story Telling." *J Clin Psychol* 10:290–2 Jl '54. * (*PA* 29:2439)
29. VAN KREVELEN, ALICE. "A Study of Examiner Influence on Responses to MAPS Test Materials." *J Clin Psychol* 10:292–3 Jl '54. * (*PA* 29:2482)
30. FINE, REUBEN. "Manual for a Scoring Scheme for Verbal Projective Techniques (TAT, MAPS, Stories and the Like)." *J Proj Tech* 19:310–6 S '55. * (*PA* 30:4570)
31. LITTLE, KENNETH B., AND SHNEIDMAN, EDWIN S. "A Comparison of the Reliability of Interpretations of Four Psychological Tests." Abstract. *Am Psychol* 10:322 Ag '55. *
32. SPIEGELMAN, MARVIN. "Jungian Theory and the Analysis of Thematic Tests." *J Proj Tech* 19:253–63 S '55. * (*PA* 30:4601)
33. PROUD, ANN P. *Response to Picture-Thematic Stimulus Material as a Function of Stimulus Structure.* Doctor's thesis, University of California (Los Angeles, Calif.), 1956.
34. SMITH, JOHN R., AND COLEMAN, JAMES C. "The Relationship Between Manifestations of Hostility in Projective Tests and Overt Behavior." *J Proj Tech* 20:326–34 S '56. * (*PA* 31:6134)
35. SPIEGELMAN, MARVIN. "A Note on the Use of Fine's Scoring System with the MAPS Tests of Children." *J Proj Tech* 20:442–4 D '56. * (*PA* 32:1648)
36. BINDON, D. MARJORIE. "Make-A-Picture Story (MAPS) Test Findings for Rubella Deaf Children." *J Abn & Social Psychol* 53:38–42 Jl '57. *
37. HOOKER, EVELYN. "The Adjustment of the Male Overt Homosexual." *J Proj Tech* 21:18–31 Mr '57. *
38. EDGAR, CLARA LEE, AND SHNEIDMAN, EDWIN S. "Some Relationships Among Thematic Projective Tests of Various Degrees of Structuredness and Behavior in a Group Situation." *J Proj Tech* 22:3–12 Mr '58. *

For reviews by Albert I. Rabin and Charles R. Strother, see 4:113; for related reviews, see 4:114.

[150]

★The Michigan Picture Test. Ages 8–14; 1953; individual; 1 form; $6.50 per set of pictures; $1.80 per 20 record blanks; $2 per manual; $9 per specimen set including the complementary *Rating Scale for Pupil Adjustment* (see 102); postage extra; (60) minutes; Gwen Andrew, Samuel W. Hartwell, Max L. Hutt, and Ralph E. Walton; Science Research Associates. *

REFERENCES

1. ANDREW, GWEN; WALTON, RALPH E.; HARTWELL, SAMUEL W.; AND HUTT, MAX L. "The Michigan Picture Test: The Stimulus Values of the Cards." *J Consult Psychol* 15:51–4 F '51. * (*PA* 26:6247)

2. HARTWELL, SAMUEL W.; HUTT, MAX L.; ANDREW, GWEN; AND WALTON, RALPH E. "The Michigan Picture Test: Diagnostic and Therapeutic Possibilities of a New Projective Test in Child Guidance." *Am J Orthopsychiatry* 21:124–37 Ja '51. * (*PA* 25:8094)
3. RINGWALL, EGAN AUGUST. *Some Picture Story Characteristics as Measures of Personality Traits of Children.* Doctor's thesis, University of Michigan (Ann Arbor, Mich.), 1951. (*Microfilm Abstr* 11:752)
4. WALTON, R. E.; ANDREW, GWEN; HARTWELL, S. W.; AND HUTT, M. L. "A Tension Index of Adjustment Based on Picture Stories Elicited by the Michigan Picture Test." *J Abn & Social Psychol* 46:438–41 Jl '51. * (*PA* 26:2199)
5. GURIN, MAIZIE G. "Differences Between Latents and Adolescents: A Psychoanalytic Study Utilizing the Michigan Picture Test." *Papers Mich Acad Sci Arts & Letters* 38:495–503 '53. *
6. GURIN, MAIZIE G. *Differences in the Psychological Characteristics of Latency and Adolescence.* Doctor's thesis, University of Michigan (Ann Arbor, Mich.), 1953.
7. CLOONAN, THEODORE F. *Objective Identification of Maladjustment in Children by Use of a Modified Projective Technique.* Doctor's thesis, Purdue University (Lafayette, Ind.), 1958. (*DA* 19:360)

WILLIAM E. HENRY, *Associate Professor of Human Development and Psychology, The University of Chicago, Chicago, Illinois.*

This test is the result of a study to evaluate the emotional reactions of children 8 to 14 years of age undertaken by the Michigan Department of Mental Health. The study involved, among other things, the development of a set of 16 TAT-like pictures. Four of the pictures are for use with boys only and four for use with girls only; thus, only 12 pictures are presented to any one child. Four core pictures may be used as a short screening test for general emotional adjustment.

This 16-card set was selected from a much larger series on the basis of the results of a number of preliminary studies. The pictures themselves are moderately realistic but yet ambiguous representations of scenes depicting intrafamilial conflicts, conflicts with authority figures, conflicts involving physical danger, sexual difficulties, school situation conflicts, feelings of personal inadequacy, confusions in self-percept, conflicts involving aggressive drives, and feelings of social inadequacy.

Responses to the test have been analyzed in terms of a number of variables. The "tension index" refers to the frequency of verbalized expressions of unresolved conflict. The score is based on seven psychological needs—love, extrapunitiveness, intropunitiveness, succorance, superiority, submission, and personal adequacy. Four of these needs were found to be useful in discriminating between groups of well and poorly adjusted children—love, extrapunitiveness, submission, and personal adequacy. Critical scores computed for the tension index show the probability that a given score will place a child within the well or poorly adjusted groups. Thus, at grade 3, a child with a tension index of

4 has a 78 per cent probability of belonging to the poorly adjusted group, and a 55 per cent probability of belonging to the well adjusted group; if the tension index is 5, the probability of poor adjustment increases.

Interscorer reliability based on ratings of two judges differs for the various needs, but for all needs at all grade levels averages .98. Similarly high reliabilities are reported for other variables, such as tense of verbs used and direction of forces. This latter variable refers to the expressed actions in the story—whether they emanate from the central figure, are directed upon the central figure, or are neutral in that no direction is indicated. Still other variables, for which trends are reported but for which no statistically significant findings have been determined, are psychosexual level, interpersonal relationships, personal pronouns, and level of interpretation.

The test, analyzed in the terms above, has also shown good results from three other projects briefly summarized. The accompanying manual reports the development of the test and the research that has been done on it. It also describes the technique of administering the pictures and the method of scoring the responses, and presents a sample analyzed case. A scoring form is provided. From the work reported to date, the *Michigan Picture Test* seems to hold considerable promise as a semi-objective test of important personality and adjustment variables for school children.

MORRIS KRUGMAN, *Assistant Superintendent in Charge of Guidance, New York Public Schools, New York, New York.*

As a rule, authors of projective tests do not utilize acceptable objective techniques for the validation of their instruments. In this respect the *Michigan Picture Test* is different; the authors apparently spared no effort in their attempt to avoid the errors of other personality test constructors. The manual appropriately summarizes their rationale and procedures.

In spite of excellent effort, however, the results are disappointing thus far. The authors hold high hopes for the test ultimately, but they are meticulously honest in interpreting their standardization data and making no exaggerated claims for currently available results.

The test consists of 16 pictures to be interpreted, four of which are for boys only and four for girls only. A core of four pictures can be

used for screening purposes. The test purports to measure emotional reactions of children 8 to 14 years of age. The pictures were carefully selected to present a minimum of trauma and to contain characters with which children of the particular age group could identify. Although 1,400 children in representative school systems and child guidance clinics in Michigan were experimented with, only 700 were included in the standardization.

An 11-item *Rating Scale for Pupil Adjustment* (see 102), filled in by teachers of regular public school classes, was used to locate children upon whom validity studies could be conducted. The upper and lower thirds of the classes, rated on the basis of "total emotional adjustment," were assumed to be, respectively, the well adjusted and the poorly adjusted children. Without in the least attempting to be facetious, this reviewer would like to ask why it is necessary to attempt to develop a complex clinical instrument that accomplishes much less effectively what a simple rating scale used by classroom teachers is assumed to do much better?

The authors selected eight variables considered by them to have high degrees of discrimination. Five of these they found to be "variables for which trends were indicated, but in which differences were not statistically significant." These were psychosexual level, interpersonal relationships, personal pronouns, popular objects, and level of interpretation. The other three are described as variables that "effectively discriminate between groups of well- and poorly-adjusted children at some, if not all, grade levels." These variables are not nearly so discriminating as this general statement would seem to indicate. Following are some specific limitations, in the authors' words, of the three variables:

Tension Index ("verbalized psychological needs") : "There will be many 'false positives' with critical scores which include about half of the well-adjusted children, but scrutiny of the particular needs a child most often expresses will help to eliminate those who are well-adjusted." In other words, not the critical score, but subjective judgment determines the state of a child's adjustment.

Verb Tense (relative emphasis on past, present, and future) : "Specific tests of these hypotheses are not yet available, but we do have evidence of the over-all relationship between tense and adjustment."

Direction of Forces (whether the central figure tends to act or be acted upon) : "This procedure was carried out for all grade levels and no significant differences were found." (Direction of forces was found to relate to adjustment but frequency of directional reference was not.) In addition, "note that although one might expect the centrifugal direction to be most commonly used by well-adjusted, and centripetal by poorly-adjusted children, this does not actually prove to be true." Well adjusted children were found to use more of both directions.

The *Michigan Picture Test,* then, has value if used by the skillful clinician as an indicator of trends in designated directions. It is an instrument that has considerable promise, but cannot, as yet, be considered a satisfactorily validated test of "emotional reactions."

J Consult Psychol 18:475–6 D '54. Laurance F. Shaffer. * No other picture-story test has been accompanied by so much data relevant to its standardization and validation. * Scoring reliability is good, but there are no data on subject response reliability. * well-prepared manual * a useful clinical tool for an age group hitherto ignored in the construction of apperception tests.

J Proj Tech 19:192–3 Je '55. Edwin S. Shneidman. * How does this test differ from, or add to, the TAT? In what ways is it an improvement over Symond's Picture Story materials? Or, over the Travis-Johnston Projection Test? Or Bellak's CAT? Further, is it sound psychological practice to prepare a different set of picture-thematic materials for each age group? And, to what extent should psychological test materials be tailor-made for specific age, ethnic, and political groups? * This reviewer feels like Dr. Robert Holt when he wrote: "So the NAT....and the UAT....are joining the CAT...., VAT....and the rest of them. Soon we'll get to the ZAT, and there I hope the new variants will stop, because zat's enough." A more severe criticism lies in the neglect of the Michigan authors to relate their new materials (no matter how good) to previous materials, especially *the* TAT. This error of omission is a conspicuous shortcoming in their project. * The authors have evidently thought about the problem of selection and know the relevant literature. In addition, they have evolved a set of seven criteria which each picture should meet. It seems disappointing, then, after all this effort that one reads in the manual that "the selection

of the areas of conflict to be sampled by the Michigan pictures was an 'armchair' process which we could only hope would be adequate ....we were developing the scoring methods and the test pictures concurrently. We were forced, therefore, to evaluate the scoring in terms of pictures which had been selected on an *a priori* basis....This fact implies the need for future revision of the test." Little is stated as to how the pictures were actually selected. * The manual is, in many ways, the best manual for a projective technique to date. There is much wisdom and many springboards for research ideas within it. It is well organized and clearly expressed. (Only in the first few chapters of the manual was I disturbed by vagueness and generalities where I sought specific information.) In many ways the manual measures up to the "Essential" standards proposed by the Cronbach Committee and in this way, too, sets a new standard for techniques of this sort. One of the "Essential" standards indicated by the Cronbach Committee is that the professional qualifications required to administer and interpret the test should be indicated. The manual under discussion does not clearly indicate these, although the manual does use the words "examiner," "clinician" and "the clinical staff"; the matter is confused, however, by the printed notice that accompanied the review copy which stated that "teachers and counselors will find the SRA *Michigan Picture Test* valuable in the study of child behavior." * In spite of the critical and negative comments above, this reviewer feels that the *Michigan Picture Test* looks interesting, seems useful, deserves a trial, presents a manual which might well be emulated, and leaves one with admiration for the authors' labors.

[151]

★The Object Relations Technique. Ages 11 and over; 1955; 1 form ['55]; manual ('55, see 3 below) ; no data on reliability; 63s. ($10) per set of 13 cards and manual, postage extra; (90) minutes; Herbert Phillipson; Tavistock Publications Ltd. (United States distributor: Free Press). *

REFERENCES
1. PHILLIPSON, H. "A Modification of Thematic Apperception Technique Based on the Psychoanalytic Theory of Unconscious Object Relations." Abstract. *B Brit Psychol Soc* (19): 28 Ja '53. *
2. O'KELLY, E. "The Object Relations Test: Some Quantitative Findings Relating to Early Separation From the Mother." *Brit Rorsch Forum* (7):23–5 N '55. *
3. PHILLIPSON, HERBERT. *The Object Relations Technique.* London: Tavistock Publications, Ltd., 1955. Pp. x, 224. (*PA* 30:5441)
4. STAUNTON, G. J. "A Comparative Analysis of Rorschach and T.A.T. Responses With Reference to a Particular Case Study." Abstract. *Brit Rorsch Forum* (6):1–4 Ap '55. *
5. ALCOCK, A. THEODORA, AND PHILLIPSON, H. "The Use of

Rorschach and Object Relations Technique in Vocational Selection Work." Abstract. *Rorsch Newsl* 1:18–9 D '56. *
6. O'KELLY, ELIZABETH. "An Investigation, by Means of the Object Relations Test, Into Some of the Effects of Early Separation From the Mother on the Personal Relationships of Adolescent Delinquent Girls." *J Mental Sci* 103:381–91 Ap '57. *

GEORGE WESTBY, *Head, Department of Psychology, The University of Hull, Hull, England.*

Among the many over-elaborated projective techniques, often of forced "originality," which followed upon the clinical popularity of the Rorschach and the TAT, few show both specificity of theoretical background and novelty of construction. The Phillipson *Object Relations Technique* can undoubtedly claim these distinctions. Moreover, since it has evolved very largely in the theoretical and practical ferment which followed recent experiments in group therapy by a number of workers at the Tavistock Clinic, London, it owes much to the latest developments of the "English" wing of the psychoanalytic school in Britain associated with Klein and Fairbairn (to be distinguished from the viewpoint of Anna Freud and Glover). It is the opinion of this reviewer that the test need not stand or fall with the "object relations" theory. From the test construction viewpoint, it is true that the development of the technique has been based upon an acceptance of the theory and not on empirical experimentation with a view to the prediction of external criteria. In this respect it is matched in the field of personality assessment only by the *Szondi Test,* which is bound even more closely to a theory which must be esoteric to the majority of present-day psychologists.

It is not appropriate in this review to do more than indicate that the underlying theoretical contribution of Fairbairn to the psychology of human motives may yet prove to be a significant step towards a true integration of the Freudian contribution with current "drive-reduction and social learning" theories. Fairbairn certainly stresses "adaptation to the social environment" as the specific subject of enquiry of the psychologist. It is certain, however, that Phillipson would scarcely be satisfied if clinical psychologists attempted to use this test (as many have indeed used the van Lennep *Four-Picture Test* and similar techniques) with eclectic theory or empirical principles taken "off the cuff." If one wishes to understand fully the purpose of the test, a thorough acquaintance is advised not only with the author's discussion in the textbook manual of the theoretical basis of the technique, but also with Fairbairn's *Psycho-Analytic Studies of the Personality* [1] or, at the very least, the summary by Money-Kyrle of object relations theory in the early chapters of *Psychoanalysis and Politics.* [2] Not unexpectedly, Phillipson, like all psychoanalytic workers in this field, lays great stress on the need for "patient accumulation of experience of unconscious dynamics" as a necessary foundation for the profitable use of this (as of all) projective techniques.

The test consists of three series of four pictures on cards of convenient size, and includes the well known TAT blank card item. Each picture of each series is designed to elicit the characteristic modes of response ("the unconscious object relations") of the subject to one of the following situations: (*a*) the one person relationship, (*b*) the two person relationship, (*c*) the three person relationship, and (*d*) a group relationship. Pilot work has also been done on a presentation of the four person relationship to cover the first sibling situation, but experience suggested, says Phillipson, that the attempt to cover this "did not outweigh the disadvantage of extending the whole series." The patience and care with which the five years of preparatory work on this test was carried out is worthy of special comment; this is in sharp contrast to the hasty productions of many self-conscious innovators in this field who have, at all costs, attempted to leap on the bandwagon with their own little drums while the circus was still attracting the crowds.

While not so unstructured as the Stern cloud pictures or the Rorschach blots, the cards have a far higher degree of ambiguity than the TAT or Symonds pictures. They are in some respects —the ambiguous sex of the figures and the "soft" artistic treatment, for instance—reminiscent of the pictures of the Jackson *Test of Family Attitudes,* except that there is, in Series C, an attempt to use subtle pastel color with a little sharp red in a manner obviously much influenced by Rorschach theory. The suggestion is made that "the introduction of colour intensifies the threats and supports in the stimulus in terms of real emotional involvement." In the B series the ambiguous shadowgraph figures are placed in very general but significant everyday environments—in a kitchen, in a bedroom, outside a house, in a public place.

The administration of the test is carefully de-

1 FAIRBAIRN, W. R. D. *Psycho-Analytic Studies of the Personality.* London: Tavistock Publications, Ltd., 1952.
2 MONEY-KYRLE, R. E. *Psychoanalysis and Politics.* London: Gerald Duckworth & Co., Ltd., 1951.

scribed. It has obviously been determined by the classical clinical attitude to individual testing, but there are a few interesting points. "It should be presented with a purpose which the subject can share," warns the author. An introductory conversational enquiry which is intended to act as a lead-in to establish rapport and guarantee productivity of response is outlined; the general nature is indicated by the question: "Will you tell me....the sort of things you really enjoy most and then those you're not so keen on, or that you really dislike?" An after-test enquiry is also recommended which follows conventional lines, except for an attempt to introduce a Rorschach-type "testing of the limits" in cases where no solution has been offered. However, the time taken by the test (an average of one and one-half hours), as Phillipson confesses, leaves little time for such extra enquiry. Indeed, perhaps a major criticism of the whole technique is that if, in addition to administration, four or five hours are spent in scoring and interpretation, the test is too expensive in time for the average clinical psychologist. It is either a luxury research instrument which may eventually lead to a more economical technique, or it is to be considered as a possible routine method of examination for those generously staffed teaching hospitals and clinics which are the overprivileged and the envied of the profession.

The manual includes a remarkably detailed case study with a full clinical background. There are full interpretations of the test protocols which throw much light on the way in which object relations theory may be used. A suggested scheme is added for scoring the themes and the "main dynamics of the tension systems." There are also half a dozen shorter case illustrations. On the other hand, normative data are at present limited to a psychiatric outpatient clinic sample of 50 patients of above average intelligence, and 40 normal adolescent girls from secondary schools. The author sees the need for further data. Unfortunately, the difficulties of research which will satisfy even the most liberal scientific criteria of reliability and validity are particularly intractable with this type of test.

The dust-jacket "blurb" claims that the pictures used in the *Object Relations Technique* have been shown to be "*particularly* suitable for use by experienced psychologists working *outside* the clinical field, in social research and in personnel selection in industry" (reviewer's italics). There are no data on validity in these fields referred to by the author. Since the test is presented in the manual exclusively as a clinical tool, it seems a pity that the publishers have felt it necessary to make such sweeping claims instead of perhaps entertaining a more realistic hope of its use as a research tool for the gathering of data upon which a useful judgment of its value outside the clinical situation could be made.

A test of this theoretically explicit type necessarily has the defect of its special merit. Those who cannot accept the object-relations brand of psychoanalytic theory will refuse to consider the practical usefulness of the instrument. In this particular case, in the reviewer's opinion, this would be regrettable because many of the special features of the test come from a notably reflective consideration of the problems which have emerged in the psychology of perception, and from the practical experience of a variety of psychologists with projective techniques over the past quarter of a century. The test could be used with a minimum of depth-psychological theory.

The summary conclusion is offered that the test has original features which may eventually justify its addition to a practical apparatus for clinical assessment and enquiry, even by those who would wish to reject the object relations theory in its present form.

For related reviews, see B338.

[152]
★The Picture Impressions: A Projective Technique for Investigating the Patient-Therapist Relationship. Adolescents and adults; 1956; individual; Forms F ['56, women], M ['56, men]; supplied free to qualified clinical and research workers; postpaid; (20-35) minutes; Lester M. Libo; Department of Psychiatry, School of Medicine, University of Maryland. *

REFERENCE
1. LIBO, LESTER M. "The Projective Expression of Patient-Therapist Attraction." *J Clin Psychol* 13:33–6 Ja '57. *

J Proj Tech 22:250 Je '58. *Steven G. Vandenberg.* This new technique is custom made to study the patient's expectations regarding the therapist. Four pictures are presented—a different set for males than for females—and four questions are asked about each story. The therapist in the line drawings which constitute the pictures seems to be wearing the short white jacket commonly worn by younger physicians in hospitals. The fact that the test is thus rather definitely structured toward therapy in such a setting may limit its usefulness in other situations. The 14 page manual recommends a simple

coding procedure in which the positive and negative attraction scores for the 4 cards are added to provide a measure of the individual's presumed attractions to his doctor. A story is only scored if it contains references to a therapist, a patient, a diagnostic or therapeutic function, the self. Misperceptions such as "The man in the suit is asking for a job. The other man is thinking of giving him the job" are not scored. There is a brief paragraph about qualitative analysis in the manual. In it perceptual distortions are listed as revealing phenomena, but no effort has been made to relate their occurrence to the patient's attitudes toward therapy. While the limitations indicated above may be regrettable, the definite structuring of the materials should result in more focused protocols. This new technique should prove useful for the purpose for which it is designed.

[153]

★The Picture World Test. Ages 6 and over; 1955–56; 1 form ('56); symbol sheet ('55); no data on reliability; $20 per set of test materials; $4 per 25 record booklets ('56); $3.50 per manual ('56); postpaid; (15–30) minutes; Charlotte Buhler and Morse P. Manson; Western Psychological Services. *

WALTER KASS, *Associate Professor of Psychology, Albert Einstein College of Medicine, Yeshiva University, New York, New York.*

The *Picture World Test* (PWT) is a projective technique purporting to tell about (*a*) motivations specific to goal-setting, conscious and unconscious, internal and external; (*b*) integrating and conflicting aspects of emotions, ambitions, and interests; (*c*) cultural and environmental influences; and (*d*) reactions to life and to the world as a whole. It is said by the authors to complement Rorschach revelations of current personality processes and *Thematic Apperception Test* (TAT) depictions of "genetic or past" forces in a person's life, and, in addition, to indicate "future directional outlook." From the case examples cited in the manual and a limited trial, this reviewer doubts the special claim on the future made by the authors for this picture world method. Future-directed and aspirational material may just as easily be derived from goals and outcomes expressed in TAT and other story telling techniques.

The test is applicable to children, adolescents, and adults, individually or in groups. Subjects write stories about a number of structured scenes which they select from a set of 12 and which they may elaborate with additional figures and objects drawn from a list of 36 diagrammatic representations; the scenes are to be interconnected in thematic sequences, according to the individual's phantasy.

Advantages of the PWT over its prototype, the *Toy World Test,* appear mainly in the group- and self-administering possibilities of a paper and pencil procedure. Like *Make A Picture Story* (MAPS), which replaces the stimulus pictures of the TAT with background sets to be populated by cutout cardboard figures, the PWT substitutes linkable background pictures to be filled with figure drawings in place of the miniature-life toy arrangements of the original *World Test.* Unlike the MAPS innovation, the PWT replaces a three-dimensional with a two-dimensional product. The authors say (but do not show) that with this exchange the PWT "offers greater potentialities for revealing the dynamics underlying adjustments to cultural pressures." But according to MAPS rationale, increased phantasy scope is secured through manipulatable material in preference to a flat graphic medium. The content of the PWT scenes may indeed enhance emergence of cultural dynamics, though it is questionable whether this format is actually superior to the original toy technique, especially with children.

The scenes, simply, clearly, and interestingly drawn, are unambiguous and predominantly reality-oriented. Dream World, the most symbolically nuanced, shows a naked woman running through an open door in a detached wooden wall toward a phallic object and the label "Shame." A preacher in a pulpit on the near side of the wall, flying saucers, an eye in the wall, and a ghoulish figure atop the wall suggest the forces of nature and morality.

Data are provided on 94 adults (53 men and 41 women), aged 18 to 85 years, 27 of whom were adequately adjusted. The remaining 67 were clinically classified as psychoneurotic, character disordered, psychotic, or brain damaged. Data are also given on 22 children (9 boys and 13 girls) 6 to 16 years of age, 10 adequately adjusted, 12 psychoneurotic. There are frequency tables on scenes selected, themes and symbols used, and story categories. The tables are sparse and distinctions between normal and clinical productions are untested and unsubstantiated. Interpretations of the sample cases cited are of the clinical kind common to all thematic techniques. There is no effort to relate test categories diagnostically with personality processes or psychopathology.

As presented, the PWT is an interesting paper and pencil modification of the *World Test* which contributes another original set of stimulus pictures to thematic testing. The innovation is a small one in technique of administration. There is great merit in the basic idea of a projective technique designed to pursue a person's concept of the world as he sees it and would wish it to be. With further development, the PWT may possibly fulfill this pursuit, especially if it helps explain how people go about creating and maintaining the worlds they thematically depict. It is insufficiently developed for valid clinical use, and is at this stage more of a good idea than a test. One wishes the authors had themselves carried out at least some of their 25 research suggestions before publishing a technique as a test. Perhaps it is in the trend of our times thus to give birth to a brain child for others to adopt and raise to maturity.

J Consult Psychol 20:237 Je '56. *Laurance F. Shaffer.* The *Picture World Test* is essentially a picture version of the well-known *World Test,* designed to explore how a person perceives and structures his world, with emphasis on his goal-setting activities. The examinee is presented with 12 small drawings of structured scenes, a large sheet of blank paper, and a chart of 36 simple symbols by which he can add persons, vehicles, buildings, and animals to the scenes. He is asked to choose any number of the scenes he wishes "to make up a world as it is or as you would like it to be; the world you like or dislike; the world of your dreams...." The examinee gums the scenes to the blank sheet, connects the scenes as he wishes, adds symbols, gives his world a name or title, and tells a story about it. The manual describes methods of interpreting the world scenes and world stories. Some data are given on the frequencies of the main story categories in relation to age and quality of adjustment. Twenty-eight illustrative case studies demonstrate the clinical use and interpretation of the test. All in all, the *Picture World Test* seems to be an interesting and challenging instrument, likely to evoke self-revealing responses of considerable clinical value.

[154]

*Rorschach. Ages 3 and over; 1921-57; variously referred to by such titles as Rorschach Method, Rorschach Test, Rorschach Ink Blot Test, Rorschach Psychodiagnostics; many variations and modifications are in use with no one method of scoring and interpreting generally accepted; unless otherwise indicated, the word "Rorschach" may be interpreted as referring to the use of Rorschach's Psychodiagnostic Plates listed as *f* below.

a) *BEHN RORSCHACH TEST. 1941-56; a parallel set of ink blots; $10 per set of cards; $3 per set of record blanks ('51); $7.50 per manual ('56); postage extra; Hans Zulliger; Hans Huber. (U.S. distributor: Grune & Stratton, Inc.) *

b) ★THE BUHLER-LEFEVER RORSCHACH DIAGNOSTIC SIGN LIST AND RECORD OF THE RORSCHACH STANDARDIZATION STUDIES FOR THE DETERMINATION AND EVALUATION OF THE BASIC RORSCHACH SCORE. 1954; $3.50 per 25 booklets, postpaid; Charlotte Buhler, Karl Buhler, and D. Welty Lefever; Western Psychological Services. *

c) HARROWER'S GROUP RORSCHACH. Ages 12 and over; 1941-45; $11 per set of the original Rorschach ink blots on Kodaslides for standard projector; $3.75 per set of 25 record blanks; postpaid; (70-90) minutes; M. R. Harrower and M. E. Steiner; distributed by Psychological Corporation.

d) HARROWER'S MULTIPLE CHOICE TEST. Ages 12 and over; 1943-45; for use with either cards or slides; $2.50 per 25 record blanks; postage extra; M. R. Harrower; distributed by Psychological Corporation. *

e) PSYCHODIAGNOSTIC INKBLOTS. 1945; a parallel set of ink blots; $5.50 per set of cards; $2 per manual; postage extra; M. R. Harrower and M. E. Steiner; Grune & Stratton, Inc. *

f) *PSYCHODIAGNOSTIC PLATES, FIFTH EDITION. 1921-54; $12 per set of cards ('54, identical with original edition copyrighted in 1921); $3 per set of 100 record blanks; $6.50 per copy of manual, fifth edition ('51 translation of German edition, '42, with the addition of a bibliography); postage extra; Hermann Rorschach; Hans Huber. (U.S. distributor: Grune & Stratton, Inc.) *

g) ★RORSCHACH COMBINED LOCATION AND RECORD FORM. 1957; 1 form; $2.75 per 25 booklets; 30¢ per specimen set; postpaid; Nicholas De Palma; the Author, Davidson County Hospital, Nashville 8, Tenn. *

h) ★THE RORSCHACH EVALOGRAPH. 1954; 1 form; $2.50 per 10 booklets, postpaid; Morse P. Manson and George A. Ulett; Western Psychological Services. *

i) ★RORSCHACH LOCATION CHARTS (BECK'S SCORING AREAS). 1951-54; 1 form ('54, identical with set copyrighted in 1951); 9.80 *fr.* ($3) per set of 10 cards, postage extra; Julian C. Davis; Hans Huber. * (U.S. distributor: Grune & Stratton, Inc.)

j) RORSCHACH METHOD OF PERSONALITY DIAGNOSIS. 1939-42; $2.95 per 35 record blanks ('42); Bruno Klopfer and Helen H. Davidson; World Book Co. *

k) ★THE RORSCHACH MINIATURE INK BLOTS: A LOCATION CHART. 1955; $2 per examiner's card; $3.50 per pad of 100 record sheets; postpaid; Morse P. Manson; Western Psychological Services. *

REFERENCES

1-147. See 40:1246.
148-598. See 3:73.
599-1219. See 4:117.
1220. KLOPFER, BRUNO. "Pseudopsychotic Reactions in Rorschach Records of Pre-School Children." Abstract. *Psychol B* 38:597 Jl '41. *
1221. IMMERGLUCK, LUDWIG. *A Comparison Between the Personality Characteristics of Adolescents With Behavior Disorders and the Personality Structures of Their Parents.* Doctor's thesis, State University of Iowa (Iowa City, Iowa), 1947.
1222. MARTIN, DOROTHY RANDOLPH. *A Comparative Study of the Rorschach Test With Aspiration Level Tests and the K-Maze.* Doctor's thesis, University of Colorado (Boulder, Colo.), 1947.
1223. ALLEE, RUTH. *Rorschach Responses of Extreme Deviation in an Experimental Stress Condition.* Master's thesis, University of Missouri (Columbia, Mo.), 1948.
1224. GUILFORD, J. P. "Some Lessons From Aviation Psychology." *Am Psychol* 3:3-11 Ja '48. *
1225. LITTELL, SUZANNE DUPUY. *A Study of the Relationship Between the Rorschach Anxiety Signs and Other Measures of Anxiety.* Master's thesis, University of Colorado (Boulder, Colo.), 1948.
1226. SHOEMAKER, H. A., AND ROHRER, J. H. "Relationship Between Success in the Study of Medicine and Certain Psy-

chological and Personal Data." *J Assn Am Med Col* 23:190–201 My '48. * (*PA* 23:951)

1227. DAVIDSON, N. "Some Aspects of the Rorschach Test." *B Nat Inst Personnel Res* 1:19–23 Jl '49. *

1228. DRYZER, E. *The Group Rorschach.* Master's thesis, Wayne University (Detroit, Mich.), 1949.

1229. LINDERFELT, F. MARGARET. *A Comparative Study of the Rorschach Protocols of Japanese and Caucasian College Students.* Master's thesis, University of Hawaii (Honolulu, Hawaii), 1949.

1230. ROOK, LEROY HUBERT. *Evidence of Change in a Group Therapy Situation as Described by the Rorschach Method.* Master's thesis, University of Oklahoma (Norman, Okla.), 1949.

1231. STAIMAN, MARTIN G. *Comparative Study of Psychoneurotic Veterans Who Continue and Discontinue Psychotherapy.* Doctor's thesis, New York University (New York, N.Y.), 1949.

1232. ABBOTT, GRETCHEN VAN CLEVE. *A Comparative Study of Adjustment Ratings of Graduate Students.* Master's thesis, Southern Methodist University (Dallas, Tex.), 1950.

1233. DOWNING, WILLARD O. *A Comparative Study of Two Different Methods of Inquiry on the Rorschach Test.* Master's thesis, University of Denver (Denver, Colo.), 1950.

1234. FINK, MARIANNE A. *Personality Differences of Acculturating Navaho Adolescent Girls as Revealed by the Rorschach Test.* Master's thesis, University of New Mexico (Albuquerque, N.M.), 1950.

1235. HORLICK, REUBEN S. *The Relationships of Psychometric Test Scores to Personality Disorders.* Doctor's thesis, New York University (New York, N.Y.), 1950.

1236. MOLISH, HERMAN B.; MOLISH, ELLEN ELSTE; AND THOMAS, CAROLINE BEDELL. "A Rorschach Study of a Group of Medical Students." *Psychiatric Q* 24:744–74 O '50. * (*PA* 26:3089)

1237. PEMBERTON, W. H. *Test Characteristics of Student Teachers Rated at the Extremes of Teaching Ability.* Doctor's thesis, University of California (Berkeley, Calif.), 1950.

1238. SCHRAM, HARRIET JEAN. *Differences on Rorschach Test Between Accepted and Non-Accepted High School Freshmen.* Master's thesis, Southern Methodist University (Dallas, Tex.), 1950.

1239. SILVERBERG, JACOB. *A Study in Body-Concept.* Doctor's thesis, University of Kentucky (Lexington, Ky.), 1950.

1240. WARE, KENNETH E. *Evaluation of a Group Rorschach Technique as a Predictor of Academic Success of Medical Students.* Master's thesis, Southern Methodist University (Dallas, Tex.), 1950.

1241. WITT, EUGENE LESTER, JR. *A Study of the Relation of Form Perception in Color on the Rorschach Ink Blot Test and Performance on the Wechsler-Bellevue Block Design Subtest.* Master's thesis, Southern Methodist University (Dallas, Tex.), 1950.

1242. ABEL, THEODORA M., AND CALABRESI, RENATA A. Chap. 13, "The People as Seen From Their Rorschach Tests," pp. 306–18, 463–90. (*PA* 26:2685) In *Life in a Mexican Village: Tepoztlán Restudied.* By Oscar Lewis. Urbana, Ill.: University of Illinois Press, 1951. Pp. xxvii, 512. *

1243. ALLISON, HARRY WILLIAM. *The Validation of Two Quantitative Measures of General Adjustments as Assessed by the Rorschach Method of Personality Diagnosis.* Master's thesis, Pennsylvania State College (State College, Pa.), 1951.

1244. ARKOFF, ABE. *An Investigation of Some Rorschach Indices of "Realistic" Behavior.* Doctor's thesis, State University of Iowa (Iowa City, Iowa), 1951.

1245. BOYD, ROBERT W. *The Use of the Multiple Choice Rorschach Test in a Study of School Attendance and School Success.* Master's thesis, Catholic University of America (Washington, D.C.), 1951.

1246. DIVNEY, HERBERT P. *A Comparative Study of the Rorschach Factors of Three Groups of Alcoholics.* Master's thesis, Catholic University of America (Washington, D.C.), 1951.

1247. DÖRKEN, HERBERT, AND KRAL, V. ADALBERT. "Psychological Investigation of Senile Dementia." *Geriatrics* 6:151–63 My–Je '51. * (*PA* 27:567)

1248. FEURFILE, DAVID. *The Validity of the Selected Signs in the Rorschach: Outgoing Adjustment, Dominance and Submissiveness.* Master's thesis, Pennsylvania State College (State College, Pa.), 1951.

1249. FINNEY, BEN C. "Rorschach Test Correlates of Assaultive Behavior." Abstract. *Am Psychol* 6:490 S '51. *

1250. GALLAGHER, JAMES J. *An Investigation Into Factors Differentiating College Students Who Discontinue Non-Directive Counseling From College Students Who Continue Counseling.* Doctor's thesis, Pennsylvania State College (State College, Pa.), 1951.

1251. GOINES, VALMORE R. *Personality Characteristics of a Certain Ethnic Group.* Doctor's thesis, Northwestern University (Evanston, Ill.), 1951.

1252. GROSSMAN, B. L. "Older People Live in Institutions." Abstract. *Int Gerontol Congr* 2:97 '51. *

1253. HARROWER, M. R., AND KRAUS, JANE. "Psychological Studies on Patients With Multiple Sclerosis." *A.M.A. Arch Neurol & Psychiatry* 66:44–57 Jl '51. * (*PA* 26:1643)

1254. HAWKINS, WILLIAM ANDREW. *Rorschach Patterns Related to Leaderless Group Discussion Behavior.* Master's thesis, Louisiana State University (Baton Rouge, La.), 1951.

1255. HERTZ, MARGUERITE R. *Frequency Tables for Scoring Responses to the Rorschach Inkblot Test, Third Edition.* Cleveland, Ohio: Press of Western Reserve University, 1951. Pp. iv, 240. * (*PA* 26:7001)

1256. INGRAM, WINIFRED. *Prediction of Aggression From the Rorschach Test.* Doctor's thesis, Northwestern University (Evanston, Ill.), 1951.

1257. JANOFF, IRMA Z. *The Relation Between Rorschach Form Quality Measures and Children's Behavior.* Doctor's thesis, Yale University (New Haven, Conn.), 1951.

1258. JOSEPH, ALICE, AND MURRAY, VERONICA F. *Chamorros and Carolinians of Saipan: Personality Studies,* pp. 143–228, 347–64, passim. Cambridge, Mass.: Harvard University Press, 1951. Pp. xviii, 381. * (*PA* 26:3359)

1259. KELLEY, PAUL. *Rorschach Measures of Affect-Adjustment in Candidates to the Religious Life.* Master's thesis, Catholic University of America (Washington, D.C.), 1951.

1260. KUHLEN, R. G. "Expansion and Constriction of Life Activities During the Adult Life Span as Reflected in Organizational, Civic, and Political Participation." Abstract. *Int Gerontol Congr* 2:115 '51. *

1261. LANGER, LEONARD HAROLD. *A Comparison of Twelve-Year-Old White and Negro Boys on the Rorschach Test.* Master's thesis, University of Southern California (Los Angeles, Calif.), 1951.

1262. LORD, EDITH. "Group-Rorschach Responses of Thirty-Five Leprosarium Patients." Abstract. *Am Psychol* 6:500 S '51. *

1263. LOTTRIDGE, DORIS SWOBODA. *A Comparative Personality Study of Philosophy and Engineering Students by Means of the Rorschach Technique.* Master's thesis, Stanford University (Stanford, Calif.), 1951.

1264. MACKAY, EDWARD A. *The Brief-Contact Method of Rorschach Administration: A Validation Study.* Master's thesis, University of Alberta (Edmonton, Alb., Canada), 1951.

1265. MEADOWS, A. W. *An Investigation of the Rorschach and Behn Tests.* Doctor's thesis, University of London (London, England), 1951.

1266. MUNGER, MANUS R. *The Differentiation of Overachievers in Engineering School by the Group Rorschach Test.* Master's thesis, Catholic University of America (Washington, D.C.), 1951.

1267. MURNEY, RICHARD G. *The Relationship Between Certain Thematic Apperception Test and Rorschach Test Scores.* Master's thesis, Catholic University of America (Washington, D.C.), 1951.

1268. NICHOLS, E. G. *A Study of Differences on the Rorschach Test Between Individuals Having Dominant Religious Values and Those Having Dominant Economic Values.* Master's thesis, Dalhousie University (Halifax, N.S., Canada), 1951.

1269. OETZEL, JAMES L., AND STERNBERG, THOMAS H. "A Personality Study of Neurodermatitis (Atopic)." Abstract. *Am Psychol* 6:493 S '51. *

1270. PICKARD, PHYLLIS M. *A Study of the More Important Traits—Assessed by the Rorschach Group Test.* Master's thesis, University of London (London, England), 1951.

1271. POMPILO, PETER T. *The Personality of Epileptics as Indicated by the Rorschach Test: A Comparison With Neurotic Subjects.* Master's thesis, Catholic University of America (Washington, D.C.), 1951.

1272. PORTER, HELEN M. *An Investigation of the Validation of Movement Responses in the Rorschach Test.* Master's thesis, University of Toronto (Toronto, Ont., Canada), 1951.

1273. RAKUSIN, JOHN M. *The Role of Rorschach Variability in the Prediction of Client Behavior During Psychotherapy.* Doctor's thesis, Pennsylvania State College (State College, Pa.), 1951.

1274. REES, W. LINFORD, AND JONES, A. M. "An Evaluation of the Rorschach Test as a Prognostic Aid in the Treatment of Schizophrenia by Insulin Coma Therapy, Electronarcosis, Electroconvulsive Therapy and Leucotomy." *J Mental Sci* 97:681–9 O '51. * (*PA* 26:2903)

1275. ROE, ANNE. "A Psychological Study of Eminent Biologists." *Psychol Monogr* 65(14):1–68 '51. * (*PA* 27:1516)

1276. ROULETTE, THOMAS GRIER. *The Validity of Selected Signs in the Rorschach: Anxiety, Compulsion, and Depression.* Master's thesis, Pennsylvania State College (State College, Pa.), 1951.

1277. SALFIELD, D. J. "Psychiatric Differential Diagnosis and Psychological Testing." Abstract. *Q B Brit Psychol Soc* 2:39 Ap '51. *

1278. SCHAEFER, EARL S. *A Comparison of Personality Characteristics of Deaf and Hearing College Students as Revealed by a Group Rorschach Method.* Master's thesis, Catholic University of America (Washington, D.C.), 1951.

1279. SCHLOSSER, JOHN R. *An Investigation of Examiner Influence on Results of Rorschach Examinations.* Doctor's thesis, Stanford University (Stanford, Calif.), 1951.

1280. SHEEHAN, JOSEPH, AND ZUSSMAN, CHARLES. "Rorschachs of Stutterers Compared With a Clinical Control." Abstract. *Am Psychol* 6:500 S '51. *

1281. SMITH, SYDNEY RUSSELL. *The Rorschach Examination and General Intelligence: A Validation Study.* Doctor's thesis, University of California (Berkeley, Calif.), 1951.

1282. SMYKAL, ANTHONY, JR. "The Significance of the Rorschach Pure Color Response." *Proc Okla Acad Sci* 32:116–21 '51. * (*PA* 27:4271)

1283. STEAD, LUCY SASSCER GORE. *A Comparative Study of Schizophrenic Signs on the Rorschach and the Wechsler-Bellevue.* Master's thesis, Stanford University (Stanford, Calif.), 1951.

1284. STEISEL, IRA M. "The Rorschach Test and Suggestibility: An Experimental Study." Abstract. *Am Psychol* 6:490 S '51. *

1285. STOPOL, MURRAY S. *An Experimental Investigation of the Consistency of Stress Tolerance and Related Rorschach Factors.* Doctor's thesis, Columbia University (New York, N.Y.), 1951. (*DA* 12:390)

1286. STORMENT, CHARLYNE TOWNSEND, AND FINNEY, BENJAMIN C. "Prediction of Violent Behavior in Neuropsychiatric Patients." Abstract. *Am Psychol* 6:490 S '51. *

1287. THOMAS, HOBART F. "A Study of Movement Responses on the Rorschach as Related to the Mechanism of Projection." Abstract. *Am Psychol* 6:500 S '51. *

1288. THOMAS, HOBART FULLER. *The Relationship of Movement Responses on the Rorschach Test to the Defense Mechanism of Projection.* Doctor's thesis, Stanford University (Stanford, Calif.), 1951.

1289. THOMPSON, LAURA. "Perception Patterns in Three Indian Tribes." *Psychiatry* 14:255–63 Ag '51. * (*PA* 26:2128)

1290. TUCKER, JOHN E. *Investigation of Criteria for Evaluating Non-Directive Psychotherapy With College Students.* Doctor's thesis, Pennsylvania State College (State College, Pa.), 1951.

1291. WHITMAN, DOROTHY. *Relationship of Certain Rorschach Indicators to a Vocational Interest Group of Male Kansas State Freshmen.* Master's thesis, Kansas State College (Manhattan, Kan.), 1951.

1292. WILEY, JOHN MASON. *The Use of a Modified Form of the Graphic Rorschach Technique With Brain Injured Subjects.* Master's thesis, University of North Carolina (Chapel Hill, N.C.), 1951.

1293. YOUMANS, CHARLES L., JR. *A Study of the Psychogenic Aspects of Ulcerative Colitis Using the Rorschach Technique.* Master's thesis, Tulane University (New Orleans, La.), 1951.

1294. ZIMMERMAN, IRLA LEE; NEWTON, BERNAUR W.; SULLIVAN, ELLEN B.; DORCUS, ROY M.; STERNBERG, THOMAS H.; AND ZIMMERMAN, MURRAY C. "An Evaluation of the Psychological Processes of the Neurosyphilitic: III, A 'Sign' Approach to the Rorschach in Neurosyphilis." Abstract. *Am Psychol* 6:500 S '51. *

1295. AINSWORTH, MARY D., AND BOSTON, MARY. "Psychodiagnostic Assessments of a Child After Prolonged Separation in Early Childhood." *Brit J Med Psychol* 25:169–201 pt 4 '52. * (*PA* 27:7845)

1296. ALEXANDER, LEO, AND AX, ALBERT F. Chap. 12, "Rorschach Studies in Combat Flying Personnel," pp. 219–43. (*PA* 27:591) In *Relation of Psychological Tests to Psychiatry.* Edited by Paul H. Hoch and Joseph Zubin. New York: Grune & Stratton, Inc., 1952. Pp. viii, 301. *

1297. ALLEN, ROBERT M.; MANNE, SIGMUND H.; AND STIFF, MARGARET. "The Influence of Color on the Consistency of Responses in the Rorschach Test." *J Clin Psychol* 8:97–8 Ja '52. * (*PA* 27:1946)

1298. ALLERHAND, MELVIN E. *Evaluation of the Chiaroscuro Determinant of the Rorschach Ink Blot Tests as an Indicator of Manifest Anxiety.* Doctor's thesis, University of Nebraska (Lincoln, Neb.), 1952. (Abstract: *Am Psychol* 7:359)

1299. ALTUS, WILLIAM D., AND ALTUS, GRACE THOMPSON. "Rorschach Movement Variables and Verbal Intelligence." *J Abn & Social Psychol* 47:531–3 Ap '52. * (*PA* 27:2698)

1300. AMES, LOUISE BATES; LEARNED, JANET; METRAUX, RUTH W.; AND WALKER, RICHARD N. *Child Rorschach Responses: Developmental Trends From Two to Ten Years.* New York: Paul B. Hoeber, Inc., 1952. Pp. xv, 310. * (*PA* 27:7066)

1301. ARONSON, MARVIN L. "A Study of the Freudian Theory of Paranoia by Means of the Rorschach Test." *J Proj Tech* 16:397–411 D '52. * (*PA* 28:2981)

1302. AXELROD, JOSEPH. *An Evaluation of the Effect on Progress in Therapy of Similarities and Differences Between the Personalities of Patients and Their Therapists.* Doctor's thesis, New York University (New York, N.Y.), 1952. (*DA* 12:329)

1303. BANDURA, ALBERT. *A Study of Some of the Psychological Processes Associated With the Rorschach White Space Response.* Doctor's thesis, State University of Iowa (Iowa City, Iowa), 1952.

1304. BARRELL, ROBERT P. "The Relationship of Various Types of Movement Responses in the Rorschach Test to Personality Trait Ratings." Abstract. *Am Psychol* 7:358 Jl '52.

1305. BARRY, JOHN R.; BLYTH, DAVID D.; AND ALBRECHT, ROBERT. "Relationships Between Rorschach Scores and Adjustment Level." *J Consult Psychol* 16:30–6 F '52. *

1306. BECK, SAMUEL J. "The Experimental Validation of the Rorschach Test: IV, Discussion and Critical Evaluation." *Am J Orthopsychiatry* 22:771–5 O '52. * (*PA* 27:5854)

1307. BECK, SAMUEL J. *Rorschach's Test: III, Advances in Interpretation.* New York: Grune & Stratton, Inc., 1952. Pp. x, 301. * (*PA* 28:926)

1308. BELL, ALICE; TROSMAN, HARRY; AND ROSS, DONALD. "The Use of Projective Techniques in the Investigation of Emotional Aspects of General Medical Disorders: I, The Rorschach Method." *J Proj Tech* 16:428–43 D '52. * (*PA* 28:2613)

1309. BENNETT, CLAYTON LEON. *An Experimental Study of Relationships Between Human Electroencephalograms and Certain Rorschach Scoring Categories.* Doctor's thesis, University of Southern California (Los Angeles, Calif.), 1952.

1310. BENTON, ARTHUR L. "The Experimental Validation of the Rorschach Test: II, The Significance of Rorschach Color Responses." *Am J Orthopsychiatry* 22:755–63 O 52. * (*PA* 27:5856)

1311. BERNSTEIN, LEONARD. *The Effects of Pre-Operative Stress Upon Rorschach Test Factors Alleged to Be Signs of Anxiety.* Doctor's thesis, Fordham University (New York, N.Y.), 1952.

1312. BLANTON, RICHARD LINN. *The Effect of Induced Anxiety on Flexibility of Set-Shifting in Rigid and Non-Rigid Subjects.* Doctor's thesis, Vanderbilt University (Nashville, Tenn.), 1952. (*DA* 12:777–8)

1313. BLANTON, RICHARD, AND LANDSMAN, TED. "The Retest Reliability of the Group Rorschach and Some Relationships to the MMPI." *J Consult Psychol* 16:265–7 Ag '52. * (*PA* 27:4241)

1314. BLECHNER, JANET ELISCU. *The Influence of Educational Conditioning on Two Scoring Factors of the Group-Administered Rorschach Test.* Doctor's thesis, University of California (Berkeley, Calif.), 1952.

1315. BLUM, GERALD S., AND MILLER, DANIEL R. "Exploring the Psychoanalytic Theory of the 'Oral Character.'" *J Personality* 20:287–304 Mr '52. * (*PA* 27:2353)

1316. BROWN, FRED; LINDNER, ROBERT; SCHAFER, ROY; SCHUMACHER, AUDREY; AND WYATT, FREDERICK. "Symposium: Problems of Content Analysis in the Rorschach." Abstract. *J Proj Tech* 16:389 S '52. *

1317. BUHLER, CHARLOTTE; LEFEVER, D. WELTY; KALLSTEDT, FRANCIS E.; AND PEAK, HORACE M. *Development of the Basic Rorschach Score: Supplementary Monograph.* Los Angeles, Calif.: Rorschach Standardization Study, 1952. Pp. iv, 71. * (*PA* 26:5602)

1318. BUKER, SAMUEL L. *A Study of Personality Variables Associated With Responses to the Achromatic Features of the Rorschach Stimulus Cards.* Doctor's thesis, Northwestern University (Evanston, Ill.), 1952.

1319. BURCHARD, EDWARD M. L. "The Use of Projective Techniques in the Analysis of Creativity." *J Proj Tech* 16:412–27 D '52. * (*PA* 28:2242)

1320. CALDEN, GEORGE. *The Relationship of Varied Test Definitions and Degrees of Ego-Involvement to Rorschach Test Performance.* Doctor's thesis, University of Michigan (Ann Arbor, Mich.), 1952. (*DA* 12:214)

1321. CALDWELL, BETTYE McD.; ULETT, GEORGE A.; MENSH, IVAN N.; AND GRANICK, SAMUEL. "Levels of Data in Rorschach Interpretation." *J Clin Psychol* 8:374–9 O '52. * (*PA* 27:5860)

1322. CAMPBELL, ELIZABETH FLETCHER. *The Effects of Colour in the Wechsler-Bellevue Block Design Subtest and in the Rorschach.* Master's thesis, University of Western Ontario (London, Ont., Canada), 1952.

1323. CARLSON, RAE. "A Normative Study of Rorschach Responses of Eight Year Old Children." *J Proj Tech* 16:56–65 Mr '52. * (*PA* 27:415)

1324. CARLSON, VIRGIL R., AND LAZARUS, RICHARD S. "A Repetition of Williams' Experiment on Stress and Associated Rorschach Factors." Abstract. *Am Psychol* 7:317 Jl '52. *

1325. CHARLES, HARVEY. *The Use of a Selected Projective Technique in the Teacher Selection Process.* Doctor's thesis, Indiana University (Bloomington, Ind.), 1952.

1326. COHEN, LEON B. *The Influence of Two Attitudinal Variables on Group Rorschach Test Performance.* Doctor's thesis, University of Michigan (Ann Arbor, Mich.), 1952. (*DA* 12:215)

1327. CORTER, HAROLD M. "Factor Analysis of Some Reasoning Tests." *Psychol Monogr* 66(8):1–31 '52. * (*PA* 27:4995)

1328. DAVIDSON, HELEN H., AND KRUGLOV, LORRAINE. "Personality Characteristics of the Institutionalized Aged." *J Consult Psychol* 16:5–12 F '52. * (*PA* 27:1875)

1329. DeVOS, GEORGE A. *Acculturation and Personality Structure: A Rorschach Study of Japanese Americans.* Doctor's thesis, University of Chicago (Chicago, Ill.), 1952.

1330. DeVOS, GEORGE. "A Quantitative Approach to Affective Symbolism in Rorschach Responses." *J Proj Tech* 16:133–50 Je '52. * (*PA* 28:2625)

1331. DÖRKEN, HERBERT, JR., AND KRAL, V. ADALBERT. "The Psychological Differentiation of Organic Brain Lesions and Their localization by Means of the Rorschach Test." *Am J Psychiatry* 108:764–70 Ap '52. * (*PA* 26:7182)

1332. DUNN, WESLEY A. "A Comparison Between Certain Rorschach Scoring Signs, College Freshman Orientation Test Scores, and Grade Point Indices." Abstract. *Am Psychol* 7:358–9 Jl '52. *

1333. ERIKSEN, CHARLES W. "Ego Strength and the Recall of Completed Versus Incompleted Tasks." Abstract. *Am Psychol* 7:316 Jl '52. *

1334. ERIKSEN, CHARLES W., AND LAZARUS, RICHARD S. "Perceptual Defense and Projective Tests." *J Abn & Social Psychol* 47:302–8 Ap '52. * (*PA* 27:2716)

1335. ERIKSEN, CHARLES W.; LAZARUS, RICHARD S.; AND STRANGE, JACK R. "Psychological Stress and Its Personality Correlates: Part II, The Rorschach Test and Other Personality Measures." *J Personality* 20:27–86 Mr '52. * (*PA* 27:2551)

1336. FERGUSON, ROBERT A. *An Investigation of the Animal Response With Particular Reference to Its Appearance on the Rorschach Inkblot Test.* Doctor's thesis, University of Kentucky (Lexington, Ky.), 1952.

1337. FILMER-BENNETT, GORDON. "Prognostic Indices in the Rorschach Records of Hospitalized Patients." *J Abn & Social Psychol* 47:502–6 Ap '52. * (*PA* 27:2878)

1338. FORER, B. R.; FARBEROW, N. L.; MEYER, M. M.; AND TOLMAN, R. S. "Consistency and Agreement in the Judgment of Rorschach Signs." *J Proj Tech* 16:346–51 S '52. * (*PA* 28:2631)

1339. FORTIER, R. *A Study of the Relation of the Response to Color and Some Personality Functions: I, The Response to Color and Ego Functions: An Effect-Color Theory; II, An Analysis of Groups of Dream Series Differing in the Frequency of Dreams in Color; III, Some Rorschach Variables Associated With the Frequency of Dreams in Color.* Doctor's thesis, Western Reserve University (Cleveland, Ohio), 1952.

1340. FOSBERG, IRVING ARTHUR. "Nationalization of Rorschach Research: A Plan for a Cooperative Research Project." Abstract. *Am Psychol* 7:359 Jl '52. *

1341. FRANK, IRVING H. *A Genetic Evaluation of Perceptual Structurization in Certain Psychoneurotic Disorders by Means of the Rorschach Technique.* Doctor's thesis, Boston University (Boston, Mass.), 1952.

1342. FRANKLE, ALLAN H. "Validity of Rorschach *M* and *H* Plus *Hd* for Predicting Fieldwork Performance of Student Social Workers." Abstract. *Am Psychol* 7:289 Jl '52. *

1343. FRIEDMAN, HOWARD. "A Comparison of a Group of Hebephrenic and Catatonic Schizophrenics With Two Groups of Normal Adults by Means of Certain Variables of the Rorschach Test." *J Proj Tech* 16:352–60 S '52. * (*PA* 28:2995)

1344. GIBBY, ROBERT G. "Examiner Influence on the Rorschach Inquiry." *J Consult Psychol* 16:449–55 D '52. * (*PA* 28:949)

1345. GIBBY, ROBERT G.; MILLER, DANIEL R.; AND WALKER, EDWARD L. "Examiner Variance in the Rorschach Protocols of Neuropsychiatric Patients." Abstract. *Am Psychol* 7:337–8 Jl '52. *

1346. GILHOOLY, FRANCIS M. *The Validity and Reliability of the Rorschach and the Thematic Apperception Tests When These Tests Are Interpreted by the Method of Blind Analysis.* Doctor's thesis, Fordham University (New York, N.Y.), 1952.

1347. GLADSTONE, ROY. "A Factor in the Degeneration of Discussions." *J Ed Psychol* 43:176–8 Mr '52. * (*PA* 27:3323)

1348. GORLOW, LEON; ZIMET, CARL N.; AND FINE, HAROLD J. "The Validity of Anxiety and Hostility Rorschach Content Scores Among Adolescents." *J Consult Psychol* 16:73–5 F '52. * (*PA* 27:1961)

1349. GRANT, MARGUERITE Q.; IVES, VIRGINIA; AND RANZONI, JANE H. "Reliability and Validity of Judges' Ratings of Adjustment on the Rorschach." *Psychol Monogr* 66(2):1–20 '52. * (*PA* 27:2724)

1350. GRAYSON, HARRY M. "The Grayson-Brentwood Rorschach Series: I, Rorschach Productivity and Card Preferences as Influenced by Experimental Variation of Color and Shading." Abstract. *J Proj Tech* 16:389 S '52. *

1351. GREMBOWICZ, EUGENE T. *Color and Affectivity in the Rorschach Test.* Doctor's thesis, Loyola University (Chicago, Ill.), 1952.

1352. GURVITZ, MILTON S., AND MILLER, JOSEPH S. A. Chap. 11, "Some Theoretical and Practical Aspects of the Diagnosis of Early and Latent Schizophrenia by Means of Psychological Testing," pp. 189–207. (*PA* 27:571) Discussion by Paul H. Hoch, pp. 215–6. In *Relation of Psychological Tests to Psychiatry.* Edited by Paul H. Hoch and Joseph Zubin. New York: Grune & Stratton, 1952. Pp. viii, 301. *

1353. HALES, WILLIAM M. "Profile Patterning and Coding of the Rorschach Test: A Preliminary Report of Research Methods and Materials." *J Consult Psychol* 16:37–42 F '52. * (*PA* 27:1964)

1354. HARROWER, MOLLY. *Appraising Personality: The Use of Psychological Tests in the Practice of Medicine,* pp. 41–80. New York: W. W. Norton & Co., Inc., 1952. Pp. xvii, 197. * (*PA* 27:6532)

1355. HAYS, WILLIAM. "Age and Sex Differences on the Rorschach Experience Balance." *J Abn & Social Psychol* 47:390–3 Ap '52. * (*PA* 27:2726)

1356. HERTZ, MARGUERITE R. Chap. 8, "The Rorschach: Thirty Years After," pp. 108–48. (*PA* 27:3555) In *Progress in Clinical Psychology, Vol. I, Sect. 1.* Edited by Daniel Brower and Lawrence E. Abt. New York: Grune & Stratton, Inc., 1952. Pp. xi, 328. *

1357. HERTZ, MARGUERITE R., AND LOEHRKE, LEAH M. "The Application of the Piotrowski and the Hughes Signs of Organic Defect to a Group of Patients Suffering From Post-traumatic Encephalopathy." Abstract. *J Proj Tech* 16:384–5 S '52. *

1358. HERTZ, MARGUERITE R., AND LOEHRKE, LEAH M. "An Evaluation of the Rorschach Method for the Study of Brain Injury." Abstract. *Am Psychol* 7:349–50 Jl '52. *

1359. HESSEL, MARTHA G., AND TRAVERS, ROBERT M. W. "Relationships Between Rorschach Performance and Student Teaching." Abstract. *Am Psychol* 7:370 Jl '52. *

1360. HOLT, ROBERT R., AND LUBORSKY, LESTER. "Research in the Selection of Psychiatrists: A Second Interim Report." *B Menninger Clinic* 16:125–35 Jl '52. * (*PA* 27:3916)

1361. HOLTZMAN, WAYNE H. "Adjustment and Leadership: A Study of the Rorschach Test." *J Social Psychol* 36:179–89 N '52. * (*PA* 27:7117)

1362. HOLZBERG, JULES D., AND BELMONT, LILLIAN. "The Relationship Between Factors on the Wechsler-Bellevue and Rorschach Having Common Psychological Rationale." *J Consult Psychol* 16:23–9 F '52. * (*PA* 27:1966)

1363. HOLZBERG, JULES D., AND CAHEN, ELEANOR R. "The Relationship Between Psychiatric Improvement and Certain Pathologic Changes in the Rorschach During Electroconvulsive

Therapy." *J Clin & Exp Psychopathol* 13:237–46 D '52. * (*PA* 28:3001)

1364. HOLZBERG, JULES D., AND HAHN, FRED. "The Picture-Frustration Technique as a Measure of Hostility and Guilt Reactions in Adolescent Psychopaths." Discussion by Goldie R. Kaback. *Am J Orthopsychiatry* 22:776–97 O '52. * (*PA* 27:5995)

1365. HOROWITZ, MILTON J. *Developmental Changes in Rorschach Test and Thematic Apperception Test Performances of Children, Six Through Nine Years of Age: An Exploratory Study.* Doctor's thesis, University of Kansas (Lawrence, Kan.), 1952.

1366. HOWIE, MARGARET M. "The Rorschach Test Applied to a Group of Scottish Children." Abstract. *Brit J Ed Psychol* 22:214–6 N '52. *

1367. HSÜ, E. H. "Further Comments on the Rorschach Response and Factor Analysis." *J General Psychol* 47:239–41 O '52. * (*PA* 27:5877)

1368. JACOBS, STEVEN M., AND GRAHAM, E. ELLIS. "A Comparison of the Rorschachs of Juvenile Auto Thieves and Juvenile Burglars." Abstract. *J Colo-Wyo Acad Sci* 4:76 O '52. *

1369. JOHNSON, ELIZABETH Z. "The Use of the Rorschach Prognostic Scale With Raven's Progressive Matrices to Predict Playtherapy Progress Among Retarded Children." Abstract. *J Proj Tech* 16:385 S '52. *

1370. KAHN, MARVIN W. *Perceptual Consistency of Rorschach Factors With Therapy Interview Responses, and Generalization Change as a Predictor of Psychotherapeutic Success.* Doctor's thesis, Pennsylvania State College (State College, Pa.), 1952.

1371. KALLSTEDT, FRANCES E. "A Rorschach Study of Sixty-Six Adolescents." *J Clin Psychol* 8:129–32 Ap '52. * (*PA* 27:1861)

1372. KASS, WALTER. *Rorschach Indications for Predicting Proficiency in the Selection of Physicians for Training in Psychiatry in a Residency Program.* Doctor's thesis, New York University (New York, N.Y.), 1952.

1373. KEEHN, J. D. "Rorschach Validation: I, A Rationale." *J Mental Sci* 98:697–706 O '52. * (*PA* 27:5880)

1374. KJENAAS, NANCY K., AND BROZEK, JOSEF. "Personality in Experimental Semistarvation." *Psychosom Med* 14:115–28 Mr–Ap '52. * (*PA* 26:6701)

1375. KLATSKIN, ETHELYN HENRY. "An Analysis of the Effect of the Test Situation Upon the Rorschach Record: Formal Scoring Characteristics." *J Proj Tech* 16:193–9 Je '52. * (*PA* 28:2644)

1376. KLETTI, LEROY. *The Agreement in Anxiety Measurement Between the Rorschach Test and the Minnesota Multiphasic Personality Inventory.* Master's thesis, University of North Dakota (Grand Forks, N.D.), 1952.

1377. KNOPF, IRWIN J. *A Study of the Effects of Recent Perceptual Training and Experience on the Rorschach Performance.* Doctor's thesis, Northwestern University (Evanston, Ill.), 1952.

1378. KOTKOV, BENJAMIN, AND MURAWSKI, BENJAMIN. "A Rorschach Study of the Personality Structure of Obese Women." *J Clin Psychol* 8:391–6 O '52. * (*PA* 27:6069)

1379. KROUT, JOHANNA; KROUT, MAURICE H.; AND DULIN, THEODORE J. "Rorschach Test-Retest as a Gauge of Progress in Psychotherapy." *J Clin Psychol* 8:380–4 O '52. * (*PA* 27:5933)

1380. LAWSON, J. L., JR. *A Rorschach Study of the Epileptic Personality.* Doctor's thesis, University of Kentucky (Lexington, Ky.), 1952.

1381. LEDWITH, NETTIE H. "Rorschach Responses of the Elementary School Child: Progress Report." *J Proj Tech* 16:80–5 Mr '52. * (*PA* 27:433)

1382. LEIMAN, CHARLES J. *An Investigation of the Perception of Movement on the Rorschach Ink-Blots.* Doctor's thesis, University of Kentucky (Lexington, Ky.), 1952.

1383. LEVI, JOSEPH, AND KRAEMER, DORIS. "Significance of a Preponderance of Human Movement Responses on the Rorschach in Children Below Age Ten." *J Proj Tech* 16:361–5 S '52. * (*PA* 28:2649)

1384. LEVY, RUTH J. "The Rorschach Pattern in Neurodermatitis." *Psychosom Med* 14:41–9 Ja–F '52. * (*PA* 26:6476)

1385. LIPTON, EDMOND, AND CERES, MILDRED. "Correlation of Clinical Improvement of Intensively Treated Psychoneurotics With Changes in Consecutive Rorschach Tests." *Psychiatric Q Sup* 26:103–17 pt 1 '52. * (*PA* 27:4489)

1386. LOEHRKE, LEAH M. *An Evaluation of the Rorschach Method for the Study of Brain Injury.* Doctor's thesis, Western Reserve University (Cleveland, Ohio), 1952.

1387. LUKE, WALTER. *The Relationship Between Suggestibility and the Rorschach Test.* Master's thesis, University of Detroit (Detroit, Mich.), 1952.

1388. McDONALD, FRANKLIN RANDOLPH. *The Effect of Differential Cultural Pressures on Projective Test Performances of Negroes.* Doctor's thesis, University of Southern California (Los Angeles, Calif.), 1952.

1389. MAGARET, ANN. "Clinical Methods: Psychodiagnostics," pp. 297–302. (*PA* 26:4799) In *Annual Review of Psychology, Vol. 3.* Edited by Calvin P. Stone and Donald W. Taylor. Stanford, Calif.: Annual Reviews, Inc., 1952. Pp. ix, 462. *

1390. MALCOM, EDWARD V. *A Study of the Validity of Individual Personality Profiles Based on Each of Four Projective Techniques.* Doctor's thesis, University of Michigan (Ann Arbor, Mich.), 1952. (*DA* 12:221)

1391. MARQUIS, DOROTHY P.; SINNETT, E. ROBERT; AND WINTER, WILLIAM D. "A Psychological Study of Peptic Ulcer Patients." *J Clin Psychol* 8:266–72 Jl '52. * (*PA* 27:6072)

1392. MARSH, JAMES T. *An Investigation of Some Examiner Influences on Productivity in the Rorschach Test.* Doctor's thesis, University of California (Los Angeles, Calif.), 1952.

1393. MARTIN, HARRY. *A Rorschach Study of Suicide.* Doctor's thesis, University of Kentucky (Lexington, Ky.), 1952.

1394. MATARAZZO, JOSEPH D., AND MENSH, IVAN N. "Reaction Time Characteristics of the Rorschach Test." *J Consult Psychol* 16:132–9 Ap '52. * (*PA* 27:2744)

1395. MATARAZZO, RUTH G.; WATSON, ROBERT I.; AND ULETT, GEORGE A. "Relationship of Rorschach Scoring Categories to Modes of Perception Induced by Intermittent Photic Stimulation—A Methodological Study of Perception." *J Clin Psychol* 8:368–74 O '52. * (*PA* 27:5887)

1396. MEHR, HELEN MARGULIES. "The Application of Psychological Tests and Methods to Schizophrenia in Children." *Nerv Child* 10:63–93 no 1 '52. * (*PA* 27:6040)

1397. MENSH, IVAN N. "The Experimental Validation of the Rorschach Test: III, Treatment of Data." *Am J Orthopsychiatry* 22:764–70 O '52. * (*PA* 27:5889)

1398. MEYER, GEORGE, AND THOMPSON, JACK. "The Performance of Kindergarten Children on the Rorschach Test: A Normative Study." *J Proj Tech* 16:86–111 Mr '52. * (*PA* 27:436)

1399. MILLER, CARMEN. *A Comparison of Personality Characteristics of High-Accident and Low-Accident Bus and Street Car Operators.* Doctor's thesis, Western Reserve University (Cleveland, Ohio), 1952.

1400. MINDESS, HARVEY. *Predicting Patients' Responses to Psychotherapy; A Preliminary Investigation of the Validity of "The Prognostic Rating Scale for the Rorschach."* Doctor's thesis, University of California (Los Angeles, Calif.), 1952.

1401. MITCHELL, MILDRED B. "Preferences for Rorschach Cards." *J Proj Tech* 16:203–11 Je '52. * (*PA* 28:2659)

1402. MONTALTO, FANNIE D. "Maternal Behavior and Child Personality: A Rorschach Study." *J Proj Tech* 16:151–78 Je '52. * (*PA* 28:2338)

1403. MURPHY, WILLIAM F. "Evaluation of Psychotherapy With Modified Rorschach Techniques." *Am J Psychother* 6:471–83 Jl '52. * (*PA* 27:3589)

1404. MYATT, MARY FRANCES. *A Study of the Relationship Between Motivation and Test Performance of Patients in a Rehabilitation Ward.* Doctor's thesis, University of Minnesota (Minneapolis, Minn.), 1952. (*DA* 12:339)

1405. NEWTON, RICHARD L. *An Investigation of Clinical Judgment: A Comparison of Results Obtained With Judgment Scales Applied to the Rorschach and to Case Material.* Doctor's thesis, University of Pittsburgh (Pittsburgh, Pa.), 1952.

1406. NORMAN, RALPH D.; LIVERANT, SHEPHARD; AND REDLO, MIRIAM. "The Influence of a Superficial Immediately Preceding 'Set' Upon Responses to the Rorschach." *J Consult Psychol* 16:261–4 Ag '52. * (*PA* 27:4266)

1407. OLTEAN, MARY. "Organic Pathology Accompanying Diabetes Mellitus as Indicated by the Rorschach." *J Proj Tech* 16:485–8 D '52. * (*PA* 28:3091)

1408. PAGE, CURTIS W., AND GLAD, DONALD D. "Experimental Use of the Rorschach and Emotional Projection Tests in the Study of Emotional Changes Coincident to Cortisone Therapy." Abstract. *J Colo-Wyo Acad Sci* 4:78–9 O '52. *

1409. PASCAL, GERALD R., AND HERZBERG, FREDERICK I. "The Detection of Deviant Sexual Practice From Performance on the Rorschach Test." *J Proj Tech* 16:366–73 S '52. * (*PA* 28:2927)

1410. PECK, CECIL P. *An Investigation of the Association-Provoking Properties and Meanings Attributed to the Rorschach Inkblots.* Doctor's thesis, University of Kentucky (Lexington, Ky.), 1952.

1411. PEÑA, CESAREO D. *Genetic Parallels of Perceptual Structurization in Cerebral Pathology as Reflected in Rorschach Test Responses.* Doctor's thesis, Boston University (Boston, Mass.), 1952.

1412. PEPINSKY, HAROLD B.; CLYDE, ROBIN J.; OLESEN, BARBARA A.; AND VAN ATTA, ELLIS L. "The Criterion in Counseling: I, Individual Personality and Behavior in a Social Group." *Ed & Psychol Meas* 12:178–93 su '52. * (*PA* 27:5942)

1413. PIOTROWSKI, ZYGMUNT A., AND ABRAHAMSEN, DAVID. "Sexual Crime, Alcohol, and the Rorschach Test." *Psychiatric Q Sup* 26:248–60 pt 2 '52. * (*PA* 27:5259)

1414. PIOTROWSKI, ZYGMUNT A., AND LEWIS, NOLAN D. C. Chap. 4, "An Experimental Criterion for the Prognostication of the Status of Schizophrenics After a Three-Year-Interval Based on Rorschach Data," pp. 51–72. (*PA* 27:586) Discussion by Joseph Zubin (pp. 100–3) and Joseph F. Kubis (pp. 105–7). In *Relation of Psychological Tests to Psychiatry.* Edited by Paul H. Hoch and Joseph Zubin. New York: Grune & Stratton, Inc., 1952. Pp. viii, 301. *

1415. PIOTROWSKI, ZYGMUNT, AND SCHREIBER, MARTIN. "Rorschach Perceptanalytic Measurement of Personality Changes During and After Intensive Psychoanalytically Oriented Psychotherapy," pp. 337–61. In *Specialized Techniques in Psychotherapy.* Edited by Gustav Bychowski and J. Louise Despert. New York: Basic Books, Inc., 1952. Pp. xii, 371. * (*PA* 27:1194)

1416. PRATT, CAROLYN. "A Validation Study of Intropunitive and Extrapunitive Signs on the Rorschach Test, Based Upon Records Given by Suicidal and Homicidal Subjects." Abstract. *Proc Ind Acad Sci* 62:296 '52. *

1417. PRATT, CAROLYN. *Validation Study of the Intropunitive and Extrapunitive Signs in the Rorschach Test.* Doctor's thesis, Purdue University (Lafayette, Ind.), 1952.

1418. RACUSEN, FRANCES RHEA. *An Exploratory Investigation of the Creativity and Productivity Variables on the Rorschach and Thematic Apperception Tests.* Doctor's thesis, State University of Iowa (Iowa City, Iowa), 1952.

1419. RICHARDS, T. W. "Personality of the Convulsive Patient in Military Service." *Psychol Monogr* 66(14):1–23 '52. * (*PA* 27:364)

1420. ROCHLIN, ISAIAH. "The Investigation, Through the Use of Projective Techniques, of Non-intellectual Factors in the Learning of Mathematics." Abstract. *Am Psychol* 7:368 Jl '52. *

1421. ROE, ANNE. "Analysis of Group Rorschachs of Psychologists and Anthropologists." *J Proj Tech* 16:212–24 Je '52. * (*PA* 28:3443)

1422. ROE, ANNE. "Group Rorschachs of University Faculties." *J Consult Psychol* 16:18–22 F '52. * (*PA* 27:2258)

1423. ROE, ANNE. "Two Rorschach Scoring Techniques: The Inspection Technique and the Basic Rorschach." *J Abn & Social Psychol* 47:263–4 Ap '52. * (*PA* 27:2760)

1424. ROHRER, JOHN H.; BAGBY, JAMES W., JR.; AND WILKINS, WALTER L. "The Reliability of Individual Inquiries and Scorings of the Rorschach." Abstract. *Am Psychol* 7:290–1 Jl '52. *

1425. ROSEN, EPHRAIM. "MMPI and Rorschach Correlates of the Rorschach White Space Response." *J Clin Psychol* 8:283–8 Jl '52. * (*PA* 27:5899)

1426. ROSEN, IRWIN C. *Parallel Researches in Sexual Psychopathology: I, A Comparison of a Group of Rapists and Controls on Certain Psychological Variables.* Doctor's thesis, University of Pittsburgh (Pittsburgh, Pa.), 1952.

1427. ROSENBERG, SELIG. *The Relationship of Certain Personality Factors to Prognosis in Psychotherapy.* Doctor's thesis, New York University (New York, N.Y.), 1952. (*DA* 12:388)

1428. SALTER, MARY D. *The Rorschach Technique: Notes Based on the Klopfer Method.* Toronto, Canada: University Bookstore, University of Toronto, [1952]. Pp. i, 77. *

1429. SAMUELS, HENRY. "The Validity of Personality-Trait Ratings Based on Projective Techniques." *Psychol Monogr* 66(5):1–21 '52. * (*PA* 27:5161)

1430. SANDERSON, HERBERT. "Card Titles in Testing the Limits in Rorschach." *J Proj Tech* 33:27–9 Ja '52. * (*PA* 26:6287)

1431. SARBIN, THEODORE R., AND FARBEROW, NORMAN L. "Contributions to Role-Taking Theory: A Clinical Study of Self and Role." *J Abn & Social Psychol* 47:117–25 Ja '52. * (*PA* 26:6111)

1432. SCHAFER, ROY. "Rorschach Imagery in Aging Psychiatric Patients." Abstract. *J Proj Tech* 16:385–6 S '52. *

1433. SCHWARTZ, EMANUEL K. "Personality Correlates of Paraplegia Indicated in the Rorschach Situation." Abstract. *J Proj Tech* 16:386 S '52. *

1434. SCHWARTZ, MILTON M. "The Relationship Between Projective Test Scoring Categories and Activity Preferences." *Genetic Psychol Monogr* 46:133–81 N '52. * (*PA* 27:4269)

1435. SHAMES, GEORGE HERBERT. *An Investigation of Prognosis and Evaluation in Speech Therapy.* Doctor's thesis, University of Pittsburgh (Pittsburgh, Pa.), 1952.

1436. SHATIN, LEO. "Psychoneurosis and Psychosomatic Reactions: A Rorschach Contrast." *J Consult Psychol* 16:220–3 Je '52. * (*PA* 27:5324)

1437. SHEPHERD, JOHN RALPH. *An Experimental Study of the Responses of Stage-Frightened Students to Certain Scoring Categories of the Group Rorschach Test.* Doctor's thesis, University of Southern California (Los Angeles, Calif.), 1952.

1438. SHERESHEVSKI-SHERE, EUGENIA, AND LASSER, LEONARD M. "An Evaluation of Water Responses in the Rorschachs of Alcoholics." *J Proj Tech* 16:489–95 D '52. * (*PA* 28:2939)

1439. SHERMAN, MURRAY. "A Comparison of Formal and Content Factors in the Diagnostic Testing of Schizophrenia." *Genetic Psychol Monogr* 46:183–234 N '52. * (*PA* 27:4473)

1440. SHNEIDMAN, EDWIN S. "The Case of Jay: Psychological Test and Anamnestic Data." *J Proj Tech* 16:297–345 S '52. * (*PA* 28:2676)

1441. SIIPOLA, ELSA, AND TAYLOR, VIVIAN. "Reactions to Ink Blots Under Free and Pressure Conditions." *J Personality* 21:22–47 S '52. * (*PA* 27:5903)

1442. SINGER, HARRY. *Validity of the Projection of Sexuality in Drawing the Human Figure.* Master's thesis, Western Reserve University (Cleveland, Ohio), 1952.

1443. SINGER, JEROME L. "The Behn-Rorschach Inkblots: A Preliminary Comparison With the Original Rorschach Series." *J Proj Tech* 16:238–45 Je '52. * (*PA* 28:2679)

1444. SINGER, JEROME L.; MELTZOFF, JULIAN; AND GOLDMAN, GEORGE D. "Rorschach Movement Responses Following Motor Inhibition and Hyperactivity." *J Consult Psychol* 16:359–64 O '52. * (*PA* 27:5904)

1445. SPIES, KATHRYN ELAINE. *A Comparison of Dream and Rorschach Content of Psychotics and Non-Psychotics.* Master's thesis, University of Chicago (Chicago, Ill.), 1952.

1446. STARER, EMANUEL. "Aggressive Reactions and Sources of Frustration in Anxiety Neurotics and Paranoid Schizophrenics." *J Clin Psychol* 8:307–9 Jl 52. * (*PA* 27:5979)

1447. STEISEL, IRA M. "The Rorschach Test and Suggestibility." *J Abn & Social Psychol* 47:607–14 Jl '52. * (*PA* 27:3563)

1448. STOTSKY, BERNARD A. "A Comparison of Remitting and

Nonremitting Schizophrenics on Psychological Tests." *J Abn & Social Psychol* 47:489–96 Ap '52. * (*PA* 27:2898)

1449. TAYLOR, KENNETH E. *Parallel Researches in Sexual Psychopathology: II, A Comparison of a Group of Pedophiliacs and Controls on Certain Psychological Variables.* Doctor's thesis, University of Pittsburgh (Pittsburgh, Pa.), 1952.

1450. THETFORD, WILLIAM N. "Fantasy Perceptions in the Personality Development of Normal and Deviant Children." *Am J Orthopsychiatry* 22:542–50 Jl '52. * (*PA* 27:5314)

1451. THETFORD, WILLIAM N. "Personality Characteristics of Schizophrenic Children Viewed Through the Rorschach Test." Abstract. *Am Psychol* 7:301–2 Jl '52. *

1452. THIESEN, J. WARREN. "A Pattern Analysis of Structural Characteristics of the Rorschach Test in Schizophrenia." *J Consult Psychol* 16:365–70 O '52. * (*PA* 27:6045)

1453. THOMAS, HOBART F. *The Relationship of Movement Responses on the Rorschach Test to the Defense Mechanism of Projection.* Doctor's thesis, Stanford University (Stanford, Calif.), 1952.

1454. TOMKINS, SILVAN S. Chap. 6, "Personality and Intelligence: Integration and Psychometric Technics," pp. 87–95. (*PA* 27:445) Discussion by Joseph Zubin, pp. 103–4. In *Relation of Psychological Tests to Psychiatry.* Edited by Paul H. Hoch and Joseph Zubin. New York: Grune & Stratton, Inc., 1952. Pp. viii, 301. *

1455. UEHLING, HAROLD F. "Rorschach 'Shock' for Two Special Populations." *J Consult Psychol* 16:224–5 Je '52. * (*PA* 27:5167)

1456. VORHAUS, PAULINE G. "Case Study of an Adolescent Boy With Reading Disability." *J Proj Tech* 16:20–41 Mr '52. * (*PA* 27:650)

1457. VORHAUS, PAULINE G. "Interpretation of Jay's Rorschach Test: The Case of Jay: Interpretations and Discussion." *J Proj Tech* 16:453–6, discussion 444–5, 462–73 D '52. * (*PA* 28:2678)

1458. VORHAUS, PAULINE G. "Rorschach Configurations Associated With Reading Disability." *J Proj Tech* 16:3–19 Mr '52. * (*PA* 27:651)

1459. VORHAUS, PAULINE G. "The Use of the Rorschach in Preventive Mental Hygiene." *J Proj Tech* 16:179–92 Je '52. * (*PA* 28:2588)

1460. WALLACE, ANTHONY F. C. *The Modal Personality of the Tuscarora Indians as Revealed by the Rorschach Test.* Smithsonian Institution, Bureau of American Ethnology, Bulletin 150. Washington, D.C.: U.S. Government Printing Office, 1952. Pp. viii, 120. * (*PA* 27:6505)

1461. WATKINS, JOHN G., AND STAUFFACHER, JAMES C. "An Index of Pathological Thinking in the Rorschach." *J Proj Tech* 16:276–86 S '52. * (*PA* 28:2686)

1462. WENAR, CHARLES. "A Comparison of Rorschach Findings on Aging Subjects With Their Psychiatric and Social Ratings." Abstract. *Am Psychol* 7:403 Jl '52. *

1463. WESTROPE, MARTHA R. *An Investigation of the Relations Among Rorschach Indices, Manifest Anxiety, and Performance Under Stress.* Doctor's thesis, State University of Iowa (Iowa City, Iowa), 1952.

1464. WHITE, MARY ALICE, AND SCHREIBER, HANNA. "Diagnosing 'Suicidal Risks' on the Rorschach." *Psychiatric Q Sup* 26:161–89 pt 2 '52. * (*PA* 27:5264)

1465. WILLIAMS, MEYER. "The Experimental Validation of the Rorschach Test: I, Experimental Correlations." *Am J Orthopsychiatry* 22:749–54 O '52. * (*PA* 27:5913)

1466. WILSON, GLEN P., JR. *Intellectual Indicators in the Rorschach Test.* Doctor's thesis, University of Texas (Austin, Tex.), 1952.

1467. WINDLE, CHARLES. "Psychological Tests in Psychopathological Prognosis." *Psychol B* 49:451–82 S '52. * (*PA* 27:3567)

1468. WIRT, ROBERT DUANE. *Ideational Expression of Hostile Impulses.* Doctor's thesis, Stanford University (Stanford, Calif.), 1952.

1469. WYATT, FREDERICK. "Prediction in the Rorschach Test." *J Proj Tech* 16:252–8 Je '52. * (*PA* 28:2693)

1470. ABEL, THEODORA M., AND WEISSMANN, SERENA. Chap. 5, "Psychological Aspects," pp. 130–65. In *Facial Deformities and Plastic Surgery: A Psychosocial Study.* By Frances Cooke Macgregor, Theodora M. Abel, Albert Bryt, Edith Lauer, and Serena Weissmann. Springfield, Ill.: Charles C Thomas, 1953. Pp. xv, 230. * (*PA* 28:6403)

1471. ALCOCK, A. T. "A Study of Mother-Child Relationships, Using the Rorschach Technique, With a Pair of Identical Twins, One Schizophrenic, the Other Healthy." Abstract. *B Brit Psychol Soc* (19):29 Ja '53. *

1472. ALLEN, ROBERT M. *Introduction to the Rorschach Technique: Manual of Administration and Scoring.* New York: International Universities Press, Inc., 1953. Pp. ii, 126. * (*PA* 28:2607)

1473. ALLEN, ROBERT M. "The M Determinant and Color in Rorschach's Test." *J Clin Psychol* 9:198–9 Ap '53. * (*PA* 28:2608)

1474. ALLEN, ROBERT M.; RAY, CHARLES D.; AND POOLE, ROBERT C. "The Levy Movement Test: Suggestions for Scoring and Relationship to Rorschach Movement Responses." *J Consult Psychol* 17:195–8 Je '53. * (*PA* 28:2609)

1475. ALLEN, ROBERT M.; STIFF, MARGARET P.; AND ROSENZWEIG, MILTON. "The Role of Color in Rorschach's Test: A Preliminary Survey of Neurotic and Psychotic Groups." *J Clin Psychol* 9:81–3 Ja '53. * (*PA* 27:7749)

1476. AMES, LOUISE B.; LEARNED, JANET; METRAUX, RUTH; AND WALKER, RICHARD. "Development of Perception in the

Young Child as Observed in Responses to the Rorschach Test Blots." *J Genetic Psychol* 82:183–204 Je '53. * (*PA* 28:6012)

1477. ARBITMAN, HERMAN D. "Rorschach Determinants in Mentally Defective and Normal Subjects." *Training Sch B* 50:143–51 N '53. * (*PA* 28:6205)

1478. ARLUCK, EDWARD W., AND BALINSKY, BENJAMIN. "Possible Shifts in Functioning Through Hypnotic Suggestion." *J Proj Tech* 17:447–54 D '53. * (*PA* 28:6013)

1479. AULD, FRANK, JR., AND ERON, LEONARD D. "The Use of Rorschach Scores to Predict Whether Patients Will Continue Psychotherapy." *J Consult Psychol* 17:104–9 Ap '53. * (*PA* 28:2701)

1480. AUSUBEL, DAVID P.; SCHIFF, HERBERT M.; AND GOLDMAN, MORTON. "Qualitative Characteristics in the Learning Process Associated With Anxiety." *J Abn & Social Psychol* 48:537–47 O '53. * (*PA* 28:6226)

1481. BARKER, G. B. "Four Rorschach Records and Case History of a Male Schizophrenic Patient." Abstract. *B Brit Psychol Soc* (19):28–9 Ja '53. *

1482. BARRELL, ROBERT P. "Subcategories of Rorschach Human Movement Responses: A Classification System and Some Experimental Results." *J Consult Psychol* 17:254–60 Ag '53. * (*PA* 28:4328)

1483. BARRON, FRANK. "Some Test Correlates of Response to Psychotherapy." *J Consult Psychol* 17:235–41 Ag '53. * (*PA* 28:4410)

1484. BATT, HAROLD VERNON. *An Investigation of the Significance of the Rorschach Z Score.* Doctor's thesis, University of Nebraska (Lincoln, Neb.), 1953.

1485. BECK, SAMUEL J. "Rorschach Test," pp. 599–610. (*PA* 27:7754) In *Contributions Toward Medical Psychology: Theory and Psychodiagnostic Methods, Vol. II.* Edited by Arthur Weider. New York: Ronald Press Co., 1953. Pp. xi, 459–885. *

1486. BECK, SAMUEL J., AND NUNNALLY, J. C. "Two Researches in Schizophrenia." Discussion by Helen D. Sargent. *Am J Orthopsychiatry* 23:223–37 Ap '53. * (*PA* 28:2984)

1487. BEIER, ERNST G. "The Effects of Rorschach Interpretations on Intellectual Functioning of Adjusted, Questionably Adjusted, and Maladjusted Subjects." *J Proj Tech* 17:66–9 Mr '53. * (*PA* 28:2612)

1488. BERGER, DAVID. "The Rorschach as a Measure of Real-Life Stress." *J Consult Psychol* 17:355–8 O '53. * (*PA* 28:6018)

1489. BERKOWITZ, MARTIN, AND LEVINE, JACOB. "Rorschach Scoring Categories as Diagnostic 'Signs.'" *J Consult Psychol* 17:110–2 Ap '53. * (*PA* 28:2616)

1490. BERLOW, NATHAN. *Psychosexual Indicators on the Rorschach Test.* Doctor's thesis, University of Michigan (Ann Arbor, Mich.), 1953. (*DA* 13:429)

1491. BILLS, ROBERT E. "Rorschach Characteristics of Persons Scoring High and Low in Acceptance of Self." *J Consult Psychol* 17:36–8 F '53. * (*PA* 28:930)

1492. BLECHNER, JANET E. "Constancy of Rorschach Movement Responses Under Educational Conditioning." *Calif J Ed Res* 4:173–6 S '53. * (*PA* 28:4332)

1493. BRADWAY, KATHERINE, AND HEISLER, VERDA. "The Relation Between Diagnoses and Certain Types of Extreme Deviations and Content on the Rorschach." *J Proj Tech* 17:70–4 Mr '53. * (*PA* 28:2620)

1494. BRANSTON, W. T. "A Study of the Rorschach Test Applied to a Group of Thirteen-Year-Old Children." *Brit J Ed Psychol* 23:67–70 F '53. *

1495. BRODY, GERTRUDE GILLENSON. "A Study of the Effects of Color on Rorschach Responses." *Genetic Psychol Monogr* 48:261–311 N '53. * (*PA* 28:7509)

1496. BROWN, FRED. "An Exploratory Study of Dynamic Factors in the Content of the Rorschach Protocol." *J Proj Tech* 17:251–79 S '53. * (*PA* 28:4335)

1497. BRUCE, J. MARSHALL, JR., AND THOMAS, CAROLINE BEDELL. "A Method of Rating Certain Personality Factors as Determined by the Rorschach Test for Use in a Study of the Precursors of Hypertension and Coronary Artery Disease." *Psychiatric Q Sup* 27:207–38 pt 2 '53. * (*PA* 28:4708)

1498. BRUDO, CHARLES S. *The Alpha Index in the Electroencephalogram and Movement Responses on the Rorschach and PMS Tests.* Doctor's thesis, Northwestern University (Evanston, Ill.), 1953. (*DA* 14:393)

1499. BUHLER, CHARLOTTE; KENDIG, ISABELLE V.; PHILLIPS, LESLIE; AND PIOTROWSKI, ZYGMUNT A. "Contributions of Projective Techniques to the Understanding of Basic Psychopathology." Abstract. *J Proj Tech* 17:381–2 S '53. *

1500. BURGESS, ELVA. *Personality Factors in Over- and Under-Achievers in Engineering.* Doctor's thesis, Pennsylvania State College (State College, Pa.), 1953.

1501. CALDEN, GEORGE. "Psychosurgery in a Set of Schizophrenic Identical Twins—A Psychological Study." *J Proj Tech* 17:200–9 Je '53. * (*PA* 28:4641)

1502. CALDEN, GEORGE, AND COHEN, LEON B. "The Relationship of Ego-Involvement and Test Definition to Rorschach Test Performance." *J Proj Tech* 17:300–11 S '53. * (*PA* 28:4337)

1503. CANTER, FRANCIS M. "Personality Factors in Seizure States With Reference to the Rosenzweig Triadic Hypothesis." *J Consult Psychol* 17:429–35 D '53. * (*PA* 28:7844)

1504. CARLSON, VIRGIL R., AND LAZARUS, RICHARD S. "A Repetition of Meyer Williams' Study of Intellectual Control Under Stress and Associated Rorschach Factors." *J Consult Psychol* 17:247–53 Ag '53. * (*PA* 28:4340)

1505. CHAPMAN, A. H. "The Rorschach Examination in a

Case of Erotomania." *J Clin Psychol* 9:195–8 Ap '53. * (*PA* 28:2894)

1506. CHAPMAN, A. H., AND REESE, D. G. "Homosexual Signs in Rorschachs of Early Schizophrenics." *J Clin Psychol* 9:30–2 Ja '53. * (*PA* 27:7928)

1507. CHAREN, SOL. "A Critique of 'An Exploratory Study of Dynamic Factors in the Content of the Rorschach Protocol.'" Letter. Reply by Fred Brown. *J Proj Tech* 17:460–4 D '53. * (*PA* 28:6021)

1508. COHART, MARY S. *The Differential Value of the Group Rorschach and the MMPI in the Evaluation of Teacher Personality.* Doctor's thesis, Yale University (New Haven, Conn.), 1953.

1509. COLLET, GRACE MARGARET. *Prediction and Communication Problems Illustrated With the Rorschach.* Doctor's thesis, Ohio State University (Columbus, Ohio), 1953. (*DA* 18:1852)

1510. COOPER, MAX. "An Evaluation of Rorschach Patterns in Headache Patients." Abstract. *Am Psychol* 8:336–7 Ag '53. *

1511. DÖRKEN, HERBERT, JR. "Projective Tests and the Consistency of the Personality Structure: A Pilot Study." *J Abn & Social Psychol* 48:525–31 O '53. * (*PA* 28:6022)

1512. EARLE, JEFFREY B. *The Diagnostic Value of the FLK Scales of the MMPI.* Master's thesis, University of Ottawa (Ottawa, Ont., Canada), 1953.

1513. ERIKSEN, CHARLES W., AND EISENSTEIN, DONALD. "Personality Rigidity and the Rorschach." *J Personality* 21:386–91 Mr '53. * (*PA* 28:2628)

1514. FABRIKANT, BEN. "Perceptual Control on the Rorschach Test." *J Clin Psychol* 9:396–7 O '53. * (*PA* 28:4429)

1515. FABRIKANT, BENJAMIN. *The Effects of an Experimental Set on Rorschach Test Performance.* Doctor's thesis, University of Buffalo (Buffalo, N.Y.), 1953. (*DA* 13:431)

1516. FISKE, DONALD W., AND BAUGHMAN, EMMETT E. "Relationships Between Rorschach Scoring Categories and the Total Number of Responses." *J Abn & Social Psychol* 48:25–32 Ja '53. * (*PA* 27:942)

1517. FORER, BERTRAM. ["An Annotated Bibliography of 28 Foreign Articles on Projective Techniques."] *J Proj Tech* 17: 373–5 S '53. *

1518. FORRER, GORDON R.; DRAPER, CHARLINE; AND GRISELL, JAMES L. "Pharmacotoxic Therapy With Atropine Sulfate: Remission in Two Cases With Rorschach Findings." *J Nerv & Mental Dis* 117:226–33 Mr '53. * (*PA* 29:1232)

1519. FORTIER, ROBERT H. "The Response to Color and Ego Functions." *Psychol B* 50:41–63 Ja '53. * (*PA* 27:7046)

1520. FRAMO, JAMES L., JR. *Structural Aspects of Perceptual Development in Normal Adults: A Tachistoscopic Study With the Rorschach Technique.* Doctor's thesis, University of Texas (Austin, Tex.), 1953.

1521. FRANKLE, ALLAN H. *Rorschach Human Movement and Human Content Responses as Indices of the Adequacy of Interpersonal Relationships of Social Work Students.* Doctor's thesis, University of Chicago (Chicago, Ill.), 1953.

1522. FRIEDMAN, HOWARD. "Perceptual Regression in Schizophrenia: An Hypothesis Suggested by the Use of the Rorschach Test." *J Proj Tech* 17:171–85 Je '53. * (*PA* 28:4650)

1523. GEORGE, C. E. "Some Unforeseen Correlates Between the Studies of Shaw and Wallen." *J Abn & Social Psychol* 48: 150 Ja '53. * (*PA* 28:948)

1524. GIBBY, ROBERT G., AND STOTSKY, BERNARD A. "The Relation of Rorschach Free Association to Inquiry." *J Consult Psychol* 17:359–64 O '53. * (*PA* 28:6027)

1525. GIBBY, ROBERT G.; MILLER, DANIEL R.; AND WALKER, EDWARD L. "The Examiner's Influence on the Rorschach Protocol." *J Consult Psychol* 17:425–8 D '53. * (*PA* 28:7524)

1526. GIBBY, ROBERT G.; STOTSKY, BERNARD A.; MILLER, DANIEL R.; AND HILER, E. WESLEY. "Prediction of Duration of Therapy From the Rorschach Test." *J Consult Psychol* 17: 348–54 O '53. * (*PA* 28:6101)

1527. GLADWIN, THOMAS, AND SARASON, SEYMOUR B. *Truk: Man in Paradise*, pp. 290–527. Viking Fund Publications in Anthropology, No. 20. New York: Wenner-Gren Foundation for Anthropological Research, Inc., 1953. Pp. 774. * (*PA* 28:8668)

1528. GLUCK, MARTIN RICHARD. *A Study of the Relationship Between the Amount of Hostility in the Content of Projective Techniques and the Amount of Hostility Expressed in Behavior.* Doctor's thesis, University of Pittsburgh (Pittsburgh, Pa.), 1953.

1529. GOERTZEL, VICTOR. *Shifts in Personality in the Rorschach Test and in Psychotherapy.* Doctor's thesis, University of Michigan (Ann Arbor, Mich.), 1953. (*DA* 13:433)

1530. GRAUER, DAVID. "Prognosis in Paranoid Schizophrenia on the Basis of the Rorschach." *J Consult Psychol* 17:199–205 Je '53. * (*PA* 28:2998)

1531. GREENBERG, N. *Psychosurgery: The Use of the Rorschach Test for Prognosis in Prefrontal Lobotomy.* Master's thesis, University of Montreal (Montreal, Que., Canada), 1953.

1532. GUERTIN, WILSON H., AND TREMBATH, WILLIAM E. "Card VI Disturbance on the Rorschachs of Sex Offenders." *J General Psychol* 49:221–7 O '53. * (*PA* 28:7787)

1533. GURVITZ, MILTON S. "Personality and Intellectual Correlates of the Aging Process as Measured by the Rorschach Technique." Abstract. *Am Psychol* 8:360 Ag '53. *

1534. HALPERN, FLORENCE. *A Clinical Approach to Children's Rorschachs.* New York: Grune & Stratton, Inc., 1953. Pp. xv, 270. * (*PA* 28:2635)

1535. HARRINGTON, ROBERT WILLARD. *Prediction of Maladap-*

tive Responses Under Conditions of Habit-Interference From Rorschach Color Responses. Doctor's thesis, Michigan State College (East Lansing, Mich.), 1953. (*DA* 14:555)

1536. HARROWER, MOLLY R. "Group Rorschach," pp. 620–4. (*PA* 27:7774) In *Contributions Toward Medical Psychology: Theory and Psychodiagnostic Methods, Vol. II.* Edited by Arthur Weider. New York: Ronald Press Co., 1953. Pp. xi, 459–885. *

1537. HEMMENDINGER, LARRY. "Perceptual Organization and Development as Reflected in the Structure of Rorschach Test Responses." *J Proj Tech* 17:162–70 Je '53. * (*PA* 28:4082)

1538. HENRY, JULES, AND SPIRO, MELFORD E. "Psychological Techniques: Projective Tests in Field Work," pp. 417–29. In *Anthropology Today: An Encyclopedic Inventory.* Edited by A. L. Kroeber. Chicago, Ill.: University of Chicago Press, 1953. Pp. xv, 966. *

1539. HILER, E. WESLEY; STOTSKY, BERNARD A.; MILLER, DANIEL R.; AND GIBBY, ROBERT G. "Rorschach Criteria for Predicting Duration of Therapy." Abstract. *Am Psychol* 8:367–8 Ag '53. *

1540. HOWARD, THOMAS W. *Physiological, Diagnostic, and Rorschach Indices of Anxiety.* Doctor's thesis, Tulane University (New Orleans, La.), 1953.

1541. IVES, VIRGINIA; GRANT, MARGUERITE Q.; AND RANZONI, JANE H. "The 'Neurotic' Rorschachs of Normal Adolescents." *J Genetic Psychol* 83:31–61 S '53. * (*PA* 28:5734)

1542. JACOBS, ROBERT, AND WILKINSON, MARGARET A. "A Brief Study of Response Types on the Multiple-Choice Rorschach as They Relate to Vocational Interests." *Yearb Nat Council Meas Used Ed* 10:25–29 '53. *

1543. JOHNSON, ELIZABETH Z. "Klopfer's Prognostic Scale Used With Raven's Progressive Matrices in Play Therapy Prognosis." *J Proj Tech* 17:320–6 S '53. * (*PA* 28:4363)

1544. JOURARD, SIDNEY MARSHALL. *A Study of Ego Strength by Means of the Rorschach Test and the Interruption of Tasks Experiment.* Doctor's thesis, University of Buffalo (Buffalo, N.Y.), 1953. (*DA* 13:435)

1545. KALDEGG, A. "German and English Personality: A Comparative Study of Individual Groups Using Projective Techniques." Abstract. *B Brit Psychol Soc* (19):29 Ja '53. *

1546. KANTOR, ROBERT E.; WALLNER, JULIUS M.; AND WINDER, C. L. "Process and Reactive Schizophrenia." *J Consult Psychol* 17:157–62 Je '53. * (*PA* 28:3002)

1547. KAUFMAN, LAWRENCE WILLARD. *Rorschach Responses Associated With Experimentally Induced Anxiety.* Doctor's thesis, Columbia University (New York, N.Y.), 1953. (*DA* 14:187)

1548. KEEHN, J. D. "Rorschach Validation: II, The Validity of Colour Shock in the Diagnosis of Neuroticism." *J Mental Sci* 99:224–34 Ap '53. * (*PA* 28:952)

1549. KEEHN, J. D. "Rorschach Validation: III, An Examination of the Role of Colour as a Determinant in the Rorschach Test." *J Mental Sci* 99:410–38 Jl '53. * (*PA* 28:4366)

1550. KELLMAN, SAMUEL. "Multiple Choice Rorschach," pp. 625–35. (*PA* 27:7778) In *Contributions Toward Medical Psychology: Theory and Psychodiagnostic Methods, Vol. II.* Edited by Arthur Weider. New York: Ronald Press Co., 1953. Pp. xi, 459–885. *

1551. KESSLER, JANE W., AND WOLFENSTEIN, CHARLOTTE M. "A Comparison of Rorschach Retests With Behavior Changes in a Group of Emotionally Disturbed Children." Discussion by Elizabeth A. Bremner. *Am J Orthopsychiatry* 23:740–54 O '53. * (*PA* 28:6159)

1552. KIRKNER, FRANK J.; WISHAM, WAYNE W.; AND GIEDT, F. HAROLD. "A Report on the Validity of the Rorschach Prognostic Rating Scale." *J Proj Tech* 17:465–70 D '53. * (*PA* 28: 6113)

1553. KLEIN, ABRAHAM, AND ARNHEIM, RUDOLF. "Perceptual Analysis of a Rorschach Card." *J Personality* 22:60–70 S '53. * (*PA* 28:4368)

1554. KOBLER, FRANK J., AND STIEL, AGNES. "The Use of the Rorschach in Involutional Melancholia." *J Consult Psychol* 17:365–70 O '53. * (*PA* 28:6355)

1555. KORNREICH, MELVIN. "Variations in the Consistency of the Behavioral Meaning of Personality Test Scores." *Genetic Psychol Monogr* 47:73–138 F '53. * (*PA* 27:6535)

1556. KOTKOV, BENJAMIN, AND MEADOW, ARNOLD. "Rorschach Criteria for Predicting Continuation in Individual Psychotherapy." *J Consult Psychol* 17:16–20 F '53. * (*PA* 28: 1030)

1557. KRATHWOHL, DAVID R. *The Prediction of Objective Test Behavior by Means of the Group Rorschach Test.* Doctor's thesis, University of Chicago (Chicago, Ill.), 1953. (Abstract: *Am Psychol* 8:382)

1558. LANDISBERG, SELMA. "Relationship of the Rorschach to the H-T-P." *J Clin Psychol* 9:179–83 Ap '53. * (*PA* 28:2645)

1559. LEDWITH, NETTIE H. "Rorschach Responses of Elementary School Children: A Normative Study." Abstract. *Am Psychol* 8:385 Ag '53. *

1560. LEIBMAN, OSCAR BERNARD. *The Relationship of Personal and Social Adjustment to Academic Achievement in the Elementary School.* Doctor's thesis, Columbia University (New York, N.Y.), 1953. (*DA* 14:67)

1561. LEVIN, MAX M. "The Two Tests in the Rorschach." Comments by W. G. Klopfer and S. J. Beck. *J Proj Tech* 17: 471–6 D '53. * (*PA* 28:6036)

1562. LEVINE, JUDITH, AND DAVIDSON, HELEN H. "Are Ab-

breviated Rorschach Records Useful?" Abstract. *Am Psychol* 8:388 Ag '53. *

1563. LODGE, GEORGE T. "A Method for the Dynamic Representation of Personality Data." *J Proj Tech* 17:477–81 D '53. * (*PA* 28:6037)

1564. LODGE, GEORGE T., AND GIBSON, ROBERT L. "A Coaction Map of the Personalities Described by H. Rorschach and S. J. Beck." *J Proj Tech* 17:482–8 D '53. * (*PA* 28:6038)

1565. LODGE, GEORGE T., AND STEENBARGER, CHARLES J. "Charting the Course of the Rorschach Interview." *J General Psychol* 48:67–73 Ja '53. * (*PA* 28:957)

1566. LOTSOF, ERWIN J. "Intelligence, Verbal Fluency, and the Rorschach Test." *J Consult Psychol* 17:21–4 F '53. * (*PA* 28:958)

1567. LUFT, JOSEPH. "Interaction and Projection." *J Proj Tech* 17:489–92 D '53. * (*PA* 28:6040)

1568. LUNDIN, WILLIAM H., AND SCHPOONT, SEYMOUR. "The Application of the Rorschach Prognostic Rating Scale to One Intensively Followed Case." *J Proj Tech* 17:295–9 S '53. * (*PA* 28:4374)

1569. MCCALL, RAYMOND J. "Psychometric Evaluation of Rorschach Records in Brain-Operated Patients." Abstract. *Am Psychol* 8:394 Ag '53. *

1570. MCFARLAND, ROBERT L.; BECKER, WESLEY; DOCTER, RICHARD; SESSIONS, ALWYN; AND ULLMANN, LEONARD. "Measures of Reality Orientation." Abstract. *Am Psychol* 8:396 Ag '53. *

1571. MANN, LESTER. *The Relation of Rorschach Indices of Extratension and Introversion to a Measure of Responsiveness to the Immediate Environment.* Doctor's thesis, University of North Carolina (Chapel Hill, N.C.), 1953.

1572. MARADIE, LOUIS JOSEPH. "Productivity on the Rorschach as a Function of Order of Presentation." *J Consult Psychol* 17:32–5 F '53. * (*PA* 28:959)

1573. MEER, BERNARD. "The Relative Difficulty of the Rorschach Cards." Abstract. *Am Psychol* 8:404 Ag '53. *

1574. MELTZOFF, JULIAN; SINGER, JEROME L.; AND KORCHIN, SHELDON J. "Motor Inhibition and Rorschach Movement Responses: A Test of the Sensory-Tonic Theory." *J Personality* 21:400–10 Mr '53. (*PA* 28:2656)

1575. MEYER, BILL THOMAS. *An Investigation of Developmental Change in the Rorschach Responses of Young Children.* Doctor's thesis, University of Nebraska (Lincoln, Neb.), 1953.

1576. MEYER, GEORGE. "Some Relationships Between Rorschach Scores in Kindergarten and Reading in the Primary Grades." *J Proj Tech* 17:414–25 D '53. * (*PA* 28:6510)

1577. MILL, CYRIL R. "Personality Patterns of Sociometrically Selected and Sociometrically Rejected Male College Students." *Sociometry* 16:151–67 My '53. * (*PA* 28:4886)

1578. MILLER, DANIEL R. "Prediction of Behavior by Means of the Rorschach Test." *J Abn & Social Psychol* 48:367–75 Jl '53. * (*PA* 28:2658)

1579. MINDESS, HARVEY. "Predicting Patients' Responses to Psychotherapy: A Preliminary Study Designed to Investigate the Validity of the 'Rorschach Prognostic Rating Scale.'" *J Proj Tech* 17:327–34 S '53. * (*PA* 28:4377)

1580. MUNROE, RUTH L. "Inspection Rorschach," pp. 611–9. (*PA* 27:7785) In *Contributions Toward Medical Psychology: Theory and Psychodiagnostic Methods, Vol. II.* Edited by Arthur Weider. New York: Ronald Press Co., 1953. Pp. xi, 459–885. *

1581. NASH, HELEN T.; MARGOLIN, JOSEPH B.; AND MACGREGOR, ROBERT. "A Method for Systematizing Rorschach Evaluation." *J General Psychol* 48:195–208 Ap '53. * (*PA* 28:963)

1582. NOWELL, ANN. "Peer Status as Related to Measures of Personality." *Calif J Ed Res* 4:37–41 Ja '53. * (*PA* 28:1514)

1583. ORANGE, ARTHUR J. "Perceptual Consistency as Measured by the Rorschach." *J Proj Tech* 17:224–8 Je '53. * (*PA* 28:4380)

1584. PAGE, MARTHA HESSEL, AND TRAVERS, ROBERT M. W. "Relationships Between Rorschach Performance and Student-Teaching." *J Ed Psychol* 44:31–40 Ja '53. * (*PA* 28:1586)

1585. PATTIE, FRANK A. "The Effect of Hypnotically Induced Hostility on Rorschach Responses." Abstract. *Am Psychol* 8:413 Ag '53. *

1586. PAULSEN, ALMA A. *Personality Development in the Middle Childhood Years, a Ten-Year Longitudinal Study of 30 Public School Children by Means of Rorschach Tests and Social Histories.* Doctor's thesis, New York University (New York, N. Y.), 1953. (*DA* 13:592)

1587. PEÑA, CESAREO D. "A Genetic Evaluation of Perceptual Structurization in Cerebral Pathology: An Investigation by Means of the Rorschach Test." *J Proj Tech* 17:186–99 Je '53. * (*PA* 28:4762)

1588. PHILLIPS, LESLIE, AND SMITH, JOSEPH G. *Rorschach Interpretation: Advanced Technique.* New York: Grune & Stratton, Inc., 1953. Pp. xiii, 385. * (*PA* 28:2666)

1589. PINNEAU, SAMUEL RICHARD. *Differences Between Normals and Various Types of Schizophrenics on a Multiple-Choice Rorschach Test.* Doctor's thesis, University of California (Berkeley, Calif.), 1953.

1590. PRICE, ARTHUR COOPER. *A Rorschach Study of the Development of Personality Structure in White and Negro Children in a Southeastern Community.* Doctor's thesis, University of Florida (Gainesville, Fla.), 1953. (*DA* 15:2578)

1591. PURCELL, CLAIRE KEPLER. *A Rorschach Study of Adjustment Prediction, Developmental Trends and Normative Data With Kindergarten Children.* Doctor's thesis, University of Nebraska (Lincoln, Neb.), 1953.

1592. RABINOVITCH, MORTIMER S. *An Experimental Investigation of Anxiety Indicators on the Rorschach Test.* Doctor's thesis, Purdue University (Lafayette, Ind.), 1953.

1593. RACUSEN, FRANCES RHEA. "An Exploratory Investigation of the Creativity and Productivity Variables on the Rorschach and Thematic Apperception Tests." Abstract. *Am Psychol* 8:417 Ag '53. *

1594. REITAN, RALPH M. "Intellectual Functions in Myxedema." *A.M.A. Arch Neurol & Psychiatry* 69:436–49 Ap '53. * (*PA* 28:3094)

1595. REITAN, RALPH M. "Psychological Factors in Essential Hypertension as Indicated by the Rorschach Test." Abstract. *Am Psychol* 8:418–9 Ag '53. *

1596. RICHARDS, T. W. "Personality Development as Reflected in Rorschach Behavior: A Case Study." Abstract. *Am Psychol* 8:420 Ag '53. *

1597. RIEMAN, GLENN W. "The Effectiveness of Rorschach Elements in the Discrimination Between Neurotic and Ambulatory Schizophrenic Subjects." *J Consult Psychol* 17:25–31 F '53. * (*PA* 28:1163)

1598. ROCKBERGER, HARRY. *The Effectiveness of a Rorschach Prognostic Scale for Predicting Results in Psychotherapy: A Study of the Relationship Between a Rorschach Prognostic Rating Scale, and the Improvement Status of Psychoneurotic and Ambulatory Schizophrenic Veterans Undergoing Individual Psychotherapy.* Doctor's thesis, New York University (New York, N.Y.), 1953. (*DA* 14:399)

1599. RODELL, CHARLES. *A Validation Study of the Rorschach Technique for the Differential Diagnosis of Psychopathic Groups.* Doctor's thesis, Pennsylvania State College (State College, Pa.), 1953.

1600. ROE, ANNE. "A Psychological Study of Eminent Psychologists and Anthropologists, and a Comparison With Biological and Physical Scientists." *Psychol Monogr* 67(2):1–55 '53. * (*PA* 28:1956)

1601. ROEHRIG, WILLIAM CRUDEN. *Eysenck's Ranking Rorschach Test Proposed as an Aid in Predicting Academic Performance.* Master's thesis, University of Florida (Gainesville, Fla.), 1953.

1602. ROGERS, LAWRENCE S., AND HAMMOND, KENNETH R. "Prediction of the Results of Therapy by Means of the Rorschach Test." *J Consult Psychol* 17:8–15 F '53. * (*PA* 28:1070)

1603. RUBIN, HAROLD, AND LONSTEIN, MURRAY. "A Cross-Validation of Suggested Rorschach Patterns Associated With Schizophrenia." *J Consult Psychol* 17:371–2 O '53. * (*PA* 28:6051)

1604. RUST, RALPH M., AND RYAN, F. J. "The Relationship of Some Rorschach Variables to Academic Behavior." *J Personality* 21:441–56 Je '53. * (*PA* 28:4858)

1605. SACKMAN, HAROLD. *An Investigation of Certain Aspects of the Validity of the Formal Rorschach Scoring System in Relation to Age, Education, and Vocabulary Score.* Doctor's thesis, Fordham University (New York, N.Y.), 1953.

1606. SANDERS, RICHARD, AND CLEVELAND, SIDNEY E. "The Relationship Between Certain Examiner Personality Variables and Subjects' Rorschach Scores." *J Proj Tech* 17:34–50 Mr '53. * (*PA* 28:2670)

1607. SANDLER, J. "A Comparative Study of Psychopaths, Using the Rorschach Test." Abstract. *B Brit Psychol Soc* (19):28 Ja '53. *

1608. SARASON, SEYMOUR B. "The Rorschach Test," pp. 223–52. In his *Psychological Problems in Mental Deficiency, Second Edition.* New York: Harper & Brothers, 1953. Pp. xi, 402. * (*PA* 28:2876)

1609. SAYONS, K., AND SAYONS, Z. "Weighted Scale and Psychogram for the Rorschach Score." *Can J Psychol* 7:60–8 Je '53. * (*PA* 28:4388)

1610. SCHAFER, ROY. "Content Analysis in the Rorschach Test." *J Proj Tech* 17:335–9 S '53. * (*PA* 28:4389)

1611. SCHNEIDER, STANLEY FRED. *The Prediction of Certain Aspects of the Psychotherapeutic Relationship From Rorschach's Test: An Empirical and Exploratory Study.* Doctor's thesis, University of Michigan (Ann Arbor, Mich.), 1953. (*DA* 13:879)

1612. SCHULMAN, IRVING. *The Relation Between the Perception of Movement on the Rorschach Test and Levels of Conceptualization: An Experimental Study and Theoretical Analysis of Thought Processes Involved in the Perception of Movement on the Rorschach Test.* Doctor's thesis, New York University (New York, N.Y.), 1953. (*DA* 14:303)

1613. SECORD, PAUL F. "An Analysis of Perceptual and Related Processes Occurring in Projective Testing." *J General Psychol* 49:65–85 Jl '53. * (*PA* 28:6053)

1614. SHATIN, LEO. "Rorschach Adjustment and the Thematic Apperception Test." *J Proj Tech* 17:92–101 Mr '53. * (*PA* 28:2675)

1615. SHEEHAN, JOSEPH G. "Rorschach Changes During Psychotherapy in Relation to Personality of the Therapist." Abstract. *Am Psychol* 8:434–5 Ag '53. *

1616. SHEPHERD, JOHN RALPH. *An Experimental Study of the Responses of Stage-Frightened Students to Certain Scoring Categories of the Group Rorschach Test.* Doctor's thesis, University of Southern California (Los Angeles, Calif.), 1953.

1617. SHERESHEVSKI-SHERE, EUGENIA; LASSER, LEONARD M.; AND GOTTESFELD, BENJAMIN H. "An Evaluation of Anatomy

Content and F+ Percentage in the Rorschachs of Alcoholics, Schizophrenics and Normals." *J Proj Tech* 17:229–33 Je '53. * (*PA* 28:4592)

1618. SIEGEL, EDWARD L. "Genetic Parallels of Perceptual Structuralization in Paranoid Schizophrenia: An Analysis by Means of the Rorschach Technique." *J Proj Tech* 17:151–61 Je '53. * (*PA* 28:4675)

1619. SILVA, JOSEPH J. *The Effect of Variation in Instructions Upon Certain Rorschach Variables in Schizophrenic and Psychoneurotic Subjects.* Doctor's thesis, Fordham University (New York, N.Y.), 1953.

1620. SILVERMAN, HERBERT. *The Prediction of Consciousness of Conflict in the Self From the Rorschach.* Doctor's thesis, University of Michigan (Ann Arbor, Mich.), 1953. (*DA* 13: 438)

1621. SOBOL, ALBERT LEO. *The Use of the Rorschach Test in Psychiatric Diagnosis and Treatment Planning.* Doctor's thesis, New York University (New York, N.Y.), 1953. (*DA* 13:1264)

1622. SOLOMON, RUTH H. Chap. 3, "Personality Adjustment to Reading Success and Failure," pp. 64–82. In *Clinical Studies in Reading, II.* Edited by Helen M. Robinson. University of Chicago, Supplementary Educational Monographs, No. 77. Chicago, Ill.: University of Chicago Press, January 1953. Pp. x, 189. *

1623. SPIELBERG, MIMI JOHNSON. *A Study of Intra-Familial Rorschach Patterns in a Rural Community.* Doctor's thesis, University of Nebraska (Lincoln, Neb.), 1953.

1624. SPOERL, DOROTHY TILDEN. " 'Category-Scoring' of the Multiple Choice Rorschach." *J Social Psychol* 38:287–91 N '53. * (*PA* 28:6054)

1625. STEINER, META. "The Rorschach Test." *Monogr Soc Res Child Develop* 16(53):34–59, 214–316 '53. * (*PA* 28:4077)

1626. STEPHENSON, WILLIAM. *The Study of Behavior: Q-Technique and Its Methodology,* pp. 293–312. Chicago, Ill.: University of Chicago Press, 1953. Pp. ix, 376. * (*PA* 28:6810)

1627. STONE, HAROLD. *The Relationship of Hostile-Aggressive Behavior to Aggressive Content on the Rorschach and Thematic Apperception Tests.* Doctor's thesis, University of California (Los Angeles, Calif.), 1953.

1628. STORMENT, CHARLYNE TOWNSEND, AND FINNEY, BEN C. "Projection and Behavior: A Rorschach Study of Assaultive Mental Hospital Patients." *J Proj Tech* 17:349–60 S '53. * (*PA* 28:4677)

1629. STOTT, WARREN WALTER. *An Evaluation of the Influence of Learning on Color and Form Responses to Ambiguous Figures.* Doctor's thesis, University of Nebraska (Lincoln, Neb.), 1953.

1630. SWARTZ, MELVIN B. *The Role of Color in Influencing Responses to the Rorschach Test: An Experimental Investigation of the Validity of the Color-Shock Hypothesis as a Sign of Neurotic Disturbance and as a Phenomenon Induced by the Color Stimulus.* Doctor's thesis, New York University (New York, N. Y.), 1953. (*DA* 13:1266)

1631. TAULBEE, EARL SELDON. *The Value of the Rorschach Test for Evaluating the Intellectual Levels of Functioning in Schizophrenics.* Doctor's thesis, University of Nebraska (Lincoln, Neb.), 1953.

1632. THALER, MARGARET. "Three Theories of Personality Applied to the Rorschach." Abstract. *J Colo-Wyo Acad Sci* 4:51 D '53. *

1633. WALKER, ROBERT G. "An Approach to Standardization of Rorschach Form-level." *J Proj Tech* 17:426–36 D '53. * (*PA* 28:6059)

1634. WALTERS, C. A. *A Study of Rorschach and Other Projective Tests as Indicators of Anxiety in Children.* Master's thesis, University of London (London, England), 1953.

1635. WALTERS, RICHARD H. "A Preliminary Analysis of the Rorschach Records of Fifty Prison Inmates." *J Proj Tech* 17:437–46 D '53. * (*PA* 28:6327)

1636. WEBER, LOUIS C. "Ethics in Administering the Rorschach Test." *J Abn & Social Psychol* 48:443 Jl '53. * (*PA* 28:2688)

1637. WERTHEIMER, MICHAEL. "On the Supposed Behavioral Correlates of an 'Eye' Content Response on the Rorschach." *J Consult Psychol* 17:189–94 Je '53. * (*PA* 28:2690)

1638. WERTHEIMER, RITA RAY. *The Relationship Between Sociometric Status, Sex, and Socio-Economic Level and Rorschach Signs of Adjustment With a Group of Adolescent Subjects.* Doctor's thesis, University of Pittsburgh (Pittsburgh, Pa.), 1953.

1639. WESTROPE, MARTHA R. "Relations Among Rorschach Indices, Manifest Anxiety, and Performance Under Stress." *J Abn & Social Psychol* 48:515–24 O '53. * (*PA* 28:6061)

1640. WILLIAMS, HAROLD L., AND LAWRENCE, JAMES F. "Further Investigation of Rorschach Determinants Subjected to Factor Analysis." *J Consult Psychol* 17:261–4 Ag '53. * (*PA* 28:4404)

1641. WIRT, ROBERT D., AND McREYNOLDS, PAUL. "The Reliability of Rorschach Number of Responses." *J Proj Tech* 17:493–4 D '53. * (*PA* 28:6064)

1642. WISHNER, JULIUS. "Neurosis and Tension: An Exploratory Study of the Relationship of Physiological and Rorschach Measures." *J Abn & Social Psychol* 48:253–60 Ap '53. * (*PA* 28:2288)

1643. ZULLIGER, HANS. "The Case of Franz and Lotti." *J Proj Tech* 17:61-5 Mr '53. * (*PA* 28:2696)

1644. ALCOCK, A. THEODORA. "Rorschach Personality Pat-

terns in Asthmatic Children." Abstract. *Brit Rorsch Forum* (4):5–6 Mr '54. *

1645. ALLEE, WAYNE L. *A Comparative Study of Modified Rorschach Techniques as Used in Evaluating the Adjustment Level of College Students.* Doctor's thesis, University of Colorado (Boulder, Colo.), 1954.

1646. ALLEN, ROBERT M. "Continued Longitudinal Rorschach Study of a Child for Years Three to Five." *J Genetic Psychol* 85:135–49 S '54. * (*PA* 29:5685)

1647. ALLEN, ROBERT M. *Elements of Rorschach Interpretation: With an Extended Bibliography.* New York: International Universities Press, Inc., 1954. Pp. 242. * (*PA* 29:2424)

1648. ALLEN, ROBERT M. "Recording the Rorschach Protocol." *J Clin Psychol* 10:195–6 Ap '54. * (*PA* 29:900)

1649. ALLERHAND, MELVIN E. "Chiaroscuro Determinant of Rorschach Test as Indicator of Manifest Anxiety." *J Proj Tech* 18:407–13 D '54. * (*PA* 29:7253)

1650. ALLISON, HARRY W., AND ALLISON, SARAH G. "Personality Changes Following Transorbital Lobotomy." *J Abn & Social Psychol* 49:219–23 Ap '54. * (*PA* 29:970)

1651. AMES, LOUISE BATES; LEARNED, JANET; METRAUX, RUTH W.; AND WALKER, RICHARD N. *Rorschach Responses in Old Age.* New York: Paul B. Hoeber, Inc., 1954. Pp. xv, 229. * (*PA* 29:637)

1652. ANDERHALTER, O. F. "An Application of Profile Similarity Techniques to Rorschach Data on 2161 Marine Corps Officer Candidates." *Proc Inv Conf Testing Probl* 1953:47–53 '54. * (*PA* 28:6770)

1653. AUSUBEL, DAVID P.; SCHIFF, HERBERT M.; AND ZELENY, MAJORIE P. "Validity of Teachers' Ratings of Adolescents' Adjustment and Aspirations." *J Ed Psychol* 45:394–406 N '54. * (*PA* 29:7981)

1654. BAKER, LAWRENCE M., AND CREAGER, JOHN A. "Rating Scale Technique Applied to Rorschach Responses." *J Clin Psychol* 10:373–5 O '54. * (*PA* 29:4027)

1655. BANDURA, ALBERT. "The Rorschach White Space Response and 'Oppositional' Behavior." *J Consult Psychol* 18:17–21 F '54. * (*PA* 28:8711)

1656. BANDURA, ALBERT. "The Rorschach White Space Response and Perceptual Reversal." *J Exp Psychol* 48:113–8 Ag '54. * (*PA* 29:4028)

1657. BAUGHMAN, E. EARL. "A Comparative Analysis of Rorschach Forms With Altered Stimulus Characteristics." *J Proj Tech* 18:151–64 Je '54. * (*PA* 29:4029)

1658. BAUGHMAN, E. EARL. "Regarding 'The Two Tests in the Rorschach' by Levin." *J Proj Tech* 18:165–8 Je '54. * (*PA* 29:4030)

1659. BECK, SAMUEL J. *The Six Schizophrenias: Reaction Patterns in Children and Adults.* American Orthopsychiatric Association, Research Monographs No. 6. New York: the Association, Inc., 1954. Pp. xi, 238. * (*PA* 29:2760)

1660. BELDEN, ARVORD W., AND BAUGHMAN, E. EARL. "The Effects of Figure-Ground Contrast Upon Perception as Evaluated by a Modified Rorschach Technique." *J Consult Psychol* 18:29–34 F '54. * (*PA* 28:8713)

1661. BERGER, DAVID. "Examiner Influence on the Rorschach." *J Clin Psychol* 10:245–8 Jl '54. * (*PA* 29:2430)

1662. BIALICK, IRVING, AND HAMLIN, ROY M. "The Clinician as Judge: Details of Procedure in Judging Projective Material." *J Consult Psychol* 18:239–42 Ag '54. * (*PA* 29:4033)

1663. BILLS, ROBERT E. "Self Concepts and Rorschach Signs of Depression." *J Consult Psychol* 18:135–7 Ap '54. * (*PA* 29:2432)

1664. BLECHNER, JANET E. "Constancy of Rorschach Color Responses Under Educational Conditioning." *J Exp Ed* 22: 293–5 Mr '54. * (*PA* 29:2433)

1665. BLECHNER, JANET E., AND CARTER, HAROLD D. "Rorschach Personality Factors and College Achievement." Abstract. *Calif J Ed Res* 5:187 S '54. *

1666. BLUM, LUCILLE HOLLANDER; DAVIDSON, HELEN H.; AND FIELDSTEEL, NINA D.; WITH THE ASSISTANCE OF LOUIS GETOFF. *A Rorschach Workbook.* New York: International Universities Press, Inc., 1954. Pp. iv, 169. (*PA* 29:4034)

1667. BOLGAR, HEDDA. "Consistency of Affect and Symbolic Expression: A Comparison Between Dreams and Rorschach Responses." Discussion by Samuel J. Beck. *Am J Orthopsychiatry* 24:538–45 Jl '54. * (*PA* 29:4036)

1668. BOREHAM, J. L. "A Rorschach Record of a Person With Homicidal Tendencies." Abstract. *Brit Rorsch Forum* (4):6–8 Mr '54. *

1669. BROCKWAY, ANN LAWLER; GLESER, GOLDINE C.; AND ULETT, GEORGE A. "Rorschach Concepts of Normality." *J Consult Psychol* 18:259–65 Ag '54. * (*PA* 29:4038)

1670. BROIDA, DANIEL C. "An Investigation of Certain Psychodiagnostic Indications of Suicidal Tendencies and Depression in Mental Hospital Patients." *Psychiatric Q* 28:453–64 Jl '54. * (*PA* 29:6019)

1671. BROIDA, DANIEL C., AND THOMPSON, GEORGE G. "The Relationship Between Certain Rorschach 'Insecurity' Hypotheses and Children's Reactions to Psychological Stress." *J Personality* 23:167–81 D '54. * (*PA* 29:5298)

1672. BUCKLE, D. F. "The Use of the Rorschach Technique in the Diagnosis of Schizophrenia." Abstract. *B Brit Psychol Soc* (22):20 Ja '54. *

1673. CALDWELL, BETTYE McD. "The Use of the Rorschach in Personality Research With the Aged." *J Gerontol* 9:316–23 Jl '54. * (*PA* 29:5419)

1674. CARR, ARTHUR C. "Intra-Individual Consistency in

Response to Tests of Varying Degrees of Ambiguity." *J Consult Psychol* 18:251–8 Ag '54. * (*PA* 29:4041)

1675. CHAMBERS, GUINEVERE S. *An Investigation of the Validity of Judgments Based on "Blind" Rorschach Records.* Doctor's thesis, University of Pittsburgh (Pittsburgh, Pa.), 1954. (*DA* 14:2399)

1676. COHEN, DAVID. "Rorschach Scores, Prognosis, and Course of Illness in Pulmonary Tuberculosis." *J Consult Psychol* 18:405–8 D '54. * (*PA* 29:7721)

1677. CORSINI, RAYMOND J., AND UEHLING, HAROLD F. "A Cross Validation of Davidson's Rorschach Adjustment Scale." *J Consult Psychol* 18:277–9 Ag '54. * (*PA* 29:4042)

1678. COX, FRANCIS N., AND SARASON, SEYMOUR B. "Test Anxiety and Rorschach Performance." *J Abn & Social Psychol* 49:371–7 Jl '54. * (*PA* 29:4043)

1679. COX, RACHEL D. "Personality Dynamics of the Well-Adjusted College Student as Revealed by the Rorschach and Thematic Apperception Tests." Abstract. *Am Psychol* 9:351–2 Ag '54. * (*J Proj Tech* 18:399 S '54. *)

1680. CRASILNECK, HAROLD B. *An Analysis of Differences Between Suicidal and Pseudo-Suicidal Patients Through the Use of Projective Techniques.* Doctor's thesis, University of Houston (Houston, Tex.), 1954. (*DA* 14:1456)

1681. CUMMINGS, S. THOMAS. "The Clinician as Judge: Judgments of Adjustment From Rorschach Single-Card Performance." *J Consult Psychol* 18:243–7 Ag '54. * (*PA* 29:4044)

1682. DANA, RICHARD H. "The Effects of Attitudes Toward Authority on Psychotherapy." *J Clin Psychol* 10:350–3 O '54. * (*PA* 29:4109)

1683. DAVIDSON, KENNETH S. *Accuracy of Self-Appraisal and Clinicians' Interpretations of Rorschach Protocols.* Doctor's thesis, University of Michigan (Ann Arbor, Mich.), 1954. (*DA* 14:1098)

1684. DUBOIS, PHILIP H., AND HILDEN, ARNOLD H. "A P Scale for the Rorschach: A Methodological Study." *J Consult Psychol* 18:333–6 O '54. * (*PA* 29:5700)

1685. DUDEK, STEPHANIE. "An Approach to Fundamental Compatibility in Marital Couples Through the Rorschach." Abstract. *J Proj Tech* 18:400 S '54. *

1686. DUDEK, STEPHANIE, AND GOTTLIEB, SOPHIE. "An Approach to Fundamental Compatibility in Marital Couples Through the Rorschach." Abstract. *Am Psychol* 9:356 Ag '54. *

1687. EICHLER, HERBERT, AND GURVITZ, MILTON S. "Research Possibilities of the Variance in the Stimulus Value of Different Editions of the Rorschach Ink Blots." Abstract. *Am Psychol* 9:359 Ag '54. *

1688. ENDACOTT, JOHN. *Methodology for the Study of Clinical Cases by the Way of Rorschach and Psychoanalytic Theories.* Doctor's thesis, University of Chicago (Chicago, Ill.), 1954.

1689. FABRIKANT, BENJAMIN. "Rigidity and Flexibility on the Rorschach." *J Clin Psychol* 10:255–8 Jl '54. * (*PA* 29:2442)

1690. FAIRCHILD, CHARLES M. *Some Personality Differences Between a Delinquent and a Non-Delinquent Group of Juveniles as Measured by the Rorschach Test.* Doctor's thesis, University of Houston (Houston, Tex.), 1954.

1691. FEINBERG, LEONARD D., AND GURVITZ, MILTON S. "The Normal Adult Rorschach." Abstract. *Am Psychol* 9:363 Ag '54. *

1692. FELDMAN, MARVIN J., AND GRALEY, JAMES. "The Effects of an Experimental Set to Simulate Abnormality on Group Rorschach Performance." *J Proj Tech* 18:326–34 S '54. * (*PA* 29:4052)

1693. FELDMAN, MARVIN J.; GURSSLIN, CAROLYN; KAPLAN, MARVIN L.; AND SHARLOCK, NIDIA. "A Preliminary Study to Develop a More Discriminating F+ Ratio." *J Clin Psychol* 10:47–51 Ja '54. * (*PA* 28:7518)

1694. FELZER, STANTON B. *A Statistical Study of Sex Differences on the Rorschach.* Doctor's thesis, Temple University (Philadelphia, Pa.), 1954. (Abstracts: *DA* 16:569, *Am Psychol* 9:364, *J Proj Tech* 18:398)

1695. FISHER, JEROME, AND GONDA, THOMAS A. "Critique of a Criterion: The Diagnostic Sensitivity of Neurologic Techniques vs. Rorschach Findings in Brain Pathology." Abstract. *Am Psychol* 9:368 Ag '54. *

1696. FLYNN, JAMES J. *Rorschach and Wechsler-Bellevue Changes Following Electric Shock Therapy in the Aged.* Doctor's thesis, Loyola University (Chicago, Ill.), 1954.

1697. FORTIER, ROBERT H. "An Appraisal of Keehn's Critique of 'The Response to Color and Ego Functions.'" *Psychol B* 51:67–9 Ja '54. * (*PA* 28:7521)

1698. GALLAGHER, JAMES J. "Test Indicators for Therapy Prognosis." *J Consult Psychol* 18:409–13 D '54. * (*PA* 29:7356)

1699. GELFAND, LEONARD; QUARRINGTON, BRUCE; WIDEMAN, HARLEY; AND BROWN, JEAN. "Inter-Judge Agreement on Traits Rated From the Rorschach." Abstract. *J Consult Psychol* 18:471 D '54. *

1700. GIBBY, ROBERT G., AND STOTSKY, BERNARD A. "Determinant Shift of Psychoneurotic and Psychotic Patients." *J Consult Psychol* 18:267–70 Ag '54. * (*PA* 29:4055)

1701. GIBBY, ROBERT G.; STOTSKY, BERNARD A.; AND HARRINGTON, ROBERT W. "A Comparison of Normals, Psychoneurotics, and Psychotics or Rorschach Determinant Shift." Abstract. *Proc Ind Acad Sci* 64:239–40 '54. *

1702. GIBBY, ROBERT G.; STOTSKY, BERNARD A.; AND MILLER,

DANIEL R. "Influence of the Preceding Test on the Rorschach Protocol." *J Consult Psychol* 18:463–4 D '54. * (*PA* 29:7278)

1703. GIBBY, ROBERT G.; STOTSKY, BERNARD A.; HILER, E. WESLEY; AND MILLER, DANIEL R. "Validation of Rorschach Criteria for Predicting Duration of Therapy." *J Consult Psychol* 18:185–91 Je '54. * (*PA* 29:2517)

1704. GOLDFARB, ALLAN. *An Experimental Study of Performance Under Stress in Relation to Intellectual Control and Expressed Self-Acceptance.* Doctor's thesis, University of Pittsburgh (Pittsburgh, Pa.), 1954. (*DA* 14:1457)

1705. GOODSTEIN, LEONARD D. "Interrelationships Among Several Measures of Anxiety and Hostility." *J Consult Psychol* 18:35–9 F '54. * (*PA* 28:8722)

1706. GRAHAM, STANLEY ROY. *Histamine Tolerance and Perceived Movement: A Study of Visually Perceived Movement as Related to Performance in the Autokinetic Effect and Rorschach Movement Responses Measured Against Histamine Tolerance.* Doctor's thesis, New York University (New York, N.Y.), 1954. (*DA* 15:1202)

1707. GRAUER, DAVID. "Homosexuality in Paranoid Schizophrenia as Revealed by the Rorschach Test." *J Consult Psychol* 18:459–62 D '54. * (*PA* 29:7645)

1708. GURVITZ, MILTON S., AND FEINBERG, LEONARD D. "Age and Intellectual Dimensions of the Normal Rorschach." Abstract. *Am Psychol* 9:387 Ag '54. * (*J Proj Tech* 18:399 S '54. *)

1709. HAMLIN, ROY M. "The Clinician as Judge: Implications of a Series of Studies." *J Consult Psychol* 18:233–8 Ag '54. * (*PA* 29:4057)

1710. HARRINGTON, ROBERT W. "Maladaptive Responses to Frustration Predicted From Rorschach Color Responses." *J Consult Psychol* 18:455–8 D '54. * (*PA* 29:7532)

1711. HAUCK, PAUL A. *Rorschach Performances of the Ute Indians.* Doctor's thesis, University of Utah (Salt Lake City, Utah), 1954.

1712. HERTZ, MARGUERITE R., AND LOEHRKE, LEAH M. "The Application of the Piotrowski and the Hughes Signs of Organic Defect to a Group of Patients Suffering From Post-Traumatic Encephalopathy." *J Proj Tech* 18:183–96 Je '54. * (*PA* 29:4553)

1713. HERTZMAN, M. Chap. 11, "The Rorschach Test," pp. 205–34, passim. In *Personality Through Perception: An Experimental and Clinical Study.* By H. A. Witkin and others. New York: Harper & Bros., 1954. Pp. xxvii, 571. * (*PA* 28:8566)

1714. HOLSOPPLE, JAMES QUINTER, AND PHELAN, JOSEPH G. "The Skills of Clinicians in Analysis of Projective Tests." *J Clin Psychol* 10:307–20 O '54. * (*PA* 29:4061)

1715. HOLTZMAN, WAYNE H.; ISCOE, IRA; AND CALVIN, A. D. "Rorschach Color Responses and Manifest Anxiety in College Women." *J Consult Psychol* 18:317–24 O '54. * (*PA* 29:5931)

1716. HURWITZ, IRVING. *A Developmental Study of the Relationships Between Motor Activity and Perceptual Processes as Measured by the Rorschach Test.* Doctor's thesis, Clark University (Worcester, Mass.), 1954. (*DA* 14:1805)

1717. INGRAM, WINIFRED. "Prediction of Aggression From the Rorschach." *J Consult Psychol* 18:23–8 F '54. * (*PA* 28:8723)

1718. ISRAËL, MARYSE. "Rorschach Responses of a Group of Adult Asthmatics." *J Mental Sci* 100:753–7 Jl '54. * (*PA* 29:4511)

1719. JAQUES, HOWARD W. *Rorschach's Erlebnistypus and Certain Manifest Behaviors in Children.* Doctor's thesis, University of Tennessee (Knoxville, Tenn.), 1954.

1720. JOHNSON, WARREN R.; HUTTON, DANIEL C.; AND JOHNSON, GRANVILLE B., JR. "Personality Traits of Some Champion Athletes as Measured by Two Projective Tests: Rorschach and H-T-P." *Res Q* 25:484–5 D '54. *

1721. JOURARD, SIDNEY M. "Ego Strength and the Recall of Tasks." *J Abn & Social Psychol* 49:51–8 Ja '54. * (*PA* 28:7222)

1722. KANTER, V. B. "A Validatory Study of a Blind Analysis and an Attempt to Integrate Rorschach Findings With Other Test Material." Abstract. *B Brit Psychol Soc* (22):22 Ja '54. *

1723. KAPLAN, BERT. *A Study of Rorschach Responses in Four Cultures.* Reports of the Ramah Project No. 6. Harvard University, Papers of the Peabody Museum of American Archaeology and Ethnology, Vol. 42, No. 2. Cambridge, Mass.: Peabody Museum, 1954. Pp. ix, 44. *

1724. KEEHN, J. D. "A Re-Interpretation of the Role Played by Colour in the Rorschach Test." *Brit J Med Psychol* 27:89–93 pts 1–2 '54. * (*PA* 28:8726)

1725. KEEHN, J. D. "'The Response to Color and Ego Functions': A Critique in the Light of Recent Experimental Evidence." *Psychol B* 51:65–7 Ja '54. * (*PA* 28:7532)

1726. KENDIG, ISABELLE V. "The Basic Rorschach Triad: A Graphic Schema of Presentation." *J Proj Tech* 18:448–52 D '54. * (*PA* 29:7288)

1727. KENNA, J. C. "The Effects of Lysergic Acid on the Rorschach." Abstract. *Brit Rorsch Forum* (5):7–8 Mr '54. *

1728. KEYES, EDWARD J. "An Experimental Investigation of Some Sources of Variance in the Whole Response to the Rorschach Ink Blots." *J Clin Psychol* 10:155–60 Ap '54. * (*PA* 29:930)

1729. KING, GERALD FRANKLIN. *A Theoretical and Experimental Consideration of the Rorschach Movement Response: Its*

Relation to the Neuropsychiatric Patient's Orientation to His Problem. Doctor's thesis, Michigan State College (East Lansing, Mich.), 1954. *(DA* 14:2127)

1730. KLOPFER, BRUNO; AINSWORTH, MARY D.; KLOPFER, WALTER G.; AND HOLT, ROBERT R. *Developments in the Rorschach Technique: Vol. I, Technique and Theory.* Yonkers, N.Y.: World Book Co., 1954. Pp. x, 726. * *(PA* 28:7533)

1731. KNOPF, IRWIN J. "The Effects of Recent Perceptual Training and Experience on Rorschach Performance." *J Clin Psychol* 10:52–6 Ja '54. * *(PA* 28:7534)

1732. KNOPF, IRWIN J., AND SPANGLER, DONALD. "Experimental Evaluation of the Rorschach as a Psychodiagnostic Instrument: I, The Use of Summary Scores." Abstract. *Am Psychol* 9:406–7 Ag '54. *

1733. KORNETSKY, CONAN. "Relationship Between Rorschach Determinants and Psychosis in Barbiturate Withdrawal Syndrome." *A.M.A. Arch Neurol & Psychiatry* 72:452–4 O '54. * *(PA* 29:5937)

1734. KORNETSKY, CONAN, AND GERARD, DONALD L. "Effect of Increasing the Number of Rorschach Responses on *Sum C* and *M:* A Note on Fiske and Baughman's Study." *J Abn & Social Psychol* 49:592–3 O '54. * *(PA* 29:5711)

1735. KOSTLAN, ALBERT. "A Method for the Empirical Study of Psychodiagnosis." *J Consult Psychol* 18:83–8 Ap '54. * *(PA* 29:2415)

1736. KRASNER, LEONARD, AND KORNREICH, MELVIN. "Psychosomatic Illness and Projective Tests: The Rorschach Test." *J Proj Tech* 18:355–67 S '54. * *(PA* 29:4515)

1737. KRUGER, ALICE KASTENBAUM. *Direct and Substitutive Modes of Tension-Reduction in Terms of Developmental Level: An Experimental Analysis by Means of the Rorschach Test.* Doctor's thesis, Clark University (Worcester, Mass.), 1954. *(DA* 14:1806)

1738. KURTZ, JOSEPHINE C., AND RIGGS, MARGARET M. "An Attempt to Influence the Rorschach Test by Means of a Peripheral Set." *J Consult Psychol* 18:465–70 D '54. * *(PA* 29:7291)

1739. KUTASH, SAMUEL B. "Personality Patterns of Old Age and the Rorschach Test." *Geriatrics* 9:367–70 Ag '54. * *(PA* 29:7055)

1740. LA FON, FRED E. *The Relationship Between Behavior on the Rorschach Test and a Measure of Self-Acceptance.* Doctor's thesis, University of Rochester (Rochester, N.Y.), 1954.

1741. LEVENTHAL, HOWARD. *The Influence of Previous Perceptual Experience on the Variance of the Rorschach W and Z Scores.* Master's thesis, University of North Carolina (Chapel Hill, N.C.), 1954.

1742. LEVINE, PHYLLIS R. "Projective Tests in a Vocational Guidance Setting." *J Counsel Psychol* 1:209–14 w '54. * *(PA* 29:7429)

1743. LIBRACH, STEPHANIE J. *Investigation of Differences Between Functioning and Non-Functioning Male Paranoid Schizophrenics by Means of the Rorschach Test.* Doctor's thesis, New School for Social Research (New York, N.Y.), 1954.

1744. LINTON, HARRIET B. "Rorschach Correlates of Response to Suggestion." *J Abn & Social Psychol* 49:75–83 Ja '54. * *(PA* 28:7536)

1745. LORD, EDITH. "Group Rorschach Responses of Thirty-Five Leprosarium Patients." *J Proj Tech* 18:202–7 Je '54. * *(PA* 29:4519)

1746. LORD, EDITH, AND HSU, FRANCIS. "Cultural Variations in Reactions to Color on the Rorschach." Abstract. *Am Psychol* 9:420 Ag '54. *

1747. LOTSOF, ERWIN J., AND CHANCE, JUNE. "Effects of Cortisone on Rorschach Performance." *J Proj Tech* 18:470–4 D '54. * *(PA* 29:7297)

1748. McARTHUR, CHARLES C., AND KING, STANLEY. "Rorschach Configurations Associated With College Achievement." *J Ed Psychol* 45:492–8 D '54. * *(PA* 29:7867)

1749. McFARLAND, ROBERT L. "Perceptual Consistency in Rorschach-Like Projective Tests." *J Proj Tech* 18:368–78 S '54. * *(PA* 29:4071)

1750. McREYNOLDS, PAUL. "The Rorschach Concept Evaluation Technique." *J Proj Tech* 18:60–74 Mr '54. * *(PA* 29:934)

1751. MANDEVILLE, PAUL FREDERICK. *A Study of the Relationship Between Responsiveness to Color on the Rorschach Examination and Impulsive Behavior.* Doctor's thesis, University of Nebraska (Lincoln, Neb.), 1954. *(DA* 14:1251)

1752. MENDOLA, VINCENT S. "The Validity of Indices of Dependency in Clinical Tests." Abstract. *Am Psychol* 9:430 Ag '54. *

1753. MENSH, IVAN N., AND MATARAZZO, JOSEPH D. "Rorschach Card Rejection in Psychodiagnosis." *J Consult Psychol* 18:271–5 Ag '54. * *(PA* 29:4073)

1754. MISCH, ROBERT C. *The Relationship of Motoric Inhibition to Developmental Level and Ideational Functioning: An Analysis by Means of the Rorschach Test.* Doctor's thesis, Clark University (Worcester, Mass.), 1954. *(DA* 14:1810)

1755. MONS, W. E. R. "Normative Study of Children's Rorschachs." Abstract. *Brit Rorsch Forum* (5):5–7 O '54. *

1756. MURRAY, DAVID COWAN. *An Investigation of the Rorschach White Space Response in an Extratensive Experience Balance as a Measure of Outwardly Directed Opposition.* Doctor's thesis, Northwestern University (Evanston, Ill.), 1954. *(DA* 14:1811)

1757. NEFF, WALTER S. "The Use of the Rorschach Test in Differentiating Between Vocationally Rehabilitable and Non-rehabilitable Groups." Abstract. *Am Psychol* 9:438–9 Ag '54. *

1758. NEFF, WALTER S., AND GLASER, NATHAN M. "Norma-

tive Data on the Rorschach." *J Psychol* 37:95–104 Ja '54. * *(PA* 28:7540)

1759. NELSON, WILLIAM DONALD. *An Evaluation of the White Space Response on the Rorschach as Figure-Ground Reversal and Intellectual Opposition.* Doctor's thesis, Michigan State College (East Lansing, Mich.), 1954. *(DA* 15:459)

1760. NEWTON, RICHARD L. "The Clinician as Judge: Total Rorschachs and Clinical Case Material." *J Consult Psychol* 18:248–50 Ag '54. * *(PA* 29:4077)

1761. PALM, ROSE, AND ABRAHAMSEN, DAVID. "A Rorschach Study of the Wives of Sex Offenders." *J Nerv & Mental Dis* 119:167–72 F '54. * *(PA* 29:2702)

1762. PATTIE, FRANK A. "The Effect of Hypnotically Induced Hostility on Rorschach Responses." *J Clin Psychol* 10:161–4 Ap '54. * *(PA* 29:940)

1763. PAULSEN, ALMA A. "Personality Development in the Middle Years of Childhood: A Ten-Year Longitudinal Study of Thirty Public School Children by Means of Rorschach Tests and Social Histories." Discussion by Judith I. Krugman. *Am J Orthopsychiatry* 24:336–50 Ap '54. * *(PA* 29:2280)

1764. PETERSON, ARNOLD O. D. "A Comparative Study of Rorschach Scoring Methods in Evaluating Personality Changes Resulting From Psychotherapy." *J Clin Psychol* 10:190–2 Ap '54. * *(PA* 29:1008)

1765. PUGH, DEREK S. "A Note on the Vorhaus Configurations of 'Reading Disability.'" *J Proj Tech* 18:478–80 D '54. * *(PA* 29:7877)

1766. RABIN, ALBERT, AND KEPECS, JOSEPH. "Personality Structure in Atopic Dermatitis: A Rorschach Study." *J General Psychol* 50:171–80 Ap '54. * *(PA* 29:4523)

1767. RABIN, ALBERT; NELSON, WILLIAM; AND CLARK, MARGARET. "Rorschach Content as a Function of Perceptual Experience and Sex of the Examiner." *J Clin Psychol* 10:188–90 Ap '54. * *(PA* 29:945)

1768. RABIN, ALBERT; PAPANIA, NED; AND McMICHAEL, ALLAN. "Some Effects of Alcohol on Rorschach Performance." *J Clin Psychol* 10:252–5 Jl '54. * *(PA* 29:2465)

1769. RABINOVITCH, M. SAM. "Physiologic Response, Perceptual Threshold, and Rorschach Test Anxiety Indices." *J Proj Tech* 18:379–86 S '54. * *(PA* 29:4083)

1770. RAPPAPORT, SIDNEY M. *An Experimental Investigation of the Effects and Persistence of Set Directed Towards Increasing Responses on the Color Variable in Rorschach.* Doctor's thesis, Temple University (Philadelphia, Pa.), 1954.

1771. REID, MELVIN P. *Emotional Stability in Stress and the Rorschach Personality Test of High School Football Players.* Doctor's thesis, Louisiana State University (Baton Rouge, La.), 1954.

1772. REITAN, RALPH M. "Intellectual and Affective Changes in Essential Hypertension." *Am J Psychiatry* 110:817–24 My '54. * *(PA* 29:1352)

1773. REITAN, RALPH M. "The Performance of Aphasic, Non-Aphasic, and Control Subjects on the Rorschach Test." *J General Psychol* 51:199–212 O '54. * *(PA* 30:3141)

1774. RICKERS-OVSIANKINA, MARIA A. "Longitudinal Approach to Schizophrenia Through the Rorschach Method." *J Clin & Exp Psychopathol* 15:107–18 Je '54. * *(PA* 29:2827)

1775. ROBERTS, LYNN K. "The Failure of Some Rorschach Indices to Predict the Outcome of Psychotherapy." *J Consult Psychol* 18:96–8 Ap '54. * *(PA* 29:2468)

1776. ROCHWARG, HERMAN. *Changes in the Structural Aspects of Perception in the Aged: An Analysis by Means of the Rorschach Test.* Doctor's thesis, Michigan State University (East Lansing, Mich.), 1954. *(DA* 16:1175)

1777. ROCKBERGER, HARRY. *The Effectiveness of a Rorschach Prognostic Scale for Predicting Results in Psychotherapy.* Doctor's thesis, New York University (New York, N.Y.), 1954.

1778. RORSCHACH, HERMANN. "Three Rorschach Interpretations." Translated by Else Sloman and Hanna Liebes. *J Proj Tech* 18:482–95 D '54. * *(PA* 29:7313)

1779. ROSENBLATT, BERNARD, AND SOLOMON, PAUL. "Structural and Genetic Aspects of Rorschach Responses in Mental Deficiency." *J Proj Tech* 18:496–506 D '54. * *(PA* 29:7497)

1780. ROSENTHAL, MELVIN. *Some Behavioral Correlates of the Rorschach Experience-Balance.* Doctor's thesis, Boston University (Boston, Mass.), 1954.

1781. ROSS, HARVEY L. *The Sources and Reliabilities of Interpretations in Rorschach Test Analysis.* Doctor's thesis, University of California (Los Angeles, Calif.), 1954.

1782. ROSVOLD, H. ENGER; ROSS, W. DONALD; AND DÖRKEN, H., JR. "The Rorschach Method as an Experimental Instrument: Review." *J Proj Tech* 18:227–32 Je '54. * *(PA* 29:4084)

1783. RULE, EVELYN T. *The Effect of Experimentally-Produced Sleep Deprivation on Projective Test Data: I, The Rorschach.* Doctor's thesis, University of Tennessee (Knoxville, Tenn.), 1954.

1784. SACKMAN, HAROLD. "An Investigation of Certain Aspects of the Validity of the Formal Rorschach Scoring System in Relation to Age, Education, and Vocabulary Score." Abstract. *Am Psychol* 9:463 Ag '54. *

1785. SAKHEIM, GEORGE A. *Suicidal Responses on the Rorschach Test: A Validation Study. Protocols of Suicidal Mental Hospital Patients Compared With Those of Non-Suicidal Patients.* Doctor's thesis, Florida State University (Tallahassee, Fla.), 1954. *(DA* 14:1253)

1786. SARASON, SEYMOUR B. *The Clinical Interaction: With Special Reference to Rorschach.* New York: Harper & Brothers, 1954. Pp. xi, 425. * *(PA* 29:896)

1787. SCHAFER, ROY. *Psychoanalytic Interpretation in Rorschach Testing: Theory and Application.* Austen Riggs Foundation Monograph Series, No. 3. New York: Grune & Stratton, Inc., 1954. Pp. xiv, 446. * *(PA* 29:2472)

1788. SCHMIDT, HERMANN O., AND FONDA, CHARLES P. "Rorschach Scores in the Manic State." *J Psychol* 38:427–37 O '54. * *(PA* 29:6041)

1789. SCHNEIDER, STANLEY F. "The Prediction of Certain Aspects of the Psychotherapeutic Relationship From Rorschach's Test: An Empirical and Exploratory Study." Abstract. *Am Psychol* 9:466 Ag '54. *

1790. SCHREIBER, HANNA, AND WHITE, MARY ALICE. "Diagnosing Organicity on the Rorschach." *Psychiatric Q Sup* 28:255–77 pt 2 '54. * *(PA* 29:7316)

1791. SHEEHAN, JOSEPH G. "Rorschach Prognosis in Psychotherapy and Speech Therapy." *J Speech & Hearing Dis* 19:217–9 Je '54. * *(PA* 29:4345)

1792. SHEEHAN, JOSEPH G.; FREDERICK, CALVIN J.; ROSEVEAR, WILLIAM H.; AND SPIEGELMAN, MARVIN. "A Validity Study of the Rorschach Prognostic Rating Scale." *J Proj Tech* 18:233–9 Je '54. * *(PA* 29:4088)

1793. SHIPMAN, WILLIAM GIBSON. *The Validity of the Interpretation of Scope and Differentiation Response to the Rorschach.* Doctor's thesis, Pennsylvania State University (University Park, Pa.), 1954.

1794. SIMS, NEIL B. *A Study of Perceptual Defense and Defensiveness on the Rorschach as Manifested by Schizophrenic Subjects.* Doctor's thesis, Purdue University (Lafayette, Ind.), 1954.

1795. SINGER, JEROME L., AND HERMAN, JACK. "Motor and Fantasy Correlates of Rorschach Human Movement Responses." *J Consult Psychol* 18:325–31 O '54. * *(PA* 29:5798)

1796. SINGER, JEROME L., AND SPOHN, HERBERT E. "Some Behavioral Correlates of Rorschach's Experience-Type." *J Consult Psychol* 18:1–9 F '54. * *(PA* 28:8898)

1797. SMITH, SYDNEY, AND GEORGE, C. E. "The Harrower Multiple Choice Rorschach: A Critique." *J Proj Tech* 18:507–9 D '54. * *(PA* 29:7320)

1798. SOLOMON, PAUL, AND ROSENBLATT, BERNARD. "A Developmental Rorschach Study of 80 Adult Mental Defectives." Abstract. *Am Psychol* 9:475 Ag '54. *

1799. SOSKIN, WILLIAM F. "Bias in Postdiction From Projective Tests." *J Abn & Social Psychol* 49:69–74 Ja '54. * *(PA* 28:7551)

1800. STEPHENSON, WILLIAM. Chap. 8, "Q-Technique and the Rorschach Test," pp. 147–56. In *The Six Schizophrenias: Reaction Patterns in Children and Adults.* By Samuel J. Beck. American Orthopsychiatric Association, Research Monographs No. 6. New York: the Association, Inc., 1954. Pp. xi, 238. * *(PA* 29:2760)

1801. STEVENS, PHYLLIS WOLFE. *The Rorschach Experience Balance as an Index of Emotional Responsiveness.* Doctor's thesis, University of North Carolina (Chapel Hill, N.C.), 1954.

1802. STEWART, G. KINSEY. *Children's Rorschachs: A Validation Study.* Master's thesis, Tulane University (New Orleans, La.), 1954.

1803. STOPOL, MURRAY S. "Rorschach Performance in Relation to Two Types of Stress." *J Consult Psychol* 18:11–5 F '54. * *(PA* 28:8734)

1804. TAULBEE, EARL S. "The Use of the Rorschach Test for Evaluating the Intellectual Levels of Functioning in Schizophrenics." Abstract. *Am Psychol* 9:481 Ag '54. *

1805. TAULBEE, EARL S., AND SISSON, BOYD D. "Rorschach Pattern Analysis in Schizophrenia: A Cross-Validation Study." *J Clin Psychol* 10:80–2 Ja '54. * *(PA* 28:7556)

1806. THOMAS, ROSS REGINALD. *Instructional Effects on Rorschach Variables in Relation to Subject Characteristics.* Doctor's thesis, Northwestern University (Evanston, Ill.), 1954. *(DA* 14:1816)

1807. VANEK, ZDENEK. *The Role of Color in Learning: An Investigation of the Role of Color in Learning and Its Relationship to the Color Rationale of the Rorschach Psychodiagnostic Test.* Doctor's thesis, New York University (New York, N.Y.), 1954. *(DA* 14:2299)

1808. VAN METRE, DOROTHY ACKERMAN. *An Investigation of the Relationship Between Inkblot Color and Certain Personality Traits.* Doctor's thesis, State University of Iowa (Iowa City, Iowa), 1954. *(DA* 14:2406)

1809. VERNON, P. E. "Problems Relating to the Validation of Rorschach and an Evaluation of Some Methods of Approach." Abstract. *Brit Rorsch Forum* (5):8–9 O '54. *

1810. VORHAUS, PAULINE G. "A Reply to Pugh's 'Note on the Vorhaus Configurations of Reading Disability.'" *J Proj Tech* 18:480–1 D '54. * *(PA* 29:7897)

1811. WALLEN, RICHARD W. "Emotional Labels and Projective Test Theory." *J Proj Tech* 18:240–7 Je '54. * *(PA* 29:4327)

1812. WARSHAW, LEON; LEISER, RUDOLF; IZNER, SANFORD M.; AND STERNE, SPENCER B. "The Clinical Significance and Theory of Sodium Amytal Rorschach Testing." *J Proj Tech* 18:248–51 Je '54. * *(PA* 29:4093)

1813. WEDEMEYER, BARBARA. "Rorschach Statistics on a Group of 136 Normal Men." *J Psychol* 37:51–8 Ja '54. * *(PA* 28:7562)

1814. WELLISCH, E. "The Rorschach Personality Index Study in Measuring Personality." Abstract. *B Brit Psychol Soc* (22):21 Ja '54. *

1815. WERTHEIMER, RITA R. "Rorschach Signs of Adjust-

ment and Their Relationship to Adolescent Sociometric Status, Socioeconomic Level, and Sex." Abstract. *Am Psychol* 9:492 Ag '54. *

1816. WHEELER, W. M. "The Psychoanalytic Theory of Object Relations and the Rorschach Technique." Abstract. *Brit Rorsch Forum* (5):4–5 O '54. *

1817. WHITMAN, ROY M. "The Use of the Rorschach Test in Schizophrenia." *Psychiatric Q Sup* 28:26–37 pt 1 '54. * *(PA* 29:2846)

1818. WILKINSON, MARGARET A., AND JACOBS, ROBERT. "A Brief Study of the Relationships Between Personality Adjustment and Vocational Interests as Measured by the Multiple-Choice Rorschach and the Strong Vocational Interest Blank." *J Ed Res* 48:269–78 D '54. * *(PA* 29:7335)

1819. WILLIAMS, HAROLD L., AND LAWRENCE, JAMES F. "Comparison of the Rorschach and MMPI by Means of Factor Analysis." *J Consult Psychol* 18:193–7 Je '54. * *(PA* 29:2484)

1820. WILLIAMS, MILTON HUGH, JR. *The Influence of Variations in Instructions on Rorschach Reaction Time.* Doctor's thesis, University of Nebraska (Lincoln, Neb.), 1954. *(DA* 14:2131)

1821. WILSON, MARY TEWKSBURY. *Regression in Perceptual Organization: A Study of Adolescent Performance on the Rorschach Test.* Doctor's thesis, Clark University (Worcester, Mass.), 1954. *(DA* 14:1819)

1822. WITKIN, H. A.; LEWIS, H. B.; HERTZMAN, M.; MACHOVER, K.; MEISSNER, P. BRETNALL; AND WAPNER, S. *Personality Through Perception: An Experimental and Clinical Study.* New York: Harper & Brothers, 1954. Pp. xxvi, 571. * *(PA* 28:8566)

1823. WRIGHT, STUART. "Some Personality Characteristics of Academic Underachievers." Abstract. *Am Psychol* 9:496 Ag '54. *

1824. WYSOCKI, B. A. *Analysis of Rorschach Responses by Objective Methods.* Doctor's thesis, University of London (London, England), 1954.

1825. ZELEN, SEYMOUR L. "Behavioral Criteria and Rorschach Measures of Level of Aspiration and Rigidity." *J Personality* 23:207–14 D '54. * *(PA* 29:5333)

1826. ZUBIN, JOSEPH. "Failures of the Rorschach Technique." *J Proj Tech* 18:303–15 S '54. * *(PA* 29:4096)

1827. ZUBIN, JOSEPH. "The Measurement of Personality." Comment by E. Lowell Kelly. *J Counsel Psychol* 1:159–64, 172–3 S '54. *

1828. *Dr. Hermann Rorschach Psychodiagnostics Bibliography: The Most Important Publications About the Rorschach Test (Until 1954).* New York: Grune & Stratton, Inc., 1955. Pp. 64. *

1829. ABRAMS, ELIAS N. "Prediction of Intelligence From Certain Rorschach Factors." *J Clin Psychol* 11:81–3 Ja '55. * *(PA* 29:7251)

1830. ABRAMS, JULES C. *A Study of Certain Personality Characteristics of Non-Readers and Achieving Readers.* Doctor's thesis, Temple University (Philadelphia, Pa.), 1955. *(DA* 16:377)

1831. ALCOCK, A. THEODORA. "The Rationale and Scoring of Movement Responses." Abstract. *Brit Rorsch Forum* (6):4–9 Ap '55. *

1832. ALCOCK, THEODORA. "The Use of the Rorschach Technique in Clinical Practice and Research—Data: Valid and Non-Valid." Abstract. *B Brit Psychol Soc* (26):13 inset My '55. *

1833. ALLEN, ROBERT M. "An Analysis of Twelve Longitudinal Rorschach Records of One Child." *J Proj Tech* 19:111–6 Je '55. * *(PA* 30:2513)

1834. ALLEN, ROBERT M. "Nine Quarterly Rorschach Records of a Young Girl." *Child Develop* 26:63–9 Mr '55. * *(PA* 30:2514)

1835. ARMITAGE, STEWART G.; GREENBERG, PAUL D.; PEARL, DAVID; BERGER, DAVID G.; AND DASTON, PAUL G. "Predicting Intelligence From the Rorschach." *J Consult Psychol* 19:321–9 O '55. * *(PA* 30:5971)

1836. ARSUAGA, ROSA AURORA. *A Comparison of Religious Attitudes of American and Latin American Catholic College Students.* Master's thesis, Fordham University (New York, N.Y.), 1955.

1837. BARD, MORTON. "The Use of Dependence for Predicting Psychogenic Invalidism Following Radical Mastectomy." *J Nerv & Mental Dis* 122:152–160 Ag '55. * *(PA* 31:1583)

1838. BARKER, G. B. "John, a Rorschach Study of a Schizophrenic at Four Stages of His Illness." *J Proj Tech* 19:271–91 S '55. * *(PA* 30:4938)

1839. BARKER, G. B. "A Study of a Child Showing Manic Depressive Mood Swings, Using Rorschach and Paintings." Abstract. *Brit Rorsch Forum* (7):14–23 N '55. *

1840. BARKER, G. B. "The Usefulness of the Rorschach Technique in Clinical Practice." Abstract. *B Brit Psychol Soc* (26):12–3 inset My '55. *

1841. BARRON, FRANK. "Threshold for the Perception of Human Movement in Inkblots." *J Consult Psychol* 19:33–8 F '55. * *(PA* 29:8629)

1842. BASH, K. W. "Einstellungstypus and Erlebnistypus: C. G. Jung and Hermann Rorschach." *J Proj Tech* 19:236–42 S '55. * *(PA* 30:4175)

1843. BAUGHMAN, E. EARL. "A Reply to Stein's 'Note on a Comparative Analysis of Rorschach Forms With Altered Stimulus Characteristics.'" *J Proj Tech* 19:466–7 D '55. * *(PA* 30:7185)

1844. BECK, S. J. "Personality Research and Theories of Per-

sonality Structure: Some Convergences." *J Proj Tech* 19:361–71 D '55. * (*PA* 30:6910)

1845. BEHN-ESCHENBURG, GERTRUD. "Working With Dr. Hermann Rorschach." *J Proj Tech* 19:3–5 Mr '55. * (*PA* 30: 1010)

1846. BENDIG, A. W., AND HAMLIN, ROY M. "The Psychiatric Validity of an Inverted Factor Analysis of Rorschach Scoring Categories." *J Consult Psychol* 19:183–8 Je '55. * (*PA* 30:2857)

1847. BENNETT, CLAYTON L. "An Experimental Study of Relationships Between Human Electroencephalograms and Certain Rorschach Scoring Categories." Abstract. *Am Psychol* 10:391–2 Ag '55. *

1848. BENT, RUSSELL J. *The Relationship of the Movement Determinant of the Rorschach Test to Autokinetic Movement.* Master's thesis, Fordham University (New York, N.Y.), 1955.

1849. BILMES, MURRAY. *Resistance to Group Influence of Various Personality Factors—as Measured by the Modification of Individual Rorschach Responses Resulting From an Intervening Group Rorschach Experience.* Doctor's thesis, New York University (New York, N.Y.), 1955. (*DA* 15:2572)

1850. BLECHNER, JANET E. "Further Explorations Into the Relationship of Rorschach to College Achievement." Abstract. *Calif J Ed Res* 6:135 My '55. *

1851. BLOOM, BERNARD L. "Prognostic Significance of the Underproductive Rorschach." Abstract. *Am Psychol* 10:325 Ag '55. *

1852. BORGATTA, EDGAR F., AND ESCHENBACH, ARTHUR E. "Factor Analysis of Rorschach Variables and Behavioral Observation." *Psychol Rep* 1:129–36 S '55. * (*PA* 30:5976)

1853. BOURGUIGNON, ERIKA E., AND NETT, EMILY WESTERKAMM. "Rorschach Populars in a Sample of Haitian Protocols." *J Proj Tech* 19:117–24 Je '55. * (*PA* 30:2706)

1854. BRECHER, SYLVIA. *The Mother-Son Relationship and Schizophrenic Reactions: An Evaluation of the Rorschach Reaction Patterns of Overprotected and Rejected Schizophrenic Patients.* Doctor's thesis, New York University (New York, N.Y.), 1955. (*DA* 15:1895)

1855. BRODY, CLAIRE M. H. *A Study of the Personality of Normal and Schizophrenic Adolescents Using Two Projective Tests: A Differentiation on the Basis of Structural and Behavioral Rigidity Using the Lowenfeld Mosaic and Rorschach Tests.* Doctor's thesis, New York University (New York, N.Y.), 1955. (*DA* 16:381)

1856. CLARKE, JOSEPH I. C., AND LODGE, GEORGE T. "Coaction Compass Positions of Normal, Neurotic, and Psychotic Individuals as Defined by Rorschach Determinant Scores: A Cross-Validation." Abstract. *Am Psychol* 10:325–6 Ag '55. *

1857. COOPER, JAMES G. "The Inspection Rorschach in the Prediction of College Success." *J Ed Res* 49:275–82 D '55. * (*PA* 30:7508)

1858. CORSINI, RAYMOND J.; SEVERSON, WINFIELD E.; TUNNEY, THOMAS E.; AND UEHLING, HAROLD F. "The Separation Capacity of the Rorschach." *J Consult Psychol* 19:194–6 Je '55. * (*PA* 30:2863)

1859. CORTNER, ROBERT H. *The Relationship of Diagnostic Criteria of the Rorschach and Szondi Tests and Psychiatric Diagnosis in a Military Population.* Master's thesis, St. Louis University (St. Louis, Mo.), 1955.

1860. CRUMPTON, EVELYN. *The Influence of Color on the Rorschach Test.* Doctor's thesis, University of California (Los Angeles, Calif.), 1955. (Abstract: *Am Psychol* 10:324)

1861. DANA, RICHARD H. "Rorschach Scorer Reliability." *J Clin Psychol* 11:401–3 O '55. * (*PA* 30:5981)

1862. DATEL, WILLIAM E. *Reliability of Interpretations and Consistency of Determinant Scoring in the Rorschach.* Doctor's thesis, University of California (Los Angeles, Calif.), 1955.

1863. DATEL, WILLIAM E., AND GENGERELLI, J. A. "Reliability of Rorschach Interpretations." *J Proj Tech* 19:372–81 D '55. * (*PA* 30:7190)

1864. DAVIDSON, HELEN H., AND GOTTLIEB, LUCILLE S. "The Emotional Maturity of Pre- and Post-Menarcheal Girls." *J Genetic Psychol* 86:261–6 Je '55. * (*PA* 30:6951)

1865. DEVOS, GEORGE. "A Quantitative Rorschach Assessment of Maladjustment and Rigidity in Acculturating Japanese Americans." *Genetic Psychol Monogr* 52:51–87 Ag '55. * (*PA* 30:7192)

1866. DUNCAN, BERTHA K. "The Ego Functions and Response to Color on the Rorschach: (1) Disturbed Children and (2) Institutionalized Children." *Trans Kans Acad Sci* 58:252–8 '55. *

1867. ECKHARDT, WILLIAM. "An Experimental and Theoretical Analysis of Movement and Vista Responses." *J Proj Tech* 19:301–5 S '55. * (*PA* 30:4565)

1868. ESCHENBACH, ARTHUR E. *The Relationship of Basic Rorschach Scoring Categories to Observed Three-Man-Group Interaction Behavior.* Doctor's thesis, University of Florida (Gainesville, Fla.), 1955. (*DA* 15:1651)

1869. ESCHENBACH, ARTHUR E., AND BORGATTA, EDGAR F. "Testing Behavior Hypotheses With the Rorschach: An Exploration in Validation." *J Consult Psychol* 19:267–73 Ag '55. * (*PA* 30:4567)

1870. FABRIKANT, BENJAMIN. "Suggestibility and the Rorschach." *J Clin Psychol* 11:309–10 Jl '55. * (*PA* 30:2873)

1871. FELZER, STANTON B. "A Statistical Study of Sex Differences on the Rorschach." *J Proj Tech* 19:382–6 D '55. * (*PA* 30:7194)

1872. FILMER-BENNETT, GORDON. "The Rorschach as a Means of Predicting Treatment Outcome." *J Consult Psychol* 19:331–4 O '55. * (*PA* 30:6024)

1873. FINNEY, BEN C. "The Diagnostic Discrimination of the 'Basic Rorschach Score.' " Abstract. *J Consult Psychol* 19:96 Ap '55. *

1874. FINNEY, BEN C. "Rorschach Test Correlates of Assaultive Behavior." *J Proj Tech* 19:6–16 Mr '55. * (*PA* 30:1338)

1875. FISHER, JEROME, AND GONDA, THOMAS A. "Neurologic Techniques and Rorschach Test in Detecting Brain Pathology: A Study of Comparative Validities." *A.M.A. Arch Neurol & Psychiatry* 74:117–24 Ag '55. * (*PA* 30:5091)

1876. FISHER, JEROME; GONDA, THOMAS A.; AND LITTLE, KENNETH B. "The Rorschach and Central Nervous System Pathology: A Cross-Validation Study." *Am J Psychiatry* 111: 487–92 Ja '55. * (*PA* 30:5702)

1877. FISHER, SEYMOUR. "Some Observations Suggested by the Rorschach Concerning the 'Ambulatory Schizophrenic.' " *Psychiatric Q Sup* 29:81–9 pt 1 '55. * (*PA* 30:7514)

1878. GEORGE, C. E. "Stimulus Value of the Rorschach Cards: A Composite Study." *J Proj Tech* 19:17–20 Mr '55. * (*PA* 30:1024)

1879. GIBBY, ROBERT G.; STOTSKY, BERNARD A.; HARRINGTON, ROBERT L.; AND THOMAS, RICHARD W. "Rorschach Determinant Shift Among Hallucinatory and Delusional Patients." *J Consult Psychol* 19:44–6 F '55. * (*PA* 29:8638)

1880. GLEASON, WALTER JAMES. "Direction of Perceived Movement in Males and Females." Abstract. *J Consult Psychol* 19:8 F '55. *

1881. GLUCK, MARTIN R. "Rorschach Content and Hostile Behavior." *J Consult Psychol* 19:475–8 D '55. * (*PA* 30:7196)

1882. GOLDMAN, ROSALINE. *Changes in Rorschach Performance and Clinical Improvement in Schizophrenia.* Doctor's thesis, Boston University (Boston, Mass.), 1955.

1883. GOODSTEIN, LEONARD D., AND GOLDBERGER, LEO. "Manifest Anxiety and Rorschach Performance in a Chronic Patient Population." *J Consult Psychol* 19:339–44 O '55. * (*PA* 30:6065)

1884. GRAHAM, STANLEY R. "Relation Between Histamine Tolerance, Visual Autokinesis, Rorschach Human Movement, and Figure Drawing." *J Clin Psychol* 11:370–3 O '55. * (*PA* 30:6066)

1885. GRAINER, HANS MARTIN. *Situational Influences on Rorschach Anatomical Responses.* Master's thesis, University of North Carolina (Chapel Hill, N.C.), 1955.

1886. GREENBERG, PAUL D.; ARMITAGE, STEWART G.; AND PEARL, DAVID. "Predicting Intelligence From the Rorschach." Abstract. *Am Psychol* 10:321–2 Ag '55. *

1887. GUTTMAN, LOUIS. "Approximate Circumplex Structures of MMPI Scores." Abstract. *Am Psychol* 10:423 Ag '55. *

1888. HAFNER, ADOLF JACK. *An Investigation of the Relationship Between Specific Setting Factors and Behavior on the Rorschach.* Doctor's thesis, Indiana University (Bloomington, Ind.), 1955. (*DA* 15:2575)

1889. HAGLUND, CARL A. *An Attempt to Differentiate Between Certain Groups of Schizophrenic and Neurotic Patients by the Use of Rorschach Composite Scores.* Doctor's thesis, New York University (New York, N.Y.), 1955. (*DA* 15:1785)

1890. HAMLIN, ROY M.; STONE, JOHN T.; AND MOSKOWITZ, MERLE J. "Rorschach Color Theories as Reflected in Simple Card Sorting Tasks." *J Proj Tech* 19:410–5 D '55. * (*PA* 30:6820)

1891. HAMMER, EMANUEL F., AND JACKS, IRVING. "A Study of Rorschach Flexor and Extensor Human Movement Responses." *J Clin Psychol* 11:63–7 Ja '55. * (*PA* 29:7281)

1892. HAND, MARY E. *The Rorschach as a Measure of Behavioral Change in Children in a Residential School for Mentally Handicapped.* Doctor's thesis, Michigan State University (East Lansing, Mich.), 1955. (*DA* 17:1585)

1893. HAUCK, PAUL A. *Ute Rorschach Performances and Some Notes on Field Problems and Methods.* Utah University, Department of Anthropology, Anthropological Papers, No. 23. Salt Lake City, Utah: University of Utah Press, July 1955. Pp. ii, 18. *

1894. HAWARD, L. R. C. "Colour Associations as a Contributing Factor to Neurotic Colour Shock." *Brit J Med Psychol* 28:183–7 Je '55. * (*PA* 30:2883)

1895. HENRY, JULES; NADEL, S. F.; CAUDILL, WILLIAM; HONIGMANN, JOHN J.; SPIRO, MELFORD E.; FISKE, DONALD W.; SPINDLER, GEORGE; AND HALLOWELL, A. IRVING. "Symposium on Projective Testing in Ethnography." *Am Anthrop* 57:245–70 Ap '55. * (*PA* 30:4397)

1896. HERTZ, MARGUERITE R., AND LOEHRKE, LEAH M. "An Evaluation of the Rorschach Method for the Study of Brain Injury." *J Proj Tech* 19:416–30 D '55. * (*PA* 30:7606)

1897. HINSON, RICHARD G. *Failure and Subject-Examiner Interaction Effects Upon Organization of Rorschach Ink-Blots.* Doctor's thesis, University of Denver (Denver, Colo.), 1955.

1898. HIRSCHSTEIN, RALPH, AND RABIN, ALBERT I. "Reactions to Rorschach Cards IV and VII as a Function of Parental Availability in Childhood." *J Consult Psychol* 19:473–4 D '55. * (*PA* 30:7199)

1899. HOHNE, H. H. *Success and Failure in Scientific Faculties of the University of Melbourne.* Melbourne, Australia: Australian Council for Educational Research, 1955. Pp. vii, 129. * (*PA* 31:3787)

1900. HOLZBERG, JULES D., AND SCHLEIFER, MAXWELL J. "An Experimental Test of the Rorschach Assumption of the

Impact of Color on the Perceptual and Associative Processes." *J Proj Tech* 19:130–7 Je '55. * (*PA* 30:2886)

1901. JENKIN, NOEL. "Some Relationships Between Projective Test Behavior and Perception." *J Clin Psychol* 11:278–81 Jl '55. * (*PA* 30:2888)

1902. JOHANNSEN, DOROTHEA E., AND BENNETT, EDWARD M. "The Personality of Diabetic Children." *J Genetic Psychol* 87: 175–85 D '55. * (*PA* 31:1514)

1903. JOHNSON, GRANVILLE B., JR. "An Evaluation Instrument for the Analysis of Teacher Effectiveness." *J Exp Ed* 23:331–44 Je '55. * (*PA* 30:3484)

1904. JOHNSON, LAVERNE C., AND STERN, JOHN A. "Rigidity on the Rorschach and Response to Intermittent Photic Stimulation." *J Consult Psychol* 19:311–7 Ag '55. * (*PA* 30:3960)

1905. KAMMAN, GORDON R., AND KRAM, CHARLES. "Value of Psychometric Examinations in Medical Diagnosis and Treatment." *J Am Med Assn* 158:555–60 Je 18 '55. * (*PA* 31:1044)

1906. KANTER, V. B. "The Use of Projective Tests in an Investigation of Patients Suffering From Duodenal Ulcers." Abstract. *Brit Rorsch Forum* (7):5–9 N '55. *

1907. KAPLAN, BERT. "Reflections of the Acculturation Process in the Rorschach Test." *J Proj Tech* 19:30–5 Mr '55. * (*PA* 30:870)

1908. KAUFMAN, MELVIN. *The Formation of Learning Sets With Mentally Retarded Children.* Doctor's thesis, University of Pittsburgh (Pittsburgh, Pa.), 1955. (*DA* 16:156)

1909. KING, GERALD F. "Rorschach and Levy Movement Responses: A Research Note." *J Clin Psychol* 11:193–7 Ap '55. * (*PA* 30:1033)

1910. KLEIN, ABRAHAM. "A Preliminary Comparative Study of Some Szondi and Rorschach Test Variables." Abstract. *J Personality* 23:499 Je '55. *

1911. KOSTLAN, ALBERT. "A Reply to Patterson." *J Consult Psychol* 19:486 D '55. *

1912. KORKES, LENORE, AND LEWIS, NOLAN D. C. "An Analysis of the Relationship Between Psychological Patterns and Outcome in Pulmonary Tuberculosis." *J Nerv & Mental Dis* 122:524–63 D '55. *

1913. KORNER, IJA N., AND WESTWOOD, DALE. "Inter-Rater Agreement in Judging Student Adjustment From Projective Tests." *J Clin Psychol* 11:167–70 Ap '55. * (*PA* 30:986)

1914. KRAEMER, DORIS R. *Some Perceptual Aspects of the Movement Responses on the Rorschach in Children.* Doctor's thesis, Yeshiva University (New York, N.Y.), 1955.

1915. KRAMER, GEORGE HARVEY, JR. *The Influence of Training and Personality Characteristics of the Examiner on Rorschach Scores.* Doctor's thesis, University of Houston (Houston, Tex.), 1955. (*DA* 16:572)

1916. KROPP, RUSSELL P. "The Rorschach 'Z' Score." *J Proj Tech* 19:443–52 D '55. * (*PA* 30:7205)

1917. LAZARUS, RICHARD S., AND OLDFIELD, MARGARET. "Rorschach Responses and the Influence of Color." *J Personality* 23:356–72 Mr '55. * (*PA* 30:1036)

1918. LEVINE, A.; ABRAMSON, H. A.; KAUFMAN, M. R.; MARKHAM, S.; AND KORNETSKY, C. "Lysergic Acid Diethylamide (LSD-25): XIV, Effect on Personality as Observed in Psychological Tests." *J Psychol* 40:351–66 O '55. * (*PA* 30:7206)

1919. LEVY, LEON H. "Movement as a 'Rhetorical Embellishment' of Human Percepts." *J Consult Psychol* 19:469–71 D '55. *

1920. LINDZEY, GARDNER, AND HERMAN, PETER S. "Thematic Apperception Test: A Note on Reliability and Situational Validity." *J Proj Tech* 19:36–42 Mr '55. * (*PA* 30:1037)

1921. LITTLE, KENNETH B., AND SHNEIDMAN, EDWIN S. "A Comparison of the Reliability of Interpretations of Four Psychological Tests." Abstract. *Am Psychol* 10:322 Ag '55. *

1922. LOFCHIE, STANLEY H. "The Performance of Adults Under Distraction Stress: A Developmental Approach." *J Psychol* 39:109–16 Ja '55. * (*PA* 29:8334)

1923. LUCAS, WINAFRED B. *The Effect of Experimentally Induced Frustration on the Rorschach Responses of Nine-Year-Old Children: A Contribution to the Study of the Effect of Set on Rorschach Responses.* Doctor's thesis, University of California (Los Angeles, Calif.), 1955. (Abstract: *Am Psychol* 10:324)

1924. McCALL, RAYMOND J., AND DOLEYS, ERNEST J., JR. "Popular Responses on the Rorschach Test in Relation to the Number of Responses." *J. Clin Psychol* 11:300–2 Jl '55. * (*PA* 30:2898)

1925. McNEELY, HAROLD ELLIS. *The Influence of Varied Instructions on the Response Adequacy of Certain Rorschach Intelligence Indicators.* Doctor's thesis, University of Nebraska (Lincoln, Neb.), 1955. (*DA* 15:628)

1926. MANN, LESTER. "The Relation of Rorschach Indices of Extraversion-Introversion to Certain Dream Dimensions." *J Clin Psychol* 11:80–1 Ja '55. * (*PA* 29:7301)

1927. MEER, BERNARD. "The Relative Difficulty of the Rorschach Cards." *J Proj Tech* 19:43–53 Mr '55. * (*PA* 30:1044)

1928. MILLER, CARMEN. "A Comparison of High-Accident and Low-Accident Bus and Street Car Operators." *J Proj Tech* 19:146–51 Je '55. * (*PA* 30:3634)

1929. MILLS, EUGENE S. "Abnormal Psychology as a Selective Factor in the College Curriculum." *J Ed Psychol* 46:101–11 F '55. * (*PA* 30:172)

1930. MINDESS, HARVEY. "Analytical Psychology and the Rorschach Test." *J Proj Tech* 19:243–52 S '55. * (*PA* 30:4584)

1931. MINSKI, LOUIS, AND DESAI, MAHESH M. "Aspects of

Personality in Peptic Ulcer Patients: A Comparison With Hysterics." *Brit J Med Psychol* 28:113–34 Je '55. * (*PA* 30:3268)

1932. MIRIN, BERNARD. "The Rorschach Human Movement Response and Role Taking Behavior." *J Nerv & Mental Dis* 122:270–5 S '55. * (*PA* 31:1455)

1933. MONS, W. E. R. "The Scoring and Rationale of Colour Responses." Abstract. *Brit Rorsch Forum* (6):16–9 Ap '55. *

1934. MURATI, JOHN DENIS. *Differences in Test Behavior Between Paranoid and Non-Paranoid Schizophrenic Groups.* Doctor's thesis, University of Wisconsin (Madison, Wis.), 1955. (*DA* 16:386)

1935. NEFF, WALTER S. "The Use of the Rorschach in Distinguishing Vocationally Rehabilitable Groups." *J Counsel Psychol* 2:207–11 f '55. * (*PA* 30:5143)

1936. NORTH, GEORGE E. *The Rorschach Intellectual Indices: An Investigation of Relationships Between Rorschach and the Wechsler-Bellevue Tests.* Master's thesis, University of Utah (Salt Lake City, Utah), 1955.

1937. ODERBERG, PHILLIP. *A Limited Test of Rorschach Reliability by Means of the Introduction of Experimental Color Stimuli.* Doctor's thesis, University of California (Los Angeles, Calif.), 1955.

1938. OGDON, DONALD POTTER. *Rorschach Relationships With Intelligence Among Familial Mental Defectives.* Doctor's thesis, University of Missouri (Columbia, Mo.), 1955. (*DA* 16:578)

1939. OLSEN, LEROY C. *Rorschach Patterns of Successful College Students.* Doctor's thesis, University of North Dakota (Grand Forks, N.D.), 1955.

1940. ORME, J. E. "Intellectual and Rorschach Test Performances of a Group of Senile Dementia Patients and of a Group of Elderly Depressives." *J Mental Sci* 101:863–70 O '55. * (*PA* 30:7532)

1941. PALMER, JAMES O. "Rorschach's Experience Balance: The Concept, General Population Characteristics, and Intellectual Correlates." *J Proj Tech* 19:138–45 Je '55. * (*PA* 30:2912)

1942. PATTERSON, C. H. "Diagnostic Accuracy or Diagnostic Stereotypy?" *J Consult Psychol* 19:483–5 D '55. * (*PA* 30:7171)

1943. PAYNE, R. W. "The Validity of the Rorschach for Psychiatric Diagnosis." Abstract. *B Brit Psychol Soc* (26):12 inset My '55. *

1944. PAYNE, R. W., AND PHILLIPSON, H. "The Clinical Usefulness of the Rorschach: A Symposium." Abstract. *Brit Rorsch Forum* (6):9–16 Ap '55. *

1945. PIOTROWSKI, ZYGMUNT A. "A Defense Attitude Associated With Improvement in Schizophrenia and Measurable With a Modified Rorschach Test." *J Nerv & Mental Dis* 122:36–41 Jl '55. * (*PA* 30:7534)

1946. PIOTROWSKI, ZYGMUNT A., AND BERG, DOROTHY A. "Verification of the Rorschach Alpha Diagnostic Formula for Underactive Schizophrenics." *Am J Psychiatry* 112:443–50 D '55. * (*PA* 30:7220)

1947. POPPLESTONE, JOHN A. "Scoring Colored Responses in Paintings." *J Clin Psychol* 11:191–3 Ap '55. * (*PA* 30:1050)

1948. POWERS, WILLIAM T., AND HAMLIN, ROY M. "Relationship Between Diagnostic Category and Deviant Verbalizations on the Rorschach." *J Consult Psychol* 19:120–4 Ap '55. * (*PA* 30:1053)

1949. PRUYSER, PAUL W., AND FOLSOM, ANGELA T. "The Rorschach Experience Balance in Epileptics." *J Consult Psychol* 19:112–6 Ap '55. * (*PA* 30:1435)

1950. QUIRK, D. *Construct Validation of Rorschach: Protocol Factors Related to Inter-Rater Disagreement.* Master's thesis, University of Toronto (Toronto, Ont., Canada), 1955.

1951. RABINOVITCH, M. SAM; KENNARD, MARGARET A.; AND FISTER, W. P. "Personality Correlates of Electroencephalographic Patterns: Rorschach Findings." *Can J Psychol* 9:29–41 Mr '55. * (*PA* 30:621)

1952. RAINIO, KULLERVO. *Leadership Qualities: A Theoretical Inquiry and an Experimental Study on Foremen.* Suomalaisen Tiedeakatemian Toimituksia, Annales Academiae Scientiarum Fennicae, Sarja-Ser. B, Nide-Tom. 95.1. Helsinki, Finland: Academiae Scientiarum Fennicae, 1955. Pp. 211. * (*PA* 31:1872)

1953. RANSOM, DOROTHY. "The Experimental Use of Electron Micrographs as a Supplement to the Rorschach Ink Blot Technique." *Psychol Rep* 1:203–20 sup 3 '55. * (*PA* 30:5998)

1954. RAY, JOSEPH BLAND. *The Meaning of Rorschach White Space Responses.* Doctor's thesis, University of Oklahoma (Norman, Okla.), 1955. (*DA* 16:580)

1955. REITAN, RALPH M. "Evaluation of the Postconcussion Syndrome With the Rorschach Test." *J Nerv & Mental Dis* 121:463–7 My '55. * (*PA* 30:5119)

1956. REITAN, RALPH M. "The Relation of Rorschach Test Ratios to Brain Injury." *J General Psychol* 53:97–107 Jl '55. * (*PA* 31:8607)

1957. REITAN, RALPH M. "Validity of Rorschach Test as Measure of Psychological Effects of Brain Damage." *A.M.A. Arch Neurol & Psychiatry* 73:445–51 Ap '55. * (*PA* 30:1438)

1958. RICHARDS, T. W. "Personality Development as Reflected in Rorschach Behavior: A Case Study." *J Proj Tech* 19:54–61 Mr '55. * (*PA* 30:733)

1959. RIGBY, MARILYN K.; WILKINS, WALTER L.; AND ANDERHALTER, O. F. "Comparisons of Profile Analyses of Rorschach Data." Abstract. *Am Psychol* 10:414 Ag '55. *

1960. ROBBERTSE, P. M. "Personality Structure of Socially Adjusted and Socially Maladjusted Children, According to the Rorschach Test." *Psychol Monogr* 69(19):1–20 '55. * (*PA* 30:6983)

1961. ROHRER, J. H.; HOFFMAN, E. L.; BAGBY, J. W., JR.; HERRMANN, ROBERT S.; AND WILKINS, W. L. "The Group-Administered Rorschach as a Research Instrument: Reliability and Norms." *Psychol Monogr* 69(8):1–13 '55. * (*PA* 30:1056)

1962. ROSS, ALEXANDER T., AND REITAN, RALPH M. "Intellectual and Affective Functions in Multiple Sclerosis." *A.M.A. Arch Neurol & Psychiatry* 73:663–77 Je '55. * (*PA* 30:3319)

1963. SAKHEIM, GEORGE A. "Suicidal Responses on the Rorschach Test: A Validation Study." *J Nerv & Mental Dis* 122: 332–44 O '55. *

1964. SALK, LEE. *The Relationship of Elaboration on the Rorschach Inquiry to Continuance in Psychotherapy.* Doctor's thesis, University of Michigan (Ann Arbor, Mich.), 1955. (*DA* 15:630)

1965. SANDLER, JOSEPH. "A Simple and Effective Test of Significance for Use With Rorschach Data." *Brit Rorsch Forum* (6):19–21 Ap '55. *

1966. SCALES, MARGARET BERON. *A Study of Intellectual Functioning in Terms of Rorschach Location Scores and Free Verbal Expression.* Doctor's thesis, Columbia University (New York, N.Y.), 1955. (*DA* 15:879)

1967. SCHMIDT, HERMANN O.; FONDA, CHARLES P.; AND LESTER, JOHN R. "Rorschach Behavior as an Index of Color Anaesthesia." *J Psychol* 40:95–102 Jl '55. * (*PA* 30:2918)

1968. SCHNEIDER, BERTRAM H. *The Effect of Varying Time Intervals on the Reproduction and Recall of Rorschach Responses on Retest.* Doctor's thesis, Michigan State University (East Lansing, Mich.), 1955. (*DA* 15:1653)

1969. SHAH, S. A. *A Study of Missionary Success and Failure Using the Inspection Rorschach Technique.* Master's thesis, Pennsylvania State University (State College, Pa.), 1955.

1970. SHATIN, LEO. "Relationships Between the Rorschach Test and the Thematic Apperception Test." *J Proj Tech* 19: 317–31 S '55. * (*PA* 30:4595)

1971. SHERMAN, MURRAY H. "The Diagnostic Significance of Constriction-Dilation on the Rorschach." *J General Psychol* 53: 11–9 Jl '55. * (*PA* 31:7970)

1972. SINGER, JEROME L., AND SUGARMAN, DANIEL A. "A Note on Some Projected Familial Attitudes Associated With Rorschach Movement Responses." *J Consult Psychol* 19:117–9 Ap '55. * (*PA* 30:1368)

1973. SISSON, BOYD D., AND TAULBEE, EARL S. "Organizational Activity on the Rorschach Test." *J Consult Psychol* 19: 29–31 F '55. * (*PA* 29:8652)

1974. SJOSTEDT, ELSIE MARIE. *A Study of the Personality Variables Related to Assaultive and Acquisitive Crimes.* Doctor's thesis, Purdue University (Lafayette, Ind.), 1955. (*DA* 15:881)

1975. SOLOMON, PAUL. "Differential Rorschach Scores of Successfully and Unsuccessfully Placed Mental Defectives." *J Clin Psychol* 11:294–7 Jl '55. * (*PA* 30:3079)

1976. SPIEGELMAN, MARVIN. "Effect of Personality on the Perception of a Motion Picture." *J Proj Tech* 19:461–4 D '55. * (*PA* 30:6831)

1977. SPITAL, CHARLES. *Prediction of Emotional Control in Children With the Rorschach Test.* Doctor's thesis, Vanderbilt University (Nashville, Tenn.), 1955. (*DA* 16:581)

1978. SPITZ, HERMAN H. *A Clinical Investigation of Certain Personality Characteristics of Twenty Adult Male Exhibitionists.* Doctor's thesis, New York University (New York, N.Y.), 1955. (*DA* 16:387)

1979. STAUNTON, G. J. "A Comparative Analysis of Rorschach and T.A.T. Responses With Reference to a Particular Case Study." Abstract. *Brit Rorsch Forum* (6):1–4 Ap '55. *

1980. STEIN, HARRY. "A Note on 'A Comparative Analysis of Rorschach Forms With Altered Stimulus Characteristics' by E. E. Baughman." *J Proj Tech* 19:465–6 D '55. * (*PA* 30:7228)

1981. STOTSKY, BERNARD A. "Differential Responses of Normals, Psychoneurotics, and Psychotics on Rorschach Determinant Shift." *J Consult Psychol* 19:335–8 O '55. * (*PA* 30:6005)

1982. STOTSKY, BERNARD A., AND LAWRENCE, JAMES F. "Various Rorschach Indices as Discriminators of Marked and Little Conceptual Disorganization Among Schizophrenics." *J Consult Psychol* 19:189–93 Je '55. * (*PA* 30:2928)

1983. SYMONDS, PERCIVAL M. "A Contribution to Our Knowledge of the Validity of the Rorschach." *J Proj Tech* 19: 152–62 Je '55. * (*PA* 30:2929)

1984. TAULBEE, EARL S. "The Use of the Rorschach Test in Evaluating the Intellectual Levels of Functioning in Schizophrenics." *J Proj Tech* 19:163–9 Je '55. * (*PA* 30:3237)

1985. THOMAS, HOBART F. "The Relationship of Movement Responses on the Rorschach Test to the Defense Mechanism of Projection." *J Abn & Social Psychol* 50:41–4 Ja '55. * (*PA* 29:7238)

1986. THOMAS, WILLIAM E. *Perceptual Structurization as a Function of Ego Strength: An Experimental Application of the Rorschach Technique.* Doctor's thesis, Michigan State College (East Lansing, Mich.), 1955.

1987. TINDALL, RALPH H. "Relationships Among Indices of Adjustment Status." *Ed & Psychol Meas* 15:152–62 su '55. * (*PA* 30:2330)

1988. TOWBIN, ALAN P. *Hostility in Rorschach Content and*

Overt Aggressive Behavior. Doctor's thesis, Yale University (New Haven, Conn.), 1955.

1989. ULETT, GEORGE. *Rorschach Introductory Manual: A Primer for the Clinical Psychiatric Worker: With Interpretive Diagram to Permit Clinical Use While Learning the Ink-Blot Technique, Second Edition.* Beverly Hills, Calif.: Western Psychological Services, 1955. Pp. 49. *

1990. VERNIER, CLAIRE M.; WHITING, J. FRANK; AND MELTZER, MALCOLM L. "Differential Prediction of a Specific Behavior From Three Projective Techniques." *J Consult Psychol* 19:175–82 Je '55. * (*PA* 30:2932)

1991. VETTER, HAROLD JOHN, JR. *The Prediction of Rorschach Content From the Psychoanalytic Theory of Obsessive-Compulsive Neurosis.* Doctor's thesis, University of Buffalo (Buffalo, N.Y.), 1955. (*DA* 15:1437)

1992. WALTON, D. "On the Validity of the Rorschach Test in the Diagnosis of Intracranial Damage and Pathology." *J Mental Sci* 101:370–82 Ap '55. * (*PA* 30:2933)

1993. WAXENBERG, SHELDON E. "Psychosomatic Patients and Other Physically Ill Persons: A Comparative Study." *J Consult Psychol* 19:163–9 Je '55. * (*PA* 30:3281)

1994. WHEELER, MARY D. "A Follow-up Study of the Case of Roddy, Reported by Dr. M. Ainsworth in March, 1952." Abstract. *Brit Rorsch Forum* (7):10–3 N '55. *

1995. WINTER, WILLIAM D. "Two Personality Patterns in Peptic Ulcer Patients." *J Proj Tech* 19:332–44 S '55. * (*PA* 30:5075)

1996. ZEICHNER, ABRAHAM M. "Psychosexual Identification in Paranoid Schizophrenia." *J Proj Tech* 19:67–77 Mr '55. * (*PA* 30:1378)

1997. ZIMMERMAN, IRLA LEE, AND OETZEL, JAMES L. "A Comparison of Infectious and Traumatic Brain Damage Utilizing Rorschach 'Signs' of Adjustment and Mental Deterioration." Abstract. *Am Psychol* 10:388 Ag '55. *

1998. ABEL, THEODORA M.; OPPENHEIM, SADI; AND SAGER, CLIFFORD J. "Screening Applicants for Training in Psychoanalytically Oriented Psychotherapy." *Am J Psychother* 10:24–39 Ja '56. * (*PA* 31:126)

1999. ABER, WALTER E. *Rorschach Patterns as Related to Sociometric Status.* Master's thesis, North Texas State College (Denton, Tex.), 1956.

2000. ALCOCK, A. THEODORA, AND PHILLIPSON, H. "The Use of Rorschach and Object Relations Technique in Vocational Selection Work." Abstract. *Rorsch Newsl* 1:18–9 D '56. *

2001. ANSBACHER, H. L. "Social Interest, an Adlerian Rationale for the Rorschach Human Movement Response." *J Proj Tech* 20:363–5 D '56. * (*PA* 32:1605)

2002. APPLEBY, LAWRENCE. *The Relationship of a Rorschach Barrier Typology to Other Behavioral Measures.* Doctor's thesis, University of Houston (Houston, Tex.), 1956. (*DA* 16: 2519)

2003. AYAD, JOSEPH MAGDY. *An Experimental Investigation of the Visual Perceptual Properties of the Rorschach Cards.* Doctor's thesis, University of Denver (Denver, Colo.), 1956.

2004. BECK, S. J.; MOLISH, HERMAN B.; AND SINCLAIR, JEAN. "Concerning Researchers' Thinking in Schizophrenia Research." *Am J Orthopsychiatry* 26:792–800 O '56. * (*PA* 32:1835)

2005. BECKER, WESLEY C. "A Genetic Approach to the Interpretation and Evaluation of the Process-Reactive Distinction in Schizophrenia." *J Abn & Social Psychol* 53:229–36 S '56. *

2006. BELL, FREDERICK B. *Some Relationships Between Rorschach Responses and Form or Color Choices.* Doctor's thesis, Purdue University (Lafayette, Ind.), 1956. (*DA* 16:2512)

2007. BENTON, ARTHUR L. "The Rorschach Test and the Diagnosis of Cerebral Pathology in Children." *Am J Orthopsychiatry* 26:783–91 O '56. * (*PA* 32:1917)

2008. BENTON, ARTHUR L. "The Rorschach Test in Epilepsy." *Am J Orthopsychiatry* 26:420–6 Ap '56. *

2009. BENVENISTE, SAMUEL J. *A Study of Shading Responses on the Rorschach Ink-Blot Test.* Doctor's thesis, University of Pittsburgh (Pittsburgh, Pa.), 1956. (*DA* 16:1171)

2010. BERCEL, NICHOLAS A.; TRAVIS, LEE E.; OLINGER, LEONARD B.; AND DREIKURS, ERIC. "Model Psychoses Induced by LSD-25 in Normals: II, Rorschach Test Findings." *Arch Neurol & Psychiatry* 75:612–8 Je '56. * (*PA* 31:6401)

2011. BERG, JACOB, AND POLYOT, C. J. "The Influence of Color on Reactions to Incomplete Figures." *J Consult Psychol* 20:9–15 F '56. * (*PA* 31:3004)

2012. BIERI, JAMES, AND BLACKER, EDWARD. "External and Internal Stimulus Factors in Rorschach Performance." *J Consult Psychol* 20:1–7 F '56. * (*PA* 31:3005)

2013. BIERI, JAMES, AND BLACKER, EDWARD. "The Generality of Cognitive Complexity in the Perception of People and Ink-blots." *J Abn & Social Psychol* 53:112–7 Jl '56. * (*PA* 32: 1610)

2014. BIRJANDI, PARVIN FARZAD. *A Rorschach Study of Psychoanalytic Proposals on Cigarette Smoking.* Doctor's thesis, University of Denver (Denver, Colo.), 1956.

2015. BLECHNER, JANET E., AND CARTER, HAROLD D. "Rorschach Personality Factors and College Achievement." *Calif J Ed Res* 7:72–5 Mr '56. * (*PA* 31:3773)

2016. BLOOM, BERNARD L. "Prognostic Significance of the Underproductive Rorschach." *J Proj Tech* 20:367–71 D '56. * (*PA* 32:1611)

2017. BOSQUET, KENNISON T., AND STANLEY, WALTER C. "Discriminative Powers of Rorschach Determinants in Children

Referred to a Child Guidance Clinic." *J Consult Psychol* 20: 17–21 F '56. * (*PA* 31:3009)

2018. BRACKBILL, GLEN A., AND FINE, HAROLD J. "Schizophrenia and Central Nervous System Pathology." *J Abn & Social Psychol* 52:310–3 My '56. * (*PA* 31:4943)

2019. BRECHER, SYLVIA. "The Rorschach Reaction Patterns of Maternally Overprotected and Maternally Rejected Schizophrenic Patients." *J Nerv & Mental Dis* 123:41–52 Ja '56. * (*PA* 31:6406)

2020. BROWN, BENJAMIN H. *The Utility of a Rorschach Derived Maturity-Immaturity Dimension in Differentiating Non-Problem From Problem Youths.* Doctor's thesis, New York University (New York, N.Y.), 1956. (*DA* 16:2521)

2021. BROWN, L. B. "English Migrants to New Zealand: A Pilot Rorschach Study." *Austral J Psychol* 8:106–10 D '56. * (*PA* 32:383)

2022. BURGESS, ELVA. "Personality Factors of Over- and Under-Achievers in Engineering." *J Ed Psychol* 47:89–99 F '56. * (*PA* 31:8811)

2023. BUTTON, ALAN D. "A Rorschach Study of 67 Alcoholics." *Q J Studies Alcohol* 17:35–52 Mr '56. * (*PA* 31:3326)

2024. CARR, ARTHUR C. "The Relation of Certain Rorschach Variables to Expression of Affect in the TAT and SCT." *J Proj Tech* 20:137–42 Je '56. * (*PA* 31:4674)

2025. CHAREN, SOL. "Regressive Behavior Changes in the Tuberculous Patient." *J Psychol* 41:273–89 Ja '56. * (*PA* 31:5000)

2026. CLEVELAND, SIDNEY E., AND FISHER, SEYMOUR. "Psychological Factors in the Neurodermatoses." *Psychosom Med* 18:209–20 My-Je '56. * (*PA* 31:5001)

2027. CLYDE, ROBIN JAMES. *An Investigation of the Construct Validity of Some Rorschach Variables.* Doctor's thesis, Ohio State University (Columbus, Ohio), 1956. (*DA* 16:1501)

2028. COAN, RICHARD. "A Factor Analysis of Rorschach Determinants." *J Proj Tech* 20:280–7 S '56. * (*PA* 31:6666)

2029. COHEN, BERTRAM D.; SENF, RITA; AND HUSTON, PAUL E. "Perceptual Accuracy in Schizophrenia, Depression, and Neurosis, and Effects of Amytal." *J Abn & Social Psychol* 52: 363–7 My '56. * (*PA* 31:4814)

2030. CONSALVI, CONRAD. *Rorschach Determinants and Intelligence: A Factor Analytic Study.* Master's thesis, Vanderbilt University (Nashville, Tenn.), 1956.

2031. COX, RACHEL DUNAWAY. *The Normal Personality: An Analysis of Rorschach and Thematic Apperception Test Responses of a Group of College Students.* *J Proj Tech* 20: 70–7 Mr '56. * (*PA* 31:3016)

2032. CRUMPTON, EVELYN. "The Influence of Color on the Rorschach Test." *J Proj Tech* 20:150–8 Je '56. (*PA* 31:4679)

2033. DAVIDS, ANTHONY; JOELSON, MARK; AND MCARTHUR, CHARLES. "Rorschach and TAT Indices of Homosexuality in Overt Homosexuals, Neurotics, and Normal Males." *J Abn & Social Psychol* 53:161–72 S '56. * (*PA* 32:2891)

2034. DÖRKEN, HERBERT, JR. "Psychological Structure as the Governing Principle of Projective Technique: Rorschach Theory." *Can J Psychol* 10:101–6 Je '56. * (*PA* 31:4682)

2035. DUNCAN, BERTHA K. "Personality Changes as Reflected in Rorschach Records Concomitant With Psychotherapy." *Trans Kans Acad Sci* 59:87–93 sp '56. *

2036. EVERETT, EVALYN G. *A Comparative Study of Paretics, Hebephrenics, and Paranoid Schizophrenics on a Battery of Psychological Tests.* Doctor's thesis, New York University (New York, N.Y.), 1956. (*DA* 16:1502)

2037. FIEDLER, MIRIAM FORSTER, AND STONE, L. JOSEPH. "The Rorschachs of Selected Groups of Children in Comparison With Published Norms." *J Proj Tech* 20:273–9 S '56. * (*PA* 31:6075)

2038. FIELDING, BENJAMIN, AND BROWN, FRED. "Prediction of Intelligence From Certain Rorschach Factors." *J Clin Psychol* 12:196–7 Ap '56. * (*PA* 31:4687)

2039. FISHER, SEYMOUR, AND CLEVELAND, SIDNEY E. "Relationship of Body Image to Site of Cancer." *Psychosom Med* 18:304–9 Jl-Ag '56. * (*PA* 31:6475)

2040. FISHER, SEYMOUR, AND MENDELL, DAVID. "The Communication of Neurotic Patterns Over Two and Three Generations." *Psychiatry* 19:41–6 F '56. * (*PA* 31:3503)

2041. FRANGLEN, SHEILA; WILLIAMS, CELIA; AND BENE, EVA M. "Symposium on the Use of the Rorschach in Various Settings." Abstract. *Rorsch Newsl* 1:1–7 My '56. *

2042. GIBSON, JAMES J. "The Non-Projective Aspects of the Rorschach Experiment: IV, The Rorschach Blots Considered as Pictures." *J Social Psychol* 44:203–6 N '56. *

2043. GOLD, DONALD LEE. *The Effect of Negative Instructions on Rorschach Symbolization.* Doctor's thesis, Columbia University (New York, N.Y.), 1956. (*DA* 16:1281)

2044. GOLDBERG, PHILIP L. *A Study of the Effect of Dependency and Other Personality Characteristics on Airmen in a Familiar Crisis Situation.* Doctor's thesis, New York University (New York, N.Y.), 1956. (*DA* 17:894)

2045. GRAYSON, HARRY M. "Rorschach Productivity and Card Preferences as Influenced by Experimental Variation of Color and Shading." *J Proj Tech* 20:288–96 S '56. * (*PA* 31:6085)

2046. HAASE, WILLIAM. *Rorschach Diagnosis, Socio-Economic Class, and Examiner Bias.* Doctor's thesis, New York University (New York, N.Y.), 1956. (*DA* 16:1283)

2047. HANFMANN, EUGENIA. "The Non-Projective Aspects of the Rorschach Experiment: III, The Point of View of the Research Clinician." *J Social Psychol* 44:199–202 N '56. *

2048. HARTOCH, ANNA. Chap. 6, "The Child's Reaction to the Rorschach Situation," pp. 153–80. In *Personality in Young Children: Vol. I, Methods for the Study of Personality in Young Children.* By Lois B. Murphy and others. New York: Basic Books, Inc., 1956. Pp. xx, 424. * (*PA* 31:2656)

2049. HENRY, EDITH M. *Situational Influences on Rorschach Response.* Master's thesis, Ohio State University (Columbus, Ohio), 1956.

2050. HENRY, EDITH M., AND ROTTER, JULIAN B. "Situational Influences on Rorschach Responses." *J Consult Psychol* 20:457–62 D '56. * (*PA* 32:1625)

2051. HOLT, ROBERT R. "Gauging Primary and Secondary Processes in Rorschach Responses." *J Proj Tech* 20:14–25 Mr '56. * (*PA* 31:3039)

2052. JOST, HUDSON, AND EPSTEIN, LEON J. "The Rorschach as a Physiological Stress." *J Clin Psychol* 12:259–63 Jl '56. * (*PA* 31:6091)

2053. KAGAN, JEROME. "Psychological Study of a School Phobia in One of a Pair of Identical Twins." *J Proj Tech* 20:78–87 Mr '56. * (*PA* 31:3346)

2054. KAHLER, CAROL. *An Exploratory Study of the Use of Action Research in Student Teaching: A Description and Analysis of the Use of Action Research in Twenty-One Off-Campus Student Teaching Situations.* Doctor's thesis, New York University (New York, N.Y.), 1956. (*DA* 16:1850)

2055. KAHN, ROBERT L.; LINN, LOUIS; AND WEINSTEIN, EDWIN A. "Personality Factors Influencing Rorschach Responses in Organic Brain Disease." Abstract. Discussion by Fred Brown. *A.M.A. Arch Neurol & Psychiatry* 76:266–7 S '56. *

2056. KAHN, SAMUEL. *Rorschach Resume: Rorschach Ink Blot Personality Testing.* Ossining, N.Y.: Dynamic Psychological Society Press, 1956. Pp. vii, 63. * (*PA* 30:5988)

2057. KALDEGG, A. "Psychological Observations in a Group of Alcoholic Patients With Analysis of Rorschach, Wechsler-Bellevue and Bender Gestalt Test Results." *Q J Studies Alcohol* 17:608–28 D '56. * (*PA* 32:648)

2058. KALDEGG, A. "Testing Alcoholics." Abstract. *Rorsch Newsl* 1:14–5 D '56. *

2059. KAPLAN, BERT, AND BERGER, STANLEY. "Increments and Consistency of Performance in Four Repeated Rorschach Administrations." *J Proj Tech* 20:304–9 S '56. * (*PA* 31:6093)

2060. KAPLAN, BERT; RICKERS-OVSIANKINA, MARIA A.; AND JOSEPH, ALICE. "An Attempt to Sort Rorschach Records From Four Cultures." *J Proj Tech* 20:172–80 Je '56. * (*PA* 31:4695)

2061. KASS, WALTER. "Projective Techniques as Research Tools in Studies of Normal Personality Development." *J Proj Tech* 20:269–72 S '56. * (*PA* 31:6096)

2062. KLINGENSMITH, STANLEY W. *A Study of the Effects of Different Methods of Structuring the Rorschach Inquiry on Determinant Scores.* Doctor's thesis, University of Pittsburgh (Pittsburgh, Pa.), 1956. (*DA* 16:2524)

2063. KLOPFER, BRUNO; with contributions by Mary D. Ainsworth, Dorothy V. Anderson, Gertrude Baker, Hedda Bolgar, Jack Fox, A. Irving Hallowell, Eileen Higham, Samuel Kellman, Walter G. Klopfer, Gertrude Meili-Dworetzki, Edwin S. Shneidman, Robert F. Snowden, Marvin Spiegelman, Marie D. Stein, Evelyn Troup, and Gertha Williams. *Developments in Rorschach Technique: Vol. II, Fields of Applications.* Yonkers, N.Y.: World Book Co., 1956. Pp. xx, 828. * (*PA* 30:7202)

2064. KNOPF, IRWIN J. "Rorschach Summary Scores in Differential Diagnosis." *J Consult Psychol* 20:99–104 Ap '56. * (*PA* 31:6099)

2065. KNOPF, IRWIN J. "The Rorschach Test and Psychotherapy." *Am J Orthopsychiatry* 26:801–6 O '56. * (*PA* 32:1628)

2066. KRAUS, ANTHONY R. "An Experiment With Blurred Exposure of Zulliger's Inkblot Slides." Abstract. *Am Psychol* 11:401 Ag '56. *

2067. KRAUS, ANTHONY R. "Shifts in the Levels of Operating Defenses Induced by Blurring of Inkblot Slides." *J Clin Psychol* 12:337–41 O '56. *

2068. LAL, RAM SURAT. "Rorschach Test and Assessment of Intelligence Under Indian Conditions." *Brit J Ed Psychol* 26: 112–6 Je '56. * (*PA* 31:6101)

2069. LAWTON, M. POWELL. "Stimulus Structure as a Determinant of the Perceptual Response." *J Consult Psychol* 20:351–5 O '56. * (*PA* 31:7938)

2070. LEVENTHAL, HOWARD. "The Effects of Perceptual Training on the Rorschach *W* and *Z* Scores." *J Consult Psychol* 20:93–8 Ap '56. * (*PA* 31:6102)

2071. LEVINE, MURRAY, AND MELTZOFF, JULIAN. "Cognitive Inhibition and Rorschach Human Movement Responses." *J Consult Psychol* 20:119–22 Ap '56. * (*PA* 31:6103)

2072. LEVY, LEON H.; BRODY, JANICE E.; AND WINDMAN, GEORGIA O. "The Relationship Between the Inferential Potential of Rorschach and TAT Protocols." *J Consult Psychol* 20: 27–8 F '56. * (*PA* 31:3049)

2073. LIGHT, BERNARD H., AND AMICK, JEAN HOLLANDSWORTH. "Rorschach Responses of Normal Aged." *J Proj Tech* 20:185–95 Je '56. * (*PA* 31:4701)

2074. LISANSKY, EDITH S. "The Inter-Examiner Reliability of the Rorschach Test." *J Proj Tech* 20:310–7 S '56. * (*PA* 31:6106)

2075. LIT, JACK. *Formal and Content Factors of Projective Tests in Relation to Academic Achievement.* Doctor's thesis, Temple University (Philadelphia, Pa.), 1956. (*DA* 16:1505)

2076. LIUTKUS, STANLEY. *Rorschach Indicators of Maturity:*

A Statistical Study of 200 Males. Doctor's thesis, Temple University (Philadelphia, Pa.), 1956. (*DA* 16:2525)

2077. LUNDIN, WILLIAM H., AND BREIGER, BORIS. "Comparison of Productivity and Fantasy on the Rorschach and Projective Movement Sequences." Abstract. *J Consult Psychol* 20:342 O '56. *

2078. LYLE, J. G. "Obsessive-Compulsive Behaviour: Problems of Rorschach Diagnosis and Classification." *Brit J Med Psychol* 29:280–6 pt 3–4 '56. *

2079. McARTHUR, CHARLES, AND HEINEMAN, ROBERT. "The Use of the Rorschach for Planning Teacher Strategy." *Yearb Nat Council Meas Used Ed* 13:156–60 '56. *

2080. McFARLAND, ROBERT L. "Two Dimensions of Test Structure in Rorschach-Like Projective Tests." *J Proj Tech* 20:398–404 D '56. * (*PA* 32:1630)

2081. MANN, LESTER. "The Relation of Rorschach Indices of Extratension and Introversion to a Measure of Responsiveness to the Immediate Environment." *J Consult Psychol* 20:114–8 Ap '56. * (*PA* 31:6110)

2082. MARADIE, LOUIS J. "The Goal-Spurt Hypothesis and the Rorschach Test." *J Consult Psychol* 20:205–10 Je '56. * (*PA* 31:6111)

2083. MARIANI, EUGENE L. *An Analysis of Relationships Between Test Behavior and Types of Defense.* Doctor's thesis, University of Houston (Houston, Tex.), 1956. (*DA* 16:1506)

2084. MARIANI, ROSE RAMSAY. *A Comparison of a Projective Test Battery With Its Component Tests.* Doctor's thesis, University of Houston (Houston, Tex.), 1956. (*DA* 16:1506)

2085. MELTZOFF, JULIAN, AND LITWIN, DOROTHY. "Affective Control and Rorschach Human Movement Responses." *J Consult Psychol* 20:463–5 D '56. * (*PA* 32:1632)

2086. MINTZ, ELIZABETH E.; SCHMEIDLER, GERTRUDE R.; AND BRISTOL, MARJORIE. "Rorschach Changes During Psychoanalysis." *J Proj Tech* 20:414–7 D '56. * (*PA* 32:1634)

2087. MOLISH, HERMAN B. "The Rorschach Test in Military Psychology and Psychiatry." *Am J Orthopsychiatry* 26:807–17 O '56. * (*PA* 32:1635)

2088. MOLISH, HERMAN B. *Schizophrenic Reaction Types as Evaluated From the Rorschach Test.* Doctor's thesis, University of Chicago (Chicago, Ill.), 1956.

2089. MORRISON, R. L. "Use of the Rorschach Test in Wormwood Scrubs." Abstract. *Rorsch Newsl* 1:5–10 D '56. *

2090. MUELLER, ALFRED D., AND LEFKOVITS, AARON M. "Personality Structure and Dynamics of Patients With Rheumatoid Arthritis." *J Clin Psychol* 12:143–7 Ap '56. * (*PA* 31:5010)

2091. MURSTEIN, BERNARD I. "The Projection of Hostility on the Rorschach and as a Result of Ego-Threat." *J Proj Tech* 20:418–28 D '56. * (*PA* 32:1636) (Abstract: *Am Psychol* 11:384)

2092. MURSTEIN, BERNARD I. *A Study of Projection of Hostility on the Rorschach and in a Stress Condition.* Doctor's thesis, University of Texas (Austin, Tex.), 1956.

2093. NITSCHE, CARL J.; ROBINSON, J. FRANKLIN; AND PARSONS, EDWARD T. "Homosexuality and the Rorschach." Abstract. *J Consult Psychol* 20:196 Je '56. *

2094. NIYEKAWA, AGNES M. "A Comparative Analysis of Foreign and American Female College Groups on Three Personality Variables: Anxiety, Level of Aspiration and Femininity." *Psychol Newsl* 7:72–91 My–Je '56. * (*PA* 31:3697)

2095. OKARSKI, JOSEPH FRANK. *Consistency of Projective Movement Responses.* Doctor's thesis, Columbia University (New York, N.Y.), 1956. (*DA* 16:1508)

2096. O'REILLY, P. O. "The Objective Rorschach: A Suggested Modification of Rorschach Technique." *J Clin Psychol* 12:27–31 Ja '56. * (*PA* 30:4585)

2097. ORME, J. E. "A Complementary Method of Assessing Rorschach Responses Applied to Groups of Senile Dementia and Elderly Depressed Patients." *Rorsch Newsl* 1:18–28 My '56. *

2098. PALM, ROSE. "Comparative Study of Symbol Formation in Rorschach Test and Dream." *Psychoanalytic R* 43:246–51 Ap '56. * (*PA* 31:5774)

2099. PALMER, JAMES O. "Attitudinal Correlates of Rorschach's Experience Balance." *J Proj Tech* 20:207–11 Je '56. * (*PA* 31:4706)

2100. PASTO, TARMO A., AND KIVISTO, PAUL. "Group Differences in Color Choice and Rejection." *J Clin Psychol* 12:379–81 O '56. *

2101. PEARLMAN, SAMUEL. "A Tentative Rorschach Frame of Reference for Superior Young Adults." Abstract. *Am Psychol* 11:400 Ag '56. *

2102. PICK, THOMAS. "A Critique of Current Methods of Rorschach Scoring." *J Proj Tech* 20:318–25 S '56. * (*PA* 31:6117)

2103. PIOTROWSKI, ZYGMUNT A. Chap. 2, "Rorschach Method in Review," pp. 16–31 D '56 (*PA* 30:7219). In *Progress in Clinical Psychology, Vol. II.* Edited by Daniel Brower and Lawrence E. Abt. New York and London: Grune & Stratton, Inc., 1956. Pp. viii, 364. *

2104. POPE, BENJAMIN, AND JENSEN, ARTHUR R. "The Rorschach as an Index of Pathological Thinking." Abstract. *Am Psychol* 11:363 Ag '56. *

2105. POTHAST, MILES DALE. *A Personality Study of Two Types of Murderers.* Doctor's thesis, Michigan State University (East Lansing, Mich.), 1956. (*DA* 17:898)

2106. PRAAG, JULES VAN. *A Rorschach and MMPI Study of a Fundamentalist Religious Sect.* Doctor's thesis, University of Denver (Denver, Colo.), 1956.

2107. RADFORD, E. "Use of the Rorschach in Industry." *Rorsch Newsl* 1:12–3 D '56. *

2108. RAVEN, J. C. "Projection as a Psychological Concept and Method of Enquiry." *Rorsch Newsl* 1:15–8 D '56. *

2109. REICHARD, SUZANNE. "Discussion: Projective Techniques as Research Tools in Studies of Normal Personality Development." *J Proj Tech* 20:265–8 S '56. * (*PA* 31:6120)

2110. RICCIUTI, HENRY N. "Use of the Rorschach Test in Longitudinal Studies of Personality Development." *J Proj Tech* 20:256–60 S '56. * (*PA* 31:6122)

2111. ROHRER, J. H., AND EDMONSON, BARBARA W. "An Experimental Study of the Effects of Individual and Group Presentation of the Rorschach Plates." *J Clin Psychol* 12:249–54 Jl '56. * (*PA* 31:6124)

2112. RYAN, WILLIAM; BOLING, LENORE; AND GREENBLATT, MILTON. "The Rorschach Test in the Evaluation of Psychiatric Treatment." Abstract. *Am Psychol* 11:361 Ag '56. *

2113. SACKS, JOSEPH M., AND COHEN, MURRAY L. "Contributions of the Rorschach to the Understanding of 'Acting-Out' Behavior." Abstract. *Am Psychol* 11:363 Ag '56. *

2114. SARBIN, ANNE. *An Analysis of the Buhler School Maturity Test as It Relates to Intelligence and Projective Test Data.* Doctor's thesis, University of Southern California (Los Angeles, Calif.), 1956.

2115. SCHAFER, ROY. "Transference in the Patient's Reaction to the Tester." *J Proj Tech* 20:26–32 Mr '56. * (*PA* 31:3073)

2116. SCHROEDER, CLIFFORD E. *Personality Patterns of Advanced Protestant Theology Students and Physical Science Students.* Doctor's thesis, Michigan State University (East Lansing, Mich.), 1956. (*DA* 18:154)

2117. SCOTT, EDWARD M. "Regression or Disintegration in Schizophrenia?" *J Clin Psychol* 12:298–300 Jl '56. * (*PA* 31:6444)

2118. SHAPIRO, DAVID. "Color-Response and Perceptual Passivity." *J Proj Tech* 20:52–69 Mr '56. * (*PA* 31:3076)

2119. SINGER, JEROME L. "The Non-Projective Aspects of the Rorschach Experiment: V, Discussion of the Clinical Implications of the Non-Projective Aspects of the Rorschach." *J Social Psychol* 44:207–14 N '56. *

2120. SINGER, JEROME L., AND OPLER, MARVIN K. "Contrasting Patterns of Fantasy and Motility in Irish and Italian Schizophrenics." *J Abn & Social Psychol* 53:42–7 Jl '56. * (*PA* 32:1868)

2121. SINGER, JEROME L.; WILENSKY, HAROLD; AND McCRAVEN, VIVIAN G. "Delaying Capacity, Fantasy, and Planning Ability: A Factorial Study of Some Basic Ego Functions." *J Consult Psychol* 20:375–83 O '56. * (*PA* 31:8506)

2122. SINNETT, E. ROBERT, AND ROBERTS, RUTH. "Rorschach Approach Type and the Organization of Cognitive Material." *J Consult Psychol* 20:109–13 Ap '56. * (*PA* 31:6132)

2123. SISSON, BOYD D.; TAULBEE, EARL S.; AND GASTON, CHARLES O. "Rorschach Card Rejection in Normal and Psychiatric Groups." *J Clin Psychol* 12:85–8 Ja '56. * (*PA* 20:4599)

2124. SMALL, LEONARD. *Rorschach Location and Scoring Manual.* New York and London: Grune & Stratton, Inc., 1956. Pp. ix, 214. * (*PA* 30:7226)

2125. SMITH, JOHN R., AND COLEMAN, JAMES C. "The Relationship Between Manifestations of Hostility in Projective Tests and Overt Behavior." *J Proj Tech* 20:326–34 S '56. * (*PA* 31:6134)

2126. SPIEGELMAN, MARVIN. "Rorschach Form-Level, Intellectual Functioning and Potential." *J Proj Tech* 20:335–43 S '56. * (*PA* 31:6136)

2127. STARER, EMANUEL. "The Use of the Kaleidoscope as an Adjunct to the Rorschach." Abstract. *J Consult Psychol* 20:466 D '56. *

2128. STAUNTON, G. J. "The Recognition and Interpretation of Perceptual Transfer in the Content Analysis of Rorschach Test Responses." Abstract. *Rorsch Newsl* 1:13–7 My '56. *

2129. STEIN, HARRY. "Developmental Changes in Content of Movement Responses." *J Proj Tech* 20:216–23 Je '56. * (*PA* 31:4716)

2130. SUTCLIFFE, J. P. "On the Methodology of Projective Testing." *Austral J Psychol* 8:180–5 D '56. *

2131. SYMONDS, PERCIVAL M., AND DUDEK, STEPHANIE. "Use of the Rorschach in the Diagnosis of Teacher Effectiveness." *J Proj Tech* 20:227–34 Je '56. * (*PA* 31:4718)

2132. TAULBEE, EARL S.; SISSON, BOYD D.; AND GASTON, CHARLES O. "Affective Ratio and 8-9-10 Per Cent on the Rorschach Test for Normals and Psychiatric Groups." *J Consult Psychol* 20:105–8 Ap '56. * (*PA* 31:6138)

2133. TAYLOR, R. S. "Use of the Rorschach Test in Wandsworth Prison." *Rorsch Newsl* 1:10–1 D '56. *

2134. THALER, MARGARET. "Notes on Three Theories of Personality Applied to the Rorschach Test." *Samīksā* 10:121–54 no 3 '56. *

2135. THALER, MARGARET. "Relationships Among Wechsler, Weigl, Rorschach, EEG Findings, and Abstract-Concrete Behavior in a Group of Normal Aged Subjects." *J Gerontol* 11:404–9 O '56. * (*PA* 31:5871)

2136. THALER, MARGARET, AND SCHEIN, EDGAR H. "Rorschach Responses of American Prisoners of War at the Time of Release From Internment." Abstract. *Am Psychol* 11:401 Ag '56. *

2137. TOLMAN, RUTH S., AND MEYER, MORTIMER M. "A Study of Patients' Identifications From Rorschach Records and

Therapists' Judgments." *J Proj Tech* 20:48–51 Mr '56. * (*PA* 31:3084)

2138. TYCKO, MILICENT. *Rorschach Responses as a Function of Exposure Time.* Doctor's thesis, New York University (New York, N.Y.), 1956. (*DA* 17:899)

2139. VAYHINGER, JOHN MONROE. *Prediction From the Rorschach of Behavior in a Group Situation.* Doctor's thesis, Columbia University (New York, N.Y.), 1956. (*DA* 16:1286)

2140. WALLEN, RICHARD W. Chap. 8, "The Rorschach Method," pp. 191–220; 266–70. In his *Clinical Psychology: The Study of Persons.* New York: McGraw-Hill Book Co., Inc., 1956. Pp. xiii, 388. * (*PA* 30:7155)

2141. WEINER, LEONARD; BROWN, EARL; AND KAPLAN, BERT. "A Comparison of the Ability of Normal and Brain Injured Subjects to Produce Additional Responses on a Second Administration of the Rorschach Test." *J Clin Psychol* 12:89–91 Ja '56. * (*PA* 30:5127)

2142. WERNER, HEINZ, AND WAPNER, SEYMOUR. "The Non-Projective Aspects of the Rorschach Experiment: II, Organismic Theory and Perceptual Response." *J Social Psychol* 44:193–8 N '56. *

2143. WETHERHORN, MITCHELL. "Flexor-Extensor Movement on the Rorschach." Abstract. *J Consult Psychol* 20:204 Je '56. *

2144. WHEELER, W. M. "Psychodiagnostic Assessments of a Child After Prolonged Separation in Early Childhood, II." *Brit J Med Psychol* 29:248–57 pt 3–4 '56. *

2145. WICKES, THOMAS A., JR. "Examiner Influence in a Testing Situation." *J Consult Psychol* 20:23–6 F '56. *

2146. WIENER, GERALD. "Neurotic Depressives' and Alcoholics' Oral Rorschach Percepts." *J Proj Tech* 20:453–5 D '56. * (*PA* 32:1655)

2147. WILLNER, ALLEN EUGENE. *The Interpretation of the Rorschach Test as a Function of Interpreter, Degree of Information, and the Subject's Personality.* Doctor's thesis, Michigan State University (East Lansing, Mich.), 1956. (*DA* 17:1385)

2148. WILSON, MARY D., AND COATES, S. "Symposium on the Use of the Rorschach in a Child Guidance Clinic and a General Hospital." Abstract. *Rorsch Newsl* 1:7–12 My '56. *

2149. WIRT, ROBERT D. "Pattern Analysis of the Rorschach." *J Clin Psychol* 12:382–4 O '56. * (*PA* 32:4211)

2150. WOLTMANN, ADOLF G. "Recent Rorschach Literature." *Am J Orthopsychiatry* 26:193–203 Ja '56. *

2151. ZEICHNER, ABRAHAM M. "Conception of Masculine and Feminine Roles in Paranoid Schizophrenia." *J Proj Tech* 20:348–54 S '56. * (*PA* 31:6458)

2152. ZIMET, CARL N., AND BRACKBILL, GLEN A. "The Role of Anxiety in Psychodiagnosis." *J Clin Psychol* 12:173–7 Ap '56. * (*PA* 31:4722)

2153. ZUBIN, JOSEPH. "The Non-Projective Aspects of the Rorschach Experiment: I, Introduction." *J Social Psychol* 44:179–92 N '56. *

2154. ZUBIN, JOSEPH. "Objective Evaluation of Personality Tests." *Am J Psychiatry* 107:569–76 F '56. *

2155. ZUBIN, JOSEPH; ERON, LEONARD D.; AND SULTAN, FLORENCE. "A Psychometric Evaluation of the Rorschach Experiment." *Am J Orthopsychiatry* 26:773–82 O '56. * (*PA* 32:1658)

2156. ZULLIGER, HANS. *Behn-Rorschach Test: Text.* Bern, Switzerland: Hans Huber, 1956. Pp. 200. (New York: Grune & Stratton, Inc., 1956.) *

2157. ADCOCK, C. J.; McCREARY, J. R.; RITCHIE, J. E.; AND SOMERSET, H. C. A. "Personality and Physique: A Rorschach Study With Maori and European Subjects." *Austral J Psychol* 9:158–89 D '57. *

2158. ALLEN, ROBERT M. "A Note on Persistent Responses in Longitudinal Rorschach Protocols." *J Proj Tech* 21:362–5 D '57. *

2159. ALLEN, ROBERT M. "The Rorschach Records of a Superior Child." *J Genetic Psychol* 91:115–8 S '57. *

2160. AMES, LOUISE BATES; WALKER, RICHARD N.; AND GOODENOUGH, EVELYN. "Old Age Rorschach Follow-Up Study." *Percept & Motor Skills* 7:68 Je '57. * (*PA* 32:2736)

2161. ARMITAGE, STEWART G., AND PEARL, DAVID. "Unsuccessful Differential Diagnosis From the Rorschach." *J Consult Psychol* 21:479–84 D '57. *

2162. AULD, FRANK, JR. "Is Beck's Sample of Rorschach Testees Representative?" *J General Psychol* 56:135–6 Ja '57. *

2163. BARKER, G. B. "Clinical Study and Rorschach Test." Abstract. *Rorsch Newsl* 2:3–8 Jl '57. *

2164. BIERI, JAMES, AND MESSERLEY, SUSAN. "Differences in Perceptual and Cognitive Behavior as a Function of Experience Type." *J Consult Psychol* 21:217–21 Je '57. *

2165. BINDON, D. MARJORIE. "Rubella Deaf Children: A Rorschach Study Employing Munroe Inspection Technique." *Brit J Psychol* 48:249–58 N '57. *

2166. BROOKS, MARJORIE, AND PHILLIPS, LESLIE. "The Cognitive Significance of Rorschach Developmental Scores." Abstract. *Am Psychol* 12:362–3 Jl '57. *

2167. BROWN, FRED. "The Present Status of Rorschach Interpretation." *J Am Psychoanalytic Assn* 5:164–82 Ja '57. *

2168. CANTER, ARTHUR. "Rorschach Response Characteristics as a Function of Color and Degree of Emotional Constriction." Abstract. *J Consult Psychol* 21:46 F '57. *

2169. CHAMBERS, GUINEVERE S., AND HAMLIN, ROY M. "Rorschach 'Inner Life' Capacity of Imbeciles Under Varied Conditions." *Am J Mental Def* 62:88–95 Jl '57. *

2170. CHAMBERS, GUINEVERE S., AND HAMLIN, ROY M. "The

Validity of Judgments Based on 'Blind' Rorschach Records." *J Consult Psychol* 21:105–9 Ap '57. *

2171. CHAREN, SOL. "Pitfalls in Interpretation of Parental Symbolism in Rorschach Cards IV and VII." *J Consult Psychol* 21:52–6 F '57. * (*PA* 32:488)

2172. CONSALVI, CONRAD, AND CANTER, ARTHUR. "Rorschach Scores as a Function of Four Factors." *J Consult Psychol* 21:47–51 F '57. * (*PA* 32:489)

2173. CROOKES, T. G. "Size Constancy and Literalness in the Rorschach Test." *Brit J Med Psychol* 30:99–106 pt 2 '57. *

2174. CUTTER, FRED. "Rorschach Sex Responses and Overt Deviations." *J Clin Psychol* 13:83–6 Ja '57. *

2175. DESAI, M. "The Rorschach in Depersonalization." Abstract. *Rorsch Newsl* 2:21–2 Jl '57. *

2176. ECKHARDT, WILLIAM. "Stimulus-Determinants of 'Shading' Responses." *J Clin Psychol* 13:172–3 Ap '57. * (*PA* 32:2892)

2177. EISNER, BETTY GROVER. *Some Psychological Differences on the Rorschach Between Infertility Patients and Women With Children.* Doctor's thesis, University of California (Los Angeles, Calif.), 1957.

2178. EPSTEIN, SEYMOUR, AND SMITH, RICHARD. "Thematic Apperception, Rorschach Content, and Judgment of Sexual Attractiveness of Women as Related to the Sex Drive in Males." Abstract. *Am Psychol* 12:383 Jl '57. *

2179. EPSTEIN, SEYMOUR; NELSON, JANE V.; AND TANOFSKY, ROBERT. "Responses to Inkblots as Measures of Individual Differences." *J Consult Psychol* 21:211–5 Je '57. *

2180. FLEISCHER, MURRAY S. *Differential Rorschach Configurations of Suicidal Psychiatric Patients: A Psychological Study of Threatened, Attempted, and Successful Suicides.* Doctor's thesis, Yeshiva University (New York, N.Y.), 1957. (*DA* 19:568)

2181. FOWLER, RAYMOND D., JR. *Psychopathology and Social Adequacy: A Rorschach Developmental Study.* Doctor's thesis, Pennsylvania State University (University Park, Pa.), 1957. (*DA* 17:1117)

2182. GRIFFIN, DOROTHY PARK. "Psychometric Scales for the Rorschach Popular Response." *J Clin Psychol* 13:283–7 Jl '57. *

2183. GRUEN, ARNO. "Rorschach: Some Comments on Predicting Structured Behavior From Reactions to Unstructured Stimuli." *J Proj Tech* 21:253–7 S '57. *

2184. HALPERN, HOWARD M. "A Rorschach Interview Technique: Clinical Validation of the Examiner's Hypotheses." *J Proj Tech* 21:10–7 Mr '57. * (*PA* 32:2896)

2185. HAYWARD, LIONEL R. C. "Some Physiological Concomitants of the Rorschach Test." Abstract. *Rorsch Newsl* 2:18–20 Jl '57. *

2186. HERSCH, CHARLES. *The Cognitive Functioning of the Creative Person: A Developmental Analysis by Means of the Rorschach Test.* Doctor's thesis, Clark University (Worcester, Mass.), 1957. (*DA* 18:296)

2187. HOOKER, EVELYN. "The Adjustment of the Male Overt Homosexual." *J Proj Tech* 21:18–31 Mr '57. * (*PA* 32:3083)

2188. JOHNSON, GRANVILLE B., JR. "An Experimental Technique for the Prediction of Teacher Effectiveness." *J Ed Res* 50:679–89 My '57. *

2189. KARSON, SAMUEL, AND POOL, KENNETH BRYNER. "The Abstract Thinking Abilities of Mental Patients." *J Clin Psychol* 13:126–32 Ap '57. * (*PA* 32:3023)

2190. KATAGUCHI, YASUFUMI. "The Development of the Rorschach Test in Japan." *J Proj Tech* 21:258–60 S '57. *

2191. KLINGENSMITH, STANLEY W. "Effects of Different Methods of Structuring the Rorschach Inquiry Upon Determinant Scores." *J Clin Psychol* 13:279–82 Jl '57. *

2192. KLOPFER, BRUNO. "Psychological Variables in Human Cancer." *J Proj Tech* 21:331–40 D '57. *

2193. KORET, SYDNEY, AND RUBIN, ELI Z. "Utilization of Projective Tests as a Prediction of Casework Movement." Discussion by Emily C. Faucett. *Am J Orthopsychiatry* 27:365–76 Ap '57. *

2194. LACY, O. W., AND NASH, DENNISON J. "The American Composer: Implications of Selected Rorschach Responses for Rôle Adjustment." Abstract. *Am Psychol* 12:407 Jl '57. *

2195. LAX, RUTH F. "An Experimental Investigation of the Influence of Color on the Perception of Movement in Ink Blots." *Psychol Newsl* 8:61–75 Ja–F '57. * (*PA* 32:2904)

2196. LEVINE, MURRAY; GLASS, HARVEY; AND MELTZOFF, JULIAN. "The Inhibition Process, Rorschach Human Movement Responses, and Intelligence." *J Consult Psychol* 21:41–5 F '57. * (*PA* 32:496)

2197. LEVITT, EUGENE E. "Alleged Rorschach Anxiety Indices in Children." *J Proj Tech* 21:261–4 S '57. *

2198. LEVY, LEON H., AND KURZ, RONALD B. "The Connotative Impact of Color on the Rorschach and Its Relation to Manifest Anxiety." *J Personality* 25:617–25 S '57. *

2199. MACHOVER, SOLOMON. "Rorschach Study on the Nature and Origin of Common Factors in the Personalities of Parkinsonians." *Psychosom Med* 19:332–8 Jl–Ag '57. *

2200. MALAN, D. H., AND PHILLIPSON, H. "The Psychodynamics of Diagnostic Procedures: A Case Study Reporting the Effects on the Patient of Psychiatric Interview and Rorschach Investigation." *Brit J Med Psychol* 30:92–8 pt 2 '57. *

2201. MARIANI, EUGENE L., AND SHEER, DANIEL E. "Relationships Between Rorschach Test Behavior and Types of Defense." Abstract. *Am Psychol* 12:383–4 Jl '57. *

2202. METRAUX, RHODA, AND ABEL, THEODORA M. "Normal and Deviant Behavior in a Peasant Community: Montserrat,

B.W.I." *Am J Orthopsychiatry* 27:167–84 Ja '57. * (*PA* 32:1510)

2203. MINDESS, HARVEY. "Psychological Indices in the Selection of Student Nurses." *J Proj Tech* 21:37–9 Mr '57. * (*PA* 32:2908)

2204. MONROE, HAROLD JAY. *A Comparative Rorschach Investigation of Functional and Non-Functional Hearing Impairment.* Doctor's thesis, University of Denver (Denver, Colo.), 1957.

2205. MOSS, C. SCOTT. "A Note on the Use of the Schizophrenic in Rorschach Content Analysis." *J Proj Tech* 21:384–90 D '57. *

2206. MURRAY, DAVID C. "An Investigation of the Rorschach White Space Response in an Extratensive Experience Balance as a Measure of Outwardly Directed Opposition." *J Proj Tech* 21:40–6 Mr '57. * (*PA* 32:2910)

2207. MURRAY, DAVID C. "White Space on the Rorschach: Interpretation and Validity." *J Proj Tech* 21:47–53 Mr '57. * (*PA* 32:2911)

2208. PAGE, HORACE A. "Studies in Fantasy—Daydreaming Frequency and Rorschach Scoring Categories." *J Consult Psychol* 21:111–4 Ap '57. *

2209. PALMER, JAMES O. "Some Relationships Between Rorschach's Experience Balance and Rosenzweig's Frustration-Aggression Patterns." *J Proj Tech* 21:137–41 Je '57. *

2210. PATTERSON, C. H. "The Use of Projective Tests in Vocational Counseling." *Ed & Psychol Meas* 17:533–55 w '57. *

2211. PIOTROWSKI, ZYGMUNT A. *Perceptanalysis: A Fundamentally Reworked, Expanded, and Systematized Rorschach Method.* New York: Macmillan Co., 1957. Pp. xix, 505. * (*PA* 32:501)

2212. POPE, BENJAMIN, AND JENSEN, ARTHUR R. "The Rorschach as an Index of Pathological Thinking." *J Proj Tech* 21:54–62 Mr '57. * (*PA* 32:2915)

2213. RABIN, A. I. "Personality Maturity of Kibbutz (Israeli Collective Settlement) and Non-Kibbutz Children as Reflected in Rorschach Findings." *J Proj Tech* 21:148–53 Je '57. *

2214. RADER, GORDON E. "The Prediction of Overt Aggressive Verbal Behavior From Rorschach Content." *J Proj Tech* 21:294–306 S '57. *

2215. RAIFMAN, IRVING. "Rorschach Findings in a Group of Peptic Ulcer Patients and Two Control Groups." *J Proj Tech* 21:307–12 S '57. *

2216. RIESS, ANNELIESE. *A Study of Some Genetic Behavioral Correlates of Human Movement Responses in Children's Rorschach Protocols.* Doctor's thesis, New York University (New York, N.Y.), 1957. (*DA* 18:668)

2217. RIESSMAN, FRANK. "Social Class and Projective Techniques." Abstract. *Am Psychol* 12:412 Jl '57. *

2218. RODGERS, DAVID A. "Sources of Variance in Students' Rorschach Interpretations." *J Proj Tech* 21:63–8 Mr '57. * (*PA* 32:2919)

2219. SACKS, JOSEPH M., AND COHEN, MURRAY L. "Contributions of the Rorschach Test to the Understanding of 'Acting-Out' Behavior." *J Nerv & Mental Dis* 125:133–6 Ja–Mr '57.

2220. SASLOW, HARRY L., AND SHIPMAN, WILLIAM G. "The Tendency of the Dörken and Kral Brain Damage Measure to Score False Positives." Abstract. *J Consult Psychol* 21:434 O '57. *

2221. SCHWARTZ, FRED, AND KATES, SOLIS L. "Behn-Rorschach and Rorschach Under Standard and Stress Conditions." *J Consult Psychol* 21:335–8 Ag '57. *

2222. SCHWARTZ, FRED, AND KATES, SOLIS L. "Rorschach Performance, Anxiety Level, and Stress." *J Proj Tech* 21:154–60 Je '57. *

2223. SCOTT, EDWARD M., AND DOUGLAS, FREDERICK. "A Comparison of Rorschach and Howard Tests on a Schizophrenic Population." *J Clin Psychol* 13:79–81 Ja '57. *

2224. SETZE, LEONARD A.; SETZE, KATUSHA DIDENKO; BALDWIN, JOAN C.; DOYLE, CHARLES I.; AND KOBLER, FRANK J. "A Rorschach Experiment With Six, Seven, and Eight Year Old Children." *J Proj Tech* 21:166–71 Je '57. *

2225. SHAH, SALEEM ALAN. "Use of the Inspection Rorschach Technique in Analyzing Missionary Success and Failure." *J Proj Tech* 21:69–72 Mr '57. * (*PA* 32:2920)

2226. SHAW, MERVILLE C., AND CRUICKSHANK, WILLIAM M. "The Rorschach Performance of Epileptic Children." *J Consult Psychol* 21:422–4 O '57. *

2227. SHIPMAN, WILLIAM G. "The Generality of Scope and Differentiation Responses to the Rorschach." *J Proj Tech* 21:185–8 Je '57. *

2228. SILVER, IRVING HERMAN. *Attitudes Toward the Self and Others of a Group of Psychoanalysands: A Determination of the Relationship Between Attitudes Toward Self and Toward Others and Human and Human-Like Responses on the Rorschach.* Doctor's thesis, New York University (New York, N.Y.), 1957. (*DA* 17:1815)

2229. SINGER, ROLAND H. *Various Aspects of Human Figure Drawings as a Personality Measure With Hospitalized Psychiatric Patients.* Doctor's thesis, Pennsylvania State University (University Park, Pa.), 1957. (*DA* 18:290)

2230. SOHLER, DOROTHY TERRY; HOLZBERG, JULES D.; FLECK, STEPHEN; CORNELISON, ALICE R.; KAY, ELEANOR; AND LIDZ, THEODORE. "The Prediction of Family Interaction From a Battery of Projective Techniques." *J Proj Tech* 21:199–208 Je '57. *

2231. SOMMER, ROBERT. "Rorschach Animal Responses and Intelligence." *J Consult Psychol* 21:358 Ag '5'. *

2232. STANFORD, MARGARET J. *A Rorschach Study of the Personality Structure of a Group of Eight Year Old Children.* Doctor's thesis, Claremont College (Claremont, Calif.), 1957.

2233. STOTSKY, BERNARD A. "Factor Analysis of Rorschach Scores of Schizophrenics." *J Clin Psychol* 13:275–8 Jl '57. *

2234. SWARTZ, MELVIN B. "The Role of Color in Influencing Responses to the Rorschach Test." Abstract. *Am Psychol* 12:383 Jl '57. *

2235. SYME, LEONARD. "Personality Characteristics and the Alcoholic: A Critique of Current Studies." *Q J Studies Alcohol* 18:288–302 Je '57. *

2236. THALER, MARGARET; WEINER, HERBERT; AND REISER, MORTON F. "Exploration of the Doctor-Patient Relationship Through Projective Techniques: Their Use in Psychosomatic Illness." *Psychosom Med* 14:228–30 My–Je '57. *

2237. TOLOR, ALEXANDER. "The Stability of Tree Drawings as Related to Several Rorschach Signs of Rigidity." *J Clin Psychol* 13:162–4 Ap '57. * (*PA* 32:2924)

2238. WATKINS, CHARLES, AND DEABLER, HERDIS L. "Responses of Chronic Schizophrenic Patients to Tachistoscopic Presentation of Rorschach Figures." *J Proj Tech* 21:404–9 D '57. *

2239. WELLS, STEPHEN. *The Relationships Between Real and Apparent Movement and Rorschach Form Perception.* Doctor's thesis, Syracuse University (Syracuse, N.Y.), 1957. (*DA* 17:1817)

2240. WERTHEIMER, MICHAEL. "Perception and the Rorschach." *J Proj Tech* 21:209–16 Je '57. *

2241. WERTHEIMER, RITA A. "Relationships Between Specific Rorschach Variables and Sociometric Data." *J Proj Tech* 21:94–7 Mr '57. * (*PA* 32:2932)

2242. WILLIAMS, CECELIA. "Differential Diagnosis in Elderly Patients Showing Depressive and Other Symptoms." Abstract. *Rorsch Newsl* 2:14–7 Jl '57. *

2243. WILLIAMS, ROBERT J., AND MACHI, VINCENT S. "An Analysis of Interperson Correlations Among Thirty Psychotics." *J Abn & Social Psychol* 55:50–7 Jl '57. *

2244. WISE, FRED. *Effects of Chronic and Stress-Induced Anxiety on Rorschach Determinants.* Doctor's thesis, Columbia University (New York, N.Y.), 1957. (*DA* 17:1603)

2245. WOHL, JULIAN. "A Note on the Generality of Constriction." *J Proj Tech* 21:410–3 D '57. *

2246. WOLF, IRVING. "Hostile Acting Out and Rorschach Test Content." *J Proj Tech* 21:414–9 D '57. *

2247. WYSOCKI, BOLESLAW A. "Assessment of Intelligence Level by the Rorschach Test as Compared With Objective Tests." *J Ed Psychol* 48:113–7 F '57. *

2248. WYSOCKI, BOLESLAW A. "Differentiation Between Introvert-Extravert Types by Rorschach Method as Compared with Other Methods." *J Psychol* 43:41–6 Ja '57. *

2249. ALTMAN, CHARLOTTE H. "Relationships Between Maternal Attitudes and Child Personality Structure." *Am J Orthopsychiatry* 28:160–9 Ja '58. *

2250. ALTUS, WILLIAM D. "Group Rorschach and Q-L Discrepancies on the ACE." *Psychol Rep* 4:469 S '58. *

2251. BAUGHMAN, E. EARL. "The Role of the Stimulus in Rorschach Responses." *Psychol B* 55:121–47 My '58. *

2252. BAUGHMAN, E. EARL, AND GUSKIN, SAMUEL. "Sex Differences on the Rorschach." *J Consult Psychol* 22:400–1 O '58. *

2253. BIERI, JAMES; BRADBURN, WENDY M.; AND GALINSKY, M. DAVID. "Sex Differences in Perceptual Behavior." *J Personality* 26:1–12 Mr '58. *

2254. BLANK, LEONARD. "Suggestions for Research With Projective Techniques." *J Proj Tech* 22:263–6 S '58. *

2255. BROOKS, MARJORIE O., AND PHILLIPS, LESLIE. "The Cognitive Significance of Rorschach Developmental Scores." *J Personality* 26:268–90 Je '58. *

2256. CARTWRIGHT, ROSALIND DYMOND. "Predicting Response to Client-Centered Therapy With the Rorschach PR Scale." Comment by W. U. Snyder. *J Counsel Psychol* 5:11–7 sp '58. *

2257. CLARK, SELBY G. "The Rorschach and Academic Achievement." *Personnel & Guid J* 36:339–41 Ja '58. *

2258. COSTELLO, C. G. "The Rorschach Records of Suicidal Patients: An Application of a Comparative Matching Technique." *J Proj Tech* 22:272–5 S '58. *

2259. DOOB, LEONARD W. "The Use of Different Test Items in Nonliterate Societies." *Public Opinion Q* 21:499–504 w 57–58 ['58]. *

2260. ELKINS, ELISE. "The Diagnostic Validity of the Ames 'Danger Signals.'" *J Consult Psychol* 22:281–7 Ag '58. *

2261. FRIEDMAN, IRA. "A Critique of Shneidman and Farberow's 'TAT Heroes of Suicidal and Non-Suicidal Subjects.'" *J Proj Tech* 22:281–3 S '58. *

2262. FRIES, MARGARET E. "Psychoanalytic Concepts and Principles Discernible in Projective Personality Tests: Workshop, 1956: 4, Application of Psychoanalytic Principles to the Rorschach Perceptanalysis in a Longitudinal Study." *Am J Orthopsychiatry* 28:61–6 Ja '58. *

2263. GRIFFIN, DOROTHY PARK. "Movement Responses and Creativity." *J Consult Psychol* 22:134–6 Ap '58. *

2264. HAFNER, A. JACK. "Response Time and Rorschach Behavior." *J Clin Psychol* 14:154–5 Ap '58. *

2265. HAMLIN, ROY M., AND POWERS, WILLIAM T. "Judging Rorschach Responses: An Illustrative Protocol." *J Clin Psychol* 14:240–2 Jl '58. *

2266. HOOKER, EVELYN. "Male Homosexuality in the Rorschach." *J Proj Tech* 22:33–54 Mr '58. *

2267. HOWARD, L. R. C., AND MARSZALEK, K. "The Munroe Check List: A Note on Its Validity in Clinical Research." *J Mental Sci* 104:483–4 Ap '58. *

2268. JOHNSON, LAVERNE C. "Rorschach Concept Evaluation Test as a Diagnostic Tool." *J Consult Psychol* 22:129–33 Ap '58. *

2269. KAGAN, JEROME; SONTAG, LESTER W.; BAKER, CHARLES T.; AND NELSON, VIRGINIA L. "Personality and IQ Change." *J Abn & Social Psychol* 56:261–6 Mr '58. *

2270. KATES, SOLIS L., AND SCHWARTZ, FRED. "Stress, Anxiety and Response Complexity on the Rorschach Test." *J Proj Tech* 22:64–9 Mr '58. *

2271. LAIR, CHARLES V. "Empathy and Its Relation to Stimulus Meaning." *J Clin Psychol* 14:175–7 Ap '58. *

2272. LANDISBERG, SELMA. "Relationship of the Rorschach to Projective Drawings," pp. 613–9. In *The Clinical Application of Projective Techniques.* Edited by Emanuel F. Hammer. Springfield, Ill.: Charles C Thomas, 1958. Pp. xxii, 663. *

2273. LEVY, EDWIN. "Stimulus-Values of Rorschach Cards for Children." *J Proj Tech* 22:293–6 S '58. *

2274. LIPTON, HERBERT; KADEN, STANLEY; AND PHILLIPS, LESLIE. "Rorschach Scores and Decontextualization: A Developmental View." *J Personality* 26:291–302 Je '58. *

2275. LOTSOF, ERWIN J.; COMREY, ANDREW; BOGARTZ, W.; AND ARNSFIELD, P. "A Factor Analysis of the WISC and Rorschach." *J Proj Tech* 22:297–301 S '58. *

2276. MATARAZZO, RUTH G.; MATARAZZO, JOSEPH D.; SASLOW, GEORGE; AND PHILLIPS, JEANNE S. "Psychological Test and Organismic Correlates of Interview Interaction Patterns." *J Abn & Social Psychol* 56:329–38 My '58. *

2277. MOLISH, HERMAN B., AND BECK, SAMUEL J. "Psychoanalytic Concepts and Principles Discernible in Projective Personality Tests: Workshop, 1956: 3, Mechanisms of Defense in Schizophrenic Reaction Types as Evaluated by the Rorschach Test." *Am J Orthopsychiatry* 28:47–60 Ja '58. *

2278. MURPHY, MARY MARTHA. "Utilization of O'Reilly's Objective Rorschach as a Screening Test for State Colony Job Applicants." *J Clin Psychol* 14:65–7 Ja '58. *

2279. MYERS, ROBERT L. *An Analysis of Sex Differences in Verbalizations and Content of Responses to the Rorschach and to the Thematic Apperception Test.* Doctor's thesis, Temple University (Philadelphia, Pa.), 1958. (*DA* 19:365)

2280. NEUHAUS, EDMUND C. "A Personality Study of Asthmatic and Cardiac Children." *Psychosom Med* 20:181–6 My–Je '58. *

2281. OKARSKI, JOSEPH F. "Consistency of Projective Movement Responses." *Psychol Monogr* 72(6):1–26 '58. *

2282. PIOTROWSKI, ZYGMUNT A. "Psychoanalytic Concepts and Principles Discernible in Projective Personality Tests: Workshop, 1956: 1, Freud's Psychoanalysis and Rorschach's Perceptanalysis." *Am J Orthopsychiatry* 28:36–41 Ja '58. *

2283. POWERS, WILLIAM T., AND HAMLIN, ROY M. "A Comparative Analysis of Deviant Rorschach Response Characteristics." *J Consult Psychol* 22:123–8 Ap '58. *

2284. PURCELL, KENNETH. "Some Shortcomings in Projective Test Validation." *J Abn & Social Psychol* 57:115–8 Jl '58. *

2285. RICHARDS, T. W. "Personal Significance of Rorschach Figures." *J Proj Tech* 22:97–101 Mr '58. *

2286. RICHARDS, T. W., AND MURRAY, DAVID C. "Global Evaluation of Rorschach Performance Versus Scores: Sex Differences in Rorschach Performance." *J Clin Psychol* 14:61–4 Ja '58. *

2287. RUESS, AUBREY L. "Some Cultural and Personality Aspects of Mental Retardation." *Am J Mental Def* 63:50–9 Jl '58. *

2288. SARASON, SEYMOUR B.; DAVIDSON, KENNETH; LIGHTHALL, FREDERICK; AND WAITE, RICHARD. "Rorschach Behavior and Performance of High and Low Anxious Children." *Child Develop* 29:277–85 Je '58. *

2289. SCOTT, EDWARD M. "A Comparison of Rorschach and Howard Ink Blot Tests on a Schizophrenic Population From a Content Point of View." *J Clin Psychol* 14:156–7 Ap '58. *

2290. SHATIN, LEO. "The Constriction-Dilation Dimension in Rorschach and TAT." *J Clin Psychol* 14:150–4 Ap '58. *

2291. SOMMER, ROBERT. "Rorschach M Responses and Intelligence." *J Clin Psychol* 14:58–61 Ja '58. *

2292. SOMMER, ROBERT, AND SOMMER, DOROTHY TWENTE. "Assaultiveness and Two Types of Rorschach Color Responses." *J Consult Psychol* 22:57–62 F '58. *

2293. SOPCHAK, ANDREW L. "Prediction of College Performance by Commonly Used Tests." *J Clin Psychol* 14:194–7 Ap '58. *

2294. TAULBEE, EARL S. "Relationship Between Certain Personality Variables and Continuation in Psychotherapy." *J Consult Psychol* 22:83–9 Ap '58. *

2295. TRIER, THOMAS R. "Vocabulary as a Basis for Estimating Intelligence From the Rorschach." *J Consult Psychol* 22:289–91 Ag '58. *

2296. WEISS, A. A. "Alternating Two-Day Cyclic Behavior Changes." *J Clin Psychol* 14:433–7 O '58. *

2297. WINTER, WILLIAM D., AND SALCINES, RAMON A. "The Validity of the Objective Rorschach and the MMPI." *J Consult Psychol* 22:199–202 Je '58. *

SAMUEL J. BECK, *Professorial Lecturer in Psychology and Psychiatry, University of Chicago and Michael Reese Hospital, Chicago, Illinois.*

To Rorschach? or not to Rorschach? The newcomer to this much debated instrument finds himself before a many-portaled quandary. Not one but several tests confront him and all bear the name Rorschach. Avid for solution of that complex riddle, the human personality, by which door shall the neophyte enter? Let us first consider the test as published by Rorschach.

His intent and his effort were empiric, experimental, and with a regard for statistics. He explicitly so states in his monograph (*285*), and in its subtitle he uses the term "experiment in perception." To test out some of his concepts, he actually did some experimenting. As a control, e.g., on the strong role played by color in the responses of epileptics, he prepared three pictures, as follows: a cat in the colors of a tree-frog; a squirrel in those of a cock; and a frog in those of a chaffinch. He describes another experiment by which he tested out his movement determinant.

Rorschach's closest co-worker and the man who took the leadership in establishing the test's clinical worth following Rorschach's untimely death—at age 37—was Oberholzer. He adhered to Rorschach's method, without deviation. Beck studied the test with Oberholzer in Zürich from March through October 1934, and has adhered to the Rorschach-Oberholzer orientation—with deviations. They are few. He has stayed, in the main, within the Rorschach-Oberholzer orientation. Closely working with Beck for many years, Molish has been utilizing his procedures and has been among the keenest exponents in solidifying the foundations for purpose of clinical interpretation. The literature has come to refer to these procedures as the "Beck system." This is a misnomer on two counts. It is not Beck's, and it is not a system. It is the Rorschach-Oberholzer nuclear test. And it has not the closed finality of a system. The procedure constantly watches for new evidence, as clinically validated, that throws light on the associations and that dictates changes in the norms and other spheres of reference whereby it guides itself. It is thus a living tool, altering in accordance with empiric evidence.

Striking out in radical independence from Rorschach's course, Klopfer has developed his "Rorschach technique." Klopfer's orientation is phenomenalist (*2063*) and as such departs

from a behavioral-empiricist approach. It is explicitly nonstatistical. The details selected by an examiner are "the result of the phenomenological analysis of the blot properties....and are, therefore, conceptually defined dimensions rather than statistically defined categories." As the reviewer sees the technique, it frees each examiner to use his own subjective judgment in processing the associations. His critique of its method, its logic, and the errors inherent therein are stated more fully elsewhere.[1] Except for the use of Rorschach's inkblot figures and some of his letter symbols, the technique has now so little in common with Rorschach's test, either in method or in some important basic presuppositions, that it represents a quite different approach. Critics of the test, however, make no distinction in their sharp, sometimes phobic, reactions to anything with the name "Rorschach" in its title. It would go far towards clearing up the present state of confusion if Klopfer and his associates ceased to identify their method by the term "Rorschach." Their technique is widely used and gives satisfying results to many clinicians. Some implications from Rorschach's thinking are no doubt comfortable in a phenomenalist bed. But it is a basic error to treat phenomenalist data as though they were behavioristic, an issue which Snygg clearly states.[2] And American psychologists, being behaviorists by training, too frequently commit just that error with their Rorschach data. What a resolution it would be of the present perplexity and confusion, both for users of the test and its critics, if the test and the technique were unmistakably distinguished not only in fact but also in name.

Before the unresolved problems of validation are considered, comment is in order concerning other schools of thought in the Rorschach test field. Hertz keeps close to structure and follows the rationale published by Rorschach, with modifications incident to her own slants. Statistics has always been a right hand to her, but she leans heavily on nomothetic method. Any research in objects of organized complexity, such as we humans are, must, after the nomothetic parameters have been set up, take the next step, to idiography. On the subject of statistics in a datum of organized complexity, see Weaver;[3]

and on its application to the Rorschach test, a paper by the reviewer (1844).

For ideas that are most original and intriguing, the newcomer should seek out Piotrowski (2211). His orientation rests soundly on the clinical observation with which he tests out his results, and the foundation stones of Rorschach's thinking on which he has built. He appears to believe in signs, however. He undertakes to depart from the "master's footsteps," but with filial loyalty he expects that his effort will really redound to the good of Rorschach's experiment. But he goes to the extreme of seeing the test as a "new science," a proposal which the reviewer fears is producing restless stirrings in its inventor's bones. Nothing in the *Psychodiagnostik*—and Piotrowski is well acquainted with it—warrants the suggestion that Rorschach had any intent other than to work within the canons of established science, experimental and psychonanalytic. Nor is it necessary to tread beyond these confines in order to use the test and its logic. Then, too, Piotrowski indulges in a bit of romanticizing when he interprets some responses within the framework of the laws of motion as in physics. All of which is too bad, since Piotrowski is one of our most reliable workers with the test. The seduction of the imagination is here carrying him to ethereal heights. For a thorough and just evaluation of Piotrowski and his "Perceptanalysis," the designation under which he subsumes his thinking, see Molish.[4]

Investigators well grounded in psychoanalytic theory will find themselves at home in Schafer's approach (1787). He emphasizes the thematic content in the associations and its significance when interpreted in accordance with psychoanalytic knowledge. He does not disregard structure, but it carries less weight in his exposition. Phillips and Smith (1588) also lean heavily on content, also as seen within the psychoanalytic frame of reference. Their interpretations appear to be, in instances, extravagant, too far removed from the evidence in their texts. They do, however, stay close to Rorschach's fundamental principles of structure with keen, fresh suggestions for exploiting the potential in them for objectivity. Sarason (1786) makes a salutary contribution in accenting the interaction between examiner and patient as affecting a test production and the ob-

1 BECK, SAMUEL J. "Statistics and the Rorschach." Book review. *Cont Psychol* 2:253–4 O '57. *
2 SNYGG, DONALD. "The Need for a Phenomenological System of Psychology." *Psychol R* 48:404–24 '41.
3 WEAVER, WARREN. "Science and Complexity." *Am Scientist* 36:536–44 O '48. *

4 MOLISH, HERMAN B. "Can a Science Emerge From Rorschach's Test?" Book review. *Cont Psychol* 3:189–92 Jl '58. *

tained results (a topic also preoccupying Schafer). This arrests the examiner's attention on his own role in the total testing process and on the need for sifting out the subjective factors which can weight heavily against validity of findings.

In the problem of validation, the confusions generated by the incompatible orientations have been long compounded by the drag on statistical thinking in psychology. This has attempted to statisticize what is probably the most complex datum in nature—the human personality—by techniques devised for what are problems of simplicity and of "disorganized complexity" (Weaver). All sorts of results have come out that have made no sense, either to the strict experimentalist or to the Rorschach test investigator. Let it be said at once and unequivocally that validation such as is sought in a laboratory experiment is not at present to be expected for whole personality findings, whether by the Rorschach test or by any other. We do not know what variables may be complicating the person's behavior and are not being reached by our available tests. Then there are the interactions of forces within the personality, interactions which play a major role in shaping the man or woman as known by others. Experimental psychology must first devise a non-Rorschach technique appropriate to test out the test's concepts, derived as these are from clinical concepts.

But how soundly based in established clinical knowledge concerning human beings are these Rorschach test principles? This is the area proper for validation of the Rorschach test. The measure of validity must be limited to indicating a *direction*. It cannot be a number such as a correlation or other coefficient. It must be a statement of a direction of the psychologic trend or process, a direction away from some one known personality group as point of reference. The patient before us is more (or less) intelligent than, more (or less) excitable than, more (or less) depressed than, more (or less) imaginative than, more (or less) self-controlled than a representative sample of our normative group. The frame of reference which the reviewer uses is the normal (*sic*) adult. One can choose any other—the feeble-minded, the schizophrenic, or the depressed. Let him only find, by statistical means, his norms for these, and use them as points of departure. The norms referred to are those for the Rorschach test variables. Rorschach arrived at

certain conclusions concerning the general psychologic significances (e.g., the color determinant as evidence of lively feeling; F+, accurate perception; and others). These conclusions require unremitting testing out. But they are problems of general psychology, and hence this validating job goes to the experimentalist. The validation of the whole characterological picture, whether described in clinical or other terms, must be done by extra-Rorschach data. After the person has been described strictly from the Rorschach test, i.e., "blind" findings, his description is compared with one obtained by another method of observation. The amount of agreement, i.e., the validity of the test, can thus be judged.

One of the abuses of the test originates in the use of cues from nontest sources to produce some of the "amazing" diagnoses which have been excitedly reported. Thus, in its earlier years, the test was uncritically applied and interpreted by methods that were little more than a speaking with tongues. The test was set to do a task for which it was not intended—that of being the final if not the sole diagnostic approach to a mental ill. As an aid towards diagnosis it can greatly facilitate the observer's task, more quickly uncover the likely major reaction patterns, eliminate false scents, and suggest hypotheses as to the depth of and the dynamics in the patient's illness. But it is always an aid to, not a substitute for, clinical diagnosis.

Another pitfall has been that of using it practically before the necessary research has been carried on for the problem presented by the personality group in question. Thus the general principles concerning the test, known from its use in, say, the neuroses, will be applied in attempting to diagnose for brain damage or for the dynamics in stuttering; or perhaps to etch some personality structure in which an industrial plant is interested, such as that of a foreman or of an executive. The empiric research must always first establish the personality pattern, in whatever group. Another principal abuse has been the aura of infallibility which some examiners generate around the test, together with the complementary readiness of their working colleagues to accept the findings. Actually, any conclusions arrived at from the test, whether in regard to separate traits in the person or the whole picture, must be looked on not as facts but as hypotheses, questions which the test asks about that person and which the

subsequent investigation is still to verify. Whatever the length and variety of one's experience, he will still make errors. Some 20 years ago this writer stated the criteria which he then considered essential to a soundly trained user of the test (*110*). These criteria still hold. They are: (*a*) broad general experience in psychopathology; (*b*) understanding of psychoanalytic theory; (*c*) use of the test in many clinical groups; (*d*) orientation in the Rorschach-Oberholzer tradition; and (*e*) a foundation in experimental psychology.

But where is the newcomer in the field to obtain this equipment? One looks first, and naturally, to the universities. The reaction to this look is a mixed one. Such information as is available indicates an extremely wide variation in the numbers of courses and hours of teaching which they provide, and in the competence of the instructors, the especial deficit being their lack of clinical sophistication. More disturbing, the reviewer detects in the universities what he can look on only as unresolved ambivalence towards the test. They seem uncertain of whether to teach it and afraid not to teach it. Behind their uncertainty are the difficulties, above noted, involved in immersing it into the laboratory's crucible. Behind their fear is its increasingly wide use throughout the United States and Europe, and their recognition of the aid that it can be as a tool in personality study. The spread is much broader than in the clinical fields of psychiatry and psychology. It includes anthropology, sociology with especial reference to delinquency, education, business, and industry, and the military services, with a scattering of interest in remoter fields e.g., forensic psychiatry and art. While the more significant clinical research must of necessity be carried on in hospitals, the basic researches are properly the tasks of the universities. Centers which can combine the two teaching resources, the clinic and the academic experimental laboratory, must provide the setups most likely to train the young student in a sound use of the test.

H. J. EYSENCK, *Professor of Psychology, Institute of Psychiatry, University of London, London, England.*

There are several difficulties in reviewing this test. The number of investigations using it must be in the thousands, and the reviewer cannot claim to have read more than a reasonably large fraction of these. Different investigators use the test in different ways and interpret it according to widely differing principles; this makes comparison of findings difficult, particularly as these principles are not always stated in detail. Statistical treatment of the data is not only frequently, but almost invariably faulty to an extent which makes interpretation impossible. Usually the statistical details given are not sufficient to recalculate the appropriate significance values. As Cronbach has pointed out in a detailed and competent analysis of the issues involved: "Perhaps ninety per cent of the conclusions so far published as a result of statistical Rorschach studies are unsubstantiated—not necessarily false, but based on unsound analysis" (*795*).

The greatest difficulty of all, however, is a lack of agreement among psychologists on a frame of reference and on the appropriate criteria for judging a test such as the Rorschach. Clinical psychologists claim that personal experience, favourable comments by users of test reports such as psychiatrists, and a general feeling of clinical usefulness are sufficient to outweigh any negative results achieved along more experimental lines, and suffice to establish the validity of the Rorschach. Experimental psychologists and psychometricians argue that, on the contrary, subjective considerations of the kind mentioned are irrelevant and only serve to establish the claims of the test to be worthy of experimental validation. They point out that many fallacious procedures have in the past received such "clinical" support—phrenology is one obvious example—and maintain that the same experimental and statistical rigour required in the verification of deductions in learning theory is necessary in the validation of Rorschach postulates also. The present review is written on the basis of this latter point of view.

The writer has recently reviewed [1] the literature of the last five years with respect to the validity of the Rorschach in its various applications and has summarised his results in a set of 10 conclusions which run as follows:

1. There is no consistent meaningful and testable theory underlying modern projective devices.
2. The actual practice of projective experts frequently contradicts the putative hypotheses on which their tests are built.
3. On the empirical level, there is no indisputable evidence showing any kind of marked relationship be-

[1] EYSENCK, H. J. "Personality Tests: 1950–55," pp. 118–59. In *Recent Progress in Psychology, Vol. 3.* Edited by G. W. T. H. Fleming. London: J. & A. Churchill, Ltd., 1959. Pp. 397.

tween global projective test interpretation by experts, and psychiatric diagnosis.

4. There is no evidence of any marked relationship between Rorschach scoring categories combined in any approved statistical fashion into a scale, and diagnostic category, when the association between the two is tested on a population other than that from which the scale was derived.

5. There is no evidence of any marked relationship between global or statistically derived projective test scores and outcome of psychotherapy.

6. There is no evidence for the great majority of the postulated relationships between projective test indicators and personality traits.

7. There is no evidence for any marked relationship between projective test indicators of any kind and intellectual qualities and abilities as measured, estimated, or rated independently.

8. There is no evidence for the predictive power of projective techniques with respect to success or failure in a wide variety of fields where personality qualities play an important part.

9. There is no evidence that conscious or unconscious conflicts, attitudes, fears, or fantasies in patients can be diagnosed by means of projective techniques in such a way as to give congruent results with assessments made by psychiatrists independently.

10. There is ample evidence to show that the great majority of studies in the field of projective techniques are inadequately designed, have serious statistical errors in the analysis of the data, and/or are subject to damaging criticisms on the grounds of contamination between test and criterion.

These conclusions are not in principle different from those obtained by other reviewers; thus Cronbach [1] has stated, "The test has repeatedly failed as a predictor of practical criteria. * There is nothing in the literature to encourage reliance on Rorschach interpretations." Similarly, Payne [2] came to the conclusions that "there is no evidence that the test is of any practical use at the moment, either for describing personality or for predicting behaviour" and "there is no evidence that the Rorschach can be used to assess whether or not individuals are well or poorly adjusted." In addition to the damning evidence regarding the validity of the Rorschach, it should perhaps also be pointed out that studies of the reliabilities of different Rorschach scores have shown these to be very low indeed. On all the usual criteria, therefore, it must be concluded that the Rorschach has failed to establish its scientific or practical value. This is becoming more widely recognised, largely as a consequence of the improved standard of Rorschach research in recent years, which has given rise to many well controlled and well analysed studies, the results of which

1 Cronbach, Lee J. "Assessment of Individual Differences," pp. 173–96. In *Annual Review of Psychology, Vol. 7.* Stanford, Calif.: Annual Reviews, 1956. Pp. x, 448. *
2 Payne, R. W. "L'utilité du test de Rorschach en psychologie clinique." *Revue de Psychologie Appliquée* 5:255–64 '55. (*PA* 31:1062)

have been uniformly negative. As a consequence many of the best known training institutions have dropped the Rorschach, while others are keeping it on only because of continued psychiatric demand.

How can the unfavourable judgment given above be reconciled with the many positive findings reported in the literature? The answer is very simply that positive findings are usually achieved in investigations which do not control adequately certain well known sources of error. Some of these errors arise through contamination; Rorschach report and diagnosis or other criterion are not derived separately but are allowed to influence each other directly or indirectly. Other methodological errors involve a failure to test findings from one population on another; this failure of cross validation leads to many positive findings which are later on negatived by other investigators using different populations or subjects. Statistical errors, as already pointed out, are frequent and give an appearance of validity and significance to data which are quite insignificant. Some investigators will compare two or more populations with respect to anything up to several hundred Rorschach scores and claim significance for a few of these which exceed the usual 5 per cent level. Such a procedure ignores the fact that out of so many comparisons you would expect a few to appear statistically significant by chance alone. In the review mentioned above, the writer has shown that quite a high correlation exists between the methodological and statistical excellence of validation studies and their negative outcome, thus supporting the belief that most of the alleged verifications of Rorschach hypotheses are achieved only through the admission of uncontrolled sources of error.

We may add to the empirical demonstration of the uselessness of the Rorschach theoretical consideration. It is claimed in favour of the Rorschach that it measures the whole personality rather than any particular aspect of it. This differentiates it sharply from scientific measuring instruments which are constructed specifically to measure one clearly identifiable attribute of reality at a time. No physicist would entertain for one minute the claims of a device said to measure the whole universe in all its salient aspects; in line with scientific tradition he relies on measuring instruments which are more restricted in their function. It may be surmised that several such restricted measuring instru-

ments could be constructed to test theories embodied in the Rorschach, and it is not impossible that these theories might in fact be verified. By putting all his eggs in one basket as it were, the Rorschach expert makes certain that none of his hypotheses can in fact be verified because none can be tested along the orthodox lines of scientific practice.

RAYMOND J. McCALL, *Professor of Psychology and Chairman of the Department, Marquette University, Milwaukee, Wisconsin.*[1]

PRESENT STATUS OF THE RORSCHACH. Despite several recent faith-shaking reports, the Rorschach remains the most widely used clinical test for the assessment of personality. It is also probably the method on which the opinions of clinicians and psychometricians are most sharply divided. Its partisans have claimed for it an almost clairvoyant power of revealing the inner structure of motive and emotion, while its more determined critics have regarded it as a fragment of clinical liturgy, having low reliability and little validity, that is worthless as a research instrument. Still, the vast majority of those who have used the test clinically are convinced that it has some objective value, particularly in the assessment of abnormality, although the metrically sophisticated among them acknowledge that careful studies have generally failed to support the claims of Rorschach enthusiasts. What controlled research has indicated at best, they say, is a qualified and limited validity which provides small basis for clinical punditry.

DESCRIPTION AND HISTORY. The material of the test is 10 symmetrical inkblots—5 in gray-black against a white ground, 2 adding a brilliant scarlet, and 3 substituting a variety of pastel shades for the gray-black. Its originator was Hermann Rorschach, a German-Swiss psychiatrist of great enterprise and invention. After several years (mostly in the period 1916–1919) of experimenting with inkblots as a diagnostic aid to the classification of patients in a public mental hospital, Rorschach became convinced that the method could be extended to the exploration of normal personality. Though he referred to his work as an "experiment" and maintained that all of its results were predominantly empirical and without theoretical foundation, he did not mean "experiment" in the

1 The reviewer is indebted to Dolores Janecky of the Milwaukee County Guidance Clinic for bibliographic assistance and to the Research Committee of Marquette University for a supporting grant.

sense of controlled observation; his mode of reasoning was actually more analytico-intuitive than inductive, and, despite the disclaimer, appears to have involved many theoretical assumptions derived from Bleulerian associationism, constitutionally oriented psychiatry, and the like. Moreover, while pointing to the need for further work with "standardized parallel series of plates and appropriate control experiments," Rorschach did not hesitate at times to make generalizations that sound anything but tentative, and to treat his limited sample as though representative of mental patients and normals generally. He felt quite sure apparently that the method laid bare the individual's "affective dynamics" and the balance of introversive and "extratensive" tendencies, and provided an intelligence test almost completely independent of previous knowledge, practice, and education. Less than a year after the publication of the *Psychodiagnostik* (1921) in which his "experiment" was described and these views set forth, Rorschach's brilliant career was cut short by his death at 37 years of age.

Though Rorschach was by no means the first to look upon responses to inkblots as revelatory of individual differences, his emphasis upon the sensitivity of the individual to certain perceptual qualities in the blots themselves (the "determinants") as the key to understanding the personality structure was indeed unique. Da Vinci and Botticelli in the 15th century had regarded ink splotches as appropriate stimuli to the painter's imagination, and Binet in the 19th century had included responses to inkblots on his intelligence scales as measures of imaginativeness. Somewhat similar uses were advocated and furthered by Dearborn and Whipple before 1910. Rorschach was probably unaware of these studies, but he pointedly cites the work of Szymon Hens (published in 1917) on similar blots as having influenced his own efforts. He adds, however, that Hens' work was "incomplete," because it was concerned only with the *content* of the interpretations and did not go beyond imagination as the source of differences. His own distinctive contribution, Rorschach felt, was in stressing the *perceptual* features of the task and in his insistence that the *formal determinants* of perception (such as color, shape, and portion of the blot responded to) revealed more of the deeper personality than did the associative content of the responses.

The appreciation of Rorschach's work was

greatly furthered by his friend, the psycho-analyst Emil Oberholzer, who edited for post-humous publication Rorschach's last paper, in which the important categories of shading and popularity were introduced. Nevertheless, the Rorschach technique was not widely accepted in European university circles in the 1920's and received only minor attention in the German-speaking world outside Switzerland. With the introduction of the test into this country and the arrival here in the 1930's of a group of ex-patriate psychologists from Germany, the situation was radically changed. Psychiatrist David Levy played an important role in this new birth of interest largely by way of his influence on Samuel J. Beck, who wrote the first doctoral dissertation on the Rorschach in this country (Columbia, 1932) and journeyed to Switzerland to study under Oberholzer. Most influential of the refugee scholars was Bruno Klopfer, who inaugurated the *Rorschach Research Exchange* (later the *Journal of Projective Techniques*) in 1936. By the mid-1930's such well known clinical specialists as Hertz and Piotrowski, in addition to Klopfer and Beck, were publishing regularly on the Rorschach. The interest of the measurement-minded was not slow to follow. In the mid-30's P. E. Vernon wrote a number of psychometrically oriented articles on the Rorschach, and prior to World War II Zubin had devised his psychometric scales for rating Rorschach responses.

It was the emergence of clinical psychology as a profession during and after the war, however, that gave the Rorschach its greatest impetus. To many clinicians, bored and irritated with the conception of the psychologist as an intelligence tester, competence in the Rorschach became a symbol of expertise in clinical diagnosis. Here was promised a means by which the psychologist could supplement, confirm, and even correct the assessment arising out of the psychiatric examination. Many psychiatrists, moreover, came to respect and depend upon this supplementation, if few sought themselves to become expert in the method.

Among psychologists, it is the clinicians, rather than the psychometricians, who are responsible for the widespread popularity of the method and who have chiefly determined the direction which its development in this country has taken. Psychometrically oriented researchers like Vernon and Burt in England and Guilford and Thurstone here have deplored the "cult" of Rorschach, while Zubin and Cronbach have written friendly but critical suggestions for making the Rorschach methodologically respectable. There is no doubt that this psychometric approach has had some influence on the enormous bulk of Rorschach research literature. In particular, it can be discerned in the studies of Sen and Sandler in England, and of Wittenborn, Adcock, Coan, Hsü, Williams, and Lawrence in this country, who have explored the factorial structure of Rorschach scores, and in the work of Allen, Baughman, Holtzman, and Siipola, who have studied most ingeniously the influence of experimental variations in test procedures on Rorschach performance. Nevertheless, in the standard Rorschach manuals statistical and experimental considerations are pretty much laid aside, and virtually all "explanation" of the psychological meaning of Rorschach test behavior is clinically, rather than empirically, derived. The original interpretive suggestions of Rorschach were based on his analysis—which was, as we have pointed out, largely intuitive rather than controlled—of the records of some 288 Swiss mental patients and 117 normals. Though tens of thousands of Rorschach tests have been administered by hundreds of trained professionals since that time, and while many relationships to personality dynamics and behavior have been hypothesized, the vast majority of these interpretive relationships *have never been validated empirically,* despite the appearance of more than 2,000 publications on the test. This holds not only for the claims made by Rorschach himself, but equally for the extensions and modifications of these advanced by Klopfer, Beck, Piotrowski, Rapaport, Loosli-Usteri, Schafer, and others. Insightful and plausible though they may be, the evidence in their favor is almost entirely subjective and impressionistic. As Wittenborn indicated in *The Third Mental Measurements Yearbook:* "What passes for research in this field is usually naively conceived, inadequately controlled, and only rarely subjected to usual standards of experimental rigor."

SCORING. In the customary method of administering the Rorschach, the examiner, after noting for each card the time of the initial response and recording verbatim the subject's description of what each of the 10 blots looks like to him, goes over his responses with the subject, endeavoring by discreet inquiry to find out just *where* in each blot the reported impression was

localized, and *what* about this area suggested this response to him. From the subject's replies to these inquiries, each response is scored for *location, determinants,* and *content.*

a) *Location* is scored as whole (W), common detail (D), or unusual detail (Dd—often subdivided in various ways). Tendency to use white space (S) as figure is also noted.

b) *Determinants* include form (F); form and color with form primary (FC), or with color primary (CF), or with form absent and color only influencing the response (C); shading or chiaroscuro similarly construed (variously abbreviated Ch, c, K, Sh, and scored Fc, cF, FK, KF, c, etc.). Form is also usually designated as good (F+) or poor (F−). Curiously, human movement (M) is scored as a determinant, even though it is obviously not present in the blots as color and form are. This reflects Rorschach's associationist leanings and his belief that we could not truly perceive movement without a kinesthetic sensation which "determined" the perception. Why those who have distinguished animal movement (FM) and inanimate movement (m) from Rorschach's M (which is confined to human or human-like movement) continue to view these as "determinants" rather than projected content remains a mystery.

c) *Content.* What the subject "sees" in the blots is classified under certain general categories, such as entire humans (H) or animals (A) or parts thereof (Hd and Ad), inanimate objects (Obj), plants (Pl), anatomy (At), sexual objects (Sex), blood (Bl), clouds (Cl), X-rays, symbols (Sym), and maps. In addition, content is usually scored for popularity (P) and sometimes, as with Rorschach himself, for originality (O).

INTERPRETATION. Though Rorschach theorists insist that no one feature of the scored responses can be interpreted by itself, and that the total configuration must be visualized holistically and dynamically, they take, both in principle and practice, certain scoring categories to reflect faithfully, if not linearly, certain tendencies or dispositions of the personality. These dispositions interact, as do their Rorschach equivalents, so that it is possible, according to the manuals, to identify from the Rorschach isolable qualities (like impulsiveness, sensitivity, intelligence) and, with even greater accuracy, the general personality constellation or global

adjustment of the individual. Let us consider certain of these identifications.

Location. W is taken as an indicator of intelligence though no research evidence supports this connection, and studies by Wittenborn (*894*), Wilson (*1466*), and E. K. Sarason (*1024*) report no relation between W and intelligence in the superior, and negative relationship between W and MA in the inferior. The hypothesized connection between D and concern for the practical and concrete is also unevidenced by research. Prevalence of Dd is supposed to be positively related to obsessive-compulsive trends, and for this there is some slight support. One cannot take this support too seriously, however, since in no case was the number of responses (R) partialed out or held constant for different subjects, and the number of Dd is known to correlate highly with R.

White space responses (S) are supposed to indicate negativistic tendencies. The evidence for this is very slight indeed, and from the few published studies one could probably make out a better case for S as a sign of indecisiveness rather than of negativism (*1655*).

Determinants. Among the "determinants," bright color was reported by Rorschach as the most sensitive indicator of affect or emotionality. Primary C responses, i.e., those in which there is no consideration of form or shape, are the "representatives of impulsiveness." CF responses are analogous to pure C but are less pathognomonic. To Rorschach they represented the urge to live outside oneself, and connoted emotional instability, irritability, sensitivity, suggestibility, and egocentricity. These characteristics of "extratension" (which is, by the way, very different from Jung's "extraversion") are found more frequently, he blandly said, in women than in men! FC responses are most common in normals and indicate the kind of emotional lability necessary to achieve environmental rapport. FC thus represents adaptive rather than egocentric affectivity, and this is said to be especially true when the form is clearly visualized (FC+).

Rorschach also described the phenomenon of "color shock," "an emotional and associative stupor" that occurs when the colored Card 8 is shown after the preceding black and white card. This, he concluded, was always a sign of neurotic repression of affect. Among signs of color shock Beck lists delay in giving response to the card, failure to respond (rejection of card), re-

duction in number of responses, lowering of form quality, and lack of popular responses.

It is difficult to deny that the chromatic cards tend to produce an affective reaction in many subjects. Several studies have shown that colored cards are significantly less likely to be adjudged neutral and more likely to contribute to expression of unpleasant emotion than equivalent cards photographically reproduced in black and white. That this tendency generalizes to other affective stimuli, or is a measure of habitual affectivity in interpersonal relations, however, is by no means self-evident. Combinations of musical tones, for example, qualify also as emotionally charged stimuli which tend to produce judgments of pleasantness—unpleasantness and other affective reactions. We do not conclude on this account that the individual's entire repertory of affectivity is implicit in his response to certain vague tonal sequences. Perhaps it is, but empirical establishment of particular connections is required before we regard this kind of proposition as more relevant to science than to poetry.

The experimental researches of Allen (*1297*), Baughman (*1657*), Crumpton (*2032*), Keehn (*1548-9*), Lazarus (*828*), Siipola (*1032*), and many others make it doubtful that color per se has very much influence on the responses of subjects to inkblots. Virtually all the signs of "color shock," for example, are elicited as frequently by equivalent achromatic cards as by the originals, and are found as often in the records of normals as neurotics.

The "lack of perceptual control" connoted by the CF and C responses seems to be an empirically identifiable factor (*895, 1215, 2172*), but it, too, applies equally to the achromatic and the chromatic cards. The studies of Wittenborn would tend to indicate further that the three kinds of color responses (FC, CF, and C) do not all pertain to the same factor or dimension of scoring. It would follow, then, that to assign a numerical value of .5 to FC, 1.0 to CF, and 1.5 to C, as is done in traditional Rorschach scoring, in order to calculate the *sum C* or "affective balance" of the individual, is not only arbitrary and supposititious but in all probability quite meaningless. There is some support for the assumed connection between CF and C scores on the one hand and ratings of impulsiveness on the other, but color responses alone distinguish the impulsive from the nonimpulsive

less clearly than they do in combination with achromatic responses (*963, 2292*).

Turning from chromatic to achromatic features of the blots, we may note that the interpretation of chiaroscuro or shading responses was suggested only tentatively by Rorschach in the paper with Oberholzer as bearing on "affective adaptability," but indicating "a timid, cautious, and hampered sort of adaptability.... and a tendency toward a fundamentally depressive disposition."

The most complicated detailing of responses to chiaroscuro is advocated by Klopfer, who distinguishes nine aspects of shading responses for purposes of scoring. Reaction to shading in general he reports as related to the way a person "handles his primary security need and derived needs for affection and belongingness." Shading taken as a sign of diffusion or undifferentiated depth (K, KF), e.g., "smoke" or "clouds," indicates "anxiety of a diffuse and free-floating nature." Shading used to produce three-dimensional vista responses (FK, or FV in Beck's system) represents an attempt to "handle his affective anxiety by introspective efforts, by an attempt to objectify his problem by 'gaining perspective' on it, by 'putting it at some distance.'" The juxtaposing of terms like "diffusion" with "diffuse anxiety," of "three-dimensional vista" with "gaining perspective" and "putting it at some distance" suggests a primitive isomorphism between Rorschach response and mental state the like of which has not been seriously advanced by anyone since Empedocles in the 5th century B.C. ("For earth is known by earth in us; water by water.") Not all interpretation of vista and diffusion is as naively metaphorical as this.

The perception of shading as *texture* is scored in the Klopfer system as c, cF, or Fc, analogous to color. The c responses indicate "an infantile, undifferentiated, crude need for affection." The "cF responses represent a relatively crude continuation of an early need for closeness....an infantile sort of dependence on others"; while Fc responses indicate "an awareness of and acceptance of affectional needs experienced in terms of desire for approval, belongingness, and response from others." All of these interpretations are, of course, pure suppositions, unencumbered by empirical considerations. When we turn to reports of research investigations, we are likely to find one study which indicates that undifferentiated shading responses are com-

moner among maladjusted than adjusted college students, which would dovetail with the "lack of perceptual control" factor identified by Wittenborn (*1215*), but which is not so evidently consistent with the finding of Cox and Sarason (*1678*) that total of c responses (c + cF + Fc) is *lower* among test-anxious subjects than among the nontest-anxious.

Such more or less conflicting results in empirical studies of the Rorschach have been noted as typical by Levy [1] who suggests that a partial explanation is to be found in the extreme variability and unreliability of the validating criteria employed, a situation also remarked on by Sargent in *The Fourth Mental Measurements Yearbook*. Thus test anxiety in students is not the same as general maladjustment, nor is either concept clearly denoted empirically. How, therefore, compare Rorschach findings for the two? If the Rorschach signs fail to accord with such constructs as "maladjustment," or with psychiatric diagnosis, ratings of social adequacy, or stated improvement under psychotherapy, this may reflect only the dubious nature of these criteria. At the same time, agreement between the Rorschach and such poorly defined criterion variables, especially where tester and "validator" share theoretical convictions and accept a common universe of clinical discourse, is likely to indicate only indeliberate collusion or, in a very special sense, correlation between persons. Herein is the weakness of "validation" by matching or by blind analysis.

Extreme emotional reaction to the achromatic cards (especially Cards 4 and 6 and to some extent Cards 5 and 7) is designated "gray black shock" (Beck) or "shading shock" (Klopfer) or "dark shock" (Piotrowski). It is said to indicate "fear of fear," "frustration of affectional needs," or an "anergic state." Neither the existence of the phenomenon nor its interpretive significance is attested to by any controlled investigation.

The F responses, or those determined by the blot contours alone, are viewed ambivalently by the Rorschach authorities. On the one hand, F is taken as the prime indicator of intellectual or rational activity, and its quality as good (F+) or poor (F−) as the chief sign of ego-strength and self-control or ego-weakness and regression. On the other hand, a preponderance of exclu-

sively form-determined responses (to the neglect of color, shading, and dynamic qualities) is generally regarded as evidence of "neurotic constriction," and this is in no way mitigated by the fact that the "form level" (F+ factor) is high. In fact, the picture of "constriction" or "coartation" is made sharper by a high proportion of F+ responses.

Certain conceptual difficulties present themselves here. In the first place, the concept of good form or F+ is a highly variable one. Beck and Klopfer, for example, use very different criteria of good form, while those of Hertz and Piotrowski are somewhat different from either and from each other. In a review published in 1950 Kimball (*974*) has nicely pointed up the problem. Comparing the lists of Beck and Hertz, Kimball found disagreement as to whether a given response was F+ or F− ranging from 11 per cent on Card 7 to 62 per cent on Card 6, and averaging 32 per cent. When Kimball had judges of varying experience rate on a 6-point scale 100 whole responses taken from these lists, there was *disagreement* in rating on 63 per cent of the responses. It would appear that the interjudge reliability of form-level estimates is disquietingly low. As much may be said for the scoring of determinants generally. (*853, 1079, 1099*)

In the second place, the distinction between form-determined (F) and dynamic responses (M) is truly an ambiguous one, since form per se is not necessarily static. In fact, Baughman showed that the silhouette equivalents of the Rorschach blots (in which peripheral form is not altered but shading variations and chromatic color are removed) elicited *more M* responses than the standard series. The relevant contrast is actually between static and dynamic *content,* and not between determinants in the sense of qualities present in the blot which are logically antecedent to perception. The so-called pure F response, then, is a shape-determined identification of a *nonmoving or static object,* and is not just the shape-determined response in itself.

Within the limits of reliability mentioned above, it does appear that form quality, as reflected in the percentage or proportion of good form and of poor form responses, bears a moderate relation to such characteristics as impulse control, reality contact, and critical judgment, though the alleged connection between F+% and intelligence has not on the whole been borne out by research (*596, 775, 1257*).

---

[1] LEVY, LEON H. "Varieties of Rorschach Research." Unpublished paper presented at the 1958 meeting of the Midwestern Psychological Association, Detroit, Michigan.

The human movement response (M) has been endowed with an almost hieratic significance by some Rorschach theorists. To Beck, Rorschach's penetration to the essence of the movement response is his greatest achievement; to Piotrowski, it is his "most original contribution to the experimental study of personality"; Klopfer regards "M's of good form level" as "signs of high intellectual capacity," of one's freedom "to use his imaginal processes to enrich his perception of the world," of "creative potential," of "inner resources upon which the person can fall back in periods of stress," and of "an inner system of conscious values."

Rorschach himself appears to have held, following J. Mourly Vold, that "fantasy" or "inner living" depended upon the actual inhibition of movement and that residues of the motor impulse would remain in the form of kinesthetic sensations or images. Though few today would take seriously the associationistic rationale which Rorschach offered for his views on M, the disposition to regard human movement responses as revealing the "creative inner life" and the deepest reaches of the personality continues. To Beck, "Producing M is, generically, the creative act"; for Piotrowski, "The M stands for the most individual and integrated strivings which dominate the individual's life."

Controlled research has failed to reveal any connection between M responses and independent ratings of creative ability, intellectual productivity and originality, or any other signs of election for salvation, psychologically speaking (1600). With brain-operated patients, Zubin (2154) showed that increase in movement responses, whether of humans or non-humans, is positively correlated with psychiatric judgments of increased anxiety, while Cox and Sarason (1678) found significantly more M among test-anxious than among nontest-anxious students. These results were not predictable from classical Rorschach theory and had little conceivable connection with intraversiveness in Rorschach's sense.

The ratio of human movement to color responses (M:ΣC) is supposed to reflect the balance of introversion-extratension, and to this "experience balance" Rorschach devoted many pages of speculation (285). Another widely used ratio is that of whole to human movement responses (W:M), indicating the relation of drive or aspiration to creative potential. Proportions greater than 2/1 in either direction for either M:ΣC or W:M are said to reflect excessive fantasy, flight into reality, too high level of aspiration, or failure to live up to capacity. Empirical studies of these ratios are few, partly because their significance is difficult to determine quantitatively, since small absolute differences (e.g., 2 versus 1 M) may cause rather large ratio differences (e.g., in W to M 4/1 versus 4/2) (795). A further impediment to research studies of these and many other suggested ratios follows from the condition noted by Sarason (1786): "When the significance attributed to each of the scores is determined by fiat and has little or no foundation in controlled research, whatever significance is attributed to their inter-relationship will probably be of very dubious validity."

The identification of animal movement, for some obscure reason designated by Klopfer "FM," with felt "impulses to immediate gratification" which "stem from the most primitive or archaic layers of the personality," represents a strenuous effort to find a place in the Rorschach for the Freudian id. Klopfer does not explain why "animal movement" should be regarded as a determinant, since such a response does not, like M, imply empathy. The suggestion that perception of animal movement is determined by "animal impulses" in us is indeed fetching, if a little preposterous.

Inanimate movement (m), beyond a maximum of one or two responses, supposedly reflects "awareness of forces outside the control of the subject, which threaten the integrity of his personality organization." These forces are naturally productive of "tension and conflict." Piotrowski thinks of m as revealing "unattainable roles," "the habit of daydreaming," and "superior intelligence." The basis on which these theories are advanced remains quite obscure.

Content. As previously noted, Rorschach himself attached relatively little significance to the content of the responses. "The problems of the experiment," he says in the Summary to the *Psychodiagnostik,* "deal primarily with the formal principles (pattern) of the perceptive process. The actual content of the interpretations comes into consideration only secondarily." The percentage of animal responses he took to be an indicator of stereotyped thinking, and repetition of content as reflecting perseverative or complex-determined thinking. Parts of humans (Hd) are seen more frequently than entire humans (H), he noted, by the anxious, the de-

pressed, and the unintelligent ; and conceptually confused ("contaminated") content is symptomatic of psychotic deterioration. The only other aspect of content in which he showed great interest was originality or popularity. Original responses (those occurring only once in a hundred records) of good form quality (O+) were regarded by Rorschach as indicators of creativity and superior intelligence, those of poor form quality as indicators of schizophrenia, feeble-mindedness, and other psychopathological conditions. At the other extreme is the popular response (P) which Rorschach dealt with very briefly but on which Beck (780) and Hertz (260) have gathered extensive, if not clearly representative, data. Zubin and his students have constructed scales for the rating of all responses along a popularity-originality continuum, and these scales have shown some utility in predicting outcome of treatment in psychosis (1152). The number of popular responses is limited, and shows high positive correlation with number of responses (R), while per cent of P is negatively correlated with R. It is desirable, therefore, to evaluate P only in relation to R, and this is seldom done (1924).

Many clinicians make far greater use of the content of responses in evaluating a record than Rorschach himself would have countenanced. Thus, Schafer's clinical analyses (749, 1787), whether diagnostically or psychoanalytically oriented, unravel every thread of symbolic or thematic significance from the content of the associations, while Klopfer indulges his penchant for extravagant isomorphism with respect to content also (1730, 2063). Burt and his student Sen (874) claim that their psychometric scaling of content yields average correlations in the .60's with pooled independent ratings of various personality traits, though Burt has never published his scales for general use. Elizur, in a model doctoral thesis (799), showed that non-experts could validly detect anxiety and hostility in subjects from the evaluation of anxious and hostile content of Rorschach responses. Sandler and Ackner (1184) in England found that certain aspects of response content related significantly to case histories of neuropsychiatric patients, while Watkins and Stauffacher (1461) in this country successfully used the content category of "deviant verbalization" to distinguish among normals, neurotics, and psychotics. Though comparatively few studies have been concerned primarily with the content of re-

sponses, the proportion of these which have shown some predictive efficacy is encouragingly high. This has moved Zubin (1827) to suggest the abandonment of the Rorschach as a weakly reliable and doubtfully valid *test* and its installation as a standardized interview, the content of which can be readily quantified and analyzed.

It is certainly doubtful that the so-called formal or perceptual scoring categories are really as independent of content as alleged by Rorschach. Movement of any type, as already noted, is content rather than form. The distinction between good and poor form is also a matter of content, specifically of how well the object "seen" fits the contour of the area responded to. Similarly, such "formal" categories as KF, FK or FV, Fk, Fc, cf are scored almost entirely from the content of the percept, e.g., "smoke," "a mountain view," "an X-ray" or "map," "a fur piece." The notion that the subject's introspections form the best basis for deciding what determines his responses is a naive one to begin with, and presently quite untenable in view of Baughman's work with altered blot stimuli (1080, 1657). Thus, few report dark color or shading as essential to the popular response "bat" on Card 1, but when these qualities are removed from the stimulus, the response "bat" is seldom given. Even the distinction between C and CF or between CF and FC is made in nearly all cases on the basis of content, e.g., "blood" or "blue of the sky" is C, "spattered blood" or "ice cream" is CF, while "red butterfly" or "green caterpillar" is FC. It may be because so many allegedly formal categories pertain really to content that the factor analysis of formal categories, as in Sen's study, yields results strikingly similar to the factor analysis of content. Very possibly the rotation of extracted formal factors brings out their content values. Rorschach's faith in the determinants as a kind of Kantian perceptual form, transcending content, remains unsupported.

Holistic or global assessments derived from the Rorschach may be clinically satisfying, but they too have not stood up well in research. Certain examiners, like Hertz (709, 810) and Schachtel (1185), using qualitative and not easily replicated methods, have had good success in identifying delinquents, neurotics, depressives, and schizophrenics from the total Rorschach, evaluated clinically. But one gathers here that the Rorschach is a simple adjunct to the extraordinary clinical acumen of some few

examiners rather than a technique in which all clinicians can share. Thus in the Michigan study of trainees in clinical psychology, Rorschach personality assessment correlated less than .30 with pooled ratings based on all sources of assessment, though two of six clinicians did well with the Rorschach (*1429*). Its failure to predict adjustment in the Armed Services has been repeatedly noted, and its utility as a general instrument for differential diagnosis is apparently very slight (*1214, 1224, 2161*).

Munroe's inspection technique (*387*) and the Davidson check list of adjustment signs (*928*) are rapid methods of evaluation which represent a compromise between the molecular and molar approaches. They have shown some value as screening devices.

FUTURE DEVELOPMENTS. In any case, the future of the traditional Rorschach will probably see greater emphasis on the content of responses —the appropriateness of content (F+ or F−), its popularity, originality, and dynamic characteristics, its expression of anxious or hostile feeling, its rich variety and conceptual clarity, or its stereotyped poverty. It should also see increasing emphasis on locating better criteria of validity for Rorschach predictions and on experimental designs which insure some cross validation of results. Lastly, if the Rorschach is viewed increasingly as an interview to be interpreted rather than a test to be scored, there should be greater emphasis on the interactional or interpersonal aspects of Rorschach administration: the effects of examiner differences, of the subject's task-set, of varying instructions, or of other aspects of the clinical interaction. Sarason and Baughman and Schafer have in their very different fashions shown the relevancy of these interpersonal considerations, but much more in the way of basic research is called for here.

Baughman's proposal (*2251*) to revise radically the procedure of inquiry may serve to objectify scoring of the standard Rorschach, especially with regard to "determinants." In view of the low reliability of determinant scores as noted to date, this might prove to be an important development.

The Harrower-Erickson and similar forms of the group Rorschach have shown reasonably good reliability but little validity either as research or screening instruments. The Harrower multiple choice Rorschach and the objective Rorschach of O'Reilly have been quite disappointing despite early favorable reports (*1797, 1961, 2096, 2297*).

Holtzman has attempted to overcome one of the great difficulties in obtaining reliable scoring of responses, viz., the variability in number of responses from one card to another, by constructing two new series of parallel blots, each consisting of 45 cards. Only one response is permitted for each card, so that the number of responses is, barring refusals, held constant. This greatly simplifies scoring and has contributed to high reliability coefficients for the determinant scores, averaging +.70 for the two alternate forms, +.84 split-half, and about +.98 for interscorer consistency. With the development of content analyses of comparable reliability, the *Holtzman Inkblot Test* may prove to be a research instrument of great value.

SUMMARY. The inkblot test devised by Rorschach has shown a high degree of clinical viability despite the general failure of empirical studies to support the sweeping claims of the Rorschach enthusiasts. The scoring systems devised for the Rorschach are various and often imperfectly conceptualized, and the interpretive significance of the categories employed is at best doubtful. Rorschach's original notion of the primary importance of the perceptual aspects of the test has not stood up at all well under research investigations, while the analysis of content (which he disparaged) has shown some promise both clinically and experimentally. Recent developments in experimental variations of the blot stimuli may eventually provide an objective and quantifiable basis for this kind of projective technique.

As the cult of the Rorschach declines, the integration of clinical methods with a critical and research orientation should advance. Among clinical psychologists few have done more than Sarason to further the appreciation of research studies. His words may serve to summarize this review. "The clinician who is not guided in his clinical work by these studies operates outside the realm of science, thereby performing a disservice to his patients as well as his profession" (*1786*).

LAURANCE F. SHAFFER, *Professor of Education, Teachers College, Columbia University, New York, New York.*

For how long does a diagnostic method stay "promising"? More than two decades ago, the present reviewer concluded one of the earliest

descriptions of the Rorschach to appear in an American psychology textbook with these words: "With further development, this method promises to be a useful one."[1] The Rorschach seemed "promising" in 1936, and many other commentators have since echoed the sentiment. Perhaps it is now time to judge the extent to which the promise has been fulfilled.

As with any other method for the appraisal of persons, the central issue about the Rorschach is its validity. Does it work? How do clinicians use it? For what purposes? To what degree are the conclusions they draw confirmed by other evidence? In spite of the protests of some Rorschachists, the validity is researchable. The user makes certain practical decisions or predictions —and he may make them objectively from scores or intuitively from global interpretations. In either case, the user has only to count his hits and misses, and he obtains evidence relevant to validity.

CLINICAL VALIDITY. Among the broad criteria of interest to psychology and psychiatry, two stand out clearly. Of any patient, we want to know two things—what's the matter with him, and will he get well? The criterion of diagnosis is therefore of great importance, as is also the criterion of improvement through treatment. These decisions are practical and realistic ones. Every day, psychologists in clinics and hospitals make inferences from the Rorschach about the diagnosis of patients and about the likelihood of their recovery.

Only in recent years have soundly designed research studies probed the validity of the Rorschach for these applications, by both score counting and global judgment methods. To review all of the research comprehensively would require a book, but it is helpful to examine a few representative studies.

In a study of the relationship of Rorschach scores to diagnosis, Knopf (2064) gathered the Rorschach records of 339 unambiguously diagnosed patients: 131 psychoneurotics, 106 psychopaths, and 100 schizophrenics. Appropriate nonparametric statistics were used to test whether 34 Rorschach summary scores differentiated the groups. Only four scores—rare details, populars, sex, and anatomy—significantly discriminated at the .05 level, and these separated only the psychopaths from the neurotics and schizophrenics. Not a single score made the

much sought distinction between the psychoneurotics and schizophrenics. Other studies have found little more. Typically, one study may find a few signs or patterns that are weakly significant, but a replication fails to confirm them (1301, 1452, 1603, 1707).

Many Rorschach workers are not surprised when scores fail to give valid diagnoses. But the method of global judgment has also been investigated. In one very competent study, Chambers and Hamlin (2169) sent a set of 5 scored Rorschach protocols to each of 20 well qualified judges, many of them eminent authorities. Each set was different, but each contained the same assortment of uncontroversially diagnosed cases—one involutional depression, one anxiety neurosis, one paranoid schizophrenia, one brain damage from neurosyphilis, and one adult imbecile. The judges were informed of the groups represented, and had the apparently simple task of assigning one protocol of the five to each diagnosis. The results exceeded chance, but did not confirm the supposition that this simplified task can be done perfectly by all competent psychologists. Mental deficiency was the easiest to judge, and was correctly identified by 18 of the 20 judges. The other four diagnoses were correctly judged in 51 per cent of the instances. To cite one typical example, involutional depression was correctly designated by 10 of the 20 judges, but was called neurosis by 4, schizophrenia by 1, brain damage by 4, and mental deficiency by 1. Global diagnosis from the Rorschach had nonchance validity, but not very much validity—far too little for the dependence that clinicians often place on it.

Other soundly designed studies have found no more global validity, and often less. Scores, profiles, and global judgments have failed to distinguish diagnostic classifications better than chance (2161). The Rorschach has shown nonchance but low agreement with criteria from psychiatric interviews (1321) and from biographical data (1714). Only about half of a group of judges matched Rorschach interpretations with Rorschach protocols better than chance (1863). Global judgments, then, fail to show either validity or reliability sufficient to the task of personality description or diagnosis.

The prediction of the outcome of treatment has fared even less well than the identification of diagnosis. In this area, also, some studies have seemed to find a little validity, only to fail in cross validation (1479, 1556). Two extensive

1 SHAFFER, LAURANCE F. The Psychology of Adjustment, p. 303. Boston, Mass.: Houghton Mifflin Co., 1936. Pp. xxii, 600. * (PA 10:2550)

studies (*1602, 1775*) of Rorschach scores and signs did not find any that were associated with therapeutic improvement. Global judgments of Rorschachs are no more valid than scores in predicting the results of treatment (*1483, 1872*). Of all the most widely employed applications of the Rorschach, the prediction of whether a patient will improve receives the least support from well designed research.

In response to the growing evidence that conventional interpretations of the Rorschach have low validity, some workers have turned to the analysis of Rorschach content. Content, of course, can be so varied that many years would be required to evaluate the merit of all such proposals. So far, the results have not been encouraging. Hostile content (*1881*) and the "eye" response supposed to indicate paranoid suspicion (*1637*) are little related to appropriate criteria. The common practice of identifying a "father" card and a "mother" card is most dubious (*2171*). In sum, there is little hope that the interpretation of Rorschach content will be a means for valid clinical appraisal.

VALIDITY AGAINST EXPERIMENTAL CRITERIA. Clinical users of the Rorschach have generally belittled attempts to relate single Rorschach scores to specific behavioral criteria. Such studies are dismissed as "atomistic," with the observation that they do not use the Rorschach in the same way as do the practical workers in hospitals and clinics. Still, it must be recognized that Rorschach himself gave specific meanings to certain scores and other authorities have followed his example. And surprisingly enough, many studies which have assessed scores against objective behavioral criteria have found results more favorable to the Rorschach than have studies which compared global judgments to clinical criteria.

Let us take the S, or white space, response as an example. Some examinees reverse figure and ground, so that "the white spaces are interpreted rather than the black or colored parts of the figure" (*285*). Rorschach wrote that such perceptions mark "stubborn, eccentric" persons who are given to "tendency to opposition" (*285*). Bandura (*1655*) had 59 high school students each rated by five teachers on personality variables such as negativism and assertiveness. The ratings were sufficiently in agreement, with reliabilities of about .80; the split-half reliability of the S scores was .84. The hypothesis was confirmed. The S scores were correlated

.34 with the ratings of negativism, an r significantly different from zero at the .01 level. This brief synopsis does scant justice to Bandura's study. He also investigated the hypothesis that S scores have different meaning for introversive and extratensive subjects, but his data gave no support to such a difference. In a similar but independent study, Ingram (*1717*) frustrated 22 college students by challenging, in an interview, their competence for their chosen vocations. The subgroup high in S differed from the low-S subjects in their initiative, resistance, and hostility in response to this attack on their self-regard. The high-S subjects, again, were more "oppositional."

Somewhat more subtle in their rationale are the studies which have dealt with the meaning of the human movement response, M, perhaps Rorschach's most novel and interesting invention. Seeing human movement in the inkblots, Rorschach hypothesized, gives evidence of kinaesthetic imagery and is therefore related to "more individualized intelligence, more creative ability, more 'inner' life....and measured, stable motility" (*285*). Some features of this remarkable intuitive hunch have been confirmed by research; others have not. The studies of Singer and Spohn (*1796*) and Singer and Herman (*1795*) offer illustrations of well conceived research on the correlates of M. The subjects of Singer and Spohn were 50 male veterans diagnosed as schizophrenic. Two tests were made. In the first test patients were rated on degree of activity during a 15-minute period in a waiting room well supplied with casual distractions. Protocols of detailed observations of waiting room behavior were rated on a scale ranging from no gross motor activity to considerable restlessness, noticing and manipulating many objects. The second test was also a motor inhibition task—writing a phrase as slowly as possible. The 50 subjects had been chosen so that 25 had high M on the Rorschach and 25 had low M. The high-M patients, as predicted, had significantly lower activity ratings and higher motor inhibition scores. The correlations, while significantly different from zero, were low; M correlated $-.23$ with activity and .29 with motor inhibition. A replication by Singer and Herman found a higher correlation, .54, between M and motor inhibition, and one of $-.27$ with waiting room activity. Further confirmation came from the finding of Levine and Meltzoff (*2071*) that cognitive inhibition is related to M, and from

that of Meltzoff and Litwin (*2085*) that M correlates .42 with the ability to inhibit laughter.

In addition to his hypotheses about M alone, Rorschach made others about the relation of movement responses to those determined by color. His M to Sum C ratio determined the experience type. A person is said to be introversive if M predominates, or extratensive if he shows more color-determined responses. The extratensive man has more "outward" life, is more immediately responsive to his environment. Mann (*2081*) has reported an ingenious experiment to study "responsiveness to the immediate environment." In a small room which contained a variety of furnishings and accessories, he administered Binet's old word naming test: "Write twenty-five words, any twenty-five words as they come to mind. Write no sentences." The task was repeated three times. An inquiry then disclosed the basis for the subject's choice of each word. A score of responsiveness to the immediate environment was the number of words determined by immediately present sights and sounds. The tetrachoric correlation between the score and the introversive-extratensive classification was −.43; the extratensives were more environment-oriented, the introversives sought their words in revery or fantasy. Mann's study was a neat validation of one of Rorschach's most subtle hypotheses, but how good was the validity? A tetrachoric r of −.43 sounds fairly substantial but, in simpler percentage figures, Mann noted that the M to Sum C ratio correctly classified the subjects 64 per cent of the time when chance would be 50 per cent. The troublesome issue here occurs again. There is validity—but not very much validity.

SOME CONCLUSIONS. The Rorschach has *some* empirical validities. Assessments based on it can exceed those made by chance, at least with respect to such variables of personality as activity level, motor inhibition, capacity for fantasy, oppositional tendency, and responsiveness to the environment. But the Rorschach is also a most imperfect instrument, not qualified to perform the tasks that many psychologists demand of it. The predictive or concurrent validity of the Rorschach is, in the areas of its best competence, perhaps of the order of .20 to .40. Its interpretation needs to be accompanied by a visual image of a correlation chart showing the relationship between two variables when r equals .2 to .4, and when from about 4 per cent to about 16 per cent of the variance is identified. The fault of

many clinicians is that they use the Rorschach as if its validity were 1.00. And, contrary to the opinions of many, the use of the Rorschach by global judgment shows poorer, not better, validity than the psychometric application of some of its scores.

In view of the relatively unfavorable evidence, why is the Rorschach held in such high esteem? Without attempting to be comprehensive, three reasons may be suggested. First, we have an intense need for a subtle and comprehensive instrument to assess personality. As recent research in social psychology shows, motivation and belief are highly related. When one has a strong need, evidence of little objective merit may be perceived as conclusive. Second, the Rorschach is projective for the examiner as well as for the examinee. One readily "reads into" the vague verbalizations of the Rorschach protocol all that one already knows and believes about the examinee. For each individual examiner, therefore, the Rorschach seems to confirm his other knowledge and he has an intuitive and personal sense of the validity of the instrument. Third, the Rorschach is not wholly without validity—it is sometimes "right." And evidence from the psychology of learning shows that a schedule of intermittent reinforcements may form as strong a habit, and one as resistant to extinction, as reinforcement on every occasion. To overcome these hazards, clinical psychologists need to be more aware of their own frailties as persons, and more aware of the fact that the scientific method of inquiry provides a means for guarding against such errors.

Still another reason for complacency about the Rorschach is that textbooks continue to cite older "research studies" which seem to affirm its validity. One widely used book, for example, contains a chapter on "validating and experimental studies with the Rorschach method" (*1171*). Many of the studies which it cites (*115, 272, 293, 753*) are notable for faulty experimental designs, poor controls, absence of appropriate tests of significance, and conclusions which transcend the data. It is instructive for any psychologist who is concerned with the Rorschach to reread such studies with a newly critical eye, and thereby to reexamine the bases of his earlier beliefs.

Within limits, the Rorschach can be improved to overcome some of its present shortcomings. Rorschach's most ingenious invention, the human movement response, provides one example.

It has an appealing and sound rationale, and the empirical evidence is relatively favorable. Why does M not have a higher validity than .2 to .4? One evident reason is that M is a distressingly poor variable when judged by standards of psychometrics. Its distribution has small variance and is badly skewed. In typical samples of persons, whether normal or disturbed, half of the M scores are 0 or 1. It is indeed a wonder that so faulty a variable correlates with anything. We can learn to make better measures of M. Barron's M-threshold scale (*1841*) is probably not the final answer, but it may point the way. Another feature that can be improved is the process of making judgments or inferences from Rorschach protocols. Hamlin (*1709*) and various collaborators have pointed out that scores provide units too simple for analysis, and that global judgments are so complex that confusion results. Intermediate units, such as responses to single cards, seem to yield better results. In many other respects, projective methods can be improved by invention and research.

In conclusion, it seems clear that the research of the past decade gives poor support to the uncritical use of *the* Rorschach. It is time that psychologists abandon this beguiling but dubious orthodoxy, and strike out in new directions which will retain some of the demonstrated values, but avoid the numerous pitfalls, of unstructured projective methods.

For a review by Helen Sargent, see 4:117; for reviews by Morris Krugman and J. R. Wittenborn, see 3:73; for related reviews, see B32, B34, B40–1, B60, B73, B79, B190, B247–8, B337, B369, B372, B402, 4:118–28 and 3:74–91.

[155]

Rosenzweig Picture-Frustration Study. Ages 4–13, 14 and over; 1944–49; also called *Rosenzweig P-F Study;* 1 form ('48); 2 levels; no data on reliability and validity; $5 per 25 tests; $1.25 per 25 record blanks ('48); postage extra; specimen set not available; Saul Rosenzweig; the Author, 8029 Washington St., St. Louis 14, Mo. *

a) FORM FOR CHILDREN. Ages 4–13; 1948; $1.25 per manual ('48, reprinted from *21*); [20] minutes.

b) REVISED FORM FOR ADULTS. Ages 14 and over; 1944–49; revised norms ('49); norms for ages 20–29 only; $1.25 per manual ('47, reprinted from *15*); [15] minutes.

REFERENCES

1–77. See 4:129.
78. LANGE, CARL J. *The Effect of Sleep Deprivation on the Rosenzweig Picture-Frustration Study.* Master's thesis, University of Pittsburgh (Pittsburgh, Pa.), 1948.
79. COWEN, JUDITH. *An Analysis of the Types of Responses Given by Negro Students at the College of the City of New York to Negro and White Aggressors as Revealed by a Modified Form of the Picture-Frustration Projective Technique.* Master's thesis, College of the City of New York (New York, N.Y.), 1949.
80. LORD, L. *A Comparison of the Tendencies Revealed by the Rosenzweig Picture-Frustration Study Between a Selected Population of Simple and Paranoid Schizophrenics.* Master's thesis, Southern Illinois University (Carbondale, Ill.), 1949.
81. EILBERT, LEO, AND SCHMEIDER, GERTRUDE R. "A Study of Certain Psychological Factors in Relation to ESP Performance." *J Parapsychol* 14:53–74 Mr '50. *
82. MCDOWELL, GLORIA MAE. *A Study of the Relationship of the Rosenzweig Picture-Frustration Response to the Scholastic Achievement of Two Hundred High School Juniors and Seniors.* Master's thesis, Pennsylvania State College (State College, Pa.), 1950.
83. TOWNER, W. C. *A Comparison of the Frustration Reactions of Delinquent and Non-Delinquent Adolescent Boys as Measured by the Rosenzweig Picture-Frustration Study.* Master's thesis, University of Washington (Seattle, Wash.), 1950.
84. BORNSTEIN, HARRY. *An Analysis of Frustration Behavior in a Puzzle-Solving Situation in Relation to Scores on the Rosenzweig Picture-Frustration Study.* Master's thesis, Fordham University (New York, N.Y.), 1951.
85. CONNERS, GEORGE ALBERT. *A Method for Investigating Frustration Reactions in Social Situations Involving Negro-White Interpersonal Relations.* Master's thesis, Tulane University (New Orleans, La.), 1951.
86. FRASCADORE, EDMUND R. *A Comparison of the Reaction to Frustration in Negro and White Children as Measured by the Rosenzweig P-F Study.* Master's thesis, Fordham University (New York, N.Y.), 1951.
87. KATES, SOLIS L. "Suggestibility, Submission to Parents and Peers, and Extrapunitiveness, Intropunitiveness, and Impunitiveness in Children." *J Psychol* 31:233–41 Ap '51. * (*PA* 26:769)
88. MENSH, IVAN N., AND MASON, EVELYN P. "Relationship of School Atmosphere to Reactions in Frustrating Situations." *J Ed Res* 45:275–86 D '51. *
89. MOORE, JACQUELINE A. *The Use of the Rosenzweig Picture-Frustration Test in Differentiating Delinquents From Non-Delinquents.* Master's thesis, Fordham University (New York, N.Y.), 1951.
90. MORRISON, EDWARD J. *An Experimental Study of Certain Factors Affecting the Validity and Reliability of the Rosenzweig P-F Study.* Master's thesis, Tulane University (New Orleans, La.), 1951.
91. PERSONS, EDWARD THOMAS. *A Study of the Relationship Between the Rosenzweig Picture-Frustration Study and Test Duration, Sims Socio-Economic Status Score, and Religion of High School Seniors.* Master's thesis, Pennsylvania State College (State College, Pa.), 1951.
92. SAWYER, GEORGE WILLIAM, JR. *A Study of the Relation Between the Allport A-S Study and the Rosenzweig P-F Study.* Master's thesis, University of Florida (Gainesville, Fla.), 1951.
93. SCOTT, JAMES STUART. *A Comparison of the Effects of Projective and Questionnaire Instructions Upon Responses to Pictures of the Rosenzweig PF Study Type.* Master's thesis, University of British Columbia (Vancouver, B.C., Canada), 1951.
94. SIEGEL, NORMA FRANCES. *An Investigation of the Interchangeable Use of the Adult Form and the Children's Form of the Rosenzweig P-F Study on Three Levels of Development.* Master's thesis, Pennsylvania State College (State College, Pa.), 1951.
95. TRONZO, RAYMOND GASPER. *The Rosenzweig Picture-Frustration Study as a Device in the Selection of Department Store Salespersons.* Master's thesis, Pennsylvania State College (State College, Pa.), 1951.
96. URBAN, HUGH BAYARD. *An Analysis of the Behavior Level of Responses by College Students to the Rosenzweig Picture-Frustration Study.* Master's thesis, Pennsylvania State College (State College, Pa.), 1951.
97. VACCARO, JOSEPH J. *A Study of Psychological Factors That Contrast the Most and Least Efficient Psychiatric Aids in a Mental Hospital.* Doctor's thesis, Fordham University (New York, N.Y.), 1951.
98. WALKER, ROBERT G. "A Comparison of Clinical Manifestations of Hostility With Rorschach and MAPS Test Performances." *J Proj Tech* 15:444–60 D '51. *
99. WALLACE, DOROTHY. *An Application of Cronbach's "Pattern Tabulation" Method to Rosenzweig's Picture-Frustration Study.* Master's thesis, University of Pittsburgh (Pittsburgh, Pa.), 1951.
100. ANGELINO, HENRY, AND SHEDD, CHARLES L. "A Comparison of Scores on the Rosenzweig Picture-Frustration Study Between Selected and Unselected School Populations." *Proc Okla Acad Sci* 33:288–92 '52. * (*PA* 29:7254)
101. DEVLIN, JOHN P. *A Study of Verbalized Self-Attitudes and Reactions to Social Frustration as Methods of Predicting Success in Brief Psychotherapy.* Doctor's thesis, Pennsylvania State College (State College, Pa.), 1952.
102. FRY, FRANKLYN D. *A Normative Study of the Reactions Manifested by College Students, and by State Prison Inmates in Response to the Minnesota Multiphasic Personality Inventory, the Rosenzweig Picture Frustration Study, and the Thematic Apperception Test.* Doctor's thesis, Pennsylvania State College (State College, Pa.), 1952. (*J Psychol* 34:27–30 Jl '52. *) (*PA* 27:2976)

103. HYBL, A. R., AND STAGNER, ROSS. "Frustration Tolerance in Relation to Diagnosis and Therapy." *J Consult Psychol* 16:163–70 Je '52. * (*PA* 27:5220)

104. KATES, SOLIS L. "Subjects' Evaluation of Annoying Situations After Being Described as Being Well Adjusted and Poorly Adjusted." *J Consult Psychol* 16:429–34 D '52. *

105. MADISON, LE ROI, AND NORMAN, RALPH D. "A Comparison of the Performance of Stutterers and Non-Stutterers on the Rosenzweig Picture-Frustration Test." *J Clin Psychol* 8:179–83 Ap '52. * (*PA* 27:2096)

106. MASON, ROBERT JOSEPH. *A Comparison of Responses on the Rosenzweig Picture-Frustration Study, the Bernreuter Personality Inventory, and a Self-Rating Form.* Master's thesis, University of Western Ontario (London, Ont., Canada), 1952.

107. MIRMOW, ESTHER L. *The Method of Successive Clinical Predictions in the Validation of Projective Techniques With Special Reference to the Rosenzweig Picture-Frustration Study.* Doctor's thesis, Washington University (St. Louis, Mo.), 1952.

108. MIRMOW, ESTHER LEE. Chap. 13, "The Rosenzweig Picture-Frustration Study," pp. 209–21. (*PA* 27:3558) In *Progress in Clinical Psychology, Vol. I, Sect. 1.* Edited by Daniel Brower and Lawrence E. Abt, New York: Grune & Stratton, Inc., 1952. Pp. xi, 328. *

109. PARKER, DONALD HENRY. *Relationship Between Reading Retardation and the Rosenzweig P-F Study.* Master's thesis, University of Florida (Gainesville, Fla.), 1952.

110. ROSENZWEIG, SAUL, AND ROSENZWEIG, LOUISE. "Aggression in Problem Children and Normals as Evaluated by the Rosenzweig P-F Study." *J Abn & Social Psychol* 47:683–7 Jl '52. * (*PA* 27:3562)

111. SCHWARTZ, MILTON M. "The Relationship Between Projective Test Scoring Categories and Activity Preferences." *Genetic Psychol Monogr* 46:133–81 N '52. * (*PA* 27:4269)

112. SMOCK, CHARLES, AND CRUICKSHANK, WILLIAM M. "Responses of Handicapped and Normal Children to the Rosenzweig P-F Study." *Q J Child Behavior* 4:156–64 Ap '52. *

113. SPACHE, GEORGE. "Personality Characteristics of Retarded Readers as Measured by the Picture-Frustration Study." Abstract. *Am Psychol* 7:376 Jl '52. *

114. STARER, EMANUEL. "Aggressive Reactions and Sources of Frustration in Anxiety Neurotics and Paranoid Schizophrenics." *J Clin Psychol* 8:307–9 Jl '52. * (*PA* 27:5979)

115. TAYLOR, MAHLON V., JR. "Internal Consistency of the Scoring Categories of the Rosenzweig Picture-Frustration Study." *J Consult Psychol* 16:149–53 Ap '52. *

116. WEINBERG, WILLIAM I. *A Study of the Relationship of the Extrapunitive Category of the Rosenzweig P-F Study to Overt Behavioral Aggression in Prisoners.* Master's thesis, University of Oregon (Eugene, Ore.), 1952.

117. ABRAMS, ELIAS N. "A Comparison of Normals and Neuropsychiatric Veterans on the Rosenzweig Picture-Frustration Study." *J Clin Psychol* 9:24–6 Ja '53. * (*PA* 27:7946)

118. BANGAS, MARY V. *Aggressive Tendencies in the Psychopathic Deviate as Measured by the Rosenzweig Picture-Frustration Study.* Master's thesis, Kent State University (Kent, Ohio), 1953.

119. BURGESS, ELVA. *Personality Factors in Over- and Under-Achievers in Engineering.* Doctor's thesis, Pennsylvania State College (State College, Pa.), 1953.

120. CANTER, FRANCIS M. "Personality Factors in Seizure States With Reference to the Rosenzweig Triadic Hypothesis." *J Consult Psychol* 17:429–35 D '53. * (*PA* 28:7844)

121. KARLIN, LAWRENCE, AND SCHWARTZ, MILTON M. "Social and General Intelligence and Performance on the Rosenzweig Picture-Frustration Study." *J Consult Psychol* 17:293–6 Ag '53. * (*PA* 28:4364)

122. KORNREICH, MELVIN. "Variations in the Consistency of the Behavioral Meaning of Personality Test Scores." *Genetic Psychol Monogr* 47:73–138 F '53. * (*PA* 27:6535)

123. MARKENSON, DAVID. *Diagnostic Effectiveness of Interpretive Tests.* Doctor's thesis, Washington University (St. Louis, Mo.), 1953. (*DA* 14:1100)

124. QUARRINGTON, BRUCE. "The Performance of Stutterers on the Rosenzweig Picture-Frustration Test." *J Clin Psychol* 9:189–92 Ap '53. * (*PA* 28:2957)

125. ROSENZWEIG, SAUL. "Rosenzweig Picture-Frustration Study," pp. 650–9. (*PA* 27:7790) In *Contributions Toward Medical Psychology: Theory and Psychodiagnostic Methods, Vol. II.* Edited by Arthur Weider. New York: Ronald Press Co., 1953. Pp. xi, 459–885. *

126. SHAPIRO, A. EUGENE. *A Comparative Evaluation of the Reactions to Frustration of Delinquent and Non-Delinquent Male Adolescents.* Doctor's thesis, New York University (New York, N.Y.), 1953. (*DA* 14:400)

127. WEISS, GEORGE. *A Study of Mothers' Responses and Mothers' Expectations of Children's Responses as Possible Factors Affecting the Actual Responses of Children on the Rosenzweig Picture Frustration Test.* Master's thesis, Kent State University (Kent, Ohio), 1953.

128. WINFIELD, DON L., AND SPARER, P. J. "Preliminary Report of the Rosenzweig P-F Study in Attempted Suicides." *J Clin Psychol* 9:379–81 O '53. * (*PA* 28:4602)

129. BROWN, ROBERT L., AND LACEY, OLIVER L. "The Diagnostic Value of the Rosenzweig P-F Study." *J Clin Psychol* 10:72–5 Ja '54. * (*PA* 28:7511)

130. CATTELL, RAYMOND B., AND SHOTWELL, ANNA M. "Personality Profiles of More Successful and Less Successful Psychiatric Technicians." *Am J Mental Def* 58:496–9 Ja '54. * (*PA* 28:6861)

131. GOODRICH, DAVID C. "Aggression in the Projective Tests and Group Behavior of Authoritarian and Equalitarian Subjects." Abstract. *Am Psychol* 9:380 Ag '54. *

132. HUSMAN, BURRIS FREDERICK. *An Analysis of Aggression in Boxers, Wrestlers, and Cross Country Runners as Measured by the Rosenzweig P-F Study, Selected TAT Pictures, and a Sentence Completion Test.* Doctor's thesis, University of Maryland (College Park, Md.), 1954. (*DA* 15:759)

133. LINDZEY, GARDNER, AND GOLDWYN, ROBERT M. "Validity of the Rosenzweig Picture-Frustration Study." *J Personality* 22:519–47 Je '54. * (*PA* 29:2452)

134. MEEK, CLINTON R. *The Effect of Knowledge of Aptitude Upon Interest Scores.* Doctor's thesis, George Peabody College for Teachers (Nashville, Tenn.), 1954.

135. PORTNOY, BERNARD, AND STACEY, CHALMERS L. "A Comparative Study of Negro and White Subnormals on the Children's Form of the Rosenzweig P-F Test." *Am J Mental Def* 59:272–8 O '54. * (*PA* 29:5895)

136. QUAY, HERBERT, AND SWEETLAND, ANDERS. "The Relationship of the Rosenzweig PF Study to the MMPI." *J Clin Psychol* 10:296–7 Jl '54. * (*PA* 29:2464)

137. SANDRA, M. ELAINE. *A Comparative Study of the Scores Obtained by Institutional Adolescent Girls on the Bell Adjustment Inventory and the P-F Test.* Master's thesis, Fordham University (New York, N.Y.), 1954.

138. SCHWARTZ, MILTON M., AND KARLIN, LAWRENCE. "A New Technique for Studying the Meaning of Performance on the Rosenzweig Picture-Frustration Study." *J Consult Psychol* 18:131–4 Ap '54. * (*PA* 29:2474)

139. SINAIKO, H. WALLACE. "Validity Information Exchange, No. 7–071: D.O.T. Code 0-75.10, Manager, Floor." *Personnel Psychol* 7:407–8 au '54. *

140. SOMMER, ROBERT. "On the Brown Adaptation of the Rosenzweig P-F for Assessing Social Attitudes." *J Abn & Social Psychol* 49:125–8 Ja '54. * (*PA* 28:7382)

141. SPACHE, GEORGE D. "Personality Characteristics of Retarded Readers as Measured by the Picture-Frustration Study." *Ed & Psychol Meas* 14:186–92 sp '54. * (*PA* 28:8001)

142. VANE, JULIA R. "Implications of the Performance of Delinquent Girls on the Rosenzweig Picture-Frustration Study." Abstract. *J Consult Psychol* 18:414 D '54. *

143. WENDLAND, LEONARD V. "A Preliminary Study of Frustration Reactions of the Post-Poliomyelitic." *J Clin Psychol* 10:236–40 Jl '54. * (*PA* 29:2911)

144. WRIGHT, STUART. "Some Personality Characteristics of Academic Underachievers." Abstract. *Am Psychol* 9:496 Ag '54. *

145. ANGELINO, HENRY, AND SHEDD, CHARLES L. "Reactions to Frustration Among Normal and Superior Children." *Excep Child* 21:215–8+ Mr '55. * (*PA* 29:8452)

146. HUSMAN, BURRIS F. "Aggression in Boxers and Wrestlers as Measured by Projective Techniques." *Res Q* 26:421–5 D '55. *

147. JENKIN, NOEL. "Some Relationships Between Projective Test Behavior and Perception." *J Clin Psychol* 11:278–81 Jl '55. * (*PA* 30:2888)

148. JOHANNSEN, DOROTHEA E., AND BENNETT, EDWARD M. "The Personality of Diabetic Children." *J Genetic Psychol* 87:175–85 D '55. * (*PA* 31:1514)

149. KORKES, LENORE, AND LEWIS, NOLAN D. C. "An Analysis of the Relationship Between Psychological Patterns and Outcome in Pulmonary Tuberculosis." *J Nerv & Mental Dis* 122:524–63 D '55. *

150. LEVITT, EUGENE E., AND LYLE, WILLIAM H., JR. "Evidence for the Validity of the Children's Form of the Picture-Frustration Study." *J Consult Psychol* 19:381–6 O '55. * (*PA* 30:5991)

151. LYON, WILLIAM, AND VINACKE, W. EDGAR. "Picture-Frustration Study Responses of Institutionalized and Non-Institutionalized Boys in Hawaii." *J Social Psychol* 41:71–83 F '55. * (*PA* 30:1039)

152. MEHLMAN, BENJAMIN, AND WHITEMAN, STEPHEN LEE. "The Relationship Between Certain Pictures of the Rosenzweig Picture-Frustration Study and Corresponding Behavioral Situations." *J Clin Psychol* 11:15–9 Ja '55. * (*PA* 29:7303)

153. MINSKI, LOUIS, AND DESAI, MAHESH M. "Aspects of Personality in Peptic Ulcer Patients: A Comparison With Hysterics." *Brit J Med Psychol* 28:113–34 Je '55. * (*PA* 30:3268)

154. PARSONS, EDWARD T. "Relationships Between the Rosenzweig P-F Study and Test Duration, Socioeconomic Status, and Religion." Abstract. *J Consult Psychol* 19:28 F '55. *

155. SMITH, LOUIS MILDE. *A Validity Study of Six Personality and Adjustment Tests for Children.* Doctor's thesis, University of Minnesota (Minneapolis, Minn.), 1955. (*DA* 16:791)

156. SUTCLIFFE, J. P. "An Appraisal of the Rosenzweig Picture-Frustration Study." *Austral J Psychol* 7:97–107 D '55. * (*PA* 31:1070)

157. ZUCKERMAN, MARVIN. "The Effect of Frustration on the Perception of Neutral and Aggressive Words." *J Personality* 23:407–22 Je '55. *

158. ANGELINO, HENRY, AND SHEDD, CHARLES L. "A Study of the Reactions to 'Frustration' of a Group of Mentally Retarded Children as Measured by the Rosenzweig Picture-Frustration Study." *Psychol Newsl* 8:40–54 N–D '56. * (*PA* 31:3290)

159. BORNSTON, FRIEDA L., AND COLEMAN, JAMES C. "The Relationship Between Certain Parents' Attitudes Toward Child

Rearing and the Direction of Aggression of Their Young Adult Offspring." *J Clin Psychol* 12:41–4 Ja '56. * (*PA* 30:5183)

160. BRESEE, CLYDE WESLEY. *Affective Factors Associated With Academic Underachievement in High-School Students.* Doctor's thesis, Cornell University (Ithaca, N.Y.), 1956. (*DA* 17:90)

161. BURGESS, ELVA. "Personality Factors of Over- and Under-Achievers in Engineering." *J Ed Psychol* 47:89–99 F '56. * (*PA* 31:8811)

162. GREY, OREVA. *An Analysis of the Frustration Pattern of a Defective-Hearing Group as Revealed by Rosenzweig's Picture-Frustration Study.* Master's thesis, Fordham University (New York, N.Y.), 1956.

163. KAMENETZKY, JOSEPH; BURGESS, GEORGE G.; AND ROWAN, THOMAS. "The Relative Effectiveness of Four Attitude Assessment Techniques in Predicting a Criterion." *Ed & Psychol Meas* 16:187–94 su '56. * (*PA* 31:5101)

164. LEWINSOHN, PETER M. "Personality Correlates of Duodenal Ulcer and Other Psychosomatic Reactions." *J Clin Psychol* 12:296–8 Jl '56. * (*PA* 31:6484)

165. McCARY, J. L. "Picture-Frustration Study Normative Data for Some Cultural and Racial Groups." *J Clin Psychol* 12:194–5 Ap '56. * (*PA* 31:4702)

166. McGUIRE, FREDERICK L. "Rosenzweig Picture Frustration Study for Selecting Safe Drivers." *US Armed Forces Med J* 7:200–7 F '56. * (*PA* 31:1054)

167. MUELLER, ALFRED D., AND LEFKOVITS, AARON M. "Personality Structure and Dynamics of Patients With Rheumatoid Arthritis." *J Clin Psychol* 12:143–7 Ap '56. * (*PA* 31:5010)

168. MURPHY, MARY MARTHA. "Social Class Differences in Frustration Patterns of Alcoholics." *Q J Studies Alcohol* 17:255:62 Je '56. * (*PA* 31:6329)

169. ROSENZWEIG, SAUL. "Projective Methods and Psychometric Criteria: A Note of Reply to J. P. Sutcliffe." *Austral J Psychol* 8:152–5 D '56. *

170. SIEGMAN, ARON W. "A 'Culture and Personality' Study Based on a Comparison of Rorschach Performance." *J Social Psychol* 44:173–8 N '56. *

171. COX, F. N. "The Rosenzweig Picture-Frustration Study (Child Form)." *Austral J Psychol* 9:141–8 D '57. *

172. GRAINE, GEORGE N. "Measures of Conformity as Found in the Rosenzweig P-F Study and the Edwards Personal Preference Schedule." Abstract. *J Consult Psychol* 21:300 Ag '57. *

173. HEDBERG, RAYMOND. "The Rosenzweig Picture-Frustration Study in Relation to Life Insurance Salesmen." Abstract. *Am Psychol* 12:408 Jl '57. *

174. KAHN, HARRIS. "Responses of Hard of Hearing and Normal Hearing Children to Frustration." *Excep Child* 24:155–9 D '57. *

175. McCARY, J. L., AND TRACKTIR, JACK. "Relationship Between Intelligence and Frustration-Aggression Patterns as Shown by Two Racial Groups." *J Clin Psychol* 13:202–4 Ap '57. * (*PA* 32:2799)

176. PALMER, JAMES O. "Some Relationships Between Rorschach's Experience Balance and Rosenzweig's Frustration-Aggression Patterns." *J Proj Tech* 21:137–41 Je '57. *

177. SCHWARTZ, MILTON M. "Galvanic Skin Responses Accompanying the Picture-Frustration Study." *J Clin Psychol* 13:382–7 O '57. *

178. SCHWARTZ, MILTON M. "The Importance of the Pictorial Aspect in Determining Performance on the Picture-Frustration Study." *J Clin Psychol* 13:399–402 O '57. *

179. SILVERSTEIN, A. B. "Faking on the Rosenzweig Picture-Frustration Study." *J Appl Psychol* 41:192–4 Je '57. *

180. SPACHE, GEORGE. "Personality Patterns of Retarded Readers." *J Ed Res* 50:461–9 F '57. *

181. SUTCLIFFE, J. P. "A Rejoinder to Rosenzweig on 'Projective Methods and Psychometric Criteria.'" *Austral J Psychol* 9:91–2 Je '57. *

182. WALLON, EDWARD J., AND WEBB, WILSE B. "The Effect of Varying Degrees of Projection on Test Scores." *J Consult Psychol* 21:465–72 D '57. *

183. BENNETT, CARSON M., AND JORDAN, THOMAS E. "Security-Insecurity and the Direction of Aggressive Responses to Frustration." *J Clin Psychol* 14:166–7 Ap '58. *

184. FOSTER, ARTHUR LEE. "The Relationship Between EEG Abnormality, Some Psychological Factors and Delinquent Behavior." *J Proj Tech* 22:276–80 S '58. *

185. FRIEDMAN, BERT. *A Study of the Szondi Assumptions of Identification Utilizing Modified Versions of the Rosenzweig P-F Study on Criminal Groups.* Master's thesis, Fordham University (New York, N.Y.), 1958.

186. SMITH, LOUIS M. "The Concurrent Validity of Six Personality and Adjustment Tests for Children." *Psychol Monogr* 72(4):1–30 '58. *

RICHARD H. DANA, *Assistant Professor of Psychology, University of Nevada, Reno, Nevada.*

FORM FOR ADULTS. Psychological testing is one expression of our culturally conceived empiricism. The *Rosenzweig Picture-Frustration Study* exemplifies those few projective instruments with rational origins. This test thus constitutes an attempted statement of Rosenzweig's frustration theory in operational terms. Elaboration of the theory by means of scoring dimensions is available in a previous review (4:129). Assessment of the adequacy of this statement of theory is the focus for this review.

The P-F test consists of 24 semi-structured, cartoon-like, two or more person stimulus situations with two caption boxes, one containing descriptive or frustrating words, the other blank for the subject's response. Test stimuli were selected to represent ego-blocking (16 items) and superego blocking (8 items). Exact selection procedures and item analyses are not reported in 20 articles dealing with description and theory. Items 2, 3, and 14 are frequently misunderstood by subjects. It is unknown whether item ambiguity is a function of uncontrolled item selection procedures. Unless the correlates of misperception are determined, the item selection procedures remain suspect.

Eight studies have examined reliability. Internal consistency coefficients have been uniformly low. To beg this question by contending the desirability of item heterogeneity is no substitute for an experimental approach to item selection. Subjects do not obtain scores which are particularly consistent over time. While it may be unrealistic to demand test-retest figures of a given magnitude, it is mandatory that such figures be available for varying periods of time and on subjects comparable to norm groups.

Administration and instructions have been systematically varied in unpublished studies to the confirmation of current practice. The scoring system may be applied with moderate agreement between independent scorers. The reported figure of 70 per cent initial agreement which augments to 85 per cent with practice compares favorably with 75 per cent for the Rorschach. That nearly one half of the discrepancies between scorers occur on only seven stimulus items (with Item 8 contributing one fourth of total scorer disagreement) again argues the need for item analysis.

Norms are reported in 26 studies for a variety of special groups. The order of normative studies has been unfortunate here. Representative, national norms predicated on adequate standardization should antedate local norms for clearly defined populations. That these national norms can now be obtained should encourage

test authors to restandardize their instruments following the examples afforded by the *Tomkins-Horn Picture Arrangement Test* and the *Wechsler Adult Intelligence Scale*. Relevant variables such as intelligence, social class, and occupation are not controlled in current norms. Separate norms have been compiled for African, Finnish, French, German, Italian, and Japanese translations (35 studies).

One score, the group conformity rating, or capacity for conformity with conventional behavior under stress, has been fixated by six studies as a particular *bête noir*. The GCR has been cited as unreliable, but nonetheless the same components are consistently identified in separate studies. Relationships are found with *Edwards Personal Preference Schedule* autonomy and *Minnesota Multiphasic Personality Inventory* dominance and achievement. This accentuates the problems of validity. Of 25 extant validity studies in English, 19 were classified as to type of validity and the studies tallied as supportive, nonsupportive, or equivocal. The results of this exercise indicate that seven predictive and congruent studies are consistently supportive; eight concurrent studies are nonsupportive or equivocal; and, of four content studies, two experimental studies are supportive and two correlation studies are nonsupportive. This leaves open the salient issue of what level of behavior is being measured, but does suggest that "validity for what?" is an appropriate question. In addition, the practice of using the P-F alone for individual prediction would not be justified on the basis of current validation.

The P-F has been a potent generator of research with 25 published studies and as many more dissertations. In approximately 25 years the P-F has demonstrated that responses to frustrating situations are measurable and have meaning consistent with other pilgrimages into the unconscious, both rational and empirical. The major shortcomings of the P-F pertain to reliability. Reliability is a function of test construction procedures employed. Systematic sampling of potential test stimuli does not really violate assumptions for projective techniques. While it is patently too late for such test construction nostrums, restandardization with a national, representative sample would seem imperative. Only with a solid nomothetic basis can idiographic techniques be maximally useful in clinical and research situations. The publication of a revised manual including all relevant re-

liability and validity data as well as scoring procedures is advisable. The P-F test lacks the breadth and sensitivity of the TAT or Rorschach. However, for the stated limited measurement purposes it is perhaps as close to a model instrument as any projective technique currently in use.

FORM FOR CHILDREN. The children's P-F has stimulated approximately 30 studies in 20 years. It was designed to parallel the adult P-F (16 similar items) with 14 ego-blocking stimulus situations and 8 superego blocking situations. Apparently there was an earlier form with more than 24 items, which the manual indicates was shortened because "it proved to add relatively little." As in the manual for the adult level, the test user must infer the criteria for item selection. The test is presented in the guise of a "game," with either examiner or subject filling in blanks for each pictured situation.

Scoring follows the format for the adult P-F, with 11 scores derived from combinations of direction of aggression (extra-, intro-, impunitive) and reaction type (obstacle-dominance, ego-defense, need-persistive). Use is made of the group conformity rating and 15 possible trend scores which indicate change during the course of the test.

Norms are presented for 256 children, aged 4-13, in two-year levels. Children aged 4-7 were tested individually in a private school; children aged 8-13 were tested in groups in public schools. No controls for intelligence, social class, father's occupation, and the like, were employed. The test user can never know the comparability of his own subjects to the standardization group on variables other than age, sex, and kind of school situation. Limited normative data have been reported for such groups as 7- to 9-year old diabetics (*148*), 10- to 14-year old institutionalized Hawaiian boys (*151*), and retarded readers (*141, 180*). Translations have been made into French, German, Italian, and Japanese.

Test reliability and scorer reliability figures are not reported and the unwarranted assumption is made that the figures for the children's form will resemble those for the adult form. Evidence for validity has been inferred from progressive age changes in P-F responses. Extrapunitive responses decrease with age; GCR, indirect expressions of hostility, and superego patterns increase with age (*110*). Trends are usable as a gross index of instability and low

frustration tolerance (*57*). Direction of aggression scores are related to differential submission to parents and peers (*87*). Need-persistence is positively associated with peer ratings for persistence, i.e., best "sticker"; [1] extrapunitiveness has some congruent validity with a problems situations test (*150*). The single study with less uniformly favorable results (*133*) has been criticized for design and statistics (*150*). Although these indications for validity are meager, their consistency should stimulate further study.

When the children's P-F is considered for clinical or research use, the tentative status of test and scorer reliability, norms, and validation must be recognized. The manual, although a distinct improvement over the manual for the adult level, should be revised to include much more of the available data. The major potential contribution of the P-F is to our knowledge of child behavior. Longitudinal studies of the P-F developmental process of specified groups of children are needed. These data could become a concrete substitute for inferences from present group norms. The most outrageous example of such inferences stems from the lumping together of private and public school children of different ages and making a continuous interpretation of changes in scoring variables as a function of age.

Rosenzweig has often stated his concern with that critical research area which attempts to determine the projective level of given responses. The problem of ambiguous level is cited to account for the results of controversial validity studies. It is known that different degrees of control can be exercised over the content of projections, especially as stimulus dimensions conform closely to everyday experience. This does not necessarily imply that such control is a function of age as the manual suggests. While assumptions concerning projective level as a function of age may legitimately be made, it should be explicitly stated that these are indeed assumptions and not facts.

Comparisons of the children's P-F with such tests as *Blacky Pictures, Children's Apperception Test,* and *Michigan Picture Test* are difficult because of extreme differences in stimulus structure. The P-F test is highly structured, limited in purpose, with a relatively objective scoring system. This makes for efficiency in measurement of subjective reactions to frustra-

tion with a necessary loss of sensitivity in other areas. It is unquestionably one of the most useful projective techniques in use with children today.

BERT R. SAPPENFIELD, *Professor of Psychology, Montana State University, Missoula, Montana.*

The P-F Study differs from many other projective tests in that its stimulus material was chosen and its scoring rationale formulated in terms of guiding hypotheses. One of these is the familiar hypothesis concerning the relation between frustration and aggression; another is Rosenzweig's hypothesis concerning the possibility of categorizing all reactions to frustration in terms of "type of reaction" and "direction of aggression."

The manual for each form describes the scoring system in sufficient detail and provides scoring samples based on responses of approximately 500 subjects to each of the 24 situations that serve as items.

There are few indications in the manuals to imply that the authors were concerned about problems of reliability or validity. The main exceptions to this statement include one mention (in the manual for the children's form) of retest reliability findings for the Adult form, and a brief discussion (also in the children's manual) relative to the "projective level from which the responses made by the subject issue." There is no mention in either manual of internal consistency, of the degree of interscorer agreement, or of the findings from validation studies.

Norms for the various categories, as reported for the children's form, are based on responses of 256 school children, aged 4 to 13. Even if this should be regarded as an adequate sample on which to base norms (provided that representativeness were also demonstrated), it is questionable whether the resulting samples are sufficiently large when the total group is subdivided into two-year age groupings. Norms for the adult form are based on responses of 236 males and 224 females, aged 20 to 29. No additional data are given concerning the composition of the adult sample.

Sixteen situations in the adult form and 14 in the children's form are intended to involve "ego-blocking," while 8 situations in each form are intended to involve "superego-blocking." The authors state that not all subjects perceive the situations as they are intended to be per-

ceived, so that an inquiry is often desirable in order to determine the appropriate basis for scoring. Better tests might have resulted if the authors had designed separate forms for ego-blocking and for superego-blocking situations, and if they had performed item analyses to insure high internal consistency among stimulus values for items retained in each of the forms.

A group conformity ratio can be computed for responses to the P-F Study; this ratio can reasonably be interpreted to indicate the degree to which a subject's reactions resemble those of the standardization group. No frequency data are provided, however, for deriving an opposite kind of interpretation (namely, the occurrence of relatively rare or idiosyncratic responses) except in the case of responses that occurred with zero frequency.

The zero-frequency information alluded to in the preceding paragraph reveals that only two cartoons (Items 4 and 6) of the adult form and only one cartoon (Item 9) of the children's form actually yielded responses scorable in all of the nine theoretically possible categories. The mean number of scoring categories not used for each of the remaining cartoons amounted to 3.0 (range 1–6) on the adult form and 3.4 (range 1–5) on the children's form. The fact that the pattern of nonused categories also varies from cartoon to cartoon on each of the forms is consistent with the findings of Taylor (*115*), which indicated low inter-item consistency.

Aside from the fact of inadequate inter-item consistency, the zero-frequency information points to another deficiency in the items. High ambiguity (maximum interindividual variation in response yield) is a desideratum for all projective tests; nearly all of the items fail to meet this ambiguity criterion, since they do not elicit all of the theoretically possible types of responses. Other projective tests may, of course, also be deficient in this regard; for example, the achromatic Rorschach blots do not yield FC, CF, or C responses.

In summary, the P-F Study can, in principle, be regarded as a highly promising projective technique, since its general design and scoring rationale are based on sound psychodynamic hypotheses. However, it appears that the test could be improved in important respects if more attention were given to the problem of item selection and to the development of internally consistent forms which assess single variables. Until such basic revisions have been made, the P-F Study will have limited usefulness either as a test or as a research instrument.

For reviews by Robert C. Challman and Percival M. Symonds, see 4:129.

[156]
The Rotter Incomplete Sentences Blank. Grades 9–12, 13–16, adults; 1950; 3 levels, 1 form; manual and standardization data based on college level only; $1.25 per 25 tests; $1.90 per manual; postpaid; specimen set not available; (20–40) minutes; Julian B. Rotter and Janet E. Rafferty (manual); Psychological Corporation. *

REFERENCES

1–6. See 4:130.
7. BERG, WILBERT ARTHUR. *Determining Validity of the Incomplete Sentences Blank Through Appraisal of Qualitative Interpretations.* Doctor's thesis, University of Missouri (Columbia, Mo.), 1952. (DA 12:504)
8. SMITH, WALTER E. *A Comparison of the Responses of Stutterers and Non-Stutterers in a College Population on the Rotter Incomplete Sentences Blank.* Master's thesis, Bowling Green State University (Bowling Green, Ohio), 1952.
9. WALTER, VERNE A. *A Comparison of the Adjustment Scores Obtained by College Freshmen Women on Two Forms of an Incomplete Sentences Blank.* Master's thesis, Bowling Green State University (Bowling Green, Ohio), 1952.
10. CLARKE, S. C. T. "The Effect of Teachers' Adjustment on Teachers' Attitudes." *Can J Psychol* 7:49–59 Je '53. * (PA 28:4958)
11. ROTTER, JULIAN B., AND RAFFERTY, JANET E. "Rotter Incomplete Sentences Blank," pp. 590–8. (PA 27:7792) In *Contributions Toward Medical Psychology: Theory and Psychodiagnostic Methods, Vol. II.* Edited by Arthur Weider. New York: Ronald Press Co., 1953. Pp. xi, 459–885. *
12. BASS, BERNARD M.; KARSTENDIEK, BARBARA; McCULLOUGH, GERALD; AND PRUITT, RAY C. "Validity Information Exchange, No. 7-024: D.O.T. Code 2-66.01, 2-66.11, 2-66.12, 2-66.23, Policemen and Detectives, Public Service." *Personnel Psychol* 7:159–60 sp '54. *
13. ROTTER, JULIAN B.; RAFFERTY, JANET E.; AND LOTSOF, ANTOINETTE B. "The Validity of the Rotter Incomplete Sentences Blank: High School Form." *J Consult Psychol* 18:105–11 Ap '54. * (PA 29:2470)
14. SECHREST, LEE B., AND HEMPHILL, JOHN K. "Motivational Variables in the Assuming of Combat Obligation." *J Consult Psychol* 18:113–8 Ap '54. * (PA 29:3144)
15. BIERI, JAMES; BLACHARSKY, EDWARD; AND REID, J. WILLIAM. "Predictive Behavior and Personal Adjustment." *J Consult Psychol* 19:351–6 O '55. * (PA 30:5974)
16. CHURCHILL, RUTH, AND CRANDALL, VAUGHN J. "The Reliability and Validity of the Rotter Incomplete Sentences Test." *J Consult Psychol* 19:345–50 O '55. * (PA 30:5980)
17. CLARKE, S. C. T., AND McGREGOR, J. R. "Teachers' Adjustment and Teachers' Achievement in University Courses." *Can J Psychol* 9:55–8 Mr '55. * (PA 30:1641)
18. TINDALL, RALPH H. "Relationships Among Indices of Adjustment Status." *Ed & Psychol Meas* 15:152–62 su '55. * (PA 30:2330)
19. BERGER, IRVING L., AND SUTKER, ALVIN R. "The Relationship of Emotional Adjustment and Intellectual Capacity to Academic Achievement of College Students." *Mental Hyg* 40:65–77 Ja '56. * (PA 31:3770)
20. LIT, JACK. *Formal and Content Factors of Projective Tests in Relation to Academic Achievement.* Doctor's thesis, Temple University (Philadelphia, Pa.), 1956. (DA 16:1505)
21. ARNOLD, FRANK C., AND WALTER, VERNE A. "The Relationship Between a Self- and Other-Reference Sentence Completion Test." *J Counsel Psychol* 4:65–70 sp '57. * (PA 32:484)
22. DEAN, SIDNEY I. "Adjustment Testing and Personality Factors of the Blind." *J Consult Psychol* 21:171–7 Ap '57. *
23. SOHLER, DOROTHY TERRY; HOLZBERG, JULES D.; FLECK, STEPHEN; CORNELISON, ALICE R.; KAY, ELEANOR; AND LIDZ, THEODORE. "The Prediction of Family Interaction From a Battery of Projective Techniques." *J Proj Tech* 21:199–208 Je '57. *
24. FITZGERALD, BERNARD J. "Some Relationships Among Projective Test, Interview, and Sociometric Measures of Dependent Behavior." *J Abn & Social Psychol* 56:199–203 Mr '58. *

For reviews by Charles N. Cofer and William Schofield, see 4:130.

To

CYRIL BURT

DESIGNED BY LUELLA BUROS

MANUFACTURED BY QUINN & BODEN COMPANY, INC., RAHWAY, NEW JERSEY
PRINTED IN THE UNITED STATES OF AMERICA

THE FIFTH MENTAL MEASUREMENTS YEARBOOK

Oscar Krisen Buros, Editor

Professor of Education and Director
The Institute of Mental Measurements, School of Education
Rutgers, The State University

THE GRYPHON PRESS

HIGHLAND PARK · NEW JERSEY

1959

EDITORIAL ASSOCIATES

Miriam M. Bryan

Barbara A. Peace

*

EDITORIAL ASSISTANT

Alfred Hall

THE FIFTH
MENTAL
MEASUREMENTS
YEARBOOK

clear that "it should be continually kept in mind that the great majority of persons having deviant profiles are not, in the usual sense of the word, mentally ill, nor are they in need of psychological treatment. Having no more information about a person than that he has a deviant profile, one should always start with the assumption that the subject is operating within the normal range." The *Atlas* then, which encourages test users to compare obtained profiles to those of mental hospital patients and contains no profiles of "normal" subjects with deviant scores, seems to add to the confusion regarding whether or not individual diagnosis is to be taken too seriously.

Another relevant question in regard to clinical use of the MMPI is whether the game is worth the candle in terms of time consumed in scoring and interpreting the test. Aside from literally scores of hours which a conscientious MMPI user must now take to acquaint himself with the theory and practice of the test, he must also spend from two to three hours checking, profiling, analyzing, and comparing each protocol in relation to the material in the manual, the *Atlas,* the *Basic Readings,* and various other MMPI researches. It is to be wondered whether the clinical psychologist who cannot, in equal or less time, get more pertinent, incisive, and depth-centered "personality" material from a straightforward interview technique, is worth his salt.

On the whole, one must have considerable respect for the great amount of time and effort that have gone into MMPI research since the first studies on it appeared in 1940. This time and effort has borne sufficient fruit to make it now appear that the instrument is quite useful for many kinds of group discrimination. About its usefulness for individual clinical diagnosis the present reviewer, for one, is still far from enthusiastic.

Warren T. Norman, *Instructor in Psychology, University of Michigan, Ann Arbor, Michigan.*

The current manual, revised in 1951, is intended to serve primarily as a "basic guide to administration and interpretation" rather than as a "general treatise on the MMPI." It provides detailed information on the item content and format, the administration, recording, and scoring of both the card and booklet forms, and procedures and norms for plotting profiles and for coding them, using Hathaway's system. In-

formation on the development and characteristics of the standard validity (in the sense of test-taking attitude) and clinical scales is brief and, in one major aspect to be discussed below, seriously inadequate. The discussion of profile interpretation, while properly cautious, is general and unsystematic and cannot serve as more than a minimal introduction to the usefulness and the problems of multiscale personality assessment with this inventory.

Test-retest stability coefficients reported range from .46 to .93 over periods of from three days to one year and cluster about a median of .76. The manual contains no table of intercorrelations among the scales of the inventory, no correlations with other personality measures, no information on internal consistency among items comprising a given scale, nor any explicit indication of the number or names of general factors of personality tapped by the several empirically derived scales.

The most serious shortcoming of the manual, however, is the absence of detailed predictive and concurrent validity information. Neither data from the original development samples nor data from subsequent studies against psychiatric diagnoses or other behavioral criteria are presented. Considerable information of this sort is now available but mostly in scattered journal articles. In short, the manual is adequate in its coverage of general test description, administration, and scoring details; it is inadequate in its report of the empirical and construct validities of the scales and ought to be revised accordingly.

Fortunately for the clinical or research user of the MMPI, many of the manual's deficiencies are compensated by other available references. The volume (*263*) of case histories compiled by Hathaway and Meehl is valuable both for purposes of training in profile interpretation and as a reference source. Hathaway and Monachesi (*438*) have reported a series of studies in predicting juvenile delinquency. A somewhat earlier monograph by Cottle (*423*) provides some technical material not covered in the test manual. But perhaps the most valuable adjunct is the Welsh and Dahlstrom collection of readings (*669*). This volume contains 66 of the most important articles on the MMPI that appeared from 1940 through 1954, plus information on the development of certain scales not previously available. In addition, it provides a

bibliography of 689 titles directly relevant to the MMPI.

Previous reviews (3:60, 4:71) have been critical concerning the predictive validity of the clinical scales for differential psychiatric diagnosis. That issue is not yet fully resolved. However, a tally of the Welsh and Dahlstrom bibliography indicates that some 70 studies were concerned with empirical validity in psychiatric classification or other behavior pathology contexts and an additional 50 or so were related to therapy and guidance.

From 80 to 90 studies have been concerned with relations of the MMPI scales to other personality measures, about 15 each to interest and attitude variables, about 35 to ability and achievement, approximately 50 to occupational, educational, and economic variables, sex, or age status, and about 65 to medical disease, drug effects, and other physical characteristics. In addition, some 17 factor analyses had been done by late 1954 and current work by Comrey (682-4, 735-41) adds further information on the internal structure of several scales. In brief, the amount of data relevant to the construct validities of the inventory's scales is impressive.

The aim of the authors to provide an instrument that will ultimately yield scores on all the important phases of personality (even from the clinician's viewpoint) may be unrealistic. Whatever the case, the aim has not thus far been fulfilled. Over 30 articles published prior to 1955 proposed new scales for the MMPI and no sign of slackening has since appeared. Some 20 studies have been concerned with the problem of response set and test-taking attitude detection.

This instrument is probably the most carefully constructed and thoroughly researched inventory available for personality assessment. It is likely to be an increasingly useful clinical tool.

For a review by Arthur L. Benton, see 4:71; for reviews by Arthur L. Benton, H. J. Eysenck, L. S. Penrose, and Julian B. Rotter, see 3:60 (1 excerpt); for related reviews, see B199, B200, B467, and 4:72.

[87]

Minnesota Personality Scale. Grades 11-16; 1941; 5 scores: morale, social adjustment, family relations, emotionality, economic conservatism; IBM; separate forms for men and women; $3 per 25; separate answer sheets must be used; $2.20 per 50 IBM answer sheets; $1.25 per set of IBM scoring stencils; 50¢ per set of hand scoring stencils; 60¢ per specimen set; postpaid; nontimed (45) minutes; John G. Darley and Walter J. McNamara; Psychological Corporation. *

REFERENCES

1-9. See 3:61.
10. HAHN, MILTON EDWIN. *An Investigation of Measured Aspects of Social Intelligence in a Distributive Occupation.* Doctor's thesis, University of Minnesota (Minneapolis, Minn.), 1942.
11. JACOBSEN, CARLYLE F. "Interest and Attitude as Factors in Achievement in Medical School." *J Assn Am Med Col* 21: 152-9 My '46. *
12. CERF, ARTHUR Z. "Minnesota Personality Scale, CE438A," pp. 601-3. In *Printed Classification Tests.* Edited by J. P. Guilford. Army Air Forces Aviation Psychology Program Research Reports, Report No. 5. Washington, D.C.: U.S. Government Printing Office, 1947. Pp. xi, 919. * (*PA* 22:4145)
13. LOVELL, GEORGE D.; LAURIE, GLORIA; AND MARVIN, DORIS. "A Comparison of the Minnesota Personality Scale and the Bell Adjustment Inventory for Student Counseling." *Proc Iowa Acad Sci* 54:247-51 '47. * (*PA* 23:5524)
14. WINBERG, WILMA C. "Some Personality Traits of Collegiate Underachievers." *Proc Iowa Acad Sci* 54:267-70 '47. * (*PA* 23:5759)
15. KELLEY, RAY R., AND JOHNSON, PAUL E. "Emotional Traits in Pacifists." *J Social Psychol* 28:275-86 N '48. * (*PA* 23:2646)
16. OWENS, WILLIAM A., AND JOHNSON, WILMA C. "Some Measured Personality Traits of Collegiate Underachievers." *J Ed Psychol* 40:41-6 Ja '49. * (*PA* 23:5014)
17. STEPAT, DOROTHY L. *A Study of Clothing and Appearance Problems in Relation to Some Aspects of Personality and Some Cultural Patterns in a Group of College Freshman Girls.* Doctor's thesis, New York University (New York, N.Y.), 1949. Pp. 181. (*Microfilm Abstr* 10:64)
18. TYLER, F. T. "Personality Tests and Teaching Ability." *Can J Psychol* 3:30-7 Mr '49. * (*PA* 23:4443)
19. COCHRAN, SAMUEL W., AND DAVIS, FREDERICK B. "Predicting Freshman Grades at George Peabody College for Teachers." *Peabody J Ed* 27:352-6 My '50. *
20. CROSBY, MARION JOSEPHINE. *Personality Adjustment, Academic Achievement and Job Satisfaction.* Doctor's thesis, Columbia University (New York, N.Y.), 1950. (*Microfilm Abstr* 10:99)
21. DARLEY, JOHN G.; GROSS, NEAL; AND MARTIN, WILLIAM E. "Studies of Group Behavior: Stability, Change, and Interrelations of Psychometric and Sociometric Variables." *J Abn & Social Psychol* 46:565-76 O '51. * (*PA* 26:3915)
22. GILBERT, HARRY B. *An Evaluation of Certain Procedures in the Selection of Camp Counselors Based on Objective Test Data as Predictive of Practical Performance.* Doctor's thesis, New York University (New York, N.Y.), 1951. (*Microfilm Abstr* 11:953)
23. NOLL, VICTOR H. "Simulation by College Students of a Prescribed Pattern on a Personality Scale." *Ed & Psychol Meas* 11:478-88 au '51. * (*PA* 27:5893)
24. GILBERT, HARRY B. "The Use of Tests and Other Objective Data in the Selection of Camp Counselors." Abstract. *Am Psychol* 7:369 Jl '52. *
25. PALUBINSKAS, ALICE L. "Personality Changes in College Women During Four Years of College Experience." *Proc Iowa Acad Sci* 59:389-91 '52. * (*PA* 28:6543)
26. PALUBINSKAS, ALICE L. *Potential Utility of the Minnesota Personality Scale in Counseling Home Economic Students at Iowa State College.* Doctor's thesis, Iowa State College (Ames, Iowa), 1952.
27. BENNETT, THELMA, AND WALTERS, JAMES. "Personal and Social Adjustment of College Home Economics Freshmen." *J Home Econ* 45:29-31 Ja '53. *
28. PALUBINSKAS, ALICE L. "A Four-Year Study of Selected Socioeducational Variables and the Minnesota Personality Scale." Abstract. *Am Psychol* 8:412-3 Ag '53. *
29. BERDIE, RALPH F. "Aptitude, Achievement, Interest, and Personality Tests: A Longitudinal Comparison." *J Appl Psychol* 39:103-14 Ap '55. * (*PA* 30:1498)
30. JOHNSON, BERNADINE. *Family Relations and Social Adjustment Scores on the Minnesota Personality Scale as Related to Home and School Backgrounds of a Selected Group of Freshman Women.* Doctor's thesis, Florida State University (Tallahassee, Fla.), 1956. (*DA* 16:1438)
31. STONE, SOLOMON. *The Contribution of Intelligence, Interests, Temperament and Certain Personality Variables to Academic Achievement in a Physical Science and Mathematics Curriculum.* Doctor's thesis, New York University (New York, N.Y.), 1957. (*DA* 18:669)

For reviews by Philip Eisenberg and John W. French, see 3:61.

[88]

Minnesota Rating Scale for Personal Qualities and Abilities, [Fourth Revision]. College and adults; 1925-38; revision of Part II of *Rating Scale for Teachers of Home Economics;* 1 form ('38); mimeographed manual ('38); no data on reliability; $1.75

per 100 scales; 25¢ per specimen set; postage extra; Clara M. Brown; University of Minnesota Press. *

REFERENCE

1. BROWN, CLARA M. *An Evaluation of the Minnesota Rating Scale for Home Economics Teachers.* Minneapolis, Minn.: University of Minnesota Press, 1931. Pp. 29.

DOROTHY M. CLENDENEN, *Assistant Director, Test Division, The Psychological Corporation, New York, New York.*

Although this rating scale was first published in 1925, and this 1938 edition represents the fourth revision, the mimeographed manual presents no statistical information, and few details are reported of the analysis of 1,400 individual ratings which the manual states was made prior to revision. There is a discussion of the general development of the instrument, suggestions for its use, and instructions for raters.

The scale consists of 20 items regarded by home economics faculty members at Minnesota as representing important personal qualities for home economics students. However, it is recommended for use with other groups. Suggested uses are "in counseling, in determining scholarship awards, and in recommending graduates for positions."

Personal qualities such as poise, voice, personal appearance, management of work, command of English, and professional attitude are included in a graphic scale which has, for each item, descriptive phrases indicating three levels. Check marks are converted to numerical values on a scale of 1 to 10. Values are added and averaged to obtain a "score."

Statements describing the qualities to be rated are in terms of observable behavior and are specific. An attempt has been made to keep all three levels equally attractive to the rater so that neither the extremes nor the average will be generally avoided. Rating all members of the group on one characteristic at a time is recommended. Anecdotal records are encouraged as supplementary information to explain a rating.

No studies of reliability are reported. This seems especially unfortunate in view of the number of ratings available to the author, and the ease with which such studies could have been made. Since rating scales have often been shown to be low in reliability, the reviewer finds absence of such information on this scale to be a serious limitation in its use. Nor is any evidence of the validity of the scale given, and one wonders, for example, to what extent teacher rating of leadership, based on observation in the classroom or department, correlates with other criteria of leadership. The same question might be asked concerning the qualities judgment, discretion, resourcefulness, and others.

As a convenient method of summarizing the observer's general impression, this scale seems to be well thought out. For use in recommending graduates, it provides a positive record of the teacher's estimate of attributes not evaluated in course grades, in place of nebulous recall at the time when a recommendation is requested. However, no evidence is presented to support acceptance of the score or its component ratings as an accurate and objective summary of the personality and behavior of the one who has been rated. Therefore, its use in counseling or in determining scholarship awards is open to question. Instruments of known reliability and validity would be more appropriate.

[89]

Mooney Problem Check List, 1950 Revision. Grades 7-9, 9-12, 13-16, adults; 1941-50; IBM for Forms JM, HM, and CM; 4 levels; manuals ('50); no norms—authors recommend the use of local norms; separate answer sheets must be used with Forms JM, HM, and CM; $1.75 per 25 tests (Forms J, H, C, A); $2.40 per 25 tests (Forms JM, HM, CM); $1.90 per 50 IBM answer sheets; 35¢ per specimen set of any one level; postpaid; (20-50) minutes; Ross L. Mooney and Leonard V. Gordon (College and Adult Forms); Psychological Corporation. *

a) JUNIOR HIGH SCHOOL FORM. Grades 7-9; 1942-50; 7 scores: health and physical development, school, home and family, money-work-the future, boy and girl relations, relations to people in general, self-centered concerns; Form J or JM ('50).

b) HIGH SCHOOL FORM. 1941-50; 11 scores: health and physical development, finances-living conditions-employment, social and recreational activities, social-psychological relations, personal-psychological relations, courtship-sex-marriage, home and family, morals and religion, adjustment to school work, the future-vocational and educational, curriculum and teaching procedures; Form H or HM ('50).

c) COLLEGE FORM. Grades 13-16; 1941-50; 11 scores: same as for High School Form; Form C or CM ('50).

d) ADULT FORM. Adults; 1950; 9 scores: health, economic security, self-improvement, personality, home and family, courtship, sex, religion, occupation; Form A.

REFERENCES

1-17. See 3:67.
18-30. See 4:73.
31. KOHRT, CARL FRED. *Problems of High-School Seniors in Douglas County, Illinois.* Master's thesis, Illinois State Normal University (Normal, Ill.), 1950.
32. McINTYRE, CHARLES JOHN. *The Validity of the Mooney Problem Check List, High School Form.* Master's thesis, Pennsylvania State College (State College, Pa.), 1950.
33. GALLAGHER, JAMES J. *An Investigation Into Factors Differentiating College Students Who Discontinue Non-Directive Counseling From College Students Who Continue Counseling.* Doctor's thesis, Pennsylvania State College (State College, Pa.), 1951.
34. TUCKER, JOHN E. *Investigation of Criteria for Evaluating Non-Directive Psychotherapy With College Students.* Doctor's thesis, Pennsylvania State College (State College, Pa.), 1951.
35. BENNETT, BRUCE L. "The Use of the Mooney Problem Check List for a College Hygiene Course." *Ed Res B* 31:231-40+ D 10 '52.
36. BROWN, CURTIS P. *The Mooney Problem Check List and*

the SRA Youth Inventory in Comparison. Master's thesis, University of Southern California (Los Angeles, Calif.), 1952.

37. FICK, REUEL L. "The Problem Check List: A Valuable Approach in Counseling." *Occupations* 30:410–2 Mr '52. * (*PA* 26:6533)

38. GARRISON, KARL C., AND CUNNINGHAM, BEN W., JR. "Personal Problems of Ninth-Grade Pupils." *Sch R* 60:30–3 Ja '52. *

39. WARDLOW, MARY E., AND GREENE, JAMES E. "An Exploratory Sociometric Study of Peer Status Among Adolescent Girls." *Sociometry* 15:311–8 Ag–N '52. * (*PA* 27:7097)

40. BATES, LAWRENCE R., AND COTTLE, WILLIAM C. "A Study of Relationships Between Measured Intelligence and Problems of Ninth Grade Pupils." *Univ Kans B Ed* 8:5–6 N '53. *

41. BROWN, WILLIAM H. "The Problems of Probation and Honor Students." *Ed Res B* 32:14–6+ Ja '53. *

42. McINTYRE, CHARLES J. "The Validity of the Mooney Problem Check List." *J Appl Psychol* 37:270–2 Ag '53. * (*PA* 28:6577)

43. TAN, HASAN. *A Survey of Student Problems With the Mooney Problem Check List in a Secondary School in Istanbul, Turkey.* Master's thesis, University of Maryland (College Park, Md.), 1953.

44. THREADCRAFT, MATTIE H. *A Comparative Study of Problems of Adolescent Boys and Girls (as Measured by the Mooney Problem Checklist) in the Arlington Vocational High School, Arlington, Georgia.* Master's thesis, Atlanta University (Atlanta, Ga.), 1953.

45. BARNES, JAMES R. *A Critical Study of the Results of the Mooney Problem Check List and the Cornell Index as a Means of Identifying Possible Cases of Psychosomatic Illness Among 400 North Carolina College Students.* Master's thesis, North Carolina College (Durham, N.C.), 1954.

46. GALLAGHER, JAMES J. "Test Indicators for Therapy Prognosis." *J Consult Psychol* 18:409–13 D '54. * (*PA* 29:7356)

47. CARR, JAMES FRANCIS, JR. *The Problem Areas of a Selected Group of Students at Florida State University as Indicated by the Mooney Problem Check List.* Doctor's thesis, Indiana University (Bloomington, Ind.), 1955. (*DA* 15:1524)

48. McCOULLOUGH, CHESTER A. *A Statistical Study of the Relationships Between Scores Obtained by 400 North Carolina College Students on the Mooney Problem Check List and the College Inventory of Academic Adjustment.* Master's thesis, North Carolina College (Durham, N.C.), 1955.

49. SIMPSON, ELIZABETH JANE. *Distinctive Personal Problems of Home Economics Students at the University of Illinois.* Doctor's thesis, University of Illinois (Urbana, Ill.), 1955. (*DA* 16:287)

50. WELLINGTON, JOHN ADAM. *Factors Related to the Academic Success of Resident Freshman Men at a Midwestern Liberal Arts College During the Academic Year 1952-1953.* Doctor's thesis, Northwestern University (Evanston, Ill.), 1955. (*DA* 16:69)

51. GROW, MILTON D. *An Analysis of Problems of Students in Selected Junior High Schools.* Doctor's thesis, Northwestern University (Evanston, Ill.), 1956. (*DA* 17:2498)

52. KOILE, EARL A., AND BIRD, DOROTHY J. "Preferences for Counselor Help on Freshman Problems." *J Counsel Psychol* 3:97–106 su '56. * (*PA* 31:5132)

53. PAQUIN, LAURENCE GILBERT. *A Plan for the Improvement of a Secondary School Program Based on an Analysis of Certain Problems of Pupils as Revealed by the Mooney Problem Check List.* Doctor's thesis, New York University (New York, N.Y.), 1956. (*DA* 17:820)

54. WALLER, LYNN T. *Use of the Mooney Problem Checklist in a Comparative Analysis of the Problems of Outstanding Students Versus Unsuccessful Students in the Eighth Grade of the Thomas Hunt Morgan School, Shoreline School District 412, Seattle, Washington.* Master's thesis, University of Washington (Seattle, Wash.), 1956.

55. GRAFF, FRANKLYN ARTHUR. *Occupational Choice Factors in Normally Achieving and Underachieving Intellectually Superior Twelfth Grade Boys.* Doctor's thesis, University of Connecticut (Storrs, Conn.), 1957. (*DA* 17:2207)

56. SINGER, STANLEY L., AND STEFFLRE, BUFORD. "Concurrent Validity of the Mooney Problem Check List." *Personnel & Guid J* 35:298–301 Ja '57. * (*PA* 32:1647)

For reviews by Harold E. Jones and Morris Krugman, see 4:73; for reviews by Ralph C. Bedell and Theodore F. Lentz of an earlier edition, see 3:67.

[90]
★**Objective-Analytic Personality Test Batteries.** Ages 11–16, adults; 1955; 18 factors: children and adults-competent assertiveness, (U.I. 16), restraint-timidity, (U.I. 17), hypomanic overcompensation, (U.I. 18), critical-dominant exactness, (U.I. 19), sociable willingness, (U.I. 20), energetic decisiveness, (U.I. 21), nervous-alert reactivity, (U.I. 22), neural

reserves vs. neuroticism, (U.I. 23), anxiety-to achieve, (U.I. 24), accurate realism vs. psychoticism, (U.I. 25), cultured introspective self-control, (U.I. 26), sociable-emotional evasiveness, (U.I. 28), sympathetic mobilization of energy, (U.I. 29), stolid super ego satisfaction, (U.I. 30), adults only-wary realism, (U.I. 31), schizoid tenacity, (U.I. 32), dourness, (U.I. 33), apathetic temperament, (U.I. 27) ; 1 form ; mimeographed tests ; 2 levels ; 3 batteries for each level ; 2 editions : group, individual ; no data on reliability ; no norms ; $3 per tape recording (7.5 ips) ; $5 per manual ; cash orders postpaid ; additional apparatus needed for various subtests ; Raymond B. Cattell, A. R. Baggaley, L. Checov, E. A. Cogan, D. Flint, W. Gruen, E. Husek, T. Meeland, D. R. Saunders, and H. Schiff ; Institute for Personality and Ability Testing. *

a) THE ADULT 18 0–A BATTERY. Ages 16 and over ; 18 factors (U.I. 16–33) ; $23.20 per set of slides.

1) *Group.* 43 tests ; $25 per set of 43 tests ; 266(300) minutes in 6 sessions.

2) *Individual.* 54 tests ; $29 per set of 54 tests ; 276(310) minutes in 7 sessions.

b) THE ADULT 12 0–A BATTERY. Ages 16 and over ; 12 factors (U.I. 16–27) ; $21.60 per set of slides.

1) *Group.* 38 tests ; $20 per set of 38 tests ; 240(280) minutes in 5 sessions.

2) *Individual.* 46 tests ; $25 per set of 46 tests ; 299(350) or 305(355) minutes in 6 sessions.

c) ADULT SINGLE FACTOR BATTERIES. Adults ; 18 factors (U.I. 16–33) ; $5 per set of testing materials for any one factor ; $23.20 per set of slides.

d) THE CHILDREN 14 0–A BATTERY. Ages 11–16 ; 14 factors (U.I. 16–26, 28–30) ; $25 per set of slides.

1) *Group.* 42 tests ; $25 per set of 42 tests ; 267(300) or 273(310) minutes in 6 sessions.

2) *Individual.* 52 tests ; $29 per set of 52 tests ; 323(350) minutes in 7 sessions.

e) THE CHILDREN 10 FACTOR 0–A BATTERY. Ages 11–16 ; 10 factors (U.I. 16, 17, 19–23, 26, 28, 29) ; 2 editions : group, individual ; $25 per set of slides.

1) *Group.* 35 tests ; $20 per set of 35 tests ; 229.25-(290) or 235.75(295) minutes in 5 sessions.

2) *Individual.* 43 tests ; $25 per set of 43 tests ; 271.25(305) or 284.25(320) minutes in 6 sessions.

f) CHILDREN SINGLE FACTOR BATTERIES. Ages 11–16 ; 14 factors (U.I. 16–26, 28–30) ; 2 editions : group, individual ; $25 per 4 sets of 47 colored and 17 black and white slides.

REFERENCES

1. CATTELL, RAYMOND B. "The Principal Replicated Factors Discovered in Objective Personality Tests." *J Abn & Social Psychol* 50:291–314 My '55. * (*PA* 30:2450)
2. CATTELL, RAYMOND B., AND GRUEN, WALTER. "The Primary Personality Factors in 11-Year-Old Children, by Objective Tests." *J Personality* 23:460–78 My '55. * (*PA* 30:2527)
3. ROSENTHAL, IRENE. *A Factor Analysis of Anxiety Variables.* Doctor's thesis, University of Illinois (Urbana, Ill.), 1955. (*DA* 16:376)
4. CATTELL, RAYMOND B. "The Conceptual and Test Distinction of Neuroticism and Anxiety." *J Clin Psychol* 13:221–33 Jl '57. *
5. CATTELL, RAYMOND B. *Personality and Motivation Structure and Measurement.* Yonkers, N.Y.: World Book Co., 1957. Pp. xxv, 948. *
6. CATTELL, RAYMOND B.; STICE, GLEN F.; AND KRISTY, NORTON F. "A First Approximation to Nature-Nurture Ratios for Eleven Primary Personality Factors in Objective Tests." *J Abn & Social Psychol* 54:143–59 Mr '57. *

H. J. EYSENCK, *Professor of Psychology, Institute of Psychiatry, University of London, London, England.*

This battery of tests is something almost entirely new in psychological measurement. It constitutes a tremendous achievement. In spite

of its many imperfections (of which Cattell himself is only too well aware and to which he draws attention at various points in the handbook which accompanies the test kit), it must be taken to mark the beginning of a new phase, a departure from the customary reliance of psychologists working in the personality field on interviews, questionnaires, and projective techniques. No judgment would be fair which leaves out of account the pioneering nature of this venture which attempts to put personality measurement on a solid, scientific basis.

The battery is based on Cattell's well known factor analytic studies, and attempts to provide measures for 18 of these factors. It is, of course, not necessary to use all the tests provided, or measure all the factors. Several different batteries, giving measures of between 10 and 18 factors, can be made up, both for children and for adults, from the set of tests provided; it is, of course, possible for the research psychologist or the clinical worker to concentrate on just one or two factors judged to be relevant to his problem.

Cattell claims three major achievements for his battery. He claims that the tests measure behaviour in actual situations instead of introspective self examination; that they are scored by keys through which all psychometricians get the same answers; and that they measure functional unities in personality structure which have been established by repeated factor analytic and experimental studies. He warns users that the tests are not as simple to administer as questionnaires; they take more time than many projective tests; and they require considerable skill and psychological knowledge for administration and interpretation.

The nature of the tests is very variable, and many would not ordinarily have been considered as personality tests at all. To name a few at random, the battery includes tests of flicker fusion, body sway suggestibility, colour-form sorting, readiness to act out animal sounds, estimation of passing time, aesthetic sense in colour planning, personal tempo, and so on and so forth. Just looking through the descriptions of the tests given in the test kit handbook will impress the reader with the tremendous range over which Cattell's choice has extended, and his ingenuity and originality in adapting these various measures to personality assessment. A whole year's course on personality measurement could easily be centred on working through this

enormous mass of material with a class of students.

Up to a point the critical evaluation of the test battery depends upon one's estimate of the factorial studies underlying the choice of tests. These studies are unrivalled from the point of view of extensiveness and technical competence. Yet the reviewer cannot wholeheartedly accept Cattell's claim to have discovered 18 independent personality traits in this work. Correlations between tests tend to be quite low on the whole, and Cattell's acceptance of factor matchings from one study to another is based on less stringent criteria than one might wish. Populations are seldom large enough to make one feel very confident about the statistical significance of the last four or five factors extracted, and the choice of populations studied has been somewhat restricted. These remarks are not criticisms so much as statements of fact; when it is realised that practically all the work has been done by Cattell himself and his associates, it will come as no surprise that no finality had been reached. Until this work is duplicated in other departments using the same tests on varying normal and abnormal populations, no final judgment is possible of Cattell's claims. That no such check has been applied can hardly be blamed on Cattell, who, it must be assumed, would like nothing better!

Two important points which the user of this battery must bear in mind are: (a) There are no norms, so that the user will have to build up his own norms as he goes along, basing them on his own group. (b) The meaning of the factors in terms of their relationships to clinical, industrial, and other outside criteria is hardly known at all; and while it would be unfair to say that here we have 18 factors in search of a criterion, it must be realised that this is a research battery of tests rather than one which can be applied directly to practical problems. Of course, Cattell himself draws attention to this restriction and does not pretend that his battery is more advanced than in fact it is. As a research instrument it can hardly be praised too highly; no comparison with existing tests can indeed be made because nothing like it exists at the moment.

Granted then that this battery constitutes a great and important achievement, the reviewer has certain nagging doubts regarding the actual use of the battery and the comparability of data from one user to another. Not all the tests spec-

ify in sufficient detail the mode of administration, or lay down methods for excluding external sources of error. As an illustration of the former difficulty, we may mention the body sway test of suggestibility. Cattell leaves it open to the user to have the suggestions made through a record or a tape recorder, or to say the words himself. The reviewer has found great differences in effectiveness of suggestion between people, and between personal and recorded suggestion. Unless this is taken into account, scores on this test will not be comparable and will in fact mean different things in different laboratories. As an example of the second objection, we may take the flicker fusion test. Anyone familiar with the detailed reviews of this phenomenon by Carney Landis will see how insufficient the instructions of this test are to rule out a wide variety of sources of error, quite apart from the fact that the instrument recommended is a very poor one for the measurement of C.F.F.!

One last point should perhaps be made. Users of personality tests are well aware of the fact that many of these techniques require them to become thoroughly acquainted with a particular set of concepts, terms, and theories. The Rorschach mythology and Murray's system of need and press are well known examples. Something of the kind is necessary here, too. No one could use these tests in any sensible way who was not thoroughly familiar with Cattell's writings and the development of the factors measured by his tests. This is probably inevitable, but it does mean a quite lengthy period of initiation to those not already in the know. The promise held out by this test battery would, in the reviewer's opinion, well justify the time and trouble taken.

[91]

★Personal Adaptability Test. Grades 11-13 and adults; 1957; 4 scores: botheredness, mental malfunctioning, physiological malfunctioning, total; 1 form; 4 editions: separate editions for men and for women, separate editions for grades 11-13 and for business; mimeographed manual; $2.60 per 25 tests; 50¢ per manual; $1.45 per specimen set; postpaid; (20-30) minutes; Guy E. Buckingham; Public School Publishing Co. *

REFERENCE

1. BUCKINGHAM, GUY E. "Making a Personal Adaptability Test." Abstract. *Am Psychol* 5:330-1 Jl '50. *

HAROLD WEBSTER, *Research Associate Psychologist, Center for the Study of Higher Education, University of California, Berkeley, California.*

The rationale for this test is based on the assumption that "abnormal personal and social behavior is the same as error in any other kind of learning." "Botheredness," as measured by the first scale, refers to irritation, annoyance, and the like, admitted by testees when confronted by shortcomings of others or themselves; botheredness is thought to precede development of the malfunctioning measured by the other two scales.

This test appears to measure a kind of neurotic syndrome well known to psychologists. It would be advantageous, therefore, to have correlations of the scales and of the total scale with other tests for measuring neurotic reactions. The combination of irritability and hypochondriasis which is measured would surely be accompanied by a decrease in ability to get along well with others, especially in certain kinds of jobs, *unless the subject decided beforehand not to reveal his irritability and hypochondriasis.* A person who above all wants acceptance by others should be able to achieve a good score on this test despite his other personality difficulties. The test may therefore be as much a measure of complaisance or obeisance as it is a measure of other kinds of adaptability. Because of this and the other limited evidence of validity, the test cannot be recommended for general use.

[92]

★The Personal and Social Development Program. Grades kgn-9; 1956; form for recording behavior incidents in 8 areas: personal adjustment, responsibility and effort, creativity and initiative, integrity, social adjustment, sensitivity to others, group orientation, adaptability to rules and conventions; 1 form; no data on reliability; $5.10 per 40 record forms; 50¢ per administrator's manual; $1.50 per teacher's guide; $2 per specimen set; postage extra; John C. Flanagan; Science Research Associates. *

EDWARD LANDY, *Director, Division of Counseling Services, Newton Public Schools, Newton, Massachusetts.*

The authors and publishers are to be commended for pioneering in the use of the "critical incident" technique to help elementary school teachers identify systematically and in proper balance the behavioral strengths and weaknesses in their pupils. This is one of the two majors aims of the *Personal and Social Development Program* and is as well done as can be reasonably expected in the light of current knowledge of personality growth and development and of the present level of sophistication now existing among elementary school teach-

ers. The major instrument for accomplishing this purpose, called the Performance Record, has been carefully constructed to be used with a minimum of time and effort. The teacher's guide is replete with easily understood and carefully selected examples of how to keep the Performance Record. The explanation offered for selecting and recording behavior also contains much that would be considered as soundly based in acceptable mental health knowledge and theory. The manual for school administrators and supervisors may prove to be a useful aid in getting teachers to accept the program and to fill out the Performance Record accurately.

This reviewer is less optimistic than the authors and publishers appear to be as to whether most, or even many, elementary school teachers would be willing to undertake the program at all. For, in spite of all the careful work done to reduce the record keeping to a minimum, it is questionable whether elementary school teachers (not under the stimulus of participating in a special tryout program) will accept the self-discipline and added clerical burden of interrupting their daily schedules to fill in the blanks or to do so after school without administrative pressure which may defeat the purpose for which the record is being kept.

The second major aim of the program is to try to get teachers to use the collected anecdotal information to encourage desirable pupil behavior. Unless this second aim can be accomplished, the first aim simply results in added clerical work. This reviewer was unable to discover any rigorous evidence as to the effectiveness of achieving the second aim by means of the Performance Record. The kind of evidence provided in the teacher's guide, as exemplified by "The Case of Martie," is of the sort which this reviewer has heard from many teachers who have never used the Performance Record or even made any effort to collect anecdotal information in any systematic way.

There are several real dangers in this program. First, it assumes far more sophistication about child growth and development and the causes and treatment of personality difficulties than most school administrators and supervisors have. Thus, teachers may be lulled into believing they are getting more expert advice from their administrators and supervisors than they really are. Second, it tends to oversimplify the problems of parent-child relationships, teacher-parent interviewing, etc. "The Case of Martie,"

as described, is an illustration of this point. Third, some teachers may start to play the roles of amateur clinical psychologists or psychiatrists.

In all fairness, however, it should be remembered that a program of this kind may be better than the alternatives of doing nothing or taking action without any understanding or data. And it should be stated that the teacher's guide does make an honest and skillful effort at developing in teachers desirable understanding and techniques useful for improving pupil behavior. Given the right kind of leadership and without overly optimistic expectations, the program would seem worth trying out.

C. GILBERT WRENN, *Professor of Educational Psychology,* and ROY D. LEWIS, *Teaching Assistant, University of Minnesota, Minneapolis, Minnesota.*

The Personal and Social Development Program consists of a 4-page performance record for each elementary school child, a 63-page teacher's guide, and a 32-page manual for school administrators. The record is a double-page spread. On one page is a chart in blue for recording incidents that are considered "Behaviors to be Encouraged" in four personal adjustment categories and four social adjustment categories. The opposite page consists of a chart in red for recording "Behaviors Needing Improving" in the same eight personal and social adjustment categories.

The total approach is an attempt to make systematic the familiar anecdotal record system by providing a list of suggested "critical incidents" under each of the categories, and to supply manuals that will help a school develop a program of attention to personality development. The manuals are persuasively written—but the concept contains several "critical concepts" with which the reviewers are concerned.

The items in each category were based upon several thousand critical incidents in pupil behavior contributed by teachers. The critical incident technique is one for which Flanagan is famous, but a serious question arises when so much dependence is placed upon the insight of teachers for what is truly "critical" in the lives of growing children. Teachers have grown mightily since the days of the Wickman study but teachers in general are still not as qualified as school psychologists and mental health specialists in the provision of penetrating

insights on significant elements in personality development. This distinction is significant, for in this program the 42 critical behaviors provide the necessary and sufficient basis for guiding a child. The incidents were not gathered for research purposes but to build a program for guiding personality development.

This suggests the second concern of the reviewers. Teachers are encouraged to talk to children after enough incidents have accumulated to suggest a "trend." The assistance given to teachers on this task is simply and clearly written, but there is too much suggestion that children must conform to the concept of personality developed in the guide. This represents a dangerous road to viewing personality development as *adjustment* and not as creative and individual patterns of growth. The author did not intend this of course, but the use of the program has this hazard.

One of the problems inherent in this plan is the same difficulty that is inherent in any anecdotal record attempt. Only the interested and cooperative teacher will "remember" to record incidents or to use them as a basis of counseling. The program makes an attack upon this problem by setting up a schoolwide plan and a common record for all to use. Not only does the program depend upon the teacher's interest and cooperation (what doesn't, of course!) ; it also rests upon the validity of the incidents recorded. The criteria for selecting a critical incident for recording are (*a*) has the child done or failed to do something *noteworthy;* (*b*) is the incident *indicative* of a child's social development, character and citizenship growth, or manners and morals; (*c*) is the behavior to be *encouraged* or does it need correction; (*d*) am I being *completely objective* in picking out the facts of my observations. It seems obvious to the reviewers that inherent in these criteria are questions which raise some doubt about the "facts" that are recorded. The italics in each instruction are the reviewers'—but each suggests a carefulness and accuracy of judgment that is truly critical. For example: What is a noteworthy behavior? What is the criterion for social development or manners and morals? Upon what basis except a personal one does the teacher determine what behaviors need correction or need to be praised? Are most persons capable of determining the extent of their objectivity?

In summary, the record and program are brave and well intentioned. Under appropriate conditions of interest, informed effort, and freedom for individual variation of both teacher and pupil behavior they could be useful adjuncts to teacher performance. The professional consultants to the program apparently think so, and they and the author are distinguished figures. It just happens that the reviewers believe that the hazards involved may outweigh the benefits. These are hazards of encapsulating behavior to be noticed within a framework of 42, or any number of, critical behaviors suggested by teachers, of quantifying and recording "facts" which are teacher opinions and values, of a uniformity of control in the school even under what are the best intentioned of efforts.

[93]

★The Personal Preference Scale. Ages 15 and over; 1947–54; 10 scores: active-inactive, sociable-individualistic, permissive-critical, consistent-inconsistent, efficient-inefficient, self-effacing-egocentric, masculine-effeminoid, feminine-masculinoid, emotionally mature-emotionally immature, socially mature-socially immature; 1 form ('51) ; guide ['53]; manual ('54, see *1* below) ; no norms below college level; 10¢ per test copy, postage extra; specimen set free; manual must be purchased separately; (20) minutes; Maurice H. Krout and Johanna Krout Tabin; Maurice H. Krout, 1938 Cleveland Ave., Evanston, Ill. *

REFERENCES

1. KROUT, MAURICE H., AND TABIN, JOHANNA KROUT. "Measuring Personality in Developmental Terms: The Personal Preference Scale." *Genetic Psychol Monogr* 50:289–335 N '54. *
2. STAGNER, ROSS; LAWSON, EDWIN D.; AND MOFFITT, J. WELDON. "The Krout Personal Preference Scale: A Factor-Analytic Study." *J Clin Psychol* 11:103–13 Ap '55. *

[94]

★The Personality Evaluation Form: A Technique for the Organization and Interpretation of Personality Data. Ages 2 and over; 1955; 1 form; mimeographed manual; $5 per 25 booklets, postpaid; specimen set not available; Charlotte Buhler and Gertrude Howard; Western Psychological Services. *

DOROTHY H. EICHORN, *Assistant Research Psychologist, Institute of Child Welfare, University of California, Berkeley, California.*

This 12-page booklet provides a clear and comprehensive outline for the summarization of case material for one individual. Objections to the form per se are relatively minor. Insufficient space is allotted for medical history. The section for developmental data consists of a list of "important age-characteristic functions and activities," followed by a yes-no column to be checked and a column for remarks. Most of these items are not usefully rated simply as present or absent; at least a 5-point scale is needed. The remarks column remedies this deficiency, but renders the yes-no column superfluous. There is a misprint in the heading of the subsection for adolescence—it should read 12 to 20

years, not 2 to 20. Section 6 carries the confusing notation, "To be filled in by Counselor," leaving one to wonder who should have filled in the previous five.

The form is purported to facilitate "interpretations and inferences based on premises generally accepted by modern clinicians and specialists in the study of personality and psychopathology." The principal device for accomplishing this objective is a section subtitled "Dynamic Data for Interpretation," organized around the concepts of the individual's needs, the environmental demands upon him, his ability to utilize and cope with reality, and his values and goals. Whether this framework will be helpful depends on the clinician's own theoretical orientation.

The manual—largely an elementary treatise on personality theory—states that the PEF is "based on well recognized dynamic concepts" but "designed for use by teachers and counselors who may have had little clinical training and experience." Neither the source of, nor the evidence for, the concepts is given. Alternative constructs are not discussed. Considerable space is devoted to descriptions of various "Need-Demand" patterns of child rearing and the behavioral results to be expected from each. These summaries lend themselves to diagnosis by the inexperienced in quite the same way as tests which may be used in "cookbook" fashion. The sections on recommendations and follow-up are replete with pious and obvious instructions such as "Every effort should be made to carry out the recommendations made" and "All available personnel and facilities in the school should be used to help maladjusted and unhappy children with their problems." A long list of possible recommendations is included. One can imagine a confused, overworked amateur poring over the list and finally choosing Number 14, "Stimulating the use of outside professional resources for the professional growth of the teachers who work with children who have problems." In both the form and the manual a point is made of distinguishing between data and interpretation. The intention is laudable, but the distinction is incomplete and may mislead the unsophisticated. No recognition is given to the fact that such items as "Home Situation: Describe briefly; adequacy for Counselee's needs" and "Record factual data: how counselee's basic needs—care, security, affection—were met" involve interpretation as well as information.

The major objection to the PEF is the encouragement which the manual gives to untrained persons to accumulate and use clinical case material. Ethically, this practice is as questionable as providing laymen with tests which may be misused. It is doubtful that many trained clinicians need the booklet. Most clinics and private practitioners have their own method of summarization, peculiar to their case loads and theoretical orientations. Those in the process of evolving a summary form might find this one helpful, at least as a model. The PEF can probably best serve as a teaching device—in practicum situations for students' appraisals which are to be reviewed by the instructor, and in the classroom as an illustration of the kinds of data which go into a clinical evaluation. The manual could be used as supplementary textual material.

J Consult Psychol 20:160 Ap '56. Laurance F. Shaffer. Described by its authors as "a technique for the organization and interpretation of personality data," the *Personality Evaluation Form* is a 12-page booklet consisting mainly of a series of headings with blank spaces for entering data, inferences, and conclusions. As an outline for case study, the form has some merit. Like all such blanks, however, it lacks flexibility. In attempting to meet the requirements of all situations and all clients, it inevitably provides too little space for some topics and too much for other less relevant issues. Somewhat dangerous is the implication that it may be used by teachers with little psychological training. Well-trained clinicians hardly need such a blank; others should not attempt its use.

[95]

The Personality Inventory. Grades 9–16 and adults; 1931–38; 6 scores: neurotic tendency, self-sufficiency, introversion-extroversion, dominance-submission, confidence, sociability; IBM; 1 form ('35); manual ('35); tentative norms ('38); $3.25 per 25; $1.50 per 50 profile sheets (no date); 25¢ per specimen set; separate answer sheets may be used; $1.75 per 50 IBM answer sheets; $1.50 per 100 Hankes answer sheets; $1 per set of hand scoring stencils; $5 per set of IBM scoring stencils; postage extra; (25) minutes; Robert G. Bernreuter; Consulting Psychologists Press, Inc. *

REFERENCES

1–71. See 40:1239.
72–259. See 4:77.
260–1. MAUNEY, JACK E. *Effect of a Social Weekend Upon the Personality of College Students, as Measured by the Bernreuter Personality Inventory.* Master's thesis, University of Florida (Gainesville, Fla.), 1947.
262. BERNARD, JESSIE; HECHT, CAROL ANN; SCHWARTZ, SYLVIA; LEVY, SYLVIA; AND SCHIELE, WILLIAM. "The Relationship Between Scores on the Bernreuter Personality Inventory and Three Indexes of Participation in a College Community." *Rural Sociol* 15:271–3 S '50. *

263. BLAIR, W. R. N. "A Comparative Study of Disciplinary Offenders and Non-Offenders in the Canadian Army, 1948." *Can J Psychol* 4:49–62 Je '50. * (PA 24:6428)

264. HAND, WILL MASON. *A Comparison and Analysis of Scores in Self and Social Adjustment Made on the California Test of Personality and the Bernreuter Personality Inventory.* Master's thesis, University of Florida (Gainesville, Fla.), 1950.

265. KLINE, NATHAN S. "Characteristics and Screening of Unsatisfactory Psychiatric Attendants and Attendant-Applicants." *Am J Psychiatry* 106:573–86 F '50. *

266. MOSS, FREDERICK JAMES, JR. *Intelligence and the Bernreuter Personality Inventory.* Master's thesis, Southern Methodist University (Dallas, Tex.), 1950

267. GEHMAN, WINFIELD SCOTT, JR. *Analysis of a Program Involving Required Psychological Counseling and Other Services for a College Population Having Serious Scholastic Difficulties.* Doctor's thesis, Pennsylvania State College (State College, Pa.), 1951.

268. GOULD, HENRY. *Relation of Certain Personality Components to Achievement in Secondary School Science.* Doctor's thesis, New York University (New York, N.Y.), 1951. (DA 12:160)

269. HUMPHREY, BETTY M. "Introversion-Extraversion Ratings in Relation to Scores in ESP Tests." *J Parapsychol* 15:252–62 D '51. * (PA 27:4109)

270. HUNT, FOLGER DEFOE. *A Study of the Relationship of Personality Scores to Level of Achievement.* Master's thesis, Ohio University (Athens, Ohio), 1951.

271. PAGE, MAUREEN. *Two Proposed Modifications of the Bernreuter Personality Inventory.* Master's thesis, Pennsylvania State College (State College, Pa.), 1951.

272. SIMES, FRANK J. *The Development of a Basis for the Selection of Resident Advisers at the Pennsylvania State College.* Doctor's thesis, Pennsylvania State College (State College, Pa.), 1951.

273. BANKS, CHARLOTTE, AND KEIR, GERTRUDE. "A Factorial Analysis of Items in the Bernreuter Personality Inventory." *Brit J Psychol, Stat Sect* 5:19–30 Mr '52. *

274. BROWN, MANUEL N. "Powell's Study on Ratings of Personality Adjustment: A Note." *Ed & Psychol Meas* 12:126–8 sp '52. * (PA 27:5859)

275. GEIST, HAROLD. "A Comparison of Personality Test Scores and Medical Psychiatric Diagnosis by the Inverted Factor Technique." *J Clin Psychol* 8:184–8 Ap '52. * (PA 27:1958)

276. GUILFORD, J. P. "When Not to Factor Analyze." *Psychol B* 49:26–37 Ja '52. * (PA 27:33)

277. LIEN, ARNOLD JUEL. "A Comparative-Predictive Study of Students in the Four Curricula of a Teacher Education Institution." *J Exp Ed* 21:81–219 D '52. *

278. MASON, ROBERT JOSEPH. *A Comparison of Responses on the Rosenzweig Picture-Frustration Study, the Bernreuter Personality Inventory, and a Self-Rating Form.* Master's thesis, University of Western Ontario (London, Ont., Canada), 1952.

279. MOFFIE, DANNIE J., AND MILTON, CHARLES R. "The Relationship of Certain Psychological Test Scores to Academic Success in Chemical Engineering." Abstract. *Am Psychol* 7:379–80 Jl '52. *

280. POE, WESLEY A., AND BERG, IRWIN A. "Psychological Test Performance of Steel Industry Production Supervisors." *J Appl Psychol* 36:234–7 Ag '52. * (PA 27:3794)

281. RICHARDSON, HELEN M., AND HANAWALT, NELSON G. "Leadership as Related to the Bernreuter Personality Measures: V, Leadership Among Adult Women in Social Activities." *J Social Psychol* 36:141–53 N '52. * (PA 27:7124)

282. WESMAN, ALEXANDER G. "Faking Personality Test Scores in a Simulated Employment Situation." *J Appl Psychol* 36:112–3 Ap '52. * (PA 27:449)

283. BRUCE, MARTIN M. "The Prediction of Effectiveness as a Factory Foreman." *Psychol Monogr* 67(12):1–17 '53. * (PA 28:5019)

284. ROSENBERG, NATHAN; IZARD, CARROLL E.; AND HOLLANDER, E. P. "Middle Category ("?") Response: Reliability and Relationship to Personality and Intelligence Variables." Abstract. *Am Psychol* 8:425 Ag '53. *

285. YOUNG, NORMAN, AND GAIER, EUGENE L. "A Preliminary Investigation Into the Prediction of Suggestibility From Selected Personality Variables." *J Social Psychol* 37:53–60 F '53. * (PA 28:571)

286. ALBIZU-MIRANDA, CARLOS. *An Experimental Study of Middle Class Bias on the Bernreuter Personality Inventory.* Doctor's thesis, Purdue University (Lafayette, Ind.), 1954.

287. BRUCE, MARTIN M. "Validity Information Exchange, No. 7-004: D.O.T. Code 0-97.61, Manager, Sales." *Personnel Psychol* 7:128–9 sp '54. *

288. BRUCE, MARTIN M. "Validity Information Exchange, No. 7-076: D.O.T. Code 5-91.101, Foreman II." *Personnel Psychol* 7:418–9 au '54. *

289. CASH, WILLIAM LEVI, JR. *Relation of Personality Traits to Scholastic Aptitude and Academic Achievement of Students in a Liberal Protestant Seminary.* Doctor's thesis, University of Michigan (Ann Arbor, Mich.), 1954. (DA 14:630)

290. GEHMAN, W. SCOTT. "Problems of College Sophomores With Serious Scholastic Difficulties." *J Counsel Psychol* 2:137–41 su '55. * (PA 30:3406)

291. GOWAN, J. C. "Relationship Between Leadership and Personality Measures." *J Ed Res* 48:623–7 Ap '55. * (PA 30:1558)

292. HOFFMAN, MARTIN L., AND ALBIZU-MIRANDA, CARLOS. "Middle Class Bias in Personality Testing." *J Abn & Social Psychol* 51:150–2 Jl '55. * (PA 30:4573)

293. KELLY, E. LOWELL. "Consistency of the Adult Personality." *Am Psychol* 10:659–81 N '55. * (PA 30:6915)

294. BRUCE, MARTIN M. "Normative Data Information Exchange, No. 26." *Personnel Psychol* 9:533–4 w '56. *

295. BURGESS, ELVA. "Personality Factors of Over- and Under-Achievers in Engineering." *J Ed Psychol* 47:89–99 F '56. * (PA 31:8811)

296. STRAIGHT, GLENN H. *Identifiable Personality Characteristics Resulting From Membership in a Conspicuous Religious Minority in Public High Schools.* Doctor's thesis, University of Nebraska (Lincoln, Neb.), 1956. (DA 17:810)

297. WITKIN, ARTHUR AARON. *The Prediction of Potentials for Effectiveness in Certain Occupations Within the Sales Field.* Doctor's thesis, New York University (New York, N.Y.), 1956. (DA 16:1718)

298. BRUCE, MARTIN M. "Validity Information Exchange, No. 10-3: D.O.T. Code 1-86.11, Salesman, Commercial Equipment and Supplies." *Personnel Psychol* 10:77–8 sp '57. *

299. BRUCE, MARTIN M. "Normative Data Information Exchange, No. 11–1." *Personnel Psychol* 11:127–8 sp '58. *

For a review by Leona E. Tyler, see 4:77; for reviews by Charles I. Mosier and Theodore Newcomb, see 40:1239; for related reviews, see 38:B358 and 36:B108.

[96]

★**Pictorial Study of Values: Pictorial Allport-Vernon.** Ages 14 and over; 1957; title on test is *The Pictorial Study;* 7 scores: aesthetic, economic, political, religious, social, theoretical, strength of liking things in general; 1 form; preliminary norms; separate answer sheets must be used; $1.95 per 20 tests; $1 per 20 answer sheets; $1 per specimen set (must be purchased to obtain manual); postage extra; (20–30) minutes; Charles Shooster; Psychometric Affiliates. *

ANDREW R. BAGGALEY, *Associate Professor of Psychology, University of Wisconsin—Milwaukee, Milwaukee, Wisconsin.*

This test represents an attempt to translate the verbal content of the Allport-Vernon-Lindzey *Study of Values* into pictorial content while continuing to measure the same processes. The six pictorial scales, with names identical to those of the SOV scales, were derived by correlating "like ratings" on a 5-point scale for 60 pictures with scores on the six SOV scales using a sample of "100 subjects." No further description of these subjects is given. By this empirical method pictures were assigned to the scales according to their "significance level" (not further specified). The *same* subjects were then scored on the pictorial scales, and correlations with their scores on the verbal scales were calculated. The author admits that these correlations, with a mean of .58, are spuriously high; however, it would obviously be better to use a cross-validation group and report the resulting correlations in future editions of the manual.

The author suggests that this version of the SOV may be useful for testees with language difficulty, and this supposition seems plausible if it can be assumed that the testees are familiar with the content of the pictures. The pictures

are rather small and in some cases indistinct or too crowded with objects. The middle category of the 5-point response scale is "for the ones you have no opinion about," and the next category is "for those you have less-than-average opinion of." These seem illogical as consecutive categories on a scale.

The reported validity of the test is based mostly on correlations with self-ratings. Intercorrelations of the pictorial scales are also given. These are roughly similar to those published on the SOV verbal scales (although the political-economic correlation is significantly *negative* for the pictures). Thus the test seems to have a moderate amount of construct validity; however, further evidence on its concurrent and predictive validity, beyond that reported for a small group of engineers, is needed before the test can be used confidently in guidance situations. No reliability data whatsoever are given! Norms are given for male and female adults and for two small groups of high school boys. Like its parent SOV, this test should probably be used for guidance rather than selection, since it seems rather easy to "fake" extreme scores on its scales.

In summary, this *Pictorial Study of Values* is an intriguing derivation from a well known test, and it holds much theoretical promise. However, continuing research along the lines indicated above is necessary before the test can be recommended for use in practical counseling work.

HARRISON G. GOUGH, *Associate Professor of Psychology, University of California, Berkeley, California.*

The goal of this test is to assess Spranger's six value types (aesthetic, economic, political, religious, social, and theoretical), using a set of 60 pictures. The criterion for assignment of a picture to a values dimension was its correlation with the relevant values score on the Allport-Vernon-Lindzey *Study of Values* in a sample of 100 "subjects" (no other designation in the manual).

The respondent checks a 5-point scale for each picture, ranging from "like best" through "have no opinion about" to "little or no liking for." An additional "genlike" score, taken from E. L. Thorndike's concept of liking for things in general, may be obtained by tallying the total number of "like best" and "like next best" responses.

With six value scales to be scored over 60 items, the number of items per scale must necessarily be small. This problem is heightened in difficulty by the fact that 11 of the pictures are scored, if at all, only for "genlike." Twenty-four items are scored on only one value scale, 17 items on two, 7 on three, and 1 item is scored on four scales.

Eighteen pictures contribute to the aesthetic score, 8 to the economic, 16 to the political, 13 to the religious, 14 to the social, and 14 to the theoretical. It seems unlikely that enough items have been included on any one of these six scales to permit reliable assessment of it. This reviewer's experience has been that, except for items having unusually high factorial homogeneity, scale reliability can seldom be maintained with less than 20 items.

The pictures seem to have been assembled in an *ad hoc,* intuitive, and unspecified way. The manual gives very little attention to the bases for the inclusion or exclusion of pictures, and it does not describe any steps taken to insure an adequate range of variation among pictures. Given the focus on "values," some of the 11 unscored pictures appear to be poor choices, and in some cases even to be incompatible with the testing instructions. For example, the instructions begin by saying: "You are looking at pictures of things that people have done. Look at Picture Number 1 and decide how much you would like to engage in that activity." Picture 15, however, merely presents a somber landscape with a road leading off toward the horizon. In general, the pictures are unattractively grouped and poorly reproduced. The author could well have invested a much greater amount of time and effort in establishing the set of stimulus materials.

This reviewer's greatest dissatisfaction, however, must be reserved for the manual, which is surely one of the most ill-prepared and inadequate manuals he has seen. The writing in it is diffuse, periphrastic, and frequently ungrammatical. Furthermore, it simply fails to provide the essential material required. For instance, no discussion of scale reliability is offered and no figures whatsoever of either test-retest or internal consistency reliability are given. One cannot help wondering what a scale reliability check of either type would have shown for the 8-item "economic" scale.

The manual is equally deficient with respect to the test's validity. The main evidence here is

taken from self-ratings of the value dimensions correlated with the subjects' *Pictorial Study of Values* scale scores. The means of the intercorrelation coefficients reported between self-ratings and scores on the six scales are approximately .18, .14, and .39 for cross-validating samples of 41, 57, and 50 cases, respectively. These coefficients are certainly too low to warrant non-research use of the test, even if the legitimacy of the self-ratings as a criterion is granted.

On the question of specific meanings (operational validity) of each scale the manual is again silent. That is, no information is presented about the question many test users consider to be the crucial one, namely, what kind of a person is it, in everyday "protocol" language, who gets a high or a low score on each of these scales? Information about such things as item selection and scale intercorrelations is of little help for inquiries of this sort. What is needed is a study of people who do in fact represent significant deviations on the scales, and a reporting of their psychodynamic and other characteristics. The manual is also weak in its presentation of norms, utilizing only three male samples (n's of 110, 57, and 41) and one female sample (n = 40).

In the reviewer's judgment, the commercial publication of this test was an unfortunate event. The initial idea—the assessment of personological values by means of pictorial stimuli—is a good one and one deserving of full research support. However, the publication of a "test" on which the necessary research study has only been started, which is entirely lacking in reliability and operational validity data, and whose manual has been badly and unclearly written is another matter. As it stands, the test reflects little credit to either publisher or author.

[97]

★**The Power of Influence Test.** Grades 2–13; 1958; seating preference sociometric test; 1 form; no data on validity; norms for grades 5–11 only; $3.50 per 50 tests; 50¢ per manual; postage extra; specimen set not available; [10–15] minutes; Roy Cochrane and Wesley Roeder; Psychometric Affiliates. *

[98]

★**Practical Policy Test.** Adults; 1948; also called *Test of Cynicism;* Form C-S; no manual; no data on reliability and validity; typewritten college norms ['48] only; 5¢ per test; free specimen set; postpaid; [10–20] minutes; Martin F. Fritz and Charles O. Neidt; Martin F. Fritz, Student Counseling Service, Iowa State College. *

REFERENCES

1. FRITZ, MARTIN F. "A Test Study of Cynicism and Idealism." *Proc Iowa Acad Sci* 53:269–72 '46. * (*PA* 23:588)
2. NEIDT, CHARLES O. "Relation of Cynicism to Certain Other Variables." *Proc Iowa Acad Sci* 53:277–83 '46. * (*PA* 23:591)
3. FRITZ, MARTIN F. "Co-variation of Cynicism and Idealism." *Proc Iowa Acad Sci* 54:231–4 '47. * (*PA* 23:5279)
4. NEIDT, CHARLES O. *Analysis of College Student Reaction to the Fritz Test of Cynicism.* Master's thesis, Iowa State College (Ames, Iowa), 1947.
5. NEIDT, CHARLES O. "Selection of the Optimal Scoring Plan for the Fritz Test of Cynicism." *Proc Iowa Acad Sci* 54: 253–62 '47. * (*PA* 23:5527)
6. FRITZ, MARTIN F. "A Short-Form Test of Cynicism." *Proc Iowa Acad Sci* 55:319–22 '48. *
7. FRITZ, MARTIN F. "Relation of the Fritz-Neidt Practical Policy Test to Freshman Entrance Tests." *Proc Iowa Acad Sci* 57:379–80 '50. *
8. NEIDT, CHARLES O., AND FRITZ, MARTIN F. "Relation of Cynicism to Certain Student Characteristics." *Ed & Psychol Meas* 10:712–7 w '50. * (*PA* 25:6425)
9. FRITZ, MARTIN F. "Statements of Cynicism Rated by College Students." *Proc Iowa Acad Sci* 58:345–9 '51. *

[99]

★**Primary Empathic Abilities.** Grades 9–16 and adults; 1957–58; 7 scores: diplomacy, industrial, with insecure people, with conscientious middle class, with lower middle class, with stable young married people, with upper social levels; Form A ('57); manual ('57); supplement ('58); no college norms; separate answer pads must be used; 29¢ per test; $1.95 per 20 answer pads; $2 per 50 profiles: high school ('57), adults ('57); $1 per specimen set (must be purchased to obtain manual); postage extra; (45) minutes; Willard Kerr; Psychometric Affiliates. *

ROBERT L. THORNDIKE, *Professor of Education, Teachers College, Columbia University, New York, New York.*

The *Primary Empathic Abilities* is an instrument designed to extend the basic idea of the *Empathy Test* by the same author to the measurement of a number of distinct empathy factors. Empathy means to the author ability to predict the actions of the "generalized other"; the distinct empathy factors are identified with specific classes of others, such as insecure people, the lower middle class, and stable young married people. The reviewer found a good deal of difficulty in rationalizing the factor names in some cases on the basis of the items keyed in the particular factor score.

The identification of seven factors was apparently based on the intercorrelations among 86 items for a population of 200 cases. When the number of variables is so large relative to the number of observations, one may expect the results of a factor analysis to be very fragile and unstable. That this was true is suggested by the fact that all but one of the seven factor scores had reliabilities below .55. The reviewer feels that the separate factors have not been demonstrated as meaningful and stable phenomena and very much suspects that they are largely artifacts of the analysis. If this be so, the results from the test seem largely meaningless.

[100]

★**Pupil Adjustment Inventory.** Grades kgn–12; 1957; ratings in 7 areas: academic, social, emotional,

physical, activities and interests, school's influence on pupil, home background; short and long forms (short form is used to identify pupils who should be rated on the long form); $2.70 per set of 35 short forms, 5 long forms, and manual; 80¢ per specimen set; postpaid; (5–15) minutes for short form, (2–5) hours for long form; Group B of the Suburban School Study Council, Educational Service Bureau, School of Education, University of Pennsylvania; Houghton Mifflin Co. *

ROBERT H. BAUERNFEIND, *Director, Test Department, Science Research Associates, Chicago, Illinois.*

This inventory is designed to provide a graphic overview of the pupil's experience and growth in seven areas. The Long Form provides 55 specific considerations to be rated. The entire form is printed on a single side of a sheet measuring 12 by 50 inches. The form could be useful in intensive programs of child study, but it is really too long and too complex for general use with all pupils in a school system. The Short Form, suggested for use with all pupils, provides 15 considerations to be rated. This form is printed on a single side of a sheet measuring 12 by 20 inches. In this format teachers and counselors are encouraged to view and interrelate all 15 ratings at the same time. In addition to blanks for the ratings, both forms have a wide margin for noting sources of information on which each rating is based.

The format is a significant plus-value for three reasons: First, it requires raters to think in terms of facts, rather than general impressions, in making their ratings. Second, it provides a much needed opportunity for school personnel to record important pupil information data on one central reference piece. Third, in the wide margin additional facts can be recorded from time to time concerning pupil behavior, interview findings, and results of recent educational tests and medical examinations.

The inventory manual is attractive and readable. Teachers and counselors will appreciate the authors' work in providing a fairly extensive review of important literature in child development and guidance.

The discussions of reliability and validity are, of necessity, somewhat weak. Our conventional concepts of reliability and validity simply do not apply to this type of form, and the authors acknowledge this point in a frank and searching way. There are, however, other points at which additional research data would be welcome. One wonders, for example, whether the scale points on each continuum were developed by any scaling technique. Several of the verbalizations for scale points appear not to be equidistant when compared with others. If the verbalizations were assigned judgmentally, it would be good to have some discussion of this development. Also, one wonders about the statement that "the *third*, or *middle* description on each scale denotes accomplishment, ability, or adjustment of the average student." Until there are confirming data, users are cautioned that this will not necessarily be the case in individual schools, or, indeed, among national samples.

This reviewer also suggests that the Short Form might better have included the three Long Form entries in the academic area—for reading, language, and mathematics. These three entries presented separately would surely be appreciated by teachers since they would add important information in the realm of the teacher's primary responsibilities.

There are theoretical problems inherent in an instrument of this type. For one thing, 15 ratings can serve only to "scratch the surface" in the appraisal of a personality. For another, there will be problems of comparability of norms or perspectives in comparing the several ratings. Nonetheless, as a central point of departure for interrelating test scores, anecdotal records, medical reports, and teachers' observations, the *Pupil Adjustment Inventory* is an excellent publication. This reviewer recommends it to any school whose pupil information is scattered or unrelated, and whose teachers are sincerely interested in pupil guidance. For such schools, the value of the form will far exceed the modest per pupil cost of the materials.

JOHN PIERCE-JONES, *Associate Professor of Educational Psychology, The University of Texas, Austin, Texas.*

This inventory is intended to identify "maladjusted" pupils needing experts' attention and to enhance teachers' understanding of children. As the manual prudently observes, the inventory is not a test, but a record form. On it a teacher notes information from divers sources (standardized tests, anecdotal records, and interviews) as ratings of a potpourri of pupil characteristics such as "language usage," "attitude toward schoolwork," "types of associates," "emotional stability," and "sexuality." Spaces exist for recording demographic facts and the sources of data used as bases for ratings.

Most routine standards of rating scale development have apparently been ignored in the con-

struction of this device. In some instances, e.g., "chronological age at grade," the traits to be rated seem to represent reasonable single dimensions, but in many cases, e.g., "hobbies and interests," several constructs have been so confounded that single rating scales are inappropriate. The descriptions of points along the scales are often phrased in ambiguous, value-laden terms, not explicitly and behaviorally. For example, the most favorable scale description of the child's attitude toward his family is "creatively active in the family group." Several of the attributes to be rated are briefly defined in a glossary. The manual presents only some 150 words concerning specific rating procedures; more detailed suggestions are given for the Long Form.

No satisfactory rationale, beyond teacher convenience, supports the development of the Short Form, and operations by which the Short Form (15 scales) was generated from the Long Form (55 scales) are not reported. There is no evidence from factorial or other analyses to justify the selection of Long Form scales appearing in the Short Form nor for the coalescences, in the Short Form, of various Long Form scales. The manual suggests that three deviant ratings on the Short Form "makes further study of a pupil by use of the Long Form advisable." Why this would be even presumptively true in the case of positive deviations from midscale ratings is unclear, and one cannot help wondering why three rather than, say, two or four negative deviations should be deemed significant. That the two forms would, generally, point to the same children as "maladjusted" is not demonstrated, although both forms are intended for identifying purposes as well as for systematizing varied data and teachers' impressions.

It seems not to have occurred to the authors of this inventory that the reliability of ratings can be assessed by other than the test-retest model which they reject. Interrater agreement has not been examined. Forty pupils' self-ratings were "significantly" correlated with teachers' ratings, but the relevance of this to reliability is not evident. A textbook definition of validity is presented, but acceptable evidence of validity is entirely absent. It is reported, however, that clinicians found the inventory "most helpful in analyzing each pupil," and it is argued that the methods of constructing the device and the reactions of school people to its use indicate its "construct validity." This reviewer's under-

standing of construct validity leads him to look for more rigorous theory and for better empirical evidence than the informal opinions of teachers and clinicians. It seems likely that many ratings afforded by this inventory may be inadequately anchored in representative objective observations. Indeed, there seems little recognition that the ratings may more accurately reflect teacher personality than child behavior. The possibility that reification of their impressions by naive or insensitive teachers may endow some children with ill-deserved reputations should surely be considered.

More disturbing than the several technical flaws are various signs of superficial and erroneous thinking about the nature of human adjustment. There is, for instance, a failure to distinguish between adjustment and the degree of the child's socialization in a matrix of culturally valued behavior. One would infer from the inventory that best adjustment includes an IQ of 140 or higher, being emulated and admired, invariable acceptance of life as worthwhile, accelerated physical maturity, general acceptance as a leader, "always (having) money to meet legitimate needs," etc. Such values need not be abjured, but to make ideal adjustment from kindergarten through high school coterminous with them is to be an apostle of the cult of conformity. Finally, there is little evidence that psychodynamic formulations influenced the development of this instrument, and it is difficult to see how "adjustment" can be conceptualized satisfactorily outside such formulations.

In the reviewer's opinion, this inventory should be viewed with great scepticism by potential users. It has been developed without elementary attention to psychometric niceties, the complexities of individual diagnosis, or the difficulties attending sophisticated thinking about adjustment. The inventory cannot be recommended for use without such extensive revision as to make it unrecognizable as the creation of the committee who produced it.

J Consult Psychol 21:507 D '57. Laurance F. Shaffer. * The content and form of the items seem sound. The *Rater's Manual* gives adequate instructions for the use of the scales and anecdotes supporting their value; it is deficient in that it provides no statistical data. The best use of the scales will be to increase the involvement of teachers in the thoughtful consideration of their pupils as persons.

[101]

*The Purdue Rating Scale for Administrators and Executives. Administrators and executives; 1950–51; 36 ratings plus factor scores; 1 form ('50); 3 editions; Report Forms A, B, C ('51); 3¢ per rating scale; 5¢ per any one report form; 25¢ per manual ('51); 35¢ per specimen set; postage extra; (15–20) minutes; H. H. Remmers and R. L. Hobson; Personnel Evaluation Research Service, Division of Educational Reference, Purdue University. *

a) REPORT FORM A. College administrators; 3 factor scores: fairness to subordinates, administrative achievement, democratic orientation.

b) REPORT FORM B. Business executives; 2 factor scores: social responsibility for subordinates and society, executive achievement; no norms for part scores.

c) REPORT FORM C. School administrators.

REFERENCES

1–7. See 4:83.
8. REMMERS, H. H., AND ELLIOTT, D. N. "The Indiana College and University Staff-Evaluation Program." *Sch & Soc* 70:168–71 S 10 '49. * (*PA* 26:2440)

JOHN P. FOLEY, JR., *President, J. P. Foley & Co., Inc., New York, New York.*

This scale is intended as an aid to the executive or administrator in discovering his job-related strengths and weaknesses, thereby providing information which can be utilized in his individual growth and development. Specifically, the scale is designed to measure subordinates' opinions of the effectiveness of executives and administrators in business and industry as well as in public schools and higher educational institutions.

The scale consists of 36 items, selected from an extensive literature survey and through personal conferences with executives, administrators, and their subordinates. These items are classified under the following ten major headings, each containing from one to ten items: intellectual balance, emotional balance, administrative leadership, administrative planning, use of funds, capacity for work, accomplishment, relations with subordinates, public relations, and social responsibility. Responses are recorded in terms of a 5-point scale which for most items consists of the terms: always, usually, sometimes, seldom, never. For certain items other, more suitable, terms are substituted. The scale is printed on the two sides of a single 8½ by 11 inch sheet, and is preceded by brief instructions. The rating process ordinarily requires 15–20 minutes.

Since the scale is to be used as a basis for self-improvement, the authors recommend that the administrator's superior not have access to the results. The administrator himself should participate voluntarily and should retain the results for his own use. In this connection, it should be noted that norms and other research data have been obtained only in situations where cooperation was voluntary on the part of the administrator rated, where all results were confidential, and where anonymity of raters was guaranteed.

In the accompanying manual, scorer reliability for each item is reported. Coefficients are stepped up by the Spearman-Brown formula. In the case of the industrial data, it is stated in a footnote in the manual that "2 vs. 2" raters were utilized, instead of the "10 vs. 10" reported in the table. The latter coefficients are obviously stepped-up estimates, although this is not made clear. In general, however, rater agreement appears to be high. Validity is discussed only in terms of content. It is maintained that no better criterion for the judgment of a subordinate's rating of his superior can be found than the judgment of that subordinate himself. The reliability and validity coefficients for scale items thus become identical.

Scoring is accomplished by plotting the mean score assigned by all raters to each item on the percentile profile chart provided in a separate report form. Three report forms are available: Form A for college and university administrators, Form B for business and industrial executives, and Form C for administrators in elementary and secondary schools. Three types of interpretation are suggested: (*a*) comparative—determination of the percentile rank for each item with reference to the appropriate normative group; (*b*) literal—selection of the descriptive scale term which most closely corresponds to the assigned mean rating for each item; and (*c*) distributive—examination of the range of ratings on each item in order to determine where disagreement exists among subordinates.

Factor analysis was applied to the data from the A and B groups mentioned above. In the business and industrial group, item intercorrelations yielded two factors, described as "social responsibility for subordinates and society" and "executive achievement." These are said to represent the twofold responsibility of an executive to "the people in his immediate and larger society" and to "his job and employers." Three factors were isolated in the college and university administration group, designated as "fairness to subordinates," "administrative achievement," and "democratic orientation." These factors are claimed to represent the tridimensional responsibility of an administrator to his staff, to his

job or superiors, and to society. A list of items from which such factors can be found, as well as corresponding percentile norms, is provided. These data, however, are available only for the group of college and university administrators.

Although the *Purdue Rating Scale for Administrators and Executives* represents a sound attempt to secure appraisal information relating to supervisory strengths and weaknesses, it is subject to a number of limitations. In most industrial and educational organizations, evaluative information is desired for administrative purposes as well as for individual development. In fact, most management development programs in business and industry clearly recognize these two major goals. The authors of the Purdue scale specifically state that the instrument should not be used for the first of these two objectives. The reviewer would concur with the statement that "inverse rating" is ordinarily an inappropriate technique for management decisions relating to placement, transfer, promotion, and compensation, but would call attention to the fact that other types of appraisal procedures can often be utilized for *both* individual development and administrative purposes.

The scale is necessarily subject to all of the limitations imposed upon a "canned" rating scale. In the reviewer's opinion, a scale which is specifically tailored to the needs of a particular organization will often prove more meaningful and of greater value. The reviewer also feels that insufficient emphasis is placed upon the training of raters. True, a bow is made in this direction through the suggestion that a "staff-meeting method" may be used in administering the scale. Other methods are also suggested, however, such as the "work-place method," which involves sending the scale to the rater along with a standard letter of instruction. Most professionals in the rating field would probably agree that poor ratings are more likely to result from attitudinal problems, such as faulty mental set or unwillingness to rate accurately, than from sheer inability to make accurate appraisals. For such reasons, the reviewer would have a real question concerning the value of canned rating procedures in most practical situations.

Careful scrutiny of the scale itself will lead to other, more specific criticisms. No attempt is made to integrate the obtained appraisals with such measurable factors as tested abilities. Nor is any provision whatever made for the appraisal of such ability factors. Yet, it is evident that

the presence or absence of varying degrees of relevant ability will most certainly influence the performance of an executive or administrator. Moreover, a particular level of a given ability will often influence the significance of an administrator's standing on another trait, as rated by his subordinates. Other criticisms relating to the content of the scale can be illustrated. In the case of Area I, Intellectual Balance, for example, it is difficult to subscribe to this designation for factors relating solely to general and specific knowledge. Area V, which is designated as Use of Funds, contains three items, dealing with employment of personnel, selection of equipment, and effort to obtain funds for subordinate improvement, respectively. What about such factors as equipment operation and maintenance, personnel utilization, and other factors relating to the maintenance of an economical and cost-conscious operation?

Within the limitations of a readymade rating scale, the present instrument can undoubtedly be utilized effectively. For most purposes, however, a carefully tailored instrument, integrated with relevant test information and administered to raters who have been carefully trained, will probably yield better appraisal results.

HERBERT A. TONNE, *Professor of Education, New York University, New York, New York.*

The authors do not assume that this scale measures administrative or executive ability. It is simply an opinion scale against which workers may measure their superiors. The scale serves this use quite well. It is easy to take. The authors have made every effort possible to assure that the scale will be used intelligently in job situations.

The only interpretive data provided are in terms of average ratings. Such measures give no evidence of the degree of rater agreement. However, the manual does encourage the administrator who is analyzed to study the tally sheet to determine to what extent there was agreement among those who rated him.

Quite wisely no attempt is made to determine a reliability coefficient for the scale as a whole. The coefficients for the individual items range from .99 for one item, as marked by collegiate raters, to .43 for another, as marked by public school raters. In general, the reliabilities are sufficiently high to be of some significance.

The reviewer questions the assumption that since the scale is concerned with the rating of a

superior by his subordinates and since the subordinates make the judgments, the validity is, therefore, the same as the reliability. As the manual indicates, we can and must question frankness and honesty; we must also question interpretation and understanding of items. However, the scale does seem as valid as is possible for such a device.

The scale should be a useful device for the evaluation of administrative and supervisory personnel if used with much care. Unfortunately, we all have overmuch a tendency to assume that a formal printed instrument is more scientific than the authors themselves claim it to be.

For a review by Kenneth L. Heaton, see 4:83.

[102]

★Rating Scale for Pupil Adjustment. Grades 3–9; 1950–53; 1 form ('53); $1.20 per 20 scales; 10¢ per manual ('53); postage extra; specimen set not available; [10] minutes; [Gwen Andrew, Samuel W. Hartwell, Max L. Hutt, and Ralph E. Walton]; Science Research Associates. *

WILLIAM E. HENRY, *Associate Professor of Human Development and Psychology, University of Chicago, Chicago, Illinois.*

The scale, based upon 11 areas of personality, was developed by the Michigan Department of Mental Health as a part of a research with the *Michigan Picture Test.* The areas—overall emotional adjustment, social maturity, tendency toward depression, tendency toward aggressive behavior, extroversion-introversion, emotional security, motor control, impulsiveness, emotional irritability, school achievement, and school conduct—are each rated on a 5-point scale. A final item lists 12 physical conditions like "unusually tall for age," "physical disfigurement," "special handicap," which may influence adjustment. These do not contribute to the score, but may be noted if they apply.

The instrument is intended for use by teachers. The ratings are made against a hypothetical total population of children of the age in question, rather than against children in the particular classroom.

A weighting system is provided to permit the derivation of a total score—the higher scores reflecting better general adjustment. No cutoff scores are available, but it is suggested that the lower portion of the scores in a class—from 25 to 33 per cent—be referred to the school psychologist for further study. Research upon the validity of the scale is reported as in progress.

One reliability study is reported. It provides a product-moment correlation of .84 between two sets of ratings of 23 children made a month apart by the same teacher.

The usefulness of such an instrument clearly depends upon the training of the rater in its use and will thus differ with teachers and school systems. This one seems a well conceived instrument, provided it is used by skilled persons primarily as a framework for recording observations.

MORRIS KRUGMAN, *Assistant Superintendent in Charge of Guidance, New York Public Schools, New York, New York.*

Originally designed for use as a validity criterion for the *Michigan Picture Test,* this rating scale can be used by classroom teachers in locating poorly adjusted children. It is recommended for schools having diagnostic and treatment services available, and is intended to improve the accuracy of referrals to such services.

Used in the recommended manner, this rating scale has merit. As the manual warns, not all children referred will necessarily be seriously disturbed, and not all disturbed children will be referred. However, even rating scales not so carefully designed as this have proven the value of systematic rating of pupil adjustment by teachers who have observed children over an extended period of time. The danger of such rating scales lies in their use without benefit of subsequent evaluation by psychologists or psychiatrists. It becomes too easy for teachers to label children, and this needs to be guarded against.

The scale consists of 11 areas of adjustment to be assigned ratings of from A (good) through E (poor) and one item dealing with physical handicaps. A system of weighted scoring is used. The authors suggest referral of the lowest quarter or third of the class, depending upon the availability of therapeutic services. A validity study is now being conducted. Results of this study are promised in forthcoming editions of the manual.

If used with appropriate safeguards, this scale can have value for the improvement of child referral procedures. It should not be used alone for personality evaluation.

[103]

★SAQS Chicago Q Sort. College and adults; 1956–57; 1 form (no date); no data on reliability; $2 per set of 10 record sheets ('56), 10 profiles ('57), cards (no

date), and manual ('56); $3 per 50 record sheets; $3 per 50 profiles; postage extra; (15–20) minutes; Raymond Corsini; Psychometric Affiliates. *

REFERENCES

1. CORSINI, RAYMOND J. "Multiple Predictors of Marital Happiness." *Marriage & Family Living* 18:240–2 Ag '56. *
2. CORSINI, RAYMOND J. "Understanding and Similarity in Marriage." *J Abn & Social Psychol* 52:327–32 My '56. * (PA 31:4536)

WILLIAM STEPHENSON, *Consulting Psychologist, 20 Brookside Drive, Greenwich, Connecticut.*

This is a set of 50 personal adjectives, such as "original," "high-strung," "sarcastic," and "excitable," to be sorted so as to describe one's self or other people. In this reviewer's opinion, the SAQS provides a straightforward introductory pack. The instructions are clear and constructive. Minor improvements might be made; for example, it scarcely seems necessary to have "sensitive" and "insensitive" together in the same pack.

The author suggests that his set of adjectives should not be expected to have general validity. What, then, is to give the SAQS scientific value? Its author suggests a wide range of uses for the pack: personality study, marital counseling, and job prediction, for example. These are important areas of psychological concern. One may ask, therefore, what is there about these adjectives that gives them scientific value? The author, we suppose, could answer in two or three different ways.

First, he has chosen the adjectives from seven personality areas (life style, intelligence, social sensitivity, emotional stability, dominance, activity, and mood), and, for this reason, the pack presumably has a certain implied general validity. That is, it can generate *explanations* of facts which, at face value, most psychologists might accept. Next, some data are provided in the form of percentile "profiles" for husband-wife Q sort correlations. However, the data are for only a few husband and wife combinations and are not norms in any sense. Third, reference is made to two papers by the author (*1, 2*) dealing with the use of the adjectives in marital counseling. For psychologists interested in such counseling, the pack, used in conjunction with these published papers, would no doubt be of some interest.

But, aside from these three indications of some validity, what justifies publication of a pack of adjectives such as SAQS? Is general validity at issue? Are norms and "profiles" necessary? Since this instrument is likely to be the forerunner of other standard packs of Q cards, such questions need to be discussed. It would seem to the reviewer that if a psychologist has a good theory, general validity is not what he is looking for, at least not general validity in the form of norms or similar kinds of data. He is more likely to want to test his theory in concrete situations, to explain what is going on, for example, between a particular husband and wife under conditions of marital stress. The focus might be on some fascinating dynamic relationships that the theory, and its operational use by way of the Q pack, had brought to light. Without such a theoretical basis, even a rag and bone merchant could put together 50 adjectives and suggest that by correlating data for husbands and wives, information would be obtained which, suitably percentiled, would—well, what?

It is important, therefore, for the author of a pack of Q cards to offer some account of the instrument's theoretical implications for the purposes for which it is recommended. If the theoretical basis is interesting and suitably exemplified, there would usually be little need to ask questions about general validity, or to give profiles or other norm-implying tables. But, at face value, there is really nothing to suggest that these particular cards will serve cogently in marital counseling, job selection, or personality study. If they will, we would all be very interested to know how they do it and why they work. Of course, any clever psychologist versed in dynamic theory and knowing the person doing the Q sort could suitably interpret it. Even in this case, however, one would like to know what there is in these adjectives that is peculiarly interesting for projective purposes.

Thus, it would seem to be incumbent upon authors of packs of Q cards to elaborate on any theory they involve in their cards, and to suggest how the theory is to be used to help the psychologist find his way about in the facts the technique reveals. The *SAQS Chicago Q Sort* would be acceptable for student training purposes and for illustrating methods of Q sorting and correlation. Wider use would require much more in the way of theoretical involvement to warrant it.

CLIFFORD H. SWENSEN, JR., *Associate Professor of Psychology, University of Tennessee, Knoxville, Tennessee.*

This test has been made available "for general experimental research use" because (according

to the author): (a) it is a convenient instrument; (b) it has unusual item characteristics; and (c) what is already known about its characteristics indicates that it is useful. The author's first claim is undoubtedly justified. The test can be given quite easily and quickly, and the correlation of one Q sort with another is accomplished quite rapidly by using the scoring form and correlation chart provided. However, the latter two justifications are not quite so apparent. Presumably the items are unusual in that they consist of words rather than sentences, and in that the words are familiar to most adults, unambiguous, unstereotyped, and representative of "seven major areas or 'factors' of personality." The author does not provide an explicit statement of how the words were selected. Neither does he indicate to what the seven factors of personality according to which he has classified the words are related. The test itself was derived from Stephenson's better known work with Q sorts, and is apparently intended as a shorter, more convenient method of getting at these same factors. The justification concerning what is already known about the test's characteristics is partially supported by evidence.

The manual cites two studies in which high agreement between husbands and wives in the sorts is related to marital happiness. However, no evidence relating the results of the sorts to personality factors is presented. In fairness to the author, it should be pointed out that he states that the test should probably not be thought of as having general validity, but as being valid for particular purposes. By particular purposes he presumably means research rather than diagnostic purposes.

Test-retest reliabilities of .81 for 27 college women and .79 for 31 college men are reported with a one week interval between administrations. Reliability studies with larger and more heterogeneous samples would be preferable.

The author presents 10 tables of norms for the intercorrelations between various kinds of sorts. One of these is the correlation between the individual's sort for Self and for Ideal Self. The remaining nine are various types of correlations between the sorts of husbands and wives. These nine are based upon 20 or more married couples. The norms for the Self-Ideal Self sort are based upon 40 college students. No additional information about the samples is provided. It would be desirable to have norms based upon larger and more heterogeneous samples,

and the manual should present more detailed information concerning the samples upon which the present norms are based. No indication of the significance of high or low intercorrelations is given, with the exception of the previously mentioned studies. Such information would be highly desirable, as would norms and validation data for other kinds of intercorrelations among sorts, and information concerning how the test was constructed.

One other minor criticism should be noted. The words are presented on very small cards that are rather difficult to handle. It would be a little easier to sort and score the cards if they were about twice their present size.

The test appears to be an easily administered research instrument, but of unknown validity for other purposes.

[104]

*SRA Junior Inventory. Grades 4–8; 1951–57; problems checklist; 5 scores: school, home, myself, people, health (Form A), general (Form S) ; 2 forms; Form S is an extensive revision of Form A rather than a parallel form; postage extra; H. H. Remmers and Robert H. Bauernfeind; Science Research Associates. *

a) FORM A. 1951; separate answer pads must be used; $9.80 per 20 tests; $2.15 per 20 answer pads; $1.20 per 20 pupil profile leaflets ('51) ; 75¢ per specimen set; (40) minutes.

b) FORM S, REVISED EDITION. 1955–57; test ('57) ; manual ('57) ; $2 per 20 tests; $1.05 per 20 profiles ('57) ; 50¢ per specimen set; (45) minutes.

REFERENCES

1. BAUERNFEIND, ROBERT H. The Development of a Needs and Problems Inventory for Elementary School Children. Doctor's thesis, Purdue University (Lafayette, Ind.), 1951.
2. RABINOVITCH, VIVIAN. The Construction and Validation of a Basic Difficulty Index for the SRA Junior Inventory. Master's thesis, Purdue University (Lafayette, Ind.), 1953.
3. NIXON, WARREN WINTERS. The Science Research Associates Junior Inventory: A Validity Study. Doctor's field study, Colorado State College of Education (Greeley, Colo.), 1954.
4. BAUERNFEIND, ROBERT H. "Measuring Children's Strength of Response to Attitude Items." Ed & Psychol Meas 15:63–70 sp '55. * (PA 30:664)
5. HERNÁNDEZ, CARLOS. The Spanish Revision of the S.R.A. Junior Inventory, Form A. Doctor's thesis, Purdue University (Lafayette, Ind.), 1958. (DA 19:354)

WARREN R. BALLER, Professor of Educational Psychology, The University of Nebraska, Lincoln, Nebraska.

Form S of this needs and problems checklist is a thoroughly revised edition of Form A (1951), and, as such, retains the desirable features of its predecessor while benefiting from changes which experience with the earlier form suggested. The wording of the items appears to be well suited to the aim of presenting children's problems in the form in which they recognize and express them. The words "I want," "I wish," "I need," "I am," "I would like," or their negatives introduce all but a small percentage

of the items. The reading level of the statements is consistent with the grade level involved.

A matter which gave the authors some concern in their interpretation of responses to the earlier form was the difficulty of determining differences in strength of feeling. This difficulty has been resolved to a considerable extent in Form S. Three response boxes of different sizes are provided for each item. The checking of the big box means "Big Problem"; the middle sized box is for indicating a "Middle-Sized Problem"; the little box is for a "Little Problem." The Fourth response choice, a circle, is to be checked to indicate no problem. The differentially-sized response box method for determining intensity of feeling is a particularly noteworthy development.

As one approach to interpretation, the authors suggest the identification of the areas in which a child's major interests and problems lie, and the differential comparison of scores in the several areas. For this purpose they suggest that values of 3, 2, and 1, respectively, be given to big-, middle-sized-, and small-box responses. A pupil profile based on national norms for each of the five problem areas is provided for depicting the resulting scores. The use of the profile chart with a problems checklist will be looked upon with some misgivings by numerous counseling psychologists and others who do not consider that interpretation based on a system of norms contributes to the best use of such an instrument. For one thing, the existence of the profile chart is an invitation to *rate* (i.e., score) pupil responses—a dubious practice when it is associated with the search for important pupil problems and interests. The authors' suggestion that each area of responses may prove to be interpretable "as a 'psychological test score'" will meet with resistance from persons who deem the functions of inventories and tests to be basically different.

In addition, in spite of evidence of the statistical reliability of the area classifications of responses, there remains the bothersome question of whether some "unlikes" have not been grouped together in such a way as to cast doubt on the meaning of profile scores. Some items in a given area appear to relate to *problems;* others in the same area seem best to be described as *interests.* The authors use the two terms. As a result, it is difficult to see what the area score for school, for example, means with both these kinds of items contributing to it.

There also seems to be room for serious doubt about whether the same profile score for different pupils will convey reasonably comparable indications of problems in view of the different point-value compositions that are possible. Conceivably, one pupil might rank high on a given area by checking many small boxes, while another pupil could receive the same score by checking a small number of large boxes. The criticism would seem all the more justified in light of the fact that the authors disregard entirely small box checking when they compute frequencies of scores for the invoicing of a class as a whole.

As another aid to interpretation, selected items have been grouped, on the basis of content analysis, into eight categories: Reading Problems, Curriculum Planning and Teaching Methods, Identifying Potential Drop-Outs, Health Problems, Relationships with Older Youngsters, Relationships with Adults, Personal Adjustment, and Objective Interests and Problems. The manual makes it clear that these are suggestive and tentative groupings. As such, they should have real value for the purpose of enlisting the interest of school nurses, attendance officers, curriculum specialists, and others in data that might point the way to desirable changes in school practices and policies.

Among the numerous good features of the inventory are the unusually complete set of directions and the inclusion in the manual of several suggestions as to how the instrument may be used. Professional workers who take the pains to read these suggestions carefully will be likely to plan for important activities which they otherwise would not have thought about. Finally, there is much about the inventory that points to its potential usefulness in important research. The authors are to be commended for suggesting a number of possibilities for further refinement of the instrument and for studies into various phases of curriculum improvement and improvement of pupil personnel services in which the inventory might advantageously be used.

J Consult Psychol 21:282 Je '57. Laurance F. Shaffer. * The revised form is clearly an improvement. It also continues to show the merits which characterized the earlier version—the good scope of technical information provided in the manual, and the modesty of the suggested interpretations.

J Counsel Psychol 4:328–9 w '57. *Laurence Siegel*. * To the extent that this inventory will be used by teachers and counselors as an evaluational tool for the purpose of stimulating discussions with students, it will serve a very useful purpose. It is doubtful, however, that the *Junior Inventory*, in its present form, deserves the refinements of scoring and profile analysis also suggested by the authors. The statistical rationale underlying the development of this inventory is simply too weak to justify the derivation and interpretation of "scores" for the five subscales. Considered as an evaluational checklist rather than as a measuring instrument, the *Junior Inventory* possesses tremendous potential for application. The items in the inventory are phrased in the youngsters' jargon since most of these items were extracted from "My Problems" essays written by elementary school children. The format of the booklet is ingenious in providing a readily comprehensible system for rating each of the self-descriptive statements as a "big problem," "middle-sized problem," "little problem" or "not a problem." By and large, the manual is well written and will be understandable to persons who might be required to administer the inventory in the absence of any specialized training in testing procedures. * There is little doubt that the perceptive teacher, and counselor, will gain much in the way of useful information about individual pupils by studying their replies to specific items. Analysis of group responses to specific items (i.e., problems) may provide a sound basis for evaluating the school's success in achieving nonacademic objectives and may well stimulate classroom discussions constituting a mental hygiene program at the elementary school level. These are, however, the limits of application of the *Junior Inventory*. Statistical considerations.... prohibit proper interpretations of scores on the five subscales. The starting point for development of clusters or subscales within the *Junior Inventory* rested upon the frequently used procedure whereby provisional clusters are hypothesized and items are grouped into these provisional clusters for the purpose of deriving subscores. The allocations of items is then verified by correlating every item with every provisional subscale. The resultant item-cluster correlations normally dictate the removal of certain items and the reassignment of others. Unfortunately this procedure was aborted in the development of the *Junior Inventory*. The em-

pirical portion of the item analysis was not iterated because the authors somehow established a rationale which prevented the expected mobility of items. This rationale is not clarified in the manual, but it is quite obvious that certain clusters were permitted to retain items which did *not* correlate substantially with the rest of the subscale! The "Myself" cluster, for example, contains at least one item with a 0.00 correlation. How many such items were retained to contaminate the subscales is not discussed in the manual. Furthermore, a usual procedure in this type of analysis is to retain only those items which correlate significantly with one or perhaps two of the subscales. The magnitudes of intercorrelations between the subscales are sufficiently high to indicate that the *Junior Inventory* contains many items which correlate with several subscales. In fact, the authors' contentions that the intercorrelations between the five areas "....are satisfactorily low to justify treating each area as an independent measure" is probably untenable. These intercorrelations range between .39 and .77 with a median value of .52. Although the data were not factor analyzed, it is probable that one general factor would account for a large portion of the total variance. And two factors, combining the "School" and "Home" clusters and the "Myself" and "People" clusters would probably remove virtually all of the variance. Thus, the data now available on the *Junior Inventory* do not justify computation of the five subscores advocated in the manual. Furthermore, since predictive validities have not yet been demonstrated, it is unlikely that one would want to score the inventory anyway. The *Junior Inventory* is a valuable supplement to general evaluational techniques in the area of personality at the elementary school level. When considered in this light, it has excellent potential. It is unlikely, however, that it can be treated as a multiscored measuring instrument at the present time.

For a review by Dwight L. Arnold of Form A, see 4:90.

[105]

*****SRA Youth Inventory.** Grades 7–12; 1949–56; problems checklist; 9 scores: school, future, myself, people, home, dates and sex, health, general, basic difficulty; IBM; 2 forms; Form S is an extensive revision of Form A rather than a parallel form; 75¢ per specimen set; postage extra; (30–40) minutes; H. H. Remmers, Benjamin Shimberg, and Arthur J. Drucker (manual for Form A); Science Research Associates. *

a) FORM A. 1949–53; listed as Forms AH and AM in publisher's catalog; IBM; 1 form ('49); manual, second edition ('53); technical supplement ('53); separate answer sheets or pads must be used; $9.80 per 20 tests; $4.50 per 100 IBM answer sheets; $2.15 per 20 hand scoring answer pads; $2.50 per set of machine scoring stencils; 50¢ per hand scoring basic difficulty key; $1.20 per 20 profile leaflets ('50) for students in grades 7–10; $1.20 per 20 profile leaflets ('49) for students in grades 9–12.

b) FORM S. 1955; only test booklet available.

REFERENCES

1-7. See 4:91.
8. BROWN, CURTIS P. *The Mooney Problem Check List and the SRA Youth Inventory in Comparison.* Master's thesis, University of Southern California (Los Angeles, Calif.), 1952.
9. DRUCKER, A. J., AND REMMERS, H. H. "Environmental Determinants of Basic Difficulty Problems." *J Abn & Social Psychol* 47:379–81 Ap '52. * (PA 27:2975)
10. DRUCKER, A. J., AND REMMERS, H. H. "A Validation of the SRA Youth Inventory." *J Appl Psychol* 36:186–7 Je '52. *
11. FICK, REUEL L. "The Problem Check List: A Valuable Approach in Counseling." *Occupations* 30:410–2 Mr '52. * (PA 26:6533)
12. WARDLOW, MARY E., AND GREENE, JAMES E. "An Exploratory Sociometric Study of Peer Status Among Adolescent Girls." *Sociometry* 15:311–8 Ag–N '52. * (PA 27:7097)
13. KEISLAR, EVAN R. "Peer Group Judgments as Validity Criteria for the SRA Youth Inventory." *Calif J Ed Res* 5:77–9 Mr '54. * (PA 28:9026)
14. WEIMER, LOIS B. *An Experiment Using the SRA Inventory With a Selected Group of Adolescents in a Latin-American Community in a Texas City.* Master's thesis, University of Wyoming (Laramie, Wyo.), 1954.
15. COOMBS, ROBERT WARREN. *The Appraisal of Personal Problems of High School Seniors.* Doctor's thesis, University of Southern California (Los Angeles, Calif.), 1955.
16. PAISIOS, JOHN P., AND REMMERS, H. H. "A Factor Analysis of the SRA Youth Inventory." *J Ed Psychol* 46:25–30 Ja '55. * (PA 29:8998)
17. DE LOPATEGUI, MIGUELINA N. *Needs and Problems of Puerto Rican High School Students Related to N Variables.* Doctor's thesis, Purdue University (Lafayette, Ind.), 1957. (DA 18:2197)
18. SPIVAK, MONROE L. "School Problems Reported by Seventh and Ninth-Grade Children Entering the Same Junior High School." *J Ed Res* 50:631–3 Ap '57. *
19. PAULEY, BERTHOLD. "Relationship Between SRA Youth Inventory Scores and School Citizenship." *Personnel & Guid J* 37:207–11 N '58. *

For reviews by Kenneth E. Clark and Frank S. Freeman of Form A, see 4:91.

[106]

★**The Science Research Temperament Scale.** Grades 12–16 and adults; 1955; title on test is *The S.R.T. Scale;* Form A; mimeographed manual ['55]; $3 per 50 tests; $1 per specimen set (must be purchased to obtain manual); postage extra; (10–30) minutes; William C. Kosinar; Psychometric Affiliates. *

REFERENCE

1. KOSINAR, WILLIAM C. *Predicting Some Aspects of Research Productivity.* Doctor's thesis, Illinois Institute of Technology (Chicago, Ill.), 1954.

JOHN D. BLACK, *President, Consulting Psychologists Press, Inc., Palo Alto, California; and Director, Counseling and Testing Services, Stanford University, Stanford, California.*

The ludicrous appearance of this test, which among other things is embellished with a hideous border reminiscent of a cheap premium certificate, may lead some subjects to think it must be a gag. A glance at the manual, which does similar violence to the most rudimentary esthetic and reproduction standards, scarcely dispels this impression. Only by reading the manual is one reassured that the SRT Scale is a serious attack on an important psychological problem.

The scale was developed "to aid in the identification of personality traits that are associated with research productivity." It is a 1-page test consisting of 37 different adjectives descriptive of human behavior presented in 42 pairs roughly equated for social desirability. Subjects check which of each pair of adjectives best describes them. The score is based on responses which successfully discriminated between the top and the bottom 10 per cent of a group of 310 research workers objectively ranked for productivity in research. The 4-page mimeographed manual provides an adequate summary of the limited data available. Decile norms are given for four male groups ranging in size from 20 to 310, and, oddly enough, for two subgroups: the most and the least productive of the 310 scientists.

The author quite properly points out that the scale "is more discriminative at its two extremes rather than in its middle range." It is interesting to note that there is almost 100 per cent overlap among the distributions of research workers, college students, and "average" high school students, and that the means of these groups are virtually identical. In other words, the scale does not discriminate between research workers and other people. Its usefulness, therefore, would appear to be confined to evaluations of men engaged in research work or persons seeking to enter it. Unfortunately, from the data presented, it does not appear to contribute materially to such evaluations.

Correlation of the scale with productivity scores of 310 research workers, including the ones on which item selection was based, is given as .28, which "is underestimative (sic) because of some curvilinearity in the scatterplot." Two cross validation studies yielded rank order correlations of .26 and .36—correlations which, because of the small n's involved are significant only when considered jointly. The author candidly acknowledges that SRT scores accounted for only 7 to 13 per cent of the variance in productivity ratings of the scientists, which is certainly disappointing in a test designed for that specific function. If the author could demonstrate that in combination with other predictive measures the SRT appreciably increases multiple correlations, this disappointment might be ameliorated. Test-retest reliability (time inter-

val not reported) is given as .76, which is also discouraging. One wonders if the item pool is too limited or too heavily weighted with a few items. The entire score actually depends on 18 adjectives; the three most frequently scored (imaginative, self-confident, and impulsive) contribute 15 of the possible 42 points on the scale.

As a research tool for investigating the personalities of research scientists, the SRT Scale probably has less to offer than a good adjective checklist with a larger repertory of descriptive words, although the forced choice technique is an interesting contribution. As a tool for selection, the scale's mediocre showing on the validity studies reported makes it of dubious value. In basic conception, the test seems sound and the author's work appears to have been carefully done. Considerably more validation and refinement is required, however, before publication of this test can be justified.

DAVID R. SAUNDERS, *Research Associate, Educational Testing Service, Princeton, New Jersey.*

According to its manual, this instrument was developed "to aid in the identification of personality traits that are associated with research productivity." It yields a single score, based on all of the 42 forced choice items included in the form, and is reported by the author to have a test-retest reliability of .76 for a sample of graduate and undergraduate students. Since such a group is, if anything, more heterogeneous with respect to "research productivity" than the groups to which this instrument would most naturally be applied, this reliability figure must be treated as an upper bound on the reliability that would be attained in a practical application. Thus, from the point of view of reliability, we are forced to be exceedingly cautious in interpreting any but the most extreme scores that may be earned by individuals.

There is evidence for the validity of scores on this scale which is of unquestionable *statistical* significance, but not of much *practical* significance. Statistical significance is readily achieved, as in this case, by carrying out validation and cross validation studies on relatively large samples. However, the manual states that "performance on the scale on cross validation accounted for 7% to 13% of the variance in scientific and technical productivity." This would be an acceptable degree of validity *only if*

there were a tremendous pool of talent from which we could select only the most extreme individuals, *and only if* we were quite unconcerned by the number of truly talented individuals who would not be selected. Such seems hardly to be the case.

In summary, in view of both the scantiness of the available data on the scale and the failure of even the data reported in the manual to justify its application to practical situations, we can only advise that its use be restricted to situations in which the scores earned by individuals genuinely do not count.

[107]

★Security-Insecurity Inventory. Grades 9–16 and adults; 1945–52; title on test is *The S–I Inventory;* 1 form ('52); $3 per 25 tests; 25¢ per scoring stencil and manual ('52); 50¢ per specimen set; cash orders postpaid; (15–25) minutes; A. H. Maslow, E. Birsh, I. Honigmann, F. McGrath, A. Plason, and M. Stein; [Consulting Psychologists Press, Inc.]. *

REFERENCES

1. MASLOW, A. H. "The Dynamics of Psychological Security-Insecurity." *Char & Pers* 10:331–44 Je '42. * (*PA* 17:206)
2. MASLOW, A. H. "Conflict, Frustration, and the Theory of Threat." *J Abn & Social Psychol* 38:81–6 Ja '43. * (*PA* 17:2737)
3. MASLOW, A. H.; HIRSH, ELISA; STEIN, MARCELLA; AND HONIGMANN, IRMA. "A Clinically Derived Test for Measuring Psychological Security-Insecurity." *J General Psychol* 33:21–41 Jl '45. * (*PA* 20:202)
4. GOUGH, HARRISON G. "A Note on the Security-Insecurity Test." *J Social Psychol* 28:257–61 N '48. * (*PA* 23:2706)
5. SMITH, HENRY CLAY. "Psychometric Checks on Hypotheses Derived From Sheldon's Work on Physique and Temperament." *J Personality* 17:310–20 Mr '49. * (*PA* 25:2916)
6. SWEETLAND, ANDERS, AND SHEPLER, BERNARD. "Unweighted Scoring Norms for the Security-Insecurity Test." *J General Psychol* 49:309–10 O '53. * (*PA* 28:7555)
7. BRESEE, CLYDE WESLEY. *Affective Factors Associated With Academic Underachievement in High-School Students.* Doctor's thesis, Cornell University (Ithaca, N.Y.), 1956. (*DA* 17:90)
8. MORRIS, ROBERT P. "An Exploratory Study of Some Personality Characteristics of Gamblers." *J Clin Psychol* 13:191–3 Ap '57. * (*PA* 32:3294)
9. BENNETT, CARSON M., AND JORDAN, THOMAS E. "Security-Insecurity and the Direction of Aggressive Responses to Frustration." *J Clin Psychol* 14:166–7 Ap '58. *
10. MEHLMAN, BENJAMIN, AND KAPLAN, JANICE E. "A Correction: A Comparison of Some Concepts of Psychological Health." *J Clin Psychol* 14:438 O '58. *

NELSON G. HANAWALT, *Professor of Psychology, Douglass College, Rutgers University, New Brunswick, New Jersey.*

The *S-I Inventory* is a product of Maslow's research program which earlier produced the *Social Personality Inventory for College Women;* although the two tests are uncorrelated by design, they are nevertheless related to each other. Specifically, the test arose from Maslow's clinical and theoretical research in emotional security. Security-insecurity is a global concept or, as Maslow expresses it, a syndrome, more precisely defined by 14 subsyndromes which were judged on the basis of clinical experience to be a part of the generic concept. Table 1 in the manual lists these subsyndromes in terms of both security and in-

security. However, there is no delusion on the part of the author that these are pure factors, for he thinks of the generic syndrome and the subsyndromes as fitting into each other like a nest of cubes.[1]

The purpose of the test is to measure feelings of security, judged by Maslow to be one of the most important determinants of mental health, if not synonymous with it, and to discover something about the individual variables which make up the syndrome of security-insecurity. On this basis he recommends its use by institutions as a general survey test to single out cases of neurotic tendencies, maladjustment, conflict, suicidal tendencies, etc. How successful the test would be for such a screening purpose is not known; at least this reviewer has found no published study where it has been evaluated in this respect. Until such studies are available, it would be advisable to use a test of better known limitations such as the *Cornell Index* or Bell's *Adjustment Inventory* for screening purposes.

Maslow makes a number of statements about the relationship of S-I and self-esteem which are interesting if they can be substantiated. In the manual he says that "a person testing low in S-I and also testing low in self-esteem will almost certainly express his neurotic tendencies in a more passive fashion, e.g., schizoid tendencies, withdrawal, fantasy, inhibition. But a person scoring equally low on S-I and scoring high in self-esteem will rather be compensating, over-aggressive, and dominating." Elsewhere [1] he says that "in Jews there is a tendency to be simultaneously high in self-esteem and low in security, while in Catholic women we find often low self-esteem joined with high security." Are these clinical hunches or are they statements based upon a systematic study? Maslow does not say. At any rate, there are some interesting research possibilities suggested in the interaction of these two tests.

Gough (*4*) demonstrated that a simple counting of the insecure answers was practically as good as Maslow's original weighted scoring. Maslow adopted Gough's system; consequently, scoring is now easy and speedy. This change in scoring system has resulted in a little confusion in the literature because the chief article describing the test (*3*) is written in terms of the old scoring where a high score indicated security. Gough found the S-I test to be unrelated to

intelligence, academic performance, or socio-economic status in his high school senior group. In comparing S-I with the *Minnesota Multiphasic Personality Inventory,* Gough found the highest correlation to be with the psychasthenic scale, which also correlates with the usual personality inventory. Maslow reports correlations of .68 and .58 with the *Thurstone Personality Schedule* and the neurotic tendency score on Bernreuter's *Personality Inventory,* respectively. Another line of research is suggested in Gough's finding that femininity in the boy is more damaging to security feeling than masculinity in the girl, and that security feeling in the girl is more vulnerable to hypochondriacal complaints than it is in the boy. In an unpublished study, the reviewer found a correlation of only .20 (n = 61, college girls) between S-I and *Pressey Interest-Attitude Test* results. Apparently, emotionally immature as well as mature people can feel secure.

The S-I test was very carefully constructed. In the description of the test (*3*), 11 attempted controls which follow good test construction principles are listed. Items were eliminated which in actual testing revealed sex, religious, self-esteem, or age differences, and the number of items representing the different subsyndromes was equalized as far as possible. Also, the items indicating security were equally divided between "yes" and "no" answers. An item analysis was made at several stages in the construction of the test to improve differentiation of secure and insecure people. The final 75 items were selected from over 300 used at various stages in construction of the test.

The reliability of the test is satisfactory. The validity, however, is not well established. Maslow depended heavily upon the clinical nature of the construction process as evidence for its validity. Of 177 college students who took the test, 88 per cent said that it was either a fairly accurate or an extremely accurate measure of their feeling of security. Maslow also cites his own experience with tested people, both in and out of the clinic, as evidence for its validity. The reviewer and some of his students have done some unpublished validity studies (1958) which are briefly reported here.

In two independent studies test scores of college girls were correlated with ratings of a house chairman (a senior selected by the college administration as being especially qualified to be in charge of a house containing about 20

---

[1] MASLOW, A. H. "Dynamics of Personality Organization, II." *Psychol R* 50:541–58 N '43. * (*PA* 18:520)

girls). Each house chairman was instructed to rate only those girls she knew well. The rank correlation coefficients (rho) were .63 (n = 25) and .50 (n = 20). The respective median scores were 19 and 15.5. In another study 26 college girls rated themselves on security-insecurity and had two friends rate them. Self-ratings and test scores correlated .51, but average ratings of the two friends and test scores correlated only .24. However, the correlation between the ratings of friend A and friend B was only .50, and that between self-rating and average friend rating, .45. Obviously the friends' ratings on security-insecurity did not mean much. In a small class of six girls which met in the reviewer's office for two semesters, and which became sort of a little club, the girls' average rankings of each other on security-insecurity and test scores showed almost perfect agreement, with only ranks 5 and 6 being reversed. Self-rating and test scores of this group of advanced psychology majors correlated .80. It is quite clear that the better the rater, and the better the rater knows the person rated, the higher the correlation between the rating and the test score. In all of the above ratings, the rater was given a mimeographed sheet with Maslow's 14 subsyndromes fully reproduced. At the bottom of the page was a linear rating scale with seven verbal descriptive categories running from "very secure" to "very insecure." The rater was instructed to indicate with a tic the appropriate place on the scale for the S.

Two other studies were made: one in a correctional home for girls and the other in a school for the deaf. Both of these groups were found to be quite insecure, as was predicted. The median scores were 37 and 36 with standard deviations of 12.7 and 9.1, respectively. Correlations with the teachers' ratings of security were positive but not significant. It is doubtful whether teachers know many of their students well enough to make a meaningful rating of security feeling.

The *S-I Inventory* is a very carefully constructed test in a very important area of human adjustment. The reliability is satisfactory, and the validity is about as good as can be expected. The means and standard deviations were quite stable in the five samples which were drawn from Douglass College students; they compared favorably with those reported by Maslow for college students. The precautions listed by the author in the manual should be studied carefully by anyone using the test. Its chief use at present would appear to be as a research tool and as an aid in the understanding of an individual in a counseling situation.

HAROLD WEBSTER, *Associate Research Psychologist, Center for the Study of Higher Education, University of California, Berkeley, California.*

This instrument was constructed by item selection based on responses of subjects known to be either secure or insecure, according to "the clinical criteria" of the late 1930's. A large number of persons were studied by means of interviews and autobiographies, which enabled the author to identify those who were either secure or insecure. After several years of this study it was possible to construct a preliminary test, composed of 349 items to be responded to by "Yes," "No," or "?" which was administered to 500 college students. The students who, according to their total test scores, were most secure and most insecure were interviewed; further validation work was undertaken; and the best 130 items were retained as a second test. This second test was administered to over 1,000 students, and after further analysis a final test of 75 items was obtained, the split-half reliability of which was .93.

The analysis which preceded the final test included procedures which minimized response bias, eliminated differences due to age, sex, religion, and, to a limited extent, culture, and balanced the test so that the 14 descriptive aspects of "the generalized unitary concept of security" would each be represented by approximately equal numbers of items.

Better than average data concerning reliability and validity are presented in the manual. It is likely that total score reliability shrinks more for new samples than is contended in the authors' interpretation; however, the reliability is likely in most cases to remain in the high .80's, which, considering the brevity of the test and the complexity of what is measured, is high enough for most purposes.

Some limitations, all of which are mentioned in the manual, may be noted. Accuracy of scores depends upon both the honesty of subjects and the adequacy of their self-knowledge. The concept, or construct, of security underlying the test was altered in order to reduce the correlation with another test developed by the same authors for measuring self-esteem in college

women. The test measures a trait similar to those measured (probably less well) by numerous other instruments, some of which are mentioned in the manual. Finally, obtained distributions are skewed so that a disproportionate number of subjects receive low (secure) scores; for such a carefully constructed test the implications of this could be important for personality theory, but the authors attempt no explanation.

On the positive side it may be said immediately that it is doubtful that there are other personality tests the authors of which have exercised such great care to insure item validity. The test can be recommended without reservations as a valid measure of security-insecurity, as this trait is described by the authors.

[108]

Self-Analysis Inventory. Adults; 1945; title on test is *"How'm I Doin'?";* interviewing aid for locating maladjustment in 37 problem areas; 1 form; no data on reliability and validity; $3.40 per 25 tests; 85¢ per specimen set; postpaid; (30–60) minutes; Harry J. Baker; Public School Publishing Co. *

WARREN R. BALLER, *Professor of Educational Psychology, The University of Nebraska, Lincoln, Nebraska.*

The *Self-Analysis Inventory* consists of a 12-page booklet of 148 items, a record blank, a handbook of suggestions for the use of the inventory, and separate leaflets of remedial suggestions applicable, respectively, to each of 37 problem areas into which the inventory items have been divided.

In the handbook the author has strongly emphasized the desirability of using the inventory as an interviewing aid rather than as a method of measurement. Many of the items of the instrument appear to be well suited to such a use: to furnish "leads....which become the basis for personal interview." For the most part, the problem areas covered are those with which a well planned personal interview with a young adult would be expected to deal. They include matters of health, and attitudes related thereto; experiences and attitudes pertaining to home; problems of growing up, marriage, peer relationships, and recreation; numerous aspects of self-appraisal; "serious personality problems" stemming from worry, fear, and the like; and miscellaneous other matters related to citizenship, school, vocations, and social interests.

As an interviewing aid, the inventory would seem not to suffer because of the absence of precise norms and evidence of validity and re-

liability. It is unfortunate, therefore, that the author went to considerable lengths in the handbook to suggest schemes for interpretation which, to be trustworthy, would have to be subjected to more validation than is in evidence. Anyone who uses these schemes now is taking a precarious step in the interpretation of data.

Specifically, the reviewer is skeptical of the 4-point scale under which responses to the inventory are classified: destructive, detrimental, doubtful, desirable. The a priori judgment that the response "being very tall makes me uncomfortable" should be classified as destructive, rather than detrimental or just doubtful, is not convincing in the absence of evidence from item analysis. And the classification of this response under the same heading with "I have a bad reputation for cruelty" begs even more for item analysis. For the user to go through the operation of transferring responses from the inventory booklet to the record blank only to arrive at a product (classification) of dubious validity may be worse than a waste of time; it may be misleading as a step in the interviewing process. To take a further step recommended by the author—totalling the number of responses in each classification to arrive at a sort of diagnostic profile—appears to be additionally risky business. The user of the inventory probably will do well to proceed cautiously with interpretation based on total scores or distributions of scores and to heed the author's suggestion that when normative data are needed the distribution of scores should be studied and "statistical tables developed accordingly." On the basis of these criticisms, the present reviewer would be much inclined to omit entirely the use of the record blank and employ only the booklet of response items, thus avoiding the problems of normative interpretation sans norms.

The claim is made in the handbook that the items of the instrument are presented in an order ranging from less serious to more serious problems, thus facilitating favorable initial attitudes on the part of the respondent—with the attendant likelihood that the favorable attitude will then persist throughout the marking of the inventory. Granting that it may be desirable to provide for this sort of progression from less serious to more serious problems, the reviewer finds it difficult to discern any such arrangement among the items. Equally difficult to accept, without supporting evidence, is the assertion that items 113 to 148 inclusive are less emo-

tionally toned than those preceding and that, since they are the later items, they will permit the respondent to finish "with the feeling he has just been expressing himself on his most recent years with their adult interests." Sample responses from this section of the inventory are: "I have always gotten by with poor ideals" (Item 118), "I get back at people by gossiping" (Item 121), "The foremen and supervisors find too much fault with me" (Item 147).

The inventory has some favorable features. As stated earlier, there is in the booklet a wealth of interviewing items which should furnish valuable "leads" to follow-up procedures. The 4-choice response scheme, which is aimed at getting evidence of intensity of feeling about each of the inventory items, is a commendable feature. Possibly equally good, if not better, results would follow from the use of four un-labeled boxes for checking—with, of course, appropriate rewording of the response items. Indeed it might be a thoroughly worthwhile research project to determine which of the two formats, the existing one or the one suggested, would pay better dividends. The title of the inventory booklet is intriguing. Whether it appeals to every user of the instrument or not, at least it represents a way of avoiding emotionally toned wording on the cover page of an interviewing aid.

JOHN W. GUSTAD, *Professor of Psychology, and Director, University Counseling Center, University of Maryland, College Park, Maryland.*

Strictly speaking, this is *not* a test. Rather, it is what its title suggests: a means for collecting subjects' self descriptions. Its primary purpose, according to the author, is to furnish the psychologist, psychiatrist, or personnel interviewer with information which will help him structure a subsequent interview. In certain respects it is like the *Mooney Problem Check List*.

The inventory consists of 12 pages containing 148 items. The items are assembled under 37 topics ranging from physical health to morals and vocational problems. It was apparently intended to cover the entire range of human problems. No time limit is assigned; 30 to 60 minutes are usually required to complete the form. Four choices are provided as alternatives in each item. This, the author feels, makes the inventory more true to life than the yes-no al-

ternative situation. Alternatives within items are arranged randomly to reduce response bias.

Scoring is done by tallying responses within topics under four headings: desirable, doubtful, deterimental, and destructive. Omitted items are to be noted and (perhaps) discussed with the client during the interview. Baker suggests, without much enthusiasm, that the items may be weighted from one to four and summed. He says, "Obviously well adjusted individuals will make much higher total scores than the poorly-adjusted on the Inventory." The reviewer wonders whether the comma after "obviously" was omitted accidentally or intentionally. In either case, the conclusion is far from obviously correct.

There are no norms presented, and the author seems to feel that, for most users, these are unnecessary. He does suggest that personnel workers may wish to develop norms for special cases. Others, however, will simply locate topics in which the subject has admitted to problems and use these as the basis for interviews.

It is difficult to evaluate this instrument within the framework of tests. It is not a test. At the same time, the claims for its usefulness relate to problems which other test developers have had to face. Baker has not faced these, and this failure makes the utility of the instrument very suspect.

He assumes, for instance, that well adjusted individuals will say that they have fewer problems than will badly adjusted ones. Nearly 40 years of research, beginning with the Woodworth inventory, have demonstrated that this assumption simply does not hold. Several studies have shown that normals will often confess to having *more* problems than will neurotics and psychotics. This being so, anyone who uses the *Self-Analysis Inventory* must face two problems: the false positives—normals who admit to many problems, and the false negatives—disturbed individuals who deny that they have problems. The existence of these groups makes the usefulness of the inventory very questionable.

There is literally no information given with respect to either the validity or the reliability of this instrument. Baker talks throughout about his successful experiences with the inventory, but this cannot be accepted as indicating validity. In one place, he says, "The author's experience....has shown that the great majority of individuals rate themselves honestly and sin-

cerely on these types of inventories." This may or may not be true. Even if true, it is *not* the great majority with whom most interviewers are most concerned; it is those with problems who may also be the ones who choose to engage in dissimulation, conscious or unconscious.

This inventory was designed as an instrument to aid the interviewer. Baker suggests that the interviewer look over the "scores" in the various problem areas and then decide whether and how much information should be given to the interviewee. If there are many problem areas, the interviewer must decide where to start. Most present day interviewers would feel uncomfortable about such a procedure, especially if they were worried about problem areas which were not admitted to. In the absence of norms, it is difficult to decide what constitutes a critical score, one which indicates a problem in a given area. This further reduces the usefulness of the inventory for its stated purpose.

In Baker's defense, it must be pointed out that the inventory was developed in 1945. A great deal has been learned since then about assessing personality. That was the year in which Meehl published his classical study of the K factor as a suppressor variable. Nevertheless, since the instrument remains on the market, its author and its publisher have the responsibility for keeping it up to date with respect to what is known about test development. This has not been done.

The reviewer finds it difficult to conceive of a situation in which this instrument would be validly applicable in terms of its stated purposes. At best, it leaves the interviewer with most or all of his original task of finding out what the problems are; at worst, in the hands of an unskilled person, it could be dangerously misleading. Unless the *Self-Analysis Inventory* is brought up to date, it should be withdrawn from circulation and sale immediately.

[109]

★Self-Perception Inventory: An Adjustment Survey With Special Reference to the Speech Situation. High school and college; 1940–54; formerly called *Personal-Social Adjustment Inventory;* 8 scores: self-centered introversion, objective introversion, self-centered extroversion, objective extroversion, self-centeredness, objectivity, introversion, extroversion; IBM; 1 form ('54); revised manual ('55); separate answer sheets must be used; 20¢ per test; 5¢ per IBM answer sheet; 5¢ per hand scoring answer sheet; 10¢ per hand scoring stencil; 20¢ per manual ('55); postpaid; [45–50] minutes; Lawrence W. Miller and Elwood Murray; University of Denver Bookstores. *

C. R. STROTHER, *Professor of Clinical Psychology, University of Washington, Seattle, Washington.*

This 45-item, multiple choice, self-rating inventory is designed to measure the following tendencies: (*a*) self-centered introversion; (*b*) objective introversion; (*c*) self-centered extroversion; and (*d*) objective extroversion. Through combination of these scores, separate ratings may also be computed on self-centeredness, objectivity, introversion, and extroversion. The items relate, principally, to attitude toward, and behavior in, situations involving verbal communication. The inventory is designed primarily for use in improving adjustment to speech situations.

The items were selected on the basis of their capacity to discriminate between the highest and lowest 10 per cent of an unspecified population of college students. Split-half reliabilities for the four basic scales range from .81 to .87 (n = 125). Percentile ranks are given for 423 college students and, separately, for 484 high school students.

Good agreement is reported between test scores of 160 students and ratings by themselves and by teachers and clinicians on the personality variables with which the test purports to deal. No information is provided on the procedure by which these estimates of agreement were arrived at. Introversion and extroversion scores on this test correlate .37 and −.38, respectively, with scores on the introversion-extroversion scale of Bernreuter's *Personality Inventory* (n = 90).

This test is vulnerable to the usual objections to self-rating inventories. The probability of contamination by the social desirability factor is high. However, disregarding the question of the meaningfulness of the scores, self-descriptive statements by the student may be of value to the speech teacher as a basis for instruction or counseling.

[110]

★The Sherman Mental Impairment Test. Adults; 1955–57; 2 scores: letter finding, reaction time; 1 form ['57]; record blank ('57); no data on reliability for reaction time score; young adult norms only; $13.50 per 100 tests; $4 per cards and manual ('56); $7 per set of 25 tests, cards, and manual; postpaid; specimen set not available; (10) minutes; Murray H. Sherman; Western Psychological Services. *

REFERENCE

1. SHERMAN, MURRAY H. "A Brief, Objective Test for the Measurement of Mental Impairment." *J General Psychol* 52: 285–96 Ap '55. * (PA 30:4598)

D. RUSSELL DAVIS, *Reader in Clinical Psychology, University of Cambridge, Cambridge, England.*

The test material consists of 10 designs, each composed of a number of letters of the alphabet and random lines mixed together. Two scores are obtained for each design: the number of letters found by the subject, and the time elapsing before the first letter is identified. The standardisation is based on the sum total of all letters given (the letter finding score), and the sum total of "reaction" times (the reaction time score).

The test has been standardised on young adults only. Both scores are claimed to distinguish normal subjects and "general medical patients" from schizophrenics, schizoid personalities, the organically impaired, and the mental defective. The letter finding score does not distinguish between organics and schizophrenics or organics and mental defectives. The reaction time score distinguishes, although not highly reliably, between organics and mental defectives but not between organics and schizophrenics.

The correlation between the letter finding score and intelligence is not significant in normal subjects, but is of the order of .50 in the patient groups. Too few data are given to evaluate these findings. One may suspect that it is partly the result of the method of selecting the samples for the standardisation. The task is an easy one for normal subjects of average intelligence, and it is possible that intelligence level becomes of importance only when it is below average. In any event, it appears difficult to make allowances for the effects of intelligence. The effect of age is not known; it is likely to be relatively large.

The test is likely to have little value in routine clinical work because of the considerations above. At most it can help in deciding between normality and impairment from whatever cause, if the subject is young and of average or above average intelligence.

WILLIAM SCHOFIELD, *Associate Professor of Psychology and Psychiatry, University of Minnesota, Minneapolis, Minnesota.*

The author's rationale for this test is that it is a measure of mental flexibility, that is, "ability to focus on two or more mental contents in an approximately simultaneous manner," and that loss of such flexibility is one index of mental impairment. The test consists of designs reproduced on cards. Each is composed of a number of alphabetic letters and random lines mixed together to constitute a geometric design of varying complexity. One item, for example, is a square. The subject is required to identify as many letters of the alphabet as he can see in each design. The administrator's instructions to the subject are given in the manual explicitly and adequately; unfortunately, the administrator is encouraged to paraphrase these excellent formal instructions as he sees fit. There is no time limit. Two scores are recorded: the total number of letters identified on the 10 test cards, and the sum of the reaction times (time from presentation of each card to identification of first letter) to the 10 cards. The author's claims of easy, simple administration and of quick, objective scoring are satisfied.

The test has been standardized exclusively on a sample of 214 young males, representing seven diagnostic groups (normals, general medical patients, schizophrenics, organics, defectives, schizoids, and emotionally unstable patients). Ranges, medians, means, and standard deviations are reported for the two scores for all seven groups. Percentage overlap statistics for the various samples would better illustrate the limitations of this test as a single differentiating or diagnostic test.

This test has the ever-sought advantages of speed, simplicity, and objectivity. It does show some relation to impairment of mental function. Its simple nature and limited range of difficulty, plus the absence of data on the precise relationship of scores to degree of impairment, make its use as a solitary measure of intellectual inefficiency inadvisable. It has promise for inclusion in a battery of other tests of different aspects of mental function.

[111]

Shipley-Institute of Living Scale for Measuring Intellectual Impairment. Adults; 1939–46; formerly called *Shipley-Hartford Retreat Scale for Measuring Intellectual Impairment;* 4 scores: vocabulary, abstractions, total, conceptual quotient; 1 form ('39); manual ('46, identical with manual copyrighted in 1940 except for title); $2 per 25 tests; 50¢ per specimen set; postpaid; 20(25) minutes; Walter C. Shipley; distributed by William U. Shipley, P.O. Box 39, Yale Station, New Haven, Conn. *

REFERENCES

1–25. See 3:95.
26. SLATER, PATRICK. "Scores of Different Types of Neurotics on Tests of Intelligence." *Brit J Psychol* 35:40–2 Ja '45. * (PA 19:966)
27. BIJOU, SIDNEY W., AND LUCIO, WILLIAM H. Chap. 8, "Measures of Mental Function for Evaluating Severity of Disturbance," pp. 133–43. In *The Psychological Program in AAF Convalescent Hospitals.* Edited by Sidney W. Bijou. Army Air Forces Aviation Psychology Program Research Reports, Report

No. 15. Washington, D.C.: U.S. Government Printing Office, 1947. Pp. viii, 256. *
28. MAGARET, ANN, AND SIMPSON, MARY. "A Comparison of Two Measures of Deterioration in Psychotics." Abstract. *Am Psychol* 2:425 O '47. *
29. WHEELER, ERMA T. *A Study of Certain Aspects of Personality as Related to the Electroencephalogram.* Doctor's thesis, University of Pittsburgh (Pittsburgh, Pa.), 1947.
30. GARFIELD, SOL L., AND FEY, WILLIAM F. "A Comparison of the Wechsler-Bellevue and Shipley-Hartford Scales as Measures of Mental Impairment." *J Consult Psychol* 12:259–64 Jl-Ag '48. * (*PA* 23:1289)
31. MAGARET, ANN, AND SIMPSON, MARY M. "A Comparison of Two Measures of Deterioration in Psychotic Patients." *J Consult Psychol* 12:265–9 Jl-Ag '48. * (*PA* 23:1407)
32. SOLOMON, JOSEPH C. "Adult Character and Behavior Disorders." *J Clin Psychopath* 9:1–55 Ja '48. *
33. BENTON, ARTHUR L., AND WESLEY, ELIZABETH L. "Preliminary Report of the Development of a Test for the Valuation of Intellectual Impairment." Abstract. *Am Psychol* 4:268 Jl '49. *
34. GRAY, CONSTANCE V. *An Investigation of the Shipley Hartford and Wechsler-Bellevue Scales and Measures of Deterioration.* Master's thesis, University of Toronto (Toronto, Ont., Canada), 1949. Pp. 35.
35. SCHERER, ISIDOR W. "The Psychological Scores of Mental Patients in an Individual and Group Testing Situation." *J Clin Psychol* 5:405–8 O '49. * (*PA* 24:3740)
36. HALSTEAD, H. "Abilities of Male Mental Hospital Patients." *J Mental Sci* 96:726–33 Jl '50. *
37. HORLICK, REUBEN S. *The Relationships of Psychometric Test Scores to Personality Disorders.* Doctor's thesis, New York University (New York, N.Y.), 1950.
38. CHODORKOFF, BERNARD, AND MUSSEN, PAUL. "Qualitative Aspects of the Vocabulary Responses of Normals and Schizophrenics." *J Consult Psychol* 16:43–8 F '52. *
39. GARFIELD, SOL L., AND BLEK, LIBBY. "Age, Vocabulary Level, and Mental Impairment." *J Consult Psychol* 16:395–8 O '52. * (*PA* 27:5739)
40. AARONSON, BERNARD S.; NELSON, SHERMAN E.; AND HOLT, SHIRLEY. "On a Relation Between Bender-Gestalt Recall and Shipley-Hartford Scores." *J Clin Psychol* 9:88 Ja '53. * (*PA* 27:7748)
41. SHIPLEY, WALTER C. "Shipley-Institute of Living Scale for Measuring Intellectual Impairment," pp. 751–6. (*PA* 27:7794) In *Contributions Toward Medical Psychology: Theory and Psychodiagnostic Methods, Vol. II.* Edited by Arthur Weider. New York: Ronald Press Co., 1953. Pp. xi, 459–885. *
42. SYDOW, DONALD WAYNE. *A Psychometric Differentiation Between Functional Psychotics and Non-Psychotics with Organic Brain Damage.* Doctor's thesis, University of Minnesota (Minneapolis, Minn.), 1953. (*DA* 13:1267)
43. WINFIELD, DON L. "The Shipley-Hartford Vocabulary Test and Pre-Trauma Intelligence." *J Clin Psychol* 9:77–8 Ja '53. * (*PA* 27:7807)
44. HORLICK, REUBEN S., AND MONROE, HAROLD J. "A Study of the Reliability of an Alternate Form for the Shipley-Hartford Abstraction Scale." *J Clin Psychol* 10:381–3 O '54. * (*PA* 29:4062)
45. HARRISON, ROSS; HUNT, WINSLOW; AND JACKSON, THEODORE A. "Profile of the Mechanical Engineer: I, Ability." *Personnel Psychol* 8:219–34 su '55. * (*PA* 30:5414)
46. BENNETT, HOWARD J. "The Shipley-Hartford Scale and the Porteus Maze Test as Measures of Functioning Intelligence." *J Clin Psychol* 12:190–1 Ap '56. * (*PA* 31:4669)
47. PARKER, JAMES W. "The Validity of Some Current Tests for Organicity." *J Consult Psychol* 21:425–8 O '57. *
48. SINES, LLOYD K. "Intelligence Test Correlates of Shipley-Hartford Performance." *J Clin Psychol* 14:399–404 O '58. *

For reviews by E. J. G. Bradford, William A. Hunt, and Margaret Ives, see 3:95.

[112]
*Sixteen Personality Factor Questionnaire. Ages 16 and over; 1949–57; title on test is *16 P.F.*; also called *The 16 P.F. Test*; 16 or 17 scores: aloof vs. warm-outgoing (A), dull vs. bright (B), emotional vs. mature (C), submissive vs. dominant (E), glum-silent vs. enthusiastic (F), casual vs. conscientious (G), timid vs. adventurous (H), tough vs. sensitive (I), trustful vs. suspecting (L), conventional vs. eccentric (M), simple vs. sophisticated (N), confident vs. insecure (O), conservative vs. experimenting (Q1), dependent vs. self-sufficient (Q2), lax vs. controlled (Q3), stable vs. tense (Q4), motivational distortion scale (optional); IBM; Forms A ('56), B ('57), C ('56); tabular supplement ['57]; mimeographed decile standardization table ['57]; separate answer sheets must be used; $2.25 per 50 answer sheets; $1.80 per 50 profiles ('56); $2.70 per 50

answer-profiles; $1 per scoring key; $6 per complete specimen set; cash orders postpaid; IBM answer sheets available on special order; R. B. Cattell, D. R. Saunders (A, B), and G. Stice (A, B); Institute for Personality and Ability Testing. *
a) FORMS A AND B. $7 per 25 tests; (40–50) minutes.
b) FORM C. $10 per 25 tests; 80¢ per supplementary manual ('56); (20–30) minutes.

REFERENCES

1–8. See 4:87.
9. GOINES, VALMORE R. *Personality Characteristics of a Certain Ethnic Group.* Doctor's thesis, Northwestern University (Evanston, Ill.), 1951.
10. LAMKE, TOM ARTHUR. "Personality and Teaching Success." *J Exp Ed* 20:217–59 D '51. * (*PA* 27:681)
11. CATTELL, R. B., AND HOROWITZ, J. Z. "Objective Personality Tests Investigating the Structure of Altruism in Relation to Source Traits A, H, and L." *J Personality* 21:103–17 S '52. * (*PA* 26:5862)
12. NEILEN, GORDON C. *A Study of the Cattell 16 PF Test by Comparison With the A. C. E. and Guilford-Martin Personality Battery.* Master's thesis, Kent State University (Kent, Ohio), 1952.
13. STICE, GLEN F., AND CATTELL, RAYMOND B. "Personality Differences Found in Small-Group Leaders Selected by Four Independent Criteria of Leadership." Abstract. *Am Psychol* 8:443 Ag '53. *
14. SUHR, VIRTUS W. "The Cattell 16 P.F. Test as a Prognosticator of Accident Susceptibility." *Proc Iowa Acad Sci* 60:558–61 '53. * (*PA* 29:3218)
15. CATTELL, RAYMOND B., AND STICE, GLEN F. "Four Formulae for Selecting Leaders on the Basis of Personality." *Human Relations* 7:493–507 N '54. * (*PA* 29:5450)
16. ERICKSON, HARLEY ELLWOOD. "A Factorial Study of Teaching Ability." *J Exp Ed* 23:1–39 S '54. * (*PA* 29:6927)
17. MONTROSS, HAROLD WESLEY. "Temperament and Teaching Success." *J Exp Ed* 23:73–97 S '54. * (*PA* 29:6302)
18. WRIGHT, STUART. "Some Personality Characteristics of Academic Underachievers." Abstract. *Am Psychol* 9:496 Ag '54. *
19. CATTELL, R. B., AND DREVDAHL, J. E. "A Comparison of the Personality Profile (16 P.F.) of Eminent Researchers With That of Eminent Teachers and Administrators, and of the General Population." *Brit J Psychol* 46:248–61 N '55. * (*PA* 30:7189)
20. ROSENTHAL, IRENE. *A Factor Analysis of Anxiety Variables.* Doctor's thesis, University of Illinois (Urbana, Ill.), 1955. (*DA* 16:376)
21. CATTELL, RAYMOND B. "Second-Order Personality Factors in the Questionnaire Realm." *J Consult Psychol* 20:411–8 D '56. * (*PA* 32:1614)
22. CATTELL, RAYMOND B. "A Shortened 'Basic English' Version (Form *C*) of the 16 PF Questionnaire." *J Social Psychol* 44:257–78 N '56. *
23. CATTELL, RAYMOND B. "Validation and Intensification of the Sixteen Personality Factor Questionnaire." *J Clin Psychol* 12:205–14 Jl '56. * (*PA* 31:6064)
24. CATTELL, R. B.; DAY, M.; AND MEELAND, T. "Occupational Profiles on the 16 Personality Factor Questionnaire." *Occupational Psychol* 30:10–9 Ja '56. * (*PA* 31:3207)
25. CATTELL, RAYMOND B. *Personality and Motivation Structure and Measurement.* Yonkers, N.Y.: World Book Co., 1957. Pp. xxv, 948. *
26. KARSON, SAMUEL, AND POOL, KENNETH BRYNER. "The Construct Validity of the Sixteen Personality Factors Test." *J Clin Psychol* 13:245–52 Jl '57. *
27. DE PALMA, NICHOLAS, AND CLAYTON, HUGH D. "Scores of Alcoholics on the Sixteen Personality Factor Questionnaire." *J Clin Psychol* 14:390–2 O '58. *
28. DREVDAHL, JOHN E., AND CATTELL, RAYMOND B. "Personality and Creativity in Artists and Writers." *J Clin Psychol* 14:107–11 Ap '58. *
29. KARSON, SAMUEL, AND POOL, KENNETH B. "Second-Order Factors in Personality Measurement." *J Consult Psychol* 22:299–303 Ag '58.

C. J. ADCOCK, *Senior Lecturer in Psychology, Victoria University of Wellington, Wellington, New Zealand.*

This test is undoubtedly a major development in the personality area. Originally based on a comprehensive factor analysis, it has been extended to three forms (plus a special form for children) and the factorisation thrice checked by independent experiment. A prodigious amount of statistical work has gone into it. No

other test covers such a wide range of personality dimensions and never before have the dimensions been so meticulously determined. It is little wonder that half a dozen foreign translations have already appeared. Nothing succeeds like success and it can be expected that there will soon be a vast amount of data available with regard to norms and correlation with criteria. The 1957 handbook already contains mean profiles for 28 occupational groups.

THE PERSONALITY FACTORS. Apart from intelligence there are 15 factors which cover a wide field. It might have been of some advantage if they could have been grouped in some way and not simply listed in haphazard order. The reviewer would like to arrange them in three groups: traits largely determined by heredity, traits largely dependent on environmental influences, and traits related to ego formation.

To the first group we might assign three factors according to the evidence of Cattell's own studies: [1]

A—Cyclothymia versus schizothymia. The essential core appears to be good-natured sociability, which this reviewer is tempted to regard as related to parental drive, possibly influenced by hormone control.
H—Parmia versus threctia. In the negative form this is characterized by shyness and timidity. It is probably related to constitutional differences in autonomic thresholds for fear response.
E—Dominance versus submission. This again would appear to be related to autonomic thresholds, this time for anger. Since Cattell found the ratio between heredity and environment for the inter-family variance to be about 10:1, the genetic factor in this trait seems fairly certain.

On the evidence of Eysenck [2] one would like to add to this group factor C, emotional stability, which Cattell considers to be similar to the former's general neuroticism, but Cattell's own evidence is to the contrary.[1] This raises some doubts about the nature of C which are reinforced by a consideration of the two second-order factors. These are designated "anxiety" and "introversion-extraversion" respectively, and appear to correspond rather closely to Eysenck's general neuroticism and "introversion-extraversion." Cattell's emotional stability factor may, therefore, be rather more a matter of learned control.

The second group would consist of eight factors:

1 CATTELL, RAYMOND B.; BLEWETT, DUNCAN B.; AND BELOFF, J. R. "The Inheritance of Personality: A Multiple Variance Analysis Determination of Approximate Nature-Nurture Ratios for Primary Personality Factors in Q-Data." Am J Human Genetics 7:122–46 Je '55. * (PA 30:2451)
2 EYSENCK, H. J. The Structure of Human Personality. London: Methuen & Co. Ltd., 1953. Pp. xix, 348. *

M—Autia versus praxernia. This might correspond to Guilford's introverted thinking or the "inner life" of the Rorschach. (The Form C description of "eccentric versus practical" is open to criticism.)
O—Guilt proneness versus confident adequacy. The description of "anxious insecurity" seems right.
Q4—High ergic tension, or "raw nerves," versus low ergic tension.
L—Protension, or paranoid tendency, versus relaxed security.
Q1—Radicalism versus conservatism of temperament.
Q2—Self-sufficiency versus group dependency. (Is this related to Riesman's "inner-directed" as opposed to "other-directed"?)
I—Premsia versus harria, or sensitivity versus toughness. This is not a constitutional toughness. Cattell associates it with "protected emotional sensitivity," whence the name.
N—Shrewdness versus naïveté, or sophistication.

All these factors are well established. O and Q4 are both appreciably correlated with the timidity factor (.41 and .35 for factor scores) and both are anxiety measures. A question may be raised as to the boundary between personality traits and interest dimensions. Radicalism and sophistication might well qualify as examples of the latter.

The third group of factors relating to ego structure might include:

G—Super-ego strength.
F—Surgency.
Q3—High self-sentiment formation.

Factors G and Q3 are both concerned with ego organization. Since the term "super-ego" is usually associated with the moral aspects of ego organization, it might be applied to both of these factors. G appears to be concerned with the setting of high standards whereas Q3 is concerned with the control of behaviour by the super-ego regardless of what its standards are. The former suggests the person who has taken refuge in the safety of "correct" behaviour, possibly as a means of obtaining parental approval or to resolve guilt. The latter suggests a well integrated personality, but the items involved appear to place little stress on the moral aspects of the super-ego. Perhaps "ego-control" might be a more suitable reference in that it does not emphasise moral aspects. Popular language would probably refer to the factor as "will."

The stress in the manual on energy and persistence as characterizing G seems to be somewhat misplaced if one judges by the items involved. It is possible, however, that we have here an obsessional need for correctness which includes a need to persist until a task is satisfactorily completed. If so, it may be related to the anal character described in Freudian litera-

ture. The fact that professional researchers are shown to have a mean sten score of only 3.4 on this factor does not accord well with this factor's being the major source of energy and persistence.

Surgency is tentatively included here because it appears to be in some way related to ego-striving. The surgent person is perhaps less inclined to be ego-involved and so able to adopt a less serious attitude towards life. This might account for the low rating of research workers on this trait. Cattell suggests that surgent people have been influenced by a more optimism creating environment. There appears to be some relation to Sheldon's viscerotonia, but the Cattell studies indicate that it is not a genetically determined trait. It includes aspects which Guilford found in his Rhathymia, but French[3] doubts whether the two can be regarded as equivalent. Cattell is inclined to favour Rhathymia as an independent factor with stress on happy-go-lucky, carefree attitudes, but he has not yet made provision for this in the 16 PF test. Further work on this factor seems desirable.

It is appropriate at this stage to ask what other personality factors have been omitted from the test since, in view of its size, it may be expected to be pretty comprehensive. Others from the Universal Index,[4] all derived from French's survey, are missing. Psychotic tendency is probably not important for the usual case for which the test will be required, and the same may be true of masculinity-femininity and autistic tendency, which should not be confused with the P.M. Autia. Self-confidence is more relevant but we need to be more certain as to how it differs from the insecurity pattern of O.

That the list of important factors is exhausted by this discussion is very unlikely. Many more will need to be added later. Some of these may not be suitable for general measurement, as, for example, sex drive. Some may be difficult to measure. One notable exception should be mentioned. This is the anal character mentioned above. A query may be raised with regard to the intelligence items. Since these consist of 13 questions in each of the A and B forms, and of 8 in the C form, they need to have a very high validity. The situation is complicated by the lack of a time limit. One is surprised that, under these conditions, 144 professional research workers get a near sten score of only 6.8, and wonders whether factors other than intelligence may not play an important part. Examination of the items suggests that some (e.g., A103, A153, B54, B153) provide some room for argument as to the right answer and random choice may lead a testee to accept the poorer alternative. In the case of B54 it is possible that highly intelligent people may be more likely to prefer the noncredited response.

VALIDITY AND RELIABILITY. Split-half reliabilities (n = 450) range from .71 to .93, ten coefficients being above .80. This is quite good; but even more pleasing is the fact that validities (based on factor loadings) range from .73 to .96 with eleven coefficients exceeding .80. For a multi-dimensional test of this kind one could not hope for much more. Evidently, despite the reputation of questionnaire methods as unreliable, this test does succeed. It should be noted, however, that the structure of the test does not require that the questions be taken at their face value. They are considered as stimulus variables, and a variable is assigned to a factor measure not because of its meaning but because of the usual mode of response to it. Of course, any questionnaire is subject to deliberate distortion and some check on this is desirable. Form C provides a motivational distortion score for this purpose. The authors believe that the best protection against such distortion is the selection of items highly loaded for a given factor but not appearing to involve it. They point out that with regard to many of the factors one pole does not appear to be morally or aesthetically more desirable than another. For the remaining factors they claim that no systematic motivational distortion has yet been experimentally found. This may be so when the test is used under circumstances where there is no high incentive to distortion, but only special studies will show whether the test can be appreciably distorted when the subject finds a need for this. No such investigation has yet been reported. In the meantime users might be advised not to use Forms A and B where motivational distortion is thought likely.

ADMINISTRATION AND SCORING. The test is very easy to give and most subjects find it interesting. Scoring can be done by hand or machine and is so simple that hand scoring is claimed to be superior for any number less than a thousand! Scores can be converted into stens

3 FRENCH, JOHN W. *The Description of Personality Measurements in Terms of Rotated Factors.* Princeton, N.J.: Educational Testing Service, 1953. Pp. 287. * (*PA* 28:5670)
4 CATTELL, RAYMOND B. "A Universal Index for Psychological Factors." *Psychologia* 1:74–85 '57. *

or deciles and, for Form C, into stanines. Appropriate information is given about each of these forms. It is to be hoped that more tests will make use of the convenient sten (standard 10-point) scale.

INTERPRETIVE DATA. In assessing the value of a personality test, an important consideration is the amount of data available with regard to the predictive significance of its scores. The tremendous effort made in conjunction with this test assures a wealth of such data. Average profiles for 28 occupation groups and 6 behavior disorders are already available. What are needed now are personality profiles for very *successful* members of various occupational groups as compared with low success members. A large scale investigation with regard to the relevance of the factors for teacher success is already under way in New Zealand and further data of this kind may be expected.

Form C has available weighted score grids for 24 major occupations. Using these, it is possible to predict success in a given occupation by the simple process of reading off the appropriate weights for each factor score, summing and consulting a 5-point table. Presumably these tables are based on typical occupational profiles and have all the weaknesses of this approach. If 80 per cent of workers in occupation X have false teeth, it does not follow that having false teeth will help one to succeed in the occupation, and a similar criticism may apply to some of the factor score requirements based on typical patterns. It is to be hoped that there will soon be profiles available based on more rigorous criteria. In the meantime, however, some guidance other than the intuition of the tester is provided.

SUMMARY. The 16 PF test bids fair to become the standard questionnaire-type personality test of the future. It provides a comprehensive range of trait scores which should be useful for occupational guidance and as a background to clinical examination. Used with due caution, it may be of help for selection purposes, but only with the motivational distortion score included. Although 16 factors may seem a lot (15 without intelligence), they are all independent, although not completely uncorrelated, and are all necessary to span the personality area involved. Indeed, a few more major factors will doubtless have to be added. The test is not, however, unwieldy and testers who are primarily concerned with only a few of the dimensions will find it well worthwhile to know some-

thing of what is happening to the other factors at the same time. Obviously this test does not take the place of a projective test like the TAT, but users of the latter would probably find an assessment of the basic dimensions of the 16 PF a valuable addition to their data.

For reviews by Charles M. Harsh, Ardie Lubin, and J. Richard Wittenborn, see 4:87.

[113]
*Social Participation Scale, 1952 Edition. Adults; 1928–52; 1 form ('52); manual ('52); $1.50 per 50 scales, postage extra; specimen set not available; administration time not reported; F. Stuart Chapin; University of Minnesota Press. *

[114]
Study of Values: A Scale for Measuring the Dominant Interests in Personality, Revised Edition. Grades 13 and over; 1931–51; 6 scores: theoretical, economic, aesthetic, social, political, religious; 1 form ('51); manual ('51); $3.80 per 35 tests; 40¢ per specimen set; postage extra; (20) minutes; Gordon W. Allport, Philip E. Vernon, and Gardner Lindzey; Houghton Mifflin Co. *

REFERENCES

1–61. See 3:99.
62–86. See 4:92.
87. JOHNSON, RALPH H., AND BOND, GUY L. "Reading Ease of Commonly Used Tests." *J Appl Psychol* 34:319–24 O '50. * (PA 26:299)
88. DIDATO, SALVATORE. *The Influence of Values, as Measured by the Allport-Vernon Study of Values, on Perceptual Estimations of Size.* Master's thesis, Catholic University of America (Washington, D.C.), 1951.
89. HORGAN, JAMES FRANCIS. *A Validation Study of the Allport-Vernon Study of Values.* Master's thesis, University of Pittsburgh (Pittsburgh, Pa.), 1951.
90. HUFFMAN, WARREN JUSTUS. *Personality Variations Among Men Preparing to Teach Physical Education.* Doctor's thesis, University of Illinois (Urbana, Ill.), 1951. (DA 12:28)
91. ANDERSON, MARY ROBERDEAU. *A Descriptive Study of Values and Interests of Four Groups of Graduate Women at the University of Minnesota.* Doctor's thesis, University of Minnesota (Minneapolis, Minn.), 1952. (DA 12:851)
92. BERNBERG, RAYMOND E. "Attitudes of Personnel Managers and Student Groups Toward Labor Relations." *J Appl Psychol* 36:291–2 O '52. * (PA 27:5456)
93. BROGDEN, HUBERT E. "The Primary Personal Values Measured by the Allport-Vernon Test, 'A Study of Values.'" *Psychol Monogr* 66 (16):1–31 '52. * (PA 27:7191)
94. EVANS, RICHARD I. "Personal Values as Factors in Anti-Semitism." *J Abn & Social Psychol* 47:749–56 O '52. * (PA 27:5090)
95. HAIGH, GERARD V., AND FISKE, DONALD W. "Corroboration of Personal Values as Selective Factors in Perception." *J Abn & Social Psychol* 47:394–8 Ap '52. * (PA 27:2441)
96. KARN, HARRY W. "Differences in Values Among Engineering Students." *Ed & Psychol Meas* 12:701–6 w '52. * (PA 27:6757)
97. KLEHR, HAROLD. "An Investigation of Some Personality Factors in Women With Rheumatoid Arthritis." Abstract. *Am Psychol* 7:344–5 Jl '52. *
98. POE, WESLEY A., AND BERG, IRWIN A. "Psychological Test Performance of Steel Industry Production Supervisors." *J Appl Psychol* 36:234–7 Ag '52. * (PA 27:3794)
99. SCHMEIDLER, GERTRUDE RAFFEL. "Personal Values and ESP Scores." *J Abn & Social Psychol* 47:757–61 O '52. * (PA 27:4909)
100. SPOERL, DOROTHY TILDEN. "The Values of the Post-War College Student." *J Social Psychol* 35:217–25 My '52. * (PA 27:3769)
101. STANLEY, JULIAN C., AND WALDROP, ROBERT S. "Intercorrelations of Study of Values and Kuder Preference Record Scores." *Ed & Psychol Meas* 12:707–19 w '52. * (PA 27:5906)
102. TOMEDY, FRANCIS JOSEPH. *The Relationship of Personality Characteristics to Measured Interests of Women Teachers of English, Social Science, Mathematics, and Physical Science in Certain Senior High Schools.* Doctor's thesis, New York University (New York, N.Y.), 1952. (DA 12:540)
103. WRENN, C. GILBERT. "The Selection and Education of Student Personnel Workers." *Personnel & Guid J* 31:9–14 O '52. * (PA 27:4782)

104. ADAMS, JOE, AND BROWN, DONALD R. "Values, Word Frequencies, and Perception." *Psychol R* 60:50–4 Ja '53. * (*PA* 28:3716)

105. BIESHEUVEL, S.; JACOBS, G. F.; AND COWLEY, J. J. "Maladjustments of Military Personnel." *J Nat Inst Personnel Res* 5:138–68 D '53. *

106. ISCOE, IRA, AND LUCIER, OMER. "A Comparison of the Revised Allport-Vernon Scale of Values (1951) and the Kuder Preference Record (Personal)." *J Appl Psychol* 37:195–6 Je '53. * (*PA* 28:3352)

107. SHORR, JOSEPH E. "The Development of a Test to Measure the Intensity of Values." *J Ed Psychol* 44:266–74 My '53. * (*PA* 28:3914)

108. STANLEY, JULIAN C. *Study of Values* Profiles Adjusted for Sex and Variability Differences." *J Appl Psychol* 37:472–3 D '53. * (*PA* 29:960)

109. STERNBERG, CARL. "Differences in Measured Interest, Values, and Personality Among College Students Majoring in Nine Subject Areas." Abstract. *Am Psychol* 8:442–3 Ag '53. *

110. STERNBERG, CARL. *The Relation of Interests, Values and Personality to the Major Field of Study in College.* Doctor's thesis, New York University (New York, N.Y.), 1953. (*DA* 13:1095)

111. BURDOCK, E. I. "A Case of ESP: Critique of 'Personal Values and ESP Scores' by Gertrude R. Schmeidler." *J Abn & Social Psychol* 49:314–5 Ap '54. * (*PA* 29:216)

112. GUILFORD, J. P.; CHRISTENSEN, PAUL R.; BOND, NICHOLAS A., JR.; AND SUTTON, MARCELLA A. "A Factor Analysis Study of Human Interests." *Psychol Monogr* 68(4):1–38 '54. *

113. MILAM, ALBERT T., AND SUMNER, F. C. "Spread and Intensity of Vocational Interests and Evaluative Attitudes in First-Year Negro Medical Students." *J Psychol* 37:31–8 Ja '54. * (*PA* 28:8027)

114. SCHLAG, MADELEINE. *The Relationship Between the Personality Preference Schedule and the Allport, Vernon and Lindzey Study of Values: A Personality Study of a Group of Medical Students.* Master's thesis, University of Washington (Seattle, Wash.), 1954.

115. STOTT, STERLING S. *A Comparison of the Authoritarian Personality F-Scale With the Allport-Vernon-Lindzey Study of Values.* Master's thesis, University of Utah (Salt Lake City, Utah), 1954.

116. BLEDSOE, JOSEPH C. "A Comparative Study of Values and Critical Thinking Skills of a Group of Educational Workers." *J Ed Psychol* 46:408–17 N '55. * (*PA* 31:3774)

117. BOUSFIELD, W. A., AND SAMBORSKI, GLORIA. "The Relationship Between Strength of Values and the Meaningfulness of Value Words." *J Personality* 23:375–80 My '55. * (*PA* 30:2448)

118. DUKES, WILLIAM F. "Psychological Studies of Values." *Psychol B* 52:24–50 Ja '55. *

119. KELLY, E. LOWELL. "Consistency of the Adult Personality." *Am Psychol* 10:659–81 N '55. * (*PA* 30:6915)

120. MAYZNER, MARK S., JR., AND TRESSELT, M. E. "Concept Span as a Composite Function of Personal Values, Anxiety, and Rigidity." *J Personality* 24:20–33 S '55. * (*PA* 30:5740)

121. ROSENTHAL, DAVID. "Changes in Some Moral Values Following Psychotherapy." *J Consult Psychol* 19:431–6 D '55. * (*PA* 30:7306)

122. STERNBERG, CARL. "Personality Trait Patterns of College Students Majoring in Different Fields." *Psychol Monogr* 69(18):1–21 '55. * (*PA* 31:1705)

123. DIDATO, S. VINCENT, AND KENNEDY, THOMAS M. "Masculinity-Femininity and Personal Values." *Psychol Rep* 2:231 Je '56. * (*PA* 31:608)

124. GOWAN, J. C. "Achievement and Personality Test Scores of Gifted College Students." *Calif J Ed Res* 7:105–9 My '56. * (*PA* 31:3783)

125. GUBA, E. G., AND GETZELS, J. W. "Interest and Value Patterns of Air Force Officers." *Ed & Psychol Meas* 16:465–70 w '56. * (*PA* 32:977)

126. HARTSHORN, ELIZABETH. "A Comparison of Certain Aspects of Student Leadership and Non-Leadership: Significant Differences on Four Psychometric Tests." *J Ed Res* 49:515–22 Mr '56. * (*PA* 31:5098)

127. LEVY, JEROME. *Reducing the Language Complexity of the Study of Values: A Revision.* Doctor's thesis, University of Denver (Denver, Colo.), 1956.

128. SCHROEDER, CLIFFORD E. *Personality Patterns of Advanced Protestant Theology Students and Physical Science Students.* Doctor's thesis, Michigan State University (East Lansing, Mich.), 1956. (*DA* 18:154)

129. SHEPHERD, JOHN R., AND SCHEIDEL, THOMAS M. "A Study of the Personality Configuration of Effective Oral Readers." *Speech Monogr* 23:298–304 N '56. * (*PA* 32:2128)

130. VAN LEEUWEN, EMIL. "Validity Information Exchange, No. 9-36: D.O.T. Code 1-57.10, Salesman, Life Insurance." *Personnel Psychol* 9:381 au '56. *

131. ANDREWS, JOHN H. M. "Administrative Significance of Psychological Differences Between Secondary Teachers of Different Subject Matter Fields." *Alberta J Ed Res* 3:199–208 D '57. *

132. FARBRO, PATRICK C., AND COOK, JOHN M. "Normative Data Information Exchange, No. 10-14." *Personnel Psychol* 10:231–2 su '57. *

133. GOWAN, J. C., AND SEAGOE, MAY. "The Relation Between Interest and Aptitude Tests in Art and Music." *Calif J Ed Res* 8:43–5 Ja '57. *

134. HALPERN, HOWARD M. "Predictive Empathy and the Study of Values." Abstract. *J Consult Psychol* 21:104 Ap '57. *

135. KAESS, WALTER A., AND WITRYOL, SAM L. "Positive and Negative Faking on a Forced-Choice Authoritarian Scale." *J Appl Psychol* 41:333–9 O '57. *

136. LEVY, JEROME. *Reducing the Language Complexity of the Study of Values: A Revision.* Doctor's thesis, University of Denver (Denver, Colo.), 1957.

137. SHOOSTER, CHARLES N. *Ability of the Allport-Vernon-Lindzey Scale to Predict Certain Pictorial Perceptions.* Master's thesis, Illinois Institute of Technology (Chicago, Ill.), 1957.

138. BARRETT, RICHARD S. "The Process of Predicting Job Performance." *Personnel Psychol* 11:39–57 sp '58. *

139. GOWAN, J. C. "Intercorrelations and Factor Analysis of Tests Given to Teaching Candidates." *J Exp Ed* 27:1–22 S '58. *

140. LEVY, JEROME. "Readability Level and Differential Test Performance: A Language Revision of the Study of Values." *J Ed Psychol* 49:6–12 F '58. *

141. NICKELS, JAMES B., AND RENZAGLIA, GUY A. "Some Additional Data on the Relationships Between Expressed and Measured Values." *J Appl Psychol* 42:99–104 Ap '58. *

142. PETERSON, TED TANGWALL. *Selecting School Administrators: An Evaluation of Six Tests.* Doctor's thesis, Stanford University (Stanford, Calif.), 1958. (*DA* 19:262)

143. SUMNER, EARL DAVID. *On the Relation of Manifest Needs to Personal Values: A Factor Analytic Study Involving R and Q Techniques.* Doctor's thesis, Wayne State University (Detroit, Mich.), 1958. (*DA* 18:2219)

N. L. GAGE, *Professor of Education, Bureau of Educational Research, University of Illinois, Urbana, Illinois.*

The hybrid vigor of this cross between American empiricism and European rationalism has made it one of the most viable of tests. This review deals mainly with aspects of the 1951 revision and the 1931 original that were not considered in earlier reviews.

According to the manual, the revision "offers certain improvements without in any way changing the basic purpose of the test or limiting its scope of usefulness." These improvements were made by introducing new questions and changing old questions on the basis of three successive item analyses, by simplifying and modernizing the wording of certain items, by making scoring more economical of time and labor, by preparing fresh norms, and by restricting the definition of the "social" value to altruistic love or philanthropy as against conjugal, familial, or religious love.

Correlations between the old and revised forms, taken two weeks apart by 50 male college students, are all, according to the manual, "significantly high." They seem low enough, however, to cause this reviewer to raise questions as to whether the meaning of the scores has not changed. That the social value has indeed been redefined is reflected by the *r* of only .31 between old and revised forms. The other *r*'s are only .48 for the theoretical, .74 for the economic, .55 for the esthetic, .45 for the political, and .75 for the religious values. Certainly these *r*'s (even if corrected for attenuation) are so low as to call for revalidation of the test in the many senses in which the old form was validated.

The split-half reliabilities of the six scores on the revised form are all higher than those on the old form, averaging .82 as against .70. (The manual is unclear as to whether the Spearman-Brown formula was applied, although it is unthinkable that it was not.) Repeat reliabilities for the revised form average .89 over a one-month interval. Whether these are superior to those obtainable with the old form is left in doubt since the authors note that the retesting with the old form took place after a greater length of time and was done with other subjects. It is regrettable that the comparisons of internal consistency and repeat reliabilities were not made with more appropriate data. If reliability is worth taking seriously, it deserves less cavalier treatment.

In discussing the correlations among values, the authors correctly point out that it is not strictly legitimate to state intercorrelations among values scores which are interdependent, in the sense that a high score on one value can be obtained only at the expense of low scores on others. Hence, as the authors recognize, the obtained intercorrelations are artifactually negative in general, and are reported merely to indicate "the *relative* degree to which various pairs of values are associated." This problem could have been circumvented to some extent, however, by scoring each value afresh for each correlation into which it entered. Thus, if value i is to be correlated with value j, the items in Part 1 consisting of forced choices between values i and j can be disregarded when the scores for values i and j are obtained; similarly, in Part 2, where 4-choice sets are to be ranked, those choices can be disregarded (in scoring for i) which represent value j. Obtained in this way, r_{ij} will not be artifactually negative.

Scoring no longer requires transferring scores for individual items to a separate score sheet. Now the subject writes his responses into boxes in the test booklet. These boxes are so arranged that the responses scored for a given value fall into the same column. Although the column for a given value shifts from one page to the next, the reviewer wonders whether this format may not make the test even more transparent than it was. The college student or college educated adult for whom the scale is primarily designed may have little trouble in seeing through this arrangement and discerning which choices represent the same kind of "personal preferences."

If he wants to fake, he gets a helping hand from this arrangement.

Response sets in psychological tests may introduce reliable but irrelevant variance. In Part 1, such a response set may come into play. Here, the subject can respond with two degrees of intensity: (*a*) with 3 and 0 if he agrees with alternative A and disagrees with B, or (*b*) with 2 and 1 if he has a slight preference for A over B. The reviewer is willing to predict that reliable individual differences will be found in the degree to which subjects use the 3-0 way of responding as against the 2-1, or less "intense," way. And the 3-0, or more intense, way of responding will probably result in a more jagged profile of values. The question arises as to whether this stylistic variable is psychologically relevant to the subject's values.

Research using the revised form has been reported in a variety of studies. Iscoe and Lucier (*106*) correlated it with the *Kuder Preference Record—Personal.* Bledsoe (*116*) found no differences in values after an intensive course in research methodology. Bousfield and Samborski (*117*) found that the religious and theoretical values correlated significantly with the frequency of associations to religious and theoretical words. Mayzner and Tresselt (*120*) found relationships between concept span and values.

In the meantime, further research with the old form has been reported. In 1952 Brogden reported a factor analysis (*93*) which yielded 10 first-order factors (general aesthetic interest, interest in fine arts, belief in "culture," anti-religious evaluative tendency, anti-aggression, humanitarian tendency, interest in science, tendency toward liberalism, theoretic interest, and "rugged individualism"), which were carefully compared with those resulting from a factor analysis reported in 1936 by Lurie (*22*).

The most impressive new findings with the old form are those reported by Kelly in his APA presidential address (*119*). Over a 20-year interval, "only 5 of the possible 12 changes [six values for each sex]....are significant. By all odds, the largest, and in fact the most significant, of all changes to be reported is that for Religious values. Both the men and women score about 5 points higher in their middle years than as young men and women....Since scores derived from the Scale of Values are relative, this shift toward higher religious values was necessarily accompanied by a downward shift on one or more of the other value scales. For the

women, most of this downward shift occurred in aesthetic values; for the men, it was about equally divided between aesthetic and theoretical values." Correlationally, the stability of values over 20 years is indicated by r's ranging from .52 (aesthetic) to .32 (social). The values measured by the *Study of Values* proved to be the most stable of the five kinds of variables (vocational interests, self-ratings on personality traits, Bernreuter and Strong personality trait scores, and attitudes) compared by Kelly.

Looking ahead to the next revision, the reviewer hopes that the authors will consider the objections raised against type concepts by Humphreys[1]; at the least, the kind of ipsative or relative scale embodied in the *Study of Values* ought to be supplemented by normative scales. Relative scales reduce everyone's profile to the same mean level, impose negative correlations among scores, and imprison predictive efforts within a possibly inappropriate model. Normative scales do not have these limitations.

At least one attempt to develop a normative test of values, in the form of Thurstone-type (equal-appearing interval) attitude scales for various values, has already been made (*107*). Although this attempt has laudable features, it served mainly to remind the reviewer of an often overlooked virtue of the Allport-Vernon-Lindzey test, namely, the impression it gives of being an intelligent test for intelligent people.

Second, the reviewer hopes that due regard will be given the results of empirical work on the organization of values, as represented by Lurie's and Brogden's factor analyses. If the authors were willing to depart from Spranger's definition of social value in the light of empirical results (low reliability), should they not also be willing to revise other values in the light of results from factor analyses? Have not Spranger's armchair speculations held sway long enough? Brogden's data were collected in 1936 and 1937; one wonders whether, had they been reported in time, his results would have influenced the authors of this 1951 revision away from Spranger's typology. For the future, at least, we have the nice question of whether the factorists should be allowed to rotate the armchair.

Finally, some account should be taken of the criticism leveled by Adams and Brown (*104*): "the Allport-Vernon test confounds to some ex-

tent two psychological dimensions which can be separated, namely *interest* and *value*. An individual can be interested in a given area even though he has a strong disagreement with individuals or institutions operating in that area. For example, a militant atheist may be very interested in religion though harboring little value for religious beliefs or experience. Because of the way in which the Allport-Vernon test is constructed and scored, it seems to us that interest and value are confounded, though no doubt these two variables are correlated to some extent."

For the present, however, the *Study of Values* will continue to serve us well. For classroom demonstration, for counseling and vocational guidance, and for research on a wide variety of psychological questions, the test is already very good. Maybe that is why we cannot help wanting it to be even better.

For reviews by Harrison G. Gough and William Stephenson, see 4:92 (1 excerpt); for a review by Paul E. Meehl of the original edition, see 3:99.

[115]

★**Temperament and Character Test.** College and adults; 1952; 11 scores: nervous, sentimental, choleric, passionate, sanguine, phlegmatic, amorphous, apathetic, emotivity, activity, perseveration; 1 form ['52]; no data on reliability and validity; no norms; $1.25 per 25 tests; 25¢ per mimeographed manual ['52]; 35¢ per mimeographed booklet of temperaments and characters ['52]; 15¢ per mimeographed descriptive booklet ['52]; 75¢ per specimen set; postage extra; French edition available; Institut pedagogique Saint-Georges, Mont-de-la-Salle, Montreal, Canada. *

[116]

★**Survey of Attitudes and Beliefs.** Grades 9–12; 1954–55; 3 scores: society, education and work, sex-marriage-family; Form AH ('54); manual ('55); $2.75 per 20 tests; $1.20 per 20 profiles ('55); 75¢ per specimen set; postage extra; (40) minutes; Leslie W. Nelson; Science Research Associates. *

DONALD T. CAMPBELL, *Professor of Psychology, Northwestern University, Evanston, Illinois.*

This test seems designed primarily as an instrument for counseling purposes with high school students rather than as a research instrument. It measures the extent to which the attitudes of students approximate those which responsible adults would like them to have toward society; education and work; and sex, marriage, and family. In several respects, it seems carefully prepared, having gone through several revisions, with both statistical editing against criterion groups and qualitative editing by panels

1 HUMPHREYS, LLOYD G. "Characteristics of Type Concepts With Special Reference to Sheldon's Typology." *Psychol B* 54:218–28 My '57. *

of educators, employers, parents, and children, followed by a standardization on a national sample of classrooms (2,923 students in 13 schools, probably all urban). Reliabilities (Kuder-Richardson formula 21) ranging from .65 to .80 are reported. Norms are provided by sex and by grade for each of the three attitude areas. No validity data are presented. Regional and social class norms are not given. No mention is made of the correlations among the three scores, which are probably as high as the reliabilities. On the other hand, the heterogeneity of content within each area cries out for more analytic subscores, factor analysis among items, or homogeneous keying. Agree and disagree items enter into all scores in about equal numbers, thus avoiding acquiescence response set.

The claim of the test instructions that there are no "right" or "wrong" answers is especially hollow in this test. The profile material for students and the discussion guides for teachers have a heavy moralizing tone, pushing for "acceptance of the expectations our society imposes upon us." Disagreement is equated with "misunderstanding of the reasons for society's expectations." The correct answers are regarded as "desirable and important to happy and productive living." When we look at the correct ("positive") answers, we see that the best citizens and educators of Contra Costa County, California (the correct answers were *not* based upon a national sample) took a *middle* position on many dimensions of attitude in which our mores are ambiguous. Thus a "negative" attitude toward high school sex includes *both* refusing to kiss on a date *and* heavy petting. Thus one should dislike a bookworm and favor compulsory education. The normative orientation thus pools for scoring purposes two opposite deviations from Contra Costa ideals. It would seem diagnostically valuable to have kept these deviations separate in the scoring system although, in general, the greatest opportunity for deviation lies in the direction of lower class customs. Girls score more positively than boys, and an increase in positive attitudes occurs from the 9th to 11th grades, followed by a drop in the 12th grade. In general, the pattern of correct answers provides an interesting sociological document.

For the purpose of discussing the answers with students, it is probably unfortunate that some of the items involve matters of fact, not of personal preference, with the factually incorrect

answer scored positively. Thus the adjusted answer is to *deny* that "self consciousness often causes people to avoid being in groups," and to deny that "people usually fear being unpopular with the opposite sex." As with so many attitude tests, this test seems least plausible when examined at the item level.

C. ROBERT PACE, *Professor of Psychology and Chairman of the Department, Syracuse University, Syracuse, New York.*

Survey of Attitudes and Beliefs is designed to identify the attitudes of high school students in three areas. Area 1, Attitude toward Society, deals with responsibilities of good citizenship and positive attitudes toward other people; Area 2, Attitude toward Education and Work, concerns beliefs about the importance of education and the responsibility to develop and use one's talents constructively; and Area 3, Attitude toward Sex, Marriage, and Family, covers understanding of acceptable sexual behavior and the role of the family. The 147 statements in the survey are approximately equally divided among the three areas. Students respond to each item by agreeing, disagreeing, or indicating an undecided attitude. The score in each area consists of the number of statements to which the student's response indicates a desirable attitude. Desirability was determined by judges.

The survey is a good and fairly typical example of a device for educational evaluation. A profile folder is provided in which students can record their scores and compare them with scores made by other students. Simple and helpful comments are given to aid the student in evaluating his score. Teachers are encouraged to find interesting items for class discussion. Guidance counselors can discuss the scores and the item responses with students who wish to talk about them. The survey is, then, a useful evaluation and teaching device; this is its chief value and its recommended use.

The survey was carefully developed, tried out, revised, criticized, and discussed by school teachers, administrators, and interested citizens over a period of several years before the present form was given to a standardization group of 2,923 students in grades 9 through 12 in 13 schools representing 7 states and all 4 geographic regions of the country. Test reliabilities, reported by grade and sex groups, are generally in the .60's and .70's, although coefficients in the .80's and .90's were obtained from a group

of 500 seniors in an earlier trial. Quite properly, the manual does not attach too much significance to the test scores, for any score which falls between the 25th and 75th percentiles is described as average, and more extreme scores are merely labeled higher or lower than average. Actually, the typical difference between the 20th and 80th percentiles is only 10 to 11 raw score points. Thus, the use of the survey as a measuring instrument is not emphasized.

Desirable scores on the survey are, ideologically, in the main stream of Riesman's other-directed man, Whyte's organization man, *McCall's* togetherness, and Norman Vincent Peale's positive thinking. These represent solid virtues, having the status of widely held objectives of high school education, although some school teachers, one hopes, may be privately glad that there are a few vigorous dissenters among the adult community.

[117]

Test of Personality Adjustment. Ages 9–13; 1931; 5 scores; personal inferiority, social maladjustment, family maladjustment, daydreaming, total; separate forms for boys and girls; $2.50 per 25 tests; 75¢ per specimen set; postage extra; (40–50) minutes; Carl R. Rogers; Association Press. *

REFERENCES

1. ROGERS, CARL R. *Measuring Personality Adjustment in Children Nine to Thirteen Years of Age.* Columbia University, Teachers College, Contributions to Education, No. 458. New York: Bureau of Publications, the College, 1931. Pp. v, 107. * (*PA* 6:1978)
2. BABCOCK, MARJORIE E. *A Comparison of Delinquent and Non-Delinquent Boys by Objective Measures of Personality.* Honolulu, H.I.: the Author, 1932. Pp. 74. * (*PA* 8:438)
3. BOYNTON, PAUL L., AND WALSWORTH, BARRIER M. "Emotionality Test Scores of Delinquent and Nondelinquent Girls." *J Abn & Social Psychol* 38:87–92 Ja '43. * (*PA* 17:3899)
4. GRUEN, EMILY W. "Level of Aspiration in Relation to Personality Factors in Adolescents." *Child Develop* 16:181–8 D '45. * (*PA* 20:2393)
5. CLARKE, HELEN JANE. "The Diagnosis of a Patient With Limited Capacity." *J Personality* 15:105–12 D '46. * (*PA* 21:3001)
6. EPSTEIN, HANS L., AND SCHWARTZ, ARTHUR. "Psychodiagnostic Testing in Group Work: Rorschach and Painting Analysis Technique." *Rorsch Res Exch & J Proj Tech* 11:23–41 no 2–4 '47. * (*PA* 22:4945)
7. CHRISTY, WILLIAM J. *A Study of Relationships Between Sociometric Scores and Personality Self-Ratings.* Master's thesis, North Texas State College (Denton, Tex.), 1949.
8. GIBSON, ROBERT L. *A Study on the Personality Pattern of Male Defective Delinquents as Indicated by the Rogers Test of Personality Adjustment.* Master's thesis, Pennsylvania State College (State College, Pa.), 1951.
9. MENSH, IVAN N., AND MASON, EVELYN P. "Relationship of School Atmosphere to Reactions in Frustrating Situations." *J Ed Res* 45:275–86 D '51. *
10. SPAETH, C. F., JR. *A Validation of Rogers' Test of Personality Adjustment.* Master's project, University of Southern California (Los Angeles, Calif.), 1952.
11. LEIBMAN, OSCAR BERNARD. *The Relationship of Personal and Social Adjustment to Academic Achievement in the Elementary School.* Doctor's thesis, Columbia University (New York, N.Y.), 1953. (*DA* 14:67)
12. NOWELL, ANN. "Peer Status as Related to Measures of Personality." *Calif J Ed Res* 4:37–41 Ja '53. * (*PA* 28:1514)
13. PRICKETT, FRANCES S. *An Analytical Study of Greene's Revision of Rogers' Test of Personality Adjustment.* Master's thesis, University of Georgia (Athens, Ga.), 1954.
14. SATTERLEE, ROBERT LOUIS. "Sociometric Analysis and Personality Adjustment." *Calif J Ed Res* 6:181–4 S '55. * (*PA* 30:6295)
15. SMITH, LOUIS MILDE. *A Validity Study of Six Personality and Adjustment Tests for Children.* Doctor's thesis, University of Minnesota (Minneapolis, Minn.), 1955. (*DA* 16:791)
16. BURCHINAL, LEE G.; HAWKES, GLENN R.; AND GARDNER, BRUCE. "The Relationship Between Parental Acceptance and Adjustment of Children." *Child Develop* 28:65–77 Mr '57. *
17. BURCHINAL, LEE; GARDNER, BRUCE; AND HAWKES, GLENN R. "Children's Personality Adjustment and the Socio-Economic Status of Their Families." *J Genetic Psychol* 92:149–59 Je '58. *
18. BURCHINAL, LEE G.; GARDNER, BRUCE; AND HAWKES, GLENN R. "A Suggested Revision of Norms for the Rogers Test of Personality Adjustment." *Child Develop* 29:135–9 Mr '58. *
19. SMITH, LOUIS M. "The Concurrent Validity of Six Personality and Adjustment Tests for Childen." *Psychol Monogr* 72(4):1–30 '58. *

DANIEL L. ADLER, *Professor of Psychology, San Francisco State College, San Francisco, California.*

This test appears in two identical editions, one published in the United States and the other in Australia. There is nothing to indicate that either varies from the original edition copyrighted in 1931, although the desiderata of test construction and the concepts of adjustment have both changed considerably since that time. In its present form, the test could, at best, be described as little more than a working tool for a pilot study of certain dimensions of child adjustment. The author's evaluation supports this view. He points out that the diagnostic scores on personal inferiority, social maladjustment, family maladjustment, and daydreaming are "not highly accurate" and that they are potentially "misleading in the case of an individual child." The major value of the test, according to the author, lies in the clinician's careful evaluation of the answers to test items, considered singly and in their relationship to one another.

The following limitations of the instrument, considered in the light of modern test sophistication, contraindicate its use for anything but further validation: (*a*) The subtest scores and the total scores have low coefficients of reliability and are reported from an inadequate sample (n = 43). (*b*) Validity is based upon correlations between subtest scores and the ratings made by "clinicians" (not otherwise identified). These correlations range from .38 to .48. (*c*) The norms, based upon 167 children of whom 52 are said to be "problem" children, constitute an obviously inadequate standardization. (*d*) The interpretations of subtest response syndromes are neither objective nor convincing. (*e*) The scoring system is cumbersome and conducive to unreliability. (*f*) The case histories, cited as examples of diagnoses based on test scores, are not likely to be extrapolated meaningfully by the rank and file test user.

Considering these shortcomings, the author would do a service to test users, students of testing, and himself by withdrawing the *Test of*

Personality Adjustment from circulation, at least in its present form.

HARRISON G. GOUGH, *Associate Professor of Psychology, University of California, Berkeley, California.*

This test seeks to measure the adequacy of the child's adjustment at home, among his peers, and in his daydreams and fantasies. Separate test booklets for boys and girls are provided, each containing skillfully probing questions grouped under six task categories. In one category, the child is asked to choose three wishes he would like to have come true from a listing including things like "to have the boys and girls like me better," "to have a different father and mother," "to have more money to spend," and "to have my father and mother love me more." In another, he checks what he considers to be the "true" answer in each multiple choice item as:

13. Do other children play mean tricks on you? (A) Never. (B) Sometimes. (C) Very often.
17. Do you wear good clothes to school? (A) I don't have any nice clothes. (B) My clothes are nice enough. (C) I have very good clothes.
21. Do you want people to like you? (A) I just can't stand it, if people don't like me. (B) I always try very hard to make people like me. (C) I don't care very much, but I'm glad when people like me. (D) I don't care a bit whether people like me or not.

Five quantitative scores are obtained for personal inferiority, social maladjustment, family maladjustment, daydreaming, and a total. Instructions for scoring are clear and precise, although the scoring methods themselves are needlessly cumbersome and awkward. The manual recommends, wisely, that the user read through the individual child's booklet in addition to examining his profile of scores.

The manual was copyrighted in 1931, and is apparently unchanged today. One would expect that a manual 28 years old would be in need of some revision, and as a matter of fact the publisher has no business continuing to issue a document as badly in need of modification as this one. Since 1931 this test has undoubtedly been given to thousands of children; systematic data are certainly available in a number of child psychology centers. It would be a relatively easy matter to compile extensive age and sex norms and validity data of both clinical and longitudinal kinds. If the publisher plans to continue selling this test, these things should be done and the manual brought up to date.

Having said this, it is my pleasant duty to return to the manual which, except for the deficiencies just noted, is a low-keyed work of art. The tone of the writing is patient and benevolent and almost necessarily implants a charitable and therapeutic attitude in the reader who is to use the test. The intercalated comments about children and their problems are deeply insightful. The cautions about test usage are in the best tradition of clinical testing. The section on interpretation goes directly to the kind of behavioral implications which the test was designed to elucidate and in which the user is presumably most interested. The manual closes with that rarity of rarities, a series of case analyses in which the author shows how the test results can be utilized in the explication and diagnosis of the individual person.

In summary, the test itself is, in this reviewer's judgment, an exemplary device. The areas covered are important ones, and the questions asked are sagacious and penetrating. The mechanics of answering and scoring could easily be simplified and improved. The test is greatly in need of revision from this standpoint. The manual is woefully lacking in information pertaining to age and sex norms, correlations of scores with other behavioral and test variables, and longitudinal implications of the test's scores. Considering the wide usage this test has had since its publication, its author and publisher have a professional obligation to bring it up to date. One would hope, however, that in doing this the really remarkable personological insight and operational relevance of the present sections on interpretation and case analysis can be retained.

For a review by C. M. Louttit, see 40:1258.

[118]

Thurstone Temperament Schedule. Grades 9–16 and adults; 1949–53; 7 scores: active, vigorous, impulsive, dominant, stable, sociable, reflective; IBM; 1 form ('49); 2 editions; manual, second edition ('53); separate answer sheets or pads must be used; $9.80 per 20 tests; 75¢ per specimen set; postage extra; (15–25) minutes; L. L. Thurstone; Science Research Associates. *
a) [FORM AH FOR HAND SCORING]. $2.15 per 20 answer pads.
b) [FORM AM FOR MACHINE SCORING]. IBM; $5 per 100 IBM answer sheets; $2.50 per set of scoring stencils.

REFERENCES

1. THURSTONE, L. L. "The Dimensions of Temperament." *Psychometrika* 16:11–20 Mr '51. * (PA 25:7327)
2. ERICKSON, HARLEY ELLWOOD. "A Factorial Study of Teaching Ability." *J Exp Ed* 23:1–39 S '54. * (PA 29:6927)
3. MONTROSS, HAROLD WESLEY. "Temperament and Teaching Success." *J Exp Ed* 23:73–97 S '54. * (PA 29:6302)
4. NATHANSON, SHERMAN NOEL. *The Relationship Between the Traits Measured by Thurstone's Temperament Schedule and Convictions for Traffic Violations Among a Group of Junior*

College Students. Master's thesis, University of Southern California (Los Angeles, Calif.), 1954.
5. KEISLAR, EVAN R. "The Validity of the Thurstone Temperament Schedule With High School Students." Abstract. *Am Psychol* 10:389–90 Ag '55. *
6. JONES, LYLE V., AND MORRIS, CHARLES. "Relations of Temperament to the Choice of Values." *J Abn & Social Psychol* 53:345–9 N '56. *
7. KUSHMAR, HOWARD S., AND CANFIELD, ALBERT A. "Validity Information Exchange, No. 9-32: D.O.T. Code 1-18.63, Order Clerk-Clerical 11 (Telephone)." *Personnel Psychol* 9: 375–7 au '56. *
8. WORPELL, DONALD FREDERICK. *A Study of Selection Factors and the Development of Objective Criteria for Measuring Success in a Co-operative General Machine Shop Training Program.* Doctor's thesis, University of Michigan (Ann Arbor, Mich.), 1956. *(DA* 17:1270)
9. DUGGAN, JOHN M. *A Factor Analysis of Reading Ability, Personality Traits and Academic Achievement.* Doctor's thesis, Yale University (New Haven, Conn.), 1957.
10. HEATH, EARL DAVIS. *The Relationships Between Driving Records, Selected Personality Characteristics and Biographical Data of Traffic Offenders and Non-Offenders: A Study of Selected Personality Characteristics and Selected Biographical Data of Motor Vehicle Traffic Offenders and Non-Offenders and the Relating of Differences Obtained to Records of Their Driving Performance.* Doctor's thesis, New York University (New York, N.Y.), 1957. *(DA* 17:1949)
11. STONE, SOLOMON. *The Contribution of Intelligence, Interests, Temperament and Certain Personality Variables to Academic Achievement in a Physical Science and Mathematics Curriculum.* Doctor's thesis, New York University (New York, N.Y.), 1957. *(DA* 18:669)
12. BRUCE, MARTIN M. "Normative Data Information Exchange, No. 11-12." *Personnel Psychol* 11:129 sp '58. *

NEIL J. VAN STEENBERG, *Research Psychologist, Personnel Research Branch, Personnel Research and Procedures Division, The Adjutant General's Office, Department of the Army, Washington, D.C.*

The schedule is designed to yield scores along seven aspects of temperament. "Temperament" the author defines as those aspects of personality which are of a relatively stable nature, as contrasted with the more ephemeral qualities, such as attitudes, opinions, and moods, which fluctuate with impact of recent experience. The seven factors are the result of analysis of scores made by normal individuals; hence, they have no intentional connection with any psychotic or neurotic classification. The schedule is self-administering and may be given with or without supervision, individually or by groups.

The schedule contains 140 items, each asking a question which is to be answered by marking "Yes," "?," or "No." The questions are presented in simple language suitable for high school students, and decisions on how to answer them are seemingly more easily reached than on some other personality tests. Items are printed in a 6-page booklet of "step-down" format, permitting the answer sheet to remain in a fixed position, and in exactly the right position for marking the answers as the pages are turned. It is by far the most ingeniously contrived testing booklet the reviewer has seen.

Interpretation of the scores is made in terms of seven traits or continua of temperament, as follows: (A) Active, (V) Vigorous, (I) Impulsive, (D) Dominant, (E) Stable, (S) Sociable, and (R) Reflective. The seven traits are derived from a factor analysis of scores in the 13 personality areas measured by the *Guilford-Martin Inventory of Factors GAMIN,* the *Guilford-Martin Personnel Inventory,* and the *Inventory of Factors STDCR.*

The reliabilities of the seven individual factor scores are relatively low; they vary from .45 to .86 with a median of .64 for four different groups. Such results can be expected where there are only 20 items per score. If seven separate scores are to be obtained, it would seem to be distinctly worthwhile to double the time of administration and the number of items.

The manual, like the schedule, is of a high standard, informative, and objectively written. It presents a number of tables of norms for various groups investigated, and includes a section which deals with the reliabilities of a profile. This section indicates the effect of possible fluctuation of individual scores, and the relative stability of the profile as a whole. By implication, the user is cautioned against too rigid interpretation of separate scores. (Again, it must be observed that the inventory should have been twice or three times as long as it is.)

In the second edition of the manual, the section on validity studies which was promised in the first edition has been added. One study gives information on the correlation of forced choice ratings by supervisors on the seven traits with the score attained by the employees on the seven scales used. Other studies using effectiveness of job performance as a criterion show the use of the schedule for predictive purposes. The subjects for the various studies were teachers, office workers, retail store sales employees, sales supervisors, and managers of small retail stores. For all groups except the office workers, *some* of the scores were valid predictors, though the particular scores which were found useful varied from study to study.

In a recent unpublished thesis, Heath (*10*) reports that Scales I, S, and R differentiated between motor vehicle traffic offenders and non-offenders. In an impressive, but yet unpublished, study made by the Psychological Service Section of Sears, Roebuck and Company,[1] a significant difference was found in scores attained on Scales A, V, I, D, and S by two groups of employees—

1 SEARS, ROEBUCK AND COMPANY, NATIONAL PERSONNEL DEPARTMENT, PSYCHOLOGICAL RESEARCH AND SERVICES. *The Five Year Predictive Validity of the Combined Retail Battery of Psychological Tests.* An unpublished study. Chicago, Ill.: Sears, Roebuck and Co., 1957. Pp. 32.

those who had received promotions in a 5-year period and those who had not. In still another unpublished doctor's thesis, Duggan (9) found considerably higher reliabilities (both test-retest and split-half) than were found in the original study. He also found what is perhaps a secondary factor which is defined by I, D, S, and A, and conjectures that this factor might best be encompassed by the term "extravert."

In conclusion, the schedule should prove useful for employment managers and counselors, though it would be desirable to have a number of additional validity studies published. Until such time as this is accomplished, advice given or action taken in nonvalidated areas must be made with caution. Meanwhile the instrument seems to be well established as an "anchor" for further research on personality and its implications.

For reviews by Hans J. Eysenck, Charles M. Harsh, and David G. Ryans, see 4:93 (1 excerpt).

[119]

★**Tulane Factors of Liberalism-Conservatism.** Social science students; 1946–55; title on test is *Tulane Factors of L-C: General Attitudinal Values Profile;* 5 scores: political, economic, religious, social, aesthetic; 1 form ('46); manual ('55); college norms only; $3 per 50 tests; $1 per specimen set (must be purchased to obtain manual); postage extra; (25–35) minutes; Willard A. Kerr; Psychometric Affiliates. *

REFERENCES

1. KERR, WILLARD A. "Untangling the Liberalism-Conservatism Continuum." *J Social Psychol* 35:111–25 F '52. * (PA 27:3426
2. VOOR, J. J. *The Relationship Between the Religious Attitude and the Conservative-Radical Attitude Among Seminarians Studying for the Catholic Priesthood.* Master's thesis, Catholic University of America (Washington, D.C.), 1953.

DONALD T. CAMPBELL, *Professor of Psychology, Northwestern University, Evanston, Illinois.*

This test, first copyrighted in 1946, seems not to have been used in any published research in spite of the popularity of the problem area. The manual cites only two studies, one by the author himself. "Liberalism" in political, economic, religious, social, and aesthetic matters is measured by from 12 to 25 Likert-type items in each category. All items are worded in the (to Kerr) "liberal" direction, thus making the test vulnerable to acquiescence response set. On the aesthetic, social, and political dimensions, Kerr's concept of "liberal" is so out of line with that of other social psychologists as to make his total scores meaningless. For example, it is aesthetically liberal to like "surrealistic" imaginative

painting, "paintings by the old masters," "colored comic cartoons," "classical music," and "humorous and novelty music." It is socially liberal both to "enjoy talking with citizens of small towns" and to believe that "whites and Negroes [should] be permitted to intermarry." It is politically liberal to believe that "congressmen try to do a good job in representing the people," that "most elected politicians are honest," and that "all races and creeds [should] have the right to vote." This heterogeneity of content calls for undone factorial analyses among the items of each scale to justify their combination into total scores, and makes difficult the interpretation of the correlations reported between total scores. On the more typical economic and religious liberalism scales, the oft-found results are replicated, e.g., Democrats are more liberal than Republicans, Jews more liberal than Catholics. Kerr's tests are in no wise superior to the older ones in demonstrating these facts, however. The lowness of the correlation (.10) between religious and economic liberalism found for 246 Tulane men is perhaps a novel and interpretable finding. Once again one is reminded that in the area of social attitudes the copyrighted tests are of inferior quality to the uncopyrighted ones.

C. ROBERT PACE, *Professor of Psychology and Chairman of the Department, Syracuse University, Syracuse, New York.*

This attitude test battery contains five subtests dealing with political, economic, religious, social, and aesthetic topics. Responses are scored on a liberal-conservative dimension. The subtests are short. The political and social subtests have 12 items each; the economic test has 13, the religious test 14, and the aesthetic test 25. To the first four subtests, responses are made by checking "Yes," "Probably Yes," "Undecided," "Probably No," or "No." To the aesthetic items, the response is made by checking "Like It Much," "Like it Some," "Don't Care," "Dislike it Some," or "Dislike it Much." Five points are given for the most liberal response (Yes) and one point for the most conservative response (No), with score weights of 4, 3, and 2 assigned to the responses in between. Intercorrelations among the five scales range from −.02 to +.40. Split-half reliabilities are adequately high for four of the scales, but low ($r = .55$) for the political scale.

The author, in the manual of instructions, de-

scribes the rationale for each of the subtests. One's reaction to these explanations will determine in large part his judgment as to the general usefulness of the test and its adequacy as a measuring device. The political subtest is described by the author as a composite. This was also the reviewer's reaction, for no clear dimension seemed to be present. On the economic scale liberalism is defined as being favorable to practices and policies commonly associated with the welfare state. The religious scale is again rather eclectic, although, generally, the liberal response is one which minimizes the importance of religion. Liberalism in the social scale is similar to the concept of social distance, with a high score given to responses which indicate that one likes different kinds of people and agrees that different kinds of people can become good citizens. The aesthetic scale simply lists a variety of items—such as Greek sculpture, hillbilly music, flowers, primitive pottery—with liberalism being defined as liking everything.

Test results are reported for 291 men enrolled in Protestant or nondenominational colleges (242 of these at Tulane University) and for 251 seminarians studying for the Roman Catholic priesthood. The test is printed on both sides of a single sheet. The typography is poor and the format is cluttered.

No relationships are reported between the results on this test and any of the hundreds of other tests and researches over the past 30 years which have dealt with similar topics or with the concepts of liberalism-conservatism or the measurement of values. If such relationships had been investigated, the meaning of scores on the test might have been established more adequately, or, as seems more likely to this reviewer, the test might not have been published. In its present state, there is little reason for using the test unless the user is curious about a lot of relationships which the test author has not investigated, or at least has not reported.

[120]

*Vineland Social Maturity Scale. Birth to maturity; 1935–53; individual; 1 form ('46); $1.80 per 25 tests; $1.25 per 39-page manual ('47); $7.75 per 682-page manual ('53, see 83 below); postage extra; $1.25 per specimen set, postpaid; (20–30) minutes; Edgar A. Doll; Educational Test Bureau. *

REFERENCES

1–58. See 3:107.
59–79. See 4:94.
80. KELLMER, MIA L. A Study of Doll's Social Maturity Scale as Applied to a Representative Sample of British Children Between the Ages of 6 and 8 Years. Master's thesis, University of London (London, England), 1951.
81. HOLLINSHEAD, MERRILL T. "Patterns of Social Competence in Older Mental Retardates." Am J Mental Def 56: 603–8 Ja '52. * (PA 26:4876)
82. CASSEL, MARGARET E., AND RIGGS, MARGARET M. "Comparison of Three Etiological Groups of Mentally Retarded Children on the Vineland Social Maturity Scale." Am J Mental Def 58:162–9 Jl '53. * (PA 28:2854)
83. DOLL, EDGAR A. The Measurement of Social Competence: A Manual for the Vineland Social Maturity Scale. Minneapolis, Minn.: Educational Test Bureau, Educational Publishers, Inc., 1953. Pp. xviii, 664. * (PA 28:4347)
84. DOLL, EDGAR A. "Vineland Social Maturity Scale," pp. 495–506. (PA 27:7765) In Contributions Toward Medical Psychology: Theory and Psychodiagnostic Methods, Vol. II. Edited by Arthur Weider. New York: Ronald Press Co., 1953. Pp. xi, 459–885. *
85. GOLDSTEIN, HERBERT. An Experiment With the Vineland Social Maturity Scale to Determine Its Utility as a Screening Aid in Vocational Placement of Mentally Retarded. Master's thesis, San Francisco State College (San Francisco, Calif.), 1953.
86. MAXFIELD, KATHRYN E., AND KENYON, EUNICE L. A Guide to the Use of the Maxfield-Fjeld Tentative Adaptation of the Vineland Social Maturity Scale for Use With Visually Handicapped Preschool Children. New York: American Foundation for the Blind, 1953. Pp. ii, 30. * (PA 29:1406)
87. REILE, PATRICIA J. A Honolulu Standardization of the Vineland Social Maturity Scale. Master's thesis, University of Hawaii (Honolulu, Hawaii), 1953.
88. ROSS, GRACE. "Testing Intelligence and Maturity of Deaf Children." Excep Child 20:23–4+ O '53. * (PA 28:4794)
89. SATTER, GEORGE, AND McGEE, EUGENE. "Retarded Adults Who Have Developed Beyond Expectation: Part I, Intellectual Functions." Training Sch B 51:43–55 My '54. * (PA 29:2662)
90. CROKE, KATHERINE. A Comparative Study of the Revised Stanford-Binet Intelligence Scale for Children, and the Vineland Maturity Scale. Master's thesis, Wisconsin State College (Milwaukee, Wis.), 1955.
91. SATTER, GEORGE. "Psychometric Scatter Among Mentally Retarded and Normal Children." Training Sch B 52:63–8 Je '55. * (PA 30:3078)
92. SATTER, GEORGE. "Retarded Adults Who Have Developed Beyond Expectation: Part III, Further Analysis and Summary." Training Sch B 51:237–43 F '55. * (PA 29:7498)
93. GOTTSEGEN, MONROE G. "The Use of the Vineland Social Maturity Scale in the Planning of an Educational Program for Non-Institutionalized Low-Grade Mentally Deficient Children." Genetic Psychol Monogr 55:85–137 F '57. *
94. ISCOE, IRA. "A Profile for the Vineland Scale and Its Clinical Applications." Abstract. Am Psychol 12:381 Jl '57. *

For reviews by William M. Cruickshank and Florence M. Teagarden, see 4:94; for reviews by C. M. Louttit and John W. M. Rothney, see 3:107 (1 excerpt); for reviews by Paul H. Furfey, Elaine F. Kinder, and Anna S. Starr of Experimental Form B, see 38:1143; for related reviews, see B121.

[121]

★A Weighted-Score Likability Rating Scale. Ages 6 and over; 1946; 10 ratings: honesty, cooperation, courtesy, responsibility, initiative, industry, attentiveness, enthusiasm, perseverance, willingness; 1 form; no data on reliability and validity; $2.50 per set of 24 scales and 12 profiles ['46], postpaid; [1–2] minutes; A. B. Carlile; the Author, 330 West 44th St., Indianapolis 8, Ind. *

[122]

★What I Like to Do: An Inventory of Children's Interests. Grades 4–7; 1954–58; 8 scores: art, music, social studies, active play, quiet play, manual arts, home arts, science; IBM; 1 form ('54); no norms for grade 7; $3 per 20 tests; separate answer sheets may be used; $5 per 100 IBM answer sheets; $1.50 per set of machine scoring stencils; 90¢ per 20 profiles ('54); 25¢ per manual ('54); 35¢ per teacher's handbook ('58); 50¢ per specimen set; postage extra; (60) minutes in 2 sessions for grade 4, (50) minutes for grades 5–7; Louis P. Thorpe, Charles E. Meyers, and Marcella Ryser Sea [Bonsall]; Science Research Associates. *

JOHN W. M. ROTHNEY, *Professor of Education, University of Wisconsin, Madison, Wisconsin.*

This inventory consists of 294 yes-no-? items designed to ascertain what pupils would like to do, would not like to do, or neither like nor dislike.

Any person who is considering the use of a test should examine the manual first for evidence of validity. There is no section on validity in the manual and no direct mention is made of the subject until one comes to the next to the last paragraph in a section entitled "Future Research." In that paragraph it is stated that, because interests are believed to shift rapidly in the intermediate grades, long range predictions from the inventory will *probably* show only limited validity. The authors state their belief that "observations of a child's current activity choices will correlate highly with his interest scores." They plan to explore this belief, based largely on the "content validity" of the items, in future research. This claim for content validity seems questionable, however, in view of the following statement which appears on page 10 of the manual. "It may come as a surprise to many parents to learn that supposed interests, claimed preferences and even activity choices may differ from the measured interests revealed by the inventory." The candor of the authors is commendable. In effect, they have warned the potential purchaser not to buy this instrument until the proposed future research has determined whether it has any kind of validity.

Sixty-four reliability coefficients (Kuder-Richardson) based on sex and age groups ranging in size from 34 to 126 are reported for the area scores. Of these 18 are .90 or greater, 36 between .80 and .89, and 10 between .70 and .79. Seven of the 8 for the art area (30 items) are below .80 and all 8 in the science area (62 items) are above .90. No mention is made of the differences in reliabilities of these area scores in the discussion of the profiles that are to be drawn from the data, and no interpretation of the table of reliability coefficients is offered. There is no evidence of stability of the scores obtained by retests over any periods of time, but there are frequent references to shifting interests of pupils at the elementary and intermediate grade levels. Thus there is no evidence that the profile obtained on one day would be repeated a day, a week, a month, or a year later. In view of this lack of evidence of stability one must

question the lengthy statements of the possible use of the inventory in classroom situations, curriculum planning, individual guidance, and parent conferences.

One hundred twelve intercorrelation coefficients among area scores are reported. Of these 4 are greater than .70, 14 lie between .60 and .69, 48 between .50 and .59, 36 between .40 and .49, and 10 between .30 and .39. The scores are not, then, highly independent but no mention is made of this matter in the discussion of profiling that is to be done with the scores. The dips and tips in a profile may not, then, indicate real differences in the areas of a child's interests.

Although there is much mention of sex differences throughout the manual and separate profiles for boys and girls are offered, an examination of the profiles reveals very few differences in sex scores. The authors report "some significant differences between the interest patterns of boys and girls" but they give no data to back up the statement. The norms used as the basis for the profiles were obtained on 3,803 fourth, fifth, and sixth grade pupils from 51 schools in 33 (unnamed) states and all 9 census geographic areas.

Space does not permit consideration of problems that children may have with particular items, the fact that only "yes" items are scored, the lack of provision for scoring of intensity of interests, the possibility of faking responses, the admitted inclusion of items of questionable readability, and many of the other common limitations of the inventory method. It seems to the reviewer that all the elaborate mechanics of this device have failed to avoid the inherent difficulties in the use of the inventory method. Good teachers will not find such an instrument useful; poor ones seem more likely to be helped by spending more time with their pupils than by manipulating the symbols that this instrument produces.

NAOMI STEWART, *Formerly Staff Associate, Educational Testing Service, Princeton, New Jersey.*

Teachers who want to adapt their classroom work to the particular interests of their pupils will find *What I Like to Do* a helpful tool if they take care to use it with a cautious eye on its limitations.

The most important of these is that the meaning of the various scores has not been established, either rationally or empirically. The score

categories were apparently not derived in any way that would support an a priori assumption that they represent genuine functional entities, and no experimental results that might help build up a picture of their meaning and relevance are given.

Another limitation is that the norms were derived from data for a comparatively small number of boys and girls in each grade. For that reason, the interest profiles are plotted in units which have a high degree of unreliability —quite apart from any question of their validity.

In light of these and other causes for concern about the scores, it would be safest for the teacher to utilize the inventory merely as a device for obtaining the pupil's reactions to a large number of activity items. The amount of valuable information to be gained from a perusal of the item responses alone should not be underestimated; in fact, the teacher's handbook describes a number of situations in which *item responses*, rather than *scores*, provided the most helpful cues to the teacher.

Unfortunately, it is not a workable solution to urge teachers to use the inventory solely at the item level. Since it is much easier to assimilate information in score form than in item form, most teachers who use the inventory at all will probably wind up making use of the scores. If they use them only in a relatively informal way as a teaching adjunct—as an aid to understanding and "reaching" difficult pupils or as a guide in selecting projects for different groups of pupils—there is little likelihood that any harm will be done. It would definitely not be advisable, however, to use the scores as the basis for administrative decisions that might in any way affect the pupil's subsequent educational placement and progress. Suggestions in the manual encouraging such use should be carefully ignored.

It would not seem desirable, either, to encourage the pupils themselves to take their scores very seriously, yet they can hardly help doing so if the profile folder is used according to the publisher's directions. These directions call for the pupils to plot their own interest profiles and discuss them with teacher and classmates, not just once but three or four times at yearly intervals, each time looking to see what changes might have occurred in the interim. Not only might this procedure cause the inventory scores to assume wholly unwarranted importance in the pupils' minds; it might also tend to

cause distortion in the scores themselves. Ordinarily, children are not likely to "slant" their answers to an interest questionnaire, but if too much fuss is made over the results the first time the inventory is administered, the responses may not be quite so spontaneously honest the second time. The profile folder is intended by the publisher to expedite longitudinal studies of interests, but its use according to the publisher's directions would seem almost bound to yield distorted results.

What I Like to Do, with its full-scale array of accessory materials, is a much more ambitious and elaborate undertaking than earlier interest inventories (see 3:52, 63) designed for use in the intermediate grades, but as a measuring device it does not seem to afford any improvement over the others. Since the inventories differ considerably in item content, probably the best basis for selecting among them is for the teacher to decide which affords the coverage that best suits her purposes.

J Consult Psychol 19:237 Je '55. Laurance F. Shaffer. * an uninspired but workmanlike job in the construction of an interest inventory for grades 4 to 6 and, by implication but without data, for grade 7 *

[123]

★**Wittenborn Psychiatric Rating Scales.** Mental patients; 1955; 9 ratings: acute anxiety, conversion hysteria, manic, depressed, schizophrenic, paranoid, paranoid schizophrenic, hebephrenic schizophrenic, phobic compulsive; 1 form; $2.75 per 25 scales; 35¢ per specimen set; postpaid; (15–25) minutes; J. Richard Wittenborn; Psychological Corporation. *

REFERENCES

1. WITTENBORN, J. R. "Symptom Patterns in a Group of Mental Hospital Patients." *J Consult Psychol* 15:290–302 Ag '51. * (PA 26:6243)
2. WITTENBORN, J. R., AND HOLZBERG, J. D. "The Generality of Psychiatric Syndromes." *J Consult Psychol* 15:372–80 O '51. *
3. WITTENBORN, J. R., AND HOLZBERG, J. D. "The Wechsler-Bellevue and Descriptive Diagnosis." *J Consult Psychol* 15: 325–29 Ag '51. *
4. WITTENBORN, J. R., AND METTLER, FRED A. "Practical Correlates of Psychiatric Symptoms." *J Consult Psychol* 15: 505–10 D '51. *
5. WITTENBORN, J. R. "The Behavioral Symptoms for Certain Organic Psychoses." *J Consult Psychol* 16:104–6 Ap '52. *
6. WITTENBORN, J. R., AND BAILEY, CLARK. "The Symptoms of Involutional Psychosis." *J Consult Psychol* 16:13–7 F '52. *
7. WITTENBORN, J. R., AND WEISS, WALTER. "Patients Diagnosed Manic Depressive Psychosis—Manic State." *J Consult Psychol* 16:193–8 Je '52. * (PA 27:5318)
8. WITTENBORN, J. R.; HERZ, MARVIN I.; KURTZ, KENNETH H.; MANDELL, WALLACE; AND TATZ, SHERMAN. "The Effect of Rater Differences on Symptom Rating Scale Clusters." *J Consult Psychol* 16:107–9 Ap '52. *
9. WITTENBORN, J. R.; HOLZBERG, J. D.; AND SIMON, B.; with the collaboration of E. K. WILK, N. TOLL, P. E. YU, A. SANTICCIOLI, C. E. BOYD, AND D. P. SCAGNELLI. "Symptom Correlates for Descriptive Diagnosis." *Genetic Psychol Monogr* 47:237–301 My '53. (PA 28:2606)
10. LORR, MAURICE. "Rating Scales and Check Lists for the Evaluation of Psychopathology." *Psychol B* 51:119–27 Mr '54. *
11. PUMROY, SHIRLEY S., AND KOGAN, WILLIAM S. "The Reliability of Wittenborn's Scales for Rating Currently Dis-

cernible Psychopathology." *J Clin Psychol* 11:411–2 O '55. *
(*PA* 30:5997)
12. Lorr, Maurice. "Orthogonal Versus Oblique Rotations."
J Consult Psychol 21:448–9 D '57. *
13. Lorr, Maurice. "The Wittenborn Psychiatric Syndromes: An Oblique Rotation." *J Consult Psychol* 21:439–44 D
'57. *
14. Lorr, Maurice; O'Connor, James P.; and Stafford,
John W. "Confirmation of Nine Psychotic Symptom Patterns."
J Clin Psychol 13:252–7 Jl '57. *
15. Wittenborn, J. R. "Rotational Procedures and Descriptive Inferences." *J Consult Psychol* 21:445–7 D '57. *

H. J. Eysenck, *Professor of Psychology, Institute of Psychiatry, University of London,
London, England.*

There are 52 symptom rating scales contained
in Wittenborn's set. These are arranged in random order and are intended to measure nine
psychiatric clusters ranging from acute anxiety
and conversion hysteria to schizophrenic excitement and paranoid condition. Each scale is composed of three or four statements so arranged
that successive statements reveal increasingly
conspicuous disorder of a particular kind. The
clusters into which the scales are grouped resulted from extensive factorial analysis of various abnormal groups. An ingenious method of
scoring makes it quite easy to obtain weighted
scores for the various clusters; these scores can
then be arranged in terms of profiles and compared with standardisation data given in the
manual.

The whole attempt is very workmanlike
throughout and in the reviewer's opinion constitutes the best available set of rating scales for
psychiatric disorders. Wittenborn has made an
attempt to deal entirely with directly observable
behaviour, and in the reviewer's experience his
claim that ratings can be readily made by psychiatrists, psychologists, nurses, or other competent observers is amply justified. The types of
behaviour included are well chosen and are indicative of close personal experience. The wording of the scales is simple and straightforward
and does not commit the "fallacy of the implied theory" so frequent in psychiatric terminology. The research background for the scale
is unusually thorough and shows a high degree
of statistical competence, somewhat unusual in
this field.

The reliability of the cluster scores is not always very high, being only .67 for Depressed
State and .76 for Paranoid Condition. The only
one to exceed .90 is for Manic State. An additional five clusters have reliabilities between .8
and .9. Wittenborn somewhat plaintively says
that these "odd-item estimates of reliability are
likely to be spuriously low because of the heterogeneity of sets of rating scales." It is curi-

ous that he should have used so old-fashioned a
method for the estimation of reliability when
more modern methods are readily available. It
is also curious that he does not give test-retest
reliabilities for the same observer, or interobserver reliabilities for different psychiatrists.
Such data would be much more relevant and interesting than odd-even reliabilities; our experience suggests that they would be somewhat
lower than the reliabilities actually quoted.

The clusters are by no means independent.
The correlation between Schizophrenic Excitement and Hebephrenic Schizophrenia is .88,
which is higher than the mean reliability of the
scales. It is difficult to see any justification for
retaining both clusters under these circumstances. There are four other correlations above
.66, most of them involving Manic State. In addition there is a correlation of .79 between
Paranoid Condition and Paranoid Schizophrenic; this correlation also is higher than the
mean reliability of the two cluster scores. Wittenborn's own evidence, therefore, suggests
that instead of nine clusters there are seven
clusters at most, and possibly only six. It seems
a great pity that no oblique factor analysis was
attempted and no second order factors established.

In summary, it may be said that the good
points of this work far outweigh the bad ones
and that, for anyone wanting to use a psychiatric rating scale, the Wittenborn scales can be
recommended as superior, on the whole, to the
available alternatives. It is to be hoped, however, that in future editions the supererogatory
scales will be dropped, second order factor analyses reported, and inter-rater reliabilities given.

Maurice Lorr, *Director, Neuropsychiatric
Research Laboratory, Veterans Benefits Office,
Washington, D. C.*

The Wittenborn scales are a procedure designed for recording currently observable behavior and symptoms of mental patients. The
52 rating scales sample patient behavior "ordinarily considered important by psychiatrists."
To reduce bias, the scales are presented in a
randomized unlabeled order. Each scale consists of three or four statements arranged so
that successive statements reveal increasing disorder. Each scale must be checked for every
patient.

The form is intended for completion by a
psychiatrist, psychologist, nurse, or other "com-

petent observer." Competence is not defined nor are data made available concerning relative reliability of the scales when used by different types of observers. Surprisingly, no instructions are provided in the manual on how observations are to be made or over what period of time. The directions only recommend the recording of currently discernible behavior. Accordingly the user is left to his own devices on such matters as to interview or not to interview the patient and to observe patient ward behavior for a couple of hours or for several weeks or months.

This issue is reflected in the reliability information provided. Odd-even estimates of cluster score reliability for 100 patients range from .67 to .92 with a median of .82. Inter-rater reliability of the cluster scores is not reported. Yet confident use of the scales by single raters demands data on inter-rater agreement levels.

The validity of the scales is not discussed. No information is given the user concerning possible concurrent validation against other psychiatric measures of psychopathology. On the other hand, no claim is made for the usefulness of the scales beyond the recording of what was observed or what changed. The cluster scores which result from factoring the scales imply, of course, a type of construct validity.

The manual presents a table of intercorrelations between the clusters based on 100 newly admitted cases. Of the 36 correlations, one third are .41 or higher. The correlation between Hebephrenic and Schizophrenic Excitement is .88. An examination reveals that all but one of the seven hebephrenic scales are included in the excitement cluster. Paranoid Condition and Paranoid Schizophrenic correlate .79. The high correlations suggest that the clusters could be combined and reduced to a substantially smaller number.

Norms for the scales are based on 1,000 consecutive admissions to a state hospital. The median cluster scores for various functional and organic diagnostic groups are also reported in the manual. There are no accompanying data descriptive of the age, sex, marital status, or educational background of the norm group. Also lacking is information as to where and how observations were made in collecting the ratings. The scoring of the form and the conversion of the raw scores into standard cluster scores is easy and rapid.

The Wittenborn instrument is the product of considerable research. It is undoubtedly one of the best developed rating schedules available to the research worker and the practical clinician in need of a procedure for recording patient behavior and symptoms. However, the manual is in need of modification. An appropriate method and optimum period of observation should be specified. Further details descriptive of the norm group and levels of inter-rater agreement on the clusters should be provided the reader. Some of the available validational data should be included.

J Consult Psychol 19:320 Ag '55. Laurance F. Shaffer. A series of 18 research articles since 1950 has reported the development and application of the Wittenborn scales. Now they are made available for general use in an attractive and convenient format. The scales are an aid to the objective description of psychiatric patients in terms of their observable symptoms. On each of 52 areas of behavior, a patient is rated by selecting the one of four statements which describes him best. The quantified ratings are turned into scores on nine factors identified by factor analytic studies. The corrected split-half reliabilities of the factor scores range from .67 to .92, with only one scale below .76; their intercorrelations are generally low. The new blank greatly simplifies the calculation of the factor scores by reducing it to the addition of digits in conveniently arranged columns and the use of a simple table. With their new convenience and availability, the scales will probably receive wider use in research. They make a valuable contribution to the knottiest problem in studies of psychopathology, the problem of the criterion.

PROJECTIVE

[124]

★**The Auditory Apperception Test.** Grades 9 and over; 1953; 1 form; no data on reliability; $25 per set of five 7-inch records (45 rpm), 25 record booklets, 25 story booklets, and manual; $5.50 per 25 record booklets; $5.50 per 25 story booklets; $3 per manual; postpaid; specimen set not available; 50(80) or (50–80) minutes in 2 sessions; Western Psychological Services. *

REFERENCES

1. STONE, D. R. "A Recorded Auditory Apperception Test as a New Projective Technique." *J Psychol* 29:349–53 Ap '50. * (PA 24:5884)
2. OVERLADE, DAN C. *A Comparison of Responses of Schizophrenics to Sounds and Pictures.* Master's thesis, Utah State Agricultural College (Logan, Utah), 1951.
3. BALL, THOMAS S., AND BERNARDONI, LOUIS C. "The Application of an Auditory Apperception Test to Clinical Diagnosis." *J Clin Psychol* 9:54–8 Ja '53. * (PA 27:7753)

KENNETH L. BEAN, *Professor of Psychology, Baylor University, Waco, Texas.*

This projective technique is similar in many ways to the well established *Thematic Apperception Test,* but with auditory rather than visual stimuli. The test consists of 10 sets of 3 sound situations. After listening to each set, the subject is asked to make up a story, using as many of the sounds as he can, telling what led up to the sounds, what is happening, and how the story ends. The material is designated as appropriate for high school, college, and adult subjects.

A tabulation of the responses of 220 college students to each set is presented in the manual under the following headings: order of sounds in stories, description of sounds, length of stories, characters named, situations, outcomes, and general observations. No real evidence of reliability or validity is furnished in the manual, nor are any sample responses interpreted with detailed description of personality dynamics revealed. The absence of detailed instructions for interpreting stories is disappointing and frustrating.

The 45 rpm discs contain many sounds that are interesting and well done, such as the dialogue in Set 3, the saw cutting in Set 5, and the typewriter in Set 8. Unfortunately, there are others so artificial in quality as to be rather unrealistic to the listener. These probably will result in a poorer quality of content in the stories elicited from subjects. Examples include the severe wind in Set 1, which the examiner probably produced by blowing and whistling simultaneously into his microphone, and the train crash in Set 6, probably similarly "faked" in the laboratory. The reviewer's hi-fi ears may be more discriminating than those of the average listener because of his past experience with music and sound effects, but it is his opinion that the ship's whistle or foghorn and the thunder or explosions could be made much more realistic by obtaining and copying available recorded sound effects now widely used in radio and television work. This viewpoint is supported by the reviewer's own tryout of 60 sound effect sequences on groups of subjects before selecting the most productive of these stimuli for his own *Sound Apperception Test,* not yet published. Realistic high fidelity sounds were found to produce much more meaningful stories than the "faked" ones the reviewer tried. With improvement in quality of the stimuli named

above, the sequences should be adequate to bring out much more interesting content than the present version of the test has produced.

The *Auditory Projective Test* of the American Foundation for the Blind is considerably different in content from the AAT, but its purpose is much the same. On the whole, its quality of recording is better, but it also is insufficiently standardized and validated. The reviewer suggests that the *Auditory Apperception Test,* after revision of the recording, may become a very valuable and interesting tool for further research using neurotics, psychotics, blind persons, and normal subjects for its validation as a diagnostic instrument. Until much further development of norms and guides for interpretation has been completed, however, the user of this test should be cautious in making any speculations regarding the significance of individual protocols on the basis of his general knowledge of projective techniques. The simultaneous construction and standardization of three or more auditory projective devices recently is a wholesome trend provided each is done thoroughly, correlated with the others, and correlated with the better established visual Rorschach and TAT.

CLIFFORD H. SWENSEN, JR., *Associate Professor of Psychology, University of Tennessee, Knoxville, Tennessee.*

The author claims that the AAT "has achieved validity and reliability comparable to those of other projective devices," but presents no data relative to either the reliability or validity of the test. He states further that "the principle claim justifying and encouraging the use of the AAT is in its productivity of useful diagnostic signs." Nowhere does the manual present such diagnostic signs. The manual does present methods for analyzing test results, but these methods are based upon work done with the *Thematic Apperception Test.* No evidence is presented to support the implicit contention that stories produced by the AAT may justifiably be interpreted in the same manner as TAT stories. In fact, evidence is produced that might suggest that the AAT stories are useless. The author refers to Tomkins who refers to Murray as saying that stories on the TAT under 140 words were nearly useless. Yet, the mean of the mean lengths of AAT stories reported in the "apperceptive norms" is 88 words. The author also reports a study of schizophrenics in which

no significant difference was found between the subjects' productivity on the AAT and the TAT in terms of mean number of responses per subject.

Norms for characters, themes, etc. referred to in the stories are presented, but these are based upon 220 college students who had no grossly deviant scores on the *Minnesota Multiphasic Personality Inventory*. It is highly questionable that such a population provides useful norms for a test designed for clinical use.

Many of the sounds used as stimuli were apparently produced by the use of sound effects. Their artificiality is quite apparent when they are played over high fidelity equipment. They sound much more authentic when played over a low fidelity reproducer.

The test appears to produce the same type of material as the TAT. Since it is less convenient to administer, depending as it does upon sound producing equipment, it probably would be preferable to use the TAT in most clinical settings. However, the AAT would probably prove useful in group situations and with subjects who have defective vision.

[125]

The Blacky Pictures: A Technique for the Exploration of Personality Dynamics. Ages 5 and over; 1950; psychosexual development; individual; 1 form; no data on reliability and validity; no norms; $11 per set of test materials and 25 record blanks; $3.50 per 25 record blanks; $1 per manual; postpaid; (35-55) minutes; Gerald S. Blum; Psychological Corporation. *

REFERENCES

1-7. See 4:102.
8. HART, ROBERT D. *An Evaluation of the Psychoanalytic Theory of Male Homosexuality by Means of the Blacky Pictures.* Doctor's thesis, Northwestern University (Evanston, Ill.), 1951.
9. HILGEMAN, LOIS M. B. *Developmental and Sex Variations in the Blacky Test.* Doctor's thesis, Ohio State University (Columbus, Ohio), 1951.
10. LINDNER, HAROLD. *An Analysis of the Psychological Characteristics of a Selected Group of Imprisoned Sexual Offenders.* Doctor's thesis, University of Maryland (College Park, Md.), 1951.
11. BLUM, GERALD S., AND HUNT, HOWARD F. "The Validity of the Blacky Pictures." *Psychol B* 49:238-50 My '52. * (*PA* 27:2707)
12. BLUM, GERALD S., AND KAUFMAN, JEWEL B. "Two Patterns of Personality Dynamics in Male Peptic Ulcer Patients as Suggested by Responses to the Blacky Pictures." *J Clin Psychol* 8:273-8 Jl '52. * (*PA* 27:6060)
13. BLUM, GERALD S., AND MILLER, DANIEL R. "Exploring the Psychoanalytic Theory of the 'Oral Character.' " *J Personality* 20:287-304 Mr '52.* (*PA* 27:2353)
14. GOLDSTEIN, STANLEY. "A Projective Study of Psychoanalytic Mechanisms of Defense." Abstract. *Am Psychol* 7:317-8 Jl '52. *
15. KLEHR, HAROLD. "An Investigation of Some Personality Factors in Women With Rheumatoid Arthritis." Abstract. *Am Psychol* 7:344-5 Jl '52. *
16. MCNEIL, ELTON B., AND BLUM, GERALD S. "Handwriting and Psychosexual Dimensions of Personality." *J Proj Tech* 16:476-84 D '52. *
17. ROSEN, IRWIN C. *Parallel Researches in Sexual Psychopathology: I, A Comparison of a Group of Rapists and Controls on Certain Psychological Variables.* Doctor's thesis, University of Pittsburgh (Pittsburgh, Pa.), 1952.
18. TAYLOR, KENNETH E. *Parallel Researches in Sexual Psychopathology: II, A Comparison of a Group of Pedophiliacs and Controls on Certain Psychological Variables.* Doctor's thesis, University of Pittsburgh (Pittsburgh, Pa.), 1952.
19. ARONSON, MARVIN L. "A Study of the Freudian Theory of Paranoia by Means of the Blacky Pictures." *J Proj Tech* 17:3-19 Mr '53. * (*PA* 28:2981)
20. ELLIS, ALBERT. "The Blacky Test Used With a Psychoanalytic Patient." *J Clin Psychol* 9:167-72 Ap '53. * (*PA* 28:2627)
21. LINDNER, HAROLD. "The Blacky Pictures Test: A Study of Sexual and Non-Sexual Offenders." *J Proj Tech* 17:79-84 Mr '53. * (*PA* 28:2975)
22. SINNETT, EARLE ROBERT. *An Experimental Investigation of the Defense Preference Inquiry for the Blacky Pictures.* Doctor's thesis, University of Michigan (Ann Arbor, Mich.), 1953. (*DA* 13:442)
23. TOBER, LAWRENCE H. *An Investigation of the Personality Dynamics and Behavior Patterns of Older People in a Mental Hospital as Measured by the Blacky Pictures and a Q-Rating Scale of Behavior.* Doctor's thesis, Western Reserve University (Cleveland, Ohio), 1953.
24. DICKSON, STANLEY. *An Application of the Blacky Test to a Study of the Psychosexual Development of Stutterers.* Master's thesis, Brooklyn College (Brooklyn, N.Y.), 1954.
25. FIELD, LEWIS WILLIAM. *Personality Correlates of College Achievement and Major Areas of Study.* Doctor's thesis, University of Houston (Houston, Tex.), 1954. (*DA* 14:1344)
26. HOGAN, VIRGINIA. *The Reliability of the Blacky Pictures With Institutionalized Senile Psychotics.* Doctor's thesis, Western Reserve University (Cleveland, Ohio), 1954.
27. SMOCK, CHARLES D., AND THOMPSON, GEORGE F. "An Inferred Relationship Between Early Childhood Conflicts and Anxiety Responses in Adult Life." *J Personality* 23:88-98 S '54. *
28. TEEVAN, RICHARD C. "Personality Correlates of Undergraduate Field of Specialization." *J Consult Psychol* 18:212-4 Je '54. * (*PA* 29:3007)
29. WINTER, WILLIAM DAVID. *The Prediction of Life History Data and Personality Characteristics of Ulcer Patients From Responses to the Blacky Pictures.* Doctor's thesis, University of Michigan (Ann Arbor, Mich.), 1954. (*DA* 14:717)
30. BERNSTEIN, LEWIS, AND CHASE, PHILIP H. "The Discriminative Ability of the Blacky Pictures With Ulcer Patients." *J Consult Psychol* 19:377-80 O '55. * (*PA* 30:6002)
31. REED, WOODROW WILSON. *Parent-Child Relationships Reflected by "The Blacky Pictures" Test.* Doctor's thesis, University of Nebraska (Lincoln, Neb.), 1955. (*DA* 15:2298)
32. WINTER, WILLIAM D. "Two Personality Patterns in Peptic Ulcer Patients." *J Proj Tech* 19:332-44 S '55. * (*PA* 30:5075)
33. BLUM, GERALD S. "Defense Preferences in Four Countries." *J Proj Tech* 20:33-41 Mr '56. * (*PA* 31:3007)
34. BLUM, GERALD S. " 'Reliability of the Blacky Test': A Reply to Charen." *J Consult Psychol* 20:406 O '56. * (*PA* 31:7899)
35. BLUMBERG, ALBERT IRWIN. *A Methodological Study of Two Approaches to the Validation of the Blacky Pictures.* Doctor's thesis, Western Reserve University (Cleveland, Ohio), 1956.
36. CHAREN, SOL. "Regressive Behavior Changes in the Tuberculous Patient." *J Psychol* 41:273-89 Ja '56. * (*PA* 31:5000)
37. CHAREN, SOL. "Reliability of the Blacky Test." Abstract. *J Consult Psychol* 20:16 F '56. *
38. CHAREN, SOL. "A Reply to Blum." *J Consult Psychol* 20:407 O '56. * (*PA* 31:7899)
39. SMITH, WENDELL, AND POWELL, ELIZABETH K. "Responses to Projective Material by Pre- and Post-Menarcheal Subjects." *Percept & Motor Skills* 6:155-8 S '56. * (*PA* 31:4715)
40. WINTER, LOUISE MORRISON. *Development of a Scoring System for the Children's Form of the Blacky Pictures.* Doctor's thesis, University of Michigan (Ann Arbor, Mich.), 1956. (*DA* 17:175)
41. WOLFSON, WILLIAM, AND WOLFF, FRANCES. "Sexual Connotation of the Name Blacky." *J Proj Tech* 20:347 S '56. * (*PA* 31:6150)
42. JACOBS, MILDRED O. *A Validation Study of the Oral Erotic Scale of the Blacky Pictures Test.* Doctor's thesis, University of Oklahoma (Norman, Okla.), 1957. (*DA* 17:1811)
43. TRENT, RICHARD D., AND AMCHIN, ABRAHAM. "An Exploration of Relationships Between Manifest Anxiety and Selected Psychosexual Areas." *J Proj Tech* 21:318-22 S '57. *
44. GRANICK, SAMUEL, AND SCHEFLEN, NORMA A. "Approaches to Reliability of Projective Tests With Special Reference to the Blacky Pictures Test." *J Consult Psychol* 22:137-41 Ap '58. *
45. RABIN, A. I. "Some Psychosexual Differences Between Kibbutz and Non-Kibbutz Israeli Boys." *J Proj Tech* 22:328-32 S '58. *

KENNETH R. NEWTON, *Associate Professor of Psychology, University of Tennessee, Knoxville, Tennessee.*

The *Blacky Pictures* are a series of 12 cartoon drawings designed to point up the psycho-

sexual development of the individual through analysis of the stories he builds around these drawings. The drawings concern a family of dogs with Blacky being the central character. In addition to Blacky, who can be of either sex, there is the mother, the father, and a sibling figure who can be either a brother or a sister. This technique was initially designed by the author as a means of investigating the psychoanalytic theory of psychosexual development. The activities portrayed in each drawing are supposedly symbolic of one of the psychoanalytic dimensions in the theory of psychosexual development. The technique and instructions are quite similar to the *Thematic Apperception Test* with the exception that as the examiner presents each card he gives a preliminary statement which tends to structure the picture somewhat for the patient. There are individual record blanks provided which contain rather complete directions for administration and space for recording the stories. After each cartoon has been presented and a story elicited, there is an inquiry or series of standardized questions that must be asked.

The author's description of the Blacky test as being a "modified projective technique" is a rather generous view of projective techniques. The cartoons themselves, the instructions involved in presenting them, and the inquiry that follows are somewhat obvious and almost directive in nature. In an attempt to obtain material on the various areas of psychosexual development, the author has structured his pictures and inquiries in such a way as to make the responses fit the theory. The interpretation of the individual's responses would quite likely yield positive findings if the subject did no more than offer affirmative or negative responses to the pictures and to the various questions of the inquiry. It seems that the patient is placed in the position of the well known defendant who has been asked, "When did you stop beating your wife?"

In his original publication, the author admits that the assumption that this test measures psychoanalytic dimensions has not been systematically explored and, therefore, that the validity of the test is still open to question. Since the hypotheses and conclusions that are drawn from the material obtained from this technique are based upon the assumption that the Blacky test is a measure of psychoanalytic dimensions, this seems to be a serious shortcoming. In the manual accompanying the series of cartoons, the author attempts to present some criteria for stories that will illustrate "strong" and "not strong" involvement in the particular psychosexual spheres. He states that the clinician's own experience with the Blacky test will enable him to develop some sort of "concept of normality" for the stories presented. In addition, he offers a sample case work-up which does little in the way of strengthening this technique in the hands of the clinician.

Although the technique was developed on adults, the author states that the *Blacky Pictures* are "well-suited for use with children." There are as yet no norms or even illustrations or examples of good or bad, strong or not strong stories for children. Children do respond readily to such a technique, but the interpretation of their responses needs further investigation.

This "modified projective technique" could be an interesting tool with which one might conceivably explore psychoanalytic concepts. However, pointing toward various concepts and making a direct effort to elicit the subject's reactions to situations involving his feelings toward various areas of psychosexual development perhaps represents a weighting of the evidence toward the theory that one wishes to prove. It seems likely that well developed and well directed questions concerning these various periods of psychosexual development might yield even more reliable results than does this "modified projective technique." That is to say, the author seems to be asking specific questions concerning specific types of situations which might just as well be handled in an interview situation without use of any cartoons or story telling. The specificity of the questions being asked in this technique seems to require a certain degree of specificity of response.

The *Blacky Pictures* attempt to portray the various spheres of psychosexual development hypothesized by the psychoanalytic school of thought. The individual's responses to the drawings and his responses to specific inquiry questions supposedly indicate the degree of his involvement in these various psychosexual spheres. Admittedly, other than the clinician's own knowledge of psychoanalytic theory, there is little in the way of normative data. At this time this technique would appear to be of little value to the practicing clinician. Its value depends upon the psychoanalytic training of the administrator, but even here there is little data available

from which one could determine a "good" or "bad" response.

J Consult Psychol 20:487–8 D '56. Samuel J. Beck. * Blum has devised a test *ad hoc* for psychoanalytic theory by the ingenious technique which activates certain of the psychoanalytically formulated unconscious traits, at the same time that it provides the defenses enabling the patient to liberate and communicate these forbidden trends—the defenses of identification and displacing. * The test has....a differentiating potency, and without a doubt it has the projective instrument value of opening a window to latent character traits. At the same time results are suspect, as I see it, by reason of a major fallacy in the technique of treating the data. This consists in the method of "scoring" each story and the other criteria as "strong" and the various gradations of "strong." The judgments are made by each examiner, without recourse to any frame of reference. Scorings must, therefore, be a function of each scorer. They can, I will concede, be made reliable as between two investigators who have worked together closely and have learned the same signs and language, in recognizing and naming the psychological traits or "dimensions." Except between two such colleagues, or for some one examiner, results are only spuriously comparable. The degree of error to which the procedure is subject is seen in Blum's own monograph: a denial of a response is construed as a repression, and since a repression involves strong emotion, the response is scored "strong." To construe denial as repression—which is a hypothesis and not a datum—is interpretation. Thus a quantitative profile is developed and is reported as *S*'s production although it is actually the examiner's interpretation of *S*'s production. This criticism touches on what is the Achilles' heel of each projective test. It dictates the need, therefore, of exploiting the objectivity potential in the test. The needed technique is that of patterning out its data into impersonal structure to be described operationally, and so creating some stable frames of reference by which the productions of any *S* can be judged, if not measured. Some of the projective tests do lend themselves more easily to such impersonal structuralization than others. But to the extent that the instrument falls short of such objectivity, it is not a test but a two-person situation, two persons—*S* and examiner, each of whom may influence the results. Schafer

has been especially emphatic concerning the interpersonal relation between examiner and subject, and the possible role of the examiner's personality in fashioning the final test picture. Brunswik writing from another theoretical viewpoint, arrives at a similar conclusion. "Since in any testing procedure the examiner constitutes part of the external stimulus situation, representative design demands that examiners should also be sampled," and he refers to the "double jeopardy of generalization." An important implication follows from these positions of Schafer and of Brunswik: projective test investigations will need to find some method of keeping the examiner factor constant, if reports by two or more persons are to be comparable. The problem becomes at this point the baby of the theorists and logicians of science. This circumstance does not, however, ease the burden of the psychologists searching personality by means of projective tests. The fact is they have so far been arriving at right answers, even if they do not know how. Their answers are bound to be that much more accurate as they are based in sound method, and as they take pains to devise such. This is where I see Blacky and his growing pains at the present. The test has the promise warranting its developing. In spite of the fallacy in the scoring procedure, its agreement with clinical theory is logically sound. It can serve, further, as an example of other *ad hoc* techniques which can be devised to explore psychoanalytic theory.

For a review by Albert Ellis, see 4:102 (3 excerpts).

[126]

*Children's Apperception Test. Ages 3–10; 1949–55; individual; 1 form; 2 editions; no data on reliability and validity; $6 per set of 10 pictures and manual of either edition; $2.50 per 25 short form record booklets ('55); postage extra; [15–50] minutes; Leopold Bellak and Sonya Sorel Bellak; C.P.S. Co. *
a) CHILDREN'S APPERCEPTION TEST. 1949–55; also called CAT; 1 form ('49); [revised] picture 2 ['51]; revised manual ('50).
b) CHILDREN'S APPERCEPTION TEST—SUPPLEMENT. 1952–55; also called CAT-S; 1 form ('52); manual ('52).

REFERENCES

1–2. See 4:103.
3. AINSWORTH, MARY D., AND BOSTON, MARY. "Psychodiagnostic Assessments of a Child After Prolonged Separation in Early Childhood." *Brit J Med Psychol* 25:169–201 pt 4 '52. * (PA 27:7845)
4. MILLAR, MARY A. *A Study of Common Stories Told by Nursery School Children on the Children's Apperception Test.* Master's thesis, University of Alberta (Edmonton, Alta., Canada), 1952. Pp. 111.
5. TOPPELSTEIN, SANFORD. *Apperceptive Norms for the Children's Apperception Test.* Master's thesis, Ohio University (Athens, Ohio), 1952.
6. BIERSDORF, KATHRYN R., AND MARCUSE, F. L. "Responses

of Children to Human and to Animal Pictures." *J Proj Tech* 17:455–9 D '53. * (*PA* 28:6019)

7. SHNEIDMAN, EDWIN S. "CAT Issue No. 2: The TAT Newsletter, Vol. 7, No. 4, December 1953." *J Proj Tech* 17:499–502 D '53. *

8. WEISSKOPF-JOELSON, EDITH A., AND LYNN, DAVID B. "The Effect of Variations in Ambiguity on Projection in the Children's Apperception Test." *J Consult Psychol* 17:67–70 F '53. * (*PA* 28:977)

9. BELLAK, LEOPOLD. *The Thematic Apperception Test and the Children's Apperception Test in Clinical Use.* New York: Grune & Stratton, Inc., 1954. Pp. x, 282. * (*PA* 29:4032)

10. BYRD, EUGENE, AND WITHERSPOON, RALPH L. "Responses of Preschool Children to the Children's Apperception Test." *Child Develop* 25:35–44 Mr '54. * (*PA* 29:5691)

11. LIGHT, BERNARD H. "Comparative Study of a Series of TAT and CAT Cards." *J Clin Psychol* 10:179–81 Ap '54. * (*PA* 29:933)

12. MAINORD, FLORENCE R., AND MARCUSE, F. L. "Responses of Disturbed Children to Human and to Animal Pictures." *J Proj Tech* 18:475–7 D '54. * (*PA* 29:7299)

13. KAGAN, MARION G. *A Preliminary Investigation of Some Relationships Between Functional Articulation Disorders and Responses to the Children's Apperception Test.* Master's thesis, Boston University (Boston, Mass.), 1955.

14. HOLDEN, RAYMOND H. "The Children's Apperception Test With Cerebral Palsied and Normal Children." *Child Develop* 27:3–8 Mr '56. * (*PA* 31:3561)

15. WHEELER, W. M. "Psychodiagnostic Assessments of a Child After Prolonged Separation in Early Childhood, II." *Brit J Med Psychol* 29:248–57 pt 3–4 '56. *

16. FURUYA, KENJI. "Responses of School-Children to Human and Animal Pictures." *J Proj Tech* 21:248–52 S '57. *

17. GINSPARG, HAROLD TVI. *A Study of the Children's Apperception Test.* Doctor's thesis, Washington University (St. Louis, Mo.), 1957. (*DA* 17:3082)

DOUGLAS T. KENNY, *Associate Professor of Psychology, University of British Columbia, Vancouver, British Columbia, Canada.*

Since its last review in *The Fourth Mental Measurements Yearbook,* three improvements or additions have occurred in this story-telling projective technique for personality evaluation: (*a*) 10 supplementary pictures, with an accompanying manual, have been added; (*b*) Bellak has published a valuable and instructive book on the interpretation of thematic material, entitled *The TAT and CAT in Clinical Use;* and (*c*) Bell's criticism that "the pictures are printed on a matt finish cardboard that soils easily" (4:103) has been partially removed in the 1952 printing of the original 10 CAT cards by having them lacquered. It is unlikely that the lacquered cards will make any basic differences in story content.

The pictures, intended for use with children between 3 and 10 years of age, contain animal figures because it is assumed that children will more readily identify with animals than humans. While the experimental findings on this assumption are ambiguous, clinical material from psychoanalysis points to its reasonableness. The pictures in the basic set were drawn with the hope that they would elicit dynamic material relating to oral conflicts, sibling rivalry, perceptions of parents, oedipal problems, and general drives and modes of responding to the world. The CAT Supplement, consisting of 10 animal scenes, was designed primarily to elicit themes "not *necessarily pertaining to universal prob-*

lems, but which occur often enough to make it desirable to learn more about them as they exist in a good many children." In general, these pictures are intended to probe fears in play situations, interpersonal problems in the classroom, fantasies about being an adult, oral themes, reactions to physical handicaps or castration fears, competitiveness to others, body image ideas, fears of physical illness, bathroom reactions, and fantasies about pregnancy. A further use of the supplement is as a play technique, particularly recommended as a means of obtaining some clinical data on children who find it hard to tell stories. In the latter use, all the supplementary cards are made available and the child's reactions to them are recorded.

Evaluating the CAT and its supplement is a difficult task because much patient research will be required before its optimal usefulness can be realized. Since little is actually known about the kinds of valid inferences that might be drawn from the thematic material that is elicited by the cards, caution must be shown in any clinical inferences based on this technique. Moreover, without a large body of accumulated research, unequivocal evaluative statements cannot be made.

In terms of the standards applied to measures of intelligence, aptitude, and achievement, the CAT and CAT-S would not be regarded as suitable for operational use. They have many technical deficiencies, some of which are meagre normative data of limited generality, no information on the reliability of clinical inferences, a paucity of validity data, and a relatively unstandardized method of administration. On the other hand, there is little doubt that, given a highly trained clinician, one can make valid and useful inferences about the personality of a child from the thematic material produced by this instrument, despite the forementioned technical weaknesses. This is not to say, of course, that this instrument will be clinically useful for all children. Research has yet to show for whom the technique will be most suitable.

In order to obtain meaningful stories for interpretation, the CAT seems to require more skill than its parent, the *Thematic Apperception Test.* It is not a good technique for the novice in test administration and interpretation. At the moment, the interpretation of CAT stories is on shifting grounds because practically nothing is known about how much of the story content reflects the deep underlying structure of the

child and how much of it mirrors the conditions immediately antecedent to the testing, the atmosphere created by the test administration, and the pictures themselves. Until a great deal more is known about how such variables operate, caution must be shown in going from the raw stories to psychological attributes of the child and then inferring from these attributes the behavior of the child. Bellak's book (9) should be of great help to the beginner in learning how to infer from raw content to psychological attributes, but of less help in getting to behavior. Of course, the latter problem is one that beclouds the use of all projective techniques, not just the CAT. As this technique requires extensive knowledge and experience in the fields of child testing, pathology, and development, one would question Bellak's statement that "the C.A.T. may be profitable in the hands of.... the social worker, and the teacher."

In summary, this technique will be of value to the experienced clinician in indicating the psychological dispositions of a child. Its valid usefulness seems to lie in providing hypotheses about a child that require checking by other procedures. The potential usefulness of the instrument could be increased if more were known about which inferences from it are valid and with what kind of children it can be most profitably used.

ALBERT I. RABIN, *Professor of Psychology, and Director, Psychological Clinic, Michigan State University, East Lansing, Michigan.*

The *Children's Apperception Test* (CAT) for children between the ages of 3–10 was designed as a sort of downward extension of the TAT. The 10 CAT cards, bearing pictures of animals in a variety of situations, are expected by the authors to reflect common problem areas and conflicts faced by children in the early developmental stages. Problems of orality, identification with parental and sibling figures, aggression, mastery, primal scene fears, and masturbation are some of the issues expected to be projected in stories told in response to the pictures. In 1952 the authors published a supplement (CAT-S) which consists of 10 additional animal pictures, not designed to elicit stories related to "universal" problems, but to relate to issues which are of a more transitory, but important, nature in the lives of many young children. Such themes as physical injury, pregnancy of the mother, social play and aggressiveness,

and teacher and peer relationships are but a few of the ones which may be projected into these pictures.

The two manuals (for CAT and its supplement) were supplemented in 1954 by a more extensive treatment (9) by the author. The manuals supply the prospective examiner with some suggestions for administration, protocols, and samples of interpretation. A record booklet is also provided to facilitate the recording and analysis of stories. Some excerpts of a larger study by Fear and Stone reporting normative data are included in the manual to the supplement. Detailed proposals for collecting norms are given in the book. However, such norms are not yet available.

As a clinical tool for use with children, the CAT enjoys considerable popularity in the United States as well as abroad. Although a good deal of research with this technique is in progress, little information concerning its reliability and validity is available. The normative data by Byrd and Witherspoon (10) are a good beginning. Also, some of the emerging research on disturbed children by Simon [1] and on cerebral palsied children by Holden (14) attest to the usefulness and vitality of this instrument.

In summary it may be stated that the CAT, like most projective techniques, is a clinical technique rather than a psychometric method. Its use by many clinicians and clinical investigators attests to its potency as a tool for the study of psychodynamics in young children. Its acceptance by the critical worker and its survival will depend upon further normative studies and carefully executed research.

For reviews by John E. Bell and L. Joseph Stone, see 4:103 (5 excerpts); for related reviews, see B63.

[127]

*Controlled Projection for Children, Second Edition.** Ages 6–12; 1945–51; individual; 1 form ('51); no data on reliability and validity; 20s. per manual ('51), postage extra; administration time not reported; John C. Raven; H. K. Lewis & Co. Ltd. *

REFERENCES

1. KALDEGG, A. "Responses of German and English Secondary School Boys to a Projection Test." *Brit J Psychol* 39:30–53 S '48. * (*PA* 24:1141)
2. RAVEN, J. C. "Establishing Typical and A-Typical Responses to a Controlled Projection Test." Abstract. *Q B Brit Psychol Soc* 1:186–7 Jl '49. *
3. BAKER, CORINNE F. *An Evaluation of the Raven Controlled Projection Test: A Multi-Technique Study.* Doctor's thesis, Western Reserve University (Cleveland, Ohio), 1950.
4. FOULDS, G. A. "Characteristic Projection Test Responses

1 SIMON, MARIA D. "Der Children's Apperception Test bei gesunden und gestörten Kindern." *Z diagnos Psychol* 2:195–219 '54.

[157]

★**Self Valuation Test.** Ages 7–15, adults; 1957; verbal and non-verbal projective test employing several stimuli simultaneously; title on test is S.V.T.; individual; 1 form ['57]; 2 levels: children, adults (separate forms for men and women); manual ['57]; 84s. per set of test materials, 100 comparison sheets, and 50 record booklets, postpaid; 20s. per 100 record booklets; 8s. 4d. per 100 comparison sheets; postage extra; specimen set not available; (5–25) minutes; John Liggett; J. & P. Bealls Ltd. *

REFERENCES

1. LIGGETT, JOHN. "A Non-Verbal Approach to the Phenomenal Self." J Psychol 43:225–37 Ap '57. *
2. LIGGETT, J. "The Simultaneous Use of Several Unstructured Stimuli in the Study of Attitudes." Abstract. B Brit Psychol Soc (35):20 My '58. *

[158]

*****Sentence Completions Test.** Ages 12 and over; 1940–57; revision of Payne Sentence Completion Blank ('29); 1 form ('53); record booklet ('47); manual ('57, see 4 below); reliability and validity data for 1940 form only; $15 per set of 25 tests, 25 record booklets, and manual; $4 per 25 tests; $4 per 25 record booklets; $7.75 per manual; postpaid; (30–60) minutes; Amanda R. Rohde; distributed by Western Psychological Services. *

REFERENCES

1–3. See 4:131.
4. ROHDE, AMANDA R. Sentence Completion Method: Its Diagnostic and Clinical Application to Mental Disorders. New York: Ronald Press Co., 1957. Pp. xii, 301. *

For reviews by Charles N. Cofer and Charles R. Strother of an earlier edition, see 4:131; for related reviews, see B358.

[159]

★**Structured-Objective Rorschach Test: Preliminary Edition.** Adults; 1958; also called S-O Rorschach Test; 15 scores (for deriving 26 traits); whole-blot (W), major details (D), minor details (Dd), white space (S), form resemblance (F), poor form resemblance (F−), human movement (M), animal movement (FM), color and form resemblance (FC), color and poor form resemblance (CF), shading (Fch), animal figure (A), human figure (H), modal responses (P), rare responses (O); IBM; 1 form; 2 editions; separate answer sheets must be used; $1.50 per set of hand scoring stencils; postage extra; scoring service available; Joics B. Stone; California Test Bureau. *
a) ILLUSTRATED EDITION. $7.50 per test; 20(30) minutes.
b) NON-ILLUSTRATED EDITION. To be used with slides or cards; $5 per 10 tests; 10¢ per IBM answer sheet; $12 per set of ink-blot cards; $11 per set of kodaslides; $1 per specimen set, postpaid; 20(30) minutes.

[160]

★**Symbol Elaboration Test.** Ages 6 and over; 1950–53; title on test is S.E.T.; 1 form ('53); manual ('50, see 1 below); $12 per set of 50 tests and manual; $10 per 50 tests; $2 per manual; postage extra; administration time not reported; Johanna Krout; C. H. Stoelting Co. *

REFERENCE

1. KROUT, JOHANNA. "Symbol Elaboration Test (S.E.T.): The Reliability and Validity of a New Projective Technique." Psychol Monogr 64(4):1–67 '50. * (PA 25:3167)

RICHARD H. DANA, *Assistant Professor of Psychology, University of Nevada, Reno, Nevada.*

Eight years have elapsed since the publication of the SET. Users of projective techniques have not responded with enthusiasm to these 11 stimulus patterns to be elaborated by drawing. This unpopularity may be due to three unstated assumptions: (*a*) symbols for basic life experiences have universal meanings, (*b*) eleven universal symbols are represented by the *particular* stimulus patterns employed, and (*c*) a drawing response to each stimulus pattern is associated with the subject's attitude toward the symbolic meaning of the stimulus.

While one may assume that symbols have fixed meanings, it is an empirical problem whether or not particular stimulus patterns actually have the meaning ascribed to them. No such experimental scrutiny of possible stimulus patterns was attempted. Similarly, relatively small differences in stimulus line placements are given important meanings, e.g., maleness versus male society, or intimate heterosexuality versus competitive heterosexuality. Item analysis would have suggested what magnitude of difference in line placements is empirically relevant. Suitable criteria could have been found in consensus of clinical judgment on other projective data.

The validation material is a curious compound of misplaced conviction and statistical miscellany. The standardization sample contained 169 subjects from five groups identified vaguely as to age, sex, and source of group. These groups included "volunteers," "normal" adults from other studies, psychiatric patients, Indian children, etc. The groups are neither comparable, representative, nor adequately described.

Blind clinical interpretations were made of each drawing. Validation data consisting of other projective and clinical material had been independently gathered in connection with other studies. Case conferences were held (whether the SET analyst contributed to these conferences is not stated) and the results compared with the blind SET interpretations. A 7-category rating scale ("complete corroboration" to "no evidence") was used. Thus, there were two sets of abstractions, each one fairly distant from the raw data. The high agreement obtained may be a function of method. This further suggests that if the pool of possible validation statements is very large and sufficiently generalized, the possibility of any single judge making unverifiable interpretations is minimized.

Two individual cases are presented as additional samples of validity. However, this process is one of "validation by suggestion." The interpretation for each drawing is made; then the subject is asked, in effect, whether or not the interpretation is correct. Social desirability, attempts to please the examiner, and generality of statements contaminate the process and substantial agreement is obtained.

Scorer reliability was approached in several ways. (a) One scorer was used and questions devised from interpretations of 15 cases. These questions were given to an independent scorer who searched the validation data for "answers." Agreement was 84 per cent. This is presented as evidence for reliable *selection* from response data. It appears merely that reliability and validity procedures are analogous, i.e., "reliability by suggestion," since data the independent scorer is to look for are at least partially indicated. (b) Reliability of the *ratings* themselves was investigated by giving paired statements (test interpretation and corresponding validation statement) to an independent scorer and asking for a judgment in one of the seven categories. Agreement was 94 per cent. (c) Reliability of the *criterion* was approached by having scorers rerate representative cases after two months. Agreement was from 82 to 98 per cent. (d) One fundamental reliability problem with projective data is agreement between two independent scorers in their specific interpretations, or reliability of the *method* of analysis. Two independent and trained scorers interpreted 10 records with 96 per cent agreement. This remarkably high figure evokes necessity for identification of scorer characteristics, complete specification of the scoring procedure, and an extension of the sample of scorers. No other projective technique has substantiated a comparable reliability claim for interpretive statements.

When the SET is evaluated as an example of test construction and clear communication of procedural detail, the results are disappointing. The most salient criticisms are: (a) Dogma was evidenced in uncritical acceptance of potentially testable hypotheses as assumptions. (b) Test stimuli were selected by fiat as opposed to experimentation. (c) The validation sample was gathered by "opportunity sampling" with no consideration for generality of results.

(d) The validation procedure itself is suspect and follows the axiom that agreement between test data and criterion is a function of the level of abstraction employed, (e) Scorer reliability procedures attempt at completeness, but results may be artificially inflated by structured scorer tasks and by inadequate identification of scorers.

However, the SET does represent increased concern with *stimulus properties* of a projective technique. The assumption of a specific symbolic meaning for each stimulus figure provides the possibility for reopening this important theoretical issue. The SET is usable only as an exploratory instrument at the same level of hypothesis testing within the single case as the DAP, the H-T-P, or the Franck test. The validation data should be disregarded. The potential usefulness for controlled research on symbols and their specific representation that may be afforded by the SET must not be overlooked.

[161]

Symonds Picture-Story Test. Grades 7–12; 1948; individual; 1 form; 2 parts (Sets A and B); Set B may be administered alone or Sets A and B together; no data on reliability; $5.25 per set of test materials, cash orders postpaid; (60–70) minutes per set; Percival M. Symonds; Bureau of Publication, Teachers College, Columbia University. *

REFERENCES

1–2. See 4:132.
3. GORLOW, LEON; ZIMET, CARL N.; AND FINE, HAROLD J. "The Validity of Anxiety and Hostility Rorschach Content Scores Among Adolescents." *J Consult Psychol* 16:73–5 F '52. * (PA 27:1961)
4. SYMONDS, PERCIVAL M., AND JENSEN, ARTHUR R. "Psychoanalytic Concepts and Principles Discernible in Projective Personality Tests: Workshop, 1956: 6, The Predictive Significance of Fantasy." *Am J Orthopsychiatry* 28:73–84 Ja '58. *

WALTER KASS, *Associate Professor of Psychology, Albert Einstein College of Medicine, Yeshiva University, New York, New York.*

The *Symonds Picture-Story Test* is a set of 20 pictures designed for administration to adolescents as a projective technique like the *Thematic Apperception Test*. Subjects are asked to make up a story for each of the pictures; the thematic content is then interpreted for personality implications. In devising the pictures and presenting quantitative and qualitative methods of analyzing story material, Symonds makes a diligent effort to forge a projective technique into a standard test. However, the mixed marriage of a psychometric approach with a polymorphous projective medium unhappily does not hold up well. The result is two parallel methods of analysis, each with its rules of rigor, which sometime supplement one another but which combine only in the author's respect for the merits of both.

In the quantitative treatment of the data, Symonds and his assistants identified and tabulated all the overtly expressed themes they could find (without regard to latent meanings or motives) in 1,680 stories told by 20 school boys and 20 school girls, 12 to 18 years of age, to 42 stimulus pictures. From a total of 10,797 themes, 1,850 occurring three or more times were culled for statistical treatment. Twenty of the 42 trial pictures were then selected for publication in the final test version.

Inventoried themes are classified as "psychological" ("eroticism," "altruism," "success," "craziness," "fatigue"); "environmental" ("punishment," "gossip," "food," "work," "appearance"); and "stylistic" ("style," "ending"). Here, for the sake of categorization, some rather arbitrary assumptions were made: "What you do to another person is psychological; what another person does to you is environmental," depending on the "character in the story taken as the point of reference." Ambivalence in the activity-passivity continuum, dynamic concepts of drive, aim, and object, and multiple aspects of the identification process are bypassed in this schema where aggression is classed as psychological and punishment as environmental, according to the rule that "what a person does is more important, in general, than what is done to him."

Frequency norms are given in terms of medians and upper and lower quartiles "for interpretation of the significance....of fantasy material." "Normal" is defined as the interquartile range. "Themes occurring with a greater frequency than the upper quartile should have special significance"; "those occurring less frequently than the lower quartile should play an exceptionally insignificant role." This, of course, tells something about popularity of thematic categories, but nothing about motivating forces at play in their production. Such quantification negates the clinical observation that it is the rare theme or rare variation of a frequent theme that often provides the clue to unique aspects of personality (e.g., as in pathognomonic responses). But this is covered in the assumption that "the only themes that are significantly found in picture-story fantasy material" are the tabulated 30 main themes and their subcategories. Absence is significant only in the case of six main themes (Family, Aggression, Economics, Punishment, Separation, Eroticism) and four subsidiary themes (Mother, Father, Death, Money)—but no others. Only themes other than those listed, in *any* frequency, are considered both rare and signficant.

The author contests the belief that thematic analysis alone can "directly enable one to interpret trends in the overt personality and behavior" as a "gratuitous assumption" that "has not passed the usual tests of validity." Comparative studies of fantasy material and personality descriptions are required. Theme counts, behavior ratings by teachers, estimates of adjustment by the author and his associates, and Sheviakov-Friedberg questionnaire self-ratings by the students were intercorrelated. The usefulness of the kind of theme counting conducted in this study is thrown into question by the author's conclusion that able clinicians often differ on meanings of designated themes, and that themes with apparently different meanings may correlate more highly than ones with the same name or similar meaning.

From a clinical viewpoint, another major weakness of Symonds' theme counting emphasis is that it not only confines significance to thematic prominence or paucity, but it also relegates interpretation to correlation with "overt personality and behavior." The projective hypothesis in clinical use is hampered by preclusion of inferences about existing personality trends imperceptible to observation. The concern shown for verifiability is certainly commendable, but it fails to recognize possibilities of verification through what is now known about thought processes in dream-work, various lapses, and ideational symptom formation. The function of fantasy in the continuum of conscious and subconscious productions is not discussed. The PST in its quantitative application is a limited tally-type or "Geiger counter" kind of instrument for detection of thematic concentrations.

The qualitative applications are actually far more extensive than the normative part of the study indicates, for Symonds also emphasizes that the essence of a projective technique is lost in a psychometric scoring approach, its value being in the "dynamically integrated picture of the inidividual" that the interpreter is able to build from the stories. He also notes that interpreter "subjectivity may consist more of incompleteness rather than inaccuracy." A chapter in *Adolescent Fantasy* (2) on "Comparison of Fantasy and Character" deals with dimensions of personality, including psychoanalytic concepts useful in interpretation (e.g., super-ego, oedipus complex, castration, masochism). A basic principle of interpretation put forth is that conflicts worked out in reality or in symptoms are usually manifested "in behavior and character, but not in fantasy"; another is that the personality may take on a character exactly opposite to the trend expressed in fantasy. Conflict kept from expression in performance will find its way into fantasy. But distinctions of the form of conflict, its origin, level of manifestation in character, symptoms, or behavior, are not differentiated for the test user. However, "principal correspondences" are noted "between the character of the stories and the character of the individuals telling them." A few contrasts are also drawn between "normal, happy," and "less well-adjusted" students.

The test pictures parallel the TAT scenes but contain more youthful figures. It is held that identifications cross age and sex lines, and the same pictures are to be given to both sexes. The possibility of homosexual identification is provided in several pictures with ambivalent attributes (A2, A4, B3) and one shadowy figure without distinctive features (B9).

Those seeking to learn about the nature of adolescence and the fantasy characteristics of this important stage of maturation will be disappointed in the slim chapter (8 pages) on "Characteristics of Adolescent Fantasy." Those who interpret fantasy material according to dynamic concepts of drives, their modifications in expression, and the ebb and flow of conscious and subconscious processes, as well as those needing norms of expressive behavior, will welcome this study as a major contribution to the field of thematic testing.

KENNETH R. NEWTON, *Associate Professor of Psychology, University of Tennessee, Knoxville, Tennessee.*

This test consists of a set of 20 drawings designed to elicit stories from adolescents that will be reflections of their fantasy life. The author has stated quite thoroughly in his manual the procedure to be followed in administering the test. The instructions, which are rather involved and time consuming, do not seem to have any advantage over a more simplified set of instructions.

All pictures involved in this technique were designed and drawn by the same artist. The author does little to defend this procedure other than to state that the stories given might to some extent be influenced by the fantasy life of the artist; he believes, however, that this is not a very important factor. In addition, the author states that he presented the artist with a list of 42 specifications for the various pictures. Then he admits that it is not possible to define how these specifications were developed. Thus, it seems the initial error of having all pictures designed by one artist is further compounded by having the list of specifications for each picture derived by one individual. Another rather consistent error in this technique is the admission that on the whole the pictures are gloomy, severe, morose, and mournful and that there is a certain similarity of expression in all faces utilized. It would seem that these consistent and influential errors would lead to considerable similarity in stories and much transfer from one picture to another.

In the author's initial attempts to standardize this technique, 42 stories were collected from each of 40 normal adolescent boys and girls of junior and senior high school ages. These 1,680 stories were analyzed for their thematic content and an attempt was made to determine norms for various types of themes and interpretations. The statement is made that these stories most successfully revealed the personality when they were interpreted dynamically. This statement is supported with the remark that the stories and their themes are those which would be expected from the findings obtained through dynamic psychology and psychoanalytic theory. This seems somewhat circuitous since any material presented by patients or subjects, when interpreted dynamically, would most likely be in keeping with the findings expected from dynamic psychology.

This is a very long-drawn projective technique which, again admittedly, is operating at its peak of efficiency only after some 20 stories have been presented by the subject. This picture-storytelling technique is apparently an extension of history taking. With this particular test and other similar ones the statement has been made that the more that is known about the individual the greater is the significance of the stories that the individual gives. Thus it seems a thorough history from the patient may very well serve in the place of such a technique. If the individual is verbal enough to give 20 or more stories in response to the pictures, it is likely that he has the verbal facility to give a thorough history which may be of greater value and which may negate the requirement of administering this test. The *Symonds Picture-Story Test* has been designed as an extension of the *Thematic Apperception Test*. It does not, however, appear to be any more adequate a tool than the TAT, except, possibly, for psychologists working exclusively with adolescents.

The manual of directions is quite thorough; however, one should not attempt to administer or interpret from this test without first referring to the author's book *Adolescent Fantasy (2)*. While there has been an attempt made to set up norms for the various findings, the clinical psychologist's experience continues to be the major validation for such a technique.

For a review by E. J. G. Bradford, see 4:132 (1 excerpt); for related reviews, see 4:133.

[162]

*Szondi Test. Ages 4 and over; 1937–52; 8 factors, 4 vectors (each vector is a total of 2 factors): homosexual, sadistic, sexual vector, epileptic, hysteric, paroxysmal vector, catatonic, paranoic, schizophrenic vector, depressive, manic, contact vector; individual or group; IBM; 1 form ('47); $5.50 per Deri manual ('49, see 11 below); $13.50 per Szondi manual ('52, see 87 below); $11 per set of 48 pictures ('47); separate answer sheets may be used; $1.80 per 50 IBM answer sheets ('51, labeled Form D); $3 per 100 profile sheets ('49, labeled Form B); $3 per 50 folders of profile sheet and table of tendency tension ('49, labeled Form A); postage extra; test must be administered "at least six, preferably ten, times with at least one day intervals between administrations"; (10–15) minutes per administration; Lipot Szondi; Hans Huber. * (U.S. distributor: Grune & Stratton, Inc.)

REFERENCES

1–64. See 4:134.

65. GEERS, JOHN BYRON. *Szondi Test Patterns in a Criminal Population.* Master's thesis, Southern Methodist University (Dallas, Tex.), 1950.

66. KELTNER, DONALD. *Comparison of Two Criminal Groups on the Szondi Test.* Master's thesis, Southern Methodist University (Dallas, Tex.), 1950.

67. SAUNDERS, ROGER. *The Effect of an Experimentally Established Frame of Reference on the Consistency of Responses on the Szondi Test.* Master's thesis, Southern Methodist University (Dallas, Tex.), 1950.

68. BALL, MAY TOWNSON. *The Relationship of Szondi Profiles of 100 Drug Addicts and the Psychoanalytic Theory of Drug Addiction.* Master's thesis, Southern Methodist University (Dallas, Tex.), 1951.

69. NEWELL, JOHN MICHAEL. *Reliability Study of the Stimulus Material of the Szondi Test.* Master's thesis, Southern Methodist University (Dallas, Tex.), 1951.

70. PATTERSON, HARRY OSCAR. *A Study of Matching Behavioral Descriptions With Szondi Pictures.* Master's thesis, University of Nebraska (Lincoln, Neb.), 1951.

71. BARRACLOUGH, PATRICIA; COLE, DAVID; AND REEB, MILDRED. "The Influence of Test Instructions on Szondi Results." *J Clin Psychol* 8:165–7 Ap '52. * (*PA* 27:1948)

72. CHANEY, JOHN W., JR. *A Validity Study of the Szondi Test: Comparison of Normal and Alcoholic Subjects in Their Preferences of Eight Szondi Portraits as Presented in Triads.* Master's thesis, Catholic University of America (Washington, D.C.), 1952.

73. DAVID, HENRY P., AND RABINOWITZ, WILLIAM. "Szondi Patterns in Epileptic and Homosexual Males." *J Consult Psychol* 16:247–50 Ag '52. * (*PA* 27:4285)

74. DAVIS, N. ELAINE, AND RAIMY, VICTOR C. "Stimulus Functions of the Szondi Cards." *J Clin Psychol* 8:155–60 Ap '52. * (*PA* 27:1954)

75. DERI, SUSAN K. Chap. 14, "The Szondi Test," pp. 222–33. (*PA* 27:3549) In *Progress in Clinical Psychology, Vol. I,*

Sect. 1. Edited by Daniel Brower and Lawrence E. Abt. New York: Grune & Stratton, Inc., 1952. Pp. xi, 328. *

76. DUDEK, FRANK J. "Determining 'Chance Success' When a Specific Number of Items Are Sorted Into Discrete Categories." *J Consult Psychol* 16:251–6 Ag '52. * (*PA* 27:3880)

77. DUDEK, FRANK J., AND PATTERSON, HARRY O. "Relationships Among the Szondi Test Items." *J Consult Psychol* 16:389–94 O '52. * (*PA* 27:5866)

78. GOLDMAN, GEORGE D. "The Validation of the Paroxysmal Vector of the Szondi Test." *J Abn & Social Psychol* 47:475–7 Ap '52. * (*PA* 27:2723)

79. GUERTIN, WILSON H., AND RABIN, ALBERT I. "The Szondi Test as a Forced-Choice Technique." *J Clin Psychol* 8:161–4 Ap '52. * (*PA* 27:1962)

80. HARROWER, MOLLY. *Appraising Personality: The Use of Psychological Tests in the Practice of Medicine,* pp. 115–38. New York: W. W. Norton & Co., Inc., 1952. Pp. xvii, 197. * (*PA* 27:6532)

81. JACKSON, VICTOR A. *Factors in Preferences for Szondi Test Pictures.* Doctor's thesis, University of Chicago (Chicago, Ill.), 1952. (Abstract: *Am Psychol* 7:347)

82. KOBLER, ARTHUR L. *An Experimental Examination of the Szondi Test as a Clinical Tool.* Doctor's thesis, University of Kansas (Lawrence, Kan.), 1952.

83. MUSSEN, PAUL H., AND KRAUSS, SHIRLEY R. "An Investigation of the Diagnostic Validity of the Szondi Test." *J Abn & Social Psychol* 47:399–405 Ap '52. * (*PA* 27:2750)

84. RABIN, ALBERT I. "Genetic Factors in the Selection and Rejection of Szondi's Pictures: A Study of Twins." *Am J Orthopsychiatry* 22:551–6 Jl '52. * (*PA* 27:5159)

85. RICHARDSON, HELEN M. "The Discriminability of the 'Drive Factors' Represented in the Szondi Pictures." *J Clin Psychol* 8:384–90 O '52. * (*PA* 27:5896)

86. SCHERER, I. W.; WINNE, J. F.; PAGE, H. A.; AND LIPTON, H. "An Analysis of Patient-Examiner Interaction With the Szondi Pictures." *J Proj Tech* 16:225–37 Je '52. * (*PA* 28:2673)

87. SZONDI, L. *Experimental Diagnostics of Drives.* New York: Grune & Stratton, Inc., 1952. Pp. x, 254. * (*PA* 27:5910)

88. WARNER, F. L. *A Szondi of Some Schizophrenic Patients Before and After Shock.* Master's thesis, Pacific University (Forest Grove, Ore.), 1952.

89. BEST, HAROLD L., AND SZOLLOSI, ETIENNE. "Recognition as a Criterion in the Szondi Test." *J Clin Psychol* 9:75–6 Ja '53. * (*PA* 27:7755)

90. BORSTELMANN, L. J., AND KLOPFER, W. G. "The Szondi Test: A Review and Critical Evaluation." *Psychol B* 50:112–32 Mr '53. * (*PA* 28:931)

91. DAVID, HENRY P.; ORNE, MARTIN; AND RABINOWITZ, WILLIAM. "Qualitative and Quantitative Szondi Diagnosis." *J Proj Tech* 17:75–8 Mr '53. * (*PA* 28:2623)

92. FLEISHMAN, MARTIN. *An Experimental Investigation of the Validity of the Szondi Test.* Doctor's thesis, University of California (Los Angeles, Calif.), 1953.

93. GORDON, LEONARD V. "A Factor Analysis of the 48 Szondi Pictures." *J Psychol* 36:387–92 O '53. * (*PA* 28:4356)

94. RAY, J. B., AND HILL, VIRGIL T. "Szondi and Matching Probabilities." *Szondi Newsl* 4:16–22 O '53. *

95. SAUNDERS, WILLIAM WINSTON. "A Methodology for the Testing of Two Assumptions Basic to Szondi Test Theory." *Szondi Newsl* 4:22–4 O '53. *

96. SIMPSON, WILLIAM H., AND HILL, VIRGIL T. "The Effects of Verbal Reward and Punishment Upon Picture Selection on the Szondi Test." *Szondi Newsl* 4:2–15 O '53. *

97. STEINBERG, ARTHUR. "Szondi's Pictures: Discrimination of Diagnoses as a Function of Psychiatric Experience and of Internal Consistency." *J Proj Tech* 17:340–8 S '53. * (*PA* 28:4397)

98. CASTON, WILLIAM FRANK. *The Szondi Test and Criminality.* Doctor's thesis, Vanderbilt University (Nashville, Tenn.), 1954. (*DA* 14:1096)

99. COHEN, JACOB, AND FEIGENBAUM, LOUIS. "The Assumption of Additivity on the Szondi Test." *J Proj Tech* 18:11–6 Mr '54. * (*PA* 29:913)

100. DAVID, HENRY P. "A Szondi Test Bibliography, 1939–1953." *J Proj Tech* 18:17–32 Mr '54. * (*PA* 29:914)

101. DERI, SUSAN K. "Introduction to This Issue." *J Proj Tech* 18:3–4 Mr '54. *

102. DERI, SUSAN K. "Differential Diagnosis of Delinquents With the Szondi Test." *J Proj Tech* 18:33–41 Mr '54. (*PA* 29:1197)

103. FLEISHMAN, MARTIN. "The Discriminative Power of Szondi's Quotient of Tendency Tension." *J Proj Tech* 18:42–6 Mr '54. * (*PA* 29:916)

104. FLEISHMAN, MARTIN. "The Discriminative Power of Szondi's Syndromes." *J Consult Psychol* 18:89–95 Ap '54. * (*PA* 29:2443)

105. GORDON, LEONARD V., AND LAMBERT, EDWARD J. "The Internal Consistency of the Szondi 'Factors.'" *J Social Psychol* 40:67–71 Ag '54. * (*PA* 29:5705)

106. HILL, VIRGIL T. *The Szondi Test With Children: A Critical Evaluation of Theory and Practice.* Doctor's thesis, University of Oklahoma (Norman, Okla.), 1954.

107. KRIMSKY, MARTIN L. "The Szondi Test in a Psychological Battery: Two Case Studies." *J Proj Tech* 18:47–59 Mr '54. * (*PA* 29:932)

108. LEFFORD, ARTHUR. *An Experimental Study of the Szondi Test Stimuli.* Doctor's thesis, New York University (New York, N.Y.), 1954. *(DA* 15:1111)

109. MOSER, ULRICH. "The Determination of the Relative Strength of Masculine-Feminine Drives by Means of the Szondi Procedure." *J Proj Tech* 18:75–88 Mr '54. * *(PA* 29:938)

110. SAUNDERS, WILLIAM W. *A Methodology for the Testing of Two Assumptions Basic to Szondi Test Theory.* Doctor's thesis, University of Oklahoma (Norman, Okla.), 1954.

111. SCHUBERT, JOSEF. "The Stimulus Value of the Szondi Pictures: A Theoretical and Empirical Study." *J Proj Tech* 18: 95–106 Mr '54. * *(PA* 29:953)

112. SHORT, PHILIP L. "Experiments on the Rationale of the Szondi Test." *J Mental Sci* 100:384–92 Ap '54. * *(PA* 29: 2477)

113. VAN KREVELEN, ALICE. "Some Effects of Subject-Examiner Interaction on Projective Test Performance." *J Proj Tech* 18:107–9 Mr '54. * *(PA* 29:963)

114. CORTNER, ROBERT H. *The Relationship of Diagnostic Criteria of the Rorschach and Szondi Tests and Psychiatric Diagnosis in a Military Population.* Master's thesis, St. Louis University (St. Louis, Mo.), 1955.

115. KLEIN, ABRAHAM. "A Preliminary Comparative Study of Some Szondi and Rorschach Test Variables." Abstract. *J Personality* 23:499 Je '55. *

116. KORKES, LENORE, AND LEWIS, NOLAN D. C. "An Analysis of the Relationship Between Psychological Patterns and Outcome in Pulmonary Tuberculosis." *J Nerv & Mental Dis* 122:524–63 D '55. *

117. PEARL, DAVID, AND JACOBS, DURAND. "Sociometric Choice and the Szondi Test." *J Clin Psychol* 11:385–8 O '55. * *(PA* 30:5996)

118. SAUNDERS, ROGER E., AND NORTH, ALVIN J. "The Effect of an Experimentally Established Frame of Reference on the Consistency of Responses on the Szondi Test." Abstract. *J Personality* 23:500 Je '55. *

119. SCOTT, EDWARD M. "An Investigation of Juvenile Profiles on the Szondi Test." *J Clin Psychol* 11:46–50 Ja '55. * *(PA* 29:7317)

120. FANCHER, EDWIN C. "A Comparative Study of Adolescents With the Szondi Test." *J Genetic Psychol* 88:89–93 Mr '56. * *(PA* 31:4685)

121. FANCHER, EDWIN C., AND WEINSTEIN, MORRIS. "A Szondi Study of Developmental and Cultural Factors in Personality: The Seven-Year-Old." *J Genetic Psychol* 88:81–8 Mr '56. * *(PA* 31:4686)

122. GRANT, RICHARD A. "Institutional Adjustment of Prison Inmates and the Szondi Paroxysmal Vector." *Szondi Newsl* 5: 8–11 Ap '56. * *(PA* 31:1393)

123. KRIMSKY, MARTIN. "The Application of the 'Shadow Method' in Szondi Test Interpretation." *Szondi Newsl* 5:3–7 F '56. * *(PA* 31:1047)

124. KRIMSKY, MARTIN. "A Szondi Profile Followed by an Epileptic Seizure." *Szondi Newsl* 5:12 Ap '56. * *(PA* 31:1569)

125. LASZLO, CARL. "On the Modification of the Szondi Test (L-Test)." *Szondi Newsl* 5:2–7 Ap '56. * *(PA* 31:1049)

126. MAHONEY, STANLEY C. "Szondi Bibliography: 1954–1955." *Szondi Newsl* 5:13–5 Ap '56. * *(PA* 31:1055)

127. RAINWATER, LEE. "A Study of Personality Differences Between Middle and Lower Class Adolescents: The Szondi Test in Culture-Personality Research." *Genetic Psychol Monogr* 54: 3–86 Ag '56. *

128. AUMACK, LEWIS. "The Szondi: Internal or External Validation?" *Percept & Motor Skills* 7:7–15 Mr '57. * *(PA* 32:4162)

129. HURLEY, JOHN R. "Psychodiagnostic Limitations of Szondi Interseries Changes." *J Clin Psychol* 13:396–9 O '57. *

130. LASSOFF, SAUL. *The Ability of the Szondi Test to Differentiate Between Law Students and Theology Students.* Doctor's thesis, University of Denver (Denver, Colo.), 1957.

131. LINGOES, JAMES C. "Minnesota Multiphasic Personality Inventory Test Correlates of Szondi Picture Preferences." *Szondi Newsl* 6:1–6 S '57. *

132. MAHONEY, STANLEY, AND KRIMSKY, MARTIN. "Validity, Interpretation, and the Szondi Test." *Szondi Newsl* 6:7–12 S '57. *

133. MORRIS, JOHN R., JR. "A Szondi Study of an Atypical Child." *Szondi Newsl* 6:6–8 D '57. *

134. PASEWARK, RICHARD ARTHUR. *The Use of Finger Paintings in Differentiating Epileptics and Paranoid Schizophrenics: An Evaluation of the Identification Hypotheses Underlying the Szondi Test.* Doctor's thesis, New York University (New York, N.Y.), 1957. *(DA* 17:1814)

135. RAY, THOMAS S., AND OLDROYD, CARL R. "Skin Resistance Changes and Individual Personality Factors as Reflected in the Szondi Test: A Pilot Study." *Szondi Newsl* 6:1–5 D '57. *

136. SILVERSTEIN, A. B. " 'Diagnosing' Szondi's Pictures." *J Proj Tech* 21:396–8 D '57. *

137. FRIEDMAN, BERT. *A Study of the Szondi Assumptions of Identification Utilizing Modified Versions of the Rosenzweig P-F Study on Criminal Groups.* Master's thesis, Fordham University (New York, N.Y.), 1958.

138. HARROWER, MOLLY. "The First Offender: A Study of Juvenile Delinquents by the Szondi Test." *Szondi Newsl* 6:1–16 Je '58. *

For reviews by Ardie Lubin and Albert I. Rabin, see 4:134; for a review by Susan K. Deri, see 3:100; for related reviews, see B418 and 4:135.

[163]

★A Test of Family Attitudes. Ages 6–12; 1952; pictorial projection; individual; no data on reliability; no norms; 12s. 6d. per manual, postage extra; (30–60) minutes; Lydia Jackson; Methuen & Co. Ltd. *

REFERENCES
1. JACKSON, LYDIA. "Emotional Attitudes Towards the Family of Normal, Neurotic and Delinquent Children." *Brit J Psychol* 41:35–51 S '50. * *(PA* 25:3740)
2. JACKSON, LYDIA. "Emotional Attitudes Towards the Family of Normal, Neurotic and Delinquent Children, Part II." *Brit J Psychol* 41:173–85 D '50. * *(PA* 25:7975)

JOHN E. BELL, *Acting Chief, Mental Health Services, United States Public Health Service, San Francisco, California.*

The *Test of Family Attitudes* is a picture-story test based on a set of seven specially designed pictures portraying situations between children and adults. The drawings represent relations likely to arouse emotion in the child. They convey impressions of maternal protection and child dependence, the child's exclusion from intimacy between the parents, adaptation to a sibling in the presence of the parents (two forms of this picture are available, one for each sex), isolation as punishment, the possibility of aggression from a father figure, the attraction of forbidden fruit, and a clash between the parents in the child's presence. The pictures are published in a convenient, small manual (5 by 7 inches), along with a description of the test, a report of an initial evaluation of its use with normal (n = 40), neurotic (n = 40), and delinquent (n = 30) boys and girls, simple instructions, and a set of standard questions to ask about each picture.

The test appears to offer little advantage over other picture-story methods, such as the TAT, CAT, and pictures used by Mallet, LeShan and LeShan, and others. Whether an examiner would find the pictures of this test more suitable than others for exploring children's experiences with their parents and consequent attitudes towards them would be a matter of taste or experience. It is evident from the pictures that the parent-child dimension of the family is more adequately represented than the sibling bond. The pictures tend to depict the parents together rather than singly.

Through a method such as this test uses, one is exploring the characteristics of an individual's memories, fantasies, feelings, and concepts about families, including his own. Action and communication vectors that actually exist in his family may be reflected, but the test offers no opportunity for verifying the authenticity of these forms of behavior. Thus, interpretations of the family life must be cautiously advanced and tested against reality through observation of other members of the family, especially as they interact. Because the test carries a title that might imply that it is a potential source of information about families, it might be well to recognize that it is essentially a test of a child's attitudes toward his parents and sibs. It does not tap attitudes of all members of a family, and thus does not yield data on habits of mind in all the various interrelationships, e.g., between parents, between parents and children. More precisely, it might be called a test of attitudes toward family rather than a test of family attitudes.

[164]

Thematic Apperception Test. Ages 4 and over; 1936–43; commonly known as TAT; individual; 1 form ('43); no data on reliability; $6 per set of test materials; 50¢ per manual ('43); cash orders postpaid; 100(120) minutes in 2 sessions 1 day apart; Henry A. Murray; Harvard University Press. * (*TAT Summary Record Blank.* 1952; $1.55 per set of 35 record blanks and manual, postage extra; 20¢ per specimen set, postpaid; Pauline G. Vorhaus; World Book Co. *)

REFERENCES

1–101. See 3:103.
102–299. See 4:136.
300. SAXE, CARL HERMAN. *A Comparison of Personality Description Obtained From the Thematic Apperception Test and From Therapeutic Contacts.* Doctor of education report, Teachers College, Columbia University (New York, N.Y.), 1947.
301. GARDNER, BURLEIGH B. "What Makes Successful and Unsuccessful Executives?" *Adv Mgmt* 13:116–25 S '48. * (*PA* 23:967)
302. McCLELLAND, DAVID C., AND ATKINSON, JOHN W. "The Projective Expression of Needs: I, The Effect of Different Intensities of the Hunger Drive on Perception." *J Psychol* 25:205–22 Ja '48. *
303. MITCHELL, DOROTHY PAULA. *The Validity of the Thematic Apperception Test and Its Implications for Group Therapy.* Master's thesis, University of Oklahoma (Norman, Okla.), 1949.
304. BRICE, BARBARA C. *A Pilot Study of the Relationship of Selected Voice Quality Deviations and Anxiety Level as Determined by the Thematic Apperception Test.* Master's thesis, Florida State University (Tallahassee, Fla.), 1950.
305. PITTLUCK, P. *The Relation Between Aggressive Fantasy and Overt Behavior.* Doctor's thesis, Yale University (New Haven, Conn.), 1950.
306. BIALICK, IRVING. *The Relationship Between Reactions to Authority Figures on the T.A.T. and Overt Behavior in an Authority Situation by Hospital Patients.* Doctor's thesis, University of Pittsburgh (Pittsburgh, Pa.), 1951.
307. BRADT, KENNETH HAROLD. *Effect of Personal Interview Upon College Grade Performance.* Doctor's thesis, Northwestern University (Evanston, Ill.), 1951.
308. CARLILE, J. ST H. *A Comparison of a Thematic Apperception Test as Applied to Neurotic and Non-Neurotic Children.* Master's thesis, University of London (London, England), 1951.
309. CHRISTENSEN, ARDEN HANS. *A Quantitative Study of Personality Dynamics in Stuttering and Nonstuttering Siblings.* Doctor's thesis, University of Southern California (Los Angeles, Calif.), 1951.
310. FIELD, WILLIAM FRANKLIN. *The Effects on Thematic Apperception of Certain Experimentally Aroused Needs.* Doctor's thesis, University of Maryland (College Park, Md.), 1951.
311. LUCE, GEORGE C. *A Study of Emotional Tone in the Thematic Apperception Test Stories of Paranoid Schizophrenics and Anxiety State Neurotics.* Master's thesis, University of Western Ontario (London, Ont., Canada), 1951.
312. MORGAN, HENRY HOLLINSHEAD. *An Analysis of Certain Structured and Unstructured Test Results of Achieving and Nonachieving High Ability College Students.* Doctor's thesis, University of Minnesota (Minneapolis, Minn.), 1951. (*DA* 12:335)
313. MURNEY, RICHARD G. *The Relationship Between Certain Thematic Apperception Test and Rorschach Test Scores.* Master's thesis, Catholic University of America (Washington, D.C.), 1951.
314. OSTERBERG, MARY N. *A Comparison of Aggression in Dreams and TAT Stories.* Master's thesis, Western Reserve University (Cleveland, Ohio), 1951.
315. ROE, ANNE. "A Psychological Study of Eminent Biologists." *Psychol Monogr* 65(14):1–68 '51. * (*PA* 27:1516)
316. SHNEIDMAN, EDWIN S.; JOEL, WALTHER; AND LITTLE, KENNETH B. "An Empirical Categorization of Psychological Test Report Items." Abstract. *Am Psychol* 6:492 S '51. *
317. SRIVASTAVA, SITAWAR SARAN. "Curative Use of T.A.T. Pictures in a Case of Mental Disorder." *Samiksa* 5:189–95 no 3 '51. * (*PA* 27:1187)
318. THURSTON, JOHN R., AND MUSSEN, PAUL H. "Infant Feeding Gratification and Adult Personality." *J Personality* 19:449–58 Je '51. * (*PA* 26:3335)
319. BEIGEL, HUGO G. "The Influence of Body Position on Mental Processes." *J Clin Psychol* 8:193–99 Ap '52. * (*PA* 27:1768)
320. BELLAK, LEOPOLD, AND ORT, EILEEN. Chap. 9, "Thematic Apperception Test and Other Apperceptive Methods," pp. 149–72. (*PA* 27:3542) In *Progress in Clinical Psychology, Vol. I, Sect. 1.* Edited by Daniel Brower and Lawrence E. Abt. New York: Grune & Stratton, Inc., 1952. Pp. xi, 328. *
321. BLUM, GERALD S., AND MILLER, DANIEL R. "Exploring the Psychoanalytic Theory of the 'Oral Character.' " *J Personality* 20:287–304 Mr '52. * (*PA* 27:2353)
322. CARLILE, JUNE ST H. "The Thematic Apperception Test Applied to Neurotic and Normal Adolescent Girls." *Brit J Med Psychol* 25:244–8 pt 4 '52. * (*PA* 27:7947)
323. CARLSEN, NORAH. *The Relationship Between Empathy and Adjustment as Shown in the Thematic Apperception Test.* Master's thesis, University of Toronto (Toronto, Ont., Canada), 1952.
324. CATTELL, R. B., AND WENIG, P. W. "Dynamic and Cognitive Factors Controlling Misperception." *J Abn & Social Psychol* 47:797–809 O '52. * (*PA* 27:5000)
325. CAUDILL, WILLIAM. "Japanese-American Personality and Acculturation." *Genetic Psychol Monogr* 45:61–102 F '52. * (*PA* 27:3466)
326. CLARK, RUSSELL A. "The Projective Measurement of Experimentally Induced Levels of Sexual Motivation." *J Exp Psychol* 44:391–9 D '52. *
327. COOK, RICHARD A. "Identification and Ego Defensiveness in Thematic Apperception." Abstract. *J Colo–Wyo Acad Sci* 4:83 O '52. *
328. DAVENPORT, BEVERLY FEST. *The Ambiguity, Universality, and Reliable-Discrimination of TAT Interpretations.* Doctor's thesis, University of Southern California (Los Angeles, Calif.), 1952.
329. DAVENPORT, BEVERLY FEST. "The Semantic Validity of TAT Interpretations." *J Consult Psychol* 16:171–5 Je '52. * (*PA* 27:5146)
330. FRY, FRANKLYN D. *A Normative Study of the Reactions Manifested by College Students, and by State Prison Inmates in Response to the Minnesota Multiphasic Personality Inventory, the Rosenzweig Picture Frustration Study, and the Thematic Apperception Test.* Doctor's thesis, Pennsylvania State College (State College, Pa.), 1952. (*J Psychol* 34:27–30 Jl '52. *) (*PA* 27:2976)
331. GARFIELD, SOL L.; BLEK, L.; AND MELKER, F. "The Influence of Method of Administration and Sex Differences on Selected Aspects of TAT Stories." *J Consult Psychol* 16:140–4 Ap '52. * (*PA* 27:2718)
332. GILHOOLY, FRANCIS M. *The Validity and Reliability of the Rorschach and the Thematic Apperception Tests When These Tests Are Interpreted by the Method of Blind Analysis.* Doctor's thesis, Fordham University (New York, N.Y.), 1952.
333. GOODMAN, MORRIS. "An Indirect Validation of a Thematic Apperception Test Scoring Manual." *J Clin Psychol* 8:149–54 Ap '52. * (*PA* 27:1960)
334. GORDON, HIRAM L. *A Comparative Study of Dream Analysis and the Thematic Apperception Test as Projective Techniques.* Doctor's thesis, Duke University (Durham, N. C.), 1952.
335. HASSOL, LEONARD; CAMERON, NORMAN; AND MAGARET, ANN. "The Production of Scattered Speech via Personalized Distraction: An Investigation of Continuity in Normal and Schizophrenic Language." Abstract. *Am Psychol* 7:351–2 Jl '52. *
336. HERMAN, GLORIA N. *A Comparison of the Thematic Apperception Test Stories of Pre-Adolescent School Children Differing in Social Acceptance.* Master's thesis, University of Toronto (Toronto, Ont., Canada), 1952.
337. HOLT, ROBERT R. "Interpretation of Jay's Thematic Apperception Test: The Case of Jay: Interpretations and Discussion." *J Proj Tech* 16:457–61, discussion 444–5, 462–73 D '52. * (*PA* 28:2678)
338. HOLT, ROBERT R. "TAT Bibliography: Supplement for 1951." *J Proj Tech* 16:114–23 Mr '52. * (*PA* 27:428)
339. HOLT, ROBERT R., AND LUBORSKY, LESTER. "Research in the Selection of Psychiatrists: A Second Interim Report." *B Menninger Clinic* 16:125–35 Jl '52. * (*PA* 27:3916)

340. HOWARD, KENNETH GILBERT. *Certain Variables in the Thematic Apperception Test.* Master's thesis, University of Western Ontario (London, Ont., Canada), 1952.

341. IVERSON, NORMAN E. *A Descriptive Study of Some Personality Relationships Underlying a Range of Speaker Confidence, as Determined by the Thematic Apperception Test.* Doctor's thesis, University of Denver (Denver, Colo.), 1952.

342. KAPLAN, HAROLD; HAUCK, HERBERT; AND KLEINMAN, MILTON L. "An Unusual Response to the Thematic Apperception Test." *Am J Psychiatry* 108:918-20 Je '52. * (*PA* 27:1969)

343. KEELY, H. W., AND GLAD, DONALD D. "The Schizophrenic Thematic Apperception Test Responses and Behavior in Acutely Psychotic and Social Remission Stages." Abstract. *J Colo-Wyo Acad Sci* 4:82 O '52. *

344. KIEFER, R. *TAT Normative Data From Common Stories Told by Normal Adult Females.* Master's thesis, University of Alberta (Edmonton, Alta., Canada), 1952.

345. KLEHR, HAROLD. "An Investigation of Some Personality Factors in Women With Rheumatoid Arthritis." Abstract. *Am Psychol* 7:344-5 Jl '52. *

346. LEVINSON, DANIEL J. "Criminality From a Sense of Guilt: A Case Study and Some Research Hypotheses." *J Personality* 20:402-29 Je '52. * (*PA* 27:3679)

347. LINDZEY, GARDNER. "Thematic Apperception Test: Interpretive Assumptions and Related Empirical Evidence." *Psychol B* 49:1-25 Ja '52. * (*PA* 27:435)

348. LOWE, WILLIAM F. "Effect of Controlling the Immediate Environment of Responses to the Thematic Apperception Test." Abstract. *Percept & Motor Skills Res Exch* 4:98 '52. *

349. McDONALD, FRANKLIN RANDOLPH. *The Effect of Differential Cultural Pressures on Projective Test Performances of Negroes.* Doctor's thesis, University of Southern California (Los Angeles, Calif.), 1952.

350. McDOWELL, JAMES V. *Developmental Aspects of Phantasy Production on the Thematic Apperception Test.* Doctor's thesis, Ohio State University (Columbus, Ohio), 1952.

351. MALCOM, EDWARD VARTAN. *A Study of the Validity of Individual Personality Profiles Based on Each of Four Projective Techniques.* Doctor's thesis, University of Michigan (Ann Arbor, Mich.), 1952. (*DA* 12:221)

352. MARQUIS, DOROTHY P.; SINNETT, E. ROBERT; AND WINTER, WILLIAM D. "A Psychological Study of Peptic Ulcer Patients." *J Clin Psychol* 8:266-72 Jl '52. * (*PA* 27:6072)

353. MASON, BETH. "Social Class and the TAT." Abstract. *Percept & Motor Skills Res Exch* 4:41 '52. *

354. MASON, BETH B. "An Experimental Investigation of the Effect of Repetition and Variation in Administration Upon the Thematic Apperception Test." Abstract. *Percept & Motor Skills Res Exch* 4:98 '52. *

355. MORGAN, HENRY H. "A Psychometric Comparison of Achieving and Nonachieving College Students of High Ability." *J Consult Psychol* 16:292-8 Ag '52. * (*PA* 27:4570)

356. PALMER, JAMES O. "A Note on the Intercard Reliability of the Thematic Apperception Test." *J Consult Psychol* 16:473-4 D '52. * (*PA* 28:964)

357. PARK, PAUL DAVID. *The Performance of Normal and Schizophrenic Adult Males on the Thematic Apperception Test in Terms of: Transcendent Reactions; Categorized Affectivity; and Verbal Enumeration.* Doctor's thesis, Yeshiva University (New York, N.Y.), 1952. (*DA* 13:1262)

358. PIOTROWSKI, ZYGMUNT A. "The Thematic Apperception Test of a Schizophrenic Interpreted According to New Rules." *Psychoanalytic R* 39:230-51 Jl '52. * (*PA* 27:5308)

359. PITTS, M. HENRY. *An Experimental Study of the Influence of Social Psychological Factors Upon Production in the Thematic Apperception Test.* Doctor's thesis, University of Chicago (Chicago, Ill.), 1952.

360. RACUSEN, FRANCES R. *An Exploratory Investigation of the Creativity and Productivity Variables on the Rorschach and Thematic Apperception Tests.* Doctor's thesis. State University of Iowa (Iowa City, Iowa), 1952. (Abstract: *Am Psychol* 8:417)

361. RICHARDS, T. W. "Personality of the Convulsive Patient in Military Service." *Psychol Monogr* 66(14):1-23 '52. * (*PA* 27:7364)

362. RITTER, ANNE M., AND ERON, LEONARD D. "The Use of the Thematic Apperception Test to Differentiate Normal From Abnormal Groups." *J Abn & Social Psychol* 47:147-58 Ap '52. * (*PA* 27:2758)

363. SAMUELS, HENRY. "The Validity of Personality-Trait Ratings Based on Projective Techniques." *Psychol Monogr* 66(5):1-21 '52. * (*PA* 27:5161)

364. SHIPLEY, THOMAS E., JR., AND VEROFF, JOSEPH. "A Projective Measure of Need for Affiliation." *J Exp Psychol* 43:349-56 My '52. * (*PA* 27:5163)

365. SHNEIDMAN, EDWIN S. "The Case of Jay: Psychological Test and Anamnestic Data." *J Proj Tech* 16:297-345 S '52. * (*PA* 28:2676)

366. SHNEIDMAN, EDWIN S., EDITOR. "The TAT Newsletter." Vol. 6, Nos. 1-4." *J Proj Tech* 16:260-5, 378-82, 510-4 Je, S, D '52. *

367. SONTAG, L. W.; CRANDALL, VAUGHN; AND LACEY, JOHN I. "Dynamics of Personality: Resolution of Infantile Dependent Need." Discussion by Harold H. Anderson. *Am J Orthopsychiatry* 22:534-41 Jl '52. * (*PA* 27:5010)

368. SUTTER, EVERETT L. *Some Audio-Mirror Effects of the Thematic Apperception Test Stories Upon Self Awareness.* Doctor's thesis, University of Texas (Austin, Tex.), 1952.

369. TERRY, DOROTHY. "The Use of a Rating Scale of Level of Response in TAT Stories." *J Abn & Social Psychol* 47:507-11 Ap '52. * (*PA* 27:2766)

370. TUMEN, ETHEL. *A Comparison of TAT Personality Readings With Psychoanalytic Findings.* Master's thesis, City College of New York (New York, N.Y.), 1952.

371. VORHAUS, PAULINE G. "Case Study of an Adolescent Boy With Reading Disability." *J Proj Tech* 16:20-41 Mr '52. *

372. WEBSTER, HAROLD. "Rao's Multiple Discriminant Technique Applied to Three TAT Variables." *J Abn & Social Psychol* 47:641-8 Jl '52. * (*PA* 27:3566)

373. WEISSKOPF, EDITH A., AND DUNLEVY, GEORGE P., JR. "Bodily Similarity Between Subject and Central Figure in the TAT as an Influence on Projection." *J Abn & Social Psychol* 47:441-5 Ap '52. * (*PA* 27:2770)

374. WILSON, CLAUDE E. "Differences Between Personal Characteristics of Students Who Have Failed in High School and Those Who Have Not Failed." *Yearb Nat Council Meas Used Ed* 9:42-50 '52. *

375. WRIGHT, CARL S. *Age and Associated Characteristics Affecting Cross-Identification of Sex on the Thematic Apperception Test.* Doctor's thesis, Western Reserve University (Cleveland, Ohio), 1952.

376. BELL, ALICE; TROSMAN, HARRY; AND ROSS, DONALD. "The Use of Projective Techniques in the Investigation of Emotional Aspects of General Medical Disorders: Part II, Other Projective Techniques and Suggestions for Experimental Design." *J Proj Tech* 17:51-60 Mr '53. * (*PA* 28:2614)

377. BERGMAN, MURRAY, AND FISHER, LOUISE A. "The Value of the Thematic Apperception Test in Mental Deficiency." *Psychiatric Q Sup* 27:22-42 pt 1 '53. * (*PA* 28:1176)

378. BERNTSON, R. K. *A Study of Adolescent Development as Reflected by the Thematic Apperception Test.* Master's thesis, Utah State Agricultural College (Logan, Utah), 1953.

379. BILLS, NORMAN. *The Personality Structure of Alcoholics, Homosexuals, and Paranoids as Revealed by Their Responses to the Thematic Apperception Test.* Doctor's thesis, Western Reserve University (Cleveland, Ohio), 1953

380. BRAMLETTE, CARL A., JR. *Some Relationships Between the Self-Concept, the Thematic Apperception Test, and Personality Adjustment.* Doctor's thesis, Duke University (Durham, N.C.), 1953.

381. BUCHER, S. *A Study of the Thematic Apperception Test Applied to a Group of Girls Aged 11 to 13 Years.* Master's thesis, University of London (London, England), 1953.

382. BURGESS, ELVA. *Personality Factors in Over- and Under-Achievers in Engineering.* Doctor's thesis, Pennsylvania State College (State College, Pa.), 1953.

383. CANTER, FRANCIS M. "Personality Factors in Seizure States With Reference to the Rosenzweig Triadic Hypothesis." *J Consult Psychol* 17:429-35 D '53. * (*PA* 28:7844)

384. CHAPIN, NED. "A Dynamic Approach to the TAT." *Psychiatric Q Sup* 27:62-89 pt 1 '53. * (*PA* 28:935)

385. COOK, RICHARD A. "Identification and Ego Defensiveness in Thematic Apperception." *J Proj Tech* 17:312-9 S '53. * (*PA* 28:4343)

386. DAVISON, ARTHUR H. "A Comparison of the Fantasy Productions on the Thematic Apperception Test of Sixty Hospitalized Psychoneurotic and Psychotic Patients." *J Proj Tech* 17:20-33 Mr '53. * (*PA* 28:2810)

387. DUNLEVY, GEORGE P., JR. *Intentional Modification of Thematic Apperception Test Stories as a Function of Adjustment.* Doctor's thesis, Purdue University (Lafayette, Ind.), 1953.

388. ERON, LEONARD D. "Responses of Women to the Thematic Apperception Test." *J Consult Psychol* 17:269-82 Ag '53. * (*PA* 28:4350)

389. FOULDS, GRAHAM. "A Method of Scoring the T.A.T. Applied to Psychoneurotics." *J Mental Sci* 99:235-46 Ap '53. * (*PA* 28:943)

390. FRY, FRANKLYN D. "Manual for Scoring the Thematic Apperception Test." *J Psychol* 35:181-95 Ap '53. * (*PA* 28:945)

391. FRY, FRANKLYN D. "TAT Scoring Blank." *J Psychol* 35:197-200 Ap '53. * (*PA* 28:946)

392. GLADWIN, THOMAS, AND SARASON, SEYMOUR B. *Truk: Man in Paradise,* pp. 209-46, 290-462, 573-651. Viking Fund Publications in Anthropology, No. 20. New York: Wenner-Gren Foundation for Anthropological Research, Inc., 1953. Pp. 774. *

393. GLUCK, MARTIN RICHARD. *A Study of the Relationship Between the Amount of Hostility in the Content of Projective Techniques and the Amount of Hostility Expressed in Behavior.* Doctor's thesis, University of Pittsburgh (Pittsburgh, Pa.), 1953.

394. GORDON, HIRAM L. "A Comparative Study of Dreams and Responses to the Thematic Apperception Test: I, A Need-Press Analysis." *J Personality* 22:234-53 D '53. * (*PA* 28:6006)

395. GREENBAUM, MARVIN; QUALTERE, THOMAS; CARRUTH, BRUCE; AND CRUICKSHANK, WILLIAM. "Evaluation of a Modification of the Thematic Apperception Test for Use With Physically Handicapped Children." *J Clin Psychol* 9:40-4 Ja '53. * (*PA* 27:7770)

396. HARRISON, ROSS. "The Thematic Apperception Test."

Monogr Soc Res Child Develop 16(53):60–88, 214–316 '53. *
(*PA* 28:4077)

397. KADIS, ASYA L.; GREENE, JANET S.; AND FREEDMAN, NORBERT. "Early Childhood Recollections—An Integrative Technique of Personality Test Data." *Am J Indiv Psychol* 10:31–42 nos 1–2 '52–53 ['53]. * (*PA* 28:910)

398. KENNY, DOUGLAS T., AND BIJOU, SIDNEY W. "Ambiguity of Pictures and Extent of Personality Factors in Fantasy Responses." *J Consult Psychol* 17:283–8 Ag '53. * (*PA* 28:4367)

399. KLINE, MILTON V. "An Hypnotic Experimental Approach to the Genesis of Occupational Interests and Choice: II, The Thematic Apperception Test (A Case Report)." *J General Psychol* 48:79–82 Ja '53. * (*PA* 28:1114)

400. KLINE, MILTON V., AND HAGGERTY, ARTHUR D. "An Hypnotic Experimental Approach to the Genesis of Occupational Interests and Choice: III, Hypnotic Age Regression and the Thematic Apperception Test—A Clinical Case Study in Occupational Identification." *J Clin & Exp Hypnosis* 1:18–31 Jl '53. * (*PA* 28:2802)

401. KNEHR, C. A.; VICKERY, A.; AND GUY, M. "Problem-Action Responses and Emotions in Thematic Apperception Test Stories Recounted by Alcoholic Patients." *J Psychol* 35:201–26 Ap '53. * (*PA* 28:1232)

402. LEVIN, BERNARD MYRON. *Predicting Progress in Psychotherapy: A Comparison of Thematic Apperception Test Results and Psychiatric Judgments.* Doctor's thesis, University of Pittsburgh (Pittsburgh, Pa.), 1953.

403. LINDZEY, GARDNER, AND GOLDBERG, MORTON. "Motivational Differences Between Male and Female as Measured by the Thematic Apperception Test." *J Personality* 22:101–17 S '53. * (*PA* 28:4372)

404. LUBORSKY, LESTER. "Self-Interpretation of the TAT as a Clinical Technique." *J Proj Tech* 17:217–23 Je '53. * (*PA* 28:4373)

405. McARTHUR, CHARLES. "The Effects of Need Achievement on the Content of TAT Stories: A Re-Examination." *J Abn & Social Psychol* 48:532–6 O '53. * (*PA* 28:6041)

406. McCLELLAND, DAVID C.; ATKINSON, JOHN W.; CLARK, RUSSELL A.; AND LOWELL, EDGAR L. *The Achievement Motive.* New York: Appleton-Century-Crofts, Inc., 1953. Pp. xxiii, 384. *

407. MARKENSON, DAVID. *Diagnostic Effectiveness of Interpretive Tests.* Doctor's thesis, Washington University (St. Louis, Mo.), 1953. (*DA* 14:1100)

408. MILL, CYRIL R. "Personality Patterns of Sociometrically Selected and Sociometrically Rejected Male College Students." *Sociometry* 16:151–67 My '53. * (*PA* 28:4886)

409. MUNSTERBERG, ELIZABETH, AND MUSSEN, PAUL H. "The Personality Structures of Art Students." *J Personality* 21:457–66 Je '53. * (*PA* 28:4064)

410. MURRAY, HENRY A. "Thematic Apperception Test," pp. 636–49. (*PA* 27:7786) In *Contributions Toward Medical Psychology: Theory and Psychodiagnostic Methods, Vol. II.* Edited by Arthur Weider. New York: Ronald Press Co., 1953. Pp. xi, 459–885. *

411. MUSSEN, PAUL H. "Differences Between the TAT Responses of Negro and White Boys." *J Consult Psychol* 17:373–6 O '53. * (*PA* 28:5888)

412. NOWELL, ANN. "Peer Status as Related to Measures of Personality." *Calif J Ed Res* 4:37–41 Ja '53. * (*PA* 28:1514)

413. ROBBINS, ARTHUR. *An Experimental Study of the Relationship Between Needs as Manifested on the Thematic Apperception Test and Kuder Preference Record Scales of Adolescent Boys.* Doctor's thesis, Columbia University (New York, N.Y.), 1953.

414. ROCK, M. L., AND HAY, E. N. "Investigation of the Use of Tests as a Predictor of Leadership and Group Effectiveness in a Job Evaluation Situation." *J Social Psychol* 38:109–19 Ag '53. * (*PA* 28:5831)

415. SARASON, SEYMOUR B. "The Thematic Apperception Test," pp. 252–9. In his *Psychological Problems in Mental Deficiency, Second Edition.* New York: Harper & Brothers, 1953. Pp. xi, 402. * (*PA* 28:2876)

416. SEN, AMYA. "A Preliminary Study of the Thematic Apperception Test." *Brit J Stat Psychol* 6:91–100 N '53. *

417. SHATIN, LEO. "Rorschach Adjustment and the Thematic Apperception Test." *J Proj Tech* 17:92–101 Mr '53. * (*PA* 28:2675)

418. SHNEIDMAN, EDWIN S. "TAT Bibliography: Supplement for 1952." *J Proj Tech* 17:109–15 Mr '53. * (*PA* 28:2677)

419. SHNEIDMAN, EDWIN S., Editor. "The TAT Newsletter, Vol. 7, Nos. 2–4." *J Proj Tech* 17:242–3, 376–9, 499–502 Je, S, D '53.

420. STONE, HAROLD. *The Relationship of Hostile-Aggressive Behavior to Agressive Content on the Rorschach and Thematic Apperception Tests.* Doctor's thesis, University of California (Los Angeles, Calif.), 1953.

421. SUTTER, EVERETT L.; KELL, BILL L.; AND McGUIRE, CARSON. "Some Audio-Mirror Effects of TAT Stories Upon Self-Awareness." Abstract. *Am Psychol* 8:444 Ag '53. *

422. WEBB, WILSE B., AND HILDEN, ARNOLD H. "Verbal and Intellectual Ability as Factors in Projective Test Results." *J Proj Tech* 17:102–3 Mr '53. * (*PA* 28:2687)

423. WEBSTER, HAROLD. "Derivation and Use of the Masculinity-Femininity." *J Clin Psychol* 9:33–6 Ja '53. * (*PA* 27:7803)

424. WEISSKOPF-JOELSON, EDITH, AND MONEY, LESTER, JR.

"Facial Similarity Between Subject and Central Figure in the TAT as an Influence on Projection." *J Abn & Social Psychol* 48:341–4 Jl '53. * (*PA* 28:2689)

425. YOUNG, RAYMOND D., JR. *The Effect of the Interpreter's Personality on the Interpretation of Thematic Apperception Test Protocols.* Doctor's thesis, University of Texas (Austin, Tex.), 1953.

426. ARMSTRONG, MARY ANN SMITH. "Children's Responses to Animal and Human Figures in Thematic Pictures." *J Consult Psychol* 18:67–70 F '54. * (*PA* 28:8710)

427. ATKINSON, JOHN W.; HEYNS, ROGER W.; AND VEROFF, JOSEPH. "The Effect of Experimental Arousal of the Affiliation Motive on Thematic Apperception." *J Abn & Social Psychol* 49:405–10 Jl '54. * (*PA* 29:4025)

428. AULD, FRANK, JR., AND ERON, LEONARD D. "Application of Guttman's Scaling Method to the TAT." Abstract. *Am Psychol* 9:323–4 Ag '54. *

429. BELLAK, LEOPOLD. "A Study of Limitations and 'Failures': Toward an Ego Psychology of Projective Techniques." *J Proj Tech* 18:279–93 S '54. * (*PA* 29:4031)

430. BELLAK, LEOPOLD. *The Thematic Apperception Test and the Children's Apperception Test in Clinical Use.* New York: Grune & Stratton, Inc., 1954. Pp. x, 282. * (*PA* 29:4032)

431. BRIGGS, DENNIE L. "A Modification of the Thematic Apperception Test for Naval Enlisted Personnel (*N-TAT*)." *J Psychol* 37:233–41 Ap '54. * (*PA* 28:8716)

432. BROIDA, DANIEL C. "An Investigation of Certain Psychodiagnostic Indications of Suicidal Tendencies and Depression in Mental Hospital Patients." *Psychiatric Q* 28:453–64 Jl '54. * (*PA* 29:6019)

433. CARR, ARTHUR C. "Intra-Individual Consistency in Response to Tests of Varying Degrees of Ambiguity." *J Consult Psychol* 18:251–8 Ag '54. * (*PA* 29:4041)

434. COX, RACHEL D. "Personality Dynamics of the Well-Adjusted College Student as Revealed by the Rorschach and Thematic Apperception Tests." Abstract. *Am Psychol* 9:351–2 Ag '54. * (*J Proj Tech* 18:399 S '54. *)

435. CRASILNECK, HAROLD BERNARD. *An Analysis of Differences Between Suicidal and Pseudo-Suicidal Patients Through the Use of Projective Techniques.* Doctor's thesis, University of Houston (Houston, Tex.), 1954. (*DA* 14:1456)

436. DANA, RICHARD H. *The Diagnostic Efficacy of a Theoretically Derived Objective Scoring System for the Thematic Apperception Test.* Doctor's thesis, University of Illinois (Urbana, Ill.), 1954.

437. DYMOND, ROSALIND F. Chap. 8, "Adjustment Changes Over Therapy From Thematic Apperception Test Ratings," pp. 109–20. (*PA* 29:4113) In *Psychotherapy and Personality Change.* Edited by Carl R. Rogers and Rosalind F. Dymond. Chicago, Ill.: University of Chicago Press, 1954. Pp. x, 447. *

438. ERON, LEONARD D., AND AULD, FRANK, JR. *A Study of TAT Stories and Sentence Completions of Subjects in Operation Hideout.* Medical Research Laboratory Report No. 243. Washington, D.C.: Bureau of Medicine and Surgery, Department of the Navy, 1954. Pp. iii, 64. *

439. GALLESE, ARTHUR J., JR., AND SPOERL, DOROTHY TILDEN. "A Comparison of Machover and Thematic Apperception Test Interpretation." *J Social Psychol* 40:73–7 Ag '54. * (*PA* 29:5703)

440. GOODRICH, DAVID C. "Aggression in the Projective Tests and Group Behavior of Authoritarian and Equalitarian Subjects." Abstract. *Am Psychol* 9:380 Ag '54. *

441. GRUMMON, DONALD L., AND JOHN, EVE S. Chap. 9, "Changes Over Client-Centered Therapy Evaluated on Psychoanalytically Based Thematic Apperception Scales," pp. 121–44. (*PA* 29:4124) In *Psychotherapy and Personality Change.* Edited by Carl R. Rogers and Rosalind F. Dymond. Chicago, Ill.: University of Chicago Press, 1954. Pp. x, 447. *

442. HAGGERTY, ARTHUR D. "A Note on the Use of an Audio-Visual Technique With the *TAT* in Psychotherapy." *J General Psychol* 51:173–4 Jl '54. * (*PA* 30:2954)

443. HERTZMAN, M. Chap. 13, "The Thematic Apperception Test," pp. 255–80, passim. In *Personality Through Perception: An Experimental and Clinical Study.* By H. A. Witkin and others. New York: Harper & Bros., 1954. Pp. xxvii, 571. * (*PA* 28:8566)

444. HOLSOPPLE, JAMES QUINTER, AND PHELAN, JOSEPH G. "The Skills of Clinicians in Analysis of Projective Tests." *J Clin Psychol* 10:307–20 O '54. * (*PA* 29:4061)

445. HUSMAN, BURRIS FREDERICK. *An Analysis of Aggression in Boxers, Wrestlers, and Cross Country Runners as Measured by the Rosenzweig P-F Study, Selected TAT Pictures, and a Sentence Completion Test.* Doctor's thesis, University of Maryland (College Park, Md.), 1954. (*DA* 15:759)

446. KENNY, DOUGLAS T. "Transcendence Indices, Extent of Personality Factors in Fantasy Responses, and the Ambiguity of TAT Cards." *J Consult Psychol* 18:345–8 O '54. * (*PA* 29:5710)

447. LaFORGE, ROLFE; LEARY, TIMOTHY F.; NABOISEK, HERBERT; COFFEY, HUBERT S.; AND FREEDMAN, MERVIN B. "The Interpersonal Dimension of Personality: II, An Objective Study of Repression." *J Personality* 23:129–53 D '54. * (*PA* 29:5313)

448. LESSA, WILLIAM A., AND SPIEGELMAN, MARVIN. *Ulithian Personality as Seen Through Ethnological Materials and Thematic Test Analysis.* University of California Publications in Culture and Society, Vol. 2, No. 5. Berkeley, Calif.: University of California Press, 1954. Pp. iii, 243–301. * (*PA* 29:757)

449. LEVINE, PHYLLIS R. "Projective Tests in a Vocational

Guidance Setting." *J Counsel Psychol* 1:209–14 w '54. * (*PA* 29:7429)

450. LIGHT, BERNARD H. "Comparative Study of a Series of TAT and CAT Cards." *J Clin Psychol* 10:179–81 Ap '54. * (*PA* 29:933)

451. LINDZEY, GARDNER, AND NEWBURG, ARTHUR S. "Thematic Apperception Test: A Tentative Appraisal of Some 'Signs' of Anxiety." *J Consult Psychol* 18:389–95 D '54. * (*PA* 29:7294)

452. McINTYRE, CHARLES J. "Sex, Age, and Iconicity as Factors in Projective Film Tests." *J Consult Psychol* 18:337–43 O '54. * (*PA* 29:5718)

453. MILAM, JAMES R. "Examiner Influences on Thematic Apperception Test Stories." *J Proj Tech* 18:221–6 Je '54. * (*PA* 29:4074)

454. MILLER, JEROME S. *The Predictive Significance of Usualness and Unusualness of Thematic Apperception Test Stories.* Master's thesis, Ohio State University (Columbus, Ohio), 1954.

455. MUSSEN, PAUL H., AND NAYLOR, H. KELLY. "The Relationships Between Overt and Fantasy Aggression." *J Abn & Social Psychol* 49:235–40 Ap '54. * (*PA* 29:1148)

456. PHILLIPSON, H. *The Development of a Rationale for the Thematic Apperception Test: A Proposed Modification of the Test Based on the Psycho-Analytic Theory of Unconscious Object Relations.* Master's thesis, University of London (London, England), 1954.

457. REEVES, MARGARET PEGRAM. *An Application of the Semantic Differential to Thematic Apperception Test Material.* Doctor's thesis, University of Illinois (Urbana, Ill.), 1954. (*DA* 14:2121)

458. RICHARDSON, STEPHEN ALEXANDER. *A Study of Selected Personality Characteristics of Social Science Field Workers.* Doctor's thesis, Cornell University (Ithaca, N.Y.), 1954. (*DA* 14:2403)

459. SHANK, KENNON. *An Analysis of the Degree of Relationship Between the Thematic Apperception Test and an Original Projective in Measuring Symptoms of Personality Dynamics of Speech Handicapped Children.* Doctor's thesis, University of Denver (Denver, Colo.), 1954.

460. SHNEIDMAN, EDWIN S. "TAT Bibliography: Supplement for 1953." *J Proj Tech* 18:111–9 Mr '54. * (*PA* 29:956)

461. SHNEIDMAN, EDWIN S., Editor. "The TAT Newsletter, Vol. 8, Nos. 1 and 2, March, June 1954." *J Proj Tech* 18:111–9, 267–8 Mr '54. *

462. SINGER, JEROME L. "Projected Familial Attitudes as a Function of Socioeconomic Status and Psychopathology." *J Consult Psychol* 18:99–104 Ap '54. * (*PA* 29:2478)

463. SOSKIN, WILLIAM F. "Bias in Postdiction From Projective Tests." *J Abn & Social Psychol* 49:69–74 Ja '54. * (*PA* 28:7551)

464. STEPHENSON, WILLIAM. *The Study of Behavior: Q-Technique and Its Methodology*, pp. 313–25. Chicago, Ill.: University of Chicago Press, 1953. Pp. ix, 376. * (*PA* 28:6810)

465. STRAUSS, F. H. "Interpretation of Thematic Test Material: A Jungian Approach." Abstract. *B Brit Psychol Soc* (23):12–3 My '54. *

466. WHITMAN, EVELYN BUSCH. "Personality of Fourth Grade Children as Measured by Modified T.A.T. and Improvisation Techniques." *Group Psychother* 7:255–61 D '54. * (*PA* 31:1081)

467. WITKIN, H. A.; LEWIS, H. B.; HERTZMAN, M.; MACHOVER, K.; MEISSNER, P. BRETNALL; AND WAPNER, S. *Personality Through Perception: An Experimental and Clinical Study.* New York: Harper & Brothers, 1954. Pp. xxvi, 571. * (*PA* 28:8566)

468. AULD, FRANK, JR.; ERON, LEONARD D.; AND LAFFAL, JULIUS. "Application of Guttman's Scaling Method to the T.A.T." *Ed & Psychol Meas* 15:422–35 w '55. * (*PA* 30:7183)

469. BARD, MORTON. "The Use of Dependence for Predicting Psychogenic Invalidism Following Radical Mastectomy." *J Nerv & Mental Dis* 122:152–160 Ag '55. * (*PA* 31:1583)

470. BORENSTEIN, BETTY A. *A Study of the Relationship Between Thematic Apperception Test Fantasy and Overt Behavior.* Doctor's thesis, University of California (Berkeley, Calif.), 1955.

471. CLARK, RUSSELL A., AND SENSIBAR, MINDA RAE. "The Relationship Between Symbolic and Manifest Projections of Sexuality With Some Incidental Correlates." *J Abn & Social Psychol* 50:327–34 My '55. * (*PA* 30:2861)

472. COWDEN, RICHARD C.; DEABLER, HERDIS L.; AND FEAMSTER, J. HARRY. "The Prognostic Value of the Bender-Gestalt, H-T-P, TAT, and Sentence Completion Test." *J Clin Psychol* 11:271–5 Jl '55. * (*PA* 30:2864)

473. DANA, RICHARD H. "Clinical Diagnosis and Objective TAT Scoring." *J Abn & Social Psychol* 50:19–24 Ja '55. * (*PA* 29:7267)

474. DANA, RICHARD H. "The Objectification of Projective Techniques: Rationale." *Psychol Rep* 1:93–102 Je '55. *

475. DAVIDS, ANTHONY; HENRY, ANDREW F.; McARTHUR, CHARLES C.; AND McNAMARA, LEO F. "Projection, Self Evaluation, and Clinical Evaluation of Aggression." *J Consult Psychol* 19:437–40 D '55. * (*PA* 30:7191)

476. ERON, LEONARD D. "Some Problems in the Research Application of the Thematic Apperception Test." *J Proj Tech* 19:125–9 Je '55. * (*PA* 30:2871)

477. ERON, LEONARD D.; SULTAN, FLORENCE; AND AULD, FRANK, JR. "The Application of a Psychometric Scoring Procedure to a Group Modification of the Thematic Apperception

Test (N-TAT)." *J Consult Psychol* 19:83–9 Ap '55. * (*PA* 30:1019)

478. ERVIN, SUSAN M. "The Verbal Behavior of Bilinguals: The Effects of Language of Response Upon the TAT Stories of Adult French Bilinguals." Abstract. *Am Psychol* 10:391 Ag '55. *

479. FESHBACH, SEYMOUR. "The Drive-Reducing Function of Fantasy Behavior." *J Abn & Social Psychol* 50:3–11 Ja '55. *

480. FINE, REUBEN. "Manual for a Scoring Scheme for Verbal Projective Techniques (TAT, MAPS, Stories and the Like)." *J Proj Tech* 19:310–6 S '55. * (*PA* 30:4570)

481. FINE, REUBEN. "A Scoring Scheme for the TAT and Other Verbal Projective Techniques." *J Proj Tech* 19:306–9 S '55. * (*PA* 30:4571)

482. GLUCK, MARTIN R. "The Relationship Between Hostility in the TAT and Behavioral Hostility." *J Proj Tech* 19:21–6 Mr '55. * (*PA* 30:1025)

483. GOLDMAN, ROSALINE, AND GREENBLATT, MILTON. "Changes in Thematic Apperception Test Stories Paralleling Changes in Clinical Status of Schizophrenic Patients." *J Nerv & Mental Dis* 121:243–9 Mr '55. * (*PA* 30:3206)

484. GOODSTEIN, LEONARD D.; MARTIRE, JOHN G.; AND SPIELBERGER, CHARLES D. "The Relationship Between 'Achievement Imagery' and Stuttering Behavior in College Males." *Proc Iowa Acad Sci* 62:399–404 '55. *

485. HARRISON, ROSS; TOMBLEN, DON T.; AND JACKSON, THEODORE A. "Profile of the Mechanical Engineer: III, Personality." *Personnel Psychol* 8:469–90 w '55. * (*PA* 31:1941)

486. HEYMANN, GARY M. *Some Relationships Among Hostility, Fantasy Aggression, and Aggressive Behavior.* Doctor's thesis, Michigan State University (East Lansing, Mich.), 1955. (*DA* 16:793)

487. HURLEY, JOHN R. "The Iowa Picture Interpretation Test: A Multiple-Choice Variation of the TAT." *J Consult Psychol* 19:372–6 O '55. * (*PA* 30:5985)

488. HUSMAN, BURRIS F. "Aggression in Boxers and Wrestlers as Measured by Projective Techniques." *Res Q* 26:421–5 D '55. *

489. JOHNSON, GRANVILLE B., JR. "An Evaluation Instrument for the Analysis of Teacher Effectiveness." *J Exp Ed* 23:331–44 Je '55. * (*PA* 30:3484)

490. KAMMAN, GORDON R., AND KRAM, CHARLES. "Value of Psychometric Examinations in Medical Diagnosis and Treatment." *J Am Med Assn* 158:555–60 Je 18 '55. * (*PA* 31:1044)

491. KANDIL, B. A. *A Study of the Thematic Apperception Test as Applied to a Group of Institutional Children.* Master's thesis, University of London (London, England), 1955.

492. KLINE, MILTON V. "Hypnodiagnosis With a Visual-Imagery Induction Technique and Modification of the House-Tree-Person and Thematic Apperception Tests." *Psychiatric Q Sup* 29:267–71 pt 2 '55. * (*PA* 31:1122)

493. LEBO, DELL. "Immediate Affective Reaction to TAT Cards." *J Clin Psychol* 11:297–9 Jl '55. * (*PA* 30:2893)

494. LICCIONE, JOHN V. "The Changing Family Relationships of Adolescent Girls." *J Abn & Social Psychol* 51:421–6 N '55. * (*PA* 30:4581)

495. LIGHT, BERNARD H. "A Further Test of the Thompson TAT Rationale." *J Abn & Social Psychol* 51:148–50 Jl '55. * (*PA* 30:4581)

496. LINDZEY, GARDNER, AND HEINEMANN, SHIRLEY H. "Thematic Apperception Test: Individual and Group Administration." *J Personality* 24:34–55 S '55. * (*PA* 30:5992)

497. LINDZEY, GARDNER, AND HERMAN, PETER S. "Thematic Apperception Test: A Note on Reliability and Situational Validity." *J Proj Tech* 19:36–42 Mr '55. *

498. LITTLE, KENNETH B., AND SHNEIDMAN, EDWIN S. "A Comparison of the Reliability of Interpretations of Four Psychological Tests." Abstract. *Am Psychol* 10:322 Ag '55. *

499. LITTLE, KENNETH B., AND SHNEIDMAN, EDWIN S. "The Validity of Thematic Projective Technique Interpretations." *J Personality* 23:285–94 Mr '55. * (*PA* 30:1038)

500. LUBIN, NATHAN M. "The Effect of Color in the TAT on Productions of Mentally Retarded Subjects." *Am J Mental Def* 60:366–70 O '55. * (*PA* 30:6093)

501. McARTHUR, CHARLES. "Personality Differences Between Middle and Upper Classes." *J Abn & Social Psychol* 50:247–54 Mr '55. * (*PA* 30:873)

502. MEYER, MORTIMER M., AND TOLMAN, RUTH S. "Correspondence Between Attitudes and Images of Parental Figures in TAT Stories and in Therapeutic Interviews." *J Consult Psychol* 19:79–82 Ap '55. * (*PA* 30:989)

503. MEYER, MORTIMER M., AND TOLMAN, RUTH S. "Parental Figures in Sentence Completion Test, in TAT, and in Therapeutic Interviews." Abstract. *J Consult Psychol* 19:170 Je '55. * (*PA* 30:2904)

504. MILLER, JEROME S., AND SCODEL, ALVIN. "The Diagnostic Significance of Usual and Unusual TAT Stories." *J Consult Psychol* 19:91–5 Ap '55. * (*PA* 30:1045)

505. MUSSEN, PAUL H., AND SCODEL, ALVIN. "The Effects of Sexual Stimulation Under Varying Conditions on TAT Sexual Responsiveness." Abstract. *J Consult Psychol* 19:90 Ap '55. *

506. NEWBIGGING, P. LYNN. "Influence of a Stimulus Variable on Stories Told to Certain TAT Pictures." *Can J Psychol* 9:195–206 D '55. * (*PA* 30:7217)

507. OHLSEN, MERLE M., AND SCHULZ, RAYMOND E. "Projective Test Response Patterns for Best and Poorest Student Teachers." *Ed & Psychol Meas* 15:18–27 sp '55. * (*PA* 30:1659)

508. Shatin, Leo. "Relationships Between the Rorschach Test and the Thematic Apperception Test." *J Proj Tech* 19: 317–31 S '55. * (*PA* 30:4595)

509. Shulman, Harold S. *Congruences of Personality Expression in Self-Conceptions, the Thematic Apperception Test, and Dreams.* Doctor's thesis, Western Reserve University (Cleveland, Ohio), 1955.

510. Spiegelman, Marvin. "Jungian Theory and the Analysis of Thematic Tests." *J Proj Tech* 19:253–63 S '55. * (*PA* 30:4601)

511. Staunton, G. J. "A Comparative Analysis of Rorschach and T.A.T. Responses with Reference to a Particular Case Study." Abstract. *Brit Rorsch Forum* (6):1–4 Ap '55. *

512. Stein, Morris I. *Thematic Apperception Test: An Introductory Manual for Its Clinical Use With Adults, Second Edition.* Cambridge, Mass.: Addison-Wesley Publishing Co., Inc., 1955. Pp. xviii, 365. * (*PA* 29:7324)

513. Ullmann, Leonard Paul. *The Definition of Stimuli in the Evaluation of Test Behavior.* Doctor's thesis, Stanford University (Stanford, Calif.), 1955. (*DA* 15:1910)

514. Vernier, Claire M.; Whiting, J. Frank; and Meltzer, Malcolm L. "Differential Prediction of a Specific Behavior From Three Projective Techniques." *J Consult Psychol* 19:175–82 Je '55. * (*PA* 30:2932)

515. Vineyard, Edwin Earle. *A Longitudinal Study of the Relationship of Differential Aptitude Test Scores With College Success.* Doctor's thesis, Oklahoma Agricultural and Mechanical College (Stillwater, Okla.), 1955.

516. Waxenberg, Sheldon E. "Psychosomatic Patients and Other Physically Ill Persons: A Comparative Study." *J Consult Psychol* 19:163–9 Je '55. * (*PA* 30:3281)

517. Zeichner, Abraham M. "Psychosexual Identification in Paranoid Schizophrenia." *J Proj Tech* 19:67–77 Mr '55. * (*PA* 30:1378)

518. Applezweig, Mortimer H.; Moeller, George; and Burdick, Harvey. "Multi-Motive Prediction of Academic Success." *Psychol Rep* 2:489–96 D '56. * (*PA* 31:5139)

519. Bellak, Leopold. "Freud and Projective Techniques." *J Proj Tech* 20:5–13 Mr '56. * (*PA* 31:1963)

520. Bentsen, Ivar Ben. *Effect of Sodium Amytal on Conventionality, Commonality of Response to the Word Association Test, and Thematic Apperception Test.* Doctor's thesis, University of California (Los Angeles, Calif.), 1956.

521. Bernstein, Lewis. "The Examiner as an Inhibiting Factor in Clinical Testing." *J Consult Psychol* 20:287–90 Ag '56. * (*PA* 31:7808)

522. Burgess, Elva. "Personality Factors of Over- and Under-Achievers in Engineering." *J Ed Psychol* 47:89–99 F '56. * (*PA* 31:8811)

523. Carr, Arthur C. "The Relation of Certain Rorschach Variables to Expression of Affect in the TAT and SCT." *J Proj Tech* 20:137–42 Je '56. * (*PA* 31:4674)

524. Child, Irvin L.; Frank, Kitty F.; and Storm, Thomas. "Self-Ratings and TAT: Their Relations to Each Other and to Childhood Background." *J Personality* 25:96–114 S '56. * (*PA* 31:7905)

525. Clark, Russell A., and McClelland, David C. "A Factor Analytic Integration of Imaginative and Performance Measures of the Need for Achievement." *J General Psychol* 55: 73–83 Jl '56. *

526. Clark, Russell A.; Teevan, Richard; and Ricciuti, Henry N. "Hope of Success and Fear of Failure as Aspects of Need for Achievement." *J Abn & Social Psychol* 53:182–6 S '56. *

527. Cleveland, Sidney E., and Fisher, Seymour. "Psychological Factors in the Neurodermatoses." *Psychosom Med* 18:209–20 My–Je '56. * (*PA* 31:5001)

528. Cox, Rachel Dunaway. "The Normal Personality: An Analysis of Rorschach and Thematic Apperception Test Responses of a Group of College Students." *J Proj Tech* 20:70–7 Mr '56. * (*PA* 31:3016)

529. Dana, Richard H. "An Application of Objective TAT Scoring." *J Proj Tech* 20:159–63 Je '56. * (*PA* 31:4680)

530. Dana, Richard H. "Cross Validation of Objective TAT Scoring." *J Consult Psychol* 20:33–6 F '56. * (*PA* 31:3019)

531. Dana, Richard H. "Selection of Abbreviated TAT Sets." *J Clin Psychol* 12:36–40 Ja '56. * (*PA* 30:4560)

532. Davids, Anthony; Joelson, Mark; and McArthur, Charles. "Rorschach and TAT Indices of Homosexuality in Overt Homosexuals, Neurotics, and Normal Males." *J Abn & Social Psychol* 53:161–72 S '56. * (*PA* 32:2891)

533. Edelstein, Ruth R. *The Evaluation of Intelligence From TAT Protocols.* Master's thesis, City College of New York (New York, N.Y.), 1956.

534. Epstein, Seymour, and Smith, Richard. "Thematic Apperception as a Measure of the Hunger Drive." *J Proj Tech* 20:372–84 D '56. * (*PA* 32:1619)

535. Fisher, Seymour, and Mendell, David. "The Communication of Neurotic Patterns Over Two and Three Generations." *Psychiatry* 19:41–6 F '56. * (*PA* 31:3503)

536. Groh, Leslie S. "A Study of Ego Integration by Means of an Index of Identification Derived from Six TAT Cards." *J Proj Tech* 20:387–97 D '56. * (*PA* 32:1358)

537. Gurel, Lee. "Quantitative Differences in Responses to Twenty Stimulus Cards of the Thematic Apperception Test." Abstract. *Am Psychol* 11:364 Ag '56. *

538. Henry, William E. *The Analysis of Fantasy: The Thematic Apperception Technique in the Study of Personality.*

New York: John Wiley & Sons, Inc., 1956. Pp. xiii, 305. * (*PA* 30:8292)

539. Heymann, Gary M. "Some Relationships Among Hostility, Fantasy Aggression, and Aggressive Behavior." Abstract. *Am Psychol* 11:391 Ag '56. *

540. Jensen, Arthur Robert. *Aggression in Fantasy and Overt Behavior.* Doctor's thesis, Columbia University (New York, N.Y.), 1956. (*DA* 16:794)

541. Jones, Richard M. "The Negation TAT: A Projective Method for Eliciting Repressed Thought Content." *J Proj Tech* 20:297–303 S '56. * (*PA* 31:6090)

542. Kagan, Jerome, and Mussen, Paul H. "Dependency Themes on the TAT and Group Conformity." *J Consult Psychol* 20:29–32 F '56. * (*PA* 31:3042)

543. Kerner, Oliver J. B. "Stress, Fantasy, and Schizophrenia: A Study of the Adaptive Processes." *Genetic Psychol Monogr* 53:189–281 My '56. *

544. Klein, Armin, Jr. *The Influence of Stimulus Material and Geographical Region on Responses to a Thematic Test.* Doctor's thesis, Columbia University (New York, N.Y.), 1956. (*DA* 16:1284)

545. LeBlanc, H. J. *The Thematic Apperception Test Applied to Army Officer Selection.* Master's thesis, University of Western Ontario (London, Ont., Canada), 1956.

546. Levy, Leon H.; Brody, Janice R.; and Windman, Georgia O. "The Relationship Between the Inferential Potential of Rorschach and TAT Protocols." *J Consult Psychol* 20: 27–8 F '56. * (*PA* 31:3049)

547. Lindzey, Gardner, and Tejessy, Charlotte. "Thematic Apperception Test: Indices of Aggression in Relation to Measures of Overt and Covert Behavior." *Am J Orthopsychiatry* 26:567–76 Jl '56. * (*PA* 31:7943)

548. McPherson, Marion White. "Speech Behavior and Egocentricity." *J Clin Psychol* 12:229–35 Jl '56. * (*PA* 31:6014)

549. Mason, Beth, and Ammons, R. B. "Note on Social Class and the Thematic Apperception Test." *Percept & Motor Skills* 6:88 Je '56. *

550. Miner, John B. "Motion Perception, Time Perspective, and Creativity." *J Proj Tech* 20:405–13 D '56. *

551. Moran, Louis J.; Fairweather, George W.; Fisher, Seymour; and Morton, Robert B. "Psychological Concomitants to Rate of Recovery From Tuberculosis." *J Consult Psychol* 20:199–203 Je '56. * (*PA* 31:6487)

552. Page, Horace A. "Studies in Fantasy: Daydreaming and the TAT." Abstract. *Am Psychol* 11:392 Ag '56. *

553. Purcell, Kenneth. "The TAT and Antisocial Behavior." *J Consult Psychol* 20:449–56 D '56. * (*PA* 32:1641)

554. Robbins, Arthur. "Emotional Status of the U.S. Soldier and Length of Tour in Korea." *US Armed Forces Med J* 7:888–94 Je '56. *

555. Sarbin, Anne. *An Analysis of the Buhler School Maturity Test as It Relates to Intelligence and Projective Test Data.* Doctor's thesis, University of Southern California (Los Angeles, Calif.), 1956.

556. Schaw, Louis C., and Henry, William E. "A Method for the Comparison of Groups: A Study in Thematic Apperception." *Genetic Psychol Monogr* 54:207–53 N '56. *

557. Semeonoff, Boris. "The Use of Projective Techniques in Selection for Counselling." Abstract. *B Brit Psychol Soc* (29):45–6 My '56. *

558. Silverstein, Arthur B. *The Expression of Acceptable and Unacceptable Needs in Thematic Apperception.* Doctor's thesis, New York University (New York, N.Y.), 1956. (*DA* 17:410)

559. Singer, Jerome L., and Opler, Marvin K. "Contrasting Patterns of Fantasy and Motility in Irish and Italian Schizophrenics." *J Abn & Social Psychol* 53:42–7 Jl '56. * (*PA* 32:1868)

560. Stone, Harold. "The TAT Aggressive Content Scale." *J Proj Tech* 20:445–52 D '56. * (*PA* 32:1650)

561. Wallen, Richard W. Chap. 9, "The Thematic Apperception Test," pp. 221–55. In his *Clinical Psychology: The Study of Persons.* New York: McGraw-Hill Book Co., Inc., 1956. Pp. xiii, 388. * (*PA* 30:7155)

562. Winch, Robert F., and More, Douglas M. "Does TAT Add Information to Interviews? Statistical Analysis of the Increment." *J Clin Psychol* 12:316–21 O '56. * (*PA* 32:4210)

563. Wyatt, Frederick, and Veroff, Joanne B. Chap. 3, "Thematic Apperception and Fantasy Tests," pp. 32–57. (*PA* 30:7238) In *Progress in Clinical Psychology, Vol. II.* Edited by Daniel Brower and Lawrence E. Abt. New York and London: Grune & Stratton, Inc., 1956. Pp. viii, 364. *

564. Young, Florene M. "Responses of Juvenile Delinquents to the Thematic Apperception Test." *J Genetic Psychol* 88:251–9 Je '56. *

565. Zeichner, Abraham M. "Conception of Masculine and Feminine Roles in Paranoid Schizophrenia." *J Proj Tech* 20: 348–54 S '56. * (*PA* 31:6458)

566. Bradley, Mary O. *The Test-Retest Reliability of the Thematic Apperception Test.* Master's thesis, Fordham University (New York, N.Y.), 1957.

567. Calogeras, Roy Cuno. *Some Relationships Between Fantasy and Self-Report Behavior.* Doctor's thesis, Columbia University (New York, N.Y.), 1957. (*DA* 17:1591)

568. Cline, Victor B.; Egbert, Robert; Forgy, Edward; and Meeland, Tor. "Reactions of Men Under Stress to a

Picture Projective Test." *J Clin Psychol* 13:141–4 Ap '57. * (*PA* 32:2889)

569. Dana, Richard H. "Norms for Three Aspects of TAT Behavior." *J General Psychol* 57:83–9 Jl '57. *

570. Epstein, Seymour, and Smith, Richard. "Thematic Apperception, Rorschach Content, and Ratings of Sexual Attractiveness of Women as Measures of the Sex Drive." *J Consult Psychol* 21:473–8 D '57. * (Abstract: *Am Psychol* 12: 383)

571. Fisher, Seymour, and Morton, Robert B. "An Exploratory Study of Some Relationships Between Hospital Ward Atmospheres and Attitudes of Ward Personnel." *J Psychol* 44:155–64 Jl '57. *

572. Fisher, Seymour, and Morton, Robert B. "Levels of Prediction From the TAT." *J Consult Psychol* 21:115–20 Ap '57. *

573. Friedman, Ira. "Objectifying the Subjective: A Methodological Approach to the TAT." *J Proj Tech* 21:243–7 S '57. *

574. Hooker, Evelyn. "The Adjustment of the Male Overt Homosexual." *J Proj Tech* 21:18–31 Mr '57. * (*PA* 32:3083)

575. Jensen, Arthur R. "Aggression in Fantasy and Overt Behavior." *Psychol Monogr* 71(16):1–13 '57. *

576. Lakin, Martin. "Assessment of Significant Role Attitudes in Primiparous Mothers by Means of a Modification of the TAT." *Psychosom Med* 19:50–60 Ja–F '57. * (*PA* 32:1407)

577. Leary, Timothy. *Interpersonal Diagnosis of Personality: A Functional Theory and Methodology for Personality Evaluation.* New York: Ronald Press Co., 1957. Pp. xix, 518. * (*PA* 31:2556)

578. Lebo, Dell, and Harrigan, Margaret. "Visual and Verbal Presentation of TAT Stimuli." *J Consult Psychol* 21: 339–42 Ag '57. *

579. Lyle, J. G., and Gilchrist, A. A. "Problems of Thematic Apperception Test Interpretation and the Diagnosis of Delinquent Trends." Abstract. *B Brit Psychol Soc* (32):21 inset My '57. *

580. Mandler, George; Lindzey, Gardner; and Crouch, Robert G. "Thematic Apperception Test: Indices of Anxiety in Relation to Test Anxiety." *Ed & Psychol Meas* 17:466–74 W '57. *

581. Scodel, Alvin. "Heterosexual Somatic Preference and Fantasy Dependency." *J Consult Psychol* 21:371–4 O '57. *

582. Scodel, Alvin, and Lipetz, Milton E. "TAT Hostility and Psychopathology." *J Proj Tech* 21:161–5 Je '57. *

583. Sherwood, Edward T. "On the Designing of TAT Pictures, With Special Reference to a Set for an African People Assimilating Western Culture." *J Social Psychol* 45:161–90 My '57. *

584. Sohler, Dorothy Terry; Holzberg, Jules D.; Fleck, Stephen; Cornelison, Alice R.; Kay, Eleanor; and Lidz, Theodore. "The Prediction of Family Interaction From a Battery of Projective Techniques." *J Proj Tech* 21:199–208 Je '57. *

585. Ullmann, Leonard P., and McFarland, Robert L. "Productivity as a Variable in TAT Protocols: A Methodological Study." *J Proj Tech* 21:80–7 Mr '57. * (*PA* 32:2928)

586. Weisskopf-Joelson, Edith; Asher, E. J.; Albrecht, Kenneth J.; and Hoffman, Martin L. "An Experimental Investigation of 'Label-Avoidance' as a Manifestation of Repression." *J Proj Tech* 21:88–93 Mr '57. * (*PA* 32:2931)

587. Davids, Anthony, and Rosenblatt, Daniel. "Use of the TAT in Assessment of the Personality Syndrome of Alienation." *J Proj Tech* 22:145–52 Je '58. *

588. Fitzgerald, Bernard J. "Some Relationships Among Projective Test, Interview, and Sociometric Measures of Dependent Behavior." *J Abn & Social Psychol* 56:199–203 Mr '58. *

589. Henry, William E., and Shlien, John M. "Affective Complexity and Psychotherapy: Some Comparisons of Time-Limited and Unlimited Treatment." *J Proj Tech* 22:153–62 Je '58. *

590. Holt, Robert R. "Formal Aspects of the TAT: A Neglected Resource." *J Proj Tech* 22:163–72 Je '58. *

591. Kagan, Jerome; Sontag, Lester W.; Baker, Charles T.; and Nelson, Virginia L. "Personality and IQ Change." *J Abn & Social Psychol* 56:261–6 Mr '58. *

592. Lindzey, Gardner. "Thematic Apperception Test: The Strategy of Research." *J Proj Tech* 22:173–80 Je '58. *

593. Lindzey, Gardner, and Kalnius, Dagny. "Thematic Apperception Test: Some Evidence Bearing on the 'Hero Assumption.'" *J Abn & Social Psychol* 57:76–83 Jl '58. *

594. Lindzey, Gardner; Tejessy, Charlotte; and Zamansky, Harold S. "Thematic Apperception Test: An Empirical Examination of Some Indices of Homosexuality." *J Abn & Social Psychol* 57:67–75 Jl '58. *

595. Lyle, J.; Gilchrist, A.; and Groh, L. "Three Blind Interpretations of a TAT Record." *J Proj Tech* 22:82–96 Mr '58. *

596. Melikian, Levon H. "The Relationship Between Edwards' and McClelland's Measures of Achievement Motivation." *J Consult Psychol* 22:296–8 Ag '58. *

597. Murstein, Bernard I. "Nonprojective Determinants of Perception on the TAT." *J Consult Psychol* 22:195–8 Je '58. * (Abstract: *Am Psychol* 12:412)

598. Murstein, Bernard I. "The Relationship of Stimulus Ambiguity on the TAT to the Productivity of Themes." Abstract. *J Consult Psychol* 22:348 O '58. *

599. Myers, Robert L. *An Analysis of Sex Differences in Verbalizations and Content of Responses to the Rorschach and to the Thematic Apperception Test.* Doctor's thesis, Temple University (Philadelphia, Pa.), 1958. (*DA* 19:365)

600. Purcell, Kenneth. "Some Shortcomings in Projective Test Validation." *J Abn & Social Psychol* 57:115–8 Jl '58. *

601. Ruess, Aubrey L. "Some Cultural and Personality Aspects of Mental Retardation." *Am J Mental Def* 63:50–9 Jl '58. *

602. Sarason, Barbara R., and Sarason, Irwin G. "The Effect of Type of Administration and Sex of Subject on Emotional Tone and Outcome Ratings of TAT Stories." *J Proj Tech* 22:333–7 S '58. *

603. Schafer, Roy. "How Was This Story Told?" *J Proj Tech* 22:181–210 Je '58. *

604. Semeonoff, Boris. "Projective Techniques in Selection for Counseling." *Human Relations* 11:113–22 no 2 '58. *

605. Shatin, Leo. "The Constriction-Dilation Dimension in Rorschach and TAT." *J Clin Psychol* 14:150–4 Ap '58. *

606. Shneidman, Edwin S. "Some Relationships Between Thematic and Drawing Materials," pp. 620–7. In *The Clinical Application of Projective Techniques.* Edited by Emanuel F. Hammer. Springfield, Ill.: Charles C Thomas, 1958. Pp. xxii, 663. *

607. Shneidman, Edwin S., and Farberow, Norman L. "TAT Heroes of Suicidal and Non-Suicidal Subjects." *J Proj Tech* 22:211–28 Je '58. *

608. Sumerwell, Harriet C.; Campbell, Mary M.; and Sarason, Irwin G. "The Effect of Differential Motivating Instructions on the Emotional Tone and Outcome of TAT Stories." *J Consult Psychol* 22:385–8 O '58. *

609. Ullmann, Leonard P. "Clinical Correlates of Facilitation and Inhibition of Response to Emotional Stimuli." *J Proj Tech* 22:341–7 S '58. *

610. Wyatt, Frederick. "A Principle for the Interpretation of Fantasy." *J Proj Tech* 22:229–45 Je '58. *

Leonard D. Eron, *Director of Research, Rip Van Winkle Foundation, Hudson, New York.*

It was the impression of the reviewer in *The Fourth Mental Measurements Yearbook* that in the busy clinic the use of the TAT was largely a luxury, since the material obtained by use of this rather "tedious and time-consuming technique" could be more efficiently obtained in a personal interview. He saw the possibility, however, that "with the development of useful scoring systems, such as that of Aron (*154*), and the establishment of empirically verified principles of interpretation, the test will achieve distinctive value as a psychodiagnostic instrument."

Over the last five years much research with the TAT has been published, but it is still doubtful that its utility as an efficient clinical tool has been established and it is uncertain whether the amount of time necessary to evaluate all the nuances of the TAT protocol could not better be spent in other pursuits in behalf of the patient. Aron's scoring system, which is an elaboration and development of the Murray scheme described in the test manual, has proved no boon to the clinician. She reports that a minimum of 10 minutes is required for scoring each story, making it hardly likely that her system can be used economically in the clinic. One complication is that needs and press are scored for everybody in the story, not just the hero. Although this may eliminate the arbitrary judgment sometimes needed in selecting a hero, it makes the whole procedure that much more unwieldy. The lack of normative and validational data, except for a few hints in studies with very small numbers which did not permit statistical differentiation of groups, as well as the questionable method used in establishing reliability of scoring categories, also makes one hesitate to recommend the Aron scoring procedure for clinical use. It is unlikely that a busy clinician could make more than an impressionistic analysis of the patient's TAT protocol, especially when it is just one of a battery of tests used in psychodiagnosis. As a timesaving device, group administration of the TAT has been attempted and it has been found that the stories yielded in group administration do not differ significantly in very many ways from stories obtained in routine individual administration (260, 497). Multiple choice answers and objective scoring have been tried (40, 477, 487), but not with too much success, at least for clinical use. In the clinic where patients usually are seen individually and where the clinician is interested in analyzing more than just one or two needs or traits which are being manipulated experimentally or otherwise, it is doubtful that the group method can be adapted in such a way that it would serve as an efficient, timesaving method and, at the same time, give sufficient information about the subject to be of value.

Benton's second condition has not been fulfilled either. Unfortunately, research has not yielded verification of principles of interpretation which have been reported as successful in the clinic. For example, the traditional "signs" of anxiety in TAT stories have been shown to have little or no relationship to independent "clinical" observation of anxiety in the subjects (451, 580). The same can be said of many other "signs" which have been reported to be clinically useful but which, on independent empirical testing, fall short of validation (204, 503).

Although the usefulness of the TAT as a routine clinical tool has not yet been demonstrated, as a research technique it has had wide and successful application. A number of scoring schemes of good reliability have been introduced (204, 473, 481) and rating scales have been developed which make TAT productions amenable to sound statistical handling without sacrificing too much in the way of clinical judgment (206, 369, 372, 468, 573). These scales have been used in a variety of investigations, both into personality processes, and into the nature of the psychological act of telling stories in response to pictures (299, 362, 438, 494, 516, 521, 529).

It cannot be assumed that, because the subject is presented with an ambiguous picture about which he is instructed to make up a story, the content of his productions will be determined solely, or even chiefly, by his own needs and attitudes. In fact, a number of studies have shown either an inverse or, at best, a curvilinear relationship between degree of ambiguity of stimulus picture and extent of personality factors involved in the response (204, 398, 446). It has been amply demonstrated that each of the pictures has its own "pull" in terms of the thematic content and emotional tone of stories told in response to it. Most of the pictures routinely elicit sad stories, and there are reliable differences among the pictures as to the degree of dysphoric affect, productivity of material, themes, level of response, need systems, etc., which they evoke (204, 206, 251, 369, 585). The outcome of the stories, however, is one variable which seems to be based more on interpersonal dynamics (204, 299). Stereotyped responses for each of the cards have been described and a fair amount of normative data is now available (147, 175, 204, 388, 538).

Aside from the stimulus properties of the cards themselves, a number of other variables extraneous to the personality content of the individual subject contribute to a determination of both the formal and the content aspects of the productions. The interaction between the examiner and the subject is important. Although it is assumed that the results are a representation of an individual's private fantasy, it has been shown that the mere presence of an examiner, whether the stories are orally administered or written down by the subject himself, is an inhibiting factor in the production of strongly emotional material on the TAT (521). However, the more the subject is made to feel that he is in a permissive, accepting, noncritical, nonevaluative situation, the more likely is he to contribute fantasies which approximate his unshared ideation and imagery. The examiner can no doubt control some of this atmosphere by the instructions he gives and the manner in which he gives them, by the extra-test comments he makes, and by his general demeanor. There are other factors, however, which are immutable and cannot be changed by the examiner, e.g., sex, age, race, social status, and intelligence. All of these variables have been shown to affect TAT productions, especially when there are differences in them between the subject and the experimenter (*331, 403, 411, 462, 501, 549*).

Quite apart from the kinds of stories elicited by different examiners is the effect of the examiner on the interpretation of the stories which are made. No systematic study of this kind of confounding has been reported, although many authors have warned of the danger of the experimenter's injecting his own theoretical bias, personality shortcomings, and predilections into the interpretations. Davenport (*329*) found little agreement among six clinical psychologists in their application of 207 statements previously rated for ambiguity, etc., to each of six records from heterogeneous subjects. The judges tended to apply statements rated as universal and loaded with psychoanalytic terminology to any subject, while avoiding use of more specific statements; and they rarely selected statements about positive assets or traits of personality, even though some of the TAT records were from normal individuals.

As in any psychological test, the cooperativeness of the subject is important, and it cannot be assumed that the "cover story" given by the examiner, e.g., "This is a test of intelligence," takes care of the attitudes, set, and preconceived notions of the subject. TAT productions have been shown to be susceptible to distortion when the subject makes a conscious effort to give a specific kind of picture of himself. Individuals can influence the diagnosis of their personalities made by experienced TAT examiners and, to some extent, can manipulate their answers in accordance with their purpose in taking the test (*298*). However, the subject need not be consciously aware of any effort to distort his stories; he may be set in such a way that it is inevitable that stories will fit in with his predominant attitudes. Differences in TAT stories have been related to physiologically controlled needs such as hunger (*302, 534*), sex (*326, 471, 505*), and sleep deprivation,[1] hypnotically produced attitudes such as sadness and criticalness,[2] and psychologically induced motivations such as need for achievement (*170*) and need for affiliation (*427*). Similarly, a number

of experiments have shown that conditions directly antecedent to the test administration will affect the productions (*496*). Although most of these studies have dealt with the effect of specific frustration (*21, 29, 258, 479, 482*), there is evidence that the immediate surroundings in general have their influence, too (*204, 281*).

Despite all these seemingly extraneous influences, there still remains a large portion of the individual's idiosyncratic, deep seated motivation that seems to be reflected in his TAT productions. However, the exact nature of this relationship between overt behavior and fantasy as represented by the TAT has yet to be delineated (*476*). Much of the research concerned with this correlation has centered around the variable of aggression and, indeed, the relationship is not uncomplicated. There is no one-to-one relationship between amount of aggressive need depicted on the TAT and the overt, or even covert, behavior of the subject. The "sign" approach advocated by a number of writers, by which one can supposedly translate what the subject says or fails to say or the way he says it to how he will act (e.g., avoidance of the gun in pictures 3 and 8 means that the subject has to inhibit strong aggressive tendencies, or the use of forceful language or the fantasying of death or failure in nonheroes signifies the tendency to act out aggression), has been demonstrated to be a failure (*547, 582*). However, when a theory of behavior is used to posit the relationship between TAT fantasy and overt behavior, results are more successful. For example, Pittluck (*305*) reasoned that both the aggressive drive and the anxiety opposing expression of this drive must be taken into account when predicting the likelihood of overt aggressive behavior in any individual. The indications of anxiety which she obtained from TAT stories included rejection or denial of aggression, excusing of the aggression by placing it in a socially acceptable context, noncompletion of aggressions planned by a fantasy character, and displacement of the aggression to nonhuman objects. These mechanisms are considered to be defensive in purpose; by their use the aggressive response becomes a compromise between aggressive impulses and the anxiety opposing their expression. It was found that the tendency to use these mechanisms in TAT stories was negatively related to the tendency to act out. The subjects who used more defense mechanisms in proportion to their out-

---

1 MURRAY, E. J. "Thematic Apperception During Sleep Deprivation." Paper read at Eastern Psychological Association, Philadelphia, 1958.
2 LEUBA, CLARENCE, AND LUCAS, CHARLES. "The Effects of Attitudes on Descriptions of Pictures." *J Exp Psychol* 35:517-24 D '45.

going, aggressive fantasies tended to act out less than the subjects who used proportionally fewer such mechanisms. In addition, the subjects who used proportionally more unmodified, primitive responses in fantasy tended to act out more than patients with proportionally fewer fantasies of this nature. Therefore, Pittluck concluded that measures of aggressive fantasy can provide direct clues to overt aggressive behavior if these measures stress not the absolute frequency of aggressive responses but the extent to which such responses are free from modifications which are the result of anxiety.

According to behavior theory, anxiety about a given behavior usually results from the association of punishment with that behavior sometime in the past. Mussen and Naylor (455) found that subjects who anticipated punishment for aggression in their TAT stories demonstrated less overt aggression than subjects who did not anticipate such punishment. A further refinement of this relationship, which makes for more efficient prediction from TAT to behavior, is found in a study by Purcell (553) who showed that anticipated internal punishment must be distinguished from retaliatory punishment since the latter variable did not differentiate antisocial from non-antisocial subjects while the former did.

This relationship between aggressive fantasy and overt behavior was more efficiently related to actual learning conditions by Lesser [3] who compared the relationship between these two variables among boys whose mothers encouraged expression of aggression as contrasted with boys whose mothers discouraged such behavior. Where aggressive behavior had maternal encouragement, there was significant positive relationship between aggression scores obtained from stories and behavioral ratings obtained from peers; but where mothers were relatively discouraging of aggression, there was a negative relationship of about the same magnitude. If both groups had been pooled, the correlation would have been no better than zero.

The foregoing studies, which have placed analysis of TAT behavior solidly in the main line of current psychological theory, seem to support a positive or representational type of relationship between fantasy and behavior. However, they have dealt only with outwardly directed aggression. An investigation by Davids,

[3] LESSER, GERALD S. "The Relationship Between Overt and Fantasy Aggression as a Function of Maternal Response to Aggression." *J Abn & Social Psychol* 55:218-21 S '57. *

Henry, McArthur, and McNamara (475) on inwardly directed aggression invokes cultural pressures to explain the negative relationship found between TAT stories and such behavior. The investigators reason that overt expression of this type of need (intra-aggression) is made difficult in western culture while its expression in fantasy is facilitated. Therefore, there would not necessarily be a relationship between the two methods of expression of this need; indeed, if the need were strong enough and it were difficult to find expression for it in overt behavior, it might very likely then be expressed in fantasy, here represented by TAT stories. This type of validation study, in which one variable at a time is rigorously defined and systematically manipulated or observed in carefully selected subjects who form clearly defined criterion groups to whom the TAT is then administered, seems to yield positive results. Other types, which depend on retrospective accounts (318, 524) or concurrent clinical evaluation (201, 204, 503), are less successful.

In summary, it seems the TAT cannot be used in the clinic as a standardized procedure in the same sense as an intelligence test, although, as one more impressionistic tool in the armamentarium of the clinician, it may have some practical utility. However, the research possibilities of the TAT are manifold. Much of what occurs in the psychological act of telling stories in response to pictures has been clearly delineated. The effect of order of presentation, picture content, presence or absence of color; the influence of the age, sex, race, intelligence, social status, etc., of both the subject and the experimenter; the immediately preceding experience, the set of the subject, the setting in which the experiment is conducted, the method of administration—all have been investigated and their effect assessed. The crucial question of just how TAT fantasy is related to overt behavior has not been so clearly demonstrated. Most of the work has been done in the area of aggression; and the consensus here is that there is a representative relationship between TAT fantasy and behavior, at least for outwardly directed aggression, if a number of modifying mechanisms such as anxiety, and other variables such as learning conditions, are taken into account. For aggression directed inward, the evidence from one study is that the relationship is compensational, and this has been tentatively related to cultural pressures prohibiting overt expression. It should be clearly understood, however, that in none of the studies relating TAT behavior to overt behavior is the obtained relationship ever high enough to permit prediction in individual cases with any degree of confidence. In clinical situations such predictions should not be made without corroboration from additional sources including other test data, interview material, and behavioral cues.

ARTHUR R. JENSEN, *USPHS Research Fellow, National Institute of Mental Health, Institute of Psychiatry, University of London, London, England.*

The TAT has now been with us for 23 years and has become one of the three or four best known and most widely used clinical psychological tests. Anyone entering the field had better begin with general reviews of the TAT literature (*181, 320, 563*), for there are now close to a thousand references on the TAT. Henry (*538*) gives a very extensive and up-to-date bibliography.

The TAT is not a test that anyone can use after merely studying the manual or a few books on interpretation. In untrained and inexperienced hands it can do more harm than good. It is a test for trained clinical psychologists. Its technique is best learned through practice in a clinical setting under the supervision of a seasoned clinician who is skilled in projective techniques. While it is possible to be a good clinician without knowing the TAT, it is not possible to use the TAT judiciously without being a good clinician. Experience with the TAT is usually gained as a part of the psychologist's clinical training, and expertness with the test seems to be associated with training along "dynamic" or psychoanalytic lines as well as experience in psychotherapy.

ADMINISTRATION. The TAT is perhaps the least standardized of all psychological tests as regards administration, scoring, and interpretation. The instructions to the subject given in Murray's original manual are roughly followed, but few clinicians ever use all 20 cards on one subject. From their own experience clinicians come to have favorite pictures and they sometimes add a few others they think relevant for the subject they are examining. Seldom are more than 10 pictures used. Clinicians have various methods for eliciting fantasy material. Some even ask the subject, "What is the one thing that could *not* be happening in this picture?" This is claimed to get at repressed psychic content better than the usual method of administration (*541*). It apparently makes little difference if the stories are obtained orally or are written by the subject, either alone or in a group (*260, 497*). The thematically "richest" TAT stories the reviewer has seen were written by subjects in a group situation (*575*).

SCORING. In addition to Murray's original schema and its later variations for scoring "needs" and "presses," there are a number of other scoring schemes (*389, 430, 473, 481*). In actual practice, however, formal scoring is little used. It is usually thought to be too time-consuming and often seems to miss the individual essence of the subject's production as well as the holistic impression the clinician wishes to obtain. In addition to the themas, attitudes, motivations, and defenses revealed in the stories, the clinician's analysis is based also on the so-called "formal" aspects, such as style, structure, the subject's complaisance with instructions, language characteristics, logical coherence, realism, bizarreness, emotional tone, productivity, and fluency. Perhaps the chief value of the schemes of scoring or tabulating various aspects of TAT productions is for students learning the TAT. Since the several scoring methods analyze the material from somewhat different angles, practice with them is a means of developing sensitivity to the many facets of TAT material that enter into interpretation.

INTERPRETATION. Rather meagre normative data on content and formal characteristics have been published (*204, 388*), but TAT interpretation is not based on the comparison of "scores" with standard norms. In practice the only "norms" are those held subjectively by the clinician from his own experience with the test. Analysis of as many as 50 to 100 TAT records may be required before one begins to have subjective "norms" for the TAT. It is largely for this reason that clinicians are reluctant to change to new sets of pictures, such as the *Symonds Picture-Story Test* or Bellak's *Children's Apperception Test,* for which subjective "norms" have not been accumulated. Murray, the inventor of the TAT, has restated and elaborated some of his ideas on interpretation (*278*), and there are now a number of good manuals on the art of TAT interpretation (*430, 512, 538*). There is no best or one authentic method of TAT interpretation. This fact is demonstrated in Shneidman's book (*290*) in which each of 15 TAT experts analyzes the same protocol and explains his own method of interpretation. The clinician brings to the task of interpretation all his psychological knowledge, clinical experience, sensitivity, and intuition. The more actual experience the examiner has had with patients, especially if gained through psychotherapy, the more knowledge he has of dynamic psychology, psychoanalysis, and other projective techniques, the more meaning will he derive from the TAT. It is generally agreed that the TAT should not be interpreted "blind," for then it is too apt to miss the mark by far and have no value in "elucidating" the case history material. TAT interpretations tend more to ring true when they are made in conjunction with the case history and with impressions gained from interviews and other tests.

RELIABILITY. The question of reliability has been quite neglected in the TAT literature.[1] Reliability of scoring, of internal consistency, of test-retest, and of interpretation must be evaluated separately.

In searching the TAT literature, the writer has found only 15 estimates of scoring reliability based on sound statistical methods and presented in the form of the product-moment correlation coefficient so as to be strictly comparable to the usual measures of test reliability. These reliability coefficients range from .54 to .91, with an average of .77. For reliability of *scoring* (i.e., interscorer agreement), these figures must be considered quite low. Scoring reliability below .80 is generally considered unacceptable in scoring essay examinations, for example.

There is a widely held misconception that split-half or internal consistency reliability is meaningless in the TAT. Actually it is no less meaningful in the case of the TAT than for any other test comprised of a number of elements which are combined into some kind of "score." A proper coefficient of internal consistency for any TAT variable may be obtained by the Kuder-Richardson formula or by a rank correlation method. When the proper technique was applied (*524*) to 10 of the major Murray TAT variables (Achievement, Aggression, Autonomy, etc.) the internal consistency reliability of the various themes ranged from −.07

to +.34, with a mean of .13. These reliabilities are typical of most internal consistency measures on the TAT (*497*). What they mean in practice is that any scoring system based on the addition of themes elicited by various pictures is fallacious. A theme on one card is not sufficiently correlated with the same theme on another card to justify an additive treatment of TAT variables. It would be like adding together pounds, gallons, and inches. Each card seems to be a unique test in itself and is correlated little, if at all, with other cards (*248*). This fact casts serious doubt on the validity of many methods of TAT interpretation.

Test-retest reliability estimates are rare and are usually more a measure of the subject's memory for his first productions. When subjects were required to make up *different* stories on retest, the reliability coefficients of only 3 out of 17 scored variables were significantly greater than zero (*497*). McClelland (*406*) reports a retest reliability (1 week interval) of .22 for his quantitatively scored *n* Achievement.

Reliability of interpretation is a more important consideration. Friedman (*573*) found the correlations (from a Q-sort) between different interpreters' ideas about the characteristics of the TAT "hero" to average .74, with a range from .37 to .88 for various protocols. This study unfortunately tells us nothing about the discriminating power of the TAT with respect to subjects, but indicates only the fact that there is some agreement between interpreters about the manifest characteristics of the central figure in the stories. Davenport (*329*) had six clinicians rate six TAT records on 207 typical interpretive statements as they applied to each record. The major finding was the lack of reliable discrimination. There was little agreement among the judges in the differential use of the statements for the six TAT records. The judges tended to apply statements rated as universal to almost any patient while avoiding the use of more specific statements. They rarely made statements about positive aspects of personality even though normal subjects were used.

VALIDITY. With such low reliability it is not surprising to find that the validity of the TAT is practically nil. But in discussing validity, one must distinguish two main classes of variables derived from the TAT protocol: thematic material and formal characteristics (style, lan-

---

[1] JENSEN, ARTHUR R. "The Reliability of Projective Techniques." *Acta Psychologica*, in press.

guage, fluency, etc.). On the criterion side one must distinguish between (a) temporary or situationally induced affects, drives, etc., and (b) relatively stable personality characteristics, traits, etc. In experimental studies there have been found significant but low correlations between certain thematic content (e.g., n Achievement, n Aggression, n Sex) and experimentally induced affects or drives (406, 497, 597). These relationships, however, have been so low and are so dependent upon particular experimental conditions as to be of no practical value in the individual clinical application of the TAT. Thematic content has not shown significant relationships to relatively stable behavioral tendencies, personality traits, or psychiatric diagnosis (204, 482, 575).

Formal aspects of the TAT show a low but significant relationship to personality characteristics and diagnostic categories (389, 473, 575). TAT material when analyzed not for its fantasy content but as a "behavior sample" (the subject's complaisance, attitude toward the examiner, degree of social inhibition, etc.) may have some predictive power. For example, adolescent boys who habitually acted out aggressively in ways regarded as taboo in school responded also to the TAT with socially tabooed content and language (575). But these relationships are tenuous; they depend upon a large number of cases for their statistical significance and are of little value in clinical prediction.

Various studies indicate that the TAT has little if any validity as a clinical test. It is generally agreed that the TAT is invalid for nosological diagnosis (181, 204, 320), although certain formal characteristics have been shown to have some relationship to certain broad diagnostic categories (389, 473). Brief, easily scored objective questionnaires, however, can do this sort of thing much more effectively than the TAT. While an objective questionnaire— the Psychosomatic Inventory—correlated .69 with pooled clinical ratings of anxiety, only 3 out of 18 commonly accepted TAT signs of anxiety correlated significantly with the clinical ratings. The highest of these correlations was .40 (451). In another study Child, Frank, and Storm (524) summarize their findings: "We have explored 10 forms of social behavior, and anxiety about each, through two techniques of data gathering. A questionnaire in which subjects rated themselves on 10 items believed relevant to each variable yielded meas-

ures of very satisfactory reliability and, for three variables for which a pertinent criterion was available, substantial validity. A group TAT using eight standard pictures relevant to our variables yielded measures of generally very low reliability, of no validity (by the same criterion applied to the questionnaire), and of no apparent relation to the corresponding measures obtained from the questionnaire." Hartman (161) made comparisons between a clinician's ratings based on the TAT and two other clinicians' ratings based on case history material. The degree of correspondence between interpretations based on the TAT and those based on the case history was barely above the chance level. The median correlations between two raters using case history material and the TAT interpreter were .19 and .28. Most of the significant correlations were based on formal characteristics of the TAT material. In terms of predictive power, Winch and More (562) found that the TAT adds nothing significant to information gained in an interview.

Murray (278) and others have argued that the real proof of the TAT would be the correspondence between TAT material and the deeper layers of personality which are revealed only in the process of psychotherapy. Murray has mentioned one case in which the TAT "adumbrated all the chief trends which five months of analysis were able to reveal." Studies based on larger samples have not found much correspondence between TAT and therapy material. Meyer and Tolman (502) sought a correspondence between attitudes concerning parents expressed in psychotherapeutic interviews and in TAT protocols. There was "no predictability from TAT to therapy as to whether or not parents were discussed, and when they were discussed, no similarity was found between those attitudes and images given in TAT stories and in psychotherapy." Saxe (233) had a TAT clinician rate a personality questionnaire tapping typical TAT variables on 20 patients. After the patients had undergone four months of psychotherapy, the therapist rated the patients on the same questionnaire. There was greater than chance (5 per cent level) agreement in only half of the cases.

If the TAT is short on actual validity, it certainly is not lacking in what might be called "subjective validity" (akin to "faith validity"). This is a feeling gained by the clinician using the TAT that it contributes something to his understanding of the case. Some psychologists have a greater capacity than others for experiencing subjective validity. This capacity seems to be associated with training and experience in psychoanalysis, psychotherapy, and projective techniques in general. The TAT also provides the clinical psychologist with the kind of dynamically interpretable material that can be appreciated by the psychoanalytically oriented psychiatrist to whom the clinician addresses his report. Thus clinicians are heard to speak of the TAT as being "useful" rather than as having validity. It is probably for these reasons that the TAT survives in clinical practice.

SUMMARY. The TAT is a nonstandardized assessment technique which is best left to clinical psychologists who have had special training in its use. While research has shown the TAT to have low reliability and negligible validity, many clinical psychologists continue to use it, apparently with some satisfaction.

For a review by Arthur L. Benton, see 4:136; for reviews by Arthur L. Benton, Julian B. Rotter, and J. R. Wittenborn, see 3:103 (1 excerpt); for related reviews, see B63, B204, B395, 4:137-41, 3:104, and 3:104a.

[165]

★Thematic Apperception Test for African Subjects. Ages 10 and over; 1953; 1 form ['53]; no data on reliability; 12s. 6d. per set of test materials, postage extra; [60-120] minutes; S. G. Lee; University of Natal Press. *

REFERENCE

1. LEE, S. G. *A Preliminary Investigation of the Personality of the Educated African by Means of a Projective Technique.* Master's thesis, University of Natal (Natal, Union of South Africa), 1949.

MARY D. AINSWORTH, *Associate Professor of Psychology, The Johns Hopkins University, Baltimore, Maryland.*

Impressed with the fruitfulness of the thematic apperception approach, Lee attempted to use the standard TAT materials for the investigation of the personality of Zulu subjects, but found that they were not adequately stimulated to imaginative production. He therefore devised his own set of pictures for use with African subjects. In order to "cross the cultural gap" and to arrive at pictorial materials that would be stimulating, he based his pictures on fantasy productions collected from Bantu inmates of a mental hospital.

His version of the TAT consists of 22 cards, 8 for males, 8 for females, and 6 (including a blank card) for both males and females. In some respects the cards impress this reviewer as being more ambiguous than the cards of the standard TAT. The faces of the figures are either highly ambiguous in expression or hidden from view. The backgrounds include little detail. The line of the drawings is more sketchy and hence less structured than that of the standard TAT drawings. On the other hand, many of the figures are portrayed in vigorous action or exaggerated posture that seems less ambiguous than that of the figures of the standard TAT and might be expected to be highly provocative of kinaesthetic empathy.

There seems to have been no attempt systematically to vary the number, sex, and apparent age of the figures in order to sample various types of relationships. Two cards, both in the female series, seem designed to elicit stories of parent-child relations, presumably from the mother's viewpoint. One card portrays a heterosexual situation. However, most of the pictures present single figures, and only six show two or more figures together.

Although the pictures were originally designed for the Zulu and contain some characteristically Zulu features, Lee reports that they have been used effectively among other African peoples (he specifies the tribes) and among both educated and uneducated subjects. Nevertheless, it may not be assumed that his *Thematic Apperception Test for African Subjects* is therefore applicable to all African peoples. The fact that 12 of the cards depict near-naked figures would undoubtedly be a disadvantage with tribes such as the Ganda of East Africa who traditionally clothe themselves from top to toe and consider it immodest to display the feet when sitting.

The 42-page manual provides in concise form an excellent guide for the administration and interpretation of a TAT-type test. The initial instructions contain all the essential points included in Murray's original instructions, but are worded more simply and might well be adapted to good effect in administering the standard TAT. Lee recommends that a recall phase be included at the conclusion of the story-telling phase, in which the subject is asked to recall as many of the pictures as he can in as much detail as possible. He further recommends a follow-up interview when the subject is asked to explain the sources of his plots.

Lee's suggestions for analysis and interpretation emphasize the form as well as the content of the story. In his suggestions for analysis, he has been influenced obviously by publications of other authors and he acknowledges his sources in his bibliography. His selection of points to be observed in analysis is commendable. Although his examples are selected from the records of the 140 African subjects to whom he has given his modification of the TAT, the manual might well serve as a useful guide to the beginner using any version of the TAT. He provides no normative material in statistical form, but lists the common responses he has obtained for each card. The manual concludes with a specimen analysis.

In short, Lee's TAT for African subjects recommends itself for the personality evaluation of individual subjects and for the investigation of culture-personality interaction among African peoples who may be presumed to be able to identify with near-naked African figures, although for some tribes either the Thompson modification of the TAT or some other special modification may be more appropriate.

[166]

Thematic Apperception Test: Thompson Modification. Negroes ages 4 and over; 1949, c1943–49; individual; 1 form ['49]; manual ('49); no data on reliability and validity; no norms; $6 per set of test materials, cash orders postpaid; (120) minutes in 2 sessions 1 day apart; Charles E. Thompson; Harvard University Press. *

REFERENCES

1–5. See 4:138.
6. WEBER, GEORGE HENRY. A Social-Psychological Schema for the Analysis of the Thompson Thematic Apperception Tests. Doctor's thesis, University of Kansas (Lawrence, Kan.), 1949.
7. COOK, RICHARD A. "Identification and Ego Defensiveness in Thematic Apperception." J Proj Tech 17:312–9 S '53. * (PA 28:4343)
8. LIGHT, BERNARD H. "A Further Test of the Thompson TAT Rationale." J Abn & Social Psychol 51:148–50 Jl '55. * (PA 30:4581)
9. KLEIN, ARMIN, JR. The Influence of Stimulus Material and Geographical Region on Responses to a Thematic Test. Doctor's thesis, Columbia University (New York, N.Y.), 1956. (DA 16:1284)

MARY D. AINSWORTH, *Associate Professor of Psychology, The Johns Hopkins University, Baltimore, Maryland.*

Thompson's purpose in modifying the TAT was to provide an instrument to facilitate a more valid clinical evaluation of Negro subjects by increasing the extent to which they can identify with the figures portrayed. His intention was to construct a series of pictures similar to those of the TAT in every respect except for changing the figures to have dark skin color and negroid features. Twenty-one of the 31 original pictures were redrawn or rephotographed (Card 13B). In the redrawing, the stimulus value of

the cards may well have been changed in respects other than the racial characteristics of the figures, for the dark backgrounds were lightened in order to provide a contrast with the dark faces, and the quality of the line was changed markedly in some of the pictures, especially in those originally reproduced from paintings, for example, Cards 2 and 7GF. Two additional and unexplained changes were made: the blank card was changed from white to gray, and Card 10 was dropped so that the complete series consists of 19 instead of 20 cards. The remaining cards (11, 12BG, 14, 15, 17GF, 19 and 20) are unchanged. The manual for the Thompson modification follows Murray's manual very closely, except for the omission of the section on analysis and interpretation of the stories.

The T-TAT differs significantly from other modifications designed for studies of culture-personality interaction,[1] in which the pictures are constructed to be appropriate to the group under investigation, not only in terms of racial characteristics of the figures portrayed, but also in features characteristic of the culture, including clothing, activities, distinctive objects, style of buildings, and so on. Henry[1] has demonstrated that such materials yield records permitting exploration of the "idiosyncratic component" of personality as well as providing data on the communal and role components.

The consensus in the literature is that the T-TAT may be useful in exploring racial attitudes and stereotypes in both Negro and white subjects. However, Thompson's contention that the T-TAT is better than the standard TAT for the clinical evaluation of individual Negroes has been challenged by other authors.

Thompson bases his claim for the superiority of the T-TAT upon a study (2) undertaken with 26 southern male Negro college students, who produced significantly longer protocols to 10 modified cards than they did to the equivalent cards of the standard version. From this and from qualitative data he concludes that the modified TAT facilitates identification and empathy in Negro subjects. Other studies with northern Negroes (4), predominantly southern Negroes (7) and white subjects (4, 7, 8) failed to demonstrate significant differences between the T-TAT and standard TAT with respect to

[1] HENRY, WILLIAM E. Chap. 8, "The Thematic Apperception Technique in the Study of Group and Cultural Problems," pp. 230–78. In *An Introduction to Projective Techniques.* Edited by Harold H. Anderson and Gladys L. Anderson. New York: Prentice-Hall, Inc., 1951. Pp. xxiv, 720. *

length of stories. No significant differences were found for "idea count" (5) or for 12 measures of ego defensiveness (7). Subjective reports (7) indicated that Negroes could identify with TAT and T-TAT figures whereas white subjects thought of the T-TAT figures as Negroes rather than "people in general."

Qualitative differences between the stories evoked by the T-TAT and standard TAT cards were noted by several authors (3, 5, 8) but these were not considered to indicate increased empathy for figures with racial characteristics similar to those of the subject. Riess, Schwartz, and Cottingham (4) claim that Negroes in our culture, unaccustomed to seeing Negroes portrayed in pictures, become self-conscious about their racial status, and that this tends to defeat the basic purpose of the projective method, and highlights social distance and racial stereotypes. Korchin, Mitchell, and Meltzoff (3) view the changed figures of the T-TAT as representing an undesirable reduction in ambiguity, which evokes attitudes toward Negro problems rather than eliciting idiosyncratic material.

Length of story seems obviously inadequate as the major criterion of the adequacy of a protocol for clinical evaluation. Qualitative differences between T-TAT and TAT productions have not been systematically studied. In the absence of studies comparing the relative thematic yield of the two versions of the test for Negro groups, similar to Mussen's study [2] using the standard TAT to compare white and Negro groups, it seems premature to conclude either that the Thompson modification is superior to the standard TAT for all Negroes or that it is a "bastardization of the projective techniques" (4).

When deciding whether to use the T-TAT or the standard version, the clinician may wish to judge whether the Negro subject in question has so little sense of social distance that the standard version may be preferable or whether he is sufficiently removed from white groups that the T-TAT seems more promising. The clinician may also be influenced by the extent to which he believes that a reflection of the subject's racial attitudes will enrich the personality evaluation to be derived from the total battery of tests or possibly impoverish the evaluation by crowding out the information about needs

and press that he relies upon the TAT to provide.

See 4:138 (3 excerpts).

[167]

★The Tomkins-Horn Picture Arrangement Test. Ages 10 and over; 1942–57; IBM; 1 form ('44); $15 per 50 tests; $25 per set of scoring materials ['57]; $4.50 per 100 scoring sheets ('57); $10 per manual ('57, see 5 below); postage extra; (30–60) minutes; Silvan S. Tomkins, Daniel Horn, and John B. Miner (manual); Springer Publishing Co., Inc. *

REFERENCES

1. TOMKINS, SILVAN S. "The Tomkins-Horn Picture-Arrangement Test." *Trans N Y Acad Sci, Series II* 15:46–50 D '52. * (PA 27:7208)
2. SJOSTEDT, ELSIE MARIE. *A Study of the Personality Variables Related to Assaultive and Acquisitive Crimes.* Doctor's thesis, Purdue University (Lafayette, Ind.), 1955. (DA 15:881)
3. TOMKINS, SILVAN S. "The Role of Tests in the United States With Particular Reference to the Tomkins-Horn Picture Arrangement Test." *Inter-Am Congr Psychol* 1:218–23 '55. *
4. TOMKINS, SILVAN S., AND MINER, JOHN B. "Contributions to the Standardization of the Tomkins-Horn Picture Arrangement Test: Plate Norms." *J Psychol* 39:199–214 Ja '55. * (PA 29:8654)
5. TOMKINS, SILVAN S., AND MINER, JOHN B. *The Tomkins-Horn Picture Arrangement Test.* New York: Springer Publishing Co., Inc., 1957. Pp. xvi, 383. * (PA 32:2926)
6. KARON, BERTRAM P. *The Negro Personality: A Rigorous Investigation of the Effects of Culture.* New York: Springer Publishing Co., Inc., 1958. Pp. viii, 184. *

DONALD W. FISKE, *Associate Professor of Psychology, University of Chicago, Chicago, Illinois.*

This "abbreviated projective test" was designed to yield material with some of the richness of the *Thematic Apperception Test* but with greater ease of administration and scoring. Each of the 25 items consists of three sketches. The subject is instructed to indicate the order for the three pictures "which makes the best sense" and to write one sentence for each picture to tell the story.

The intended function of the technique is not made explicit. There is a passing comment that it was "originally designed for purposes of selection and guidance of industrial personnel," but later "redesigned for more general use." However, the emphasis in the book implies that the authors are concerned with clinical diagnosis, with case studies. The content of the pictures reflects the development of the procedure —14 of the 25 items portray a shop setting. The odd distribution over content areas does not clarify the problem of the appropriate utilization of the instrument. The authors indicate that they attempted to sample three areas: social orientation, optimism-pessimism, and level of functioning.

The highly commendable and unique feature of this test's development was its administration to a representative "normal" sample (n =

2 MUSSEN, PAUL H. "Differences Between the TAT Responses of Negro and White Boys." *J Consult Psychol* 17:373–6 O '53. * (PA 28:5888)

1,500) of the United States population. A vocabulary test administered at the same time made it possible to publish norms for various groups identified by intelligence as well as by age, education, and other demographic characteristics. Hundreds of abnormals were also tested, but less representatively.

Although the administration is simple, the scoring is exceedingly complex. It is based on a clinical rationale that diagnosis must be based on responses which are rare for the subject's group, as determined by his age, IQ, and education. Thus, the authors practically throw away all information contained in "common" responses or patterns (occurring with frequencies greater than 5 per cent). They do, however, have conformity keys indicating popular tendencies, but these are "intended primarily for research purposes." They also note that cross-cultural comparisons should be based on modal tendencies for groups.

Hand scoring and interpretation are said to take only an hour, but scoring on an IBM accounting machine requires 20 minutes per subject. At the time the normative study was conducted, the scoring of individual records was so cumbersome that group statistics are reported rather than frequency distributions of scores for individuals.

Once the scoring of a single protocol has identified the pertinent keys from the 655 specified patterns, the trained psychologist can proceed with an essentially clinical interpretation. If he wishes, he may use the subject's qualitative sentences in this step.

In spite of the enormous amount of work expended on the PAT, adequate psychometric analyses have not been reported in the book which serves as manual. No alternate form is available and the authors dismiss as inappropriate the investigation of internal consistency, although at one point they imply that the correlation between items is very low.

Two studies of stability are reported, with three weeks and three years between administrations: 33 and 45 per cent, respectively, of the responses changed on retest. The authors make the dubious interpretation that the test is sensitive to personality changes over a three-year period but fail to grasp the serious weakness implied by the large change over three weeks. (No data on changes in pattern are reported.)

The authors note that over plates or items the smaller the modal response, the more frequently such modal responses changed. Although they do not report data on this point, there is reason to expect that the more atypical a subject's response, the more likely it is to be changed.[1] Thus, the rare responses and the rare patterns are probably the least stable. But it is just these on which the authors base their scoring and interpretation! They are well aware of changes in a subject from day to day, but they make no provision for distinguishing momentary tendencies from enduring dispositions.

The manual is especially deficient on the problem of validity. A few sentences are devoted to one study which found correlations with independently assessed personality characteristics that were in the expected directions but low and "too weak to be diagnostically useful." Pertinent but not definitive evidence is presented in the patterns associated with each of the several abnormal groups.

The exposition in the book is not concise and clear. No sample protocols are presented.

This procedure is one of several recent innovations which attempt to apply current knowledge and technical developments to personality assessment. While the work on norms is commendable, the technique has not been investigated sufficiently to justify its use for any purpose except methodological research. The use of ordered and objectively scored responses to approach thematic material is a step in the right direction, but this study indicates the high cost of this method.

JOHN W. GITTINGER, *Field Representative, Society for the Investigation of Human Ecology, Forest Hills, New York.*

The *Tomkins-Horn Picture Arrangement Test* is an ingenious group projective personality test, adapted for machine scoring, utilizing simple social and work situations. The test consists of 25 plates, each containing three sketches which can be combined into a variety of sequences or "a story that makes sense" by the subject. The subject is asked to arrange the three pictures and to write three sentences explaining the selected sequence. It is the subject's selection of one of a variety of possible sequences that makes it possible to measure the projective nature of the test. Theoretically, the test is concerned with the personality or dynamic meaning revealed by the selection of sequence

1 FISKE, DONALD W. "The Constraints on Intra-Individual Variability in Test Responses." *Ed & Psychol Meas* 17:317-37 au '57. *

rather than with the best, most common, or most conventional sorting. In fact, the emphasis in the development of the keys has been on the rare response.

Although the authors indicate that their inspiration was the *Thematic Apperception Test,* their model was the Picture Arrangement subtest of the Wechsler-Bellevue. Based on their observations that personality factors seemed to influence Picture Arrangement scores on the Wechsler-Bellevue, they developed their series of highly structured interpersonal relationships mainly in work situations. Though the authors state that the test was originally designed for use with industrial personnel, it is not clear why, with the broadening of its use, the concentration on work situations rather than the relatively more versatile interpersonal situations used by the Wechsler-Bellevue has been retained. The book-manual presents a highly systematic and orderly description of how the test was developed and how the 655 scoring patterns were derived.

In evaluating the test as published, there only can be admiration for the care with which the standardization population was selected, the methods by which the keys were constructed, and the detail in which the mechanical results are reported. Some exception will undoubtedly be taken to the discussion of reliability because it is somewhat unique and certainly unconventional. The authors argue that some of the change noted in a test-retest situation must be attributable to personality changes over time, and that, if the test is sensitive to changes in personality, less stability would be expected over longer retest intervals. They have, however, stated their case convincingly and, while the argument may be controversial, it certainly is not unscientific.

The rationale for the test is presented in but 21 pages of the 383-page book. These pages are filled with provocative but tantalizing and at times highly elusive comments. To a very large extent, the average reader will finish the presentation somewhat confused about what the test purports to measure. In spite of the fact that the test is claimed to be uncommitted to "any contemporary theory of personality," the composition and interpretation of the keys depends upon some type of conceptual framework which is nowhere clearly explained. The presentation of the descriptive terms for the keys, their definitions, and their relationship to one another does not show the same care and precision that characterizes the material on the construction of the test.

To a large extent the PAT is a well constructed projective device whose meaning and purpose is obscure. Its immediate clinical application is limited, but as a research tool it has much implied promise. It is hoped that future research can contribute to transforming the test from a clever measuring device to a well rounded clinical instrument.

WAYNE H. HOLTZMAN, *Associate Professor of Psychology, and Associate Director, The Hogg Foundation for Mental Health, The University of Texas, Austin, Texas.*

Inspired by the *Thematic Apperception Test,* the *Picture Arrangement Test* (PAT) was constructed as an extension of the well known picture arrangement method in the testing of intelligence. The test is comprised of 25 plates, each containing three simple, cartoon-like drawings. The subject is instructed to indicate the order in which the three situations make the best sense and to write three brief sentences, one for each drawing, explaining the situation. The same central figure is depicted in every drawing, making it possible for the subject to project some of his own personality into the short story he formulates. The three drawings are shown at angles of 120 degrees to minimize spurious effects due to position and order of presentation. Use of standard test booklets and simple instructions makes it possible to administer the PAT to any number of subjects at one time.

The majority of the plates emphasize the work situation of a laborer in an industrial setting. Other drawings were chosen to obtain information about social orientation, optimism-pessimism, and level of functioning with respect to the "relative strength of thinking, phantasy, affect, and behavior in the economy of the individual." Time for test administration is typically one hour but may take as long as 10 hours in several sessions for some psychotic patients.

One highly significant aspect of the PAT from a methodological point of view is the extent to which its authors have developed an empirical system for scoring complex patterns of response. Numerous individuals have sung the praises of configural scoring, pattern analysis, or clinical-global treatment of information as opposed to the use of single isolated scores. But few, if any, have achieved the degree of success in the actual employment of such pattern scoring as Tomkins and Miner. Of the almost infinite number of permutations that are possible when all 25 plates are considered simultaneously, only those combinations which seemed plausible for interpretive purposes on a priori grounds were examined empirically for frequency of occurrence in the normative sample. Wisely focusing upon the rare response patterns rather than hoping to find meaningful data in every response of every subject, Tomkins and his colleagues have painstakingly developed 96 conformity keys, 559 content keys, and 12 keys designed to detect undue effects of position or order. Special techniques have been developed for efficient pattern scoring so that a given protocol can be hand scored by a clerk in about 45 minutes.

A second highly commendable feature of the PAT is the use of a representative nationwide sample of 1,500 subjects for the establishment of norms. Tomkins was fortunate in having the resources of the Gallup Poll for standardization of his test. His extensive norms for different ages, educational levels, and degrees of intelligence as measured by a short vocabulary test are probably the best that can be reasonably obtained and surpass by far the usual standard for projective techniques. In addition to the primary normative sample, data were obtained from 755 abnormal subjects in 84 different clinics and mental hospitals.

In spite of an elaborate, complex scoring system based on a well developed rationale and an adequate normative sample, the interpretation of an individual test record leaves much to be desired. Test-retest reliability is not high, nor are any studies cited that demonstrate the validity of the PAT.

Basic to the interpretation of the pattern norms is the assumption that the situation depicted by the drawing placed last in sequence on any given plate is the significant one with respect to the respondent's personality. For example, if the subject invariably ends his arrangement with the hero working when other endings might have been just as plausible, it is inferred that the subject has high general interest in work. While the content keys may seem reasonable enough on an a priori basis to merit serious consideration, interpretation of the PAT will remain largely speculative until further research is undertaken dealing with their validity

with respect to the subject's personality. It is one thing to classify patterns of response according to the subject's preferences and quite another matter to draw valid inferences about his personality.

Personnel & Guid J 36:289–90 D '57. Leonard D. Goodstein. This is a fascinating but frustrating book presenting a new *standardized* projective test of personality * contains a brief theoretical paper dealing with the rationale of projective personality tests in general and the PAT in particular, a long and extremely confusing description of the development and standardization of the PAT, a discussion of the techniques of administering and scoring the PAT, together with a presentation of the interpretative significance of the several PAT scores. * Norms are not only available for single plates but also for *patterns* or *keys* which are scored over several plates by means of special answer sheets and scoring templates. These patterns or keys are based upon the authors' *a priori* interpretations of certain consistencies in theme from plate to plate; for example, the High General Work Interest Key (Pattern 217) showing "a preference for physical work" is scored over 14 plates, involving 34 different arrangements. Depending upon the subject's education, intelligence, and age (the three breakdowns for the pattern norms), a score of 9 or 10 on the High General Work Key would be regarded as *interpretable,* that is given by less than five per cent of the normal standardization group. There is no data, unfortunately, on the responses of the pathological groups on these keys. This is an extremely frustrating book to read especially for the first time. The organization is very weak and quite confusing; there is detailed discussion of the significance of certain scores (pp. 83–93) before the techniques for obtaining the scores are explained. Nowhere is there a simple, straight-forward, organized description of the procedures and steps involved in administering, scoring, and interpreting an individual PAT protocol. The tables are poorly labeled (especially those for the pattern norms), difficult to follow without a careful prior reading of the text, and inconsistent in the type of data presented (the plate norms are in percentages while the pattern norms are in actual frequencies). Many of these problems could have been eliminated by careful editing. There is no discussion of the problem of the *validity*, that is, the non-test behavioral correlates, of the PAT nor is any evidence on this point presented except for the data on the differences between the normal and patient response frequencies on each plate. Whether or not high or low scores on the High General Work Interest Key are related to occupational success or any other behavior index still remains a problem for empirical solution. It is the reviewer's hope that the difficulties and obscurities of the text will not limit its use or that of the PAT. Here is a new and quite different approach to projective personality assessment and one that may live up to the publisher's enthusiastic statement that this is the beginning of "a new era of projective testing."

[168]

*The Toy World Test. Ages 2 and over; 1941–55; formerly called *The World Test;* individual; 1 form ('49); 4 sets of test materials differing in number of pieces, materials used, and country where manufactured; $75 per American set; $90 per American-French set; $90 per German set; $130 per French set; $2 per 25 record blanks ('55); $1.50 per manual ('49); postage extra; (20–45) minutes; Charlotte Buhler; distributed by Joyce B. Baisden, 4570 Mont Eagle Place, Los Angeles 41, Calif. *

REFERENCES

1–6. See 4:147.
7. BOLGAR, HEDDA, AND FISCHER, LISELOTTE K. "Personality Projection in the World Test." *Am J Orthopsychiatry* 17:117–28 Ja '47. * (*PA* 21:2317)
8. FISCHER, LISELOTTE K. "A New Psychological Tool in Function: Preliminary Clinical Experience With the Bolgar-Fischer World Test." *Am J Orthopsychiatry* 20:281–92 Ap '50. * (*PA* 25:2453)
9. FISCHER, LISELOTTE K. "The World 'Test,' " pp. 62–76. (*PA* 25:6869) In *Projective and Expressive Methods of Personality Investigation* ("*Diagnosis*"). Edited by Werner Wolff. New York: Grune & Stratton, Inc., April 1950. Pp. ii, 76. *
10. BUHLER, CHARLOTTE. "The World Test." *J Child Psychiatry* 2:2–3 sect 1 '51. * (*PA* 26:2743)
11. BUHLER, CHARLOTTE. "The World Test: A Projective Technique." *J Child Psychiatry* 2:4–23 sect 1 '51. * (*PA* 26:2741)
12. BUHLER, CHARLOTTE. "The World Test: Manual of Directions." *J Child Psychiatry* 2:69–81 sect 1 '51. * (*PA* 26:2743)
13. BUHLER, CHARLOTTE, AND CARROL, HELEN SARA. "A Comparison of the Results of the World Test With the Teacher's Judgment Concerning Children's Personality Adjustment." *J Child Psychiatry* 2:36–68 sect 1 '51. * (*PA* 26:2742)
14. LUMRY, GAYLE KELLY. "Study of World Test Characteristics as a Basis for Discrimination Between Various Clinical Categories." *J Child Psychiatry* 2:24–35 sect 1 '51. * (*PA* 26:2751)
15. BUHLER, CHARLOTTE. "National Differences in 'World Test' Projection Patterns." *J Proj Tech* 16:42–55 Mr '52. * (*PA* 27:352)
16. PASCAL, GERALD R. Chap. 11, "Gestalt Functions: The Bender-Gestalt, Mosaic and World Tests," pp. 185–90. (*PA* 27:3559) In *Progress in Clinical Psychology, Vol. I, Sect. I.* Edited by Daniel Brower and Lawrence E. Abt. New York: Grune & Stratton, Inc., 1952. Pp. xi, 328. *
17. WENAR, CHARLES. "The Effects of a Motor Handicap on Personality: III, The Effects on Certain Fantasies and Adjustive Techniques." *Child Develop* 27:9–15 Mr '56. * (*PA* 31:3594)

L. JOSEPH STONE, *Professor of Child Study, Vassar College, Poughkeepsie, New York.*

The *Toy World Test,* like most other projective devices, can be considered a "test" only in a special sense. To the extent to which it permits or invites free expressive use of the materials, i.e., invites projection, it defies standardization in the usual understanding of that term; to the extent that fixed classification and quasi-standardization is carried out, the special qualities of idiosyncratic personality portrayal inherent in projective methods may be sacrificed. Investigators have stationed themselves at different points on the imaginary line that can be drawn between the horns of this dilemma. In the test itself the alternative emphases are evident in the ways in which it has been handled by its originator, Lowenfeld, who does not call it a test, and by Buhler, whose approach is the subject of this review. A use of the same materials that is comparable in many ways to Buhler's but follows a different approach to standardization and scoring is that of Bolgar and Fischer (7–9).

The earliest version of the miniature toys used in the test is lost in antiquity. However, the first organized approach to a "world on the floor" is found in H. G. Wells' *Floor Games* [1] in which there are descriptions and photographs of the elaborate miniature constructions like stage sets which he designed for (and with?) his children.

Klein and other child analysts first used miniature toys for the purpose of eliciting fantasy as a substitute for the free associations which children could not be instructed to supply. This approach was first systematized by Lowenfeld, who, like Klein, considers Lowenfeld's *World Technique* [2] to be primarily a psychotherapeutic instrument. Lowenfeld has published her findings with the procedure and her instructions for its systematic use; she has also circulated an unpublished revision for the use of American investigators in adapting the approach and materials to the American scene in a cooperative investigation now under way. Somewhat different versions of the use of miniature toys have been worked out by Erikson [3] in his *Dramatic Productions Test,* Murphy [4] in her *Miniature Life Toys,* and others.

Buhler observed the "world play" material in 1935 at Lowenfeld's Institute of Child Psychology in London and proposed a standardiza-

1 WELLS, H. G. *Floor Games.* London: F. Palmer, 1911.
2 LOWENFELD, MARGARET. "The World Pictures of Children: A Method of Recording and Studying Them." *Brit J Med Psychol* 18:65–101 pt 1 '39. * (*PA* 13:3897)
3 HOMBURGER [ERIKSON], ERIK. "Configurations in Play: Clinical Notes." *Psychoanalytic Q* 6:139–214 '37. (*PA* 11:4564)
4 MURPHY, LOIS BARCLAY. *Personality in Young Children: Vol. I, Methods for the Study of Personality in Young Children.* New York: Basic Books, Inc., 1956. Pp. xx, 424. *

tion. The first effort along these lines was represented by the Van Wylick dissertation [5] published in 1937 in Vienna under the direction of K. Wolff. In recent years Buhler has instigated or supervised a series of standardization studies. Her current prescribed set of materials, renamed the *Toy World Test* to distinguish it from her newly developed *Picture World Test,* consists of 160 or 300 wooden items, less elaborate, colorful, and varied than the Lowenfeld materials; she has departed from the use of sand and water which Lowenfeld considers essential. In Buhler's approach the children use the toys on the floor or table.

Buhler's standardization, which has gone through several stages, now includes a fixed, reproducible form of the materials (produced by the Los Angeles Crippled Children's Society) not subject to whims of toy manufacturers, standardized instructions and recording procedures, and, most important of all, the interpretation of the results in terms of "signs." In such an approach the projective requirements are met by permitting the child (or adult) to use the materials with considerable freedom ("Now you may play"), while the requirements of standardization are met by "scoring"—which is to say, more accurately, sorting or classifying—various aspects of the completed productions under the heading of several signs. First, the number of "elements" used (i.e., kinds of toys, such as men, women, trees, and animals) are recorded; next, the presence of A-Signs (aggressions), CDR-Signs (distortions, including closed-in areas, disarrangements, and rigid arrangements), and S-Signs (symbolic arrangements in which important qualitative material is revealed), is judged and recorded. In addition, although the manual, oddly enough, does not include the definition of E-Signs, it is apparent from the score sheet and from various published articles that this sign (empty, or relatively sparse and unpopulated worlds) is also intended as an important indicator.

Briefly, A-Signs alone are said to indicate superficial and perhaps temporary problems; E-Signs may indicate retardation or various kinds of emotional disturbance; CDR-Signs are held to be "more significant symptoms of deep emotional disturbances....present in all psychoneurosis and psychosis cases in children and adults." Of the latter, R-Signs are considered

5 VAN WYLICK, M. *Die Welt des Kindes in seiner Darstellung.* Vienna: Gerold, 1937.

the gravest: except with the very young and the mentally deficient, their use indicates obsessive compulsive trends, with deep anxiety. Beyond the use of these standardized signs as descriptive entities, interpretation includes qualitative consideration of the subject's remarks and elaboration in his play.

In summarizing a series of studies carried out under her supervision, Buhler (6) compared 30 normal (N) children, 117 problem (P) children, and 27 retarded (R) children in 174 American and European cases. In comparing their productions, using the criterion of no symptoms (subvarieties of Signs) as against "symptoms," she found critical ratios of differences among the groups as follows: N and P, 3.58; N and R, 3.50; P and R, .70. A criterion of two or more symptoms increased the critical ratio for P and R to 1.99 but somewhat lowered the others.

Lumry (6) examined four different groups of children of 25 each: normal, stuttering, withdrawing, and retarded. The mean numbers of symptoms in these four groups were .32, 2.32, 2.52, and 2.52, respectively, leading to the conclusion that "the frequency of appearance of symptoms is of clinical importance in differentiating the well adjusted child and the one who has certain psychological difficulties, but does not provide a quantitative basis for differential diagnosis." Certain symptoms were found to be particularly significant. For example, no normal child showed the symptom "no men and women," while this was found among 50 per cent of the children with psychological problems.

These and related studies suggest that while the sign approach as used by Buhler and her coworkers is approaching the stage where considerable reliance may be placed on the quantitative "scoring," it has not yet reached that point of statistical validation generally required of tests primarily quantitative in nature. It seems to the reviewer that one essential stage has been omitted in the attempt to make this projective material quantitatively manipulable. In none of the studies is there any evidence of the reliability of the scoring or of the clinical skill or training required to make these classificatory judgments. Since the presence of even two "symptoms" may be important, the criteria for assigning a symptom score should be much more precise if critical quantitative use is to be made of them. Their usefulness as clinical indicators or signposts in the understanding of the individual child is, of course, another matter.

[169]

*The Travis Projective Pictures. Ages 4 and over; 1949–57; revision of *The Travis-Johnston Projective Test: For the Exploration of Parent-Child Relationships;* 1 form ['57] ; directions sheet ['57] ; no data on reliability and validity; no norms; $8.50 per set of 29 pictures, postage extra; administration time not reported; [Lee E. Travis] ; Griffin-Patterson Co. Inc. *

REFERENCES

1–3. See 4:142.
4. TRAVIS, LEE EDWARD, AND SUTHERLAND, LAVERNE DEEL. Chap. 25, "Suggestions for Psychotherapy in Public School Speech Correction," pp. 805–31. In *Handbook of Speech Pathology.* Edited by Lee Edward Travis. New York: Appleton-Century-Crofts, Inc., 1957. Pp. vii, 1088. *

EDWIN S. SHNEIDMAN, *Co-Principal Investigator, Central Research Unit, V.A. Center, Los Angeles, California.*

If a psychological test can be defined as consisting of a set of stimuli and, *in addition,* having accrued to it some normative data, reliability data, and conceptual notions (all subsumed under the purview of some general personality theory), then the *Travis Projective Pictures* is not a test, nor does Travis make any attempt to indicate otherwise. The reviewer telephoned the author and asked him about his materials. He said that the pictures were simply a set of stimulus materials; that there had never been a manual; that he had made no effort at norms or standards. He did indicate that the pictures had been given to around 150 school children and that the examiners "got some very fine responses." He stated that a number of speech correctionists—a field in which Travis has an international reputation—had "picked up" the materials and that the materials were being used mainly as an adjunct to speech therapeutic processes.

An interesting feature of the set of materials —which consist of freehand drawings of either one or two children and one or two adults "in various situations and relationships centering in some important and potentially troublesome areas of the socializing process of the child"— is that the pictures are focused around specific parent-child problem areas, such as punishment, hostility, parent-child rivalry, and toilet training. This is consistent with current thinking in some thematic test circles about the special advantages of using stimulus materials which focus on specific psychodynamic areas. The only reference to these materials appears in Travis' recent text on speech pathology (4).

The suggestions for administration are quite flexible. Travis indicates:

As a rule children respond well verbally to the pictures. They are instructed simply to tell a story about a picture. The speech therapist can make the situation a group or an individual one as time and circumstances warrant. Also, she can use a picture only, or she can present a picture while the child is doing something else, such as working with clay, playing with puppets, or playing a role in sociodrama. Although the cards are numbered, they need not necessarily be used in numerical order. The experienced therapist will choose the picture that fits best into the forward flowing process of therapy.

Travis does well in calling his materials *Travis Projective Pictures* rather than a test. One can hardly argue with an author who presents a set of stimulus materials and makes no special claims for them. *Caveat emptor.*

For a review by Robert R. Holt of the original edition, see 4:142.

[170]

★The Tree Test. Ages 9 and over; 1949–52; 1 form ('52) ; manual ('52, see 1 below) ; no data on reliability and validity; 15.95 *Sw. fr.* ($4.50) per manual, postage extra; [5–10] minutes; Charles Koch; Hans Huber. * (U.S. distributor: Grune & Stratton, Inc.)

REFERENCES

1. KOCH, CHARLES. *The Tree Test: The Tree-Drawing Test as an Aid in Psychodiagnosis.* Berne, Switzerland: Hans Huber, 1952. Pp. 87. * (PA 27:3137)
2. TOLOR, ALEXANDER. "The Stability of Tree Drawings as Related to Several Rorschach Signs of Rigidity." *J Clin Psychol* 13:162–4 Ap '57. * (PA 32:2924)

For related reviews, see B251.

[171]

*Twitchell-Allen Three-Dimensional Personality Test. Ages 3 and over (sighted and sightless) ; 1948–58; formerly called *Twitchell-Allen Three-Dimensional Apperception Test;* 1 form ('48) ; revised manual ('58) ; revised record blank ('58) ; $62 per set of testing materials, 50 recording blanks, and manual; $2 per manual; postage extra; (60) minutes; Doris Twitchell-Allen; C. H. Stoelting Co. *

REFERENCES

1. TWITCHELL-ALLEN, DORIS. "A 3-Dimensional Apperception Test: A New Projective Technique." Abstract. *Am Psychol* 2:271–2 Ag '47. *
2. STARER, EMANUEL. "An Examination of the Responses of a Group of Young Normal Female and a Group of Female Psychotic Patients on the Three-Dimensional Apperception Test." *J Clin Psychol* 9:47–50 Ja '53. * (PA 27:7944)
3. FEIN, LEAH GOLD, AND ALLEN, DORIS TWITCHELL. "Parts of Speech Ratio: A Maturational and Diagnostic Index to Personality Function." *Psychol Newsl* 9:162–6 '58. *

For a review by Edward Joseph Shoben, Jr., see 4:143.

[172]

Visual Motor Gestalt Test. Ages 4 and over; 1938–46; commonly called *Bender Gestalt Test;* individual; 1 form ('46) ; manual ('38, see 5 below) ; no data on reliability; $1.10 per set of cards and directions for administering ('46) ; $3.80 per manual; postpaid; [10] minutes; Lauretta Bender; American Orthopsychiatric Association, Inc. * ($2 per pad of 50 scoring sheets

['51] ; $7.25 per manual, *The Bender-Gestalt Test* ('51) ; postage extra; Gerald R. Pascal and Barbara J. Suttell; Grune & Stratton, Inc.)

REFERENCES

1–8. See 3:108.

9–42. See 4:144.

43. BENDER, LAURETTA. Chap. 6, "The Bender Gestalt Test and Analysis," pp. 136–42, passim. In *Chamorros and Carolinians of Saipan: Personality Studies*. By Alice Joseph and Veronica F. Murray. Cambridge, Mass.: Harvard University Press, 1951. Pp. xviii, 381. *

44. DINWIDDIE, FRANK W. *A Comparative Study of the Bender-Gestalt Records of Two Groups of Alcoholics*. Master's thesis, Catholic University of America (Washington, D.C.), 1951.

45. HALPERIN, SIDNEY L. "A Study of the Personality Structure of the Prisoner in Hawaii." *J Clin & Exp Psychopathol* 12:213–21 S '51. * (*PA* 27:1331)

46. PEEK, ROLAND M., AND QUAST, WENTWORTH. *A Scoring System for the Bender-Gestalt Test*. Hastings, Minn.: Roland M. Peek (Box 292) or Minneapolis, Minn.: Wentworth Quast (2810 42nd St.), 1951. Pp. iii, 72. * (*PA* 27:1183)

47. SUTTELL, BARBARA JANE. *The Development of Visual-Motor Performance in Children as Estimated by the Bender-Gestalt Test*. Master's thesis, University of Pittsburgh (Pittsburgh, Pa.), 1951.

48. ADDINGTON, MILTON C. "A Note on the Pascal and Suttell Scoring System of the Bender-Gestalt Test." *J Clin Psychol* 8:312–3 Jl '52. * (*PA* 27:5851)

49. ADDINGTON, MILTON C. *Some Aspects of the Reliability and Validity of the Bender-Gestalt Test*. Doctor's thesis, University of Tennessee (Knoxville, Tenn.), 1952.

50. BARKLEY, BILL J. *A Study Comparing the Performance of Brain Damage Cases on the Bender Visual Motor Gestalt Test and a Tactual-Kinesthetic Version of the Same*. Doctor's thesis, Western Reserve University (Cleveland, Ohio), 1952.

51. BENDER, LAURETTA. *Child Psychiatric Techniques: Diagnostic and Therapeutic Approach to Normal and Abnormal Development Through Patterned, Expressive, and Group Behavior*, pp. 50–103. Springfield, Ill.: Charles C Thomas, 1952. Pp. xi, 335. *

52. BENSBERG, GERARD J. "Performance of Brain-Injured and Familial Mental Defectives on the Bender Gestalt Test." *J Consult Psychol* 16:61–4 F '52. *

53. BORKO, HAROLD. *A Factor-Analytic Study of the Minnesota Multiphasic Personality Inventory Using a Transpose Matrix (Q-Technique)*. Doctor's thesis, University of Southern California (Los Angeles, Calif.), 1952.

54. DEMING, BURTON. *A Study of the Emotional Adjustment of Functional Articulation Cases as Indicated by the Bender-Gestalt Test*. Master's thesis, University of Oklahoma (Norman, Okla.), 1952.

55. DOSIER, CHARLOTTE H. *The Bender-Gestalt Test as an Instrument for the Differentiation of Subcategories of Schizophrenia*. Doctor's thesis, University of Colorado (Boulder, Colo.), 1952.

56. FELDMAN, IRVING S. *Psychological Differences Among Moron and Borderline Mental Defectives as a Function of Etiology: I, Visual-Motor Functioning*. Doctor's thesis, University of Pittsburgh (Pittsburgh, Pa.), 1952.

57. GOBETZ, WALLACE. *A Quantification, Standardization, and Validation of the Bender-Gestalt Test on an Adult Population in Terms of Its Ability to Differentiate Normal and Psychoneurotic Levels of Adjustment*. Doctor's thesis, New York University (New York, N.Y.), 1952.

58. GUERTIN, WILSON H. "A Factor Analysis of the Bender-Gestalt Tests of Mental Patients." *J Clin Psychol* 8:362–7 O '52. * (*PA* 27:5874)

59. HOLLON, THOMAS HARRY. *The Relationship of the Visual-Motor Gestalt Function to Mental Age*. Master's thesis, Catholic University of America (Washington, D.C.), 1952.

60. MYATT, MARY FRANCES. *A Study of the Relationship Between Motivation and Test Performance of Patients in a Rehabilitation Ward*. Doctor's thesis, University of Minnesota (Minneapolis, Minn.), 1952. (*DA* 12:339)

61. PASCAL, GERALD R. Chap. 11, "Gestalt Functions: The Bender-Gestalt, Mosaic and World Tests," pp. 185–90. (*PA* 27:3559) In *Progress in Clinical Psychology, Vol I, Sect. 1*. Edited by Daniel Brower and Lawrence E. Abt. New York: Grune & Stratton, Inc., 1952. Pp. xi, 328. *

62. SACKS, JAMES. *A Study of Normal and Paranoid Schizophrenic Responses to the Tachistoscopic Presentation of the Bender Gestalt Test*. Master's thesis, University of Chicago (Chicago, Ill.), 1952.

63. SAMUELS, HENRY. "The Validity of Personality-Trait Ratings Based on Projective Techniques." *Psychol Monogr* 66(5):1–21 '52. * (*PA* 27:5161)

64. SUCZEK, ROBERT F. *Reliability, Generality, and Some Personality Correlates of Bender Gestalt Responses*. Doctor's thesis, University of California (Berkeley, Calif.), 1952.

65. SUCZEK, ROBERT F., AND KLOPFER, WALTER G. "Interpretation of the Bender Gestalt Test: The Associative Value of the Figures." *Am J Orthopsychiatry* 22:62–75 Ja '52. *

66. SUTTELL, BARBARA J., AND PASCAL, GERALD R. " 'Regression' in Schizophrenia as Determined by Performance on the Bender-Gestalt Test." *J Abn & Social Psychol* 47:653–7 Jl '52. * (*PA* 27:3707)

67. ZOLIK, E. *The Reproduction of Visuo-Motor Gestalten by Delinquent and Nondelinquent Children*. Master's thesis, Catholic University of America (Washington, D.C.), 1952.

68. AARONSON, BERNARD S.; NELSON, SHERMAN E.; AND HOLT, SHIRLEY. "On a Relation Between Bender-Gestalt Recall and Shipley-Hartford Scores." *J Clin Psychol* 9:88 Ja '53. * (*PA* 27:7748)

69. BLUM, RICHARD H., AND NIMS, JERRY. "Two Clinical Uses of the Bender Visual-Motor Gestalt Test." *U S Armed Forces Med J* 4:1592–9 N '53. * (*PA* 29:4035)

70. BOSSOM, J. *The Effect of Certain Variables Upon Recall: A Study of the Bender-Gestalt Test*. Master's thesis, New York University (New York, N.Y.), 1953.

71. CALDEN, GEORGE. "Psychosurgery in a Set of Schizophrenic Identical Twins: A Psychological Study." *J Proj Tech* 17:200–9 Je '53. * (*PA* 28:4641)

72. CURNUTT, ROBERT H. "The Use of the Bender Gestalt With an Alcoholic and Non-Alcoholic Population." *J Clin Psychol* 9:287–90 Jl '53. * (*PA* 28:2896)

73. GOBETZ, WALLACE. "A Quantification, Standardization, and Validation of the Bender-Gestalt Test on the Normal and Neurotic Adults." *Psychol Monogr* 67(6):1–28 '53. * (*PA* 28:4354)

74. HANVIK, LEO J. "A Note on Rotations in the Bender Gestalt Test as Predictors of EEG Abnormalities in Children." *J Clin Psychol* 9:399 O '53. * (*PA* 28:4361)

75. HUTT, MAX L. "Revised Bender Visual-Motor Gestalt Test," pp. 660–87. (*PA* 27:7776) In *Contributions Toward Medical Psychology: Theory and Psychodiagnostic Methods, Vol. II*. Edited by Arthur Weider. New York: Ronald Press Co., 1953. Pp. xi, 459–885. *

76. KATES, SOLIS L., AND SCHMOLKE, MERTON F. "Self-Related and Parent-Related Verbalizations and Bender-Gestalt Performance of Alcoholics." *Q J Studies Alcohol* 14:38–48 Mr '53. * (*PA* 28:1231)

77. PEEK, ROLAND M. "Directionality of Lines in the Bender-Gestalt Test." *J Consult Psychol* 17:213–6 Je '53. * (*PA* 28:2665)

78. ROBINSON, NANCY MAYER. "Bender-Gestalt Performances of Schizophrenics and Paretics." *J Clin Psychol* 9:291–3 Jl '53. * (*PA* 28:3024)

79. SWENSEN, C. H., AND PASCAL, G. R. "A Note on the Bender-Gestalt Test as a Prognostic Indicater in Mental Illness." *J Clin Psychol* 9:398 O '53. * (*PA* 28:4678)

80. TAYLOR, GERRY M. *A Study of the Validity of the Pascal and Suttell Scoring System for the Bender-Gestalt Test*. Master's thesis, Baylor University (Waco, Tex.), 1953.

81. THORNTON, SAM M. *A Clinical Evaluation of the Bender-Gestalt Test*. Master's thesis, Ohio University (Athens, Ohio), 1953.

82. CURNUTT, ROBERT H., AND LEWIS, WILLIAM B. "The Relationship Between Z Scores on the Bender Gestalt and F+% on the Rorschach." *J Clin Psychol* 10:96–7 Ja '54. * (*PA* 28:7515)

83. GUERTIN, WILSON H. "A Factor Analysis of Curvilinear Distortions on the Bender-Gestalt." *J Clin Psychol* 10:12–7 Ja '54. * (*PA* 28:7525)

84. GUERTIN, WILSON H. "A Transposed Analysis of the Bender Gestalts of Brain Disease Cases." *J Clin Psychol* 10:366–9 O '54. * (*PA* 29:4550)

85. GUERTIN, WILSON H. "A Transposed Factor Analysis of Schizophrenic Performance on the Bender-Gestalt." *J Clin Psychol* 10:225–8 Jl '54. * (*PA* 29:2789)

86. HAMMER, EMANUEL F. "An Experimental Study of Symbolism on the Bender Gestalt." *J Proj Tech* 18:335–45 S '54. * (*PA* 29:4058)

87. KORCHIN, SHELDON J., AND BASOWITZ, HAROLD. "The Tachistoscopic Bender-Gestalt Test." Abstract. *Am Psychol* 9:408 Ag '54. *

88. LINDSAY, JOHN. "The Bender-Gestalt Test and Psychoneurotics." *J Mental Sci* 100:980–2 O '54. * (*PA* 29:7708)

89. LONSTEIN, MURRAY. "A Validation of a Bender-Gestalt Scoring System." *J Consult Psychol* 18:377–9 O '54. * (*PA* 29:5717)

90. PARKER, JAMES W. "Tactual-Kinesthetic Perception as a Technique for Diagnosing Brain Damage." *J Consult Psychol* 18:415–20 D '54. * (*PA* 29:7778)

91. PEIXOTTO, H. E. "The Bender Gestalt Visual Motor Test as a Culture Free Test of Personality." *J Clin Psychol* 10:369–72 O '54. * (*PA* 29:4081)

92. SATTER, GEORGE, AND MCGEE, EUGENE. "Retarded Adults Who Have Developed Beyond Expectation: Part II, Non-Intellectual Functions." *Training Sch B* 51:67–81 Je '54. * (*PA* 29:2663)

93. SLOCOMBE, EDNA ELIZABETH. *The Relation of Certain Aspects of Anxiety to Performance on the Bender Visual-Motor Gestalt Test*. Doctor's thesis, University of Michigan (Ann Arbor, Mich.), 1954. (*DA* 14:1260)

94. TERRY, JAMES H. *A Study of the Diagnostic Validity of a Five-Second Presentation of the Bender Gestalt Test*. Doctor's thesis, University of Denver (Denver, Colo.), 1954.

95. ABRAMSON, H. A.; WAXENBERG, S. E.; LEVINE, J.; KAUFMAN, M. R.; AND KORNETSKY, C. "Lysergic Acid Diethylamide (LSD-25): XIII, Effect on Bender-Gestalt Test Performance." *J Psychol* 40:341–9 O '55. * (*PA* 30:7182)

96. BYRD, EUGENE. *The Clinical Validity of the Bender Ges-*

talt Test With Children: A Developmental Comparison of Children in Need of Psychotherapy and Children Judged Well-Adjusted. Doctor's thesis, Florida State University (Tallahassee, Fla.), 1955. (*DA* 15:1254)

97. COWDEN, RICHARD C.; DEABLER, HERDIS L.; AND FEAMSTER, J. HARRY. "The Prognostic Value of the Bender-Gestalt, H-T-P, TAT, and Sentence Completion Test." *J Clin Psychol* 11:271–5 Jl '55. * (*PA* 30:2864)

98. GOODSTEIN, LEONARD D.; SPIELBERGER, CHARLES D.; WILLIAMS, JOHN E.; AND DAHLSTROM, W. GRANT. "The Effects of Serial Position and Design Difficulty on Recall of the Bender-Gestalt Test Designs." *J Consult Psychol* 19:230–4 Je '55. * (*PA* 30:2880)

99. GREENBAUM, RICHARD S. "A Note on the Use of the Word Association Test as an Aid to Interpreting the Bender-Gestalt." *J Proj Tech* 19:27–9 Mr '55. * (*PA* 30:1027)

100. GUERTIN, WILSON H. "A Transposed Analysis of the Bender-Gestalts of Paranoid Schizophrenics." *J Clin Psychol* 11:73–6 Ja '55. * (*PA* 29:7649)

101. HALPIN, VIRGINIA G. "Rotation Errors Made by Brain-Injured and Familial Children on Two Visual-Motor Tests." *Am J Mental Def* 59:485–9 Ja '55. * (*PA* 29:7487)

102. KAMMAN, GORDON R., AND KRAM, CHARLES. "Value of Psychometric Examinations in Medical Diagnosis and Treatment." *J Am Med Assn* 158:155–60 Je 18 '55. * (*PA* 31:1044)

103. KELLER, JAMES E. "The Use of a Bender Gestalt Maturation Level Scoring System With Mentally Handicapped Children." Discussion by Winifred Ingram. *Am J Orthopsychiatry* 25:563–73 Jl '55. * (*PA* 30:4791)

104. KLEINMAN, BERNARD. *A Study of Factors Involved in the Reproduction of Bender Designs in Normal and Schizophrenic Subjects.* Doctor's thesis, University of Oklahoma (Norman, Okla.), 1955. (*DA* 15:2569)

105. LACHMANN, FRANK MICHAEL. *Perceptual-Motor Development in Children Retarded in Reading Ability.* Doctor's thesis, Northwestern University (Evanston, Ill.), 1955. (*DA* 15:1900)

106. McPHERSON, MARION WHITE, AND PEPIN, LORETTA A. "Consistency of Reproductions of Bender-Gestalt Designs." *J Clin Psychol* 11:163–6 Ap '55. * (*PA* 30:1040)

107. MARK, JOSEPH C., AND MORROW, ROBERT S. "The Use of the Bender-Gestalt Test in the Study of Brain Damage." Abstract. *Am Psychol* 10:323 Ag '55. *

108. PEEK, ROLAND M., AND OLSON, GORDON W. "The Bender-Gestalt Recall as an Index of Intellectual Functioning." *J Clin Psychol* 11:185–8 Ap '55. * (*PA* 30:1048)

109. ROSENTHAL, DAVID, AND IMBER, STANLEY D. "The Effects of Mephenesin and Practice on the Bender-Gestalt Performance of Psychiatric Outpatients." *J Clin Psychol* 11:90–2 Ja '55. * (*PA* 29:7314)

110. RUSSELL, IVAN LEE. *The Visual Motor Function as Related to Child Growth and Reading Development.* Doctor's thesis, University of Michigan (Ann Arbor, Mich.), 1955. (*DA* 15:532)

111. SONDER, SYLVIA L. "Perceptual Tests and Acute and Chronic Status as Predictors of Improvement in Psychotic Patients." *J Consult Psychol* 19:387–92 O '55. * (*PA* 30:6187)

112. TAYLOR, JAMES R., AND SCHENKE, LOWELL W. "The Bender Visual-Motor Gestalt Test as a Measure of Aggression in Children." *Proc Iowa Acad Sci* 62:426–32 '55. *

113. VATOVEC, EDWARD A. *A Validation Study of the Bender-Gestalt Test.* Master's thesis, Kent State University (Kent, Ohio), 1955.

114. WAXENBERG, SHELDON E. "Psychosomatic Patients and Other Physically Ill Persons: A Comparative Study." *J Consult Psychol* 19:163–9 Je '55. * (*PA* 30:3281)

115. WISSNER, FRED. *The Improvement of a Clinic Population Undergoing Psychotherapeutic Treatment: Pascal and Suttell's Quantification of the Bender-Visual Motor Gestalt Test as a Predictive Instrument in Psychotherapy.* Doctor's thesis, New York University (New York, N.Y.), 1955. (*DA* 15:1910)

116. BOWLAND, JOHN A., AND DEABLER, HERDIS L. "A Bender-Gestalt Diagnostic Validity Study." *J Clin Psychol* 12:82–4 Ja '56. * (*PA* 30:4554)

117. BYRD, EUGENE. "The Clinical Validity of the Bender Gestalt Test With Children: A Developmental Comparison of Children in Need of Psychotherapy and Children Judged Well-Adjusted." *J Proj Tech* 20:127–36 Je '56. * (*PA* 31:4673)

118. CRASILNECK, H. B., AND MILLER, CARMEN. "Performance on the Bender Under Hypnotic Age Regression." Abstract. *Am Psychol* 11:364 Ag '56. *

119. EVERETT, EVALYN G. *A Comparative Study of Paretics, Hebephrenics, and Paranoid Schizophrenics on a Battery of Psychological Tests.* Doctor's thesis, New York University (New York, N.Y.), 1956. (*DA* 16:1502)

120. INGLIS, J.; SHAPIRO, M. B.; AND POST, F. " 'Memory Function' in Psychiatric Patients Over Sixty, the Role of Memory in Tests Discriminating Between 'Functional' and 'Organic' Groups." *J Mental Sci* 102:589–98 Jl '56. * (*PA* 31:7926)

121. JACOBS, BEVERLY BLOM. *Study of Performances on the Bender-Gestalt for Possible Differentiation Between Brain-Damaged, Deaf, and Normal Children.* Master's thesis, Emory University (Emory University, Ga.), 1956.

122. KALDEGG, A. "Psychological Observations in a Group of Alcoholic Patients With Analysis of Rorschach, Wechsler-Bellevue and Bender Gestalt Test Results." *Q J Studies Alcohol* 17:608–28 D '56. * (*PA* 32:648)

123. MEHLMAN, BENJAMIN, AND VATOVEC, EDWARD. "A Validation Study of the Bender-Gestalt." *J Consult Psychol* 20:71–4 F '56. * (*PA* 31:3056)

124. MORTENSON, RODNEY H. *An Investigation of the Use of the Bender Gestalt Test as a Device for Screening Mentally Retarded Children.* Master's thesis, Claremont College (Claremont, Calif.), 1956.

125. MURRAY, EDWARD J., AND ROBERTS, FRANCIS J. "The Bender-Gestalt Test: In a Patient Passing Through a Brief Manic-Depressive Cycle." *US Armed Forces Med J* 7:1206–8 Ag '56. * (*PA* 31:3058)

126. POPPLESTONE, JOHN A. "Variability of the Bender Gestalt Designs." *Percept & Motor Skills* 6:269–71 D '56. * (*PA* 31:6118)

127. SCOTT, EDWARD M. "Regression or Disintegration in Schizophrenia?" *J Clin Psychol* 12:298–300 Jl '56. * (*PA* 31:6444)

128. SHAW, MERVILLE C., AND CRUICKSHANK, WILLIAM M. "The Use of the Bender Gestalt Test With Epileptic Children." *J Clin Psychol* 12:192–3 Ap '56. * (*PA* 31:5037)

129. TOLOR, ALEXANDER. "A Comparison of the Bender-Gestalt Test and the Digit-Span Test as Measures of Recall." *J Consult Psychol* 20:305–9 Ag '56. * (*PA* 31:7979)

130. WINTER, WILLIAM D., AND FREDERICKSON, WILBUR K. "The Short-Term Effect of Chlorpromazine on Psychiatric Patients." *J Consult Psychol* 20:431–4 D '56. * (*PA* 32:1876)

131. AARONSON, BERNARD S. "The Porteus Mazes and Bender Gestalt Recall." *J Clin Psychol* 13:186–7 Ap '57. * (*PA* 32:2882)

132. BAROFF, GEORGE S. "Bender-Gestalt Visuo-Motor Function in Mental Deficiency." *Am J Mental Def* 61:753–60 Ap '57. * (*PA* 32:3038)

133. CLAWSON, AILEEN. *The Bender Visual Motor Gestalt Test as an Index of Emotional Disturbance in Children.* Doctor's thesis, University of Houston (Houston, Tex.), 1957.

134. CRASILNECK, HAROLD B., AND MICHAEL, CARMEN MILLER. "Performance on the Bender Under Hypnotic Age Regression." *J Abn & Social Psychol* 54:319–22 My '57. *

135. GOLDBERG, FRANKLIN H. "The Performance of Schizophrenic, Retarded, and Normal Children on the Bender-Gestalt Test." *Am J Mental Def* 61:548–55 Ja '57. * (*PA* 32:2894)

136. KEEHN, J. D. "Repeated Testing of Four Chronic Schizophrenics on the Bender-Gestalt and Wechsler Block Design Tests." *J Clin Psychol* 13:179–82 Ap '57. * (*PA* 32:3167)

137. NADLER, EUGENE B. "Prediction of the Sheltered Shop Work Performance of Individuals With Severe Physical Disability." *Personnel & Guid J* 36:95–8 O '57. *

138. OLIN, TOM D., AND REZNIKOFF, MARVIN. "Quantification of the Bender-Gestalt Recall: A Pilot Study." *J Proj Tech* 21:265–77 S '57. *

139. PARKER, JAMES W. "The Validity of Some Current Tests for Organicity." *J Consult Psychol* 21:425–8 O '57. *

140. QUAST, WENTWORTH. *Visual-Motor Performance in the Reproduction of Geometric Figures as a Developmental Phenomenon in Children.* Doctor's thesis, University of Minnesota (Minneapolis, Minn.), 1957.

141. REZNIKOFF, MARVIN, AND OLIN, TOM D. "Recall of the Bender-Gestalt Designs by Organic and Schizophrenic Patients: A Comparative Study." *J Clin Psychol* 13:183–6 Ap '57. * (*PA* 32:3189)

142. SHAPIRO, M. B.; FIELD, JACK; AND POST, F. "An Enquiry Into the Determinants of a Differentiation Between Elderly 'Organic' and 'Non-Organic' Psychiatric Patients on the Bender Gestalt Test." *J Mental Sci* 103:364–74 Ap '57. *

143. STEWART, HORACE F., JR. "A Note on Recall Patterns Using the Bender-Gestalt With Psychotic and Non-Psychotic Patients." *J Clin Psychol* 13:95–7 Ja '57. *

144. TAMKIN, ARTHUR S. "The Effectiveness of the Bender-Gestalt in Differential Diagnosis." *J Consult Psychol* 21:355–7 Ag '57. *

145. TOLOR, ALEXANDER. "Structural Properties of Bender-Gestalt Test Associations." *J Clin Psychol* 13:176–8 Ap '57. * (*PA* 32:2925)

146. TRIPP, CLARENCE A. *Some Graphomotor Features of the Bender Visual-Motor Gestalt Test in Relation to Delinquent and Non-Delinquent White Adolescent Males.* Doctor's thesis, New York University (New York, N.Y.), 1957. (*DA* 18:671)

147. VITANZA, ANGELO A. *A Comparative Study of Selected Psychological and Physiological Measures to Evaluate Psychiatric Conditions.* Doctor's thesis, New York University (New York, N.Y.), 1957. (*DA* 18:671–2)

148. WOHL, JULIAN. "A Note on the Generality of Constriction." *J Proj Tech* 21:410–3 D '57. *

149. EBER, MILTON. *A Bender Gestalt Validity Study: The Performance of Mentally Retarded Children.* Doctor's thesis, Florida State University (Tallahassee, Fla.), 1958. (*DA* 18:296)

150. HANNAH, LEWIS D. "Causative Factors in the Production of Rotations on the Bender-Gestalt Designs." *J Consult Psychol* 22:398–9 O '58. *

151. KOPPITZ, ELIZABETH MUNSTERBERG. "The Bender Gestalt Test and Learning Disturbances in Young Children." *J Clin Psychol* 14:292–5 Jl '58. *

152. KOPPITZ, ELIZABETH MUNSTERBERG. "Relationships Between the Bender Gestalt Test and the Wechsler Intelligence Test for Children." *J Clin Psychol* 14:413–6 O '58. *

153. OLIN, TOM D., AND REZNIKOFF, MARVIN. "A Compari-

son of Copied and Recalled Reproductions of the Bender-Ge-stalt Designs." *J Proj Tech* 22:320–7 S '58. *
154. PEEK, ROLAND M., AND STORMS, LOWELL H. "Judging Intellectual Status From the Bender-Gestalt Test." *J Clin Psychol* 14:296–9 Jl '58. *
155. SCHON, MARTHA, AND WAXENBERG, SHELDON E. "Effect of Hypophysectomy on Bender-Gestalt Test Performance." *J Clin Psychol* 14:299–302 Jl '58. *
156. STENNETT, R. G., AND UFFELMANN, RUTH. "The Bender Gestalt Test: Manner of Approach." *Can J Psychol* 12:184–6 S '58. *
157. STEWART, HORACE, AND CUNNINGHAM, SAM. "A Note on Scoring Recalled Figures of the Bender Gestalt Test Using Psychotics, Non-Psychotics and Controls." *J Clin Psychol* 14: 207–8 Ap '58. *

158. TOLOR, ALEXANDER. "Further Studies on the Bender-Gestalt Test and the Digit-Span Test as Measures of Recall." *J Clin Psychol* 14:14–8 Ja '58. *
159. TUCKER, JOHN E., AND SPIELBERG, MIMI J. "Bender-Gestalt Test Correlates of Emotional Depression." Abstract. *J Consult Psychol* 22:56 F '58. *
160. ZOLIK, EDWIN S. "A Comparison of the Bender Gestalt Reproductions of Delinquents and Non-Delinquents." *J Clin Psychol* 14:24–6 Ja '58. *

For reviews by Arthur L. Benton and Howard R. White, see 4:144; for related reviews, see B330, 4:145, 3:109, and 40:B843.

ENGLISH

REVIEWS BY *Janet G. Afflerbach, M. A. Brimer, Robert S. Cathcart, John C. Daniels, Charlotte Croon Davis, Clarence Derrick, John S. Diekhoff, Jerome E. Doppelt, Reginald Edwards, Leonard S. Feldt, James A. Fitzgerald, J. Raymond Gerberich, Neil Gourlay, A. N. Hieronymus, Worth R. Jones, Gerald V. Lannholm, Constance M. McCullough, Richard A. Meade, Bernadine Meyer, John Nisbet, Stanley Nisbet, Osmond E. Palmer, Robert C. Pooley, Winifred L. Post, Roger A. Richards, J. A. Richardson, S. C. Richardson, Holland Roberts, Louise B. Scott, Geraldine Spaulding, John M. Stalnaker, Ruth Strickland, Cleveland A. Thomas, M. J. Wantman, D. K. Wheeler, and Louis C. Zahner.*

[173]
A.C.E.R. English Usage Tests. Ages 10–13.0; 1951; Form C ['46]; 2 parts: word usage, sentences; 3s. per 10 tests of either part; 1s. per scoring key; 4s. 9d. per manual ['50]; 6s. 3d. per specimen set; postpaid within Australia; 30(40) minutes; Australian Council for Educational Research. *

J. A. RICHARDSON, *Professor of Special Education, The University of British Columbia, Vancouver, British Columbia, Canada.*

Two aspects only of English usage are covered by these tests—familiarity with certain basic rules of grammar and word usage (Part 1) and recognition of correct or most effective sentence structure (Part 2). No attempt is made to assess skill in the use of vocabulary or punctuation or skill in free expression in composition. These are at least equally important aspects of English usage.

The two parts have limited value. The items of the first are classified under nine diagnostic categories. This part indicates the pupil's recognition knowledge, not the extent to which he will actually use correct word and grammar forms in practice. Correlations of .48 and .74 are given as evidence of the degree of correspondence between scores on this subtest and functional usage, the criterion being the school marks in formal grammar of two groups of sixth grade children. Quite apart from the fact that the criterion (as thus baldly stated) is inadequate, no attempt is made to interpret, for

the teacher for whose use the test is intended, the significance of the correlational figures.

The same criticism is applicable to Part 2, Sentences, save that here the position is worse inasmuch as no indication at all is given of the correspondence between test success and effective written or oral expression. The item type used in this subtest—selection of the correct or most effective sentence structure from four alternative sentences—suggests that such correspondence would be low. In the writer's opinion, a much more effective test of knowledge of sentence structure is that used in the *Schonell Diagnostic English Tests* in which the testee is required himself to join given simple sentences together into a single complex sentence.

It follows from what has been written that the statistical information given on the tests is in some respects most inadequate. There are no validity figures apart from the correlations mentioned. One assumes that content validity is claimed from the manual statement (regarding the word usage test) that the items chosen "are based mostly upon errors made in children's speech and writing" and "have been shown by preliminary item analyses to discriminate between children who use words and phrases correctly and those who do not." However, no supporting figures are given. Content validity is not mentioned with respect to the sentence test. Test score stability is indicated by test-retest correlations and probable errors for one grade level only; no evidence is presented, nor is any available from the test constructors, on internal consistency. Although the subtests are both timed, there is no comment on the effects, if any, of the time limit on test performance.

On the credit side, the *English Usage Tests* were standardized, with rigorous regard for accepted sampling procedures, on 30,000 children from nearly 600 Australian schools. Maximum information is provided for the teacher with grade norms and age norms by sex for each Australian state in the form of scale scores and centile ranks. Interpretation of these statistics is adequate. Layout of tests and manuals is a model of clarity.

Despite these commendable points, the tests appear to have only limited practical value. They attempt assessment of only two aspects of English usage, ignoring others at least as important. Even within their limited coverage, they indicate only the pupil's recognition knowledge, not necessarily the extent to which he himself uses the correct English forms in his writing. The teacher, wanting to assess the "English usage ability" of his class, should use these tests, if at all, with the greatest caution and with full appreciation of their limitations.

[174]

*American School Achievement Tests, Part 3, Language and Spelling. Grades 4–6, 7–9; 1941–58; 2 scores: language, spelling; Forms D ('55), E ('56), F ('57), G ('58) ; Forms D, E, F are essentially the same as Forms A, B, C copyrighted 1941–43; 2 levels; revised battery manuals ('58) ; $2 per 25 tests; 35¢ per specimen set of either level; postpaid; 32(45), 37(47) minutes for Intermediate, Advanced Battery; Willis E. Pratt and Robert V. Young; Public School Publishing Co. *

M. A. BRIMER, *Senior Lecturer in Educational Psychology, University College, Ibadan, Nigeria.*

At both the intermediate and advanced levels, separately timed subtests of language and spelling are presented. The language test is made up of five sections measuring usage, punctuation, capitalization, sentence recognition, and grammar; there are 65 items in all at the intermediate level and 73 at the advanced. The authors state that they have deliberately restricted content to the "tools of learning" because these are susceptible to objective testing and because their treatment is relatively constant throughout the country, and that they have drawn their material from research studies of common errors and from a large number of textbooks.

It would seem that objectivity has been a less limiting factor in the choice of content than suitability for the multiple response form. It may be that the authors have confused the two things. Language usage is probably more influenced by the prompting offered by a choice of responses than most skills; and in these tests, where the majority of the items require a choice from two alternatives, the prompting is considerable. The validity of this section as a measure of spontaneous usage is probably much lower than the representation of common errors suggests. Unprompted completion items are much more suitable for this purpose. Again, the use of the multiple choice form in the punctuation section, where the nature of the omitted punctuation has to be identified, removes the skill tested from the function involved in inserting the correct mark in a certain place. A small criticism here also is that the dots lining up the item with the answer are aligned with, and too close to, the period at the end of the sentence, possibly leading to confusion.

The capitalization and sentence recognition items arouse little comment, except that 10 items devoted to capitalization seem too much for a test of this length and that sentence recognition is more appropriately tested within continuous prose than by discrete phrases and clauses as it is here. The grammar section is very liberally interpreted and depends more heavily upon comprehension than the authors recognise. The grammar is too formal and would be better tested as usage. Some of the items involve dubious solutions. In one case, the authors have confused the logical with the grammatical object, and their use of the word "predicate" to refer to the verb alone, and not to its extension, would be authoritatively challenged.

The spelling test is composed of 50 items in which three common misspellings are used as alternatives to the right answer. There is a considerable body of feeling amongst teachers, not altogether unjustified, against the use of wrong spellings in spelling tests. Certainly, for a child who uses a common misspelling and encounters it in a test situation where it appears in print, reinforcement of the error is not unlikely to occur.

The evaluation of an attainment test intended for classroom use must take into account the adequacy of its proposed function, as well as the effectiveness of the tasks chosen to serve that function. Insofar as the concern for objectivity has undesirably restricted the content of this test, the function proposed is inadequate. Within the restricted range of tasks determined by the authors' limited interpretation of "objectivity," the representation of skills tested will suffice, though the proportionate contribution of the various skills to the total score might be challenged. Evidence in the manual of a close correspondence between results on this test and on other tests providing a more comprehensive range of English language tasks would go some way to moderate the criticism of the test's limited function.

It seems rather a pity that, after taking considerable pains to establish content validity, the authors did not think it worthwhile to correlate the tests with others which depend less upon the multiple choice form of response. There seem grounds for supposing that the test's validity measured in this way would be lower than the content validity suggests. The authors claim that the tests may be used to furnish data for remedial programmes. The limited content and length of the language sections and the absence of data or guidance on their diagnostic use suggests that teachers would be unwise to use these instruments for determining even general disabilities.

For tests of this length employing multiple choice items without correction for chance scoring, the reliabilities assessed by intercorrelating the various forms are substantial and adequate. This is probably attributable to the effectiveness of the distracting alternatives, since the authors do not report having analysed the items for internal consistency.

The norms, professedly tentative, are based on too few cases for the age and grade ranges they are supposed to cover. They are based on median scores of children in the various grades and do not appear to have been adequately smoothed, so that, for example, in the norms for the advanced level, within the score range 48 to 52 an increase of a single point of raw score is accorded between 2 and 4 months of age increase, and there is a reversal in the trend of change. While the practice of comparing a child's performance with the performance of children of different ages and grades may still be acceptable to teachers, modern tests should attempt to provide alternative norms which are more precise in their information.

As a rough guide to the relative level of the language and spelling skills of a group of children, these tests will appeal to teachers who are not too fastidious over administration. The experienced teacher will prefer tests in which the items correspond more closely to actual classroom skills, which can more justifiably claim to provide diagnostic information, and which do not sacrifice validity for quick scoring and easy administration.

CLARENCE DERRICK, *Associate Professor of English and Humanities, University of Florida, Gainesville, Florida.*

There may be poorer tests than this one, and there certainly ought to be better ones.

The test contains six parts: Correct Usage (20 items), Punctuation (10 items), Capitalization (10 items), Sentence Recognition (10 items), Grammar (15 and 23 items), Spelling (50 items). It yields only two scores, however, one in language and one in spelling.

Correct usage is tested by asking pupils to select the correct completion for a presented sentence. Example: "I hope your mother says that you....go. a) may, b) can." The items avoid most of the disputable points although the importance of the "may-can" and the "in-into" distinctions could be argued. Most of the errors are so gross that the test is more likely to be an indicator of incompetence than proof of competence. Since all but 3 of the 80 items in the correct usage sections of the four forms examined were 2-choice items and since there is no correction for guessing, scores are inflated by chance success.

Punctuation is tested by having students indicate which punctuation mark (apostrophe, comma, period, quotation marks, question mark) is missing from the sentences presented. Since most of the items are not really 5-choice items, chance can again unduly affect scores. In the sentence "It is John's ball," for example, how many students would think a comma, an extra period, quotation marks, or a question mark were needed? Since the capitalization section has a similar format, the criticism that not all the options really function again applies. Sentence recognition is tested by deciding whether a group of words is or is not a sentence —more 2-choice items.

The grammar section requires familiarity

with grammatical terminology which may not be (should not be?) covered in a course of study for the fourth or fifth grade. Item 52 in Advanced Form E is surprising: "Which sentence is the topic sentence, that is, tells what the paragraph is about? a) one b) two c) four d) five." The examinee looks in vain for any paragraph to which the item might be referring and, not finding any, is understandably confused. Finally it dawns on him that there is an assumption (erroneous) that a topic sentence is necessarily the first sentence!

Spelling is tested with completion-type items with variant spellings. Example: "She....he would go. a) siad b) said c) saed d) sead." It would be interesting to check item analyses to discover how many of these variants are actually functioning. (According to Gates' *List of Spelling Difficulties in 3876 Words*,[1] the most common misspelling of "said" is "sed.")

The test makes use of a carbon, self-scoring technique that reduces the labor of scoring and is intriguing to pupils. It has, however, some limitations. For one, if the pupil does not mark heavily enough, the scorer may have to mark the test over so that the responses can be determined. For another, the test cannot be reused.

Like the test, the Teacher's Manual is inadequate. The manual informs the user that these tests "do not purport to be diagnostic tests," but three sentences later explains that from the results obtained on each part of the tests it is possible "to determine the general disabilities which each pupil may have." Too frequently essential data are missing. Specifically what techniques were used to compute reliability? What is meant by "checking" the original norms data against scores of 3,589 pupils in 44 school districts in 17 states and Canada? What schools? How checked?

In presenting evidence regarding the curricular validity of the test, the manual explains that the content is based on analyses of five texts, some state courses of study, and some research studies. The texts are of 1950 vintage, but the research studies are dated 1930, 1935, and 1938. Linguists have done a good deal of talking and writing since the 1930's.

From reading the manual, the reviewer gets the impression that the battery of which this test is a part was developed for a specific region (Erie County, Pennsylvania), and subse-

quently the norms were modified in some unexplained way. Because data are lacking, test users would be justified in questioning the meaning of the norms. The norms table translates uncorrected raw scores into grade and age norms. Test users who do not know the limitations of these kinds of norms should read Flanagan's discussion of grade and age equivalents in *Educational Measurement*.[2]

On all counts, the language usage test of the *American School Achievement Tests* is hardly adequate. Use it if you must; but, if you have an option, search for a test without the limitations of this one.

For reviews by J. Raymond Gerberich and Virgil E. Herrick of the complete battery, see 1; for a review by Ralph C. Preston of an earlier edition, see 4:1; for reviews by Walter W. Cook and Gordon N. Mackenzie (with Glen Hass), see 3:1.

[175]

*Barrett-Ryan English Test. Grades 7–13; 1926–57; Forms 1 ('56), 2 ('56), 3 ('29), 4 ('40), 5 ('44), 6 ('44), 1946, 1948, 1954 ['55], 1955 ('56); revised manual ('56); norms: Forms 1 ['57], 2 ['57], 1946 ['46], 1948 ['48], 1954 ['56], 1955 ['57]; no data on reliability for Forms 1, 2, 1946, 1948, 1954, 1955; $1.40 per 25 tests, postage extra; 50¢ per specimen set, postpaid; 50(55) minutes; E. R. Barrett, Teresa M. Ryan, M. W. Sanders (1, 2, 1955), H. E. Schrammel (1946, 1948, 1954, manual), and E. R. Wood (manual); Bureau of Educational Measurements. *

REFERENCE

1. ANDERSON, MARY R., AND STEGMAN, ERWIN J. "Predictors of Freshman Achievement at Fort Hays Kansas State College." *Ed & Psychol Meas* 14:722–3 w '54. * (PA 29:7952)

J. RAYMOND GERBERICH, *Director, Bureau of Educational Research and Service, and Professor of Education, University of Connecticut, Storrs, Connecticut.*

Ten forms of this English test are now in print. The earliest four forms were designed for use in grades 7–12 and college, but grades 7 and 8 are not listed in the specifications for any of the six later forms and a further cutback to eliminate the college level is embodied in the 1955 and 1956 forms. "College" presumably was intended to apply only to freshmen, inasmuch as the norm tables do not provide for any higher levels.

Five purposes are listed for the tests: to classify students into sections, to discover weaknesses of individual students, to standardize work, to measure achievement, and to motivate

1 GATES, ARTHUR I. *A List of Spelling Difficulties in 3876 Words*. New York: Bureau of Publications, Teachers College, Columbia University, 1937. Pp. 166.

2 LINDQUIST, E. F., EDITOR. *Educational Measurement*. Washington, D.C.: American Council on Education, 1951. Pp. xix, 819. *

learning. Later in the manual, five uses, by implication based on the purposes previously stated, are enumerated. Uses included here but not anticipated in the purposes are: checking the efficiency of instruction, assigning school marks, and analyzing class weaknesses. It seems clear to the reviewer that uses should reflect purposes to a much greater degree than is apparent here. The lack of more coherence seems to evidence a rather traditional conception of test purposes and perhaps less than optimum care in phrasing important ideas.

Brief comments are made about content validity and some evidence is given on concurrent and predictive validity in the manual. Content validity is dealt with in one 3-line paragraph that merely lists sources of content employed and judgments sought—content of "leading textbooks and courses of study" and criticisms from "teachers and supervisors on earlier editions of the test." Correlation coefficients of .70 with an unspecified "battery of entrance tests" and of .58 and .59 with results from two specified intelligence tests furnish evidence on concurrent validity. Correlation coefficients of .66, .55, and .50 with three measures of subsequent scholastic success are presented as evidence of predictive validity. No mention is made of when these correlational data were obtained, of the age or grade groups on which they were based, or of the meaning, in either the statistical or the practical sense, of the coefficients. Only three short paragraphs of the manual are devoted to this most important characteristic of a good examination.

Split-half and alternate form reliabilities are reported. Split-half coefficients, listed as falling in the .80 to .89 range and seemingly not stepped up by use of the Spearman-Brown formula, were obtained "before the final equating of the different forms." Intercorrelations among Forms 1, 2, and 3 are reported as ranging from .76 to .85, whereas the sole reference to equivalence of other forms is found in the statement that coefficients range from .88 to .96. The latter is almost incredibly high. That these "other forms" are not very recently published seems probable, inasmuch as an earlier 4-page undated manual listing norms for Forms 1 to 3, all published originally during or before 1929, carries precisely the same statement.

It seems apparent that the 7-line statement about reliability is extremely inadequate. Pupil samples used in obtaining the data are not char-

acterized by any indications of size, range of talent, geographical representation, testing dates, or, except for editions in print by 1929, forms of the test. Nor is any information given about the central tendency and variability of scores for these samples.

The 2-column format of the test booklets is uniformly poor, if one accepts as a norm the format of tests put out by the 10 or so companies publishing such instruments most widely. The type font is small, probably 9-point, and not easily read; in many instances the bold face type used to identify options is hardly distinguishable from the regular roman type. Material is frequently set without adequate leading between lines. Spacing is irregular and seemingly without pattern.

In printing the scoring keys, no attention was given to the vertical spacing of items in groups, so the scorer must vary the vertical positioning of strip keys from page to page and even from column to column instead of being able to align top edges of keys and test folders uniformly.

The various test forms seem to have similarities not much greater than chance in such matters of form and style as headings, examples, and even directions to the pupils. For example, the first part of the test is introduced in six different ways in the first six of the current forms. Examples, or sample items, also seem to be used according to whim rather than design. Forms 4 and 5 do not employ any examples, to represent one extreme. Form 3, nearest to the opposite extreme, presents examples for all parts and for all sections except one. The other forms take varying intermediate positions on this characteristic. Copyright dates also are not uniformly treated.

Circumlocutions, ambiguities, and even grammatical errors seem to be common in the directions to pupils. In the directions for Part 3, Form 1946, for example, pupils are instructed under certain circumstances to place "a '11' in the parenthesis." Almost without exception, the word "parenthesis" is used to represent the *pair* of curved lines. A further example is that directions for the second item of each pair in Part 2, Form 1955, seem to ask the pupil to indicate the *wrong* reason for a grammatical *error* he noted in the preceding item.

Two generalizations about the parts and sections of these test forms seem to be well founded. First, there is no pattern, no guiding principle, no coherence observable when the various forms are compared one with another. Second, there is no trend, no directional tendency, no transition away from or toward any type of content or testing technic observable when the forms are considered in their chronological sequence. In well standardized tests that occur in a sequence, especially when a sequence in a dynamic area has endured for a period of years, one might expect to find a pattern modified over a period of time by a trend.

Three item varieties seem to be most widely used: a plus-minus version of the basic alternate response type, a multiple choice variety with either three or four options, and a classification type of matching exercise. Form 3 uses only the plus-minus item, whereas Forms 1946 and 1948 discard it entirely in favor of multiple choice and matching varieties. Most of the other forms combine two or even all three of these types.

Although many of the test parts employ these item varieties in their simplest or basic form, some test parts present situations in which two related items appear in sequence. In one type of part dealing with a combination of functional and formal grammar, where the first of two plus-minus items is on usage and the second is on grammar controlling the usage, it seems rather strange to find that two negative answers can be expected on occasion to occur together, i.e., to find that the pupil is expected to indicate that the grammatical rule stated *does not* apply to an *error* observed. Somewhat similarly, another type of part on grammar combines by pairs a plus-minus item on correct usage and a 3-option multiple choice item on formal grammar controlling the usage. A third variation of this type of pattern combines two 3-option multiple choice items, one on usage and one on formal grammar, in a sequence or related pair. In Part 2 of Form 1946, the second item in each of three pairs contains an irrefutable, logical clue to the answer, although the clue leads to the *right* answer only if the right answer was given for the preceding usage item. Less definite clues, again misleading in some instances, appear in some other pairs of items.

Functional and formal grammar occur together in some test parts, as in several illustrations above, and separately in others. The distinctly formal grammar loading varies from around one fourth of the total scoring points in Forms 1-2 and 3-6 to more than 40 per cent in

Forms 1946 and 1948. The formal grammar items cover identification of predicate adjectives used as subjective complements, infinitive phrases, participial phrases, and present perfect passive tenses, as well as the less technical issues involving number, person, and parts of speech.

Form 1946 differs significantly from all other forms in having 160 items whereas a total of 150 items is otherwise standard. The last 20 items of Form 1946, with one exception, require two answers each. Scoring instructions specify one half point for each correct answer, ignoring the need for variation from this pattern for the one item and failing to specify what should be done with fractional scores. The front of each booklet lists the possible score of 150 on one line (160 for Form 1946), provides a space for the "number wrong and omitted" on a second line, and provides a space for "FINAL SCORE" on the third line. The implication seems to be that omissions and wrong answers should enter into the scoring. However, it appears that the "FINAL SCORE," or total number of correct answers, is to be obtained in the scoring process, so incorrect answers and omissions are incidental or else are used only by the careful scorer of his own volition in checking for accuracy.

Two tables are presented in the manual for the conversion of raw scores to percentile ranks for each grade from 7 through 13. Although the norms are reported to "be based on the scores made by 196,097 students in a large number of schools located in all parts of the country," the total number accounted for in the one table where subtotals are listed is only 195,997. The discrepancy of 100, not in itself of much consequence, was apparently carried forward from what appears to be the first, and perhaps the only other, edition of the manual, which the reviewer found in his files. The 1929 norms reported in the first manual were based on "143,633 scores made by students in the two previous years" and shown as 143,533 by subtotals, whereas the 1956 edition norms are based on these same data plus 53,464 scores of high school pupils in 1939 and 1940 and of college freshmen from 1937 to 1941.

The older edition of the manual reports end-of-year norms for 5,126 and 5,325 pupils from grades 7 and 8 respectively and shows medians of 81.3 and 86.5 for the two grades in that order. The 1956 manual bases its comparable norms for these two grades on precisely the same number of cases, but shows medians of 87 and 91 respectively. Furthermore, comparable scores for the 10th percentile are from 4 to 5 points higher in the 1956 manual than in the earlier version and approximately the same degree of discrepancy appears at the 90th percentile. Similar discrepancies in medians occur for all of the other grades, but the inclusion in the 1956 norms of the additional 53,464 scores mentioned above makes further direct comparisons impossible.

The 1956 manual reports that end-of-year norms and midyear norms are based on the 196,097 scores referred to above. The sole explanation of how this was accomplished is found in the statement that midyear norms were "statistically computed" from end-of-year data.

Some form of derived score customarily stands between raw scores and percentile ranks when scores on several parallel forms of a test are given comparability in the standardization process. A crude alternative for standardized tests would be to compute percentile ranks separately for the several forms by the use of essentially comparable normative groups. When the inconsistencies in norms noted above are viewed in the light of the attempt in these tests to give comparable meaning to raw scores, the reviewer cannot but feel that the norms are, and indeed must be, quite unreliable. The situation is not unlike that in which a teacher attempts to assign equivalent meaning to a passing mark of, say, 70, and also to every other percentage mark from 1 to 100, on several different tests.

Several interesting and rather puzzling questions may be raised in brief summary. Are norms based on pupil scores from testing done during 1927–29 and 1937–41 likely to be reliable in 1958? Are coefficients of equivalency as high as .88 to .96 more likely to be the result of a very highly consistent series of short, parallel tests than of a wide range of talent in the pupil samples on which they are based? Are test forms having wide variations in content and types of items and exercises likely to result in raw scores that are comparable? It seems to the reviewer that a negative answer to each of these questions must be given. He is forced to conclude, therefore, that these English tests do not stand up well under the careful scrutiny that modern standards of test construction demand.

[176]

*Barrett-Ryan-Schrammel English Test, New Edition. Grades 9–13; 1938–54; 6 scores: grammar, sentence, punctuation, vocabulary, pronunciation, total; IBM; Forms DM, EM ('54); manual ('54); no data on reliability for grade 9 and part scores; $3.50 per 35 tests; separate answer sheets may be used; $1.70 per 35 IBM answer sheets; postage extra; 35¢ per specimen set, postpaid; 60(70) minutes; E. R. Barrett, Teresa M. Ryan, and H. E. Schrammel; World Book Co. *

REFERENCE
1. MARTIN, RICHARD RALPH. *An Investigation of the Effectiveness of an Entrance Test Battery for Predicting Success in Law School.* Doctor's thesis, Temple University (Philadelphia, Pa.), 1954. (*DA* 16:575)

LEONARD S. FELDT, *Assistant Professor of Education, State University of Iowa, Iowa City, Iowa.*

According to the manual, this test was designed to survey student proficiency in the essential mechanics of English, to diagnose deficiencies in this area, and to facilitate grouping and placement in high school and college classes. There is little factual evidence made available to the user to demonstrate that the test performs any of these functions with greater validity than a reasonably good teacher-made examination.

In defense of test content the authors state that items are based on the "common content of leading textbooks and courses of study." How many and which ones is not specified. Criticisms by teachers and supervisors of earlier editions of the test were considered, as was a study of student errors. No bibliographic reference is made to this study, however; hence its adequacy must be accepted on faith. The authors do not indicate that they consulted published research on the nature and frequency of student errors in written language. Thus the manual contains no factual evidence which would allow the potential user to evaluate the appropriateness of content.

Usefulness as a placement instrument can be claimed for any achievement test. What is required to support this claim is evidence that the instructional program is facilitated by assignment on this basis. Even more important, the user needs evidence that placement of students on the basis of test scores is more fruitful than placement on the basis of previous grades in English or some other inexpensive alternative. No such evidence is presented in the manual.

The claims of diagnostic potential are also without proof, and careful analysis of the test itself does not support such claims. Language mechanics—correct spelling, proper punctuation, appropriate capitalization, and proper choice of word forms—is a heterogeneous body of skills, and the mastery of one will not increase the student's mastery of another. For effective diagnosis, a number of items must be included on each type of problem situation. The one item on agreement of a pronoun with its antecedent and the two items on the hyphen are obvious examples of coverage inadequate for individual diagnosis. The publisher should have specifically warned against such use rather than encouraged it.

In the reviewer's opinion, the test includes far too many items (67) on the academic aspects of language—identification of parts of speech and parts of sentences and specification of the rules governing various situations—and too few items (52) involving functional mechanics. The latter group includes no items on capitalization and spelling. Surely many teachers would have sacrificed willingly the vocabulary and pronunciation items for a greater number of items involving common problems of written expression.

A number of criticisms may be leveled at the reporting of the reliability data in the manual. Most serious, perhaps, is the absence of reliability estimates for grade 9 total score and for the various subtests at all levels. Since differential interpretations and diagnoses from subtest scores are clearly encouraged, this oversight is to be deplored. Even the estimates of total score reliability (.85 to .95 for a single grade) are of little value, since the groups on which the estimates are based are not described. The wide fluctuations in the numbers of cases (42 to 257) suggest the subjects were not randomly chosen from the standardization groups.

Midyear percentile ranks for subtest and total scores are separately tabled for each of grades 9–13. Except for these norms and beginning-of-year norms for college freshmen, percentile ranks for all other testing dates must be interpolated by the user. This might represent a considerable inconvenience for the high school principal who wished to administer the test at the beginning of the year for placement purposes or for the classroom teacher who wished to test both at the beginning and the end of the year to measure growth. Unfortunately, even the meaningfulness of the midyear norms may be seriously questioned, since only the vaguest of descriptions is given of the norms groups. While the number of cases is

impressive (32,641 high school students), test users should be wary of "national" norms that are based on samples drawn from "a large area of the country."

In summary, this reviewer does not regard this instrument as a good test of proficiency in English mechanics. The user is required to accept it more on faith than on evidence, and faith is not a trustworthy criterion for test selection.

CLEVELAND A. THOMAS, *Principal, Francis W. Parker School, Chicago, Illinois.*

Although this test seems as useful as most objective tests in the field of English, certain weaknesses must be noted. In the first place, although Test 1 is called functional grammar, many teachers would not agree that it is based on functional grammar but rather on the familiar formal grammar. It will, therefore, test knowledge of grammar in a vacuum, that is, in a way not necessarily related to speech and writing. This relationship has been constantly demonstrated by studies of the connection between the study of formal grammar and skill in speech and writing. Similarly, the subtest on the sentence is actually a test of the grammar of the sentence. There is no effort to test the student's skill in the construction of sentences. The punctuation test seems to be a reasonable selection of the conventions of punctuation. In the vocabulary items, the authors have avoided the usual trap of asking for synonyms when exact synonyms do not exist. However, there is no indication of the bases for the selection of the words included, so that just how much of a test of vocabulary this subtest actually is remains doubtful. The items on pronunciation represent an ingenious method of getting as close to pronunciation as is probably possible in an objective test. But it seems dubious, at least to this reviewer, that demonstration of knowledge of syllabication and accent placement necessarily indicates correct pronunciation.

In summary, this reviewer would urge the inclusion of work in sentence construction and items of appropriateness similar to those developed in the English achievement test of the College Entrance Examination Board in order to gain some measure not only of knowledge of the mechanics of English, but also of skill in their use. It also seems regrettable that the full contexts used in previous editions of the test (in which the items were based on several selections of paragraph length) have been deserted. A fuller context for some items in the present test would be more desirable. In general, it seems likely that this test will appeal more to those who teach formal grammar as a separate subject than to those whose interest is in whether students can speak and write creditably. Even the former type of teacher may have difficulty, however, because she will not be able to use with real reliability anything except the total score. Since only the total score is reliable, the test does not lend itself to use with the part scores. In spite of the objections noted above, the test will probably give as good an overall measure of the mechanics of English as other tests.

For reviews by G. Frederic Kuder, Robert C. Pooley, and Charles Swain Thomas of the original edition, see 40:1267.

[177]

*California Language Test, 1957 Edition. Grades 1–2, 3–4.5, 4–6, 7–9, 9–14; 1933–58; previous edition (see 4:151) still available; subtest of the *California Achievement Tests;* 4 scores: mechanics of English, spelling, total, handwriting; IBM for grades 4–14; 5 levels; battery manual ('57) for each level; technical report ['58]; separate answer sheets may be used in grades 4–14; 4¢ per IBM answer sheet; 7¢ per Scoreze answer sheet; 20¢ per hand scoring stencil; 10¢ per survey data sheet ('52); postage extra; 50¢ per specimen set of any one level, postpaid; Ernest W. Tiegs and Willis W. Clark; California Test Bureau. *
a) LOWER PRIMARY. Grades 1–2; Forms W ('57), X ('57); $2.10 per 35 tests; (27–40) minutes.
b) UPPER PRIMARY. Grades 3–4.5; Forms W ('57), X ('57); $2.45 per 35 tests; 30(40) minutes.
c) ELEMENTARY. Grades 4–6; IBM; Forms W ('57), X ('57), Y ('57), Z ('57); $2.80 per 35 tests; 20¢ per machine scoring stencil; 38(50) minutes.
d) JUNIOR HIGH LEVEL. Grades 7–9; IBM; Forms W ('57), X ('57), Y ('57), Z ('57); $2.80 per 35 tests; 60¢ per machine scoring stencil; 30(40) minutes.
e) ADVANCED. Grades 9–14; IBM; Forms W ('57), X ('57), Y ('57); $2.80 per 35 tests; 40¢ per machine scoring stencil; 36(50) minutes.

REFERENCES

1. REID, T. JAMES, AND CONQUEST, GEORGE R. "A Survey of the Language Achievement of Alberta School Children." *Alberta J Ed Res* 1:39–52 Je '55. *
2. SANGSTER, C. H. "An Evaluation of the Effectiveness of a Standardized Test of Language." *Alberta J Ed Res* 2:186–202 S '56. *
3. SOPCHAK, ANDREW L. "Prediction of College Performance by Commonly Used Tests." *J Clin Psychol* 14:194–7 Ap '58. *

CONSTANCE M. McCULLOUGH, *Professor of Education, San Francisco State College, San Francisco, California.*

This is a survey test with considerable emphasis upon diagnostic uses of the pupils' responses. A "Diagnostic Profile" on the back of each pupil's booklet provides a graphic picture of his attainments and, by means of shaded areas, the location of scores typical of pupils a grade below or a grade above him. In the examiner's manual, a "Diagnostic Analysis of Learning Difficulties" classifies the errors and lists the test items which deal with particular areas.

The 56-page manual has been done with impressive care and detail. The novice is guided in the meaning of tables and scores as well as being given careful directions for administering the tests. In addition to data on reliability and norms, the concept of "anticipated achievement grade placement" is presented. This is defined as the "norm performance of a nation-wide sample of students in the same school grade and having comparable chronological age and mental ability characteristics." Graphs present separately the curves for mechanics of English and spelling scores for children in different grades whose IQ's vary from 80 to 135. While this seems very significant for use in subjects which are largely developed in school, it seems rather misleading to present such a means of interpretation for the mechanics of English score when word usage is included in the score. Considering the wide variations of knowledge of good usage with which children come to school, the little that intelligence has to do with it, the little that teachers have to do for some children and the much they have to do for others, and the importance of ear training (indeed, parrotting), the presence of word usage in the score makes such a chart an interesting statistical feat rather than anything of value to the teacher of usage. (My parakeet uses good English and learns fast—and has only a bird brain.)

The 1957 Technical Report on the *California Achievement Tests* is as good as an elementary course in test construction and standardization. It describes in detail the way in which the tests were standardized, how the results were treated, and why certain methods were used.

The batteries for the first four grades are introduced as "games," giving a cheerful slant to an old form of torture. The authors wisely have the teacher read aloud the sentences in the lower primary tests, so that the reading difficulty is minimized or removed. The vocabulary of the tests is well controlled, but, as every teacher knows, there are always some children who cannot read the test of their grade level even though it is relatively easy. For such chil-

dren, the teacher might well read or have another pupil read aloud the passages of the
higher test batteries, or administer a test for a
lower grade. Otherwise, the test will be a reading test instead of a language test.

The mechanics tests present successive sentences, sometimes in a running text, with numbers over certain words or at crucial points. One
response (right or wrong or multiple choice)
is required for a line; thus, each answer space
at the right of the page is in perfect alignment
with a crucial point. Narrative form, letter
form, and unrelated sentences are used. Unfortunately, clues to correct responses may be
deduced in certain instances by the surrounding material. If, for example, all sentences
begin with a capital except one and the first
word of this sentence is numbered as crucial,
it is pretty clear that this should have a capital,
too.

The spelling test for the first four grades is
a dictated test, the first five words of which
provide handwriting samples for the grading of
the child's handwriting by a scale in the answer
key. The words are well chosen and are representative of useful words at the levels tested.
Unfortunately, the authors do not provide suggestions for the possible diagnostic value of
such a test or show the types of spelling errors
that indicate kinds of spelling difficulties and
needs.

Beginning with the elementary level, the tests
are called tests (not games) and are machine
scorable as well as hand scorable. The spelling
test at this level presents rows of four words,
any one of which may be misspelled. Thus 120
words are reviewed by the pupil. The words include samplings of different vocabulary levels:
the words "most" and "dispatch" are in the
same test. Thus the teacher can see the height
as well as the depth of a student's spelling ability and need.

The handwriting test in the upper level tests
is a 2-minute test in which the pupil writes a
sentence containing all the letters of the alphabet.

On the backing sheet of the Scoreze answer
sheet, the point being tested in each item is indicated. Thus the teacher who wishes to chart
a student's strengths and weaknesses can do so
as he marks the paper.

The repetition of certain basic items at successive levels of the test means that the high
school teacher will not be alerted to such

things as misuse of the possessive with gerund
while the student is still writing and saying,
"I wish I had of knowed." This is a well constructed battery for survey purposes, and its
many suggestions for diagnosis give the teacher
some ideas for teaching on the basis of the
results.

WINIFRED L. POST, *Instructor in English,
Dana Hall, Wellesley, Massachusetts.*

Each test consists of two main sections: the
first includes three subtests on capitalization,
punctuation, and word usage; the second tests
spelling. Each of the five tests also offers an
optional measure of penmanship.

Because capitalization and spelling are almost completely subject to arbitrary rules, the
tests in these areas will be more uniformly
satisfying to English teachers than the tests of
either punctuation or usage. Some English
teachers may question the heavy stress on capitalization, at least at the advanced level, but all
will agree that the capitalization sections measure skillfully, efficiently, and thoroughly—
through the use of increasingly complex sentences—the student's ability to apply all important rules for capitalization.

In the punctuation sections, almost all the
items are confined to those areas of punctuation which are governed by rules. Many teachers may feel that any full-scale testing of skill
in punctuation, at least for the high school
grades, ought to pose some problems which a
student can solve only by awareness of just
what punctuation the intended meaning of the
sentence requires. And certainly any high school
test ought to include some testing of ability to
use the semicolon and possibly the dash.

The third section, word usage, has the drawback throughout the series of the 2-choice item
which is wide open to guessing. Items on each
test range from a choice between literate and
illiterate English to choices involving fairly
subtle distinctions in idiom. Even the most difficult items, however, demand only a knowledge
of rules and, increasingly for grades 7 and
over, a familiarity with grammar terminology.

For measuring students in grades 1–8, these
tests are skillfully constructed with ingeniously
contrived equivalence among their many forms.
They are easy to administer and score as well
as highly practical for any school which wants
separate scores in capitalization, punctuation,

word usage, and spelling. For some English teachers, the title *California Language Test* may be misleading. The manual calls the capitalization, punctuation, and word usage sections tests of "Mechanics of English," a phrase which accurately and modestly defines their scope and purpose. They measure with precision and efficiency only those areas of language in which rules of right and wrong are final arbiters. They leave untested judgment, sensitivity, and ability to solve problems by grasp of meaning rather than by remembered rules. According to the manual, each of these tests is "designed for adequate measurement throughout the full range of ability found in almost any school group." Yet, in the test for grades 9–14, there is little attempt to test such important problems in language as the dangling element, the misplaced word, phrase, or clause, the squinting modifier, the lack of parallel structure, faulty comparisons, missing or illogical transitions, and illogical metaphor. The *College Entrance Examination Board Achievement Test in English Composition* has already shown that these areas in language can be tested validly and reliably by objective test techniques. Therefore, in the judgment of this reviewer, no test which fails to reckon significantly with these elements of language can rightly claim that it is testing "the full range of ability" of students in grades 9–14.

For reviews by Gerald V. Lannholm and Robert C. Pooley of the 1950 edition, see 4:151; for reviews by Harry A. Greene and J. Paul Leonard of an earlier edition, see 40:1292. For a review by Charles O. Neidt of the complete battery, see 2; for reviews by Warren G. Findley, Alvin W. Schindler, and J. Harlan Shores of the 1950 edition, see 4:2; for a review by Paul A. Witty of the 1943 edition, see 3:15; for reviews by C. W. Odell and Hugh B. Wood of an earlier edition, see 40:1193; for a review by D. Welty Lefever, see 38:876.

[178]
College English Test: National Achievement Tests. Grades 12–13; 1937–43; 7 scores: punctuation, capitalization, language usage, sentence structure, modifiers, miscellaneous principles, total; Forms A ('42, identical with test copyrighted in 1937 except for minor changes), B ('41); directions sheet for Form A ('43), directions sheet for Form B ('42, identical with sheet copyrighted in 1937 except for minor changes); teachers' guide ['44]; no norms for part scores; $3.75 per 25 tests; 50¢ per specimen set; postage extra; 45(50) minutes; A. C. Jordan; Acorn Publishing Co. *

OSMOND E. PALMER, *Associate Professor, Office of Evaluation Services, Michigan State University, East Lansing, Michigan.*

The two forms are parallel in form and quite close in content, except as noted in the subsequent discussion. The test must be hand scored. In the punctuation section, the student is to insert the proper marks and enclose them in parentheses (for easier identification by the rater?). In the capitalization section, the words which need to be capitalized are to be underlined. The next three sections require the student to draw a line under the best of four sentences. (It would be much simpler merely to circle the letter of the right response.) The last section requires matching; the letter of the right response is written before the item.

The 4-page teachers' guide covers a whole series of English tests, but only one brief descriptive paragraph (and the corrected odd-even reliability figure .88) can be taken as referring specifically to the *College English Test*. The directions, space for recording class scores, the answer keys, and the norms are all contained on a single sheet. The norms are not convincing. They are given in median scores by month for grades 11–13. Each month at the high school level shows exactly a one-point increase over the month before. The college norms begin one point above the highest high school figure and increase by one or two points a month for nine months. Even if the test had been more carefully constructed and had a higher reliability, it could not measure progress as minutely as this.

The test, in parts at least, is unrealistic and arbitrary, occasionally careless, and not completely consistent from one form to the other. One item in each form tests for punctuation of a Biblical reference. Form A requires "1 Sam. IX. 13" and Form B, "Deut. 5:11–21." In one answer, the items in a bibliography entry are separated by commas; in the other, by periods. In Form B, the key calls for three commas in "The French king Henry IV of Navarre ruled from 1589–1610." With respect to capitalization, the student is expected to know that a Latin sentence, when it appears on the Great Seal of a state, would have every word capitalized and how to treat the "whereases" in a formal declaration. At the other extreme, he is tested for the capitalization of "I" and "United States," both of which appear properly capitalized in other parts of the same section. One form calls for the capitalization of "western" in the phrase "the western part of the state"; both forms insist that "spring" in "South American Spring" is capitalized.

Part 3, Language Usage, is quite different in the two forms. This is probably due to the fact that in the earlier Form A so many of the right answers are unnatural—"Them who failed, we also praised"; "Let us fellows go, for we are better than they"; and "Can you tell me if I may go, or will I have to see to [sic] the principal." Occasionally, there would seem to be two acceptable answers. For examples: "Lincoln's assassination caused much trouble" or "An act that caused much trouble was the assassination of Lincoln"; "Can you tell me if it is raining," "Can you tell me whether it is raining," or "Can you tell me whether or not it is raining?" In one case the attempt to test for who-whom led to a confusion in the keying. This is supposed to be right: "Tell him that whomever we see coming will be the man whom we are instructed to arrest." Both forms reject a one-he sequence in favor of one-one. Form B does not test for so many out of the way points and its sentences are a little less awkward, but some responses are still dubious.

The sections on sentence structure and modifiers illustrate some of the same difficulties and introduce a new one. In order to get the four choices of response, the authors frequently test for two different things simultaneously—a matter of emphasis plus the one-one sequence; tense plus order; shall-will plus can-may.

Some of the "Principles" which form the key list in the last section are not mutually exclusive, so that a student could well mark one of several responses. For instance, an "incorrect use of the expletive there" might also be an example of an "unnecessary change of subject." An "unnecessary change of subject" might also involve a "lack of parallel structure." An "incomplete comparison" could also be an "illogical comparison." It is a little hard to make a distinction between "lack of parallel correlative elements" and "lack of parallel structure for parallel ideas," or between "incorrect co-ordination" and "unnecessary double-barreled co-ordinating construction."

Because this test does not reflect current language practices and because it is not carefully made, it could well be allowed to go out of print.

For reviews by Constance M. McCullough and Robert W. Howard of Form A, see 40: 1269.1.

[179]

*Cooperative English Test: Lower and Higher Levels. Grades 7–12, 11–16; 1940–56; IBM; 3 tests available as separates and in a single booklet edition; no specific manual; general Cooperative manual ('51); descriptive folders [Mechanics and Effectiveness of Expression, '56; Reading Comprehension, '51]; norms ['40]; separate answer sheets must be used with Form Z, optional with other forms; postage extra; Cooperative Test Division, Educational Testing Service. *

a) SINGLE BOOKLET EDITION : LOWER AND HIGHER LEVELS. Grades 7–12, 11–16; 7 scores: mechanics of expression, effectiveness of expression, vocabulary, speed of comprehension, level of comprehension, total comprehension, total; IBM; Forms T ('50 or '51, same as test copyrighted in 1943), Y (Lower Level, '51—same as test copyrighted in 1948), Higher Level, '48), RX ('49), Z ('53, same as test copyrighted in 1951) ; 2 levels; directions for hand scoring answer sheets ['49] ; $4.95 per 25 tests; $1.95 per 25 IBM answer sheets; 60¢ per set of scoring stencils; 120(130) minutes.

b) TEST A, MECHANICS OF EXPRESSION. Grades 7–16; IBM; Forms T ('43), X ('47), Y ('50, revision of Forms Q and R; same as test copyrighted in 1948), Z ('53) ; $2.50 per 25 tests; $1 per 25 IBM answer sheets; 25¢ per scoring stencil; 40(45) minutes; Geraldine Spaulding (T, X, Y), Herbert Danzer (X), W. W. Cook (Y), Janet Afflerbach (Z), Miriam M. Bryan (Z), and Paula Thibault (Z).

c) TESTS B1 AND B2, EFFECTIVENESS OF EXPRESSION : LOWER AND HIGHER LEVELS. Grades 7–12, 11–16; IBM; Forms T (Lower Level, '43; Higher Level, '51—same as test copyrighted in 1943), X ('47), Y (revision of Forms Q and R; Lower Level, '50—same as test copyrighted in 1948; Higher Level, '48), Z ('53) ; $2.75 per 25 tests; $1 per 25 IBM answer sheets; 25¢ per scoring stencil; 40(45) minutes; Geraldine Spaulding (T, X, Y), Miriam M. Bryan, Janet Afflerbach (Y, Z), Catherine Dodd (Z), and Paula Thibault (Z).

d) TESTS C1 AND C2, READING COMPREHENSION : LOWER AND HIGHER LEVELS. Grades 7–12, 11–16; 4 scores: vocabulary, speed of comprehension, level of comprehension, total; IBM; Forms R ('50, same as test copyrighted in 1941), T (Lower Level, '43; Higher Level, '50—same as test copyrighted in 1943), Y ('48), Z ('53) ; 2 levels; directions for hand scoring ['49] ; $3.25 per 25 tests; $1 per 25 IBM answer sheets; 25¢ per scoring stencil; 40(45) minutes; Frederick B. Davis, Mary Willis (T), Clarence Derrick (Y), Harry R. Neville (Y), Jeanne M. Bradford (Y), Geraldine Spaulding (Y), and Charlotte Croon Davis (Z).

REFERENCES

1–2. See 40:1276.
3–31. See 3:120.
32–84. See 4:155.
85. HESTON, JOSEPH C. "The Graduate Record Examination vs. Other Measures of Aptitude and Achievement." *Ed & Psychol Meas* 7:618–30 au '47. * (PA 22:3210)
86. LINDSAY, REX B. *Predicting Success in the Lower Division at the University of Utah.* Master's thesis, University of Utah (Salt Lake City, Utah), 1947.
87. MURPHY, HAROLD D., AND DAVIS, FREDERICK B. "College Grades and Ability to Reason in Reading." *Peabody J Ed* 27:34–7 Jl '49. *
88. BERNER, WILLIAM. *An Evaluation of the Freshman Testing Program at Southern Methodist University.* Master's thesis, Southern Methodist University (Dallas, Tex.), 1951.
89. KNICKERBOCKER, K. L. "Placement of Freshmen in First-Quarter English." *J Higher Ed* 22:211–5+ Ap '51. * (PA 26:520)
90. WELSH, MARY L. *A Comparison of Two Psychological Examinations in Predicting Academic Success of Ohio Univer-*

sity Students. Master's thesis, Ohio University (Athens, Ohio), 1951.

91. *Final Report on the 1951 National College Freshman Testing Program.* Princeton, N.J.: Cooperative Test Division, Educational Testing Service, [1952]. Pp. i, 27. *

92. ANDREW, DEAN C. "Predicting College Success of Non-High-School Graduates." *Sch R* 60:151–6 Mr '52. *

93. FREDERIKSEN, NORMAN. "The Influence of Timing and Instructions on Cooperative Reading Test Scores." *Ed & Psychol Meas* 12:598–607 w '52. * *(PA* 27:6741)

94. FREEHILL, MAURICE F. "Student Self-Estimates as Guidance in Selecting Courses." *Col & Univ* 27:233–42 Ja '52. *

95. LIEN, ARNOLD JUEL. "A Comparative-Predictive Study of Students in the Four Curricula of a Teacher Education Institution." *J Exp Ed* 21:81–219 D '52. *

96. VORDENBERG, WESLEY. "How Valid Are Objective English Tests?" *Engl J* 41:428–9 O '52. *

97. WELCH, W. BRUCE. *An Examination of the Usability of Selected Standardized Tests of Mental Ability and Achievement for College Groups With Atypical Socio-Economic Status.* Doctor's thesis, Indiana University (Bloomington, Ind.), 1952.

98. ANDERSON, SCARVIA B. "Prediction and Practice Tests at the College Level." *J Appl Psychol* 37:256–9 Ag '53. * *(PA* 28:6583)

99. BARRETT, DOROTHY M. "Correlation of Survey Section of Diagnostic Reading Tests and of Test C2: Reading Comprehension With College History Grades." *J Ed Res* 46:465–9 F '53. * *(PA* 28:1461)

100. CARLIN, LESLIE C. "A Longitudinal Comparison of Freshman-Senior Standing." *J Ed Res* 47:285–90 D '53. * *(PA* 28:6586)

101. COLEMAN, WILLIAM. "An Economical Test Battery for Predicting Freshman Engineering Course Grades." *J Appl Psychol* 37:465–7 D '53. * *(PA* 29:1562)

102. JENSON, RALPH E. "Predicting Scholastic Achievement of First-Year Graduate Students." *Ed & Psychol Meas* 13:322–9 su '53. * *(PA* 28:4833)

103. KERN, DONALD WARREN. *The Prediction of Academic Success of Freshmen in a Community College.* Doctor's thesis, New York University (New York, N.Y.), 1953. *(DA* 15:85)

104. MORTVEDT, AUDREY R. *Relative Effectiveness of a Local English Test, the ACE L-Score, Cumulative Grade Average, and the Cooperative General Culture Test in the Selection of Upper-Class Regent's Scholarship Winners.* Master's thesis, University of Nebraska (Lincoln, Neb.), 1953.

105. RUSSON, ALLIEN R. *The Prediction of Scholastic Achievement of Business Education Majors at the College Level.* Doctor's thesis, University of California (Los Angeles, Calif.), 1953.

106. SATZ, MARTIN ALLEN. *The Relationship Between Eleven Independent Variables and Academic Performance in Nine Social Science Areas at the University of Washington.* Doctor's thesis, University of Washington (Seattle, Wash.), 1953. *(DA* 14:635)

107. SPAULDING, GERALDINE. "A Note on the Interpretation of Scaled Scores for Form Z of the Cooperative English Test." *Ed Rec B* 61:72–4 Jl '53. * *(PA* 28:4863)

108. VOTAW, DAVID F., AND LAFORGE, PAULA K. "Rapid Hand Scoring of Cooperative English Tests." *Jun Col J* 24:214–8 D '53. *

109. WEBB, SAM C., AND MCCALL, JOHN N. "Predictors of Freshman Grades in a Southern University." *Ed & Psychol Meas* 13:660–3 w '53. * *(PA* 28:6598)

110. BOLTON, EURI BELLE. "The Predictive Value of the Columbia and the Michigan Vocabulary Tests for Academic Achievement." *Peabody J Ed* 32:9–21 Jl '54. * *(PA* 29:7954)

111. CHAPPELL, TOLAN L.; CALLIS, ROBERT; RENZAGLIA, GUY A.; AND SPOHRER, MYRON A. "The Differential Prediction of Achievement at the University of Missouri." *Ed & Psychol Meas* 14:724–5 w '54. * *(PA* 29:7955)

112. FREEHILL, MAURICE F. "The Co-operative English Test in Academic Counseling." *Col & Univ* 29:244–52 Ja '54. *

113. GUAZZO, EUGENE J., JR. *Predicting Academic Success of Architecture Students.* Master's thesis, Alabama Polytechnic Institute (Auburn, Ala.), 1954.

114. LAYTON, WILBUR L. "The Relation of Ninth Grade Test Scores to Twelfth Grade Test Scores and High School Rank." *J Appl Psychol* 38:10–1 F '54. * *(PA* 29:1570)

115. MARTIN, RICHARD RALPH. *An Investigation of the Effectiveness of an Entrance Test Battery for Predicting Success in Law School.* Doctor's thesis, Temple University (Philadelphia, Pa.), 1954. *(DA* 16:575)

116. SEIGLE, WILLIAM F. "Prediction of Success in College Mathematics at Washburn University." *J Ed Res* 47:577–88 Ap '54. * *(PA* 29:2982)

117. BOYD, JOSEPH DON. *The Relative Prognostic Value of Selected Criteria in Predicting Beginning Academic Success at Northwestern University.* Doctor's thesis, Northwestern University (Evanston, Ill.), 1955. *(DA* 15:1780)

118. BUCKTON, LAVERNE, AND DOPPELT, JEROME E. "Freshman Tests as Predictors of Scores on Graduate and Professional School Examinations." *J Counsel Psychol* 2:146–9 su '55. * *(PA* 30:3453)

119. CHAHBAZI, PARVIZ. "The Prediction of Achievement in a College of Agriculture." *Ed & Psychol Meas* 15:484–6 w '55. * *(PA* 30:7754)

120. CHAPMAN, HAROLD MARTIN. *The Prediction of Freshman Scholarship From a Combination of Standardized Test Scores and High School Grades.* Doctor's thesis, University of Houston (Houston, Tex.), 1955. *(DA* 15:1201)

121. GUSTAD, JOHN W., AND FISH, JANICE P. "The Use of the Cooperative Mechanics of Expression Test in Classification at the College Freshman Level." *Ed & Psychol Meas* 15:436–40 w '55. * *(PA* 30:7761)

122. HAYNES, JERRY O. *Some Predictive Factors of Academic Success in Two Curricula of a Land-Grant College.* Master's thesis, Alabama Polytechnic Institute (Auburn, Ala.), 1955.

123. MELTON, RICHARD S. "Differentiation of Successful and Unsuccessful Premedical Students." *J Appl Psychol* 39:397–400 D '55. * *(PA* 30:7769)

124. MULLINS, CECIL J. "The Effect of Reading Ability on Two Standardized Classification Tests." *J Ed Psychol* 46:189–92 Mr '55. * *(PA* 30:1627)

125. POUNDS, RALPH L. "Prediction of Academic Success at the University of Cincinnati, Teachers College: Progress Report II." *Yearb Nat Council Meas Used Ed* 12(pt 2):12–31 '55. *

126. ROYER, J. EVERETT. *Selection and Use of Certain Factors Significant in Predicting Achievement of Students in First-Semester Accounting at the University of Miami, 1950–1953.* Doctor's thesis, Indiana University (Bloomington, Ind.), 1955.

127. SKUBA, MICHAEL. "An Analysis of English Errors and Difficulties Among Grade Ten Students in the Smoky Lake School Division." *Alberta J Ed Res* 1:15–23 D '55. *

128. ANDERSON, RODNEY EBON. *The Use of Entrance Tests in the Differential Prediction of Freshman College Achievement, and the Effect of an Item Analysis on the Efficiency of the Predictive Batteries.* Doctor's thesis, Indiana University (Bloomington, Ind.), 1956. *(DA* 16:1234)

129. HOUK, CLIFFORD C. *An Investigation of the Relationship Between General Chemistry 3 at Ohio University and Various Measures of Achievement.* Master's thesis, Ohio University (Athens, Ohio), 1956.

130. SMITH, GEORGE B. *Who Should Be Eliminated? A Study of Selective Admission to College.* University of Kansas Publications, Kansas Studies in Education, Vol. 7, No. 1. Lawrence, Kan.: School of Education, the University, December 1956. Pp. 28. *

131. TRAXLER, ARTHUR E. "Reliability of Cooperative Achievement Tests for Independent Secondary School Pupils." *Ed Rec B* 68:64–8 Jl '56. * *(PA* 31:8853)

132. WEBB, SAM C. "Differential Prediction of Success in Graduate School." *J Ed Res* 50:45–54 S '56. * *(PA* 31:6685)

133. FRICKE, BENNO G. "Speed and Level Versus Rate and Accuracy of Reading." *Yearb Nat Council Meas Used Ed* 14:73–7 '57. *

134. HENDERSON, HAROLD L. "Predictors of Freshmen Grades in a Long Island College." *Ed & Psychol Meas* 17:623–7 w '57. *

135. HEWER, VIVIAN H. "Vocational Interest-Achievement-Ability Interrelationships at the College Level." *J Counsel Psychol* 4:234–8 fall '57. *

136. MANUEL, HERSCHEL T. "Aptitude Tests for College Admission." *Yearb Nat Council Meas Used Ed* 14:20–7 '57. *

137. RICHARDS, JAMES M., JR. "The Prediction of Academic Achievement in a Protestant Theological Seminary." *Ed & Psychol Meas* 17:628–30 w '57. *

138. BARRETT, RICHARD S. "The Process of Predicting Job Performance." *Personnel Psychol* 11:39–57 sp '58. *

139. BERRY, CHARLES A., AND JONES, ARLYNNE L. "The Predictive Value of the Tests of the National Freshman Testing Program for Grambling College Freshmen." *Negro Ed R* 9:23–33 Ja '58. *

140. GOWAN, J. C. "Intercorrelations and Factor Analysis of Tests Given to Teaching Candidates." *J Exp Ed* 27:11–22 S '58. *

141. JENSEN, VERN H., AND CLARK, MONROE H. "A Prediction Study of Cooperative English Test Scores." *Personnel & Guid J* 36:635–6 My '58. *

142. MOORE, CHARLES W. *Some Relationships Between Standardized Test Scores and Academic Performance in the College of Business Administration of the University of Houston.* Doctor's thesis, University of Houston (Houston, Tex.), 1958. *(DA* 19:356–7)

For a review by Chester W. Harris of Forms S, T, Y, and RX, see 4:155; for reviews by J. Paul Leonard, Edward S. Noyes, and Robert C. Pooley of Forms R, S, and T, see 3:120. For reviews by Robert Murray Bear and J. B. Stroud of the reading test, see 3:497.

[180]

*Coordinated Scales of Attainment: English. Grades 4, 5, 6, 7, 8; 1946–54; subtest of *Coordinated Scales of Attainment;* 3 scores: punctuation, usage, capitalization; IBM; Forms A ('46), B ('49); 5 levels; directions for administering ['52]; battery manuals (A, '54; B, '49); separate answer sheets must be used;

$1.70 per 25 tests; $1 per 25 IBM scorable answer sheets; 25¢ per scoring stencil; $1 per specimen set; postage extra; (45) minutes; Dora V. Smith; Educational Test Bureau. *

For a review by Alvin W. Schindler of the complete battery, see 4:8; for reviews by Roland L. Beck, Lavone A. Hanna, Gordon N. Mackenzie (with Glen Hass), and C. C. Ross of batteries 4–8, see 3:6.

[181]

*Correctness and Effectiveness of Expression. High school, college; 1944–57; subtest of *Tests of General Educational Development*; IBM; 2 levels, 2 forms: high school, Form B ('44), college, Form B ('43); revised manuals: high school level ('56), college level ('54); $2.50 per 25 tests of either level; separate answer sheets must be used; $1 per 25 IBM answer sheets; 50¢ per specimen set; postage extra; (120) minutes; prepared by Examination Staff of United States Armed Forces Institute; Veterans' Testing Service, American Council on Education. *

For a review by Charlotte W. Croon of the college level, see 3:122. For a review by Robert J. Solomon of the complete battery, see 27; for a review by Gustav J. Froehlich of Form B, see 4:26; for reviews by Herbert S. Conrad and Warren G. Findley, see 3:20.

[182]

★Cotswold Junior English Ability Test. Ages 8–9; 1949–52; forms A ['49], B ['52]; 9s. per 20 tests; 5½d. per single copy; 1s. per manual; postage extra; C. M. Fleming; Robert Gibson & Sons (Glasgow), Ltd. *
a) JUNIOR ENGLISH A. Form A ['49]; manual ['49]; 28(35) minutes.
b) JUNIOR ENGLISH B. Form B ['52]; manual ['52]; 35(45) minutes.

M. A. BRIMER, *Senior Lecturer in Educational Psychology, University College, Ibadan, Nigeria.*

Though the norms for both forms of this test extend from 8-0 to 9-11 years and the tests are similar, they differ in difficulty and in some of the processes tested. Form A has 51 scored items and Form B, 70. The mean raw score on Form A at age 8-11 is 30, while on Form B it is 22. Thus the author is quite right to recommend Form A for 8-year-old and Form B for 9-year-old children. Both forms of the test and the tasks included are part of the outcome of the author's own researches into the basic primary school subjects, which she reports separately.[1] The items were selected after having been tried out and analysed for difficulty and internal consistency. Items found to

1 FLEMING, C. M. *Research and the Basic Curriculum.* London: University of London Press Ltd., 1946. Pp. vii, 120. *

be ambiguous after scrutiny of children's responses were discarded.

In each form there are six separately timed subtests covering reading comprehension, language usage, written composition, short term recall of material read, and accuracy in transcription. There is a progressive increase in difficulty throughout the tests and a well developed unity of the parts. The reading comprehension links the content by making each paragraph part of a single story. This has the merit of reducing the artificiality of the testing situation and of aiding the orientation of young children when they are required to adjust rapidly from one task to another. Teachers of English in primary schools will recognise that, both in this respect and in the skills emphasised, the test is adjusted to the standpoint of the classroom.

On the back cover of the booklet there is a short practice test which adequately familiarises the children with the type of material they will encounter in the test proper, and with the kind of responses they will be required to make. The practice is necessary since the children are required to read the instructions for themselves in the test proper. An example preceding each subtest would undoubtedly have helped a great deal to extend discrimination to the lower ability ranges where the test is at present most weak.

There are rather more selective response items than necessary and more direct questions with single word answers than are desirable. Children grasp completion items rather more readily than those involving selective underlining, and the response made has the advantage of completing a unit of sense, which is a desirable exercise in itself. As a general rule, tests for classroom use should avoid testing techniques which are not a function of the skill being tested.

Instructions for administration are clear and leave little to chance, and despite their similarity to the usual classroom exercises, the scoring of the items remains objective. Marking takes a little longer than with many objective tests and a certain amount of judgment is required of the marker.

The reliability of Form A has been estimated at .97 by the split-half technique and at .94 by the test-retest technique. The figure of .97 confirms the success of the system of item selection used in producing high internal consistency.

The figure of .94 indicates that the whole procedure of administering, working, and scoring the test produces highly consistent results on two occasions. The reliability of Form B is not reported, but the similarity of the two forms and the fact that Form B is longer suggests that it will prove to be at least as reliable as Form A. No evidence of validity is reported in the manual, but reference is made to *Research and the Basic Curriculum* as the basis of the form and content of the test.

The norms for both forms are presented as standardised scores with a mean of 100, a standard deviation of 15, and a normalised distribution. These have the effect of comparing each child's performance with that of a representative group of English children of the same age. Neither form is at its best at the lower extreme of its range. The lower 10 per cent of 8-year-old children make scarcely any score. Norms are provided from 8-0 to 10-0 years, but Form A at least is restricted at the top of its range. It would be better to employ the test well within the limits of its range.

In summary, this is a test to be recommended for classroom use, particularly to those teachers who wish to have tests closely related to classroom exercises. It is rare to find a test of this nature standardised on such a large population.

JOHN C. DANIELS, *Lecturer in Education, University of Nottingham, Nottingham, England.*

It is claimed by the author that these tests have been "devised to measure....the mastery of vocabulary....and the comprehension and use of what is commonly called English" of 8-year-olds. The two tests consist of six subtests, all timed separately. For example, in Form B, subtests 1 and 2 are reading comprehension tests of the type in which the child reads a story silently and then answers five questions on the text. In this case the passages for subtests 1 and 2 are two halves of one longer story. Subtest 3 consists of a story with missing words to be found and underlined in a column to the right of the text. After this, the child is to compose and write out in full two sentences about the story. Subtest 4 consists of direct questions, with answers to be recalled, on the story of subtest 3, plus a test in which the child has to find and underline certain synonyms for words underlined in the text of another story. Subtest 5 is a spelling test, the words to be spelt being read out aloud and their use illus-

trated in sentences. Subtest 6 consists of deciding which of 10 sentences are "commands" and copying these in full, marks being subtracted for errors of copying.

The author explains the rationale of the test in her work *Research and the Basic Curriculum*. It is, she claims, based upon "careful analysis of the difficulties in reading and the processes used in written composition." Certainly the validity of the tests must rest upon the validity of Fleming's analysis, for it is otherwise difficult to see how this empiricist mish-mash of tests could give valid estimates of any recognisable factor other than a rather rough and ready estimation of *g*. Norms are given as standardised scores, with age allowances, having a mean of 100 and, apparently, a standard deviation of 15.

So much depends upon 8- and 9-year-olds being sufficiently "test-trained" to be able to follow the detailed plan of work which has to be carefully controlled by the teacher that, since no reliability coefficients are quoted, your reviewer must be allowed to venture the opinion that retest reliability would be found to be low. The complexity of the testers' and markers' tasks will also militate against high reliability. However, since there is a grave shortage of good tests of general "scholastic" ability at this age level, these tests will no doubt find many satisfied users.

[183]

*Cotswold Measurement of Ability: English. Ages 10–12.5; 1947–54; 6 forms: labeled Series 2 ['47], 3 ['49], 4 ['51], 5 ['52], 6 ['53], 7 ['54]; incomplete norms for Series 2-5; 9s. per 20 tests; 5½d. per single copy; 1s. per manual (dates as for tests) for any one series; postage extra; 35(50) minutes; C. M. Fleming and J. W. Jenkins (manual for Series 2); Robert Gibson & Sons (Glasgow), Ltd. *

M. A. BRIMER, *Senior Lecturer in Educational Psychology, University College, Ibadan, Nigeria.*

These tests are designed as measures of attainment in English at the stage of transfer from primary to secondary schools in England and Wales. They are produced annually for use by education authorities in their selection procedures, and distribution is restricted during this critical, initial use. They are eventually released and published with norms based on quite large numbers of English children. While the original function remains in evidence to the extent that the greater discrimination occurs above the mean, the tests have nevertheless sufficient range for general classroom measurement.

The tests have been constructed on the evidence derived from the author's own researches into the difficulties children encounter in reading and the processes by which written composition takes place. Each test is made up of about 112 scored items arranged in four separately timed subtests. The tasks presented are essentially of functional English, concentrating upon reading comprehension and composition. The reading comprehension relies a great deal, perhaps too much, on inference from context. The complexity of the inference gradually increases since, although questions follow each paragraph, the paragraphs continue the theme and the questions integrate material from the preceding paragraphs. Composition is tested analytically by selective response, completion type items within a continuous prose passage, and by the arrangement of sentences into a sensible order, after first selecting them from among others to be relevant to a given theme. These two tasks probably approach as close to an objective assessment of written composition as it is possible to get. Vocabulary is tested within the context of a sentence and spelling is tested with a completion item which avoids the pitfalls of employing misspellings as distractors or phonetic spellings as clues. An interesting exercise in precise expression is also included, in which the children are required to select two sentences which mean most nearly the same as a given model.

The tests are intended to be used with the arithmetic and mental ability tests of their batteries, which justifies the placing of the practice test for the English test on the back cover of the arithmetic booklet. Nevertheless, it does inconvenience those users who wish to employ the tests separately, since it is necessary to give the practice test if the norms are to be strictly applicable. On the back covers of the English booklets, short tests of visual acuity are presented. No great precision of measurement is attempted, since they are intended as indications of the children's effectiveness with the size of type used in the tests rather than as measures in their own right. No norms or other form of guidance is given for the interpretation of performance.

The administration is strictly controlled and presents no difficulties apart from the placing of the practice test referred to above. Marking is objective but rather laborious since no mark column is provided and composite marks are sometimes accorded to the same response.

The norms are presented in the form of standardised scores with a mean of 100 and a standard deviation of 15. In effect, they compare the child's performance with that of a representative group of English children of the same age. The scores are grouped into decile ranks for ready interpretation.

The tests are well constructed and cover processes which teachers consider important and which are often missing from other tests of English. The continuity of a single theme throughout each test reduces the artificiality of the testing situation. The tests have well established norms and adequate reliability. More information on the construction of the tests and more extensive guidance to teachers on the interpretation of the scores would improve the manuals.

S. C. RICHARDSON, *Lecturer in Psychology, Hillcroft College, Surbiton, Surrey, England.*

This test is in six forms which are roughly similar. Each is developed around comprehension passages and groups of sentences. Questions follow each section. Items other than comprehension items (spelling and vocabulary questions, for instance) are related to the themes of the passages. The great advantage of this design, in the reviewer's opinion, is that it avoids the use of short, disconnected items which make up most objective tests and which must, to some extent, favour the nonperseverative candidate. Some questions demand sustained thought and the capacity to build up and use mental content. Writing capacity is tested to some extent by a question requiring an answer six sentences long, though the material is not original.

The material of the tests seems likely to be independent of any particular teaching method and should be suitable for children from any school. The grammatical and syntactical questions have been chosen to test some of the points of difficulty revealed by research into the nature of children's errors in writing English. The tests have good reliabilities and have been standardised on large groups of children. Practice material and "warming-up" questions are supplied.

One type of item, occurring in only one form of the test, might perhaps be criticised. This is one where the child is asked to write four lines of verse from memory. The product is scored for spelling and punctuation. This question must surely yield material varying widely in difficulty, with a tendency for the abler children to produce more difficult material.

It would be useful to know more about the criteria of external validity mentioned in the manual. In the absence of exact information, the test seems a good measure of the ability to understand English and, to a lesser extent, of the ability to use it. It is notoriously difficult to construct a good, objectively scored English test. The criticisms which apply to many tests of this kind are (a) that they instigate undesirable teaching methods and (b) that they test only the more mechanical aspects of English ability. The Cotswold test, in the reviewer's opinion, avoids the first of these difficulties and goes some way towards overcoming the second.

[184]

*English: Every Pupil Scholarship Test. Grades 2-4, 5-6, 7-8, 9-12; 1926-58; new form usually issued each January and April; 4 levels; norms available following testing program; no data on reliability; 4¢ per test; 4¢ per scoring key; postage extra; 40(45), 50(55) minutes for grades 2-8, 9-12; Bureau of Educational Measurements. *

[185]

*English IX-XII: Achievement Examinations for Secondary Schools. High school; 1951-53; Forms 1 ('51), 2 ('52), 3 ('53); no specific manual; series manual ('57); no data on reliability and validity; norms: Forms 1 ['52], 2 ['53], 3 ('53); 10¢ per specimen set; postage extra; [60-90] minutes; Educational Test Bureau. *
a) FORMS 1 AND 3. Grades 9, 10, 11, 12; 10¢ per test.
b) FORM 2. Grades 9-10, 11-12; $2.75 per 25 tests.

[186]

★English IX-XII: Midwest High School Achievement Examinations. Grades 9, 10, 11, 12; 1955-57; Forms A ('55), B ('57); 4 levels; no specific manual; no data on reliability; norms: [A, '55; B, '57]; 10¢ per test, postage extra; Form A: 60(65) minutes; Form B: 90[95] minutes; Educational Test Bureau. *

ROGER A. RICHARDS, *Assistant in Secondary Curriculum, New Jersey State Department of Education, Trenton, New Jersey.*

The most serious shortcoming of these tests is the total lack of information about them. The prospective user is not even told how much time is required to administer the tests. A single sheet of paper folded to make a 4-page brochure is entitled "Manual," but the data generally contained in such a publication are not provided. The so-called "Rationale" might better be referred to as a thumbnail sketch of the history of American education (and not a very

good sketch). The statement labeled "Purpose" is as follows:

The purpose of these High School Achievement Examinations is to motivate efforts of accomplishments by the students. A less easily arrived at purpose is that of motivating thinking ability. However, these Examinations make a real effort to stimulate thinking ability based on mastery of contents resulting from efforts of work.

How they make that effort is a mystery to this reviewer, and the publishers are apparently content to let it remain that way to all readers. The manual—which apparently serves science, mathematics, history, and language tests as well as those under review here—states that the "norms are established at the end of each school year." But how they are established is not divulged. The terms "validity" and "reliability" are not mentioned in the manual.

The reviewer infers that the tests are intended to provide a basis for grading students at the end of a year's work in English. That they are worthless for such a purpose would be quite obvious to almost any teacher who looked at a copy of any one of them. In order to construct any test to measure achievement in a course, one must start with a knowledge of the course. If he is to include some spelling words, he must select them from those which the students have supposedly learned during the term. If he is to ask questions about literature, he must base them on the literary works which the students have read. Unfortunately, we are not told anything about the type of English course upon which these tests are based. The reviewer hopes that no such course exists, and he is reasonably confident that it does not.

The provision of two forms for each grade leads one to hope that the forms might be equivalent. But an examination of the contents leads the reviewer to suspect that the two forms for any grade are quite different. Again, the publishers have chosen not to clarify this point.

With so many basic deficiencies, these tests do not warrant the space that would be required to consider some of the more detailed matters such as item writing, format, and scoring. In the opinion of the reviewer the tests do not warrant serious consideration for use as evaluation instruments. English teachers who are looking for good standardized tests would do well to continue their search.

[187]

★English Progress Tests A-F. Ages 8, 9, 10, 11, 12, 13; 1952-57; 1 form; 6 levels; 7s. per 12 tests; 8d. per single copy; 1s. per manual of any one test; postage extra; A. F. Watts (*a*, *c*, *f*) and M. A. Brimer (*b*, *d*, *e*); published for the National Foundation for Educational Research in England and Wales; Newnes Educational Publishing Co. Ltd. *

a) ENGLISH PROGRESS TEST A. Age 8; 1952; 1 form ['52]; manual ['52]; no data on reliability; 39(45) minutes.

b) ENGLISH PROGRESS TEST B. Age 9; 1956–57; 1 form ['56]; manual ['57]; (45) minutes.

c) ENGLISH PROGRESS TEST C. Age 10; 1952; formerly called *English Grading Test 3;* 1 form ['52]; manual ['52]; no data on reliability; (55) minutes.

d) ENGLISH PROGRESS TEST D. Age 11; 1956; 1 form ['56]; manual ['56]; provisional norms; (45) minutes.

e) ENGLISH PROGRESS TEST E. Age 12; 1956; 1 form ['56]; manual ['56]; provisional norms; (45) minutes.

f) ENGLISH PROGRESS TEST F. Age 13; 1953; 1 form ['53]; manual ['53]; no data on reliability; (55) minutes.

NEIL GOURLAY, *Professor of Education, University of the Witwatersrand, Johannesburg, Union of South Africa.*

The series is "designed to provide a continuous assessment of English skill from 8–14." There is a test and manual for each age level. Various skills are involved: vocabulary, spelling, reading comprehension, rewording of sentences, direct and reported speech, punctuation, and several others. Vocabulary and spelling enter into all the tests, but only a limited sample of the other skills is tested at each level, the sample varying appropriately from age to age.

Most of the tests would appear to have been well standardised and, where the standardisation might be inadequate, this has been stated. The standardisation procedure adopted enables the user to convert raw scores to transmuted scores, which, for the age group concerned, are distributed with mean 100 and SD 15. Age corrections can then be applied to obtain standardised scores for all ages *within* the age group. A difficulty arises for the teacher using the tests with pupils whose ages range over two or more of the age groups. If an allowance is to be made for age, the teacher has little option but to use standardised scores; and, since the standardisation of each form is limited to an age group, two or more forms of the test will therefore be required. This has certain obvious disadvantages. It is in fact doubtful whether much is gained by the method of standardisation adopted. A set of age norms for each form of the test would probably have increased the tests' usefulness.

A certain amount of the scoring is subjective. This is a disadvantage, but it is compensated for by the increased scope of the items which must improve validity.

There is no doubt that the series is well constructed and can be recommended to teachers and other test users. But, as stated above, a simpler form of standardisation would probably have increased its usefulness.

STANLEY NISBET, *Professor of Education, University of Glasgow, Glasgow, Scotland.*

These tests are designed to "give teachers an idea of the progress a pupil has so far made in mastering the English language." They cover reading comprehension, vocabulary, sentence construction, written expression, punctuation, spelling, and simple grammatical usage.

A special feature is their preference for "free" responses, which require the pupil to write a word or a sentence, and the consequent avoidance of strictly "objective" items (e.g., multiple choice). The manuals give guidance to markers, with examples of acceptable and unacceptable answers. This characteristic helps the tests to give adequate credit to pupils whose teachers have followed "more liberally conceived programmes," as opposed to those who teach English too mechanically. On the other hand, much is left to the subjective judgment of the marker; the reviewer quite often found it difficult to decide whether certain answers on scripts were acceptable or not.

Kuder-Richardson (formula 20) reliability coefficients are quoted for Tests B, D, and E only. They are high (around .95) and indicate that, provided the same person marks all the scripts in a group, a satisfactorily stable assessment is obtained. We do not know, however, to what extent different markers would agree in assessing the same scripts. The reliability quoted merely assures us that the self-consistency of the single marker on a single occasion is high enough not to impair the inherent stability of the test, which is itself high.

Test B was standardized on a representative sample of about 4,500 children. Figures are not provided for the other tests. In the case of Tests D and E, users are warned that the standardizing sample was too small to make the norms trustworthy. The layout of the norms in the manuals is clear, but there is a lack of uniformity in the way in which they are presented in the different manuals. This is probably due to the fact that the tests were produced at different times and by two different authors. If a new edition is contemplated, it would be helpful if a uniform presentation were adopted. It is only fair to say, however, that no great importance is claimed for these norms.

The reviewer has doubts about several small details in some of the marking keys, but on the whole they are clear enough.

It may be concluded that the tests can be recommended for internal classroom use as being preferable to most English tests of a more mechanical type. They have been constructed, often ingeniously, to discover whether pupils can in fact *use* English. The norms, however, should be treated with great caution or not used at all, and, in the absence of strict precautions to ensure consistency among markers, the tests should not be used for any external purpose (e.g., grading pupils or comparing schools or classes).

[188]
*English Survey Test: Ohio Scholarship Tests: Ohio Senior Survey Tests.** Grade 12; 1935–54; 6 scores; grammar, spelling, capitalization, punctuation, sentence structure, total; Forms A ('53), B ('54); mimeographed battery manual ['53]; no data on reliability; 4¢ per test; 50¢ per battery teacher's manual ('35); cash orders postpaid; 150(160) minutes; Mary H. Hutchison; Ohio Scholarship Tests. *

For reviews by Charlotte W. Croon Davis and J. Paul Leonard of the original edition, see 3:125.

[189]
★English Test (Adv.).** Ages 12–13; 1954–58; forms 1 ['54], 2 ['57], 3 ['58]; distribution restricted to directors of education; 8s. 3d. per 12 tests; 9d. per single copy; 1s. 7d. per manual; postage extra; 50(55) minutes; published for National Foundation for Educational Research in England and Wales; Newnes Educational Publishing Co. Ltd. *
a) ENGLISH TEST (ADV.) 1. 1954–55; manual ['55]; G. A. V. Morgan.
b) ENGLISH TEST (ADV.) 2. 1957; manual ('57).
c) ENGLISH TEST (ADV.) 3. 1958; manual ('58).

[190]
*English Test: Municipal Tests: National Achievement Tests.** Grades 3–6, 6–8; 1938–56; subtest of *Municipal Battery;* 5 scores: language usage-words, language usage-sentences, punctuation and capitalization, expressing ideas, total; 2 forms; 2 levels; no data on reliability; no norms for part scores; $1.75 per 25 tests; 50¢ per specimen set of either level; postage extra; 30(35) minutes; Robert K. Speer and Samuel Smith; Acorn Publishing Co. *
a) GRADES 3–6. 1938–55; Forms A ('55, identical with test copyrighted in 1938), B ('39); directions sheet ('38).
b) GRADES 6–8. 1938–56; Forms A ('52, identical with test copyrighted in 1938), B ('56, identical with test copyrighted in 1939); directions sheets (A, '38; B, '39).

For a review by J. Murray Lee of the complete battery, see 18; for a review by Ralph C. Preston, see 4:20; for reviews by A. M. Jordan

of the complete battery for grades 6–8 and Hugh B. Wood of the batteries for grades 6–8, see 40:1191.

[191]
*English Test: National Achievement Tests.** Grades 3–8, 7–12; 1936–57; 2 forms; 2 levels; no norms for part scores; 50¢ per specimen set of either level; postage extra; (40) minutes; Robert K. Speer and Samuel Smith; Acorn Publishing Co. *
a) GRADES 3–8. 1936–38; 7 scores: capitalization, punctuation, language usage (sentences), language usage (words), expressing ideas, letter writing, total; Forms A ('38), B ('38); directions sheet ('38); no data on reliability; $2.50 per 25 tests.
b) GRADES 7–12. 1936–57; 7 scores: word usage, punctuation, vocabulary, language usage (sentences), expressing ideas, expressing feeling, total; Forms A, B ('52, identical with tests copyrighted in 1938); directions sheets (A, '57; B, '52); teachers' guide ['44]; no data on reliability for Form B; $3 per 25 tests.

For a review by Winifred L. Post, see 4:162; for a review by Harry A. Greene, see 3:126.

[192]
★English Test 2.** Ages 12–13; 1952; 1 form ['52]; 8s. 6d. per 12 tests; 9d. per single copy; 1s. per manual ['52]; postage extra; 60(65) minutes; G. A. V. Morgan; published for the National Foundation for Educational Research in England and Wales; Newnes Educational Publishing Co. Ltd. *

REGINALD EDWARDS, *Lecturer in Educational Psychology, University of Sheffield, Sheffield, England.*

This test was produced in response to a demand from teachers of children between 12 and 14 who attend secondary modern schools—that is, those who academically fall below the 80th percentile. A panel of teachers cooperated in its production. A reasonable attempt has been made to sample what is usually taught to children of this age, bearing in mind that each school is autonomous in this respect. The test covers: selective and inventive vocabulary, reported speech, grammatical usage, knowledge of idiom and conventional patterns of language, sentence joining, punctuation, reading comprehension, poetry completion, spelling, and the use of the dictionary. The test contains 120 items in two separately timed sections. The time limits are said to be generous in order that slow readers will not be unduly penalised. In fact, the second half of the test is found by children to be much harder than the first, so that the limits for the second half are none too generous for children of average ability.

The first section consists of 15 questions dealing with idiomatic expression, 15 on vocabulary and meaning, and 30 on grammatical rules, usages, punctuation, etc. For its kind, this is a most useful section, though it could be argued that each individual usage might be tested separately, and tested in a better way. The second half of the test is heavily concentrated on exercises based upon a dictionary extract (20 items) and passage comprehension and sentence completion items. This section might well be a test of verbal intelligence.

Although intended for secondary modern school children, the test was standardized upon "two complete age groups of pupils attending all types of secondary school" in two areas, one rural and one urban. Thus, the standardization population included the academically brightest 20 per cent. This procedure is still useful with a single age group, but some care is necessary in its extension. After two years, the academically gifted will pursue a much different course than the less gifted, and, as is known, measured verbal intelligence among the less gifted will tend to decline in comparison with that of those pursuing a more academic course. The standardization showed the expected sex difference in favour of girls which exists between ages 10 and 13. In this case, a significant difference of 7.5 points of raw score was found, but separate norms for boys and girls are not available. Although more boys than girls (1,920 against 1,841) were included in the standardization group, the table of norms gives the mean raw score at the middle of the age range as 69. The reported mean scores are boys, 62.47 and girls, 69.97. These facts detract from the value of the norms provided.

It still remains to be asked, what does the test measure? One of the declared aims of the National Foundation for Educational Research is to produce verbal intelligence tests, English attainment tests, linked ability and attainment tests, and diagnostic tests in basic subjects. Certainly this test cannot be used diagnostically, save in a rough and ready way, as it contains too few items of most kinds to be sufficiently diagnostic. Equally, it can scarcely be a verbal intelligence test, though, on the basis of factor analysis of material analogous to that in the test, its items are said to have "high loadings in a factor representing verbal ability." Indeed, from these facts the test's validity is argued. But a knowledge of the wide range of item difficulty and of the test's sampling of vocabulary and comprehension would enable anyone to guess at this high loading on verbal ability. It would seem, therefore, that this is a test

which measures a composite of ability and attainment. As such, its usefulness outside its country of origin must be limited. However, in England, it satisfies teachers who feel that it measures the kind of teaching that goes on in school, where spelling, punctuation, and sentence structure are still important in a subject commonly called "English."

S. C. RICHARDSON, *Lecturer in Psychology, Hillcroft College, Surbiton, Surrey, England.*

This test is intended for secondary modern school children. The questions were suggested by a panel of teachers and appear to be fairly closely related to the teaching methods most commonly used in these schools. Children taught in a different way may be at some disadvantage in the test.

The test includes questions on spelling, vocabulary, sentence construction, and comprehension. There is also a section testing the ability to use a dictionary. Many of the items are nicely designed to give objective scoring without appearing too artificial. In some, the candidate is required to construct a fairly long sentence out of given material.

It seems to the writer a pity that one or two of the questions have a social class bias. No middle class child, however backward in English, is likely to give as a correct answer, "Someone has taken Mary's pencil off of her," or "the man....is the one who learnt me to swim," though, with a predominantly working class group, such items may have validity. Since, in some circumstances, tests influence teaching methods and content, it also seems regrettable that so many of the questions favour the depressing form of English teaching which consists in training children in the use of clichés ("fall between two stools" and "show the white feather," for examples). The poetry completion section is perhaps open to criticism on the ground that the poem is a fairly hackneyed one and some children may already know it by heart.

Apart from some very indirect factorial evidence, there is nothing to show, objectively, exactly what the test measures. The authors suggest that it measures "mechanical English" (spelling and punctuation) and "comprehension and creativity" (reading comprehension and writing). This last claim seems to the writer a trifle optimistic. It seems to rest chiefly on the poetry completion items. The difficulty of testing this ability objectively does not seem to have been solved in the test and it should probably be used in conjunction with an essay paper if a full measure of English ability is required.

The test has reasonably generous time limits and high scores should not depend to a great extent on speed. It has a high (Kuder-Richardson) reliability, and gives a good spread of raw scores. Since British tests of English for the 12–14 age group are relatively scarce, it will be a useful addition.

CLEVELAND A. THOMAS, *Principal, Francis W. Parker School, Chicago, Illinois.*

The content of this test is sufficiently different from American tests that extensive attention must be paid to it. Section I of the test is made up of 60 consecutive items with no time breaks but only simple directions for the various parts of the section. Vocabulary is tested by asking students to select the proper item from among six to match a definition. Students are also asked to select one idiomatic use from among six to fit the context of a given sentence. Ability to handle indirect quotations is tested by asking the student to fill in blanks in an indirect quotation on the basis of a previously stated direct quotation. Ability to combine ideas is tested by asking the student to join two or three short sentences into one. In the spelling sections, one form of a word is given and the student is asked to write the proper form of the given word in a sentence. Punctuation is tested by asking the student to supply the proper mark at designated spots in given sentences.

Section 2 includes an extract from a dictionary for use in answering a series of questions. Spelling is tested by giving some letters of a word in a sentence and asking the student to write the whole word, for example, st_p_d for "stopped." The section also includes short passages followed by comprehension questions such as "Find the *four* words, occurring *together* in the passage, which mean nearly the same as 'still to come.'"

This is an interesting test which attempts to put the emphasis squarely on the use of the language rather than on knowledge about it. American teachers and testers may feel that some parts of the test will not test what they are supposed to test. For instance, the example of the reading comprehension item above raises the question of whether reading comprehension

of the passage or only of the specific items within the passage is actually being tested. The test will not render specific diagnosis of the various aspects tested, but only a total score. It should be of interest to any teacher of English as evidence of British emphases. It would also be useful to the experimentally minded or to those who would like to measure their students against British students.

[193]

★English Tests 1, 3–8. Ages 10–11; 1951–58; 7 forms; distribution restricted to directors of education; 7s. 6d. per 12 tests; 8d. per single copy; 1s. 7d. per manual; postage extra; G. A. V. Morgan (*a–d*) and M. A. Brimer (*e*); published for National Foundation for Educational Research in England and Wales; Newnes Educational Publishing Co. Ltd. *
a) ENGLISH TEST 1. 1951–58; form 1 ['51]; manual ['58]; 45(50) minutes.
b) ENGLISH TEST 3. 1952–53; form 3 ['52]; manual ['53]; 50(55) minutes.
c) ENGLISH TEST 4. 1953–57; form 4 ['53]; manual ('57); 40(45) minutes.
d) ENGLISH TEST 5. 1954–55; form 5 ['54]; manual ('55); no norms for ages 11-6 to 11-11; 50(55) minutes.
e) ENGLISH TEST 6. 1955–56; form 6 ['55]; manual ('56); no norms for ages 11-10 to 11-11; 50(55) minutes.
f) ENGLISH TEST 7. 1956–57; form 7 ['56]; manual ('57); 50(55) minutes.
g) ENGLISH TEST 8. 1957–58; form 8 ['57]; manual ('58); 50(55) minutes.

[194]

*English Usage: Every Pupil Test. Grades 3–4, 5–6, 7–9, 10–12; 1929–58; new form usually issued each December and April; 4 levels; norms available following testing program; no data on reliability; 3¢ per test; 1¢ per scoring key; cash orders postpaid; 40(45) minutes; Ohio Scholarship Tests. *

For a review by J. R. Gerberich of the 1946 forms, see 3:127.

[195]

★Greene-Stapp Language Abilities Test: Evaluation and Adjustment Series. Grades 9–13; 1952–54; 5 scores: capitalization, spelling, sentence structure, punctuation, usage; IBM; Forms AM ('52), BM ('53); manual ('54); no norms for grade 13; separate answer sheets must be used; $6.40 per 35 tests; $1.70 per 35 IBM answer sheets; postage extra; 35¢ per specimen set, postpaid; 80(95) minutes in 2 sessions; Harry A. Greene and Helen I. Stapp; World Book Co. *

REFERENCE

1. CROOK, FRANCES E. "Interrelationships Among a Group of Language Arts Tests." *J Ed Res* 51:305–11 D '57. *

RICHARD A. MEADE, *Professor of Education, University of Virginia, Charlottesville, Virginia.*

This test is designed to measure proficiency in five areas of language study. It is administered in two periods of 50 and 45 minutes, respectively. The directions seem clear, and it should not be difficult for any teacher who has read them with care to give the test. The test may be machine scored; however, a convenient stencil is furnished for hand scoring.

The manual is an adequate one. It gives understandable directions for scoring and treats well the kinds of interpretation of results which are possible. Raw scores obtained may be easily converted by the use of tables into percentile ranks and standard scores. There is also a clear section on the use of the results and suggestions for conducting remedial work. In general, these suggestions are clear, but, in a few instances, they are vague. Also, the contents of the test should never determine the objectives of a classroom. Test items may be based on content which a given class or pupil should not attempt. Hence, remedial work should relate only to those items that are in accord with goals already set without regard to the content of this test.

Characteristics of the group upon which the test was standardized are given in the manual, and users are warned to interpret results in the light of this information. This point is an excellent one for a manual to make, and teachers should consider it with care.

The capitalization, spelling, and punctuation subtests are adequate and are geared to actual performance at this level. However, the subtests on sentence structure and so-called applied grammar and on usage and so-called applied grammar are open to some question. In both these subtests, there is more stress on grammatical understanding than on ability to identify correct or incorrect structure and usage. The only way the subject can indicate that a sentence is incorrect is to assign a grammatical reason for the error; he receives no credit unless he evidences this knowledge. Hence, the user must decide whether or not it is his purpose to test thorough grammatical knowledge that includes the full understanding of standard terminology.

In addition, the subtest on usage takes no note of colloquial (informal) usage. About one third of the items involve usages that many authorities would consider correct for informal language purposes. There is no direction to the subject to tell him that the test is based on very formal usage. English teachers themselves differ in their points of view about correct usage. So, here again, the user must decide whether this test is in keeping with his own philosophy.

All in all, the *Greene-Stapp Language Abili-*

ties Test is a well constructed test that adequately covers the areas it includes. If the user takes into account the two points made above about grammar and usage, he should find this test convenient and usable in terms of his purposes.

OSMOND E. PALMER, *Associate Professor, Office of Evaluation Services, Michigan State University, East Lansing, Michigan.*

A lot of work has gone into these tests but the results are dubious.

The manual is unusually complete and even has suggestions for analyzing the errors a student makes and for correcting them. The tests seem to have been constructed after good tryouts. They were standardized on an adequate population; reliabilities (fair) were found; and standard scores were established which allow direct comparison with Terman-McNemar IQ's and with other tests in the series.

Each of the five parts of the test is long enough to give a fairly detailed picture of the student's mastery. But all sections do not seem to do an equally good job. The section on capitalization covers its area pretty thoroughly. That on punctuation is likewise quite thorough, but it is not quite as meaningful. A word in a sentence is underlined and the student is given a choice of four marks of punctuation which might be used before, after, or within the word. A fifth choice is that no punctuation is necessary. In half the cases, the choice probably reduces itself to comma (or period) or nothing. In addition, where two spots in a sentence are marked, the same punctuation is required at both spots. The correct decision at one point automatically ensures a correct answer at the other; but it is here, in the omission of one of two necessary commas, that students frequently err.

The spelling section is not so carefully worked out as these two. The setup itself is a little disturbing. Each item consists of four words printed horizontally across the whole width of the page. One or none of these words may be correctly spelled. Since it is easier to glance down a column than to span a page, the good speller may be tempted to see how often the correctly spelled word is the first response in an item. In this manner he could get 10 of the 45 items without looking at three of the four words tested. The misspellings are supposed to have been taken from student papers, but a number of them look so strange that it is doubtful if many students will even recognize them. There is a fair representation of words testing for final *e,* final *y, al* plus *ly,* and doubling. For some reason there are no examples of *ie-ei* words. Also, some of the more commonly misspelled words are missing: grammar, separate, athletics, arctic. There would have been room for these, for about 10 words are needlessly (?) repeated with different spellings in different items, and a few that appear are expendable: voucher, statistics, millinery, embroidery.

What one learns about a student from the two remaining sections, Sentence Structure and Applied Grammar, and Usage and Applied Grammar, is ambiguous. Each item in the sentence structure test has as its stem a sentence. The first response is always, "The sentence is correct." The other three, which suggest ways in which the sentence may be corrected, are an assortment of about 25 statements used, in set patterns or randomly, throughout the 38 items. In fewer than half the cases are these three foils homogeneous or do they all have relevance to the point being tested for in the sentence. For instance, in Item 3, Form AM, the sentence "He wants us to appreciate fully what he has done for this community" is correct. Two of the responses, suggesting corrections of a dangling participle or a dangling gerund, do not seem to have much relevance to this sentence. Nor does the third seem much more apropos: "Leave out a word or phrase that repeats an idea." In 9 cases out of 11 (both forms) when the response "Leave out an unnecessary conjunction before a relative pronoun" is used, there is no such combination in the sentence. This means that a student can eliminate one or two responses simply because they cannot apply to the situation. It also means that if he does pick one of these nonrelevant responses, he is confused by something other than what the item seems to be testing. For diagnosis it also suggests an analysis of the wrong responses for each student individually to find out exactly what is bothering him. Does he mistake an infinitive for a gerund? Does he know what a verbal is?

Test 5, Usage, has the same arrangement as the sentence structure test, but the student has to consider only the one word underlined in the sentence. There is a greater variety in the responses, but some 25 are used frequently. Here,

too, the foils are frequently not to the point. For example, the sentence "Everyone should prepare *his* lessons on time" obviously tests for agreement in number between pronoun and antecedent. The first response, which calls for agreement in gender, is either irrelevant or misleading—how is a student to know whether only girls are involved? The second introduces the problem of the antecedents of reflexive pronouns. And the third response jumps to: "A pronoun used with a gerund to show ownership should be in the possessive case."

Aside from the need here, too, to analyze wrong answers to find a student's specific weaknesses, there is another difficulty. Most of the responses are statements of principle, such as, "The present tense should be used for facts permanently true," and, "The nominative case should be used after a copulative or linking verb." The student undoubtedly assumes that these statements are true and needs to decide only if they are relevant. But of the specific statements introduced as responses, only 9 (5 of these being right answers) of 41 in both forms of the test are correct statements. Eleven might be true of some sentences in some contexts, but 21 are not true for the sentence tested for or for any sentence. Since, throughout the sentence structure test and in most cases here, the student did not have to question the accuracy of the responses, he may fail to do so in the case of these 30-odd responses. Does this help to make the usage test the hardest part of the tests?

If these are speeded tests, and the reviewer's guess is they are (he would estimate that it would take at least 120 minutes instead of 80 to finish them), several other problems are introduced. They may be easier than the 50th percentile difficulties (about 44 per cent correct for 9th graders and about 60 per cent for 12th) reflected in the total score norms would indicate. The reliability, too, figured as it was on the split-half formula, may be spuriously high. The main problem, however, is the significance of the scores. The difference between two scores may be due to a greater knowledge of the matters tested, or it may be due merely to speed. Does the 12th grader get a higher percentage of items attempted right than the 9th grader, or did he simply get more right because he answered more items?

These tests, if carefully used, can tell us

something about our students, but others should prove more fruitful.

[196]

★**Hoyum-Schrammel English Essentials Tests.** Grades 3-4, 5-6, 7-8; 1955-56; Forms A ('55), B ('55), C ('56), D ('56); 3 levels: primary, intermediate, advanced; manual ['56]; no data on reliability for Forms C and D; $1.25 per 25 tests, postage extra; 25¢ per specimen set of any one level, postpaid; 40(50) minutes; Vera Davis Hoyum and H. E. Schrammel; Bureau of Educational Measurements. *

WORTH R. JONES, *Assistant Professor of Education, University of Cincinnati, Cincinnati, Ohio.*

Forms for the primary grades consist of parts covering sentence recognition, capitalization, punctuation, correct usage, and alphabetization. Forms for grades 5–8 consist of parts covering sentence recognition, capitalization, punctuation, correct usage, and reference materials, such as guide words and an index.

No publication date is indicated in the manual, which contains reliability data and limited information for Forms A and B of the tests. Data for Forms C and D are not given. The manual is extremely brief in its explanation of the development of the tests. Although the statement is made that the tests may be used for both survey and diagnostic purposes, the norms are based only on total scores. These norms were computed from the scores made by 22,485 pupils located in "many representative" schools in "twenty-three different states." No further information on this point is included.

Reliability coefficients for Forms A and B are reported as ranging from .87 to .96, and the standard error of scores, from 2.8 to 6.3. Reliability data are based on results obtained from pupils in "a number" of schools, located in Arkansas, Colorado, Kansas, and Nebraska. An adequate description of the reliability studies is lacking.

The authors' description of attempts to establish the validity of the tests also leaves much to be desired. The content of the tests is reportedly based on the common content of 11 sets of leading textbooks, with items "somewhat in proportion as they were stressed in these sources." The authors assert that criticisms from teachers, supervisors, and test construction specialists were carefully considered in the making of revisions and improvements, although such individuals are not otherwise identified.

An examination of the tests reveals the following technical and editorial errors:

a) Form C, grades 3-4, Part 2, Item 16: The word "be" has been omitted from the sentence.

b) Form A, grades 7-8, Part 3, Item 37: The word "though" evidently should be "thought."

c) Form A, grades 7-8, Part 4, Item 58: "The students [1. choose 2. chose 3. choosed] Carl as team captain." Although "chose" is the desired answer, is it not true that "choose" might be equally correct, depending upon the context?

d) Form D, grades 7-8, Part 6: The example is incorrectly marked. The correct answers should be 12 and 20 rather than 12 and 22.

e) Sections pertaining to capitalization require the pupils to identify letters in heavy type. It is questionable as to whether there is enough distinction between the heavy type and the light type in some of the items.

f) It is the opinion of the reviewer that the directions for marking the punctuation sections on the forms for the primary grades probably will confuse the students. For example, Form C, grades 3-4, uses the term "parentheses" to refer to both brackets and parentheses. At all levels these sections require the pupil to refer to a single list of answers before marking each item. Much time might be wasted through this procedure. It appears highly possible that ease of marking has been sacrificed for ease of scoring.

Because of the inadequacies of the manual, the lack of data on reliability for Forms C and D, the poor format, and the errors within the tests, the reviewer is unwilling to recommend these tests to prospective users.

RUTH STRICKLAND, *Professor of Education, Indiana University, Bloomington, Indiana.*

Each of the tests covers sentence recognition, capitalization, punctuation, and certain aspects of usage. The remainder of each test deals with the use of reference and resource materials. No attention is given to word meanings, writing style, or spelling.

The tests of sentence recognition follow an identical pattern from grade 3 through grade 8. They test recognition of fragments, run-on sentences, and simple sentences—mainly declarative. There is relatively little difference in maturity and complexity between the sentences for the primary grades and those for the advanced grades. The content dealt with at the three test levels differs little.

Part 2 of each test deals with capitalization. In each case the letter to which the child is to respond is indicated in darker type. The child is not asked to find an error in a sentence or to look at the sentence as a whole—the way he would experience it in his own writing. He is told to respond only to the one letter in heavy type in the context of the sentence. Because the dark type differs in size from the rest of the type, it is, in a few instances, difficult to locate the letter to which attention is called.

Knowledge of punctuation is tested in Part 3 of each test. The answer choices for the section are listed at the beginning of the section. Parentheses or brackets appear at the point which is to be tested. It appears likely that many children will receive considerably higher scores on this subtest because attention is directed to a specific spot, whether it calls for punctuation or not. The child might not have recognized the need for attention at that point had he not been called upon to consider it.

Part 4 of each test deals with usage. In the test for grades 3 and 4 common verb errors, double subjects, and a few other common errors are included. The two final items of Forms A and B which link a pronoun with a noun as a double subject seem very difficult for this level. Forms C and D for grades 3 and 4 have an added part dealing with contractions and possessives. These do not appear in Forms A and B.

The usage section of each of the intermediate forms contains 50 items, some of which test the same elements which appear in the easier tests. Again at this level a new Part 4 dealing with contractions, possessives, and plurals appears in Forms C and D but not in Forms A and B.

The final section of the tests for grades 3 and 4 and Forms C and D for grades 5 and 6 deals with alphabetization. Directions are clearly stated so that children ought to have little difficulty with these items.

Forms A and B of the intermediate test have two sections which do not appear in Forms C and D. Part 5 of Forms A and B deals with reference materials. Section A is concerned with the use of guide words as one finds them in a dictionary and Section B with the use of an index. The questions dealing with the index would be difficult for many pupils of grades 5 and 6.

The four forms of the intermediate test differ considerably in difficulty and in content. Forms C and D appear distinctly easier and more within the scope of the majority of pupils of this age than do Forms A and B.

Part 5 of Forms A and B of the tests for grades 7 and 8 deals with reference materials. It is essential that children learn to use reference resources easily and effectively but there is some question as to whether these skills fall

within the scope of an English test. Also the items dealing with reference materials in Forms C and D of this test seem distinctly easier than those of Forms A and B. Part 6 of Forms C and D is concerned with the location of authors and topics in card index drawers.

At all grade levels, the directions for the test are to be read by the pupils. This adds considerably to the difficulty for many pupils at grades 3 and 4. At each grade level there is a great deal to cover in a 40-minute period.

What really constitutes skill and power in the use of language is not touched upon here. The ability to express an idea or a series of ideas in organized, clear cut sentences and well-knit paragraphs and to set them down in a form which will carry meaning to a reader is in no way measured in these tests.

[197]

*The Iowa Tests of Educational Development: Test 3, Correctness and Effectiveness of Expression.** Grades 9–13; 1942–58; IBM; Forms X-3S, Y-3S ('52); examiner's manual ('58); battery manual ('54); pupil profile leaflet, fourth edition ('58); profile card (no date); separate answer sheets must be used; $3 per 20 tests; $5 per 100 IBM answer sheets; 50¢ per hand and machine scoring stencil; 50¢ per specimen set; 50¢ per battery manual; postage extra; 60(70) or 40(50) minutes (class period version); prepared under the direction of E. F. Lindquist; Science Research Associates. *

For reviews by J. Murray Lee and Stephen Wiseman of the complete battery, see 17; for a review by Eric F. Gardner of Forms X-2 and Y-2, see 4:17; for reviews by Henry Chauncey, Gustav J. Froehlich, and Lavone A. Hanna of Forms X-1 and Y-1, see 3:12.

[198]

Modern English Usage Test. Grades 9–16 and adults; 1949–50; IBM; Form A ('49); manual ('50); no data on reliability and validity; separate answer sheets must be used; $4 per 25 tests; 50¢ per specimen set; cash orders postpaid; 40(50) minutes; Antonia Bell Morgan; Aptitude Associates. *

HOLLAND ROBERTS, *Director, Academic Freedom Committee, San Francisco, California.*

The author has designed this test to cover a very wide field: conversation and written English in secondary schools, colleges and universities, business schools, and business and industry. The manual states that it has been standardized nationwide on 3,283 high school students and 171 male high school graduates, 63 holding the bachelor's degree, and 67 with unspecified advanced degrees.

The test consists of 130 sentences, with one

or more words underlined to indicate some point of usage. The student is asked to mark each sentence T for "correct" or F for "incorrect."

Interested teachers will find a number of problems in considering what the test offers, as little or no information is provided on a number of key questions: how the test was constructed, how the standardization was done, and how the test is to be used in improving usage in teaching programs. In particular, there is no reference to authority for the choice of the 130 usage items which make up the body of the test nor any indication that the author recognized or made use of the important studies in the field of English usage issued by the National Council of Teachers of English and other authoritative and scholarly organizations. There is no reference to any authority anywhere in the manual, scoring key, or test. The result is general confusion. Colloquialisms and idiomatic English are accepted at times and rejected at others for undisclosed reasons. Positive positions are taken on cases of divided usage, and even against generally accepted usage: "It's up to you and *I* to set a good example" is considered acceptable usage, but not "Bill has worked here longer than *I*."

The use of the nominative in "Who do you have in mind?" is rejected, although it is in almost universal use and is given as established by Leonard in *Current English Usage* and Marckwardt and Walcott in *Facts About Current English Use,* and approved by Kennedy in *English Usage* as "natural" and "almost inevitable." In the *Oxford English Dictionary* it is called "common in colloquial use" and Shakespeare, Southey, and Hardy are cited in support. At times it is not clear what usage is in question, as in the sentence: "He will *succeed* if he continues to work hard." The author does not accept this usage but gives no reason. A number of cases of divided usage are included such as: "Ben talks *like* he knew everything." The author of the test accepts this usage, although Leonard and Kennedy report it as "disputable" and the Oxford dictionary notes that it is "generally condemned as vulgar or slovenly."

Finding ways to rationalize such diverse unilateral decisions would tax the ingenuity of the nimblest. Most teachers and supervisors will prefer to use the *Cooperative English Test* or make their own teaching tests which place major emphasis upon learning the large body of accepted usage and subordinate the debatable usages which illustrate the ebb and flow of change and the presence all about us of different levels of language.

For a review by Walter N. Durost, see 4:170.

[199]

★The New Purdue Placement Test in English. Grades 11–16; 1931–55; 8 scores: punctuation, grammar, sentence structure, reading (study), reading (pleasure), vocabulary, spelling, total; IBM; Forms D, E ('55); preliminary manual ('55); only norms are tentative grade 13 norms for total score; separate answer sheets or booklets must be used; $2.70 per 35 tests; $1.35 per 35 IBM answer sheets; $2.10 per 35 answer booklets; 42¢ per machine scoring stencil; 60¢ per specimen set; postage extra; 65(75) minutes; G. S. Wykoff, J. H. McKee, and H. H. Remmers; Houghton Mifflin Co. *

REFERENCES

1–9. See 4:173.
10. JOHNSON, A. PEMBERTON. "Counseling Engineering Freshmen." *Ed & Psychol Meas* 13:133–44 sp '53. * (*PA* 28:1566)
11. SEVERANCE, KATHERINE M. *The ACE and the Purdue English Placement Tests as Predictors of Academic Success at Baylor University.* Master's thesis, Baylor University (Waco, Tex.), 1953.
12. BAKER, PAUL CLEO. *Experiments in Variable Selection for Prediction of Academic Achievement.* Doctor's thesis, Purdue University (Lafayette, Ind.), 1955. (*DA* 15:2565)
13. DUNGAN, EARL WILLIAM. *An Evaluation of the Orientation Test Battery at Dickinson State Teachers College for Purposes of Prediction and Counseling.* Doctor's field study, Colorado State College of Education (Greeley, Colo.), 1955.
14. BONNER, LEON WILLIAM. *Factors Associated With the Academic Achievement of Freshmen Students at a Southern Agricultural College.* Doctor's thesis, Pennsylvania State University (State College, Pa.), 1956. (*DA* 17:266)

GERALD V. LANNHOLM, *Program Director, Educational Testing Service, Princeton, New Jersey.*

The authors of the *New Purdue Placement Test in English* state that its primary purpose is "to sample the knowledge possessed by high school seniors or college freshmen of what is called 'good English.' " An examination of the content of the test reveals that the authors were either unnecessarily modest in this claim or had in mind a much broader concept of "knowledge" than that used by this reviewer. While it is clear that knowledge is required to respond correctly to the test exercises, the successful examinee must also be able to apply such knowledge.

The names of the various parts of the test indicate the general areas covered: recognition of grammatical errors, punctuation, sentence clearness and effectiveness, reading, vocabulary, and spelling. In each of the first three of these parts, the authors employ a 2-response (right or wrong) type of exercise. In the first part, the examinee is to study each of the 30 sentences and indicate whether or not it contains an error in grammar. In the second, he is to decide, for each of 45 sentences, whether or not it is punctuated correctly. In the third, he is to indicate, for each of 30 sentences, whether or not it is clear and effective. In none of these parts is he asked to identify the error or to supply a correction. To measure reading ability, two reading selections (constituting the fourth and fifth parts, respectively) with 14 four-choice questions based on each are presented. In the vocabulary part, the examinee is required to indicate which of the five words given for each of 45 key words means most nearly the same as the key word. The spelling part includes 45 items, each of which is made up of three different words plus the word "none"; the examinee is to select the misspelled word, if any, in each item. Each of the seven parts has its own time limit, with 65 minutes being allotted for the 225 items in the total test. The answer sheet provides space for recording the score on each part.

Labeled a "preliminary edition," the manual nevertheless represents a fairly complete job. It contains considerable information to assist the prospective user in evaluating the usefulness of the test for his particular purpose, directions for administering and scoring the test, and interpretative data, the source of which is described in some detail. The data, all based on the use of the test at Purdue University, include percentile and T score norms for total score, estimated reliability coefficients and standard errors of measurement for part scores and total score, intercorrelations among the part scores and total score, and correlations of the test scores with scores on a number of other tests.

The authors report that the principal use of the test scores has been for placement in English courses. While they do not present direct evidence on the effectiveness of the test scores alone for that purpose, they cite correlations between the test scores and grades in English courses for freshmen at Purdue University assigned to English courses at three different levels on the basis of their scores on this test and other data. Raw correlation coefficients ranging from .08 to .34 were obtained for the separate courses. Corrected for restriction of range in test scores, the estimated correlations ranged from .84 to .86. The authors' statement that "the validity of this test is near .85" may be misleading to readers who do not realize that validity is a specific rather than a generalized concept.

Without the information given in the manual, some might be inclined to underestimate the quality of this test on the basis of the overemphasis on error recognition, the use of the right-wrong item type, the relatively small sampling of specific skills within ability areas, and the lack of exercises requiring the student to produce good writing. Although this reviewer believes that the prospective user should always examine any test before making a decision on its quality, this test demonstrates the soundness of the adage which says that "the proof of the pudding is in the eating." The evidence presented indicates that the test has a high degree of effectiveness for the placement of college freshmen in English courses.

M. J. WANTMAN, *Visting Director of Educational Measurement and Research, University of Malaya, Singapore.*

The primary purpose of this test is stated as being "to sample the knowledge possessed by high school seniors or college freshmen of what is called 'good English.' " The test is specifically designed for use in the placement of freshmen students at Purdue in advanced English, standard English, and remedial English classes. The test seems to be adequate for placement purposes.

The typography of the test and its format are not impressive. The type in Parts 2, 4, and 6, covering punctuation, reading, and vocabulary, is small. The booklet is stapled at the top of the long side of the pages rather than at the side.

Either IBM answer sheets or the "self-marking answer booklets" must be used. There is no provision for recording answers in the test booklet. The layout of the IBM answer sheet is good, but that of the self-marking answer sheet is crowded, particularly for the vocabulary part. The printing of the names of the parts on both the IBM answer sheets and the self-marking answer booklets would have minimized the possibility of a student's marking his answers in the wrong place.

The directions for administering the test are clear and straightforward. A student is allowed to work on a particular part only during the time announced for that part. It may be difficult to proctor students to be sure they are conforming to this instruction since neither the pages of the test booklet nor the parts of the answer sheets are labeled with large distinguishing marks.

The norms reported are marked "tentative" —which indeed they should be. They are based on 1,310 and 1,306 first year students at Purdue for Forms D and E, respectively. The cases for Form D include 1,037 men and 273 women; the Form E norms are based on 1,029 men and 277 women. Separate norms are provided for men and women because "it has been found that, on the average, women in the first year of college score higher on this test than do men."

The table of norms presents raw scores, percentile ranks, and T scores. The T scores have been normalized so that they should not be interpreted in terms of standard deviation units. For example, a raw score of 195 for a man on Form E is reported as a T score of 64. A T score of 64 implies the student is 1.4 standard deviations above the mean for men on this test. A raw score of 195 for a man on Form E is, in fact, almost 2.7 standard deviations above the mean for men. Another apparent weakness in the norms is the lack of comparability of results for the two forms. A raw score of 195 for a man on Form D, for example, is converted into a T score of 77. The authors enumerate other important reasons why "caution in the use of these norms is strongly recommended," and indicate that new norms will be published.

The reliabilities reported were computed by the Kuder-Richardson formula 20. The directions for administering the test suggest that speed is a factor ("An error of a few seconds in the time allowed may mean a difference of several points in a score.") in spite of the claim that "the test has more the nature of a power test than of a rate or speed test." While the latter statement is no doubt true, speed is enough of a factor to make the Kuder-Richardson reliabilities overestimates. If Forms D and E are really equivalent, parallel forms reliabilities would be a better indication of reliability.

Since the time limits for the various parts range from 7 minutes to 11 minutes, the reliabilities of the scores, as might be expected, are not high enough to warrant the use of the part scores. The reliabilities reported for Part 3, Sentence Clearness and Effectiveness, and Parts 4 and 5, Reading, are the lowest, being .68, .80, and .77, respectively, for Form E. The standard errors are relatively large. In Part 4, for example, where the maximum possible score is 15, the standard error is 1.83. The re-

liabilities reported for total scores are adequate. They are .94 and .96 for Forms D and E, respectively.

In spite of a suggestion made early in the manual that the test was not designed as a predictive device, the authors later present as evidence of validity correlations between test scores and grades in English courses and between test scores and first semester grade point index. The correlations reported have a modal value in the neighborhood of .30, which, when the correlations are corrected for restricted range, rises to the neighborhood of .80. The data presented suggest that .80 highly overestimates the correlational value. It is probably somewhere between .30 and .80.

The correlations between total scores on the test and a "Verbal Factor Score" (no indication of the source of this score is given) for various groups of students suggest that these two values are measures of the same thing. For the groups in which the number of cases is over 200, the correlations range from .8676 to .9035. The reporting of coefficients of correlations to four decimal places is amazing when it is noted that one such 4-decimal place value is based on 14 cases and when cognizance is taken of the known competence in statistics of at least one of the authors.

The *New Purdue Placement Test in English* is a good test for measuring the "fundamentals of English." Even though there are still a few items for which the answers are probably controversial, the authors seem to have succeeded in not being "too doctrinaire in attitude, neither too liberal nor too conservative." The evidence of validity for English placement and for predicting success in first year performance at Purdue is strong enough to warrant universities' using this test for these purposes at their institutions provided they establish their own norms and determine evidence of validity based on their own students.

[200]

★SRA Achievement Series: Language Arts. Grades 2–4, 4–6, 6–9; 1954–57; title on some tests for grades 2–6 is *How Should We Say This?*; 2–3 scores: capitalization-punctuation, grammatical usage, spelling (grades 4–9 only); IBM for grades 4–9; Forms A, B; 3 levels; technical supplement, second edition ('57); separate answer sheets must be used in grades 4–9; 50¢ per teacher's handbook ('55); 50¢ per administrator's manual ('56); $1 per technical supplement; postage extra; Louis P. Thorpe, D. Welty Lefever, and Robert A. Naslund; Science Research Associates. *

a) GRADES 2–4. Forms A ('55), B ('57); examiner's

manual, second edition ('57) ; $1.70 per 20 tests ; $1 per scoring stencil ; (105) minutes in 2 sessions.

b) GRADES 4–6. IBM; Forms A ('54), B ('56) ; examiner's manual ('56) ; $2 per 20 tests ; $5 per 100 IBM scorable answer sheets ; $1 per set of machine scoring stencils ; 50¢ per hand scoring stencil ; 75(90) minutes.

c) GRADES 6–9. IBM; Forms A ['55], B ('56) ; examiner's manual ('56) ; prices same as for grades 4–6 ; 60(75) minutes.

CONSTANCE M. MCCULLOUGH, *Professor of Education, San Francisco State College, San Francisco, California.*

These tests constitute a basic literacy measure for the grades concerned, in the form of a proofreading test of capitalization, punctuation, usage, and (for grades 4–6 and 6–9 only) spelling. The punctuation, capitalization, and usage items are strewn throughout a series of stories so that the examinee is required to be aware of all three types of error. The points of error are numbered, and correspondingly numbered items on the right hand side of the pages present two or more possibly correct answers from which to choose. Narrative materials are used in the spelling tests for grades 4–6 and 6–9, crucial words underlined, and multiple choice spelling versions given in the right hand margin.

These tests have much in their favor. The Examiner Manual offers clear directions for administering the tests and classifying the items for scoring.

The Teacher's Handbook provides some interpretation of scores and suggestions for follow-up of deficiencies. The Manual for the School Administrator explains that item selections were based on analysis of textbooks, courses of study, expert opinion, and research studies. Tables in the manual show a breakdown of the actual intent of each item. The Technical Supplement is a veritable textbook on the construction and standardization of the tests, the manner in which the batteries were equated, and the procedure followed for establishing norms. It is important to note that the norms are based upon May testing, and require a different interpretation if the tests are to be given at another time of year. Reliability coefficients on total usage items and combined capitalization and punctuation items range from .78 to .91, and seem to be slightly lower for the higher levels within each battery.

Needless confusion is avoided by the fact that the examinee makes only one kind of response throughout the entire test. The narra-

tive material includes personal letters, business letters, and even poetic form, as well as conversation. The subject matter reflects natural child life at the levels tested. The most basic errors are tested more than once, so that a more dependable diagnosis is possible. Forms A and B, slightly different in subject matter, are utterly identical in the types of item tested and the order of their occurrence.

On the negative side it might be mentioned that the narrative form and the mixture of types of item mean a more complicated kind of answer key and pupil inconvenience in finding the space intended for answers. Although the vocabulary of the tests is relatively easy for the grade levels concerned, there will doubtless be some children for whom the test is one of reading ability rather than language. Such children should have the items read to them or be given the next easier test.

Test users should know that the tests at each level are more discriminating at lower score levels than at higher score levels. As a basic literacy test, the test contains few niceties which would characterize the high scorers. On the other hand, some of the niceties are actually no longer disputed usages and probably reflect educational lag rather than linguistic truth. Examples are : *can* for *may,* come *and* see, every*one* —*they,* and off *of.* For the teacher who wishes to identify a child's specific needs, the omission of some errors, like "ain't," seems unfortunate.

The spelling test reflects spelling ability at a difficulty level rather than a child's ability to spell demons common to all educational levels. The test does not provide a way of diagnosing the kinds of spelling error the pupil makes. The presence of "to, two, too" and "they're, their, there" under usage instead of under spelling seems odd.

In general, the tests have been constructed with admirable care and concern for the purposes of possible users.

WINIFRED L. POST, *Instructor in English, Dana Hall, Wellesley, Massachusetts.*

All three tests in this series measure skills in capitalization, punctuation, grammar, and usage. One form of the test for grades 4–6 and both forms of the test for grades 6–9 measure skill in spelling in a separate section.

The test for grades 2–4 consists of four passages, mainly narrative, on such subjects as pet dogs, pet birds, or birthday parties. The print is large, the instructions are simple, and the opening page is inviting. Throughout the test portions of the text are underlined, and either one or two alternatives are offered for each underlined portion. The student indicates his choice by a mark in his test booklet. The items range in difficulty from a choice between "had brang" and "had brought" to a choice between "they" and "he" to refer to the pronoun "everyone."

The test for grades 4–6 is in form like that for grades 2–4, except that it offers the option of a separate answer sheet for machine scoring, and, in Form B, provides a section which tests ability to spot spelling errors in a continuous passage. The other sections of the test also consist of continuous passages, still mainly narrative, but with heavy use of dialogue and letters for testing skills in punctuation. The variety of problems offered in punctuation is an evident strength of the test, though thoughtful English teachers may question the assumption that even the allegedly quoted informal conversation of children must adhere to ultra-conservative standards of formal "good English." The grammar-usage items range in difficulty from a choice between illiterate and literate English to rather subtle distinctions between restrictive and nonrestrictive elements. Those items which require a student to read fairly long, fairly complex groups of words and then indicate whether or not these groups of words form a complete sentence will be warmly received by all English teachers. This test, unlike the test for grades 2–4, assumes that the student has some knowledge of common technical terms and that he will be able to select the correct term to describe underlined groups of words.

The test for grades 6–9 differs from that for grades 4–6 mainly in the increased complexity of the reading material and the inclusion of descriptions and evaluations as well as narratives. Like the lower level test, this one includes a separate spelling section requiring the student to find spelling errors in context. All four sections preceding the spelling section present a rich variety of items on punctuation, grammar, usage, and capitalization. Here, too, the items range in difficulty from a choice between "We *seen* him" and "We *saw* him" to a choice between "try *and*" and "try *to*."

The title for these tests is misleading. "Mechanics of English" would be a less pretentious and a more precisely descriptive title for tests which, within the sharply defined areas of capitalization, punctuation, grammar, usage, and spelling, measure admirably what they set out to measure. Ease of administration, ease of scoring—either by schools themselves or by the scoring service offered by SRA—the provision of complete data for interpreting scores for individual students and evaluating them in the light of norms based on carefully selected groups of public school students, the carefully and ingeniously contrived equivalence of forms, the attractive format, and the use of intrinsically interesting materials are the outstanding strengths of these tests. Teachers who are alive to recent developments in the teaching of language will especially welcome the use of connected material which forces the student throughout the test to reckon with a total context rather than to deal with isolated sentences. English teachers whose concept of language teaching includes more than those situations governed by a hard and fast rule of right and wrong will find these tests excellent as far as they go, but may wish to supplement them with other items which seek to test judgment, awareness of meaning as sometimes the sole determiner of what punctuation needs to be used, where a word or phrase or clause should be put in its sentence, when words or phrases can be deleted without loss of meaning, or when the relationship of ideas in a sentence requires the subordination of one of two clauses within the sentence. English teachers trained in testing may cavil over the considerable number of items in this test which offer the student only two choices; and the teachers who want the separate skills in mechanics of English measured in separate sections will prefer the *California Language Test*. In the opinion of this reviewer, however, one of the outstanding advantages of these tests is the very fact that the student is not told to look for only one kind of problem in each section. He must have the flexibility to deal with many kinds of language problems within each section of the test; this is closely in line with the realities of meaning, language, and the written word.

For reviews by Warren G. Findley and Worth R. Jones of the complete battery, see 21.

[201]

★**Scholastic Achievement Series: English-Spelling.** Grades 2.5–3, 4–6, 7–9; 1954–55; various titles used by publisher; for Catholic schools; subtest of *Scholastic Achievement Series;* 4 scores: punctuation and capitalization, correct usage, English total, spelling;

IBM for grades 4–9; 2 forms; 3 levels; separate answer sheets may be used in grades 4–9; $1.75 per 35 IBM scorable answer sheets; 24¢ per scoring stencil; 50¢ per specimen set of any one level; postage extra; (40–50) minutes; Oliver F. Anderhalter, R. Stephen Gawkoski, and John O'Brien; Scholastic Testing Service, Inc. *

a) PRIMARY TEST. Grades 2.5–3; Forms A ('54, identical with English-spelling tests of complete battery copyrighted in 1953), B ('55); battery manual ('55); $2.70 per 35 tests.

b) ELEMENTARY TEST. Grades 4–6; IBM; Forms A ('54), B ('55); battery manual ('55); $3.75 per 35 tests.

c) ADVANCED TEST. Grades 7–9; IBM; Forms A ('54), B ('55); battery manual ('55); $3.75 per 35 tests.

GERALDINE SPAULDING, *Consultant, Educational Records Bureau, New York, New York.*

The manuals provided with these tests are those prepared for the complete battery, with a separate manual for each level. The text of the three manuals is the same except for the descriptions of test content and directions for administering. The figures in tables giving reliability and related data are the same in the primary and elementary manuals, but, without explanation, the corresponding table in the advanced manual gives different figures. Several varieties of reliability index are shown, but each represents the median of a number of single-grade indices. There is no indication of how much variation in reliability there was from grade to grade. The median split-half reliabilities given in the primary and elementary manuals are .90 for total English score and .91 for spelling score; those in the advanced manual are .91 for total English and .95 for spelling. More detailed information on reliability, grade by grade, would be more useful than the variety of indices given.

The manuals do give relatively complete information on the procedures of construction and standardization. Detailed directions for administering, scoring, and tabulating are given. The instructions to the examiner for some of the spelling tests are rather muddled, but examiners will doubtless know how to proceed. There is an error in the directions (for use when answers are marked in the booklets) for Test 1A, elementary level: "select its number as the answer" should read "select its *letter* as the answer."

The choice of content is based on the analysis of the courses of study in a large number of Catholic schools. The content of the English tests, reflecting that analysis, would appear to confirm the need for a special test for Catholic schools, since the emphasis differs from that found in most achievement batteries. A rather superficial difference (as far as measurement is concerned) is that some of the sentences used to provide testing situations are on religious subjects. A more fundamental difference is in the weight given to formal matters of language in the elementary and advanced tests. The primary English test consists only of subtests on punctuation, capitalization, and correct usage; but at the two higher levels, three more subtests are added to these parts, all dealing with information *about* language—knowledge of rules, statements of principles, identification and classification of conventional linguistic elements, and information about specific techniques of writing and speaking. Non-Catholic schools would probably consider this kind of material greatly overemphasized in the tests.

The usage tests employ the conventional technique of requiring the examinee to choose between a right and a wrong word or form of word given in a sentence. The chief problem in such items is that of devising sentences in which the wrong choice is not too farfetched. Even when the grammatical distinction involved is a suitable one, the specific sentence, using the wrong choice, sometimes looks very artificial. A number of items in Test 3 exhibit this defect. In usage items, the wrong choices ought to conform to *real* uneducated or childish patterns of speech, and should not have a "manufactured" look. One might expect that item analysis would reveal defects of this kind, but even if it did not, it is doubtful that such items are really testing what the test is designed to measure.

In general design and printing, the test booklets are clear and reasonably attractive, though conservative. The grade-equivalent conversion tables are printed in very small type, but this, unfortunately, is a defect common to many achievement batteries. The machine scorable answer sheets fall far short of the standard of the booklets. The small letters identifying choices are blurred and barely legible. The conversion tables on the Form A answer sheet are in microscopic type and are almost completely illegible. The tables on the Form B answer sheet are in larger and clearer type, but on neither form are the tables conveniently placed for machine scoring. These deficiencies should be corrected in later printings.

In general, the content of the capitalization, punctuation, and usage sections is conventional, and the kind of item used presents no innovations. The tests, presumably, correspond more closely in emphasis, and probably in grade placement of topics, to the curriculum of Catholic schools than do tests designed primarily for use in public schools.

RUTH STRICKLAND, *Professor of Education, Indiana University, Bloomington, Indiana.*

Each of the tests contains a section dealing with punctuation. These sections are satisfactorily graduated in difficulty, but all of them call upon children to take note of certain designated points. There is no means of ascertaining whether children would recognize these as points needing attention if they were proofreading their own writing. The subtests on capitalization, on the other hand, do require children to locate and mark the points at which capital letters are needed.

The test for grades 2 and 3 also contains a correct usage section that deals mainly with common verb errors and homonyms.

The test for grades 4–6 includes a two-part section dealing with various aspects of grammar: sentences, phrases, clauses, parts of speech, and syntax. A great deal more knowledge of abstract grammar—parts of speech, definitions, and syntax—is called for here than is now thought desirable for these grades by many authorities in the field of English. Test 3 is concerned with correct usage. Parts of it deal with common errors and parts of speech with refinements which, in teaching practice, are often left for a slightly later age. Test 4 is concerned with oral and written English. The attention here is centered on structure, definition, and the mechanics of writing.

The test for grades 7–9 starts with punctuation and capitalization, as do the others. Test 2A deals with sentences, phrases, and clauses. Test 2B is concerned with parts of speech and syntax. Again, in both of these sections, an unusually extensive knowledge of abstract, structural grammar is called for—far more than many authorities advocate for this level. Test 3 deals with correct usage and reflects more closely what most teachers of English would expect children of these ages to know. In fact, it would be quite an easy test for children of this level who have experienced the emphasis on correct usage that is commonly thought good for elementary and junior high school age young people. In Test 4, on oral and written

English, the 22 multiple choice questions deal mainly with form and definition.

Each test in the series ends with a section on spelling consisting of 35 dictated words.

At all grade levels, the directions for the tests are given orally to the pupils. Scoring keys are provided with all testing materials. Grade equivalents are provided for each test in convenient conversion scale form following each test in the booklet. All grade placements are in terms of tenths of a year. Corresponding percentile ranks are also given. Scores on the various subsections are not convertible into grade equivalents but do have diagnostic value. Diagnostic profiles can be plotted from them.

These tests raise some fundamental and truly amazing questions. Is a child in the middle grades who knows how many parts there are in "every" paragraph or friendly letter, who can fit together a definition of a homonym or synonym, and who knows *exactly* how many inches of margin to leave at the right side of a page, through that knowledge a writer? Can one learn to speak or write through definitions and mechanics alone? Of what does growth in the use of English consist?

Growth in expressing ideas through clear, well organized writing is in no way touched upon in any part of any of the tests. English is treated throughout the tests as a machine or a jigsaw puzzle, not a living, organic language. One could designate and name every bone and muscle that makes up the human frame and still know nothing about a human being as a living, breathing entity. In these tests English is treated as an unrelated mass of discrete parts without color or motion or life. In no way is it approached as a means of communication. It would appear that a child could pass these tests with perfect scores and still be unable to put on paper, between an initial capital and a final period, anything that would be worth writing or reading.

Research on the teaching of grammar makes it fairly clear that grammar, as it is handled in the tests for grades 4 to 9, is little if at all used by children. Much that is covered here would be of value only to superior 10th to 12th grade students who are headed for college. It would have no significance for the majority of high school students at any level. Use of these tests can only yield results which are unrelated to the measurement of skill and power in the use of language.

For reviews by William E. Coffman and James R. Hayden of the complete battery, see 23.

[202]

★**Survey Tests of English Usage.** Grades 9–13; 1947–49; Forms E ('47), H ('48), S ('49) for use at the beginning of either semester; Forms G ('47), N ('48), T ('49) for use during the second semester; Forms J, K ('49) based on the book *Self-Aids in English Usage;* title on Forms T, N, and G is *Achievement Test of English Usage;* no manual; directions sheet (no date); teacher's remedial sheet ('47); tentative norms for Form J; no data on reliability and validity; 90¢ per 30 tests of any one form; postage extra; 25¢ per specimen set, postpaid; (35–40) minutes; L. J. O'Rourke; Psychological Institute. *

[203]

*Tressler English Minimum Essentials Tests, Revised Edition.** Grades 8–12; 1932–56; IBM; Forms A ('54, identical with test copyrighted in 1941 except for changes in 4 items), AM ('56, machine scoring edition of Form A), B ('41), C ('41); manual ['55, identical with sheet copyrighted in 1941 except for minor changes]; separate answer sheets must be used with Form AM; $1.75 per 25 tests; 5¢ per IBM answer sheet; 25¢ per machine scoring stencil; 30¢ per specimen set; postpaid; (40–50) minutes; J. C. Tressler; Public School Publishing Co. *

COMPOSITION

[204]

*College Entrance Examination Board Achievement Test in English Composition.** Candidates for college entrance; 1943–58; for more complete information, see 599; IBM 60(80) minutes; program administered by Educational Testing Service for the College Entrance Examination Board. *

REFERENCES
1–6. See 4:178.
7. NEWMAN, SIDNEY H.; FRENCH, JOHN W.; AND BOBBITT, JOSEPH M. "Analysis of Criteria for the Validation of Selection Measures at the United States Coast Guard Academy." *Ed & Psychol Meas* 12:394–407 au '52. * (*PA* 27:6159)
8. DYER, HENRY S. *College Board Scores.* New York: College Entrance Examination Board [1953]. Pp. xxiii, 70. * (*PA* 28:4936)
9. OLSEN, MARJORIE A. "The Predictive Effectiveness of the College Entrance Examination Board English Composition Test." Abstract. *Am Psychol* 8:411 Ag '53. *
10. WEBB, SAM C., AND MCCALL, JOHN N. "Predictors of Freshman Grades in a Southern University." *Ed & Psychol Meas* 13:660–3 w '53. * (*PA* 28:6598)
11. College Entrance Examination Board. *English Composition: A Description of the English Composition Test of the College Entrance Examination Board.* Princeton, N.J.: the Board, June 1954. Pp. 35. * (*PA* 29:1443)
12. MILLER, PETER M. "An Analysis of Error-Types Used in the Interlinear Exercise of the College Entrance Examination Board's English Composition Test." *Yearb Nat Council Meas Used Ed* 11:19–22+ '54. *
13. DYER, HENRY S., AND KING, RICHARD G. *College Board Scores: Their Use and Interpretation, No. 2.* New York: College Entrance Examination Board, 1955. Pp. viii, 192. * (*PA* 30:1616)
14. ELEY, EARLE G. "Should the General Composition Test be Continued? The Test Satisfies an Educational Need." *Col Board R* (25):9–13 w '55. *
15. PEARSON, RICHARD. "Should the General Composition Test be Continued? The Test Fails as an Entrance Examination." *Col Board R* (25):2–9 w '55. *
16. SWINEFORD, FRANCES. "Reliability of an Interlinear Test of Writing Ability." *Sch & Soc* 81:25–7 Ja 22 '55. *
17. College Entrance Examination Board. *A Description of the College Board Achievement Tests.* Princeton, N.J.: Educational Testing Service, 1956. Pp. 133. * (*PA* 31:1745)
18. FISHMAN, JOSHUA A. *1957 Supplement to College Board*

Scores No. 2. New York: College Entrance Examination Board, 1957. Pp. vi, 206. Paper. *
19. EVENSON, A. B., AND SMITH, D. E. "A Study of Matriculation in Alberta." *Alberta J Ed Res* 4:67–83 Je '56. *
20. FRENCH, JOHN W. "Validation of New Item Types Against Four-Year Academic Criteria." *J Ed Psychol* 49:67–76 Ap '58. *

For a review by Charlotte Croon Davis of earlier forms, see 4:178.

[205]

★**College Entrance Examination Board Advanced Placement Examination: English Composition.** High school seniors desiring credit for college level courses; 1954–58; for more complete information, see 600; 180(200) minutes; program administered by Educational Testing Service for the College Entrance Examination Board. *

ROBERT C. POOLEY, *Professor of English and Chairman, Department of Integrated Liberal Studies, University of Wisconsin, Madison, Wisconsin.* [Review of Form FBP.]

This test is designed for the use of colleges to evaluate students who have taken advanced courses in English composition in schools, and are seeking recognition of this work at the college level in the form of advanced standing or credit upon admission. It is therefore set at a level above ordinary college entrance tests. Unlike tests which deal with subject content areas, this test is not objective in character, and relies upon the skill of readers within the procedure set up to insure a reasonable degree of objectivity.

In a period of three hours the candidate is required to write three essays of one hour each. One of these calls for the ability to read, understand, and evaluate a critical passage of an advanced nature, pointing out and evaluating the effectiveness of the rhetorical aspects of the passage. Another calls for the thoughtful response to the implications of a quotation, in which a student may display his own resources from reading and experience. The third is a constructive development of one of several topic statements or ideas.

Inasmuch as the power to write effectively is the end result of instruction in composition, this test is aimed at the very heart of the skills and abilities to be tested. It is centered upon the power to think, organize, and compose English expository prose, and upon this power alone. To the extent that the quotations and topics arouse the optimum response from the candidates and permit the fullest display of their competence, the test is as nearly perfect for its purpose as any test can be. However, since it is not objective in nature, its true validity rests upon the impartiality of judgment of the readers.

Having been devised by independent committees of school and college teachers, the test was administered in 1957 to properly qualified high school students and a cross section of college freshman students from colleges representative of those the high school students might enter. The papers were mixed without identification before going to the readers. The chief reader read a sample of examination booklets and prepared tentative standards for each section. These standards were discussed in a training session with the corps of readers to establish a uniform interpretation of the standards. Each essay was read only once, but different readers were assigned to the separate essays, so that each book was read by three readers. Essays were rated on a 15-point scale, the raw scores were distributed, and by analysis of the chief reader were converted to grades on a 5-point scale: 5 (high honors), 4 (honors), 3 (creditable), 2 (pass), 1 (fail). In the 1957 examination 61 high school students, or 9 per cent of the high school group achieved grade 5, high honors; not one of the college sample achieved this grade. Although the college sample was only a little over 10 per cent of the size of the high school group, the failure of anyone of this group to achieve grade 5 is indicative of the high level set for the evaluation of advanced standing in composition.

Provided the same procedures are followed in subsequent years in reading and evaluation, this test can be highly commended for testing precisely what it intends to test, for setting a high level of performance and challenge to the candidate, and for establishing a basis of evaluation which is confirmed by cross reference to a college level sample of students. The growing concern for the advancement of superior students, and the difficulty of establishing fair and equitable procedures for the granting of advanced standing or credit on the campuses of many different institutions make this test particularly desirable as one yielding a nationally established set of grades which are reported to the college of the candidate's choice and are there interpreted and utilized as the proper authorities decide.

[206]

★Sequential Tests of Educational Progress: Essay Test. Grades 4–6, 7–9, 10–12, 13–14; 1957; Forms A, B, C, D; 4 levels; $1 per 20 tests; $4.25 per manual

of any one level; $5 per specimen set; postage extra; 35(40) minutes; Cooperative Test Division, Educational Testing Service. *

a) LEVEL 4. Grades 4–6; Forms 4A, 4B, 4C, 4D.
b) LEVEL 3. Grades 7–9; Forms 3A, 3B, 3C, 3D.
c) LEVEL 2. Grades 10–12; Forms 2A, 2B, 2C, 2D.
d) LEVEL 1. Grades 13–14; Forms 1A, 1B, 1C, 1D.

REFERENCE

1. BLACK, DONALD B. "A Note on the Use in Alberta of the Sequential Tests of Educational Progress: Essay Test." *Alberta J Ed Res* 4:172–80 S '58. *

JOHN S. DIEKHOFF, *Dean, Cleveland College, Western Reserve University, Cleveland, Ohio.*

Teachers of English composition at any school level will agree that the best way to judge a student's ability to write is to read something he has written. They will also agree that any teacher's judgment of a single brief composition is not very reliable. The simple experiment of having every English teacher in a school or department grade the same set of student papers always has disturbing results and makes the point for most of us.

The formulators of the STEP essay tests recognize that writing is the test of writing. They provide essay topics at four levels: grades 4-6, grades 7-9, grades 10-12, and the freshman and sophomore years of college. For each level there are four forms of the test, i.e., four sets of essay topics, so that students may be tested more than once. There are careful instructions for the administration of the tests, sample essays on each topic ranked in terms of their quality, and instructions for scoring the essays and translating numerical scores into percentile ranks, and the like.

"The problem," say the directions for scoring, "is to score papers in such fashion that an independent scorer will come up with the same results." Indeed this is the problem. The sample essays with their assigned scores, to which essays on the same topics may be compared, and the eminently sensible instructions for the test reader constitute the attempt to solve this problem.

Accepting as he does the assumption that the best test of writing is writing, this reviewer does not see how it could be done much better. The essay topics are appropriate to the several school levels. The sample essays present clear differences in quality—one wishes student themes were always so clearly "high," "low," or "middle." The test reader is warned against his preconceptions of identifiable students, against letting "neatness" become a criterion in judging papers written under test conditions, against his "pet peeves," and happily against fruitless interminable rereading of papers difficult to score.

At bottom, however, these tests are essay tests. Assigning numerical scores, converting those scores into percentile ranks, recording them on the student's "profile," and comparing them with national and local norms will not make the test reader's critical judgment more exact. The sample essays, the *caveats* for the test reader, and the awareness that he is working with nationally used tests ought to make him more careful, however.

JOHN M. STALNAKER, *President, National Merit Scholarship Corporation, Evanston, Illinois.*

The STEP essay test requires a student to spend 35 minutes writing on a single topic which is specified. There are 16 tests, four forms at each of the four grade levels. Each test booklet consists of eight pages. The first page gives general directions which are identical for all levels whether it be the fourth grade or the sophomore in college. The second page gives six or eight lines of explicit directions for the writing and of course is different in each of the 16 forms. The student is not told the length that his essay should be but he is told after he has spent five minutes planning that he will have 30 minutes to complete the writing. The remainder of the test booklet consists of five ruled blank pages for the actual writing.

In addition to the test booklets there are four handbooks—one for each of the four grade levels but these are identical except for the sample comparison essays which are given on pages 9-17. One handbook contains the comparison essays for all four forms of one grade level.

The essays are to be evaluated by the classroom teachers who are given instructions to read them on a 7-point scale. The planning committee felt that it was concerned only with recommending broad criteria for judgment in reading. The committee suggested three factors to be evaluated in the reading: originality of thought, 50 per cent; style, 30 per cent; and convention, 20 per cent. Five comparison essays are given for each form: one graded 6 (high), one graded 2 (low), and three graded 4 (middle). The teacher is instructed to match the essay she is grading against the most com-

parable comparison essay and assign the appropriate grade.

Tables are given to translate the raw score into a converted score for which percentile ranks are given. These are based on the publisher's norming program of 5,000 students in grades 4 to 14, each of whom took two forms of the preliminary essay test.

The tests were developed from questions written by teachers, but it is stated that the final responsibility for the design and development rests with the ETS staff. The topics require personal narrative, exposition, argument or persuasion, and analysis of a problem or a situation.

Some statistics are given. Reading reliabilities for the selected experts who did the reading for the norms are low, ranging from .50 to .73, and score reliabilities are reported ranging from .50 to .62. The relationship between the essay test and the objective STEP test on writing ability is reported as ranging from .61 to .70, or about the same as the relationship between one essay test and another.

Some additional information on reader reliability might be helpful. A simple distribution of the scores assigned is itself frequently revealing. What is the reading reliability for the average classroom teacher who has no instruction other than that given in the handbook?

It is obvious that this is not a test of the usual type. Its use is limited. The scores must be cautiously interpreted in the light of the quality of the reading, and the general lack of reliability.

In the promotional literature about this test it is said that "means should be found to encourage English teachers....by making available some standardized essay materials. The STEP essay tests are planned to satisfy a part of this need." There is much to be done in improving the teaching of English and, if this effort helps, we should favor it. There are, of course, other approaches which may be fruitful.

LOUIS C. ZAHNER, *Head, English Department, Groton School, Groton, Massachusetts.*

Few teachers, administrators, or businessmen who employ the product of schools and colleges would deny that written composition is deteriorating. The wholesale substitution of objective tests for essay examinations in all subjects may well be a major cause of the deterioration; for testing influences teaching to a degree little short of control. For this reason, if for no other, the test here reviewed deserves use wide enough to establish it as a permanent part of testing programs, and thoughtful enough to provide its sponsors with data for its continuing improvement—improvement that does not convert it into a straddle between essay and objective tests, but strengthens it as the straightforward "free response" essay test it now is. If this latest attempt to establish an essay examination goes the way of its predecessors and becomes the last, a decisive battle may well have been lost.

This test is exactly what it claims to be—an examination in composition. It examines the testee's ability to write by setting him an assignment in writing. The subjects set, moreover, are on the whole realistic and well selected at each level to provide pupils with natural subjects about which they can be expected to have something of their own to say. The test has the same sort of solid validity as that of a swimming test that requires the testee to swim in the water; it is not concerned about how the details of his anatomy as measured on land correlate with those of other swimmers of known ability.

But similar tests have been killed by two disorders that have come to be considered congenital: the difficulty and expense of administration and reading; and the "unreliability," or lack of uniformity, in the reading.

This test meets the first difficulty quite simply: it is locally administered and read. The only expense is that of the teacher's time. Once the reader has examined the handbook, this should not be excessive. The scoring is on a 7-point scale; the essay topics are not structured, and hence do not require meticulous point-by-point checking of details of content. The handbook provides full conversion tables, norms, and instructions for conversion of scores into percentiles.

The second difficulty—reliability of reading —is more menacing. The method used is to give the reader sample answers with which to match the answers of his students. These samples have been selected and scored by a representative group of experienced teachers, who arrived at their conclusions in meetings at which they had ample opportunity for full discussion of criteria and standards of reading in general and for reconciling differences of opinion in the scoring of individual essays. The handbook gives also the figures for the reliability of the reading achieved by this group of experienced teachers. They are impressive. But it must be remembered that the reading of even this select group had to be carefully standardized and controlled, and that uniformity of reading was achieved through a somewhat intricate process carried on under unusually favorable circumstances.

It is doubtful whether local readers of the test can be expected to achieve uniformity among themselves or with the group that scored and selected the sample answers. The user of the test is guided by only a very few samples and an analysis of them so meager as to be negligible. The only scores illustrated by samples are 6, 4, and 2. The highest score, 7, is not illustrated, nor are 5, 3, and the lowest, 1.

From one to three samples are given for each score. The analytical comments are of little help. None are given on samples scored 6 or 2. The most voluminous, all on samples scored 4, run: "Thought O.K.; mechanics weak," or "An average in thought, style, and mechanics." There is nothing on such matters as organization or, in fact, on any other elements of composition.

What a reader needs to know as he attempts to "match" his papers with the samples is not *how* a committee of experts agreed to score an essay, but *why* they agreed to score it as they did. Here the committee could well follow the example set by Noyes, Sale, and Stalnaker in a monograph [1] published in 1945.

Provision of more divergent samples and fuller, more searching analysis of samples would serve two essential purposes: it would make for reading that would tie in with greater reliability to the published norms and percentiles; and it would give a teacher a clearer idea about what qualities the experienced and highly qualified teachers who made up the reading committee consider to be desirable in composition and its teaching.

Even without such a full support of analysis of sample answers to establish more uniform reading, the test is likely to prove stimulating to a class and useful to a teacher.

1 NOYES, EDWARD SIMPSON; SALE, WILLIAM MERRITT, JR.; AND STALNAKER, JOHN MARSHALL. *Report on the First Six Tests in English Composition: With Sample Answers From the Tests of April and June 1944.* Princeton, N.J.: College Entrance Examination Board, 1945. Pp. 72. *

For reviews by Robert W. B. Jackson and Wilbur L. Layton of the complete battery, see 24.

[207]
★Sequential Tests of Educational Progress: Writing. Grades 4–6, 7–9, 10–12, 13–14; 1956–57; IBM; Forms A, B ('57); 4 levels; manual ('57); battery directions ('57); no data on reliability of Form B; separate answer sheets must be used; $3.95 per 20 tests; $1 per 20 IBM scorable answer sheets; 45¢ per scoring stencil; $1 per manual; $1 per battery technical report ('57); $1.25 per specimen set; postage extra; 70(90–100) minutes; Cooperative Test Division, Educational Testing Service. *

a) LEVEL 4. Grades 4–6; Forms 4A, 4B.
b) LEVEL 3. Grades 7–9; Forms 3A, 3B.
c) LEVEL 2. Grades 10–12; Forms 2A, 2B.
d) LEVEL 1. Grades 13–14; Forms 1A, 1B.

CHARLOTTE CROON DAVIS, *Test Research Service, Bronxville, New York.*

Approximately 50 educators participated directly in the construction of the STEP writing tests: a steering committee of 5, a planning committee of 5, 14 test authors, including members of the planning committee, and 32 critical reviewers. The test materials were prepared at workshop sessions lasting several weeks. Committees of teachers designed the tests; items were written by subcommittees of teachers; other teachers served as critics; test experts gave technical assistance. These cooperative procedures have advantages and drawbacks. They are excellent for educating test users, fostering good public relations, and gaining acceptance and effective advertising for the tests. On the other hand, they are expensive and time-consuming. More serious is the fact that creative work of this kind done by committees tends to be neither very poor nor conspicuously good; it reflects the compromises inevitable in committee functioning. Usually a better test is produced if committees serve in advisory capacities, where they are invaluable, and some one competent, experienced individual has responsibility and authority. In the reviewer's opinion, these general observations are borne out by a careful examination of these tests.

In addition to the objective tests under review here, the STEP battery contains essay tests of writing, in which the examinees write compositions on assigned topics and which, scored by a semiobjective method, are said to produce reliable results. With this provision for tests of writing in which the examinees actually write, it might have been advisable to limit the objective tests to those aspects of expression that can be directly measured by ob-

jective methods. Techniques of measuring the abilities to "think critically in writing," "write material appropriate for a given purpose," and "write effectively" used in tests in which the examinees do *no* writing are necessarily indirect. They measure primarily other skills, more or less closely related to these abilities.

Whether or not these tests measure writing ability, they definitely appear to measure reading ability. Each form consists of 8 to 10 selections written by pupils, each followed by several items based on the selection. The amount of reading per item is large. For example, one selection in Form 1A with its 8 items has about 1,000 words, or 125 words per item. Many items depend on such recognized reading skills as getting the main idea of a selection, following its structure, or deciding which statements need supporting evidence. It seems to the reviewer that these tests must substantially overlap the reading tests in the battery.

The selections are well chosen to provide variety, face validity, and difficulty suitable to the four levels. Whether the authors were wise to use largely pupil assignments that had been graded *poor or failing* is dubious. The explanations preceding some selections of how they came to be written are helpful and could have been given more often; e.g., a setting for "Black Blaze" in Form 1A might have clarified Items 13 and 14. With only 60 items per test, coverage of the wide field of English expression is necessarily thin in spots; e.g., spelling, an important skill in the intermediate grades, is touched on by just two or three items in Form 4A, none in 4B.

On the whole, the items are clear and direct and require the application of information or skills to new material. They can be classified into two general types: (*a*) those that test only *correctness* of expression, in which three of the four choices are clearly incorrect, (an exception is 4A, Part I, Item 1, which has two correct choices, only one of which is keyed) and (*b*) those that require selecting the most appropriate or effective choice. Ideally, in the second type the examinee should not be able to rule out distractors as "mechanically" incorrect. However, many items of this type are really mixtures of effectiveness and correctness. This double-barreledness may be almost inevitable if the number of choices cannot be varied to fit the point tested and if the items are not to have more than one defensible answer. Nevertheless, some items, especially at the higher levels, seem to the reviewer to include two defensible choices or to have *no* choice that seems just right or particularly good; e.g., 4B-I-9, -II-8; 3A-I-21; 3B-I-19, -II-15; 2A-II-1; 2B-I-19, -II-2, -3, -5, -8; 1A-I-9, -II-8; 1B-I-3, -II-7, -10. Some items overlap or give clues to the answers to other items: e.g., 4B-I-9, -13; 3A-I-7, -10, -12; 3B-I-8, -10; 3B-II-20, -21; 2B-I-16, -17; 2B-I-25, -28. Systematic review of the test materials by one or two experienced critics during the construction process should have called attention to most of these items at a time when they could conveniently have been revised or abandoned.

The statistical framework for the tests received expert attention. The items were pretested and analyzed; the eight forms were equated both horizontally (Form A with Form B at each level) and vertically (Level 4 with Level 3, Level 3 with Level 2, etc.), and all raw scores converted to a single scale. The norms are based on a national sample scrupulously chosen to be representative. They are presented by grades and are in the form of percentile bands which automatically indicate the accuracy of the scores. For example, the chances are about two out of three that a fifth grader who obtains a score of 250 will have a true percentile rank somewhere between 35 and 60. Parallel form coefficients are not provided.

The directions for administration and scoring, which are the same for most of the tests in the battery, are well presented but are questionable in certain respects. Parts I and II may be given at different sessions. As the examinees are free to use extra time at the end of the second session to return to Part I, they are also free to improve their Part I scores by changing their answers as a result of consultation or study about particular items during the time between sessions. The instruction to guess on "too difficult" items is necessary, since the score is the number right, and it is regarded as effective since the *average* number of omissions in the 100-case samples used for estimating reliability was very low. However, this does not insure that an *individual* pupil, unwilling to guess even when told to do so, may not fail to mark a sizable number of items. A scoring method that corrected for *failure* to guess might minimize the effect of this personality factor or lack of testwiseness.

Some examinees might benefit from directions specific to these tests. They could be told to read each selection before attempting the accompanying items and could be made aware, through samples, that there may be items in which the keyed response is to leave the point under consideration just as it is expressed in the selection (some naive pupils feel that some change must be needed or the point would not be brought up), and items like 1B-I-8, in which *all* the choices are at least partially correct and the last choice, which includes the other three, is keyed.

Although, on the whole, the format of the tests is satisfactory, the arrangement would be more convenient for the examinee if all choices, no matter how short, were placed in a single column, B directly under A, etc., and if the items based on a selection always appeared on the same page as the selection or on the facing page.

Probably the most notable feature of these tests is that they are available at four levels, with a single, continuous score scale. Regarded as a whole, they should provide, within the limitations of the individual forms, a valuable standardized instrument for measuring a pupil's growth over many years in the abilities tested. The tests should also be useful for evaluating classes, grades, and larger groups on the basis of the norms supplied. Although the tests might be improved both in general design and in specific content, the authors are to be commended for making progress in testing some of the important but hard-to-measure skills related to good writing.

JOHN M. STALNAKER, *President, National Merit Scholarship Corporation, Evanston, Illinois.*

The STEP test in writing is designed "to measure comprehensively the full range of skills involved in the process of good writing," a rather heavy assignment for a 70-minute objective test. There are two forms of the test at each of four grade levels (4-6, 7-9, 10-12, 13-14), or eight tests in all. There is a 12-page set of directions for administering and scoring, a 36-page manual for interpreting scores, and a 60-page technical report which covers all STEP tests except the essay test.

Each 12-page test booklet contains 60 questions for which the student selects the best answer from among four choices. An IBM type answer sheet is used. The questions concern a passage, the sentences of which are numbered. In general, 8 to 10 brief passages are included in each of the tests. The test is divided into two parts, each requiring 35 minutes of testing time. The time is said to be ample for most pupils. The single score is the number of items answered correctly.

Most of the items propose several revisions of a sentence in the passage, but some of the items concern spelling and mechanics. The test is said to cover organization, conventions, critical thinking, effectiveness, and appropriateness. Most of the passages are intentionally quite poorly written. One must sympathize with the student who is sensitive to the written word and to style, for the reading of such passages and the options given for change can constitute an ordeal.

In the manual for interpreting scores, a good deal of space is given to converting scores and interpreting the results. The statement is made that *"there is no such thing as an absolute score on a test"* by which apparently is meant that a score on a specific test does not necessarily reflect precisely the true ability of the person tested. Users are encouraged to interpret the converted test scores by percentile bands (confidence intervals) in which one score is said to lie between say the 51st and the 72nd percentiles.

Individual score norms are given for the various grades. They are based in some instances on relatively small numbers of students (under 200). Validity is said to be insured because qualified persons have constructed the tests—a highly questionable statement, especially in this type of test.

Form A is, in general, slightly less reliable than the other tests in the series. No reliability data are given for Form B. Test scores correlate with the verbal factor scores of an aptitude test between .68 and .83.

Some of the claims made for the test would appear to have been written with an eye on sales promotion rather than on any evidence reported. On the other hand, the test, while offering nothing new or distinctive in test construction, appears to have been prepared with care, by competent people using approved procedures. It will doubtless yield results of value in many classrooms.

Louis C. Zahner, *Head, English Department, Groton School, Groton, Massachusetts.*

This is not a test *in* writing. Whether it can legitimately be called a test *of* writing is debatable. A more accurately descriptive, though somewhat unwieldy, title would be "A Test in the Recognition of Appropriate Usage, and of Logical and Effective Written Expression." It falls somewhere between a test of proofreading and one of editing. It requires more than a proofreader's correction of errors in mere mechanics, and less than an editor's or author's revision; for the editor or author has to produce his own rewording for what he himself considers to be weak spots, while this test demands only the selection of the most effective of several ready-made versions for spots already pinpointed.

Put another way, this is an objective test of what is essentially a subjective process; for all writing of whatever sort is "creative," a melding of content and forms according to some design—"design" in the sense not only of artistic and effective shaping, but of purpose.

In the piecemeal dealing with details to which an objective test of expression must resort, the quality of the thought and design of the composition as a whole is lost sight of. This is perhaps unavoidable: appraisal of the qualities of a complete composition would convert the test into one of reading. But the omission poses a stubborn question. If writing is the union of whole thought and design, can proficiency in the art be appraised by a test that touches on neither? The question is particularly embarrassing for a test of writing that requires no writing at all on the part of the testee.

In spite of this, it may still prove to be true, when validity studies have been completed, that most proficient writers will do well on this test and most poor writers badly. But this is not to say that all who score high are proficient writers, or that all who score low are defective writers. All racehorses are quadrupeds, but not all quadrupeds are racehorses.

Within the limits set any test in composition by the requirements of objective testing, this is a strong test, well conceived and well executed. Its use of student writing as a base is realistic. Its coverage of the details of structure, usage, rhetoric, and logic is wide and nicely attuned to the grade levels tested.

This test and its companion piece, the STEP

essay test, may well complement each other. The writing test has coverage of details of composition, and built-in reliability of scoring. But it loses sight of a work as a whole, and is questionable in its validity. The essay test, on the other hand, is questionable in the reliability of its scoring, and it pays little attention to the many details of the "skills" of written composition. It does, however, have built-in validity, and it emphasizes the appraisal of the testee's work as a whole. As complementary parts of a program in testing written composition, a program in which each would tend to correct the mistakes of the other, they would be a strong combination. Such a program would have to be local: while the writing test, which is machine scorable, can be used in a program of any geographical extent, the essay test, which is locally read, might be impracticable for use in any unit larger than a city school system.

Taken singly, this test at least indicates how much a student knows about the skills of written composition, even though it leaves open the question of whether or not he can apply them in practice; and it directs the attention of student and teacher alike to the importance of details.

For reviews by Robert W. B. Jackson and Wilbur L. Layton of the complete battery, see 24.

LITERATURE

[208]
★**American Literature: Every Pupil Scholarship Test.** High school; 1958; new form usually issued each April; norms available following testing program; no data on reliability; 4¢ per test; 4¢ per scoring key; postage extra; 60(65) minutes; Bureau of Educational Measurements. *

[209]
*American Literature: Every Pupil Test.** High school; 1934–58; new form usually issued each April; norms available following testing program; no data on reliability; 3¢ per test; 1¢ per scoring key; cash orders postpaid; 40(45) minutes; Ohio Scholarship Tests. *

[210]
★**Center-Durost Literature Acquaintance Test: Evaluation and Adjustment Series.** Grades 11–13; 1953, c1952–53; IBM; Form AM ('53); manual ('53); no college norms; separate answer sheets must be used; $3.60 per 35 tests; $1.40 per 35 IBM answer sheets; postage extra; 35¢ per specimen set, postpaid; 40(50) minutes; Stella S. Center and Walter N. Durost; World Book Co. *

REFERENCE
1. DUROST, WALTER N. "Issues in the Measurement of Literature Acquaintance at the Secondary-School Level." *J Ed Psychol* 43:31–44 Ja '52. * (PA 26:7210)

HOLLAND ROBERTS, *Director, Academic Freedom Committee, San Francisco, California.*

This test illustrates some complex problems which educators face in attempting to measure cultural values. The authors state in the manual that "the test is designed to measure one's acquaintance with worth-while literature" focusing "attention on the fact that there are thoughts, feelings and convictions that are an essential part of Anglo Saxon culture"; further, that "to be without at least an acquaintance with literature embodying these traditions is to lack an essential element of literacy."

They consider that the test serves "as a survey instrument" and "as an instructional device," and specify four specific uses: (*a*) "to survey the literature acquaintance of high school students and college freshmen" and to establish the 85 books sampled in the test as "a basic reading list for both high school and college freshmen classes"; (*b*) to guide the teacher of literature in placing emphasis in the class work; (*c*) to stimulate and measure breadth of reading in club work; and (*d*) to stir adults in extension classes to fill in gaps in their reading.

To achieve these important objectives, students are asked to identify 65 short quotations of a few sentences or lines by matching each with one of three titles printed below. American and English literature are about equally represented in the 53 prose and 12 poetry samples chosen for the test and strike a balance between the classics and modern writing.

In deciding whether this test is a valuable tool, teachers and supervisors will be interested in examining some of its basic assumptions: (*a*) that our high schools should concentrate on a small specific body of writing which our students ought to know, or they will lack "an essential element of literacy"; (*b*) that American secondary schools should concern themselves primarily with the development of "Anglo Saxon culture" and "traditions" to the virtual exclusion of most of world literature; (*c*) that a rigid, limited test of ability to identify small pieces dissected from literature should be used to evaluate and so set the basic pattern for teaching literature; (*d*) that the test measures something significant—something more than casual acquaintance with the literature from which the samples are taken; (*e*) that the books from which the selections were taken represent "worthwhile" reading for our high school juniors and seniors and college fresh-men living in our modern world.

The testmakers supply little evidence other than traditional authority to support these basic assumptions. Today as the world grows daily more unified and the peoples of every nation are reaching out to each other to make man-kind one family, both the general public and educational leaders are advocating that our schools recognize in their teaching that our na-tions has its origins in many peoples and cul-tures. They see Anglo Saxon culture and its rich literature as one of many notable contribu-tions to our worldwide heritage. Teachers and the public are moving away from preoccupa-tion with traditional English and American lit-erature to concern themselves with some of the contributions of world literature. The great books of French, Spanish, Scandinavian, Ger-man, Jewish, Italian, Slavic, African, Indian, Arabian, and Chinese literature are vital read-ing for our youth if they are to take their places among the cultured peoples of Latin America, Europe, Africa and Asia.

The authors have given two places in their test to Louisa May Alcott, with quotations from *Little Women* and *An Old Fashioned Girl,* but they have found no room for Cervantes' *Don Quixote* or any other repre-sentative of Spanish letters. There are two titles by Edna Ferber and two by Booth Tarkington, but none by Dumas, Hugo, Heine, Mann, Lager-lov, Nexo, Gogol, Chekhov or Tolstoi. Inter-cultural relations are increasing in importance today for all people and especially for those nations who hold a major position in world affairs. Curriculum makers, parents, and our youth are proposing that secondary English classes explore the possibilities of world litera-ture for contributing to one world at peace, with liberty and justice for all. From the view-point of the United Nations, a literature ac-quaintance test which gives no hint that not-able books by Tagore, Sophocles, Pushkin, Turgenev, Voltaire, Rousseau, Anderson, Omar Khayyam, Confucius, and Lao-tse exist might, to paraphrase the manual, be said to lack some "essential elements of literacy."

However, even if the test were more exactly entitled "An *Anglo American* Literature Ac-quaintance Test," it would still be subject to sharp criticism. Some of the literature included is too juvenile for high school juniors and sen-iors. *Treasure Island, Ivanhoe, Rip Van Win-*

kle, Kidnapped, Call of the Wild, Little Women and *The Deacon's Master Piece* are commonly read anywhere from the fifth grade through junior high school. Others, like *The Little Min-ister* and *Gone with the Wind,* are of doubtful literary value. A few notable pieces such as Milton's *L'Allegro* have been found by several generations of English teachers to be beyond the experience and outside the interests of many 17-year-olds.

On the whole, curriculum makers and the College Entrance Examination Board have been moving rapidly away from the narrow con-fines of a rigid test based on the identification of minute pieces of writing toward the broader and deeper perspective of understanding and assimilating the central meanings of literature for our generation. In this respect the test pre-sents other unresolved problems. Is there any certainty that recognition of the source of a quotation means that the student has either read the book or poem or assimilated its sig-nificant meanings? He may have skimmed over it, seen a movie or read a comic book version, read a review or summary, or picked up enough names and factual information about it from casual discussion to pass the test. As the au-thors note in the manual, "Many of the [po-etry] quotations are as familiar as proverbs." On the other hand, what reason do we have to say that failing to identify one short, often un-important quotation from a book or poem is proof that the student has not read and under-stood it? How can we know that the episodes selected by the testmakers are, as they have stated, "unforgettable if one has read the books"? No studies are cited or evidence given to support this view. On both these counts the test is subject to question.

A standardized measuring instrument should serve the purposes of a changing, growing edu-cational program if it is itself to pass the basic test of utility; it should not attempt to dominate it, and it should not stereotype the educational process. This test restricts and cramps the teaching of literature. It has neither the depth nor the scope to meet the crisis in American education and culture.

For the present we must continue to rely on such unstandardized tests of acquaintance with literature as listing by students of read-ing done, accompanied by informal annotations, informal and formal dramatizations of novels and stories and plays, interviews with students on their reading, biographical histories of student reading experiences, and class, club, and small group discussions that apply to the issues of our day the significant meaning of the wide scope of our heritage of English, American, and world literature.

A precise instrument would be valuable, but the important thing is to keep clearly before us the objective of the teaching of literature—the firing of young minds for the never ending search for the best that has been felt and said and thought, and its use in improving the world in which we live and the world we are building.

[211]

★College Entrance Examination Board Advanced Placement Examination: Literature. High school seniors desiring credit for college level courses; 1954–58; for more complete information, see 600; 180(200) minutes; program administered by Educational Testing Service for the College Entrance Examination Board. *

JOHN S. DIEKHOFF, *Dean, Cleveland College, Western Reserve University, Cleveland, Ohio.* [Review of Form FBP.]

This test depends for its value on the critical judgment and consistency of its readers. It is made up of three essay questions of kinds familiar to college students in literature and therefore appropriate for the purposes of the test. Each essay is graded, on a 15-point scale, on different categories to which the student's attention has been specifically directed. All three essays are weighted equally in obtaining the total score. As with other tests among the Advanced Placement Examinations, final test grades of 5, representing highest honors, to 1, fail, are reported.

One question asks for critical comment on a contemporary lyric that the reviewer is unable to identify. The question gives some guidance by suggesting points to be discussed; perhaps it suggests too many points. The poem is not one that the reviewer would choose for the purpose, but there is plenty for the student to understand and to discuss, and it will serve.

A second question asks for comment on a brief narrative passage, so familiar to the reviewer that there is risk that it will also be familiar to some students. Some may have studied it. Indeed, it is included with detailed analytical questions in a widely used college freshman anthology. Here again, specific questions are asked to focus the student's comment on particular aspects of the writer's technique; but the student is also asked to call upon his

knowledge of other literature for the discussion of the advantages and limitations of a specified literary device.

The final question requires the student to draw entirely upon what he has read in the past. A genre is specified and an approach to its discussion, but the books to be drawn upon for illustration are not specified. The reviewer is pleased at the assumption that the student has done some private reading and that he should be encouraged to comment on it.

All in all, the examination gives the student an opportunity to show that he knows how to read literature of different types and to demonstrate the extent of his reading. Knowledgeable test scorers should be able to judge whether or not he has achieved college competence in literature and colleges should be willing to trust their judgment.

[212]

★English Language and Literature: National Teacher Examinations. College seniors and teachers; 1940–58; for more complete information, see 538; IBM; 80(90) minutes; Educational Testing Service. *

For reviews by William A. Brownell, Walter W. Cook, and Lawrence G. Derthick of the entire series, see 538; for a review by Harry N. Rivlin of an earlier edition, see 4:802.

[213]

★English Language and Literature: Teacher Education Examination Program. College seniors preparing to teach secondary school; 1957; for more complete information, see 543; IBM; 80(95) minutes; Educational Testing Service. *

For a review by Walter W. Cook of the entire series, see 543.

[214]

*English Literature: Every Pupil Test. High school; 1934–58; new form usually issued each April; norms available following testing program; no data on reliability; 3¢ per test; 1¢ per scoring key; cash orders postpaid; 40(45) minutes; Ohio Scholarship Tests. *

[215]

*The Graduate Record Examinations Advanced Tests: Literature. College seniors and graduate students; 1939–56; for more complete information, see 601; IBM; 180(200) minutes; Educational Testing Service. *

ROBERT C. POOLEY, *Professor of English and Chairman, Department of Integrated Liberal Studies, University of Wisconsin, Madison, Wisconsin.* [Review of Form EGR.]

Designed for the evaluation of students having completed a four-year undergraduate program of liberal studies, with a major or minor in English literature and with some correlative work in modern European literatures, this test was prepared under the auspices of a committee of six members appointed from a panel nominated by the Modern Language Association of America. The test consists of 229 individual exercises in sequence to be performed in three hours' time. All questions are of the multiple choice type, providing in a few instances three choices, in many, four choices, and in the majority, five choices. Answers are recorded by special pencil on a numbered answer sheet for machine scoring.

Although the parts are not marked off by separating enumeration, this examination consists of six recognizable divisions: (*a*) knowledge of specific works of literature and their authors, approximately 35 per cent of the total; (*b*) interpretation of meaning from passages of verse, requiring no previous knowledge although recognition of the passage and its context undoubtedly assists the interpretation, about 11 per cent; (*c*) identification of the author or title of a work from a specific passage, in which pure memory or recall is subordinated to selection on the basis of content and qualities of style exhibited in the passages, which are about equally divided between prose and verse, about 9 per cent; (*d*) ability to read, understand, interpret, and give judgments of value concerning content and structure of verse, about 14 per cent; (*e*) understanding and evaluation of prose passages of literary criticism, including the ability to relate critical judgments to a wide variety of specific authors and works, about 13 per cent; (*f*) evaluation of poetry on the basis of poetic qualities, including value judgments of diction, metrics, consistency, and emotional tone, about 18 per cent.

The content as a whole is of a very high order, apparently most thoroughly sifted and weighed prior to selection to offer a fair and reasonable measure of attainment in knowledge, skills, judgments, and appreciations in literature truly representative of English, American, and continental traditions. The specific exercises are carefully worded to avoid ambiguity, yet are sufficiently mature and technical to test the well trained, widely read student. Most successful is the balance between factual knowledge of literature and literary persons, and ability to recognize and deal critically with literary values. For the purposes of such a test as this the balance between knowledge and

power is extremely important, and has been very well achieved. In matters of detail it is difficult to satisfy everyone. Some of the facts selected to test knowledge seem overspecific, yet they may be defended as specific to very widely read selections. In the selection of particular authors and works for fact and judgment the test represents a very conservative tradition of courses in literature; the student who has followed such a conservative pattern of courses will have an advantage over others.

The chief adverse criticism is addressed to the imbalance between verse and prose in the content of the examination. It is heavily weighted to verse, and correspondingly weak in literary judgments of fiction, both novel and short story, the informal essay, and drama as a literary type. The student who by personal taste or fortunate pressure has applied himself to the poetic tradition in literature will reap his reward in this test.

In total, however, the test is excellent, and is well designed for the purpose of evaluating the attainment in literature of an applicant to a graduate school. Within the limits imposed by objective techniques in testing, this test comes as close as is reasonable and presently possible to a fair evaluation of knowledge of literature in the Anglo-American tradition, and of power to deal independently with literature and to arrive at sound value judgments in literature.

For a review by Harold Seashore of the entire series, see 601.

[216]

*Interpretation of Literary Materials.** High school, college; 1944–57; subtest of *Tests of General Educational Development;* IBM; 2 levels, 2 forms: high school, Form B ('44), college, Form B ('43); revised manuals: high school level ('56), college level ('54); $2.50 per 25 tests of either level; separate answer sheets must be used; $1 per 25 IBM answer sheets; 50¢ per specimen set; postage extra; (120) minutes; prepared by Examination Staff of United States Armed Forces Institute; Veterans' Testing Service, American Council on Education. *

For a review by Robert J. Solomon of the complete battery, see 27; for a review by Gustav J. Froehlich of Form B, see 4:26; for reviews by Herbert S. Conrad and Warren G. Findley, see 3:20.

[217]

*The Iowa Tests of Educational Development: Test 7, Ability to Interpret Literary Materials.** Grades 9–13; 1942–58; title on Form Y-3S is *Interpretation of Literary Materials;* IBM; Forms X-3S, Y-3S ('52); examiner's manual ('58); battery manual ('54);

pupil profile leaflet, fourth edition ('58); profile card (no date); separate answer sheets must be used; $3 per 20 tests; $5 per 100 IBM answer sheets; 50¢ per hand and machine scoring stencil; 50¢ per specimen set; 50¢ per battery manual; postage extra; 50(60) or 40(50) minutes; prepared under the direction of E. F. Lindquist; Science Research Associates. *

For reviews by J. Murray Lee and Stephen Wiseman of the complete battery, see 17; for a review by Eric F. Gardner of Forms X-2 and Y-2, see 4:17; for reviews by Henry Chauncey, Gustav J. Froehlich, and Lavone A. Hanna of Forms X-1 and Y-1, see 3:12.

[218]
*Literature: Every Pupil Scholarship Test. Grades 7–8, 9–12; 1928–58; new form usually issued each January and April; 2 levels; norms available following testing program; no data on reliability; 4¢ per test; 4¢ per scoring key; postage extra; 40(45) minutes; Bureau of Educational Measurements. *

[219]
*Literature Test: National Achievement Tests. Grades 7–12; 1937–57; 5 scores: recognizing effects, recognizing qualities, analyzing moods, miscellaneous facts, total; Forms A ('44, identical with test copyrighted in 1937), B ('54, identical with test copyrighted in 1939); directions sheet for Form A ('44), directions sheet for Form B ('57, identical with sheet copyrighted in 1939 except for minor changes); teachers' guide ['44]; no data on reliability for Form B; no norms for part scores; $3 per 25 tests; 50¢ per specimen set; postage extra; 40(50) minutes; Robert K. Speer and Samuel Smith; Acorn Publishing Co. *

For reviews by H. H. Giles and Robert C. Pooley, see 40:1304.

SPEECH

[220]
★The Graduate Record Examinations Advanced Tests: Speech. College seniors and graduate students; 1953; available only in the Institutional Testing Program of *The Graduate Record Examinations* (see 601); IBM; 180(200) minutes; Educational Testing Service. *

For a review by Harold Seashore of the entire series, see 601.

[221]
★Weidner-Fensch Speech Screening Test. Grades 1–3; 1955; individual; Forms A, B; hectographed manual; no data on reliability; $3.50 per examiner's kit including 50 record blanks; $1 per 20 record blanks; postage extra; [20] minutes; William E. Weidner and Edwin A. Fensch; Psychometric Affiliates. *

ROBERT S. CATHCART, *Associate Professor of Speech, and* LOUISE B. SCOTT, *Assistant Professor of Speech, Los Angeles State College, Los Angeles, California.*

This test purports to "screen out children with speech difficulties from those who have normally developed speech." It uses 33 simple pictures in a 4-page booklet to which "children suspected of defective speech" are asked to respond. The pictures are so designed and arranged that "the eleven consonant sounds which are most often defective in children" will be tested in their initial, medial, and final position in word forms. A record sheet for each form includes the question to go with each picture, the word response desired, the sound being tested, and space in which to score the response.

This test is easy to understand and simple to administer, requiring no previous testing experience or special equipment. It can be completed in less than 10 minutes. A single booklet can be used a number of times with only a record sheet needed for each new subject. Unfortunately, the test's simplicity and economy are not matched in validity and reliability. The data furnished in the test manual do not establish its validity and reliability, and a careful examination of the test itself reveals weaknesses which create doubts about the test's ability to screen out consistently articulatory problems.

One weakness of this test has to do with the pictures which are used to get word responses. To work properly, the pictures must always elicit the *same* desired response, that is, a picture of a dog for the final "g" sound and a goat for the initial "g" sound. Ideally, the "name" of the picture should be obvious to all children and the word response elicited should be so simple that the desired sound can be clearly distinguished. In the Weidner-Fensch test there are a number of pictures which do not get the desired response. For example, there is a picture of a baby in a baby carriage to which most children would respond "baby carriage"; however, the response desired is "buggy," to the test for the medial "g" sound. Another picture is of a horse-drawn coach of Louis XIV vintage to which TV era children would respond "stage coach," but the sound to be assessed is the final "dz" sound as in "carriage." Random applications of the test to first and third grade children revealed four pictures in each form to which *no child ever gave the desired response.* Add to this further problems which would obviously be created by regionalism (a "violin" is a "fiddle" in some regions and there is no "r" sound in a Boston "car") and socioeconomic differences (some upper-middle class children did not recognize the wringer-type "washing machine" used for the medial "sh" sound), and one has reason to doubt the validity of the test.

There are some data in the manual about the construction and validating procedures used by the authors but it is not specific or detailed. They state that the pictures selected were originally presented to 474 children in the first, second, and third grades, after which nine picture changes were made and tried out with 87 other children. Then the revised test was given to 321 similar children. The authors then concluded that "all object items now have high specific word recall recognition value," a statement which is hardly warranted by the data presented. Other vague and unsupported statements like "recognition is a bit higher in the third than in lower grade levels" do little to establish confidence in their validating procedures. Reliability is not mentioned in the manual.

One can infer from the manual that the test is to be given by a "therapist" because this word is used when information about scoring the test is presented; however, the word "examiner" is used in four other places with no explanation or clarification. One can hardly conceive of a trained speech therapist who would need a test like this to locate sound difficulties; and if it is to be applied by the "untrained" classroom teacher, then there is the problem of his ability to recognize misarticulated sounds when he hears them. This latter point presents an even greater problem when one notes that a number of words in the test call for difficult sound blends and syllabics (e.g., shirt, star, flag, and bottle). In words like these it would be very hard for the untrained ear to detect just what sound was causing the difficulty.

Finally, one could question the selection of "the eleven consonant sounds which are most often defective" because such common sound problems as "n" and "ng" are omitted; whereas sounds like "s" and "r," which are common problems in the first grade but become less so in the third grade, are included.

All in all, the Weidner-Fensch test seems to have been constructed without rigorous experimental procedures and without a basic understanding of the problems involved in standardizing a general speech test. Its use and value appear severely limited by these shortcomings.

SPELLING

[222]
★A.C.E.R. Spelling Test (Form C). Grades 3–4, 4–5, 5–6, 6–7, 7; 1946–51; 1 form; 5 levels; 3s. 6d. per manual ['51]; postpaid within Australia; (30) minutes; Australian Council for Educational Research. *

J. A. RICHARDSON, *Professor of Special Education, The University of British Columbia, Vancouver, British Columbia, Canada.*

The form of these tests is rather an unusual one. Complete sentences are dictated to the pupils, but only some of the words are marked. The children are aware from the instructions that spelling is being tested but do not know which of the words they write will actually be scored. This seems to the reviewer to be, on the whole, a better method of testing spelling than the more usual one employed in the very widely used 1935 A.C.E.R. spelling tests where the examiner dictates each successive word in the list, uses it in a given illustrative sentence, and then repeats the word. The first method—writing the words in context—approximates more closely the practical situation of composition or letter writing.

The 1946 tests are intended for use in all six Australian states on the apparent assumption that the words chosen are equally appropriate throughout the continent. An even more dubious procedure in construction was the selection of words for preliminary trial from two American lists. Even though these lists were supplemented by "some typically Australian words" (no further information being provided) and by "a group of difficult words from a commercially published spelling book," there must still be a major doubt concerning the content validity of the tests. This, incidentally, is the only validity referred to in the manual. Though the tests were constructed and used for the A.C.E.R. curriculum survey of 1946, no further information concerning them has subsequently appeared. There is a similar lack of information on the internal consistency of the tests.

As with all of the attainment tests used in the 1946 survey, the sample of 30,000 children from nearly 600 schools throughout Australia is more than adequate. Grade norms only, in the form of 15-point scale scores and centile rank equivalents, are provided. It is a pity that steps have not been taken, subsequent to the original standardisation, to provide age and age-in-grade norms to give these spelling tests the comprehensive coverage in respect to norms which is such a useful feature of other A.C.E.R. tests.

The manual presenting the spelling lists falls short of the usual high standard of A.C.E.R. publications. Although it contains useful general information on the significance of test scores, on the devising of the 15-point scale, and, in an appendix, on basic statistical concepts, unfortunately it does not give by any means sufficient details about the tests with which it is concerned—their validity, the interpretation of scores, and their usefulness to teachers. Moreover, the manual is marred by inferior technical production—crowded pages and poor print.

In short, although the tests appeal to the reviewer as a well devised and effective means of testing proficiency in spelling, they are recommended only with some reservations. More information is needed about validity and the significance and usefulness of the scores; further work to provide more comprehensive norms for the tests is also desirable. At present, with only meagre manual information as the basis for judgment, the teacher is probably justified in his preference for the 1935 A.C.E.R. spelling tests (see 40:1309).

D. K. WHEELER, *Senior Lecturer in Education, University of Western Australia, Nedlands, Australia.*

These tests consist of five sentence lists, of which lists A, B, and C are intended for grades 4, 5, and 6 in four Australian states and grades 3, 4, 5 in Queensland and Western Australia; list D is for grade 7 in South Australia and grade 6 in Western Australia and Queensland; and list E is for grade 7 in Queensland. In all, there are 33 sentences containing 102 different words to be marked (55–60 words in any one sentence list). Over 75 per cent of the words are common to any two consecutive lists.

The scored words were derived from four sources: Coleman's [1] list of 3,017 words; Horn's [2] basic writing vocabulary of 10,000 words, "typically Australian words" (*wallaby, boomerang, eucalypts, corroboree,* and *black-*

fellows); and difficult words from a commercially published spelling book. No good reasons are given for the insertion of any "typically Australian" words, or for these words in particular. Why *wallaby* rather than *kangaroo? Eucalypts* is probably used more often in California than in Australia. *Blackfellows* (equivalent of "niggers") is suspect in terms of human relations programs.

Of the 97 general words, 67 are found in Coleman's list, though doubt is likely to arise about their random selection when *pour* and *powder* (listed together in Coleman) appear in the same sentence in the test. These 67 words are also found in Horn's list. Of the remaining 30 words, 20 are in or above Horn's first 5,000, and 9 are not listed. Presumably these 9 are derived from the commercial speller. It is difficult to see why words should be chosen at random from Horn's list. Surely a standardized test at the elementary level would have considerably more curricular validity if it sampled only the first three or four thousand most frequently used words. Coleman's list gives neither frequency nor difficulty, but the average grade placement of 34 of the 38 words common to lists A, B, C is, according to Gates,[3] 6.3.

If the three lists are considered separately, there is the same high proportion of less frequently used words. Only 50 per cent are in Horn's first 3,000. From 30 to 40 per cent are in or above the fourth thousand for the grade indicated by Rinsland,[4] or else are not listed as used in the grade for which the list is intended. List D has 25 words (of 60) in or above Horn's fifth thousand, and 6 not listed; list E has 28 words in or above the fifth thousand, and 9 not listed. List D has 16, and list E, 23 words not listed in Rinsland's basic vocabulary of 25,000 words. No reasons are given why these words should be included.

The manual suggests that the random selection of words from comprehensive spelling lists should serve to make the lists for each grade fairly representative of the children's spelling vocabulary. The above data cast some doubt on this statement and hence on the validity of the words in these lists of sentences.

All standardized spelling tests suffer from limited usefulness in the direction and appraisal of instruction, but these have two particular

1 COLEMAN, WILLIAM H. *A Critique of Spelling Vocabulary Investigation.* Colorado State Teachers College, Education Series No. 12. Greeley, Colo.: the College, 1931. Pp. 119.
2 HORN, ERNEST. *A Basic Writing Vocabulary: 10,000 Words Most Commonly Used in Writing.* University of Iowa Monographs in Education, Series 1, No. 4. Iowa City, Iowa: the University, 1926. Pp. 225.

3 GATES, ARTHUR I. *A List of Spelling Difficulties in 3876 Words.* New York: Bureau of Publications, Teachers College, Columbia University, 1937. Pp. 166.
4 RINSLAND, HENRY D. *A Basic Vocabulary of Elementary School Children.* New York: Macmillan Co., 1945. Pp. 636.

drawbacks: (*a*) the fact that the words represent only a small sampling of those on the lists which children tested are required to learn; and (*b*) the low social usefulness of many of the words tested. To what extent they test general spelling ability, as distinct from ability to spell these particular words, is a moot point. Lists A, B, and C are probably useful as a rough indication of how children stand compared with other children in the same state (since most states use one list throughout). The usefulness of lists D and E is more doubtful.

[223]

*Coordinated Scales of Attainment: Spelling. Grades 4, 5, 6, 7, 8; 1946-54; subtest of *Coordinated Scales of Attainment;* IBM; grade 4: Forms A ('46), B ('49); grades 5-8: Forms A, B ('49); 5 levels; directions for administering ['52] for each level; battery manuals (A, '54; B, '49); separate answer sheets must be used; $1.90 per 25 tests; $1 per 25 IBM scorable answer sheets; 10¢ per scoring stencil; 50¢ per specimen set; postage extra; (45) minutes; James A. Fitzgerald; Educational Test Bureau. *

For a review by Alvin W. Schindler of the complete battery, see 4:8; for reviews by Roland L. Beck, Lavone A. Hanna, Gordon N. Mackenzie (with Glen Hass), and C. C. Ross of batteries 4-8, see 3:6.

[224]

*Graded Word Spelling Test. Ages 5-15; 1950-55; Forms A, B ['50]; no data on reliability; no norms; 3s. per 12 tests; 4d. per single copy; 1s. 6d. per manual ['55]; postage extra; [15-40] minutes; Fred J. Schonell; Oliver & Boyd Ltd. *

JOHN NISBET, *Lecturer in Education, University of Aberdeen, Aberdeen, Scotland.*

The 100 words in each of the two forms of the test are arranged in groups of 10, the first group covering attainment at age 5-6, the next group at age 6-7, and so on up to age 14-15. Administration is oral, subjects writing the words on a blank sheet of paper as the tester first reads out the word, then the word "embedded in an explanatory sentence," and finally the word repeated. It is left to the tester to invent explanatory sentences; skill in inventing these sentences may affect scores.

The manual includes no data on construction or reliability, but a personal communication from the author gave the following information. A pool of words drawn mainly from the author's Essential Spelling List was given to approximately 2,000 English children, about 200 in each age group from 5-15 years. After elimination of words which were unsuitable in terms of statistical criteria, 10 words were

chosen for each age group, each word having been spelled correctly by 45 to 55 per cent of the age group. The last 20 words include more difficult words to allow headroom for the ablest (e.g., miscellaneous, hydraulic). Reliability (test-retest on 195 children, age unspecified) was .96. Since girls scored higher than boys on the average, the author considered giving separate norms for boys and girls; but having checked scores from some 10,000 children, he suggests that separate norms would merely add 1 or 2 months of score to boys' scores and subtract 3 or 4 months from girls' scores between the ages of 7 and 13 years.

It is unfortunate that these data were not included in the manual, for their absence suggests a less systematic construction. The merit of the test is that it can be administered without expense to an entire class at one time, and that the "spelling quotient" is simple to calculate and easy to understand. Spelling standards, however, vary considerably between areas and over quite short periods of time; and as the representativeness of the standardisation group is uncertain, the norms may not be generally valid. The nature of the construction of the test complicates any revision of test norms with changing standards. Nevertheless, the lists provide a convenient rough check on spelling attainment between ages 8 and 12, and are widely used for this purpose in Britain.

[225]

*Lincoln Diagnostic Spelling Tests. Grades 5-8, 8-12 or 9-12; 1941-57; 2 editions; (30-40) minutes; A. L. Lincoln.
a) [EDUCATIONAL RECORDS BUREAU EDITION.] Grades 5-8, 8-12; 4 forms; 2 levels; manual ('51); 6¢ per test; postage extra; Educational Records Bureau. *
  1) *Lincoln Intermediate Spelling Test.* Grades 5-8; Forms A, B, C ('49, identical with tests published in 1947 and 1948), D ('49).
  2) *Lincoln Diagnostic Spelling Test [Advanced].* Grades 8-12; Forms 1 ('49, identical with test copyrighted in 1941), 2 ['42], 3 ['43], 4 ['44].
b) LINCOLN DIAGNOSTIC SPELLING TESTS [PUBLIC SCHOOL PUBLISHING COMPANY EDITION]. Grades 5-8, 9-12; 2 forms; 2 levels; manual ('56); tentative norms; $2.25 per 25 tests; 50¢ per specimen set; postpaid; Public School Publishing Co. *
  1) *Intermediate.* Grades 5-8; Forms A, B ('56, same as Forms A, B of the *Lincoln Intermediate Spelling Test* published in 1947 and 1948).
  2) *Advanced.* Grades 9-12; Forms A, B ('56, same as Forms 1, 2 of *Lincoln Diagnostic Spelling Test* published in 1941 and 1942).

REFERENCES
1. TOWNSEND, AGATHA. "A Study of the Lincoln Diagnostic Spelling Test." *Ed Rec B* 38:49-53 Je '43. *
2. LUNTZ, LESTER. "A Comparison of Results Obtained With Dictation and Multiple-Choice Spelling Tests." *Ed Rec B* 65: 76-84 F '55. * (*PA* 29:7866)

For reviews by Walter Scribner Guiler and George Spache, see 4:202–3.

[226]

★**Phonovisual Diagnostic Spelling Test: A Test for All Consonant Sounds and the 17 Fundamental Vowel Sounds.** Grades 3 and over; 1949; 1 form; no data on reliability; no norms; 75¢ per 50 tests; 10¢ per single copy; cash orders postpaid; administration time not reported; Lucille D. Schoolfield and Josephine B. Timberlake; Phonovisual Products, Inc. *

[227]

Spelling and Vocabulary: Every Pupil Test. Grades 3–4, 5–6, 7–9, 10–12; 1948–58; new form usually issued each December and April; 4 levels; norms available following testing program; no data on reliability; 3¢ per test; 1¢ per scoring key; cash orders postpaid; 40(45) minutes; Ohio Scholarship Tests. *

[228]

★**Spelling Errors Test.** Grades 2–4, 5–6, 7–8; 1948–55; 1 form ['55]; 3 levels; 25¢ per set of record blank ['55] and manual ['55]; postage extra; [15] minutes; George Spache; the Author, University of Florida, Gainesville, Fla. *

REFERENCE

1. LAMPARD, DOROTHY M. "A Study of Spelling Disabilities in Grades Four, Five, and Six." *Alberta J Ed Res* 1:48–59 D '55. *

[229]

Spelling: Every Pupil Scholarship Test. Grades 3, 4–6, 7–8, 9–12; 1928–58; new form usually issued each January and April; 4 levels; norms available following testing program; no data on reliability; 4¢ per test; 4¢ per scoring key; postage extra; 15(20), 30(35) minutes for grades 3–8, 9–12; Bureau of Educational Measurements. *

[230]

Spelling Test: National Achievement Tests. Grades 3–4, 5–8, 7–9, 10–12; 1936–57; 2 forms; 4 levels; no data on reliability; $1.25 per 25 tests; 50¢ per specimen set of any one level; postage extra; (25) minutes; Robert K. Speer and Samuel Smith; Acorn Publishing Co. *
a) GRADES 3–4. 1936–57; Forms A ('57, identical with test copyrighted in 1939), B ('39); directions sheet ('39).
b) GRADES 5–8. Same as for *a*.
c) GRADES 7–9. Same as for *a*.
d) GRADES 10–12. 1936–56; Forms A ('56, identical with test copyrighted in 1939), B ('39); directions sheet for Form A ('42, identical with sheet copyrighted in 1939), directions sheet for Form B ('39).

JAMES A. FITZGERALD, *Professor of Education, University of Scranton, Scranton, Pennsylvania.*

The sources and the objectives of the vocabulary of these spelling tests are not stated by the authors, nor is the validity of the tests indicated. However, an analysis of one of the two forms for each level indicates that they have a degree of curricular validity. Forty-seven of the 50 words in Form B, grades 3–4, are included among the 2,650 words most commonly written by children and adults in Fitzgerald's *A Basic Life Spelling Vocabulary.*[1] All 50 are in Horn's adult list[2] of 10,000 words. All are included in Rinsland's *A Basic Vocabulary of Elementary School Children.*[3]

Twenty-six of the 60 words in Form A, grades 5–8, are in Fitzgerald's vocabulary; 57 are in Horn's (53 among his most common 5,000 words); and 56 are in Rinsland's.

Forty-nine of the 60 words in Form B, grades 7–9, are among Horn's 10,000, but only 36 are within the 5,000 most useful words of adult writing. On this level, a list of 60 words of which 24 are beyond the most common 5,000 and 11 beyond the most common 10,000 words of adult writing may be criticized on the basis of curricular validity. In addition, some prospective test users may be concerned because 15 of these 60 words are not found in Rinsland's vocabulary.

Many of the 60 words presented in Form A, grades 10–12, may be questioned on the basis of utility. Only 26 of these words are in Horn's list of 10,000. In other words, 34 are not within the 10,000 most common words in adult writing. Only 11 are among Horn's most common 5,000; 49 of the 60 are beyond the 5,000 most useful words in adult writing. Thirteen are not included in the Thorndike-Lorge *Teacher's Word Book of 30,000 Words.*[4] If the purpose of the test is to test pupils upon words generally useful in writing, the value of the test is questionable because some of these words will seldom, if ever, be used in writing by ordinary individuals. Therefore, although the tests have curricular validity on the two lower levels, their validity is low at the two higher levels.

No manual is presented, but norms are provided for each test at each level. The purpose of the tests is not stated, but it may be inferred from the accompanying norms that the objective is to rate the spelling ability of individuals.

The manner of administering the tests is clearly described. Each word to be spelled is to be pronounced, read in a prepared sentence, and pronounced a second time. Some sentences, however, do not clearly indicate the meaning of words. Examples of such sentences are: "Call

1 FITZGERALD, JAMES A. *A Basic Life Spelling Vocabulary.* Milwaukee, Wis.: Bruce Publishing Co., 1951. Pp. 161.
2 HORN, ERNEST. *A Basic Writing Vocabulary: 10,000 Words Most Commonly Used in Writing.* University of Iowa Monographs in Education, First Series No. 4. Iowa City, Iowa: the University, 1926. Pp. 225.
3 RINSLAND, HENRY D. *A Basic Vocabulary of Elementary School Children.* New York: Macmillan Co., 1945. Pp. 636.
4 THORNDIKE, EDWARD L., AND LORGE, IRVING. *The Teacher's Word Book of 30,000 Words.* New York: Bureau of Publications, Teachers College, Columbia University, 1944. Pp. xiii, 274.

a *physician* at once," "The new *tariff* is too high," "He is *altogether* too bold," and "Be less *equivocal* in your answers." From these sentences, it would be difficult, if not impossible, for pupils who were unacquainted with the words to infer the meanings of *physician, tariff, altogether,* or *equivocal.*

Unfortunately, many pupils on all levels will find that insufficient room is allowed for writing the words in the blanks. This defect can be very easily corrected by the publisher.

Despite their limitations, these tests have value for determining the comparative spelling abilities of pupils in a class or in different schools in a district. The two comparable forms at each level should have some value for determining the spelling progress of individuals, particularly on the two lower levels where the validity of the word lists is highest.

For a review by W. J. Osburn, see 38:1161.

[231]

*Traxler High School Spelling Test. Grades 9–12; 1937–55; Forms 1 ('55, same as 1937 test), 2 ('55, same as 1937 test), 3 ('55, same as 1940 test) ; manual ('55) ; norms based upon testing in private schools in 1937–40; $1.75 per 25 tests; 50¢ per specimen set; postpaid; administration time not reported; Arthur E. Traxler; C. A. Gregory Co. *

For a review by Henry D. Rinsland, see 4:212.

[232]

*Wellesley Spelling Scale. Grades 9–16; 1944–57; IBM; Forms 1 ('57, identical with test copyrighted in 1944 except for one item), 2 ('57, identical with test copyrighted in 1944) ; manual ('57) ; $1.75 per 35 tests; separate answer sheets may be used; 3¢ per IBM answer sheet; 20¢ per scoring stencil; postage extra; 25¢ per specimen set, postpaid; (15–20) minutes; Thelma G. Alper and Edith B. Mallory; California Test Bureau. *

REFERENCE
1. ALPER, THELMA G. "A Diagnostic Spelling Scale for the College Level: Its Construction and Use." *J Ed Psychol* 33: 273–90 Ap '42. * (PA 17:932)

JANET G. AFFLERBACH, *Editor, Professional Examination Service, American Public Health Association, New York, New York.*

The *Wellesley Spelling Scale* is a compact and practical test of 50 items of the multiple choice type. The examinee chooses among one correct spelling and three incorrect spellings of a word for which a context setting is supplied. The answer sheet is well designed, with more than usual precaution taken to insure the use of proper norms in interpreting the score. A simple scoring key is provided, the same for both forms. An unusually com-

plete manual contains a detailed description of the construction and purposes of the test, precise directions for administering and scoring it, and sensible suggestions for interpreting the test results.

The choice of key words is excellent. Among them are examples of generally accepted "pitfalls" to avoid in spelling, including the formation of the past tense from the present (occur-red), of adverbs from adjectives (definite-ly), and of "agent-devoting" nouns from verbs (descend-ants). The very "everydayness" of the key words enhances the practicality of the tests for the classroom teacher. Here the student meets the kind of words he is likely to need in ordinary personal or business writing. No attempt has been made to include bizarre, "spelldown" favorites, highly technical terms, or new words of uncertain status.

However, to judge the scale on the merits of words included rather than of words omitted is the chief concern. These scales are obviously a good tool with which to discover poor spellers and to determine the type of remedial instruction that is needed. The scales are also valuable in determining the amount of progress made after a specific course of spelling instruction. The availability of two forms makes such measurement a practical possibility. With the two forms very well balanced in choice of key words, the test user can be confident of coverage of similar rules and exceptions regardless of which form he selects.

The reviewer found only three items to which exception could be taken. In Item 44, Form 1, the exclusion of *criticising* as a correct spelling is debatable. Certainly a spelling allowed by Webster's unabridged dictionary should be accounted for in the scoring key. The appearance of *affect* (Item 14, Form 1) and *effect* (Item 6, Form 2) with identical choices places undue emphasis upon what is basically a problem in vocabulary rather than in spelling since the speller must be able *first* to discriminate from contextual clues between the two and *secondly* to spell the words correctly. This is not true of other words in the scale.

The value of the *Wellesley Spelling Scale* for the purposes indicated is not diminished to any significant extent by the specific criticisms noted. The instrument, with its thorough and attractive accessory materials, represents a sensible answer to the need for a practical ready-made measuring device in spelling for grades 9 through 13.

For reviews by Henry D. Rinsland and Guy M. Wilson, see 3:157.

VOCABULARY

[233]

★**Durost-Center Word Mastery Test: Evaluation and Adjustment Series.** Grades 9–12; 1951–52, c1950–52; 3 scores: vocabulary, vocabulary in context, use of context; IBM; Form AM ('51); manual ('52); separate answer sheets must be used; $4.15 per 35 tests; $1.70 per 35 IBM answer sheets; postage extra; 35¢ per specimen set, postpaid; 60(80) minutes in 2 sessions 2 to 7 days apart; Walter N. Durost and Stella S. Center; World Book Co. *

A. N. HIERONYMUS, *Associate Professor of Education, State University of Iowa, Iowa City, Iowa.*

ORGANIZATION AND CONTENT. This test consists of two parts. Part 1 is a 100-item multiple response vocabulary test. Part 2—to be administered "several days, preferably a week" later—is an exact duplicate of Part 1, with the notable exception that each item is preceded by a sentence in which the word to be defined is employed in context. Part 1 provides a measure of general vocabulary; Part 2, a measure of the knowledge of words when they are used in contextual material. A third score is obtained as the difference between the two part scores. This difference score, labeled Use of Context, is intended to yield evidence on "the extent to which the student is able to learn the meanings of unknown words by seeing them in typical context situations."

As a general vocabulary test, Part 1 is highly satisfactory. Words were selected so as to be representative with respect to source, parts of speech, and social utility, and they were submitted to an adequate tryout. Distributions of tryout item difficulty indexes are presented and appear to be close to ideal.

While norms and evaluational evidence are presented for Part 2, the authors recommend basing instructional follow-up primarily on the results from Part 1 and Use of Context scores.

RELIABILITY. Both alternate form and split-half within-grade reliability coefficients are reported for one community. In view of the generally recognized superiority of alternate forms reliability data, one wonders why the split-half coefficients were even reported, and, more particularly, why the standard errors of measurement were based on split-half coefficients rather than on alternate forms data.

Reliability data are conspicuously absent for the Use of Context score which the authors term "perhaps the most significant measure to be derived" from the test. The logic of assessing the extent to which an individual is able to learn the meaning of unknown words from context is very appealing. Obtaining scores on this ability would appear to be the main reason for giving this particular test. Important scores for which norms are provided should be accompanied by reliability coefficients. Also missing are correlations between part scores; such correlations would shed light on the reliability or lack of reliability of the Use of Context scores. The only empirical evidence bearing on the behavior of these scores is in the form of correlations with IQ, which are .24, .02, −.11, and −.24 for grades 9, 10, 11, and 12, respectively.

INTERPRETATION OF RESULTS. The standardization was conducted in 1950 as a part of the standardization of the Evaluation and Adjustment Series. No information is given about methods of selecting the norms sample. The numbers of pupils (2,405 to 3,880 per grade), schools (54), and states (24) involved are given. The median CA's and IQ's supplied are of dubious value.

Standard scores and percentile ranks are supplied for Parts 1 and 2 for fourth- and ninth-month testing in each of the four grades. Percentile norms for Use of Context difference scores are given for all grades combined.

No provision is made for measuring growth. Since identical standard score distributions are used for each grade level, growth must be inferred from change in status. All the user can conclude from such data is that a given student gained more than or less than others with the same initial score.

A case is made for comparing scores made on the Durost-Center test with those on an intelligence test "with the idea of making further use of the two measures in a diagnostic and remedial sense." This would seem to be carrying the notion of expectancy too far, especially since obtained correlations between the vocabulary scores and IQ's run about as high as the correlations between equivalent forms of so-called tests of intelligence.

OVERALL EVALUATION. As a vocabulary test, either Part 1 or Part 2 is eminently satisfactory.

A second score probably adds little important knowledge about the student. The difference between the part scores (Use of Context) is probably too unreliable to be of much significance.

[234]

*The Inglis Tests of English Vocabulary. Grades 9–16; 1923–51; Forms A, B ('51, identical with forms copyrighted in 1923, 1924, except for change in format), C ('27); directions sheets (A, '23; B, '24; C, '27); no norms for grades 14–16; $3 per 30 tests, postpaid; specimen set not available; (40) minutes; Alexander Inglis; Form C completed by Ralph W. Walter; Ginn & Co. *

REFERENCES

1–7. See 3:163.
8. DOWNING, C. M. "A Lower Extension of the Inglis Tests of English Vocabulary." *Engl Leaflet* 32:21–30 F '33. *
9. LANGSAM, ROSALIND S. *A Factorial Analysis of Reading Ability.* Doctor's thesis, New York University (New York, N.Y.), 1941.
10. UHRBROCK, RICHARD STEPHEN. "Construction of a Selection Test for College Graduates." *J General Psychol* 41:153–93 O '49. * (PA 24:4874)

For a review by Henry D. Rinsland, see 3:163.

[235]

*The Iowa Tests of Educational Development: Test 8, General Vocabulary.** Grades 9–13; 1942–58; IBM; Forms X-3S, Y-3S ('52); examiner's manual ('58); battery manual ('54); pupil profile leaflet, fourth edition ('58); profile card (no date); separate answer sheets must be used; $3 per 20 tests; $5 per 100 IBM answer sheets; 50¢ per hand and machine scoring stencil; 50¢ per specimen set; 50¢ per battery manual; postage extra; 22(30) minutes; prepared under the direction of E. F. Lindquist; Science Research Associates. *

For reviews by J. Murray Lee and Stephen Wiseman of the complete battery, see 17; for a review by Eric F. Gardner of Forms X-2 and Y-2, see 4:17; for reviews by Henry Chauncey, Gustav J. Froehlich, and Lavone A. Hanna of Forms X-1 and Y-1, see 3:12.

[236]

★New Standard Vocabulary Test. Grades 7–12; 1955–58; reprinted from the Educational Edition of the *Reader's Digest*; IBM; Forms A ('55), B ('56), C ('56), D ('57), E ('57), F ('58); manual ('58); $2.50 per 35 tests; $3 per 100 IBM answer sheets; 30(35) minutes; Miriam M. Bryan, Janet G. Afflerbach, and Herbert A. Landry; Educational Department, Reader's Digest. *

RICHARD A. MEADE, *Professor of Education, University of Virginia, Charlottesville, Virginia.*

This vocabulary test consists of 125 four-response multiple choice items. The words represent a sampling from the Thorndike-Lorge word list [1] and also from words that have come

1 THORNDIKE, EDWARD L., AND LORGE, IRVING. *The Teacher's Word Book of 30,000 Words.* New York: Bureau of Publications, Teachers College, Columbia University, 1944. Pp. xiii, 274.

into general use since the creation of that list.

Of the four forms reviewed, two are designed for administering in the fall and the other two in the spring. It is the purpose of the test to provide a means for discovering the extent of vocabulary growth of pupils during the school year. In addition, pupil achievement may be compared with that of the large group of pupils upon whom the test was standardized.

The test is quite simple in both administration and scoring. An adequate manual provides clear directions and suggestions for using, scoring, and interpreting results. The test provides teachers of grades 7–12 with a simple, reliable, and usable test.

OSMOND E. PALMER, *Associate Professor, Office of Evaluation Services, Michigan State University, East Lansing, Michigan.*

These tests originated in vocabulary quizzes of the Student Guide section of the *Reader's Digest Educational Edition,* but they were prepared by test experts on the basis of the Thorndike-Lorge 30,000 word list and more recent words, and extensively tried out. From the tryouts the better items were chosen and comparable forms developed on the basis of 5,000–8,000 students per form. Large and small school systems in all parts of the country were used. The reliability of the tests is satisfactory and the norms seem reasonable, showing an improvement at the median of from 5 to 7 points between testings with fall and spring forms and from 6 to 10 points between one grade and the next.

There are 125 words in each form, presented in short phrases. The student is to choose from among four responses the response which most nearly corresponds to the meaning of the underlined word in the phrase. The time allowed for each test, 30 minutes, seems too short, for even college students often fail to finish 50-word vocabulary tests in 15 minutes.

These tests may be used to assess a student's individual progress, his standing in his class, and his wealth of vocabulary as compared to national averages. The words chosen seem fair enough, considering the grade range involved. The words range from easy to difficult and there do not seem to be too many at either extreme.

The authors' claim of careful tryout and careful selection of items seems borne out by inspection. In many cases the choice of foils for a word is ingenious. In general, the authors have avoided the trap of making the responses harder than the word being tested. In only a few cases can one quarrel with the right answer or the value of the foils. These are minor objections and there are few of them to raise. The tests should serve as a convenient and reliable measure of vocabulary growth.

[237]

★Purdue Industrial Supervisors Word-Meaning Test: Purdue Personnel Tests. Supervisors; 1952; 1 form; preliminary manual; $2.50 per 25 tests, postage extra; 50¢ per specimen set, postpaid; 15(20) minutes; Joseph Tiffin and Donald A. Long; distributed by University Book Store. *

REFERENCES
1. LONG, DONALD A. *Construction of an Industrial Vocabulary Test.* Master's thesis, Purdue University (Lafayette, Ind.), 1952.
2. SAWYER, JACK. *Self-Insight and Supervisory Performance.* Doctor's thesis, Purdue University (Lafayette, Ind.), 1955. (*DA* 15:1892)

JEROME E. DOPPELT, *Assistant Director, Test Division, The Psychological Corporation, New York, New York.*

This instrument is designed to determine the relative ability of supervisors to understand words which may appear in material directed to them. The test includes 60 four-choice vocabulary items of the synonym type, administered in 15 minutes. The preliminary manual gives a table of percentiles based on "180 industrial supervisors in a variety of plants." The odd-even reliability of the test, apparently determined for the same industrial supervisors, was found to be .92. Means and standard deviations are not given.

It is noted on the test booklet that "this test consists of words found in printed material that had been distributed to industrial supervisors." The attempt to achieve a certain amount of face validity by this method of selection is, of course, commendable. There is, however, no reason to believe that such words, in themselves, guarantee a suitable measuring instrument. More important for the test user is evidence that the test is effective in discriminating among supervisors. Unfortunately, such evidence is not given in the current (1952) manual, which states that "validity studies are now in process and will be published as soon as available."

There is a need for additional information on this test. The lack of validity data is a crucial weakness. Further normative and reliability data for groups that are not as broadly defined as "supervisors in a variety of plants" would

also be helpful. Until such information is available and can be evaluated, the reviewer feels the test cannot be recommended for use.

BERNADINE MEYER, *Assistant Professor, School of Business Administration, Duquesne University, Pittsburgh, Pennsylvania.*

This test is designed "to determine the relative ability of supervisors (or prospective supervisors) to understand those words which may appear in material directed to them." The test consists of 60 words, for each of which the testee is to select one of four possible definitions.

Directions for taking the test are readily understandable and easy to follow, as are also the directions for administering. The test user is entitled to more information about the construction of the test than is given in the manual. The manual states that the test was constructed from an original list of 500 words taken from the *Supervisors' Memory Jogger.* However, it does not tell how the 500 words were selected or why the Jogger was used. There is an implication that the Jogger contains the same vocabulary found in other written materials directed to industrial supervisors, but there is no evidence offered to support this implication.

The manual further states that the list of 500 words was reduced to 60 words by "a series of pooled judgment and internal consistency item analysis steps" described by one of the test authors in a Master's thesis. Since the probability that test users will read this thesis is extremely remote, the manual should describe the steps and indicate whose judgment was involved.

No information is given concerning the method used to select the words given as possible definitions. In some cases the test tests knowledge of the meaning of one or more of the words given as possible definitions. For instance, the word to be defined in Item 13 is "impracticable." Given as possible definitions are: "implacable," "plausible," "infeasible," and "imaginable." One might know the meaning of the word "impracticable" but be unable to answer correctly because he does not know the meaning of "implacable," "plausible," and "infeasible."

Percentile rank equivalents for raw scores are provided. The manual states that "these norms are based on 180 industrial supervisors in a variety of plants." Again, there is need for additional information: Were these experienced or beginning supervisors? How were they selected? Were they readers of the *Supervisors' Memory Jogger?* How much variety was there in the plants involved?

Reliability of the test, estimated on odd-even items, is reported as .92 for a group of 180 industrial supervisors, presumably the supervisors in the normative group. Validity studies for the test are reported only as being in process.

All in all, this is a simple, easily administered, easily scored test. However, with only sketchy information concerning test construction and with validity undetermined, one cannot enthusiastically endorse it.

[238]

★**Quick-Scoring Vocabulary Test: Dominion Tests.** Grades 9–13; 1958; preliminary manual; Forms A, B; $1 per 25 test-answer sheets; 10¢ per scoring key; 75¢ per complete specimen set; postage extra; 20(30) minutes; Department of Educational Research, Ontario College of Education, University of Toronto; distributed by Guidance Centre. *

[239]

Survey Test of Vocabulary. Grades 3–12; 1931–48; Forms X4 ('40), Z4 ('48); no manual; key-norms sheets (no dates); no data on reliability; $1.95 per 50 tests, postage extra; 25¢ per specimen set, postpaid; 20(25) minutes; L. J. O'Rourke; Psychological Institute. *

REFERENCES
1. See 3:167.
2. STEAD, WILLIAM H., AND OTHERS. *Occupational Counseling Techniques: Their Development and Application.* New York: American Book Co., 1940. Pp. ix, 273. *
3. JANUS, SIDNEY. *The Prediction of Learning Ability for Certain Types of Mechanical Skill.* Doctor's thesis, George Washington University (Washington, D.C.), 1944.
4. LITTLETON, ISAAC T. "Prediction in Auto Trade Courses." *J Appl Psychol* 36:15–9 F '52. * (PA 26:7256)

For reviews by Verner M. Sims and Clifford Woody, see 3:167.

[240]

Vocabulary: Every Pupil Scholarship Test. High school; 1935–58; new form usually issued each January and April; norms available following testing program; no data on reliability; 4¢ per test; 4¢ per scoring key; postage extra; 40(45) minutes; Bureau of Educational Measurements. *

[241]

Vocabulary Test: National Achievement Tests. Grades 3–8, 7–12; 1939–57; 2 forms; 2 levels; 50¢ per specimen set of either level; postage extra; (15) minutes; Robert K. Speer and Samuel Smith; Acorn Publishing Co. *
a) GRADES 3–8. Forms A ('57, identical with test copyrighted in 1939), B ('40); directions sheets (A, '43; B, '40); no data on reliability; $2 per 25 tests.
b) GRADES 7–12. 2 scores: vocabulary, word discrimination; Forms A ('51, identical with test copyrighted in 1939), B ('54, identical with test copyrighted in 1939); directions sheet for Form A ('51, identical with sheet copyrighted in 1939), directions sheet for Form B ('40); teachers' guide ['44]; no data on reliability for Form B; $2 per 25 tests.

For a review by Clifford Woody, see 3:168.

FINE ARTS

REVIEWS BY *Kenneth L. Bean, Paul R. Farnsworth, William S. Larson, Robert W. Lundin, James Mainwaring, Kate Hevner Mueller, Orville Palmer, and Herbert D. Wing.*

ART

[242]

Horn Art Aptitude Inventory. Grades 12–16 and adults; 1939–53; 2 scores: scribbling and doodling, imagery; 1 form ('51); [revised] manual ['53]; scoring booklet ('51); $5 per 50 tests; 50¢ per manual; postage extra; (50) minutes; Charles C. Horn; C. H. Stoelting Co. *

ORVILLE PALMER, *Test Development Division, Educational Testing Service, Princeton, New Jersey.*

The *Horn Art Aptitude Inventory* is a straightforward two-part performance test. Part 1, a "scribble and doodle exercise," asks the examinee to sketch a total of 20 familiar objects (e.g., a house, six circles, a book, and

a corkscrew) in small scale on one 8½ by 11 inch page of the test booklet. The student is told to work as rapidly as he can; each of the 20 exercises is timed and highly speeded: 4 seconds, 3 seconds, 10 seconds, etc.

In Part 2, Imagery, the examinee is furnished 12 rectangles, 2¾ by 3½ inches, each containing a number of "key" lines intended to function as "springboards" or as the basis of a composition incorporating the lines. The rectangles may be rotated as the student desires in his search for a "picture." No time limit is indicated for this portion of the test.

Rating scales are furnished for both parts, similar in nature to the once familiar penmanship rating scales. For Part 1, two examples each of excellent, average, and poor work are furnished for each exercise. For Part 2, one sample each of excellent, average, and poor work is furnished for each exercise.

To assist the test administrator in grading the tests, several paragraphs on such pertinent matters as order, clarity of thought and presentation, and originality are included. The author suggests that the rating scales and informative paragraphs permit the test to be graded with reliability. He cites intercorrelations from .83 to .86 among ratings of 21 test papers by two art teachers and by a lay person with no art training; for another group of 20 test papers, he reports the correlation between ratings by an art teacher and by a layman as .79. An alternate form reliability of .76 is reported, based on scorings by two art teachers of two forms of the test taken by 70 applicants for admission to art school.

No study of sufficient size to establish statistical validity is offered, though two small studies are cited, neither conducted within the present decade. In one of these, test scores are compared with faculty ratings of 52 art school graduates, with a resultant correlation coefficient of .53. In a similar situation, a validity of .66 was obtained with a group of 36 high school seniors enrolled in special art classes. As would be expected, the test's correlation with measures of intelligence is quite low.

As a brief sketch-pencil test, the examination has several merits. Part 1 tests a kind of dexterity and aptness at quick sketching and neat rendering which would be desirable in architecture students or in anyone doing caricature or other kinds of simple illustration. To some degree both parts test originality, imagination, compositional sense, neatness, and general sketching competence. The examination does not, of course, test color sense, aptitude for work in oils and watercolor, and the like.

A number of other drawbacks must be mentioned. In Part 2, the small rectangles necessitate cramped, miniature work. The key lines may prove stultifying rather than stimulating to some examinees. This portion of the test may demand mere cleverness, a kind of puzzle solving skill, as much as real originality.

The three groupings and specimen sketches furnished for rating purposes are not wholly convincing; some of the sample sketches are less than clear-cut in their distinction between excellent and average performance. An instruc-

tor might resolve the three-part rating scale with greater confidence into an "indicates competence" and "suggests incompetence" dichotomy which would be sufficient for art instructors desiring to section beginning art classes into more and less "gifted" or "advanced" groups.

The test in itself is not a sufficient testing instrument on which to base decisions regarding rejection or admission to art school or art departments, nor broad or sensitive enough for art scholarship awarding purposes. As a preliminary instrument, it should have value in furnishing clues as to the presence or absence of several desirable kinds of art aptitude.

For a review by Edwin Ziegfeld, see 3:171.

MUSIC

[243]

★Aliferis Music Achievement Test: College Entrance Level. Entering freshman music students; 1954, c1947–54; may be administered using piano, but tape recording is recommended; 4 scores: melody, harmony, rhythm, total; 1 form ('54); $3 per 20 tests; 50¢ per scoring key ('54); $9.50 per tape recording (7½ ips); $3 per manual ('54); $3.75 per specimen set; postage extra; (40–45) minutes; James Aliferis; University of Minnesota Press. *

REFERENCES

1. Aliferis, James, and Stecklein, J. E. "The Development of a College Entrance Test in Music Achievement." *J Res Music Ed* 1:83–96 fall '53. *
2. Aliferis, James, and Stecklein, John E. "Measurement of Music Achievement at College Entrance." *J Appl Psychol* 39:263–72 Ag '55. * (*PA* 30:4211)
3. Stecklein, John E. "Relationship of Instrument to Music Achievement Test Scores." *Yearb Nat Council Meas Used Ed* 13:146–50 '56. *
4. Stecklein, John E., and Aliferis, James. "The Relationship of Instrument to Music Achievement Test Scores." *J Res Music Ed* 5:3–15 sp '57. *
5. Williams, Raymond E. *The Measurement and Prediction of Cooperating Teacher Effectiveness in Music Teacher Education.* Doctor's thesis, University of Illinois (Urbana, Ill.), 1958. (*DA* 19:1023)

Herbert D. Wing, *Principal, City of Sheffield Training College, Sheffield, England.*

In each question the candidate is asked to choose which musical notation out of four matches a melody, harmony, or rhythm he has heard played. The piano is used for the testing, having been chosen after careful consideration since "its general use by musicians and general acceptance as representative of the complete tonal realm were thought to more than compensate for its inadequacies."

The instructions to the candidates are given orally and are fully set out in the manual. The music is recorded on a standard tape played at 7½ ips or it may be played on the piano; in the interests of standardisation the former is obviously to be preferred. The test took about 45–50 minutes when it was applied by the reviewer to a group of 31 college freshmen. The majority of these students found it difficult. The marking was easy and straightforward.

The students' scores for each section and for the total may be compared with tables of geographical or national norms. These norms are based on the testing of 1,768 students, a figure which leads one to regard the tables with confidence. The reliability for the total score is given as .88. This is reasonably high for a test of a musical nature which cannot hope to reach the level of reliability of tests of mere sensory acuity. Validity coefficients, based on correlation with one and two year music course grades, are reported as falling between .25 and .57 for the sectional tests, and between .53 and .61 for the total. In this matter it is thought that Aliferis does himself less than justice since, with the above group of college freshmen, the reviewer obtained a correlation of .73 between this test and his own test of musical intelligence. If this figure of .73 were corrected for the reliabilities of the two tests, the resulting validity coefficient would be one of the highest recorded for a music test. Shortage of time prevented the reviewer from carrying out any extended work in this direction, but sufficient was done to justify the conclusion that further investigation on validity would pay handsome dividends to the author of the test.

This is a well documented and thoroughly prepared and developed test of a good scientific standard. It may be used with confidence for the purpose and at the level intended by the author, i.e., measuring "at the college entrance level....the music student's power of auditory-visual discrimination of melodic, harmonic, and rhythmic elements and idioms."

If a test achieves what the author claims for it, the reviewer should end with a congratulatory remark to this effect. However, for the benefit of future research in the field of musical testing, it may be added that the validation against the reviewer's test of general musical aptitude would appear to indicate that the test is likely to be highly saturated with the general factor for music. If this is true, the test might well prove to be a sound diagnostic test of general musical aptitude at college level. The author states that when the test is used as a test of general aptitude, the results should be combined with at least three other kinds of information: practical performance, IQ level, and Seashore test performance. The reviewer's work with this test, however, indicated that the validity fell rather than rose when the last of these three was added. It must be admitted that these results were obtained with a comparatively small group $(n = 31)$ and that experiments on a larger scale might produce rather different figures. However, all this should prove a fruitful field of investigation for some future psychologist interested in music.

[244]

Conrad Instrument-Talent Test. Ages 6 and over; 1941; 6 scores: pitch, tempo, rhythm, harmony, tone recognition, total; 1 form; no data on reliability and validity; $3 per set of 100 grading sheets and manual; $1 per 100 grading sheets; postage extra; piano and electric metronome essential for administration; Jacques W. Conrad; Mills Music, Inc. *

HERBERT D. WING, *Principal, City of Sheffield Training College, Sheffield, England.*

This test is mainly concerned with selecting the musical instruments which a given child might most profitably study. It consists of three parts: (*a*) five listening tests of musical aptitude; (*b*) a questionnaire on scholastic and musical interests; and (*c*) a consideration of the shape of the pupil's hand, lips, and jaw.

The ear tests are given by means of the piano and the electric metronome. Some deviation from a strictly standardised administration is inevitable in that the supervisor is given somewhat imprecise instructions, such as hold a note "four slow beats," "play at moderato tempo," or "slightly accent" the notes. Then, the actual instructions which are to be given to the candidates are not given in full, as is usual in test procedure. When the reviewer gave the tests to a group of student music teachers, they found the ear tests of interest; however, they were unwilling to accept that a choice could be made of the better harmony between two 3-note chords, for, they maintained, a given chord can only be harmonically judged according to its context. They often found difficulty, too, in assigning a hand, lip, or jaw type, for, as in so many typologies, many of those actually met seemed to be of a mixed type.

The information obtained from the testing is to be interpreted by means of a number of charts which have been built up as a result of Conrad's experience as a teacher and an instrumentalist—the introduction tells us that he "has mastered nineteen instruments."

Although the test is described as a "scientific

test," there seems to have been no use made of the normal scientific procedures for evaluating a test in terms of coefficients of reliability and validity and of making sure that these values are statistically significant. This is a great pity. It would indeed be interesting to see how tests consisting of five 2-choice items (as do the ear tests) measured up to these criteria. It would be even more interesting to see what scientific support there is for the assumption that a liking for geography is linked with ability in harmony, or of history to that of tone recognition. The present reviewer attempted to obtain a statistically significant validity coefficient for the "percentages of talent required" section, but failed. However, it is for the author of the test and not the reviewer to establish such a figure; until he does so, the test should not be used for serious guidance.

[245]

★**Drake Musical Aptitude Tests.** Ages 8 and over; 1954–57; Forms A, B ('54); 2 tests: musical memory (identical with *Drake Musical Memory Test*), rhythm; forms for *Rhythm Test* are "unequivalent forms," differing in difficulty; manual, second edition ('57); $5.95 per LP microgroove 12-inch record (33⅓ rpm); $6 per 100 answer sheets; $6.95 per specimen set; cash orders postpaid; (30–40) minutes for music students, (70–80) minutes for nonmusic students; Raleigh M. Drake; Science Research Associates. *

REFERENCE

1. GORDON, EDWIN. *A Study to Determine the Effects of Training and Practice on Drake Musical Aptitude Test Scores.* Doctor's thesis, State University of Iowa (Iowa City, Iowa), 1958. (*DA* 19:487)

See also references for 3:175.

ROBERT W. LUNDIN, *Associate Professor of Psychology, Hamilton College, Clinton, New York.*

The tests attempt to measure objectively two fundamental components of musical ability: musical memory and rhythm. The two forms of each test can be given separately or together; the author advises giving both forms to insure best results. Reliabilities for both tests are generally good, ranging in most cases in the .80's and .90's. The tests tend to be superior to other currently available tests such as the *Seashore Measures of Musical Talent* and the *Kwalwasser-Dykema Music Tests.*

Ample practice exercises are provided before the tests proper are taken. The number of each test item is announced on the phonograph record to prevent the subject from losing his place. This has always been a problem on the Seashore tests, particularly when young subjects are involved.

The instructions for administration presented in the manual and on the record blanks are somewhat involved, particularly for the musical memory test. In each item of this test melodies played on the piano are compared as to sameness, or change in notation, key, or tempo. This might cause difficulty for some subjects, particularly if they are young or naive as to musical terminology. A wide range of difficulty is presented, and the harder items will prove a challenge for the most musically sophisticated individuals.

The rhythm test is really a test of tempo or ability to "keep time." In each item a particular beat is given, and the listener counts to himself at the same rate. Following the cessation of the presented beat, the listener continues to count until told to stop. He then writes the number he has reached at that point. In Form B of this test a more difficult problem is presented, the subject being required to continue to count at the rate of the original beat while a distracting beat is presented.

Drake reports remarkably good validities using an external criterion of "talent" which is defined in terms of expression in playing and rapidity in learning music. Considering the omnibus nature of this criterion, the results are sometimes surprising. The validity coefficients reported in the manual range from .31 to .91, with a median coefficient of .59. This is certainly better than those reported for other current tests of this type. One cannot help but wonder how the validities might compare if more specific ratings were used for various kinds of musical performance as well as for work in music theory courses.

The reported correlations between the rhythm test and the test by a similar name in the Seashore battery are low, ranging from .02 to .11. It would appear that two different variables are being measured by these two tests. Further information concerning the relationship between the ability to keep rhythm measured by the Drake test and the rhythmic discrimination of the Seashore test might be worth having. Drake does not report comparable correlations between his test of musical memory and the Seashore tonal memory test. However, this reviewer has found the relationships to be moderately high.

The intercorrelations between the two Drake tests are also quite low, yet both correlate well with the general criterion used for validation.

Drake suggests that these two factors along with pitch discrimination (which he does not measure) make up musical aptitude. Further information concerning the validity of this hypothesis might be helpful. This reviewer's impression is that these two tests actually involve a number of different musical behaviors.

The vast majority of research on these tests (see references in manual) has, by the way, been done by their author. It would be interesting to know how these findings agree with those of some independent investigators.

In general, it would seem that these tests are a valuable and much needed addition to the field of musical aptitude measurement. On the basis of evidence so far reported, they are superior to others previously available.

JAMES MAINWARING, *Formerly Lecturer in Psychology and Music, Dudley Training College, Birmingham, England.*

The Drake tests measure ability to remember two-bar melodies and to maintain mentally a given metronomic pulse, first with and then without distraction. They may be given to groups not exceeding 30 children or 60 adults, preferably by a musician. The instructions are comprehensive and clear, the recorded voice and examples are distinct, the scoring is quick, and the instructions for converting scores into percentile ranks and thence into categories of relative musical aptitude are simple. The conciseness of the tests, their ease of administration, and their evolution from the author's long experience in this field make them both practical and authoritative.

Before commenting on the tests in detail, it is necessary to stress Drake's own comment that they "do not measure all factors of the inherent or acquired type....neither are they measures of creative or interpretative abilities." He claims, however, that they are "as pure and as functional as might have been hoped for from a multiple-factor analysis study of 'musical aptitude.'"

In the musical memory test the subjects hear a two-bar melody which they then must recall for comparison with other melodies. If the new melody is the same as the first one, they put S in the appropriate answer box; the same melody in a new key is indicated by K, a change in time by T, and a change of notes by N. Though good practice examples are given on the record, some further illustration of what the test calls

"transposition" and "change of time" would seem desirable, since in transposition *all* the notes are changed and the change of time is not a change of tempo but of rhythmic structure. A slightly longer interval after the melody to be remembered might also improve this test.

The chief criticism of this reviewer is of the second rhythm test. In Form A, a metronome beats while a voice counts, "One, two, three, four." The subject must continue counting silently, at this rate, until the voice says "Stop!" and then write down the number reached. In Form B, the subject has to do this against a new and distracting pulse which he must try to ignore. The author accepts the two principles that a test of musical aptitude "should approximate life-like musical situations," and that musicians must *feel* rhythm strongly enough to resist distractions. The reviewer is of the opinion that while it is necessary to resist such tendencies as undue acceleration, or to continue to feel the pulse when complex rhythmic figures are superimposed on it, musicians have to respond to a new pulse in a normal musical situation rather than resist it.

Many factors in musical aptitude can, in the reviewer's opinion, be adequately assessed only by individual tests;[1] however, when these are impracticable, the tests under review must rank high among existing group tests of relative aptitude for general musical training.

For a review by William S. Larson of the Drake Musical Memory Test, *see 3:175; for reviews by Paul R. Farnsworth and James L. Mursell, see 40:1330; see 38:1083 (1 excerpt).*

[246]

★The Farnum Music Notation Test. Grades 7–9; 1953; 1 form; tentative norms; $6.75 per set of 12-inch record (78 rpm), manual, scoring key, and 50 test blanks; $1.50 per 25 test blanks; 35¢ per specimen set of manual and test blank; postpaid; (20–25) minutes; Stephen E. Farnum; Psychological Corporation. *

REFERENCE

1. BENTLEY, RICHARD R. *A Critical Comparison of Certain Music Aptitude Tests.* Doctor's thesis, University of Southern California (Los Angeles, Calif.), 1955. (Abstract: *Calif J Ed Res* 7:139)

KENNETH L. BEAN, *Professor of Psychology, Baylor University, Waco, Texas.*

The material consists of 40 relatively simple 4-measure melodic phrases not familiar to the listener and four similar sample exercises, the first of which is the beginning of "America," and the other three unfamiliar. These are re-

1 MAINWARING, JAMES. "The Assessment of Musical Ability." *Brit J Ed Psychol* 17:83–96 Je '47.

corded, with instructions and announced item numbers, on two sides of a 78 rpm disc. Test blanks given to subjects, in a group or individually, have the same phrases in notation, but with a change in one of the four measures. The task is to indicate in the answer spaces the number of the measure in which the change occurs. Practice exercises make the task and manner of answering unmistakably clear. This test is classed as a readiness test to predict success in musical instruction in junior high school, but it can be understood by fifth or sixth graders if they have had individual music lessons or if the elementary school has placed some emphasis upon learning to read music.

The material covers a sufficiently wide range of difficulty to serve the purpose for which it is intended. Some of the changes in the melodic line are radical departures involving more than one note and a deviation of several scale steps from the written notes, while others alter only one note by one step or change the time values. There are no complex rhythmic changes, such as may be found in a somewhat similar section of Gaston's *Test of Musicality*.

The lack of sufficient variety in the content appears to be a disadvantage of Farnum's test. Some real and perhaps insurmountable limitations of an individual student would not be likely to show up on such a brief sample of musical behavior. The *Watkins-Farnum Performance Scale* is an inadequate criterion against which to validate this test, because of the similarity of tasks on both, and also because of the limited aspects of achievement evaluated by the Watkins-Farnum scale. The pitch, time, and tonal memory parts of the *Seashore Measures of Musical Talent* show low to moderate correlations with the Farnum, and this is the best evidence presented by the author of some degree of validity for his brief screening device. The Seashore tests do not require reading of notes, and the tasks are somewhat different; therefore, high correlations would not be expected.

While this reviewer would prefer more basic measures of aptitude that would tap more aspects of talent, such as the Seashore battery would furnish, he recognizes the need in some school situations to supplement the basic measures with a brief evaluation of musical achievement such as the Farnum test provides. This more thorough procedure would enable teachers of public school music to give counseling

help to students and parents if extended study of music is or ought to be considered. Since its reliability is high, further long range study of the predictive value of the Farnum test should be undertaken in order better to establish its validity.

WILLIAM S. LARSON, *Chairman, Music Education Department, Eastman School of Music, University of Rochester, Rochester, New York.*

The examinee has a 4-page printed score of 4 trial melodies and 40 relatively simple 4-measure test melodies before him. The directions and the accompanying trial examples from the record explain and illustrate how the test is to be taken. Each musical example of both the trial and regular test melodies has one measure different from the notation of the printed score. There are four blank squares printed at the right of each example; the examinee is to follow the score as the example is played and mark his answer by checking the square which corresponds to the measure played incorrectly. The examinee does not need to specify whether the mistake is in melody or in rhythm. An analysis of the test shows that 33 of the 40 test examples have melodic errors, 6 have rhythmic errors, and only one has errors in both melody and rhythm. The test is well constructed and easily administered. Split-half reliabilities reported separately for boys and girls in grades 7–9 range from .78 to .91. Norms for these grades are given in percentiles, with separate norms for boys and girls, and with different tables covering students with and without special music instruction as well as the group as a whole.

The author explains in the manual that the purpose of the test is to provide a prognostic measure which will help a music staff select students who will profit most from instrumental training. He considers the test to be a "readiness" test on the premise that those who are proficient in the fundamentals of music notation will be the best prospects for instrumental instruction. In other words, the author considers that a score on his test is "not a measure of native ability" but rather a reflection of the "aptitude of the student to profit from the common core of musical experience plus his developed skill coming from special tutelage."

This reviewer finds himself in the position of disagreeing with the author's interpretation of the test's true function. Practically all students, by the time of their entrance into junior high school, have had adequate opportunities in their regular music classes to acquire a knowledge of the rudiments of music which include all the elements of notation found in the test. Actually, the test makes greater demands on musicality than on knowing notation as such; it has exacting and determinative requirements in musical imagery, which is a complexity of various musical talents.

The more musical students in junior high school, because of their talent and interest, are apt to be drawn toward special musical instruction not regularly given to all, instruction such as that secured in the glee club or in private or class lessons. It is likely that the higher scores made by these students who have had special instruction can be accounted for better by a natural or planned selection operating to place these children in special music classes than, as the author believes, by the fact that they have had more experience with notation. In the light of this discussion, the reviewer considers that this test is, in effect, more of a talent test than a readiness test. The elementary knowledge of notation required is simply an intellectual, informational tool, analogous to the basic acquaintance with the English language needed to take an intelligence test.

Consideration of the musical examples of the test with reference to the norms will confirm the basis for this reviewer's standpoint. An analysis of the 40 test items shows that the examples are structurally very simple, both melodically and rhythmically. Only a very few of the 40 examples have any chromatic tones. Most of the examples are of the simplest kind in 3/4, 4/4, and 6/8 time; a few examples have notation with the equally divided beat, but there is nothing more difficult than that in the test. The significant point is that the simple factual knowledge of notation required in this test is generally taught as such and with little difficulty to most children in regular music classes in the grades. But the musical imagery involved in following and checking the musical score in order to discover errors in simple melodies is an exacting requirement resting on musical talent, and quite a different matter.

The scores are not corrected for guessing. The norms show that a student in the eighth grade with an expected chance score of 10 has a surprising percentile rank of 13 to 15 (the scores for girls generally are somewhat higher than for boys); to acquire a score at the median, the eighth grader needs only 5 to 8 correct answers above this chance score of 10; and if he answers half of the remaining examples (15 of 30) above this chance score, he ranks near the 80th percentile. Surely the simple factual material of notation does not account for the difficulty of the test; it is more reasonable to consider the complex demands of musical imagery as being the real determinant of the test scores.

In summary, the reviewer considers the *Farnum Music Notation Test* primarily a type of musical talent test depending on musical imagery, rather than a test which rests on the student's experience in the use of music notation. The reviewer believes that a measure of knowledge of music notation can be secured in simpler ways which are divorced from demands of musical talent; and, that even though they might be more time-consuming, there are less devious and probably more effective and conclusive ways of measuring talent in the interest of selecting students who will profit most from instrumental instruction.

[247]

The Graduate Record Examinations Advanced Tests: Music. College seniors and graduate students; 1951; available only in the Institutional Testing Program of *The Graduate Record Examinations* (see 601); IBM; 105(125) minutes; Educational Testing Service. *

WILLIAM S. LARSON, *Chairman, Music Education Department, Eastman School of Music, University of Rochester, Rochester, New York.* [Review of Form ZGR.]

This is a multiple choice test of 160 items requiring 105 minutes of working time. It is one of the few GRE Advanced Tests administered in less than the customary 3-hour period.

The content of the test, considered in a broad sense, falls into the general realm of musicology. The test has mainly to do with form and analysis, theory, and history of music of all periods from ancient to modern; a limited number of questions about instrumentation and orchestration are included. In other words, the test is devoted to the scholarly side of music: there is no provision for measuring the musical achievement of the executant or practical musician, an aspect of musical ability which is admittedly unadaptable to measurement by objective test methods. The test might more appropriately be called an "Advanced Test in Musicology" or an "Advanced Test in Musical Knowledge" than an "Advanced Test in Music."

When this test is used as an index of musical achievement in the selection of students for graduate study, it should be realized that a good test score indicates a measure of the student's breadth of knowledge about music but does not necessarily indicate high musical performance or fine sensitivity to music. If the test is given as a comprehensive examination to gain information for educational guidance of graduate students or as part of a qualifying examination for admission to candidacy for an advanced degree, it has further shortcomings. Since only total scores are reported back to colleges, it is not possible to determine in which areas of musical knowledge the student has peculiar strengths and weaknesses.

Statistical information for this test is not complete. Correlations between the test and the *Graduate Record Examinations Aptitude Test* are given for 44 college seniors, these being .69 with the verbal and .18 with the quantitative scores on the aptitude test. Reliability data are completely lacking. Percentile tables are given for first semester, first year graduate students and for second semester seniors. The norms for graduate students are not of practical value because the number of cases for whom data are reported is so small: there are only 58 graduate students from 10 colleges, 3 of which have 74 per cent of the total of 58 students. It is unlikely that a particular college would want to consider only these three colleges, either individually or collectively, as being representative in serving as a yardstick for comparative purposes. The norms for college seniors are somewhat better, being based on the scores of 354 second semester college seniors from 86 colleges. Here again, however, is an uneven representation, half of the scores coming from 18 of the 86 colleges. Possibly the best evaluation that can be made of a candidate's score is in terms of the scores made by others in his local group.

From the writer's experience as a music educator who has served on a large number of graduate examination committees, he judges that the test would be a difficult one even for selected graduate students, and that few undergraduates, including the limited number having history of music or musicology as their majors, would be able to do very well on it. Because of its difficulty the test can best be adapted to use

for musicology majors at the Master's and Doctor's degree levels and possibly for other doctoral candidates who have a minor in musicology. The test gives evidence of the finest scholarship on the part of those who provided the questions, and it is so beautifully constructed that it also reflects credit on those who assisted in its formulation. It is regrettable that a test so well prepared seems to be destined for limited use.

For a review by Harold Seashore of the entire series, see 601.

[248]

★Kwalwasser Music Talent Test. Grades 4-6, 7-16 and adults; 1953; 1 form; 2 levels: Forms B (grades 4-6), A (grades 7 and over); no data on reliability and validity; $4.75 per set of record (78 rpm), manual, and 100 record blanks; (15) minutes; Jacob Kwalwasser; Mills Music, Inc. *

PAUL R. FARNSWORTH, *Professor of Psychology, Stanford University, Stanford, California.*

A stopwatch check shows that the *Kwalwasser Music Talent Test* takes only 10 minutes of a subject's time. Hence, this measure can claim brevity as an asset. Only three sets of norms are offered, one for Form B and two for Form A (junior high school, and senior high school and college). Form B presents 40 items, each with three tones given and then repeated with a change in either pitch, time, loudness, or rhythm. Form A, the more difficult test, is built on the same plan but has 50 items. The change magnitudes in Form B range as follows: pitch, 15 to 70 cents; time, 15 to 40 per cent; rhythm not quantified; and loudness, 3 to 10 decibels. The corresponding magnitudes in Form A are: pitch, 5 to 70 cents; time, 5 to 40 per cent; and loudness, 2 to 10 decibels. The items are presented in forced choice manner in which the subject must determine, from between two possible variables given, whether a change has occurred in pitch, rhythm, loudness, or time.

Kwalwasser presents no validity data of any sort and seems content to rest his case on face validity. It can be assumed, however, that persons with musical interests and training will score above the published norms. At least one of the reviewer's classes in the psychology of music (n = 33) yielded a median score at the 86th percentile. Kwalwasser declares, without supporting evidence, that training has little or no effect upon his test's scores. He also rules out intelligence, sex, and nationality as possible score modifiers.

Perhaps an even more shocking omission than the absence of validity data is the lack of reliability figures. The reviewer attempted to remedy this fault in a small way by finding the reliability of the scores of 55 college students who came from a large class in general psychology. There was no reason to suspect that this group was not typical of many college populations although their median score was at the 60th percentile. The split-half reliability coefficient for this group was .48.

Few will deny that many musical aptitude tests are so long that they bore not only the students who take them but even the music teachers who attempt to use them. This fact, however, should not have led an experienced test constructor to market a test so brief as to have extremely low reliability. And is it asking too much of any testmaker who plies his trade in the year 1958 (or even in 1953 when the test in question was copyrighted) that his test manual present data on reliability and validity? Professional ethics most assuredly demands a negative answer.

KATE HEVNER MUELLER, *Professor of Education, Indiana University, Bloomington, Indiana.*

Kwalwasser's new test has the advantage of being short, requiring only from 10 to 15 minutes to administer. Loudness, pitch, rhythm, and time are the variables, and both the method and the materials used represent only technical improvements on the Seashore originals.

There are two forms, Form B being slightly easier. Form A provides separate norms for grades 7-9 and for "senior high school and college." "Norms" are given in terms of percentiles, but there is no indication of how or where and on what numbers these percentile scores were obtained. The experimenter is advised simply to "explain" the meaning of pitch, time, rhythm, and loudness changes; no standardized directions are given. There are no data on either the reliablity or the validity of the test.

In his manual, the author claims that the uninstructed child "may be accurately tested for musical talent" and that what is being tested is "auditory potential, and not the influence of training." Since such claims need extensive research for their support, the usefulness of the

present test remains as yet an unknown quantity.

[249]

★Music Education: National Teacher Examinations. College seniors and teachers; 1957-58; for more complete information, see 538; IBM; 80(90) minutes; Educational Testing Service. *

For reviews by William A. Brownell, Walter W. Cook, and Lawrence G. Derthick of the entire series, see 538; for a review by Harry N. Rivlin of an earlier edition, see 4:802.

[250]

Musical Aptitude Test: Series A. Grades 4-10; 1950; 4 scores: rhythm, pitch, melody, total; IBM; 1 form; separate answer sheets must be used; 3¢ per IBM answer sheet; 20¢ per either hand or machine scoring stencil; postage extra; $3 per manual, postpaid; piano essential for administration; (40-50) minutes; Harvey S. Whistler and Louis P. Thorpe; California Test Bureau. *

REFERENCES

1. WHISTLER, HARVEY S., AND THORPE, LOUIS P. "Testing for Musical Talent." *Ed Music Mag* 31:16-7+ Mr-Ap '52. *
2. BENTLEY, RICHARD R. *A Critical Comparison of Certain Music Aptitude Tests.* Doctor's thesis, University of Southern California (Los Angeles, Calif.), 1955. (Abstract: *Calif J Ed Res* 7:139)

ROBERT W. LUNDIN, *Associate Professor of Psychology, Hamilton College, Clinton, New York.*

The purpose of this test is simple and straightforward: "to measure an individual's aptitude for the study of music." Based on the assumption that the basic elements of all music are rhythm, pitch, and melody, the test sets out to measure the student's ability to recognize rhythm and pitch as utilized in melodic patterns. The extent to which the student comprehends these musical units is taken to reveal his aptitude, or lack of aptitude, for the study of music.

One of the merits of this test, and also one of its deficiencies, is that it uses real life situations in music. The musical stimuli are played to the subject on a piano by the test administrator. The musical scores are provided in the manual of instructions. Although quite admirable in theory, this technique of test administration presents certain hazards. All pianos do not sound alike even when they are in tune; all people do not interpret musical stimuli in exactly the same manner. No tempo markings are indicated on the musical scores so it is possible for some administrators to play the test items faster than others might; accents are not marked in the rhythm tests. Errors in playing can easily be made, even though the music is simple enough to read. The players are told to repeat an item if they make a mistake. This may help or hinder the subject; in any event it invalidates the item. If these tests were recorded on standard discs so that a regularity of presentation were assured, the reliabilities (and validities) might be appreciably improved.

The test results are presented in a diagnostic profile on which are plotted the combined score for the two rhythm tests, the score for the two pitch tests, the score on the melody test, and the total score. No attempt is made to weight individual subtest scores in the total score. Separate norms are available for each of grades 4–10. The tests, then, are aimed at selecting talent among school children at ages when they would be most likely to take up the study of voice or of a musical instrument. They are too easy to be of much value for adults or children who have already had extensive musical experience.

The Kuder-Richardson reliability coefficients reported are only fair, ranging from .64 for the melody test to .87 for the total score. The validity coefficients for the total score, obtained from teachers' estimates of talent and from number of years in band, orchestra, chorus, and glee club, range from .19 to .56.

The rationale behind the tests appears to be a good one: behavior is measured using stimuli in musical situations. However, the chances of getting the best predictive results seem to be unfortunately marred by the failure to use standard stimuli in these days of good recording techniques and reproducing apparatus. Improvements in testing procedure could be expected to result in musical situations much more "real" than those which are likely to be provided by an individual interpreter on an untuned piano.

For a review by William S. Larson, see 4:228.

[251]

Seashore Measures of Musical Talents, Revised Edition. Grades 4–16 and adults; 1919–56; 6 scores: pitch, loudness, time, timbre, rhythm, tonal memory; IBM; 1 form: Series A ('39); Series B ('39) discontinued; revised manual ('56); no adult norms; $14 per set of three 12-inch records (78 rpm), 50 IBM answer sheets, scoring key, and manual; $2.20 per 50 IBM answer sheets; 60¢ per manual; postpaid; (60) minutes; Carl E. Seashore, Don Lewis, and Joseph G. Saetveit; Psychological Corporation. *

REFERENCES

1-55. See 40:1338.
56-101. See 3:177.
102-117. See 4:229.
118. HARRISON, LOMA. *Application of Certain Seashore Measures of Musical Talent and the Kuder Preference Record to the*

Building of a Music Program in Borger High School. Master's thesis, North Texas State College (Denton, Tex.), 1949.
119. FARNUM, S. E. *Prediction of Success in Instrumental Music.* Doctor's thesis, Harvard University (Cambridge, Mass.), 1950.
120. WILSON, WILLIAM E. *Use of the Seashore Measures of Musical Talent in the Prediction of Certain Academic Grades for Music Students at the Pennsylvania State College.* Master's thesis, Pennsylvania State College (State College, Pa.), 1950.
121. EBERLY, JOHN W. *The Aptitude of Elderly People for Learning the Piano.* Doctor's thesis, University of Nebraska (Lincoln, Neb.), 1952.
122. KIESZ, THELMA D. *A Statistical Study Based on Seashore Musical Talent Scores as Collated With Motility, Steadiness, and Equilibrium Test Scores.* Master's thesis, Syracuse University (Syracuse, N.Y.), 1953.
123. LUNDIN, ROBERT W. *An Objective Psychology of Music*, pp. 201-9. New York: Ronald Press Co., 1953. Pp. ix, 303. * (PA 28:590)
124. EDMONDSON, HAROLD S. *The Seashore Measures of Musical Talents as a Prognostic Guide in Language Rehabilitation for Persons With Aphasia.* Doctor's thesis, University of Michigan (Ann Arbor, Mich.), 1954. (DA 14:735)
125. CHRISTY, LEO J. *A Study of the Relationships Between Musicality, Intelligence, and Achievement.* Doctor's thesis, Indiana University (Bloomington, Ind.), 1956. (DA 17:373)
126. GOWAN, J. C., AND SEAGOE, MAY. "The Relation Between Interest and Aptitude Tests in Art and Music." *Calif J Ed Res* 8:43-5 Ja '57. * (PA 32:296)

For reviews by John McLeish and Herbert D. Wing, see 4:229; for reviews by Paul R. Farnsworth, William S. Larson, and James L. Mursell, see 3:177.

[252]

★**Test of Musicality, Fourth Edition.** Grades 4–12; 1942–58; 1 form; $10 per set of LP 12-inch records ('58, 33⅓ rpm), test blank, scoring key, and manual ('57); 5¢ per test blank ('57); postage extra; [25–35] minutes; E. Thayer Gaston; Odell's Instrument Service. *

REFERENCE

1. BENTLEY, RICHARD R. *A Critical Comparison of Certain Music Aptitude Tests.* Doctor's thesis, University of Southern California (Los Angeles, Calif.), 1955.

PAUL R. FARNSWORTH, *Professor of Psychology, Stanford University, Stanford, California.*

According to the author, the major change from the third to the present fourth edition of Gaston's *Test of Musicality* rests in the recording; that is, the four 78 rpm records of the third edition have been replaced in the fourth edition by a single long-playing disc. In the introduction of his manual Gaston agrees to a need for the so-called sensory tests of an earlier day. But in this present test he checks rather on the pupil's perceptual abilities—what results in considerable part from musical training.

The *Test of Musicality*, an omnibus 40-item affair, has been standardized for the sexes separately for ages 9, 10–11, 12–13, 14–15, and 16–18; and for grades 4, 5–6, 7–8, 9–10, and 11–12. Actually, only 39 items are scored, number 18 being merely a query as to the instrument the pupil would most like to play.

The first 17 questions are scored independently of the rest and separate norms are offered for this portion of the test. The items constitute an interest test which presents such questions as "Do you have a piano in your home?" and "Would you like to be a musician?" Unfortunately, it cannot be told from the manual whether or not these items enter into the validity and reliability data for the entire test.

A phonograph presents the remaining test items. The directions are easily comprehended, not at all like those of the older Seashore Sense of Consonance measure, where those taking the test were invariably so confused that they identified consonance with preference. The tonal portion of Gaston's test opens with five items which tap the ability to find a given tone in a chordal complex. The next five items have to do with sight reading where possible note and rhythmic changes must be detected. These are followed by five Kwalwasser-Dykema-like tonal movement phrases in need of resolution, and lastly by seven items in each of which a short melody is repeated from two to six times either in the same form or with different note or rhythmic patterns.

On the last page of the test blank the music teacher is given the opportunity to gather data concerning the pupil's voice register, the instrument he plays, and his IQ. There are also spaces for self ratings on his general health, school attendance, lip texture, condition of teeth, type of fingers, and personality characteristics. Before the test is given the teacher may, if she wishes, record her impression of the pupil's musicality.

Corrected split-half reliabilities are excellent at all ages. But as is too often the case with music tests, the validity picture is muddy. The author presents a table in terms of what he calls "chi-square r" which purports to disclose the degree of association between a five-point teacher rating and score on his test. The reviewer puzzled over the table for some time and then showed it to a well known Stanford statistician who also failed to make sense out of it. However, with the first portion of the test a measure of musical interests it can be practically guaranteed that a statistical study would show pupils who impress the music supervisor as being most musical to possess the higher Gaston test scores. And, because of the nature of the test's tonal stimuli, one would expect to find a correlation of considerable magnitude with amount of musical training.

There is little novelty in Gaston's test. Yet it is carefully constructed and has been standardized on a sizeable population. The teacher who distrusts her ratings and obtains comfort from music tests should give this test a trial.

Kate Hevner Mueller, *Professor of Education, Indiana University, Bloomington, Indiana.*

Gaston's test has been several years in the making but is only now available in the truly convenient form of one long playing record which is complete with spoken directions to the listeners, practice exercises which are corrected and explained, a convenient printed test blank and scoring mask, and norms carefully established for all parts of the test, by grade and by sex, on many thousands of children.

The 4-page test booklet begins with a self rating scale for the subject in which a numerical score is obtained by adding the credits earned for having lessons on any instrument, playing in band, having others in the home who play or sing, etc. No differentiation is made for the different instruments, e.g., lessons on the piano give the same credit as lessons on a ukelele, although, especially at the high school levels, weighting for lessons on such instruments as the piano, cello, and flute would increase the sensitivity of the scale.

The test items are of three kinds: (*a*) listening to a melody of from four to eight measures, and comparing it with the printed notation to check any difference in pitch or rhythm; (*b*) listening to a brief melody which lacks the final closing measure, and deciding whether the final note should be higher or lower than the semifinal; (*c*) listening to a melody which is repeated several times, and discriminating the character of the alternation in pitch or rhythm.

The test is intrinsically interesting, and is rightly named as a test of general musicality, of sensitivity to and interest in music. The range of difficulty is remarkable for so short a test. The reliability of .88 to .90 is good for any recorded test of 40 items which requires uninterrupted attention from the subjects for 15 minutes at a time, and where a momentary lapse of attention cannot be corrected, as in a visual test. So far the validity has been established only on the basis of teacher ratings, but it seems statistically satisfactory.

This test is short, convenient, pertinent, and well constructed. The wide use which it deserves will further develop its value to the public schools from grade 4 through high school.

[253]

★**Watkins-Farnum Performance Scale: A Standardized Achievement Test for All Band Instruments.** Music students; 1942–54; individual; score sheet ('54) for each instrument; $1.50 per 100 score sheets; $4 per manual ('54); postpaid; [20–30] minutes; John G. Watkins and Stephen E. Farnum; Hal Leonard Music, Inc. *

REFERENCES

1. WATKINS, JOHN GOODRICH. *Objective Measurement of Instrumental Performance.* Columbia University, Teachers College, Contributions to Education, No. 860. New York: Bureau of Publications, the College, 1942. Pp. x, 98. * (*PA* 17:334)
2. FARNUM, STEPHEN E. *The Prediction of Success in Instrumental Music.* Doctor's thesis, Harvard University (Cambridge, Mass.), 1950.

HERBERT D. WING, *Principal, City of Sheffield Training College, Sheffield, England.*

In this test a series of musical exercises of increasing difficulty are presented for sight reading and the level of performance is judged by checking the number of mistakes made in playing. Any one error in a bar of music cancels the mark for that bar and counts as minus one from the total possible score for that piece. Errors are looked for in pitch, tempo, length of note, expression, slurs, rests, pauses, and repeats. The student is stopped when he has failed to score in two consecutive exercises.

The instructions to the candidates are fully written out and the tempo for the playing is indicated by metronome figures. The metronome is stopped after the student has begun playing an exercise. Details of how errors are to be assessed are given; the process has been found not to be too difficult for the average experienced teacher of music. The test must, of course, be administered individually. It took the reviewer some 30 minutes for assessing each of several moderately competent instrumentalists.

The marks obtained by the candidates are converted to letter grades from a table which gives the marks in terms of the number of years the instrument has been studied. The tables are based on "thousands of scores from the schools in one city." How many thousands is not stated, nor is the meaning of the four letter grades explained. This is a very sad omission. The grade of B seems to correspond to the average level of performance; this would mean that the usual 5-point scale of the psychologists (with C as the average) has been made into a 4-point scale by combining the top two grades (A and B) and changing the usual lettering of the others by one step. All this seems more diplomatic than psychological and rather out of keeping with the standard of this test.

The reliabilities claimed range from .87 to .94. Validity coefficients, based on correlation with instructors' ratings, lie in the region of .68 to .87. These are extremely good figures for any music test.

A considerable amount of work has evidently been done in preparing, standardising, and simplifying a process which is common enough amongst musicians in examining performing ability. The test should not only be of great practical value in schools in arranging the children in the orchestra or assessing the merit of newcomers, but should also provide a valuable scale for assessing practical ability where this is required in investigations into musical aptitude. It is hoped that the authors will be able to extend their test to cover the stringed instruments at some not too distant future date. It is also hoped that when this is done, one of the more normal 5-point scoring scales will be adopted (e.g., A, 10 per cent; B, 20 per cent; C, 40 per cent; D, 20 per cent; E, 10 per cent) and that the precise value of each of these grades will be given in terms of percentiles or some other generally accepted standard.

For related reviews, see 3:1228.

[254]

*****Wing Standardized Tests of Musical Intelligence, [Revised Edition].** Ages 8 and over; 1939–58; 8 scores: chord analysis, pitch change, memory, rhythmic accent, harmony, intensity, phrasing, total; 1 form ['57]; 2 types of tape recordings: standard, long playing in either 7½ ips or 3¾ ips; directions for administering ['58]; English answer booklet ['50], American answer booklet ['58]; norms for tests 1–3 available upon request; 84s. per set of standard tape recording, 40 answer booklets, scoring stencil, and manual ['57]; 63s. per set of 3¾ ips tape recording, 40 answer booklets, scoring stencil, and manual; 8s. per manual; 15s. per 100 answer booklets; postpaid within U.K.; German and French editions available; edition for the blind available; (50–60) minutes; H. D. Wing; distributed by National Foundation for Educational Research in England and Wales. *

REFERENCES

1–6. See 4:230.
7. WING, HERBERT. "Some Applications of Test Results to Education in Music." *Brit J Ed Psychol* 24:161–70 N '54. * (*PA* 29:6188)
8. BENTLEY, RICHARD R. *A Critical Comparison of Certain Music Aptitude Tests.* Doctor's thesis, University of Southern California (Los Angeles, Calif.), 1955. (Abstract: *Calif J Ed Res* 7:139)
9. FRANKLIN, ERIK. *Tonality as a Basis for the Study of Musical Talent.* Goteborg, Sweden: Gumperts Förlag, 1956. Pp. 193. * (*PA* 31:636)
10. WHITTINGTON, R. W. T. "The Assessment of Potential Musical Ability in Secondary School Children." *J Ed Psychol* 48:1–10 Ja '57. * (*PA* 32:4632)

For a review by John McLeish of an earlier edition, see 4:230; for related reviews, see 4:231.

FOREIGN LANGUAGES

REVIEWS BY *Ralph Bedell, Nelson Brooks, John A. Cox, Jr., Harold B. Dunkel, Konrad Gries, Walter V. Kaulfers, Charles R. Langmuir, Herschel T. Manuel, Kathleen N. Perret, Herbert Schueler, Geraldine Spaulding, Mary E. Turnbull, and Clarence E. Turner.*

ENGLISH

[255]

★**Diagnostic Test for Students of English as a Second Language.** Applicants from non-English countries for admission into American colleges; 1953; 1 form; manual ['53]; no data on reliability; no norms; separate answer sheets must be used; $3.50 per 10 tests; $1 per 10 answer sheets; 45¢ per specimen set; postpaid; 60(65) minutes; A. L. Davis; Educational Services. *

NELSON BROOKS, *Associate Professor of French, Yale University, New Haven, Connecticut.*

This is a pencil and paper test on a number of frequently used patterns of form and order in which vocabulary plays a minor role and sound no role at all. Each item offers a choice of three ways of writing a short utterance in English, two of which are unacceptable. All the items use English only. Some of the choices are wrong because the suggested forms are impossible: "severals," "gooder," "tooths," "mights," "absenced." Other choices are wrong because the words as given do not fit accepted patterns of English syntax: "in his coffee sugar he uses," "resemble to," "wants on time breakfast," "pair of shoe," "can to write," "had the tailor a coat make," "doesn't he can't." A third type of wrong answer results when the suggested forms—correct in themselves—are fitted into the entire utterance: "It is (hardly) (very) (much) difficult to write on a grain of rice"; "She buys (her own clothes) (his own clothes) (its own clothes)"; "If he had seen you, he (would have spoken) (would speak) (will have spoken) to you." In the opinion of this reviewer, only the last named type of distractor is allowable, although this renders invalid nearly a third of the test.

The issue is an old one, but can never be dismissed from the testmaker's mind: are the parts which the testee is asked to fit together all to be genuine, though sometimes incompatible, or must he distinguish between genuine and spurious parts as well? Beyond the questions of intellectual integrity and fair play there is the matter of wrong learning by the testee. There is no need to learn a thing wrong in order eventually to learn it right, and it is gratuitous on the part of the testmaker to assume wrong learning by the testee as a matter of course. To ask that such a standard of high-mindedness be applied to this test is merely to ask that all of it be as good as the larger part of it is.

There are some misprints, two of them serious. In Item 132 of the student's booklet the first choice is not accompanied by its code letter A, and for Item 127 the key indicates A as the correct answer; it should be C. In Item 14 there are two possible correct answers, "I hope he will go" and "I hope he would go," both being perfectly acceptable English.

In scoring, one-half of the number of wrong answers is to be deducted from the number right in arriving at a final evaluation. Missing answers are not counted at all. Neither of these facts is mentioned in the instructions to the student, though both are very likely to influence his performance on this or any other test and hence affect the accuracy of measurement.

No table of norms is provided, but the test is said to have been given to hundreds of students from foreign countries. Experience at the American Language Center of the American University has shown that students with scores of 125 or better are ready for college work, those between 100 and 125 need considerable extra training, and those between 40 and 80 need full time instruction in English.

While this test will doubtless serve to separate in a general way those who know English well from those who do not, the impression persists that this could be done with far greater accuracy if the test were based upon a more systematic analysis of the patterns of English, and if it included some work with English sounds—surely a matter of prime importance to those who intend to study in American classrooms.

HERSCHEL T. MANUEL, *Professor of Educational Psychology, The University of Texas, Austin, Texas.*

This test illustrates the type of measuring instrument which is developed to meet a need in a particular situation and then made available to other users without sufficient descriptive material on which the new user can base an independent judgment of its value. The test "has been given to hundreds of students from foreign countries," apparently with satisfactory results.

The test consists of 150 multiple choice items which are for the most part short sentences in which the student is to choose the best of three words or phrases—for example, "They meet (at) (to) (on) eight o'clock." The ability tested is primarily acquaintance with English idioms rather than extent of vocabulary, comprehension of reading material, or understanding of spoken language. Although ability to do college work depends upon much more than ability with the English language, and although ability with the English language is much more than acquaintance with idioms, the mastery of idiomatic usage, in the opinion of the reviewer, is undoubtedly an important variable in itself and an important index of progress toward general mastery of the language.

The method of selecting items (letter from author) was one of "checking all available texts for materials, having our teachers submit possible questions and criticising what we had done." Validity (same source) was based upon a comparison of test results with class scores. No item analyses or validity coefficients are given.

There is no indication in the available material that a method of comparative linguistic analysis such as that used by Lado was used in selecting items. There is, however, a classification of items on the answer sheet under 10 heads—pronouns, nouns, adjectives and adverbs, ellipses, prepositions, word order, verbs, tenses and voice, verbals, and idiomatic vocabulary. Thus, to a certain degree, the test does, as the title suggests, provide an opportunity to discover types of errors. Because of the small number of items in each division no attempt should be made to find part scores, or at least to regard them as reliable. Indeed, the author

makes no suggestion that part scores should be found; he does express an interest in using the results for lesson planning.

The format of the test is good except that perhaps something more should be done to facilitate keeping the right place on the answer sheet. (The reviewer once found himself shifting to a new column on the answer sheet when going to a new page in the test booklet!) The answer sheet is double, having a carbon paper insert which records the student's responses on the second sheet. The second sheet is preprinted to show the correct answers.

The Spearman-Brown split-half reliability (author's letter) is amazingly high (.96, *n* not reported), the range of scores is wide (31–145), and the mean score (103.5) is well below the total possible score. The author gives certain scores which have been found, by "experience at the American Language Center of the American University," to indicate corresponding degrees of preparation for college work.

In summary, the reviewer regards the test as useful in the practical situation for which it was empirically developed, but lacking in published information which would enable other testers to evaluate it for their own situations and use it most profitably. In addition, the reviewer would like to see more attention given to what the test measures as distinguished from the use which may be made of the scores. We need to know more about the relation of idiom mastery to other phases of language ability.

[256]

*English Examinations for Foreign Students. Applicants from non-English language countries for admission to American colleges; 1947–56; 3 booklets; manual ['56]; practice booklet ['47]; norms ['51]; separate answer sheets must be used except with *b;* 10–19 tests, $3.50 each; one set of 12-inch records (78 rpm) provided with orders of 10–50 tests; postpaid; 270(305) minutes in 2 sessions; published for the College Entrance Examination Board; Educational Testing Service. *

a) BOOK 1. 4 scores: reading comprehension, aural comprehension, pronunciation, total; Form VFS; 140(155) minutes.

b) BOOK 2, [ENGLISH COMPOSITION]. Forms A, B ['47, also labeled Form VFS]; no norms; 40(45) minutes.

c) BOOK 3. Title on test is *English Examination for Foreign Students (Including a Test of Non-Verbal Reasoning)* ; 2 scores: scientific vocabulary, nonverbal reasoning; Form VFS; 90(105) minutes.

RALPH BEDELL, *Specialist for Higher Education Programs, United States Office of Education, Washington, D.C.*

The large number of foreign students on our campuses and the still larger numbers to come are challenging some of our best educators to examine English with a new perspective —a view through the eyes of intelligent people whose first language is a language other than English.

The teaching of English as a foreign language presents many pedagogical and practical problems. To watch an intelligent adult struggling for the first time to learn English with its many nuances, its incessant flow of idioms, its casual disregard for grammar, is enough to bring out the best in any teacher. Is it any wonder that the student often turns to us who use English and asks, "Are there no rules?" And perhaps we whose first language is English might ask, "Who among us can say that he has learned English well?"

The trends of the times, nevertheless, bring constant pressure on our friends overseas to learn English. Since World War II, English has become the language of most of the scholars, business men, and officials throughout the free world. To many millions overseas success in learning English is the avenue to becoming well informed. The ability to use and understand English is especially important to keep abreast of modern technology. American colleges and universities are being pressed as never before to meet the English problems of foreign students, and one of the major chapters in any book of American higher education might be the success with which this is being done.

The *English Examination for Foreign Students* is designed to help select those whose English is sufficiently well advanced to permit profitable pursuit of college level courses in which the language of instruction is English. Further, the examination may be of considerable use to teachers of English as a foreign language in adjusting instruction to the needs of students.

The examination measures silent reading and auditory comprehension. The former is tested through sections on English vocabulary, recognition of correct and incorrect grammatical forms, and comprehension of sentences and short passages in English. Most of the vocabulary, sentence, and paragraph items sample words and ideas from everyday experience. There is a separate section, however, on scientific vocabulary, which includes words from elementary mathematics, physics, and chemistry. The large number of foreign students wishing to study the sciences in English speaking

colleges and universities makes this section especially significant. The items testing paragraph comprehension place emphasis upon reading for detail and understanding of ideas. The paragraphs are short samples of those found in the first year of college history, social studies, and literature.

Auditory comprehension is tested through written questions based upon spoken passages played on phonograph records. The 16 spoken passages vary in length from about one quarter of a minute to about two minutes. Eleven paragraphs are spoken in a male voice and five in a female voice. At the conclusion of each paragraph the student is given time to mark multiple choice items which test recall of detail, understanding of ideas, or general significance of the paragraph. The number of such test items for each paragraph varies from one to six depending upon the length and content of the paragraph. The student is permitted to listen to the spoken paragraph only once and the test is so arranged that he cannot see the questions on a paragraph until after he has heard the paragraph spoken. After listening to a paragraph, the student answers the questions on it before proceeding to the next paragraph in the test.

Subordinate to the reading and auditory sections is a test purporting to measure the student's pronunciation of English words through his recognition of rhymes and correct accentuation. The student is asked to indicate whether or not the same sound is found in such pairs of words as *won—sun, did—ride,* and *air—bear.* Accentuation is tested by numbering the syllables of words and asking the student to indicate the number of the syllable most heavily accented. While these are strikingly clever devices for obtaining paper and pencil measures of pronunciation, tests of this type may at best be expected only to identify those whose pronunciation is very poor or who cannot relate their pronunciation to the printed word; that is, those who pass this test may still be in need of improvement in pronunciation.

The Test of Non-Verbal Reasoning, is obviously not intended as a measure of English attainment, but is designed to be helpful in determining the student's aptitude for school or college work independent of his proficiency in English. This test measures the ability of a student to determine the relationship that exists among a group of four line diagrams and select from a second group of diagrams the one that fits in with the relationship found in the first group.

The examination may be administered by anyone trained in the use of group tests of educational achievement. The publisher provides instructions for administration which are unusually complete and are clearly and precisely written. As some foreign students may have difficulty in following directions in English, and may not be generally familiar with testing procedures, it is desirable to have one or more proctors to assist the supervisor of the examination. The publisher recommends one proctor for each 20 students.

All persons who administer this examination will need to give it careful study in advance. The publisher recommends that each student who is to take the examination receive the practice book at least one week before the examination date with the direction to study it carefully. The practice book contains an answer sheet and questions like the ones in the examination. Correct answers are given to permit the student to check his work. The practice book does not contain any reference to the essay or auditory portions of the examination. This is not considered a serious fault, however, as the student will almost certainly have greater need for the very useful practice on other sections of the examination.

For administration of the aural comprehension section, it is necessary to have an electric phonograph that will play records at 78 revolutions per minute. The publishers provide a special phonograph needle with the records, and the use of this needle is recommended. The recordings are of good quality and can be understood when played on an ordinary phonograph. It is necessary, however, to have an advance tryout of the phonograph in the room where the examination is to be given to make sure the acoustics of the room are such that all students can hear the records distinctly.

The examination is published in one form only, except for the essay portion which is in two forms. Those who administer the examination will therefore need to exercise special care to see that no copy of it gets into unauthorized hands.

The scoring of the examination is objective except for the essay portion. The student marks an answer sheet which may be a copy of that supplied by the publisher, or an IBM or other similar answer sheet. With the exception of the essay portion, each copy of the examination may be reused by providing replacement answer sheets.

The publisher furnishes norms for each section of the examination (except for the essay portion) and for a composite score on reading comprehension, aural comprehension, and punctuation. The norms are based upon 507 foreign students tested at universities in the United States and abroad. There is no further description of these students. No data on the reliability and validity of the examination are available. Users of the examination are advised to conduct their own standardization and validation research.

The examination, especially those portions that deal with English, may have considerable use for groups of foreign students who are currently enrolled in colleges or universities in addition to those who are applicants for college entrance. A skilled teacher of English for foreign students may be able to make a number of inferences from responses to the questions of the examination that will be helpful in teaching. Pending further research, the examination should not, however, be considered suitable for individual counseling. The absence of sufficient validating data on the Test of Non-Verbal Reasoning makes this portion, especially, of little value unless an institution can obtain research on the predictive value of this test for its own students. Institutions lacking such research will be well advised to use one of the well standardizing nonverbal tests otherwise available for which validation data are available.

The examination originally was sponsored by the College Entrance Examination Board and the United States Department of State. It was first administered in 1947, and has found limited use since that time in colleges and universities, some divisions of the Armed Forces, and foreign affiliates of industrial corporations. It is a great pity that a test which is so well constructed and for which there is so much need should not be sufficiently well standardized and validated to warrant much wider use.

JOHN A. COX, JR., *Research Psychologist, Personnel Laboratory, Wright Air Development Center, Lackland AFB, Texas.*

This battery of tests gives every appearance of being a well planned and carefully prepared set of measures. It is rather complete, giving information about the examinee's ability to read English, compose in English, and comprehend spoken English, and about his intellectual level. The printed materials are well organized and editorially clean. The material presented orally is equally well prepared. There is no doubt that these tests were prepared by experts in the field of test construction.

Apart from the conversion tables, there is no indication of statistical analysis. No reliability estimates are presented. No validity information is given. In fact, the user is told that no validity studies are planned. Rather he is advised to validate the instrument for his own use. At least the publishers do not make unsubstantiated claims of validity for the instrument. There is no mention of the interrelationships among the several part scores, leaving the user to guess (or determine for himself) the utility of two or more part scores combined. This seems a waste of the data collected on the normative sample.

Strictly on the basis of subjective judgment, this examination bears the marks of a fine instrument. The user must be prepared to undertake validation studies and intercorrelation analysis along with the computation of reliability estimates before he will have the commonly accepted objective criteria to evaluate the instrument.

CHARLES R. LANGMUIR, *Director of Special Projects, The Psychological Corporation, New York, New York.*

Neither a foreign student adviser nor a foreign student is ever likely to forget the experience of this examination. A week prior to the scheduled testing the student works through nine pages of instructions and sample test questions. On the day of the test he appears for two sessions, totaling 4 hours and 50 minutes of working time plus incidental administration time.

In the first 60 minutes he is presented with Section A (Reading Comprehension), consisting of 35 vocabulary opposites, 10 vocabulary completion, and 20 two-choice usage items, followed by 25 paragraph reading questions based on seven passages. Section B (Aural Comprehension) uses the next 80 minutes. The student listens to 16 recorded passages and answers 50 four-choice questions. The paragraphs are spoken by several voices at rates varying from 130 to 160 words per minute. The simplest statement consists of two sentences, totaling 33 words, spoken in 15 seconds. The longest passage, between 300 and 400 words in length, is spoken in 2 minutes. The material has a descriptive-literary-philosophical character. After listening to a passage, the student turns the page to find the questions, which may vary in number from one to six. The first session ends with Section C, a 20-minute test of "pronunciation comprehension," consisting of 30 true-false rhymes and 30 words to mark for syllabic accent.

The second session opens with Section D, an essay part. The student has 15 minutes in which to write one or two sentences responsive to each of four statements and a related question. In the next 25 minutes he writes an essay of about 125 words on an assigned topic. The testing is concluded with a 30-minute test of 60 scientific vocabulary items (Section E) and a 60-minute nonverbal reasoning test (Section F) composed of two timed parts, 30 minutes for 30 three-by-three Penrose-Raven-type matrices, and 30 minutes for 60 two-choice figure classification items.

This is an impressive amount of business to find out whether a foreign student can read English and understand spoken English at a level sufficient to meet the demands of American colleges. Unfortunately, the examiner has a lot more work to accomplish before he discovers that he is not going to find out. First, he has to score four sides of two special hand scoring answer sheets, writing the scores in widely separated, unlabeled spaces on opposite sides of the answer sheets. The scores for Sections A, B, and C are then added, and the composite score is recorded on the front side of the first answer sheet. The five part scores and the composite score for the first three parts can then be looked up on six pages of conversion tables to get the six converted scores. These are presumably written down somewhere not identified. There are no scoring boxes of any kind on the answer sheets. These converted scores are now looked up in another table to get the percentile ranks, which are based on "foreign students tested at universities in this country and abroad" (n = 507). There is no other relevant information, except possibly that the converted scores are derived by a linear equating to an arbitrary scale of the raw scores of 119 foreign students tested somewhere. The publisher says the converted scores are "considerably more meaningful and much easier for interpretive work."

The examiner will reach this point much sooner if he is thoughtful enough to invent some way to register the key on the answer sheet. The keys supplied the purchaser are made by an unsteady hand—or by a steady hand with unsteady scissors—out of pieces of manila folders. Lines are ruled in pencil. The labeling is pen-and-ink, holograph. Scoring directions are omitted. If the examiner is planning a repeat performance with the reusable test booklets, he should design his own answer sheets and keys from scratch. The publisher says that replacement answer sheets are not available. The publisher recommends standard IBM answer sheets "or any other appropriate type devised or secured by the institution." It had better be devised by the institution since no standard IBM answer sheet will be in any way appropriate.

The second session involves the examiner in other difficulties. The essay section is not scorable. The publisher supplies no information, not even examples for normative or scale comparison, but does make one suggestion: "that the consensus of opinion of a group of readers be used in determining this score, but ETS leaves the method of scoring and the use of this score entirely to the discretion of the test user."

A scientific vocabulary test might have some utility in advising foreign students, especially if the choice of items were based on their specific differential content validity. The publisher offers no information about the ideas which generated this collection of science vocabulary. No rational basis is evident from an inspection of the items.

The final hour of the second session is given over to the nonverbal reasoning test. It is clearly not a part of the English examination, but is given with it "because most colleges would like an indication of the applicant's general reasoning ability." The normative and validity information required for such use by most colleges turns out to be some percentiles computed from 497 "foreign students tested at universities in this country and abroad." Who, where, level of education, age, sex, etc., are not mentioned.

About 200 words on the interpretation of scores accompanies the percentile table. The statements imply a powerful validity, e.g.,

"Scores of less than 40 on Reading Comprehension, Aural Comprehension, or Pronunciation suggest the need for special work in these areas," and "Candidates with (composite) scores above 50 will probably not be handicapped in their college work because of an English deficiency." No data in support of any validity statement are supplied, not even the intercorrelation of the parts, the reliabilities of the scores, or group differences of any kind. No follow-up studies are cited. In fact, it is not even known what kind of performance would be demonstrated by typical students whose native language is English. This situation is not likely to improve. The publisher states, "No additional normative studies are contemplated."

The test was put together immediately after the war with financial support of the State Department, and was published in its present form in 1947 by the College Entrance Examination Board for restricted rental. In 1951 it was made available by sale of materials to institutions and with the tacit understanding that the strict security conventional with College Board materials would be preserved. The materials supplied to current purchasers are apparently remainders from the original stock. The three test booklets are printed by offset on poor quality paper from a mediocre typescript much reduced. The reading paragraphs, for example, are printed in lines 7 inches long and packed 8 lines to the inch. The recorded material is presented on eight sides of four 12-inch discs, to be played at 78 rpm. The records are not packaged for storage. The pressings received for review were substandard in every respect.

[257]

English Language Test for Foreign Students. Applicants from non-English language countries for admission into American colleges; 1951; Form A; tentative norms; separate answer sheets must be used; 25¢ per test; 5¢ per answer sheet; $1 per set of scoring stencils; $1.30 per specimen set; postage extra; 120-(125) minutes; Robert Lado; George Wahr Publishing Co. *

REFERENCES

1–2. See 4:234.
3. LADO, ROBERT. "Improvements in Foreign Language Tests." *Univ Mich Sch Ed B* 24:3–5 O '52. *

JOHN A. COX, JR., *Research Psychologist, Personnel Laboratory, Wright Air Development Center, Lackland AFB, Texas.*

According to the author, this test measures "control of the English language by foreign students." The test contains 134 items of four types and requires no more than two hours' time to administer. The first part (40 items) is labeled "Structure"; the second (54 items), "Pronunciation." In both these parts the questions are in the form of multiple completion type items. In this form three alternatives are given, any combination of which, including "none," may be correct. The second part also contains 14 items with four and five choices consisting of syllabicated words whose accented syllables must be identified. The third part (40 items) is labeled "Vocabulary," and the items are, once again, in the multiple completion form. The format of the test is good and the booklet is editorially clean. Excellent sample items are presented separately for each part.

Special answer sheets are used and must be hand scored. Scoring stencils are provided which should make obtaining the raw scores (number correct) quite easy. A table for converting the raw scores to "per cent correct" is printed on the back page of the answer sheet.

The manual contains simple and satisfactory directions for administering the test and for scoring. There is a bare mention of using the time taken to finish as a separate score. The validity and reliability of this score are not discussed. A chance-half reliability coefficient is reported as .95 for the per cent correct score (based on 41 cases). Validity is implied by a table giving behavior descriptions of candidates scoring at various per cent levels. Thus, a testee earning a score falling between 90 to 100 per cent is described as follows: "This student is carrying a full time load and doing very good work in freshman English." This table is also based on 41 cases. The author implies that his test possesses "content" validity, but he gives no direct evidence of this. As evidence of validity, he presents the fact that this test correlates .89 with the average of scores from three other tests, two of which are "aural." This seems to be a type of construct validity. No information is given as to the size or character of the sample on which the relationship was found. This critic feels that more useful information would have been obtained by correlating scores from this test with those from each of the other three tests separately. The author's position that performance on the test is highly related to aural English proficiency possibly would be better supported by such data. Certainly, the author's position that this "silent test" measures "aural control" is still open to question.

In general, this test appears to be a satisfac-

tory instrument for measuring proficiency in the comprehension of written English, but the evidence presented by the author that it is such an instrument is very weak. In truth, there are no norms given. There is a minimum of "validity" information, none of which is of the predictive variety. What little information is given is based on an undefined sample of 41 cases. The author's statement that the test has been thoroughly pretested should be verified in the manual by presenting results of the "pretesting." On the basis of the information given, the *English Language Test for Foreign Students* can be recommended for use only in an experimental way, not for any practical purposes such as selection of students for a training program.

For a review by Clarence E. Turner, see 4:234.

[258]
★An English Reading Test for Students of English as a Foreign Language. College entrants; 1956; 1 form; no data on reliability; 10 or more tests, 10¢ each; 18¢ per specimen set; postpaid; 30(35) minutes; Harold V. King and Russell N. Campbell; Washington Publications. *

RALPH BEDELL, *Specialist for Higher Education Programs, United States Office of Education, Washington, D.C.*

The test, developed in connection with the authors' work in the Costa Rican-American Cultural Center, measures certain aspects of silent reading comprehension in English. It is intended for use with students whose first language is other than English. Until further research is available this test, at best, is likely to be no more than a minor aid to a good teacher.

The test consists of 50 multiple choice items, of which 32 measure primarily paragraph comprehension. The remainder appear to measure ability to comprehend very short sentences, but they probably measure vocabulary also. The paragraph comprehension items measure principally reading for detailed information. Throughout the test, a student may refer from questions to paragraphs; consequently, scores may be more indicative of ability to search out details in a paragraph than of ability to recall what has been read. All items are concerned with common everyday words, expressions, and ideas; there is no attempt to measure any aspect of specialized subject matter fields. *

The test may be administered by any teacher. The printed directions are so abbreviated that the student may not fully understand how he is to answer the questions unless the teacher enlarges upon them. The 30-minute time limit is designed to cut off extremely slow students rather than to enforce speed as an element of the test.

Scoring is done by multiplying the number of correct answers by 2 to obtain a percentage of the total items answered correctly. A key is provided. An interpretive table is given which describes scores for various percentages. For example, those who score in the range 70–80 per cent are said to "have no trouble in reading newspapers and magazines. May need a dictionary to read literary material."

The authors state that the interpretations are "based on the scores obtained by students on all levels of ability in the experimental try-outs." This quotation is the total published information available on the tryout group. There is not available in any published source the number or level of students included. No distribution of scores is available. Therefore, this test is without norms in the generally accepted sense. Although the authors state that the test includes "only items of the highest validity and reliability," no published evidence on either of these points is available.

The test is likely to be useful to teachers in institutions that have a sufficient number of students to establish their own normative data and research on validity. The extent to which the test would be useful would be revealed by these data and research studies. The absence of an alternative form greatly increases the chance that the test will be invalidated by copies getting into unauthorized hands or by knowledge of the items becoming too generally known.

JOHN A. COX, JR., *Research Psychologist, Personnel Laboratory, Wright Air Development Center, Lackland AFB, Texas.*

The 50-item test is proposed as a measure of reading skill among foreign students. The first 18 questions are multiple choice items testing knowledge of vocabulary and ability to select words and phrases which are logical in terms of the context given. Each is in the form of an incomplete sentence as a stem with four alternatives to complete the stem correctly. The other 32 questions are reading comprehension type items based on five paragraphs. The test is not intended as a speed test, but a time limit of 30 minutes is recommended "to insure comparable results." The answers are to be marked

in the test booklets. A folding key is provided which should make hand scoring simple and fast. The score is per cent correct.

While taking the test, this reviewer found several faulty items. One item depends on the word "defray" and another on the word "rift." These words seem rather esoteric for most English usage, but they may fit into the scheme of difficulty the authors used in item selection. Another question seems to have two perfectly good answers. Answers to some of the reading comprehension items do not require ever having seen the paragraph. Other items require reasoning from information given in the paragraph, a factor which is not primarily a matter of comprehension. At least one item (Item 22) is ambiguous.

No manual is furnished. Information about the test is printed on the back of the front and back covers of the test booklet. No instructions are given for administration. No statistical analysis is presented. No reliability estimates are reported. Validity is implied in the form of descriptions of language and reading behavior to be expected from persons earning various "per cent right" scores. However, no information as to how these descriptions were arrived at is given. Norms are in the same condition. There is simply a statement that "over five hundred" students were used as the basis for the behavioral descriptions. There is also an implication that some sort of item analysis was performed. The authors say that "only items of the highest validity and reliability" were included, but no description of the techniques used in determining item validities and reliabilities is given. It is recommended that 70 (per cent right) be used as a cutoff score for entry into college. Nothing is said of the relationship between the two parts or item types.

In conclusion, this test seems too short for use as a screening device for college entrance. An instrument for diagnosis in areas of English proficiency would need to be longer and more reliable than one for selection, so this test should not be used for diagnosis. In an experimental situation (such as in a thesis where scores would be used for information but not as a basis for making practical decisions that would affect individuals) the need for accuracy is not so important. This test might be used in such an experimental program. Any other use would require that it be lengthened and the items made cleaner with respect to the points made above. A manual providing administrative directions and properly reported normative information, reliability data, and validity data would be most useful.

[259]

★**English Usage Test for Non-Native Speakers of English.** Non-native speakers of English; 1955–57; Forms A ['55], B ['57]; directions sheet for Form A ['55], directions sheet for Form B ['57]; no data on reliability; no norms; distribution is restricted to the International Cooperation Administration or the International Educational Exchange Service of the U.S. Department of State; separate answer sheets must be used; Form A: 60(65) minutes, Form B: 75(80) minutes; A. L. Davis and Kenneth Croft; Washington Publications. *

[260]

★**Examination in Structure (English as a Foreign Language).** Entering foreign college freshmen; 1947; Forms A, B, C; mimeographed directions sheet ['47]; no data on reliability; no norms; separate answer sheets must be used; 15¢ per test; 3¢ per answer sheet; 50¢ per scoring stencil; $1 per specimen set; postage extra; 60(65) minutes; English Language Institute, University of Michigan; distributed by Wahr's Book Store. *

[261]

*Test of Aural Comprehension.** Applicants from non-English language countries for admission into American colleges; 1946–57; Forms A, B, C ('46); separate answer sheets must be used; 10¢ per test; 2¢ per answer sheet; 50¢ per set of scoring stencils; $1.50 per manual ('57); $1 per specimen set; postage extra; (40) minutes; Robert Lado; distributed by George Wahr Publishing Co. *

HERSCHEL T. MANUEL, *Professor of Educational Psychology, The University of Texas, Austin, Texas.*

This test consists of 60 three-choice items. The examiner reads a sentence (sometimes two or more sentences) and the student marks a picture, a phrase, or a sentence to indicate his understanding of what is read. For example, in one of the more difficult items the examiner reads the sentence "Had John been sincere he would have told me the truth," and the student marks one of the three sentences: "(*a*) John was sincere; (*b*) John told the truth; (*c*) John did not tell the truth."

The test is said to measure "understanding of spoken English by persons whose native language is not English." Apparently this understanding of spoken English is regarded as an index of a student's "control of English" in general. This is in contrast to the Davis *Diagnostic Test for Students of English as a Second Language,* in which the knowledge of written English idioms is the basis of measurement. The point is not that Lado and Davis think they are measuring the same aspects of language

ability but that they use different approaches to accomplish the same purpose—the measurement of the adequacy of the English of foreign students. Idioms are not lacking in Lado's test, but the student is required only to indicate his understanding of the language used and not to judge (as in the Davis test) which of different expressions is best.

Instead of taking samples of English at random, Lado has constructed items which present special comprehension difficulties to foreign students. Thus a foreign student might have difficulty distinguishing the sounds "sixty" and "sixteen," interpreting a phrase such as "tear up a paper," or interpreting a preposition like "on," which may have meanings somewhat different from those of the corresponding word in the native language. It would be interesting to know how the results of such a test correlate with the results of the usual test of reading. Although this information is not given, the reviewer believes that the approach to testing through a comparative analysis of different languages is a promising one. Lado's *Linguistics Across Cultures*[1] is a key to understanding this point of view.

The format of the test is good and the test is easy to score. "Proficiency" norms and "progress" norms, stated in simple terms, reflect experience with the test in the English Language Institute.

Data on reliability and validity are rather meager. The coefficient of reliability based upon administration of Forms A and C to the same students (.87) and the split-half reliability of Form A (.88) are satisfactory for a test of 60 items, but low enough to suggest the possibility of considerable error in measuring an individual student if only one form is used. The validity coefficient of .85 (*n* not given) resulting from the correlation of test scores and composite teacher judgments is good. It should be pointed out, however, that the statistics appear to be based solely upon results achieved in the English Language Institute where the test was developed. The test consumer would like to know how the test would perform in another setting.

It is clear that more information is needed for an independent evaluation of the test and for optimum use of the results. From the standpoint of test construction one may question why

1 LADO, ROBERT. *Linguistics Across Cultures: Applied Linguistics for Language Teachers.* Ann Arbor, Mich.: University of Michigan Press, 1957. Pp. 141.

the last 10 items in Form B are much longer than corresponding items in the other forms, whether the items chosen for the test reflect equally the learning difficulties of students of different mother tongues, and why the raw scores are converted to percentages of items correct rather than to standard scores or percentiles. However, in spite of the questions which may be raised, the reviewer believes that the test will be useful in judging the ability of foreign students to work in English speaking colleges and that it represents a significant approach to the evaluation of this ability. He hopes that the author will develop additional tests on the basis of comparative linguistic analysis, and that the relation of these tests to other tests and to general English proficiency will be shown.

CLARENCE E. TURNER, *Professor of Romance Languages, Rutgers University, New Brunswick, New Jersey.*

This test is devised to measure understanding of spoken English by persons not natives of that language, and has been developed largely in working with and for foreign born students in American academic institutions. Unlike the same author's *English Language Test for Foreign Students,* it does not seek either to measure pronunciation or to sample range of vocabulary. The present test may be thought of very roughly as an elaboration for the ear of the excellent structure portion of the other test, with the inclusion of a few items testing sound discrimination, and of a larger number of items testing not range of vocabulary but comprehension of vocabulary signals embodied in two-word verbs, prefixes, and the like.

There can be little doubt that the student's status will have been pretty clearly determined by the time he has finished following Mrs. Smith, Mary, John, and Charles through their deceptively basic activities. He will have met many of the characteristic problems which offer little difficulty to the native speaker of familiar English but which torment the learner of that idiom. He will have dealt with progressive tenses, contractions, *do* and *going* as auxiliaries, concealed negation, concealed subordination, contrary-to-fact conditions with negative result, nouns used as adjectives, *not any* with elements interposed, two-word verbs, adjectives and adverbs, auxiliary *had* with participle understood, and so on through a long list of

genuine problems ingeniously pinpointed. He will have shown whether he can catch the operative *when?* or *who?* in a question containing a few natural but distracting irrelevancies. He will have had to sense interrogation from structure in a question read with falling inflection. He will have sorted out *sinking* from *singing* and *thinking,* and *milk chocolate* from *chocolate milk.* The last two items alone would make a fair little pocket test.

The author has again shown that he is a keen analyst of language and a shrewd maker of tests. One can quarrel only with a few details. The Charles of the examiner's manual, evidently a sneaky fellow, turns up as Carlos in the test booklet in several items of Forms B and C. Even decent Mr. Smith passes as Dr. Smith in the test booklet, Form B, Part 2, Item 17. If we are told, "The man's horse is crossing the river," does it necessarily follow that the owner is not on the horse's back? If not, Form B, Part 1, Item 15, has two possible answers. "The boy is giving the rat a cat" pinpoints English by isolating it utterly from experience, but it is scarcely a fair item in a test where no other sentence does comparable violence to common sense. Finally, there is inconsistency concerning the flashback presentation of past action. In Form A, Part 1, Item 17, "The girl used the telephone" is not to be matched with the picture of a girl using a telephone, but rather with that of one walking away from the phone. "The girl has used the telephone" would seem a better verbalization of this. Again, in Form B, Part 1, Item 5, "Where did he put his hat? He put it on the table" is to be matched with the picture of a man walking away from hat and table, rather than with a flashback of the action being performed. But in Form C, Part 1, Item 16, "He opened the door of his room" is supposed to match a picture of a man actually engaged in opening a door. Here there is admittedly no other possible matching, but the items are inconsistent with each other, and the whole matter is confusing. How does one visualize the pastness of a past action? Is there a valid general visual difference between "She used the phone" and "She is using the phone"? Perhaps tense cannot be shown pictorially with any accuracy in cases like these.

There is fascination and instruction in this test for users or lovers of language, and anyone requiring an instrument to determine whether a handicap exists in the aural comprehension of English need look no further.

[262]
★**Test of Aural Perception in English for Latin-American Students.** Latin-American students of English; 1947–57; 1 form ('57); separate answer sheets must be used; 4¢ per answer sheet ('47) ; $1.50 per manual ('57) ; postage extra; (60) minutes; Robert Lado; distributed by George Wahr Publishing Co. *

FRENCH

[263]
*College Entrance Examination Board Achievement Test in French.** Candidates for college entrance with 2–4 years high school; 1901–58; for more complete information, see 599; IBM; 60(80) minutes; program administered by Educational Testing Service for the College Entrance Examination Board. *

REFERENCES

1–7. See 4:237.
8. COLLEGE ENTRANCE EXAMINATION BOARD. *Foreign Languages: A Description of the College Board Tests in French, German, Latin, and Spanish.* Princeton, N.J.: the Board, April 1954. Pp. 31. * (PA 29:1444)
9. EVENSON, A. B., AND SMITH, D. E. "A Study of Matriculation in Alberta." *Alberta J Ed Res* 4:67–83 Je '58. *

For a review by Walter V. Kaulfers of earlier forms, see 4:237.

[264]
★**College Entrance Examination Board Advanced Placement Examination: French.** High school seniors desiring credit for college level courses; 1954–58; for more complete information, see 600; 2 scores : language, literary; IBM in part; 3 parts in 2 booklets; 180(200) minutes; program administered by Educational Testing Service for the College Entrance Examination Board. *

[265]
★**Cooperative French Listening Comprehension Test.** 2–5 semesters high school or college; 1955; Forms A, B; $12.50 per tape recording (3¾ or 7½ ips) ; $3.25 per 25 answer booklets; 25¢ per scoring stencil; $1 per manual; postage extra; 30(40) minutes; Nelson Brooks; Cooperative Test Division, Educational Testing Service. *

REFERENCE

1. SPAULDING, GERALDINE. "A Brief Study of the Cooperative French Listening Comprehension Test." *Ed Rec B* 68:61–3 Jl '56. * (PA 31:8847)

WALTER V. KAULFERS, *Professor of Education, University of Illinois, Urbana, Illinois.*

This relatively advanced standardized test of ability to understand spoken French can be administered either orally or by means of tape recordings. It claims to serve four purposes : to help determine a student's general ability in aural comprehension, to help locate weaknesses requiring attention, to provide a basis for ability grouping in French, and to afford examinees an objective measure of their relative achievement in comparison with that of other students.

To serve these purposes, the test is divided into four parts totaling 42 items of the 5-answer multiple choice type. The 10 items in Part 1 involve phonetic discrimination. In his answer booklet the examinee indicates which of five statements he hears spoken either by the examiner reading from the manual or by the voice recorded on tape. The second part requires the listener to check the best response, out of five in his answer booklet, to each of 10 questions posed in French.

Part 3 is essentially a 10-item completion test. The examinee indicates which of five answers best completes a statement or sentence spoken in the foreign language. The last part consists of 12 questions involving the comprehension of passages of 100–175 words in length. Here the examinee is required to select the best of five answers to each question.

The entire test, including the oral directions to students, is in French. The directions for each part are also printed in French in the answer booklet, so that the examinee can follow them as they are delivered orally. However, since the recorded version sometimes varies from the printed version of the directions (e.g., *je lirai* on tape versus *on lira* in print), some students may find these discrepancies momentarily distracting. Only if the script is to be read from the manual instead of broadcast is a knowledge of French absolutely essential on the part of the examiner.

The reliability coefficient of .87 indicates that the test is more accurate for the purposes which it claims to serve than "homemade" tests are likely to be. Correlations between teacher ratings of their pupils' ability to understand spoken French and scores made by the pupils on the test range from .42 to .79. There is reason to believe that the tape recorded version is much more valid for examinees who have frequently heard French spoken by different individuals than it is for students who have rarely heard anyone but their teacher speak the language.

The recordings, which use standard Parisian French, are generally satisfactory. Except in Part 4, where a woman speaker is introduced in the dialogue passages, the same male voice continues throughout. The delivery is clear and at a moderate pace. In a few cases elisions occur where a native speaking at this deliberate rate might not be likely to make them. Occasionally, the attempt to speak clearly does not necessarily facilitate comprehension. The French *sonner*, for example, comes out sounding very much like *son nez*. These limitations, as well as the discrepancies between the printed and oral directions, however, are minor. It should be easy for the publishers to correct them on the master tape. Examiners can avoid them by reading the script from the manual instead of using the recordings. In this case, however, comparison of results with the norms will not be fair, since norms are based on administration of the test via recordings exclusively.

Scoring is done by means of a stencil. The test is not scorable by machine. Because raw scores must be totaled and then translated into converted scores, a double checking of tests by two people is recommended.

Norms are available for public secondary schools, independent secondary schools, and colleges. High school students who have had less than three years of French, however, are likely to find the test discouragingly difficult unless they have been enrolled in intensive courses giving special attention to the spoken language. Because over 80 per cent of secondary school students take only two years of French, the examination will probably be useful primarily for purposes of advanced guidance-placement in college.

A less advanced test is needed to appraise the increasing amount of oral work being done in the first and second years of high school French. At this level the directions and choice of answers should probably be in English rather than in the foreign language. Otherwise the examination would be almost as much a test of comprehension in silent reading as of ability to understand the spoken language. To a certain extent this criticism applies even to the present relatively advanced form of the test.

If the scope of the present examination were extended somewhat it could be used as an aid in vocational placement. To this end a greater variety of voices and at least the commoner dialectal variations should be included. To this end also, comparison norms obtained from native speakers in France (e.g., by administering the recorded test to 100 students of the *première classe* in three or four widely separated *lycées* or *collèges*) would be desirable. The comparison norms could serve as a life criterion in answering the question "How far have the examinees progressed toward understanding spoken French as well as educated natives?"

It is an unfortunate limitation of foreign language tests published to date that their norms allow for little but an intramural interpretation. They do not tell us how well the examinee is qualified to get along in an exclusively foreign language environment. At best they usually tell us only whether the student has "covered" enough, or been exposed enough, in previous courses to make him eligible to sit in a more advanced classroom. Although the *Cooperative French Listening Comprehension Test* comes much closer to being a real-life performance test than most achievement examinations produced to date, the limitations noted in the preceding paragraphs still prevent it from fulfilling this qualification completely.

KATHLEEN N. PERRET, *Interpreter, Department of Conference Services, Interpretation Division, United Nations, New York, New York.*

The testing of aural comprehension has been a vexed question ever since the inception of the standardized testing movement, and while the difficulties have been attributable in part to technical problems, the general attitude of the public toward foreign languages has also accounted in no small measure for the dearth of aural comprehension tests. Fortunately, the development of disc and tape recordings has opened up vast horizons in the testing field at a time when it is more important than ever before to verify actual achievement and to ensure that the schools are doing their job properly.

The *Cooperative French Listening Comprehension Test,* on tape, came like a breath of fresh air as the reviewer read the scripts through. It has so many virtues that it seems carping to pick up the relatively minor shortcomings, and the criticisms that follow should be read with this comment in mind.

The test includes four types of listening situation: phonetic discrimination, comprehension of isolated questions, sentence completion, and comprehension of conversation and conversational narrative as contained in four passages running from 50 to 75 seconds in length. After the instructions are read out, the tape is started and the test begins. From this moment on, the entire material, questions and answers, is in French. Before starting on the questions, the speaker first reads an introductory passage that is largely a restatement of the directions on the cover page so that the student has about 2 minutes to accustom his ear to the voice. Throughout the test the answers are all of the multiple choice type.

The Examiner's Manual, a 28-page booklet, gives ample statistical and historical background, as well as copious directions for administration and scoring. Presented in a smart kit with scoring key and explanatory leaflets, it also contains the complete script for the two forms, so that the test may be given "live" if necessary.

The phonetics of French probably offer more difficulty to the English speaking student than any other European language. Obviously, the student must be trained to distinguish between *il veut* and *ils veulent,* or between *allais* and *allez,* or between *je, j'ai* and *j'y,* to name some typical cases, and the 10 questions in Part 1 should give definite indication of the weaknesses or strengths of the student's grasp of fundamental French sounds. This is a particularly difficult type of question to construct, for not only must the decoy responses be plausible but they must offer a sequence of sounds reasonably similar to that of the correct response. At the same time, they should not degenerate into a pure vocabulary test, the common flaw in earlier tests. Item 7 in Form B, where some valid distractors might have been built on *entendre,* is thus too limited in its decoys. On the other hand, Item 2 in Form A, "Elle a quitté la cuisine," with decoys based on *quitte, quitta,* and *quittait* in various combinations with *la cuisine* and *la cousine,* is a good example of the best items in Part 1.

The first part of the test consists largely of phrases or very short sentences. Parts 2 and 3, which consist of sentences of varying length, provide a useful transition to the lengthy material in Part 4. The difference in approach in Parts 2 and 3, apart from purely functional considerations, serves to enliven the material and exploit the element of spontaneous recall. There are some items in these two parts, however, which are open to technical criticism. In Form A, Items 27 and 29 may depend largely on vocabulary. In particular, Item 29, which reads, "J'entends sonner. Je décroche le récepteur et je dis...." uses one key word which is at the very top of the Vander Beke list (*décrocher*) and one (*récepteur*) which does not appear in the list at all. The key word *dérapa*

in Item 30 does not appear in the Vander Beke list either. The same comment applies to Item 24 in Form B, where the key word is *contrôleur.* Otherwise the items are varied in tone and style and reflect an awareness of the commonest types of student error.

Part 4, consisting of four passages, clearly bears the stamp of contemporary conversational style. Interestingly enough, much of the material has been selected from Voice of America broadcasts, although two passages in Form A and one in Form B are taken from contemporary books and publications. Each form contains one historical-cultural narrative, one purely conversational passage, one personal anecdote or personal experience passage, and one travelogue narrative. Both forms use a male voice for two passages, a male and female voice for the conversational passage, and a female voice for the travelogue or cultural-type narrative. The voices are extremely clear and typical in their pronunciation and intonation.

Part 4 offers a considerable range of difficulty. Technically, the construction of the responses and the distractors in this part seems weaker than in any other part of the test. For example, in Form A, four decoys for Item 40 will be automatically eliminated if the student knows the answer to Item 42, while three decoys for Item 41 can be eliminated in the light of the answer to Item 40. A certain amount of inference might enter into the responses to Items 31 and 32 and to Item 39, in view of the responses required for Items 37 and 38. In Form B, the only negative response among the decoys for Item 33 happens to be the correct one, and the response marked as correct for Item 35 is open to question. Lastly, Item 40 is not quite fair because the only clear indication of the correct answer comes in the introduction to the passage which is read but once, while everything else is read twice.

As a general comment on style, it must be said that some of the language, although grammatically correct, smacks of translation from English; but, apart from this and certain minor errors, the test as a whole is impressive, particularly when set against the previous work done in the field. The two forms are, according to the publisher, comparable in range of difficulty and content. It is the opinion of the reviewer that Form A, particularly in Part 4, is somewhat easier than Form B.

Few of the earlier aural comprehension tests

in any language were divorced to any considerable degree, if at all, from the visual approach and, on rereading now, they have a slightly archaic air. A notable exception to this is Part I of the *Lundeberg-Tharp Audition Test in French,* Part I (on phonetic accuracy); although it consists largely of words rather than phrases, thus simplifying the problem, many of the decoys are nevertheless extremely well chosen. The remainder of the test, however, is not so advanced in content or technique. The *Columbia Research Bureau Aural French Test,* despite the highly literary nature of many of the items, is interesting in that it includes pictures, a device that has many obvious advantages and might be further explored in testing aural comprehension.

In preparing an aural comprehension test, many authorities feel it is better to use the literary vocabulary characteristic of classroom texts. Others argue that, even with the usual textbook, enough vocabulary commonly used in conversation can be extracted to make a useful test. This reviewer rather thinks that what is needed is not a new and different course of study but more imagination in devising stimulating tests that will present the material available in current textbooks in a lighter and more contemporary style. In that respect, the test under review is a shining example.

Today there is a growing realization of the importance of teaching the student to speak as well as to read and write a language. This will not be satisfactorily accomplished in this country, however, until American schools begin to achieve the type of results obtained in European and British institutions. This means that, on the very first day of the first semester of French, teachers must begin developing the ability to speak and must use English themselves only when it is absolutely unavoidable. With such discipline, after three years of high school or two years of college French, every student should be able to express himself with some degree of fluency and, as techniques for teaching pronunciation tricks to overcome special hurdles such as *eu* and *u* become more widely used, with some ease and elegance. In these circumstances, this test will prove of increasing value. If, at times, the pronunciation used in the tapes is almost too French, as in Item 23 of Form A, where it takes a fine ear to hear the *ce* in the "J'aime bien ce chapeau"— this may provide a healthy shock to the Ameri-

can student whose penchant for wresting a loud "uh" out of every mute *e* has been the bane of many a teacher's existence.

The test is sound and well constructed and, what is perhaps more appealing, fresh and new in feeling and remarkably free of the visual approach. It constitutes a major breakthrough in the field of testing aural comprehension and, in addition to providing a valid measure of achievement, it should serve to set new standards for teacher and pupil alike.

[266]

★**First Year French Test.** High school and college; 1956; Form A; no manual; no data on reliability; tentative norms (no date); $1.20 per 25 tests, postage extra; 25¢ per specimen set, postpaid; 40(45) minutes; Minnie M. Miller, Jean Leblon, and Marguerite Rice Crain; Bureau of Educational Measurements. *

NELSON BROOKS, *Associate Professor of French, Yale University, New Haven, Connecticut.*

This 90-item test contains eight sets of directions and nine different procedures. The student is asked to match isolated words in two languages (paix-peace), to identify similar sounds as represented in printed words (the *i* of "midi" and the *y* of "type"), to match equivalents in two languages as they appear in statements ("Il will come bientôt."), to complete sentences in French ("Comment _____-vous ce matin?"), and to read with comprehension two prose passages (edited) of 20-odd lines. In 65 items the student makes a choice of four suggested answers, in 5 he separates true from false, and in 20 he must write one or two words in French. Twenty four items are concerned principally with matters of structure and 5 items with information that is other than linguistic. Sound is dealt with in 10 items, though only in terms of printed symbols.

All tests should measure subject matter rather than technique; for this reason everything possible should be done to make directions clear and procedure simple. This test needs considerable revision in this regard. In the attempt to present the entire test on two sides of a sheet the size of typewriter paper, very small type has been used, in which the difference between ordinary and boldface type, an important matter in some items, is not easily distinguished. In Part I numbers are used for both items and choices; the use of letters for the latter would have made things less confusing for the testee. Part 2, by far the most difficult from the point of view of technique, has no example and depends upon the selection of letters which boldface type does not make sufficiently clear. Directions and arrangement in Part 3 are especially puzzling. "In the parenthesis before each word place the number of the word which has the *same* vowel sound as the vowel in the first word." In no case do the parentheses immediately precede a word, and in some cases the choices have two syllables and hence two vowel sounds. The wording of the first sentence in Part 7 is most unfortunate: "Read this passage carefully and then do the statements below." Even in American English, one does not "do" a statement.

Some points are covered twice: the problem in Item 31 is the same as that in 28, and Item 62 is essentially the same as 53. In some parts the test puts a high value upon what is relatively unimportant, if not detrimental, to the beginner. Part 1 is a lexicography test involving the matching of isolated words in two languages, something to be minimized at all costs by the beginner. The items in Part 4 employ a procedure which has done as much to negate successful language learning in America as any other practice one can think of. This is the arbitrary mixing of two languages within the confines of the same utterance, a behavior pattern that is characteristic only of speakers whose language is in a serious state of disintegration. (This is reflected in items of the type: "Je him ai vu.") The textbooks, the tests, and the teaching procedures that encourage the learner to link two languages at a less-than-complete-utterance level are the result of a colossal misunderstanding of the nature of language behavior. Whatever may be the dictates of economy in printing and whatever may be the heritage of learning traditions that compound the mother tongue with the language being studied, it is by now perfectly clear that the learning of a second language that may—at least in part—replace the mother tongue must be done in terms of *separating* the two rather than binding them tightly and permanently together. Early levels of language learning in American schools and colleges cannot greatly improve until they are freed from the fetters of textbooks, tests, and teachings that employ this practice.

In Parts 7 and 8, the precise indication of the origin of the passages used (author, editor, publisher, and page) disqualifies these items for use in a "standardized" test. A test is either based upon knowledge of certain chosen materials known to and studied by the testee, or upon certain general linguistic facts for which one candidate has presumably had no more special preparation than any other. Accurate measurement can hardly be expected to result from performance with materials on which some candidates have had long and careful drill and some none at all, especially when this fact is made so explicit.

Some items in this test are to be commended. Many of the completion and comprehension exercises that involve only French are good; so is the use of recall as well as recognition. But the matching of isolated words in the manner of a bilingual dictionary, the use of single utterances composed of two languages, and the study of "pablumized" prose are pedagogical misdeeds which early levels of language teaching and testing cannot too soon renounce.

Mary E. Turnbull, *Formerly Head of Test Production, Educational Testing Service, Princeton, New Jersey.*

This is a good, neatly printed, and carefully edited test of various aspects of French that should be covered during a first year course.

Part 1, a vocabulary test, consists of 19 French words, for each of which the appropriate English translation must be chosen from four possibilities, and then 6 French words or expressions, each with four possible French definitions. A good group of basic nouns, verbs, adjectives, and adverbs is included and the distractors are intelligently selected to entice the uncertain student. The words seem carefully arranged in order of difficulty, the French definitions at the end of the part being much harder than the words tested at the beginning.

Parts 2 and 3 are very short but good tests of pronunciation. In Part 2 the student must select from a column of given words the word containing the same sound as the boldfaced letters in each of five given words. In each of the five items of Part 3 the correct answer must be a word having the same vowel sound as the first word given. Again, good distractors are supplied; these should really test the student's ability to discriminate between the correct and incorrect sound.

Part 4 tests knowledge of five French verbs, since the student must complete each given French sentence by choosing the French word or words which best translate the boldfaced English word or expression included in the sentence. Basic verbs are tested and the choices should all seem logical or attractive to some pupils.

Part 5 consists of 20 French sentences, each of which is to be completed by one of four given French choices. This part tests vocabulary (especially verbs), grammar (a good variety of elementary points), and some geographical knowledge of France. In this part there occurs the rare (for this test) case of a missing accent (Item 53).

Part 6 consists of a French paragraph that includes a number of English words or expressions. For each of these English portions the student is to write the corresponding French word or words on dotted lines provided below. In two cases (Items 62, 63) the grammar or vocabulary tested has already been tested in the preceding part (Items 53, 42). Correct spelling influences the points given for this part. Scoring this part will require more time than that necessary for scoring a straight objective test, but having the student do some writing in French is well worthwhile.

Part 7 is a French paragraph-reading test with five multiple choice and five true-false questions. The selection is a rather difficult one, but the questions based on it are quite simple. The reader who skims through the paragraph, getting the gist but not necessarily understanding each word, will probably get a better score on this part than the more conscientious reader who may spend too much time on the paragraph.

Part 8 consists of a fairly difficult passage from *Les Misérables* on which are based 10 French questions that require only very short answers to be written in French. Again, the questions are very simple as compared with the passage and only one or two words will answer each. A careful reading of this selection will give the answers to Items 53 and 55 in an earlier part.

The *First Year French Test* is an interesting test of the basic elements of achievement in elementary French. It should be useful to both teachers and pupils in classroom situations where an unspeeded measure is desired.

[267]

*French I and II: Achievement Examinations for Secondary Schools. 1 or 2 years high school; 1951–53; Forms 1 ('51), 2 ('53); no specific manual; directions sheets [1, '51; 2, '53]; no data on reliability; Form 1 norms ['52]; no norms for Form 2; 10¢ per test, postage extra; (60–90) minutes; Lee Stark; Educational Test Bureau. *

For a review by Elton Hocking of Form 1, see 4:239.

[268]

★French I and II: Midwest High School Achievement Examinations. 2 years high school; 1953–55; Forms A ('55), B ('53), identical with Form 2 of *French I and II: Achievement Examinations for Secondary Schools*); no specific manual; directions sheet ['55]; series manual ('57); no data on reliability; no norms; 10¢ per test, postage extra; 45(65–95) minutes; Lee Stark (A); Educational Test Bureau. *

MARY E. TURNBULL, *Formerly Head of Test Production, Educational Testing Service, Princeton, New Jersey.* [Review of Form A.]

The test begins somewhat ruggedly for the student with a 15-minute Reading Examination, consisting of 12 items based on three historical articles. Both articles and items are in French. Unfortunately, the articles, especially the first one, present well known facts, with the result that many of the succeeding items can be answered without reference to the article. More variety in content, closer attention to accents (cf. Article 1, line 7, *Pétain;* Item 6, choice C, *maîtres;* Item 7, choice A, *très*), and more care in wording the questions (inclusion of *quoique* in Item 10 makes A the only possible answer) would have improved this section.

Section 2, Civilization and Culture Identification, tests knowledge of French geography, history, and the arts by means of 23 items to be answered in 10 minutes. These are interesting and varied, but they are marred by careless errors in spelling (Item 26, *gouvernement*) and omissions of accents (four are omitted from the sample item alone).

Section 3, Vocabulary Examination, consists of two parts for which 10 minutes in all are allowed. Part 1 gives 20 short French sentences in which the italicized words are to be translated; more than half of the words tested are nouns. Many of the items show a distressing lack of correlation between the italicized words and the given translations (e.g., Item 40, where *du* is italicized but ignored in all choices; Item 47, where *ma* receives similar treatment; and particularly Item 51, where "formidable" is the only word in italics but where "wonderful team" is supposed to be the correct answer). In some items the definite article is translated in the given choices whether it is italicized or not; in others the article is ignored even though it is italicized. The word *entrer* is misspelled in the sample item. Part 2 is much more difficult than Part 1 and tends to be a test of reasoning powers rather than vocabulary. There are 10 items, each consisting of five French words or phrases; in each item the one word or phrase "which least follows the pattern set by the other words" is to be selected. In Item 61, where the correct answer is E, the choices have been labeled A, B, C, D, and 1; and in Item 62 choice B is needlessly capitalized and only choice A is given without the definite article.

Section 4, Aural Examination, allows 15 minutes for two parts, a definition series and an anecdote series. In this section the teacher reads the definitions and the anecdotes "ONLY ONCE." The answer choices to the 15 definitions are in French (although the example gives English choices), whereas the questions based on the French anecdotes are in English. Part 1 gives some interesting definitions that test knowledge of Paris as well as geography, history, and straight vocabulary. Part 2 consists of three historical anecdotes. These appear in order of difficulty, but the student of history may find the correct answers easy to select without paying much attention to the French. Again in this section careless errors appear in the test copy. In Item 66 *gouvernement* is again misspelled; two choices are capitalized in Item 75 while the other three are not; and the first choice in Item 80 is not labeled. For Item 82 "by" is included in the premise of the item and repeated at the beginning of choice B; and in choice C of Item 90 "Gauls" is not capitalized.

Section 5, a 10-minute Grammar Examination, consists of 20 items, each with four or five possible French translations of a given English expression or sentence. This section occasionally becomes a vocabulary test (cf. Items 101, 103, 104, 106, and 111). The adjective *prêt(e)* accounts for two errors in this section, being given no accent in the sample item and the wrong accent in Item 103.

Section 6, Matching Famous Personalities of the Current and Historical Scene, allows 5 minutes for selecting from a list of 20 names the name of the individual who best fits each of 11 given descriptions. Emphasis here seems to be on the arts.

Space for the answer is provided beside each test question; there is a neatly printed scoring key. The directions are adequate, and examples are given for all but the last section of the test. Time limits seem appropriate for each section, except possibly for the Aural Examination, where 15 minutes, if this includes the time taken by the teacher to read the definitions and the anecdotes, may not give the student sufficient time to answer the questions.

No norms are currently available for the test. The manual gives a short review of the changing purposes of the American High School during the past 50 years (!) and also states the purpose of the Midwest High School Achievement Examination—to motivate efforts of accomplishment and to motivate thinking ability. There are no data concerning validity and no reliability coefficients.

French I and II is an interesting test in which a good variety of elements of achievement in French language, history, and culture are included; the inclusion of an aural test is especially praiseworthy. The test could be useful for student motivation as well as for checkup on teaching emphasis on the different phases of the subject. It could be improved by careful editing which would eliminate the numerous proofreading errors and by a rearrangement of the various sections in order of difficulty.

[269]
★**French: Teacher Education Examination Program.** College seniors preparing to teach secondary school; 1957; for more complete information, see 543; IBM; no data on reliability; no norms; 80(95) minutes; Educational Testing Service. *

For a review by Walter W. Cook of the entire series, see 543.

[270]
*****The Graduate Record Examinations Advanced Tests: French.** College seniors and graduate students; 1939–58; for more complete information, see 601; IBM; 180(200) minutes; Educational Testing Service. *

WALTER V. KAULFERS, *Professor of Education, University of Illinois, Urbana, Illinois.* [Review of Form GGR.]

This 3-hour objective, machine scorable examination is not to be confused with the *Graduate Record Examinations Advanced French Test*, which requires only 1¾ hours. The purpose of Form GGR is fourfold: (*a*) to aid in assessing the qualifications of college majors in French for graduate work, and in predicting their success in graduate study; (*b*) to serve as part of a comprehensive departmental examination or proficiency examination for college seniors; (*c*) to assist in guiding and placing advanced students transferring from other institutions; and (*d*) to help in evaluating curriculum and instruction in French at the college level by providing a common yardstick comparable for all examinees.

Except for the directions to students, the 200 5-response multiple choice items comprising the test are entirely in French. Approximately one eighth deal with the history, geography, and civilization of France (including a few items on architecture, music, painting, science, and products). Since this section is brief, considering the range of coverage, only the highlights of French history and civilization are included. Some of these should be familiar to examinees from other sources besides offerings in French.

About two-fifths of the examination stresses comprehension and interpretation of passages of prose and poetry varying in length from 90 to approximately 300 words. The remainder— nearly half the test—measures knowledge of literary history and terminology, and ability to identify important figures and characters in French literature, including some from the postwar period.

A conscious effort has been made to measure sensitivity to style and literary values, and to test ability to follow the development of an author's thoughts as well as to draw proper inferences. An idea of the nature of the examination can be obtained from the following excerpts from directions selected at random:

Line 13 means....
Verses 10 and 11 convey the idea of....
In line 12, the *il* refers to....
Of the dates assigned below which one is clearly false?
Which of the lettered words or phrases is nearest in meaning to the underlined word in the sentence?
The name of a character from literature is given and followed by five suggested descriptions of the character. Select the best characterization.

The content of the examination has apparently been based on expert judgment regarding items of French literature, history, and civilization commonly included in college French courses and the syllabi, readings, or departmental tests accompanying them. As a general measure of ability to read and interpret French literature, and of knowledge of the highlights of French history, literature, and civilization, Form GGR leaves little to be desired.

It is not, however, a diagnostic test. In its present form only a very time-consuming analysis of each examinee's answer sheet would indicate whether a relatively low score on the test were attributable to inability to read and interpret literary selections, to inadequate knowledge of French literary history, to ignorance of the vocabulary of literary criticism, or to a lack of acquaintance with French culture outside the field of literature. This is a significant limitation, since for the guidance and placement of students in graduate courses such knowledge is almost imperative.

Although the answer sheets could easily be redesigned to yield diagnostic subscores, there is no question but that this would seriously complicate machine scoring. Until a convenient method for recording diagnostic subscores as well as the overall achievement score is devised, however, the examination should be used only in connection with other measures, such as grades in previous courses, or ratings by the candidates' major professors.

Because ability to understand and use the spoken language is now a common objective of instruction in the modern languages, Form GGR must obviously be supplemented by tests of aural comprehension and rating scales of ability to speak French if an adequate evaluation of a candidate's ability to do graduate work in courses making extensive use of the spoken language is to be obtained. Form GGR does not distinguish between students who are well prepared to hold their own in courses conducted entirely in French, and those who by virtue of previous training are qualified only to enter courses conducted in English where use of the foreign language is limited almost exclusively to silent reading of assigned works outside of class. The latter type of offering is by no means extinct.

Now that communication with French *lycées, collèges,* and *universités* is readily possible, scores obtained from an administration of the test to 200–300 representative students in France would be of considerable value in helping to appraise both the validity and the real life significance of the examination.

To date Form GGR has not been used widely enough to yield representative norms or dependable measures of statistical reliability. Estimates of reliability furnished by the Educational Testing Service range between .93 to .96. These estimates, however, need confirmation from a wider tryout of the test than has so far been possible. For some of the uses suggested for the examination, such as retesting of students to measure growth, more than one 3-hour form of the test would be desirable.

Like nearly all standardized tests, this examination follows the ladder principle of progressing from easy to difficult as a means of determining how high an examinee can climb. All test results are translated into 3-digit scaled scores ending in zero. These range from approximately 200 to 950. Eventually, when enough data have been assembled from a wider administration of the test, the scaled scores should make it possible to tell whether a candidate's performance on the French examination was higher or lower than his performance on another test relative to the same group of examinees. The Educational Testing Service is also in process of developing norms for particular levels and types of institutions.

For a review by Harold Seashore of the entire series, see 601.

[271]
★Second Year French Test. High school and college; 1956; Form A; no manual; no data on reliability; tentative norms (no date); $1.20 per 25 tests, postage extra; 25¢ per specimen set, postpaid; 40(45) minutes; Minnie M. Miller, Jean Leblon, and Marguerite Rice Crain; Bureau of Educational Measurements. *

GERALDINE SPAULDING, *Consultant, Educational Records Bureau, New York, New York.*

From the point of view of subject matter, the content of this test is, for the most part, well chosen. Since the total of 95 items includes a little bit of everything, there is necessarily rather limited coverage of any one area. However, the test yields only a total score, and makes no attempt to provide differential measures in various phases of achievement.

Though the subject matter content is satisfactory, a number of criticisms can be made of the formal characteristics of the test. First of all, the chief consideration in the design of the test sheet seems to have been economy in the use of paper—an economy that is costly in terms of resulting difficulties for both examinee and scorer. The entire test is printed on the two sides of a single 8½ by 11 inch sheet, with very small type. Many of the spaces provided for students to write in their answers are barely large enough for a legible response by a student having small, neat handwriting. The response parentheses provided for the multiple choice

items are small and very close together, and are at the left of the item, which is awkward. The cramming of so much material onto a single sheet results in unreasonable difficulties for both examinee and scorer.

There are several shortcomings in the directions. There is at present no manual, and perhaps none would be needed, at least for presentation of administering and scoring instructions, if the test directions and key were complete and clear. But the directions are involved, none too clear, and not always complete, so that procedure is not made plain to either examinee or scorer.

With respect to the techniques of item writing, the multiple choice items are well constructed. The decoys are suitable and the correct answers clear-cut, with one or two exceptions. Five of the 25 reading questions are true-false items. In the 10 items of Part 6, the student supplies the appropriate verb form, in context, writing out the form himself. In the remaining 30 items, the student also writes out the answers; but it is difficult to see what is gained by this, since most of the 30 items are so restricted, either in the directions or in the wording of the question, that relevant answers are limited to a small number of choices, usually only two. Such items have no clear advantages over items in which the choice of an answer is indicated by code, as in the ordinary fixed choice item. They have definite disadvantages when it comes to scoring. Even if questions are phrased so that answers *can* be single words, anyone with scoring experience knows that there is no limit to the number of variant answers that examinees can think of—including many borderline answers to the simplest question, requiring judgment in deciding whether or not to give credit. Coded choice items eliminate such scoring problems, and reduce those due to illegible writing.

Items requiring spontaneous answers have their place in tests not designed for machine scoring, and in many situations, especially in language tests, are probably more valid than coded choice items. But for the sake of reliability of scoring, items with answers written out by the student should be confined to situations where the examinee really must "think up" the answer, as in Part 6 of this test. They are inadvisable if the question lends itself readily to the coded choice form.

With respect to statistical data, the test is

not really ready for general use at the present time. The potential user is not furnished any data with the test on its reliability and validity, or on the procedures followed in its construction. However, a personal letter from the publisher gives the following information: reliability, .93; item difficulty, about 50 (range 25–65); discrimination index, about 23 for most of the items (range 20–45). A sheet of tentative norms accompanying the test gives a percentile table, but without information on the source or number of the scores used in preparing the table. It is indicated that new norms are being gathered, but they are not available at the present writing.

In summary, this test, yielding a single score of acceptable reliability, has possibilities of usefulness for the classroom teacher who scores his own tests, if he is willing to cope with scoring problems and to interpret the results without the help of adequate, and adequately defined, norms. The selection of content is, in general, good, and the questions, aside from reservations about the forms in which some of them are cast, are free from most of the common defects.

However, the printing and format, as well as the form of some of the questions, impose difficulties on both the examinee and the scorer. Because of these features, the test is not well adapted to large scale use with centralized scoring.

CLARENCE E. TURNER, *Professor of Romance Languages, Rutgers University, New Brunswick, New Jersey.*

This is a useful little test for its purposes. Its immediately striking characteristics are compactness and eclecticism.

Its 95 items cover four columns, two on each side of a single sheet. Some crowding inevitably results, and the print is quite fine. Good editing and printing have, however, protected clarity in the main. The authors have husbanded their testing time as carefully as their space, so that few items (scarcely over four) are so easy as to test nothing much, and the distractors are quite consistently of the sort which operate.

The authors have clearly tried to make the test reflect the variety which exists in teaching methods and emphases. There is something here for almost every taste. For example, vocabulary is tested in terms of English equivalents (22 items) and French (3 items). Reading comprehension of three well chosen passages is tested in three different ways, by brief answers in French to questions in French (12 items), by brief answers in English to questions in English (8 items), and by marking statements in French true or false (5 items). There are questions on civilization to reflect that normal component of the second year curriculum. Grammar (30 items) is tested by completions in French of French sentences, one third of them multiple choice and the rest guided completion by the student. Even pronunciation (one is tempted to say the most fundamental and least tested of language skills) is dealt with in the form of matching vowel sounds (5 items). More could be done in this area, and should be done if relative importance is the criterion.

The authors may be said, then, to have sought a common center of second year curricula, and to have moved a hair's breadth to the left of it. A minimum of teachers should find this test objectionably unrelated to what they are doing.

A few details invite reproach. Item 8 has two correct answers, since *entendre* may mean "to intend" in certain contexts. Item 44 has an inoperative option, since *suis allé* can not follow *j',* and might better be replaced by *irais,* the incorrect form most attractive to students in such a sentence. Item 76 has a pronoun with no clear antecedent. Item 81, "Est-ce que l'apprenti est intelligent?" seems to invite a value judgment and may militate against the more thoughtful student. To be sure, the text has described the apprentice as *leste et éveillé,* but it can be argued that he is not behaving very intelligently at the moment in question. Finally, why not in Part 6 simply call for the correct verb forms (which the key gives) instead of for the "subjunctive, if needed"? The student is left not knowing whether to write anything when the subjunctive is not needed, and perhaps feeling that verbs in the indicative are somehow not very important.

Can it be said that this trim and useful instrument promises to function equally well at school and college level? In the absence of statistical evidence we can only guess. The guess here recorded is that it fits the secondary somewhat better than the college situation. Its use at the end of the third college semester might be indicated.

GERMAN

[272]

*College Entrance Examination Board Achievement Test in German. Candidates for college entrance with 2–4 years high school; 1901–58; for more complete information, see 599; IBM; 60(80) minutes; program administered by Educational Testing Service for the College Entrance Examination Board. *

REFERENCES

1–3. See 4:244.
4. COLLEGE ENTRANCE EXAMINATION BOARD. *Foreign Languages: A Description of the College Board Tests in French, German, Latin, and Spanish.* Princeton, N.J.: the Board, April 1954. Pp. 31. * (PA 29:1444)
5. KING, RICHARD G. "The German Test—Good, Bad, or Indefinite?" *Col Board R* (23):444–8 My '54. *
6. HOLLMANN, WERNER. "The German Achievement Test of the College Board." *German Q* 31:128–32 Mr '58. *

HAROLD B. DUNKEL, *Professor of Education, The University of Chicago, Chicago, Illinois.* [Review of Form FAC.]

The German test of the CEEB series of achievement tests possesses all the usual virtues of that organization's examinations. The 110-item test achieves a reliability of .93 for students having two years of German and .94 for those having three years (as estimated by a modified form of the Kuder-Richardson formula 20). As is the practice of the CEEB, a considerable amount of detailed information concerning the number of students completing various portions of the material, the skewness of the distribution, the standard error of measurement, and the like is provided.

The test itself consists of five sections. In the first section of 20 items, the student is asked to select from among the offered responses that remark which a person in a situation already briefly sketched in German is most likely to make. The second section of 15 items consists of questions on three short reading passages. The third section of 30 items involves picking the proper German translation for parts of given English sentences. The fourth section of 25 items calls for supplying an omitted word or phrase in a given German sentence; and the fifth section of 20 items contains German passages with individual words or phrases underlined, for which English equivalents are to be selected. In this section there are also a few incomplete German statements about the passage which are to be completed by making a choice from four German possibilities offered for each.

The test was competently written and meticulously edited. Knowing from personal experience how difficult suitable passages are to find,

this reviewer was particularly impressed by the felicity of the German passages used.

Within the range it covers, the examination is an extremely competent job. As it stands, it probably includes just about what teachers and students expect to appear on a "College Board." This very fact gives considerable food for reflection. The prestige of these examinations has always been great, and their content has undoubtedly influenced the thinking of students and teachers in regard to what is important in any academic field of study for the college oriented. The influence of these tests will undoubtedly increase still more as more and more schools come to rely on them as at least partial dams to stem the probable flood of students.

Under these circumstances, one may perhaps find fault, not with what the test includes, but rather with what it excludes. What is not measured by so influential a test will probably receive shorter and shorter shrift in the classroom. The varied and stupendous difficulties in measuring on a national scale such objectives as the aural-oral skills or that area commonly labeled "culture and civilization" are familiar. One readily understands why a national testing organization approaches them gradually and gingerly. But the neglect of these areas is something which both the College Entrance Examination Board and teachers who prepare students for these examinations should keep in their minds and on their consciences.

For a review by Herbert Schueler of earlier forms, see 4:244.

[273]

★College Entrance Examination Board Advanced Placement Examination: German. High school seniors desiring credit for college level courses; 1954–58; for more complete information, see 600; 2 tests; 180(200) minutes; program administered by Educational Testing Service for the College Entrance Examination Board. *
a) GERMAN 3. At least 3 years high school; IBM in part; 2 parts.
b) GERMAN 4. At least 4 years high school; 2 scores: aural comprehension and composition, literary composition.

HERBERT SCHUELER, *Professor of Education, and Director of Teacher Education, Hunter College, New York, New York.* [Review of Form FBP-DLC2.]

These two examinations, administered in 1957 as part of the CEEB Advanced Placement Program, are searching, difficult tests of understanding and use of the language. Unfortunately, the small number of candidates taking these examinations did not warrant the usual careful analysis of the results by the CEEB; this review, therefore, is based on one individual's opinion without the help of inferences to be drawn from such an analysis.

The tests were prepared to correspond to college courses at two different levels: German 3, to test primarily for the ability to understand and use the language; and German 4, to test knowledge of German literature as well. The difficulty level of each examination is at least up to the standard of competence expected in corresponding first-rate college courses. If the scores are reliably derived, there should be little hesitancy on the part of colleges in accepting the results for credit and advanced placement.

Both tests have an aural comprehension section in which the student responds to oral passages recorded on tape. In German 3 this section is a version of the CEEB *German Listening Comprehension Test,* featuring several voices, both male and female, in short repeated sentences to which the student responds in a series of multiple choice items, and in connected passages and dialogues requiring free response answers to oral questions. In the main, the material is presented clearly and in standard German, although one of the male voices is guilty of certain nonstandard regionalisms in pronunciation. Certain passages in the script are marred by a stilted, noncolloquial language. A transatlantic telephone dialogue, for example, between a man and his sweetheart making plans for their marriage is so unlikely in its polite formality of idiom and in its unemotional presentation as to sound utterly ridiculous. Most of the aural material is of acceptable quality, however.

The aural comprehension section of German 4 presents a single, 15-minute presentation by one voice of a comparative analysis of two works of literature. The student listens to the material, as if in a college lecture hall, and is asked to take "reasonably complete" notes, either in German or in English, during a single hearing of the material. These notes represent the student's total response to the aural section of the examination. (In view of wide variation in what constitutes acceptability in lecture note taking, and the wide range of acceptable individual differences in this activity, it is diffi-cult to conceive of commonly acceptable standards of rating for this question.)

The nonaural portion of the German 3 examination requires the answering in English of various reading comprehension items, the translation into English of a passage in German, and the writing of three compositions, one in English, and two in German. The stimuli used for the two German compositions are particularly noteworthy—a sequence of cartoon drawings and an English outline of suggested content. In German 4 the nonaural portion requires first the retelling in German of the story of an episode from a work of one of the six authors read in preparation for the examination, and then, based on selections from the authors read, the kind of literary analysis, in English, characteristic of this level of work in a college class in German literature. The nonaural portions of both the German 3 and German 4 tests present sound, testable material, and the student's controlled and free responses should furnish sufficient evidence of his command of the German language and of German literature. Whether the analysis of the student's response yields, in truth, accurate evidence of his competence depends, of course, on the quality of the rating. Each of these examinations is rated by a committee of readers who are expected to agree in advance on the criteria for rating. The instruction sheets to readers and the report of the chief reader on the procedures used for the examinations reveal a commendable regard for the necessity of establishing and following defensible and agreed criteria and standards. This reviewer is concerned, however, about the practice, evidently followed for all the advanced placement tests in 1957, of having each essay read by only one reader. While it is true that different readers read different essays in each booklet, with the result that at least two readers participated in the total rating of each booklet, the fact remains that each partial score was based on the unchecked judgment of a single reader. There is abundant evidence to indicate the fallibility of any given individual's ratings of free, written responses, no matter how thorough the prerating briefing. Since the bulk of each of these examinations is nonobjective, the necessity for achieving maximum objectivity in rating free responses should be obvious. It is this reviewer's opinion that the CEEB practice in this regard does not have sufficient checks and safeguards, however excellent the examinations themselves may be.

[274]

First Year German Test. High school and college; 1933; Form A; mimeographed directions sheet ['33]; tentative high school norms; $1.20 per 25 tests, postage extra; 25¢ per specimen set, postpaid; 40(45) minutes; J. R. Aiken and Cora Held; Bureau of Educational Measurements. *

HERBERT SCHUELER, *Professor of Education, and Director of Teacher Education, Hunter College, New York, New York.*

This short, 100-item, 40-minute test is intended to provide a measure of vocabulary recognition, reading comprehension, and command of elementary structure for students in first year college and first year high school classes. No distinction between the college and high school levels is suggested by the authors.

Part 1 consists of 35 vocabulary items in which the student is asked to choose one of three English translation alternatives of single German words. This section has several evident weaknesses: the words to be tested are not presented in context, and 15 of the items use an obvious, similar sounding misleader (like *Esel*-easel) as one of the three alternatives. This reviewer doubts whether this section provides a sufficiently searching measure of vocabulary recognition, and believes that an item analysis of a representative number of student responses will reveal serious shortcomings in many of the items.

Part 2 presents five German sentences, each of which is to be matched with a sentence of similar meaning to be chosen from among a group of 10 German alternatives. This section is unnecessarily cumbersome and time-consuming for the five items it covers. It actually represents, in an awkwardly camouflaged form, five 2-alternative items, in which the wrong answer in each case is a rather obvious misleader.

Part 3 requires the student to supply a missing word or expression in 40 short German sentences, with the English translation of the missing word supplied in each case. The majority of the items deal with verb forms; several require more than one word to be filled in. As is inevitable with such items, they vary greatly in difficulty and in the number of possibilities of error presented.

Part 4 consists of a single paragraph relating a German anecdote, followed by 20 true-false

statements in German. The inclusion of but one short reading selection and the use of the outmoded true-false items, make this section both inadequate in scope and possibly insufficiently discriminating in the few short measures it offers.

A short manual accompanying the test offers percentile norms secured from 191 students in first year classes of 12 high schools. No norms are given for college students. Reliability coefficients were obtained on the basis of but 50 high school and 44 college cases. These are given as .84 and .94, respectively.

This is an unambitious and somewhat archaic test. It is neither long enough, comprehensive enough, nor discriminating enough to be useful in any but informal, casual applications.

[275]

***German I and II: Achievement Examinations for Secondary Schools.** 1 or 2 years high school; 1951–53; Forms 1 ('51), 2 ('53); no specific manual; directions sheets [1, '51; 2, '53]; no data on reliability; norms: Forms 1 ['52], 2 ['53]; 10¢ per test, postage extra; (60–90) minutes; Emma Marie Birkmaier; Educational Test Bureau. *

[276]

★German I and II: Midwest High School Achievement Examinations. 2 years high school; 1953–55; Forms A ('55), B ('53, identical with Form 2 of *German I and II: Achievement Examinations for Secondary Schools*); no specific manual; directions sheet ['55]; no data on reliability; no norms; 10¢ per test, postage extra; (60) minutes; Gilbert C. Kettlekamp (A); Educational Test Bureau. *

HAROLD B. DUNKEL, *Professor of Education, The University of Chicago, Chicago, Illinois.*

According to the 4-page manual which accompanies this series of tests, they seemingly are intended to serve some special educational purpose. Since, however, the language in which this explanation is couched is something less than felicitous, the precise point is not clear. The first sentence, "The purpose of the American High School has had varying influences from time to time," is fairly illustrative of the difficulty which a reader has in figuring out just what is meant.

Be that as it may, the German test under review is of a familiar type, containing sections on reading, vocabulary, aural comprehension, and grammar, for a total of 87 items to be completed in an hour of testing time. It is too bad that the effort and expense which went into the manual were not devoted to matters more relevant to this test, especially since no useful information is given there. A sheet for tallying the distribution of class scores and a sheet of norms in terms of quartiles for several tests in the series are furnished with the manual. Unfortunately, German is not one of the tests covered by this list of quartiles, though this omission is a small loss since, even for those tests for which quartiles are supplied, no information is given concerning the number or type of student (or of institution) on which they are based. No estimate of reliability is provided. Thus, the teacher giving this test has only the equivalent of a homemade test since he has no data concerning its quality as a measuring device and no basis for comparing the performance of his own pupils with that of other groups. The question then is, apart from his having saved himself trouble by purchasing it rather than constructing it, whether he has as good a test as he would have built himself.

The sections on vocabulary and grammar (of 34 and 15 items, respectively) are perhaps no worse than what the average teacher would prepare, though they include some items with poor distractors and some with clumsy ones, and one item in which the wrong word is italicized and hence for which none of the offered responses is correct.

The reading section seems, however, poorer than the average teacher who was not in too much of a hurry might have come up with. In general, the section provides inefficient testing since often a whole paragraph must be read to answer one item which hangs on a single sentence. There are misprints, clumsy or dubious responses, and the other familiar shortcomings of the inexpertly prepared and insufficiently edited test. No attempt was made, even a priori, to arrange the items in order of ascending difficulty; hence the poorer students will never get to what seems probably the easiest item in this part, the last one. This entire section needs thoroughgoing revision before it should be used by anyone.

That a section endeavoring to measure aural comprehension is included is a welcome gesture in the direction of the aural-oral skills. In this instance, however, one doubts whether this section constitutes more than such a gesture. Without the reading's being standardized through being recorded on tape or disc, variations among the readers (especially with the additional visual and other clues which readers fall into unconsciously under these circumstances) certainly will not produce results which are comparable. The additional fact that each reader must work out his own timing within each aural part—with the probable result that readers will not work it out in advance and simply blunder through under the dubious inspiration of the moment—will raise further hob with the reliability of the results, as does one item with clumsy English and one item where English idiom permits two answers.

In sum, the reader has, at best, the equivalent of a test he could himself make the night before. If he is experienced and careful, he could probably make a better one. If he is spending money, he would do better to purchase, say, the *Cooperative German Test.*

GREEK

[277]
*College Entrance Examination Board Achievement Test in Greek. Candidates for college entrance; 1901-58; available only in the March testing program; for more complete information, see 599; IBM; 2 tests (candidate takes only one): Attic Prose, Homer and Attic Prose; 60(80) minutes; program administered by Educational Testing Service for the College Entrance Examination Board. *

KONRAD GRIES, *Associate Professor of Classical Languages and Chairman of the Department, Queens College, Flushing, New York.* [Review of Form FAC.]

The comments of this reviewer on the CEEB Latin test (see 280) apply in principle also to the CEEB test in Greek, although here he has found no slips or errors, and only one doubtful item (Item 50 in the test on Homer, where too much is read into the Greek).

The test comes in two versions: one on Attic prose for those candidates who have followed the traditional Greek course, the other on Homer and Attic prose for candidates from those schools which introduce Homer at an early stage. Both versions have two parts: a short one, limited to 8 or 10 items, and a longer one with 57 or 58 assorted questions based on three passages. In the "old-style" test all of the passages are Xenophontic, whereas in the other test the first passage is identical with the first passage in the old-style test and the second and third passages are from *Odyssey* and *Iliad.* The two versions differ mainly in their first, and minor, part, where the eight items of the old-style test include four in which synonyms or synonymous expressions are to be chosen and four where the correct Greek translation of an

English phrase or clause is to be indicated, while the 10 items of the other test are simple vocabulary items. In either case, the sampling is much too small.

As only 32 and 36 students, respectively, took this test in March 1957, statistics are limited to a reporting of score distributions.

HEBREW

[278]

★Uniform Achievement Tests. Grades 1, 2, 3; 1951(?) ; 1 form; 3 tests; manual; teacher's mimeographed supplement; record blank; no data on reliability; no norms; 25¢ per test, postage extra; Jewish Education Committee of New York; the Committee. *
a) HEBREW LANGUAGE. (60–75) minutes.
b) JEWISH LIFE AND OBSERVANCES. (45–55) minutes.
c) THE JEWISH PEOPLE. (55–65) minutes.

ITALIAN

[279]

*College Entrance Examination Board Achievement Test in Italian. Candidates for college entrance with 2–4 years high school; 1924–58; available only in the March testing program; for more complete information, see 599; IBM; 60(80) minutes; program administered by Educational Testing Service for the College Entrance Examination Board. *

LATIN

[280]

College Entrance Examination Board Achievement Test in Latin. Candidates for college entrance with 2–4 years high school; 1901–58; for more complete information, see 599; IBM; 60(80) minutes; program administered by Educational Testing Service for the College Entrance Examination Board.

REFERENCES
1–2. See 4:250.
3. COLLEGE ENTRANCE EXAMINATION BOARD. *Foreign Languages: A Description of the College Board Tests in French, German, Latin, and Spanish.* Princeton, N.J.: the Board, April 1954. Pp. 31. * (PA 29:1444)

KONRAD GRIES, *Associate Professor of Classical Languages and Chairman of the Department, Queens College, Flushing, New York.* [Review of Form FAC.]

This test, like other CEEB tests, consists entirely of multiple choice items. There are 94 items, each with four choices, arranged in three parts.

The first part consists of 15 vocabulary items and two derivative items, each item being given in isolation. The words involved are not particularly abstruse; a second year student should know all but three or four. The suggested an-

swers are clever and sound, though one might quibble about Item 5: *curo;* the key designates "look out for" as the correct answer, but one could make out a good case for "want" (cf., e.g., Tibullus 1.1.58 *non ego laudari curo*). It is doubtful whether much is proved by so limited a sampling of the candidates' vocabulary, especially in view of the high frequency of most of the items. In any case, the practice of word matching here employed is reprehensible in itself.

The second part contains 22 items. In each an English phrase or sentence is translated in four different ways, only one of which is correct. Presumably meant to test recognitional knowledge of forms, syntax, and idiom, it is complicated by occasional vocabulary problems. Again, there would seem to be no functional value: college students of Latin will hardly be called upon to correct each other's written Latin, and under what other circumstances would they be likely to see the plethora of impossible Latinity contained in these two pages?

The last part, with 55 items, is based on three Latin passages, each a self-contained unit of about 20 lines, with occasional vocabulary aids. These three passages represent approximately the kind and the level of the Latin read respectively in the second, the third, and the fourth years of secondary school, the first being a straightforward prose narrative, the second (also in prose) involving ideas of a literary nature, and the third presenting a Vergilian episode from Valerius Flaccus in hexameters. The obvious difficulty of the second and third passages seems confirmed by the results achieved when the test was given in March 1957.

The aggregate of the items may aptly be described as a fruit salad, a vivid term used by Harold B. Dunkel in reviewing the *CEEB Achievement Test in Latin Reading* in *The Fourth Mental Measurements Yearbook.* There are items on syntax, on morphology, on derivation, on word and phrase translation, on content (both factual and interpretive), on poetry, and on scansion. It is not surprising that the candidates, given only one hour for the whole test and forced in this part to change their basis of operation almost from item to item, "found this test of greater than middle difficulty." Taken individually, on the other hand, these items are fair enough, provided the Latin itself has been understood, although several sore spots must be pointed out. In Item 44 the correct answer is B, not C, as indicated in the key. In Item 53 the correct answer, "Trajan.... did not want Hadrian to become emperor, but Plotina did," involves a straining of the Latin (*sine aliqua quidem voluntate Traiani*). Item 81, which calls upon the candidates to find a "symbolically....emotional counterpart" to a quoted phrase in one of four suggested lines, is completely beyond the reviewer. In Item 86, on *dapibus coeptis,* the answer given as correct, "only at this point do they really begin the banquet," is hardly right in view of the preceding *dum vincitur....prima fames....omnis aula silet.* In Item 93, where the correct answer is undoubtedly the one indicated by the key, the question itself speaks of a "dramatic effect" which is absent in all four suggested answers. And in Item 94, where the candidates are required to choose which of four lines "illustrates the quality of poetry defined by *duriora*" (with a good reference to the literary discussion contained in the second Latin passage), it is again difficult to identify the "hardness" of the line labeled correct by the key. The reviewer finds it euphonious.

Statistics on the 3,004 candidates who took the test in March 1957, are given in a test analysis bulletin. Whatever their interpretation, the test in itself is not one to inspire confidence in its ability to determine that rather nebulous conception "achievement in Latin," which is, by the way, not adequately defined in any literature connected with the test that the reviewer has seen.

For a review by Harold B. Dunkel of earlier forms, see 4:250.

[281]
★College Entrance Examination Board Advanced Placement Examination: Latin. High school seniors desiring credit for college level courses; 1954–58; for more complete information, see 600; 2 levels in 1 booklet: Latin 4 (candidates who present the advanced Vergil course), Latin 5 (candidates who have studied 2 of the following fields: prose, lyric poetry, comedy); 180(200) minutes; program administered by Educational Testing Service for the College Entrance Examination Board. *

[282]
*First Year Latin: Every Pupil Scholarship Test. 1 year high school; 1926–58; new form usually issued each January and April; norms available following testing program; no data on reliability; 4¢ per test; 4¢ per scoring key; postage extra; 40(45) minutes; Bureau of Educational Measurements. *

[283]
★Kansas First Year Latin Test. 1, 2 semesters high school; 1935–56; 2 levels; mimeographed manual ('56); $1.20 per 25 tests, postage extra; 25¢ per specimen set, postpaid; 40(45) minutes; Helen Pearson; Bureau of Educational Measurements. *
a) TEST I, FORM A, FIRST SEMESTER. 1956.
b) TEST I, FORM B, SECOND SEMESTER. 1956.

[284]
*Latin I and II: Achievement Examinations for Secondary Schools. 1 or 2 years high school; 1951–53; Form 1 ('51); no specific manual; no data on reliability; norms ['52]; 10¢ per test, postage extra; (60) minutes; Margaret M. Forbes; Educational Test Bureau. *

[285]
*Latin I and II: Every Pupil Test. 1 or 2 years high school; 1929–58; new form usually issued each December and April; norms available following testing program; no data on reliability; 3¢ per test; 1¢ per scoring key; cash orders postpaid; 40(45) minutes; Ohio Scholarship Tests. *

[286]
★Latin I and II: Midwest High School Achievement Examinations. 2 years high school; 1953–55; Forms A ('55), B ('53, identical with Form 2 of *Latin I and II: Achievement Examinations for Secondary Schools;* no specific manual; no data on reliability; no norms; 10¢ per test, postage extra; Form A: 60(65) minutes; Form B: 90(95) minutes; Margaret M. Forbes; Educational Test Bureau. *

SPANISH

[287]
*College Entrance Examination Board Achievement Test in Spanish. Candidates for college entrance with 2–4 years high school; 1902–58; for more complete information, see 599; IBM; 60(80) minutes; program administered by Educational Testing Service for the College Entrance Examination Board. *

REFERENCES
1–3. See 4:259.
4. COLLEGE ENTRANCE EXAMINATION BOARD. *Foreign Languages: A Description of the College Board Tests in French, German, Latin, and Spanish.* Princeton, N.J.: the Board, April 1954. Pp. 31. * (*PA* 29:1444)

[288]
★College Entrance Examination Board Advanced Placement Examination: Spanish. High school seniors desiring credit for college level courses; 1954–58; for more complete information, see 600; 180(200) minutes; program administered by Educational Testing Service for the College Entrance Examination Board. *

[289]
*The Graduate Record Examinations Advanced Tests: Spanish. College seniors and graduate students; 1946–58; for more complete information, see 601; IBM; 180(200) minutes; Educational Testing Service. *

For a review by Harold Seashore of the entire series, see 601.

[290]
★Kansas Second Year Spanish Test. High school and college; 1953; Form A; no college norms; $1.20

per 25 tests, postage extra; 30¢ per specimen set, postpaid; 40(45) minutes; Helen Johnson; Bureau of Educational Measurements. *

[291]
★Spanish and Latin American Life and Culture.
2 years high school or 1 year college; 1956; Form A;
mimeographed directions sheet; tentative norms; $1.20
per 25 tests, postage extra; 25¢ per specimen set, postpaid; 40(45) minutes; Minnie M. Miller and Beulah
Aiken; Bureau of Educational Measurements. *

KATHLEEN N. PERRET, *Interpreter, Depart-
ment of Conference Services, Interpretation
Division, United Nations, New York, New
York.*

This test is designed to test students completing two years of high school or one year of
college Spanish in the geography, history, government, art, literature, science, and customs
of Spain and Latin America. It consists of 100
questions in English broken down into three
sections. Part 1, consisting of 25 items, requires the student to write the answer in English (the student is told that one half point will
be counted for spelling); Part 2, is made up
of three groups of 10 questions each, the answers to which are to be selected from three
lists of 15 possible replies; Part 3 gives 45 incomplete sentences, each followed by three
choices of an English word or phrase to complete the text.

The authors display an obvious knowledge
of the mechanics of testing, but the sum total
of their efforts on this test is neither enlightened nor inspiring. What is more, Part 1 contains something which, to the reviewer's mind,
is a totally unacceptable feature—the proviso
that spelling count so heavily. This, after all,
purports to be a test on a foreign civilization.
How, in the circumstances, can the correct
or incorrect spelling of the answer to Item 3
("October 12") or to Item 13 ("green") be
considered pertinent or valid?

Despite the all-embracing content coverage
announced, geography and history account for
approximately one third and one fifth, respectively, of the items, although much of this subject matter is certainly covered elsewhere in
the normal high school or college curriculum.
Cultural items, the catch-all category, constitute about two fifths of the test, leaving 5 per
cent to be apportioned among the categories of
art, literature, and science. There may be some
question about the fine points of this breakdown, but the general distribution is unmistak-
able. It is depressing to feel that students in

this field are confined to such an austere and
trivial diet.

Examining the items in more detail, is it
really useful to include 10 questions of the
"What is the capital city" type? Surely a student knowing one or two capital cities is likely
to know a fair proportion of the others as well;
if teachers of Spanish are concentrating in so
large measure on this type of material, it is a
great pity. So many other items come to mind
that might have been included on music, dance,
and agriculture, to name only a few areas.
Finer differentiation could certainly have been
achieved by more items in neglected fields.
There is another facet of the tests which seems
questionable, namely the emphasis on Mexico
(about 28 items, as compared with about 18 on
Spain). Admittedly, it is difficult for teachers
and testers to weigh the relative merits of the
contributions of Spain and Latin America and
to apportion time available fairly and sensibly.
The mass of information is so overwhelming
that it might be better to devote no time to this
field at all if enough space cannot be allocated
for the program to make it meaningful. But, if
time is to be spent on this work, deeper and
more lasting results might be achieved by using
Spain as the starting point and developing understanding by later comparing and contrasting
Spain with Latin America. To dismiss the all-
pervading influence of Spain in so few items
scattered over a wide field, while paying lip
service to Latin America through a mass of
items on its geography, serves no purpose, except perhaps to give the student an abiding dislike for "culture" and prevent him from pursuing these studies in later life.

In summary, the reviewer feels that the end
product falls far short of the ambitious goal
set by the authors. Much of the substance of
the test has undoubtedly been conditioned by
what is actually being taught. Even so, the
range of content could have been considerably
broader. The reliability and validity data reported in the manual are not sufficiently impressive to outweigh the many shortcomings of the
test content. Before using the test, teachers
would be well advised to consider carefully
whether this is indeed a test suited to their
needs.

[292]
*Spanish I and II: Achievement Examinations
for Secondary Schools. 1 or 2 years high school;
1951–53; Forms 1 ('51), 2 ('53); no specific manual;
directions sheets [1, '51; 2, '53]; no data on reliability;

norms: Forms 1 ['52], 2 ('53); 10¢ per test, postage extra; (60–90) minutes; Emma Marie Birkmaier (2); Educational Test Bureau. *

[293]

★Spanish I and II: Midwest High School Achievement Examinations. 2 years high school; 1951–55; Forms A ('51, title on test is *Spanish I and II: Achievement Examinations for Secondary Schools*), B ['52, identical with Form 2 of *Spanish I and II: Achievement Examinations for Secondary Schools*]; no specific manual; directions sheet ['55]; no data on reliability; Form A norms ['55]; no norms

for Form B; 10¢ per test, postage extra; Form A: 35(60) minutes; Form B: 45(90) minutes; Educational Test Bureau. *

[294]

★Spanish: Teacher Education Examination Program. College seniors preparing to teach secondary school; 1957; for more complete information, see 543; IBM; no data on reliability; no norms; 80(95) minutes; Educational Testing Service. *

For a review by Walter W. Cook of the entire series, see 543.

INTELLIGENCE

REVIEWS BY *C. J. Adcock, Charlotte E. K. Banks, Nancy Bayley, Cyril Burt, Lee J. Cronbach, John T. Dailey, Reginald R. Dale, John C. Daniels, Frederick B. Davis, Raleigh M. Drake, Walter N. Durost, Norman Eagle, George A. Ferguson, Joshua A. Fishman, John P. Foley, Jr., Hanford M. Fowler, Elizabeth D. Fraser, Frank S. Freeman, Gustav J. Froehlich, Eugene L. Gaier, Henry E. Garrett, Wilson H. Guertin, J. P. Guilford, Nelson G. Hanawalt, Mary Haworth, Alfred B. Heilbrun, Jr., A. W. Heim, Duncan Howie, Cyril J. Hoyt, J. A. Keats, D. Welty Lefever, Roger T. Lennon, John Liggett, James Lumsden, James Mainwaring, William B. Michael, T. R. Miles, John E. Milholland, G. A. V. Morgan, Louis C. Nanassy, Charles O. Neidt, John Nisbet, Raymond C. Norris, Gerald R. Patterson, E. A. Peel, D. A. Pidgeon, A. E. G. Pilliner, M. L. Kellmer Pringle, Albert I. Rabin, James H. Ricks, Jr., Cyril A. Rogers, Arthur B. Royse, C. Sanders, I. David Satlow, William B. Schrader, William Sloan, I. Macfarlane Smith, Julian C. Stanley, Naomi Stewart, Norman D. Sundberg, Calvin W. Taylor, Erwin K. Taylor, Florence M. Teagarden, W. Wesley Tennyson, David V. Tiedeman, Leona E. Tyler, F. W. Warburton, Alexander G. Wesman, John M. Willits, R. Winterbourn, and Alfred Yates.*

GROUP

[295]

★A.C.E.R. Advanced Tests AL and AQ. College and superior adults; 1953–55; 1 form ['53]; 2 tests; mimeographed manual ['55]; 3s. per 10 tests; 6d. per scoring key ['54]; 4s. 6d. per manual; 5s. 3d. per specimen set; postpaid within Australia; manual by D. Spearritt; Australian Council for Educational Research. *
a) TEST AL. Linguistic; 1 form ['53]; 25(35) minutes.
b) TEST AQ. Quantitative; 1 form ['54]; 30(40) minutes.

DUNCAN HOWIE, *Professor of Psychology, The University of New England, Armidale, Australia.*

These tests are designed as high level intelligence tests to discriminate levels of general ability in students who are completing secondary education or entering university or similar tertiary education. Although the subtests appear as separates, with AL a test of ability to reason with linguistic material and AQ a test of ability to reason with quantitative material mainly of an arithmetical nature, they are intended not as measures of distinct abilities but as two approaches to a measure of general

alertness from two differing media. There are 28 items in Test AL, ranging over analogies, opposites, letter series, and proverb types of problems. Test AQ consists of 25 items, comprising number series, number matrices, and arithmetical problems.

The manual gives a quite comprehensive account of the development of the test with completely adequate instructions for its administration at a level suited to teachers or others who have had the usual sort of elementary training in testing. A brief but valuable technical supplement gives the basic statistical data for the more expert.

The direct data for standardization are from 500 students (309 first year students in teachers colleges in Victoria and 191 seniors in a single high school). Provisional norms could have been drawn from these data for the guidance of those interested in using the test in relation to its objectives, for example, for comparing groups of students of comparable age and educational level. The publishers, however, adopted a more elaborate and more indirect procedure. Scores from AL-AQ were indirectly standardized against scores from the *A.C.E.R. Higher Test M*. This in turn was directly standardized at the 18 years plus level, but indirectly standardized at the 13–14 year levels against another A.C.E.R. test. Further, ML-MQ IQ's between the ages of 14 and 18 were arrived at by interpolation. In these circumstances, the IQ norms given in the AL-AQ manual for each 3-month age interval from 15.0 to 18.9 could appear misleadingly authoritative.

The publishers are careful to point out that these IQ's, derived by means of normalized standard scores for each age interval with mean at 100 and standard deviation of 15 points, are not to be confused with Binet type IQ's. The possibility of such confusion in itself raises a question as to whether anything is gained by perpetuating the by no means illuminating IQ concept at these later age and higher ability levels. The publishers' justification would appear to be that, recognizing that educationalists in general are still so sold on the IQ, it was thought advisable, as they put it, "to conform with current practice." In view of the danger that these indices can so easily be considered without reference to the conditions under which they were obtained, and bearing in mind the indirect nature of the standardization, it is unfortunate that the publishers have seen fit to pay so much respect to current practice or current prejudice.

Evidence of validity is confined to correlations between AL and a standardized A.C.E.R. English achievement test and between AQ and a similarly standardized A.C.E.R. mathematics test. Intercorrelations are reported for three groups of men and three groups of women in teachers colleges in three states. For the men the means of the correlations are: AL and English, .54; AQ and mathematics, .66. The respective means for the women are .65 and .70. The implications of these correlations would appear to be that AL-AQ correlates with measures of abilities which are of importance in academic achievement. Presumably, as the subtests are not designed as measures of distinct abilities, the differences between the relationships with verbal and mathematical tests are not being advanced as justification for using AL as a test of verbal ability and AQ as a test of mathematical ability. It would, however, have been of interest if correlations between AL and mathematics and AQ and English had

been given. As the purpose of AL-AQ is to discriminate general ability levels in higher educational groups, one would wish to see further evidence of its validity in this respect, e.g., its relation to success or failure in senior high school, teachers college, or university work.

There is an increasingly acute need in Australia for an adequately standardized test with clear evidence of validity for selection and guidance at higher secondary and tertiary levels. The AL-AQ combination is a promising step in this direction and is, in fact, the best available Australian test for these purposes. It must be recognized, though, that the information from it should be used tentatively because its standardization implies no more than a basis of comparison and its validity remains to be shown. The data for direct standardization and evidences of the degree of the test's validity will accrue if it is used, as it deserves to be used, sufficiently extensively and intensively in research programmes in student selection and guidance.

[296]

*A.C.E.R. Advanced Test B40. Ages 13 and over; 1940–53; title on test is *Adult Test (B40)*; 1 form ['40]; mimeographed manual ['53]; 5s. per 10 tests; 2s. per manual; 2s. 6d. per specimen set; postpaid within Australia; 55(65) minutes; Australian Council for Educational Research. *

REFERENCES
1. Cook, P. H. "Criteria for the Selection of Personnel Officers." *B Ind Psychol & Personnel Prac* 2:28–37 Je '46. * (PA 20:4761)
2. Hohne, H. H. "The Prediction of Academic Success." *Austral J Psychol* 1:38–42 Je '49. *
3. Hohne, H. H. *Success and Failure in Scientific Faculties of the University of Melbourne*. Melbourne, Australia: Australian Council for Educational Research, 1955. Pp. vii, 129. * (PA 31:3787)

C. Sanders, *Professor of Education and Dean of the Faculty, University of Western Australia, Nedlands, Australia.*

Mental tests should meet the dictates of recognisable validity, sound construction and standardisation, acceptable reliability, and serviceable usage. If the *A.C.E.R. Advanced Test B40* is rated on the extent of its usage during and since the war, then it qualifies, in terms of its catalogue description, as a test of "general ability (intelligence)" for students in colleges and universities—at least in Australia.

Test B40 is designed to discriminate among students aged 15 years and over. When the A.C.E.R. moved into test construction at this level, it began by adapting the *Otis Self-Administering Tests of Mental Ability* to Australian conditions. This enabled Otis Higher C to be used in standardising Test B40, the first major Australian test of the advanced type.

Test B40 contains 77 verbal and quantitative items. Its directions are simple, its administration is straightforward, and its marking is reasonably easy. By means of conversion tables the raw scores from the test can be converted to IQ's on a range varying from 85 to 145.

The IQ as a measure of ability is well entrenched in Australia even though in "advanced" tests of the B40 type it is largely a misnomer, being more accurately a quantitative index or estimate of scholastic aptitude. On this assumption, and despite acceptance of the test by qualified people in Australia, B40 has not yet graduated beyond the experimental stage. For example, in a restandardisation of Otis Higher C by the A.C.E.R. some years ago, the conclusion was reached that the original Australian norms were too low and that the B40 IQ's, based on the Otis Higher C norms, were underestimated by about 3 points at the lower end of the range and 5 points at the upper end. In consequence, a reexamination of the B40 norms is to be undertaken. Meantime, the manual, containing directions, norms, and scoring key, remains tentative, and is supplied in duplicated form with the printed tests.

Although the original reliability and validity studies were based on only 74 cases, a split-half reliability coefficient of .89 and a validity coefficient of .80 with Otis Higher C were obtained. The test was widely employed during the war to assess various student groups as well as applicants for the public services, and the results it produced at that time were accepted as reasonably reliable.

Despite its present defects, including its tentative standardisation and impermanent manual, the *A.C.E.R. Advanced Test B40* is a useful comparative instrument for assessing groups of college and university students. However, in using it for such purposes the point should be kept in mind that the results it so far has produced may be somewhat conservative.

[297]

*A.C.E.R. Higher Test M. Ages 13 and over; 1944–55; formerly called *A.C.E.R. General Ability Test: Advanced M;* 3 scores: linguistic, quantitative, total; 1 form ['48]; 2 parts; revised mimeographed manual ['55]; 3s. per 10 tests; 9d. per scoring key; 6s. 6d. per manual; 7s. 6d. per specimen set; postpaid within Australia; manual by D. Spearritt; Australian Council for Educational Research. *
a) [PART ML.] Linguistic; 15(25) minutes.
b) [PART MQ.] Quantitative; 20(30) minutes.

C. SANDERS, *Professor of Education and Dean of the Faculty, University of Western Australia, Nedlands, Australia.*

Like its more advanced counterpart, *A.C.E.R. Advanced Tests AL and AQ,* Higher Test M yields two scores, L and Q, which can be taken separately or together. Part ML consists of linguistic or verbal relation items, and Part MQ of quantitative or number relation items. The comprehensive manual of directions gives substantial information about the history of the test and the various ways in which it may be employed. Each of the scores and the total score can be converted to estimates of IQ.

The test has been standardised in various ways and, although imperfection is easier to attain than perfection, the impression gained is that the work in general has been competently and ingeniously performed, and that the test and its subtests are reasonably valid and reliable. However, at the upper end of the scale the norms are based entirely on males—service trainees in one state—and adjustments have had to be made to allow for the performance of females.

Considerable information is given as to the interrelations of Test M, and its subparts L and Q, with other measures. A correlation of .63 is reported between L and Q. This, in the circumstances, is rather high, and indicates internal overlap to a greater extent than apparently is present in tests AL-AQ, between which the correlation is stated to be .45. However, ML-MQ correlates .76 with AL-AQ and .84 with the *A.C.E.R. Intermediate Test D.* Part ML correlates .66 with AL and Part MQ .73 with AQ. These latter coefficients are fairly good in view of the fact that tests AL and AQ are designed for a population aged 15 years and over.

The results of a factor analysis of ML-MQ and other variables are reported and interesting occupational norms in terms of raw scores are provided. As far as occupational differences are concerned, farmers and university students produced the widest variations. Farmers yielded mean 15.47, SD 7.2, on ML, and mean 15.24, SD 7.5, on MQ. The figures for university students were: ML—mean 31.0, SD 3.3; MQ—mean 30.84, SD 5.0.

As an experimenter among university students, the reviewer confesses a partiality towards the approach to mental testing adopted by the A.C.E.R. in its preparation of tests ML-MQ and AL-AQ. At a meeting of the

Australian and New Zealand Association for the Advancement of Science held at Brisbane in 1951, he pointed out, in a paper dealing with omnibus tests of the Advanced N type, how differences between groups of individuals who are verbally or nonverbally minded are concealed in total raw scores, or under the canopy of the IQ's obtained from raw scores. On this point he emphasised the opinion that reported differences in the mean IQ's of men and women students at the college and university level were probably due "in greater measure to the nature of the tests themselves and to the social and educational background of the sexes" than to other causes.

In the construction of the present tests, the A.C.E.R. seems to have paid some attention to the sort of criticism just mentioned. Tests of the ML-MQ type, despite difficulties in construction and some deficiencies in standardisation, have the advantage of variety and flexibility, and avoid the need to employ a test battery when such a procedure is inconvenient. Moreover, in the Australian context, the best scholastic predictors at the higher levels have been found to be tests of verbal relation and number relation, rather than other tests. However, the intrinsic worth of ML-MQ and AL-AQ will not be fully known until they have been more widely employed than so far has been the case.

[298]

★A.C.E.R. Intermediate Tests C and D. Ages 10–14.0; 1939–53; 1 form; 2 tests; 3s. 9d. per 10 tests; postpaid within Australia; Australian Council for Educational Research. *

a) TEST C. 1939–53; formerly called A.C.E.R. General Test C; 1 form ['52]; mimeographed manual ['53]; 4s. per manual; 6d. per scoring key; 4s. 9d. per specimen set; 35(45) minutes.

b) TEST D. 1947–51; 1 form ['47]; 3s. 6d. per manual ['51]; 1s. per scoring key; 4s. 9d. per specimen set; 30(50) minutes.

REFERENCES

1. DUNN, S., AND SPEARRITT, D. "A Comparative Study of the Reliability of Some Verbal and Non-Verbal Intelligence Tests." Austral J Psychol 7:169–74 D '55. * (PA 31:1030)
2. DUNN, S. S., AND BROWNLESS, V. T. "Differences in Test and Retest Responses of a Group of Children to a Verbal and a Non-Verbal Test." Austral J Psychol 8:84–7 Je '56. * (PA 31:7910)

JAMES LUMSDEN, *Lecturer in Psychology, University of Western Australia, Nedlands, Australia.*

These tests are designed to assess the general aptitude for school work of children in Australian schools. Normalized standard score norms, called "IQ's" (mean 100, SD 15), are provided for the age range 10.0–14.0 years but

the authors point out that the norms at the extremes of the range may be inaccurate. Norms for Test D are based on 300 to 600 subjects at each 6-month age interval. Norms for Test C were obtained by indirect standardization from Test D for the upper ages and from the A.C.E.R. *Junior B Test* for the lower ages. Indirect standardization is not theoretically valid, but the experience of test users indicates that marked variations in "IQ" from one test to the other are not more frequent than usual.

The items are of the well tried Otis type: verbal analogies, number series, letter series, vocabulary, arithmetical problems. Item discrimination between high and low scorers on the original item pool was used to select items for the final test. Quarrying the recognized item types in this way is unlikely to produce a great test but it will rarely produce a bad one.

The reliability coefficients for Test D, as determined by test-retest, split-half, and Kuder-Richardson methods, range from .91 to .96. Validity has been determined by correlation with standardized reading and arithmetic achievement tests. The resulting coefficients (for a slightly restricted sample) range from .21 to .70, indicating that Test D can be expected to predict the results in formal school subjects with reasonable accuracy. No direct evidence concerning its validity for educational guidance or placement is given, but it can be inferred to be high. Reliability and validity data are provided with adequate supporting explanation in the manual for Test D but similar data are not given for Test C.

It is not clear whether Test C is intended to be strictly parallel to Test D. The method of norming and the omission of details about validity for Test C would suggest that this is so, but the correlation between the tests (given to a restricted sample on the same occasion) is only .81. One would expect some explanation from the authors concerning its lowness; however, their only statement is that the value "would almost certainly be lower than the immediate test-retest coefficient for Test C."

Intermediate Test D is a first rate test. Work by the reviewer indicates that it has no superior in Australia for educational prediction. The manual is a model achieving a nice balance between brevity, clarity, and technical completeness. The manual for Intermediate Test C is quite unsatisfactory and rather gives the impression that the test was hurriedly prepared to provide an alternative when the use of Intermediate Test D was undesirable.

[299]
*A.C.E.R. Junior A Test.** Ages 8.6–12.0; 1946–53; formerly called *General Test T;* 1 form ['46]; [revised] mimeographed manual ['53]; 6s. per 10 tests; 1s. 6d. per scoring key; 2s. 6d. per manual; 4s. 6d. per specimen set; postpaid within Australia; 30(40) minutes; Australian Council for Educational Research. *

R. WINTERBOURN, *Professor of Education, The University of Auckland, Auckland, New Zealand.*

This group test consists of 75 items, including the usual analogies, problems, similarities, best reasons, substitutions, arithmetic, and sequence arrangement types. Twenty-one of the items are nonverbal, mostly pictorial. These occur at intervals throughout the test, thus possibly helping to sustain the interest of the less verbally inclined children. At the same time, some users of the test have claimed that certain of these items are so attractive that they tend to distract the attention of some children. This is, of course, a subjective opinion. Another criticism is that the test, printed on seven foolscap-sized pages with the 75 items arranged without a break, may appear rather formidable to some children.

Since the test is intended for use with young children (although norms are provided for ages 8-6 to 12-0, the test is said to be most useful within the age range 9–11) directions are very clear and full, and are related to suitable practice examples. Scoring keys and easily read conversion tables are provided.

The test has been standardized so that the mean IQ for each age group is 100 and the SD 15. The standard error of measurement suggests reasonable limits of IQ variation. It is recommended that each score be interpreted in terms of an IQ range instead of being represented by a single IQ. This is a useful lesson for those teachers and others who still tend to think in terms of a rigidly fixed IQ. No IQ's are given beyond 135. It is claimed that the test discriminates satisfactorily among average and poorer than average children beyond 11 years of age but not among the brighter ones.

Certain possible shortcomings and limitations are apparent, but they are not of a major nature. The test's overall usefulness as an aid to grouping and classifying in schools has been demonstrated by its popularity for many years.

[300]
★**A.C.E.R. Junior B Test.** Ages 8.6–12.0; 1948–49; title on test is *General Ability Test: A.C.E.R. Junior B;* 1 form ['48]; mimeographed manual ['49]; no data on reliability and validity; no norms; distribution restricted; 5s. 3d. per 10 tests; 6d. per scoring key; 6s. 6d. per manual; 7s. 6d. per specimen set; postpaid within Australia; 35(60) minutes; Australian Council for Educational Research. *

REFERENCE
1. DUNN, S., AND SPEARRITT, D. "A Comparative Study of the Reliability of Some Verbal and Non-Verbal Intelligence Tests." *Austral J Psychol* 7:169–74 D '55. * (PA 31:1030)

R. WINTERBOURN, *Professor of Education, The University of Auckland, Auckland, New Zealand.*

Unlike the Junior A Test, this verbal group test of 65 items is broken down into five subtests, each with its own time limit. This arrangement overcomes one of the minor criticisms leveled at Junior A, i.e., that the test may appear quite formidable to some pupils. A further related point is that the practice examples are also broken into two groups, one being given before the first three subtests and the other before the last two. The subtests cover synonyms, problems, analogies, number series, and arithmetical problems.

Norms cover the ages 8-0 to 12-0. As for Junior A, there is an upper limit of 135 IQ. Easily used keys and conversion tables are supplied.

Validity coefficients ranging from .67 to .77 have been obtained between Junior B and the *A.C.E.R. Junior Non-Verbal Test.* Between Junior B and Intermediate Test D, correlations ranging from .75 to .85 have been obtained.

Test-retest and Kuder-Richardson reliability data are reported for the complete test and for the separate subtests. Retesting of 160 fifth grade Melbourne children after one week yielded a total score *r* of .86; retesting of 107 children after one year yielded a total score *r* of .88.

A Thurstone centroid analysis (*n* = 152 fifth grade Victorian children) of the intercorrelations found between Junior B and the A.C.E.R. arithmetic and reading achievement tests revealed loadings of .82 on what is called a general ability factor and .31 on a factor "which appears to be a reasoning factor of some kind."

This test has many features to commend it. It measures up quite well to the standard of test construction established by the A.C.E.R., a standard which is by no means reached by all test constructors. It should be apparent that the test's merit lies in the field of grouping and classifying rather than in that of individual assessment.

[301]
★A.C.E.R. Junior Non-Verbal Test. Ages 8.6–12.0; 1949–53; 1 form ['49]; [revised] mimeographed manual ['53]; 10s. per 10 tests; 1s. per scoring key; 3s. 6d. per manual; 5s. 6d. per specimen set; postpaid within Australia; 34(60) minutes; manual by D. Spearritt; Australian Council for Educational Research. *

REFERENCE
1. DUNN, S., AND SPEARRITT, D. "A Comparative Study of the Reliability of Some Verbal and Non-Verbal Intelligence Tests." *Austral J Psychol* 7:169–74 D '55. * (*PA* 31:1030)

D. A. PIDGEON, *Senior Officer, Test Services, National Foundation for Educational Research in England and Wales, London, England.*

This test is composed of 60 items which are divided into four separately timed subtests of 15 items each—time sequences, block series, diagrammatic analogies, and matrices. Each subtest is preceded by a page of practice examples illustrating the principle involved in that particular subtest; all instructions are given orally. The test is printed on rather cumbersome foolscap paper and the heavy type used does not give a particularly pleasing appearance.

Exceptional care was taken over the construction of the test, the choice of the four item types employed being based on research findings. A battery of nonverbal tests was given to a group of 167 fourth grade children in five Melbourne schools and the results submitted to factor analysis. The item types finally selected were those with high loadings on the general factor and negligible loadings on the verbalisation factor, thus producing items that presumably depend little on verbal ability for their solution.

The test has been well standardised on an effectively random sample of children attending all types of schools from the whole of Australia. The reliability coefficients quoted (average approximately .90) are not so high as might be desired, probably due in part to the fact that the test contains only 60 items. The manual, however, suggests that test results should be recorded in terms of an "IQ range," determined from the probable error of measurement, the value of which is given for three levels of raw score. In evidence of the test's validity, correlations ranging from .60 to .81 are quoted both with a verbal test and with another nonverbal test. The mean of the correlations with eight arithmetic and reading tests given to 152 Victorian fifth grade children is

.34. No evidence, however, is provided on the value of the test for predicting future school work, or on the possible results of remedial education.

There is no doubt that this is a well made test, but, in the light of recent research, one is bound to question its value for educational guidance. The evidence from research disagrees with the implication in the manual that remedial work is possible only with children whose nonverbal scores are significantly above their scores on a verbal test and not with those unfortunates who obtain low scores on both types of test. If, as the manual states, "a verbal test cannot be expected to give a satisfactory assessment of the general ability of children who are handicapped by poor ability in reading," then it is an unwarranted assumption to think that a nonverbal test will do instead. The results of factorial analyses indicate clearly that nonverbal tests such as this measure group or specific factors of their own besides "g," and it is difficult to see why the ability to discover relationships among pictorial or other nonverbal materials should predict school work which is, for the most part, verbal.

If an adequate reason can be found for obtaining a reliable measure of the "nonverbal" ability of young school children, this test will provide that measure; as an indication of the ability of children to reason, within the context of the usual school subjects, it is difficult to see how it, or any other nonverbal test of a similar type, can replace a verbal one. Certainly, as an indication of a child's potential for learning school work, the scores on this test should be used with extreme caution, if at all.

[302]
★APT Performance Test. Adults; 1954–57; Forms A, B ('54); 2 tests; manual ['57]; distribution restricted to clients; $4 per 50 tests; specimen set available upon request; postpaid; 5(10), 10(15) minutes for verbal, quantitative tests; Bentley Barnabas; Associated Personnel Technicians. *

[303]
*Academic Aptitude Test: Non-Verbal Intelligence: Acorn National Aptitude Tests. Grades 7–16 and adults; 1943–57; 4 scores: spatial relations, physical relations, graphic relations, total; 1 form ('57, identical with test copyrighted in 1944); directions sheet ('43); no norms for part scores; $3.75 per 25 tests; 25¢ per manual ('44); 50¢ per specimen set; postage extra; 26(45) minutes; Andrew Kobal, J. Wayne Wrightstone, and Karl R. Kunze; Acorn Publishing Co. *

For a review by William B. Schrader, see 4:274.

[304]

*Academic Aptitude Test: Verbal Intelligence: Acorn National Aptitude Tests. Grades 7–16 and adults; 1943–52; 4 scores: general information, mental alertness, comprehension of relations, total; 1 form ('52, identical with test copyrighted in 1943 except for minor changes); directions sheet ('43); $3.75 per 25 tests; 25¢ per manual ('45); 50¢ per specimen set; postage extra; 40(45) minutes; Andrew Kobal, J. Wayne Wrightstone, and Karl R. Kunze; Acorn Publishing Co. *

For a review by William B. Schrader, see 4:275; for a review by Marion A. Bills, see 3:215.

[305]

*Adaptability Test. Job applicants; 1942–54; Forms A, B ('42); revised manual ('54); $2.45 per 20 tests; 50¢ per specimen set; postage extra; 15(20) minutes; Joseph Tiffin and C. H. Lawshe; Science Research Associates. *

REFERENCES

1–3. See 3:216.
4. KAHN, D. F. *An Analysis of Factors Related to Life Insurance Selling.* Doctor's thesis, Purdue University (Lafayette, Ind.), 1948. *(PA 24:2884)*
5. PRED, GORDON D. *A Comparison of the Test Performance of "Good" and "Poor" Industrial Supervisors.* Master's thesis, Purdue University (Lafayette, Ind.), 1948.
6. STROMBERG, ELEROY L. "Testing Programs Draw Better Applicants." *Personnel Psychol* 1:21–9 sp '48. * *(PA 22:4157)*
7. GIESE, WILLIAM JAMES. "A Tested Method for the Selection of Office Personnel." *Personnel Psychol* 2:525–45 w '49. * *(PA 24:4278)*
8. HADLEY, J. M., AND KAHN, D. F. "A Comment on Wallace's Note on 'Factors Related to Life Insurance Selling.'" *J Appl Psychol* 33:359–62 Ag '49. * *(PA 24:2882)*
9. KAHN, D. F., AND HADLEY, J. M. "Factors Related to Life Insurance Selling." *J Appl Psychol* 33:132–40 Ap '49. * *(PA 24:357)*
10. LAWSHE, C. H. "How Can We Pick Better Supervisors?" *Personnel Psychol* 2:69–73 sp '49. * *(PA 23:5071)*
11. WALLACE, S. RAINS, JR. "A Note on Kahn and Hadley's 'Factors Related to Life Insurance Selling.'" *J Appl Psychol* 33:356–8 Ag '49. * *(PA 24:2884)*
12. POE, WESLEY A., AND BERG, IRWIN A. "Psychological Test Performance of Steel Industry Production Supervisors." *J Appl Psychol* 36:234–7 Ag '52. * *(PA 27:3794)*
13. ROSENSTEEL, RICHARD K. *A Validation of a Test Battery and Biographical Data for the Selection of Machine Operator Trainees.* Master's thesis, Bowling Green State University (Bowling Green, Ohio), 1953.
14. PATTON, WENDELL M., JR. "Studies in Industrial Empathy: III, A Study of Supervisory Empathy in the Textile Industry." *J Appl Psychol* 38:285–8 O '54. * *(PA 29:6378)*
15. ALBRIGHT, LEWIS E. "Validity Information Exchange, No. 9-44: D.O.T. Code 0-66.93, Seed Analyst." *Personnel Psychol* 9:522–3 w '56. *
16. ALBRIGHT, LEWIS EDWIN. *The Development of a Selection Process for an Inspection Task.* Doctor's thesis, Purdue University (Lafayette, Ind.), 1956. *(DA 16:2201)*

JOHN M. WILLITS, *Business and Industrial Psychologist, 566 Everett Ave., Palo Alto, California.*

"Designed to measure....adaptability or mental alertness" in job applicants—to differentiate rapid learners from other persons better suited to simple, routine jobs—this test is itself an example of adaptation—to the time pressures so typical in employment offices. In 20 minutes it can be made to yield a composite measure of several "factors" of intelligence, derived from Thurstone's analysis. This spiral-omnibus test's 35 items would be judged to sample at least two verbal factors, two numeri-

cal factors, and one spatial factor. Thus it averages, at most, only seven items per factor! And yet data in the manual indicate this single, composite measure to be reasonably reliable (with coefficients clustering around .8) and probably valid, to a degree, for many jobs in business and industry.

Let us assume that, like very many employment managers today, we are still having to settle for only 20 minutes' testing time in which to measure mental ability. Does this test represent the *best* available use of that amount of time?

In reply we may ask: "How specific are the demands of the different job openings, in terms of intelligence factors utilized?" For the differential placement of applicants, we would do well to weigh the feasibility of measuring *several separate* factors in the allotted 20 minutes. In that time, the *Short Employment Tests* would yield three separate measures—verbal knowledge, computational speed and accuracy, and visual-perceptual speed and accuracy—with at least as much reliability and validity. Or, from the 10 factored tests of the newly published *Employee Aptitude Survey,* we could assemble literally dozens of different 3-test batteries, each requiring only 20 minutes but each tailored to the requirements of a different job or family of jobs—again with no loss statistically.

The 8-page revised manual for the *Adaptability Test* makes specific mention of the *Technical Recommendations for Psychological Tests and Diagnostic Techniques,* and it reflects many of those recommendations. This manual states clearly the use for which the test is intended. It indicates, though rather obscurely (by the designation "Level B" and a fragmentary quote from the reference just mentioned), the required qualifications for administering and using the test. It describes very briefly, yet clearly, the procedures of administering, scoring, and interpreting. It discusses the essential topics of item selection, comparability of forms, reliability (by two methods), and validity (both intrinsic and predictive). It stresses the importance of accumulating local norms and setting local cutting scores. And it warns that this test presumably measures only a portion of the significant factors in success on any given job.

The manual reports that items "were retained on the basis of an internal consistency item analysis," but it gives little information on the method of analysis or the size of the resulting coefficients. Validity correlations ranging from .73 to .79 are reported with three other mental tests: Ohio State, Otis Self-Administering, and Wonderlic. The latter two of these resemble the *Adaptability Test* in pattern and in length.

Predictive validity of the test is indicated by means of expectancy tables for four employee populations, but three of these populations are only vaguely described. There are no data on ranges of age, education, experience, etc. Confidence limits are reported for all four tables, but score means and sigmas are not. The validating criteria are described in some detail, but there is no mention of the adequacy or the reliability of these criteria, which are chiefly ratings. Nor is there mention of the possibility of criterion contamination by test results.

Equivalence of the two forms is supported by data on average discrimination values and difficulty levels for one population, and by score means and sigmas for four other populations. Two of these populations are too small for this purpose (*n*'s of about 20 and 40), and it is not surprising that their means and sigmas vary widely.

Reliability evidence is apparently based on the same four populations, with neither the populations nor the testing conditions being adequately described. Though the manual specifically recommends "retesting of doubtful cases," there are no data on stability of retest scores nor on time elapsed between alternate forms reliability runs. Sigmas of score distributions are given for the reliability samples, but means are not. (Such means, if estimated from those of the form equivalence data, appear to vary widely.) There are no data on the error of measurement at different score levels. In justification of its split-half reliability data, the manual states that "this test is essentially a power test," but no data support this statement.

Norms, both in percentiles and in sigma units, are given for 12 populations, with adequate supporting statistics on their score distributions but with only minimal qualitative descriptions of their characteristics. Population sizes range from 32 to 6,000, with three *n*'s below 50 and six over 600. Three of the largest normative populations are each composed of several potentially unlike subgroups, e.g., applicants of one firm combined with present employees of another firm in a different industry. No data are presented to justify such group-

ings. The manual merely states that the "jobs are similar" and that the score distributions of the subgroups either showed "no significant difference" or that "there was a significant but not a practical difference."

The *Adaptability Test* undertakes to measure a composite of several intelligence factors in a single score, within a short time limit demanded by many employment situations today. But several such factors can now be measured separately in as little time and with as much precision. The test manual is well planned, touching on most of the topics currently deemed essential—but touching rather lightly on many of them. There are numerous gaps in supporting statistical evidence and in the essential qualitative descriptions of normative populations. The test is now 16 years old, and the current manual is four. More of the needed data doubtless will be found in the manual's next edition.

For reviews by Anne Anastasi and Marion A. Bills, see 3:216.

[306]

*Advanced Personnel Test. High-level employees in business; 1926–52; Form H ('52, identical with Form H of *Miller Analogies*, copyrighted in 1950); no data on reliability and validity when used in business; no business norms; distribution restricted and test administered at specified licensed testing centers; details may be obtained from publisher; examination fee, $1; 50(55) minutes; W. S. Miller; Psychological Corporation. *

For a review by John T. Dailey, see 352; for reviews by J. P. Guilford and Carl I. Hovland, see 4:304.

[307]

★Advanced Test N. Ages 15 and over; 1951–52; title on manual is *General Test N;* 1 form ['51]; mimeographed manual ['52]; no data on reliability and validity; distribution restricted; 6s. per 10 tests; 1s. 9d. per manual; 2s. 3d. per specimen set; postpaid within Australia; 50(65) minutes; Australian Council for Educational Research. *

A. E. G. PILLINER, *Lecturer in Education, University of Edinburgh, Edinburgh, Scotland.*

The item construction in this test bears witness to the painstaking thoroughness and technical skill that has come to be associated with the tests issued by the Australian Council for Educational Research. There is an almost complete absence of ambiguity, which is a noteworthy achievement with items of this quite high level of difficulty.

The test proper is preceded by a practice test in two parts. The first consists of seven items to which the answers are given, together with explanations of the reasoning by which these answers are reached. In the second, there are 15 items, presented without answers, which the testees work through at approximately the same rate as that required in the test proper. Five and 10 minutes, respectively, are allowed for the two parts of the practice test.

For the test proper, which consists of 76 items, the time allowance is 50 minutes. The items include analogies, number series, classi-fication, 3 x 3 matrices, and problems of vari-ous kinds. More than half of the test is verbal, about one quarter is nonverbal, and the rest is numerical. The various item types are scat-tered throughout the test rather than being grouped together. This means that a separate instruction has to be given with many items, so that the test is rather long in relation to the number of items it contains. What advantages the constructors claim for this way of ordering the items is not known.

There appears to be no manual of instruc-tions. Instead, four mimeographed sheets are supplied, providing instructions for administra-tion, norms, and the answer key. While each of these is clear in itself, the general effect is one of inadequacy. No information is given about reliability or validity, and we are not told what purpose the test is intended to serve. These omissions are unfortunate, since the result of entering the conversion table with a given raw score is a single "approximate IQ," the inter-pretation of which is puzzling since it is de-rived from a test with very mixed content. It would be useful to have a validity coefficient, or at least to know the views of the test con-structors who, presumably, had in mind some particular purpose for which the "approximate IQ" resulting from performance on this hetero-geneous test was thought to have sufficient validity.

No direct information is presented about the group of testees who worked the test for standardisation purposes. We are told, how-ever, that the test was normed against Form C of the Higher Examination of the *Otis Self-Administering Tests of Mental Ability,* so that the IQ's from the two tests are approximately comparable. In the absence of reliability and validity data for *Advanced Test N,* it would have been useful to quote its correlation with Otis Higher C. Since the standardisation group

must have worked both tests, this correlation should be available.

The test is difficult in terms of the Otis Higher C population on which the norms are indirectly based. For testees of 18 plus, a raw score of 25 gives an approximate IQ of 100. Thus there is ample headroom and good dis-crimination in the upper ability levels, though, in the absence of validity coefficients, what this discrimination means cannot be assessed. For testees between 13 and 18, age allowances are provided, those for the younger testees being startlingly large. A 13-year-old testee with a raw score of 11 or 12, for example, obtains an IQ of about 100. For young testees, therefore, re-sponses made at random may give sizeable, though quite meaningless, IQ's.

To sum up: *A.C.E.R. Advanced Test N* is a heterogeneous collection of unusually well con-structed items which will undoubtedly challenge even high ability testees. The reliability of the test and its general purpose supported by valid-ity data are not given. IQ's obtained with it for younger testees should be accepted with re-serve.

This reviewer has little doubt that this test will prove a useful instrument to those whose concern it is to measure adult ability, especially at its upper level, once the A.C.E.R. has ex-panded the somewhat meagre information at present available about the test.

C. SANDERS, *Professor of Education and Dean of the Faculty, University of Western Aus-tralia, Nedlands, Australia.*

In view of the complete lack of information about the purpose, construction, standardiza-tion, reliability, validity, and limitations of *Ad-vanced Test N,* it is difficult to recommend it. The accompanying 4-page manual tells us noth-ing at all about the test, its development, or its intended uses. The directions to supervisors are set out on the first page of the manual; two fur-ther pages contain tables to convert raw scores to IQ's in a range from IQ 77 (5 items cor-rect) to IQ 140 (70 items correct); and the last page provides the scoring key.

The test contains 76 items consisting of analogies, opposites, meanings, codes, number series, arithmetical problems, matrices, and space-form items. Test N is, therefore, a con-glomerate type of measure. It is described as a "general" test; this presumably means a test of general ability rather than a test for general use. In construction, it resembles a "general aptitude" test produced by the A.C.E.R. during the war and subsequently discontinued after trial.

One assumes that it remains listed because there is a certain demand for it by Australian public service and similar authorities. But far more information about the test should be supplied to justify its inclusion in the standard catalogue of the A.C.E.R., even though its sale is reported to be "restricted."

[308]

*American Council on Education Psychological Examination for College Freshmen.** Grade 13; 1924-54; 3 scores: quantitative, linguistic, total; IBM; Editions 1947, 1948, 1949, 1952, 1954; manual ('50); no data on reliability and validity; norms: 1947 Edition ('48), 1948 Edition ('49), 1949 Edition ('50), 1952 Edition ('53), 1954 Edition ('55); separate answer sheets must be used; $2.95 per 25 tests; $1 per 25 IBM answer sheets; 50¢ per set of scoring stencils; postage extra; 38(65) minutes; 1947 and earlier editions by L. L. Thurstone and Thelma Gwinn Thurstone; later editions prepared by publisher from materials developed by the Thurstones; Cooperative Test Division, Educational Testing Service. *

REFERENCES

1-48. See 40:1377.
49-143. See 3:217.
144-276. See 4:277.
277. Dodson, Mary H. *A Study in Shorthand and Typewriting Prognosis.* Master's thesis, University of Kentucky (Lexington, Ky.), 1943.
278. Solomon, Lewis E. *Some Relationships Between Reading Ability and Degree of Academic Success in College.* Doctor's thesis, University of Colorado (Boulder, Colo.), 1944.
279. Guinn, Mary P. *Aids for the Prognosis of Success in Typewriting.* Master's thesis, Kansas State Teachers College (Pittsburg, Kan.), 1948.
280. Silver, Charles E. *A Comparison of the Scores Made by College Reading Problem Cases on the California Short-form Test of Mental Maturity and Form I of the Wechsler-Bellevue Scales.* Master's thesis, Bowling Green State University (Bowling Green, Ohio), 1950.
281. Veon, Dorothy H. *The Relationship of Learning Factors Found in Certain Modern Foreign-Language Aptitude Tests to the Prediction of Shorthand Achievement in College.* Stillwater, Okla.: Division of Commerce, Oklahoma Agricultural and Mechanical College, 1950. Pp. 74. *
282. Berner, William. *An Evaluation of the Freshman Testing Program at Southern Methodist University.* Master's thesis, Southern Methodist University (Dallas, Tex.), 1951.
283. Hanson, Anna J. *An Analysis of "Drop Out" Students at Montana State University.* Master's thesis, Montana State University (Missoula, Mont.), 1951.
284. Huffman, Warren J. *Personality Variations Among Men Preparing to Teach Physical Education.* Doctor's thesis, University of Illinois (Urbana, Ill.), 1951. (DA 12:28)
285. Peterson, Leander H. *A Study of the Relative Validity of Q, L, and Total Scores of the American Council on Education Psychological Examination for Entering Freshmen.* Master's thesis, Chico State College (Chico, Calif.), 1951.
286. Welsh, Mary L. *A Comparison of Two Psychological Examinations in Predicting Academic Success of Ohio University Students.* Master's thesis, Ohio University (Athens, Ohio), 1951.
287. *Final Report on the 1951 National College Freshman Testing Program.* Princeton, N.J.: Cooperative Test Division, Educational Testing Service. [1952]. Pp. i, 27. *
288. Altus, William D. "Personality Correlates of Q-L Variability on the ACE." *J Consult Psychol* 16:284-91 Ag '52. * (PA 27:4237)
289. Angoff, William H. "Equating of the ACE Psychological Examinations for High School Students." Abstract. *Am Psychol* 7:287 Jl '52. *
290. Barrett, Dorothy M. "Differential Value of Q and L Scores on the ACE Psychological Examination for Predicting Achievement in College Mathematics." *J Psychol* 33:205-7 Ap '52. * (PA 26:7231)
291. Berdie, Ralph F., and Layton, Wilbur L. "Predicting Success in Law School." *J Appl Psychol* 36:257-60 Ag '52. * (PA 27:3839)
292. Bolton, Euri Belle. "Predictive Value for Academic Achievement of the A.C.E. Psychological Examination Scores." *Peabody J Ed* 29:345-60 My '52. *
293. Carrillo, Lawrence W., Jr., and Reichart, Robert R. "The Use of a 'Caution Factor' to Increase the Predictive Value of the A.C.E. Examination for Students of Engineering." *J Ed Res* 45:361-8 Ja '52. * (PA 27:2989)
294. Frederiksen, Norman, and Schrader, W. B. "The ACE Psychological Examination and High School Standing as Predictors of College Success." *J Appl Psychol* 36:261-5 Ag '52. * (PA 27:3786)
295. Freehill, Maurice F. "Student Self-Estimates as Guidance in Selecting Courses." *Col & Univ* 27:233-42 Ja '52. *
296. French, John W.; Tucker, Ledyard R.; Newman, Sidney H.; and Bobbitt, Joseph M. "A Factor Analysis of Aptitude and Achievement Entrance Tests and Course Grades at the United States Coast Guard Academy." *J Ed Psychol* 43:65-80 F '52. * (PA 26:7233)
297. Hanna, Joseph V. "Use of Speed Tests in Guidance." *Occupations* 30:329-31 F '52. *
298. Isaacson, Lee E. "Predictors of Success for Cooperative Occupational Education Classes in Kansas City, Missouri, High Schools." Abstract. *Am Psychol* 7:379 Jl '52. *
299. Johnson, Gordon. *An Analysis of Six Theories as to the Origin of Delinquent Behaviour.* Master's thesis, University of British Columbia (Vancouver, B.C., Canada), 1952.
300. Krathwohl, David R.; Ewing, T. N.; Gilbert, W. M.; and Cronbach, Lee J. "Prediction of Success in Architecture Courses." Abstract. *Am Psychol* 7:288-9 Jl '52. *
301. Lien, Arnold Juel. "A Comparative-Predictive Study of Students in the Four Curricula of a Teacher Education Institution." *J Exp Ed* 21:81-219 D '52. *
302. Newman, Sidney H.; French, John W.; and Bobbitt, Joseph M. "Analysis of Criteria for the Validation of Selection Measures at the United States Coast Guard Academy." *Ed & Psychol Meas* 12:394-407 au '52. * (PA 27:6159)
303. O'Neal, Charles E., and Cottle, William C. "A Comparison of Freshman Entrance Scores for Successful and Unsuccessful Football Scholarship Candidates at the University of Kansas." *Univ Kans B Ed* 7:21-3 N '52. *
304. Rasmussen, Elmer M. *A Study of the Changes in Tested General Intelligence of Students Between the Freshman and Senior Years as Measured by the ACE Psychological Examination for College Freshmen.* Doctor's thesis, University of Nebraska (Lincoln, Neb.), 1952.
305. Roesel, Hilde A. *The Value of the American Council on Education Psychological Examination in Assessing the Scholastic Potential of Entering Freshmen.* Master's thesis, East Tennessee State College (Johnson City, Tenn.), 1952.
306. Slater, Margaret M. *The Meaning of A.C.E. Scores of Students at Bowling Green State University.* Master's thesis, Bowling Green State University (Bowling Green, Ohio), 1952.
307. Traxler, Arthur E. "Reliability and Validity of the Scores on the Six Parts of the American Council on Education Psychological Examination." *Ed Rec B* 58:71-8 F '52. * (PA 26:7238)
308. Weiss, Irving. "Prediction of Academic Success in Dental School." *J Appl Psychol* 36:11-4 F '52. * (PA 26:7296)
309. Williams, John E., and Gerken, C. d'A. "'Verbal Factor' and 'Number Factor'—A Study of Two Tests." *Proc Iowa Acad Sci* 59:397-401 '52. * (PA 28:6599)
310. Anderson, Rose G. "Do Aptitudes Support Interests?" *Personnel & Guid J* 32:14-7 S '53. * (PA 28:4495)
311. Anderson, Scarvia B. "Prediction and Practice Tests at the College Level." *J Appl Psychol* 37:256-9 Ag '53. * (PA 28:6583)
312. Arn, Elmer H. R. *The Prediction of Academic Success in Ten Selected Science Areas at the University of Washington.* Doctor's thesis, University of Washington (Seattle, Wash.), 1953. (DA 13:495)
313. Bentz, V. J. "A Test-Retest Experiment on the Relationship Between Age and Mental Ability." Abstract. *Am Psychol* 8:319-20 Ag '53. *
314. Carlin, Leslie C. "A Longitudinal Comparison of Freshman-Senior Standing." *J Ed Res* 47:285-90 D '53. * (PA 28:6586)
315. Coleman, William. "An Economical Test Battery for Predicting Freshman Engineering Course Grades." *J Appl Psychol* 37:465-7 D '53. * (PA 29:1562)
316. Deridder, Lawrence M. "Relation Between Gross Scores on the A.C.E. and Academic Success." *J Ed Res* 46:353-8 Ja '53. * (PA 28:1558)
317. Drake, L. E., and Thomas, W. F. "Forecasting Academic Achievement in the College of Engineering." *J Eng Ed* 44:275-6 D '53. * (PA 29:1564)
318. Durnall, Edward J., Jr. "A Testing Program for Junior College for Women." *Jun Col J* 23:261-7 Ja '53. *
319. Hale, Peter P. "ACE Results of 72 Public Law 16 Teacher Trainees." *Sch & Soc* 77:41-3 Ja 17 '53. *
320. Hardaway, Charles. "Orientation Tests and Freshmen Scholarship." *Teach Col J* 25:10-1 O '53. *
321. Hendrix, O. R. "Predicting Success in Elementary Accounting." *J Appl Psychol* 37:75-7 Ap '53. * (PA 28:1479)
322. Herke, Mary L. *The Value of Three Measures in Predicting Academic Success for Graduate Students of Bowling*

Green State University. Master's thesis, Bowling Green State University (Bowling Green, Ohio), 1953.

323. JOHNSON, A. PEMBERTON. "Counseling Engineering Freshmen." *Ed & Psychol Meas* 13:133–44 sp '53. * (*PA* 28:1566)

324. KERN, DONALD W. *The Prediction of Academic Success of Freshmen in a Community College.* Doctor's thesis, New York University (New York, N.Y.), 1953. (*DA* 15:85)

325. LINS, L. J., AND PITT, HY. "The 'Staying Power' and Rate of Progress of University of Wisconsin Freshmen." *Col & Univ* 29:86–99 O '53. *

326. MALLOY, J. P. *The Prediction of College Achievement With the Life Experience Inventory.* Doctor's thesis, University of Nebraska (Lincoln, Neb.), 1953.

327. MANUEL, HERSCHEL T. "Expectancy Tables for Predicting Academic Success." *Yearb Nat Council Meas Used Ed* 10: 66–72 '53. *

328. MERRILL, REED M., AND HEATHERS, LOUISE B. "A Comparison of the Wechsler-Bellevue and ACE Tests on a University Counseling Center Group." *J Consult Psychol* 17:63–6 F '53. * (*PA* 28:1570)

329. MILAM, OTIS H. *A Study of the Relationship Between High School Grades, American Council on Education Psychological Examination for College Freshmen Scores, a Combination of the Two, and Grades Earned During the First Semester at Marshall College.* Master's thesis, Marshall College (Huntington, W.Va.), 1953.

330. MORTVEDT, AUDREY R. *Relative Effectiveness of a Local English Test, the ACE L-Score, Cumulative Grade Average, and the Cooperative General Culture Test in the Selection of Upper-Class Regent's Scholarship Winners.* Master's thesis, University of Nebraska (Lincoln, Neb.), 1953.

331. SAMENFELD, HERBERT W. "Predicting College Achievement." *J Higher Ed* 24:432–3 N '53. * (*PA* 28:6595)

332. SATZ, MARTIN A. *The Relationship Between Eleven Independent Variables and Academic Performance in Nine Social Science Areas at the University of Washington.* Doctor's thesis, University of Washington (Seattle, Wash.), 1953. (*DA* 14:635)

333. SCHWINGER, WILLIAM A. *The Predictive Efficiency of the ACE Test for Sociology I in the College of Nursing at Niagara University.* Master's thesis, Niagara University (Niagara Falls, N.Y.), 1953.

334. SEVERANCE, KATHERINE M. *The ACE and the Purdue English Placement Tests as Predictors of Academic Success at Baylor University.* Master's thesis, Baylor University (Waco, Tex.), 1953.

335. SOIKA, GEORGE R. *Effect of Warm-Up on Performance of the ACE Q-L Subtests.* Doctor's thesis, George Peabody College for Teachers (Nashville, Tenn.), 1953.

336. SOPER, MERWIN E. *The Value of the ACE Psychological Examination and the Purdue Pegboard Test of Manual Dexterity in Predicting High School Typewriting Grades.* Master's thesis, Drake University (Des Moines, Iowa), 1953.

337. SWENSON, LLOYD G. *An Investigation of the Areas Measured by Selected Psychological and Sociological Instruments.* Doctor's field study, Colorado State College of Education (Greeley, Colo.), 1953.

338. TOWNSEND, AGATHA. "A Study of the American Council on Education Psychological Examination, 1952 Edition." *Ed Rec B* 60:53–60 F '53. * (*PA* 28:1577)

339. WARD, WILLIAM D. *An Investigation of the Predictability of Academic Success of the A.C.E. and Certain Factors Measured by the Johnson Temperament Analysis.* Doctor's thesis, Bradley University (Peoria, Ill.), 1953. (*DA* 13:518)

340. WEBB, SAM C., AND MCCALL, JOHN N. "Predictors of Freshman Grades in a Southern University." *Ed & Psychol Meas* 13:660–3 w '53. * (*PA* 28:6598)

341. ANDERSON, MARY R., AND STEGMAN, ERWIN J. "Predictors of Freshman Achievement at Fort Hays Kansas State College." *Ed & Psychol Meas* 14:722–3 w '54. * (*PA* 29:7952)

342. BASS, BERNARD M., AND COATES, CHARLES H. "Validity Information Exchange, No. 7-082: R.O.T.C. Cadets." *Personnel Psychol* 7:553–4 w '54. *

343. BOLTON, EURI BELLE. "The Predictive Value of the Columbia and the Michigan Vocabulary Tests for Academic Achievement." *Peabody J Ed* 32:9–21 Jl '54. * (*PA* 29:7954)

344. CASEY, JOHN E. *An Investigation of the Effect of Increasing the Homogeneity of Response Patterns on the General Culture Test on Its Correlation With the American Council on Education Psychological Examination and the Interpretation of Data Test.* Doctor's thesis, Indiana University (Bloomington, Ind.), 1954.

345. CHAPPELL, TOLAN L.; CALLIS, ROBERT; RENZAGLIA, GUY A.; AND SPOHRER, MYRON A. "The Differential Prediction of Achievement at the University of Missouri." *Ed & Psychol Meas* 14:724–5 w '54. * (*PA* 29:7955)

346. DI VESTA, FRANCIS J. "Subscore Patterns on ACE Psychological Examination Related to Educational and Occupational Differences." *J Appl Psychol* 38:248–52 Ag '54. * (*PA* 29:6268)

347. FITZGIBBON, THOMAS J. *The Prediction of Academic Success of Freshmen at Bradley University.* Doctor's thesis, Bradley University (Peoria, Ill.), 1954. (*DA* 14:1170)

348. FREEHILL, MAURICE F. "The Co-operative English Test in Academic Counseling." *Col & Univ* 29:244–52 Ja '54. *

349. FRITZ, MARTIN F. "Q and L Difference Scores on the

A.C.E. Test." *Proc Iowa Acad Sci* 61:356–7 '54. * (*PA* 30: 3458)

350. GRAHAM, WARREN R. "Identification and Prediction of Two Training Criterion Factors." *J Appl Psychol* 38:96–9 Ap '54. * (*PA* 29:1798)

351. GUAZZO, EUGENE J., JR. *Predicting Academic Success of Architecture Students.* Master's thesis, Alabama Polytechnic Institute (Auburn, Ala.), 1954.

352. HANER, CHARLES F. "Wonderlic, Wesman P.C.T., and A.C.E.: A Comparison of Three Group Intelligence Tests." *Proc Iowa Acad Sci* 61:358–60 '54. * (*PA* 30:3460)

353. HENDRIX, O. R. " 'A Note' Acknowledged." *J Appl Psychol* 38:9 F '54. * (*PA* 29:1451)

354. HOERRES, MARY ANN, AND O'DEA, J. DAVID. "Predictive Value of the A.C.E." *J Higher Ed* 25:97 F '54. * (*PA* 28:8079)

355. HOLT, WELDON G. *Relationships Between the ACE and the Wesman Personnel Classification Test.* Master's thesis, University of Kansas (Lawrence, Kan.), 1954.

356. HOYT, DONALD P., AND NORMAN, WARREN T. "Adjustment and Academic Predictability." *J Counsel Psychol* 1:96–9 su '54. * (*PA* 29:3043)

357. JACOBS, ROBERT. "A Note on 'Predicting Success in Elementary Accounting.' " *J Appl Psychol* 38:7–8 F '54. * (*PA* 29:1456)

358. LEE, PHYLLIS J. *The Effectiveness of a Test Battery in Predicting Chemistry Grades.* Master's thesis, Alabama Polytechnic Institute (Auburn, Ala.), 1954.

359. MALECKI, GERALD S. *Effectiveness of the College Entrance Board Scholastic Aptitude Test, American Council on Education Psychological Examination, and High School Average for Predicting First Semester Scholarship at Fordham College.* Master's thesis, Fordham University (New York, N.Y.), 1954.

360. MARTIN, RICHARD R. *An Investigation of the Effectiveness of an Entrance Test Battery for Predicting Success in Law School.* Doctor's thesis, Temple University (Philadelphia, Pa.), 1954. (*DA* 16:575)

361. MURRAY, THOMAS. *An Analysis of First Year Chemistry Marks at the University of Scranton in Relation to High School Chemistry Marks, High School Quintile Standings and American Council on Education Test Scores.* Master's thesis, University of Scranton (Scranton, Pa.), 1954.

362. ROGO, ROBERT A. *The Relationship of Scores of the Diagnostic Reading Tests: Survey Section and the American Council on Education Psychological Examination, to First Semester Freshman Honor Point Averages for Students in the College of Arts and Sciences at the University of Detroit.* Master's thesis, University of Detroit (Detroit, Mich.), 1954.

363. SCHMITZ, ROY M., AND HOLMES, JOHN L. "Relationship of Certain Measured Abilities to Freshman Engineering Achievement," pp. 32–42. (*PA* 29:1584) In *Selection and Counseling of Students in Engineering.* Edited by Wilbur L. Layton. Minnesota Studies in Student Personnel Work, No. 4. Minneapolis, Minn.: University of Minnesota Press, 1954. Pp. iv, 89. *

364. SEASHORE, HAROLD. "Tenth Grade Tests as Predictors of Twelfth Grade Scholarship and College Entrance Status." Comment by David V. Tiedeman. *J Counsel Psychol* 1:106–15 su '54. * (*PA* 29:3054)

365. SEIGLE, WILLIAM F. "Prediction of Success in College Mathematics at Washburn University." *J Ed Res* 47:577–88 Ap '54. * (*PA* 29:2982)

366. SKARD, ØYVIND; AURSAND, INGER MARIE; AND BRAATEN, LEIF J. "Development and Application of Tests for University Students in Norway: A Report on Parts of a Research Project." *Psychol Monogr* 68(12):1–54 '54. * (*PA* 29:7971)

367. SPRING, LAURENCE E. *The American Council on Education Psychological Examination for College Freshmen as a Predictive Measure for Student Selection in Five Curriculums at the Buffalo State Technical Institute.* Master's thesis, University of Buffalo (Buffalo, N.Y.), 1954.

368. STONE, JOICS B. "Differential Prediction of Academic Success at Brigham Young University." *J Appl Psychol* 38: 109–10 Ap '54. * (*PA* 29:3057)

369. WASHBURNE, NORMAN F., AND ANDREW, DEAN C. "Relation of Scholastic Aptitude to Socioeconomic Status and to a Rural-to-Urban Continuum." *J Appl Psychol* 38:113–5 Ap '54. * (*PA* 29:3059)

370. AHMANN, J. STANLEY. "Prediction of the Probability of Graduation of Engineering Transfer Students." *J Exp Ed* 23:281–8 Je '55. * (*PA* 30:3451)

371. ANDERSON, LEONE; RANKIN, RICHARD; RICHARDSON, JOY; SASSENRATH, JULIUS; AND THOMAS, JULIUS. "Differential Methods of Solving Selected Problems on the ACE Psychological Examination." *J Exp Ed* 24:133–40 D '55. * (*PA* 31:8803)

372. BAKER, PAUL C. *Experiments in Variable Selection for Prediction of Academic Achievement.* Doctor's thesis, Purdue University (Lafayette, Ind.), 1955. (*DA* 15:2565)

373. BERTRAND, JOHN R. "Relation Between High School Average Grade and Academic Achievement of Agricultural Students, Agricultural and Mechanical College of Texas." *Col & Univ* 30:166–81 Ja '55. * (*PA* 31:3771)

374. BOLIN, BYRON J. "A Comparison of Raven's Progressive Matrices (1938) With the ACE Psychological Examination and the Otis Gamma Mental Ability Test." Abstract. *J Consult Psychol* 19:400 O '55. *

375. CHAPMAN, HAROLD M. "The Prediction of Freshman

Achievement From a Combination of Test Scores and High School Grades." Abstract. *Am Psychol* 10:373 Ag '55. *

376. CHAPMAN, HAROLD M. *The Prediction of Freshman Scholarship From a Combination of Standardized Test Scores and High School Grades.* Doctor's thesis, University of Houston (Houston, Tex.), 1955. (*DA* 15:1201)

377. COLLINS, CHARLES C. *The Relationship of Breadth of Academic Interest to Academic Achievement and Academic Aptitude.* Doctor's thesis, Stanford University (Stanford, Calif.), 1955. (*DA* 15:1782)

378. DUNGAN, EARL W. *An Evaluation of the Orientation Test Battery at Dickinson State Teachers College for Purposes of Prediction and Counseling.* Doctor's field study, Colorado State College of Education (Greeley, Colo.), 1955.

379. GRATER, HARRY, AND THALMAN, W. A. "A Statistical Analysis of the Relationship Between American Council on Education Psychological Examination Ratings and Grade-Point Averages." *J Ed Res* 49:07–10 D '55. * (*PA* 30:7759)

380. HAYNES, JERRY O. *Some Predictive Factors of Academic Success in Two Curricula of a Land-Grant College.* Master's thesis, Alabama Polytechnic Institute (Auburn, Ala.), 1955.

381. JACKSON, ROBERT A. "Prediction of the Academic Success of College Freshmen." *J Ed Psychol* 46:296–301 My '55. * (*PA* 30:6333)

382. KLUGH, HENRY B., AND BENDIG, A. W. "The Manifest Anxiety and ACE Scales and College Achievement." Abstract. *J Consult Psychol* 19:487 D '55. *

383. KRAMAR, EDWARD J. J. *The Relationships of the Wechsler-Bellevue and A.C.E. Intelligence Tests With Performance Scores in Speaking and the Brown-Carlsen Listening Comprehension Test.* Doctor's thesis, Florida State University (Tallahassee, Fla.), 1955. (*DA* 15:2599)

384. MALLOY, JOHN. "The Prediction of College Achievement With the Life Experience Inventory." *Ed & Psychol Meas* 15:170–80 su '55. * (*PA* 30:3462)

385. MALLOY, JOHN P.; WYSOCKI, BOLESLAW; AND GRAHAM, LEO F. "Predicting Attrition-Survival in First Year Engineering." *J Ed Psychol* 46:217–21 Ap '55. * (*PA* 30:1624)

386. MELTON, RICHARD S. "Differentiation of Successful and Unsuccessful Premedical Students." *J Appl Psychol* 39:397–400 D '55. * (*PA* 30:7769)

387. MULLINS, CECIL J. "The Effect of Reading Ability on Two Standardized Classification Tests." *J Ed Psychol* 46:189–92 Mr '55. * (*PA* 30:1627)

388. MUTH, MARTHA JEAN. *Attitude Toward Mathematics as a Function of the Discrepancy Between Q and L Scores of the A.C.E.* Master's thesis, University of Florida (Gainesville, Fla.), 1955.

389. NAPP, FREDERICK P. *Forecasting Scholastic Achievement at Eastern New Mexico University on the Basis of Scores on the American Council on Education Psychological Examination.* Master's thesis, Eastern New Mexico University (Portales, N.M.), 1955.

390. PAUK, WALTER J. *An Analysis of Certain Characteristics of Above-Average and Below-Average Male and Female Readers at the Ninth-Grade Level.* Doctor's thesis, Cornell University (Ithaca, N.Y.), 1955. (*DA* 16:285)

391. POUNDS, RALPH L. "Prediction of Academic Success at the University of Cincinnati, Teachers College: Progress Report II." *Yearb Nat Council Meas Used Ed* 12(pt 2):12–31 '55. *

392. REILLY, WILLIAM J. *The Efficiency of the A.C.E. in Predicting English One and Two Grades in the College of Arts and Sciences at Niagara University.* Master's thesis, Niagara University (Niagara Falls, N.Y.), 1955.

393. ROYER, J. EVERETT. *Selection and Use of Certain Factors Significant in Predicting Achievement of Students in First-Semester Accounting at the University of Miami, 1950-1953.* Doctor's thesis, Indiana University (Bloomington, Ind.), 1955.

394. SCHULZ, R. E., AND CALVIN, ALLEN D. "A Failure to Replicate the Finding of a Negative Correlation Between Manifest Anxiety and ACE Scores." *J Consult Psychol* 19:223–4 Je '55. * (*PA* 30:2919)

395. SHEA, JOSEPH AUGUSTINE. *Predictive Value of Various Combinations of Standardized Tests and Subtests for Prognosis of Teaching Efficiency.* Catholic University of America, Educational Research Monograph, Vol. 19, No. 6. Washington, D.C.: Catholic University of America Press, Inc., June 1, 1955. Pp. xi, 44. *

396. SUPEAU, GERALD A. *Norms and Correlations of Scores Between the A. C. E. Psychological Examinations and Freshman Grades Received in History One and Two in the College of Arts and Sciences of Niagara University From 1948 to 1953.* Master's thesis, Niagara University (Niagara Falls, N.Y.), 1955.

397. TRAXLER, ARTHUR E. "Comparative Value of Certain Mental Ability Tests for Predicting School Marks in Two Independent Schools." *Ed Rec B* 65:65–75 F '55. * (*PA* 29:7976)

398. TRAXLER, ARTHUR E. "Relationship of Certain Predictive Measures to Achievement in First-Year French and Latin." *Ed Rec B* 66:73–7 Jl '55. * (*PA* 30:5181)

399. ANDERSON, RODNEY E. *The Use of Entrance Tests in the Differential Prediction of Freshman College Achievement, and the Effect of an Item Analysis on the Efficiency of the Predictive Batteries.* Doctor's thesis, Indiana University (Bloomington, Ind.), 1956. (*DA* 16:2344)

400. ANNESER, ROBERT. *An Evaluation of Scholastic Aptitude in Predicting Senior Level Achievement at Ohio University.* Master's thesis, Ohio University (Athens, Ohio), 1956.

401. BEAVER, ALMA P. "Psychometric Data and Survival in a College of Nursing." *Psychol Rep* 2:223–6 Je '56. * (*PA* 31:1738)

402. BOYER, LEE E., AND KOKEN, JAMES E. "Admissions Test as Criteria for Success in College." *J Ed Res* 50:313–5 D '56. * (*PA* 32:2095)

403. BOYER, ROSCOE A. *A Study of the Academic Success of Undergraduate Students as Identified by Aptitude Test Profiles.* Doctor's thesis, Indiana University (Bloomington, Ind.), 1956. (*DA* 15:89)

404. BRAGG, EMMA W. "A Study of Student Withdrawal at W.U.'" *J Ed Psychol* 47:199–202 Ap '56. *

405. CAPELLINI, JOHN, JR. *Norms and Relative Validity of the A.C.E. in Prediction of Scholastic Accomplishment of Freshmen in the College of Business Administration at Niagara University in the Fall Semester of 1955-1956.* Master's thesis, Niagara University (Niagara Falls, N.Y.), 1956.

406. FRICK, J. W., AND KEENER, HELEN E. "A Validation Study of the Prediction of College Achievement." *J Appl Psychol* 40:251–2 Ag '56. * (*PA* 31:6674)

407. HENDERSON, HAROLD L. "Prediction of Academic Success." *Psychol Rep* 2:321–2 S '56. * (*PA* 31:3784)

408. KEELER, HAROLD J. *Predicting Teacher Effectiveness of Graduates of the State University of New York Teachers Colleges.* Doctor's thesis, Cornell University (Ithaca, N.Y.), 1956. (*DA* 17:545)

409. NORTH, ROBERT D. "A Comparison of the Cooperative School and College Ability Tests: College Ability Test, and the American Council Psychological Examination: Reliabilities, Intercorrelations, and Correlations With the Diagnostic Reading Tests." *Ed Rec B* 67:65–72 F '56. * (*PA* 31:3800)

410. POLLARD, JAMES R. *The Significance of Quantitative and Linguistic Abilities for Academic Performance and High School Adjustment.* Doctor's thesis, University of Missouri (Columbia, Mo.), 1956. (*DA* 16:2089)

411. SMITH, GEORGE B. *Who Should Be Eliminated? A Study of Selective Admission to College.* University of Kansas Publications, Kansas Studies in Education, Vol. 7, No. 1. Lawrence, Kan.: School of Education, the University, December 1956. Pp. 28. Paper. *

412. TRAXLER, ARTHUR E. "Should SCAT Scat ACE? A Comparison Between the Cooperative School and College Ability Tests, Form 1A, and the American Council on Education Psychological Examination, 1948 College Freshman Edition, as to Difficulty and Value for Predicting School Marks." *Ed Rec B* 67:51–63 F '56. * (*PA* 31:3817)

413. VAN DER JAGT, E. R., AND MESNER, D. M. "Predictability of Success in College Courses, by Accelerating and Non-Accelerating Students as Measured by Scores Made by Entering Freshmen on A.C.E. and Cooperative Reading Test." *Sci Ed* 40:327–32 O '56. *

414. WEBB, SAM C. "The Prediction of Achievement for First Year Dental Students." *Ed & Psychol Meas* 16:543–8 w '56. *

415. WINING, MARY H. *Prediction of First Year Mathematics Grades at Central Washington College of Education With the ACE Psychological Examination.* Master's thesis, Central Washington College of Education (Ellensburg, Wash.), 1956.

416. ANGOFF, WILLIAM H. "The 'Equating' of Non-Parallel Tests." *J Exp Ed* 25:241–7 Mr '57. *

417. BRICE, MARSHALL M. "A Comparison of Subjective Predictions With Objective Predictions of College Achievement." *Col & Univ* 32:347–53 sp '57. *

418. CHANSKY, NORMAN M., AND BREGMAN, MARTIN. "Improvement of Reading in College." *J Ed Res* 51:313–7 D '57. *

419. GOWAN, J. C. "Intelligence, Interests, and Reading Ability in Relation to Scholastic Achievement." *Psychol Newsl* 8:85–7 Mr–Ap '57. * (*PA* 32:3346)

420. HENDERSON, HAROLD L. "Predictors of Freshmen Grades in a Long Island College." *Ed & Psychol Meas* 17:623–7 w '57. *

421. HEWER, VIVIAN H. "Vocational Interest-Achievement-Ability Interrelationships at the College Level." *J Counsel Psychol* 4:234–8 fall '57. *

422. HOLT, WELDON G.; OTTMAN, DONALD K.; AND COTTLE, WILLIAM C. "Evidenced Relationships Between the 'ACE' and the Wesman Personnel Classification Test." *J Ed Res* 51:71–7 S '57. *

423. KIM, KI SUK. *The Use of Certain Measurements of Academic Aptitude, Study Habits, Motivation, and Personality in the Prediction of Academic Achievement.* Doctor's thesis, Louisiana State University (Baton Rouge, La.), 1957. (*DA* 18:150)

424. KLUGMAN, SAMUEL F. "Agreement Between Two Tests as Predictors of College Success." *Personnel & Guid J* 36:255–8 D '57. *

425. LARSEN, TORA M. *A Study of the Student Personnel Records at East Carolina College as Relates to Prediction in Elementary Accounting.* Doctor's thesis, University of Minnesota (Minneapolis, Minn.), 1957. (*DA* 18:1304)

426. LOWRY, CARMEN E. *The Prediction of Academic Success in a Private Liberal Arts College for Negroes.* Doctor's thesis, University of Texas (Austin, Tex.), 1957. (*DA* 17:2500)

427. MANUEL, HERSCHEL T. "Aptitude Tests for College Admission." *Yearb Nat Council Meas Used Ed* 14:20–7 '57. *

428. NORTH, ROBERT D. "A Further Report on the Cooperative College Ability Test." *Ed Rec B* 69:60–2 F '57. * (*PA* 32:2119)

429. STONE, SOLOMON. *The Contribution of Intelligence, In-*

terests, Temperament and Certain Personality Variables to Academic Achievement in a Physical Science and Mathematics Curriculum. Doctor's thesis, New York University (New York, N.Y.), 1957. (*DA* 18:669)

430. ALTUS, WILLIAM D. "Q-L Variability, MMPI Responses, and College Males." *J Consult Psychol* 22:367–71 O '58. *

431. BARRETT, RICHARD S. "The Process of Predicting Job Performance." *Personnel Psychol* 11:39–57 sp '58. *

432. BERRY, CHARLES A., AND JONES, ARLYNNE L. "The Predictive Value of the Tests of the National Freshman Testing Program for Grambling College Freshmen." *Negro Ed R* 9: 23–33 Ja '58. *

433. EVENSON, A. B., AND SMITH, D. E. "A Study of Matriculation in Alberta." *Alberta J Ed Res* 4:67–83 Je '58. *

434. GOWAN, J. C. "Intercorrelations and Factor Analysis of Tests Given to Teaching Candidates." *J Exp Ed* 27:1–22 S '58. *

435. MOORE, CHARLES W. *Some Relationships Between Standardized Test Scores and Academic Performance in the College of Business Administration of the University of Houston.* Doctor's thesis, University of Houston (Houston, Tex.), 1958. (*DA* 19:356)

436. PHILLIPS, JOHN C. "Normative Data Information Exchange, No. 11-6." *Personnel Psychol* 11:271 su '58. *

437. SOPCHAK, ANDREW L. "Prediction of College Performance by Commonly Used Tests." *J Clin Psychol* 14:194–7 Ap '58. *

438. SPILKA, B., AND KIMBLE, GLORIA. "Personality Correlates of Q-L Differentials on the ACE." Abstract. *J Consult Psychol* 22:142 Ap '58. *

439. VINCENT, LEWIS. "A Comparison of the Quantitative Items of the A.C.E. Psychological With Similar Items in the Cooperative School and College Abilities Tests." *Yearb Nat Council Meas Used Ed* 15:144–9 '58. *

HANFORD M. FOWLER, *Professor of Education, University of Toronto, Toronto, Ontario, Canada.*

Whereas the *Cooperative School and College Ability Tests* (SCAT) may be likened to a lusty newborn infant, still unproved but crying for research attention, the *American Council on Education Psychological Examination for College Freshmen* (ACE) should be considered a venerable gentleman of demonstrated worth who is now looking forward to an early retirement. Undoubtedly, ACE is one of the oldest and most respected psychological instruments on the market. Its continued use by many institutions across the country attests its value and its usefulness. Evidence of the great research interest in ACE may be found in the large number of references to it in the research literature. But like all members of an older generation, worthy and respected though they may be, ACE must soon give way to other younger, more modern, possibly more vigorous, instruments. No doubt many will prefer to remain with ACE as long as it is available and will regret its passing.

Although ACE seems destined to be superseded by SCAT, it is quite different from SCAT in a number of ways. Primarily, ACE is a psychological test of mental abilities and not a measure of "school-learned abilities," as is SCAT. This reviewer must confess that although he suspects there are differences between the two, the exact nature of these differences escapes him. Probably the best way to get

at least a superficial knowledge of what ACE measures is to examine the test itself.

According to the manual, which has not been revised since 1950, "the examination consists of the six tests that have been used for several years." These are: arithmetical reasoning, 20 items; figure analogies, 30 items; number series, 30 items; same-opposite, 50 items; completion (vocabulary), 30 items; and verbal analogies, 40 items. The first three subtests make up the Q-score or quantitative score; the last three, the L-score or linguistic score.

The latest edition of ACE (1954), like earlier editions, is accompanied by a norms bulletin which is separate from the manual. This bulletin gives a list of the colleges which reported scores to the Cooperative Test Division and the results of the statistical analyses of these scores. The norms data consist of mean scores of individual colleges and universities and percentile ranks corresponding to the Q, L, and total scores. Also included in the bulletin are equivalent scores for the 1948, 1949, 1952, and 1954 college editions.

Strong features of the ACE are: its authorship and sponsorship (the Thurstones, who were the original authors, are well known for their work in the factorial analysis of psychological tests, and the Cooperative Test Division provides as good a sponsorship as can be found in the country); its use of the Q and L scores which, although they may not be factorially pure, provide at least the elements of a differential guidance along the lines of what appear to be the two chief correlates of success in high school and college; its good construction and sound, if somewhat conservative, treatment of mechanical features, such as printing, and format; the adequate statistical treatment; and the reporting service which has kept users informed of results currently being obtained by colleges across the country.

On the other hand, the weaknesses of ACE outnumber the strengths, and some of them are serious. Before these are discussed, it might be pointed out that in the last ten years or so there has been a considerable decline in the number of institutions using ACE and in the number of students whose scores were reported. In 1947, 293 colleges reported scores of 65,276 freshmen, whereas in 1954 these numbers had dropped to 186 and 26,603. It would be interesting to determine why so many colleges have stopped using ACE. Some, perhaps because of increasing awareness of weaknesses in ACE, may have decided to use another test, possibly SCAT after it became available.

Adverse criticism of ACE may be applied to the following aspects of the test: weaknesses in the norms; relatively low validity; absence of reporting of criterion statistics such as reliability and validity estimates; limitations in possible score interpretation; and deficiencies in basic characteristics of a good college aptitude test such as a convenient length of administration time and a suitable difficulty level. Other complaints which have been voiced by Berdie and others (263) relate to deficiencies in the Q score, to the adulterated nature of the part scores, and to the extensive overlap between the part scores as evidenced by reported high correlations between L and Q.

Those who believe that the worth of an aptitude test depends upon how adequately its scores can be interpreted in an individual situation will undoubtedly be unhappy about the norms for ACE. In the first place, no attempt has been made to present what might be called national norms. The norming samples, consisting of colleges who have reported scores, are accidental, not planned. The test user must feel very insecure about the norms, especially if he finds it difficult to identify the position of his own institution in the doubtful classification of colleges on which the norms are based. Secondly, there is no attempt to provide data, or instructions, which might help users to construct local norms. Surely the essence of usefulness of a standardized test is the provision of information which will make the test readily interpretable and abundantly meaningful in the local situation! Possibly soundly constructed national norms, if they were available, would provide some users with all the yardsticks they need; some users would prefer local norms; others might like both. ACE provides neither.

The validity of ACE has been questioned for some time. In particular, the Q scores have failed to measure up under the relentless scrutiny of the research worker. More serious than the low validity which has been reported frequently is the lack of consistency in the reported validity coefficients. Scientists are concerned more by inconsistent results than by consistently unsatisfactory results; in the latter case at least they know what to do. Berdie, Dressel, and Kelso (263) report that "correlations with total point average vary from .25 to

.66. Within any particular subject area there is marked variation from .08 to .44." Studies such as this lead us to conclude that the validity of ACE is an uncertain quantity for institutions generally. The new user is forced to embark upon a time-consuming preliminary study to demonstrate validity in the local situation.

No reference is made in any of the norms bulletins to reliability estimates or validity estimates. This omission appears to be inexcusable in a modern test which has advanced well beyond the experimental stages. No doubt many studies have been completed. The publishers should summarize and present the salient features of these results. In a study designed to equate scores of the 1952 and 1954 editions, summary statistics are presented for a group of 511 students from one school system, but these results can hardly be considered representative of any large group of colleges.

Because of the lack of adequate norms, and for other reasons, it is not possible to get a clear-cut interpretation of the meaning of the Q and L scores. In the first place, it is difficult to believe that the sum of scores of three tests, which on the surface at least appear to be quite dissimilar, can reflect the type of homogeneity or psychological purity which makes test interpretation easy. Also, the content of the tests is not directly related to the content of the typical college curriculum. Perhaps most distressing is the absence of any sort of conversion score or standardized score to render the scores meaningful; reliance upon raw scores and uncertain norms is an open invitation to misuse of the scores. The absence of any kind of profile and of warnings about possible misinterpretations, such as the common mistake of considering scores as points rather than as intervals, contribute to the general picture of inadequacy.

Other deficiencies limiting the usefulness of ACE are the absence of comparable forms, the single difficulty level, and the amount of time it takes for administration. There are very few exceptions to the rule that all good tests require comparable forms if for no other reason than to provide double testing and an average of scores to reduce errors of measurement. The fact that ACE has only one difficulty level is particularly serious in a country which has a wide divergence of university standards. It has been said that the graduates of some American universities can just barely meet the entrance requirements of others. If this is so, it is obvious that ACE cannot be suitable for all institutions. Administration time is another factor which should be given careful consideration. Even though it is granted that validity is the ultimate criterion of a test's value, validity has little more than academic interest if a test is not used. ACE requires 58 minutes to administer after the general instructions have been read and all preliminary preparations have been completed. In these days of 50-minute college periods a test has to be really good before the layman is convinced that it is worth an hour or more of testing time.

All things considered, it must be concluded that ACE has pretty well outlived its usefulness. Its disadvantages greatly outweigh its advantages. This is not to deny that many colleges have made good use of the test, and may still find it useful. Much depends upon the individual situation. Those who have developed local norms, and have evidence of validity in the local situation, can rest content. But as a college aptitude test for general use ACE is lacking too much in too many ways. Fortunately what appears to be a worthy substitute (SCAT) is now available.

WILLIAM B. MICHAEL, *Director, The Testing Bureau, and Professor of Psychology and Education, University of Southern California, Los Angeles, California.*

Resembling in many respects the forms prepared for high school students, the *American Council on Education Psychological Examination for College Freshmen* (ACE) consists of six subtests. From the 120 items in the three subtests Completion, Same-Opposite, and Verbal Analogies a verbal score is obtained, and from the 80 items in the subtests Arithmetic, Figure Analogies, and Number Series a quantitative score is derived. Neither the verbal nor the quantitative section approximates factorial purity—a fact that is supported not only by a correlation of .54 between the two parts for a large sample of examinees (reported in a pamphlet upon norms and equating procedures accompanying the 1954 edition of the examination), but also by an inspection of the diversified content of the items themselves. Simply stated, the instrument furnishes an indication of general scholastic aptitude in which verbal reasoning and numerical abilities are primarily required.

Widely used by colleges for purposes of ad-

mission, placement, and guidance, the various forms of the examination offer satisfactorily reliable part and total scores. In addition, normative data in terms of percentile ranks have been carefully prepared for each of the forms and are issued routinely to authorized testing personnel. Other commendable features are found in the relative ease of administration, the simplicity of scoring, and the existence of numerous practice items at the beginning of each subtest.

From a negative standpoint the lack of validity data in the manual and in the bulletins containing normative information cannot be overlooked. Another limiting characteristic would appear to be the predominance of a speed factor, especially in the instance of the sections yielding a quantitative score. Since the items are arranged in order of difficulty, it might be anticipated, particularly for parts contributing to the quantitative score, that much validity might be lost in view of the fact that several of the more difficult items capable of discriminating between potentially bright and dull students would not be reached by examinees of either ability level. Thus, the scores realized would fail to distinguish in a too adequate fashion important amounts of individual differences in ability. Concerning the speed factor in this test, it was informally reported about five years ago by a discussant in the audience of a professional meeting of measurement workers that when the verbal and quantitative scores were combined in a regression equation to predict success in an engineering curriculum in a college in upstate New York, a negative (suppressor) weight for the quantitative scores arose. When the time limits were extended at the discretion of the examiner to approximate power conditions, substantial increments in predictive validity coefficients occurred.

It is interesting to note that both the *Cooperative School and College Ability Test* (SCAT), recently developed by the Cooperative Test Division of the Educational Testing Service more or less as a substitute for the ACE series, and the *College Qualification Test* (CQT), lately prepared by the Psychological Corporation, contain items that reflect somewhat more specific types of learning experiences in the high school curriculum than do the ACE forms. Moreover, both the SCAT and the CQT more nearly approximate the readily defensible power condition than do the rather speeded ACE counterparts. Since the interpretative materials and statistical data in the manual and in the special bulletins for the SCAT are unusually complete and, likewise, since the manual for the CQT is excellent in virtually every respect, one may anticipate that the ACE college series will soon be displaced, even though the examination, assured of a prominent position in the history of psychological testing, has been a reliable and serviceable instrument upon which many meaningful normative data have been collected.

For reviews by W. D. Commins and J. P. Guilford of an earlier edition, see 3:217; for reviews by Jack W. Dunlap and Robert L. Thorndike, see 40:1377; for reviews by Anne Anastasi and David Segel, see 38:1037.

[309]

*American Council on Education Psychological Examination for High School Students. Grades 9–12; 1933–54; 3 scores: quantitative, linguistic, total; IBM; Editions 1946, 1947, 1948, 1953; manual ['54]; no data on validity; separate answer sheets must be used; $3.25 per 25 tests; $1 per 25 IBM answer sheets; 50¢ per set of scoring stencils; postage extra; 35(65) minutes; 1947 and earlier editions by L. L. Thurstone and Thelma Gwinn Thurstone; later editions prepared by publisher from materials developed by the Thurstones; Cooperative Test Division, Educational Testing Service. *

REFERENCES

1–2. See 40:1378.
3–9. See 3:218.
10–11. See 4:278.
12. LAYTON, WILBUR L. "The Relation of Ninth Grade Test Scores to Twelfth Grade Test Scores and High School Rank." *J Appl Psychol* 38:10–1 F '54. * (PA 29:1570)

WILLIAM B. MICHAEL, *Director, The Testing Bureau, and Professor of Psychology and Education, University of Southern California, Los Angeles, California.*

Although the last annual release of the *American Council on Education Psychological Examination for High School Students* (ACE) was in 1953, various annual forms of the test are still being widely used. Two parts, Same-Opposites (consisting of 50 antonym-synonym multiple choice items) and Completion (made up of 60 items in which a definition of a word is followed by five letters, one of them being the initial letter of the word desired), furnish a verbal, or linguistic, score. The other two parts, Arithmetic (including 20 thought problems cast in multiple choice form) and Number Series (containing 30 different sequences of seven numbers each followed by five alternative numbers, one of which continues correctly the pattern formed by the series), yield a

quantitative score. Despite the appearance of several competitive instruments during the past few years, including the sequel to ACE, the *Cooperative School and College Ability Test* (SCAT), ACE is still a highly useful and, even by today's improved procedures of test construction and standardization, a noteworthy test reflecting the high level of workmanship that the Thurstones employed in the building of initial forms and that the Cooperative Test Division of the Educational Testing Service continued after 1948.

Among many of the positive features of the various forms that are reported in the manual are the high reliabilities of the total scores (between .89 and .93) and the relatively high reliabilities for the part scores (between .87 and .92 for the verbal section and between .75 and .91 for the much shorter quantitative section), the presentation of tables of equivalent scores and percentile ranks for each of the various forms, a detailed description of the composition of the sample from which norms were derived, and additional statistical data regarding grade-to-grade shifts in mean and variability of scores, and the magnitudes of the standard errors of measurement for 8th and 12th grade groups. Additional advantages of the series include ease of administration and of scoring.

On the somewhat less positive side has been the lack of any mention in the manual as to the predictive validity, or, for that matter, to any kind of validity of the examination. It would seem that since such a large number of high school counselors and administrators have employed this test as a basis for placement and for prognostication of scholastic success either in a high school college preparatory program or in subsequent college work, certain information pertaining to validity either would have been reported within the body of the manual itself or would have been cited in a set of references to various appropriate journal articles, bulletins, or reports. In terms of the interest that the Thurstones have exhibited for a factorial approach to the study of intelligence, it has been somewhat disconcerting, perhaps, to note from the intercorrelations between scores on the verbal and quantitative sections the lack of factorial purity of the subtests—a circumstance that is apparent from an inspection of the nature of the items themselves. It would appear that a rather general measure of scholastic aptitude, or symbolic thinking, embracing verbal comprehension, word fluency, general reasoning, and numerical facility, has been achieved that, with the probable exception of the test in arithmetic, does not indicate specific attainment, or achievement, in high school courses.

Another characteristic of the test that is of concern to many, including the reviewer, has been the importance of speed of response to the realization of a high score. Since speed is such a decisive factor in the examination, it would seem desirable that examinees be advised somewhat more emphatically in the directions regarding the importance of working as rapidly as possible, of not spending too much time on any one item, and of not diverting attention to checking or double checking their work as they progress through each subtest. In light of some informal and not too well controlled observations that the reviewer made a number of years ago involving the analysis of responses on answer sheets of several small groups of high school seniors (residing for the most part in neighborhoods of middle socio-economic level), it seemed that an increment of perhaps 25 per cent in working time on each test part would lead to the situation in which almost 90 per cent of the items in the two verbal sections would be attempted and perhaps 70 per cent of the items on the two quantitative parts would be tried. Of course, what is needed is a series of empirical validation studies in which not only mental set regarding speed of response is varied, but also different amounts of time are allowed for various parts of the examination.

It is interesting to compare briefly some of the characteristics of ACE and SCAT. It would appear that the latter test tends to reflect to a slightly greater extent the examinee's educational development and classroom experiences rather than the more generalized aspects of scholastic aptitude found in ACE. Although it is reasonable to hypothesize that the approach followed in SCAT might lead to somewhat higher predictive validities, comparative studies, which undoubtedly are forthcoming, are needed. In taking both tests, the reviewer noted that for SCAT, as compared with ACE, the significance of the speed factor was less (but still present); that the directions, content of the items, and layout appeared less threatening; and that the items were less difficult and more closely related to one's everyday reading and

learning experiences. There is no doubt that the manual for SCAT is decidedly easier to interpret and that the normative procedures—especially in view of the introduction of confidence intervals—are much more meaningful than those reported for the ACE forms. In addition, tables are available for equating ACE scores to those of SCAT. Moreover, an excellent Technical Report containing detailed information upon reliability, validity, equating procedures, and normative data is available and will be augmented from time to time.

In summary, it may be said that the *American Council on Education Psychological Examination for High School Students* is a satisfactorily reliable instrument for which considerable normative information is available. However, the lack of validity data and the element of undue speed required for attainment of a high score pose reservations concerning its use. In view of the existence of other competitive instruments such as SCAT, for which considerable data upon reliability, validity, norms, and equating procedures are already available and for which an excellent manual replete with interpretative data exists, it seems only a matter of a few years before the ACE series will cease to be used.

For a review by Carl I. Hovland of an earlier edition, see 3:218; for a review by A. H. Turney, see 40:1378; for a review by V. A. C. Henmon, see 38:1038.

[310]

Army General Classification Test, First Civilian Edition. Grades 9–16 and adults; 1940–48; also called AGCT; IBM; 1 form ('47, identical with Form 1a ('40) of the Army Edition); 2 editions; revised manual ('48); separate answer pads or sheets must be used; $10.80 per 20 tests; 75¢ per specimen set of either edition; postage extra; 40(50) minutes; original test prepared by Personnel Research Section, The Adjutant General's Office, War Department; Science Research Associates. *

a) [HAND SCORING EDITION.] 1947–48; Form AH ('47); $2.35 per 20 answer pads.

b) [MACHINE SCORING EDITION.] 1947–48; IBM; Form AM ('47); $5 per 100 IBM answer sheets; $1 per set of scoring stencils.

REFERENCES

1–14. See 3:219.
15–29. See 4:280.
30. JOHNSON, RALPH H., AND BOND, GUY L. "Reading Ease of Commonly Used Tests." *J Appl Psychol* 34:319–24 O '50. * (PA 26:299)
31. MASON, CHARLES F. *Intelligence and Mental Illness.* Doctor's thesis, Purdue University (Lafayette, Ind.), 1950. (DA 15:2296)
32. FERSON, REGIS F. *The Probabilities of Success in Trade Training as Estimated by Standardized Tests.* Doctor's thesis, University of Pittsburgh (Pittsburgh, Pa.), 1951.
33. FRUCHTER, BENJAMIN. "Orthogonal and Oblique Solutions of a Battery of Aptitude, Achievement and Background

Variables." *Ed & Psychol Meas* 12:20–38 sp '52. * (*PA* 27: 6180)

34. FULK, BYRON E., AND HARRELL, THOMAS W. "Negro-White Army Test Scores and Last School Grade." *J Appl Psychol* 36:34–5 F '52. * (*PA* 26:6925)

35. BERNARD, JACK. *Selection of Technical School Students: An Investigation of the Relationship Between Certain Personality Characteristics, Interests and Abilities, and Success in a Radio and Television Curriculum.* Doctor's thesis, New York University (New York, N.Y.), 1954. (*DA* 15:631)

36. CHAPPELL, TOLAN L.; CALLIS, ROBERT; RENZAGLIA, GUY A.; AND SPOHRER, MYRON A. "The Differential Prediction of Achievement at the University of Missouri." *Ed & Psychol Meas* 14:724–5 w '54. * (*PA* 29:7955)

37. DUBOIS, PHILLIP H., AND WATSON, ROBERT I. "Validity Information Exchange, No. 7-075:D.O.T. Code 2-66.23, Policeman." *Personnel Psychol* 7:414–7 au '54. *

38. GLASER, ROBERT, AND JACOBS, OWEN. "Predicting Achievement in Medical School: A Comparison of Preclinical and Clinical Criteria." *J Appl Psychol* 38:245–7 Ag '54. * (*PA* 29:6271)

39. BARNETTE, W. LESLIE, JR. "Diagnostic Features of the AGCT." *J Social Psychol* 42:241–7 N '55. * (*PA* 31:1019)

40. CHAPPELL, TOLAN L. "Note on the Validity of the Army General Classification Test as a Predictor of Academic Achievement." *J Ed Psychol* 46:53–5 Ja '55. * (*PA* 29:8993)

41. MULLINEAUX, JEWEL E. "An Evaluation of the Predictors Used to Select Patrolmen." *Pub Personnel R* 16:84–6 Ap '55. *

42. PATTERSON, CECIL H. *Test and Background Factors Related to Drop-Outs in an Industrial Institute.* Doctor's thesis, University of Minnesota (Minneapolis, Minn.), 1955. (*DA* 15: 1024)

43. OTTERNESS, WILLIAM B.; PATTERSON, C. H.; JOHNSON, R. H.; AND PETERSON, LENNIS R. "Trade School Norms for Some Commonly Used Tests." *J Appl Psychol* 40:57–60 F '56. * (*PA* 31:3803)

44. PATTERSON, C. H. "The Prediction of Attrition in Trade School Courses." *J Appl Psychol* 40:154–8 Je '56. * (*PA* 31: 6680)

45. WOLINS, LEROY, AND PERLOFF, ROBERT. "The Factorial Composition of AGCT 'Subtests' Along With College Aptitude Items and High School Grades." Abstract. *Am Psychol* 11:449 Ag '56. *

46. BARRETT, RICHARD S. "The Process of Predicting Job Performance." *Personnel Psychol* 11:39–57 sp '58. *

For a review by John T. Dailey, see 4:280; see 3:219 (1 excerpt).

[311]

★**The Business Test.** Clerical workers; 1952–56; Form A ['52]; mimeographed manual ['56]; no data on reliability; no norms; $2.50 per 25 tests; 35¢ per specimen set; postage extra; 10(15) or (10–25) minutes; Edward N. Hay; Aptitude Test Service. *

LOUIS C. NANASSY, *Professor of Business Education, Montclair State College, Upper Montclair, New Jersey.*

This is a verbal test of mental ability or quickness of learning, with the emphasis placed on perceiving relationships and solving problems. It consists of 35 items, mostly multiple choice, of a nonquantitative, nonmathematical nature, using a simple vocabulary; it may be used as either an untimed or a timed test.

According to the manual, the test was designed to overcome the disadvantage of some similar tests which, by reason of having many difficult words, penalize good workers, particularly foremen, whose education may not be high. Also according to the manual, a high proportion of clerical jobs require no particular vocabulary, so the test is also suitable for use in the selection of clerical employees.

Clear and concise directions are given for administering and scoring the test. It requires only a short period of time to take—10 to 25 minutes at the most. The test papers may be collected at the end of the 10 minutes; or, as an alternate procedure, at the end of 10 minutes the applicant may draw a line under the last item completed and then continue working until all items are completed. If only one score is desired, the 10-minute score is claimed to be sufficient.

For validation of the test, 67 clerical supervisors and 98 operating foremen of seven gas companies were tested. On the basis of the results, it was concluded that even if a company used no other tests to assist in determining who should be promoted from the ranks into the management organization, this short test, easy to obtain and easy to use, could make a significant contribution.

Perhaps the title *Business Test* is a misnomer. The items have little relationship to business situations and processes. In effect, the test is a simple intelligence test, with possible usefulness in evaluating people in numerous lines of work.

JAMES H. RICKS, JR., *Assistant Director, Test Division, The Psychological Corporation, New York, New York.*

When a test reaches the age of 6 years (as indicated by its copyright date) with neither reliability data nor anything approaching adequate norms in its manual, it can claim the serious attention of reviewers and prospective users only if some important, even though still hypothetical, virtue distinguishes it from its competitors. The distinctions which this test appears to possess are few and the evidence for them is scant. Three specific differences from "the typical intelligence test" are cited in the manual:

a) "There are no quantitative or mathematical items." This is true, but verbal mental ability scores uncontaminated by quantitative material may be obtained in short times from such tests as the *Short Employment Tests* and the *Thurstone Test of Mental Alertness.*

b) "It does not require an extensive vocabulary." Probably true, so far as inspection indicates, but not supported by reference to any evidence such as the Thorndike-Lorge frequency counts. The statement is equally applicable to the verbal score on the *Wesman Personnel Classification Test.* And neither argument nor evidence is adduced in support of the idea that verbal intelligence is better measured for employment purposes by analogies and other "reasoning" items than by a straight vocabulary test.

c) "It is designed to be used either as an untimed or a timed test." This statement is no less true of the *Wonderlic Personnel Test,* but its implications deserve further examination. It is not stated what elements of design qualify a test to be used on both a timed and an untimed basis. Presumably the difficulty range of the items is relevant to its use without time limit, but no information on item difficulties is provided.

Operationally, such a statement as the third one must mean that a score obtained within a time limit or a score obtained with unlimited time may be used. Actually, the manual suggests recording three scores, viz., the total time required, the number right in 10 minutes, and the total number of items answered correctly. In one of the validation studies, the score used is the sum of the second and third of these, equivalent to twice the number of points earned in 10 minutes plus the number earned after that limit (neither rationale nor data are offered in defense of this procedure). And in the recommended "Selection Scores" table offered in lieu of norms, there is no indication as to *which* of the four types of score was used!

In support of the test's usefulness, the information obtained from the manual plus two letters to the publisher consists of a correlation coefficient of .80 with the *Wonderlic Personnel Test* and a report indicating that supervisors rated "Best" by their superiors average higher than those rated "Middle" who in turn average higher than those rated "Poorest." No indications of the overlap among the groups nor of the significance of the differences are provided.

The manual observes that "some of the well known tests are familiar to applicants because they are so widely used." *The Business Test* may well continue to enjoy its advantage on this count.

[312]

★California Analogies and Reasoning Test. Grades 10–13; 1958; IBM; Forms A, B; $4.20 per 35 tests; separate answer sheets may be used; 5¢ per IBM answer sheet; 20¢ per set of hand and machine scoring stencils; postage extra; 50¢ per specimen set, postpaid; 40(50) minutes; Claude Mitchell; California Test Bureau. *

[313]

*California Short-Form Test of Mental Maturity. Grades kgn–1, 1–3, 4–8, 7–9, 9–13, 10–16 and adults;

1938–57; 7 scores: spatial relationships, logical reasoning, numerical reasoning, verbal concepts, language, nonlanguage, total; IBM for grades 4 and over; 1957 S-Form ('57); 6 levels; manual ('57) for each level; supplement ['50]; technical report ('57); $3.15 per 35 tests; separate answer sheets may be used in grades 4 and over; 4¢ per IBM answer sheet; 7¢ per Scoreze answer sheet; 20¢ per hand scoring stencil; 40¢ per machine scoring stencil; postage extra; 50¢ per specimen set of any one level, postpaid; Elizabeth T. Sullivan (except *e*), Willis W. Clark, and Ernest W. Tiegs; California Test Bureau. *
a) PRE-PRIMARY. Grades kgn–1; S-Form ('57); (29–40) minutes.
b) PRIMARY. Grades 1–3; S-Form ('57); (42–55) minutes.
c) ELEMENTARY. Grades 4–8; S-Form ('57); 47–49(60) minutes.
d) JUNIOR HIGH. Grades 7–9; S-Form ('57); 51–52(65) minutes.
e) SECONDARY. Grades 9–13; S-Form A ('57); 52–53(65) minutes.
f) ADVANCED. Grades 10–16 and adults; S-Form ('57); 52–53(65) minutes.

REFERENCES

1. SILVER, CHARLES E. *A Comparison of the Scores Made by College Reading Problem Cases on the California Short-form Test of Mental Maturity and Form I of the Wechsler-Bellevue Scales.* Master's thesis, Bowling Green State University (Bowling Green, Ohio), 1950.
2. LEACH, KENT W. "Intelligence Test Scores of Michigan Ninth-Grade Pupils." *Univ Mich Sch Ed B* 24:6–9 O '52. *
3. POE, WESLEY A., and BERG, IRWIN A. "Psychological Test Performance of Steel Industry Production Supervisors." *J Appl Psychol* 36:234–7 Ag '52. * (*PA* 27:3794)
4. RALEIGH, WILLIAM H. *A Study of the Relationships of Academic Achievement in Sixth Grade With the Wechsler Intelligence Scale for Children and Other Variables.* Doctor's thesis, Indiana University (Bloomington, Ind.), 1952.
5. TAYLOR, EDWARD A. "Some Factors Relating to Social Acceptance in Eighth-Grade Classrooms." *J Ed Psychol* 43:257–72 My '52. * (*PA* 27:3770)
6. BREGOLI, ELMO J. *An Item Analysis of the Vocabulary Sub-Test of the California Short-Form Test of Mental Ability.* Master's thesis, Boston College (Chestnut Hill, Mass.), 1953.
7. O'NEIL, WILLIAM J. *An Item Analysis of the Numerical Quantity Section, Test 6, of the California Short-Form Test of Mental Ability.* Master's thesis, Boston College (Chestnut Hill, Mass.), 1953.
8. COWNE, LESLIE. "A Study of the California Short Form Test of Mental Maturity." *Ed Rec B* 62:67–75 F '54. * (*PA* 28:8070)
9. BLIESMER, EMERY P. "A Comparison of Results Obtained With Various Types of Capacity Tests Used With Retarded Readers." *Yearb Nat Council Meas Used Ed* 12(pt 1):60–2 '55. *
10. NORTH, ROBERT D. "The California Short-Form Test of Mental Maturity: Further Reliability and Correlation Data." *Ed Rec B* 65:59–64 F '55. * (*PA* 29:7307)
11. FOWLER, WILLIAM L. *A Comparative Analysis of Pupil Performance on Conventional and Culture-Controlled Mental Tests.* Doctor's thesis, University of Michigan (Ann Arbor, Mich.), 1956. (*DA* 17:91)
12. MITCHELL, JAMES V., JR. "A Comparison of the Factorial Structure of Cognitive Functions for a High and Low Status Group." *J Ed Psychol* 47:397–414 N '56. *
13. FOWLER, WILLIAM L. "A Comparative Analysis of Pupil Performance on Conventional and Culture-Controlled Mental Tests." *Yearb Nat Council Meas Used Ed* 14:8–19 '57. *
14. KLUGMAN, SAMUEL F. "Agreement Between Two Tests as Predictors of College Success." *Personnel & Guid J* 36:255–8 D '57. *
15. MOULY, GEORGE J., AND EDGAR, MARY. "Equivalence of IQ's for Four Group Intelligence Tests." *Personnel & Guid J* 36:623–6 My '58. *

CYRIL BURT, *Emeritus Professor of Psychology, University of London, London, England.*

This is an abridgement of the earlier *California Test of Mental Maturity,* and is described as "an instrument for appraising mental development or mental capacity." The whole scale comprises six booklets of increasing difficulty designed to cover the entire range of school grades from the preprimary to the adult level. Each booklet contains seven subtests which sample four main areas of mental activity (termed "mental factors"): spatial relations, logical reasoning, numerical reasoning, and verbal concepts.

The results obtained are intended to serve both normative and analytical purposes. The norms are given in terms of mental ages and IQ's; the analysis is effected by means of individual profiles, constructed graphically, which provide mental ages and IQ's for the four "factors" and for the language and nonlanguage sections of the test. In general, both the items and the format of the new 1957 edition remain much as before. But the content of the various subtests has been checked and revised, the norms have been evaluated afresh, and additional data on reliability and validity have been incorporated in the manuals (which now extend to 28 or 32 pages).

The items selected for the several levels and the resulting norms have been carefully articulated, in the hope that the IQ's both for the test as a whole and for the language and nonlanguage components will prove comparable when the pupil passes from the more elementary stages to the later levels. To check the articulation, correlations (analogous to reliability coefficients based on "parallel forms") have been computed by applying tests for adjacent levels to the same groups.

The variety of content and the high proportion of nonverbal problems even at the upper levels are commendable features. The directions for administering and scoring the tests are lucid and complete. The material presented (pictures, diagrams, and reading matter) is, on the whole, clearly printed, though the type size is rather small in the booklet for the youngest children. On the other hand, the discussions of methods to be used for calculating the various IQ's and for constructing the individual profiles seem needlessly long and overelaborate. An examiner who requires a detailed explanation of the meaning of "IQ" would scarcely be prepared to follow the detailed steps for converting the raw test data into a profile with 16 linear scales. Most teachers would probably prefer a short practical manual giving essential instructions for administering the particular test they intended to use and a separate introductory pamphlet explaining the theoretical

basis of the whole series and summarizing the evidence for the reliability and validity of the different levels. This would avoid much of the repetition in the present manuals.

In the original form, the conceptual framework for the *California Test of Mental Maturity* was that of the Stanford-Binet scale. The fuller version has been in use for over 20 years. The experience and the mass of data thus accumulated have been freely utilized in progressively improving the shortened series. The outcome is one of the best sets of group tests at present available. The reliability has been assessed by various methods. With the Kuder-Richardson formula 21 the reliability of the total scores varies between .87 and .89 at most grade levels, but at the secondary stage (as one might expect) it is appreciably higher. The validity coefficients consist of observed and corrected correlations with the Stanford-Binet and WISC, and with group intelligence tests. They vary far more widely, averaging about .75. But correlations of this nature are not very informative.

The intercorrelations between the measurements for the four "mental factors" are positive at every stage, and usually range from .30 to .60 (without correction for selection), except for those between "spatial relationships" and "verbal concepts," which are far lower. Evidently a general cognitive factor dominates the picture. This supports the authors' claim that the test, taken as a whole, provides an excellent instrument for assessing general "capacity." But to state that it also measures "development" and to designate it as a test of "maturity" seems tantamount to adopting two alternative interpretations of "intelligence" which are not altogether consistent. Certainly there is very little evidence for claiming that it may likewise be used to measure distinct mental processes.

To begin with, the mere fact that similar types of tests are repeated stage after stage does not guarantee that the same special aptitudes are being assessed throughout the child's school life or that these particular types of tests really depend on the same mental factors or functions at different ages. At the preprimary stage the tests yielding the highest reliability (.66) are the subtests for spatial relationships; at the secondary stage they are the subtests for verbal concepts (.92). Such a result, together with what is already known about the progressive differentiation of mental capacities, seems merely to imply that for the younger ages the best measures of general capacity are to be obtained with nonverbal material and for the older with verbal problems. Specialization is usually a relatively late phenomenon; and even with older children the chief value of nonverbal tests is to counteract any special disabilities that might otherwise impair the value of the test as a whole.

In any case, two or three subtests, lasting in all for only 7 to 15 minutes, would scarcely suffice to yield a reliable and valid assessment for the so-called special "factors." Indeed, the reliability coefficients recorded for the separate assessments are nearly all fairly low (.50 to .75, but higher for the secondary group); much of this must really be reliability as measures of general capacity. Moreover, little or nothing is actually known as to how these particular "factors" would affect different types of school work. No doubt, in a few exceptional cases, especially at the later stages, the construction of a differential profile for some particular pupil will prove informative. But, from the practical standpoint of the teacher, the names given to the factors and the detailed instructions for their measurement in terms of separate mental ages or IQ's might encourage him to fancy that he can extract far more information out of the test results than is actually the case. These minor criticisms, however, in no way affect the general merits of the test as a whole.

For reviews of the California Test of Mental Maturity *and its adaptations, see 4:282, 3:223, 40:1384, and 38:1042.*

[314]

*California Test of Mental Maturity, 1957 Edition. Grades kgn–1, 1–3, 4–8, 7–9, 9–13, 10–16 and adults; 1936–57; 8 scores: memory, spatial relationships, logical reasoning, numerical reasoning, verbal concepts, language, nonlanguage, total; IBM for grades 4 and over; 1 form ('57); 6 levels; manual ('57) for each level; supplement ['50]; technical report ('57); $5.25 per 35 tests; separate answer sheets may be used in grades 4 and over; 4¢ per IBM answer sheet; 7¢ per Scoreze answer sheet; 40¢ per set of hand scoring stencils; 60¢ per set of machine scoring stencils; postage extra; 50¢ per specimen set, postpaid; Pre-Primary: 48(70) minutes; Primary: 67(90) minutes; Elementary: 84–88(110) minutes; Junior High School: 88–90(115) minutes; Secondary: 90–(115) minutes; Advanced: 90–92(115) minutes; Elizabeth T. Sullivan, Willis W. Clark, and Ernest W. Tiegs; California Test Bureau. *

REFERENCES

1–5. See 40:1384.
6–15. See 3:223.
16–39. See 4:282.
40. ARNOLD, E. REX. *The Diagnostic Possibilities of the California Test of Mental Maturity.* Master's thesis, North Texas State College (Denton, Tex.), 1948.
41. CARL, PAULINE M. *California's Test of Mental Maturity as a Means of Detecting Cases of Reading Disability.* Master's thesis, Kansas State Teachers College (Pittsburg, Kan.), 1948.
42. JACKSON, B. J. *The Relationship Between Certain Mental Characteristics and Achievement.* Master's thesis, North Texas State College (Denton, Tex.), 1948.
43. AMERICAN GAS ASSOCIATION, PERSONNEL COMMITTEE. *Personnel Testing in the Gas Industry.* New York: the Association, January 1952. Pp. 10. *
44. BOGER, JACK H. "An Experimental Study of the Effects of Perceptual Training on Group I.Q. Test Scores of Elementary Pupils in Rural Ungraded Schools." *J Ed Res* 46:43–52 S '52. * (*PA* 27:5414)
45. CLARK, WILLIS W. "Evaluating School Achievement in Basic Skills in Relation to Mental Ability." *J Ed Res* 46:180–91 N '52. * (*PA* 27:6149)
46. DRISCOLL, JUSTIN A. *Factors in Intelligence and Achievement: A Study of the Factor Pattern Resulting From Analysis of the Scores of Boys in Junior Year of High School on Intelligence and Achievement Tests.* Catholic University of America, Educational Research Monographs, Vol. 16, No. 7. Washington, D.C.: Catholic University of America Press, Inc., June 15, 1952. Pp. viii, 56. * (*PA* 27:3330)
47. WELCH, W. BRUCE. *An Examination of the Usability of Selected Standardized Tests of Mental Ability and Achievement for College Groups With Atypical Socio-Economic Status.* Doctor's thesis, Indiana University (Bloomington, Ind.), 1952.
48. CLARK, WILLIS W. "Sex Differences in Mental Abilities Among Students of High Intelligence." *Calif J Ed Res* 5:90–3 Mr '54. * (*PA* 28:8559)
49. HAMMER, EMANUEL F. "Comparison of the Performances of Negro Children and Adolescents on Two Tests of Intelligence, One an Emergency Scale." *J Genetic Psychol* 84:85–93 Mr '54. * (*PA* 28:8659)
50. SCHWELLENBACH, JOHN A. "An Experiment in Predicting the Ability of Eighth Grade Students to Work Simple Algebra Problems." *Calif J Ed Res* 5:36–41 Ja '54. * (*PA* 28:7998)
51. SHELDON, WILLIAM D., AND MANOLAKES, GEORGE. "A Comparison of the Stanford-Binet, Revised Form L, and the California Test of Mental Maturity (S-Form)." *J Ed Psychol* 45:499–504 D '54. * (*PA* 29:7318)
52. SWEENEY, FRANCIS J. "Intelligence, Vocational Interests and Reading Speed of Senior Boys in Catholic High Schools of Los Angeles." *Calif J Ed Res* 5:159–65 S '54. * (*PA* 29:4656)
53. ALTUS, GRACE T. "Relationships Between Verbal and Nonverbal Parts of the CTMM and WISC." *J Consult Psychol* 19:143–4 Ap '55. * (*PA* 30:1008)
54. COMREY, ANDREW L., AND HIGH, WALLACE S. "Validity of Some Ability and Interest Scores." *J Appl Psychol* 39:247–8 Ag '55. * (*PA* 30:5278)
55. MCCALL, JOHN R. *Sex Differences in Intelligence: A Comparative Factor Study.* Washington, D.C.: Catholic University of America Press, Inc., 1955. Pp. viii, 65. * (*PA* 30:4171)
56. MANOLAKES, GEORGE, AND SHELDON, WILLIAM D. "The Relation Between Reading-Test Scores and Language-Factors Intelligence Quotients." *El Sch J* 55:346–50 F '55. * (*PA* 29:8918)
57. MARSHALL, THOMAS A. *Analysis of Predictive Value for Pupils in a Single Third Grade From Scores Based on the California Test of Mental Maturity.* Master's thesis, Fresno State College (Fresno, Calif.), 1955
58. SMITH, THOMAS WOOD, AND CAFFREY, JOHN. "Comprehension of Written Language (Reading) and Oral Language (Auding) as Related to 'Cultural Bias' on the Davis-Eells Games and the California Test of Mental Maturity." Abstract. *Am Psychol* 10:382–3 Ag '55. *
59. ALTUS, GRACE T. "Some Correlates of the Davis-Eells Tests." *J Consult Psychol* 20:227–32 Je '56. * (*PA* 31:6053)
60. BLIESMER, EMERY P. "A Comparison of Results of Various Capacity Tests Used With Retarded Readers." *El Sch J* 56:400–2 My '56. * (*PA* 31:5140)
61. CALIFORNIA TEST BUREAU, DIVISION OF PROFESSIONAL SERVICES; WITH THE ASSISTANCE OF JAMES C. COLEMAN. *California Test of Mental Maturity: Summary of Investigations Number Three.* Hollywood, Calif.: California Test Bureau, 1956. Pp. 30. * (*PA* 31:7287)
62. GALLAGHER, JAMES J.; BENOIT, E. PAUL; AND BOYD, HERBERT F. "Measures of Intelligence in Brain Damaged Children." *J Clin Psychol* 12:69–72 Ja '56. * (*PA* 30:5093)
63. MARSHALL, THOMAS A. *Analysis of Predictive Value for Pupils in a Single Third Grade From Scores Based on the California Test of Mental Maturity.* Master's thesis, Fresno State College (Fresno, Calif.), 1956.
64. SHANNER, WILLIAM M. "Relationships Between Norms for Mental Maturity and Achievement Tests." *Calif J Ed Res* 7:15–21 Ja '56. * (*PA* 30:7775)
65. SMITH, THOMAS WOOD. *Auding and Reading as Sources of Cultural Bias in the Davis-Eells Games and the California Test of Mental Maturity.* Doctor's thesis, University of Southern California (Los Angeles, Calif.), 1956.

66. SMITH, THOMAS WOOD. "Comparison of Test Bias in the Davis-Eells Games and the CTMM." *Calif J Ed Res* 7:159–63 S '56. * (*PA* 31:6135)

67. TATE, MERLE W., AND VOSS, CHARLOTTE E. "A Study of the Davis-Eells Test of Intelligence." *Harvard Ed R* 26: 374–87 fall '56. * (*PA* 32:1347)

68. McHUGH, ANN F. *An Investigation of the Reliability and Concurrent Validity of Two Levels of the California Test of Mental Maturity, Short Form.* Doctor's thesis, Fordham University (New York, N.Y.), 1957.

69. NICHOLSON, ALICE. *Background Abilities Related to Reading Success in First Grade.* Doctor's thesis, Boston University (Boston, Mass.), 1957.

70. OWEN, JASON CAMILLOUS. *A Study of the Prognostic Value of Certain Measures of Intelligence and Listening Comprehension With a Selected Group of Elementary Pupils.* Doctor's thesis, University of Missouri (Columbia, Mo.), 1957. (*DA* 19:484)

71. TOPETZES, NICK JOHN. "A Program for the Selection of Trainees in Physical Medicine." *J Exp Ed* 25:263–311 Je '57. *

72. COOPER, JAMES G. "Predicting School Achievement for Bilingual Pupils." *J Ed Psychol* 49:31–6 F '58. *

73. NICHOLSON, ALICE. "Background Abilities Related to Reading Success in First Grade." *J Ed (Boston)* 140:7–24 F '58. *

FRANK S. FREEMAN, *Professor of Psychology, Cornell University, Ithaca, New York.*

The 1957 edition of this group test of intelligence is an improved version of earlier editions, but it is unchanged in respect to underlying structure and basic psychological rationale. "The major effort of this revision," state the manuals, "has been devoted to a re-evaluation and improvement of the norms, with special attention given to the articulation of successive levels."

As in all previous editions, the types of subtests included at all age levels are based upon the original psychological analysis, by one of the test's authors,[1] of the operations involved in the Stanford-Binet scale. It is to be noted that this was not a factorial analysis; yet the derived "mental factors" are strikingly similar to the statistically derived factors utilized in the tests of "primary mental abilities", which followed some years later.

Technically, there is much to recommend this sequence of scales. The authors provide a considerable amount of useful data in the manuals. The standardization population appears to be quite satisfactory as to numbers (25,000 originally, "checked against 100,000 additional cases"), geographic distribution, and stratification. At each level, tables are given showing percentage contribution of variance to language, nonlanguage, and total scores of each "mental factor" (memory, spatial relations, logical reasoning, numerical reasoning, and verbal concepts). From these tables the qualified user may draw his own inferences and better interpret individual test profiles. The data on reliability are as complete and as satisfac-

tory as those generally found with the sounder tests—high coefficients for total score and for the two major divisions, language and nonlanguage, and moderate to high coefficients for individual subtests. Anyone planning to use these scales should examine the reliability tables since the coefficients are not uniform for all age and grade levels. Still another type of reliability study, presented in place of alternate forms data, is given in a discussion of "articulation." The procedure here was to test "one and two school grades below and one and two grades above the recommended grade levels for the various tests. The equivalent Language and Non-Language raw scores for the level of the test being articulated were then computed for each consecutive Language and Non-Language raw score of the test level being used within its recommended range. The design of these studies specified that the raw scores coincide, test for test, within one standard error of measurement on either test." No data are presented to show the actual approximation to coincidence obtained, though we may assume, presumably, that the stated criterion of correspondence was satisfied.

Intercorrelations among subtests are given at each level. These range from very low (e.g., between spatial relationships and verbal concepts) to moderately high (e.g., between memory and verbal concepts), thus indicating various degrees of communality and independence of mental operations being tested by the several parts.

Instructions for administering and scoring are clear. Tables for converting scores into percentile ranks, mental ages, and estimated grade equivalents are quite satisfactory. The profiles are well designed.

The manuals state that these tests yield a "normal distribution of intelligence quotients, with a mean of 100 and a standard deviation of 16 for the unselected general population." However, the "Summary of Investigations Number Three" provides tables of *median* IQ's and standard deviations for grade levels, but not for age levels. Nor do the manuals or the "Summary" state explicitly the method used in deriving the mean (or median) of 100 IQ and the SD of 16. By experimental testing of the standardization population and item analysis? By the deviation IQ technique? In the "Summary" there is a suggestion, however, that the latter method was employed.

[1] SULLIVAN, ELIZABETH T. "Psychographic Representation of Results of the Stanford Revision of the Binet-Simon Tests." *J Delinquency* 10:284–5 Ja '26.

The major criticism of the technical information available for these scales has to do with data on their validity. The "Summary" lists five criteria.

a) Intercorrelations with other intelligence tests, both group and individual. On the whole, the coefficients resulting from these validating studies, which were carried out by investigators other than the authors of the scales, are satisfactory or even high, especially in the case of the Stanford-Binet and the Wechsler scales. But these tables of intercorrelations and their explications do not always provide essential statistical data such as probable (or standard) errors of the coefficients, number of subjects used, range of ages and of grades, and range of ability. But the "Summary" does include a bibliography which provides the sources from which the intercorrelations were obtained.

b) Correlations with achievement tests. These coefficients compare very favorably with those obtained with other tests, but here again some essential indices are lacking, much as in (*a*) above. Where grade levels are given, they are, for the most part, 7 and higher. Since these scales are intended for use beginning in the kindergarten, and primarily for educational guidance and placement, it is highly desirable to have data on reliability and validity (especially in terms of school achievement and prediction) separately at every age and grade level.

c) Intercorrelations among parts of the test itself. These have already been commented on above.

d) Distinguishing between "different kinds of mental maturity." This criterion has been studied in terms of intercorrelations between language and nonlanguage sections of the scales. The correlations are in the neighborhood of .5 and .6, indicating that these two principal sections are measuring abilities which are markedly similar in some respects but, at the same time, different in others. This criterion has also been studied in terms of correlations with arithmetic and reading achievement test results. As would be expected, the language sections correlate much higher (.50–.82) than do the nonlanguage sections (.26–.36).

e) Factor analytic evaluation. A table of factor loadings, based on the Thurstone centroid method and expressed in terms of percentages, indicates that the language factors, from preprimary through the advanced level, contribute from about 37 to 48 per cent of total common factor variance, while the nonlanguage factors contribute from about 53 to 62 per cent.

On the whole, these 1957 scales provide fuller and more significant standardization and evaluative data than did their predecessors; hence, they are more valuable than the earlier editions. But more data on them are needed to demonstrate the extent to which they are valid in educational selection, prediction, and guidance at each of the several age and grade levels. Data are needed, also, regarding validity and reliability of the tests when used with groups of individuals at each of the several levels of ability—that is, with the mentally deficient, the slow, the average, the superior, and the gifted. It has long been known that a test does not necessarily yield equally sound results at all levels along the scale of mental ability. When these additional data are supplied, the value of these scales will be enhanced.

JOHN E. MILHOLLAND, *Associate Professor of Psychology, and Chief, Evaluation and Examinations Division, Bureau of Psychological Services, University of Michigan, Ann Arbor, Michigan.*

The physical and practical aspects of this test are particularly appealing. The booklets seem to be sturdy enough to withstand repeated use, almost all the pictures are clear, and the general format is conducive to accurate following of directions by testees. Directions for administering are well written and easy for the tester to follow, scoring is simple for any of the three methods of registering answers, and provisions for collating results and recording normative equivalents are well organized. For handy filing, the back page of the test booklet or answer sheet contains a profile of subscores as well as the record of all raw scores and pupil information data.

The various levels of the tests were articulated in standardization by giving two tests to each school grade. One was the regular test for that grade, the other, the test for the level immediately below or above. The results of this procedure were taken account of in the norming so that IQ's and mental ages for successive levels would be comparable.

Another basis for comparability was produced by adjusting the norms to obtain a normal distribution of IQ's with a standard deviation of 16 at each level. Thus, a person who maintains the same relative position in the group will have a constant IQ.

The manuals give reliability coefficients and standard errors of measurement for certain single grades as well as for certain grade ranges for each of the six levels of the test. Three different methods of estimating reliability were used at various places: the split-half correlation, stepped up by the Spearman-Brown formula; Kuder-Richardson formula 21; and the Rulon split-half formula. All these are equivalence estimates and tend to be spuriously high if the test is speeded. The subtests are in fact timed, but the authors assert in the directions for administration that the test is a power test and that the time limis are "ample for examinees to reach the effective limits of their abilities." No data on the degree of speededness are presented in the manuals, and we can only hope that speededness has not seriously inflated the reliabilities.

For the total score, the single grade reliabilities for grades 1, 2, 5, 8, 12, and college freshmen are all above .90. For the language score, based on four subscores, these single grade reliabilities range from .80 to .95, with a median of .89; for the nonlanguage score, based on seven or eight subscores, the range is .83 to .96, median. 91. The five subscores (memory, spatial relationships, logical reasoning, numerical reasoning, and verbal concepts), perseveratingly called "factors" by the authors, have reliabilities ranging from .55 to .92; 10 of the 30 are below .80. We are probably safe in saying that the language, nonlanguage, and total scores are sufficiently reliable for describing individual pupils; the subscores generally are not.

The manuals state that the original *California Tests of Mental Maturity* were designed to correlate with the Stanford-Binet. Herein, it is said, lies one of the chief claims for validity. One study is cited in which this correlation is .88, and the claim is made that several other studies have yielded even higher values. Correlations with a number of other intelligence tests are also reported.

The manuals do not report data on the relation between the CTMM and school achievement. This is rather odd, since the WXYZ series of the *California Achievement Tests* is supposed to have been anchored to the CTMM. Some correlations of an earlier edition of the test with school grades and with previous forms

of the *California Achievement Tests* are, however, reported in a 1956 publication (*61*). These are in the usual ranges, .50 to .70, with an occasional higher one. The language, nonlanguage, and total scores of the CTMM seem, then, to exhibit satisfactory validities against intelligence and achievement measures.

For more than 20 years, reviewers in this *Yearbook* and elsewhere have criticized the authors of the CTMM for using the term "factors" for scores derived from tests whose development was not based on factor analyses. The authors have shown no disposition to discontinue the practice, possibly because they may have some claim to chronological priority in the use of the word. It is nonetheless unfortunate that the confusion continues. In the present series of manuals, explanations are given that the factors about which the CTMM were built are "logical constructs based on assumptions about higher mental processes, e.g., numerical reasoning, rather than the mathematical factors of a factor analytic method." It is further asserted that, although the entire series has been submitted to numerous factor analyses, "the mathematical factors have not proved as meaningful nor as practically useful as the original logical constructs, the 'mental factors.'" Concrete evidence is, however, lacking as to the meaning and practical usefulness of the "factors." Opinions are given, it is true, as to the importance of certain "factors" in certain areas of endeavor, but no factual information is presented for the use of the subscores. Nevertheless, throughout the manuals the impression is left that the unique and most valuable feature of the test is the availability of a profile of "factor" scores. The only validation of the "factors" appears in the manual for the junior high level and consists of a table of correlations between CTMM subscores and appropriate scores on the *Holzinger-Crowder Uni-Factor Tests* and on the *SRA Primary Mental Abilities*. For example, intercorrelations between CTMM and PMA subscores are as follows (the second figure in each case is the coefficient corrected for range and attenuation): Verbal Concepts and PMA Verbal Meaning, .69 (.89); Verbal Concepts and PMA Word-Fluency, .33 (.47); Spatial Relationships and PMA Space, .32 (.77); Logical Reasoning and PMA Reasoning, .46 (.92); Numerical Reasoning and PMA Number, .27 (.51). These data may be used either to support the contruct validity of the CTMM "factors" or to ttack the authors' position that the CTMM 'factors" are more meaningful than factor-analytic ones.

There does seem to be sufficient research available to warrant the use of separate language and nonlanguage scores from the test.

To summarize, the test is an excellent and usable test of general intelligence and has real value for comparing an individual's verbal and nonverbal abilities. However, as long as the authors persist in emphasizing the use of the "factor" scores in the face of lack of research evidence, the use of the CTMM by classroom teachers should be discouraged unless they are sophisticated enough not to be taken in by the "Diagnostic Profile" or are supervised by someone who is.

See 4:282 (1 excerpt); for a review by Henry E. Garrett of an earlier edition, see 3:223 (2 excerpts); for reviews by Raymond B. Cattell and F. Kuhlmann, see 40:1384 (1 excerpt); for reviews by W. D. Commins, Rudolph Pintner, and Arthur E. Traxler, see 38:1042.

[315]

Cattell Intelligence Tests. Mental ages 4–8, 8–11, 11–15, 15 and over; 1930–52; 4 levels; no data on reliability and validity; Scales 1–3: manual, third edition ('52); 10s. per 25 tests; 6d. per single copy; 7s. 6d. per complete specimen set; postage extra; R. B. Cattell; George G. Harrap & Co. Ltd. *
a) SCALE O (DARTINGTON SCALE). Mental ages 4–8; 1933; identical with Scale 1 of *IPAT Culture Free Intelligence Test*; individual; 1 form; 63s. 6d. per set of 50 tests, cards, and manual; (45) minutes.
b) SCALE 1 (NON-VERBAL), NEW EDITION, REVISED. Ages 8–11; 1930–52; Forms A, B ('35) ; (45) minutes.
c) SCALE 2, NEW EDITION, REVISED. Mental ages 11–15; 1930–35; Forms A, B ('35) ; (90) minutes.
d) SCALE 3, NEW EDITION, REVISED. Mental ages 15 and over; 1930–35; Forms A ('35), B ('30) ; (90) minutes.

REFERENCES

1–4. See 3:228.
5. ROHAN, J. C. "A Study of the Binet and Cattell Systems of Intelligence Testing in a Colony for Mental Defectives." *J Mental Sci* 87:192–207 Ap '41. * (PA 15:3190)
6. HALSTEAD, H., AND CHASE, V. E. "Review of a Verbal Intelligence Scale on Military Neurotic Patients." *Brit J Med Psychol* 20:195–201 pt 2 '44 (issued F '45). * (PA 19:2066)
7. SLATER, PATRICK. "Scores of Different Types of Neurotics on Tests of Intelligence." *Brit J Psychol* 35:40–2 Ja '45. * (PA 19:966)
8. SMITH, CHRISTINA A. *Mental Testing of Hebridean Children in Gaelic and English.* With "A Statistical Analysis" by D. N. Lawley. Publications of the Scottish Council for Research in Education, [No.] 27. London: University of London Press, Ltd., 1948. Pp. 42. *
9. UHRBROCK, RICHARD STEPHEN. "Construction of a Selection Test for College Graduates." *J General Psychol* 41:153–93 O '49. * (PA 24:4874)
10. CATTELL, RAYMOND B. "The Fate of National Intelligence: Test of a Thirteen-Year Prediction." *Eug R* 42:136–48 O '50. * (PA 25:2896)
11. FITT, A. B., AND ROGERS, C. A. "The Sex Factor in the Cattell Intelligence Tests, Scale III." *Brit J Psychol* 41:186–92 D '50. * (PA 25:8085)
12. TIZARD, J.; IN COLLABORATION WITH N. O'CONNOR AND J. M. CRAWFORD. "The Abilities of Adolescent and Adult High-
Grade Male Defectives." *J Mental Sci* 96:888–907 O '50. * (PA 25:5421)
13. MOORE, B. G. R., AND PEEL, E. A. "Predicting Aptitude for Dentistry." *Occupational Psychol* 25:192–9 Jl '51. * (PA 26:3675)

I. MACFARLANE SMITH, *Lecturer in Education, University of Durham, Newcastle, England.*

This series of intelligence tests was first published in 1930. There were originally three scales, Scale 1 for mental ages 8–11, Scale 2 for mental ages 11–15, and Scale 3 for mental ages 15 and over. Scale O for mental ages 4–8, an individual test, was published in 1933 as the *Dartington Scale.*

The *Dartington Scale* has not been revised. It consists of eight subtests, totaling 96 pass or fail items—Substitution (pictorial), Line's Test, Mazes, Selecting Named Objects, Following Directions, Wrong Pictures, Riddles, and Similarities (pictorial and diagrammatic). The content is reasonably appropriate for young children, being varied, interesting, and attractive and not overweighted with verbal or scholastic material. But the standardization is scarcely adequate, the norms being based on the scores of only 117 children, of which 20 was the largest group for any year. The sample was of approximately average ability according to the Binet and other scales.

Scales 1, 2, and 3, which are group tests, were revised in 1935. Considerable alterations were made as a result of the experience gained in the intervening five years. Preliminary practice sheets were introduced. These are probably of value as "shock-absorbers," but since the time allowed for practice is only 5 minutes, the sheets are scarcely sufficient to counteract the effects of differences in test sophistication, which is one of the reasons given for providing practice tests. Scale 1 was made entirely nonverbal, replacing the previous Scale 1 which was predominantly verbal. Though somewhat more difficult to administer, this test is now much fairer to children coming from widely differing educational environments. In Scales 2 and 3 various items were improved and time allowances were revised. Thus, in Scale 3 two subtests were shortened by 1 minute, and one subtest by 2 minutes.

The new scales have been extensively standardized, Scale 1 on more than 6,000 children, Scale 2 on 7,500 children, and Scale 3 on more than 3,000 adults. Each scale is available in two forms, parallel in construction and equal in difficulty. The manual contains very adequate tables of norms, but no data on reliability or validity. It also contains a statement of the aims and guiding principles which were followed in constructing the tests. One of these was to diminish the effects of verbal facility as far as was compatible with the retention of high g saturation. Yet, in spite of this declared aim, the tests for the two upper scales are almost entirely verbal in form. Of the possible marks for Scales 2 and 3, totaling 151 in each, only 8 are for nonverbal items. Hence, both these scales give a very great advantage to subjects possessing high verbal ability. It would seem very desirable to alter the title of the tests for Scales 2 and 3 to "verbal intelligence test" or simply "verbal test." This is all the more necessary since the manual contains a section headed "The Meaning of the Results" which is misleading when applied to Scales 2 and 3. The section includes a quotation from Spearman in which the meaning of general ability or g is explained. Cattell then writes, "The above discussion helps us more clearly to interpret the results of the tests. They measure this pure general ability." If the tests for Scales 2 and 3 were called verbal tests, there would be less likelihood of the scores being interpreted as measures of general ability or g. Also, there is much to be said for following Spearman's lead and dropping the term "intelligence" altogether from the titles of all tests of ability. This policy was adopted in 1950 by the National Foundation for Educational Research in England and Wales, and more recently by Moray House.

Apart from stating that the items were arranged in order of increasing difficulty, the manual provides no information about the methods of test construction or item analysis employed. A recent paper by R. T. Green[1] suggests that the methods of item analysis and selection have not been entirely satisfactory. According to Green:

An item analysis of a well-established intelligence test [Cattell IIIA] using data provided by highly intelligent subjects shows that not only are some items poor indicators of intelligence as measured by the test as a whole, but that other items are good indicators of lack of intelligence. It is suggested that this defect....is inherent in the original selection of the officially correct items on subjective a priori grounds.

No doubt this criticism could be made of many other widely used intelligence tests, constructed about or before 1930.

[1] GREEN, R. T. "An Item Analysis of the Cattell IIIA Intelligence Scale." Abstract. B Brit Psychol Soc (35):A17 My '58. *

Cattell must be commended for having provided a wide range of test material covering mental ages from 4 upwards, and for having secured very adequate standardization data for his Scales 1, 2, and 3. The tests have been very widely used and the main criticism,[2] voiced from time to time, that the IQ's have not been comparable with those obtained from other tests, has been due to the fact that the standard deviation of the IQ's has been in the region of 25. Cattell has consistently maintained that this high standard deviation is the correct one. It is a matter for regret that psychologists have not been able to agree on this matter since so many British users of tests have now become accustomed to the lower standard deviation of 15 employed by N.F.E.R. and Moray House.

For a review by Godfrey H. Thomson, see 40:1386.

[316]
Chicago Non-Verbal Examination. Ages 6 and over; 1936-47; administered orally or in pantomime; 1 form ('36); $3.50 per 25 tests; $1.20 per set of manual ['47] and scoring keys; $1.25 per specimen set; postpaid; 25(40-50) minutes; Andrew W. Brown, Seymour P. Stein, and Perry L. Rohrer; Psychological Corporation. *

REFERENCES
1. BROWN, ANDREW W. "The Development and Standardization of the Chicago Non-Verbal Examination." J Appl Psychol 24:36-47, 122-9 F, Ap '40. * (PA 14:3774, 4767)
2. BROWN, ANDREW W., AND COTTON, CAROL B. "A Study of the Intelligence of Italian and Polish School Children From Deteriorated and Non-Deteriorated Areas of Chicago as Measured by the Chicago Non-Verbal Examination." Child Develop 12:21-30 Mr '41. * (PA 15:3486)
3. JOHNSON, ELIZABETH HUGHES. "The Effect of Academic Level on Scores From the Chicago Non-Verbal Examination for Primary Pupils." Am Ann Deaf 92:227-33 My '47. *
4. ALLEN, ROBERT M., AND BESSELL, HAROLD. "Intercorrelations Among Group Verbal and Non-Verbal Tests of Intelligence." J Ed Res 43:394-5 Ja '50. * (PA 24:4841)
5. EWING, R. M. The Standardization of the Chicago Non-Verbal Examination on English-Speaking School Children Living in Nova Scotia. Master's thesis, Acadia University (Wolfville, N.S., Canada), 1950. Pp. 79.
6. LAVOS, GEORGE. "The Chicago Non-Verbal Examination: A Study in Re-Test Characteristics." Am Ann Deaf 95:379-86 S '50. *
7. ROPER, GEORGE E. Study of the Use of the Chicago Non-Verbal Examination in a Rural Psychiatric Clinic. Master's thesis, Acadia University (Wolfville, N.S., Canada), 1952. Pp. 59.
8. NEWLAND, T. ERNEST, AND LAWRENCE, WILLIAM C. "Chicago Non-Verbal Examination Results on an East Tennessee Negro Population." J Clin Psychol 9:44-7 Ja '53. * (PA 27:7718)
9. LAVOS, GEORGE. "Interrelationships Among Three Tests of Non-Language Intelligence Administered to the Deaf." Am Ann Deaf 99:303-13 My '54. * (PA 29:4596)
10. LEVINE, BERT, AND ISCOE, IRA. "The Progressive Matrices (1938), the Chicago Non-Verbal and the Wechsler Bellevue on an Adolescent Deaf Population." J Clin Psychol 11:307-8 Jl '55. * (PA 30:3334)

RALEIGH M. DRAKE, *Professor of Psychology, Kent State University, Kent, Ohio.*

This test was designed to minimize the English language factor in testing children from

[2] This point has been very fully discussed by Godfrey H. Thomson in The 1940 Mental Measurements Yearbook.

ge 6 through the adult level. It is not a culture ree test in which most environmental influ-nces have been eliminated. On the contrary, t is very much culture bound and would be nappropriate in cultures dissimilar to ours. Even in the United States not all of the picto-rial objects would be equally familiar to chil-lren in different parts of the country and some pictures are now out of date. A more serious feature is that many of the pictures are so small and vaguely drawn that the picture object or meaning is difficult to determine.

The test has been standardized with both verbal and pantomime directions. The stand-ardization group numbered 3,778 with verbal directions and 2,260 with pantomime directions, respectable numbers for tests constructed in 1936. Although the sample was all from Chi-cago or nearby schools, reasonable attention was given to representativeness; in this respect, the test should be equal to most other general ability tests.

The reliability of .89 (split-half, corrected) reported for a group of 334 children aged 8 to 13 inclusive seems to be spuriously high, con-sidering that the test correlates above .70 with age for a group with a similar age range. Since it is a point scale attempting to cover an ex-tremely wide age range, most of the items are either too easy or too difficult for the average testee, a factor which in effect reduces the length of the test and therefore its reliability. Validity data show correlations of from .51 with mental ages on the *Kuhlmann-Anderson Intelligence Test* with chronological age con-stant, to .67 with IQ's on the *Otis Self-Ad-ministering Tests of Mental Ability* with an age range from 8 to 15 years. With age par-tialled out, this would probably be reduced to about .50. Correlations with the Stanford-Binet are not reported, although data from at least two groups were available showing average IQ's from the two tests to be almost identical. Although the averages were almost the same, there was an average difference in individual scores of 9.0 in one group and 7.3 in the other. Since SD's for ages 6 to adult vary from 17.6 to 22.2, compared to 12.5 to 19 for the Stanford-Binet, there is a general tendency for the Chicago IQ equivalents (reported as stand-ard scores in the manual) to run higher for scores above the mean and lower for scores below the mean. The farther the score is from the mean the greater is this tendency. There-

fore, IQ's obtained from either test would have to vary considerably from those obtained from the other. A similar variability would occur if the same child were to be retested several times at different ages. Likewise, the IQ's (standard scores) from the test given with verbal direc-tions are not directly comparable to scores re-sulting from the use of pantomime directions, SD's at various ages averaging almost 3 points higher under the latter procedure. On the av-erage, there is about a 7-months' difference be-tween MA's derived from the same raw score under the two types of directions. The separate standardization takes care of some of this variability, but not all. The test was never given to the same group under both types of direc-tions and no direct comparison of scores is therefore possible. If the test with pantomime directions is to be used for testing the deaf and for non-English speaking children, which is re-ported as its main function, this rather large nonequivalence either to the verbal directions form or to the Stanford-Binet or any other test could be a serious disadvantage. Other tests also suffer from this same variability, of course, which is a common source of error in interpret-ing all converted IQ's.

Considering the demands made upon it (one test is expected to measure sensitively a com-plex ability like intelligence from age 6 to the adult level in 25 minutes of working time and 80 test items, plus two substitution tests), the results are not too disappointing. Nonetheless, the test is in need of considerable restandardiz-ing, lengthening, and redrawing before it can be depended upon for individual diagnosis.

For reviews by Robert G. Bernreuter, Myrtle Luneau Pignatelli, and S. D. Porteus, see 40: 1387.

[317]

★Classification Test 40-A. Job applicants; 1957; 1 form; preliminary mimeographed manual; no data on reliability; no norms; separate answer sheets must be used; PPA member agency: 10–49 tests, 54¢ each; others, 68¢ each; $2 per specimen set; postpaid; 50-(60) minutes; Public Personnel Association. *

[318]

*College Entrance Examination Board Scholas-tic Aptitude Test. Candidates for college entrance; 1926–58; for more complete information, see 599; 2 scores: verbal, mathematical; IBM; 180(240) min-utes; program administered by Educational Testing Service for the College Entrance Examination Board. *

REFERENCES

1–22. See 4:285.
23. MYERS, ROBERT COBB. "Biographical Factors and Aca-

demic Achievement: An Experimental Investigation." *Ed & Psychol Meas* 12:415–26 au '52. * *(PA* 27:6158)

24. NEWMAN, SIDNEY H.; FRENCH, JOHN W.; AND BOBBITT, JOSEPH M. "Analysis of Criteria for the Validation of Selection Measures at the United States Coast Guard Academy." *Ed & Psychol Meas* 12:394–407 au '52. * *(PA* 27:6159)

25. PRESTON, RALPH C., AND BOTEL, MORTON. "The Relation of Reading Skill and Other Factors to the Academic Achievement of 2048 College Students." *J Exp Ed* 20:363–71 Je '52. * *(PA* 27:2967)

26. ALLISON, ROGER B., JR. "Comparison of Reading Comprehension Items and Verbal Items From the Scholastic Aptitude Test." Abstract. *Am Psychol* 8:311 Ag '53. *

27. DYER, HENRY S. "Does Coaching Help?" *Col Board R* (19):331–5 F '53. * *(PA* 28:1559)

28. WEBB, SAM C., AND McCALL, JOHN N. "Predictors of Freshman Grades in a Southern University." *Ed & Psychol Meas* 13:660–3 w '53. * *(PA* 28:6598)

29. MALECKI, GERALD S. *Effectiveness of the College Entrance Board Scholastic Aptitude Test, American Council on Education Psychological Examination, and High School Average for Predicting First Semester Scholarship at Fordham College.* Master's thesis, Fordham University (New York, N.Y.), 1954.

30. OLSEN, MARJORIE A., AND SCHRADER, WILLIAM B. "A Comparison of Item Types in the College Board Scholastic Aptitude Test." Abstract. *Am Psychol* 9:445 Ag '54. *

31. PEARSON, RICHARD. "Equating the Scholastic Aptitude Test." *Col Board R* (23):449–50 My '54. *

32. SEASHORE, HAROLD. "Tenth Grade Tests as Predictors of Twelfth Grade Scholarship and College Entrance Status." Comment by David V. Tiedeman. *J Counsel Psychol* 1:106–15 su '54. * *(PA* 29:3054)

33. BOYD, JOSEPH D. *The Relative Prognostic Value of Selected Criteria in Predicting Beginning Academic Success at Northwestern University.* Doctor's thesis, Northwestern University (Evanston, Ill.), 1955. *(DA* 15:1780)

34. FRENCH, JOHN W. "An Answer to Test Coaching: Public School Experiment With the SAT." *Col Board R* (27):5–7 fall '55. * *(PA* 31:2107)

35. PARRES, JOHN G. *Prediction of Academic Success in the Undergraduate Schools of the University of Pennsylvania.* Doctor's thesis, University of Pennsylvania (Philadelphia, Pa.), 1955. *(DA* 15:2105)

36. COLLEGE ENTRANCE EXAMINATION BOARD. *A Description of the College Board Scholastic Aptitude Test.* Princeton, N.J.: Educational Testing Service, 1956. Pp. 64. * *(PA* 31:1745)

37. LEVINE, RICHARD L., AND ANGOFF, WILLIAM H. "The Effect of Practice on Scores on the Scholastic Aptitude Test of the College Entrance Examination Board." Abstract. *Am Psychol* 11:423 Ag '56. *

38. ANGOFF, WILLIAM H. "The 'Equating' of Non-Parallel Tests." *J Exp Ed* 25:241–7 Mr '57. *

39. EVENSON, A. B., AND SMITH, D. E. "A Study of Matriculation in Alberta." *Alberta J Ed Res* 4:67–83 Je '58. *

40. FEENEY, MARY MARTHA. *Scores on SAT-V and Survey of Study Habits and Attitudes as Predictors of Achievement in a College for Women.* Master's thesis, Fordham University (New York, N.Y.), 1958.

41. FRENCH, JOHN W. "Validation of New Item Types Against Four-Year Academic Criteria." *J Ed Psychol* 49:67–76 Ap '58. *

42. GUMMERE, JOHN F. "Scholastic Aptitude Test Scores of SEB Member Schools." *Sch & Soc* 86:197–8 Ap 26 '58. *

JOHN T. DAILEY, *Program Director, American Institute for Research, Washington, D.C.*

This test consists of five sections, each with a 30-minute time limit. The first three, containing mixtures of completion items, opposites, analogies, and paragraph comprehension exercises, are scored together as a verbal subtest; the last two, designated as Arithmetic Reasoning, although they include considerable algebra and elementary geometry, are scored as a mathematical subtest. Standard scores are available separately for the two subtests.

While a considerable number of applicants will not finish within the time allowed, the manual suggests that the test is essentially unspeeded because the items are arranged in order of difficulty. Several analyses indicate that the tests do appear for the most part to lack "speed-edness" since most of the items omitted seem to be beyond the level of the candidate. The two subscores are of adequate reliability to be used separately, the reported reliabilities being in the vicinity of .90. Standard errors of measurement are given for raw and scaled scores.

A tremendous amount of normative and analytical data regarding the test are published in the manuals. In addition, there are a very large number of validity studies for different schools with many different kinds of groups and criteria. The usual pattern of validities is found against course grades. Particular attention is given to the problem of test-retest effect and to the susceptibility of the test to "cram schools." Studies indicate it is relatively "cram resistant."

The large amount of normative data available in the manuals is probably the most valuable aspect of the test. For example, the *1957 Supplement to College Board Scores No. 2* contains 32 pages of norms for various types of candidates. Results are shown separately for public schools and independent schools, and for all schools, for preliminary and final candidates; boys and girls; students in liberal arts, engineering, and other curricula; transfer students; and college sophomores.

The test is essentially a conventional, general abstract "intelligence" test at the bright adult level. This can probably be said with equal truth of any of its competitors. It does a very effective job of estimating liberal arts scholarship potential and should be interpreted as just that and used accordingly in deciding on admission of a given applicant. The primary value of the test lies in the availability of annual forms, adequate security, and extremely voluminous normative and analytical statistical data.

For a review by Frederick B. Davis of earlier forms, see 4:285.

[319]

★College Placement Test. College entrants; 1957; 3 scores: verbal, quantitative, total; IBM; Form 1 ['57]; preliminary manual; $1 per student when scored by publisher; separate answer sheets must be used; $9.80 per 20 tests; $5 per 100 IBM answer sheets; 50¢ per either hand or machine scoring stencil; 35¢ per manual; $1.50 per specimen set; postage extra; 180-(200) minutes; Science Research Associates.*

GUSTAV J. FROEHLICH, *Assistant Director, Bureau of Institutional Research, University of Illinois, Urbana, Illinois.*

The *College Placement Test* is a power test of scholastic ability, designed to be adminisered in one session of 3 hours or less. It is similar in form and content to a number of currently available group intelligence tests for high school seniors and college freshmen. The test consists of 150 multiple choice items. The first half yields a verbal score; the last half, a quantitative score.

The verbal part is essentially a reading test consisting of 37 verbal relations items (synonyms, antonyms, analogies, sentence completions) and 38 paragraph comprehension questions based on reading passages from college social studies and biological sciences materials. The quantitative part of the test has 38 items involving the interpretation of various tables, graphs, figures and charts, and a 37-item high school mathematics reasoning test including algebra and geometry.

CPT scores, when used in conjunction with the interpretative data given in the test manual, yield useful predictions of college success. Hence, this test is essentially a guidance instrument which can be helpful to both college admissions officers and high school counselors in advising those who have college aspirations. It is not a "placement" test in the sense that it would provide a direct basis for assignment to advanced courses or to noncredit remedial courses.

The internal validity of the test is apparent. The content and language of the test items appear to be consistent with college performance situations. Reading passages, tables, graphs, figures, and charts are such as one would expect to find in college textbooks and references. The construction, analysis, and refinement of the test items were undertaken by three individuals whose competence as test construction specialists is unquestioned. All of the items were pretested on appropriate experimental groups and were selected on the basis of their difficulty level and internal consistency. The items are presented in the test in approximate order of difficulty and are arranged in blocks of similar item types.

The test shows a high positive correlation ($r = .68$, based on 590 cases) with the *Army General Classification Test*. The CPT has also demonstrated factorial validity, yielding measures of three separate factors of intelligence—general, language (more appropriately called reading comprehension), and quantitative ability.

Research studies have shown the feasibility of establishing equivalencies between total raw scores on the CPT and standard scores on the AGCT; and similarly, with standard scores on the *Selected Service College Qualification Test*. These equivalencies, along with percentile norms, are shown in the manual. Tentative equivalencies between raw V and Q scores and standard V and M scores, respectively, on the *Scholastic Aptitude Test* of the College Entrance Examination Board program are also shown in the manual, but further confirmation studies are necessary before these part score equivalences can be accepted as having been established.

From the percentile norms it can be inferred that the CPT has a great amount of "ceiling" (the 99th percentile for college freshmen begins at a total raw score of 118, out of a possible 150). As a matter of fact, as of the date of the manual, no perfect score had been recorded. On the other hand, the test probably has an inadequate "floor" for some college groups. There are a number of instances of record where the total raw score has been found to be below 30, the "chance" score on a 150-item five choice test.

It is the contention of its publishers, and rightly so, that the predictive validity of the CPT must be established for each different type of college and university—ideally for each institution separately. To this end the publishers have expressed a willingness to cooperate in such studies with any college or university interested to do so. To date, there have been only a limited number of such studies, but the results warrant the statement that the predictive validity of the test is as good as, or better than, most other currently available single predictive indices of overall academic success in college.

It has been shown that for Purdue University the total score on the CPT correlates .57 with freshman grade-point index, as compared with a correlation of .40 between high school rank and grade-point index. As a matter of fact, each one of the subtests was found to have a higher zero order correlation with grade-point index than the .40 found for high school rank. The Purdue study also showed that the test has a higher predictive validity than the *Purdue Orientation Tests*—a battery of three tests constructed especially for use on the Purdue campus.

Available studies of the reliability of CPT scores show total score reliabilities to be in the low .90's, V and Q score reliabilities in the middle .80's, and coefficients for the four different subtests ranging from the low .70's to the high .80's. The verbal relations subtest (Items 1–28) consistently shows the lowest subtest reliability. Taking into account the fact that the population tested to obtain the above reliability coefficients is a relatively homogeneous one, and also the fact that the inflationary effect of speed is entirely eliminated, it appears that adequate reliability has been demonstrated.

The test is entirely objective and provides for the use of a separate electrographic answer sheet. A special scoring stencil enables the answer sheet to be either machine or hand scored with a minimum of effort. Directions for administration and scoring are clear, concise, and adequate.

The only real objection this reviewer has is with respect to the format and choice of type for Items 29 through 66. These pages are too crowded, and the type for the reading passages is too small. The layout is conducive to unnecessary mental fatigue, and may prove to be an unnecessary stumbling block to those having even a minor visual deficiency. Similarly, the explanatory materials under the weather map and the detail in the airline schedule are hard to read.

The *College Placement Test* can provide useful predictions of college success in a variety of institutions when used by trained counselors and guidance personnel who are conscious of the pitfalls inherent in the use of any predictive index which is significantly better than a chance guess, but is still subject to considerable statistical "error." Its predictive validity has been demonstrated for a limited number of institutions; but further studies for a larger number of schools should be made. At the same time additional studies to determine the predictive efficiency of this test when used in combination with high school rank are in order. Finally, the validity of the V and Q score as predictive indices for specific curricular areas should be explored further.

DAVID V. TIEDEMAN, *Associate Professor of Education, Harvard University, Cambridge, Massachusetts.*

The *College Placement Test* is a power test which most college students are reported to finish in less than 2 hours. The verbal section consists of an approximately equal number of vocabulary items (synonyms, antonyms, analogies, and sentence completions) and of questions regarding comprehension of written material. Paragraphs are similar to textbook material encountered in several areas of college study. The quantitative section consists of an approximately equal number of items requiring the interpretation of data (tables, graphs, figures, and charts) and of items requiring quantitative reasoning of an algebraic and geometric kind when formulas are supplied. There are 75 items in each section. Perhaps it is this small number of items that makes the split-half reliability coefficients of the section scores only about .87 in a sample of college students. The standard error of measurement of each score is not reported.

The paragraph comprehension items and the data interpretation items are representative of the tasks facing college students in their courses. But the inclusion of these types of item material gives the factor structure of the test a peculiar cast. The reported factor analysis of four subscores (derived by scoring separately the two types of verbal material and the two types of quantitative material) indicates a definite "general" factor in all four tests with subsidiary Q (quantitative ability) and L (language ability) factors. But Q is more oriented by the data interpretation subtest than by the arithmetic reasoning subtest, and paragraph comprehension has a slight loading on the Q factor. L, on the other hand, is primarily oriented by paragraph comprehension; verbal relations and data interpretation have equal but secondary loadings on this factor. Thus, some caution should surround placing the V and Q scores of this test in the same system as the L and Q scores of the *American Council on Education Psychological Examination* and the V and N scores of the *College Qualification Tests.*

The manual treats in some detail (e.g., intercorrelations, multiple correlations, and factor analysis) four subscores which are not recommended for general use. This suggests that two verbal subtest scores and two quantitative subtest scores may have been under consideration at some time during the development of the test but that the four subtests were finally judged to be too interdependent to warrant separation into more than two sections.

With the "general" factor running through the CPT so definitely, it is somewhat surprisng to find that the few predictive validity co-efficients reported for the total score do not press nearer to .60 more frequently than they do. For the most part, validity coefficients for the total score run from .40 to .57.

The publishers have taken great pains to tie the CPT total score in with standard scores of the *Army General Classification Test* and with standard scores of the *Selective Service College Qualification Test*. The CPT is well anchored to a generally understood median of the AGCT and of the SSCQT. There is one trouble, how-ever. CPT and AGCT are reported to correlate to the extent of only .68 in one sample. The standard error of estimating an AGCT score from a CPT score is 73 per cent of the standard deviation of the AGCT scores in this case. Thus, the CPT does not give a very good esti-mate of an AGCT score even though equi-per-centile points are very well equated. The corre-lation of CPT and SSCQT is not reported. This does not matter so much for the purpose of selection as it does for the purpose of coun-seling.

The manual presents a table for converting V and Q scores on this test into equivalent V and M scores on the *Scholastic Aptitude Test*. Correlations between supposedly similar scores on the CPT and SAT are not reported; inter-pretation of the table of equivalencies should await the report of such correlations.

The manual for the CPT was designated as "preliminary" as of September 1957. In these circumstances, it is advisable for colleges to experiment with the test before making it oper-ational. With the CPT, experimentation may proceed either independently or in collabora-tion with the publisher since the test is offered either for sale in the usual manner or as part of a service including scoring, development of local norms, and planning of local validity stud-ies. Since the V and Q scores of the test are of seeming relevance for study in college, the test is likely to have at least some predictive validity in most colleges, as is suggested by the several predictive validity studies already re-ported.

Until the results of such experimentation are made available by the publisher or others, this test is of little or no help to a high school pupil in relation to his planning of college attend-ance. The reviewer would not yet make appli-cation of experience with the AGCT, the SSCQT, the ACE, or the SAT to the inter-pretation of scores on the CPT in individual cases. The translation of experience with these tests into the scores of the CPT is probably justifiable if the purpose is selective admission to college.

[320]

★College Qualification Tests. Candidates for col-lege entrance; 1955–58; also called CQT; 6 scores: verbal, numerical, science information, social science information, total information, total; IBM; Forms A, B ('56); 2 editions; manual ('57); supplement ('58); distribution of Form B restricted to colleges and uni-versities; separate answer sheets must be used; post-paid; George K. Bennett, Marjorie G. Bennett, Wim-burn L. Wallace, and Alexander G. Wesman; Psycho-logical Corporation. *
a) COMBINED BOOKLET EDITION. $5 per 25 tests; $3.50 per 50 IBM answer sheets; 60¢ per specimen set; 80(105) minutes.
b) SEPARATE BOOKLET EDITION. $2.50 per 25 tests; $1.90 per 50 IBM answer sheets; 90¢ per specimen set.
1) *Test V*. Verbal; 15(25) minutes.
2) *Test N*. Numerical; 35(45) minutes.
3) *Test I*. 3 scores: science information, social sci-ence information, total; 30(40) minutes.

GUSTAV J. FROEHLICH, *Assistant Director, Bu-reau of Institutional Research, University of Illinois, Urbana, Illinois.*

The *College Qualification Tests* are a series of three ability tests developed for use by col-lege admissions officers and guidance personnel. High school counselors may also find the test data helpful in advising those who want to go on to college.

Test V, Verbal, consists of 75 vocabulary items—50 synonyms and 25 antonyms. Test N, Numerical, contains 50 items, drawing on arith-metic, algebra, and geometry. It is aimed at con-ceptual skill in simple mathematics, not at com-putational or clerical speed. Test I, Informa-tion, has 75 items and yields, in addition to the overall information score, a separate science in-formation score (based on 38 items drawn from the fields of biology, chemistry, and phys-ics), and a separate social studies information score (based on 37 items drawn from the fields of economics, geography, government, and his-tory).

Even though the tests are timed, they appar-ently function as power tests in that the time limits seem to be generous enough to permit all those who actually have college ability to attempt all of the items.

Everywhere throughout the test booklets and the manual there is evidence of careful plan-ning, rigid adherence to the principles of good test construction, and adequate experimenta-tion and research prior to putting the tests on the market. The mechanics of the tests—format, wording, type, and directions—are well executed.

It is the contention of the authors and publishers, and rightly so, that the approach to meaningful norms is through specific identification of the institutions and the individuals which make up the norms sample. Thus, a number of different sets of norms are in order, broken down not only by sex, but by type of institution and by curriculum. To this end, in addition to general percentile norms for college freshmen given separately for men and women, the manual contains the special sets of norms for freshmen in different types of colleges and universities and for freshmen in different types of curricula.

The most important single characteristic of a test is its validity. The *College Qualification Tests* were developed to serve as predictors of academic success in college courses. The elaborate table of validity coefficients reported (correlations between raw test scores and first semester college grade-point averages) indicates that the tests can serve a useful purpose by yielding estimates of probable success in the first semester of college which are significantly better than chance guesses. Furthermore, it is immediately evident from this table that the validity of the tests varies from one institution to another. Hence, it is suggested that each college which plans to use the tests extensively should develop its own set of norms. One factor which strongly influences test validity thus determined is the reliability of course grades; this, we know, varies considerably from institution to institution and from curriculum to curriculum within a given institution.

The manual reports both reliability coefficients and standard errors of measurement based upon a sampling of students whose score means and variances are comparable to those of the normative population. The reliabilities are adequate—in the middle .90's for the total score and from the high .70's through the low .90's for the subtests. No data are shown for the more homogeneous populations represented in the several special sets of norms.

The verbal and numerical tests are similar to those found in a number of currently available group intelligence tests at the freshman college level. The information test represents the conviction of the authors that a measure of educational background which the student brings to college will be indicative of his future learning and will be a more effective predictive index than high school grades, which are subject to considerable unreliability. Some justification for this is evident from the fact that a number of the validity coefficients reported for the information subtests are higher than those usually reported for rank in high school class.

The *College Qualification Tests* are well constructed instruments. They should be useful to college admission officers and high school counselors.

A. E. G. PILLINER, *Lecturer in Experimental Education, University of Edinburgh, Edinburgh, Scotland.*

For general layout and clarity of presentation of items, this pair of parallel tests is outstandingly good. Scoring, by whichever method is chosen, is simple. The manual is not only explicit in stating the purpose of the tests and in detailing the considerations which have guided the constructors in their work, but also presents a wealth of statistical information by the study of which the extent of their success in achieving their goals can be assessed. The instructions for administration are a model of clarity and conciseness.

The basic principles were laid down by an advisory committee of psychologists and educationists, "having responsibility for the college student at the time of entrance," who listed a number of requirements to be met in constructing tests to be used for selecting college students. Their main points are: (a) the tests should be broadly predictive of college success and suitable for many curricula; (b) they should stress power rather than speed; (c) they should serve several purposes, namely, selection, placement, and counseling; (d) comparability of tests should be ensured by having them normed on the same population; (e) the times and places of their administration should be at the discretion of the colleges using them; and (f) for reasons of security, the use of at least one form of the tests should be restricted to the colleges.

It may be said at once that the tests do in fact meet many of these requirements. The manual indicates that the committee's points (d), (e), and (f) have been successfully covered. By working through the tests himself, this reviewer was able to confirm their point (b). With regard to point (a), the validity coefficients published in profusion in the manual demonstrate that, provided one accepts first semester grade-point averages as an adequate criterion of college success, the tests predict as well as might be expected in a variety of different situations. This reviewer must, however, record his agreement with Guilford, who, discussing a previous test published by the Psychological Corporation, wrote, "Those of us who train students beyond the M.A. level know well that there are often great discrepancies in both directions between grade-getting abilities and capacities for independent thinking and research" (see 4:304).

With regard to point (c), this reviewer, while sympathising with the constructors' intention to make the tests multipurpose, must confess to some doubts as to the success likely to be achieved. For selection purposes, subject to what has been said about the adequacy of the present criterion, the tests appear to be efficient. For the kindred tasks of placement and counseling, the evidence is less convincing. Short of an *ad hoc* experiment which, while easy to design could scarcely be carried out in a democratic country, it is difficult to see how really convincing evidence could be obtained in relation to one specific test or battery of tests. We can never know what a student's grades might have been in a group of studies other than that he has in fact undertaken. Nevertheless, something might emerge indirectly from a comparison of the grade scores of students who had accepted advice based on their performances on the several parts of this series with the grade scores of students who had not done so.

As for psychometric quality: (a) The tables of norms in the manual show that each form successfully exercises discrimination over the whole range of already accepted students tested —no mean achievement within a total testing time of 80 minutes. The tests, that is, possess the first prerequisite of a selection instrument. (b) Having regard to the nature of the groups tested, reliability (internal consistency) is high, ranging from .95 for the verbal test to .80 for the social studies subtest, with .97 overall. So far as they go, these figures are satisfactory, but it would have been useful to know also the parallel-forms reliability. (c) Validity, as already mentioned, is reasonably high. The mean of the 24 validity coefficients based on total score is .55. (d) The intercorrelations among the parts range from .71 for verbal and social

studies to .45 for numerical and social studies. (e) CQT correlates quite well with other scholastic aptitude tests, for example, .78 with the ACE and .82 with SCAT.

Few institutions using these tests will fail to find among the 11 sets of percentile norms (8 of these for men and women separately) that most appropriate to their requirements. Even so, test users are rightly urged to develop their own local norms which, to quote from the manual, "are, of course, more important for a particular school than are any published norms."

To sum up: the presentation of these tests and of their manual is technically excellent. So far as their limited objective of predicting grade-point averages goes, they are at least the equal of other tests having the same purpose. They should prove useful in selecting college students, but the claim that they can assist in counseling and placing in courses needs (and, it is hoped, will receive) confirmation.

DAVID V. TIEDEMAN, *Associate Professor of Education, Harvard University, Cambridge, Massachusetts*.

Test V consists of 75 vocabulary items requiring identification of synonyms or antonyms. The V score correlates highly with the L score of the *American Council on Education Psychological Examination* (ACE) and with the verbal score of the *Cooperative School and College Ability Tests* (SCAT).

Test N consists of 50 items requiring application of arithmetical, algebraic, and geometrical concepts. The N score correlates highly with the quantitative score of the SCAT, but the correlation of the CQT-N score with the ACE-Q score is only around .55.

Test I, Information, consists of 38 questions of a "scientific" nature and 37 questions of a "social studies" nature. Each of these tests correlates reasonably well with its counterpart in the *Cooperative General Achievement Test, Form XX*. Study of Test I reveals, however, that the subject does not have to reason very much with the concepts of either science or social studies to answer the questions. He will either have the answer to a question at his fingertips or not. The science items demand information accumulated in biology, chemistry, and physics. The social studies items demand information of an economic, geographical, legal, or political nature. Amount of information in either science or social studies correlates with first semester grade average as well as V or N scores do. Because of the relatively high correlation of scores of information about science and social studies with scores of either V or N, however, scores on these tests of information will add very little to the predictive efficiency of V and N scores. In addition, the slight variation of the average score in science and social studies information according to the degree program in which a freshman is enrolled suggests that these scores of science and social studies information will not be terribly useful in advising about degree programs. The scores are, of course, relevant for assessing the amount of information a student has stockpiled in each of these areas and hence *may* be indicative of interest in the area. But perhaps it might be easier and more valid to ask directly about interest in the fields. Hence the reviewer is of the opinion that Test I is not too useful.

Statistics on Forms A and B are reasonably comparable but the reviewer is more concerned about the "somewhat more perceptible" difference in averages for the total score of Test I than are the authors. In the first place, the difference in averages on the two forms is significant in the case of both men and women. The averages do not differ only randomly. Secondly, the difference in averages for men is 1.5 points, for women 1.8 points. Since the standard deviations for the two forms are similar in the data for either men and women, these differences indicate that the Form B distribution is almost everywhere 1.5 points above the Form A distribution for men and 1.8 points above the Form A distribution for women. The consequences of these circumstances can be illustrated in terms of the general norms for college freshmen. For men, in the percentile range from 5 to 95 inclusive, there are four percentile rank classes which are designated by a single score on Test I. The percentile rank of a score on Form B which should really be in one of these percentile rank classes will actually appear to be 5 percentile ranks higher. The same advantage of 5 percentile ranks will be associated with approximately one half of the scores in the 11 percentile rank classes which are defined by 2 raw score points and with approximately one third of the scores in the 4 percentile rank classes defined by 3 raw score points. The situation is even worse in the data for women. Finally, the differences in average

scores of Forms A and B for Test I are between four and five tenths of the standard error of measurement for a score obtained either by a man or by a woman. This is too great an eliminable bias to leave in the interpretation of a true score on either Form A or B of Test I. In the case of Test I, scores on either form are not "directly comparable with scores earned on the other form." This does not negate the other conclusion that any differences "are still small enough so that averages based on combined scores yield sufficiently representative data to warrant merging the distributions."

Test V, Test N, Test I, and total scores are quite reliable. The science and social studies scores, however, are less reliable as the manual warns.

The CQT are offered to colleges for the purposes of selective admissions, placement in sections, and counseling. Since the CQT scores correlate with first semester grade average in several colleges to as high a degree as one usually obtains for such tests, a college would probably increase its pool of desired students by using the tests for the purpose of selective admissions *provided* the college considered its circumstances like the specified circumstances of the 14 colleges for which data are briefly reported. The manual provides no information of relevance for sectioning classes except for those colleges which have previously sectioned classes on the basis of the ACE or SCAT. The manual provides norms for freshmen *intending* to study for the A.B. or B.S. degree or to study in programs of business, education, engineering, technical fields, or nursing. Therefore, the tests are of some slight use in counseling with regard to the competition a student might face under several alternatives. However, the distributions of scores for those pursuing the several alternatives overlap too much to permit fine distinctions of this kind. The extensive norms and the completeness with which data on predictive validity are reported mean that the CQT are an important source of information in counseling with regard to ability to pursue collegiate study.

The CQT will be sold to high schools. Although norms are extensive and based on large numbers of cases, high school counselors should realize that only the 37 institutions listed in the manual are represented. In addition, counselors must rely upon their own prototypes of these institutions because no characteristics of an educational kind are associated with the norms save for the test scores themselves.

Psychometrically the tests are quite sound. Technically, the manual, test booklet, answer sheet, and scoring stencil are fine. Adequate time limits are provided for each test. Many mistakes will be made in getting the science and social studies scores in Test I by hand. In addition, the reviewer does not consider Test I to be very useful. Nevertheless, the CQT are ready for use by anyone capable of understanding the cautions the publisher explicitly incorporates throughout the manual. An informed person can immediately use these tests for any purpose for which they are offered, viz., selective admission to college, placement of students in sections (provided the ACE or SCAT was formerly used for this purpose), and counseling of high school students about college intentions and, to a slight degree, of college students about degree programs.

[321]

★Concept Mastery Test. Grades 15–16 and graduate students; 1956, c1950; IBM; Form T ('56); manual ('56); separate answer sheets must be used; $3 per 25 tests; $1.90 per 50 IBM answer sheets; 35¢ per specimen set; postpaid; (35–45) minutes; Lewis M. Terman; Psychological Corporation. *

REFERENCES

1. THORNDIKE, ROBERT L. "An Evaluation of the Adult Intellectual Status of Terman's Gifted Children." *J Genetic Psychol* 72:17–27 Mr '48. * (PA 22:4836)
2. BAYLEY, NANCY, AND ODEN, MELITA H. "The Maintenance of Intellectual Ability in Gifted Adults." *J Gerontol* 10:91–107 Ja '55. * (PA 30:2583)
3. BARTHOL, RICHARD P., AND KIRK, BARBARA A. "The Selection of Graduate Students in Public Health Education." *J Appl Psychol* 40:159–63 Je '56. * (PA 31:6666)
4. TAYLOR, DONALD W. "Variables Related to Creativity and Productivity Among Men in Two Research Laboratories." In *The Identification of Creative Scientific Talent.* Edited by Calvin W. Taylor. Salt Lake City, Utah: University of Utah Press, 1958.

J. A. KEATS, *Senior Lecturer in Psychology, University of Queensland, Brisbane, Australia.*

Perhaps the most interesting point about the *Concept Mastery Test* is that it is a by-product of Terman's extensive studies of gifted children and of these same children in adult life. The test is a high level verbal test for adults. It is untimed, but usually takes about 40 minutes to complete.

The test contains two types of items. In the first part are standard synonym-antonym items which rely for their difficulty on rather unusual vocabulary. Those in the second part are items of the analogy type, but this form is used with number items as well as verbal problems covering general knowledge and relationships between terms. The title "concept mastery"

seems too broad to cover such restricted content. Coverage of what the reviewer understands by this title would require a battery of tests and the result would not be summarized in a single score. Terman concedes this point but claims that the test gives as good an indication of a person's ability to deal with abstract concepts as can be obtained in this limited time. In such circumstances, it would seem better to choose a more precise title.

The correlation between the two parts is .76 for the subjects of the Stanford Gifted Study for whom the test was intended. This figure is probably not very much below what the parallel forms reliability of either part computed separately would be; thus, a single score is justified. Reliability was found to lie between .86 and .94 using a parallel form of the test. With the gifted subjects, similar figures were obtained after a lapse of 12 years.

The test distinguishes clearly between adults of different educational levels and has shown the usual validity for such tests as predictors of success in university courses. Correlations between CMT and a number of other tests are provided in the manual.

Because of the two simple forms of presenting the problems, the need for complicated and detailed instructions is largely removed. Directions to be stressed deal entirely with the requirements for machine scoring and not with explanation of item forms.

Norms in the form of percentile ranks in 5 per cent intervals are provided for four groups of subjects. However, those based on the gifted subjects are the only norms obtained from a sample of more than 200 cases. Thus, the only satisfactory norms from the point of view of stability are for a rather special group. This lack of suitable norms limits the usefulness of the test.

It is interesting to note how many of the gifted subjects obtained high scores on a test requiring a wide background of information and knowledge of rare words. However, the claim that the test is "a measure of ability to deal with abstract ideas" needs further substantiation. The test may have value as a selection and guidance instrument, but the prospective user would have to carry out more preliminary standardization and validation work than would be required if he were to use some other tests currently available.

CALVIN W. TAYLOR, *Professor of Psychology, University of Utah, Salt Lake City, Utah.*

Since no intellectual test was available that met the needs of Terman's follow-up studies of the gifted, the *Concept Mastery Test* was devised to reach into the stratosphere of adult intelligence by use of synonyms, antonyms, and verbal analogy items. From data presented in the manual, it would seem that the test served its purpose well.

In the follow-up studies Form A was administered in 1939–40 and Form T (earlier called Form B) in 1951–52. Form T, which is now being marketed, was designed to match all except the most difficult items in the earlier Form A and to extend the scale downward, making it suitable for wider use as a selection and a counseling tool. The items are arranged in order of difficulty and use concepts from a variety of fields.

The new claims for Form T are that it is suitable for testing college juniors and seniors, graduate students, and adults who are being considered for research, executive, and other unusually demanding jobs. Percentile norms are presented solely for specially selected groups and for one group of graduate students, with only means and standard deviations presented for college juniors and seniors. There is little doubt, however, that a wide variability in scores would occur on juniors, seniors, or graduate students.

Although the test deals with verbal concepts and abstractions, the examinee merely has to recognize such concepts, not to produce them. The author readily admits that this test does not tap all the kinds of intellect. He has stated that some aspects of intelligence, such as creative intelligence or the ability to make new mental constructs, are so elusive that man has been unable so far to map or quantify them adequately.

Donald Taylor (4) found that Form T correlated only .11 with undergraduate grades in the last two years and failed to correlate significantly with any supervisory ratings in research laboratories for creativity, productivity, originality, quality of work, or quantity of work. The test correlated at least moderately with the Owens-Bennett *Test of Mechanical Comprehension,* the *Test for Productive Thinking,* and the *Test for Selecting Research Personnel,* the highest correlation being with the least valid part of the last test. Every score

from the above three tests had significant validities with the supervisor's creativity rating, while the *Concept Mastery Test* failed to have a significant validity. Apparently, the *Concept Mastery Test* is better in earlier academic situations and tends to lose some validity against later criteria. The main positive evidence known to the reviewer of the test's validity for the newly advertised purposes, as distinct from the Terman study purposes, is indirect evidence through its correlates. The evidence of validity for the initial purposes may or may not be very highly related to its new uses on advanced students and for predicting certain criteria of job success.

In summary, from its careful construction and from direct and indirect evidence, the *Concept Mastery Test* is apparently an excellent test for its initial purpose of measuring, at a high level and over a wide range, the ability to recognize (not necessarily produce) verbal concepts and abstractions. However, the available evidence casts some doubt on whether or not it works nearly as well in predicting upper division and graduate success and productivity and creativity on the job in science and other high level fields.

[322]

★**Cooperative School and College Ability Tests.** Grades 4–6, 6–8, 8–10, 10–12, 12–14; 1955–57; also called SCAT; 3 scores: verbal, quantitative, total; IBM; 5 levels (labeled forms); directions for administering ('57); record blank ('57); separate answer sheets must be used; $3.95 per 20 tests; $1 per 20 IBM answer sheets; 45¢ per scoring stencil; 40¢ per profiles ('57); $1.25 per specimen set; postage extra; 70(95) minutes; Cooperative Test Division, Educational Testing Service. *

a) SCHOOL ABILITY TEST. Grades 4–6, 6–8, 8–10, 10–12; 2 forms, 4 levels.

1) [*Level 5.*] Grades 4–6; Forms 5A, 5B ('56).
2) [*Level 4.*] Grades 6–8; Forms 4A, 4B ('56).
3) [*Level 3.*] Grades 8–10; Forms 3A, 3B ('56).
4) [*Level 2.*] Grades 10–12; Forms 2A, 2B ('55).

b) COLLEGE ABILITY TEST. Grades 12–14; 4 forms.

1) [*Level 1.*] Grades 12–14; Forms 1A, 1B, 1C, 1D ('55); Forms 1C and 1D available only by special arrangement for use with students in college.

REFERENCES

1. NORTH, ROBERT D. "A Comparison of the Cooperative School and College Ability Tests: College Ability Test, and the American Council Psychological Examination: Reliabilities, Intercorrelations, and Correlations With the Diagnostic Reading Tests." *Ed Rec B* 67:65–72 F '56. * (*PA* 31:3800)
2. TRAXLER, ARTHUR E. "Should SCAT Scat ACE? A Comparison Between the Cooperative School and College Ability Tests, Form 1A, and the American Council on Education Psychological Examination, 1948 College Freshman Edition, as to Difficulty and Value for Predicting School Marks." *Ed Rec B* 67:51–63 F '56. * (*PA* 31:3817)
3. MANUEL, HERSCHEL T. "Aptitude Tests for College Admission." *Yearb Nat Council Meas Used Ed* 14:20–7 '57. *
4. NORTH, ROBERT D. "A Further Report on the Cooperative College Ability Test." *Ed Rec B* 69:60–2 F '57 .* (*PA* 32:2119)
5. EVENSON, A. B., AND SMITH, D. E. "A Study of Matriculation in Alberta." *Alberta J Ed Res* 4:67–83 Je '58. *

6. Gremillion, Benedict Joseph. "The Cooperative School and College Ability Test as a Screening Instrument for the Mathematics Proficiency Examination." *J Social Psychol* 47: 149–51 F '58. *

7. Vincent, Lewis. "A Comparison of the Quantitative Items of the A.C.E. Psychological With Similar Items in the Cooperative School and College Abilities Tests." *Yearb Nat Council Meas Used Ed* 15:144–9 '58. *

Frederick B. Davis, *Professor of Education, and Director, Educational Clinic, Hunter College, New York, New York; and Director, Test Research Service, Bronxville, New York.*

The *Cooperative School and College Ability Tests* (SCAT) are intended primarily to aid in estimating the capacity of students in grades 4–14 to undertake additional schooling. Four operational skills are measured: Part 1, getting the meaning of isolated sentences (15 minutes); Part 2, performing numerical computations rapidly (20 minutes); Part 3, associating meanings of isolated words (10 minutes); Part 4, solving arithmetic problems (25 minutes). Parts 1 and 3 are combined to obtain a verbal score, Parts 2 and 4 to obtain a quantitative score, and all four parts to obtain a total aptitude score. The total score is influenced a little more by the verbal than by the quantitative parts.

The design of the test is such that it is likely to be moderately useful for many educational purposes but not especially useful for any one particular purpose. For predicting school grades, it is likely to be less accurate than previous grades in the same subject; for comparing school achievement in any given subject with potential capacity in that subject, it is likely to be less revealing than a test of basic psychological traits; for comparing the verbal and numerical or the verbal and quantitative reasoning aptitudes of one individual, it is likely to be less sensitive and less analytic than a pair of highly specialized tests.

Some interesting data regarding the predictive validity of the test are now available. In grades 9 and 11 the average correlations of SCAT verbal scores with English grades, of SCAT quantitative scores with mathematics grades, and SCAT total scores with grades in social studies and in science are about .50 to .55. In grade 7 analogous correlations (based on smaller samples) run as high as .65 to .70. Teachers of fifth grade in seven different schools rated pupils at the end of the academic year in defined verbal and quantitative abilities. The correlations of these ratings with SCAT verbal and quantitative scores were about .70 if the data from one school, which yielded

markedly atypical results, are excluded. In all of these studies the SCAT scores were obtained at the beginning of the school year and the grades or ratings at the end of the school year. The SCAT scores were not made known in the schools during the year.

Directions for administration are provided in a neat 12-page brochure. All forms of the test at each of the five levels are given with the same time limits, answer sheets, and directions (with minor additions for the Level 5 tests, which have more answer spaces than items in Parts 1 and 3). There are advantages in this standardization of materials. If the test is given in one session, the directions recommend a 5-minute recess after Part 2. Since only one side of one answer sheet is used, a student who obtains helpful information during the recess can improve his score by changing answers and filling in spaces he left blank. To prevent this, the directions state: "It is preferable that groups of students going to the rest room be accompanied by a proctor in order to prevent discussion of specific test topics." There is no mention of this problem in the directions for giving the test in two sessions, although under these circumstances almost all students can obtain information enabling them to improve their scores. The boldest, most sophisticated, and least conscientious will avail themselves of this opportunity to the greatest extent. Recognition of this tends to engender in many students, parents, and educators unfavorable attitudes toward testing.

The scoring of SCAT is straightforward, but the need for locating and deleting (by erasure or the use of scotch tape) all multiple answer marks makes it tedious. Moreover, the recommended procedures will not cope with the practice (common among sophisticated examinees) of placing inconspicuous dots in one or more answer spaces for a given item in addition to blackening one of the spaces heavily. The best practical way of handling the problem of multiple marking is to include a correction for chance success in the scoring. This eliminates the need for scanning answer sheets prior to hand scoring and reduces the amount of scanning needed prior to machine scoring to the relatively simple matter of cleaning messy answer sheets. It also reduces greatly the likelihood that an examinee who spends the last few moments making marks at random to all the items he has not read will thereby improve his score. As a result, another source of unfavorable attitudes toward testing in students, parents, and educators is removed. Unfortunately, a correction for chance success is not used in scoring SCAT.

Considerable effort has been devoted to making possible the meaningful interpretation of scores. The degree of success attained rests mainly on the utility of the converted scores, the percentile bands, and the norms. Three scales have been developed, one for all verbal scores, one for all quantitative scores, and one for all total-aptitude scores. Thus, verbal converted scores are serviceably equivalent regardless of the form or level used; similarly, quantitative and total-aptitude converted scores. However, converted scores in verbal, quantitative, and total aptitude are not comparable with one another. Consequently, comparison of a given student's verbal and quantitative converted scores is conveniently possible only by converting them, in turn, into percentile ranks in an appropriate reference group. In practice, this is done by using the individual score norms to plot the student's percentile bands on the SCAT Student Profile. Some test users may feel that, since all the converted scores are not comparable, the conversion of raw scores directly to percentile bands (or percentile ranks) would be more economical of time and sacrifice little in ease of interpretation.

Percentile bands replace the more familiar percentile ranks for reporting SCAT scores. For example, a ninth grade student who obtains a quantitative converted score of 283 has a percentile band of 29–55. This method of reporting scores certainly emphasizes the lack of precision in some test scores. Whether it is more useful to test users than the reporting of percentile ranks with the standard error of measurement in terms of percentiles at various percentile ranks is doubtful. Each percentile band was obtained by laying off on both sides of the middle of a score category one standard error of measurement and taking the two points thus defined as the ends of the band. However, the resulting bands are not 68 per cent confidence intervals; the chances that a student's true aptitude standing is included by his percentile band are less than 68 out of 100 by an amount that cannot be exactly determined from the data. One reason for this is that the standard errors of measurement are spuriously small because they are based on reliability coefficients

of *speeded* tests computed by Kuder-Richardson formula 20. In accordance with the basic plan of SCAT, the degree of speededness is greater for the quantitative than for the verbal parts. Data in the Technical Report indicate that at some grade levels as few as 48 per cent complete Part 2 and 60 per cent Part 4, and Parts 1 and 3 are completed by as few as 65 per cent and 80 per cent, respectively. Quite a different impression is given test users by the statement in the Directions for Administering and Scoring: "The subtests are relatively unspeeded; all but the slowest students can complete them in the time limits allowed." Examinees may also get an erroneous mind-set from the following sentence in the general directions: "If you work at average speed you will have plenty of time to read and answer all of the questions."

The SCAT Student Profile makes possible a comparison of a student's verbal and quantitative percentile bands. If the standard errors of measurement had been obtained by a more appropriate procedure and were the same for the two scores being compared, the technique recommended on the profile for identifying differences between verbal and quantitative scores that may be regarded as indicative of true differences in aptitude standing would so identify differences significant at the 16 per cent level, or better. In practice, the recommended technique so identifies some differences that do not meet this standard.

The samples on which the fall percentile norms are based were carefully constructed to be representative of students in grades 4–14, in American schools and colleges willing to participate in testing programs. It is rare to find normative groups that so well conform to their characterizations.

Other aids for interpreting scores are provided, including norms for school averages, tables of comparable scores for SCAT and the high school (1953) and college (1952) editions of the *American Council on Education Psychological Examinations,* and probability tables for estimating verbal and mathematics scores on the *College Entrance Examination Board Scholastic Aptitude Test* of students with specified SCAT converted scores.

Finally, it may be said that the items in SCAT are, in general, well written and well edited.

HANFORD M. FOWLER, *Professor of Education, University of Toronto, Toronto, Ontario, Canada.*

The *Cooperative School and College Ability Tests* (SCAT) were designed "to aid in estimating the capacity of a student to undertake the next higher level of schooling." The two functions chosen for measurement, verbal and quantitative, presumably relate closely to skills which are essential to success in school and college.

Although the SCAT series resembles the *American Council on Education Psychological Examination* (ACE) in a number of ways, SCAT is strictly not a replacement for ACE. For one thing, the five levels of SCAT extend from the second year at college down through grade 4. ACE is for college freshmen and high school students only. There are other differences with respect to the tests themselves and the way in which they were developed. It is unlikely that the two series measure the same elements. On the other hand, the general purpose of the tests is probably the same. Those who have found usefulness in ACE may expect to find the same type of utility in SCAT.

The purpose of ACE is to measure what has been called scholastic aptitude or general intelligence; the authors of SCAT make no direct reference to intelligence but prefer to consider their tests measures of "school-learned abilities." They claim that SCAT measures "specific developed abilities rather than abstract, hard-to-explain psychological traits." However, in practice, SCAT will probably be used in much the same way as ACE has been used: for identifying the overachiever and the underachiever; for counseling the individual student; for comparing average abilities of different groups of students; and so on.

In outward appearance and attractiveness SCAT is as good as any test which this reviewer has seen. The series appears in attractive 7½ by 10½ inch booklets with clear printing, well spaced items, and a pleasing use of colour; the separate answer sheets have an equally attractive format. To assist the administration of the tests, no less than three manuals are provided: one contains directions for administering and scoring; one gives information, directions and illustrations to help in interpreting the scores; and one describes the procedure followed in the various experimental and norms programmes and gives statistical information

describing the characteristics of SCAT and its relationships with ACE and with the *Scholastic Aptitude Test* (SAT). And there is even more to come! The publishers promise supplements in which will be reported the results of various studies now being conducted to determine predictive validity. All of this is very impressive, but it costs money. The test consumer who must pay the shot has a right to ask what value is being received for prices which are inflated far beyond those of the good old days of the 5-cent test. How does SCAT measure up with respect to validity, reliability, and standardization?

VALIDITY. No studies as yet have been reported which provide evidence of the predictive validity of SCAT; no evidence is available in the manual. Readers of the manual must infer their own estimates of validity from information relating to the construction of the test, which indeed is detailed and complete, and from fragmentary evidence of the concurrent validity of the test. Such inferences lack the conviction of data-based estimates. Fortunately, information on predictive validity of SCAT will be published in a forthcoming supplement, a draft of which has been made available to the writer. The results reported in the supplement are definitely favourable. Certainly the reported validity coefficients are at least as high as, and occasionally considerably higher than, similar coefficients reported for other tests of this type. We must conclude that on the evidence presently available SCAT shows promise of being an efficient measure of future scholastic success. Some of the coefficients in the lower grades, above .80 in a few cases, impressed this reviewer as being almost suspiciously high. However, the coefficients of the higher grades are generally lower than those in the lower grades. Two other considerations must be kept in mind: (*a*) when numbers are very small, as they were in a number of schools, high coefficients turn up with surprising regularity even if samples are drawn from a population in which the true relationship is zero; (*b*) great variation in the results appeared from school to school, which means that individuals are faced with the necessity of investigating the validity of the tests in their own local situations.

RELIABILITY. To the extent that validity depends upon reliability, the prospects for SCAT are good. Kuder-Richardson (formula 20) estimates of reliability for the total score are at least .95 in all grades; the reliabilities of the verbal scores are at least .92 in all grades; and the reliabilities of the quantitative scores are .90 or greater in three of the five grades (5, 7, 9, 11 and 13) used in the reliability study, the lowest estimate being .88 in grade 5. Readers who are more familiar with between-forms estimates of reliability should not be overimpressed by the size of the reported coefficients for two reasons: (a) consistency estimates as given by the Kuder-Richardson formula 20 tend to be considerably higher than between-forms estimates of reliability; (b) the reliability for an individual school at a particular grade level would tend to be lower than those reported for the heterogeneous experimental sample. The manual which gives no between-forms comparisons says that "the results should characterize the B forms reasonably well, since the A and B forms are very similar in content"; it promises more information on the equivalence of forms "as soon as there are sufficient data based on the administration of two forms of SCAT to the same students."

NORMS. A characteristic of modern standardized test construction is the care with which the norms are produced. The days of accidental sampling are definitely past. The development of SCAT provides no exception to this enlightened trend. Great care was taken to obtain a truly representative national sample in developing norms by grade for the interpretation of scores of individual students in grades 4 through 14, and school mean norms for the interpretation of mean scores of administrative groups of students in grades 4 through 12. Since only 12 students per school were tested at the college level it was not considered advisable to publish mean norms for grades 13 and 14.

Despite the use of the most modern statistical procedures to ensure representativeness, national norms have value only to the extent that they add required meaning in score interpretation. Much depends upon the way the test scores are going to be used. Are nationwide comparisons profitable? In general, the most meaningful test score interpretation involves a state or local community comparison rather than a national comparison based on results obtained from a large, despairingly heterogeneous, group. Local norms are more valuable than national norms for many test users. In the Manual for Interpreting Scores SCAT recognizes this

trend by providing detailed instructions for the construction of local norms.

Evidence of the need for local norms is provided by the results of the administration of SCAT in 1956 to 8,852 Ontario students in grade 13 as part of the Atkinson Study of the Utilization of Student Resources (Department of Educational Research, Ontario College of Education). Large discrepancies appear between the Ontario results and the norms reported in the manual for 1,134 students in 97 colleges tested in the fall of the grade 14 year (it is assumed that Ontario grade 13, which leads to senior matriculation, would correspond to the first college year of universities which have junior matriculation admissions policies). At the extreme upper ends of the distributions the differences are not great, but at the middle and at the lower ends of the distributions the differences are so large that the use of the American norms would be completely unsuitable for this group. It is true that Ontario students in grade 13 are generally considered to be a highly selected group, but the fact remains that Ontario norms would be required for interpreting the scores of Ontario students in the Ontario situation. Indeed, for this particular group the efficiency of the test is seriously reduced by the marked piling up of scores at the top ends of the distributions. The distribution of the verbal scores is reasonably satisfactory, but the quantitative scores and, as a result, the total scores, show a very marked negative skew. The mathematical items are much too easy for this group. Additional evidence that the numerical items do not provide sufficient ceiling for top level students is contained in the Technical Report which says that "it should be noted that the quantitative sections of levels 1, 2 and 3 are so similar as to warrant considering them alternate forms."

STRONG POINTS. Among the excellent features of SCAT are: the use of equated conversion scores (not intelligence quotients) which permit comparison of scores not only from form to form but also from level to level—a feature which teachers in the elementary and secondary schools will find particularly attractive; the provision of profiles to assist score interpretation; the emphasis through the use of percentile bands upon the fallibility of test scores; and the lack of speededness in the subtests which makes it possible for all but the slowest students to complete them in the time limits allowed. In general, the technical recommendations for psychological tests which have been endorsed by the American Psychological Association, the American Educational Research Association, and the National Council on Measurements Used in Education have been followed.

SOME WEAKNESSES. Besides weaknesses in the national norms and limitations uncovered by the validity study, there are other deficiencies in SCAT. In the first place, a number of doubts are raised by the quantitative score: in the upper grades the items are apparently too easy, at least for superior students; in the first semester of grade 4 they are too difficult. The validity study shows disturbingly high intercorrelation coefficients between the quantitative score and the verbal score, particularly in the lower grades. One wonders whether the quantitative subtests are indispensable and whether their omission would greatly reduce the effectiveness of the test. A second matter of concern is the amount of time that is required to administer SCAT. Those who hoped that ACE would be replaced by a test which could be administered in a single college period are doomed to disappointment; it takes two full college periods to administer SCAT. Thus, the lack of speededness in the subtests has been obtained only at a considerable sacrifice in another direction.

USES OF SCAT. In accordance with the modern conception that a test is a tool to assist in the solution of an educational problem, rather than just a toy or a device for tagging a student, one may say that any test has value to the extent that it is used meaningfully in the schools. Reference has already been made to some possible uses of SCAT; the publishers suggest seven ways in which the individual test results can be used and four ways to employ results from classes, grades, departments, schools, and other groups. But SCAT measures ability only; it is not a measure of achievement in the ordinary sense of that word. Teachers and counselors are well aware that diagnosis and the proper choice of remedial treatment depend upon knowledge of student ability *and* student achievement. Users of SCAT will welcome the appearance of the *Sequential Tests of Educational Progress* (STEP) which are reviewed in another part of this Yearbook. SCAT-STEP should prove to be a useful team. STEP indicates a student's achievement and SCAT indicates his ability to achieve. The fact

that the norming population for SCAT includes exactly the same students as the norming population for STEP greatly increases the value of the team for purposes of score interpretation.

SUMMARY. Undoubtedly, SCAT is a superior test series. It clearly shows the result of careful planning, an excellent experimental programme, and the use of sound, up-to-date statistical procedures. It is the type of test that could hardly be produced without the cooperation of many individuals, the assistance of technical experts, and the backing of a well financed organization blessed with all the necessary facilities for the construction of a nationally standardized instrument. There is certainly room for improvement; changes will no doubt be introduced as more data on the usefulness, as well as the limitations, of the test become available. At the moment it is relatively untried. It is tempting to commit oneself to a definite prediction of a rosy future for this test; but scientific caution warns that the data are for the most part still not in.

JULIAN C. STANLEY, *Professor of Education, University of Wisconsin, Madison, Wisconsin.*

This series of well standardized "scholastic aptitude" tests will be especially useful to those teachers and administrators who want to compare Mary's scores in grade 8, say, with Henry's in grade 9, or Henry's on Level 5A with his own later scores on Level 3B. A single common score scale for all levels, forms, and subtests (verbal and quantitative) makes such comparisons possible. Furthermore, through the norms, scores on the *Cooperative School and College Ability Tests* (SCAT) can be compared with scores on the *Sequential Tests of Educational Progress* (STEP) of the same publisher.

Each form has four parts yielding separate verbal, quantitative, and total scores. Part 1 contains 25 or 30 incomplete sentences, for each of which one word must be supplied from among the five options offered. Part 2 consists of 25 arithmetic computation items. "None of these" is the fifth option for every one of the items in this part. Part 3 has 25 or 30 vocabulary items of the definition recognition type. Part 4 contains 25 arithmetic reasoning items. By alternating A, B, C, D, E with F, G, H, J, K, as option labels, the authors help prevent purely clerical slips. If a student looks up from

Item 16 in the booklet with, say, G in mind as the correct answer, he cannot mark Item 15 or Item 17 by mistake because neither will have a G among the options.

The verbal raw score is the sum of the raw scores on Parts 1 and 3. The quantitative raw score is the sum of the raw scores on Parts 2 and 4. The total raw score is simply the sum of the raw scores on all four parts. No correction for chance is employed. Raw scores may be changed to "converted scores" by reference to a simple table on the back of the appropriate scoring stencil. Percentile rank equivalents of converted scores appear in the Manual for Interpreting Scores; these are expressed as bands, to emphasize the standard error of measurement of the scores and to facilitate intra- and inter-individual score comparisons.

Grades for which the various levels are recommended overlap intentionally. Because format, instructions, time limits, and answer sheets are identical for all levels and forms, testers are encouraged to use several levels simultaneously for testing a given group. The least able students, as judged by prior information, can be handed a lower level than the average students, who in turn may receive a lower level than the brightest students.

The hitherto standard procedure of retesting the lowest and highest scorers on a test can largely be avoided by careful advance determination of the optimum level for each testee. For a test with plenty of "floor" and "ceiling" for everyone, we aim, as a rule of thumb, for levels such that each testee will get about half the items right, corrected for chance. For 100 5-option items this would be a number-right score of 60 if all 100 items were marked. On Level 5A such a total score yields a converted score of 254, not far above the median of the grade 5 norms near the beginning of the school year. Roughly, we may assume that a given level is most suitable for average students at the beginning of the midgrade for which it is specified: Level 5 for grade 5, Level 4 for grade 7, Level 3 for grade 9, etc.

Oddly, instructions concerning "guessing" for SCAT differ from those for STEP, which encourage the student to try every item. The SCAT booklet states: "You may answer questions even when you are not perfectly sure that your answers are correct. Your score will be the number of correct answers you mark." Undoubtedly, testees will interpret the words "per-fectly sure" in various ways, depending upon their gambling propensities. Some will mark every item, even though they do not know much. Others will omit all but the ones about which they are virtually certain. Caution versus recklessness sometimes produces anomalous individual results. For example, sheer chance marking of the 50 quantitative items of Level 5A should yield, on the average, a converted score equivalent to the 21–40th percentile band for grade 4, while not marking the questions at all yields the 0–21st band. STEP avoids this common source of test invalidity by do-guess instructions (but thereby, of course, may increase chance variance); only force of habit seems to have prevented the authors of SCAT from utilizing a similar procedure.

Though the test items appear to have been constructed at least as carefully as were those in competing tests, quite a few of them would have benefited appreciably from the personal ministrations of a meticulous editor. The reviewer found a considerable number of not-quite-ideal stems and options in the verbal sections of the highest levels (1C and 1D). Quantitative items and the verbal items below Levels 1C and 1D seem better edited.

The Manual for Interpreting Scores and the Technical Report are both excellent. The former gives the typical test administrator considerable help, while the latter supplies further technical information that both he and the more statistically trained user will appreciate.

No comparable-forms reliability coefficients are available yet for SCAT. Kuder-Richardson (formula 20) coefficients vary from .88 for the quantitative raw score of Level 5A for fifth graders tested in the norms program to .96 for the total raw score of Level 4A in grade 7. As the Technical Report cautions, these figures are usually overestimates for individual schools, which are invited to compute their own estimates of reliability and are shown how to do so.

Since much of the rationale and standardization of SCAT is similar to that of STEP, the reader interested in SCAT is hereby encouraged to consult the STEP reviews in this volume also.

Overall, the 12 synchronized members of the SCAT series, each with two subtests, represent a new application and downward extension of the *American Council on Education Psychological Examination* and other scholastic aptitude tests with which Educational Testing

Service has had much experience. They provide verbal, quantitative, and total scores based much more on power than speed. Test users who desire other intellective scores, such as nonlanguage or spatial, must supplement SCAT. Those who want a carefully devised, well standardized series of intelligence tests that can be used flexibly over many grades and related via norms to the STEP achievement test series should give the *Cooperative School and College Ability Tests* careful consideration.

[323]

★Cotswold Junior Ability Tests. Ages 8–9; 1949–51; Forms A ['49], B ['51]; no data on validity; 11s. per 20 tests; 6½d. per single copy; 1s. per manual; postage extra; C. M. Fleming; Robert Gibson & Sons (Glasgow), Ltd. *
a) JUNIOR MENTAL ABILITY A. Form A ['49]; manual ['49]; 30(40) minutes.
b) JUNIOR MENTAL ABILITY B. Form B ['51]; manual ['51]; 35(45) minutes.

[324]

*Cotswold Measurement of Mental Ability. Ages 10–12.5; 1947–54; title on manual is *Cotswold Measurement of Ability;* Series 1 and 2 entitled *Cotswold Mental Ability Test;* 6 forms: labeled Series 2 ['47], 3 ['50], 4 ['50], 5 ['52], 6 ['53], 7 ['54]; incomplete norms for Series 2–5; 7s. per 20 tests; 5½d. per single copy; 1s. per manual (dates as for tests) for any one series; postage extra; Series 2–5: 35(45) minutes; Series 6–7: 30(40) minutes; C. M. Fleming (except test booklet for Series 2) and J. W. Jenkins (Series 2); Robert Gibson & Sons (Glasgow), Ltd. *

A. W. HEIM, *Medical Research Council, Psychological Laboratory, University of Cambridge, Cambridge, England.*

The six Cotswold tests (Series 2–7) are broadly similar in form. They have a preliminary practice page for which 5 minutes are allowed; the practice items are identical throughout the six series. Each test consists of five subtests with verbal or numerical biases, each of them having a time limit of either 5 or 10 minutes. Most questions are multiple choice, the child being asked to underline the correct solution among the five presented.

The principal item types employed consist of analogies, classification items, series, and arithmetical and verbal problems involving deductive reasoning and instruction following. In Series 2, 3, and 4, one subtest consists of a simple table showing the number of children in three school classes who, for instance, sing, dance, and paint. The subject is asked eight questions whose answers demand interpretation of the table. The questions become progressively harder and the eighth question struck the reviewer as ambiguous. Apart from this,

the problem seems admirably suitable for test purposes and a welcome change from the hackneyed, often artificial, type of test problem.

Series 5 and 6 include subtests which require the child to copy contrived foreign-looking words and phrases. In the reviewer's opinion this is a retrogressive step: the task assesses accuracy only—and is as demanding of the scorer as of the subject! The traditional virtues of objectivity and speed of marking are largely lost with such items.

In general, the method of scoring is not ideal. Since in several of the subtests the subject is required to *underline* his solution, the correct answers naturally come in different positions all over the page. In the marking key for the more recent tests, these solutions are printed in positions which correspond to their place on the test paper. Even so, scoring must still be slower than is desirable.

The most serious criticism of the test booklets concerns the preliminary practice sheet. There is no indication that this has to be *correctly* completed by *all* subjects before they embark on the test proper. This implies that children who are most in need of preliminary examples—the slow starters, the nervous, and those lacking in test sophistication—will gain the least benefit. Moreover, there are in the practice sheet no examples of "double analogies" nor of table interpretations. The reviewer feels strongly that the child should meet in the test proper only the types of problem with which he has familiarised himself in preliminary examples.

There are several individual items, notably (and inevitably) among the classification problems, whose cogency is questionable, despite the statement in the manuals that "the correctness of each response was determined after analysis of pupils' replies, and ambiguous questions were discarded." Furthermore, a few problems are misleadingly worded, e.g., those in Series 2, 3, and 4 that ask such things as "Which is the *first* letter of the alphabet which occurs only once in the word ECCENTRICITY?" (Reviewer's italics.)

Each series has its own manual containing directions for general procedure and oral instructions, marking keys for the five subtests, tables of standardised scores, and notes on the background of the tests, their construction, standardisation, validity, and reliability. These notes are overbrief. The explanation of the standardised scores is rendered needlessly difficult by careless errors in several of the manuals.

Apart from these objections, however, and the regrettable lack of any diagrammatic or pictorial items, the tests are well thought out and agreeably varied and the instructions in the manuals are clearly expressed. It is useful to have six almost parallel tests within the 10–12 age range.

[325]

★Daneshill Intelligence Test. Ages 9.5–11.5; 1950–51; 1 form ['51]; 8s. 6d. per 25 tests; 6d. per single copy; 1s. per manual ('50); postage extra; 45(60) minutes; R. MacDonald; University of London Press Ltd. *

A. W. Heim, *Medical Research Council, Psychological Laboratory, University of Cambridge, Cambridge, England.*

The preface to the manual informs the reader that the test "is the result of a project arising out of discussions and lectures on the assessment of children's abilities during the period 1948–50 in Daneshill Training College. * It formed the growing point for the course in Educational Psychology." That this project proved useful for the students in training is readily believable. It would, however, be surprising if the exercise had resulted in a wholly satisfactory test of intelligence. There are, in effect, a good many criticisms to make, both of the test proper and of the manual.

To consider the latter first, the information given on test standardisation is quite inadequate. It is not clear how many children of what ages were used; for test reliability, only the split-half technique was employed—with an unspecified number of cases. There are literally no data at all on the validation of the test against an external criterion. It is not even clear whether the test was retested after having been altered in the light of item analysis findings.

Tables for converting scores into IQ's are presented for ages 10-0 to 10-11. Earlier in the manual, however, is a note stating that "by extrapolation the table may be extended to include the ages 9:6 to 11:6." This procedure consists of adding (or subtracting) one year to the age and adding (or subtracting) 6 from the IQ then found. No explanation is offered of this system but a warning is given that "such extrapolation must not be carried beyond the ages 9:6, 11:6."

The test booklet consists of 95 items, the vast majority of which score one point if correctly answered. The theoretical maximum test score is 100 marks. The questions cover verbal or numerical series, analogies, codes, classifications, directions, mixed (true-false) sentences, and reasoning problems. There are no preliminary examples for the subject to work through and the child is told to "ask no questions." The wording of some of the test problems is ambiguous, as, for example, in the problems which say, "A certain number is out of place in each of the following." The offending number is in fact one that has no place in the given set of numbers at all. Finally, there is some rather slipshod thinking in the actual problems themselves, notably in the classification questions and in the so-called "sames" and "opposites."

The reviewer would suggest that the training of students and the publishing of tests should be kept separate or, at the least, that tests arising in the course of student training should be allowed more than two years in which to mature.

F. W. Warburton, *Lecturer in Educational Psychology, University of Manchester, Manchester, England.*

This test is the outgrowth of a project concerning the assessment of children's abilities which was carried on during the period 1948–1950 in Daneshill Training College. The purpose of the project was to give students in training "some insight into the methods employed for measuring intelligence," and "a knowledge of statistical techniques applied to psychological investigations." These two objects were no doubt fulfilled, but they scarcely justify the publication of this rather amateurish test.

The general instructions to the children are clear, but no practice test is provided. The explanations preceding the individual sections are sometimes unambiguous, for example: "Look at this mixed sentence. Men fat are all. True. False. The sentence when rearranged is not true so FALSE has been underlined. Do the same in the following." In another section, no instruction is given.

The test is entitled "intelligence test" although it includes a few items which would usually be found in attainment tests, such as arithmetical sums and geographical comparisons. The key contains a typographical error in which "give" instead of "girl" is listed as the answer. The correct response to "What word begins with D and means the opposite of AD-MIRE" is given as "Dislike." "Despise" might well be acceptable. The manual contains adequate instructions to supervisors. Conversion tables for ages 10-0 to 10-11, based on the analysis of as many as 5,078 scripts, are provided. The authors suggest that the tables may be extended to include the ages of 9-6 to 11-6 by extrapolation, a risky procedure. The reliability coefficient is fairly satisfactory. Unfortunately, no validities are given.

The 150 items were selected from an original pool of 300 items. There 150 items were given a trial on a group of 312 children from primary schools in Nottinghamshire. The test was refined on the basis of an analysis of the items in terms of "success and difficulty." (Unfortunately, indices of consistency were apparently not included among the selection criteria.) The resulting new edition of the test was tried out on a similar group of 127 children.

The Daneshill test clearly cannot supplant tests published by Moray House and the National Foundation for Educational Research, or Schonell's *Essential Intelligence Test*.

[326]

★Davis-Eells Test of General Intelligence or Problem-Solving Ability. Grades 1–2, 3–6; 1953, c1952–53; title on test is *Davis-Eells Games;* Form A ('53); 2 levels; directions for administering ('53); 85¢ per manual ('53); postage extra; 35¢ per specimen set of either level, postpaid; Allison Davis and Kenneth Eells; World Book Co. *

a) PRIMARY. Grades 1–2; $4.35 per 35 tests; (60) minutes in 2 sessions for grade 1; (90) minutes in 3 sessions for grade 2.

b) ELEMENTARY. Grades 3–6; $4.80 per 35 tests; (100–120) minutes in 2 sessions.

REFERENCES

1. SURRATT, CAROLYN. *Cultural Factors in Children's Solutions of Verbal Problems.* Master's thesis, University of Chicago (Chicago, Ill.), 1946.
2. ATAULLAH, KANIZ. *Cultural Influences on Children's Solution of Verbal Problems.* Doctor's thesis, University of Chicago (Chicago, Ill.), 1950.
3. HESS, ROBERT D. *An Experimental Culture-Fair Test of Mental Ability.* Doctor's thesis, University of Chicago (Chicago, Ill.), 1950.
4. GLADSTEIN, GERALD A. *Cultural Factors in an Experimental Test of Intelligence.* Master's thesis, University of Chicago (Chicago, Ill.), 1951.
5. WEISS, MARCIA. *The Validity of Non-Verbal Problems From a Culture-Fair Test for Middle and Lower-Class School Children.* Master's thesis, University of Chicago (Chicago, Ill.), 1952.
6. EELLS, KENNETH. "Some Implications for School Practice of the Chicago Studies of Cultural Bias in Intelligence Tests." *Harvard Ed R* 23:284–97 fall '53. *
7. STENQUIST, JOHN L., AND LORGE, IRVING. "Implications of Intelligence and Cultural Differences; As Seen by a Test-User; As Seen by a Test-Maker." *Teach Col Rec* 54:184–93 Ja '53. * (PA 27:6423)
8. GEIST, HAROLD. "Evaluation of Culture-Free Intelligence." *Calif J Ed Res* 5:209–14 N '54. * (PA 29:5291)
9. RICHIE, ALICE. "A Comparison of the Kuhlmann-Anderson With the Davis-Eells Intelligence Tests in a Fifth Grade." Abstract. *Calif J Ed Res* 5:186 S '54. *
10. ANGELINO, HENRY, AND SHEDD, CHARLES L. "An Initial Report of a Validation Study of the Davis-Eells Tests of Gen-
eral Intelligence or Problem-Solving Ability." *J Psychol* 40: 35–8 Jl '55. * (PA 30:2854)
11. CAFFREY, JOHN, AND SMITH, THOMAS WOOD. "Preliminary Identification of Some Factors in the Davis-Eells Games." Abstract. *Am Psychol* 10:453–4 Ag '55. *
12. COLEMAN, WILLIAM, AND WARD, ANNIE W. "A Comparison of Davis-Eells and Kuhlmann-Finch Scores of Children From High and Low Socio-Economic Status." *J Ed Psychol* 46:465–9 D '55. * (PA 31:3779)
13. JUSTMAN, JOSEPH, AND ARONOW, MIRIAM. "The Davis-Eells Games as a Measure of the Intelligence of Poor Readers." *J Ed Psychol* 46:418–22 N '55. * (PA 31:3791)
14. MACRAE, JOHN M. "A Comparison of Davis-Eells and Stanford-Binet Scores at Different Socio-Economic Levels." Abstract. *Calif J Ed Res* 6:133 My '55. *
15. PAPANIA, NED; ROSENBLUM, SIDNEY; AND KELLER, JAMES E. "Responses of Lower Social Class, High-Grade Mentally Handicapped Boys to a 'Culture Fair' Test of Intelligence—The Davis-Eells Games." *Am J Mental Def* 59:493–8 Ja '55. * (PA 29:7494)
16. ROSENBLUM, SIDNEY; KELLER, JAMES E.; AND PAPANIA, NED. "Davis-Eells ('Culture-Fair') Test Performance of Lower-Class Retarded Children." *J Consult Psychol* 19:51–4 F '55. * (PA 29:8722)
17. SAWREY, JAMES M. "The Predictive Effectiveness of Two Non-Verbal Tests of Intelligence Used in the First Grade in the Santa Clara County Schools." Abstract. *Calif J Ed Res* 6:133 My '55. *
18. SMITH, THOMAS WOOD, AND CAFFREY, JOHN. "Comprehension of Written Language (Reading) and Oral Language (Auding) as Related to 'Cultural Bias' on the Davis-Eells Games and the California Test of Mental Maturity." Abstract. *Am Psychol* 10:382–3 Ag '55. *
19. ALEXANDER, ETHEL B. *A Study of the Davis-Eells Test of General Intelligence and Problem-Solving Ability in Selected Elementary Schools in Greensboro, North Carolina.* Master's thesis, Agricultural and Technical College (Greensboro, N. C.), 1956.
20. ALTUS, GRACE T. "Some Correlates of the Davis-Eells Tests." *J Consult Psychol* 20:227–32 Je '56. * (PA 31:6053)
21. FOWLER, WILLIAM L. *A Comparative Analysis of Pupil Performance on Conventional and Culture-Controlled Mental Tests.* Doctor's thesis, University of Michigan (Ann Arbor, Mich.), 1956. (DA 17:91)
22. LEVINSON, BORIS M. "Note on the Davis Eells Test of General Intelligence." *Psychol Rep* 2:242 S '56. * (PA 31: 3048)
23. LUDLOW, H. GLENN. "Some Recent Research on the Davis-Eells Games." *Sch & Soc* 84:146–8 O 27 '56. * (PA 31:7947)
24. RUSSELL, IVAN L. "The Davis-Eells Test and Reading Success in First Grade." *J Ed Psychol* 47:269–70 My '56. * (PA 32:2125)
25. SMITH, THOMAS WOOD. *Auding and Reading as Sources of Cultural Bias in the Davis-Eells Games and the California Test of Mental Maturity.* Doctor's thesis, University of Southern California (Los Angeles, Calif.), 1956.
26. SMITH, THOMAS WOOD. "Comparison of Test Bias in the Davis-Eells Games and the CTMM." *Calif J Ed Res* 7:159–63 S '56. * (PA 31:6135)
27. TATE, MERLE W., AND VOSS, CHARLOTTE E. "A Study of the Davis-Eells Test of Intelligence." *Harvard Ed R* 26:374–87 fall '56. * (PA 32:1347)
28. ZWEIBELSON, I. "Test Anxiety and Intelligence Test Performance." *J Consult Psychol* 20:479–81 D '56. * (PA 32: 1659)
29. CLARK, GLYNN E. *A Comparison of the Performance of Selected Pupils on the Davis-Eells Test and the Otis Test of Mental Ability.* Doctor's thesis, Washington University (St. Louis, Mo.), 1957. (DA 17:807)
30. FOWLER, WILLIAM L. "A Comparative Analysis of Pupil Performance on Conventional and Culture-Controlled Mental Tests." *Yearb Nat Council Meas Used Ed* 14:8–19 '57. *
31. FRANDSEN, ARDEN N., AND GRIMES, JESSE W. "Age Discrimination in Intelligence Tests." *J Ed Res* 51:229–33 N '57. *
32. KNIEF, LOTUS M. *An Investigation of the Cultural Bias Issue in Intelligence Testing.* Doctor's thesis, State University of Iowa (Iowa City, Iowa), 1957. (DA 17:1951)
33. LOVE, MARY I., AND BEACH, SYLVIA. "Performance of Children on the Davis-Eells Games and Other Measures of Ability." *J Consult Psychol* 21:29–32 F '57. * (PA 32:952)
34. COOPER, JAMES G. "Predicting School Achievement for Bilingual Pupils." *J Ed Psychol* 49:31–6 F '58. *
35. RUESS, AUBREY L. "Some Cultural and Personality Aspects of Mental Retardation." *Am J Mental Def* 63:50–9 Jl '58. *
36. STILLWELL, LOIS. *A Study of the Davis-Eells Games: A Group Test of Intelligence for Use in the Elementary Schools.* Master's thesis, Kent State University (Kent, Ohio), 1958.

CYRIL BURT, *Emeritus Professor of Psychology, University of London, London, England.*

This is a group intelligence test in pictorial form. No reading is required. The directions, expressed in colloquial language, are read by an examiner called the "game leader." To break tension, the solving of the problems is preceded by 3 minutes of physical exercise (waving arms or patting stomach and head), and letting the pupils "laugh as much as they wish," and throughout the test the "atmosphere" is to be kept "relaxed."

The material is based on a conception of general intelligence as "the sum total of the skills of thinking, work habits, and other factors which determine how well any given individual will be able to solve important kinds of intellectual problems that face him in life." The items have been selected so as to cover a wide variety of tasks which will "parallel the real-life problems of children more closely than most intelligence-test items in the past." The problems are often exceedingly ingenious. The pictures are drawn in semihumorous style, and are usually about 2½ or 3 inches square: the size is thus larger than is commonly adopted, and therefore should impose no handicap even on children with relatively poor vision. The whole procedure is "child oriented"; and, as the type of test material, the method of administration, and the title on the pupil's booklet all imply, the pupils are meant to regard their task rather as a game than as a formal test or school examination.

Tables are appended enabling the user to convert scores to IQ's. The authors, however, prefer the phrase "Index of Problem Solving Ability (I.P.S.A.)" as less vague, less misleading, and more meaningful than the older term. Two types of reliability coefficient are reported: (a) a split-half coefficient, which yields a reliability averaging about .82 for grades 2 to 6, and somewhat less for grade 1; and (b) a coefficient of stability, assessed by giving the test a second time to the same group after an interval of a couple of weeks: this was apparently possible for two grades only, and yielded a coefficient of .72 for grade 2 and .90 for grade 4.

The authors contend that the validity of the test is best "indicated by a careful analysis of its nature and of the nature of the problem-solving ability which it seeks to measure," not by the usual statistical comparison with scores from other tests, since these may actually be less effective than the test to be evaluated. The principle is excellent, but its practical consequences are not very successfully fulfilled. The definition stating the results of the analysis is far too loose

for scientific purposes. "Intelligence" in the technical sense is ordinarily regarded as a mental capacity; and the phrase "skills of thinking" is at once too narrow and too broad to specify its nature with precision. The child's work habits and the other factors affecting his efficiency —his emotional attitudes, the effort he makes, and so on—call rather for separate assessment. The mere fact that the analysis of the test appears to correspond with the analysis of the capacity tested cannot of itself guarantee the test's validity: the ideal criterion would be the accuracy with which it predicts the subsequent performances of the child in the fields defined; failing that, the next best standard would be the assessments of a teacher, known to be a competent judge, who has systematically observed each child's progress and performance in the past. It is curious that American investigators make far less use of teachers' opinions than British.

An inspection of the actual material raises doubts as to whether the tasks presented are in fact as varied, as realistic, and as important as was intended. Experience and results already gained with similar pictorial tests indicate that, with increasing age, the scores obtained tend more and more to depend on special aptitudes, special experience, and special interest; indeed, with older children, a purely pictorial test yields as one-sided an assessment as a purely verbal test with the younger.

Presenting tests as games is an excellent device with the younger and duller pupils. But with British children aged 9 and upwards better results are secured when tests of intelligence are given quite frankly as an internal examination in which every pupil is expected to take the problems seriously and do his utmost to answer even the more difficult problems. To insist that the tests should be preceded by amusing exercises during which pupils are encouraged to "laugh as much as they wish" and that the problems should be tackled in a state of relaxation is scarcely likely to ensure that they do their best. Indeed, on making an actual trial, the reviewer finds that with British pupils this method of approach tends to reduce the reliability to .60 or less. The test material assumes a familiarity with the conventions of the strip cartoon (e.g., musical notation to represent sounds emerging from a child's mouth); and is thus bound to handicap the less sophisticated children from rural areas. The stylized exaggerations and would-be comicality of the drawings, amounting at times almost to caricature, tend to induce a mood of frivolity and frequently to obscure the real nature of the problem.

These criticisms apply far more strongly to some items than to others. If, as a provisional criterion, we take the total score for the test as a whole, preliminary trials would seem to indicate that the component items differ widely in validity, and that the grading in difficulty is very uneven. There appears, therefore, to be an urgent need for a more thorough item analysis before the test can be regarded as having reached a final or a satisfactory form.

RALEIGH M. DRAKE, *Professor of Psychology, Kent State University, Kent, Ohio.*

This reviewer is very much in favor of culture free, culture fair performance and other such tests which attempt to get a more direct measurement of mental capacity, mental potential, mental energy, or intelligence. To the extent that scores are influenced by environmental and training factors, our tests are subject to error and equivocal interpretation. The purpose of the *Davis-Eells Games* is to eliminate one of these spurious factors—socioeconomic differences and inequities. The original data report that this purpose was accomplished, but replications done elsewhere fail to verify these results (*10, 15, 20, 23, 33*).

A recent study (*36*) which this reviewer supervised, obtained similar results. The *California Test of Mental Maturity* was compared directly with the Davis-Eells on two groups, one a high socioeconomic group and the other a low socioeconomic group. The Davis-Eells consistently gave lower IPSA-scores (these are really IQ scores and are as directly equivalent to IQ's as are scores on any of the numerous tests which try to convert their scores to IQ's) than did the CTMM, but the Davis-Eells showed as much difference between the high and low socioeconomic groups as did the CTMM. This indicates that the Davis-Eells is not achieving anything in the way of an advantage as far as culture fairness is concerned. In view of the fact that the IQ's are approximately 7.5 points lower, it would appear that the Davis-Eells is culturally unfair to all subjects to about this extent. The reliability computed for this study is reported as .79. This is not so high as the reliability reported for

CTMM or other tests. Validity was checked in two schools against the individual ratings of seven different teachers:

Teacher	1	2	3	4	5	6	7
Davis-Eells	.16	.49	.53	.42	.68	.63	.40
CTMM	.77	.73	.86	.93	.70	.71	.60

Correlations with the arithmetic test of the *Iowa Tests of Basic Skills* gave .41 and .51 for two groups while the CTMM gave r's of .61 and .67 for the same two groups. Correlations with the *California Reading Test* gave .36 and .41 for these same groups, while the CTMM gave .71 and .69, respectively. Thus, as a predictive instrument, the Davis-Eells is less valid than the CTMM with two criteria, teacher's ratings and scores on standardized achievement tests.

Another study (*34*) with native Indian children in Guam produced very similar results. Here the average IQ (IPSA) was about 16.6 points lower than with the CTMM. Most studies report that IQ's obtained with the Davis-Eells run lower than those obtained with other tests, and the test differentiates as much between high and low socioeconomic groups as do the general verbal tests which it was intended to improve upon. Some children in the Guam study had scores on the Davis-Eells as much as 51 points below their scores on the CTMM. If the Davis-Eells scores alone had been used, serious misclassification or interpretation of an individual child might have resulted. It appears that in attempting to eliminate socioeconomic influences, a significant portion of the test's intended capacity to discriminate differences in intelligence has been partialled out.

Additional comments are that it is difficult to administer because it requires a great deal of oral directions and as much as 90 minutes of working time (grade 2). Scoring is slow and tedious. Several items have strong emotional loadings: (*a*) a boy being spanked by his father, (*b*) three tough boys lying in wait to beat up another boy, (*c*) a boy being spanked for breaking a window, and (*d*) a girl crying because she thinks she hasn't a Christmas present. The directions for administering the arithmetical reasoning problem are not entirely clear to all children, with the result that some miss all of this section. A severe strain is put upon the attention span of young children. There is one favorable aspect—children like the test because of its gamelike nature.

J. P. GUILFORD, *Professor of Psychology, University of Southern California, Los Angeles, California.*

The purpose of this test as stated by the authors is "to measure fairly and accurately as possible the ability of children to solve problems of a kind interesting and important to them." The specification of "fairly" refers to the conviction of the authors that most tests of intelligence are biased in favor of children from the higher socioeconomic levels. In the selection of items considerable attention was given to ensure that they were equally within the sphere of experience of all groups.

This criterion was largely responsible for eliminating all need for reading on the part of examinees, the items being presented pictorially and the instructions for each item being given orally. Pictorial material also lends itself to intrinsic interest. An effort is made to maintain a "game" atmosphere throughout the test. Although the test can be given to groups of children, the long oral instructions make administration very cumbersome. The test is inefficient in view of the time it takes for the levels of reliability achieved (about .8 for split-half estimates and .7 and .9 for test-retest estimates in grades 2 and 4).

There are 47 items in a 16-page booklet at the primary level and 62 items in a 20-page booklet at the elementary level. One kind of item asks the child to make a judgment as to what is going on in a picture in which usually two or more individuals are in some kind of interaction. This would seem to this reviewer to measure something in the area of social intelligence, mainly ability for social cognition. Another kind of item shows three similar scenes in each of which a child is attempting to perform a task, the examinee being asked to say which child is acting most wisely. This would seem to measure an ability to evaluate behavior; hence it is also in the area of social intelligence, and possibly in the area of concrete intelligence, too, since objects are dealt with as well as individuals. In other kinds of items abilities more like those involved in conventional intelligence tests appear to be tested. In items involving coins and the counting of sums of money, probably some numerical facility is measured and possibly some foresight in dealing with symbols. Other items are essentially verbal analogies presented in pictorial form. The objects involved are so familiar that probably

little verbal comprehension is measured, but the ability to see relationships between concepts should be assessed.

If this reviewer's guesses are correct, we have here a measure of something rather different from the usual intelligence test. Correlations with several forms of the *Otis Quick-Scoring Mental Ability Tests* are in the region of .4 to .6. Correlations with scholastic achievement tests are mostly in the range of .1 to .5, depending upon the subject.

The authors insist that the test measures problem solving ability. There is no empirical evidence presented to support this contention. Items were chosen for the supposed purpose merely by expert inspection. Except for the items involving coins, the items seem to this reviewer to be not so much in the nature of problems calling for solution as situations calling for cognition. Cognitions play their parts in solving problems, but more important is productive thinking. The latter seems to be of little importance in answering the items of this test. Perhaps the authors should have defined problem solving in an unusually broad sense. The term is likely to be interpreted more narrowly by the test user.

The test was obviously developed with great care and industry. The items went through several analytical studies. Norms are based upon large and well selected samples, except for the fact that no rural children were included.

Raw scores are transformed into the familiar IQ scale, but the authors properly urge that a scale score not be interpreted as a conventional IQ, that is, as to psychological meaning. It is unfortunate, for this and for other reasons mentioned earlier, that the term "general intelligence" appears in the title of the test. In fact, the entire title seems inappropriate.

In view of the efforts to achieve comparable scores for children of all socioeconomic groups, it is unfortunate that the authors do not present some comparative scores obtained from those different groups. It would not be surprising to find some differences after all. Such differences would probably be small, for in the area of social intelligence, which the reviewer believes to be stressed in the test, the social groups should be much more alike than they are on verbal intelligence.

For related reviews, see B140.

[327]

★**Deeside Picture Puzzles.** Ages 6.5–8.5; 1956–58; 1 form ('56); 15s. per 25 tests; 8d. per single copy; 3s. 6d. per manual ('58); postage extra; 25.5(75) minutes; W. G. Emmett; George G. Harrap & Co. Ltd. *

CHARLOTTE E. K. BANKS, *Lecturer in Psychology, University College, London, England.*

This test has been designed to measure the ability of children between the ages of 6-6 and 8-6. It contains 100 items in seven sections, with problems in following directions, classification, picture series, perception of mirror images and simple relations, and number series. It thus covers a slightly wider sample of cognitive processes than the N.F.E.R. *Picture Intelligence Test I.*

With the exception of attempts to draw sea, rivers, and mountains, the drawings are very clear and unambiguous, though peculiarly unaesthetic to the adult eye. The author has drawn up an excellent teachers' handbook, giving directions for administering and scoring, data concerning reliability, and suggestions for the use of the conversion table and norms.

The test was standardised on a complete year-group of 9,951 children between the ages of 7-1 and 8-2. Standard scores are given in the conversion table for each month between the ages of 6-6 and 8-6. The scores are based on norms having a mean of 100 and a standard deviation of 15. Mental ages are also given for the use of clinical psychologists. Intelligence quotients for children younger than 6-6 years and older than 8-6 years may be found by extrapolation, using a simple formula provided in the handbook.

The reliability of the test, determined by Ferguson's formula 29, is given as .97. The 100 items in the test were chosen from an original set of 250 items on the basis of item analysis. Little information, however, seems to be available about the validity of the test.

M. L. KELLMER PRINGLE, *Lecturer in Education, and Deputy Head, Department of Child Study, University of Birmingham, Birmingham, England.*

This recently designed test is closely similar to the *Moray House Picture Intelligence Test,* though it is in some aspects inferior to it. Of its seven sections, Following Directions, Doesn't Belong, Sequences, Matching, Mirror Images, Analogies, and Series, six are identical with six of the nine Moray House subtests; however,

the layout of the latter is clearer and more generous. A number of the drawings in the Deeside test have too much detail for children of the age for which the test is intended, and a high proportion of the items (32 out of a total of 100) consist of educational symbols, such as letters, numbers, and clockfaces. The title of the test is thus rather misleading since a third of its content probes children's readiness to cope with reading and number work. For example, in Section 1 the following instructions are given: "There are five numbers. Put a cross on the number that is smaller than all but the third number" or "There are five sums. Put a cross on the sum that is wrong [i.e., five addition sums, the wrong one being 7 and 9 makes 17]." Or "Put crosses on the *two* words [out of a total of six words] which are spelt wrong." Similarly, in Section 2 an odd number has to be picked from among four even ones, and, from among six small clockfaces, the one showing a half hour instead of the full hour has to be crossed out. In the matching section, the logic of some items is rather unconvincing.

The Teacher's Handbook gives clear directions for administering and scoring the test.

Though quite a useful and well standardised addition to the available nonverbal tests for this age group, this reviewer fails to see that as a new test it has any special merits or purpose. Both the Moray House and the N.F.E.R. picture intelligence tests are superior in design and layout and at least equally well standardised. If the author of the *Deeside Picture Puzzles* is deliberately aiming at exploring the early stages of children's educational attainments, it is nowhere explicitly stated. This would constitute a departure from other tests of this type, in which case some interpretative guidance should be given to its users. Lastly, it is regrettable that the old label "mentally defective" for IQ's below 70 should be perpetuated in the Teacher's Handbook when the term "educationally subnormal" is officially (and with beneficial effects) current in our educational system.

[328]

★**Detroit General Intelligence Examination.** Grades 7–12; 1938–54; consists of 8 of the 10 subtests used to get an intelligence score in the *Detroit General Aptitudes Examination;* Form A ('54, identical with subtests copyrighted in 1938); revised manual ('54); $3.25 per 25 tests; 65¢ per specimen set; postpaid; 31(45) minutes; Harry J. Baker and Paul H. Voelker; Public School Publishing Co. *

[329]

*[Detroit Intelligence Tests.] Grades 2–4, 5–8, 9–16; 1924–56; 3 levels; $2.75 per 25 tests; 40¢ per specimen set of any one level; postpaid; Harry J. Baker; Public School Publishing Co. *

a) PUBLIC SCHOOL PRIMARY INTELLIGENCE TEST. Grades 2–4; 1954–56; revision of *Detroit Primary Intelligence Test;* Forms A, B ('54, identical with Forms C, D copyrighted in 1924 except for minor changes) ; manual ('56) ; (45) minutes.

b) DETROIT ALPHA INTELLIGENCE TEST. Grades 4–8; Forms S, T ('54, same as tests published in 1941) ; revised manual ('54) ; 32(45) minutes.

c) DETROIT ADVANCED INTELLIGENCE TEST. Grades 9–16; 1924–42; Forms V, W ('25) ; manual ('42) ; 29(40) minutes.

REFERENCES

1–2. See 4:288.

3. SAWYER, CLIFFORD R. *A Comparison of the Detroit and Kuhlmann-Anderson Intelligence Tests as Applied in the Grand Forks Public Schools.* Master's thesis, University of North Dakota (Grand Forks, N.D.), 1931. Pp. 60.

4. KELLY, PRICE O. *Comparative Validity and Reliability of Four Intelligence Tests in the Ninth Grade.* Master's thesis, University of Kentucky (Lexington, Ky.), 1933. Pp. 63.

5. NEMZEK, CLAUDE L., AND DE HEUS, JOHN H. "The Prediction of Academic and Non-Academic Marks in Junior High Schools." *Sch & Soc* 50:670–2 N 18 '39. * (*PA* 14:1598)

6. BAILEY, ALBERT E. *The Relative Validity of Ten Different Intelligence Tests.* Doctor's thesis, University of Washington (Seattle, Wash.), 1942.

7. MILLER, LYLE L. *An Analysis of the Predictive Values of the Section of the Detroit Advanced Intelligence Test.* Master's thesis, University of Southern California (Los Angeles, Calif.), 1944.

8. BARNOWE, THEODORE J. *The Influence of Scoring Technique and Construction on the Validity of Mental Tests.* Doctor's thesis, University of Washington (Seattle, Wash.), 1946.

9. CARLILE, A. B. "Predicting Performance in the Teaching Profession." *J Ed Res* 47:641–68 My '54. * (*PA* 29:3063)

10. FOWLER, WILLIAM L. *A Comparative Analysis of Pupil Performance on Conventional and Culture-Controlled Mental Tests.* Doctor's thesis, University of Michigan (Ann Arbor, Mich.), 1956. (*DA* 17:91)

11. FOWLER, WILLIAM L. "A Comparative Analysis of Pupil Performance on Conventional and Culture-Controlled Mental Tests." *Yearb Nat Council Meas Used Ed* 14:8–19 '57. *

For a review by W. Line, see 40:1393.

[330]

★The Dominion Group Test of Intelligence. Ages 13 and over; 1945; adaptation of Form B of the advanced level of *Group Test of Learning Capacity: The Dominion Tests* for Australian use; Form B ['45]; mimeographed manual ['45]; 5s. per 10 tests; 1s. per scoring key; 2s. per manual; 3s. 6d. per specimen set; postpaid within Australia; 30(45) minutes; Australian Council for Educational Research. *

[331]

★Doppelt Mathematical Reasoning Test. Graduate students and employees; 1958, c1954; IBM; Form A ('54) ; manual ('58) ; distribution restricted and test administered only at specified licensed testing centers; details may be obtained from publisher; 50(60) minutes; Jerome E. Doppelt; Psychological Corporation. *

[332]

★Easel Age Scale. Grades kgn–1; 1955; 1 form; $3.75 per set of testing materials; no formal testing time since paintings are produced during regular class sessions; Beatrice Lantz; California Test Bureau. *

NAOMI STEWART, *Formerly Staff Associate, Educational Testing Service, Princeton, New Jersey.*

The *Easel Age Scale* is a valuable new tool for understanding young children and deserves to be widely accepted. With the use of the scale, free tempera (calcimine) paintings produced by kindergarten and primary grade children in the course of their ordinary classroom activity can be scored in such a way as to yield reliable and valid measures of the children's mental maturity. The children are not subjected to any of the stresses that are sometimes involved in "taking a test." In fact, it is essential to the validity of the results that the children be under no strain and that each child feel free to paint as and what he wishes.

All that is required is an easel (or several), large paper (approximately 18 by 24 inches) of newsprint quality, long handled brushes with bristles around ¾ inches wide and 1 or 1½ inches long, paints in six designated colors, and —most important—a classroom atmosphere in which easel painting of a free character is a normal part of the day's activity. The teacher simply dates each picture as the child produces it and puts it away for scoring at her leisure.

The *Easel Age Scale* recognizes that children often produce paintings that are primarily expressions of their feelings and not attempts to express their ideas. Such paintings are not representative of a child's mental and physical maturity, and are not suitable for scoring. The manual gives a number of carefully developed criteria for identifying paintings of this nature —called "Q," for questionable, paintings—and 12 illustrations in full color which exemplify various features of "Q" productions. Teachers are urged to study each child's easel paintings and score the *best* of the paintings done during each period of observation. Paintings that qualify for scoring are rated independently on four separate counts: form, detail, meaning, and relatedness. The manual gives clear directions for rating each of these dimensions and also provides two dozen full color samples of children's paintings, for each of which is given its rating on form, detail, meaning, and relatedness, its easel score and the corresponding easel age, and the chronological age of the child who produced the painting.

The easel score, which is the sum of the four separate ratings, has a very satisfactory test-retest reliability (.95) and a surprisingly high scoring reliability (.94), even when used by comparatively inexperienced raters. The score converts to an easel age that correlates rather closely with mental ages derived from such instruments as the *Goodenough Intelligence Test,* the *Pintner-Cunningham Primary Test,* and the *California Test of Mental Maturity.*

Throughout the manual, emphasis is placed on using the scale in a developmental context. As already indicated, safeguards are included to make sure that only representative paintings are scored by the teacher. In addition, teachers are urged to maintain growth records on each child, making a minimum of three evaluations a year, based on paintings produced at the beginning, middle, and end of the year. In this context, and in light of the careful directions and illustrations for scoring the paintings, even inexperienced teachers should be able to obtain valid results.

In addition to its value as a measure of the mental maturity of young children, the *Easel Age Scale,* as the manual clearly explains and illustrates, has the important advantage of increasing the teacher's understanding of the child as a whole. The scale should undoubtedly be in the possession of every kindergarten and primary grade teacher who has, or can arrange for, facilities for making easel painting part of the regular class activity.

FLORENCE M. TEAGARDEN, *Emeritus Professor of Psychology, University of Pittsburgh, Pittsburgh, Pennsylvania.*

The author describes the *Easel Age Scale* as a "rating scale for studying the growth and adjustment of kindergarten and primary grade children, as well as somewhat older mentally retarded children." Over 10 years went into this study, involving the examination of more than 6,000 pictures painted at the easel by children of ages 4 to 9 in the Los Angeles area. Unfortunately, the statistical treatment does not reflect anything like the number of paintings studied. Further statistical studies are, however, promised. The author's claim for the reliability of the scale is based upon a study of pictures by 37 children who made two or more paintings within a month in 1945. The test-retest coefficient of reliability was found to be .95. The validity of the scale was determined by comparing pictures made by 112 children and their ratings on the *Goodenough Intelligence Test.*

Directions for administering the scale require that the rater examine a picture first to determine whether the child has primarily expressed his feelings and emotions rather than ideas. Such paintings of emotions are called "Q" (Questionable) because from them one cannot necessarily determine the child's maturity. No data are given as to the validation of the assumption of "emotions." Twelve samples are given of Q pictures. Certainly in a few of these the clinician can recognize some of the usual diagnostic signs, such as great use of color, restrictions within boundaries, meticulous detail, and the like. However, since no data are given as to the age, intelligence, or other evidences of emotionality for the children who made the samples, one might feel hesitant to discard a painting as a Q painting from these meager details.

If the person using the scale decides that a picture is not a Q picture, then he proceeds to examine and score it for each of these items in order: Form, on a 7-point scale; Detail, on a 7-point scale; Meaning (to the adult), on an 8-point scale; and Relatedness (beginning of depth perception) on an 8-point scale. The highest possible score in each of these categories is assigned pictures in which recognizable objects are portrayed in action. Twenty-four pictures are scored as samples.

Norms are based on analysis of the paintings of 1,329 children ranging in chronological age from 4-6 to 9-6. We are not told how the raw scores were converted into easel age equivalents. At some places along the normative scale an increase of a single raw point raises the easel age equivalent by 3 months; in some places by 2 months; and in some places by 1 month. The possible raw scores run from 2 through 30, with easel age equivalents from below 4-0 through 8-6 plus.

The progression of mental ability and representative drawing in a more or less *para passu* manner is an intriguing subject to the clinical and research psychologist. The author has added more material to the field. Her attempt to measure form, detail, meaning, and relatedness—each leading ultimately to representation of action—is good. The reproduced paintings are interesting. The reported statistics do not add greatly to the value of the study.

[333]

*The Essential Intelligence Test. Ages 7-12; 1940-52; c1940-48; title on manuals is *Essential Junior Intelligence Test;* Forms [A] ('40), B ('49); Form A manual ['40], Form B manual ['49]; revised norms ['52] for Form B; 25–49 tests, 5*d.* each; 6*d.* per single copy; 1*s.* 6*d.* per manual for either form; postage extra; 45(60) minutes; Fred J. Schonell and R. H. Adams; Oliver & Boyd Ltd. *

R. WINTERBOURN, *Professor of Education, The University of Auckland, Auckland, New Zealand.*

Form A of this verbal test of general intelligence has now been in use for 18 years, Form B for almost 10 years. During this time the two forms have been very widely applied, particularly in Great Britain, but also in other countries, notably Australia and New Zealand. It can fairly be said that they have withstood the test of time.

Face validity appears to be good. The 100 items are grouped in 18 sections, thus avoiding what must be for some children the formidable appearance of an unbroken sequence of a large number of items. Eleven practice items familiarize the child with all types of questions he will find. They are worked through orally with the examiner. Directions to both children and examiner are clear. The aim is to create a puzzle solving attitude in the former.

Item types include sentence completions (multiple choice and the filling of gaps), recognition of similarities, differences, and opposites, number and letter sequence completions, arithmetical problems, and other problems.

Because of the increasing test sophistication of British children, a restandardization is about to be carried out in Great Britain. An Australian standardization of Form A is now available.

A recently calculated split-half reliability coefficient (208 children, ages unspecified) is .94 (communication from the author). A split-half coefficient of .92 based on a small group of 66 11-year-olds and a test-retest coefficient of .92 (retest after one year on an unspecified group) were reported earlier for Form A. An intercorrelation of .95 is reported between Forms A and B.

The tests have measured up quite well to statistical evaluation and practical use in schools. Articles appearing in the *British Journal of Educational Psychology* from time to time, referring to the use of these tests along with others, indicate that they have proved to be satisfactory means of assessing general intelligence. One suspects that they are more valid for children in the middle and higher age groups than for 7- and 8-year-olds. It is to be hoped that more precise statistical data will be made available to confirm or reject this suspicion.

For a review by F. W. Warburton, see 4:290.

[334]

★**General Verbal Practice Test G1.** Ages 10–11; 1954; to be given at least 3 weeks before administering a verbal intelligence test in order to equalize coaching effects; 1 form ['54]; distribution restricted to directors of education; 4s. 6d. per 12 tests; 6d. per single copy; 6d. per manual ['54]; postage extra; 45(50) minutes; published for National Foundation for Educational Research in England and Wales; Newnes Educational Publishing Co. Ltd. *

[335]

Goodenough Intelligence Test. Grades kgn–3; 1926; also called *Draw-a-Man;* 1 form; $1.50 per 35 children's drawing sheets; $3.25 per manual (see 1 below); postage extra; specimen set not available; (10) minutes; Florence L. Goodenough; World Book Co. *

REFERENCES

1–60. See 4:292.
61. PETERSON, JOSEPH, AND TELFORD, C. W. "Results of Group and Individual Tests Applied to the Practically Pure-Blood Negro Children on St. Helena Island." *J Comp Psychol* 11:115–44 D '30. * (*PA* 5:1576)
62. TSAO, D. F. *A Comparative Study of Drawing Ability in English Children in the Goodenough Scale.* Master's thesis, University of London (London, England), 1935.
63. MAURER, KATHARINE M. "Measuring Leadership in College Women by Free Association." Abstract. *Am Psychol* 2:334 Ag '47. *
64. BEYER, FRANCES N. *The Goodenough Measurement of Intelligence Used in a Comparison of the Test Results of the Deaf Children and the Normal Hearing Children.* Master's thesis, MacMurray College for Women (Jacksonville, Ill.), 1949.
65. BENDER, LAURETTA. "The Goodenough Test (Drawing a Man) in Chronic Encephalitis in Children." *J Child Psychiatry* 3:449–59 O '51. *
66. ANSBACHER, H. L. "The Goodenough Draw-A-Man Test and Primary Mental Abilities." *J Consult Psychol* 16:176–80 Je '52. * (*PA* 27:5141)
67. BRITTON, JOSEPH H. "Influence of Social Class Upon Performance on Draw-A-Man Test." Abstract. *Am Psychol* 7:304 Jl '52. *
68. COBB, KATHARINE. "Measuring Leadership in College Women by Free Association." *J Abn & Social Psychol* 47:126–8 Ja '52. * (*PA* 26:6178)
69. DEJESÚS, CRUZ. *A Study of the Language Development and Goodenough I.Q. of Puerto Rican Preschool Children in New York.* Master's thesis, Fordham University (New York, N.Y.), 1952.
70. McHUGH, ANN F. *The Effect of Preceding Affective States on the Goodenough Draw-A-Man Test of Intelligence.* Master's thesis, Fordham University (New York, N.Y.), 1952.
71. MARQUIS, DOROTHY P.; SINNETT, E. ROBERT; AND WINTER, WILLIAM D. "A Psychological Study of Peptic Ulcer Patients." *J Clin Psychol* 8:266–72 Jl '52. * (*PA* 27:6072)
72. ANASTASI, ANNE, AND DEJESÚS, CRUZ. "Language Development and Nonverbal IQ of Puerto Rican Preschool Children in New York City." *J Abn & Social Psychol* 48:357–66 Jl '53. * (*PA* 28:2471)
73. GLOWATSKY, EDWARD. "The Verbal Element in the Intelligence Scores of Congenitally Deaf and Hard of Hearing Children." *Am Ann Deaf* 98:328–35 My '53. * (*PA* 28:7921)
74. HANVIK, LEO J. "The Goodenough Test as a Measure of Intelligence in Child Psychiatric Patients." *J Clin Psychol* 9:71–2 Ja '53. * (*PA* 27:7773)
75. JOHNSON, GRANVILLE B., JR. "Bilingualism as Measured by a Reaction-Time Technique and the Relationship Between a Language and a Non-Language Intelligence Quotient." *J Genetic Psychol* 82:3–9 Mr '53. * (*PA* 27:7648)
76. PAPAVASSILIOU, I. TH. "The Validity of the Goodenough Draw-A-Man Test in Greece." *J Ed Psychol* 44:244–8 Ap '53. * (*PA* 28:2663)
77. REICHENBERG-HACKETT, WALLY "Changes in Goodenough Drawings After a Gratifying Experience." Discussion by Esther Katz Rosen. *Am J Orthopsychiatry* 23:501–17 Jl '53. * (*PA* 28:2667)
78. TUSKA, SHIRLEY A. *Developmental Concepts With the Draw-A-Person Test at Different Grade Levels.* Master's thesis, Ohio University (Athens, Ohio), 1953.
79. BLISS, MONTE, AND BERGER, ANDREW. "Measurement of Mental Age as Indicated by the Male Figure Drawings of the Mentally Subnormal Using Goodenough and Machover Instructions." *Am J Mental Def* 59:73–9 Jl '54. * (*PA* 29:4253)
80. BRITTON, JOSEPH H. "Influence of Social Class Upon Performance on the Draw-A-Man Test." *J Ed Psychol* 45:44–51 Ja '54. * (*PA* 28:7208)

81. HARRIS, ROBERT E., AND FISHER, JEROME. "Closure Phenomena (Prägnanz) in Social Interaction." Abstract. *Am Psychol* 9:390–1 Ag '54. *

82. HAWARD, L. R. C., AND ROLAND, W. A. "Some Inter-Cultural Differences on the Draw-A-Man Test: Goodenough Scores." *Man* 54:86–8 Je '54. *

83. DORIS, ROBERT E. *The Relationship of the Goodenough Draw-A-Man Test to the Wechsler Intelligence Scale for Children: A Study With Mentally Retarded Children in Fresno County, California.* Master's thesis, Fresno State College (Fresno, Calif.), 1955.

84. GUNZBURG, HERBERT C. "Scope and Limitations of the Goodenough Drawing Test Method in Clinical Work With Mental Defectives." *J Clin Psychol* 11:8–15 Ja '55. * (*PA* 29:7280)

85. HAWARD, L. R. C., AND ROLAND, W. A. "Some Inter-Cultural Differences on the Draw-A-Man Test: Part II, Machover Scores." *Man* 55:27–9 F '55. *

86. HAWARD, L. R. C., AND ROLAND, W. A. "Some Inter-Cultural Differences on the Draw-A-Man Test: Part III, Conclusion." *Man* 55:40–2 Mr '55. *

87. NORMAN, RALPH D., AND MIDKIFF, KATHERINE L. "Navaho Children on Raven Progressive Matrices and Goodenough Draw-A-Man Tests." *Southw J Anthrop* 11:129–36 su '55. * (*PA* 30:4426)

88. BAILEY, ROBERT B. *A Study of Predicting Academic Success in Elementary School Reading From Projective Tests.* Doctor's thesis, University of Oklahoma (Norman, Okla.), 1956. (*DA* 16:1397)

89. BRENNER, ANTON, AND MORSE, NANCY C. "The Measurement of Children's Readiness for School." *Papers Mich Acad Sci, Arts & Letters* 41:333–40 '56. *

90. MURPHY, MARY MARTHA. "A Goodenough Scale Evaluation of Human Figure Drawings of Three Non-Psychotic Groups of Adults." *J Clin Psychol* 12:397–9 O '56. * (*PA* 32:4199)

91. DENNIS, WAYNE. "Performance of Near Eastern Children on the Draw-A-Man Test." *Child Develop* 28:427–30 D '57. *

92. HERRON, WILLIAM G. *The Effect of Preceding Affective States on the Goodenough Drawing Test of Intelligence.* Master's thesis, Fordham University (New York, N.Y.), 1957.

93. HUNT, BETTY, AND PATTERSON, RUTH M. "Performance of Familial Mentally Deficient Children in Response to Motivation on the Goodenough Draw-A-Man Test." *Am J Mental Def* 62:326–9 S '57. *

94. JONES, ALLAN W., AND RICH, THOMAS A. "The Goodenough Draw-A-Man Test as a Measure of Intelligence in Aged Adults." *J Consult Psychol* 21:235–8 Je '57. *

For a review by Naomi Stewart, see 4:292.

[336]

*The Graduate Record Examinations Aptitude Test.** College seniors and graduate students; 1949–58; for more complete information, see 599; 2 scores: verbal, quantitative; IBM; 150(170) minutes; Educational Testing Service. *

REFERENCES

1–2. See 4:293.

3. SAUM, JAMES A. *Selection Techniques and Their Application in the Stanford School of Education.* Doctor's thesis, Stanford University (Stanford, Calif.), 1951.

4. CROSBY, DONALD W. "The Development of a Test of Academic Aptitude for Superior College Students." Abstract. *Calif J Ed Res* 4:185–6 S '53. *

5. SCHULTZ, MARGARET K., AND ANGOFF, WILLIAM H. "The Development of New Scales for the Aptitude and Advanced Tests of the Graduate Record Examinations." Abstract. *Am Psychol* 8:430 Ag '53. *

6. MANUEL, HERSCHEL T. "A Study of an Examination for Admission to Candidacy for the Doctorate in Education." *Yearb Nat Council Meas Used Ed* 11:15–8 '54. *

7. SCHULTZ, MARGARET K., AND ANGOFF, WILLIAM H. "The Development of New Scales for the Aptitude and Advanced Tests of the Graduate Record Examinations." *J Ed Psychol* 47:285–94 My '56. * (*PA* 32:2127)

8. CAPPS, MARIAN P., AND DeCOSTA, FRANK A. "Contributions of the Graduate Record Examinations and the National Teacher Examinations to the Prediction of Graduate School Success." *J Ed Res* 50:383–9 Ja '57. * (*PA* 32:937)

9. ROBINSON, DONALD W. "A Comparison of Two Batteries of Tests as Predictors of First Year Achievement in the Graduate School of Bradley University." *Yearb Nat Council Meas Used Ed* 15:118–27 '58. *

JOHN T. DAILEY, *Program Director, American Institute for Research, Washington, D.C.* [Review of Form EGR.]

This is a test of general scholastic ability suitable for use at the college senior or gradu-

ate school level. It is designed to accompany the Advanced Tests, which are comprehensive achievement tests in 16 different fields of study, and the Area Tests for the social sciences, humanities, and material sciences. The first part of the Aptitude Test consists of verbal reasoning questions (opposites, analogies, and completion) plus paragraph reading comprehension. These together make up the verbal score. The second part of the test includes various kinds of quantitative mathematical materials, such as questions on arithmetic reasoning, on algebraic problems, and on the interpretation of graphs, diagrams, and descriptive data. These give the quantitative score. Scores are reported as 3-digit scaled scores with the third digit always a zero. This is necessary since one raw score point represents 10 or more points of scaled score.

The reliability of each part of the test is reported as .92, which is adequate for the two parts of the test to be used separately when desired.

In content the test parallels most other scholastic aptitude tests from the junior high school level up. Essentially, it measures verbal reasoning ability, vocabulary-reading comprehension, and arithmetic achievement. Statistics quoted in the manual indicate that the test correlates substantially with the specific advanced tests. Validities are not available in the manual. They would, perhaps, be superfluous since the pattern of validities of this test should be highly predictable; at any rate, validity figures should be about the same as those obtained with any similar test commonly used at the graduate school level.

Extremely voluminous normative material is supplied in several manuals. Normative data are available for a large number of categories of applicants. Results on the Aptitude Test are reported separately for those subjects taking each of 16 advanced tests. As always, those taking the education test score lowest of all. It is of interest to note that psychologists, who are one of the highest scoring groups on the *Miller Analogies Test,* score at about the median for the various groups on the Aptitude Test. Exploring the reasons for this might prove interesting.

In summary, the Aptitude Test is an adequately constructed and well calibrated test of general scholastic potential that should be useful when used in combination with the Area

Tests and the Advanced Tests. It will be of less utility when used alone, becoming then only another general scholastic aptitude test although specifically slanted in terms of difficulty level for a high level school or graduate student population.

For reviews by J. P. Guilford and Carl I. Hovland of Forms XGR and YGR, see 4:293. For a review by Harold Seashore of the entire series, see 601.

[337]

★Group Selective Test No. 1. Ages 10–12.0; [1940]; I form; no data on reliability and validity; out of print; 31(45) minutes; M. M. Lewis; University of London Press Ltd. *

T. R. MILES, *Lecturer in Psychology, University College, Bangor, Wales.*

The instruction manual contains no details as to where or how this test was standardised, no reliability coefficient, and no record of any attempt at validation by means of external criteria. Its avowed purpose is to grade children "according to their ability to profit by higher education of the type which, at present, is provided in secondary schools"; but as to its effectiveness we are told only that in both urban and rural districts it has been found to give "satisfactory" results. Such a claim is far too vague to be convincing; in addition, the evaluative word "profit" brings in issues other than psychological ones. Whether a child has "profited" by his education can be determined only if there is broad agreement as to what is "profitable." This raises social and moral questions on which the psychologist, as such, has no special authority to pronounce.

With regard to individual items, the layout and explanation in the first part (Changing Patterns) seem to me very unsatisfactory; words and diagrams are interspersed in such a way that some of the time one has to read vertically instead of horizontally, and even then the result is anything but plain English. The reviewer is also uneasy about Part 4 (Reasoning), where on two occasions the correct answer is given as "I cannot tell," the data being insufficient for any conclusion to be drawn. "No answer possible" might perhaps have been a preferable formula. A notice at the top of the page says, "Underline *I cannot tell*, if that is your answer"; but is this cryptic remark sufficient to reassure the very conscien-

tious child? Reluctance to say "I cannot tell" may vary according to a child's temperament and training; ability to overcome this reluctance is not purely a cognitive task.

A more serious criticism might perhaps be levelled at some of the items in Part 5. Each item contains five pictures, four of which tell a coherent story. The pictures are to be numbered in the correct order, the fifth being left blank. Far too many of these stories, it seems to the reviewer, are suggestive of what may be called a "bourgeois" background; they are taken from events in the social life of the British upper-middle classes—running water from a tap, parcels arriving by post, an elegant lady with an umbrella, and, above all, a boy having a bath and then going to bed in pyjamas. Has not the author overlooked the fact that at least some of the children taking the test may have no running water in their houses, let alone a bathroom, and that the use of pyjamas, even nowadays, may not be by any means universal? Part 5 seems to exemplify the danger that upper-middle class test setters may inadvertently overload tests with upper-middle class items.

One further caution should be given. When verbal and performance scores are discrepant, users of the test would do well to consider each in isolation; it may not always be meaningful to sum the two. A specific ability on the performance side is not unknown, and there may be children, particularly those suffering from the syndrome known as dyslexia or developmental aphasia (involving, briefly, failure to recognise words at sight and failure of spatial orientation), who show high reasoning ability but are quite at a loss when it comes to grasping the spatial relationships in some nonverbal items.

In general, I am hesitant to recommend the widespread use of this test. To investigate a child's powers of reasoning and abstraction by the occasional use of some such test may well be informative; but a simple numerical score, based on the number of "correct" answers, should not, by itself, be given much weight when major decisions about a child's future are involved. Since it is far from clear precisely what tests of this kind are supposed to be measuring (if indeed they are a measure of anything at all), it is dangerous to take for granted that they measure it efficiently.[1]

1 Since this review was prepared the publisher has indicated that the test is now out of print.

[338]

★**Group Test 75.** Ages 12–13; 1957; 1 form ['57]; mimeographed manual ['57]; no data on reliability and validity; separate answer sheets must be used; 27s. per 12 tests; 1s. 6d. per 12 answer sheets; 2s. 3d. per set of scoring key and manual; 2s. 3d. per specimen set; postage extra; 20(35) minutes; National Institute of Industrial Psychology. *

[339]

*****Group Tests 33 and 33B.** Ages 14 and over; 1923–56; forms 33 ['23]; 33B ['56]; mimeographed manuals [form 33, '50; form 33B, '56]; no data on reliability and validity; 5s. per 12 tests; 1s. 3d. per manual; 1s. per specimen set; postage extra; 29(35) minutes; National Institute of Industrial Psychology. *

REFERENCES

1–2. See 4:295.
3. MITCHELL, J. H. "An Experiment in the Selection of Sales Managers." *Occupational Psychol* 12:308–318 au '38. * (*PA* 13:500)
4. HOLLIDAY, FRANK. "An Investigation Into the Selection of Apprentices for the Engineering Industry." *Occupational Psychol* 14:69–81 Ap '40. * (*PA* 14:3710)
5. SLATER, PATRICK. "Some Group Tests of Spatial Judgment or Practical Ability." *Occupational Psychol* 14:40–55 Ja '40. * (*PA* 14:2644)
6. HOLLIDAY, FRANK. "A Further Investigation Into the Selection of Apprentices for the Engineering Industry." *Occupational Psychol* 15:173–84 O '41. * (*PA* 16:732)
7. HOLLIDAY, FRANK. "A Survey of an Investigation Into the Selection of Apprentices for the Engineering Industry." *Occupational Psychol* 16:1–19 Ja '42. * (*PA* 16:2823)
8. HOLLIDAY, FRANK. "The Relation Between Psychological Test Scores and Subsequent Proficiency of Apprentices in the Engineering Industry." *Occupational Psychol* 17:168–85 O '43. * (*PA* 18:1835)
9. ORTON, R., AND MARTIN, D. R. "Psychiatric Screening of Medical Students." *Lancet* 255:321–3 Ag 28 '48. *
10. TOZER, A. H. D., AND LARWOOD, H. J. C. "An Analysis of Intelligence Test Scores of Students in a University Department of Education." *Brit J Psychol* 44:347–58 N '53. * (*PA* 28:6597)
11. TOZER, A. H. D., AND LARWOOD, H. J. C. "The Changes in Intelligence Test Score of Students Between the Beginning and End of Their University Courses." *Brit J Ed Psychol* 28:120–8 Je '58. *

[340]

Group Test 90A. Adults; 1947–48; 1 form ['48]; no data on reliability and validity; mimeographed manual ['48]; 5s. per 12 tests; 1s. per single copy; 1s. 6d. per manual; postage extra; 20(30) minutes; National Institute of Industrial Psychology. *

JOHN LIGGETT, *Lecturer in Applied Psychology, University of Durham, Newcastle, England.*

This paper and pencil test of verbal intelligence consists of four separate sets of problems, each set requiring 5 minutes of working time. The first set employs items requiring the correct synonym or antonym of a given word to be selected from among five alternatives; the second requires the selection of correct "analogies" from among five possible choices; the third consists of jumbled sentences whose meaning (when the sentences are mentally rearranged) can be completed by only one of five given words; the last consists of straightforward sentences whose meaning can be completed by only one of five given words. There is supervised practice for each subtest.

Norms are given for ages 20–25 for an un-

selected group and for subjects who had previously attended a secondary grammar school. Information on distributions of scores up to 60 years of age is supplied on request to the publisher. This supplementary information shows that the test has been administered to 7,000 temporary civil servants, aged 20–60 years, drawn from all educational levels. These subjects were to some extent a selected group in that they had been displaced from their ordinary occupations by the upheaval of the war years. Results are subdivided according to level of school originally attended. The figures show that the decline of scores with age is a perfectly linear one. No norms have been compiled for children of school age since the test has been mainly used for industrial purposes. The lack of norms for children is unfortunate since the test is a competently produced one with good item variety, and it is easy to administer and score. It should find considerable usefulness as a measure of verbal ability in normal subjects.

[341]

*****Group Test of Learning Capacity: Dominion Tests.** Grades kgn–1, 4–6, 7–9, 10–12 and adults; 1934–56; formerly called *Group Test of Intelligence*; 2 forms; 4 levels; 45¢ per specimen set of primary, intermediate, or advanced level; postage extra; Department of Educational Research, Ontario College of Education, University of Toronto; distributed by Guidance Centre. *

a) PRIMARY. Grades kgn–1; 1934–56; Forms A, B ('56); administration of both forms is recommended; revised manual ('56); norms ('50); $1.80 per 25 tests; (50) minutes in 2 sessions.

b) JUNIOR. Grades 4–6; 1940–56; Forms A, B ('56); revised manual ('56); norms ('52); $1.20 per 25 tests; 35¢ per specimen set; 25(45) minutes.

c) INTERMEDIATE. Grades 7–9; 1934–56; 2 editions.
1) *Subtest Edition.* 1934–56; Forms A, B ('34); revised manual ('56); norms ('52); $1.80 per 25 tests; 37(50) minutes.
2) *Omnibus Edition.* 1950–56; Forms A, B ('50); revised manual ('56); norms ('52); $1.20 per 25 tests; 30(45) minutes.

d) ADVANCED. Grades 10–12 and adults; 1939–55; Forms A, B ('39); revised manual ('55); norms ('54); $1.20 per 25 tests; 10¢ per scoring key; 30(45) minutes.

For a review by W. G. Emmett, see 4:294; for a review by F. T. Tyler, see 3:231.

[342]

*****The Henmon-Nelson Tests of Mental Ability, Revised Edition.** Grades 3–6, 6–9, 9–12; 1931–58; previous edition (see 4:299) still available; Forms A ('57), B ('58); 3 levels; manual ('57) for each level; $3 per 35 tests; 42¢ per specimen set of any one level; postage extra; 30(35) minutes; Tom A. Lamke and M. J. Nelson; Houghton Mifflin Co. *

REFERENCES

1–25. See 4:299.

26. DODSON, MARY H. *A Study in Shorthand and Typewriting Prognosis.* Master's thesis, University of Kentucky (Lexington, Ky.), 1943.

27. JOHNSON, RALPH H., AND BOND, GUY L. "Reading Ease of Commonly Used Tests." *J Appl Psychol* 34:319–24 O '50. * (PA 26:299)

28. BARBE, WALTER, AND GRILK, WERNER. "Correlations Between Reading Factors and IQ." *Sch & Soc* 75:134–6 Mr 1 '52. *

29. LIEN, ARNOLD JUEL. "A Comparative-Predictive Study of Students in the Four Curricula of a Teacher Education Institution." *J Exp Ed* 21:81–219 D '52. *

30. TURNER, G. H., AND PENFOLD, D. J. "The Scholastic Aptitude of Indian Children of the Caradoc Reserve." *Can J Psychol* 6:31–44 Mr '52. * (PA 26:6935)

31. JUSTMAN, JOSEPH, AND WRIGHTSTONE, J. WAYNE. "A Comparison of Pupil Functioning on the Pintner Intermediate Test and the Henmon-Nelson Test of Mental Ability." *Ed & Psychol Meas* 13:102–9 sp '53. * (PA 28:1567)

32. SMITH, VAUGHN E. *Correlation Between the Intelligence Quotients as Determined by the Henmon-Nelson Tests of Mental Ability and Achievement of Two Hundred and Fifty Graduates From Tony High School, Tony, Wisconsin.* Master's thesis, Wisconsin State College (Superior, Wis.), 1953.

33. CARLILE, A. B. "Predicting Performance in the Teaching Profession." *J Ed Res* 47:641–68 My '54. * (PA 29:3063)

34. RANDALL, ROGERS E. "Correlation of Henmon-Nelson Tests of Mental Ability With the National Achievement General Science Test." *Sch Sci & Math* 54:635–6 N '54. *

35. LAMKE, TOM ARTHUR. "The Revision of the Henmon-Nelson Test of Mental Ability." *Yearb Nat Council Meas Used Ed* 12(pt 1):78–80 '55. *

36. FOWLER, WILLIAM L. *A Comparative Analysis of Pupil Performance on Conventional and Culture-Controlled Mental Tests.* Doctor's thesis, University of Michigan (Ann Arbor, Mich.), 1956. (DA 17:91)

37. LAMKE, TOM ARTHUR. "The Standardization of the Henmon-Nelson Revision." *Yearb Nat Council Meas Used Ed* 13:42–4 '56. *

38. MITCHELL, JAMES V., JR. "A Comparison of the Factorial Structure of Cognitive Functions for a High and Low Status Group." *J Ed Psychol* 47:397–414 N '56. *

39. FOWLER, WILLIAM L. "A Comparative Analysis of Pupil Performance on Conventional and Culture-Controlled Mental Tests." *Yearb Nat Council Meas Used Ed* 14:8–19 '57. *

D. WELTY LEFEVER, *Professor of Education, University of Southern California, Los Angeles, California.*

CHANGES PRODUCED BY THE REVISION. In this revision of the *Henmon-Nelson Test of Mental Ability* a number of the weaknesses of the earlier edition have been remedied. The tests are much more attractive in typography, design, and quality of paper used. The items are more easily read, the provision for recording the responses is less confusing to the eye, and the manual is more complete and helpful. The revision retains the outstanding virtue of quick and easy scoring through the use of the Clapp-Young self-marking device which requires no separate scoring key. The pupil's responses are recorded on the reverse side of the test page by the action of a carbon backing. When the scorer removes the perforated edging and pulls the carbon backing away, the correct responses are clearly indicated.

In the revised edition, the range of grade levels from 3 through 12 has been assigned to three batteries (3–6, 6–9, 9–12), in place of the former two batteries (3–8, 7–12). This change has greatly improved the matching of item difficulty with the range of ability of the pupils at each grade level.

TEST CONTENT. The content of this edition is substantially the same as that of the original tests. Items from the earlier edition were revised and retained or discarded in accordance with an item analysis based on a national sample which included 77 communities in 24 states.

Each test is composed of a scrambled sequence of 90 five-choice items arranged in order of difficulty without regard to the exact character of the items. As a number of critics have remarked regarding the earlier edition, the test contains a "hodge-podge" of item types including vocabulary, sentence completion, word classification, logical selection, disarranged sentences, interpretation of proverbs, verbal analogies, mixed spelling, series completion, design analogies, and arithmetic reasoning. The content is heavily weighted with items measuring various types of verbal ability. However, the history of mental testing has indicated substantial correlations between such test content and scholastic success.

AUTHORS' RATIONALE FOR THE TEST. A potential user of the *Henmon-Nelson Tests of Mental Ability* must answer an important question for himself: Will a relatively short test (90 items in 30 minutes) carrying a heavy verbal emphasis and yielding a single score serve the purposes for which an intelligence test is being administered? Several pages in the manuals are devoted to the rationale underlying the authors' approach to this problem. According to the authors, research findings support the position that "factored" tests or multiscore tests have not predicted scholastic success any better than tests producing a single global score. Subtests in multiscore batteries which apparently have little to do with success in a given subject matter field often yield higher correlations with grades in that field than do the subtests which, because of the nature of their content, ought to be the best predictors. This reviewer finds considerable merit in the interpretation of background research presented in the manual. If a single predictor of school success is needed which can be given in less than a class period and scored with a minimum of time and effort, serious consideration should be given the Henmon-Nelson test. On the other hand, if guidance involving some differentiation among aptitudes is required and if a profile showing the strengths and weaknesses of each counselee is desired, a more complex test battery will be more appropriate. A test yielding a single score may not offer much diagnostic help leading to remedial instruction. In selecting such a test, however, the correlations reported between the subtests and appropriate criteria of success (such as grades) should be examined with care to be sure that a sufficient gain in predictive power is likely to counterbalance the greater cost in material, student time, and scoring time, and the greater expertness required for interpretation.

EVIDENCE FOR VALIDITY. The manual for each test summarizes the data available concerning the validity and reliability of the revised tests. The correlations reported as measures of validity are remarkably similar for the three grade levels.

Evidence for congruent validity is presented in the form of correlations with several well known tests of intelligence. The median coefficient for all levels is .76; the range is .50 to .84. Theoretically, these correlations should be discounted somewhat because of the presence of a common factor, chronological age. However, test manuals reporting correlations between mental ages or raw scores as well as IQ's (such as those for the *Lorge-Thorndike Intelligence Tests* and the *Differential Aptitude Tests*) do not support this suggestion.

Concurrent validity is rather well established by correlations between Henmon-Nelson IQ's and achievement test scores and between IQ's and teachers' grades. The median coefficient for total achievement battery scores versus IQ is .79 (range, .64 to .85). Average grades and IQ produced a median r of .60, with a range of .09 to .74.

In the light of the authors' contention that a single score will predict scholastic success as well as a more elaborate battery, perhaps the most interesting evidence of validity is the series of correlations between Henmon-Nelson IQ's and achievement test scores or teachers' grades for separate subject matter areas. Following are the medians of the correlations reported at the various grade levels: IQ and reading scores, .76; IQ and arithmetic or mathematics scores, .65; IQ and work-study scores, .72; IQ and science scores, .69. Teachers' grades and IQ's produced these median coefficients: English or reading, .64; mathematics, .53; science, .71. These correlations show a fairly homogeneous predictive potential for diverse areas of academic achievement. Since all of these data were obtained after the revision was completed, the number and quality of validity measures reported seems praiseworthy.

EVIDENCE FOR RELIABILITY. The reliability of the revised tests is reported in terms of odd-even correlations for each grade level and form. Correlations between Form A and Form B are given for grades 3, 6, and 12. The evidence for reliability is definitely satisfactory since the coefficients are consistently within the range of acceptable values. The median of the 24 odd-even reliability coefficients reported is .94; the range of values is .90 to .97. The six interform correlations range from .87 to .94, with a median of .91. The differences in reliability coefficients produced by the two approaches seem to demonstrate the presence, to some degree at least, of a speed factor. If further research should indicate that the scores of some pupils are affected by the present time limit, this reviewer would urge that more time be allowed. Too much concern has been given in some quarters to convenience and expediency at the possible sacrifice of the full value that tests can give.

STANDARDIZATION PROCEDURES. The authors deserve special commendation for the excellent plan for determining the norms of the test. They have achieved the rare distinction of clearly defining the population on which the norms are based and of selecting the norming sample in a way that permits an estimate to be made of the sampling error. Cluster sampling was employed and 250 school systems were selected at random from a master file in the Bureau of the Census after 8 strata for size of system and 48 strata representing the several states had been set up. Within each system, a school was selected at random; and within the school, a classroom in the range of grades 3–6. Then classrooms were selected for the 6–9 and 9–12 ranges because they represented the classrooms into which the children tested in the 3–6 range would go as they progressed through school. More than 96 per cent of the classrooms selected by the sampling process actually participated in the study. This is a remarkable achievement in itself and gives the norming sample employed unusual significance.

Tables are furnished in the manuals so that raw scores can be translated into percentile ranks by grade level groups, into mental ages, into grade equivalents, and into deviation IQ's. In the first edition of the manual a number of inconsistencies in IQ values occurred as the authors endeavored to obtain satisfactory articulation between successive test levels. The grade equivalent scale inadvertently slipped out of position during the process of producing better articulation. These discrepancies are being remedied and will undoubtedly be corrected by the time this review is published.

DIFFICULTY OF THE TESTS. In general the level of item difficulty appears to be satisfactory except for some evidence of insufficient ceiling for the 3–6 and the 6–9 tests. In order for a student aged 12 years 6 months (the age at which a raw score equivalent of a grade placement at the middle of grade 6 yields an average IQ and thus, apparently, the average CA for the middle of grade 6) to have an IQ of 130, 87 items would need to be answered correctly. This would leave only three more items for possible "ceiling." With an IQ of 140, only one item would be "left." A similar check on the norms for the middle of the ninth grade and the 6–9 test indicates that at this average CA, an IQ of 130 requires 85.5 correct answers while an IQ of 140 calls for 89. On the other hand, the 9–12 test requires only 79 items right for an IQ of 130 at a CA of 204 months, while an IQ of 140 is based on 83 right answers. Thus, the 9–12 test apparently allows the gifted pupil more opportunity to answer one more item correctly.

The scoring key shows no evidence of a "response bias." The correct answer is distributed among the response positions approximately equally.

More detailed suggestions for the use of test results, prepared for each grade level, would be valuable. Perhaps a special manual on the use of intelligence test measures would be more appropriate than more bulky examiners' manuals.

SUMMARY. The revised edition of the *Henmon-Nelson Tests of Mental Ability* represents a distinct improvement over the earlier edition. It is greatly improved in format, in the usefulness of the examiners' manuals, in the evidence for validity, and especially in the care with which the standardization was conducted. For many purposes a relatively short intelligence test yielding a single score will be satisfactory. As the basis for predicting success in academic subjects, the Henmon-Nelson offers reliable help. It may not be as valuable in diagnosing special problems in learning, in vocational counseling, or in working with the mentally re-

tarded. The heavy emphasis on verbal content may produce results somewhat unfair to the nonacademic student. The potential user of an intelligence test should assess his objectives with care before deciding which type of test is best for him.

LEONA E. TYLER, *Professor of Psychology, University of Oregon, Eugene, Oregon.*

The revision of these widely used tests exemplifies the application of the newest technology of mental measurement to one of our oldest testing problems. The aim was to produce short, self-administering, easily scored instruments that would have maximum predictive validity in school situations. The effort was eminently successful, and the complete, clearly written manuals for the different grade levels present us with the evidence we need for evaluating and interpreting the results.

The reader cannot fail to be impressed with the care that was taken in (*a*) selecting items and matching them so that the different forms and levels would be truly equivalent, (*b*) sampling the total school population in a way that would insure that the norms would be truly representative of this population, and (*c*) collecting and reporting evidence of several different kinds with regard to reliability and validity. Scores can be expressed as mental ages, as percentiles, or as deviation IQ's equated to those on the Stanford-Binet. The grade equivalents of the raw scores are also reported. Any teacher should be able to administer and score the tests. Any educator with a moderately complete background in measurement and statistics should be able to interpret scores correctly.

The most serious question that is likely to be raised with regard to it is whether it does not imply adherence to a theory that intelligence is a single, unitary trait after factor analysis has made such a theory untenable. During the 1940's and the 1950's the trend has been toward batteries based on factor analysis and away from single-score tests. In the manual the authors face this problem and examine the usefulness of single measures of academic ability as compared with profiles of separate factors. The evidence they assemble indicates that the single-score test still does a better job in the school situation than the multiple factor tests do—and with a much smaller investment of testing time. What best predicts school success in any of the special subject areas seems to be whatever it is that the different factors have in common rather than what is distinctive about them. If this general intellectual capacity is what we wish to measure, then it would seem advantageous to measure it directly.

The revised Henmon-Nelson tests are carefully planned, carefully constructed, readily interpretable instruments designed to do one thing and do it well. They should find widespread acceptance in elementary and secondary schools.

J Consult Psychol 22:241 Je '58. *Laurance F. Shaffer.* * The content....is based on an extensive item analysis of the older tests, and the equivalence of the Forms A and B is well established. The....manuals....give impressively favorable data about reliability, congruent validity with other tests, and concurrent and predictive validity with achievement measures. * The standardization is a model of precise method, using a predetermined sample of 250 classrooms stratified by state and size of school system. The manual closes with a persuasive argument for the use of omnibus tests, rather than of tests with factor scores, for the prediction of school achievement. In all, the revised Henmon-Nelson impresses the reviewer as a scholarly example of the best in test construction, and as a remarkably efficient instrument for its length.

For a review by H. M. Fowler of the previous edition, see 4:299; for reviews by Anne Anastasi, August Dvorak, Howard Easley, and J. P. Guilford, see 40:1398 (1 excerpt).

[343]
*IPAT Culture Free Intelligence Test. Ages 4–8, 8–13 and average adults, grades 10–16 and superior adults; 1933–58; title on test is *Test of g: Culture Free;* 3 levels; cash orders postpaid; Raymond B. Cattell and A. K. S. Cattell (2, 3); Institute for Personality and Ability Testing. *

a) SCALE 1. Ages 4–8; 1933–50; identical with the *Cattell Intelligence Tests, Scale O: Dartington Scale;* individual in part; 1 form ('50); mimeographed manual ['50]; no data on reliability; $3.50 per 25 tests; $3 per set of cards for classification test; 25¢ per scoring key; 50¢ per manual; 75¢ per specimen set; (30) minutes.

b) SCALE 2. Ages 8–13 and average adults; 1949–58; Forms A ('57), B ('56); $3.30 per 25 tests; separate answer sheets may be used; $1.80 per 50 answer sheets; 50¢ per hand scoring key; $1.20 per manual ['58]; $1.75 per specimen set; 14(30) minutes.

c) SCALE 3. Grades 10–16 and superior adults; 1950; Forms A, B; mimeographed manual ['50]; no data on reliability; prices same as for Scale 2; 14(30) minutes.

REFERENCES

1–2. See 4:300.
3. GIBSON, Q. H. "Intelligence Tests and University Careers of Medical Students." *Lancet* 255:323–4 Ag 28 '48. *
4. CORDOVA, F. A. *A Comparison of the Performance of a Bilingual Group on a "Culture Free" Test Administered in English and in Spanish.* Master's thesis, Fordham University (New York, N.Y.), 1951.
5. SCHWARTZ, IRVING H. *A Validation Study of the Culture-Free Intelligence Test (A Measure of "G"), Scale 3.* Master's thesis, University of Florida (Gainesville, Fla.), 1951.
6. ANASTASI, ANNE, AND CORDOVA, FERNANDO A. "Some Effects of Bilingualism Upon the Intelligence Test Performance of Puerto Rican Children in New York City." *J Ed Psychol* 44:1–19 Ja '53. *
7. BENSBERG, GERARD J., AND SLOAN, WILLIAM. "The Use of the Cattell Culture Free Test With Mental Defectives." *Am J Mental Def* 59:499–503 Ja '55. * (PA 29:7476)
8. CATTELL, RAYMOND B. "A Note on Dr. Sloan's Evidence Regarding the Value of Culture-Free Intelligence Tests." *Am J Mental Def* 59:504–6 Ja '55. * (PA 29:7480)
9. KEEHN, J. D., AND PROTHRO, E. TERRY. "Non-Verbal Tests as Predictors of Academic Success in Lebanon." *Ed & Psychol Meas* 15:495–8 w '55. * (PA 30:7765)
10. MARQUART, DOROTHY I., AND BAILEY, LOIS L. "An Evaluation of the *Culture Free Test* of Intelligence." *J Genetic Psychol* 86:353–8 Je '55. * (PA 30:6905)
11. FOWLER, WILLIAM L. *A Comparative Analysis of Pupil Performance on Conventional and Culture-Controlled Mental Tests.* Doctor's thesis, University of Michigan (Ann Arbor, Mich.), 1956. (DA 17:91)
12. FOWLER, WILLIAM L. "A Comparative Analysis of Pupil Performance on Conventional and Culture-Controlled Mental Tests." *Yearb Nat Council Meas Used Ed* 14:8–19 '57. *
13. COOPER, JAMES G. "Predicting School Achievement for Bilingual Pupils." *J Ed Psychol* 49:31–6 F '58. *

I. MACFARLANE SMITH, *Lecturer in Education, University of Durham, Newcastle, England.*

This series of intelligence scales has the same aims as Cattell's original *Culture-Free Test* published in 1944: (*a*) to ensure the highest possible validity, (*b*) to ensure freedom from contamination by cultural learning effects, and (*c*) to provide adequate reliability.

The same principles of test construction have been employed in all three scales, though Scale 1 is not so exactly comparable as Scales 2 and 3, for only half of its eight subtests can be described as "culture free." Scales 2 and 3 each consist of four subtests involving different types of relation eduction. The first three subtests are of familiar types—series, classification, and matrices, but the fourth subtest, called Conditions, involves a novel type of "topological" reasoning.

Many of the criticisms made in *The Fourth Mental Measurements Yearbook* have been met in the most recent edition of the tests and manuals. Thus, answer sheets have been provided for Scales 2 and 3. Also, the latest edition of the manual for Scale 2 contains full information about the test, including data on validity and reliability and very comprehensive tables of norms to suit the requirements of different types of user. Data on validity are presented in the form of saturations with Thurstone's second order general ability factor or Spearman's "g." Correlations with "g" for the four subtests are .53, .68, .89, and .99. Data on reliability are presented in two ways. Immediate test-retest correlations on the full test were .82 and .85 on American and British samples, respectively. Consistency coefficients (split-half, corrected to full length) are reported as .70, .86, .87, and .92 for "four different groups." Since the actual testing time for one form alone is 14 minutes for Scales 2 or 3, the figures for validity and reliability are probably as high as could be expected. Thus, when sufficient time is available, it is desirable to give both forms. There is a useful device for testing groups containing individuals at different levels of test sophistication. Form A can be regarded as a training run; the score is based on Form B only. (The norms for Form B are applicable only when Form A has been given first.)

Scale 1 was standardized on only 117 children, 20 being the largest group for any age. These were selected as being "approximately of average ability according to the Binet and other scales." Scale 2 was standardized on 4,328 pupils, sampled from various regions of the United States and Britain. Scale 3 was standardized on 886 school pupils and 600 students from three universities or colleges. Thus, the standardization of Scale 2 is much more satisfactory than that of Scale 1 or Scale 3.

Attention has frequently been drawn to the fact that the standard deviation of IQ's obtained from Cattell's tests is very much higher than that of IQ's obtained from most other tests. This difference has sometimes created difficulty and misunderstanding when it has been necessary to compare scores on Cattell's tests with scores obtained on other tests. The new manual for Scale 2 should be helpful in this connection since the authors have provided tables of norms based on different standard deviations. One table gives the ordinary or classical IQ based on the actual sigma of 24.4 points of IQ. Another gives a normalized standard score based on a sigma of 24. A third gives a normalized standard score based on a sigma of 16. The third table makes it possible to compare readily the results of the culture free tests with IQ's obtained from many other tests. (British users have become accustomed to a standard deviation of 15 which is used both by the National Foundation for Educational Research and by Moray House.) The manual also contains tables giving percentiles for scores obtained when the tests are administered both with and without a time limit. These tables of norms are a valuable addition to the information provided in previous manuals.

Many psychologists have criticised the term "culture free" on the ground that it is not possible to produce an intelligence test which is entirely culture free. In the most recent manual, the authors have gone some way towards meeting this criticism by introducing the term "culture fair" as an alternative, which many will find more acceptable. Certainly there are grounds for claiming that the tests are relatively culture fair, for no significant differences were discovered in the performances of American, Australian, French, and British samples. On the other hand, norms were slightly different in some other countries, but it is possible that these differences were due to sampling artefacts. A striking finding is that when the tests were given twice to a complete age-group of 10 years in a city of 300,000 (retest interval, 14 years), no significant difference was obtained either in mean or standard deviation. This result contrasts with that obtained with other tests, e.g., the Binet test which, when used in the Scottish survey, showed an increase of 2.28 points of IQ over a period from 1932 to 1947.

The authors have to be commended for devising and developing these tests which have been shown to be relatively free from the influence of cultural factors. For this reason alone, the tests are likely to find many applications. On theoretical grounds, they are probably more effective tests of "g" than other culture fair tests such as *Progressive Matrices,* which put the whole emphasis on one particular type of subtest. On the other hand, the Cattell culture free tests necessitate more careful administration and timing than *Progressive Matrices,* which is normally given without a time limit.

For reviews by Raleigh M. Drake and Gladys C. Schwesinger, see 4:300.

[344]
*Jenkins Non-Verbal Test. Ages 10–14.0; 1949–53; adaptation of *Non-Verbal Test I* for Australian use; title on test is *A Scale of Non-Verbal Mental Ability;* 1 form ['49]; manual ['53]; 10s. per 10 tests; 1s. per scoring key; 3s. 6d. per manual; 5s. 6d. per specimen set; postpaid within Australia; 24(45) minutes; Australian Council for Educational Research. *

REFERENCES
1–3. See 4:307.
4. DUNN, S., AND SPEARRITT, D. "A Comparative Study of the Reliability of Some Verbal and Non-Verbal Intelligence Tests." *Austral J Psychol* 7:169–74 D '55. * (*PA* 31:1030)

5. DUNN, S. S., AND BROWNLESS, V. T. "Differences in Test and Retest Responses of a Group of Children to a Verbal and a Non-Verbal Test." *Austral J Psychol* 8:84–7 Je '56. * (*PA* 31:7910)

For a review by Cyril A. Rogers, see 356; for a review by E. A. Peel of the original edition, see 4:307.

[345]

*Junior Scholastic Aptitude Test, Revised Edition. Grades 7–9; 1935–59; 2 scores: verbal, numerical; IBM; Forms A, B, C ('57) ; manual ('59) ; separate answer sheets must be used; tests rented only; $1 per student, postage extra; fee includes scoring and reporting service; 60(80) minutes; Secondary Education Board (original edition) ; Geraldine Spaulding (revised edition) ; Educational Records Bureau. *

REFERENCES

1–3. See 3:233.
4. TRAXLER, ARTHUR E. "Twelve Years of Experience With the Junior Scholastic Aptitude Test." *Ed Rec B* 59:79–92 Jl '52. * (*PA* 27:2996)
5. TRAXLER, ARTHUR E., AND TOWNSEND, AGATHA. "Relationship of Differences Between Verbal and Numerical Aptitude to Differences in Achievement in English and Mathematics." *Ed Rec B* 61:61–5 Jl '53. * (*PA* 28:4865)
6. TRAXLER, ARTHUR E. "Comparative Value of Certain Mental Ability Tests for Predicting School Marks in Two Independent Schools." *Ed Rec B* 65:65–75 F '55. * (*PA* 29:7976)
7. TRAXLER, ARTHUR E. "Relationship of Certain Predictive Measures to Achievement in First-Year French and Latin." *Ed Rec B* 66:73–7 Jl '55. * (*PA* 30:5181)
8. SPAULDING, GERALDINE. "A Brief Account of the Preparation of New Editions of the Junior Scholastic Aptitude Test." *Ed Rec B* 70:71–3 Jl '57. *
9. SPAULDING, GERALDINE. "A Preliminary Report on the Reliability of the Revised Edition of the Junior Scholastic Aptitude Test." *Ed Rec B* 71:55–6 F '58. *
10. SPAULDING, GERALDINE. "Reliability and Other Data on the Revised Edition of the Junior Scholastic Aptitude Test, Forms A, B, and C." *Ed Rec B* 72:75–9 Jl '58. *

[346]

★Kelvin Measurement of Ability in Infant Classes. Ages 5–8; 1935; 1 form ['35] ; 9s. per 20 tests; 5½d. per single copy; 6d. per manual ['35] ; postage extra; administration time not reported; C. M. Fleming ; Robert Gibson & Sons (Glasgow), Ltd. *

[347]

★The Kingston Test of Intelligence. Ages 10–12; 1953–54; 1 form ('53) ; practice sheet ['53] ; 10s. per 25 tests; 6d. per single copy; 2s. 6d. per manual ('54) ; postage extra; 33(78) minutes; M. E. Highfield; George G. Harrap & Co. Ltd. *

A. W. HEIM, *Medical Research Council, Psychological Laboratory, University of Cambridge, Cambridge, England.*

This group test consists of a preliminary practice sheet (for which 30 minutes are allowed) and a test booklet consisting of five separate sections. Each section has a different maximum score and a different time limit. The five sections are as follows: numerical series, verbal analogies, diagrammatic analogies, classification of a kind, and arrangement (of three words) "in order of size or intensity." Sections 2, 3, and 4 are made up of questions of the multiple choice type, each accompanied by four solutions from which the correct one is to be chosen.

In the reviewer's opinion, this test is unsatisfactory from several points of view. For many of the multiple choice problems the "correct" solution is quite indefensible. This is true especially of the two sets of analogies, which contain some very odd reasoning. Section 4, described above as "classification," consists of 16 statements of the following form: "Honey is always useful, desirable, plentiful, of value." (The illustrations in this review are drawn from the preliminary practice sheet.) The subject is instructed to "underline the word which may be *sometimes* true but is not *always* so." There are three objections to this problem: (*a*) The question is expressed in a confusing and misleading manner. (*b*) Its form is in fact different from that used in the test proper. (*c*) In so far as the statement has any meaning, "desirable" would be as good (and bad) an answer as "plentiful"—the intended solution.

The deviser's logic has again let him down in the word arrangement section. Here the subject is asked to arrange in order words whose meanings often differ in *kind* as well as in *degree*. There are some factual errors in addition to logical errors, e.g., "The River is *still*, rushing, slow, rippling" (reviewer's italics). Cogent reasoning is lacking to at least as great an extent in the diagrammatic questions. It is felt that many items in this test might well penalise the brighter and more thoughtful child.

The only information given on validation is as follows: "The test was validated internally by item analysis, and a check on its discriminatory value was made by applying it to grammar school and secondary modern populations." The first of these assertions is not validation at all ; the second, as it stands, gives virtually no information.

The layout of the test is appalling; the paper is of poor quality; the test booklet can be used once only ; the marking key is so arranged that the scorer shall combine maximum time with minimum accuracy. The test might be useful for a psychologist wishing to conduct investigations on experimental neurosis in children.

[348]

Kuhlmann-Anderson Intelligence Tests, Sixth Edition. Grades kgn, 1, 2, 3, 4, 5, 6, 7–8, 9–12; 1927–52; 9 levels (labeled booklets K, A, B, C, D, E, F, G, and H) ; 1 form ('52, the same as 1942 edition) ; directions for administering ('52) ; handbook ('52) ; master manual ('52) ; $2.40 per 25 tests of any one level ; 35¢ per handbook (free with first order) ; $2.50 per master manual ; postage extra; $1 per specimen set (does not include master manual), postpaid; 25–30

(40–45) minutes; F. Kuhlmann and Rose G. Anderson; Personnel Press, Inc. *

REFERENCES

1–15. See 40:1404.
16–40. See 3:236.
41–50. See 4:302.
51. JOHNSON, RALPH H., AND BOND, GUY L. "Reading Ease of Commonly Used Tests." *J Appl Psychol* 34:319–24 O '50. * (*PA* 26:299)
52. SPAULDING, GERALDINE. "The Effects on the Kuhlmann-Anderson Intelligence Test Results of Changing From the 1940 Mental Age Norms to the Revised 1942 Norms." *Ed Rec B* 60:61–7 F '53. * (*PA* 28:1574)
53. RICHIE, ALICE. "A Comparison of the Kuhlmann-Anderson With the Davis-Eells Intelligence Tests in a Fifth Grade." Abstract. *Calif J Ed Res* 5:186 S '54. *
54. BLIESMER, EMERY P. "A Comparison of Results Obtained With Various Types of Capacity Tests Used With Retarded Readers." *Yearb Nat Council Meas Used Ed* 12(pt 1):60–2 '55. *
55. CANTONI, LOUIS J. "High School Tests and Measurements as Predictors of Occupational Status." *J Appl Psychol* 39:253–5 Ag '55. * (*PA* 30:4722)
56. HINKELMAN, EMMET ARTHUR. "Relationship of Intelligence to Elementary School Achievement." *Ed Adm & Sup* 41:176–9 Mr '55. * (*PA* 30:1622)
57. LEON, JOHN F. *An Experimental Study Comparing Matched Bilingual and Monolingual Groups on the Kuhlmann-Anderson Intelligence Test in Fifth Grade of One School in East Los Angeles.* Master's thesis, University of Southern California (Los Angeles, Calif.), 1955.
58. TRAXLER, ARTHUR E. "Comparative Value of Certain Mental Ability Tests for Predicting School Marks in Two Independent Schools." *Ed Rec B* 65:65–75 F '55. * (*PA* 29:7976)
59. TRAXLER, ARTHUR E. "Relationship of Certain Predictive Measures to Achievement in First-Year French and Latin." *Ed Rec B* 66:73–7 Jl '55. * (*PA* 30:5181)
60. BLIESMER, EMERY P. "A Comparison of Results of Various Capacity Tests Used With Retarded Readers." *El Sch J* 56:400–2 My '56. * (*PA* 31:5140)
61. NORTH, ROBERT D. "Relationship of Kuhlmann-Anderson IQ's and Stanford Achievement Test Scores of Independent School Pupils." *Ed Rec B* 68:53–60 Jl '56. * (*PA* 31:8837)
62. LOVE, MARY I., AND BEACH, SYLVIA. "Performance of Children on the Davis-Eells Games and Other Measures of Ability." *J Consult Psychol* 21:29–32 F '57. * (*PA* 32:952)
63. NASH, PHILIP G. "Comparison of IQ's Derived From Two Different Tests." *Calif J Ed Res* 8:23–6 Ja '57. * (*PA* 32:954)
64. TRAXLER, ARTHUR E. "Some Data on the Lorge-Thorndike Intelligence Tests Among Independent School Pupils." *Ed Rec B* 69:63–9 F '57. * (*PA* 32:2131)
65. NORTH, ROBERT D. "The Interpretation of Otis Quick-Scoring Mental Ability Test IQ's in Relation to Kuhlmann-Anderson IQ's, ACE Scores, and Independent School Norms." *Ed Rec B* 71:47–54 F '58. *

For reviews by Henry E. Garrett and David Segel, see 4:302; for reviews by W. G. Emmett and Stanley S. Marzolf of an earlier edition, see 3:236; for a review by Henry E. Garrett, see 40:1404; for reviews by Psyche Cattell, S. A. Courtis, and Austin H. Turney, see 38:1049.

[349]

★Kuhlmann-Finch Tests. Grades 1, 2, 3, 4, 5, 6, 7–9, 10–12; 1951–57; IBM for grades 4–12; 1 form ('57, identical with tests copyrighted in 1951 or 1952); 8 levels (Tests 1, 2, 3, 4, 5, 6; Junior High School Test; Senior High School Test); manual, second edition ('56); $2.95 per 25 tests; separate answer sheets may be used in grades 4–12; $2.40 per 50 IBM scorable answer sheets; 25¢ per hand or machine scoring stencil; $1.25 per manual; postage extra; $1.50 per complete specimen set, postpaid; 25(40), 30(45) minutes for grades 1–9, 10–12; Frank H. Finch; American Guidance Service, Inc. *

REFERENCES

1. COLEMAN, WILLIAM, AND WARD, ANNIE W. "A Comparison of Davis-Eells and Kuhlmann-Finch Scores of Children From High and Low Socio-Economic Status." *J Ed Psychol* 46:465–9 D '55. * (*PA* 31:3779)
2. FRANDSEN, ARDEN N., AND GRIMES, JESSE W. "Age Discrimination in Intelligence Tests." *J Ed Res* 51:229–33 N '57. *
3. MOULY, GEORGE J., AND EDGAR, MARY. "Equivalence of

IQ's for Four Group Intelligence Tests." *Personnel & Guid J* 36:623–6 My '58. *

WALTER N. DUROST, *Director of Educational Services, Pinellas County Public Schools, Clearwater, Florida.*

Evidence concerning the validity of the *Kuhlmann-Finch Tests* is very meager. Briefly stated, the argument is that low intercorrelations among subtests coupled with a gain in score with increase in age constitute sufficient evidence of validity for a test of intelligence. True, if a test does not show gains in score through the age range where growth is obviously to be expected, then it cannot be a measure of mental ability. However, the reverse is not necessarily true. That the given test measures intelligence and not some other growth parameter rests solely on the face validity of the test, not increase in score with age.

In the manual for the *Kuhlmann-Finch Tests* much is made of the fact that this test is true to the tradition established by the work of Kuhlmann, who died in 1941. In the years since Kuhlmann was making his important and noteworthy contributions to mental measurement, it has become increasingly evident that measures of intelligence must demonstrate validity for something and not validity in general. For the most part, such tests are used to predict school learning capacity. This capacity measure is desirable in order that such things as the following may be accomplished: (*a*) the identification of slow learning and talented children for whom curriculum modification is needed; (*b*) the detection of children with mental potential not being realized in their school output; and (*c*) the determination of a community's capacity to reach or exceed national achievement test norms. In fairness to these tests, it must be said that few extant intelligence tests provide more convincing and definitive evidence of their usefulness along the lines indicated.

There is much that is left to be inferred from the information given in the manual concerning scaling procedures. The use of the deviation IQ is a positive step forward and one which the earlier *Kuhlmann-Anderson Intelligence Tests,* still widely used, would do well to emulate.

Insufficient evidence is presented to permit evaluation of the standardization of the test. Apparently the normative group was a stratified sample, but the bases for stratification seem to be the opinions of "such agencies as those operating statewide testing programs." No information is given as to conditions of participation in the standardization program.

Reliability information is reasonably adequate and the authors are to be commended for giving reliability information for separate single-year ranges. However, the reliability population was "a systematically drawn unused subsample of that [national standardization] group." This means that a substantial increase in heterogeneity must surely have arisen because the cases came from many different communities widely distributed geographically.

While using the median of subtest scores as the test average is an admirable technique devised many, many years ago, it works best for hand scored tests. Because of the need to get subtest scores for each of the five tests included, the test is very time-consuming to score by machine.

This is the worst looking test published by a major test publisher which the reviewer has ever seen. The art work is poor, and the printing off color, blurred, and oftentimes almost illegible. The IBM answer sheet enclosed with the material sent for review is a locally printed sheet which could not conceivably score accurately in an IBM test scoring machine. The use of a separate booklet for each grade is good for the first two or three grades, but is a waste of time and effort beyond grade 3.

The intent in publishing these tests, obviously, was to compete with or replace the good but ancient Kuhlmann-Anderson. There have been improvements by way of simplification of administration and the adoption of a more modern method of obtaining an index of brightness, but these gains are offset by obvious shortcomings in other areas.

HENRY E. GARRETT, *Professor Emeritus of Psychology, Columbia University, New York, New York.*

This is a battery of eight test booklets planned to cover the range of intelligence from grade 1 through high school. Each booklet contains five subtests. The first two booklets, intended for the first two grades, contain only nonverbal material—pictures and diagrams; the third booklet has one verbal test and four nonverbal tests; and the other five booklets have three of the five subtests in verbal form. The format of the tests follows that of the Kuhlmann-Anderson tests. Pictures and diagrams are well

drawn, and the material is interesting and clear. The tests are timed, but are essentially power tests.

Validity is said to be a matter of test rationale and to depend upon certain principles in the selection and placement of test items. Most of these procedures are well known: increase in percentage passing with age, low inter r's and high criterion r's, homogeneity of test material over the age range, freedom of test items from specific training, objectivity in directions and scoring, and power rather than speed. For the K-F tests the main criterion appears to have been regular increase in per cent passing with age. When tests are well chosen and have been studied experimentally and item analyzed, as these have, this criterion is probably sufficient.

The K-F tests are well standardized. The original standardization sample consisted of approximately 10,000 children. In this and subsequent testing, the range of difficulty in each test was found to be suitable and the discriminative power of the items high. Boys and girls did about equally well on the tests. In one group of 197 13-year-olds, the correlations of test scores with an index of cultural status ranged from .19 to .27 for various types of test material. This is taken as evidence that the tests are not simply the products of culture. No correlations with criteria are given, as the author believes the tests to be validated sufficiently through their method of construction.

Evidence for reliability is found in the fact that the tests do not show increases in score under unlimited time, and in the high split-half correlations. Within-age reliability coefficients for ages 6–17 range from .86 to .92 for samples of from 110 to 250 pupils.

Norms for the K-F tests are in terms of median MA's and IQ's. The median MA is the chronological age corresponding typically to the median of the five point scores earned on the subtests. The IQ is a deviation or standard score in a distribution with a mean of 100 and a standard deviation of 16. Percentile ranks corresponding to standard score IQ's are provided. The median MA is an acceptable index of general level when the subtests correlate highly so that an average is based upon composite measures of a common ability. The manual reports intercorrelations for Test 6 ranging from .16 to .56, with a median of about .40. A median MA from these tests is, then, acceptable only as a rough index of general ability. A weighted composite of the five subtest scores in terms of a measured general factor would have been better—at least theoretically.

The rules offered in the manual for determining the median MA and the deviation IQ are unnecessarily confusing. In the paragraph on finding the MA, for example, the X marking the median score on the sample profile is mentioned as being referred to in the paragraph "immediately above"; the reference is in the paragraph following; on the sample record chart the IQ is never actually located; and the girl in the illustration is referred to variously as Mary Joan L—and Mary J. Smith. It is interesting to note that while the Heinis growth units are mentioned in the manual, probably in deference to Kuhlmann, they are not actually used.

As a supplement to group verbal tests or the Stanford-Binet, the *Kuhlmann-Finch Tests* are undoubtedly useful over the range of elementary and high school grades. They correspond closely to the *Kuhlmann-Anderson Intelligence Tests,* and are virtually alternate forms. The tests should have greatest value as measures of general level. They are not designed to be used in differential diagnosis of scholastic strengths and weaknesses.

CHARLES O. NEIDT, *Professor of Educational Psychology and Measurements and Chairman of the Department, University of Nebraska, Lincoln, Nebraska.*

The tests consist of five types of items divided into eight sequential levels with no duplication of content. The eight levels are presented in separate test booklets. Each of the five subtests in the eight booklets contains from 20 to 24 items. Performance on the tests is expressed as "standard IQ" and as mental age. The "standard IQ" is based upon the median score on the five subtests. Age units paralleling the Heinis mental growth unit curve were used in constructing the tests.

Evidence of the validity of these tests has been assembled following Kuhlmann's rationale that intercorrelations among subtests should be neither high nor low, tests should include items which will discriminate between the levels of ability found at successive ages, and test scores should be free from cultural influence. Data supporting these contentions are presented in the manual along with differences between median standard scores of adjacent age groups.

Reliability of the tests is based upon split-half estimates, correlations between scores from the administration of adjacent booklets, and retesting after a 6-month interval. The reliability coefficients reported are relatively high for a 25-minute test. Although the subtests are timed, speed is not an important factor in performance on these tests.

The standard deviation of the IQ's yielded by the tests is 16. Since most derived IQ's have a standard deviation of 15, some variation in interpretation of results will be necessary for test users who have become accustomed to interpretation based upon a standard deviation of 15. Fifteen would have been a better choice than 16 for the standard deviation.

In the section of the manual entitled "Relationships to Other Tests," means and standard deviations obtained from administering the Kuhlmann-Finch and the Kuhlmann-Anderson tests to two samples are shown. Whereas these data demonstrate similarity of the two overall distributions of IQ's, they can hardly be said to demonstrate relationship. Correlation would have been a more appropriate technique for showing relationship between the two series of scores.

The directions for administering and scoring the tests are clearly stated, and the general format of the tests is good. The organization of the manual could be improved by more effective grouping of the data presented. Tables 2 and 3 in the manual appear twice. There is little question that the content of these tables contributes to understanding the tests, but repetition of the material seems unnecessary.

In summary, the *Kuhlmann-Finch Tests* are based upon extensive item analysis data and are highly usable in terms of the availability of booklets for each grade level and their ease of administration and scoring. A less favorable aspect of these tests is the paucity of standardization cases at the lower age levels.

[350]

★The Lorge-Thorndike Intelligence Tests. Grades kgn–1, 2–3, 4–6, 7–9, 10–12; 1954–57; IBM for grades 4–12; Forms A, B ('54); 5 levels; Levels 3–5: 2 tests (nonverbal, verbal), 2 editions (consumable, reusable) of each test; manual ('57) for each level; technical manual ('57); Levels 1–2: $3 per 35 tests; Levels 3–5: $2.40 per 35 tests, separate answer sheets must be used with re-usable edition, $1.20 per 35 IBM answer sheets, 21¢ per hand scoring stencil; 12¢ per technical manual; 60¢ per specimen set of any one level; postage extra; Spanish directions available for nonverbal batteries; Irving Lorge and Robert L. Thorndike; Houghton Mifflin Co. *

a) LEVEL 1, NONVERBAL BATTERY. Grades kgn–1; (35) minutes in 2 or 3 sessions.
b) LEVEL 2, NONVERBAL BATTERY. Grades 2–3; (35) minutes.
c) LEVEL 3. Grades 4–6; IBM.
   1) *Verbal Battery.* 34(44–49) minutes.
   2) *Nonverbal Battery.* 27(37–42) minutes.
d) LEVEL 4. Grades 7–9; IBM.
   1) *Verbal Battery.* 34(44–49) minutes.
   2) *Nonverbal Battery.* 27(37–39) minutes.
e) LEVEL 5. Grades 10–12; IBM.
   1) *Verbal Battery.* 34(44–49) minutes.
   2) *Nonverbal Battery.* 27(37–39) minutes.

REFERENCES

1. ROSNER, BENJAMIN. *Community Socioeconomic Status in Mental Organization.* Doctor's thesis, Columbia University (New York, N.Y.), 1955.
2. KNIEF, LOTUS M. *An Investigation of the Cultural Bias Issue in Intelligence Testing.* Doctor's thesis, State University of Iowa (Iowa City, Iowa), 1957. (DA 17:1951)
3. NORTH, ROBERT D. "A Preliminary Report on the Reliability of the Lorge-Thorndike Intelligence Tests, Level 4, Verbal Battery, and Correlations With IQ's on the Otis Quick-Scoring Mental Ability Tests." *Ed Rec B* 69:71–2 F '57. * (PA 32:2120)
4. OWEN, JASON C. *A Study of the Prognostic Value of Certain Measures of Intelligence and Listening Comprehension With a Selected Group of Elementary Pupils.* Doctor's thesis, University of Missouri (Columbia, Mo.), 1957. (DA 19:484)
5. TRAXLER, ARTHUR E. "Some Data on the Lorge-Thorndike Intelligence Tests Among Independent School Pupils." *Ed Rec B* 69:63–9 F '57. * (PA 32:2131)
6. TRAXLER, ARTHUR E. "A Further Note on the Reliability of the Lorge-Thorndike Intelligence Tests With Independent School Pupils." *Ed Rec B* 71:57–8 F '58. *

FRANK S. FREEMAN, *Professor of Psychology, Cornell University, Ithaca, New York.*

This 1957 version of the *Lorge-Thorndike Intelligence Tests* is among the best group tests available, from the point of view of the psychological constructs upon which it is based and that of statistical standardization.

These scales utilize test materials that are both verbal and nonverbal in character in the three highest levels, but are entirely nonverbal in the two lowest (kindergarten and grades 1–3). The authors' position, however, is that both types of materials test "abstract intelligence," defined as "ability to work with ideas and relationships among ideas." Although the authors are not concerned with presenting or insisting upon a formal definition of intelligence, they do state that the following mental processes are descriptive of intelligent behavior and are sampled by their tests: (*a*) dealing with abstract and general concepts; (*b*) interpretation and use of symbols; (*c*) dealing with relationships among concepts and symbols; (*d*) flexibility in the organization of concepts and symbols; (*e*) utilizing one's experience in new patterns; and (*f*) utilizing "power" rather than speed in working with abstract materials. (It is noteworthy that, in this description of intelligent behavior, Lorge and Thorndike have, wisely the reviewer believers, utilized the views

and theories of the late distinguished psychologists, Lewis M. Terman and C. Spearman.)

The statistical methods and analyses used in selecting individual items and in developing the scales as a whole are thoroughly presented in the manual. To begin with, each item was correlated (biserial or a value estimated from Flanagan's table) with scores on the subtest of which it is a part. For all the items finally retained, the median correlations range from .43 to .70, most of them (46 of 58 coefficients) being between .43 and .59. Although these coefficients are far from unity, they are high enough to warrant the conclusion that a sufficient number of items, thus positively correlated, will provide a satisfactory sampling of the psychological operations common to all of them.

The standardization population consisted of 136,000 children in 44 communities in 22 states. The communities were selected on the basis of "a composite of factors which have been found to be related to the measured intelligence of children in the community." These factors were: per cent of adult illiteracy, number of professional workers per thousand in the population, per cent of home ownership, and median home rental value. By these means, it was possible to obtain an appropriate stratified sample of American communities which were rated socio-economically as very high, high, average, low, and very low. With few exceptions, all pupils from the kindergarten through high school were tested in each community.

The composite distribution of scores from this large and representative sample population was used for the determination of IQ equivalents for each age group in terms of the familiar and widely used deviation IQ. The authors followed the now widely accepted practice of assuming a mean IQ of 100 and a standard deviation of 16 IQ points. Unlike some other current scales, the steps used in arriving at the deviation IQ's for each age group are fully presented in the manual for these tests.

Having obtained data from communities of varied and specified socio-economic levels, Lorge and Thorndike are able to present a valuable table of median IQ's for each age group within each of these five levels. Separate medians are given for the verbal and for the nonverbal scales. The value of this table would be enhanced if an index of dispersion were also given for each age and type of community.

Even so, however, these data are valuable not only in showing community differences but also in revealing the fact that both the verbal and the nonverbal IQ's exhibit the same general pattern in relation to community levels. That is, almost without exception, the higher the community's socio-economic rating, the higher are the median IQ's at each of the age levels. This fact has an important bearing on the contention of some educators and psychologists that verbal tests of intelligence are "culturally unfair" to individuals in the lower socio-economic groups.

Evidence of reliability of the scales is presented in several ways. Alternate forms correlate rather well (.76 to .90) at all levels, but the verbal scales for levels 3, 4, and 5 yield the highest coefficients, namely: .90, .86, and .86. All of these coefficients are the more significant since, in each instance, they were computed on the population of a single grade. Thus they were computed in accordance with a very desirable statistical practice, one which does not yield spuriously high reliability coefficients. The odd-even reliabilities are very high (.88 to .94), with one exception (Level 2, nonverbal, $r = .59$). About this the authors say: "At this level, an *odd-even* reliability coefficient is really not meaningful, since there is a systematic alternation between geometric and pictorial items in subtests 2 and 3." In that case, it seems to the reviewer that this method should not have been used at this level, especially since inspection of the test items shows that a different and more appropriate adaptation of the split-half technique could have been devised.

Standard errors of measurement in terms of IQ points are given as an additional and highly desirable estimate of the tests' reliabilities. The data of this table are useful, showing the SE to be within a reasonable number of points, especially in the middle score range and, more particularly, in the case of the verbal scales. The value of this table of standard errors of measurement is somewhat vitiated, however, by the fact that the data are based upon "only a modest number of cases" at each of the score levels, with the actual findings "smoothed by fitting a curve by eye to the observed points." The standard errors, therefore, must for the present be accepted as tentative estimates.

The validity of an intelligence test, it is well recognized, is more difficult to evaluate and demonstrate than is its reliability. The manual of the Lorge-Thorndike scales presents only a modest number of statistics on validity, and, in addition, a better than ordinary (as far as test manuals are concerned) discussion of what the authors call "rational" validity. This, presumably, is validity which cannot be demonstrated by statistics derived from experimental or empirical findings, but which the prospective user is asked to accept on the basis of "a rational analysis of what [psychological processes and test materials] should appropriately be included" in the tests.

Under rational validity the authors include "content" validity and "construct" validity. The first of these is what used to be called disparagingly, "face" validity, that is, a rational analysis of *materials* appropriate for inclusion in a test. This analysis will determine what particular types of items shall be used. Basically, every test author must begin this way, but he must go well beyond content validity as a criterion. Such a criterion, after all, will insure only the appropriateness of what might be called the raw materials. These have to be organized and refined in order to test the mental processes to be evaluated. Furthermore, the long history of intelligence testing provides all psychologists with abundant information regarding the most useful types of test materials with which to start.

The second type of rational validity, called "construct" validity, refers to the mental *processes* utilized by the test. The question is: Do these tested processes "correspond well with the concept or construct which the test is designed to measure"? In other words, does the test measure and evaluate intelligence by means of operations that are consistent with the test authors' definition and analysis of what intelligent behavior is? The Lorge-Thorndike construct and analysis are given earlier in this review.

It is clear that the answer to the question of whether a psychological test is valid with regard to content and construct will depend upon the psychological insights of qualified and expert judgment. This is reasonable. But the ultimate, the basic, value of a test of intelligence (or of any other psychological test) is its "functional" validity. The question here is, how well does it work in situations for which it is intended? How well does it select, differentiate, and predict? The manual of the Lorge-Thorndike scales provide only very meager data in answer to these questions, namely, a correlation of .67 between these tests (given at the beginning of grade 9) and the "average achievement" of 214 pupils at the end of the grade. In itself, this correlation is highly satisfactory, but more studies of "predictive" validity are needed throughout the grade ranges of the scales.

Another answer to the foregoing questions is found in what the authors call "concurrent" validity, that is, "correlation of test scores with other types of measures obtained before or at the same time that the test is given." As evidence of this type of validity, one study is cited: the correlation between Lorge-Thorndike IQ's and Stanford grade-equivalents in reading was .87, while that between IQ and average grade equivalents in arithmetic was .76 for 171 sixth grade pupils. These are encouraging findings; more such data are needed covering the entire grade range.

There are still other data on validity—correlations with other tests ("congruent" validity) and intercorrelations of subtests, though the latter data are not cited under the caption validity. Lorge-Thorndike test scores were correlated with those of four other group tests, as well as with the Stanford-Binet and the WISC. With few exceptions, the coefficients were .60 or higher (46 coefficients out of 52). Thus, all of the tests used will yield rankings that correspond reasonably well. With one exception correlations with the Stanford-Binet and the WISC were quite high (.63, .54, .71, .77). These are especially noteworthy because two of the coefficients (.63 and .54) were based on first grade children only while the other two were found with children in grades 7–9. In each instance, however, the number of cases was very small. The reviewer believes that in all studies of congruent validity too much emphasis is placed upon correlation coefficients and too little (almost none) upon the distribution, mean, and standard deviation of differences in ratings (MA's and IQ's) obtained with the tests employed. Reports on congruent validity would be much more meaningful and significant if this deficiency were corrected.

Intercorrelations among subtests of a scale should be given as evidence of its validity, perhaps, indirectly, of its construct validity; for unless the correlation coefficients support the concept or concepts upon which the test is presumably constructed, it cannot be said that the test exhibits construct validity, although

the correlations in themselves do not necessarily demonstrate such validity. In the case of the Lorge-Thorndike scales, construct validity requires that the subtest intercorrelations be quite marked. Intercorrelations among the subtests range from .30 (number series with vocabulary) to .70 (sentence completion with vocabulary). Eight (of 21) intercorrelations are .50 or higher; five are in the .40's; six in the .30's; and two in the .20's. It appears, therefore, that we may infer that the extent of mental processes common to the subtests is appreciable in most instances, moderate in a few, and very limited in at least two. However, when the verbal and nonverbal batteries are taken as a whole and these two major divisions are correlated (each correlation being restricted to a single grade), the coefficients are much more convincing, ranging from .54 to .70, all but two being in the .60's.

On the whole, the Lorge-Thorndike series is among the sounder group instruments available, from the point of view of psychological insights (with regard to both content and concepts of intelligence) shown in selecting and developing the materials, and from the point of view of statistical analysis of the standardization data. The major deficiency, so far as available data are concerned, is the lack of adequate data on predictive and concurrent validity.

JOHN E. MILHOLLAND, *Associate Professor of Psychology, and Chief, Evaluation and Examinations Division, Bureau of Psychological Services, University of Michigan, Ann Arbor, Michigan.*

This test is admirable for the clarity with which its objective is stated and for the restraint exercised in the claims made for what it will do. It is frankly labeled an intelligence test, and we are told that it is a test of abstract intelligence, defined as "the ability to work with ideas and the relationships among ideas." There is, of course, no precise objective criterion for this definition, so one is forced to rely upon indirect evidence, inspection of the items, and the professional reputations of the authors for the assessment of this kind of validity. All three lines of evidence are confirmatory.

The suggestions made in the manual for the use of the results are reasonable and practical and do not rely upon exorbitant claims for what the test is measuring. The authors recommend administering both the verbal and nonverbal batteries in grades for which both are available, and state that "the functions are sufficiently similar so that, for most pupils, it will be appropriate to average the I.Q.'s from the two batteries to yield a single more comprehensive and more reliable estimate of intellectual ability. However, in about 25 per cent of cases, the two forms will yield I.Q.'s differing by as much as 15 points. In these cases, the difference may have practical significance in relation to a pupil's reading level, school achievement, or vocational planning."

With the possible exceptions of Word Knowledge and Arithmetic Reasoning, the subtest titles simply describe the types of items they contain. This should certainly reduce any temptation to try to interpret subtest scores, and, in keeping with this point of view, the authors present no subtest norms. It is gratifying to see that they do not expect to provide more than one usable score in 27 to 35 minutes of working time.

The standardization sample included more than 136,000 children in 44 communities in 22 states. Since participation by a community was on a volunteer basis, some bias may remain in the norms. Reliabilities are estimated by alternate forms correlations within single grades. This procedure tends to produce estimates which are lower than split-half estimates because of daily fluctuations in pupil performance and because any degree of speededness in the test inflates split-half estimates. The alternate forms reliabilities for the various levels and batteries range from .76 to .85. For comparison, split-half (odd-even) reliabilities of the tests are also given. With two exceptions the estimates are all above .90. One exception is .59 for a test in which there was systematic alternation of item types. One wonders why in this case items were not taken in units of two.

The examiner's manuals seem to be especially well adapted for use by classroom teachers. They contain directions for administration, suggestions for using the test, and tables of norms. The two paragraphs explaining the use of the standard error of measurement should probably be expanded. As they stand, these paragraphs might be more confusing than helpful to a great many teachers.

The details of construction, standardization, and validation of the tests are contained in the technical manual. Much of this information should be at hand in any testing program, and

the reviewer hopes that at least one technical manual accompanies every test order filled by the publishers. Parts of it are excellent, and some information given (on item-test correlations and mean IQ's by socio-economic levels, for example) is frequently not found in test manuals. Despite these strengths, the technical manual leaves much to be desired. Some of the data seem to have been hastily or ill-advisedly collected and inadequately analyzed. The odd-even reliabilties, which are presumably given for comparison with the alternate-forms reliabilities which the authors advocate, are based on samples different from the ones on which the alternate-forms reliabilities were computed. There are some correlations reported with Stanford-Binet scores which are based on 20 cases (with extremely restricted range) and 34 cases, and one with WISC based on 39 cases. In the factor analysis reported, the reliabilities were used as communality estimates, yet the obtained communalities for three of the seven tests differed from the reliabilities by .12. These discrepancies may not have materially altered the factor loadings, but certainly iteration would have made the analysis neater. Also in connection with the factor analysis, a report of the multiple r between the verbal and nonverbal factors and the appropriate subtests would have provided useful evidence bearing on validity.

The formula on page 9, incidentally, is for the complement of the reliability, not the reliability.

The Lorge-Thorndike tests should be accorded a place among the best of our group intelligence tests. They are well designed, easily administered and scored, and, what is especially noteworthy, the uses recommended for them are reasonable and defensible.

D. A. PIDGEON, *Senior Officer, Test Services, National Foundation for Educational Research in England and Wales, London, England.*

The authors of this series of tests have attempted the commendable task of providing, for a wide age range, measures of "abstract intelligence" defined as "the ability to work with ideas and the relationships among ideas." To say that they have produced a number of excellent tests does not mean that they have necessarily succeeded in their task. Nevertheless, one may be impressed by the way the tests have been presented in a compact series arranged to suit the most fastidious of test users.

Apart from the examiner's manual supplied for each test level, a technical manual is provided giving detailed information on such points as item selection, norming, reliability, and validity. It is difficult to find fault with the construction of the tests, and, clearly, considerable care was taken to norm them on a sample that fully represented the complete United States population of children falling within the tests' age range. The norms are presented in a variety of ways—as grade percentiles, grade equivalents, age equivalents, and IQ equivalents, the last named assuming a population mean of 100 and a standard deviation of 16. Since the "IQ's" are not derived from any consideration of mental age, it seems a pity that the term "intelligence quotient" has been retained even if qualified by the word "equivalent." It also seems a pity that some agreement, preferably international, could not be made to standardise the value adopted for the standard deviation. English test users, for example, are now becoming familiar with normalised scores having a mean of 100 and an SD of 15.

Standard errors of measurement calculated from the differences between scores on Forms A and B show, as might be expected, that somewhat greater precision is obtained at intermediate score levels, hence it is recommended that users retest with a lower or higher level test if the scores obtained fall below or above stated values. Alternate-forms reliability coefficients range from about .79 for the tests of Levels 1 and 2, which use pictorial material, to about .87 for the verbal tests of Levels 3, 4, and 5. These values can be regarded as satisfactory, if rather on the low side.

No test, however reliably constructed and normed, is of value unless it can also be shown to serve adequately the purpose for which it is intended. The technical manual devotes nearly four pages to the question of validity and yet gives little direct evidence that is specifically related to the uses suggested for the tests, namely, "Formation of Class Groups," "Grouping within Class," "Setting Standards of Expectancy for the Individual Pupil," "Educational Guidance," and "Vocational Guidance." One of the reasons for this may be the confusion existing about what the tests are really measuring. Although, in the section on construct validity, the authors imply that they have taken an operational approach to the definition of "intelligence" and although, in discussing the selection of items, they state that their tests "have been designed to measure reasoning ability," in discussing the uses of the tests they use the words "intelligence," "scholastic aptitude," and "general mental ability" indiscriminately to imply some mental function that controls or limits the scholastic performance of pupils.

Certainly, for separating children into relatively homogeneous ability groups, a single test which correlates highly with most attainments is of positive value; correlations with reading and average arithmetic grade equivalents (.87 and .76, respectively) derived from the *Stanford Achievement Test*, indicate that the Lorge-Thorndike tests will adequately serve this purpose. But, for "setting standards of expectancy," tests are needed which will predict future scholastic performance. Only one study is cited, based on 214 cases and giving a correlation of .67 between Lorge-Thorndike (Level 4) given at the beginning of the ninth grade and average achievement at the end of the ninth grade. The manual does not state whether actual achievement at the beginning of the grade predicts end-of-year achievement any better or worse than this.

The test user is also encouraged to use the nonverbal battery with the retarded reader, since, it is argued, this procedure will enable an estimate to be obtained of mental ability which is "uninfluenced by specific disability in reading." However, no evidence is supplied to support this statement, and, since factorial studies have clearly demonstrated that nonverbal tests measure specific or group factors of their own besides "g," one may well doubt their value for predicting ability to read, or indeed for predicting any scholastic performance. Again, it is stated elsewhere that the difference between performance on the verbal and nonverbal batteries "may be useful in revealing significant facts about reading achievement, school progress, or vocational prospects." However, the manuals do not state what these facts are, nor is any evidence supplied to enable the test user to make his own judgment.

It should be made clear that, in this reviewer's opinion, this is an excellent series of tests, well designed and constructed, admirably printed and presented, and equipped with highly satisfactory norms. It can also be said that the tests provide reliable measures of verbal reasoning and nonverbal reasoning. In their use, however, extreme caution should be taken to see that the scores are only interpreted in this way and that no assumptions are made about their measuring mental capacity. It is to be hoped that the authors will subsequently provide evidence more directly relevant to the uses they suggest for the tests, especially uses relating to the prediction of achievement.

[351]

★Manchester General Ability Test (Senior) 1. Ages 13–15; 1952; 1 form ['52]; practice test ['52]; no data on validity; 10s. 6d. per 25 tests; 7d. per single copy; 2s. per 25 practice tests; 1d. per single copy; 9d. per manual ['52]; postage extra; 45(60) minutes; Stephen Wiseman; University of London Press Ltd. *

A. E. G. PILLINER, Lecturer in Education, University of Edinburgh, Edinburgh, Scotland.

The constructors of the Manchester General Ability Test have paid Moray House tests the compliment of rather closely following their layout, both in test and manual. Since MGAT is designed for use in English secondary schools, this similarity is an advantage to those testees and testers to whom the pattern of tests like the Moray House tests is familiar.

The MGAT covers the ages of 14 and 15, thus spanning a gap in the existing range of tests in current use in England. According to the manual, it is "more appropriately to be used in the secondary grammar school and the upper ability levels of the secondary modern school" since it provides "a measure of ability in the verbal and academic field." We are not told, however, what specific purpose it is intended to serve in measuring this ability, that is, to what use the quotients obtained with it are to be put in the schools.

The constructors are to be congratulated on the instructions for administration, which are admirably lucid. Those for markers, while equally clear and designed to minimise scoring errors, are possibly a little too rigid. Many of the test items are answered by inserting a number in brackets at the end of the item line. Since in most of the other tests currently used in Great Britain the correct response is underlined, it may happen that some children, accustomed to the latter method of answering, will inadvertently use it here also. If they do so, they cannot receive credit since the instructions state quite specifically: "No credit should be allowed for answers other than those appearing here." This is not only unduly "tough" but

conceivably may reduce the reliability and validity of the test also.

Standardisation is based on the performance of an approximately complete English county authority age group of 4,175 children. British custom is followed in arranging the conversion table to give standardised scores ("quotients") with a mean of 100 and a standard deviation of 15. Users of the test are rightly warned that quotients so obtained are not strictly comparable with Binet-type quotients, but wrongly informed that the quotients from this test are comparable with those derived from other group tests of intelligence having the same standard deviation. With the same test, the mean quotients of complete year groups of children, each from a different English authority, range from 94 to 106 approximately. Age allowance varies also among authorities. Only if the different tests have been standardised on the same year group of children does one achieve strict comparability of quotients.

A study of the conversion table reveals that at the median age for the standardisation group the raw scores at the 15th, 50th, and 84th percentiles are approximately 10, 23, and 40, respectively. These figures suggest that the test is too difficult. While "headroom" is always desirable, there is probably too much here. The highest raw score against which an entry occurs in the unextrapolated portion of the table is 81. We are not told the raw score standard deviation (a defect which should be corrected) but the figures suggest that it is not high, so that discrimination will be adversely affected in some parts at least of the raw score range. On the other hand, there is a raw score range of 20 between the 84th and 97.5th percentiles, so that in this region discrimination will be good. Nevertheless, it would seem that the all-round measuring quality of the test would be improved by easing it by some 12–15 raw score points.

Internal consistency coefficients of .95 ("boosted" split-half) and .93 (Kuder-Richardson) are quoted. These are low for a test of this kind, and appear to confirm the view that the test is too difficult. Unfortunately, no test-retest reliability coefficients are reported.

One purpose of the short preliminary test provided is to give the children practice "in doing particular types of questions which might be unfamiliar to them." This purpose is scarcely achieved since (a) the mode of presentation of some of the item types in the practice test differs from that of the corresponding item types in the test proper, and (b) one item in the practice test has no counterpart in the test proper. The main virtue of the preliminary test, its effect as a "shock absorber," remains, but its items should be recast.

Approximately two thirds of the 100 items in the test proper, for which the time allowed is an uninterrupted 45 minutes, are conventional in type. Same and opposites, straight analogies, series, insertion of missing figures in multiplication sums, and classifications are all included. In addition, there are some items based on rectangular tables which, while differing in detail, are generally similar in that the child must grasp the whole problem presented by each table in order to answer the items based on it. The construction of these tables and items shows considerable ingenuity. A set of anagrams which the child has to solve with the help of a brief description (GERNE is a colour) is included.

In constructing tests for children younger than those for whom this test is intended, it is usual to follow the principle of grading the blocks of items and the items within the blocks from easy to difficult. While the item order is decided in most cases by some such statistical measure of difficulty as proportion passing, the experienced test constructor usually has a fairly good a priori notion of what the outcome of the statistical evidence will be. It is arguable that it is less important, with tests for older testees, to adhere to this principle, though this reviewer would maintain that it is a sound rule in general. An a priori impression derived in the absence of statistical evidence is that some of the early items in the test proper are more difficult than some of the later items. For instance, Items 1–8, in which the testee has to discover either a synonym or an antonym of a given word, appear to be among the most difficult items in the test, making considerable demands on vocabulary. A child weak in this respect might suffer discouragement which could affect adversely his performance on the remainder of the test.

Synonym-antonym items, intended to trap the unwary testee, succeed only too frequently in enmeshing the unvigilant test constructor. The flexibility of the English language is such that, given the right contexts, many words can mean "nearly the same as" or "nearly the opposite of" a given word. With items designed

for more mature or high ability testees the danger of this kind of ambiguity is increased. Testees with the highest awareness of the possibilities suffer most. It is not enough to attempt to resolve ambiguities by the greater frequency of choice of one particular alternative. If a single testee can see a response legitimately alternative to that popularly chosen, the item needs modifying. These reflections are prompted by the fact that with the possible exception of one item, the writers of the synonym-antonym items in MGAT appear to have avoided the trap successfully. The exception is Item 1, in which the given word is PERMIT and among the alternative responses appear the words ALLOW and DENY. The synonym is certainly valid, and will be most frequently chosen, but may there not be a small minority of testees who, while seeing the synonym ALLOW, will also see DENY as a possible antonym? "To deny entry" is certainly the opposite of "to permit entry."

There is a minor defect in the preamble to Items 9–15. It begins, "In the table below, some numbers appear once only, some twice...." In the table only one number appears once only. This inaccuracy may confuse some testees.

Items 16–22, based on a rectangular table which must be completed from given clues, seem admirable if one admits the principle that the trick of completing the table must be mastered before any of the items can be answered successfully. An item analysis might well indicate a tendency towards an "all or none" response to this set. The wording of Item 20, which reads, "How much less did Peter earn?" is defective in that it relates back to the previous item, "What were Stanley's earnings for the week?" which is disconcerting.

The letter series, Items 37–48, presents no unusual features with the exception of Item 45: A, C, F, J, O, ( ) ( ). In order to complete this successfully, one must start again at the beginning of the alphabet, a situation which is not covered by the instructions.

In the instructions for the final set of items the testee is told first that "in each of the following questions there are three items which are alike in some way," and next that he must "find out which are the three which go together." This is unfortunate, since "alike" and "go together" do not necessarily mean the same, and the double-barreled attempt to clarify the instructions may have the opposite effect. A cup, a plate, and a saucer are alike in that all three are made of porcelain, or that all three are containers. On the other hand a cup, a saucer, and a spoon are also alike in that they go together to constitute the set of utensils customarily employed in drinking tea. (All four objects are named in Item 92.)

It was stated earlier that the test includes a set (eight items) of anagrams. These appear to be open to criticism on two grounds, one particular and minor, the other general and major. The first relates to a discrepancy between the layout of the instructional example: "GERNE is a colour. Answer (GREEN)"; and that of the test items: MERMAN is a tool. Write it correctly here (   ). Why not repeat in the test items the layout in the example, thus avoiding the questionable "it"? More seriously, is the inclusion of items of this type desirable? What aspect of general ability do they test? Is not the "seeing" which leads to their rapid solution rather a specialized ability? It is clear from the special instructions preceding these items ("Do not spend too much time on these questions") that the test constructors are aware that these items are time consuming for these testees who do not "see" the solution rather quickly. How will such testees interpret the warning?

There are few tests which are beyond criticism, and, apart from the last one most of the criticisms made here are of a minor nature and can be taken into account in later editions. The general impression of this reviewer is that the test, as a whole, is good. Most of its material has a priori validity, the instructions in general are clear and concise, and, above all, working through it is more enjoyable than is the case with too many objective tests. If its a priori validity is confirmed by follow-up studies, this test is recommended to those requiring estimates of the general ability of testees of the age range it is designed to cover.

[352]

Miller Analogies Test. Candidates for graduate school; 1926-52; Forms G ('47), H ('50), J ('52); Form H is also published under the title *Advanced Personnel Test* for use in business; revised manual ('52); supplement to manual ('56); distribution restricted and test administered at specified licensed testing centers; details may be obtained from publisher; 50(55) minutes; W. S. Miller; Psychological Corporation. *

REFERENCES

1-16. See 4:304.
17. CURETON, EDWARD E.; CURETON, LOUISE W.; AND BISHOP, RUTH. "Prediction of Success in Graduate Study of Psychology

at the University of Tennessee." Letter. *Am Psychol* 4:361-2 Ag '49. *
18. STAFFORD, JOHN W. "The Prediction of Success in Graduate School." Abstract. *Am Psychol* 6:298 Jl '51. *
19. STREIT, L. ROBERT. *A Comparison of Miller Analogies Test Scores With Undergraduate and Graduate Grade-Point Averages of Graduate Students.* Master's thesis, Southern Methodist University (Dallas, Tex.), 1951.
20. BERDIE, RALPH F., AND LAYTON, WILBUR L. "Predicting Success in Law School." *J Appl Psychol* 36:257-60 Ag '52. * (PA 27:3839)
21. COCKRUM, LOGAN V. "Predicting Success in Training for the Ministry." *Relig Ed* 47:198-202 My-Je '52. *
22. STROWIG, RONALD W. *Predictive Values of the Miller Analogies Test for Master's Degree Students in Education.* Doctor's thesis, Stanford University (Stanford, Calif.), 1952.
23. FAHEY, GEORGE L. "Discriminatory Capacity of the University of Pittsburgh Examination Among Graduate Students in Psychology." *Am Psychol* 8:204-6 My '53. *
24. JENSON, RALPH E. "Predicting Scholastic Achievement of First-Year Graduate Students." *Ed & Psychol Meas* 13:322-9 su '53. * (PA 28:4833)
25. TRONCA, WILLIAM F. *A Study of the Validity and Reliability of Forms H and J of the Miller Analogies Test.* Master's thesis, Fordham University (New York, N.Y.), 1953.
26. WATTERS, G. V., AND PATERSON, D. G. "Miller Analogies Test Scores and Ratings of PhD's in Psychology." *Am Psychol* 8:89-90 F '53. * (PA 28:227)
27. DURNALL, EDWARD J., JR. "Predicting Scholastic Success for Graduate Students in Education." *Sch & Soc* 80:107 O 2 '54. * (PA 30:3456)
28. GLASER, ROBERT, AND JACOBS, OWEN. "Predicting Achievement in Medical School: A Comparison of Preclinical and Clinical Criteria." *J Appl Psychol* 38:245-7 Ag '54. * (PA 29:6271)
29. BUCKTON, LAVERNE, AND DOPPELT, JEROME E. "Freshman Tests as Predictors of Scores on Graduate and Professional School Examinations." *J Counsel Psychol* 2:146-9 su '55. * (PA 30:3453)
30. HOUNTRAS, P. T. *Factors Associated With the Academic Achievement of Foreign Graduate Students at the University of Michigan.* Doctor's thesis, University of Michigan (Ann Arbor, Mich.), 1955.
31. MEER, BERNARD, AND STEIN, MORRIS I. "Measures of Intelligence and Creativity." *J Psychol* 39:117-26 Ja '55. * (PA 29:9102)
32. MEER, BERNARD; STEIN, MORRIS I.; AND GEERTSMA, ROBERT. "An Analysis of the Miller Analogies Test for a Scientific Population." *Am Psychol* 10:33-4 Ja '55. * (PA 30:3658)
33. WARD, JOE H., JR. "Use of Electronic Computers in Psychological Research." Letter. *Am Psychol* 10:826-7 D '55. *
34. ARMSTRONG, HUBERT C. "The Prediction of Success in Graduate School Based on Undergraduate Records and the Miller Analogies Test." Abstract. *Calif J Ed Res* 7:129 My '56. *
35. HOUNTRAS, PETER T. "The Use of the Miller Analogies Test in Predicting Graduate Student Achievement." *Col & Univ* 32:65-70 fall '56. *
36. BRAMS, JEROME MARTIN. *The Relationship Between Personal Characteristics of Counseling Trainees and Effective Communication in Counseling.* Doctor's thesis, University of Missouri (Columbia, Mo.), 1957. (DA 17:1510)
37. HYMAN, SIDNEY R. "The Miller Analogies Test and University of Pittsburgh PhD's in Psychology." *Am Psychol* 12:35-6 Ja '57. * (PA 32:947)
38. SMITH, L. M. "Correlates of the Miller Analogies Test." *Sch & Soc* 85:286-7 O '57. *
39. DUNNETTE, MARVIN D., AND KIRCHNER, WAYNE K. "Validation of Psychological Tests in Industry." *Personnel Adm* 21:20-7 My-Je '58. *
40. FELDMAN, MARVIN J. "A Comparison of Miller Analogy Test Scores." *J Counsel Psychol* 5:149-50 su '58. *
41. PETERSON, TED T. *Selecting School Administrators: An Evaluation of Six Tests.* Doctor's thesis, Stanford University (Stanford, Calif.), 1958. (DA 19:262)
42. PEPINSKY, HAROLD N. "A Comparison of Miller Analogy Test Scores." *J Consult Psychol* 5:149-50 su '58. *
43. ROBINSON, DONALD W. "A Comparison of Two Batteries of Tests as Predictors of First Year Achievement in the Graduate School of Bradley University." *Yearb Nat Council Meas Used Ed* 15:118-27 '58. *
44. VOTAW, DAVID F. "Validity of Estimates of Success in Graduate School Based on Miller Analogies Test Scores." *Yearb Nat Council Meas Used Ed* 15:150-6 '58. *

JOHN T. DAILEY, *Program Director, American Institute for Research, Washington, D.C.*

The *Miller Analogies Test* is designed to measure scholastic aptitude at the graduate level. One of the earliest tests of its kind, it has in its several forms enjoyed steadily increasing use over a period of more than thirty years.

Considerable statistical data are furnished in the manual regarding the test. Alternate form reliabilities range between .85 and .89 for sizable samples of senior and graduate students; odd-even reliabilities, of course, run higher. The correlations between the test and the subject matter tests among the Graduate Record Examinations are for the most part between .75 and .80. The test also correlates in the low .80's with the Verbal factor in the Graduate Record Examinations.

It might, therefore, be concluded that the test has nothing to offer over and above a good vocabulary test; and yet, close examination of the test and analysis of available validity data seem to contraindicate this. The test itself is pitched at such a high difficulty level that it probably has more ceiling than any other test of its kind. For a highly selected group, such as graduate students, this could have a very positive effect in maximizing reliability and validity. The high ceiling on the test is a compounding of highly abstruse subject matter plus often very complex analogies. It is not likely that either a straight subject matter or a straight vocabulary test could have as much discrimination at extremely high levels. Some penalty is, however, paid for these advantages. Psychologically and educationally the test is extremely loosely structured and is a hodgepodge of subject matter from practically all fields, making it a very difficult test to interpret psychologically or educationally.

The manual reports the results of several validity studies. As is usual for tests of this sort, fairly high validity coefficients are found against measures of scholastic achievement. Relatively little data are available regarding the validity of this test as compared with other good predictive tests; however, some studies indicate that the test may offer validity over and above that offered by a combination of other commonly used tests, by course grades, or by other criteria. As always happens with tests of this type, the validity becomes progressively lower as one departs farther and farther from course grades as criteria.

The manual gives normative data for several groups of students in various subject matter fields. Of special interest is a 1956 supplement to the manual which reports several studies involving graduate students in education. Here, various institutions show tremendous variation in score distribution, and all show markedly lower scores for education students than those reported in the manual for students in other areas of graduate study. Of all groups for whom norms are provided, the psychologists score highest. This may be a function of greater operational use of the test in selection of the students in the normative group. It could also be influenced by the balance of subject matter in the test.

This test is undoubtedly subjected to the tightest security control for any test of its kind. The manual states that the test should not be used in mass testing situations and should be given only in small groups with highly trained proctors; the same manual, however, points out that the test is practically self-administering. Close examination of the test and the available statistics indicate that the test should be about as self-administering as anything in its field. The extreme emphasis on security should be a minus factor in the value of the test for most consumers.

The *Miller Analogies Test* is a well constructed test of general academic scholarship potential with a difficulty pitched at a high graduate student level. Its high difficulty level, together with its loading with highly abstruse subject matter, probably allows for greater validity than is likely for other criteria of academic graduate scholarship. However, the nature of this contribution has not been adequately explored and the excessive security of the test make its exploration more difficult.

[353]
*Moray House Intelligence Tests. Ages 8.5–10.5, 10–12, 12–14, 13.5–17.5; 1930–58; 4 levels; distribution restricted to education authorities; 2s. 9d. per 25 practice tests for *b* or *c*; postage extra; Department of Education, University of Edinburgh; University of London Press. *

a) MORAY HOUSE JUNIOR REASONING TEST 2 FOR NINE-YEAR-OLDS. Ages 8.5–10.5; 1947–58; former tests in series called *Moray House Junior Intelligence Tests;* 1 form ['58]; 13s. per 25 tests; 8d. per single copy; 1s. 6d. per manual ['58]; 45(104) minutes in 2 sessions.

b) MORAY HOUSE VERBAL REASONING TEST 61. Ages 10–12; 1930–58; former tests in series called *Moray House Intelligence Tests;* 1 form ['58]; 9s. 6d. per 25 tests; 6d. per single copy; 1s. 6d. per manual ['58]; practice test: 10(15) minutes; test: 45(50) minutes.

c) MORAY HOUSE VERBAL REASONING TEST (ADV.) 10. Ages 12–14; 1940–56; 1 form ['56]; prices same as for *b* above; practice test: 10(15) minutes; test: 45(50) minutes.

d) MORAY HOUSE ADULT TEST 1. Ages 13.5–17.5; 1952; title on test is *Intelligence Test (Adult) 1;* 1 form ['52]; prices same as for *b* above; 45(50) minutes.

REFERENCES

1–2. See 3:241.
3. THOMSON, G. H. "The Distribution of Intelligence Among University and College Students." *Brit J Ed Psychol* 15:76–9 Je '45. * (*PA* 20:333)
4. DEMPSTER, J. J. B. "Symposium on the Effects of Coaching and Practice in Intelligence Tests: III, Southampton Investigation and Procedure." *Brit J Ed Psychol* 24:1–4 F '54. * (*PA* 28:8718)

For a review by Patrick Slater of earlier forms, see 3:241.

[354]

*New Rhode Island Intelligence Test. Ages 3–6; 1923–55; identical with *Rhode Island Intelligence Test* ('23) except for slight changes in some drawings; 1 form ('55, combination of Forms A and B of original edition); no manual; directions for administering ('55); tentative norms; $2.15 per 25 tests; 25¢ per specimen set; postpaid; [30] minutes in 2 sessions; original test by G. E. Bird and Clara R. Craig; new edition by G. E. Bird and G. L. Betts; Public School Publishing Co. *

REFERENCES

1. TOWN, CLARA HARRISON. "A Mass Mental Test for Use With Kindergarten and First Grade Children." *J Appl Psychol* 6:89–112 Je '22. *
2. BIRD, GRACE E. "An Intelligence Test for Children From Three to Six." Abstract. *Psychol B* 20:97–8 F '23. *
3. BIRD, GRACE E. "The Rhode Island Intelligence Test." *J Ed Res* 8:397–403 D '23. *
4. POULL, LOUISE E. "Clinical Values of the Rhode Island Intelligence Test and the Town Picture Game." *J Appl Psychol* 11:68–72 F '27. *
5. SANGREN, PAUL V. "Comparative Validity of Primary Intelligence Tests." *J Appl Psychol* 13:394–412 Ag '29. * (*PA* 3:4324)
6. HUGGETT, A. J. "An Experiment in Reading Readiness." *J Ed Res* 32:263–70 D '38. *

RAYMOND C. NORRIS, *Associate Professor of Psychology, George Peabody College for Teachers, Nashville, Tennessee.*

The directions for administering the test indicate that the two parts (forms) are to be administered at separate sittings and the two MA estimates averaged before establishing the ratio IQ. The parts are apparently made as nearly parallel as possible by having directly equivalent items in the two forms. For instance, while Part 1 contains comparisons of pairs of objects calling for the identification of the bigger, faster, colder, heavier, etc., the items in Part 2 call for identification of the smaller, slower, warmer, lighter, etc. Each part consists of six subtests dealing with properties and qualities of common objects, identification of missing parts, recognition of family members, identification of common household and sports activities, identification of stereotypes, and ability to make discriminations among similar and different patterns.

All items consist of line drawings of people or objects to be marked over by the subject. While the quality of the drawings is not high and some pictures appear dated, it seems likely that any child familiar with the concepts can make a response.

Available norms are sketchy and based on a sample of unknown size and character. Local norms would have to be established before either the mental age or intelligence quotient scores could be interpreted.

[355]

★New South African Group Test. Ages 8–11, 10–14, 13–18; 1931–56; 3 scores: verbal, nonverbal, total; IBM; Forms A, B ['55]; 3 levels; mimeographed manual ['55]; mimeographed supplement ('56); separate answer sheets must be used; 43s. 2d. per 100 tests; 5s. 10d. per 100 IBM answer sheets; 7d. per scoring stencil; 1s. 6d. per manual; specimen set not available; postage extra; Afrikaans edition available; 70(75) minutes; National Bureau of Educational and Social Research under the auspices of South African Psychological Association; National Bureau of Educational and Social Research. *
a) JUNIOR. Ages 8–11.
b) INTERMEDIATE. Ages 10–14.
c) SENIOR. Ages 13–18.

[356]

*Non-Verbal Tests. Ages 8 to 11–0, 10 to 12–11, 10 to 11–11, 12 to 13–11; 4 levels; postage extra; published for National Foundation for Educational Research in England and Wales; Newnes Educational Publishing Co. Ltd. *
a) NON-VERBAL TESTS 1–2. Ages 10 to 12–11; 1947–51; title on test is *A Scale of Non-Verbal Mental Ability;* 2 forms; use of the practice exercise, *Preliminary Practice Test 1* ['50], is optional; no data on validity; distribution is restricted to directors of education; 8s. 6d. per 12 tests; 10d. per single copy; 3s. per 12 practice exercises; 4d. per single copy; 2s. 9d. per manual; practice exercise: 10(15) minutes; test: 30(35) minutes.
 1) *Non-Verbal Test 1.* 1947–51; test ['49]; revised manual ['51]; provisional norms ['51] for administration with practice exercise for ages 10–2 to 11–1 only; Welsh ['54], Arabic ['48], and Hindi ['57] editions available; J. W. Jenkins.
 2) *Non-Verbal Test 2.* 1948–51; test ['49]; revised manual ['51]; provisional norms for administration with practice exercise for ages 10–3 to 11–2 only; English-Welsh and Welsh-English editions ['58] available; D. M. Lee and J. W. Jenkins.
b) NON-VERBAL TEST 3. Ages 10 to 11–11; 1953–58; 1 form ['53]; separate answer sheets must be used; 16s. 6d. per 12 tests; 1s. 6d. per single copy; 1s. 6d. per 12 answer sheets; 1s. per revised manual ['58]; 50(60) minutes; I. Macfarlane Smith (manual), B. Calvert (test).
c) NON-VERBAL TEST 4. Ages 12 to 13–11; 1951; 1 form ['51]; no data on reliability and validity; 7s. 6d. per 12 tests; 8d. per single copy; 1s. per manual ['51]; 40(50) minutes.
d) NON-VERBAL TEST 5. Ages 8 to 11–0; 1953–57; 1 form ['53]; revised manual ('57); 10s. 6d. per 12 tests; 1s. per single copy; 1s. per manual; Hindi edition (no date) available; 20(40) minutes; D. A. Pidgeon.

REFERENCES

1–3. See 4:307.
4. JONES, W. R. "The Language Handicap of Welsh-Speaking Children: A Study of Their Performance in an English Verbal Intelligence Test in Relation to Their Non-Verbal Mental Ability and Their Reading Ability in English." *Brit J Ed Psychol* 22:114–23 Je '52. * (*PA* 27:2197)

CYRIL A. ROGERS, *Senior Lecturer in Psychology, University College of Rhodesia and Nyasaland, Salisbury, Southern Rhodesia.* [Review of Tests 1–3.]

These three tests have been designed to furnish a measure of nonverbal intelligence within the age range of 10–12 years. Practice exercises are included with each of the tests, and the directions for administration are outlined clearly and are easy to follow. The norms are logically arranged and simple to read.

Non-Verbal Test 1 employs five separately timed subtests embodying different principles of classification, ordered sequence, and nonverbal analogy. The norms, which straddle a range of from 10-0 to 12-11, have been standardised with a mean of 100 and a standard deviation of 15 points; they are therefore statistically, although not necessarily psychologically, the equivalent of IQ scores. There are two procedures for administering the test, the first without preliminary practice exercises and the second with practice exercises which can be administered within 15 minutes.

Apart from mentioning the size and age range of the sample, no information is given on the group which furnished norms for the first procedure. However, it is given that the provisional norms for the second procedure are based on an urban sample of 842 boys and 777 girls. The manual shows that there is a small sex difference in mean raw scores which favours the girls, but whether or not this is significant is not indicated. The test reliability, as determined by the split-half technique, was found to be .95, although the sample on which this was based is not described. Neither are there any data given to indicate validity.

A Welsh version of the test has been prepared and an inspection of the norms shows that children tested through the medium of the Welsh language obtain considerably lower scores than do English children tested in English. An Arabic version has been employed in the Sudan, but Scott's (3) findings indicate that such adaptations are of little value when compared with tests developed on the spot. No norms are available for the Arabic adaptation.

Non-Verbal Test 2 was designed as a parallel form of Test 1 although the correlation between the two is not given in the manual. Certainly the norms established for Test 2 (using practice exercises) indicate that it is either considerably more difficult than Test 1, or

else the sampling has been fundamentally different. The first explanation seems the more likely, but, in the absence of descriptive data, one cannot be sure. Sex differences in mean score are more marked on Test 2 than Test 1, but the significance of these is not explored. As with the first test, no information is given concerning the relation of the scale to other well established tests of intelligence, nor are factorial studies cited which may throw some light on its validity. The publisher's test catalogue reports a reliability coefficient of .92 established on retesting 861 children after an interval of one week. This information should be given in the test manual.

Non-Verbal Test 3, originally planned for use with Maori children, contains 96 carefully designed items requiring the completion of a pattern within a square, or the completion of a series of diagrams or numerals. The manual claims that the test may be used: (*a*) to discover children "whose intelligence does not find adequate expression through verbal channels," (*b*) to test children who are having reading or other linguistic difficulties, and (*c*) to investigate the "intellectual capacities" of children in widely differing cultural groups. No evidence is given in the manual in support of these claims. Although the test probably has validity for the first two uses, its validity in widely differing cultural groups must be questioned.

The only validation reported on an external criterion is a correlation of .81 with Raven's *Progressive Matrices* based upon 86 pupils. No information on reliability is presented in the manual where it should be. The publisher's test catalogue reports an unidentified reliability coefficient of .95. Neither of these correlation coefficients can be interpreted properly without further information about the groups tested and identification of the statistical formulas employed. Provisional norms for each month from 10-6 to 12-0 years are presented without explanation as to their meaning. From information published elsewhere,[1] it appears that the norms are normalized scores with a mean of 100 and a standard deviation of 15. Yet it seems unlikely that such norms can be very well founded when they are presented separately for each of 19 age groupings and there were only 413 children tested in the normative group. Be-

1 PIDGEON, D. A., AND YATES, ALFRED. "The Use of Tests in the Classroom (5)." *B Nat Found Ed Res* (7):6–11 Mr '56. *

cause of the small sample and the lack of information about the normative group and the standardised scores, these provisional norms are of questionable value.

CONCLUSION. It is surprising that the National Foundation for Educational Research is willing to publish tests with so little information about their construction, reliability, validity, norming, and limitations. Although some of this information can be gleaned from other sources, it is essential that it be included in the manuals to the tests. As they stand, it is difficult to conceive of manuals which could be less complete. Until the information is readily available, these nonverbal tests cannot be recommended for general use in schools. Further studies are needed to demonstrate their usefulness in particular situations. Such studies should be made or reported by the publisher.

For a review by E. A. Peel of the original edition, see 4:307.

[357]

★**Nufferno Tests of Speed and Level.** Mental ages 11 and over; 1956; 5 tests; 4s. 6d. per 25 sheets; 15s. per set of level cards; 2s. 6d. per specimen set; postage extra; W. D. Furneaux; distributed by National Foundation for Educational Research in England and Wales. *

a) NUFFERNO SPEED TESTS. 5 scores: speed (stressed or unstressed), speed range, speed slope, stress speed-gain, accuracy; 2 tests; 7s. per manual ['56].

　1) *Nufferno Sheet 1: Test GIS/14E.36.* Mental ages 11–15; Forms A(1), A(2) on 1 sheet; (15) minutes.

　2) *Nufferno Sheet 2: Test GIS/14E.36.* Mental ages 13 and over; Forms A(2), B(1); (20) minutes.

b) NUFFERNO LEVEL TESTS. 3 tests; 5s. per manual ['56.]

　1) *Nufferno Level Test Cards: Test IL/2(AB)36.* Mental ages 11 and over; individual; 2 scores: personal level, situation level; 1 form ['56]; (40) minutes.

　2) *Nufferno Sheet 3: Test GL/2C.46.* Adults with IQ's 100 and over; 1 form ['56]; (40) minutes.

　3) *Nufferno Sheet 4: Test GL/3A.35.* Mental ages 11 and over; 1 form ['56]; (40) minutes.

REFERENCES

　1. BLEWETT, D. B. "An Experimental Study of the Inheritance of Intelligence." *J Mental Sci* 100:922–33 O '54. * (*PA* 29:6909)

　2. FURNEAUX, W. D. "The Nufferno Tests." *B Nat Found Ed Res Engl & Wales* (6):32–6 N '55. *

　3. SHAPIRO, M. B., AND NELSON, E. H. "An Investigation of the Nature of Cognitive Impairment in Co-operative Psychiatric Patients." *Brit J Med Psychol* 28:239–56 pt 4 '55. * (*PA* 30:6185)

JOHN LIGGETT, *Lecturer in Applied Psychology, University of Durham, Newcastle, England.*

In the *Nufferno Tests of Speed and Level* an ingenious attempt has been made to assess separately the many different mental operations (such as speed, persistence, and accuracy) which contribute to intelligence test performance. The basic material is of conventional type (Thurstone letter series items), but there are several novel features in the mode of administration and in the treatment of results.

For the individual form of the level test, the material is a pack of cards of playing card size, each with a single letter series problem printed on it. The pack is divided into several sections each of which contains a group of problems whose difficulty steadily increases from very easy to very difficult. The individual cards are presented until two successive failures are made. The remaining (i.e., the more difficult) cards in that group are then discarded and a second cycle is begun. This too, is discontinued when the problems become too difficult. The number of these more or less equivalent cycles which are presented depends on the time available for testing and the reliability of measurement which is required. The scoring system is such that the maximum score possible is the same no matter how few or how many cycles have been completed and so it is perfectly possible for the slow, persistent but accurate worker to obtain a higher score than one who is fast but lacks persistence. In addition to discarding the "too difficult" items, the "too easy" items are also omitted from the second and subsequent cycles. The omission of too easy and too difficult items is very easily made by observing a simple system involving code letters and numbers printed on the back of the cards. These omissions, in addition to saving time, have the effect of equalising such motivational factors as discouragement.

In the group form of the level test, printed forms are used instead of "playing cards," but the problems are of the same letter series type and are arranged in the same cyclic form employed in the individual method.

The speed tests also employ letter series items, but all the items within a given form are of approximately equal difficulty. The total testing time is broken into a number of short timed periods or subsections. If the majority of answers within any subsection turn out to be wrong, that period is ignored for scoring purposes since, as the author explains, only times associated with correct responses should be taken into account. A scoring system is employed which gives maximum weighting to those subsections having the greatest proportion of correct answers. The speed tests may be administered under two different conditions —either unstressed (at the subject's own comfortable rate) or stressed (when the subject is asked to perform as quickly as possible and a stop watch is prominently displayed). Several methods of dealing with the speed scores are described in the manual in which the author presents his views on the theoretical aspects of speed measurement. According to the author, speed measurement cannot be made easily with little expenditure of time. "Strictly speaking," he says, "it calls for the use of specialised apparatus, in the laboratory." The author, however, "has found it possible....to devise a method for obtaining true speed scores, without special equipment, under group-test conditions, and without great loss of accuracy. Both testing and scoring, however, make special demands." He goes on to say that "testing requires the continuous active participation of the invigilator during the whole time that testing is in progress, and scoring requires a knowledge of how to use a table of logarithms." Certainly the schedule of instructions is a formidable one.

The manual summarises results obtained on both speed and level tests by a large number of normal and abnormal subjects. These results suggest that the tests may prove very useful in educational selection and in differential diagnosis. Psychotics have shown, for example, abnormal slowness on the speed tests, whereas neurotics have shown no such slowness. Interesting data is presented comparing speed under stressed and unstressed conditions. University students seeking psychological help showed a slower speed under stressed conditions, whereas normal subjects showed an increase of speed. Impressive normative data are presented for the level tests for groups such as normal adult males, university students, and school children from various types of schools.

There are unfortunate defects in the manual in spite of its attractive and useful looseleaf format. Explanations of procedure are not as clear as they could be. This is all the more unfortunate since the tests involve relatively complicated procedures and rest on much close theoretical argument. A great deal of searching backwards and forwards through the pages could have been avoided by a little repetition of procedural instructions. Convenience in use is more important than brevity in a manual. The presentation of the author's "Theory of Speed and Accuracy Measurements" could be improved. A number of theoretical concepts are introduced with scant explanation or justification. Some of the references are difficult of access and an important one has yet to appear. The status of the theory on which these tests rest can, of course, be established only by time, controversy, and much empirical work. But there can be little doubt that the Nufferno tests will come to occupy an important place in the equipment of psychologists, both clinical and educational. The tests are original, pointed, and skillfully designed. They are an important contribution to cognitive measurement.

E. A. PEEL, *Professor of Education, University of Birmingham, Birmingham, England.*

THE SPEED TESTS. The basic ideas underlying these tests are sound and the attempt to disengage speed, accuracy, and persistence is helpful. The tests are designed to measure speed and accuracy under stressed and unstressed conditions. Stress is brought about by telling the subject to work as fast as he can. The tests may be given individually or to groups. The essential technique in the speed tests is to count up the time devoted to successful solution of the items. These are composed of letter series to be completed by the next letter required. Times are converted to their logarithms and tables of percentile scores are provided, for both speed and accuracy, for groups of university students, normal adults, neurotics, and schizophrenics.

Accuracy of testing is measured by standard errors of estimates. A table in the manual gives correlations between different scores (speed, accuracy, etc.) after correction for reliability. The more technically minded reader might also like to see the reliabilities and the raw correlations between the tests.

The theoretical foreword and the tests themselves form a useful contribution in the field of ability testing, particularly in teasing out two variables which intelligence testers are usually content to leave undisturbed. But what an exercise is provided in the pages given over to descriptions and instructions! Here the reader needs to be tough minded indeed, for he is tossed like a shuttlecock backwards and forwards from page to page, from one set of symbols to another. The author has a penchant for never finally clearing up any particular point at any one place. The whole booklet is littered far too much with numerico-literal symbols. This part of the booklet really ought to be simplified if it is to be workable for less vigorous readers.

THE LEVEL TESTS. The author first discusses the interrelation of speed, accuracy, and continuance (persistence), and then takes up more fully the relationship between persistence and intelligence scores. We are given to understand that the personal level score is a measure of the level of intelligence at a constant level of subjective difficulty. The Nufferno concept of personal level of intelligence as the way in which persistence is affected by the test seems to be meaningful in the test situation. It is measured individually by Test IL/2(AB)36 by giving a series of short cycles of items of increasing difficulty so that items of similar difficulty appear in different cycles. The purpose is to ensure that the testee is asked to do only items that are neither too easy nor too hard for him. The items are not speeded; the author claims that under these conditions the persistent, accurate worker may obtain more marks than one who works fast, but lacks persistence.

A group test GL/3A.35 provides a similar measure in group test form. The items consist of letter series problems.

The author provides tables of norms for adults, university students, and school pupils for both individual and group tests, but he has not provided norms for abnormal groups. The instructions take less out of the reader than those for the speed tests. However, the author would also do well here to streamline them a little and perhaps use a simpler system of test nomenclature. The author's concept of personal level requires more attention from research workers. These tests should be tried out, particularly at the research level, in order to verify his findings. They could also be of use in individual cases where the usual intelligence tests have produced anomalous results.

[358]

★The Ohio Penal Classification Test. Penal institutions; 1952–54; 5 scores: block counting, digit-symbol, number series, memory span, total; Forms F ('54, women), PP ('52, men); manual ('52); separate answer sheets must be used; $1.95 per 20 tests; $1 per 20 answer sheets; $1 per specimen set (must be purchased to obtain manual); postage extra; 14.5(25–35) minutes; DeWitt E. Sell; Psychometric Affiliates. * (Form PP is also sold for industrial use under the title

Ohio Classification Test with a 1957 copyright; manual by the original author, Robert W. Scollay, and Leroy N. Vernon.)

NORMAN EAGLE, *School Psychologist, Public Schools, Fort Lee, New Jersey.*

The Ohio Classification Tests are group administered, nonverbal, paper and pencil measures of adult mental ability. There are two "forms" of the *Ohio Penal Classification Test* (for use in prisons), and one "form" of the *Ohio Classification Test* (for use in industry). Each test is composed of four subtests. The first three subtests are identical for all forms; Form PP of the OPCT and the single form of OCT are identical throughout. Test 1 consists of counting blocks in a pile perceived at an oblique angle; it is supposed to measure spatial perceptive aptitude and reasoning capacity. Test 2 is an original digit-symbol task purporting to measure perception and associative learning speed. Test 3, requiring the completion of 20 number series arranged in order of increasing difficulty, is designed to measure number facility and reasoning. Test 4 consists of 10 drawings of common objects whose names the subject is required to write, from recall, after a brief exposure; this test is supposed to measure "both apperception and memory."

The purpose of the tests, as stated in the manual, is to provide a group test of adult mental ability "which would circumvent as far as possible the verbal factors in general intelligence which are overemphasized in widely used group intelligence tests and which would emphasize altitude or power rather than speed." The authors hope, in this way, to avoid penalizing the "uncultured and uneducated" for their verbal deficiencies. In removing the verbal factor, however, the authors have restricted the interpretation of what their tests measure to something less, or more specific, than general intelligence. The intellectual areas tapped are spatial and numerical reasoning, and visual associative learning and memory. The justification for such an excision of general intelligence would lie in showing that this test can predict success at certain tasks with greater facility than can more highly verbal tests. Unfortunately, this is not demonstrated by the evidence reported. In addition, all of the subtests are by no means power tests. Thus, there is considerable doubt as to whether the objectives of the tests have been realized.

The manuals for the two tests are practically

identical, the principal difference being in the more extensive interpretative data given in the manual for the OCT. The directions for administration leave much to be desired. On both the OCT and the OPCT, Test 1 is completely exposed while the examiner gives rather lengthy instructions for taking it. Examinees who finish Test 1 in the OCT early may gain some advantage from the fact that the digit symbols of Test 2 are clearly exposed. In this same test the directions call for turning "to" Test 3, whereas actually what is required is to invert the page. The directions for the digit-symbol test in both tests are, in the opinion of this reviewer, inadequate. Not all of the samples are exhausted in the practice, a situation which may lead to uncertainty as to where to begin the test. Test 4 suffers from not having a definite time interval during which the figures are exposed, as well as from failing to take into account the wide range of attention which may be present. This test is also qualitatively scored in that examinees may call the objects by different names, requiring scorer judgment and interpretation. Only little assistance is given by the manual on this problem. For these reasons, as well as the fact that this test correlates only .36 with the sum of the standard scores of the other three subtests, it probably would be better to exclude this test in favor of one drawing more on reasoning capacity.

The standardization population on which the test statistics are based consisted of 550 prisoners ranging in age from 17 to 30 years, with a mean of 23 years, and a white-Negro ratio of 7 to 3. The test was also administered to 107 ninth grade boys, and the mean scores of the two groups compared. The manual states in one place that the difference between these scores is *not* significant at the 2 per cent level of confidence; in another place it is admitted that the difference obtained *is* significant at the 5 per cent level. Also provided are standard score percentile norms for women factory workers ($n = 40$), male factory workers ($n = 100$), factory workers being considered for higher positions ($n = 65$), sales and managerial applicants ($n = 162$), "middle management men" ($n = 44$), graduate engineers ($n = 22$), and upperclass scientific and technical students ($n = 93$). No further information on the composition of these groups is given. While the provision of norms for these special groups demonstrates that the authors are aware of

the inapplicability of the original norms to other than a selected prison population, the small size of most of these groups and the complete lack of identifying information still leaves the interpretation of nonprison population scores in doubt.

The manual states that "the 4 subtests of the *Ohio Classification Test* have already been extensively 'judged' by 'experts' to measure intelligence." There is no further elaboration, though some substantiation or reference would seem to be called for after such a declaration. The manual reports a correlation (presumably product-moment) of .79 between the OCT and Wechsler-Bellevue full scale for 155 prisoners, and a rank order correlation of .93 between these tests based on only 10 prisoners. However, correlations with other tests, including the *Minnesota Paper Form Board Test* and the *American Council on Education Psychological Examination for College Freshmen*, based on nonprison groups show relationships of a much lower order. One table in the manual shows the relationship between mean OCT standard scores and years of schooling; however, the interpretation of this relationship as evidence for test validity is clouded by indications that schooling affects IQ scores. A correlation of .34 is reported between OCT scores and average rate of salary increase, and it is claimed that this "is significant at the 1% level." This may be true, but it means that the correlation is significantly different from *zero correlation,* and in itself does not indicate a high degree of relationship. Further correlations are provided with merit rankings and average hourly earnings of industrial workers, but the numbers of subjects involved are so small as not to merit further comment. A test-retest reliability of .87, with a standard error of measurement of 5.76 IQ points, is reported for a prison sample of 138. Again, we do not know the range of scores or composition of the group upon which these statistics are based.

The *Ohio Penal Classification Test* may serve some function as a group test in the specific situation out of which it developed and for which it was designed, though the absence of the verbal factor may reduce its predictive ability in certain occupational areas, even within the prison setting. For nonprison situations the test does not seem to be applicable in its present form. In any case, the manuals and the test booklet for the *Ohio Classification Test* should be completely overhauled and the manuals printed in a type which can be read without the aid of a magnifying glass.

[359]
*Ohio State University Psychological Test. Grades 9–16 and adults; 1919–58; 4 scores: same-opposites, analogies, reading comprehension, total; IBM; Forms 18 ('33), 19 ('35), 20 ('37), 21 ('40), 22 ('43), 23 ('47), 24 ('50), 25 ('54), 26 ('58); mimeographed instructions and norms published separately as Ohio College Association Bulletins and Ohio High School Bulletins; high school norms for Forms 18–24 for total score only; college norms for Form 22 for reading comprehension and total score only; no norms for grades 14–16 or adults; separate answer sheets or pads must be used; high school prices: 5¢ per test booklet (Forms 23–26), 5¢ per answer pad, 5¢ per IBM answer sheet (Forms 21–26 only); college prices: 10¢ per test booklet (Forms 23–26), 8¢ per test booklet (Forms 18–22), 6¢ per answer pad, 6¢ per IBM answer sheet (Forms 21–26 only); 5¢ per IBM scoring stencil for both levels; postage extra; instructions and norms bulletins free; specimen set free to qualified school personnel; scoring service available at 4¢ per answer sheet, postage extra; (120) minutes; Herbert A. Toops; Ohio College Association. * (Form 21 also published in 2 editions by Science Research Associates: Forms AH (hand scoring edition), AM (machine scoring edition); $9.80 per 20 tests of either edition; $2.35 per 20 answer pads; $5 per 100 IBM answer sheets; 75¢ per specimen set; postage extra.)

REFERENCES

1–28. See 3:244.
29–51. See 4:308.
52. KIRK, HARRY A. The Relation Between Intelligence Rating and Achievement in Shorthand and Typing. Master's thesis, Kent State University (Kent, Ohio), 1942.
53. EDBERG, GEORGE. The Validity of High School General Educational Development Tests and the Ohio Psychological (Form 21) Test in Predicting Chances of College Success for Students Who Have Had Less Than a High School Education. Master's thesis, University of North Dakota (Grand Forks, N.D.), 1948.
54. JOHNSON, RALPH H., AND BOND, GUY L. "Reading Ease of Commonly Used Tests." J Appl Psychol 34:319–24 O '50. * (PA 26:299)
55. LAYTON, WILBUR L. Factors Associated With Grades in the First Course in Psychology. Doctor's thesis, Ohio State University (Columbus, Ohio), 1950.
56. WELSH, MARY L. A Comparison of Two Psychological Examinations in Predicting Academic Success of Ohio University Students. Master's thesis, Ohio University (Athens, Ohio), 1951.
57. HANNA, JOSEPH V. "Use of Speed Tests in Guidance." Occupations 30:329–31 F '52. *
58. NEWMAN, SLATER E.; DUNCAN, CARL P.; BELL, GRAHAM B.; AND BRADT, KENNETH H. "Predicting Student Performance in the First Course in Psychology." J Ed Psychol 43:243–7 Ap '52. * (PA 27:3178)
59. HENDRIX, O. R. "Predicting Success in Elementary Accounting." J Appl Psychol 37:75–7 Ap '53. * (PA 28:1479)
60. JENKINS, JAMES J. "Some Measured Characteristics of Air Force Weather Forecasters and Success in Forecasting." J Appl Psychol 37:440–4 D '53. * (PA 29:1642)
61. KINZER, JOHN R., AND KINZER, LYDIA GREENE. "Predicting Grades in Advanced College Mathematics." J Appl Psychol 37:182–4 Je '53. * (PA 28:3209)
62. SAMENFELD, HERBERT W. "Predicting College Achievement." J Higher Ed 24:432–3 N '53. * (PA 28:6595)
63. CARLILE, A. B. "Predicting Performance in the Teaching Profession." J Ed Res 47:641–68 My '54. * (PA 29:3063)
64. CASH, WILLIAM L., JR. Relation of Personality Traits to Scholastic Aptitude and Academic Achievement of Students in a Liberal Protestant Seminary. Doctor's thesis, University of Michigan (Ann Arbor, Mich.), 1954. (DA 14:630)
65. CONNER, HAROLD T. An Investigation of Certain Factors for the Selection and Guidance of Prospective Students Entering a School of Public Health. Doctor's thesis, University of North Carolina (Chapel Hill, N.C.), 1954.
66. HOYT, DONALD P., AND NORMAN, WARREN T. "Adjustment and Academic Predictability." J Counsel Psychol 1:96–9 su '54. * (PA 29:3043)
67. KINZER, JOHN R., AND KINZER, LYDIA GREENE. "Some

Bases for Predicting Marks in Advanced Engineering Mathematics." Ed Res B 33:13–8 Ja 13 '54. *
68. SCHMITZ, ROY M., AND HOLMES, JOHN L. "Relationship of Certain Measured Abilities to Freshman Engineering Achievement," pp. 32–42. (PA 29:1584) In Selection and Counseling of Students in Engineering. Edited by Wilbur L. Layton. Minnesota Studies in Student Personnel Work, No. 4. Minneapolis, Minn.: University of Minnesota Press, 1954. Pp. iv, 89. *
69. BOYD, JOSEPH D. The Relative Prognostic Value of Selected Criteria in Predicting Beginning Academic Success at Northwestern University. Doctor's thesis, Northwestern University (Evanston, Ill.), 1955. (DA 15:1780)
70. CHAHBAZI, PARVIZ. "The Prediction of Achievement in a College of Agriculture." Ed & Psychol Meas 15:484–6 w '55. * (PA 30:7754)
71. LAYTON, WILBUR L. "Construction of a Short Form of the Ohio State University Psychological Examination." Yearb Nat Council Meas Used Ed 12(pt 1):81–5 '55. *
72. MUNGER, PAUL F., AND GOECKERMAN, ROBERT W. "Collegiate Persistence of Upper- and Lower-Third High School Graduates." J Counsel Psychol 2:142–5 su '55. * (PA 30:3416)
73. ALLUISI, EARL A. "Maintaining Test Validity by Selectively Scoring a Short Form." Psychol Rep 2:57–8 Mr '56. * (PA 31:65)
74. ANNESER, ROBERT. An Evaluation of Scholastic Aptitude in Predicting Senior Level Achievement at Ohio University. Master's thesis, Ohio University (Athens, Ohio), 1956.
75. BOYER, LEE E., AND KOKEN, JAMES E. "Admissions Test as Criteria for Success in College." J Ed Res 50:313–5 D '56. * (PA 32:2095)
76. CHAHBAZI, PARVIZ. Prediction of Achievement in New York State College of Agriculture at Cornell University. Doctor's thesis, Cornell University (Ithaca, N.Y.), 1956. (DA 17:562)
77. HOUK, CLIFFORD C. An Investigation of the Relationship Between General Chemistry 3 at Ohio University and Various Measures of Achievement. Master's thesis, Ohio University (Athens, Ohio), 1956.
78. HEWER, VIVIAN H. "Vocational Interest-Achievement-Ability Interrelationships at the College Level." J Counsel Psychol 4:234–8 fall '57. *
79. RICHARDS, JAMES M., JR. "The Prediction of Academic Achievement in a Protestant Theological Seminary." Ed & Psychol Meas 17:628–30 w '57. *
80. STACKHOUSE, HENRY A. An Analysis of Factors Associated With the Use of the Ohio State Psychological Test Administered Under Two Different Conditions in the Missouri College Aptitude Testing Program. Doctor's thesis, University of Missouri (Columbia, Mo.), 1957. (DA 17:2925)

CYRIL J. HOYT, Associate Professor of Education, and W. WESLEY TENNYSON, Assistant Professor of Education, University of Minnesota, Minneapolis, Minnesota.

The Ohio State University Psychological Test is a verbal test of scholastic ability based upon college grade level as a criterion. This test is comprised of three subtests for which centile norms are available for each of grades 9 through 12, and for college freshmen. The subtests consist of 30 same-or-opposite items, 60 word analogy items, and 60 reading comprehension items based on ten paragraphs. The subject matter of the reading paragraphs may be classified as six passages concerned with natural science and mathematics, two concerned with social science material, and two consisting of literary descriptions. All items of the test are of the multiple choice variety with five suggested responses.

Form 25, a worklimit or power test requiring approximately two hours for its administration, includes 78 items from Form 23 selected for having the highest correlations with one year cumulative point-hour ratios for approximately 4,000 college freshmen. These 78 items are currently in use at the University of Minnesota as a time limit test known as the *Minnesota Scholastic Aptitude Test*. The other 72 items of Form 25 are new items which have been selected for their high correlations with the ability to earn high college grades.

The items of OSUPT were given careful trials and study before they were incorporated in the published form. Distractors for items were formulated by college students responding to the items presented in completion form. Those student-supplied answers which showed negative correlations with the criterion of college grade-point average were used as distractors in a multiple choice tryout form. Such selection of distractors helped to assure the test-maker that no alternative responses were so near to the correct choice that the item's correlations with the criterion were lowered by the inclusion of the distractors. Application of these item analysis techniques has resulted in high validity on a limited set of items, and a general avoidance of validity retrogression, common among tests which have been in use for a period of time.

At Ohio State University, in 1952–53, Form 24 showed a correlation of .58 with first semester grades of 1,158 freshmen of both sexes; and in 1953–54, a correlation of .60 for 1,491 freshmen. The corresponding correlations for Form 25 were not available to the reviewers, though previous experience with other forms would indicate that this magnitude can be expected for this latest revision. No information is given on the magnitude of the correlations of the subtest scores with the criterion. Reliability coefficients were not provided on Form 25; however, the test authors report a satisfactory level of reliability of the total score on earlier forms.

Percentile norms for Form 25 are based upon 1,346 ninth graders, 826 tenth graders, 1,578 eleventh graders, 3,164 twelfth graders, and an unstated number of college freshmen. The secondary school norms were derived from the 1954–55 Ohio High School Intelligence Test Survey. The college norms are tentative.

The OSUPT has been refined over the years by means of repeatedly applying item selection procedures based upon a general ability to earn college grades regardless of any specialization in the college curriculum. This seems in keeping with the idea of continuing general education, at least through the 14th year. Technical

and other schools will probably find it advantageous to supplement the OSUPT with tests of quantitative reasoning and other special ability tests.

As a test designed to measure college aptitude, the *Ohio State University Psychological Test* is particularly useful in providing accurate differentiations in ability in the upper half of the general high school senior population from which most college freshmen are drawn. Form 25 benefits from the exacting test construction procedures employed in the development of earlier forms. It should serve well its intended purpose.

For a review by George A. Ferguson of Form 24, see 4:308; for a review by J. P. Guilford of Form 21, see 3:244; for reviews by Louis D. Hartson, Theos A. Langlie, and Rudolf Pintner of Form 20, see 38:1051.

[360]

★An Orally Presented Group Test of Intelligence for Juniors. Ages 8–11; 1952; 1 form; 3s. 6d. per manual, postage extra; (75–100) minutes in 5 sessions; J. Cornwell; Methuen & Co. Ltd. *

REFERENCES

1. CORNWELL, J. *The Construction, Standardisation, and Validation of an Orally Presented Group Test of Intelligence for Children Between the Ages of Eight and Eleven.* Master's thesis, University of Birmingham (Birmingham, England), 1950.
2. CORNWELL, J. "An Orally Presented Group Test of Intelligence for Juniors." *Ed R* 3:212–21 Je '51. *

ELIZABETH D. FRASER, *Lecturer in Psychology, University of Aberdeen, Aberdeen, Scotland.*

This unpretentious little book presents a rather unusual type of group test designed for children between 8 and 11 years of age, and intended to be given by teachers in the classroom situation. It is administered orally, the teacher writing the sample items on the blackboard and demonstrating, also on the board, the method of recording answers. The child writes his answers on a simple sheet of ruled paper. The whole procedure resembles an ordinary classroom lesson rather than a special test occasion. This is claimed to have two advantages: (*a*) it arouses no "test-anxiety" and (*b*) the oral presentation makes each item a separate challenge to the child, possibly resulting in a more sustained effort throughout the test, especially in the case of easily distracted pupils.

The test consists of five short subtests of the verbal type, each containing 20 items. Subtest 1 involves the recognition of same and opposite word relations; subtest 2 requires the child to say whether a given statement is always true, always false, or sometimes true and sometimes false; subtest 3 consists of items requiring a kind of riddle-solving with a choice of answers, for example, "What often falls but is never damaged? Is it fruit, glass, a chimney, or snow?"; subtest 4 is composed of the familiar pick-out-the-one-that-is-different items; and subtest 5 involves the carrying out of simple instructions, e.g., "Put three crosses side by side on the line and draw a ring round the middle one." The subtests take 15 or 20 minutes each to administer. It is intended that they should be given on separate occasions in order to maintain concentration and avoid fatigue.

The preliminary work (*1*) on the development of the test has been admirably done and is a model for other test constructors to follow. The original test of 270 items in nine subtests was first tried out on a representative sample of 300 children aged 7 to 12. As a result of this trial the instructions were tightened up, timing was adjusted, the clearly unsuitable items were eliminated, and the remainder of the items were arranged in order of difficulty. A second try-out on a similar group of 600 children led to an analysis of the internal validity of each item, the selection of the most discriminating items, a further revision of the order of difficulty, and the calculation of correlations among the subtests. The five most satisfactory subtests, each containing the 20 most satisfactory items, were thus selected, and the test in this form was finally given to a standardisation sample of 4,150 children aged 8 to 12 in a representative sample of Birmingham schools. Norms are given in the form of IQ's, but are in fact based on standard scores with mean 100 and SD 16.5 (SD of Stanford-Binet, Form L, at 10 years of age).

The standardisation sample, in spite of its size, cannot be regarded as completely adequate since it is drawn entirely from a very large industrial city and contains no rural children at all. More widespread application of the test is obviously required.

The reliability quoted for the test (a split-half correlation based on 200 children in the 10–11 age group) is very high—.95. It must be remembered, however, that, on this occasion, the test was administered by training college students with some knowledge of the theory and practice of mental testing and some appreciation of the pitfalls of an orally presented

test. One might expect a somewhat lower figure when the test is given by relatively unsophisticated teachers.

The only data available on validity are correlations with two other well known tests. The correlation with the *Simplex Junior Intelligence Test* (n = 200 Birmingham children aged 9–11) is .91. With a much smaller group of 50 children of indeterminate composition, the correlation with the Stanford-Binet was .85.

The aim of the author has been to provide a test which is easily given by teachers in the classroom setting and which will enable them to make a preliminary classification of children into groups broadly homogeneous with respect to intelligence. It is also intended to aid in the assessment of children who are backward readers, and who may be penalised in the more usual written tests of intelligence. Carefully administered and properly interpreted, the test may prove of considerable use and great interest to enquiring teachers. The reviewer would suggest, however, that the author might find a shorter and less unwieldy title for his test.

[361]
*Otis Quick-Scoring Mental Ability Tests. Grades 1.5–4, 4–9, 9–16; 1936–54; tests for grades 4 and over are revisions of *Otis Self-Administering Tests of Mental Ability;* IBM for grades 4–16; 3 levels; separate answer sheets may be used with Forms AM, BM, CM, DM; $1.25 per 35 IBM answer sheets; 20¢ per machine scoring stencil; postage extra; 35¢ per specimen set of any one level, postpaid; Arthur S. Otis; World Book Co. * For latest edition and references, see 362.
a) ALPHA TEST. Grades 1.5–4; 1936–39; the same test booklet may be used to administer the verbal test, non-verbal test, or both; 3 scores: non-verbal, verbal, total; Forms A ('36), B ('38); manual ('39); $3.20 per 35 tests; 20(25), (30) minutes for non-verbal, verbal.
b) BETA TEST. Grades 4–9; 1937–54; IBM; Forms A ('37), B ('39), CM ('39), DM ('39); manuals (A and B, '37; CM and DM, '54); $2.30 per 35 tests (Forms A, B); $2.80 per 35 tests (Forms CM, DM); 30(35) minutes.
c) GAMMA TEST. Grades 9–16; 1937–54; IBM; Forms AM ('37), BM ('37), C ('39), D ('39); manuals (AM and BM, '54; C and D, '39); $2.30 per 35 tests (Forms C, D); $2.80 per 35 tests (Forms AM, MM); 30(35) minutes.

For a review by Frederic Kuder, see 3:249; for reviews by F. Kuhlmann and C. Spearman, see 40:1413 and 40:1427; for reviews by Psyche Cattell and R. Pintner, see 38:1053 (2 excerpts).

[362]
*Otis Quick-Scoring Mental Ability Tests, New Edition. Grades 1.5–4, 4–9, 9–16; 1936–54; previous edition (see 361) still available; IBM for grades 4 and over; 3 levels; manual ('54) for each level; sep-

arate answer sheets may be used in grades 4 and over; $1.25 per 35 IBM answer sheets; 20¢ per machine scoring stencil; postage extra; 35¢ per specimen set of any one level, postpaid; Arthur S. Otis; World Book Co. *

a) ALPHA SHORT FORM. Grades 1.5–4; 1936–54; Form AS ('52); $2.70 per 35 tests; (35) minutes.

b) BETA TEST. Grades 4–9; 1937–54; IBM; Forms EM, FM ('54); $2.80 per 35 tests; 30(35) minutes.

c) GAMMA TEST. Grades 9–16; 1937–54; IBM; Forms EM, FM ('54); $2.80 per 35 tests; 30(35) minutes.

REFERENCES

1–9. See 3:249.
10. KERR, GEORGE. "Aptitude Testing for Secondary Courses: An Essay in Control Under War-Time Difficulties." *Occupational Psychol* 16:73–8 Ap '42. * *(PA* 16:3290)
11. WITTENBORN, J. R., AND LARSEN, R. P. "A Factorial Study of Achievement in College German." *J Ed Psychol* 35:39–48 Ja '44. * *(PA* 18:2613)
12. DAVIS, W. ALLISON, AND HAVIGHURST, ROBERT J. "The Measurement of Mental Systems: Can Intelligence Be Measured?" *Sci Mo* 66:301–16 Ap '48. * *(PA* 22:3381)
13. PEEL, E. A. "Symposium on Selection of Pupils for Different Types of Secondary Schools: VI, Evidence of a Practical Factor at the Age of Eleven." *Brit J Ed Psychol* 19:1–15 F '49. *
14. ALLEN, ROBERT M., AND BESSELL, HAROLD. "Intercorrelations Among Group Verbal and Non-Verbal Tests of Intelligence." *J Ed Res* 43:394–5 Ja '50. * *(PA* 24:4841)
15. HURD, ARCHER W. *Factors Influencing Student Success in Medical Education, Exhibits 614–7.* Richmond, Va.: Bureau of Educational Research and Service, Medical College of Virginia, August 1950. Pages not numbered. *
16. BARNETTE, W. LESLIE, JR. "Occupational Aptitude Patterns of Selected Groups of Counseled Veterans." *Psychol Monogr* 65(5):1–49 '51. * *(PA* 26:2794)
17. BARRON, EMERSON M., AND DONOHUE, H. H. "Psychiatric Aide Selection Through Psychological Examinations: A Preliminary Report of the Screening of Applicants at the Arkansas State Hospital." *Am J Psychiatry* 107:859–65 My '51. * *(PA* 27:697)
18. LENNON, ROGER T. *A Comparison of Results of Three Intelligence Tests.* Test Service Notebook, No. 11. Yonkers, N.Y.: World Book Co., [1951]. Pp. 4. *
19. PURDY, BENJAMIN F. *A Study of Certain Tests and Personal History Factors as Predictors of Job Success for a Group of Clerical Workers.* Master's thesis, Southern Methodist University (Dallas, Tex.), 1951.
20. BOGER, JACK H. "An Experimental Study of the Effects of Perceptual Training on Group I.Q. Test Scores of Elementary Pupils in Rural Ungraded Schools." *J Ed Res* 46:43–52 S '52. * *(PA* 27:5414)
21. FRUCHTER, BENJAMIN. "Orthogonal and Oblique Solutions of a Battery of Aptitude, Achievement and Background Variables." *Ed & Psychol Meas* 12:20–38 sp '52. * *(PA* 27:6180)
22. SLUTZKY, JACOB E.; JUSTMAN, JOSEPH; AND WRIGHTSTONE, J. WAYNE. "The Use of a Group Intelligence Test as a Screening Device for the Selection of Mentally Retarded Children for Placement in Special Classes." *Am J Mental Def* 57:106–8 Jl '52. * *(PA* 27:3776)
23. ANDERSON, SCARVIA B. "Prediction and Practice Tests at the College Level." *J Appl Psychol* 37:256–9 Ag '53. * *(PA* 28:6583)
24. CROUCH, MILDRED S. *The Relative Value of the Differential Aptitude Tests and the Otis Quick-Scoring Mental Ability Test for Predicting Scholastic Success.* Master's thesis, Tennessee Agricultural and Industrial University (Nashville, Tenn.), 1953.
25. RIDLEY, WALTER N. *Prognostic Values of Freshman Tests Used at Virginia State College.* Doctor's thesis, University of Virginia (Charlottesville, Va.), 1953. *(DA* 14:1042)
26. DELANCY, ELMER O. *A Study of Three Psychological Tests as Related to Reading Achievement in Grade One American School Reading Readiness Test, Form A; SRA Primary Mental Abilities, Primary Form; Otis Quick-Scoring Mental Ability Tests, Alpha Test: Form A.* Doctor's thesis, Pennsylvania State University (University Park, Pa.), 1954.
27. "Comparison Between Terman IQ's and Otis IQ's for a Group of Independent School Boys." *Ed Rec B* 66:78–9 Jl '55. * *(PA* 30:5235)
28. BARNES, PAUL J. "Prediction of Achievement in Grades 1 Through 4 From Otis Quick-Scoring Mental Ability Tests: Alpha Short Form." *Ed & Psychol Meas* 15:493–4 w '55. * *(PA* 30:7750)
29. BOLIN, BYRON J. "A Comparison of Raven's Progressive Matrices (1938) With the ACE Psychological Examination and the Otis Gamma Mental Ability Test." Abstract. *J Consult Psychol* 19:400 O '55. *
30. MITCHELL, JAMES V., JR. "A Comparison of the Factorial Structure of Cognitive Functions for a High and Low Status Group." *J Ed Psychol* 47:397–414 N '56. *
31. ZWEIBELSON, I. "Test Anxiety and Intelligence Test Performance." *J Consult Psychol* 20:479–81 D '56. * *(PA* 32:1659)
32. "A Note on Comparison of Correlations With Grades of Otis IQ's and Terman IQ's in an Independent School for Boys." *Ed Rec B* 69:73–4 F '57. *
33. CLARK, GLYNN E. *A Comparison of the Performance of Selected Pupils on the Davis-Eells Test and the Otis Test of Mental Ability.* Doctor's thesis, Washington University (St. Louis, Mo.), 1957. *(DA* 17:807)
34. LENNON, ROGER T., AND SCHUTZ, RICHARD E. *A Summary of Correlations Between Results of Certain Intelligence and Achievement Tests.* Test Service Notebook, No. 18. Yonkers, N.Y.: World Book Co., 1957. Pp. 4. *
35. LONG, JAMES R. *Academic Forecasting in the Technical-Vocational High School Subjects at West Seattle High School.* Doctor's thesis, University of Washington (Seattle, Wash.), 1957. *(DA* 17:1951)
36. NICHOLSON, ALICE. *Background Abilities Related to Reading Success in First Grade.* Doctor's thesis, Boston University (Boston, Mass.), 1957.
37. NORTH, ROBERT D. "A Preliminary Report on the Reliability of the Lorge-Thorndike Intelligence Tests, Level 4, Verbal Battery, and Correlations With IQ's on the Otis Quick-Scoring Mental Ability Tests." *Ed Rec B* 69:71–2 F '57. * *(PA* 32:2120)
38. SPEER, GEORGE S. "Validity Information Exchange, No. 10-13: D.O.T. Code 0-88.31, Ship Pilot." *Personnel Psychol* 10:201 su '57. *
39. WELLMAN, F. E. "Differential Prediction of High School Achievement Using Single Score and Multiple Factor Tests of Mental Maturity." *Personnel & Guid J* 35:512–7 Ap '57. * *(PA* 32:4631)
40. MOULY, GEORGE J., AND EDGAR, MARY. "Equivalence of IQ's for Four Group Intelligence Tests." *Personnel & Guid J* 36:623–6 My '58. *
41. NICHOLSON, ALICE. "Background Abilities Related to Reading Success in First Grade." *J Ed (Boston)* 140:7–24 F '58. *
42. NORTH, ROBERT D. "The Interpretation of Otis Quick-Scoring Mental Ability Test IQ's in Relation to Kuhlmann-Anderson IQ's, ACE Scores, and Independent School Norms." *Ed Rec B* 71:47–54 F '58. *

D. WELTY LEFEVER, *Professor of Education, University of Southern California, Los Angeles, California.*

The new edition of the *Otis Quick-Scoring Mental Ability Tests* includes a shorter form of the Alpha Test (grades 1–4), in which the number of items has been reduced from 180 to 90, two new forms of the Beta Test (grades 4–9), and two revised forms of the Gamma Test (high school and college). The Beta and Gamma tests were developed from the Intermediate and Higher Examinations, respectively, of the *Otis Self-Administering Tests.*

The Alpha Short Form is composed of 45 sets of four pictorial forms, representing objects or designs. Each set of four pictures is treated as a nonverbal item, in which the pupil marks the picture which does not belong logically in the group, because it differs in kind, as a rabbit among domestic fowl, or because it differs in design or pattern. The same 45 items are transformed into a verbal test by requiring the pupil to follow such teacher-read directions as: "Mark the drawing that is just below the chain with the oval-shaped links."

As stated in the manual for each of the three tests, the purpose seems highly abstract and somewhat out of step with a modern definition of intelligence: "to measure mental ability— thinking power or the degree of maturity of the mind." However, in the Beta and Gamma manuals the definition is given a more operational character by the qualification that "any test which involves the use of language can measure mental ability only to the extent to which we may assume that pupils of the same age have had approximately the same opportunity to learn * In a given community in which all children have (such) opportunities, it is reasonable to assume that a pupil who progresses rapidly in school and learns much has a greater mental ability for his age than one who progresses less rapidly and learns less." This reviewer has no quarrel with such an assumption but he does object to the use of pupil acceleration and retardation as the direct criterion for selecting items for a mental ability test. The manuals for the Alpha Short Form and for the parent tests of Beta and Gamma indicate that in the construction of the preliminary editions two contrasting groups were employed in the validation, a "good group" and a "poor group." Twenty or more years ago school progress may have furnished a fairly meaningful criterion for judging intelligence, but this is no longer true because of marked changes in promotional policies in many school systems. Certainly the statement made in the Beta and Gamma manuals that "the actual rate of progress of pupils through school is the most appropriate criterion of the....test" cannot be justified.

The present reviewer is also unhappy with the use of the term "validity" in this quotation from the Gamma manual: "The validity of each item of the Higher Examination was investigated by finding the biserial coefficient of correlation between the item and the total score on the test." Such correlations are measures of internal consistency and should be considered primarily indicators of reliability.

In content, the Beta and Gamma tests parallel closely the parent tests. The self-administering approach is maintained. The directions for answering sample items are read by the pupils. The examiner explains the rather detailed instructions for manipulating the answer sheet.

The Beta and Gamma tests each yield a single score which summarizes the 80 items, including word meaning, verbal analogies, scrambled sentences, interpretation of proverbs, logical reasoning, number series, arithmetic reasoning, and design analogies. More than two thirds of the 80 items of the Beta Test measure some

form of verbal competence. There is considerable evidence in the literature on group intelligence tests indicating that a single score reflecting a considerable emphasis on the use of verbal symbols will predict school success about as well as a more complex pattern of scores.

School personnel in using such a "single-variable" test of scholastic aptitude should guard against an oversimplified interpretation of this score for even the academically oriented pupil, and should be especially cautious in applying the test findings to children with clinical problems or to those who need remedial help in reading and in the language arts. The abilities of the pupil whose interests and talents are distinctly along "nonbookish" lines may be incorrectly appraised by this type of test.

Split-half reliability coefficients are reported for one of the new forms of each test. For Alpha the odd-even coefficients are .87 and .88 for two samples. The median grade level coefficient for Form EM of Beta is .93, the coefficients ranging from .84 to .95. For Form EM of Gamma split-half reliabilities of .92, .91, and .92 are reported for grades 10, 11, and 12, respectively. These data seem to indicate a satisfactory level of reliability. However, some evidence of a speed factor is shown in the fact that the median of 12 correlations between two older forms of Beta, A versus B, was only .80. The author accounts for the considerably higher odd-even coefficients on the grounds of the instability of the pupils. Since no data are given regarding the time interval between the administration of the two forms, it is difficult to disprove his contention; however, the most probable reason appears to be the necessity for completing 80 items in 30 minutes.

The size of the standard error of measurement reported for apparently the same sample of data differs in the Beta and Gamma manuals. Reference is made in each manual to 465 pupils in grades 4–9, but in the Beta manual the error of measurement is reported as 4.0 points while in the Gamma manual the value is 3.0 points.

The standardization of the new forms of each of the three tests is apparently based chiefly on comparisons with the earlier forms of the tests. The statements in the manuals are vague; no clear definition is given of the nature of the normative population nor of the normative sample. There are few facts given to support the author's statement that "the norms should not be thought of as necessarily representative of any particular section of the country but rather as representative of the country as a whole."

A count of the number of times the correct answer is assigned to each response position reveals a distinct response bias for the Beta and Gamma tests. For example, in Beta the correct answer is in the "a" position only 3 times out of an expected 16 times. The chi square value for Beta responses is 25.4; the similar chi square for Gamma is 15.4. Both values result in the rejection of the hypothesis of equal assignment of correct answers to the five possible response positions at well beyond the one per cent level.

In addition to the rather vague and incomplete account of the manner in which the norms were derived for the new forms, the most serious weaknesses of the revised tests appear to be the lack of percentile norm tables of any description and the failure to furnish normative data on the comparability of the two new forms for each level. The manuals are very brief. More detailed suggestions for teachers, counselors, and supervisors on the applications of the tests to instructional and guidance problems would be helpful. More recent evidence concerning the validity of Gamma is to be desired, as well as more extensive recent data for the predictive power of both Beta and Gamma tests.

Most of the above criticisms have been directed at the amount of information furnished the user of the tests rather than against the quality or value of the tests themselves. The *Otis Quick-Scoring Mental Ability Tests,* as the title implies, do furnish a short and easily scored indicator of scholastic aptitude. Such a measure, if interpreted with care, can be useful to both teacher and counselor by revealing within fairly broad limits of accuracy the probable level of academic achievement for a majority of pupils.

ALFRED YATES, *Senior Research Officer, National Foundation for Educational Research, London, England.*

This new series comprises three tests: the Alpha Short Form is designed for grades 1–4; Beta, suitable for grades 4–9, is a revision of the Intermediate Examination of the *Otis Self-Administering Tests of Mental Ability;* and Gamma, intended for high schools and colleges, is a revision of the Higher Examination of the older series.

The avowed purpose of the tests is to measure mental ability defined as "thinking power or the degree of maturity of the mind." The author states that in making up the tests the aim has been to choose items which depend as little as possible on schooling, except that in the Beta and Gamma tests questions on vocabulary and arithmetic reasoning, recognised as being largely measures of achievement, are included.

A number of specific applications of the tests are suggested. The first of these is to discover which pupils are capable of doing better school work than they are doing and to discover which pupils may be attempting work beyond their capacity. In the light of recent evidence concerning the distribution of achievement ratios or of the differences between tests of ability and achievement, it would seem that this application of the test should be treated with some reserve. A high score on a test of this kind does not necessarily imply that a pupil can be expected to distinguish himself in some particular branch of school work. For this purpose— and indeed for several of the other purposes listed in the manuals accompanying the tests— standardised tests of attainment in the various school subjects would seem to be more serviceable.

In certain circumstances, however, tests such as the ones included in this series can be used with advantage. If it is required, for example, to segregate pupils into relatively homogeneous groups for teaching, administrative, or research purposes, tests of this kind can afford a satisfactory rough classification. They would be especially advantageous in circumstances in which little is known about the pupils' previous attainments or at the outset of a new type of course, when knowledge of previous attainments is not necessarily predictive of the likelihood of success.

The reliability coefficients quoted for these tests are not strikingly high. The quoted values vary according to the test examined and the grade of the children concerned. For the Alpha test coefficients of .87 and .88 (split-half, with the Spearman-Brown correction) are reported for two samples of third grade pupils. The standard error for this test is 4 points. In other words, the "true score" of one child in 20 is likely to depart from his obtained score by more than plus or minus 8 points of standardised score. It is clear, therefore, that the results of applying such a test should be interpreted cautiously. The coefficients quoted for the Beta test average .91, and the standard error is again quoted as 4 points. The comparable figures for the Gamma test are .88 and 3 points, respectively.

The evidence concerning the validity of the test for predictive purposes is somewhat slender. It is indeed doubtful whether, for the normal purposes of classification and guidance within a school, teachers are likely to find the tests more serviceable than measures of attainment and their own judgments of their pupils' progress. The tests are obviously serviceable instruments, however, for the purposes of coarse classification when this has to be carried out without access to relevant information about children's previous educational progress.

For a review by Frederic Kuder of the previous edition, see 3:249; for reviews by F. Kuhlmann and C. Spearman, see 40:1413 and 40:1427; for reviews by Psyche Cattell and R. Pintner, see 38:1053 (2 excerpts).

[363]

Otis Self-Administering Tests of Mental Ability. Grades 4–9, 9–16; 1922–29; Forms A ('22), B ('22), C ('28), D ('29); 2 levels: intermediate examination, higher examination; manual ('28); interpretation chart ('22); no data on reliability for Forms C and D; $2.25 per 35 tests, postage extra; 35¢ per specimen set, postpaid; 20(25) or 30(35) minutes; Arthur S. Otis and Thomas N. Barrows (D, intermediate C); World Book Co. * For later editions, see 361–2.

REFERENCES

1–71. See 3:250
72. ISAACS, ARCHIE. *Evaluation of the Items of the Otis Self-Administering Test in Terms of High-School English Marks.* Master's thesis, College of the City of New York (New York, N.Y.), 1928. Pp. 60.
73. TOLL, CHARLES H. "Scholastic Aptitude Tests in Amherst College." *Sch & Soc* 28:524–8 O 27 '28. * (PA 3:512)
74. DESSOTNEKOFF, NATHAN. *The Improvement of the Otis S.A. Intelligence Test and Marks in High School English.* Master's thesis, College of the City of New York (New York, N.Y.), 1929. Pp. 19.
75. RIESS, BERNARD. *The Otis Self Administering Test as a Predictive Measure of Success in High School.* Master's thesis, College of the City of New York (New York, N.Y.), 1929.
76. SEAGOE, MAY V. "Prediction of Achievement in Foreign Languages." *J Appl Psychol* 22:632–40 D '38. * (PA 13:2725)
77. TEEPE, ELIZABETH A. *"Speed" and "Power" on a Test of Mental Ability as Related to Age and Sex of Subject.* Master's thesis, George Washington University (Washington, D.C.), 1938. Pp. 40.
78. GARRISON, K. C. "The Use of Psychological Tests in the Selection of Student-Nurses." *J Appl Psychol* 23:461–72 Ag '39. * (PA 13:6426)
79. ACHARD, F. H., AND CLARKE, FLORENCE H. "You *Can* Measure the Probability of Success as a Supervisor." *Personnel* 21:353–73 My '45. *
80. HARTSON, L. D. "Influence of Level of Motivation on the Validity of Intelligence Tests." *Ed & Psychol Meas* 5:273–83 au '45. * (PA 20:2500)
81. COOK, P. H. "Criteria for the Selection of Personnel Officers." *B Ind Psychol & Personnel Prac* 2:28–37 Je '46. * (PA 20:4761)
82. OXLADE, M. "An Experiment in the Use of Psychological Tests in the Selection of Women Trainee Telephone Mechanics."

B Ind Psychol & Personnel Prac 2:26–32 Mr '46. * (PA 20:4838)
83. WALKER, K. F., AND OXLADE, M. N. "A Tentative Battery of Tests for the Selection of Women for Cotton Textile Spinning." *B Ind Psychol & Personnel Prac* 2:6–27 Je '46. * (PA 20:4871)
84. KUSHNER, ROSE ESTRIN. *The Relationship Between Content of an Adult Intelligence Test and Intelligence Test Score as a Function of Age.* Columbia University, Teachers College, Contributions to Education, No. 933. New York: Bureau of Publications, the College, 1947. Pp. vii, 59. * (PA 22:621)
85. LANIGAN, MARY A. "The Effectiveness of the Otis, the A.C.E. and the Minnesota Speed of Reading Tests for Predicting Success in College." *J Ed Res* 41:289–96 D '47. * (PA 22:2748)
86. FREEMAN, KENNETH H. "Predicting Academic Success in Admissions Work." *Jun Col J* 19:33–5 S '48. *
87. OXLADE, M. N. "Selection Tests for Power-Sewing Machine Operators." *B Ind Psychol & Personnel Prac* 4:26–36 Je '48. * (PA 23:1486)
88. ABT, LAWRENCE EDWIN. "A Test Battery for Selecting Technical Magazine Editors." *Personnel Psychol* 2:75–91 sp '49. * (PA 23:5099)
89. ROSENZWEIG, SAUL; WITH THE COLLABORATION OF KATE LEVINE KOGAN. *Psychodiagnosis: An Introduction to Tests in the Clinical Practice of Psychodynamics,* pp. 32–3. New York: Grune & Stratton, Inc., 1949. Pp. xii, 380. * (PA 23:3761)
90. WIGHTWICK, BEATRICE. *The Effect of Retesting on the Predictive Power of Aptitude Tests.* Doctor's thesis, New York University (New York, N.Y.), 1949.
91. YELA, MARIANO. "Application of the Concept of Simple Structure to Alexander's Data." *Psychometrika* 14:121–35 Je '49. * (PA 24:1066)
92. ZAKOLSKI, F. C. "Studies in Delinquency: I, Personality Structure of Delinquent Boys." *J Genetic Psychol* 74:109–17 Mr '49. * (PA 23:4925)
93. EDMONSON, LAWRENCE D. *Comparative Analyses of a Test Battery Used for the Prediction of Scholastic Success at the University of Missouri.* Doctor's thesis, University of Missouri (Columbia, Mo.), 1949. (Microfilm Abstr 9:64)
94. SUPER, DONALD E. *Appraising Vocational Fitness By Means of Psychological Tests,* pp. 107–14. New York: Harper & Brothers, 1949. Pp. xxiii, 727. * (PA 24:2130)
95. HOLMES, FRANK J. "Validity of Tests for Insurance Office Personnel." *Personnel Psychol* 3:57–69 sp '50. * (PA 24:5490)
96. JOHNSON, RALPH H., AND BOND, GUY L. "Reading Ease of Commonly Used Tests." *J Appl Psychol* 34:319–24 O '50. * (PA 26:299)
97. PORUBEN, ADAM, JR. "A Test Battery for Actuarial Clerks." *J Appl Psychol* 34:159–62 Je '50. * (PA 25:3995)
98. BAIR, JOHN T. "Factor Analysis of Clerical Aptitude Tests." *J Appl Psychol* 35:245–9 Ag '51. * (PA 26:3067)
99. OXLADE, M. N. "Further Experience With Selection Tests for Power-Sewing Machine Operators." *B Ind Psychol & Personnel Prac* 7:27–37 Mr '51. * (PA 25:7713)
100. VACCARO, JOSEPH J. *A Study of Psychological Factors That Contrast the Most and Least Efficient Psychiatric Aids in a Mental Hospital.* Doctor's thesis, Fordham University (New York, N.Y.), 1951.
101. CASE, HARRY W. "The Relationship of Certain Tests to Grades Achieved in an Industrial Class in Aircraft Design." *Ed & Psychol Meas* 12:90–5 sp '52. * (PA 27:6106)
102. JOHNSON, GORDON. *An Analysis of Six Theories as to the Origin of Delinquent Behaviour.* Master's thesis, University of British Columbia (Vancouver, B.C., Canada), 1952. Pp. 190.
103. MOFFIE, DANNIE J., AND MILTON, CHARLES R. "The Relationship of Certain Psychological Test Scores to Academic Success in Chemical Engineering." Abstract. *Am Psychol* 7:379–80 Jl '52. *
104. BRUCE, MARTIN M. "The Prediction of Effectiveness as a Factory Foreman. *Psychol Monogr* 67(12):1–17 '53. * (PA 28:5019)
105. JOHNSON, GRANVILLE B., JR. "Bilingualism as Measured by a Reaction-Time Technique and the Relationship Between a Language and a Non-Language Intelligence Quotient." *J Genetic Psychol* 82:3–9 Mr '53. * (PA 27:7648)
106. SEASHORE, HAROLD G. "Validation of Clerical Testing in Banks." *Personnel Psychol* 6:45–56 sp '53. * (PA 28:1670)
107. BRUCE, MARTIN M. "Validity Information Exchange, No. 7-004: D.O.T. Code 0-97.61, Manager, Sales." *Personnel Psychol* 7:128–9 sp '54. *
108. BRUCE, MARTIN M. "Validity Information Exchange, No. 7-076: D.O.T. Code 5-91.101, Foreman II." *Personnel Psychol* 7:418–9 au '54. *
109. HANES, BERNARD, AND HALLIDAY, R. W. "Unfavorable Conditions in Intelligence Testing." *J Genetic Psychol* 85:151–4 S '54. * (PA 29:5708)
110. SEASHORE, HAROLD. "Tenth Grade Tests as Predictors of Twelfth Grade Scholarship and College Entrance Status." Comment by David V. Tiedeman. *J Counsel Psychol* 1:106–15 su '54. * (PA 29:3054)
111. BARBE, WALTER B. "Reading Improvement and Group Intelligence Test Scores." *Sch & Soc* 82:72–3 S 3 '55. * (PA 30:4550)
112. BRUCE, MARTIN M. "Normative Data Information Exchange, No. 30." *Personnel Psychol* 9:541–2 w '56. *

113. BEAMER, GEORGE C., AND BONK, EDWARD C. "Reliability of Mental Ability Tests." *J Counsel Psychol* 4:322 w '57. *
114. BRICE, MARSHALL M. "A Comparison of Subjective Predictions With Objective Predictions of College Achievement." *Col & Univ* 32:347–53 sp '57. *
115. BRUCE, MARTIN M. "Validity Information Exchange, No. 10-3: D.O.T. Code 1-86.11, Salesmen, Commercial Equipment and Supplies." *Personnel Psychol* 10:77–8 sp '57. *
116. DU MAS, FRANK M. "A Manifest Structure Analysis of the Otis Intelligence Test." Abstract. *Am Psychol* 12:429–30 Jl '57.
117. GUNNELL, DOROTHY C., AND NUTTING, RUTH E. "Prediction of Achievement in Schools of Nursing." *Calif J Ed Res* 8:184–91 S '57. *
118. HECHT, ROBERT, AND BRUCE, MARTIN M. "Normative Data Information Exchange, No. 10-40." *Personnel Psychol* 10:532 w '57. *
119. LAWRENCE, P. J. "Contributions to Intelligence Testing and the Theory of Intelligence: III, A Study of Cognitive Error Through an Analysis of Intelligence Test Errors." *Brit J Ed Psychol* 27:176–89 N '57. *
120. SAUNDERS, WM. J., JR. "Normative Data Information Exchange, No. 10-26." *Personnel Psychol* 10:360 au '57. *
121. SAUNDERS, WM. J., JR. "Normative Data Information Exchange, No. 10-27." *Personnel Psychol* 10:361 au '57. *
122. SHAH, SALEEM A. *An Investigation of Predictive Ability in Hospital Personnel and University Students.* Doctor's thesis, Pennsylvania State University (State College, Pa.), 1957. (*DA* 18:288–9)
123. DU MAS, FRANK M., AND MACBRIDE, KING. "A Manifest Structure Analysis of the Otis S-A Test of Mental Ability, Higher Examination: Form B." *J Appl Psychol* 42:269–72 Ag '58. *

For a review by Frederic Kuder, see 3:250.

[364]

*Personnel Research Institute Classification Test. Adults; 1943–54; formerly called *Classification Test For Industrial and Office Personnel;* Forms A ('47, revision of 1943 form), B ('47); revised manual ('54); $3 per 25 tests; 50¢ per specimen set; cash orders postpaid; 15(20) minutes; Jay L. Otis, Evelyn Katz (A), Robert W. Henderson (A), Mary Aiken (A), David J. Chesler (B), and Gardner E. Lindzey (B); Personnel Research Institute. *

[365]

★Personnel Research Institute Factory Series Test. Applicants for routine industrial positions; 1950–56; Form B ('50); mimeographed manual ('56); no data on validity; $3 per 25 tests; 35¢ per specimen set; cash orders postpaid; 10(15) or 15(20) minutes; Jay L. Otis and Alfred H. Exton; Personnel Research Institute. *

[366]

★Personnel Tests for Industry. Trade school and adults; 1945–54; 3 tests; 35¢ per specimen set including manual for *Oral Directions Test;* postpaid; Psychological Corporation. *
a) PTI-VERBAL TEST. 1952–54; Forms A ('52), B ('52); preliminary manual ['54]; $1.70 per 25 tests; 5(15) minutes; Alexander G. Wesman.
b) PTI-NUMERICAL TEST. 1952–54; Forms A ('52), B ('52); preliminary manual ['54]; $1.70 per 25 tests; 20(25) minutes; Jerome E. Doppelt.
c) PTI-ORAL DIRECTIONS TEST. 1945–54; Form S ('54); preliminary manual ['54]; 2 types of recordings: LP microgroove 12-inch record (33⅓ rpm), tape recording (3.75 ips); $12 per set of scoring key, 100 answer sheets, manual, and either record or tape recording; $4 per 100 answer sheets; Spanish edition on tape available; (15) minutes; Charles R. Langmuir.

ERWIN K. TAYLOR, *President, Personnel Research and Development Corporation, Cleveland, Ohio.*

The PTI is a short, low-level intelligence battery of which three tests have been published at the time of this writing. These are a 5-minute Verbal Test, a 20-minute Numerical Test, and a 15-minute Oral Directions Test.

"The content of the tests," according to the manual, "was selected so as to appear reasonable to adult applicants and employees." In the writer's opinion, the items of the verbal and the numerical tests seem somewhat less academic in their terminology than is true of many available intelligence tests. On the other hand, it cannot be said that the PTI has achieved this objective to a markedly greater degree than a number of others on the market.

VERBAL TEST. With a time limit of 5 minutes for 50 items, one might question the publisher's claim that this is primarily a power rather than a speed test. The items covered are synonyms, information, classification, and "recognition of essentials." By the latter, we presume that the publisher means such items as "A team always has (A) equipment, (B) uniforms, (C) schedules, (D) members." Two forms of the test are available, and judging from the means and sigmas on nine populations (ranging in size from n = 33 to n = 171), an excellent job of equating the forms has been done.

Alternate form reliabilities range from .73 to .92. Normative data are presented for six industrial and three educational samples. These range in size from 80 to 237. The normative data are characterized by wide variation from sample to sample. The means of the groups vary from 15.8 for applicants for factory jobs in a southern textile mill to 37.1 for mechanical apprentices in an Ohio paper mill. The first percentile of the latter group is equivalent to the 72nd percentile of the former group. The manual, which shows admirable restraint in all respects, remarks, "It is generally recognized that the most appropriate norms are those which the test user develops from the testing of his own groups. The norms given in manuals are useful primarily as general reference points until local norms are developed." Save for the fact that this precludes small organizations from using tests, as well as rendering the use of tests questionable for positions that do not exist in large numbers, this advice seems sound.

The validity data presented are somewhat more extensive than those found in most manuals, even though they are not too impressive. Most of the data, unfortunately, are derived from training rather than job performance criteria. However, the test does show enough promise to justify its use on an experimental basis for the selection of low-level production workers. The reader should note, however, that the test has a rather low ceiling and is not likely to discriminate well among graduates of a four-year academic high school. No relationship with age is provided in the manual, but considering the speed factor, the reviewer would venture to predict that a rather substantial negative correlation exists.

NUMERICAL TEST. Each form of the Numerical Test consists of 30 open-ended items. The testees are required to calculate and write in the correct answer. The items are a combination of the arithmetic reasoning and number skills so that the testee needs first to determine the arithmetic process or processes appropriate to the problem and then to do the necessary computations correctly. Either of these processes will of course, if improperly done, yield an incorrect answer. The correlations between the two tests for nine populations ranged from .73 to .92. Normative data are available on the same populations as for the Verbal Test.

The comments above with reference to the Verbal Test are equally pertinent here. In Form B of the Numerical Test, Items 2 and 7 employ similar numerical values so that the answer to one provides a clue to the answer to the other. In Item 17 of this form, a contractor estimates that he will pay 65 per cent for labor, 10 per cent for overhead, and the remainder of a contract for material. The absence of a profit margin divests this item of reality—either that or this is a type of contractor completely unfamiliar to the writer. Item 29 in this form requires the computation of the area of a rhomboid. Knowledge of geometry, as well as an inference with reference to what may be a right angle, is needed to solve it.

ORAL DIRECTIONS TEST. This, like a television movie, is a truncated re-release of a longer version originally published in 1946. The test contains 39 scorable items. It is available either on a 12-inch long playing record or on a 300-foot standard magnetic tape to be played at the rate of 3¾ inches per second. A unique feature of the tape is the recording of the test on both tracks so that it may be used without rewinding. A special answer sheet is provided on which the examinee records his responses. The writer listened to the test from the magnetic tape recording. He found this to be of excellent quality, clarity, and auditory comprehensi-

bility. With adequate sound reproducing equipment and good testing facilities, its use in a group testing situation should present no problems.

Like the other tests in the battery, the Oral Directions Test has a quite low ceiling and appears to be suitable for use only with populations whose socioeconomic and educational status would be expected to fall below the general population average. While the normative data are presented for nine populations, five male and four female, varying in number from 23 to 522, only five percentile points are presented. Since only one form of the test is available, only split-half reliabilities are reported. These range from .82 to .94. The test is paced rather than timed, therefore the usual objections to split-half reliability for timed tests do not apply in this case. No validation data with reference to this form of the test are given in the preliminary manual. The test is, however, undoubtedly of value in getting a rough estimate of the intelligence of semiliterates and of individuals with educational handicaps.

The entire battery is characterized by its low ceiling and the simplicity of its items. It is appropriate, therefore, primarily as a rejection device for rather low level positions in either factory or office.

For reviews by Charles D. Flory, Irving Lorge, and William W. Turnbull of the original edition of the Oral Directions Test, *see 3:245.*

[367]
★Picture Intelligence Test 1. Ages 7 to 8-1; 1955; 1 form ['55]; no data on validity; 10s. per 12 tests; 1s. per single copy; 1s. per manual; postage extra; 22(45) minutes; Joan E. Stuart; published for the National Foundation for Educational Research in England and Wales; Newnes Educational Publishing Co. Ltd. *

CHARLOTTE E. K. BANKS, *Lecturer in Psychology, University College, London, England.*

This 60-item test consists of problems in classification, picture series, and perception of simple relations. The test is entirely in pictures, with no writing of any kind. The drawings, although sometimes rather difficult for adults to decipher, are nevertheless fairly simple, and presumably suitable for children of this age.

There is an excellent manual giving detailed instructions for the administration and scoring of the test and also data on reliability, standardisation, and use of the tables which are provided for the purpose of converting raw scores into standard scores.

The test was originally constructed for testing 8-year-old children in the Population Investigation Committee's sample—a sample of children born in the first week of March 1946. Unfortunately, the results of this survey have not been published. The test has also been used for testing the 7–8 year age group in the National Survey in 1955. Again, the results of this survey are unfortunately not yet in print, but the reviewer understands from a private communication that the norms obtained scarcely differed from those given in the published manual.

The sample on which the test was standardised consisted of 4,350 children between the age of 6-9 and 8-3 in an urban and a rural area of Great Britain. It is on these results that the norms are based. Mental ages are not used. Each child's score is converted to a standard score and compared with those of children of his own age. The standard scores for each age group have a mean of 100 and a standard deviation of 15, thus corresponding in mean and spread to intelligence quotients as generally understood.

Reliability, calculated by Kuder-Richardson formula 20, is given as .92. Unfortunately, there seem to be no data available for assessing the validity of the test.

M. L. KELLMER PRINGLE, *Lecturer in Education, and Deputy Head, Department of Child Study, University of Birmingham, Birmingham, England.*

The test is designed for a narrow age band, namely the first year in the junior school. In contrast to other so-called picture tests, it really does consist of pictures only; neither patterns, letters, nor numbers are introduced. Moreover, the design and layout of the pictures are excellent: they are boldly and clearly drawn, well spaced out, and devoid of fussy detail which tends to be confusing to young children. The test has three sections: the first contains 15 items of the "doesn't belong" type; the second is made up of 20 items of the "sequence" and "series" type; and the third has 25 analogy items. Throughout, the items are of the multiple choice type. Each section has a separate, clearly marked practice page and the end of each section is indicated clearly. Perhaps the only drawback is that this very clarity facili-

tates copying; this point is stressed in the manual.

The directions for the administration of the tests are commendably brief and concise, and teachers will be appreciative of the fact that the total working time occupies just one school period. The manual also contains a well set out answer key and a table for the conversion of raw scores into standardised scores. These have been arranged so as to have a mean of 100 and a standard deviation of 15. It is explained that the standardised scores are similar to IQ's in their numerical distribution, but differ from them in that they are not arrived at through consideration of mental age. "Each child is assessed by comparing him with a representative sample of children of exactly the same age."

The test has been constructed with care. The most discriminative items and the most satisfactory method of administration were determined after preliminary drafts had been given three tryouts. It would have been of interest to know the number of children involved in the preliminary trials. For the final standardisation, the test was administered to 4,350 children between the ages of 6-9 and 8-3 in two areas, one urban and the other rural. The reliability coefficient, obtained by the Kuder-Richardson formula 20 from a random sample of 200 scripts, is .92. No data are given concerning the test's validity or its correlation with other tests.

The only serious criticism is for sins of omission. Nowhere is there a warning that a score of less than 70 does not necessarily mean that the child is educationally subnormal. Neither is there any indication that the author is aware of the unreliability of a nonverbal group test for predicting long term educable capacity for such young children, particularly if a child be emotionally disturbed or in any other way atypical. Lastly, in view of the fact that the National Foundation for Educational Research has during the past two or three years been reframing test design and rethinking test policy, it is surprising that there is no indication in the manual of the purpose for which this test was designed.

There is little doubt, however, that *Picture Intelligence Test 1* is carefully constructed, attractively designed, well laid out, and easy to administer. In addition, having been recently standardised, it must be considered one of the best nonverbal group tests of intelligence available in this country for children 7 to 8 years of age.

[368]

Pintner General Ability Tests: Verbal Series.
Grades kgn–2, 2–4, 4–9, 9–12 and over; 1923–46; IBM for grades 4 and over; 4 levels; 35¢ per specimen set of any one level; separate answer sheets may be used for grades 4 and over; $1.70 per 35 IBM answer sheets; 40¢ per set of matching scoring stencils; postage extra; Rudolf Pintner, Bess V. Cunningham (*a*), and Walter N. Durost (*a*, *b*); World Book Co. *

a) PINTNER-CUNNINGHAM PRIMARY TEST. Grades kgn–2; 1923–46; Forms A ('38, revision of *Pintner-Cunningham Primary Mental Test,* '23), B ('39), C ('46); manual ('46); $3.05 per 35 tests; (20–25) minutes.

b) PINTNER-DUROST ELEMENTARY TEST. Grades 2–4; 1940–41; 3 scores: picture content (Scale 1), reading content (Scale 2), total; Forms A ('40), B ('41); manual ('41); $4.20 per 35 tests of Scale 1; $3.25 per 35 tests of Scale 2; (45) minutes per scale.

c) PINTNER INTERMEDIATE TEST. Grades 4–8; 1931–42; a revision of *Pintner Intelligence Test* ('31); IBM; Forms A ('38), B ('39); directions for administering ('42); interpretation manual ('39); $3.55 per 35 tests; 25¢ per interpretation manual; 45(55) minutes. *

d) PINTNER ADVANCED TEST. Grades 9–12 and over; 1938–42; IBM; Forms A ('38), B ('39); directions for administering ('42); interpretation manual ('39); $3.55 per 35 tests; 25¢ per interpretation manual; 55(65) minutes.

REFERENCES

1–13. See 3:255.
14. KIRKPATRICK, FORREST H. "Four Mental Tests and Freshman Marks." *J Higher Ed* 11:38–9 Ja '40. * (PA 14:3215)
15. TILTON, J. W. "The Relation Between IQ and Trait Difference as Measured by Group Intelligence Tests." *J Ed Psychol* 38:343–52 O '47. * (PA 22:2066)
16. JORDAN, A. M. "Efficiency of Group Tests of Intelligence in Discovering the Mentally Deficient." *H Sch J* 31:73–94 Mr–Ap '48. *
17. LENNON, ROGER T. "The Relation Between Intelligence and Achievement Test Results for a Group of Communities." *J Ed Psychol* 41:301–8 My '50. * (PA 25:3391)
18. LENNON, ROGER T. *A Comparison of Results of Three Intelligence Tests.* Test Service Notebook, No. 11. Yonkers, N.Y.: World Book Co., [1951]. Pp. 4. *
19. DARCY, NATALIE T. "The Performance of Bilingual Puerto Rican Children on Verbal and on Non-Language Tests of Intelligence." *J Ed Res* 45:499–506 Mr '52. * (PA 27:1827)
20. DRISCOLL, JUSTIN A. *Factors in Intelligence and Achievement: A Study of the Factor Pattern Resulting From Analysis of the Scores of Boys in Junior Year of High School on Intelligence and Achievement Tests.* Catholic University of America, Educational Research Monographs, Vol. 16, No. 7. Washington, D.C.: Catholic University of America Press, Inc., June 15, 1952. Pp. viii, 56. * (PA 27:3330)
21. JUSTMAN, JOSEPH, AND WRIGHTSTONE, J. WAYNE. "A Comparison of Pupil Functioning on the Pintner Intermediate Test and the Henmon-Nelson Test of Mental Ability." *Ed & Psychol Meas* 13:102–9 sp '53. * (PA 28:1567)
22. McCALL, JOHN R. *Sex Differences in Intelligence: A Comparative Factor Study.* Washington, D. C.: Catholic University of America Press, Inc., 1955. Pp. viii, 65. * (PA 30:4171)
23. LENNON, ROGER T., AND SCHUTZ, RICHARD E. *A Summary of Correlations Between Results of Certain Intelligence and Achievement Tests.* Test Service Notebook, No. 18. Yonkers, N.Y.: World Book Co., 1957. Pp. 4. *

For reviews by Stanley S. Marzolf and D. A. Worcester, see 3:255; see 40:1416 (3 excerpts).

[369]

★**Primary School Verbal Intelligence Test 1.**
Ages 8 to 10-6; 1953–58; adaptation of *A.C.E.R. Junior A* and *A.C.E.R. Junior B*; 1 form ['53]; re-

vised manual ('58); 5s. 6d. per 12 tests; 6d. per single copy; 1s. per manual; postage extra; 30(40) minutes; D. A. Pidgeon; published for the National Foundation for Educational Research in England and Wales; Newnes Educational Publishing Co. Ltd. *

JOHN NISBET, *Lecturer in Education, University of Aberdeen, Aberdeen, Scotland.*

The demands of selection for secondary education in Britain have ensured a plentiful supply of group tests of intelligence for the 10–12 age range. Less attention has been given to the age range 8–10, and this test should be welcomed as providing a soundly constructed measure for this younger group. The data given in the manual, though brief, are sufficient to show that the construction and standardisation (based on a sample of over 6,000) have been thoroughly and competently done. In technical aspects of construction, the test appears to satisfy the highest standards.

Three criticisms, however, make the reviewer hesitate to give an unqualified recommendation for its use.

Firstly, the test assumes a mastery of reading. Obviously, group tests should not be used with backward readers at this age level. At age 8-0, the child scoring at the mean on this test has only 20 items right out of 85, and norms given for lower raw scores at this age (for example, a score of 4 equals a standardised IQ-like score of 81) have little significance because of reading difficulties. But even at later ages and higher levels of ability, reading skill will influence score to an extent which is hardly justified by the implications of the title "verbal intelligence." Therefore, users should be cautious in interpreting the meaning of "verbal intelligence" applied to a score in this test. The print, however, is larger and clearer than in other tests constructed in England and hitherto available for this age range, such as the *Essential Intelligence Test* and *Simplex Junior Intelligence Tests.*

Secondly, the child who is familiar with tests will have a marked advantage on this test. The back page of the test booklet is a practice sheet with 11 items which are to be worked and checked under the teacher's supervision in the first 10 minutes. Once the practice test has been done, there are no worked examples in the test proper. The types of item are not grouped in sections but are mixed throughout the test, so that an analogy may be followed by a coding item, with a reasoning problem following that. The child must therefore retain the examples of the practice test clearly in mind throughout. Speed of working counts heavily, for only 30 minutes are allowed for the 85 items. The competitive setting in which intelligence tests have frequently been used has influenced some teachers to devote classroom time to coaching for objective tests. The form of this test is liable to encourage such coaching. A longer practice session, detailed instructions, worked examples throughout the test, and a more generous time limit would be necessary to minimise the advantage of the "sophisticated" child.

Finally, almost all the items are in multiple choice form, where each alternative is numbered and the child writes the number of the correct answer in a space at the end of the line. This seems to introduce an undesirable complication, apparently only for ease of marking. (The instructions add that if a child underlines the correct answer instead of writing the number, he is not to be penalised.)

On balance, the test is to be recommended as a measure of educational aptitude, provided that the user remembers that it is more affected by the teaching and training which has preceded it than are similar verbal intelligence tests constructed for older age groups.

F. W. WARBURTON, *Lecturer in Educational Psychology, University of Manchester, Manchester, England.*

This test was constructed "with a view to supplying teachers with an up-to-date verbal intelligence test for use in primary school." It is intended to be suitable for the age range 8 to 11. The present conversion table covers the age range 8-0 to 10-6 only, an omission which should be rectified by now, as the test was first published in 1953.

Most of the items were taken from the Junior A and Junior B tests of the Australian Council for Educational Research which have already been satisfactorily analysed. After a trial the 71 items considered most suitable were selected from these tests and combined with 14 original items to make an 85-item test.

The conversion table is based on the scores of a very large sample of 6,419 children. Lawley's method was used to give standardised scores with mean of 100 and standard deviation of 15. These scores are similar to intelligence quotients in their numerical distribution, but, as the manual points out, they differ in that

they are not arrived at through consideration of mental age.

Satisfactory content validities have been obtained. Unfortunately, test-retest reliabilities have not been obtained, but Kuder-Richardson formula 20 gives a value of .97 (n = 330). The standard error of the scores is 2.5, a very satisfactory result.

This test has already been used in a large number of individual schools, and three or four authorities give it to all children as part of their record card programme. There would appear to be no reason why it should not be used more extensively with advantage. It gives every indication of being a useful addition to the rather small number of reliable mental tests available in Britain and of providing the up-to-date verbal intelligence test that the author claims it to be.

[370]

*Progressive Matrices. Ages 5 and over; 1938-56; 3 levels; postage extra (postpaid); J. C. Raven; H. K. Lewis & Co. Ltd. * (U.S. distributor: Psychological Corporation.)

a) PROGRESSIVE MATRICES (1938), 1956 REVISION. Ages 6 and over; 1938-56; title on test is *Standard Progressive Matrices: Sets A, B, C, D, and E;* 1 form ('56, identical with test copyrighted in 1938 except for change in one item and order of items); revised manual ('56); no norms for individual administration for ages 14 and over; separate answer sheets must be used; 168s. ($12.50) per 25 (10) tests; 7s. 6d. ($1.50) per 25 (50) answer sheets; 20s. per scoring key; 7s. 6d. per 50 record booklets (no date); 3s. 6d. (75¢) per manual; 17s. 6d. ($2.25) per specimen set; (60) minutes.

b) COLOURED PROGRESSIVE MATRICES (1947), 1956 REVISION. Ages 5-11 and mental patients and senescents; 1947-56; individual, ages 5-8; 1 form ('56, subtest Sets A and B same as subtest Sets A and B of the *Progressive Matrices, 1938* except for color); revised manual ('56); record booklet (no date); separate answer sheets must be used for group administration; 189s. ($13.50) per 25 (10) tests; $1.50 per 50 answer sheets; 5s. (75¢) per manual; 18s. 6d. ($2.60) per specimen set; [30] minutes; also distributed by George G. Harrap & Co. Ltd.

c) PROGRESSIVE MATRICES (1947). Ages 11 and over; 1943-47; 2 editions; 1 form ('47); 7s. 6d. per 50 record booklets (no date); no data on reliability and validity.

1) *Set 1*. For use either as a practice test for Set 2 or as a rough screening test; no norms; 50s. per 25 tests; 5s. ($2.50) per specimen set; (10) minutes.

2) *Set 2*. For use either as "a test of intellectual capacity" when used without a time limit or as "a test of intellectual efficiency" when used with a time limit ("usually of 40 minutes"); distribution is restricted to registered users who after signing an agreement and paying an annual service fee may borrow tests for indefinite periods at 150s. per set of 25 tests or for 4 weeks at 20s. per set of 25 tests; 7s. 6d. per 100 record forms; specimen set not available; 147s. per 25 tests; 15s. per single copy; [40] minutes.

REFERENCES

1–8. See 40:1417.
9–21. See 3:258.
22–53. See 4:314.
54. ESHER, F. J. S. "Short Tests of Low-Grade Intelligence: II." *Occupational Psychol* 15:112–9 Jl '41. * (*PA* 16: 1712)
55. SLATER, PATRICK. "Tests for Selecting Secondary and Technical School Children." *Occupational Psychol* 15:10–25 Ja '41. * (*PA* 15:3177)
56. SLATER, PATRICK, AND BENNETT, ELIZABETH. "The Development of Spatial Judgment and Its Relation to Some Educational Problems." *Occupational Psychol* 17:139–55 Jl '43. *
57. GIBSON, Q. H. "Intelligence Tests and University Careers of Medical Students." *Lancet* 255:323–4 Ag 28 '48. *
58. ORTON, R., AND MARTIN, D. R. "Psychiatric Screening of Medical Students." *Lancet* 255:321–3 Ag 28 '48. *
59. HEIM, A. W. "Learning in Intelligence Test Performance." Abstract. *Q B Brit Psychol Soc* (3):120–1 Ja '49. * Reply by John C. Raven: (3):197–8 Jl '49. * Rebuttal by A. W. Heim: (3):219–20 O '49. *
60. KLONOFF, HARRY. *An Exploratory Study and Analysis of the Wechsler-Bellevue Intelligence Scale and the Raven Progressive-Matrices.* Master's thesis, University of Toronto (Toronto, Ont., Canada), 1951.
61. TAIBL, RAYMOND MARTIN. *An Investigation of Raven's "Progressive Matrices" as a Tool for the Psychological Evaluation of Cerebral Palsied Children.* Doctor's thesis, University of Nebraska (Lincoln, Neb.), 1951.
62. DESAI, MAHESH. "The Test-Retest Reliability of Progressive Matrices Test." *Brit J Med Psychol* 25:48–53 pt 1 '52. * (*PA* 27:1177)
63. JOHNSON, ELIZABETH Z. "Sex Differences and Variability in the Performance of Retarded Children on Raven, Binet and Arthur Tests." *J Clin Psychol* 8:298–301 Jl '52. * (*PA* 27: 5981)
64. JOHNSON, ELIZABETH Z. "The Use of the Rorschach Prognostic Scale With Raven's Progressive Matrices to Predict Playtherapy Progress Among Retarded Children." Abstract. *J Proj Tech* 16:385 S '52. *
65. LINGWOOD, JOAN. "Test Performances of ATS Recruits From Certain Civilian Occupations." *Occupational Psychol* 26: 35–46 Ja '52. * (*PA* 26:6567)
66. O'CONNOR, N. "The Prediction of Psychological Stability and Anxiety-Aggressiveness From a Battery of Tests Administered to a Group of High Grade Male Mental Defectives." *J General Psychol* 46:3–17 Ja '52. * (*PA* 27:2055)
67. TURNER, G. H., AND PENFOLD, D. J. "The Scholastic Aptitude of Indian Children of the Caradoc Reserve." *Can J Psychol* 6:31–44 Mr '52. * (*PA* 26:6935)
68. WILSON, LOLITA. *A Comparison of the Raven Progressive Matrices (1947) and the Performance Scale of the Wechsler Intelligence Scale for Children for Assessing the Intelligence of Indian Children.* Master's thesis, University of British Columbia (Vancouver, B.C., Canada), 1952.
69. BROMLEY, D. B. "Primitive Forms of Response to the Matrices Test." *J Mental Sci* 99:374–93 Jl '53. * (*PA* 28:4101)
70. HOPKINS, BARBARA, AND ROTH, MARTIN. "Psychological Test Performance in Patients Over Sixty: I, Paraphrenia, Arteriosclerotic Psychosis and Acute Confusion." *J Mental Sci* 99:451–63 Jl '53. * (*PA* 28:4655)
71. JOHNSON, ELIZABETH Z. "The Clinical Use of Raven's Progressive Matrices to Appraise Potential for Progress in Play Therapy: A Study of Institutionalized Mentally and Educationally Retarded Children." Discussions by Anna S. Elonen and Thorleif G. Hegge. *Am J Orthopsychiatry* 23:391–405 Ap '53. * (*PA* 28:2865)
72. JOHNSON, ELIZABETH Z. "Individual Patterns of Emotional Functioning in Children of Comparable I.Q.'s—Implications for Education." *Am J Mental Def* 57:681–6 Ap '53. * (*PA* 28:1187)
73. JOHNSON, ELIZABETH Z. "Klopfer's Prognostic Scale Used With Raven's Progressive Matrices in Play Therapy Prognosis." *J Proj Tech* 17:320–6 S '53. * (*PA* 28:4363)
74. LEVINE, BERT D. *The Progressive Matrices 1938 and Its Relationship With Certain Subtests of the Wechsler-Bellevue Intelligence Scale.* Master's thesis, University of Texas (Austin, Tex.), 1953.
75. ROTH, MARTIN, AND HOPKINS, BARBARA. "Psychological Test Performance in Patients Over Sixty: I, Senile Psychosis and the Affective Disorders of Old Age." *J Mental Sci* 99:439–50 Jl '53. * (*PA* 28:4671)
76. SYDOW, DONALD W. *A Psychometric Differentiation Between Functional Psychotics and Non-Psychotics With Organic Brain Damage.* Doctor's thesis, University of Minnesota (Minneapolis, Minn.), 1953. (*DA* 13:1267)
77. ALLEBACH, NANCY L. *Raven's Colored Matrices and Tests of Primary Mental Abilities With Young Children.* Master's thesis, Pennsylvania State University (State College, Pa.), 1954.
78. GABRIEL, K. R. "The Simplex Structure of the Progressive Matrices Test." *Brit J Stat Psychol* 7:9–14 My '54. * (*PA* 29:2445)
79. LEVINE, BERT, AND ISCOE, IRA. "A Comparison of Raven's Progressive Matrices (1938) With a Short Form of the Wechsler-Bellevue." Abstract. *J Consult Psychol* 18:10 F '54. *
80. MARTIN, ANTHONY W., AND WIECHERS, JAMES E. "Raven's Colored Progressive Matrices and the Wechsler In-

telligence Scale for Children." *J Consult Psychol* 18:143–4 Ap '54. * (*PA* 29:2457)
81. RICHARDSON, ELIZABETH J., AND KOBLER, FRANK J. "Testing the Cerebral Palsied." *Excep Child* 21:101–3+ D '54. * (*PA* 29:6108)
82. SATTER, GEORGE, AND MCGEE, EUGENE. "Retarded Adults Who Have Developed Beyond Expectation: Part I, Intellectual Functions." *Training Sch B* 51:43–55 My '54. * (*PA* 29:2662)
83. BOLIN, BYRON J. "A Comparison of Raven's Progressive Matrices (1938) With the ACE Psychological Examination and the Otis Gamma Mental Ability Test." Abstract. *J Consult Psychol* 19:400 O '55. *
84. BOLTON, FLOYD B. "Experiments With the Raven's Progressive Matrices—1938." *J Ed Res* 48:629–33 Ap '55. * (*PA* 30:1013)
85. CRAWFORD, AGNES. "An Analysis of Children's Wrong Answers on Raven's Progressive Matrices Test, 1938." Abstract. *B Brit Psychol Soc* (26):2 inset My '55. *
86. DESAI, MAHESH M. "The Relationship of the Wechsler-Bellevue Verbal Scale and the Progressive Matrices Test." Abstract. *J Consult Psychol* 19:60 F '55. *
87. GREEN, MEREDITH W., AND EWERT, JOSEPHINE C. "Normative Data on Progressive Matrices (1947)." *J Consult Psychol* 19:139–42 Ap '55. * (*PA* 30:1026)
88. JORDAN, THOMAS E. *The Utility of the Coloured Progressive Matrices.* Doctor's thesis, Indiana University (Bloomington, Ind.), 1955. (*DA* 15:1554)
89. KEEHN, J. D., AND PROTHRO, E. TERRY. "Non-Verbal Tests as Predictors of Academic Success in Lebanon." *Ed & Psychol Meas* 15:495–8 w '55. * (*PA* 30:7765)
90. LEVINE, BERT, AND ISCOE, IRA. "The Progressive Matrices (1938), the Chicago Non-Verbal and the Wechsler-Bellevue on an Adolescent Deaf Population." *J Clin Psychol* 11:307–8 Jl '55. * (*PA* 30:3334)
91. NORMAN, RALPH D., AND MIDKIFF, KATHERINE L. "Navaho Children on Raven Progressive Matrices and Goodenough Draw-a-Man Tests." *Southw J Anthrop* 11:129–36 su '55. * (*PA* 30:4426)
92. SATTER, GEORGE. "Retarded Adults Who Have Developed Beyond Expectation: Part III, Further Analysis and Summary." *Training Sch B* 51:237–43 F '55. * (*PA* 29:7498)
93. STACEY, CHALMERS L., AND CARLETON, FREDERICK O. "The Relationship Between Raven's Colored Progressive Matrices and Two Tests of General Intelligence." *J Clin Psychol* 11:84–5 Ja '55. * (*PA* 29:7321)
94. STACEY, CHALMERS L., AND GILL, MARIE R. "The Relationship Between Raven's Colored Progressive Matrices and Two Tests of General Intelligence for 172 Subnormal Adult Subjects." *J Clin Psychol* 11:86–7 Ja '55. * (*PA* 29:7322)
95. WALTON, D. "The Validity and Interchangeability of Terman-Merrill and Matrices Test Data." *Brit J Ed Psychol* 25:190–4 N '55. * (*PA* 30:7233)
96. WAMBA, DONALD E., AND MARZOLF, STANLEY S. "Use of Eye Movements as a Response Indicator in Testing the Physically Handicapped." *J Clin Psychol* 11:405–7 O '55. * (*PA* 30: 6007)
97. BARRATT, ERNEST S. "The Relationship of the Progressive Matrices (1938) and the Columbia Mental Maturity Scale to the WISC." *J Consult Psychol* 20:294–6 Ag '56. * (*PA* 31: 7893)
98. CASTETTER, JOELLEN S. *An Empirical Investigation of the Item Characteristics, Validity, and Reliability of Raven's Progressive Matrices Test (1938).* Master's thesis, Indiana University (Bloomington, Ind.), 1956.
99. CURR, W., AND GOURLAY, N. "Differences Between Testers in Terman-Merrill Testing." *Brit J Stat Psychol* 9:75–81 N '56. *
100. GWYNNE JONES, H. "Comments on 'The Validity and Interchangeability of Terman-Merrill and Matrices Test Data' by D. Walton." *Brit J Ed Psychol* 26:141 Je '56. * (*PA* 31: 6086)
101. KNEHR, CHARLES A. "Progressive Matrices Findings Associated With Cerebral Histopathology." *Percept & Motor Skills* 6:249–54 D '56. * (*PA* 31:6098)
102. STRUHS, ISABEL. *The Relation Between the Raven Progressive Matrices Test and the Stanford-Binet in a Group of Gifted Children.* Master's thesis, Fordham University (New York, N.Y.), 1956.
103. BUCKLOW, MAXINE, AND DOUGHTY, PATRICIA. "The Use of Aptitude Tests in Clerical Employment: The Selection of Accounting Machinists." *Personnel Pract B* 13:35–44 S '57. *
104. GASKILL, P. Chap. 9, "Tests of Ability and Attainments: Pilot Experiments in Selection and Guidance," pp. 188–212. In *Educational Guidance and the Deaf Child.* Edited by A. W. G. Ewing. Manchester, England: Manchester University Press, 1957. Pp. xiii, 345. *
105. HALL, JULIA C. "Correlation of a Modified Form of Raven's Progressive Matrices (1938) With the Wechsler Adult Intelligence Scale." *J Consult Psychol* 21:23–6 F '57. * (*PA* 32:267)
106. JORDAN, THOMAS E., AND BENNETT, CARSON M. "An Item Analysis of the Coloured Progressive Matrices (1947)." *J Consult Psychol* 21:222 Je '57. *
107. ORME, J. E. "Non-Verbal and Verbal Performance in Normal Old Age, Senile Dementia, and Elderly Depression." *J Gerontol* 12:408–13 O '57. *
108. QUALTERE, THOMAS J. *An Investigation of the Relation-

ship Between Visual Figure-Background Disturbance and Performance on Raven's Progressive Matrices Test in Cerebral Palsy Children. Doctor's thesis, Syracuse University (Syracuse, N.Y.), 1957. (*DA* 17:1708)

109. RAVEN, JOHN C. "The 1956 Revision of the Matrices Tests." Abstract. *B Brit Psychol Soc* (32):3 inset My '57. *

110. SULLIVAN, ARTHUR. "Measurement of Intelligence in Different Environments." *B Maritime Psychol Assn* 6:18–23 D '57. *

111. WYSOCKI, BOLESLAW A. "Assessment of Intelligence Level by the Rorschach Test as Compared With Objective Tests." *J Ed Psychol* 48:113–7 F '57. *

112. BURKE, HENRY R. "Raven's Progressive Matrices: A Review and Critical Evaluation." *J Genetic Psychol* 93:199–228 D '58. *

113. KASPER, SIDNEY. "Progressive Matrices (1938) and Emotional Disturbance." Abstract. *J Consult Psychol* 22:24 F '58. *

114. SPERRAZZO, GERALD, AND WILKINS, WALTER L. "Further Normative Data on the Progressive Matrices." *J Consult Psychol* 22:35–7 F '58. *

115. TUDDENHAM, READ D.; DAVIS, LOUIS; DAVISON, LESLIE; AND SCHINDLER, RICHARD. "An Experimental Group Version for School Children of the Progressive Matrices." Abstract. *J Consult Psychol* 22:30 F '58. *

For reviews by Charlotte Banks, W. D. Wall, and George Westby, see 4:314; for reviews by Walter C. Shipley and David Wechsler of the 1938 edition, see 3:258; for a review by T. J. Keating, see 40:1417.

[371]

★**Proverbs Test.** Grades 5–16 and adults; 1954–56; 2 scores: abstract, concrete; general manual ('56); clinical manual ('56); $4.50 per set of 10 tests of all forms, cards, manuals and scoring keys; postage extra; specimen set not available; Donald R. Gorham; Psychological Test Specialists. *

a) BEST ANSWER FORM. 1 form ('56); separate answer sheets must be used; $2.50 per 25 tests; $2.50 per 100 answer sheets; (20–40) minutes.

b) [CLINICAL FORM.] Forms 1 ('54), 2 ('56), 3 ('56); individual; $1 per 25 tests; (10–30) minutes.

REFERENCES

1. GORHAM, DONALD R. "A Proverbs Test for Clinical and Experimental Use." *Psychol Rep* 2:1–12 sup 1 '56. * (*PA* 31:1037)

2. GORHAM, DONALD R. "Use of the Proverbs Test for Differentiating Schizophrenics From Normals." *J Consult Psychol* 20:435–40 D '56. * (*PA* 32:1849)

3. POUNDERS, C. J. *A Study of the Proverbs Test as a Measure of the Abstract Level of Concept Formation.* Master's thesis, Baylor University (Waco, Tex.), 1956.

4. ELMORE, CLYDE M., AND GORHAM, DONALD R. "Measuring the Impairment of the Abstracting Function With the Proverbs Test." *J Clin Psychol* 13:263–6 Jl '57. *

EUGENE L. GAIER, *Assistant Professor of Psychology, Louisiana State University, Baton Rouge, Louisiana.*

In the *Proverbs Test,* the subject either freely explains the meaning of each of 12 proverbs (individual Forms 1–3) or selects the best explanation among four presented choices for each of 40 items (group multiple-choice form). According to the author, the test makes use of "the universal appeal of proverbs to all age levels and to the mentally disturbed as well as to normal populations....[and] effectively taps verbal comprehension, particularly in the area of abstraction."

The presented norms are based on a standardization procedure with a series of samples totaling 1,345 children and adults. Scores equivalent to educational levels from the fifth grade through college are presented, as well as tentative norms for the clinical use of the test in the evaluation of schizophrenia.

The validity coefficients, based on correlations with other tests of "known" factorial content, indicate that the *Proverbs Test* is a measure of verbal comprehension.

Three principal uses of the test have been reported (clinical evaluation, clinical research, and screening and survey) and the author states that it can be used as a "rapid objective method for the appraisal of level of abstract verbal functioning" as well as an index of verbal functioning during psychotherapy. It is also indicated to be a sensitive measure of temporary intellectual impairment associated with severe emotional disturbance or schizophrenic disorganization.

Although industrial and counseling psychologists may find that the group form will provide a short and rapidly scored measure of verbal abstraction, it would be best to exercise caution in interpreting these scores as definitive measures of all that is claimed in the manual. The test is very short, the measures of reliability are based on small mixed samples (especially the Air Force enlistees), and the validity measures appear overinterpreted. As an ancillary index of verbal abstraction or gross differentiation of normals and schizophrenics, the individual forms should yield rich qualitative materials.

ALFRED B. HEILBRUN, JR., *Assistant Professor of Psychology, State University of Iowa, Iowa City, Iowa.*

This test seeks to measure the subject's verbal comprehension ability by requiring him to define the meaning of proverbs. Two modes of presentation are available. The clinical test consists of three parallel forms with 12 proverbs each. Scoring samples are provided to aid in evaluating the quality of the free responses on a 3-point abstractness scale. The multiple choice test contains 40 items and both an abstract and a concrete score are derived. Correlations between the clinical and multiple choice tests range from .81 when a single clinical form is used to .90 when the three are combined. These figures compare favorably to the tests' respective reliability coefficients (clinical test, .79, .88, .92 using one, two, and all three forms;

multiple choice test, .88), suggesting that it is as safe to interchange the two modes of testing as to rely on inferences from either.

The *Proverbs Test* has some potential merit as a verbal comprehension measure. This task probably holds more intrinsic interest than most intellectual tests. The multiple choice form has been administered to a substantial range of subjects from the fifth grade level (about 10 years of age) through college seniors with increasing mean scores and normal score distributions at each level increment resulting.

Certain aspects of the scoring procedures need clarification, however. Concerning the clinical form, Gorham states that the scoring system was derived *empirically* using certain a priori principles "as the author attempted to evaluate the answers of the original normative population." This would seem more like a judgmental derivation and one in which only one judge determined the scoring weights. In defining these a priori principles the manual stipulates: "Rationality of the abstractions was not considered; bizarre or autistic conceptions were given the same value as more usual responses as long as they met the criteria of converting the concrete symbolism of the proverb into concepts." Yet an examination of the 114 scoring samples of "adequate" responses fails to provide a single example of such irrational responses. Thus the examiner is left with the problem of how to score obviously incorrect yet conceptualized responses. Finally, the "validity" of the scoring values for each item was determined by the point biserial correlation of that item with scores on the total item pool. It should be pointed out that this procedure is better described as an internal consistency check rather than validation (i.e., correlation with an external criterion). A minimal correlation of .35 was selected as the criterion for item inclusion which means that an item could account for only about 12 per cent of the total item pool variance and still be retained.

Other questions which should be raised concern the operations involved in demonstrating the test's diagnostic utility. Starting with Goldstein's notion that the "abstract attitude" is impaired in schizophrenia, the performances of 100 hospitalized chronic schizophrenics were compared with those of 100 Air Force enlistees. These groups were matched in pairs on the basis of sex, education, and intelligence. Matching for intellectual level was attempted by pairing performance on the Word Knowledge Test of the Airman Classification Battery. Since vocabulary tests have been shown to be relatively insensitive to intellectual impairment in schizophrenia, such a measure would appear to be a poor estimate of present functional intelligence in the psychotic group. The effect of using a vocabulary test for matching would be systematically to match normals with less functionally intelligent schizophrenics. To the extent that performance on the *Proverbs Test* is negatively correlated with age at older age levels, the failure to match for age and the likelihood that the chronic schizophrenic group was older on the average than the normal group would also tend to increase spuriously the discriminative power of the test.

It also seems important to note the failure to control for the hospitalization variable. The effects of presumably prolonged institutionalization (the schizophrenics are described as chronic) should tend to depress performance on psychometric tasks because of altered motivational, attentional, and interest levels. Again, spuriously high discrimination would result.

Considering the above criticisms, the finding that classification on the basis of the most effective cutting score leads to only 77.5 per cent discrimination between basic airmen and hospitalized chronic schizophrenics does not lend confidence to the test's diagnostic use at the present time.

As a promising beginning, the *Proverbs Test* warrants further refinement and more rigorous investigation of its clinical or research utility.

[372]

★Purdue Non-Language Test. Grades 9–12 and adults; 1957–58; Forms A, B ('57); preliminary manual ('58); $1.75 per 20 tests; 30¢ per specimen set; postage extra; 25(30) minutes; Joseph Tiffin, Alin Gruber, and Kay Inaba; Science Research Associates. *

[373]

*Quick-Scoring Test of Learning Capacity: Dominion Tests. Grades 7–9, 10 and over; 1934–58; quick scoring edition of *Group Tests of Learning Capacity: Dominion Tests;* Forms A, B ('58); 2 levels; preliminary manual ('58) for each level; separate answer sheets must be used; $1.75 per set of 25 tests, 25 answer sheets, and manual; $1 per 50 answer sheets; 10¢ per scoring key; 75¢ per complete specimen set of either level; postage extra; 30(40) minutes; Department of Educational Research, Ontario College of Education, University of Toronto; distributed by Guidance Centre. *

a) INTERMEDIATE. Grades 7–9; 1958.

b) ADVANCED. Grades 10 and over; 1955–58; revised norms ('55).

[374]

★Reasoning Tests for Higher Levels of Intelligence. College entrants; 1954; 1 form; group norms only; 8d. per test; 2s. per manual ['54]; postage extra; 55(60) minutes; C. W. Valentine; Oliver & Boyd Ltd. *

REGINALD R. DALE, *Lecturer in Education, University College of Swansea, Swansea, Wales.*

Designed especially for use in the selection of entrants to universities and teachers' training colleges, this test provides an assessment of general "reasoning ability" at a high level. Section A has 4 items involving inductive reasoning; Section B consists of 12 items of symbolic logic based partly on problems set in old logic papers, all the suggested solutions from which the candidate must choose being provided by the author. It is primarily a power test, the time limit being liberal. The items have a touch of humour reminiscent of the author, and students appear to enjoy attempting the problems; this is an important merit if other motivation is lacking.

A determined attempt is made to validate the test by using such criteria as the degree results of students and comparison of test results with a hierarchy of student groups. The validation outcome is good enough to give confidence to users, though neither the author nor the reviewer will be satisfied until further testing provides still larger numbers and wider representation in the subgroups. Two principal difficulties are apparent here. First, many subgroups, varying in sex, university and training college background, and intelligence level are essential. Second, the degree criterion is a difficult one, as the standard of a First Class Honours degree, for example, is inclined to vary from one university department to another. None the less, the difference between the means for First and Second Class Honours graduates is significant at the two per cent level, between Second and Third Class at the five per cent level, and between Second Class and Pass graduates at the one per cent level.

With regard to norms, the author claims that as his purpose is "to provide a college or university department with a further basis on which to select entrants, all each will need will be comparative estimates among its own applicants. Hence there is no absolute necessity for a wise standardisation and absolute norms." The provision of the present group norms is certainly sufficient to make the test valuable, but its value would be considerably increased if national norms could be provided for training college students of both sexes and for graduates in different faculties or faculty subgroups. There is evidence, for example, that a higher level of g is needed for success in physical science and mathematics than for success in literary subjects in the arts faculty, and there are other differences of this kind.

A split-half reliability coefficient reported for one group of men is .83. This figure is depressed by the fewness of the items and by the highly selected nature of the group.

This test is a welcome and praiseworthy attempt to break away from the conventional approaches in this area. As a pioneer effort, it achieves undoubted success. Like all pioneer efforts, it will in due course be improved upon. It will undoubtedly be widely used in Great Britain; its experimental use in the United States is recommended for cross-fertilisation purposes, even though there are at present no American norms. Those who use this test for selection will naturally bear in mind the importance for some subjects of those special abilities which have little weight in the test. Nor is it decrying the test to remind educationists that, among the highly selected applicants for university entry in Great Britain, temperamental factors and motivation are even more important than a further assessment of "reasoning ability," useful though this is for the border zone.

[375]

Revised Beta Examination. Grades 7–12 and adults; 1931–57; revision of *Army Group Examination Beta* ('20); nonlanguage; 1 form ('35); 2 editions; revised manual ('57); $4.20 per 25 tests; 35¢ per specimen set; postpaid; French edition available; 15(30) minutes; 1946 revision by Robert M. Lindner and Milton Gurvitz; D. E. Kellogg and N. W. Morton; Psychological Corporation. *

REFERENCES

1–4. See 40:1419.
5–9. See 3:259.
10. MURPHY, LAURA WHITE. "The Relation Between Mechanical Ability Tests and Verbal and Non-Verbal Intelligence Tests." *J Psychol* 2:353–66 '36. * (PA 11:3928)
11. MORTON, N. W. "Mental Age Norms for Revised Beta Examination." Abstract. *B Can Psychol Assn* 1:10–1 D '40. *
12. ROSS, LAURENCE W. "Results of Testing Machine-Tool Trainees." *Personnel J* 21:363–7 Ap '43. * (PA 17:2459)
13. WILLIAMS, H. M.; HAFEMEISTER, NORMAN; AND WEGMAN, MARGARET. "An Analytical Study of Scores on Stanford-Binet, Revised Army Beta, and School Achievement Tests." *Am J Mental Def* 53:617–20 Ap '49. * (PA 24:2687)
14. ZAKOLSKI, F. C. "Studies in Delinquency: I, Personality Structure of Delinquent Boys." *J Genetic Psychol* 74:109–17 Mr '49. * (PA 23:4925)
15. ELIAS, JACK Z. *Non-Intellective Factors in Certain Intelligence and Achievement Tests: An Analysis of Factors in Addition to the Cognitive Entering Into the Intelligence and Achievement Scores of Children at the Sixth Grade Level.* Doctor's thesis, New York University (New York, N.Y.), 1951. (*Microfilm Abstr* 11:558)
16. YERBURY, EDGAR C.; HOLZBERG, JULES D.; AND ALESSI, SALVATORE L. "Psychological Tests in the Selection and Place-

ment of Psychiatric Aides." *Am J Psychiatry* 108:91–7 Ag '51. *

17. BLUETT, CHARLES G. "Normative Data for the Alpha-Beta-Gregg Battery." *J Clin Psychol* 8:237–45 Jl '52. * (PA 27:5857)

18. KNAPP, WILLIAM. *A Study of the Quality of Slowness of Two Groups of Psychotic Patients as Demonstrated by Performance on the Revised Beta Examination.* Doctor's thesis, Western Reserve University (Cleveland, Ohio), 1952.

19. MOORE, JOSEPH E., AND ROSS, LAURENCE W. "The Changing of Mental Test Norms in a Southern Industrial Plant." *J Appl Psychol* 37:16–7 F '53. * (PA 28:1625)

20. LAVOS, GEORGE. "Interrelationships Among Three Tests of Non-Language Intelligence Administered to the Deaf." *Am Ann Deaf* 99:303–13 My '54. * (PA 29:4596)

21. LAVOS, GEORGE. "Sex Differences on the Revised Beta Examination." *J Consult Psychol* 18:375–6 O '54. * (PA 29:5714)

22. STOTSKY, BERNARD A. "Vocational Tests as Measures of Performance of Schizophrenics in Two Rehabilitation Activities." *J Clin Psychol* 12:236–42 Jl '56. * (PA 31:6447)

23. WOODS, WALTER A., AND TOAL, ROBERT. "Subtest Disparity of Negro and White Groups Matched for IQs on the Revised Beta Test." *J Consult Psychol* 21:136–8 Ap '57. *

For reviews by Raleigh M. Drake and Walter C. Shipley, see 3:259; for reviews by S. D. Porteus and David Wechsler, see 40:1419.

[376]

★**SRA College Classification Tests.** College entrants; 1958; 6 scores: English usage, mathematics usage, social studies reading, natural science reading, word usage, composite; IBM; Form A ('58); manual ('58); separate answer sheets must be used; tests rented only; $1 per student; fee includes scoring and reporting service; 170(200) minutes; Science Research Associates. *

[377]

★**SRA Tests of Educational Ability.** Grades 4–6, 6–9, 9–12; 1957–58; 5 scores (4 in grades 6–12): language, reasoning, quantitative, total, nonreading total (grades 4–6); 1 form, 3 levels; separate answer sheets must be used; $7 per 20 tests of any one level; $6 per 100 IBM answer sheets; 50¢ per scoring stencil; 35¢ per manual; $1 per revised technical supplement ('58); $2 per specimen set of any one level; postage extra; L. L. Thurstone and Thelma Gwinn Thurstone; Science Research Associates. *

a) GRADES 4–6. 1958; manual ('58); 26(52) minutes.
b) GRADES 6–9. 1958; manual ('58); 42(67) minutes.
c) GRADES 9–12. 1957–58; manual ('57); 27(45) minutes.

JOSHUA A. FISHMAN, *Director of Research, College Entrance Examination Board, New York, New York.* [Review of test for grades 9–12.]

This is the first test in what is planned as a five-test series covering the range of school grades from kindergarten through grade 12. It is a group test designed to provide an estimate of aptitude for current school work, and requires a test administrator for the reading of instructions and for the accurate timing of its four parts. The test consists of 110 items, which are subdivided as follows: 20 word grouping items (find the word that does *not* belong with the other four); 30 synonyms; 30 letter-series items (what letter should come next in this series: abx, cdx, efx, ghx?) taken from *SRA*

Primary Mental Abilities for ages 11–17; and 30 number-judgment items. The first two item types, though separately timed, are combined to yield an L (language) score. The letter-series items yield an R (reasoning) score, and the number-judgment items, a Q (quantitative) score. A total score is also derived from all 110 items. The test is nicely printed, in reusable booklets with heavy paper covers. The answer sheet and the scoring stencil are both designed for either hand or machine scoring. A manual of directions and a separate technical supplement are available. The answer sheet permits a direct translation of raw scores into percentile ranks and AQ's ("ability quotients"), the latter being standard scores similar to deviation IQ's except that their comparison is with other pupils at the same *grade* (rather than *age*) level.

Some users may find unsatisfactory the directions in the manual which caution that the person administering the test "should be thoroughly familiar....with principles of group testing," without implying what these principles might be or what sources might be used in order that one might become familiar with these principles. The manual makes embarrassed mention of error of measurement without specifying its magnitude for this test. All in all, however, the manual, answer sheet, scoring stencil, and the explanatory sections of the test are at appropriate levels of clarity and readability. The relatively minor lapses such as those indicated above (as well as the fact that the instructions may seem to some to imply a correction for guessing although there is none) can be corrected easily in future editions.

The publishers emphasize that the test was constructed so as to maximize the short term prediction of academic grades. Due to this emphasis on an external, global criterion, item selection was necessarily less concerned both with internal consistency and with differential prediction. As a result, the reliability of the test is somewhat *lower* (in the .80's for the part scores and in the middle or high .80's for the total score) and the intercorrelations among the parts are *higher* (.63 between Q and L, and .65 between Q and R) than might have been attained had other criteria been kept to the fore. An impressive array of validity studies is reported in which intercorrelations between the TEA and other tests (intelligence, educational development, educational achievement) as well as between TEA scores and school marks are shown. The general conclusions from the validity studies would seem to be that the test as a whole and particularly the L section is as good a predictive instrument as one might seek of the 45–50 minute variety. The R and Q sections, however, do not seem to be functioning particularly well, there being several instances where the L section correlates higher with course grades and with scores on other tests—instances where one would expect the other sections to excel. The R and Q sections are, of course, serving face validity functions and adding to the entire test length and to the improved reliability and validity that accompanies greater length.

Although the test was not designed for differential purposes, both the technical supplement and the manual of directions defend the differential interpretation of part scores when they are at least 20 percentile points apart. The advisability of such interpretations seems open to question in view of the somewhat low part score reliabilities and validities (particularly the validities of Q and R) and the high intercorrelations among part scores. In any case, the advisability of differential interpretations should be demonstrated via appropriately designed studies rather than merely persuasively argued. The norming of the TEA was accomplished by equipercentile equating of its raw scores to the 1957 revised norms for the *Iowa Tests of Educational Development.* This stopgap approach to norms should also be improved upon, particularly in the light of the fact that the correlations between these two tests are not convincingly high (.71 for L, .51 for R, .62 for Q), nor are they as high as between the TEA and other tests cited by the publisher.

No special claim is made by the publisher as to the suitability of the TEA for college guidance or selection purposes. There would seem to be no reason to prefer it for such purposes to the 3-hour *SRA College Placement Test,* the Psychological Corporation's 80-minute *College Qualification Test* or the Educational Testing Service's 70-minute *Cooperative School and College Ability Tests.* For educational guidance and evaluation purposes in grades 9–12 the TEA seems generally inferior to Forms 1A and 2A of SCAT in conjunction with reliability, part score intercorrelations, and norming. Nevertheless, the TEA seems to be a quite adequate instrument for estimating current academic ability of a global nature. Various desirable technical improvements in future editions, as well as the preparation of a parallel form, would greatly enhance the substantial value which it already possesses.

WILLIAM B. MICHAEL, *Director, The Testing Bureau, and Professor of Psychology and Education, University of Southern California, Los Angeles, California.* [Review of test for grades 9–12.]

Designed to furnish a means for estimating a student's current ability to do high school work, the *SRA Tests of Educational Ability* (abbreviated as TEA) yield a total score and three part scores in subtests designated as Language (L), Reasoning (R), and Quantitative (Q). Although the total time for administration of the examination is expected to approximate 45 minutes, the short total working time of only 27 minutes (which, from the standpoint of the manual's stated preference for a power condition, might better have been 30 or 32 minutes) is distributed in the following manner: 10 minutes for Language which consists of two parts—word-grouping, a 20-item verbal test of a reasoning nature requiring 4 minutes and vocabulary, a 30-item synonym test taking 6 minutes; 6 minutes for Reasoning, a 30-item letter series test taken from the *SRA Primary Mental Abilities;* and 11 minutes for Quantitative, which is made up of 30 multiple choice items involving numerical skills and judgments concerning numerical relationships.

The content of the easy-to-read manual is directed primarily toward the problems of planning for a test session, of administering and scoring the examination, and of forming profiles and interpreting test results. To obtain information regarding validity, reliability, the intercorrelations of test parts, and the development of normative data, one is required to consult the carefully prepared technical supplement that was issued November 1957. Even though the technical supplement is clearly written, detailed in its coverage, and judiciously modest in its tone, the data upon which one must formulate judgments regarding reliability and validity are somewhat meager in view of the limited number of different high schools employed (five in the Chicago area), the possible lack of representativeness of these schools, the number of grade levels considered (usually only the 9th and 12th grades), and the size of each of the samples involved (varying between 16 and 214 depending upon the subject or cluster of subjects with the grades of which scores on subtests were correlated). Although the publishers probably intend to release additional reliability and validity data as they become available and to revise the norms periodically, one cannot help but conclude that the release of TEA was somewhat premature.

Considering the data reported as tentative, it would appear that the reliabilities of the part scores (averaging about .80 or slightly above) and the total score (approximating .90) are satisfactory, although the estimates for the single form were based on internal consistency approaches for which the control of the speed factor was not entirely defensible. Initial concurrent validity data are quite promising with respect to the extent of correlation of the scores of each of the subtests with grades in specific courses and with total grade average, as well as with scores on other tests such as parts of the *Iowa Tests of Educational Development,* the *SRA Achievement Series,* and the Kuhlmann-Anderson mental age score.

Although some degree of differential predictability is apparent in the validity coefficients of the three parts with respect to different high school courses, it would appear, as stated in the technical supplement, that other test batteries developed primarily in a factor-analytic setting would tend to attain a higher degree of differential efficiency, for the authors have intended and contended that the TEA score is, essentially, a predictor of general achievement. (Additional evidence pertaining to the general nature of TEA is apparent in the reported intercorrelations of .57, .63, and .65 between L and R, L and Q, and R and Q part scores, respectively.)

Nevertheless, the normative data are portrayed as profiles containing the three part scores (L, R, and Q) and the total score at each of four grade levels in terms both of percentile ranks and of an ability quotient in which the mean is 100 and the standard deviation is 15. Through use of Flanagan's equipercentile method of equating, score standards for TEA were supposedly made comparable with those of ITED, which along with TEA, was administered in 1957 to 300 students at each grade level from 9 to 12 in two public high schools judged (on the basis of previous ITED performance) to be of average level (one in Texas and the

other in Pennsylvania). Although the reviewer is optimistic of the eventual utility of the instrument in light of the initial validity data reported and in view of the previous excellent work of the Thurstones with experimental versions of the tests in TEA, he would feel much more comfortable if the standardization had already been carried out on a large number of samples representative of different geographical areas, of different types of educational programs, and of different philosophies of education—samples in which boys and girls were always treated separately.

In summary, TEA offers the advantages of being a conveniently administered, readily scored, and (potentially) easily interpreted device for prediction of high school achievement. However, until additional data concerning reliability and validity are obtained, until several parallel forms are devised, and especially until the standardization process is extended to diversified samples of high school boys and girls throughout the United States, the degree of confidence that can be placed in the interpretation of the scores will be somewhat less than that which can be given to other competitive instruments currently available.

E. A. Peel, *Professor of Education, University of Birmingham, Birmingham, England.* [Review of test for grades 9–12.]

The purpose of these three tests is to provide an estimate of students' current potentiality for school success. For this purpose the authors have chosen short timed tests of language, reasoning, and number work. The first is made up of a 4-minute test of choosing the unlike word from sets of five words and a 6-minute vocabulary test using multiple choice technique. The reasoning test, timed to six minutes, consists of items requiring the completion of letter series, and the third test is one of number and simple arithmetical computation requiring 11 minutes. The whole test is accompanied by a comprehensive manual of directions and a technical supplement providing statistical and psychometric information of value to the specialist. The layout of the answer sheets and the marking stencil is good.

For use as a predicting device, the subtests are better combined to give a total measure. Inspection of the correlations between the subtests and teacher grades readily demonstrates that the language and quantitative (arithmetic) tests do not differentiate markedly between allied school subjects. This is perhaps not surprising in tests of such similar format even though the language and quantitative tests clearly make use of elements of attainment as well as ability. On the whole, the quantitative subtest seems, by casual inspection of the subscore versus grades correlations, to predict mathematical subject grades less well than the language test predicts language subject grades. This is a tendency often noticed in English 11+ selection and it seems that we have yet to devise a satisfactory number and space test to predict secondary school mathematical achievement. These opinions are confirmed by inspecting a shorter table where median correlations are set out. Here we see, in the case of 12 correlations with mathematics and science grades, that the language subtest is superior to both the reasoning and quantitative subtests in predicting mathematics and science achievement. The reliability figures given include some correlations which are perhaps rather low for this kind of test, although no doubt they are affected by the homogeneity of the sample of persons tested and the shortness of the tests.

All the material and information is so efficiently set out that instances to criticise are rare, but it might help the routine worker if, in the two sections on page three of the manual devoted to a description of the three subtests, the subtests were mentioned in the same order as used in the scheme of testing, and if the two parts of the language test were given in the same order as in the test itself. In the technical supplement, it would help the specialist if some standard deviations were given. This would apply particularly to those who wish to use this test outside the United States. The whole question of correlation is so bound up with homogeneity and distribution of scores that we need more than comments through the text that this or that group was more or less homogeneous.

In spite of these criticisms, the tests as a whole should provide a useful single predictor of secondary school potentiality, both for research work and for routine guidance.

[378]

*SRA Verbal Form. Ages 12 and over; 1946–56; formerly called *SRA Verbal Classification Form;* abbreviated adaptation of *Thurstone Test of Mental Alertness* which is an abbreviated adaptation of *American Council on Education Psychological Examination for High School Students,* 1940 Edition; 3 scores: quantitative, linguistic, total; Forms A ('47), B ('55);

manual, second edition ('56); $2.75 per 20 tests; 50¢ per specimen set; postage extra; 15(25) minutes; Thelma Gwinn Thurstone and L. L. Thurstone; Science Research Associates. *

[379]

★The Scholarship Qualifying Test. Juniors and seniors seeking college scholarships; 1956–58; test administered annually in October at participating secondary schools; 2 scores: verbal, quantitative; IBM; supervisor's manual ('57); examination fee, $1; fee includes the reporting of scores; scores for juniors reported only to secondary schools; 120(140) minutes; program administered by Educational Testing Service for the College Entrance Examination Board. *

LEE J. CRONBACH, *Professor of Education and Psychology, University of Illinois, Urbana, Illinois.* [Review of Form FSQ.]

The growing national awareness of the wasted talent of young people who cannot afford higher education has led to establishment of dozens of scholarship programs. Fair comparison of candidates requires a standard and unfamiliar test, and since the same pupil is eligible for numerous scholarships, a unified testing service for many if not all programs has become a necessity. A new form of the *Scholarship Qualifying Test,* prepared by the Educational Testing Service under the sponsorship of the College Entrance Examination Board, is given throughout the country each fall. A small fee is charged pupils, except for a limited number of top candidates named by the principal. Seniors who take the test are considered for about 20 different scholarship programs. Test scores are returned to the school for guidance purposes.

Form FSQ (1957) consists of 60 verbal items (sentence completion, analogies, reading comprehension) and 50 quantitative items (arithmetic reasoning, data interpretation). Nearly all students finish the verbal part, but over half fail to complete the quantitative items. Omissions are numerous, indicating that poor performance reflects unwillingness to try mathematical items as much as it does the effect of the time limit. As its purpose requires, the test is quite difficult, difficulty being attained mostly by subtlety. In the verbal section, words are rarely more unfamiliar than "prosaic" and "synopsis." But each multiple choice item contains numerous plausible, near-correct answers, and the student who is unwilling to make painstaking comparisons will fare badly. The reading section includes difficult adult reading material, and the comprehension questions are penetrating. A pupil with facility in commonplace algebra, ability to comprehend intricate problems, and patience in carrying out successive steps can earn a high score in the quantitative section. Very few items require geometric knowledge or specialized algebraic skills.

A primary requisite in a scholarship test is that it have a healthy effect on student attitudes and on the curriculum. This test stands up well on both counts. A student who fails to qualify for an award will have little excuse to offer save that others did better work. The questions are patently fair. If parents demand that the school do something to increase their son's chance of winning an award, the best "cramming" would be that sort of training in reading and reasoning which will also make him a better college prospect. (In this respect, the test by another publisher which replaced the SQT in the 1958 National Merit Scholarship testing is inferior. Some items in the new test call for knowledge of crammable grammatical rules, and the use of uncommon words in its verbal section makes almost reasonable the conduct of the reviewer's young acquaintance who prepared for the competition by reading through a dictionary.) The SQT seems to require more persistence and thoughtfulness than most mental tests, but no college teacher will regret having students of the sort who take this test in stride. The test is designed for steady pacers. The intuitive, nonconformist hare, darting here and there after brilliant ideas, will be left behind, but so will the drudging tortoises of academic life.

An unpublished memorandum prepared by Frances Swineford provides technical data on the test. Scores are reported for each section on a scale from 10 (chance) to 70 (perfect). Scaled scores for one year are equated to those from previous years. The argument for a distinctive scale is that, in a test not applied to a representative sample, standard scores would be of little use. The difficulty of the test is indicated by the fact that the midpoint of the verbal range comes at the 83rd percentile for the 256,-000 pupils taking the test. The distribution is skewed, providing best discrimination in the upper portions of the range. Only one pupil in the entire sample earned a perfect verbal score, which suggests that the authors have been clever beyond necessity in concealing their correct answers. The test reliability is around .90 —a respectable figure, especially since a second test is generally used to select final scholarship

winners. Here if ever, however, is a test for which one needs a separate report of the standard error of measurement in each portion of the range instead of an overall reliability. The test surely measures less accurately in the lower part of the range than elsewhere.

There are some risks in the system which this test represents. Principals find that the pupils they nominate to take the test without charge are often outscored by pupils who volunteer and pay a fee. There is need to make sure that all possible winners do take the test. A different problem arises from the application of the test to pupils who perform badly. Literally thousands of pupils who take the test earn chance-level scores on one or both sections. Such a discouraging experience is unprofitable for all concerned. Could not a short practice booklet profitably be used in the school both to prepare pupils for the items to be used and to help determine who should take the test?

For use in guidance, schools are provided with a booklet giving a brief summary of the meaning of the test, including a scale for making conversions to the scales of the *Scholastic Aptitude Test* and *Cooperative School and College Ability Tests*. It is better to return test scores to the school than to waste the information obtained. The recent announcement that the test will be opened to juniors indicates an apparent intention to feature the test for guidance purposes. This will require a more extensive manual reporting correlational information, particularly on the differential validity or significance, if any, of the separate subtest scores. Though the SQT appears excellent for separating the very best college prospects from the merely very good, no guidance program should use this as its principal test; other tests suited to the wider range of college-bound students or to the entire student body will give more useful information.

ROGER T. LENNON, *Director, Division of Test Research and Service, World Book Company, Yonkers, New York.* [Review of Forms ESQ and FSQ.]

In October 1956, the Educational Testing Service initiated for the College Entrance Examination Board administration to high school seniors of the *Scholarship Qualifying Test* (SQT). SQT had as its primary aim the selection of students "to be given further consideration for the award of scholarships"; and, secondarily, provision of information useful in the educational guidance of students. In 1956 and 1957 SQT was used as the preliminary selection instrument in the National Merit Scholarship Program. Scores of examinees were reported to the various scholarship programs in which the examinees were participating and to the examinees' high schools; the respective scholarship programs made such use of the scores as they saw fit. In 1956, 166,581 examinees took SQT, in 1957, 255,887, and in 1958 well over 300,000. Beginning in 1959 the SQT is to be replaced by the *Preliminary Scholastic Aptitude Test* of the College Entrance Examination Board.

The first two forms of the *Scholarship Qualifying Test,* ESQ and FSQ, accessory materials, and information (exceptionally detailed in many respects) concerning technical characteristics of the tests have been made available to the reviewer, and form the basis for the comments which follow. Forms ESQ and FSQ are parallel forms in every important detail, and the comments pertain equally to both.

GENERAL DESCRIPTION. SQT yields two scores, Verbal and Quantitative, the former based on a 60-item subtest and the latter on a 50-item subtest, each subtest requiring 60 minutes' testing time. The 60 verbal items are divided equally among analogies, double definitions, and reading comprehension items; the quantitative section comprises 30 arithmetic reasoning and 20 data-interpretation items. The test is completely objective; all items are multiple choice, five-option items, with responses recorded on an IBM answer sheet. From the standpoint of content, SQT blazes no new trails but sticks to tried-and-true types of material for prediction of college success.

The reading comprehension part of the verbal subtest consists of four selections, ranging in length from about 200 to 400 words, each selection followed by from four to six questions. The content is largely drawn from scientific sources, presumably of a kind that college students will have to read. Questions assess ability to locate information, to draw inferences, to relate elements of information, and to understand the explicit information given. Item validity data, in the form of biserial correlations, presented in the technical report, both for the reading and the other parts of the verbal subtest, indicate a satisfactory degree of internal consistency, very few of the reported values falling below .30.

The quantitative subtest is fundamentally an arithmetic reasoning test, supplemented by exercises on interpretation of charts and tables; it makes few demands on mathematical skills acquired in any secondary level mathematics courses. Data in the technical report indicate that the quantitative section as a whole is rather more difficult than might be desired, and likewise appears to have more of a speed component than this reviewer would consider optimum for the purposes. Item validity data do, however, indicate that most of the items in the quantitative subtest have satisfactory discriminative capacity.

On the basis of a careful reading of a large proportion of the individual items, this reviewer judges them to be, on the whole, clear, unambiguous, and well written. The instructions to the examinees likewise seem entirely adequate, and the general directions for administration of the program, for maintenance of security of materials, etc., conform to the College Entrance Examination Board's customary high standards in these respects.

RELIABILITY. Kuder-Richardson formula 20 estimates of reliability are presented for both Form ESQ and Form FSQ, for all sections of the test, for the V score, the Q score, and total score. Estimates are reported for three independent populations chosen to represent different parts of the range of scores. The median estimate of reliability of the V score is approximately .87, of the Q score approximately .84, and of the total score .91—somewhat low, perhaps, for tests of this length and lower than might be hoped for, in view of the importance of the decisions made on the basis of the results.

INTERPRETIVE INFORMATION. The primary purpose of SQT, the identification of potential recipients of scholarships, may be achieved with little or no normative data, a mere ranking of candidates being sufficient for the purposes of most scholarship programs. For realization of the guidance values of SQT, however, additional interpretive information is called for. Such interpretive, or normative, data are provided in the form of percentile ranks corresponding to V and Q scores for the total group tested; tables indicating scores on ETS' *Scholastic Aptitude Test* and ETS' *Cooperative School and College Ability Tests* corresponding to SQT scores; and estimated percentile ranks for a representative national sample of 12th grade students, based on equating of SQT to SCAT. Additionally, a bulletin that accompanied reports of 1956 examination results to schools presented estimates of probability of admission to certain CEEB colleges corresponding to selected SQT scores. These data on equivalent scores on SAT and SCAT are presented with appropriate expressions of caution and with emphasis on the point that the conversions are not exact; it is pointed out that the estimated SAT or SCAT equivalent is not to be regarded with the same confidence as if it were derived directly from the test in question.

For educational guidance purposes it is also suggested, though again with appropriate reservations, that the counselor consider relative performance on the verbal and quantitative scores. Since correlations averaging slightly more than .60 are reported between the V and Q scores, the differential validity power of the two measures is probably quite limited. Interpretation of such differences is clouded also by systematic sex differences on both the V and the Q tests.

VALIDITY. The treatment of validity in the published material accompanying the test is indeed scant. The bulletin for the 1957 test asserts that, "The Verbal and Quantitative scores are measures of aptitude for learning verbal and quantitative types of material involved in many college courses. Such measures have been found to be useful and reliable in predicting success in academic work"; and this, as far as this reviewer could note, is the only reference to validity in the materials. Inasmuch as SQT was first administered in 1956 to students who did not complete their first year in college until June 1958, it was, obviously, impossible to obtain empirical predictive validity data in time for inclusion in any of the materials seen; but one would have felt more comfortable had the material included data on the correlation between SQT and other measures concerning whose predictive worth there are research findings—particularly when such correlations must have been available. In the absence of predictive data the reviewer must base his opinion as to the validity of SQT as a predictor of college success on consideration of the content of the test and its surface resemblance to other instruments whose predictive validity is better known. On this tenuous basis, the reviewer considers SQT to be of about the same order of predictive validity as, say, SAT, ACE, or the Ohio State psychological examination.

The validity of SQT for purposes other than identification of scholarship award winners— that is, for guidance purposes in the high school—is likewise entirely presumptive in character. The reviewer judges SQT to be no better for high school guidance purposes than measures of similar abilities in widespread use in high school and probably less valuable for these purposes than the better of the multi-factor batteries.

Is SQT a fair and efficient instrument for the identification of worthy recipients of college scholarship assistance? This is a question not to be answered solely, and perhaps not even primarily, on the basis of the technical characteristics of the test. What types of high school students should society seek to encourage through scholarship aid to pursue their education? Is the notion of a single selection instrument for all scholarship candidates, regardless of the type of collegiate program they may be interested in pursuing, a sound approach? Does the SQT type of instrument, minimizing the influence of specific attainment in any high school course, have harmful consequences on the motivation of high school students? These are the types of questions that come quickly to mind as ones that must be answered before a satisfactory answer can really be offered to the opening question in this paragraph. Pending answers to these larger questions, this reviewer concludes that SQT does a reasonably effective job of identifying high school students having the ability to "succeed" in college, when that success is measured by conventional criteria, such as grade-point average or end-of-course examinations.

[380]

★Scholastic Mental Ability Tests. Grades kgn–1, 2–3, 4–9; 1953–54; various titles used by publisher; for Catholic schools; IBM for grades 4–9; 3 levels; 2 editions; 50¢ per specimen set of any one level of either edition; postage extra; Oliver F. Anderhalter; Scholastic Testing Service, Inc. *

a) LONG FORM. Grades kgn–1, 2–3, 4–9; 1953–54; 1 form; 3 levels.

1) *Pre-Primary Test*. Grades kgn–1; 1954; Form A; $3.50 per 35 tests; (50–60) minutes.

2) *Primary Test*. Grades 2–3; 1953–54; 6 scores: linguistic, non-linguistic, total, logical reasoning, numerical reasoning, fluency; Form A ('53); manual ('54); $3.25 per 35 tests; (50–60) minutes.

3) *Elementary Test*. Grades 4–9; 1954; scores same as for Primary Test; IBM; Form A; $3.50 per 35 tests; separate answer sheets may be used; $1.75 per 35 IBM scorable answer sheets; 24¢ per set of scoring stencils; 36(60) minutes.
b) SHORT FORM. Grades 2–3, 4–9; 1955; 2 levels.
1) *Primary Test*. Grades 2–3; Short Form A; $2.60 per 35 tests; (30–40) minutes.
2) *Elementary Test*. Grades 4–9; IBM; Short Forms A, B; $3 per 35 tests; $1.75 per 35 IBM scorable answer sheets; 12¢ per scoring stencil; 26(35) minutes.

WALTER N. DUROST, *Director of Educational Services, Pinellas County Public Schools, Clearwater, Florida.*

The *Scholastic Mental Ability Tests* are intended for use in Catholic parochial schools only. This was determined only after a diligent search of the manuals for the several levels of this series. Why an *intelligence* test for parochial schools only? The argument runs somewhat as follows.

Intelligence tests administered to a national cross-sectional group are not appropriately administered to parochial school children because such populations may be selected groups, and may have had instruction differing in quality and kind. Such factors would obviously influence intelligence test results. The author presents evidence that in at least one midwestern diocese the less able children (children below 90 IQ) tend to drop out of the parochial school population and, presumably, return to public school. If it were claimed that the test was designed to be paired with a valid measure of parochial school achievement standardized on the same group, this argument would bear considerable weight with the writer. No such evidence seems to be present.

As to validity, the argument is made that the construct validity of a test is to a considerable extent established if it can be shown that there is a gain in raw score from one age to a successively higher age group. This comparison is made in age groups differing by three months, and it is shown that there are consistent differences in mean raw score. That there would be similar differences in any other physical measure taken for similarly differing age groups is not mentioned. This argument for establishing the validity of a mental ability measure falls down completely unless it is demonstrated on logical grounds that the subtests do in fact measure mental traits which are largely independent of school instruction rather than some other phase of the individual's development. From this point of view, it would be very hard to justify the validity of using, as this test does, an arithmetic reasoning test which might be taken from any standardized achievement test.

Under concurrent validity, correlations are given with the Kuhlmann-Anderson and Otis Alpha tests, these being .75 and .78, respectively, for small single grade populations. There is no evidence that these are corrected for attenuation, and it would be the writer's judgment that these correlations are "run of the mine" for intercorrelations of intelligence measures at this grade level.

In one manual at least, the validity of the mental tests is discussed in terms of the nomenclature adopted for the evaluation of tests in the APA *Technical Recommendations for Psychological Tests and Diagnostic Techniques*. For example, the content validity of the picture classification test at the primary level is defended on the basis that a survey of currently marketed intelligence tests indicate that a similar subtest is found in 75 per cent of these tests, and that picture similarities tests have "long been recognized as containing a large amount of 'g' factor, or general intelligence." The defense of the content validity of the other tests at the primary level is similarly vague.

Throughout the discussion of the construction and standardization of the tests, phrases such as "research has long pointed to the fact that," "this test is a valuable measure of 'mental alertness,'" and "similarities tests have long been recognized as containing a large amount of general intelligence" appear. There is no documentation of these claims.

Assuming that someone in a position of authority in a parochial school system wishes seriously to consider this test for use in his school, the question is whether it is a good test from other points of view. It is not exactly a bad test, but one does not have to search too diligently to find things to criticize about the items themselves or about the procedures used in scaling and norming the test.

For example, Item 11 in the primary level picture arrangement test shows a sequence having to do with baseball. The artwork in this illustration is extremely bad, and the figures are very hard to distinguish. Regardless of this, it seems improbable that children in the second and third grade, especially girls, would know enough about baseball to arrange the pictures in correct sequence. This undoubtedly explains why this sequence is next to last in this particular test. Many other pictures in this test are so poorly drawn that their meaning is ambiguous.

In Primary Short Form A, Test 3 is a verbal classification test. There is one sample question plus five other examples, answers to which are given to the children taking the test. In all five of these examples the right answer is in the fourth or last position. It is also in the fourth or last position in 4 of the remaining 10 items in the actual test. It would hardly seem that this could occur by chance allocation of correct answer positions, especially since not a single item has the correct answer in the first position.

Other ambiguous or incorrect items were noted throughout the tests. While a majority of the items seem to be fairly satisfactory as well as one can tell without having the item statistics at hand, each subtest examined had one or two items that were open to serious criticism. The manuals leave much to be desired by way of explicit description of what was actually done in the construction of these tests. For example, each of the manuals states that "tetrachoric coefficients of correlation were computed, based on the relation of test item to total score of the test. This index is a measure of the item reliability, and was used since increasing the reliability of the test should tend also to improve the validity." It is hoped that "the test" refers to each *subtest* separately, but there is no indication that this is true. Furthermore, such indices are hardly reliability coefficients of individual items, but rather measures of the extent to which the item discriminates between more able and less able individuals, which is evidence of validity of a sort.

The mechanics of the test (scoring, layout on the page, etc.) are reasonably adequate. The answer sheet is evidently a locally printed sheet. The copy which came in the specimen set used for review would not score accurately in the test scoring machine available. The spacing between the answer spaces is just a very small amount too large, a type of deviation that is cumulative from the bottom to the top of the sheet as it is inserted in the machine.

The authors are to be commended for abandoning the ratio IQ, which certainly is outmoded, in favor of the deviation IQ, but no attempt has been made to adjust for changes in the standard deviation of standard scores from age to age.

ALEXANDER G. WESMAN, *Associate Director, Test Division, The Psychological Corporation, New York, New York.*

These tests are offered as intelligence tests yielding mental age and IQ for linguistic, nonlinguistic, and total ability, and separate scores for logical reasoning, numerical reasoning, and fluency at the primary and elementary levels; only nonlinguistic MA and IQ are provided for the preprimary level.

The preprimary test consists of five pictorial subtests dealing with object naming, identification of object characteristics, identification of missing elements, following oral directions, and object classification. The total number of items is 77.

The primary test consists of seven subtests: picture classification, picture arrangement, number series, classification (verbal), word and sentence formation, arithmetic reasoning, and vocabulary (synonyms). There are 112 items. A short form, which omits the picture arrangement section, is also available.

The elementary test is composed of seven subtests: picture similarities, picture arrangement, number series, inference (syllogisms), word arrangement, arithmetic reasoning, and vocabulary. A short form eliminates the picture and word arrangement tests. The numbers of items are 145 and 110, respectively.

In some ways, it would be easier to review this series one level at a time. Comparison of the manuals for the three levels simultaneously (or, for that matter, of the regular and short form manuals at a single level) reveals startling inconsistencies and leads to confusion. This is especially so since much of the content in any one manual is clearly intended to describe the entire series. For example, the elementary manual (long form) reports "no item was retained which yielded an average tetrachoric coefficient of less than .30." The elementary manual (short form) says "no item was retained if the average coefficient obtained from the several grades taking each item fell below .25." The preprimary manual says "the index of brightness used in the Scholastic Test of Mental Ability is the conventional 'quotient' IQ." The primary manual discusses the limitation imposed by the slackening of intelligence in the teens (how many teenagers are in grades 2 and 3?) and concludes, "the Scholastic Mental Ability Test uses a deviation IQ rather than a quotient IQ." The elementary manual (long form) states that 13,642 children entered into the norms determination; one must read the short form manual to learn that all these students were attending Catholic elementary schools.

The above contradictions and omissions are not isolated; additional instances abound. The net impression on the reader is that the manuals were prepared at different times by someone who changed his mind and failed to correct or amend what had been written earlier.

RELIABILITY. The author's treatment of reliability is both unorthodox and confusing. The preprimary manual states that "coefficients are reported for separate grade levels as well as for the combined group." The latter coefficients are not presented, which is just as well. In the regular edition primary and elementary manuals both "single-year" and "year-span" coefficients are reported. The former are the medians of the coefficients obtained for each grade; the year-span coefficients are based on all grades combined. In the short form manual for the primary level, coefficients are shown for each grade, but not for the combined group; the short form elementary manual reports the median and range of single-grade coefficients as well as interform reliability for grades 4, 6, and 8 and for these three grades combined.

Except for the interform reliability mentioned above, all coefficients are based on split-half correlation. With the preprimary and primary tests such estimates, when based on a single grade, may be reasonable. However, the elementary test is used to cover grades 4 to 9. We are informed that the test is primarily a power test (the evidence to support this claim is dubious). The absence of speededness is a necessary condition if split-half reliability coefficients are to be justifiable. Since the time limits for fourth grade and ninth grade students are the same, it seems clear that either the test has a large speed component with fourth grade students or ninth grade students finish in a fraction of the allotted time. Thus, one must conclude either that inappropriate coefficients of reliability are reported for (at least) the fourth grade, or that the test is a poor instrument at the ninth. One might be able to select a horn of this dilemma if data concerning the standard deviations were reported for the samples on which reliability coefficients were computed.

The presentation of reliability coefficients based on a sample of pupils from all six grades combined is unfortunate. The scholastic aptitude of fourth grade pupils is not ordinarily compared with that of ninth graders; the effect of presenting coefficients for combined groups is merely to delude the unwary reader into over-estimating the reliability of the instrument.

VALIDITY. The material offered to document the validity of the test is poorly organized. Coefficients of correlation with well known instruments such as the Otis, Kuhlmann-Anderson, and Terman-McNemar tests appear in the manuals for the short forms, but not in the manuals for the regular forms. Means and standard deviations accompany some of the coefficients, but are unfortunately absent in places where they are vital to understanding. For example, the same coefficient is reported with Terman-McNemar scores for grade 6 students and for students in grades 5, 6, and 7 combined; a single standard deviation figure is given, presumably for the combined group, but not for the single-grade group.

The only evidence of predictive validity is a series of five coefficients with reading and achievement tests as criteria. With only 9 months intervening between the predictor and criteria, and with objective test scores rather than teacher grades being predicted, the predictive validity must be regarded as undistinguished.

There is discussion of construct and content validity, but no evidence to convince an informed reader.

TIME LIMITS. One of the fascinating features of the series is the casual attitude with respect to time limits. At several points in the preprimary directions the examiner is told to allow "about 5 seconds" for each item. In the primary manual we find "allow 5 to 10 seconds." This kind of informality is hardly consistent with standardized test procedures.

USES OF THE TESTS. The flavor of the manuals is epitomized for this reviewer by the statements offered in the preprimary manual on how to use the test. "Should a pupil be unusually bright or dull, or mischievous, or unusual in any respect, intelligence tests give information not possible through other means." "The results of the tests should assist the counselor in advising the pupil concerning the selection of suitable courses in school work, and concerning the selection of occupations within his ability level." Note that this manual is intended for use with kindergarten and first grade pupils!

SUMMARY. The *Scholastic Mental Ability Tests* were developed primarily for use in Catholic schools. Aside from the restriction of the standardization population to such schools, there is nothing to make the use of the tests more appropriate in Catholic schools than in any others. The manuals are largely uninformative if not outright bewildering. Until there is a better organized, more consistent, more convincing, more informative set of manuals offered for this series, Catholic schools (and non-Catholic schools) would do far better to use instruments such as the Metropolitan Readiness, Pintner, Kuhlmann-Anderson, or Thorndike-Lorge tests—to name but a few.

[381]

★Schrammel General Ability Test. Grades 9 and over; 1953–55; based in part upon the *Army Group Examination Alpha* and revisions; IBM; Forms A ('53), B ('55), C ('56); manual ('55); no data on reliability and validity for Form C; no norms for grades 14–16; no norms for Form C; $1.50 per 25 tests; separate answer sheets may be used; 85¢ per 25 IBM answer sheets; 30¢ per set of either hand or machine scoring stencils; postage extra; 35¢ per specimen set, postpaid; 50(60) minutes; H. E. Schrammel; Bureau of Educational Measurements. *

HENRY E. GARRETT, *Professor Emeritus of Psychology, Columbia University, New York, New York.*

This general ability test is an adaptation and revision of the *Army Group Examination Alpha* which was used widely in World War I. First revised and published with norms for public schools in 1920, the present tests have passed through several revisions to reach their current form. The examination is planned to be an entrance and placement test for college freshmen. It also provides norms for, and is said to have usefulness in, evaluating candidates for graduate school entrance. In the reviewer's opinion, however, the test is too limited in range and difficulty for the latter purpose.

The test contains 150 multiple choice items subdivided into five parts of 25–40 items each. Part 1 is vocabulary; Part 2, number series completion; Part 3, verbal analogies; Part 4, information; and Part 5, arithmetic problems. Each part is allotted 10 minutes of working time, but an examinee may continue on with the next section if he finishes one before time is called. The test is one of both speed and

power, but the difficulty level is not very high. The format gives the impression of being crowded. There are too many items on a page and this makes reading difficult. The important parts of the directions could be made to stand out more. An examiner must search through the printed directions and could easily miss an important detail.

A single correlation coefficient of .65 between test scores and the one-year grades of 110 college freshmen is offered as evidence of validity. Reference is made to validity data obtained with previous editions. In view of the mass of material available on Army Alpha, the present test, which is much like Army Alpha, can probably be taken as having validity in the college screening situation. As implied above, its validity for use with advanced students is questionable.

Reliability coefficients for groups of high school seniors and college freshmen range from .87 to .94. These compare favorably with coefficients derived from comparable group tests of intelligence.

Nearly 12,000 high school students and 2,400 college freshmen and graduate students contributed to the norms. Separate percentile norms are presented for each high school grade, for college freshmen, and for graduate students (small groups). In addition to the percentile ranks, "IQ's" may be read from a table for raw scores ranging from "less than 56" to 150. These IQ's are said to "parallel very closely" Stanford-Binet IQ's. The author does not explain the derivation of his IQ's. Presumably they are deviation (standard) scores in a distribution with mean 100 and SD 16. The reviewer was unable completely to verify this. More detail here would clarify the procedure.

This is an intelligence test of mostly verbal materials and is not of a very high level of difficulty. According to the author, it is intended for use in classifying and sectioning entering students and also in individual counseling. The test should be useful in screening and selection but less valuable in individual guidance. It is neither comprehensive enough nor varied enough in content for other than a very preliminary approach to vocational or educational guidance. Its use above the college freshman level is not recommended.

[382]

★Schubert General Ability Battery. Grades 12–16 and adults; 1946–53; 5 scores: vocabulary, analogies, arithmetic problems, syllogisms, total; 1 form ('46); revised mimeographed manual ('53); 1–99 tests, 15¢ each, postage extra; 16(25) or 32(40) minutes; Herman J. P. Schubert; the Author, 500 Klein Road, Route 2, Buffalo 21, N.Y. *

WILLIAM B. SCHRADER, *Director, Statistical Analysis, Educational Testing Service, Princeton, New Jersey.*

This test provides a measure of general ability based on vocabulary (50 items), verbal analogies (35 items), arithmetic problems (15 items), and logical reasoning (15 items). It is intended to be suitable for use in industry as well as in educational situations. It is well printed, although one spelling error slipped through in Item 24 of Part 1. The manual contains much relevant information.

With respect to test development, the author does not make it clear why he chose the particular item types used nor how he arrived at the relative weight given each part in determining the total score. Considerable stress is placed on the role of item analysis in developing the test, but the particular method of analysis used is not described. The items seem to be well written, except that Items 10 and 12 of the verbal analogies part tend to give each other away. Two serious flaws in the manual are that the directions give the candidate no information concerning whether a correction for guessing is made, and that there is no indication as to whether the candidates are to be informed in advance about the time limit for each part.

A discussion of score interpretation must take note of the fact that the test may be administered in several ways. Specifically, if 4-minute time limits are used for each part, the author regards this as a speeded test; if 8-minutes are allowed for each part, the author regards it as a power test. No data on per cent finishing the test within either time limit are reported. The author suggests that there are advantages to be gained by comparing the performance of a person who takes the test under both time limits, noting such things as amount of tension due to inner conflict, perseverance, and caution. It is unfortunate that this dual time limit approach to interpretation is recommended by the author without any specific evidence.

No data are given on the reliability of part scores; and since the author estimates the reliability of the total score by an internal consistency method, the only useful reliability co-efficients reported are for the 8-minute time limit. These are .86 for 68 high school senior boys and .93 for 143 high school senior girls. The fact that two of the part scores contain only 15 items each and that some stress is placed on part scores in score interpretation make the need for part score reliability data acute. The development of a parallel form would make it possible to supply these data.

A number of interesting norms tables are presented. The adult-male table is based on 461 cases described as randomly selected from the adult-male population of the Great Lakes region. No statement is made, however, as to how the sample was obtained. High school norms are based on results in a single school; norms for college entrants, on results in a single university; and norms for graduate students in education, also on results in a single university. The distributions indicate that the tests are reasonably suitable in difficulty for these groups. Norms for the 4-minute time limit are given for factory workers, foremen, executives, store managers, wholesale salesmen, and office clerks. However, since these samples were evidently obtained independently of each other, comparisons across occupations must be made with caution. In the absence of reliability data for these scores, much of the value of the norms is lost as far as individual score interpretation is concerned.

Several correlational studies relating scores to high school and college grades and to scores on other tests are reported. The two verbal parts show reasonably high correlations with other tests and with appropriate course grades. Arithmetic, when given with a 4-minute time limit, yielded a disappointingly low coefficient (.25) with college mathematics grades. Results for the logical reasoning part are difficult to evaluate, but the evidence so far available is not encouraging. Total scores seem to show moderate correlations with other tests and with college grades on the basis of the limited evidence given.

On the whole, this test is well made and should be useful in industrial applications. It is fair to say, however, that the superstructure of interpretation has gone beyond the foundation of empirical studies, with the consequent danger that unwarranted interpretations of individual performance will be made. The inclusion of a logical reasoning section appears to be the only original feature of this test, and the brevity of this part seems likely to limit its differential value.

[383]

★Ship Destination Test. Grades 9 and over; 1955–56; general reasoning; IBM; Form A ('55); separate answer sheets must be used; $2 per 25 tests; 10¢ per single copy; 3¢ per IBM answer sheet; 50¢ per scoring stencil; 25¢ per manual ('56); postage extra; 15(20) minutes; Paul R. Christensen and J. P. Guilford; Sheridan Supply Co. *

REFERENCE

1. HILLS, JOHN R. "Factor-Analyzed Abilities and Success in College Mathematics." *Ed & Psychol Meas* 17:615–22 w '57. *

C. J. ADCOCK, *Senior Lecturer in Psychology, Victoria University of Wellington, Wellington, New Zealand.*

This test is based on factorial studies of reasoning ability. According to the manual, in two studies it had the highest loading of the tests analysed on the general reasoning factor (.51 and .56). It is a disguised arithmetical reasoning test but has practically no loading on the number factor.

In evaluating a test of this kind, two distinct questions must be kept in mind. The first relates to the authenticity and importance of the factor measured; the second, to the efficiency of the test in measuring this factor. With regard to the former we have to note that the general reasoning factor was first found by Thurstone among his primary mental abilities when it was named "restrictive reasoning." Zimmerman [1] made a new orthogonal rotation of the same data and found the reasoning factor in more clearly defined form which corresponded with the Army Air Force's "general reasoning" and was so named. Ahmavaara [2] has developed a technique of "transformation analysis" by means of which he has been able to make direct comparisons of factors found in different analyses. Making a comprehensive survey in this way, he found general reasoning to be a factor of the "second certainty class" with a mean variance value of .35. (For comparison, the number factor has a mean variance of .85.) The later work of Guilford would possibly raise this figure somewhat.

Naive users of the *Ship Destination Test* should be quite clear that general reasoning is not by any means a measure of general intelligence, nor is it even a general measure of reasoning capacity. This latter is probably manifested in three chief forms: verbal (deduction), analogical, and arithmetical. It is the last which is measured by the present test. It has a loading (.36) also on a factor involving the ability to handle complicated procedures, and one wonders whether the relative importance of these factors may not vary with level of ability in the same way that a simple intelligence test becomes largely a function of perceptual speed when administered to superior subjects. In working the test, one gets the impression that the ability to maintain a multiple set is very important. Some indication of the degree to which personality factors may have loadings on the test would also be useful. The handling of several variables under speed conditions is likely to be emotionally disturbing for some people.

VALIDITY. The only real measure of validity with this type of material is construct validity, based on the factor analysis. There is no pure criterion with which one can correlate it. It is interesting, however, to check on the predictive capacity for various purposes. According to the manual, the test results correlated significantly with course grades ($n = 116$) in nautical astronomy (.36), physics (.40), geometry and calculus (.39), algebra and trigonometry (.25), and descriptive geometry (.26). One industrial validity figure (.55) is reported, based on correlation of rank order of performance of 20 operations analysts in an aircraft manufacturing organization. If such coefficients are further confirmed, the test will certainly merit inclusion in diagnostic batteries.

TEST STRUCTURE. The test is ingenious in form. It provides a large number of items with the minimum of descriptive material. The homogeneous nature of the items favours a high level of reliability. By Kuder-Richardson formula 21, this ranges from .86 to .95. The saturation with other factors is kept to a minimum.

There appear, however, to be one or two weaknesses with regard to structure. The instructions require the subject to calculate the time required for a ship to travel between two stated points under certain conditions of wind and current. The quickest route is not asked for and the testee may, therefore, assume that routes which are spatially equivalent will require similar time. Unfortunately, this is not always so (e.g., Items 49, 50, 54, 56, and 57),

1 ZIMMERMAN, WAYNE S. "A Revised Orthogonal Rotational Solution for Thurstone's Original Primary Mental Abilities Test Battery." *Psychometrika* 8:77–93 Mr '53. *
2 AHMAVAARA, YRJÖ. *On the Unified Factor of Mind,* pp. 130–2. Helsinki, Finland: Finnish Academy of Science and Letters, 1957. Pp. 176. *

and a wrong answer is possible despite formal compliance with the instructions. The difficulty arises with regard to the allowances to be made for changes of direction. If the testee understands that complete reversal of direction should be avoided if possible and that no turns should be made until essential, ambiguous solutions will be avoided. Instructions to this affect, however, would probably change the norms and modify factorial composition. Some further research might raise both reliability and validity.

SUMMARY. This test is a useful addition to our tests of special abilities. Reliability and validity merit its inclusion in a comprehensive aptitude battery. It is probably the best available measure of the factor involved, but testers should be careful not to confuse the general reasoning ability with intelligence.

[384]

★The Simplex GNV Intelligence Tests. Ages 11–12.0; 1952–57; title on tests is, say, for form 1, *The Simplex Intelligence Test GNV 1;* forms 1 ('52), 2 ('54), 3 ('54), 4 ('55), 5 ('56), 6 ('57); manual for each form (dates as for tests); no data on reliability and validity; distribution of forms 4–6 restricted to Educational Committees; 9s. per 25 tests; 6d. per single copy; 1s. per manual; postage extra; 60(70) minutes; C. A. Richardson; George G. Harrap & Co. Ltd. *

REFERENCES

1. SHUTTLEWORTH, CLIFFORD W. "Tests of Technical Aptitude." *Occupational Psychol* 16:175–82 O '42. *
2. NISBET, JOHN D. "Contributions to Intelligence Testing and the Theory of Intelligence: IV, Intelligence and Age: Retesting With Twenty-Four Years' Interval." *Brit J Ed Psychol* 27:190–8 N '57. *

[385]

The Simplex Group Intelligence Scale. Ages 10 and over; 1922–39; 1 form ('34); no data on reliability; tentative norms; 12s. 6d. per 25 tests; 2s. 6d. per scoring stencil; 1s. 3d. per manual ('39); 4s. 3d. per specimen set; postage extra; 90(95) minutes; C. A. Richardson; George G. Harrap & Co. Ltd. *

JAMES MAINWARING, *Formerly Lecturer in Psychology and Music, Dudley Training College, Birmingham, England.*

One of the early intelligence tests, and using still earlier test material, the Simplex scale has survived over 15 reprints. It consists of 26 subtests of six questions each. They are divided into two similar groups of 10 subtests each and a more difficult group of 6 subtests. Each group includes various classifications, analogies, and vocabulary tests. The data are verbal and numerical. No pictorial material is included except that used in a reversed similarity test. The third group of subtests includes a memory test, requiring the recognition of 6- to 8-digit numbers printed in reverse, and a rather difficult

vocabulary test. This last subtest hardly seems consistent with one of the stated aims of the test, that is, "it is directed to the estimation of the child's *natural mental endowment,* which is independent of teaching."

The test has two other specific aims. The first is to avoid the necessity of more than the briefest preliminary directions, and to achieve this "the tests are so worded and arranged as to provide their own instructions." The second is to avoid interruption of the test. For this reason, individual subtests are not timed, and subjects who complete the series before the allotted 90 minutes have a page on which to express their views of the test. This page is not scored.

The choice of this very comprehensive test will depend on how much significance is attached to the absence of the time factor and the absence of pictorial data in an instrument designed to assess relative inherent mental capacity.

[386]

[The Simplex Junior Intelligence Tests.] Ages 7–14; 1932–51; 2 forms; postage extra; 45(50) minutes; C. A. Richardson; George G. Harrap & Co. Ltd. *

a) THE SIMPLEX JUNIOR INTELLIGENCE SCALE. 1932; test ['32]; 6s. per 25 tests; 6d. per single copy; 8d. per manual.

b) THE SIMPLEX JUNIOR 'A' INTELLIGENCE TEST. 1950–51; title on test is *The Simplex Junior 'A' Test;* test ('50); no data on reliability and validity; 9s. per 25 tests; 6d. per single copy; 1s. per manual ('51).

REFERENCES

1–2. See 4:322.
3. CURR, W., AND GOURLAY, N. "Differences Between Testers in Terman-Merrill Testing." *Brit J Stat Psychol* 9:75–81 N '56. * (*PA* 32:1617)

ARTHUR B. ROYSE, *Lecturer in Psychology, The University of Hull, Hull, England.*

These are alternate forms, each comprising 100 completion type items. Items were rather arbitrarily chosen, some from existing tests, no particular novelty being claimed or achieved.

The chief claims made are that the tests are easily administered, are suitable for all children from 7 to 14, are valid measures of general intelligence, and are thoroughly standardised. The first two claims are obviously valid and, in these respects, the tests compare favourably with similar tests. Although it is possible that the second two claims are also valid, evidence to support them is not sufficiently rigorous.

Test-retest reliability for the first test is good (.95) but no measure is given for the Junior A, reliability apparently being assumed on the basis that they are alternate forms. This latter claim, however, is not based on correlation between scores but on the less reliable criterion of reasonable comparability of mental ages for identical raw scores. Validity for the Junior Intelligence Scale is claimed solely on the basis of a correlation of .93 with teacher estimates of intelligence. No attempt has been made to establish content validity either by item analysis or by demonstration of correlations or comparison of factor patterns with other intelligence tests. No follow-ups have been made and no attempt has been made to show effective prediction of variables other than teacher estimates.

Standardisation was thorough in that the whole relevant school population of a large English urban area—some 12,000 children—was used. Unfortunately, the only norms given are mental ages corresponding to 5-point intervals of raw score. As neither means and standard deviations nor percentile ranks for each age group are given, it is difficult, in the absence of knowledge of correlations with similar tests, to compare the resultant IQ's with IQ's from other tests.

In all, this is just one more intelligence test which presents no new features and which, although offering the virtues of ease of administration and wide applicability, is not sufficiently validated. As a result, major difficulties are encountered both in attaching precise meaning to the obtained IQ's and in utilising the IQ's for comparative or predictive purposes.

[387]

Sleight Non-Verbal Intelligence Test. Ages 6–10; 1931; 1 form; no data on reliability; tentative norms; 15s. per 25 tests; 8d. per single copy; 1s. per manual; postage extra; 20(75) minutes; George F. Sleight; George G. Harrap & Co. Ltd. *

JOHN C. DANIELS, *Lecturer in Education, University of Nottingham, Nottingham, England.*

The reviewer has used this test frequently with 7- and 8-year-old groups, and, unfortunately, is far from satisfied about its validity and reliability when given under ordinary classroom conditions. Children of this age, since they are naturally cooperative and relatively strange to the necessary, though alien, rigour of group test procedure, need a great deal of unobtrusive but thorough supervision or they will either not produce their best work or, alternatively, produce the freely offered work of other children.

Group testing, especially when such compli-

cated instructions as accompany this test have to be given, is quite unsuitable for young children. It is recognized, however, that often the shortage of time available for testing may seem to indicate a group test as the only possibility. When given by teachers with little testing experience, however, the results are often quite useless. For this reason, both retest reliability and validity are to be doubted, in spite of the author's claim that "only tests of proved reliability have been included."

M. L. KELLMER PRINGLE, *Lecturer in Education, and Deputy Head, Department of Child Study, University of Birmingham, Birmingham, England.*

The test was first published in 1931 and, though it has been reprinted several times, it has been neither revised nor restandardised. This is all the more regrettable as it is still widely used in this country. Moreover, there are several signs betraying its age. Some of the drawings have an old fashioned air about them, especially the cars, lorries, and articles of clothing. It is still argued in the manual that both "genius" and subnormality can be detected by the use of this nonverbal group test as early as "the upper infant class and the lower junior school classes." And it is claimed that "most existing tests depend on the child's power to read and write," which is no longer true.

The test consists of 10 nonverbal subtests, all of which are preceded by practice items. Each subtest is timed. The layout of the test is rather cramped, particularly for subtests 2, 6, and 8; the individual pictures should be larger and the number of rows of pictures per page needs to be reduced. In the reviewer's experience, young and dull children tend to become confused even on the practice items; this is made worse by the fact that no numbers or letters are attached to the rows so that the examiner cannot give additional guidance to those who have lost their places. The simplified instructions for testing lower age groups or backward classes are useful, but for such children the total testing time required (though two sittings can be used with younger children) seems rather excessive (about 75 minutes; slightly longer with infant classes, provided the examiner "is perfectly familiar with the instructions"). To facilitate marking, the scoring key could be set out more clearly and systematically, especially for subtests 2, 3, 5, and 6.

On the back of the test's title page is a form "for the entry of additional particulars which may be relevant to the examiner," especially to one "investigating special cases of backwardness, etc." Though still useful, nowadays this portion is rarely filled in because some form of record card has been adopted by most local authorities and its completion by schools is obligatory.

The most serious criticisms must be leveled against the lack of information regarding the construction, standardisation, and reliability of the test. In the manual it is merely stated that "only tests of proved reliability in the measurement of intelligence have been included" and that "the items originally devised for the various tests were in the first place treated experimentally." However, no details are given about the numbers of items devised and tried out, nor about the number of children involved. Again, it is not stated what criteria were used in calculating coefficients of item discriminating power. All that is said is that "the data resulting from this preliminary survey was used to eliminate items which were not diagnostic, and to range the remainder in order of difficulty." The information on the standardisation is similarly vague and inadequate. Neither the mean nor the standard deviation nor reliability values are stated, the possibility of sex differences is not discussed, and no test validity is given either in terms of other tests of intelligence or of independent estimates of general ability. And perhaps most serious of all, the norms are still described as being "only tentative" in the current manual reprinted in 1957.

In view of this lack of information and the age of the test itself, one must be very hesitant in using it as a valid and reliable measure of intelligence.

[388]
★The Southend Test of Intelligence. Ages 10–12; 1953; 1 form; 10s. per 25 tests; 6d. per single copy; 2s. 6d. per manual; postage extra; 30(60) minutes in 2 sessions; M. E. Hebron and W. Stephenson (test); George G. Harrap & Co. Ltd. *

JAMES MAINWARING, *Formerly Lecturer in Psychology and Music, Dudley Training College, Birmingham, England.*

An analysis of a group of representative standard intelligence tests, comprising over 1,000 questions, reveals that 75 per cent of the questions depend essentially on two mental processes: the eduction of some relation or

principle of classification, and the arrangement, selection, or rejection of items in accordance with this educed principle. The Southend test has the merit of isolating these two processes in five sharply graduated tests, three of classification and two of analogies. In three of the tests the processes are further isolated by being applied to shapes and patterned groups, in which the principle of relationship has to be sought very deliberately.

The manual is commendably clear, comprehensive, and concise. The construction and standardization of the test are described in less than a hundred words.

A practice period of 30 minutes, followed by a break of 15 minutes, helps to counteract the possibility that some testees may have had previous experience with similar tests while others have not. Each test is timed by a stop watch. Five minutes are allowed for the first and second tests together, for the third test, and for the fourth; the fifth is allotted 15 minutes.

Except for the possible criticism that the test should have included questions in which the aforementioned processes are applied to numerical data, the Southend test has everything to recommend it.

[389]
*Test of Word-Number Ability. Grades 10–16; 1939–57; Form K formerly called *Word-Number Test of Scholastic Aptitude,* Form A; 3 scores: word, number, total; IBM; Forms K, L ('55); manual ('57); college norms for entering freshmen only; tentative high school norms; distribution of Form L restricted to colleges; separate answer sheets must be used; $2.50 per 30 tests; 3½¢ per IBM answer sheet; 30¢ per set of scoring stencils; 25¢ per specimen set; cash orders postpaid; 40(50) minutes; H. T. Manuel, James Knight (K), J. A. Floyd (K), R. C. Jordan (K), Lulu Vinson (L), Marjorie L. Bagley (L), and B. F. Johnson, Jr. (L); Steck Co. *

REFERENCE
1. MANUEL, HERSCHEL T. "Aptitude Tests for College Admission." *Yearb Nat Council Meas Used Ed* 14:20–7 '57. *

I. DAVID SATLOW, *Chairman, Department of Accounting and Distributive Education, Thomas Jefferson High School, Brooklyn, New York.*

This test is a revision and extension of the *Word-Number Test of Scholastic Aptitude* for high school and college. It is designed to measure ability in two areas: verbal and numerical. The test is set up attractively in an 8-page booklet, and consists of two 20-minute parts.

Part 1 presents 90 multiple response vocabulary and analogy items, judiciously distributed in alternating groups of five questions. The vocabulary questions require the selection of a word having a meaning similar to or related to that of a given word or phrase. The analogy questions call for selecting a fourth word which bears the same relation to the third word that the second bears to the first. In the words of the manual, the framers of the test hope to provide "a partial measure of the extent and richness of vocabulary, the ability to see relations between concepts presented by words, and the ability to reason with verbal materials."

Part 2 consists of 45 questions designed to measure abilities to deal with fractions, decimals, and per cents in simple functional situations, to do some elementary algebra, and to apply mathematical reasoning.

Two forms of the test have been issued—Form K, usable at either senior high school or college, and Form L, which is available to colleges only. Both forms are similar as to scope of content and range of difficulty. According to the manual, the only reason for restricting the distribution of Form L is "to make it possible for a college to use the test without repeating a form already administered to the same students in high school."

Even though the guidance values of these tests are, in the opinion of this reviewer, the most significant aspect, one can well conceive of individual schools desiring to use test results for purposes of comparison with other groups. For such institutions, the published norms may prove of value.

JOHN M. WILLITS, *Business and Industrial Psychologist, 566 Everett Ave., Palo Alto, California.*

This test and its manual appear well suited to their assigned task: educational and vocational guidance in senior high school and college. The test yields part scores on two mental ability factors, verbal ability and numerical ability. These scores and their weighted total are reported to correlate about .8 with widely used college aptitude tests, and about .6 with grades of college freshmen. Odd-even reliabilities (corrected) are in the vicinity of .9.

The manual is almost a model in form and content. But its greatest strength is related to its chief weakness, and both its strength and its weakness apparently result from its being designed for users with minimal experience in testing. The manual's strength lies in the clarity and completeness of its text. One assumes,

though specific statement is not found, that it was written primarily for secondary school officials or teachers who are not highly expert in test administration and interpretation. Its paragraphs teem with homely advice and suggestions on unglamorous but essential points that have long been routine to "old hands" in testing, e.g., proper atmosphere of a testing session, equipment and procedures for accurate timing, other duties of examiners during a testing session, control of the close of a session, how to score tests accurately, why a correction for guessing, why the Spearman-Brown formula, obtained scores and errors of estimate, limitations of "national" norms and of other normative samples as reported, uses of local norms, and factors other than mental ability in educational guidance. The 13-page manual clearly and convincingly discusses all these and numerous other extremely practical considerations for the tyro in testing—matters basic to the sound utilization of tests, and thus not replaceable by any amount of test theory or statistical lore. There is consistent emphasis throughout the manual on restraint and caution and on limitations and precautions consonant with the test's conservative title.

But the manual's weakness seems to derive from its very unity of purpose. If written mainly for test users with minimal experience in testing, its authors seem to feel, why should our manual include statistical data that would tax their comprehension? Thus, in the manual's five tables of correlation coefficients there is nary a mean nor a sigma! For all of the four tables of norms, the reader who wants means or sigmas must estimate them from percentiles. Sample sizes are omitted from one of these tables of norms, and also from a very usable expectancy table which shows test scores in relation to college freshman grades. This latter table also reveals nothing about confidence limits for its data. Statistical data such as these should be included for the users who can interpret them, even though many others may choose or may have to ignore them.

The manual makes no mention of correlation between the test's two part scores, nor of the reasoning behind the unequal weighting of part scores in the total score. One of the test's two forms is restricted to use at the college level to permit retesting at that level without duplication. But, though stability of scores is mentioned, no test-retest data or other statistics on stability are offered.

The various normative groups, all student populations, are adequately described for the most part, but there is no mention of sex distribution or of sex differences in score. The latter question is significant, particularly in relation to scores on the numerical part. One fourth of the numerical items require basic algebra. With algebra currently an elective in many high schools and more colleges, we may anticipate that fewer girls than boys elect it—and that, in consequence, there is considerable sex difference in scores on Part 2 of the test.

The norms for college freshmen have been equated, via the "national" norms of the *American Council on Education Psychological Examination for College Freshmen*, to distributions of student scores in a composite of some 269 colleges in various parts of the United States. The high school normative population was sampled from 15 schools all located in one state (Texas), but well distributed as to size of school and location within the state.

In summary, the *Test of Word-Number Ability*, true to its title, is modestly competent in its field of high school and college guidance, educational and vocational. Its manual is very well tailored to the needs of test users who are less than expert in test administration and interpretation, but it omits most of the supporting statistical evidence necessary for a critical evaluation of the correlations and norms which it reports.

For a review by Jane Loevinger of an earlier edition, see 4:333.

[390]
★**Tests AH4 and AH5.** Ages 10 and over, 13 and over; 1955–56; 1 form, 2 levels; separate answer sheets must be used; postpaid within U.K.; A. W. Heim; distributed by the National Foundation for Educational Research in England and Wales. *
a) TEST AH4: GROUP TEST OF INTELLIGENCE. Ages 10 and over; 1955; 1 form ['55]; no norms for age 10; 12s. 25 tests; 4s. per 25 answer sheets; 1s. 6d. per set of scoring key and manual ['55]; 2s. 6d. per specimen set; 20(30–45) minutes.
b) TEST AH5: GROUP TEST OF HIGH-GRADE INTELLIGENCE. Ages 13 and over; 1956; 1 form ['56]; 17s. per 25 tests; 5s. per 25 answer sheets; 2s. per set of scoring key and manual ['56]; 3s. 3d. per specimen set; 40(60–70) minutes.

REFERENCES
1. HEIM, A. W. "An Attempt to Test High-Grade Intelligence." *Brit J Psychol* 37:70–81 Ja '47. * (*PA* 21:2036)
2. HEIM, A. W., AND BATTS, V. "Upward and Downward Selection in Intelligence Testing." *Brit J Psychol* 39:22–9 S '48. * (*PA* 24:1060)
3. HEIM, A. W. "Learning in Intelligence Test Perform-

ance." Abstract. *Q B Brit Psychol Soc* (3):120–1 Ja '49. * Reply by John C. Raven: (3):197–8 Jl '49. * Rebuttal by A. W. Heim: (3):219–20 O '49. *
4. CANE, V. R., AND HEIM, A. W. "The Effects of Repeated Retesting: III, Further Experiments and General Conclusions." *Q J Exp Psychol* 2:182–97 pt 4 '50. *
5. HEIM, A. W., AND WALLACE, J. G. "The Effects of Repeatedly Retesting the Same Group on the Same Intelligence Test." *Q J Exp Psychol* 2:19–32 F '50. * (*PA* 25:6938)
6. WALLACE, JEAN G. "The Intelligence Testing of University Staff and Students." Abstract. *Q B Brit Psychol Soc* 1:285–6 Ja '50. *
7. WALLACE, JEAN G. "Results of a Test of High-Grade Intelligence Applied to a University Population." *Brit J Psychol, Gen Sect* 43:61–9 F '52. * (*PA* 26:7239)
8. WATTS, KATHLEEN P. "Influences Affecting the Results of a Test of High-Grade Intelligence." *Brit J Psychol* 44: 359–67 N '53. * (*PA* 28:5659)
9. WATTS, KATHLEEN P. "The Effect of a University Training in Mathematics on the Scores in an Intelligence Test." *Brit J Ed Psychol* 24:32–7 F '54. * (*PA* 28:9048)
10. HEIM, A. W. "Adaptation to Level of Difficulty in Intelligence Testing." *Brit J Psychol* 46:211–24 Ag '55. * (*PA* 30:5748)
11. WATTS, KATHLEEN P. "Intelligence Test Performance From 11 to 18: A Study of Grammar School Girls." *Brit J Ed Psychol* 28:112–9 Je '58. *

GEORGE A. FERGUSON, *Professor of Psychology, McGill University, Montreal, Canada.* [Review of Test AH4.]

This test is a measure of general intelligence for adults and for children over 10 years of age. It is divided into two parts. Part 1 consists of 65 items of the common verbal and numerical type, opposites, analogies, number series, following directions, arithmetic problems, and synonyms. Part 2 is an assortment of nonverbal items, figure analogies, figure series, superimpositions, sames, and subtractions. The author is concerned with the adjustment of the subject to the testing situation, and much emphasis is placed on the proper completion of the preliminary practice exercises. Time limit for each part is 10 minutes. Separate answer sheets, not adapted to machine scoring, are used. Scoring is done with a marking key.

The test manual provides norms based on three groups: (*a*) 3,407 industrial subjects, (*b*) 726 university students, and (*c*) groups of school children, ages 11 to 16. No conversion tables to percentiles or normalized standard scores are provided. A 5-point letter grade system based on the percentages 10, 20, 40, 20, 10 is used. Although norms for university students are given, the test is not suitable as a test of intelligence at the university level because the items are too easy. The mean score reported for university students is 96. A peculiarity of the normative data given in the manual is that the mean score for adults is 47, whereas the mean score for 11-year-old grammar school children is 60. Indeed, the average adult is not much above the 10th percentile for the 11-year-old group. This may mean, contrary to the claim in the manual, that the adult group used in the standardization is not representative of the adult population.

Test-retest reliability with one-month interval between testings is .92. Indications are that the test conforms to accepted standards of reliability and discriminatory capacity for average or below average groups.

While AH4 appears to be a fairly well constructed and useful test, it has few distinguishing features, if any, which would commend it in preference to numerous other group tests of intelligence. In many respects it is perhaps no better and no worse than many other tests. In the testing of school children in Britain, it has no characteristics which would recommend it in preference to the thoroughly standardized Moray House tests of intelligence. The non-verbal part has nothing to commend it, other perhaps than variety, in preference to the *Progressive Matrices*. It is improbable that AH4 will have much application in North America where many not dissimilar tests are available. An incidental observation is that the art work in Part 2 is amateurish, a fault which probably does not detract from the merits of the test as a measure of intelligence.

J. A. KEATS, *Senior Lecturer in Psychology, University of Queensland, Brisbane, Australia.* [Review of Test AH5.]

This is a general intelligence test to be used "with selected, highly intelligent [adult] subjects." It is claimed by the author that most intelligence tests discriminate between such subjects mainly on the basis of the speed with which they can do the items. Presumably, the present test is not intended to be speeded and, if not, should be a more valid measure of intelligence.

The test consists of two separately timed parts. Part 1 consists of verbal analogies, number series, ordering words according to meaning, and recognizing double meanings for one word. This part may be expected to be a good measure of academic aptitude. Some ingenious devices are used to obtain difficult and discriminating items which do not require knowledge of out of the way terms. Item 35 seemed to the reviewer to be unfortunate in that the correct answer (as keyed) could be obtained by the "clang" "manner is to matter" response.

Part 2 consists of diagram items in the form of clock problems, reversed and rotated figure problems, and problems requiring recognition of patterns and common characteristics. These items are similar to those in standard "non-verbal" tests which are usually regarded as good measures of general ability. The items involving the recognition of patterns seem very time-consuming to the reviewer and may well introduce an element of speed into this part.

The correlation between these two parts has been computed on five occasions with resulting coefficients of .49, .50, .52, .52, and .62. The reviewer does not agree that "it is satisfactory that the association is in fact always positive and significant." Such low correlations are hardly in keeping with the claim that "marked discrepancy between a subject's Part 1 score and his Part 2 score is unusual." The fact that these correlations are much lower than the reliability of either part suggests that the parts are measuring different attributes.

There has been a great deal of empirical work done with this test. The retest reliability with at least several months' interval between testing has been examined many times. For selected adults this measure was never less than .80, and in the majority of occasions a value greater than .90. was obtained. These figures indicate that reasonably stable attributes are being measured. The figures for the separate parts are not much smaller than this.

As might be expected, validity studies are confined to correlations with other intelligence tests and to predictions of academic success. The coefficients reported in the manual range from .27 to .54 for various prediction criteria. These values do not seem to be much if at all higher than values obtained with other tests. None of the six studies reported gives the validities for the two parts. This omission is the more surprising since separate norms and reliability coefficients are provided. In view of the relatively low correlation between the parts it is not impossible that one of the parts alone is contributing most of the validity. Correlations with other tests of general intelligence lie mainly in the range .55 to .65.

Again, separate correlations for the two parts are not provided. No estimate of the effect of practice is given although the data for such an estimate must have been available from the reliability studies. It is well known that performance on items of the kind used in Part 2 is influenced to a considerable extent by practice.

The manual also contains details for the testing procedure, standard instructions, and norms which have been established for three well defined groups by means of very adequate samples. Five letter ratings are provided: A, B, C, D, and E. These ratings correspond to the top 10 per cent, the next 20 per cent, the middle 40 per cent, the next 20 per cent, and the bottom 10 per cent, respectively. Scores corresponding to these ratings would have been estimated more accurately by some method such as that of Keats [1] which provides for smoothing the raw frequency distribution.

AH5 has been very thoroughly prepared according to a certain theoretical position concerning the nature of abilities. Whether or not a particular worker agrees with this position, he would probably not agree with a practice which leads to less precision in prediction—the practice of including items of Part 2 with those of Part 1 in a single score. This could lead to a lowering of the efficiency of prediction. The prospective user would probably be better served by treating the two parts as separate tests.

The test seems to have wide application for testing adults of high ability in English-speaking countries.

[391]
*Thurstone Test of Mental Alertness, Revised Edition. Grades 9–12 and adults; 1943–53; abbreviated adaptation of *American Council on Education Psychological Examination for High School Students*, 1940 Edition; 3 scores: quantitative, linguistic, total; Forms A ('52), B ('53); manual, third edition ('52); separate answer pads must be used; $9.80 per 20 tests; $2.15 per 20 answer pads; 75¢ per specimen set; postage extra; 20(25) minutes; Thelma Gwinn Thurstone and L. L. Thurstone; Science Research Associates. *

Joshua A. Fishman, *Director of Research, College Entrance Examination Board, Inc., New York, New York.*

This is a 1952 revision of the 1943 instrument reviewed in *The Third Mental Measurements Yearbook*. The 1952 revision, like the 1943 edition, is virtually self-administering, except for an 11-item practice section and a few clarifying instructions. The test now has 126 items, or an increase of 28 over the 1943 version. As in the 1943 edition the items are arranged in spiral order and in order of increasing difficulty. The item types, as before, are word definitions, same-opposite, arithmetic, and number series completion. The test yields an

L(inguistic) score, derived from the first two item types, a Q(uantitative) score, derived from the second two item types, and a total score.

The examiner's manual now presents percentile rank norms for a variety of occupational groups as well as for high school students. The high school norms reported are for the same 3,820 pupils in nine high schools that served in norming the 1943 edition. The number of cases in each of the four high school years is not reported although separate norms are given for each year. In some instances the norming populations seem to be either insufficient in size or restricted in location; in others, desirable information concerning the populations is not reported. In addition, the norms for all but business executives and stockmen-and-clerical workers are reported only up to the 90th percentile. This seems to be due to the fact that the new 126-item edition was administered only to these two groups. For the other groups, norms developed from administrations of the 1943 edition are presented and the claim is advanced that they may be used as good estimates of the eventual norms for the revised test. Inasmuch as the revised forms contain 28 items more than the earlier edition, the publishers admit that this will cause a difference in the "upper end of the scale." For this reason, all percentile tables based on results from the earlier edition are reported up to the 90th percentile only. More complete norms based on the revised test were promised when the 1952 version first appeared. If these have been compiled, they have not yet been released. All in all, the norms produce a makeshift impression.

The reliability and validity data presented are also far from the highest professional standards. Reliability coefficients are given for the 1943 version only. Although correlations between the 1943 and 1952 versions are reported, as well as correlations between the 1943 version and the college form of the *ACE Psychological Examination* (a surprisingly low .68), no reliability findings or estimates for the 1952 version proper are given. In view of the fact that the latter is more than 25 per cent longer than the former, it is probable that its reliability is as great as or slightly greater than that reported for the former, namely, .95 for split-halves corrected by the Spearman-Brown formula. On the other hand, it is questionable whether this is the proper method for estimat-

1 Keats, J. A. *A Statistical Theory of Objective Test Scores.* Melbourne, Australia: Australian Council for Educational Research, 1951. Pp. viii, 48.

ing reliability for such a highly speeded test. The validity findings are reported in a manner which makes it unclear whether they pertain to the 1943 or the 1952 version. The studies are largely based upon "t-tests" for the significance of the differences between mean TMA scores of groups (pertinent to the norm populations) that have been rated "good" or "poor" on "general effectiveness," "cooperation," and "sales mindedness." The differences reported are significant at the .05 level or better. "Accuracy," "ability to work under pressure," and "cooperation" ratings are related to TMA scores via biserial correlations, and the average of 8-months' sales for managers of small retail stores is related to TMA scores via the Pearson product moment correlation. With the exception of the biserial between "cooperation" and TMA (for 27 clerical workers), the other correlations are significantly greater than zero at the .01 level. On the other hand, the TMA failed to discriminate between "good" and "poor" retail store employees on "sales ability" and only the Q score did so on ratings for "customer service." A number of these validity studies are based on a very small sample (*n*'s of 17, 19, 22, 23, and 27 are the lowest that are reported while the highest are 232, 173, and 169) and, in the absence of any data on the test's standard error of measurement, it is difficult to venture any opinion concerning the practical significance of the differences between means that prove to be statistically significant. The publishers summarize the section on the validity studies described above with the statement "It appears that the *Thurstone Test of Mental Alertness* has validity in predicting on-the-job success in positions which require flexibility, versatility, and resources for solving problems. Where such performance expectations do not exist, the TMA does not prove to be discriminating." The reviewer feels that none of the criterion ratings employed are clearly indicative of on-the-job flexibility, versatility, and resources for solving problems but that they are all rather easily seen as related to conformity with the expectations of the rater. The publishers seem to have concluded that the TMA is a test of mental alertness because it is named such. They then consider any variable significantly related to test performance as being a result of (or an aspect of) some type of mental alertness. Thus they claim that "the difference....between a cooperative and a non-co-

operative employee is to a major degree a difference in adaptiveness and versatility," or that "*sales ability* [for managers of small retail stores] is highly related to mental flexibility and versatility as measured by the *Thurstone Test of Mental Alertness.*" The trouble with all of this is not only that the distinctions between cognitive and noncognitive aspects of flexibility, adaptiveness, versatility, etc., are lost, but that the direct relevance of the TMA to even the cognitive aspects of these characteristics is never seriously probed. Finally, no evidence is presented concerning the validity of the TMA in any educational setting. For educational guidance purposes there certainly seems to be no reason to prefer the TMA to either the 60-minute *ACE Psychological Examination for High School Students,* the 75-minute *Cooperative School and College Ability Tests,* or the 45-minute *SRA Test of Educational Ability.*

To summarize, the principal advantages of this test remain, as in 1943, its brevity, ease of administration, ease of scoring, and compactness. Its greatest shortcoming is in the area of the meaning of its scores. Both the norms and the validity data are inadequate and the conceptual rationale for the test is unclear. The publishers claim that the TMA was "designed to measure an individual's capacity for acquiring new knowledge and skills." This claim is modest enough but the evidence advanced in support of its realization is unnecessarily oblique. It is certainly unacceptable to rest one's claim that this is a test of mental alertness on the observation that "like electricity, 'mental alertness' is easier to measure than to define or explain." The publishers venture the definition that "mental alertness" refers to "the kind of thinking flexibility and versatility an individual possesses that makes it possible for him to adjust to new situations." Although they are free to define this construct as they see fit, they have not demonstrated that the test is clearly related to the construct, however it may be defined.

For reviews by Anne Anastasi and Emily T. Burr of an earlier edition, see 3:265.

[392]

★The Tomlinson Junior School Test. Ages 7–12.0; 1953; 1 form; no data on reliability and validity; test booklets not required since the test is orally presented using black board examples; 2s. per 25 answer sheets; 1s. 6d. per manual; postage extra; [80-90] minutes; T. P. Tomlinson; University of London Press Ltd. *

JOHN C. DANIELS, *Lecturer in Education, University of Nottingham, Nottingham, England.*

This test has been designed primarily for classifying "the children of the 7–8 years agegroup on their transfer to the junior school." It is a test for "streaming" children in the junior school, though it can, apparently, also be used at the 11–12 years age level for streaming in the secondary modern school.

Its special attraction is its cheapness, a quality stemming from the fact that the testee "expends" only one quarto size answer sheet for writing down the answers to about 120 questions. Each test question is read orally by the tester to the children, though before the testing session the teacher has to prepare five fairly substantial sets of "blackboard material." The test is given in two sections. In form, Section 2 is a replication of Section 1. Each section contains eight subtests with the following titles: Obeying Instructions, Definitions, Number Series, Opposites, Reasoning, Classification, Selection, and Analogies. When the reviewer gave the test to about 40 ten-year-olds, the total testing time added up to 2 hours 2 minutes—a formidable period for tester and tested. All the test items consist of questions of the classical intelligence test type, but they have been so carefully selected from the point of view of item consistency that the reviewer found no quarrel with the interpretation of any items. This is a record for this type of test.

The scores are converted directly into what the manual calls "IQ's." In the conversion table, IQ's are given only for scores at 10-point intervals, which makes it necessary to interpolate for practically every child's score. This makes this part of the testing unnecessarily cumbersome. Indeed, it is not made clear whether these "IQ's" once obtained are IQ's in the strict sense or standardized scores. No standard deviation for an unselected population is given.

No doubt this test will give reliable scores if properly administered, but the validity of tests given in this way is open to some doubt.

[393]

*Verbal and Non-Verbal Test 1. Ages 12 to 13-11; 1951–53; 1 form ['51]; either 54–item *Practice Test 1* ['51] or 22-item *Practice Test 1A* should precede administration of test by 1 week; no data on validity; 8s. 6d. per 12 tests; 9d. per single copy; 5s. per 12 copies of *Practice Test 1*; 6d. per single copy; 2s. 6d. per 12 copies of *Practice Test 1A*; 3d. per single copy; 2s. 6d. per manual ['51]; postage extra; practice test: [10–15] minutes; test: 40(45) minutes; published for

National Foundation for Educational Research in England and Wales; Newnes Educational Publishing Co. Ltd. *

T. R. MILES, *Lecturer in Psychology, University College, Bangor, Wales.*

Although the manual gives detailed instructions for the administration and marking of this test, the crucial issues on the theoretical side receive no discussion at all. This seems to the reviewer a serious omission. By implication, the authors clearly want us to regard this test as a test of intelligence (whatever that means), but we are left completely in the dark as to what theoretical basis, if any, they had in mind in constructing it. Do they believe, for instance, that Spearman's application of factorial analysis to the study of intelligence constitutes a major scientific discovery? The existence of *g* or other factors is neither an agreed truth which can be taken for granted, nor an agreed blind alley comparable to, say, phlogiston; but one looks in vain in the manual for either an expression of acceptance or an unambiguous disclaimer. In the absence of any universally accepted theoretical basis for the study of intelligence, users of this test would be wise, in the reviewer's opinion, to treat the results as a general guide rather than as an accurate measure of some identifiable character trait. Those who are not statistically minded should also remember that, although the test is said to have a Kuder-Richardson reliability coefficient of .98, this figure relates to the consistency of item scores within the test. It does not and cannot mean—except by a verbal quibble—that the test is to that extent *a reliable measure of intelligence.*

A further difficulty is this. It is apparently assumed either that the administrator, the test situation, and all words and diagrams in the test booklet are emotionally neutral to the child, or else that emotional influences do not seriously affect performance on cognitive tasks. One continually wants to know whether the test was supervised by the child's regular teacher, whether the supervisor showed signs of worry at conforming strictly to the timetable, whether the child thought of the situation as a "special occasion," whether the test contains any words or symbols which in a free association test would have produced "blockage," and so on. Some brief reference to such problems should surely have been included; the absence of any such reference confirms one's general impression that those responsible for test construction have not, for the most part, taken such problems seriously enough.

A third general problem which this test has failed to solve is that of alternative methods of classification. In Test 1, for instance, the child has to delete the odd word from groups of four words, e.g., "milk butter cheese water." In some cases, the most suitable method of classification does not admit of serious dispute, but this is not invariably so. Thus in Item 6 ("eiderdown quilt blanket pillow"), the correct answer is given as pillow, presumably since it does not cover us, whereas the others do; but why not blanket, since it is the only one that is not padded? In Item 9 ("rosy red crimson scarlet"), the correct answer is given as rosy (the only adjective derived directly from a noun?), but why not red (the genus word), as opposed to the others which are species of red? It is hard to see, in general, by what right anyone can claim that his particular method of classification is the only correct one.

Apart from these three general difficulties, the reviewer's only other adverse criticisms are minor ones. The complete test is perhaps on the long side, with the result that there is too much of a premium on speed. Knowledge that the game commonly known as "tennis" should strictly be called "lawn tennis" (Test 5, Item 9) seems to the reviewer an unfair requirement, and he should certainly question the assumption that the word "quilt" (Test 1, Item 6) is universally known. There is a misprint on page 1 ("If your pencil points breaks"), and when the child is told on page 2 and elsewhere to underline "the words that are 'different,'" the use of inverted commas around "different" seems to the reviewer incorrect. Dark type or italics would provide the requisite emphasis.

On the credit side, mention should be made in particular of the fact that the instruction manual for this test (and for others in the same series) is addressed primarily to the teacher, who must therefore share the responsibility for assessing the results. It is very desirable, in my opinion, that the psychologist should take the teacher into his confidence in this way; the more the psychologist can be looked upon as a *consultant* rather than as a suspect authority figure, the better for everyone.

Other commendable features in this test are (*a*) that the problem of practice and coaching is squarely faced, and (*b*) that the somewhat

unsatisfactory concept of "mental age" is no longer used in the scoring. As regards (*a*), two preliminary practice tests are available which are to be given a week or so beforehand. The teacher is required to go through all the different kinds of items with the class so that the general principles in each type of test are understood and the need for speed is appreciated. As for (*b*), the familiar procedure is adopted of converting the raw scores, with an allowance for age, into standard scores with mean 100 and standard deviation 15. A child's score is thus primarily an indication of his position in relation to other children of the same age.

This review has concentrated mainly on what the reviewer takes to be the defects of this test, but it would be unfair to conclude without paying tribute to the painstaking work which has clearly gone into its construction. The reviewer's main worry is a general one. Although he does not dispute the value of *individual* intelligence tests, such as those of Terman and Wechsler, as a standardised form of interview, he has some doubts as to whether, in view of the difficulties already mentioned, large scale multiplication of *group* intelligence tests justifies the amount of labour involved. There are so many profitable paths which psychological research can follow that one has to be all the more careful in trying to avoid the blind alleys.

[394]

★**Verbal Capacity Sampler.** Male adults; 1950–52; Form AH ('51); mimeographed manual ('52); 10¢ per test; 25¢ per scoring stencil; 25¢ per manual; 35¢ per specimen set; postage extra; 5(10) minutes; Byron B. Harless and Gerald P. Bodily (test); Gerald P. Bodily (manual); Byron Harless & Associates, Inc. *

[395]

Verbal Intelligence Test. Grades 12–16 and applicants for executive positions; 1948–51; formerly called *Verbal Intelligence Test for Business Executives;* 1 form ('50, identical with test copyrighted in 1948); manual ('49); supplement ('51); no data on reliability; $2.50 per 25 tests; 50¢ per specimen set; cash orders postpaid; 20(25) minutes; William J. Morgan and Antonia Morgan; Aptitude Associates. *

JOHN P. FOLEY, JR., *President, J. P. Foley and Company, Inc., New York, New York.*

This test is printed in blue ink on the inside spread of a folded booklet, the front of the booklet providing space for identifying personal data and the back of the booklet containing the instructions as well as a sample exercise. In each of five sets of items, two columns of words are given. Column A consists of 10 words, Column B of 12 words. For each of the 10 words in Column A the subject is to select the word in Column B which is either most nearly similar or most nearly opposite in meaning. The number of the chosen word is then placed in the appropriately numbered answer space. The total possible score is thus 50.

The scoring sheet provided to the test user consists of a regular test booklet with correct answers overprinted in red. Instructions and norms are provided in a 2-page lithoprinted sheet carrying a 1949 copyright and in a 3-page lithoprinted supplement carrying a 1951 copyright. The 1949 sheet presents decile norms on 259 business executives, ranging in age from 23 to 48 years, with a median age of 36. Annual salaries within the group ranged from $4,500 to $12,000, with a median of $7,400. The group is said to constitute a "representative sample" and to have been "selected from a wide variety of business and industrial concerns." In the 1951 instructions and norms, two normative tables are supplied, one giving percentile equivalents of the scores made by a "random sample" of 312 high school graduates, aged 20 to 49, and the other the percentile equivalents of scores made by a "random sample" of 575 college graduates, ranging in age from 20 to 49.

No reliability data whatever are reported. Data relating to validity are inadequate. The following evidences of validity are claimed or reported: (a) Significantly higher scores are obtained by college graduates than by high school graduates. (b) Correlations with the *Henmon-Nelson Test of Mental Ability* for 334 unspecified cases ranged from .67 to .84 in four studies, although no information is provided on the range of ability or on other group characteristics that might affect these correlations. (c) A correlation of .83 with the V score on the Thorndike CAVD is reported for 43 unspecified cases. (d) Executives earning higher salaries are said to obtain higher test scores, although no supporting data are cited. There are no references given to published reports of any of these studies.

From the 1949 sheet of instructions and norms one learns that the *Verbal Intelligence Test* is designed for business executives. It would seem that most of the validation procedures utilized are not particularly relevant to industrial criteria. In the 1951 "manual," the test is described as "a test of mental ability for adults." This is misleading in the sense that only verbal ability of a limited nature is tested. The elementary nature of the instructions for administration and scoring suggests that the test is designed for use by psychologically untrained and unsophisticated persons. It is thus all the more liable to misuse and misinterpretation. The authors deserve credit, however, for calling attention to the fact that, in the selection of applicants for executive responsibilities, "many factors must be considered such as work attitudes, interests, vocational history, specialized training and education as well as the results of aptitude tests." It is also true, of course, that such factors must be considered in the selection of clerks, typists, administrative assistants, and all other types of personnel.

On the whole, the data relating to norms, reliability, and validity are clearly inadequate in the case of this test. Use of the instrument should be predicated upon local investigation of its validity and reliability, as well as upon the collection of local norms. It would be difficult, however, to justify the use of this test when other instruments, such as certain forms of the *Wonderlic Personnel Test,* are already available for rapid screening purposes.

For a review by William B. Schrader, see 4:329.

[396]

★**Verbal Test (Adv.) 1, 2, and 3.** Ages 12 to 13-11; 1954–58; forms 1 ['54], 2 ['57], 3 ['58]; no data on validity; distribution restricted to directors of education; 8s. 3d. per 12 tests; 9d. per single copy; 1s. 6d. per 12 practice tests; 2d. per single copy; 1s. 7d. per manual; postage extra; practice test: 10(15) minutes; D. A. Pidgeon; published for National Foundation for Educational Research in England and Wales (a); Newnes Educational Publishing Co. Ltd. *
a) VERBAL TEST (ADV.) 1. 1954–55; practice test ['54]; manual ('55); 50(60) minutes.
b) VERBAL TEST (ADV.) 2. 1957; practice test ['57]; manual ('57); 45(55) minutes.
c) VERBAL TEST (ADV.) 3. 1958; practice test ['58]; manual ('58); 45(55) minutes.

[397]

*Verbal Tests 1–2, 4–8.** Ages 10–11; 1951–58; 7 forms; no data on reliability for form 4; no data on validity; distribution restricted to directors of education; 6s. 6d. per 12 tests; 7d. per single copy; 1s. 3d. per 12 practice tests (dates same as for tests except 7B); 2d. per single copy; 1s. 7d. per manual; postage extra; form 1: 50(75) minutes; forms 2, 4–7: 45(65) minutes; I. Macfarlane Smith (a–d) and M. A. Brimer (e); published for National Foundation for Educational Research in England and Wales; Newnes Educational Publishing Co. *
a) VERBAL TEST 1. 1951–53; form 1 ['51]; manual ('53).
b) VERBAL TEST 2. 1952–53; form 2 ['52]; manual ['53]; no norms for ages 11-7 to 11-11.

c) VERBAL TEST 4. 1953; form 4 ['53]; manual ['53];
norms ['54].
d) VERBAL TEST 5. 1954-55; form 5 ['54]; manual
('55); no norms for ages 11-6 to 11-11.
e) VERBAL TEST 6. 1955-57; form 6 ['55]; manual ('57).
f) VERBAL TEST 7. 1957-58; forms 7A ['57], 7B ['57];
practice test ['58] for form 7B; manual (7A, '57; 7B,
'57).
g) VERBAL TEST 8. 1957-58; forms 8A ['57], 8B ['58];
manual (8A, '58; 8B, '58).

[398]
Vocabulary Tests. Ages 10-15; 1931-35; 1 form
['31]; 5 tests; manual ('35, same as manual copyrighted in 1931); no data on reliability; 4s. 6d. per 25
copies of any one test; 3d. per single copy; 2s. per
manual; postage extra; 50(60) minutes per test 1 day
apart; Frank Watts; University of London Press
Ltd. *
a) VOCABULARY TEST NO. 1, 100 COMMON NAMES.
b) VOCABULARY TEST NO. 2, 100 COMMON CLASS NAMES.
c) VOCABULARY TEST NO. 3, 100 COMMON VERBS.
d) VOCABULARY TEST NO. 4, 100 COMMON ADJECTIVES
(LIST A).
e) VOCABULARY TEST NO. 5, 100 COMMON ADJECTIVES
(LIST B).

JOHN NISBET, *Lecturer in Education, University of Aberdeen, Aberdeen, Scotland.*

The items in the first three of this series of
100-item tests are open questions; those in the
last two are a type of multiple choice item.
Norms are in the form of average scores (both
sexes together) at each age from 10 through
15. The standardisation groups, which are not
precisely described, vary in number from 2,857
for Test 1 to 1,898 for Test 3. No data on
construction are given. Instructions are very
brief, and the key gives few alternatives for
answers to the open-ended questions. The tests
are difficult, the average score, except on Test
1, reaching the 50 per cent correct mark only
at about age 15.

The author suggests that the tests "will provide measures of intelligence similar to those
obtained by the ordinary type of intelligence
tests," and he himself has used them in his
basic research on the relation of vocabulary to
general mental growth in adolescence.[1] However, the tests seem unsuited for use as measures of general ability or even as measures of
vocabulary for several reasons—their length,
the inadequacy of instructions for administration and scoring, and the vagueness of data on
construction and standardisation. Also, a number of the items are surprisingly dated. For
example, Item 59 in Test 2: Common Class
Names, asks "What do we call carbolic powder,
Condy's fluid and chloride of lime?"

[1] WATTS, A. F. *The Language and Mental Development of
Children.* London: George G. Harrap & Co. Ltd., 1944. Pp.
354.

The tests would require revision of certain
out of date terminology and new item analysis
and standardisation before they could be accepted as a useful vocabulary assessment at a
fairly advanced level. They could be used more
appropriately as teaching aids to help focus
pupils' attention on the finer point of verbal expression, rather than as tests.

[399]
Wesman Personnel Classification Test. Grades 8-
16 and adults; 1946-51; 3 scores: verbal, numerical,
total; Forms A ('46), B ('47); revised manual ('51);
$1.70 per 25 tests; 35¢ per specimen set; postpaid;
28(35) minutes; Alexander G. Wesman; Psychological Corporation. *

REFERENCES

1-3. See 4:331.
4. GILBERT, HARRY B. "The Use of Tests and Other Objective Data in the Selection of Camp Counselors." Abstract. *Am
Psychol* 7:369 Jl '52. *
5. WILLIAMS, JOHN E., AND GERKEN, C. D'A. " 'Verbal Factor' and 'Number Factor'—A Study of Two Tests." *Proc Iowa
Acad Sci* 59:397-401 '52. * (*PA* 28:6599)
6. HANER, CHARLES F. "Wonderlic, Wesman P.C.T., and
A.C.E.: A Comparison of Three Group Intelligence Tests."
Proc Iowa Acad Sci 61:358-60 '54. * (*PA* 30:3460)
7. HOLT, WELDON G. *Relationships Between the ACE and
the Wesman Personnel Classification Test.* Master's thesis, University of Kansas (Lawrence, Kan.), 1954.
8. PERRINE, MERVYN WILLIAM. "The Selection of Drafting
Trainees." *J Appl Psychol* 39:57-61 F '55. * (*PA* 30:1725)
9. BAIER, DONALD E., AND DUGAN, ROBERT D. "Normative
Data Information Exchange, No. 2." *Personnel Psychol* 9:265-
6 su '56. *
10. BAIER, DONALD E., AND DUGAN, ROBERT D. "Tests and
Performance in a Sales Organization." *Personnel Psychol* 9:
17-26 sp '56. * (*PA* 31:5169)
11. HOLT, WELDON G.; OTTMAN, DONALD K.; AND COTTLE,
WILLIAM C. "Evidenced Relationships Between the 'ACE' and
the Wesman Personnel Classification Test." *J Ed Res* 51:71-7
S '57. *

*For reviews by John C. Flanagan and Erwin
K. Taylor, see 4:331; see 3:253 (1 excerpt).*

[400]
Wonderlic Personnel Test. Adults; 1939-45;
Forms D and F are adaptations, for business and industrial use, of *Otis Self-Administering Tests of Mental Ability, Higher Form;* Forms A ('42), B ('42),
D ['39], F ['39]; manual ('45); $8 per 100 tests and
manual; 50¢ per manual; postage extra; 12(20) minutes; E. F. Wonderlic; Wonderlic Personnel Test
Co. *

REFERENCES

1-2. See 40:1415.
3-9. See 3:269.
10. JACOBSEN, CARLYLE F. "Interest and Attitude as Factors
in Achievement in Medical School." *J Assn Am Med Col* 21:
152-9 My '46. *
11. LINDZEY, GARDNER E. "Four Psychometric Techniques
Useful in Vocational Guidance." *J Clin Psychol* 2:157-60 Ap
'46. * (*PA* 20:3899)
12. ROBERTS, WILLIAM H. "Test Scores and Merit Ratings
of Graduate Engineers." Abstract. *Am Psychol* 1:284 Jl '46. *
13. FISKE, DONALD W. "Validation of Naval Aviation Cadet
Selection Tests Against Training Criteria." *J Appl Psychol* 31:
601-14 D '47. * (*PA* 22:2770)
14. CHESLER, DAVID J. "The Wonderlic Personnel Test as a
Predictor of Scores on the American Council on Education Examination." *J Clin Psychol* 4:82-5 Ja '48. * (*PA* 22:5566)
15. CAPWELL, DORA F. *Psychological Tests for Retail Store
Personnel.* Pittsburgh, Pa.: Research Bureau for Retail Training, University of Pittsburgh, 1949. Pp. 48. * (*PA* 25:3449)
16. GLASER, ROBERT. "A Methodological Analysis of the Inconsistency of Response to Test Items." *Ed & Psychol Meas*
9:727-39 w '49. * (*PA* 26:2747)
17. KNAUFT, EDWIN B. "A Selection Battery for Bake Shop
Managers." *J Appl Psychol* 33:304-15 Ag '49. * (*PA* 24:2850)
18. LINDZEY, GARDNER. "Remarks on the Use of the Won-

derlic Personnel Test as a 'Pre-Test.'" *J Clin Psychol* 5:100–2 Ja '49. * *(PA* 23:5522)

19. DOUB, BETTY ALLEN. "Better Clerks Can Be Hired With Tests." *Personnel J* 29:102–3 Jl-Ag '50. * *(PA* 25:2074)

20. DULSKY, STANLEY G., AND KROUT, MAURICE H. "Predicting Promotion Potential on the Basis of Psychological Tests." *Personnel Psychol* 3:345–51 au '50. * *(PA* 25:3452)

21. HAY, EDWARD N. "A Warm-Up Test." *Personnel Psychol* 3:221–3 su '50. * *(PA* 25:2078)

22. HOLMES, FRANK J. "Validity of Tests for Insurance Office Personnel." *Personnel Psychol* 3:57–69 sp '50. * *(PA* 24:/5490)

23. HOLMES, FRANK J. "Validity of Tests for Insurance Office Personnel, II." *Personnel Psychol* 3:217–20 su '50. * *(PA* / 25:2079)

24. MILLER, RICHARD B. "Reducing the Time Required for Testing Clerical Applicants." *Personnel J* 28:364–6 Mr '50. * / *(PA* 24:4872)

25. WECHSLER, IRVING R. "The Personal Factor in Labor Mediation." *Personnel Psychol* 3:113–32 su '50. * *(PA* 25:| 2089)

26. BLAKEMORE, ARLINE. "Reducing Typing Costs With Aptitude Tests." *Personnel J* 30:20–4 My '51. * *(PA* 25:7749)

27. HAY, EDWARD N. "Mental Ability Tests in Clerical Selection." *J Appl Psychol* 35:250–1 Ag '51. * *(PA* 26:3071)

28. LANEY, ARTHUR R., JR. "Validity of Employment Tests for Gas-Appliance Service Personnel." *Personnel Psychol* 4: \ 199–208 su '51. * *(PA* 26:1735)

29. MEYER, HERBERT H. "Factors Related to Success in the Human Relations Aspect of Work-Group Leadership." *Psychol Monogr* 65(3):1–29 '51. * *(PA* 25:7132)

30. AMERICAN GAS ASSOCIATION, PERSONNEL COMMITTEE. *Personnel Testing in the Gas Industry.* New York: the Association, January 1952. Pp. 10. *

31. HAY, EDWARD N. "Some Research Findings With the Wonderlic Personnel Test." *J Appl Psychol* 36:344–5 O '52. * *(PA* 27:5446)

32. JENNINGS, EUGENE EMERSON. "The Motivation Factor in Testing Supervisors." *J Appl Psychol* 37:168–9 Je '53. * *(PA* 28:3330)

33. SEASHORE, HAROLD G. "Validation of Clerical Testing in / Banks." *Personnel Psychol* 6:45–56 sp '53. * *(PA* 28:1670)

34. "Validity Information Exchange, No. 7-094: D.O.T. Code 7-80.120, Beginner Mechanics." *Personnel Psychol* 7:572 w '54. *

35. BASS, BERNARD M.; KARSTENDIEK, BARBARA; McCULLOUGH, GERALD; AND PRUITT, RAY C. "Validity Information Exchange, No. 7-024: D.O.T. Code 2-66.01, 2-66.11, 2-66.12, 2-66.23, Policemen and Detectives, Public Service." *Personnel Psychol* 7:159–60 sp '54. *

36. GROHSMEYER, FREDERICK A., JR. *Validation of Personnel Tests for a Paper Mill.* Doctor's thesis, Purdue University / (Lafayette, Ind.), 1954. *(DA* 14:1796)

37. HANER, CHARLES F. "Wonderlic, Wesman P.C.T., and A.C.E.: A Comparison of Three Group Intelligence Tests." *Proc Iowa Acad Sci* 61:358–60 '54. * *(PA* 30:3460)

38. HAY, EDWARD N. "Comparative Validities in Clerical Test-| ing." *J Appl Psychol* 38:299–301 O '54. * *(PA* 29:6351)

39. KNAUFT, EDWIN B. "Validity Information Exchange, No. 7-070: D.O.T. Code 0-72.21, Manager, Retail Food." *Personnel Psychol* 7:405–6 au '54. *

40. McCARTY, JOHN J. "Validity Information Exchange, No. 7-077: D.O.T. Code 5-92.621, (Foreman II)." *Personnel Psychol* 7:420–1 au '54. *

41. McCARTY, JOHN J.; WESTBERG, WILLIAM C.; AND FITZPATRICK, EUGENE D. "Validity Information Exchange, No. 7-091: D.O.T. Code 5-92.621, (Foreman II)." *Personnel Psychol* 7:568–9 w '54. *

42. RUSMORE, JAY, AND MARTIN, FRED. "Validity Information Exchange, No. 7-053: D.O.T. Code 1-37.34, Clerk-Typist." *Personnel Psychol* 7:289 su '54. *

43. SKARD, ØYVIND; AURSAND, INGER MARIE; AND BRAATEN, LEIF J. "Development and Application of Tests for University Students in Norway: A Report on Parts of a Research Project." *Psychol Monogr* 68(12):1–54 '54. * *(PA* 29:7971)

44. WESTBERG, WILLIAM C.; FITZPATRICK, EUGENE D.; AND McCARTY, JOHN J. "Validity Information Exchange, No. 7-073: D.O.T. Code 1-37.32, Typist." *Personnel Psychol* 7:411–2 au '54. *

45. WESTBERG, WILLIAM C.; FITZPATRICK, EUGENE D.; AND McCARTY, JOHN J. "Validity Information Exchange, No. 7-074: D.O.T. Code 1-37.32, Typist." *Personnel Psychol* 7:413 au '54. *

46. WESTBERG, WILLIAM C.; FITZPATRICK, EUGENE D.; AND McCARTY, JOHN J. "Validity Information Exchange, No. 7-087: D.O.T. Code 1-37.32, Typist." *Personnel Psychol* 7:561–2 w '54. *

47. YOUNG, MARY B. *The Predictive Value of the Wonderlic Personnel Test and the Minnesota Clerical Test in the Selection of Clerical and Telephone Sales Workers.* Master's thesis, Boston University (Boston, Mass.), 1954.

48. BARNABAS, BENTLEY. "The Apt Performance Tests for Screening in Business Situations." *Trans Kans Acad Sci* 58: 419–23 '55. *

49. BARNABAS, BENTLEY. "A Study of Speed-Power and Verbal-Quantitative Scores for the Personnel Test." *Trans Kans Acad Sci* 58:111–4 '55. *

50. CUOMO, SYLVIA, AND MEYER, HERBERT H. "Validity In-

formation Exchange, No. 8-19: D.O.T. Code 6-78.632, **Floor** Assembler." *Personnel Psychol* 8:270 su '55. *

51. FITZPATRICK, EUGENE D., AND McCARTY, JOHN J. "Validity Information Exchange, No. 8-35: D.O.T. Code 9-00.91, Assembler VII (Electrical Equipment)." *Personnel Psychol* 8: 501–4 w '55. *

52. HARDING, F. D. "Validity Information Exchange, No. 8-23: D.O.T. Code 1-18.84, Collection Clerk." *Personnel Psychol* 8:378 au '55. *

53. HARRISON, ROSS; HUNT, WINSLOW; AND JACKSON, THEODORE A. "Profile of the Mechanical Engineer: 1, Ability." *Personnel Psychol* 8:219–34 su '55. * *(PA* 30:5414)

54. WEAVER, HERBERT B., AND BONEAU, C. A. "Equivalence / of Forms of the Wonderlic Personnel Test: A Reliability Study." Abstract. *Am Psychol* 10:473 Ag '55. *

55. GOLDHOR, HERBERT. "Validity Information Exchange, No. 9-33: D.O.T. Code 1-20.01, Librarian Assistant." *Personnel Psychol* 9:378 au '56. *

56. KUSHMAN, HOWARD S., AND CANFIELD, ALBERT A. "Validity Information Exchange, No. 9-32: D.O.T. Code 1-18.63, Order Clerk-Clerical 11 (Telephone)." *Personnel Psychol* 9: 375–7 au '56. *

57. McCARTY, JOHN J., AND FITZPATRICK, EUGENE D. "Validity Information Exchange, No. 9-26: D.O.T. Code 5-92.621, (Foreman II)." *Personnel Psychol* 9:253 su '56. *

58. WALKER, FRANCIS C. "Normative Data Information Exchange, No. 3." *Personnel Psychol* 9:267 su '56. *

59. WEAVER, H. B., AND BONEAU, C. A. "Equivalence of / Forms of the Wonderlic Personnel Test: A Study of Reliability and Interchangeability." *J Appl Psychol* 40:127–9 Ap '56. * *(PA* 31:6143)

60. McCARTY, JOHN J. "Normative Data Information Exchange, No. 10-19." *Personnel Psychol* 10:241 su '57. *

61. McCARTY, JOHN J. "Normative Data Information Exchange, No. 10-28." *Personnel Psychol* 10:362 au '57. *

62. McCARTY, JOHN J. "Validity Information Exchange, No. 10-14: D.O.T. Code 1-33.01, Secretary." *Personnel Psychol* 10: 202–3 su '57. *

63. McCARTY, JOHN J. "Validity Information Exchange, No. 10-15: D.O.T. Code 1-33.01, Secretary." *Personnel Psychol* 10: 204–5 su '57. *

64. ALBRIGHT, LEWIS E.; GLENNON, J. R.; AND SMITH, WALLACE J. "Normative Data Information Exchange, No. 11-8." *Personnel Psychol* 11:273 su '58. *

65. BARRETT, RICHARD S. "The Process of Predicting Job Performance." *Personnel Psychol* 11:39–57 sp '58. *

66. BRIDGMAN, C. S.; SPAETHE, M.; AND DIGNAN, F. "Validity Information Exchange, No. 11-21: D.O.T. Code 8-09.11, Sliced-Bacon Scaler; 8-09.11, Sliced-Bacon Packer, II." *Personnel Psychol* 11:264–5 su '58. *

67. GLENNON, J. R.; SMITH, WALLACE J.; AND ALBRIGHT, LEWIS E. "Normative Data Information Exchange, No. 11-7." *Personnel Psychol* 11:272 su '58. *

68. PHILLIPS, JOHN C. "Normative Data Information Exchange, No. 11-9." *Personnel Psychol* 11:274 su '58. *

For reviews by H. E. Brogden, Charles D. Flory, and Irving Lorge, see 3:269.

INDIVIDUAL

[401]

*Benton Visual Retention Test, Revised Edition. Ages 8 and over; 1946–55; individual; Forms C, D, E ('55); $4.50 per set of test materials, 50 record blanks ('55), and manual ('55), postpaid; 5(10) minutes; Arthur L. Benton; distributed by Psychological Corporation. *

REFERENCES

1–3. See 4:360.

4. WHARTON, LYLE H. *Effect of Stress-Produced Anxiety on Rorschach, Draw-A-Person, and Visual Performance.* Doctor's thesis, State University of Iowa (Iowa City, Iowa), 1953. *(DA* 13:1268)

5. KOLSTOE, OLIVER P. "A Comparison of Mental Abilities of Bright and Dull Children of Comparable Mental Ages." *J Ed Psychol* 45:161–8 Mr '54. * *(PA* 29:2270)

6. LACHMANN, FRANK M. *Perceptual-Motor Development in Children Retarded in Reading Ability.* Doctor's thesis, Northwestern University (Evanston, Ill.), 1955. *(DA* 15:1900)

7. NASH, JOHN. "The Diagnosis of Brain Damage by Psychological Techniques: A Review of the Literature and Present Status." *B Maritime Psychol Assn* 4:32–46 '55. * *(PA* 30:8440)

8. WAHLER, H. J. "A Comparison of Reproduction Errors Made by Brain-Damaged and Control Patients on a Memory-For-Designs Test." *J Abn & Social Psychol* 52:251–5 Mr '56. * *(PA* 31:3571)

NELSON G. HANAWALT, *Professor of Psychology, Douglass College, Rutgers University, New Brunswick, New Jersey.*

The manual states that this is "a clinical and research instrument designed to assess memory, perception and visuomotor functions." This statement is somewhat misleading since the test is one of memory for designs, not of memory in general. Memory in general becomes more and more difficult to assess by any single method or material after the age of 6 years as witnessed by the decreasing intercorrelations of memory tests with increasing age up to the adult level. Also, it is difficult to see how this is a perceptual test, since there is no mechanism to separate memory and perception unless Administration C, which does not measure memory at all, is also given. There is a good possibility that this test (as well as other memory for designs tests) could be improved by using Administration C (copying the design) as the learning method and taking the measurement of error of memory from the copies rather than from the stimulus figures. This method would give a much better measure of what the subject saw (perception) as distinguished from what he remembered, and would assist greatly in separating these two functions from drawing and motor ability.

A number of criticisms of the first edition of this test, reported in *The Fourth Mental Measurements Yearbook,* have been met in the new edition. The test now has 10 designs in place of 7. Better standardization for a normal population is indicated, but not at all adequately described, in the manual. Unfortunately, much of the data one would wish to have at hand in considering a test is not in the manual. One is referred to the American Documentation Institute for such things as population description, number of subjects, sex differences, statistical methods, reliability of the test, and the correlation among the three different forms of the test. For instance, a correlation of about .7 is reported between scores on the test and intelligence, but no indication is given as to the number or character of cases or the kind of "standard intelligence scales" used.

The new error scoring system introduced in this edition appears to add little to the previous, and still used, "number correct" score. Wahler (8) has published an analysis of "error" scores, comparing normal and brain damaged cases. In none of the different types of error was

there a significant difference of proportion in the two groups, although several types of error were suggestive for further study. Copying the designs in the learning period would help eliminate some of the problems encountered in this work, such as the difficulty of not knowing whether the subject saw the peripheral figures which he did not reproduce. Size differences of peripheral and central figures also appear to be a promising lead. Copying the designs in the learning period would help determine whether this was a perceptual or a memory factor. Rotational errors are still another promising lead, but the test as designed does not separate the perceptual from the memory factors. Obviously a bizarre drawing is an important bit of evidence. Having the subject draw the design in the learning period would enable one to tell whether the subject saw the bizarre figure in the stimulus or whether it was entirely a matter of memory. The delayed recall test which Benton promises for the future also would appear to be a good addition to the test. In short, it is possible that better distinction beween perceptual, memory, and motor factors would help make a more precise distinction between normal and brain damaged cases.

The author admits that the validity of the test for diagnosing brain injury (the real purpose of the test) is not well established in this difficult field. His claim that, if the appropriate cutoff is used, the test will pick out 40 to 50 per cent of the brain damaged cases and include only about 4 per cent of normals, is about the same as that made for other memory for design tests. This reviewer tried the test on a small sample of 22 delinquent youths at the New Jersey Diagnostic Center. The 9 female and 13 male subjects ranged in age from 8 to 18 years, with a median age of 12.5. Wechsler-Bellevue IQ's ranged from 72 to 124, with a median of 95.5. Only the new error scoring was used. When scores were equated for age and intelligence according to the tables in the manual, only one subject did better than expected, 6 were within normal expectation, 2 were questionable, 3 were suggestive of brain damage, and 10 gave strong indication of brain damage. There were no obviously bizarre responses. One might conclude from the distribution of scores alone that the sample was drawn from a brain damaged population. In fact, the distribution was almost identical with that for Benton's sample of 100 brain injured patients, of whom 43 per cent were reported to have scored borderline or normal and 57 per cent defective. In the reviewer's sample 41 per cent were borderline or normal and 59 per cent defective. Although the correlations were positive, he found no significant correlations of "good memory" with either IQ or reading test score. The scoring instructions were found to be adequate and clear.

It is quite possible that the above sample of delinquents had a higher percentage of brain damage than the normal population, but it was a sample of the usual type of delinquents whose Wechsler-Bellevue scores were available, and not a sample of neurological cases. Most of the subjects were below their expected reading level. The above study is not a criticism of Benton's test in particular, but rather a criticism of all tests of memory for design as being specifically related to brain damage. There is no indication at present that any of the psychological tests for brain damage can separate out the neurological factors from the general environmental-developmental factors in test performance for most subjects (7). Certain striking cases keep hope alive and this is as it should be.

The revised edition of the *Benton Visual Retention Test* is an improvement over the first edition, but it is still in an experimental stage. It is probably as good as any of the three or four tests of this type which are currently being used to diagnose brain damage.

For reviews by Ivan Norman Mensh, Joseph Newman, and William Schofield of the original edition, see 4:360; see 3:297 (1 excerpt).

[402]

★Columbia Mental Maturity Scale. Mental ages 3–12; 1954; 2 scores: MA, IQ; individual; 1 form; $34 per examiner's kit including 100 record blanks; $1.10 per 100 record blanks; $4.75 per carrying case; postage extra; (15–30) minutes; Bessie B. Burgemeister, Lucille Hollander Blum, and Irving Lorge; World Book Co. *

REFERENCES

1. STROTHER, C. R. "Evaluating the Intelligence of Children Handicapped by Cerebral Palsy." *Crippled Child* 23:82–3 '45.
2. MILLER, ELSA, AND ROSENFELD, G. B. "The Psychological Evaluation of Children With Cerebral Palsy and Its Implication in Treatment." *J Pediatrics* 41:613–21 '52.
3. MILL, CYRIL R., AND TURNER, CHARLES J. "The Measurement of Primary Mental Abilities by the Columbia Mental Maturity Scale." Abstract. *J Consult Psychol* 19:472 D '55. *
4. ROSENBLUM, JEROME. *The Intellectual Evaluation of the Cerebral Palsied With the Columbia Mental Maturity Scale.* Master's thesis, University of North Carolina (Chapel Hill, N.C.), 1955.
5. BARRATT, ERNEST S. "The Relationship of the Progressive Matrices (1938) and the Columbia Mental Maturity Scale to the WISC." *J Consult Psychol* 20:294–6 Ag '56. * (PA 31:7893)

6. CANTER, ARTHUR. "The Use of the Columbia Mental Maturity Scale With Cerebral Palsied Children." *Am J Mental Def* 60:843–51 Ap '56. * (PA 31:5019)
7. GUSLOFF, RICHARD F. *Comparability of Columbia Mental Maturity Scale Quotients.* Master's thesis, Illinois State Normal University (Normal, Ill.), 1956.
8. JOHNSON, G. ORVILLE; NEELY, JAMES H.; AND ALLING, ROGER L. "A Comparison of the 1937 Revision of the Stanford-Binet (Form L) and the Columbia Scale of Mental Maturity." *Excep Child* 22:155–7+ Ja '56. * (PA 31:3562)
9. LANTZ, BEATRICE, AND WOLF, RUTH. "The Columbia Mental Maturity Scale and the Stanford-Binet With Cerebral Palsied Children." *Calif J Ed Res* 7:183–5 S '56. * (PA 31:6521)
10. TAYLOR, EDWARD A. "The Columbia Mental Maturity Scale as a Screening Test for Special Classes." Abstract. *Calif J Ed Res* 7:131 My '56. *
11. MAY, W. THEODORE, AND PERRY, HAROLD W. "The Relationship Between the Stanford-Binet (Form L) Vocabulary and the Columbia Mental Maturity Scale in a Group of Mentally Retarded Children." *Am J Mental Def* 62:330–3 S '57. *
12. SHONTZ, FRANKLIN C. "Evaluation of Intellectual Potential in Hemiplegic Individuals." *J Clin Psychol* 13:267–9 Jl '57.
13. COOPER, JAMES G. "Predicting School Achievement for Bilingual Pupils." *J Ed Psychol* 49:31–6 F '58. *

[403]

*Detroit Tests of Learning Aptitude. Ages 3 and over; 1935–55; 20 scores: pictorial absurdities, verbal absurdities, pictorial opposites, verbal opposites, motor speed and precision, auditory attention span (for unrelated words, for related syllables), oral commissions, social adjustment A, visual attention span (for objects, for letters), orientation, free association, memory for designs, number ability, social adjustment B, broken pictures, oral directions, likenesses and differences, total; individual; 1 form ('35); manual ('35); revised record booklet ('39); supplementary norms ('55); no data on reliability for part scores except for auditory attention span for unrelated words; $6.50 per set of test materials; $3.60 per 25 record booklets; postpaid; (60–95) minutes; Harry J. Baker and Bernice Leland; Public School Publishing Co. *

For a review by F. L. Wells, see 3:275; for reviews by Anne Anastasi and Henry Feinberg of an earlier edition, see 38:1058 (1 excerpt).

[404]

★The Griffiths Mental Development Scale for Testing Babies From Birth to Two Years. 1951–55; individual; 6 scores: locomotor, personal-social, hearing and speech, eye and hand, performance, total; 1 form ('54); revised record booklet ('55); tentative norms; test materials sold only to persons taking author's lecture course; 495s. fee for course and set of test materials; 20s. per manual ('54, see 2 below); postage extra; (20–40) minutes; Ruth Griffiths; the Author, Child Development Research Centre, 47 Hollycroft Ave., London, N.W. 3, England. *

REFERENCES

1. GRIFFITHS, R. "A New Approach to the Assessment of General Mental Development in Infancy," pp. 68–70. Abstract. In *Proceedings and Papers of the Twelfth International Congress of Psychology Held at the University of Edinburgh, July 23rd to 29th, 1948.* Edinburgh, Scotland: Oliver and Boyd Ltd., 1950. Pp. xxviii, 152. *
2. GRIFFITHS, RUTH. *The Abilities of Babies: A Study in Mental Measurement.* London: University of London Press Ltd., 1954. Pp. x, 229. * (PA 29:76)
3. GRIFFITHS, RUTH. "Testing the Very Young." Abstract. *B Brit Psychol Soc* (29):40–1 My '56. *

NANCY BAYLEY, *Chief, Section on Child Development, Laboratory of Psychology, National Institute of Mental Health, National Institutes of Health, Public Health Service,*

United States Department of Health, Education, and Welfare, Bethesda, Maryland.

This is a carefully considered, well worked out British scale in which the author has made use of other infant scales (mostly from the United States) as a basis for her first selections of items and their age placements. After the preliminary selections and fairly extensive pretesting and observation of infants, she grouped the tests into five scales: locomotor, personal-social, hearing and speech, eye and hand, and performance. Items were arranged in the order of increasing difficulty and selected in such a way that there are three for each week during the first year and two for each week during the second year. They are equally distributed into the five categories, with 31 items in each for the first year and 21 in each for the second. The scale thus contains a total of 260 items, 52 for each scale category.

In the final standardization sample, 571 infants were selected to give an occupational distribution of fathers similar to that used by Goodenough. The number of cases at each month ranged from 16 to 31. Sixty babies were given a second test after an average interval of 30 weeks (range, 7 to 70 weeks). By counting each item in the first year as one third of a week and in the second year as one half of a week, Griffiths obtains a cumulative point score that is a mental age, and from this computes a ratio IQ or "GQ" (general intelligence quotient). Because the standard deviations of these GQ's were so large during the first eight months, an adjustment was applied for these ages by adding 8 weeks to both the MA and CA before computing the IQ. By this procedure, the SD's of the GQ's at all ages are approximately 12 points, and the average SD for the total sample is 12.1 points. By an appropriate pro-rating of mental age units to items within each of the five categories, quotients for them may be derived in the same way. With an SD of just 12 points, the range of quotients is rather restricted: for the total population of 571 infants Griffiths found the scores to range "between a little over 60 and a little below 140." As a test of validity, the author gives the correlation between first and second test of 60 cases, which is .87. For this *r* there is no control either of the ages of the subjects or the time interval between tests.

In addition to detailed directions for giving and scoring the tests and some excellent recom-

mendations about the general procedures, there are chapters concerned with interpretation of the test results, including "Profile Studies of Normal Infants," and "Differential Diagnosis of Mental Handicap in Special Cases." Although the author several times cautions against accepting as final, scores for a single test on the young infants, she is optimistic about the scores' general usefulness both in predicting later levels of intelligence and in the diagnostic use of the five category profiles. She does say, however, that more studies need to be made to test both general prediction and the reliability and validity of the profiles. She makes use of individual cases to illustrate points. Where changes occur on repeat tests, they are usually attributed to intervening therapy or other specific conditions. In fact, the predictive usefulness of both the general quotient and the category quotients cannot be known until more systematic studies have been made on test-retest comparisons.

The scale impresses the reviewer as a very good, well worked out test of the developmental status of English children. The number of cases studied at any one age seems small, but care is evident in the preliminary trials and means by which items were selected; and this has resulted in a clear stable progression of scores with age. The test should not be applied to children in other countries, however, without some necessary adaptations. Both test materials and the language and idiomatic phrasing of the test procedures are in many instances peculiarly English. Although there is no statement to this effect in the text of the book, those who have tried to buy the testing materials have been told that Dr. Griffiths will sell them only to persons who have been trained by her in their use.

[405]

Intelligence Tests for Children. Ages 1.5–15; 1945–58; formerly called *Intelligence Tests for Young Children;* individual; 1 form ('53); no data on reliability; 8s. 6d. per manual (see 5 below); postage extra; 7s. 6d. per set of test materials; (30–45) minutes; C. W. Valentine; Methuen & Co. Ltd. *

REFERENCES

1–3. See 4:343.
4. VALENTINE, C. W. *Intelligence Tests for Children, Fifth Edition.* London: Methuen & Co., Ltd., 1953. Pp. xiii, 84. *
5. VALENTINE, C. W. *Intelligence Tests for Children, Sixth Edition.* London: Methuen & Co. Ltd., 1958. Pp. xiii, 87. *

ELIZABETH D. FRASER, *Lecturer in Psychology, University of Aberdeen, Aberdeen, Scotland.*

Although elaborate and expensive apparatus does not necessarily add to the value of a test, it does have one advantage, especially in the case of individual tests of intelligence: it tends to keep the test in the hands of people who are competent to administer it and to interpret the results correctly and with due caution. In this test, Valentine dispenses with all but the very minimum of apparatus and recommends the test for teachers and even for "the intelligent parent who knows nothing of intelligence tests." This could be unwise even if the content of the test were new. But Valentine has constructed the test largely from items appearing in other tests, some of which, e.g., the Terman-Merrill revision of the Binet Scale, are in constant use by psychologists. The widespread application of the Valentine test in the hands of untrained people might well invalidate the later work of more competent testers.

The test claims to cater to children from 1½ to 15 years of age. It follows the pattern of the Stanford-Binet in that it has a set of tasks (varying in number from 6 to 10) to be performed at each age level. Instructions are given concerning the administration of the tests, the scoring of items, and the calculation of IQ.

On the question of standardisation, however, very little information is given. Although the items are derived from other tests, some of them well standardised and validated, these items were originally given in a different context. Moreover, Valentine has altered the presentation and the scoring of many of them before incorporating them in his test. Ideally, each item and certainly each test as a whole should have been tried out on a large representative sample of children. In fact, the sample was neither very large nor possibly very representative of British children. It consisted of 414 children aged between four and eight, who "were nearly all in unselected Infant and Junior Schools, almost all in or near Birmingham, except for a group of about 25 who were in a rural area. Of the Birmingham Schools, one was in a poor district and provided about 175 of the children. (Thirteen decidedly subnormal children in this school were not included in the results.) Three schools were in suburban districts and provided about 65 children. The remainder of about 150 were in fairly average schools, about a score being in Nursery Schools." No tryout of the tests for children up to 15 (tests introduced in the third edition and extended in the present edition) is

reported by Valentine, and no reliability figures are quoted for the test as a whole at any age.

To sum up, the reviewer doubts the wisdom of publishing tests of this kind designed for unskilled testers, yet using material similar to or identical with that found in other tests used routinely by trained people. Even if this objection were disallowed, much work on standardisation would have to be done before the tests could be recommended.

G. A. V. MORGAN, *Senior Psychologist, North Wales Child Guidance Clinics, Denbighshire, North Wales.*

This set of individual tests of ability is clearly a grandchild of the Binet family and has the advantages and defects of the original. Many items are in fact adapted from the Burt and Stanford revisions of the Binet. Nevertheless, it must be judged not as a new revision, but as a compendium of tests for practical use by teachers.

This scale is not likely to be acceptable to the educational psychologist as a substitute for the WISC or traditional Terman-Merrill. It may, however, meet a need one sometimes feels, in brief preliminary testing of the very young and dull child, for items linking the Gesell and Merrill-Palmer type of "developmental" assessments with the introductory items of a Binet scale. It seems simpler, though less systematic for this purpose, than the Cattell scale.

The tests are varied and interesting in content, with some ingenious new items. They sample the usual range of functions forming the composite "general ability" which is useful to the clinician despite its factorial complexity. Verbal bias is about as heavy as in the Terman-Merrill.

The great weakness of this scale is its standardization. Items adapted from existing Binet revisions have age placements agreeing with the originals for ages 3-6 to 9. Actual trials of items on children between 5 and 7 confirmed, on the whole, the appropriateness of placement. For tests for ages 1-6 to 3-0, the author correctly remarks that he cannot feel the same confidence. Here, items from Gesell, Merrill-Palmer, and Terman-Merrill scales follow their original age placement, but the new scaling has not been empirically checked. The scale is least trustworthy for ages 11 to 15. In extending the scale upward, the author has adapted several

105

nd Ballard's verbal reasoning
n, but has reported no restand-
ese items. One cannot feel
neir placement according to origi-
ngs since (*a*) the original standardiza-
ons are about 40 years old, with no guarantee
that they were representative even then, and
(*b*) the tests have been considerably modified,
e.g., adapted from written to oral form.

Elsewhere, too, modifications have been made
in items, but no evidence is given to show the
effect on item placement or discrimination.

Whilst sympathizing with the difficulties of
standardizing an individual scale widely, one
must criticize the weaknesses of the tryout sample. Restricted to ages 5 to 8, it was drawn
from a small number of schools in the single
city of Birmingham. The standardization cannot be regarded as representative.

Unfortunately, no measure of the test's reliability is quoted. It should be possible to derive
a Kuder-Richardson estimate from the standardization data. In the hands of an experienced
tester, the reliability of score should be as high
—at least between the ages of 3 and 11—as for
the Stanford scales.

An excellent feature of the test is the inclusion of 10 items at each age level up to 3 and
8 at each age level from 3-6 to 8. This widens
the sampling of items and should improve reliability. By using starred items forming 50 per
cent of each group, one can quickly establish
the child's approximate level before testing in
detail.

Predictive validity of the scale must be presumed to be similar to that of mental age scales
which it resembles.

Two points of policy adopted by the author
appear controversial. He implies that testers
may use material (e.g., pictures) *"similar"* to
that described in the manual or construct their
own material according to brief specifications.
This seems to leave the way open to unnecessary variations in standard. Normative samples
of correct and incorrect responses to items are
not given on the grounds that (as in the Terman-Merrill manual) these are usually overelaborate and possibly indefensible. Omitting
scoring samples certainly simplifies instructions,
but it may open the door to personal interpretations by individuals, especially teachers, likely
to vary widely in testing experience and skill.

From the practical point of view, one would
recommend that the test materials requiring

manipulation be stronger (thick cardboard or
thin plywood). The present ones are flimsy. It
would also be more convenient if envelopes
containing test material were assembled in a
looseleaf booklet similar to that of the Terman-
Merrill test.

Valentine, with his wide knowledge of the
psychology of early childhood, has succeeded
in producing a simple and varied scale for individual administration. It has marked weaknesses in standardization. Nevertheless, it
should enable the skillful teacher to make a
broadly correct assessment of the ability of
pupils between 5 and 10 whilst observing them
as individuals. Thus, it covers a period when
group tests are inappropriate or can well be
supplemented. The Valentine tests are not acceptable as a substitute for the educational psychologist's chief tools, but they may be a useful auxiliary for rapid "screening" of young
children.

*See 4:344 (2 excerpts), 4:345 (4 excerpts),
and 3:283 (2 excerpts).*

[406]

★The Leiter Adult Intelligence Scale. Adults;
1956–57; includes *The FR-CR Test, Partington's
Pathways Test, The Leiter Adaptation of Arthur's
Stencil Design Test,* and *The Leiter Adaptation of the
Painted Cube Test;* 3 scores: language, nonlanguage,
total; individual; 1 form ['56]; $29 per set of test
materials; $5 per 100 record booklets ['57]; $2 per
manual ['56]; postage extra; (40–60) minutes; Russell
Graydon Leiter; C. H. Stoelting Co. *

REFERENCE

1. LEITER, RUSSELL GRAYDON. "The Leiter Adult Intelligence Scale." *Psychol Service Center J* 3:1–52 D '51. *

[407]

★Leiter International Performance Scale: Arthur Adaptation. Ages 2–12; 1952–55; individual;
may be administered by pantomime; 1 form ['52]; test
materials consist of Trays 1 and 2 (ages 2–12) of the
Leiter International Performance Scale; manual
('52); $130 per set of test materials, 100 record blanks,
carrying case, and manual; $5 per 100 record blanks
['55]; $4 per manual; postage extra; (30–60) min-
utes; Grace Arthur; C. H. Stoelting Co. * For references, see 408.

[408]

*Leiter International Performance Scale. Ages
2–18; 1936–52; individual; 1 form ('48); manual in 2
parts: Parts 1 ('48), 2 ('50, see 27 below); $187.50
per set of test materials, 100 record blanks, carrying
case, and manual; $5 per 100 record blanks ('48); post-
age extra; specimen set not available; [30–60] minutes; Russell Graydon Leiter; C. H. Stoelting Co. *

REFERENCES

1–25. See 4:349.
26. LEITER, RUSSELL G. *Performance Tests for Measuring
Native Intelligence.* Master's thesis, University of Southern
California (Los Angeles, Calif.), 1929.
27. LEITER, RUSSELL GRAYDON. "Part II of the Manual for

the 1948 Revision of the Leiter International Performance Scale." *Psychol Service Center J* 2:259-343 D '50. *

28. ARNOLD, GWEN F. "A Technique for Measuring the Mental Ability of the Cerebral Palsied." *Psychol Service Center J* 3:171-8 S '51. *

29. BENSBERG, GERARD J., AND SLOAN, WILLIAM. "Performance of Brain-Injured Defectives on the Arthur Adaptation of the Leiter." *Psychol Service Center J* 3:181-4 S '51. *

30. ARTHUR, GRACE. *The Arthur Adaptation of the Leiter International Performance Scale.* Washington, D.C.: Psychological Service Center Press, 1952. Pp. viii, 73. *

31. BEVERLY, LOUISE, AND BENSBERG, GERARD J. "A Comparison of the Leiter, the Cornell-Coxe and Stanford-Binet With Mental Defectives." *Am J Mental Def* 57:89-91 Jl '52. * (PA 27:3620)

32. TATE, MIRIAM E. "The Influence of Cultural Factors on the Leiter International Performance Scale." *J Abn & Social Psychol* 47:497-501 Ap '52. * (PA 27:2763)

33. EVANS, MILDRED L. *A Comparison of the Performance of Mentally Defective Children on the Leiter International Performance Scale and the Stanford-Binet.* Master's thesis, Pennsylvania State University (State College, Pa.), 1954.

34. BURNS, PEARL PRATT, *The Value of the Leiter Scale in Testing Mexican-American Children.* Master's thesis, University of Southern California (Los Angeles, Calif.), 1955.

35. ORGEL, ARTHUR R., AND DREGER, RALPH MASON. "A Comparative Study of the Arthur-Leiter and Stanford-Binet Intelligence Scales." *J Genetic Psychol* 86:359-65 Je '55. * (PA 30:6907)

36. BIRCH, JANE R., AND BIRCH, JACK W. "Predicting School Achievement in Young Deaf Children." *Am Ann Deaf* 101:348-52 S '56. * (PA 31:6634)

37. GALLAGHER, JAMES J.; BENOIT, E. PAUL; AND BOYD, HERBERT F. "Measures of Intelligence in Brain Damaged Children." *J Clin Psychol* 12:69-72 Ja '56. * (PA 30:5093)

38. PEISNER, EARL FREDERICK. *The Validity of the Leiter International Performance Scale in Measuring the Intelligence of Selected Superior Children.* Doctor's thesis, Oregon State College (Corvallis, Ore.), 1956.

39. SHARP, HEBER C. "A Comparison of Slow Learner's Scores on Three Individual Intelligence Scales." *J Clin Psychol* 13:372-4 O '57. *

40. ALPER, A. E. "A Comparison of the Wechsler Intelligence Scale for Children and the Arthur Adaptation of the Leiter International Performance Scale With Mental Defectives." *Am J Mental Def* 63:312-6 S '58. *

41. COOPER, JAMES G. "Predicting School Achievement for Bilingual Pupils." *J Ed Psychol* 49:31-6 F '58. *

42. SHARP, HEBER C. "A Note on the Reliability of the Leiter International Performance Scale 1948 Revision." *J Consult Psychol* 22:320 Ag '58. *

For a review by Gwen F. Arnold, see 4:349 (1 excerpt); for a related review, see 40:B989.

[409]

***Nebraska Test of Learning Aptitude.** Ages 4-10; 1941-55; standardized for both hearing and deaf children; individual; 1 form ('41); revised manual ('55); record blank ['41] with norms for deaf children, record blank ['55] with norms for hearing children; $52 per set of test materials including an aluminum carrying case, postage extra; (50-60) minutes; Marshall S. Hiskey; the Author, 5640 Baldwin, Lincoln, Neb. *

REFERENCES

1-3. See 3:289.

4. See 4:353.

5. LUDLOW, MARJORIE E. *A Comparison of the Nebraska Test of Learning Aptitude for Young Deaf Children and Form L of the Revised Stanford-Binet.* Master's thesis, Pennsylvania State College (State College, Pa.), 1942.

6. MACPHERSON, JANE GAERTNER. *A Comparison of Scores of Deaf and Hearing Children on the Hiskey Test of Learning Ability and on Performance Scales.* Master's thesis, Washington University (St. Louis, Mo.), 1945.

7. PERRY, JUNE A. *A Comparative Study of the Ontario and Nebraska Tests for the Deaf.* Master's thesis, Wisconsin State College (Milwaukee, Wis.), 1947.

8. DAVIS, KATHRYN A. *A Study of the Performance of Hearing Children and Deaf Children on the Nebraska Test of Learning Aptitude for Young Deaf Children.* Master's thesis, Southern Illinois University (Carbondale, Ill.), 1952.

9. ROSS, GRACE. "Testing Intelligence and Maturity of Deaf Children." *Excep Child* 20:23-4+ O '53. * (PA 28:4794)

10. WALSH, ROSALINE. *The Prognostic Value of the Merrill-Palmer Mental Tests and the Nebraska Test of Learning Aptitude for Pre-School Deaf Children.* Master's thesis, University of Buffalo (Buffalo, N.Y.), 1954.

11. HISKEY, MARSHALL S. "A Study of the Intelligence of Deaf and Hearing Children Through a Comparison of Performances on the Separate Standardizations of the Nebraska Test of Learning Aptitude." *Am Ann Deaf* 101:329-39 S '56. * (PA 31:6544)

12. HISKEY, MARSHALL S. "Norms for Children With Hearing for the Nebraska Test of Learning Aptitude." *J Ed Res* 51:137-42 O '57. *

WILLIAM SLOAN, *Superintendent, State Colony and Training School, Pineville, Louisiana.*

This is a revision of a test originally published in 1941. The primary additions are instructions and norms for hearing children. Also, the materials have been somewhat streamlined and are not so bulky. There are still 11 types of tests using 124 individual parts. However, they fit compactly into an easily carried case.

Present norms on deaf children are apparently based on the 1941 data. The test was standardized on 466 deaf children from ages 4 to 10. Except for the four year group (10 children), the number at each age ranged from 42 to 117. All the subjects were residents of schools for the deaf in several midwestern states. With few exceptions all the children in each school who fell within the ages 4 to 10 were included in the sample. Since the norms were obtained on institutionalized deaf children, the question must be raised concerning the possible deviation in intelligence of this sample from the total population. No data on this point are included. An item analysis yields correlations ranging from .63 to .84 for each group of items with the entire scale, i.e., part-whole correlations. Split-half reliability is reported as .96.

Validity is based mainly upon per cent passing at varying ages. For the deaf, no outside criterion is used. The author's reluctance to use "mental age" is understandable, since he feels this may lead to false comparisons with Binet MA's. However, his calling the score on this test a "learning age" is less clear since no evidence is adduced which would indicate a meaningful relationship to any of a variety of "learning" tasks. This is in spite of his assertion that the items involve tasks similar to those which a deaf child must perform in school. Curiously enough, a correlation of .829 between Nebraska and Binet scores on 380 hearing children is reported. Hiskey says in the manual, "If one accepts the Stanford-Binet as a useable criterion, this correlation is evidence of high validity and indicates that the *Nebraska Test of Learning Aptitude* can be used with confidence as a measure of intelligence."

The total score on the test is the median of the scores on the subtests taken. This has some advantages. Chance successes and failures, or accidental "spoiling" of an item will not invalidate the whole test. Also, special disabilities (e.g., motor disorders) are not unduly penalized if a few items are omitted. The instructions for pantomime administration are thorough. A few practice sessions will make the test relatively easy to administer for the experienced psychometrician. Abbreviated versions of the test are described but are not recommended if the entire scale can be given. Since a median score is used, the fewer the number of items on which it is based, the greater the possibility of errors. Separate directions and norms for hearing children are included along with an easily used record blank and simple instructions for obtaining the median "learning age." The materials are colorful and attractive to children and have much of the flavor of a game.

This test is a useful addition to the clinician's tools but more evidence needs to be forthcoming on its relation to other tests used with deaf children, such as the Arthur, Ontario, Chicago Non-Verbal, etc. Also, the question of "mental age" or "learning age" should be resolved on the basis of experimental evidence. In the meantime, it is felt to be a valuable instrument in shedding light on children with special problems, e.g., hearing, motor disability, speech defects, foreign language, or other communication problems.

For a review by Mildred C. Templin of an earlier edition, see 4:353.

[410]
★**Non-Verbal Intelligence Tests for Deaf and Hearing Subjects.** Ages 3–16; 1939–58; 2 forms ('58, Scales P, Q); $80 (572s.) per set of testing materials, manual, and 100 scoring forms; $3.50 (26s.) per manual ('58); $1.50 (10s.) per 100 scoring forms; postage extra; Dutch and German editions available; (45) minutes; J. Th. Snijders and N. Snijders-Oomen; J. B. Wolters, Groningen, Holland. *

[411]
The Northwestern Intelligence Tests: For Measuring Adaptation to the Physical and Social Environment. Ages 13–36 weeks; 1943–51; revision of *Gilliland-Shotwell Intelligence Scale* ('43) by A. R. Gilliland and Anna M. Shotwell; individual; 1 form (labeled Test B); Test A (ages 4–12 weeks) is out of print; $2.80 per set of 35 record blanks ('51) and manual ('51); 40¢ per specimen set; postage extra; (20–30) minutes; A. R. Gilliland; Houghton Mifflin Co. *

NANCY BAYLEY, *Chief, Section on Child Development, Laboratory of Psychology, National Institute of Mental Health, National Institutes of Health, Public Health Service, United States Department of Health, Education, and Welfare, Bethesda, Maryland.*

Each of these tests contains 40 items, arranged approximately in order of difficulty. The items cover, in general, the same behaviors that are to be found in other tests of infant development, but they utilize slightly different test materials and criteria for passing or failing. There is a strong component of motor coordinations, ranging from degrees of finger-thumb opposition to sitting and crawling. There are tests of visual and auditory reactivity, vocalizations, and of social responsiveness, as tested by interactions with adults. Some items would be classed as adaptive.

Although there are some interesting items that have not been included in other scales (e.g., "feels cardboard" and "moves head in flight movement" from cotton held against nose), the directions for giving and scoring are often ambiguous and difficult to follow.

The standardization was made on a large sample, 1100 infants for Test A and 214 for Test B. But over half of the first sample was composed of infants in institutions. The Test B sample is more in line with accepted usage, though it still includes a proportionately large number (36 of 214) of institutional infants. Until we have better information about the environmental effects of institutions on the development of infants, the scores of such infants are not appropriate for setting up norms.

Computation of the IQ appears to be based on a rule of thumb method that results in a normal distribution of IQ's with mean of 100, SD 14. The derivation of this method is not given.

Split-half reliability for Test A, corrected by the Spearman-Brown formula, is .84. Some validation was attempted for the scale but it is not described except to say that "in general a close agreement has been found" with a few Cattell and Stanford-Binet tests. A mean difference of 3.8 IQ points was found between Test A and these other tests, but the ages at testing and the numbers tested are not given. The Test B population is described as having a mean IQ of 100, SD 16.

Since Gilliland's death there apparently has been nothing further done with the test standardization. The printed forms still give the author as a source for securing test equipment.

The test, as it stands, may be used as a basis for further standardization or research, but it does not seem to this reviewer to be in a form that can be recommended for general application.

For a review by Mildred C. Templin, see 4:354 (1 excerpt).

[412]

*The Porteus Maze Test. Ages 3 and over; 1914–55; individual; 2 scores: quantitative, qualitative; 1 form; 3 editions and 1 supplement; Stanley D. Porteus. *

a) VINELAND REVISION. Ages 3 and over; 1914–21; 1 form ('21); 13 mazes: years 3–12, 14, adult 1, 2; manual ['21]; $11 per set of manual and 100 mazes of any one level; 90¢ per 100 copies of any one maze; postage extra; (15–60) minutes; C. H. Stoelting Co.

b) VINELAND REVISION: NEW SERIES. Ages 3 and over; 1914–50; 1 form ('33); 12 mazes: years 3–12, 14, adult 1; $11.50 per set of 100 copies of each maze; $4.10 per manual ('50, see 50 below); $1.15 per 100 mazes of any one level; (15–60) minutes; Psychological Corporation.

c) PORTEUS MAZE EXTENSION. Ages 14 and over; 1953–55; for use only as a supplement to the *Vineland Revision: New Series;* 1 form ('53); 8 mazes: years 7–12, 14, adult; no adult norms; $7.75 per set of 100 copies of each maze; $2.10 per manual ('55, see 74 below); $1.15 per 100 mazes of any one level; (25) minutes; Psychological Corporation.

d) BRITISH EDITION. Ages 3 and over; 1914–52; 1 form ('52, same as the *Vineland Revision: New Series* copyrighted in 1933 except for format); 12 mazes: years 3–12, 14, adult 1; 5s. per 100 mazes of any one level; 5s. per 100 score sheets ('52); 6s. per manual ('52); postage extra; [15–60] minutes; George G. Harrap & Co. Ltd. *

REFERENCES

1–56. See 4:356.
57. JARRETT, R. FITZROY. "Some Observations on Social Capacity: Application of the Porteus Maze Tests to 100 Borstal Lads." *Lancet* 211:1059–60 N 20 '26. *
58. McDONALD, JANE REGINA. *A Comparative Study of Deaf Children by Means of the Kohs Block Designs and Porteus Maze.* Master's thesis, Ohio State University (Columbus, Ohio), 1931.
59. GRAJALES, M. C. *Porteus' Qualitative Maze Test as a Measure of Delinquency.* Master's thesis, Fordham University (New York, N.Y.), 1945.
60. ARNOLD, GWEN F. "A Technique for Measuring the Mental Ability of the Cerebral Palsied." *Psychol Service Center J* 3:171–8 S '51. *
61. FOULDS, G. A. "Temperamental Differences in Maze Performance: Part II, The Effect of Distraction and of Electroconvulsive Therapy on Psychomotor Retardation." *Brit J Psychol, Gen Sect* 43:33–41 F '52. * (*PA* 26:7159)
62. DOCTER, RICHARD FLOYD. *Delinquent vs. Non-Delinquent Performance on the Porteus Qualitative Maze Test.* Master's thesis, Stanford University (Stanford, Calif.), 1952.
63. MYATT, MARY FRANCES. *A Study of the Relationship Between Motivation and Test Performance of Patients in a Rehabilitation Ward.* Doctor's thesis, University of Minnesota (Minneapolis, Minn.), 1952. (*DA* 12:339)
64. O'CONNOR, N. "The Prediction of Psychological Stability and Anxiety-Aggressiveness From a Battery of Tests Administered to a Group of High Grade Male Mental Defectives." *J General Psychol* 46:3–17 Ja '52. * (*PA* 27:2055)
65. PORTEUS, S. D. *The Porteus Maze Test Manual.* London: George G. Harrap & Co., Ltd., 1952. Pp. 64. *
66. PORTEUS, S. D. "A Survey of Recent Results Obtained With the Porteus Maze Test." *Brit J Ed Psychol* 22:180–8 N '52. * (*PA* 27:5158)
67. SYDOW, DONALD WAYNE. *A Psychometric Differentiation Between Functional Psychotics and Non-Psychotics With Organic Brain Damage.* Doctor's thesis, University of Minnesota (Minneapolis, Minn.), 1953. (*DA* 13:1267)
68. DOCTER, RICHARD F., AND WINDER, C. L. "Delinquent vs. Nondelinquent Performance on the Porteus Qualitative Maze Test." *J Consult Psychol* 18:71–3 F '54. * (*PA* 28:8865)
69. FOULDS, G. A. "Comment on Professor Porteus's Paper: 'Maze Test Qualitative Aspects.'" *Brit J Med Psychol* 27:252 pt 4 '54. *
70. PORTEUS, S. D. "Maze Test Qualitative Aspects." *Brit J Med Psychol* 27:72–9 pts 1 and 2 '54. * (*PA* 28:8730)
71. SATTER, GEORGE, AND McGEE, EUGENE. "Retarded Adults Who Have Developed Beyond Expectation: Part I, Intellectual Functions." *Training Sch B* 51:43–55 My '54. * (*PA* 29:2662)
72. SMALL, KALMAN. *Planning as a Non-Intellective Component of Intelligent Behavior.* Doctor's thesis, Columbia University (New York, N.Y.), 1954. (*DA* 14:1814)
73. MINSKI, LOUIS, AND DESAI, MAHESH M. "Aspects of Personality in Peptic Ulcer Patients: A Comparison With Hysterics." *Brit J Med Psychol* 28:113–34 Je '55. * (*PA* 30:3268)
74. PORTEUS, STANLEY D. *The Maze Test: Recent Advances.* Palo Alto, Calif.: Pacific Books, 1955. Pp. 71. * (*PA* 30:1051)
75. SATTER, GEORGE. "Retarded Adults Who Have Developed Beyond Expectation: Part III, Further Analysis and Summary." *Training Sch B* 51:237–43 F '55. * (*PA* 29:7498)
76. BENNETT, HOWARD J. "The Shipley-Hartford Scale and the Porteus Maze Test as Measures of Functioning Intelligence." *J Clin Psychol* 12:190–1 Ap '56. * (*PA* 31:4669)
77. PORTEUS, S. D. "Porteus Maze Test Developments." *Percept & Motor Skills* 6:135–42 Je '56. *
78. PURCELL, KENNETH. "A Note on Porteus Maze and Wechsler-Bellevue Scores as Related to Antisocial Behavior." *J Consult Psychol* 20:361–4 O '56. * (*PA* 31:7960)
79. STOTSKY, BERNARD A.; SACKS, JOSEPH M.; AND DASTON, PAUL G. "Predicting the Work Performance of Psychiatric Aides by Psychological Tests." *J Counsel Psychol* 3:193–9 fall '56. * (*PA* 31:8251)
80. AARONSON, BERNARD S. "The Porteus Mazes and Bender Gestalt Recall." *J Clin Psychol* 13:186–7 Ap '57. * (*PA* 32:2882)
81. FOOKS, GILBERT, AND THOMAS, ROSS R. "Differential Qualitative Performance of Delinquents on the Porteus Maze." *J Consult Psychol* 21:351–3 Ag '57. *
82. PORTEUS, S. D. "Maze Test Reactions After Chlorpromazine." *J Consult Psychol* 21:15–21 F '57. * (*PA* 32:735)
83. PORTEUS, S. D., AND BARCLAY, JOHN E. "A Further Note on Chlorpromazine: Maze Reactions." *J Consult Psychol* 21:297–9 Ag '57. *
84. GIBBENS, T. C. N. "The Porteus Maze Test and Delinquency." *Brit J Ed Psychol* 28:209–16 N '58. *

For reviews by C. M. Louttit and Gladys C. Schwesinger, see 4:356; for related reviews, see 4:357, 38:B453, and 36:B210.

[413]

Revised Stanford-Binet Scale. Ages 2 and over; 1916–37; revision of *Stanford-Binet Scale* ('16); individual; Forms L ('37), M ('37); manual ('37); $22 (105s.) per set of test materials; $4.20 (12s. 6d.) per 35 (25) record booklets ('37) of either form; $2.10 (5s.) per 35 (25) abbreviated record booklets ('37) for either form; $4.50 (12s. 6d.) per manual; postage extra; (30–90) minutes; Lewis M. Terman and Maud A. Merrill; Houghton Mifflin Co. (English distributor: George G. Harrap & Co. Ltd.) *

REFERENCES

1–134. See 40:1420.
135–351. See 3:292.
352–493. See 4:358.
494. LUDLOW, MARJORIE E. *A Comparison of the Nebraska Test of Learning Aptitude for Young Deaf Children and Form L of the Revised Stanford-Binet.* Master's thesis, Pennsylvania State College (State College, Pa.), 1942.
495. EATTELL, ELEANOR A. *The Terman-Merrill Intelligence Scale in Testing Institutionalised Epileptics.* Master's thesis, University of London (London, England), 1945.
496. HIGHFIELD, MIRIAM E. *The Diagnostic Significance of the Terman-Merrill Scale.* Master's thesis, University of London (London, England), 1945.
497. RAY, JOSEPH BLAND. *An Analysis of the Differential Performance on the Stanford-Binet Scale, Form L, of Mental Defective and Normal Children.* Master's thesis, University of Oklahoma (Norman, Okla.), 1949.
498. CLARKE, F. R. *A Comparative Study of the WISC and Revised Stanford-Binet, Form L, in Relation to Scholastic Achievement on a Fifth Grade Population.* Master's thesis, Pennsylvania State University (State College, Pa.), 1950.
499. DEAN, DOUGLAS ARTHUR. *A Factor Analysis of the Stanford-Binet and SRA Primary Mental Abilities Battery at the First Grade Level.* Doctor's thesis, Pennsylvania State College (State College, Pa.), 1950.
500. PRICE, ARTHUR COOPER. *A Preliminary Study in Statistical Comparison of the Revised Stanford-Binet Intelligence Test Form L With the Wechsler Intelligence Scale for Children Using the Ten Year Age Level.* Master's thesis, University of Florida (Gainesville, Fla.), 1950.

501. SCOTT, GORDON R. *A Comparison Between the Wechsler Intelligence Scale for Children and the Revised Stanford-Binet Scales.* Master's thesis, Southern Methodist University (Dallas, Tex.), 1950.

502. WINTER, WILLIAM NELSON. *An Investigation of the Relationship Between Scatter on the Stanford-Binet Test and Adjustment to Society by Children of Average Intelligence.* Master's thesis, University of Maryland (College Park, Md.), 1950.

503. BIRCH, JACK WILLARD. *An Investigation of the Utility of Certain Short Forms of the Terman-Merrill Revision of the Stanford-Binet Tests of Intelligence.* Doctor's thesis, University of Pittsburgh (Pittsburgh, Pa.), 1951.

504. BUGDEN, C. W. *The Stanford-Binet and the Wechsler Intelligence Scale for Children: A Correlational Study.* Master's thesis, Dalhousie University (Halifax, N.S., Canada), 1951. Pp. 32. *

505. GLENN, ROBERT THOMAS. *A Comparison of Intelligence Quotients Derived by the Leiter International Performance Scale and the 1937 Stanford Revision of the Binet.* Master's thesis, University of Pittsburgh (Pittsburgh, Pa.), 1951.

506. PASTOVIC, JOHN J., AND GUTHRIE, GEORGE M. "Some Evidence on the Validity of the WISC." *J Consult Psychol* 15:385-6 O '51. * (*PA* 26:7008)

507. POWELL, JOAN A. *A Comparison of the Stanford-Binet (1937 Revision, Form L) and Wechsler Intelligence Scale for Children at Different Age and Intellectual Levels.* Master's thesis, University of British Columbia (Vancouver, B.C., Canada), 1951. Pp. 63. *

508. RAPAPORT, IRENE. *A Comparison of Performance on the Wechsler Intelligence Scale for Children and the Revised Stanford-Binet Scale.* Master's thesis, University of Pittsburgh (Pittsburgh, Pa.), 1951.

509. WAGNER, WINIFRED K. *A Comparison of Stanford-Binet Mental Ages and Scaled Scores on the Wechsler Intelligence Scale for Children for Fifty Bowling Green Pupils.* Master's thesis, Bowling Green State University (Bowling Green, Ohio), 1951.

510. "1951 Norms for Independent-School Populations on the Terman-Merrill Revision of the Stanford-Binet Scale." *Ed Rec B* 58:85-6 F '52. *

511. ALDERICE, E. T., AND BUTLER, A. J. "An Analysis of the Performance of Mental Defectives on the Revised Stanford-Binet and the Wechsler-Bellevue Intelligence Scale." *Am J Mental Def* 56:608-14 Ja '52. * (*PA* 26:4872)

512. BERK, ROBERT L. "Coaching in an Institution for Defective Delinquents: An Evaluation by Means of the Critical Incident Technique." *Am J Mental Def* 56:615-21 Ja '52. *

513. BEVERLY, LOUISE, AND BENSBERG, GERARD J. "A Comparison of the Leiter, the Cornell-Coxe and Stanford-Binet With Mental Defectives." *Am J Mental Def* 57:89-91 Jl '52. * (*PA* 27:3620)

514. COHEN, BERTRAM D., AND COLLIER, MARY J. "A Note on the WISC and Other Tests of Children Six to Eight Years Old." *J Consult Psychol* 16:226-7 Je '52. * (*PA* 27:5145)

515. DENNY, E. C. "Stanford-Binet Testing and Re-Testing." *Yearb Nat Council Meas Used Ed* 9:37-41 '52. *

516. DUNSDON, M. I. *An Application of the Myers-Gifford Response Pattern Scoring Scheme to the Terman-Merrill Records of Children.* Doctor's thesis, University of London (London, England), 1952.

517. ELWOOD, MARY ISABEL. "Changes in Stanford-Binet IQ of Retarded Six-Year-Olds." *J Consult Psychol* 16:217-9 Je '52. * (*PA* 27:5233)

518. FARTHING, MADELINE. *A Factor Analysis of the Revised Stanford-Binet at Two Age Levels.* Doctor's thesis, University of California (Berkeley, Calif.), 1952.

519. FEIFEL, HERMAN. "An Analysis of the Word Definition Errors of Children." *J Psychol* 33:65-77 Ja '52. * (*PA* 26:6266)

520. JOHNSON, ELIZABETH Z. "Sex Differences and Variability in the Performance of Retarded Children on Raven, Binet and Arthur Tests." *J Clin Psychol* 8:298-301 Jl '52. * (*PA* 27:5981)

521. KURETH, GENEVIEVE; MUHR, JEAN P.; AND WEISGERBER, CHARLES A. "Some Data on the Validity of the Wechsler Intelligence Scale for Children." *Child Develop* 23:281-7 D '52. * (*PA* 28:954)

522. MANOLAKES, GEORGE, AND SHELDON, WILLIAM D. "A Comparison of the Grace Arthur Revised Form II, and the Stanford-Binet, Revised Form L." *Ed & Psychol Meas* 12:105-8 sp '52. * (*PA* 27:5886)

523. MUSSEN, PAUL; DEAN, SANFORD; AND ROSENBERG, MARGERY. "Some Further Evidence on the Validity of the WISC." *J Consult Psychol* 16:410-1 O '52. * (*PA* 27:5891)

524. RALEIGH, WILLIAM H. *A Study of the Relationships of Academic Achievement in Sixth Grade With the Wechsler Intelligence Scale for Children and Other Variables.* Doctor's thesis, Indiana University (Bloomington, Ind.), 1952.

525. RIGGS, MARGARET M., AND BURCHARD, KATHRYN A. "Intra-Scale Scatter for Two Kinds of Mentally Defective Children." *Training Sch B* 49:36-44 Mr '52. * (*PA* 27:523)

526. ROBERTS, J. A. FRASER, AND MELLONE, MARGARET A. "On the Adjustment of Terman-Merrill I.Q.'s to Secure Comparability at Different Ages." *Brit J Psychol, Stat Sect* 5:65-79 Je '52. * (*PA* 27:2759)

527. SACKS, ELINOR L. "Intelligence Scores as a Function of Experimentally Established Social Relationships Between Child and Examiner." *J Abn & Social Psychol* 47:354-8 Ap '52. * (*PA* 27:2761)

528. SANDERCOCK, MARIAN G., AND BUTLER, ALFRED J. "An Analysis of the Performance of Mental Defectives on the Wechsler Intelligence Scale for Children." *Am J Mental Def* 57:100-5 Jl '52. * (*PA* 27:3640)

529. STROMER, WALTER F. "An Adaptation of the Stanford-Binet Test of Intelligence, Form M, for Use by a Blind Examiner." Abstract. *J Colo-Wyo Acad Sci* 4:77 O '52. *

530. TATHAM, LOUISE JEANETTE. *Statistical Comparison of the Revised Stanford-Binet Intelligence Test—Form L With the Wechsler Intelligence Scale for Children Using the Six and One-Half Year Level.* Master's thesis, University of Florida (Gainesville, Fla.), 1952.

531. WARINNER, ELLEN M. *A Comparison of Test Performance of Dull Children on the Revised Stanford-Binet and the Wechsler-Intelligence Scale for Children.* Master's thesis, University of Chicago (Chicago, Ill.), 1952.

532. DUNCAN, JOHN O. "Correlation Between the Wechsler-Bellevue and Stanford-Binet Vocabulary Lists." *Med Tech B* 4:45-7 Mr-Ap '53. * (*PA* 28:4348)

533. DUNSDON, M. I. "A Comparison of Terman Merrill Scale Test Responses Among Large Samples of Normal Maladjusted and Backward Children." *J Mental Sci* 99:72031 O '53. * (*PA* 28:6004)

534. DUNSDON, M. I., AND ROBERTS, J. A. FRASER. "The Relation of the Terman-Merrill Vocabulary Test to Mental Age in a Sample of English Children." *Brit J Stat Psychol* 6:61-70 N '53. *

535. FITT, A. B. *The Stanford-Binet Scale: Its Suitability for New Zealand.* New Zealand Council for Educational Research, Studies in Education Series No. 14. Christchurch, New Zealand: Whitcombe & Tombs Ltd., 1953. Pp. 32. *

536. GIBSON, FREDERICK J. *Correlation Study of the 1937 Revision of the Stanford-Binet Scale, Form L, With the Performance Items of the Wechsler-Bellevue Intelligence Scale, Adult, Form I.* Master's thesis, Boston College (Chestnut Hill, Mass.), 1953.

537. HOLLAND, GLEN A. "A Comparison of the WISC and Stanford-Binet IQ's of Normal Children." *J Consult Psychol* 17:147-52 Ap '53. * (*PA* 28:2638)

538. JOHNSON, ELIZABETH Z. "Individual Patterns of Emotional Functioning in Children of Comparable I.Q.'s—Implications for Education." *Am J Mental Def* 57:681-6 Ap '53. * (*PA* 28:1187)

539. KURETH, GENEVIEVE. *Correlation of the Subtests of the Wechsler Intelligence Scale for Children With the Revised Stanford-Binet For Five and Six Year Olds.* Master's thesis, University of Detroit (Detroit, Mich.), 1953.

540. MCNEMAR, QUINN. "Note on Elwood's Study of IQ Changes." *J Consult Psychol* 17:153 Ap '53. * (*PA* 28:2653)

541. RAPPAPORT, SHELDON R. "Intellectual Deficit in Organics and Schizophrenics." *J Consult Psychol* 17:389-95 O '53. * (*PA* 28:6365)

542. SCARR, ELIZABETH H. "Changes in Terman-Merrill I.Q.s With Dull Children: A Test of the Roberts-Mellone Adjustments." *Brit J Stat Psychol* 6:71-6 N '53. * (*PA* 28:7548)

543. SIEVERS, DOROTHY J., AND NORMAN, RALPH D. "Some Suggestive Results in Psychometric Testing of the Cerebral Palsied With Gesell, Binet, and Wechsler Scales." *J Genetic Psychol* 82:69-90 Mr '53. * (*PA* 27:7974)

544. SLUTZKY, JACOB E.; JUSTMAN, JOSEPH; AND WRIGHTSTONE, J. WAYNE. "Screening Children for Placement in Special Classes for the Mentally Retarded: A Preliminary Report." *Am J Mental Def* 57:687-90 Ap '53. * (*PA* 28:1528)

545. TERMAN, LEWIS M., AND MERRILL, MAUD A. "1937 Stanford-Binet Scales," pp. 510-21. (*PA* 27:7798) In *Contributions Toward Medical Psychology: Theory and Psychodiagnostic Methods, Vol. II.* Edited by Arthur Weider. New York: Ronald Press Co., 1953. Pp. xi, 459-885. *

546. TRIGGS, FRANCES ORALIND, AND CARTEE, J. KEITH. "Pre-School Pupil Performance on the Stanford-Binet and the Wechsler Intelligence Scale for Children." *J Clin Psychol* 9:27-9 Ja '53. * (*PA* 27:7800)

547. BAKER, C. T.; NELSON, V. L.; AND SONTAG, L. W. "General Versus Specific Areas of Ability in IQ Change." Abstract. *Am Psychol* 9:325 Ag '54. *

548. BORUSZAK, RUBY J. *A Comparative Study to Determine the Correlation Between the IQ's of the Revised Stanford Binet Scale, Form L, and the IQ's of the Wechsler Intelligence Scale for Children.* Master's thesis, Wisconsin State College (Milwaukee, Wis.), 1954.

549. CURETON, EDWARD E. "Mental Age Equivalents for the Revised Stanford-Binet Vocabulary Test." *J Consult Psychol* 18:381-3 O '54. * (*PA* 29:5696)

550. DAVIDSON, JACK FREDERICK. *A Preliminary Study in Statistical Comparison of the Revised Stanford-Binet Intelligence Test Form L With the Wechsler Intelligence Scale for Children Using the Fourteen Year Level.* Master's thesis, University of Florida (Gainesville, Fla.), 1954.

551. EVANS, MILDRED L. *A Comparison of the Performance of Mentally Defective Children on the Leiter International Performance Scale and the Stanford-Binet.* Master's thesis, Pennsylvania State University (State College, Pa.), 1954.

552. GODFREY, L. LARUE. *The Stanford-Binet Intelligence Scale in Appraising Reading Readiness.* Master's thesis, Utah State Agricultural College (Logan, Utah), 1954.

553. JONES, LYLE V. "Primary Abilities in the Stanford-

Binet, Age 13." *J Genetic Psychol* 84:125-47 Mr '54. * (*PA* 28:8725)

554. KARDOS, M. SERAPHIA. *A Comparative Study of the Performance of Twelve-Year-Old Children on the WISC and the Revised Stanford-Binet, Form L, and the Relationship of Both to the California Achievement Tests.* Master's thesis, Marywood College (Scranton, Pa.), 1954.

555. KESTON, MORTON J., AND JIMENEZ, CARMINA. "A Study of the Performance on English and Spanish Editions of the Stanford-Binet Intelligence Test by Spanish-American Children." *J Genetic Psychol* 85:263-9 D '54. * (*PA* 29:7290)

556. LEHMANN, MARGARET M. *The Basis of Teacher's Choice Between Two Intelligence Tests in an Elementary School.* Master's thesis, Ohio University (Athens, Ohio), 1954.

557. MATYAS, R. P. *A Longitudinal Study of the Revised Stanford-Binet and the WISC.* Master's thesis, Pennsylvania State University (State College, Pa.), 1954.

558. MILLER, VELMA J. *A Critical Analysis of Standardized Vocabulary Tests to Determine Those Most Valid for Use With the Macmillan Readers.* Master's thesis, Bowling Green State University (Bowling Green, Ohio), 1954.

559. PAPANIA, NED. "A Qualitative Analysis of the Vocabulary Responses of Institutionalized, Mentally Retarded Children." *J Clin Psychol* 10:361-5 O '54. * (*PA* 29:4272)

560. RICHARDSON, ELIZABETH J., AND KOBLER, FRANK J. "Testing the Cerebral Palsied." *Except Child* 21:101-3+ D '54. * (*PA* 29:6108)

561. SATTER, GEORGE, AND MCGEE, EUGENE. "Retarded Adults Who Have Developed Beyond Expectation: Part I, Intellectual Functions." *Training Sch B* 51:43-55 My '54. * (*PA* 29:2662)

562. SHELDON, WILLIAM D., AND MANOLAKES, GEORGE. "A Comparison of the Stanford-Binet, Revised Form L, and the California Test of Mental Maturity (S-Form)." *J Ed Psychol* 45:499-504 D '54. * (*PA* 29:7318)

563. ARNOLD, FRANK C., AND WAGNER, WINIFRED K. "A Comparison of Wechsler Children's Scale and Stanford-Binet Scores for Eight- and Nine-Year Olds." *J Exp Ed* 24:91-4 S '55. * (*PA* 30:8121)

564. BAKER, CHARLES T.; SONTAG, LESTER W.; AND NELSON, VIRGINIA L. "Specific Ability in IQ Change." *J Consult Psychol* 19:307-10 Ag '55. * (*PA* 30:4169)

565. BIRCH, JACK W. "The Utility of Short Forms of the Stanford-Binet Tests of Intelligence With Mentally Retarded Children." *Am J Mental Def* 59:462-84 Ja '55. * (*PA* 29:7258)

566. BLIESMER, EMERY P. "A Comparison of Results Obtained With Various Types of Capacity Tests Used With Retarded Readers." *Yearb Nat Council Meas Used Ed* 12(pt 1):60-2 '55. *

567. CALHOUN, FRANKLIN J. *The Florida State-Binet Intelligence Scale for the Physically Handicapped.* Doctor's thesis, Florida State University (Tallahassee, Fla.), 1955. (*DA* 15:1254)

568. CROKE, KATHERINE. *A Comparative Study of the Revised Stanford-Binet Intelligence Scale for Children, and the Vineland Maturity Scale.* Master's thesis, Wisconsin State College (Milwaukee, Wis.), 1955.

569. DUNSDON, M. I. "The Application of Vocabulary Tests to a Large Sample of Children." Abstract. *B Brit Psychol Soc* (26):22 inset My '55. *

570. DUNSDON, M. I., AND ROBERTS, J. A. FRASER. "A Study of the Performance of 2,000 Children on Four Vocabulary Tests: I, Growth Curves and Sex Differences." *Brit J Stat Psychol* 8:3-15 My '55. * (*PA* 30:3363)

571. KATZ, ELIAS. "Can the Mental Abilities of the Cerebral Palsied be Measured?" *Calif J Ed Res* 6:3-8 Ja '55. * (*PA* 29:7766)

572. McCULLOCH, THOMAS L.; RESWICK, JOSEPH; AND WEISSMANN, SERENA. "Studies of Word Learning in Mental Defectives: II, Relation to Scores on Digit Repetition, the Stanford-Binet, M, and the WISC Verbal Scale." *Am J Mental Def* 60:140-3 Jl '55. * (*PA* 30:4797)

573. MacRAE, JOHN M. "A Comparison of Davis-Eells and Stanford-Binet Scores at Different Socio-Economic Levels." Abstract. *Calif J Ed Res* 6:133 My '55. *

574. MARQUART, DOROTHY I., AND BAILEY, LOIS L. "An Evaluation of the *Culture Free Test* of Intelligence." *J Genetic Psychol* 86:353-8 Je '55. * (*PA* 30:6905)

575. ORGEL, ARTHUR R., AND DREGER, RALPH MASON. "A Comparative Study of the Arthur-Leiter and Stanford-Binet Intelligence Scales." *J Genetic Psychol* 86:359-65 Je '55. * (*PA* 30:6907)

576. RICHARDS, B. W. "Intelligence Survey of a Mental Deficiency Institution." *Brit J Med Psychol* 28:267-70 pt 4 '55. *

577. SATTER, GEORGE. "Psychometric Scatter Among Mentally Retarded and Normal Children." *Training Sch B* 52:63-8 Je '55. * (*PA* 30:3078)

578. SMITH, WILLIAM L. *The Establishment of a Grade Reading Level by the Stanford-Binet Intelligence Test.* Master's thesis, Utah State Agricultural College (Logan, Utah), 1955.

579. SONTAG, L. W.; BAKER, CHARLES T.; AND NELSON, VIRGINIA L. "Personality as a Determinant of Binet Performance." *Inter-Am Congr Psychol* 1:291-7 '55. *

580. STACEY, CHALMERS L., AND CARLETON, FREDERICK O. "The Relationship Between Raven's Colored Progressive Matrices and Two Tests of General Intelligence." *J Clin Psychol* 11:84-5 Ja '55. * (*PA* 29:7321)

581. STACEY, CHALMERS L., AND GILL, MARIE R. "The Relationship Between Raven's Colored Progressive Matrices and Two Tests of General Intelligence for 175 Subnormal Adult Subjects." *J Clin Psychol* 11:86-7 Ja '55. * (*PA* 29:7322)

582. STANLEY, JULIAN C. "A Note Concerning Brown's 'On the Constancy of the I.Q.'" *J Ed Res* 48:545-7 Mr '55. * (*PA* 30:1062)

583. STANLEY, JULIAN C. "Statistical Analysis of Scores From Counterbalanced Tests." *J Exp Ed* 23:187-207 Mr '55. * (*PA* 30:1919)

584. WALTON, D. "The Validity and Interchangeability of Terman-Merrill and Matrices Test Data." *Brit J Ed Psychol* 25:190-4 N '55. * (*PA* 30:7233)

585. BLIESMER, EMERY P. "A Comparison of Results of Various Capacity Tests Used With Retarded Readers." *El Sch J* 56:400-2 My '56. * (*PA* 31:5140)

586. CURR, W., AND GOURLAY, N. "Differences Between Testers in Terman-Merrill Testing." *Brit J Stat Psychol* 9:75-81 N '56. *

587. ESHLEMAN, EDITH R. "Detroit Beginning First Grade Test Compared With Stanford Binet." *J Ed Res* 49:543-6 Mr '56. * (*PA* 31:5144)

588. GALLAGHER, JAMES J.; BENOIT, E. PAUL; AND BOYD, HERBERT F. "Measures of Intelligence in Brain Damaged Children." *J Clin Psychol* 12:69-72 Ja '56. * (*PA* 30:5093)

589. GEHMAN, ILA H., AND MATYAS, RUDOLPH P. "Stability of the WISC and Binet Tests." *J Consult Psychol* 20:150-2 Ap '56. * (*PA* 31:6082)

590. JONES, H. GWYNNE. "Comments on 'The Validity and Interchangeability of Terman-Merrill and Matrices Test Data' by D. Walton." *Brit J Ed Psychol* 26:141 Je '56. * (*PA* 31:6086)

591. JOHNSON, G. ORVILLE; NEELY, JAMES H.; AND ALLING, ROGER L. "A Comparison of the 1937 Revision of the Stanford-Binet (Form L) and the Columbia Scale of Mental Maturity." *Excep Child* 22:155-7+ Ja '56. * (*PA* 31:3562)

592. KATZ, ELIAS. "The Pointing Scale Method: A Modification of the Stanford-Binet Procedure for Use With Cerebral Palsied Children." *Am J Mental Def* 60:838-42 Ap '56. * (*PA* 31:5029)

593. LANTZ, BEATRICE, AND WOLF, RUTH. "The Columbia Mental Maturity Scale and the Stanford-Binet Test With Cerebral Palsied Children." *Calif J Ed Res* 7:183-5 S '56. * (*PA* 31:6521)

594. LEVINSON, BORIS M. "Note on the Davis Eells Test of General Intelligence." *Psychol Rep* 2:242 S '56. * (*PA* 31:3048)

595. LUMSDEN, J. "Revised Stanford-Binet Norms." *Austral J Psychol* 8:174-9 D '56. * (*PA* 32:271)

596. O'CONNOR, N., AND VENABLES, P. H. "A Note on the Basal Level of Skin Conductance and Binet I.Q." *Brit J Psychol* 47:148-9 My '56. * (*PA* 31:4374)

597. SEDAL, V. S. *The Stanford-Binet With Nine to Ten Year Old Children Whose Knowledge of English Is Inadequate.* Master's thesis, University of Toronto (Toronto, Ont., Canada), 1956.

598. STRUHS, ISABEL. *The Relation Between the Raven Progressive Matrices Test and the Stanford-Binet in a Group of Gifted Children.* Master's thesis, Fordham University (New York, N.Y.), 1956.

599. WARBURTON, F. W. "The Roberts-Mellone Corrections for Terman-Merrill I.Q.s." Abstract. *B Brit Psychol Soc* (28):71 Ja '56. *

600. WATERS, THOMAS J. "Qualitative Vocabulary Responses in Three Etiologies of Mental Defectives." *Training Sch B* 53:151-6 O '56. * (*PA* 31:8274)

601. WOLF, WILLIAM CHARLES, JR. *The Relationship Between Intelligence and Reading Success of Selected Elementary School Children.* Master's thesis, Ohio University (Athens, Ohio), 1956.

602. BARRATT, ERNEST S., AND BAUMGARTEN, DORIS L. "The Relationship of the WISC and Stanford-Binet to School Achievement." Abstract. *J Consult Psychol* 21:144 Ap '57. *

603. BECK, ELIZABETH J. *Item Analysis of Stanford-Binet Performance of Institutional Children in Comparison With the Standardization.* Master's thesis, Fordham University (New York, N.Y.), 1957.

604. DUNSDON, M. I., AND ROBERTS, J. A. FRASER. "A Study of the Performance of 2,000 Children on Four Vocabulary Tests: II, Norms, With Some Observations on the Relative Variability of Boys and Girls." *Brit J Stat Psychol* 10:1-16 My '57. *

605. FROMM, ERIKA; HARTMAN, LENORE DUMAS; AND MARSCHAK, MARIAN. "Children's Intelligence Tests as a Measure of Dynamic Personality Functioning." *Am J Orthopsychiatry* 27:134-44 Ja '57. * (*PA* 32:1621)

606. GOODEY, D. J. *The Diagnostic Uses of the Reading Test of the Stanford-Binet Intelligence Scale.* Master's thesis, Utah State University (Logan, Utah), 1957.

607. HARLOW, JUSTIN E., JR.; PRICE, ARTHUR COOPER; TATHAM, LOUISE J.; AND DAVIDSON, JACK F. "Preliminary Study of Comparison Between Wechsler Intelligence Scale for Children and Form L of Revised Stanford Binet Scale at Three Age Levels." *J Clin Psychol* 13:72-3 Ja '57. *

608. KENT, NORMA, AND DAVIS, D. RUSSELL. "Discipline in the Home and Intellectual Development." *Brit J Med Psychol* 30:27-33 pt 1 '57. * (*PA* 32:3997)

609. LEVINSON, BORIS M. "Re-Evaluation of the Revised Stanford-Binet Form L Vocabulary as a Test of Intelligence for the Kindergarten and Primary School Child." Abstract. *Am Psychol* 12:380 Jl '57. *

610. LIVINGSTON, JEROME STANLEY. *An Evaluation of a Photographically Enlarged Form of the Revised Stanford-Binet Intelligence Scale for Use With the Partially Seeing Child.* Doctor's thesis, New York University (New York, N.Y.), 1957. (*DA* 18:1866)

611. MAY, W. THEODORE, AND PERRY, HAROLD W. "The Relationship Between the Stanford-Binet (Form L) Vocabulary and the Columbia Mental Maturity Scale in a Group of Mentally Retarded Children." *Am J Mental Def* 62:330–3 S '57. *

612. SHARP, HEBER C. "A Comparison of Slow Learner's Scores on Three Individual Intelligence Scales." *J Clin Psychol* 13:372–4 O '57. *

613. WALTON, D., AND BEGG, T. L. "Cognitive Changes in Low-Grade Defectives." *Am J Mental Def* 62:96–102 Jl '57. *

614. CLARKE, A. D. B. "The 1937 Revision of the Stanford-Binet Scale—A Critical Appraisal." *B Brit Psychol Soc* (35): 11–3 My '58. *

615. COLLMANN, R. D., AND NEWLYN, D. "Changes in Terman-Merrill IQs of Mentally Retarded Children." *Am J Mental Def* 63:307–11 S '58. *

616. HISKEY, MARSHALL S., AND SADNAVITCH, JOSEPH M. "Minimizing Exaggerated Changes in Binet Ratings of Retarded Children." *Excep Child* 25:16–20 S '58. *

617. KATZ, ELIAS. "The 'Pointing Modification' of the Revised Stanford-Binet Intelligence Scales, Forms L and M, Years II Through VI: A Report of Research in Progress." *Am J Mental Def* 62:698–707 Ja '58. *

618. LEVINSON, BORIS M. "Reevaluation of the Revised Stanford-Binet Scale, Form L Vocabulary as a Test of Intelligence for the Kindergarten and Primary School Child." *J Genetic Psychol* 93:237–48 D '58. *

619. LIVINGSTON, JEROME S. "Evaluation of Enlarged Test Form Used With the Partially Seeing." *Sight-Saving R* 28:37–9 sp '58. *

620. PORTWOOD, PETER F. "Progress Report on the Sheffield E.S.N. Study." Abstract. *B Brit Psychol Soc* 34:61 Ja '58. *

MARY R. HAWORTH, *Assistant Professor of Psychology, Michigan State University, East Lansing, Michigan.*

Twenty-one years elapsed between the appearance of the original Stanford-Binet scale in 1916 and the revision by Terman and Merrill in 1937. An equally long interval of time has now passed, making a further revision imperative. Some of the pictures and objects (e.g., woodburning stoves and steam engines) are so out of date as to unduly penalize all but the brighter child with an interest in historical oddities. The current TV and space conscious culture has "juggled" vocabulary items into new positions in the hierarchy of difficulty, so that a longer presentation is often necessary to secure the required sequence of failures. Sweeping postwar population shifts, the higher standard of living, and possible changes in the general educational level of the nation all suggest that the original normative data may not adequately represent the population today.

In spite of its old fashioned tinge and the healthy competition of another now widely used child test (*Wechsler Intelligence Scale for Children*), the Stanford-Binet continues to serve as the standard and generally accepted criterion against which other tests are validated. Most comparative studies of the WISC and the Stanford-Binet attest to the latter's greater discriminative value at both the higher and lower mental levels. It is still the best available instrument for adequately measuring the in-

tellectual abilities of children below school age and of mentally defective children and adults with mental levels below six or seven years. The lowest possible IQ on the WISC is 46 and the lowest "mean test age" is five years, two months. This means that a mentally defective child of that level would have to be 11 years of age before the most minimal testing could be accomplished. The Stanford-Binet, on the other hand, will yield mental ages as low as two years. Consequently a discrimination can be made between custodial, trainable, and educable cases at a much earlier age.

With the WISC coming into more widespread use with children, certain advantages and disadvantages of the Stanford-Binet, as an age scale, should be pointed out. While the same intellectual functions may not be tapped at each age level, any individual child will have an opportunity to confront a suitable variety of tasks over the usual span of several year levels. The alternate form of the Stanford-Binet is a distinct advantage. The all-or-none method of scoring is essential to the Stanford-Binet's schema and is not only easier to master but also more objective than the varying degrees of credit allowed throughout the WISC. Nevertheless, valuable qualitative data may be overlooked when responses are not scored for different levels of success.

The length of administration for the Stanford-Binet varies widely and may put too great a strain on a child for the little additional information that may be gained in establishing an accurate upper limit. In the process, the child could conceivably be subjected to as many as 11 consecutive failures, while on a point scale his failures would be scattered throughout the test.

The fluctuation in the standard deviations of the Stanford-Binet at different age levels, with the consequent variation in the meaning of the IQ, is a concept not easily grasped by some users of the test. But for any individual child, rate of mental growth from test to retest, and the relationship of his own mental age to his own chronological age have very real meaning in terms of present expectations and educational placement quite irrespective of his relative position among his peers.

An age scale is necessarily postulated on the assumption of a fairly regular and progressive increase in mental growth. Recent reports of longitudinal studies [1] suggest that such regularity is no more to be expected for intellectual development than for gains in height or weight. This maturational phenomenon might not have been detected but for age scales serving as the yardsticks against which to measure each child's idiosyncratic mental growth pattern. Point scales will not readily yield discriminating data concerning the unevenness of development, since the performance of each child is measured against that of his age group in terms of a predetermined and uniform mean and standard deviation at each age level. To refer back to the raw scores achieved at successive ages by each child would be inadequate since there is no provision in a point scale for equal, or proportionate, increments of increase from year to year, either within each subtest or for the scale as a whole.

There are no separate verbal and performance scales on the Stanford-Binet, but short forms of either type can be derived at the lower age levels. At least four items not requiring speech from the subject can be located at each half-year or year level through the first six years. A somewhat shorter scale of items requiring no speech on the part of either the subject or the examiner can be used with the deaf. The blind can be tested through all age levels by combining verbal items from Forms L and M (Interim Hayes-Binet). Recently a "pointing scale" (592) has been extracted for use with cerebral palsied children which employs only items requiring the subject to point to the correct response.

The administration and scoring of the present form of the test would be greatly facilitated if each test item in the manual were followed by its scoring criteria. The rationale and qualitative aspects for all the items could then be placed in a separate section.

It is highly unlikely that the perfect intelligence test will ever be devised. In the meantime, testing must be done and evaluations must be made. Some variation of the Binet-type test will probably continue to be the tool that best meets this clinical need.

NORMAN D. SUNDBERG, *Director, University Child Guidance Clinic and Associate Professor*

[1] BAYLEY, NANCY. "Individual Patterns of Development." *Child Develop* 27:45–74 Mr '56.
CORNELL, ETHEL L., AND ARMSTRONG, CHARLES M. "Forms of Mental Growth Patterns Revealed by Reanalysis of the Harvard Growth Data." *Child Develop* 26:169–204 S '55.

of Psychology, University of Oregon, Eugene, Oregon.

The grand old test has had to bow to an upstart. There is no doubt that the *Wechsler Intelligence Scale for Children* has usurped much of the field of individual intelligence testing of children. However, there is a lot of kick in the old Stanford-Binet yet. The appearance of WISC has precipitated a number of studies comparing the two tests which lead to the following conclusions: (a) Correlations between WISC and Stanford-Binet range from the .60's to .90's. (b) The WISC Verbal Scale, as expected, correlates more highly with the Stanford-Binet than the Performance Scale. (c) WISC IQ's tend to run a few points lower than Stanford-Binet IQ's except at the lowest levels, and they do not disperse as widely. These findings may be caused partly by the fact that the Stanford-Binet mean was intentionally set a little above 100 to correct for the urban sampling bias; also, the WISC standard deviation was set at 15 whereas the average Stanford-Binet standard deviation is 16.4. The differences are larger than might be expected for these reasons, but still they are not large enough to alter most practical judgments. Both tests predict school achievement about equally well.

An informal survey of psychologists in several clinics and school systems leads the reviewer to hypothesize that the WISC is definitely much more popular than the Stanford-Binet. The WISC probably accounts for at least 75 per cent of the individual intelligence testing of children. It is almost exclusively used for children from grades 3–8 and above this age the adult Wechsler tests predominate. On the other hand, the Stanford-Binet is still preferred with (a) young children, i.e., preschoolers or first graders, (b) children suspected of being considerably retarded, and (c) very gifted children. Frequent complaints about the Stanford-Binet concern the outmoded items, the lack of a performance score, and the awkwardness of the nonserial item arrangement.

What about the Stanford-Binet in the future? It was 21 years between the 1916 and 1937 versions; at this writing 21 more years have gone by. Fortunately some of the deficiencies are being corrected. Through the kindness of Merrill, the reviewer has had the opportunity to learn more about Form L-M which will probably be published by the time this Yearbook comes off the press. It is not a new scale nor a restandardization: it is a combination of the best items from Forms L and M. These are the items which display all four of the following characteristics: a substantial correlation with the rest of the scale, an increase in per cent passing with increasing age, proper location, and no discernible effect from cultural changes. Two thirds of these items are in the present Form L. Item modification has been kept to a minimum. The vocabulary has been rearranged in order of difficulty as determined by results on more than 5,000 cases tested in the 1950's, such words as "Mars" and "juggler," for example, now coming earlier in the test. IQ tables will incorporate corrections for inequalities in standard deviations at different ages. These changes will meet several of the criticisms of the test. Many psychologists will see it as unfortunate that the serial order of presentation of items could not have been instituted more broadly, thereby enhancing the efficiency and ease of administration. Undoubtedly there will be criticisms of the reordering of items without a restandardization; further research will be needed to check whether these changes will affect norms. Desirable as a large scale revision of the test would have been, there is a great deal of value in the intention of this Form L-M: to bring the Stanford-Binet up to date while still keeping it equivalent to the 1937 form, thus preserving the basic meaning of the test over the years. If this goal is achieved, the new version will be especially valuable for use in long range follow-up studies of the future. The reviewer's guess is that this test, which reflects the genius of Terman, will be standing as a memorial to him for several more decades to come.

A word about the Stanford-Binet in relationship to the whole field of psychological assessment. It is undoubtedly true that there will continue to be a great need for general intelligence tests like the Stanford-Binet. However, such tests are becoming less and less the dominating figures they once were. The *Zeitgeist* calls on psychologists to help with the making of decisions on a wider and wider variety of situations. The purposes for which tests are used vary so much that validity is no longer the simple matter it was once thought to be. We often expect too much of any single measure. In any important decision we use a complex combination of information data. Perhaps the limitations of the Stanford-Binet and other tests stem more from our ignorance of criterion situations and decision making processes than from test construction per se. It is against the decision matrix of the school and the clinic that the Stanford-Binet must be evaluated. Individual studies in separate situations are woefully inadequate for grasping the larger meaning and usefulness of tests. It would seem appropriate for test publishers and professional organizations to take it as their responsibility to collect, collate, and distribute information on intelligence tests, as is being done with some interest and personality tests. This need is particularly important with regard to interpretation and application of tests. Test manuals should be issued from time to time which give much more attention to the "pay-off" end of testing, rather than emphasizing just the beginning.

For a review by Boyd R. McCandless, see 4:358; see 40:1420 (3 excerpts); for reviews by Francis N. Maxfield, J. W. M. Rothney, and F. L. Wells, see 38:1062; for related reviews, see B149, 3:293–4, 40:B1093, and 38: B497.

[414]

*Wechsler Adult Intelligence Scale. Ages 16 and over; 1939–55; revision of Form 1 of *Wechsler-Bellevue Intelligence Scale;* individual; 14 scores: verbal (information, comprehension, arithmetic, similarities, digit span, vocabulary), performance (digit symbol, picture completion, block design, picture arrangement, object assembly), total; 1 form ['55]; $21 per set of test materials, 25 record booklets ('55), and manual ('55); $1.70 per 25 record booklets; 80¢ per 25 supplementary [record] sheets ('55); $2.75 per manual; postpaid; (40–60) minutes; David Wechsler; Psychological Corporation. *

REFERENCES

1. DOPPELT, JEROME E., AND WALLACE, WIMBURN L. "The Performance of Older People on the Wechsler Adult Intelligence Scale." Abstract. *Am Psychol* 10:338–9 Ag '55. *
2. DOPPELT, JEROME E., AND WALLACE, WIMBURN L. "Standardization of the Wechsler Adult Intelligence Scale for Older Persons." *J Abn & Social Psychol* 51:312–30 S '55. * (*PA* 30: 4320)
3. WESMAN, ALEXANDER G. "Standardizing an Individual Intelligence Test on Adults: Some Problems." *J Gerontol* 10:216–9 Ap '55. * (*PA* 30:1923)
4. ANASTASI, ANNE. "Age Changes in Adult Test Performance." *Psychol Rep* 2:509 D '56. * (*PA* 31:4016)
5. BALINSKY, BENJAMIN, AND SHAW, H. WESTCOTT. "The Contribution of the WAIS to a Management Appraisal Program." *Personnel Psychol* 9:207–9 su '56. * (*PA* 31:8949)
6. COHEN, JACOB. "A Comparative Factor Analysis of WAIS Performance for Four Age Groups Between Eighteen and Eighty." Abstract. *Am Psychol* 11:449 Ag '56. *
7. COLE, DAVID, AND WELEBA, LOIS. "Comparison Data on the Wechsler-Bellevue and the WAIS." *J Clin Psychol* 12:198–9 Ap '56. * (*PA* 31:4675)
8. DOPPELT, JEROME E. "Estimating the Full Scale Score on the Wechsler Adult Intelligence Scale From Scores on Four Subtests." *J Consult Psychol* 20:63–6 F '56. * (*PA* 31:3024)
9. HALL, JULIA C. "Two Degrees of Overt Psychiatric Disturbance and Differences Among Subtest Scores of the Wechsler Adult Intelligence Scale (WAIS)." Abstract. *Am Psychol* 11: 357 Ag '56. *
10. JONES, H. GWYNNE. "The Evaluation of the Significance of Differences Between Scaled Scores on the WAIS: The Perpetuation of a Fallacy." *J Consult Psychol* 20:319–20 Ag '56. * (*PA* 31:7928)

11. ROBERTSON, J. P. S., AND BATCHELDOR, K. J. "Cultural Aspects of the Wechsler Adult Intelligence Scale in Relation to British Mental Patients." *J Mental Sci* 102:612–8 Jl '56. * (*PA* 31:7965)

12. BLACKBURN, HAROLD L., AND BENTON, ARTHUR L. "Revised Administration and Scoring of the Digit Span Test." *J Consult Psychol* 21:139–43 Ap '57. *

13. COHEN, JACOB. "A Factor-Analytically Based Rationale for the Wechsler Adult Intelligence Scale." *J Consult Psychol* 21:451–7 D '57. *

14. COHEN, JACOB. "The Factorial Structure of the WAIS Between Early Adulthood and Old Age." *J Consult Psychol* 21: 283–90 Ag '57. *

15. DANA, RICHARD H. "A Comparison of Four Verbal Subtests on the Wechsler-Bellevue, Form I, and the WAIS." *J Clin Psychol* 13:70–1 Ja '57. *

16. EISDORFER, CARL; BUSSE, EWALD W.; COHEN, LOUIS D.; AND GREENBERG, GEORGE. "The WAIS Performance of a Piedmont Aged Sample." Abstract. *Am Psychol* 12:374–5 Jl '57. *

17. HALL, JULIA C. "Correlation of a Modified Form of Raven's Progressive Matrices (1938) With the Wechsler Adult Intelligence Scale." *J Consult Psychol* 21:23–6 F '57. * (*PA* 32:267)

18. HIMELSTEIN, PHILIP. "A Comment on the Use of the Abbreviated WAIS With Homeless Men." *Psychol Rep* 3:440 S '57. * (*PA* 32:4178)

19. HIMELSTEIN, PHILIP. "A Comparison of Two Methods of Estimating Full Scale IQ From an Abbreviated WAIS." *J Consult Psychol* 21:246 Je '57. *

20. HIMELSTEIN, PHILIP. "Evaluation of an Abbreviated WAIS in a Psychiatric Population." *J Clin Psychol* 13:68–9 Ja '57. *

21. HOOKER, EVELYN. "The Adjustment of the Male Overt Homosexual." *J Proj Tech* 21:18–31 Mr '57. * (*PA* 32:3083)

22. ISON, M. GAIL. "The Effect of 'Thorazine' on Wechsler Scores." *Am J Mental Def* 62:543–7 N '57. *

23. KARSON, SAMUEL; POOL, KENNETH B.; AND FREUD, SHELDON L. "The Effects of Scale and Practice on WAIS and W-B I Test Scores." *J Consult Psychol* 21:241–5 Je '57. *

24. LEVINSON, BORIS M. "The Socioeconomic Status, Intelligence, and Psychometric Pattern of Native-Born White Homeless Men." *J Genetic Psychol* 91:205–11 D '57. *

25. LEVINSON, BORIS M. "Use of the Abbreviated WAIS With Homeless Men." *Psychol Rep* 3:287 Je '57. * (*PA* 32: 4189)

26. MCNEMAR, QUINN. "On WAIS Difference Scores." *J Consult Psychol* 21:239–40 Je '57. *

27. MAXWELL, EILEEN. "Validities of Abbreviated WAIS Scales." *J Consult Psychol* 21:121–6 Ap '57. *

28. NADLER, EUGENE B. "Prediction of the Sheltered Shop Work Performance of Individuals With Severe Physical Disability." *Personnel & Guid J* 36:95–8 O '57. *

29. OLIN, TOM D., AND REZNIKOFF, MARVIN. "The Use of Doppelt's Short Form of the Wechsler Adult Intelligence Scale With Psychiatric Patients." *J Consult Psychol* 21:27–8 F '57. * (*PA* 32:500)

30. STERNE, DAVID M. "A Note on the Use of Doppelt's Short Form of the WAIS With Psychiatric Patients." Abstract. *J Consult Psychol* 21:502 D '57. *

31. WIENER, GERALD. "The Effect of Distrust on Some Aspects of Intelligence Test Behavior." *J Consult Psychol* 21:127–30 Ap '57. *

32. DUNNETTE, MARVIN D., AND KIRCHNER, WAYNE K. "Validation of Psychological Tests in Industry." *Personnel Adm* 21: 20–7 My–Je '58. *

33. FINK, STEPHEN L., AND SHONTZ, FRANKLIN C. "Inference of Intellectual Efficiency From the WAIS Vocabulary Subtest." *J Clin Psychol* 14:409–12 O '58. *

34. GRAHAM, E. E., AND KAMANO, D. "Reading Failure as a Factor in the WAIS Subtest Patterns of Youthful Offenders." *J Clin Psychol* 14:302–5 Jl '58. *

35. GRIFFITH, RICHARD M., AND YAMAHIRO, ROY S. "Reliability-Stability of Subtest Scatter on the Wechsler-Bellevue Intelligence Scales." *J Clin Psychol* 14:317–8 Jl '58. *

36. HOWELL, ROBERT J.; EVANS, LAVON; AND DOWNING, LESTER N. "A Comparison of Test Scores for the 16–17 Year Age Group of Navaho Indians With Standardized Norms for the Wechsler Adult Intelligence Scale (Arizona and New Mexico)." *J Social Psychol* 47:355–9 My '58. *

37. KASPER, SIDNEY. "Progressive Matrices (1938) and Emotional Disturbance." Abstract. *J Consult Psychol* 22:24 F '58. *

38. LEVINSON, BORIS M. "Cultural Pressure and WAIS Scatter in a Traditional Jewish Setting." *J Genetic Psychol* 93:277–86 D '58. *

39. LIGHT, MORTON L., AND CHAMBERS, WILLIAM R. "A Comparison of the Wechsler Adult Intelligence Scale and Wechsler-Bellevue II With Mental Defectives." *Am J Mental Def* 62:878–81 Mr '58. *

40. OLIN, TOM D. "The Use of Age-Scaled Scores on the Determination of IQ Equivalents on the Wechsler Adult Intelligence Scale." *Psychol Newsl* 9:154–9 Mr–Ap '58. *

41. WECHSLER, DAVID. *The Measurement and Appraisal of Adult Intelligence, Fourth Edition.* Baltimore, Md.: Williams & Wilkins Co., 1958. Pp. ix, 297. *

42. WHITMYRE, JOHN W., AND PISHKIN, VLADIMIR. "The Abbreviated Wechsler Adult Intelligence Scale in a Psychiatric Population." *J Clin Psychol* 14:189–91 Ap '58. *

NANCY BAYLEY, *Chief, Section on Child Development, Laboratory of Psychology, National Institute of Mental Health, National Institutes of Health, Public Health Service, United States Department of Health, Education, and Welfare, Bethesda, Maryland.*

This is a revision and restandardization of Form I of the *Wechsler-Bellevue Intelligence Scale.* The Psychological Corporation has collaborated with Wechsler in carrying out a large scale testing of a nationwide sample of 1,700 adults selected to match the 1950 United States census. The sampling procedure for the principal sample took into account occupation, age, sex, education, urban-rural, geographic, and racial variables. The entire testing program appears to have been carried out with great care, not only for the sample tested but also for the testing procedures, including the use of experienced testers who were carefully supervised in order to insure that their testing procedures would be comparable. An additional sample of 475 older persons (persons 60 years of age and over) was also included in the testing.

The tests themselves have been changed primarily in the direction of adding more ceiling, thus increasing the range in scores of some of the subtests, and of clearing up ambiguities both in test items and in their scoring. There is evidence that the changes in the new form have been made on the basis of wide experience with the original scale, including the suggestions that have been made in the many published reports on its use.

The resulting scale is an all-round improvement of a good instrument. The reliabilities both of the subtests and the total scales have been improved, and the upper range of IQ's has been extended about 10 points. Thus the scale is more discriminating among the highly intelligent, as well as being a more generally satisfactory and reliable instrument.

It is interesting to note that in the WAIS the curve of intelligence by age is somewhat different than in the 1939 Wechsler-Bellevue. In the new scale the scores start lower at 16 years, gain their maximum a little later, and remain high from 20 to 34 years, with a more gradual decline with age after 34. These differences may be the result of both a generally improved instrument and a better standardization sample.

WILSON H. GUERTIN, *Clinical Psychologist.*
Veterans Administration Hospital, Knoxville,
Iowa.

While critically reviewing the new *Wechsler*
Adult Intelligence Scale one might be struck
by the absence of a brief, explicit statement as
to what the test is designed to do. However,
workers in mental measurement are so familiar
with the Wechsler intelligence scales that it
suffices to describe the present revision in terms
of its differences from its noble ancestors.

Only a few readers will need the orientation
that the WAIS is designed to be a broad-sam-
pling, wide range of ability, individual test of
adult intelligence. Norms are provided for ages
from 16 to 75 and for IQ's ranging from 45 to
159 for the young adult.

Six verbal and five performance areas are
sampled by subtests to provide a point-scale indication of intelligence. Raw scores on the various subtests are converted directly into standard scores in order to facilitate intercompari-
sons. Thus, the various subtests provide indices
of impairment from sensory, motor, and other
special disabilities. Missing subtest scores are
easily prorated to provide full scale estimates
of IQ when special disabilities make it desirable to omit some of the subtests. Brief forms
of the test are easily obtained by giving a few
subtests and prorating the ones omitted.
Wechsler persists in asserting that subtest
score patterns may provide useful diagnostic
indicators.

The WAIS is a revision of the original
Wechsler-Bellevue Intelligence Scale. Only the
vocabulary subtest is entirely new. A few new
items have been added to the other subtests.
Troublesome and ambiguous items in the W-B
have been replaced. All of the subtests except
Digit Span have been lengthened slightly. However, the overall change in content is not great.
Some changes in administration and scoring
have been made. The spiral-bound, large-type
manual of directions seems serviceable and convenient. The quality of the test material is comparable to that of earlier issues.

Wechsler reports a full scale reliability of
.97. Tables in his new book show reliability
for the WAIS subtests to be greater than those
for the W-B on 9 of the 11 subtests. However,
comparison of the coefficients of reliability is
hazardous since they came from two samples.
Several small sample studies of agreement
between the WAIS and the W-B are reported.

Full scale scores seem to be significantly higher
for the W-B by 3 or 4 IQ points. In the old
age range the differences are likely to be
greater. The differences are attributable to differences in the standardization samples used
with the two tests. Wechsler, quite justifiably,
places more confidence in the more adequate
WAIS standardization.

Correlation between the WAIS and the *Re-*
vised Stanford-Binet Scale was .85. Correlation with Raven's *Progressive Matrices* was .72.
In the latest revision of Wechsler's book (*39*)
there are no data showing the relation between
the Wechsler scales and external criteria such
as school success, although such data were included in the previous edition. Such criteria
are weak and it would appear that Wechsler
has come to depend upon the traditional acceptance of his instruments rather than external criteria of validity. Wechsler is not alone
in thinking that the care taken in construction
of a test and its underlying rationale are often
the best evidence that it will be effective in
measuring what it purports to measure.

Wechsler admits being unable to present convincing evidence for the effectiveness of his
deterioration measures and for the diagnostic
strength of subtest pattern analysis. Over the
years the positive diagnostic studies have been
repeatedly offset by the negative findings of
other researchers. Wechsler's ideas for evaluating psychiatric pathology continue to be intriguing even though weakly supported by research. Arbitrary psychiatric diagnoses and
classificatory systems as well as poor sampling
techniques continue to plague us and obscure
small but real systematic differences.

The WAIS standardization sample of 2,175
individuals is twice that used for the W-B.
Furthermore, the careful selection of a stratified sample appears to have produced a sample
quite representative of the American population. The variables controlled were age, sex,
urban-rural, location, race, occupation, and education. This represents a marked improvement over the W-B standardization sampling.
One is encouraged to accept these new norms
unconditionally for general clinical application.

Factor analytic discussion of the WAIS is
included in Wechsler's latest revision. It would
appear that the factorial constitution of the subtests is quite simple. The major factors seem
to be a verbal and a nonverbal factor. In addition, there is a memory factor.

The 577-item bibliography in Wechsler's book is testimony to the amount of research interest in the scales. The WAIS is still quite new but what has been demonstrated with the W-B should, in time, be demonstrated to hold true for the WAIS, also, since they differ so little from one another. The W-B has been viewed rather critically by a few writers but seldom, if ever, have they compared the instrument unfavorably with other adult intelligence measures.

The WAIS is a clear improvement over the earlier, well received Wechsler scales. For the time being, at least, the WAIS stands alone with very little competition. It can be expected to take its place as a paragon of intelligence tests and will serve as a criterion of validity for nearly all newly proposed measures of intelligence.

For reviews by Murray Aborn and William D. Altus of an earlier edition, see 4:361; for a review by Robert I. Watson, see 3:298; for a review by F. L. Wells, see 40:1429 (2 excerpts); for related reviews, see 4:362, 3:299–301, and 40:B1121.

[415]

Wechsler-Bellevue Intelligence Scale. Ages 10 and over; 1939–47; individual; 2 forms; $1.70 per 25 record booklets ('47) of either form; postpaid; (40–60) minutes; David Wechsler; Psychological Corporation. * For revised edition, see 414.
a) FORM 1. 1939–47; out of print except for record forms and some replacement parts.
b) FORM 2. 1946–47; catalog states that "Form 2 is the retest instrument for the WAIS as well as for Form 1"; 14 scores: verbal (general information, general comprehension, digit span, arithmetic, similarities, vocabulary), performance (picture arrangement, picture completion, block design, object assembly, digit symbol), total; $19˙ per set of test materials, 25 record booklets ('47), and manual ('46); $2.25 per manual.

REFERENCES

1–2. See 40:1429.
3–121. See 3:298.
122–371. See 4:361.
372. FISHBEIN, SILVIA. *An Evaluation of the Wechsler-Bellevue Intelligence Tests for Use on the College Level.* Master's thesis, Temple University (Philadelphia, Pa.), 1941.
373. GRAJALES, M. C. *Portcus' Qualitative Maze Test as a Measure of Delinquency.* Master's thesis, Fordham University (New York, N.Y.), 1945.
374. WHEATLEY, MABEL MARIE. *Primary Mental Abilities of Deaf Children.* Doctor's thesis, University of Maryland (College Park, Md.), 1947.
375. GOLDSTEIN, M. J. "Standardisation for South Africa of the Wechsler-Bellevue Adult Intelligence Scale." *B Nat Inst Personnel Res* 1:3–7 N '48. *
376. HANER, CHARLES F., AND WEBB, WILSE B. "Quantification of the Wechsler-Bellevue Vocabulary." *Proc Iowa Acad Sci* 55:323–8 '48. *
377. MEIER, LORAINE D. *A Critical Analysis of Scores, Accumulated From the Presentation of the Wechsler-Bellevue Intelligence Scale to Adolescent and Adult Deafened Individuals.* Master's thesis, Washington University (St. Louis, Mo.), 1948.
378. RAINE, LOIS MARGARET. *An Investigation of Changes in Performance Level With Repetition on the Wechsler-Bellevue Intelligence Scale.* Master's thesis, University of Colorado (Boulder, Colo.), 1948.
379. FOX, CHARLOTTE, AND BIRREN, JAMES E. "Some Factors Affecting Vocabulary Size in Later Maturity: Age, Education, and Length of Institutionalization." *J Gerontol* 4:19–26 Ja '49. *

380. HOWELL, ROBERT J. *An Analysis of the California Capacity and Wechsler Bellevue Intelligence Tests.* Master's thesis, University of Utah (Salt Lake City, Utah), 1949.
381. JUI, ALICE HONG-ZOEN. *The Use of Wechsler-Bellevue With the Hard of Hearing Pupils.* Master's thesis, MacMurray College for Women (Jacksonville, Ill.), 1949.
382. CARSE, DOROTHY. *A Study of the Relationships Between the Wechsler-Bellevue Intelligence Scale and the Kuder Preference Record-Personal.* Master's thesis, North Texas State College (Denton, Tex.), 1950.
383. CLARKE, F. R. *A Comparative Study of the WISC and Revised Stanford-Binet, Form L, in Relation to Scholastic Achievement on a Fifth Grade Population.* Master's thesis, Pennsylvania State University (State College, Pa.), 1950.
384. COHEN, EDWIN. "Is There Examiner Bias on the Wechsler-Bellevue?" *Proc Okla Acad Sci* 31:150–3 '50. * (*PA* 27:417)
385. HORLICK, REUBEN S. *The Relationships of Psychometric Test Scores to Personality Disorders.* Doctor's thesis, New York University (New York, N.Y.), 1950.
386. LEVINE, L. S. *Psychometric Patterns in Psychiatric Diagnosis.* Doctor's thesis, Stanford University (Stanford, Calif.), 1950.
387. O'DELL, PERRY L. *Psychometric Patterns of the Wechsler-Bellevue Intelligence Scale Subtests as an Indicator of Schizophrenic Syndromes.* Master's thesis, North Texas State College (Denton, Tex.), 1950.
388. SILVER, CHARLES E. *A Comparison of the Scores Made by College Reading Problem Cases on the California Short-form Test of Mental Maturity and Form I of the Wechsler-Bellevue Scales.* Master's thesis, Bowling Green State University (Bowling Green, Ohio), 1950.
389. SMYKAL, A., AND WILSON, M. O. "Wechsler-Bellevue Subtest Score Changes Resulting From Electric Convulsive Therapy." *Proc Okla Acad Sci* 31:148–9 '50. * (*PA* 27:589)
390. WITT, EUGENE LESTER, JR. *A Study of the Relation of Form Perception in Color on the Rorschach Ink Blot Test and Performance on the Wechsler-Bellevue Block Design Subtest.* Master's thesis, Southern Methodist University (Dallas, Tex.), 1950.
391. ALTUS, WILLIAM D. "The Relation of Intelligence to Adjustment." Abstract. *Am Psychol* 6:490 S '51. *
392. BOTWINICK, JACK, AND BIRREN, JAMES E. "Differential Decline in the Wechsler-Bellevue Subtests in the Senile Psychoses." *J Gerontol* 6:365–8 O '51. * (*PA* 26:4134)
393. EVERSON, RICHARD REESE. *Senescent Decline on the Wechsler-Bellevue in Relation to Organic Brain Damage, Schizophrenia, and Psychoneurosis.* Master's thesis, University of Pittsburgh (Pittsburgh, Pa.), 1951.
394. FOSTER, CHARLES. *W-B Data as Indices of Aptitude for Law and Engineering—A Contribution to Vocational Counseling.* Doctor's thesis, University of Southern California (Los Angeles, Calif.), 1951.
395. HODGSON, GERALD L. "The Psychometric Pattern of the Mexican Delinquent." Abstract. *Am Psychol* 6:499 S '51. *
396. KING, DORIS MARIE. *A Comparative Study of the Wechsler-Bellevue Scores of Negro and White Prison Inmates.* Master's thesis, Southern Methodist University (Dallas, Tex.), 1951.
397. KLONOFF, HARRY. *An Exploratory Study and Analysis of the Wechsler-Bellevue Intelligence Scale and the Raven Progressive-Matrices.* Master's thesis, University of Toronto (Toronto, Ont., Canada), 1951.
398. LEVINE, LOUIS S. "The Diagnostic Utility of Qualitative Responses to Wechsler-Bellevue Test Items." Abstract. *Am Psychol* 6:499–500 S '51. *
399. NEWTON, BERNAUR W.; ZIMMERMAN, IRLA LEE; SULLIVAN, ELLEN B.; DORCUS, ROY M.; STERNBERG, THOMAS H.; AND ZIMMERMAN, MURRAY C. "An Evaluation of the Psychological Processes of the Neurosyphilitic: II, The Wechsler-Bellevue Scale." Abstract. *Am Psychol* 6:500 S '51. *
400. OPPENHEIM, HENRY. *Diagnostic Limitations of the Adult Wechsler-Bellevue Intelligence Scale in Cerebral Pathology.* Master's thesis, University of North Carolina (Chapel Hill, N.C.), 1951.
401. POWELL, JOAN A. *A Comparison of the Stanford-Binet (1937 Revision, Form L) and Wechsler Intelligence Scale for Children at Different Age and Intellectual Levels.* Master's thesis, University of British Columbia (Vancouver, B.C., Canada), 1951.
402. REICH, H. *The Applicability of Regression Equations to the Bellevue Adult Scale in Diagnosis of Schizophrenia.* Master's thesis, Brooklyn College (Brooklyn, N.Y.), 1951.
403. SCHILLO, RICHARD J. *Wechsler-Bellevue Results of Normals and Neurotics With Obsessive-Compulsive Features.* Master's thesis, Catholic University of America (Washington, D.C.), 1951.
404. STEAD, LUCY SASSCER GORE. *A Comparative Study of Schizophrenic Signs on the Rorschach and the Wechsler-Bellevue.* Master's thesis, Stanford University (Stanford, Calif.), 1951.
405. WIGGINS, JACK G., JR. *A Comparative Study of the Performances of Prison Inmates on a Group and on an Individual Intelligence Test.* Master's thesis, Southern Methodist University (Dallas, Tex.), 1951.
406. ALDERDICE, E. T., AND BUTLER, A. J. "An Analysis of the Performance of Mental Defectives on the Revised Stanford-

Binet and the Wechsler-Bellevue Intelligence Scale." *Am J Mental Def* 56:608–14 Ja '52. * (*PA* 26:4872)

407. BERK, ROBERT L. "Coaching in an Institution for Defective Delinquents: An Evaluation by Means of the Critical Incident Technique." *Am J Mental Def* 56:615–21 Ja '52. *

408. BINKS, VIRGINIA M.; FOSTER, DESMOND V.; ADAMS, NICHOLAS A.; AND TRIGGS, FRANCES. "The Relationship of Reading Skills as Learned in Grades 4–College Freshman Years to Verbal and Performance Scores on an Individual Intelligence Test." Abstract. *Am Psychol* 7:376–7 Jl '52. *

409. BIRREN, JAMES E. "A Factorial Analysis of the Wechsler-Bellevue Scale Given to an Elderly Population." *J Consult Psychol* 16:399–405 O '52. * (*PA* 27:5771)

410. CAMPBELL, ELIZABETH FLETCHER. *The Effects of Colour in the Wechsler-Bellevue Block Design Subtest and in the Rorschach.* Master's thesis, University of Western Ontario (London, Ont., Canada), 1952.

411. COHEN, JACOB. "A Factor-Analytically Based Rationale for the Wechsler-Bellevue." *J Consult Psychol* 16:272–7 Ag '52. * (*PA* 27:4251)

412. COHEN, JACOB. "Factors Underlying Wechsler-Bellevue Performance of Three Neuropsychiatric Groups." *J Abn & Social Psychol* 47:359–65 Ap '52. * (*PA* 27:2818)

413. CORSINI, RAYMOND J., AND FASSETT, KATHERINE K. "The Validity of Wechsler's Mental Deterioration Index." *J Consult Psychol* 16:462–8 D '52. * (*PA* 28:936)

414. CORSINI, RAYMOND J., AND FASSETT, KATHERINE K. "Wechsler-Bellevue Age Patterns for a Prison Population." Abstract. *Am Psychol* 7:402 Jl '52. *

415. CORTER, HAROLD M. "Factor Analysis of Some Reasoning Tests." *Psychol Monogr* 66(8):1–31 '52. * (*PA* 27:4995)

416. CORTES, CARLOS F. *The Use of the Wechsler-Bellevue Scale With Spanish-Speaking Students.* Master's thesis, University of Wyoming (Laramie, Wyo.), 1952.

417. DAVIS, PAUL C. *A Factor Analysis of the Wechsler-Bellevue Intelligence Scale, Form I, in a Matrix With Reference Variables.* Doctor's thesis, University of Southern California (Los Angeles, Calif.), 1952. (Abstract: *Am Psychol* 7:296)

418. DELATTRE, LOIS, AND COLE, DAVID. "A Comparison of the WISC and the Wechsler-Bellevue." *J Consult Psychol* 16:228–30 Je '52. * (*PA* 27:5147)

419. DEVONSHIRE, MARION E. *An Experimental Study of Abbreviated Forms of the Wechsler-Bellevue With a Group of Dull Normals.* Master's thesis, University of Texas (Austin, Tex.), 1952.

420. ENGEN, TRYGG. *A Comparison of Performance on the Wechsler-Bellevue Intelligence Scale and Success in the Engineering College.* Master's thesis, University of Detroit (Detroit, Mich.), 1952.

421. FINKELSTEIN, MELVILLE; GERBOTH, RENATE; AND WESTERHOLD, RUTH. "Standardization of a Short Form of the Wechsler Vocabulary Subtest." *J Clin Psychol* 8:133–5 Ap '52. * (*PA* 27:1956)

422. GAINER, WILLIAM L. *A Study of the Ability of the Wechsler-Bellevue Sub-Tests to Discriminate Between the Mental Levels of Delinquent Negro Boys.* Master's thesis, College of the Pacific (Stockton, Calif.), 1952.

423. GERMAIN, GEORGE L. *The Use of Z Scores in Place of the Regular Weighted Scores on the Wechsler-Bellevue Intelligence Scale, Form I.* Master's thesis, University of Detroit (Detroit, Mich.), 1952.

424. GIEDT, HELEN MOORE. *The Influence of Aphasia on Wechsler-Bellevue Scatter Patterns.* Doctor's thesis, University of Southern California (Los Angeles, Calif.), 1952.

425. GRAHAM, E. ELLIS. "Wechsler-Bellevue and WISC Scattergrams of Unsuccessful Readers." *J Consult Psychol* 16:268–71 Ag '52. * (*PA* 27:4564)

426. GRIFFITHS, JACK STEWART. *The Effect of Experimentally Induced Anxiety on Certain Subtests of the Wechsler-Bellevue.* Doctor's thesis, University of Kentucky (Lexington, Ky.), 1952. (*DA* 18:655)

427. GURVITZ, MILTON S. "Some Defects of the Wechsler-Bellevue." *J Consult Psychol* 16:124–6 Ap '52. *

428. GURVITZ, MILTON S., AND MILLER, JOSEPH S. A. Chap. 11, "Some Theoretical and Practical Aspects of the Diagnosis of Early and Latent Schizophrenia by Means of Psychological Testing," pp. 189–207. (*PA* 27:571) Discussion by Paul H. Hoch, pp. 215–6. In *Relation of Psychological Tests to Psychiatry.* Edited by Paul H. Hoch and Joseph Zubin. New York: Grune & Stratton, 1952. Pp. viii, 301. *

429. HALL, K. R. L. "Conceptual Impairment in Depressive and Organic Patients of the Pre-Senile Age Group." *J Mental Sci* 98:256–64 Ap '52. * (*PA* 27:572)

430. HARROWER, MOLLY. *Appraising Personality: The Use of Psychological Tests in the Practice of Medicine,* pp. 81–97. New York: W. W. Norton & Co., Inc., 1952. Pp. xvii, 197. * (*PA* 27:6532)

431. HELMICK, JOHN S. "Reliability or Variability?" *J Consult Psychol* 16:154–5 Ap '52. * (*PA* 27:2727)

432. HERRING, FRED H. "An Evaluation of Published Short Forms of the Wechsler-Bellevue Scale." *J Consult Psychol* 16:119–23 Ap '52. * (*PA* 27:2728)

433. HILDEN, ARNOLD H.; TAYLOR, JAMES W.; AND DUBOIS, PHILIP H. "Empirical Evaluation of Short W-B Scales." *J Clin Psychol* 8:323–31 O '52. * (*PA* 27:5876)

434. HOLZBERG, JULES D., AND BELMONT, LILLIAN. "The Relationship Between Factors on the Wechsler-Bellevue and Rorschach Having Common Psychological Rationale." *J Consult Psychol* 16:23–9 F '52. * (*PA* 27:1966)

435. KUTASH, SAMUEL B. "Interpretation of Jay's Wechsler-Bellevue Scale: The Case of Jay: Interpretations and Discussion." *J Proj Tech* 16:445–9, discussion 444–5, 462–73 D '52. * (*PA* 28:2678)

436. MALOS, HERBERT BERNARD. *Some Psychometric Evaluations of Epilepsy.* Doctor's thesis, University of Minnesota (Minneapolis, Minn.), 1952. (*DA* 12:396)

437. MANDLER, GEORGE, AND SARASON, SEYMOUR B. "A Study of Anxiety and Learning." *J Abn & Social Psychol* 47:166–73 Ap '52. * (*PA* 27:2743)

438. MEE, ELIZABETH ANN. *A Psychometric Study of Diffuse and Focal Cerebral Pathology Groups.* Doctor's thesis, University of Minnesota (Minneapolis, Minn.), 1952. (*DA* 12:338)

439. MERRILL, REED M., AND HEATHERS, LOUISE B. "Centile Scores for the Wechsler-Bellevue Intelligence Scale on a University Counseling Center Group." *J Consult Psychol* 16:406–9 O '52. * (*PA* 27:5890)

440. MERRILL, REED M., AND HEATHERS, LOUISE B. "Deviations of Wechsler-Bellevue Subtest Scores From Vocabulary Level in University Counseling-Center Clients." *J Consult Psychol* 16:469–72 D '52. * (*PA* 28:961)

441. MOLDAWSKY, STANLEY, AND MOLDAWSKY, PATRICIA CORCORAN. "Digit Span as an Anxiety Indicator." *J Consult Psychol* 16:115–8 Ap '52. * (*PA* 27:2747)

442. MONROE, JACK J. "The Effects of Emotional Adjustment and Intelligence Upon Bellevue Scatter." *J Consult Psychol* 16:110–4 Ap '52. * (*PA* 27:2748)

443. MORAN, L. J.; MORAN, F. A.; AND BLAKE, R. R. "An Investigation of the Vocabulary Performance of Schizophrenics: I, Quantitative Level." *J Genetic Psychol* 80:97–105 Mr '52. * (*PA* 27:581)

444. MORAN, L. J.; MORAN, F. A.; AND BLAKE, R. R. "An Investigation of the Vocabulary Performance of Schizophrenics: II, Conceptual Level of Definitions. *J Genetic Psychol* 80:107–132 Mr '52. * (*PA* 27:582)

445. PIZZAT, FRANK J. *Factor Analysis Patterns on the Wechsler-Bellevue Test of Adult Intelligence: Their Effectiveness in Discriminating Clinical Groups.* Doctor's thesis, University of Pittsburgh (Pittsburgh, Pa.), 1952.

446. PURCELL, CLAIRE KEPLER. "The Relationship Between Altitude—I.Q. Discrepancy and Anxiety." *J Clin Psychol* 8:82–5 Ja '52. * (*PA* 27:1978)

447. RICHARDS, T. W. "Personality of the Convulsive Patient in Military Service." *Psychol Monogr* 66(14):1–23 '52. * (*PA* 27:7364)

448. SCHNADT, FREDERICK. "Certain Aspects of Wechsler-Bellevue Scatter at Low IQ Levels." *J Consult Psychol* 16:456–61 D '52. * (*PA* 28:967)

449. SCHOFIELD, WILLIAM. "Critique of Scatter and Profile Analysis of Psychometric Data." *J Clin Psychol* 8:16–22 Ja '52. * (*PA* 27:1979)

450. SHANNON, WALTER, AND ROSSI, PHILIP D. "Suggestions for Efficient Presentation of the Wechsler-Bellevue Object-Assembly Sub-Test." *J Clin Psychol* 8:413–5 O '52. * (*PA* 27:5902)

451. SHNEIDMAN, EDWIN S. "The Case of Jay: Psychological Test and Anamnestic Data." *J Proj Tech* 16:297–345 S '52. * (*PA* 28:2676)

452. STARER, EMANUEL. "Aggressive Reactions and Sources of Frustration in Anxiety Neurotics and Paranoid Schizophrenics." *J Clin Psychol* 8:307–9 Jl '52. * (*PA* 27:5979)

453. STORRS, SIBYLL VIOLET. *An Evaluative Comparison of the United States Employment Service General Aptitude Test Battery and the Wechsler Bellevue Intelligence Scale.* Master's thesis, University of Florida (Gainesville, Fla.), 1952.

454. STOTSKY, BERNARD A. "A Comparison of Remitting and Nonremitting Schizophrenics on Psychological Tests." *J Abn & Social Psychol* 47:489–96 Ap '52. * (*PA* 27:2898)

455. VORHAUS, PAULINE G. "Case Study of an Adolescent Boy With Reading Disability." *J Proj Tech* 16:20–41 Mr '52. * (*PA* 27:650)

456. WEBB, WILSE B. "Corrections for Variability: A Reply." *J Consult Psychol* 16:156 Ap '52. *

457. YEATS, LEWIS CLIFFORD. *The Wechsler-Bellevue Adult Intelligence Scale as an Instrument for Predicting the Effects of Prefrontal Lobotomy.* Master's thesis, University of Western Ontario (London, Ont., Canada), 1952.

458. ARMSTRONG, RENATE GERBOTH. "A Comparison of the Comprehension Subtests of the Wechsler Bellevue Intelligence Scale, Forms I and II." *J Clin Psychol* 9:172–6 Ap '53. * (*PA* 28:2611)

459. BERKOWITZ, BERNARD. "The Wechsler-Bellevue Performance of White Males Past Age 50." *J Gerontol* 8:76–80 Ja '53. * (*PA* 28:657)

460. BERNSTEIN, RACHEL, AND CORSINI, RAYMOND J. "Wechsler-Bellevue Patterns of Female Delinquents." *J Clin Psychol* 9:176–9 Ap '53. * (*PA* 28:2963)

461. BIESHEUVEL, S.; JACOBS, G. F.; AND COWLEY, J. J. "Maladjustments of Military Personnel." *J Nat Inst Personnel Res* 5:138–68 D '53. *

462. BOTWINICK, JACK. "Wechsler-Bellevue Split-Half Subtest Reliabilities: Differences in Age and Mental Status." *J Consult Psychol* 17:225–8 Je '53. * (*PA* 28:2619)

463. CORSINI, RAYMOND J., AND FASSETT, KATHERINE K. "Intelligence and Aging." *J Genetic Psychol* 83:249–64 D '53. * (*PA* 28:7317)

464. DeMartino, Hugo A. *The Wechsler-Bellevue Intelligence Scale as a Predictor of Success in a College of Engineering.* Master's thesis, University of Detroit (Detroit, Mich.), 1953.

465. DeStephens, William P. "Are Criminals Morons?" *J Social Psychol* 38:187–99 N '53. * (*PA* 28:6294)

466. Dore, John J., Jr. *Performance on the Wechsler-Bellevue Intelligence Scale and Success in the College of Arts and Sciences at the University of Detroit.* Master's thesis, University of Detroit (Detroit, Mich.), 1953.

467. Dörken, Herbert, Jr., and Greenbloom, Grace C. "Psychological Investigation of Senile Dementia: II, The Wechsler-Bellevue Adult Intelligence Scale." *Geriatrics* 8:324–33 Je '53. * (*PA* 28:2359)

468. Duncan, John O. "Correlation Between the Wechsler-Bellevue and Stanford-Binet Vocabulary Lists." *Med Tech B* 4:45–7 Mr-Ap '53. * (*PA* 28:4348)

469. Fellers, Gloria L. *A Response-Category Analysis of Wechsler-Bellevue Intelligence Scale, Form I, Vocabulary Responses.* Master's thesis, Bowling Green State University (Bowling Green, Ohio), 1953.

470. Gibson, Frederick J. *Correlation Study of the 1937 Revision of the Stanford-Binet Scale, Form L, With the Performance Items of the Wechsler Bellevue Intelligence Scale, Adult, Form I.* Master's thesis, Boston College (Chestnut Hill, Mass.), 1953.

471. Haggerty, Arthur D. "The Intellectual Functioning of a Post-Institutional Group." *J Genetic Psychol* 83:303–6 D '53. * (*PA* 28:7816)

472. Henning, Richard L. *An Investigation of Sex Differences on the Weighted Subtest Scores of the Wechsler-Bellevue Intelligence Scale for Adults, Form I.* Master's thesis, Bowling Green State University (Bowling Green, Ohio), 1953.

473. Hopkins, Barbara, and Roth, Martin. "Psychological Test Performance in Patients Over Sixty: I, Paraphrenia, Arteriosclerotic Psychosis and Acute Confusion." *J Mental Sci* 99:451–63 Jl '53. * (*PA* 28:4655)

474. Jastak, Joseph. "Ranking Bellevue Subtest Scores for Diagnostic Purposes." *J Consult Psychol* 17:403–10 D '53. * (*PA* 28:7530)

475. Knopf, Irwin J.; Murfett, Betty J.; and Milstein, Victor. "A Comparative Study of the Wechsler-Bellevue Form I and the WISC." Abstract. *Am Psychol* 8:380 Ag '53. *

476. Levine, Bert D. *The Progressive Matrices 1938 and Its Relationship With Certain Subtests of the Wechsler-Bellevue Intelligence Scale.* Master's thesis, University of Texas (Austin, Tex.), 1953.

477. Love, Leonore Rice. *An Analysis of Wechsler-Bellevue Items Score for Assessing the Clinical Significance of Variability of Performance.* Doctor's thesis, University of California (Los Angeles, Calif.), 1953.

478. Luchins, Abraham S., and Luchins, Edith H. "Effects of Varying the Administration of the Digit Symbol Subtest of the Wechsler-Bellevue Intelligence Scale." *J General Psychol* 49:125–42 Jl '53. * (*PA* 28:6039)

479. McLean, Orison S. *Divergent Scores on the Wechsler-Bellevue Intelligence Scale as Indicators of Learning Ability Among Institutionalized Subjects.* Doctor's thesis, University of Kentucky (Lexington, Ky.), 1953.

480. Mainord, Willard A. "Some Effects of Sodium Amytal on 'Deteriorated' Schizophrenics." *J Consult Psychol* 17:54–7 F '53. * (*PA* 28:1329)

481. Maksimczyk, Walter J. *A Comparison of Performance on the Wechsler-Bellevue Intelligence Scale and Success in a College of Commerce and Finance.* Master's thesis, University of Detroit (Detroit, Mich.), 1953.

482. Marks, Melvin R. "A Criticism of the Use of the Wechsler-Bellevue Scale as a Diagnostic Instrument." *J General Psychol* 49:143–52 Jl '53. * (*PA* 28:6045)

483. Markwell, Earl D., Jr.; Wheeler, William M.; and Kitzinger, Helen. "Changes in Wechsler-Bellevue Test Performance Following Prefrontal Lobotomy." *J Consult Psychol* 17:229–31 Je '53. * (*PA* 28:2744)

484. Mattar, J. C. *A Study of the Performance of Multiple Sclerosis Patients on the Wechsler-Bellevue.* Master's thesis, University of Ottawa (Ottawa, Ont., Canada), 1953.

485. Mech, Edmund. "Item Analysis and Discriminative Value of Selected Wechsler-Bellevue Subtests." *J Ed Res* 47:241–60, 260a–260b D '53. * (*PA* 28:6046)

486. Merrill, Reed M., and Heathers, Louise B. "A Comparison of the Wechsler-Bellevue and ACE Tests on a University Counseling Center Group." *J Consult Psychol* 17:63–6 F '53. *

487. Norman, Ralph D. "Sex Differences and Other Aspects of Young Superior Adult Performance on the Wechsler-Bellevue." *J Consult Psychol* 17:411–8 D '53. * (*PA* 28:7541)

488. Patterson, C. H. *The Wechsler-Bellevue Scales: A Guide for Counselors.* Springfield, Ill.: Charles C Thomas, Publisher, 1953. Pp. viii, 146. * (*PA* 28:2664)

489. Rappaport, Sheldon R. "Intellectual Deficit in Organics and Schizophrenics." *J Consult Psychol* 17:389–95 O '53. * (*PA* 28:6365)

490. Roth, Martin, and Hopkins, Barbara. "Psychological Test Performance in Patients Over Sixty: I, Senile Psychosis and the Affective Disorders of Old Age." *J Mental Sci* 99:439–50 Jl '53. * (*PA* 28:4671)

491. Rothstein, Harvey Jones. *A Study of the Qualitative Aspects of the Wechsler-Bellevue Intelligence Scale.* Doctor's thesis, Columbia University (New York, N.Y.), 1953. (*DA* 14:1813)

492. Rubin, Harold. "A Quantitative Study of the H-T-P and Its Relationship to the Wechsler-Bellevue Scale." Abstract. *Am Psychol* 8:426–7 Ag '53. *

493. Sievers, Dorothy J., and Norman, Ralph D. "Some Suggestive Results in Psychometric Testing of the Cerebral Palsied With Gesell, Binet, and Wechsler Scales." *J Genetic Psychol* 82:69–90 Mr '53. * (*PA* 27:7974)

494. Stanley, Julian C. "Why Wechsler-Bellevue Full-Scale IQ's Are More Variable Than Averages of Verbal and Performance IQ's." *J Consult Psychol* 17:419–20 D '53. * (*PA* 28:7553)

495. Strange, Frank B., and Palmer, James O. "A Note on Sex Differences on the Wechsler-Bellevue Tests." *J Clin Psychol* 9:85–7 Ja '53. * (*PA* 27:7796)

496. Vanderhost, Leonette; Sloan, William; and Bensberg, Gerard J., Jr. "Performance of Mental Defectives on the Wechsler-Bellevue and the WISC." *Am J Mental Def* 57:481–3 Ja '53. * (*PA* 27:6629)

497. Walters, Richard H. "Wechsler-Bellevue Test Results of Prison Inmates." *Austral J Psychol* 5:46–54 Je '53. * (*PA* 29:1219)

498. Watson, Robert I. "Wechsler-Bellevue Intelligence Scale for Adolescents and Adults," pp. 530–44. (*PA* 27:7802) In *Contributions Toward Medical Psychology: Theory and Psychodiagnostic Methods, Vol. II.* Edited by Arthur Weider. New York: Ronald Press Co., 1953. Pp. xi, 459–885. *

499. Winne, John F. "An Alternate Form of the Series Completion Test." *J Clin Psychol* 9:321–7 O '53. * (*PA* 28:4405)

500. Wolff, Sidney J. "Clinical Application of the Wechsler-Bellevue Intelligence Scale for the Clinical Psychology Technician." *Med Tech B* 4:49–51 Ja–F '53. *

501. Adcock, C. J.; McCreary, J. R.; Ritchie, J. E.; and Somerset, H. C. A. "An Analysis of Maori Scores on the Wechsler-Bellevue." *Austral J Psychol* 6:16–29 Je '54. * (*PA* 29:5524)

502. Allen, Robert M.; Thornton, Thomas E.; and Stenger, Charles A. "Ammons and Wechsler Test Performances of College and Psychiatric Subjects." *J Clin Psychol* 10:378–81 O '54. * (*PA* 29:4022)

503. Bacon, Coleen Shaner. *A Comparative Study of the Wechsler-Bellevue Intelligence Scale for Adolescents and Adults, Form I, and the Wechsler Intelligence Scale for Children at the Twelve-Year Level.* Master's thesis, University of North Dakota (Grand Forks, N.D.), 1954.

504. Butler, Alfred. "Test-Retest and Split-Half Reliabilities of the Wechsler-Bellevue Scales and Subtests With Mental Defectives." *Am J Mental Def* 59:80–4 Jl '54. * (*PA* 29:4040)

505. Carment, D. W. *Differences in the Behavior Patterns and in the Wechsler-Bellevue Test Performances Between Psychopaths With Normal Electroencephalograms and Psychopaths With Abnormal Electroencephalograms.* Master's thesis, University of Toronto (Toronto, Ont., Canada), 1954.

506. Cook, Murray. *The Relationship Between Susceptibility to Secondary Motivation and Test Performance in Schizophrenics.* Doctor's thesis, New York University (New York, N.Y.), 1954. (*DA* 18:2197)

507. Corrie, C. C.; Fogel, J.; and Frank, G. H. "A Critique on Research With the Wechsler-Bellevue Test in Differential Psychodiagnosis." Abstract. *Am Psychol* 9:350–1 Ag '54. *

508. DeMartino, Hugo A. "The Wechsler-Bellevue Intelligence Scale as a Predictor of Success in a College of Engineering." *Papers Mich Acad Sci, Arts & Letters* 39:459–65 '54. *

509. Flynn, James J. *Rorschach and Wechsler-Bellevue Changes Following Electric Shock Therapy in the Aged.* Doctor's thesis, Loyola University (Chicago, Ill.), 1954.

510. Goolishian, H. A., and Foster, Austin. "A Note on Sex Differences on the Wechsler-Bellevue Test." *J Clin Psychol* 10:298–9 Jl '54. * (*PA* 29:2447)

511. Guertin, Wilson H. "The Effect of Instructions and Item Order on the Arithmetic Subtest of the Wechsler-Bellevue." *J Genetic Psychol* 85:79–83 S '54. * (*PA* 29:5706)

512. Gurvitz, Milton S. "An Experimental Evaluation of Judgment as Measured by the Comprehension Subtest of the Wechsler-Bellevue." Abstract. *Am Psychol* 9:386–7 Ag '54. *

513. Hollingsworth, Berneice H. *An Investigation of the Correlation Between the Wechsler Intelligence Scale for Children and the Durrell-Sullivan Reading Capacity Test.* Master's thesis, University of Denver (Denver, Colo.), 1954.

514. Kelley, Eileen. *A Study of the Relative Contributions of the Eleven Subtests to the Full Scale Wechsler-Bellevue Score.* Master's thesis, Bowling Green State University (Bowling Green, Ohio), 1954.

515. Knopf, Irwin J.; Murfett, Betty J.; and Milstein, Victor. "Relationships Between the Wechsler-Bellevue Form I and the WISC." *J Clin Psychol* 10:261–3 Jl '54. * (*PA* 29:2449)

516. Levine, Bert, and Iscoe, Ira. "A Comparison of Raven's Progressive Matrices (1938) With a Short Form of the Wechsler-Bellevue." Abstract. *J Consult Psychol* 18:10 F '54. *

517. Levreault, Lionel P. *Diagnosis of Idiopathic Epilepsy by Means of the Wechsler-Bellevue Scattergram.* Master's thesis, Ohio University (Athens, Ohio), 1954.

518. McLean, Orison S. "Divergent Scores on the Wechs-

ler-Bellevue Scale as Indicators of Learning Ability." *J Clin Psychol* 10:264–6 Jl '54. * (*PA* 29:2161)

519. MARTIN, STEPHAN B., AND WERTHEIMER, MICHAEL. "A Bibliography of Recent Work on the Wechsler-Bellevue." *Psychol Newsl* 6:10–38 S–O '54. * (*PA* 31:3053)

520. PTACEK, JAMES E., AND YOUNG, FLORENCE M. "Comparison of the Grassi Block Substitution Test With the Wechsler-Bellevue in the Diagnosis of Organic Brain Damage." *J Clin Psychol* 10:375–8 O '54. * (*PA* 29:4082)

521. RHODERICK, WAYNE A. *An Item Analysis of Wechsler-Bellevue Intelligence Scale, Form I Subtests.* Master's thesis, College of the Pacific (Stockton, Calif.), 1954.

522. RUSSELL, GEORGE E. "Wechsler-Bellevue Vocabulary Subtest Items: Revised Order of Words." *Med Tech B* 5:143–8 Jl-Ag '54. * (*PA* 29:950)

523. SATTER, GEORGE, AND MCGEE, EUGENE. "Retarded Adults Who Have Developed Beyond Expectation: Part I, Intellectual Functions." *Training Sch B* 51:43–55 My '54. * (*PA* 29:2662)

524. STACEY, CHALMERS L., AND SPANIER, S. WILLIAM. "Differential Responses Among College Students on the Vocabulary Subtest of the Wechsler Intelligence Scale." *J Ed Psychol* 45: 29–35 Ja '54. * (*PA* 28:7552)

525. THURSTON, JOHN R., AND CALDEN, GEORGE. "Intelligence Factors in Irregular Discharge Among Tuberculosis Patients." Abstract. *J Consult Psychol* 18:404 D '54. *

526. VANE, JULIA R., AND EISEN, VIRGINIA W. "Wechsler-Bellevue Performance of Delinquent and Nondelinquent Girls." *J Consult Psychol* 18:221–5 Je '54. * (*PA* 29:2753)

527. YOUNG, FLORENE M., AND COLLINS, JOHN J. "Results of Testing Negro Contact-Syphilitics With the Wechsler-Bellevue Intelligence Scale." *J Social Psychol* 39:93–8 F '54. * (*PA* 28:8929)

528. ANGERS, W. P. *A Psychometric Study of Institutionalized Epileptics on the Wechsler-Bellevue.* Doctor's thesis, University of Ottawa (Ottawa, Ont., Canada), 1955.

529. BRADWAY, KATHERINE, AND BENSON, STANLEY. "The Application of the Method of Extreme Deviations to Rapaport's Wechsler-Bellevue Data." *J Clin Psychol* 11:285–91 Jl '55. * (*PA* 30:2859)

530. BRESSLER, MILDRED BLOOM. *A Study of an Aspect of Concept Formation in Brain-Damaged Adults With Aphasia.* Doctor's thesis, New York University (New York, N.Y.), 1955. (*DA* 16:568)

531. BROWN, MORONI H., AND BRYAN, G. ELIZABETH. "The Interpretation of the Wechsler-Bellevue Intelligence Scale in Terms of Altitude Scores." Abstract. *Am Psychol* 10:431 Ag '55. *

532. BROWN, MORONI H., AND BRYAN, G. ELIZABETH. "Sex Differences in Intelligence." *J Clin Psychol* 11:303–4 Jl '55. * (*PA* 30:2860)

533. BRYAN, GERALDINE E. *A Study of the Performance of Adolescents With Diagnosed Brain Damage on the Wechsler-Bellevue Intelligence Scale, Form One.* Master's thesis, University of Utah (Salt Lake City, Utah), 1955.

534. COHEN, JACOB. "The Efficacy of Diagnostic Pattern Analysis With the Wechsler-Bellevue." *J Consult Psychol* 19:303–6 Ag '55. * (*PA* 30:4557)

535. DESAI, MAHESH M. "The Relationship of the Wechsler-Bellevue Verbal Scale and the Progressive Matrices Test." Abstract. *J Consult Psychol* 19:60 F '55. *

536. DILLER, JULIET C. "A Comparison of the Test Performances of Male and Female Juvenile Delinquents." *J Genetic Psychol* 86:217–36 Je '55. * (*PA* 30:7485)

537. FORSTER, CECIL R. *The Relationship Between Test Achievement and Success in Training of a Selected Group of Tuberculosis Patients.* Doctor's thesis, New York University (New York, N.Y.), 1955. (*DA* 15:1201)

538. FRANK, G. H.; CORRIE, C. C.; AND FOGEL, J. "An Empirical Critique of Research With the Wechsler-Bellevue in Differential Psychodiagnosis." *J Clin Psychol* 11:291–3 Jl '55. * (*PA* 30:2877)

539. HALLBERG, MARGARET C. *A Study of the Characteristics of Mentally Competent Offenders as Revealed by Vocabulary Scatter on the Wechsler-Bellevue Intelligence Scale (Form 1).* Master's thesis, University of Alberta (Edmonton, Alta., Canada), 1955.

540. HORWITZ, MURRAY; DELLA PIANA, GABRIEL M.; GOLDMAN, MORTON; AND LEE, FRANCIS J. "Veridicality of Attitudes Toward Authority and Effects on Learning." Abstract. *Am Psychol* 10:336 Ag '55. *

541. HOWELL, ROBERT J. "Changes in Wechsler Subtest Scores With Age." *J Consult Psychol* 19:47–50 F '55. * (*PA* 29:8429)

542. HOWELL, ROBERT J. "Sex Differences and Educational Influences on a Mental Deterioration Scale." *J Gerontol* 10: 190–3 Ap '55. * (*PA* 30:2887)

543. IPSON, WILLIAM M. *The Relationship Between the Critical Frequency of Flicker and Performance on the Wechsler-Bellevue Intelligence Scale.* Master's thesis, University of Utah (Salt Lake City, Utah), 1955.

544. JACKSON, C. V. "Estimating Impairment on Wechsler Bellevue Subtests." *J Clin Psychol* 11:137–43 Ap '55. * (*PA* 30:1030)

545. KAMMAN, GORDON R., AND KRAM, CHARLES. "Value of Psychometric Examinations in Medical Diagnosis and Treatment." *J Am Med Assn* 158:555–60 Je 18 '55. * (*PA* 31:1044)

546. KELLEY, EILEEN. *A Study of the Relative Contributions of the Eleven Subtests to the Full Scale Wechsler-Bellevue*

Score. Master's thesis, Bowling Green State University (Bowling Green, Ohio), 1955.

547. KRAMAR, EDWARD JOHN JOSEPH. *The Relationships of the Wechsler-Bellevue and A.C.E. Intelligence Tests With Performance Scores in Speaking and the Brown-Carlsen Listening Comprehension Test.* Doctor's thesis, Florida State University (Tallahassee, Fla.), 1955. (*DA* 15:2599)

548. LEVINE, A.; ABRAMSON, H. A.; KAUFMAN, M. R.; AND MARKHAM, S. "Lysergic Acid Diethylamide (LSD-25): XVI, The Effect on Intellectual Functioning as Measured by the Wechsler-Bellevue Intelligence Scale." *J Psychol* 40:385–95 O '55. * (*PA* 30:6904)

549. LEVINE, BERT, AND ISCOE, IRA. "The Progressive Matrices (1938), the Chicago Non-Verbal and the Wechsler-Bellevue on an Adolescent Deaf Population." *J Clin Psychol* 11: 307–8 Jl '55. * (*PA* 30:3334)

550. LOTT, W. J. *Characteristics of High Standing University Students on the Wechsler-Bellevue Adult Intelligence Scale.* Master's thesis, University of Alberta (Edmonton, Alta., Canada), 1955.

551. LOVE, DEBORAH B. *Brain Damage and Wechsler-Bellevue.* Master's thesis, Howard University (Washington, D.C.), 1955.

552. MATARAZZO, RUTH G. "The Relationship of Manifest Anxiety to Wechsler-Bellevue Subtest Performance." Abstract. *J Consult Psychol* 19:218 Je '55. *

553. MATARAZZO, RUTH GADBOIS. *The Effect of Anxiety Level Upon Motor Learning, Level of Aspiration, and Wechsler-Bellevue Subtest Performance.* Doctor's thesis, Washington University (St. Louis, Mo.), 1955. (*DA* 15:877)

554. MEER, BERNARD, AND STEIN, MORRIS I. "Measures of Intelligence and Creativity." *J Psychol* 39:117–26 Ja '55. * (*PA* 29:9102)

555. MEER, BERNARD; STEIN, MORRIS I.; AND GEERTSMA, ROBERT. "An Analysis of the Miller Analogies Test for a Scientific Population." *Am Psychol* 10:33–4 Ja '55. * (*PA* 30: 3658)

556. NORTH, GEORGE E. *The Rorschach Intellectual Indices: An Investigation of Relationships Between Rorschach and the Wechsler-Bellevue Tests.* Master's thesis, University of Utah (Salt Lake City, Utah), 1955.

557. PLUMB, GALEN R., AND CHARLES, DON C. "Scoring Difficulty of Wechsler Comprehension Responses." *J Ed Psychol* 46:179–83 Mr '55. * (*PA* 30:1049)

558. PRICE, JOHN R., AND THORNE, GARETH D. "A Statistical Comparison of the WISC and Wechsler-Bellevue, Form I." *J Consult Psychol* 19:479–82 D '55. * (*PA* 30:7221)

559. RABIN, A. I.; KING, G. F.; AND EHRMANN, J. C. "Vocabulary Performance of Short-Term and Long-Term Schizophrenics." *J Abn & Social Psychol* 50:255–8 Mr '55. * (*PA* 30:1361)

560. SATTER, GEORGE. "Retarded Adults Who Have Developed Beyond Expectation: Part III, Further Analysis and Summary." *Training Sch B* 51:237–43 F '55. * (*PA* 29:7498)

561. SLOAN, WILLIAM, AND NEWMAN, J. ROBERT. "The Development of a Wechsler-Bellevue II Short Form." *Personnel Psychol* 8:347–53 au '55. * (*PA* 30:7838)

562. WARD, JOE H., JR. "Use of Electronic Computers in Psychological Research." Letter. *Am Psychol* 10:826–7 D '55. * (*PA* 30:6510)

563. WEISGERBER, CHARLES A. "A Note on Diamond's Method of Scoring the Wechsler-Bellevue Intelligence Scale for Vocational Aptitude." *J Clin Psychol* 11:311 Jl '55. * (*PA* 30:3591)

564. ALLEN, ROBERT M.; THORNTON, THOMAS E.; AND STENGER, CHARLES A. "The Full-Range Picture Vocabulary Test Compared With Two Short Forms of the Wechsler Scale." *J Ed Res* 50:133–7 O '56. * (*PA* 32:933)

565. BARRY, JOHN R.; FULKERSON, SAMUEL C.; KUBALA, ALBERT L.; AND SEAQUIST, MAURICE R. "Score Equivalence of the Wechsler-Bellevue Intelligence Scales, Forms I and II." *J Clin Psychol* 12:57–60 Ja '56. * (*PA* 30:4553)

566. BREIGER, BORIS. "The Use of the W-B Picture Arrangement Subtest as a Projective Technique." Abstract. *J Consult Psychol* 20:132 Ap '56. *

567. CALDWELL, MARK B., AND DAVIS, JULIAN C. "A Short Form of the Wechsler-Bellevue Intelligence Scale Form II for a Psychotic Population." *J Clin Psychol* 12:402–3 O '56. * (*PA* 32:4168)

568. DAVIS, PAUL C. "A Factor Analysis of the Wechsler-Bellevue Scale." *Ed & Psychol Meas* 16:127–46 sp '56. * (*PA* 31:6072)

569. EVERETT, EVALYN G. *A Comparative Study of Paretics, Hebephrenics, and Paranoid Schizophrenics on a Battery of Psychological Tests.* Doctor's thesis, New York University (New York, N.Y.), 1956. (*DA* 16:1502)

570. FORTSON, CHARLES B. *A Study of the Comparability of Forms I and II of the Wechsler-Bellevue Intelligence Scale When Used With Clinically Normal Negro Adults.* Master's thesis, Atlanta University (Atlanta, Ga.), 1956.

571. FRANK, GEORGE H. "The Wechsler-Bellevue and Psychiatric Diagnosis: A Factor Analytic Approach." *J Consult Psychol* 20:67–9 F '56. * (*PA* 31:3032)

572. FRY, LOIS M. "A Predictive Measure of Work Success for High Grade Mental Defectives." *Am J Mental Def* 61:402–8 O '56. *

573. FRYE, U. CASSIAN. *The Relevancy of the SRA Primary Mental Abilities Test and the SRA Reading Record to Ninth*

Grade Achievement in a Catholic Boys' High School. Master's thesis, St. Louis University (St. Louis, Mo.), 1956.

574. GOOLISHIAN, H. A., AND RAMSAY, ROSE. "The Wechsler-Bellevue Form I and the WAIS: A Comparison." *J Clin Psychol* 12:147–51 Ap '56. * *(PA* 31:4691)

575. GUERTIN, WILSON H.; FRANK, GEORGE H.; AND RABIN, ALBERT I. "Research With the Wechsler-Bellevue Intelligence Scale: 1950–1955." *Psychol B* 53:235–57 My '56. * *(PA* 32:492)

576. INGLIS, J.; SHAPIRO, M. B.; AND POST, F. "'Memory Function' in Psychiatric Patients Over Sixty, the Role of Memory in Tests Discriminating Between 'Functional' and 'Organic' Groups." *J Mental Sci* 102:589–98 Jl '56. * *(PA* 31:7926)

577. KALDEGG, A. "Psychological Observations in a Group of Alcoholic Patients With Analysis of Rorschach, Wechsler-Bellevue and Bender Gestalt Test Results." *Q J Studies Alcohol* 17:608–28 D '56. * *(PA* 32:648)

578. MARIANI, ROSE RAMSAY. *A Comparison of a Projective Test Battery With Its Component Tests.* Doctor's thesis, University of Houston (Houston, Tex.), 1956. *(DA* 16:1506)

579. MILNE, G. G. "Deterioration and Over-Learning." *Austral J Psychol* 8:163–73 D '56. *

580. MURPHY, DONALD B., AND LANGSTON, ROBERT D. "A Short Form of the Wechsler-Bellevue and the Army Classification Battery as Measures of Intelligence." Abstract. *J Consult Psychol* 20:405 O '56. *

581. NEURINGER, CHARLES. *A Statistical Comparison of the Wechsler-Bellevue Intelligence Scale, Form I and the Wechsler Adult Intelligence Scale for a College Population.* Master's thesis, University of Kansas (Lawrence, Kan.), 1956.

582. O'NEILL, JOHN J., AND DAVIDSON, JOANN L. "Relationship Between Lipreading Ability and Five Psychological Factors." *J Speech & Hearing Dis* 21:478–81 D '56. * *(PA* 31:4907)

583. PLANT, WALTER T., AND SAWREY, JAMES M. "A Preliminary Review of the Data for 1,000 College Undergraduates Individually Tested With the Wechsler-Bellevue Scale, Form I." Abstract. *Calif J Ed Res* 7:130 My '56. *

584. PURCELL, KENNETH. "A Note on Porteus Maze and Wechsler-Bellevue Scores as Related to Antisocial Behavior." *J Consult Psychol* 20:361–4 O '56. * *(PA* 31:7960)

585. ROBINOWITZ, RALPH. "Performances of Hospitalized Psychiatric Patients on the Kent Emergency Test and the Wechsler-Bellevue Intelligence Scale." *J Clin Psychol* 12:199–200 Ap '56. * *(PA* 31:4711)

586. RUBIN-RABSON, GRACE. "Item Order and Difficulty in Four Verbal Subtests of the Bellevue-Wechsler Scale." *J Genetic Psychol* 88:167–74 Je '56. *

587. SCARBOROUGH, B. B. "Some Mental Characteristics of Southern Colored and White Venereal Disease Patients as Measured by the Wechsler-Bellevue Test." *J Social Psychol* 43:313–21 My '56. *

588. SHIER, DAVID A. *An Exploratory Study of the Use of the Wechsler-Bellevue and the Rotter Tests to Determine Common Personality Patterns for Retarded Readers.* Master's thesis, Sacramento State College (Sacramento, Calif.), 1956.

589. THALER, MARGARET. "Relationships Among Wechsler, Weigl, Rorschach, EEG Findings, and Abstract-Concrete Behavior in a Group of Normal Aged Subjects." *J Gerontol* 11:404–9 O '56. * *(PA* 31:5871)

590. TOLOR, ALEXANDER. "A Comparison of the Bender-Gestalt Test and the Digit-Span Test as Measures of Recall." *J Consult Psychol* 20:305–9 Ag '56. * *(PA* 31:7979)

591. TOLOR, ALEXANDER. "The Wechsler-Bellevue Scale in Clinical Diagnosis: Some Aspects of Its Use in Clinical Diagnosis." *U S Armed Forces Med J* 7:192–9 F '56. * *(PA* 31:1071)

592. ZIMET, CARL N., AND BRACKBILL, GLEN A. "The Role of Anxiety in Psychodiagnosis." *J Clin Psychol* 12:173–7 Ap '56. * *(PA* 31:4722)

593. BAYLEY, NANCY. "Data on the Growth of Intelligence Between 16 and 21 Years as Measured by the Wechsler-Bellevue Scale." *J Genetic Psychol* 90:3–15 Mr '57. *

594. BROWN, MORONI H., AND BRYAN, G. ELIZABETH. "The Altitude Quotient as a Measurement of Intellectual Potential." *J Clin Psychol* 13:137–40 Ap '57. * *(PA* 32:2654)

595. BRYAN, G. ELIZABETH, AND BROWN, MORONI H. "A Method for Differential Diagnosis of Brain Damage in Adolescents." *J Nerv & Mental Dis* 125:69–72 Ja–Mr '57. *

596. DANA, RICHARD H. "A Comparison of Four Verbal Subtests on the Wechsler-Bellevue, Form I, and the WAIS." *J Clin Psychol* 13:70–1 Ja '57. *

597. DAVIS, JULIAN C. "The Scatter Pattern of a Southern Negro Group on the Wechsler-Bellevue Intelligence Scale." *J Clin Psychol* 13:298–300 Jl '57. *

598. DELLI COLLI, PASCAL. *The Rationale of the Wechsler-Bellevue Picture Arrangement Subtest, Form I.* Master's thesis, University of Ottawa (Ottawa, Ont., Canada), 1957.

599. GASKILL, P. Chap. 9, "Tests of Ability and Attainments: Pilot Experiments in Selection and Guidance," pp. 188–212. In *Educational Guidance and the Deaf Child.* Edited by A. W. G. Ewing. Manchester, England: Manchester University Press, 1957. Pp. xiii, 345. *

600. GILGASH, CURTIS A. "Effects of Thorazine on Wechsler Scores of Adult Catatonic Schizophrenics." *Psychol Rep* 3:561–4 D '57. *

601. GOETZINGER, C. P., AND ROUSEY, C. L. "A Study of the Wechsler Performance Scale (Form II) and the Knox Cube

Test With Deaf Adolescents." *Am Ann Deaf* 102:388–98 N '57. *

602. GOODSTEIN, LEONARD D., AND FARBER, I. E. "On the Relation Between A-Scale Scores and Digit Symbol Performance." *J Consult Psychol* 21:152–4 Ap '57. *

603. HALL, JULIA C. "Reliability (Internal Consistency) of the Wechsler Memory Scale and Correlation With the Wechsler-Bellevue Intelligence Scale." *J Consult Psychol* 21:131–5 Ap '57. *

604. KARSON, SAMUEL, AND POOL, KENNETH BRYNER. "The Abstract Thinking Abilities of Mental Patients." *J Clin Psychol* 13:126–32 Ap '57. * *(PA* 32:3023)

605. KEEHN, J. D. "Repeated Testing of Four Chronic Schizophrenics on the Bender-Gestalt and Wechsler Block Design Tests." *J Clin Psychol* 13:179–82 Ap '57. * *(PA* 32:3167)

606. MINDESS, HARVEY. "Psychological Indices in the Selection of Student Nurses." *J Proj Tech* 21:37–9 Mr '57. * *(PA* 32:2908)

607. MURPHY, K. P. Chap. 11, "Tests of Abilities and Attainments: Pupils in Schools for the Deaf Aged Twelve," pp. 252–77. In *Educational Guidance and the Deaf Child.* Edited by A. W. G. Ewing. Manchester, England: Manchester University Press, 1957. Pp. xiii, 345. *

608. PARKER, JAMES W. "The Validity of Some Current Tests for Organicity." *J Consult Psychol* 21:425–8 O '57. *

609. SCHNEYER, SOLOMON. "A Short Form of the Wechsler-Bellevue Scale, Form II, for Alcoholic Outpatients." *Q J Studies Alcohol* 18:382–7 S '57. *

610. SULLIVAN, ARTHUR. "Measurement of Intelligence in Different Environments." *B Maritime Psychol Assn* 6:18–23 D '57. *

611. TOPETZES, NICK JOHN. "A Program for the Selection of Trainees in Physical Medicine." *J Exp Ed* 25:263–311 Je '57. *

612. WHITEMAN, MARTIN, AND JASTAK, JOSEPH. "Absolute Scaling of Tests for Different Age Groupings of a State-Wide Sample." *Ed & Psychol Meas* 17:338–46 au '57. *

613. ANGERS, WILLIAM P. "A Psychometric Study of Institutionalized Epileptics on the Wechsler-Bellevue." *J General Psychol* 58:225–47 Ap '58. *

614. ARMITAGE, STEWART G., AND PEARL, DAVID. "Wechsler-Bellevue Changes Over Time." *J Clin Psychol* 14:22–4 Ja '58. *

615. FISHER, GRANVILLE C. "Selective and Differentially Accelerated Intellectual Dysfunction in Specific Brain Damage." *J Clin Psychol* 14:395–8 O '58. *

616. GRIFFITH, RICHARD M., AND YAMAHIRO, ROY S. "Reliability-Stability of Subtest Scatter on the Wechsler-Bellevue Intelligence Scales." *J Clin Psychol* 14:317–8 Jl '58. *

617. HILER, E. WESLEY. "Wechsler-Bellevue Intelligence as a Predictor of Continuation in Psychotherapy." *J Clin Psychol* 14:192–4 Ap '58. *

618. LIGHT, MORTON L., AND CHAMBERS, WILLIAM R. "A Comparison of the Wechsler Adult Intelligence Scale and Wechsler-Bellevue II With Mental Defectives." *Am J Mental Def* 62:878–81 Mr '58. *

619. McKEEVER, WALTER F., AND GERSTEIN, ALVIN I. "Validity of the Hewson Ratios: Investigation of a Fundamental Methodological Consideration." Abstract. *J Consult Psychol* 22:150 Ap '58. *

620. MAHRER, ALVIN R., AND BERNSTEIN, LEWIS. "A Proposed Method for Measuring Potential Intelligence." *J Clin Psychol* 14:404–9 O '58. *

621. MUNDY-CASTLE, A. C. "Electrophysiological Correlates of Intelligence." *J Personality* 26:184–99 Je '58. *

622. PLANT, WALTER T., AND RICHARDSON, HAROLD. "The IQ of the Average College Student." *J Counsel Psychol* 5:229–31 fall '58. *

623. SINES, LLOYD K. "Intelligence Test Correlates of Shipley-Hartford Performance." *J Clin Psychol* 14:399–404 O '58. *

624. TREHUB, ARNOLD, AND SCHERER, ISIDOR W. "Wechsler-Bellevue Scatter as an Index of Schizophrenia." *J Consult Psychol* 22:147–9 Ap '58. *

625. WOLFENSBERGER, WOLF P. "Construction of a Table of the Significance of the Difference Between Verbal and Performance IQ's on the WAIS and the Wechsler-Bellevue." *J Clin Psychol* 14:92 Ja '58. *

For reviews by Murray Aborn and William D. Altus, see 4:361; for a review by Robert I. Watson, see 3:298; for a review by F. L. Wells, see 40:1429 (2 excerpts); for related reviews, see B332, 4:362, 3:299–301, and 40:B1121.

[416]

Wechsler Intelligence Scale for Children. Ages 5–15; 1949; downward extension of Form 2 of *Wechsler-Bellevue Intelligence Scale;* also called WISC; individual; 15 scores: verbal (information, comprehension, arithmetic, similarities, vocabulary, digit span—optional), performance (picture completion, picture arrangement, block design, object assembly, mazes—

optional, coding), total; 1 form; record booklet (revised slightly in 1958 but dated 1949) $22 per set of test materials, 25 record booklets, and manual; $2.10 per 25 record booklets; $1.20 per 25 WISC Maze Tests, an alternate subtest which may be used in place of Coding; $2.50 per manual; postpaid; (40–60) minutes; David Wechsler; Psychological Corporation. *

REFERENCES

1–22. See 4:363.
23. ORR, KENNETH N. *The Wechsler Intelligence Scale for Children as a Predictor of School Success.* Master's thesis, Indiana State Teachers College (Terre Haute, Ind.), 1950.
24. PRICE, ARTHUR COOPER. *A Preliminary Study in Statistical Comparison of the Revised Stanford-Binet Intelligence Test Form L With the Wechsler Intelligence Scale for Children Using the Ten Year Age Level.* Master's thesis, University of Florida (Gainesville, Fla.), 1950.
25. SCOTT, GORDON R. *A Comparison Between the Wechsler Intelligence Scale for Children and the Revised Stanford-Binet Scales.* Master's thesis, Southern Methodist University (Dallas, Tex.), 1950.
26. PASTOVIC, JOHN JOSEPH. *A Validation Study of the Wechsler Intelligence Scale for Children at the Lower Age Level.* Master's thesis, Pennsylvania State College (State College, Pa.), 1951.
27. THOMPSON, GRACE M. "W. I. S. C. Patterns of a Selective Sample of Dull Bilingual Children." Abstract. *Am Psychol* 6:493–4 S '51. *
28. THRONE, JOHN MARSHALL. *A Short Form of the Wechsler-Bellevue Intelligence Test for Children.* Master's thesis, University of Florida (Gainesville, Fla.), 1951.
29. WAGNER, WINIFRED K. *A Comparison of Stanford-Binet Mental Ages and Scaled Scores on the Wechsler Intelligence Scale for Children for Fifty Bowling Green Pupils.* Master's thesis, Bowling Green State University (Bowling Green, Ohio), 1951.
30. WINPENNY, NAOMI. *An Investigation of the Use and the Validity of Mental Age Scores on the Wechsler Intelligence Scales for Children.* Master's thesis, Pennsylvania State College (State College, Pa.), 1951.
31. ALTUS, GRACE THOMPSON. "A Note on the Validity of the Wechsler Intelligence Scale for Children." *J Consult Psychol* 16:231 Je '52. * (PA 27:5140)
32. BINKS, VIRGINIA M.; FOSTER, DESMOND V.; ADAMS, NICHOLAS A.; AND TRIGGS, FRANCES. "The Relationship of Reading Skills as Learned in Grades 4–College Freshman Years to Verbal and Performance Scores on an Individual Intelligence Test." Abstract. *Am Psychol* 7:376–7 Jl '52. *
33. COHEN, BERTRAM D., AND COLLIER, MARY J. "A Note on the WISC and Other Tests of Children Six to Eight Years Old." *J Consult Psychol* 16:226–7 Je '52. * (PA 27:5145)
34. DELATTRE, LOIS, AND COLE, DAVID. "A Comparison of the WISC and the Wechsler-Bellevue." *J Consult Psychol* 16:228–30 Je '52. * (PA 27:5147)
35. GRAHAM, E. ELLIS. "Wechsler-Bellevue and WISC Scattergrams of Unsuccessful Readers." *J Consult Psychol* 16:268–71 Ag '52. * (PA 27:4564)
36. HAGEN, ELIZABETH P. *A Factor Analysis of the Wechsler Intelligence Scale for Children.* Doctor's thesis, Columbia University (New York, N.Y.), 1952. (DA 12:722)
37. KURETH, GENEVIEVE; MUHR, JEAN P.; AND WEISGERBER, CHARLES A. "Some Data on the Validity of the Wechsler Intelligence Scale for Children." *Child Develop* 23:281–7 D '52. * (PA 28:954)
38. MUHR, JEAN P. *Validity of the Wechsler Intelligence Scale for Children at the Five and Six Year Level.* Master's thesis, University of Detroit (Detroit, Mich.), 1952.
39. MUSSEN, PAUL; DEAN, SANFORD; AND ROSENBERG, MARGERY. "Some Further Evidence on the Validity of the WISC." *J Consult Psychol* 16:410–1 O '52. * (PA 27:5891)
40. RALEIGH, WILLIAM H. *A Study of the Relationships of Academic Achievement in Sixth Grade With the Wechsler Intelligence Scale for Children and Other Variables.* Doctor's thesis, Indiana University (Bloomington, Ind.), 1952.
41. REIDY, MARY ELIZABETH. *A Validity Study of the Wechsler-Bellevue Intelligence Scale for Children and Its Relationship to Reading and Arithmetic.* Master's thesis, Catholic University of America (Washington, D.C.), 1952.
42. SANDERCOCK, MARIAN G., AND BUTLER, ALFRED J. "An Analysis of the Performance of Mental Defectives on the Wechsler Intelligence Scale for Children." *Am J Mental Def* 57:100–5 Jl '52. * (PA 27:3640)
43. SCHWITZGOEBEL, ROLAND R. *The Predictive Value of Some Relationships Between the Wechsler Intelligence Scale for Children and Academic Achievement in Fifth Grade.* Doctor's thesis, University of Wisconsin (Madison, Wis.), 1952.
44. TATHAM, LOUISE JEANETTE. *Statistical Comparison of the Revised Stanford-Binet Intelligence Test—Form L With the Wechsler Intelligence Scale for Children Using the Six and One-Half Year Level.* Master's thesis, University of Florida (Gainesville, Fla.), 1952.
45. TURNER, G. H., AND PENFOLD, D. J. "The Scholastic Aptitude of Indian Children of the Caradoc Reserve." *Can J Psychol* 6:31–44 Mr '52. * (PA 26:6935)
46. WARINNER, ELLEN M. *A Comparison of Test Performance of Dull Children on the Revised Stanford-Binet and the Wechsler-Intelligence Scale for Children.* Master's thesis, University of Chicago (Chicago, Ill.), 1952.
47. WILSON, LOLITA. *A Comparison of the Raven Progressive Matrices (1947) and the Performance Scale of the Wechsler Intelligence Scale for Children for Assessing the Intelligence of Indian Children.* Master's thesis, University of British Columbia (Vancouver, B.C., Canada), 1952.
48. ALTUS, GRACE T. "W.I.S.C. Patterns of a Selective Sample of Bilingual School Children." *J Genetic Psychol* 83:241–8 D '53. * (PA 28:7207)
49. BLAKEMORE, JOHN R. *A Comparison of Scores of Negro and White Children on the Wechsler Intelligence Scale for Children.* Master's thesis, College of the Pacific (Stockton, Calif.), 1953.
50. DELP, HAROLD A. "Correlations Between the Kent Egy and the Wechsler Batteries." *J Clin Psychol* 9:73–5 Ja '53. * (PA 27:7764)
51. ESTES, BETSY WORTH. "Influence of Socioeconomic Status on Wechsler Intelligence Scale for Children: An Exploratory Study." *J Consult Psychol* 17:58–62 F '53. * (PA 28:940)
52. GLOWATSKY, EDWARD. "The Verbal Element in the Intelligence Scores of Congenitally Deaf and Hard of Hearing Children." *Am Ann Deaf* 98:328–35 My '53. * (PA 28:7921)
53. GRAHAM, E. ELLIS, AND SHAPIRO, ESTHER. "Use of the Performance Scale of the Wechsler Intelligence Scale for Children With the Deaf Child." *J Consult Psychol* 17:396–8 O '53. * (PA 28:6449)
54. HITE, LORAIN. *Analysis of Reliability and Validity of the Wechsler Intelligence Scale for Children.* Doctor's thesis, Western Reserve University (Cleveland, Ohio), 1953.
55. HOLLAND, GLEN A. "A Comparison of the WISC and Stanford-Binet IQ's of Normal Children." *J Consult Psychol* 17:147–52 Ap '53. * (PA 28:2638)
56. HOLLOWAY, HAROLD DAVID. *Effects of Training Upon, and Relationships Between, Two Standard Child Intelligence Tests.* Doctor's thesis, State University of Iowa (Iowa City, Iowa), 1953. (DA 13:884)
57. KNOPF, IRWIN J.; MURFETT, BETTY J.; AND MILSTEIN, VICTOR. "A Comparative Study of the Wechsler-Bellevue Form I and the WISC." Abstract. *Am Psychol* 8:380 Ag '53. *
58. KURETH, GENEVIEVE. *Correlation of the Subtests of the Wechsler Intelligence Scale for Children With the Revised Stanford-Binet for Five and Six Year Olds.* Master's thesis, University of Detroit (Detroit, Mich.), 1953.
59. RACHIELE, LEO D. *A Comparative Analysis of Ten Year Old Negro and White Performance on the Wechsler Intelligence Scale for Children.* Doctor's thesis, University of Denver (Denver, Colo.), 1953.
60. SCHOLL, GERALDINE. "Intelligence Tests for Visually Handicapped Children." *Excep Child* 20:116–20+ D '53. * (PA 28:6455)
61. STEMPEL, ELLEN FLAUM. "The WISC and the SRA Primary Mental Abilities Test." *Child Develop* 24:257–61 S–D '53. * (PA 29:4089)
62. TRIGGS, FRANCES ORALIND, AND CARTEE, J. KEITH. "Pre-School Pupil Performance on the Stanford-Binet and the Wechsler Intelligence Scale for Children." *J Clin Psychol* 9:27–9 Ja '53. * (PA 27:7800)
63. VANDERHOST, LEONETTE; SLOAN, WILLIAM; AND BENSBERG, GERARD J., JR. "Performance of Mental Defectives on the Wechsler-Bellevue and the WISC." *Am J Mental Def* 57:481–3 Ja '53. * (PA 27:6629)
64. WECHSLER, DAVID, AND WEIDER, ARTHUR. "Wechsler Intelligence Scale for Children," pp. 522–9. (PA 27:7804) In *Contributions Toward Medical Psychology: Theory and Psychodiagnostic Methods, Vol. II.* Edited by Arthur Weider. New York: Ronald Press Co., 1953. Pp. xi, 459–885. *
65. BACON, COLEEN S. *A Comparative Study of the Wechsler-Bellevue Intelligence Scale for Adolescents and Adults, Form I, and the Wechsler Intelligence Scale for Children at the Twelve-Year Level.* Master's thesis, University of North Dakota (Grand Forks, N.D.), 1954.
66. BORUSZAK, RUBY J. *A Comparative Study to Determine the Correlation Between the IQ's of the Revised Stanford Binet Scale, Form L, and the IQ's of the Wechsler Intelligence Scale for Children.* Master's thesis, Wisconsin State College (Milwaukee, Wis.), 1954.
67. CALDWELL, MARCUS B. *An Analysis of Responses of a Southern Urban Negro Population to Items on the Wechsler Intelligence Scale for Children.* Doctor's thesis, Pennsylvania State University (University Park, Pa.), 1954.
68. CARLETON, FREDERICK O., AND STACEY, CHALMERS L. "Evaluation of Selected Short Forms of the Wechsler Intelligence Scale for Children (WISC)." *J Clin Psychol* 10:258–61 Jl '54. * (PA 29:2438)
69. DAVIDSON, JACK FREDERICK. *A Preliminary Study in Statistical Comparison of the Revised Stanford-Binet Intelligence Test Form L With the Wechsler Intelligence Scale for Children Using the Fourteen Year Level.* Master's thesis, University of Florida (Gainesville, Fla.), 1954.
70. GAULT, UNA. "Factorial Patterns of the Wechsler Intelligence Scales." *Austral J Psychol* 6:85–9 Je '54. * (PA 29:5704)
71. HENDRIX, RUBY. *A Study of the Revision of the Wechsler Intelligence Scale With Particular Reference to Laymen's Concepts of Intelligence.* Master's thesis, University of Texas (Austin, Tex.), 1954.

72. HOLLINGSWORTH, BERNEICE H. *An Investigation of the Correlation Between the Wechsler Intelligence Scale for Children and the Durrell-Sullivan Reading Capacity Test.* Master's thesis, University of Denver (Denver, Colo.), 1954.

73. HOLLOWAY, HAROLD D. "Effects of Training on the SRA Primary Mental Abilities (Primary) and the WISC." *Child Develop* 25:253–63 D '54. * *(PA* 29:7284)

74. KARDOS, M. SERAPHIA. *A Comparative Study of the Performance of Twelve-Year-Old Children on the WISC and the Revised Stanford-Binet, Form L, and the Relationship of Both to the California Achievement Tests.* Master's thesis, Marywood College (Scranton, Pa.), 1954.

75. KNOPF, IRWIN J.; MURFETT, BETTY J.; AND MILSTEIN, VICTOR. "Relationships Between the Wechsler-Bellevue Form I and the WISC." *J Clin Psychol* 10:261–3 Jl '54. * *(PA* 29:2449)

76. KOLSTOE, OLIVER P. "A Comparison of Mental Abilities of Bright and Dull Children of Comparable Mental Ages." *J Ed Psychol* 45:161–8 Mr '54. * *(PA* 29:2270)

77. KRALOVICH, ANNE M. *The Effect of Bilingualism on Intelligence Test Scores as Measured by the Wechsler Intelligence Scale for Children.* Master's thesis, Fordham University (New York, N.Y.), 1954.

78. LEHMANN, MARGARET M. *The Basis of Teacher's Choice Between Two Intelligence Tests in an Elementary School.* Master's thesis, Ohio University (Athens, Ohio), 1954.

79. MARTIN, ANTHONY W., AND WIECHERS, JAMES E. "Raven's Colored Progressive Matrices and the Wechsler Intelligence Scale for Children." *J Consult Psychol* 18:143–4 Ap '54. * *(PA* 29:2457)

80. MATYAS, R. P. *A Longitudinal Study of the Revised Stanford-Binet and the WISC.* Master's thesis, Pennsylvania State University (State College, Pa.), 1954.

81. SCHONHORN, ROBERT. "A Comparative Study of the Differences Between Adolescent and Child Male Enuretics and Non-Enuretics as Shown by an Intelligence Test." *Psychol Newsl* 6:1–9 S-O '54. * *(PA* 31:3369)

82. SMITH, LOUIS M., AND FILLMORE, ARLINE R. "The Ammons FRPV Test and the WISC for Remedial Reading Cases." Abstract. *J Consult Psychol* 18:332 O '54. *

83. STARK, ROSEMARY. *A Comparison of Intelligence Test Scores on the Wechsler Intelligence Scale for Children and the Wartegg Drawing Completion Test With School Achievement of Elementary School Children.* Master's thesis, University of Detroit (Detroit, Mich.), 1954.

84. TRIGGS, FRANCES ORALIND; CARTEE, J. KEITH; BINKS, VIRGINIA; FOSTER, DESMOND; AND ADAMS, NICHOLAS A. "The Relationship Between Specific Reading Skills and General Ability at the Elementary and Junior–Senior High School Levels." *Ed & Psychol Meas* 14:176–85 sp '54. * *(PA* 28:8005)

85. YOUNG, F. L. *The Reliability and Validity of the Wechsler Intelligence Scale for Children as Applied to British School Children of Primary School Age.* Master's thesis, University of London (London, England), 1954.

86. YOUNG, FLORENE M., AND BRIGHT, HOWARD A. "Results of Testing 81 Negro Rural Juveniles With the Wechsler Intelligence Scale for Children." *J Social Psychol* 39:219–26 My '54. * *(PA* 29:4094)

87. ABRAMS, JULES C. *A Study of Certain Personality Characteristics of Non-Readers and Achieving Readers.* Doctor's thesis, Temple University (Philadelphia, Pa.), 1955. *(DA* 16:377)

88. ALTUS, GRACE T. "Relationships Between Verbal and Nonverbal Parts of the CTMM and WISC." *J Consult Psychol* 19:143–4 Ap '55. * *(PA* 30:1008)

89. ARMSTRONG, RENATE GERBOTH. "A Reliability Study of a Short Form of the WISC Vocabulary Subtest." *J Clin Psychol* 11:413–4 O '55. * *(PA* 30:5972)

90. ARNOLD, FRANK C., AND WAGNER, WINIFRED K. "A Comparison of Wechsler Children's Scale and Stanford-Binet Scores for Eight- and Nine-Year Olds." *J Exp Ed* 24:91–4 S '55. * *(PA* 30:8121)

91. ATCHISON, CALVIN O. "Use of the Wechsler Intelligence Scale for Children With Eighty Mentally Defective Negro Children." *Am J Mental Def* 60:378–9 O '55. * *(PA* 30:6079)

92. BECK, HARRY S., AND LAM, ROBERT L. "Use of the WISC in Predicting Organicity." *J Clin Psychol* 11:154–8 Ap '55. * *(PA* 30:1202)

93. BURKS, HAROLD F., AND BRUCE, PAUL. "The Characteristics of Poor and Good Readers as Disclosed by the Wechsler Intelligence Scale for Children." *J Ed Psychol* 46:488–93 D '55. * *(PA* 31:3777)

94. CARLETON, FREDERICK O., AND STACEY, CHALMERS L. "An Item Analysis of the Wechsler Intelligence Scale for Children." *J Clin Psychol* 11:149–54 Ap '55. * *(PA* 30:1018)

95. DORIS, ROBERT E. *The Relationship of the Goodenough Draw-A-Man Test to the Wechsler Intelligence Scale for Children: A Study With Mentally Retarded Children in Fresno County, California.* Master's thesis, Fresno State College (Fresno, Calif.), 1955.

96. DUNSDON, M. I. "The Application of Vocabulary Tests to a Large Sample of Children." Abstract. *B Brit Psychol Soc* (26):22 inset My '55. *

97. DUNSDON, M. I., AND ROBERTS, J. A. FRASER. "A Study of the Performance of 2,000 Children on Four Vocabulary Tests: I, Growth Curves and Sex Differences." *Brit J Stat Psychol* 8:3–15 My '55. * *(PA* 30:3363)

98. ESTES, BETSY WORTH. "Influence of Socioeconomic Status

on Wechsler Intelligence Scale for Children: Addendum." *J Consult Psychol* 19:225–6 Je '55. * *(PA* 30:2872)

99. McCULLOCH, THOMAS L.; RESWICK, JOSEPH; AND WEISSMANN, SERENA. "Studies of Word Learning in Mental Defectives: II, Relation to Scores on Digit Repetition, the Stanford-Binet, M, and the WISC Verbal Scale." *Am J Mental Def* 60:140–3 Jl '55. * *(PA* 30:4797)

100. NEWMAN, J. ROBERT, AND LOOS, FRANK M. "Differences Between Verbal and Performance IQ's With Mentally Defective Children on the Wechsler Intelligence Scale for Children." Abstract. *J Consult Psychol* 19:16 F '55. *

101. PRICE, JOHN R., AND THORNE, GARETH D. "A Statistical Comparison of the WISC and Wechsler-Bellevue, Form I." *J Consult Psychol* 19:479–82 D '55. * *(PA* 30:7221)

102. SOSULSKI, MICHAEL C. *A Comparison of the Performance of Matched Pairs Old-Dull and Young-Bright Children on Some Items of the Wechsler Intelligence Scale for Children.* Master's thesis, University of Saskatchewan (Saskatoon, Sask., Canada), 1955.

103. STACEY, CHALMERS L., AND CARLETON, FREDERICK O. "The Relationship Between Raven's Colored Progressive Matrices and Two Tests of General Intelligence." *J Clin Psychol* 11:84–5 Ja '55. * *(PA* 29:7321)

104. STANLEY, JULIAN C. "Statistical Analysis of Scores From Counterbalanced Tests." *J Exp Ed* 23:187–207 Mr '55. * *(PA* 30:1919)

105. YALOWITZ, JEROME M., AND ARMSTRONG, RENATE GERBOTH. "Validity of Short Forms of the Wechsler Intelligence Scale for Children (WISC)." *J Clin Psychol* 11:275–7 Jl '55. * *(PA* 30:2937)

106. ALTUS, GRACE T. "A WISC Profile for Retarded Readers." *J Consult Psychol* 20:155–6 Ap '56. * *(PA* 31:6568)

107. BARRATT, ERNEST S. "The Relationship of the Progressive Matrices (1938) and the Columbia Mental Maturity Scale to the WISC." *J Consult Psychol* 20:294–6 Ag '56. * *(PA* 31:7893)

108. CROFTS, IRENE E. *A Comparison of Urban and Rural Responses to the Wechsler Intelligence Scale for Children.* Master's thesis, University of Manitoba (Winnipeg, Man,, Canada), 1956.

109. GEHMAN, ILA H., AND MATYAS, RUDOLPH P. "Stability of the WISC and Binet Tests." *J Consult Psychol* 20:150–2 Ap '56. * *(PA* 31:6082)

110. RICHARDSON, HELEN M., AND SURKO, ELISE F. "WISC Scores and Status in Reading and Arithmetic of Delinquent Children." *J Genetic Psychol* 89:251–62 D '56. *

111. ROBINOWITZ, RALPH. "Learning the Relation of Opposition as Related to Scores on the Wechsler Intelligence Scale for Children." *J Genetic Psychol* 88:25–30 Mr '56. * *(PA* 31:4710)

112. WALKER, HARRY A. *The Wechsler Intelligence Scale for Children as a Diagnostic Device.* Master's thesis, Utah State Agricultural College (Logan, Utah), 1956.

113. BARRATT, ERNEST S., AND BAUMGARTEN, DORIS L. "The Relationship of the WISC and Stanford-Binet to School Achievement." Abstract. *J Consult Psychol* 21:144 Ap '57. *

114. DUNSDON, M. I., AND ROBERTS, J. A. FRASER. "A Study of the Performance of 2,000 Children on Four Vocabulary Tests: II, Norms, With Some Observations on the Relative Variability of Boys and Girls." *Brit J Stat Psychol* 10:1–16 My '57. *

115. HARLOW, JUSTIN E., JR.; PRICE, ARTHUR COOPER; TATHAM, LOUISE J.; AND DAVIDSON, JACK F. "Preliminary Study of Comparison Between Wechsler Intelligence Scale for Children and Form L of Revised Stanford Binet Scale at Three Age Levels." *J Clin Psychol* 13:72–3 Ja '57. *

116. ISON, M. GAIL. "The Effect of 'Thorazine' on Wechsler Scores." *Am J Mental Def* 62:543–7 N '57. *

117. KELLER, JAMES E. "The Relationship of Auditory Memory Span to Learning Ability in High Grade Mentally Retarded Boys." *Am J Mental Def* 61:574–80 Ja '57. * *(PA* 32:3046)

118. KENT, NORMA, AND DAVIS, D. RUSSELL. "Discipline in the Home and Intellectual Development." *Brit J Med Psychol* 30:27–33 pt 1 '57. * *(PA* 32:3997)

119. LAIRD, DOROTHY S. "The Performance of Two Groups of Eleven-Year-Old Boys on the Wechsler Intelligence Scale for Children." *J Ed Res* 51:101–7 O '57. *

120. MURPHY, L. J. Chap. 10, "Tests of Abilities and Attainments: Pupils in Schools for the Deaf Aged Six to Ten," pp. 213–51. In *Educational Guidance and the Deaf Child.* Edited by A. W. G. Ewing. Manchester, England: Manchester University Press, 1957. Pp. xiii, 345. *

121. SHARP, HEBER C. "A Comparison of Slow Learner's Scores on Three Individual Intelligence Scales." *J Clin Psychol* 13:372–4 O '57. *

122. STROUD, J. B. "The Intelligence Test in School Use: Some Persistent Issues." *J Ed Psychol* 48:77–86 F '57. *

123. STROUD, JAMES B.; BLOMMERS, PAUL; AND LAUBER, MARGARET. "Correlation Analysis of WISC and Achievement Tests." *J Ed Psychol* 48:18–26 Ja '57. * *(PA* 32:4623)

124. VOLLE, FRANK O. "A Proposal for 'Testing the Limits' With Mental Defectives for Purposes of Subtest Analysis of the *WISC* Verbal Scale." *J Clin Psychol* 13:64–7 Ja '57. *

125. WHATLEY, RUTH G., AND PLANT, WALTER T. "The Stability of W.I.S.C. IQ's for Selected Children." *J Psychol* 44:165–7 Jl '57. *

126. WILLIAMS, ROBERT J., AND MACHI, VINCENT S. "An Analysis of Interperson Correlations Among Thirty Psychotics." *J Abn & Social Psychol* 55:50–7 Jl '57. *

127. ALPER, A. E. "A Comparison of the Wechsler Intelligence Scale for Children and the Arthur Adaptation of the Leiter International Performance Scale With Mental Defectives." *Am J Mental Def* 63:312–6 S '58. *

128. COOPER, JAMES G. "Predicting School Achievement for Bilingual Pupils." *J Ed Psychol* 49:31–6 F '58. *

129. FINLEY, CARMEN J., AND THOMPSON, JACK. "An Abbreviated Wechsler Intelligence Scale for Children for Use With Educable Mentally Retarded." *Am J Mental Def* 63:473–80 N '58. *

130. KOPPITZ, ELIZABETH MUNSTERBERG. "Relationships Between the Bender Gestalt Test and the Wechsler Intelligence Test for Children." *J Clin Psychol* 14:413–6 O '58. *

131. LOTSOF, ERWIN J.; COMREY, ANDREW; BOGARTZ, W.; AND ARNSFIELD, P. "A Factor Analysis of the WISC and Rorschach." *J Proj Tech* 22:297–301 S '58. *

132. MATTHEWS, CHARLES GEORGE. *Differential Performances of Non-Achieving Children on the Wechsler Intelligence Scale.* Doctor's thesis, Purdue University (Lafayette, Ind.), 1958. (*DA* 19:878)

133. PORTWOOD, PETER F. "Progress Report on the Sheffield E.S.N. Study." Abstract. *B Brit Psychol Soc* 34:61 Ja '58. *

ELIZABETH D. FRASER, *Lecturer in Psychology, University of Aberdeen, Aberdeen, Scotland.*

In the WISC, as in the Wechsler adult scales, the concept of mental age is abandoned, a step deplored by many who stress the developmental aspect of intelligence, but hailed by those who have long objected to the defects and inconsistencies of this method of arriving at intelligence quotients.

In WISC, a child's performance is compared not with that of children older or younger than himself, but only with that of his own age group: the IQ given him is simply a convenient way of expressing his score in terms of the mean and standard deviation of his peers. This method has certain clear advantages. In the first place, it ensures equal means and standard deviations (100 and 15 respectively) at all ages—in contrast to the Stanford-Binet where SD's range from 12.5 at age 6 to 20.0 at age 12. With equal SD's direct comparison of IQ's of children of different ages is a much simpler affair. In the second place, it is particularly useful in the upper age levels, where the mental age concept begins to break down, and hypothetical mental ages of 22 years and over have previously had to be called into play.

On the other hand, this system throws great onus on the standardisation sample at each age level, especially in the case of the two extremes tested by the WISC, the 5-year-old and the 15-year-old groups. If a child's performance is to be related to that of a sample of his age group, then that sample must be adequate in number and fully representative; further, the sampling of his and their performance on the test must be adequate.

On the first count, there is good reason to believe that the WISC standardisation samples are as a whole a fair cross section of white American children—the manual provides a moderate amount of information about the selection of the sample—but with only 100 boys and 100 girls in each age group the sampling of very bright and very dull children at any one level must necessarily be somewhat scanty. In the Stanford-Binet, with much the same size of sample at each age, for the purposes of norms the numbers are supplemented by those in the age groups above and below.

On the second count, it appears from the manual that in the lowest age groups and especially in the duller members of these age groups, the sampling of test performance is far from adequate. A child of 5-0 to 5-3 does not have to perform at all in order to secure an IQ of 57 on the Verbal Scale and one of 55 on the Performance Scale. Even for an IQ of 80 on the Verbal Scale, a very small sample of his ability is tested. By contrast, the Stanford-Binet at this age taps a much wider range of performance.

The reliability coefficients quoted for the WISC are commendably high, .88 at age 7½, .96 at 10½ and again at 13½ for the Verbal Scale, and .86 at 7½, .89 at 10½ and .90 at 13½ for the Performance Scale, giving overall coefficients .92, .95, and .94 at those ages for the full scale. These are corrected split-half coefficients.

No validity figures for the test are quoted in the manual, and for information on this vital point and on the correlations between WISC and other tests, the user must refer to the rapidly growing literature, which contains many reports of relatively small scale investigations, which in general suggest that WISC and Stanford-Binet correlate fairly highly (.8 plus) and differ little in their ability to predict academic attainment.

The WISC has several very attractive features. It is easy to give, the material is compact and very accessible, and the testing time varies much less than in the Stanford-Binet. These are important practical points for those engaged in routine testing. WISC has the advantage of two scores, Verbal and Performance, and discrepancies between these scores may be of great value to the clinician and to the school.

For use in Great Britain, many items in the WISC are inappropriate as they stand, and a working party of the British Psychological Society has suggested a number of alterations based on the combined testing experience of some of its members. These amendments have been generally adopted, but so far have not been fully standardised. A great deal of work remains to be done on the development of norms before the test can be unreservedly recommended for British children.

To sum up: For testing children who are not outstandingly bright or markedly dull, the WISC is a convenient, reliable instrument which uses up-to-date material intrinsically interesting to the child; for very young children, and for children at the extreme ranges of intelligence, this reviewer still recommends the Stanford-Binet.

GERALD R. PATTERSON, *Assistant Professor of Psychology, University of Oregon, Eugene, Oregon.*

This instrument undoubtedly represents one of the major contributions to the field of intelligence testing with children in the last two decades. Although the standardization is limited to the white population, attention given to obtaining a representative sample makes this one of the better standardized individual tests. Equally rigorous attention has been given to some aspects of reliability with split-half coefficients in the .80's and .90's reported for the verbal and performance sections, and reliabilities in the .90's for the full scale. Needed, however, is information on test-retest consistency over varying lengths of time. This close attention to many of the problems of test construction, plus the use of up-to-date, inherently interesting materials makes it probable that this will be one of the main tools in the psychologists' armamentarium.

One of the features that is particularly appealing is the amount of information available for decision making when using scaled data from 12 subtests. This procedure is consistent with Wechsler's assumption that he is measuring not only a general *g* factor but in addition a set of unspecified group factors. Factor analytic studies of both his previous scales for adults, and the present test for children, indicate that at best only a few dimensions are being tapped (*36, 70*). If the subtests on the WISC did, in fact, measure different factors, perhaps we would have an even better contribution to the psychologist in search of more information about his client.

To some extent the work initiated with the adult scales on patterning has carried over to the children's scale, and with the same equivo-

cal results (*34, 35, 48, 106*). For those tending to psychologize the WISC subtest in the same fashion applied to the adult scales, it should be noted that the scales are related but not equivalent. Although the relationship between IQ's on the adult and children's forms is high, all of the assumptions of equivalence are not met (*75, 101*). The assumption of equivalence is even more tenuous when comparing subtests; here only a few of the correlations reach the .70 range (*101*).

The order of items within subtests correlates very well with a ranking of the items in order of difficulty in a research report by Carleton (*94*). However, in spite of the fact that order is maintained, several clinicians, including the writer, have noted that there seem to be abrupt shifts in some of the subtests from easy to rather difficult material. Research supports this impression showing that the distribution of item difficulty is in general bimodal; that is, the items tend to be either easy or difficult with inadequate sampling of moderately difficult items (*94*).

Within a short span of time, the scale has been subjected to a variety of samples and clinical groups including the deaf (*53*), organics (*92*), Negroes (*91*), and mentally defective children (*42, 46, 63, 100*). Although only one study [1] involving cross-cultural comparisons was noted, it will be surprising if others are not made.

An impressive number of studies have been aimed at validating the WISC particularly as it relates to other measures of intelligence. Respectable relationships have been shown with such tests as *Progressive Matrices* (*79, 103, 107*), *California Test of Mental Maturity* (*88*), *SRA Primary Mental Abilities* (*61*), *Arthur Point Scale of Performance Tests* (*33*), *Full-Range Picture Vocabulary Test* (*82*), and with school achievement (*31, 39, 41*).

With the exception of the age group 5-7 years, the relationship between the Stanford-Binet and the WISC is reported consistently in the range .70 to .90 (*46, 55, 90, 115*). Harlow and others (*115*) with 30 6½-year-olds, and Triggs (*62*) with 46 5-year-olds, report lower relationships (.48 to .64). These findings perhaps reflect a tendency for many psychologists to use the Stanford-Binet at the lower age

[1] ORTAR, G. "Yitsuv mivhan Wechsler liladim b'Israel." *M'gamot* 4:87-100 '52-53. (PA 28:2662)

levels and the WISC for children seven years and older.

As might be expected, the Verbal and Full Scale IQ's on the WISC generally correlate higher with the Stanford-Binet than do the Performance IQ's. Within the average and high ranges of intelligence, one typically finds higher Binet than WISC scores. The discrepancies are particularly marked for the younger age groups and at the higher levels of intelligence (37, 62, 115). On the basis of a slightly smaller standard deviation used for the WISC, one would predict some discrepancies particularly at the extremes in intelligence. However, the discrepancies should not be of the magnitude reported nor should they necessarily vary as a function of age. It should be noted that at these younger ages the standard deviation on the Binet is actually smaller, leading to predictions which are directly opposite to results obtained in the literature. This problem merits further consideration, meanwhile calling for cautious interpretation of results at certain age levels and ranges of intellectual functioning.

The WISC, with some exceptions, is technically a satisfying instrument. The preliminary evidence now available indicates that the test will probably satisfy the major requirements of internal consistency, reliability, and validity. Presenting the psychologist with scaled information about the child's functioning in several areas is certainly a step in the right direction. What we need at this point is an individual test that provides information from factorially independent areas of intellective functioning. Such a test would serve the dual purpose of providing a variety of independent sources of information about the individual child and probably have greater predictive utility for many areas of behavior.

ALBERT I. RABIN, *Professor of Psychology and Director of Psychological Clinic, Michigan State University, East Lansing, Michigan.*

This "downward extension" of the *Wechsler Adult Intelligence Scale,* the adequacy of its standardization, and some of its advantages and disadvantages, were reviewed with a high degree of competence in *The Fourth Mental Measurements Yearbook.* Although, psychometrically, it was considered (and still is) a well standardized and thoughtfully devised test, some of the reviewers felt that the final place of WISC would be determined by the research

done with it. A fair amount of research data is now available.

The problem of validity has been attacked primarily through correlation with older, standardized intelligence tests. High correlations with the Wechsler-Bellevue Form I were obtained ($r = .87$) by Delattre and Cole (34) and Price and Thorne (101). However, correlations were insufficient to meet the criteria for test "equivalence" (101). Correlations between WISC and W-B with defectives are somewhat lower: .72, .54, and .77 on the Full, Verbal, and Performance Scales, respectively (63). The WISC Verbal mean IQ was found to be significantly higher than that of the W-B. In a similar comparison, Knopf and others (75) obtained a higher total WISC IQ as well. An analysis of the subtest correlations further supports the thesis of dissimilarity between the two tests. Generally, the equivalence of the two tests in *individual* cases is very much to be doubted.

WISC correlations with the time honored Stanford-Binet are quite high (37). Yet, despite this fact, sizable discrepancies (5 to 13 points) between the IQ's of 5- and 6-year-olds have been noted. The WISC IQ's tend to be the lower ones. Especially of questionable validity are Picture Arrangement and Coding with children at the lower age range. Although Holland (55) found no relationship between age and IQ discrepancies, Harlow and others (115) obtained lower correlations with 6-year-olds as compared with ages 10 and 14. Most studies report higher Verbal IQ correlations with the Binet than for Performance IQ's.

Barratt and Baumgarten (113) report that the Verbal and Full Scales compare well with the Binet in their prediction of achievement in reading and arithmetic. Estes (51) also reports similar r's (.50's and .60's) with achievers and nonachievers. High r's between the WISC and a variety of other tests such as *Progressive Matrices, California Test of Mental Maturity* and *Columbia Mental Maturity Scale* are also reported in the literature.

The flexibility of the WISC as a research tool has stimulated a good deal of research with special clinical groups (organics, feebleminded, etc.), ethnic (Negro, Mexican) and socioeconomic classes. It probably will continue to be employed as a research tool because of its advantages as a point-scale; it will, like its W-B predecessor, be used to some extent "clinically" as a tool for diagnosis and description of non-intellective factors as well. However, the chief desideratum still remains—that of further investigation of the reliability and validity of this instrument. More longitudinal studies such as the ones reported by Estes (which cast some doubt on the reliability of the WISC) and school achievement prediction studies are needed for the better scientific delineation of this test.

For the present it may be stated that although, in general, the WISC measures the same thing as the Wechsler-Bellevue and the Stanford-Binet, its sensitivity and discrimina-

tion at the lower end of the age range (5-6 years) and at the higher end (14-15 years) are inferior to those of the time honored instruments. Serious difficulties in diagnosis of mental deficiency and discrimination within that category are noted. Probably a refinement of the scale, especially at the lower end, would add greatly to its usefulness. Also, more research will aid in establishing the place of this test more solidly as a psychometric and clinical tool.

For reviews by James M. Anderson, Harold A. Delp, and Boyd R. McCandless, see 4:363 (1 excerpt).

MATHEMATICS

Reviews by *Dorothy C. Adkins, Paul Blommers, Stanley Clark, Frances E. Crook, William Curr, Paul L. Dressel, Reginald Edwards, Harold P. Fawcett, Gordon Fifer, Eric F. Gardner, Joseph Justman, Theodore E. Kellogg, Tom A. Lamke, William Harrison Lucow, Albert E. Meder, Jr., Harold E. Moser, Stanley Nisbet, Robert D. North, Lynnette B. Plumlee, H. Vernon Price, James H. Ricks, Jr., Charles S. Ross, Myron F. Rosskopf, Marion F. Shaycoft, Emma Spaney, Harry L. Stein, George W. Sturrock, John Sutherland, J. Fred Weaver, J. Wayne Wrightstone, and Jack Wrigley.*

[417]

*College Entrance Examination Board Achievement Test in Advanced Mathematics. Candidates for college entrance; 1936-58; for more complete information, see 599; IBM; 60(80) minutes; program administered by Educational Testing Service for the College Entrance Examination Board. *

REFERENCES

1-4. See 4:367.
5. College Entrance Examination Board. *Mathematics: A Description of the College Board Tests in Intermediate and Advanced Mathematics.* Princeton, N.J.: the Board, September 1954. Pp. 27. * (*PA* 29:2957)
6. Douglas, Edwin C. "College Board Examinations and Curriculum Change." *Math Teach* 50:305-8 Ap '57. *
7. Evenson, A. B., and Smith, D. E. "A Study of Matriculation in Alberta." *Alberta J Ed Res* 4:67-83 Je '58. *

For a review by Paul L. Dressel, see 4:367.

[418]

*College Entrance Examination Board Achievement Test in Intermediate Mathematics. Candidates for college entrance; 1936-58; for more complete information, see 599; IBM; 60(80) minutes; program administered by Educational Testing Service for the College Entrance Examination Board. *

REFERENCES

1-2. See 4:368.
3. College Entrance Examination Board. *Mathematics: A Description of the College Board Tests in Intermediate and Advanced Mathematics.* Princeton, N.J.: the Board, September 1954. Pp. 27. * (*PA* 29:2957)
4. Douglas, Edwin C. "College Board Examinations and Curriculum Change." *Math Teach* 50:305-8 Ap '57. *
5. Evenson, A. B., and Smith, D. E. "A Study of Matriculation in Alberta." *Alberta J Ed Res* 4:67-83 Je '58. *

For a review by Paul J. Blommers of earlier forms, see 4:368.

[419]

★College Entrance Examination Board Advanced Placement Examination: Mathematics. High school seniors desiring credit for college level courses; 1954-58; for more complete information, see 600; 2 scores: objective, total; IBM in part; 180(200) minutes; program administered by Educational Testing Service for the College Entrance Examination Board. *

REFERENCE

1. Douglas, Edwin C. "The College Entrance Examination Board's Examination for Advanced Placement in Mathematics." *Math Teach* 50:458-61 O '57. *

Paul L. Dressel, *Director of Evaluation Services, Michigan State University, East Lansing, Michigan.* [Review of Form FBP.]

Part 1 of this examination is made up of 30 multiple choice items for which 60 minutes of working time are permitted. Part 2 is a free answer section composed of 10 problems, for which 120 minutes is allowed. Scores on Part 1 $(R - W/4)$ are translated to a scale of 1 to 15. Each of the 10 questions on Part 2 is rated on a 15-point scale. The maximum total score, 10 Part 1 + 2 Part 2, is 450. In the 1957 administration, observed scores ranged from 6 to

432, with a mean of 184.5 and a standard deviation of 94.5. These scores were finally translated to a scale of 1–5, 5 indicating high honors and 1 indicating failure, the scale being determined by comparison with the performance of college students who took the test. Presumably, this sequence of transformations was dictated in part by the committee of mathematicians who made and scored the examination and in part by the desirability of reporting scores for all fields on the same basis, but it seems unnecessarily complicated.

The reliability of Part 1, obtained by Kuder-Richardson formula 20 is reported as .80. This is identical with the correlation reported between Part 1 and Part 2. No evidence on the reliability of ratings or scores is presented for Part 2. Item statistics demonstrate a lack of easy items. This indication of difficulty is reinforced by evidence that over 25 per cent of the scores on Part 1 were in the chance area.

The test is unduly difficult, not primarily because the actual tasks demanded involve anything novel, but because many of the functions chosen present unnecessary complications. Whether based on the desire to make the very best student aware of his limitations or on an overoptimistic conception of results of college work in analytic geometry and calculus, the difficulty may have the unfortunate effect of discouraging advanced placement candidates and programs in mathematics. In this connection it should be emphasized that test difficulty and standards are by no means identical. Because of the high percentage of scores in the chance area it is difficult to be sure just how high the standards are, even though the 3 rating is so determined that about 50 per cent of a group of college students fall below it. What is here a matter of concern is that the reaction will be to difficulty rather than to standards.

The test is largely traditional in content. Although the brochure describing the program recommends alterations in mathematics courses in grades 9–11 to give more attention to objectives involving aspects of deductive reasoning both in mathematical and in life situations, there is nothing in this examination which would make it apparent to teacher or student that the committee preparing this examination was really concerned with such objectives. Instead, the emphasis appears to have been on the inclusion in the examination of as many as possible of the processes and types of problems commonly found in calculus textbooks. Perhaps this is inevitable if the examination is to create the necessary favorable reactions to the program among members of college mathematics staffs. However, it may encourage the development of 12th grade courses emphasizing problem solution rather than basic understandings, a development hardly consistent with the recommendations for courses for the preceding years.

In summary, the examination is an unnecessarily difficult one which covers thoroughly the topics and problems of analytic geometry and differential and integral calculus. Students receiving a 5 or a 4 rating should certainly be granted advanced placement and, depending on the quality of work in a particular college, those with a 3 rating deserve consideration for such placement. This, after all, is the purpose of the examination.

[420]
*Cooperative General Achievement Tests: Test III, Mathematics. Grade 12 and college entrants; 1937–56; manual uses the subtitle *A Test of General Proficiency in the Field of Mathematics;* 3 scores: terms and concepts, comprehension and interpretation, total; IBM; Forms XX ('53, revision of Form X), YZ ('51, revision of Forms Y and Z); no norms for part scores; high school norms same as those published in 1938; separate answer sheets must be used; $2.95 per 25 tests; $1 per 25 IBM answer sheets; 25¢ per scoring stencil; 35¢ per battery manual ('56); $1 per specimen set; postage extra; 40(50) minutes; Paul J. Burke (XX); Cooperative Test Division, Educational Testing Service. *

For a review by John F. Randolph of earlier forms, see 3:316. For a review by Max D. Engelhart of the complete battery, see 6; for a review by Paul L. Dressel of earlier forms, see 4:5; for a review by John V. McQuitty, see 3:3.

[421]
Cooperative Mathematics Tests for Grades 7, 8, and 9. Grades 7–9; 1938–50; 5 scores: skills, facts-terms-concepts, application, appreciation, total; IBM; Forms X ('47), Y ('48); no specific manual; descriptive sheet ('50, same as sheet copyrighted in 1940; general Cooperative manual ('51); norms ['40]; $3.25 per 25 tests; separate answer sheets may be used; $1 per 25 IBM answer sheets; 25¢ per scoring stencil; postage extra; $1 per specimen set, postpaid; 80(85) minutes; Vernon Price (X) and Bernice Orshansky (Y); Cooperative Test Division, Educational Testing Service. *

REFERENCES
1–2. See 40:1433.
3. See 3:305.
4–5. See 4:370.
6. JUSTMAN, JOSEPH, AND FORLANO, GEORGE. "The Performance of Academic and Vocational High School Pupils on the Cooperative Mathematics Test." *Math Teach* 45:267–8 Ap '52. *

GORDON FIFER, *Research Psychologist, Test Research Service, Bronxville, New York; and Lecturer in Education, Hunter College, New York, New York.*

Forms X and Y have been in print for over 10 years and have been widely used during this time. Although the test represents a somewhat traditional approach to the measurement of mathematical ability, it is hoped that it will be continued in print and that the publisher will provide revised norms and interpretative materials. There will always be a need for measuring instruments designed to evaluate the achievement of specific skills and knowledges.

The face validity of the test is excellent. Part 1, Skills, has a reasonably good coverage of the fundamental operations that most pupils should be expected to acquire by the time they reach the seventh or eighth grade. Part 2, Facts, Terms, and Concepts, is somewhat brief, containing only 30 items, but it covers many of the essential outcomes expected at this level. Possibly the least adequate section of the test is Part 3, Application. Most of the items in this section are similar to the arithmetic reasoning items that appear in arithmetic tests year after year. Perhaps the very fact that this type of item has been repeated so often is an indication of its having some validity. Part 4, Appreciation, would be more appropriately called "interpretation," since most of the items measure the ability to interpret numerical data and symbols. Many of the most interesting items are in this section of the test.

The format of the test is, in general, quite good. The type used is legible, the items are well spaced on the pages, and the item sequence is easy to follow. However, the repetition of item numbers opposite each choice not only seems unnecessary at this level but also tends to clutter the pages. In addition, on a test containing so much numerical data, it would be desirable to use capital letters (A, B, C, D, E) rather than numbers to identify the choices. Organization of the test so that the four parts have separate time limits forces the examinee to give an appropriate amount of time to each test area. This is certainly a desirable provision if the part scores are to be at all reliable.

Very little information is given about the standardization of the test and most of the data that are supplied were derived from earlier forms. The percentile norms would be much more useful if some descriptive information about the schools participating in the standardization were provided. It is extremely unfortunate that no separate manual has ever been prepared for use with this test. The materials provided for use with the various Cooperative tests are much too general to be of value to the person untrained in measurement. Further, the comments on the interpretation of percentile scores and on uses of the tests are superficial and inadequate. The mention of the standard error of measurement is haphazard and confusing, and no explanation is given regarding the use of the standard error confidence intervals in interpreting the percentile scores.

No reliability or validity data are supplied for Forms X and Y. Since these two forms were obviously carefully developed as parallel forms of the same test, it seems incredible that the publisher has never obtained a parallel-forms reliability estimate. One is forced to fall back on the data supplied for Form P, copyrighted in 1939. These data indicate reasonably good reliability estimates for the earlier form, which supposedly is comparable to Forms X and Y.

This mathematics test could be of value to any teacher or counselor interested in evaluating student mastery of many of the basic skills, facts, concepts, terms, and applications of mathematics that are taught prior to or during grades 7, 8, and 9. The test is aimed more at fundamental skills than at meaningful interpretations or applications, but it would be of considerable value in selecting pupils ready for the algebra sequence and pupils in need of remedial work. The supplementary materials provided are fragmentary and incomplete. The usability and interpretability of the test would be immeasurably increased by the publication of a separate manual that synthesized and amplified the many bits of information now provided on separate sheets. A technical report of some kind is needed that would provide data on reliability and validity.

For a review by M. L. Hartung of earlier forms, see 3:305; for reviews by Richard M. Drake, Judson W. Foust, and G. M. Ruch, see 40:1433.

[422]

Davis Test of Functional Competence in Mathematics: Evaluation and Adjustment Series. Grades 9–12; 1951–52, c1950–51; IBM; Forms AM ('51), BM ('52); manual ('51); separate answer sheets must be used; $4.15 per 35 tests; $1.40 per 35 IBM answer sheets; postage extra; 35¢ per specimen set, postpaid; 80(90) minutes; David J. Davis; World Book Co. *

REFERENCES

1. PITTS, RAYMOND J. "Relationship Between Functional Competence in Mathematics and Reading Grade Levels, Mental Ability, and Age." *J Ed Psychol* 43:486–92 D '52. * (*PA* 27:7383)
2. MIRES, KATHERINE C. "General Mathematics for College Freshmen." *Math Teach* 50:513–6 N '57. *

PAUL L. DRESSEL, *Director of Evaluation Services, Michigan State University, East Lansing, Michigan.*

On the whole, this test would seem to be a useful instrument, appealing to many teachers in that the exercises depart only modestly from the formal patterns of much mathematics testing. The functional competence which the test attempts to measure involves somewhat less of the practical application to problems having real significance to the student than one might assume from the title. Consumer problems are included, but, although there are exercises and novel twists which require a degree of insight and understanding, most of the material is quite reminiscent of textbook exercises. The items have been carefully selected to cover the areas and objectives stated in the manual. The two forms have been equated with care and the statistical procedures in selecting items, in developing standard scores, in determining reliability, and in norming are adequate. Validity would seem to be justifiably assumed because of the criteria used in selecting the problems.

There are, however, a few inconsistencies and misleading statements in the manual. Thus the manual, page 2, speaks of "the objectives measured" as though a score would be provided for each objective. Again, on page 7, there is a statement that "this measure....permits the teacher to determine how well the student has succeeded in mastering those objectives" which are covered by the test. Only on page 8, finally, is it definitely stated, "The test, however, is not designed as a diagnostic instrument: it does not furnish analytical measures of the individual student's mastery of the various aspects of the subject." The manual also claims for the test the measurement of such objectives as: (*a*) "Is he mathematically conditioned for satisfactory adjustment to a first job in business?" (*b*) "Does he have a basis for dealing intelligently with the main problems of the consumer?" (*c*) "Can he analyze given facts or assumptions and draw valid conclusions from those assumptions?" These are indeed large orders which the test does not and could not deliver.

There could be a modest statement to the effect that these objectives have been considered in selecting the materials included in the test, but they should not be listed as "objectives measured."

In the discussion of the use of test results, it is claimed that the test "may reasonably be assumed to be prognostic of success in later work in the field of mathematics." No substantiating evidence is available. Neither is there any evidence to relate achievement to the amount of mathematics taken, although the equating of the scores to standard scores on the *Terman-McNemar Test of Mental Ability* does permit account to be taken of ability.

The test is adequate. The manual is slightly immodest in its claims.

TOM A. LAMKE, *Coordinator of Research, Iowa State Teachers College, Cedar Falls, Iowa.*

Based on objectives set forth by the Commission on Post-War Plans of the National Council of Teachers of Mathematics, on other objectives mentioned in the professional literature, and on textbook analysis, this test was designed to "determine the student's general level of functional competence in mathematics" throughout the high school years. The test is administered in two 40-minute periods, and contains 80 multiple choice items. Format of test and manuals is satisfactory.

For the most part the test questions deal with matters in everyday life requiring competence in mathematics, or with fundamental mathematics skills or concepts. Certain questions require understandings somewhat removed from some high school mathematics courses. For example, to answer one question correctly, the student must know that stubs of checks should be filled out before rather than after the checks have been used. The keyed answer to another question of this type states that the installment plan cost is always more than the cash price of an article. Before using the test the test user should assure himself, by taking the test, that his view of functional mathematics accords with that of the test author.

In spite of the fact that some care was taken in item and test construction, split-half test reliabilities are generally in the .80's. No indication is given of the form or forms used in establishing the single-form reliabilities reported.

The standard error of measurement is reported as ranging from 4.9 to 5.9 standard score points. In the ninth grade the result is that in the middle score range the percentile band covering the standard score plus and minus the standard error of score is an undesirable 30 to 40 percentile points. The manual does well to point out the importance of the standard error of measurement; perhaps even more conservative and detailed statements might have been used.

Middle and end-of-year percentile norms are supplied for grades 9 through 12. Data given for the norms groups comprise only number, median age, and median intelligence score (all by grade), and the statement that the students came from 31 schools in 19 states. No evidence is presented showing that the standardizing group resembles a defined larger population in important respects, nor is there any indication that the standardizing group is a statistically based sample of some larger population. It is, then, difficult to know just how to generalize from the norms group to a population which is of practical importance.

Standard scores are supplied for the test which are related to standard scores on the *Terman-McNemar Test of Mental Ability.* The statement is made that a comparison of the student's standard score on the Davis test with his Terman-McNemar standard score will indicate the extent and direction of the difference between his mathematics achievement and mental maturity level. Such a comparison is suspect for the same reason that the reported norms are of dubious value. The relationship between mental maturity and mathematics scores found in the group used to norm the mathematics test is not one that would necessarily hold in a statistically based sample of some important parent population of high school students.

This test will be most useful to those subscribing to the objectives of mathematics education set forth by the Commission on Post-War Plans of the National Council of Teachers of Mathematics. The test norms are neither much better nor much worse than those for other tests of this kind; very likely the most useful norms will be those established by a local school system or several cooperating systems over a period of time. As is usual with subject matter tests, the test user should assure himself that test content accords with his own curriculum to an acceptable degree. The best way he can do this is to take the test himself. If he finds the content appropriate for his own courses—and in many cases he will—the convenience of giving and scoring a published test which has been constructed with attention to technical considerations may argue for the use of this test in preference to teacher made tests.

[423]

*General Mathematics: Every Pupil Scholarship Test.** High school; 1926–58; new form usually issued each January and April; norms available following testing program; no data on reliability; 4¢ per test; 4¢ per scoring key; postage extra; 40(45) minutes; Bureau of Educational Measurements. *

[424]

★General Mathematics: Midwest High School Achievement Examinations.** High school; 1955–57; Forms A ('55), B ('57, identical with Form 2 of *General Mathematics III: Achievement Examinations for Secondary Schools* copyrighted in 1952); no specific manual; series manual ('57); no data on reliability; norms: [A, '55; B, '57]; 10¢ per test, postage extra; Form A: 60(65) minutes; Form B: 90[95] minutes; Joy Hamrin (A) and J. R. Schunert (B); Educational Test Bureau. *

[425]

*General Mathematics III: Achievement Examinations for Secondary Schools.** High school; 1951–53; Forms 1 ('51), 3 ('53); no specific manual; no data on reliability; norms: Forms 1 ['52], 3 ('53); 10¢ per test, postage extra; [60–90] minutes; J. R. Schunert (1) and Wallace M. Bernards (3); Educational Test Bureau. *

[426]

*General Mathematical Ability.** High school; 1944–57; subtest of *Tests of General Educational Development;* IBM; Form B ('44); revised manual ('56); $2.50 per 25 tests; separate answer sheets must be used; $1 per 25 IBM answer sheets; 50¢ per specimen set; postage extra; (120) minutes; prepared by Examination Staff of United States Armed Forces Institute; Veterans' Testing Service, American Council on Education. *

[427]

*The Graduate Record Examinations Advanced Tests: Mathematics.** College seniors and graduate students; 1939–57; for more complete information, see 601; IBM; 180(200) minutes; Educational Testing Service. *

REFERENCE

1. SCHULTZ, MARGARET K., AND ANGOFF, WILLIAM H. "The Development of New Scales for the Aptitude and Advanced Tests of the Graduate Record Examinations." *J Ed Psychol* 47: 285–94 My '56. * (*PA* 32:2127)

ERIC F. GARDNER, *Professor of Education and Psychology, University of Syracuse, Syracuse, New York.*

This test consists of 75 multiple choice items. The items are, in general, well constructed and measure mathematical competence over a wide range of ability. The reliability is high, .95 for a normative group, with a standard deviation of 181.

Of special interest are some of the methods of interpreting scores on the Graduate Record Examinations. Both scaled scores and percentile scores are used. All conversions from raw scores to scaled scores are done by means of equations expressing linear relationships between raw and scaled scores. This process does not change either the shape of the raw score distribution or the rank order of scores within the distribution. Initially, scales were established for advanced tests so that 500 was the mean scaled score on each particular test for a group of college seniors majoring in the field covered by the test, and the standard deviation of their scores was 100.

In 1952 a new method of deriving scales for advanced tests was introduced. An examination of the aptitude scores for candidates taking different advanced tests showed marked differences with respect to level and range of ability from one field to another. The new scales were devised to take into account differences among subject matter groups in aptitude test performance. A group consisting of 2,095 graduating seniors, 686 women and 1,409 men from 11 different colleges, was used as a scaling population. Each student took the verbal and quantitative parts of the Aptitude Test as well as the advanced test in his own particular field. For each advanced test subgroup, regression coefficients were determined for predicting advanced test scores from a linear combination of verbal and quantitative aptitude test scores. Estimations were then made of the raw score mean and variance of the entire standardization group of 2,095 on each advanced test, utilizing the regression coefficients and also the measured differences between the entire group and each advanced test subgroup on the two aptitude test scores. The estimates of the raw score mean and variance of the entire standardization group on the advanced mathematics test were used in linear transformations to obtain scaled scores with a mean of 500 and a standard deviation of 100 for the entire standardization group. Hence, the new mean scaled score earned by the normative subgroup taking the advanced mathematics test was a larger value than 500 due to its superior performance on the Aptitude Test as compared with the candidates in many of the other fields. In 1954 a revision of the advanced mathematics test was made and comparable scaled scores were obtained, using the same basic procedure.

It should be pointed out that the present scaling procedure does not claim to give comparability of achievement. A score of 600 on the mathematics test does not represent the same level of achievement in mathematics that a score of 600 on the literature test represents in that field. Attempts have been made to adjust achievement scores for differences in ability only among the several groups.

It should also be noted that the scaling of the mathematics test would tend to be somewhat unreliable in view of the small number of cases ($n = 81$ for the original scaling) and the low multiple correlation coefficient of .47 between advanced mathematics test scores and the two aptitude predictors. In the extreme case, where the multiple correlation is zero, the scale resulting would be identical with one obtained by the original method of scaling the Graduate Record Examinations.

Although the reviewer is well aware of the great advantages in having comparability from one subject to another for subtests in an achievement test battery where students take all subjects, he is not convinced that there are equal merits in the application of the present scaling procedure. There are certain advantages in being able to interpret a score of 500 as the mean performance of mathematics majors on the advanced mathematics test rather than as the estimated average score of the entire group, most of whom were not mathematics majors. It seems to the reviewer that this application of statistical eruditeness to remove differences in ability between majors in the various fields results in scores which convey less useful information.

Well written pamphlets, including the Handbook for Deans and Examiners, the Score Interpretation Handbook for Deans and Advisors, and Summary Statistics, are available to describe the program, including the appropriate use of the tests. There is also a report on a study of the practices in 377 institutions participating in the GRE Institutional Testing Program 1955–1956, which provides useful information for institutions using the Graduate Record Examinations.

In general, the *Graduate Record Examinations Advanced Tests: Mathematics* is a sound examination which deserves serious consideration from those who wish to test the mathematical achievement of their graduating mathematics majors and those who wish objective information to assist them in recommending graduate work involving mathematical competence.

For a review by Harold Seashore of the entire series, see 601.

[428]
*The Iowa Tests of Educational Development: Test 4, Ability to Do Quantitative Thinking. Grades 9–13; 1942–58; IBM; Forms X-3S, Y-3S ('52); examiner's manual ('58); battery manual ('54); pupil profile leaflet, fourth edition ('58); profile card (no date); separate answer sheets must be used; $3 per 20 tests; $5 per 100 IBM answer sheets; 50¢ per hand and machine scoring stencil; $3 per complete specimen set; postage extra; 65(75) or 40(50) minutes; prepared under the direction of E. F. Lindquist; Science Research Associates. *

For reviews by J. Murray Lee and Stephen Wiseman of the complete battery, see 17; for a review by Eric F. Gardner of earlier forms, see 4:17; for reviews by Henry Chauncey, Gustav J. Froehlich, and Lavone A. Hanna, see 3:12.

[429]
*Junior High School Mathematics Test: Acorn Achievement Tests. Grades 7–9; 1942–52; 4 scores: concepts, problem analysis, problems, total; Forms A ('52, identical with test copyrighted in 1942 except for minor changes), B ('42); directions sheet ('42); teachers' guide ['44]; no norms for part scores; $2.75 per 25 tests; 50¢ per specimen set; postage extra; 52(60) minutes; Harry Eisner; Acorn Publishing Co. *

MYRON F. ROSSKOPF, *Professor of Mathematics, Teachers College, Columbia University, New York, New York.*

The test's purpose is to furnish a measure of a junior high school student's (*a*) mastery of correct concepts of measures, elementary geometry, and elementary algebra; (*b*) ability to analyze a problem; and (*c*) skill in carrying through the solution of a problem. The 4-page manual and answer key give meager information concerning validity, reliability, and norms. No information concerning variability is given.

The two forms are intended to be parallel, and perhaps they do give comparable scores. It is doubtful, however, that they test the same concepts, since a problem on one form often involves the inverse operation of its corresponding problem on the other. For example, a question in Form A requires a student to find the distance in miles between two cities, given the scale of the map and the scale measurement in inches between them. The supposedly parallel question in Form B requires the computation of the scale used when the scale measurement and the actual distance are given. Although the two problems are intimately related, it is clear one tests in a multiplication and the other in a division situation.

The test problems, which are reasonably well written, are representative of the subject matter contained in typical junior high school textbooks. One might say that the two forms are excellent examples of teacher-made tests. They do not, however, qualify as standardized tests because of the inadequacy of the statistical data for satisfactory interpretation of student scores.

For a review by William Betz, see 3:310.

[430]
★Kansas Mathematics Test, Revised Edition. Grades 9–13; 1937(?)–55; 2 scores: arithmetic, algebra; IBM; Forms A ('53), B ('55); manual ('55); $1.45 per 25 tests; separate answer sheets may be used; 85¢ per 25 IBM answer sheets; 30¢ per scoring stencil; 50(60) minutes; H. E. Schrammel; Bureau of Educational Measurements. *

PAUL BLOMMERS, *Professor of Education, State University of Iowa, Iowa City, Iowa.*

According to both the catalog and the manual, this test is intended for determining the level of mathematical proficiency of students completing high school or entering college. The test is organized into two parts: the first deals with the fundamental operations applied to integers and to common and decimal fractions, with per cents, and to some extent with arithmetic reasoning; the second deals with elementary algebraic manipulation and the solution of simple equations, and includes a few of the usual type of verbal problem found in beginning algebra or general mathematics texts. The two forms are almost perfect paraphrases of one another. On the whole the exercises are traditional and textbookish in character and setting, and require at most a rather low level of proficiency. Granting the difficulty level of the test to be appropriate for graduating high school or entering college students (the median for the latter group is reported as about half the highest possible score), it would seem to follow that the proficiency level currently demanded of such students must be disturbingly low.

No evidence is reported regarding the validity of this test for such possible uses as the selection of promising students of mathematics, the counseling of students, the identification of mathematically deficient students and of their particular deficiencies, or the placement of students within a first year college mathematics program. The only statement contained in the manual regarding validity is to the effect that the test is based on the judgment of competent high school and college mathematics instructors, on textbook content studies, and on studies of student errors on previous editions. Thus its validity as a measure of the mathematical proficiency level of graduating high school and entering college students is largely a judgmental issue. This being the case, it can only be said that this test does not assess the type of insights and understandings which in this reviewer's judgment ought to rank high among the important outcomes of high school mathematics instruction.

The reliability is reported as .87 for a sample of 650 beginning college students, a value which should be reasonably adequate though information is lacking as to the experimental design employed in arriving at this estimate.

Percentile norms for both parts and for the total score are given for high school and college students. The high school norms are wholly inadequate, being based on only 87 students. The college norms are based on the performance of 1,295 entering freshmen, but no description is given as to the type of college involved. An indication of the inadequacy of the high school norms is to be found in the fact that the reported high school median is 11 points higher than that reported for entering college students. This phenomenon, incidently, is explained by the remark that the scores on which high school norms are based were submitted by schools which had classes studying general mathematics, whereas most of the students involved in the establishment of the college norms had never had such a course. This suggests that the type of college for which the college norms might be appropriate is one which requires little or no training in mathematics for admission. The inadequacy of the high school norms is further illustrated by the fact that for Part 1 a higher than possible score is reported as the 99th percentile. It is also stated in the manual that the norms may be used for interpreting both individual and group scores, a claim clearly impossible of accomplishment with a single set of norms. Furthermore, no description of the type of group for which they conceivably might be appropriate is given.

In summary, this test appears to deal with only a highly limited segment of a sound high school mathematics program and with this at a rather elementary level. Its stated purpose is so general as to be vague, leaving little to be said regarding its validity. Its reliability is probably reasonably adequate. For all practical purposes the high school norms are too inadequately determined to justify reporting. The college norms are based on a more adequate sample of students but are probably unique to certain types of colleges.

[431]

*Mathematical Literacy for High School Seniors: A Test of Basic Skills and Abilities. Grade 12; 1946–53; 4 scores: terms and formulas, computational skills, solving problems, total; Forms A, B ['52]; mimeographed manual ['53]; no data on reliability; 3¢ per test; cash orders postpaid; 60(70) minutes; Ohio Scholarship Tests. *

[432]

*Mathematics: Every Pupil Test. Grades 7–8; 1930–58; new form usually issued each December and April; norms available following testing program; no data on reliability; 3¢ per test; 1¢ per scoring key; cash orders postpaid; 40(45) minutes; Ohio Scholarship Tests. *

[433]

★Mathematics: National Teacher Examinations. College seniors and teachers; 1940–58; for more complete information, see 538; IBM; 80(90) minutes; Educational Testing Service. *

For reviews by William A. Brownell, Walter W. Cook, and Lawrence G. Derthick of the entire series, see 538; for a review by Harry N. Rivlin of an earlier edition, see 4:802.

[434]

★Mathematics: Teacher Education Examination Program. College seniors preparing to teach secondary school; 1957; for more complete information, see 543; IBM; 80(95) minutes; Educational Testing Service. *

For a review by Walter W. Cook of the entire series, see 543.

[435]

★Mathematics Test (Adv.). Ages 12–14.0; 1954–58; form 1 adapted from an experimental edition by A. F. Watts and J. E. Stuart; title on form 1 is *Arithmetic Test (Adv.)* 1; forms 1 ['54], 2 ['57], 3 ['58]; manuals ('57–58); distribution restricted to directors of education; 8s. 3d. per 12 tests; 9d. per single copy; 1s. 7d. per manual; postage extra; prices include British purchase tax; 50(55) minutes; D. A. Pidgeon (1); published for National Foundation for Educational Research in England and Wales; Newnes Educational Publishing Co. Ltd. *

[436]

Mathematics Test 1. Ages 12 to 13-11; 1951–52; 1 form ('51); norms ['52]; 9s. per 12 tests; 10d. per single copy; 1s. 8d. per manual ['52]; postage extra; 65(70) minutes; I. Macfarlane Smith; published for National Foundation for Educational Research in England and Wales; Newnes Educational Publishing Co. Ltd. *

JACK WRIGLEY, *Lecturer in the Teaching of Mathematics, Institute of Education, University of London, London, England.*

This test is an interesting attempt to provide a standardised objective test of elementary mathematics for British secondary modern pupils. Secondary modern schools are nonselective and very varied in character. Since their inception, they have not been subject to the influence of standardised examinations, and have been free to experiment and develop in their own way. This has led to great differences in the mathematics curricula of these schools. In consequence, it is difficult to design a single test equally suitable for all such schools. The principle adopted here has evidently been one of "minimum essentials," that is, that the test content should reflect only the basic parts of a mathematical curriculum for secondary modern schools. The test implies a syllabus which would be the basis of a mathematics curriculum, but by no means the whole of the curriculum. A test produced by such a principle might be dull, confined to uninteresting essentials. But this pitfall has been avoided; the test is interesting and stimulating and could hardly have a restrictive influence. The subject matter is modern in outlook and reflects the present trend towards realistic mathematics. In addition to mechanical arithmetic items, there are some sensible problems and attempts to measure whether the child can read simple tables, graphs, and diagrams.

The test was standardised on a sample of 6,911 pupils in the age range 12-0 to 13-11, attending all types of schools in an urban and rural area. The standardised scores produced (mean 100 and SD 15) resemble standardised scores derived from an intelligence test. However, with any test of this type, significant differences will occur between schools in average score and in rate of development; thus, a test score should be interpreted cautiously. A significant sex difference of 6.08 in mean raw scores was found in favour of boys, yet the conversion table does not separate boys from girls.

In summary, this is an interesting, well produced test employing a modern approach to mathematics for the average child. The test samples a wide field of elementary mathematics and is not restrictive in character. It is adequately standardised, but any score derived should be used with care. A high score would almost certainly imply good teaching and good ability, but a low score might be due to lack of knowledge not indicative of either bad teaching or lack of ability. In other words, the principle of "minimum essentials" has not been fully implemented. Nevertheless, the test constructors are to be congratulated for a bold attempt at an almost impossible task.

[437]
*The Morgan Achievement Test in Mathematics for Employee Selection. Adults; 1942–46; 1 form ('46, identical with *Rogers Achievement Test in Mathematics for Technical and Industrial Schools* copyrighted in 1942); directions sheet ['46]; no data on reliability and validity; $2.50 per 25 tests; 50¢ per specimen set; cash orders postpaid; 30(35) minutes; William J. Morgan; Aptitude Associates. *

MARION F. SHAYCOFT, *Program Director, American Institute for Research, Washington, D.C.*

"Morgan Achievement Test in Arithmetic" would perhaps be a somewhat better name for this test, since none of the problems requires anything beyond eighth grade arithmetic. The 54 items are about equally divided among addition, subtraction, multiplication, and division problems. Problems involving whole numbers, decimals, and common fractions are all included. Half the items simply call for arithmetic computation while the other half involve simple arithmetic reasoning problems—problems in which it is necessary to decide what computational procedure to use and then to apply it correctly. The problems are couched in terms of industrial and trade applications.

The manual consists of three typed pages which contain a description of the test, instructions for administration, instructions for scoring, and percentile norms. According to the description of the test which appears in the manual, it is designed to measure the ability to "use simple arithmetic and mathematics in the solution of practical problems * [It] is especially useful in selecting apprentices and employees for skilled and semi-skilled trades and occupations with technical and industrial companies." The test, it is said, can be used for "any occupation which requires the employee to deal with numbers and figures, whether by computation or by measurement." This latter statement is highly questionable. There is little or no reason to believe that the ability to measure, which can be conceived as a kind of task in spatial perception, is highly related to the ability to compute accurately. Ability to compute is measured by the test; ability to measure is *not*.

The manual gives no indication about reliability or validity of the test, or about the manner of construction. Percentile norms based on "a random sample of 1479 industrial workers engaged in skilled and semi-skilled trades whose work required computation and measurement in arithmetic and mathematics" are presented. The manual suggests using the 50th percentile as the critical score for employment in relevant occupations. The development of private norms is also suggested. For comparison with the percentile norms described above, percentile norms based on 1,133 grammar school graduates, ages 16 to 25, who were applicants for unskilled employment, are also presented. The norms for this group are systematically lower, as might be expected.

The manual suggests ranking the examinees on their scores, because "comparison by ranks are useful in the analysis and classification of different vocational groups." Just what advantages are to be derived from this procedure that cannot be more simply and better obtained from raw scores or percentiles is not at all clear.

Thirty minutes testing time is allowed; this probably represents a degree of speeding.

The test is suitable for group administration. The directions for administration, though brief, are adequate, except for the omission of specific instructions to the examinee on how to handle decimals—for instance, whether to round off answers to a specified number of decimal places. This omission could lead to some confusion. The scoring instructions are adequate. However, the key, which is a copy of the test with the answers overprinted in red, would not lend itself to efficient scoring of a large number of tests—despite the fact that the manual says that "the test can be given just as easily to hundreds in a group as to a single individual."

Some of the diagrams, which are not very clearly drawn or labeled, contribute little to the solution of the problems. In general, the items are clearly worded, although one or two are deficient in this respect.

In summary, the *Morgan Achievement Test in Mathematics* is a test designed for personnel selection in industry and trade which appears to give some indication of facility in handling arithmetic problems. Its major deficiency is its very inadequate manual, the contents of which fail at many points to meet the standards presented in the American Psychological Association's *Technical Recommendations for Psychological Tests and Diagnostic Techniques* (1954).

[438]

★Sequential Tests of Educational Progress: Mathematics. Grades 4–6, 7–9, 10–12, 13–14; 1956–57; IBM; Forms A, B ('57); 4 levels; manual ('57); battery directions ('57); battery technical report ('57); no data on reliability of Form B; separate answer sheets must be used; $3.95 per 20 tests; $1 per 20 IBM scorable answer sheets; 45¢ per scoring stencil; $1 per manual; $1 per battery technical report; $1.25 per specimen set; postage extra; 70(90–100) minutes; Cooperative Test Division, Educational Testing Service. *

a) LEVEL 4. Grades 4–6; Forms 4A, 4B.
b) LEVEL 3. Grades 7–9; Forms 3A, 3B.
c) LEVEL 2. Grades 10–12; Forms 2A, 2B.
d) LEVEL 1. Grades 13–14; Forms 1A, 1B.

PAUL L. DRESSEL, *Director of Evaluation Services, Michigan State University, East Lansing, Michigan.*

As described in the prospectus the mathematics tests of the STEP battery were developed around a set of concepts derived from vertical analysis of the mathematics curriculum. Mastery of these concepts is tested by problems which require understanding and application in the context of situations of practical significance to the student. It is evident that considerable care and much ingenuity went into the selection of problems, and particularly into adjusting the level of understanding and application to the various grade levels. The tests do, to a remarkable degree, test understanding and application rather than rote recall.

Despite this, some exception may be taken to certain materials in the tests. The tests at level 4, particularly in Part 2, are very heavily dependent upon reading skills. This is verified by data in the Technical Report which shows that at grade 4 the correlation of scores on Form A with verbal scores on the two lower level forms of SCAT (.74 and .70) is greater than with SCAT quantitative scores (.64 and .58). Some of this is inevitable because of the emphasis placed on practical situations, but in many cases the reading material is entirely gratuitous. For example, in Part 2 of Form 4A, Item 16 uses eight lines of reading simply to pose a question as to the meaning of a Roman numeral. This tendency to use superfluous material is found in a few items at all levels. Other items are based on assumptions which may trip up the particularly critical student. Thus, in Part 1 of Form 3A, Item 21 involves the length of time required for a father and son to mow the lawn together, given the time required for each separately. The answer seems to assume the availability of two mowers whereas the usual family will probably have but one. In an item in Part 1 of Form 3B, the student is expected to identify an ellipse as being more like a track in a school stadium than the route of a transatlantic ship. Since the latter may travel great circle routes, the keener student might readily and rightly regard the arc of a circle as being closer to an ellipse than the usual track layout. In Items 16 and 17, Part 1, Form 3B, the popular use of the word "average" is questionable in a test which places a premium on critical mindedness. Indeed, the student who knows that the mode is also an average would find the first of these items ambiguous. These examples, rather than indicating general carelessness in test construction, indicate the very real difficulties in devising or finding practical problems and posing them in unambiguous fashion.

A casual check of content indicates that the testing of various concepts has been carefully balanced in the separate tests and between the various forms. In Form 1B, the initial item involving the Colson numerical notation may, in its novelty and probable difficulty, be an unfortunate choice for the first item of the test.

The Directions, Manual, and Technical Report give in unusual and commendatory detail the necessary information for understanding and interpreting the tests. The overlapping of testing objectives at the various levels, which provides continuity in measurement, and the relation of the series to SCAT offer particularly valuable features for measurement of progress and of achievement in relation to ability. One notable and regrettable omission is the failure to provide for the teacher a chart showing the concepts and abilities tested by the various objectives. Despite the obvious difficulties of and ambiguities in such a classification, it might be helpful to teachers for group diagnostic purposes and influential in focusing instruction more definitely on these concepts and abilities by pointing out specific examples of their meaning and practical significance. Unfortunately, not all teachers are able to do this for themselves. It is in this beneficial influence on teaching that the reviewer would see the greatest value of these tests.

GORDON FIFER, *Research Psychologist, Test Research Service, Bronxville, New York; and Lecturer in Education, Hunter College, New York, New York.*

The STEP mathematics tests represent an ambitious attempt to provide measures of achievement in mathematics that meet some of the criteria of evaluation long requested by educators. The test outline and the basic items are the contribution of a committee of 16 mathematics teachers from all parts of the United States. The tests are designed to measure basic mathematical concepts from the fourth grade of elementary school through the second year of college in an integrated sequence.

FACE VALIDITY. As is true of most arithmetic and mathematics tests, the face validity of the tests is good. In general, the essential aspect of each item is the measurement of an important mathematical concept or skill. One major deficiency in terms of content, however, is the highly verbal character of these tests. This is particularly apparent at the lowest level. Perhaps many mathematical problems faced in life are couched in reasonably verbal terms, but the authors went out of their way to create excessively verbal statements in an effort to pose problems attractive to young pupils. It is doubtful that this is either desirable or justifiable. Data in the Technical Report indicate that scores on the STEP tests have significantly higher correlations with verbal scores on SCAT (.70 and .74) than with quantitative scores on SCAT (.58 and .64) at the fourth grade level. Further, at grade 12 the correlations with verbal score on SCAT run as high as .64.

With regard to the selection of topics and the quality of the items, this series ranks high when compared with competing achievement tests. It is outstanding in terms of measuring understanding as opposed to rote memory, application of principles and skills, abilities involved in interpreting and understanding as opposed to rote memory. Of course, as with any test, one can find deficiencies. For example, five items on Form 3A, representing one tenth of the test, require knowledge of the value of pi (π). It is questionable that one tenth of the mathematical knowledge acquired by the end of the ninth grade is adequately represented by these items. On the other hand, no item in Form 3B can conceivably be said to require this knowledge. It would have been better to divide these items more evenly between the two forms.

FORMAT. The test format is attractive and the type used quite legible. Identical directions and time limits for all forms at all levels permit the use of different forms and levels in the same testing situation. The paging of the test booklets, however, is poor. Large parts of some pages are blank, while many items are squeezed into a format that lists choices horizontally rather than vertically. This is particularly undesirable at level 4, designed for use as low as grade 4. In this connection, it is highly debatable whether a separate answer sheet can be used with any degree of success with average fourth grade classes. In fact, the standardization data indicate that possibly over 33 per cent of the fourth graders obtained no more than chance scores and that fewer than 10 per cent got as many as 12 items right. These really inadequate results for the fourth grade may be due to the use of the separate answer sheet and to the overly verbal nature of the test.

STANDARDIZATION. The standardization of STEP approaches the highest standards of educational measurement. It is recognized that at certain levels some of the sample sizes are small, but the techniques of sampling, equating, and norming apparently were not only appropriate but also quite carefully carried out. The norms provided are comprehensive, representative, and usable. One deficiency which may be noted is that on some forms the sequence of items permits some of the easiest items to appear near the end of a test. Since the items are arranged in groups, each group relating to a particular problem or situation, they cannot, of course, be presented in absolute order of difficulty; however, one wonders whether, in some cases, a better ordering of the sets themselves might not have been devised. The low achievers in any group are unnecessarily penalized if some of the easiest items appear near the end of a test that is, for them, speeded.

RELIABILITY AND VALIDITY. Reliability coefficients reported for the four levels, as determined by Kuder-Richardson formula 20, run from .83 to .89. These values are rather disappointing for reliabilities estimated this way. Parallel-forms reliability coefficients will probably be provided in the future. There may be some trouble estimating these, however, since in spite of the claims of the publisher to the contrary, the A and B forms at each level do not have parallel content and are not as comparable as one might wish with respect to difficulty.

At present no empirical validity data are reported. The publishers indicate that these will be made available as soon as possible in supplements to the Technical Report.

INTERPRETABILITY AND USABILITY. The supplementary materials provided for teachers and counselors represent a definite contribution to educational measurement. Educational Testing Service has made tremendous advances in its organization and presentation of materials for aiding the person untrained in measurement. The handling of the standard error of measurement without the usual difficult terminology is excellent. The emphasis upon local norms is highly desirable, and the rather detailed procedure outlined for the accumulation of local norms is good. The directions provided for obtaining raw scores, converted scores, and percentiles are clear and well illustrated, and many helpful suggestions and warnings are provided in regard to interpretations of the percentile scores.

SUMMARY. The STEP mathematics tests represent a significant addition to modern educational evaluation. At all levels the tests measure mathematical competence comprehensively and functionally, if somewhat too verbosely. Persons interested in measuring achievement in particular units or courses will have to rely on traditional measures, but the educator concerned with general mathematical facility in realistic and significant situations will welcome this series.

TOM A. LAMKE, *Coordinator of Research, Iowa State Teachers College, Cedar Falls, Iowa.*

The mathematics tests in the STEP series are part of an ambitious attempt to measure "critical skills and understandings that lie at the heart of each major subject matter field." Four levels of the tests are available in this "continuous and integrated series of tests, aimed at the critical outcomes of education." While the series is nominally designed for grades 4–14, the least difficult mathematics test is too difficult for most fourth grades. The tests were designed "to provide an instrument for the overall evaluation of an individual or a class with respect to achievement in the broad mathematical objectives of general education."

The 50 test items for each form and level

give evidence of a good deal of imagination and thought, although some items may be more topical than necessary. The test booklets are attractive. Good use is made of the two-color format, not only in the tests but also in answer sheets and manuals. The manual and technical report are clearly written and often commendably complete.

VALIDITY. It is usually difficult to obtain agreement on the kinds of specifics to be examined when devising tests for a general education program. The publisher attempted this by unusually extensive committee work and critical reviews. Very likely the objectives tested are those supported by a majority of authorities in the field at this time. Very likely, too, some authorities will disagree with the approach exemplified by the test questions. In general, the questions seem to this reviewer to test concepts generally associated with mathematics in general education.

Some suggestions in the manual relevant to validity are rather broad. While the manual states that high test scores imply little trouble in handling the specific content of the average high school mathematics course, no evidence is given that this is true; no correlations are provided between test scores and high school mathematics grades. Again, the manual suggests that one use of the tests is the comparison of a student's general mathematics ability, as measured by STEP, with his mathematics capacity, as measured by the *School and College Ability Test* (SCAT). If there is any evidence that STEP measures developed ability, as contrasted with SCAT, which measures capacity, it is not given. Examination of the test content makes this claim seem somewhat improbable.

The manual has suggestions designed to help teachers use the test scores. In the case of Albert, who has unusually high SCAT, and STEP science and mathematics scores, the suggestion is that "the counselor wants to investigate very carefully with Albert the wisdom of taking prelaw, as his parents suggest, instead of a [college] course emphasizing science and mathematics. Of course, the wise counselor will consider many factors other than standing on the STEP tests." Some of the factors are listed. Nevertheless, the implication seems to be that Albert may be wrong if he takes prelaw—more wrong than he would be if he majors in science or mathematics. If data supporting this implication exist, they are not given. In the realm

of speculation, it is possible that Albert would do as well in law as in science or mathematics; he might become a supreme court justice, governor, or secretary of state.

RELIABILITY. Reliability derived by Kuder-Richardson formula 20 is reported for Form A. An odd technique, where both universe and sample statistics are employed in the formula, is used; the effect is to make the reported reliability higher than it would be had the formula been used as it is usually employed. Reliabilities are as high as might be expected from a 50-item test designed for the grade ranges used; nevertheless, the coefficients, reported as .83, .84, .83, and .89 for the four levels, leave something to be desired for individual counseling. The caution is well included that within a single school reliability may be somewhat smaller. Reliabilities are not reported for Form B, which is supposed to be parallel to Form A; such figures should be supplied, as should also alternate-forms reliabilities.

NORMS. There may be a fundamental question about the real usefulness of national norms based on a sample of the entire population for which a test is designed when that population is very heterogeneous; nevertheless, there seems to be a demand for them. If they are provided, the job should be well done. The STEP norms were derived from a random sample of schools where superintendents would cooperate in giving the tests in grades 4–12. No statement is made to indicate how many of the superintendents originally contacted were willing to cooperate. In such a case, perhaps the best argument which can be used is that the group which did cooperate resembles the total population in important relevant respects. In this case the argument is not pursued very far. The group used for norming in the grades had approximately the same regional distribution as the population (save for grade 5, where the proportions in the norms group add up to 110 per cent). No information is provided concerning other relevant variables like size of school or socioeconomic status. Because the norms group is not a statistically based sample of the entire population, some such data should be given. Since a similar process was followed in obtaining norms at the college level, similar criticisms apply. As the manual states, "The important thing is that the general characteristics of a norms group must be clearly specified, in order for the percentile ranks derived from it to be useful." It does not appear that this dictum was followed very well. The use of scores as bands instead of points in the norms tables is commendable.

SUMMARY. These are probably the best available published tests of competence in the mathematics of general education. The user should nevertheless assure himself that the testmakers' concept of general education coincides with his own. The format is attractive. The technical work, while frequently good, leaves the following shortcomings to be corrected: (*a*) Reliability for Form B and alternate forms reliability for Forms A and B are not given. (*b*) The norms groups are insufficiently described, with the result that a sounder, more detailed argument is needed to prove that the norms groups are representative of the general population. (*c*) No evidence is given for certain implied or suggested uses of test scores. (*d*) The test is too difficult for most fourth graders.

For reviews by Robert W. B. Jackson and Wilbur L. Layton of the complete battery, see 24.

[439]

*Snader General Mathematics Test: Evaluation and Adjustment Series. Grades 9–13; 1951–54, c1950–51; IBM; Forms AM ('51), BM ('52); manual ('51); expectancy chart ['54]; separate answer sheets must be used; $4.15 per 35 tests; $1.40 per 35 IBM answer sheets; postage extra; 35¢ per specimen set, postpaid; 40(50) minutes; Daniel W. Snader; World Book Co. *

For reviews by Paul J. Blommers and Howard F. Fehr, see 4:378.

[440]

Test of Mathematical Fundamentals for Grades 7 to 12. Grades 7–12; 1944; 1 form; no data on reliability and validity; mimeographed manual ['44]; tentative norms; $1 per 25 tests; 20¢ per specimen set (must be purchased to obtain manual); postage extra; 25(30) minutes; H. R. Beattie; distributed by Guidance Centre. *

FRANCES E. CROOK, *Assistant Professor of Education, McGill University, Montreal, Canada.*

This test of "mathematical fundamentals" includes 60 items covering only the four fundamental operations in computation with whole numbers, fractions, and decimals, and the first two cases in percentage. There are also seven simple problems, most of them involving per cents. The stated purpose of the test is to determine "general level of mathematical achievement" as well as to "locate weaknesses in some

particular phase of mathematical fundamentals."

Since the test is very highly speeded (according to the manual, "very few students will complete the test within the time allotted") its value as a diagnostic instrument is limited. Moreover, the choice of examples and their arrangement would make it difficult to use the test for diagnosis of the difficulties of a class or of individuals. The test's value is probably greater for estimating the general level of achievement in basic computational skills.

The rather small norming sample of 1,790 students in grades 7–12 was chosen in an unspecified way from a "survey of representative schools in Ontario." It is said to include students from commercial, shop, and general classes in large and small schools, both urban and rural. Norms are presented in percentile form for each grade and show the expected leveling off of growth after the ninth grade. The test appears to have been intended mainly for the first year of high school, since about a third of the students tested were in the ninth grade.

There is no indication of the time of year for which the norms are given and it is stated that they are to be regarded as tentative. The author apparently intended to build up further norms from the voluntary submission of test scores by users, a method which has severe limitations. Moreover, the manual is now several years old and it should be possible to provide more than tentative norms in 1958.

The test format is poor in the light of present-day standards. The test could easily be arranged for scoring with fan-type or stencil key, but neither is provided. In the content of the items there are signs of a somewhat outdated point of view and lack of care in planning. Ragged decimals (as in the subtraction problem $9.173 − 4.62$) are included at the computational level rather than in an exercise which requires some understanding of the need for rounding in any practical situation involving such numbers. Another subtraction example is set up in this form: $1.34 − 29c$. In the items involving fractions, no denominators other than powers of 2 are to be found.

In summary, it may be said that this test might be of use in Ontario schools, and possibly elsewhere, for measuring a rather limited aspect of arithmetical skill. It could be improved by better choice of items, by arranging the items in a form that would make scoring easier, and by providing much more complete statistical information than that to be found in the present manual.

ALGEBRA

[441]

*Advanced Algebra: Achievement Examinations for Secondary Schools.** High school; 1951–53; Forms 1 ('51), 2 ('52), 3 ('53); no specific manual; no data on reliability; norms: Forms 1 ['52], 2 ['53], 3 ('53); 10¢ per test, postage extra; (60–90) minutes; Donovan A. Johnson (1) and Harvey O. Jackson (3); Educational Test Bureau. *

[442]

★Advanced Algebra: Midwest High School Achievement Examinations.** High school; 1952–55; Forms A ('55), B ('52, identical with Form 2 of *Advanced Algebra: Achievement Examinations for Secondary Schools;* no specific manual; no data on reliability; norms [A, '55; B, '57]; 10¢ per test, postage extra; 60(65) minutes; Daymond J. Aiken (A); Educational Test Bureau. *

EMMA SPANEY, *Associate Professor of Psychology, Queens College, Flushing, New York.* [Review of Form A.]

Although there is a 4-page folder labeled "Manual" which is provided with the test materials, this is not specific to Advanced Algebra, nor is it the kind of manual which gives pertinent information about validity, reliability, and norms. It is rather an impassioned oration against the "progressive movement" in education as perceived by the author, and a plea for a return to emphasis on "mastery of subject contents and student effort." A separate descriptive sheet defines the purpose of the Midwest series as "to motivate efforts of accomplishments by the students. A less easily arrived at purpose is that of motivating thinking ability....based on mastery of contents resulting from efforts of work."

Part 1 consists of 24 multiple choice items dealing with fundamental operations, finding values of unknowns when verbal conditions on these are given, finding roots of given equations, and identifying graphs of functions with their descriptions. Part 2 consists of 20 multiple choice items covering factoring, finding values of expressions, logarithms, determinants, solving equations, progressions, and graphs. Part 3 consists of 11 verbal problems, which are to be worked out in the test booklet, involving primarily the solution of various types of equations. In terms of the stated purpose for the series, the items do not seem to be especially thought-provoking!

The arrangement of items on the page is satisfactory, and their sequence is quite clear; however, the type face is such that several of the exponents are hard to identify on first reading. In Part 1, groups 1, 2, and 3 each present six items, the answers to which must be selected from among nine choices. Since some of the choices can be eliminated fairly easily, this sometimes results in 2- or 3-choice items. In terms of difficulty, some of the items are out of order, especially in Part 3.

The test can be quite easily administered and scored. No appropriately spaced fan key is provided, but the sophisticated test user will have no difficulty in preparing his own. He will, however, want to establish his own correct answers, there being several errors on the scoring sheet that accompanies the test.

A sheet of norms (end of the school year) gives the "perfect score" and the quartiles for all the subject matter areas in the series. There is no indication of the number of students on whom the norms are based, and no description or enumeration of the schools from which they come. Anyone using the test should be prepared to set up local norms.

In view of the many shortcomings in test content and technical information, the teacher looking for a test in this subject matter area may well conclude that some other test will better meet his needs.

[443]

★Blyth Second-Year Algebra Test: Evaluation and Adjustment Series.** 4 semesters high school; 1953–54; IBM; Forms AM, BM ('53); manual ('54); expectancy chart ['54]; $3.25 per 35 tests; separate answer sheets may be used; $1.40 per 35 IBM answer sheets; postage extra; 35¢ per specimen set, postpaid; 45(55) minutes; M. Isobel Blyth; World Book Co. *

PAUL BLOMMERS, *Professor of Education, State University of Iowa, Iowa City, Iowa.*

According to the manual, this test was "designed to measure the extent to which students have achieved the important objectives of a second year course in high school algebra." These objectives were established on the basis of a survey of commonly used textbooks, of typical courses of study, and of other publications dealing with secondary school mathematics. The objectives were further subjected to the scrutiny of the members of the Commission on Post-War Plans of the National Council of Teachers of Mathematics. The exercises built to measure the objectives thus established suggest that little if any change has occurred in the past 25 to 30 or more years in the emphasis placed on the content covered in second year high school algebra courses. Teachers of such courses will find that the exercises of this test provide a reasonably adequate sampling of the content of such courses as they are usually taught today.

On the whole, the exercises are of good quality. Though it would seem possible for the student who has memorized the rules of algebraic manipulation to perform adequately on this test without ever having achieved much insight into or understanding of their logical bases, nevertheless the test is still superior to many mathematics tests in the measurement of such insights and understandings. Moreover, the exercises used stood the test (statistically, with respect to difficulty and validity) of what should have been a reasonably adequate tryout with 633 students who were completing courses in second year algebra. Only two items, both appearing in Form BM, are mathematically faulty, Item 21 because no correct answer is given, and Item 33 because more than one correct answer is given. In both cases, however, the keyed response may possibly be defended as best among the answers given.

The raw scores on this test, like those of other tests in the Evaluation and Adjustment Series are readily converted into standard scores which for the normative or reference group (3,884 high school students from 72 communities who were completing a second year algebra course) are normally distributed with mean and standard deviation having the same values as those of the IQ's for this reference group as measured by the *Terman-McNemar Test of Mental Ability*. A table of percentile norms in terms of the standard score scale and based on this reference group is given in the manual. This table is cited as appropriate for evaluating not only individual achievement but also the average score for a class. The manual fails to point out that the percentile ranks reported in this table of norms cannot be interpreted as the percentile ranks of such class averages.

The fact that the standard scores have the same mean and standard deviation for the reference group as do IQ scores for this group makes it possible to relate either individual or class performance on the algebra test to expected performance as reflected by IQ. This, of course, requires the use of the appropriate test of mental ability as well as of proficiency in algebra.

The reliability is reported separately for students in each of five communities. The coefficients (odd-even item correlations corrected by the Spearman-Brown formula) range from .82 to .92. While this algebra test is somewhat lower in reliability than the associated *Terman-McNemar Test of Mental Ability* it is probably as reliable as most algebra tests of similar length.

On the whole, this test appears to be of good quality, and it should provide for a reasonably sound assessment of degree of mastery of content of second year high school algebra as it is typically taught. The two forms are built to the same specifications and are equivalent in interpretation without simply paraphrasing one another. The reliability and norms appear to be reasonably adequate. The accompanying manual is quite complete and provides helpful suggestions for using the results.

Myron F. Rosskopf, *Professor of Mathematics, Teachers College, Columbia University, New York, New York.*

Although the test purports to secure data on understanding concepts, study of the 55 items in each form indicates that information concerning possession of skills only is obtained.

The manual gives a clear, concise description of the test, directions for administering and scoring it, and suggestions for using the results. Both percentile norms and standard scores are provided. Information concerning the development of the test and its reliability and validity leaves one quite confident that the test was carefully constructed.

The test items of both forms are well chosen. The printing is clear; the spacing makes for ease of reading; the arrangement is systematic. All figures that appear show careful drawing and good reproduction. There are no bizarre items; the items appear as typical textbook exercises or problems. In short, a student should feel quite comfortable taking the test.

In summary, this is an excellent test for a teacher who wishes to determine whether his students possess the skills of second year algebra.

[444]

*California Algebra Aptitude Test. High school; 1940–58; 1 form ('58, identical with test copyrighted in 1940) ; [revised] manual ('58, essentially the same as manual copyrighted in 1950) ; $2.25 per 25 tests; 55¢ per specimen set; postpaid; 50(55) minutes; Noel Keys and Muriel McCrum; American Guidance Service, Inc. *

For a review by William G. Mollenkopf, see 4:385; for a review by David Segel, see 3:320.

[445]

★Diagnostic Test in Basic Algebra. 2, 3 semesters high school; 1956; 1 form; 2 levels: Parts 1, 2; no data on reliability; no norms; 5s. per 10 tests; 3s. per scoring key; 4s. per manual; 11s. 6d. per specimen set; postpaid within Australia; (30–90) minutes; John H. Henshaw; Australian Council for Educational Research. *

STANLEY CLARK, *Professor of Education, University of Saskatchewan, Saskatoon, Saskatchewan, Canada.*

This is the first of a projected series of tests to be used for diagnosis in algebra and in other branches of mathematics. Since the emphasis is placed upon the exercise of the simple but fundamental mechanical and manipulative skills, verbal problems are few in number and arithmetical computation is kept to a minimum. The questions are of the traditional type and may be solved mentally, although space is provided for figuring. Some types of expressions which one might expect to fall within the scope of the test are not considered. Negative terms, for example, do not appear in the sections dealing with the multiplication and division of monomials. Several problems involve the use of the English monetary system.

Part 1 is intended for use during the first year of algebra and beyond. Six topics are included: the expression of very simple mathematical statements in symbolic form; the evaluation of algebraic expressions; the addition and subtraction of monomials; the multiplication of monomials; simplification involving the removal of parentheses; and the division of monomials by monomials.

Although Part 2 is designed for the second year of algebra and beyond, much of its content is included in first year courses in algebra on this continent. This part of the test assists in the diagnosis of the student's skill in expressing simple mathematical statements as equations; in solving first degree equations in one unknown; in elementary factoring, and in finding the product of two binomials.

Each item contains two problems of approximately equal difficulty which depend for their solution upon the application of the same principle. The appropriate principle differs somewhat from item to item within each topic. The author assumes that a student understands the process if he gets both parts of an item correct and that he needs remedial instruction if he misses both. Interpretation of the situation in which the student gets one part right and the other wrong presents difficulties and requires further investigation by the teacher.

Administration of the test is left to the discretion of the teacher although some suggestions are offered in the manual. The test may be adapted to different teaching situations: students may be administered the relevant group of items after a particular topic has been taught, or, if the circumstances warrant it, they may be required to work through either part in its entirety. There are no norms since the test is not designed to yield a measure of achievement. Validation of the test is based upon the care taken in constructing items which will reveal the presence or absence of the pertinent algebraic skills and upon its demonstrated usefulness in individual and group diagnosis. No mention is made of its reliability although the consistency of performance on part and topic scores might profitably be investigated. Remedial exercises are contained in the booklet Aids to Algebra, comprising 150 sets of 5 problems, each set being conveniently keyed to the test. A parallel form of the test for retesting after corrective instruction is not available.

Diagnosis of student difficulties and the provision of remedial instruction are important but frequently neglected aspects of high school teaching. The construction of instruments to facilitate this work is commendable. The materials reviewed above should be of value for the busy teacher in the setting for which they were devised. The *Diagnostic Test in Basic Algebra* is, however, more an instructional aid than a standardized test. Any competent teacher of algebra should be able to produce a comparable collection of problems if he is willing to devote the time to the task.

[446]

*Elementary Algebra: Achievement Examinations for Secondary Schools. High school; 1951–53; Forms 1 ('51), 2 ('52), 3 ('53) ; no specific manual; no data on reliability; norms: Forms 1 ['52], 2 ['53], 3 ('53) ; 10¢ per test, postage extra; (60–90) minutes; Donovan A. Johnson (1, 2) and Lyle M. Eakins (3) ; Educational Test Bureau. *

[447]
*Elementary Algebra: Every Pupil Test. High school; 1929–58; new form usually issued each December and April; norms available following testing program; no data on reliability; 3¢ per test; 1¢ per scoring key; cash orders postpaid; 40(45) minutes; Ohio Scholarship Tests. *

[448]
★Elementary Algebra: Midwest High School Achievement Examinations. High school; 1955–57; Forms A ('55), B ('57); no specific manual; no data on reliability; norms [A, '55; B, '57]; 10¢ per test, postage extra; Form A: 60(65) minutes; Form B: 90[95] minutes; Daymond Aiken (A) and J. N. Weiss (B); Educational Test Bureau. *

LYNNETTE B. PLUMLEE, *Personnel Research and Testing Division, Sandia Corporation, Albuquerque, New Mexico.* [Review of Form A.]

The manual for the Midwest High School Achievement Examinations gives the rationale for this series, justifying an emphasis "on mastery of subject contents and student effort" in the interest of "motivating thinking ability." The practice of presenting a rationale is one which might well be adopted more generally by test publishers. A further desirable step, not taken for tests in this battery, would be an evaluation of the extent to which the rationale is met by the content of the individual test. In the case of the elementary algebra test, the aim of mastery of subject content seems to be met, with the majority of the items testing rules of algebraic operations and definitions. The aim of motivating thinking ability could have been better achieved had questions been used which are less commonly found in textbooks and therefore less subject to specific learning by the student. Virtually all of the word problems are variations on traditional tasks. A better basis for motivating the student and giving meaning to algebra would be found in problems which require the student to apply his knowledge to tasks which are new to him.

Little information is given in the manual regarding the construction of the test. However, in a letter from the publisher it is noted that the tests in this series were developed in response to the request of superintendents and principals who wanted tests which would help evoke from the student "thought process to give deeper and more significant meaning to that which he does know." The content of the test is based primarily on the author's own teaching experience, following the publisher's instruction to make the content independent of any one textbook and to include contents generally included in the present day textbooks. The test appears to cover the traditional course in algebra quite well, although there seems to be a disproportionate emphasis on signed numbers at the expense of other important topics such as proportion, variation, quadratic formulas, and complex fractions, which are covered only slightly or not at all.

In the same letter to the reviewer, the publisher indicates that items are not arranged in difficulty order on the grounds that difficulty ordering is not useful in a test intended for review purposes rather than for ability rating. This is reasonable if timing is adequate. The 1-hour time allowance for this test seems adequate for only the better students; however, the publisher notes that "these are power tests and thus do not depend on accuracy of timing. In general it was suggested to the schools to allow at least enough time for 90% of the students to complete." It was not made clear where these instructions to the schools are provided, since they are not given in the manual. It is also not clear what effect these instructions had on the norms which are provided.

Norms information consists of raw scores corresponding to the 25th, 50th, and 75th percentiles. According to the publisher, the norms are based on the administration of Form A in the spring of 1956, with the bulk of the cases coming from Minnesota. Though the number of cases on which the norms are based is not given, it is presumed that it was adequate for stability; another administration in the spring of 1957 did not change the percentiles. Since no information is given on the representativeness of the norms population sample, the user may well use caution in applying the norms to his own students. The norms information which is available does, however, indicate that the range in item difficulty is sufficient to measure both the strong and the weak student.

The format of the test is generally good, with clear print and adequate scratchwork space for the most part. The directions will probably cause no difficulty to the student, though an example illustrating the method of answering the multiple answer items might be helpful. The use of multiple options in common for each of three sets of six items in Part 1 saves space but makes it more difficult to provide answer options based on common errors of operation.

In summary, the test has a worthwhile aim,

but one which might better have been met by questions requiring more understanding and thought on the part of the student. However, it can well be used as a test of the student's mastery of algebraic operations and concepts. The norms information should be used with caution in view of lack of information on its general applicability.

[449]

*First Year Algebra: Every Pupil Scholarship Test. 1 year high school; 1926–58; new form usually issued each January and April; norms available following testing program; no data on reliability; 4¢ per test; 4¢ per scoring key; postage extra; 40(45) minutes; Bureau of Educational Measurements. *

[450]

★Illinois Algebra Test. 1, 1.5, 2 semesters high school; 1956–58; formerly called *Chicago Algebra Test;* 1 form ('58, identical to test copyrighted in 1956 except for title and minor change in 1 item) ; 3 levels: Tests 1, 2, 3; manual ('58) ; mimeographed analysis of errors sheet ('58) ; $1.75 per 25 tests ; 60¢ per specimen set; postpaid; 37(40) minutes; Charles H. Schutter; C. A. Gregory Co. *

STANLEY CLARK, *Professor of Education, University of Saskatchewan, Saskatoon, Saskatchewan, Canada.*

This test is in reality three tests, designed for use at the end of one, one and a half, and two semesters of high school algebra, respectively.

The problems are of the conventional type, involving use of the manipulative and mechanical skills; the verbal items are stereotyped and few in number. Outcomes such as the ability to employ and interpret graphs and the understanding of the vocabulary of algebra are not measured. Most of the numerical coefficients are integers; decimal fractions are not used at all. Expressions involving powers beyond the second are rare. Students are required to produce the answers, a procedure which has considerable merit. The time limits are ample for most students. The tests are easy to administer.

The tests are fairly short, 20 to 21 items per test. The manual, however, speaks of each test as having 24 to 30 items. These latter figures are misleading since they were obtained by counting the two roots of a quadratic equation or the two solutions of simultaneous equations as two separate items.

The author departs from the usual procedure of giving correct answers unit weighting and scores items 1 to 8 points "according to the algebraic knowledge and skill needed to answer them." The method of determining the weights is not explained. It is difficult to understand why a student should receive 7 points for a single simple subtraction, as in the second answer to Item 15, Test 1.

Information about validity is meagre; the term "validity" does not appear in the manual. The manual contains an outline of the topics included at each level but fails to say anything about the construction of the test, the experimental editions, if any, item analysis, item difficulty, and the like. The standardization group is not described in any way.

Reliability coefficients found by use of one of the Kuder-Richardson formulas are .97, .94, and .96 for the three levels, respectively. These are questionably high for such short tests. Furthermore, the Kuder-Richardson formulas have been developed upon the assumption that the test items have unit weight, a condition which does not hold here.

The author and publishers have failed to make available to prospective users detailed information respecting the construction, validity, and reliability of the test, and to furnish an accurate description of the individuals upon whom it was standardized. These are responsibilities which cannot be lightly disregarded. The technical imperfections of this instrument stand out in bold relief when it is compared with such other instruments as the *Seattle Algebra Test* and the *Lankton First Year Algebra Test.*

THEODORE E. KELLOGG, *Admissions Officer and Assistant Professor of Education, University of Minnesota, Minneapolis, Minnesota.*

This test was developed as a measure of the fundamentals of algebra. Although the test contains a good sampling of standard textbook problems, it does not sample beyond this. The algebra student taking it will encounter little if any need to generalize his knowledge of algebra, nor will he need to deal with "new" algebraic situations. The verbal problems in the test may be solved by routine type-form procedures.

The manual makes no mention of the validity of the test except to point out that an examination of eight standard texts shows "that a common body of algebraic concepts is measured by these tests." The content included in the test is mentioned only in general terms. Kuder-Richardson reliabilities of .97 (first semester), .94 (midterm second semester), and .96 (second semester) are reported. No data are reported as to what extent the test may operate as a speed test. This information is important in view of the apparent difficulty of the test and the fact that the Kuder-Richardson formula provides an overestimate of reliability if any substantial number of items cannot be attempted during the time limits of a test.

The manual states that the items on the test are weighted "according to the knowledge and skill needed to answer them." Such a statement, in the absence of any criteria or quantitative data, is of minimum help to the prospective test user. The manual points out that since each test has 100 points, a pupil's score may be considered as "percent of mastery" in the particular content area. It is somewhat difficult to reconcile this rather absolute concept with the fact that on Test 3, for example, a student with 46 per cent mastery by the above definition would receive a percentile rank of 81 and a grade of B if suggestions in the manual were followed. In the writer's opinion the manual for this test suggests a somewhat ambiguous concept in "percent of mastery."

The norms provided include percentile ranks for each of the three tests. However, the meaning of these ranks is not clear since no description of the normative group is given. Minimum essentials, in the writer's opinion, would be data regarding the size of the group, the ability of the group, and the population from which the group was drawn. The norms suggest that the tests may have limitations as relates to adequate measurement of the full range of ability found in the typical algebra class. On Test 1, for example, 50 per cent of the points on the test are associated with percentile ranks ranging from 75 to 100. On Test 3, 50 per cent of the points are associated with percentile ranks ranging from 85 to 100. At the other end of the scale, 25 per cent of the points on Test 3 are associated with percentile ranks ranging from 1 to 50.

The test manual suggests letter grades which may be associated with the various percentile ranks. The assumptions underlying the assignment of grades are very important and these should be provided if such suggestions are to be used wisely. It is of interest to note that on Test 3, for example, a score of 6 points (which could represent a single item) would correspond to a grade of D on the suggested scale. Similarly a student earning 58 per cent of the points on Test 3 would receive a percentile rank

of 93 and a corresponding grade of A. Thus, on Test 3, 42 per cent of the points are functioning for 7 per cent of the norms group.

Certain details pertaining to the printing and writing of the test should be mentioned. The student does his work and writes his answers in the test booklet. In several instances, the answer blanks are too short for the necessary response, e.g., Item 5, Test 3, and Item 17, Test 1. Some item directions could be improved, e.g., a division problem (Item 21, Test 1) which states, "Leave answer on top without re-writing." In some cases the unknown is printed in front of the response line and in others it is not, e.g., Item 20, Test 1. In some items space allocation implies that the response line is to serve as a fraction line, e.g., Item 10, Test 2.

The results of this test could be considerably more useful if additional information could be provided on such matters as the following: reliability, validity, difficulty level of items, discrimination indices, characteristics of the norms group, and assumptions and criteria relating to the weighting of items.

[451]

*Lankton First-Year Algebra Test: Evaluation and Adjustment Series. 1 year high school; 1951-54, c1950-51; IBM; Forms AM ('51), BM ('52); manual ('51); expectancy chart ['54]; separate answer sheets must be used; $3.60 per 35 tests; $1.40 per 35 IBM answer sheets; postage extra; 35¢ per specimen set, postpaid; 40(50) minutes; Robert Lankton; World Book Co. *

EMMA SPANEY, *Associate Professor of Psychology, Queens College, Flushing, New York.*

According to the manual, this test was constructed "to measure the extent to which students have achieved the important objectives of a high school course in first year algebra." Operationally, this has been translated into understanding and using the language of algebra and "acquiring habits, attitudes, and appreciations through algebra as a way of thinking."

Selection of content was based on analyses of textbooks, courses of study, and other pertinent publications. A detailed outline of the content distribution of items in each form is provided for the test user. This is particularly helpful to the teacher desiring to examine the validity of the test for his particular situation because a column has been provided for the comparison of his own course of study and the test outline. The items are of the 5-choice single correct answer type and are in general clearly presented.

The test booklet is a 6-page folder, fan-folded so that the direction "Go on to the next page" in the lower right hand corner of each page is appropriate. The type face is sufficiently large and quite clear. The test is easily administered.

Students are instructed to answer questions even when not perfectly sure of the correct answer, but to avoid wild guessing. However, they are not told that the tests will be scored for number right only. With the growing level of sophistication of test takers and our increasing information about individual differences in response-set preferences, the author may wish to revise these directions in the future.

The tests were standardized on 3,183 students in 57 schools in 22 states. Their median chronological age was 15 years, 1 month; their median Terman-McNemar IQ was 106, with a standard deviation of 12.5. Raw scores on the algebra test were accordingly converted to normalized standard scores with mean 106 and SD 12.5, thus equating algebra performance to estimated ability level. Percentile equivalents of these standard scores are provided. Since this standard score system is used for the entire Evaluation and Adjustment Series, the comparison of a given student's performances in various areas is possible.

An expectancy chart, based on a random sample of 300 students in the standardization group, shows the typical relationship between mental ability as measured by the Terman-McNemar, Pintner, or Otis tests of mental ability and achievement as measured by the algebra test, and should be useful in the early identification of students who are likely to have difficulty in the course, and in the identification of "over" and "under" achievers.

A distribution of difficulty indices for items in each form is given in the manual. It would appear from this that the inclusion of a few very easy "icebreaker" items might be considered, since the difficulties of the first items in the two forms are 86 and 80, respectively, and the mean Terman-McNemar IQ of the tryout group was given as 111. The mean validity indices for the two forms are .44 and .40 respectively—certainly more than adequate.

Split-half reliabilities of .84 and .87 were obtained from 155 beginning algebra students in

one community and from 134 in a second community. Since the test is not essentially highly speeded, this technique may be properly used. An alternate forms reliability of .81 was obtained from 90 students, with an interval of less than a week between administrations.

The equivalence of the two forms was carefully controlled not only with regard to content, but also in terms of difficulty and validity indices. As a check, a rotation-of-forms administration was made, and the distributions of scores were found to be comparable.

These forms are very good illustrations of carefully constructed and standardized tests. The accompanying manual and aids to interpretation are well calculated to prove useful to the alegbra teacher whose interest in his students warrants the use of these devices.

For a review by Stanley Clark, see 4:394.

[452]

*Seattle Algebra Test: Evaluation and Adjustment Series. 1 semester high school; 1951-54; IBM; Forms AM ('51), BM ('52) ; manual ('51) ; expectancy chart ['54] ; separate answer sheets must be used; $3.05 per 35 tests; $1.40 per 35 IBM answer sheets; postage extra; 35¢ per specimen set, postpaid; 40(50) minutes; Harold B. Jeffery, Earl E. Kirschner, Philip Stucky, John R. Rushing, David B. Scott, and Otie P. Van Orsdall; World Book Co. *

ALBERT E. MEDER, JR., *Vice Provost and Dean of the University, Rutgers, The State University, New Brunswick, New Jersey.*

This test is intended for use at the end of one term of instruction in elementary algebra. The manual includes an accurate description of the nature and content of the test and the basis on which it was developed, and an adequate discussion of reliability and equivalence of forms, as well as directions for administering, scoring, interpreting, and using the test.

In the manual it is stated that "most elements measured may be justified both in terms of frequency of inclusion in commonly used textbooks and on the basis of expert judgment as to importance." The reviewer has no doubt that the first part of the statement is correct; he wishes, however, to demur with respect to a few points from the alleged expert judgment: (*a*) It is unimportant that students know some of the vocabulary items covered; in particular, there is too much stress on "literal" versus "numerical" factors, terms, etc. (*b*) The items on order of operation are artificial; no mathematician in his senses would write the expressions used without appropriate signs of aggregation. (*c*) The items on use of parentheses are exaggerated. (*d*) In one item the result of substituting in "the temperature formula" is $21\frac{1}{9}°$ and all the distractors also contain fractions with denominator 9. It is submitted that no one measures temperatures in ninths of a degree. This item is unreal.

It must be noted that these criticisms apply at most to a half dozen items. It is doubtful that a student's score would be seriously affected by these defects.

The reviewer is pleased to note that the items in Part D, which measures what he considers to be the most important aspect both of the test and of instruction in elementary algebra, are unusually good. Parts B and C are generally good. Part A is adequate, but weaker than the other parts. With the exception of Part D, the test is rather mechanical.

On the whole, the strengths of this test far outweigh its weaknesses, and its use is recommended.

ARITHMETIC

[453]

*A.C.E.R. Arithmetic Tests: Standardized for Use in New Zealand. Ages 9–12; 1946–57; same as corresponding parts of the *A.C.E.R. Arithmetic Tests;* Form C ['46]; 4 tests: multiplication, subtraction, division, addition; manual ['57]; no data on reliability; 7*s.* 6*d.* per 25 tests; 3*s.* per specimen set; postage extra; 16(40) minutes; manual by A. E. Fieldhouse; tests by Australian Council for Educational Research; New Zealand Council for Educational Research. *

REFERENCES
1. HOHNE, H. H. *Success and Failure in Scientific Faculties of the University of Melbourne.* Melbourne, Australia: Australian Council for Educational Research, 1955. Pp. vii, 129. * (*PA* 31:3787)
2. BUCKLOW, MAXINE, AND DOUGHTY, PATRICIA. "The Use of Aptitude Tests in Clerical Employment: The Selection of Accounting Machinists." *Personnel Pract B* 13:35–44 S '57. *

[454]

*A.C.E.R. Number Test. Ages 13.5 and over; 1942–55; 1 form ['52]; mimeographed manual ['55]; 4*s.* per 10 tests; 1*s.* per set of scoring keys ['42]; 3*s.* 6*d.* per manual; 4*s.* 9*d.* per specimen set; postpaid within Australia; 10(15) minutes; manual by D. Spearritt; Australian Council for Educational Research. *

For a review by Leslie M. Haynes of the original edition, see 4:399.

[455]

★American School Achievement Tests: Arithmetic Readiness. Grades kgn–1; 1941–55; 1 form ('55, identical with the numbers test of the Primary Battery I of *American School Achievement Tests* copyrighted in 1941); directions sheet ['55]; no data on validity; $2.75 per 25 tests; 35¢ per specimen set; post-

paid; administration time not reported; Robert V. Young, Willis E. Pratt, and Frank Gatto; [Public School Publishing Co.] *

HAROLD E. MOSER, *Director of College Test Services, State Teachers College, Towson, Maryland.*

This test suffers from a confusion of purposes. Although it currently is called a "readiness" test, it was originally designed as an achievement test. In addition, the authors propose values for the test as a diagnostic tool. Now a test that sets out to do all of these things is likely to reveal some important internal contradictions and inconsistencies. There are evidences of both in this test.

The test is a reprint, under the new title Arithmetic Readiness, of the numbers test from the 1941 edition of Primary Battery I of the *American School Achievement Tests.* The reliability coefficient of the 1941 numbers tests was only .76 and so the authors have doubled the length of the original test by combining the numbers tests from Form A and Form B of the ASAT. Items from the two tests are not mixed; each test is scored separately and the final score is determined by averaging the scores on Tests A and B. Other than a leaflet containing directions and a record chart, there is no manual for the readiness test. The reader is referred to the manual for Primary Battery I of the ASAT for data on validity and reliability.

The test user may well ask himself whether the administration of two equivalent forms of a primary grade achievement test in arithmetic yields results similar to those of a number readiness test or a diagnostic test. This question brings us to the source of the confusions mentioned earlier. Knowing that a pupil has not attained a mathematical objective is not equivalent to knowing that he is ready for formal training in that area. Two examples may be cited from Test A. (*a*) Four of the 34 items in this test require pupils to find answers to these combinations: $8 + 8$, $5 + 9$, $8 - 2$, $14 - 8$. Correct responses to these items will certainly provide evidence of one kind of achievement, but will failure to respond correctly indicate readiness to learn these more difficult facts? (*b*) Two items in Test A require the pupils to interpret Roman numerals up to XI. For what first grade experiences are these items measures of readiness?

A study of the test discloses little evidence

of diagnostic value. In educational literature the term diagnostic test usually refers to a test which systematically explores a limited range of abilities or understandings. In such a test, each item calls for an exercise of the ability under conditions that vary in complexity and subtlety. The test thus provides a profile of the limits of a pupil's capacity to work effectively in a given area.

The achievement survey test must sacrifice this intensive analysis for the wider coverage of content. This fact is reflected in the present test. In Test A, for example, there is but one item to measure the pupil's ability to extend the number series from a given value when counting by ones; there is one similar item for counting by twos. This frequency is adequate for survey purposes but it offers little in the way of diagnosis.

The raw scores on the test are converted into age and grade norms. Again, it should be noted that these norms have been taken from the 1941 achievement tests. In current practice, readiness and diagnostic test scores are seldom converted into age and grade norms. Such normative data do not provide the kinds of information a teacher needs.

Still more examples could be cited to point up the confusions that arise from overlapping purposes, but they hardly seem necessary. The test was originally devised as a short survey test covering some of the more traditional content found in grade 1. Whatever value this test possesses still lies in this area. It will contribute little to diagnosis or to information about arithmetic readiness in the senses in which these terms are most often used.

[456]
*American School Achievement Tests, Part 2, Arithmetic. Grades 4-6, 7-9; 1941-58; 3 scores: computation, problems, total; Forms D ('55), E ('56), F ('57), G ('58); Forms D, E, F are essentially the same as Forms A, B, C copyrighted 1941-43; 3 levels; battery manuals ('58); $2 per 25 tests; 35¢ per specimen set of either level; postpaid; 50(60), 60(70) minutes for Intermediate, Advanced battery; Willis E. Pratt and Robert V. Young; Public School Publishing Co. *

JOSEPH JUSTMAN, *Assistant Director, Bureau of Educational Program Research and Statistics, New York Public Schools, New York, New York.* [Review of Forms D, E, F.]

These tests are designed to measure some of the conventional computational and problem solving skills in arithmetic. Although presented as completely new instruments, evidently Forms D, E, and F are identical with Forms A, B, and C, respectively, except for minor changes in a few items. The manuals accompanying the tests are also relatively unchanged.

While test content has remained the same, the format has been revised. The test is now presented in the form of a 10 by 14½ inch booklet, and a carbon strip marking device has been introduced. The large size may be rather unwieldy in some school situations.

The test content leaves much to be desired. No attempt is made to test concepts, relationships, judgments, or inferences, all of which are looked upon as important outcomes of a modern arithmetic program. When considered in relationship to the scope of the present-day program of meaningful arithmetic, the tests are very narrowly conceived. Courses of study and textbooks have changed markedly in the past 10 to 15 years; these tests have not.

Little attempt has been made to restandardize the tests or to provide more complete normative data. Items were originally selected through administration of a sample of items in a single county in Pennsylvania. The test norms are hardly representative. The original intermediate level manual merely stated that the age and grade norms were based on median scores obtained by approximately 1,000 pupils in grades 3 to 7 inclusive, enrolled in schools ranging in size from small rural schools to schools in urban districts having populations of 5,000 or more. There was no indication of the geographical distribution of the schools involved, nor of the relative number of cases among the types of schools. The original advanced level manual was equally vague about "approximately 2,000 pupils in grades 6 to 9." Both "new" manuals carry virtually the same new sentence—"In 1955, norms were further checked against the scores of 3,589 pupils in 44 school districts located in 17 states and Canada." It would be a rare coincidence if exactly the same number of pupils had been tested in grades 3-7 and in grades 6-9. Yet, no indication is given that the entire range of grades 3-9 was included. Perhaps more surprising is the fact that almost no change in norms was found necessary, in spite of changes in course content over the many years that had elapsed and the change in test format.

Test reliabilities were determined by correlating scores on equivalent forms of the test. At the intermediate level, reliabilities range from

.86 to .92 ($n = 100$); at the advanced level, however, reported reliabilities are too low to be considered satisfactory, ranging from .73 to .82 ($n = 293$).

The "new" manuals also carry forward the extravagant claims for the diagnostic value of the tests made in the earlier editions. The paucity of items dealing with any given process limits the use of the tests to survey purposes.

It is very difficult to understand why the major faults of the test have not been corrected in the current edition. Much the same criticisms have been made in previous *Mental Measurements Yearbooks*—poor standardization, inadequate norms, and low reliability. Although the revision in format is a step in the right direction, the failure to reformulate test content in the light of changing curricula makes these tests unsuitable for use in other than a very traditional arithmetic program.

J. FRED WEAVER, *Director of Graduate Studies, and Associate Dean, School of Education, Boston University, Boston, Massachusetts.* [Review of Forms D, E, F.]

The arithmetic subtests of each battery seek to provide separate measures of the two most commonly recognized components of arithmetic ability: computation and problem solving. Mathematical concepts and understandings, which are receiving increasing emphasis in modern programs, are not measured as such.

The compactness of the test format is advantageous in a sense but is not without its disadvantages. For each form all test items, along with their corresponding 4-choice answers and answer boxes, are contained on a single test sheet printed on both sides. At the intermediate level this involves a 40-item computational subtest and a 20-item problem solving subtest; at the advanced level, a 43-item computational subtest and a 23-item problem solving subtest are involved. Each test sheet is relatively large (approximately 10 by 15 inches) and somewhat inconvenient to use. The computational and problem solving subtests are separately timed, yet the end of the former test appears on the same side of the sheet as the beginning of the latter. Even though pupils who finish the computational test in less than the allotted time may not formally begin the problem solving subtest until instructed to do so, they undoubtedly will be scanning the problem solving items in advance. This will vitiate the controlled

timing to an undetermined extent. Factors such as these, coupled with relatively poor typography in general, leave the actual test sheets with much to be desired from the standpoint of effective format.

The manuals give somewhat more information than is the case at times regarding the construction and validation of the tests, their reliability, the development of norms, and the like. Nevertheless, omissions and ambiguities are much in evidence. An attempt is made to establish the curricular validity of the items in each subtest of each form, but an inadequate framework for the analysis of content has been used in this connection. Furthermore, no data are presented regarding aspects of statistical validity, such as indices of difficulty and discriminating power.

The reported reliability coefficients are based on between-forms correlations. At the intermediate level, these range from .90 to .92 for computation and from .86 to .89 for problem solving. At the advanced level, however, the corresponding ranges are .79 to .82 and .73 to .80. No standard errors of measurement are reported to supplement the reliability coefficients. Furthermore, no information is given regarding the grade level distribution of the sample used in determining the reliability of each test. The same is true of the samples used in establishing and verifying the conventional grade and age norms, which are the only types of norms reported. All these factors, coupled with other less important inadequacies, prevent the manuals from rising above the commonplace.

In regard to individual test items, the manual asserts that the distractors for each item represent the three incorrect answers found to be most frequently given, and that each item in any test form was matched with an item of "exactly the same difficulty" in each of the other two forms. These are desirable features. However, even a rather superficial examination of the individual test items in each form reveals some disturbing things.

First, consider this situation observed in connection with the computation subtest of the intermediate test. In Form D, three items deal with the multiplication of common fractions or mixed numbers. In Form E, there is just one such item and that is a more difficult one than any of the three in Form D. In Form F there is *no* item dealing with multiplication of common fractions or mixed numbers. Other similar differences among forms are in evidence.

Next, consider these two items taken from the advanced test: (*a*) "What is the area of a triangle with a 12 ft. base and a 30 ft. altitude?" and (*b*) "What is the area of a right triangle whose base is 7 ft. and height is 9 ft.?" The first item appears in the Form E *computation* subtest; the second item is in the Form D *problem solving* subtest. Also consider the item in the Form F *computation subtest* which asks: "Which of these figures is a right triangle?" and then shows four geometric forms from which the correct answer is to be selected. Things such as these make one wonder just how validly the respective subtests actually measure computation and problem solving!

The final point to be mentioned in this review opens a definite question regarding the test norms. Specifically, consider the problem solving subtest of the intermediate test, which is to be used in grades 4–6. According to the table of norms, only two of the raw scores—15 and 16 (items correct out of a possible 20)—yield grade-equivalents at the sixth grade level (6.4 and 6.9, respectively). A situation such as this points to some serious inadequacy in the test or the derived norms.

In summary, the arithmetic tests of the *American School Achievement Tests* exhibit very little, if anything, that would significantly commend their use. Almost any other standardized test of arithmetic achievement designed for these grade levels could be used with a greater degree of confidence.

For reviews by J. Raymond Gerberich and Virgil E. Herrick of the complete battery, see 1; for a review by Ralph C. Preston of an earlier edition, see 4:1; for reviews by Walter W. Cook and Gordon N. Mackenzie (with Glen Hass), see 3:1.

[457]

★Analytical Survey Test in Computational Arithmetic. Grades 7–12; 1930–57; Forms 3, 4 ('57); mimeographed manual ('57); $2.25 per 25 tests; 35¢ per specimen set; postpaid; 40(50) minutes; H. C. Christofferson and W. S. Guiler; C. A. Gregory Co. *

EMMA SPANEY, *Associate Professor of Psychology, Queens College, Flushing, New York.*

The purpose of this test as given in the manual is "to measure achievement in only the abstract computational phase of arithmetic. Wherever such a measure is needed—the seventh grade through college, in the public school, private school or trade school, on the farm, in the factory or business office—this test will give a quick survey."

The test contains 50 items divided into five parts of 10 items each: Operations with Whole Numbers, Fractions and Mixed Numbers, Decimals, Practical Measurements, and Percentage. The problems are given in boldface type, and the student is asked to work them out right on the same page. There is enough space for most students—it is the unusual one who will write so large that he will feel cramped for space. The key contains all answers which are to be credited as correct. This reviewer would question the advisability of giving full credit for answers not in lowest terms, e.g., $94\frac{80}{8}$%, as listed on the key.

Although the parts are timed, the manual states that "in each of these areas five basic processes are included and for each of these processes equivalent examples, a and b, are given. These are so arranged that the very slow worker would have time to work one of each, and the fast worker possibly two of each in the time allotted. The time allowance is generous because this is not a speed test." Students who finish a part before time is called may go on to the next part. Since the overall time is constant, the manual states that the total score should be given greater weight than any part score when comparison with norms is made.

Median grade norms for each part and the total score are provided for each of grades 7 through 12, and total score medians are given for grades 13 and 14. The norms are based on 8,456 seventh graders and 7,819 eighth graders in statewide experimentation; and upon "several high school and college groups" and "college freshmen and sophomores, largely those preparing to be teachers in the elementary schools." The number of cases in grades beyond the eighth is not given. Additional percentile scores, 10th, 25th, 75th, and 90th, are given for total score for grades 7 and 8.

In terms of the groups which might use this test as enumerated in the first paragraph of this review, the norms are sadly lacking, since no trade school, farm, factory, or business office norms are furnished. If the test is to be offered for large scale screening purposes, a machine scorable edition would be preferable to the present comparatively cumbersome, hand scorable forms. It might also be advisable to consider cutting the working time down, since screening batteries cannot usually afford to give 40 minutes to arithmetic computation alone.

[458]
*Arithmetic Essentials Test. Grades 3, 4, 5, 6, 7, 8, 9–12; 1949–56; grades 3–8: Forms A ('52), B ('53); grades 9–12: Forms A ('53), B ('54); 7 levels; no manual; class analysis sheets ('52–56); no data on reliability and validity; no norms; $1.80 per 30 tests; 25¢ per specimen set of any one level; cash orders postpaid; [30] minutes; James T. Shea; Steck Co. *

J. WAYNE WRIGHTSTONE, *Director, Bureau of Educational Research, New York Public Schools, New York, New York.*

Each test in this series consists of 40 computational examples and 10 verbal problems, except for the grade 9-12 test which contains 100 items. These tests have no manual and provide no norms or data on reliability and validity. The author states that these tests "were designed along the latest idea of local *norms*" and that "if a grade of 70 is the prevailing requirement in a school, then the same grade of 70 would be the norm for the test" in that school. This assumption would be considered outmoded and archaic by most modern test technicians.

Each test is provided with a class analysis blank for making a tabulation of the specific difficulties of individuals and the group to serve as a basis for remedial work. Since each type of difficulty is represented by one test item only, the results will be disappointing. At least three or four samples of a given type must be provided in order to give a reliable diagnosis of pupil difficulties.

The test exercises are strictly limited to the conventional types of arithmetical computations and verbal problems. One of several objections to the content of the tests is the use of "ragged" columns of decimals. Since this type of exercise is rarely encountered in real life, the test is perpetuating a type of arithmetical exercise which present-day textbook writers and curriculum experts have discarded. Another objection is that the tests have ignored some important objectives of a modern arithmetic curriculum. There is no attempt to measure concepts and understandings associated with a meaningful approach to instruction in arithmetic.

In view of the lack of data on reliability, validity, norms, and item analysis, and the emphasis upon formal and restricted objectives of the arithmetic curriculum, these tests can be re-garded only as practice exercises or informal tests which the teacher might use in stressing computation and problem solving. Furthermore, the content of some of the examples should be revised in accord with modern instructional practices in the elementary and junior high school curriculum. These tests fail to meet the minimum standards of the Committees on Achievement Test Standards of the American Educational Research Association and the National Council on Measurements Used in Education. The tests may be used for informal evaluation of the limited objectives indicated. They are inappropriate for testing the achievement of the various objectives in the modern arithmetic curriculum.

For reviews by Foster E. Grossnickle and Charles S. Ross of the original edition, see 4:400.

[459]
*Arithmetic: Every Pupil Scholarship Test. Grades 4–6, 7–8; 1928–58; new form usually issued each January and April; 2 levels; norms available following testing program; no data on reliability; 4¢ per test; 4¢ per scoring key; postage extra; 50(55) minutes; Bureau of Educational Measurements. *

[460]
*Arithmetic: Every Pupil Test. Grades 3, 4, 5–6; 1930–58; new form usually issued each December and April; norms available following testing program; no data on reliability; 3¢ per test; 1¢ per scoring key; cash orders postpaid; 40(45) minutes; Ohio Scholarship Tests. *

[461]
★Arithmetic Progress Test. Ages 9 to 10-8, 10 to 11-6; 1952–58; 2 levels; 2 forms; 5d. per single copy; postage extra; G. A. V. Morgan (b); published for the National Foundation for Educational Research; Newnes Educational Publishing Co. Ltd. *
a) ARITHMETIC PROGRESS TESTS B1 AND B2. Ages 9 to 10-8; 1958; Tests B1, B2 ['58]; manuals ('58) for each form; 4s. 3d. per 12 copies; 1s. per manual; 40(45) minutes.
b) ARITHMETIC PROGRESS TESTS C1 AND C2. Ages 10 to 11-6; 1952–58; Tests C1 ['52], C2 ['53]; revised manuals ('58) for each form; 4s. per 12 copies; 9d. per manual; 30(40) minutes.

WILLIAM CURR, *Lecturer in Education, University of Birmingham, Birmingham, England.* [Review of Tests C1 and C2.]

These tests measure arithmetic attainment in the last two years of the English junior school. Test C1 (formerly designated "C") is now reissued with a revised manual. The two forms are closely parallel but C2 is easier than C1. There are no practice items. Each test has two 15-minute sections ("mechanical" and "problem" arithmetic) of 25 items each. Basic concepts and number facts are not tested, and fractions appear only in problems. Work on denominate quantities is kept within realistic limits and requires reduction through only two or three steps. Problems are chiefly single operation, and are realistic, simple, and concisely stated. They involve a fair degree of computational skill. It is a pity (though it reflects the practice of many schools) that a test at this age level should include no items calling for approximation. The suggested use of the tests for diagnosis would be limited by the absence of any check on the work of earlier years, but the tests are obviously directed mainly at the brighter half of the two top age groups in the primary school (the lower quartile for age 10 on C1 is 5 items correct). With age allowances applied, mean scores range on C1 from 22 per cent correct at 10-0 to 34 per cent at 11-6, and on C2 from 34 per cent to 56 per cent.

The 4-page, quarto sized booklets have a very crowded front cover, which bears the test identification, scoring panel, personal data, instructions to the subject, and the first 8 of the 25 mechanical items. Accuracy of timing is apt to suffer with one third of the first 15-minute section of the test openly displayed during the whole process of distributing booklets, giving instructions, and completing seven personal entries. A similar disadvantage is the fact that the first half of the separately timed problems section faces page 2 of the mechanical section. Type face and layout are clear and there is ample space for answers, though not always for working. The instructions allow this to be done in the margin, but this procedure may penalise some children and tend to introduce copying errors.

In the mechanical section, operational symbols are omitted, and the need to refer to the verbal instruction above the problem is distracting. In the problem sections, "labels" are provided in the answer brackets. This is an ideal practice, though admittedly in some cases it may give a clue to the magnitude of the answer (for example, in cost problems where the £ sign is omitted). The repetition of item numbers beside answer brackets aids scoring, which is exceptionally speedy, the key being admirably clear and unambiguous.

Directions for administration follow the familiar NFER pattern. The printed instructions to the subject are brief and readable. In one item, milk consumption in pints per week

is to be converted to gallons per month; the lunar month, however, as assumed by the scoring key, is perhaps the obvious interpretation.

Standardisation of C1 is based on over 3,000 children aged 10-2 to 11-3 (less than the range of the norms) and Kuder-Richardson (formula 20) reliability is given as .96 ($n = 180$). Reliability data are usefully translated in the manual in terms of errors of measurement. No standardisation data are given for C2. On both tests the norms transform every raw score directly into a "transmuted score" (mean 100, SD 15) and these are also grouped into a 5-point literal scale. Optional age allowances for every month from 10-0 to 11-6 are offered. Discrimination is fine; over most of the range, one unit of standard score is roughly equal to a unit of raw score. The upper half of the ability range is particularly well spread.

These are very carefully prepared tests, showing a high standard of test production. Some improvements in layout would facilitate administration. They are excellent for grading and rough diagnosis within the upper half of the ability range in the final two years of junior school, but, for work with backward pupils at these levels, they are of more limited value because of their difficulty and their omission of the more elementary skills.

JOHN SUTHERLAND, *Senior Lecturer in Education, Moray House Training College, Edinburgh, Scotland.* [Review of Tests C1 and C2.]

These tests are open tests (that is, available to individual teachers) designed for the purpose of estimating the progress made by pupils in the last two years of the primary school course.

There are two sections in each test, one consisting of 25 items on mechanical arithmetic and the other containing 25 items on problem arithmetic. Fifteen minutes are allowed for each section. The mechanical arithmetic covers knowledge of the four fundamental processes together with a knowledge of the tables (money, length, weight, capacity, and time). The items in the problem section cover the same ground, but herein the problems are stated verbally rather than numerically. In addition, a few items involving vulgar fractions and simple proportion are included.

The manuals of instructions give detailed instructions for administration and marking, both of which follow the straightforward standard pattern for most such tests. What is termed a "Transmutation Table" is provided in each manual, by which raw scores are converted into transmuted scores which are measured on a scale with a mean of 100 and a standard deviation of 15. Another table gives a list of age allowances which may be added to the transmuted score if it is desired to take age differences into account when making score comparisons. These two tables are very simple and straightforward and have a great deal to commend them. Literal mark equivalents (A, B, C, D, E) are also provided, but there seems to be little to commend them.

The manual tells us that C1 was standardised on a representative sample of 3,201 children aged 10-2 to 11-3. The reliability of the test, measured by Kuder-Richardson formula 20, is .96, giving a standard error of measurement of 2.8. Test C2 has norms based on more than 3,200 pupils. No measure of reliability is provided for this test. In neither manual is the standardisation population precisely defined. This, together with the small numbers on which the norms are based, takes from the value of the transmuted scores. Though it is implied that the tests are parallel, a strict comparison between the transmuted scores obtained on each is not possible and any comparison with national norms must be made only within very broad limits.

The syllabus covered by the tests is what is generally accepted as the minimum requirement for all pupils completing a primary education in Britain. It is the sort of material tested in the fairly generally applied secondary school selection tests, and the transmuted scores with age allowances are measured on a scale similar to that on which intelligence and attainment quotients are measured. Therefore, with the qualifications indicated in the previous paragraph, they can serve as a guide to the teacher who is thinking in terms of these selection examinations and who may have to submit estimates of his pupils' abilities.

The question of age allowances on such tests is, of course, a very controversial one. It is argued that since performance on a school attainment test is to a large extent the product of the teaching which the child has received, the young child who has had the same teaching as the older child and is given an age allowance in addition has a decided advantage. Further, it is

pointed out that scores without age allowances are better predictors of future school success.

On the other hand, the child's performance does not depend solely on teaching and the group on which the test has been standardised must certainly have included younger children having the benefit of teaching given to older children so that the age allowances will allow more for differences which are independent of teaching. Again, in follow-up studies which show that scores without age allowances are better predictors, the criterion is usually one in which no allowance is made for age. This must vitiate the results. When attempting to select pupils with the greatest future potential, it seems wise to take steps to allow for the full recognition of the ability of the younger pupils in a class. Thus, the balance of the argument would appear to be in favour of age allowances.

The test itself might be criticised on two grounds. It appears to be rather short for accurate assessment, and a slight crowding of scores at the top would appear to indicate a lack of ceiling with the present time allowances. However, the reliability coefficient reported for C1 is as high as those for many longer tests; so if the test is used internally to assess progress as suggested in the manual, it is probably quite long enough and the lack of headroom is probably not a serious fault. In fact, to the busy teacher whose primary task is teaching and not assessment, the shorter time involved in testing and scoring will be counted as a positive asset.

The two tests, therefore, are useful tests for internal use by the individual teacher wishing some indication of the progress of his pupils, particularly with reference to the secondary school selection tests. For accurate assessment, however, a longer test with norms based upon a larger and more precisely defined population would be necessary.

[462]
*Arithmetic Test: Fundamental Operations: Dominion Tests. Grades 4-8; 1934-56; Forms A, B ('34); manual ('48); $1.20 per 25 tests; 10¢ per manual; 10¢ per scoring key; 40¢ per complete specimen set; postage extra; 35(45) minutes; Department of Educational Research, Ontario College of Education, University of Toronto; distributed by Guidance Centre. *

HARRY L. STEIN, *Professor of Education, University of British Columbia, Vancouver, British Columbia, Canada.*

This test, originally published in 1934, is still unrevised as to content. It is widely used in

Ontario but less widely used in the other provinces of Canada. Revised norms were published in 1948 and a new format of the manual was prepared in 1956. The new norms are based upon an Ontario sample of 7,000 children in grades 4–8. A feature of the revised norms is the separate ratings for small schools (1–4 teachers) and larger schools (5 or more teachers). However, the small number of pupils in the samples for some of the grades might cause concern regarding the reliability of the norms. Curricular validity of the test is based mainly upon the programme of studies followed in Ontario.

The test was reviewed in *The Third Mental Measurements Yearbook* by C. L. Thiele who questioned its use (as suggested by the authors) for both placement and diagnostic purposes. This criticism is even more serious today since curricular changes, even since 1948, have altered the grade placement of many of the computational aspects of arithmetic. The norms might, therefore, be quite inappropriate for schools other than those of the province of Ontario.

It would be well to reiterate the criticism that diagnosis on the basis of a limited number of test items in each of the designated areas (fundamental operations, weights and measures, fractions, etc.) is precarious. The instrument is essentially a survey test; for diagnostic purposes, it should be supplemented by a much more analytical instrument such as the *Diagnostic Tests in Arithmetic Fundamentals* by the same publishers.

Individual grade reliabilities vary from .87 at the fourth grade level to .94 at the sixth grade level. The original manual states that "the reliability of the test is greater in the higher grades because more examples are attempted by the pupils." The diagnostic function of the test at the earlier levels would be negated if many of the items were not attempted by the pupils.

In summary, then, the test will provide a useful basis for class to class comparison, and for individual assessment provided that local norms are prepared. It would be unrealistic to use it for diagnostic purposes. Thiele's review in *The Third Mental Measurements Yearbook* is recommended reading.

For a review by C. L. Thiele, see 3:332.

[463]

*Arithmetic Test (Fundamentals and Reasoning): Municipal Tests: National Achievement Tests.** Grades 3–6, 6–8; 1938–56; subtest of *Municipal Battery;* 6 scores: computation, number comparisons, comparisons, problem analysis, problems, total; 2 forms; 2 levels; no data on reliability; no norms for part scores; $2.75 per 25 tests; 50¢ per specimen set of either level; postage extra; 60(70) minutes; Robert K. Speer and Samuel Smith; Acorn Publishing Co. *
a) GRADES 3–6. 1938–56; Forms A ('38), B ('56, identical with test copyrighted in 1939); directions sheets (A, '38; B, '39).
b) GRADES 6–8. 1938–54; Forms A ('51, identical with test copyrighted in 1938 except for minor changes), B ('54, identical with test copyrighted in 1939); directions sheets (A, '51; B, '39).

For reviews by Foster E. Grossnickle and Charles S. Ross, see 4:406. For a review by J. Murray Lee of the complete battery, see 18; for a review by Ralph C. Preston, see 4:20; for reviews by A. M. Jordan of the complete battery for grades 6–8 and Hugh B. Wood of the batteries for grades 6–8, see 40:1191.

[464]

*Arithmetic Test: National Achievement Tests.** Grades 3–8; 1936–55; 2 forms; 2 tests; no data on reliability; no norms for part scores; $2.50 per 25 tests; 50¢ per specimen set; postage extra; Robert K. Speer and Samuel Smith; Acorn Publishing Co. *
a) FUNDAMENTALS. 1938–55; 4 scores: fundamentals-speed, number comparisons, fundamentals-skills, total; Forms A ('55, identical with test copyrighted in 1938), B ('38); directions sheet ('38); (55–85) minutes.
b) REASONING. 1936–54; 5 scores: comparisons, problem analysis, finding problem key, problems, total; Forms A ('50, identical with test copyrighted in 1938), B ('54, identical with test copyrighted in 1938 except for Item 6, Part 4); directions sheet ('38); (40) minutes.

For reviews by R. L. Morton and Leroy H. Schnell, see 40:1449; for reviews by William A. Brownell and W. J. Osburn, see 38:889.

[465]

★Arithmetic Tests 1–2, 4–7, 7E.** Ages 10 to 11-11; 1951–57; 7 forms; distribution restricted to directors of education; postage extra; 6s. 6d. per 12 tests; 7d. per single copy; 1s. 7d. per manual; G. A. V. Morgan (a–d) and M. A. Brimer (e); published for National Foundation for Educational Research in England and Wales; Newnes Educational Publishing Co. Ltd. *
a) ARITHMETIC TEST 1. 1951–54; form 1 ['51]; revised manual ('54); 40(45) minutes.
b) ARITHMETIC TEST 2. 1952–55; form 2 ['52]; revised manual ['55]; norms ['53]; 50(55) minutes.
c) ARITHMETIC TEST 4. 1954–57; form 4 ['53]; manual ('57); 50(55) minutes.
d) ARITHMETIC TEST 5. 1954–55; form 5 ['54]; manual ('55); no norms for ages 11-10 to 11-11; 50(55) minutes.
e) ARITHMETIC TEST 6. 1955–56; form 6 ['55]; manual ('56); no norms for ages 11-10 to 11-11; 50(55) minutes.

f) ARITHMETIC TEST 7. 1957; form 7 ['57]; 50(55) minutes.
g) ARITHMETIC TEST 7E. 1957; form 7E ['57]; 48(55) minutes.

[466]

★**Basic Number Skills Test for Employee Selection.** Job applicants; 1951–52; 1 form ('51); manual ('52); $2.50 per 25 tests; 50¢ per specimen set; cash orders postpaid; 60(65) minutes; William J. Morgan and Antonia Morgan; Aptitude Associates. *

DOROTHY C. ADKINS, *Professor of Psychology and Chairman of the Department, University of North Carolina, Chapel Hill, North Carolina.*

This 50-item test covers various numerical operations from simple addition to problems concerning carpeting floors and figuring income taxes. Since it is in completion form, its three pages must be hand scored. An error in test construction is that several problems depend upon answers to preceding ones, two even requiring referral to a problem on the reverse side of a page. One hour is allowed, although clearly some subjects would complete the test in less time. The test administrator is instructed to record any time less than an hour on the front page of the test, since "this time may serve as a qualitative index in evaluating the score." Preferred quantitative techniques for coping with individual differences in computational speed have been available for many years.

The authors state that various forms of the test have been tried out on thousands of cases. Without presenting any evidence of empirical validity, however, they state that the test is designed to test applicants for positions calling for skill in computation and practical arithmetic, that it is also useful for classifying employees in such jobs, and that it is relevant to any job that involves thinking in terms of dollars and cents. There follows a list of 21 occupations, such as accountant, business manager, economist, lawyer, and nutritionist, to which the test is said to apply. Decile norms are presented for 144 male high school graduates, aged 20 to 48; for 262 male college graduates with B.A. or B.S. degrees, aged 21 to 55; and for 116 male college graduates with majors in mathematics, accounting, or statistics, aged 21 to 57. All of these samples are referred to as random, almost certainly erroneously so.

In a misleading section on "BNST as an Index of Intelligence," the authors note that many experiments have demonstrated the very high relationship between scores on intelligence tests and the ability to solve problems in arithmetic.

They cite three correlations (based on 88, 22, and 25 cases, respectively) between the BNST and tests presumed to measure one or more aspects of intelligence.

As for reliability, the authors discuss this in connection with the possible desirability of using only the odd-numbered items (plus Item 6, presumably because Item 11 depends upon it!). They report that in a number of experimental runs the reliability coefficients (stepped-up odd-even coefficients?) varied from .90 to .94, and they seem to take great comfort from the fact that these coefficients were statistically significant. About the only consolation this reviewer derived was assurance that the size of the various samples must have been at least from 5 to 7 (depending upon whether the 5 per cent or the 1 per cent level of significance was demanded and assuming a 2-tailed test of the hypothesis that the population *r* equals zero).

MARION F. SHAYCOFT, *Program Director, American Institute for Research, Washington, D.C.*

This is a one-hour test consisting of 50 items measuring the ability to do arithmetic computation and to solve arithmetic problems. It is designed for high school and college graduates who are applicants for positions which call for skill in computation and practical arithmetic. According to the manual, "it is relevant to any job that involves thinking in terms of dollars and cents, as in calculating costs, profits or losses; taking in or spending money; and keeping accounts." The test is also described as "very useful for classifying employees in such jobs," although no instructions are given on how to use the test for this purpose.

Most of the test items appear satisfactory. A few, however, are either awkwardly or ambiguously worded. Instructions specify that decimal points are to be carried to four places but rounded off to two. This seems pointless and time wasting. A more serious difficulty with these instructions is that they fail to tell the examinee *how* to round, and then penalize him for using a reasonable procedure.

The manual presents percentile norms for "a random sample of 144 male high school graduates, ages 20 to 48"; for "a random sample of 262 male college graduates with B.A. or B.S. degrees, ages 21 to 55"; and for "a random sample of 116 males, college graduates, ages 21 to 57, all of whom had majored in mathematics, accounting, or statistics." Since the norms samples are said to be random, it is unfortunate that no supporting details are given as to how they were randomized. Furthermore, the populations are not defined adequately in terms of their sources. Are they job applicants or current employees? Are they in one organization or in several? The manual does not say. No norms tables are presented for women, but it is reported that they "obtain scores 20 percentiles lower than men of equivalent education" (except women who have majored in mathematics, accounting, or statistics). More detailed information clarifying the nature of the entire distributions of women's scores would be helpful.

It is reported that no significant age differences in regard to test score were found, over the age range 20 to 59. But this statement is difficult to interpret since the numbers of cases involved are not given. Some relationship might reasonably be expected, since the test appears to be somewhat speeded. Many examinees would not have time to finish within the allotted hour. The test is described in the manual as "a test of power as well as speed."

Odd-even reliability coefficients of .90 to .94 are reported, but neither the size nor the character of the samples is indicated. Since the test appears to be speeded, and since the halves were apparently not separately timed, the reliability coefficients reported are almost certainly spuriously high.

No evidence is presented concerning the validity of the test as a predictor of success in any of the jobs for which it is claimed to be a suitable selection tool. Nor are data presented to support the claim that the test is "useful for classifying employees."

In summary, the *Basic Number Skills Test for Employee Selection* is a test with considerable face validity, but one for which the descriptive information and empirical evidence that would permit the prospective user to evaluate its appropriateness for his own needs is either lacking or very inadequately reported. In other words, the most glaring deficiency of the test lies not in its content but in the vagueness and misleading character of some of the information presented in the manual, as indicated by its many departures from the standards presented in the American Psychological Association's *Technical Recommendations for Psychological Tests and Diagnostic Techniques.*

[467]

***A Brief Survey of Arithmetic Skills, Revised Edition.** Grades 5–12, 7–12; 1947–53; 3 scores: computation, reasoning, total; Forms A, B ('53); 2 editions; 20(25) minutes; Arthur E. Traxler. *

a) [EDUCATIONAL RECORDS BUREAU EDITION.] Grades 5–12; preliminary manual ['53]; norms ('53); no norms for Form B; postage extra.

b) [C. A. GREGORY CO. EDITION.] Grades 7–12; manual ('53); $2 per 25 tests; 35¢ per specimen set; postpaid.

REFERENCE

1. TRAXLER, ARTHUR E. "Reliability and Validity of a Brief Survey of Arithmetic Skills, Revised Edition." *Ed Rec B* 62: 76–84 F '54. * (PA 28:8004)

H. VERNON PRICE, *Professor of Mathematics and Astronomy, and Head of Mathematics in University High School, State University of Iowa, Iowa City, Iowa.*

Each form of the test consists of two parts. Part 1 contains 40 problems arranged in four cycles of 10 problems. Each cycle consists of one problem of each of the following kinds: addition, subtraction, multiplication, division, addition of fractions, subtraction of fractions, multiplication of fractions, division of fractions, placing the decimal point in multiplication, and placing the decimal point in division. Part 2 contains 10 reasoning problems. The time limits are 12 minutes for Part 1 and 8 minutes for Part 2.

The reliability coefficients, derived in a number of ways, center around .80. Norms are based on a substantial number of cases and seem to be quite adequate. The same tests, carrying norms for grades 5–12, are published by Educational Records Bureau.

The items of Part 1 are typical mechanical problems of varying degrees of difficulty. The time limit of 12 minutes to solve 40 items is quite short. It is doubtful if the very best students could do more than react to each problem and hurry on to the next; there isn't time to stop to meditate. In other words, a premium is placed on mechanical skill and speed—understanding is minimized, if not erased.

The items of Part 2 appear to be thought-provoking and to encompass an unusually wide range of difficulty for so short a test. A number of the exercises are type problems, however, and sufficient familiarity with the type is a distinct advantage in terms of speed.

The purpose of the test is to measure, in a short period of time, the achievement of pupils in the intermediate and upper grades and in high school in the skills of arithmetic. Because the test is so short and all items receive the same weight, one wonders if the discriminating factor is not speed rather than skill or any other attribute.

For reviews by William A. Brownell and Henry Van Engen of the original edition, see 4:409.

[468]

*California Arithmetic Test, 1957 Edition. Grades 1-2, 3-4.5, 4-6, 7-9, 9-14; 1933-57; subtest of the *California Achievement Tests;* 3 scores: reasoning, fundamentals, total; IBM for grades 4-14; 5 levels; battery manual ('57) for each level; technical report ('57); $2.80 per 35 tests; separate answer sheets may be used in grades 4-14; 4¢ per IBM answer sheet; 7¢ per Scoreze answer sheet; 20¢ per hand scoring stencil; 60¢ per machine scoring stencil; postage extra; 50¢ per specimen set of any one level, postpaid; Ernest W. Tiegs and Willis W. Clark; California Test Bureau. *
a) LOWER PRIMARY. Grades 1-2; Forms W ('57), X ('57); (39-50) minutes.
b) UPPER PRIMARY. Grades 3-4.5; Forms W ('57), X ('57); 54(65) minutes.
c) ELEMENTARY. Grades 4-6; IBM; Forms W ('57), X ('57), Y ('57), Z ('57); (80) minutes.
d) JUNIOR HIGH LEVEL. Grades 7-9; IBM; Forms W ('57), X ('57), Y ('57), Z ('57); 78(90) minutes.
e) ADVANCED. Grades 9-14; IBM; title on test is *California Mathematics Test;* Forms W ('57), X ('57), Y ('57); 72(80) minutes.

REFERENCE

1. PETA, STEPHEN BENJAMIN. "An Evaluation of Arithmetical Competence in the Junior High Schools of Lethbridge." *Alberta J Ed Res* 2:114-28 Je '56. *

ROBERT D. NORTH, *Assistant Director, Educational Records Bureau, New York, New York.*

The item content and essential features of the 1957 edition of the California arithmetic and mathematics tests are very similar to those of the corresponding tests of the 1950 series. Some items have been rearranged among subtests and forms, and some new items have been introduced. The primary level of the 1950 series was revamped to make the upper primary level of the 1957 edition, while the new lower primary level is an addition to the series. The length and timing of the comparable levels of the two series are about the same.

At each level, scores are obtained in reasoning and fundamentals, on the component sections of the subtests, and on the test as a whole. The results may be interpreted in terms of grade, age, and percentile norms, as well as in relation to the pupil's anticipated grade placement scores derived from his "intellectual status index" which is a function of his IQ and CA.

The Kuder-Richardson (formula 21) reliability coefficients, based on 200 cases at each of the grades 2-12, range from .72 to .93 for the reasoning scores, .70 to .95 for the fundamentals scores, and .84 to .97 for the total scores. The majority of the coefficients for the fundamentals and total scores are above .90. Reliabilities below .80 are reported for grades 2, 4, 5, and 7 in reasoning and for grades 4, 5, and 6 in fundamentals. No reliability data are given for the lower primary level for the first grade.

The articulation of these tests through a 14-grade span is advantageous for measuring growth from year to year in the basic arithmetic skills, but coverage of the typical content of mathematics courses from the seventh grade upward is sacrificed in attaining this objective. For any courses at or above the level of elementary algebra, the content validity of the tests is poor.

Throughout the various levels, the *California Arithmetic Test* offers little challenge to the more capable pupils, and weak students can obtain fair scores with a minimum of knowledge and average luck in guessing. For example, a fourth grade child taking the elementary level in the fall could get an arithmetic grade score of 3.7 and a percentile rank of 30 if he knew the meaning of the plus, minus, division, multiplication, and cents signs and had only chance success on the rest of the items. Furthermore, the coarse "percentile" scale would yield him another 10 points if one additional item were misscored in his favor, or if he knew, for example, that $4 + 2 = 6$. No correction is made for guessing though alternate norms based on corrected scores are available from the publisher.

Among the praiseworthy aspects of the series are the ease of scoring, diagnostic leads afforded by the item classification and difficulty data, coordinate norming with the *California Test of Mental Maturity,* and the attractive appearance of the booklets and supplementary materials.

The tests are appropriate for use as measures of basic arithmetic skills for the general run of public school pupils, provided that the normative ratings are interpreted cautiously. Other tests, such as those in the Stanford and Cooperative series, are more suitable for brighter pupils, especially for those who are preparing to go on to college.

For a review by Robert L. Burch of the 1950 edition, see 4:411; for reviews by C. L. Thiele and Harry Grove Wheat of an earlier edition, see 40:1459; for a review by W. A. Brownell, see 38:893. For a review by Charles O. Neidt of the complete battery, see 2; for reviews by Warren G. Findley, Alvin W. Schindler, and J. Harlan Shores of the 1950 edition, see 4:2; for a review by Paul A. Witty of the 1943 edition, see 3:15; for reviews by C. W. Odell and Hugh B. Wood of an earlier edition, see 40: 1193; for a review by D. Welty Lefever, see 38:876.

[469]

*Coordinated Scales of Attainment: Arithmetic. Grades 4, 5, 6, 7, 8; 1946–54; subtest of *Coordinated Scales of Attainment*; 2 scores: computation, problem reasoning; IBM; Forms A ('46), B ['49]; 5 levels; directions for administering ['52]; battery manuals (A, '54; B, '49); separate answer sheets must be used; $1.90 per 25 tests; $1 per 25 IBM scorable answer sheets; 10¢ per scoring stencil; 50¢ per specimen set; postage extra; (80) minutes; Leo J. Brueckner; Educational Test Bureau. *

For a review by Alvin W. Schindler of the complete battery, see 4:8; for reviews by Roland L. Beck, Lavone A. Hanna, Gordon N. Mackenzie (with Glen Hass), and C. C. Ross of Batteries 4–8, see 3:6.

[470]

★Cotswold Junior Arithmetic Ability Test. Ages 8–9; 1949–52; Forms A ['49], B ['52]; 9s. per 20 tests; 5½d. per single copy; 1s. per manual; postage extra; C. M. Fleming; Robert Gibson & Sons (Glasgow), Ltd. *
a) JUNIOR ARITHMETIC A. Form A ['49]; manual ['49]; 28(35) minutes.
b) JUNIOR ARITHMETIC B. Form B ['52]; manual ['52]; 40(50) minutes.

WILLIAM CURR, *Lecturer in Education, University of Birmingham, Birmingham, England.*

These two tests extend the age range of the Cotswold arithmetic tests down to 8 years. The forms are not parallel. The six separately timed subtests of Form A cover number concepts (enumeration, ordination, etc.) and notation, basic number facts, simple mechanical operations, vocabulary (shorter, bigger, difference, total, etc.), money, and length. In Form B, concepts are omitted, mechanical work covers a much greater range, and a 4-item subtest on common fractions is included.

The content is meaningful and realistic and corresponds well to the work of the first half of the primary school. The 99 items of Form A and 137 items of Form B cover this wide field representatively, though inevitably rather thinly in some areas (for example, Form A has 2 items on notation, 12 number facts, and 6 verbal problems). The pictorial and verbal items to test early number concepts and the problems on number vocabulary enhance the value of the tests. Zeros and common errors are well covered. Though limited by the sparseness of the coverage, these are useful diagnostic screening tests. A diagnostic analysis chart would be helpful to classroom teachers who use the test in this way.

The level and gradient of difficulty is satisfactory, and fatigue is slight. The verbal text requires a reading age of about 7 years. Time allowances are reasonable, except in the sections requiring reading and drawing. The meticulous child—despite the instruction to "draw any shapes you like"—can be much handicapped by attempting to reproduce the aesthetically but awkwardly asymmetrical boats.

Layout of the 8-page small-quarto booklet is ideal: front cover—identification, child's name, instructions to pupil (admirably contrived in words of one syllable); back cover—practice test; and one page for each timed subtest. Type face for digits is excellent. Working space is generally adequate except in the items requiring drawings. For the problems, there is no indication of where the answer is to be placed. Operational signs are regrettably omitted in the mechanical work, and the provision of "labels" in the answer brackets (— s — d) would avoid the awkward and ambiguous question form used in Form A to indicate reduction: "How many shillings and pennies had she?" The answer "one shilling and three pennies" is not provided for in the key, though this answer form is allowed in similar items in Form B. In the table of norms, the representation of years and months as if they were decimal fractions (e.g., 9.11) is confusing.

The brief manuals give simple and adequate directions for administration but there are a few ambiguities. For example, for Form A the teacher is asked to "read aloud the instructions for each test as it is reached"—but there are no introductory instructions for each subtest, and to read aloud each *item* would be prohibitively slow and involve "pacing" of those subtests using verbal material. In the practice test, "Draw nine trees" is followed by instructions to mark "the third tree" and "the fourth tree"; instructions to "draw nine trees *in a row*" would be better.

Scoring is quick, simple, and objective, the layout of the keys being parallel to that of the test items. In Form A, there is no indication that verbal answers to verbal problems should be accepted though the instructions do not forbid them. Norms are in the form of "standardised scores" (presumably of mean 100 and standard deviation 15) for each month of age between 8-0 and 9-11 (10-0 in Form B). Ages and standard scores are the marginal entries; raw scores are in the body of the table. This makes some interpolation necessary. Scores for each month group are well spread out. Form A was standardised on 16,000, and reliabilities are .99 (split-half, $n = 203$) and .93 (test-retest, $n = 92$). Item validity was checked by the upper and lower thirds technique; no details are given. No standardisation data are given for Form B.

These are useful tests to assess readiness for the work of the second half of the junior school. Most of the defects noted in Form A have been corrected in Form B, but the latter gives poorer coverage of the earliest stages of number.

GEORGE W. STURROCK, *Educational Psychologist, Dundee Education Committee, Dundee, Scotland.*

The tests, which are junior counterparts of the Cotswold tests for educational guidance at the 11 plus stage, are in two versions: Form A, said to be for children of age 8 on their last birthday, and Form B, for children of age 9 on their last birthday. Both give norms in the form of standardised scores for children from 8-0 to 10-0 (8-0 to 9-11 for Form A). Form A takes 28 minutes of working time and contains 99 items; Form B takes 40 minutes and contains 137 items. Form A was standardised on 16,000 pupils; the standardisation figure is not given for Form B. From the norms, it appears that both tests are suitable instruments of measurement for the age group 8-0 to 10-0, except that Form A does not provide headroom for the very bright older pupils. However, the difference between the tests and their relationship to one another is not made plain in the manuals, the only literature supplied by the publishers.

On examining the tests themselves, the main difference observed is that Form B contains a much larger proportion of formal sums and is far less verbal generally than Form A (B is

80 per cent formal and A 50 per cent). The original aim of Form A was to measure "the understanding of number, and the mastery of the vocabulary and the processes of arithmetic." This would explain its excessively verbal appearance. The appearance of Form B some years later suggests that Form A proved oververbal and that mastery of arithmetic was thought to be measured better through sums than through the verbalisation of arithmetical situations. At the same time, more sums of a slightly higher order of difficulty were added in Form B.

Both tests are divided into six subtests, each designed to cover a different section of an arithmetic syllabus based generally on the Beacon arithmetic scheme. It should be possible from an examination of a pupil's script to detect his strengths and weaknesses in each of the subtests, and then to take steps to make up the deficiencies. But some doubt arises as to what the total scores mean and whether total scores on Forms A and B are comparable. Inspection suggests that they would be far from comparable because of the above noted very verbal nature of Form A; but before a positive statement could be made, a factor analysis of the two forms in a battery of English and other arithmetic tests would be necessary.

The test layout is not altogether satisfactory. As is usual with printed tests known to the reviewer, the figures are much smaller than the child of 8 is accustomed to write. There is insufficient space for the drawings of boats and planes in Form A (and the drawing of the boats is too difficult, anyway). Then, short division sums are printed for an answer above the dividend. This is not universal practice. The instructions are not sufficiently exact nor is the layout, particularly of Form A, designed to prevent fast working pupils from going on to the next subtest when they have finished one. There are insufficient instructions about whether "working" in the problem sums is allowed and, if it is, where it is to be done.

The norms are expressed in standardised scores, mean 100, sigma 15. Too much interpolation is required in converting the scores. Standardised scores are reported at 2-point intervals in the range between 90 and 110, and at 3-, 4-, and 5-point intervals beyond these limits. The test constructor's difficulty has apparently been the very wide range of raw scores. This could be gotten over by printing raw scores in the margin and standardised scores in the body of the table. The tester would rather use the big table which this would involve, than interpolate. And a teacher would much rather have an arithmetic age than a standardised score.

To sum up: Form B is preferable to Form A because, in the reviewer's opinion, it is less contaminated with verbal ability and it has a rather higher ceiling. Both forms could be used to obtain ratings for a cumulative record card, where all that is required is a rough grading on a nationally known and standardised test; both could indicate weaknesses to be probed by individual diagnostic tests. It would be unsafe to compare classes (and thereby teachers and schools) on the basis of the test because of the vagueness of the instructions and the amount of verbal material in both forms, particularly Form A. Both forms could profit by a thorough revision of instructions, layout, and presentation of norms, and by the providing of more information about the validity of the whole tests and the subtests.

[471]

*Cotswold Measurement of Ability: Arithmetic. Ages 10–12.5; 1947–54; 6 forms: labeled Series 2 ['47], 3 ['49], 4 ['50], 5 ['52], 6 ['53], 7 ['54]; incomplete norms for Series 2–5; 9s. per 20 tests; 5½d. per single copy; 1s. per manual (dates as for tests) for any one series; postage extra; 35(45) minutes; C. M. Fleming and J. W. Jenkins (manual for Series 2); Robert Gibson & Sons (Glasgow), Ltd. *

For a review by W. L. Sumner of Series 1–4, see 4:412.

[472]

★Diagnostic Tests and Self-Helps in Arithmetic. Grades 3–12; 1955; orally administered in part; 1 form; no data on reliability; no norms; 50¢ per set of tests; 2¢ per test; 2¢ per record blank; 25¢ per manual; postage extra; 85¢ per specimen set, postpaid; administration time not reported; Leo J. Brueckner; California Test Bureau. *
a) SCREENING TESTS. Grades 4–6, 5–6, 6, 7 and over; Tests I–IV: whole numbers, fractions, decimals, general arithmetic.
b) DIAGNOSTIC TESTS. Grades 3, 4, 5, 6, 7; Tests 1–2: addition facts, subtraction facts; Tests 3–9(I): multiplication facts, division facts, uneven division facts, addition, subtraction, and multiplication of whole numbers, division by one-place numbers; Tests 9(II)–13: division by one-place numbers, division by two-place numbers, regrouping fractions, addition of like fractions, subtraction of like fractions; Tests 14–21: addition of unlike fractions, subtraction of unlike fractions, multiplication of fractions, division of fractions, addition of decimals, subtraction of decimals, multiplication of decimals, division of decimals; Tests 22–23: percentage, operations with measures.

HAROLD E. MOSER, *Director of College Test Services, State Teachers College, Towson, Maryland.*

The complete series of tests consists of 4 screening tests and 23 diagnostic tests. The diagnostic tests are keyed to the screening tests. On the reverse side of each diagnostic test is a page of self-help exercises that match the items in the diagnostic test.

The diagnostic tests are computational power tests. Each deals with one operation and contains sets of examples arranged in a carefully graded sequence of skills with one new complexity added at a time. Pupil weakness in a given operation will be exposed at a "breaking point," which is defined as that level of difficulty at which two or more similar items are missed. This point, the author indicates, is where remedial work should begin.

The self-help provided is based on what is sometimes called the "cookbook" technique. One or more of the examples from the test is solved by the standard algorism and, where appropriate, the procedural steps employed in reaching the solution are summarized beside it. Pupils are told to study the examples and to rework the exercises in the test according to pattern.

The entire set of tests covers all areas of the fundamental operations with whole numbers, common fractions, and decimals that are taught in grades 3–8. The tests are recommended for either individual or class diagnosis. An individual record sheet is available for those who keep case histories. The author recommends that each screening test be repeated after the related diagnostic tests and remedial work have been completed.

The manual provides suggestions for the effective use of the test results. The author recommends the use of supplementary diagnostic procedures, such as pupil observation and oral interview, when the underlying difficulties are not clearly revealed by the test. The manual also provides a list of "the most common faults" in operations with whole numbers, common fractions and decimals. Users of the *California Arithmetic Test* will find a table keying the items from the fundamentals test to the DTSA to facilitate the identification of related elements.

These tests are intended as instructional materials and no national or local norms are provided. The materials will be useful to those who are concerned solely with the ability to compute accurately with the conventional algorisms. For these users the tests will supply useful information about the varieties of computational complexities that can, or cannot, be handled effectively.

It is unfortunate that a test with such a restricted function should carry the unqualified title of "Diagnostic Tests." Any implication that the discovery and elimination of errors in the mechanics of computation is the essence of diagnosis falls far short of current thinking. Teachers attempting diagnosis in this narrow and oversimplified frame of reference will, in many instances, find themselves treating the symptoms rather than the causes. A comprehensive approach to diagnosis ought to furnish answers to questions such as the following:

a) Does the pupil have the meanings and understandings to function adequately in the area?

b) At what level of thinking is he attempting to operate? Is the level appropriate to his intellectual calibre, powers of concentration, and depth of perception?

c) For this pupil, are the mechanical operations ends in themselves, or a means to quantitative thinking? For example, does the pupil divide only when the situation is set up for him, or does he readily recognize, in their social settings, those quantitative situations that call for division as a means of arriving at a conclusion?

d) How dependent is he upon rigid forms or "steps" in procedure? Must he use paper, pencil, and thinking routines for all computations—even where the numbers have properties that suggest laborsaving shortcuts?

e) What are the limitations in the pupil's technical skills? What are the limits of the complexities in computation that he is equipped to handle accurately and with reasonable speed? Is his ability to compute adequate for his powers of thinking?

It is not presumed, of course, that the answers to all of these questions can be obtained through the application of one paper-pencil test any more than a complete medical diagnosis can be effected with the sole aid of a clinical thermometer. On the other hand, a test that supplies answers to but one of five important questions pertinent to arithmetical diagnosis ought not to mislead teachers into believing that they have, in one instrument, a complete answer to their needs in arithmetic diagnosis.

[473]

*Diagnostic Tests in Arithmetic Fundamentals: The Dominion Tests, Revised Edition. Grades 2, 3, 4, 5, 6; 1945–57; 1 form ('53); 5 levels; mimeographed manual ('55) for each level except *b, g,* and *h;* no data on reliability; $1.35 per 25 tests; 25¢ per manual; 30¢ per specimen set of any one level; postage extra; Department of Educational Research, Ontario College of Education, University of Toronto; distributed by Guidance Centre. *

a) GRADE 2, ADDITION-SUBTRACTION. (87–110) minutes in 4 sessions.

b) GRADE 3, ADDITION-SUBTRACTION-MULTIPLICATION. Revised manual ('55); (70–95) minutes in 3 sessions.

c) GRADE 4, PART 1, ADDITION-SUBTRACTION. 100(120) minutes in 5 sessions.

d) GRADE 4, PART 2, MULTIPLICATION-DIVISION. (90–110) minutes in 4 sessions.

e) GRADE 5, PART 1, ADDITION-SUBTRACTION-MULTIPLICATION-DIVISION. 80(100) minutes in 4 sessions.

f) GRADE 5, PART 2, FRACTIONS (ADDITION-SUBTRACTION). 90(110) minutes in 3 sessions.

g) GRADE 6, PART 1, ADDITION-SUBTRACTION-MULTIPLICATION-DIVISION. Manual ('53); 60(75) minutes in 2 sessions.

h) GRADE 6, PART 2, FRACTIONS-DECIMALS. Manual ('53); 75(95) minutes in 3 sessions.

JOHN SUTHERLAND, *Senior Lecturer in Education, Moray House Training College, Edinburgh, Scotland.*

There are in this series tests at five levels to be set in the spring term of the second to sixth year at school or the fall term following. In the lower tests up to grade 4, part of each test is administered orally at a fixed speed indicated in the instructions and part of it is left for the child to do in a fixed time. The later tests can be tackled by the child on his own.

The grade 2 test contains items testing addition without bridging the 10 and subtraction without borrowing. The grade 3 test covers addition involving bridging the 10, subtraction involving borrowing, and multiplication by single digit numbers up to five. The grade 4 test is in two parts, Part 1 dealing with addition and subtraction, and Part 2 with multiplication and division up to multiplication by a 2-digit number and division by a single digit number. Some of the addition columns here seem to be unnecessarily long. It is stated in the instruction booklet that the column additions are based on the assumption that the child will add up. There is no guarantee that the child will do so even if he is so instructed.

The grade 5 test covers all four basic processes in Part 1 and addition and subtraction of vulgar fractions in Part 2. The layout of the fractions with the fractions to be added or subtracted set one below the other would seem strange to most British children. The grade 6 test covers the same ground together with addition and subtraction of decimals. The examples on decimals involve a great deal of computation and tell the tester very little about the child's knowledge of decimals. In addition and subtraction of decimals, nothing new is introduced except putting the point in the answer below the column of points above. No understanding of decimals is tested until the child tackles multiplication and division.

For each process at each stage norms are provided both in percentile ranks and on a 9-point letter scale. From these norms it seems quite clear that the tests are designed to pick out those children who are becoming retarded. There is very little spread of scores above the median.

There are two points which must be borne in mind in using these tests and the norms. In the first place, the knowledge of arithmetic possessed by a child is very dependent upon the syllabus and the teaching methods in the school that he attends. There is, for example, a movement today towards concentrating on giving the child an understanding of the basic processes in the first two years and leaving drilling in these processes until the third and later years. Pupils taught in this way might well be handicapped in the grade 2 and 3 tests. Those using the tests must, therefore, select the tests which are suited to the stage the children they are teaching have reached and not necessarily the tests corresponding to the age of the children.

Secondly, these tests are group tests with fixed times. Thus, while they will tell the teacher how his pupils compare with other pupils at the same stage both in regard to accuracy and speed, and while they will also indicate the particular type of item with which the child has difficulty, the information cannot be compared with that provided by an individually administered test. In such a test, there are normally no time limits and the highly skilled tester can use the test as he sees fit and supplement it where necessary. Only in this way is it possible to obtain detailed information about the individual child's difficulties.

This series of tests, administered according to the instructions, should prove a valuable aid to teachers in identifying the more obvious difficulties of pupils not holding their own. Points

which require reteaching or additional drill or practice will show up, but pupils with more complex difficulties will need to be referred to a person with more specialised knowledge who, with the help of a test such as the *Schonell Diagnostic Arithmetic Test* or the above tests used as individual tests without time limits, can make a more detailed diagnosis.

For a review by Leo J. Brueckner of the original edition, see 3:341.

[474–5]

★Diagnostic Tests in Vulgar Fractions, Decimal Fractions and Percentages. Ages 10–14; 1956; 14 subtest scores; 1 form; no norms; 25–49 tests, 7d. each; 8d. per single copy; 2s. per manual; postage extra; 66.5(80) or (60–90) minutes in 2 sessions 1 day apart; Fred J. Schonell, J. Richardson, and K. P. O'Connor; Oliver & Boyd Ltd. *

REGINALD EDWARDS, *Lecturer in Educational Psychology, University of Sheffield, Sheffield, England.*

In preparing this test of 232 items, the authors analysed each of the three processes (vulgar fractions, decimal fractions, and percentages) into its basic components, and considered the logical steps necessary for their mastery. Preliminary testing revealed a certain amount of duplication of the steps involved in some processes, but it is safe to say that the final tests contain no duplication whatsoever. Each kind of difficulty that can be encountered, save only those due to the use of extremely large and frightening numbers beloved of some of the older textbooks, has one and only one item which might reveal it. Diagnosis, in the case of an individual child, should therefore be made in a broad area only; in the case of a group, frequent incorrect responses to a single item might well be diagnostic of group weaknesses in this particular process.

There are four subtests in vulgar fractions, five in decimal fractions, and five in percentages. Since the items follow a logical skill mastery pattern, the number of items varies from subtest to subtest. The authors indicate that items are placed in order of difficulty in so far as that does not cut across the logical development of the tests. The important work of analysis was carried out on 200 children (age not given) who had completed two years' work in vulgar and decimal fractions and one year in percentages. Preliminary investigations were carried out on 500 children between the ages of 11 and 14, the amount of study devoted to these topics not being disclosed. Reliability was determined by test-retest of a relatively homogeneous group of 100 children of age 13. Lowest and highest reliabilities only are quoted, these being .83 and .94. No indication is given of the interval between test and retest, nor the kind of teaching in the interim. There is a useful manual with instructions for giving the tests, an analysis of the steps involved in the correct solution of each item, and an analysis of the errors of 250 children on each item.

The tests are meant to be diagnostic of the progress which children make after teaching and of the difficulties which individuals in the class are encountering. Teaching can then be directed to overcoming such difficulties. Equally, knowledge of the kind of errors made should enable the teacher to decide in advance the kind of teaching which might prevent their arising. The authors suggest further that the tests can be used to indicate the attainment level of children coming into the class from different schools, which seems to imply that they should be useful in the first year of a secondary school, when children are approximately 12 years old. That would be a year earlier than the age of children upon whom they were standardised, and there is no guarantee that the condition of the standardisation group at the time of testing (two years' study of vulgar and decimal fractions and one year of percentages) will have been fulfilled. It is the reviewer's opinion that relatively few children of 12 will be able to fulfill this condition.

In fact, the authors appear to be advising teachers that if they do not wish to use the test for its proper purpose, they can use it as an attainment test, even though no norms are given for such a use. This seems to be a most dubious procedure, and is hardly conducive to the further training of teachers in the use of properly constructed tests. The majority of teachers in primary and secondary schools in England have received little training in the use of diagnostic tests, and tend to regard them as tools for the psychologist rather than for the practising teacher. Among the few who do make use of them, there may well be a tendency to overdiagnose. It is vitally important, therefore, that the test constructors be specific in their instructions and intentions.

In the giving of the tests, two notes of caution must be sounded. It is advised that no more than two or three of the subtests be given in any one day, that is, at the most, about 20 minutes of testing time. Testing may be spread out over several days or even more widely. This is an important condition to observe, since there are some enthusiastic teachers who must be restrained from seeking to know everything about each child in the very first few days of secondary school life. Again, it is suggested that the test be used with children between the ages of 11 and 14. This is largely because, in the past, it has been traditional for English children to be introduced to vulgar and decimal fractions at about the age of 10, and to percentages a year later. During recent years there has been a growing tendency to remove from the primary schools the teaching in decimal fractions and percentages, and to reduce the time spent on the teaching of vulgar fractions. This would suggest that the test must be used with discretion, and with more regard to the condition of "two years' teaching in fractions and decimals and one year in percentages" than to any consideration of age or grade placement.

It is this reviewer's opinion that this is a most useful diagnostic test, a necessary adjunct for a skillful teacher. Its greatest merit lies in its thorough analysis of all the operations encountered in a mastery of the three processes; with this analysis, a good teacher would increase in skill and in the elimination of mistakes among pupils. Unfortunately, at the moment we do not possess sufficient good teachers of arithmetic and mathematics, and many indifferent teachers are called upon to teach the subject. With the help of such tests as this, and training in their use, the indifferent teacher can be helped to recognize the kind of errors into which his pupils fall and to improve their computational accuracy. But, in the light of the scantiness of training in the use of diagnostic tests which many have received, if this is to be done, it is most important that interpretation instructions should be more detailed than those supplied and, above all, that the test should be represented as a diagnostic test, and not as a test which can be used in any one of a variety of ways at the whim of the individual teacher.

[476]

Graded Arithmetic-Mathematics Test. Ages 7-21; 1949; 1 form ['49]; 5s. per 25 tests; 3d. per single copy; 1s. 3d. per manual ['49]; postage extra; 20(25) minutes; P. E. Vernon; University of London Press Ltd. *

STANLEY NISBET, *Professor of Education, University of Glasgow, Glasgow, Scotland.*

The test consists of 75 questions, the earlier ones being purely arithmetical and the later ones bringing in algebra, geometry, and trigonometry at levels corresponding to the ages at which these subjects are usually taught in British schools. The item gradient is very steep indeed: the first question requires adding 5 and 3; the last concerns the equation of a parabola. "Arithmetic-Mathematics Ages" are worked out on the principle used in Binet testing. There are five items for each year of mental age, beginning at 6.0. The A-M age is, therefore, six years plus one fifth of a year for each correct response. As in Binet testing, time is saved by finding a suitable starting point for each child, and by ending the test as soon as a whole group of five items is failed. The instructions given for this are reasonable and adequate.

Information is given about the reliability (corrected odd-even coefficients, averaging .88) and about the standardization procedure. The latter is not clearly enough explained, and would appear to rest on assumptions which require more justification than they receive in the manual. "Representative sampling at all ages," we are told, "was hardly practicable. For the most part, therefore, [the test] has been standardised against Mental Ages or Reading Ages." This seems to imply that the relationship between A-M score and mental or reading age can be worked out directly without reference to chronological age. This is surely doubtful, especially if one also disputes the claim which seems to be made earlier in the manual that this is as much a test of ability in arithmetic and mathematics as a test of knowledge. Surely the year of school life (school grade) a pupil has reached—which is largely a matter of chronological age—must be a considerable factor in determining his score on a test like this.

According to the manual, this test is intended "primarily for use in Educational and Child Guidance Clinics, where it is important to know the standing of the child in the main school subjects as well as his Mental Age." The test is well designed for this purpose, enabling the tester to gauge the pupil's level quickly and with the minimum of trouble. The grading it provides is coarse, but it should be adequate for preliminary or diagnostic procedures. It should show quickly, for instance, whether a pupil is significantly retarded in arithmetic or

mathematics (though, in the light of the criticism above concerning chronological age, it appears doubtful whether it could detect ability far in advance of chronological age). The test may also be used as a group test for school and class surveys, but not "in a competitive situation." Its very wide attainment range makes it a useful general purpose instrument for survey work, though it will not give fine discrimination at any particular level. It is doubtful, however, if the test can be recommended to class teachers for general use; the reviewer would certainly hesitate to accept the suggestion in the manual and use the test "for providing A-M Ages or Quotients which can be entered on cumulative record cards."

[477]

★Group Test of Speed and Accuracy in Arithmetic Computation: Dominion Tests. Grades 5–10; 1955–56; 3 scores: speed, accuracy, achievement; Forms A ('55), B ('55); mimeographed preliminary manual ('56); $1.20 per 25 tests; 10¢ per manual; 20¢ per complete specimen set; postage extra; 22(35) minutes; Department of Educational Research, Ontario College of Education, University of Toronto; distributed by Guidance Centre. *

FRANCES E. CROOK, *Assistant Professor of Education, McGill University, Montreal, Canada.*

This test provides a measure of achievement, speed, and accuracy in the four fundamental operations with whole numbers. Each of the four subtests is separately timed. The last page of the test booklet contains directions for computing raw scores for each part of the test and a profile chart on which can be plotted the percentile rank for achievement, speed, and accuracy in the fundamental operations.

The items in the various subtests do not seem to be arranged in order of difficulty or in any pattern according to type, and they do not include as wide a variety of items as would seem desirable. If the test is to be used for the wide range of grades for which it is designed, a greater range of difficulty is needed and more attention should be paid to the arrangement of items.

The manual is carefully prepared and contains, in addition to the directions for administration and scoring, some information concerning the Ontario schools used in the standardization of the test, spring percentile norms for grades 5 to 10, tables showing between-forms reliability, and examples illustrating the diagnostic use of the test profiles. The manual also includes a brief discussion of the size of the between-forms reliability coefficients obtained, including an explanation of the low values found for the accuracy scores on all of the subtests. However, no mention is made and no explanation given of the equally noteworthy fact that the mean scores on the whole test increase from 10 to 12 points with each successive grade, *except* between grades 8 and 9, where there is a drop of 2 points.

In general, the test appears to have been carefully prepared for a rather limited purpose. It could be useful to those attempting to survey achievement or diagnose difficulty in computation with whole numbers.

WILLIAM HARRISON LUCOW, *Associate Professor of Education, University of Manitoba, Winnipeg, Manitoba, Canada.*

The test offers nothing new in the way of content, but it does yield three pertinent scores: achievement, speed, and accuracy.

Percentile norms are provided for each grade for each subtest and for total achievement, speed, and accuracy scores. The standardization involved 11,000 public school pupils in Ontario, Canada. No validity data appear in the 1956 preliminary edition of the manual. Estimates of between-forms reliabilities for individual grades range from .85 to .92 for total scores in achievement and from .87 to .91 for total scores in speed. Because of the narrow spread of scores, the reliabilities for accuracy are much lower, ranging from .47 to .76.

Scoring is time-consuming, and is aggravated by the absence of a stencil. There is an error in the key for Item 21 in the multiplication test. Item 12 in the division test might present an ambiguity to the scorer; with zero remainder, there is a tendency for the testee not to complete the last step of the division process. This could be obviated if the tests were not expendable, and the answer sheet called for the answer plus remainder.

This could be a useful test. The subtests provide diagnostic data for remedial work, and the profiles for each pupil indicate whether achievement, speed, or accuracy requires added attention.

[478]

★**Madden-Peak Arithmetic Computation Test: Evaluation and Adjustment Series.** Grades 7 and over; 1954–57; 6 scores: addition and subtraction, multiplication and division, common fractions, decimal fractions-mixed decimals-percentages, mental compu-

tation and estimation, total; IBM; Forms AM, BM ('54); manual ('56); reliability data for part scores for grade 11 only; 2 sheets of supplementary norms ['57]; no norms for grades 13 and over; $3.25 per 35 tests; separate answer sheets may be used; $1.40 per 35 IBM answer sheets; 20¢ per machine scoring stencil; postage extra; 35¢ per specimen set, postpaid; 49(60) minutes; Richard Madden and Philip Peak; World Book Co. *

THEODORE E. KELLOGG, *Admissions Officer and Assistant Professor of Education, University of Minnesota, Minneapolis, Minnesota.*

The format of this test is quite good but the fact that the six pages fold together, and that when a separate answer sheet is used, each test page must be folded to match the answer key, seem to present unnecessary mechanical difficulties which could be avoided by a booklet arrangement. Some distraction also results from the fact that responses for alternate items are keyed "a" through "d" and then "e" through "h." The "not given" response for each item is coded as "NG" but the definition of "NG" is given only in the original instructions. In Part 4 it would seem better to place those items pertaining only to decimal placement together rather than mixing them with items where choice of digit is also required.

While the test manual is very comprehensive, it could be greatly improved by better organization and by greater conciseness in writing. Some information is unnecessarily hidden (e.g., difficulty level) and some is scattered with inadequate cross referencing (e.g., equivalence of forms). Some tables are not self-descriptive (e.g., 6 and 13). Explanations pertaining to interpretation of results are good in some instances, and inadequate in others (e.g., the use of stanines).

The 9th, 10th, and 11th grade norms groups are well described, with data given according to sex, ability, mathematics courses taken, and curriculums followed. The extent to which the norms groups may reflect the national school population is not equally well defined. The norms are reported as percentile ranks for total scores and part scores (grades 7–8 tentative, and grades 9–11), stanine levels for total scores (grades 7–11), and "standard scores" for total scores (grades 9–11). Supplemental norms for grades 9–12 are provided, but the norms group is not described. The appropriateness and value of the stanine transformation are discussed much too briefly to insure proper use of the levels derived in this way. The term "standard score" is somewhat a misnomer as used in the test manual, for the transformation used involves the conversion of raw score distributions to a distribution of IQ scores (*Terman-McNemar Test of Mental Ability*). The usual standard score derives from a transformation using the mean and standard deviation. Although the conversion does provide one type of comparability to other scores similarly transformed, the reviewer feels it adds little to the interpretation of the results of the test being reviewed. The "standard score" here provided is extremely difficult to interpret in view of the relationship between this test and the intelligence test used (reported as $r = .64$ in one sample). The fact that the "standard score" is interpreted in relation to the IQ score, with both scores drawn from the same numerical range, adds to this difficulty.

The reliability of the test is reported for grade 11 only. The two groups used were small ($n = 92, 131$) and probably necessarily biased with respect to the basic norms group because of the restriction in grade level. Reliability coefficients are sufficiently high for total score, but for several of the part scores they are in the .70's and in one instance in the low .60's (which seems unduly low for this type of test).

The validity of the test is described largely in terms of selection of content. This selection is adequate within the restrictions imposed by the small number of items dealing with each type of skill. Correlations between this test and the computation subtest of the *Stanford Achievement Test: Arithmetic* are also reported (.77 and .82). The small number of items in each part (12, 14, 16, 15, and 16 in the respective parts) inevitably restricts the diagnostic function the test is purported to provide. It is also of interest to note that six of nine "judges" from business, industry, and government rated Part 3 of the test (Common Fractions) as "Unrelated to Success" or "Desirable" in contrast to the greater importance assigned to the other areas measured.

Although the forms of this test are said to be interchangeable, alternate forms reliability data provided in the manual indicate that correlations between total scores on the two forms range from .86 to .94. An alternate forms coefficient of .50 is reported for one part score. In the writer's opinion these coefficients pose some question as to the degree of equivalence between the two forms.

Little or no information is provided in the manual as to item discrimination indices, item difficulty level, and the effectiveness of distractors. This latter point is important where few items are involved, as in the parts of this test, and there is no correction for guessing.

The publisher is to be commended for objective reporting and interpretation of data pertaining to the test. The data provided in the manual suggest that the test is most adequate for use in grades 9, 10, and 11. The appropriateness of the test for lower levels and for adults is not so clearly defined. Although the manual indicates a wide variety of uses for the test, it would seem, on the basis of data provided, to be best suited for achievement testing at the levels already indicated and less useful as a diagnostic or prognostic instrument. It seems clear that considerably more confidence may be placed in total scores than in those for the various parts.

ALBERT E. MEDER, JR., *Vice Provost and Dean of the University, Rutgers, The State University, New Brunswick, New Jersey.*

This test is described by the publisher as "a reliable measure of the skills needed in performing the basic operations of arithmetic." It is intended for use chiefly at the high school and adult levels, but may also be used in grades 7 and 8.

It is stated in the manual that nine personnel directors of business, industry, and governmental services judged each item of the test as to the need for the ability tested by the item. They considered practically all items in Parts 1, 2, and 4 to be essential, but little of Part 3; there was great variation in opinion with respect to individual items in Part 5, which calls largely for mental computation of the same skills tested in Parts 1–4. The judgments on individual items in Part 5, however, were generally consistent with the judgments expressed on Parts 1–4.

The description of the test seems accurate. It seems to be a good test of arithmetic computation. As indicated, it includes computations that many persons will not consider particularly important. Part scores are, therefore, probably more significant than total scores. A high score on any part should indicate functional competence with respect to the skills tested in that part. The manual is unusually complete.

[479]

★**Milne Arithmetic Test.** Standards 2–8 (ages 7–17); 1946–54; based upon F. T. Milne's *Witwatersrand Test;* Forms A, B ['46]; 2 tests; manual ['54]; no data on reliability; postage extra; specimen set not available; National Bureau of Educational and Social Research. *
a) FUNDAMENTAL PROCESSES. 4 scores: addition, subtraction, multiplication, division; 21*s.* 2*d.,* 21*s.* 8*d.* per 100 copies of Forms A, B; 16(20) minutes.
b) MECHANICAL COMPUTATION AND PROBLEMS. 2 scores: computation, problems; 7*s.* 6*d.,* 5*s.* per 100 copies of Forms A, B; 20(25) minutes.

[480]

★**New York Test of Arithmetical Meanings.** Grades 1.5–2.0, 2.5–3.0; 1956; 1 form; 2 levels; $3.70 per 35 tests for grades 1.5–2.0; $3.10 per 35 tests for grade 2.5–3.0; postage extra; 50¢ per specimen set, postpaid; (60) minutes in 2 sessions; J. Wayne Wrightstone, Joseph Justman, Morris Pincus, and Ruth H. Lowe; World Book Co. *

CHARLES S. ROSS, *Editor-in-Chief, Silver Burdett Company, Morristown, New Jersey.*

This standardized testing program in arithmetic for the first two grades consists of two tests in a single booklet for each of two levels. Test 1 at each level consists of "pre-measurement concepts" or measurement items. Test 2 consists of numerical concepts or items requiring use of numerical processes, with a few exceptions which require general information only.

The tests themselves are carefully and professionally prepared, appear to be easy to administer, and avoid reading difficulties by relying entirely on pictures and oral directions. The drawings which make up the tests, however, are not of high quality and the small size of many of the pictured objects may create difficulties for immature children. A few items are poor technically: for example, some items requiring use of ordinals give the child no clue as to which end of a row is considered the beginning of it.

In their presentation of the program in the examiner's manual, the authors speak of testing "essential" concepts. There is a real question, however, as to the essentiality of some of the items for future success in arithmetic, and particularly as to the success of these tests in providing a balanced survey of the child's arithmetical development.

Test 1 for Level One, for instance, contains such items as the following:

a) Four pairs of mittens of different sizes are pictured hanging from a line. The child is asked to identify the baby's mittens.
b) Four sailboats are pictured in perspective and

the child is asked to identify the boat which is farthest away.
c) Four boys are pictured pulling four carts each of which has a package on it. The packages are identical. From the ease of pulling the carts, as indicated by the angle at which the boys are leaning forward as they pull, the child is supposed to identify the lightest package.

Other items in this part of the test involve terms of position and comparison, as *under, outside, most, longest,* and items requiring estimation of size and shape. The term *fit* is tested in the sense that gloves fit the hand. The concept that a pile of rubber balls weighs less than a pile of bricks, rocks, or sand, is also tested.

Many of these items are related only obscurely to arithmetic instruction or content and cannot be justified as "essential concepts" necessary to future progress in arithmetic. It appears that concern over selecting items that can be pictured, and therefore can be used in a test for children having little reading ability, may have influenced the inclusion of some of the items.

The items for Test 2 at each level should be carefully scrutinized by potential users for curricular validity. In the test for Level One, for instance, the children are expected to have some concepts of multiplication and division, including finding a fractional part of a group. The inclusion of multiplication, division, and the partition idea of division in the first grade will mean that these items are outside the experience of many, if not most, first grade children.

No one can surely say what represents an accurate cross section of "essential" arithmetical concepts from which future success in arithmetic can be predicted and on which one can base a well balanced remedial program. Nevertheless, it is safe to say that the items in these tests do not represent such a cross section. Of 114 items in the four tests for both levels, 57, or one half, are on "pre-measurement" concepts or matters of general information. In the arithmetic course in grades 3–8, no such emphasis on measurement and general information exists.

Standardized tests have an influence on curriculum and on teaching emphasis that test authors frequently fail to recognize. Some users of these tests will be tempted to put into the first and second grade arithmetic program much more emphasis on "pre-measurement concepts" of dubious instructional value than the present program includes. They will do this, not for sound curriculum reasons, but because the authors of this test, in searching for items that are usable, warped the test out of all resemblance to a sensible and balanced arithmetic program. The same test users, or others, will be tempted to put partition division into the first grade program merely because the test for that grade calls for it, and despite the fact that much must be done to get the child ready for this concept before the process is introduced. At the same time, users of this test will be tempted to reduce the emphasis on number meanings, meaning of the processes, and development of other basic understandings because the test does not appear to emphasize them.

These shortcomings are not confined to the standardized test under discussion. The makers of standardized tests generally—and this includes both authors and publishers—have a responsibility to the curriculum. It is not the function of test makers to make tests and simultaneously remake the curriculum. Rather, it should be the responsibility of test makers to leave the curriculum unrestricted. This means selecting test items which in themselves represent a balanced curriculum. It also means trying to select items which are universally included in the curriculum—not items which only radically new or completely outmoded courses include. Unless test makers assume this responsibility, standardized tests may unintentionally restrict curriculum development and impede progress in instruction.

[481]

*Primary Arithmetic: Every Pupil Scholarship Test.** Grades 1, 2–3; 1935–58; new form usually issued each January and April; 2 levels; norms available following testing program; no data on reliability; 4¢ per test; 4¢ per scoring key; postage extra; (60) minutes; Bureau of Educational Measurements. *

[482]

*Revised Southend Attainment Test in Mechanical Arithmetic.** Ages 7–15; 1939–50; 1 form ['50]; 2 parts: Sheets 1, 2; manual ('50); withdrawn; George G. Harrap & Co. Ltd. *

For a review by Stephen Wiseman of the original edition, see 3:352.

[483]

★SRA Achievement Series: Arithmetic.** Grades 2–4, 4–6, 6–9; 1954–57; title on some tests for grades 2–6 is *Let's Figure This Out;* 3 scores: reasoning, concepts and usage, computation; IBM for grades 4–9; Forms A, B; 3 levels; technical supplement, second edition ('57); separate answer sheets must be used in grades 4–9; 50¢ per teacher's handbook ('55); 50¢ per administrator's manual ('56); $1 per technical supplement; postage extra; Louis P. Thorpe, D. Welty

Lefever, and Robert A. Naslund; Science Research Associates. *
a) GRADES 2–4. Forms A ('55), B ('57); examiner's manual, second edition ('57); $1.70 per 20 tests; $1 per scoring stencil; (170) minutes in 3 sessions.
b) GRADES 4–6. IBM; Forms A ('54), B ('56); examiner's manual ('56); $2 per 20 tests; $5 per 100 IBM scorable answer sheets; $1 per set of machine scoring stencils; 50¢ per hand scoring stencil; 120–(150) minutes in 2 sessions.
c) GRADES 6–9. IBM; Forms A ['55], B ('56); examiner's manual ('56); prices same as for grades 4–6; 120(150) minutes in 2 sessions.

ROBERT D. NORTH, *Assistant Director, Educational Records Bureau, New York, New York.*

As components of the new SRA Achievement Series, these arithmetic tests have many desirable characteristics, such as attractive format, lucid directions, interesting items, and comprehensive accessory materials. The conversational style of the directions is a refreshing change from the staid phraseology that has become typical of standardized tests.

Each of the levels yields subtest scores in arithmetic reasoning, arithmetic concepts, and arithmetic computation. No provision is made for a total or average arithmetic score in the norms tables or on the profile charts. The tests consist of 108 items in the 2–4 grade booklets, 113 items in the 4–6 grade booklets, and 135 items in the 6–9 grade booklets. (The tests for grades 1–2 had not been published at the time this review was prepared.)

The difficulty ranges of the items appear to be approximately comparable to those of the corresponding levels of the Stanford arithmetic tests, but the larger number of items in the SRA tests provides more extensive coverage. For example, the Stanford arithmetic test (advanced) contains 45 reasoning and 43 computation items, while the SRA test for grades 6–9 has 50 reasoning, 35 concepts, and 50 computation items.

Considering the length of the subtests, the Kuder-Richardson (number 21) reliabilities reported in the Technical Supplement are in most instances quite low. Only the sixth grade arithmetic reasoning and the eighth and ninth grade computation reliabilities are as high as .90. The reliabilities for second and third grade computation are only .54 and .64, respectively, and the sixth grade concepts reliability is only .68. Of the other 24 reliability coefficients reported, 9 are in the range .75 to .79, and 15 are in the range .80 to .89. While some allowances should be made for the fact that the Kuder-Richardson formulas tend to yield conservative estimates of reliabilities, most of the reported coefficients are still low enough to indicate that considerable caution should be used in interpreting the scores of individual pupils on these tests.

Data on construct validity are given in the supplement in terms of intercorrelations in the matrix of scores of the complete battery and the results of a factor analysis of this matrix. The intercorrelations of the three arithmetic scores in the three batteries range from .44 in grade 4 up to .79 in grade 9, indicating that the communality is substantial. The factor loadings show that the communality is attributable mainly to the factors of "general achievement" and "quantitative accuracy and principles," with the "symbolic language" factor carrying some weight in the concepts and computation tests in the battery for grades 2–4.

The predictive validity data consist of correlations between eighth grade scores on the SRA arithmetic test and ninth grade course marks, grade point averages, and scores on the *Iowa Tests of Educational Development* for several hundred pupils in two Illinois schools. Evidently the scores on the three parts of the arithmetic test were added for these studies, since the subtest results are not reported separately. The correlations between the arithmetic scores and grade point averages are .73 and .66 in the two schools, and the correlations with general mathematics and algebra grades in one school are .48 and .58, respectively. It is interesting to find that the correlations of the arithmetic scores with English, general science, and social science grades in the same school range from .65 to .70. Of course, it is not known whether the higher correlations with the course grades outside of the arithmetic area are attributable to test characteristics or to the marking systems. The correlation of the SRA arithmetic scores with the ITED quantitative thinking scores is reported to be .69.

In the reasoning subtests, the situational approach is used, which involves describing the general problem and then basing several items on that problem. This approach is advantageous in that the types of errors made by the students may be identified. On the other hand, the items interlock to a certain extent, and an erroneous answer on one item may cause the student to lose credit for several of the following items. A further disadvantage of this arrangement in the tests for grades 4–6 and 6–9

is that pupils must turn back to a preceding page to get the data necessary for answering some of the items, which is inconvenient when the booklets are properly folded back for answer sheet alignment.

On the whole, however, the technical standards of these tests and the supplementary materials are commendable. The student motivational appeal of the series is considerably better than that of most currently available arithmetic tests. In company with the other tests in the SRA battery, these arithmetic measures are valuable contributions to the evaluation of general achievement at the elementary school level.

J. FRED WEAVER, *Director of Graduate Studies and Associate Dean, Boston University School of Education, Boston, Massachusetts.*

The arithmetic subtests of each battery seek to provide separate measures of arithmetic computation, arithmetic reasoning, and numerical or arithmetic "concepts." Many arithmetic achievement tests do not attempt to measure the last of these as a separate factor or ability. The test authors and publishers are to be commended for taking cognizance of the need for a separate concepts measure.

At each level, reasoning is measured in relation to groups of problems organized around several social situations rather than in relation to more or less isolated problems, each with its own social setting. The approach used here in the reasoning subtest has much to commend it.

Whenever an arithmetic test seeks to measure so-called concepts per se, that test is inviting criticism on at least two counts: criticism regarding the inclusion of certain test items as measures of conceptual learning, and criticism regarding the absence of any test items relating to various phases of conceptual learning. The concepts subtest at each level will not escape criticism on either count. For example, there are those persons who will say, in effect: "Just because a pupil can tell that in an example such as $85 \div 5 = 17$, the 85 is the dividend, this doesn't mean that he necessarily comprehends the concept of dividend. Why didn't the test measure his understanding of the difference between 'measurement' and 'partitive' division?"

Criticisms like the above are inevitable whenever an attempt is made to measure concepts as such. Rather than debate or argue about what has and what has not been included among the concepts items, it will be better for the user to try to interpret this separate measure in light of the authors' definition of "concepts" as implied by the nature of the items per se.

An unusually large number of helpful supplementary materials are available to the user of this arithmetic test series. Among these, special mention should be made of the following: (a) the Manual for the School Administrator, which includes a detailed breakdown of the arithmetic skills and abilities measured by each subtest at each level; (b) the Teacher's Handbook, which offers suggestions for developing arithmetic skills and abilities on the basis of knowledge of arithmetic test results; and (c) the Technical Supplement, which gives varied and detailed statistical data relevant to the arithmetic subtests—their validity, reliability, and the like. All supplementary materials, as well as the test booklets themselves, appear in a most acceptable format.

Raw scores on each arithmetic subtest may be interpreted in relation to grade-equivalent norms and percentile norms by grade and semester. No more or less conventional age-equivalent norms are included in the examiner's manual, however.

It is difficult to understand why such a limited sampling of items appears in the concepts subtest at level 4–6. At this level the reasoning subtest includes 49 items and the computation subtest, 44 items, while the concepts subtest has only 20 items. However, the concepts subtest at both levels 2–4 and 6–9 includes 35 items. This limited sampling may be responsible, at least in part, for the following two conditions. On the one hand, in relation to grade-equivalent norms the concepts subtest at level 4–6 has a tabled ceiling of 9.0, whereas the other two subtests at this level have tabled ceilings that range from 9.7 to 10.0 (depending on test form). This lower tabled ceiling for the concepts subtest corresponds to 20 items correct out of a possible 20 items. The tabled ceilings for the reasoning and computation subtests correspond to a number of correct items that is less than the maximum possible score in each case.

On the other hand, the grade-equivalent norms for the concepts subtest seem to discriminate almost too greatly at the fifth grade range on one subtest form and at the sixth grade range on the other subtest form. On Form A, only two raw scores (11 and 12)

place the pupil within the fifth grade range (5.3 and 5.6, respectively); and on Form B, only two raw scores (14 and 15) place the pupil in the sixth grade range (6.3 and 6.7, respectively).

All in all, however, the SRA arithmetic tests have much to commend them. In light of the fact that from a curricular standpoint the validity of a test for a specific situation is a relative rather than an absolute matter, no categorical recommendation for use of the SRA arithmetic tests can be made. However, these tests do merit serious study and consideration when important aspects of arithmetic achievement in grades 2–9 are to be measured in a particular situation by means of a standardized instrument.

For reviews by Warren G. Findley and Worth R. Jones of the complete battery, see 21.

[484]

★Scholastic Achievement Series: Arithmetic. Grades 2.5–3, 4–6, 7–9; 1954–55; various titles used by publisher; for Catholic schools; subtest of *Scholastic Achievement Series;* 3 scores: computation, reasoning, total; IBM for grades 4–9; 2 forms; 3 levels; 50¢ per specimen set of any one level; postage extra; Oliver F. Anderhalter, R. Stephen Gawkoski, and John O'Brien; Scholastic Testing Service, Inc. *

a) PRIMARY TEST. Grades 2.5–3; Forms A ('54), B ('55); battery manual ('55); $2.25 per 35 tests; 43-(55) minutes.

b) ELEMENTARY TEST. Grades 4–6; IBM; Forms A ('54), B ('55); battery manual ('55); $2.90 per 35 tests; separate answer sheets may be used; $1.75 per 35 IBM scorable answer sheets; 24¢ per scoring stencil; 53(65) minutes.

c) ADVANCED TEST. Grades 7–9; IBM; Forms A ('54), B ('55); battery manual ('55); $2.90 per 35 tests; separate answer sheets may be used; $1.40 per 35 IBM scorable answer sheets; 12¢ per scoring stencil; 53-(65) minutes.

JOSEPH JUSTMAN, *Assistant Director, Bureau of Educational Program Research and Statistics, New York Public Schools, New York, New York.*

The content of these tests designed for use in Catholic schools does not differ markedly from the more conventional materials ordinarily appearing in arithmetic achievement tests of this type. Although the tests are relatively traditional in tone, some attempt has been made to incorporate materials reflecting a modern approach to the teaching of arithmetic. Thus, items are included that measure concepts about fractions, decimals, and the number system, but the tests fail to touch upon the relationships, judgments, and generalizations that the modern arithmetic program emphasizes. Since courses of study used in Catholic schools representing half of the dioceses in the country were analyzed before developing sample items, one may conclude that the tests reflect existing practice in such schools. Many public school systems, particularly those whose arithmetic curricula stress the development of understandings, would find that these tests are not effective measures of their objectives.

The tests differ from other arithmetic tests now on the market in that the subtests generally contain several more items. The level of difficulty of each subtest is also somewhat higher. Another unusual feature is the extensive use, in the elementary and advanced tests, of "not given" as one of the answer choices.

Administration is described adequately in the manuals. Evidently, the test is designed to be given in a single sitting. Many elementary and junior high school pupils may find that the long working time called for constitutes a burden. However, there seems to be no reason why administration cannot be broken up into two periods. Students may be troubled, too, by the small size of type used, particularly in the elementary and advanced batteries.

Three types of reliability coefficients (odd-even, Kuder-Richardson, and parallel forms) were determined for each grade level. However, only the median for each of these three coefficients is presented in the manual. These single-year coefficients vary widely. Although most are high enough for all practical purposes, particularly when the total test score is to be considered, some are much too low to be considered satisfactory. Thus, the median parallel forms coefficient reported for the arithmetic reasoning section of the advanced tests is only .77, reflecting a degree of dependability ordinarily considered inadequate even for group testing.

In general, these tests appear to be slightly better than the average tradition oriented arithmetic tests now available, but they fall far short of providing a measure of the arithmetic program now offered by many school systems. In view of the restricted normative population and the limited content, it does not appear likely that these tests are suitable for wide use in public school situations. Catholic schools, however, may find them admirably suited to their needs.

CHARLES S. ROSS, *Editor-in-Chief, Silver Burdett Company, Morristown, New Jersey.*

These separately published tests in arithmetic are also published in battery form for Catholic schools together with tests in religion, English, and spelling. A reading test is published separately.

The authors claim for the tests that they meet a "long-standing need for standardized tests geared to the Catholic elementary school program." Although the authors admit that a separate test in religion would meet the specific testing need, they feel that there are advantages in standardizing tests in other areas of instruction over a common (Catholic school) population. They state, "Aside from other curricular differences which could be noted, the effects of cultural differences....call for a distinct set of norms to serve as standards of achievement in Catholic schools." The implication that Catholic school achievement in arithmetic, for example, is either markedly lower or markedly higher than achievement in public schools is not substantiated by available evidence. In fact, it is contrary to available evidence. Other than the normative group, there is nothing about the arithmetic tests that marks them as Catholic.

The tests themselves consist of several parts at each level. A time allowance is suggested for each part. Although each test differs in some respects, the primary, elementary, and advanced tests are sufficiently alike so that an analysis of one test will suffice for this review.

The advanced test for grades 7–9 has four parts. Although the test is supposed to be for use in three grades, there are no ninth grade items in it, and all but two or three of the items are within the experience of a seventh grade student who has completed a modern seventh grade course. Therefore, the only progress that could be measured from the seventh to the ninth year would be progress resulting from familiarity with old subject matter, not progress achieved by mastering new subject matter.

The first three parts of the test call for computation with whole numbers, decimals, and fractions. The student is to do his work in the space provided, find the correct answer among the five alternatives provided, and write the letter of the correct answer on the line provided for it. In many instances enough working space has not been provided. The items are poorly set up for working purposes. For instance, examples having decimal points in them are insufficiently letterspaced, so that figures in the multiplier are not under the correct figures in the multiplicand. The authors require students to add tenths, hundredths, and thousandths in a single example—a situation that is mathematically unsound and that does not occur in life. Some examples are set up so that what would normally be the multiplicand is in multiplier position, as: $.28 \times .3$. Examples having unusual fractions are included. For instance, the pupils multiply $\frac{7}{11}$ by $14\frac{1}{3}$, with a product of $9\frac{4}{33}$. This section of the test has many serious faults.

The fourth part of the test is called "Arithmetic Reasoning." For a test that is seriously offered for sale to schools and whose authors state that "emphasis is again placed on problem types that might be encountered in real life situations," the fourth part of this test is almost incredibly wide of the mark. Consider, for instance, the following examples from Form A: Item 4 states, "The cost of constructing an oil line for 28 miles was $420.00." This oil line cost $15 per mile! Item 5 reads, "A utility plant uses 2106 gallons of fuel a year. If it takes 234 gallons of fuel to produce the power of 1 ton of coal, how many tons of coal would be needed to produce power for the utility plant?" This "utility plant" generates the power for its customers for a year on 9 tons of coal! Item 8 has a typist typing $22\frac{2}{3}$ words per minute, when the minimum rate for high school graduation is about 60 words per minute. Item 10 reads, "Jack weighs 154.2 pounds with his coat on. If his coat consists of 23 square inches of leather weighing .07 pounds per square inch, how much does Jack weigh alone?" Aside from the puerility of the situation, how could anyone conceive of a leather coat whose dimensions would be no more than 2 inches by $11\frac{1}{2}$ inches? Item 24 states that "the spoke of a bicycle wheel is 14 inches in diameter." Item 27 speaks of "a farm of rectangular shape" that is "90 feet by 132 feet." Items 35–37 give the wholesale and retail price of "pork" as 62¢ and 79¢ respectively and of "beef" as 81¢ and 92¢ respectively! The items assume that the customer can save money by buying pork and beef at wholesale.

Items 38–41 depend upon a line graph, which, incidentally, is out of proportion. The graph gives the following statistics on coal production of three states in dollars: Kentucky, $200,000; Georgia, $100,000; Illinois, $325,000

(approx. from chart). These figures are ridiculously low and were obviously pulled out of thin air by the item writer. Item 38, based on the chart, reads, "From Figure 2, if coal sells for $50 per ton, how many fewer tons of coal did Georgia produce than did Kentucky?" In Item 39, the already fabulous and fictitious price of coal goes up to $50.86 per ton!

Instructional material, including tests, must maintain professional standards, including intellectual and factual integrity. Items of the kind quoted above have no place in the schoolroom and reflect on the workmanship and integrity of purpose of the tests in which they appear. Since it appears difficult to justify separate norms in arithmetic for Catholic schools, it is difficult to see what contribution these tests make to the field of testing in arithmetic.

For reviews by William E. Coffman and James R. Hayden of the complete battery, see 23.

[485]

***Schonell Diagnostic Arithmetic Tests.** Ages 7–13; 1936–57; 1 form ('47); 12 subtests; 25–49 tests, 7d. each; 8d. per single copy; 2s. per manual ('57); postage extra; Fred J. Schonell; Oliver & Boyd Ltd. *

REFERENCES
1–2. See 40:1461.
3. See 3:350.
4. SCHONELL, FRED J., AND SCHONELL, F. ELEANOR. *Diagnosis and Remedial Teaching in Arithmetic.* Edinburgh, Scotland: Oliver & Boyd Ltd., 1957. Pp. ix, 198. *

JOHN SUTHERLAND, *Senior Lecturer in Education, Moray House Training College, Edinburgh, Scotland.*

This test has 12 subtests. The first four cover 100 basic number combinations in addition, subtraction, and multiplication, and 90 basic combinations in division. In each case the combinations are arranged in approximate order of difficulty. Subtest 5 covers miscellaneous, more difficult combinations in the above four processes. These subtests are followed by a series of tests in graded addition, subtraction, multiplication, and division (three tests in division). The last subtest consists of 40 items in mental (or problem) arithmetic.

The items in subtests 6–11 are arranged in very carefully graded steps with four items allotted to each step. For example, in the graded subtraction subtest, the first few items involve subtraction of a single digit number from a 2-digit number; in the second four, a 2-digit number is subtracted from another 2-digit number, and so on. Borrowing is introduced at

Item 17. Thus, if a sharp increase in the number of errors should take place after Item 17, we might with some justification suspect that the child's difficulty was connected in some way with borrowing. The items in the other processes are similarly graded.

The test on problem arithmetic (subtest 12) is not nearly so useful as the others. It is limited in its use by the facts that it uses the British system of measurement and that it is heavily dated. This subtest, however, is not an integral part of the test; it is a little doubtful what it tests, and, in many ways, the rest of the test is probably better used without it.

The most satisfactory results can be obtained by using the test in conjunction with the author's *Diagnosis of Individual Difficulties in Arithmetic*. This book contains a complete description of the tests, instructions for administration, and a very detailed discussion of the interpretation of results. Tables showing the average number of sums correct in unlimited time, average time in minutes taken to complete each subtest, and average number of items correct in certain fixed times for children of age 8 to 13 or 14 are provided. The book also includes chapters on the causes of backwardness in arithmetic and on remedial teaching.

The test may be used to obtain three rather different measures of the child's arithmetic achievements: (*a*) It may be used in a purely diagnostic or clinical sense to discover more precisely the nature of the child's difficulty in arithmetic. (*b*) It may be used to estimate speed of working in the various number combinations and the four basic processes. (*c*) A combined measure of accuracy and speed may be derived by using the time limits indicated on the front page of the test booklet and the table of norms in the book.

It is when used in the first way by a skilled tester working with an individual child that the test is at its best. Used as a truly diagnostic test, the reviewer knows of no better. When it is used in this way, there are no time limits and the subtests may be used in any order at the discretion of the tester. They may be supplemented by further similar items at critical points in the testing and the child may also be asked to work the items aloud. In this way it is usually possible to arrive at a fairly precise estimate of the nature of the child's difficulty.

It is also possible to allow students training to be teachers to use this test after a period of careful training. The test can be most helpful in giving such students significant insights into the way in which a child's mind works.

It is, however, rather doubtful if it is possible to design a test which will serve equally well the three functions mentioned above and it is perhaps better not to attempt it. There are tests which are specifically designed to test speed and accuracy which, because of this, do it better.

Briefly then, the test is an excellent diagnostic test when used by a skilled tester with an individual child. It is also useful in giving intending teachers some understanding of the child's difficulties in arithmetic.

For a review by C. Ebblewhite Smith of an earlier edition, see 40:1461.

[486]

*The Staffordshire Arithmetic Test. Ages 7–15; 1938–58; Sheet 1 is revision of *Revised Southend Attainment Test in Mechanical Arithmetic;* 1 form; Sheets 1 ['50], 2 ['58]; no data on reliability; 5*s.* per 50 copies of either sheet; 3*s.* 6*d.* per manual ('58); 3*s.* 8*d.* per specimen set of Sheet 1; 3*s.* 8*d.* per specimen set of Sheet 2; postage extra; administration time not reported; M. E. Hebron; George G. Harrap & Co. Ltd. *

For a review by Stephen Wiseman of the original edition, see 3:352.

[487]

*Stanford Achievement Test: Arithmetic. Grades 3–4, 5–6, 7–9; 1922–55; subtest of *Stanford Achievement Test;* 2 scores: arithmetic reasoning, arithmetic computation; IBM; postage extra; 35¢ per specimen set of any one level of either edition, postpaid; Truman L. Kelley, Richard Madden, Eric F. Gardner, Lewis M. Terman, and Giles M. Ruch; World Book Co. *

a) [HAND SCORING EDITION.] Grades 3–4, 5–6, 7–9; 3 levels; manual ('53).

1. *Elementary Arithmetic Test.* Grades 3–4; 1953, c1952–53; Forms J, K ('53); $2.20 per 35 tests; 55(65) minutes in 2 sessions.

2. *Intermediate Arithmetic Test.* Grades 5–6; 1953–55, c1952–55; Forms J ('53), K ('53), L ('54), M ('55); $2.75 per 35 tests; 70(80) minutes in 2 sessions.

3. *Advanced Arithmetic Test.* Grades 7–9; 1953–55, c1952–55; Forms J ('53), K ('53), L ('54), M ('55); $2.75 per 35 tests; 70(80) minutes in 2 sessions.

b) [MACHINE SCORING EDITION.] Grades 5–6, 7–9; IBM; Forms JM ('53), KM ('53), LM ('54); manual ('53); $4 per 35 tests; $1.50 per 35 IBM answer sheets; 40¢ per set of machine scoring stencils; 70(80) minutes in 2 sessions.

1. *Intermediate Arithmetic Test.* Grades 5–6.

2. *Advanced Arithmetic Test.* Grades 7–9.

REFERENCES
1. See 4:419.
2. GOWAN, J. C. "Intercorrelations and Factor Analysis of Tests Given to Teaching Candidates." *J Exp Ed* 27:1–22 S '58. *

For a review by Robert L. Burch of the previous edition, see 4:419. For a review by N. L. Gage of the complete battery, see 25; for reviews by Paul R. Hanna (with Claude E. Norcross) and Virgil E. Herrick of the previous edition, see 4:25; for reviews by Walter W. Cook and Ralph C. Preston, see 3:18.

[488]

★**Survey Test of Arithmetic Fundamentals: Dominion Tests.** Grades 3–5, 5–8; 1957–58; Forms A, B ('57) ; 2 levels ; no data on reliability ; $1.20 per 25 tests ; 25¢ per scoring key ; 10¢ per manual of either level ; 75¢ per complete specimen set of either level ; postage extra ; 35(45) minutes ; Department of Educational Research, Ontario College of Education, University of Toronto ; distributed by Guidance Centre. *
a) GRADES 3–5. 7 scores : addition, subtraction, multiplication, division, measurement, fractions, total ; manual ('58).
b) GRADES 5–8. 5 scores : whole numbers, fractions, decimals and percentage, measurement, total ; preliminary manual ('58).

FRANCES E. CROOK, *Assistant Professor of Education, McGill University, Montreal, Canada.*

Of the 80 items in the test for grades 3 to 5, 60 cover the four operations with whole numbers and 20 are concerned with measurement and fractions. The test for grades 5 to 8 includes items involving computation with whole numbers, fractions, decimals, per cents, and measures.

The items are said to conform strictly to the arithmetic curriculum outlined in the course of study for Ontario schools, but no outline of the test content and its relation to the course of study is provided. The items are arranged in order of their introduction into the curriculum and also, to the maximum degree consistent with curricular order, in order of difficulty. Such an arrangement would be very satisfactory if another factor had not been introduced— putting the items in cyclic order, with items involving the operations of addition, subtraction, multiplication, and division, and then a measurement item following one another. This order is designed to make the test more useful as a diagnostic instrument, but the consequence is that the items are not effectively arranged in order of either difficulty or curricular emphasis. The test is scored with a stencil key ; and although the use of the test for diagnostic purposes requires separate scoring of the various parts, the mechanical arrangement of the test makes this fairly easy to do.

The final edition of the test was administered for standardization purposes in a random sampling of Ontario schools. Percentile norms are given for each of the subtests and for the total score, for each grade and, somewhat unnecessarily, for boys and girls separately. No evidence is given in the manual as to the reliability of the test or of the subtests, or as to the comparability of the forms, although the manual states that "the forms may be regarded as equivalent."

The test could be of value in Ontario schools and in other systems with similar grade placement of arithmetic topics for both survey and diagnostic purposes in the field of arithmetic computation. However, the arrangement of the test for diagnostic purposes may lessen its value as a survey instrument. The present lack of information about reliability is a more serious deficiency.

[489]

***Tests of Mechanical Arithmetic.** Ages 7 to 8-8, 8 to 9-2, 8 to 10-0 ; 3 forms ; 3*d.* per single copy ; 6*d.* per manual ; postage extra ; published for the National Foundation for Educational Research in England and Wales ; Newnes Educational Publishing Co. Ltd. *
a) NUMBERS IA AND IB. Ages 8 to 10-0 ; 1949–50 ; forms 1A ['49], 1B ['49] ; manual ['50] ; 2*s.* 3*d.* per 12 tests ; 3*d.* per single copy ; 30(35) minutes ; Miriam E. Highfield.
b) NUMBERS IC AND ID. Ages 8 to 9-2 ; 1951–57 ; forms 1C ['52], 1D ['52] ; manual ['57] ; 25(30) minutes ; [G. A. V. Morgan].
c) NUMBERS 2A AND 2B. Ages 7 to 8-8 ; 1958 ; forms 2A, 2B ('58) ; 30(35) minutes.

GEORGE W. STURROCK, *Educational Psychologist, Dundee Education Committee, Dundee, Scotland.* [Review of Forms 1A–1D.]

Forms 1A and 1B, two exactly parallel tests, were originally devised to match children for scholastic attainment in connection with research into rewards and punishments. The tests were observed to give a normal distribution at the age range 8½ years to 9½ years and were standardised on over 5,000 children within that range. They were then published as attainment tests in mechanical arithmetic for ages 8 to 10. The original purpose of the tests explains the inclusion of fractions which are normally outside the curriculum for that age. Forms 1C and 1D, also exactly parallel, were devised later in the same style but for a narrower age range (8-0 to 9-2).

Forms 1A and 1B consist of 30 sums in

mechanical (formal) arithmetic and Forms 1C and 1D of 26 similar sums. The layout is good, the only criticism being that there is not enough room for the children's answers. The instructions for Forms 1C and 1D are much more detailed than those for the earlier version and might better be used in giving Forms 1A and 1B.

The norms for Forms 1A and 1B are set out in two useful tables, one giving arithmetic ages and the other standardised scores (mean 100, SD 15). Norms for Forms 1C and 1D are given in another form. Raw scores are first converted into "transmuted scores" and then, by age allowances, into "standardised scores." Transmuted scores are said "to enable the teacher to compare any child's score with the mean scores of a representative sample of children of *exactly* the same age." The reviewer does not understand this statement. The transmuted scores appear to be merely the standardised scores of children aged 8 years, 8 months.

The criticisms are minor. The tests will admirably serve the following purposes in English schools: (*a*) to arrange the children in a class in order of merit in formal arithmetic; (*b*) to show the general standing of a class in relation to other classes; and (*c*) to diagnose the weaknesses of a class as a whole.

JACK WRIGLEY, *Lecturer in the Teaching of Mathematics, Institute of Education, University of London, London, England.*

These tests have been carefully constructed and adequately standardised on representative samples of English children so that the available norms should be as accurate as is possible with tests of this kind.

The mechanical aspects of arithmetic which are usually covered in British primary schools appear in the tests, but it is particularly important to realise the limitations of this type of test. The test constructors have deliberately restricted themselves to sampling only the purely mechanical elements in arithmetic. Any arithmetical quotient derived from these tests should be used with caution. Stress on the mechanical elements in arithmetic teaching varies from district to district. The norms, for example, would not be applicable in Scotland or in Ireland.

Each particular type of operation in arithmetic is represented by only one or two questions in the tests, and, with little effort, great

changes in score could be produced by intensive teaching. Such efforts, however, would be largely misplaced because there is much more to the understanding and use of arithmetic than the purely mechanical processes measured here. Used wisely, the tests could have a diagnostic value, though that is clearly not their primary aim.

In summary, this series of objective mechanical arithmetic tests is useful only in Britain and is very limited in scope. Used wisely, the tests could help a teacher check the standards of achievement of her class and the efficiency of teaching. They could also be used to measure the amount of stress put on mechanical elements in arithmetic in different districts. There remains the possibility of misuse. Real arithmetic teaching involves so much more than the mechanical elements stressed in these tests. If it is desired to measure arithmetic ability in general, they should certainly be supplemented by other less restrictive tests. Even so, the tests give a rough guide to an individual child's ability in arithmetic and could be useful in guidance work by psychologists.

[490]

★The Tiedeman Arithmetical Knowledge and Information Test. Grades 7-13; 1957; Forms A, B; mimeographed manual; $4 per 25 tests; postpaid; specimen set not available; 50(60) minutes; H. R. Tiedeman; Western Psychological Services. *

JAMES H. RICKS, JR., *Assistant Director, Test Division, The Psychological Corporation, New York, New York.*

This test is intended for use as "a survey test of arithmetical knowledge and information for grades 7 through 13" and "an instrument for the selection and classification of applicants for jobs....in which....arithmetic fundamentals are important." There are 90 items in each form, sampling command of the four fundamental operations; many of the items include fractions, decimals, percentages, and units of measurement. Answers are written on the test itself in designated spaces; there are no multiple choice items. There is adequate working space for the numerical examples, but not for all of the 13 verbally stated problems in each form.

Among tests intended for surveying students' knowledge of arithmetic, perhaps no other covers precisely the range of this one with precisely the same balance of content. At any specific level, however, better standardized, better printed, equally well planned and less expensive tests are available. It hardly seems worthwhile, therefore, to detail at length such good features of this test as the high reliability and the ease of administration and scoring or such bad features as the crowded format, the absence of information on the sources of the norms and on the equivalence of the forms, the occasional incorrect answers on the scoring key, and the misprinting of at least one example in such a way as to make it nearly impossible to tell what operations are to be performed with what numbers.

Most of the other tests serving the second purpose stated above require less time than this one. Since there are no norms for any business or industrial (or even any adult) population and no data bearing on the validity of this test as a predictor of success in learning or performing any type of work, further discussion of its suitability for employment testing seems premature.

This *is* an arithmetic test, and as such it cannot be denied a certain utility. Teachers may want to consider using it in the classroom as a supplement to their own tests or to the exercises provided with most textbooks. It should be satisfactory for exercise purposes where the particular content is appropriate and when a few corrections have been made on the test blank and in the scoring key. Much more evidence is needed before it can be considered seriously for any other use.

GEOMETRY

[491]

★Chicago Plane Geometry Test. .5, 1, 1.5, 2 semesters high school; 1957; 1 form; 4 levels: Tests 1–4; $2 per 25 tests; 35¢ per specimen set; postpaid; 37(40) minutes; Charles H. Schutter; distributed by C. A. Gregory Co. *

LYNNETTE B. PLUMLEE, *Personnel Research and Testing Division, Sandia Corporation, Albuquerque, New Mexico.*

These tests are designed to serve as midterm and final examinations for the first and second semesters of plane geometry and are thus intended for classroom use rather than for predictive purposes. The author is to be commended on checking the coverage of his test against six textbooks published since 1947, for listing these textbooks in the manual, and for describing in general terms in the manual the concepts covered by each of the tests. He should, however, have included in the manual information concerning the construction and the validation of the test in terms of his objectives.

The content is that of the traditional course in plane geometry. While there are items requiring the student to apply his knowledge in situations he probably has not met before, the majority of the items seem to measure the ability to operate in familiar textbook situations. Many mathematics teachers will be happy to see the inclusion of items requiring the student to supply part or all of a formal proof, though the proofs are generally familiar ones.

The manual gives no description of the population samples on which reliability and norms data are based. In a letter to the reviewer, however, the author describes the samples as being made up largely of sophomores in some high schools considered to be "typical cross-sections of the Chicago school system," with classes for the slow as well as for the gifted represented. In applying the norms to test results, users should bear in mind the fact that the items are for the most part of the free answer type. Some standardization of scoring is achieved by listing acceptable variations in response in the scoring information, and the author states that he has found that proof items are scored about the same by different readers; however, it seems likely that different interpretations of the scoring instructions will result in more lenient scoring by some test users than by others. Such differences will have an undetermined effect on the applicability of the norms.

From further information supplied by the author, it appears that the difficulty upon which the weighting of the items was based was determined on subjective grounds but checked by an analysis of errors on the test. It seems likely that a very similar ranking of students would be achieved by scoring on a point per item basis, though the allowance of more points for the proof items may be desirable.

The range of scores obtained by the norms group suggests that item difficulty is appropriate for measuring the knowledge of both the weak and the strong student. Letter grade equivalents are provided for percentile scores. This helps lessen the likelihood of treating a score of 70 out of 100 points as minimum passing, but it would seem desirable to provide more explanation of how such equivalents were derived, in order that the user can judge the applicability to his own situation.

In summary, the tests will probably be useful in checking the student's knowledge of the concepts of geometry and his ability to handle familiar proofs, but they seem less likely to measure the student's ability to use his knowledge of these concepts in solving unfamiliar problems or in handling original proofs.

[492]
*Geometry: Every Pupil Test. High school; 1929–58; new form usually issued each December and April; norms available following testing program; no data on reliability; 3¢ per test; 1¢ per scoring key; cash orders postpaid; 40(45) minutes; Ohio Scholarship Tests. *

[493]
*Plane Geometry: Achievement Examinations for Secondary Schools. High school; 1951–53; Forms 1 ('51), 2 ('52), 3 ('53); no specific manual; no data on reliability; norms: Forms 1 ['52], 2 ['53], 3 ('53); 10¢ per test, postage extra; [60–90] minutes; J. R. Schunert (1, 2) and Emil J. Berger (3); Educational Test Bureau. *

[494]
*Plane Geometry: Every Pupil Scholarship Test. High school; 1926–58; new form usually issued each January and April; norms available following testing program; no data on reliability; 4¢ per test; 4¢ per scoring key; postage extra; 40(45) minutes; Bureau of Educational Measurements. *

[495]
★Plane Geometry: Midwest High School Achievement Examinations. High school; 1955–57; Forms A ('55), B ('57); no specific manual; series manual ('57); no data on reliability; norms: [A, '55; B, '57]; 10¢ per test, postage extra; Form A: 60(65) minutes; Form B: 90(95) minutes; John B. Anglin (A) and Ethel Saupe (B); Educational Test Bureau. *

HAROLD P. FAWCETT, *Professor of Education, The Ohio State University, Columbus, Ohio.* [Review of Form A.]

Approximately two thirds of the 62 items in this test deal with geometric relationships, interpreting data, and analysis of geometric figures. The remaining one third deal with a knowledge of geometric facts.

A stated purpose of this test is to "motivate efforts of accomplishments by the students." Another purpose is "to stimulate thinking ability." The ratio of the number of questions which require thinking as compared with the number which require only a knowledge of geometric facts is consistent with this purpose. The test does seem to evaluate thinking ability more thoroughly than do many other achievement tests in plane geometry.

The test includes items which seem repre-

sentative of the geometric facts and concepts which are currently emphasized in plane geometry. The content is, however, limited entirely to the context of geometry. The test includes no attempt to measure the ability of the students to apply the reasoning power developed through the study of plane geometry to nongeometric situations. Such transfer is one of the basic reasons for the inclusion of geometry in a curriculum and should not be neglected. The measurement and stimulation of thinking ability would have been enhanced by including appropriate items from such fields as science, engineering, and everyday life. As an achievement test, the only apparent advantage of this test over a well constructed teacher made test seems to be the time saving factor; this advantage can be outweighed by the advantages of the teacher made test in content coverage and the testing for transfer of training.

Since a new form of the test is contemplated every year or every other year, the test is not standardized and norms are not available until the end of the school year. The test is expendable and is not produced with quick scoring keys as are most standardized tests. There is no specific manual other than the series manual which is noticeably lacking in information about the test and serves little purpose. No mention is made of reliability or validity, or of how the test was developed. One advantage of the test is that, when Form B is available, it will be reserved for the end of the year, while Form A will be slated for use during the year, presumably at the end of the first semester. The authors state that "forms not reserved for the end of the year render value in motivation, and also in checking emphasis on varying phases of subject-matter contents."

In summary, this test seems to evaluate thinking ability better than many achievement tests in plane geometry, but is limited to the evaluation of this outcome within the context of geometry, neglecting transfer of training. The evaluation of the extent to which the student is familiar with geometric facts follows the usual pattern. There is a definite need for information on reliability, validity, how the tests were developed, and how the norms were established. In short, a specific manual for this test needs to be developed. The test seems to be in the process of development and should, in time, with study and revisions, become a good instrument for the evaluation of achievement in plane geometry.

[496]
Schrammel-Reed Solid Geometry Test. High school; 1950–52; Forms A ('50), B ('51); mimeographed manual ['50]; tentative high school norms; typed college norms ['52]; $1.20 per 25 tests, postage extra; 25¢ per specimen set, postpaid; 50(55) minutes; H. E. Schrammel and Virginia M. Reed; Bureau of Educational Measurements.

H. VERNON PRICE, *Professor of Mathematics and Astronomy, State University of Iowa, and Head of Mathematics in University High School, Iowa City, Iowa.*

Each form of the test consists of 55 true-false items and 42 five-response multiple choice items. A time limit of 50 minutes is specified for each form. In the opinion of this reviewer, the time limit is much too short and the test may actually measure speed rather than knowledge.

"Form A of the test was used in the 1950 Every Pupil Testing Program and 11 different schools reported their scores. Form B was used in the 1951 Testing Program and 16 different schools reported their scores. The 27 schools from which the scores were received were located in 6 different states." These schools reported scores earned by 207 pupils (an average of less than 8 per school) and the entire distribution of these scores formed the basis for the norms which are listed. In other words, the two forms were treated as though they were one and a single table of percentile norms was prepared. The table lists raw scores and percentiles only; no attempt is made to convert to standard scores.

No information is given to show that the two forms give identical results. However, the authors' apparent assumption that the two forms may be treated as one may not be as strange as it seems. Of the 55 true-false items in each form, 12 are identical from one form to the other, and 37 are identical with the change of only a word or two. Of the 42 multiple choice items, 3 are identical except for the rearrangement of responses, and 37 are exactly the same except for the replacement of one or two foils and/or a minor change of a number in the problem.

It appears that Form A was written first and Form B constructed from it by means of the minor changes already noted. As a result, many of the items of Form B are poorly worded and this form, in general, is inferior to Form A.

The distribution of items over the normal solid geometry course appears to be excellent; the only exception noted by this reviewer was the fact that six items were devoted to the prismatoid, a relatively unimportant polyhedron which is deemphasized by most authors and completely omitted by some. About one half of the items are of the pure memory, recall type. Perhaps 20 per cent require some real thinking.

The most serious drawback, in the opinion of the reviewer, is the careless manner in which a number of items are written or edited. For example, one item which has a rather obvious answer has that answer listed incorrectly in the key; in six other cases, either none or several of the responses are correct; in three others, the exercise as stated cannot be answered at all; and in still another (this one true-false), the truth or falsity depends upon a definition which varies from textbook to textbook.

One of the examples given is as follows: "The number of sides of a quadrilateral is 1. two 2. four 3. five 4. six 5. eight." The answer is 2, which means *four*. Unfortunately, there are similar items in the test itself.

The authors pay no attention whatever to the principles governing approximate computation. In some cases, measurements of *one* significant digit are multiplied and an answer containing *five* such digits is keyed as correct.

One expects to find minor defects in any test and it is far more difficult to prepare a test than it is to criticize. However, in the opinion of this reviewer, the Schrammel-Reed test contains too many questionable items to be recommended for use with a solid geometry class.

[497]
*Seattle Plane Geometry Test: Evaluation and Adjustment Series. 1 semester high school; 1951–54; IBM; Forms AM ('51), BM ('52); manual ('51); expectancy chart ['54]; separate answer sheets must be used; $3.60 per 35 tests; $1.40 per 35 IBM answer sheets; postage extra; 35¢ per specimen set, postpaid; 40(50) minutes; Harold B. Jeffery, S. L. Merriam, Clifton T. Smith, Roy D. Kellogg, and Richard E. Bennett; World Book Co. *

HAROLD P. FAWCETT, *Professor of Education, The Ohio State University, Columbus, Ohio.*

The two forms of this test are so nearly equivalent that it will suffice to review only Form AM. This test is composed of 45 multiple choice items and is divided into four parts. According to the manual, the test has been designed to measure "the achievement of students in the important objectives of a high school course in beginning plane geometry." The authors do not state what these important objectives are, but they do assert that a first semester geometry test should "measure progress" in the following four areas: (*a*) the student's understanding of terms used in beginning geometry; (*b*) his recognition of fundamental construction; (*c*) his application of numerical measurement to geometric figures; and (*d*) his ability to think clearly and logically in reaching a geometric conclusion.

The 12 vocabulary items in Part A seem to test a representative sample of geometric terms. Part B contains 11 constructions which the students are required to analyze. Three of these problems are based on practical situations. In Part C, Computations, the 10 items concern various problems involving angles and sides of geometric figures. Some of the items in this section require only recall of geometric facts and are not of a problem solving or computational nature. Part D contains questions concerned with the interpretation of data from geometric figures. One of the important objectives for teaching geometry is the development of clear, logical reasoning ability and the transfer of training in this area. This test has no problems in reasoning which involve nonmathematical situations or reasoning in the applied sciences. The only problems of a practical nature included in the test are the three mentioned previously.

This test was carefully developed and is free of errors in its construction. The manual, describing its nature, development, and use, is quite complete.

In summary, the *Seattle Plane Geometry Test* is a good, though generally factual, test involving questions in the areas of vocabulary, construction, computation, and reasoning. It is conveniently administered and scored. Although the test adequately covers geometric facts and skills, not enough attention is given to the fundamental aspects of proof and to the transfer of clear, logical reasoning to nonmathematical and applied science areas.

[498]
Shaycoft Plane Geometry Test: Evaluation and Adjustment Series. 1 year high school; 1951-54, c1950-51; IBM; Forms AM ('51), BM ('52); manual ('51); expectancy chart ['54]; separate answer sheets must be used; $3.60 per 35 tests; $1.40 per 35 IBM answer sheets; postage extra; 35¢ per specimen

set, postpaid; 40(50) minutes; Marion F. Shaycoft; World Book Co. *

For reviews by Harold P. Fawcett and Cyril J. Hoyt (with Theodore E. Kellogg), see 4:433.

[499]
Solid Geometry: Achievement Examinations for Secondary Schools. High school; 1951-53; Forms 1 ('51), 2 ('52), 3 ('53); no specific manual; no data on reliability; norms: Forms 1 ['52], 2 ['53], 3 (53); 10¢ per test, postage extra; (60-90) minutes; Donovan A. Johnson (1, 2) and Emil J. Berger (3); Educational Test Bureau. *

[500]
★Solid Geometry: Midwest High School Achievement Examinations. High school; 1952-55; Forms A ('55), B ('52, identical with the still-in-print Form 2 of *Solid Geometry: Achievement Examinations for Secondary Schools*); no specific manual; no data on reliability; Form A norms ['55]; no norms for Form B; 10¢ per test, postage extra; Form A: (110) minutes; Form B: 60[65] minutes; Paul Jorgenson (A); Educational Test Bureau. *

TRIGONOMETRY

[501]
Rasmussen Trigonometry Test. High school and college; 1940; Forms A, B ['40]; mimeographed directions sheet; $1.20 per 25 tests, postage extra; 25¢ per specimen set, postpaid; 40(45) minutes; Otho M. Rasmussen; Bureau of Educational Measurements. *

LYNNETTE B. PLUMLEE, *Personnel Research and Testing Division, Sandia Corporation, Albuquerque, New Mexico.*

The possible uses of the results of this test are listed in the manual as follows: determining student achievement, checking efficiency of instruction, assigning marks, analyzing student weaknesses, and motivating student effort. To serve these uses adequately, a test should presumably test not only knowledge of the factual content of trigonometry, such as formulas and definitions, but also the ability to work with trigonometric facts in solving triangles and in meeting other situations new to the student where trigonometry is required. The majority of the items in the *Rasmussen Trigonometry Test* test only knowledge of formulas and other facts and few require the student to go beyond recall and recognition or simple algebraic manipulation of learned formulas.

The manual indicates that the selection of items was based on an examination of "a number of leading textbooks." The names of the texts are not given. However, some coverage seems to be sacrificed through unnecessary duplication, within each form, of facts tested.

The author is to be commended on having had the test reviewed by other teachers in the field. However, it should be noted that each form contains one key error (Form A, Item 73; Form B, Item 32) and that Form B contains one item (Item 77) which is mathematically unsound and another (Item 29) which cannot be answered because of a typographical error.

Correlations of test scores with term average, grades on homework, and average score on class tests are given for 33 (Form A) and 34 (Form B) college students. A letter from the publisher indicates that the Rasmussen test was administered at the end of the term, but it does not make clear whether the examinees were students of the author of the test. If the validity data were obtained on scores made by the author's students, correlations with grades for other students might be expected to be lower.

Odd-even reliability coefficients of .87, .90, and .93, obtained for a high school group on Form A and for a college class on Forms A and B, respectively, are provided. These figures may be spuriously high if the test is as speeded as it appears to be to the reviewer. The timing seems inadequate, especially for high school students, for a test in which items are not arranged in difficulty order. An alternate forms coefficient of .75 is reported, but no information is given regarding the population involved.

Norms are given for high school and college, based on 472 and 67 cases, respectively. According to the publisher, the tests were "built equivalent" on the basis of "error data....available from experimental studies. Norms were based on scores made on Form A. Later the two forms were given to the same group to find the degree of difficulty to be the same." Without more specific data, the reviewer would still question whether scores on the two forms are sufficiently equal to permit the use of a single set of percentile equivalents.

The instructions for interpreting results are not entirely clear or particularly helpful. They warn against the use of college norms but suggest that the high school norms be used for both college and high school since the "distribution pattern is practically the same." They go on to state: "Class median scores....which are at or near the 50%-ile are to be considered average according to the distribution of scores made by the large group. Other scores are either high or low in proportion to the degree of their deviation from the 50%-ile norm."

Letter grade equivalents are provided for percentile scores. While this may help lessen the practice of treating a score of 70 out of 100 items as minimum passing, more explanation of how such equivalents were derived should be provided in order that the teacher might judge their applicability to his own situation.

In summary, the usefulness of the test seems limited by its restriction largely to questions of fact. As a test of trigonometric facts it seems adequate, though probably speeded. A major weakness of the test is its manual, which appears to have been inadequately reviewed.

MISCELLANEOUS

REVIEWS BY *Dorothy C. Adkins, Janet G. Afflerbach, Dwight L. Arnold, John D. Black, William A. Brownell, James E. Bryan, Gale W. Clark, Dorothy M. Clendenen, Walter W. Cook, Lawrence G. Derthick, Benno G. Fricke, Edward B. Greene, Edward N. Hay, William E. Henry, Clifford E. Jurgensen, E. F. Lindquist, Irving Lorge, James Lumsden, Bernadine Meyer, Clarence H. Nelson, Jacob S. Orleans, Harry N. Rivlin, I. David Satlow, Harold Seashore, Leona E. Tyler, Wimburn L. Wallace, and Henry Weitz.*

BUSINESS EDUCATION

[502]

*Bookkeeping: Achievement Examinations for Secondary Schools. High school; 1951–53; Forms 1 ('51), 3 ('53); no specific manual; no data on reliability; norms: Forms 1 ['52], 3 ('53); 10¢ per test, postage extra; [60–90] minutes; Helen L. Haberman; Educational Test Bureau. *

[503]

*Bookkeeping: Every Pupil Scholarship Test. High school; 1926–58; new form usually issued each January and April; norms available following testing program; no data on reliability; 4¢ per test; 4¢ per scoring key; postage extra; 50(55) minutes; Bureau of Educational Measurements. *

[504]

★**Bookkeeping: Midwest High School Achievement Examinations.** High school; 1952–55; Forms A ('55), B ('52, identical with Form 2 of *Bookkeeping: Achievement Examinations for Secondary Schools*); no specific manual; no data on reliability; norms: [A, '55; B, '57]; 10¢ per test, postage extra; 60(65) minutes; Lois E. Hastings (A); Educational Test Bureau. *

I. David Satlow, *Chairman, Department of Accounting and Distributive Education, Thomas Jefferson High School, Brooklyn, New York.*

The test is fairly representative of the theory covered in the first year of bookkeeping. The arithmetic phase, unfortunately, is not sufficiently representative either in scope or weight; only 4 of the 164 items deal with arithmetic.

There is no evidence of any attempt at validation, a step that would have eliminated much of the vagueness, ambiguity, and inaccuracy that characterizes the test in its present form. A significant number of questions are not sufficiently clear. A number of the questions are susceptible to several responses. Items 2, 52, and 56 are answerable by *all* choices. Items 95, 98, 100, and 137 are answerable in ways that are at variance with the key. Items 15, 88, 90, 120, 147, and 148 contain inaccuracies. In the absence of scoring directions, the rater does not know whether any penality is to be imposed for guessing or whether any deviation from the language of the scoring key is acceptable.

The editing is somewhat haphazard. Ordinary rules of English grammar are overlooked. In Section 1, the student is asked to "choose the word or words which best completes [sic] the statements below." Question 4 likewise ignores the rule governing the agreement of subject and predicate, "Assets which the average American family possess." The language employed might be improved so that the test would measure the acquistion of bookkeeping knowledge and skill more reliably. The terms "payment" in Item 139, "merchandise" in Item 142, and "charged" in Item 52 tend to mislead the student.

There appears to be a decided lack of uniformity in the construction of the multiple choice questions in Section 1. Twenty-four questions offer three possible responses, 11 offer four choices, 2 present five choices, and one double question calls for two responses out of four choices. Section 2 omits all question numbers from the answer column, thus making it difficult to answer 25 questions that span across seven inches of printed line space. In Section 4, column 2 appears underneath column 1, which in turn is broken up into two columns. For *each* of the 25 items in column 2, the student is compelled to refer to column 1 and to select *one* of *nine* classifications. Even the systematic student will find it necessary to spend an inordinate amount of time identifying each of the 25 items. Notably lacking are sample questions—an element that is taken for granted as a *sine qua non* of test construction.

The test may serve the purpose of a specific teacher in a specific classroom; in its present form it is not recommended for usage on a mass scale. At best the test is based solely on the acquisition of specific knowledges and skills. It does not attempt to measure the ability to interpret the learning outcomes of the study of bookkeeping. Several questions aim at breadth of coverage, but none aims at depth. No records and reports are presented for interpretation, nor are materials presented in increasing order of difficulty. Thus, the test fails to measure the attainment of some important objectives of bookkeeping instruction, and measures quantity and not quality of what it does seek to ascertain.

[505]

★**Bookkeeping I: Every Pupil Test.** 1 year high school; 1939–58; new form usually issued each April; norms available following testing program; 3¢ per test; 1¢ per scoring key; cash orders postpaid; 40(45) minutes; Ohio Scholarship Tests. *

[506]

★**Bookkeeping Test: National Business Entrance Tests.** Grades 12–16 and adults; 1938–57; for complete battery, see 515; 1 form; 2 editions; general information ['56]; no data on reliability; postpaid; 120(130) minutes; Joint Committee on Tests of the United Business Education Association and the National Office Management Association; United Business Education Association. *
a) [general testing series.] Form 19-52 ('55); manual ('55); correction manual ['55]; no adult norms; 50¢ per test.
b) [official testing series.] Administered only at NBET Centers which may be established in any community; Form 18-42 ('54); manual ('54); norms ['57]; examination fee, $1; specimen set not available.

For reviews by Harvey A. Andruss and Ray G. Price of the 1946 Form, see 3:368. For reviews by Edward N. Hay, Jacob S. Orleans, and Wimburn L. Wallace of the entire series, see 515; for a review by Paul S. Lomax of the 1946 Form, see 3:396.

[507]

★**Business Education: National Teacher Examinations.** College seniors and teachers; 1956-58; for more complete information, see 538; IBM; 80(90) minutes; Educational Testing Service. *

For reviews by William A. Brownell, Walter W. Cook, and Lawrence G. Derthick of the entire series, see 538; for a review by Harry N. Rivlin of an earlier edition, see 4:802.

[508]

*****Business Fundamentals and General Information Test: National Business Entrance Tests.** Grades 12-16 and adults; 1938-57; for complete battery, see 515; 1 form; 2 editions; general information ['56]; no data on reliability; postpaid; 45(55) minutes; Joint Committee on Tests of the United Business Education Association and the National Office Management Association; United Business Education Association. *
a) [GENERAL TESTING SERIES.] Form 19-51 ('55); manual ('55); correction manual ['55]; no adult norms; 50¢ per test.
b) [OFFICIAL TESTING SERIES.] Administered only at NBET Centers which may be established in any community; Form 18-41 ('54); manual ('54); norms ['57]; available free when any one of the tests in the series is ordered.

For reviews by Vera M. Amerson and C. C. Upshall of the 1946 Form, see 3:369. For reviews by Edward N. Hay, Jacob S. Orleans, and Wimburn L. Wallace of the entire series, see 515; for a review by Paul S. Lomax of the 1946 Form, see 3:396.

[509]

*****Business Relations and Occupations: Achievement Examinations for Secondary Schools.** High school; 1951-53; Forms 1 ['51], 3 ('53); no specific manual; no data on reliability; norms: Forms 1 ['52], 3 ('53) 10¢ per test, postage extra; [60-90] minutes; A. Donald Beattie (3); Educational Test Bureau. *

[510]

★**Business Relations and Occupations: Midwest High School Achievement Examinations.** High school; 1952-55; Forms A ('55), B ('52, identical with Form 2 of *Business Relations and Occupations: Achievement Examinations for Secondary Schools*); no specific manual; no data on reliability; norms: [A, '55; B, '57]; 10¢ per test, postage extra; 60(65) minutes; A. Donald Beattie (A); Educational Test Bureau. *

[511]

*****General Office Clerical Test (Including Filing): National Business Entrance Tests.** Grades 12-16 and adults 1948-57; for complete battery, see 515; 1 form; 2 editions; general information ['56]; no data on reliability; postpaid; 120(130) minutes; Joint Committee on Tests of the United Business Education Association and the National Office Management Association; United Business Education Association. *
a) [GENERAL TESTING SERIES.] Form 19-53 ('55); manual ('55); correction manual ['55]; no adult norms; 50¢ per test.
b) [OFFICIAL TESTING SERIES.] Administered only at NBET Centers which may be established in any community; Form 18-43 ('54); manual ('54); examination fee, $1.25; norms ['57]; specimen set not available.

For reviews by Arnold E. Schneider and C. C. Upshall of the 1946 Form, see 3:379. For reviews by Edward N. Hay, Jacob S. Orleans, and Wimburn L. Wallace of the entire series, see 515; for a review by Paul S. Lomax of the 1946 Form, see 3:396.

[512]

Hiett Simplified Shorthand Test (Gregg). 1-2 semesters high school; 1951; IBM; Forms A, B; mimeographed; $1.95 per 25 tests; separate answer sheets may be used; 85¢ per 25 IBM answer sheets; 30¢ per hand scoring stencil; postage extra; 45¢ per specimen set, postpaid; (50) minutes; Victor C. Hiett and H. E. Schrammel; Bureau of Educational Measurements. *

GALE W. CLARK, *Instructor in Business, Western Michigan University, Kalamazoo, Michigan.*

The two forms of the test are substantially alike, the only differences being in content and dictation rate. There are some errors on Form A, but they are adequately indicated on the scoring key for that form of the test.

Each form has four parts, the first consisting of the dictation of material to be used in answering questions presented in the final part of the test. Here the student is required to "take" dictation for five minutes at approximately 80 words per minute on Form B and approximately 60 words per minute on Form A. The second activity consists of a series of longhand and shorthand presentations of statements. For each statement the student must select the incorrectly written shorthand character (if any), or indicate that the sentence is correctly written. The third part of the test is divided into three sections. Section A presents a shorthand character for which four longhand transcripts are provided; the student selects the correct longhand equivalent. Section B is a reverse pattern of Section A in that a longhand word is presented and four shorthand characters are given from which the student selects the appropriate character. The small changes in characters in this section will be very confusing to many excellent shorthand students, especially those who have been taught to improvise characters when in doubt. Section C consists of 20 incomplete statements in shorthand from which the final characters are omitted. In each case the final character must be chosen from a selection of four endings. The fourth part is a group of 25 true-false questions based on the original dictation and requiring the student to determine from the dictation whether each statement presented is true or false. Questions in this part of the test could be answered by an attentive student even though he has no knowledge of shorthand. It is not necessary to quote the material exactly and many students could remember enough details to answer the questions.

The dictation at the beginning is too rapid for most first semester students and for many second semester students. Of course, this may be in interpretation of progress, but such progress depends upon teaching methods designed to build speed. This reviewer believes that the test would not be a fair examination for first semester students on the secondary school level, but that it would be quite satisfactory for students on the college level. Unfortunately, the norms provided are based entirely on the performance of high school students.

In taking the test, the student may record his answers either on the test blank or on a separate answer sheet. Because directions for both methods are presented on the test blank, careful explanation on the part of the administrator is necessary to insure that the examinee understands exactly which directions are to be followed and which are to be disregarded.

A good feature is the possibility of using the same test copies several times if separate answer sheets are used. However, there may be discrepancies between scores when different answering methods are used, especially since the test is timed.

Because of the rate discrepancy between Form A and Form B, the two forms cannot be used interchangeably. Actually, the two forms are at different levels. Teachers should select the form to be used depending on the progress of the class. The author suggests the use of Form A for first semester students and Form B for second semester students. There are no end-of-year norms for Form A.

Properly administered, the test is easily scored with a minimum of error. Scores may be interpreted in terms of percentile ratings and letter grade equivalents. Provision for the latter is unusual but helpful, especially to beginning teachers. The specific interpretation of such grades must, of course, serve only as a guide; the grade equivalents should not be considered an austere grading scale. With the qualifications noted, the test should be fairly

good for two of its stated purposes, determining achievement and checking instruction. It is probable that college teachers will find it much more reliable than secondary teachers. The test should be used only as a general guide for assigning marks. The reviewer doubts its motivational characteristics.

[513]

Kimberly-Clark Typing Ability Analysis. Grade 12 and adults; 1942; 3 scores: speed, accuracy, total; 1 form; $3.75 per 25 tests, postage extra; 25¢ per specimen set, postpaid; administration time not reported; Clifford E. Jurgensen; [the Author], 6101 Oliver Ave. South, Minneapolis 19, Minn. *

REFERENCES
1. JURGENSEN, CLIFFORD E. "A Test for Selecting and Training Industrial Typists." Ed & Psychol Meas 2:409–25 O '42. * (PA 17:1350)
2. GIESE, WILLIAM JAMES. "A Tested Method for the Selection of Office Personnel." Personnel Psychol 2:525–45 W '49. * (PA 24:4278)

For a review by E. G. Blackstone, see 3:383.

[514]

*Machine Calculation Test: National Business Entrance Tests. Grades 12–16 and adults; 1941–57; for complete battery, see 515; 1 form; 2 editions; general information ['56]; no data on reliability; postpaid; 120(130) minutes; Joint Committee on Tests of the United Business Education Association and the National Office Management Association; United Business Education Association. *
a) [GENERAL TESTING SERIES.] Form 19-54('55); manual ('55); correction manual ['55]; no adult norms; 50¢ per test.
b) [OFFICIAL TESTING SERIES.] Administered only at NBET Centers which may be established in any community; Form 18-44 ('54); manual ('54); norms ['57]; $1 per examinee; specimen set not available.

DOROTHY C. ADKINS, *Professor of Psychology and Chairman of the Department, University of North Carolina, Chapel Hill, North Carolina.*

The test is intended for key-driven machine operators, but the use of any machine, electric or hand operated, is permitted. The order in which the parts are taken varies with the kind of machine used. The examinee is directed to note on the test booklet the kind of machine used, but it is not clear who does what with the information. It seems to have no bearing on the norms presented by the authors, a situation which is particularly strange because, although the test is said not to be a "speed-spurt" test, a bonus of one point is given for each minute saved in the 2-hour time period.

The test must be scored by hand. In an effort to present problems that will appear practical (such as those involving adding sales figures vertically and horizontally to obtain branch totals and monthly totals or those requiring computation of total time worked for each of several employees from weekly time cards), scoring convenience is sacrificed. Although the service sold with the official series includes scoring, inconvenient, time-consuming scoring is expensive no matter where it is done. The scoring instructions for some of the problems also imply dual penalties for errors in certain problems such as those requiring the extension of invoice items and addition of the extensions. An incorrect extension entails, say, a 1-point penalty and then an additional 4-point penalty for the wrong total.

Percentile norms for secondary school and college students are available. For the general series edition, the total n's were 486 and 142, respectively; the table for the official series tests omits the n's.

In a sales brochure on the National Business Entrance Tests entitled "What About Reliability and Validity?" it is variously noted that the tests are "prepared by specialists and reviewed by qualified office executives," that "originally, such tests were validated by administering them to experimental and control groups in offices and schools," that "since then the general form of the tests has been retained, in order to perpetuate the qualities which make them reliable and valid," that every step is taken to insure having tests which *are* valid and reliable, and that the Joint Committee on Tests "employs, as consultant, a nationally recognized expert in test construction and measurement." It is to be regretted that more specific reference to empirical evidence of reliability and validity was not presented in the bulletins available for review.

For a review by Elizabeth Fehrer of the 1946 Form, see 3:384. For reviews by Edward N. Hay, Jacob S. Orleans, and Wimburn L. Wallace of the entire series, see 515; for a review by Paul S. Lomax of the 1946 Form, see 3:396.

[515]

*National Business Entrance Tests. Grades 12–16 and adults 1938–57; 1 form; 3 editions; 6 tests (also listed separately); general information ['56]; no data on reliability; postpaid; Joint Committee on Tests of the United Business Education Association and the National Office Management Association; United Business Education Association. *
a) [GENERAL TESTING SERIES.] 1 form; 6 tests; manual ('55); correction manual ['55]; no adult norms; 50¢ per test.
1) *Machine Calculation Test.* 1941–56; Form 19-54 ('55); 120(130) minutes.

2) *Typewriting Test.* 1941–56; Form 19-56 ('55); 120(130) minutes.
3) *Business Fundamentals and General Information Test.* 1938–56; Form 19-51 ('55); 45(55) minutes.
4) *Bookkeeping Test.* 1938–56; Form 19-52 ('55); 120(130) minutes.
5) *General Office Clerical Test (Including Filing).* 1948–56; Form 19-53 ('55); 120(130) minutes.
6) *Stenographic Test.* 1938–56; Form 19-55 ('55); 120(130) minutes.
b) [SHORT FORM SERIES.] 1 form; no data on reliability; no norms; 50¢ per test.
1) *Typewriting Test.* 1 form ('55); 45(55) minutes.
2) *Stenographic Test.* 1 form ('55); directions sheet ('55); (60) minutes.
c) [OFFICIAL TESTING SERIES.] Administered only at NBET Centers which may be established in any community; 1 form; 6 tests; manual ('54); norms ['57]; specimen set not available.
1) *Machine Calculation Test.* 1941–57; Form 18-44 ('54); examination fee, $1; 120(130) minutes.
2) *Typewriting Test.* 1941–57; Form 18-46 ('54); examination fee, $1; 120(130) minutes.
3) *Business Fundamentals and General Information Test.* 1938–57; Form 18-41 ('54); available free when any one of the tests in the series is ordered; 45(55) minutes.
4) *Bookkeeping Test.* 1938–57; Form 18-42 ('54); examination fee, $1; 120(130) minutes.
5) *General Office Clerical Test (Including Filing).* 1948–57; Form 18-43 ('54); examination fee, $1.25; 120(130) minutes.
6) *Stenographic Test.* 1938–57; Form 18-45 ('54); correction manual ('54); examination fee, $1.25; (125–135) minutes.

REFERENCES

1–9. See 40:1476.
10. See 4:453.

EDWARD N. HAY, *Chairman of the Board, Edward N. Hay and Associates, Inc., Philadelphia, Pennsylvania.*

These tests have been designed to evaluate skills necessary to five basic office jobs—stenography, typewriting, machine calculation, bookkeeping, and general office work (including filing). The committee states that these measurements of achievement can be utilized in (*a*) evaluating the status of high school or college business students compared with the performance of students in other schools; (*b*) evaluating the effectiveness of teachers; (*c*) screening prospective employees; and (*d*) granting proficiency certificates to examinees who have passed one or more of the tests satisfactorily.

Although there are no alternative forms available, there are two similar series of tests. The General Testing Series for which no proficiency certificates are given is intended for school and office use. The Official Testing Series is available only for administration at National Business Entrance Test Centers. These test centers can be set up by interested individuals with the only apparent qualification being that of an established minimum of five examinees for each center. In 1955, there existed 92 such centers in the United States and Canada.

If the Official Testing Series is administered by a recognized testing center, then a grading service is provided. On this basis, it might be wise to use only this series, for the scoring appears time-consuming and somewhat complicated for a rapid evaluation of the measured skills. The criterion for passing these tests appears to be somewhat tenuous for, according to the Committee, it rests primarily on the discretion of the administrator or the needs of the local business population. It seems that this is proficiency measured only by the qualifications demanded by schools, employers, etc., rather than a true delineation of proficiency in the basic skills evaluated. Perhaps, with more research, the criticism will become unwarranted.

The Committee states that the validity and reliability of the tests have been established by research workers and competent authorities. Statistical data are not reported; therefore, people who contemplate using this service should request the information to evaluate the tests properly. Although three doctoral dissertations which are said to have evolved around the predictive validity of different tests in the series are mentioned, no implications of these findings are reported. Validity and reliability coefficients would be a sound background on which to base the Committee's plea for better business education.

In the explanatory manual, there is a suggestion that users clinically appraise scores obtained on the various tests as they relate to one another, and specifically as they relate to those on the *Business Fundamentals and General Information Test*. The implication is that this latter test is a basic measure of intellectual capacity and that achievement on it should be used in making judgments regarding quality of instruction, motivation of examinees, and examinees' efficiency in use of capacities. It would appear that such an interpretative approach should be used with utmost caution—if at all.

JACOB S. ORLEANS, *Lecturer in Psychology, Southern Regional Division, University of Nevada, Las Vegas, Nevada.*

The prospective user of such a series of tests, or of any one of the separate tests, looks first

for evidence of predictive validity. The validity of these tests rests on the accuracy with which they predict the success of the examinee on the job, if not in merely securing a job. There is no "manual of directions" in the usual sense of the term. The administrator's manual contains the instructions for administering all but the stenography test. There is a separate manual for administering that test. A correction manual contains scoring keys and instructions for scoring. There is also a set of stapled sheets with such headings as "Origin of the Tests," "Who Benefits From These Tests?," "Your Testing Center," "What Are the NBETests?," "General Information About the Tests," "Percentile Norms," "Growth and Trends of NBET," "What About Reliability and Validity?," a list of 92 testing centers at which "official" testing has taken place, and registration and order forms.

All the information furnished on both validity and reliability is contained in this short paragraph:

National Business Entrance Tests are prepared by specialists and reviewed by qualified office executives. Originally, such tests were validated by administering them to experimental and control groups in offices and schools. Since then the general form of the tests has been retained, in order to perpetuate the qualities which make them reliable and valid. The Joint Committee on Tests is aware of the importance of these factors and takes every step to insure having tests which *are* valid and reliable. It employs, as consultant, a nationally recognized expert in test construction and measurement.

The users of the tests are asked to accept on faith the claim that the persons who prepared the first series of the tests were "specialists" and that the office executives who reviewed them were "qualified"; that the first series of tests was found to have adequate predictive validity; that retaining the general form of the tests has maintained their validity and reliability over the years; that "every step [taken] to insure having tests which *are* valid and reliable" has actually resulted in predictive validity; and that the efforts of the nationally recognized expert who serves as a consultant maintain the predictive validity of the tests. In short, the test user is asked to take the predictive validity of the tests on faith. No information is given concerning the sources of the types of tasks or other content in the tests other than such general statements as that "the calculating machine operator must be able to handle a variety of computations rapidly and accurately as well as to maintain a satisfactory, sustained pace. Hence the test is made up of samplings of computational work common to many offices." The fact that the content of the tests is extensive and appears to be representative of office tasks is not very helpful to the user who should be given evidence—for instance, in the form of the frequency of occurrence of certain tasks and their importance for job success.

The announcement leaflet for the tests lists the following purposes and values of the series: "For improving educational programs in the schools; for upgrading vocational business education; for in-service training of younger teachers; for more effective evaluation of school business curricula; give evaluation device with national norms; give uniform grading of tests; give Certificates of Proficiency to those who qualify; give reliable criteria for measuring vocational training outcomes." It may well be that the tests can be used validly and reliably to perform these functions, but in nothing accompanying the tests do the publishers present any evidence to show that this is so. Nor is the test user told how the tests can be employed to serve these purposes.

The customary manuals accompanying published tests present information about the tests and the purposes they are intended to serve, and evidence to show that they can serve these purposes; descriptions of the tests, the source of the content, and the method of preparation; norms, the sources of the norms, and the interpretation of scores; and suggestions for using the test results. There is no such manual available for the NBET tests. Instead, the prospective user is presented with some 16 pages of what is essentially advertising matter—except for a 1-page table of percentile norms and a page on the interpretation of scores. The norms are based on 7,875 secondary school skill tests and 1,278 college tests. It is not clear whether this means 7,875 secondary school graduates and 1,278 college graduates, or whether the numbers include those who have not yet been graduated from these levels. No information is given concerning the geographical distribution of the examinees on whom the norms are based, nor the types of schools from which they come —public or private, general or commercial. Since suggestions are given concerning the interpretation of group averages, it would be helpful to have differential norms for different types of schools. The number of examinees on whose scores the norms are based varies for the college group from 115 on the *General Office Clerical Test* to 652 on the *Business Fundamentals and General Information Test*. For the secondary group the numbers vary from 486 on the *Machine Calculation Test* to 6,661 on the *Business Fundamentals and General Information Test*. There is no evidence that, despite the differences in the groups on whom the norms are based, the norms are comparable. The suggestions for interpreting the test scores obviously assume such comparability.

It is suggested that the score on the *Business Fundamentals and General Information Test* be used as a criterion for the evaluation of scores on the other tests—something like using an individual's mental test status to evaluate his achievement status: "A student scoring at only the 30th percentile in a skill test and at about the same in the Business Fundamentals and General Information Test is scoring in skill up to our expectation for her (or him)." No argument and no data are offered to explain this criterion or to support the validity of it.

The *Business Fundamentals and General Information Test* consists of 100 multiple choice questions. The scoring is quite objective. Each item is allowed 1 point, and the total score is 100 points. With the exception of parts of the *General Office Clerical Test,* the other tests, being performance tests, are of necessity liable to some subjectivity of scoring. Detailed instructions for scoring are given which should go a long way to make the scoring objective. Specified amounts of score are allowed for the various parts of each task. There may be some rationale for the total score allowed for each test; if so, it is not explained. There is apparently no reason that the total possible score on the *Bookkeeping Test,* for instance, should not be 120 points or 180 points or 360 points, rather than the 240 actually allowed. Except for the *Stenographic Test* and the *Business Fundamentals and General Information Test,* the total score is the same for all the tests, 240 points.

Despite the apparent attempt at comparability reflected in having the maximum score the same for four of the tests, the 50th percentile scores differ by large amounts from test to test. The table of percentile norms lists a "passing score" for each of the five skill tests. No mention is made, nor any explanation given, of the reason for the "passing score," or of how it was derived. The table also contains a row of figures showing the "per cent passed" for each test—the per cents varying for the secondary group from 77 per cent on the *General Office Clerical Test* to 44 per cent on the *Machine Calculation Test,* and, for the college group, from 94 per cent on the *General Office Clerical Test* to 40 per cent on the *Machine Calculation Test.*

For lack of information it is difficult, if at all possible, for the prospective user of any of these tests to judge their value for him. That is most unfortunate. It is likely that the tests are good ones and that they can serve important purposes in a valid manner and with high reliability. When a large amount of time and effort has gone into the preparation of tests, as has apparently been true of the NBET tests, it is unfortunate that the information is lacking which the prospective user needs to satisfy himself that they are good tests.

WIMBURN L. WALLACE, *Director, Professional Examinations Division, The Psychological Corporation, New York, New York.*

The National Business Entrance Tests (NBET) comprise a battery of six tests intended to assess the proficiency of students in high schools and colleges in clerical areas. Five are skill tests and one covers general information and fundamentals. Original forms issued in 1937 were called the *National Clerical Ability Tests.* In 1947 the program was taken over by the joint sponsorship of the United Business Education Association and the National Office Management Association.

Two parallel series of tests, the official and the general, are available. The official series (currently the "1800 series") is restricted to program use in established testing centers. Students may take any number of the six tests but must include the Business Fundamentals and General Information Test. For a modest fee the central agency provides all materials, instructions, scoring services, and proficiency certificates for the official series. Schools or employers may purchase the general series (currently the "1900 series") for practice or screening testing; no scoring service or certificates are provided with it.

The test booklets and materials for both series are well designed and attractively printed. Directions for administration are meticulously clear and precise. Procedures for conducting the official series are described in adequate detail. In other words, the mechanics of the testing program are very well conceived and executed. Literature describing the program is somewhat overly promotional to be consistent with the dignity it should reflect. The user of the general series might be somewhat handicapped by the complex, awkward, time-consuming, arduous system of scoring.

Percentile norms are provided for each series. Separate norms are shown for secondary schools and for colleges on each test. The population for the norms for the official series is described only as "all participants in the National Business Entrance Testing program who have used the 1800 series tests." Numbers of cases, mean scores, and standard deviations are not reported. Suggested passing scores for the five skill tests are given, but there is no indication of the basis for the selection of these cutoff points. This is a serious omission of information. Until recently, proficiency certificates were granted or withheld depending upon attainment of the passing score, but the current procedure is to report raw scores to the local test center administrator who issues the certificates in the light of local situations.

Norms for the general series are based on all the candidates tested in NBET centers in 1955. The table shows number of cases and passing score for each category as well as the percentile equivalents of the raw scores. Although explanation and illustrations are provided for the interpretation of percentile scores, little or nothing is said about the interpretation of the test results themselves. Apparently one has to be somewhat familiar with the contents of the tests in order to understand the significance of particular scores on them.

The fact that the manual provides no data at all on reliability, validity, form equivalence, or score consistency is the greatest deficiency in this battery of tests. While content validity might be claimed as most appropriate for this type of instrument, the opportunities for studies of concurrent validity with grades in appropriate courses and of predictive validity with employment records should not be neglected. Mention is made in the manual of the existence of doctoral dissertations involving such research, but none of the results are reported. There is no excuse for failure to supply other statistics. Data must be readily available for estimations of reliability, and the existence of the parallel series makes the investigation of interform consistency and reliability feasible.

In summary, the NBET is a well designed battery of tests in clerical areas. The testing program uses a restricted series of the tests and is excellently organized in its mechanical aspects. The alternate series is available for purchase and has the same high standards of clarity in format and procedures, but the scoring method is complex and difficult. The most serious defect in the battery is the lack of any data in the manual concerning the reliability, validity, or interform consistency of the tests. This omission prevents a complete evaluation of the psychometric quality of the instruments.

For a review by Paul S. Lomax of the 1946 edition, see 3:396. For reviews of individual tests, see 506, 508, 511, 514, 522, 526, 3:368–9, 3:379, 3:384, 3:391, and 3:394.

[516]

★Office Worker Test 30-A. Office workers; 1956–58; 11 scores: reading, vocabulary, reasoning, arithmetic, checking, filing, spelling, punctuation, usage, information, total; 1 form ('56); preliminary mimeographed manual ('56); norms ('58); separate answer sheets must be used; PPA member agency: 10–49 tests, 38¢ each; others, 46¢ each; $2 per specimen set; postpaid; 90(100) minutes; Public Personnel Association. *

[517]

★Personnel Research Institute Test of Shorthand Skills. Stenographers; 1951–54; title on test is *Otis and Laurent Test of Shorthand Skills;* 2 scores: transliteration, transcription; Forms A, B ('51); tentative norms; $3.75 per 25 tests; 50¢ per set of scoring key and manual ('54); $1 per specimen set; cash orders postpaid; (20–35) minutes; [Jay L. Otis and Harry Laurent]; Personnel Research Institute. *

[518]

★SRA Typing Adaptability Test. High school and adults; 1954–56; formerly called *Columbia-Southern Typing Test;* 3 scores: time, error, total; 1 form ('56); manual ('56); no data on reliability; tentative norms; $2 per 20 tests; $2 per 20 typing forms; 75¢ per specimen set; postage extra; (45) minutes; Mary Tydlaska and Clem White; Science Research Associates. *

GALE W. CLARK, *Instructor in Business, Western Michigan University, Kalamazoo, Michigan.*

This test is designed to measure the adaptability of the typist in using a variety of typing skills to perform competently on the job. The test is presented in a 4-page folder of general directions given to the typist. The typing is done in a second 4-page folder. A third 4-page folder describes the test and gives directions for administering and scoring it and interpreting test results.

Test 1 requires the reproduction of a rough draft into an acceptable manuscript. The directions are given on the first page of the instructions while the test is presented on the second page. Although the test is very adequate insofar as testing the ability of the typist to type a corrected manuscript is concerned, it is inconvenient to use because of the necessity of turning from page 1 to page 2 to be sure that directions are being followed. Test 2 requires the student to transfer tabular material from page 3 of the test folder to page 3 of the typing forms folder, following directions printed on page 1 of the former. Again, considerable manipulating of pages is required. The job required by this test may be presented differently in various training programs; the directions do not take this into account. Test 3 requires the writing of five names and addresses in alphabetical order according to an example provided.

The typist is carefully instructed that the individual tests are not timed, but that a record will be made of the amount of time needed to complete the whole test. This procedure is good; however, some typists might work faster if they knew that time is considered in the scoring.

Not all phases of typing skill are tested, but this is a good measure of performance ability except in straight copy work. The chief criticism of the test is that of organization. Directions are difficult to follow when they are placed elsewhere than with the problem. This is an especially important consideration when one of the aims of the test is to test "the ability to follow directions."

EDWARD B. GREENE, *Supervisor of Personnel Testing, Chrysler Corporation, Detroit, Michigan.*

The test measures ability to follow directions and type quickly and accurately. The examinee is asked (*a*) to make a corrected copy of a fairly difficult letter with corrections shown in longhand, (*b*) to copy material containing dates and costs on a printed form with lined columns, and (*c*) to rearrange five names and addresses and type them in alphabetical order. The examinee is told to erase all errors and advised that he will be penalized 1 point for each corrected error and 2 points for each uncorrected error. He is told that the total amount of time spent will be included in the score, but no time limits are set. Ten minutes are allowed for the silent reading of directions. After reasonable questions are answered, the starting time is recorded. In large groups each examinee may record his own finishing time; with individuals or small groups the recording is done by the examiner.

Detailed directions for finding the error score are given in the manual. Time and error scores are added for a total score. For example, a person who makes 4 errors and finishes the work in 12 minutes has a total score of 16, a very superior score. Average scores, based on a group which is not described as to number or characteristics, range from 28 to 37. Scores of 48 and over are very inferior. Another table gives mean scores and standard deviations for groups of 50 students, applicants, and employees. The students took almost twice as long to complete the test and made almost twice as many errors as the employees. No indications are given of the practice effects of this test. The writer suspects that the scores might go up a great deal for some examinees on a retest.

This test appears to be very useful as a short screening test which is easy to administer and can be scored by a careful clerk in about two minutes. The emphasis on speed in determining the total score is probably not realized by most examinees, and one's speed often varies with the time of day and the amount of coffee recently drunk.

[519]

*The Seashore-Bennett Stenographic Proficiency Tests: A Standard Recorded Stenographic Work-sample. Adults; 1946–56; Forms B-1, B-2 ('46); revised manual ('56); 3 types of recordings: 4 standard 12-inch records (78 rpm), LP microgroove 12-inch record (33⅓ rpm), 2 tapes (3.75" per sec.); distribution is restricted to business firms; $19.50 per set of script, manual, 100 summary charts, and standard records; $13.50 per set of script, manual, 100 summary sheets, and either the microgroove record or a set of tape recordings; $2 per 100 summary charts; 35¢ per manual; postpaid; (65–70) minutes; Harold Seashore and George K. Bennett; Psychological Corporation. *

REFERENCES

1. See 4:455.
2. "Comparative Performances of Different Groups on the Seashore-Bennett Stenographic Proficiency Test." *Test Service B* (50):6 Je '56. *
3. McCarty, John J. "Normative Data Information Exchange, No. 10-41." *Personnel Psychol* 10:533 w '57. *

For a review by Harold F. Rothe, see 4:455; for a review by Ann Brewington, see 3:386.

[520]

★Shorthand Aptitude Test. High school; 1953–54; 1 form ['53]; mimeographed manual ['54]; 5s. per 10 tests; 3s. per manual; 3s. 6d. per specimen set; postpaid within Australia; 31(45) minutes; manual by V. Brownless and S. Dunn; Queensland Department of Public Instruction; Australian Council for Educational Research. *

JAMES LUMSDEN, *Lecturer in Psychology, University of Western Australia, Nedlands, Australia.*

The test consists of material similar to the first four subtests of the *Turse Shorthand Aptitude Test*. There is a saving in testing time of approximately 25 per cent.

Reliability data are not reported in the manual. Since the test is recommended only for prediction of a single criterion which is unambiguously assessed, this is not serious, though researchers may be interested in the extent to which failure of prediction arises from random error or systematic bias.

Validity was determined by a follow-up study of 239 Queensland girls given the test on entry to a shorthand course. Test results were correlated with shorthand examination marks obtained after three terms ($n = 200$) and after five terms ($n = 155$). This test yielded slightly higher correlations than the Turse. The validity coefficients (.54 and .69) indicate that the test has sufficient predictive power to be of considerable assistance in selection for shorthand courses. It was notable that Test 3, phonetic association, gave correlations almost as high as the total test on both occasions. It would seem that this subtest, requiring less than one third of the time, could be substituted for the total test, particularly if considered alongside other data routinely available, e.g., group intelligence test scores. The manual very sensibly recommends that users develop expectancy tables based on a follow-up of their own cases and gives an example which clearly reveals the predictive power of the test.

Centile norms are provided based on the results of a sample of about 500 Queensland girls with an average age of approximately 13 years, 3 months. Such norms would be of little use to the user and the adoption of the recommendation concerning local expectancy tables should make it unnecessary ever to use them.

The test gives every appearance of being soundly constructed. No extravagant claims are made in the manual which, apart from the lack of reliability data, is adequate. Its use by those willing to develop expectancy tables is recommended. Further work on the test should produce further savings in testing time without reducing validity.

[521]

*Shorthand I: Every Pupil Test. 1 year high school; 1938–58; new form usually issued each April; norms available following testing program; no data on reliability; 25¢ per set of teacher's dictation sheets, cash orders postpaid; 36(45) minutes; Ohio Scholarship Tests. *

[522]

*Stenographic Test: National Business Entrance Tests. Grades 12–16 and adults; 1938–57; for complete battery, see 515; 1 form; 3 editions; general information ['56], no data on reliability; postpaid; Joint Committee on Tests of the United Business Education Association and the National Office Management Association; United Business Education Association. *

a) [GENERAL TESTING SERIES.] Form 19-55('55); manual ('55); correction manual ['55]; no adult norms; 50¢ per test; 120(130) minutes.

b) [SHORT FORM SERIES.] 1 form ('55); directions sheet ('55); no data on reliability; no norms; 50¢ per test; (60) minutes.

c) [OFFICIAL TESTING SERIES.] Administered only at NBET Centers which may be established in any community; Form 18-45 ('54); manual ('54); norms ['57]; examination fee, $1.25; specimen set not available (125–135) minutes.

EDWARD B. GREENE, *Supervisor of Personnel Testing, Chrysler Corporation, Detroit, Michigan.*

The authors state that the purpose of this test is to measure "ability to take dictation and transcribe it under office conditions." Although these are two quite separate operations, the test yields only one overall score. One cannot tell, therefore, whether a candidate is deficient in both ability to take notes and ability to type, or only in one of these abilities. The reviewer has found that separate scores are highly desirable both for selection and training.

There are two long forms and one short form of the *Stenographic Test*. The two long forms appear to be similar but no data are furnished to show their reliability or comparability. Each form consists of 13 letters. The shortest letter contains about 80 words, and the longest about 190 words. Numbers are very rare in these letters. The short form was not received. It contains only five letters and allows 10 minutes for dictation and 45 minutes for transcription. No data are given to show its reliability or relation to the long forms.

All the letters are to be read aloud by an examiner at a rate of just 80 words a minute. The results would doubtless be more significant if the rate were varied from 60 to 100 words

per minute, and if a phonograph record or other sound device were used for dictation. The test is preceded by a short practice dictation, after which the examinee is allowed to check her notes with a printed copy of the material.

The text from which the examiner dictates indicates the amount to be read each 15 seconds, the words to be spelled out, and the punctuations and capitals to be dictated. The total dictation time is 20 minutes. However, after each group of three or four letters, two minutes are allowed for rest, answering questions, and redictation "of any reasonable request." Variations among examiners on what are reasonable requests will occur. Some examiners will probably be much more lenient than others even after considerable training.

After the last letter has been dictated, there is a 5-minute rest period. Then the examinees are furnished with printed names and addresses to go with the letters they have taken. Dictionaries are made available. Ninety minutes are allowed to type an original and one or two carbons of each letter. This requires a typing rate of only about 19–20 words per minute.

In scoring, errors are deducted from the maximum points for each letter. The shortest letters have 9 points maximum and the longest, 22. The total is 180. If the total deductions for a letter exceed its maximum, the item is given a zero. Sixteen correctable types of errors are listed with penalties ranging from 1 to 3 points; 13 noncorrectable types of errors cause rejection of the whole letter. There are a considerable number of situations where the scorer must use judgment, such as: "Transcripts must make the sense intended by the test administrator, but the words dictated and those transcribed need not be identical in all cases," and "Be especially lenient with commas, avoiding penalties on them if possible."

In the 1955 use of Series 19-50, 2,501 secondary school students and 407 college students took the *Stenographic Test*. Resulting percentile norms indicate median scores of 78 for the secondary school students and 102 for the college students. Norms for 1957 show medians of 83 and 106. In both cases, a cutoff score of 75 is recommended for determining the recipients of proficiency certificates. This would allow one to be certified even when half the letters were rejected or 105 points were deducted. This seems to be a rather low standard.

The test is not recommended for either business schools or personnel offices because there are excellent separate typing and stenographic tests already available. In spite of these many criticisms, the *Stenographic Test* is probably as good as any of the tests on the market which use this combined testing procedure. However, the reviewer believes that test accuracy has been sacrificed in the attempt to simulate office conditions.

For reviews by Ann Brewington and Elizabeth Fehrer of the 1946 Form, see 3:391. For reviews by Edward N. Hay, Jacob S. Orleans, and Wimburn L. Wallace of the entire series, see 515; for a review by Paul S. Lomax of the 1946 Form, see 3:396.

[523]

★**Test for Typing Skill.** Typists; 1952; Forms A, B; no data on reliability; $1.50 per set of each form, manual, directions sheet, and norms, postage extra; 8(20) minutes; Edward N. Hay; Aptitude Test Service. *

BERNADINE MEYER, *Assistant Professor, School of Business Administration, Duquesne University, Pittsburgh, Pennsylvania.*

Entitled a *Test for Typing Skill,* this is actually nothing more than an 8-minute timed writing from straight copy. The typist copies the material line for line, making no changes and no erasures.

The test is designed for use in selecting typists for office work, particularly beginners. The test user should bear in mind that the test is only a measure of speed and accuracy in copying from typed material; it does not measure ability to do such things as type from rough drafts or arrange tabular reports or business letters, and it is not intended for use with applicants for positions where such skills are necessary.

The test has other limitations. It does not test an applicant's ability to type numbers or the special characters on the keyboard, such as the "$" or the "%." The ability to type numbers and special characters is generally less well developed, particularly in beginning typists, than the ability to type the letters of the alphabet.

The typist's speed is reported in net words per minute (after 10 words have been deducted for each error). An accuracy ratio is determined by dividing by total strokes typed the total strokes typed less a penalty of 50 strokes (10 words) for each error. It seems to this reviewer that the use of net words per minute with the error penalty, along with an accuracy ratio, measures accuracy twice and does not really measure speed. A better measure of speed would result from the use of either gross words per minute with no penalty for errors or correct words per minute with one word deducted for each error.

Directions for taking the test are simple and clear; so are the directions for administering and scoring it. The reviewer would add a suggestion that the typist might be given two 8-minute writings, one from each form, and the better of the two writings scored. Some time could be saved in the scoring process if the test copy showed the word count instead of the stroke count.

The suggestions for interpreting the test results are less satisfactory. Norms are provided for speed and accuracy scores, but they are based upon the performance of only 132 unselected women clerical applicants on the West Coast in 1952. A larger normative group spread over a wider geographic area is needed. Thirty words per minute is suggested as the minimum speed for hiring. This speed seems low; one must remember, however, that it is in terms of net words per minute and that it covers a writing time of eight minutes.

In summary, the reviewer feels that this test will serve its purpose if the test user will bear in mind its limitations and the fact that its results are reported in terms of net words per minute.

[524]

★**Typewriting I and II: Every Pupil Scholarship Test.** 1 or 2 years high school; 1928–58; new form usually issued each January and April; norms available following testing program; no data on reliability; 4¢ per test; 4¢ per scoring key; postage extra; 42(50) minutes; Bureau of Educational Measurements. *

[525]

*Typewriting I: Every Pupil Test.** 1 year high school; 1938–58; 2 scores: speed, performance; new form usually issued each April; norms available following testing program; no data on reliability; 3¢ per test; 1¢ per scoring key; cash orders postpaid; 35(40) minutes; Ohio Scholarship Tests. *

[526]

*Typewriting Test: National Business Entrance Tests.** Grades 12–16 and adults; 1941–57; for complete battery, see 515; 1 form; 3 editions; general information ['56]; no data on reliability; postpaid; Joint Committee on Tests of the United Business Education Association and the National Office Management Association; United Business Education Association. *
a) [GENERAL TESTING SERIES.] Form 19-56 ('55); manual ['55]; no adult norms; 50¢ per test; 120(130) minutes.

b) [SHORT FORM SERIES.] 1 form ('55); no manual; no data on reliability; no norms; 50¢ per test; 45(55) minutes.

c) [OFFICIAL TESTING SERIES.] Administered only at NBET Centers which may be established in any community. Form 18-46 ('54); manual ('54); norms ['57]; examination fee, $1; specimen set not available; 120(130) minutes.

CLIFFORD E. JURGENSEN, *Assistant Vice President in Charge of Personnel, Minneapolis Gas Company, Minneapolis, Minnesota.*

This is a work sample test simulating common office jobs such as typing letters and memos (albeit from running printed copy), filling in form letters, setting up and typing tabulated material, and typing from corrected handwritten draft. It requires typing envelopes, making carbon copies, using letterheads and other printed forms, and the like. The test is scored on form and arrangement of typed material, accuracy, speed, and ability to follow instructions. A total score is obtained by summing the various part scores.

The manual states that the test was prepared by specialists and reviewed by qualified office executives, that it was originally validated with experimental and control groups in offices and schools, and that the general form of the test has been retained in subsequent editions "in order to perpetuate the qualities which make them reliable and valid." No statistics or other pertinent evaluative data are given. In fact, the entire discussion of reliability and validity requires only eight lines in the manual. Inasmuch as forms of this test have been available since 1937, the reader may well raise an eyebrow regarding this lack of basic information.

Although evaluative data are absent, the tests do create a generally favorable impression. The nature of the typing tasks is likely to make sense to the typical office manager because they closely approximate jobs being done daily by office typists. Scoring procedures are also likely to make sense to persons not technically trained in test procedures. Variable penalties are assigned to different types of errors, the size of penalty appearing to correlate with the difficulty in correcting the error and the seriousness of the error from usual office standards. Test parts which would not be usable in an office situation are given a penalty equal to the total point value assigned to the item. This type of scoring raises a question of reliability. For example, a word omitted at the end of a line is penalized

1 point whereas that same omission from the middle of a line is penalized up to 40 points. Thus, chance exerts considerable influence on the score.

Although detailed instructions are given for penalizing different types of errors, it nevertheless appears that scoring may be highly subjective. For example, different scorers may differ in their opinion as to what is messy appearance or poor form. Also, how is the examiner to know whether carbon smudges are due to carelessness of the testee or to factors not controllable by the testee such as improper handling of materials by packers, shippers, test monitors, and others?

In former years certificates of proficiency were issued by the official scoring staff for those examinees who passed the test. Henceforth, such certificates will be issued to examinees whose tests are graded by the scoring staff, but each school will determine which of its examinees have passed. This procedure makes possession of a certificate of proficiency meaningless, for a certificate will henceforth indicate unspecified achievement on a typing test for which validity and reliability are unknown.

In summary, this test is likely to appear highly practical to persons untrained in testing, but evidence is lacking to indicate whether this impression is right or wrong. The publishers should immediately replace the informational (and sales) manual with one which gives at least a minimum of statistical data useful for evaluative purposes. Whatever the reason for absence of statistical data, a test which has been available as many years as this, and is as widely used as this, should be considered suspect in the absence of any information on validity and reliability.

For reviews by E. G. Blackstone and Beatrice J. Dvorak of the 1946 Form, see 3:394. For reviews by Edward N. Hay, Jacob S. Orleans, and Wimburn L. Wallace of the entire series, see 515; for a review by Paul S. Lomax of the 1946 Form, see 3:396.

[527]

★United Students Typewriting Tests, Volume 14. 1, 2, 3, 4 semesters; 1932–58; 1 form ('58); 4 levels; directions sheet ['58] for each level; no data on reliability; $2.10 per 30 tests; $1.50 per specimen set; postpaid; 35–36(40) minutes; Committee on Tests, UBEA Research Foundation; United Business Education Association. *

COMPUTATIONAL AND SCORING DEVICES

[528]

★**The Bowman I.Q. Kalculator.** 1957; for calculating IQ's from MA's and CA's between 4 and 22; $1 per calculator, postage extra; Personnel Press, Inc. *

[529]

Hankes' Answer Sheets. Special answer sheets and scoring services available on three tests; 1946; postage extra; E. J. Hankes; Testscor. *

a) STRONG VOCATIONAL INTEREST BLANK. $2.25 per 50 answer sheets; $1 for scoring one Hankes' answer sheet for 48 scales on Form M or 28 scales on Form W; $1.20 for scoring one IBM answer sheet or for scoring directly from test booklet; individual report forms furnished as part of scoring service.

b) THE PERSONALITY INVENTORY. $1.50 per 50 answer sheets; 35¢ for scoring one Hankes' answer sheet; 40¢ for scoring one IBM answer sheet or for scoring directly from test booklet; $1.25 per 50 individual report forms; only raw scores reported.

c) MINNESOTA MULTIPHASIC PERSONALITY INVENTORY. $1.90 per 50 answer sheets; 45¢ for scoring one Hankes' answer sheet; 50¢ for scoring one IBM answer sheet or for scoring directly from test booklet; individual report forms furnished as part of scoring service.

REFERENCES

1–5. See 4:466.
6. CUADRA, CARLOS A. "A New Technique for Rapid Item Analysis." *J Appl Psychol* 40:187–8 Je '56. * (PA 31:5330)

[530]

*IBM Test Scoring Machine. For scoring IBM answer sheets; 1937–58; model Type 805 ('37); manual ('54); rents for $600 per year, $900 when equipped with the Graphic Item Counter; taxes extra; rental fees to colleges and universities are 16⅔ per cent lower; standard answer sheets printed on one side vary in price from $13 per 1,000 when minimum of 500 are purchased to $6.25 per 1,000 when 25,000 or more are purchased; the corresponding prices for standard answer sheets printed on two sides vary from $19 to $9.50; mechanical pencils (filled with electrographic lead) vary from $4 per dozen to $39 per gross; $6 per box of 432 electrographic leads; $5 per 1,000 graphic item count records; $2.25 per 100 special carbons for use with graphic item count records; postage and freight charges extra; International Business Machines Corporation. *

REFERENCES

1–14. See 40:1492.
15–36. See 3:397.
37. McQUITTY, JOHN V. "The Integration of the Test Scoring Machine and Tabulating Equipment in a Program of Progress Tests and Comprehensive Examinations," pp. 106–10. In *Proceedings of the Educational Research Forum, Endicott, New York, August 26–31, 1940.* New York: International Business Machines Corp., [1941]. Pp. 127. *
38. BICE, RAYMOND C. "More Effective Use of Machine-Scored Examinations." Letter. *Am Psychol* 2:179 My '47. * (PA 21:3770)
39. DRAKE, LEWIS E. "A Method for Machine Scoring the Card Form of the MMPI." *J Ed Res* 41:139–41 O '47. * (PA 22:2149)
40. ENGELHART, MAX D. "Suggestions for Writing Achievement Exercises to Be Used in Tests Scored on the Electric Scoring Machine." *Ed & Psychol Meas* 7:357–74 au '47. * (PA 22:3642)
41. MOUNT, GEORGE E. "An Efficient Method of Obtaining Counts for Computing the Interrelation of Test Items." *J Appl Psychol* 31:634–7 D '47. * (PA 22:2430)
42. WOLFLE, DAEL. "Testing Is Big Business." *Am Psychol* 2:26 Ja '47. *

43. DRESSEL, PAUL L. "Problems and Procedures in Administering Comprehensive Examinations," pp. 60–3. In *Educational Research Forum Proceedings, Endicott, New York, August 25–29, 1947.* New York 22: International Business Machines Corporation, 1948. Pp. 96. *
44. GERBERICH, J. RAYMOND. "Use of Punched-Card and Test-Scoring Machines at the University of Connecticut," pp. 50–9. In *Educational Research Forum Proceedings, Endicott, New York, August 25–29, 1947.* New York 22: International Business Machines Corporation, 1948. Pp. 96. *
45. RUFF, WILLIAM H. "Saving Time by Machine Scoring." *Pub Personnel R* 9:143–5 Jl '48. * (PA 22:5578)
46. SCHAEFER, WILLIS C. "A Simplified Procedure for Item Analysis of Examination Material," pp. 64–70. In *Educational Research Forum Proceedings, Endicott, New York, August 25–29, 1947.* New York: International Business Machines Corporation, 1948. Pp. 96. *
47. TRAXLER, ARTHUR E. "A Procedure for Overprinting Answer Sheets for Hand Scoring Which Might Be Adapted to Local Scoring." *Ed & Psychol Meas* 8:65–7 sp '48. * (PA 22:3703)
48. WOOD, RAY G. "Functions of the Test Scoring Machine in the Testing Program of the Ohio Department of Education," pp. 15–20. In *Educational Research Forum Proceedings, Endicott, New York, August 25–29, 1947.* New York: International Business Machines Corporation, 1948. Pp. 96. *
49. BRIGHT, H. F. "Mechanical Test Scoring in San Angelo College." *Jun Col J* 20:9–12 S '49. *
50. BRADLEY, PHILIP H. "Speaking for International Business Machines." *Proc Inv Conf Testing Probl* 1953:169–72 '54. * (PA 28:6774)
51. TRAXLER, ARTHUR E. "The IBM Test Scoring Machine: An Evaluation." *Proc Inv Conf Testing Probl* 1953:139–46 '54. * (PA 28:6816)

For a review by Arthur E. Traxler, see 3:397; for reviews by John G. Darley and H. T. Manuel, see 40:1492.

EDUCATION

[531]

★**Academic Freedom Survey.** College students and faculty; 1954; 3 scores: student, faculty, total; 1 form; hectographed manual; $1 per 25 tests; $1 per specimen set (must be purchased to obtain manual); postage extra; [15] minutes; manual by Paul Slivnick; Academic Freedom Committee, Illinois Division, American Civil Liberties Union; Psychometric Affiliates. *

[532]

★**Attitude Toward Student Ratings of Instruction.** Student ratings of teachers; 1939; 1 form ['39]; mimeographed; directions sheet ['39]; no data on reliability and validity; 2¢ per scale, postpaid; [10] minutes; Personnel Evaluation Research Service, Division of Educational Reference, Purdue University. *

[533]

The Case of Mickey Murphy: A Case-Study Instrument in Evaluation, [Third Edition]. Teachers; 1942–55; 3 scores: interpretation of data, hasty conclusions, planning; IBM; Form T ['55]; manual ('55); norms ['55]; separate answer sheets must be used; $5 per 25 tests; 50¢ per 25 IBM answer sheets; postage extra; specimen set not available; (90–120) minutes; Warren R. Baller; University of Nebraska Press. *

REFERENCES

1. LYNCH, WILLIAM W., JR. *The Development of Proficiency in Educational Psychology.* Doctor's thesis, Yale University (New Haven, Conn.), 1950.
2. BALLER, WARREN R., AND BAKER, ROBERT L. "Revision of an Instrument for Measurement of Knowledge of Human Behavior." *J Ed Res* 51:623–8 Ap '58. *

DWIGHT L. ARNOLD, *Professor of Education, Kent State University, Kent, Ohio.*

Although the authors are not completely

clear as to whether this test measures "knowledge of" or "characteristics of a person's thinking about" human behavior and development, the *Case of Mickey Murphy* appears to be a worthwhile attempt to measure an important aspect of professional behavior, the ability to interpret information about children.

The test consists of the case records of an actual 14-year-old boy, interspersed with 150 multiple choice questions which give scores in three areas: (*a*) avoiding hasty conclusions (66 items), (*b*) interpretation of data (23 items), and (*c*) formulating plans of action (61 items). Reliabilities of .79, .68, and .75 for the three parts are reported for a group of 188 women students. With 124 teachers reliabilities of .87, .64, and .81 were obtained. While these indicate significance for group measurement, the highest ones are barely adequate to recommend the test for individual use.

Validity of the test is based on the nature of the material and the judgment of 11 professors of educational psychology on whose judgment "correct" scores were determined. No positive relation was found between scores and number of graduate hours, or with years of experience in teaching. However, one group of advanced students in psychology of adolescence and one group of guidance students scored significantly higher as groups than did teachers in service or undergraduates in educational psychology. Instructors in educational psychology scored distinctly higher than any other group on all three parts. Since the "case" deals with school problems in a school setting, it would seem desirable to utilize teachers as well as child study and guidance people from the schools in the search for clearer validity for this instrument.

The absence of a trained counselor in the "case" will make it less and less applicable to our better high schools. Validity of such an instrument must eventually be related somehow to what persons actually do with actual children. Experience with early studies in critical thinking and interpretation of data would suggest that Part 2, especially, may be rather closely related to reading comprehension. Certainly correlations of the part scores with various factors such as school ability and cross validation through studies in other situations are needed.

The test would be more adequate if the correct responses were not so nearly all in single types of response. In Part 1, all 66 items are in one response category, "insufficient evidence"; in Part 2, 19 items out of 23 require the response "contradicted by data"; and in Part 3, 46 items out of 61 are properly responded to by "disagree." In taking and scoring the test, the writer felt that too much weight was given to different interpretations of the word "uncertain." He felt that in Part 1 he was penalized for not being more "uncertain," while in Part 2 he was penalized for being "too uncertain." It may be that more emphasis is needed on the usefulness or value of certain assumptions and less on the degree of certainty.

The area dealt with by this test is an important one that needs more study than has so far been given it. While the *Case of Mickey Murphy* is not yet ready for widespread use in individual measurement, it does have promise as an instructional device. And it should certainly be used in further research regarding teacher understanding of child growth and development.

For a review by Frank S. Freeman of the second edition, see 4:794.

[534]

*Diagnostic Teacher-Rating Scale. Grades 4–12; 1938–52; ratings by pupils; originally published in 1938 for use in grades 4–8; 8 ratings: liking for teacher, ability to explain, kindness-friendliness-understanding, fairness in grading, discipline, work required, liking for lessons, total; 2 parts (Area Scale; Diagnostic Check List, Forms A, B) in a 4-page folder; folder ('55, identical with scale copyrighted in 1938 except for format) ; manual ('52) ; no data on reliability and validity; tentative norms ['38] based on use in grades 4–8; $2.20 per 25 scales; 35¢ per specimen set; postpaid; administration time not reported; Mary Amatora; C. A. Gregory Co. *

REFERENCES

1–2. See 4:795.
3. AMATORA, MARY. "Can Elementary School Children Discriminate Certain Traits in Their Teachers?" *Child Develop* 23: 75–80 Mr '52. * (*PA* 27:7411)
4. AMATORA, MARY. "Some Teacher Personality Traits Analyzed." *Peabody J Ed* 31:91–6 S '53. * (*PA* 28:8098)
5. AMATORA, MARY. "Teacher Rating by Younger Pupils." *J Teach Ed* 5:149–52 Je '54. * (*PA* 30:3473)
6. AMATORA, MARY. "Highs and Lows in the Teacher Personality." *J Ed Res* 48:693–8 My '55. * (*PA* 30:1637)
7. AMATORA, MARY. "Grade-Level Similarities and Differences in Teacher Personality." *Sch & Soc* 79:25–8 Ja 23 '54. * (*PA* 30:3472)

DOROTHY M. CLENDENEN, *Assistant Director, Test Division, The Psychological Corporation, New York, New York.*

This scale, designed to measure the attitudes of elementary pupils toward their teachers, was originally published in 1938. The 1952 manual states that it is for use with any group in grades 4–12, and presents tentative norms in terms of percentile equivalents of average ratings. Although the author requests the cooperation of users in establishing better norms, the manual has no evidence of research on the effectiveness of the scale in improving teacher-pupil relationships. The manual does not present details on the construction and standardization of the instrument, nor coefficients of reliability or validity, although this information may be found in a journal article (*1*) which, incidentally, is not listed with the more recently published references in the manual but which should probably be read by the prospective user.

The instrument consists of an Area Scale, and a Diagnostic Check List which has two parallel forms, A and B. All are printed in a 4-page booklet, with the Area Scale appearing in identical form on pages 1 and 3. The directions for administration imply that the Area Scale is given prior to the Check List, but do not state this specifically. For the suggested use of Form B as a follow-up some months after using Form A, separate sheets might be preferable to a single booklet.

Seven questions such as "How kind, friendly, and understanding is your teacher?" constitute the Area Scale. The pupil rates the teacher on a 5-point scale from "the best" to "the worst." The average rating on each item and an average total score are converted to percentile ratings.

The Diagnostic Check List has seven statements, scaled by the Thurstone method, for each of the seven general areas. The pupil may check several items; the median item number of the items marked is used to enter the table of scale values to find the pupil's rating of the teacher in this area. The teacher's score for the area is the median of the scale values so determined for all pupils in the class. Scores may range from 1.2 to 10.8, and any score above 6.0 is regarded as favorable. There is a Teacher's Score Sheet which requests information regarding education, age, number of years in the teaching field, and the like, yet the manual presents no information regarding the significance of these facts in interpreting the teacher's scores.

The assumption is made that if one measures the attitude of pupils reliably, validity is established, since opinions are being sought rather than an estimate of qualities actually possessed by the teacher. That this is adequate validity in a scale designed for teacher improvement seems open to question. It is pointed out in the article referred to previously that when 68 pupils were asked to express their attitudes on the Area Scale toward the best and poorest teachers they had known, no overlapping existed in average ratings. The article also states that correlations ranging from −.09 to .61 were found between supervisor's attitudes and pupils' attitudes. The author seems to feel that pupil judgment is the more valid estimate of teacher characteristics. Certainly it is with respect to pupils' liking for teacher, but is it necessarily so with respect to such items as appropriateness of amount of work required?

Reliability was established by a "split-test" procedure for the Area Scale, using 31 teachers and 610 pupils, and for the Diagnostic Check List by correlating Form A with Form B in one school with 300 children. The range of reliabilities on the Area Scale is from .86 to .96. The range on the check list is from .72 to .81. A comparison with reliabilities from a test-retest situation would be of interest to one who feels that pupil reactions to a teacher may vary from week to week.

It seems appropriate to mention that while the directions for administration convey the impression of anonymity of response ("Do not write your name on this sheet"), it is suggested that each child be given a code number in order to use the results "to establish better support with individual pupils where lack of such appears evident in the replies." This reviewer feels it would be better not to combine two purposes—that of securing frank evaluations on a group basis and that of learning of specific instances of inadequate understanding between the teacher and a particular pupil. Pupils may become alert to the presence of identifying numbers on the scale, or become sensitive to a teacher's use of information acquired from the scale. When this happens, the probability of securing frank responses on future questionnaires is unlikely.

While the claims made in the manual are modest and results obtained from the scale may be quite helpful to teachers who are concerned, as they should be, with the reactions toward them of those they teach, much more detailed and complete information should be presented in the manual. This seems clearly to be an instrument which, though published in 1938, is still in the experimental stage.

[535]

★**Educational Interest Inventory.** Prospective students of education; 1958; 10 scores: counselor, elementary teacher, high school teacher, elementary principal, high school principal, superintendent of schools, supervisor, psychologist, research worker, college professor; IBM; 1 form ['58]; manual ['58]; no data on reliability; separate answer sheets must be used; $12 per 25 tests; $1.75 per 25 IBM answer sheets and profiles ['58]; $1.80 per set of scoring stencils; 75¢ per specimen set; cash orders postpaid; [30–45] minutes; Percival M. Symonds, Arthur R. Jensen, Gordon Fifer, and Robert Drummond; published for Cooperative Center for Educational Administration; Bureau of Publications, Teachers College, Columbia University. *

[536]

★**Faculty Morale Scale for Institutional Improvement.** College faculty; 1954–56; 1 form ('54); hectographed manual ['56]; $3 per 50 tests; $1 per specimen set (must be purchased to obtain manual); postage extra; [12] minutes; A Local Chapter Committee, American Association of University Professors; Psychometric Affiliates. *

[537]

*****The Graduate Record Examinations Advanced Tests: Education.** College seniors and graduate students; 1946–58; for more complete information, see 601; IBM; 180(200) minutes; Educational Testing Service. *

REFERENCES

1–2. See 4:797.

HARRY N. RIVLIN, *Dean of Teacher Education, Board of Higher Education, New York, New York.* [Review of Form CGR.]

This test is designed for use in evaluating a college graduate's qualifications for graduate work in education. The test consists of 200 multiple choice items taken from the various areas of study ordinarily included in the undergraduate teacher education sequence: social foundations of education, philosophy of education, educational psychology, and curriculum and methods. There are no items directly related to experience as a student teacher or as a classroom teacher.

The test items are well selected and clearly written. The grouping of all of the items in which the testee is to select the least desirable choice instead of the customary best answer spares the testee the confusion and possible misinterpretation that occur when negative and positive choices are intermingled. Most of the items are concerned with the ability to interpret and to apply information rather than with the ability merely to recall information. Whenever questions deal with judgment rather than facts, there is a risk that more than one answer can be defended as the best one. There are remarkably few items in which the key is challengeable.

Because so many of the items call for maturity, intelligence, insight into education, and judgment rather than for specific knowledge, an inspection of the test suggests that a capable college graduate who has had little work in education should get a higher score than would another student who has completed a full undergraduate education sequence but is less capable as a college graduate. Few of the items reflect the skill or the insight which is gained as the result of classroom teaching rather than from college studies. To the extent to which student teaching is accepted as a major part of undergraduate teacher education programs, the GRE education test falls short of measuring achievement as a basis for predicting success in graduate studies.

The test does not differentiate between elementary education majors and secondary education majors. The curriculum and methods questions are those which are common to both fields or which apply more often to elementary education than to secondary education. While secondary education students may find that their courses did not cover some of the test items, elementary education students will not find themselves similarly handicapped.

The absence of part scores reduces the value of the tests for placement purposes or for program planning at the graduate school. It is thus impossible to tell from the reported scaled scores whether the student is superior in such an area as educational psychology or whether he needs additional study before being ready for advanced work.

For a review by Harold Seashore of the entire series, see 601.

[538]

*****National Teacher Examinations.** College seniors and teachers; 1940–58; tests administered annually in February at centers established by the publisher; tests may also be locally administered by arrangement; IBM; administrator's manual ['58]; Common Examinations with or without 1 Optional Examination: $7 for full-time students, $11 for other candidates; Common Examinations with 2 Optional Examinations: $9 for full-time students, $13 for other candidates; 1 or 2 Optional Examinations: $6 for all candidates; fee includes 2 reports of scores designated at time of application; $1 per additional report; Educational Testing Service. *
a) COMMON EXAMINATIONS. 6 scores: professional information, social studies-literature-fine arts, science and mathematics, English expression, nonverbal reasoning, weighted total; 185(210) minutes.
b) OPTIONAL EXAMINATIONS. Candidates elect 1 or more tests; 11 tests: Education in the Elementary School, Early Childhood Education, Biology and General Sci-

ence, English Language and Literature, Industrial Arts Education, Mathematics, Chemistry-Physics and General Science, Social Studies, Physical Education, Business Education, Music Education; 80(90) minutes per test.

REFERENCES

1-43. See 4:802.
44. KANDEL, I. L. "The Teacher's Right to Be Ignorant: Apropos of the Criticisms of the National Teacher-Examinations." *Sch & Soc* 51:753-6 Je 22 '40. Reprinted: *Bus Ed World* 22:377-80 Ja '42. *
45. TULLY, ALICE G. *A Study to Evaluate the Resuts of the Tests Administered to Graduates of the Rhode Island College of Education in the National Teacher Examination Program During the Period 1940-1950.* Master's thesis, Rhode Island College of Education (Providence, R.I.), 1952.
46. BENSON, ARTHUR L. "The National Teacher Examinations in 1954." *J Teach Ed* 5:244-8 S '54. * (PA 30:3476)
47. DELANEY, ELEANOR C. *Teacher Selection and Evaluation: With Special Attention to the Validity of the Personal Interview and the National Teacher Examinations as Used in One Selected Community (Elizabeth, New Jersey).* Doctor's thesis, Columbia University (New York, N.Y.), 1954. (DA 14:1334)
48. SHEA, JOSEPH AUGUSTINE. *Predictive Value of Various Combinations of Standardized Tests and Subtests for Prognosis of Teaching Efficiency.* Catholic University of America, Educational Research Monograph, Vol. 19, No. 6. Washington, D.C.: Catholic University of America Press, Inc., June 1, 1955. Pp. xi, 44. *
49. CAPPS, MARIAN P., AND DECOSTA, FRANK A. "Contributions of the Graduate Record Examinations and the National Teacher Examinations to the Prediction of Graduate School Success." *J Ed Res* 50:383-9 Ja '57. * (PA 32:937)

WILLIAM A. BROWNELL, *Dean, School of Education, University of California, Berkeley, California.* [Review of Forms CNT, ENT, and FNT.]

The 1958 edition of the *National Teacher Examinations* comprises a total of 12 separate test booklets. The largest of these, entitled Common Examinations and intended as the name implies "to measure general knowledge and ability requisite to effective teaching" at whatever level, consists of 5 separate tests. The other 11 test booklets, Optional Examinations, are for use in specialized professional areas. All tests are completely objective in character.

Customarily students and candidates for teaching positions take the Common Examinations and one or more of the Optional Examinations. Time allowances are such that few can complete any of the tests or subtests, a fact which probably assures discrimination. On the other hand, the imposition of time limits introduces the factor of speed or quickness of response into test scores and thus beclouds their interpretation as measures of power. It is only fair, however, to point out that the directions given to candidates include advice concerning the effects of undue haste and guessing.

Copies of the examinations and other materials are made available to school superintendents and responsible persons in colleges for 30 days to permit study of their contents in order to determine their usefulness for the particular purposes for which they are being considered. Every precaution is taken to prevent the tests from falling into the hands of students and other persons who may make unfair or unwise use of them. The examinations are given nationwide once a year, usually in February, in approved centers, and are administered by persons who are especially chosen for the purpose. Answer sheets are forwarded to the Educational Testing Service for scoring.

COMMON EXAMINATIONS. The Common Examinations are designed on the assumption that "prospective teachers should be able to demonstrate reasonable competence with respect to professional knowledge, general culture, English usage, and mental ability."

All items are of the best answer type, five alternatives being furnished in each instance, thus presumably reducing the chances of lucky "hits." (Appropriate formulas are also employed on test scores to reduce still more the effect of chance.) The attempt has been made —and with considerable success—to avoid purely factual items, or, stated positively, to require the application of knowledge in new ways. In the test on professional information, for example, a classroom situation is described and the best (or the least desirable) of five procedures is to be identified. When the understanding of terms, such as "readiness for learning," is being tested, the alternatives describe practices, one of which more closely than any other is in accordance with the most acceptable meaning of the term. The subtest on organization (Test B) calls for the exercise of judgment in ordering a series of related sentences. Test C (Social Studies, etc.) perhaps contains more items of simple fact than any of the other four tests in the Common Examinations. Tests D and E (Science and Mathematics, and Non-Verbal Reasoning) are especially good in the demands they make upon "the higher mental processes."

Scores on the various parts of the Common Examinations are scaled, so that comparisons can be made among them for a given student; and comparisons for groups, say, in a given institution, can be made from year to year. The scaled scores are furnished to colleges and superintendents upon the candidate's request.

Critical questions to be raised (even if they cannot be satisfactorily answered) concerning the content of the Common Examinations are: (a) How adequate is the sampling in each test? and (b) What are the "correct" answers for several of the items?

The test on professional information contains 105 items. Sixteen of these relate to statistics and measurement, e.g., the meaning of IQ and MA, of coefficients of correlation, of a test of significance, of percentiles. Are 16 items too many or too few? And what is the cutoff point for the difficulty of acceptable items? That is to say, how difficult may items be and still be included? In the same test, the alternatives designated as "correct" for a number of items, are certainly debatable. To the reviewer, in such instances another of the five alternatives is equally as good as, if not better than, the one approved.

While question (b) is less relevant to the other tests in the Common Examinations, question (a) is still pertinent. For instance, are 30 items enough to measure skill in language usage, 15 enough to measure the ability to organize sentences in logical order, and 20 enough to measure mathematical ability? And is a desirable level of difficulty represented in each test? Answers to these questions are obviously based upon judgment, something that cannot be escaped even in the preparation of objective tests. Yet, for the Common Examinations (and the Optional Examinations as well) it can be said that the judgment exercised is about as good as we are likely to get. Those in charge of constructing the tests have not limited their resources to their own opinions, as will be explained below.

OPTIONAL EXAMINATIONS. Separate tests are available for: Education in the Elementary School; Early Childhood Education; Biology and General Science; English Language and Literature; Industrial Arts Education; Mathematics; Chemistry, Physics, and General Science; Social Studies; Physical Education; Business Education; and Music Education.

The first two tests named, Education in the Elementary School and Early Childhood Education, are similar in form, organization, and type of item to the professional information test in the Common Examinations. The fields represented seem to be pretty well sampled, though a few items are open to question. Some of the "correct" answers seem to be no better than their alternatives; several call for factual knowledge alone, though not too many to throw either test out of balance; and a few, perhaps

intentionally, appear to be so easy as to be answerable without professional preparation.

The test on biology and general science (120 items) has six sections, each with its set of directions. Five sections, while requiring knowledge of subject matter, are for the most part devoted to problems of teaching this subject matter. The remaining section, an incomplete analogies test, is directly on subject matter. An expert in this field, at the request of the reviewer, examined the test and reported: (a) that the general level of difficulty is too low ("If this is all teachers need to know, Heaven help us!"), (b) that there is too much emphasis on verbalized, rote-memorized information, and (c) that there are too many questionable "correct" answers. These criticisms from a single individual are included here for what they may be worth. Their validity must be assessed in conjunction with the opinions of other experts who assisted in preparing the test. Yet, it is to be noted that this expert, like all the others to be mentioned, is involved in the preparation of teachers and is a staff member in education.

Another expert was asked to evaluate the test on English language and literature (125 items, all multiple choice). While he commented favorably upon the sections involving knowledge of literature and the ability to read and interpret literary passages, he nevertheless was convinced (a) that too many of the items relating to teaching methodology could be answered by persons of little sophistication and (b) that many more items relating to the English language (its history, structure, etc.) should have been included since the test purports to assay knowledge in this area.

No expert in the industrial arts being available, this inexpert reviewer can say only that he regards this test as covering the area well, with adequate balance among its various parts.

In general, the expert consulted by the reviewer in connection with the mathematics test (85 items) was favorably impressed. He regarded the first section (35 items) relating to instructional methods as a valuable part of the test. As for the remaining 55 items (on content), most of the questions are restricted to topics usually treated in secondary mathematics courses (including arithmetic, algebra, and plane and solid geometry) with only 6 having to do with the concepts of trigonometry, analytic geometry, and calculus. The predominance of questions on algebraic concepts he viewed as desirable, but believed it an error to include so little on such topics as inequalities, binomial expansion, sequence and series, determinants, complex numbers, and the binary and other number systems. The same local expert examined the test in chemistry, physics, and general science (120 items) and made similar comments concerning it.

The expert consulted about the test on the social studies (105 items) regarded the sections which measure knowledge of content, and the distribution of these items among the various subjects in this area, as well done, except for a tendency to test at too low a level. ("Certainly not very many of these questions should be missed if the applicant has an A.B. degree with a major in social studies, and is held to high scholastic standards.") It can be argued that the publishers have the answer for this criticism in the results obtained on the test. The expert reported considerable dissatisfaction with the questions on instructional methodology, objecting particularly to questions in which the alternatives are not parallel or in which more than one alternative properly may be selected.

The cooperating expert for the test on music education (120 items) was quite unhappy about it. He objected (a) that the test is superficial and assesses minimum preparation in many facets of music and educational practices in the teaching of music (only two items have to do with stringed instruments, and the field of harmony and composition is but "gently scratched") and (b) that the apparent assumption that there is one best way of teaching music is completely invalid; instead, views vary considerably. ("To reach the same responses as those of the testmakers one must have the same frame of reference.")

This reviewer is incompetent to pass on the merits of the tests on physical education (105 items) and business education (125 items). Since expert colleagues were not available to evaluate them, he suggests that those who contemplate use of these tests examine them ahead of time, in the light of the criticisms for the other Optional Examinations dealt with above.

It is apparent that the Optional Examinations, even more than the Common Examinations, are achievement tests; that is, they measure the amount of knowledge, or usable knowledge, that has been acquired, presumably under instruction in college. (The test items in general, save for the mathematics test, are derived from collegiate rather than from secondary education.) It follows that individual differences in depth and extent of study in each of the specialized areas will be reflected in scores. Such differences in scores are to be expected, and they may well be desirable. On the other hand, one must protect oneself in interpreting the *significance* of these differences. There is no assurance that the highest scorers in subject matter tests will be better able to teach their subjects than will those who have done somewhat less well on the tests. And low scorers may be unsuccessful because of lack of opportunity in their college careers to take enough courses in a given subject to make a good showing on tests. Their deficiencies may not be permanent and may not, therefore, indicate that they will be incompetent as teachers. Rather, their shortages may be rather easily corrected—and of course they should be corrected. The Optional Examinations will help identify persons of the latter type, with corresponding advantages to counseling them in their educational programs provided that they take the tests early enough.

GENERAL COMMENTS. When a new test is to be developed, the appropriate professional association is asked to suggest a panel of expert consultants. From this panel a committee is selected, to outline test content and to write items for the first edition. In the appointment of the committee an effort is made to choose representatives from all sections of the country, state and local systems, and teacher education institutions. The items are then subjected to careful screening and to statistical analysis on the basis of returns from the first administration of the test. The cooperation of outstanding professional leaders in the development of tests has the obvious value of extending the range, and probably of improving the quality, of the judgments which enter into the formulation of the final instruments.

There is evidence, beyond the use of expert opinion in test preparation, that the tests are valid. For one thing, according to one research report, they discriminate between good and poor candidates for teaching positions. For another, according to another report, candidates with fewer than four years of college work in general score lower than do college graduates, who in turn score lower than those with the master's degree, and so on through later stages of schooling.

In his review in *The Fourth Mental Measurements Yearbook,* Rivlin states, "Few examinations have been the center of greater controversy," pointing out that in the first years of their history "more than 68 articles were published explaining, defending, and attacking them." That they have not yet come into general use is attested by data in the 1956–57 Annual Report of the Educational Testing Service. Figures in this report show that "the total number tested in all teacher examinations" increased from 12,197 in 1948–49 to only 24,921 in 1956–57. This increase over a period of nine years is not large; and, in comparison with the hundreds of thousands of students and teachers who for one reason or another might well have been tested, the number actually tested in 1956–57 was very small. True, according to the 1958 Bulletin of Information for Candidates dozens of school systems and superintendents in 41 states and the District of Columbia are expected "to encourage or require applicants for teaching positions to submit" their scores on the *National Teacher Examinations;* and some 400 teacher education institutions are listed as having the same intent. It must be that there is more encouragement than requirement.

One wonders why the *National Teacher Examinations* are not more widely used, especially in view of the common reliance upon objective tests prepared and standardized as carefully as are these. Possible reasons are: cost, time demands on students (many of whom may be reluctant to take the tests), the shortage of teachers (with consequent less concern about their qualifications), and local and state regulations which prevent making the use of the tests obligatory. It is possible that there is a more fundamental objection, one which relates to the limited function that the tests serve.

No false or exaggerated claims are made for the *National Teacher Examinations.* In the 1958 Bulletin of Information for Candidates it is stated that the Common Examinations are supposed to "measure knowledge and ability" in the five areas tested, and the Optional Examinations, "to provide opportunity for candidates to demonstrate mastery of the subject matter they wish to teach." In a word, they assess knowledge, and knowledge only. (The "ability" tested has to do only with the application of this knowledge to verbally described situations.) The fact that they seem to do this to good effect does not appear to have proved a powerful argument for their general adoption. And perhaps it is not really a powerful argument, for many will be satisfied with other evidence of subject matter mastery, such as is represented in transcripts of college credits.

While knowledge of subject matter is an *essential* ingredient in the make-up of teachers, it is not the only one. Knowledge of subject matter does not correlate very highly with teacher effectiveness, whatever the criterion, and therefore is not a good predictive measure of teacher effectiveness. (This condition is, of course, a statistical artifact since those who take the examinations, college graduates, represent a limited and upper level of knowledge of subject matter.) Other requisite ingredients in teacher competence are knowledge and understanding of children and of youth and the ability to set up favorable learning conditions, to mention but two. Obviously, scores on the *National Teacher Examinations* have little to reveal at these and similar points.

What has just been said is not intended to reflect too seriously on the worth of the tests under review, if one but remembers their announced purposes. In refusing to use a bushel basket to measure the temperature of boiling water, one does not deny *all* value to the bushel basket; one merely recognizes its appropriateness for certain ends and its inappropriateness for others. So it is with the *National Teacher Examinations.* What they do, they do quite well; but their sphere of helpfulness is restricted. For those who want test scores on the knowledge of subject matter and of educational theory college students and teachers have acquired, these instruments are probably the best now available. At the same time, users of the tests will need to supplement the information they provide with data from other sources if they hope to have the full measure of the actual or potential competence of teachers.

WALTER W. COOK, *Dean, College of Education, University of Minnesota, Minneapolis, Minnesota.* [Review of Forms CNT, DNT, and GNT.]

DESCRIPTION OF BATTERY. The *National Teacher Examinations* (NTE) are a battery of achievement tests designed to measure "some of the knowledges and abilities expected of teachers." These tests have been administered annually since 1940 to seniors in teacher education institutions and to others, including experienced teachers, who wished to be considered for teaching appointments in school systems that encourage applicants to supply scores as part of their credentials.

Two sets of tests are included in the NTE battery, the Common Examinations, which are tests of professional information, general cultural background, facility in English expression, and nonverbal reasoning ability for individuals preparing for any type of teaching position, and the Optional Examinations from which the candidate may elect to take one or two in the fields that he is best prepared to teach. Separate Optional Examinations are now provided at the elementary level for candidates prepared to teach throughout the entire eight grades of elementary school and for those specializing in primary level teaching. At the secondary school level new optional tests have been introduced in recent years in the special and vocational subjects, including music education, physical education, business education, and industrial education, in addition to the tests in the academic fields. All of the tests are objective, composed almost entirely of multiple choice items. Responses are recorded on machine scorable answer sheets.

SCORES AND SCORE INTERPRETATION. All NTE tests are administered at examination centers and returned to the Educational Testing Service for scoring, following the careful procedures for which this organization is famous. Reports of scores are made to the candidate and to any school system or teacher education institution which he designates. The score on each of the examinations is expressed as a scaled score which may range in value from 30 to 90 with an average of about 60. No further information about this score system was located, nor was the rationale for it explained in any of the literature available to the reviewer.

The custom of computing a total score for the Common Examinations raises a question about the NTE scoring procedures. This total score is obtained by weighting the separate tests according to a formula designed to simulate the weights given to the tests that comprised the earlier and longer NTE batteries. Presumably this procedure is followed so that the scores of individuals who take the battery at various times may be compared, but no other evidence is presented as to the merits of the particular weighting scheme used.

For the interpretation of scores by school officials and by the candidate himself, a number of percentile tables are provided. New tables are prepared each year based on the scores of all individuals tested in the nationwide administration. The rather notable differences found in the mean scores on the various Common Examinations for individuals preparing to teach in various fields suggest that separate percentile tables for these groups would be much more useful in many situations than those now provided for the quite heterogeneous total group of examinees.

CONSTRUCTION OF THE TESTS. A detailed analysis of the content of all 15 tests of the current NTE battery would require broader competencies than are represented in one reviewer. The following comments on the construction of the tests are based on a general appraisal of the quality of test items and of behaviors which it seems likely that they measure, with most attention to the test of professional information.

The quality of item writing in the three forms examined was good, with few flaws detected. According to the test construction procedures described in correspondence with the reviewer, the planning and, at least for the initial forms, the actual item writing for the professional information test and for the various Optional Examinations were done by test development committees composed of individuals active in the preparation or selection of teachers. These committees were selected from panels nominated by national professional associations in the pertinent fields. The balance of the tests, i.e., the general culture, English expression, and nonverbal reasoning tests were prepared by the ETS test development staff. While this distribution of responsibility for test development between specialists in the subject matter tested, in teacher supervision, and test construction presumably provided a balance of perspectives in the selection of what was to be tested, the appraisal of the tests by the potential user would be facilitated by a statement in outline or other form of the plans agreed upon for each test. The restrictions placed on the distribution of examination copies of the NTE make such a statement of the content and behavioral objectives presumed to be measured particularly desirable.

The need for careful understanding of the test content by the test user is, perhaps, most clearly evident in the professional information test. The problems involved in sampling the professional knowledge to be expected of teachers are great. When one considers that the professional information test will be taken by individuals who expect to teach various subjects at both the elementary and secondary school levels; who have been prepared in institutions which may emphasize different educational philosophies; and who are being considered for positions in school systems with different social atmospheres and following varying educational practices; there are obvious difficulties in selecting material for a test of professional information that will be generally appropriate. Some indications of the outline used in constructing this test are given by the titles of the four sections into which this examination was divided in all forms before the latest. These include Education as a Social Institution, Child Development and Educational Psychology, Guidance and Measurement in Education, and General Principles and Methods of Teaching, with testing time distributed almost equally among these four sections. These section divisions do not appear in the most recent form (GNT), perhaps because difficulties were encountered in the classification of application items. One of the desirable features of this test is that a definite attempt seems to have been made to include such application items, although the result may be that more than one answer may be defensible for some items, depending on the way the situation cited is viewed. There has perhaps been some avoidance of areas which are likely to be controversial. This could be reinforced by the practice of selecting items for subsequent forms of each test on the basis of their discrimination in earlier administrations with total test scores used as a criterion. Such a procedure might unfortunately lead to testing a "least common denominator" of professional information.

The tests of English expression, general culture, and nonverbal reasoning are quite close relatives of other tests developed or distributed by ETS. Much of the comment made by reviewers of the *Cooperative General Culture Test* in past issues of this yearbook, for example, would apply to the NTE general culture tests.

RELIABILITY. Reliability data for one form of each of the NTE tests were reported in a supplementary leaflet. Coefficients for the Common Examinations were computed by a special procedure devised by Angoff for speeded tests. The reliability coefficients for this series were rather low, ranging from .86 to .90. For the weighted total score, however, a coefficient of .96 was reported. Reliability coefficients for the Optional Examinations were higher, being .91 or more, except for the mathematics test and three of the special field options which were less reliable, perhaps because of greater homogeneity in the group tested. No information about the variability of the scores in the samples on which any of the reliability coefficients were based was given. If one assumes that the typical NTE user will be comparing scores made by selected and rather homogeneous groups of candidates, such as applicants for a particular position, variability information for the groups on which the reliability data is based is essential. A tabulation of the standard errors of measurement for each score scale is also needed. At present, no caution is given to keep the unknowing test user from making finer discriminations than the tests justify.

VALIDITY. Of fundamental concern also is the need for information about the relevance of NTE scores for the main purpose of using the NTE battery, the selection of teachers. Though considerable care has been taken in all of the literature distributed about the NTE to point out that other factors related to teaching effectiveness, notably personal characteristics and experience, are not measured by these tests, it is clearly assumed that the knowledges and abilities measured are important for effective teaching. The relevance of the battery for selection purposes is based on the judgment of professionally competent individuals. Considering the great variety of teaching positions for which candidates have been tested by the NTE, it is unfortunate that no follow-up of subsequent teaching performance of individuals tested has been reported by the publisher.

SUMMARY. To summarize, the NTE measures certain types of information and abilities that many would agree to be important factors in teaching success. Many years of experience have gone into the construction of this battery, which in its present form represents the results of a series of adaptations to the requirements of the colleges and school systems that use it.

Where potential teachers receive their professional preparation in a variety of institutions, some of which are quite unfamiliar to the school officials, NTE scores may well provide useful information about the students' background. But the use of the NTE by a particular school system in the selection of teachers ought to depend on a careful examination of the tests in the light of its own teaching philosophy and practices, and on a carefully planned experimental study of the use of the test scores in that system.

The early fear expressed by some critics that the NTE would have a stifling effect on teacher education does not seem to have been borne out in practice. In fact, one of the chief uses made of the NTE battery, apart from for selecting teachers, has been for evaluating the achievement and abilities of senior students in teacher education institutions. The extent to which the introduction of the new *Teacher Education Examination Program* (see 543), that has been designed more specifically for institutional evaluation purposes, will affect this use of the battery remains to be seen.

One of the less publicized but perhaps one of the most valuable uses of the NTE at the present time would be for self-appraisal on the part of prospective teachers who are seriously interested in evaluating their competencies in the areas measured. The usefulness of the battery for this purpose could be considerably enhanced by the provision of more adequate interpretative materials for individual score analysis.

LAWRENCE G. DERTHICK, *United States Commissioner of Education, Office of Education, Department of Health, Education, and Welfare, Washington, D.C.* [Review of Forms CNT, ENT, and FNT.]

The *National Teacher Examinations* are designed to provide objective measurements of some of the knowledge and abilities expected of teachers. The examinations, inaugurated in 1940, are focused on the individual student. However, they do provide information to teacher education institutions in determining the needs of the students as a group as well as the needs of the institution. It is the responsibility of the candidate to register for the examinations which are administered in a one-day session on the same date throughout the country. Each candidate receives a copy of his scores on the examinations, and, upon his request, the results may be made available to authorized recipients.

The examinations, revised at frequent intervals and offered annually, are of two types: the Common Examinations, designed to measure professional information, cultural background, verbal facility, and nonverbal reasoning, which are taken by all candidates; and the Optional Examinations, covering 11 teaching fields, from which the candidate can elect no more than two.

Little evidence is available on the validity of the examinations largely because the studies which have been undertaken by ETS normally are not reported. The early controversies concerning the validity, however, have all but disappeared—which might be an indication that those who make use of the test results are now interpreting them in the context for which they were intended, i.e., the candidates' understanding of educational theory and specific subject material—the only validity claimed by the authors.

The reliability of the various parts of the battery is high, especially in view of the homogeneity of the population tested. In a recent study, reliabilities for both the Common and the Optional Examinations were reported in the high .80's and low .90's. Similarly, the intercorrelations for the Common Examinations were found to be fairly substantial, ranging from .46 between English expression and science and mathematics to .79 between social studies, literature, and fine arts, and professional information. Although the battery is not designed as a differential guidance instrument, some of the differences among the intercorrelations suggest possibilities for limited use in that area.

There are a number of features about the examinations which are worthy of special note. With few exceptions, the test items are well constructed and test largely for understanding in the different fields rather than rote recall of information. This feature is enhanced by the frequent reissuing of the examinations, which makes it possible to alter the test items to conform with changes which may occur in teaching methodologies and objectives. In these respects, the examinations have improved markedly over the years.

Further, the national system of administering the examinations and the security measures employed in the administration are highly commendable features. Because of the extensiveness of their use, the scores in any one school system or institution can be interpreted in the light of national averages and percentiles. In addition, the difficulties of assuring confidential handling of the test materials, constantly present in any testing program, have been minimized by a rigid control system.

The results of the NTE, used in conjunction with additional information such as college records, supervised teaching recommendations, and faculty evaluations, can be a valuable instrument to aid teacher training institutions, school boards, and administrators in appraising teaching ability.

For a review by Harry N. Rivlin of an earlier edition of the entire series, see 4:802.

[539]

★A Pupil's Rating Scale of an Instructor. High school and college; 1952–57; 1 form ('57, identical with scale copyrighted in 1952); no manual; no data on reliability and validity; $2.75 per 100 scales, postage extra; [5–10] minutes; Russell M. Eidsmoe; Morningside College, Sioux City, Iowa. *

[540]

★SRA Educators Opinion Inventory. Teachers; 1953; 19 ratings: work demands, working conditions, curriculum materials, pay, benefits, friendliness and cooperation of fellow employees, relations with immediate superior, confidence in administration, confidence in school board members, technical skills of immediate superior, effectiveness of school administration, adequacy of communication, personal freedom and community relations, security of job and work relations, professional satisfaction, identification with the school and its program, adequacy of provision for pupil individual differences, opportunity for growth and advancement, reactions to the inventory; Form AT; no manual; no data on reliability; separate answer sheets must be used; test materials rented for survey purposes; postage extra; [40–60] minutes; Science Research Associates. *

[541]

★A Self Appraisal Scale for Teachers. Teachers; 1957; 1 form; no data on reliability; no norms; 50¢ per scale, postpaid; [30–40] minutes; Howard Wilson; Administrative Research Associates. *

[542]

★The Teaching Evaluation Record. Supervisory ratings of teachers; 1953; 1 form; no data on reliability; $5 per 20 records, postage extra; specimen set not available; Dwight E. Beecher; Educators Publishing Co. *

[543]

★Teacher Education Examination Program. College seniors preparing to teach; 1957; IBM; 1 form; $5 per student for any 2 tests; $6 per student for professional examination and any 2 field tests; postpaid; Educational Testing Service. *

a) GENERAL PROFESSIONAL EXAMINATIONS. 7 scores: foundations of education, child development and educational psychology, guidance and measurement, instructional methods, English, history-literature-fine arts, science and mathematics; 185(245) minutes.
b) TEACHING FIELD TESTS. 11 tests: Early Childhood Education, Elementary School Education, English Language and Literature, Social Studies, Biological Science, Physical Science, Mathematics, French, Spanish, Industrial Arts, Physical Education; 80(95) minutes per test.

WALTER W. COOK, *Dean, College of Education, University of Minnesota, Minneapolis, Minnesota.* [Review of Form FTC.]

The *Teacher Education Examination Program* (TEEP) might be described as "old wine in new bottles," with the *National Teacher Examinations* (NTE) as the "old wine." Like the NTE, from old forms of which it was constructed, the TEEP is divided into two main parts, the General Professional Examinations, corresponding to the NTE Common Examinations, and Teaching Field Tests, which, like the NTE Optional Examinations, are intended to cover the more common elementary and secondary teaching fields.

The TEEP was apparently introduced because the scheduling arrangements and per student cost of the NTE made it impractical for many teacher education institutions that wanted to test entire groups of students. Also, a more detailed score breakdown on the professional phase of the student's preparation than the NTE provides would be desirable for evaluation purposes. The scheduling arrangements for the TEEP were therefore made much more flexible than those for the NTE and, with the assumption of responsibility for administering the tests by the institution and the elimination of individual score reporting services, the per student cost was reduced by about 45 per cent.

Because the TEEP tests are much the same as the tests in the NTE battery that has been reviewed in this and previous *Mental Measurements Yearbooks*, attention will be given in this review to the usefulness of the TEEP battery for its intended purposes. A variety of uses for the test scores are suggested in a bulletin addressed to school officials. Several of these uses involve the comparison of an individual student's ability, either with that of fellow students or with that of the norms group. None of the General Professional Examinations has a reliability coefficient above .84, and the four tests of professional education, with reliability coefficients ranging from .61 to .67, are clearly too unreliable for individual score comparisons. Despite these low reliability coefficients, the use of these scores to identify differential abilities of students is also suggested. With intercorrelations ranging from .40 to .65, in some cases almost as large as the average reliabilities of the two measures, the reliability of score differences would be quite low, and consequently the comparison of scores on the separate phases of professional education most questionable. The use of a combined score for the four professional areas has been recommended by the publishers in correspondence with colleges which make use of the tests, and although the reliability of this measure (.88) is better than for the separate tests, it is still not as high as one would expect for such an important measure of student achievement. Furthermore, the use of the combined score was not anticipated in the preparation of normative data, so no percentile tables are provided for it. Certain of the teaching field tests, particularly those in English language and literature and social studies, are sufficiently reliable for the individual scores to be meaningful, but for most of the tests the comparisons suggested could only be made with great caution.

The low reliability of a number of the TEEP tests would not, of course, prevent their use for the evaluation of group achievement in the areas measured. For this purpose the distributions of college mean scores on the various tests provide useful comparative data. Unfortunately, the usefulness of these distributions, and indeed of all the present TEEP normative data, is hampered by the fact that they were based on the scores of students in a variety of types of colleges. Eastern state teachers colleges comprised the largest share of the institutions included in the norms group, but a scattering of liberal arts colleges and university groups was also included. The known differences in kinds of students attending such institutions and in the curricula offered would argue for the presentation of tables based on more homogeneous groups.

The recommendation that passing or qualifying scores be established, presumably for use in making administrative decisions about continuing or graduating students in a teacher preparatory program, seems most dubious at the present state of the TEEP. While cautions are given about the dangers in using single scores in this manner, because of the errors of measurement in the tests, the recommendation that an average score be used to avoid this problem runs clearly into the difficulty of justifying any particular combination of scores. The statement that some tests can be allowed to contribute more than others to such an average skirts too quickly some of the problems which would need to be considered in validating the battery for measuring achievement in a particular teacher education program. Since no validity data have been presented for the TEEP, institutions using this battery must rely on their own examination of the tests, and on any experience that they may have had in the use of NTE results, in making decisions as to how, if at all, the scores can be validly used for qualifying purposes.

In summary, the TEEP battery was designed to meet an apparent need on the part of teacher education institutions for a battery of tests which would provide more useful scores for evaluative purposes than the NTE does and which could be administered at more convenient times and at less cost than the NTE. While the administrative requirements appear to be better satisfied by the new test program, it is questionable whether the TEEP scores now available provide any more information than the NTE did for individual students, and the normative data are no better. Until the reliability of the TEEP tests, especially of the professional education tests, is improved, the TEEP will be useful primarily for evaluating the achievements of groups of students. Unfortunately for this purpose, the percentile tables now available only permit comparisons of performance with a rather poorly defined group of institutions.

[544]
★A Test on Adult Attitudes Toward Children. Classes in child development, teachers, and parents; 1957; 1 form; directions sheet ['57]; $1.50 per 25 tests; 25¢ per specimen set; cash orders postpaid; (15) minutes; David F. Votaw; Steck Co. *

[545]
★What Would *You* Do? Perplexing Incidents in Human Relations. Teachers; 1955; Form A; norms and scoring key are not provided since users are expected to adapt the test to meet local needs and values; no manual; no data on reliability; $5.25 per 35 tests; 25¢ per test; cash orders postpaid; (35-45) minutes; Willard S. Elsbree and others; Bureau of Publications, Teachers College, Columbia University. *

[546]

*The Wilson Teacher-Appraisal Scale. Rating of
instructors by students in grades 7-9, 10-16; 1948-57;
1 form; 2 levels; no manual; no data on reliability; no
norms; $1.50 per 50 scales; sample scale free; postpaid;
[10-15] minutes; Howard Wilson; Administrative Research Associates. *

a) JUNIOR EDITION. Grades 7-9; 1948-57; 1 form ('57,
identical with form copyrighted in 1948).

b) [COLLEGE EDITION.] Grades 10-16; 1957; 1 form.

ETIQUETTE

[547]

★The New Century Social Conduct Test. Grades
9 and over; 1939-45; 1 form ('45); no manual; no
data on reliability and validity; no norms; $2.50 per
50 tests, postage extra; administration time not reported; Century School Crafts. *

[548]

★Parsons Social Comprehension Test. Grades 9-
12; 1953; Form A; mimeographed manual; $1.20 per
25 tests, postage extra; 25¢ per specimen set, postpaid;
(40-50) minutes; Verlin Parsons; Bureau of Educational Measurements. *

[549]

*Test on Social Usage. High school and college;
1935-57; based on the authors' book As Others Like
You; Forms A, B ('57); no manual; $2 per 25 tests;
10¢ per specimen set; postage extra; administration
time not reported; Margaret Stephenson and Ruth
Millett; McKnight & McKnight Publishing Co. *

HANDWRITING

[550]

*Ayres Measuring Scale for Handwriting. Grades
2-8; 1912-40; also called Ayres Handwriting Scale:
Gettysburg Edition; 2 scores: quality, speed; 1 form
['17]; no data on reliability; additional norms ['40]
published by Public School Publishing Co.; 25¢ per
scale, postage extra; 2¢ per record blank ['40, published by Public School Publishing Co.], postpaid;
2(10-15) minutes; Leonard P. Ayres; Cooperative
Test Division, Educational Testing Service. *

REFERENCES

1-9. See 4:475.

For a review by Worth J. Osburn, see 4:475.

[551]

★Evaluation Scales for Guiding Growth in Handwriting. Grades 1, 2, 3, 4, 5, 6, 7, 8-9; 1958; no manual; 45¢ per scale; $3.25 per specimen set of all scales;
postpaid; Frank N. Freeman; Zaner-Bloser Co. *

HEALTH

[552]

*Cornell Medical Index—Health Questionnaire.
Ages 14 and over; 1949-56; medical questionnaire to
be used by examining physician; separate forms ('49)
for men and women; revised manual ('56); no data on
reliability; $2.50 per 50 questionnaires; $1 per 50 diag-

nostic sheets ['53]; specimen set free; postpaid; Spanish edition available; (10-30) minutes; Keeve Brodman, Albert J. Erdmann, Jr., and Harold G. Wolff;
Cornell University Medical College. *

REFERENCES

1. HOLMES, THOMAS H. Chap. 6, "Multidiscipline Studies of
Tuberculosis," pp. 65-152. In Personality, Stress, and Tuberculosis. Edited by Phineas J. Sparer. New York: International
Universities Press, Inc., 1956. Pp. xviii, 629. *
2. BARD, MORTON, AND WAXENBERG, SHELDON E. "Relationship of Cornell Medical Index Responses to Postsurgical Invalidism." J Clin Psychol 13:151-3 Ap '57. * (PA 32:2884)

[553]

★Elementary Health: Every Pupil Scholarship
Test. Grades 6-8; 1933-58; new form usually issued
each January and April; norms available following
testing program; no data on reliability; 4¢ per test; 4¢
per scoring key; postage extra; 30(35) minutes;
Bureau of Educational Measurements. *

[554]

Gill-Schrammel Physiology Test. High school;
1936-37; Forms A ('36), B ('37); directions sheet
['37]; $1.45 per 25 tests; 25¢ per specimen set; post-
paid; 40(45) minutes; Ethan M. Gill and H. E.
Schrammel; Bureau of Educational Measurements. *

CLARENCE H. NELSON, Professor, Office of
Evaluation Services, Michigan State University, East Lansing, Michigan.

This test has three parts. Part 1 in each form
is made up of 52 true-false items, Part 2 consists of 22 5-response multiple choice items,
and Part 3 has 28 matching items. The neat
preciseness with which the two forms have
been constructed to parallel each other in outward form looks impressive indeed. Closer
scrutiny, however, reveals a number of shortcomings in this test.

But in fairness to the test authors as well as
to potential users, how does one evaluate a test
written more than 20 years ago covering a
subject that is rapidly changing? Since physiology is closely associated with biochemistry
and new discoveries in biochemistry are constantly being made, a great deal of new knowledge has been added to the field of physiology
in recent years. An attempt at listing even a
few of these new developments will point up
the dynamic character of the field. It will also
indicate why a textbook or test that is more
than 20 years old is out of date.

At the time it was written, this test covered
some of the major aspects of physiology as
then taught, and the testing techniques used
were generally accepted as fairly adequate.
Several of the then leading textbooks served
as the basis for the test content and the test
was further validated by being checked by science teachers, supervisors, and test construction specialists. These reviewers were not suffi-

ciently critical, however, to detect several poorly worded items. In Form A, Item 5, if "human" body is meant, it should be so stated. In Item 19, the word "only" tends to prejudice the answer. In Item 29, "lean" meat would have improved the item. In Item 56, "wall" is keyed as the correct answer, but only plant cells have walls. For Item 77 (as for Item 59, Form B) the keyed answer "thyroxin" is so nearly like "thyroid" in the item that the answer practically falls into place automatically. The same can be said regarding the keyed answers to Items 82 and 97 in Form A and 90 in Form B.

In Form B, Item 2 contains two ideas. A good true-false item should contain but a single idea. Item 63 is inaccurate. There are many kinds of salts which do not contain sodium. If table salt is meant, the item should so state. Item 65 could have several answers among those listed. Fish oils are certainly a valuable source of vitamins. It would appear that the distractors for Item 73 would be practically nonfunctional. Item 84 is inaccurate from the standpoint of grammar. As stated, it would call for a singular answer, but the keyed answer is "capillaries."

According to better test writing practices, a list of possible responses in a set of matching type items should be homogeneous. If names are to be matched, the list should consist exclusively of one kind of name, e.g., names of people, names of processes, or names of structures, but not all three. Moreover, there should be grammatical homogeneity. Nouns, verbs, and adjectives should not appear in the same list, nor should singulars and plurals be included together, nor proper names mixed with common nouns. The matching items in this physiology test violate the foregoing rules of test writing.

According to the manual the *Gill-Schrammel Physiology Test* "covers the basic facts and principles commonly included in a thorough physiology course. Its aim is to measure knowledge outcomes." In recent years a more far-reaching concept of testing has evolved. In the better types of measuring instruments, testing mainly for the names of structures and processes has become incidental to testing for understanding, the ability to interpret data, and the ability to apply what has been learned in the appraisal of real life situations related to the area of study. This does not mean that fundamental knowledge is no longer of any importance. Fundamental knowledge becomes more essential than ever. It forms the basis for ability to do critical thinking, and the extent to which students have mastered this basic material will become apparent in their performance on thought questions which embody, in incidental fashion, these fundamentals in the presentation of the problem situations.

Since the course content of physiology veritably teems with dynamic problem situations, there is little reason why a test in this area should consist largely of items which merely call for names of things. If there is a sufficient market for a high school physiology test to justify revision of this one or the construction of a completely new one, the new version should be made to reflect the vital, functional, problem-oriented character of this subject.

[555]

*Health and Safety Education Test: National Achievement Tests. Grades 3–6; 1947–56; 5 scores: good habits, cause and effect, facts, application of rules, total; Form A ('56, identical with test copyrighted in 1947); directions sheet ('47); no data on reliability; $2.75 per 25 tests; 50¢ per specimen set; postage extra; 40(45) minutes; Lester D. Crow and Loretta C. Ryan; Acorn Publishing Co. *

CLARENCE H. NELSON, *Professor, Office of Evaluation Services, Michigan State University, East Lansing, Michigan.*

This test reflects careful workmanship in its construction. The division into four parts (1, Good Health and Safety Habits; 2, Cause and Effect in Relation to Health and Safety; 3, Facts About Health and Safety; and 4, Application of Health and Safety Rules) indicates that the authors were cognizant of several types of outcomes of health and safety education and that they made a deliberate attempt to measure each type of outcome. It is particularly gratifying to find in the test a section that embodies application. This section could have been enhanced, however, by increasing its length. The 10 application situations presented are excellent, but had the authors included 25 such situations the test might have been even better.

Easy-to-read type and adequate spacing of the items contribute to good format in this test. Norms are supplied for each grade level. The scoring procedure appears to be a little cumbersome. It is regrettable that no data on reliability or validity accompany this test; these data should be made available.

One distinctive and noteworthy feature of this test is the personalized manner in which many of the items are written. The pupil is made to feel that he or she is being addressed individually in items such as the following from Part 1:

4. When dirt or a cinder gets into your eye
   A rub your eye to push it out
   B let the tears wash it out
   C have it removed by a person who knows how
7. If you must cross a busy street while roller skating
   A remove skates before crossing
   B skate across quickly
   C skate across slowly

This personalized feature gets away from the stilted artificiality which tends to make some school work distasteful or uninteresting to children. The application items in Part 4 are also thoughtfully designed to appeal to children by posing lifelike situations using names of boys and girls. For example:

Problem 7. Jane fainted in the school yard. Alice wanted to carry Jane into the building. Rose ran to get Jane a drink. Elsie laid Jane flat on her back. The best first aid given Jane was by
   A Alice   B Rose   C Elsie

Test items of this sort enable pupils taking the test to demonstrate understanding by applying what they have learned to new nontextbook situations. Moreover, test taking can become a pleasant experience rather than an onerous one when interesting situations are presented in the test exercises.

Despite a few minor shortcomings that have been pointed out, the *Health and Safety Education Test* reflects skillful and imaginative craftsmanship and is on the whole an excellent test.

[556]

*Health Education and Hygiene: Every Pupil Test. Grades 7–9; 1935–58; new form usually issued each December and April; norms available following testing program; no data on reliability; 3¢ per test; 1¢ per scoring key; cash orders postpaid; 40(45) minutes; Ohio Scholarship Tests. *

[557]

*Health Education Test: Knowledge and Application: Acorn National Achievement Tests, Revised Edition. Grades 7–13; 1946–56; 3 scores: knowledge, application, total; Form A ('56, identical with test copyrighted in 1946 except for minor changes); directions sheet ('56, identical with sheet copyrighted in 1946); $3 per 25 tests; 25¢ per manual ('47); 50¢ per specimen set; postage extra; 40(45) minutes; John H. Shaw and Maurice E. Troyer; Acorn Publishing Co. *

REFERENCE

1. SHAW, JOHN H., AND TROYER, MAURICE E. "The Development of a New Test in Health Education." *J Sch Health* 17: 216–9 O '47. *

For reviews by H. H. Remmers and Mabel E. Rugen, see 3:421.

[558]

★Health Knowledge Test for College Freshmen: National Achievement Tests. Grade 13; 1956; 1 form; $4 per 25 tests; 25¢ per manual; 50¢ per specimen set; postage extra; 40(45) minutes; A. Frank Bridges; Acorn Publishing Co. *

REFERENCES

1. KILANDER, H. F. "Health Knowledge of High School and College Students." *Res Q* 8:2–32 O '37. *
2. BRIDGES, FRANK. "Health Knowledge Test for College Freshmen." *J Sch Health* 24:218–21 O '54. *
3. BOYDSTON, DONALD N.; SELLS, JAMES A.; AND WHELAN, ROBERT F. "A Comparison of Scores on a Health Knowledge Test of College Veterans and Non-Veterans." *J Sch Health* 26: 220–2 S '56. *

JAMES E. BRYAN, *Foreign Quarantine Division, United States Public Health Service, New York, New York.*

The manual for this test lists nine purposes, among which is this one: "To assist in appraising the teacher, the methods used, the curriculum, and the teaching material." This purpose alone is a big order—one that few, if any, of the tests so far constructed in this area can claim to fulfill. The test under review certainly cannot.

The manual reports that the 13 areas covered by the 100 items, and the percentage of items devoted to each of the areas, were determined by a jury of college health educators. The emphasis ranges from a high of 16 items on nutrition to a low of a single item on current health. The latter would seem most inadequate. As the title implies, the test is concerned only with knowledge of health facts; there is no attempt to test understandings.

The test is scored by reference to a code word, any response preceded by any letter in that word being correct. Since anyone who knows the word can score the test, the need for a scoring key is eliminated. Unfortunately, it may be just as convenient for the testee to decipher the code word as it is for the teacher to use it. The arrangement of items in order of difficulty should make it rather easy for an alert student to "crack" the code.

The norms presented in the manual are based on the scores of "3,062 college freshmen in 25 colleges and universities in 17 different states." The normative group is not further described. The table gives percentile ranks and T score values for raw scores, at intervals of 5, with ranks of 0 and 100 for raw scores of 20 and 80, respectively. There are no directions for finding values for scores not shown in the table.

There is a rating scale in the manual for use in translating the student's score into an overall evaluation of his health education background. The scale bands range from a score of 73 or better, interpreted as indicating excellent background in health education, to a score of 28 or below, indicating poor background. No explanation is given as to how the values were determined.

The directions printed on the test booklet include this sentence: "There are four possible answers for each of the following test items." The use of the term "possible answers" is unfortunate, for there are several items that give at least two correct responses. Some of them, like Item 28, are obvious: "Today, man can expect to live:....x. To 65 years, n. To 70 years." Anyone who lives to 70 years [keyed as correct] must have lived to 65 years. Others have multiple correct responses that are not so easily detected. For example, Item 48 reads: "Foods containing iron should be included in the diet for: a. The formation of hemoglobin [keyed as correct]....f. The repair of body tissue." Item 87 reads: "The immunization against rabies for human beings is: a. The Pasteur treatment [keyed as correct]....k. The vaccination." These items may well be confusing to the student who knows that blood is a tissue and that the formation of hemoglobin is, therefore, a repair of a body tissue; or that the Pasteur treatment is a series of vaccinations. And it can be strongly argued that at least one item (31) has four correct responses. This item reads: "It would be vastly to the advantage of the next generation if those about to marry were to have: h. An examination for venereal disease, x. An examination by a psychiatrist, u. A complete general examination [keyed as correct], z. An examination for tuberculosis." Surely the correct answer includes all of the others.

Some items have no completely correct response, i.e., Item 69: "The colon is the name used to denote:....n. The large intestine [keyed as correct], p. The cecum." The colon is one of the three parts of the large intestine, as is also the cecum. And several items have responses that immediately permit the testee to eliminate certain of them, thus decreasing the number of effective foils. For example, in Item 57, "Syphilis is one of the diseases: h. We cannot completely control, e. We could completely control...." Any student can see that one of the responses quoted has to be correct. He can ignore the other two.

The cases cited by no means include all of the items that are subject to adverse criticism. The test could be improved if the stems were rewritten so as to pose the questions more directly, and the responses rewritten so that they are parallel and mutually exclusive, and do not overlap either with other responses within the item or with responses in other items.

In spite of the criticisms made, the content coverage is, on the whole, good. The mediocrity of the instrument is largely due to the method of handling materials in both the test and the manual, and to the failure to include certain strategic information in the manual. There is no reason why these shortcomings cannot be remedied. Until such time as this is done, the reviewer is of the opinion that the test will not particularly impress college health instructors.

[559]

*Health Practice Inventory. Grades 12–16 and adults; 1943–52; 14 scores: personal health, nutrition, dental health, physical activity, rest-sleep-relaxation, communicable disease, chronic disease, stimulants and depressants, mental health, family health, consumer health, community health, safety education, total; 1 form ('52); manual ('52); no data on reliability of subtests; norms for grades 11–14 only; no norms for safety education score; 1–99 tests, 15¢ each; cash orders postpaid; 50¢ per specimen set, postpaid; (30–40) minutes; Edward B. Johns and Warren L. Juhnke; Stanford University Press. *

REFERENCES

1–2. See 3:423.
3. MASLEY, JOHN W. *An Analysis of Certain Factors Related to the Health Knowledge and Health Habits of College Freshmen Women.* Doctor's thesis, Pennsylvania State College (State College, Pa.), 1950.
4. JUHNKE, WARREN L. *A Revision on Further Validation of the Johns Health Practice Inventory.* Master's thesis, University of California (Los Angeles, Calif.), 1951.

JAMES E. BRYAN, *Foreign Quarantine Division, United States Public Health Service, New York, New York.*

Both the *Health Practice Inventory* and the accompanying manual have been revised and considerably enlarged since they were reviewed in *The Third Mental Measurements Yearbook.*

The new manual reports respectable reliability coefficients of .87, .88, and .86, based on data on the original inventory, and .84, .73, and .87, based on data on the revised inventory. There is no information regarding the method of arriving at these figures. The description of the validation is essentially the same as in the earlier manual. The principal change in the manual is the inclusion of norms tables—one table for the inventory as a whole, and separate tables for each of the areas covered except safety education. The norms are based on "scores obtained from a sampling of high schools, a college, and one university." Nothing is said about size or geographic distribution of the normative sample.

The revised inventory contains 100 items as compared to 36 in the earlier edition. The items cover 13 areas: personal health; nutrition; dental health; physical activity and recreation; rest, sleep, and relaxation; prevention and control of communicable disease; prevention and control of chronic disease; stimulants and depressants; mental health; family health; consumer health; community health; and safety education. Coverage is quite comprehensive, even if an occasional item appears in the wrong area.

The body of the inventory is arranged according to areas, and area and total scores are obtained. Provision is made in the booklet for recording the scores and for charting a profile of the individual's health practices. Each of the questions has five responses: never, rarely, sometimes, usually, and always, numbered 1 to 5 if the best practice is indicated by "always," and 5 to 1 if the best practice is indicated by "never." The number of the response is its numerical value for scoring purposes. If responses are recorded directly on the inventory, the scoring is simple addition. If separate answer sheets are used, five scoring keys are necessary, making the scoring cumbersome whether done by hand or by machine.

There are certain specific criticisms concerning the handling of parts of the inventory. For example, can Item 31, "Do you awake in the morning feeling refreshed after your usual night's sleep?" be considered an inquiry into a health practice or a state of mind? And Item 47, "Do you take a laxative (or enema) if you have abdominal pain?" seems more closely related to the correct handling of an acute abdominal condition than to the prevention or control of chronic disease. In the section on stimulants and depressants, the lumping together of headache preventives (or remedies) and sleep-preventive patent medicines (presumably benzedrine or drugs of similar qualities) is unfortunate. In view of recent trends toward increased use of such items as narcotics, tranquilizers, and marihuana, questions on their use might well be included here. Although it can be argued that annual medical and dental examinations, tuberculin tests or x-ray examinations, and urine examinations are related to consumer health since the patient buys these services from his physician, dentist, or laboratory, they would seem to this reviewer to fall more logically in the areas of personal health and dental health.

Despite these small criticisms, the reviewer is of the opinion that the authors have done much to eliminate the defects of the earlier inventory. The increased number of items permits both wider coverage and the use of questions that suggest remedial action, making this a much more useful instrument.

For a review by Thomas Kirk Cureton of the original edition, see 3:423.

[560]

*Health Test: National Achievement Tests. Grades 3–8; 1937–57; 5 scores: recognizing best habits, health comparisons, causes and effects, health facts, total; Forms A ('49, identical with test copyrighted in 1938 except for Item 1, Part 3), B ('57, identical with test copyrighted in 1938 except for Item 20, Part 1); no data on reliability; no norms for part scores; directions sheet for Form A ('49, identical with sheet copyrighted in 1938), directions sheet for Form B ('38); $2.50 per 25 tests; 50¢ per specimen set; postage extra; (40) minutes; Robert K. Speer and Samuel Smith; Acorn Publishing Co. *

BENNO G. FRICKE, *Assistant Chief, Evaluation and Examinations Division, and Assistant Professor of Psychology, University of Michigan, Ann Arbor, Michigan.*

Prospective users of this test are supplied no information on the validity, reliability, or comparability of the two forms. Furthermore, they are not provided information on the composition of the norm groups, or the method used to select them. Nor are they furnished any data on the construction of the test. It is safe to say that authors Speer and Smith have failed to supply most of the crucial bits of information a test user (and test reviewer!) needs in order to arrive at a satisfactory judgment of the test's utility, or, perhaps more accurately, a judgment favorable to the test. Obviously the critical comments made by Jacob S. Orleans in *The Fourth Yearbook* have not been acted upon.

Since norms for the four part scores are not given, it is impossible for the test user to draw

valid inferences about the differential performance of each pupil. And since the correlations
among the parts also are not given, it is impossible to know how independent they are. An inspection of the items leads the reviewer to
doubt that relatively independent scores are
obtained. In general, test producers should
make provision for no more than a single total
score for an area unless they can demonstrate
that an adequate description of test takers requires more than one score. It should not be
necessary for test users to discover whether or
which part scores are worth having.

The division of the items into the four parts
might be questioned on nonstatistical grounds
as well. For example, in Form A, Item 1 in
Part 4, Health Facts, reads:

> It is proper to
> d. spit on the sidewalk
> h. stick gum on a chair
> a. wet the end of a pencil with one's tongue
> i. refuse to use someone else's handkerchief

While refusing to use someone else's handker-
chief is a desirable practice children should
develop, the item does not appear to tap a fact
so much as a habit, which would be more appropriately tested under Part 1, Recognizing
Best Habits.

Perhaps even more serious, the 80-item test
purports to be useful for pupils in grades 3 to
8. It is highly unlikely that most of the items
would be appropriate for most of the pupils
for whom the test is intended. While it is possible that some kind of analysis was done to
determine item difficulty, the arrangement of
items does not seem to follow the popular "least
to most difficult item" order.

Probably most pupils, particularly those in
the lower grades, are confused by the designations preceding the response alternatives. They
are not consistently a, b, c, d, or 1, 2, 3, 4,
or anything else. For example, for Item 3 in
Part 1 the alternatives are designated as n, o,
p; but for Item 1 in Part 4 the alternatives are
d, h, a, i. The jumble of letters provides the
basis for a scoring scheme: the correct answer
to Item 1 in Part 4 is i, and to Item 3 in Part 1,
n. While this scheme may facilitate matters for
the test scorer, it probably complicates the situation for young and dull pupils at least. Gim-
micks such as this one may serve to contaminate scores unnecessarily with a general test
ability or general intelligence, and conceal what
is desired, namely a measure of health achieve-

ment. Before leaving the topic of response alternatives, it is worth noting that most items
have one or two alternatives that are so obviously wrong that few if any pupils would bite
on them. Insufficient attention seems to have
been given to plausibility of decoys.

In light of the above, a close look at the
norms, especially those for grades 3 and 4, discloses some interesting material. The median
performance of pupils at grade 3-0 is 25 on
Form A and 22 on Form B. The chance average for Form A is 21; for Form B, 20. The
reviewer by tossing a die and marking response
alternatives at random (i.e., the questions and
answers were not read) obtained raw score
totals higher than the grade 3-0 medians on
both forms in the first "taking" of the test!
Such high performance *by chance alone* is certainly undesirable. Obviously many pupils obtain scores which are in the "chance average"
range. It seems important to stress that a pupil
with very little health knowledge, but with
some general ability (to eliminate one or two
obviously incorrect alternatives) and with some
good luck, could obtain substantially higher
than the norm at most grade levels; but a pupil
with limited general ability or reading ability,
or with some bad luck, might obtain a score
below the norm even though his true health
achievement would be average for his grade.

If there is a need for expertly constructed
standardized achievement test materials in areas
such as health, and it appears that there is, despite the fact that not all schools in the nation
have the same objectives and offering, it would
seem that test item files or folios similar to that
prepared by Dressel and Nelson [1] in the science
area, instead of tests, should be prepared and
sold to school systems. From this file teachers
might select and duplicate those items that are
relevant and appropriate for their course and
grade level. Highly standardized, nationally
available achievement tests are probably of
greatest value when there is a highly standardized curriculum throughout the nation;
when school programs differ, these differences
should be reflected in the tests given to pupils.
But the tailor-made tests might still retain some
of the "national-standardization" features if
test item producers would supply item difficulty
levels. An oversimplified example may have

1 DRESSEL, PAUL L., AND NELSON, CLARENCE H., EDITORS. *Questions and Problems in Science: Test Item Folio No. 1.* Princeton, N.J.: Cooperative Test Division, Educational Testing Service, 1956. Pp. xvi, 805.

value: if a teacher selected 40 "Desirable Health Practices" test items each having a difficulty level of 75 per cent, the teacher would expect the average test score for her class to be 30 if her class is at the norm; an average raw score of less than 30 would indicate that her class was below average. Test producers, with the stimulation and cooperation of test users, might well consider using some of the techniques employed successfully by builders of prefabricated houses and unfinished furniture. The difficult and technical aspects should be in the hands of competent test authors and publishers, but the final assembly and finishing touches should be made by teachers and administrators who are familiar with the local situation.

One final matter deserving of critical comment lies in the note on the back side of the sheet, "Teachers Directions, Class Record, Answer Form and Norms," designed to accompany Form A. It is addressed to school administrators and teachers and says: "You can assist the health movement by mailing a copy of this Class Record Form to Professor Robert K. Speer, New York University, Washington Square East, New York, N.Y. Descriptions of effective teaching devices you have used will also be useful to the research staff." There are a number of other things worth doing that would benefit the health movement and educational and psychological measurement much more, and these include not using this health test unless it is improved and pertinent research conducted and reported.

For a review by Jacob S. Orleans, see 4:485.

[561]

★**High School Health: Every Pupil Scholarship Test.** High school; 1938(?)–58; new form usually issued each April; norms available following testing program; no data on reliability; 4¢ per test; 4¢ per scoring key; postage extra; 40(45) minutes; Bureau of Educational Measurements. *

[562]

*****Kilander Health Knowledge Test: Evaluation and Adjustment Series.** High school; 1936–51; IBM; Forms AM, BM ('51); manual ('51); separate answer sheets must be used; $3.60 per 35 tests; $1.40 per 35 IBM answer sheets; postage extra; 35¢ per specimen set, postpaid; 40(50) minutes; H. F. Kilander; World Book Co. *

REFERENCES
1. KILANDER, H. F. "Health Knowledge of High School and College Students." *Res Q* 8:3–32 O '37. *
2. TRICE, ETHEL W. *A Study of the Health Knowledge of College Students in Louisiana.* Master's thesis, Louisiana State University (University Station, Baton Rouge, La.), 1946.

3. MASLEY, JOHN W. *An Analysis of Certain Factors Related to the Health Knowledge and Health Habits of College Freshmen Women.* Doctor's thesis, Pennsylvania State College (State College, Pa.), 1950.

See 40:1503 (2 excerpts).

[563]

★**Physical Education: National Teacher Examinations.** College seniors and teachers; 1954–58; for more complete information, see 538; IBM; 80(90) minutes; Educational Testing Service. *

For reviews by William A. Brownell, Walter W. Cook, and Lawrence G. Derthick of the entire series, see 538; for a review by Harry N. Rivlin of an earlier edition, see 4:802.

[564]

★**Physical Education: Teacher Education Examination Program.** College seniors preparing to teach secondary school; 1957; for more complete information, see 543; IBM; 80(95) minutes; Educational Testing Service. *

For a review by Walter W. Cook of the entire series, see 543.

[565]

★**Physical Education Tests.** College women; 1955; 1 form ['55] mimeographed; 7 tests: badminton, basketball, bowling, field hockey, softball, tennis, volley ball; no manual; no data on reliability; norms ['55]; $10 per set of 7 tests, postpaid; fee includes permission to reproduce the test materials; specimen set not available; [40] minutes; Gail M. Hennis; the Author, Department of Physical Education, Woman's College, University of North Carolina, Greensboro, N.C. *

REFERENCE
1. HENNIS, GAIL M. "Construction of Knowledge Tests in Selected Physical Education Activities for College Women." *Res Q* 27:301–9 O '56. *

[566]

*****Sex Knowledge Inventory, Experimental Edition.** Sex education classes in high school and college and adults; 1950–56; 1 form; 2 tests (labeled Forms X and Y); cash orders postpaid; Gelolo McHugh; Family Life Publications, Inc. *
a) SEX KNOWLEDGE INVENTORY: FOR MARRIAGE COUNSELING. 1950–52; Form X ('50); manual ('50); tentative norms ('52); separate answer pads must be used; 1–10 tests, 85¢ each; $1 per 10 answer pads; $2.75 per specimen set (must be purchased to obtain manual); [45] minutes.
b) SEX KNOWLEDGE INVENTORY: VOCABULARY AND ANATOMY, SECOND REVISION. 1950–56; Form Y ('55); directions sheet ['55]; tentative norms ['56]; no norms for part scores; $2.25 per 25 tests; $1.20 per specimen set including 10 tests.

REFERENCE
1. PARMER, CHARLES H. *The Relation Between Scores on the McHugh Inventory and Self-Ratings of Marital Satisfaction.* Doctor's thesis, Pennsylvania State College (State College, Pa.), 1953.

For a review by Albert Ellis, see 4:488 (1 excerpt).

[567]

★**[Winsberg Tests: Examinations for Physical Education Major Students.]** College; 1952; IBM;

1 form ['52] ; mimeographed ; 15 tests : badminton, basketball, body mechanics, bowling, canoeing, folk dancing, golf, hockey, rhythms, soccer, softball, stunts and tumbling, swimming, tennis, volleyball ; no manual ; no data on reliability and validity ; no norms ; 20¢ per test ; $1.25 per set of 15 tests ; postpaid ; 30-[35] minutes ; Shirley Winsberg ; Department of Physical Education for Women, State University of Iowa, Iowa City, Iowa. *

HOME ECONOMICS

[568]

*Clothing: Every Pupil Scholarship Test. High school ; 1927–58 ; new form usually issued each April ; norms available following testing program ; no data on reliability ; 4¢ per test ; 4¢ per scoring key ; postage extra ; 40(45) minutes ; Bureau of Educational Measurements. *

[569]

*Foods: Every Pupil Scholarship Test. High school ; 1927–58 ; new form usually issued each April ; norms available following testing program ; no data on reliability ; 4¢ per test ; 4¢ per scoring key ; postage extra ; 40(45) minutes ; Bureau of Educational Measurements. *

[570]

★Johnson Home Economics Interest Inventory. College women majoring in home economics ; 1955 ; 14 scores : clothing merchandising, designing, county extension work, food product promotion, food service directing, social welfare and public health work, home service, hospital dietetics, interior decorating, journalism or radio, restaurant or tearoom managing, secondary school teaching, textile testing, work with young children ; IBM ; 1 form ; 2 editions ; separate answer pads or answer sheets must be used ; 72¢ per test ; $1 per 20 profiles ; 65¢ per manual ; postage extra ; $1.95 per specimen set, cash orders postpaid ; (60) minutes ; Hildegarde Johnson ; Iowa State College Press. *

a) FORM H FOR HAND SCORING. 28¢ per set of answer pads.

b) FORM MS FOR MACHINE SCORING. 65¢ per 20 IBM answer sheets ; $18 per set of scoring stencils.

REFERENCES

1. JOHNSON, HILDEGARDE. *Techniques for Determining the Professional Interests of Home Economists.* Doctor's thesis, Iowa State College (Ames, Iowa), 1950.
2. JOHNSON, HILDEGARDE. "Development of a Home Economics Interest Inventory." *J Appl Psychol* 36:338–41 O '52. * (PA 27:4735)
3. BEAVERS, IRENE. *Vocational Interests of Certain Home Economics Extension Personnel.* Master's thesis, Iowa State College (Ames, Iowa), 1953.
4. COZAD, MARTHA S. *Validity of Scoring Keys for Johnson Home Economics Interest Inventory.* Master's thesis, Iowa State College (Ames, Iowa), 1955.
5. FIFE, PATRICIA B. *Cluster Analysis of Fourteen Occupational Keys of the Johnson Home Economics Interest Inventory.* Master's thesis, Iowa State College (Ames, Iowa), 1955.
6. SCHOLL, PHYLLIS C. *Stability of Johnson Home Economics Interest Inventory Scores From Freshman to Senior Year.* Master's thesis, Iowa State College (Ames, Iowa), 1955.

JOHN D. BLACK, *President, Consulting Psychologists Press, Inc., Palo Alto, California; and Director, Counseling and Testing Services, Stanford University, Stanford, California.*

Differential measurement of the vocational interests of women has not achieved the impressive refinement which Strong and others have brought to the measurement of men's interests. Some students of the problem have begun to doubt that equal success is possible with females. It is encouraging, therefore, to observe the excellent results of Hildegarde Johnson in the differential measurement of the interests of diverse workers in the field of home economics.

The *Johnson Home Economics Interest Inventory* is designed to help women who have already selected home economics as their field to refine their choice within that area ; it is not suited for general use with all women. The test consists of 300 items covering activities and characteristics pertinent to jobs in home economics to which subjects respond with five degrees of feeling from "like very much" to "greatly dislike," or by rank ordering. It provides 14 empirically derived scales, each of which attempts to differentiate the interests of a particular group of home economists from all other home economists.

The research on which the inventory is based shows care and sophistication. A pool of 448 items was administered to women employed in different activities and settings in the home economics field. Most of the 14 criterion groups numbered about 100, though a few were quite small, e.g., n's of 54, 59, and 69. The manual describes each group in detail. Item weights were derived and the 300 items which differentiated best among the criterion groups were retained. The author found surprisingly little overlap between scores of the criterion groups on their scales with scores obtained by a "home-economists-in-general" group. Only one scale has been cross validated, but it held up very well. Split-half reliabilities range from .79 to .93 for all scales but one.

A rather complicated profile sheet gives norms for each scale based largely on the criterion group for that scale. In some cases these n's are less than 50. The reverse side of the sheet gives norms based on 460 Iowa State College freshmen majoring in home economics. The manual for the test is complete and detailed but a trifle prolix and difficult to read.

Unfortunately, most psychometrists will not be enthusiastic about this inventory. While the directions are easy to follow, the handscoring edition is a pin punching operation with answer pads eight pages thick printed on heavy stock. Scoring is a demanding chore : each test requires two answer pads, each of which consists of two separate parts which must be unstapled for response counting. Each scale requires two counting operations: first, one counts punches falling in the circles and subtracts these from 150; then one counts punches falling in the squares and adds these to the remainder. This entire operation is then repeated for the other answer pad and the results of the two pads are totaled for each of the 14 scales. The entire operation takes an experienced scorer at least 30 minutes, and the excessive numbers of additions and subtractions invite significant errors. Machine scoring is equally formidable, requiring 56 stencils.

The magnitude of some of the scale intercorrelations raises the question of whether an equally useful but less cumbersome inventory might result if some scales were combined. For example, interior decorating and design correlate .85 with each other, and .86 and .87, respectively, with clothing merchandising. These three scales correlate with hospital dietetics −.81, −.94, and −.76, respectively. In all, 10 intercorrelations have absolute values greater than .80, and 26 exceed .63.

Obviously the inventory should have a great deal of further work done on it, particularly in cross validating the scales, obtaining more adequate norms, and, hopefully, improving and simplifying the responding and scoring methods. The work so far accomplished certainly justifies additional research and may stimulate needed improvement in other tests for less specialized measures of the vocational interests of women.

Leona E. Tyler, *Professor of Psychology, University of Oregon, Eugene, Oregon.*

As a general rule, interest tests have been most useful when they encourage testees and those who counsel them to chart broad general directions rather than to decide on specific occupations. As Strong puts it, "My test will tell a young person whether he ought to head toward Seattle or toward Los Angeles. It will not tell him for sure whether he belongs in Hollywood, Pasadena, or Long Beach."

The *Johnson Home Economics Interest Inventory* departs from this precedent. Its aim is to help girls who have already chosen home economics as a major to make definite career choices within this broad area. It would be possible to muster cogent arguments for such an interest blank in this particular field because such a large proportion of girls in high school and college share a general feminine interest pattern that fits in well with a home economics major. A test that would help such people make a more specific choice would be very useful. How well does the Johnson blank serve this purpose?

Each of the 14 scores (see above) is made up of items that differentiate between women in the given occupation and those in the other occupations. The items themselves seem to have been chosen with unusual care after a careful analysis of work done by home economists in various situations. The reliability of each scale compares favorably with that of other interest tests. The format, scoring arrangements, and interpretive information are excellent. One particularly good feature is the inclusion on the interest chart of shaded areas that lead to an immediate indication of whether the testee scores higher in any particular occupation than do other home economists not in this specialty.

With all these good points, however, there are some inadequacies serious enough that the test must still be considered a research instrument rather than a practical tool. A score on any interest scale of this type represents a comparison between an individual and an occupational group. The groups on which these particular scales are based are small (100 or fewer in all but one case) and it is doubtful how representative they are of their respective professions. Apparently, only 1,262 out of approximately 3,000 persons who were asked to participate returned their blanks. Furthermore, the norm groups are made up of the same persons whose responses determined the scoring keys. Only one of the scales (county extension agents) has been cross validated. The fact that in this instance the results for the cross validating group were very similar to those for the norm group does constitute some evidence that the scale is indeed valid. But this needs to be demonstrated rather than assumed for the other scales.

Used cautiously and in accordance with the admonitions the author gives in the manual, the test may serve to *suggest* careers for a girl to consider. The danger is that persons not fully aware of the limitations outlined will place more confidence in the inventory than they should when important life decisions are being made.

In brief, this is a soundly conceived, well designed, clearly explained interest test that needs to have more research done on it before it can be considered acceptable for general use.

[571]

*Minnesota Check List for Food Preparation and Serving, Third Edition. Grades 7–16 and adults; 1938–51; 1 form ('51); mimeographed manual ('45); no data on reliability; no norms; $1.75 per 100 scales; 25¢ per specimen set; postage extra; administration time not reported; Clara Brown Arny; University of Minnesota Press. *

See 40:1509 (1 excerpt).

[572]

★Scales for Appraising High School Homemaking Programs. Pupils, teachers, community members, and administrators; 1953; 1 form; 3 scales; mimeographed manual; $2.50 per set of manual and 10 copies of each scale; 75¢ per specimen set; postage extra; administration time not reported; Clara Brown Arny and Sara Blackwell; University of Minnesota Press. *
a) SCALE 1, THE CURRICULUM.
b) SCALE 2, REFERENCE AND ILLUSTRATIVE MATERIALS.
c) SCALE 3, SPACE AND EQUIPMENT.

INDUSTRIAL ARTS

[573]

★Garage Mechanic Test. Automobile mechanics; 1956; Form A; manual ['56]; no data on reliability; $1.50 per 25 tests; 30¢ per specimen set; postage extra; administration time not reported; P. L. Mellenbruch; Educational Test Bureau. *

[574]

★Industrial Arts Education: National Teacher Examinations. College seniors and teachers; 1947–58; for more complete information, see 538; IBM; 80(90) minutes; Educational Testing Service. *

For reviews by William A. Brownell, Walter W. Cook, and Lawrence G. Derthick of the entire series, see 538; for a review by Harry N. Rivlin of an earlier edition, see 4:802.

[575]

*Industrial Arts: Every Pupil Scholarship Test. High school; 1926–58; new form usually issued each April; norms available following testing program; no data on reliability; 4¢ per test; 4¢ per scoring key; postage extra; 40(45) minutes; Bureau of Educational Measurements. *

[576]

★Industrial Arts: Teacher Education Examination Program. College seniors preparing to teach secondary school; 1957; for more complete information, see 543; IBM; 80(95) minutes; Educational Testing Service. *

For a review by Walter W. Cook of the entire series, see 543.

LISTENING COMPREHENSION

[577]

★Brown-Carlsen Listening Comprehension Test: Evaluation and Adjustment Series. Grades 9–13; 1953–55; IBM; Forms AM ['53], BM ('55); expectancy chart ['54]; $1.80 per 35 IBM test-answer sheets; 20¢ per set of scoring keys; 30¢ per manual ('55); postage extra; 50¢ per specimen set, postpaid; (45–50) minutes; James I. Brown and G. Robert Carlsen; World Book Co. *

REFERENCES

1. BROWN, JAMES I. *The Construction of a Diagnostic Test of Listening Comprehension.* Doctor's thesis, University of Colorado (Boulder, Colo.), 1948.
2. BROWN, JAMES I. "The Construction of a Diagnostic Test of Listening Comprehension." *J Exp Ed* 18:139–46 D '49. * (PA 24:4812)
3. BROWN, JAMES I. "The Measurement of Listening Ability." *Sch & Soc* 71:69–71 F 4 '50. * (PA 25:3382)
4. BROWN, JAMES I. "Teaching Listening Through Listening-Type Tests." *Col Engl* 13:224–5 Ja '52. *
5. BROWN, JAMES I. "How Teachable Is Listening?" *Ed Res B* 33:85–93 Ap 14 '54. *
6. PUBLICOVER, PHYLLIS R. *Listening Efficiency of College Students With High-Frequency Hearing Loss.* Master's thesis, Utah State Agricultural College (Logan, Utah), 1954.
7. BROWN, JAMES I. "Evaluating Student Performance in Listening." *Ed* 75:316–21 Ja '55. * (PA 29:7838)
8. KRAMAR, EDWARD J. J. *The Relationships of the Wechsler-Bellevue and A.C.E. Intelligence Tests With Performance Scores in Speaking and the Brown-Carlsen Listening Comprehension Test.* Doctor's thesis, Florida State University (Tallahassee, Fla.), 1955. (DA 15:2599)
9. STILL, DANA S. *The Relationship Between Listening Ability and High School Grades.* Doctor's thesis, University of Pittsburgh (Pittsburgh, Pa.), 1955. (DA 15:1761)
10. HABERLAND, JOHN A. *An Investigation of Listening Ability in College Freshmen.* Doctor's thesis, Northwestern University (Evanston, Ill.), 1956. (DA 17:303)
11. HABERLAND, JOHN A. "Listening Ability in College Freshmen." *Sch & Soc* 84:217–8 D 22 '56. *
12. STARK, JOEL. *An Investigation of the Relationship of the Vocal and Communicative Aspects of Speech Competency With Listening Comprehension.* Doctor's thesis, New York University (New York, N.Y.), 1956. (DA 17:696)
13. HABERLAND, JOHN A. "Speaker Effectiveness and the Brown-Carlsen Listening Test." *Sch & Soc* 86:198–9 Ap 26 '58. *

E. F. LINDQUIST, *Director of Iowa Testing Programs, State University of Iowa, Iowa City, Iowa.*

With the *Brown-Carlsen Listening Comprehension Test,* as with the *Sequential Tests of Educational Progress: Listening,* the local examiner reads the stimulus materials to the examinees, and the examinee marks the responses on a separate answer sheet (in the B-C test, the responses are printed on the answer sheet itself, rather than in a separate booklet). Accordingly, the B-C test shares with STEP Listening all of the serious limitations of this mode of presentation of the stimulus materials (see 578 for reviewer's review of STEP Listening). Aside from its more limited grade range (9–13), the B-C test differs from STEP Listening primarily in that its contents look somewhat less like those of a silent reading comprehension test, or appear to be more directly and exclusively concerned with those aspects of listening comprehension which distinguish it from silent reading comprehension. However, no satisfactory evidence of validity of the test, either in the form of a carefully developed rationale or of experimental data proving that the test measures anything not measured by a silent reading test, is found in the single manual provided. Furthermore, the section of the manual on "Interpretation of Results" consists only of a brief discussion of wholly general characteristics of percentile ranks and of standard scores, and the section on "Using the Test Results" contains no suggestions that could not apply as well to an achievement test in any other area—that is, no suggestions specific to the problem of how to use the results from this particular test in improving listening comprehension (as contrasted to silent reading comprehension).

Form AM of the test was constructed in the usual manner on the basis of a preliminary tryout and item analysis followed by an independent standardization program. No information is given in the manual on the numbers of items tried out or retained. The "equivalent" Form BM was produced by the dubious procedure of (a) administering an apparently untried test of 96 items to a random half of a sample, the other half of which took Form AM, (b) discarding 20 items from the experimental test on the basis of item data from this sample so as to match the remaining 76 items as closely as possible with the 76 items in Form AM with respect to difficulty and validity, (c) rescoring the retained items for the same sample, and using the data from this sample to establish equivalence tables for Form AM and the test (Form BM) consisting of the retained items.

The norming procedures for the B-C test are no more satisfactory than for STEP Listening. The sample for establishing the norms for grades 9–12 involved a total of only 25 schools, representing only 16 states—no claim of nationwide representative sampling being made. The college norms are based on a sample of 300 freshmen, no indication being given of the number and nature of the colleges involved. Under these circumstances, one can have little confidence in the rule of thumb suggested in the manual that a difference of 10 standard score points in the score on this and other independently standardized tests is "sufficiently large to warrant careful consideration," since differences of this magnitude might be attributable to differences in the norms alone.

IRVING LORGE, *Professor of Education, and Executive Officer, Institute of Psychological Research, Teachers College, Columbia University, New York, New York.*

The *Brown-Carlsen Listening Comprehension Test* is the first, or very nearly the first, of the tests to evaluate the comprehension of the spoken word. The test contains 76 items grouped into five parts: Immediate Recall (17 items), Following Directions (20 items), Recognizing Transitions (8 items), Recognizing Word Meanings (10 items), and Lecture Comprehension (21 items). Of these five parts, the sections on transitions and lecture comprehension get closest to the evaluation of listening comprehension; the sections on immediate recall, following directions, and word meanings are more like the subtests of well known intelligence tests. Further, the subtests on immediate recall and following directions tend to overemphasize memory for numbers and the numerical ordering of things, and mental arithmetic of a trivial sort. Of the first 37 items, at least 29 are based on numbers.

The genuine invention in the test is the recognition of transitions, i.e., whether a spoken sentence is introductory, transitional, concluding, or none of these. Skill in recognizing transitions can be a significant component in *useful* listening skills. The longest section of the test is the lecture section—about twelve minutes of continuous discourse followed by questions of *"reflective,* or *critical,* listening," i.e., questions of general import and influence as well as the usual ones about detail.

The listening test is read by the teacher or the administrator. This tactic obviates the use of tape or record at the expense of lack of control, of rate of presentation or of emphasis, in speaking the stimulus material. The variation from speaker to speaker should affect not only the reliability of the results but also the dependability of the norms.

The authors report good item-test consistency indexes. The criterion, however, overemphasizes the principal component in the total test—and, to the extent that it does, lessens the value of the analysis of listening skills for the making of the separate parts. The current manual reports that the norming group consisted of about 2,000 students at each of four grades: 9, 10, 11, and 12. These 8,000 students, moreover, had been given the Terman-McNemar intelligence test. In view of this large sample with intelligence test scores, it seems strange that the manual makes no reference to the correlations (for these samples) between the listening scores and the Terman-McNemar IQ's. In Table 6, the reported correlations between the Brown-Carlsen test and mental ability are based on samples of sizes from 52 to 150 students, but the correlations are not always based on the total listening score. They are usually given against parts of the listening test, usually early experimental sections. This unusual pattern of reporting is continued for the relation between listening and reading comprehension test results. It is difficult to assess the validity of a listening test except in terms of its relation to reading comprehension or school success—and even then, tests and criteria are saturated with general intelligence. Guidance counselors, indeed, will miss the needed auxiliary evidence on the relation between the *difference* between reading and listening comprehension scores and intellectual level—evidence which would enable them to make fuller use of the test results.

Within grades reliability, on the basis of within-form (Spearman-Brown) estimates, is about .86, and, on a between-form basis, about .78. The test probably covers too wide a range of grades to be as generally discriminating in grades 11 and 12 as in grades 9 and 10.

Historically, the test represents a first attempt at measuring an important educational objective and component of scholastic success. Especially valuable are the subsections on recognizing transitions and lecture comprehension. If these two parts were extended, they would lead to a more useful evaluation and guidance test. It is hoped that the test will be improved and that the manual will be revised by excluding from it the correlations that were collected in the early development phases and by including data from the more substantial standardization and those so tantilizingly suggested in the expectancy chart.

[578]

★**Sequential Tests of Educational Progress: Listening.** Grades 4-6, 7-9, 10-12, 13-14; 1956-57; IBM; Forms A, B ('57); 4 levels; manual ('57); separate directions ('57) for each form at each level; no data on reliability of Form B; separate answer sheets must be used; $3.20 per 20 tests; $1 per 20 IBM scorable answer sheets; 45¢ per scoring stencil; $1 per directions; $1 per manual; $1 per battery technical report; 35¢ per specimen set; postage extra; (90-100) minutes; Cooperative Test Division, Educational Testing Service. *

a) LEVEL 4. Grades 4-6; Forms 4A, 4B.
b) LEVEL 3. Grades 7-9; Forms 3A, 3B.
c) LEVEL 2. Grades 10-12; Forms 2A, 2B.
d) LEVEL 1. Grades 13-14; Forms 1A, 1B.

REFERENCE

1. NORTH, ROBERT D. "An Evaluation of the STEP Listening Test for the Independent School Testing Program." *Ed Rec B* 72:61-7 Jl '58. *

E. F. LINDQUIST, *Director of Iowa Testing Programs, State University of Iowa, Iowa City, Iowa.*

The construction and administration of a *standardized* test of listening comprehension presents serious difficulties not typically encountered with standardized tests in other areas, such as silent reading comprehension. Foremost among these difficulties is the control of variable factors in the presentation of the stimulus materials to the examinees. The authors of STEP Listening have dismissed the use of tape or disc recordings and of sound moving pictures as impracticable, and have employed the technique of having the local examiner read the stimulus materials and the associated multiple choice comprehension questions to the examinees. The examinees are provided with printed copies of the suggested *answers* (only) to the questions, and mark on separate answer sheets what they regard as the best answer to each question. STEP Listening at each level consists of 12 to 13 passages (25 seconds to over 3 minutes in length), about half of which are informational articles, stories or anecdotes, and poems such as typically constitute a silent reading comprehension test or are found in school readers. The other half of the test exercises are more obviously sampled from listening situations, and consist of short talks of an argumentative or persuasive character, and oral directions, instructions, and explanations.

The examiner's manual instructs the examiner to devote some preliminary practice to reading the test passages. Even so, considerable variation must be expected from examiner to examiner in the extent to which they aid or facilitate the listener's comprehension by appropriate emphasis, phrasing, and intonation, by proper use of pauses, by clear and distinct enunciation, by intentional or unintentional emphasis on the *correct* responses to the questions, etc. Examiners will also differ, perhaps markedly, in their ability to create and maintain a serious and closely attentive attitude on the part of the examinees, or in ability to maintain discipline in the face of unexpected distractions or unfortunate interpretations or reactions to the materials read. Considerable skill in presentation and more than average disciplinary control may be required, for example, to avoid an undesirable group reaction to the reading of some of the poetry selections, or, for example, to the passages beginning, "Students, teachers, friends! I should say fellow students, fellow teachers, and fellow friends because I fit into all of these," or "As I stand before you this morning, I do it with great humility," or "A students, B students, C students, and D students, and my friends! As you know, I am running for the office of President of the Student Council."

How seriously these variables will actually affect test performances, and hence affect the comparability of results from examiner to examiner and from school to school, or the comparability of the results with the norms provided, is something that can only be determined empirically through research studies specifically designed for these particular test materials. Since the passages are all of a type that could be administered as a silent reading test, it would seem particularly desirable to administer equivalent forms of these materials to the same examinees under both listening and reading conditions, and determine as objectively and precisely as possible to what extent reading and listening comprehension as defined by these materials consist of common and specific factors. No evidence of the kinds suggested, needed to establish the validity of these tests, is presented in the test manuals. Incidentally, these variable factors associated with the examiner make it particularly important that reliability data be of the equivalent forms (with independent examiners) type, but the reliability coefficients reported are the internal consistency type only.

The Directions for Administering and Scoring seem to be very competently prepared. The typography and format of all the materials are of excellent quality. Within the limitations of any listening comprehenison test constructed according to the same general formula, these tests themselves and the auxiliary materials provided with them are well done.

The norms provided with all of the STEP tests leave much to be desired, and this is particularly true of the norms for the listening test. In norming any achievement test, the school (or school system) rather than the examinee, should be considered as the unit of sampling. For a test provided with percentile norms for school averages (which is true of the other STEP tests), it would seem reasonable to demand that the 95 per cent confidence interval for the 50th percentile should not extend beyond the 45th and 55th percentiles. Assuming a normal distribution of school averages, this would require a random sample of at least 225 schools or school systems, or, with strictly representative and unbiased sampling from nine geographical regions of the United States, a sample of well over 150 schools or school systems. Furthermore, to secure high comparability of the norms from grade to grade and level to level, the norms for all levels should be based on the *same* school systems. These norming standards have been observed by at least one competing test battery. In contrast with this, the number of schools participating in the STEP Listening norming program at each grade level ranges from 17 in grade 7 to 32 in grade 5. Furthermore, very few of the schools participating at one level participated at the other levels, also. These schools were not well distributed by geographical regions. In fact, three out of the nine major geographical regions in the United States were totally unrepresented in the norms sample for most grades. It is significant, also, that the schools used to standardize STEP Listening were all different from those used to establish norms for the other tests in the STEP battery, although an effort was made to adjust the Listening norms in relation to those on the other tests on the basis of SCAT scores.

How biased these small samples of schools are, due to self-selection in recruiting, is difficult to determine, but there is a suggestion that considerable bias may be present. In arranging for the program, letters were written to 2,402 school superintendents requesting the participation of their schools in norming and pretesting. Of these, 425 replied affirmatively to the first general request, of which only 175 (out of 356 requested) replied affirmatively to a later more specific request for participation in the norming program only. This ratio of the number of schools agreeing to participate in the norming program to the numbers of schools randomly selected and requested to do so compares very unfavorably with similar data for other achievement test batteries. (The data here presented concerning the adequacy of the norming sample are not all contained in any of the STEP manuals, but were in part supplied to the writer by the editor of the tests. The writer feels that the ETS editorial staff deserves highest commendation for its professional attitude in supplying the reviewer with needed information, but feels that more of these facts should have been made generally available in the Technical Report.)

A major shortcoming of the STEP battery is that no comparable scales have been provided for the various tests in the battery. Unfortunately, the similarity in appearance of the various converted score scales that are supplied, and the manner in which they are presented in the manuals, make it easy for the test user to infer mistakenly that the scales are actually comparable, and it seems likely that many users will attempt to employ the scales as if they were comparable. This lack of comparable scales makes it impossible also to compute and provide norms for a composite score on the entire battery. Such a composite, if provided, would undoubtedly have relatively high validity as a predictor of future scholastic achievement.

The title of the STEP battery strongly implies that it may be employed in the measurement of *growth*. Presumably, this was the original intention of the test authors, and plans were originally developed and informally announced for a new method of scaling the tests that would provide comparable scales for all tests from grades 4–14. Apparently, these original plans proved unsound and had to be abandoned. Yet, the original title, *Sequential Tests of Educational Progress*, has been retained, even though it contains an implied promise to the user that is not fulfilled.

IRVING LORGE, *Professor of Education, and Executive Officer, Institute of Psychological Research, Teachers College, Columbia University, New York, New York.*

The *Sequential Tests of Educational Progress: Listening* reflect the growing awareness of teachers and educators of the importance of comprehension of the spoken word not only

as an educational objective but also as a fundamental means for learning from teaching. Comprehending the heard passage basically involves the same kinds of questions that are involved in comprehending the printed word—questions of getting the detail, understanding general significance, making inferences and applications, and evaluating mood, intent, and accuracy. Essentially the difference is that in the listening situation, the stimulus vanishes. In reading, the text usually can be reread.

In the series of STEP listening tests, the rate at which the passage is spoken is not under control. Reading times for each selection are suggested only. "The exact amount of time allowed for the various selections of the test is left to the judgment of the teacher." Thus variation in rate of presentation and in speaker's emphasis may affect significantly an individual candidate's performance. The anticipated variation in rate and other factors may affect adversely reliability, validity, and norms.

Essentially, each level and form of the STEP listening tests consists of about a dozen passages to be read, each of which is followed by about a half dozen questions to be answered. The passages are considered to be like those usually spoken to pupils and students. They usually are, but it must have been apparent that sometimes the student must listen to lectures considerably longer than the times suggested in the STEP listening tests. If the suggested timing is followed, the speaking time per passage ranges from about twenty-five seconds to about four and a half minutes, with the modal passage time from one to two minutes. In terms of the objectives stated by the teachers and educators, this makes for relatively short listening comprehension situations. Among high school and college students the expectation should be for significantly longer listening time and for more questions.

The format of the tests seems to be unnecessarily redundant in that each candidate must have a test booklet *and* a separate answer sheet to record his responses. Indeed, the printed versions of the choices for each question may make the simulus a joint reading and listening task.

The reported reliability, as estimated from Kuder-Richardson formula 20, of Form A is about .90 within a single grade. Raw scores are converted to a special scale for each STEP test. The scale was constructed by assigning the score of 300 to a raw score midway between a "chance" score and a maximum score on Level 1, and a score of 230 to a mean chance score on Level 4. The converted score may have some kind of meaning for the very low scores; for scores in the upper ranges, however, the interpretations must be quite arbitrary. The interpretation of STEP listening scores requires going from raw score to converted score to percentile rank for each grade to obtain some estimate of significance. While such a process may lead to the abandonment of the concept of arbitrary mean and standard deviation, the little gain is not worth the labor.

The tests were well prepared, adequately item analyzed and well normed. The difference in mean converted score from grade to grade is about 5 converted score points which is equivalent to about five questions or raw score points between grades. The meaning of the differences between grades is not related to what schools teach; rather the gains seem to parallel gains in intelligence scores. The correlations with intelligence (SCAT-V) average around .75 within grades—an anticipated result in view of the nature of the test. Schoolmen and guidance workers have a right to expect data about the correlations between the STEP listening tests, intelligence, and reading.

Harry Goldstein [1] has demonstrated that the disparity between measures of reading comprehension and listening comprehension is related to level of intelligence. He reported that listening comprehension is always superior to reading comprehension regardless of the rate of presentation of the spoken and printed materials, and that the higher the level of intelligence, the smaller the superiority of listening over reading. The STEP tests, of course, are relatively new, but it seems that the fullest value of the STEP listening tests can come only from the full set of interrelations.

In summary, the STEP listening tests are well made, as ETS tests usually are. The principal limitations are that listening comprehension is restricted to passages requiring not more than five minutes of listening time, and that the data necessary to evaluate the difference between a student's reading comprehension and listening comprehension are not cur-

rently provided. For face validity, at the senior high school level and at the college level, longer passages requiring longer listening times seem to be needed.

For reviews by Robert W. B. Jackson and Wilbur L. Layton of the complete battery, see 24.

MISCELLANEOUS

[579]

★How Well Can You Read Lips? Deaf and hard of hearing children and adults with a reading level of third grade or over; 1946; Forms A, B ['46] on a 16 mm. film; manual ['46]; norms ['46]; no norms for Form B; $125 per film; $4.50 daily on rental basis; 45(60) minutes; Jean Utley; [American Film Registry]. *

REFERENCES

1. UTLEY, JEAN L. *Development and Standardization of a Motion Picture Achievement Test of Lip Reading Ability.* Doctor's thesis, Northwestern University (Evanston, Ill.), 1946.
2. DICARLO, LOUIS M., AND KATAJA, RAYMOND. "An Analysis of The Utley Lipreading Test." *J Speech Disorders* 16: 226–40 S '51. * (*PA* 26:2860)

[580]

★What Do You Know About Photography? Photography students; 1953; 1 form; hectographed; no data on reliability; 15¢ per test; 25¢ per scoring key; 25¢ per directions sheet; 75¢ per specimen set; cash orders postpaid; administration time not reported; Martin M. Bruce and Jack Bernard; [15–20] minutes; Martin M. Bruce. *

PHILOSOPHY

[581]

*The Graduate Record Examinations Advanced Tests: Philosophy. College seniors and graduate students; 1939–56; for more complete information, see 601; IBM; 180(200) minutes; Educational Testing Service. *

For a review by Harold Seashore of the entire series, see 601.

PSYCHOLOGY

[582]

★Engle Psychology Test: Evaluation and Adjustment Series. High school; 1952–54, c1950–53; IBM; Forms AM, BM ('52); manual ('53); expectancy chart ['54]; separate answer sheets must be used; $4.15 per 35 tests; $1.40 per 35 IBM answer sheets; postage extra; 35¢ per specimen set, postpaid; 40(50) minutes; T. L. Engle; World Book Co. *

HAROLD SEASHORE, *Director, Test Division, The Psychological Corporation, New York, New York.*

Engle analyzed the contents of seven textbooks in psychology designed for high schools

1 GOLDSTEIN, HARRY. *Reading and Listening Comprehension at Various Controlled Rates.* Contributions to Education, No. 821. New York: Bureau of Publications, Teachers College, Columbia University, 1940. Pp. 69.

to provide him with a "blueprint" for this achievement test. Four of the seven books have titles which suggest emphasis on human relations and personal adjustment; the other three, with more standard titles, probably are also oriented to the same themes, but with a more solid scientific core. Engle's test contains a mixture of psychology as science, as mental hygiene, and as a guide to competence in interpersonal relations. There are science items testing for physiological and behavioral facts (facts about the cortex, genetics, scientific method, and intelligence). There are items on practical behavior (what to say if you are asked by a boy how you like his coat which you don't like). It is hard to say whether this is the right content for a high school course in psychology. It does seem apparent, however, that Engle has undertaken a straightforward and workmanlike development of an achievement test based on content he found to be acceptable in the late 1940's. The test rationale, technical data, and applications presented are good examples of American Psychological Association and American Educational Research Association recommendations.

The test is adequately reliable for evaluation of individuals and groups. The two forms are demonstrated to be equivalent. The norms are anchored to the ability level of the normative sample in terms of the examinees' scores on a group intelligence test. Norms are based on about 1,100 students in 32 schools in 20 states. The difference in mean scores between students in one-semester courses and those in two-semester courses is about two points of raw score. Does the test emphasize first-semester content? What goes on in two-semester courses? One set of norms is provided.

The anchoring referred to in the paragraph above deserves comment. In the Evaluation and Adjustment Series, the publisher employs a plan for relating the scores on each test to all others through anchoring all of them to the *Terman-McNemar Test of Mental Ability.* This test presumably was chosen because it is a good all-around predictor of academic achievement. In the case of the Engle test the median IQ of the standardization sample was 106, so the average *raw score* on the Engle test was converted to a standard score, not of 100, but of 106; similarly the obtained Engle standard deviation was equated to the obtained Terman-McNemar standard deviation of 14.

The standard score assigned a person on the basis of his raw score is an estimate of the score he would have secured if the test *had been* standardized in a situation in which psychology had been studied by a true cross section of the whole school population as defined by the T-M IQ's. These standard scores, then, permit comparisons across the several tests when a student or a class takes more than one test in the Evaluation and Adjustment Series.

The correlation coefficient between T-M IQ and the Engle test is reported as .77. The standard score on the Engle test permits the teacher to estimate whether a particular student whose Terman-McNemar IQ is known has achieved above, at, or below his expectancy as determined by the T-M IQ. On a separate sheet, the publisher provides an Expectancy Chart based on 186 random cases from the standardization population. (Why all 1,100 cases were not used, to provide more stability of the cell entries, is not clear to the reviewer.) By entering the table with a student's IQ, one can obtain an estimate of his expected Engle score. Such data, the descriptive literature points out, are useful both in individual counseling and in determining beforehand the level of achievement the teacher might expect from a class for which he has IQ data based on the Terman-McNemar, Otis, or Pintner tests.

The use of standard scores as an intermediate step between raw scores and, say, percentile ranks, creates problems. The plan in the Evaluation and Adjustment Series is intended to permit one to say, for example, that a score of 110 on Test A is as far above the average of a typical student's performance as is a score of 110 on Test B. However, one cannot state that this score of 110 on Test A is a good or poor performance in the particular subject field of Test A for students who choose to study subject A. One needs also to know what kind (level) of students normally elect to study in the field covered by Test A. Therefore, for each test in the Evaluation and Adjustment Series, percentile equivalents derived from the norming populations are provided. A standard score of 100 on the Engle, for instance, yields a percentile rank of 34. This datum and the related data in the expectancy table show that a person with an IQ of about 100 could expect to rank at about the 34th percentile on the

Engle test at the end of a course in psychology. If a teacher had a class with an average IQ of about 100 (and taught them the same kind of psychology as he did to other classes), he should expect the average end-of-course standard score on the Engle test to be about at the 34th percentile on the published norms.

The manual does not suggest that the Engle test be used to assign course grades, although it does emphasize the evaluation of individual achievement. The test's main role might be to provide the teacher a chance to compare the achievement of his students with that of students in other schools. The reviewer wonders if any college professors have used this test at the beginning of a course as a basis for discussion and as an interesting introduction for the students. This reviewer also would like to see the scores of equally able students who had not elected to take a formal course in psychology.

The teaching of psychology in high schools seems to be increasing and we probably should not assume that the contents of such courses have been stabilized as of the 1940's. Engle probably should consider revising his test fairly soon.

[583]

*The Graduate Record Examinations Advanced Tests: Psychology. College seniors and graduate students; 1939–56; for more complete information, see 601; IBM; 180(200) minutes; Educational Testing Service. *

HAROLD SEASHORE, Director, Test Division, The Psychological Corporation, New York, New York.

The relationship of this test to the whole Graduate Record Examinations series and the technical points such as reliability, scaled scores, and norms are discussed elsewhere (601) by this reviewer.

Content validity is a central problem in achievement testing. If this test is intended as a comprehensive examination to evaluate seniors at the end of college or applicants at entrance to graduate programs in psychology, one must ask whether the items cover the field properly. Is the test adequate with respect to (a) level of difficulty of items, (b) proportion of items allocated to the many subfields within psychology, and (c) relevance of each item within the subfields? Obviously content validity is to a large degree a matter of expert judgment. The advisory committee of psychologists who helped make this test surely is an eminent group.

Consider level of difficulty. The test makers must first accept the judgments of the committee as to difficulty of items. Beyond this we can look at the test statistics. The manuals and bulletins do not provide any detailed information on this point. The published data are in scaled score form; none are in raw score form.

The norms are based on majors who were in graduate school or were seeking graduate school admission; one wonders how some could have learned so little in college to secure as few as 40–50 right answers on a 248-item test. One could get a score of about 50 by chance! One can understand the absence of near-perfect scores because as undergraduates these students would not be expected to have covered all aspects of psychology. From conversion tables provided this reviewer, it appears that for the graduate candidates $(n = 1375)$ the raw score at the 1st percentile is 43 and at the 99th percentile, 195; the raw score at the 10th percentile is 85 and at the 90th percentile, 171. The median raw score is 130. The maximum possible raw score is 248 points.

Allocation of items among the various fields of psychology is also a judgmental variable. For the current form, no detailed analysis is presented. The reviewer feels the coverage is good. Section 1 includes 117 5-choice items which tap general psychology mainly through what might be called technical vocabulary and basic definitions. Section 2 has 131 items in 11 parts, each purporting to appraise knowledge and understanding of basic concepts and methodology. In these parts, students coming from different psychology departments may have different degrees of success, depending upon the courses offered or chosen. But the coverage is broad; it is not so detailed that a potential rat maze psychologist can complain that the items on psychometrics are unfair, or the budding clinician that the memory items are just endless detail. In each part the questions are preceded by a short presentation, such as the setup of an experiment, an excerpt from a theoretical discussion, digests of cases, or tables of data. Although there is considerable overlap among them, the several parts seem to emphasize these topics: experimental design, general theory and systems, learning, theory and research, social research in industry, abnormal psychology, psychophysics, industrial training, human factors in industry, interpretation of clinical case data, social theory, and psychometrics. Knowledge of statistics is appraised by items scattered among the parts.

In general, emphasis is on inferences from the information presented, which inferences in turn depend upon considerable breadth and depth of knowledge. Without revealing items, the following example will illustrate: "Which of the following children is most likely to do well in college?" There are no percentile ranks or IQ's in the table, but the answer can be found if one understands means and sigmas and has some ideas of abilities required in colleges. On the matter of coverage and allocation among fields the reviewer concludes that the committee has covered the fields broadly and has emphasized understanding of major concepts rather than memory.

The foregoing conclusion also pertains to the third point listed above: relevance of items within the subfields. The reviewer can only observe that the material for each subfield of psychology does not seem to be unreasonably esoteric or local. The items involving psychometrics, this reviewer's specialty, seem to be appropriate and reasonably probing for an end-of-college examination.

The reliability of the test is satisfactory. The norms are based on about 1,400 cases at the graduate candidate level and about 600 at the college senior level.

None of the bulletins and manuals provided the reviewer discusses validity or presents any validity data, nor is a bibliography of published articles presented. Although acceptable on the basis of content validity, the test certainly must have generated some studies which by now could have appeared in the ETS reports. As an admissions test, the test must justify itself as a predictor of the next levels of training. It remains to be shown whether whatever the test measures is genuinely relevant to graduate level achievement. By now this test should have generated studies which would illuminate the relation to graduate success of the amount of undergraduate psychological training. Do those who have high scores because they are presumably bright students with many courses do better in graduate school than those scoring lower who may be bright students with little psychology and much more related mathematics, biology, or anthropology?

For a review by Harold Seashore of the entire series, see 601.

[584]

Hogan Psychology Test. High school and college; 1951; IBM; Forms A, B ['51]; no high school norms for Form B; $1.20 per 25 tests; separate answer sheets may be used; 85¢ per 25 IBM answer sheets; 30¢ per scoring stencil; postage extra; 25¢ per specimen set; postpaid; 50(55) minutes; Irene Hogan and H. E. Schrammel; Bureau of Educational Measurements. *

HAROLD SEASHORE, *Director, Test Division, The Psychological Corporation, New York, New York.*

This is a poorer than ordinary end-of-year test for a course in psychology. Each year at least a thousand professors make objective tests to measure the desired outcomes of the year of instruction. This reviewer believes that students are better measured by most of these than they would be by Hogan's test.

Over two thirds of the items are in the true-false format. This item type might be satisfactory when measuring cut and dried facts, as in spelling and in details of history; it is treacherous and confusing when complex concepts are the content and when contingent facts are relevant.

There is no reason why this should be called a standardized test. It is normed on 127 cases for Form A at the high school level and on about one hundred cases each for Forms A and B at the college level. The manual is far below reasonable technical standards.

Revision of the test and writing of a new manual are not recommended.

RECORD AND REPORT FORMS

[585]

★**Blum-Fieldsteel Development Charts.** Birth to 72 months; 1952–53; based upon *Gesell Developmental Schedules;* individual; 1 form ('52); 2 charts: Cumulative Record of Functional Behavior, Cumulative Record of Motor Behavior; manual ('53); $3.90 per 35 sets of charts, postage extra; 20¢ per specimen set, postpaid; Lucille Hollander Blum and Nina D. Fieldsteel; World Book Co. *

REFERENCE

1. BLUM, LUCILLE HOLLANDER. "Do They Catch Up?" *Q J Child Behavior* 4:66–79 Ja '52. *

[586]

★**The Cassel Developmental Record.** Birth to death; 1954; profile of 6 areas of development (physiological, emotional, psycho-sexual, intellectual, social, educational) and average development; individual; 1 form; 75¢ per 25 charts; $1.25 per manual; $1.50 per specimen set; postpaid; Russell N. Cassel; C. A. Gregory Co. *

WILLIAM E. HENRY, *Associate Professor of Human Development and Psychology, University of Chicago, Chicago, Illinois.*

The *Cassel Developmental Record* is primarily a form upon which may be recorded conclusions related to the stages of development of individuals in six areas: physiological, emotional, psychosexual, intellectual, social, and educational. The form is arranged on a basic axis of chronological age, from prenatal to 109 years and 11 months. Each of the six areas is similarly arrayed to parallel the age axis and is itself given a basic age axis—physical age, emotional age, and so on. Each of these areas is further subdivided into stages called by either common sense or research based designations. Thus, the physiological area is subdivided into the stages of infancy, childhood, and so forth, through the oldest stage, identified as senility. The emotional development area is subdivided on general psychological grounds, and the psychosexual area on primarily psychoanalytic psychosexual stages. Social development is identified in such terms as "socially dependent," "socially organized play," and "interdependency emergence"; and educational development is described in terms of the expected school activities for the various ages.

The form includes an average total developmental age defined as the average of the "ages" decided upon in each of the main areas. Cassel recommends the preparation of a profile made merely by drawing a line connecting the age of each area, at about 3-year intervals, and sees the profiles so developed as a kind of cumulative record of developmental progress.

Since the various areas are arrayed against the same age axis, a straight line profile automatically becomes "typical" at all age levels, and deviation from this in any direction or any area becomes either under- or over-development. It is through this mechanism that Cassel identifies the six patterns which he reports as occurring with some frequency upon use of the form—typical, over-development, under-development, unbalanced development (bright), unbalanced development (retarded), and oscillating.

The form is in no sense a test or a rating scale, and all information needed for its use is to be gathered from other sources—interviews, observations, tests, school records, and the like. The manual accompanying the form provides a guide to its use, with a suggested bibliography in each of the six areas and a discussion of the six frequently observed profiles.

The proper use of the form undoubtedly hinges upon the user's need for some simple cumulative profile and upon his readiness to assume the same developmental stages as Cassel has identified. These stages seem entirely appropriate—at least to the extent that the available research upon which they are based will permit. It is proposed that the instrument would be useful in guidance, presumably in schools or similar institutions where the person rated remains for some years. The subdivisions are understandably far more numerous below age 20 than above, and thus perhaps one would find the form more productive for these younger ages. The proper use would also seem to depend upon the fullness of data available upon the subject, and upon the ability of the user to describe these data meaningfully in the terms provided on the form. With these conditions, the form would seem a very useful short and yet pointed summary of a person's personal development.

[587]

★**A Pre-School Record Form.** Ages 2–5; 1940–52; ratings in 5 areas: gross motor development, language, general emotional development, social adjustment to adults, social adjustment to children; 1 form ['52]; 1s. per record form; 1s. 6d. per manual ['52]; postage extra; Agatha H. Bowley; E. & S. Livingstone Ltd. *

For related reviews, see 3:776 (2 excerpts).

RELIGIOUS EDUCATION

[588]

★**Attitude Inventory.** Grades 5–12; 1952–54; religious attitudes; Forms X, Y ('52); manual ('54); $2.50 per 35 tests, postage extra; (30–40) minutes; Walter O. Kraeft, Oliver E. Graebner, Elmer F. Pflieger, and Ernest E. Yunghans; Concordia Publishing House. *

REFERENCE

1. YUNGHANS, ERNEST E. "Constructing an Attitude Inventory." *Lutheran Ed* 87:318–24 Mr '52. *

[589]

★**Bible History Tests.** Grades 5–8; 1952–53; for Catholic schools; 1 form; 4 tests; 1-page manuals ('53) for each test; norms for grade 8 only; $1.25 per 25 tests, postage extra; specimen set free; 45(50) minutes per test; John A. O'Brien and Gaston Benedict; Loyola University Press. *

a) FORM A: FROM ADAM TO MOSES.
b) FORM B: FROM JOSUE TO THE ROMAN CONQUEST.
c) FORM C: THE BIRTH, CHILDHOOD, AND PUBLIC LIFE OF CHRIST.
d) FORM D: THE PASSION, DEATH, AND RESURRECTION OF CHRIST.

[590]

Peters Biblical Knowledge Test. Grades 9–16 and adults; 1948; Form A; 2 parts; $1.20 per 25 tests of either part, postage extra; 25¢ per specimen set, postpaid; 60(65) minutes per part; Frank C. Peters; Bureau of Educational Measurements. *

a) TEST I, OLD TESTAMENT.

b) TEST II, NEW TESTAMENT.

JANET G. AFFLERBACH, *Test Editor, Professional Examination Service, American Public Health Association, New York, New York.*

This test is in reality two tests, one covering the Old Testament and the other, the New Testament. Each test consists of four parts: a 5-choice multiple choice section of 85 items; a true-false section of 30 items; a matching exercise with 20 items; and a slight variation of the matching exercise with 15 items.

The Manual of Directions (a misnomer, since the only directions for administering the tests are supplied in the test booklet itself) contains a short statement of the nature and purposes of the tests, data concerning their validity and reliability, and brief recommendations for the interpretation of test scores. Percentile norms are provided for each test separately, for "all high school" students and for each of the four college grades.

These tests are intended to measure content knowledge of the Bible. This has been accomplished with a limited degree of success. With great assiduity the author has avoided controversial, doctrinal, and theological issues. One can only wish that he had not felt so restricted by his test title that items on Biblical commentary and criticism, analysis of authorship, history of the printing of the Bible as a *book*, recent discoveries revealing new knowledge of Bible origins (Dead Sea scrolls), etc., could logically have been included. As it is, the tests are tests of knowledge about what the Bible says, not how it says it, what it is, or how it came to be.

Despite recommendations by the author that these tests be used in pre- and post-course testing, they are much too "course oriented" to be used to good advantage at any time other than *after* the completion of an intensive course in Bible content. The items have the definite flavor of Bible quiz program material and not of content coverage expected in the general Bible survey course. High school pupils coming to the test with the usual surface "highlighting" sequences of church school curricula may be totally unprepared for the rather obscure settings in which many of the most familiar Biblical personages are encountered.

The tests display what this reviewer considers an ill-advised emphasis. For example, in the Old Testament test, omission of any material for the period from the Creation to the Fall is difficult to justify. The same test has only one item on Jacob (a rather unworthy one, at that) but four to six items each on Abraham, Moses, David, Isaiah, Joseph, Job, Daniel, and Ruth, and unexpectedly, eight items on Elijah. There are 12 items on the Book of Psalms and two items on Proverbs and Ecclesiastes. These are the only books about which items are the only ones which deal with the books per se and not with characters or events described therein.

Similar imbalance is shown in the New Testament test. Three items concern Festus (who tried Paul) while only three deal directly with the miracles of Christ; and there are three items on Cornelius (the centurion converted by Peter) and only two concerning the actual birth story of Christ. John the Baptist is the subject of 11 items, including two which ask for the names of his father and his mother; and there are at least 28 items which concern Paul, his writings and his missionary journeys. Very little else of the New Testament, outside the gospels, is touched upon. A greater number of items in this test deal with the books as writings of specific authors and call for the location of familiar passages. Since the New Testament test does not contain so many obscure references, it appears to be less difficult than the Old Testament test.

The tests give several indications of poor editing and careless proofreading. The directions preceding the several parts are generally unsatisfactory. Especially confusing are those for Part 3 of Test I where the titles of the two column headings are *reversed*. Throughout the directions reference is made to the "parenthesis" in which answers are to be marked. In the multiple-choice sections the ambiguous phrase "correct part" is used for "correct choice."

Typographical errors abound. The reviewer counted 15 misspellings without too serious searching, most of them of proper names. A spelling error that reduces Item 145 in Part 4 of Test II to an absurdity turns Paul's "conversion" into Paul's "conversation."

There are numerous inconsistencies and peculiarities in style and arrangement. There is no evident policy regarding the capitalization of words referring to any member of the deity or the placement of choices with numerical values in ascending or descending order. An especially disconcerting practice in Test II is the spelling out of choices which would ordinarily call for Arabic numerals. This is particularly cumbersome (and is contrary to generally accepted usage in referring to scriptural texts) in Item 62 where chapter locations are written as "chapter one," "chapter two," etc. In Test II also scriptural references are broken so that the chapter designation is separated from the name of the book.

Haphazard grammatical construction makes many wrong choices flagrantly nonsensical. Disagreement in number of noun mentioned in stem and appositive noun in choices, disagreement in gender between pronouns in stem and nouns in choices, and general grammatical incompatability of choices with stem encourage the immediate discarding of many choices.

There are several content inaccuracies. In Test I, Item 63 describes Psalm 119 as written "according to the alphabet." Actually, in this "acrostic psalm" the initial letters of successive verses follow the order of the Hebrew alphabet. Item 75 is a 3-choice item since choices 3 and 4 and choices 2 and 5 are in essence identical. The keyed answer is 4, which cannot possibly be defended as the *only* correct answer. In Test II, Item 10 assigns the Sermon on the Mount to Matthew 5 only, whereas it is actually recorded in Matthew 5, 6, and 7. In Item 131 Demetrius is identified as a goldsmith, whereas he is called a silversmith in Acts 19:24.

Only two items, both in Test I, are controversial. Item 12 asks for the author of the Proverbs. Authorities ascribe the *latter* part of the book to authors other than Solomon (the keyed answer). Item 104 asks for the Fourth Commandment—but the numbers by which the commandments are known will vary with the denominational persuasion of the testee.

In summary, the *Peters Biblical Knowledge Test* is so constructed as to provide such an exhaustive survey of specific details of Bible content that it is less useful for the average high school or introductory college course than for the preseminary or seminary student specializing in Bible study. However, the distorted emphasis in regard to content, careless proofreading, and the generally poor item construction make the test such a poor professional product as to seriously detract from its value as a device for measuring achievement in Biblical knowledge at any level.

[591]
★**Religion Test for Grades Two and Three.** Grades 2–3; 1951–52; for Catholic schools; Forms A ('52), B ('57); manual ['52]; $1.25 per 25 tests; postage extra; specimen set free; 52(65) minutes; M. Providencia; Loyola University Press. *

[592]
★**Religion Test for High Schools.** Grades 9–12; 1953–55; for Catholic schools; 4 scores: the Creed, the Commandments, the Means of Grace, total; IBM; Forms A, B, C, D ('55); manual ['55]; separate answer sheets may be used; $2.10 per 25 tests; $2 per 100 IBM answer sheets and key; postage extra; specimen set free; 45(55) minutes; Austin G. Schmidt and O. F. Anderhalter; Loyola University Press. *

SAFETY EDUCATION

[593]
★**Lauer Driver Reaction Inventory.** Drivers; 1948–57; revision of *Driving Attitude Inventory;* Forms A, B, C ['57]; $1.25 per 20 tests; $1.25 per specimen set; postage extra; (10–15) minutes; A. R. Lauer; Iowa State College Press. *

REFERENCES
1. AGAN, RAYMOND J. "A Comparison of Attitude Scores Made on the Conover Attitude Inventory Before and After a Course in Driving." *Proc Iowa Acad Sci* 57:357–9 '50. *
2. HANNUM, T. E.; HELMSTADTER, GERALD C.; LAUER, A. R.; AND SOULE, DAVID H. "An Empirical Study of Scoring Methods for the Conover Driving Attitude Inventory." *Proc Iowa Acad Sci* 57:385–6 '50. *

[594]
★**Road Test Check List for Passenger Car Drivers.** Passenger car drivers; 1955; 1 form; instruction and scoring sheet; wooden cylinder driving jerk recorder essential for administration (may be constructed or purchased from AAA); no data on reliability; 30¢ per 25 checklists; postage extra; specimen set free; (30) minutes; Amos E. Neyhart; published jointly by American Automobile Association and Institute of Public Safety, Pennsylvania State University. *

[595]
★**Rogers-Lauer Driver Rating Inventory.** Drivers; 1935–57; formerly called *Rogers-Lauer Driver Training Inventory;* 3 scores: behavior patterns, basic skills, total; 1 form ('56); directions sheet ['57]; $1.25 per 20 scales, postage extra; $1.25 per specimen set, cash orders postpaid; (5–10) minutes; A. R. Lauer; Iowa State College Press. *

SOCIOECONOMIC STATUS

[596]
The American Home Scale. Grades 8–16; 1942; socio-economic status; 5 scores: cultural, aesthetic, economic, miscellaneous, total; 1 form; mimeographed manual; $3 per 50 tests; $1 per specimen set (must be purchased to obtain manual); postage extra; (35–50)

minutes; W. A. Kerr and H. H. Remmers; Psychometric Affiliates. *

REFERENCES

1–7. See 3:417.
8. GOUGH, HARRISON G. "A Short Social Status Inventory." J Ed Psychol 40:52–6 Ja '49. * (PA 23:4499)
9. FINCH, F. H., AND HOEHN, A. J. "Measuring Socio-Economic or Cultural Status: A Comparison of Methods." J Social Psychol 33:51–67 F '51. * (PA 26:830)

For reviews by Henry S. Maas and Verner M. Sims, see 3:417.

[597]

★Sims SCI Occupational Rating Scale. Grades 9–16 and adults; 1952; social class identification; Form A; $1.30 per 35 tests, postage extra; 20¢ per specimen set, postpaid; (25) minutes; Verner M. Sims; World Book Co. *

REFERENCES

1. SIMS, VERNER M. "The Social Class Affiliation of Students in a Southern State University." J Social Psychol 32:163–75 D '50. * (PA 25:7096)
2. SIMS, VERNER M. "The Social-Class Affiliations of a Group of Public School Teachers." Sch R 59:331–8 S '51. *
3. SIMS, VERNER M. "A Technique for Measuring Social Class Identification." Ed & Psychol Meas 11:541–8 w '51. * (PA 27:5800)
4. SIMS, VERNER M. "Some Correlates of Social-Class Identification Among High-School and College Students." Sch R 60: 160–3 Mr '52. *
5. SIMS, VERNER M. "Relations Between the Social-Class Identification and Personality Adjustment of a Group of High School and College Students." J Social Psychol 40:323–7 N '54. * (PA 29:7190)
6. SIMS, VERNER M. "The Relation of Occupational Tolerance to Intelligence and Social Affiliation." J Social Psychol 40: 17–21 Ag '54. * (PA 29:6205)
7. FRIEDHOFF, WALTER H. Relationships Among Various Measures of Socio-Economic Status, Social Class Identification, Intelligence, and School Achievement. Doctor's thesis, State University of Iowa (Iowa City, Iowa), 1955. (DA 15:2098)
8. BRESEE, CLYDE W. Affective Factors Associated With Academic Underachievement in High-School Students. Doctor's thesis, Cornell University (Ithaca, N.Y.), 1956. (DA 17:90)
9. OVERS, ROBERT P., AND ST. CLAIR, NORMAN E. "The Social Class Identification of 1038 Western New York Students." J Ed Res 51:185–90 N '57. *
10. RABINOWITZ, WILLIAM, AND ROSENBAUM, IRA. "A Failure in the Prediction of Pupil-Teacher Rapport." J Ed Psychol 49: 93–8 Ap '58. *

HENRY WEITZ, *Associate Professor of Education, and Director, Bureau of Testing and Guidance, Duke University, Durham, North Carolina.*

This instrument is "designed to reveal the level in our social structure....with which a person unconsciously identifies himself." The examinee rates 42 occupations as employing people who generally belong to the same social class as the examinee and his family or to a higher or lower class. Provision is made for "don't know" or "don't care to answer" ratings. The scale is scored in such a way as to indicate the class (lower working to upper) with which the examinee identifies.

Reliability coefficients reported in the manual range from .95 (split-half) for a wide range sample of high school and college students to .82 (test-retest) for a narrower range sample of college students retested after an interval of four months. These reliabilities are adequate for group measurement and approach adequacy for individual measurement.

Validity of the scale is reported in terms of the differentiation it can make between groups estimated as coming from different social classes such as fraternity and sorority pledges and non-pledges, different types of school populations, and groups defined by parent's occupation. Studies of this sort reported in the manual and in subsequent journal articles seem to indicate that the scale is effective in making such differentiations.

In terms of both the time allotted for testing and the nature of the items, the scale would seem to be usable with groups as young as beginning high school students, with no limitation on its use with more mature or sophisticated groups.

The evidence given in the manual to support the notion that the scale measures *unconscious* identification is based upon the degree to which sophisticated subjects reported that they knew what the scale was getting at. Only one out of 69 college students had a feeling that the scale was measuring more than it seemed to be.

The author suggests that, in its present form, the scale's principal use will be in research although there is some suggestion that it may be useful in clinical situations concerned with vocational and personal adjustment. These latter possibilities seem interesting and worth pursuing.

This reviewer finds it difficult to estimate the kind of psychological behavior being sampled by this scale. If we look upon any psychometric device as a means of observing behavior, we must be able to say that the sample represented by the score is indicative of a general universe of behavior segments. Yet the data provided with this scale make it difficult to imagine the way in which particular examinees or groups are likely to behave if their scale scores indicate that they "unconsciously identify" with a given social level. To the extent that other users of the scale may have the same difficulty as the reviewer, this scale has limited usefulness.

[598]

*The Social Status Scale, 1952 Revision. Socioeconomic status; 1933–52; checklist for rating the living room of a home; 1 form ('52); no data on reliability and validity for 1952 revision; no norms for 1952 revision; $1.50 per 50 scales, postage extra; F. Stuart Chapin; University of Minnesota Press. *

REFERENCES

1. CHAPIN, F. STUART. "A Quantitative Scale for Rating the Home and Social Environment of Middle Class Families in an

Table of Contents

* * * * *

Contributing Test Reviewers

* * * * *

C. J. ADCOCK, Senior Lecturer in Psychology, Victoria University of Wellington, Wellington, New Zealand

DOROTHY C. ADKINS, Professor of Psychology, and Chairman of the Department, University of North Carolina, Chapel Hill, North Carolina

DAN L. ADLER, Professor of Psychology, San Francisco State College, San Francisco, California

JANET G. AFFLERBACH, Editor, Professional Examination Service, American Public Health Association, New York, New York

LOIS GRIMES AFFLERBACH, Serials Librarian, Queens College, Flushing, New York

MARY D. AINSWORTH, Associate Professor of Psychology, The Johns Hopkins University, Baltimore, Maryland

ANNE ANASTASI, Professor of Psychology, Fordham University, New York, New York

HOWARD R. ANDERSON, Professor of Education, and Dean, University School of Liberal and Applied Studies, The University of Rochester, Rochester, New York

DWIGHT L. ARNOLD, Professor of Education, Kent State University, Kent, Ohio

THEO. A. ASHFORD, Professor of Chemistry, Saint Louis University, Saint Louis, Missouri

ANDREW R. BAGGALEY, Associate Professor of Psychology, The University of Wisconsin—Milwaukee, Milwaukee, Wisconsin

BENJAMIN BALINSKY, Associate Professor of Psychology, Bernard M. Baruch School of Business and Public Administration, The City College, New York, New York

WARREN R. BALLER, Professor of Educational Psychology, The University of Nebraska, Lincoln, Nebraska

CHARLOTTE E. K. BANKS, Lecturer in Psychology, University College, London, England

FRANK BARRON, Associate Research Psychologist, Institute of Personality Assessment and Research, University of California, Berkeley, California

ROBERT H. BAUERNFEIND, Director, Test Department, Science Research Associates, Chicago, Illinois

BRENT BAXTER, Director of Agencies Research, Prudential Insurance Company, Newark, New Jersey

NANCY BAYLEY, Chief, Section on Child Development, Laboratory of Psychology, National Institute of Mental Health, National Institutes of Health, Public Health Service, United States Department of Health, Education, and Welfare, Bethesda, Maryland

KENNETH L. BEAN, Professor of Psychology, Baylor University, Waco, Texas

HAROLD P. BECHTOLDT, Associate Professor of Psychology, State University of Iowa, Iowa City, Iowa

SAMUEL J. BECK, Professorial Lecturer, Departments of Psychology and Psychiatry, The University of Chicago; and Associate, Michael Reese Hospital; Chicago, Illinois

RALPH BEDELL, Specialist for Higher Education Programs, United States Office of Education, Washington, D.C.

JOHN E. BELL, Acting Chief, Mental Health Services, United States Public Health Service, San Francisco, California

GEORGE K. BENNETT, President, The Psychological Corporation, New York, New York

RALPH F. BERDIE, Professor of Psychology, and Director, Student Counseling Bureau, University of Minnesota, Minneapolis, Minnesota

HARRY D. BERG, Professor, Office of Evaluation Services, Michigan State University, East Lansing, Michigan

ÅKE BJERSTEDT, Department of Psychology, University of Lund, Lund, Sweden

JOHN D. BLACK, President, Consulting Psychologists Press, Inc., Palo Alto, California; and Director, Counseling and Testing Services, Stanford University, Stanford, California

PAUL BLOMMERS, Professor of Education, State University of Iowa, Iowa City, Iowa

BENJAMIN S. BLOOM, University Examiner, The University of Chicago, Chicago, Illinois

JOAN BOLLENBACHER, Supervisor of Appraisal Services, Cincinnati Public Schools, Cincinnati, Ohio

EDWARD S. BORDIN, Professor of Psychology, University of Michigan, Ann Arbor, Michigan

ARTHUR H. BRAYFIELD, Professor of Psychology and Head of the Department, Pennsylvania State University, University Park, Pennsylvania

M. A. BRIMER, Senior Lecturer in Educational Psychology, University College, Ibadan, Nigeria

NELSON BROOKS, Associate Professor of French, Yale University, New Haven, Connecticut

WILLIAM A. BROWNELL, Dean, School of Education, University of California, Berkeley, California

JAMES E. BRYAN, Foreign Quarantine Division, United States Public Health Service, New York, New York

N. DALE BRYANT, Associate Professor of Psychology, University of Houston, Houston, Texas

CYRIL BURT, Emeritus Professor of Psychology, University of London, London, England

DONALD T. CAMPBELL, Professor of Psychology, Northwestern University, Evanston, Illinois

JOHN B. CARROLL, Professor of Education, Harvard University, Cambridge, Massachusetts

FRANK P. CASSARETTO, Professor of Chemistry, Loyola University, Chicago, Illinois

ROBERT S. CATHCART, Associate Professor of Speech, Los Angeles State College, Los Angeles, California

E. G. CHAMBERS, Assistant Director of Research in Industrial Psychology, Psychological Laboratory, Cambridge, England

RUTH CHURCHILL, Professor of Education and Psychology, Antioch College, Yellow Springs, Ohio

CHERRY ANN CLARK, The Meyers Clinic, Los Angeles, California

GALE W. CLARK, Instructor in Business, Western Michigan University, Kalamazoo, Michigan

J. F. CLARK, Professor of Applied Psychology, New South Wales University of Technology, Kensington, New South Wales, Australia

STANLEY CLARK, Professor of Education, University of Saskatchewan, Saskatoon, Saskatchewan, Canada

DOROTHY M. CLENDENEN, Assistant Director, Test Division, The Psychological Corporation, New York, New York

CHARLES N. COFER, Professor of Psychology, University of Maryland, College Park, Maryland

WILLIAM E. COFFMAN, Director, Test Development Division, Educational Testing Service, Princeton, New Jersey

ANDREW L. COMREY, Associate Professor of Psychology, University of California, Los Angeles, California

WALTER W. COOK, Dean, College of Education, University of Minnesota, Minneapolis, Minnesota

WILLIAM C. COTTLE, Professor of Education, The University of Kansas, Lawrence, Kansas

JOHN A. COX, JR., Research Psychologist, Personnel Laboratory, Wright Air Development Center, Lackland AFB, Texas

LEE J. CRONBACH, Professor of Education and Psychology, University of Illinois, Urbana, Illinois

FRANCES E. CROOK, Assistant Professor of Education, McGill University, Montreal, Canada

WILLIAM CURR, Lecturer in Education, University of Birmingham, Birmingham, England

W. GRANT DAHLSTROM, Associate Professor of Psychology, University of North Carolina, Chapel Hill, North Carolina

JOHN T. DAILEY, Program Director, American Institute for Research, Washington, D.C.

REGINALD R. DALE, Lecturer in Education, University College of Swansea, Swansea, England

RICHARD H. DANA, Assistant Professor of Psychology, University of Nevada, Reno, Nevada

JOHN C. DANIELS, Lecturer in Education, University of Nottingham, Nottingham, England

CHARLOTTE CROON DAVIS, Test Research Service, 12 Normandy Road, Bronxville, New York

D. RUSSELL DAVIS, Reader in Clinical Psychology, University of Cambridge, Cambridge, England

FREDERICK B. DAVIS, Professor of Education, and Director, Educational Clinic, Hunter College, New York, New York; and Director, Test Research Service, Bronxville, New York

JAMES DEESE, Associate Professor of Psychology, The Johns Hopkins University, Baltimore, Maryland

CLARENCE DERRICK, Associate Professor of English and Humanities, University of Florida, Gainesville, Florida

LAWRENCE G. DERTHICK, United States Commissioner of Education, Office of Education, Department of Health, Education, and Welfare, Washington, D.C.

JOHN S. DIEKHOFF, Dean, Cleveland College, Western Reserve University, Cleveland, Ohio

JEROME E. DOPPELT, Assistant Director, Test Division, The Psychological Corporation, New York, New York

RALEIGH M. DRAKE, Professor of Psychology, Kent State University, Kent, Ohio

PAUL L. DRESSEL, Director of Evaluation Services, Michigan State University, East Lansing, Michigan

LYDIA A. DUGGINS, Associate Professor and Director of Reading Services, University of Bridgeport, Bridgeport, Connecticut

HAROLD B. DUNKEL, Professor of Education, The University of Chicago, Chicago, Illinois

S. S. DUNN, Officer-in-Charge, Test Division, Australian Council for Educational Research, Melbourne, Australia

WALTER N. DUROST, Director of Educational Services, Pinellas County Public Schools, Clearwater, Florida

HENRY S. DYER, Vice President in Charge of Research, Educational Testing Service, Princeton, New Jersey

NORMAN EAGLE, School Psychologist, Public Schools, Fort Lee, New Jersey

ROBERT L. EBEL, Vice President for Testing Programs and Services, Educational Testing Service, Princeton, New Jersey

REGINALD EDWARDS, Lecturer in Educational Psychology, University of Sheffield, Sheffield, England

DOROTHY H. EICHORN, Assistant Research Psychologist, Institute of Child Welfare, University of California, Berkeley, California

ALBERT ELLIS, Consulting Psychologist, 333 West 56th St., New York 19, New York

MAX D. ENGELHART, Director, Division of Student Examinations, Chicago Public Schools, Chicago, Illinois

LEONARD D. ERON, Director of Research, Rip Van Winkle Foundation, Hudson, New York

ANNA S. ESPENSCHADE, Professor of Physical Education, University of California, Berkeley, California

H. J. EYSENCK, Professor of Psychology, Institute of Psychiatry, University of London, London, England

PAUL R. FARNSWORTH, Professor of Psychology, Stanford University, Stanford, California

HAROLD P. FAWCETT, Professor of Education, The Ohio State University, Columbus, Ohio

LEONARD S. FELDT, Assistant Professor of Education, State University of Iowa, Iowa City, Iowa

GEORGE A. FERGUSON, Professor of Psychology, McGill University, Montreal, Canada

ROBERT H. FERRELL, Assistant Professor of History, Indiana University, Bloomington, Indiana

JAMES A. FIELD, JR., Professor of History, Swarthmore College, Swarthmore, Pennsylvania

GORDON FIFER, Research Psychologist, Test Research Service, Bronxville, New York; and Lecturer in Education, Hunter College, New York, New York

WARREN G. FINDLEY, Assistant Superintendent for Pupil Personnel Services, Atlanta Public Schools, Atlanta, Georgia

JOSHUA A. FISHMAN, Director of Research, College Entrance Examination Board, New York, New York

DONALD W. FISKE, Associate Professor of Psychology, The University of Chicago, Chicago, Illinois

JAMES A. FITZGERALD, Professor of Education, University of Scranton, Scranton, Pennsylvania

JOHN P. FOLEY, JR., President, J. P. Foley and Company, Inc., New York, New York

HANFORD M. FOWLER, Professor of Education, University of Toronto, Toronto, Ontario, Canada

ELIZABETH D. FRASER, Lecturer in Psychology, University of Aberdeen, Aberdeen, Scotland

WAYNE A. FREDERICK, Social Studies Department, Isidore Newman School, New Orleans, Louisiana

NORMAN FREDERIKSEN, Director of Research, Educational Testing Service, Princeton, New Jersey

FRANK S. FREEMAN, Professor of Psychology, Cornell University, Ithaca, New York

JOHN W. FRENCH, Research Associate, Educational Testing Service, Princeton, New Jersey

BENNO G. FRICKE, Assistant Chief, Evaluation and Examinations Division, and Assistant Professor of Psychology, University of Michigan, Ann Arbor, Michigan

CLIFFORD P. FROEHLICH, Professor of Education, University of California, Berkeley, California

GUSTAV J. FROEHLICH, Assistant Director, Bureau of Institutional Research, University of Illinois, Urbana, Illinois

BENJAMIN FRUCHTER, Associate Professor of Educational Psychology, The University of Texas, Austin, Texas

N. L. GAGE, Professor of Education, University of Illinois, Urbana, Illinois

EUGENE L. GAIER, Assistant Professor of Psychology, Louisiana State University, Baton Rouge, Louisiana

ERIC F. GARDNER, Professor of Education and Psychology, University of Syracuse, Syracuse, New York

HENRY E. GARRETT, Professor Emeritus of Psychology, Columbia University, New York, New York

J. RAYMOND GERBERICH, Director, Bureau of Educational Research and Service, and Professor of Education, University of Connecticut, Storrs, Connecticut

CECIL A. GIBB, Professor of Psychology, Canberra University College, Canberra, Australia

JOHN W. GITTINGER, Field Representative, Society for the Investigation of Human Ecology, Forest Hills, New York

MARVIN D. GLOCK, Professor of Educational Psychology, Cornell University, Ithaca, New York

HARRISON G. GOUGH, Associate Professor of Psychology, University of California, Berkeley, California

NEIL GOURLAY, Professor of Education, University of the Witwatersrand, Johannesburg, Union of South Africa

EDWARD B. GREENE, Supervisor of Personnel Testing, Chrysler Corporation, Detroit, Michigan

KONRAD GRIES, Associate Professor of Classical Languages and Chairman of the Department, Queens College, Flushing, New York

RICHARD E. GROSS, Associate Professor of Education, Stanford University, Stanford, California

WILSON H. GUERTIN, Supervisor, Research Unit, Psychology Service, Veterans Administration Hospital, Knoxville, Iowa

J. P. GUILFORD, Professor of Psychology, University of Southern California, Los Angeles, California

JOHN W. GUSTAD, Professor of Psychology, and Director, University Counseling Center, University of Maryland, College Park, Maryland

JOHN H. HAEFNER, Professor of Social Studies Education, State University of Iowa, Iowa City, Iowa

ELIZABETH HAGEN, Assistant Professor of Education, Teachers College, Columbia University, New York, New York

NELSON G. HANAWALT, Professor of Psychology, Douglass College, Rutgers, The State University, New Brunswick, New Jersey

PHILIP L. HARRIMAN, Professor of Psychology, Bucknell University, Lewisburg, Pennsylvania

DALE B. HARRIS, Professor, and Director, Institute of Child Development and Welfare, University of Minnesota, Minneapolis, Minnesota

J. THOMAS HASTINGS, University Examiner; Director, Unit on Evaluation, Bureau of Educational Research; and Professor of

Education; University of Illinois, Urbana, Illinois

MARY HAWORTH, Assistant Professor of Psychology, Michigan State University, East Lansing, Michigan

EDWARD N. HAY, Chairman of the Board, Edward N. Hay and Associates, Inc., Philadelphia, Pennsylvania

JAMES R. HAYDEN, Assistant Superintendent, New Bedford Public Schools, New Bedford, Massachusetts

DAVID K. HEENAN, Assistant Professor, Department of Humanities, and Office of Evaluation Services, Michigan State University, East Lansing, Michigan

ALFRED B. HEILBRUN, JR., Assistant Professor of Psychology, State University of Iowa, Iowa City, Iowa

A. W. HEIM, Medical Research Council, Psychological Laboratory, University of Cambridge, Cambridge, England

WILLIAM E. HENRY, Associate Professor of Human Development and Psychology, The University of Chicago, Chicago, Illinois

VIRGIL E. HERRICK, Professor of Education, The University of Wisconsin, Madison, Wisconsin

A. N. HIERONYMUS, Associate Professor of Education, State University of Iowa, Iowa City, Iowa

WALKER H. HILL, Associate Professor, Office of Evaluation Services, Michigan State University, East Lansing, Michigan

JAMES R. HOBSON, Director of Child Placement, Brookline Public Schools, Brookline, Massachusetts

WAYNE H. HOLTZMAN, Associate Professor of Psychology and Associate Director, The Hogg Foundation for Mental Health, The University of Texas, Austin, Texas

JOHN E. HORROCKS, Professor of Psychology, The Ohio State University, Columbus, Ohio

CLARK W. HORTON, Consultant in Educational Research, Dartmouth College, Hanover, New Hampshire

CARL I. HOVLAND, Sterling Professor of Psychology, Yale University, New Haven, Connecticut

DUNCAN HOWIE, Professor of Psychology, The University of New England, Armidale, Australia

CYRIL J. HOYT, Associate Professor of Education, University of Minnesota, Minneapolis, Minnesota

LLOYD G. HUMPHREYS, Professor of Psychology, University of Illinois, Urbana, Illinois

ROBERT W. B. JACKSON, Professor of Educational Research and Director of the Department, University of Toronto, Toronto, Canada

JOHN R. JENNINGS, Research and Testing Officer, New Zealand Department of Education, Wellington, New Zealand

ARTHUR R. JENSEN, USPHS Research Fellow, Institute of Psychiatry, University of London, London, England

RICHARD JESSOR, Associate Professor of Psychology, and Director, Clinical Training Program, University of Colorado, Boulder, Colorado

A. PEMBERTON JOHNSON, Assistant Director, Counseling Center, Newark College of Engineering, Newark, New Jersey

CECIL D. JOHNSON, Task Leader, New Classification Techniques, Personnel Research Branch, The Adjutant General's Office, Department of the Army, Washington, D.C.

PALMER O. JOHNSON, Professor of Education, University of Minnesota, Minneapolis, Minnesota

ROBERT A. JONES, Assistant Director, Testing Bureau, University of Southern California, Los Angeles, California

WORTH R. JONES, Assistant Professor of Education, University of Cincinnati, Cincinnati, Ohio

CLIFFORD E. JURGENSEN, Assistant Vice President in Charge of Personnel, Minneapolis Gas Company, Minneapolis, Minnesota

JOSEPH JUSTMAN, Assistant Director, Bureau of Educational Program Research and Statistics, New York Public Schools, New York, New York

WALTER KASS, Associate Professor of Psychology, Albert Einstein College of Medicine, Yeshiva University, New York, New York

MARTIN KATZ, Assistant Director, Evaluation and Advisory Service, Educational Testing Service, Princeton, New Jersey

RAYMOND A. KATZELL, Professor of Psychology and Management Engineering, New York University, New York, New York

WALTER V. KAULFERS, Professor of Education, University of Illinois, Urbana, Illinois

J. A. KEATS, Senior Lecturer in Psychology, University of Queensland, Brisbane, Australia

THEODORE E. KELLOGG, Admissions Officer, and Assistant Professor of Education, University of Minnesota, Minneapolis, Minnesota

E. LOWELL KELLY, Professor of Psychology, University of Michigan, Ann Arbor, Michigan

DOUGLAS T. KENNY, Associate Professor of Psychology, University of British Columbia, Vancouver, British Columbia, Canada

DAVID R. KRATHWOHL, Research Coordinator, Bureau of Educational Research, and Professor of Education, Michigan State University, East Lansing, Michigan

RUSSELL P. KROPP, Associate Professor of Education, Florida State University, Tallahassee, Florida

MORRIS KRUGMAN, Assistant Superintendent in Charge of Guidance, New York Public Schools, New York, New York

ALBERT K. KURTZ, Professor of Psychology, University of Florida, Gainesville, Florida

TOM A. LAMKE, Coordinator of Research, Iowa State Teachers College, Cedar Falls, Iowa

EDWARD LANDY, Director, Division of Counseling Services, Newton Public Schools, Newton, Massachusetts

CHARLES R. LANGMUIR, Director of Special Projects, The Psychological Corporation, New York, New York

GERALD V. LANNHOLM, Program Director, Educational Testing Service, Princeton, New Jersey

WILLIAM S. LARSON, Chairman, Music Education Department, Eastman School of Music, The University of Rochester, Rochester, New York

WILBUR L. LAYTON, Associate Professor of Psychology, and Assistant Director, Student Counseling Bureau, University of Minnesota, Minneapolis, Minnesota

J. MURRAY LEE, Professor of Elementary Education and Chairman of the Department, Southern Illinois University, Carbondale, Illinois

D. WELTY LEFEVER, Professor of Education, University of Southern California, Los Angeles, California

ROGER T. LENNON, Director, Division of Test Research and Service, World Book Company, Yonkers, New York

ROY D. LEWIS, Teaching Assistant, University of Minnesota, Minneapolis, Minnesota

JOHN LIGGETT, Lecturer in Applied Psychology, University of Durham, Newcastle, England

E. F. LINDQUIST, Director of Iowa Testing Programs, State University of Iowa, Iowa City, Iowa

IRVING LORGE, Professor of Education, and Executive Officer, Institute of Psychological Research, Teachers College, Columbia University, New York, New York

MAURICE LORR, Director, Neuropsychiatric Research Laboratory, Veterans Benefits Office, Washington, D.C.

WILLIAM HARRISON LUCOW, Associate Professor of Education, University of Manitoba, Winnipeg, Manitoba, Canada

JAMES LUMSDEN, Lecturer in Psychology, University of Western Australia, Nedlands, Australia

ROBERT W. LUNDIN, Associate Professor of Psychology, Hamilton College, Clinton, New York

RAYMOND J. McCALL, Professor of Psychology and Chairman of the Department, Marquette University, Milwaukee, Wisconsin

R. W. McCULLOCH, Chief Psychologist and Superintendent of Special Schools, Tasmanian Education Department, Hobart, Tasmania, Australia

CONSTANCE M. McCULLOUGH, Professor of Education, San Francisco State College, San Francisco, California

D. W. McELWAIN, Professor of Psychology, University of Queensland, Brisbane, Australia

CHRISTINE McGUIRE, Assistant Professorial Lecturer in the Social Sciences, and Examiner, The University of Chicago, Chicago, Illinois

JAMES MAINWARING, Formerly Lecturer in Psychology and Music, Dudley Training College, Birmingham, England

M. JACINTA MANN, Instructor in Mathematics, Seton Hill College, Greensburg, Pennsylvania

JOHN MANNING, Associate Professor, Department of Humanities, and Office of Evaluation Services, Michigan State University, East Lansing, Michigan

HERSCHEL T. MANUEL, Professor of Educational Psychology, The University of Texas, Austin, Texas

JAMES MAXWELL, Visiting Professor of Education, Teachers College, Columbia University, New York, New York

RICHARD A. MEADE, Professor of Education, University of Virginia, Charlottesville, Virginia

ARTHUR W. MEADOWS, Head, Department of Psychology, University of Adelaide, Adelaide, Australia

I. G. MEDDLETON, Deputy Head, Research Department, University of Queensland, Brisbane, Australia

ALBERT E. MEDER, JR., Vice Provost and Dean of the University, Rutgers, The State University, New Brunswick, New Jersey

P. L. MELLENBRUCH, Professor of Psychology, University of Kentucky, Lexington, Kentucky

BERNADINE MEYER, Assistant Professor, School of Business Administration, Duquesne University, Pittsburgh, Pennsylvania

WILLIAM B. MICHAEL, Director, The Testing Bureau, and Professor of Psychology and Education, University of Southern California, Los Angeles, California

WILLIAM J. MICHEELS, Professor of Industrial Education and Chairman of the Department, University of Minnesota, Minneapolis, Minnesota

T. R. MILES, Lecturer in Psychology, University College, Bangor, Wales

JOHN E. MILHOLLAND, Associate Professor of Psychology, and Chief, Evaluation and Examinations Division, Bureau of Psychological Services, University of Michigan, Ann Arbor, Michigan

G. A. V. MORGAN, Senior Psychologist, North Wales Child Guidance Clinics, Denbighshire, Wales

JOHN B. MORRIS, Associate Professor of Psychology, and Director of Institutional Research, The University of Mississippi, University, Mississippi

HAROLD E. MOSER, Director of College Test Services, State Teachers College, Towson, Maryland

KATE HEVNER MUELLER, Professor of Education, Indiana University, Bloomington, Indiana

CHARLES T. MYERS, Associate in Test Development, Educational Testing Service, Princeton, New Jersey

LOUIS C. NANASSY, Professor of Business Education, Montclair State College, Upper Montclair, New Jersey

LEO NEDELSKY, Associate Professor of Physical Sciences, The University of Chicago, Chicago, Illinois

CHARLES O. NEIDT, Professor of Educational Psychology and Measurements and Chairman of the Department, The University of Nebraska, Lincoln, Nebraska

CLARENCE H. NELSON, Professor, Office of Evaluation Services, Michigan State University, East Lansing, Michigan

KENNETH R. NEWTON, Associate Professor of Psychology, University of Tennessee, Knoxville, Tennessee

JOHN NISBET, Lecturer in Education, University of Aberdeen, Aberdeen, Scotland

STANLEY NISBET, Professor of Education, University of Glasgow, Glasgow, Scotland

VICTOR H. NOLL, Professor of Education, Michigan State University, East Lansing, Michigan

WARREN T. NORMAN, Instructor in Psychology, University of Michigan, Ann Arbor, Michigan

RAYMOND C. NORRIS, Associate Professor of Psychology, George Peabody College for Teachers, Nashville, Tennessee

ROBERT D. NORTH, Assistant Director, Educational Records Bureau, New York, New York

MARY ELLEN OLIVERIO, Associate Professor of Education, Teachers College, Columbia University, New York, New York

JACOB S. ORLEANS, Lecturer in Psychology, Nevada Southern Regional Division, University of Nevada, Las Vegas, Nevada

C. ROBERT PACE, Professor of Psychology and Chairman of the Department, Syracuse University, Syracuse, New York

ORVILLE PALMER, Test Development Division, Educational Testing Service, Princeton, New Jersey

OSMOND E. PALMER, Associate Professor, Office of Evaluation Services, Michigan State University, East Lansing, Michigan

GERALD R. PATTERSON, Assistant Professor of Psychology, University of Oregon, Eugene, Oregon

E. A. PEEL, Professor of Education, University of Birmingham, Birmingham, England

KATHLEEN N. PERRET, Interpreter, Department of Conference Services, Interpretation Division, United Nations, New York, New York

THEODORE G. PHILLIPS, Assistant Dean, Amundsen Branch, Chicago City Junior College, Chicago, Illinois

D. A. PIDGEON, Senior Officer, Test Services, National Foundation for Educational Research in England and Wales, London, England

JOHN PIERCE-JONES, Associate Professor of Educational Psychology, The University of Texas, Austin, Texas

A. E. G. PILLINER, Lecturer in Education, University of Edinburgh, Edinburgh, Scotland

LYNNETTE B. PLUMLEE, Personnel Research and Testing Division, Sandia Corporation, Albuquerque, New Mexico

ROBERT C. POOLEY, Professor of English, and Chairman, Department of Integrated Liberal Studies, The University of Wisconsin, Madison, Wisconsin

WINIFRED L. POST, Instructor in English, Dana Hall, Wellesley, Massachusetts

H. VERNON PRICE, Professor of Mathematics and Astronomy, and Head of Mathematics in University High School, State University of Iowa, Iowa City, Iowa

M. L. KELLMER PRINGLE, Lecturer in Education, and Deputy Head, Department of Child Study, University of Birmingham, Birmingham, England

ALBERT I. RABIN, Professor of Psychology, and Director, Psychological Clinic, Michigan State University, East Lansing, Michigan

JOHN A. RADCLIFFE, Lecturer in Psychology, University of Sydney, Sydney, Australia

S. A. RAYNER, Assistant Registrar, University of Queensland, Brisbane, Australia

H. H. REMMERS, Professor of Psychology and Education, Purdue University, Lafayette, Indiana

MAYNARD C. REYNOLDS, Associate Professor of Educational Psychology, University of Minnesota, Minneapolis, Minnesota

ROGER A. RICHARDS, Assistant in Secondary Curriculum, New Jersey State Department of Education, Trenton, New Jersey

J. A. RICHARDSON, Professor of Special Education, The University of British Columbia, Vancouver, British Columbia, Canada

S. C. RICHARDSON, Lecturer in Psychology, Hillcroft College, Surbiton, Surrey, England

JAMES H. RICKS, JR., Assistant Director, Test Division, The Psychological Corporation, New York, New York

EDWARD G. RIETZ, Instructor in Chemistry, Wright Junior College, Chicago, Illinois

HARRY N. RIVLIN, Dean of Teacher Education, Board of Higher Education, New York, New York

HOLLAND ROBERTS, Director, Academic Freedom Committee, San Francisco, California

HELEN M. ROBINSON, Associate Professor of Education, The University of Chicago, Chicago, Illinois

CYRIL A. ROGERS, Senior Lecturer in Psychology, University College of Rhodesia and Nyasaland, Salisbury, Southern Rhodesia

BENJAMIN ROSNER, Assistant Professor of Education, Rutgers, The State University, New Brunswick, New Jersey

CHARLES S. ROSS, Editor-in-Chief, Silver Burdett Company, Morristown, New Jersey

MYRON F. ROSSKOPF, Professor of Mathematics, Teachers College, Columbia University, New York, New York

JOHN W. M. ROTHNEY, Professor of Education, The University of Wisconsin, Madison, Wisconsin

ARTHUR B. ROYSE, Lecturer in Psychology, University of Hull, Hull, England

C. SANDERS, Professor of Education and Dean of the Faculty, University of Western Australia, Nedlands, Australia

BERT R. SAPPENFIELD, Professor of Psychology, Montana State University, Missoula, Montana

I. DAVID SATLOW, Chairman, Department of Accounting and Distributive Education, Thomas Jefferson High School, Brooklyn, New York

DAVID R. SAUNDERS, Research Associate, Educational Testing Service, Princeton, New Jersey

DOUGLAS E. SCATES, Professor of Education, University of Florida, Gainesville, Florida

WILLIAM SCHOFIELD, Associate Professor of Psychology and Psychiatry, University of Minnesota, Minneapolis, Minnesota

FRED J. SCHONELL, Professor of Education, University of Queensland, Brisbane, Australia

WILLIAM B. SCHRADER, Director, Statistical Analysis, Educational Testing Service, Princeton, New Jersey

HERBERT SCHUELER, Professor of Education, and Director of Teacher Education, Hunter College, New York, New York

LOUISE B. SCOTT, Assistant Professor of Speech, Los Angeles State College, Los Angeles, California

HAROLD SEASHORE, Director, Test Division, The Psychological Corporation, New York, New York

S. B. SELLS, Professor of Psychology, Texas Christian University, Fort Worth, Texas

LAURANCE F. SHAFFER, Professor of Education, Teachers College, Columbia University, New York, New York

MARION F. SHAYCOFT, Program Director, American Institute for Research, Washington, D.C.

EDWIN S. SHNEIDMAN, Co-Principal Investigator, Central Research Unit, V. A. Center, Los Angeles, California

VERNER M. SIMS, Professor of Psychology, University of Alabama, University, Alabama

WILLIAM SLOAN, Superintendent, State Colony and Training School, Pineville, Louisiana

DONALD E. P. SMITH, Chief, Division of Reading Improvement Services, and Associate Professor of Education, University of Michigan, Ann Arbor, Michigan

I. MACFARLANE SMITH, Lecturer in Education, University of Durham, Newcastle, England

ROBERT J. SOLOMON, Assistant Director, Test Development Division, Educational Testing Service, Princeton, New Jersey

GEORGE D. SPACHE, Professor of Education, and Head, Reading Laboratory and Clinic, University of Florida, Gainesville, Florida

EMMA SPANEY, Associate Professor of Psychology, Queens College, Flushing, New York

GERALDINE SPAULDING, Consultant, Educational Records Bureau, New York, New York

DONALD SPEARRITT, Senior Research Assistant, Australian Council for Educational Research, Melbourne, Australia

JOHN M. STALNAKER, President, National Merit Scholarship Corporation, Evanston, Illinois

ROY W. STANHOPE, Senior Lecturer in Science Education, Sydney Teachers' College, University Grounds, Sydney, Australia

JULIAN C. STANLEY, Professor of Education, The University of Wisconsin, Madison, Wisconsin

RUSSELL G. STAUFFER, Director, The Reading-Study Center, University of Delaware, Newark, Delaware

HARRY L. STEIN, Professor of Education, The University of British Columbia, Vancouver, British Columbia, Canada

WILLIAM STEPHENSON, Consulting Psychologist, 20 Brookside Drive, Greenwich, Connecticut

NAOMI STEWART, Formerly Staff Associate, Educational Testing Service, Princeton, New Jersey

L. JOSEPH STONE, Professor of Child Study, Vassar College, Poughkeepsie, New York

RUTH M. STRANG, Professor of Education, Teachers College, Columbia University, New York, New York

RUTH STRICKLAND, Professor of Education, Indiana University, Bloomington, Indiana

C. R. STROTHER, Professor of Clinical Psychology, University of Washington, Seattle, Washington

GEORGE W. STURROCK, Educational Psychologist, Dundee Education Committee, Dundee, Scotland

FREDERICK H. STUTZ, Professor of Education, Cornell University, Ithaca, New York

NORMAN D. SUNDBERG, Director, University Child Guidance Clinic, and Associate Professor of Psychology, University of Oregon, Eugene, Oregon

DONALD E. SUPER, Professor of Education, Teachers College, Columbia University, New York, New York

J. P. SUTCLIFFE, Senior Lecturer in Psychology, University of Sydney, Sydney, Australia

JOHN SUTHERLAND, Senior Lecturer in Education, Moray House College of Education, Edinburgh, Scotland

CLIFFORD H. SWENSEN, JR., Associate Professor of Psychology, University of Tennessee, Knoxville, Tennessee

PERCIVAL M. SYMONDS, Professor Emeritus of Education, Teachers College, Columbia University, New York, New York

CALVIN W. TAYLOR, Professor of Psychology, University of Utah, Salt Lake City, Utah

ERWIN K. TAYLOR, President, Personnel Research and Development Corporation, Cleveland, Ohio

FLORENCE M. TEAGARDEN, Emeritus Professor of Psychology, University of Pittsburgh, Pittsburgh, Pennsylvania

W. WESLEY TENNYSON, Assistant Professor of Education, University of Minnesota, Minneapolis, Minnesota

CLEVELAND A. THOMAS, Principal, Francis W. Parker School, Chicago, Illinois

ALBERT S. THOMPSON, Professor of Education, Teachers College, Columbia University, New York, New York

ROBERT L. THORNDIKE, Professor of Education, Teachers College, Columbia University, New York, New York

DAVID V. TIEDEMAN, Associate Professor of Education, Harvard University, Cambridge, Massachusetts

HERBERT A. TONNE, Professor of Education, New York University, New York, New York

AGATHA TOWNSEND, Associate Professor of Education, State Teachers College, Kutztown, Pennsylvania

ROBERT M. W. TRAVERS, Professor of Educational Psychology and Head of the Department, University of Utah, Salt Lake City, Utah

ARTHUR E. TRAXLER, Executive Director, Educational Records Bureau, New York, New York

MARY E. TURNBULL, Formerly Head of Test Production, Educational Testing Service, Princeton, New Jersey

WILLIAM W. TURNBULL, Executive Vice President, Educational Testing Service, Princeton, New Jersey

CLARENCE E. TURNER, Professor of Romance Languages, Rutgers, The State University, New Brunswick, New Jersey

MERVYN L. TURNER, Research Assistant, Australian Council for Educational Research, Melbourne, Australia

LEONA E. TYLER, Professor of Psychology, University of Oregon, Eugene, Oregon

RALPH W. TYLER, Director, Center for Advanced Study in the Behavioral Sciences, Stanford, California

B. H. VAN ROEKEL, Associate Professor of Teacher Education, Michigan State University, East Lansing, Michigan

NEIL J. VAN STEENBERG, Research Psychologist, Personnel Research Branch, Personnel Research and Procedures Division, The Adjutant General's Office, Department of the Army, Washington, D.C.

MAGDALEN D. VERNON, Professor of Psychology, University of Reading, Reading, England

PHILIP E. VERNON, Professor of Educational Psychology, Institute of Education, University of London, London, England

VERNA L. VICKERY, Associate Professor of Education, Mississippi State University, Starkville, Mississippi

S. RAINS WALLACE, Director of Research, Life Insurance Agency Management Association, Hartford, Connecticut

WIMBURN L. WALLACE, Director, Professional Examinations Division, The Psychological Corporation, New York, New York

M. J. WANTMAN, Visiting Director of Educational Measurement and Research, University of Malaya, Singapore

F. W. WARBURTON, Lecturer in Educational Psychology, University of Manchester, Manchester, England

NEIL D. WARREN, Professor of Psychology and Head of the Department, University of Southern California, Los Angeles, California

WILLARD G. WARRINGTON, Associate Professor, Office of Evaluation Services, Michigan State University, East Lansing, Michigan

J. FRED WEAVER, Director of Graduate Studies, and Associate Dean, School of Education, Boston University, Boston, Massachusetts

HAROLD WEBSTER, Research Associate Psychologist, Center for the Study of Higher Education, University of California, Berkeley, California

HENRY WEITZ, Associate Professor of Education, and Director, Bureau of Testing and Guidance, Duke University, Durham, North Carolina

ALEXANDER G. WESMAN, Associate Director, Test Division, The Psychological Corporation, New York, New York

GEORGE WESTBY, Head, Department of Psychology, University of Hull, Hull, England

D. K. WHEELER, Senior Lecturer in Education, University of Western Australia, Nedlands, Australia

HAYDN S. WILLIAMS, Assistant Superintendent of Technical Education, Education Department, Perth, Australia

JOHN M. WILLITS, Business and Industrial Psychologist, Palo Alto, California

HERBERT D. WING, Principal, City of Sheffield Training College, Sheffield, England

R. WINTERBOURN, Professor of Education, The University of Auckland, Auckland, New Zealand

STEPHEN WISEMAN, Director, School of Education, University of Manchester, Manchester, England

C. GILBERT WRENN, Professor of Educational Psychology, University of Minnesota, Minneapolis, Minnesota

J. WAYNE WRIGHTSTONE, Director, Bureau of Educational Research, New York Public Schools, New York, New York

JACK WRIGLEY, Lecturer in the Teaching of Mathematics, Institute of Education, University of London, London, England

ALFRED YATES, Senior Research Officer, National Foundation for Educational Research, London, England

LOUIS C. ZAHNER, Head, English Department, Groton School, Groton, Massachusetts

Preface

* * * * *

IF THE reader were to take time to read through the introductions to previous volumes in this series, he might well come away with the impression that *The Mental Measurements Yearbook* is something of a tenacious publication. It seems always to have had financial difficulties and never to have quite been able to meet the schedule of publication dates anticipated for it! Indeed, this has been and, I fear, continues to be the case. It is to the credit of the friends (and sometimes even the foes) of the Editor who have encouraged and inspired him for so long and in so many ways, and of the many test reviewers and publishers who have made his work possible that the series has had that tenacity and that it has succeeded in winning a place in the working library of many a test user.

It has been the purpose of this series to assist test users of all kinds—educators, teachers, personnel workers, psychiatrists, psychologists, sociologists, and others—in locating and in evaluating tests and books on testing. The present volume represents the eighth publication [1]

in this service to test users which began 24 years ago with the publication of a 44-page unannotated bibliography of tests called *Educational, Psychological, and Personality Tests of 1933 and 1934*. Since that time many changes have taken place, some more slowly than we would have liked and some more rapidly than anticipated. The volumes have constantly increased in size and improved in format. More and more tests have been listed. Books and excerpts from book reviews in journals, features not part of the original publications, have been introduced and have grown successively in number. Original test reviews, again not envisioned in the original volumes, have been introduced and increased in number with each succeeding volume. The story of the initiation and growth of the series has been told in detail in the Introduction to *The Nineteen Forty Mental Measurements Yearbook*. For the present, suffice it to say that, prior to the publication of this volume, tests had stood trial in better than 2,100 reviews under the competent scrutiny of more than 1,000 pairs of reviewing eyes; more than 9,000 references on the development, use, and limitations of specific tests had been documented and published; and more

[1] Buros, Oscar K. *Educational, Psychological, and Personality Tests of 1933 and 1934.* Rutgers University Bulletin, Vol. 11, No. 11; Studies in Education, No. 7. New Brunswick, N.J.: School of Education, Rutgers University, May 1935. Pp. 44. Paper. Out of print. *

Buros, Oscar K. *Educational, Psychological, and Personality Tests of 1933, 1934, and 1935.* Rutgers University Bulletin, Vol. 13, No. 1; Studies in Education, No. 9. New Brunswick, N.J.: School of Education, Rutgers University, July 1936. Pp. 83. Paper. $0.50. * For reviews, see 40:B856, 38:B325, and 36:B46.

Buros, Oscar K. *Educational, Psychological, and Personality Tests of 1936: Including a Bibliography and Book Review Digest of Measurement Books and Monographs of 1933–36.* Rutgers University Bulletin, Vol. 14, No. 2A; Studies in Education, No. 11. New Brunswick, N.J.: School of Education, Rutgers University, August 1937. Pp. 141. Paper. $0.60. * For reviews, see 40:B857 and 38:B326.

Buros, Oscar Krisen, Editor. *The Nineteen Thirty Eight*

Mental Measurements Yearbook of the School of Education, Rutgers University. New Brunswick, N.J.: Rutgers University Press, 1938. Pp. xv, 415. Out of print. * For reviews, see 40:B858.

Buros, Oscar Krisen, Editor. *The Nineteen Forty Mental Measurements Yearbook.* Highland Park, N.J.: Gryphon Press, 1941. Pp. xxv, 674. Out of print. * For reviews, see 4:B70 and 3:788.

Buros, Oscar Krisen, Editor. *The Third Mental Measurements Yearbook.* New Brunswick, N.J.: Rutgers University Press, 1949. Pp. xv, 1047. $12.50. * For reviews, see 4:B71.

Buros, Oscar Krisen, Editor. *The Fourth Mental Measurements Yearbook.* Highland Park, N.J.: Gryphon Press, 1953. Pp. xxv, 1163. $18.00. * For reviews, see B84.

than 2,000 books on testing and related fields had been cited and evaluated in more than 3,400 excerpted journal reviews.

OBJECTIVES

The objectives of *The Mental Measurements Yearbooks* have remained basically unchanged since their first statement in *The Nineteen Forty Yearbook*. For the section "Tests and Reviews" these include: to make readily available comprehensive and up-to-date information on recent tests published in all English-speaking countries, hundreds of frankly critical test reviews which will assist test users to make more discriminating selections of the standard tests which will best meet their needs, and comprehensive and accurate bibliographies of references on specific tests; to impel authors and publishers to place fewer but better tests on the market and to provide test users with detailed and accurate information about their tests at the time that they are first placed on the market; to suggest to test users better methods of arriving at their own appraisals of both standard and nonstandard tests in light of their particular values and needs; to stimulate reviewers—and others to a lesser extent—to reconsider and think through more carefully their beliefs and values relevant to testing; to inculcate upon test users a keener awareness of both the values and dangers which may accompany the use of standard tests; and to impress test users with the desirability of suspecting all standard tests—even those prepared by well known authorities—unaccompanied by data on their construction, validation, use, and limitations.

The objectives of the section "Books and Reviews" continue to be: to make readily available comprehensive and up-to-date bibliographies of recent books on measurements and closely associated fields published in all English-speaking countries, evaluative excerpts from hundreds of journals in this country and abroad which will assist test users to make more discriminating selection of books for study and purchase, and important and provocative statements which though appearing in book reviews have considerable value entirely apart from a consideration of the book under review; to call attention to books which are not being reviewed but which probably merit review; and to improve the quality of book reviews by stimulating review editors to make greater effort to choose competent reviewers who will contribute frankly critical reviews and by stimulating reviewers to "take their responsibilities more seriously" by refusing to review books which they cannot appraise competently and honestly.

The Editor will perhaps be forgiven if, after a 24 year period, he wonders to what extent these objectives have been and are being met. It is easy to look back over the period since the first publication in this series and to note that a great number of high quality tests have been published, that more publishers are including more detailed information about their tests in manuals, that tests are being more widely used (with, it is hoped, more recognition of the need for discriminating use) by more sophisticated users, and that the quality of test and book reviews has steadily increased. It would, of course, be presumptuous to conclude that *The Mental Measurements Yearbooks* are responsible for these changes. Yet it does not seem too much to say that the series, particularly since the introduction of critical test reviews 21 years ago, has made some contribution to these trends. Reviews have sometimes pleased and sometimes antagonized; they have been ignored by some and acted upon by others. They have sometimes induced authors and publishers to reexamine their work; we have sometimes induced reviewers to reexamine theirs. Despite our best efforts to insure fairness and balance of opinion, we have undoubtedly published some reviews which lacked fairness because they were either too harsh or too lenient. These characteristics are extremely difficult to judge objectively. In most such cases, we think that reviewers have erred in being too lenient rather than too harsh. On the whole, though, reviewers have given credit for work well done and have been reasonable and constructive in their criticism.

Whatever the influence of the yearbook series, it is a fact that the testing industry has grown tremendously both in quality and quantity of production in the past quarter century. It seems to us that this growth alone has made some assistance in sorting through the many test titles available more and more vital. To the extent that *The Mental Measurements Yearbook* has helped busy teachers, personnel workers, psychologists, and others to be acquainted with and form some opinions concerning tests existing in their areas, to the extent that it has caused authors and publishers to be more aware of the needs and expectations of the test-purchasing public, to the extent that it has furnished some organized information on existing tests and books where less was available before—to this extent it has achieved its goal of being of service to test users.

THE FIFTH YEARBOOK

The Fifth Mental Measurements Yearbook covers a seven-year period—1952 through 1958. The volume was scheduled originally for publication in 1956, three years after the publication of *The Fourth Yearbook.* Unfortunately, sales were not high enough to permit this schedule to be carried out.

The Fifth Yearbook is a completely new work which supplements rather than supplants the earlier volumes in the series. It attempts to list all commercially available tests—educational, psychological, and vocational—published as separates in English-speaking countries, and all measurements books published in English-speaking countries, in the period 1952 through 1958. Although it includes reviews of a few older tests which either were not previously reviewed or were reviewed by only one or two persons, the emphasis here as in previous volumes is upon tests and books which have been published or revised since the appearance of the last yearbook. Therefore, in order to obtain comprehensive coverage of tests and books currently being sold, users should consult at least the last three *Mental Measurements Yearbooks.*

TESTS AND REVIEWS

The section "Tests and Reviews" contains listings of 957 tests, 698 original test reviews by 350 reviewers, 48 excerpts from test reviews in 16 journals, and 6,468 references on the construction, use, and limitations of specific tests. Fifty two per cent of the 957 tests are reviewed by one or more reviewers; 21 per cent by two or more reviewers; and 3 per cent by three or more reviewers. Some of these tests have been reviewed in earlier yearbooks. Many tests available only as part of restricted testing programs are again listed and, in some cases, reviewed. Substantial coverage is given to tests of British, Australian, Canadian, New Zealand, and South African origin.

In terms of page allotments, the content coverage of *The Fifth Yearbook* is quite similar to that of *The Fourth Yearbook.* Somewhat more attention has been given to the sections

covering achievement batteries, nonprojective personality tests, English, foreign languages, group intelligence tests, mathematics, miscellaneous areas, reading, science, and social studies. Multi-aptitude batteries have been moved from the section on vocations where they appeared in *The Fourth Yearbook* and assigned a separate category of their own. In *The Fourth Yearbook,* excerpts from reviews of books dealing with specific tests were presented in the test section immediately following the listing of the test; in this volume, all such excerpts appear in the book section.

BOOKS AND REVIEWS

The section "Books and Reviews" lists 485 books on measurements and closely related fields, along with 535 excerpts from book reviews in 81 journals. The range of books is the same as in *The Fourth Yearbook* except that books on the use of interviewing and statistical methods in education and psychology have been omitted. The practice of publishing excerpts from practically all reviews located has been discontinued in order to reduce costs and to allow for expansion of the test review section. This yearbook attempts only to present a representative coverage of the reviews received by a given book.

REVIEWERS

Test reviewers for *The Fifth Yearbook,* like those for previous volumes, were selected with special attention to their particular fields of interest and competency. The response to invitations to review was most gratifying. Better than 75 per cent of those asked to participate in the project expressed a willingness—in an encouraging number of cases, an eagerness—to do so. The Editor was fortunate to be able to count among the reviewers for *The Fifth Yearbook* many "old hands" who have consistently and conscientiously contributed to the quality of volumes in the series.

SUGGESTIONS TO TEST REVIEWERS

Reviewers were asked to write evaluative, frankly critical reviews. To that end, they were sent the following suggestions for reviewing tests.

1) Reviews should be written with the following major objectives in mind:

    a) To provide test users with carefully prepared appraisals of tests for their guidance in selecting and using tests.

    b) To stimulate progress toward higher professional standards in the construction of tests by commending good work, by censuring poor work, and by suggesting improvements.

c) To impel test authors and publishers to present more detailed information on the construction, validity, uses, and possible misuses of their tests.

2) Reviews should be concise, the average review running from 300 to 700 words in length. The average length of the reviews written by one person should not exceed 800 words. Except for reviews of achievement and multifactor batteries, to which restrictions regarding length do not apply, longer reviews should be prepared only with the approval of the editors.

3) Reviews should be frankly critical, with both strengths and weaknesses pointed out in a judicious manner. Descriptive comments should be kept to the minimum necessary to support the critical portions of the review. Criticism should be as specific as possible; implied criticisms meaningful only to testing specialists should be avoided. Reviews should be written primarily for the rank and file of test users. An indication of the relative importance and value of a test with respect to competing tests should be presented whenever possible. If a reviewer considers a competing test better than the one being reviewed, the competing test should be specifically named.

4) If a test manual gives insufficient, contradictory, or ambiguous information regarding the construction, validity, and use of a test, reviewers are urged to write directly to authors and publishers for further information. Test authors and publishers should be held responsible for presenting adequate data in test manuals—failure to do so should be pointed out. For comments made by reviewers based upon unpublished information received personally from test authors or publishers, the source of the information should be clearly indicated.

5) Reviewers will be furnished with the bibliographic entries which will precede their reviews. Information presented in the entry should not be repeated in reviews unless such repetition appears desirable.

6) The use of sideheads and centered heads is optional with reviewers. For an example of the use of the headings, see Herbert S. Conrad's review of test 9 in *The Fourth Mental Measurements Yearbook.*

7) Each review should conclude with a paragraph presenting a concise summary of the reviewer's overall evaluation of the test.

8) A separate review should be prepared for each test. Each review should begin on a new sheet. The test and forms reviewed should be clearly indicated. Your name, title, position, and address should precede each review, e.g.: John Doe, Professor of Education and Psychology, University of Maryland, College Park, Maryland. The review should begin immediately after the address.

9) All reviews should be typed in triplicate. *Two copies* of each review should be submitted to *The Mental Measurements Yearbook; one copy* should be retained by the reviewer.

10) If for any reason a reviewer thinks he is not in a position to write a frankly critical review in a scholarly and unbiased manner, he should request the editors to substitute other tests for review.

11) Reviewers may not invite others to collaborate with them in writing a review unless permission is secured from the editors.

12) Each test will be reviewed by two or more persons in order to secure better representation of various viewpoints. Noncritical content which excessively overlaps similar material presented by another reviewer may be deleted. Reviews will be carefully edited, but no important changes will be made without

the consent of the reviewer. Galley proofs (unaccompanied by copy) will be submitted to reviewers for checking.

13) The editors reserve the right to reject any review which does not meet the minimum standards of the yearbook series.

HOW TO USE THIS YEARBOOK

The reader who wishes to get maximum value out of *The Fifth Mental Measurements Yearbook* may find the following suggestions and explanations helpful.

1) *Table of Contents.* The Table of Contents may be consulted first to get an overall picture of the volume's contents and the classification plan used. The Table of Contents lists all the headings and the main subheadings under which tests are classified in the section "Tests and Reviews."

2) *Classified Index of Tests.* After examining the Table of Contents, the reader may find it profitable to turn to the Classified Index of Tests at the end of the volume. The Classified Index, an expanded table of contents of the section "Tests and Reviews," presents a complete list of all tests and reviewers represented in this volume.

3) *Page and Entry Numbers.* Page numbers appear in the running heads next to the inside margins. Entry numbers (i.e., the numbers assigned to specific tests and books) appear in the running heads next to the outside margins. The entry numbers on facing pages represent the first and last tests or books listed on those pages. The Table of Contents refers to page numbers; cross references and the indexes refer to entry numbers. Except when using the Table of Contents, the reader will have no need to use page numbers.

4) *Stars, Asterisks, and Ellipses.* A star preceding an entry indicates a new book or test not previously listed in this series of yearbooks and bibliographies. An asterisk preceding an entry indicates a book or test which has been revised or supplemented in some way since being last listed. An asterisk following a book entry, a test entry, or a test reference indicates that the entry or reference was prepared from a first-hand examination of the publication in question. Asterisks and ellipses in quotations and excerpts indicate omissions; asterisks indicate a break in the continuity of reading, and ellipses indicate continuity of reading.

5) *Citations for Cross References.* Cross references to reviews and references in this and

earlier volumes are frequently made. Cross references should be interpreted thus: "see 416" refers to test entry 416 in this volume; "see 4:87" refers to entry 87 in *The Fourth Mental Measurements Yearbook;* "see 38:B51" refers to book entry B51 in *The Nineteen Thirty Eight Mental Measurements Yearbook;* and "see 36:B210" refers to book entry B210 in *Educational, Psychological, and Personality Tests of 1936.*

6) *Test Entries.* For each test, an attempt has been made to present in the bibliographic entry the following information in the order given:

a) TITLE. The test titles are printed in boldface type. Secondary and series titles are set off from main titles by a colon. Subtest or booklet titles are printed in small capital letters. When the titles on the test booklet and the test manual differ, the better known title is used.

b) DESCRIPTION OF THE GROUPS FOR WHICH THE TEST IS INTENDED. The grade, chronological age, or semester range is usually given. "Grades 1B, 1A, 2–3, 4–12, 13–17" indicates that there are five test booklets: a booklet for the first half of grade 1, a booklet for the second half of grade 1, a booklet for grades 2 and 3, a booklet for grades 4 to 12 inclusive, and a booklet for undergraduate and graduate students in colleges and universities. "First, second semesters" indicates that there are two test booklets: one covering the work of the first semester, the other covering the work of the second semester. "1, 2 semesters" indicates that the second booklet covers the work of the two semesters.

c) DATE OF COPYRIGHT OR PUBLICATION. The inclusive range of copyright dates (or publication dates if not copyrighted) for the various forms, accessories, and editions of a test is reported. When the publication date differs from the copyright date, both dates are given; e.g., "1948, c1946–48" means that the test was copyrighted both in 1946 and in 1948 but was not published until 1948.

d) PART SCORES. The number of part scores is presented along with their titles or descriptions of what they presumably represent.

e) INDIVIDUAL OR GROUP TEST. All tests are group tests unless otherwise indicated.

f) MACHINE SCORABLE TESTS. Tests which may be scored by the *IBM Test Scoring Machine* (see 530) are marked "IBM."

g) FORMS, PARTS, AND LEVELS. All available forms, parts, and levels are listed with the most recent date of publication.

h) RELIABILITY AND VALIDITY. The complete absence of data in a test manual is indicated.

i) COST OF TESTS. Price information is believed to be correct as of late 1958. Although every precaution has been taken to ensure accuracy, some prices may be in error and other prices may have changed. For full and up-to-date information on test prices, the latest catalogs of test publishers should be consulted.

j) TIME. The number of minutes of actual working time allowed examinees and the approximate length of time needed for administering a test are reported whenever obtainable. The latter figure is always enclosed in parentheses. Thus, "50(60) minutes" indicates that the examinees are allowed fifty minutes of working time and that a total of sixty minutes is needed to administer the test.

k) AUTHOR. For most tests, all authors are reported. In the case of tests which appear in a new form each year, only authors of the most recent forms are listed. Names are reported exactly as printed on test booklets. Names of editors are not reported for tests edited by two or more persons.

l) PUBLISHER. The full name of the publisher or distributor is reported for each test. For addresses of the publishers, see the Publishers Directory and Index.

7) *Test References.* All known references, published and unpublished, on the construction, validity, use, and limitations of each test are reported immediately after the test entry. These references are arranged in chronological order by year of publication and alphabetically by authors within years. The test bibliographies are believed to be fairly complete through 1958; a few references for 1959 are included. In order to assist students who wish to do selected reading on a particular test, references are given to abstracts in *Psychological Abstracts.* For example, "(*PA* 32:301)" refers to abstract 301 in Volume 32 of *Psychological Abstracts.*

8) *Original Test Reviews.* Original test reviews of a particular test are arranged in alphabetical order by reviewers. Cited references which are also references for the test under review are indicated by the use of italic numbers in parentheses. Cited references which are not among the test references are indicated by the use of superscripts which refer to footnotes.

9) *Excerpted Test Reviews.* Excerpts from test reviews first published elsewhere appear immediately after the original test reviews in alphabetical order by journal. In general, only critical comments have been excerpted.

10) *Cross References to Test Reviews.* Cross references to reviews in earlier yearbooks of the same or earlier editions of tests and to related reviews in this volume follow the original and excerpted reviews.

11) *Book Entries.* The books listed in the section "Books and Reviews" are arranged in alphabetical order by authors with anonymous books preceding the others. Rather complete bibliographic information is presented for each book.

12) *Classified Index of Books.* A roughly classified index presented at the beginning of the section "Books and Reviews" will assist the reader to locate books on a particular subject. In addition to using this index, readers are urged to skim over titles and excerpts in search of works which might otherwise be overlooked.

13) *Book Reviews.* Excerpts from book reviews first published elsewhere are arranged

under each book in alphabetical order by journals. In general, only critical comments were excerpted.

14) *Cross References to Book Reviews.* Cross references to reviews of the same or earlier editions of books either in this volume or in earlier volumes follow the excerpted reviews.

15) *Catchwords.* The running heads include catchwords to assist readers in the location of particular materials.

16) *Indexes.* The book contains five indexes: the previously mentioned Classified Index of Tests, in which tests related to a given area are grouped; the Periodical Directory and Index, the major purpose of which is to serve as a key to the abbreviations used for journal titles from which excerpts have been taken; the Publishers Directory and Index, which furnishes the addresses of test and book publishers; the Index of Titles, wherein any test or book included in *The Fifth Yearbook* can be quickly located if its exact title is known; and the Index of Names, which lists the names of all authors, editors, and others mentioned in test entries, book entries, references, reviews, cross references, and footnotes. Detailed information on the use of each index is contained in the italic matter preceding the index.

FUTURE PLANS

In all probability *The Fifth Mental Measurements Yearbook* will mark another turning point in this series. The books cannot continue to grow larger and still retain the convenience of a single-volume work. A multi-volume work would be more costly and would not appear practical. Yet, tests continue to be published and researched at an ever-increasing rate, so that there is no reason to suppose that future yearbooks would not grow larger and larger if allowed to continue on their present course. Editorial and printing costs have increased phenomenally, even since *The Fourth Yearbook*. Since our policy has been to publish no journal excerpts and few, if any, data on tests or test references which have not been examined by the Editor, the drain on his time has become no small issue. In short, if the yearbook series were to continue with all of its present features, some of its comprehensiveness would have to be sacrificed.

For these reasons, it has been decided to eliminate from *The Sixth Yearbook* all bibliographies for specific tests. This decision will be regretted by those who have found the bibliographies useful; the Editor sympathizes with those users who have found the yearbooks a help in their quest for comprehensive bibliographies on given tests. However, from the standpoint of the objectives of the series, test references would appear to be one of the least essential features of the volumes.

Secondly, our present practice of presenting rather extensive review coverage of tests published in Australia, Canada, England, New Zealand, and the Union of South Africa will be discontinued. We hope, however, to continue listing tests published in other English-speaking countries and to review a few foreign tests which appear to be of special interest to test users in the United States.

Other economies may be found necessary, but these are all that are contemplated at present. With these changes, it is hoped that the yearbook will be more manageable in size and time and money requirements. Every effort will be made to reduce the time interval between volumes to three years. Consequently, our target date for *The Sixth Yearbook* is 1962.

Yearbook readers may also be interested in knowing that we are now preparing a comprehensive bibliography of titles and basic information on all tests published in English-speaking countries. This booklet, to be entitled *Tests in Print,* is scheduled for publication in 1960. *Tests in Print* will serve as something of an index to *The Mental Measurements Yearbooks* since it will refer users to more complete information and reviews of tests to be found in the five yearbooks published to date. It is hoped that *Tests in Print* may become a bi- or tri-annual publication appearing in those years when the yearbook is not published.

ACKNOWLEDGMENTS

I am deeply grateful to the numerous individuals, journals, and organizations which have cooperated with us in the preparation of this book. It has been most heartening that so many persons have been willing to take time from their busy schedules to participate in this cooperative enterprise by reviewing tests. To these reviewers, I wish to express my thanks for their important contributions. Thanks are also due to the editors who permitted us to reproduce excerpts from book reviews in their journals and to the test publishers who provided specimen sets of their tests for review purposes.

Many persons have worked at various times as members of my office and editorial staff during the seven years this volume has been in preparation. My editorial assistant, Mr. Alfred Hall, prepared practically all of the test entries in this volume. My editorial associates, Mrs. Miriam M. Bryan and Miss Barbara A. Peace, made important contributions in their editing of test reviews. I am most grateful to these three coworkers for their assistance in preparing this volume.

Special mention should be made of the valuable services of Mrs. Doris G. McCan and Mrs. Ruth G. Thurlow, two part-time members of my staff who have worked on three successive *Mental Measurements Yearbooks*. Mrs. McCan and Mrs. Thurlow have done just about everything which needs to be done in an editorial office. Along with Miss Peace, they also have been responsible for proofreading the entire volume. Because of the painstaking care and thoroughness with which they have undertaken every task assigned to them, the volume is definitely better than it would have been without their help. It is with considerable warmth that I express my thanks to these veterans of three yearbooks.

Among the others to whom thanks are due are the following: Mrs. Susanne Anderson, Mrs. Helen Foster, Mrs. Josephine Herge, Mrs. June Lo Castro, Mr. Warner H. Thurlow, Mr. Richard J. Wood, and Mrs. Minnie Yale. I also wish to acknowledge my indebtedness to my wife Luella for her valuable assistance in the preparation and production of this volume.

Rutgers University has played an important part in making possible the preparation of this volume. The School of Education has assisted the project by providing office space in its Institute of Mental Measurements and has given encouragement and support in many other ways.

For the first time, the dedication of this volume is being used to honor an outstanding scholar in mental measurements. It is with special pleasure that I dedicate this volume to a great man, Sir Cyril Burt.

Oscar Krisen Buros

New Brunswick, N.J.
May 20, 1959

THE FIFTH
MENTAL
MEASUREMENTS
YEARBOOK

Tests and Reviews

*   *   *   *   *

ACHIEVEMENT BATTERIES

REVIEWS BY *Benjamin S. Bloom, William E. Coffman, William C. Cottle, Frederick B. Davis, Max D. Engelhart, Warren G. Findley, Benno G. Fricke, N. L. Gage, J. Raymond Gerberich, James R. Hayden, Virgil E. Herrick, Cyril J. Hoyt, Robert W. B. Jackson, Robert A. Jones, Worth R. Jones, David R. Krathwohl, Wilbur L. Layton, J. Murray Lee, Roger T. Lennon, G. A. V. Morgan, Charles O. Neidt, Victor H. Noll, Jacob S. Orleans, H. H. Remmers, Douglas E. Scates, Verner M. Sims, Robert J. Solomon, W. Wesley Tennyson, William W. Turnbull, and Stephen Wiseman.*

[1]

*American School Achievement Tests. Grades 1, 2–3, 4–6, 7–9; 1941–58; 4 levels; 2–4 parts (Parts 1–3 of Forms D, E, F are essentially the same as Forms A, B, C copyrighted 1941–43); Parts 1–3 are available as separates; postpaid; Willis E. Pratt, Robert V. Young (Parts 1–3), Miriam E. Wilt (a), and Clara Cockerille (Part 4); Public School Publishing Co. *

a) PRIMARY BATTERY I. Grade 1; 5 scores: reading (word recognition, word meaning, total), numbers, total; Forms D ('55), E ('56); manual ('55); $2.25 per 25 tests; 35¢ per specimen set; (35) minutes in 2 sessions.

b) PRIMARY BATTERY II. Grades 2–3; 9 scores: reading (sentences and words, paragraphs, total), arithmetic (computation, problems, total), language, spelling, total; Forms D ('55), E ('56), F ('57); separate Parts 1 (reading), 2 (arithmetic, language, spelling); revised manual ('58); $2.75 per 25 sets of 2 parts; 35¢ per specimen set; 65(85) minutes in 2 sessions.

c) INTERMEDIATE BATTERY. Grades 4–6; 1942–58; 11 scores: same as for Primary Battery II plus social studies, science; Forms D ('55), E ('56), F ('57), G ('58); separate Parts 1 (reading), 2 (arithmetic), 3 (language and spelling), 4 (social studies and science); revised manual ('58); $4.75 per 25 sets of Parts 1–4 (complete battery); $3.70 per 25 sets of Parts 1–3 (partial battery); 50¢ per specimen set (complete battery); 55(200) minutes in 4 sessions for complete battery.

d) ADVANCED BATTERY. Grades 7–9; 1947–58; 11 scores: same as for Intermediate Battery; Forms D (Parts 1, 55; 2–3, '56; 4, '57), E (Parts 1–3, '56; 4, '57), F

('57), G ('58): separate Parts 1–4 same as for Intermediate Battery; revised manual ('58); prices same as for Intermediate Battery; 177(220) minutes in 4 sessions for complete battery.

J. RAYMOND GERBERICH, *Director, Bureau of Educational Research and Service, and Professor of Education, University of Connecticut, Storrs, Connecticut.* [Review of Forms D, E, F.]

Two significant additions to this battery of general achievement tests have been made since publication of its first forms in 1941. The first consisted of an upward extension, in 1947, to provide advanced level tests for grades 7–9. The second involved an extension in scope, in 1957, to provide tests in science and the social studies at the intermediate and advanced levels.

Primary Battery I, for grade 1, has three parts—word recognition, word meaning, and number. In Primary Battery II, for grades 2 and 3, two parts each deal with reading (sentence, word, and paragraph meaning), arithmetic (computation and problem solving), and expressive language (usage and spelling). The

Intermediate and Advanced Batteries, for grades 4–6 and 7–9 respectively, add two parts for the content subjects (social studies and science) to essentially the same six parts in the reading, arithmetic, and language skills areas. Time requirements vary from 35 and 85 minutes for the Primary Batteries, each to be given in two sittings, to the 200 and 220 minutes for the Intermediate and Advanced Batteries, each scheduled for four sittings.

Several types of evidence suggest that the content tests were not originally included when the D to F forms of the Intermediate and Advanced Batteries were projected. The manuals for these tests first appeared separately as single-stapled sets of photo-offset reproductions. The norms are based on only 300 pupils at one level and on 550 pupils at the other. The publication dates—1957 for all forms—are not in harmony with the 1955 and 1956 copyrights for other parts of Forms D and E. As a result, the content areas are not well integrated into the two higher level batteries.

Four purposes are listed for the batteries. Measurement of pupil progress, a common stated purpose at all four levels, is difficult to envision as an appropriate purpose for pupils in the first half of grade 1. The second purpose at the primary and intermediate levels, assistance in the classification of pupils, becomes assistance in the individualization of instruction at the advanced level. The third purpose, providing data for remediation, appropriately is broadened from emphasis on reading for grade 1 to include the expressive language arts at the higher levels. The fourth purpose, which is diagnosing "knowledge of specific concepts" at grade 1, becomes, with minor modifications, diagnosing "knowledge of specific computations and problem-solving ability" at the three other levels. To the reviewer, the phrase "knowledge of specific computations and problem-solving ability" conveys little if any meaning psychologically. It represents the kind of jargon, he believes, that gives rise to much criticism of educators and of professional education.

Validity of the test batteries at all four levels depends upon analyses of curricular and related materials. Word lists, modern textbooks, modern courses of study, and, particularly at the higher levels, studies of course content initiated by the authors were used in the selection of basic test content. Test items and exercises were administered to representative pupil groups in

tryout form. The usual indices of item difficulty and discriminative power, as well as error counts and certain other analytical procedures, were then applied as a basis for assembling the final test forms. Items were often assigned to parallel forms on the basis of identical or closely similar difficulty indices. In short, commonly accepted steps of procedure for insuring content validity and item discriminating power appear to have been well and carefully followed in the construction of the tests.

Evidence concerning reliabilities of the test parts appears in two forms—coefficients of internal consistency and coefficients of equivalence. Stepped-up split-half coefficients, reported only for the two Primary Batteries and the content parts of the Intermediate and Advanced Batteries, range from .71 to .96, with a median value of .91. Two of the 21 coefficients are below .80 and two others are below .85. Such coefficients are usually considered to be too low to justify the use of test scores in making important decisions about individual pupils.

Coefficients of equivalence are variously reported for the higher level batteries. For the intermediate and advanced levels, a surprising if not startling situation appears in the 36 intercorrelations equally divided between, and identically patterned at, the two levels—Form D versus Form E, Form D versus Form F, and Form E versus Form F for each of the six language and arithmetic parts. The 18 coefficients for the Intermediate Battery range from .86 to .94, with a median of .90, whereas the comparable coefficients for the Advanced Battery range from .73 to .86, with a median of .81. The widely differing medians and especially the complete lack of overlap between the two sets of coefficients can be explained in several ways: (a) the Intermediate Battery may be distinctly more reliable than the Advanced Battery, (b) some significant and presumably unrecognized bias may have existed in the samples on which the coefficients were based, or (c) computational errors may have been made in obtaining the coefficients. Of these, the first explanation seems least likely. However, if the coefficients for the Advanced Battery are accepted at face value, practically none of the parts seems to be sufficiently reliable to warrant the use of individual pupil scores in the fulfillment of the four purposes of the tests.

The coefficients of internal consistency and of equivalence were determined by the use of samples ranging from 100 to 325 in size. Except for the three coefficients reported for Primary Battery I, in which case all of the pupils in the sample were necessarily in grade 1, the range of talent is not specified. If the 2-grade range for Primary Battery II and the 3-grade range for the higher level batteries are represented in the coefficients, the reliability data can easily be overinterpreted. Any reason for the use of two separate samples of 325 each for the coefficients of the content parts of the Intermediate and Advanced Batteries is difficult to infer.

In general, the format of the tests is excellent. Primary Battery I appears in one 4-page folder of convenient size, but the approximately 10 by 14¾ inch folders, two for Primary Battery II and four each for the higher level batteries, may be somewhat too long for easy manipulation. One disharmony in this pattern appears in the Part 4 (social studies and science) booklet of Form D of the Advanced Battery. This booklet is only 10 inches in length and is reproduced by a photo-offset or comparable process from copy typed in capital letters, whereas all of the other forms are printed in capitals and lower case type. The arrangement of test content is excellent. Parallel test forms include identical numbers of items in the various parts and sections. The spacing and pagination of parts and sections in parallel forms are also very similar. Except for Primary Battery I, where a columnar arrangement of response positions appears, a 2-column format with item stems, options, and response positions in a "run-on" or paragraph arrangement is typical.

Items types are primarily of the multiple choice variety with either three or four options, although several alternate response item varieties are employed in some of the language usage parts and sections. In Primary Battery I, oral stimuli are given by the examiner for two parts and pictorial stimuli are employed for many items in two parts. Typical paper and pencil items restricted to verbal and numerical stimuli are used entirely at the three higher levels. Understandably, the paragraph meaning and arithmetic problem solving parts consist of items or item groups based on reading paragraphs and problem situations; otherwise, most of the items are unitary and self-contained. The items in all parts of the batteries at all four levels are well and carefully written. They appear to embody usual recommendations for writing objective achievement test items.

Directions and sample items in the booklets are well organized and clear. The manual also provides detailed and, in general, carefully written directions to the examiner for test administration. Scoring is facilitated by use of a self-marking technic that results in the occurrence of all correct answers in designated cells printed on the inside, or sealed, booklet pages. After the booklet seals are broken, the number of correct answers for each part is obtained by a simple counting process. Although the counting is simple enough, marks for the right answers do not seem to the reviewer to be clearly enough defined for optimum ease and accuracy of scoring. A wrong answer appears in otherwise blank space and is consequently easily seen. However, a correct answer, which appears as an "X" mark in a small printed rectangle and which is superimposed over the printed letter or symbol that identifies it, is not so readily apparent.

Several typographical errors in the manuals and test booklets can be troublesome if not discovered in advance. For example, "30" should be "40" in Item 28 in the instructions for oral stimuli to be given by the examiner for the numbers test in Form E of Primary Battery I. A wrong response is keyed as correct for Item 18 of the spelling test in Form E of the Advanced Battery. At least two other minor typographical errors occur, but they seem unlikely to have a direct influence on the scores.

Grade and age norms are provided for all four of the batteries. Statements in the test manuals do not specify how pupil samples used in establishing norms were chosen or even precisely how large the samples were. In general, pupils came from schools ranging in size from small rural to large urban and from homes in industrial, agricultural, and residential areas. Norms seem to be based on more than 10,000 pupils (the sample for the original Forms A and B) in grades 1 and 2 for Primary Battery I, on a similar minimum number of pupils in grades 1–4 for Primary Battery II, on about 1,000 pupils in grades 3–7 for the skills tests of the Intermediate Battery, and on approximately 2,000 pupils in grades 6–9 for the skills tests of the Advanced Battery. The content tests at the two higher levels are provided with norms based on considerably smaller samples.

Rather than employing the more realistic concept of essential equivalence, each of the four manuals reports that the various forms of the test are "practically identical." Norms for the

A and B forms and the later D and E forms were found to be "exactly equal," according to the manual for Primary Battery I. Such precision seems hardly credible to the reviewer. The other three manuals merely report that the norms for the older forms were "checked against" the scores of 3,589 pupils from 44 school districts located in 17 states and Canada. It seems apparent that only a fraction of these 3,589 pupils took the battery at any one of the three levels.

The three higher level batteries, each involving more than one test booklet, make no provision for assembling the individual pupil scores derived from the parts, the subject areas, and the total test, or for profiling these scores on a single form that can be filed in the pupil's cumulative record folder. However, a record chart leaflet in each battery manual provides a line on which to record for each pupil grade equivalents for the parts and the reading and arithmetic subtotals and age equivalents for the total battery. It also provides space for entering frequency distributions of grade equivalents obtained by pupils in a class on the various parts.

In summary, the reviewer believes that these tests embody some highly professional and some quite crude applications of technics for constructing and standardizing a series of general achievement test batteries for grades 1 through 9. The technics of content analysis and of item analysis used in validating the tests appear to be at a high level of competence. Certainly the test items are technically good and their organization into test parts, forms, and levels is in general systematic and skillful. The format of the tests and the printing of the tests and manuals are good. Directions for administering and scoring are adequate except in a few minor details.

Weaknesses of the batteries occur primarily in certain portions of the manuals and in the planning of underlying statistical work, the reviewer believes. The four purposes listed in rather similar ways at all four levels seem not to be well conceived, well integrated, or well depicted in the manuals. They savor of afterthoughts rather than of basic guides to test planning. Data on test reliability seem to be hit-or-miss rather than systematically planned and integrated. Desirable information on range of talent, methods of choosing samples, and standard or probable errors of measurement is not given. There is reason to suspect sampling bias

or even computational errors in some of the reliability coefficients reported. Some of the test parts, perhaps even major portions of one battery, seemingly are not sufficiently reliable to warrant their use in attaining some of the stated purposes. Norms appear to be of questionable reliability, and some statements in the manuals about the equating of test forms and equivalence of scores from different test forms seem to be indefensible.

Although the reviewer has noted what he believes to be a number of major weaknesses, they may be primarily after-the-fact rather than basic. If new and systematic reliability data were obtained, if revised norms were prepared on the basis of carefully defined pupil samples, and if the manuals were rewritten and carefully edited, the reviewer believes that the test batteries could be expected to rank among the best of their type. It is possible, however, that he is placing too much confidence in the validity of the instruments and the technical excellence of test items.

VIRGIL E. HERRICK, *Professor of Education, University of Wisconsin, Madison, Wisconsin.* [Review of Forms D, E, and F.]

The *American School Achievement Tests* cover grades 1 through 9 with four separate test batteries.

The test booklets are self-correcting and printed on what appears to be a medium quality of paper. They are approximately 10 x 15 inches in size. The publisher may be forced to use this size in order to maintain the convenience of the self-correcting feature, but the size makes the booklets difficult for both pupils and teachers to handle. The general format of the tests does not reveal the same consideration and finish present in some other tests, and, in the primary tests the quality of the drawing seems of low grade. A great deal more care and technical skill should go into the development of the booklets which accompany the various batteries.

The populations used for standardization consisted of groups of between 300 and 8,000 children "in 44 school districts, located in 17 states and Canada." Pretesting seems to have been done entirely in a single county in Pennsylvania. It is hardly likely that these children, their backgrounds of experience, the instructional materials to which they have been exposed, or the promotion policies of the schools they attend are representative of educational programs gen erally in the United States. From the population descriptions given, it is difficult to tell how valid the tests and their norms are for use in many portions of the United States.

Curricular validation is based on the examination of commonly used texts and a very limited sample of courses of study. This validation seems limited and should be evaluated carefully by any school system which contemplates using these tests on a comprehensive basis. The reliability coefficients reported for the separate tests range between .72 and .96. Most of the *r*'s are based on alternate forms but the .96 is a split-half coefficient. These figures, while adequate for the test as a whole, create the impression that the reliabilities for individual grades would be equally high. This is not so and probably should be explained in the manuals.

The reviewer was struck with the use of almost identical statements in the manuals at all levels to report on the comparability of different test forms, namely—"Each item was so perfectly balanced in one form with corresponding items in the other two forms that the same age and grade norms were found for all three forms: D, E, and F. The three forms may be said to be practically identical." To anyone who has had experience in trying to develop different forms of the same test, this "perfect" record seems almost too good to be true. In any case, the blanket use of this extreme statement suggests some carelessness in the development of the manuals.

Primary Battery I for grade 1 consists of three tests: word recognition, word meaning, and numbers. The two tests which are classified as reading can hardly be considered as such in the usual sense. It may be noted also that the difference between a grade equivalent of 2.0 and one of 2.4 is only two raw score points on the word recognition test. Apparently, the successful recognition of two additional words is considered to represent the work of the first half of the second grade. The major value of the test at this level is its unique feature of oral presentation of the items and its use of a fairly large number of items to cover the areas tested.

Primary Battery II for grades 2 and 3 includes tests in sentence and word meaning (30 items), paragraph meaning (30 items), arithmetic computation (40 items), arithmetic problems (12 items), language (25 items), and spelling (30 items). Each form consists of two parts, enabling the administration of the battery to be accomplished in two sittings.

While time does not permit in this review, a careful study should be made of the 30 items which are intended to cover the sentence and word meaning achievement for the work of the usual second and third grade. For most second grade children, reading vocabulary consists of from 600 to 2,000–3,000 words. Yet, according to the grade equivalent norms, the passing of five items beyond the grade equivalent of 1.9 apparently represents the work of the second grade. Six additional items correct in paragraph meaning, three in arithmetic problems, and three in language usage represent expected achievement for the same period in the respective areas. Success or failure on one test item can change the child's grade placement by as much as five months on some of the tests.

One added difficulty in handling the Primary Battery II test booklet was noted in the arithmetic computation test. The column addition examples are placed on the page in such a way that the child is forced to turn his booklet around to compute the answers. This may cause some confusion in the administration of the test.

The Intermediate Battery for grades 4–6 includes tests on sentence and word meaning (40 items), paragraph meaning (40 items), arithmetic computation (40 items), arithmetic problems (20 items), language (65 items covering correct usage, punctuation, grammar, capitalization, and sentence recognition), spelling (50 items), social studies (40 items), and science (40 items). These tests cover many of the common curriculum areas of the elementary school, and, for many teachers, would probably represent most of what is being taught. The tests are arranged in four parts and are intended to be administered in four sittings.

Perhaps the most questionable tests in this battery are the short subtests in language which cover such topics as capitalization in 10 items. The major value of the language tests will be in the total score. A teacher will not be able to use the subtest results to diagnose the instructional needs of individual children. The subtest on sentence recognition seems to be the least discriminating of the language tests.

The newest tests of this battery are in Part 4, which covers social studies and science. Anyone who has worked on building a test of achievement for elementary schools in a content area like social studies or science realizes how difficult, if not how impossible, a task it is. These tests are primarily directed at covering factual information and make little pretense of testing other aspects of comprehension and problem solving. In the social studies test, the content is restricted to historical and geographical aspects of the United States and South America. Little attention is given to characteristic climatic regions, Canada, Europe, Africa, Asia, etc. (which usually are the concern of the fourth and sixth grades) or to the general area of civics. The importance of common and persistent problems of human living in giving focus to social studies does not seem to be recognized.

Many of the same objections can be raised about the science test. Little effort is made to test anything other than science information. It is very difficult to know what actually is included in the science program of the middle grades. Most of the test items are well constructed; some, however, need to be examined to determine whether each response choice is plausible enough to make it an actual choice on the part of some children.

The Advanced Battery, covering grades 7–9, includes the same type of tests and four-part arrangement as the Intermediate Battery. The paragraph meaning test seems to be most adequate in measuring comprehension at the detail level. Few of the items deal with inference, organization, purpose, or the evaluation aspects of reading comprehension. These qualities should be of major importance at the level of the Advanced Battery. The paragraphs also seem limited in range of reading material presented. No poetry is used. The arithmetic computation test does not explore the area of arithmetical concepts except insofar as these concepts are necessary for computation. Six items deal with algebra. The language and spelling tests are similar to those used in the Intermediate Battery and have the same advantages and disadvantages. The social studies and science tests attempt an almost impossible task of trying to cover in 40 items what is attempted in these areas in these grades. The curricular validity of these two tests seems questionable and the reviewer would urge that any school system study them carefully to determine their appropriateness for the particular school program.

In summary, the *American School Achievement Tests* have one great convenience—the self-correcting aspect of the booklets. Many will find the test booklets awkward to use and to file.

The norms are limited to grade and age equivalents and, while probably usable for cross-grade and cross-school comparisons, they do not seem to be adequate for evaluating the performance of individual children. The curricular validation of these tests, while having much in common with that of many other achievement batteries, needs great improvement, both in the quality of the curricular analysis and in its representativeness for all kinds of elementary school children and programs. The reviewer feels that this battery does not represent our best practice in the field of achievement testing.

For a review by Ralph C. Preston of an earlier edition, see 4:1; for reviews by Walter W. Cook and Gordon N. Mackenzie (with Glen Hass), see 3:1. For reviews by M. A. Brimer and Clarence Derrick of the language test, see 174. For reviews by Joseph N. Justman and J. Fred Weaver of the arithmetic test, see 456. For a review by Agatha Townsend of the reading test, see 621.

[2]

*California Achievement Tests, 1957 Edition. Grades 1–2, 3–4.5, 4–6, 7–9, 9–14; 1934–58; previous edition (see 4:2) still available; 11 scores: reading vocabulary, reading comprehension, reading total, arithmetic reasoning, arithmetic fundamentals, arithmetic total, mechanics of English, spelling, language total, total, handwriting; IBM for grades 4–14; 5 levels; tests in reading, language, and arithmetic available as separates; manual ('57) for each level; battery profile ('57); technical report ('57); separate answer sheets may be used in grades 4–14; 4¢ per IBM answer sheet; 7¢ per Scoreze answer sheet; 60¢ per set of hand scoring stencils; $2.50 per set of anticipated achievement calculators ('58, grades 1–12) by William M. Shanner; postage extra; technical report free; 50¢ per specimen set of any one level, postpaid; can be administered in 2 sessions; Ernest W. Tiegs and Willis W. Clark, California Test Bureau. *
a) LOWER PRIMARY. Grades 1–2; Forms W ('57), X ('57); $4.90 per 35 tests; 89(110) minutes.
b) UPPER PRIMARY. Grades 3–4.5; Forms W ('57), X ('57); $5.25 per 35 tests; 124(145) minutes.
c) ELEMENTARY. Grades 4–6; IBM; Forms W ('57), X ('57), Y ('57), Z ('57); $5.60 per 35 tests; $1.20 per set of machine scoring stencils; with answer sheets: 160(175) minutes, without answer sheets: 144(165) minutes.
d) JUNIOR HIGH LEVEL. Grades 7–9; IBM; Forms W ('57), X ('57), Y ('57), Z ('57); $5.60 per 35 tests; $1.60 per set of machine scoring stencils; with answer sheets: 178(190) minutes, without answer sheets: 162 (180) minutes.
e) ADVANCED. Grades 9–14; IBM; Forms W ('57), X ('57), Y ('57); $5.60 per 35 tests; $1.40 per set of machine scoring stencils; with answer sheets: 178(190) minutes, without answer sheets: 163(180) minutes.

REFERENCES

1. See 40:1193.
2–4. See 3:15.
5–12. See 4:2.

13. CLARK, WILLIS W. "Evaluating School Achievement in Basic Skills in Relation to Mental Ability." *J Ed Res* 46:180–91 N '52. * (*PA* 27:6149)

14. BURRALL, LUCILLE. *A Study of Internal or Trait Variability in Achievement of Pupils at the Fifth Grade Level.* Doctor's thesis, Pennsylvania State College (State College, Pa.), 1953.

15. BURRALL, LUCILLE. "Variability in Achievement of Pupils at the Fifth Grade Level." *Calif J Ed Res* 5:68–73 Mr '54. * (*PA* 28:9038)

16. SCHWELLENBACH, JOHN A. "An Experiment in Predicting the Ability of Eighth Grade Students to Work Simple Algebra Problems." *Calif J Ed Res* 5:36–41 Ja '54. * (*PA* 28:7998)

17. BUEGEL, BETTY LaVETTA. *An Analysis of the Coefficients of Reliability and Errors of Measurement of the California Achievement Tests in Reading, Arithmetic, and Language as Used in the Fourth, Fifth, and Sixth Grades of Four Public Schools in a City of North Dakota.* Master's thesis, University of North Dakota (Grand Forks, N.D.), 1955.

18. MANOLAKES, GEORGE, AND SHELDON, WILLIAM D. "The Relation Between Reading-Test Scores and Language-Factors Intelligence Quotients." *El Sch J* 55:346–50 F '55. * (*PA* 29:8918)

19. SATTER, GEORGE. "Psychometric Scatter Among Mentally Retarded and Normal Children." *Training School B* 52:63–8 Je '55. * (*PA* 30:3078)

20. TAIT, ARTHUR T. "A Comparative Study of Five Major Achievement Tests." *Calif J Ed Res* 6:99–106 My '55. * (*PA* 30:1633)

21. SCOTT, HELEN E., AND WILSON, GUY M. "A Critical Examination of Spelling Words in One Speller in Relation to Four Standardized Tests in Spelling." *J Ed Res* 49:331–43 Ja '56. * (*PA* 31:3658)

22. SHANNER, WILLIAM M. "Relationships Between Norms for Mental Maturity and Achievement Tests." *Calif J Ed Res* 7:15–21 Ja '56. * (*PA* 30:7775)

CHARLES O. NEIDT, *Professor of Educational Psychology and Measurements and Chairman of the Department, University of Nebraska, Lincoln, Nebraska.*

In the 1957 edition of the *California Achievement Tests,* completely new norms have been established; upper and lower primary level batteries have been developed; some subtests have been revised and many have been lengthened; some changes in format have been made; and an elaborate procedure for estimating anticipated achievement has been developed. Many features of former editions have been retained: two principal scores are reported in each of the basic skill areas of reading, arithmetic, and language from grades 1 through 14; performance is summarized in profile form; and grade placement, percentile, and age norms are provided. The manuals for this edition also contain a section called "Diagnostic Analysis of Learning Difficulties" which is designed for identification of specific types of errors on the test items.

The 1957 edition was standardized on a stratified sample representing 341 school systems in the 48 states. Since all pupils in the standardization groups were also administered the *California Test of Mental Maturity,* control of mental age was possible. By means of dual standardization procedures, the authors have provided norms representing the typical performance of pupils throughout the United States. In the standardization of the battery, extensive provisions for selecting an unbiased sample

were followed. Pupils in adjacent grades were not tested in the same school system. The final norm group was based upon random sampling of pupils within each substratum rather than upon random sampling of schools. Whereas such careful sampling procedures do result in a nationwide average which is relatively stable, the heterogeneity of educational conditions makes the interpretation of deviations from the norms somewhat difficult. In the opinion of this reviewer, additional normative data based upon geographic regions would be an aid in interpreting the test results.

One of the major weaknesses of the 1950 edition was the wide range of achievement represented in the primary battery. Division of this range (grades 1–4.5) into a lower primary level and an upper primary level represents an important improvement in the 1957 edition. Elimination of the written directions in the arithmetic test at the lower primary level is also a desirable feature.

Frequent reference to the use of the tests for the diagnosis of learning difficulties is made throughout the manuals. Whereas the diagnostic profile and the diagnostic analysis of learning difficulties do reflect areas of weakness, the number of items within each category is small. The authors recognize this limitation and suggest that the analysis be used only to identify areas for further study. Little evidence has been presented, however, to indicate that the categories represent separate factors of achievement.

The directions for administering the test are clearly stated and the format of the manuals and test booklets is outstanding. Availability of both Scoreze and separate machine scored answer sheets, as well as alternate forms of the tests, contributes to the tests' usability.

The continued use of the reading, arithmetic, and language classification of test content at the advanced level is a limitation of the *California Achievement Tests.* This classification has the effect of obscuring the measurement of educational objectives classified according to typical subject matter content. Teachers and counselors using the advanced battery for educational planning will have difficulty relating the test results to courses available in most secondary schools.

The provision of the "anticipated achievement" charts constructed in terms of grade placement allows for comparing the achievement of pupils of various levels of mental ability with the achievement of pupils of comparable mental ability in the same grade for the standardization group. This procedure may be satisfactory for assessing the achievement expectation in terms of pupils of comparable mental ability, but it cannot be thought of as an indication of the extent to which a child's needs are actually being met. Anticipated achievement scores, however, do provide an empirical basis for appraising the relative progress of children at differing levels of mental functioning and as such contribute to the interpretability of the test results.

The thoroughness with which the authors report empirical evidence regarding the construction of the tests is noteworthy. Reliability coefficients are uniformly high for the various levels and the item discrimination data are indicative of the efficient functioning of nearly all items. Coefficients of correlation between scores on the new edition and other standardized achievement test scores reflect a high degree of construct validity.

In summary, the 1957 edition of the *California Achievement Tests* represents a well constructed achievement test battery designed to measure the basic fundamentals of reading, mathematics, and language from grades 1 through 14. This test battery has many desirable features and can be recommended for the measurement of general achievement at the grade levels indicated.

For reviews by Warren G. Findley, Alvin W. Schindler, and J. Harlan Shores of the 1950 edition, see 4:2; for a review by Paul A. Witty of the 1943 edition, see 3:15; for reviews by C. W. Odell and Hugh B. Wood of an earlier edition, see 40:1193; for a review by D. Welty Lefever, see 38:876. For reviews by Constance M. McCullough and Winifred L. Post of the language test, see 177; for reviews by Gerald V. Lannholm and Robert C. Pooley of the 1950 edition of the language test, see 4:151; for reviews by Harry A. Greene and J. Paul Leonard of an earlier edition, see 40:1292. For a review by Robert D. North of the arithmetic test, see 468; for a review by Robert L. Burch of the 1950 edition of the arithmetic test, see 4:411; for reviews by C. L. Thiele and Harry Grove Wheat of an earlier edition, see 40:1459; for a review by W. A. Brownell, see 38:893. For reviews by John C. Flanagan and James R. Hob-

son *of the 1950 edition of the reading test, see 4:530; for a review by Frederick B. Davis of an earlier edition, see 40:1563; for reviews by Ivan A. Booker and Joseph C. Dewey, see 38: 1110.*

[3]

*California Basic Skills Tests. Grades 4–6, 7–9 1933–54; hand scoring edition of Forms AA and DL of the *California Achievement Tests, 1950 Edition* (see 4:2; for the 1957 Revision, see 2) except for the spelling tests which are from the *Progressive Achievement Tests* (see 3:15) ; 10 scores: vocabulary, reading (comprehension, total), arithmetic (reasoning, fundamentals, total), mechanics of English and grammar, spelling, total language, total; Forms 1, 2 ('54) ; 2 levels $4.90 per 35 tests, postage extra; 50¢ per specimen se of either level, postpaid; Ernest W. Tiegs and Willi W. Clark; California Test Bureau. *
a) ELEMENTARY. Grades 4–6; manual ('54) ; (120) minutes.
b) INTERMEDIATE. Grades 7–9; manual ('54) ; (155) minutes.

For reviews, see 2.

[4]

*California Tests in Social and Related Sciences. Grades 4–8, 9–12; 1946–55; IBM; 2 forms; levels; 3 parts; $2.80 per 35 copies of any one part separate answer sheets may be used; 4¢ per IBM answer sheet; 7¢ per Scoreze answer sheet; 20¢ per set o hand scoring stencils; postage extra; 75¢ per specimen set of either level, postpaid; Georgia Sachs Adams John A. Sexson, and (for various parts of the advance battery) William E. Keeley, William B. Melchior, an Vesperella E. Ott; California Test Bureau. *
a) ELEMENTARY. Grades 4–8; 1946–53; formerly calle *Progressive Tests in the Social and Related Sciences* 23 scores; Forms AA, BB ('53) ; 3 parts; manua ('53) ; 150–170(180) minutes in 2 sessions.
  1) *Part 1, Social Studies I.* 8 scores; 50–60(70 minutes.
  2) *Part 2, Social Studies II.* 8 scores; 50–60(70 minutes.
  3) *Part 3, Related Sciences.* 7 scores; 40–50(60 minutes.
b) ADVANCED. Grades 9–12; 1954–55; 28 scores; Form AA ('54), BB ('55) ; 3 parts; manual ('54) ; 170(190 minutes in 2 sessions.
  1) *Part 1, American History Through the War Be tween States.* 8 scores; 45(55) minutes.
  2) *Part 2, American History Since the War Be tween States.* 8 scores; 45(55) minutes.
  3) *Part 3, Related Sciences.* 12 scores; 80(90) min utes.

DAVID R. KRATHWOHL, *Research Coordinato Bureau of Educational Research, and Profes sor of Education, Michigan State University East Lansing, Michigan.*

ELEMENTARY LEVEL. These tests, a revisio of the *Progressive Tests in Social and Relate Sciences,* were very thoroughly reviewed i their original form in *The Fourth Mental Meas urements Yearbook.* In this review it remain to note what changes have been made an whether these correct the faults previously found.

Except for the revision of about 5 per cent of the items, particularly those criticized in earlier reviews, the replacement of less than 2 per cent of the items, and the dropping of 15 items from Test 4, the test items are identical to those in the previous edition. All flaws in items specifically noted in the previous review have been removed. The new format is much more attractive as well as more functional. The only criticism of format is that a few items are split across columns, though none across pages. Forms AA and BB have been made equivalent; a single scoring key applies to both.

Additional information is available on the norming population. From 24,740 tests given in grades 4–8, a stratified sample was drawn with specified characteristics as follows: (a) mean IQ of 100, with standard deviation of 16, and (b) 70 per cent making normal progress through the grades, 20 per cent retarded one half year or more, 10 per cent accelerated one half year or more. Though the sampling appears heavily western and midwestern, the stratification procedure would tend to eliminate certain regional biases and, to the extent the sampling for IQ was nationally representative, would enforce a greater representativeness.

Reliability coefficients are now available on the subtest scores. As might be expected, some of them are quite low. In the fourth grade, the range of reliabilities for a single form is from .62 to .87, with a median of .76; in the eighth grade the range is greater, from .50 to .92, but the median is higher, .82. A new diagnostic profile for all 23 scores and subscores appears both on the back of each booklet and on the answer sheet. Profiles are plotted in terms of percentile scores. However, since the profile unit is a standard score unit, the differences at the extremes are spread. Thus, the teacher will not mistake large percentile differences at midrange for large real differences.

The test directions formerly assigned time limits only to the three major parts. In an earlier review Gerberich (4:23) noted that Tests 2, 4, and 6, the end tests in the time blocks, frequently had many untried items. The new directions include comments within time blocks such as, "After 33 minutes have passed, tell the pupils they should be starting on Test 2—Section A." While this will help the student to pace himself, these directions are not strong enough to

make him leave Test 1 unfinished, do Test 2, and come back to the former if there is time. Thus, the cumulation of unfinished items will probably continue. It should be alleviated somewhat in Test 4 by the elimination of 15 of its former 75 items.

Overall, the level of workmanship has been raised in the revised tests by the correction of item flaws, the improved format, and the improved and expanded manual. The subscores are still too unreliable for reference except as gross clues in individual interpretation, particularly at the lower grade levels. If Gerberich's review was correct on time limit problems, these may have been somewhat lessened, but it is questionable that they are solved. The norms still show decile jumps for 2-point changes in test score. Particularly at the lower grade levels, the percentile equivalents of chance scores run from the 30th to 50th percentiles, which is too high. While one cannot help but be sympathetic to the author's problem of providing the user with a maximum of information in the shortest possible time, it is questionable whether providing so many scores without more clearly warning the teacher about their possible misinterpretation is wise. The well developed profile almost invites overinterpretation of the score differences.

While the revision of the elementary form is an improvement, it is regrettable that the revision was not sufficiently far reaching to make it comparable to the much better done revision of the advanced level.

ADVANCED LEVEL. Because these tests are entirely new since the last Yearbook, they are reviewed more intensively. The tests were designed to measure achievement in three general areas: (a) United States history and government, (b) physical science, and (c) biological science. There are three parts, each yielding two scores. Two of the three parts (four scores) are concerned with United States history and government (57 per cent of the 410 four-distractor multiple choice items—12 subscores): Part 1 covers American history through 1876; and Part 2, 1877 to the present. Both parts are organized around three strands: (a) economic growth and development, (b) social and cultural life, and (c) development of political democracy. The third part, designed for use with general science courses, deals with physical science (17 per cent of the items, 4 subscores) and biological science (26 per cent of the items, 6 subscores). The biology section has sufficient range for use during or at the end of the senior high school course in biology. A number of items test more than mere memory of facts, an important feature of this test.

Several means of assuring validity are reported in the manual. Courses of study, current leading textbooks, and research studies on the content of required high school courses were consulted in the preliminary selection and organization of content. More items were constructed than needed, and item analysis statistics were obtained on them. "Expert" judgment from 9 college professors, 24 supervisors and curriculum workers, and 50 classroom teachers was used in selecting the items testing the most significant and important concepts and information. Finally, correlations with other standardized achievement tests were computed. These correlations, ranging from .46 to .74, are substantial. The methods of validation seem to indicate more careful workmanship than the elementary battery. Since, as the manual indicates, there is more agreement as to what constitutes important content in the physical and biological sciences than there is in the social sciences, potential users should examine the content carefully to determine its validity for their purposes.

Reliability coefficients, obtained by using both forms, range from .91 to .96 for the various parts. Few teachers, however, will be likely to have over six hours of testing time available. Single form reliabilities for the social science tests are acceptable (.83 to .89) and not atypical for tests in the social science areas; the .81 for physical science and the .86 for biological science are, however, somewhat lower than would be expected in these areas. In reporting norms for the subscores, the authors are to be congratulated on having switched from percentiles used in the elementary form to a high (top 16 per cent), average (68 per cent), and low (bottom 16 per cent) categorization of scores. But reliability coefficients especially developed for this score system are still too low for individual interpretation in many instances (.62–.94, median of .79, for various subscores in single grade, i.e., 9 or 10, and .70–.91, median of .80 for various subscores in grouped grade, i.e., 10–12, situations).

The manual claims that 90 per cent of the examinees should finish within the time limits, so that the test will be a power test. It indicates that the remaining 10 per cent will have completed all the items they are capable of doing within the time limits. This would suggest that items are arranged in order of difficulty, which does not appear to be true, making the second of the two statements too strong. Unlike the elementary level test, specific time limits are set on each subtest so that untried items do not cumulate in the last test of the testing period.

Percentile norms are given for the 6 test and 22 subtest scores. Approximately 3,000 students in 13 states from all parts of the nation contributed to the norms. IQ's of the normative group increase with the grades from 101.5 at the 9th grade to 105.0 at the 12th grade. Schools may wish to compare the selectivity of their dropouts with these data to determine the fit of the norms.

As indicated previously, recommended practice in interpretation suggests use of three rank classifications (high, average, and low) for the subscores for individual interpretations, but percentiles are given for class subscore interpretation. Suggestive of even cruder interpretation of subscores is a table showing the likelihood for specified reliability levels that the true score of a person in either the high or low category is likely to be on the opposite side of the median from his category. While it is questionable that this is an interpretation a teacher is likely to want to make, it does point the way toward a more conservative, and probably more accurate, interpretation of the data.

The level of workmanship for the advanced level test is markedly better than that for the elementary level. If the teacher judges the content measured to be appropriate, and interprets the scores within the limits suggested in the manual, these will be a valuable addition to her measures of achievement.

For reviews by Harry D. Berg and J. Raymond Gerberich of an earlier edition of the elementary level, see 4:23.

[5]

*Contemporary Affairs: Every Pupil Test. Grades 7–12; 1939–58; new test usually issued each December and April; norms available following testing program; no data on reliability; 3¢ per test; 1¢ per scoring key; cash orders postpaid; 40(45) minutes; Ohio Scholarship Tests. *

[6]

*Cooperative General Achievement Tests. Grad 12 and college entrants; 1937–56; 3 tests, 3 scores for each test: terms and concepts, comprehension and interpretation, total; IBM; Forms XX ('53, revision o Form X), YZ ('51, revision of Forms Y and Z); n norms for part scores; high school norms same as those published in 1938; separate answer sheets must be used; $2.95 per 25 tests; $1 per 25 IBM answer sheets; 25¢ per scoring stencil; 35¢ per manual ('56); $1 per specimen set; postage extra; 40(50) minutes for any one test; Cooperative Test Division, Educational Testing Service. *

a) TEST 1, SOCIAL STUDIES. Manual uses the subtitle *A Test of General Proficiency in the Field of Social Studies;* Jeanne M. Bradford (XX).

b) TEST 2, NATURAL SCIENCE. Manual uses the subtitle *A Test of General Proficiency in the Field of Natural Science;* Paul J. Burke (XX).

c) TEST 3, MATHEMATICS. Manual uses the subtitle *A Test of General Proficiency in the Field of Mathematics;* Paul J. Burke (XX).

REFERENCES

1–9. See 4:5.
10. LINDSAY, REX B. *Predicting Success in the Lower Division at the University of Utah.* Master's thesis, University of Utah (Salt Lake City, Utah), 1947.
11. DeGOOYER, MELVIN HENRY. *Validation of the Cooperative General Achievement Test in Mathematics at the University of Utah.* Master's thesis, University of Utah (Salt Lake City, Utah), 1948.
12. RALPH, SALLY. *The Prediction of Success in the College of Pharmacy at the University of Utah.* Master's thesis, University of Utah (Salt Lake City, Utah), 1948.
13. STEWART, NAOMI; BRYAN, MIRIAM M.; AND BURKE, PAUL J. "Correction for Guessing in the Scoring of Pretests: Effect Upon Item Difficulty and Item Validity Indices," pp. 31–45. In *The Seventh Yearbook of the National Council on Measurements Used in Education, 1949–1950.* Fairmont, W.Va.: the Council, Fairmont State College, 1950. Pp. v, 55, xi. *
14. FARBER, ROBERT HOLTON. *Guidance Implications of the Freshman Testing Program at DePauw University.* Doctor's thesis, Indiana University (Bloomington, Ind.), 1951.
15. ANDREW, DEAN C. "Predicting College Success of Non-High-School Graduates." *Sch R* 60:151–6 Mr '52. *
16. KRATHWOHL, DAVID R.; EWING, T. N.; GILBERT, W. M.; AND CRONBACH, LEE J. "Prediction of Success in Achitecture Courses." Abstract. *Am Psychol* 7:288–9 Jl '52. *
17. CARLIN, LESLIE C. "A Longitudinal Comparison of Freshman-Senior Standing." *J Ed Res* 47:285–90 D '53. * (*PA* 28:6586)
18. RUSSON, ALLIEN R. *The Prediction of Scholastic Achievement of Business Education Majors at the College Level.* Doctor's thesis, University of California (Los Angeles, Calif.), 1953.
19. ANDERSON, MARY R., AND STEGMAN, ERWIN J. "Predictors of Freshman Achievement at Fort Hays Kansas State College." *Ed & Psychol Meas* 14:722–3 w '54. * (*PA* 29:7952)
20. ANNESER, ROBERT. *An Evaluation of Scholastic Aptitude in Predicting Senior Level Achievement at Ohio University.* Master's thesis, Ohio University (Athens, Ohio), 1956.
21. BERRY, CHARLES A., AND JONES, ARLYNNE L. "The Predictive Value of the Tests of the National Freshman Testing Program for Grambling College Freshmen." *Negro Ed R* 9:23–33 Ja '58. *

MAX D. ENGELHART, *Director, Division of Student Examinations, Chicago Public Schools, Chicago, Illinois.*

The first forms of the *Cooperative General Achievement Tests* were published in 1937. The early forms tended to emphasize recall of specific details of subject matter while the more recent forms have sought to measure general proficiency in social studies, natural science, and mathematics. Form XX is a revision of Form X, and Form YZ was derived from Forms Y and Z. These new forms are accompanied by an Examiner's Manual, dated 1956, which is worthy of special commendation for its completeness.

The tests are appropriate for use toward the end of high school or at the beginning of the college freshman level. Each Part 1, containing

exercises measuring understanding of terms and concepts, requires 15 minutes, while each Part 2, measuring comprehension and interpretation of paragraphs, tables, or charts, requires 25 minutes. The total working time for each test is 40 minutes. All of the test items are 5-response multiple choice exercises with one answer correct for each. The answer sheets may be hand or machine scored. Each raw score, or total number of correct answers, is converted to a scaled score by means of the conversion tables printed in the margins of the answer sheets. Percentile rank norms are reported in the manual for each of the high school years and for college freshmen.

Emphasis is given in the manual to the usefulness of the tests for guidance and placement. The limitations of the tests are frankly stated. It seems to this reviewer that the tests should yield data decidedly useful to high school counselors offering advice to students with respect to future educational plans. In view of the increasing amount of scholarship testing and the growing practice of admitting students to colleges and universities on the basis of admissions tests rather than in terms of transfer of high school credits alone, the tests may be useful in identifying likely candidates and in giving high school students experiences with the taking of tests less rigorous, perhaps, but similar to those later encountered. Since the three tests are rather highly correlated, differences in their scaled scores need to be quite large to identify areas of strength or weakness or to justify efforts to offer differential predictions with respect to the fields in which proficiency is measured. Using correlations given in the manual between the three tests and the ACE, this reviewer undertook a very minor factor analysis study. In the case of Form XX, the social studies, natural science, and mathematics tests had first factor loadings of .86, .85, and .83; ACE had a loading of .87. The first factor residual varied from −.03 to +.02. In the case of Form YZ, the first factor loadings were .85, .87, .81, and .86, respectively. The first factor residuals varied from −.06 to +.05. While it may be inferred from these data that the tests and the ACE are all measuring much the same basic abilities, the two forms of the mathematics test have the largest specific variances, .21 and .26.

The manual mentions that the tests may be used for admissions purposes. It is possible that certain colleges might find them useful in this way. Where this is the case, the advice of the manual should be heeded: "Effective use of the tests in this manner will depend on the extent to which the school or college studies the relationship between success and test scores in its own situation." It should also be stated that wise use of the test scores for admission purposes should also involve consideration of other data concerning the candidates for admission—measures of general scholastic aptitude and of proficiency in English, high school records, and the like. Even if not used as one of the bases for admission, the administration of these tests on entrance to college may yield data useful for placement and for guidance. Where a college has a program of required general courses, as is exemplified by the general courses of our Chicago City Junior College and a number of higher institutions, these tests could be used as a means of identifying students who should be assigned to lower level, or remedial, courses in the fields relevant to the areas tested. Similarly, students earning relatively high scores might be permitted to waive the corresponding required general courses and enroll in more advanced courses in the same field. The tests would possibly be more useful for this purpose if, instead of a single test in natural science, there were separate tests measuring proficiency in physical science and in biological science. Even though such tests might well be highly correlated, separate tests would be more acceptable to the instructors in these fields. It would also be helpful in such a situation to have a proficiency test in the area of the humanities.

One of the admirable features of the manual is the section devoted to the content validity of these tests. In the case of Part 1 of Test 1, Social Studies, it is reported that United States history, world history, government, and economics are each represented by about one fifth of the 35 exercises. Fourteen per cent and six per cent of the exercises are relevant to sociology and to geography. In the case of this test, and the others of this battery, one wonders if the test is not more fair to students who have had courses in each of these fields and are the type of students who are college bound. While many of the exercises of Part 1 of the social studies test evaluate the ability to associate terms and their definitions, other exercises evaluate understandings of important relationships. Exercises of the latter type are more evident in Form YZ than in Form XX. Part 2 of Form

XX contains 32 exercises following paragraphs a bar graph, and a table of numerical data. Certain of these exercises evaluate such desirable intellectual skills as recognition of the author's basic attitude, purpose, or motivation; the identification of assumptions; recognition of need for additional data; and identification of the consequences of different courses of action Part 2 of Form YZ differs in not having exercises involving interpretation of a graph and a table, but does have exercises requiring interpretation of a topographic map and a genealogical chart. While the latter may be of interest only to prospective history majors, the series of exercises requiring students to discriminate between contrasting points of view with respect to aid to Europe seems especially timely and worthwhile in its demand for critical thinking Background knowledge, in addition to that contained in the selections preceding the exercises contributes to the solution of a number of them This is not undesirable since it helps to make such tests more acceptable to instructors who tend to feel that tests pertaining to quoted materials are "nothing more than reading tests." There are, however, very few items answerable by 12th grade students on the basis of background knowledge alone without reference to the paragraph, graph, or table. Paul Dressel in reviewing earlier forms for *The Fourth Mental Measurements Yearbook* (4:5) suggested that "a more meaningful vocabulary section would be obtained by testing in Part 1 for the meaning of key words in the reading selections given in Part 2." Possibly so, but this reviewer prefers the present organization since the students have the advantage of context cues. A separate Part 1, ranging over important concepts and understandings of a field, again appeals to instructors who value acquisition of knowledge as a major goal and who, unfortunately, are not satisfied with tests which emphasize the evaluation of "critical thinking." In any case, vocabulary background knowledge, reading comprehension, and critical thinking skills are reasonably well balanced in the current forms of the social studies test.

According to the manual, practically all of the 36 exercises of Part 1 of Test 2, Natural Science, "attempt to determine whether the student is able to recall important facts and definitions in the realm of science." It is reported with respect to Form XX that 13 of the exercises are in biology, 7 in chemistry, 11 in physics and 5 in derived sciences. Similar data are reported for Form YZ. In the judgment of this reviewer, the items of Part 1 of Form XX are almost entirely "vocabulary" items, while only half the items of Part 1 of Form YZ deserve this label. In defense of the vocabulary items it should be said, however, that the terms whose meanings are tested for are generally important terms, an understanding of which is requisite for achievement in the natural science field. With respect to Part 2 the manual states, "In addition to testing the ability to read and understand scientific material, certain of the items also test the ability to reason scientifically from given data and the ability to perform computational operations commonly found in scientific materials." This reviewer agrees that this is true to the extent to which such measurement can be accomplished by 24 exercises. It is unfortunate, however, that two of the exercises of Part 2 of Form XX do not contribute to this goal. Exercise 6 begins "Each of the following is an example of a chemical change EXCEPT" and then lists "accumulation of iron ore deposits" as the exception. The selection states, "There is some reason to believe that certain bacteria which have the property of precipitating iron oxide from iron salts cause the accumulation of iron in such concentration that it can be profitably mined." Possibly the exercise writer meant merely the accumulation of the iron oxide precipitated, but the total process certainly involves chemical change. Exercise 7 begins "Bacteria do not ordinarily decompose living organisms because...." and is completed by "living organisms resist destruction by bacteria." This is almost a tautology. Certainly a better answer would be an explanation of *why* bacteria do not decompose living organisms.

In the manual it is indicated that the 36 items on terms and concepts of Part 1 of the mathematics test are distributed over arithmetic, algebra, plane geometry, solid geometry, and trigonometry. Only six or seven items pertain to terms or concepts taught in the last two subjects named. According to the manual, "Part II contains 25 items based on tables, graphs, reading passages, and diagrams. Most of these items require the solution of arithmetic and simple algebraic problems involving data presented in tabular and graphical form; a few require the type of reasoning used in a geometry course." After listing objectives for secondary school mathematics instruction formulated by the Joint Com-

mission of the Mathematical Association of America and the National Council of Teachers of Mathematics, the manual shows the percentage distribution of the exercises of the entire test over these objectives for Forms XX and YZ, respectively, as follows: (*a*) number and computation, 13, 18; (*b*) geometric form and space perception, 35, 30; (*c*) graphic representation, 11, 6; (*d*) elementary analysis, 9, 10; (*e*) logical thinking, 7, 15; (*f*) relational thinking, 16, 17; and (*g*) symbolic representation and thinking, 9, 4. The more extended definitions of objectives (*d*) and (*e*) are "Elementary Analysis—manipulative techniques of algebra" and "Relational Thinking—functions and variables in the form of equations, graphs, tables, and verbal formulas." This is an especially fine example of the presentation of evidence with respect to the content validity of a test. Such analyses should be the rule in the test manuals of all standardized achievement tests.

While almost all of the items of both Forms XX and YZ of the mathematics test are well constructed, a few minor criticisms seem justified. In Part 2 of Form XX, a histogram presents a distribution of annual incomes. One of the five exercises begins "The average yearly income of all the families in the town is...." and the answer keyed as correct is "impossible to determine from the data given." It is not impossible to compute the average from per cent frequencies read from the histogram, although it is probable that only gifted students would attempt to do so. In an excellent series of six items pertaining to five fundamental laws of arithmetic expressed in terms of a, b, and c, the sixth exercise begins "The symbols a, b, and c used in the paragraph above could represent...." and the answer keyed as correct is "the number of persons in a class." The answer should be written "the numbers of persons in three classes" and the item stem should refer to laws 1 and 3 and not the entire paragraph, since these laws pertain to addition and do not involve multiplication. An alternative would be to revise the item stem to read, "The symbol a, b, or c in the paragraph above." In Part 1 of Form YZ, Item 9 begins, "Which one of the following values is not included in the range represented by $2 \pm \frac{1}{2}$?" It would be more precisely stated if the word "inclusive" were added. The distractors of Item 18 in the same part seem much too obviously incorrect. A student need not know how to solve the problem of the difference between two areas so long as he knows the difference between a perimeter and an area since all of the incorrect answers contain the word "perimeter." In Part 2 of Form YZ, a floor plan of a house is given. It would help the students to solve one of the exercises if the front of the house were identified in the floor plans.

Comparison of Forms XX and YZ of each of the tests with the earlier Forms X and Y reveals improvement in a number of respects. The format of the tests has definitely been improved by much more attractive title pages. The labeling of answers to each exercise as (A), (B), (C), (D), and (E) is much less forbidding than the former labeling, e.g., 13–1, 13–2, 13–3, 13–4, and 13–5, though this reviewer prefers periods after the letters rather than parentheses around them. No provision is made on the answer sheets of Forms XX and YZ for the recording of information concerning the student's background of courses in each field. Such data are indispensable in interpreting a student's score. There is empty space on each answer sheet in which a table could be provided for the entry by the student of this information. In the revisions resulting in Forms XX and YZ less discriminating items and items of inappropriate difficulty have been eliminated. In some instances new exercises have been substituted and the phraseology of other items and their answers improved. The tests have been reduced in length; only the current forms of the mathematics test seem to be quite speeded, and this may be more apparent than real since students may tend to omit mathematics exercises with whose content they are quite unfamiliar. If this hypothesis is correct, provision of more time would not result in higher scores; the hypothesis should be investigated.

Reliability coefficients ranging from .86 to .92 are reported, as well as the corresponding standard errors of measurement for raw scores and for scaled scores. As has been indicated earlier, intercorrelations of the tests of the battery are high, ranging from .63 to .75. Data are reported with respect to speededness. The categories "Per cent completing the test," "Per cent completing 75 per cent of the test," and "Number of items reached by 80 per cent of the candidates" would be more meaningful if it were explained that if a student answers the last item, no matter how many items he has omitted within the test, he is considered to have completed the test. Item difficulty indices and item discrimina-

tion indices are reported. The item difficulty indices are the "Delta values" used at Educational Testing Service. In the opinion of this reviewer, distributions of the per cents of correct response to the items would be more meaningful to the typical administrator of the tests. Only 10 per cent of all of the items in both forms of each of the tests have item-test correlations of less than .30, and only 3 per cent are between .10 and .19.

In addition to evidences of the content validity, the manual reports correlations with various scores on the *Cooperative English Test,* the ACE, and the *Cooperative Contemporary Affairs Test.* All of these correlations are substantial—14 of the 42 reported are in the range .70 to .77, 15 are in the range .60 to .69, 10 are in the range .50 to .59, and only 3 are below .50, two of .49 and one of .46. Much lower correlations are reported between earlier forms of these tests and marks in courses at Brooklyn College. This is attributed to selection and the fact that the average marks in a field represented a variety of course patterns. If course marks at Brooklyn College are typical of marks in other higher institutions, their unreliability is also a factor in attenuating the correlations.

Percentile rank norms for college freshmen are based on the results of testing a random sample of 6,027 freshmen drawn from the 15,-000 freshmen in 129 colleges participating in the 1955 National College Freshman Testing Program. The names of these colleges and a classification of their types are reported. Most are small liberal arts colleges, a few are teachers colleges, and a few are junior colleges. Only a few are colleges in large cities. Fifty-five per cent of the students in the sample were attending church controlled colleges, 31 per cent were attending private colleges, and only 13 per cent were attending publicly controlled colleges. The manual is to be commended for providing the information needed in judging the representativeness of the norms sample so that the user of the tests will not conclude that the norms apply to all college entrants throughout the United States.

The high school percentile rank norms are based on data collected in the late 1930's in a representative sample of 40 high schools in 12-grade systems of the East, Middle West, and West. According to the manual, high school norms for later forms of the test were obtained by equating each new form to the most recent of the previous forms. In view of this information, the high school norms should not be considered as applying to a representative sample of contemporary high school students. It is probable that changes have occurred in recent years, especially in the larger cities, and possibly in general. For example, in standardizing recent forms of the quite similar GED tests, Bloom found significant differences between the 1943 and 1955 national levels of peformance of high school seniors.[1]

Lacking norms relevant to colleges of different types and norms pertaining to contemporary high school students, users of the tests will be wise to employ the reported norms with caution and to develop and use local norms as suggested in the manual.

In conclusion, it should be emphasized that Forms XX and YZ of the *Cooperative General Achievement Tests* are superior tests with an outstanding test manual. Although certain limitations have been noted, they are outnumbered by the merits mentioned. These forms and future forms of this battery should be increasingly used for the purposes earlier discussed.

For a review by Paul L. Dressel of Forms T, X, and Y, see 4:5; for a review by John V. McQuitty of Forms S and T, see 3:3. For a review by Harry D. Berg of Test 1, Forms S and T, see 3:596. For a review by Palmer O. Johnson of Test 2, Forms S and T, see 3:548. For a review by John F. Randolph of Test 3, Forms S and T, see 3:316.

[7]

*Cooperative General Culture Test. College; 1930–56; 6 scores: social studies, literature, science, fine arts, mathematics, total; IBM; Forms A ('54), B ('55) ; general Cooperative manual ('51) ; norms ['54] for grade 14 only ; separate answer sheets must be used; $4.95 per 25 tests; $1.95 per 25 IBM answer sheets; 60¢ per set of scoring stencils ; 35¢ per manual ('56) ; postage extra ; 150(160) minutes ; prepared by the publisher from materials developed by the faculty of the University of Minnesota; Cooperative Test Division, Educational Testing Service. *

REFERENCES

1–2. See 40:1184.
3–16. See 3:4.
17–26. See 4:6.
27. ANDERSON, BERT D. "The Sophomore General Culture Tests and Student Knowledge of Cultural Facts." *J Ed Psychol* 45:359–64 O '54. * (*PA* 29:6265)
28. MARTIN, RICHARD RALPH. *An Investigation of the Effectiveness of an Entrance Test Battery for Predicting Success in Law School.* Doctor's thesis, Temple University (Philadelphia, Pa.), 1954. (*DA* 16:575)
29. STONE, JOICS B. "Differential Prediction of Academic Success at Brigham Young University." *J Appl Psychol* 38:109–10 Ap '54. * (*PA* 29:3057)

1 BLOOM, BENJAMIN S. "The 1955 Normative Study of the Tests of General Educational Development." *Sch R* 64:110–24 Mr '56.

30. BUCKTON, LAVERNE, AND DOPPFLT, JEROME E. "Freshman Tests as Predictors of Scores on Graduate and Professional School Examinations." *J Counsel Psychol* 2:146–9 su '55. * (*PA* 30:3453)
31. SHEA, JOSEPH AUGUSTINE. *Predictive Value of Various Combinations of Standardized Tests and Subtests for Prognosis of Teaching Efficiency.* Catholic University of America, Educational Research Monograph, Vol. 19, No. 6. Washington, D.C.: Catholic University of America Press, Inc., June 1, 1955. Pp. xi, 44. *
32. WEBB, SAM C. "Differential Prediction of Success in Graduate School." *J Ed Res* 50:45–54 S '56. * (*PA* 31:6685)
33. GOWAN, J. C. "Intelligence, Interests, and Reading Ability in Relation to Scholastic Achievement." *Psychol Newsl* 8:85–7 Mr–Ap '57. *
34. RICHARDS, JAMES M., JR. "The Prediction of Academic Achievement in a Protestant Theological Seminary." *Ed & Psychol Meas* 17:628–30 w '57. *
35. GREMILLION, BENEDICT JOSEPH. "The Cooperative School and College Ability Test as a Screening Instrument for the Mathematics Proficiency Examination." *J Social Psychol* 47:149–51 F '58. *

BENJAMIN S. BLOOM, *University Examiner, The University of Chicago, Chicago, Illinois.*

This test has been repeatedly reviewed in *The Mental Measurements Yearbook* but without visible effect. It would be simplest, and in some ways fairest, for the reviewer to suggest that the reader refer to the appropriate reviews in previous yearbooks. However, the reviewer is attempting to address both the test authors and the test users. He is certain the test authors have read the previous reviews. Perhaps one more review will do what the previous ones have not.

Previous reviews have all cited this test for excellence from the measurement point of view but questioned its value from an educational viewpoint on the basis that the test sampled little more than a miscellaneous collection of specific facts. The reviewer finds that in its more recent forms the test has deteriorated even from the standpoint of measurement, the reliabilities reported for eight of the ten sections of Forms A and B being .85 or lower, with three of the ten below .80.

In this day of pretesting examination material, it is hard to justify such low reliabilities, since one might have expected that care in test construction, careful selection of items on the basis of pretest results, and some reworking of questions would yield sufficiently high reliabilities. The test authors are also concerned about this point since they state that "the reliabilities obtained indicate that only the total score in either form of the test is sufficiently reliable for individual interpretation. Part scores should be used only for group comparisons or for obtaining rough clues of individual weakness."

Since we have already backed into this review by concerning ourselves with the test's statistical properties before considering its validity and value from an educational point of view, we perhaps should stay at this task for another few paragraphs.

Table 6 of the manual for Forms A and B reports correlations between the *Cooperative General Culture Test* and course grades as one index of validity. One wonders why the authors report these data since only one of the 13 correlations reported is above .50 (.52 for mathematics) and the data were collected in 1947 and 1948 while the present tests were copyrighted in 1954 and 1955. Here again the test authors come to the reader's rescue by pointing out that these results "should be interpreted with caution since the present forms of the test are not strictly parallel to the earlier forms."

Table 8 in the manual reports a correlation of .77 between total scores on Form B and the *Cooperative English Test* and a correlation of .78 between total scores on Form B and the *Cooperative Contemporary Affairs Test*. Although the part scores do not correlate this highly, one is a bit surprised to learn from the test authors that "the pattern of correlations obtained is what one would expect. None of the correlations is so high as to indicate that tests or parts of tests are measuring essentially the same thing." Validity is never established by the independence of tests, but some doubt is cast on the need for three tests when one correlates .77 and .78 with the other two.

Slightly more creditable data are provided in Table 10 which summarizes correlations with two-year college grade averages. Although the correlations range from .24 to .70, the average correlation is .57, suggesting that the total score on the test is substantially related to college grade averages.

The test authors claim that in Forms A and B "emphasis has been placed on the understanding of important basic concepts and the application of this understanding in the solution of specific problems," and, further, that "although they contain the same number of parts as their immediate predecessors (Forms XX and YY), they differ from them in that less emphasis is placed on knowledge of isolated subject matter."

This reviewer attempted to discern the truth of this claim that a hitherto immovable instrument had actually shifted toward covering some of the more complex learning outcomes by applying the classifications of the *Taxonomy of Educational Objectives* [1] to Form XX and Form

1 BLOOM, BENJAMIN S., Editor. *Taxonomy of Educational Objectives: Handbook 1, Cognitive Domain.* New York: Longmans, Green & Co., 1956. Pp. 207.

A with results as shown in Table 1. (Form B was not included since it is parallel to Form A.) Since the reviewer was also charged with the task of reviewing the Area Tests of the Graduate Records Examinations, these were also included in the analysis. Although a second judge might differ somewhat in his classification of these items, it is doubtful that the differences would be sufficiently great to make the comparison shift markedly.

Table 1

Percentage of Test Items in Each of the Major Categories of the *Taxonomy of Educational Objectives.*

	Cooperative General Culture Test		Graduate Record Examinations
Objectives	Form XX	Form A	The Area Tests
1.00 Knowledge			
1.10 Knowledge of specifics	92	76	26
1.20 Knowledge of ways and means of dealing with specifics	3	4	10
1.30 Knowledge of the universals and abstractions in a field	4	8	6
2.00 Comprehension	—	10	48
3.00 Application	1	2	7
4.00 Analysis	—	—	3
5.00 Synthesis	—	—	—
6.00 Evaluation	—	—	—
	100%	100%	100%

It is evident from this classification that Form A covers a greater range of educational objectives than Form XX. However, both tests still are most heavily weighted in knowledge, 99 per cent of the items in Form XX and 88 per cent of the items in Form A falling in this general category. That there is room for further development here is suggested by the fact that only 42 per cent of the items in the Area Tests fall in this category. In the more complex objectives, Form A appears to have a considerably larger proportion of items than does Form XX. However, this is somewhat deceptive, since two thirds of the items concerned with the more complex objectives are from a single section, the literature comprehension section, while the remaining one third is distributed over the social studies, science, mathematics, and fine arts sections. It is interesting to note that 48 per cent of the items in the Area Tests are classified as items testing comprehension.

There is little doubt that the *Cooperative General Culture Test* still represents an extensive sample of items testing knowledge which may be learned in the first two years of college or through extensive reading. If the educational objectives of a college include more than the acquisition of information, the *Cooperative*

General Culture Test can, therefore, serve only a limited purpose; the college must plan either to include other tests to sample its other objectives or to secure evidence in some other way than by testing. The fact that many colleges still find this test useful is attested by the list of 188 colleges which made use of it in the 1954 National College Sophomore Testing Program.

The test writers summarize the situation very well when they say that "proficiency in the basic academic areas includes more than can be measured by the *Cooperative General Culture Test* * Scores on these tests should be supplemented by information of other types if a more comprehensive evaluation of proficiency in an area is desired."

For a review by John V. McQuitty of Forms Y and XX, see 4:6; for reviews by Benjamin S. Bloom and H. T. Morse of Form W, see 3:4; for reviews by Lavone A. Hanna, Edward S. Jones, and Hilda Taba of Form P, see 40:1184; for a review by F. S. Beers of Form 1936, see 38:871.

[8]
★**Current Affairs: Every Pupil Scholarship Test.** High school; 1935–58; new form usually issued each January and April; norms available following testing program; no data on reliability; 4¢ per test; 4¢ per scoring key; postage extra; 40(45) minutes; Bureau of Educational Measurements. *

[9]
*****General Scholarship Test for High School Seniors.** Grade 12; 1930–58; new form usually issued each January; 6 scores: English, history, mathematics, science, reading-language, total; Form 2-58 ['58]; no manual; norms available following testing program; no data on reliability and validity; 10¢ per test; cash orders postpaid; 150(155) minutes; Ohio Scholarship Tests. *

For a review by C. C. Ross of the 1947 edition, see 3:14.

[10]
★**The Graduate Record Examinations: The Area Tests.** Sophomore year college through graduate school; 1954; available only in the Institutional Testing Program of the Graduate Record Examinations (see 601) ; 3 scores: social science, humanities, natural science; IBM; 225(255) minutes; Educational Testing Service. *

REFERENCE
1. LANNHOLM, GERALD V. "Development of a College-Level General Achievement Battery." *Yearb Nat Council Meas Used Ed* 12(pt 1):44–9 '55. *

BENJAMIN S. BLOOM, *University Examiner, The University of Chicago, Chicago, Illinois.*

The Area Tests of the Graduate Record Examinations represent one of the highest developments in the present art of achievement test construction. These tests give testimony to the skill with which modern test constructors are able to take a set of specifications of the educational objectives or outcomes of general education and translate them into examination questions which are valid and at the same time interesting and imaginative. The student taking these examinations should find the experience exciting whether or not he makes a high score. In some cases the examination experience should open to the student vistas which he did not perceive before. One might even expect some students, after taking the examinations, to elect courses, to do reading, and to seek learning experiences of which they were previously unaware or even disdainful.

The tests are noteworthy in that they present typical problems in the fields of social sciences, humanities, and natural sciences, and then pose questions which are natural and appropriate to these problems. The questions characteristically move from the simple to the complex, from the surface phenomena to the core or heart of the problem. The overworked metaphor "peeling an onion" is appropriate to describe the kind of thinking required from the immediately observable to deeper and deeper layers of the matter.

The descriptive material on the social science test claims that it attempts to appraise students with regard to such objectives as: understanding of fundamental terms and concepts; acquaintance with basic facts and trends; understanding of cause-and-effect relationships; ability to identify central issues and underlying assumptions; ability to recognize the adequacy of data; ability to draw warranted conclusions; ability to compare and contrast points of view; and ability to apply appropriate outside information. Surprisingly enough, the test questions do in fact sample these particular understandings and critical abilities as they relate to the subject matter of sociology, history, government, and economics.

The description of the humanities test claims that it places stress on such abilities as the following: to interpret verbal and other modes of expression and to compare texts; to recognize formal elements and their relationship; to recognize the function of a work of art; to recognize the nature, use, and importance of medium and technique; to recognize organizing principles in an art; to recognize characteristics in design and style of a historical period, a particular movement, or an artist; to understand relationships and aspects of similarity and difference in art forms; and to understand the bases on which critical judgments and ethical decisions are made. It should not surprise the reader by now to learn that the test lives up to its blurb and that it skillfully samples these abilities, as well as the student's basic knowledge in relation to literature, ethics, philosophy, painting, sculpture, architecture, music, and miscellaneous arts. In the humanities, especially, the testmaker has made use of excellent illustrative material. The painting used is a color reproduction, the work of sculpture is seen in four views so that the student can get some of the effects of the three-dimensional qualities of the statue, the architectural plan is seen from several different perspectives, and the music is presented in a descriptive passage and in musical notation form. One is certain that if the testers could have presented live or recorded music, they would have done so.

The natural science test is intended to sample the student's ability to understand and interpret basic principles and concepts; to recall, use, and interpret common symbols and terms; to identify the problem suggested by given evidence; to understand symbolic, graphic, and verbal presentation and be able to translate from one to another; to interpret data and judge its reliability; to identify the implications of changed conditions in a situation; to evaluate ways of verifying a hypothesis; to recognize the limitations of scientific procedures; to detect assumptions implicit in conclusions, courses of action, and the like; and to explain a phenomenon in terms of qualitative and quantitative principles. The test does in actuality sample these types of competence in relation to material drawn from the fields of physics, chemistry, biology, astronomy, and geology.

After writing what must to some readers appear to resemble the hyperbole of a Hollywood press agent extolling the merits of the most recent Grade B movie or the unusual characteristics of a new actress, this reviewer checked once again to determine whether he too had been guilty of exaggerated praise. The adjectives might be revised slightly, but the Area Tests do live up to their advanced billing.

The tests are so good that one wonders whether undergraduate education prepares students for the kinds of material and problems sampled by the tests. Some evidence bearing on this is available in the very extensive summary

statistics reported for the Graduate Record Examinations. The relationship between the Area Tests and appropriate parts of the Aptitude Test ranges from .61 to .76, suggesting that aptitude at present plays a very important role in determining test performance. It is also of interest to note that the correlations among the different parts of the Area Tests tend to be somewhat lower, averaging about .50. Thus, it would seem that for the particular college senior populations reported, the student with characteristically high scores on the three tests was in the minority as compared with seniors who had high scores in one of the Area Tests and moderate or low scores on another.

Another bit of evidence on this point is that college seniors who have majored in humanities or natural sciences, respectively, tend to make scores on the appropriate test which are 50 to 100 points (one-half to one standard deviation) above those of college seniors who have not majored in the relevant field. Incidentally, college seniors who have not majored in the field tested receive scores which are about the same as college sophomores. The exception to this is the social science test in which the college seniors are about 50 points (one-half standard deviation) above the college sophomores. What is being suggested here is that it may take some years before the colleges (at least those represented in the normative data reported) prepare their students to the level tested by the Area Tests.

If this critic is correct about the discrepancies between general education in American colleges and the Area Tests, it would seem desirable to organize the reporting of results so as to help the colleges appraise more precisely the results of the learning experiences. At the present time only total scores are reported, and students with identical scores may have quite different knowledge and skills. For example, of two students with the same score on the test in natural science, one may have made all of his score on the physical science items while the other may have made all of his score on the biological science items. Part scores would, of course, not have as high reliability as the present total scores but would offer ways of summarizing the 260 items so that the results would provide a basis for more detailed appraisals of growth in the broad outcomes of education in the liberal arts.

FREDERICK B. DAVIS, *Professor of Education, and Director, Educational Clinic, Hunter College, New York, New York; and Director, Test Research Service, Bronxville, New York.*

The Area Tests are designed "to assess the broad outcomes in education in the liberal arts from the [college] sophomore year through the first year of graduate study." Separate tests in social science, the humanities, and natural science are printed in a single booklet; mathematics is not covered. The social science test includes 110 items on terms, concepts, and interpretation of data. The humanities test comprises 75 items on philosophy, literature, music, painting, sculpture, and architecture. It requires more specific knowledge of facts than either of the other tests. The natural science test also consists of 75 items, covering the fields of biology, chemistry, physics, geology, and astronomy. Thirty of the items are essentially definitions of terms and thus test specific knowledge; the other 45 items accompany passages or tables.

Attempts to measure the outcomes of a liberal education in 3¾ hours of testing time are bound to seem presumptuous even if carried out with all possible skill. Granting this, the reviewer can consider whether the tests yield scores useful for less ambitious purposes. Each test measures a combination of factual knowledge and ability to interpret material in its own field. One cannot be sure, therefore, whether an examinee's performance is attributable mainly to the former or to the latter. Factual knowledge is more directly influenced by quality of teaching and diligence of application than is the ability to comprehend and interpret. Because of the ambiguous nature of the scores, their interpretation is difficult. Certainly they should be used with great caution for assigning grades to students, for evaluating teaching success, or for comparing curricula. Without doubt, the scores do indicate with serviceable accuracy the ability of a student to continue his education.

If comparisons are made of a given student's scaled scores (reported as 3-digit figures) in the three fields tested, differences among them should be interpreted only if they are larger than the following: Social Science versus Humanities, 72; Social Science versus Natural Science, 65; Humanities versus Natural Science, 75. Smaller differences should be regarded as chance fluctuations.

Many of the items are ingenious and well conceived. In the humanities test, photographs of a piece of sculpture, a painting, a building, and music scores serve as the bases for questions that add realism and interest. A topographical map is used to good effect in the social science test. Some items are unnecessarily wordy; this often seems to arise from an effort to make an item testing a simple association of names or terms look as though it tested an "application" or "general principle." A very few items appear to include more than one defensible answer or to have no reasonably adequate answer.

The level of difficulty of the social science and humanities tests seems good. On the natural science test about 10 per cent of both sophomores and seniors obtain scores no greater than chance would most likely provide; this test probably does not determine the rank order of the lowest 20 per cent of either of these groups (especially the women) with reasonable accuracy. The reviewer's impression that a large proportion of the items in the social science test depend on general information rather than on information specific to courses in the area is supported by the fact that, as a group, seniors majoring in the social sciences do slightly less well on the social science test than do seniors majoring in the other two areas. This fact may also indicate that students majoring in the humanities and in the natural sciences tend to be superior in general reading ability.

A special bulletin on the use of the Graduate Record Examinations by colleges and universities is interesting. Whether it is a good practice to publicize some of the ways in which the tests are used is a moot question.

For a review by Harold Seashore of the entire series, see 601.

[11]

The Gray-Votaw-Rogers General Achievement Tests. Grades 1–3, 4–6, 5–9, 7–9; 1934–51; IBM for grades 5–9; 4 forms; 2 editions; $1.50 per 100 profiles; cash orders postpaid; Hob Gray, David F. Votaw, and J. Lloyd Rogers; Steck Co. *
a) [COMPLETE EDITION.] Grades 1–3, 4–6, 7–9; 4 forms; 3 levels; manuals ('48); $3 per 25 tests; 25¢ per specimen set of any one level.
1) *Primary.* Grades 1–3; 6 scores: reading comprehension, reading vocabulary, spelling, arithmetic reasoning, arithmetic computation, total; Forms Q ('48), R ('48), S ('50), T ('50); (75) minutes, 35(55) minutes in 2 sessions.
2) *Intermediate.* Grades 4–6; 11 scores: same as Primary level plus elementary science, language, litera-

ture, social studies, health and safety; Forms Q
('48), R ('48), S ('50), T ('50); 120(150) minutes
in 4 sessions.

3) *Advanced*. Grades 7–9; 11 scores: same as Intermediate level; Forms Q ('48), R ('48), S ('50),
T ('50); 120(150) minutes in 2 sessions.

b) ABBREVIATED EDITION. Grades 5–9; 1939–51; 7
scores: elementary science, social studies, literature,
language, reading, arithmetic, total; IBM; Forms U,
V, W, X ('51); manual ('51); $2.50 per 25 tests;
separate answer sheets may be used; $1.25 per 50 hand
scoring answer sheets; $1.75 per 50 machine scoring
answer sheets; 15¢ per hand scoring stencil; 30¢ per
set of machine scoring stencils; 25¢ per specimen set;
68(80) minutes in 2 sessions.

REFERENCES

1. See 40:1187.
2–4. See 3:9.
5. FRUCHTER, BENJAMIN. "Orthogonal and Oblique Solutions
of a Battery of Aptitude, Achievement and Background Variables." *Ed & Psychol Meas* 12:20–38 sp '52. * (PA 27:6180)

WARREN G. FINDLEY, *Assistant Superintendent for Pupil Personnel Services, Atlanta Public Schools, Atlanta, Georgia.*

The *Gray-Votaw-Rogers General Achievement Tests* are the same measures that were so
thoroughly and competently analyzed by Anderhalter in *The Fourth Mental Measurements
Yearbook*. This reviewer would like especially
to direct the reader's attention to that review
so that he may dispense with unnecessary repetition of the detailed commentary, in which he
concurs. Certain major points will inevitably
be stated again in this review as part of a balanced and rounded treatment.

These tests, in their present form, have then
stood since 1948–51. Historically, their development can be traced from a 1935 offering of
the senior authors, which has been modified in
successive editions to the present coverage from
grades 1–9. The primary battery for grades
1–3, yields five part scores in reading comprehension, reading vocabulary, spelling, arithmetic
reasoning and arithmetic computation. Beginning at grade 4, five additional part scores may
be obtained for language, literature, social studies, science, and health and safety. The abbreviated edition for grades 5–9 omits spelling, and
health and safety, and telescopes the two separate arithmetic sections into one.

The present offering may be commended for
its clear format, including use of large type in
the primary battery. The questions are clearly
and unambiguously stated, a strength doubtless
enhanced by the extensive preliminary item
analyses. There is a balanced coverage of the
total curriculum, including health and safety.
A number of constructive features in the manual and accessory materials deserve mention.

The profile chart contains extra columns for
relating achievement to age and grade placement, use of which is explained in the manual.
The chart also bears on its face short vertical
lines indicating graphically the error of measurement in the various scores. The tone of recommendations and admonitions in the manual
on use of tests and test results is generally good.
The notion of norms for upper and lower
thirds of the modal grade populations is worth
pondering. Direct personal supervision of the
norming operations eliminates one source of
errors that might affect norms.

On the other hand, there would be general
agreement that the norms sample of 2,160 is
insufficient as described. The reliabilities of
the separate part scores are generally too low
to warrant evaluation of relative strengths and
weaknesses of individual children within a single grade. In general, the account of developmental and statistical procedures is so condensed as to be unclear. The manual might also
be expanded to keep pace with the demands of
modern test users for greater amplification of
ideas for use of tests and test results. Without
this the classroom teacher may well be unable
to relate the incomplete illustrations of possible
test uses in the manual to her previous training and experience in adapting teaching methods to pupil deficiencies. The statistical methods
proposed for analysis of group results, involving the standard deviation, are unnecessarily
complicated and will be applied by few without
the help of specialists. Although the tests will be
discussed subject by subject and level by level
later in this review, mention should be made
of the textbookish character of many questions
in science and social studies, where applications
of knowledge or cause-and-effect relations
might better have been tested. Finally, this battery stops with grade 9 with no indication of
the relation of the achievement on these tests to
further achievement in school. This is to be
accounted a limitation in view of the growing
pressure for continuous measurement of educational growth through secondary school and
junior college.

The tests will be quite universally criticized
for the inadequacy of the norms sample and its
description. Correspondence with one of the
senior authors evoked only reiteration of the
statements in the manual that Anderhalter
questioned. In a day when sampling procedures
have reached a high degree of refinement and

test publishers go to great lengths to obtain adequate samples of geographical regions, size of communities, and numbers of different schools and school systems, an undefined sample of 2,160 children must be deemed plainly inadequate for the standardization of a test battery over a range of nine grades. By good fortune, norms on such a sample might prove comparable to those based on more rigorous procedures, but the prospective new user cannot fairly be asked to assume that risk—a very real and serious risk of wrong administrative evaluation of a school population's achievement, or wrong placement of school children for instruction.

The manual and accessory materials are significant elements in any test offering. By what they claim and do not claim, the descriptions of technical procedures followed, and the quality of their recommendations and explanations of test use, they markedly enhance or limit the usefulness of the tests they accompany. The manuals and accessory materials of the Gray-Votaw-Rogers tests are good but scant, and frequently tax unduly the reader's sophistication in educational measurement. Scoring has been made direct and easy, but this reviewer would prefer to have scorers advised to count the number wrong and omitted as a check on the number right. Once the number right on a test has been established, the converted score is immediately determined and one may proceed directly to charting a pupil's achievement on a profile showing his achievement on comparable scales on all parts of the test. A clear illustration is given, but too briefly. Educational age and grade are calculated and shown to be 3 to 6 months above present placement. The proposal already made in the manual that a second set of lines in color be drawn to show class average achievement is not illustrated and no general evaluation of the pupil's achievement is expressed. Later, in another illustration achievement data for several children in a single class are interpreted and related to chronological age to suggest advancement to a higher grade for two in the class. This matter of adjustment of placement to achievement and age is gaining increased public attention and needs to be presented thoroughly. What of the child with high average achievement for his grade but specific weakness in, say, arithmetic? What is to be done in favored schools or school systems where most of the students in all grades

are above the national average and will go on to college? The authors may well prefer to leave this to local decision, but their proposals may receive greatest attention by new and relatively untrained test users. A full exploration and explanation is needed here.

Elsewhere in the manual clear concise statements are made on several points which trouble many test users. Cogent explanations are given of why per cent right cannot be taken as the basis for comparing scores, how widely high and low pupils in normal classes vary in achievement, how much to worry about practice effect when test forms are repeated, why language usage and arithmetic tests lend themselves better to diagnostic and remedial use than do tests in the other subjects. This reviewer would question the emphasis on answering all questions, regardless of whether one knows an answer, and not skipping. This is a perennial discussion point among test specialists. Most would favor a more elaborate instruction recommending that the pupil answer any question to which one answer seems best even if not sure, but to proceed without answering if he feels he has no basis for a decision. Insistence on not skipping can inhibit pupils who try to weigh fine points and do not feel free to proceed because of inability to give a sure answer to a particular question.

The emphasis on use of the standard deviation in describing group variation is unwarranted. The percentile system is increasingly well understood, and teachers can learn to use medians and quartiles effectively for the same purposes for which test specialists use means and standard deviations. Graphical aids are also important. The placing of vertical lines on charts to show probable errors of scores is a step in the right direction. In the next edition, it would be well to consider using a "score band," as is done in the *Sequential Tests of Educational Progress,* which is a range of scores that indicates, by overlapping or not overlapping a similar "band" in each other subject, whether or not the scores in the various subjects differ enough to be considered significantly different. It would help, too, if the lines on the chart showing grade norms were less prominent. They imply an evenness of growth in different areas which is unwarranted. Provision of a form or procedure for showing achievement year after year by the same pupil would do more to build use of the cumulative record approach than incidental recommendation of cumulative records in the manual.

The speededness of tests is a matter of considerable concern. As Anderhalter pointed out, the values of reliability coefficients calculated by the split-half method tend to be spuriously inflated if tests are speeded. This reflects itself in uncertainty as to whether children have done themselves full justice on a test because of the working rate they have adopted. Test builders now generally prefer tests to permit the great majority of pupils examined to finish in the time allowed. This is because *speed* in test performance is imperfectly correlated with *power* to handle progressively more advanced or more difficult material in the subject, which is the generally accepted goal of instruction in most subjects. We can only infer that time limits have been set with this goal in mind from the fact that the manual reports that two trial time limits were used in deriving the test norms. As an indirect measure of speededness this reviewer has sometimes applied the criterion that a test may be assumed to be speeded if median scores in the norms run below 50 per cent right —after allowing for average chance success— in the highest grade for which the test is offered. Application of this criterion would suggest that half of the tests are speeded, while medians of many others barely exceed 50 per cent right in the highest grade. In some cases, there is another possible explanation, but it is significant that spelling is the only test that is not indicated as speeded at any level and the spelling test is a dictation exercise in which all pupils get to answer all questions.

To measure satisfactorily the achievement of poor learners in a grade, chance scores achievable by random guessing need to yield grade equivalents well below the lowest grade for which the test is offered. The manual directs the examiner to stop pupils who thus mark their answers, but this is difficult to assure in crowded classrooms. The tests in this battery in arithmetic and spelling are generally free from this problem because answers must be written out and the chance number right is zero. At the primary level, the reading comprehension test yields chance scores for the end of both second and third grades that are less than a grade below the grade at which testing takes place. If testing is done early in these grades, the vocabulary test is also inadequate on this count. On the Intermediate Test, the chance score is at the fourth grade level in literature, and at the third grade level in all other tests except the two in arithmetic. On the Advanced Test, all the chance scores are one or more grades below the norm for beginning seventh grade. On the Abbreviated Edition, for grades 5–9, the chance scores are at fifth grade level in language and literature and at beginning fourth grade level or higher in all other tests. On this count, then, of measuring poor learners, only the Advanced Test, for grades 7–9, may be considered adequate. On the other tests, many poor learners can earn as good scores by random marking as by efforts to find and mark correct answers.

On the other hand, all the tests afford adequate scope for measurement of superior pupils. All the tests in the Primary Test provide a score margin of more than two grades beyond the end of grade 3, although those above 5.2 are extrapolated. The same may be said of all tests in the Intermediate Test, with the extrapolation beginning at 9.0. The Advanced Test and the Abbreviated Edition provide similarly adequate clearance at the top of the scales for all tests although grade equivalents for scores above 9.0 are extrapolated rather than established.

The commentary which follows is just one reviewer's evaluation of the test content. There is, however, no substitute for such evaluation. The content of a test is basic to its validity for any use. The reader is advised to make a similar appraisal by himself of this or any other achievement battery he may consider for use in his classes.

PRIMARY TEST. The several tests at this level have the merit of good content, presented in large type for clear perception. The reading passages are appropriate to this age child. The vocabulary test is well designed to measure understanding, in that each word is defined by a simpler synonym, by category, use, or association. The spelling words are appropriately simple and the arithmetic problems are real and comprehensible. This reviewer, however, is coming increasingly to question all arithmetic tests where reading and abstract symbolism are required at the primary level. It would seem preferable to lengthen the reading comprehension and vocabulary tests to make them adequately reliable and unspeeded, possibly omit spelling, and limit arithmetic testing to oral problems to be answered by marking out pictorial representations of answers. It would also seem essential to set the time limits for the reading comprehension test the same at all three grade levels. With greater time allowed for the silent reading exercises in grade 3 than in grade 2, as at present, a superior reader in grade 2 cannot achieve as high a score as an equally competent reader tested in grade 3.

INTERMEDIATE TEST. The reading comprehension, vocabulary, spelling, and arithmetic tests have the same virtues as their counterparts in the Primary Test. The language test employs simple 2-choice items appropriate to this level and the usages tested are fair and significant. The test on health and safety includes a worthwhile set of items with major emphasis on knowing what is best to do in described situations. The science test contains a strong factual emphasis, but the questions deal with pertinent knowledge. The social studies test comprises largely a miscellany of factual items and definitions. The literature test samples knowledge of books and stories that can best be evaluated by a committee of librarians and teachers. With the wide and free reading we encourage, a sufficient variety must be offered so that each child will have an opportunity to show the scope of his reading. The reviewer particularly questions the requirement that pupils respond to all questions on the literature test without skipping. Since most readers will have read less than half the books, chance marking will predominate and lead to dubious interpretations.

ADVANCED TEST. Much of what is said concerning the Intermediate Test also characterizes the Advanced Test. The reading comprehension test presents interesting and significant content, but there is a peculiar emphasis on material requiring quantitative reasoning. Most test specialists consider that emphasis should be carried almost wholly by the arithmetic tests. The vocabulary and spelling tests continue to carry a wholesome balance of well constructed items. The arithmetic tests offer advanced problems suitable for testing those able to apply their understandings at a high level. The language test appears inadequate: fully 70 per cent of the items are drawn from the Intermediate Test and seem to imply lack of growth in this area. The test might well have been broadened to cover felicity and effectiveness of expression, rather than mere correctness at the level used in the Intermediate Test. In many cases,

more than two choices might have been presented or the pupil might have been presented sentences with four places marked from which to choose which, if any, required a revision or correction. The health and safety test has a less satisfactory balance than the one in the Intermediate Test in that more questions have to do with factual content of uncertain value than with applications. The science test is dominated by questions requiring recognition of facts or definitions. A full 75 per cent of the questions are of this sort and few demand applications or cause-and-effect judgments. With the currently growing emphasis on science in elementary schools, this test may be said already not to be sufficiently advanced in emphasis. The social studies test suffers even more from an emphasis on encyclopedic knowledge without regard to application or cause-and-effect judgments. Hasty evaluation by this reviewer would classify 59 of the 66 items on one form of this test as matters of fact or terminology. The literature test samples reading more familiar to this reviewer than that sampled in the Intermediate Test but appropriately diverse to evaluate readers fairly broadly.

ABBREVIATED EDITION. This test may be said to share the virtues and limitations of the Advanced Test, just described. It is organized to yield subtotals for Knowledge Subjects and Tool Subjects, a helpful subgrouping for some purposes of comparison and emphasis.

SUMMARY. This test offering has many commendable features, but these might well be developed more fully. The manual might be expanded in two directions: (a) to present clearer evidence of details of standardization procedure, more adequate norms and reliability data, and (b) to spell out more fully the ways in which the test results may be used, and with less elaborate statistical techniques. The test questions are generally excellent and the curriculum coverage is comprehensive, yet balanced. The test on health and safety is a helpful element not present in a number of other achievement batteries. In the tests of science and social studies the emphasis on encyclopedic knowledge might well be replaced by more on applications and cause-and-effects relations.

DOUGLAS E. SCATES, *Professor of Education, University of Florida, Gainesville, Florida.*

These tests have gone through a number of stages, the present edition being the fourth.

Fairly conspicuous shortcomings of earlier editions, pointed out by reviewers, seem to have been taken care of. Anderhalter's systematic and discerning review of the present edition set forth a number of criticisms along with certain strengths. The present writer is in agreement with the points made by Anderhalter; they will not therefore be repeated here. The reader is referred to *The Fourth Mental Measurements Yearbook* (4:12) for their informative presentation.

There are, however, other perspectives from which tests such as these can be viewed. Accepting the various specific and more or less technical points previously indicated, we may look directly at the fundamental question: Do these tests call for and give evidence of the kind of education America aspires for its young people to have? By virtue of the complexity of life, a simple categorical answer will not be expected. We will need to bring in certain background by way of establishing a frame of reference for our judgment.

It was 40 years ago that a committee of the National Education Association published [1] its "Cardinal Principles" setting forth, for all levels of education, seven "main objectives." The present writer can well recall that when he first encountered these objectives he could not translate them into schoolroom terms: they were too foreign to anything he had ever known in public education. He is fully convinced, however, that during the intervening period many school teachers have succeeded in translating them and are actually teaching for the large purposes heralded by the unusual vision of that document. It seems fair to inquire: What, meanwhile, have testmakers been doing?

Midway along the span of intervening years, the distinguished historian and scholar, Charles A. Beard, was asked by the Educational Policies Commission to prepare a carefully considered, fundamental statement on the peculiar function of education in contemporary American democracy.[2] He wrote:

Effecting the promises of American democracy....involves the dissemination of knowledge, the liberation of the mind, the development of skills, the promotion of free inquiries, the encouragement of the creative or inventive spirit, and the establishment of wholesome attitudes toward order and change. [pp. 77–78] * Knowl-

edge alone does not present imperatives of conduct; nor kindle aspiration for the good life. * The selection of knowledge to be disseminated and emphasis placed on courses of study are ethical choices. [p. 81] * Public education is charged with....keeping alive the spirit necessary to the functioning of democracy. [p. 88] * Society is concerned with all of culture, with the moral code that holds its members together. * And upon education is laid an obligation to see that the youth of the land possess the cultural values which sustain society, hold the conflicts of politics and economy within bounds, and enrich life itself. [p. 95]

According to widespread testing practices, all that is necessary to guarantee the possession of this rich spectrum of human abilities, and to provide reassurances to serious minded adults who have the future at heart, is for the pupil to recognize that he is expected to move his pencil up and down a few times in the space (let us say) below the printed D rather than below A, or B, or C. Our test technology thus accomplishes the magnificent metamorphosis of living, pulsating objectives into objective objectives! If the richly complex sounds of a recorded symphony can be reproduced through a vibrating needle, would anyone try to deny that the destiny of a generation of young people can be revealed through the momentary flutter of a pencil point—a little to the right, or a little to the left?

Of course, nobody would use tests in this way; or at least that is what we are told. Well, *what else do they do?* When the master teacher has invested years of effort, rich resourcefulness, energy beyond measure, and hours of self-questioning and evaluation, all in the effort to see that education for his pupils, at least as far as his strength and skill will extend, "guards those virtues of the race that are vouchsafed to the humblest—industry, patience, self-denial, and consideration for others, and at the same time stimulates the more imperial gifts of imagination, originality, and invention by which the treasures of mankind are enlarged and enriched," [3] who will provide the test, or any "substitute" evaluation precedure, by which his teaching success is attested as convincingly and excitingly as when his pupils make a high score on a standard spelling test? Who will? When, in the story, the Little Red Hen asked "Who will?" the answer came in chorus, "Not I."

In our own day, four national groups [4] have cooperated in defining desirable educational

1 National Education Association, Commission on the Reorganization of Secondary Education. *Cardinal Principles of Secondary Education.* Bureau of Education, Bulletin 1918, No. 35. Washington, D.C.: Government Printing Office, 1918. Pp. 32.
2 Educational Policies Commission. *The Unique Function of Education in American Democracy.* Washington, D.C.: the Commission, 1937. Pp. 129.
3 *Ibid.,* p. 71.
4 Educational Testing Service, United States Office of Education, Department of Elementary School Principals, and the Russell Sage Foundation.

outcomes of elementary education.[5] "Why do we send our children to school? What do we expect them to learn?" The purpose was to produce a set of *practical* objectives, those which were *measurable*—for the project was initiated by a testmaking agency, and the contributors were instructed to "lay down useful guidelines for the building of tests."

It is interesting to note that this committee, charged specifically to prepare objectives for the use of testmakers, set forth its outcomes under four different categories: knowledge, abilities, attitudes, and utilization. The first category includes understanding. The second embraces a broad area: skill in all routine performances, problem solving, resourcefulness, critical mindedness, judgment. The third deals with aspects of affect: the interplay of "will" and emotion; interests, drives, wants, motives; attitudinal orientation; loyalties. The fourth concerns the integration and practical application of what one knows, or is able to manage in smaller units. What does he do when confronted with situations calling for decision and action? How does he interpret and respond to complex life situations?

We describe these four classes of outcome for any subject area to indicate their breadth—for even the first category goes well beyond the range of many (most?) available tests.

The categories representing substantive areas also are of broad compass. The social and emotional development of the individual is a separate, specific area for attention, coordinate with such usual areas as language and mathematics, and receiving, in turn, outcomes of the four classes indicated above. So also the following are treated as major areas of learning: ethical standards, values, and behavior; the individual in his face-to-face relations with others; esthetic development (both appreciation and expression). What we might ordinarily call "citizenship education" is here dealt with as four separate and distinct major areas.

Thus far, we have been developing background for our judgment. We find that the thinking of educational leaders in 1918, in 1937, and in our present postwar era emphasizes the same breadth, the same quality of educational responsibility, simply divided up differently into different lists of subcategories. If

further substantiation is needed, we may recall that Pestalozzi impressed on the scroll of history his convictions of education as being not mere lesson learning, but education of the head, the heart, and the hand. Our mind may journey further: Herbart, early last century, emphasized the importance of a variety of interests, and stated that education must take its orientation from the ethics of its society. We are intrigued by this continuing emphasis on the dynamic and the orienting. Our inquiring mind takes another leap; pushing back over two millenniums of tangled European struggle, we become aware that the ancient civilization of the Hebrews occupies a peculiarly prominent place in the pages of world history—far out of proportion to its size or military or economic importance. And we recall that its educational system was centered on religious law, ethics, and morals.

We look now at the tests before us—and wonder. Not that we would raise question concerning the technical competence with which the tests were put together. But we recognize that in those schools where these tests are used they will constitute the chief formal index of success in reaching educational objectives—in preparing the oncoming generation of Americans for their broad responsibilities as citizens. We review once again the formulations of objectives set forth by careful thinkers. We cannot help but pause. There is much to think about.

For a review by Oliver F. Anderhalter, see 4:12; for a review by Roland L. Beck of an earlier edition, see 3:9; for reviews by Joseph E. Moore and C. C. Ross, see 40:1187.

[12]
*Group Achievement Test: Dominion Tests, 1934 Edition. Grade 8; 1934–56; Forms A, B ('34); 2 parts; revised manual ('56); $1.45 per 25 tests; 20¢ per complete specimen set; postage extra; 76(85) minutes; Department of Educational Research, Ontario College of Education, University of Toronto; distributed by Guidance Centre. *
a) PART 1. 3 scores: spelling, language usage, paragraph reading; 33(45) minutes.
b) PART 2. 2 scores: arithmetic computation, arithmetic reasoning; 43(50) minutes.

[13]
★Group Achievement Tests: Niagara Edition: Dominion Tests. Grade 8; 1949–56; 2 forms; 5 tests; preliminary mimeographed battery manual ('50); experimental urban profile ('51); experimental rural profile ('51); 50¢ per specimen set of complete battery (must be purchased to get battery manual); postage extra; F. W. Minkler, C. Howitt, C. R. MacLeod, W. A. Marshall, M. F. Pummell, N. Wightman, and

5 KEARNEY, NOLAN C. *Elementary School Objectives: A Report Prepared for the Mid-Century Committee on Outcomes in Elementary Education.* New York: Russell Sage Foundation, 1953. Pp. 189. *

the Department of Educational Research, Ontario College of Education, University of Toronto; distributed by Guidance Centre. *

a) TEST 1, VOCABULARY. 1949–50; Forms A, B ('49); manual ('50); $1.10 per 25 tests; 20¢ per complete specimen set; 25(35) minutes.

b) TEST 2, DIAGNOSTIC PARAGRAPH COMPREHENSION. 1950; 4 scores: errors (general significance, detail, inference), achievement; Forms A, B ('50); $1.45 per 25 tests; 10¢ per manual ('50); 25¢ per complete specimen set; 30(40) minutes.

c) TEST 3, ENGLISH GRAMMAR. 1949–56; Forms A, B ('49); $1.10 per 25 tests; 10¢ per manual ('50); 20¢ per complete specimen set; 35(40) minutes.

d) TEST 4, SPELLING. 1950; Forms A, B; $1.10 per 25 tests; 10¢ per manual ('50); 20¢ per complete specimen set; (20–30) minutes.

e) TEST 5, ARITHMETIC COMPUTATION. 1950; Forms A, B; $1.45 per 25 tests; 20¢ per complete specimen set; 35(45) minutes.

[14]

★**High School Fundamentals Evaluation Test.** Grades 9–12; 1955–56; 6 scores: reading (vocabulary, comprehension), history and social studies, science, mathematics, total; IBM; Forms A, B ('55); manual ('55); record blank ('56); $3.50 per 25 tests; separate answer sheets may be used; $1.25 per 50 hand scoring answer sheets; 4¢ per IBM answer sheet; 15¢ per hand scoring key; 30¢ per machine scoring stencil; 25¢ per specimen set; cash orders postpaid; 120(180) minutes in 3 sessions; David F. Votaw; Steck Co. *

VICTOR H. NOLL, *Professor of Education, Michigan State University, East Lansing, Michigan.*

The battery under review is one of the most recent additions to the field of survey batteries for secondary grades. It includes tests on reading vocabulary, reading comprehension, history and social studies, science, and mathematics. The tests are printed in one booklet and are simple to administer and score. The format is attractive, the material is of good quality, and, in general, the makeup of the battery gives a favorable impression.

There are 290 items in the complete battery; all items are in multiple choice form, varying from 3-response to 5-response. The number of items right in each part is converted to a scale score ranging from 15 to 85, the basis for which is nowhere explained. The total score is the mean of the scale scores on the five parts. Norms for part and total scores are given in means and standard deviations for grades 9–12 inclusive; percentile norms by grades are provided for part but not for total scores. Norms are based on 1,013 cases from four high schools, only two of which are identified.

The author states that the tests were not planned as individual course tests but rather to measure the "accumulated 'capital' of fundamental knowledge and its applications that sur-

vive in high school students as a result of educational experiences." More specifically, he states the purposes of the battery to be the general achievement evaluation of the entire high school, discovery of "strong" and "weak" areas in the scholastic program, discovery of "strong" and "weak" areas in individual students, and location of gifted students.

These purposes seem quite modest and reasonable, as far as the subject matter of the test goes and insofar as a 2-hour battery can provide an overall measure of achievement of one to four years of work in high school. If the "strong" and "weak" areas are areas in fact, one cannot have a serious difference with this claim. It is to the author's credit that he does not make assertions regarding any diagnostic values of his tests, a claim often made to interest prospective users and one sometimes not justified by the facts.

The content of the battery was chosen from outlines submitted by "high school teachers who had been named by their supervisors as outstanding" and "high school textbooks in current use." Vocabulary test material was chosen "from literary, science, and social science books recommended for grades 9, 10, 11, and 12." Reading comprehension selections were chosen from original or noncurrent materials in an effort "to insure that no student would have encountered the materials previously." In the other three parts, the wide range of topics tested was chosen from textual materials, current literature, and everyday living.

It is claimed that in the mathematics test the elements of geometry and trigonometry included "are largely those that are brought into the students' useful control earlier than the time of formal courses in such subjects." This statement seems open to serious question. Examination of items in this part of the battery shows some which it is extremely doubtful that many students would know or learn before instruction. Examples are questions dealing with congruent triangles, logarithms, straight line equations, and the trigonometric functions of angles.

The science test is said to emphasize knowledge of science and ability to see simple applications of it. Most of the questions, however, seem not to deal with applications but with knowledge of facts, such as the direction of a compass needle, the number of legs an insect has, and the composition of meteors. There are actually few items in this part that seem to call for anything more than recall of rather specific information. To a lesser degree, the same may be said of the items in the test on history and social studies. Again, to cite a few examples, such factual information as the year the gold rush began, what pulls a jinricksha, the state in which the Twin Cities are located and the year the Panama Canal was completed is tested by the items in this part of the battery.

Items were retained if they discriminated positively between the upper 27 per cent and the lower 27 per cent of the tryout sample (no minimum discriminating index limit is mentioned), and if they showed increasing percentage of successful responses from grades 9–12. Experience has shown that if test items are chosen only on the basis of such statistical criteria, a preponderance of factual items often is the result. A few very easy items were retained even though these criteria were not met, but there is no indication that items were retained because they satisfied curricular criteria even though not necessarily meeting the statistical ones.

Taken altogether, the content of the last three tests in the battery is not distinguished and seems little above the level that could be found in many good locally made tests. The first two tests, Reading Vocabulary and Reading Comprehension, are probably the best in the battery. They appear to function best, also, as shown by correlations with grade-point average in the one sample of 138 high school students for whom data are reported.

Validity of the battery rests upon the curricular sources and correlations with grade-point average already mentioned. The statements concerning curricular bases for construction are so vague as to source, scope, and representativeness as to be of little use to the critical user. The correlation of grade-point average with score on Reading Vocabulary is .64; with Reading Comprehension, .73; with History and Social Studies, .42; with Science, .51; and with Mathematics, .58. The correlation between scores on the total battery and grade-point average is .81. These relationships are high as such correlations go. It is unfortunate that similar correlations upon larger and more representative samples are not available.

Reliabilities, given for each test by grade and for all grades combined, and for the total battery by grades, are in the form of corrected odd-even correlations. They range from a low of .61 for Reading Comprehension in grade 9 to a high of .96 for History and Social Studies in each of grades 10, 11, and 12. The reliabilities for total scores for each grade range from .88 to .95; and for all grades combined, from .84 to .97. All coefficients of internal consistency for total score in any grade or for any one test in all grades are .84 or above. For both forms of the test, the coefficient for total score for all grades combined is .96. With the exceptions noted, these reliabilities are very satisfactory.

As is true of any survey battery, this battery is limited in its usefulness by the wide range it attempts to cover. Inevitably in such a situation there must be many items, especially in the content areas of mathematics and science, that many 9th and 10th graders will have had little or no opportunity to learn. If they have had the opportunity, it must be largely a chance occurrence or the result of a special interest. On the other hand, much in such batteries must be "baby stuff" to a good 12th grader, to say nothing of a gifted one. This is not to imply that such batteries serve no useful function. They do, though perhaps a more limited one, in both range and level of content, than is often realized. Certainly, they cannot, as the author himself makes clear, take the place of tests in the separate subjects. They can only serve as a rather coarse screen for differentiating individuals in the secondary school program who differ in the grosser and more obvious ways from each other.

Although this battery has a number of good features, it would be much better if the author were more explicit as to the nature and scope of the source materials upon which it is based and the basis of selection and the nature of the normative population. It would also be better if they would use a larger and more representative population. There is room, too, for considerable improvement in the quality of the items with reference to the stated objective of testing ability to apply knowledge.

VERNER M. SIMS, *Professor of Psychology, University of Alabama, University, Alabama.*

Quoting its author, the *High School Fundamentals Evaluation Test* (FET) was "planned to measure the accumulated 'capital' of fundamental knowledge and its applications that survive in high school students as a result of educational experiences. * The very poor-scholarship students are separated one from another in order; individual students within the gifted group likewise are separated on the score scale." The test is recommended by the author for the following purposes: (a) general achievement evaluation of the entire high school, (b) discovery of "strong" and "weak" areas in the scholastic program, (c) discovery of "strong" and "weak" areas in individual students, and (d) location of gifted students.

This is a 2-hour test, possible of administration in three sittings, covering vocabulary, reading comprehension, history and social studies, science, and mathematics. It yields a total score and five subscores.

The content of the test gives the impression that its author conceives the function of the American high school to be that of teaching young people to read, to figure, and to remember a multiplicity of minutia from the sciences. On the surface, the reading tests (vocabulary and comprehension) would appear to be the best feature of FET, although the reading comprehension score is reported in the manual as the least reliable of the part scores. More than two thirds of the items on history and social studies are concerned with the names of people, places, dates, events, the definition of words, and the identification of specific functions of the several branches of our government. At least one third of the items in the science test are limited to the definition of technical terms. All of this would perhaps be helpful in selecting people for quiz programs; but the abilities to apply principles, to see relationships, causal and otherwise, and to interpret data of various sorts—abilities which some might consider important—are touched on lightly or not at all. Success in the mathematics test, in spite of the author's claim, appears to favor students who have studied formal algebra and geometry; and whether one likes it or not, there are in our public high schools today many who graduate without such ennobling experiences. Adding to these limitations a disregard of the humanities and the arts, one comes up with a doubtful measure of the "general achievement of the entire high school."

Data summarized in the manual indicate that considerable work went into the preparation of the test, but they are not too helpful in its evaluation. As evidence of "content validity"

the author states that the "valuable stockpile of material" from which the test was built came from "high school teachers [unidentified] who had been named by their supervisors [unidentified] as outstanding" and from "high school textbooks in current use" at places not named. As evidence of "concurrent validity" it is reported that in a Dallas, Texas, high school 12 of 13 gifted students identified by the tests were "confirmed as such by the faculty or personnel director" and "all gifted students indicated by the test in the smaller [unnamed] high schools were confirmed." In addition, for a San Marcus, Texas, high school relatively high correlations between grade-point average and scores on FET are given without any indication of the grade range of the students involved. Under the heading "Item Survival" we find that only items which favored the high 27 per cent over the low 27 per cent of groups (their size and nature not reported) and showed a "climb" through grades 9–12 were retained.

Coefficients of reliability for subtest and total scores are reported for both forms of the test. These were estimated by the split-half method for a population the size and nature of which again are not given. It presumably represented a range of four grades, however, since coefficients were also estimated from these estimates for the restricted range of each grade. If one can assume that the coefficients were obtained from an adequate sample, the total test appears to have satisfactory reliability for ordinary use, except perhaps in grade 9, where the estimated coefficient is only .88. The coefficients are not high, however, if one proposes to separate not only "poor-scholarship" but gifted students "one from another in order." In the 12th grade alone are the reported coefficients as high as .95.

Many of the subtests, particularly in the lower grades, yield estimated coefficients which appear to be too low for such a purpose as the "discovery of 'strong' and 'weak' areas in individual students." In grades 9 and 10, for instance, one half of the estimated coefficients are below .80 and only 5 of the 20 coefficients given for the two grades are above .90.

Raw scores on both the total test and the subtests are converted to equivalent scores, the kind not stated, but a guess would be that they are either linear or normalized transformations. Centile equivalents for these scores for each grade constitute what the author rather generously labels national norms since they are based on a sample of 1,013 students selected from four high schools, two from Texas and the other two not identified. The sample included students from the four grades, 9–12, the numbers per grade ranging from 160 in the 9th to 296 in the 12th.

All of the above may be interpreted to mean that in the reviewer's opinion if the author's goal was to develop an adequate measure of the fundamental learnings which "survive in high school students as a result of educational experiences," it was achieved in FET only in a limited way.

[15]

★High School Placement Test. Entering freshmen; 1955–58; various titles used by publisher; for Catholic schools; IBM; Forms A ('55), B ('58); $17.50 per 35 tests; 10¢ per IBM answer sheet; 40¢ per set of scoring stencils; 50¢ per specimen set; postage extra; Scholastic Testing Service, Inc. *
a) FORM A. 1955; Tests 1–6 identical with tests in the elementary level of the *Scholastic Mental Ability Tests;* separate answer sheets may be used; 1¢ per pupil record card; 114(135) minutes; Oliver F. Anderhalter, Ruth Colestock, and R. Stephen Gawkoski.
b) FORM B. 1958; distribution is restricted to colleges and universities; 8 scores: general ability, verbal ability, quantitative ability, arithmetic, mechanics of language, reading, religion, total; separate answer sheets must be used; no data on reliability and validity; no norms; 130(180) minutes.

WILLIAM C. COTTLE, *Professor of Education, The University of Kansas, Lawrence, Kansas.* [Review of Form A.]

These tests, intended for use with eighth graders entering Catholic high schools, require 114 minutes actual testing time. They cover mental ability, reading (vocabulary, comprehension, and rate), English, spelling, arithmetic reasoning, and religion. Raw scores are translated directly into percentiles based on 2,132 eighth grade students applying for admission to 17 Catholic high schools in the spring of 1955. There are no separate norms for each sex and there is no way to determine whether the normative group is representative of all students entering the approximately 2,000 Catholic high schools in the United States.

In addition to percentile scores, it is possible to translate the mental ability score into IQ or MA. Two small studies (n=282, n=266) show correlations of .77 and .82, respectively, between the mental ability test and the *Otis Quick-Scoring Mental Ability Test* and the *Terman-Mc-Nemar Test of Mental Ability.* This and the

content and construct validity evidence seem to indicate that the battery will be useful as a rough screening test for placing entering ninth graders. It will, however, need to be supplemented by at least an interest inventory, and more evidence of concurrent validity needs to be provided.

Reliabilities reported range from .93 for the mental ability test to .75 for the religion test. These split-half reliabilities may be low because of heterogeneity of items within a test or because of the brevity of a given test. Test time limits range from 26 minutes for mental ability to 8 minutes for spelling. The number of items per test ranges from 110 for mental ability to 35 for spelling, with the median at 55 items.

The tests are easy to administer and to score. There are hand scored and machine scored forms. Probably no one will need the hand scored form because the machine scoring stencils can be used more easily for hand scoring since the raw score is the number of right answers.

This battery offers promise for placing beginning students in Catholic high schools. It will need to be used with caution until further research substantiates validation data and until local norms are developed. It needs to be supplemented by an interest inventory, biographical data, and elementary school records.

ROBERT A. JONES, *Assistant Director, Testing Bureau, University of Southern California, Los Angeles, California.* [Review of Form A.]

Compiled from several existing tests of the publisher and restandardized as a battery, the *High School Placement Test,* Form A, yields seven scores derived from nine tests and a general mental ability score based on information from five tests. Although certain positive features indicative of sound workmanship are to be found in the format, content, and functional aspects of several of the items and in the clarity and detail of the directions for administration and scoring, unfortunately the marked limitations of the battery with respect to normative and validity data, the level of estimated reliabilities, and the inadequate control of the possible influence of certain types of response sets pose serious obstacles as to the overall utility of the instrument.

Particularly inadequate is the section of the manual concerned with normative samples, the data for which furnish no breakdown as to sex, no grade level equivalents, no mean scores for the various tests, and no rationale for the selection of the geographical areas utilized. Thus, on the general mental abilities portion, it would be of particular value in the interpretation of normative data, as well as validity characteristics, to be able to assess the contribution of each part to the total score through having the raw score means as well as the variances and the intercorrelations of the parts given.

Perhaps even more dissatisfying are the sections of the manual pertaining to validity and reliability. In addition to the previously mentioned lack of intercorrelations of various part scores, the evidence for predictive validity, although encouraging, is extremely limited, as indicated by the reporting of only three contingency coefficients relative to a sample of questionable representativeness. Although on a priori grounds the content of the various sections appears satisfactory to the reviewer, evidence relative to content validity should have been presented. Moreover, the data listed under concurrent validity actually seem to be more closely related to construct, or possibly, congruent validity (e.g., the correlation of scores on the examination with those of the *Terman-McNemar Test of Mental Ability*). Finally, whatever data might be available elsewhere as to the validity of the scale should have been included. Although the publishers are to be commended for presenting both split-half and alternate-form estimates of reliability of scores on all parts except religion (for which two forms were not available at the time of publication of the manual), the values, with the exception of the tests of mental ability and spelling, are too low to be considered acceptable.

Possibly influencing the estimates of reliability may be the presence of response sets associated with the frequency with which certain alternatives are keyed as being correct. For example, in Test 9, Punctuation, choice *d,* representing the need for no punctuation, is not used as the correct answer for any one of the 30 items. In contrast, for Test 13, Arithmetic Reasoning, alternative *e,* signifying the absence of a right answer in the other alternatives, is used as the correct response in 15 of 41 items. A highly inaccurate computer could conceivably receive credit for 15 correct items and place relatively high at the 60th centile.

Just as the test in arithmetic reasoning is much too difficult for the intended group, those on reading vocabulary and spelling, and possibly reading comprehension and religion, seem too easy for efficient discrimination between individuals. Disconcerting also is the fact that the reading rate score is based entirely on two self report facts that easily could be misstated deliberately.

In summary, since the information concerning norms, validity, and reliability for the test battery is considerably inferior to that provided for competing tests, and since the possibility exists for deleterious response sets, the reviewer would hesitate to make substantial use of the battery until further improvements are effected in its standardization and reported in a revised manual and until modifications are made in certain groups of items to minimize the possible operation of response sets.

[16]

★**Iowa Tests of Basic Skills.** Grades 3–9; 1955–56 15 scores: vocabulary, reading comprehension, language (5 scores), work-study skills (4 scores), arithmetic skills (3 scores), total; IBM; Forms I ('55), ('56); separate answer sheets must be used; 60¢ per test; $3 per 35 MRC answer sheets; 42¢ per set of MRC stencils; $5.40 per 35 sets of IBM answer sheets grades 3–5: $1.47 per set of IBM stencils; grades 6–9 $1.68 per set of IBM stencils; 42¢ per teacher's manual ('56); 75¢ per administrator's manual ('56); 42¢ per IBM manual ('56); 75¢ per 35 profiles ('55); 75¢ per 35 pupil report folders ('55); $3 per specimen set postage extra; 279(325) minutes in 4 sessions; under the direction of E. F. Lindquist and A. N. Hieronymus; Houghton Mifflin Co. *

VIRGIL E. HERRICK, *Professor of Education University of Wisconsin, Madison, Wisconsin*

The present edition of the *Iowa Tests of Basic Skills* represents a significant improvement in achievement test development. The two decades of test experience gained in the development of successive forms and editions of the old *Iowa Every-Pupil Tests of Basic Skills* is reflected in the quality of the curriculum research done, the adequacy of the technical validation of items, and the convenient easy-to-use format of this new edition. From the point of view of the reviewer, the present edition represents a distinct advance over the old editions.

These tests are devised to test functional skills of children in grades 3–9 in the areas of vocabulary, reading comprehension, language skills, work-study skills, and arithmetic. These areas and their subdivisions are common to every elementary school curriculum and represent important and common objectives of every elementary school teacher.

This test battery cannot be considered as an

achievement battery in the usual sense of measuring knowledge in the common content areas of the elementary school curriculum such as social studies, geography, science, and health. The focus of these tests is on the evaluation of the *generalized* intellectual skills and abilities involved in vocabulary, reading comprehension, language, work-study skills, and arithmetic, not on content achievement per se. The makers of the tests argue that the measurement of these basic intellectual skills is far more valuable for use in the improvement and individualization of instruction and educational guidance than is the assessment of the acquisition of specific information in school subjects. The reviewer agrees that such skills tests are more generally usable and that they cover common educational abilities important in most if not all of the curriculum areas of the elementary school. Devotion to common learning skills and abilities is a distinctive and valuable characteristic of the Iowa tests, with the exception of the arithmetic tests and perhaps the vocabulary test. To claim, however, that just because a test is primarily concerned with *abilities* and not with *content* it is automatically a better test for the individualization of instruction and for educational guidance is missing an essential point about instruction, namely, that proper individualized instruction and guidance requires good information on both abilities and content achievement and that tests in both of these areas are necessary to proper educational evaluation.

A second point should be made in all fairness to other general tests of achievement. No good test of achievement in subject areas like social studies, literature, science, or geography would necessarily limit its concern to the acquisition of specific information. Any adequate appraisal instrument in a content area would want to consider, in addition to the child's specific information, the breadth and depth of his knowledge and comprehension in the area and his competency in using related intellectual tools and skills. These new tests of the basic skills are open to the criticism of not paying enough attention to the appraisal of those intellectual processes and skills which are a part of the process of "knowing and comprehending" and those which are a part of any process of "critical thinking" or "scientific method." A third common intellectual ability not considered in these tests lies in the area of "creative thinking"—"imagination" or "creativity." A final question

might be raised in respect to the limitation of the language skills tests to vocabulary, reading comprehension, spelling, capitalization, punctuation, and usage. There are other language skills involved in writing, speaking, and listening which are basic to learning but which are not included in the present test battery.

The reviewer grants the difficulty of devising adequate tests in the above areas of generalized intellectual skills. He wishes, however, to underscore the need for the rapid expansion of tests into additional areas of the intellectual skills, the need for more adequate tests of knowledge and comprehension in content areas, and the need for using *both* kinds of tests for individualization and guidance. This discussion does not, however, ignore the point frequently made by the authors of the Iowa tests that more adequate achievement tests and norms need to be devised by the staffs and resources of local school systems. The variations in the instructional programs of individual school systems make satisfactory generalized achievement tests difficult if not impossible to devise and validate.

The organization of the *Iowa Tests of Basic Skills,* while providing a single test booklet for all skill areas and for all grades, is around one continuous test in each area for all grades. Children in a specific grade begin and stop at different points in this continuous test. Curriculumwise, this feature of the tests makes excellent sense. It emphasizes the universality of the key skill objectives and the importance of continuity in measurement of their development. This procedure, however, creates some difficulties in the giving of instructions to enable the child to use such a comprehensive and complex test booklet, and in making sure that answer forms and procedures are appropriately related to the proper test item. For children in the lower grades, the instructions for writing one's name on the test form in an IBM code may be more difficult than the test itself.

Because of the length of the tests, one would expect the reliability coefficients to be high and they are. They range from .84 to .96 for the major tests and from .70 to .93 for the subtests. The composite reliabilities for the whole test range from .97 to .98 for the different grades. These correlations are sufficiently high for individual diagnosis and prediction. These data were derived from scores obtained at the beginning of the school year. One would expect that coefficients obtained from midyear and end-of-year testings would be even higher.

Intercorrelations among the various subtests range from .37 to .83, with the average ranging from .60 to .70. As one would expect, the tests of vocabulary and reading comprehension have the highest intercorrelation with all other subtests, indicating a heavy loading of all subtests with vocabulary and reading skills. This suggests that a factor analysis of these data would reveal that 2 to 3 skills are really being tested rather than 5 to 11. The intercorrelations suggest further that not much would be left after the effect of the vocabulary and reading skills was removed.

A major strength of this new battery is its curricular validation. Besides the usual widespread administration of sample test items and the establishment of discrimination and difficulty indexes, extremely careful identification and definition of the skill processes being tested was done before test items were devised. This aspect of test development is not usually undertaken with such care, and the authors are to be commended for the way the curricular validation of their test items was done. School staffs attempting to improve their curriculum in the skill areas could use with profit the definitions of the skill objectives developed by the Iowa staff. These curricular analyses are found in the Teacher's Manual and form a basis for helping teachers plan remedial or corrective instruction following evaluation. Here each basic skill is analyzed, the test items related to it identified, and corresponding teaching suggestions made.

Two types of norms are provided: grade norms and percentile norms within grade. Pupil profile charts are provided for each child in order that growth in skills can be plotted. While these performance profiles can be very useful, few teachers are able to interpret them. Too often simple straight line assumptions are made about growth and fallacious conclusions are drawn about low points or high points on the curve and what these mean for instruction. This, however, is a problem confronting all test profiles and is not limited to the Iowa tests and their procedures.

One valuable aspect of the norms is their development for beginning-of-year, middle-of-year, and end-of-year performance. Thus the teacher may use them with confidence at these different periods of the school year to interpret her test findings. The authors are very wise in separating the norms for school averages from those for individual pupils. These norms provide different levels of information and cannot be used for the same purpose. It is very easy to mix them up.

In previous editions, the local character of the Iowa test populations—Iowa school children—was criticized. It is claimed that the sample used with this edition was drawn from the *total sample* of all public school children in the United States in grades 3 through 9. Every effort was made to get a representative sample of this population; there is every assurance that those responsible for this test battery have achieved this goal as well as any test group in America. This comprehensive population base increases the users' confidence in the standardization of test items, the stability and representativeness of the norms, and the comparability of the two forms of the test.

The vocabulary test is placed first in the battery in order to start the child with a test which is easy to take from the standpoint of mechanics and which is not directly related to specific instruction. The stimulus words are selected from the Thorndike and Rinsland lists, as are the words in most other vocabulary achievement tests. About equal attention is paid to nouns, verbs, and adjectives. This weighting corresponds to what we know about vocabulary growth in young children. A total of 114 words is used to cover the vocabulary knowledge of children in grades 3–9: 31 words for grade 3, 37 for grade 4, 42 for grade 5, 4[5?] for grade 6, 47 for grade 7, and 47 for grades 8 and 9. While limited, this sample still is more adequate than that employed in many similar tests. The authors defend their sampling by claiming that the understanding of all of the four response words is being checked at the same time, thus making a total of around 200 words actually being tested for each child. This test has been criticized because the response words are sometimes more difficult than the word whose meaning is being tested. The authors claim that this is not important. There i[s] some logic in their argument, but the reviewe[r] still feels that this characteristic does not improve the quality of the test.

The most important criticism in regard to th[e] testing of vocabulary is that major attention [is] paid to understanding the meanings of word[s] while little attention is given to the evaluatio[n] of tools involved in word recognition and verification. This battery purports to test "basic skills" and not meaning or content aspects of the child's development. Yet, in the area of vocabulary development, it is more of a test of experiential background or intelligence than basic skills.

The test of reading comprehension is designed to evaluate the specific comprehension skills involved in grasping details and purpose, analyzing organization, and evaluating a reading selection. This test covers 19 pages in the test booklet, each grade covering from 7 to 9 reading selections and 59 to 98 exercises. The reading selections, while mostly narrative, include poetry selections in grades 3, 4, 5, and 6. Most of the items for grades 3, 4, and 5 deal with comprehension of details; the test section for 6, 7, 8, and 9 includes increasing numbers of purpose, organization, and evaluation items. One question which might be considered is why better balance in the different types of comprehension items is not maintained at all grade levels. Certainly in grades 3–5, children should be able to recognize purpose and organization in a reading selection and to evaluate what they read. In defense of the large number of items dealing with details, it should be said that most such items go beyond recognition of facts to understanding and drawing inferences from the reading selections.

The language skills tests cover the four areas of spelling, capitalization, punctuation, and usage. While the authors recognize the value of the unitary test to appraise these aspects of language skills, they claim that no one test could pay adequate attention to all aspects of these four skills. The basic type of item used is the "find the error" question. While this item type has high reliability and permits the presentation of a large number of choice situations, it tends to emphasize the editorial aspect of language use and not the dynamic, functional, creative aspect which exists when one writes.

All of the language subtests are well constructed. Their content has been carefully checked against the available research studies and leading language arts texts. The important aspects of each area are covered by appropriate test items; one can only question whether sufficient attention is paid to certain common and persistently used language skills. At present, however, there is little research available

which would be of much help in making this judgement.

The section on work-study skills is unique in that it attempts measurement in a skill area not taught formally as a subject in elementary schools. These tests are designed to evaluate the child's ability to use graphic materials, reference materials, tables, and maps. These, unfortunately, are materials which are inadequately dealt with in many school programs. They will, therefore, present special difficulties to children whose school curriculum is thus impoverished. The map tests tend to become complicated and confusing, although a real attempt has been made to improve these materials in the new forms. The test on reference materials is adequate but not as distinctive as the other two tests in this area.

The arithmetic section is divided into two parts—arithmetic concepts and problem solving. The subtest on concepts, while making adequate use of common number situations to present key concepts of arithmetic, deals more with the content of arithmetic than with intellectual skills. The problem solving subtest gets closer to the major purpose of the test battery. However, no attempt is made to cover the common computational aspects of arithmetic; one should not attempt to use the arithmetic tests for assessment in this area. Again, this test will be found difficult by children in schools where routine computational skills are emphasized at the expense of understanding. The problem situations in the problem solving subtest are heavily loaded in the direction of situations which involve money. While it is true that most of the situations in which children use arithmetic skills involve the cost of objects and the purchase of materials, the reviewer wonders if it is necessary to use the proportion of problems of this kind to cover adequately the key problem solving skills in arithmetic.

The current edition of the *Iowa Tests of Basic Skills* represents a real improvement over past editions. While the bulky test booklets may prove cumbersome and complex for young children to handle and use, the advantages of economy and flexibility may outweigh these disadvantages. The real strength of the tests is in their curricular validity, careful construction, provision of adequate norms based on a national sample, and high reliabilities. The manuals provide the teacher with excellent help in using test results to improve instruction. These advantages outweigh the disadvantages of length and time necessary for administration. The tests, for their purposes, are among the best available at this time.

G. A. V. MORGAN, *Senior Psychologist, North Wales Child Guidance Clinics, Denbighshire, Wales.*

The first impression made on a British reviewer by the *Iowa Tests of Basic Skills* is of the extensive research and tremendous technical experience and expertness which have gone into their construction. He tends to feel that by comparison he is in the paleotechnic era of test construction. Later he begins to wonder if too high a price is paid for technical excellence.

The *Iowa Tests of Basic Skills* battery is a development of the well known *Iowa Every-Pupil Tests of Basic Skills,* but with significant improvements. Instead of coming in two forms, elementary and advanced, the present tests are "multi-level." One continuous, homogeneous test for each skill is divided into overlapping segments, each segment forming the appropriate test for one of the grade levels from grade 3 to grade 9. This has the marked advantage of providing each grade with a test correctly pitched in difficulty and discriminating power, as modern test theory would require, whilst allowing the overlap necessary to take up the full spread of scores and permit the anchoring of each set of grade norms to the common scale.

Another useful result is that all tests are now compactly assembled in a single booklet, one for each of the two forms of the battery. These reusable booklets should be very convenient and economical. The same testing time is needed on each test regardless of grade, which means that several different age groups can be tested simultaneously. All test materials and manuals are soundly and attractively turned out, and it is an excellent idea to have separate manuals for teachers and administrators. One would suggest that the covers of the booklets might with advantage be made sturdier and possibly protected with plastic material.

Responses to items are marked only on a separate answer sheet (or sheets) which can be hand or machine scored. An apparently comprehensive electronic scoring and reporting service is offered which should remove all labour from large scale testing. An excellent feature of the hand scoring procedure is that one scoring mask serves for each grade, with conversion tables printed on each mask to minimize clerical errors in scoring.

The Iowa tests are "evaluative," that is, defined as measuring generalised educational skills over a wide range of ability rather than mastery of specific facts or topics. The tests measure generalised skills because they must be applicable in schools with widely varying curricula. They cover the basic subjects which are educationally the most important. The reviewer agrees, from his own experience, that this is the correct approach for a wide-range test of attainment. The skills covered are: vocabulary, reading, language, work-study skills, and arithmetic.

Reading is based on comprehension of paragraphs. The test very commendably emphasizes reading for meaning and aims at covering several aspects of comprehension—the main ones described being reminiscent of I. A. Richards' subdivision of meaning into sense, feeling, tone, and intention. Functionally, however, the items appear to measure the main components of comprehension: vocabulary and verbal inference. The total score probably represents level of comprehension, with an element of speed.

Language skills are, rather curiously, limited to spelling, capitalization, punctuation, and usage. The "find-the-error" item type (detecting the one error or the lack of error among a number of choices) is used throughout. This type seems much nearer the real life situation than the usual multiple choice item offering the correct choice among errors. Even so, the demands of item form seem, to a British reviewer, to restrict considerably the flexibility and range of a language attainment test. The language section also appears to be overweighted with capitalization and punctuation. The capitalization subtest seems repetitive and the punctuation subtest at times appears to rely on rather mechanical, "textbook" detail. The reviewer is not convinced that, useful as they are, these subtests fully measure the control of expression and sense of sentence structure which punctuation exists to serve.

The usage test (grammatical errors in single words) also appears limited in range and sometimes rather "textbookish" in character. What is lacking is some assessment of expression and control of coherent language such as has been developed in semi-objective form (see 187 and 193 for examples) by workers in the United Kingdom, the present writer among them, in response to educational criticisms of standardized tests. The language section is the most open to the criticism that it might encourage a restricted approach in teaching and seems to sacrifice the most to the demands of objective form and rapid scoring.

Nevertheless, experience suggests that, together with reading comprehension and vocabulary, the language tests should form a composite yielding a reasonable measure of language attainment.

The inclusion of work-study skills—map reading, reading graphs and tables, and use of reference materials—is most commendable. These skills are indeed relevant to basic educational aims in modern society. Explicit teaching of these skills is certainly neglected in Britain and tends to be, it seems, in the United States. Minor criticisms are that maps appear at times overcrowded with detail, that some items requiring the interpretation of several maps simultaneously may be ambiguous, and that some complex items for advanced grades may depend more on inference and juggling of item alternatives than on grasp of concepts underlying attainment in geography or social studies.

An excellent feature of the arithmetic section is the subtest on arithmetic concepts. This is intended to assess the knowledge of fundamental relationships and experiences in number which form the basis of the modern approach to arithmetic. A wide range of mathematical experiences is very ingeniously tested. Computation is encountered in meaningful form in the problems subtest, although one gets the impression that the range of topics in this subtest is rather narrow, with an undue emphasis on money at the expense of items on capacity, weight, and measures. Mechanical computation is correctly excluded because of difficulties in testing this adequately over a wide age range and in order to discourage rote number routine and drilling in computation. A drawback of the arithmetic section, however, is the considerable verbal content. This may penalise pupils who have a good grasp of arithmetic, as shown in computation and oral work, but who are specifically backward in reading.

One unintended consequence of the need for separate answer sheets and fairly elaborate instructions may well be the introduction into the test of a factor of test-comprehension or clerical ability, such as Vernon [1] found in his researches

on selection for the British Armed Forces. This may prevent the dull and backward pupil from registering on the test. Similarly, because of the verbal bias of the tests and the response set to item form and answer sheet, one might expect the test-form factors which are only partly relevant to the main aim of the test.

As a composite, the tests measure basic general educational attainment—the British psychologist's "verbal-educational" factor. Inspection of the inter-test correlations available suggests a general factor heavily loaded on vocabulary, with possibly small group factors, e.g., clerical-mechanical English in the punctuation and capitalization subtests, numerical ability in the arithmetic skills test, and map and graph skills in work-study skills test. The high inter-test correlations resulting from the verbal-educational and formal factors would militate against differential use of subtests.

Technically, the tests are beyond criticism. Items selected from three times as many tryout items were carefully edited for educational and statistical acceptability. Standardization of the test is excellent. It is based on a sample as near as humanly obtainable to a true random sample of United States schools (74,000 pupils in 213 school systems) and merits the claim that it is nationwide.

The use of grade-equivalent scores seems strange to a British reviewer used to age norms and standard scores, but this procedure is the best adapted to American educational practice. Ingenious scaling allows any score to be meaningfully interpreted in terms of a common scale of grade-equivalents ranging from grades 3 to 9. The system of norms is simple and effective, the first digit in each score representing grade level and the second the month of school year in that grade. Individual percentile norms for each grade record relative status within the grade. Percentiles for school means should also be very useful for comparative purposes. Nevertheless, it is difficult to see how grade norms can be related to age norm standard scores on ability tests.

Reliability coefficients seem very satisfactory in relation to the length of the tests—though those quoted are split-half estimates, and test-retest measures might run lower. Some subtests have reliabilities so near their correlations with other tests that score differences between them would need to be large to be reliable. Correla-

1 Vernon, Philip E. *The Structure of Human Abilities.* London: Methuen & Co. Ltd., 1950. Pp. xii, 160.

tion between the two forms of the test is not explicitly reported, but it should be high.

An excellent feature of the teachers' manual is the analysis and tabulation of educational aims or functions of test areas and even of individual items. Nevertheless, it should be borne in mind that this is a test of general attainment. Broad skill areas and individual subtests can be compared within limits of the reliability of differences between scores, but care is required in using single items or groups of items for diagnostic purposes.

It seems a pity that standard errors for varying score levels are not quoted, as they were for the older Iowa tests.

Predictive validity is not quoted, but is claimed to be as much as for the older Iowa tests, which were very adequate for prediction of status in high school and first year university courses.

The Iowa tests are very well constructed and standardized, with an excellent background in fundamental research and understanding of educational aims. The language tests tend to lack width and imagination; too high a price may have been paid here for the advantages of technical efficiency in objective response form and rapid scoring. Nevertheless, the reviewer would strongly recommend the tests as a whole as the best of their kind and a model of test construction. One wishes that a similar comprehensive battery were available to psychologists and teachers in Britain.

H. H. REMMERS, *Professor of Psychology and Education, Purdue University, Lafayette, Indiana.*

No battery of achievement tests intended for civilian uses has been constructed with greater technical sophistication, greater adequacy of statistical base, and greater use of previous research.

Validation is based on "all the commonly used principles" of validation of test content, curricular and statistical. Reliability was sought by making each test "long enough to provide a *sound* basis for drawing inferences about individual pupils, without regard to the consequent length of the complete battery," a criterion which has worked out, on the average, to 25 minutes per test, with a range of from 17 minutes for vocabulary to 80 minutes for workstudy skills.

Within-grade split-half reliability coefficients for the total battery scores, each based on 500 cases, are reported as .97 for grade 3 and .98 for all other grades. Subtest reliabilities are generally in the .80's. The manual gives an excellent brief discussion of reliability and especially of the standard error of measurement.

The massive norms population—11,000 to 13,000 per grade—was intended to constitute a stratified random sample of communities in eight geographical regions. The only large deviations from census data are shortages of rural children in the east north central region and of children from south central urban communities of 100,000 and over. The latter deficit, particularly, may possibly have depressed the norms a bit, since this deficit is a total one. No south central community of 100,000 or over is included and it is in this size community that educational quality is likely at a maximum for the region.

On the horns of the dilemma of grade norms versus age norms, the authors chose grade norms. Their rationale ("By so doing, we make the comparison of local achievement to national achievement one in which the crucial element—length of time pupils are available for systematic instruction—is held constant.") arouses doubts, unless "available" is used in a Pickwickian sense. The realities of, say, a Mississippi cotton belt school and one in Evanston, Illinois, make equation of grades in this sense a more than dubious semantic hazard. Modal-age grade norms, such as used in the *Stanford Achievement Test,* seem preferable.

This stricture, however, is at least somewhat compensated for by the scaling method used, that is, the equi-percentile definition of equivalent performance, using an "anchor" or "linking" test as the basis for scaling. Thus a pupil's achievement can be related to grades above and below his grade status.

Anyone familiar with group "intelligence" tests will know that their content and the present battery have very much in common. It would be interesting to obtain the correlation between the two. It would likely be close to the geometric mean of the reliabilities involved.

This characteristic of the battery is desirable since it is related to some of the mythology surrounding the IQ in the minds of too many teachers. Quite obviously, the content of this battery is *taught* and *learned,* not something "in the genes." Thus there will be few preconceptions that "native ability" is being measured by these

Urban Community: A First Approximation to the Measurement of Socio-Economic Status." *J Ed Psychol* 19:99–111 F '28. * (*PA* 2:1927)

2. CHAPIN, F. STUART. "Socio-Economic Status: Some Preliminary Results of Measurement." *Am J Sociol* 37:581–7 Ja '32. * (*PA* 6:1124)

3. CHAPIN, F. STUART. *Measurement of Social Status by the Use of the Social Status Scale, 1933.* Minneapolis, Minn.: University of Minnesota Press, 1933. Pp. 16.

4. DICKENS, DOROTHY. "Living Rooms of Low-Income Farm Families of Mississippi." *J Home Econ* 29:702–9 D '37. *

5. GUTTMAN, LOUIS. "A Revision of Chapin's Social Status Scale." *Am Sociol R* 7:362–9 Je '42. *

6. LUNDBERG, GEORGE A., AND FRIEDMAN, PEARL. "A Comparison of Three Measures of Socioeconomic Status." Discussion by Genevieve Knupfer and Robert K. Merton. *Rural Sociol* 8:227–42 S '43. * (*PA* 18:539)

7. GORDON, MILTON M. "The Logic of Socio-Economic Status Scales." *Sociometry* 15:342–53 Ag–N '52. * (*PA* 27:7136)

TESTING PROGRAMS

[599]

*College Entrance Examination Board Admissions Testing Program. Candidates for college entrance; students in grades 10–11 may take examinations, for practice and information, as "preliminary candidates"; 1901–58; tests administered at centers established by the publisher; IBM; examination fees: $7 for morning session (*Scholastic Aptitude Test*), $9 for afternoon session (achievement tests), $16 for both morning and afternoon sessions; fees include the reporting of scores to 3 schools designated at time of application; $1 per additional report; program administered by Educational Testing Service for the College Entrance Examination Board. * See separate test entries referred to below for additional information, references, and reviews.

a) SCHOLASTIC APTITUDE TEST. See 318; 1926–58; tests administered 6 times annually (Ja, F, Mr, My, Ag, D); 2 scores: verbal, mathematical; Form FSA3 ['57] used in March testing program; test analysis booklet ('57); descriptive booklet ('56); 180(240) minutes.

b) ACHIEVEMENT TESTS. 1901–58; tests administered 4 times annually (Mr, My, Ag, D); candidates elect 1–3 tests as specified by individual college requirements; 13 tests: Biology (see 723), Chemistry (see 742), English Composition (see 204), French (see 263), German (see 272), Greek (see 277), Italian (see 279), Latin (see 280), Intermediate Mathematics (see 418), Advanced Mathematics (see 417), Physics (see 749), Social Studies (see 786), Spanish (see 287); test analysis booklet ('57); descriptive booklet ('56); 60(80) minutes per test.

REFERENCES

1–9. See 4:526.

10. DYER, HENRY S. *College Board Scores.* New York: College Entrance Examination Board [1953]. Pp. xxiii, 70. * (*PA* 28:4936)

11. DYER, HENRY S., AND KING, RICHARD G. *College Board Scores: Their Use and Interpretation, No. 2.* New York: College Entrance Examination Board, 1955. Pp. viii, 192. * (*PA* 30:1616)

12. FISHMAN, JOSHUA A. *1957 Supplement to College Board Scores No. 2.* New York: College Entrance Examination Board, 1957. Pp. vi, 206. *

For reviews of individual tests, see 272, 277, 280, 318, 418, 725, 742, 749, 4:178, 4:237, and 4:367.

[600]

★College Entrance Examination Board Advanced Placement Examinations. High school seniors desiring credit for college level courses; 1954–58; tests administered annually in May at centers established by the publisher; IBM in part; 12 tests: English Composition (see 205), Literature (see 211),

American History (see 812), European History (see 813), French (see 264), German (see 273), Latin (see 281), Spanish (see 288), Mathematics (see 419), Biology (see 726), Chemistry (see 743), Physics (see 750); supervisor's manual ('58); examination fee for 1 or more tests, $10; fee includes reporting scores to college which candidate plans to attend; test booklets sent to college; 180(200) minutes; program administered by Educational Testing Service for the College Entrance Examination Board. * See separate test entries referred to above for additional information, references, and reviews.

For reviews of individual tests, see 205, 211, 273, 419, 726, 743, 750, and 812.

[601]

*The Graduate Record Examinations. College through graduate school; 1937–58; IBM; 2 programs; Educational Testing Service. * See separate test entries referred to below for additional information, references, and reviews.

a) NATIONAL PROGRAM FOR GRADUATE SCHOOL SELECTION. Graduate school entrants; 1942–58; tests administered 4 times annually (November, January, April, July) at centers established by the publisher; supervisor's manual ['58]; examination fees: $8 for morning session (Aptitude Test), $9 for afternoon session (Advanced Tests), $14 for both morning and afternoon sessions; fees include reporting of scores to 3 schools designated at time of application; $1 per additional report; postpaid.

1) *Aptitude Test.* See 336; 1949–58; 2 scores: verbal, quantitative; 150(170) minutes.

2) *Advanced Tests.* 1939–58; candidates elect 1 test as specified by individual college requirements; 16 tests: Biology (see 727), Chemistry (see 746), Economics (see 800), Education (see 537), Engineering (see 923), French (see 270), Geology (see 748), Government (see 835), History (see 818), Literature (see 215), Mathematics (see 427), Philosophy (see 581), Physics (see 754), Psychology (see 583), Sociology (see 842), Spanish (see 289); 180(200) minutes per test.

b) INSTITUTIONAL TESTING PROGRAM. College and graduate school; 1937–58; tests available for institutional testing at any time except during weeks National Program for Graduate School Selection is scheduled; institution must agree to test all students in at least one administration group; 3 parts; $3 per any 1 test (Area Tests, Aptitude Test, an Advanced Test); $5 per any 2 tests; $7 per any 3 tests; postage extra; fees include scoring service; administration must be completed within 1 week.

1) *The Area Tests.* See 10; 1954; 3 scores: social science, humanities, natural science; 225(255) minutes.

2) *Aptitude Test.* See *a*1 above.

3) *Advanced Tests.* Same as *a*2 above plus Music (see 247), Scholastic Philosophy (see 4:506), Speech (see 220); 105(125) minutes.

REFERENCES

1–24. See 4:527.

25. VAUGHN, K. W. "The Graduate Record Examination as an Aid in the Selection of Medical Students." *J Assn Am Med Col* 21:129–46 My '46. * (*PA* 21:296)

26. ABERNETHY, JULIUS. *A Study of Undergraduate and Graduate Records and Corresponding Graduate Record Examination Scores of 537 University of North Carolina Graduate Students, 1947–1949, With Special Studies of English, Modern Language, and Social Science Students.* Master's thesis, University of North Carolina (Chapel Hill, N.C.), 1950.

27. FINDLEY, WARREN G. "Development and Evaluation of Objective Tests for Advanced Specializations." Abstract. *Am Psychol* 7:292 Jl '52. *

28. JONES, EDWARD S. "Some Results of Requiring the Grad-

uate Record Examination of All Seniors." *Ed Rec* 33:105–10 Ja '52. * (*PA* 28:6589)

29. WALLACE, ANITA D. *The Predictive Value of the Graduate Record Examination at Howard University.* Master's thesis, Howard University (Washington, D.C.), 1952.

30. HERKE, MARY L. *The Value of Three Measures in Predicting Academic Success for Graduate Students of Bowling Green State University.* Master's thesis, Bowling Green State University (Bowling Green, Ohio), 1953.

31. KING, DELBERT W. *Graduate Record Examination Scores and Grade-Point Averages of Graduate Students at the College of the Pacific.* Master's thesis, College of the Pacific (Stockton, Calif.), 1953.

32. SCHULTZ, MARGARET K., AND ANGOFF, WILLIAM H. "The Development of New Scales for the Aptitude and Advanced Tests of the Graduate Record Examinations." Abstract. *Am Psychol* 8:430 Ag '53. *

33. OSBORNE, R. TRAVIS, AND SANDERS, WILMA B. "Variations in Graduate Record Examination Performance by Age and Sex." *J Gerontol* 9:179–85 Ap '54. * (*PA* 29:6283)

34. WHITE, ELIZABETH L. *The Relationship of the Graduate Record Examination Results to Achievement in the Graduate School at the University of Detroit.* Master's thesis, University of Detroit (Detroit, Mich.), 1954.

35. CONWAY, MADONNA T. *The Relationship of the Graduate Record Examination Results to Achievement in the Graduate School at the University of Detroit.* Master's thesis, University of Detroit (Detroit, Mich.), 1956.

36. SCHULTZ, MARGARET K., AND ANGOFF, WILLIAM H. "The Development of New Scales for the Aptitude and Advanced Tests of the Graduate Record Examinations." *J Ed Psychol* 47:285–94 My '56. * (*PA* 32:2127)

HAROLD SEASHORE, *Director, Test Division, The Psychological Corporation, New York, New York.*

This review presents an overall description of the components of the *Graduate Record Examinations*. Detailed reviews of most of the separate tests are presented elsewhere in the volume.

I. THE THREE GROUPS OF TESTS. The original GRE series, introduced in 1937, included eight Profile Tests: Verbal Factor, Mathematics, Physics, Chemistry, Literature, Fine Arts, Biology, and Social Studies. It was intended that these tests would be taken by students from all major fields to provide comprehensive measures of general educational achievement in the liberal arts and sciences and aptitude for graduate work. Of course, a student was expected to score higher in his major field than in others.

By 1949 the first two Profile Tests had been replaced by a new pair, now called the Aptitude Test, the components being labeled Verbal Ability and Quantitative Ability. The other Profile Tests were dropped in 1954 and a new series, the Area Tests, was introduced. The Area Tests comprise three separate tests: Social Science, Humanities, and Natural Science. The Aptitude Test and the Area Tests together are the successors, then, to the original eight components of the Profile Tests.

In 1941 the first 16 Advanced Tests, each covering a major field of college study, were made available. This series has undergone considerable revision in the intervening years. The fields currently covered are: biology, chemistry, economics, education, engineering, French, geology, government, history, literature, mathematics, (music), philosophy, physics, psychology, (scholastic philosophy), sociology, Spanish, and (speech). Tests for the three fields in parentheses are included in the Institutional Testing Program but not in the National Program for Graduate Student Selection. For most of the tests 3 hours of testing time are allowed; for music and scholastic philosophy the time is 105 minutes.

The GRE series, it is seen, is designed to provide comprehensive measurement. How are the tests used? What are some of their common features?

II. THE PROGRAMS. These are restricted tests; that is, to insure their integrity, they are released only under rigidly controlled conditions and only to college and university administrators. New forms are made from time to time. Apparently their use in selective admissions is not in such a competitive situation that annual forms are needed. No statements on frequency of revisions or new editions are made in the literature provided this reviewer. Most of the current tests date from the mid-50's; the Educational Testing Service informed the reviewer that many new editions are scheduled for 1958–61. Test copies are not sold; rather a test service is sold and charged for on a per capita basis. The tests are released to contracted examiners for two types of programs.

A. NATIONAL PROGRAM FOR GRADUATE STUDENT SELECTION. Dates for examinations are set far in advance. Over 200 centers are listed. A Bulletin of Information for Candidates tells how to register for the tests and gives other useful background information. Depending on their own purposes and the requirements imposed by institutions, candidates select, for one testing day, the Aptitude Test and one of the Advanced Tests, or just the Aptitude Test, or just one of the Advanced Tests. The Area Tests are not given as part of the national program.

The "paper work" associated with the taking of tests on the scheduled dates seems to be of a high order. In its administration the program is similar to that of the College Entrance Examination Board. Besides presenting all the needed administrative facts, the Bulletin of Information for Candidates also describes the nature of the tests, gives samples of item types, and offers suggestions for the examinee. Example: "General review....may help....but to attempt to 'cram'....would be futile."

Who are tested in the national program? By and large the examinees are seniors and college graduates who are applying for admission to graduate schools which require one or more of the tests in the GRE series. In some institutions enrolled graduate students are required to take the test for counseling and planning purposes or when they are being evaluated formally for candidacy for a degree.

B. INSTITUTIONAL TESTING PROGRAM. This program provides institutions an opportunity to test whole classes, departments, or other administrative groups on their own time schedule and at a lower fee. The Aptitude Test and Advanced Tests are the same as for the national program. The same general conditions of control apply. The Area Tests, not given in the national program, play a large role in the undergraduate institutional programs.

A particular institution wishing to evaluate its "product" might decide that all seniors shall take the Aptitude Test and the Area Tests and one of the Advanced Tests—or any desired combination of these several parts. Some colleges have used the tests at the sophomore and junior levels. Graduate colleges or departments may require the appropriate advanced test, given under institutional program rules, as a component in the comprehensive evaluation of candidates for the Master's degree.

While the national program is designed primarily for securing scores on particular persons for decision making with respect to admission to graduate departments, the institutional program is primarily used for assessment of the effectiveness of undergraduate instruction, for comparative studies of institutions, and for counseling of undergraduates, particularly seniors. The Educational Testing Service provides, as part of its fee, certain summary statistics on the groups which are tested by an institution.

III. TECHNICAL CONSIDERATIONS. The various manuals and bulletins provide technical information. Since the reviewers of the separate tests will consider the data pertaining to that test, here the reviewer presents only descriptions and evaluations which are relevant to all of the tests.

A. RELIABILITY. Reliability coefficients for the Aptitude Test and the Advanced Tests are computed by means of Angoff's Case II, which yields coefficients of internal consistency similar to those obtained from the Kuder-Richardson formula 20. For the Area Tests the latter formula was used. Standard errors of measurement are provided. A footnote explains that for five tests reliability data have not been assembled; this is a surprising report since the publisher at least could compute coefficients on a few hundred cases used in the norming of the tests. Of the 19 coefficients reported, 15 are .90 or better and the others are in the .80's. The standard error of measurement ranges from 22 to 52 scaled score units, with 16 under 40.

The descriptions and tables of data on reliability do not describe the sample—institutions, classes used, number of cases, and sex. The SD's of the samples, however, are provided. Nine are from 90 to 110, thus approximating 100 which is the desired SD on the particular system of scaled scores used; four of the SD's are over 130.

B. THE SCALED SCORE SYSTEM. The GRE tests are all reported in a system of scaled scores based on a mean of 500 and a SD of 100. Two purposes are cited: to provide comparability of scores on the several tests and on the forms of a given test, and to provide direct normative meaning. The first point is well taken. The second goal is achieved only to an unimportant degree. The only time one can properly use the scaled scores directly as norms is when one judges his own sample to be similar to the original norms group described below. The conversion of raw scores to scaled scores is made on the basis of the scaling, in 1952, of the scores of 2,095 seniors in 11 colleges and universities: Antioch, Buffalo, Detroit, Iowa, Lehigh, Miami, Muhlenberg, New Rochelle, St. Louis, Tulane, and Vanderbilt.

Each of these seniors took the Aptitude Test and the Advanced Test in his major field. But the scaled scores established for each major field test are not based directly on the raw scores of the students who majored in that field; there is an intermediate step which can add considerably to the confusion of the typical test user. The scaled scores for the biology test, for example, are derived by relating the original distribution of obtained raw scores on the advanced biology test to the Aptitude Test scores of these same biology majors. The effect of this "anchoring" to the Aptitude Test is that the scaled scores are supposed to report performance "as if" a true cross section (as defined by the Aptitude Tests) of the whole senior class had majored in each of the fields for which a test was developed. A score of 500 on the physics test, for example, does not mean the average score of the original group of students who majored in physics. A score of 500 in physics is an estimate of the score which would be obtained by physics majors who have a score at or close to 500 on the Aptitude Test.

The purpose of this equating is to secure comparability of scores. Comparable scores among the Advanced Tests for an individual student are hardly needed since he will generally take only one of these tests. The comparability which has been gained among the three scores a given student normally receives (two scores on the Aptitude Test and a score on one of the Advanced Tests) hardly seems worth the complexity, especially since a 500, for example, on the Aptitude Test does not really mean the same as 500 on any one of the Advanced Tests. A person with exactly 500 on the verbal and quantitative subtests is called average in scholastic aptitude as defined by the original senior normative group; but if he has a score of 500 also in his major field test, say physics, one cannot say he is also average in physics. One can only say, "If a true cross section of seniors did major in physics, then we would estimate that this student's achievement in physics would be average." In fact, since physics students tend to be above average in academic ability as commonly appraised, a reported scaled score of 500 in physics doubtless places the recipient well below average among physics majors. However, the original raw scores of the major groups on the Aptitude Test are not reported in the manuals, so one cannot observe the adjustments directly.

Because the scaled scores are anchored to the performance of the original senior classes on the Aptitude Test, it follows that graduate students who are both self-selected and institution-selected have scaled scores which typically are well above 500. For 764 graduate students, for example, the scaled scores for the advanced physics test run from about 440 at the 10th percentile rank to about 800 at the 90th percentile rank and to top scores in the 900's. On the advanced psychology test, the median score of 1,375 students is about 570. The median score of education students on their test is about 490.

Parenthetically one should note that this elaborate anchoring and adjusting of scores to

account for differences in aptitudes among groups of majors was accomplished from scores of 2,095 seniors assorted among 16 major fields. Some of the groups must have been rather small since the average group size was 130 students and some fields must have been more popular than others. The manual, further, does not report the correlations between the Advanced Tests and the Aptitude Test for the groups on which the adjusted scaled scores were computed. In another part of the manual such r's are provided for different samples (n's from 45 to 341); it seems, however, from the mean scores that these students are of lower ability than the original sample. Seven of the inter-r's between the Advanced Tests and the verbal score on the Aptitude Test are .74 or over; four are lower. For the quantitative score, the largest r is .64 and .10 r's range from .36 to .62. For five tests no r's are given for lack of cases, which seems odd when one reads in one manual that over 22,000 students took the Advanced Tests in a recent year.

In summary of this point, we suggest that the GRE system of equating scores on the several Advanced Tests to the scores of 16 subgroups of the 2,095 seniors on the Aptitude Test is a psychometric refinement which is certainly confusing to the everyday user. Fortunately the everyday user can ignore the theory of the scaling procedure; his individual evaluations can be derived from percentile tables based on the populations in which he is interested.

c. NORMS. Norms in percentile form are presented in the bulletins for the national and the institutional programs. As is appropriate, the bulletins suggest that because of differences in purposes in using the tests, each institution's norms are probably most appropriate.

For the Aptitude Test, norms derived from about 5,200 seniors in 75 colleges are given separately by sex and for both sexes combined. The mean scores of 444 on V and 452 on Q are considerably below the means of the seniors on which the scaling of the tests was used. Norms based on scores of about 4,700 first year graduate students who were examined under the institutional plan are also presented. Since these means are 472 for V and 482 for Q, one concludes that this sample of selected and self-selected graduate students in 32 institutions is below the ability level of the original reference group composed of whole classes of seniors. However, the approximately 15,500 candidates who were examined under the national program show mean scores of 545 for V and 542 for Q. The Aptitude Test norms for these students are separately presented for 16 majoring groups.

For the Area Tests, norms are provided by sex and for each of the three tests on the basis of about 15,000 college seniors, presumably whole classes, in 192 colleges. Similar norms derived from a sample of about 5,500 sophomores are shown. A sample of about 2,200 first year graduate students also provide norms.

For each of the Advanced Tests, norms based on institutional program samples, both seniors and first year graduate school students,

are presented. More important are the norms computed from candidates under the national program, since these persons were by and large actively applying for admission to graduate school for acceptance as degree candidates. For the 16 tests, n's range from 263 to 1,382, except for a smaller group in Spanish.

The manuals for both the institutional and the national programs properly stress the need for local standards. The n's for the samples presented are satisfactory and the norms are fresh, 1955–1957.

For reviews of individual tests, see 10, 215, 220, 247, 270, 336, 427, 537, 583, 727, 754, 818, and 835.

MULTI-APTITUDE BATTERIES

REVIEWS BY *Dorothy C. Adkins, Anne Anastasi, Harold P. Bechtoldt, Ralph F. Berdie, John B. Carroll, Ruth Churchill, Andrew L. Comrey, Norman Frederiksen, Clifford P. Froehlich, Benjamin Fruchter, Lloyd G. Humphreys, Albert K. Kurtz, E. A. Peel, H. H. Remmers, Donald E. Super, Philip E. Vernon, and S. Rains Wallace.*

[602]

*[Aptitude-Intelligence Tests.] Adults; 1947–57; former title, *Factored Aptitude Series,* still on test booklets; *a–n:* 1 form ('56); 15 tests; supplement ('57); 20¢ per test; $10 per manual ('56); postage extra; French edition available for tests *a–n,* Spanish edition available for tests *c–d, f–h, j–m;* Joseph E. King; Industrial Psychology. *
a) OFFICE TERMS. 5(10) minutes.
b) SALES TERMS. 5(10) minutes.
c) TOOLS. 5(10) minutes.
d) NUMBERS. 5(10) minutes.
e) PERCEPTION. 5(10) minutes.
f) JUDGMENT. 5(10) minutes.
g) PRECISION. 5(10) minutes.
h) FLUENCY. 6(10) minutes.
i) MEMORY. 5(10) minutes.
j) PARTS. 5(10) minutes.
k) BLOCKS. 5(10) minutes.
l) DIMENSION. 5(10) minutes.
m) DEXTERITY. 3(5) minutes.
n) MOTOR. $15 per motor apparatus ['47]; 6(10) minutes.
o) FACTORY TERMS. 1957; 10(15) minutes.

HAROLD P. BECHTOLDT, *Associate Professor of Psychology, State University of Iowa, Iowa City, Iowa.*

The previous review of this aptitude series in 1953 by D. W. Lefever (see 4:712) covers the background and the composition of the tests very well. This reviewer wishes to state his opinion that the 15 separate measures defin-

ing the 8 "factors" appear to be well designed, to be printed nicely on good stock, and to be arranged so as to be reasonably interesting to young adults. The content is such that some "face validity" might be expected.

The tests, and especially the manual, are designed for industrial applications, and only passing references are made to the use of these materials for vocational counseling and guidance in the high schools or colleges. Accompanying the publisher's notes on the development and use of the tests are a series of "company research studies" in which "emphasis is placed on the cost reduction implications, achieved by scientific personnel evaluations." In this connection the authors present, in four separate studies, examples of their comments and recommendations to the company for which the study was carried out. The four studies involve chemical engineers, file clerks, route salesmen, and women assemblers, with a range of 50 to 82 cases per study.

STRONG POINTS. The strongest point of the *Factored Aptitude Series* is the generally adequate test construction procedures. As indicated in a 1953 report entitled Development of

Job-Tests Program, the development of the items involved careful consideration of the distribution of difficulty indices, measures of internal consistency, magnitude of the item-score correlations, and the relative effectiveness of the four alternatives for the separate items. The reliabilities as reported seem reasonably adequate for short 5-minute tests. The ranges of the distributions of scores are such as to permit fairly effective discrimination between individuals from an industrial viewpoint.

A second important consideration is the extremely simple format of the test scoring, recording, and weighting devices. In terms of simplicity, the "hiring summary worksheets" represent the closest approximation this reviewer has yet seen to a "cookbook" for industrial personnel clerks. In view of our general ignorance as to the variables important to the prediction of behavior, a third point might be the emphasis upon a combination of testing and interviewing procedures for the selection, placement, promotion, and transfer of employees.

WEAK POINTS. The most conspicuous weak point in this program is the entirely inadequate evidence supporting the claims made by the publisher. Evidence as to the accuracy of these claims surely would be found in the manual if such evidence were available. The few items of data offered neither justify the statements made nor indicate any superiority of this program over that of competing testing programs.

In the 1953 publisher's notes, the intercorrelations among the tests are reported as having an average value of .35 with specific tests showing intercorrelations from .05 to .50. Correlations between the tests and certain other tests are listed with the numbers of cases. The results, in general, are consistent with the correlations among similar tests in various journals. Selected correlations, termed "Validation Statistics," are also reported by job-test areas in the 1953 notes. These "validity" correlations for tests retained in the "job area" batteries range from .56 for the numbers test against a criterion of rated job performance as a numbers clerk to .26 for the test of perception against rated performance as an instructor. The numbers of cases shown for the "validation" data range from 1,465 semiskilled workers to 113 writers. Since these correlations apparently were computed on groups combined from different companies in different jobs, the variables influencing these indices include every source of variance in an industrial installation. The absence of data in the manual as to the intercorrelations of these tests on these same subjects precludes an accurate evaluation of the differences between validity coefficients.

The lack of statistical tests of significance, together with a surprising faith in the stability of the means of the arrays of these bivariate distributions, represents a situation which the reviewer thought was disappearing in industrial psychology. Nonlinear correlations indicated in a 1957 report entitled How to Tailor Personnel Tests to Your Company Operation could be based upon samples of as few as 40 cases. As any psychologist can determine in a few minutes, tests of nonlinearity (using the F distribution) are not very sensitive with samples of this size. It is also simple to demonstrate that the direction as well as the magnitude of any nonlinearity index found in one sample can be expected to vary markedly from that in another sample of 40 cases. There are several indications that the weights used to determine the "qualification grades" represent the "expert guesses or hypotheses" of a group of two or more industrial psychologists. Such hypotheses are, of course, understandable and necessary in the initial stages of theoretical or empirical formulations. However, presenting these "guesses" as established relations with no more evidence than is contained in the manual is hard to justify.

Besides the absence of acceptable statistical support for the general statements, a further serious limitation is the lack of evidence as to the cross validation of these tests and test batteries. On three of the four company research studies, the "correlations, score classifications, and weights" are not released. Instead, scatterplots of four to seven qualification levels with 9-point job efficiency ratings are offered. However, even these data are not acceptable because, as an accompanying statement in the manual indicates for one group, "since this is the group of engineers on whom the tests are validated, the plot is somewhat biased." Most psychologists would probably say with Cureton that such data are more aptly described as "baloney." [1] The only study for which cross validation data are provided is a 1956 report made by the Transformer Engineers Company,

1 CURETON, EDWARD E. "Validity, Reliability, and Baloney." *Ed & Psychol Meas* 10:94–6 '50.

Pasadena, California, and furnished to the publisher. This report indicates the correlations between merit ratings and the tools, precision, and motor tests of .42, .23, and .44, respectively. The means and standard deviations are also shown. "The correlation between the weighted score and merit rating was .30." For a sample of 57 cases, the correlation of .30 is significant at the 5 per cent level. However, the publisher, for some unknown reason, recommends that this company use the weighted score, which has a correlation of .30 with the criterion, instead of the tools or motor tests alone, which show correlation coefficients with the criterion of .42 and .44. The contrast is great between the elaborate set of guesses reflected in this program and Meehl's demonstration of how empirical data can be used to provide a "good cookbook" approach even in the more difficult area of prediction in clinical psychology.[2]

It is to be hoped that, in the future, additional studies will be reported in which the data provide acceptable evidence as to the usefulness of the weighting and testing procedures which have been recommended so confidently.

A further serious weakness, in the opinion of this reviewer, is the level of psychological sophistication indicated by the emphasis in developing tests on a "present employee" basis and applying the results to applicants with the justification that "the psychological traits are a constant (are matured by the age of 20 and remain fairly static after that time)." It seems strange in 1957–58 to find industrial psychologists confusing "trade test" procedures with "predictive test" procedures. Surely the available evidence as to the effects of training or experience on the job upon test performance is such that the statements in the manual can be considered hard to explain.

In summary, the tests themselves are well designed. Furthermore, the publisher has an appreciation of the low order of skill and knowledge to be expected of clerical help in a personnel department. The materials are written in a beautifully simple fashion. The vocabulary and stylistic form of the manual represents the journalistic "fourth grade education" approach carried to an extreme. An industrial concern might well use these tests in their own long term *research* program, but this re-

2 MEEHL, PAUL. "Wanted—a Good Cookbook." *Am Psychol* 11:263–72 '56.

viewer cannot recommend the tests for the selection or classification of job applicants.

For a review by D. Welty Lefever of an earlier edition, see 4:712 (1 excerpt).

[603]

*Detroit General Aptitudes Examination. Grades 6–12; 1938–54; assembled from *Detroit Mechanical Aptitudes Test, Detroit Clerical Aptitudes Test,* and *Detroit Advanced Intelligence Test;* 20 scores: intelligence, mechanical, clerical, total, and 16 subtest scores; Form A ('38); revised manual ('54, identical with manual copyrighted in 1941 except for minor changes); $3.40 per 25 tests; 35¢ per copy of *Ayres Measuring Scale for Handwriting;* 40¢ per manual; 65¢ per specimen set; postpaid; 60(90) minutes; Harry J. Baker, Alex C. Crockett, and Paul H. Voelker; Public School Publishing Co. *

For reviews by G. Frederic Kuder, Irving Lorge, and John Gray Peatman, see 40:1654.

[604]

★Differential Ability Tests. Ages 10–17 (standards 5–10); 1951; 9 tests; mimeographed manual ['51]; separate answer sheets must be used for *b, c,* and *d;* 5s. per 100 answer sheets; postage extra; specimen set not available; Afrikaans edition available; 201 (470) minutes in 4 sessions 1 day apart; National Bureau of Educational and Social Research. *
a) [LANGUAGE TESTS.] 3 forms; 3 tests; 16s. 9d. per 100 tests except Form B of the *Silent Reading Test (Paragraphs: Senior)* which is 15s. 8d. per 100 tests; 58(75) minutes.
    1. *Silent Reading Test (Paragraphs: Senior).* Forms A, B, C ['51]; 18(25) minutes.
    2. *Silent Reading Test (Vocabulary: Senior).* Forms A, B, C ['51]; 10(15) minutes.
    3. *English Usage Test (Senior).* Forms A, B, C ['51]; 30(35) minutes.
b) [GENERAL ABILITY TESTS.] 2 forms; 2 tests; 48(60) minutes.
    1. *Verbal Reasoning Test.* Forms A, B ['51]; 13s. 3d. per 100 copies of Form A; 17s. 3d. per 100 copies of Form B; 20(25) minutes.
    2. *Non-Verbal Reasoning.* Forms A, B ['51]; 18s. 9d. per 100 copies of Form A; 17s. 4d. per 100 copies of Form B; 28(35) minutes.
c) ARITHMETIC TEST. 2 scores: mechanical arithmetic, problems; Forms A, B ['51]; 16s. 7d. per 100 copies of Form A; 16s. 1d. per 100 copies of Form B; 30(35) minutes.
d) [TESTS OF SPECIFIC ABILITIES.] Form A; 3 tests; 65(100) minutes.
    1. *Memory Test.* Form A ['51]; 21(35) minutes.
    2. *Space Perception.* Form A ['51]; 26(40) minutes.
    3. *Mechanical Comprehension Test.* Form A ['51]; 18(25) minutes.

[605]

*Differential Aptitude Tests. Grades 8–12; 1947–58; IBM; Forms A, B ('47); 8 tests in 7 booklets; manual, second edition ('52); supplement ('58); directions for administration ['52, reprinted from manual]; separate answer sheets must be used; $1.90 per 50 IBM answer sheets; $1.25 per set of hand scoring stencils; $1.40 per set of machine scoring stencils; $1.25 per 50 profiles ['53]; $2 per manual; $3 per specimen set; $1.75 per casebook ('51, see 29 below); postpaid; 186(240) minutes; George K. Bennett, Harold

G. Seashore, and Alexander G. Wesman; Psychological Corporation. *

a) VERBAL REASONING. $3 per 25 tests; 30(40) minutes.

b) NUMERICAL ABILITY. $2.25 per 25 tests; 30(35) minutes.

c) ABSTRACT REASONING. $3 per 25 tests; 25(30) minutes.

d) SPACE RELATIONS. $3.50 per 25 tests; 30(40) minutes.

e) MECHANICAL REASONING. $3.75 per 25 tests; 30(35) minutes.

f) CLERICAL SPEED AND ACCURACY. $3 per 25 tests; 6(15) minutes.

g) LANGUAGE USAGE. 2 scores: spelling, sentences; $3 per 25 tests; 35(45) minutes.

REFERENCES

1-28. See 4:711.

29. BENNETT, GEORGE K.; SEASHORE, HAROLD G.; AND WESMAN, ALEXANDER G. Counseling From Profiles: A Casebook for the Differential Aptitude Tests. New York: Psychological Corporation, 1951. Pp. 95. * (PA 26:3399)

30. KERMEEN, BARBARA G. A Factor Analysis of the Differential Aptitude Tests and a Factor Analysis of the Kuder Preference Record, Vocational. Master's thesis, University of California (Berkeley, Calif.), 1951.

31. SHELDON, F. A. Validation of the Differential Aptitude Tests in a Selected High School Population. Master's thesis, Stanford University (Stanford, Calif.), 1951.

32. "Results of the Space Relations, Mechanical Reasoning, and Clerical Speed and Accuracy Tests of the Differential Aptitude Test Battery in Six Public Schools." Ed Rec B 58:79-84 F '52. * (PA 26:7240)

33. BENNETT, GEORGE K.; SEASHORE, HAROLD G.; AND WESMAN, ALEXANDER G. "Aptitude Testing: Does It 'Prove Out' in Counseling Practice?" Occupations 30:584-93 My '52. * (PA 27:1240)

34. DOPPELT, JEROME E., AND WESMAN, ALEXANDER G. "The Differential Aptitude Tests as Predictors of Achievement Test Scores." J Ed Psychol 43:210-7 Ap '52. * (PA 27:3784)

35. FRUCHTER, BENJAMIN. "Orthogonal and Oblique Solutions of a Battery of Aptitude, Achievement and Background Variables." Ed & Psychol Meas 12:20-38 sp '52. * (PA 27:6180)

36. GLASER, ROBERT. "The Reliability of Inconsistency." Ed & Psychol Meas 12:60-4 sp '52. * (PA 27:5523)

37. HODGES, JOHN M. Primary Mental Abilities vs. Differential Aptitude Tests. Master's thesis, Illinois State Normal University (Normal, Ill.), 1952.

38. MELEIKA, LOUIS K. Intra-Individual Variability in Relation to Achievement, Interest, and Personality. Doctor's thesis, Stanford University (Stanford, Calif.), 1952.

39. STINSON, PAIRLEE J. A Statistical Analysis of the Differential Aptitude Tests for the Purpose of Predicting First Semester Grade Averages of a Freshman High School Group. Master's thesis, Oklahoma A. & M. College (Stillwater, Okla.), 1952.

40. WESMAN, ALEXANDER G. "The Differential Aptitude Tests." Personnel & Guid J 31:167-70 D '52. * (PA 27:6201)

41. WILLIAMS, NANCY. "A Study of the Validity of the Verbal Reasoning Subtest and the Abstract Reasoning Subtest of the Differential Aptitude Tests." Ed & Psychol Meas 12:129-31 sp '52. * (PA 27:5914)

42. BEAMER, GEORGE C.; PENDER, FRANCES RUSSELL; AND PARTON, NORMA WEST. "Selection of Teachers of Homemaking." J Home Econ 45:98-100 F '53. * (PA 27:7412)

43. CROUCH, MILDRED S. The Relative Value of the Differential Aptitude Tests and the Otis Quick-Scoring Mental Ability Test for Predicting Scholastic Success. Master's thesis, Tennessee Agricultural and Industrial University (Nashville, Tenn.), 1953.

44. SEASHORE, HAROLD G. "Tests in the Tenth Grade as Predictors of Graduating Status and Status on College Entrance Tests." Abstract. Am Psychol 8:431-2 Ag '53. *

45. YOUNG, DOROTHY M. The Use of the Differential Aptitude Scores in Predicting Success in Certain School Subjects in Schools in New Castle, Pennsylvania. Master's thesis, Kent State University (Kent, Ohio), 1953.

46. "Validity Information Exchange, No. 7-065: D.O.T. Code 5-92.411, Foreman II." Personnel Psychol 7:301 su '54. *

47. "Validity Information Exchange, No. 7-094: D.O.T. Code 7-80.120, Beginner Mechanics." Personnel Psychol 7:572 w '54. *

48. "Validity Information Exchange, No. 7-095: D.O.T. Code 7-94.112 and 7-94.100, Tool and Die and Machinist Apprentice." Personnel Psychol 7:573 w '54. *

49. "Validity Information Exchange, No. 7-096: D.O.T. Code 9-03.01, Riveter Assistants (Rivet-Buckers)." Personnel Psychol 7:574 w '54. *

50. FROEHLICH, C. P., AND MOSER, W. E. "Do Counselees Remember Test Scores?" J Counsel Psychol 1:149-52 fall '54. * (PA 29:6245)

51. GLASER, ROBERT, AND JACOBS, OWEN. "Predicting Achievement in Medical School: A Comparison of Preclinical and Clinical Criteria." J Appl Psychol 38:245-7 Ag '54. * (PA 29:6271)

52. HALL, ROBERT C. A Study of the Relationships Among Certain Occupational Groups in Performance on the Differential Aptitude Test Battery. Doctor's thesis, University of Connecticut (Storrs, Conn.), 1954. (DA 15:84)

53. SEASHORE, HAROLD. "Tenth Grade Tests as Predictors of Twelfth Grade Scholarship and College Entrance Status." Comment by David V. Tiedeman. J Counsel Psychol 1:106-15 su '54. * (PA 29:3054)

54. BENNETT, GEORGE K. "The D.A.T.—A Seven-Year Follow-Up." Test Service B (49):1-4 N '55. * (PA 30:7751)

55. HARRISON, ROSS; HUNT, WINSLOW; AND JACKSON, THEODORE A. "Profile of the Mechanical Engineer: 1, Ability." Personnel Psychol 8:219-34 su '55. * (PA 30:5414)

56. JENSON, RALPH E. "Using Multiple Aptitude Measures to Improve Guidance in a Secondary School System," pp. 29-50. In Fourth Annual Western Regional Conference on Testing Problems, March 4, 1955. Princeton, N.J.: Educational Testing Service, [1955]. Pp. iv, 87. * (PA 30:1617)

57. PAUK, WALTER J. An Analysis of Certain Characteristics of Above-Average and Below-Average Male and Female Readers at the Ninth-Grade Level. Doctor's thesis, Cornell University (Ithaca, N.Y.), 1955. (DA 16:285)

58. PERRINE, MERVYN WILLIAM. "The Selection of Drafting Trainees." J Appl Psychol 39:57-61 F '55. * (PA 30:1725)

59. SCHULMAN, J. A Comparison Between 9th and 12th Grade Students on Self-Estimates of Abilities and Objective Scores on the Differential Aptitude Tests. Doctor's thesis, New York University (New York, N.Y.), 1955.

60. SEASHORE, HAROLD. "Cross-Validation of Equations for Predicting CEEB-SAT Scores From DAT Scores." J Counsel Psychol 2:229-30 fall '55. *

61. STOUGHTON, ROBERT W. The Differential Predictive Values of the Differential Aptitude Tests in the Connecticut Technical Schools. Doctor's thesis, University of Connecticut (Storrs, Conn.), 1955. (DA 15:1355)

62. VINEYARD, E. E. A Longitudinal Study of the Relationship of Differential Aptitude Test Scores With College Success. Doctor's thesis, Oklahoma A. & M. College (Stillwater, Okla.), 1955.

63. WOLKING, WILLIAM D. "Predicting Academic Achievement With the Differential Aptitude and the Primary Mental Abilities Tests." J Appl Psychol 39:115-8 Ap '55. * (PA 30:1636)

64. "Predicting CEEB-SAT Status From Grade 10 Scores on the Differential Aptitude Tests." Test Service B (50):4 Je '56. *

65. BENNETT, GEORGE K.; SEASHORE, HAROLD G.; AND WESMAN, ALEXANDER G. "The Differential Aptitude Tests: An Overview." Comments by Donald E. Super. Personnel & Guid J 35: 81-93 O '56. * (PA 31:8809)

66. ELTON, CHARLES F., AND MORRIS, DONALD. "The Use of the D.A.T. in a Small Liberal Arts College." J Ed Res 50: 139-43 O '56. * (PA 32:941)

67. HALSEY, HUGH. The Predictive Value of Certain Measures Used in Selecting Freshmen for the Technical Curricula in a Community College. Doctor's thesis, New York University (New York, N.Y.), 1956. (DA 17:542)

68. McCLINTIC, STANLEY A. The Prognostic Value of Selected Sub-Tests of the Differential Aptitude Test for Programming Students in 9th Grade Foreign Language Classes. Master's thesis, Claremont College (Claremont, Calif.), 1956.

69. BRAYFIELD, ARTHUR H., AND MARSH, MARY MARKLEY. "Aptitudes, Interests, and Personality Characteristics of Farmers." J Appl Psychol 41:98-103 Ap '57. *

70. HALL, ROBERT C. "Occupational Group Contrasts in Terms of the Differential Aptitude Tests: An Application of Multiple Discriminant Analysis." Ed & Psychol Meas 17:556-67 w '57. *

71. STEWART, LAWRENCE H. "Does Knowledge of Performance on an Aptitude Test Change Scores on the Kuder?" J Counsel Psychol 4:161-4 su '57. *

72. DUNNETTE, MARVIN D., AND KIRCHNER, WAYNE K. "Validation of Psychological Tests in Industry." Personnel Adm 21: 20-7 My-Je '58. *

73. LAYTON, WILBUR L., AND SWANSON, EDWARD O. "Relationship of Ninth Grade Differential Aptitude Test Scores to Eleventh Grade Test Scores and High School Rank." J Ed Psychol 49:153-5 Je '58. *

74. MARTENS, W. LEON. "Normative Data Information Exchange, No. 11-3." Personnel Psychol 11:131-2 sp '58. *

75. MENDICINO, LORENZO. "Mechanical Reasoning and Space Perception: Native Capacity or Experience." Personnel & Guid J 36:335-8 Ja '58. *

76. SMITH, D. D. "Abilities and Interests: I, A Factorial Study." Can J Psychol 12:191-201 S '58. *

77. VINEYARD, EDWIN E. A Longitudinal Study of the Relationship of Differential Aptitude Test Scores With College Success." Personnel & Guid J 36:413-6 F '58. *

JOHN B. CARROLL, *Professor of Education, Harvard University, Cambridge, Massachusetts.*

The *Differential Aptitude Tests* represent an attempt to measure a number of relatively distinct abilities thought to be of prime importance in assessing the potentialities of high school students. While each test has satisfactory reliability and validity in its own right, the tests are intended ordinarily to be administered as a total battery—not all on one day, but at least within a relatively short span of time. (Several possible testing schedules are suggested in the manual.) The tests are completely objective. Reusable test booklets are utilized, all answers being recorded on separate IBM answer sheets.

The term "differential" implies not only that the tests measure *different* abilities but also that differences in score level within a single individual's profile are likely to be significant and interpretable. In constructing the battery, the authors banked heavily upon the results of the various researches which have been done on the dimensions of human ability, that is, researches utilizing the statistical techniques of factor analysis. Nevertheless, they were not as intent upon constructing "pure" tests of the various dimensions as they were upon constructing highly reliable, valid, and useful tests. In some cases, therefore, the separate tests measure a combination of factors of ability; the counselor needs to be aware of what each test measures. The following paragraphs describe the tests and indicate the *probable* factorial composition of each, based largely upon Fruchter's (*35*) study.

Verbal Reasoning presents a series of verbal analogies items which probably measure a combination of the "verbal ability" and "deductive reasoning" factors. In any event it is a good measure of the student's ability to handle complex logical relationships which can be stated in verbal terms, and, in this sense, it is largely a measure of "intelligence" as this is ordinarily conceived.

Numerical Ability presents a series of relatively simple numerical problems requiring a minimum of arithmetic reasoning. It is thus chiefly a measure of mental computational skill (or, in factor analysis jargon, the "number" ability), but it also may measure specific educational achievement in simple mathematics because it contains some problems involving square and cube roots, solving proportions, and evaluation of fractions.

Abstract Reasoning requires the student to indicate which of a series of choices properly carries out the logical development exhibited by a sequence of figures. It was intended to be a nonverbal measure of reasoning ability. This intention was well realized in the test, but factorial studies show that to some extent it is also a measure of the student's ability to visualize spatial patterns and shapes; this undoubtedly explains some of its correlation with another test, Space Relations.

Space Relations utilizes the familiar "unfolded paper boxes" technique and measures chiefly the ability to visualize objects and forms in two or three dimensions.

Mechanical Reasoning asks the subject to answer simple questions in what someone has called "barnyard physics," based on pictures showing thrown balls, gears, levers, propellers, etc. It probably measures a combination of "mechanical experience" and ability to visualize in two or three dimensions.

Clerical Speed and Accuracy requires the subject to make quick comparisons of arbitrary patterns of letters and numbers; it measures what has usually been called the "perceptual" factor—more specifically, the ability to scan visual materials rapidly and locate designated items.

The spelling subtest of Language Usage requires the subject to indicate whether each of 100 words is spelled right or wrong. In addition to a component of verbal knowledge, this subtest probably contains a highly specific component of spelling ability. The second subtest of Language Usage asks the student to find "errors" (grammar, punctuation, or spelling) in a series of English sentences. Like the spelling subtest, this subtest measures both general verbal knowledge and a specific factor, knowledge of "correct" English usage.

Super, in his review of multifactor guidance tests (*65*), considers only two of the currently available batteries "ready for use in counseling": the *Differential Aptitude Tests* and the United States Employment Service's *General Aptitude Test Battery*. If this accolade is justified, and the reviewer thinks it is, the DAT battery merits serious consideration for use in high school testing programs. Super's implicit assumption—a correct one—is that a test is not merely the test booklet, the answer sheet, the scoring key, and the other paraphernalia one has to purchase in order to use the test, but something more: the product of careful, scientific research in test construction, norming, and validation. One purchases a great deal of this in the DAT; in fact, Super warns that the counselor is likely to feel overwhelmed by the literally hundreds—even thousands—of validity coefficients and other statistics which are available to the user of this test if he wants to go to the trouble of collecting them all. The DAT is probably one of the few tests the data on which are so voluminous that they have had to be deposited in the American Documentation Institute. But the publishers of the DAT can hardly be criticized for making too *much* data available, and they cannot be criticized for failing to offer materials to help the counselor learn how to use the test, for they have indeed done this illuminatingly in their 1951 *Counseling From Profiles: A Casebook for the Differential Aptitude Tests* (29.) Even with respect to making the available validity data digestible, they have done an admirable job of summarization and presentation in their manual, which is a model of organization, comprehensiveness, and clarity. They have even presented a full bibliography of relevant research publications by others who have studied the DAT; one is struck by the fact, however, that the text of their manual makes no direct reference to any research not done "in the house."

The authors have done such a thorough and technically satisfactory job that a reviewer finds it hard to make himself appear sufficiently critical. With one or two possible exceptions, the tests are excellent in format, item construction, standardization, validation, and just about every other aspect which is regarded as important in the testing fraternity. Just as an example of the fine points to which the authors have attended, note the completeness with which validity data are reported: date test taken, date and grade in which course marks reported, number of cases, correlation coefficients for each test. No question here about whether the validities are "concurrent" or "predictive"! Most are clearly predictive, that is, derived in a situation where the test was given a considerable number of months before the course grades were collected and thus having a bearing on the guidance decisions that might have been taken at the time the tests were given.

Since the tests, manuals, and associated data so clearly meet high standards of technical excellence, the reviewer shall utilize the remaining space to raise some questions—some of them possibly quibbling, others dead serious.

He is intrigued first by problems of test construction and test content. One would suppose that item analysis techniques had been used in the original construction of the tests or at least in the construction of equivalent forms, but no statement to this effect can be found. We have no assurance that there are no "dead-wood" items nor items with debatable answers. As a matter of fact, the reviewer is already on record [1] as having raised serious questions about the sentence subtest of Language Usage, which appears to him to be based on obsolete norms of English usage. For example, Item 13 of that test (Form A) is keyed so as to require that the sentence "Is it I whom they are calling?" be regarded as correct, and, in Item 5, "It is me" is keyed as wrong. But in *Teaching English Usage,* Pooley points out that "it is me" has been accepted usage for hundreds of years and deserves no class time. When the reviewer filled out the test in the light of Pooley's standards, his raw score was 66 out of a possible 90, which is equivalent to a percentile of 94. It is probable that many students with excellent grasp of language usage are getting a number of items wrong because their standards are several decades in advance of those on which the test was apparently based.

There has been debate as to whether the DAT is truly *differential,* i.e., do the tests really measure different abilities? To be sure, the intercorrelations are only low to moderate, and the authors have computed statistics to show "the proportion of differences between the standardized test scores on any pair of tests which are in excess of the chance proportion." These proportions range, for boys, from .29 to .52, and for girls, from .20 to .48. For both sexes combined and for all pairs of tests, it works out that only about 37 per cent of all possible differences are beyond those expected by chance. We can put a favorable light on this result by saying that in the long run we can expect about 10 of the 28 possible differences between pairs of test scores for one individual case to be significant. Thus, a *typical* profile can be expected to be "flat" except for 1 or 2 deviant scores (1 deviant score producing 7 significant differences, 2 deviant scores producing 12 or 13 significant differences depending upon whether the 2 deviant scores them-

1 CARROLL, JOHN B. "An Evaluation of Language Tests From the Standpoint of the Psychology of Language," pp. 75–80. *Ninth Yearbook of the National Council on Measurements Used in Education,* 1952.

selves are significantly different from each other). Even this amount of difference is enough to provide some leverage in differential counseling; the differences, of course, are more or less equally likely to occur in different parts of the profile. But is this not less than we have a right to expect from so long a test battery? Is there not still an undue amount of overlap and high correlation between tests? Although meaningful comparisons are impossible to make because of the lack of readily available data, it would seem that the *General Aptitude Test Battery* or even the *Flanagan Aptitude Classification Tests* offer more in the way of differential diagnosis *as such*. Many of the DAT tests, incidentally, correlate well with their opposite numbers in the *General Aptitude Test Battery*. The overlap of abilities apparently measured by the subtests of the DAT is sometimes disturbing, and it will take experience and training on the part of the counselor to use the profiles wisely.

Of course, any multifactor battery like the DAT tends to be handicapped by the fact that even if truly independent aptitudes exist, the differences between them are obscured by common educational experiences and by degrees of motivation for school learning and for test taking which more or less uniformly make for a high, medium, or low level of performance on a series of tests. There is not much chance that *any* set of differential tests designed chiefly for general educational guidance, as the DAT is, would not be substantially affected by these influences.

The authors make much of the fact that the DAT battery is a group of tests, each of which is valid and useful in itself; they appear to advise against the combination of weighted scores. In the notable controversy about "clinical" versus "statistical" prediction they are on the side of "clinical" prediction. Paradoxically, this position prevents them from displaying some of the undoubted powers of the test in affording statistical prediction from weighted combinations of scores. In the whole array of validity coefficients presented there is not a single multiple correlation. The authors hesitate to get the counselor into what might appear to be needless complexities, but in view of the high importance to the individual of such decisions as whether to plan emphasis on liberal or on technical studies, would it not be possible to provide the counselor with simple ways of

combining scores in order to make predictions of superior accuracy? At all events, it is hoped that the authors' remarks about score combinations will not deter the development of prediction equations in local situations.

At the present time, it can be said that, considering the tests themselves and all the supporting data, the DAT constitutes the best available foundation battery for measuring the chief intellectual abilities and learned skills which one needs to take account of in high school counseling.

NORMAN FREDERIKSEN, *Director of Research, Educational Testing Service, Princeton, New Jersey.*

At the time the *Differential Aptitude Tests* were introduced, the multidimensional nature of mental ability was well recognized. Tests were appearing which measured the "primary" mental abilities. The authors of the DAT recognized the need for aptitude tests which produced scores for separate abilities, but they rejected the pure factor test idea. Instead they sought test types which were not necessarily pure in a factorial sense but which had demonstrated their usefulness in a variety of situations and which could readily be interpreted by teachers and counselors.

Eight tests, printed in seven reusable test booklets, are included in the battery. All are power tests except Clerical Speed and Accuracy. Answers are recorded on IBM answer sheets which may be scored by hand or by machine. The time allowances permit all eight tests to be administered in six class periods. Alternate forms of all tests are available.

The 50 items of Verbal Reasoning are analogies, but they are unusual in that both the first and the last elements of the analogy are omitted. The task is to choose the appropriate words, from options provided, to complete the analogy. The items are probably more complex, factorially, than the usual analogy item. The particular item type would seem to require verbal ability and reasoning; in addition, some of the items depend on a background of information. Still other items seem to require flexibility, since they contain words which are homonyms spelled alike, and it may be necessary to reject one meaning of a word in order to find another which permits an interpretation consistent with a correct answer.

There are 40 multiple choice arithmetic items

in Numerical Ability. The option "none of these" is employed each time, which decreases the likelihood that an estimating technique or some other short cut method can be employed in taking the test. Factorially, the test probably measures both number and reasoning factors. Some of the items are straight computation items involving the adding, subtracting, multiplying, and dividing of whole numbers, decimals, and fractions. Other problems seem to require reasoning, although the form of the items resembles the purely computational type.

The 50 items in Abstract Reasoning all employ abstract figures. The operation of a principle is portrayed in a sequence of four figures and the task is to choose from five additional figures the one which logically follows in the sequence. The drawings are reasonably large and are clearly printed. Size estimations or other difficult visual discriminations are not required in order to solve the problems.

The items employed in Space Relations are of the type called surface development, but with the added feature that the solid figures which comprise the options may be rotated to various positions in space. The task is to indicate all the solid figures which can be made from the pattern. All items involve three- rather than two-dimensional space. Drawings are large, and finding the correct answers does not depend upon visual discrimination.

Mechanical Reasoning is a new form of the Bennett *Test of Mechanical Comprehension*. Each item depicts the operation of a physical principle by means of a drawing, and is accompanied by a question such as, "Which man must pull harder to lift the weight?" Three choices are presented: A, B, and a third option such as, "If either, mark C." (C is the correct answer only 11 times for the 68 items in Form A.) This type of test has been widely used in military classification work and has been shown to be of value for predicting a variety of occupational and training criteria. Factorially, the test is probably quite complex.

Clerical Speed and Accuracy is the only test in the battery which is speeded. Each item in the booklet presents five pairs of symbols such as 2y, 5y, 57, 37, and y3; one of the pairs is underlined. The same pairs are printed above the answer spaces on the answer sheet, but in a different order. The task is to find the pair which was underlined and to mark the answer space below it. There are two separately timed

parts, each containing 100 items. The test is supposed to measure speed of response in a simple perceptual task.

The spelling subtest of Language Usage includes 100 words; the task is to indicate whether each word is spelled right or wrong. The choice of words and incorrect spellings is based on Gates' work on spelling difficulties. In order to minimize the effects of a possible acquiescent response set, the correctly spelled words were carefully selected to be effective items when presented in the correct form.

In the sentences subtest of Language Usage 50 sentences are included, each of which is broken into five parts by slant lines. The task for each sentence is to mark the answer positions corresponding to those parts which contain errors in grammar, punctuation, or spelling. The number of errors per sentence may vary from 0 to 5. Thus the test contains the equivalent of 250 2-choice items of a "correct-incorrect" sort; the operation of an acquiescent response set on this test is therefore a distinct possibility.

For each form of the DAT, norms are presented for boys and girls separately at each grade level from 8 through 12. There are thus 20 norms tables in all. The norms table is entered with the raw score for a particular test, and the corresponding percentile rank for the grade and sex group is found.

The number of cases on which each norms table is based ranges from 2,100 to 7,400 for Form A and from 350 to 1,075 for Form B. Over 100 school systems, from all the major geographic regions of the country, are involved. The manual does not go into details about size of communities and types of schools, but detailed tables may be obtained from the American Documentation Institute.

Profile sheets are provided for plotting the eight scores for each person. Scores are to be plotted on the basis of percentiles. The percentile values are positioned to correspond to a standard score scale, and such a scale is printed on the profile sheet, for those who wish to convert to standard scores.

The profile chart is set up so that one inch of vertical distance is equal to 10 standard score units, or one standard deviation. The arrangement makes possible a simple rule for evaluating approximately the significance of the difference between two scores earned by a student. If the vertical distance between two scores is one inch or more, it is reasonable to assume that the student is really better in one of the abilities than the other; but if the distance is less than half an inch, it is highly probable that the abilities do not really differ. This is a very simple device which helps the counselor to make cautious interpretations.

When the DAT was first released in 1947, the manual was printed in looseleaf format so that pages could be added as the results of validity studies became available. Reports of such studies were issued in such numbers that when the manual was revised in 1952 it was necessary to present validity data in summary form. The current manual therefore contains frequency distributions of validity coefficients for the most common educational criteria and summary tables which contain the correlations (but not means and standard deviations) for all the studies completed so far. The original tables may be obtained from the American Documentation Institute.

All the validity coefficients are apparently reported: none is omitted because it happened to be low. The results strikingly verify the statement in the manual that there is no "validity of a test" but there are many validities describing the relation between test scores and various more fallible or less fallible criteria. The user of the test is encouraged to use local data for the development of expectancy tables in order to find out how the test works in his own situation. Examples of expectancy tables and how they can be constructed and used are included.

Validity studies summarized in the manual employ as criteria high school grades (including courses taken up to four years after testing), achievement test scores, college grades, and educational and vocational placement after graduation from high school. All studies reported as predictive validity studies are strictly that; that is, the tests were administered prior to the time when the criterion measures were earned.

It is impossible to summarize the wealth of validity studies within the scope of this review. There is ample evidence of the usefulness of DAT scores in a wide variety of situations. Course grades are predictable, and achievement test scores even more so (presumably because of their greater reliability). DAT scores appear to differentiate groups tested in high school who went on to various educational and voca-

tional careers (although measures of dispersion of score distributions are not presented). There is even evidence that the tests might be useful at the college freshman level, in certain institutions, for predicting freshman grades.

The question might legitimately be raised as to how "differential" the tests are, especially for predicting academic criteria. The distributions of validity coefficients are quite similar for high school courses, whether English, mathematics, science, or social studies. The three best predictors for all four of these course areas are Verbal Reasoning, Numerical Ability, and the sentences part of Language Usage. Since the summary tables do not present means, it is impossible to tell how well one could discriminate on the basis of level; but with relatively minor variations the same abilities are involved in all four course areas. For such courses as shorthand and typing the clerical and spelling tests show predictive value, and for industrial arts and mechanical drawing the spatial and mechanical reasoning tests may be related to grades. But even in such courses as bookkeeping, business arithmetic, physical education, health, home economics, and music the sentences test often shows high predictive value. High school teachers can apparently recognize ability to write grammatically correct sentences on an examination, regardless of the name of the course!

Reliability was determined by the split-half method for all tests except the highly speeded Clerical Speed and Accuracy; the reliability of this test was determined by the use of alternate forms. Reliabilities were separately computed for boys and for girls at each grade level from 8–12. The reliabilities are predominantly quite satisfactory: in the high .80's and low .90's. One test, Mechanical Reasoning, is apparently less suitable for girls than for boys; its reliability for girls ranges from .69 to .73. So far as reliability is concerned, the tests are equally good at grades 8 through 12. Standard errors of measurement are presented for each test by grade and by sex.

As might be expected with a test battery of this sort, the intercorrelations are not as low as one might desire. For boys, the mean intercorrelation coefficients range from .06 to .62, and for girls, from .12 to .67. (Some test batteries claimed to measure pure factors have intercorrelations about as high.) A table of the "proportion of differences in excess of the chance proportion" of differences between scores on pairs of tests is included. For boys, these proportions range from .29 (the verbal reasoning and sentences tests) to .52 (the space relations and spelling tests). For girls, the proportions range from .20 to .48. The proportions involving the mechanical reasoning test are all low (.20 to .24), presumably because this test is relatively unreliable for girls. As described above, the instructions for using profile charts provide a rule of thumb for deciding which differences are the ones which are large enough to be considered "in excess of chance."

Evidence from validity studies and from intercorrelations suggests that fewer than eight variables could be used without loss in predictive value, and with some increase in ease of interpretation.

Correlations of DAT with a great variety of other tests are presented. Correlations with tests of general intelligence are high enough to suggest that administration of such a test is unnecessary if DAT scores are available. Scores on the *Kuder Preference Record* are for the most part unrelated to the DAT ability measures—evidence that interest measures should not be used in lieu of ability measures (and vice versa). The information given should be useful to those who are considering the choice of a test battery; more generally, it throws light on the nature of the abilities measured by DAT.

The DAT manual is a model which other test publishers might well emulate. It presents a great deal of information clearly and without the annoying omissions which so often make it difficult or impossible to interpret statistical data in test manuals. One cannot help feeling that this is an honest and complete description of all the relevant findings, both favorable and unfavorable, which resulted from a great deal of research. Much of this work has been done by Psychological Corporation staff members, but the bibliography of 91 references also includes work by many other workers.

The authors do not hesitate to take space in the manual to instruct when they consider it desirable, and the result is a manual which is not only useful in understanding the DAT but also might well be used as supplementary reading for courses in measurement.

Some publishers of multifactor test batteries advocate use of combinations of certain scores for specific purposes. For example, methods may be recommended for weighting and combining scores to yield IQ equivalents or measures of scholastic aptitude. The DAT authors do not advocate such a procedure; instead they strongly urge the practice of counseling from profiles. They have prepared a booklet, *A Casebook for the Differential Aptitude Tests* (29), which presents DAT profiles and other information about a variety of student problems and which shows how counseling from profiles can be done. Such a clinical approach has merit, and the clinical approach, in fact, must be used in many situations. But in order to take full advantage of a multitest battery, one should also employ statistical methods to discover how best to combine scores for use in certain important and recurring problem situations. Some reference in the manual to multiple regression methods would have been desirable.

The tests are technically of very high quality, and there is ample evidence that they can be usefully employed in a wide variety of educational selection, placement, and guidance areas. This reviewer does not hesitate to recommend the *Differential Aptitude Tests* for use in testing programs at the secondary school level.

For reviews by Harold Bechtoldt, Ralph F. Berdie, and Lloyd G. Humphreys, see 4:711; see 3:620 (1 excerpt).

[606]

★**Differential Test Battery.** Ages 11 to "top university level" (range for Test 1 extends downward to age 7); 1955; 1 form; 12 tests in 7 booklets; no data on validity; 6s. 5d. per battery manual; 69s. 9d. per specimen set; postpaid in the U.K.; 136.5(200) minutes; J. R. Morrisby; distributed by the National Foundation for Educational Research in England and Wales. *

a) TEST 1, COMPOUND SERIES TEST. Ages 7 and over; "mental work power"; separate answer sheets must be used; 32s. 3d. per test; 5s. 7d. per 25 answer sheets; 3s. 6d. per set of scoring key and manual; 30(40) minutes.

b) GENERAL ABILITY TESTS. Ages 11 and over; 3 tests; 32s. 3d. per 25 tests; 11s. 9d. per set of scoring stencils and manual for all 3 tests.

　1) *Test 2, General Ability Tests: Verbal.* 12(20) minutes.

　2) *Test 3, General Ability Tests: Numerical.* 29(40) minutes.

　3) *Test 4, General Ability Tests: Perceptual.* 23 (35) minutes.

c) TEST 5, SHAPES TEST. Ages 11 and over; spatial ability; separate answer sheets must be used; 7s. 6d. per test; 6s. 4d. per 25 answer sheets; 5s. 10d. per set of scoring stencil and manual; 10(15) minutes.

d) TEST 6, MECHANICAL ABILITY TEST. Ages 11 and over; separate answer sheets must be used; 5s. 7d. per test; *6s. 4d.* per 25 answer sheets; *3s. 10d.* per set of scoring key and manual; 15(20) minutes.

e) SPEED TESTS. Ages 11 and over; 6 tests in a single booklet; no specific manual; no data on reliability; provisional norms; *48s. 6d.* per 25 tests; 17.5(30) minutes.

1) *Test 7 (Speed Test 1), Routine Number and Name Checking.*
2) *Test 8 (Speed Test 2), Perseveration.*
3) *Test 9 (Speed Test 3), Word Fluency.*
4) *Test 10 (Speed Test 4), Ideational Fluency.*
5) *Test 11 (Speed Test 5), Motor Speed.*
6) *Test 12 (Speed Test 6), Motor Skill.*

E. A. PEEL, *Professor of Education, University of Birmingham, Birmingham, England.*

According to the author, this battery represents an attempt to assess mental ability by a method that will "enable the more subtle differences between persons to be readily observed, and....show the nature of a person's mental ability structure in perspective, in the round." The tools chosen for this purpose indicate Morrisby's views about the structure of intelligence. First there is a general intelligence test which reminds one a little of a matrices test. Then there are three general ability tests dealing, respectively, with verbal, numerical, and perceptual material; a shapes test, whose purpose is to measure the spatial element; a mechanical ability test, which deals with more *km* abilities; and, finally, six speed tests of number and name checking, perseveration along the lines of the traditional copying of *s*'s and reversed *s*'s, word and ideational fluency, and motor speed and skill. The tests themselves are well produced. The manuals for the battery and for each of the several tests give adequate instructions for administering and scoring and percentile norms for appropriate age groups.

In spite of the abundance of information provided so far, however, Morrisby has failed to produce the kind of information that is essential in guiding pupils into different kinds of educational programs and into different types of vocations. For example, he reports no correlations between the tests and relevant criteria. Here he might do well to look at the technical supplement produced by the Thurstones for the *SRA Tests of Educational Ability,* in which correlations between the tests and criteria for many schools and subjects are provided so that the would-be user can judge for himself the validity of any claim that the tests differentiate as suggested. Furthermore, Morrisby does not give any data about the reliability of his test or about the standard deviations of the scores at the various age levels—statis-

tics which should certainly be provided with such a battery.

The reviewer cannot conceive of the use of these tests at the moment except in experimental and research situations. When information now lacking is forthcoming, then one can judge how useful the battery will be in school and vocational guidance.

DONALD E. SUPER, *Professor of Education, Teachers College, Columbia University, New York, New York.*

This English battery, first published in 1955, is based on the factorial structure of mental and other abilities as revealed by psychological research, particularly in Great Britain, but also in America. Thus, the American test user will encounter familiar types of tests of verbal, numerical, abstract (perceptual), and mechanical reasoning, of spatial visualization, perceptual speed and accuracy (number and name checking), and even of manual speed and dexterity (dotting and tracing); he will also find tests of types more often used in Britain than here, namely, perseveration, word fluency, and ideational fluency. As the latter types have been more useful in laboratory studies than in educational and vocational prediction, one may be inclined to question their value in a battery designed for school and college use, but that is a question to be answered by validity data.

The first test, the Compound Series Test, is a nonverbal intelligence test designed to cover the age range 7 to 22, a wider range than the other tests in the battery. It is essentially an ingenious paper and pencil version of the familiar bead stringing performance test. Morrisby suggests that it measures "mental workpower," i.e., persistence and concentration in the performance of an intellectual task, but whether or not the test measures anything other than what performance tests of intelligence generally measure is apparently a matter of conjecture. Time limits vary with age, being 20, 25, or 30 minutes, and the test is said to be a power test, but examination of the norms shows increasing scores with increasing time, which suggests that speed does play a part. It is noteworthy that the correlations between scores on this test and school grades are, on the whole, about as high as those between the more typical verbal and numerical intelligence tests and school grades. This may prove to be a most useful nonverbal test.

The General Ability Tests are three in number: Verbal, Numerical, and Perceptual. Each has three parts, the first in each case stressing speed and the last stressing comprehension; the total score weights the parts in such a way as to deemphasize speed somewhat. The perceptual test is comparable to some American abstract reasoning tests, but in each test there is evidence of ingenuity in item construction. This test is designed for use with, and standardized on, students from age 11 to age 22, as are all the tests which follow.

The Shapes Test is intended to measure spatial visualization, the "K" factor in Britain, defined as mental manipulation of perceptual figures. The items are unusual, and, although designed to minimize the use of adventitious clues, seem to this reviewer to depend upon a principle the seeing of which is a matter of intelligence, and which, if seen, changes the nature of the trait measured from complex mental manipulation to a very simple form. The trick seems to be to imagine a pin placed in the white dot occurring in each of the three shapes and mentally to let the shape rotate or fall into position around that point: the answer is then immediately obvious. But whether or not the trick is discovered is left up to the subject. Morrisby states that the ability measured by this test is not developed before about age 11, about half of that age group making zero scores; this is perhaps a defect arising from depending entirely upon one type of item with no apparent item gradient.

The Mechanical Ability Test is based on the now familiar Bennett-type item. Among the speed tests, the routine number and name checking tests, combined to give one score, otherwise resemble American tests of this type. Perseveration, Word Fluency, Ideational Fluency, Motor Speed, and Motor Skill are made up of familiar types of items and need no additional comment.

The general manual points out that the psychological interpretation of the test results must at present be limited since there is little information on which to base it. But the author proceeds, injudiciously in this reviewer's judgment, to suggest that "a great deal can be done by considering subjectively the nature of the functions measured by the various tests and judging a priori their likely interrelationships with other variables such as those we need to predict." He goes on to state, quite properly,

that "the test variables do not always behave in the way we might expect." Obviously, normative and validity data are needed.

Reliability data, it may be noted, seem adequate. The author has taken speed into account in determining reliability, and the coefficients are up to standard.

Norms leave a great deal to be desired, which may be understandable in a new test and can be excused if the author is proceeding apace to collect better norms. All the tests in the battery have "general," "grammar school," and "university" norms. At present the general norms for the Compound Series Test are based on what is "considered to be a representative sample" of nearly 3,000 boys and girls aged 7 to 15, extrapolated to provide norms for ages 6 and 16. The reasons for so thinking regarding representativeness are not given, leaving the potential user to accept the norms on faith or to reject them on the basis of sad experience. The general norms for the bulk of the battery are based on "about 800 boys and girls from secondary modern and grammar schools," essentially junior and senior high school students of all types. The grammar school (or, in American terms, junior and senior high school, college preparatory only) norms are based on "771 boys and a few girls"; it is not claimed that they are a representative sample, and the possibility of sex differences is noted but not examined. The university norms are based on 214 apparently assorted but undescribed students of both sexes, with no account taken of sex differences or of sampling.

Obviously, the norms leave a great deal to be desired before a British user can use them with any confidence, and they are of no value to a possible American user (for whom they are not intended). There is no way of knowing how representative the samples are, and sex differences, always noted on tests of mechanical reasoning and generally on tests of verbal, numerical, spatial, and perceptual abilities, are not taken into account. It is no exaggeration to say that the norming of the battery still remains to be done.

Validity has been considered in only two ways: the logic of the item writing and construction, and correlation with grades. There has been, as yet, no attempt to check the adequacy of Morrisby's spatial items, for example, by ascertaining their correlation with other, thoroughly studied tests of spatial visualization. It is this reviewer's expectation that this spatial test will not correlate as highly with existing spatial tests as they do among themselves, while the verbal and several of the other tests will probably yield the usual interform reliabilities. Hence one cannot simply accept Morrisby's recommended use of a priori judgment.

The predictive validity data are still very limited, but they are rather encouraging so far as they go. Correlations with school grades are available for what we would call 115 10th grade and 79 11th grade college preparatory high school boys, for the compound series, verbal, numerical, perceptual, shapes, and mechanical tests, and, in the case of the 11th graders, for the ideational fluency test as well. The first four tests are reasonably good predictors of grades in all subjects, the median r for the first test, for example, being .38 and all but two r's being .30 or higher. English grades are predicted best by the verbal and numerical tests, mathematics grades by the compound series and perceptual tests, and physics by the mechanical, shapes, and perceptual tests, these highest r's ranging from .36 to .80. It is noteworthy that the ideational fluency test is unrelated to any of the three subjects for which validity coefficients were obtained (English, French, and mathematics). This raises again the question of just what use a counselor or admissions officer will make of the scores on this and the other laboratory, or typically unvalidated, tests.

Manufacture of the tests, manuals, and scoring keys is quite uneven. Test booklets and answer sheets (hand scoring) are generally well printed and on suitable stock. But the holes in the scoring stencils are often imperfectly spaced and alignment in scoring is difficult to verify, no aids being provided in the form of guide lines or guide holes. The administrators' manuals are well printed but weakly bound; the use of red and black inks to differentiate explanatory material from oral directions is a helpful innovation. Mimeographed supplementary manuals and a variety of binding devices, including one with a frustrating plastic string tie-binder, give one the impression of an ill thought out profusion of materials which is not entirely justified but persists nevertheless. As one who has often decried the expenditure of more energy on merchandising than on validation by some test publishers, this reviewer hesitates to recommend more attention to packaging, but this battery would benefit by it.

In summary: this is an interestingly conceived and at points ingeniously devised multifactor battery which builds on both British and American factor analysis and test construction work. British in origin and designed for use in Britain, it has not been standardized in a way which makes it usable for practical purposes in North America, but it includes some well designed tests which may recommend it to persons conducting certain types of research in this country. The Compound Series Test, in particular, might well be exploited in America. The manual makes some unwarranted assumptions, and neither standardization nor validation has progressed far enough in Great Britain for effective use to be possible there as yet. However, the battery looks promising, and it is to be hoped that more adequate norms, studies of the relationships between these tests and others whose meaning and validity are better established, and studies of the predictive value of the tests for larger numbers of individuals in a greater variety of criterion situations (including academic subjects and occupations) will in due course be forthcoming.

PHILIP E. VERNON, *Professor of Educational Psychology, University of London, Institute of Education, London, England.*

This battery, though the first of its type to be published in England, is similar to the *General Aptitude Test Battery* or, since it disclaims factorial purity, the Psychological Corporation *Differential Aptitude Tests.* Insufficient information is available wherewith to judge the reliabilities, validities, adequacy of norming, or usefulness of the tests for any purpose. The present manual merely contains the administration and scoring instructions and norms. While a more extensive manual is promised for the future, more than two years have already gone by since the original publication. A duplicated "Preliminary Notice" by the author does little more than describe the tests and give some correlations between the first half dozen tests and grammar school examination grades of 15- and 16-year-old boys. On the basis of these figures, there would appear to be slightly better differential prediction of different school subject grades than is generally obtained by the DAT or *SRA Primary Mental Abilities.*

The battery consists of tests in 7 areas and yields 12 scores. It occupies 139 minutes of working time, but probably takes over 3 hours to administer, since the oral instructions are rather elaborate. The various types of tests may be described as follows:

a) Compound Series Test—a nonverbal reasoning test based on the completion of bead patterns. This is novel and ingenious, though its use of colored patterns possibly handicaps the color defective.

b) General verbal ability tests: three subtests—identification of synonyms and antonyms, classification of similar words, and construction of analogies.

c) Number ability tests: three subtests—checking additions and multiplications, completion of number series, and completion of number matrices. No reason is given for combining N and I tests in the same total score.

d) Perceptual ability tests: three subtests—identification of identical shapes, classification of similar figures, and selection of analogous figures. Again, the combination of perceptual speed and nonverbal reasoning tests seems curious.

e) Shape judging test—identification of reversed shapes. This is probably a sound test of S factor, but it is too difficult for younger and duller children.

f) Mechanical comprehension test—a test similar to the Bennett *Test of Mechanical Comprehension,* but with four- and five-choice items. This test, too is somewhat lacking in discrimination at the lower end.

g) Speed tests: a series of six separately scored tests—number and name checking (clerical speed); perseveration in letter writing; word completion; ideational fluency revealed through words and drawing; motor speed (similar to a dotting test); and motor coordination in drawing lines along narrow paths. No reason is given for expecting motor perseveration to be predictive of anything.

A somewhat irritating feature is the frequent alternation between black and red pencils, presumably with the object of preventing testees from working outside the time limits. This should hardly be necessary with good invigilation. Otherwise, administrative instructions and preliminary practice material are good, and the tests are well printed throughout. Tests 1, 5, and 6 employ booklets which can be reused with fresh answer sheets. Scoring, by means

of stencils, appears reasonably convenient, but might well take 15 minutes per testee. Tables are provided for converting raw scores to scaled scores (0–20) and scaled scores into equivalent T scores, percentiles, or standard IQ's, for each age group from 11 plus to 16 plus. There are also scaled score norms for grammar school and college students.

In conclusion, the tests seem to be generally well constructed, and they may be of considerable potential value in educational and vocational guidance. But no overall evaluation is possible in the absence of a proper manual.

[607]

★**Employee Aptitude Survey.** Ages 16 and over; 1952–58; IBM; 10 tests; battery manual ('58); Lockheed manual ('57); manual ['58] for each test; $2.50 per 25 test-answer sheets; postage extra; $2.50 per complete specimen set; 50¢ per specimen set of any one test; postpaid; G. Grimsley (*a–h*), F. L. Ruch (*a–g, i, j*), N. D. Warren (*a–g*), J. S. Ford (*a, c, e–g, j*); Psychological Services, Inc. *
a) TEST 1, VERBAL COMPREHENSION. 1952–58; IBM; Forms A, B ('56); 5(10) minutes.
b) TEST 2, NUMERICAL ABILITY. 1952–58; IBM; Forms A ('52), B ('56); 10(15) minutes.
c) TEST 3, VISUAL PURSUIT. 1956–58; IBM; Forms A ('56), B ('57); 5(10) minutes.
d) TEST 4, VISUAL SPEED AND ACCURACY. 1952–58; IBM; Forms A ('52), B ('56); 5(10) minutes.
e) TEST 5, SPACE VISUALIZATION. 1952–58; IBM; Forms A, B ('57); 5(10) minutes.
f) TEST 6, NUMERICAL REASONING. 1952–58; IBM; Forms A, B ('57); 5(10) minutes.
g) TEST 7, VERBAL REASONING. 1952–58; IBM; Forms A, B ('57); 5(10) minutes.
h) TEST 8, WORD FLUENCY. 1953–58; Forms A, B ('53); 5(10) minutes.
i) TEST 9, MANUAL SPEED AND ACCURACY. 1953–58; I form ('53); 5(10) minutes.
j) TEST 10, SYMBOLIC REASONING. 1956–58; IBM; Forms A, B ('57); 5(10) minutes.

DOROTHY C. ADKINS, *Professor of Psychology and Chairman of the Department, University of North Carolina, Chapel Hill, North Carolina.*

The *Employee Aptitude Survey* is comprised of nine 5-minute tests and one 10-minute test. This series has many convenient features: each test is on a single 8½ by 11 inch sheet; the time required is very short; scoring, in most cases possible by IBM scoring machine, is facilitated by stencils for right and wrong responses; norms for various job categories for each test as well as for a cross-section of the working population are provided; alternate forms, together with special retest norms, are available; separate manuals for each test report validation studies.

The general manual states that the series was

withheld from general industrial use for several years until the tests' validities against job performance could be established. To this end, it acknowledges the support of the United States Air Force, Lockheed Aircraft Corporation, Northrop Aviation, AiResearch Manufacturing Company, University of Southern California School of Engineering, and Los Angeles City College Department of Engineering.

The authors have developed this battery on the principle that "maximum validity per minute of testing time is achieved through a battery of short, mutually independent tests." The tests in the battery, together with some reference variables, were given to 90 high school boys and factor analyzed. Little information about the analysis is given in the materials accompanying the tests, but the two to four highest loadings of each of nine tests on nine factors are tabulated. The 10th test (Test 9), Manual Speed and Accuracy, correlated so low with the others that it was excluded from the analysis.

In general, alternate-forms reliability coefficients are presented, in several cases for two groups. The reporting of reliability indices as well seems unnecessary for the sophisticated and possibly misleading for the naive.

For several of the tests correlations with other standardized tests, including the *Otis Employment Test*, the *California Test of Mental Maturity*, and Bennett's *Test of Mechanical Comprehension*, are given. Unwarranted inferences are drawn from some of these correlations; e.g., the conclusion that, because the new test called Numerical Ability correlates .53 with the Bennett test, numerical ability has been shown to be an important ingredient of mechanical aptitude.

The separate examiner's manuals accompanying the different tests summarize validity data, which, altogether, form a rather impressive array. A number of the 50-odd correlations with measures other than standardized tests represent relationships with measures of success in training courses—proficiency tests, teacher evaluations, or pass-fail criteria—rather than measures of success in job performance as such. Nevertheless, a few studies were based upon job performance criteria, and information on the predictability of indices of success in training programs is distinctly better than no validity data at all.

Also provided for each test are raw score equivalents for the following centile points: 90,

75, 60, 55, 50, 45, 40, 25, 10. These norms are based on groups of subjects that differ somewhat from test to test. In all cases, norms for the "general population" are reported. Several of the tests have norms for such groups as general college students, general graduate engineers, accountants, high school students, and so on. Charts presenting norms for several additional groups for the six tests used by Lockheed Aircraft Corporation (Tests 1, 2, 4, 5, 6, and 7) are contained in a Manual for Interpreting the Employee Aptitude Survey published by that company. The authors are careful to urge each user of the tests to explore their validity in his own situation.

The bulletin How to Use the Employee Aptitude Survey contains a table of suggested cutting scores on tests recommended for various occupations. This covers 29 occupational titles, several of which do not seem to correspond to the jobs for which validity or normative data are provided elsewhere. This table is presented immediately after mention of the validation of the various tests against actual job performance criteria, and it is said that "the table of recommended tests and minimum acceptable scores....is based on the results of this long-range research program." One is at first led to believe that all of the recommendations concerning which tests to use and what cutting points are appropriate are based upon empirical validation research specific to the occupation in question and against measures of actual job success. While the authors doubtless have in their files some additional unreported research results, one can scarcely avoid the thought that, in at least some instances, they were applying the "rule of thumb" that they recommend at the end of this bulletin. Here they note that "it is common practice to set the cutting score at some raw score value between the 10th and 25th centiles for the particular occupational group in question." They further remark that, when a battery of tests is used, cutting scores between the 10th and 15th centiles are "usually most realistic." It may be reasonable to suppose, then, that where they lacked validity data but had occupational norms they applied the foregoing rule. It could even be that where they lacked both validity data and norms for a particular occupation they used their best judgment, based upon performance of similar occupational groups. Such procedures may be quite defensible and helpful, but in any case the methods followed should be clearly indicated.

Among other materials presented are tables of the coefficients of independence among the tests in the battery for four samples. These are in keeping with the authors' emphasis on unique tests.

The reviewer was disappointed to see a bulletin entitled Estimating Otis IQ from Employee Aptitude Survey Tests. Why anyone would want to administer an aptitude battery and then attempt to estimate such a defective index as the IQ for adults is incomprehensible.

A brief description and critique of each test follows.

Test 1, Verbal Comprehension, consists of 30 four-choice vocabulary items, with a ceiling that appears undesirably low. The authors will doubtless improve or replace some of the items. In a few cases, a good one-word answer does not seem possible. Thus "magnitude" does *not* mean the same as "minuend," since the latter is a particular kind of magnitude. Nor, except archaically, can "soil" be regarded as equivalent to "loam." "Rancorous" and "indignant" also have quite different connotations. The alternate-forms reliability coefficient of .83 seems unnecessarily low, especially since it was based on a wide range sample of 535 job applicants. With the 90th centile falling at 27 or above for 8 of the 15 groups for which norms are provided, it is clear that the test difficulty could well be increased.

Test 2, Numerical Ability, contains three separately timed parts: 25 items based on fundamental arithmetic operations with no larger than 3-digit numbers; 25 items involving operations with decimals and percentages; and 25 items involving simple fractions. The one-page arrangement of three parts intended to have separate time limits may well prove faulty. A "cycle omnibus" arrangement of the items with one time limit might be preferable. The reliability coefficients for the total and the three parts are not stated but can be computed from the indices of reliability that are given (.96 for the total score). The test probably could be improved if the answers followed the common plan of arranging numerical answers in ascending or descending numerical order.

Test 3, Visual Pursuit, contains 30 items patterned after the well known visual maze form. Several validation studies against training course grades are reported, along with one study against a pass-fail criterion for engineering students at the end of their first year. These studies, together with norms for "a general population," industrial leadmen, high school seniors, and freshman engineering students, do not clearly substantiate such a statement as, "The test is also useful in the selection of personnel for certain very specific clerical positions such as card-punch operators and similar jobs in which a major task component involves the scanning of paper-work." Either the substantiating data should be reported or the statement should be more cautious.

Test 4, Visual Speed and Accuracy, is a 150-item test modeled after the *Minnesota Clerical Test,* with which it correlated to the extent of .82 for a heterogeneous group of 89 job applicants. It uses various admixtures of digits, letters, and other familiar typewriter symbols (such as $, #, %, ., *, -, 1), and an occasional fraction. Alternate-forms and test-retest coefficients of from .84 to .87 are reported, along with several empirical validity studies. From a table of median scores for different occupational groups, the authors conclude that persons in job categories requiring heavy, detailed paper work obtained relatively high scores on this test. It is then curious to note that a "top management" group has scores rather similar to those of "employed stenographers" and that "college students" exceed both these groups as well as two engineering groups. It would seem that this test could bear further study.

Test 5, Space Visualization, is a 50-item block counting test with reported alternate-forms reliabilities of .87 and .89. Surprisingly enough, freshman engineering students and college students in general show almost identical norms.

Test 6, Numerical Reasoning, contains 20 number series items. A large proportion of the items that the reviewer tested were defective in that the rule for the progression that the test constructor intended could not be established until after the available answers had been inspected. Thus in the series 5 4 3 6 9 8 7 ?, the answer could be 14 (as keyed) or 10. To be sure, 10 is not among the answers presented, but this is no excuse for including annoyingly ambiguous items. The general principle, is, of course, that the rule of progression should be inducible by the time the end of the series is reached. This defect in the items may indeed account for the rather low reliability figures reported for this test: .76 (test-retest) for 90 high school males, and .60 (alternate-forms) for 335 freshman engineering students.

Test 7, Verbal Reasoning, contains six sets of five items each, each set consisting of conclusions to be judged as true, false, or uncertain upon the basis of four or five simple factual statements. One might suppose that errors within each set would be substantially correlated, thus lowering the reliability per item. Alternate-forms coefficients of .79 for 90 high school males and .70 for 335 freshman engineering students were obtained.

Test 8, Word Fluency, is of the familiar form with 75 spaces for words beginning with a designated letter. Alternate-forms reliability for the 335 engineering students was .75. No predictive validity data are given for this test.

Test 9, Manual Speed and Accuracy, involves the familiar task of placing a pencil dot in as many as possible of a series of O's within the time allowed. Reported retest reliability for 335 engineering students is .79. Only "general population" norms (for an unspecified n) are presented.

Test 10, Symbolic Reasoning, is a 30-item test containing items of the sort "$X < Y < Z$, therefore $X < Z$." The subject marks them true, false, or uncertain. Reported reliability coefficients are .68 and .69. The authors state that repeated studies have shown that mean scores of engineers and engineering students are distinctly superior to the general population mean. Norms for these three groups and for general college students and high school seniors are presented. With the 90th centile for graduate engineers at 21 (maximum score being 30) and the distribution for the general population positively skewed (as evidenced by the mean falling at the 61st centile), the test probably could be improved by adjustment of the item difficulties.

S. RAINS WALLACE, *Director of Research, Life Insurance Agency Management Association, Hartford, Connecticut.*

This is a battery of 10 short (nine have 5-minute time limits and one has a 10-minute limit) paper and pencil tests. It represents an attempt to achieve "maximum validity per minute" by taking advantage of findings which indicate that the addition to a battery of many tests having relatively unique variance enhances predictive validity to a much greater extent than the shortening of tests (with concomitant reduction in reliability) reduces it. The intercorrelations among the tests and a factor analysis (the latter, unfortunately, based on only 90 cases) support the contention that the tests are substantially independent. They have been standardized for a variety of occupational groups.

The authors provide an examiner's manual for the battery and a brochure entitled How to Use the Employee Aptitude Survey. In both of these documents there is a refreshing insistence on the importance of establishing predictive validity before using a test as a selection device. Recognition is also explicitly made of the fact that "the validity of a particular test for a particular job depends upon the specific requirements for that job in a specific organization," and potential users are urged to validate the component tests against job performance in their own organizations. However, in describing procedures for such validation, the major emphasis is placed on concurrent validities, although it is admitted that predictive validation "permits more accurate validation in the long run."

Furthermore, validity data given for each of the tests are based upon very small samples. The criteria employed are typically not measures of job performance but, instead, ratings, course or test grades, etc., which are notoriously (and spuriously) predictable. The populations are only too often freshman engineers, drafting students, or commerce students. When actual workers are studied, the validities are concurrent rather than predictive. In the case of one test (Word Fluency) no validities are reported, yet cutoff scores are recommended for three occupations.

In general, both the battery manual and the brochure represent excellent jobs of describing the test battery and its construction, and of providing a sound basis for its use and interpretation. Unfortunately, one has the feeling that the authors have violated some of their own tenets in their eagerness to establish a basis for the battery's wide and varied use. For example, the brochure presents a table of suggested cutting scores for 29 different occupations, including electrical engineers, junior executives, sales persons, inspectors, etc. A closer examination of this table in conjunction with the separate manuals for each of the tests raises some doubts about the manner in which the cutoff scores were derived. One thing which immediately strikes the eye is that the tests and cutoff scores suggested for electrical engineers, mechanical engineers, and aeronautic engineers are practically identical. One must wonder why, in this case, the heading "engineers" would not have sufficed, particularly since the individual test manuals indicate that the basic validity data were derived from the performance of some 90 freshman engineering students in their first year. Examination of the cutoff scores in conjunction with the normative tables given for each test for 251 "general graduate engineers" reveals that the recommendation is (with some very minor deviations) to cut off the bottom 25 per cent on each of the six tests recommended for engineering occupations. These tests are named, Verbal Comprehension, Numerical Ability, Visual Pursuit, Visual Speed and Accuracy, Space Visualization, and Symbolic Reasoning. Since the intercorrelations of these tests are demonstrably low, it seems surprising that cutoffs for maximum efficiency would be so similar. Also, while a recommended cutoff at the 25th centile might appear conservative, its use for each of six relatively independent tests might well produce a prohibitively low selection ratio, even in a period of recession. This could produce a very bad effect unless the validity of the suggested battery is much higher than any evidence presented would suggest. The authors give no warnings about this point.

For selecting sales persons, five tests are recommended. None of the appropriate manuals provides validity data for such occupations, but examination of the norms for 253 security salesmen and 302 sales representatives reveals that the suggested cutoff scores fall at about the 10th centile for each of the tests recommended (Verbal Comprehension, Numerical Ability, Visual Speed and Accuracy, Verbal Reasoning, and Word Fluency). One is led to the conclusion that the recommendations regarding tests and cutoff scores for the various occupations were reached through a process of arbitrary rules coupled with the authors' professional judgment about which of the occupations lend themselves most readily to prediction.

In summary, this is an outstandingly well thought out and well constructed battery of tests based upon unusually competent analysis. The format, instructions, and scoring keys are uniformly excellent. It deserves the attention of anyone who has a selection problem, particularly for a wide variety of occupations. The warnings of the authors concerning the importance of specific predictive validation of each test and the development, accordingly, of cutoff scores also deserve attention—more attention than they have received from the authors themselves.

[608]

★Flanagan Aptitude Classification Tests. Grades 12–16 and adults; 1951–56; also called FACT; 14 tests; manual ('53); $2.55 per 20 tests; 60¢ per 20 classification sheets ('53); 30¢ per examiner's manual ('53); 30¢ per technical supplement ('54); 40¢ per counselor's booklet ('53); 25¢ per manual for interpreting scores ('56); 25¢ per student's booklet for interpreting scores ('53); 50¢ per personnel director's booklet ('53); $3 per educational specimen set; $5.75 per industrial specimen set; postage extra; 210(328) minutes in 2 sessions; John C. Flanagan; Science Research Associates. *

a) FACT 1A, INSPECTION. Form A ('53); 6(12) minutes.

b) FACT 2A AND 2B, CODING. Forms A ('53), B ('54); 10(30) minutes.

c) FACT 3A AND 3B, MEMORY. Forms A ('53), B ('54); 4(5) minutes.

d) FACT 4A, PRECISION. Form A ('53); 8(15) minutes.

e) FACT 5A, ASSEMBLY. Form A ('53); 12(18) minutes.

f) FACT 6A, SCALES. Form A ('53); 16(28) minutes.

g) FACT 7A, COORDINATION. Form A ('53); $2\frac{2}{3}$(8) minutes.

h) FACT 8A, JUDGMENT AND COMPREHENSION. Form A ('53); (35–40) minutes.

i) FACT 9A, ARITHMETIC. Form A ('53); 10(20) minutes.

j) FACT 10A, PATTERNS. Form A ('53); 20(28) minutes.

k) FACT 11A, COMPONENTS. Form A ('53); 20(24) minutes.

l) FACT 12A, TABLES. Form A ('53); 10(15) minutes.

m) FACT 13A AND 13B, MECHANICS. Forms A ('53), B ('54); 20(25) minutes.

n) FACT 14A, EXPRESSION. Form A ('53); (35–45) minutes.

REFERENCES

1. LATHAM, ALBERT J. Job Appropriateness: A One-Year Follow-up of High School Graduates. Doctor's thesis, University of Pittsburgh (Pittsburgh, Pa.), 1948.
2. VOLKIN, LEONARD. A Validation Study of Selected Test Batteries Applied to Fields of Work. Doctor's thesis, University of Pittsburgh (Pittsburgh, Pa.), 1951.

HAROLD P. BECHTOLDT, *Associate Professor of Psychology, State University of Iowa, Iowa City, Iowa.*

The *Flanagan Aptitude Classification Tests* (FACT) is one of the newest and most elaborately organized of the aptitude batteries. Fourteen tests are available in Form A, and three tests in Form B. According to the manual, additional tests are being prepared to increase the accuracy of coverage of the job elements in a number of occupations.

Each test is prepared in a separate booklet

of the self-scoring (carbon transfer) type which requires the responses to be made in the test booklet. There are extensive practice materials, to be presented by the examiner, which should reduce the possibility of misunderstanding the test instructions. The test items are obviously the product of a very competent test construction staff. Accompanying the several test booklets is a series of rather extensive pamphlets for examiners, counselors, personnel directors, and students, together with a Technical Supplement summarizing the available data. The separate printing of these materials allows the test purchaser considerable flexibility in planning an order.

The Examiner Manual indicates that the battery "has been developed in an effort to establish a standard classification system for describing those aptitudes that are important for successful performance of particular occupational tasks." The two suggested uses, for vocational counseling and for the selection and placement of employees, are discussed in detail in the Counselor's Booklet and the Personnel Director's Booklet. The "aptitude" feature of these tests is emphasized in striking fashion by the omission, in the suggested procedures, of any trade or achievement tests for occupational placement and of any academic performance measures for counseling high school or college students. In view of the uniformly high correlations regularly reported between past performance and future performance in both of these areas, such omissions would seem serious in terms of "predicting successful performance."

The instructions to the examiner are quite detailed and very clearly prepared. Time limits and suggested schedules for the complete battery and for portions of the battery are provided. The use of several timed practice trials in the tests Precision and Coordination is an interesting innovation as well as a possible motivating device. A few specific suggestions to the examiner as a result of the reviewer's trial of the instructions are as follows: (*a*) More emphasis should be given to the unusual procedure for circling, rather than erasing, a response to be changed. (*b*) The omission of a question by marking a vertical line should also be emphasized, when appropriate. (*c*) In Coordination, the instructions to try to control both speed and accuracy might well be emphasized more. The time (40 seconds) allowed on

the second and third trials is twice as long as the time for the first practice trial. (*d*) In the Patterns Test, the example for Part 2 contains both an upsidedown (flopping) movement and a rotation of 90 degrees, although the instructions refer only to the upsidedown movement.

The scoring formulas and procedures are sufficiently simple to justify having the examinees exchange booklets and score them. For most tests the score is the total number of correct responses; for three tests there is a correction. Differential weighting of separate performances is required for two of the tests. Convenient conversion tables for translating raw scores to stanine scores are provided. In addition, an "answer grid" for the determination of occupational stanine scores (minus and plus values are shown for many of the occupations) provides a very convenient summary sheet for scores on the several tests.

The number of tests in the individual occupational "batteries" varies from two (usually Tests 8 and 14) to seven. The frequency with which a given test enters into the prediction equations for 30 occupations is indicated on the Aptitude Classification Sheet. Test 2, Coding, is used in only two occupational equations while Test 14, Expression, is involved in 15 occupational equations and Test 8, Judgment and Comprehension, in 22. Since Coding must precede Test 3, Memory, its use is actually required for 10 occupations.

Although the authors point out correctly that differential weighting does not markedly increase the validity of a composite score when the number of tests combined is large, the application of the principle of equal weights to small batteries of two to seven tests seems hardly appropriate. In fact, the authors repeatedly use multiple correlation coefficients (with differential weights, not unit weights) as evidence of the usefulness of the batteries.

The rationale offered for the aptitude battery involves an implicit rejection of the miniature job sample approach and the primary mental factor approaches. The authors prefer an intermediate procedure, said to start from a job element approach based on "a comprehensive list of critical behaviors involved in the job or jobs being studied." In the Technical Supplement, these critical behaviors are stated to be the ones that "really make a difference with respect to on-the-job success and failure." The selection of these behaviors, however, seems to be based on the opinions of a few industrial psychologists. The classifications of these behaviors into job elements are then "tested" in some unspecified way. It is also claimed, without supporting evidence, that this "very practical origin" of the job element approach makes possible a type of generalization and application which is excluded by the more strictly empirical approach of the job sample and primary factor procedures. (This is the first time this reviewer has seen the factor approach *criticized* for its "almost exclusive reliance on empirical validation studies.") The authors further claim that using the job element approach tends to make the personnel research worker more of a "professional worker" than a "technician."

At a time when clinical testing seems to be becoming more objective and empirical, the established emphasis on "demonstrated empirical relations" in industrial personnel work apparently is here being modified toward more emphasis on so-called professional or clinical judgment and opinion. Further evidence of such a shift can be seen in the discussion of the data offered in support of claims of prediction of "successful performance" reviewed below.

The data provided in the Technical Supplement and in the booklets for counselors and personnel directors are chiefly summaries of three large scale testing programs carried out in the Pittsburgh public high schools in 1947, 1951, and 1952, involving 1,500, 500, and 1,563 seniors, respectively. The first two of these studies provided evidence as to the adequacy of the test materials and furnished data for two follow-up studies, one by Latham (*1*) and the other by Volkin (*2*). The third provided the data for the calculation of standard scores, and intercorrelations among the 14 tests. The median intercorrelation coefficient is .29, with three tests (Assembly, Scales, and Patterns) accounting for all but one of the intercorrelations of .50 or higher. The highest intercorrelation, .69, is between Coding and Memory, which essentially are 2-response measures from different trials of the same general task.

Reliability coefficients, as well as standard errors for three stanine ranges, are provided for both Form A and Form B tests, with test-retest procedures used for the speeded tasks. The authors carefully point out that the standard errors of measurement on some of the tests are fairly substantial and that the sample sizes in several cases are not large. The lowest reli-

ability coefficient is for Mechanics, Form A, which contains only four mechanical problems with a total of 20 questions. Since Form B of this test has been made longer and less difficult, the two forms are not parallel. The claims as to comparability of the Form A and Form B series, with the exception of the mechanics test, seem reasonable. No explicit statement is made as to the computation of the reliability coefficients for "representative combined scores," but the slight increase in the coefficient over the most reliable of the several components suggests that the generalized Kuder-Richardson formulation for the reliability of a composite was used. In general, the separate reliability coefficients seem high enough to warrant serious consideration of stanine score differences of about 2.0.

Although the authors apparently question placing much reliance on empirical validation studies, they do mention the data regarding the predictive value of test scores for various types of performance. Volkin (*2*) in his 3-year follow-up of the 1947 testing program obtained positive correlations significant at the 1 per cent level for 6 out of 10 comparisons, the number of cases in the several comparisons ranging from 15 to 275. The validity coefficients using the unit nominal weights of the aptitude classification sheet are in every case considerably lower than the multiple correlation coefficients computed with optimum (beta) weights. Since the occupational combinations of Volkin were based on "tests selected at the time of initial testing as likely to be most important for the work fields," it is interesting that the authors, in the Personnel Director's Booklet, suggest that the currently recommended (but somewhat different) sets of tests will result in more accurate predictions than those reported by Volkin. If this point is sound, would it not seem reasonable for the publishers to have recomputed the validity coefficients using the currently recommended tests and weights?

During World War II, Flanagan pioneered the classic personnel research study in which nearly 1,100 airmen were given a complete aptitude battery and then sent without restriction into pilot training. The justification for this drastic action was that in no other way could the usefulness of the tests for pilot selection be unambiguously determined. It would seem nearly as important to provide similarly unequivocal data when predictions are to be made in 30 occupations. If the students had been tested on the complete battery and then followed up for three to five years, we could determine which of the many possible combinations would give the greatest likelihood of successful prediction. It would then not be necessary to use "educated guesses" concerning the similarities of the FACT tests to other published tests and the comparability of criterion measures in a variety of studies in formulating the recommended batteries for different occupations.

Probably most personnel psychologists would like also to obtain unbiased estimates of the predictive usefulness, if any, added to a set of tests by guidance and counseling procedures. Such unbiased estimates should be obtained after the test "validities" are determined and in such a way that the test and counseling contributions to "successful prediction" can be evaluated. Yet, in the Counselor's Booklet we find discussions of counseling failures on the one-year follow-up study written as though the tests were used prior to the "validity" determinations in suggesting occupational goals to the Pittsburgh high school students. Such discussions are indeed relevant to the evaluation of statements justifying current counseling procedures. However, the data so obtained cannot provide unbiased estimates of the accuracy of predictions determined from the tests alone or from the combination of tests and interviews.

In summary, the *Flanagan Aptitude Classification Tests* constitute a well designed series worthy of serious consideration for a guidance program. The test battery is judged as comparable to other available batteries for such a purpose. Although the data are considered by this reviewer as inadequate justification for many of the claims made, no other battery of tests currently available is free of this fault.

RALPH F. BERDIE, *Professor of Psychology, and Director, Student Counseling Bureau, University of Minnesota, Minneapolis, Minnesota.*

The concepts underlying the development of this battery of tests and the vast amount of relevant psychometric experience of the author suggest that the FACT battery should be of use to vocational counselors. The results of two studies, cited in the manual, involving approximately 1,000 Pittsburgh high school students, suggest that the scores derived from the tests are related to subsequent educational and voca-

tional history. The published information, however, is only suggestive and, although promising, provides a rather tenuous basis for using the battery.

The battery itself is based upon the work of Flanagan and his colleagues in the United States Army Air Force during World War II. Different tests were given to half a million persons and the scores compared to performance and achievement in a variety of military occupations. The tests included in the FACT battery can be considered as lineal descendants of the Air Force tests.

Many of the tests are quite different from those used in similar batteries. In the inspection test, for instance, each item consists of 15 different pictures of the same object; the examinee must respond to the imperfections in some of the pictures. The coding test presents brief codes to be learned and simple words or phrases to be translated into code. The memory test consists of items which measure the subject's ability to remember the codes previously learned. The precision test requires the subject to draw a line in the narrow area between two concentric circles without crossing either circle; this is done first with one hand, and then with both hands at the same time. The assembly test consists of pictures of the component parts of an object, and the subject is required to select from five objects pictured that one which consists of the components presented.

In the scales test the subject answers questions based on two graphs. In the coordination test he must draw a pencil line in the areas lying between rather large incomplete concentric circles without touching the figures; this test requires both hand and arm movement. The judgment and comprehension test items consist of a paragraph followed by multiple choice questions based in part upon the content of the paragraph. The arithmetic test includes simple and combined addition and subtraction items involving both numbers and less meaningful abstract symbols (x's), and multiplication and division of numbers. The pattern test requires the subject to reproduce simple pattern outlines and to reproduce the outlines with the figures reversed.

The components test consists of items, each of which presents a set of simple figures and a number of more complicated figures; the subject is required to determine which simple figure is contained within each complex figure.

The tables test requires the subject to answer questions, making use of first, a numerical table, and secondly, an alphabetical table. The mechanics test presents pictures of relatively simple mechanical components and the subject must answer questions pertaining to possible uses and functions of the components. The expressions test is a true and false type English examination of both grammatical usage and sentence structure.

Although only 4 of the 14 tests have items that appear to be of a verbal nature, these 4 tests (Coding, Memory, Judgment and Comprehension, and Expression) use about 37 per cent of the entire testing time. Conspicuously absent are some of the more traditional verbal items, particularly relatively simple vocabulary items, same-opposite items, and items of the analogy type. As these missing item types have in the past frequently proved to be the best predictors of academic achievement, particularly at the college level, one might suspect that the FACT battery may not prove to be useful for this purpose. Flanagan reports that seven additional tests are being prepared for publication and that these will include more tests of interest to persons concerned with predicting college success.

The items included in the FACT battery tend to be similar in type to the work sample test items which bear a direct relationship to many skilled and semiskilled jobs. The job orientation of the author is well illustrated by his attempt to make the test scores meaningful through the use of the concept of job elements. Flanagan studied a number of occupations making use of the critical incident technique and defined 21 job elements which provide information on the tasks which he thinks determine success and failure in the occupations most frequently encountered by high school graduates. These job elements were used in selecting the tests to be included in the battery as well as in arriving at estimates as to the test score patterns appropriate for most jobs.

The author and the publishers have made available a profusion of manuals for test users, but the content of each manual tends to be pretty much the same as that of the other manuals. The Examiner Manual provides a brief description of the tests and instructions for administering and scoring them. Another manual, Interpreting Test Scores, presents the results of follow-up studies with mean scores

for specific groups. A Technical Supplement describes the concepts underlying the development of the battery and the job element approach used in constructing the tests, and summarizes the information about validity, reliability, and norms. The Counselor's Booklet contains job descriptions of 30 occupations, recommendations regarding the tests to be used for each of the different occupations, and suggestions for the interpretation and use of the tests. The Personnel Director's Booklet contains essentially the same information but changed somewhat from an educational orientation to a business orientation. Finally, a bulletin for students, entitled Your FACT Scores and What They Mean, presents much of the same information, including the occupational descriptions. This bulletin cannot be substituted for the counseling provided by a qualified counselor.

The validity of the battery is suggested by the study done on 1,000 Pittsburgh high school students, which shows that students following different educational and vocational paths have different profiles. Other than this study, no additional validity data have been presented by the author, and no other published studies regarding this battery of tests have been found. Quite relevant, however, is the information about the parent Air Force battery of tests and a study by Thorndike and Hagen provides quite conclusive evidence that the scores on tests identical to or very similar to those used in the FACT battery do differentiate among persons upon the basis of occupational careers. The Thorndike-Hagen study, soon to be published in full, suggests also that test scores are not related to success on a job, as shown either by salary or self-ratings, but only to differentiations among persons in different jobs. One must conclude that as much evidence regarding the validity of these scores is available as is true for other tests at comparable stages of developments; nevertheless, the validity evidence now available warrants only cautious counseling guidance and counseling use of these tests.

The tests are relatively elaborate and complex in terms of administration and timing. When all 21 tests are finally available, they will require at least 7 hours of testing time. For many of the tests, as much time is involved in preparing the person to do the test exercises as in taking the items themselves. Whether or not this is the best use of testing time is a question.

The scoring of the tests will present a real problem if they are used in large groups. Machine scoring is not yet available. Machine scorable answer sheets are being prepared, along with single booklet editions. The present test booklets are not reusable; compared to similar tests they are relatively expensive. In those schools where counselors are reluctant to have students score their own tests—and there is much justification for this attitude—the difficulty of mass scoring now presents an almost insoluble problem.

The author's adaption of the stanine concept from his work in the Army Air Force requires more justification than he provides. Most teachers, and many counselors, are only now grasping the meaning of percentiles and standard scores. To confuse this problem now by introducing stanines may be statistically and psychologically sound, but in terms of practical problems of in-service training in test use, some real problems may be encountered.

The tests were standardized on a group of Pittsburgh public high school seniors and the norms are based on scores of these pupils. Nothing in the manual indicates how representative this group of Pittsburgh students is of United States students in general, and no attempt is made to provide norms on a nationwide sample. Whether one uses percentiles or stanines, one should know much about the nature of the group from which these scores were derived. It is hoped that more normative information will soon be available, as the author has promised.

The intercorrelations of the tests are low. Only 7 of the 91 coefficients are as high as .50 and the median coefficient is .29. The tests seem to be reasonably independent. The reliability coefficients of the 14 tests vary from .26 to .86. Standard errors of measurement are provided to help the more sophisticated counselor interpret the test scores. In general, the reliabilities of the tests in the FACT battery appear to be somewhat lower than reliabilities of tests in comparable batteries. The median reliability coefficient for the *Differential Aptitude Tests* as presented in its manual is .89. For FACT, reliability coefficients are presented not only for the individual tests but also for the combined occupational stanine scores. These coefficients range from .83 to .93.

In summary, this battery of tests is relatively long, difficult to administer and to handle, and expensive. These characteristics are unimportant if the validity and usefulness of the tests warrant the expenditure of time, effort, and money. The present evidence suggests that eventually this battery may be proved of satisfactory validity, but at the present time, as with so many other tests, one must warn the test user to approach these scores with somewhat more than the usual amount of skepticism, and with the hope that during the next few years the author will be able to present information that will reduce the need for such doubt.

JOHN B. CARROLL, *Professor of Education, Harvard University, Cambridge, Massachusetts.*

The *Flanagan Aptitude Classification Tests* comprise a group of tests, each with its own separate booklet, intended to measure a number of independent abilities which its author thinks likely, on the basis of professional judgment and previous research, to be relevant to various jobs, vocations, and professions. Materials accompanying the tests offer ingenious and easily used procedures for obtaining special scores that are supposed to be predictive of success in 30 different occupations or job fields. The orientation is distinctly towards vocational counseling and personnel selection at the high school senior level and above. On the whole, the intercorrelations among the tests are quite low.

The tests are designed to measure what the author calls "critical job elements," i.e., elements in jobs which "really make a difference with respect to on-the-job success and failure." In this way, the author feels he has been able to strike a happy balance between the miniature job sample approach and the "primary mental factor" approach. The former of these approaches he regards as impractical because it would require work samples for a very large number of jobs, while the latter approach, he believes, relies too heavily on "empirical validation studies," to the extent that "the personnel research worker becomes almost entirely a technician rather than a professional worker." In Flanagan's opinion, the testmaker or the personnel worker who uses the "job element" approach has the opportunity to call upon all his powers of observation and understanding of the abilities and performances that make for success in work. It is difficult, however, to see just how this view differs from that of the factor analyst, who is just as anxious as Flanagan to understand the nature of the abilities required in different jobs and to learn the extent to which they are relevant. If the job element approach discloses abilities which the factor analyst had not envisaged, it is the fault only of the factor analyst's creative imagination or perception, not of his analytic model. Flanagan's "critical job element" approach is factor-analytic thinking in a slightly new guise, and it does not in any way preclude the need for careful and extensive validation studies, however tiresome such studies may seem.

Flanagan's total program calls for the publication of 21 FACT tests in all, but at this writing only 14 are available, 3 of them with alternate forms. Planned for later publication are tests of vocabulary, reasoning, planning, ingenuity, alertness, tapping, and carving. No explanation is given for delaying the publication of these tests, some of which might conceivably be more generally useful than some of the first 14 tests; the battery is short on purely intellectual tests.

One is inclined to feel that the author would have been well advised to delay the publication of some of the tests until they had been subjected to considerable revision or validation. There is no evidence that the items in the various tests were selected through analyses of item difficulty and item validity. We are told that a 27-test battery was developed and experimentally administered in 1947, and that 11 revised tests underwent preliminary tryouts with about 500 high school senior boys in 1951; thereafter, we find only that the 14 tests currently available were administered in their "final" form to a sample "representative of all Pittsburgh Public High School seniors" in December 1952. The published stanine norms are based on this latter sample, but the results sometimes belie the author's claim that the tests produce "a satisfactory spread among those tested." For example, the raw scores on the 120-item Test 6, Scales, have a mean of 17.9 and a standard deviation of 12.0! The distribution is highly skewed, and the test is highly speeded. As another example, it appears that scores on Test 13, Mechanics, are largely chance (mean score is 6.5; each of the 20 items has 5 alternatives). This test involves questions on drawings of fairly complicated pieces of mechanical equipment which would be gen-

erally unfamiliar to most examinees—even those with a mechanical bent. Test 13, in fact, has a split-half reliability of only .26 and an alternate-form reliability of .59, despite its 20-minute time limit. The fact that this test has low intercorrelations with other tests in the battery is hardly spectacular.

The reported reliabilities of the subtests seldom exceed .80, but these are excused on the ground that the subtest scores are intended to be combined in teams of from two to seven scores in accordance with the scheme worked out for this purpose (the Aptitude Classification Sheet). Since some of the resulting "vocational aptitude scores" are shown to have high reliabilities and useful validity coefficients, we may tentatively accept the author's judgment, but with the reservation that the reliabilities could probably have been improved in many of the subtests by standard test construction techniques.

Solely on the basis of careful perusal of the tests themselves, this reviewer judges that the currently available subtests are extremely uneven in quality. Test 1, Inspection, is highly speeded and might be a reasonably good measure of some sort of perceptual ability involved in factory inspection tasks and the like, except that the "inspection" of a parade of little pictures on a piece of paper is a far cry from the real task in a factory. It correlates only .22 with the DAT clerical speed and accuracy test, at least in one sample. Test 2, Coding, suffers from the fact that its task is ambiguous: subjects can succeed either by quickly memorizing the codes or by being nimble in referring to them. Most subjects will probably be lazy and try to rely on looking them up; thus they will be ill prepared for Test 3, Memory, which, unheralded, asks the examinee to demonstrate his memory for the codes. The reliability of .55 does not speak well for the test. Test 4, Precision, is a paper and pencil performance test of fine coordination ability; what has to be demonstrated, however, is that this kind of task is really similar to the finger and tweezer precision tasks actually encountered in industry. On the surface, Test 5, Assembly, looks as if it would measure the so-called spatial visualization factor, and perhaps it really does ($r =$ .59 with Space Relations, DAT); the task of matching up pictured 3-dimensional forms in terms of alphabetical symbols seems overly distracting, however. Even the practice items are at a high level of difficulty.

We have already mentioned the poor score spread on Test 6, Scales. For the individual without special training, the task of reading values from 2-dimensional graphs and from a chart of polar coordinates will be very difficult; the situation is not helped by very fine, close printing and excessive photographic reduction. For those who know how to read graphs and scales, the test is really a measure of "carefulness." Test 7, Coordination, is another paper and pencil performance test, this time measuring a grosser kind of hand-arm coordination than Test 4, with which it intercorrelates .39 (in the 1952 standardization sample). Test 8, Judgment and Comprehension, seems to be a combined reading comprehension and practical judgment test. It has poor score spread (mean 15.2, SD 3.8, 24 items) and poor reliability (.65), and seems not to be worth the investment of 35 minutes or more of testing time. Its factorial complexity would probably make score interpretations problematical; many of the items are ambiguous and open to question. Test 9, Arithmetic, is similar to number ability tests found in other batteries; it displays reasonably good test characteristics in view of its 10-minute working time. Test 10, Patterns, is a paper and pencil performance test probably measuring a combination of spatial ability and carefulness; it is reminiscent of the copying test in the *MacQuarrie Test for Mechanical Ability* but requires closer visual attention. Test 11, Components, is reminiscent of the Gottschaldt figures test, but again, it is quite difficult and taxing; furthermore, one would be hard pressed to conceive a job in which the ability to detect a specified visual pattern within a larger field would be critical (except perhaps in detecting military camouflage!). Test 12, Tables, would be a good measure of the perceptual speed factor if its reliability were more satisfactory; it correlates .40 with the DAT clerical speed and accuracy test. Test 13, Mechanics, has already been commented on as being too difficult and specialized for the ordinary test taking population. Test 14, Expression, is a reasonably satisfactory test of knowledge of grammatical "rules" and sensitivity to the more superficial aspects of good English writing; it correlates .68 with DAT Language Usage—Part II (Sentences).

So much for the tests themselves. There is not so much to say about the validation of the tests because this is up to now more in the realm of plan than of reality. The author has adopted the strategy of making the test widely available at the outset and planning extensive periodic follow-up studies. The results of the one validity study reported in the Technical Supplement are of moderate promise, however, even if we restrict our attention to the coefficients based on "equal weights." Success in sales, electrical work, structural work, and mechanical work can be predicted with validity coefficients of .45 to .65. The validities for college work are low, however, and probably reflect the fact that the battery contains few tests of the conventional college aptitude type. It will take a major effort over a period of years to provide adequate validation data for the FACT tests. But the basic material to be validated is of such dubious quality, on the whole, that one wonders whether the author might not better serve the cause of multifactor testing by stopping to make judicious revisions of the tests before undue amounts of time and money are expended in standardizing the current series.

In this light, it is hard to understand the air of assurance which seems to be adopted by the author (or his publishers or editors) in setting forth elaborate procedures for combining scores, interpreting score profiles, and using the tests in personnel selection. The extensive studies made by Super and by Ghiselli of the general problem of predicting occupational success cannot make one overwhelmingly confident that occupational guidance is a simple matter of making judicious mixtures of "critical job elements" whereby to match men and jobs. For all of Flanagan's earnest exhortations to personnel workers to seek to apply superior wisdom and psychological insight to the understanding of the behavior of men working on tasks, one is faced with the fact that Flanagan's own insight has its dim moments. Consider the test in the present series called Memory (Test 3), which figures in the vocational aptitude scores for accountant, businessman, office clerk, humanities professor, lawyer, nurse, physician, salesperson, secretary, and writer. According to the description provided, "This test measures ability to remember the codes learned in Test 2." And what are those codes? A series of arbitrary alphabetical and numeral symbols which might represent "office room numbers of departments," "delivery truck routes," etc. While we might grant that such a kind of memory could be useful to an accountant, a nurse, or a physician, it would hardly be regarded as "critical" to them—and certainly not to a "humanities professor" or a "writer."

One may go so far as to characterize the FACT tests as sleek and even handsome in format and appearance. The scoring device involving a carbon insert is ingenious and will have many advantages, although it was noticed that on some of the tests the carbon was not heavy enough to produce a clear carbon impression on the scoring grid.

Because of the somewhat undeveloped state of some of the tests and the rather weak validation data available to date, the *Flanagan Aptitude Classification Tests* should be regarded as constituting an interesting research instrument which may potentially develop into a useful counseling tool.

[609]

General Aptitude Test Battery. Ages 16 and over; 1946–58; test battery developed for use in the occupational counseling program of the United States Employment Service and released in 1947 for use by State Employment Services; titles on tests are *GATB Book 1, GATB Book 2, GATB Part 8*; 9 scores (12 tests): intelligence, verbal, numerical, spatial, form perception, clerical perception, motor coordination, finger dexterity, manual dexterity; IBM except Part 8 and apparatus tests; Forms A ['52], B ['53]; manual ('58) in 3 sections; directions for administering ['52] apparatus tests; mimeographed record blank ['52] for apparatus tests; profile ['56]; aptitude pattern card ['57]; tests available to nonprofit institutions for counseling purposes; testing services free of charge when program is conducted through the facilities of State Employment Service offices; institutions using their own facilities must purchase tests and employ testing supervisors trained by U.S.E.S.; details may be secured from local and state offices, through which all orders must be cleared; separate answer sheets must be used; $9.50 per 500 IBM answer sheets; specimen set not available; 49(135) minutes; United States Employment Service.

a) BOOK 1. 4 tests: name comparison, computation, three-dimensional space, vocabulary; $14 per 100 copies of Form A; $15 per 100 copies of Form B; postpaid; Government Printing Office.

b) BOOK 2. 3 tests: tool matching, arithmetic reasoning, form matching; $10 per 100 copies of Form A; $12 per 100 copies of Form B; postpaid; Government Printing Office.

c) PART 8. 1 test: mark making; $2.75 per 100 tests; postpaid; Government Printing Office.

d) PEGBOARD. 2 tests: place, turn; $20.50 per set of test materials; postpaid; distributed by Specialty Case Manufacturing Co. and Warwick Products Co.

e) FINGER DEXTERITY BOARD. 2 tests: assemble, disassemble; $9.65 per set of test materials; postpaid; distributed by Specialty Case Manufacturing Co. and Warwick Products Co.

REFERENCES

1–33. See 4:714.
34. ODELL, CHARLES E. "Cooperative Research in Aptitude Test Development." *Ed & Psychol Meas* 9:396–400 au '49. * (PA 26:3050)
35. BIERBAUM, WILLIAM B. *The Prediction of Scholastic Success of Graduate Students in Psychology by Means of the United States Employment Service General Aptitude Test Battery.* Master's thesis, University of Florida (Gainesville, Fla.), 1951.
36. MORGAN, MARCELLUS. *An Evaluation of the United States Employment Service General Aptitude Test Battery for the Field of Forestry.* Master's thesis, University of Florida (Gainesville, Fla.), 1951.
37. ASHE, MARGARET R. *Predicting Scholastic Success at Texas State College for Women Through the Use of the General Aptitude Test Battery: An Inquiry Based on a One Year's Study.* Master's thesis, Texas State College for Women (Denton, Tex.), 1952.
38. BOULGER, JOHN R. *The Generalized Distance Function and Differential Aptitude Testing.* Doctor's thesis, University of Minnesota (Minneapolis, Minn.), 1952. (DA 13:254)
39. DVORAK, BEATRICE J.; FOX, FRANCES C.; and MEIGH, CHARLES. "Tests for Field Survey Interviewers." *J Marketing Res* 16:301–6 Ja '52. *
40. ISAACSON, LEE E. "Predictors of Success for Cooperative Occupational Education Classes in Kansas City, Missouri, High Schools." Abstract. *Am Psychol* 7:379 Jl '52. *
41. O'CONNOR, N. "The Prediction of Psychological Stability and Anxiety-Agressiveness From a Battery of Tests Administered to a Group of High Grade Male Mental Defectives." *J General Psychol* 46:3–17 Ja '52. * (PA 27:2055)
42. RALPH, RAY B., AND TAYLOR, CALVIN W. "The Role of Tests in the Medical Selection Program." *J Appl Psychol* 36:107–11 Ap '52. * (PA 27:674)
43. STORRS, SIBYLL V. *An Evaluative Comparison of the United States Employment Service General Aptitude Test Battery and the Wechsler Bellevue Intelligence Scale.* Master's thesis, University of Florida (Gainesville, Fla.), 1952.
44. STORRS, SIBYLL. "Evaluative Data on the G.A.T.B." *Personnel & Guid J* 31:87–90 N '52. * (PA 27:6164)
45. TAYLOR, EDWIN S. *The Prediction of Scholastic Success of Engineering Seniors With the General Aptitude Test Battery.* Master's thesis, University of Florida (Gainesville, Fla.), 1952.
46. BOULGER, JOHN R. "The Generalized Distance Function and Differential Aptitude Testing." Abstract. *Am Psychol* 8:324 Ag '53. *
47. GERBER, VERNON R. *Prediction of College Success From the General Aptitude Testing Battery.* Master's thesis, University of Toledo (Toledo, Ohio), 1953.
48. JEX, FRANK B., AND SORENSON, A. GARTH. "G.A.T.B. Scores as Predictors of College Grades." *Personnel & Guid J* 31:295–7 F '53. * (PA 28:1565)
49. MALECKI, HENRY R. *An Investigation of the Validity of the General Aptitude Test Battery for the Vocational Guidance of High School Graduates.* Doctor's thesis, Purdue University (Lafayette, Ind.), 1953.
50. MAPOU, ALBERT. "Development of General Working Population Norms for the USES General Aptitude Test Battery." Abstract. *Am Psychol* 8:401–2 Ag '53. *
51. MORGAN, JOSEPH P. *Investigation Into the Use at Senior High School Level of the U.S. Employment Service General Aptitude Test Battery.* Master's thesis, Boston College (Chestnut Hill, Mass.), 1953.
52. SCHENKEL, KENNETH F. *Tabulator Operator Selection, Emphasizing Relationships Among Aptitudes, Interests, Proficiency, Job- and Vocational-Satisfaction.* Doctor's thesis, University of Minnesota (Minneapolis, Minn.), 1953. (DA 13:1251)
53. "Validity Information Exchange, No. 7-050: D.O.T. Code 0-98.07, Manager, Insurance Office." *Personnel Psychol* 7:285 su '54. *
54. ANDERSON, MARY R. "Standardization of the General Aptitude Test Battery for Three Certification Areas at Stephens College." *Trans Kans Acad Sci* 57:354–65 S '54. *
55. MINNESOTA STATE EMPLOYMENT SERVICE. "Validity Information Exchange, No. 7-052: D.O.T. Code 1-25.64, Tabulating-Machine Operator." *Personnel Psychol* 7:287–8 su '54. *
56. MINNESOTA STATE EMPLOYMENT SERVICE. "Standardization of the GATB for the Occupation of Tabulating Machine Operator." *J Appl Psychol* 38:297–8 O '54. * (PA 29:6358)
57. UNITED STATES EMPLOYMENT SERVICE. "Validity Information Exchange, No. 7-001: D.O.T. Code 0-13.10, Dentist." *Personnel Psychol* 7:125 sp '54. *
58. UNITED STATES EMPLOYMENT SERVICE. "Validity Information Exchange, No. 7-002: D.O.T. Code 0-33.27, Nurse." *Personnel Psychol* 7:126 sp '54. *
59. UNITED STATES EMPLOYMENT SERVICE. "Validity Information Exchange, No. 7-003: D.O.T. Code 0-50.22, Chemist Assistant." *Personnel Psychol* 7:127 sp '54. *
60. UNITED STATES EMPLOYMENT SERVICE. "Validity Information Exchange, No. 7-006: D.O.T. Code 1-02.01, Bookkeeping-Machine Operator I." *Personnel Psychol* 7:132 sp '54. *
61. UNITED STATES EMPLOYMENT SERVICE. "Validity Information Exchange, No. 7-008: D.O.T. Code 1-06.02, Teller." *Personnel Psychol* 7:135 sp '54. *
62. UNITED STATES EMPLOYMENT SERVICE. "Validity Information Exchange, No. 7-013: D.O.T. Code 1-36.04, Survey Worker." *Personnel Psychol* 7:143 sp '54. *

63. UNITED STATES EMPLOYMENT SERVICE. "Validity Information Exchange, No. 7-015:D.O.T. Code 1-37.12, Stenographer; 1-37.32, Typist." *Personnel Psychol* 7:146 sp '54. *
64. UNITED STATES EMPLOYMENT SERVICE. "Validity Information Exchange, No. 7-020:D.O.T. Code 1-42.01, Central-Office Operator." *Personnel Psychol* 7:155 sp '54. *
65. UNITED STATES EMPLOYMENT SERVICE. "Validity Information Exchange, No. 7-025:D.O.T. Code 4-52.760, Pilot-Control Operator." *Personnel Psychol* 7:161 sp '54. *
66. UNITED STATES EMPLOYMENT SERVICE. "Validity Information Exchange, No. 7-026:D.O.T. Code 4-75.010, Machinist." *Personnel Psychol* 7:162 sp '54. *
67. UNITED STATES EMPLOYMENT SERVICE. "Validity Information Exchange, No. 7-027:D.O.T. Code 4-97.010, Electrician." *Personnel Psychol* 7:163 sp '54. *
68. UNITED STATES EMPLOYMENT SERVICE. "Validity Information Exchange, No. 7-028:D.O.T. Code 4-97.910, Electrician, Airplane." *Personnel Psychol* 7:164 sp '54. *
69. UNITED STATES EMPLOYMENT SERVICE. "Validity Information Exchange, No. 7-029:D.O.T. Code 5-25.110, Carpenter." *Personnel Psychol* 7:165 sp '54. *
70. UNITED STATES EMPLOYMENT SERVICE. "Validity Information Exchange, No. 7-030:D.O.T. Code 5-30.210, Plumber." *Personnel Psychol* 7:166 sp '54. *
71. UNITED STATES EMPLOYMENT SERVICE. "Validity Information Exchange, No. 7-031:D.O.T. Code 6-06.450, Cheese Wrapper." *Personnel Psychol* 7:167 sp '54. *
72. UNITED STATES EMPLOYMENT SERVICE. "Validity Information Exchange, No. 7-032:D.O.T. Code 6-12.341, Wrapper Layer and Examiner, Soft Work; 6-12.351, Wrapper Layer." *Personnel Psychol* 7:168 sp '54. *
73. UNITED STATES EMPLOYMENT SERVICE. "Validity Information Exchange, No. 7-033:D.O.T. Code 6-27.560 Through 6-27.589, Special Sewing Machine Operators, Garment; 6-27.530 Through 6-27.539, Standard Sewing Machine Operators, Garment." *Personnel Psychol* 7:169 sp '54. *
74. UNITED STATES EMPLOYMENT SERVICE. "Validity Information Exchange, No. 7-034:D.O.T. Code 6-54.052, Bomb-Fuse-Parts Assembler." *Personnel Psychol* 7:170 sp '54. *
75. UNITED STATES EMPLOYMENT SERVICE. "Validity Information Exchange, No. 7-035:D.O.T. Code 6-99.166, Electric-Motor Assembler." *Personnel Psychol* 7:171 sp '54. *
76. UNITED STATES EMPLOYMENT SERVICE. "Validity Information Exchange, No. 7-036:D.O.T. Code 7-00.020, Mounter; 7-00.016, Mounter I." *Personnel Psychol* 7:172 sp '54. *
77. UNITED STATES EMPLOYMENT SERVICE. "Validity Information Exchange, No. 7-037:D.O.T. Code 7-05.901, Outboard-Motor Assembler III." *Personnel Psychol* 7:173 sp '54. *
78. UNITED STATES EMPLOYMENT SERVICE. "Validity Information Exchange, No. 7-038:D.O.T. Code 7-16.900, Decorator, Hand." *Personnel Psychol* 7:174 sp '54. *
79. UNITED STATES EMPLOYMENT SERVICE. "Validity Information Exchange, No. 7-039:D.O.T. Code 8-04.10, Fruit Sorter." *Personnel Psychol* 7:175 sp '54. *
80. UNITED STATES EMPLOYMENT SERVICE. "Validity Information Exchange, No. 7-040:D.O.T. Code 8-09.01, Laborer, Poultry." *Personnel Psychol* 7:176 sp '54. *
81. UNITED STATES EMPLOYMENT SERVICE. "Validity Information Exchange, No. 7-041:D.O.T. Code 8-09.11, Slaughtering and Meat Packing Workers." *Personnel Psychol* 7:177 sp '54. *
82. UNITED STATES EMPLOYMENT SERVICE. "Validity Information Exchange, No. 7-042:D.O.T. Code 8-49.01, Bindery Workers." *Personnel Psychol* 7:178 sp '54. *
83. UNITED STATES EMPLOYMENT SERVICE. "Validity Information Exchange, No. 7-043:D.O.T. Code 8-53.01, Table Worker." *Personnel Psychol* 7:179 sp '54. *
84. UNITED STATES EMPLOYMENT SERVICE. "Validity Information Exchange, No. 7-044:D.O.T. Code 9-68.01, Packer, Tea Bag." *Personnel Psychol* 7:180 sp '54. *
85. UNITED STATES EMPLOYMENT SERVICE. "Validity Information Exchange, No. 7-046:D.O.T. Code 0-15.01, 0-16.01, 0-17.01, 0-19.01, Engineer." *Personnel Psychol* 7:280-1 su '54. *
86. UNITED STATES EMPLOYMENT SERVICE. "Validity Information Exchange, No. 7-047:D.O.T. Code 0-25.10, Pharmacist." *Personnel Psychol* 7:282 su '54. *
87. UNITED STATES EMPLOYMENT SERVICE. "Validity Information Exchange, No. 7-048:D.O.T. Code 0-26.10, Physician." *Personnel Psychol* 7:283 su '54. *
88. UNITED STATES EMPLOYMENT SERVICE. "Validity Information Exchange, No. 7-049:D.O.T. Code 0-30.02, Teacher, Nursery School." *Personnel Psychol* 7:284 su '54. *
89. UNITED STATES EMPLOYMENT SERVICE. "Validity Information Exchange, No. 7-051:D.O.T. Code 1-17.02, File Clerk II." *Personnel Psychol* 7:286 su '54. *
90. UNITED STATES EMPLOYMENT SERVICE. "Validity Information Exchange, No. 7-054:D.O.T. Code 1-44.12, Ticket Agent (Reservation Clerk)." *Personnel Psychol* 7:290 su '54. *
91. UNITED STATES EMPLOYMENT SERVICE. "Validity Information Exchange, No. 7-056:D.O.T. Code 2-38.20, Nurse, Practical." *Personnel Psychol* 7:292 su '54. *
92. UNITED STATES EMPLOYMENT SERVICE. "Validity Information Exchange, No. 7-057:D.O.T. Code 4-35.720, Upholsterer II." *Personnel Psychol* 7:293 su '54. *
93. UNITED STATES EMPLOYMENT SERVICE. "Validity Information Exchange, No. 7-058:D.O.T. Code 4-44.010, Compositor, Hand." *Personnel Psychol* 7:294 su '54. *
94. UNITED STATES EMPLOYMENT SERVICE. "Validity Information Exchange, No. 7-059:D.O.T. Code 4-48.010, Cylinder-Press Man; 4-48.030, Web-Press Man." *Personnel Psychol* 7:295 su '54. *
95. UNITED STATES EMPLOYMENT SERVICE. "Validity Information Exchange, No. 7-060:D.O.T. Code 4-84.012, Shipfitter." *Personnel Psychol* 7:296 su '54. *
96. UNITED STATES EMPLOYMENT SERVICE. "Validity Information Exchange, No. 7-061:D.O.T. Code 4-88.622, Sheet Metal Worker." *Personnel Psychol* 7:297 su '54. *
97. UNITED STATES EMPLOYMENT SERVICE. "Validity Information Exchange, No. 7-062:D.O.T. Code 5-81.010, Automobile Mechanic." *Personnel Psychol* 7:298 su '54. *
98. UNITED STATES EMPLOYMENT SERVICE. "Validity Information Exchange, No. 7-063:D.O.T. Code 5-83.123, Calculating-Machine Serviceman." *Personnel Psychol* 7:299 su '54. *
99. UNITED STATES EMPLOYMENT SERVICE. "Validity Information Exchange, No. 7-066:D.O.T. Code 6-14.171, Boarder II; 6-14.173, Boarding-Machine Operator." *Personnel Psychol* 7:302 su '54. *
100. UNITED STATES EMPLOYMENT SERVICE. "Validity Information Exchange, No. 7-067:D.O.T. Code 6-88.627, Forming-Press Operator." *Personnel Psychol* 7:303 su '54. *
101. UNITED STATES EMPLOYMENT SERVICE. "Validity Information Exchange, No. 7-068:D.O.T. Code 8-98.71, Record Pressman." *Personnel Psychol* 7:304 su '54. *
102. UNITED STATES EMPLOYMENT SERVICE. "Validity Information Exchange, No. 7-072:D.O.T. Code 1-18.33, Claims Taker; 0-68.71, Employment Interviewer." *Personnel Psychol* 7:409-10 au '54. *
103. UNITED STATES EMPLOYMENT SERVICE. "Validity Information Exchange, No. 7-080:D.O.T. Code 8-27.77, Carding Machine Operator." *Personnel Psychol* 7:427 au '54. *
104. UNITED STATES EMPLOYMENT SERVICE. "Validity Information Exchange, No. 7-081:D.O.T. Code 8-53.51, Laborer (Fireworks)." *Personnel Psychol* 7:428 au '54. *
105. UNITED STATES EMPLOYMENT SERVICE. "Validity Information Exchange, No. 7-083:D.O.T. Code 0-39.93, Dietitian." *Personnel Psychol* 7:555 w '54. *
106. UNITED STATES EMPLOYMENT SERVICE. "Validity Information Exchange, No. 7-088:D.O.T. Code 5-83.411, Radio Repairman I." *Personnel Psychol* 7:563-4 w '54. *
107. UNITED STATES EMPLOYMENT SERVICE. "Validity Information Exchange, No. 7-092:D.O.T. Code 6-19.041, Spinner, Ring Frame." *Personnel Psychol* 7:570 w '54. *
108. UNITED STATES EMPLOYMENT SERVICE. "Validity Information Exchange, No. 7-093:D.O.T. Code 7-00.070, Light-Bulb Assembler." *Personnel Psychol* 7:571 w '54. *
109. WISE, ROBERTA M. *The Educational Significance of the General Aptitude Test Battery for Howard University School of Pharmacy.* Master's thesis, Howard University (Washington, D.C.), 1954.
110. BLACKBURN, JESSIE B. *The Use of the General Aptitude Test Battery Recorded Interviews in Vocational Counseling.* Master's thesis, Oregon State College (Corvallis, Ore.), 1955.
111. DVORAK, BEATRICE J. "New G.A.T.B. Occupational Aptitude Pattern: Norm Structure." *Voc Guid Q* 3:110-2 su '55. *
112. GJERNES, OSCAR. *The Use of the General Aptitude Test Battery to Predict Success for Students in Professional Courses in Agriculture and Chemical Technology.* Master's thesis, North Dakota Agricultural College (Fargo, N.D.), 1955.
113. MADDEN, GORDON J. *The Standardization of the General Aptitude Test Battery and Development of Selection Aptitude Test Battery for Student Nurse.* Master's thesis, Marquette University (Milwaukee, Wis.), 1955.
114. MAPOU, ALBERT. "Development of General Working Population Norms for the USES General Aptitude Test Battery." *J Appl Psychol* 39:130-3 Ap '55. * (PA 30:1720)
115. SORENSON, GARTH, AND SENIOR, NOEL. "Changes in GATB Scores With College Training." *Calif J Ed Res* 6:170-3 S '55. * (PA 30:6340)
116. TRAEGER, CARL. *Effectiveness of the United States Employment Service General Aptitude Test Battery in Employment Counseling of High-School Seniors.* Doctor's thesis, University of Wisconsin (Madison, Wis.), 1955.
117. UNITED STATES EMPLOYMENT SERVICE. "Validity Information Exchange, No. 8-01:D.O.T. Code 0-13.10. Dentist." *Personnel Psychol* 8:105-6 sp '55. *
118. UNITED STATES EMPLOYMENT SERVICE. "Validity Information Exchange, No. 8-02:D.O.T. Code 0-34.10, Veterinarian." *Personnel Psychol* 8:107-8 sp '55. *
119. UNITED STATES EMPLOYMENT SERVICE. "Validity Information Exchange, No. 8-05:D.O.T. Code 1-38.01, Stock Clerk II." *Personnel Psychol* 8:113 sp '55. *
120. UNITED STATES EMPLOYMENT SERVICE. "Validity Information Exchange, No. 8-06:D.O.T. Code 2-42.20, Nurse Aide." *Personnel Psychol* 8:114 sp '55. *
121. UNITED STATES EMPLOYMENT SERVICE. "Validity Information Exchange, No. 8-07:D.O.T. Code 4-25.030, Dressmaker." *Personnel Psychol* 8:115 sp '55. *
122. UNITED STATES EMPLOYMENT SERVICE. "Validity Information Exchange, No. 8-08:D.O.T. Code 4-44.010, Compositor, Hand and Machine." *Personnel Psychol* 8:116-7 sp '55. *
123. UNITED STATES EMPLOYMENT SERVICE. "Validity Information Exchange, No. 8-10:D.O.T. Code 6-27.513, Seamer." *Personnel Psychol* 8:120 sp '55. *
124. UNITED STATES EMPLOYMENT SERVICE. "Validity Information Exchange, No. 8-11:D.O.T. Code 6-57.174, Pressman." *Personnel Psychol* 8:121 sp '55. *

125. UNITED STATES EMPLOYMENT SERVICE. "Validity Information Exchange, No. 8-12:D.O.T. Code 8-53.01, Laborer; 7-68.015, Filling-Machine Operator II; 9-68.20, Labeler, Hand; 9-68.10, Laborer, Container Capping; 9-68.30, Packer II; 9-68.20, Stamper II." *Personnel Psychol* 8:122–3 sp '55. *

126. UNITED STATES EMPLOYMENT SERVICE. "Validity Information Exchange, No. 8-15:D.O.T. Code 5-30.010, Pipe Fitter; 5-30.210, Plumber." *Personnel Psychol* 8:264–6 su '55. *

127. UNITED STATES EMPLOYMENT SERVICE. "Validity Information Exchange, No. 8-18:D.O.T. Code 6-14.341, Pairer (Hosiery)." *Personnel Psychol* 8:269 su '55. *

128. UNITED STATES EMPLOYMENT SERVICE. "Validity Information Exchange, No. 8-20:D.O.T. Code 8-12.10, Stripper, Hand (Tobacco)." *Personnel Psychol* 8:271 su '55. *

129. UNITED STATES EMPLOYMENT SERVICE. "Validity Information Exchange, No. 8-21:D.O.T. Code 1-04.01, Clerk, General; 1-05.01, Clerk, General Office; 1-25.02, Billing Machine Operator; 1-25.13, Comptometer Operator." *Personnel Psychol* 8:375–6 au '55. *

130. UNITED STATES EMPLOYMENT SERVICE. "Validity Information Exchange, No. 8-22:D.O.T. Code 1-18.65, Stock Chaser II." *Personnel Psychol* 8:377 au '55. *

131. UNITED STATES EMPLOYMENT SERVICE. "Validity Information Exchange, No. 8-24:D.O.T. Code 4-35.720, Upholsterer II." *Personnel Psychol* 8:379–80 au '55. *

132. UNITED STATES EMPLOYMENT SERVICE. "Validity Information Exchange, No. 8-25:D.O.T. Code 6-24.234, Decorator." *Personnel Psychol* 8:381 au '55. *

133. UNITED STATES EMPLOYMENT SERVICE. "Validity Information Exchange, No. 8-28:D.O.T. Code 0-97.61, Manager, City District." *Personnel Psychol* 8:493 w '55. *

134. UNITED STATES EMPLOYMENT SERVICE. "Validity Information Exchange, No. 8-29:D.O.T. Code 6-14.235, Stocking Inspector I." *Personnel Psychol* 8:494 w '55. *

135. UNITED STATES EMPLOYMENT SERVICE. "Validity Information Exchange, No. 8-30:D.O.T. Code 6-24.235, Straw Hat Sewing Machine Operator I; 6-27.530 through 6-27.539, Standard Sewing Machine Operators, Garment; 6-27.560 through 6-27.589, Special Sewing Machine Operators, Garment." *Personnel Psychol* 8:495–6 w '55. *

136. UNITED STATES EMPLOYMENT SERVICE. "Validity Information Exchange, No. 8-31:D.O.T. Code 6-66.361, Paster." *Personnel Psychol* 8:497 w '55. *

137. UNITED STATES EMPLOYMENT SERVICE. "Validity Information Exchange, No. 8-32:D.O.T. Code 7-35.100, Routeman." *Personnel Psychol* 8:498 w '55. *

138. UNITED STATES EMPLOYMENT SERVICE. "Validity Information Exchange, No. 8-33:D.O.T. Code 8-66.01, Fettler." *Personnel Psychol* 8:499 w '55. *

139. UNITED STATES EMPLOYMENT SERVICE. "Validity Information Exchange, No. 8-34:D.O.T. Code 9-00.91, Assembler, Dry Cell Battery." *Personnel Psychol* 8:500 w '55. *

140. DVORAK, BEATRICE J. "Advantages of the Multiple Cut-Off Method." *Personnel Psychol* 9:45–7 sp '56. * (*PA* 31:5188)

141. DVORAK, BEATRICE J. "GATB in Foreign Countries." *J Appl Psychol* 40:197–200 Je '56. * (*PA* 31:6726)

142. DVORAK, BEATRICE J. "The General Aptitude Test Battery." Comments by Donald E. Super. *Personnel & Guid J* 35:145–54 N '56. *

143. SAMUELSON, CECIL O. "The General Aptitude Test Battery in Predicting Success of Vocational School Students." *J Ed Res* 50:175–82 N '56. * (*PA* 32:958)

144. UNITED STATES EMPLOYMENT SERVICE. "Validity Information Exchange, No. 9-3:D.O.T. Code 0-30.11, Teacher." *Personnel Psychol* 9:106 sp '56. *

145. UNITED STATES EMPLOYMENT SERVICE. "Validity Information Exchange, No. 9-6:D.O.T. Code 1-57.40, Claims Examiner." *Personnel Psychol* 9:111 sp '56. *

146. UNITED STATES EMPLOYMENT SERVICE. "Validity Information Exchange, No. 9-8:D.O.T. Code 2-32.15, Beauty Operator." *Personnel Psychol* 9:113–4 sp '56. *

147. UNITED STATES EMPLOYMENT SERVICE. "Validity Information Exchange, No. 9-9:D.O.T. Code 3-48.94, Artificial-Breeding Technician." *Personnel Psychol* 9:115 sp '56. *

148. UNITED STATES EMPLOYMENT SERVICE. "Validity Information Exchange, No. 9-10:D.O.T. Code 4-19.332, Mender; 6-19.331, Burler." *Personnel Psychol* 9:116 sp '56. *

149. UNITED STATES EMPLOYMENT SERVICE. "Validity Information Exchange, No. 9-11:D.O.T. Code 4-55.030, Stillman." *Personnel Psychol* 9:117 sp '56. *

150. UNITED STATES EMPLOYMENT SERVICE. "Validity Information Exchange, No. 9-12:D.O.T. Code 4-97.010, Electrician." *Personnel Psychol* 9:118–9 sp '56. *

151. UNITED STATES EMPLOYMENT SERVICE. "Validity Information Exchange, No. 9-13:D.O.T. Code 4-97.910, Electrician, Airplane." *Personnel Psychol* 9:121–2 sp '56. *

152. UNITED STATES EMPLOYMENT SERVICE. "Validity Information Exchange, No. 9-15:D.O.T. Code 5-53.235, Central-Office Repairman." *Personnel Psychol* 9:124 sp '56. *

153. UNITED STATES EMPLOYMENT SERVICE. "Validity Information Exchange, No. 9-16:D.O.T. Code 5-80.100, Airplane Mechanic." *Personnel Psychol* 9:125 sp '56. *

154. UNITED STATES EMPLOYMENT SERVICE. "Validity Information Exchange, No. 9-17:D.O.T. Code 6-12.043, Stemmer, Machine (Tobacco)." *Personnel Psychol* 9:126–7 sp '56. *

155. UNITED STATES EMPLOYMENT SERVICE. "Validity Information Exchange, No. 9-18:D.O.T. Code 7-57.501, Presser, Hand." *Personnel Psychol* 9:128 sp '56.

156. UNITED STATES EMPLOYMENT SERVICE. "Validity Information Exchange, No. 9-20:D.O.T. Code 9-57.21, Continuous Towel Roller; 9-57.21, Flatwork Catcher; 9-57.21, Flatwork Feeder; 9-57.21, Flatwork Folder." *Personnel Psychol* 9:130 sp '56. *

157. UNITED STATES EMPLOYMENT SERVICE. "Validity Information Exchange, No. 9-22:D.O.T. Code 0-50.04, X-Ray Technician." *Personnel Psychol* 9:248 su '56. *

158. UNITED STATES EMPLOYMENT SERVICE. "Validity Information Exchange, No. 9-23:D.O.T. Code 2-42.20, Nurse Aide." *Personnel Psychol* 9:249–50 su '56. *

159. UNITED STATES EMPLOYMENT SERVICE. "Validity Information Exchange, No. 9-24:D.O.T. Code 4-80.010, Sheet-Metal Worker." *Personnel Psychol* 9:251 su '56. *

160. UNITED STATES EMPLOYMENT SERVICE. "Validity Information Exchange, No. 9-25:D.O.T. Code 5-03.552, Assembly-man I; 5-03.562, Assembler; 5-03.572, Engine-Installation Assembler; 5-03.572, Rigger I." *Personnel Psychol* 9:252 su '56. *

161. UNITED STATES EMPLOYMENT SERVICE. "Validity Information Exchange, No. 9-27:D.O.T. Code 6-27.513, Seamer." *Personnel Psychol* 9:255–6 su '56. *

162. UNITED STATES EMPLOYMENT SERVICE. "Validity Information Exchange, No. 9-28:D.O.T. Code 7-00.904, Assembler, Electrical Accessories II." *Personnel Psychol* 9:257 su '56. *

163. UNITED STATES EMPLOYMENT SERVICE. "Validity Information Exchange, No. 9-29:D.O.T. Code 7-13.043, Fishing-Rod Assembler." *Personnel Psychol* 9:258 su '56. *

164. UNITED STATES EMPLOYMENT SERVICE. "Validity Information Exchange, No. 9-30:D.O.T. Code 8-04.10, Peeler, Hand." *Personnel Psychol* 9:259 su '56. *

165. UNITED STATES EMPLOYMENT SERVICE. "Validity Information Exchange, No. 9-37:D.O.T. Code 4-01.100, Baker (Bake. Prod.); 4-01.400, Baker (Hotel & Rest.)." *Personnel Psychol* 9:383 au '56. *

166. UNITED STATES EMPLOYMENT SERVICE. "Validity Information Exchange, No. 9-38:D.O.T. Code 5-86.514, Multiple-Photographic-Printer Operator." *Personnel Psychol* 9:384 au '56. *

167. UNITED STATES EMPLOYMENT SERVICE. "Validity Information Exchange, No. 9-39:D.O.T. Code 8-42.01, Take-Off Man (Paper Goods)." *Personnel Psychol* 9:385 au '56. *

168. UNITED STATES EMPLOYMENT SERVICE. "Validity Information Exchange, No. 9-40:D.O.T. Code 8-42.01, Scrapper (Paper Goods)." *Personnel Psychol* 9:386 au '56. *

169. UNITED STATES EMPLOYMENT SERVICE. "Validity Information Exchange, No. 9-42:D.O.T. Code 0-30.11, Teacher, Grade or Grammar School; 0-31.01, Teacher, High School." *Personnel Psychol* 9:518–9 w '56. *

170. UNITED STATES EMPLOYMENT SERVICE. "Validity Information Exchange, No. 9-43:D.O.T. Code 0-46.01, Clothes Designer." *Personnel Psychol* 9:520–1 w '56. *

171. UNITED STATES EMPLOYMENT SERVICE. "Validity Information Exchange, No. 9-48:D.O.T. Code 6-66.311, Tile Sorter; 6-66.361, Paster." *Personnel Psychol* 9:528–9 w '56. *

172. UNITED STATES EMPLOYMENT SERVICE. "Validity Information Exchange, No. 9-49:D.O.T. Code 6-85.060, Welder, Spot." *Personnel Psychol* 9:530 w '56. *

173. NICKSICK, THEODORE, JR. *Relationship Between Aptitudes and Major Fields of Study.* Doctor's thesis, North Texas State College (Denton, Tex.), 1957. (*DA* 17:1030)

174. UNITED STATES EMPLOYMENT SERVICE. "Validity Information Exchange, No. 10-1:D.O.T. Code 0-65.20, Director, Funeral; 0-65.10, Embalmer." *Personnel Psychol* 10:73–4 sp '57. *

175. UNITED STATES EMPLOYMENT SERVICE. "Validity Information Exchange, No. 10-2:D.O.T. Code 1-25.13, Comptometer Operator." *Personnel Psychol* 10:75–6 sp '57. *

176. UNITED STATES EMPLOYMENT SERVICE. "Validity Information Exchange, No. 10-4:D.O.T. Code 2-26.32, Cook (Hotel & Rest.)." *Personnel Psychol* 10:79 sp '57. *

177. UNITED STATES EMPLOYMENT SERVICE. "Validity Information Exchange, No. 10-6:D.O.T. Code 5-83.322, Knitting-Machine Fixer." *Personnel Psychol* 10:81 sp '57. *

178. UNITED STATES EMPLOYMENT SERVICE. "Validity Information Exchange, No. 10-7:D.O.T. Code 7-00.971, Toy Train Assembler; 9-13.01, Assembler (Toys and Games)." *Personnel Psychol* 10:82–3 sp '57. *

179. UNITED STATES EMPLOYMENT SERVICE. "Validity Information Exchange, No. 10-8:D.O.T. Code 8-04.10, Laborer; 8-04.10, Vegetable Picker." *Personnel Psychol* 10:84–5 sp '57. *

180. UNITED STATES EMPLOYMENT SERVICE. "Validity Information Exchange, No. 10-9:D.O.T. Code 8-04.10, Corn-Husking Machine Operator; 8-04.10, Corn-Cutting Machine Operator." *Personnel Psychol* 10:86–7 sp '57. *

181. UNITED STATES EMPLOYMENT SERVICE. "Validity Information Exchange, No. 10-10:D.O.T. Code 8-04.10, Peeling-and-Coring-Machine Operator." *Personnel Psychol* 10:88 sp '57. *

182. UNITED STATES EMPLOYMENT SERVICE. "Validity Information Exchange, No. 10-11:D.O.T. Code 8-57.51, Cementer." *Personnel Psychol* 10:89 sp '57. *

183. UNITED STATES EMPLOYMENT SERVICE. "Validity Information Exchange, No. 10-18:D.O.T. Code 4-48.010, Cylinder-Press Man; 4-48.040, Embossing-Press Operator; 4-48.041, Engraving-Press Operator; 4-48.050, Offset-Press Man; 4-48.011, Overlay Cutter; 4-48.020, Platen-Press Man; 4-48.030, Web-Press Man." *Personnel Psychol* 10:209–12 su '57. *

184. UNITED STATES EMPLOYMENT SERVICE. "Validity Information Exchange, No. 10-19:D.O.T. Code 4-88.018, Cold Mill

Operator; 4-88.018, Hot Mill Operator; 6-94.821, Payoff Operator; 6-94.822, Rewind Operator; 6-94.205, Slitting-Machine Operator II." *Personnel Psychol* 10:213–4 su '57. *

185. UNITED STATES EMPLOYMENT SERVICE. "Validity Information Exchange, No. 10-20:D.O.T. Code 6-88.807, Crusher Inspector; 6-88.808, Mill-End Inspector; 6-88.801, Mill Inspector; 6-88.806, Pipe & Coupling Sizer; 6-88.804, Pipe Walker; 6-88.808, Thread Inspector." *Personnel Psychol* 10:215–7 su '57. *

186. UNITED STATES EMPLOYMENT SERVICE. "Validity Information Exchange, No. 10-21:D.O.T. Code 8-10.25, Nut Sorter I." *Personnel Psychol* 10:218 su '57. *

187. UNITED STATES EMPLOYMENT SERVICE. "Validity Information Exchange, No. 10-22:D.O.T. Code 9-68.01, Bagger II; 9-68.30, Bag Sealer; 9-68.30, Packer II; 9-68.01, Weigher II." *Personnel Psychol* 10:219–21 su '57. *

188. UNITED STATES EMPLOYMENT SERVICE. "Validity Information Exchange, No. 10-23:D.O.T. Code 9-68.35, Packer (Agric.)." *Personnel Psychol* 10:222–4 su '57. *

189. UNITED STATES EMPLOYMENT SERVICE. "Validity Information Exchange, No. 10-26:D.O.T. Code 4-32.100, Cabinetmaker I." *Personnel Psychol* 10:345 au '57. *

190. UNITED STATES EMPLOYMENT SERVICE. "Validity Information Exchange, No. 10-27:D.O.T. Code 5-83.444, Electronics Technician." *Personnel Psychol* 10:346 au '57. *

191. UNITED STATES EMPLOYMENT SERVICE. "Validity Information Exchange, No. 10-28:D.O.T. Code 6-19.635, Weaver." *Personnel Psychol* 10:347–8 au '57. *

192. UNITED STATES EMPLOYMENT SERVICE. "Validity Information Exchange, No. 10-29:D.O.T. Code 6-41.940, Paper Sorter and Counter." *Personnel Psychol* 10:349–50 au '57. *

193. UNITED STATES EMPLOYMENT SERVICE. "Validity Information Exchange, No. 10-30:D.O.T. Code 6-94.515, Coil Assembler; 8-93.41, Unit Assembler; 8-94.51, Unit Assembler." *Personnel Psychol* 10:351 au '57. *

194. UNITED STATES EMPLOYMENT SERVICE. "Validity Information Exchange, No. 10-32:D.O.T. Code 7-68.831, Candy-Wrapping Machine Operator II." *Personnel Psychol* 10:354 au '57. *

195. UNITED STATES EMPLOYMENT SERVICE. "Validity Information Exchange, No. 10-45:D.O.T. Code 1-04.01, Copy Holder; 1-10.07, Proofreader; 1-10.07, Reader, First II." *Personnel Psychol* 10:494–5 w '57. *

196. UNITED STATES EMPLOYMENT SERVICE. "Validity Information Exchange, No. 10-48:D.O.T. Code 1-18.31, Employment Clerk." *Personnel Psychol* 10:500–1 w '57. *

197. UNITED STATES EMPLOYMENT SERVICE. "Validity Information Exchange, No. 10-55:D.O.T. Code 4-73.520, Pantographer." *Personnel Psychol* 10:516 w '57. *

198. UNITED STATES EMPLOYMENT SERVICE. "Validity Information Exchange, No. 10-56:D.O.T. Code 5-17.010, Patternmaker, Metal; 5-17.020, Patternmaker, Wood." *Personnel Psychol* 10:517 w '57. *

199. UNITED STATES EMPLOYMENT SERVICE. "Validity Information Exchange, No. 10-57:D.O.T. Code 5-24.010, Bricklayer." *Personnel Psychol* 10:518 w '57. *

200. UNITED STATES EMPLOYMENT SERVICE. "Validity Information Exchange, No. 10-58:D.O.T. Code 5-51.010, Powerhouse Engineer I." *Personnel Psychol* 10:519 w '57. *

201. UNITED STATES EMPLOYMENT SERVICE. "Validity Information Exchange, No. 10-59:D.O.T. Code 6-27.512, Glove Sewer." *Personnel Psychol* 10:520 w '57. *

202. UNITED STATES EMPLOYMENT SERVICE. "Validity Information Exchange, No. 10-60:D.O.T. Code 7-03.040, Insulation-Blanket Maker." *Personnel Psychol* 10:521–2 w '57. *

203. HAY, JOHN E. "The GATB at Work in Vocational Counseling." *Voc Guid Q* 6:174–6 su '58. *

204. UNITED STATES EMPLOYMENT SERVICE. "Validity Information Exchange, No. 11-1:D.O.T. Code 0-50.01, Medical Technologist." *Personnel Psychol* 11:97–8 sp '58. *

205. UNITED STATES EMPLOYMENT SERVICE. "Validity Information Exchange, No. 11-4:D.O.T. Code 5-80.100, Airplane Mechanic." *Personnel Psychol* 11:105 sp '58. *

206. UNITED STATES EMPLOYMENT SERVICE. "Validity Information Exchange, No. 11-10:D.O.T. Code 6-66.311, Tile Sorter; 8-66.01, Tile Placer; 6-66.361, Paster." *Personnel Psychol* 11:121–3 sp '58. *

207. UNITED STATES EMPLOYMENT SERVICE. "Validity Information Exchange, No. 11-11:D.O.T. Code 0-01.20, Accountant, General; 0-01.60, Auditor." *Personnel Psychol* 11:237–9 su '58. *

208. UNITED STATES EMPLOYMENT SERVICE. "Validity Information Exchange, No. 11-12:D.O.T. Code 4-76.040, Tool-and-Die Maker." *Personnel Psychol* 11:240–1 su '58. *

209. UNITED STATES EMPLOYMENT SERVICE. "Validity Information Exchange, No. 11-19:D.O.T. Code 5-83.411, Radio Repairman; 5-83.416, Television Service and Repairman." *Personnel Psychol* 11:260–2 su '58. *

ANDREW L. COMREY, *Associate Professor of Psychology, University of California, Los Angeles, California.*

The *General Aptitude Test Battery* (Form B-1001) was reviewed in *The Fourth Mental*

Measurements Yearbook. Forms B-1002A and B-1002B constitute a revised battery in which separate answer sheets have been introduced for paper and pencil tests 1–7. The revised battery consists of 12 separately timed objective tests: (1) Name Comparison, 6 minutes; subject compares two names which may or may not differ slightly, and judges them to be identical or different; similar to traditional clerical speed and accuracy tests. (2) Computation, 6 minutes; subject does addition, subtraction, multiplication, and division; similar to the common numerical ability test. (3) Three-Dimensional Space, 6 minutes; a three-dimensional figure is shown flattened into two dimensions; subject chooses among several drawings the one which shows how the figure would look in three dimensions. (4) Vocabulary, 6 minutes; four words are given; subject picks two that are synonyms or two that are antonyms, whichever is available. (5) Tool Matching, 5 minutes; a test drawing of a tool is accompanied by several similar drawings and one identical drawing, which the subject must identify; similar to the traditional perceptual speed test. (6) Arithmetic Reasoning, 7 minutes; subject solves the usual thought problem in arithmetic. (7) Form Matching, 6 minutes; subject must find a figure in a second group which is identical to each test figure in the first group. (8) Mark Making, paper and pencil, 10 seconds; the subject makes an underlined quotation mark in each square. (9) Place, apparatus, 15 seconds; using both hands, subject transfers pegs from one set of holes to another; three trials. (10) Turn, apparatus, 30 seconds; using the preferred hand, subject inverts and replaces pegs. (11) Assemble, apparatus, 90 seconds; subject picks up a rivet with the preferred hand, puts a washer on it with the other hand, and places the assembly in a preassigned hole. (12) Disassemble, apparatus, 60 seconds; subject does the reverse of what he did in Part 11.

Tests C and G of the original Form B-1001 have been dropped in the new edition because they apparently did not add to what was accomplished alone by Part K of Form B-1001, identical to Part 8 in the new editions. Part F in the old edition was dropped also, because Part H, or Part 3 in the new edition, could do about as well alone. Otherwise, the 12 tests in the two-form new edition are virtually alternate forms of corresponding tests in the old edition, being identical for Parts 8–12.

Factor studies of Form B-1001 provided the basis for isolation of nine factors for which scores are derived from the 12 test scores. These factors, and the equally weighted parts used to measure them are: (G) intelligence, 3, 4, 6; (V) verbal aptitude, 4; (N) numerical aptitude, 2, 6; (S) spatial aptitude, 3; (P) form perception, 5, 7; (Q) clerical perception, 1; (K) motor coordination, 8; (F) finger dexterity, 11, 12; and (M) manual dexterity, 9, 10. Factor, or aptitude, scores, are expressed for each subject in scaled form.

Reliability data, unfortunately, are given only for the factor aptitude scores, rather than for the individual tests. Reliabilities based on combined test-retest data from several studies totaling about 500 males and 500 females are in the .80's for G, V, N, and S; in the .70's for P, Q, K, and M; and in the .60's for F. Alternate-form reliabilities for Parts 1–7 are generally in the .80's. Most of the reliability studies cited are based upon student rather than working groups. It is to be expected that reliabilities for individual tests would be lower than reliabilities for composite aptitude scores. Those for Parts 11 and 12 particularly are too low.

Normative data have been collected on 4,000 workers, typical of the general working population, according to the 1940 census, with respect to age, sex, educational, occupational, and geographical distribution. These excellent data are for Form B-1001, however, rather than for the revised forms. Extrapolations for B-1002 have been made upon the basis of administering B-1001 and B-1002A to smaller student groups. Norms for B-1002B are in turn extrapolated from the extrapolated results for B-1001A by giving both forms to other student groups. With the vast data collection facilities of the United States Employment Service, it would seem reasonable to expect direct norms on the B-1002 forms themselves, although probably no great differences would be found. A very considerable amount of valuable data is given on the test performance of different occupational groups.

Data on validity are being continuously collected for this battery of tests. The various state employment offices collaborate with the USES in validating the test battery in local work situations. As far as possible, the validation procedure for each new situation is to carry out an aptitude oriented job analysis followed by the development of a suitable criterion of proficiency. Production records, earnings, work samples, and ratings may be used. The test battery is administered. Validity data are obtained in the form of a tetrachoric correlation between criterion and aptitude scores. Concurrent and longitudinal designs are utilized, although the latter type is relatively uncommon, except with student groups. On the basis of the statistical finding and other considerations, critical aptitudes are selected for the occupation and cutting scores determined for each aptitude. This is done in such a way as to eliminate about one third of the individuals. Where possible, cross validation is undertaken, although this has not been common so far. An attempt is made to fit the occupation into an already established occupational aptitude pattern (a set of two to four aptitudes with cutting scores) of which there are 22 at present. Thus, if the occupation in question shares two of three, or three of four critical aptitudes with an established occupational aptitude pattern, with cutting scores within 10 points, it is grouped with that particular pattern. If not, it is held out for later grouping with a new pattern, and may be used singly in the meantime.

These procedures represent a very rough compromise with practical realities and are probably justified with the amount of information now available. More precise procedures should be adopted eventually. For example, the cutting score approach should be replaced except where minimum aptitude levels are shown to exist and compensatory effects in other aptitudes are shown to be lacking. At present, cutting scores are established too arbitrarily. Such coarse grouping of occupations should be stopped and more aptitudes should be considered in making an evaluation.

Over 50 per cent of the occupations considered in counseling are placed in one of the 22 established occupational aptitude patterns merely on the basis of job analysis and armchair thinking, although the entire structure is being placed more and more upon an empirical basis as additional validation data are collected. Unfortunately, the reporting of validity studies is not complete, being confined to tabular summarization of validity coefficients and a few other data. Studies are carried out by local office personnel under conditions which probably fail to meet scientific standards in many instances. Tetrachoric coefficients are used with small samples, in spite of the large sampling error. It seems safe to conclude, however, that validation has reached the point where these tests can definitely be said to have considerable value in many work situations. The amount of information now available is only a fraction of what is needed; nevertheless it is extensive in comparison with what is available for other tests.

The foundation of factorial studies upon which this multiple factor battery is based leaves much to be desired. Several exploratory studies using relatively small numbers of variables and trainee groups were carried out about 1942, yielding 11 factors of which only 9 are presently used. Many more carefully designed factorial studies on a larger scale, including a wide variety of variables, are needed to verify the basic factorial structure. These studies should attempt particularly to clarify the nature of the GATB general intelligence factor. This factor is defined by three tests which are also used to define other factors, introducing artificial dependence between aptitude scores. More evidence is needed to be certain that a system of correlated ability factors would not be superior.

The factorial coverage of this battery is not great enough. While Guilford has recently pointed to the existence of at least 40 ability factors, only about 9 are covered here. Furthermore, all the tests are speeded, every paper and pencil test correlating over .4 with the perceptual speed test. The apparatus tests have lower correlations, but their reliabilities are also lower. Although the manual emphasizes the importance of personality factors in job success and the necessity of taking them into account in counseling, no thought of developing tests in these areas seems contemplated. In fact, the tendency has been to narrow the factor content of the battery rather than to enlarge it. The reviewer would recommend, therefore, *continuing* factorial analyses of the GATB tests together with newer experimental tests with the constant objective of increasing the technical excellence and the factorial coverage of the battery.

In summary, one can scarcely help but be impressed with the tremendous amount of effort and thought which has gone into the development and validation of these tests. The manual is generally very complete, giving extremely meticulous directions for the use of the tests, validity information, reliability information, test development information, correlations between tests and with other tests, and instructions for administration which even list errors commonly made by subjects and what to do about them. Although the GATB is somewhat short on factor analytic foundation and too narrow factorially at present, certainly in the vast test program of the USES we have one of the main hopes for developing a legitimate and effective empirical science of selection and guidance by means of psychological tests.

CLIFFORD P. FROEHLICH, *Professor of Education, University of California, Berkeley, California.*

It is a unique experience to prepare a review of a test about which so many data are available. Dvorak and her associates in the United States Employment Service have shown considerable sophistication in the standardization of this battery and in gathering validity data, both concurrent and predictive.

The comprehensive looseleaf manual has the advantage that new data have been added as they have been acquired. Unfortunately, the constant addition of data and subsections has resulted in a conglomerate for which no adequate index is available. It is not an easy document to use.

The outstanding characteristic of this multi-factored aptitude test is that a person's scores can be compared with 23 occupational aptitude patterns. These patterns are believed to be pertinent to about 500 occupations. In nearly 250 of them the patterns were empirically established; the others were included upon the basis of judgments made from job analysis data. If the developers continue their present practices, additional data bearing on the relationship of occupational aptitude patterns to specific occupations will be made available from time to time.

The occupational norms are designed on the assumption that about one third of the employees in a given job are regarded as unsatisfactory. This may be a valid assumption, but this reviewer believes that the Minnesota Employment Stabilization Research Institute data indicate that the percentage would vary with labor market conditions. There is the possibility that this test could be used to deter some persons from entering occupations in which they could compete successfully in certain labor markets.

The USES has wisely established the policy that the GATB is a "controlled" test, i.e., not available except with approval of the Service or its affiliated state employment services. However, in some instances known to this reviewer, the control has interfered with the battery's most efficient and effective use by schools. The USES has prepared excellent materials to train counselors in the proper use of the battery and has fostered institutes for the training of counselors. There is, however, much room for improvement in the procedures for making this battery available to qualified counselors working in agencies other than public employment services.

A summary evaluation of this battery must include these points: (a) the test developers have made only modest and fair claims regarding its reliability and validity; (b) adequate data are now available to support its use in vocational counseling; and (c) as usual, further research is recommended. At this writing, the battery can be recommended for use in counseling and selection of persons 16 years and older.

LLOYD G. HUMPHREYS, *Professor of Psychology, University of Illinois, Urbana, Illinois.*

The *General Aptitude Test Battery* (GATB) of the United States Employment Service (USES) constitutes one of the best known of the factored aptitude test batteries, even though it is not available for general use. There are 12 tests in the battery which are combined to measure the following factors: intelligence (G), verbal aptitude (V), numerical aptitude (N), spatial aptitude (S), form perception (P), clerical perception (Q), motor coordination (K), finger dexterity (F), and manual dexterity (M).

There are many desirable features of this battery. The tests are generally well selected and constructed. The most important feature is the mass of data which have been accumulated concerning the use of GATB. Such data are of primary importance for selection or guidance purposes. As long as the battery covers the major functions or factors, the manner in which this is accomplished is relatively unimportant. Distributions of item difficulties and correlations of items with total

score, within rather wide limits, contribute relatively little to the effectiveness of the tests in use. The location of the test vectors in the battery is of even less importance. If adequate data on reliability, stability, and validity are available on factor scores obtained from the unrotated principal components of an aptitude battery, these "arbitrary" scores will be completely satisfactory for personnel selection or vocational guidance purposes.

FACTOR SCORE DEFICIENCIES. Thus there is little profit in speculating about the selection of item type "A" rather than "B." Of substantially greater importance is the omission of an important function or factor from the battery. An error of the latter type in GATB is the lack of any measure of mechanical information or comprehension. A great deal of data are available concerning the importance of this function in vocational predictions. The argument that mechanical information is not an aptitude is not convincing. One can rest the case for mechanical information in the statement "It works." In addition, the position that general vocabulary measures aptitude while specialized vocabulary measures achievement is logically unsound.

The inclusion of a general factor in GATB, and the way in which it is measured, is also worthy of note. The introduction of a general factor measure is somewhat rare in the post-Thurstone era. The present use of both a general factor and group factor measures in the same battery is unfortunate. The reviewer has no objection to a measure of "g" as such. As a matter of fact, a general factor is clearly indicated in aptitude test data. Since "g" is always composed of the group factors which define it, however, it is statistically superfluous to measure both.

The decision to measure the general factor may have been dictated by the reluctance of users to give up the intelligence test to which they had become accustomed. The present measure of "g" is close to the centroid of intelligence tests—components are vocabulary, spatial relations, and arithmetic reasoning—and is technically sound in itself. But this does not make the procedure as a whole desirable. The first two components of the measure of intelligence also appear as separate factor measures, and the third is used with numerical operations to measure the number factor. The part-whole correlations involving intelligence and these three group factor measures are very high and together almost completely determine the variance of the intelligence test. The only information furnished by the measure of the general factor is the difference between the functions measured by arithmetic reasoning and numerical operations. This is ordinarily a useful distinction to make, but the procedure used to make it here is certainly awkward. A desire for psychological realism might suggest the use of a general factor measure in future aptitude batteries, but some other solution is required.

DEFICIENCIES IN ANALYSIS. There is a high level of professional competence involved in the development of GATB. The reviewer has selected certain practices for adverse criticism, but this does not detract from an overall favorable evaluation.

For most problems of prediction, the multiple regression model is preferable statistically to the multiple cutoff procedure for combining two or more tests. Nevertheless, to predict many criteria from a single battery and to minimize computational difficulties for relatively untrained people, multiple cuts can easily be defended. One cannot defend, however, the publication of unshrunken validities. If the cuts are made after inspecting the joint distributions of tests and criteria the multiple cutoff procedure will produce substantially more shrinkage than will multiple regression. The reviewer is willing to state dogmatically that the only sample too small for the use of cross validation is one in which there would be zero degrees of freedom available in the split samples. In all other cases and particularly for small n's cross validate!

Interpretation of published validation data is also complicated by the choice of the statistic used to relate pass-fail on the multiple cutoff to the criterion. The test analyst in the USES typically uses a dichotomous criterion, even if continuous data are available, and describes the relationship between tests and criterion with the tetrachoric correlation. This statistic is not acceptable. It tells one what the product-moment correlation would be if both variables were continuously and normally distributed. Since the multiple cutoff procedure results inevitably in a dichotomous predictor variable, depending on the nature of the criterion variable, the analyst has available only two correlation coefficients from which to choose. Neither is the

tetrachoric. If he wishes to predict a dichotomous criterion, he should report a phi coefficient; if he wishes to predict a continuous criterion, he should report a point biserial.

The combination of the two errors discussed above, use of unshrunken tetrachoric validity coefficients, has produced some remarkably high values. One's feeling that they are too high to be true is probably correct. On the other hand, relatively high correlations can be expected when one is working in the full range of human talent.

It was mentioned earlier that a substantial amount of both concurrent and predictive validation had been accomplished. The only possible reason for obtaining concurrent validity on a selection and guidance battery is a need for quick results. Concurrent validity can and should be replaced as quickly as possible by predictive validity. At one point a USES publication implies that concurrent can be substituted for predictive because, empirically, the former coefficients are on the average no higher than the latter. This is insufficient empirical justification. In addition to differences in size, pattern of validities could differ in the two cases, i.e., concurrent validation may select the wrong variables for predictive use. On a priori grounds one might expect this error to be more serious with motivational and personality variables than with ability variables, but empirical demonstration is lacking. The USES research program may well have the relevant data. It would be useful to analyze those data from this point of view.

THE MANUALS. The mass of data referred to, including both concurrent and predictive validation results, does not appear in the manuals, but much has been published in the professional literature. The reviewer has no quarrel with these practices. The authors of this battery have different practical and ethical problems than the authors of commercial tests. On the practical side the tests are used by interviewers to refer job applicants to potential employers. It is debatable whether adding the "why" to the "how" would help this function. On the ethical side, they are responsible primarily to their organization for their products, not to a diffuse consuming public. There is then an acceptable double standard for writing test manuals, though only a single standard for professional competence.

There may be objections in certain quarters

to the cut and dried instructions for use of the battery contained in the manuals. There are two aspects to this question. One, the job to be done, has already been alluded to. On this score, since the function of the battery is as much selection as guidance, rigidity is desirable. The second has to do with what the counselor can add to the information furnished by the tests. The weight of the evidence here is that the counselor is more apt to degrade than to improve test information unless his area of decision making is sharply circumscribed. Thus, a military type standardized operating procedure, though politically unrealistic for other batteries, would probably improve their effectiveness in use.

CONCLUSIONS. For purposes of summary, three conclusions have been drawn about the GATB. These are worded conservatively, though with no intent to damn with faint praise. The frame of reference is other similar batteries. (a) The tests of the GATB were selected and constructed as well as most. (b) The GATB has been validated and otherwise analyzed as well as or better than most. (c) If interviewers follow instructions, the GATB battery is used more effectively than most.

For reviews by Milton L. Blum, Edward B. Greene, and Howard R. Taylor, see 4:714.

[610]

★Holzinger-Crowder Uni-Factor Tests. Grades 7–12; 1952–55; 5 scores: verbal, spatial, numerical, reasoning, scholastic aptitude; IBM; Forms AM ('52), BM ('53); manual ('55); separate answer sheets must be used; $6.40 per 35 tests; $3.90 per 35 sets of IBM answer sheets; 50¢ per set of right keys for hand or machine scoring; 30¢ per set of item elimination keys for machine scoring; postage extra; 50¢ per specimen set, postpaid; 40.5(90) minutes in 2 sessions; Karl J. Holzinger and Norman A. Crowder; World Book Co. *

REFERENCES

1. MITCHELL, BLYTHE C. "The Relation of High School Achievement to the Abilities Measured by the Holzinger-Crowder Uni-Factor Tests." *Ed & Psychol Meas* 15:487–90 w '55. * (PA 30:7771)
2. CROWDER, NORMAN A. "The Holzinger-Crowder Uni-Factor Tests." Comments by Donald E. Super. *Personnel & Guid J* 35:281–8 Ja '57. * (PA 32:2103)
3. NORTH, ROBERT D. "The Holzinger-Crowder Uni-Factor Tests: Profile, Reliability, and Correlation Data Based on Independent School Results." *Ed Rec B* 69:53–9 F '57. * (PA 32:2121)

ANNE ANASTASI, *Professor of Psychology, Fordham University, New York, New York.*

The four factor scores yielded by this battery are derived from nine tests. The verbal score is based on Word Meaning and Odd Words, both tests requiring the discrimination of word meanings. The spatial factor is meas-

ured by two tests, Boots and Hatchets, in which the subject must determine whether the two boots or hatchets, respectively, in each item are viewed from the same side or different sides. The two tests measuring numerical ability, Mixed Arithmetic and Remainders, call for simple computational skills. The reasoning score is based on three tests utilizing verbal, numerical, and spatial content. These tests include: Mixed Series, consisting of number-letter series completions; Figure Changes, composed of figure analogies items; and Teams, presenting a series of syllogisms concerned with overlapping membership on different athletic teams. The spatial and numerical tests are highly speeded; the verbal and reasoning tests measure predominantly power. Answers on the nine tests are recorded on two answer sheets, each used in a different testing session. An individual profile chart is provided on the reverse side of one of the answer sheets.

Norms for each of the four factor scores are in the form of end-of-year percentiles for each of grades 7–12. The normative sample was obtained from 38 schools located in 28 communities in 7 states, the number of cases in each grade varying from 827 to 2,562. December norms derived by linear interpolation from the June standardization data are available on request from the publisher, as are separate sex norms. In the derivation of the latter, significant but slight mean differences in favor of girls were found in the verbal factor; larger significant differences favoring the boys were obtained on the spatial factor. Sex differences in the numerical and reasoning factors were small and inconsistent but tended to favor girls.

Percentile scores are plotted on a normalized percentile chart, in which a half inch is approximately equal to the standard error of a score. Similarly, the standard error of the difference between scores on any two factors corresponds to a little less than three fourths of an inch. The manual recommends that these distances be used in interpreting scores. Being based on $\pm$ 1 SE, however, these values correspond to a rather low confidence level. It might be noted that, with the scale employed, 1 inch designates a significant deviation at the .03 level within a single factor, and 1½ inches a significant difference at the .02 level between factors. Since these significance levels are closer to the usual standards and correspond to easily measured distances on the graph, they would appear preferable to the limits suggested in the manual.

Alternate-form reliabilities for the four factor scores, computed on single-grade groups, ranged from .758 to .951. Split-half reliabilities of verbal and reasoning scores (neither of which depends appreciably on speed) are all above .90 except for a single value of .88. Validity was investigated through correlations with achievement tests and teachers' grades in a variety of courses. Most of the coefficients are based on concurrent validity, although a few measure predictive validity. With few exceptions, the verbal factor yielded the highest correlations and the spatial factor the lowest, regardless of the nature of the course—a finding indicative of little differential validity. Moreover, the correlations of any one factor tended to vary more among schools or communities than among criteria. With regard to absolute size, the correlations with the verbal factor compare favorably with corresponding correlations obtained with common group intelligence tests. With numerical and reasoning factors, the median correlations are generally in the .40's and .50's. The spatial factor yields few correlations at this level, except in predominantly manual vocational courses.

On the basis of a large number of available validity coefficients, a regression equation was derived for a scholastic aptitude score, in which the largest weight is given to the verbal score, progressively smaller weights are given to reasoning and numerical scores, and the spatial factor is omitted. This composite score, for which percentile norms are also provided, yields somewhat higher validities than generally found with intelligence tests. At the same time, the correlations of the scholastic aptitude score with each of several common group intelligence tests are about as high as the correlations ordinarily found between any two intelligence tests. Similar regression equations have been worked out for predicting achievement in mathematics, science, social studies, and English.

That the four factor scores do not represent independent measures is indicated by the substantial intercorrelations among them. The medians of these correlations in 36 single-grade groups range from .31 to .53. Nevertheless, in view of the high reliability of the factor scores, it is estimated that approximately 40 per cent of intra-individual score differences are in excess of chance. On this basis, the use of profiles would seem justified, although the meager evidence for differential validity makes the diagnostic interpretation of such profiles doubtful.

The battery was evidently developed by means of factorial analyses, although the procedure and findings are not clear. A table of factor loadings, based on earlier forms of the nine tests, seems to show a remarkably close approximation to simple structure. Each test has virtually zero loadings (none above .11) on three of the factors, while loadings on the fourth are all over .78 and two are over 1.00! Without information regarding the method of factor analysis employed and what other tests (if any) were factorized in the battery, it is difficult to evaluate these factor loadings. It would probably have been better not to try to cover the relevant factorial research in the manual, but rather to insert a reference to a published source where the detailed data should be made available.

On the whole, however, the manual provides a well organized, effective presentation of essential facts. It is clear, helpful, and intelligible to the unsophisticated test user, and yet sufficiently informative for the technically oriented reader. The construction and evaluation of this test reveal the characteristic thoroughness and soundness which we have come to expect from its publisher. These qualities are evident in the careful choice of appropriate statistical techniques, the full presentation of data, and the objective and cautious interpretation of results. Special mention should be made of the use of regression equations to find composite scores, a procedure which represents the most effective way of predicting complex criteria from multiple aptitude batteries.

Despite their technical merits, in actual operation the *Holzinger-Crowder Uni-Factor Tests* do not appear to be substantially superior to other available multiple factor batteries or intelligence tests. The lack of convincing evidence of differential validity highlights the principal shortcoming of the battery. Nor does the derivation of composite scores raise the validity much above that obtained with other instruments. The chief difficulty probably stems from the limited nature of the test content. Although a variety of item types and materials is included, it would seem that the battery leaves untapped intellectual functions which may be important in academic achievement. The tests

concentrate unduly on relatively simple processes and routine intellectual skills. Even the
three reasoning tests demand little complex or
original thought. It is also noteworthy that, in
the regression equation for the composite science score, the numerical factor does not appear. Apparently the type of quantitative thinking required in science is not covered by those
tests.

The original formulation of items would have
profited from a more imaginative approach.
The authors' rather compulsive justification for
the inclusion of the spatial tests reveals a
fundamental weakness in their choice of test
content. Thus they write that "inclusion of
spatial tests stems more from the repeated
emergence of a spatial component in factor-
analysis studies of mental measures than from
any evidences of substantial utility of the
spatial factor, as measured by the Holzinger-
Crowder or other tests, for predicting success
in various educational or occupational endeavors." Of course the reason such a spatial factor
emerged in the early factorial research of Holzinger, Thurstone, and others is that spatial
tests were included in the batteries. More recent research with other types of tests, as
cited for example in Guilford's "The Structure
of Intellect," [1] has revealed many other more
promising factors. The present battery exemplifies the all-too-common practice of *ex post
facto* validation, in which tests are chosen without adequate reference to the behavior domain
to be measured, and validity coefficients are
subsequently computed against criteria within
that domain. A more productive approach would
be to begin with a "job analysis" of the area to
be investigated and then develop tests to predict the most important behavior functions
within that area.

BENJAMIN FRUCHTER, *Associate Professor of
Educational Psychology, The University of
Texas, Austin, Texas.*

This battery of nine general aptitude tests
yields scores in four aspects of mental ability
useful for educational and ultimately vocational guidance. The verbal factor is represented by Word Meaning and Odd Words; the
spatial factor by Boots and Hatchets; the
numerical factor by Mixed Arithmetic and Remainders; and the reasoning factor by tests

1 GUILFORD, J. P. "The Structure of Intellect." *Psychol B*
53:267–93 Je '56. *

called Mixed Series, Figure Changes, and
Teams.

Considering the wide variety of item types
that have been developed in recent years to
measure spatial abilities, the tests used to measure the spatial factor are rather limited in
structure and scope. The task they set is to determine whether the two members of a pair of
pictured boots or hatchets are viewed from the
same or different sides. From the point of view
of validity, the correlations of the factor scores
derived from these tests with academic grades
and achievement tests are as high as or higher
than those obtained with other spatial scores.
Teams, a test in syllogistic form, is likely to be
difficult for some students in the lower grades,
but it probably gives needed "top" to the reasoning scores for some of the brighter students
in the upper grades.

The manual is unusually complete and has
much useful information. There are, however,
almost no data concerning the individual tests,
the norms, reliability, validity, and other data
being reported for the factor scores only. The
norms furnished in the manual are end-of-year
percentile ranks by grades for the four factor
scores and the total scholastic aptitude score.
They are based on approximately 10,000 cases
from 28 communities in 7 states. Since neither
the communities and states nor the basis for selecting them are specified, one suspects that
some sections of the country may not be represented. A table for converting percentile
ranks to stanine scores is furnished.

A formula is provided for weighting the
verbal, numerical, and reasoning scores to yield
a scholastic aptitude score, intended to be comparable to the single score derived from a general intelligence test. Norms are provided for
this general score and a table is furnished for
estimating Terman-McNemar IQ's from them.
Weights are given for predicting achievement
in science, social studies, English, and mathematics. Only for the last named subject are
the weights much different than for the general
scholastic aptitude score, in which the verbal
score receives the highest weight, followed by
the reasoning and numerical scores, with the
spatial score not being weighted since it does
not contribute significantly. The validities of
the factor scores for teachers' marks and
achievement test scores follow a similar pattern. The prescribed weights are derived from

averages and it is suggested that each school develop its own regression weights.

Validity information is reported in the form of correlations between factor scores and teachers' marks for a number of subjects, as well as correlations with other standardized tests. While the degree of independence between factors is good relative to most batteries of this type, the correlation between factors is still appreciable. The reported median correlation of the verbal score with the other three scores is .44, the spatial .37, the numerical .45, and the reasoning .50.

In a relatively short testing time (two class periods) this battery yields four reliable factor scores useful for educational guidance at the secondary level. The scores are as independent as any derived from this type of scholastic aptitude battery. Preliminary results show good validity for the verbal, spatial, numerical, and reasoning scores. The tests can be efficiently administered and scored. A score for predicting general scholastic aptitude can be derived from the factor scores and corresponding IQ's can be estimated. Additional work needs to be done in gathering normative and validity data for educational and vocational guidance.

PHILIP E. VERNON, *Professor of Educational Psychology, Institute of Education, University of London, London, England.*

This battery raises afresh the question of the superiority of differential aptitude or factor-based tests over the general scholastic aptitude or intelligence test. As one would expect from the senior author, the subtests have been chosen after extensive research, not merely for their high saturations with their own factor, but also for their low overlap with other factors. The nine subtests are combined to yield separate scores for verbal, spatial, numerical, and reasoning factors. Each of the tests shows good reliability, the mean parallel-form coefficient being .86. The median factor score intercorrelation for several one-grade populations is .44. The authors calculate that 40 per cent of the differences between paired factor scores should exceed chance expectation, so that the battery should be adequate for differential predictive or counseling purposes.

However, the manual also summarizes the results of 90 comparisons between factor scores and tests or teachers' marks in a variety of school subjects, and these show a disappointing lack of differentiation. In almost all subjects, V has the highest correlations, followed closely by R; N shows lower correlations, though these rise somewhat with mathematics courses and, curiously enough, with foreign languages; while S seldom makes any useful contribution, except possibly to geometry and to some vocational courses. Thus it is found that a scholastic aptitude total score, based on $5V + N + 3R$, gives almost as good predictions of achievement in any area as do differentially weighted combinations. Likewise, the median correlations of the four factors with a number of intelligence tests are .79 (V), .35 (S), .55 (N) and .63 (R), and there appear to be no marked variations in these figures at different age levels. The logical inference would seem to be that it is the verbal intelligence component of the tests $(g + v)$ which alone contributes to educational prediction, and that the 40 per cent of significant score differences derive almost wholly from the specific variance of the tests (s factors), which is educationally irrelevant.

As against this interpretation, it may be noted that standard intelligence tests seldom yield as high correlations with any achievement criterion as do one or the other of the factor scores, though this may be due merely to chance variations. However, the authors further point out that the patterns of correlations with any one school subject vary markedly, and often significantly, in different school groups, and suggest that the educational counselor should work out for himself the most appropriate profiles, or weighted combinations, of scores for his own local criteria. In the present writer's view it has still to be demonstrated whether regression equations based on specific courses are sufficiently stable or consistent to yield better predictions than a single equation for all courses (or maybe two equations—one for linguistic, and one for quantitative courses). It is only when very much more varied batteries are used, incorporating tests of previous attainment and of interest in particular subjects, that any real gain in differential prediction is achieved.

Except in the reasoning tests, the content is rather narrow; i.e., the tests cannot claim to provide representative samplings of the factors concerned. Nevertheless the battery is superior to those which provide only one test per factor or aptitude. It will be apparent that the fairly low factor intercorrelations may have arisen less because these are pure factor tests than because there are differences in speed conditions and form of response, and because the reasoning tests use predominantly symbolic or nonverbal materials.

Within the limitations noted, this battery may be accepted as a well constructed and thoroughly standardized and validated instrument, one of the good ones of its kind. The manual is one of the most informative the writer has met.

[611]

★The Jastak Test of Potential Ability and Behavior Stability. Grades 7–9; 1958; 10 scores: coding, picture reasoning, arithmetic, vocabulary, space series, social concept, verbal reasoning, number series, space completion, and spelling; 6 derived scores: language, reality, motivation, psychomotor, intelligence, capacity; 1 form; $4.25 per 25 tests; $1.50 per manual; $1 per set of scoring keys; postage extra; $1.50 per specimen set, postpaid; 65(90) minutes; J. F. Jastak; Educational Test Bureau. *

[612]

★The Multi-Aptitude Test. College courses in testing; 1955; miniature battery of 10 tests for instructional use; Forms A, B; $1.25 per study kit; 10 or more study kits, 90¢ each; postpaid; 35(50–60) minutes; Edward E. Cureton, Louise Witmer Cureton, and students; Psychological Corporation. *

REFERENCE
1. WESMAN, ALEXANDER G. "A Test Battery for Teaching Tests and Measurements." *Yearb Nat Council Meas Used Ed* 13:76–8 '56. *

H. H. REMMERS, *Professor of Psychology and Education, Purdue University, Lafayette, Indiana.*

This test battery is admirably designed to serve its intended purpose—to provide an instructional device "which can be used both to familiarize students and laymen with the more usual kinds of ability measures and to provide material for practice in test administration, scoring, and analysis."

The 10 tests, which range in length from 8 to 30 items, cover vocabulary, general information, arithmetic, number series, figure classification, mechanical comprehension, word recognition, scrambled letters, checking, and paper formboard. Testing time ranges from 1 to 5 minutes per test. A variety of scoring devices have purposely been included.

The authors suggest that the test may be used to supplement instruction in a variety of courses in statistics, measurement, and evaluation and to serve as illustration for lectures to lay groups. So far as cognitive functions are concerned, the battery can admirably serve these purposes.

The manual is usefully detailed and relevant. The rationale of construction and the scoring, standardization, and psychological meaning of the tests are clearly explained. Tables of illustrative statistical data give information on mean scores, standard deviations, interform reliability coefficients, comparative difficulties of the two forms, practice effects, sex differences, and illustrative centile and standard score norms, all based on a group of 113 college students.

The battery represents a very useful idea competently and carefully implemented with psychological and statistical sophistication of a high order. It is an excellent instructional tool to teach the measurement of cognitive functions.

[613]

★Multiple Aptitude Tests. Grades 7–13; 1955; 13 scores: 9 tests plus combinations of tests *a*, *b*, and *c* (verbal comprehension), *d* and *e* (perceptual speed), *f* and *g* (numerical reasoning), *h*, *i*, and *j* (spatial visualization); IBM; 1 form; $24.50 per 35 sets of 9 tests; separate answer sheets may be used; 8¢ per set of IBM answer sheets; 60¢ per set of either hand or machine scoring stencils; postage extra; $1.75 per complete specimen set, postpaid; 175.5(220) minutes in 3 sessions for complete battery; David Segel and Evelyn Raskin; California Test Bureau. *

a) WORD MEANING. $2.45 per 35 tests; 12(20) minutes.
b) PARAGRAPH MEANING. $3.50 per 35 tests; 30(35) minutes.
c) LANGUAGE USAGE. $2.45 per 35 tests; 25(30) minutes.
d) ROUTINE CLERICAL FACILITY. $2.45 per 35 tests; 6.5 (10) minutes.
e) ARITHMETIC REASONING. $2.45 per 35 tests; 30(35) minutes.
f) ARITHMETIC COMPUTATION. $2.45 per 35 tests; 22 (35) minutes.
g) APPLIED SCIENCE AND MECHANICS. $4.55 per 35 tests; 30(35) minutes.
h) SPATIAL RELATIONS—TWO DIMENSIONS. $3.50 per 35 tests; 8(10) minutes.
i) SPATIAL RELATIONS—THREE DIMENSIONS. $3.50 per 35 tests; 12(15) minutes.

REFERENCES
1. MENDENHALL, GEORGE V. *A Statistical Investigation of the Interrelationships in the Multiple Aptitude Tests.* Master's project, University of Southern California (Los Angeles, Calif.), 1952.
2. SEGEL, DAVID. "The Multiple Aptitude Tests." Comments by Donald E. Super. *Personnel & Guid J* 35:424–34 Mr '57. * (PA 32:1645)

RALPH F. BERDIE, *Professor of Psychology and Director of Student Counseling Bureau, University of Minnesota, Minneapolis, Minnesota.*

This battery consists of nine tests which provide nine separate scores, which in turn yield scores on four basic factors. The tests are designed primarily for secondary school students, and the authors state the strategic time for testing is in grade 8 or 9, with further possibilities for testing during the latter half of grade 10 and in grades 11 and 12. The absence of an alternate form presents a retesting problem. The tests have been designed mainly as tools to be used by school counselors who assist students with problems involving educational and vocational decisions. The tests and the standardization process appear to be as well conceived as for similar batteries, but because of their relative youth, they have not been subjected to the same kind of examination through research and use as have older batteries. The item types in the tests are identical with item types in traditional tests.

The word meaning test consists of a 60-item simple multiple choice vocabulary test, with the student instructed to select the one of four alternatives which is synonymous with the key word. The paragraph meaning test consists of eight paragraphs, each of about 100 words and each followed by from four to nine brief multiple choice questions based upon the content of the preceding paragraph. The language usage test consists of 60 discrete brief sentences, each divided into four parts. Some of these parts contain errors in spelling, grammar, punctuation, or capitalization, and the student is to identify sections in which errors are found.

The routine clerical facility test consists of 90 pairs of names and numbers, among which the student is to identify the pairs which are similar and different. The arithmetic reasoning test consists of 35 arithmetic problems presented verbally and involving simple arithmetic computations. The arithmetic computation test consists of 35 brief problems presented numerically and involving addition, subtraction, multiplication, division, and percentage.

The applied science and mechanics test consists of drawings of 52 simple mechanical arrangements or practical situations, each accompanied by one or more sets of questions of the multiple choice type. The two spatial relations tests present 25 simple drawings each. The first test consists of 2-dimensional drawings of completed figures accompanied by sets of segments of figures, and the student is instructed to select that set of segments which will form the completed figure; the second test presents 3-dimensional drawings of completed figures accompanied by sets of "unfolded" patterns, and the student is required to select that pattern

which when properly assembled will form the 3-dimensional figure.

Each of these item types has appeared in earlier tests, and the authors of the *Multiple Aptitude Tests* use for evidence of validity for their tests the assumed or demonstrated validity of the earlier tests. Certainly they are justified to some extent in doing this, and the many substantial correlations between the *Multiple Aptitude Tests* and the earlier tests suggest that the new tests tend to measure much the same things measured by the earlier tests. For instance, correlations between the word meaning test and other tests of verbal ability extend from .48 through .96. One correlation between the paragraph meaning test and the reading vocabulary score of the *California Achievement Test* is .99. A correlation between the *Barrett-Ryan-Schrammel English Test* and the language usage test is .81. The clerical scores on the *Multiple Aptitude Tests* and the *Minnesota Clerical Test* correlate between .53 and .99. One correlation between the arithmetic reasoning score and the numerical score of the *Differential Aptitude Tests* is .96. A correlation between the applied science and mechanics score and the score on the *Test of Mechanical Comprehension* is .93 (in fairness, it should be stated that for another group this correlation is .26). The correlations between scores on the spatial relations test and on other tests are somewhat lower, however, ranging from —.07 to .70. Thus, the correlations between scores on the *Multiple Aptitude Tests* and on tests that tend to have similar kinds of items confirm the similarity of the tests, and the evidence for validity of the earlier tests suggests, but certainly does not demonstrate, that the new tests have comparable validity.

Reliability coefficients and standard errors of measurement for each of the nine *Multiple Aptitude Tests* are presented for each sex by grade, from grade 7 through grade 13. Thus, for each test 14 reliability coefficients are available. All of these coefficients, except for the routine clerical facility test, were calculated by Kuder-Richardson formula 21; those for the clerical score were based on test-retest. The coefficients for the word meaning test range from .81 to .92, with a median of .90. Coefficients for the paragraph meaning test range from .74 to .85, with a median coefficient of .81. The range of coefficients for the language usage test is from .86 to .91, with a median of

.89, and for the routine clerical facility test the correlations range from .75 to .94, with a median of .87. The coefficients for the arithmetic reasoning test range from .84 to .90, with a median coefficient of .87, and the range of coefficients for arithmetic computation is from .88 to .98. The range of coefficients for the applied science and mechanics test is from .66 to .88, with a median coefficient of .76; for the 2-dimension spatial relations test, from .83 to .89, with a median coefficient of .88; and for the 3-dimension spatial relations test, from .71 to .82, with a median of .77. Thus, it appears that the word meaning, language usage, and arithmetic computation tests have very good reliability; but that reliability for paragraph meaning, arithmetic reasoning, applied science and mechanics, and spatial relations is not as good.

The paragraph meaning test is a short test when one considers the length of test needed to get a reliable reading score. It well might be that for some of these tests with lower than desired reliabilities an extension in the length of the test might be warranted.

The authors are to be commended for including the standard errors of measurement for raw scores for each of the tests by sex and by grade. The careful test user will find this information useful in making more careful interpretations of the score.

The intercorrelations of some of the tests are quite high. More important than the intercorrelations of the tests, however, are the intercorrelations of the four factor scores: verbal comprehension, based upon scores on the tests for word meaning, paragraph meaning, and language usage; perceptual speed, based upon the language usage score and the routine clerical facility score; numerical reasoning, based upon the scores on tests of arithmetic reasoning and arithmetic computation; and spatial visualization, based upon scores on the test for applied science and mechanics and the two spatial relations tests. Reliability coefficients and standard errors of measurement are provided for these factor scores, the former ranging from .91 to .95. Since these coefficients were based upon large groups of students drawn from grades 7 through 13, and thus were derived from a much more heterogeneous group than were the reliability scores for individual tests, the two cannot be directly compared.

The correlations between factor scores range from −.10 to .73. Some interesting and confusing sex differences are apparent here. For instance, for the males the correlation between factor one and factor two is −.10; for the females it is .70. When information regarding the relationships between tests is summarized, it is obvious that the tests are far from independent from one another and that some of them to a large extent measure overlapping abilities. The factor structure of the battery is complex, and factor analysis information perhaps will be of less help in determining what the validity of the battery is than will information derived from prediction studies.

The authors base much of their evidence for validity of these tests upon correlations between test scores and school grades. An abundance of these data is presented in the manual, and an effective profile method of presenting the information is used. For instance, the correlations between grades in algebra and each of the nine tests for boys range from .06 to .39, the highest correlation being with score on the arithmetic computation test. The correlations between physics grades and test scores for boys range from .21 to .47, the highest correlation being with the paragraph meaning test. As is true with all such correlations for tests similar to these, the correlation between grades and scores is disappointingly low, being hardly ever higher than .50 and usually no higher than .40. In most cases, the patterns of correlations are in the expected differences, but in some cases they are not.

Unfortunately, one cannot tell from the information presented in the manual whether the tests were given at the beginning or at the end of the school year. Thus, one does not know whether the information presented here pertains to predictive validity or concurrent validity.

Although no information is presented in the manual concerning the validity of these tests as determined by a vocational criterion, the authors have made available to the reviewer a study done in one large company where test scores were related to ratings of success made by supervisors for a great variety of occupations in that company. Although these scores appear to have little, if any, relationship with rated success, the mean scores of persons doing different kinds of work tended to vary in the expected direction. In other words, again we have evidence that tests such as these perhaps cannot predict how successful men will be on a job, but rather can serve to differentiate among persons who enter in and are minimally successful in different occupations.

The authors have done much to assist the school counselor as he uses the tests. An extended profile facilitates the visual presentation of the test scores and, more importantly, a convenient means is provided for determining the statistical significance of differences between scores. Counselors frequently work with students who have, for example, a percentile score of 40 on word meaning and 60 on arithmetic reasoning, and they must help the student decide whether his word meaning ability really is superior to his arithmetic reasoning ability, or whether this is a chance fluctuation. Segel has been concerned with this problem for many years, and in the *Multiple Aptitude Tests* he and Raskin have presented a convenient means for the counselor to make inferences concerning the meaning of test score discrepancies.

Another counseling aid, this one of more questionable usefulness, is the transparent profile provided for the tests. This profile allows the student's scores to be plotted on a semi-transparent chart and then compared with the profiles of groups of students who have done well and who have done poorly in various subjects. Segel was one of the earliest psychologists to see the counseling use of expectancy tables, and a comprehensive series of these is presented in the manual. Counselors cannot assume, however, that the data in the manual will necessarily be useful for predicting success or failure in their schools; each school will probably find that it must use its own data in deriving its expectancy tables and success and failure profiles. For those counselors who have enough ambition and energy to construct similar devices based upon their local information, the methods suggested in the manual will be most helpful.

In summary, the *Multiple Aptitude Tests* are a very new series of tests that have as yet been subjected to little careful scrutiny through research and use. The authors have done a careful job of test construction and standardization, and the finished tests do not look inferior to the similar tests that are available. Unfortunately, the tests themselves seem to have nothing that other tests do not have. Inevitably, one will want to compare these tests with the *Differential Aptitude Tests,* which, as of this date, have the advantage because of the greater amount of research data accumulated during recent years. The authors of the *Multiple Aptitude Tests* have some interesting ideas regarding the counseling use of these tests, and their work has been carefully and rigorously done.

BENJAMIN FRUCHTER, *Associate Professor of Educational Psychology, The University of Texas, Austin, Texas.*

This battery of differential aptitude tests is designed for use with secondary level students to aid in counseling them concerning the choice of appropriate school curricula, to give them some information concerning their relative strengths and weaknesses in four scholastic aptitude areas, and to yield information on how they compare with other students in these areas. It is based, as are a number of other differential aptitude test batteries, on the results of the extensive factor analytic studies of intellectual abilities and aptitudes that have been carried out during the past 20 years.

The authors have done a professional job of developing the test battery and providing the materials necessary for its efficient use and interpretation. The principal limitation is that only one form is so far available. The tests come in nine separate booklets; if desired, parts of the battery can be selected for administration. Fall norms, based on approximately 11,000 cases widely distributed over the country, are provided. These are given in percentiles and T scores, by sex, for each grade. In addition, differential percentile norms, by sex, for grades 7–9 and 10–12, are furnished for comparing a given examinee's aptitude scores with the scores of others of similar intelligence.

Several types of validation data are furnished in the manual. The correlations of each test in the battery with a number of other widely used intelligence and scholastic aptitude tests are reported. The usefulness of this type of validity data for most test users is very limited and often open to misinterpretation. Its location in an appendix rather than its present prominent position would probably be preferable.

A more direct type of validation data is represented by the correlation of the test scores with teachers' grades. The correlations of scores on the separate tests with school marks for males in 16 school subjects and for females in 15 school subjects are given in tabular and graphical form. These correlations are overall values with no indication given of how much they would fluctuate from time to time or place to place. The mean standard scores on the nine tests for the highest and lowest 10 per cent of the students in each subject, and the significance of the differences between them, are reported. The profiles for these mean scores are presented in graphical form for the various school subjects. An ingenious transparent profile, on which may be entered the scores for a given student, is placed over the graphs to determine the school subjects for which his aptitude score profile is in accord with averages of the top 10 per cent or the bottom 10 per cent of the validation group.

One advantage of this type of test battery over the more conventional intelligence test is that it yields differential information in several areas of ability. Inspection of the factor intercorrelation matrix given in the manual indicates that there is considerable relationship among performances on the verbal comprehension, numerical reasoning, and spatial visualization factors. The authors explain this, in part, by pointing out that "items were selected on the basis of the highest possible correlation with the test in which they were placed, without regard to whether or not they were incidentally measuring some other ability." In other words, the emphasis in construction was on internal consistency of the tests rather than on purity of factors. The reviewer factor analyzed the corrected intercorrelation matrix for males by the centroid method. After rotation of axes his results agreed closely with factor analysis results reported by the authors.

With the exception of Routine Clerical Facility, all of the tests are power tests and their reported reliabilities were appropriately computed by Kuder-Richardson formula 21. The reliability of the speeded clerical test was computed by the test re-test method on scores obtained one week apart. The average reliabilities of the separate tests, for grades 7 through 13, range from .72 to .92. In addition to the reliability coefficients, the standard errors of measurement both for raw scores and for standard scores (T scores) are provided for each sex at each grade level. The reliabilities for the four factor scores, derived by combining appropriate test scores, range from .91 to .95.

In summary, this is a battery of differential aptitude tests for counseling at the secondary level. The mechanics for administration, scoring, and interpretation are well worked out and the necessary auxiliary materials are provided. The test and factor scores have satisfactory reliability for use in individual counseling. Some information is furnished concerning the validity of the scores for several school subjects. These data should be regarded as suggestive rather than definitive since no indication is given concerning how much these values may be expected to fluctuate under varying conditions. The results of the factor analysis, the correlation profiles for various school subjects, and the reliability of differences between scores for tests of different factors indicate that the differential approach upon which the battery is based is a sound one.

This promising battery is not as far along in its development as some of its competitors since only one form is available, end-of-year norms are not furnished, and validation data are not extensive or detailed.

[614]

*SRA Primary Mental Abilities. Grades kgn–2, 3–6, 7–12; 1946–58; IBM for ages 11–17; 3 levels; postage extra; L. L. Thurstone and Thelma Gwinn Thurstone; Science Research Associates. *
a) FOR AGES 5 TO 7. Grades kgn–2; 1946–53; formerly called Tests of Primary Mental Abilities for Ages 5 and 6; 6 scores: verbal, perception, quantitative, motor, space, total; 1 form ('53); manual, third edition ('53); supplement ('53); $3 per 20 tests; 50¢ per specimen set; (60–80) minutes in 2 sessions 1 day apart.
b) ELEMENTARY: AGES 7 TO 11. Grades 3–6; 1948–56; 5 factor scores (verbal, space, reasoning, perception, number), IQ, nonreading IQ, reading aptitude, arithmetic aptitude, and 4 part scores; Form AH ('48); manual, second edition ('54); supplement ('54); profile ('54); separate answer pads must be used; $9.80 per 20 tests; $2.15 per 20 answer pads; 90¢ per 20 interpretation folders ('54); 90¢ per 20 short form interpretation folders ('54); 75¢ per specimen set; 39(60) minutes in 2 sessions.
c) INTERMEDIATE: AGES 11 TO 17. Grades 7–12; 1947–58; 6 scores: verbal, spatial, reasoning, number, word-fluency (optional), total; IBM; Forms AH ('47, hand scored), AM ('48, machine scored); manual, third edition ('58); separate answer pads or answer sheets must be used; $9.80 per 20 tests; $5 per 100 IBM answer sheets; $2.15 per 20 answer pads; $3 per set of machine scoring stencils; 60¢ per 20 profiles; 75¢ per specimen set; 21(35–45) or 26(40–50) minutes.

REFERENCES

1–10. See 40:1427.
11–60. See 3:225.
61–102. See 4:716.
103. WHEATLEY, MABEL M. Primary Mental Abilities of Deaf Children. Doctor's thesis, University of Maryland (College Park, Md.), 1947.
104. AVAKIAN, SONIA A. An Investigation of Trait Relationships Among Six-Year-Old Children. Doctor's thesis, Fordham University (New York, N.Y.), 1951.
105. OLSON, DONALD J. A Study of the Iowa Tests of Educational Development and the SRA Primary Mental Abilities in the Montana State Wide Cooperative Testing Program. Master's thesis, Montana State University (Missoula, Mont.), 1951.
106. ANSBACHER, H. L. "The Goodenough Draw-A-Man Test

and Primary Mental Abilities." *J Consult Psychol* 16:176–80 Je '52. * (*PA* 27:5141)

107. BECHTEL, RAYMOND. *A Study of Thurstone's Primary Mental Abilities Test.* Doctor's thesis, St. John's University (Brooklyn, N.Y.), 1952.

108. CORTER, HAROLD M. "Factor Analysis of Some Reasoning Tests." *Psychol Monogr* 66(8):1–31 '52. * (*PA* 27:4995)

109. HODGES, JOHN M. *Primary Mental Abilities vs. Differential Aptitude Tests.* Master's thesis, Illinois State Normal University (Normal, Ill.), 1952.

110. HUTCHEON, JAMES F. *The Application of the Primary Mental Abilities Test to Mental Defectives.* Doctor's thesis, State University of Iowa (Iowa City, Iowa), 1952. (*DA* 12:587)

111. JOHNSON, RALPH W. *SRA Primary Mental Abilities vs. Algebra Aptitude: A Study.* Master's thesis, Illinois State Normal University (Normal, Ill.), 1952.

112. McKEE, JOHN P. "The Tests of Primary Mental Abilities Applied to Superior Children." *J Ed Psychol* 43:45–56 Ja '52. * (*PA* 26:7235)

113. MARQUIS, FRANCIS N. *A Study of Reading Ability in Its Relation to the SRA Primary Mental Abilities Test.* Doctor's thesis, University of Missouri (Columbia, Mo.), 1952. (*DA* 12:518)

114. MICHELI, GENE S. *The Relationship Between Speed of Concept Formation and Five "Primary Mental Abilities."* Master's thesis, Fordham University (New York, N.Y.), 1952.

115. MOODY, CAESAR B., JR. *The SRA Primary Mental Abilities Test in Relation to School Marks and Other Tests.* Doctor's thesis, University of North Carolina (Chapel Hill, N.C.), 1952.

116. ROBERTS, S. OLIVER, AND ROBINSON, JAMES M., SR. "Intercorrelations of the Primary Mental Abilities Tests for Ten-Year-Olds by Socioeconomic Status, Sex, and Race." Abstract. *Am Psychol* 7:304–5 Jl '52. *

117. ROCHLIN, ISAIAH. "The Investigation, Through the Use of Projective Techniques, of Nonintellectual Factors in the Learning of Mathematics." Abstract. *Am Psychol* 7:368 Jl '52. *

118. TOWNSEND, AGATHA, AND SPAULDING, GERALDINE. "The SRA Primary Mental Abilities Tests in the Independent-School Testing Program." *Ed Rec B* 58:58–70 F '52. * (*PA* 26:7237)

119. BURRALL, LUCILLE. *A Study of Internal or Trait Variability in Achievement of Pupils at the Fifth Grade Level.* Doctor's thesis, Pennsylvania State College (State College, Pa.), 1953.

120. CHAMBERS, JAMES R. *A Study of the Use of the Primary Mental Abilities Test With Negro Students in Mining, Rural, Urban, and Industrial Areas of West Virginia.* Master's thesis, West Virginia University (Morgantown, W.Va.), 1953.

121. DRAKE, JOHN D. *An Investigation of the Reliability of the SRA Primary Mental Abilities Test for Ages Eleven to Seventeen.* Master's thesis, Fordham University (New York, N.Y.), 1953.

122–3. HOLLOWAY, HAROLD D. *Effects of Training Upon, and Relationships Between, Two Standard Child Intelligence Tests.* Doctor's thesis, State University of Iowa (Iowa City, Iowa), 1953. (*DA* 13:884)

124. SCHAIE, K. WARNER; ROSENTHAL, FRED; AND PERLMAN, ROBERT M. "Differential Mental Deterioration of Factorially 'Pure' Functions in Later Maturity." *J Gerontol* 8:191–6 Ap '53. * (*PA* 28:2376)

125. SCHMIDT, LOUIS G. "Primary Mental Abilities and Occupational Choices." *J Ed Res* 47:297–300 D '53. * (*PA* 28:6174)

126. STEMPEL, ELLEN FLAUM. "The WISC and the SRA Primary Mental Abilities Test." *Child Develop* 24:257–61 S–D '53. * (*PA* 29:4089)

127. TRUMBULL, RICHARD. "A Study of Relationships Between Factors of Personality and Intelligence." *J Social Psychol* 38:161–73 N '53. * (*PA* 28:5589)

128. TYLER, LEONA E. "Changes in Children's Scores on Primary Mental Abilities Tests Over a Three-Year Period." Abstract. *Am Psychol* 8:448–9 Ag '53. *

129. ZIMMERMAN, WAYNE S. "A Revised Orthogonal Rotational Solution for Thurstone's Original Primary Mental Abilities Test Battery." *Psychometrika* 18:77–93 Mr '53. *

130. ALLEBACH, NANCY L. *Raven's Colored Matrices and Tests of Primary Mental Abilities With Young Children.* Master's thesis, Pennsylvania State University (University Park, Pa.), 1954.

131. ANASTASI, ANNE, AND DRAKE, JOHN D. "An Empirical Comparison of Certain Techniques for Estimating the Reliability of Speeded Tests." *Ed & Psychol Meas* 14:529–40 au '54. *

132. BAKER, EMILY H. *An Analysis of Four Aspects of Elementary School Geography.* Doctor's thesis, St. Louis University (St. Louis, Mo.), 1954.

133. BLEWETT, D. B. "An Experimental Study of the Inheritance of Intelligence." *J Mental Sci* 100:922–33 O '54. * (*PA* 29:6909)

134. BURRALL, LUCILLE. "Variability in Achievement of Pupils at the Fifth Grade Level." *Calif J Ed Res* 5:68–73 Mr '54. * (*PA* 28:9038)

135. DELANCY, ELMER O. *A Study of Three Psychological Tests as Related to Reading Achievement in Grade One American School Reading Readiness Test, Form A: SRA Primary Mental Abilities, Primary Form: Otis Quick-Scoring Mental Ability Tests, Alpha Test: Form A.* Doctor's thesis, Pennsylvania State University (University Park, Pa.), 1954.

136. HERZBERG, FREDERICK, AND LEPKIN, MILTON. "A Study of Sex Differences on the Primary Mental Abilities Test." *Ed & Psychol Meas* 14:687–9 w '54. * (*PA* 29:7283)

137. HOLLOWAY, HAROLD D. "Effects of Training on the SRA Primary Mental Abilities (Primary) and the WISC." *Child Develop* 25:253–63 D '54. * (*PA* 29:7284)

138. KOCH, HELEN L. "The Relation of 'Primary Mental Abilities' in Five- and Six-Year-Olds to Sex of Child and Characteristics of His Sibling." *Child Develop* 25:209–23 S '54. * (*PA* 29:6913)

139. KOLSTOE, OLIVER P. "A Comparison of Mental Abilities of Bright and Dull Children of Comparable Mental Ages." *J Ed Psychol* 45:161–8 Mr '54. * (*PA* 29:2270)

140. SCHMIDT, LOUIS G., AND ROTHNEY, J. W. M. "Relationship of Primary Abilities Scores and Occupational Choices." *J Ed Res* 47:637–40 Ap '54. * (*PA* 29:3004)

141. SHALLOE, M. PARACLETA. *A Study of the S.R.A. Primary Mental Abilities Battery as a Means of Educational Guidance in Selected Schools.* Doctor's thesis, Fordham University (New York, N.Y.), 1954.

142. BERDIE, RALPH F. "Aptitude, Achievement, Interest, and Personality Tests: A Longitudinal Comparison." *J Appl Psychol* 39:103–14 Ap '55. * (*PA* 30:1498)

143. BOND, GUY L., AND CLYMER, THEODORE W. "Interrelationship of the SRA Primary Mental Abilities, Other Mental Characteristics, and Reading Ability." *J Ed Res* 49:131–6 O '55. * (*PA* 30:7752)

144. MEREDITH, PHILIP. *The Thurstone Primary Mental Abilities and Academic Achievement in the Junior Forms of an English Grammar School.* Master's thesis, University of Manchester (Manchester, England), 1955. (Abstract: *Brit J Ed Psychol* 27:222)

145. MILL, CYRIL R., AND TURNER, CHARLES J. "The Measurement of Primary Mental Abilities by the Columbia Mental Maturity Scale." Abstract. *J Consult Psychol* 19:472 D '55. *

146. POOLER, MARY H. "Prediction of School Success Through the Use of the SRA Test of Primary Mental Abilities for Ages 5 to 7 Administered at the Kindergarten or First Grade Level." *Yearb Nat Council Meas Used Ed* 12(pt 2):76–81 '55. *

147. SATTER, GEORGE. "Psychometric Scatter Among Mentally Retarded and Normal Children." *Training Sch B* 52:63–8 Je '55. * (*PA* 30:3078)

148. SCHAIE, K. WARNER, AND STROTHER, CHARLES R. "Age Changes in the Primary Mental Abilities in a Group of Superior Older People." Abstract. *Am Psychol* 10:339 Ag '55. *

149. WELLINGTON, JOHN A. *Factors Related to the Academic Success of Resident Freshman Men at a Midwestern Liberal Arts College During the Academic Year 1952–1953.* Doctor's thesis, Northwestern University (Evanston, Ill.), 1955. (*DA* 16:69)

150. WOLKING, WILLIAM D. "Predicting Academic Achievement With the Differential Aptitude and the Primary Mental Abilities Tests." *J Appl Psychol* 39:115–8 Ap '55. * (*PA* 30:1636)

151. BRUCE, MARTIN M. "Normative Data Information Exchange, No. 4." *Personnel Psychol* 9:268–70 su '56. *

152. FRYE, U. CASSIAN. *The Relevancy of the SRA Primary Mental Abilities Test and the SRA Reading Record to Ninth Grade Achievement in a Catholic Boys' High School.* Master's thesis, St. Louis University (St. Louis, Mo.), 1956.

153. MITCHELL, JAMES V., JR. "A Comparison of the Factorial Structure of Cognitive Functions for a High and Low Status Group." *J Ed Psychol* 47:397–414 N '56. *

154. ROGERS, CARL A. *Measuring Intelligence in New Zealand: A Re-standardisation of Thurstone's Primary Mental Abilities (or Intermediate Test) for Ages 11 to 17 Years.* Auckland University College, Monograph Series No. 2. Auckland, New Zealand: Pilgrim Press, 1956. Pp. 127. (*PA* 32:2658)

155. SHINN, EDMOND O. "Interest and Intelligence as Related to Achievement in Tenth Grade." *Calif J Ed Res* 7:217–20 N '56. * (*PA* 31:8844)

156. KAMIN, LEON J. "Differential Changes in Mental Abilities in Old Age." *J Gerontol* 12:66–70 Ja '57. * (*PA* 32:4021)

157. LONG, JAMES R. *Academic Forecasting in the Technical-Vocational High School Subjects at West Seattle High School.* Doctor's thesis, University of Washington (Seattle, Wash.), 1957. (*DA* 17:1951)

158. WELLMAN, F. E. "Differential Prediction of High School Achievement Using Single Score and Multiple Factor Tests of Mental Maturity." *Personnel & Guid J* 35:512–7 Ap '57. * (*PA* 32:4631)

159. THURSTONE, THELMA GWINN. "The Tests of Primary Mental Abilities." Comments by Donald E. Super. *Personnel & Guid J* 35:569–78 My '57. * (*PA* 32:3909)

160. SMITH, D. D. "Abilities and Interests: I, A Factorial Study." *Can J Psychol* 12:191–201 S '58. *

161. WALTERS, RICHARD H. "The Intelligence Test Performance of Maori Children: A Cross-Cultural Study." *J Abn & Social Psychol* 57:107–14 Jl '58. *

NORMAN FREDERIKSEN, *Director of Research, Educational Testing Service, Princeton, New Jersey.*

The tests of *SRA Primary Mental Abilities*

are direct descendants of the tests used in the factor studies performed with high school and college students by L. L. Thurstone at the University of Chicago in the 1930's. An experimental edition called *Tests for Primary Mental Abilities,* published in 1938, provided measures of seven factors and required 222 minutes to administer; another edition, published in 1941, required 240 minutes. A shorter version, requiring 120 minutes, was published in 1943. The present high school level tests represent a further abbreviation of the test battery and require 40 to 50 minutes to administer. Other test batteries for lower age groups have appeared which are also intended to measure separate mental abilities.

ITEM TYPES. In the present battery, five factors are measured at each level. Only two of these factors, however, are common to all three levels—verbal meaning and space. The 7–11 and 11–17 tests measure in common two additional factors—reasoning and number. The fifth factor at the 11–17 level is word fluency. The two lower level batteries measure in common the perceptual speed factor (in addition to verbal meaning and space). Factors measured only at the 5–7 level are motor and quantitative factors. The latter is thought to differentiate into the reasoning and number factors at higher ages.

Tests bearing the same name at different levels do not necessarily involve the same types of items. The verbal meaning factor is measured at the 5–7 level by requiring the child to choose the picture corresponding to a word or idea stated orally. At the 7–11 level, the same factor is measured partly by a printed synonyms test and partly by a picture choosing test. At the 11–17 level, the factor is measured entirely by a printed synonyms test.

The space factor is measured at the 5–7 level by two subtests, one which requires finding "the rest of the square" and one which requires the child to complete a simple line drawing to make it like another drawing. At the 7–11 level, only the "find the rest of the square" type of item is used, while at the 11–17 level the task is to identify all the figures like the first figure in the row, when some of the figures are mirror images and all have been rotated into positions unlike the first.

Reasoning at 7–11 is measured by two subtests: which word does not belong? and which

picture does not belong? At 11–17, reasoning is measured by a letter series test.

The number factor is measured at both the 7–11 and 11–17 levels by addition tests. At 7–11, numbers are to be added and the answer written down. At 11–17, the task is to indicate whether the answer given is right or wrong.

Perceptual ability is measured at both levels (5–7 and 7–11) by similar tasks: find the picture exactly like the first picture.

The quantitative factor, measured only at the 5–7 level, involves marking pictures to show understanding of quantitative relationships, e.g., "mark the largest dog" and "Bobby and Billy want to dig. How many shovels do they need?" The motor ability factor, also measured only at the 5–7 level, is based on a test of how many lines the child can draw in the time allowed.

Word fluency, which occurs only at the 11–17 level, requires the examinee to write as many words beginning with a designated letter as he can in five minutes.

TIMING. The 5–7 test requires a little over an hour, preferably in two sessions on successive days. From 60 to 75 minutes are required for the 7–11 tests; again two sessions are recommended. The 11–17 tests require only 26 minutes of actual working time for the 5 scores, the overall testing time being 40 to 50 minutes. At the 5–7 level, only the perceptual speed and motor tests are timed (1½ and 1 minute, respectively, are allowed); the other tests are not speeded. At 7–11, the perception and number tests are speeded tests, and at 11–17 all tests are speeded. Thus scores at different levels which bear the same name may be measured not only by different types of items but also under different conditions with regard to speededness.

FORMAT. The test booklets are generally attractive and the arrangement convenient. The 5–7 booklet makes use of small pictures at the tops of pages and opposite certain items to assist the children in locating the proper place in the booklet. The cover of this particular test booklet is used as a profile chart, which makes a rather uninteresting cover for a six-year old.

The 7–11 booklet has a plastic ring binding and step-down pages so that an answer sheet can be inserted in the back in such a way as to align the answer spaces with the items. The answer sheet spacing does not permit the alignment to be made very accurately, although the lack of coincidence is probably not great enough to disturb a child seriously. The number test is printed on the answer sheet itself. The answer sheet may be opened to reveal a scoring stencil which is automatically marked by means of carbon paper. This method should result in quicker and more accurate scoring than would be possible by using a separate stencil.

The 11–17 booklet employs an IBM answer sheet whose columns correspond to the items on the pages of the test booklet and which can be aligned with the items quite accurately. Item numbers on booklet and answer sheet are adjacent when positioned properly, which should reduce errors resulting from putting answer marks in the wrong place.

The tests are obviously the work of competent people. The items appear to be good and the instructions clear. From the standpoint of test construction one can find little fault with the tests of SRA Primary Mental Abilities.

THE MANUALS. The examiners' manuals and technical supplements at the 5–7 and 7–11 levels were last revised in 1954. A new manual, dated May 1958, has just appeared for the 11–17 tests, the previous manual having been issued in 1949. A number of improvements characterize the 1958 manual which the publishers might well emulate in revisions of the lower level test manuals. In the new manual, references to pertinent research accompany claims which are made, and the list of references at the end is reduced from 91 to 21 references—references which are really appropriate. More statistical information about the 11–17 test has been added, especially validity data.

DESCRIPTIONS OF ABILITIES MEASURED. In the 5–7 and 7–11 manuals the description of each test includes a sample item and gives an interpretation in terms of school subjects or of occupations in which one is likely to do well if he is high in the ability measured. In describing verbal meaning at the 5–7 level, for example, the manual states that older children high in this ability usually do well in English, history, and foreign languages, and, as adults, are likely to succeed as secretaries, librarians, teachers, and executives. No evidence is presented to support such statements, and, in the case of executives at least, the statement vastly oversimplifies the problem. The vocational guidance implications of such statements are

disturbing, especially in view of the absence of any evidence that a high verbal score earned at age 5 to 7 on the PMA is associated with a high verbal score on an acceptable measure of verbal ability at college age.

The description of the verbal meaning factor in the 5–7 manual also states that "young children high in V should....learn to read easily, to communicate their ideas well, and to comprehend oral directions." One would not think of quarreling with this statement but for the data presented in the accompanying technical supplement. Correlations and beta weights are given for the prediction of scores on the Chicago Reading Tests in the second grade from PMA scores in the first grade. The correlations are .35 for V and .49 for Q, and the beta weights are .085 and .358 respectively. The text attributes the low weight for V to restriction in range of ability, but this interpretation is not borne out by data presented in the technical manual.

In the new 1958 manual for the 11–17 age level, such overenthusiastic descriptions of the traits measured do not occur. In revising the manual's description of word fluency, for example, the description was changed from "the ability to write and talk easily" to "the ability to produce words easily," which, in view of the nature of the test, is much more defensible. The more objective descriptions of abilities, without implication that high scores are associated with success in specific jobs, are to be preferred.

RELIABILITY. The reliabilities reported in the 5–7 technical supplement are split-half reliabilities, even for the highly speeded perceptual speed test. The reliabilities range from .77 for verbal meaning to .96 for perceptual speed. Reliability of the motor test is not reported. The reliabilities reported for the 7–11 level tests are based on Kuder-Richardson formula 20 (or 21 for the speeded perception and number tests). The correlations range from .79 to .95. The 1949 manual for 11–17 reported "Spearman-Brown" reliabilities ranging from .87 to .96. In the revised manual, these reliabilities are again reported (except that the reliability for word fluency is omitted); in addition, reliabilities obtained by Anastasi and Drake (131) by correlating separately timed halves are reported. These later correlations, based on a method which is more appropriate for speeded tests, yielded somewhat lower reliabilities ranging from .72 to .90. Anastasi, in reviewing the PMA in *The Fourth Mental Measurements Yearbook,* criticized the manual for using internal consistency methods for estimating reliability of speeded tests. The reliability data she and Drake provided are presented in the new manual; the 10-year-old split-half data are, however, still included.

INTERCORRELATIONS. At the 5–7 level, the intercorrelations among the five scores range from .51 to .73, and are described as "low to moderate." The .73 correlation is between verbal and quantitative scores. One might question whether the scores should be referred to as measures of "separate mental abilities." At the 7–11 level the intercorrelations among the main subtests are lower, ranging from .10 to .63. The question of how separate the abilities are is still pertinent, however. One of the two parts of the test of verbal ability, for example, correlates higher with one of the reasoning subtests than with the other verbal subtest. The two parts of the reasoning test correlate .46 with each other; this is lower than the correlation of .63 reported between verbal and reasoning abilities.

The new 11–17 manual reports six intercorrelation studies, including four from the 1949 manual. The median values range from .13 to .50; the correlation between verbal and reasoning abilities remains fairly high even at this age level. A table of "proportion of differences in excess of chance" which is included in the new manual helps in the interpretation of reliabilities and intercorrelations. The entries in the table represent the proportion of differences between scores on two tests which are so large that they cannot reasonably be attributed to chance. The median intercorrelations and the Anastasi-Drake reliabilities were used in computing the values. The proportions range from .27 (for number-word fluency) to .37 (for verbal-number). Tables such as this might well be added to the manuals at the other two levels whenever revisions are made.

If only a quarter to a third of the differences between pairs of scores are great enough to be attributable to something other than chance, it would be wise to provide the test user with appropriate information as to how big a difference must be before he should pay attention to it. In the manuals much is made of the usefulness of scores on the separate mental abilities in guidance and placement, but nowhere is

there a word of advice about a difference being so small that it should be ignored.

NORMS. The norms are based on fairly large numbers of cases, but the manuals leave much to be desired as to descriptions of the groups. The 5–7 technical supplement states that the PMA 5–7 was administered to 1,200 children whose ages ranged from 5 to 8; no further description of the children is given. Another table of means and standard deviations of raw scores for 263 first graders is given, again with no description of the group beyond the age range. Similarly, the technical supplement for the 7–11 tests states the age range of the 4,744 children used in the standardization, but gives no other description.

The revised 11–17 manual gives considerably more information than the 1949 manual it replaces. The old manual indicates that 18,000 students, a "random sampling" of junior and senior public high school students, were used. In the new manual, the 18,000 students are identified as Chicago students, and several other groups which contributed to revision of the norms are mentioned. The groups are predominantly from large cities, although the West Virginia sample presumably includes schools from small communities.

The revised norms are substantially different from those of 1949. Verbal meaning scores which would have been at the 50th percentile on the old norms place a student below the 35th percentile for most age groups on the 1958 norms. For reasoning and number scores, the differences are in the same direction but not quite as great. The correction for the space score is of comparable magnitude but in the opposite direction. Only for word fluency are the differences between the old and new norms tables minor.

Sex differences are not discussed in the technical supplements for levels 5–7 and 7–11. The new 11–17 manual reports data from a 1954 study by Herzberg and Lepkin (*136*) dealing with sex differences. The study showed that at age 17 there were significant sex differences on four of the five tests, differences between means which were separated by 10 or more percentile points in the region of the scale where they occurred. A study of 14-year olds done by Rogers (*154*) in 1956 also showed significant differences between sexes. No sex differentiated norms are presented however.

The profile sheet for 5–7 permits a profile

to be drawn on the basis of the five raw scores earned. The side entries permit translation to mental age, and directions are given for computing quotient scores, analogous to IQ's, for each score and for a total score. The weights used for determining the total quotient score provide an estimate of a Stanford-Binet IQ. At the 7–11 level the profile sheet is similarly interpreted in terms of mental age and quotient scores. A computation form is provided for weighting certain scores properly to get estimates of IQ for children who can read and for children who cannot, and also for reading aptitude and arithmetic aptitude quotients. At the 11–17 level, the profiles may be translated into either percentiles or quotients, although the former is recommended.

None of the profiles or manuals gives any indication of how big a difference should be before it can reasonably be attributed to something other than chance, although teachers, parents, and students are encouraged to use differences in scores as a basis for decisions on educational or occupational problems.

VALIDITY. Validity data of various sorts are presented in the three manuals. Correlations with intelligence tests such as the Stanford-Binet and Kuhlmann-Anderson are high. At the 5–7 levels, single tests such as those for verbal and reasoning ability correlate as high as .75 with Binet IQ's, with multiple correlations in the .80's. When the Binet is given a year after the PMA, the correlation is almost as large. Correlations with reading readiness tests are above .50. At the 7–11 level the correlations with IQ's are slightly lower. High correlations with reading and arithmetic tests are also reported. Both the technical supplements present regression equations for predicting Stanford-Binet IQ's. At the 7–11 level, regression equations are included for predicting reading age and arithmetic grade equivalent. This use of regression equations is an excellent way to take advantage of the fact that several abilities are measured in the battery. The inclusion in the 7–11 interpretation folder of convenient computing forms capitalizes more fully on the advantages of the multifactor test battery.

Validity data at the 11–17 level include correlations with the United States Employment Service *General Aptitude Test Battery,* the *Iowa Tests of Educational Development,* the Otis test, the ACE examination, the Kuhlmann-Anderson, and with grades in a variety of courses. Multiple correlations with tests of general intelligence or scholastic aptitude are high. On the basis of results found in the literature, the formula $2V + R$ is suggested as a measure of scholastic aptitude.

CHANCE SCORES. In general the raw scores which are likely to occur are well out of the chance score level, but there are a few exceptions. The 5–7 perception test has 30 four-choice items. If a child answered the items randomly he would be expected by chance to get about seven right. A raw score of seven is equivalent to a mental age of five, according to the information on the profile sheet. The 7–11 verbal test contains 73 four-choice items, so that a child who responded entirely by guessing might be expected to get 18 right. This raw score is equivalent to an MA of eight years, four months.

On the profile sheet for the 11–17 tests, percentiles are presented for each age from 11 to 17. Some of the tests are apparently too difficult for 11-year-olds; chance scores are quite high—above the 50th percentile for verbal scores and the 25th for reasoning scores. A correction for guessing is employed for the 11–17 space and number tests but not for the verbal and reasoning tests.

LONGITUDINAL STUDIES. In view of the long history of the Primary Mental Abilities, one might expect to find in a recent manual information on the correlations among levels. Such longitudinal studies apparently have not been made. The descriptions of the abilities strongly imply that an ability with a particular name is the same whether measured at 5 or at 17 years of age. The fact that item types and conditions of testing, particularly speededness, may vary considerably with test level suggests, on the other hand, that the abilities may not be the same. Longitudinal studies which result in correlations across levels are needed to answer questions of this sort.

SUMMARY. The PMA tests are sound and well constructed, and, if the scores are properly used, the tests could be of considerable value to teachers and school administrators. The outstanding needs, in this reviewer's opinion, are for (*a*) words of caution about insignificant differences between scores on a profile chart, and some graphic means of calling the user's attention to this problem; and (*b*) longitudinal studies to help determine to what extent the same ability is measured at different levels by tests bearing the same name.

ALBERT K. KURTZ, *Professor of Psychology, University of Florida, Gainesville, Florida.*

EFFECT OF PREVIOUS REVIEWS. Previous reviewers of *SRA Primary Mental Abilities* listed a number of highly specific criticisms (some major, some minor) of the tests. They did not all agree on all of these criticisms, nor does the present reviewer, although he feels that the great majority of them are justified. Since the appearance of *The Fourth Mental Measurements Yearbook,* the manuals and profiles have all been revised. (So have some of the test booklets and technical supplements.) Thus, there has been opportunity to make changes. The present reviewer's analysis leads him to conclude that some action has been (or already had been) taken with respect to the following earlier criticisms:

a) Reliability coefficients are inadequately reported, incorrectly computed, or omitted. This is still true for the two younger age groups, but the manual for ages 11–17 also cites recent figures based on separately timed halves.

b) Little evidence concerning validity is given and the recommendations for interpretation go far beyond available evidence for empirical validity. At the two lower levels, the only validity figures are correlations with other tests. At the 11–17 level, correlations with high school and college grades and ratings are also reported. No correlations with vocational success are reported. Discussions of the importance of certain factors in various occupations continue. It seems doubtful that the earlier reviewers would regard the present validity data as justifying these discussions.

c) No separate sex norms are given nor are data on sex differences included. Two tables in the age 11–17 manual show 10 of the 20 reported sex differences to be significant at the 1 per cent level, yet separate norms are not given at any age.

d) The authors have almost completely ignored the significance of individual differences and recent advances regarding influence of maturation. It is a matter of opinion as to whether or not this remains true.

e) Guidance counselors and parents may easily draw erroneous conclusions from some of the statements made. The definition of W has been changed from "the ability to write and talk easily" to "the ability to produce words easily," but the other allegedly misleading statements remain.

f) All editions yield only a single score for each factor. This is true (and the present reviewer feels properly so) for most subtests, although two part scores are available for V and for R at ages 7–11.

g) The authors indicate that V and P are prognostic of reading readiness, but they do not give evidence to support the claim or indicate how the scores should be combined. The manual cites two studies, each showing that V, P, and Q are related to subsequent reading achievement. Combination of scores is now explained and illustrated, using scores on V, P, and Q.

h) The motor test at ages 5–7 could better be described as a test of ability to manipulate a pencil. The manual says it "is important in learning to use a pencil properly."

i) The subject should print his name and other data before taking the word fluency test for ages 11–17 in order to eliminate cheating. This printing is now inconsistently done *before* the test on Form AM, but *after* it on Form AH. (May 1958 Manual.)

j) The manual says there are 60 number items; actually, there are 70. The manual now omits this statement.

The present reviewer may have overlooked something, but, as far as he could tell, the following additional criticisms have been rejected or ignored in revising the PMA materials.

k) No figures are given on test-retest reliability. This is still true.

l) There is no information on correlations between tests of the same factors at different levels. This is still true.

m) It is most misleading to suggest that single short tests can supply relatively pure measures of the factors. This is still implied.

n) The norm samples are inadequately described and insufficient information is given to determine their representativeness. This is still true.

o) Tests of W should be dropped because of little evidence for relevance in educational or vocational guidance. This test is still used.

p) Tests of perceptual speed should have been added at the upper levels. This has not been done.

q) Memory tests were excluded "because they take too long to administer." They are still excluded.

r) The authors recommend percentiles instead of (normalized) IQ. They still do in the two advanced levels.

s) The change from the earlier sliding scale of percentiles to 1950 MA units (all treated as equal) represents a deterioration in test construction. The MA units are still used.

t) Profile sheets should indicate how large a deviation must be to be meaningful. This has not been done, although a table showing the proportion of differences in excess of chance for pairs of PMA subtests is included in the manual for ages 11–17.

u) The authors fail to say whether the child should be encouraged to guess and to recommend what should be done if he cannot come to a decision. These points have not been clarified.

v) Speed is too prominent in the tests. The tests are unchanged.

w) A better method should be used to evaluate effect of speed on the tests. The same method is used.

x) The manuals do not suggest that regression techniques be used to obtain measures from which the effect of a general factor has been eliminated. This is still true.

y) No report is given of factorial investigation from which the tests at the 5–7 level were developed. This report is still delayed.

Enough of earlier reviews; it is time for the present review to begin.

GENERAL. The test items are well written. The directions are almost always clear. The tables of quotients (IQ's) and precomputed weights are excellent. Testing time is short—

probably too short. Most of the cited reliability coefficients are faulty (see *a* above), the best current estimates of the reliabilities of five subtests being .72, .75, .83, .87, and .90—obviously far lower than most test specialists would desire. With respect to the most important single characteristic of any test, we simply do not yet know much about the validities of these tests. Norms are not separated by sex and norm groups are inadequately described. Statements in the manuals and on the profiles tend to foster misinterpretations.

AGES 5–7. The 24-page test booklet and the directions for administering the test are very nicely coordinated. With the possible exception of lack of guessing instructions, everything connected with the mechanics of administering the tests seems well designed to get the child to respond as well as he is able. It is only after the child has recorded all his answers that we encounter any trouble. While technically correct, the directions for scoring are unnecessarily confusing. The neophyte (and all users start out as such) cannot tell at a glance which pages are to be scored, nor is he told what a perfect score is on any subtest. It would be simple to give the latter information (which would result in both faster and more accurate scoring of good papers) and to put some circles, squares, and other designs around the numbers of the pages to be scored, tying these symbols in to the spaces where the raw scores are recorded.

After the five raw scores are obtained, recorded, and plotted as a profile, "weights" for four of the scores are copied, added, and used in obtaining a mental age. Here arises the mystery of why the motor score vanishes. The motor score has no "weights" beside it and is not used further. The user may wonder why he should bother testing for motor if it isn't good enough to put in the total. Perhaps he should be told.

Most unfortunately, there still are remarkably few figures on the really important characteristics of the tests. Their reliabilities are unknown, the only set of figures being subject to the criticism in *a* above.

As to validity, these subtests can be so weighted as to give a multiple *r* of around .70 to .80 with Stanford-Binet. They can also be weighted to give a multiple *r* of around .50 with scores on reading tests. Further, the quantitative score correlates around .77 with arithmetic achievement of 75 children measured three

months later. More validity data should be available for a widely used test first copyrighted in 1946, even if the manual did come out in 1953.

Norms (the same for both sexes) are given in MA units only. (See *c* and *s* above.)

The manual helpfully provides and discusses a full-page sample interpretation. Unfortunately, the present reviewer believes that both he and some of the earlier reviewers will feel that the criticism in *e* above still applies. The interpretations should be much more conservative—at least until we have data to justify them.

The *Learning to Think Series,* by the same author and publisher, which was so thoroughly criticized in earlier reviews of this test, is still recommended in the manual.

AGES 7–11. At this level, there is a test booklet and separate answer sheet, readily scorable in "about three minutes." The selection of abilities to be tested is good, and there should be no problems connected with giving or scoring the tests.

Again, we encounter trouble with respect to test statistics. Only one set of reliability coefficients is given. Most were computed by Kuder-Richardson formula 20, but for some peculiar reason K-R 21 was used for two "tests in which speed is of major importance." This is highly inappropriate since *all* K-R formulas are inapplicable to speed tests. It is too bad we know so little about the reliabilities of these tests.

The validity data consist solely of correlations with other tests. As was true at ages 5–7, these subtests can be so weighted as to give a multiple *r* of around .70 to .80 with Stanford-Binet or Kuhlmann-Anderson IQ. The verbal score based on words (Vw) also correlates around .75 with reading tests; and a regression equation gives a multiple *r* of around .60 with an arithmetic test. Most, if not all, of these figures are concurrent validities. It seems that nothing is known about how well these tests will *predict* anything at some future time. This statement has important implications concerning the use of the tests in counseling and guidance. (See *b* and *e* above.)

In one of the two tables of intercorrelations, after we exclude the part scores, the correlations run from .10 to .63 with a median of .34. In the other, no total scores are given for V and R, so after we eliminate the correlations between Vw and Vp and between Rw and Rf, the other 19 correlations run from .34 to .73 with a median of .46. Both these sets of correlations seem far too high for tests which are supposed to measure relatively independent factors. (Remember that if we could correct these correlations for attenuation, they would be higher by an unknown amount.)

Norms (the same for both sexes) are given in MA units only, just as was true at the 5–7 year level. As was true at the younger ages, the recommended interpretations frequently do not seem justified by the available data. Because both the verbal and reasoning scores are divided into two parts, as well as a total, the five factors yield nine separate scores to be plotted on profiles. This is, indeed, a large superstructure to be erected on a foundation about which so little is known.

AGES 11–17. The same test booklet can be used with either hand scored or machine scored answer sheets. The two sets of directions for giving the tests are very conveniently presented in two parallel columns. The only criticism, and it is a minor one, centers on the statement, "If necessary, explain....that once a word has been used, it is incorrect to...." The optional nature of this may result in slightly different scores on the word fluency test. This subtest is hand scored on both answer sheets. The scoring directions for all subtests are simple and clear.

Whereas the other manuals were revised in 1953 and 1954, the one for ages 11–17 was revised in 1958. It is well prepared, starting with "an overview" and a very complete table of contents and ending, not with a 64-item, largely unused bibliography (as was true at the earlier ages) but with one of 21 recent items, every one of which is referred to in the text.

One of the earlier reviewers, Anastasi, is responsible for the only correct reliabilities that have yet been reported for these tests. She and Drake computed the reliabilities and got much lower figures [1] than the incorrectly computed figures previously reported. In the case of the space subtest, the effect was catastrophic, the figure changing from .96 to .75. The manual concedes the correctness of these lower figures. It would be even better if something were done to raise them. Specifically, the application of the general form of the Spearman-Brown

formula for lengthening tests shows that the reliabilities of V and R could be raised to .95 and those of S, N, and W to .90 by nearly tripling the present working time of 26 minutes while only doubling the present overall testing time of 40 to 50 minutes. If these scores are to be used for guidance or any other worthwhile purpose, it is imperative that some such steps be taken to make them reliable.

It is, of course, even more important that the scores be valid. Several hundred correlations between PMA subtests and other test scores are given. Usually V and R, the most reliable subtests, show the highest correlations. The reader may be interested in knowing that an arithmetic reason test correlates negligibly higher with V than with either N or R. There are about six studies in which school grades are correlated with PMA scores. In one of them, the PMA tests were taken about two years *after* the grades were given. Since the usual purpose is prediction of achievement rather than of PMA scores, such correlations are not very helpful. In at least one other study, the tests were given first, as they should be. Let us temporarily define validity as the correlation between the high school grades and whatever PMA subtest shows the highest correlation with the grades. So defined, the 13 high school validities run from .22 to .66, the median being .48. In four instances, the correlation with V was not computed; in six of the other nine, V gave the highest correlation. Stated differently, this PMA correlates reasonably well with high school grades; the verbal test, alone, would do nearly as well.

There are only two validity studies not relating to test scores or to ordinary high school grades. One used multiple correlation to predict ratings of progress in three vocational high school courses (auto mechanics, electric wiring, and woodworking). The validities were only .31, .38, and .17, respectively. The other study attempted to predict college grades from PMA tests administered in the 12th grade. "Correlations with grades in a variety of college courses were inconsistent and low." Reasons are given for both these failures to predict.

There are six sets of intercorrelations of the subtests. These correlations run from .10 to .55 with a median of .31. Thus, they are a little, but not much, lower than those for the preceding age group.

Sex differences are clearly revealed in two

1 Even these figures are perhaps not so low as they should be. Anastasi and Drake used boys in the 11th and 12th grades. Reliabilities within a single grade would almost certainly be lower.

tables and in the text. Ten of the 20 differences are significant at the 1 per cent level of confidence, the significant differences running from about 2 to 6 points. This largest difference means that the average boy has a percentile of about 45, while the average girl has one of 65. Separate sex norms are needed, but still not provided. (See *c* above.)

The May 1958 "Profile" is a single sheet with no directions or explanations on it and not much in the manual. It gives "Percentiles" at one side and "Quotients" at the other, the former being recommended as more meaningful for almost all uses. The present reviewer would disagree, but this is a matter on which there are differences of opinion. (See *r* and *s* above.) By omitting the directions and explanations which were printed on earlier editions of the profile, the authors have left the teacher, parent, or student somewhat bewildered, but they have eliminated some of the force of criticisms *b, e, m,* and *r* above.

OVERALL EVALUATION. This is not an excellent test battery, but it is a good one. Most of its defects were pointed out in earlier *Mental Measurements Yearbooks*. It is objective, easy to administer, and has high face validity. But its reliability is low at ages 11–17 and unknown, and probably very low, at the younger ages. Its validity is no better than that of many other tests. It correlates fairly well with achievement test scores and some high school grades; it does not correlate with vocational training ratings or with college grades. (The test may be much better or worse than this sentence implies; the chief defect is that there are so few studies of its predictive value.)

The theoretical rationale underlying the test is sound. It may well be that an excellent test can be developed upon this foundation. Until the reliabilities are improved and satisfactory validity data are available, the potential user should investigate other possibilities also. The present reviewer is not familiar with competing tests at ages 5–7. At ages 7–11, almost any reliable intelligence (or other) test with a large verbal component should do as well as the PMA in predicting school achievement. At ages 11–17, this simple procedure would also work, but a better procedure would be to use a competing battery about which more information is available, such as the *Differential Aptitude Tests*. Although these require more time for administration and have higher average in-

tercorrelations, the latter is in part due to their much higher reliability. They also have validities which are known and which are much higher than the few available for the *SRA Primary Mental Abilities* test batteries.

[615]

*Yale Educational Aptitude Test Battery. Grades 9–16; 1946–53; 7 scores: verbal comprehension, artificial language, verbal reasoning, quantitative reasoning, mathematical aptitude, spatial relations, mechanical ingenuity; IBM in part; 1 form; 7 tests in 3 booklets (tests 3, 4, and 7 in booklet entitled "Single Booklet Edition," '46; tests 1, 2, 5, and 6 in booklet entitled "Second Single Booklet Edition," '47; practice booklet, '47); mimeographed directions ('47); descriptive bulletin ('53); profile ('47); norms ('47); separate answer sheets must be used; $1.75 per set of test booklets, answer sheets, and profile; $2.50 per set of scoring stencils; $2.50 per battery with scoring service; postage extra; (60–70) minutes per test; Albert B. Crawford and Paul S. Burnham; distributed by Educational Records Bureau. *

REFERENCES

1–7. See 4:718.
8. CRAWFORD, ALBERT B., AND BURNHAM, PAUL S. "Freshman Aptitude Tests: How Yale Predicts Undergraduate Scholastic Performance." *Yale Scientific Mag* 23:9–10+ O '48.
9. MCCARTHY, MARY VITERBO. *An Empirical Study of the Personality Profiles Characterizing Differential Quantitative and Linguistic Ability.* Catholic University of America, Studies in Psychology and Psychiatry, Vol. 8, No. 4. Washington, D.C.: Catholic University of America Press, 1953. Pp. viii, 45. * (*PA* 28:4043)
10. SKARD, ØYVIND; AURSAND, INGER MARIE; AND BRAATEN, LEIF J. "Development and Application of Tests for University Students in Norway: A Report on Parts of a Research Project." *Psychol Monogr* 68(12):1–24 '54. * (*PA* 29:7971)
11. BURNHAM, PAUL S. *Entrance to a University College: An Exploratory Study.* Christchurch, New Zealand: Canterbury University College, 1955.

ANNE ANASTASI, *Professor of Psychology, Fordham University, New York, New York.*

Originally developed as an integrated series of aptitude tests for use in the educational counseling of Yale freshmen, this battery has recently been made available for wider distribution. The current form has evolved through some 15 years of systematic research with both Yale students and secondary school boys. It consists of seven tests, grouped into two booklets (but labeled "single booklet edition"!), to be administered in separate testing sessions. The tests are:

Test 1, Verbal Comprehension, requiring the identification of synonyms, antonyms, and inappropriate words; Test 2, Artificial Language, calling for a demonstration of linguistic facility; Test 3, Verbal Reasoning, comprising logical inference, deductive judgment, and similar functions; Test 4, Quantitative Reasoning, calling for the manipulation of hypothetical data and the derivation of principles analogous to but different from those met in the natural sciences; Test 5, Mathematical

Aptitude, requiring the performance of various tasks with equations; Test 6, Spatial Relations, including block counting, projections, and other item types that utilize two-dimensional representations of three-dimensional figures; and Test 7, Mechanical Ingenuity, requiring the solution of problems in gear or pulley movements, structural stability, and other mechanical operations.

Raw scores on each of the seven tests can be converted into standard scores with mean 50 and SD 10, as well as into percentile equivalents. The norms provided for these conversions were obtained on approximately 2,000 students tested in 13 secondary schools. Most of these subjects were in eastern private preparatory schools. No information regarding sex or grade level of the normative sample is given, although personal communication with the test distributors revealed that most of the subjects were 10th grade boys. Percentile norms on Yale freshmen may be obtained on request. These norms are offered only as suggestive data, test users being urged by the authors to develop their own local norms. It is stated (4, 8) that, with appropriate modifications in norms, the battery can be used effectively from the 10th grade to the college freshman level. In general, amount of previous education exerts maximum influence on the two tests (Verbal Comprehension and Mathematical Aptitude) which, in some respects, are similar to the CEEB Scholastic Aptitude Test. At the other extreme, grade means exhibit the least change in Tests 6 and 7, Spatial Relations and Mechanical Ingenuity, although relevant job experience (as in the course of military service) is reflected in superior performance on these tests (4, 8).

It is reported that split-half reliability coefficients of .92 to .96 have been found for each of the seven tests with different populations and educational levels, although detailed data are not given. Kuder-Richardson coefficients on two samples in grades 10–12 fell between .75 and .97 (6). Retests over a two-year interval (some involving closely similar but not identical tests) yielded stability coefficients of .56 to .82, most being in the .60's (4). Intercorrelations of the seven tests in a Yale freshman class of approximately 850 students ranged from .19 to .64, with a mean of .41 (4). Very similar patterns of correlations were obtained in other Yale freshman classes and among secondary school students, although the correlations tended to run higher in the latter population.

Differential validity of each part of the Yale battery has been checked principally against grades in appropriate college courses. The large majority of these validity coefficients fall between .45 and .65, while correlations with inappropriate courses (for example, scores on Mathematical Aptitude with English grades) are reported as generally under .20, many being statistically insignificant. For purposes of educational counseling, the authors recommend a classification of the tests into three overlapping groups: Tests 1, 2, and 3 indicating aptitude for the liberal arts; Tests 3, 4, and 5 for pure science and mathematics; and Tests 5, 6, and 7 for technological studies such as engineering.

Certain limitations of the test in its present form obviously stem from its having been designed for restricted use. There is, for example, no manual in the usual sense, the necessary information being provided in a 4-page descriptive booklet and another leaflet containing general directions, time limits, and norms. Although the descriptive booklet presents a concise, objective, and well balanced picture of the technical characteristics of the battery, the reader must consult Chapter 5 of *Forecasting College Achievement* (4) for supporting data. Even this source omits much relevant material; reference is made repeatedly to a projected second volume which has not appeared. Two recent publications concerned with the use of these tests in other countries are of some interest. Burnham (11) has described the application of parts of the battery to a small group of secondary school boys in New Zealand. Data on differential validity, intercorrelations, and factorial analysis of a Norwegian adaptation of the battery are reported by Skard and others (10).

In appearance, the test booklets fall short of the "deluxe" standards attained by some commercial tests, although the reproduction of test items is sufficiently clear. Another minor detail concerns the numbering of test parts which is now quite confusing, especially since Arabic and Roman numerals are used inconsistently to refer to the same parts. Finally, the preparation of a unified and fuller manual would be of considerable assistance to the potential general user of the battery.

With regard to the more basic requirements of test construction, the Yale battery represents an outstanding achievement. Available data on its reliability and validity indicate unusual promise for differential prediction of academic performance in broad curricular areas. In its objectives, this battery falls between traditional achievement tests and such multiple factor batteries as the *SRA Primary Mental Abilities,* but it appears to be closer to the latter than to the former. Although the research leading to its development was initiated more than two decades ago, the Yale battery reflects important current trends in test development in its use of a multiple aptitude profile and in its emphasis on the measurement of reasoning. Closely allied to the latter characteristic is the relatively extensive coverage of aptitudes relevant to science. And of special interest in this connection is the content of the quantitative reasoning test which requires the analysis of imaginary scientific data.

RUTH CHURCHILL, *Professor of Education and Psychology, Antioch College, Yellow Springs, Ohio.*

The *Yale Educational Aptitude Battery,* developed in the 1940's by Crawford and Burnham at Yale University, is one of the small number of aptitude batteries available. The distinctive characteristic of these batteries is the attempt to sample a range of abilities significant for educational and vocational guidance by means of a group of tests all standardized on the same population. Most of the aptitude batteries, however, such as the *Flanagan Aptitude Classification Tests* are designed for general vocational guidance and sample abilities widely. They include many perceptual, manual, and motor tests, so that skills needed for a wide variety of jobs, clerical and skilled as well as professional, are tapped. The Yale battery is the only one specifically designed with the question of educational, rather than vocational, guidance at both the high school and the college levels clearly in mind.

In the descriptive bulletin, the following statements made concerning the aim of the Yale tests clearly illustrate the concentration on educational guidance:

The purpose of this battery may....be defined as the provision of a series of differential measures severally pointing towards comparative *learning capacity in one direction or another.* * Tests I, II, and III appraise scholastic promise for the Liberal Arts—English, languages, history, economics and related (Verbal) subjects. Tests III, IV, and V point towards comparative

ability, or lack of it, for the physical (Quantitative) sciences and mathematics. Tests V, VI and VII measure aptitude for technological studies, such as engineering.

From the practical standpoint, the major problem in the use of this battery is that of time. The practice booklet takes 2 hours, and the typical time limit for each of the seven tests is 45 minutes. When time is allowed for distribution and collection of materials for each test, the total time for the battery is about eight hours, including the practice booklet but exclusive of rest periods. Conceivably the test can be given in one day, but three half-day testing sessions would be better, or students can be requested to complete the practice booklet before the day of testing. It is also possible to give the test without the use of the practice booklet and with longer time limits (about one hour) for each individual test. Again a full day is necessary. In a letter to the reviewer, Arthur Traxler gives some indication of the amount of use of the test in the past few years. Each year about 15 to 18 schools and colleges have used the test. He feels that its limited use has been the result of the amount of time needed to give the battery.

Over and above practical considerations involved in using a test or battery of tests, one of the first major considerations is the reliability of the various tests. The explanatory materials available indicate that split-half correlations adjusted by the Spearman-Brown formula range from .92 to .96 for the various tests, with a median of .94. These are for an unnamed sample of unknown size. In a study by Jacobs (6), Kuder-Richardson reliability coefficients for two groups of high school students (grades 10–12) ranged from .91 to .97 for all the tests except Test 5 for which the coefficients were .87 to .88 and Test 7 for which they ranged from .75 to .85. This reviewer obtained Kuder-Richardson formula 21 reliability coefficients ranging from .87 to .95 for Tests 1–7 (Test 2 omitted) for a group of 319 students entering Antioch College in September 1957. The two reliability coefficients below .90 for this group were .87 for Test 5 and .89 for Test 7. Thus, the reliability of the battery, with the possible exception of Test 7, seems adequate then in both high school and college populations.

The questions linked to the suitability of the battery for various groups are the difficulty level of the various tests and the availability of norms based on known groups. The test is recommended for use throughout the high school and college years. Jacobs presents data which indicate that the tests are somewhat difficult for an independent school 10th grade group (median percentage right on any one test is 25 per cent), but that they are not too difficult (median percentage right, 37 per cent) for a 12th grade group. For the group of 319 students entering Antioch College in 1957 the median percentage right on any one test was 44 per cent. Four of the six tests were close to 50 per cent in difficulty for this group while two, Mathematical Aptitude and Mechanical Ingenuity, were difficult for it. While the high difficulty level of the test may be a disadvantage at the high school level, it is one of the test's greatest advantages at the college level. The tests of the battery are sufficiently difficult to permit distinguishing differences among superior college students; the reviewer has found few other aptitude tests which do so.

The norms furnished are based on "some 2000 students in 13 secondary schools. These were mostly eastern private preparatory institutions which as a group ranked at approximately the sixty-third percentile on the independent-school norms for general scholastic aptitude prepared by the Educational Records Bureau." Other norms referred to in the descriptive bulletin as being available are based on Yale freshmen. These norm groups have two serious shortcomings. First, they include no women. Both the Jacobs study and Antioch data indicate that women do better than the men in the verbal tests but poorer in the quantitative and technical tests. Second, the norm group of secondary school students (and that for college students, for that matter) is a highly selected one. Independent school norms in general run higher than public high school norms, and the students upon whom the reported norms are based were selected even for an independent school group. Norms based on both sexes (or given separately by sex) and on more typical high school and college groups would be desirable. Of course, the ideal solution is the development of local norms; for even when norms based on a range of groups are available, it is difficult to find the exact set most appropriate to each particular situation.

Crawford and Burnham (4) point out that they have compromised between a battery which attempts to measure factors in as pure a form as possible and one which stresses relevance to needs for prediction in educational guidance. The intercorrelations among the Yale tests are evidence of this compromise between factorial purity and everyday relevance in complex situations. In most cases, the intercorrelations are low enough to suggest that the various tests of the battery do measure somewhat independent variables. Although each test is a composite of several subtests and thus can scarcely be pure factorially, as Crawford and Burnham point out, factor analyses by them did indicate three factors in addition to a residual factor labeled "general scholastic ability": verbal-linguistic facility, quantitative-mathematical reasoning, and spatial-mechanical aptitude.

Data on the validity or usefulness of such a test battery as the Yale can be of many kinds. What are the relationships of these tests to other tests and to relevant course grades? What studies are there of the usefulness of the test profile in educational guidance? What discussion is there of these profiles in counseling? Again, it is clear that *Forecasting College Achievement* rather than the materials provided with the battery must be considered the manual for the test. The descriptive bulletin summarizes validation studies in one paragraph, emphasizing correlations between test scores and appropriate and inappropriate college grades. It states, "Coefficients in general ranged from about .45 to .65 or higher, between test scores and *appropriate* criteria of subsequent academic grades; from .10 or less to about .20 with *inappropriate* criteria." The paragraph concludes with a reference to the cumulative validation studies in *Forecasting College Achievement*.

In this work, the validation studies are amplified, but the above statement from the manual is a good summary of the studies dealing with the prediction of course grades. Unfortunately the only material presented on the usefulness of the *profile* of test scores consists of a comparison of profiles for groups of 1944 Yale freshmen entering the liberal arts and the engineering curricula and the presentation of a few individual profiles together with relevant material on their later academic performance at Yale.

Over the course of 10 years' use, this reviewer has collected data on the usefulness of the Yale battery. Some of this is formal data of the sort to be hoped for in manuals; some of it is informal data based on acquaintance with the test. The net result of this long acquaintance has been a decided impression that the test is useful for the purposes for which it was designed.

In summary, the *Yale Educational Aptitude Test Battery* is a well constructed, carefully standardized, thorough, difficult battery which is well designed for use at the college level. At a time when everyone is concerned about our best college students, such a test should be extremely useful. If norms for the test and studies of the test are scanty, these shortcomings can be traced to the fact that the test has had far too few users, which can in turn be traced to the length of administration time required. Unfortunately, a thorough, comprehensive job of differential testing cannot be done in an hour or so. Although the requirement that the tests be used as a complete battery is a wise one (otherwise the essential value of a battery is lost), one possible compromise might shorten the length of the battery without

weakening it. Test 1, Verbal Comprehension, and Test 5, Mathematical Aptitude, are very similar to the two parts of the *Scholastic Aptitude Test* of the College Entrance Examination Board. In fact, in some of the research on the Yale battery they have been used interchangeably. In colleges which use the *Scholastic Aptitude Test,* why could not the SAT be substituted for Tests 1 and 5 of the Yale battery, thus shortening the battery by an hour and a half to two hours? Perhaps, this compromise should be considered by the Educational Records Bureau.

In a way it is a sad commentary on guidance programs when one day's time cannot be found for gathering information which may improve decisions for four or more years of education. With the latest Office of Education figures reporting that only 40 per cent of entering freshmen graduate at the end of four years, surely there is room for improving educational guidance at the college level. Everything about the *Yale Educational Aptitude Test Battery* indicates that it is an excellent instrument for this task.

READING

REVIEWS BY *Janet G. Afflerbach, Lois Grimes Afflerbach, Joan Bollenbacher, N. Dale Bryant, Reginald R. Dale, James Deese, Clarence Derrick, Jerome E. Doppelt, Lydia A. Duggins, S. S. Dunn, Henry S. Dyer, Robert Ebel, Leonard S. Feldt, Eric F. Gardner, Marvin D. Glock, Neil Gourlay, J. Thomas Hastings, A. N. Hieronymus, Walker H. Hill, James R. Hobson, Carl I. Hovland, Duncan Howie, Russell P. Kropp, Charles R. Langmuir, Roy D. Lewis, R. W. McCulloch, James Maxwell, Louis C. Nanassy, Stanley Nisbet, Victor H. Noll, S. A. Rayner, Maynard C. Reynolds, Helen M. Robinson, Benjamin Rosner, Fred J. Schonell, Donald E. P. Smith, George D. Spache, Russell G. Stauffer, Harry L. Stein, Ruth M. Strang, Agatha Townsend, Arthur E. Traxler, B. H. Van Roekel, Magdalen D. Vernon, Verna L. Vickery, D. K. Wheeler, Stephen Wiseman, C. Gilbert Wrenn, and J. Wayne Wrightstone.*

[616]

A.C.E.R. Silent Reading Tests. Grades 3–8 and adults (Part 1, Form B only); 1933–57; Forms A, B ['33]; 5 tests; 18s. per 10 copies of all tests; 3s. 6d. per manual ['34]; 5s. per specimen set; postpaid within Australia; Australian Council for Educational Research. *

a) PART 1, WORD KNOWLEDGE. 3s. per 10 tests; 8(10) minutes. (An Adult Form B ['54, identical to grades 3–8 Form B except for directions] is also available; 9d. per set of mimeographed instructions ['57] and 18-year-old norms ['54].)

b) PART 2, SPEED OF READING. 3s. per 10 tests; 3(5) minutes.

c) PART 3, READING FOR GENERAL SIGNIFICANCE. Optional; 4s. per 10 tests; 6(10) minutes.

d) PART 4, READING TO NOTE DETAILS. 4s. per 10 tests; 10(15) minutes.

e) PART 5, READING FOR INFERENCE. Optional; 4s. per 10 tests; 6(10) minutes.

FRED J. SCHONELL, *Professor of Education, University of Queensland, Brisbane, Australia.*

The standardisation of this test was carried out in 1933 on approximately 33,000 state school children in 469 schools throughout Australia. It would seem that the standardisation was adequately done and that careful statistical measures were employed in connection with the test. However, due to the fact that there is evidence of a slight move forward in silent reading abilities in several Australian states, it would seem that there is a need for a more recent standardisation.

The reliability of each part was determined by retesting 1,800 children in grades 3–8. It seems a pity, however, that the retesting was done on successive days. It is a more realistic procedure to allow a somewhat greater interval on which to base the reliability of a test.

An examination of the intercorrelations among the various parts of the test shows that there is a fairly close correspondence among them; this is a fair indication that they are measuring valid aspects of reading ability. It is also suggested that a shorter form of the test may be given by omitting Parts 3 and 5. The evidence is that these may be omitted without any appreciable decrease in reliability.

Raw scores have been changed to scale scores for each of the five subtests so that educational ages may be obtained. Centile graphs are also given, but, again, it is doubtful whether these are of any great value to the ordinary class teacher. Grade norms are also provided. These may be used for obtaining the position of an individual child in the grade or for determining the standing of a grade as a whole. Norms are given separately for each state.

[617]

A.C.E.R. Silent Reading Test, Form C. Grades 4–6; 1946–50; Form C ['46]; 3 parts; 12s. per 10 tests of all parts; 2s. per scoring key; 5s. per manual ['50]; 8s. per specimen set; postpaid within Australia; Australian Council for Educational Research. *
a) PART I, WORD KNOWLEDGE. 3s. per 10 tests; 10(20) minutes.
b) PART 2, SPEED OF READING. 4s. per 10 tests; 6(15) minutes.
c) PART 3, READING FOR MEANING. 5s. 6d. per 10 tests; 20(30) minutes.

REFERENCE
1. WHEELER, D. K. "Reading Speed of W.A. Children." *Educand* 2:4–9 N '54.

FRED J. SCHONELL, *Professor of Education, University of Queensland, Brisbane, Australia.*

Part 1, Word Knowledge, is a vocabulary test consisting of 100 words of increasing difficulty in 5-choice multiple choice form. There are eight practice examples. Part 2, Speed of Reading, consists of a story of 2,950 words, preceded by a short practice passage. In each 50 words there are 47 words of prose and 3 words in brackets from which one must be chosen for completion of the sentence. Although the comprehension aspect of this subtest has been kept to a minimum, it is, nevertheless, a test of both speed and comprehension. Part 3, Reading for Meaning, is composed of paragraphs of varied context and increasing difficulty. Testees answer two questions on each paragraph.

It is suggested that the subtests should be given in the order of their standardisation: Speed of Reading, Reading for Meaning, Word Knowledge. They have been carefully compiled and constitute a very useful battery for measuring the reading abilities of children between the ages of 9 and 12. They were standardised in 1946 on 30,000 children from nearly 600 schools in the six states. The only possible weakness may derive from the fact that teachers gave the tests. For purposes of standardisation, it is always advisable to have tests given by trained workers.

The scoring method is straightforward and the form of interpretation of scores sound and well based. Care has been taken in the calculation and presentation of norms. Five types are provided—grade norms, grade medians, age norms, age medians, and age-in-grade norms—separately for each state.

Both age and grade norms are given on a 15-point scale, but it is doubtful whether many primary teachers ever use a 15-point scale in marking. Hence, the scale scores will not be particularly meaningful to them. Again, while results from these tests are extremely useful for those engaged in surveys and counseling work, it is unlikely that teachers make much use of centile grading. The class teacher who wishes to discover the level of attainment of his children in reading wants a readily understood scale presented in terms of reading age or grade level, even if there is a small element of error attachable to such a measure. It is difficult to see why separate norms for boys and girls are given in the age norms, but not in the grade norms—surely the same sex differences still operate.

However, these are minor criticisms and the tests may be strongly recommended. They are sound, reliable measures and the standardisation reveals very thorough statistical work.

D. K. WHEELER, *Senior Lecturer in Education, University of Western Australia, Nedlands, Australia.*

Because of its availability the reviewer has used this test in schools, but with reservations, particularly about Part 1, Word Knowledge. In similar vocabulary tests it is usual, and seems good practice, to follow the test words by similar parts of speech. In at least 40 per cent of these examples this is not done.

Despite the fact that it is not a test of ability to follow instructions, there are items likely to mislead. In many cases, distractors are words which in context could be closely associated with the test word, e.g., "large" (test word) has as one choice "man"; "separate" has "chaff." The test is not one of visual discrimination; yet "thorough" has as choices "trough" and "tough." Finally, there are 17 items where one choice belongs in the schoolboy howler or boner class. "Colt" has as a choice "frozen"; "signature" has "young swan"; "escalator" both "horse-rider" and "Alpine climber"; "surplus" has "clerical collar"; "chicanery" has "inferior coffee." English teachers will object to "lie back" being taken as the correct answer for "recline" when "rest" is also included as a choice, and teachers generally will object to "storehouse" given for "silo" or "brute" for "thug." Purists may well object to other items such as 24, 79, and 93.

Part 2, Speed of Reading, is a 2,950-word selection. Forty-seven words of continuous prose are followed by three words in parentheses under one of which a line must be drawn to make best sense. According to the manual, all words are within the vocabulary of the fourth grade child and the difficulty of comprehension has as far as possible been kept constant throughout. The writer applied the Lorge and the Dale-Chall readability formulas to words 1294–1403 and 2213–2310. Both readability measures indicated a sixth grade level.

Part 3, Reading for Meaning, consists of 30 paragraphs (19 to 83 words long) of varied content and increasing difficulty, each with two multiple choice questions. About half of the questions are concerned with the main idea ("This story tells you about" or "The best name for this story is"). About one sixth are concerned with detail and about one third require inferences to be made. Occasionally, both questions ask much the same thing (e.g., 39 and 40, 45 and 46).

Answers are checked on test papers and marked with a key. Some care should be exercised with the keys, as the one sent for review needed taking to pieces and rearranging before use. The general format of the tests is good, the cover page of each test being devoted to instructions and adequate practice examples.

Part 1 might be better set out to avoid the difficulty for middle school children of following a question clear across the page. The manual is comprehensive and contains descriptions, detailed instructions, and norms.

In the manual it is suggested that "until experimental evidence is available as to whether the order of administration of the tests is important, it is recommended that they be given in the order followed in the original standardization," that is, 2, 3, 1. As 12 years have passed since the test was first published, either this evidence should be forthcoming or the tests should be renumbered in the proper sequence.

The norms were derived in 1946 from a sample of 30,000 children in 600 schools in six Australian states. Raw scores are converted to normalized standard scores. Age and grade norms are adequate and detailed. There is no provision for a total reading score. The speed test has no norms in terms of rate, only in terms of correct answers from which one can derive rate norms, assuming all children get all answers correct.

Three paragraphs in the manual are devoted to validity. For Part 1, no details are given as to how words were "chosen from the Thorndike and other word lists and subjected to experimental testing." "Only the most satisfactory items were retained. The test can therefore be regarded as a valid measure of a child's ability to select synonyms within the range of general vocabulary." In view of previous remarks about Part 1, it would be of interest to know the criteria by which the items were judged satisfactory. Part 2 exhibits face validity for similar material rather self-consciously culture oriented. Reading for meaning is a blanket term which here at least covers reading for main ideas, for detail, and for inference. Whether the weighting in these areas is deliberate or accidental is not known.

Reliability is given as .93 for Part 1 (split-half), .82 for Part 2 (parallel-forms), and .91 for Part 3 (split-half). The numbers on which these reliabilities are based (149, 134, 151) seem small in view of the extensive sampling, and no indication is given of the age and grade ranges of the samples for which they were computed. The inference is that the standard error of measurement is constant over the total range. Experience would suggest it is not.

Parts 1 and 3 could be used anywhere, subject to the objections made to Part 1. Part 2 is so Australian in its flavour and includes so many local words (boomerang, wallaby, bull-roarer, etc.) that its use is restricted to Australian schools.

As the reading test most easily available to Australian teachers, this is, in parts, in need of revision.

[618]
*A.C.E.R. Silent Reading Tests: Standardized for Use in New Zealand. Ages 9–12; 1934–55; 1 form; manual ['55] ; 3 parts; 2s. 3d. per specimen set; postage extra; manual by A. E. Fieldhouse; tests by Australian Council for Educational Research; New Zealand Council for Educational Research; distributed by Educational Books. *
a) PART 1, WORD KNOWLEDGE. Same as corresponding part of *A.C.E.R. Silent Reading Test;* Form C ['46] ; 6s. 3d. per 25 tests; 10(20) minutes.
b) PART 2, SPEED OF READING. Same as corresponding part of *A.C.E.R. Silent Reading Test;* Form B ['34] ; 6s. 3d. per 25 tests; 3(10) minutes.
c) PART 3, READING FOR MEANING. Same as corresponding part of *A.C.E.R. Silent Reading Test;* Form C ['46] ; 12s. 6d. per 25 tests; 20(35) minutes.

[619]
*Achievement Test in Silent Reading: Dominion Tests. Grades 1, 2, 2–3, 3–4, 4–6, 5–6; 1941–57; postage extra; Department of Educational Research, Ontario College of Education, University of Toronto; distributed by Guidance Centre. *
a) PRIMARY. Grade 1; 1941–53.
1) *Type 1, Word Recognition.* 1941–53; Forms A, B ('41) ; revised manual ('57) ; $1.10 per 25 tests; 20¢ per complete specimen set; 10(20) minutes.
2) *Type 2, Phrase and Sentence Reading.* 1941–53; Forms A, B ('41) ; revised manual ('53) ; $1.45 per 25 tests; 20¢ per complete specimen set; 20(30) minutes.
3) *Type 3, Paragraph Reading.* 1943–53; 1 form ('43) ; $1.35 per 25 tests; 25¢ per manual ('45) ; 30¢ per specimen set; 30(40) minutes.
4) *Type 4, Diagnostic Test in Word Recognition.* 1943–53; 1 form ('45) ; $1 per 25 tests; 25¢ per manual ('45) ; 30¢ per specimen set; 30(40) minutes.
b) TYPE 1, VOCABULARY. Grades 2–3, 4–6; 1943–56; Forms A, B ('43) ; 2 levels; $1.10 per 25 tests; 10¢ per manual ('53) for each level; 20¢ per complete specimen set of either level; (30) minutes.
c) TYPE 2, DIAGNOSTIC TEST IN PARAGRAPH READING. Grades 2, 3–4, 5–6; 1943–56; 2 forms; 3 levels; 10¢ per manual ('53) for each level; $1.45 per 25 tests; 25¢ per complete specimen set of any one level; 30(40) minutes.
1) *Grade 2.* 1943–55; Forms A, B ('43).
2) *Grades 3–4.* 1946–56; Forms A, B ('46).
3) *Grades 5–6.* 1948–53; Forms A, B ('48).

HARRY L. STEIN, *Professor of Education, University of British Columbia, Vancouver, British Columbia, Canada.*

This battery was carefully reviewed in *The Third Mental Measurements Yearbook* by Mc-Kim. Since that time three tests have been added: a Diagnostic Test of Word-Analysis Skills for grade 1, administered individually;

a Diagnostic Test in Paragraph Reading for grades 3–4; and a similar test for grades 5–6.

Two important comments should be added to those made by McKim. First, of the 10 tests in the battery, 5 are labeled as diagnostic tests. As such, they should be administered at the beginning of the year rather than at the end, as are the achievement tests. In this way, their diagnostic function could be put to valuable use by teachers through a well designed program of remedial work. To this end, of course, norms should be established for the beginning of the year. Secondly, users of these tests should be careful to note that the fact that the tests are titled "The Dominion Tests" should not be interpreted as meaning that the tests are necessarily standardized on pupils in all provinces of the Dominion of Canada.

The norms for these tests were revised in 1953. Test users may obtain from the publishers an insert for the manual. This insert includes percentile norms, grade norms, and error norms, and replaces two norms tables in the manual. The new norms are based upon the administration of the tests to some 7,000 pupils in the province of Ontario. One might question the adequacy of the sampling for individual grades in both rural and urban schools.

Some attempt has been made in the revised insert (June 1953) to explain how the error levels for the paragraph reading tests were determined. However, for the lay reader, the wording of this explanation is not very clear. In any event, from a normative standpoint, the value for the teacher of this aspect of the test may be very limited. To make a diagnosis by the method suggested entails more than a modest amount of clerical work, and if the reliability of the diagnosis is low because of the rough estimation of level obtained, the game may not be worth the candle. The table of norms should, however, be very valuable for a general diagnosis of the nature of errors crudely classified, as they are in the error norms, as "Beginnings," "Middles," "Endings," "Reversals," and "Configurations." A machine scoring method of counting these errors would save the teacher a good deal of time.

In spite of the limited sampling, the tests in the primary battery are maintaining a high degree of internal consistency. The latest manual reports reliabilities for Types 3 and 4 of .90 and .94. In the earlier manual the reported reliabilities were .96 and .95.

As a whole, the battery is a strong one and should continue to serve a useful purpose. The format continues to be excellent and the curricular validity acceptable. For local use, the norms should be considered only as a rough guide to level of achievement.

MAGDALEN D. VERNON, *Professor of Psychology, University of Reading, Reading, England.*

This battery, which has been prepared for the group testing of silent reading in grades 1–6 in Canadian schools, falls into two parts. The first part, intended to test the achievement of first graders in the mechanics of reading, includes tests of the ability to match pictures against single words, phrases and short sentences, and paragraphs. The words, selected from books in use in some Canadian schools, are arranged in order of difficulty as given in Gates' *Reading Vocabulary for Primary Grades.* This method of selection must make somewhat difficult the comparison of reading performance in schools which do and schools which do not use these books, since some of the words appear far too difficult for 6- and 7-year-old children unless they have been taught them specifically. However, it is probable that written group tests for children of this age can give no more than a very rough assessment of achievement for any individual child, though they may be valuable for measuring the general level of achievement of a whole class or grade.

This criticism applies more strongly to the fourth of the grade 1 tests, the Diagnostic Test in Word Recognition. This is intended to show, from the pattern of errors made by individual children, whether they tend to make most mistakes in the endings, middles, or beginnings of words; to substitute words with the same letters in a different order; or to substitute words of the same general shape. The children may then be given special drill in overcoming a particular type of error. Now, even supposing that the grade 1 child manages to cope with such a group test adequately, there is no evidence that he will consistently make one of these types of error rather than other types, or indeed that this differentiation of types of error has any particular significance with regard to difficulties in reading. Before any remedial measures are applied, any child who makes a large number of errors of any kind should be given individual reading tests designed to diagnose the fundamental nature of his difficulties—to show, for instance, if he has learnt to analyse words phonetically and blend the phonetic units.

The second part of the battery, containing tests for grades 2–6, consists of two types of tests in paragraph reading—vocabulary and diagnostic tests. No information is given as to how the words for the vocabulary tests were selected, except that they were "constructed and standardized with the active assistance and advice of experienced public school teachers." Many of the words are most unlikely to be within the comprehension of children with the ages given. However, since the child has to choose one word out of four that "goes best" with the test word, he can guess to a certain extent from general similarity of meaning.

No explanation is given as to why this type of test was chosen for assessing reading achievement; nor do its results appear to have been correlated with those of the second type, Diagnostic Tests in Paragraph Reading, or with other measures of reading ability. The diagnostic tests, however, appear to be the most valuable type of test in the battery. The child's answers to questions on the paragraphs read are designed to show if he can grasp the general topic of the paragraph, pick out some important details, and make simple inferences from what he reads. Clearly, all these processes are essential to the development of efficient reading once the child has acquired the fundamental mechanics, and it is important to detect whether a child fails in any one of them. But it would seem advisable to supplement these tests by one designed to determine whether failures were due to inability to read a sufficient number of the words of the paragraphs, or to failure to understand the words or sentences contained in them. Again, individual tests for cases of failure would be most desirable to discover the exact cause of difficulty.

It is unfortunate that the directions, score norms, and methods of standardization are given only in separate manuals for each test. There is no general explanation as to how the tests were designed, how they should be used, and what is the general significance of results on the separate tests or of differences in performance on the several tests. There seems to be some danger that individual teachers may use the tests appropriate to the grades they are teaching in a mechanical fashion, chalking up the error scores of each child and then automatically drilling him in the task in which he seems least efficient. It is to be hoped that when the format of all the test instructions has been revised, a comprehensive manual will be prepared explaining just what is the significance of the results of each test in relation to the others, and what conclusions can be drawn from such results. Moreover, such a manual could contain a more systematic presentation of instructions, answer keys, and norms; a description of the standardization process; and a report of calculations of reliability and internal consistency. The standardization appears to have been carried out satisfactorily on an adequate number of rural and urban children, for whom separate norms are given. Reliability and internal consistency are high, but the separate manuals of directions and their supplementations and revisions are so confused and unsystematic in presentation that it is difficult to understand the rationale of the tests and to follow the method and results of their standardization.

This battery of tests, therefore, requires a more systematic presentation of the explanatory material before it can be finally assessed. In particular, we need to know more about how and for what specific purposes the tests were designed and how the material was selected. At the present moment, the Diagnostic Tests in Paragraph Reading are the most satisfactory; the others are open to numerous criticisms.

For a review by Henry P. Smith, see 4:529; for a review by Margaret G. McKim, see 3:476.

[620]
*American School Achievement Tests, Part 1, Reading. Grades 2–3, 4–6, 7–9; 1941–58; 3 scores: sentence and word meaning, paragraph meaning, total; Forms D ('55), E ('56), F ('57), G ('58); Forms D, E, F essentially the same as Forms A, B, C copyrighted 1941–43; 3 levels; 35¢ per specimen set of any one level; postpaid; Willis E. Pratt and Robert V. Young; Public School Publishing Co. *
a) PRIMARY BATTERY II. Grades 2–3; revised battery manual ('55); $1.75 per 25 tests; 25(35) minutes.
b) INTERMEDIATE BATTERY. Grades 4–6; revised battery manual ('58); $2 per 25 tests; 25(35) minutes.
c) ADVANCED BATTERY. Grades 7–9; revised battery manual ('58); $2 per 25 tests; 30(40) minutes.

RUSSELL G. STAUFFER, *Director, The Reading-Study Center, University of Delaware, Newark, Delaware.* [Review of Forms D, E, F.]

The teachers' manual accompanying Primary Battery II says:

The....tests....are designed to measure pupil achievement as early as the beginning of the second year of school and as late as the end of the third year of school attendance. Results....may serve a 4-fold purpose: (*1*) to measure pupil progress, (*2*) to assist in the classification of pupils, (*3*) to furnish data for remedial programs in the language arts, and (*4*) to diagnose pupil's knowledge of specific computations and problem-solving ability.

A similar statement of purposes appears in the manuals for the Intermediate and the Advanced Batteries. To appraise the extent to which the tests fulfill the purposes, the reviewer not only worked through each test but studied carefully the additional statements about how the test accomplishes the purposes.

The sentence and word meaning and the paragraph meaning items cover a wide range in vocabulary and in interest areas. In the paragraph meaning section certain questions can be answered without reading the story; for example, "The squirrel likes to eat....nuts." Many of the items require answers other than the parroting of facts, and this is good. The strategy is to present paragraphs followed by multiple choice questions. Many alert readers may soon discover not only that reading the questions first makes the reading of the paragraph more purposeful but that some questions can be answered without reading the paragraph. The items seem to do everything the authors claim for them. As is frequently the case with reading tests of this type, the reader has to read as many running words in the questions as he does in the paragraphs.

In the vocabulary section many of the correct answers cannot be obtained unless the sentence introducing the item is read. This is commendable. Some of the items involve opposites and would require no sentence setting. The more difficult items are not merely confusing items, but seem to reflect a good measure of breadth and depth of word knowledge.

The ceiling for Primary Battery II is quite adequate. The grade equivalents of the maximum possible scores are consistently more than two grades above the highest grade level for which the tests are designed. In the Advanced Battery the sentence and word meaning section requires 26 out of 40 items correct to achieve a score of 6.9. Only eight additional items are required to cover the entire grade range for which the battery is designed—grades 7–9. This is mighty thin selecting; it leaves only five additional items with which to run a score from 9.9 to 11.9. The Advanced Battery has enough bottom to test even the poorest student, but not enough top to test even the good student and certainly not the best student. The same is true of the Intermediate Battery.

This might lead one to believe that the Intermediate and Advanced Batteries would be especially useful as aids to remedial instruction, but this is hardly the case. The authors are right when they say the tests "do not purport to be diagnostic tests." As always, however, a study of items missed by a pupil might be helpful as a partial inventory of needs.

The statements made in the manual about how the tests can be used to classify pupils should be interpreted with similar caution. If pupils are to be grouped on the basis of test scores, reading instruction levels would in many instances be either too high or too low. Standardized test scores tend to overrate the instructional level of average and slow learners and underrate that of superior readers. Results could be used, though, as one source of information for grouping. Test constructors should be especially sensitive to false notions about the possibility of homogeneous grouping and should not suggest it even by implication.

Using test results to measure individual pupil progress is fraught with danger as long as the only norms provided are based on results obtained in large group testing situations. There is nothing wrong with this method of standardization if it is understood that the norms are not based on the results of individual testing. Much of the widespread misuse of norms as standards seems directly attributable to erroneous claims made by testmakers, either directly or by implication, for the use of test results.

According to the manual, curricular validation was thought by the authors to be most feasible because of the lack of adequate criteria for other types of validation. Therefore, the vocabulary of all the tests was "checked against widely used word lists and commonly used textbooks." Only the Thorndike Word List is mentioned as having been used, and there is no indication as to which of the Thorndike lists it was. Reference to word lists might have yielded greater validity evidence: those of Rinsland, Gates, Horn, and Spache, for example. Some of the published vocabulary studies of commonly used basal readers might have provided better validation material than an examination of textbook materials.

The authors state that their "sentences of necessity include many very simple words (a, and, the, to, do, etc.)." What is really meant is frequently occurring words. There is a sharp difference between "simple" and "difficult" words, especially insofar as learning to read is concerned. It is the feeling of this reviewer that it would be helpful if such statements as the following did not occur in test manuals: "Some more difficult words have been included in order fully to test the abilities of better pupils." What test will ever fully test abilities of any student? This is a trap for unsophisticated test users.

Some standardized tests currently on the market have been standardized on populations of half a million pupils, with as many as 100,000 cases at a particular level; the various batteries of the *American School Achievement Tests* were standardized on 1,000 to 10,000 cases only. The manual reports that the population used was stratified according to school size and socioeconomic location—agricultural, industrial, and residential areas. Apparently there was no stratification according to IQ distributions, acceleration and retardation, and ethnic groups. Testmakers in general could render greater service by being more attentive to more accurate measures of worthwhile aspects of the skill processes in reading for meaning and in concept development.

The time allowances for the tests tend to place emphasis on speed. Timed tests make for comparability of scores. However, emphasis on speed of reading is undesirable, especially at the primary level. It would be better to have a separate section on speed of reading if a measure of speed is wanted.

In summary, the reading tests of the *American School Achievement Tests* are useful for a general survey of reading achievement. They are interesting and attractive, and can be administered and scored easily. They can be used to compare large groups, but are of little or no value for diagnostic purposes. This reviewer would recommend that consideration be given to making the vocabulary section more closely related to the comprehension section. This might permit the teacher to note discrepancies between knowledge of terms and ability to use these in context.

AGATHA TOWNSEND, *Associate Professor of Education, State Teachers College, Kutztown, Pennsylvania.* [Review of Forms D, E, F.]

Certain general features of format and layout are common to all three levels. The tests are printed on a carbon-backed sheet which removes the necessity for a separate answer sheet while still retaining some advantages for quick scoring. The pupil is faced with a sheet approximately 10 by 15 inches, printed on both sides. The size may be inconvenient for some pupils to handle, and since the test parts are divided without regard to the size of the sheet, folding the booklet in half will not be a satisfactory solution. The situation for the scorer is even more troublesome. He will need a working space large enough to accommodate a sheet 20 by 15 inches. If he starts to score Form D of the intermediate test, he will probably begin by counting down the columns on the first page; but he must shift to counting only the bottom segment of the columns on the second, without, it may be added, any guide lines or instructions to keep him out of trouble in column three, where the sentence and word meaning score meets the paragraph meaning score with no division whatever. The test must be refolded before the scores can be recorded on the front, and there is no provision for removing the front portion for filing.

The format of the test apparently has been revised several times, though the norms take no cognizance of any effect this revision may have had on pupil performance. Between 1955, when Form D of Primary Battery II was published, and 1956 when Form E was issued, the shift was made to the oversized sheet, the choices in the sentence and word meaning test received identifying letters and were printed in line instead of vertically, and the answering procedure was changed so that instead of marking an answer space immediately after his choice the pupil marked the space corresponding to the letter of his selection. From Form E to Form F a (desirable) change was made from small letters to capitals in this identification. Somewhat similar changes were made in the intermediate and advanced tests, and it is noticeable that the type for Form F of the Advanced Battery is more reduced and compressed than that on the other two current forms. Unfortunately, even close similarity of test content may not be enough to ensure comparability to the extent that the same norms can be applied to different

forms, and this doubt arises especially with respect to the test for grade 2, where the changes are quite marked.

The organization seems to reflect an oversimplified concept of the nature of reading. Only two kinds of skills are tested—word meaning and paragraph meaning. In structure, these tests parallel the reading tests of other widely used batteries. An attempt has been made to improve over the usual synonym type vocabulary test by the use of an incomplete sentence technique, and the authors underline this step by naming this part "Sentence and Word Meaning."

In view of the multiple aims of reading instruction in the primary and intermediate grades, such an approach has definite limitations. The authors recognize these, but it is doubtful whether the test as it stands fulfills their aims of measuring pupil progress in reading achievement. They point out, quite correctly, that the tests are not designed for diagnosis of individual difficulties, but this statement is buried in a paragraph which aims at quite the opposite—a paragraph which implies that the language arts tests permit one "to determine the general disability which a pupil may have." It does seem as if a better reading test would result if some recognition were given to the changing aims and character of reading instruction from the primary, to the intermediate, to the junior high school grades. As it stands, solution to the problem of assuring continuity in measurement has taken the form of "more of the same."

The authors have provided more information about the tryout and selection of items than most producers. Each manual includes details on the selection of words, the appearance of the words in widely used textbook series, and their location on the Gates and Thorndike lists, and similar data on the vocabulary of the paragraphs.

The authors should have eliminated item writing errors like ending a sentence stem with an "a" only to have one of the choices read "engineer" or "office." More serious is the kind of extraneous difficulty introduced when an item is phrased awkwardly or obscurely. Can a second grader handle a sentence like Item 15 in Form D (Primary Battery II) which says, "A minute is the same kind of measure as....an hour"? Is it accurate to say, as in Item 12 of Form E (Advanced Battery) "One who belongs to a land is called a....native"? Test items cannot always be included merely because they seem to meet difficulty standards on tryout.

With all their care for item selection, the authors have evidently not given equal thought to item placement. How, otherwise, would one find Items 31 and 32, with their paragraph, in Form D of the Intermediate Battery, reappearing as Items 47 and 48, at the very end of Form E of the Advanced Battery? In Form D of the Intermediate Battery, again, the last two items (39 and 40) appear as Items 45 and 46, just before the end of Form E of the Advanced Battery.

Normative data are not nearly so complete as are data on item tryout, and it is not clear, either, to what extent normative populations are identical with experimental groups. The manuals for both the intermediate and advanced batteries refer to the norms as "tentative," but no such indication appears on the norms table. Since the number of cases is not given in the table, it is not possible to tell if the entries are based on a rechecking of the norms which occurred in 1955.

Reliability information, based on test-retest with different forms, is given for groups of about 100 to 200 cases for the various levels. These reliabilities are moderately high, and should probably prove adequate for group survey.

Evidence favorable to the test series is found in the careful description of item construction and selection, and in the care with which the different forms have been improved as one followed another. Reliability data are probably satisfactory, though reliability and norms information seem to be based on a rather small number of cases. Scoring should be reasonably easy, though more attention should be given to scoring problems in the manuals.

Some flaws in item construction, possibly inadequate scaling of items, and rather sparsely described norms seem to be the chief technical limitations. When these are added to the basic problem of determining whether or not the concept of reading expressed throughout the test is satisfactory—which is a major question indeed—it is doubtful if the battery can be highly recommended.

For reviews by J. Raymond Gerberich and Virgil E. Herrick of the complete battery, see 1; for a review by Ralph C. Preston of an *earlier edition, see 4:1; for reviews by Walter W. Cook and Gordon N. Mackenzie (with Glen Hass), see 3:1.*

[621]

★**American School Reading Tests.** Grades 10-13; 1955; various titles used by publisher; 3 scores: vocabulary, reading rate, comprehension; Forms A, B; tentative norms; $2.80 per 25 tests; separate answer booklets may be used; $1.75 per 25 answer booklets; 50¢ per specimen set; postpaid; 65(80) minutes; Willis E. Pratt and Stanley W. Lore; Public School Publishing Co. *

HENRY S. DYER, *Vice President in Charge of Research, Educational Testing Service, Princeton, New Jersey.*

This is a conventional type of reading test which yields three conventional scores—one on vocabulary, one on reading rate, and one on reading comprehension. It contains the usual types of material for this purpose. In selecting the materials for the sections on vocabulary and on reading rate, the authors have paid careful attention to the frequency of the words used as given in the "Thorndike Word List" and have taken account of this information in equating the two forms.

The format of the test itself is good: the type is legible and the directions to students are clear and uncomplicated. The directions for administering and scoring the test are also simple and straightforward.

The content of the test leaves something to be desired. In the opinion of this reviewer, both the vocabulary section and the reading comprehension section are, in general, measuring only the more superficial aspects of the reading process. There is little attempt in the vocabulary section to test the student's sensitivity to the fine shades of meaning which are likely to be of critical importance in differentiating between an adequate student and one who is highly perceptive. Furthermore, too many of the questions in the paragraph reading section depend too heavily on key words in the text itself. A quick glance back often yields the correct answer; there is little attempt to see whether the student has grasped the significance of what he has read or whether he can demonstrate understanding of the concepts given by using them in his own thinking. In short, it seems to this reviewer that this test hardly samples the kinds of student responses that are, or should be, involved in really effective reading.

The technical information given in the manual accompanying the test is in many respects inadequate. There is essentially no evidence presented on the validity of the test. The claim that the test should be useful in selecting students for college, for instance, is not supported by any data to show how well the scores correlate with college performance. The manual reports reliability data based on a sample of 100 cases "from approximately 1,000 cases in typical schools," but gives no information on the range of ability in the sample. The percentile norms are admittedly "tentative"—so tentative, indeed, that they are likely to be of little help in interpreting the scores. No data other than those drawn from the Thorndike list are given on the characteristics of the items.

Finally, there is one serious piece of misdirection in the manual: the user of the test is directed to obtain a total percentile rank on the test by averaging the percentile ranks of the scores on each of the three parts. It is hard to imagine a procedure more unsound or more calculated to give a meaningless result.

DONALD E. P. SMITH, *Chief, Division of Reading Improvement Services, and Associate Professor of Education, University of Michigan, Ann Arbor, Michigan.*

Reading tests which limit their announced coverage to two or three grades are uncommon. Most purport to span five grades or more, thus often yielding poor estimates at either extreme. This test is designed for use with grades 10 through 13. It is very doubtful, however, that it is "sufficiently easy to allow for some success by even the poorest tenth grade pupil." The easiest vocabulary items, for example, are "lattice" and "perjury." The test might better be limited to college freshmen.

Its purposes are three: to provide diagnostic information, to aid in remedial instruction, and to predict college success. No evidence is provided to indicate whether those purposes have been realized. The two equivalent forms each include three sections, a 72-item vocabulary test, a timed reading passage followed by 20 multiple choice questions, and a reading comprehension section of 10 paragraphs and 50 questions. A self-scoring answer sheet is provided. Administration time, with time limits for each part "experimentally determined," is 65 minutes.

The authors report that sample items were tried out with a thousand students in grades 8–13. Of 300 vocabulary items, 144 were retained; of 28 paragraphs, 20 were retained; of 60 questions on the timed readings, 40 were retained. Norms and reliability data are reported on the same population. Without cross validation, such data are spurious, of course, and lead to such inflated reliability coefficients (parallel forms) as .953 and .978.

A number of other problems suggest that "the buyer beware." For example, the manual states that a total score should be derived by averaging the subject's percentile rank on the subtest scores, at best a questionable procedure. The grade norms are apparently based upon less than 200 cases, since the 1,000 normative cases were spread over six grades. One is surprised to find a percentile rank of 100 reported. While the reading paragraphs consist of textbook material, that hardly provides the curricular validity claimed for them.

In general, the manual is well written and the choice of content is very good. Vocabulary items were selected from the "Thorndike Word List" (not otherwise identified) and data are provided to illustrate the broad range of difficulty sampled. With few exceptions, distractors on the vocabulary items are common words, as they should be. Some obvious clues are provided, however. The most flagrant is the difference in length of the choices: in nearly every case, the longest choice is the correct one.

The authors apparently made a good start toward constructing a reading test appropriate for college freshmen, but not for high school students. Its similarity in design to several other well established tests (*e.g.,* the Survey Section of the *Diagnostic Reading Tests*) raises the question of whether it will make any unique contribution to measurement. The answer to that question must wait until the test is properly validated.

[622]
California Reading Test, 1957 Edition. Grades 1–2, 3–4.5, 4–6, 7–9, 9–14; 1933–58; previous edition (see 4:411) still available; subtest of the *California Achievement Tests;* 3 scores: vocabulary, comprehension, total; IBM for grades 4–14; 5 levels; battery manual ('57) for each level; 1957 technical report ['58]; separate answer sheets may be used in **grades 4–14**; 4¢ per IBM answer sheet; 7¢ per Scoreze answer sheet; 20¢ per hand scoring stencil; 40¢ per machine scoring stencil; 10¢ per survey data sheet ('52); postage extra; 50¢ per specimen set of any one level, postpaid; Ernest W. Tiegs and Willis W. Clark; California Test Bureau. *
a) LOWER PRIMARY. Grades 1–2; Forms W, X ('57); $2.45 per 35 tests; 23(35) minutes.

b) UPPER PRIMARY. Grades 3–4.5; IBM; Forms W, X ('57); $2.80 per 35 tests; 40(50) minutes.
c) ELEMENTARY. Grades 4–6; IBM; Forms W, X, Y, Z ('57); $3.15 per 35 tests; 48–50(60) minutes.
d) JUNIOR HIGH LEVEL. Grades 7–9; IBM; Forms W, X, Y, Z ('57); $3.15 per 35 tests; 66–68(80) minutes.
e) ADVANCED. Grades 9–14; IBM; Forms W, X, Y ('57); $3.15 per 35 tests; 66–68(80) minutes

REFERENCES

1. CARMICHAEL, ANNE, AND REES, ROBERT E. "A Survey of Reading Achievement in Alberta Schools." *Alberta J Ed Res* 1:18–33 Mr '55. *
2. COULL, WILLIAM H. "A Normative Survey of Reading Achievement of Alberta Children in Relation to Intelligence, Sex, Bilingualism, and Grade Placement." *Alberta J Ed Res* 2:18–29 Mr '56. *
3. YOUNG, CAMPBELL. "A Qualitative Analysis of Reading Achievement in Edmonton Schools." *Alberta J Ed Res* 2:135–50 S '56. *
4. LONG, JAMES R. *Academic Forecasting in the Technical-Vocational High School Subjects at West Seattle High School.* Doctor's thesis, University of Washington (Seattle, Wash.), 1957. (*DA* 17:1951)
5. SOPCHAK, ANDREW L. "Prediction of College Performance by Commonly Used Tests." *J Clin Psychol* 14:194–7 Ap '58. *

For reviews by John C. Flanagan and James R. Hobson of the 1950 edition, see 4:530; for a review by Frederick B. Davis of an earlier edition, see 40:1563; for reviews by Ivan A. Booker and Joseph C. Dewey, see 38:1110. For a review by Charles O. Neidt of the complete battery, see 2; for reviews by Warren G. Findley, Alvin W. Schindler, and J. Harlan Shores of the 1950 edition, see 4:2; for a review by Paul A. Witty of the 1943 edition, see 3:15; for reviews by C. W. Odell and Hugh B. Wood of an earlier edition, see 40:1193; for a review by D. Welty Lefever, see 38:876.

[623]

★**Chapman Reading Comprehension Test.** Grades 5–12; 1924–53; formerly called *Chapman Unspeeded Reading Comprehension Test;* Form A ('53, same as test copyrighted in 1924); directions for administering ('53, norms same as in 1924 manual); no data on reliability and validity; $1.30 per 25 tests, postage extra; 40¢ per specimen set, postpaid; 30(40) minutes; J. C. Chapman; Educational Test Bureau. *

RUSSELL P. KROPP, *Associate Professor of Education, Florida State University, Tallahassee, Florida.*

This instrument appraises reading comprehension by presenting to the examinee 31 short statements, each about two sentences in length, in the second half of each of which the examinee crosses out that word that makes the statement absurd.

A 4-page fold accompanying the test includes directions for administering and scoring and a table of norms. No evidence concerning reliability and validity is presented here or elsewhere.

The raw score can be transformed to a verbal rating, a percentile rank, a standard score, or a reading age. The verbal rating is simply an adjectival description of the score in nine classifications from highest to lowest. The verbal ratings correspond to nine percentile ranks ranging from 95 to 5, and to nine standard scores ranging from 126 to 74. Reading age is determined from a separate table.

In addition to the already apparent weaknesses in the norms, the following criticisms can be made. First, the total number of cases in the normative group is not given. Second, the number of cases tested at each grade level is not given. Third, there is no indication of the grade range of the normative group; consequently, one cannot determine whether or not some of the equivalent scores are extrapolated. In fact, the normative group is not identified or described in any way whatsover except for the implication that they were tested during the midyear in grade. The absence of such information nearly renders the instrument useless.

A passage following the table of norms reads, in part, as follows: "Suppose, for example, that a ninth grade pupil gets 22 right. This is a 'Medium high' score, is at the 66th percentile, and is a standard score of 107, which is expected of a ninth grade pupil with a 'Standard IQ' of 107." This interpretation is clearly not warranted. It implies that intelligence and reading comprehension are, or should be, perfectly related. The error is extremely serious since it is the only suggested interpretation.

This test of only 31 items is designed for use over a range of eight grades. If adequate information were presented about its reliability, validity, and norming, the test might be used in screening situations where information concerning only the grossest kind of discrimination was tolerable. The reviewer believes, however, that the instrument would be of extremely limited usefulness under any circumstances.

[624]

★**Commerce Reading Comprehension Test.** Grades 12–16 and adults; 1956–58; IBM; 1 form ('56); mimeographed manual ['58]; tentative norms ['56, '58]; separate answer sheets must be used; 25¢ per test; $4 per 100 IBM answer sheets; 25¢ per either hand or machine scoring stencil; 20¢ per specimen set; postpaid; 60(65) minutes; Irma T. Halfter and Raymond J. McCall; Department of Psychological Testing, De Paul University. *

[625]

★**Davis Reading Test.** Grades 11–13; 1956–58; IBM; Forms 1A, 1B, 1C, 1D ('57); manual ('58); separate answer sheets must be used; $3.50 per 25 tests; $1.90 per 50 answer sheets; 35¢ per scoring stencil and manual for any one form; 50¢ per specimen set; postpaid;

40(55) minutes; Frederick B. Davis and Charlotte Croon Davis; Psychological Corporation. *

BENJAMIN ROSNER, *Assistant Professor of Education, Rutgers, The State University, New Brunswick, New Jersey.*

The *Davis Reading Test* is a carefully planned and constructed reading comprehension test designed to appraise the overall reading ability of high school students in grades 11 and 12 and college freshmen. The test is an operational extension of the senior author's earlier analysis of the factors involved in reading comprehension. Accordingly, the items have been constructed to measure ability to: (*a*) answer questions explicitly answered in a passage; (*b*) weave together ideas in a passage and grasp its central thought; (*c*) draw inferences from a passage about its contents and the author's point of view, purpose, or intent; (*d*) recognize the tone or mood of a passage and the literary devices used by its author; and (*e*) follow the structure of a passage. In less well constructed tests, the items may degenerate into pure measures of word knowledge. In the *Davis Reading Test* the verbal difficulty level of the items appears to have been carefully controlled so that the items are more clearly measures of the reading skills cited above.

The Davis test is available in four forms, each form yielding two scores—one for speed and one for level of comprehension. While both scores measure essentially the accuracy of understanding (a global interpretation of the reading factors cited above), the speed score also provides an index as to the relative speed with which students can read and understand the passages in the test booklet. Both scores are obtained from a single administration of the test with a single 40-minute time limit. This is accomplished by dividing the 80 items in the test into, in effect, two 40-item subtests. (No statistical evidence is presented to document the equivalence of the two halves, but the test construction procedures adopted in establishing the two subtests would tend to ensure their equivalence.) Because almost all examinees are reported able to reach the first 40 items, the score on the first subtest provides the level score; because very few examinees have sufficient time to complete the total test, the score on the entire test furnishes a measure of speed.

Directions for administering and scoring the tests, and for interpreting the test results are clearly presented in the manual. The single time limit makes the test practically self-administering; however, the additional time required for the distribution and collection of materials and the reading of directions extends the total testing time somewhat beyond the time limits of most regularly scheduled high school classes. From a practical point of view, it would be more convenient to have the time limits such that the test could be administered within the limits of a single class period. Loss in the precision of measurement would probably be negligible.

Percentile norms for grades 11 and 12, and for college freshmen are provided for both level and speed scores. In general, geographical distribution and size of the norming sample are adequate. It is hoped, however, that future manuals will present norms for separate geographical regions and for different kinds of collegiate institutions.

Scores on the *Davis Reading Test* are translated into individual percentiles rather than presented in percentile "bands" as are scores on the STEP reading tests. While the confidence interval presents a more reasonable appraisal of student performance in terms of "true" scores, the current consumer of test information does not possess the minimally necessary statistical sophistication to appreciate this new approach. The point estimate (single percentile rank), together with tables controlling the interpretation of score differences, is probably less confusing. For this reason current consumers are likely to find the Davis scores more easily interpretable.

Mean reliability estimates (alternate-form) of the level score are .74, .77, and .80 for grades 11 and 12, and college freshmen, respectively. These are adequate but not overly impressive. For the speed score the estimates are .84, .85, and .88 for the same grades. These are more acceptable. The averages of the correlations between level and speed (from two different forms) are .74 for grade 11, .77 for grade 12, and .80 for college freshmen. When these correlations are considered in terms of the reliabilities of the two scores, interpretations of differences are rather questionable. Incidentally, inspection of the effective score range at the three grade levels suggests that the test might be useful at the college sophomore level and that appropriate norms should be developed.

Evidence on statistical validity is good. Correlations with high school and college English grades average approximately .5. Congruent validity estimates are much higher; e.g., the correlation with the STEP reading test is about .80. In almost every instance the speed score has greater predictive and congruent validity than does the level score. In all likelihood the greater statistical validity of the speed score is accounted for by its higher reliability. Considering the correlation between speed and level scores and the greater reliability and statistical validity of the speed score, this reviewer questions the need for both scores. On the other hand, the ease with which both scores are obtained may warrant their computation.

Considering the importance of reading comprehension as a determinant of success in high school and collegiate programs, the *Davis Reading Test* should provide useful information for high school and college guidance personnel. The item construction, the clarity of the manual, and the cautious approach of the authors in the interpretation of test score differences are particularly impressive.

[626]

★**Developmental Reading Tests.** Grades 1.5, 1.5–2.5, 2.5–3; 1955; 1 form; 3 parts; 3 levels; no specific manual; no data on reliability; no norms; $2 per 35 tests of any one part of any one level, postage extra; 40¢ per specimen set, postpaid; 10(15), 15(20) minutes for Parts 1, 2–3; [Guy L. Bond, Theodore Clymer, and Cyril Hoyt]; Lyons & Carnahan. *

a) PRIMER READING. Grade 1.5; 3 parts.
  1) *Part 1, Basic Vocabulary.* Form PV-A.
  2) *Part 2, General Comprehension.* Form PG-A.
  3) *Part 3, Specific Comprehension.* Form PS-A.

b) LOWER PRIMARY READING. Grades 1.5–2.5; 3 parts.
  1) *Part 1, Basic Vocabulary.* Form LV-A.
  2) *Part 2, General Comprehension.* Form LG-A.
  3) *Part 3, Specific Comprehension.* Form LS-A.

c) UPPER PRIMARY READING. Grades 2.5–3; 3 parts.
  1) *Part 1, Basic Vocabulary.* Form UV-A.
  2) *Part 2, General Comprehension.* Form UG-A.
  3) *Part 3, Specific Comprehension.* Form US-A.

[627]

★**Diagnostic Reading Test: Pupil Progress Series.** Grades 1.9–2.1, 2.2–3, 4–6, 7–8; 1956–57; various titles used by publisher; some subtests also appear in *Scholastic Diagnostic Reading Test* for Catholic schools; IBM for grades 4–8; 2 forms; 4 levels; manual ('57) for each form of each level; $4.55 per 35 tests; separate answer sheets may be used in grades 4–8; $1.75 per 35 IBM answer sheets; 20¢ per set of scoring stencils; 50¢ per specimen set of any one level; postage extra; Oliver F. Anderhalter, R. Stephen Gawkoski, and Ruth Colestock; Scholastic Testing Service, Inc. *

a) PRIMARY TEST I. Grades 1.9–2.1; 10 scores: vocabulary (3 subscores), rate, comprehension (3 subscores), total; Forms A ('56), B ('57); (40–60) minutes.

b) PRIMARY TEST II. Grades 2.2–3; 11 scores: vocabulary (3 subscores), rate, comprehension (5 subscores), total; Forms A ('56), B ('57); 40(60) minutes.

c) ELEMENTARY TEST. Grades 4–6; 11 scores: vocabulary (3 subscores), rate, comprehension (5 subscores), total; IBM; Forms A ['56], B ('57); (60) minutes.

d) ADVANCED TEST. Grades 7–8; 14 scores: vocabulary (4 subscores), rate, comprehension (6 subscores), total; IBM; Forms A ['56], B ('57); (60) minutes.

[628]

★**Elementary Reading: Every Pupil Scholarship Test.** Grades 4–6, 7–8; 1928–58; new form usually issued each January and April; 2 levels; norms available following testing program; no data on reliability; 4¢ per test; 4¢ per scoring key; postage extra; 15(20) minutes; Bureau of Educational Measurements. *

[629]

*Elementary Reading: Every Pupil Test.** Grades 4–6; 1936–58; new form usually issued each December and April; 2 parts; norms available following testing program; no data on reliability; 3¢ per test; 1¢ per scoring key; cash orders postpaid; Ohio Scholarship Tests. *

a) GENERAL ABILITY. 19(30) minutes.

b) SPEED AND COMPREHENSION. 2 scores: speed, comprehension; 6(10) minutes.

[630]

*Gates Advanced Primary Reading Tests.** Grades 2.5–3; 1926–58; Forms 1, 2, 3 ('58); 2 tests; manual ('58); series supplement ('58); $1.35 per 35 copies; 40¢ per specimen set of either test; cash orders postpaid; 40(60) minutes; Arthur I. Gates; Bureau of Publications, Teachers College, Columbia University. *

a) TYPE AWR, WORD RECOGNITION. 15(25) minutes.

b) TYPE APR, PARAGRAPH READING. 25(35) minutes.

REFERENCES

1. GATES, ARTHUR I. *The Improvement of Reading: A Program of Diagnostic and Remedial Methods, Third Edition.* New York: Macmillan Co., 1947. Pp. xxi, 657. * (*PA* 22:3195)
2. MILLER, VELMA J. *A Critical Analysis of Standardized Vocabulary Tests to Determine Those Most Valid for Use With the Macmillan Readers.* Master's thesis, Bowling Green State University (Bowling Green, Ohio), 1954.
3. WARE, FLORENCE EDNA. "Effect on Reading Achievement of Under-Testing Pupils in Low Third Grade." *Calif J Ed Res* 7:22–4 Ja '56. * (*PA* 30:7698)

For reviews by Virginia Seavey and George Spache of an earlier edition, see 3:484.

[631]

*Gates Basic Reading Tests.** Grades 3.5–8; 1926–58; Tests GS, UD, and ND scored for percentage of attempts correct; Forms 1, 2, 3 ('58); 5 tests; manual ('58); series supplement ('58); $1.35 per 35 copies of any one test; 40¢ per specimen set of any one test; cash orders postpaid; 30(85), 24(85) minutes for grades 3–4, 5–8; Arthur I. Gates; Bureau of Publications, Teachers College, Columbia University. *

a) TYPE GS, READING TO APPRECIATE GENERAL SIGNIFICANCE. 10(15), 8(15) minutes for grades 3–4, 5–8.

b) TYPE UD, READING TO UNDERSTAND PRECISE DIRECTIONS. 10(15), 8(15) minutes for grades 3–4, 5–8.

c) TYPE ND, READING TO NOTE DETAILS. 10(15), 8(15) minutes for grades 3–4, 5–8.

d) TYPE RV, READING VOCABULARY. (20) minutes.

e) TYPE LC, LEVEL OF COMPREHENSION. (20) minutes.

REFERENCES

1–5. See 40:1539.
6–7. See 3:485.
8. HARRIS, CHESTER W. "An Exploration of Language Skill Patterns." *J Ed Psychol* 39:321–36 O '48. * (*PA* 23:1755)

S. S. DUNN, *Officer-in-Charge, Test Division, Australian Council for Educational Research, Melbourne, Australia.*

The series contains three speed and accuracy tests—Reading to Appreciate General Significance (GS), Reading to Understand Precise Directions (UD), and Reading to Note Details (ND). Two additional tests—Reading Vocabulary (RV) and Level of Comprehension (LC) —are power tests. Three forms, stated to be equivalent, are provided for each test, but evidence of equivalence is not given in the manual.

While there is a need to separate the "how to use the test" material from the technical information, the decision to place it in a manual supplement published separately has dangers. If it makes these data less accessible it encourages teachers to use the tests in faith and contributes nothing to their proper understanding of the tests. In any case, statements and recommendations in the manual which are presumably based on technical information should be cross referenced to the appropriate page in the supplement. Only by close reading does one come across the reference to the existence of the supplement on the second last page of the manual.

The decision to use material of fairly uniform difficulty in the three speed tests poses a problem when the test is supposed to be useful over five and a half grades. If it is not too difficult for grade 4 then it must appear somewhat childish for grade 8. Is there any educational advantage in trying to make the same test cover such a large range? A look at the accuracy norms bears witness to the difficulty of the tests for the younger children.

The appearance of the test papers is excellent with type faces that should offer no problems in readability. The bold type used in LC to distinguish questions from paragraphs could have been extended with benefit to GS and ND. Adequate spacing, and the use of blue lines to divide passages, adds to the total appearance.

The directions for administration are not easy to follow. It is not clear in the manual what is required. There is a note on the front of the two power test booklets labeled "To the Teacher" from which one gets an inkling of what to do, but is it desirable for the pupils to read an instruction such as "The pupils should be kept working vigorously, but they should have as much time as they need to try every exercise"?

For Reading Vocabulary and Level of Comprehension, the standard correction for guessing is applied. There is no instruction on how to handle corrections involving one half point. For example, the correction for 14 wrong is one quarter of 14 or 3½. Does one subtract 3 or 4? No reason is given for not correcting tests UD and GS which have multiple choice answers. The use of a separate "accuracy score" (see later comment) is not a substitute if one believes a correction for guessing is desirable.

For the three speed tests two sets of norms are given, one for 8 minutes (recommended administration time for grades 5 and above) and one for 10 minutes (recommended time for grades 3 and 4). The small differences between the norms for lower reading ages leads one to wonder whether the advantages in using the two times are sufficient to compensate for the dangers of looking at the wrong table.

The general discussion on reliability is useful, but the author fails to provide the reader with examples of the use of the standard error of measurement. The standard errors of individual test scores appear only in the technical supplement, and it would probably surprise teachers to realise the size of changes which could occur on retesting, especially amongst the more able older children. Thus, children scoring 38 on test ND have a reading grade of 8.8 and a reading age of 14.0, but on a retest one in three could be expected to score outside the range 38 ± 4, i.e., outside the reading grade range of 7.5 to 10.2 and the reading age range of 12-10 to 15-6. Such changes must be expected when the growth curve for an ability is flattening out. In these circumstances, the use of reading grades and reading ages becomes artificial in the same way the use of mental ages does for adolescents and adults.

Likewise, the discussion on checking the differences between scores on two tests for significance is useful, but the single table dealing with significance of differences is oversimplified and probably misleading. From the information in the supplement, the reliabilities of differences can be estimated for various pairs of tests and range from zero to .60. It is highly improbable that the standard deviations of differences between pairs of tests are such as to compensate for these different reliabilities and produce approximately equal standard errors of differences for different pairs of tests. Nor is the reader given any indication of level of significance used to decide whether differences are "unreliable," "fairly reliable," or "quite reliable."

The use of accuracy scores is interesting, but one wonders whether the reliability of these scores on each test is such as to justify the use of three separate accuracy scores rather than a more reliable combined score. No evidence on the reliability of the accuracy scores is provided.

The section on improving reading abilities is a useful one and draws on Gates' wide experience.

In summary, the tests are attractively presented. The use of the same material over several grades raises problems. The use of grade percentiles is a valuable addition to the reading grades and reading ages, but the use of the latter for higher grades and older ages is of doubtful value. The provision of a table setting out differences needed for significance in variations among test scores is to be commended, but the value of the present table is questionable. The hints on helping children with reading difficulties are helpful.

For reviews by George Spache, Herbert F. Spitzer, and T. L. Torgerson of an earlier edition, see 3:485; for reviews by Joseph C. Dewey and James R. Hobson of the Gates Silent Reading Tests, see 40:1539 (1 excerpt).

[632]

*Gates Primary Reading Tests. Grades 1–2.5; 1926–58; 3 scores: word recognition, sentence reading, paragraph reading; Forms 1, 2, 3 ('58); 3 tests; manual ('58); series supplement ('58); $1.35 per 35 copies of any one test; 40¢ per specimen set of any one test; cash orders postpaid; 50(80) minutes; Arthur I. Gates; Bureau of Publications, Teachers College, Columbia University. *

a) TYPE PWR, WORD RECOGNITION. 15(25) minutes.
b) TYPE PSR, SENTENCE READING. 15(25) minutes.
c) TYPE PPR, PARAGRAPH READING. 20(30) minutes.

REFERENCES

1–7. See 3:486.
8. WARE, FLORENCE EDNA. "Effect on Reading Achievement of Under-Testing Pupils in Low Third Grade." *Calif J Ed Res* 7:22–4 Ja '56. * (*PA* 30:7698)
9. PRINGLE, M. L. KELLMER, AND NEALE, M. D. "A Note on the Use of the Schonell and Gates Reading Tests in the First Year of the Junior School." *Brit J Ed Psychol* 27:135–41 Je '57. *

For reviews by William S. Gray and George Spache of an earlier edition, see 3:486.

[633]

*Gates Reading Survey. Grades 3.5–10; 1939–58; 5 scores: speed and accuracy, accuracy, vocabulary, level of comprehension, total; Forms 1, 2, 3 ('58); manual ('58); series supplement ('58); $2.35 per 35 tests; 40¢

per specimen set; cash orders postpaid; (50–60) minutes; Arthur I. Gates; Bureau of Publications, Teachers College, Columbia University. *

REFERENCES

1. GATES, ARTHUR I. *The Improvement of Reading: A Program of Diagnostic and Remedial Methods, Third Edition.* New York: Macmillan Co., 1947. Pp. xxi, 657. * (*PA* 22:3195)
2. WEST, DORAL N. "Reducing Chance in Test Selection." *Personnel & Guid J* 36:420–1 F '58. *

For reviews by Dorothy E. Holberg and Herbert F. Spitzer of an earlier edition, see 3:487.

[634]

*High School Reading Test: National Achievement Tests. Grades 7–12; 1939–52; 6 scores: vocabulary, word discrimination, sentence meaning, noting details, interpreting paragraphs, total; Forms A ('52, identical with test copyrighted in 1939 except for minor changes), B ('51, identical with test copyrighted in 1940 except for Item 4, Part 3); directions sheet for Form A ('45), directions sheet for Form B ('51, identical with sheet copyrighted in 1940); general teachers' guide ['44]; no norms for part scores; $3.75 per 25 tests; 50¢ per specimen set; postage extra; (40) minutes; Robert K. Speer and Samuel Smith; Acorn Publishing Co. *

VICTOR H. NOLL, *Professor of Education, Michigan State University, East Lansing, Michigan.*

This test was adequately reviewed in *The Third Mental Measurements Yearbook* (3:488) and *The Fourth Mental Measurements Yearbook* (4:536). As noted above, no changes of any importance have been made since these reviews were written. The present reviewer is in agreement with what was said about the test in the earlier reviews. Consequently, little more need be said except to make a few additional observations. The statement that "these tests were....based primarily upon the National Survey of Instruction in English for Secondary Schools, Bulletin No. 17, U.S. Department of Interior, Office of Education, and publications of the National Council of Teachers of English" as sole evidence of validity is of little or no value to the prospective user. For one thing, the first reference is of doubtful value for anyone constructing a reading test for use in today's schools if for no other reason than that it is now more than a quarter century since it was published. For another, it contains little that would contribute to the validity of a test such as this. The second reference is meaningless in this instance since it gives no information as to *what* publications of the National Council were used.

Another observation of interest to this reviewer has to do with the equivalence of Forms A and B of the test. The norms were established on 9,000 pupils said to be representative of different sizes of schools and parts of the country. These were checked against returns of thousands of additional pupils and "were found to be accurate." A comparison of norms for the two forms raises serious questions regarding this statement. It is obvious that the forms are not eqivalent. Perhaps most disturbing is the fact that at some points in the scale Form A seems the more difficult and at others, the easier. The range of differences between median scores on the two forms at various grade levels is from 4 points in favor of Form A to 13 points in favor of Form B.

As stated in previous reviews, the tests have some attractive features but these are marred by what must be regarded as inexcusable carelessness in their standardization. Poor workmanship makes the critical, discriminating user of standardized tests take a doubting or suspicious attitude toward all of them and hurts most the careful, conscientious producer who is doing his best to develop tests that will not be subject to such criticisms. Unfortunately, the consumer, who is often relatively unsophisticated in these matters and who may not know what to look for, is likely to be unaware of the serious differences between two tests, both appealing in content and format but very unequal in the quality of work and the attention to sound principles that have gone into their development.

For a review by Holland Roberts, see 4:536; for a review by Robert L. McCaul, see 3:488.

[635]
Holborn Reading Scale. Ages 5.5–11.0; 1948; 2 scores: word recognition, comprehension; individual; 1 form ['48] no data on reliability; 3s. per 25 tests; 2d. per single copy; 1s. 6d. per manual; postage extra; [20–30] minutes; A. F. Watts; George G. Harrap & Co. Ltd. *

REFERENCE
1. WATTS, A. F. *The Language and Mental Development of Children.* London: George G. Harrap & Co. Ltd., 1944. Pp. 354. *

STANLEY NISBET, *Professor of Education, University of Glasgow, Glasgow, Scotland.*

This test consists of 33 sentences arranged in increasing order of difficulty with respect both to mechanical elements and to comprehensibility. The sentences have been so chosen that the gradient in mechanical difficulty is steep but linear, each sentence representing a reading age three months higher than the preceding sentence. A child is given the test sheet and asked to read aloud from the beginning. He is stopped after his fourth mistake, and his reading age determined from figures in the margin opposite the sentence in which the mistake occurs. The scale thus enables the tester to make a rough assessment of a child's reading level in a remarkably short time and without calculations. The same sentences are also used to test comprehension, the manual containing 33 questions, one to be asked about each sentence.

This is quite obviously a sound test. It could hardly be otherwise, taken as it is from Watts' excellent book *The Language and Mental Development of Children (1)*. Such a useful measuring instrument, however, deserves a new and more carefully produced manual, specially written for users of the test. As it is, the relevant paragraphs have merely been lifted verbatim from the book. Not only do they read a little unnaturally by themselves but—a much more serious fault—they do not give clear and adequate instructions to the user.

First of all, he is not told how to obtain a score for comprehension. Presumably the reading ages given in the margin opposite the sentences refer only to mechanical reading, and the comprehension score is simply the total number of questions answered correctly. Secondly, no norms are given for comprehension, although it is assumed in the discussion that comparisons can be made between a child's performances in mechanical reading and comprehension. Thirdly, the graph on which are plotted average scores on mechanical reading for some two thousand children is not so clearly interpreted as it might be, and it contains two errrors. Finally, no mention is made in the manual of test reliability or validity, or of the relationship of the test to other tests.

To sum up: this is already a good test, but it could be a better one with a completely new and adequate manual.

For a review by C. M. Fleming, see 4:537.

[636]
★**Kelley-Greene Reading Comprehension Test: Evaluation and Adjustment Series.** Grades 9–13; 1953–55, c1952–55; 5 scores: paragraph comprehension, directed reading, retention of details, reading rate, total; IBM; Forms AM ('53), BM ('55); manual ('53); expectancy chart ['54]; no college norms; separate answer sheets must be used; $5.35 per 35 tests; $1.70 per 35 IBM answer sheets; postage extra; 35¢ per specimen set, postpaid; 63(75) minutes in 2 sessions; Victor H. Kelley and Harry A. Greene; World Book Co. *

REFERENCE
1. CROOK, FRANCES E. "Interrelationships Among a Group of Language Arts Tests." *J Ed Res* 51:305–11 D '57. *

RUSSELL P. KROPP, *Associate Professor of Education, Florida State University, Tallahassee, Florida.*

There are three parts to the *Kelley-Greene Reading Comprehension Test.* Test 1, Paragraph Comprehension, consists of nine paragraphs, each approximately eight sentences in length, dealing with science and social science topics. Five items follow each paragraph and they call for generalization and inference from the paragraph. Twenty minutes are allowed. Test 2, Directed Reading, consists of three reading passages, each 26 to 28 sentences long, dealing with science and social science content. Each passage is timed separately, 3 minutes being provided for the initial reading and 8 minutes for answering the 24 items that follow the passage. The examinee is permitted to refer back to the passage during these 8 minutes. A measure of reading rate can also be obtained from Test 2. Test 3, Retention of Details, consists of 35 items dealing with the passages in Test 2. Ten minutes are allowed.

The total test is built around seven objectives of reading comprehension: skimming to locate answers to specific questions, critical reading to identify details, selecting the central theme of a passage, generalizing from statements, drawing inferences, summarizing passages, and remembering materials that were read for a purpose. These objectives are important in reading comprehension; their appraisal demands a rather carefully constructed test. The reviewer believes that these objectives have been met in large measure by the authors. However, a separate score is not given for each objective. Nevertheless, the test is commendable from the standpoint of carrying out the purposes for which it was built. It is technically adequate with regard to its construction, standardization, and norming. The weakest part is Test 3, Retention of Details. This weakness is due to the utter detail tested.

The directions for administration are complete and clear. The authors recommend that the test be taken on two successive days. They also recommend that when the test is given in one day a break of at least 15 minutes occur between Tests 1 and 2. No information is provided about whether these two kinds of administration lead to different scores, nor is the user informed about the kind of administration used in collecting the normative data.

Two sets of reliability data were computed, one on 10th grade groups and the other on 12th grade groups. Reliabilities are satisfactory except for Test 3, for which the coefficient is lower than one might expect.

The intercorrelations among the three tests are moderately high, thus indicating that each has much in common with the others.

Concurrent validity information is presented dealing with the relationships between the three tests and the *Terman-McNemar Test of Mental Ability* and other tests in the Evaluation and Adjustment Series. Relationships between the Kelley-Greene and other reading comprehension tests in subject matter fields and language sections of intelligence tests would be more useful. The reviewer can understand the value of having available a series of tests normed on the same groups and having available the intercorrelations of these tests, but he is aware too of the value of having information about the relationships between a particular test and other tests of the same kind that are not necessarily published by the same company.

The normative information apparently was gathered with care and thoroughness and it is quite adequate for high school groups. However, no normative data are provided for the interpretation of scores achieved by college freshmen. The Kelley-Greene is a better than average reading comprehension test that will justifiably be used extensively in the public schools.

MAGDALEN D. VERNON, *Professor of Psychology, University of Reading, Reading, England.*

This group test of reading comprehension is designed to test four competencies: (*a*) selecting the central idea and summarizing the gist of a paragraph; (*b*) reading carefully and skimming for details; (*c*) generalizing and drawing inferences from what is read; and (*d*) remembering details for subsequent recall. The first subtest is mainly concerned with (*a*) and (*c*), but there are also questions about single details. Moreover, since most of the multiple choice questions can be answered by selecting a single sentence from the paragraph, a piecemeal approach to the paragraph is almost inevitable. In the reviewer's opinion, the only satisfactory manner of measuring a reader's ability to summarize or to extract the main argument of a paragraph is to require him to reproduce it in his own words. In the first place, the gist of a paragraph necessarily requires a longer statement than can conveniently be presented in the form of multiple choice questions. Secondly, a reader cannot demonstrate that he has really grasped the gist unless he can formulate it himself. Merely matching one sentence against another can be done without any real assimilation of the content as a coherent whole. Naturally, numerous difficulties are encountered in standardizing the scoring of statements written by the reader; but they are not insuperable. A test of formulation would be immeasurably superior in demonstrating whether the reader had obtained a real idea of the content he has read.

The same comment is equally apposite to the testing of remembering and recall. We know that in some cases the reader may retain a coherent general impression of what he reads; but in others he may forget or modify considerably the ideas of the original, or may retain certain details only. No allowance is made for the different types of error in Test 3. Test 2 requires the reader to locate single sentences that answer questions on the details of three simple passages relating to the social and physical sciences. Test 3 asks him to recall rather similar details from the same passages. In the first place, it is not made clear to the reader whether or not his memory for this material is going to be tested, though the initial instructions hint at it. In the second place, in order to obviate the difficulty that the reader may not have time to read the whole of each of the passages in Test 2, the questions on these passages are rotated in Test 3 (Item 1 is on passage 1, Item 2 on passage 2, and so on). Thus, if he did in fact acquire and retain impressions of the general gist of these passages, these impressions might be hopelessly confused by the rotation of the questions in Test 3. All in all, both these subtests emphasize the mechanical rote remembering of details, rather than an intelligent and coherent grasp of the passages as a whole. It also seems possible that subjects with special knowledge of the contents of the passages might have some advantage over those who have none.

Lastly, norms are given only for the total scores on each of the three subtests, and there are no separate norms for the different types of item in Test 1, relating to (a), (b), and (c)

above. Thus, it would be difficult to ascertain whether a reader was relatively proficient or deficient in understanding the general gist of a passage, or in drawing conclusions and making inferences from it. His final score would be determined mainly by his rote memory for detail.

Split-half reliability coefficients for the three subtests vary from .71 to .96 and the calculated standard errors of measurement are reasonably small. It is stated that validity indices were calculated for each item in the original tryout of the test, and that valid items were selected for the final form; but no measure of validity is quoted. The test was correlated with tests of intelligence, listening comprehension, and written English usage, but naturally the correlations were only moderate.

This test attempts to test comprehension and remembering of the content of simple material relating to the social and physical sciences; but it is doubtful whether it tests adequately anything more than the assimilation and remembering of factual detail.

[637]

★The Kingston Test of Silent Reading. Ages 7–11; 1953–54; 1 form ('53); 5s. per 25 tests; 3d. per single copy; 2s. 6d. per manual ('54); postage extra; 20(30) minutes; M. E. Highfield; George G. Harrap & Co. Ltd. *

NEIL GOURLAY, *Professor of Education, University of the Witwatersrand, Johannesburg, Union of South Africa.*

This test consists of a simple prose passage of about 600 words in which 50 words have been omitted. The task of the testee is to write down as many of these as he can in 20 minutes. Various other methods for measuring reading comprehensions have been used, but at the reading age levels for which the Kingston test is intended (7 to 12 years)—and particularly over the first half of this range—the Kingston technique is probably as good as most.

Since the missing words do not show any apparent increase in difficulty as one proceeds from the beginning to the end of the passage, speed of working must play an important part in performance on this test. It might, therefore, be regarded as more of a speed test than a power test—unlike Schonell's reading comprehension tests, for example, where the provision of a number of short paragraphs of steadily increasing difficulty ensures that test performance is decided more by the intrinsic difficulty of filling in the missing words and less by the speed factor.

The manual's account of the standardisation of the test is far from clear. The author states that the test was standardised on a population of 2,000 children "nearing the end of their second year in the primary junior school." The reader is informed that "the sigma of the raw scores is 13, but the conversion table is based on a sigma of 15" in order to facilitate "a comparison of a pupil's reading quotient, or R.Q., with his I.Q." Apparently the assumption was made that the reading quotients of the 2,000 children were distributed with a standard deviation of 15, and with this assumption it would, of course, be a simple matter to derive the reading age equivalents of all the raw scores 1–50. The assumption, however, is very dubious. The author tries to justify the procedure by claiming that smaller representative groups at age levels from 7 to 10 obtained mean scores comparable to those for the derived reading ages.

Reliability, as measured by the split-half method, is reported as .98 for pupils aged 8½ years or more. A high figure like this is to be expected with a test in which speed plays such a large part. A parallel-forms reliability coefficient would not be so high. The author, however, does not provide a parallel form of the test.

There is no doubt that the chief weakness of the test is the uncertainty which must exist in regard to the accuracy of the standardisation. The test could not be recommended for use in a situation requiring accurate norms.

MAGDALEN D. VERNON, *Professor of Psychology, University of Reading, Reading, England.*

This is a group test of comprehension in silent reading. Children are given a complete story with words missing at intervals; they have to supply the missing words. It is a test of the ability to recognize the words of the story, to comprehend their meaning and that of the sentences in which they occur, to demonstrate the possession of a vocabulary including the missing words, and to reason out which are the most appropriate words to be inserted. Thus, a good performance on the test requires an adequate degree of all these abilities; and indeed test performance correlates fairly highly with performance on word recognition, vocabulary, and intelligence tests. Again, failure on the test may be due to deficiency in any of these abili-

ties, and therefore further testing or study would be necessary to determine where the deficiency lay. The author states that about four per cent of junior school children may be unable to score at all, and that these children should be tested individually with a graded word reading test. But the range of scores up to a reading age of eight years is a narrow one, and children below this reading age should also be given tests of the mechanics of reading.

The format of the test is unsatisfactory, since the text is printed in two columns on each of two pages and the child has to enter his answers in four different columns. The tester is warned that he should check to see whether the answers are being entered opposite the right numbers. There seems to be no reason other than economy of paper why the test should not be printed in a single column, a format much more familiar to most children and much easier to work with.

For British children with reading ages from 8½ to 12 years this test should provide a reasonably satisfactory measure of general proficiency in reading, though it will give little indication as to ability to comprehend the gist of a whole passage. Supplementary testing would be required to estimate this ability as well as to locate deficiencies in word recognition at lower reading ages.

[638]
*Lee-Clark Reading Test, 1958 Revision. Grades 1, 1–2; 1931–58; Forms A, B ('58); 2 levels; manual ('58) for each level; $2.80 per 35 tests, postage extra; 25¢ per specimen set, postpaid; (20–30) minutes; J. Murray Lee and Willis W. Clark; California Test Bureau. *
a) PRIMER. Grade 1; 4 scores: auditory stimuli, visual stimuli, following directions, total.
b) FIRST READER. Grades 1–2; 6 scores: same as for primer level plus completion, inference.

For a review by Ruth Lowes of an earlier edition of the primer level, see 3:490.

[639]
★Nelson-Lohmann Reading Test: Coordinated Scales of Attainment. Grades 4, 5, 6, 7, 8; 1946–54; identical with reading sections of *Coordinated Scales of Attainment;* IBM; Forms A, B ('53, identical with tests copyrighted in 1946 and 1949 except for title); 5 levels; directions for administering ('53); battery manuals (A, '54; B, '49); separate answer sheets must be used; $1.90 per 25 tests; $1 per 25 IBM scorable answer sheets; 25¢ per scoring stencil; postage extra; 75¢ per complete specimen set, postpaid; (45) minutes; Ethel V. Nelson (A), Victor L. Lohmann (A), and Marvin J. Van Wagenen (B); Educational Test Bureau. *

For a review by Alvin W. Schindler of the complete battery, see 4:8; for reviews by Roland L. Beck, Lavone A. Hanna, Gordon N. Mackenzie (with Glen Hass), and C. C. Ross, see 3:6.

[640]
*Primary Reading: Every Pupil Scholarship Test.** Grades 1, 2–3; 1935–58; new form usually issued each January and April; 2 levels; norms available following testing program; no data on reliability; 4¢ per test; 4¢ per scoring key; postage extra; (45), 15(20) minutes for grades 1, 2–3; Bureau of Educational Measurements. *

[641]
*Primary Reading: Every Pupil Test.** Grades 2–3; 1936–58; new form usually issued each December and April; norms available following testing program; no data on reliability; 3¢ per test; 1¢ per scoring key; cash orders postpaid; 15(30) minutes in 2 sessions; Ohio Scholarship Tests. *

For reviews by William S. Gray and Virginia Seavey of earlier forms, see 3:493.

[642]
*Primary Reading Test: Acorn Achievement Tests.** Grades 2–3; 1943–57; 5 scores: word recognition, words-similar meaning, word meaning-opposites, story-paragraph-sentence meaning, total; Forms A ('57, identical with test copyrighted in 1943), B ('43); manual ('43); directions sheet ('43); no norms for part scores; $2.75 per 25 tests; 25¢ per manual; 50¢ per specimen set; postage extra; 31(40) minutes; Winifred E. Stayton, Frances C. Ranson, and Roland L. Beck; Acorn Publishing Co. *

For a review by Alice N. Jameson, see 3:495.

[643]
*The Purdue Reading Test.** Grades 7–16; 1928–53; identical with test copyrighted in 1928 except for minor changes; IBM; Forms AM, BM ('52); no manual; no data on reliability; norms ['53]; 10¢ per test; separate answer sheets may be used; 15¢ per specimen set; postpaid; H. H. Remmers, John M. Stalnaker, and P. C. Baker; distributed by State High School Testing Service for Indiana. *

For a review by Albert J. Harris, see 3:496.

[644]
★Purdue Reading Test for Industrial Supervisors: Purdue Personnel Tests.** Supervisors; 1955; Form A; preliminary manual; $5 per 25 tests, postage extra; 50¢ per specimen set, postpaid; 25(35) minutes; Joseph Tiffin and Roy Dunlap; distributed by University Book Store. *

REFERENCE

1. Dunlap, Roy D. *A Reading Comprehension Test for Industrial Supervisors.* Doctor's thesis, Purdue University (Lafayette, Ind.), 1955. (DA 16:375)

Jerome E. Doppelt, *Assistant Director, Test Division, The Psychological Corporation, New York, New York.*

The test consists of 14 reading passages with either two or three multiple choice items per passage. The content of the passages centers around factory and industrial situations in an effort to make the material acceptable to the intended examinees. The time limit of 25 minutes is evidently not sufficient to make the test a power measure.

This instrument is described as "particularly useful in identifying supervisors who are in need of developmental reading instruction or, if such instruction cannot be given, as a guide to management in writing material that supervisors are expected to read." Although these two objectives are laudable, there is no evidence that the test is helpful in the accomplishment of either one.

At the present time, there is a preliminary manual which includes a table of norms based on 137 industrial supervisors representing all levels from first line supervisors to plant superintendents. Reliability was estimated by applying the Kuder-Richardson formula 20 to the scores of a group of supervisors who finished the test and then correcting the coefficient for the increased range of scores when all supervisors are included. The resulting coefficient was .83. When a modification developed by Horst was applied to the K-R formula, the coefficient rose to .91. However, it must be noted that the group for which reliability was estimated was very heterogeneous and it is doubtful whether such reliability could be expected in a single plant.

For validity, the manual simply reports a correlation with another reading test. A communication from one of the test authors states that a revised manual will contain the report of a study in which scores on the test were found to be significantly related to job performance ratings.

There is no evidence to indicate this test is more suitable for accomplishing its purposes than a vocabulary test which could be administered in considerably less time. The technical data supporting the test do not resolve doubts as to its value in specific industrial situations. The reviewer feels there is, as yet, no good reason for recommending the use of this instrument.

Louis C. Nanassy, *Professor of Business Education, Montclair State College, Upper Montclair, New Jersey.*

This 38-item test is designed to assist in measuring the paragraph comprehension of industrial supervisors. It is self-administering and is easily scored, the score being simply the number of correct answers.

An estimate of the reliability, based on several computations, would seem to indicate that when the test is used with typical industrial supervisors and covers the full range of reading ability found in such a group, the reliability is in the neighborhood of .90. The only estimate of validity presently reported is a correlation of .81 between scores made by 137 supervisors on this test and on the paragraph comprehension part of the *Nelson Silent Reading Test*.

The test is well constructed, with vocabulary and subject matter appropriate for industrial supervisors. The format and copy make for readability and ease in administering. Instructions are exceptionally clear.

The test gives every indication of fulfilling the specific purpose for which it was constructed. When a more comprehensive analysis of reading ability is desired, the use of the *Purdue Word-Meaning Test for Industrial Supervisors* with this test is recommended.

[645]

*Reading Comprehension: Cooperative English Test: Lower and Higher Levels, C1 and C2. Grades 7–12, 11–16; 1940–53; 4 scores: vocabulary, speed, level, total; IBM; Forms R ('50, same as test copyrighted in 1941), T (Lower Level, '43; Higher Level, '50—same as test copyrighted in 1943), Y ('48), Z ('53); 2 levels; no specific manual; general Cooperative manual ('51); descriptive folder ['51]; directions for hand scoring ['49]; norms ['40]; separate answer sheets must be used with Form Z, optional with other forms; $3.25 per 25 tests; $1 per 25 IBM answer sheets; 25¢ per scoring stencil; postage extra; 40(45) minutes; Frederick B. Davis, Mary Willis (T), Clarence Derrick (Y), Harry R. Neville (Y), Jeanne M. Bradford (Y), Geraldine Spaulding (Y), and Charlotte Croon Davis (Z); Cooperative Test Division, Educational Testing Service. *

REFERENCES

1–2. See 40:1564.
3–17. See 3:497.
18–37. See 4:547.
38. COCKRUM, LOGAN V. "Predicting Success in Training for the Ministry." *Relig Ed* 47:198–202 My–Je '52. *
39. FREDERIKSEN, NORMAN. "The Influence of Timing and Instructions on Cooperative Reading Test Scores." *Ed & Psychol Meas* 12:598–607 w '52. * (*PA* 27:6741)
40. ARN, ELMER H. R. *The Prediction of Academic Success in Ten Selected Science Areas at the University of Washington.* Doctor's thesis, University of Washington (Seattle, Wash.), 1953. (*DA* 13:495)
41. BARRETT, DOROTHY M. "Correlation of Survey Section of Diagnostic Reading Tests and of Test C2: Reading Comprehension With College History Grades." *J Ed Res* 46:465–9 F '53. * (*PA* 28:1461)
42. JENSON, RALPH E. "Predicting Scholastic Achievement of First-Year Graduate Students." *Ed & Psychol Meas* 13:322–9 su '53. * (*PA* 28:4833)
43. BOLTON, EURI BELLE. "The Predictive Value of the Columbia and the Michigan Vocabulary Tests for Academic Achievement." *Peabody J Ed* 32:9–21 Jl '54. * (*PA* 29:7954)
44. FITZGIBBON, THOMAS J. *The Prediction of Academic Success of Freshmen at Bradley University.* Doctor's thesis, Bradley University (Peoria, Ill.), 1954. (*DA* 14:1170)
45. MUNRO, JAMES J. R. *The Predictive Value of Entrance Reading Test Scores at the University of Washington.* Doctor's thesis, University of Washington (Seattle, Wash.), 1954. (*DA* 14:1179)
46. BOYKIN, LEANDER L. "The Reading Performance of Some Negro College Students." *J Negro Ed* 24:435–41 fall '55. * (*PA* 30:7666)
47. CHAHBAZI, PARVIZ. "The Prediction of Achievement in a College of Agriculture." *Ed & Psychol Meas* 15:484–6 w '55. * (*PA* 30:7754)
48. HAYNES, JERRY O. *Some Predictive Factors of Academic Success in Two Curricula of a Land-Grant College.* Master's thesis, Alabama Polytechnic Institute (Auburn, Ala.), 1955.
49. McGOLDRICK, DAVID T. *A Correlation Between Scores Attained on the Cooperative Reading Test and Grades Achieved in English One and Two by Freshmen Entering the School of Business, Niagara University From 1951 to 1953, to Ascertain the Value of the Test as a Prediction and to Establish Norms.* Master's thesis, Niagara University (Niagara Falls, N.Y.), 1955.
50. BRAGG, EMMA W. "A Study of Student Withdrawal at 'W.U.'" *J Ed Psychol* 47:199–202 Ap '56. *
51. BRESEE, CLYDE W. *Affective Factors Associated With Academic Underachievement in High-School Students.* Doctor's thesis, Cornell University (Ithaca, N.Y.), 1956. (*DA* 17:90)
52. CHAHBAZI, PARVIZ. *Prediction of Achievement in New York State College of Agriculture at Cornell University.* Doctor's thesis, Cornell University (Ithaca, N.Y.), 1956. (*DA* 17:562)
53. HENDERSON, HAROLD L. "Prediction of Academic Success." *Psychol Rep* 2:321–2 S '56. * (*PA* 31:3784)
54. VAN DER JAGT, E. R., AND MESNER, D. M. "Predictability of Success in College Courses, by Accelerating and Non-Accelerating Students as Measured by Scores Made by Entering Freshmen on A.C.E. and Cooperative Reading Test." *Sci Ed* 40:327–32 O '56. *
55. FRICKE, BENNO G. "Speed and Level Versus Rate and Accuracy of Reading." *Yearb Nat Council Meas Used Ed* 14:73–7 '57. *
56. HENDERSON, HAROLD L. "Predictors of Freshmen Grades in a Long Island College." *Ed & Psychol Meas* 17:623–7 w '57. *
57. LARSEN, TORA M. *A Study of the Student Personnel Records at East Carolina College as Relates to Prediction in Elementary Accounting.* Doctor's thesis, University of Minnesota (Minneapolis, Minn.), 1957. (*DA* 18:1304)
58. LOWRY, CARMEN E. *The Prediction of Academic Success in a Private Liberal Arts College for Negroes.* Doctor's thesis, University of Texas (Austin, Tex.), 1957. (*DA* 17:2500)

For reviews by Robert Murray Bear and J. B. Stroud of Forms R, S, and T, see 3:497. For reviews by J. Paul Leonard, Edward S. Noyes, and Robert C. Pooley of Forms R, S, and T of the complete battery, see 3:120.

[646]

*Reading Comprehension Test: National Achievement Tests [Speer and Smith]. Grades 3–8; 1938–57; 4 scores: following directions, sentence meaning, paragraph meaning, total; Forms A ('57, identical with test copyrighted in 1938), B ('38); directions sheet ('38); no data on reliability; no norms for part scores; $2.50 per 25 tests; 50¢ per specimen set; postage extra; (30) minutes; Robert K. Speer and Samuel Smith; Acorn Publishing Co. *

For a review by James R. Hobson, see 3:498.

[647]

★Reading Comprehension Test: National Achievement Tests [Crow, Kuhlmann, and Crow]. Grades 4–6, 4–9; 1953–57; Form A ('57); 2 levels; 25¢ per manual ('54); 50¢ per specimen set of either level; postage extra; 30(35) minutes; Lester D Crow, Martha J. Kuhlmann, and Alice Crow; Acorn Publishing Co. *

a) GRADES 4–6. Identical with the first 88 items of the 130-item test for grades 4–9; reliability and normative data based upon the 130-item test for grades 4–9; $2.50 per 25 tests.

b) GRADES 4–9. Form A ('57, identical with test copyrighted in 1953); $3 per 25 tests.

[648]

***Reading Test (Comprehension and Speed):
Municipal Tests: National Achievement Tests.***
Grades 3–6, 6–8; 1938–57; subtest of *Municipal Battery;* 5 scores: following directions, sentence meaning, paragraph meaning, reading speed, total; 2 forms; 2 levels; no data on reliability; no norms for part scores; $2.75 per 25 tests; 50¢ per specimen set of either level; postage extra; Robert K. Speer and Samuel Smith; Acorn Publishing Co. *
a) GRADES 3–6. 1938–57; Forms A ('54), B ('55) identical with tests copyrighted in 1938 and 1939; directions sheets (A, '57; B, '39); 33(38) minutes.
b) GRADES 6–8. 1938–54; Forms A ('50), B ('54) identical with tests copyrighted in 1938 and 1939; directions sheets (A, '38; B, '39); 32(37) minutes.

For a review by J. Murray Lee of the complete battery, see 18; for a review by Ralph C. Preston, see 4:20; for reviews by A. M. Jordan and Hugh B. Wood of the complete battery for grades 6–8, see 40:1191.

[649]

★SRA Achievement Series: Reading. Grades 2–4, 4–6, 6–9; 1954–57; title on some tests for grades 2–6 is *What Is This About?;* 2 scores: comprehension, vocabulary; IBM for grades 4–9; Forms A, B; 3 levels; technical supplement, second edition ('57); separate answer sheets must be used in grades 4–9; 50¢ per teacher's handbook ('55); 50¢ per administrator's manual ('56); $1 per technical supplement; postage extra; Louis P. Thorpe, D. Welty Lefever, and Robert A. Naslund; Science Research Associates. *
a) GRADES 2–4. Forms A ('55), B ('57); examiner's manual, second edition ('57); $1.70 per 20 tests; $1 per scoring stencil; 90(130) minutes in 2 sessions.
b) GRADES 4–6. IBM; Forms A ('54), B ('56); examiner's manual ('56); $2 per 20 tests; $5 per 100 IBM scorable answer sheets; $1 per set of machine scoring stencils; 50¢ per machine scoring stencil; 65(80) minutes.
c) GRADES 6–9. IBM; Forms A ['55], B ('56); examiner's manual ('56); prices same as for grades 4–6; 70(80) minutes.

N. DALE BRYANT, *Associate Professor of Psychology, University of Houston, Houston, Texas.*

Reading is only one of four areas covered by the *SRA Achievement Series.* Like the rest of the tests in series, the reading test has three separate tests that are used at different grade levels. Each test consists of five stories of graduated difficulty. Following each story are two types of questions which yield the two test scores. The first score is Reading Comprehension, and the items contributing to this score require the reader to (*a*) locate specific information and overall meaning, (*b*) locate information in several places and compare the information in order to select a correct response, and (*c*) locate information and draw logical conclusions or inferences from it. The second score is Reading Vocabulary, and items

contributing to it refer to underlined words in the stories. The items require the reader to either (*a*) select the literal meaning of a specific underlined word when only one of the alternatives in the item gives a correct definition, or (*b*) select the correct meaning of the word as it is used in the story when all of the item choices give correct literal definitions of the word but only one has the shade of meaning used in the context.

While the difficulty level of the stories is not given, the Technical Supplement indicates that difficulty was controlled by regulating sentence length, sentence complexity, and concept load, as well as by using standard vocabulary lists. It seems likely that the difficulty of the first story in each test is slightly below the 2.5, 4.5, or 6.5 minimum grade level for which the test is supposed to be appropriate. The Technical Supplement does indicate that *items* are included that are above the highest grade level for which the test is designed, and this logically implies that the difficulty level of the last story is above the upper ranges of 4.9, 6.9, or 9.9 indicated.

Reliabilities are reported only for Form A, and, while considerable care was exercised in developing Form B so that it would be equivalent and would have equivalent norms, there is no direct evidence that a student making a particular score on Form A would make a very similar score on Form B. Evidence does show that both forms give the same general distribution of scores. The reported estimates of Kuder-Richardson formula 21 reliability, particularly the figures for grades 4–6 and 6–9, are high enough to warrant the use of the test scores in dealing with individuals. The subtest coefficients are generally in the .80's. A split-half estimate of reliability would probably be a little higher but an alternate-form reliability estimate might be lower, depending upon the equivalence of the two forms.

The tests are designed to measure reading ability, and this is further defined as reading comprehension and reading vocabulary. Certainly, reading speed is one aspect of reading that is not evaluated, and it is a particularly important aspect at the sixth to ninth grade level. Flexibility in adjusting speed and technique to suit the purpose of reading and the difficulty of the material being read is another aspect of reading, particularly important at this level, which is not covered. In addition to these untested components, which limit the validity of this test of reading, the more specific validity of a test of reading comprehension is also suspect. The task of reading comprehension is generally one of reading and understanding material at the time. When a student is allowed to go back and seek the answer to a question, a different variable is added. This skill is usually called scanning or one type of skimming. The time limits are liberal, and the Technical Supplement states that "It was frequently observed....that pupils were expending considerable effort to secure the answers to items in the reading tests, going back again and again to the stories."

The reading comprehension score is made up of items that the examinee gets correct because he understood the story when he read it and remembers it when he encounters the item; however, it also consists of items dealing with points which are not comprehended during the initial reading but which are answered correctly after rereading, possibly again and again, with the question in mind. To the extent that scanning or rereading contributes to the test score, the test is less valid as a measure of reading comprehension in the day to day sense of understanding what one reads as one reads it. This reduces the validity only partially, however, since pupils may sometimes reread on their own and since the ability to get information when looking for it is probably related to getting information in the normal reading situation. To the extent that reading comprehension is defined to include the ability to locate information that has been used in a question, the test is more valid.

The validity of the reading vocabulary subtest seems to be closely related to the understanding of both the literal meaning and shades of meaning of words in context. Yet, here again, the testing situation, which supplies direction for rereading, tends to produce a variation from the normal reading situation. The result may be a less valid measure of vocabulary use as it occurs in normal reading. However, even for measuring normal vocabulary use, the test appears to be more valid than many vocabulary measures which use words out of context.

In conclusion, the reading comprehension and reading vocabulary subtests of the SRA reading tests are carefully constructed, frequently item analyzed and revised, and rela-tively reliable measures. However, the equivalence of the Forms A and B should be demonstrated for individuals rather than just for groups. If understanding during normal reading is the ability the test is trying to reflect, high validity for the tests may be questionable. Going from items back to the stories for repeated rereadings could introduce variance not perfectly related to the content validity.

CLARENCE DERRICK, *Associate Professor of English and Humanities, University of Florida, Gainesville, Florida.*

The reading tests in this series are good; the accessories are excellent.

Users of the SRA reading tests obtain two scores—reading comprehension and reading vocabulary. Bargain hunters who expect more scores per penny are warned to ask whether the part scores which some tests purport to yield in multiplicity are sufficiently reliable to be meaningful. The authors of these tests are to be commended for supplying only scores which can be statistically defended.

The tests differ from many reading tests in two respects. First, the reading selections are relatively long—about twice the length of the passages in most reading tests; second, all vocabulary items are based on words in the selections. Both of these characteristics make sense and will undoubtedly be featured in sales promotion. The reviewer, however, through his own research [1] into the effects of passage length upon the measurement of reading comprehension, is convinced that good tests measuring a wide variety of important reading skills can be constructed using short reading selections. Vocabulary in context has advantages, but the technique necessarily limits sampling. A price is paid by using the vocabulary-in-context approach.

The tests are relatively unspeeded and require two class periods to administer. This may be a limitation in some situations. The reading tests in the *Sequential Tests of Educational Progress* also require two periods, but the STEP tests provide a usable score from a single period, a feature lacking in the SRA reading tests. This reviewer's chief criticism is that, at the second to the fourth grade level, pupils are confronted with questions to be answered

1 DERRICK, CLARENCE. *Three Aspects of Reading Comprehension as Measured by Tests of Different Lengths.* Research Bulletin No. 53-8. Princeton, N.J.: Educational Testing Service, 1953. Pp. vi, 176. *

"Yes," "No," or "We can't tell." The distribution between "No" and "We can't tell" is too sophisticated a concept for the age group.

The six manuals are models of completeness. There is a manual for school administrators featuring a detailed analysis of the skills being tested; a manual for test technicians which discusses the rationale of the series, national standardization, reliability, validity (including factor analysis data), and equating; three manuals for examiners (one for each level) containing instructions for administering and scoring; and a teacher's handbook with a discussion of norms, use of profiles, and some suggested procedures for developing comprehension skills.

Both percentile and grade equivalent norms are available. There are separate percentile norms for each semester of each grade, and the extrapolation of grade equivalents is limited to one year above and below the grades tested. Each test is designed so that it "does not contain easy items suitable for the seriously retarded student to answer correctly, and only a few items for the low-average learner to handle successfully." (The authors recommend, for example, that retarded students in grade 5 be given the test prepared for the grade 2-4 level.) As a result of the gradient selected for these tests, grade equivalents have a stability lacking in less carefully designed tests where an extra item or two correct will greatly increase a pupil's grade placement score. The norming procedures are described in such detail that the sophisticated test user has a clear idea of what the norms mean, and the less sophisticated can appreciate that the authors have done their job thoroughly and well.

The authors of this series have certainly taken seriously the suggestions of the Committee on Test Standards of the American Educational Research Association as set forth in *Technical Recommendations for Achievement Tests,* January 1955. It is hoped that many test users will have the interest and training to make use of the information supplied to them in the manuals and other accessories in this series.

In summary, there are reading tests as good as the SRA reading tests; there are few or none so fully documented and supported by helpful accessory materials.

For reviews by Warren G. Findley and Worth R. Jones of the complete battery, see 21.

[650]

★**Scholastic Diagnostic Reading Test.** Grades 1–3, 4–6, 7–9; 1953–55; various titles used by publisher; for Catholic schools; some subtests also appear in *Diagnostic Reading Tests: Pupil Progress Series* for non-Catholic schools; IBM for grades 4–9; 2 forms; 3 levels; manual ('55) for each level; no data on reliability for specific grade levels; separate answer sheets may be used in grades 4–9; $1.75 per 35 IBM scorable answer sheets; 50¢ per specimen set of any one level; 24¢ per set of scoring stencils; postage extra; Oliver F. Anderhalter, Ruth Colestock, and R. Stephen Gawkoski; Scholastic Testing Service, Inc. *

a) PRIMARY TEST. Grades 1–3; 1953–55; 12 scores: vocabulary (3 subscores), rate, comprehension (5 subscores), total; Forms A ('53), B ('55); $3.25 per 35 tests; (30–40) minutes.

b) ELEMENTARY TEST. Grades 4–6; 1953–55; 14 scores: knowledge and use of sources (4 subscores), rate, comprehension (6 subscores), total; IBM; Forms A ['53], B ('55); $3.65 per 35 tests; 42(60) minutes.

c) ADVANCED TEST. Grades 7–9; 1935–55; 14 scores: same as for *b;* IBM; Forms A, B ('55); $3.75 per 35 tests; 42(60) minutes.

RUSSELL G. STAUFFER, *Director, The Reading-Study Center, University of Delaware, Newark, Delaware.*

The purpose of this test is twofold: to help the teacher identify students who are deficient in reading and to provide assistance in the establishment of a remediation program by pointing out areas in reading in which students function at a low level.

To this reviewer it seems that the title of the test is faulty. The word "diagnostic" implies an exhaustive analysis of individual differences in ability to use particular skills. Since such an analysis cannot be accomplished with the use of this test, it would be more accurate to call the test a "reading inventory."

Even a cursory examination of the subparts of the test, regardless of levels, quickly shows that the test is not designed as a clinical device for use in diagnosing severe reading disability. Therefore, the reviewer also protests the use of the words "remediation" and "deficient." The former implies "remedial" with all its connotations of disability and the need for special help, while the latter similarly implies major shortcomings.

The purposes might better read then: to help the teacher identify students who need additional training in certain skills, and to provide assistance in more adequately individualizing reading instruction.

That the test is made available in a series is good, especially if users at any one level will become familiar with what skills are tested at the other two levels. The better a teacher grasps the pattern of the hierarchy of skills and the continuity of development, the better she will be able to differentiate instruction. Since the purpose of the test is to encourage teachers to use the results to plan and motivate learning, the additional study would be especially helpful.

The word recognition test at the primary level is not a true measure of a pupil's ability to recognize words on his own. As an experienced first grade teacher can substantiate, beginning pupils can do much better when someone else reads the words and all they need to do is locate the words, as is true in this test. Word to content relation tends to be a better measure of word recognition ability since it requires the pupil to do his own reading. Here, of course, the meaningful picture clues facilitate recognition, so that once again the task is not as demanding as recognizing words in isolation.

To this reviewer it would seem that there are many other skills more useful and necessary at the primary level than rate of reading. Reading is a mental process involving thinking and versatility of adjustment. Judgment about rate is usually determined, at least in part, by the reader's purpose for reading. In this test the pupil is admonished to read "as fast as you can, but try to remember what you read." Given only such a vague purpose, the pupil has no alternative but to try to soak up everything so as to be prepared for the test that follows. Furthermore, he is told that if he finishes all four of the stories before he is told to stop, he may go back and read the stories again. This forecast of comprehension events to follow should slow the pupil down to a rote memorization pace if the previous warning did not. Then, to boot, Recalling Information, which follows, is strictly a measure of facts, most of them unimportant to either plot development or plot outcome.

The Elementary and Advanced Tests are sounder and more useful. The sections covering knowledge and use of sources are especially good. Many teachers may be alerted to skills that need to be taught when they study these sections. Also, the number of items per section is larger than in the Primary Test.

In the higher level tests Rate of Reading for Meaning merits many of the criticisms given about that section in the Primary Test. The instructions do not urge the reader to "remem-ber"; neither do they establish "purposes" for reading. Rereading is again encouraged.

While rereading is an important reading-study skill, it is not what is being appraised here. In Form A of the Elementary Test (grades 4–6), 17 of the 20 questions start with "the chipmunk('s)" and then proceed to ask a fact about chipmunks. The other three questions also ask for factual information but at least vary the style of the question asking. Knowlege of facts is important, it is true, but never that important. Skillful readers need to know how to size up a situation, evaluate a title, make hypotheses, read to confirm or refute conjectures, alter hypotheses, evaluate outcomes or data, and use ideas or information gained. In all of this, facts are important—but getting them is only one part of the process.

A good feature of the Elementary and Advanced Tests is that they offer scores for the same 10 parts, subtotal, and total categories for grades 4–9. This is a good way to stress continuous growth of all students at all grade levels with respect to basic skills.

In summary, the *Scholastic Diagnostic Reading Test* is useful for a more specific survey of some of the skills of reading. It points up certain skills that might be overlooked otherwise. As an inventory of needs for improved individualization of instruction, the test may be very useful. It is not a diagnostic test in the same sense that it diagnoses a disability. The Elementary and Advanced Tests are particularly useful. The Primary Test leaves much to be desired.

ARTHUR E. TRAXLER, *Executive Director, Educational Records Bureau, New York, New York.*

The format and typography of the test booklets and manuals are generally good, although a few of the pictures in the Elementary and Advanced Tests are too small and indistinct to be easily read.

Raw scores on all tests and subtests at each level are translated into grade equivalents. These equivalents may be graphed on an individual profile form on the cover page of the test booklets. Each raw score is simply the number right, even in subtests consisting of yes-no items. This procedure allows chance scores to yield substantial grade equivalents. For instance, in Test 1 of the elementary battery, pure guessing would on the average yield a grade equivalent of about 5.5—a rather respectable score for a fourth grade pupil.

The grade equivalents are based on nationwide testing in Catholic schools. No evidence is presented to support the use of the same grade equivalents when responses are entered in booklets and when they are recorded on answer sheets. This procedure may be questioned, since research has often shown that more time is required to record responses on answer sheets than to enter them in the booklets.

Because of their brevity, the grade equivalent scales for some of the subtests are necessarily coarse. In some places, one item makes a difference of more than one grade in a pupil's score.

The deciles and the 5th and 95th percentiles of the grade scores are reported for each half year from the end of grade 1 through the first half of grade 9. Such norms are desirable but their use requires an extreme amount of interpolation by test users. In fact, in certain brief subtests, no percentile ranks may be obtained without interpolation. The presentation of only certain percentiles is common practice, but it causes test users much loss of time. Tables showing all percentiles, or the percentile ranks of all scores, should be prepared.

Since all three levels were administered in the spring for normative purposes, the percentile norms for the first half of each grade must have been found by interpolation—a somewhat hazardous procedure.

The percentile tables for the Primary Test indicate that this test is somewhat too easy for grade 3. In two of the subtests, the grade equivalent which corresponds to a perfect score yields a percentile rank of about 60 in the last half of the third grade.

The small amount of validity data reported is reasonably favorable. A correlation of .67 between comprehension scores and reading grades of sixth grade pupils is rather high for this kind of relationship.

Split-half and alternate-forms reliabilities for single grades are about what one would expect for tests of these lengths. The reliabilities of two of the three main scores average about .90, which may be regarded as satisfactory. The median of the reliability coefficients reported for the rate score is only .76, which is hardly high enough to indicate usefulness of the rate measure in the study of individuals. The probable reason for the rather low reliability of the

rate score is the brevity of the rate test. The rate score in the primary test is based on a two-minute interval; the one in the intermediate and advanced tests is derived from a total of one and one-half minutes of reading time. In order to obtain a rate reliability of .80 to .90, at least three minutes of reading time is generally required.

The reliabilities of the subtests, ranging from .62 to .94 with a median of about .77, are as high as could be expected for scores based on 10 to 20 items. Nevertheless, the rather low reliabilities of at least half of the subtests cast doubt upon their value for individual diagnosis. The diagnostic worth of the subtests could more readily be ascertained if information were available about their intercorrelation.

Raw score equivalence data indicate that the means and standard deviations of the scores yielded by Forms A and B tend to be closely similar. There is an obvious error in the mean rate score for grade 4 reported on page 15 of the manual for the Elementary Test. This is the only printing error noted.

SUMMING UP. Since this purportedly diagnostic reading test was standardized on a nationwide sampling of Catholic pupils, it is very probably one of the most useful available reading tests for Catholic schools. The test has a number of desirable features which would commend it to public schools and independent schools outside the Catholic group. The items are well constructed, the directions are clearly written, the tests are well printed, and the manuals contain a good deal of helpful statistical data.

On the other hand, there are several disadvantages for the general user. No public school norms are available; the reliability of one of the main scores, the rate of reading score, is rather low; and the value of the subtest diagnostic scores is open to question because of their somewhat low reliability and doubtful independence. This reviewer recognizes the special contribution made by the *Scholastic Diagnostic Reading Test,* but for general use he questions whether it offers any advantages over such well known tests as *Reading Comprehension: Cooperative English Test,* the *Diagnostic Reading Tests,* and the *Iowa Silent Reading Tests.*

[651]

*The Schonell Reading Tests. Ages 5–15, 6–9, 7–11, 9–13; 1942–55; individual in part; 1 form; tests are reproduced in full in 6 below; tests R5, R6, and R7 not available as separates; 2s. 9d. per 12 copies of any one test; 1s. 6d. per manual of instructions and norms ['55]; 6s. 6d. per copy of *The Psychology and Teaching of Reading, Third Edition,* ('51, see 5 below) which serves as the complete manual for *a;* 25s. per copy of *Backwardness in the Basic Subjects, Fourth Edition,* ('51, see 4 below) which serves as the complete manual for *b–g;* postage extra; Fred J. Schonell; Oliver & Boyd Ltd. *

a) TEST R1, GRADED WORD READING TEST. Ages 5–15; 1942; also called *Graded Reading Vocabulary Test;* individual; (5–15) minutes.

b) TEST R2, SIMPLE PROSE READING TEST. Ages 6–9; 1942; also called *My Dog Test;* individual; (3–8) minutes.

c) TEST R3, SILENT READING TEST A. Ages 7–11; 1942; 9(15) minutes.

d) TEST R4, SILENT READING TEST B. Ages 9–13; 1942; 15(20) minutes.

e) TEST R5, TEST OF ANALYSIS AND SYNTHESIS OF WORDS CONTAINING COMMON PHONIC UNITS. Individual; (5–15) minutes.

f) TEST R6, TEST OF DIRECTIONAL ATTACK ON WORDS. Individual; (5–10) minutes.

g) TEST R7, VISUAL WORD DISCRIMINATION TEST. Individual; (10–15) minutes.

REFERENCES

1–3. See 4:552.
4. SCHONELL, FRED J. *Backwardness in the Basic Subjects, Fourth Edition.* Edinburgh, Scotland: Oliver & Boyd Ltd., 1951. Pp. xix, 566.
5. SCHONELL, FRED J. *The Psychology and Teaching of Reading, Third Edition.* Edinburgh, Scotland: Oliver & Boyd Ltd., 1951. Pp. 156.
6. SCHONELL, FRED J., AND SCHONELL, F. ELEANOR. *Diagnostic and Attainment Testing: Including a Manual of Tests, Their Nature, Use, Recording and Interpretation, Third Edition.* Edinburgh, Scotland: Oliver & Boyd Ltd., 1956. Pp. viii, 192.
7. PRINGLE, M. L. KELLMER, AND NEALE, M. D. "A Note on the Use of the Schonell and Gates Reading Tests in the First Year of the Junior School." *Brit J Ed Psychol* 27:135–41 Je '57. *

R. W. McCULLOCH, *Chief Psychologist and Superintendent of Special Schools, Tasmanian Education Department, Hobart, Tasmania, Australia.*

The three tests of reading comprehension (Tests R2, R3, and R4) cover successive difficulty levels from age 6 through age 13, while Test R1 is an individual attainment test in word recognition for ages 5–15. Test R1 is composed of 100 words divided into 10 words per year from ages 5–13 and 10 words for the two years 14 and 15. The 100 words were selected from 300 words administered individually to approximately 60 children in each of the 10 age groups. They are arranged in continuous order of difficulty, the easiest word being read correctly by 55 per cent of children aged 5 and the most difficult being read correctly by 45 per cent of children aged 14–15. The words have no special connection with any method of reading teaching. The test appears to be equally useful in schools following the look-and-say, whole sentence, or phonic methods, or a combined method. The test has been used repeatedly, even at monthly intervals, to check progress, without any practice effect being detected.

Test R2 is designed for pupils of reading age 6–9 and is scored for speed, accuracy, and comprehension. The story to be read is sufficiently interesting to keep average readers of ages 6–9 trying. To its credit, it can also hold the interest of the older backward reader, though the printing and layout are of the type that is usually provided for the younger child. The norms—always weak in reading tests for children near the age at which they begin to read—have been revised by the author to give separate norms for Paragraph 1 (based on a 5- to 6-year-old vocabulary), for Paragraphs 1 and 2, and for Paragraphs 1, 2, and 3. This improves the test's value for use with the very poor reader.

Tests R3 and R4, silent reading tests, consist of a number of paragraphs, each followed by questions, instructions, or multiple choice problems. Answer sheets are separate. The questions in these tests of comprehension come very close to the kinds of questions which arise in natural reading situations. The requirement of writing a single word in answer to some questions has been criticized as possibly penalizing the slow writer. This may be true, but, to the tester, this disadvantage is balanced by the added information given by the nature of the word chosen.

Tests R5, R6, and R7 constitute a set of diagnostic tests aimed at identifying whether or not any or all of a large number of specific difficulties are operative in individual cases. Test R5 is a diagnostic test of graded words containing most of the common phonic combinations and families. The test consists of two parts. The first 60 words contain regular combinations of vowels and consonants together with the common vowel digraphs such as *ai, ee,* and consonantal digraphs like *ck, gr,* and *sh.* The last 30 words are polysyllabic and are designed to reveal the testee's ability to read regular words that require syllabification, such as "forget" and "contented." The test's prime purpose is the diagnosis of weaknesses in the auditory or phonic elements of word recognition. Its value lies in its qualitative rather than its quantitative results; the application of standardisation procedures would have been pointless.

Test R6, designed to cover directional attack on words, consists of 12 groups of words. Each group comprises four words which contain the same letters but in different positions. The test rapidly identifies the pupil who has not stabilized his ability to look at words carefully from left to right and to differentiate among words of similar but slightly different structure. Test R7 is directed at weaknesses in the perception of visual patterns of words. Its usefulness is mainly as a supplement to Tests R1 and R6.

The tests form an integral part of the books mentioned in the test entry preceding this review. This makes it clear that the author designed the tests for teachers and specialists who intended to use them in conjunction with actual reading programs, whether group or individual. He assumes that those administering the tests will have access to considerably more detail about each child than is provided by the tests alone, and he emphasizes (particularly in relation to Tests R5, R6, and R7) that the insight, caution, and background of the tester play as important a part as does the test itself. Viewed in this context the group tests provide a coverage, both in age range and in competences tested, which is adequate for surveys carried out as preliminaries to the design of group instructional programs in reading, or as appraisals of group instructional programs already in operation. The diagnostic tests are sufficiently comprehensive in the aspects of reading which they probe to lead the diagnostician into the careful consideration of personal history and environmental factors which the author rightly sees as an essential part of the diagnostic procedure. The diagnostic tests achieve comprehensiveness in spite of the absence of tests requiring auditory discrimination between words, the matching of printed words and words heard, and the comprehension of ideas differentiated only by punctuation, word position, or choice of phrasing. Although they are adequate in the way mentioned, Tests R5, R6, and R7 are supported in the Schonell books only by the all too brief chapters on the clinical evaluation of the complex factors which may underlie the failures revealed by the tests. This is the most critical weakness in the series of books and tests which the Schonells and their assistants have issued since 1942.

In summary, it may be said that the fulfilment of the overall plan implicit in the series of books and tests has been brought closer by the extra explanatory material and the restandardizations reported in the latest editions of the books. As they stand, they provide a convenient and reliable testing kit for the teacher or specialist who is experienced and sensitive. For the learner, the tests, particularly the diagnostic tests, require supplementing by more case reports.

For a review by M. L. Kellmer Pringle, see 4:552; for a review by Edith I. M. Thomson, see 3:499.

[652]

★Sentence Reading Test 1. Ages 7-6 to 11-1; 1956; 1 form ['56] no data on validity; 1s. 9d. per 12 tests; 2d. per single copy; 1s. per manual; postage extra; 15(25) minutes; A. F. Watts; published for National Foundation for Educational Research in England and Wales; Newnes Educational Publishing Co. Ltd. *

REGINALD R. DALE, *Lecturer in Education, University College of Swansea, Swansea, England.*

This test assesses the ability of children aged 7-6 to 11-1 to read and understand incomplete sentences and to choose the correct completion word out of five supplied. There are 35 graded sentences. The standardisation is well done, though users should be told whether "a specially chosen sample of primary schools" includes schools representing the necessary proportion of educationally subnormal children, etc., and also children from private schools. In tests of the future, even more attention may be paid to proportions of occupational class in the standardisation sample. Reliability is high, but users are rightly warned that errors at the extremes of the range are "not inconsiderable." It would have been valuable and reassuring for users if an item analysis had been provided, as a careful inspection of the items leaves one with the feeling that the grading of both the sentences and the completion words, though by no means absent, might have been improved.

As a child could give one correct answer in five by guessing, the author examined statistically how this effect might be minimised in the scoring. Discarding the total raw score and "rights minus weighted wrongs" methods, he concluded that the best method was to discount "correct" answers occurring after a gap of five consecutive wrong answers. On the whole, the reviewer agrees that, with the given test, this method of marking is an improvement on the raw scores and will give a valid result, but it is overstating the case a little to claim that the gap "successfully segregated 'chance' scores from scores contributing to a measure of reading ability."

This test is cheap, simple in method, short, and easy to administer. The answering procedure for the pupils is the same throughout and should cause no undue difficulties. Marking is also simple and quick but it would have been useful for a machine scoring method to have been provided for users who test very large numbers of pupils. The imperfections are slight in relation to the value of the test. Though no data are provided on the difficult question of validity, this reviewer is of the opinion that the test will prove to be a valuable means of assessing the comparative silent reading standards of individuals and groups.

STEPHEN WISEMAN, *Director, School of Education, University of Manchester, Manchester, England.*

The test consists of 35 (unrelated) incomplete sentences for which the subject has to choose the correct final word from five alternatives. The response is made by underlining the correct word. The test is printed on both sides of a single sheet. The format of the test, although extremely simple and inexpensive by American standards, is excellent. Fourteen of the 35 items come on the first side of the sheet, in adequately bold sans-serif type face. The remaining 21 items are in smaller type. The items are graded in difficulty and 15 minutes is allowed for the test after two examples have been worked. The range of difficulty can best be demonstrated by quoting the first and last items:

    1. Come with me to the shops to buy some (fire, water, stone, sweets, motors).
    35. The political dangers of monopoly seem to have been much (exasperated, excised, exaggerated, expropriated, expostulated).

Raw scores are converted to standardised scores with a mean of 100 and a standard deviation of 15—the common British method for primary school group tests. The standardisation sample consisted of 7,776 boys and girls aged 7-6 to 11-1. The population was drawn from a "specially chosen sample of primary schools"; no other details are given. Clearly, a large number of schools was involved, since British primary schools are small by American standards, and there are relatively few with more than a three or four stream entry. It would have been more satisfactory, however,

to give more information about how the sample was drawn, and particularly, about the regions from which it came. Reading ability may well vary considerably from one area to another and it is not unconnected with dialect and differences in speech habits. Standardisations were done for "each year group separately, after which inconsistencies between the tables for adjacent months of age, resulting from differences between segregated year groups, were smoothed out." Although figures are given in the manual showing that girls in the sample had a significantly higher mean score than the boys at each age level, separate conversion tables are not provided. Inspection of the conversion table shows that the effect of age on score is greater at the younger months, being nearly twice as great at the 8-5 to 8-9 level as at 10-5 to 10-9 (approximately .7 points of standardised score change per month of age as against .4).

The reliability figures of .91 to .97 (test-retest after one week, $n = 243$), for a test of 35 items and 15 minutes' time, are extremely good, giving standard errors of score between 2.7 and 4.5. The short interval between test and retest should, however, be noted. Test-retest after one year yielded coefficients of .82, .89, and .88 for groups of seven-, eight-, and nine-year-olds, respectively. No Kuder-Richardson coefficient is reported.

One of the most interesting aspects of the manual is the suggested correction for chance scoring. An analysis of item responses "indicated that a gap of five consecutive wrong answers successfully segregated 'chance' scores from scores contributing to a measure of reading ability." Correlations between "corrected" and "uncorrected" scores were .98 or .99, and a study of the test-retest results after one year showed that the correction had no effect on reliability. One could wish that Watts had included more detailed information about the analysis of answer patterns which led to this correction. It is a most interesting technique, one which might perhaps be further developed. One wonders, however, whether the "gap" should be constant over the whole of this very wide ability range, and what the effect on validity would be for different groups of children. No guidance is given to the test marker as to what to do with a gap consisting of four wrong answers and one omitted item. In view of the instructions to the children ("Do not worry if you cannot do some of the sentences. Just do what you can."), there might be a certain degree of injustice done to some subjects by varying interpretations of the instructions.

[653]

★Sequential Tests of Educational Progress: Reading. Grades 4-6, 7-9, 10-12, 13-14; 1956-57; IBM; Forms A, B('57); 4 levels; manual ('57); battery directions ('57); battery technical report ('57); no data on reliability of Form B; separate answer sheets must be used; $3.95 per 20 tests; $1 per 20 IBM scorable answer sheets; 45¢ per scoring stencil; $1 per manual; $1 per battery technical report; $1.25 per specimen set; postage extra; 70(90-100) minutes; Cooperative Test Division, Educational Testing Service. *

a) LEVEL 4. Grades 4-6; Forms 4A, 4B.
b) LEVEL 3. Grades 7-9; Forms 3A, 3B.
c) LEVEL 2. Grades 10-12; Forms 2A, 2B.
d) LEVEL 1. Grades 13-14; Forms 1A, 1B.

ERIC F. GARDNER, *Professor of Education and Psychology, University of Syracuse, Syracuse, New York.*

The *Sequential Tests of Educational Progress* are a series of achievement tests measuring learning in seven fields (essay writing, listening comprehension, reading comprehension, writing, science, mathematics and social studies) from the fourth grade through the sophomore year of college. This review is restricted to an examination of the reading comprehension test.

The items were constructed with an intent to assess the following skills: ability to reproduce ideas, ability to translate ideas and make inferences, ability to analyze motivation, ability to analyze presentation, and ability to criticize. Fortunately, no attempt to present separate scores for each of these functions was made. A single score based on the number right is obtained.

Each form of the reading test contains a number of passages of various types, such as directions, announcements, letters, poetry, essays, and speeches. Following each passage is a series of items relating to that passage. There are 70 items of the 4-choice multiple choice type at each level.

Reliability coefficients were computed by an estimate of internal consistency obtained from a single administration of each level (battery) to a single grade. Form 1A was administered to grade 13, Form 2A to grade 11, Form 3A to grade 8, and Form 4A to grade 5. The reliability indices (Kuder-Richardson formula 20) were around .90. As pointed out in the Technical Report, these are slight overestimates of

reliability within a classroom. Of special interest is the attempt to incorporate the standard error of measurement in the score itself by advocating the use of a confidence interval rather than a single point to interpret a student's score. This is a very worthwhile emphasis and should assist in helping teachers avoid making decisions on small score differences, which could have readily arisen by chance.

The validity of the STEP reading comprehension test, as well as that of most other reading tests, is essentially content validity. It is based upon the judgment of the people who constructed the items and built the tests. No information on concurrent or predictive validity is reported, although such information is promised as soon as it may become available.

The norms were obtained from a large sample selected with a view to adequate geographical representation. Both percentile norms for individual scores and percentile norms for the means of the schools included in the normative group are presented. Considerable stress is placed upon the construction of local norms.

In conclusion, the STEP reading test appears to be another technically well constructed test whose basic merits have yet to be demonstrated. This reviewer fails to see where the statement "The Sequential Tests of Educational Progress (STEP) are a new set of achievement tests of a *new kind*" has been substantiated. The criteria set forth for STEP are desirable, but they have been accepted by test constructors for many years and utilized in the construction of most of the currently used achievement test batteries.

JAMES R. HOBSON, *Director of Child Placement, Brookline Public Schools, Brookline, Massachusetts.*

These reading tests are at each level one of a battery of tests of basic skills and understandings and ability in applying them in new situations. They more or less cut across narrowly conceived subject matter lines and attempt to measure educational development and progress in fundamental skill areas rather than subject achievement in the usual sense. Earlier test series which have had some of the same goals in mind would include the *Iowa Every-Pupil Tests of Basic Skills,* the *Iowa Tests of Educational Development,* and, to a degree, the *Cooperative English Test* and the *Diagnostic Reading Tests.* The major goal of the last named series is different, of course, but there is considerable similarity in some of the concepts and methods of implementing them.

A careful reading of the Technical Report, the Manual for Interpreting Scores, and the Directions for Administering and Scoring, and, finally, an item by item and form by form perusal of the tests themselves leave this test consumer and critic with two main generalizations: The conception and development of this test series is an excellent illustration of the scientific method in action; and the end result represents an outstanding professional achievement.

There are several aspects of this undertaking and of its finished product which are worthy of comment. To begin with, a planning committee for each skill area to be tested was chosen with the help of national professional organizations. The members of each planning committee in turn surveyed curriculum and course objectives in their respective geographical areas and arrived at some common agreement at to what it was important to measure at each level. They also took the responsibility for choosing other educators to assist in writing the tests, with due consideration to competence, experience level, geographical location, and type of school representation. Finally, for the actual item writing, all groups were assembled in workshop situations. The tremendous advantages engendered by such an approach to the problem and by the face to face writing and evaluation of test items and exchange of ideas are evident in the propriety of the test items at the different levels and the essential harmony in the overall pattern.

The technical steps taken in producing the final test forms leave little to be desired. The planning foresight, and anticipation of flaws and difficulties in the construction of these instruments show what can be expected when specialists in classroom teaching, curriculum planning, and test construction come together in a professional endeavor which is essentially noncommercial in nature. For example, instead of the usual two preliminary administrations for item analysis and standardization there were separate administrations for item analysis, horizontal as well as vertical equating, and norming the final forms. In many test construction endeavors either steps 1 and 2 or steps 2 and 3 are combined.

In the pretesting program for purposes of item analysis, the respective difficulties of all items were determined not only for the grade for which the test was intended, but in some cases for adjacent grades as well. Next, the effectiveness of every item in discriminating between top ranking and low ranking students was determined. This is, of course, the heart of the content validity of any test. Finally, the pretesting item analysis furnished data on the plausibility of the alternatives to the correct answers, which is such an essential factor in the effectiveness of measurement of all test items of the multiple choice type.

An interesting innovation in the interpretation of STEP scores is the percentile band or confidence interval for any score, based upon the standard error of measurement of a specific score in a given test in a particular class. While this doubtless salves the test construction statistician's conscience and sounds a necessary warning to the literal-minded test user, it is not an unmixed blessing in that it can create as many problem as it solves. After working for 25 years to develop instruments and techniques to give teachers and parents practical methods for interpreting percentile ratings, grade norms, and the like, this reviewer shudders at the thought of trying to interpret a converted score of 290 on a level 2 reading test in terms of a percentile band of 44–74 (manual, page 20), although a recently published student report form does a very good piece of work in this respect albeit the illustrated directions deal with percentile bands only one third as large as the one cited above. It is much easier to interpret a percentile rank of 59, emphasizing the importance of the fact that this is only one item of evidence and that no important decision can be made on the basis of such scanty evidence alone. Incidentally, this reviewer was not able to determine from any data presented specifically how the table of intervals for determining percentile bands was derived. Obviously the range of scores, the shape of the distribution, and the size of the standard error of measurement are the important factors. In view of the completeness and excellence of the presentation in every other respect, however, it was not difficult to take this on faith.

It is not clear why a 2-point "score group" was used in all of the individual score norms tables unless it was so that the percentile rank of a score group would *not* fall on a converted score. A 1-point score group, while making the tables twice as long, would narrow the percentile band by 2 to 4 points in the case of any given score, which would seem desirable to this reviewer. In setting up local norms, it would, of course, be easy to do this if desired.

The maintenance of similarity in the nature and overall pattern of the reading tests at all four levels is clearly illustrated by the fact that the tests look exactly alike and that the number of test items, the directions, and the time limits are identical. To anyone who has ever tried to "run a three-ring circus" by testing pupils of different grades, perhaps those new to the system, in the same room, these identities would constitute a great convenience. The content, of course, becomes progressively more difficult, the skills more complex, and the understandings more mature. These factors amply justify the use of the term "sequential."

In summary, the STEP reading tests are a broadly conceived, expertly planned, scientifically executed, efficiently packaged series whose innate validity will be demonstrated in the crucible of use. This series, over its entire grade and area range, may well prove to be the most useful and authoritative scholastic measuring instrument to be developed in many years.

STEPHEN WISEMAN, *Director, School of Education, University of Manchester, Manchester, England.*

The aim of the STEP series is ambitious— to measure, by means of tests at four levels, all grades from 4 to 14 in each of seven learning fields, of which reading is one; and to do so by "testing ability to apply learning rather than just 'play it back.'" To the British reviewer the format of the tests is impressive, and, to some extent, formidable. In addition to eight tests, with accompanying answer sheets and scoring stencils, he is provided with a prospectus, directions for administering and scoring, a manual for interpreting scores, a technical report, and specimens of a class record, a score distribution sheet, a student profile, a student report, a supplement to the test catalogue, and an order form.

Each of the reading tests consists of 14 comprehension passages, followed by five multiple choice items, each with four alternatives. This makes a very tidy and symmetrical job, but there seems little other virtue in having exactly five questions on each item. Many times when

reading the tests, the reviewer was struck by the obvious wealth of other possible items which might stem from a fairly long extract, and marveled at the discipline which sternly rejected all but the chosen.

The reading material is well varied, including extracts from poems and plays as well as letters, children's stories, technical passages, newspaper articles, and the like. The poetry in the lower grades tends to be somewhat sentimental and trite at times, but this is perhaps difficult to avoid. The reviewer particularly admired some of the passages in the level 1 tests, but could not help contrasting the complexity and sophistication of the extracts and the relative simplicity (or even naiveté) of some of the questions. This gives a rather misleading appearance to the tests at this level: it does not follow that because a student gets a good score on Test 1B, he is capable of coping with confidence with such material as "They told me, Heraclitus, they told me you were dead." The reading material in the tests at this level would be admirable for sixth forms in this country, but one suspects that the items would be much too easy to give an adequate ceiling.

The testmakers have endeavoured to divide items equally among "five major reading-for-comprehension skills": ability to reproduce ideas, ability to translate ideas and make inferences, ability to analyse motivation, ability to analyse presentation, and ability to criticise. The reviewer has made no systematic attempt to check this claim of content validity, but he suspects that the last-named skill at least carries less weight than some of the others. It would be surprising if this were not so.

Nine criteria for the selection of passages are listed in the manual. It is unfortunate that in a test manual in the field of English the English usage should be suspect. Criterion 3 reads: "Materials should be crucial in value (e.g., a selection on how to build a model airplane would be preferable to directions for navigating the Yangtze River)." The meaning of "crucial" is (O.E.D.) "decisive, critical."

Directions for administering the reading tests are exactly the same for all tests at all levels. Thus, one can test a "mixed" group containing students taking tests of different forms and at different levels. This is a great convenience, but when one considers the difference in educational level between the dull fourth grader and the bright college sophomore, one wonders whether the same instructions can be equally effective over such a wide range of comprehension. The vocabulary level is not uniformly low enough for the bottom end, while the length and detail of instructions (and the common "example" used) is likely to be irksome to the top end.

The technical report gives a good deal of information about the construction of the series as a whole, but it is not always clear in detail. Three different samples of children were used for pretesting, for equating, and for norming. All these samples were apparently drawn from the school systems of willing superintendents in a "random sample of superintendents of school systems throughout the nation." The lack of representativeness caused by refusal to participate is recognised, and this is a necessary limitation which must be accepted.

In pretesting the reading tests, 4,000 students in each of grades 5, 8, 11, and 13 were given four forms of each level (each form being administered to a random quarter of the sample). Analysis was based on a 200-case random sample for each form in each grade, and items analysed for difficulty and for discrimination between high and low 100-case subgroups. With 1,000 cases for each form one might have expected rather larger samples to be used for analysis. No information is given on the level of discrimination demanded.

Two hundred twenty-two schools and 41 colleges took part in the programme to equate the tests in the series "horizontally" and "vertically," i.e., to determine the comparability of Forms A and B at the same level and the relationship between different levels. For the vertical equating, pairs of successive grades were used, with random halves in each classroom taking successive levels of Form A. In addition, every student took a "link test," parallel in content and "straddling the two levels of difficulty."

The score scale derived for the series from the programme results is a curious one to British eyes. The scores run from the 220's up to 380, with 230 as the "mean chance score" on level 4 and 300 as the score midway between chance and maximum at level 1. No distributions are given of raw scores or standardised scores—a great pity, for the experienced test-maker can learn a great deal from such distributions.

In order to learn more about the score scale,

the reviewer plotted raw score against standard score for all forms of the reading tests at all levels. The curves for levels 1, 2, and 3 are broadly similar and roughly parallel ogives. Level 4 is quite different, being practically a straight line from raw score 10 to 50, and then gently curving off to become almost asymptotic to the maximum score level. Thus Forms 4A and 4B do not appear to be of the same test "family" as the others. The difference can, perhaps, best be illustrated by considering what raw score is necessary on each test to give a scaled score of 260:

Level:	1A	1B	2A	2B	3A	3B	4A	4B
Raw Score:	19	17	23	23½	29	31	51	49

Notice the large jump from level 3 to level 4; this means a large jump in difficulty between these levels, large enough indeed to justify an additional test to straddle the gap. This table also shows some small discrepancies between alternative forms. In parts of the score, scale differences are extremely large. The graph lines for Forms 3B and 4B actually cross at a raw score of 68, but this is so near the maximum that one would hesitate to draw strong conclusions from it. The difference between Forms 1A and 1B is, however, most marked. Form 1B is consistently more difficult than Form 1A, and this difference in difficulty increases as we go up the scale. Beyond a raw score of 55, Form 1B appears to be more difficult than Form 1A by an amount greater than the difference in difficulty between Form 1A and Form 2A! This may well prove to be a blessing in disguise, since Form 1B will give a much higher ceiling than Form 1A and thus give the tester more flexibility. It does, however, raise some doubts as to the efficiency of the equating programme.

Content validity is assumed as a result of the method of item selection and analysis. Correlations with verbal, quantitative, and total scores on the *Cooperative School and College Ability Test* (SCAT) are given by grades and test forms, and are of the expected magnitude. They run from .77 to .87, with .51 for SCAT—V, .74 for SCAT—Q, and .71 to .85 for SCAT—T. No factor analysis data or other evidence on construct validity are given.

Reliability data are restricted to Form A (Why?) and to calculations based on Kuder-Richardson formula 20 (Why?). In addition (or subtraction) to this, in calculating K-R 20, smaller samples were used for Σpq than for the test SD. After the care taken in selecting samples for tryout, equating, and norming, the lack of any attempt to estimate alternate forms reliability—and even more so, test-retest reliability—seems extraordinary. The coefficients reported, .91, .92, .90, and .95 for Levels 1–4, respectively, seem low to British eyes for a test of 70 minutes. Here one is handicapped by lack of precise knowledge of the range of ability in grades as compared with age groups; but in view of the suggestion of lack of parallelism between the A and B forms, the omission of *any* reliability check on Form B seems inexcusable.

In summary, these reading tests seem to be useful and efficient, and no doubt will be found acceptable in schools. The scale and level of publication is impressive, and quite incommensurable with the lack of data on reliability and validity. Whether it is worth correcting raw scores to scaled scores in order to arrive at percentile levels seems to the reviewer highly debatable: the time and energy devoted to this could have been better spent, perhaps, on fuller analysis of the finished product before presenting the tests for publication.

For reviews by Robert W. B. Jackson and Wilbur L. Layton of the complete battery, see 24.

[654]

★**Silent Reading Test.** Standards 1–3 (ages 7–10), 4–8 (ages 10–15); 1947–54; 3 tests; manual ['54]; no data on reliability; specimen set not available; National Bureau of Educational and Social Research. *
a) PARAGRAPHS. Standards 1–3, 4–8; 2 forms; 2 levels; 20(30) minutes.
   1) [*Elementary.*] Standards 1–3; Forms A, B ['47]; 13s. 10d. per 100 tests.
   2) *Junior.* Standards 4–8; Forms A, B ['47]; 16s. 10d., 18s. 5d. per 100 copies of Forms A, B.
b) VOCABULARY. Standards 1–3, 4–8; 3 forms; 2 levels; 10(15) minutes.
   1) [*Elementary.*] Standards 1–3; Forms A, B, C ['47]; 13s. 10d. per 100 tests.
   2) *Junior.* Standards 4–8; Forms A, B, C ['47]; 15s. 1d., 17s. 5d., 16s. 10d. per 100 copies of Forms A, B, C.
c) SPEED. Standards 1–3, 4–8; 2 forms; 2 levels; 4(7) minutes.
   1) [*Elementary.*] Standards 1–3; 1947–54; Forms A, B ['47]; 11s. 4d., 13s. 4d. per 100 copies of Forms A, B.
   2) [*Junior.*] Standards 4–8; 1947–54; Forms A, B ['47]; 16s. 10d. per 100 tests.

[655]

The Standard Reading Tests. Reading ages up to 9–0; 1958; individual; 1 form; 12 tests; manual (see *1* below); no data on reliability; 8s. 6d. per 50 record blanks (published by Philip & Tacey Ltd.); 21s. per manual; postage extra; administration time not reported for Tests 1–11; J. C. Daniels and Hunter Diack; Chatto & Windus Ltd. *

a) TEST 1, THE STANDARD TEST OF READING SKILL.
b) TEST 2, COPYING ABSTRACT FIGURES.
c) TEST 3, COPYING A SENTENCE. No norms.
d) TEST 4, VISUAL DISCRIMINATION AND ORIENTATION TEST. No norms.
e) TEST 5, LETTER-RECOGNITION TEST. No norms.
f) TEST 6, AURAL DISCRIMINATION TEST. No norms.
g) TEST 7, DIAGNOSTIC WORD-RECOGNITION TESTS. 8 tests; no norms.
h) TEST 8, ORAL WORD-RECOGNITION TEST. No norms.
i) TEST 9, PICTURE WORD-RECOGNITION TEST. No norms.
j) TEST 10, SILENT PROSE-READING AND COMPREHENSION TEST. No norms.
k) TEST 11, GRADED SPELLING TEST.
l) TEST 12, GRADED TEST OF READING EXPERIENCE. (20) minutes.

REFERENCE
1. DANIELS, J. C., AND DIACK, HUNTER. *The Standard Reading Tests.* London: Chatto & Windus Ltd., 1958. Pp. 215. *

[656]

***Stanford Achievement Test: Reading.** Grades 3–4, 5–6, 7–9; 1922–55; subtest of *Stanford Achievement Test;* 2 scores: paragraph meaning, word meaning; IBM; 2 editions; postage extra; 35¢ per specimen set of any one level of either edition, postpaid; Truman L. Kelley, Richard Madden, Eric F. Gardner, Lewis M. Terman, and Giles M. Ruch; World Book Co. *
a) [HAND SCORING EDITION.] Grades 3–4, 5–6, 7–9; 3 levels; $2.20 per 35 tests; directions for administering ('53).
   1) *Elementary Reading Test.* Grades 3–4; Forms J ('53), K ('53), L ('54); 33(45) minutes.
   2) *Intermediate Reading Test.* Grades 5–6; Forms J ('53), K ('53), L ('54), M ('55); 37(45) minutes.
   3) *Advanced Reading Test.* Grades 7–9; Forms J ('53), K ('53), L ('54), M ('55); 37(45) minutes.
b) [MACHINE SCORING EDITION.] Grades 5–6, 7–9; IBM; Forms JM ('53), KM ('53), LM ('54); 2 levels; $3.35 per 35 tests; $1.25 per 35 IBM answer sheets; 20¢ per machine scoring stencil; 37(40) minutes.
   1) *Intermediate Reading Test.* Grades 5–6.
   2) *Advanced Reading Test.* Grades 7–9.

HELEN M. ROBINSON, *Associate Professor of Education, The University of Chicago, Chicago, Illinois.*

The reading tests are a portion of a larger battery of tests, but are printed separately. They are designed to measure two aspects of reading achievement: comprehension and word meaning. Thus, these tests may be described as survey tests in contrast to diagnostic tests, which offer several subtest scores.

At each level the paragraph meaning section begins with simple sentences and progresses to longer and more difficult paragraphs. In each paragraph one to four words are omitted, and a blank with a number appears in place of the word. Following the paragraph each number is listed with four alternatives to replace it. There are 40 to 50 separate items. The vocabulary section uses sentence completion for 38 to 50 words. The sentences may define the word or ask for a synonym.

The format of the tests is good and the type is clear. Directions for administering and scoring are unambiguous. The latest revision has eliminated the necessity for writing the answers; hence the score is not contaminated by handwriting and spelling.

Norms are based on 350,000 pupils selected from "all areas of the country, all types of school systems, and all socioeconomic levels." Two types of norms are provided: first, modal-age grade norms, recommended for interpretation of the scores of an individual; and second, total-group grade norms for interpretation of group averages. The modal-age norms are given in percentiles for the beginning, middle, and end of the year. The two sets of norms are especially useful to teachers because they permit comparison of a class with a national norms group and comparison of each pupil with others at his grade level. The manual reports that since the norms beyond grade 10.0 are extrapolated, grade scores are to be interpreted with caution.

The claim for validity of the tests is based on the "content of the typical elementary school curriculum," in addition to extensive experimentation prior to publication. While it is always desirable to have a figure representing validity if some criterion is available, the reviewer prefers that a test be based on the curriculum rather than correlated with teacher's marks or with an another reading test which may not be recent. Split-half reliabilities of the two parts for grades 3–9 range from .82 to .92, with half of them over .90. The reliability, therefore, is satisfactory.

Unfortunately, the paragraph meaning section relies entirely on selecting words to fit the context. Hence, pupils who have had considerable experience and instruction in using context clues are likely to earn higher scores, even though they can read less well than other pupils who have had no such instruction. Furthermore, the technique of filling in blanks with words definitely limits the range of comprehension abilities which can be measured. An examination of the skills required in this section reveals that in most cases filling in the blanks correctly depends on getting the facts or details and securing implied meanings. Notably lacking, especially at the upper levels, is the demand for getting main ideas, following directions, drawing conclusions, determining bias, and recognizing the feelings of those who

are described. Surely most reading curricula state broader goals than merely reading for fact and inference. In general, the paragraphs appear to cover content of interest to pupils of the age levels for which the tests are intended; selections from such content areas as arithmetic, social studies, and science are included.

The manual states that "these are not speed tests," but also that *"under no conditions* should the time limits be extended." Even though the time limit may be generous, speed becomes a factor in individual cases. A more accurate measure of comprehension is a power test such as the Gates reading survey tests in which no pupil is penalized by limited time, and in which speed of reading is measured by a separate test for that purpose.

In spite of the limitations noted, these tests are undoubtedly among the best survey tests of reading achievement for the elementary grades. The format and content, the standardization and norms, the ease of administering and scoring—all contribute to the conclusion that this is a dependable gross measure of reading achievement.

AGATHA TOWNSEND, *Associate Professor of Education, State Teachers College, Kutztown, Pennsylvania.*

Long experience marks the Stanford reading test in many ways—experienced authorship, continuity in publication over a period of almost 30 years, a backlog of statistical study probably unequalled by that for any other test, and (decidedly not the least important factor) a group of users fully familiar with the test and its predecessors. In at least one respect maturity has brought conservatism. The test maintains a limited pattern for reading testing —concentrating on word and paragraph meaning. While skillful item writing has inserted a great deal of reasoning into this rather simple situation, test users seeking a broader picture of reading in grades 5 and above may want to supplement the reading test with the study skills tests in the intermediate and advanced batteries or with other similar measures.

In spite of limitations of test content, however, the Stanford holds a position of importance in the testing program which is very hard to duplicate. This position it holds primarily for these reasons: (a) It can be used either with or without the rest of the battery. (b) It exists in five comparable forms for each level.

(c) Its scoring system facilitates the comprehensive longitudinal study of growth in reading skills over a wide grade range. (d) The results within these limits are unusually dependable.They probably justify fully the remark in the manual that "inability to measure all the outcomes of education should not deter one from measuring those functions for which there are suitable measures."

The modal age norms in which the Stanford results are expressed have certain quite well defined characteristics. They are described in a number of published articles on the Stanford, but they are not described in the manuals as clearly and as consistently as they should be. Specifically, the most complete descriptions of the norms are in the manuals for the complete batteries. The manual for the elementary reading test, for instance, reprints the first part of the explanation given in the battery manual, but omits the rest. Moreover, one of the best statements on the norms is not contained in any of the manuals, but in a 4-page folder addressed to school administrators and teachers. The fact that the publishers have recognized the need for the special brochure is perhaps the best indication that some reworking of the descriptions in the manuals is needed.

The test manuals have other limitations. For example, they have omitted the discussion of what is in the reading parts, which is a section of the manual for the whole battery. They also omit much of the careful description of the construction and tryout of the items, the establishment of reliability, the basis for selecting normative populations, and so on. In all these ways, the manuals do not permit the reading test to stand alone in quite the way it should.

In summary, the Stanford reading test has a number of strong advantages. Schools which limit the testing of general achievement to alternate years should take advantage of the separate printing of the reading test in the off-years, in order to provide greater continuity of the record reading progress through the grades. The testing of reading may well be extended beyond this program, of course; but the use of a consistent plan will permit comparison of reading achievement with progress in other fields, and also the measurement of reading growth through a single score system.

For a review by James R. Hobson of the previous edition, see 4:555; for a review by

Margaret G. McKim, see 3:503. For a review by N. L. Gage of the complete battery, see 25; for reviews by Paul R. Hanna (with Claude E. Norcross) and Virgil E. Herrick of the previous edition, see 4:25; for reviews by Walter W. Cook and Ralph C. Preston, see 3:18.

[657]
*Techniques in Reading Comprehension for Junior-Senior High School: Every Pupil Test. Grades 7–12; 1937–58; new form usually issued each December and April; norms available following testing program; no data on reliability; 3¢ per test; 1¢ per scoring key; cash orders postpaid; 32(40) minutes; Ohio Scholarship Tests. *

For reviews by Ivan A. Booker and James M. McCallister of earlier forms, see 3:505.

[658]
*Williams Primary Reading Test. Grades 1, 2–3; 1926–55; Forms C, D ('55); 2 levels; manual ('55); $2 per 25 tests; 30¢ per specimen set of either level; postpaid; (25–35) minutes; Allan J. Williams; Public School Publishing Co. *
a) PRIMARY I. Grade 1.
b) PRIMARY II. Grades 2–3.

For a review by Alice N. Jameson of the original edition, see 3:508.

MISCELLANEOUS

[659]
★Doren Diagnostic Reading Test of Word Recognition Skills. Grades 1–9; 1956; 12 scores: letter recognition, beginning sounds, whole word recognition, words within words, speech consonants, ending sounds, blending, rhyming, vowels, sight words, discriminate guessing, total; 1 form; no norms for subtest scores; $3.50 per 25 tests; $1.25 per manual; postage extra; $1.40 per specimen set, postpaid; (180) minutes in 3 sessions; Margaret Doren; Educational Test Bureau. *

B. H. VAN ROEKEL, *Associate Professor of Teacher Education, Michigan State University, East Lansing, Michigan.*

The most striking characteristic of this instrument is its comprehensiveness and attention to detail. The content of the 11 subtests is based on an analysis of the word recognition skills presented in the first three books of five widely used basic reading series. Although commonly used textbooks are not necessarily the best criterion for the selection of test content, the fact that considerable care is exercised in the selection of content for most basic reading series supports the contention that Doren's procedure for determining test content has considerable merit.

The skills which the test purports to measure include letter recognition, beginning sounds, whole word recognition, words within words, speech consonants, ending sounds, blending, rhyming, vowels, sight words, and discriminate guessing. The subtest measuring each of these skills has two or more parts, which, combined, make a voluminous instrument that requires about 3 hours when administered in its entirety.

The manual discusses a variety of topics, including the nature of diagnosis, the construction and arrangement of the test, instructions for administering and scoring the test, technical data concerning the test, and suggestions for remedial activities. The manual does not include directions for giving the test but states that "the examiner should read those printed on the test form and encourage the children to follow the words from their own papers." The examiner is not restricted to the printed directions and is at liberty to amplify them.

The manual confuses the issue of norms. Doren states: "In an achievement test, the number of correct responses is the measure of the degree of success. In a diagnostic test, it is the mistakes which an individual makes that will indicate his areas of need, and an exact identification of the types of errors will direct the examiner to specific remedial work." The manual has a table of mean scores for each of grades 1–4, supposedly representing the normal rate of growth in reading skills in the first four years. In essence, the mean scores for each grade level are not different from grade norms except that in this case the mean scores are expressed as raw scores rather than as grade norms. The raw score equivalents of grade norms on any achievement test are as much a measure of rate of growth as are the grade level mean scores on this test.

An overall validity coefficient of .90 is reported for the test, with reading achievement scores of children in the first four grades on the *Coordinated Scales of Attainment* serving as a criterion. Validity coefficients are reported for each grade level as well. Reliability coefficients for the various subtests range from .53 to .88. No information is given concerning the normative group or the method of determining reliability.

The design and quality of the test items themselves leave much to be desired. For example, Test B of Unit II, Beginning Sounds, consists of a series of sentences and specifies that pupils must encircle the one of three rhyming words which in each case best com-

pletes the sentence. This is as much a matter of context and sight vocabulary as it is of initial sounds. Unit X supposedly checks a child's ability to recognize sight words and his ability to sound out an unfamiliar word. Each item begins with a word of nonphonetic spelling followed by three words or nonsense syllables, one of which represents the phonetic spelling of the initial word. The pupils are to encircle the phonetic spelling of the initial word. This is hardly a measure of a child's fund of sight words. The deficiencies among the items of some of the other units are equally serious.

Many of the limitations of this test are inherent in the fact that this is a group test. Many of the criticisms previously mentioned would not hold if it were an individual test. As a group instrument, it should be used with considerable discretion.

VERNA L. VICKERY, *Associate Professor of Education, Mississippi State University, Starkville, Mississippi.*

This test consists of 390 items divided among 11 units, each unit purporting to measure a specific word recognition skill required for independent reading. The units are said by the author to be arranged in the order of the introduction of word recognition skills into the reading program "insofar as such introduction of skills has a time placement in the teaching of reading." Since the skills tested and the order of their presentation are based on an analysis of the skills taught in five widely used and highly respected series of primary readers, the claim to overall content validity is probably justified.

Norms as generally presented with achievement tests are not available. The author states that since this test is designed to measure deficiencies in specific areas of word recognition, an indication by norms of level of attainment is neither necessary nor desirable. With this point of view the reviewer would disagree, being of the opinion that the availability of more extensive interpretative data would do much to increase the usefulness of the test.

The test booklet is attractive in format. The manual is clearly and simply written and contains a section on remedial techniques for use in correcting the various deficiencies that may be revealed. Administration and scoring of the test and interpretation of the test results require a considerable amount of time; however, since the test is designed to be diagnostic, it would necessarily be longer and more time-consuming than tests of the survey type.

In spite of the deficiencies noted, the test should be of value to primary teachers, and to teachers of children in need of remedial help in the middle grades as well. The test will provide information concerning a child's word recognition problems and suggestions for remediation which the teacher, especially the skillful one, should be able to put to good use.

[660]

*Durrell Analysis of Reading Difficulty, New Edition. Grades 1-6; 1937-55, c1933-55; individual; 1 form ('55); no data on reliability; reading paragraphs ('55); tachistoscope and cards ('55); manual ('55); $3.70 per examiner's kit including 5 record booklets ('55), postpaid; $3.75 per 35 record booklets, postage extra; (30-90) minutes; Donald D. Durrell; World Book Co. *

REFERENCES

1-2. See 4:561.

James Maxwell, *Visiting Professor of Education, Teachers College, Columbia University, New York, New York.*

The requirements of diagnostic tests of reading are very largely determined by the nature of the reading task itself, so that all such tests follow much the same pattern. This test does not diverge radically from the established pattern. The core of the test is two sets of paragraphs, one set for oral and the other for silent reading, accompanied by tables of norms and checklists for recording observations of reading difficulties. Norms are expressed for each of grades 1-6 on three levels (low, medium and high), these being sufficiently precise for the purpose of the test. Unfortunately, however, the norms are based upon speed of reading alone; there are no norms for level of comprehension, which is, nevertheless, tested, and the diagnosis of this aspect of reading comes to depend almost entirely on the checklists of difficulties.

A praiseworthy feature is the inclusion of a set of graded paragraphs for listening comprehension, this giving useful information not always included in diagnostic reading tests.

Other major subtests are word and letter recognition exercises, the presentation being mainly by means of a simple tachistoscope included in the test kit. The child's visual recognition of words is adequately tested, as is his auditory recognition of letters, but there are no tests of the child's methods of word attack,

e.g., syllabication or phonic analysis of the complete word. There are also checklists for the pupil's medical, psychological, and educational records.

The test material is thoroughly prepared and well arranged, and the instructions clear. The checklists of difficulties are perhaps rather too extensive for easy recording while the test is being administered, but they are comprehensive and become quite manageable with practice. The reading paragraphs are well chosen and graded, and the word lists are adequately comprehensive. The weakness of the test lies in the unsatisfactory norms for paragraph reading and the inadequacy of standardized tests of word attack.

George D. Spache, *Professor of Education, and Head, Reading Laboratory and Clinic, University of Florida, Gainesville, Florida.*

This is a battery of tests designed for the observation of the reading performances of individuals varying from nonreading to sixth grade levels. The tests are intended for the use of experienced teachers or those specifically trained in their administration and interpretation.

The battery opens with an oral reading test that permits observation of reading errors and reading speed. Comprehension is measured by questions involving merely recall of the details. The author suggests that testing begin at the child's actual reading level and that at least three paragraphs should be used. Since there is only a single paragraph at each reading level, it is impossible to follow these directions and secure an adequate sample with individuals reading below the third grade level. Thus, if we assume that the reading selections represent specific grade levels, which is doubtful, the test will function adequately only as a measure of the simplest type of oral reading above primary levels.

The second subtest, a silent reading test, offers norms for speed and parrot-like recall. No questions involving any type of comprehension are offered. The purpose is to permit direct comparison of oral and silent reading abilities since the child reads selections and answers questions which are presumably comparable to those in the preceding test. As in the oral reading test, the examiner cannot secure an adequate sample for individuals reading below the third grade level. Since many pupils could recall the details of these selections without actual comprehension, the test's adequacy as a measure of silent reading is doubtful, as is its comparability with the oral reading test. Apparently, the author assumes that any type of recall or interpretation is a thorough measure of comprehension and is equivalent to any other type. For some reason, several questions on imagery are offered for two of the eight reading selections. Similar questions are to be phrased by the teacher for the other selections. The purpose of these questions and their significance in cases of reading difficulty is not clear.

The third subtest, a listening test, is really an adaptation of an oral reading test offered in the earlier edition of the battery. In revising the test, the author has merely downgraded each oral reading selection by one grade and devised a group of recall questions. Just how this revision was justified or just what is measured by this test in its present form is not clarified by the author. The directions indicate that if the child can answer all the questions on the single paragraph for his grade level (?), his reading difficulty is not due to lack of comprehension. Apparently this arbitrarily scaled test is intended to function as a measure of potential for reading comprehension.

The next subtest measures quick word recognition and delayed word analysis techniques with the use of a hand tachistoscope. This is probably the most original and functional test in the entire battery, provided the examiner can manipulate it properly.

New tests added to the current edition include six measures of the visual and auditory characteristics of letters and words. These should be useful measures of phonic skills even among individuals of higher reading levels than the primary level for which they are recommended. A new learning rate test is also included, in which the child's ability to learn isolated words by an abbreviated visual method is presumably evaluated. The lack of norms, the ignoring of the influence of the child's intellectual level, and the use of an inadequate number of words to challenge children of higher capacities, all tend to make this test of little practical value in its present form.

Supplementary tests of written spelling and speed of handwriting are offered. Spelling errors are to be noted and combined with those from oral reading, but these errors are not carefully defined or described, nor are all significant types noted.

The nature or size of the population on which these tests were standardized is not revealed, nor are there any data on the reliability or validity of any of the tests. Apparently the user is to assume that all of the tests are highly valid, dependable and consistent, despite the serious limitations we have noted above. As the author suggests, probably the outstanding contributions of this battery are the checklists for guiding the observation of various reading performances. For the most part, these checklists are detailed and fairly complete. They should be particularly useful for relatively inexperienced reading teachers and clinicians. It is regrettable that the accompanying tests with which the checklists are to be used do not offer a more adequate foundation.

For a review by Helen M. Robinson of the original edition, see 4:561; for reviews by Guy L. Bond and Miles A. Tinker, see 40:1533; for a review by Marion Monroe, see 38:1098.

[661]

Durrell-Sullivan Reading Capacity and Achievement Tests. Grades 2.5–4.5, 3–6; 1937–45; 5 scores: word meaning, paragraph meaning, total, spelling (optional), written recall (optional); 2 levels; 2 tests; 25¢ per battery manual ('45); postage extra; 50¢ per specimen set of either level, postpaid; Donald D. Durrell and Helen Blair Sullivan; World Book Co. *

a) PRIMARY TEST. Grades 2.5–4.5; Form A ('37); 2 tests published in 1 booklet; directions for administering ('39); $4.60 per 35 tests.
  1) *Reading Capacity Test.* (30–50) minutes.
  2) *Reading Achievement Test.* 30(40) minutes; optional tests, (15–20) minutes.

b) INTERMEDIATE TEST. Grades 3–6.
  1) *Reading Capacity Test.* Form A ('37); directions for administering ('37); $3 per 35 tests; 35(50) minutes.
  2) *Reading Achievement Test.* Forms A ('37), B ('44); directions for administering ('45); $3.50 per 35 tests; 30(40) minutes; optional tests, (15) minutes.

REFERENCES

1–4. See 4:562.
5. MILLER, VELMA J. *A Critical Analysis of Standardized Vocabulary Tests to Determine Those Most Valid for Use With the Macmillan Readers.* Master's thesis, Bowling Green State University (Bowling Green, Ohio), 1954.
6. BLIESMER, EMERY P. "A Comparison of Results Obtained With Various Types of Capacity Tests Used With Retarded Readers." *Yearb Nat Council Meas Used Ed* 12(pt 1):60–2 '55. *
7. BOND, GUY L., AND CLYMER, THEODORE W. "Interrelationship of the SRA Primary Mental Abilities, Other Mental Characteristics, and Reading Ability." *J Ed Res* 49:131–6 O '55. * (PA 30:7752)
8. BLIESMER, EMERY P. "A Comparison of Results of Various Capacity Tests Used With Retarded Readers." *El Sch J* 56:400–2 My '56. * (PA 31:5140)
9. OWEN, JASON C. *A Study of the Prognostic Value of Certain Measures of Intelligence and Listening Comprehension With a Selected Group of Elementary Pupils.* Doctor's thesis, University of Missouri (Columbia, Mo.), 1957. (DA 19:484)

JAMES MAXWELL, *Visiting Professor of Education, Teachers College, Columbia University, New York, New York.*

These tests are constructed on the proposition that reading disability can be detected by differences between scores on a test of reading achievement and a parallel test of equivalent difficulty and of similar content that requires no reading. Each test contains a subtest on word meaning and one on paragraph meaning. In the nonverbal, or reading capacity, test, the questions are answered by the selection of the appropriate picture.

The selection of the material, words and paragraphs, seems to be adequate for the purpose and suited to the abilities of the children for whom the tests are intended. Credit must be given for the avoidance of excessive use of nouns in the word list, and for the close correspondence between the verbal and nonverbal material; though the pictures seem rather small (1 inch square), the authors state this gives no difficulty. The test envelopes contain adequate apparatus for administration and the instructions for administering and scoring are detailed and clear.

The least satisfactory feature of the tests is the manual. Objective data and selling points tend to be confused. Reliability coefficients corrected for attenuation (Is this justified?) are given "for a representative sampling of cases." These are of the order of .85 and "should inspire confidence in the use of these tests." The reviewer feels .95 is more inspiring. The vital score is the difference between the two sets of tests, as it is on this that the validity hinges. The data given are rather vague. A correlation of .85 is given for "a population from which all children over age for their grade have been eliminated." This also "inspires confidence...." The lower part of the distribution of differences is given; but the nature of the total distribution of differences and the interpretation of cases whose achievement is higher than their capacity are sidestepped. The authors state that the "true" correlation is still a matter for further research. More extensive and precise data would more effectively inspire confidence in the tests than do the authors' beliefs.

The underlying concept of this test is an interesting one. The exact paralleling of the content and structure of the two tests, one verbal and the other nonverbal, is ingenious and logi-cal, but not necessarily psychologically valid. It is not clearly established that the abilities required to accomplish successfully the non-verbal test are those underlying reading achievement. And is this particular nonverbal test the most valid predictor available? The two component tests are themselves sufficiently well constructed to provide the basis for fuller investigation of the underlying thesis. Perhaps final judgment should be suspended till this thesis is more fully corroborated.

For a review by Helen M. Robinson, see 4:562; for reviews by William S. Gray and Marion Monroe of the original edition, see 38:1099 (1 excerpt).

[662]

*Gates Reading Diagnostic Tests. Grades 1–8; 1926–53; individual; Forms 1, 2 ('42); revised manual ('53); the author's *The Improvement of Reading, Third Edition* (see *3* below) is necessary for administration; no data on reliability and validity; 55¢ per test; 20¢ per record blank ('45); 10¢ per set of tachistoscopic cards; 45¢ per manual; $1.50 per complete specimen set; cash orders postpaid; [60–90] minutes; Arthur I. Gates; Bureau of Publications, Teachers College, Columbia University. *

REFERENCES

1–3. See 3:510.
4–5. See 4:563.

GEORGE D. SPACHE, *Professor of Education, and Head, Reading Laboratory and Clinic, University of Florida, Gainesville, Florida.*

This battery of tests is intended for individual diagnosis of reading difficulties. The tests themselves are of 1942 vintage. The manual bears a 1953 copyright date, but differs in no essential detail from earlier editions.

In general, the tests are simple enough for classroom teachers or inexperienced clinicians to give. Their interpretation is likewise simple and apparently obvious. Thus, ease of administration and interpretation contribute to the face validity of the battery. However, a number of the separate tests are of questionable validity. Moreover, the interpretations suggested by the author are misleading or even erroneous.

The tendency to a superficial interpretation of the child's performance is first found in the opening instructions in the manual. Here the author suggests that the grade score derived from each test may be rated "low" or "very low" when compared to some such criterion as actual grade placement, mental grade level, or average score on a group of the other tests. On page 29 of the manual, the author offers a table to facilitate this rating of test performance.

This tendency to ignore the actual reliability of the tests in the battery is present in the manual in two other instances. Despite published and unpublished data on the various tests, no reliability coefficients are offered. In addition, highly detailed tables of norms are offered for every test, giving the implication that each and every score is highly accurate, dependable, and discriminative. This attitude is in sharp contrast to current test construction practices of interpreting the significance of a difference between two scores only in terms of the accuracy of both scores and the degree of error of estimate present in both measures.

The first section of the battery is an oral reading test of seven paragraphs, the last three of which are highly artificial and stilted. They do not resemble any reading materials this reviewer has ever seen that are commonly used with children. Furthermore, this test is administered without any estimate of comprehension, thus rewarding the child who is skillful in word calling with an excessively high estimate of functional oral reading level. As a result of these limitations, it is probable that the oral reading test functions as a measure of ability to read (?) this esoteric material rather than as a test of general oral reading ability. It is also doubtful that the intensive analysis of reading errors on this test suggested by the author is realistically related to the child's true reading performance with ordinary materials.

The second test offered is called Oral Vocabulary. This is mislabeled since it measures auditory vocabulary, not the usable speaking vocabulary of the child. These vocabularies are not identical in breadth, depth, or fluency. Therefore, the test does not function as a general measure of the child's vocabulary but as an indication of his level of auditory comprehension of word meanings. It would be correctly interpreted as a measure of potential for development of the child's speaking vocabulary rather than as an actual test of this latter ability.

A third test measures the pupil's tendency to make reversals in a series of readily reversible words. It is based on the questionable assumption that this artificial situation is representative of or related to the child's usual reading error tendencies. Current theories of the etiology of reading disability decry the tendency to overemphasize the importance of any one type of reading error. Contrary to the author's suggestions, reversals have not been found to bear any consistent relationship to eye, hand, or cerebral dominance. They are most properly interpreted as an immaturity of the left-to-right orientation in reading found in severely retarded readers functioning on primary levels, regardless of age or neurological conditions.

Another section offers tests of phrase and word perception and word analysis. These may well function, as they are intended to, as measures of phrase reading, sight word vocabulary, and methods of word attack. An oral spelling test is also included. In the reviewer's opinion, a written spelling test would be more valuable in revealing word analysis patterns, knowledge of word structure, and the like, particularly if a careful analysis of written spelling errors were made.

The battery ends with a group of subtests measuring visual and auditory perception techniques. These tests will aid in the analysis of the primary child's phonic skills and knowledge —his ability to recognize, to hear, and to use the sound qualities of words, letters, and letter combinations.

In addition to the specific limitations noted above, there are other serious omissions in this battery of diagnostic reading tests. No attempt is made to measure reading comprehension, to contrast oral and silent reading skills, or to compare oral and silent reading ability with auditory comprehension. No effort is made to evaluate potential for reading growth by measuring comprehension of spoken language. The only suggestion in this connection is a reference to the Stanford-Binet intelligence test, which is of questionable value in reading retardation cases. Finally, the majority of the subtests are useful only with individuals reading at primary levels. In general, the battery is serviceable to those classroom teachers and clinicians who, in working with individuals reading on primary levels, are concerned only with the word calling, word recognition, and phonic skills of their pupils.

For a review by Worth J. Osburn, see 4:563; for related reviews, see 4:564; for a review by T. L. Torgerson, see 3:510.

[663]

Individual Reading Test. Ages 5.6–8.6; 1935–36; individual; 1 form ['35]; 3 tests: oral word reading, comprehension, speed; no data on reliability; 7s. 6d. per set of cards; 2s. 6d. per manual ['36]; postpaid within

Australia; administration time not reported; L. W. Allen; Australian Council for Educational Research. *

R. W. McCulloch, *Chief Psychologist and Superintendent of Special Schools, Tasmanian Education Department, Hobart, Tasmania, Australia.*

The 12-page manual includes description, directions, and norms. It is accompanied by a set of cards which comprise all the printed material required for using the test. The purchaser, however, must provide 10 common articles, ranging from a piece of rag to a cardboard box, for use with the printed material.

The norms were derived during 1935 from the performance of 1,000 South Australian children aged 5-6 to 9-11 who had been taught reading according to the curriculum then followed in South Australia. The handbook reproduces that curriculum; it differs only slightly from present-day reading curricula of the various education departments of Australia and New Zealand, though a review of the present-day validity would be timely.

The test has three sections: word reading, reading comprehension, and speed of reading. All sections are administered individually and the speed of reading test has a time limit of one minute. The word reading section is composed of 100 graded words (from "can" to "valetudinarian") arranged in five sizes of print. The reading comprehension section requires the child to carry out the instructions printed on 30 cards, most of which refer to the materials provided by the tester. The speed of reading section is based on a 500-word story entitled "Tom and His Dog."

The norms are given for chronological age and for period of school attendance. For education systems other than those in South Australia the latter is the set of most value.

Because of its brevity, ease of administration, and close relationship to school curricula, the test is the most useful of those available in Australia for those who wish to test only in the first three grades of the elementary school. However, for those whose testing extends over the whole of the elementary school, a test which covers all grade levels is more convenient. The *Schonell Reading Tests* and *Gates Reading Diagnostic Tests* are, therefore, to be preferred by them.

[664]
★McGuffey Diagnostic Reading Test. Grades 4-6; 1955; 5 scores: syllables, sound value recognition, vocabulary, appreciation, understanding; Form A; no data on reliability; $2.50 per 25 tests, postage extra; $1 per specimen set, postpaid; 81(110) minutes in 2 sessions; Ullin W. Leavell; Educational Test Bureau. *

[665]
★Primary Reading Profiles, [Revised Edition]. Grades 1, 2; 1953–57; 6 scores: reading aptitude, auditory association, word recognition, word attack, reading comprehension, total; 1 form ('57); 2 levels; manual ('57) for each level; $3.60 per 35 tests, postage extra; 40¢ per specimen set, postpaid; (95–100) minutes in 3 sessions; James B. Stroud and Albert N. Hieronymus; Houghton Mifflin Co. *

James R. Hobson, *Director of Child Placement, Brookline Public Schools, Brookline, Massachusetts.*

A rather unique feature of these tests is the built-in readiness or aptitude test which is Test 1 at each level. It is assumed that this test is a measure of readiness for the following year's work in reading; otherwise, it would seem somewhat futile to measure aptitude for reading at the close, rather than at the beginning— particularly in first grade.

On the front cover of each test booklet is an individual profile chart on which the pupil's score on each of the five tests and the composite score for Tests 3, 4, and 5 are to be plotted. Each of the levels was standardized on a widely scattered school population of over a thousand pupils, described by the authors as "nationwide."

Previous to the 1956 standardization, tryout administrations for item analysis purposes were given. In each case almost exactly one third of the original test items were discarded as being unsuitable. The items retained were answered correctly by from 25 per cent to 94 per cent of the tryout sample for Level One and by 20 per cent to 89 per cent for Level Two. Reliability coefficients calculated by both the Spearman-Brown and Kuder-Richardson formulas ranged from .86 to .98 for the composite score and for all subtests, with the exception of Test 1 at each level. These are .77 for Level One and .69 for Level Two.

Although about two and one half pages in the manual for each level are devoted to a discussion of various aspects of validity (content, construct, congruent, concurrent), the only actual evidences of validity produced are: (a) Fairly complete data on the level of difficulty and commonality of use of the words in the various subtests, according to such recognized criteria as the Gates, Krantz, Stone, and Thorndike-Lorge word lists; (*b*) Correlation coefficients between raw scores and both IQ and MA, as determined by administration of the *Revised Stanford-Binet Scale* (form not specified). These correlations, based on 130 first grade and 85 second grade pupils, are fairly normal for the first grade, reaching .53 for Test 1 raw score and MA, and .60 for composite raw score (Tests 3, 4, and 5) and MA. For the second grade the coefficients between the same variables were .49 and .48, respectively.

This reviewer does not see the utility of Test 1 as a sort of a built-in aptitude test. It is not stated that it indicates aptitude for reading the following year, which would seem to be its chief claim to usefulness. It lacks both the validity and the reliability to perform the function of picking out potential or actual cases of reading difficulty through the size of the discrepancy between aptitude and achievement scores. This, in the reviewer's opinion, can be done much better by taking stock of the discrepancy between reading achievement and mental age on a good individual intelligence test, together with observation of sensory abilities and development of other skills and concepts—numbers, for example. A separate aptitude or readiness test long enough to have greater reliability and to include other aspects of reading aptitude would serve a more useful purpose. Test 1 correlations with the *Gates Reading Readiness Tests* (.23 for Level One) and with the composite of Tests 3, 4, and 5 of its own battery (.40 and .43 for Levels One and Two, respectively) cast considerable doubt on its essential validity. It would certainly have very little value as a predictor of subsequent reading achievement.

The auditory association test at each level is cleverly designed and measures a most important primary reading skill too often neglected in standardized tests at these levels. Considerable ingenuity is also displayed in devising word attack tests, each item of which requires the child to complete the meaning of a short paragraph by choosing from pictorial or contextual clues a word which is within his oral and meaning vocabulary but which very probably is not yet within his sight recognition vocabulary.

The reliability data have little value. In the case of each level they are based upon a "representative sample" consisting of about a third of the cases in the tryout sample several years ago. The statement is made that "because only the best of the tryout items were selected for the final test, these coefficients are probably lower than they would have been had they been computed on the basis of an odd-even scoring of items on the tests taken by the standardization sample." This is a gratuitous assumption which is not necessarily so. Shortening the test by discarding about one third of the items would tend to reduce the size of the coefficients, other things being equal. On the other hand, if the items were arranged without reference to order of difficulty in the tryout sample and then were arranged in order of difficulty in the final test, such arrangement would tend to raise the coefficients as calculated by the Spearman-Brown formula.

In the opinion of this reviewer, Tests 2, 3, 4, and 5 of each level are good solid tests with essential content validity for the tasks they attempt to perform, as might be expected from such competent authors. The inclusion in each battery of a brief aptitude test of questionable validity, low reliability, and unclear purpose detracts from its essential value. With the exception of the standardization data, which are somewhat on the scanty side, the other technical data do not appear to have been derived in any planned, consistent manner but seem to have been somewhat improvised from data which were already available. The answer to the criticism of the standardization data would, of course, be to standardize on one's own school population.

VERNA L. VICKERY, *Associate Professor of Education, Mississippi State University, Starkville, Mississippi.*

This is a battery of five tests designed to measure a pupil's aptitude for reading and his reading progress. The authors suggest that the battery may be given whenever pupils have completed the appropriate readers described as being in the basal series; the percentile norms, however, are described as being based on the results of children completing the first and second grades, with no reference to the portion of the basal series completed or supplementary reading accomplished.

A distinctive feature of the battery is a listening comprehension test which purports to measure aptitude for reading. This subtest provides a carefully devised set of 32 items measuring the pupil's general information, reasoning ability, memory span, ability to draw conclusions, and ability to arrange events in correct sequence. An examination of the content of this subtest reveals that the authors are tapping an extremely difficult but very significant area for measurement in primary reading.

The chief value of this battery as compared with other reading tests is that reading aptitude and reading achievement are measured within the same test. In addition to the obvious administrative value of this technique, both the aptitude and achievement scores have been standardized on the same population, making for greater comparability of norms.

The technical information in the manual is presented with such clarity as to increase the classroom teacher's understanding and interpretation of test results. The item analysis data indicate that the items selected met the established criteria in regard to content, range of difficulty, and discriminative value. Reasonably adequate reliability and validation data are presented, except that no data are presented to show the relationships between achievement on these tests and on other reading tests.

The *Primary Reading Profiles* constitute a worthwhile contribution to the field of reading aptitude and achievement at the early primary levels. The format of the battery is quite good, and the material used and techniques recommended combine to provide tests which are at once interesting to children and useful to teachers. The provision of the profile makes for ease of interpretation. It should go without saying, of course, that the teacher who considers this battery for use in her own classroom should make a careful study of the content of each subtest to note its validity for her particular program of study.

[666]

*Reading Diagnostic Record for High School and College Students. High school and college; 1938-52; 1 form ('52); directions sheet ('52); 10 or more copies, 30¢ each; 35¢ per single copy; cash orders postpaid; Ruth Strang, Margaret M. Conant, Margaret G. McKim, and Mary Alice Mitchell; Bureau of Publications, Teachers College, Columbia University. *

MARVIN D. GLOCK, *Professor of Educational Psychology, Cornell University, Ithaca, New York.*

This is an individual diagnostic record folder designed for the recording of the various interests, attitudes, and experiences of a student which are related to his reading performance. The booklet is divided into 12 sections and

forms are provided for listing different kinds of data. Typical of these are provisions for biographical history, results of standardized tests, a summary of scholastic achievement, reading interests and attitudes, and information about work-study skills. One section is devoted to oral reading paragraphs for diagnosing specific reading difficulties. There is also space for summarizing data, stating, recommendations, indicating procedures used, and suggesting a follow-up program.

The folder provides a vehicle for the systematic gathering of pertinent information. Sufficient data are mandatory for diagnosis and remediation and the booklet becomes a continuous and convenient permanent record of important information. This information becomes more useful if the clinician uses the sheet of directions. The author presents helpful suggestions for diagnosis.

The inclusion of oral reading paragraphs in the booklet may be questioned, especially since standardized oral reading tests are available. However, their presence makes the results available as a part of the permanent record. Although no norms are given, this is really unimportant in terms of the use to which the paragraphs are put. Oral reading is helpful to determine the reader's deficiencies in such areas as word attack skills, phrasing, and expression. A good reader should make few if any errors.

The record is too lengthy for general use in high school and college. Work involved in recording so much information will probably preclude the busy teacher from using it with groups of students. This is not to say that any part of the record is unnecessary. If there is time for attention to individual students, the record should prove to be an invaluable aid.

DONALD E. P. SMITH, *Chief, Division of Reading Improvement Services, and Associate Professor of Education, University of Michigan, Ann Arbor, Michigan.*

This is a 21-page interview guide, the implied purpose of which is to facilitate the gathering of information relative to the reading problem of high school and college students. Spaces are provided for identification and family data, a summary of intelligence and school achievement test results (to be gathered, presumably, from school records), medical reports (four of the five headings concern vision), reading background and interests, and present reading status. The latter includes an oral reading test designed to reflect the kinds of errors the subject makes. No scoring key or norms are provided. Next a series of questions are asked to test comprehension of the passages read orally. Finally, space is provided for writing in recommendations, procedures used, and follow-up.

The booklet may be useful for training teachers to look for information on correlates of reading difficulty. The authors state that their method for data gathering is "clinical." The term "clinical," as used here, seems to mean an indirect approach to finding answers. For example, take this statement: "In various ways during the interview the counselor will indirectly learn the student's attitude toward reading. It cannot be obtained by asking, 'What is your attitude toward reading?'"

While this reviewer would agree that much of the information to be gathered is interesting, it seems to be largely irrelevant to the reading problem. If one knows that a boy's father is a laborer, that there are no books in his home, that his IQ score is 90, that he doesn't like reading (most poor readers don't and they'll tell you so when you ask them if they think it won't hurt your feelings), and that he has failed English and social studies over the past several years, what, then, does one know about the cause of his reading problems?

When this form was first published in 1938, it probably reflected diagnostic procedures of that day, at least procedures of a "clinically" oriented shop. Today, with the advent of knowledge about the role of cognition in reading, the importance of physical development, the variety of perceptual skills involved, and the interaction between personality structure and reading styles, the present form appears to be dated despite its revision in 1952.

For reviews by Robert Murray Bear and Carolyn M. Welch of the original edition, see 3:509; for a review by Henry D. Rinsland, see 40:1535 (3 excerpts).

[667]

★Roswell-Chall Diagnostic Reading Test of Word Analysis Skills. Grades 2–6; 1956–58; individual; Forms 1, 2 ('56); manual ('56); supplement ('58, reprint of 1 below); $2.58 per 35 tests; 50¢ per specimen set; postpaid; [5–10] minutes; Florence G. Roswell and Jeanne S. Chall; Essay Press. *

REFERENCE
1. CHALL, JEANNE S. "The Roswell-Chall Diagnostic Reading Test of Word Analysis Skills." *Reading Teacher* 11:179–83 F '58. *

BYRON H. VAN ROEKEL, *Associate Professor of Teacher Education, Michigan State University, East Lansing, Michigan.*

This test was developed to help teachers identify specific weaknesses of pupils having difficulty with word recognition. It is intended to supplement standardized silent and oral reading tests.

It was the intent of the authors to provide a simple, practical instrument for the classroom teacher and this they have done. The test is administered individually and requires about five minutes per pupil. It is designed primarily for children who are reading at approximately the second to sixth grade level; it is functional for children of any age or grade who have difficulty with word recognition. It is easy to administer and anyone qualified to teach reading in the elementary school should have no difficulty using this instrument.

The scope and content of the five subtests is open to question. The test purports to measure "basic skills" which "provide the teacher with an estimate of the pupil's strengths and weaknesses in word recognition." Herein lies the major weakness of this instrument. It measures knowledge of certain elements which are essential to word attack but it does not measure the ability to apply this knowledge.

Subtest 1 includes all of the consonants, except q and x, and 10 of the consonant blends. The pupil is asked to give the sound of each of the elements in this section. No rationale or evidence is cited to support the inclusion of certain blends in contrast to others which might have been included. It is unfortunate that some common blends such as *br, bl, cl, fr, gr,* and *gl* have been excluded. More adequate coverage of the blends could have been effected without materially influencing the time or complexity of administration.

Subtest 2 consists of three parts: (*a*) ten monosyllabic words with short vowel sounds, (*b*) two sentences composed of monosyllabic words, a majority of which contain the short vowel sound, and (*c*) the five vowels in isolation. The pupil is to read the words and sentences and say the long and short sounds of the vowels. It is highly conceivable that the words in the first two parts of this subtest would be in the sight vocabulary of pupils reading at low third grade level. Experience tells us that it is not unusual for poor readers to glibly give the long and short vowel sounds. Hence, this test is of little value in determining the ability to apply knowledge of vowel sounds in word attack.

The third subtest consists of five pairs of words such as pin and pine, cut and cute, and supposedly measures the ability to apply the rule of silent *e*. This appears to be as much a measure of sight vocabulary as it is a measure of the ability to apply the rule.

Subtest 4 deals with vowel combinations including both digraphs and diphthongs. Two of the words (*harm* and *cart* in Form 1 and *part* and *hard* in Form 2) represent the influence of the letter *r* on vowel sounds rather than vowel combinations. This section is subject to the same criticism as the third.

The fifth subtest, Syllabication, includes two compound words and six polysyllabic words. The usual rules of syllabication are applicable in the case of each word and the directions provide for diagnosis of errors in pronunciation.

The manual makes no reference to reliability or validity although such information has been published elsewhere (*1*). Reliability coefficients of the subtests, based on scores on equivalent forms, are as follows: Subtest 1, single consonants, .78, consonant combinations, .81; subtest 2, .99; subtest 3, .84; subtest 4, .93; and subtest 5, .86. The reliability of the total test is reported to be .98. These data are based on a limited sample of 52 pupils enrolled in a remedial reading service and ranging in grade placement from third through eleventh grade. Since reliability coefficients are a function of rank, one would naturally expect a poor eleventh grade reader to consistently rank above a poor third grade reader. Hence, it is difficult to say that the individual part scores are sufficiently reliable to identify, with confidence, a pupil's specific weaknesses in word recognition.

Three different populations were used to obtain validity coefficients: (*a*) two second grade classes averaging at grade 2.1 in overall reading ability, (*b*) two fifth grade classes averaging at grade 5.9 in overall reading ability, and (*c*) the 52 clinic cases previously mentioned, averaging at grade 4.3 in overall reading ability.

The total scores on the Roswell-Chall for each of the groups were correlated with appropriate levels of various standardized silent and oral reading tests. The validity coefficients for the various groups range from .64 for the clinic group to .92 for the second grade group when using standardized silent reading tests as criteria. Since various levels of the reading tests of the *Metropolitan Achievement Tests* were used for the clinic group and the *New York Test of Reading Growth* was used for the second grade group, it is difficult to pass judgment on the discriminative quality of the test. Apparently it is not as valid for the group for which it is intended as it is for children making normal progress in reading.

There are no norms for this test. Scoring is somewhat subjective and the results are qualitative. The manual states that "if a child misses more than half the items on any subtest, it may be assumed either that he has a special deficiency in this area, or has not received instruction and therefore needs systematic work."

The title of this test is a misnomer. In the main, it measures knowledge of certain phonetic elements rather than skills in word analysis. The classroom teacher will find this instrument helpful but incomplete. Although it does not reflect careful test construction, it will function as an informal inventory of certain elements essential to word recognition.

[668]

★SRA Achievement Series: Language Perception. Grades 2–4; 1954–57; title on test is *Are These The Same?*; 3 scores: auditory discrimination, visual discrimination, sight vocabulary; Form A ('55); examiner's manual, second edition ('57); technical supplement, second edition ('57); 40¢ per 20 tests; 50¢ per teacher's handbook ('55); 50¢ per administrator's manual ('56); $1 per technical supplement; $1 per scoring stencil; postage extra; (60) minutes; Louis P. Thorpe, D. Welty Lefever, and Robert A. Naslund; Science Research Associates. *

For reviews by Warren G. Findley and Worth R. Jones of the complete battery, see 21.

[669]

★Silent Reading Diagnostic Tests: The Developmental Reading Tests, Experimental Form. Grades 3 and over; 1955; 20 scores; 1 form; $4 per 20 tests, postage extra; 40¢ per specimen set, postpaid; 39(65) minutes; Guy L. Bond, Theodore Clymer, and Cyril J. Hoyt; Lyons & Carnahan. *

[670]

★Stanford Diagnostic Phonics Survey, Research Edition. High school and college; 1956–58; test of ability to relate printed sounds to spoken sounds; IBM; 1 form ('56); preliminary manual ('58); distribution restricted to research and experimental use; separate answer sheets must be used; $2.75 per 25 tests and 1 examiner's booklet ('56); $1.25 per 50 IBM answer sheets; $1 per manual and hand or machine scoring stencil; postage extra; $1 per specimen set, cash orders postpaid; (30–45) minutes; Grace M. Brown and Alice B. Cottrell; distributed by Consulting Psychologists Press, Inc. *

ORAL

[671]

★Gilmore Oral Reading Test. Grades 1–8; 1951–52; 3 scores: accuracy, comprehension, rate; individual; Forms A, B ('52); $1.70 per set of reading paragraphs ('51); $2.10 per 35 record blanks; 50¢ per manual ('52); postage extra; 50¢ per specimen set, postpaid; (15–20) minutes; John V. Gilmore; World Book Co. *

REFERENCE
1. GILMORE, JOHN V. *The Relationship Between Oral Reading Habits and Oral and Silent Reading Comprehension.* Doctor's thesis, Harvard University (Cambridge, Mass.), 1950.

LYDIA A. DUGGINS, *Associate Professor and Director of Reading Services, University of Bridgeport, Bridgeport, Connecticut.*

This is an instrument designed to measure three aspects of oral reading competency: pronunciation, comprehension, and rate of reading. A separate score is obtained for each of these. The two forms of the test are not exactly equal in difficulty, but tables of equivalent scores are provided for use in comparing initial and final scores.

The test is comprised of 10 paragraphs which form a continuous story about episodes in a family group. Each form is introduced with a picture of the characters, intended to aid the examiner in establishing rapport and in making the testing more like a normal reading activity. There are five comprehension questions on each paragraph, to be asked and answered orally following the reading of the paragraph. A record blank for each pupil provides for the recording and classification of errors as the reading proceeds, the time required for reading each paragraph, and the responses made to the comprehension questions.

According to the manual, three variables were considered in the gradation of the paragraphs: vocabulary, sentence structure, and interest. Vocabulary was regulated by an increase in the number of words per paragraph, the selection of words of appropriate and evenly increasing difficulty, and the controlled use of polysyllabic words. Sentence difficulty was judged by sentence length and per cent of complex sentences. An effort was made to include materials that were within the experiences of and would be of interest to pupils at

the various grade levels. The gradation appears to have been successfully accomplished.

The comprehension questions following each paragraph are of the recall type. The questions refer to information specifically given in the paragraph; no attempt is made to test for interpretation going beyond the paragraph. Increasing skill in comprehension is related to the increasing difficulty of materials rather than to variation in the type of question asked. This, the author assumes, "differentiates readers of varying degrees of comprehension skill." It also enables the teacher to score the responses to the questions with greater objectivity.

The types of errors to be noted on the record blank were arrived at as the result of a study of error frequency based on data obtained from an initial administration of the test to 446 pupils in grades 1 through 8 in a single Massachusetts community and through an analysis of published oral reading tests. Statistical evidence of the validity of the test was obtained from a comparison of the scores made by 24 fifth grade pupils of the same age on this test and on Gray's *Standardized Oral Reading Paragraphs* and the oral reading test from the *Durrell Analysis of Reading Difficulty.* Correlations ranging from .39 to .80 are reported, with the highest correlations for accuracy and the lowest for speed.

Since this test is designed to aid in a detailed analysis of an individual's oral reading ability, emphasis is put on methods of analyzing performance rather than on interpretative data for comparing individual performance with group performance. However, for those desiring such information, performance ratings for accuracy, comprehension, and rate are provided, as are grade equivalents and standard scores for accuracy and comprehension. These data are based on the results of a standardization program involving 1,620 pupils in five states.

One of the outstanding advantages of the *Gilmore Oral Reading Test* is that no special training is required to administer it satisfactorily. The manual contains specific and clear directions for administration and scoring. A basal level is established as the paragraph on which the pupil makes no more than two errors. A ceiling paragraph is established as that on which he makes 10 or more errors.

The reading paragraphs for both Forms A and B are included in the same spiral-bound booklet which is substantial in construction and can be used over and over. The examiner needs only to replace the supply of record blanks, which makes for economy in cost of administering. The record blank is especially well constructed, providing in addition to the items already mentioned, space for comment on test behavior, a summary checklist of difficulties, and space for entering silent reading test data. The provision for recording both oral and silent reading test data in one place facilitates the evaluation of the child's reading needs.

This test can be used, then, for the analysis of individual or group performance in accuracy, comprehension, and rate of oral reading, and for comparison of this performance with a national norm. It can be used also to provide information concerning the specific weaknesses in these three areas for purposes of more efficient small group instruction to meet common needs. The reviewer is of the opinion that the face validity of the test is so obvious that the scanty statistical evidence of validity should not be a deterrent to its use.

MAYNARD C. REYNOLDS, *Associate Professor of Educational Psychology, University of Minnesota, Minneapolis, Minnesota.*

In each of its two forms, the stimulus material of the *Gilmore Oral Reading Test* consists of 10 paragraphs which form a continuous story, and a picture which portrays the characters in the story. The paragraphs are arranged in order of difficulty, from easy to hard. Five recall type comprehension questions, to be asked upon the completion of the reading of each paragraph, are furnished by the author. The examiner makes a detailed record of a pupil's performance on a blank which permits the recording of errors according to eight categories of error type, the computing of "performance rating" for accuracy, comprehension, and rate of reading, and the summarizing of reading difficulties. Norms, in terms of grade equivalents, are provided for accuracy and comprehension.

The extensive manual includes information concerning the development and standardization of the test, details with respect to the vocabulary difficulty and grammatical construction of each of the paragraphs, suggestions for the interpretation of test results, and a selected bibliography of materials useful in planning the oral reading program. The standardization

population included 1,620 pupils from five states in grades 1 through 8. Analysis of the results of a fifth grade sample on the Gilmore test and similar tests by Gray and Durrell indicates that the accuracy scores on these several tests are quite comparable (correlations of .77, .80, and .73 are reported), but that correlations among comprehension and rate scores tend to be low. Alternate-forms correlations for groups of second, fifth, and seventh grade pupils indicate high reliability for the accuracy scores (.89, .85, and .84), and lower reliability for comprehension (.68, .67, and .52) and rate (.95, .72, and .59), particularly for older pupils. Kuder-Richardson coefficients are approximately the same for accuracy (.88, .86, and .89) and somewhat higher for comprehension (.82, .78, and .78).

Teachers and reading diagnosticians will probably prefer this test over most other tests of similar type. The proper use of the test will, of course, depend on the experience and training of the examiner, but as compared with most other oral reading tests, this one can be administered and scored in quite objective fashion.

[672]

★Leavell Analytical Oral Reading Test. Grades 1–10; 1952–53; individual; Forms A, B ('52); manual ('53); no data on reliability; $1.25 per 25 reading booklets, postage extra; 50¢ specimen set, postpaid; administration time not reported; [Ullin W. Leavell]; Educational Test Bureau. *

LYDIA A. DUGGINS, *Associate Professor and Director of Reading Services, University of Bridgeport, Bridgeport, Connecticut.*

The *Leavell Analytical Oral Reading Test* is an individual test designed to yield an oral reading placement that is comparable to that yielded by a silent reading test. It gives, in addition, information regarding the type of errors the child makes in word perception. Provision is made for recording rate of reading and comprehension. The test does not yield separate scores in these three factors, but rather a composite score in which each of these factors is weighted.

The test materials include a reading section and a record section for each of the two forms. The reading section is reusable. Directions for administering and scoring the test are presented in a manual and made clear by examples at each step.

The material of the reading section consists of a series of paragraphs of increasing difficulty built around the history of a horse (Form A) and a dog (Form B). These should have high enough interest value to the child to encourage his best performance on the test. The range of the test (grades 1–10) should increase its usefulness in the evaluation of gifted readers in the primary and elementary grades where the group tests administered often do not measure the superior child's skills.

One of the desirable features of the test is the organization of the record section. Specific directions for recording errors in word perception are given on the front of the individual record, making it possible for a less skilled examiner to refer to them readily. The comprehension section gives acceptable answers to the comprehension questions, making for greater objectivity in scoring these responses. Space is provided at the end of each paragraph for recording reading time, errors in word perception, and correct answers to comprehension questions. A summation of scores is presented for time, errors, comprehension, and total test.

A less desirable feature is the ambiguity of the section of the manual devoted to the standardization of the test and the scantiness of the statistical data given. So far as this reviewer can determine, a group of 25 children, aged 8 to 16, comprised a combined standardization and norms group. The standardization procedure involved individual testing with the Leavell test and an uncertain combination of oral and silent reading tests, and a comparison of the mean scores on the various tests. The publishers base their claims for comparability of forms, comparability of the Leavell test to the silent reading tests, and significance of differences of scores from grade to grade on these mean scores, and present 100-step grade score equivalents! There is no evidence of the reliability of the test for individual children.

It is rather difficult to imagine that the *Leavell Analytical Oral Reading Test* would justify the necessary time of administration by an inexperienced teacher who could secure comparable scores on a silent reading test in much less time. The major value of this test should lie in the observation and analysis of a child's difficulties, and little attention, other than the careful and convenient directions for recording such difficulties, is given to this matter, either in the manual or on the record form. The child's final score represents a composite of achievements and difficulties rather than an analysis of them. However, in the hands of a skilled observer who understands the significance of the types of errors made by a child, the comparable forms, interesting reading content, and ease and objectivity of administration would make this test a useful supplement to group tests for individual diagnosis and for research purposes. It does not have the subjectivity of scoring of the usual oral reading test; on the other hand, neither does it have the comprehensiveness of diagnostic information such tests are expected to yield.

MAYNARD C. REYNOLDS, *Associate Professor of Educational Psychology, University of Minnesota, Minneapolis, Minnesota.*

The test consists of nine brief paragraphs which are to be read orally by the child. The paragraphs, organized to make a continuous story, range in difficulty from very simple (beginning readers) to difficult (high school students). Following the reading of each paragraph, the child is asked a set of comprehension questions. The examiner must record reading errors, reading time, and responses to the comprehension questions. Each paragraph is assigned three subscores, the sum of which gives a paragraph score. The total score is then converted into a grade score. There are no norms for part scores. Very little information is given regarding the standardization.

Many teachers and reading diagnosticians like to use a brief oral reading test as part of their diagnostic procedure. Others prefer to use selections from a series of graded readers. The consistent use of a simple oral reading test like the *Leavell Analytical Oral Reading Test,* even though the test may be extremely limited, does allow for greater objectivity of analysis than does the simple procedure of "reading from a book." If such a test is used, however, it should be realized that the evaluation of performance is still highly subjective.

A great many weaknesses in the Leavell test can be cited, most of them reflecting gaps in the manual. For example: No clear statement of the difficulty of the paragraphs is given. There are no data on the reliability of individual scores. The analysis and interpretation of errors and of speed and comprehension scores is left entirely to the examiner. The norms provided are little better than none at all. It is reported that the mean grade scores for 25 children ages 8 to 16 on the two forms of the test were closely comparable and that these mean scores were nearer the mean grade score of an unknown mixture of scores on two silent reading tests for the same population than was the mean score on the Gray oral reading test. Unfortunately, no information is given concerning the comparability of scores earned by *individuals* on the various tests.

We must hope that further information will be incorporated in the manual. Until this is done, those who use the Leavell test will need to do so in highly informal, subjective ways.

[673]

Oral Diagnostic Test of Word-Analysis Skills, Primary: Dominion Tests. Grades 1–2; 1947; individual; no data on reliability; no norms; 1 form; $1 per 25 record booklets; 15¢ per set of word slide cards and sleeve; 25¢ per manual; 45¢ per specimen set; postage extra; [20–40] minutes; Department of Educational Research, Ontario College of Education, University of Toronto; distributed by Guidance Centre. *

S. A. RAYNER, *Assistant Registrar, University of Queensland, Brisbane, Australia.*

As Smith pointed out in *The Fourth Mental Measurements Yearbook,* this instrument could best be regarded as an informal checking device worthy of commendation as a pioneer effort. Now that the test has been available for more than a decade, it must be asked whether it has fulfilled its original purpose and what further data on it has been collected.

There is no evidence to show that any development has occurred since 1947. The original manual has not been modified in any way; it does not yet provide norms; and it lacks evidence on reliability and validity. If the criteria suggested by the A.E.R.A.'s *Technical Recommendations for Achievement Tests* were used to evaluate this test, it would not rate highly.

It is not readily apparent from either the manual or the test that this is a diagnostic instrument which will enable the relatively inexperienced teacher to locate the specific difficulties of a particular pupil. The lack of any norms is a major weakness. If the test is used with a child in grade 2, a considerable number of mistakes can apparently be expected; but, without norms, the tester cannot tell whether reading development is normal for a child of this age, grade, and mental ability or whether there is either a specific or a general reading disability.

A second major weakness is that generalizations based on the errors in relatively few items

of the one type will almost certainly be highly unreliable. Since children will answer known words correctly without any formal analysis, the number of words tackled as an exercise in word analysis will be far smaller than the 100 items ostensibly in the test. In addition, children in grade 2 may not make any serious effort at analysis of the longer and more difficult words. It is almost certain that this test attempts to cover too wide a range of material in too few items to be a reliable diagnostic instrument.

The recommended system of coding errors and of analysing the results appears cumbersome and suggestions for remedial work must be found in a list of reference books published between 1935 and 1940.

This reviewer is of the opinion that the following weaknesses make the *Oral Diagnostic Test of Word-Analysis Skills* unsuitable for classroom use by the teacher: (*a*) lack of norms which makes interpretation difficult; (*b*) a cumbersome system of classifying errors; (*c*) lack of modern suggestions for remedial work; and (*d*) the certainty that there will be relatively few discriminating items for any one normal grade group and hence that the reliability for diagnostic purposes will often be low.

However, if any author should be interested in developing a new test of word analysis skills, he might do worse than to use this test as a starting point.

For a review by Nila Banton Smith, see 4:565.

[674]

★**Oral Word Reading Test.** Ages 7–11; 1952; individual; 1 form ['52]; 4s. per set of 1 test, 50 record blanks, and manual ['52]; 2s. 6d. per 50 record blanks; postage extra; specimen set not available; administration time not reported; A. E. Fieldhouse; New Zealand Council for Educational Research; distributed by Educational Books. *

S. A. RAYNER, *Assistant Registrar, University of Queensland, Brisbane, Australia.*

An oral word recognition test is so generally recognized as being among the most valuable means of estimating the language development of children in their first or second year at school that the construction of such a test to suit a particular culture (such as that of New Zealand) is a valuable service to the educational system. However, since it is highly probable that the English speaking children of New Zealand (for whom this test is specifically designed) may not differ greatly in vocabulary from those of Australia or England, consideration should be given to whether the *Oral Word Reading Test* is superior to the best overseas tests.

None of the 50 words chosen for the test is peculiar to New Zealand; in particular, there are none of the Maori words so widely used in that country. Neither the content nor the format of the test gives any obvious clue to the country of origin. Like other word reading tests, the words are arranged in ascending order of difficulty; the size of type becomes smaller as the words become more difficult. Each child's responses are checked on a separate record form.

The 16-page manual contains directions for administration and scoring and also provides norms. These are based on a total of 5,000 children, made up of 200 boys and a similar number of girls from each half-year age group from 6 to 11 years. Norms are provided for each group. Beyond these age ranges there are norms for bright younger children and dull older children. The table of norms suggests that the test is more steeply graded in difficulty than are similar tests from England.

Few details about the construction and standardization of the test are given in the manual. A brief technical appendix on the choice of words and the selection of children for the standardization sample would have added to its value. The stability reliability, based on a sample of 150 children aged 8-6 to 8-11 retested at an interval of one week, was found to be .98; this can be regarded as remarkably high for a test of this length. However, since the test would commonly be used with children a year younger than this, data on the reliability of the test with 7-year-old children should also be obtained.

No specific information is provided on validity. At least two methods are open to the author: test scores could be compared with an external criterion such as teacher's ratings; or the scores could be compared with those on a similar test designed by another person.

The gradient of difficulty of the *Oral Word Reading Test* for Queensland children has been tested by a method devised by Keats. He found that many of the words were rarely used by 9-year-old children in Queensland and that the easiest words on the list were probably at the

7-year-old level. This suggests that the test is more difficult than the best known British tests.

This reviewer is not able to comment on the suitability of the *Oral Word Reading Test* for New Zealand schools. However, the evidence on the gradient of difficulty of the items suggests that the Australian tester should continue to use the Hull or the Schonell test in preference to the New Zealand test.

D. K. WHEELER, *Senior Lecturer in Education, University of Western Australia, Nedlands, Australia.*

This word recognition test consists of 50 words arranged in approximate order of difficulty on a card which the child is required to read to the tester.

The author points out the difficulties of satisfactory discrimination at the highest and lowest levels with a 50-word test and says that it discriminates reasonably well at ages 7 to 11 years but gives a relatively reliable indication only of high attainment at age 6 and of low attainment at age 11. Reliability is given as .98 for test-retest of 150 children aged 8-6 to 8-11. In view of the remarks about lack of consistency at the ends of the distribution in this middle age range, reliability figures for other ages would be welcomed. The manual states that the N.Z.C.E.R. hopes to collect further information to check the norms, which should, meanwhile, be considered as tentative. This statement was made nearly seven years ago but no further information has been received.

For each half-year group from 6 to 11 years inclusive, score ranges are given for each tenth (called "attainment groups" with 10 designating the highest tenth) of the normative population. Norms are given for boys and girls separately on the ground that results suggest consistent sex differences, but there are also combined norms. It might be helpful to indicate to the classroom teacher where sex norms might be used and where composite norms would be appropriate.

The manual gives good and detailed general and particular instructions about giving the test and recording the results on the record form. Furthermore, it is cautious about the interpretation of scores, warning that too much must not be read into a single score.

This test was designed to determine the level of the child's attainment in word recognition. What it does with high reliability is to provide a means of comparing his attainment in recognizing these particular 50 words with that of other children throughout the age range of the test. Whether it does determine the level of attainment in word recognition generally is dependent on the extent to which these words are a representative sample of words which the child is likely to have to recognize. No information is given as to how the original 290 words were selected, on what criteria were used in reducing them to 90, and on how these 90 were in turn reduced to 50. As a test user, the reviewer would like to know for this, as for all such tests, the criteria for selection of words.

For an experienced reading teacher well versed in the literature of his subject, this could be a useful test of word recognition and attack. Being standardized (for New Zealand children whose mother tongue is English), it will serve, with other tests, for grouping for reading instruction and determining disability. Teachers using it would do well to heed the instructions about interpretation.

READINESS

[675]

*American School Reading Readiness Test. First grade entrants; 1941–55; 9 scores: vocabulary, discrimination of letter forms, discrimination of letter combinations, word selection, word matching, discrimination of geometric forms, following directions, memory of geometric forms, total; Form D ('55, identical with Form A except for slight changes in some drawings) ; manual ('55, identical with manual copyrighted in 1941 except for minor changes) ; $2.75 per 25 tests; 35¢ per specimen set; postpaid; (45) minutes; Willis E. Pratt, Robert V. Young, and Carroll A. Whitmer; Public School Publishing Co. *

REFERENCES

1. Pratt, Willis E. *The Construction of a Group Test of Reading Readiness.* Doctor's thesis, University of Pittsburgh (Pittsburgh, Pa.), 1940.
2. Pratt, Willis E. "A Study of the Differences in the Prediction of Reading Success of Kindergarten and Non-Kindergarten Children." *J Ed Res* 42:525-33 Mr '49. * (*PA* 23: 5753)
3. Delancy, Elmer O. *A Study of Three Psychological Tests as Related to Reading Achievement in Grade One American School Reading Readiness Test, Form A; SRA Primary Mental Abilities, Primary Form; Otis Quick-Scoring Mental Ability Tests, Alpha Test: Form A.* Doctor's thesis, Pennsylvania State University (University Park, Pa.), 1954.

Joan Bollenbacher, *Supervisor of Appraisal Services, Cincinnati Public Schools, Cincinnati, Ohio.*

This test contains 60 items distributed among eight subtests, covering visual discrimination, vocabulary, ability to copy forms from memory, and ability to follow directions. Pupils react favorably toward this test. It can be ad-

ministered conveniently to 10 pupils at a time, and possibly up to 15 if the group is capable. No time limits have been assigned, but the entire test can be given easily within an hour, including time for a 15-minute recess.

The illustrations in the test generally are clear, but minor criticisms can be made of several of the subtests. The varying sizes and shapes of the blocks containing letter combinations and words contribute to a somewhat confusing format on two of the pages. The geometric forms also could be larger.

The test for following directions contains 12 blocks, each with identical pictures of a boy, a girl, a ball, a book, and an airplane. Perhaps the authors had good reason for using the same pictures with varying directions for each item ; nevertheless, this test requires special alertness on the part of the examiner to be sure the pupil does not lose his place or does not mark twice in the same block.

The necessity for a child to understand a different set of instructions for each of the eight subtests poses a question as to whether or not the test, with a subtest specifically devoted to ability to follow directions, may be overemphasizing this purpose. Directions could, perhaps, have been simplified to some extent had similar subtests, such as Discrimination of Letter Combinations and Recognition of Words been combined, or had they at least followed one another.

The test manual, in addition to giving the customary directions for administering and scoring, provides some background information on the concept of reading readiness, a description of the procedures used in constructing the test, data on reliability and validity, and norms for interpreting scores. The manual has copyright dates of 1941 and 1945. Since a review of this test in *The Third Mental Measurements Yearbook* refers to the same normative data, apparently no further reliability and validity studies have been made.

Reliability, determined by the odd-even method, is reported as .95. Because of the great variability in performance of young children, information concerning test-retest reliability should also be provided.

Predictive validity data are based on testing 196 kindergarten and nonkindergarten pupils, all of about the same mental age, for reading readiness and intelligence, and testing six months later for reading achievement. A validity coefficient of .53 was found for both kindergarten and nonkindergarten homogeneous groups. By formula, a validity coefficient of .77 was estimated for a heterogeneous kindergarten group and one of .68 for the nonkindergarten heterogeneous group.

On the basis of the validity data, weights were computed for the subtests, and separate tables for kindergarten and nonkindergarten groups provided for converting raw scores into weighted scores. The negative weights which resulted for several of the tests are mentioned in a footnote. A statistical technique, no matter how defensible, in which higher raw scores receive lower predicted reading grades needs more explanation than a mere footnote to satisfy most teachers. It should be noted also that these data are based on test results for 196 pupils. Further validity studies would be appropriate to verify these findings.

Intelligence tests for the normative groups are mentioned, but the data are not reported in the manual. The reader is referred to an unpublished dissertation, a reference which may not be too accessible.

In view of the increasing size of first grade classes, teachers need a reading readiness test which is valid, reliable, and not too time consuming to administer. In spite of some shortcomings, the *American School Reading Readiness Test* might meet this need, especially if additional validity data were gathered. It is regrettable that further validity studies were not made in the period from 1941 to 1955.

HELEN M. ROBINSON, *Associate Professor of Education, The University of Chicago, Chicago, Illinois.*

This test is intended for use at the beginning of the first grade of school before reading instruction has started. The purpose of the test is to predict success in learning to read, and by implication, to locate difficulties which may impede early progress.

The test is composed of eight parts designed to estimate vocabulary development, visual discrimination, ability to follow directions, and skill in copying forms from memory. The content is similar to that of most other tests of reading readiness, except that auditory discrimination and information are not included. However, only 6 to 10 items are used in each subtest, with a total of 60 items. Thus the number of items is too small to provide reliable subtests. This may account for the fact that the manual makes no suggestions for readiness instruction based on weaknesses in areas measured by the subtests.

Form D is essentially the same as Form A, published in 1941. The booklet for form D is somewhat larger and the pictures are clearer; a few substitutions have been made so that all pictures will be of objects and scenes familiar to children today. Slight rearrangements which have been made in the format of some of the tests should make them easier for young children to use. The manual makes no statement concerning the changes or the adequacy of the old norms for the new form.

The first form of the test was validated by comparing scores on the test with reading attainment on the *Gates Primary Reading Tests* administered six months after the readiness test. The manual describes the original sample to which the readiness test was given as including 1,091 pupils in districts "ranging in size from small rural school districts to large urban schools." No further description is given to determine how representative this sample was of the general population. The reading tests were administered to only 196 pupils from 12 rooms in three "typical school districts" in the original sample. Both the size of the validation sample and the lack of information concerning its distribution are limitations which create many doubts concerning the validity of the test and of the norms supplied. Furthermore, the group of 196 appears to have been divided again into pupils who had had kindergarten experience, and those who had had none. The correlation coefficients between each subtest and the criterion test for the kindergarten group ranged from .22 to .43, and from .17 to .46 for the nonkindergarten group.

This reading readiness test is unique in that the total score is not just a sum of the parts. Instead, each subtest has been weighted by the multiple correlation technique. This method of using weighted scores often yields maximal prediction, providing that the sample is sufficiently large. In this instance, there is considerable doubt about the sample size.

A second unique feature of the test is that the norms "predict" actual reading achievement from grades 1.2 to 3.2 plus. While the manual cautions against prediction "with *absolute* accuracy," the norms are given in such a way as to imply such accuracy. Other tests, such as the *Metropolitan Readiness Tests* or Monroe's *Reading Aptitude Tests,* interpret the scores as high, average, and low, or select a cutoff point below which pupils are not likely to learn to read. The gross interpretations of the last two tests seem to be much more realistic. However, a multiple correlation of .53 is reported for homogeneous groups, which represents validity nearly as high as that reported by the other tests using the more flexible interpretations.

A coefficient of reliability of .91 is reported by correlating odd with even items. This figure is higher than those reported by most reading readiness tests.

The *American School Reading Readiness Test* appears to be worth further study because it may be a better predictor than those tests more frequently used in schools. At present, however, school personnel should choose reading readiness tests with more dependable norms, based on samples with wider distributions. Furthermore, teachers should be able to determine specific as well as general weaknesses in order to provide differentiated reading readiness experiences and instruction.

For reviews by David H. Russell and Paul A. Witty, see 3:513.

[676]

*Group Test of Reading Readiness: The Dominion Tests. Grades kgn, kgn–1 ; 1949–55 ; 2 editions ; postage extra ; Department of Educational Research, Ontario College of Education, University of Toronto ; distributed by Guidance Centre. *
a) [LONG FORM.] Grades kgn–1 ; 1949–51 ; 6 scores : discrimination of objects-symbols-words, listening-remembering-observing, familiarity with word forms, memory for word forms, motor coordination, total ; Forms A, B ('49) ; mimeographed manual ('51) ; profile ('51) ; $1.70 per 25 tests ; 25¢ per set of 10 flash cards of either form ; 70¢ per specimen set including both forms, flash cards, and manual ; (30–50) minutes in 2 sessions.
b) [SHORT FORM.] Grade kgn ; 1954–55 ; 2 editions ; $1.10 per 25 tests ; 25¢ per specimen set of either edition including all forms and manual.
1) *Subtest Type.* Forms A, B, C ('54) ; manual ('54) ; norms ('54) ; 11(19) minutes.
2) *Omnibus Type.* Forms A, B ('54) ; manual ('55) ; norms ('54) ; 12(17) minutes.

N. DALE BRYANT, *Associate Professor of Psychology, University of Houston, Houston, Texas.*

The *Group Test of Reading Readiness* is a name given to three separate tests of the Dominion Tests series. Each of the three is designed to accomplish the same purpose : to predict at the end of kindergarten or at the beginning of the first grade the reading performance each student will achieve by the completion of the first grade.

The first subtest in the Long Form is designed to measure the ability to discriminate objects, symbols, and words. Five letters, objects, symbols, or words are presented, and the child marks an "X" through the one that is different. Subtest 2 is designed to measure ability to listen, remember, and observe well. Each item consists of four pictures from which the child must select and put an "X" on the picture that fits a story told by the test administrator. The third subtest is designed to measure the ability to discriminate between words and familiarity with word forms. In this subtest four words are presented, and the child draws a ring around the two words that are alike. Subtest 4 is planned to measure the ability to observe and remember word forms and to discriminate these forms from memory. Each of these items consists of a picture and six words, one of which is the name of the object in the picture. The examiner holds up a card with the correct word on it. The child is asked to remember the word and, when the card is no longer visible, to draw a ring around the correct word. This subtest gives an advantage to a child with some word familiarity. The final subtest is designed to measure motor coordination and the ability to observe and reproduce details of simple drawings. Each item consists of a simple figure or design. The child is asked to copy it.

The Short Form—Omnibus Type yields a single score obtained from 16 items similar to those in the first and third subtests of the Long Form. Each item consists of four to five symbols or random combinations of letters. The child marks an "X" through the two or three that are alike.

The Short Form—Subtest Type contains items of the same type as those in the omnibus test, but the items are grouped into two homogeneous subtests of eight items each. Separate directions are provided for each subtest, and two subtest scores are obtained.

Scoring of the Long Form is easy except for the fifth subtest which requires judgment of how adequately the child reproduces a drawing. The manual gives specific and rather comprehensive directions, including examples of correct and incorrect reproduction. The short forms are administered item by item, a method which provides closer control over children in their following directions. The type of item is easier to administer and score than items in some sections on the Long Form. Similar items on the Long Form had the highest subtest correlation with the total score.

The reported alternate-forms reliabilities of the Long Form subtest scores suggest that the subtest scores would be more suitable for making group comparisons than for making decisions about specific individuals. The intercorrelations between the subtests are roughly proportional to their reliabilities, and all subtests seem to be reflecting much the same thing. The high degree of internal consistency suggests that when the total score is used alone, there is little loss in information as compared with the use of the subscores. Of course, extreme deficiencies on any subtest should be noted, as such differences might represent misunderstood directions or some actual deficiency. In addition to providing subtest scores, the Long Form is rich in opportunity for clinical interpretation. While over the entire group, subtest scores and clinical interpretation may add little to the prediction achieved by the total score, extreme cases might provide valuable insights and suggestions for remedial work. Similarly, subtest scores averaged for an entire class may provide useful guides to the teacher.

For the Short Form, the manual reports alternate-forms reliabilities of .63 for Omnibus Type and .77 for Subtest Type. The higher reliability of the latter test is borne out in the higher correlations of this test with the Long Form. It seems likely that the higher reliability is due, at least in part, to the fact that the two types of items are separated and separate directions are given with each type. In addition, there are twice as many examples as there are in the Omnibus Type, and two extra minutes are used for administration. Subtest reliabilities for the Subtest Type range from .57 to .80 for Test 1 and from .57 to .72 for Test 2. Once again, equivalence and reliability data warrant the use of the subtest scores for group work, but use of them to make decisions about individuals unsupported by other evidence should be avoided. The total score for the Subtest Type might, however, justifiably be used with individuals. The use of two forms should be

considered if higher reliability for individual work is desired.

A correlation of about .50 is reported between the Long Form total score (test administered prior to first grade training) and a measure of reading achievement at the end of the first grade training. In view of the lapse of time, the effect of variation in instruction, and the lack of perfect reliability, this is a substantial validity. However, it does not account for most of the criterion variance.

The manual repeatedly recommends that the test be used only in conjunction with an intelligence test. However, no correlation is reported between the readiness test and an intelligence test, nor are multiple correlations for validity coefficients given. It is quite possible that the test measures much the same thing as an intelligence test, and the use of both this readiness test and an intelligence test may be no better than using one instrument alone. In the various item analyses that have been done on this test, selection of items which show high correlation with the criterion but low correlation with the intelligence test (if such items exist) would have insured the development of a test that fits the stated purpose, "to measure certain factors of reading readiness which are not completely covered by an intelligence test."

No direct validities are reported for the short forms. However, since correlations with the Long Form (.65 to .70 for the Omnibus Type and .74 to .77 for total score on the Subtest Type) are close to the estimated reliability, most of the validity reported for the Long Form is probably retained by the shorter tests.

In conclusion, these tests are useful, moderately valid measures of reading readiness. The Subtest Type of the Short Form appears well suited for use as a quick screening device in conjunction with other data. The major handicap in using and evaluating the tests is the absence of information about how they relate to intelligence measures and other variables used in predicting readiness.

[677]

*The Harrison-Stroud Reading Readiness Profiles. Grades kgn–1; 1949–56; individual in part; 7 scores: using symbols, making visual discriminations (2 parts), using the context, making auditory discriminations, using context and auditory clues, giving the names of letters; 1 form ('56); 6 tests in 4 booklets; manual ('56); no data on reliability; $3.75 per 35 tests, postage extra; 80¢ per specimen set, postpaid; (80–90) minutes in 3 sessions; M. Lucile Harrison and James B. Stroud; Houghton Mifflin Co. *

REFERENCES

1. Mosbo, Alvin O. *A Study of the Harrison-Stroud Reading Readiness Tests in Relation to Achievement in First Grade Reading, and of Pupil Growth in Specific Readiness Skills in the Public Schools of Davenport, Iowa.* Doctor's field study, Colorado State College of Education (Greeley, Colo.), 1953.
2. Spaulding, Geraldine. "The Relation Between Performance of Independent School Pupils on the Harrison-Stroud Reading Readiness Tests and Reading Achievement a Year Later." *Ed Rec B* 67:73-6 F '56. * (PA 31:3812)

S. S. Dunn, *Officer-in-Charge, Test Division, Australian Council for Educational Research, Melbourne, Australia.*

The immediate impression gained by looking at the tests is excellent. The use of coloured boxes and the spacious layout of the questions is likely to attract the child's interest. The general directions to the tester show a good appreciation of the steps necessary to obtain a valid score for an individual, and the specific directions are precise and should cause no difficulties. The provision of scoring stencils independent of the manual would probably speed up marking, but the present method may have the advantage of forcing the teacher to a more detailed study of each individual's performance.

A detailed study of the manual, however, leaves the impression that the authors are more at home with children than with measurement theory. At no place in the manual is there any evidence of the reliability of the tests or of their intercorrelations, yet this evidence is crucial if one is going to try to interpret differences between scores on individual tests as the authors do. In particular, the authors encourage users to give meaning to differences in scores on Test 2a and Test 2b without any indication of the size of difference needed for significance. In practice, the majority of differences would almost certainly be due to "error" in the tests. The interpretation given to the illustrative profile on page 6 of the manual is certainly using differences which are probably chance fluctuations.

Also, when one is making use of a profile approach, the matter of norms is important. In its first edition, this test appeared with norms based on 221 pupils in one middle western city in the United States. The number has been increased to 1,400 pupils—32 communities in 28 states using at least 5 different reading programmes. Does the reading programme have any effect on the norms? We are not told. The desirability of an individual education authority developing its own norms is not mentioned. A local expectancy table would be even better. The discussion about validity is not helpful.

Evidence of high internal consistency discrimination indexes is presented, but this only points to the likelihood of high reliability. One is asked to take on faith the content validity of the test. One would like some evidence that tests labeled Using Symbols, Using the Context, Making Auditory Discriminations, etc. are in fact measuring these abilities as they relate to reading readiness and that they are not unduly influenced by such a factor as ability to follow directions and to understand what the tester wants.

The method given of computing mental age is appropriate only for tests such as the Binet, using an age scale method of norming. For the WISC and most group tests it would be incorrect. And why compute MA at age of entry to the grade and not at the time the readiness test is taken? Presumably it is then that the decision about classifying the children is going to take place. Overseas experience (Scotland, New Zealand, Australia) should lead reading experts to question the validity of the statement that a mental age of 6-4 to 6-6 is necessary for successfully learning to read.

In the section on interpretation of test results no reference is made to the fact that the result on Test 6, Giving the Names of Letters, depends almost entirely on specific teaching whether by teacher or parent and that, in this regard, the test differs from the other five tests. A low score on this test would seem relatively unimportant if the other five scores are high. A high score on the other hand is unlikely without satisfactory scores on the other tests. The result on this test could well be treated as additional information of value in the same way that mental age is.

In practice, then, the test may be found to be useful, but the authors should endeavour to improve the manual by providing evidence on reliability and validity, and they should use this information to help users properly interpret the test profile.

For a review by William S. Gray of an earlier edition, see 4:568.

[678]

Lee-Clark Reading Readiness Test, 1951 Revision. Grades kgn-1; 1931-51; 4 scores: letter symbols, concepts, word symbols, total; 1 form ('51, identical to test copyrighted in 1943); manual ('51); $3.15 per 35 tests, postage extra; 25¢ per specimen set, postpaid; (20) minutes; J. Murray Lee and Willis W. Clark; California Test Bureau. *

JAMES R. HOBSON, *Director of Child Placement, Brookline Public Schools, Brookline, Massachusetts.*

The 1931 edition of this test was the first of the better known tests in the field, and the 1943 and 1951 revisions, with two subtests and a diagnostic profile added, have preserved its usefulness and widespread acceptance.

The general purpose of the test is to predict a child's ability to learn to read, with concomitant dividends in the form of data for initial intraclass grouping, some indication of how long formal reading instruction should be deferred if need be, and a rough analysis of the general readiness area in which a child may be deficient. These purposes are accomplished through four subtests measuring recognition of likenesses; discrimination of differences; experiential background, including understanding vocabulary; and ability to discriminate among similar but different letter and word forms. That these purposes are accomplished with as high a degree of validity as is reported in a fairly sizable body of research by a test which takes less than 20 minutes to administer is a tribute to the ability of the authors and their understanding of the field of beginning reading.

Reliability coefficients obtained on split halves by the Spearman-Brown formula range from .83 to .94 on the subtests, with .92 for the total score, as based on 170 entering first grade pupils. Research data reported by others, as well as by the authors of the test, show coefficients of correlation between scores on various editions of the test and other reading tests that are substantial enough to indicate a fair degree of predictive validity. In practically every instance the criterion reading test was also correlated with either teachers' ratings or group intelligence tests, and in every instance but one the *Lee-Clark Reading Readiness Test* yielded a higher coefficient.

Norms for the 1951 Revision are based on 5,000 entering first graders with median CA 6-0 and median IQ 100, with sigma 16. Norms for near the end of the kindergarten year are based on a different population not further described. Considerable supplementary information of value in determining degree of reading readiness—grade placement equivalents of scores, expectation of success and of failure of various scores—are also provided.

This is an excellent test, considering its brevity and ease of administration. After using it for more than 20 years in the last month of kindergarten, this reviewer can report that in practice it is very effective in screening out those children with gross and usually rather obvious hindrances to success in beginning reading, such as mental immaturity, deprivation in experiential background, nervous instability resulting in short interest and attention span, and gross sensory handicaps. It sometimes serves to give evidence of excellent ability and probable success in reading on the part of children who, lacking somewhat in physical size, social forwardness, manual dexterity, or oral verbosity, have not previously been rated high by their teachers.

Neither the test itself nor any of the technical data presented in the manual would appear to support the rather elaborate normative and interpretative tables. These are attractive and logical enough; but in the absence of any experimental support or statistical verification, it must be assumed that they have been more or less subjectively derived and that their validity for such exact and detailed analysis is in question. We have found that a more valid method of diagnosis is to determine a critical score (35 out of 64 in our situation) below which the chances of success in first grade reading have proved to be poor and to follow up the 5 per cent of the children thus screened out with an individual reading aptitude test (Monroe) and an individual psychological examination (Stanford-Binet). These data, together with an individual 4-page personality profile kept from the beginning of the year by the kindergarten teacher, furnish the material for diagnosis. It jars this reviewer to see the term "diagnostic" applied to a profile based on a test measuring three or four rather general aspects of reading readiness and requiring only 12 to 15 minutes of working time. "Analytic" might be a less presumptuous term.

This is a superior screening test with surprising reliability and validity for its purpose, considering its brevity. Its total administration time of 15 to 20 minutes makes it particularly convenient to administer in one sitting in kindergarten or first grade and gives it a definite advantage in this respect over such widely used tests as the Gates, Metropolitan, Harrison-Stroud, and Murphy-Durrell tests, which require from 50 to 90 minutes and two or three sittings to administer. It saves time from those who do not need detailed diagnosis which can be used on those who do. In the absence of other objective data it serves as a good rough measure for initial grouping, but its scores should not be interpreted too minutely and it should be followed up by additional diagnostic instruments.

For reviews by Marion Monroe Cox and David H. Russell of the 1943 edition, see 3:517.

[679]

Murphy-Durrell Diagnostic Reading Readiness Test. First grade entrants; 1949, c1947–49; 3 scores: auditory, visual, learning rate; Part 3 individual in part; 1 form ('47); manual ('49); $3.05 per 35 tests; $2.20 per set of flash cards ['49]; postage extra; 35¢ per specimen set, postpaid; Parts 1–2: (60) minutes; group administration of Part 3: (20) minutes; individual administration of Part 3: (5–10) minutes; Helen A. Murphy and Donald D. Durrell; World Book Co. *

REFERENCES

1–2. See 4:571.
3. NICHOLSON, ALICE. *Background Abilities Related to Reading Success in First Grade.* Doctor's thesis, Boston University (Boston, Mass.), 1957.
4. NICHOLSON, ALICE. "Background Abilities Related to Reading Success in First Grade." *J Ed* (Boston) 140:7–24 F '58. *

JOAN BOLLENBACHER, *Supervisor of Appraisal Services, Cincinnati Public Schools, Cincinnati, Ohio.*

This test is designed to measure what the authors consider three critical areas in learning to read. It is, accordingly, divided into three parts, testing auditory discrimination, visual discrimination, and learning rate, respectively.

It seems appropriate to consider each of the subtests separately, since the manual states that there is no provision for finding a total score on the test. There is, however, space provided on the front cover of the test booklet for recording total score and percentile. An inconsistency of this type is confusing to a teacher.

The auditory test, consisting of 84 picture items, takes about 30 minutes to administer. The manual indicates that the test is for group use, but contains no information as to the appropriate size of the group. The reviewer has found, however, that no more than six children can be handled properly, since the test requires the children to pay close attention in order to distinguish separate sounds in spoken words. In the general directions, the manual suggests that "it is important to enunciate very clearly and follow directions exactly," but fails to stress the effect of variations in administration on the reliability of the test. The manual reports a reliability coefficient of .96, based on correlating the odd and even items. Since this

is a test for young children whose attention wanders easily and since it depends on the ability of the examiner to enunciate, the test user would have more confidence in a reliability coefficient based on a test-retest procedure.

Evidence that inattention is, indeed, a matter for concern was provided in a test tryout conducted by the reviewer. Given to a capable class of 25 pupils by a trained examiner under optimum conditions, the auditory test, which employs the scoring formula of the number of items right minus twice the number of items wrong, yielded zero scores for 12 of the pupils. On the visual test the lowest score for the same group was 30 (49th percentile). The manual admonishes the examiner to check individual pupils who have zero scores, having them respond orally, to determine whether there is an actual weakness or whether inattention was a determining factor in the test result. If such a procedure is necessary, a question as to whether this should be a group or an individual test might legitimately be raised.

The visual test contains 52 items, half of which involve perception of letters and half, perception of words. The items are presented by the examiner on flash cards, and the pupils must select the matching letter or word among five choices for each item. This test takes about 30 minutes. The odd-even reliability is .95.

The learning rate test consists of 10 words presented in a 20-minute teaching situation to groups of 10 pupils. Later the same day each pupil is tested individually three times on his ability to recognize the words. His score is the number of words he recognizes on the third testing. In a first grade class of present-day size, it would take a teacher the greater part of three days to complete the test. The manual suggests that the teacher provide seatwork exercises for pupils while they are not being tested. This is easier said than done. Even in a class where all pupils had attended kindergarten, this would require quite a degree of independence on the pupils' part and quite a quantity of seatwork.

The manual states that the validity of the learning rate test "stems from the closeness with which the test situation resembles the actual typical word-learning situation in the first grade." The manual furnishes no data regarding the relationship of the learning rate scores to subsequent scores on reading achievement tests, commenting that "it is felt that the closeness of the logical relationship between rate of learning words and reading achievement is so great as to make such data superfluous." (This reviewer believes that data on the predictive validity of a test scarcely could be considered superfluous.) Nevertheless, the manual indicates that this test can provide a meaningful evaluation of pupil performance and suggests that pupils be divided into four groups on the basis of their scores on this test. It is regrettable that data regarding the reliability and the error of measurement on this 10-item test have been omitted. Such data are significant, particularly since groupings such as these sometimes become permanent labels, and more often when they are dignified by a somewhat misleading title such as "learning rate."

In brief, this reviewer does not recommend this test for group use in the first grade.

S. S. Dunn, *Officer-in-Charge, Test Division, Australian Council for Educational Research, Melbourne, Australia.*

For this test there is no empirical evidence for validity. The argument for validity runs thus: (*a*) Clinical studies on 4,000 children show that failure in reading is mainly due to lack of auditory discrimination, lack of visual discrimination, and improper adjustment to learning rate (no reference to any publication is given). (*b*) Tests of auditory discrimination, visual discrimination, and learning rate are prepared. (*c*) Low scores on any of these tests is indicative of lack of readiness for reading.

There seems to be fairly general agreement on the importance of visual and auditory discrimination in learning to read. But can we be sure that the Murphy-Durrell tests bearing these names measure these abilities and not irrelevant ones? For instance, in the auditory discrimination test the first practice example requires the pupil to place his finger on a picture of a garden while the examiner says: "Listen—go—garden. Does garden sound like go at the beginning? Yes, so we shall mark it with a large cross, like this!" Now unless the child has already played this "game" before, he could well say that "go" and "gar" are not the same beginning sounds. There are 12 practice examples and one hopes that all children understand the task before starting. But it is quite possible that only the quick learners understand

what is required. Some evidence, then, that this group test is a valid measure of auditory discrimination, in the form of a correlation with a more direct measure of auditory discrimination obtained individually, would be welcome.

In the visual discrimination test the teacher holds up a card with a letter or a word on it and the children find the matching letter or word on the test paper. In a large class the distance from the stimulus of the nearest and furthest child could be of considerable importance in clear recognition. And what of people suffering from some visual defect? Those tests of visual discrimination in which the stimulus is on the child's test would seem to provide more standard conditions.

The learning rate test is most time-consuming. Only 10 subjects are taught at a time and then tested individually three times during the day. The conditions are far from standard for each individual. The other children in the class doing seatwork exercises are going to be most unusual individuals if they pay no attention to the oral, blackboard, and testing activities of the test group. The aim of a simple "work-sample test" is appealing, but surely the classroom teacher can quickly find out who are fast learners and who are slow learners from her normal observations. In any case it would seem a waste of time to use this third test with those whose scores on tests 1 and 2 are low.

Reliability figures are given only for tests 1 and 2 and these are split-half coefficients. With young children test-retest or parallel-forms figures would be more satisfactory. No table of intercorrelations between the tests is given. This is essential information when tests are purporting to be measuring different abilities.

The usefulness of norms for a test of this type is debatable, but the information given is insufficient to enable a teacher to decide whether or not her group can legitimately be compared with the normative group. Would it not be possible and more meaningful to provide some sort of expectancy table which relates readiness scores to ability to read a passage of given difficulty "X" months after the test?

The teacher who uses the test as a learning experience for the children may find that it gives her insights into the state of readiness of individual children and even helps in the development of these skills. Her own observations of her everyday tasks may, however, be just as useful.

[680]

★Reading Readiness Test. Grades kgn-1; 1957; 1 form; $2.50 per 25 tests; 25¢ per specimen set; cash orders postpaid; (20) minutes; David F. Votaw and Peggy Lou Moses; Steck Co. *

REFERENCE

1. BANHAM, KATHARINE M. "Maturity Level for Reading Readiness: A Check List for the Use of Teachers and Parents as a Supplement to Reading Readiness Tests." Ed & Psychol Meas 18:371-5 su '58. *

[681]

★Scholastic Reading Readiness Test. Grades kgn-1; 1953; various titles used by publishers; for Catholic schools; Form A; manual ['53]; $3.20 per 35 tests; 50¢ per specimen set; postage extra; (30-45) minutes; Oliver F. Anderhalter and Ruth Colestock; Scholastic Testing Service, Inc. *

[682]

★Webster Reading-Readiness Test. Grades kgn-1.5; 1950; 5 scores: verbal discrimination, memory of word forms, auditory discrimination, vocabulary and comprehension, total; 1 form; manual ['50]; 24¢ per test; 36¢ per manual kit; postpaid; (30-40) minutes; Clarence R. Stone and Mary Nila; Webster Publishing Co. *

SPECIAL FIELDS

[683]

*Interpretation of Reading Materials in the Natural Sciences. High school, college; 1944-57; subtest of Tests of General Educational Development; IBM; 2 levels; 2 forms: high school, Form B ('44); college, Form B ('43); revised manuals: high school level ('56), college level ('54); $2.50 per 25 tests of either level; separate answer sheets must be used; $1 per 25 IBM answer sheets; 50¢ per specimen set; postage extra; (120) minutes; prepared by Examination Staff of United States Armed Forces Institute; Veterans' Testing Service, American Council on Education. *

For a review by Robert J. Solomon of the complete battery, see 27; for a review by Gustav J. Froehlich of Form B, see 4:26; for reviews by Herbert S. Conrad and Warren G. Findley, see 3:20.

[684]

*Interpretation of Reading Materials in the Social Studies. High school, college; 1944-57; subtest of Tests of General Educational Development; IBM; 2 levels; 2 forms: high school, Form B ('44); college, Form B ('43); revised manuals: high school level ('56), college level ('54); $2.50 per 25 tests of either level; separate answer sheets must be used; $1 per 25 IBM answer sheets; 50¢ per specimen set; postage extra; (120) minutes; prepared by Examination Staff of United States Armed Forces Institute; Veterans' Testing Service, American Council on Education. *

For reviews by W. E. Hall and C. Robert Pace of the college level, see 3:528. For a review by Robert J. Solomon of the complete battery, see 27; for a review by Gustav J. Froehlich of Form B, see 4:26; for reviews by Herbert S. Conrad and Warren G. Findley, see 3:20.

[685]

*The Iowa Tests of Educational Development: Test 5, Ability to Interpret Reading Materials in the Social Studies. Grades 9-13; 1942-58; title on Form Y-3S is Interpretation—Social Studies; IBM; Forms X-3S, Y-3S ('52); examiner's manual ('58); battery manual ('54); pupil profile leaflet ('58); profile card (no date); separate answer sheets must be used; $3 per 20 tests; $5 per 100 IBM answer sheets; 50¢ per scoring stencil; $3 per complete specimen set; postage extra; 60(70) or 40(50) minutes; prepared under the direction of E. F. Lindquist; Science Research Associates. *

For reviews by J. Murray Lee and Stephen Wiseman of the complete battery, see 17; for a review by Eric F. Gardner of earlier forms, see 4:17; for reviews by Henry Chauncey, Gustav J. Froehlich, and Lavone A. Hanna, see 3:12.

[686]

*The Iowa Tests of Educational Development: Test 6, Ability to Interpret Reading Materials in the Natural Sciences. Grades 9-13; 1942-58; title on Form Y-3S is Interpretation—Natural Sciences; IBM; Forms X-3S, Y-3S ('52); examiner's manual ('58); battery manual ('54); pupil profile leaflet, fourth edition ('58); profile card (no date); separate answer sheets must be used; $3 per 20 tests; $5 per 100 IBM answer sheets; $2.15 per 20 answer pads; 50¢ per scoring stencil; $3 per complete specimen set; postage extra; 60(70) or 40(50) minutes; prepared under the direction of E. F. Lindquist; Science Research Associates. *

For reviews by J. Murray Lee and Stephen Wiseman of the complete battery, see 17; for a review by Eric F. Gardner of earlier forms, see 4:17; for reviews by Henry Chauncey, Gustav J. Froehlich, and Lavone A. Hanna, see 3:12.

SPEED

[687]

★Tinker Speed of Reading Test. Grades 7-16 and adults; 1955, c1947-55; Forms 1 ('55), 2 ('55); mimeographed manual ('55); norms for college sophomores on 5-, 10-, and 30-minute tests only; $5 per 25 tests; 50¢ per specimen set; postage extra; any time limit from 4(15) to 30(40) minutes; Miles A. Tinker; University of Minnesota Press. *

LEONARD S. FELDT, Assistant Professor of Education, State University of Iowa, Iowa City, Iowa.

This test was developed by the author in connection with his long series of experiments on the effects of typographical and illumination variations on reading speed. It is published primarily for other experimenters in this field and for college and high school reading instructors in need of a rate measure. Since the number of potential users in the first category is undoubtedly very small, its publication is of most consequence to those in the second.

The test consists of 450 independent, 30-word items (usually one sentence, sometimes two) set in pseudo-paragraphs of five items each. The student is instructed to read with all possible speed and, as a comprehension check, to look for and cross out the one word near the end of each item which "spoils the meaning." For this technique the author is indebted to the *Chapman-Cook Speed of Reading Test* and the *Michigan Speed of Reading Test*. The comments of the reviewer of these instruments on this technique are worth careful consideration by the potential user of this test.

There are two main strengths to this instrument. First, it provides sufficient homogeneous material to permit a relatively long test (30 minutes), if the user desires one. Second, the author has gone to considerable trouble to produce two forms which were equated item by item in the mean reading time and mean reading errors of a group of 55 subjects. The resultant forms, though not exactly equal in difficulty, are very closely matched. The availability of such equated forms should facilitate the assessment of changes in reading speed, an important measurement problem in remedial reading programs.

The principal weaknesses of the test are the deficient norms, the inadequate reliability data, and the absence of correlations with other types of rate measures. The only norms provided are based on groups of 96 to 135 sophomores of the University of Minnesota. Norms are presented for 5-, 10-, and 30-minute tests, but the data are clearly inadequate for the interpretation of the scores of high school students. Moreover, without additional evidence, one cannot assume that the norms are suitable for college students at other institutions. Since performance on rate tests depends to some extent on the type of comprehension check employed and the nature of the reading material, evaluation of pupil performance in words per minute will not permit the examiner to use normative data available from other sources. Thus, every user must expect to compile his own norms, a responsibility which a publisher might well recommend but should hardly demand.

Parallel-form reliabilities ranging from .76 to .93 are reported for 18 groups which are not described in any respect. Apparently, the coefficients apply to a 30-minute test, although this is not clearly specified. Since 5-minute and 10-minute tests are specifically suggested, reliability data for tests of these lengths should have been made available for all grade levels. It should be noted, in this regard, that recent investigations strongly indicate the Spearman-Brown formula does not provide accurate estimates of the reliability of shortened and lengthened rate tests. Estimates of such reliabilities must be empirically determined.

The author states that the test was constructed to provide a measure of speed of reading uncomplicated by comprehension difficulties —an end achieved by the use of only the most common words and sentences of unsophisticated thought content. Many reading specialists may not consider this a virtue. The goal of many college programs is not the unqualified increase of reading speed, but the selective use of speed, depending upon the nature and purpose of the reading. This test is clearly unsuited for measurement of this objective. High school and college teachers might well be concerned with the relationship of performance on this test to that on rate tests involving other kinds of material and other kinds of comprehension checks. They might also question the relationship to performance on reading materials which do present comprehension problems. The latter situation is our primary concern, after all. No data are presented on these points, however.

The potential user will have to weigh the strengths of this test against its weaknesses. Both are obvious. With more comprehensive norms and more thorough reliability analyses the instrument could be far more useful than it now is.

STUDY SKILLS

[688]
★Brown-Holtzman Survey of Study Habits and Attitudes. High school and college; 1953-56; IBM; 1 form ('53); revised manual ('56); separate answer sheets must be used; $2 per 25 tests; $1.90 per 50 IBM answer sheets; 50¢ per set of either hand or machine scoring stencils and manual; 60¢ per specimen set; postpaid; (25-35) minutes; William F. Brown and Wayne H. Holtzman; Psychological Corporation. *

REFERENCES
1. HOLTZMAN, WAYNE H., AND BROWN, WILLIAM F. "Study Habits and Attitudes in the Prediction of Academic Success." Abstract. Am Psychol 8:369 Ag '53. *

2. BROWN, WILLIAM F., AND HOLTZMAN, WAYNE H. "The Importance of Study Habits and Attitudes in the Scholastic Achievement of High School and College Students." Abstract. *Am Psychol* 9:341-2 Ag '54. *

3. HOLTZMAN, WAYNE H.; BROWN, WILLIAM F.; AND FARQUHAR, W. G. "The Survey of Study Habits and Attitudes: A New Instrument for the Prediction of Academic Success." *Ed & Psychol Meas* 14:726-32 w '54. * (PA 29:7962)

4. BROWN, WILLIAM F., AND HOLTZMAN, WAYNE H. "A Study-Attitudes Questionnaire for Predicting Academic Success." *J Ed Psychol* 46:75-84 F '55. * (PA 30:1503)

5. PAUK, WALTER J. *An Analysis of Certain Characteristics of Above-Average and Below-Average Male and Female Readers at the Ninth-Grade Level.* Doctor's thesis, Cornell University (Ithaca, N.Y.), 1955. (DA 16:285)

6. SIE, GEORGIANA D. W. *The Relationship of Two Experimental Measures of Student Motivation to Academic Success in College.* Doctor's thesis, State University of Iowa (Iowa City, Iowa), 1955. (DA 15:1556)

7. BROWN, WILLIAM F., AND HOLTZMAN, WAYNE H. "Use of the Survey of Study Habits and Attitudes for Counseling Students." *Personnel & Guid J* 35:214-8 D '56. * (PA 31:8766)

8. AHMANN, J. STANLEY, AND GLOCK, MARVIN D. "The Utility of Study Habits and Attitudes Inventory in a College Reading Program." *J Ed Res* 51:297-303 D '57. *

9. CHANSKY, NORMAN M., AND BREGMAN, MARTIN. "Improvement of Reading in College." *J Ed Res* 51:313-7 D '57. *

10. KIM, KI SUK. *The Use of Certain Measurements of Academic Aptitude, Study Habits, Motivation, and Personality in the Prediction of Academic Achievement.* Doctor's thesis, Louisiana State University (Baton Rouge, La.), 1957. (DA 18:150)

11. KRUMBOLTZ, JOHN D., AND FARQUHAR, WILLIAM W. "The Effect of Three Teaching Methods on Achievement and Motivational Outcomes in a How-to-Study Course." *Psychol Monogr* 71(14):1-26 '57.

12. AHMANN, J. STANLEY; SMITH, WILLIAM L.; AND GLOCK, MARVIN D. "Predicting Academic Success in College by Means of a Study Habits and Attitude Inventory." *Ed & Psychol Meas* 18:853-7 w '58. *

13. FEENEY, MARY M. *Scores on SAT-V and Survey of Study Habits and Attitudes as Predictors of Achievement in a College for Women.* Master's thesis, Fordham University (New York, N.Y.), 1958.

14. GARCIA, DOLORES, AND WHIGHAM, NEIL. "Validity of SSHA Administered Before and After College Experience." *Ed & Psychol Meas* 18:845-51 w '58. *

JAMES DEESE, *Associate Professor of Psychology, The Johns Hopkins University, Baltimore, Maryland.*

This inventory is designed to identify students whose study habits and attitudes are not those of students who do well in academic work and, in addition, to provide a basis for aiding such students through counseling and remedial work with study methods. Furthermore, the inventory may be used to predict academic success for high school and college populations.

The 75 items on the inventory differ somewhat from those usually found in study inventories. In preliminary administrations during the selection and validation of items, the authors found that items probing "study attitudes" were in general more highly related to superior grades than items designed to assess the mechanics of studying. The manifest contents of some of the items are aimed at anxiety before and during tests and, in some instances, at general personality characteristics. The result is that the inventory is very heavily pointed in the direction of assessing motivation for study and attitudes towards academic work. This emphasis provides the most unique and valuable aspect of the inventory.

The data accumulated during validation are very encouraging, though the authors themselves are cautious about the test's predictive use because of its dependence upon frankness of responding. Perhaps the most encouraging aspect of these data is not the size of the obtained coefficients, but the indication that, to a surprising degree, what the inventory measures is independent of scholastic aptitude as measured by the *American Council on Education Psychological Examination for College Freshmen.* The inventory substantially increases the correlation with grades when used in conjunction with the ACE. One curious feature of the validation data is that the correlations between single-semester grade-point averages and SSHA scores are consistently higher for college students in Texas (.39 to .66) than for those from other parts of the country (.27 to .37).

The only serious deficiency in the manual is the sketchiness with which information about the counseling keys is given. On the keys themselves we are informed that the items indicated are items to which the student's response is different from that of students who obtain high grades. While little information about the selection of items used for scoring is necessary to the user, most people giving the test will want to know more than they are told in the manual about the items selected for the counseling key. Indeed, many counselors will be interested in the responses to items not included on the counseling keys.

In summary, this inventory or survey is a unique and valuable contribution to the techniques for assessing student habits of work and motivation for study. It is more suited for uncovering attitudinal and motivational difficulties than any other published study inventory, and its use is particularly recommended where such difficulties are the prime concern. In addition, its value for research on counseling and remedial teaching must not be overlooked.

C. GILBERT WRENN, *Professor of Educational Psychology,* and ROY D. LEWIS, *Teaching Assistant, University of Minnesota, Minneapolis, Minnesota.*

This instrument is designed "to furnish an inventory of study habits and attitudes to serve as a foundation for self-improvement." It consists of a series of statements which are to be responded to in terms of the extent to which they represent actions and attitudes of the person responding. In addition to the scoring key, a special counseling key is provided which permits identification of items to which the response given is different from that most frequently given by students of high scholastic achievement.

The instrument has been standardized on high school students and college freshmen. Correlations between scores and one-semester grade-point averages for college freshmen range from .27 to .66 for men, and from .26 to .65 for women. Correlations for the high school students are somewhat lower. Reliability coefficients seem satisfactory, ranging from .79 to .95 for different groups and different methods.

Correlations between this test and the *American Council on Education Psychological Examination for College Freshmen* are consistently low according to the authors. Multiple correlation coefficients based upon the ACE and the SSHA in combination indicate an increase in the predictive efficiency over either instrument used singly. For example, the weighted average coefficient between grades and ACE scores of women college freshmen rose from .53 to .61 when the SSHA was used in combination. If the test were to be used as a selection device it can be assumed that students would tend to respond in the approved direction and that the predictive efficiency of the instrument would be effected.

The recommended uses as seen by the authors, while fairly clear cut, appear to be a bit ambitious. As either a screening instrument or a diagnostic instrument the test must assume both complete frankness of response and a fairly high degree of memory accuracy on the part of the student. In the use of the SSHA for research, an uncontrolled variable of interest or motivation shows up. In one study (*3*) reported by the authors the correlations between grades and test scores were considerably higher for persons showing interest in their scores than for persons who did not show such interest. Another variable is revealed in a study by Krumboltz and Farquhar (*11*) in which students showing a preference for cognitive-type, teacher directed instructors *increased* their SSHA scores after taking a how to study course, whereas students in the same course preferring a student-centered type of instruction *lowered* their scores.

The development procedure for this test was extremely well conceived. Items were chosen on the basis of interviews with students and each item was then empirically validated as to its applicability to the problem. The manual is unusually complete with considerable technical data reported for both college and high school groups.

The instructions state that the student can be helped to obtain an understanding of how to study properly and to learn many of his study faults. These reviewers feel that there is an implication in the instructions that the student will be helped simply by responding honestly. Although there is the possibility of insight through exposure to such information, there is no evidence to support such a thesis.

Tenth grade students should be able to read the test readily. The terms used are generally easy to understand. The statements to be responded to are fairly concise and should create no problem.

In general, the reviewers feel that this instrument is well grounded, easy to understand, and can be an excellent source of study habit and attitude information for use by student and counselor. The basis for interpretation, however, assumes that the student will respond frankly and that he is capable of understanding and reporting his own motivations and attitudes toward studying and academic activities. This assumption may be questioned on the basis of present knowledge in this area. While the instrument may be used to advantage since it has been carefully constructed, use of it will require good judgment and a rigorous application of limiting factors inherent in self-reports of any kind. It is *not* a test and any user of it should fully understand the difference between a test and an inventory or a survey of self-reports.

[689]

★**California Study Methods Survey.** Grades 7–13; 1958; 5 scores: attitudes toward school, mechanics of study, planning and system, total, verification; IBM; 1 form; $3.50 per 35 tests; separate answer sheets may be used; 5¢ per IBM answer sheet; 40¢ per set of hand and machine scoring stencils; postage extra; 50¢ per specimen set, postpaid; scoring service available; (35–50) minutes; Harold D. Carter; California Test Bureau. *

REFERENCES

1. CARTER, HAROLD D. "Methods of Learning as Factors in the Prediction of School Success." *J Psychol* 26:249–58 Jl '48. * (*PA* 23:1439)
2. CARTER, HAROLD D. "Correlations Between Intelligence Tests, Study Methods Tests, and Marks in a College Course." *J Psychol* 30:333–40 O '50. * (*PA* 25:3383)
3. CARTER, HAROLD D. "What Are Some of the Basic Prob-

lems in Analysis of Study Techniques?" *Calif J Ed Res* 2:170–4 S '51. *
4. CARTER, HAROLD D. "Cross-Validation of a Study Methods Test." *Calif J Ed Res* 4:32–6 Ja '53. * (PA 28:1553)
5. CARTER, HAROLD D. "Development of a Diagnostic Scoring Scheme for a Study Methods Test." *Calif J Ed Res* 6:26–32 Ja '55. * (PA 29:7841)
6. CARTER, HAROLD D. "Some Validity Coefficients for Study Test Scores." *Calif J Ed Res* 7:212–6 N '56. * (PA 31:8812)
7. CARTER, HAROLD D. "The Mechanics of Study Procedures." *Calif J Ed Res* 9:8–13 Ja '58. *

[690]

Cooperative Dictionary Test. Grades 7–12; 1951–52; 5 scores: alphabetizing, spelling, pronunciation, meaning, total; IBM; Form A ('51); manual ('52); directions sheet ('52); no data on reliability for grades 8, 10–11; no norms for part scores, no norms for grades 8, 10–11; separate answer sheets must be used; $2.50 per 25 tests; $1.50 per 25 IBM answer sheets; 45¢ per scoring stencil; postage extra; 30(40) minutes; S. D. Melville, Clarence Derrick (manual), and Frances Swineford (manual); Cooperative Test Division, Educational Testing Service. *

A. N. HIERONYMUS, *Associate Professor of Education, State University of Iowa, Iowa City, Iowa.*

ORGANIZATION AND CONTENT. This test employs an ingenious, convenient design. The items are printed on both sides of an IBM answer sheet. A 4-page reusable leaflet contains instructions to the student and two composite pages of selected entries from an established dictionary. The entries very adequately represent the many situations for which a dictionary may be used.

The 50 items cover almost every conceivable skill in the use of the dictionary. The first 20 items deal with alphabetization within a framework of four pairs of guide words; this subtest is accompanied by reliability data but no norms. The remaining 30 items yield three scores based on 10 items each, somewhat misleadingly called pronunciation, meaning, and spelling. However, after the teacher obtains these scores, she is at a complete loss as to what to do with them; no norms or other data are provided.

In order to measure most of the uses which people *can* make of the dictionary, many items deal with skills of marginal social utility, such as the meaning of the abbreviations *Colloq.* and *Dial.* On the other hand, people most often use the dictionary for looking up the pronunciation, meaning, and spelling of words. Pronunciation is represented by several items; spelling and meaning are not so well represented. Only one item deals directly with spelling; other items classified under spelling deal with irregular plurals, irregular verb forms, and the like. Only 3 of the 50 items on the test are concerned directly with the interpretation of meaning.

Whether this should be considered a disadvantage depends upon the purposes for which the test is given.

NORMS. Percentile norms, provided for grades 7, 9, and 12 only, are based on results in only seven schools in five communities. The criteria of selection are not provided, nor are any further data which would allow the user to determine whether this is a meaningful normative sample to employ in evaluating the results from his school. Different schools tested pupils at different levels (only three schools tested in grade 7), but the norms were "adjusted so as *to reflect the performance of the students in all seven schools.*" The authors recommend the use of local norms. In view of the inadequacy of the normative sample, schools should take this recommendation seriously.

Schools are encouraged to compute class medians and compare them with the medians for the normative groups. This will almost inevitably result in misinterpretations. Class medians are not distributed in the same way as pupil scores. In recommending this type of comparison, the authors are encouraging schools to misinterpret the standing of their classes.

Item analysis data are provided which allow schools to compare group performance on individual items with that of the normative sample. It is suggested that follow-up instructions begin with the types of items missed most frequently by the group, the implication being that these identify the skills which most need attention. The rank order of the difficulty of items in a test depends on many factors. Very often the most difficult items are difficult because of faulty construction or because they represent skills which are seldom used or needed. It is doubtful that follow-up instruction on the use of the dictionary should start, for example, with tracing the etymology of words. Yet, in almost every class, this is quite likely to be the most difficult skill measured by this test. The second suggested criterion for selecting points for study, to begin with items which are fundamental to the use of the dictionary, would seem to be much more defensible.

TECHNICAL DATA. The section in the manual dealing with technical data is quite complete. Kuder-Richardson (formula 20) reliability coefficients are provided for scores which are accompanied by norms. Intercorrelations of part and total scores are shown, as are speededness data. Difficulty and discrimination data are supplied. No statistical evidence of validity is given, but none would seem to be crucial to evaluating the test.

OVERALL EVALUATION. This is a skillfully constructed test, possibly overemphasizing dictionary skills of marginal social utility. The norms must be regarded as inadequate.

[691]

★Evaluation Aptitude Test. Candidates for college and graduate school entrance; 1951–52; 5 scores: neutral syllogisms, emotionally toned syllogisms, total, emotional bias, indecision; 1 form ('52); manual ('52); $1.95 per 20 tests; $1 per specimen set (must be purchased to obtain manual); postage extra; 50(55) minutes; DeWitt E. Sell; Psychometric Affiliates. *

J. THOMAS HASTINGS, *University Examiner; Director of Unit on Evaluation in Bureau of Educational Research; Professor of Education, University of Illinois, Urbana, Illinois.*

A name like *Evaluation Aptitude Test* (EAT) demands a brief description of the stimulus-response content before comments or appraisals are meaningful. The task set for the examinee is to evaluate 36 conclusions each of which is based upon two premises. The evaluation (response) consists of checking each conclusion as logically sound or unsound, or of marking "o" to indicate uncertainty. The first 18 of these syllogisms deal with premises and conclusions which are obviously unreal since a nonsense word is used in the second premise. These first 18 are spoken of as "affectively neutral" because one cannot judge the conclusion from prior knowledge of fact. The other 18—matched one for one with the first group on syllogistic mood and keyed response —deal with social, political, and economic statements and are spoken of as "affective" since the examinee's prior opinions presumably may support or conflict with the syllogistic conclusion.

It should be obvious that in either set of 18 (Part A and Part B, respectively) the examinee who knows anything of syllogistic form may convert each to its equivalent type of general statement (e.g., "All A's are B's. Some C's are A's. Therefore,.....") and then ignore both the nonsense word and the prior opinion, if any.

The author suggests that the test be used in college or graduate school entrance examination batteries as an aid in diagnosis, educational guidance, and selection. Since the operational attack on the items (conversion to general syllogism of all, some, none) by the respondents is indeterminable, diagnosis or selection on the basis of logical validity would be a poor risk. Since no data are presented on the effectiveness of this task for predicting deductive reasoning required in educational situations, there is no possibility of diagnosing or selecting on the basis of empirical validity.

If one wants to diagnose or select on critical thinking and problem solving abilities, he is faced with a shortage of instruments with demonstrated validity. Short of developing his own, he may have to use *cautiously* a published test. However, certain other tests (e.g., *Watson-Glaser Critical Thinking Appraisal*) should certainly be considered before this one.

Norms are given in terms of percentiles for high school seniors (n = 165) and for college seniors (n = 158) on Part A, Part B, and the total score. Only two high schools and two colleges (both small) were used in norming. The person considering using the test should recognize that the author's statement that the norms "can be considered reliably indicative of the probable distribution of evaluation aptitude in high school and college seniors" expresses at most a hope—not a well founded claim. The norms for the other two scores—Index of Discrepancy (proportion of responses in Part B which disagree with responses to paired items in Part A) and Index of Indecision (proportion of omits)—are based upon college seniors only. Furthermore, the five scores are so interdependent that use of all five might be more confusing than helpful, especially to the test user who is less than highly trained in measurement.

The EAT is certainly not ready at present for distribution to school and college guidance people or selection officers. Although this reviewer has serious doubt that more data on relevant points will demonstrate that the test is useful for the purposes stated, such data should be collected and presented if the test is to be offered to consumers. Neither the stated general purposes nor the suggested specific applications are supported convincingly in the data currently presented in the manual.

WALKER H. HILL, *Associate Professor, Office of Evaluation Services, Michigan State University, East Lansing, Michigan.*

"Evaluation aptitude" is defined in the manual as "the capacity to appraise data accurately; to draw correct inferences from given premises; to think 'straight' or without emotional bias." In view of the range of thinking abilities which this definition seems to suggest, it is rather a letdown to find that the *Evaluation Aptitude Test* is simply a 36-item test of ability to judge the validity of syllogisms.

The test is in two parts. Part A includes 18 syllogisms in various moods and figures. The required judgments are: "sound" (conclusion follows), "unsound" (conclusion does not follow), or "uncertain." Part B is a corresponding set of syllogisms, identical in mood and figure, and therefore in keyed answers, but differing in content. The correspondence is such that Parts A and B are printed in parallel columns, with each item directly opposite its counterpart.

The different content of the two parts is the central feature of the test. The syllogisms in Part A deal with supposedly neutral material. They all concern relationships between candies, confections, and "twangs." Students are not expected to have any feelings, biases, or prior knowledge about the relation of twangs and candies. Part B, on the other hand, deals with such terms as politicians, liberals, conservatives, radicals, Communists, and labor leaders, about which students are expected to have biases and preconceptions.

By comparing scores and responses to corresponding items on the two parts, one can presumably judge the effect of emotionally toned material on a student's ability to reason deductively. In addition to the two part scores and a total score, two "indices" are obtained: a "discrepancy index," which represents the percentage of instances in which two corresponding items are answered differently, regardless of correctness, and an "indecision index," which is the percentage of the total number of items answered "uncertain."

On the theory (said by the author to be a "well-recognized" fact) that the ideological biases of most people can be classed as liberal or conservative, the items in Part B are so constructed that half of them are intended as "traps" for unwary liberals and half as "traps" for unwary conservatives.

It is clear that considerable care has gone into the design of the instrument, and not a little ingenuity. One can seriously question, however, whether the result really justifies the effort, for even the most reasonable claims which can be made for it rest on some shaky

assumptions, and claims actually made for it go far beyond what is reasonable.

The author recognizes that some students may have little or no emotional bias concerning the items in Part B. Yet he says that since the two parts are "comparable in every respect other than their affective character," only bias and chance can produce discrepancies between the two parts. There are other possibilities. Surely some Part B items are easier for some people simply because they have meaningful content. In others the content becomes such a tangle of verbiage as to make them quite difficult. Take, for example, this item in Part B:

> If some qualified by education to hold public office are not politicians, and some democratically elected congressional representatives are politicians; then some democratically elected congressional representatives are not qualified by education to hold public office.

This is the corresponding item in Part A:

> If some candies are not confections, and some twangs are confections; then some twangs are not candies.

The former is loaded all right, but there is more than one kind of loading. Is it attitude toward politicians that makes the difference? Indeed, one can even have misgivings about the *neutrality* of Part A. Granted that it has the appearance of having a pretty low emotional level, this reviewer detected in himself an incipient prejudice against "twangs" by the time he had read about them 18 times.

Examination of the test immediately raises the question of how it would be answered by students who have had a course in logic. Might they not apply mechanically the rules for valid and invalid syllogisms, without paying any attention to the content? The author has recognized this possibility and has investigated it. But he seems to overstate the case. Because a group of students made different part scores before they took such a course and equal part scores after its completion, he concludes: "Evaluating syllogisms correctly by the application of rules learned by rote memory does not denote rational comprehension or increased evaluation aptitude. For this reason the EAT as an aptitude test is meaningless for any person who has had training in deductive logic." He does not say how he knows that the application of rules learned by rote memory is the only outcome of the logic course.

There is no evidence of any investigation of the extent to which students may recognize the parallelism of the two parts. Such recognition would, of course, vastly affect the scores. It is more likely for students who have studied logic, but is possible for others as well. This possibility could easily be eliminated by rearranging the sequence so that like items do not appear opposite each other.

The format of the test is otherwise acceptable. However, the manual is published in a lithoprinted form in which the type size is so reduced as to make it almost unreadable.

A test of this kind has potential usefulness, which in the present instance falls regrettably short of realization. It must be recognized, however, that, even if this were a very good test, the kind of reasoning it involves is but a limited aspect of "straight thinking." To equate it with the thinking required of "leaders in the social sciences who can think 'straight' or without emotional bias" is little short of ludicrous.

[692]

*The Iowa Tests of Educational Development: Test 9, Use of Sources of Information.** Grades 9-13; 1942-58; IBM; Forms X-3S, Y-3S ('52); examiner's manual ('58); battery manual ('54); pupil profile leaflet, fourth edition ('58); profile card (no date); separate answer sheets must be used $3 per 20 tests; $5 per 100 IBM answer sheets; 50¢ per scoring stencil; $3 per complete specimen set; postage extra; 27(35) minutes; prepared under the direction of E. F. Lindquist; Science Research Associates. *

For reviews by J. Murray Lee and Stephen Wiseman of the complete battery, see 17; for a review by Eric F. Gardner of earlier forms, see 4:17; for reviews by Henry Chauncey, Gustav J. Froehlich, and Lavone A. Hanna, see 3:12.

[693]

★A Library Orientation Test for College Freshmen, 1955 Edition.** Grade 13; 1950-55; 1 form ('55); manual ['55]; no data on reliability; no norms; separate answer sheets must be used; $4.50 per 35 tests; $1.25 per 35 answer sheets; 50¢ per specimen set; cash orders postpaid; (50-60) minutes; Ethel M. Feagley, Dorothy W. Curtiss, Mary V. Gaver, and Esther Greene; Bureau of Publications, Teachers College, Columbia University. *

JANET G. AFFLERBACH, *Editor, Professional Examination Service, American Public Health Association, New York, New York; and* LOIS GRIMES AFFLERBACH, *Serials Librarian, Queens College, Flushing, New York.*

This little test of only 80 items provides an excellent two-way look: backwards for an assessment of the effectiveness of the high school library program and forwards toward a broadening and strengthening of the college library program to meet student needs. Strong emphasis is put on the most important tool of the library, the card catalog, three of the nine parts of the test dealing with this subject. Of the six other parts, four deal with specific reference tools and two with definitions of bibliographical terms. Noticeably absent are the dictionary and encyclopedia play type of item. One must assume that college freshmen know some reference tools and these two are probably the most familiar.

Part 1 is an exercise in matching terms and their respective meanings. The range of terms covered is quite wide. There are not only the usual parts-of-a-book terms, but also types-of-books terms, such as anthology, atlas, and gazeteer. Definitions of types of materials, such as biography, document, and periodical, might have been included as well.

Part 2 shows a typical catalog card with its component parts: author, title, publisher, paging, bibliography, tracings, etc. Each of the parts is given a number, and students choose their answers from the numbered "points of information." While the points exhibited are all testworthy, this section could be enlarged to include such problems as ascertaining from the card whether the book is an English translation or deciding from a subject card what the correct call slip entry should be. There may be some confusion for students in the abundance of numerical figures on the sample card and the test item numbers, which are placed immediately below the card. Could the points of information be given letters of the alphabet instead?

Part 3 is designed to test ability to choose from a list of 19 standard subject headings the one heading most appropriate for each of several book topics or titles. The headings are familiar, ordinary, and workable. Of course, students must know how to use the broad and obvious headings and the system of subdivisions of headings. Regrettably, there seems to be no way in objective tests to discover how students would proceed to find material on new, unusual, or specific topics like atomic submarines, witchcraft, or Dead Sea Scrolls.

Part 4 presents a problem in alphabetizing sample card catalog headings, according to filing rules printed at the head of the problem. This is an excellent approach in miniature to the organization of the catalog.

A good review of important reference tools

in a single field is found in Part 5, where students are to indicate in which of eight familiar reference books they would expect to find the answers to several questions about literature. Since the field of literature is so well provided with reference tools, and since the college student's first encounter with the library is usually by way of English composition and literature classes, it is not a bad idea to devote one whole section of the test to this single subject area. However, one wishes that the student's knowledge of reference material in science and social studies could also be tested.

Part 6 presents the same kind of problem as does Part 5, but covers the more general biographical tools. Responses to the questions included should reveal very well whether students have grasped the distinctive features of each reference book.

Knowledge of several periodical indexes, the *Book Review Digest,* and the *Cumulative Book Index* is tested in Part 7. This part deals mainly with general indexes; e.g., although the *Education Index* is listed, nothing so specialized as the *Art Index* or the scientific abstracting and indexing tools is included.

A group of references from a periodical index is reproduced as the problem in Part 8. Certain parts of the references (title, name of periodical, volume number, date, etc.) are numbered and students must answer questions from these numbered parts. The *Readers' Guide to Periodical Literature* inevitably becomes the freshman's favorite reference tool and this section of the test is a good exercise in the use of all periodical indexes of the *Readers' Guide* type.

Part 9 is a matching exercise to test the student's knowledge of general bibliographical abbreviations, such as *ca., ibid.,* and *q.v.* Although the abbreviations are well chosen, one might wish that the emphasis was more on ability to interpret than on ability to recognize them.

All in all, this test should go far in meeting the purposes set by the test authors: to discover to what extent and in what areas college freshmen need instruction in using the resources of the library, to help freshmen recognize their own deficiencies in the use of the library, and to provide data that can be used as a basis for a program of library instruction to meet the needs of the group tested.

J. WAYNE WRIGHTSTONE, *Director, Bureau of Educational Research, New York Public Schools, New York, New York.*

These test exercises were prepared for: (*a*) discovering to what extent and in what areas college freshmen need instruction in using the resources of a college library; (*b*) diagnosing the strengths and weaknesses of college freshmen in the use of the library; and (*c*) providing data that can be used as a basis for a program of library instruction fitted to the needs of the particular student group.

The manual contains no data on reliability and validity and no norms; hence, the test cannot be considered standardized. The test consists of questions requiring definition of terms related to library usage; interpretation of information on a catalog card; selection of appropriate subject headings in a catalog; arrangement of headings in a card catalog; selection of literature reference books appropriate to a given question; knowledge of sources of biographical information; choice of appropriate book and periodical indexes; interpretation of information in periodical indexes; and definition of abbreviations (such as *ibid., et al.,* and *op. cit.*) frequently found in books.

These various test exercises have face validity as measures of important knowledge that a college freshman should acquire in learning how to use the resources of a library. The authors have attempted to make the exercises as closely parallel to real situations in the library as possible by including, for example, a reproduction of an actual catalog card. The reference books, indexes, and sources of biographical information included are those most frequently used. The section dealing with interpretation of information in periodical indexes contains a reproduction of actual references that an individual would find in *Readers' Guide to Periodical Literature.*

Although the test has some shortcomings with respect to the reliability of diagnosing specific library usage skills because of the limited number of exercises, the results would probably be valuable to the librarian or teacher in counseling the student about improving his specific abilities in using the resources of a library. The authors state that colleges which used earlier forms of the test reported it to be useful for excusing from introductory library instruction students who made a satisfactory score (arbitrarily determined) and for discovering the extent of student progress through administering the test at the beginning and at the end of a period of instruction in library skills.

As a nonstandardized test of knowledge about library resources, this test is probably superior to an informal test constructed by a local librarian. It is unfortunate that evidence has not been presented to show that the items have been analyzed by technically accepted methods and that norms and data on reliability and validity have not been collected and presented.

[694]

★Logical Reasoning. Grades 9–16 and adults; 1955; IBM; Form A; no adult norms; separate answer sheets must be used; $3.75 per 25 tests; 20¢ per single copy; 3¢ per IBM answer sheet; 50¢ per scoring stencil; 25¢ per manual; postage extra; 20(25) minutes; Alfred F. Hertzka and J. P. Guilford; Sheridan Supply Co. *

REFERENCE

1. HILLS, JOHN R. "Factor-Analyzed Abilities and Success in College Mathematics." Ed & Psychol Meas 17:615–22 w '57. *

DUNCAN HOWIE, *Professor of Psychology, The University of New England, Armidale, Australia.*

This test has resulted from factorial researches at Guilford's laboratory which have confirmed and clarified Thurstone's earlier identification of a factor he called "deduction." The factor may generally be described as involving "sensitivity to logical relationships in the testing of the correctness or incorrectness of a conclusion." The authors call it "logical evaluation." The test consists of two parallel parts, each of 20 items covering "the 15 valid syllogistic forms." Each item presents two propositions and requires the subject to choose from among four alternatives the logically correct conclusion. Considerable care has been taken to insure that the "herrings" have a near-appropriate smell, i.e., that each of them is at least plausible. The general format and conditions of administration make the test a straightforward one to give. The time limit for each of the parts is 10 minutes.

Standardization is based on two populations: the first, 402 high school students distributed over grades 10, 11, and 12 and ranging in age from 14 to 20 years with mean age of 16.5; the second, 509 college students about 90 per cent of whom were below 30 years of age. In view of the wide age scatter, it is unfortunate, particularly in the case of the high school group, that information is not given as to the

possible relationships between age level and test score. Norms are presented for each group in standard C scores and in centile ranks equivalent to raw scores.

Reliabilities are reported for both groups at about .90 for the whole test and about .80 for each of the parts. The main evidence of validity is of factorial or internal validity. The test is said to have a loading of .50 in the logical evaluation factor. Evidences of external or criterion validity are somewhat confusing and decidedly less encouraging. For example, correlations are reported with grades in various mathematics courses ranging from .04 to .42 with a mean of .26.

The reviewer agrees with the authors that this aspect of reasoning ability is one that has been almost entirely neglected in intelligence tests and that the time has come to take it seriously. In this perspective, the test is of unquestionable value as a research instrument for further validation studies. That it should be so used is clearly the authors' intention. It is perhaps necessary, however, to caution prospective users that, at this stage, the test cannot be used as other than a research instrument.

CHARLES R. LANGMUIR, *Director of Special Projects, The Psychological Corporation, New York, New York.*

The test consists of 40 formal syllogisms separated into two comparable parts of 20 items. Ten minutes are allowed for each part. An additional 10 minutes are required for students to read the instructions and to become familiar with the item type. A typical item is:

Some women are mothers.
All women are females.

Therefore:
A. All mothers are females.
B. All females are women.
C. Some females are mothers.
D. Some women are not mothers.

The correct answer is the *one* conclusion which follows from the *two* premises. Statements which reformulate a single premise, statements which are consistent, but not necessary, and statements that are invalid make up the distractors. This reviewer's reasoning found two correct conclusions for Items 14, 23, 27, and 35, a questionable distractor in Item 11, and a questionable introduction of a term in the keyed conclusion which is not in the premises of Item 5. The keyed answers are best in the sense of being "logically stronger," but the instructions ask only for a correct conclusion without revealing the existence of such formal distinctions.

Subjective experience with intensive study of the items suggests that the test may be highly speeded for naive subjects. It would be helpful to have information in the manual about the speed-power element. A little practice with syllogisms and the tricky distractions introduced by common language symbols may have a marked effect on speed and accuracy in taking the test.

Centile equivalents are supplied for 402 San Diego high school students evenly distributed in grades 10, 11, and 12, and, separately, for 509 San Diego State College students, principally freshmen and sophomores. The mean total score for the high school group was 23, with standard deviation of 8. In the college group, the mean was 27; standard deviation, 6.5. Sex differences are reported to have been small. The reliability of scores is estimated to be about .80 for a single part and .90 for the full test. The extent to which these estimates are inflated by speed effects is not discussed. The test is scored by the formula rights plus one quarter of the omits. This algebraic device is used to avoid the "many negative scores" that occur with the formula R − W/3.

Some productive research results could develop from experiments with this test and variations of it. The item material is notably homogeneous and might, therefore, be particularly useful in studying the effectiveness of instruction. It would be interesting, for example, to know whether there are individuals who cannot be taught to overcome the distracting influence of semantically loaded common language in syllogisms that are substantively identical, in the logical sense, with syllogisms not containing irrelevant semantic distractions. We can expect to find a distribution of empirical difficulty values for items of identical logical complexity. Some important clues to the components of reasoning abilities might emerge.

[695]

★**Pictographic Self Rating Scale.** High school and college; 1955–57; Experimental Form A ('55); manual ('57); no college norms; separate answer sheets must be used; $2.50 per 25 tests; $1.25 per 25 answer sheets; 50¢ per specimen set; postage extra; (35) minutes; Einar R. Ryden; Acorn Publishing Co. *

REFERENCES
1. ROMANOWSKI, WALTER V. *The Revision and Factor Analysis of a Pictographic Self Rating Scale.* Doctor's thesis, Purdue University (Lafayette, Ind.), 1955.
2. SALES, ROBERT C. *A Validity Study of a Pictographic Self-Rating Scale.* Master's thesis, Purdue University (Lafayette, Ind.), 1955.

[696]

★**SRA Achievement Series: Work-Study Skills.** Grades 4–6, 6–9; 1954–57; 2 scores: references, charts; IBM; Forms A, B; 2 levels; technical supplement, second edition ('57); separate answer sheets must be used; $2 per 20 tests; $4.50 per 100 IBM scorable answer sheets; 50¢ per hand scoring stencil; 50¢ per teacher's handbook ('55); 50¢ per administrator's manual ('56); $1 per technical supplement; postage extra; specimen set not available; Louis P. Thorpe, D. Welty Lefever, and Robert A. Naslund; Science Research Associates. *
a) GRADES 4–6. Forms A ['54], B ('56); examiner's manual ('56); $1 per set of machine scoring stencils; 92(125) minutes in 2 sessions.
b) GRADES 6–9. Forms A ('55, identical with test copyrighted in 1954 except for change in format), B ('56); examiner's manual ('56); 50¢ per machine scoring stencil; 70(90) minutes.

ROBERT L. EBEL, *Vice President for Testing Programs and Services, Educational Testing Service, Princeton, New Jersey.*

The test for grades 4–6 consists of 82 multiple choice items administered in two periods. It includes 19 items on the use of a table of contents (21 minutes), 17 items on the use of an index (21 minutes), 20 items on the use of reference materials (15 minutes), and 26 items on reading graphs and tables (35 minutes). The test for grades 6–9 consists of 94 items, administered in a single 90 minute period. It includes 20 items on the use of references (10 minutes), 10 items on the use of a table of contents (8 minutes), 15 items on the use of an index (12 minutes), and 49 items on the reading of graphs, tables, and maps (40 minutes).

All of the items are four alternative, multiple choice items. They require the examinee to demonstrate his ability to apply the various work-study skills. Sample tables of contents, indexes, tables, graphs, and maps are used as the basis for the questions. The sample indexes, particularly those in Form A of the tests, are rather highly organized under major headings and subheadings. This disturbs the alphabetical arrangement of the entries. For example, to find a reference on *Television programs* one must look not under *Television,* or *Programs,* but under *Home entertainment.*

Most of the questions on the indexes and the tables of contents require the examinee to use these reference materials as guides to the location of information. This is as it should be. A few questions require the student to draw inferences concerning the nature of that information. One, for example, requires the examinee to infer the name of the inventor of the steamboat from certain entries in an index. Another departure from direct relevance is found in items which, instead of asking where to find certain facts, ask what information will be found on certain pages.

Each section of the tests is provided with one or more fore-exercises designed to explain to the student exactly what the test requires him to do. This is a desirable feature, especially in tests for the lower grades. In the sections on charts, however, these fore-exercises may actually do considerable teaching of the skill which the remainder of the test is designed to measure, and may therefore make the test partly a measure of ability to learn.

The test publishers have provided a very complete and attractive set of reference materials. The examiner's manual includes general instructions for use of the test battery, directions for administration and scoring, and grade and percentile norms for the tests. The inclusion of a list of correct responses was a convenience to the reviewer and should also be helpful to teachers in making effective use of the tests. A manual for the school administrator describes the nature of the tests and presents a classification of items according to the work-study skills being measured. The attempt to provide such a content analysis of the test is highly commendable; however, the authors have not been as successful in their analysis of this test as in other areas covered in the battery. The difficulty appears to be that the listed work-study skills do not correspond closely to the tasks presented in the test items. This results in suggestions that each item is measuring a multiplicity of skills. For example, one question asks on which page one should begin reading to find certain information. This item is listed as measuring five skills:

1. Ability to locate desired information with the aid of a table of contents.
2. Ability to use clues to arrangement and location of reference information, such as the alphabet, guide words as in the dictionary, page, figures, and table numbers, chapter headings, etc.
3. Ability to select and interpret main and subordinate ideas.

4. Ability to infer from and to see implications of facts given.
5. Ability to generalize from facts given.

This analysis of the diverse functions of a fairly simple item seems overelaborated.

A useful teachers' handbook provides aids to the interpretation of test scores and suggestions for follow-up action on the basis of the test results. These essential steps in the effective utilization of test results are too often slighted or omitted entirely from the accessory materials provided with standardized tests.

The excellent technical supplement gives evidence of careful attention to test construction, standardization, and analysis. The raw score quartiles indicate that, in general, the tests are appropriate in difficulty for the groups tested and give reasonably wide distributions of scores.

The section on validity places appropriate emphasis on the importance of content validity. It also presents an extensive and instructive factor analysis of the scores for the entire battery. This is an excellent example of the use of factor analysis to support the construct validity of each of the tests in the battery. The analysis revealed that all four of the tests in the battery were measuring a general achievement factor. Three of them also appeared to be measuring group achievement factors which corresponded to the content of three of the tests. Only the work-study skills did not yield a group factor. This may be a reflection of the diversity of tasks included in the test. It may be a reflection of the fact that no organized curriculum for the development of work-study skills is followed in most schools. It may be due to some other influence. In any case it suggests that scores on a work-study skills test do not have the kind of independence shown by arithmetic, reading, and language test scores. Hence, it raises a question of the appropriateness of work-study skills tests in achievement batteries at this level.

Most teachers and curriculum specialists readily agree that it is an important objective of elementary education to develop work-study skills. But there is thus far little if any evidence that these study skills can be, or are being, developed independently of other achievements. The immediate consequence of this excellent study is to cast some doubt on the desirability of including a study skills test in a general achievement test battery.

RUTH M. STRANG, *Professor of Education, Teachers College, Columbia University, New York, New York.*

As stated in the manual, this test measures ability to select and discriminate among reference sources; to use the table of contents, index, and other clues to the location of information; to see relationships and to infer and generalize from facts given; and to obtain information from, note relationships among, discern trends among, and make inferences from data presented in graphs, maps, and tables.

Emphasis is placed on the true-to-life, situation approach. However, some conflict may be noted between the objectives of providing life-like situations and meeting the demands of objective measurement; some of the items seem contrived just for test purposes. For example, some of the items dealing with the table of contents pose problems one would not naturally solve by going to the table of contents. Similarly, some of the information that pupils are expected to obtain from graphs and charts seems trivial and too labored.

The tests for grades 4–6 are introduced in story form, followed by clear, simple directions. In the tests for grades 6–9 the directions are given in a brief straightforward way. The time is ample to give every pupil opportunity to demonstrate his ability.

The number and regional distribution of the normative sample seems adequate, except that the proportion of rural to urban is lower than in the general population. It is pointed out, however, that differences between urban and rural have been decreasing in recent years. Since the test is most appropriately used for diagnosing rather than for grading, for teaching rather than for testing, high standards of general reliability are not so necessary as is the establishment of validity.

Efforts to establish validity have included reference to commonly stated goals and objectives, three minor studies of predictive value, and extensive factorial analysis. Although the content of the test is similar to that of other current tests in this area, it covers only one aspect of study skills—performance of the objective type; it is not at all concerned with the more basic psychological factors involved in effective study methods. For the predictive studies, the manual reports correlations of .66 and .68 between scores obtained by two groups of eighth

grade pupils and grade-point averages computed a half year and a year later, respectively; and .70 between scores obtained by an eighth grade group and composite scores on a battery of achievement tests administered a year later. These limited predictive studies are described as "encouraging."

It is recommended in the manual that, in order to gain a complete picture of the pupil's ability in this area, the test user examine the pupil's responses to items involving study skills in other subtests in the series. The Teacher's Handbook suggests not only an analysis of the kind of errors made by an individual or a class, but also classroom procedures and projects for developing these study skills. It is with respect to the use of this test that the *SRA Achievement Series* is particularly strong.

There is a question, however, as to whether the study skills test is worth taking time to administer. Since the main objective is the understanding of the pupils' study skills, the teacher might obtain similar and more specifically usable information by asking pupils questions based on the tables of contents and indexes of the books they are using. In the same way he could direct pupils' attention to the interpretation of charts, graphs, and tables in the context of the books they are studying. However, as an introduction, the second part of the test, with its appealing situations for analysis, would arouse the pupils' interest in these special study skills, uncover difficulties in perception and seeing relationships, and lead to application to similar tasks in their daily assignments. At best, the teaching of study skills requires a more searching psychological analysis of methods and patterns effectively used by pupils of different ages and abilities. As in so many instances, tests are being constructed before the field has been sufficiently defined and analyzed.

For reviews by Warren G. Findley and Worth R. Jones of the complete battery, see 21.

[697]

★Spitzer Study Skills Test: Evaluation and Adjustment Series. Grades 9–13; 1954–55; 6 scores: dictionary, index, graphs-tables-maps, sources of information, note taking, total for subtests 1–4; IBM; Forms AM ('54), BM ('55); manual ('54); no college norms; separate answer sheets must be used; $5 per 35 tests; $1.65 per 35 IBM answer sheets; postage extra; 35¢ per specimen set, postpaid; 75(90) minutes in 2 sessions for subtests 1–4 only; 105(135) minutes in 3 sessions; Herbert F. Spitzer; World Book Co. *

REFERENCE
1. CROOK, FRANCES E. "Interrelationships Among a Group of Language Arts Tests." *J Ed Res* 51:305–11 D '57. *

JAMES DEESE, *Associate Professor of Psychology, The Johns Hopkins University, Baltimore, Maryland.*

This test is designed to measure achievement in five specific areas of study skills: (*a*) using the dictionary, (*b*) using the index, (*c*) understanding graphs, tables, and maps, (*d*) locating sources of information, and (*e*) organizing facts in note taking. Each of these areas constitutes a subtest; the fifth subtest is specified as "optional." The test can be administered in two ordinary school periods (or three if the fifth subtest is employed).

The manual presents tables for converting raw scores on each of the five subtests to percentile ranks and standard scores. The standard scores are scaled with a mean of 106 and a standard deviation of 13.0. A number of recommendations are presented for the interpretation and use of test scores. The user is cautioned that the norms themselves may represent undesirably low achievement, the implication being that typical high school students do not receive adequate instruction in these particular study skills. Hints for remedial teaching are given for those subtests on which class achievement is very low.

Reasonably complete information concerning the development of the test is presented. Item analysis was accomplished with data obtained from 2,400 high school students in four high schools. Neither the location of these schools nor the distribution of the sample among them is mentioned. Mean values of difficulty and validity indices for items in all but the fifth subtest are presented for each of the final forms. These are the only data reported for the final forms.

For the standardization study 5,000 students in 17 high schools in 14 states were tested with the preliminary forms of the test. Again, there is no information in the manual concerning the distribution of those tested, nor is there any information about the number of cases for whom data were obtained for each of the forms. One very useful aspect of the validation data is that correlations between scores on each of the first four subtests and a number of other measures, including Terman-McNemar IQ's and scores on other tests in the Evaluation and Adjustment Series, are presented. The manual states

that these four subtests "measure substantially different aspects of study skills." The correlations between them, ranging from .26 to .60, are about typical of the correlations between achievement tests at large. Reliability coefficients obtained by the split-half method on preliminary Form 1 (later Form AM) are satisfactory for the first three subtests, but low for the fourth subtest. No data on reliability are presented for the fifth subtest because "interdependence of items in Test 5 made it inappropriate to obtain a measure of reliability by the same method."

While the standardization is less than completely satisfactory, it is not unsatisfactory. The classroom teacher or counselor has something to gain in using the measure of study skills provided by this test rather than a completely unstandardized test. The chief drawback to the test is the considerable time required for administration.

[698]

★Stanford Achievement Test: Study Skills. Grades 5–6, 7–9; 1953–54, c1952–54; items identical to those in study skills section of *Stanford Achievement Test;* IBM; 2 levels; manual ('53); separate answer sheets must be used; $2.75 per 35 tests; $1.25 per 35 IBM answer sheets; 20¢ per machine scoring stencil; postage extra; 35¢ per specimen set of either level, postpaid; 40(50) minutes; Truman L. Kelley, Richard Madden, Eric F. Gardner, Lewis M. Terman, and Giles M. Ruch; World Book Co. *
a) INTERMEDIATE STUDY SKILLS TEST. Grades 5–6; 1953, c1952–53; Forms JM, KM ('53).
b) ADVANCED STUDY SKILLS TEST. Grades 7–9; 1953–54, c1952–54; Forms JM ('53), KM ('53), LM ('54).

ROBERT L. EBEL, *Vice President for Testing Programs and Services, Educational Testing Service, Princeton, New Jersey.*

Almost all of the items in this test are of the application type in which the student must demonstrate his ability to make practical interpretations or uses of the data presented in charts, tables, maps, dictionaries, indexes, and other sources of information. There is one item in each form which requires identification of a root word from among several combined forms. These items can be justified on the ground that the root word entry in a dictionary frequently includes information that is useful in understanding or using the combined form. On the other hand, it seems doubtful that ability to identify the root word (which is always shorter than and part of the combined forms) in these items really indicates possession of the skill in using the dictionary it is intended to test.

A striking characteristic of the items in both forms is the brevity of the responses. Ordinarily they consist of a single word or numerical value. Economy of words in an objective test item is highly commendable, and tends to yield high reliability per unit of testing time. On the other hand, there are certain inferences, conclusions, and recommendations which cannot be expressed adequately in one word responses. The exclusion of such items may limit the sampling of relevant tasks somewhat.

Part 1 in both tests includes two charts and one table, with five questions based on each. The questions on the line graphs, and to a lesser extent on the bar graphs, tend to be quite similar. Sometimes the effort to make them different leads to rather artificial questions, e.g., "How many papers did Joe sell on Wednesday and Tuesday together?" (The preceding question had asked, "How many papers did Joe sell on Wednesday?") It is reasonable to suppose that scores on such closely related items would be highly related. This raises the question of whether one would not obtain a better indication of ability to interpret charts and graphs by using a wider variety of examples with fewer questions on each. An alternative would be to seek greater complexity in the information presented in the charts.

Excellent norms of two types, modal-age grade norms and total-group grade norms, are available for both tests. The manual makes clear that grade equivalents above 10.0 have been obtained by extrapolation. Since there is no study skills test in the elementary or primary batteries, it seems likely that grade scores below 5.0 were also obtained by extrapolation. Grade scores for the intermediate test in the 5.0 to 6.9 range, and for the advanced test in the 7.0 to 9.9 range were obtained directly. Other grade scores for each test in the 5.0 to 9.9 range were derived from a norm line based on K-score equating.

Percentile norms for the various modal-age groups indicate that both tests are appropriate in difficulty and give good score distributions. Reliability coefficients in the high .80's on both tests are very good for tests of this length. The manual is careful to point out that the reliability of scores for a single class, or even for a single school system, would probably be somewhat lower than the reported values, which are based on pupils from numerous school systems.

The manual has detailed directions for administering and scoring the test, and for interpreting the scores. Reference is made to a more extensive manual for the complete battery which includes test descriptions, suggestions for the use of test results, information on test construction and standardization, and a brief discussion of the K-scores.

The validity of tests of this type depends largely upon the competence and skill of the test constructors. The primary requirement is that the tests possess content validity. This must be built into the tests, and cannot ordinarily be demonstrated convincingly by any routine statistical procedures. In particular, the typical validity study involving a correlation of test scores with school grades is of little value in demonstrating the validity of tests like those under review.

On the other hand, there are troublesome problems of test content and test design which relate to the question of test validity. Is it appropriate and useful to group diverse test items based on graphs, tables, maps, dictionaries, indexes, encyclopedias, and other sources of information into a single test yielding a single score? Study skills seem not to be considered important enough by curriculum builders to deserve substantial direct allocations of time in the school program. Do they, nevertheless, deserve a place on a par with reading, language, and arithmetic in an achievement battery? Is there any evidence that the use of study skills tests contributes to the improvement of these skills? Or, is there evidence that a well worked out program for developing study skills will be reflected by greater than normal score gains on these tests from grade to grade? Is a study skills test something more than a short, indirect indication of general educational achievement?

The asking of these questions is not intended to imply any special shortcomings of the Stanford tests. In comparison with other similar tests they have a number of excellent qualities and few deficiencies. The point is that more attention should be paid by the authors and publishers of all such tests to their basic meaningfulness (construct validity) and educational utility. A section on validity in the manual would provide an opportunity and an incentive to marshal whatever evidence there is on these questions.

RUTH M. STRANG, *Professor of Education, Teachers College, Columbia University, New York, New York.*

The directions for administering the test are precise and definite except for the introductory statement: "This is a test to show how much you have learned"—presumably about study skills. Actually, the test is limited to skills involved in reading graphs, charts, and maps, and several location of information and word recognition skills.

The test has three parts: Part 1, Reading Charts and Tables; Part 2, Map Reading; and Part 3, Using the Dictionary, Sources, and Index. The test does not presume to measure broader psychological aspects of study methods such as approach to an assignment, concentration, and remembering. In fact, we do not have enough understanding of the study process used by different students to construct a satisfactory study test encompassing these factors.

Parts 1 and 2 of the intermediate forms are high in interest. They test relationships as well as separate facts. The choice of content is practical and sound. Part 3 of Form JM is less satisfactory because of the difficulty of understanding the directions. Part 3 of Form KM tests the same kind of location of information and word recognition skills in a less complicated way. The intent is good, but some children who have the study skills may get tangled up in the test directions and form. The skills in Part 3 might be better tested informally through "work samples" rather than forced into the mold of multiple choice tests.

The advanced test measures the same types of study skills and is interesting and ingenuously constructed.

The conversion of raw scores into total-group grade norms, modal-age grade norms, and percentile norms is clearly and adequately described. The variety of norms permits interpretation for various purposes. The percentile norms, expressed in terms of grade scores for modal-age groups, make possible a comparison of the scores of a pupil with scores of other pupils of the same grade status; the modal-age norms permit comparison with scores of pupils of a given age in a given grade. According to the manual, "the use of the total group average as the norm for evaluation of an individual's performance sets an unduly low standard for the majority of pupils and, in the long run, is likely to encourage acceptance of

an unnecessarily low level of achievement." Thus, accelerated pupils and the larger group of retarded pupils are both eliminated from the modal-age norms group.

According to the manual, the corrected split-half reliability coefficients range from .87 to .89 for both the intermediate test and the advanced test. These are single grade coefficients. However, for a small sample ($n = 89$) of fifth graders in independent schools the coefficient of correlation was lower than the reliability reported for the same grade in the manual—.70 as compared with .87. Any group with less than average variability might be expected to have lower correlations.

No attempt seems to have been made to ascertain the validity of the test by comparing test results with pupils' observed functioning in study skills in classroom situations.

In summary, the test is useful for ascertaining a group's ability to interpret certain kinds of maps and graphs, and to locate information and recognize certain words. The title of the test, however, is misleading in that the test does not tap the psychological aspects of study such as motivation, problem solving, and the use of knowledge gained, nor does it measure habits and attitudes of study characteristic of able students.

For a review by N. L. Gage of the complete battery, see 25.

[699]

A Test of Study Skills. Grades 4–9; 1940–41; IBM; Forms A, B ('40); directions sheet ('40); reliability data based on preliminary edition; no norms; separate answer sheets must be used; $2.50 per 30 tests; 1½¢ per IBM answer sheet; 30¢ per scoring stencil; 25¢ per specimen set; cash orders postpaid; 60(70) minutes; J. W. Edgar and H. T. Manuel; Steck Co. *

MARVIN D. GLOCK, *Professor of Educational Psychology, Cornell University, Ithaca, New York.*

The test is in two parts. Part 1, Finding and Understanding Printed Materials, is concerned with the location of sources of information and the intelligent utilization of the type of materials found in common references. Questions are of the 5-response multiple choice type. Part 2, Critical Thinking in the Use of Printed Materials, consists of a series of paragraphs, accompanied by multiple choice questions the pupils' understanding of which is checked by questions that may be answered by Yes or No, or by a phrase to the effect that the answer is impossible to arrive at from the facts given. To label the skill required to answer the questions in this part as critical thinking may well be questioned, since a number of the items do nothing more than check main ideas and details.

A major weakness of the test is its design for such a wide range of grade levels, the sampling for any particular grade being, as a result, severely limited. Much of the test will be so difficult for many fourth graders that little information will be gained about the study habits they should have mastered. Likewise, the test will have too low a ceiling for able pupils in the upper grades.

No norms of any kind are provided either in the manual or elsewhere. Information concerning test reliability is limited to the reporting of a coefficient of .92, determined by correlating the scores of 72 pupils in grades 4, 6, and 8 on two forms of an earlier edition of the test. Content validity is claimed on the basis of the careful selection of items. The authors, however, are frank in acknowledging weaknesses in content. They also acknowledge the fact that certain study processes can be tested only indirectly through a recall of information. It is possible, for example, for a pupil to answer correctly the question "Where should the light be placed for a left-handed boy writing a letter at night?" He might, however, place the light over his left shoulder.

When this test is compared with the study skills tests of some of the newer achievement test batteries, it is difficult to see why any school official would select it. Since the batteries are designed for a much narrower grade range, the study skills tests at the various levels provide a wider sampling of skills in a larger number of study areas; and language, content, format, and size of print can be adjusted from level to level to suit pupils of a particular age. Finally, with most achievement test batteries, pupil profiles are furnished on which strengths and weaknesses in various areas can be easily observed. For the test under consideration profiles are not available.

For a review by Douglas E. Scates, see 3:542.

[700]
*Watson-Glaser Critical Thinking Appraisal. Grades 9–16 and adults; 1942–56; revision of *Watson-Glaser Tests of Critical Thinking;* 6 scores: inference, assumptions, deduction, interpretation, arguments, total; IBM; Forms AM ('52), BM ('52, booklet with printer's mark WGCTA:BM-2 is a slight revision of booklet WGCTA:BM-1) ; manual ('52) ; no data on reliability of the current forms; norms ('56) ; separate answer sheets must be used; $4.15 per 35 tests; $1.40 per 35 IBM answer sheets; postage extra; 35¢ per specimen set, postpaid; (40–50) minutes; Goodwin Watson and Edward Maynard Glaser; World Book Co. *

REFERENCES
1–3. See 3:544.
4. BREMBECK, WINSTON L. *The Effects of a Course in Argumentation on Critical Thinking Ability.* Doctor's thesis, University of Wisconsin (Madison, Wis.), 1947.
5. BREMBECK, WINSTON L. "The Effects of a Course in Argumentation on Critical Thinking Ability." *Speech Monogr* 16: 177–89 S '49. * (PA 24:4486)
6. CANTER, RALPH R., JR. "A Human Relations Training Program." *J Appl Psychol* 35:38–45 F '51. * (PA 25:7152)
7. BROWNELL, JOHN ARNOLD. "The Influence of Training in Reading in the Social Studies on the Ability to Think Critically." *Calif J Ed Res* 4:28–31 Ja '53. * (PA 28:1466)
8. BLEDSOE, JOSEPH C. "A Comparative Study of Values and Critical Thinking Skills of a Group of Educational Workers." *J Ed Psychol* 46:408–17 N '55. * (PA 31:3774)
9. COOK, JOHN. "Validity Information Exchange, No. 8-13: D.O.T. Code 0-17.01, Electrical Engineer." *Personnel Psychol* 8:261–2 su '55. *
10. HOLLENBACH, JOHN W., AND DE GRAAF, CLARENCE. "Teaching for Thinking." *J Higher Ed* 28:126–30 Mr '57. *
11. ENNIS, ROBERT H. "An Appraisal of the Watson-Glaser Critical Thinking Appraisal." *J Ed Res* 52:155–8 D '58. *

WALKER H. HILL, *Associate Professor, Office of Evaluation Services, Michigan State University, East Lansing, Michigan.*

This test, compared with the 1942 edition, has been shortened and refined through experimentation and analysis. The five subtests which have been retained are clearly pertinent to most definitions of "critical thinking." The directions are simplified, and the format is greatly improved. An earlier "objectivity score" has been dropped.

Two parallel forms are provided, each containing 99 items. The five subtests are: (*a*) Inference (20 items), (*b*) Recognition of Assumptions (16 items), (*c*) Deduction (25 items), (*d*) Interpretation (24 items), (*e*) Evaluation of Arguments (14 items). The authors properly urge caution in the use of subtest scores, even when both forms of the test are used.

Both "neutral" and "emotionally toned" items are included, but it is recognized that the impact of the latter will vary with different groups. The authors now advise teachers who are interested in studying the effect of feeling or prejudice on critical thinking to identify for themselves those items which are likely to have a loading for their particular groups.

A significant change has been made in the design of the assumptions subtest. Formerly this test called for *selection* of an assumption from three suggested statements, with a fourth alternative: "None of the above assumptions is made." In the new test one must decide for each statement whether it is or is not assumed. This seems to be a change for the better.

As much as the authors have improved the test, they have not solved all the problems inherent in this area of testing. In the inference subtest they feel it necessary to require use of "certain commonly accepted knowledge or information which practically every person knows." This is a loophole which makes it possible to question the key to certain items, depending on what one considers to be commonly accepted knowledge.

The interpretation subtest permits the use of two types of judgment. The pattern here is a short paragraph followed by a number of proposed conclusions. In some cases each conclusion must be judged independently of the others. In other cases the conclusions are alternative explanations of a set of facts. When this is true, and is recognized, it is immediately apparent that none of the conclusions can follow beyond a reasonable doubt, and it is not necessary to judge each one on its own merit. This discrepancy may or may not have been intended, but it seems to introduce a heterogeneity (involving more than one kind of ability) that is questionable in a short subtest.

In the last subtest each argument is given in support of an answer to a question. The testee is instructed to "try not to let counter-arguments or your own attitude toward the question influence your judgment." This is a misleading instruction. Undoubtedly it is intended to mean: Do not let your own answer to the question keep you from recognizing a strong argument on the other side. But it also means something else. One of the questions, for example, is this: "Should infants be fed by regular schedule rather than whenever they seem to be hungry?" The answer "Yes; a regular schedule is easier for the parents" is supposed to be judged a weak argument. Why? Because the welfare of the infant should be considered more important than the convenience of the parents. The reviewer agrees—which is to say that in this respect he shares the authors' attitude toward the question. There are several instances of this kind. While the reviewer finds the keyed answers quite acceptable, he believes they *do* involve attitudes and that this will be recognized by some students, particularly those who are critical thinkers.

Though the keyed answers throughout the test are said to represent the unanimous judgment of 35 selected persons, this reviewer remains unsatisfied with several and would stoutly challenge a few. In part this reflects the above-mentioned loophole in the first subtest; in other cases it involves the interpretation of individual items. And, though the two forms are said to be carefully equated, there seems to be a significantly larger number of questionable items in Form BM than in Form AM.

The authors have prepared an excellent manual for users of the test. In addition to a description of the test and discussion of its uses, the manual includes percentile norms for high school and college students (based, however, on a regrettably limited college population), tables of technical data, and reports on validity and reliability. While reliability data for the current forms are not given, rough estimates can be made from the data reported for preceding experimental editions. A discussion of the meaning of critical thinking and its relation to other abilities is especially valuable. A useful list of references is included.

If, as this reviewer believes, critical thinking is a central goal of education, serious efforts to understand it and appraise it must be encouraged. The number of such efforts has been growing in recent years, and the *Watson-Glaser Critical Thinking Appraisal* is one of the useful instruments for this purpose. The difficulties mentioned in this review concern certain details, but are not intended to obscure the instrument's generally high quality.

CARL I. HOVLAND, *Sterling Professor of Psychology, Yale University, New Haven, Connecticut.*

The Watson-Glaser test is a conscientious, imaginative effort to provide appraisal in a most difficult area—that of "critical thinking." Five subtests are employed to evaluate the capacity of the individual to draw correct inferences, recognize assumptions, draw appropriate deductions, interpret data, and evaluate arguments. The authors vary the subject matter to which the reasoning process is applied in an interesting manner—some of their items employ content which is abstract and noncontroversial, and other items, parallel in logical structure, involve issues of a controversial character to which many individuals react with emotion and prejudice. Critics of the test may still feel, however, that it does not include sufficient representation of the more subtle aspects of critical thinking, such as those involved in identification of one's own latent premises or in the differentiation of sources of information possessing varying degrees of credibility.

The tests have found useful application both for selection purposes in schools and industry and for evaluation of the effectiveness of programs of instruction. The latter application will undoubtedly be of increasing importance in view of present-day emphasis on improving instruction in scientific reasoning. The authors also suggest the utilization of the test for diagnosis of difficulties in thinking and as a teaching aid. References to researches which have used the test for various of these purposes are cited in the test manual.

Within the last few years the authors have reworked many of the items, basing their modifications on criticisms, expert opinion, and experience gained during the last decade of use. About 40 per cent of the items have been changed.

In addition, the authors have accumulated a more substantial collection of cases upon which to base their norms. The norms printed in the manual are quite sketchy, being based on miscellaneous samples of students in various high schools and colleges. Mimeographed materials which supply somewhat more extensive norms, including norms for adult groups and graduate students in various fields, are available from the publisher. There is still, of course, nothing like national norms available, although additional cases are constantly being secured.

While the two forms of the tests were standardized in a manner intended to provide equivalent scores, there are differences ranging up to 6 points between scores on the two forms so that specification of which form was used is a desirable procedure in individual testing. In evaluation work it is also quite critical to take the form used into account because otherwise increases or decreases may spuriously be attributed to the educational experience being evaluated. A dittoed table of equivalent scores is provided by the authors but it is not stated on what basis this was developed or upon what groups the equivalence is based.

Moderately high reliabilities of .79 to .84 are reported on a preliminary edition for small samples of high school students, based on estimates utilizing split-half and interform methods. (The 19 least reliable items were deleted in the final edition.) The size of these correlation coefficients is, of course, a function of the range of scores, and it is possible that for some purposes higher reliability coefficients might be obtained when testing more heterogeneous populations. By the nature of the test, however, the most frequent utilization will probably involve populations of restricted range, and hence only moderate reliability is to be expected. Reliability is a problem particularly in studies evaluating the effectiveness of educational programs where the reliability of change scores will be very low indeed since the range of changes typically represents only a fraction of the range of the test scores themselves.

The assessment of the validity of a test of this type is a most difficult matter. The authors state that "several high school science teachers were asked to identify their students who appeared markedly able or markedly poor in ability to reason accurately and to think logically. The test distinguished significantly between the two groups." Correlations of from .33 to .52 for four different classes are reported between teacher's ratings and total scores on the test. Similarly, with groups of 15 research chemists, 12 biologists, 18 engineers, and 15 accountants, there was a significant difference between those who were rated in the top and bottom halves of the group by their supervisors. Converted into correlation form, this relationship may not be very impressive. It is also true that since the theoretical relationship between critical thinking and other measures of intelligence is not established, it is difficult to assess whether the correlation of .70 reported between this test and the *Terman-McNemar Test of Mental Ability* means that the Watson-Glaser test is measuring a single major aspect of intelligence or is just another form of intelligence test. (The reliability of the critical thinking test itself is only around .80.) The authors themselves state that the test differs considerably from an intelligence test and is not an intelligence test as such.

Practice effects appear to be relatively slight. The average improvement for a group of secondary students retested after a week was only 0.6 points, as compared with the 6 point difference in scores mentioned above for alternate forms of the test.

This is a very promising test for use on an experimental basis for selection purposes and for research on the effects of instructional procedures on critical thinking. Development of tests in this area is an extremely difficult undertaking. As a consequence we cannot expect to find as precise measurement here as in less complex areas. The test is not yet thoroughly enough standardized to permit the use of scores on it in any absolute way for determining the adequacy of a testee's skill in critical thinking.

Nevertheless, compared with other less well developed tests which are springing up on all sides with items selected as measures of critical thinking largely on a priori considerations, the Watson-Glaser test is a quite effective instrument.

For a review by Robert H. Thouless of the original edition, see 3:544 (1 excerpt).

SCIENCE

REVIEWS BY *Theo. A. Ashford, Frank P. Cassaretto, Max D. Engelhart, Elizabeth Hagen, Clark W. Horton, Palmer O. Johnson, William Harrison Lucow, M. Jacinta Mann, Leo Nedelsky, Theodore G. Phillips, Edward G. Rietz, Roy W. Stanhope, Julian C. Stanley, Robert M. W. Travers, Mervyn L. Turner, and Willard G. Warrington.*

[701]
★Biology and General Science: National Teacher Examinations. College seniors and teachers; 1940–58; for more complete information, see 538; IBM; 80(90) minutes; Educational Testing Service. *

For reviews by William A. Brownell, Walter W. Cook, and Lawrence G. Derthick of the entire series, see 538; for a review by Harry N. Rivlin of an earlier edition, see 4:802.

[702]
★Chemistry, Physics, and General Science: National Teacher Examinations. College seniors and teachers; 1940–58; for more complete information, see 538; IBM; 80(90) minutes; Educational Testing Service. *

For reviews by William A. Brownell, Walter W. Cook, and Lawrence G. Derthick of the entire series, see 538; for a review by Harry N. Rivlin of an earlier edition, see 4:802.

[703]
*Cooperative General Achievement Tests: Test II, Natural Science. Grade 12 and college entrants; 1937–56; manual uses the subtitle *A Test of General Proficiency in the Field of Natural Science;* 3 scores: terms and concepts, comprehension and interpretation, total; IBM; Forms XX ('53, revision of Form X), YZ ('51, revision of Forms Y and Z); no norms for part scores; high school norms same as those published in 1938; separate answer sheets must be used; $2.95 per 25 tests; $1 per 25 IBM answer sheets; 25¢ per scoring stencil; 35¢ per battery manual ('56); 50¢ per specimen set; cash orders postpaid; 40(50) minutes; Paul J. Burke (XX); Cooperative Test Division, Educational Testing Service. *

For a review by Palmer O. Johnson of earlier forms, see 3:548. For a review by Max D. Engelhart of the complete battery, see 6; for a

review by Paul L. Dressel of earlier forms, see 4:5; for a review by John V. McQuitty, see 3:3.

[704]
*Coordinated Scales of Attainment: Science. Grades 4, 5, 6, 7, 8; 1946–54; subtest of *Coordinated Scales of Attainment;* IBM; grades 4, 7: Forms A ('46), B ('49); grades 5–6, 8: Forms A, B ('49); 5 levels; directions for administering ['52]; battery manuals (A, '54; B, '49); separate answer sheets must be used $1.90 per 25 tests; $1 per 25 IBM scorable answer sheets; 10¢ per scoring stencil; 50¢ per specimen set; postage extra; (20) minutes; Victor C. Smith; Educational Test Bureau. *

For a review by Alvin W. Schindler of the complete battery, see 4:8; for reviews by Roland L. Beck, Lavone A. Hanna, Gordon N. Mackenzie (with Glen Hass), and C. C. Ross of Batteries 4–8, see 3:6.

[705]
*Elementary Science and Health: Every Pupil Test. Grades 4–6; 1935–58; new form usually issued each December and April; norms available following testing program; no data on reliability; 3¢ per test; 1¢ per scoring key; cash orders postpaid; 40(45) minutes; Ohio Scholarship Tests. *

[706]
★Elementary Science: Every Pupil Scholarship Test. Grades 5–8; 1926–58; new form usually issued each January and April; norms available following testing program; no data on reliability; 4¢ per test; 4¢ per scoring key; postage extra; 40(45) minutes; Bureau of Educational Measurements. *

[707]
*Elementary Science Test: National Achievement Tests. Grades 4–6; 1948–55; 6 scores: practical applications, cause and effect relationships, miscellaneous facts, simple identifications, evaluation of statements, total; Form A ('55, identical with test

copyrighted in 1948 except for a minor change in Item 9, Part 2) ; directions sheet ('55) ; no data on reliability; no norms for part scores; $2.75 per 25 tests ; 50¢ per specimen set; postage extra; 35(40) minutes ; Lester D. Crow and W. L. Shuman; Acorn Publishing Co. *

WILLIAM HARRISON LUCOW, *Associate Professor of Education, University of Manitoba, Winnipeg, Manitoba, Canada.*

This test has definite value in spite of its shortcomings. The neglect of science teaching in the elementary schools is an ever-present problem due mainly to mental blocks in teachers with regard to the subject. This test provides a means of assessing the extent to which the children have been able to attain scientific knowledge incidentally in situations where their science education has been neglected.

Part 1 purports to measure "Practical Applications" of science. Few of the items do this ; rather, they tap miscellaneous bits of information. Of the three alternatives in the multiple choice items, the two to be rejected are not always plausible nor even related to scientific knowledge. Part 2, Cause and Effect Relationships, contains more items that live up to their purpose, but many are simply factual. Part 3, Miscellaneous Facts, draws on biology, astronomy, geology, and mechanics, with an emphasis on plants and animals quite appropriate at this level. Part 4, Simple Identifications, presents a mental hurdle in the change from multiple choice items to a confusing type of matching exercise. Part 5, Evaluation of Statements, is a true-false array, again confusing in structure. "Problem Situation A" is followed by five endings to the introductory statement to be declared true or false; "Problem Situation B" is followed by five complete statements ; and "Problem Situation C" consists of 10 independent problems.

Validity is claimed to be achieved by consideration of the latest courses of study and recent textbooks on elementary science. The heterogeneous nature and often nonexistent offerings in elementary science make such validity questionable with respect to any local administration. Nevertheless, the curricular content covered by the test is a good indication of what *should* be taught. Reliability, not published, but according to the publisher, is .91 as determined by the odd-even method and the Spearman-Brown formula. Norms are supplied in the form of percentiles for grades 3 to 7, although the test is designed for grades 4 to 6

inclusive. Directions, a class record form, the answer key, and the norms all come printed on a single sheet. No norms are presented for the five subtests.

Apart from the significance mentioned above, there is little to commend this test. Improvement might be achieved by eliminating the parts and presenting the items all in multiple choice form as one homogeneous test.

[708]
*General Science: Every Pupil Scholarship Test. High school; 1926–58; new form usually issued each January and April; norms available following testing program; no data on reliability; 4¢ per test; 4¢ per scoring key; postage extra; 40(45) minutes ; Bureau of Educational Measurements. *

[709]
*General Science: Every Pupil Test. 1, 2 semesters high school; 1929–58; new form usually issued each December and April; norms available following testing program; no data on reliability; 3¢ per test; 1¢ per scoring key; cash orders postpaid; 40(45) minutes ; Ohio Scholarship Tests. *

[710]
★General Science: Midwest High School Achievement Examinations. High school; 1955–57; Forms A ('55), B ('57) ; no specific manual; no data on reliability; norms: [A, '55; B, '57] ; 10¢ per test, postage extra; Form A: 60(65) minutes ; Form B: 90(95) minutes ; Victor C. Smith (A), Jennings O. Johnson (B), and George R. Otto (B) ; Educational Test Bureau. *

[711]
*General Science III: Achievement Examinations for Secondary Schools. High school; 1951–53; Forms 1 ('51), 2 ('52), 3 ('53) ; no specific manual; no data on reliability; norms: Forms 1 ['52], 2 ['53], 3 ('53) ; Forms 1, 2: 10¢ per test, Form 3: $2.75 per 25 tests; 10¢ per specimen set; postage extra; [60–90] minutes ; Victor C. Smith; Educational Test Bureau. *

[712]
*General Science Test: National Achievement Tests. Grades 7–9; 1936–50; 7 scores: general concepts, identifications, men of science, definitions, uses of objects, miscellaneous facts, total; Forms A ('50, identical with test copyrighted in 1936 except for minor changes), B ('50, identical with test copyrighted in 1939) ; directions sheet ('50) ; no data on reliability; no norms for part scores; $2.75 per 25 tests; 50¢ per specimen set; postage extra; (35) minutes ; Robert K. Speer, Lester D. Crow, and Samuel Smith; Acorn Publishing Co. *

ROBERT M. W. TRAVERS, *Professor of Educational Psychology and Head of the Department, University of Utah, Salt Lake City, Utah.*

Rarely does one find a test which illustrates all of the errors which such instruments may manifest. The reviewer has often thought of preparing such an instrument to be used as a teaching device in courses in tests and measurements. However, it seems that the test considered here would be satisfactory for such purposes.

First, the explanatory sheet which is provided for the teacher is as uninformative as if it had been written with the deliberate intent of keeping secret the purpose, design, and statistical characteristics of the test. Careful consideration of the matter suggests that the test is not the result of any concerted effort at careful planning, but rather is it a motley collection of items, some of which are derived from obsolete sources. The publisher provides a statement of purpose which runs as follows: "This test measures the student's knowledge of scientific concepts; ability to identify objects from illustrations; recognition of important men of science; ability to define scientific terms; knowledge of uses of objects; and mastery of scientific facts." After reading this statement, the reviewer expected to find test items which would really measure the pupil's ability to "recognize important men of science" and which would determine whether the pupil could identify the portrait of a bearded figure as that of Francis Galton. Of course, items of this kind are not to be found. Instead, the pupil is asked to pair famous men of science with their discoveries. Again, "knowledge of uses of objects" hardly represents a useful category of test items, but rather is it a license to write a wide range of different items. In summary, the test shows no evidence of having been developed according to a well thought-out plan.

Sometimes apparently unplanned tests may still have merit because the authors had in their thoughts a plan which they never described in the manual. With this in mind the reviewer turned to a study of the test items themselves. A quick reading of the items revealed that any misgivings already entertained were fully justified. Several questions have multiple right answers while some have none. In one item the right answer is that gravity pulls towards the center of the earth, and a supposedly wrong answer is that gravity is a force that pulls towards the sun. In this case the correct answer is not precisely stated; but if it is accepted as the right answer, the supposedly wrong answer is also right. Some of the items are hilarious in their use of the English language. The reviewer particularly enjoyed reading the item which begins "The boiling point of the fahrenheit thermometer is...." (The lower case f is in the test, but even Mr. fahrenheit might have had difficulty in making a thermometer boil.) Then there is the item which together with the correct answer reads "Pressure is exerted by air because air has weight." This is a rather sad distortion of the fact that air exerts pressure because the molecules of the gas have both mass and velocity.

Another disturbing fact is that some of the items represent an outlook on science which was typical of the last century rather than the present one. For example, the notion that the ether is a substance comes from the pre-relativity era. Another example of this type of outmoded thinking is represented by items which ask the student to agree with the proposition that science is a search for truth. It is doubtful whether any modern philosopher would find such a naive outlook acceptable.

Information on reliability is notable by its absence. The so-called norms provide median scores for each month within the seventh, eighth, and ninth grades, but no indication is given of the range of scores. Also, there is no information on the number of children who took the test to provide the norm group and no indication of the characteristics of the population, whether from a large city school system or a rural school. The use of the norms provided would involve the interpretation of a meaningless score in terms of a meaningless standard.

The real mystery to the reviewer is how this test has stayed on the market for nearly 20 years. Will all guilty parties consider themselves hereby reprimanded.

For reviews by Francis D. Curtis and G. W. Hunter, see 40:1602.

[713]

*The Iowa Tests of Educational Development: Test 2, General Background in the Natural Sciences. Grades 9–13; 1942–58; IBM; Forms X-3S, Y-3S ('52); Examiner's manual ('58); battery manual ('54); pupil profile leaflet, fourth edition ('58); profile card (no date); separate answer sheets must be used; $3 per 20 tests; $5 per 100 IBM answer sheets; 50¢ per scoring stencil; $3 per complete specimen set; postage extra; 60(70) or 40(50) minutes; prepared under the direction of E. F. Lindquist; Science Research Associates. *

For reviews by J. Murray Lee and Stephen Wiseman of the complete battery, see 17; for a review by Eric F. Gardner of earlier forms, see 4:17; for reviews by Henry Chauncey, Gustav J. Froehlich, and Lavone A. Hanna, see 3:12.

[714]

★**Physical Science: Teacher Education Examination Program.** College seniors preparing to teach secondary school; 1957; for more complete information, see 543; IBM; 80(95) minutes; Educational Testing Service. *

For a review by Walter W. Cook of the entire series, see 543.

[715]

*****Read General Science Test: Evaluation and Adjustment Series.** Grades 9–13; 1951–54, c1950–51; IBM; Forms AM ('51), BM ('52); manual ('51); expectancy chart ['54]; separate answer sheets must be used; $3.90 per 35 tests; $1.35 per 35 IBM answer sheets; postage extra; 35¢ per specimen set, postpaid; 40(50) minutes; John G. Read; World Book Co. *

REFERENCE

1. READ, JOHN G. "Construction and Evaluation of a New General Science Test." *Sci Ed* 35:262–6 D '51. *

For reviews by Benjamin S. Bloom and John S. Richardson, see 4:628.

[716]

★**Sequential Tests of Educational Progress: Science.** Grades 4–6, 7–9, 10–12, 13–14; 1956–57; IBM; Forms A, B ('57); 4 levels; manual ('57); battery directions ('57); battery technical report ('57); no data on reliability of Form B; separate answer sheets must be used; $3.95 per 20 tests; $1 per 20 IBM scorable answer sheets; 45¢ per scoring stencil; $1 per manual; $1 per battery technical report; $1.25 per specimen set; postage extra; 70(90–100) minutes; Cooperative Test Division, Educational Testing Service. *
a) LEVEL 4. Grades 4–6; Forms 4A, 4B.
b) LEVEL 3. Grades 7–9; Forms 3A, 3B.
c) LEVEL 2. Grades 10–12; Forms 2A, 2B.
d) LEVEL 1. Grades 12–14; Forms 1A, 1B.

PALMER O. JOHNSON, *Professor of Education, University of Minnesota, Minneapolis, Minnesota.*

The STEP science tests comprise four levels extending from the fourth grade in the elementary school through the second year in college. The tests constitute a new approach to the construction of achievement tests. They are designed to measure how well students can make use of what they have learned in the classroom. Generally, educational growth in science includes two main aspects: (*a*) the understanding and retention of basic scientific concepts, and (*b*) the development of the ability to use the basic concepts in the solution of scientific problems. In these tests it is assumed that by measuring the second aspect one measures also the first. Accordingly, the test situation is a problem situation.

Each test is comprised of sets of multiple choice objective questions. Each set is based on a single problem situation, the problems included being those deemed to be of concern in the everyday life and interests of the students. The tests in the series presumably progress from lower to more advanced levels. As an example, an analysis of Part 1, Form 4A, reveals the organization of the test around five situations: (1) Fun at Camp, (2) Sick in Bed, (3) Bicycle Ride, (4) The Jackson Garden, and (5) A Trip to the Moon. The 30 test situations are distributed between the physical (16) and the biological (14) sciences. At the uppermost end of the sequence, in Part 1 of Form 1A, the 30 problems can be classified among five different sciences as follows: 1–10, conservation and agriculture; 11–16, chemistry; 17–20, physics; 21–26, biology (health); and 27–30, geology.

Interspersed among the problem situations in the various levels, there are attempts to test understandings of the scientific method, including abilities to identify and define a scientific problem, to suggest hypotheses, to select validating procedures, to interpret data and draw conclusions, to evaluate claims or statements, and to reason quantitatively and symbolically.

For the tryout of the test materials a plan was adopted which aimed to secure samples of students similar to those for whom the final forms were intended. A roster of superintendents of school systems supplied by the U.S. Office of Education constituted the sampled population of public schools. At the college level almost every college in the nation was asked to participate. However, all of the subsequent samples were drawn from the groups that indicated a willingness to participate. No statement is made of the number of refusals. However, from the lists of participating schools provided it is observed that schools in 29 states participated although some states were represented by only a single school system, and that the 33 participating colleges were dispersed among 21 states. Approximately 4,000 students were tested in each of grades 5, 8, 11, and 13. Not knowing the representative qualities of schools included makes it very hazardous to use the norms reported.

Critical appraisal of STEP must await the results of their use in the schools and colleges for which they were designed and upon special studies of the relationship between these tests and measures of other academic performances. Every reasonable attempt has been made to create a high standard product and the problem has been attacked in a practical spirit.

Certainly the emphasis upon testing problem solving ability and the continuity of measurement of this important outcome over long periods is to be highly commended. The tests should be especially useful as instruments in developing integrated, graduated, and well articulated programs of science particularly designed for general educational purposes. As they are used, evidence resulting from carefully controlled study should reduce to secondary importance reliance on the judgment of the teachers who constructed them and on statistics based on fragmentary data whose representativeness has still to be established. The STEP tests go hand in hand with the kind of curricular organization which should increase the efficiency of learning experiences.

JULIAN C. STANLEY, *Professor of Education, University of Wisconsin, Madison, Wisconsin;* M. JACINTA MANN, *Instructor in Mathematics, Seton Hill College, Greensburg, Pennsylvania.*

Booklets and answer sheets for all levels have the same excellent format and directions and do not designate the grades to which they are most applicable, so it is easy to use two or even more levels for testing a single class, or to test several grade groups together. A common score scale spans all levels and forms, making it possible, for example, to compare Mary's score of two years ago on Level 4, Form A, with her current score on Level 3, Form B, or either of Mary's scores with Susan's performance on Level 1, Form A. Since STEP is well articulated with the *Cooperative School and College Ability Tests* (SCAT), a school system can, by using these two batteries, meet a large percentage of its standardized testing needs and have much more comparable scores than separately prepared tests provide.

The STEP science tests are relatively unspeeded (two 35-minute periods of working time for 60 four-option multiple choice items). They have "do-guess" instructions: "You will make your best score by answering *every* question because your score is the number of correct answers you mark." It seems desirable to minimize the influence of quickness and differential gambling propensity in these ways. Options for odd-numbered items are labeled A, B, C, and D and for even-numbered items E, F, G, H, an ingenious stratagem to reduce careless errors in marking the separate answer sheet.

Sampling of scientific knowledge is broad and comprehensive. Blocks of as many as ten and as few as three items are based upon a single situation, usually one commonly experienced by the age group for which the level is primarily designed. Titles of some blocks at the lowest level are "Fun at Camp," "Sick in Bed," "Bicycle Ride," "The Jackson Garden," and "A Trip to the Moon." Under the first we read: "Jack, Bobby, Joe, and Harry went to a summer camp. At the camp many interesting things happened to them." This introduction is followed by seven questions, each dealing with some aspect of the camp.

Employing familiar situations for the blocks of items must tend to enhance interest and motivation, making the testing situation less formal and abstract than ordinarily found. It appears to lower the novelty of the material, however, thereby reducing the level of the mental operations required to answer a given item correctly. The reviewers found many of the items difficult to classify according to the *Taxonomy of Educational Objectives* [1] because it seems likely that the rather typical points involved might have been taught explicitly in some classes but not others. For example, Item 2 in Part 1 of Test 4A deals with why we see a lightning flash before we hear the thunder it produces: "Bobby said that it was because light travels faster than sound." Some fourth graders will already have heard this very illustration discussed in class or on television, while others will not, and the mental processes of successful answerers from the two groups may be quite different. Items from a test rooted in common curricular materials may rank lower in the Taxonomy than would similar items based upon novel content.

When all items of all forms of the science tests were classified by the reviewers according to the Taxonomy, several interesting conclusions emerged. The first concerns comparability of the various forms. If parity between the taxonomical classifications of any two forms is used as the criterion, all four pairs of forms are seen to be quite satisfactorily comparable. For any given Forms A-B pair, the number of items classified at each of the various major levels of the Taxonomy is very nearly the same.

1 BLOOM, BENJAMIN S.; ENGELHART, MAX D.; FURST, EDWARD J.; HILL, WALKER H.; AND KRATHWOHL, DAVID R. *Taxonomy of Education Objectives: The Classification of Educational Goals: Handbook I, Cognitive Domain.* New York: Longmans, Green & Co., Inc., 1956. Pp. xiii, 207. *

The tabulations reveal further that there is a general tendency for the number of higher taxonomical classifications to increase as one goes from the lower to higher level tests. This suggests not only that more difficult matter is being tested but also that a higher type of mental process is required to make the correct response.

When classifications are made of the list of "abilities being tested" as given in the manual and these classifications are compared with those of the items, little congruency is evident. The abilities are at a much higher level than the test items. According to the manual, only 10 per cent of the items are designed to test abilities which are classified in the 1.00 ("knowledge") category. Yet at the three lower test levels over 75 per cent of the items, and at the highest test level about 50 per cent of the items, are classified in the 1.00 category. Furthermore, although many of the abilities can be classified in the 5.00 ("synthesis") and 6.00 ("evaluation") categories, practically no items of any form have these taxonomical classifications. Other classifiers might differ appreciably from the reviewers in categories assigned, but the general conclusions would probably hold. The STEP science series is as high level, Taxonomy-wise, as other such tests (and probably higher than many), but it exhibits the rather usual discrepancy between "noble" objectives and "less noble" items.

The great amount of reading these tests require is somewhat disturbing, especially since more than a little of it does not seem essential to answering the item correctly, even though the test authors do have an explicit rationale for their long contexts. An especially pertinent example is the stem of Item 25 in Part 2 of Level 4A: "George liked to play in the sandbox. The sand glistened in the sunlight. Betty said that sand is useful to people in the making of glass. George wondered how you could see through sand. How do you think sand can be used to make glass?" Though the items have, in general, been edited at least as well as those in most other achievement tests, the meticulous efforts of a highly insightful editor could have improved the wording of the stems and options of quite a few items materially.

Especially noteworthy insofar as the entire STEP series is concerned are: the development of the various levels and forms, with a common score scale for all; the provision for the "band"

interpretation of scores (the band for any score representing the area within one standard error of measurement of the score); and the integral relationship of the series to the SCAT series. So far lacking are statistical evidence of validity and alternate forms reliability coefficients; these should be provided in supplements to the Technical Report.

Overall, the STEP science tests meet excellently the need for a well planned, coordinated survey series stressing application of common curricular material to familiar situations. By being more *a la carte* than most batteries, STEP provides virtually everyone, from the least technically informed classroom teacher to the most statistically oriented measurement specialist, with instruments he can use and understand.

ROBERT M. W. TRAVERS, *Professor of Educational Psychology and Head of the Department, University of Utah, Salt Lake City, Utah.*

The STEP science tests are outstanding in the care and thought with which they have been planned. They are designed to measure ability to identify and define scientific problems, suggest or screen hypotheses, select valid procedures, interpret data and draw conclusions, evaluate critically claims or statements made by others, and reason quantitatively and symbolically. The percentage of items representing each objective is given in the manual, together with the percentage in each of the content fields of biology, chemistry, physics, astronomy, geology, and meteorology. A novel specification is that the situations presented by the items should cut across four areas, namely, the economic, social, cultural, and home. The manual also clearly states the possible uses for the tests. While there is nothing very original here, teachers may still find the statement a source of ideas.

The items measure a considerable number of distinct thinking skills as well as the extent to which factual information has been acquired.

The reviewer selected Form 3A for a study of content accuracy. In Part 1, Item 13 implies that a solution made by adding one gram of iodine to 50 grams of alcohol can be considered a 2 per cent solution. Ordinarily a 2 per cent solution by weight would be made by dissolving one gram of iodine in 49 grams of alcohol. In Part 2, Item 14 shows a confusion between absolute number of deaths from various causes and death rate. The question appears to ask about the number of deaths but the answers refer to death rates. In this same part Item 19 implies that planes are pressurized primarily to prevent nosebleeds and related troubles. This is probably a very minor reason for pressurization. Equalization of pressure in the ear chambers and the possibility of flying at relatively high altitudes without oxygen certainly are more important reasons. In Item 24 the picture of the crescent moon lying on its side with the points of the crescent in the horizontal plane rather than in the vertical is quite amusing.

A review of the tests by competent scientists would have caught these and other errors. In fairness, however, one should say that the number of errors in the particular test studied in detail is no greater than the number generally found in tests of science. In addition, an incorrect item here and there is not going to be of great influence on the score of a test and will not necessarily make an otherwise well planned test into a poor instrument. This set of tests is in many ways so far ahead of the others known to the writer that his comments on the items should not discourage test users.

The items appear to be rather unnecessarily long winded. This is a result of the fact that each one of a series of items is often woven into a story, presumably to make the test more interesting. For example, Item 27 in Part 1, which, stated in its simplest form, would read "Why does the water heat first at the top of a water heater even though this is farthest from the heating element?" is presented as a part of a story about Alice who was puzzled by this fact. The story almost doubles the length of the item stem. This verbiage is so trivial that it is hard to believe that it adds interest value to the test. There is also another matter to be considered in this unnecessary wordiness. Surely it must result in an unnecessarily high weighting of the score with the verbal factor. A study needs to be conducted to determine the effect of introducing this story telling element. The reviewer's guess is that it would be found to have deleterious value.

Statistical data on the tests are reported with thoroughness in the manual and in the Technical Report. Kuder-Richardson formula 20 was used for the computation of reliability coefficients for Form A. The publishers state that it is reasonable to infer that similar results might be expected with Form B; however, since the

two forms at each level are not matched item by item, a cautious attitude should be adopted regarding this inference. Various data indicate that level of difficulty of the tests is satisfactory. The norms are described in considerable detail, although, it is feared, in language that the typical science teacher will not understand. The norms for all tests in the series are based on samples of equal ability in terms of the SCAT tests. Every effort was made to obtain a sample that was widely distributed over the entire country. While it is possible that some attempt may have been made to control in the norms population the quality and amount of instruction to which the pupils had been exposed in the content area, the reviewer could not find such information in the data provided.

Much would have been gained from the point of view of the consumer if a simpler and more concise presentation of the statistical and interpretive data had been provided with the more technical details relegated to an appendix where they would be available to technically trained personnel. That the tests have been thoughtfully planned and standardized is clear, but every consumer does not want to have to read through the entire procedure in order to find the data which he needs. The Technical Report in particular is such that real questions may be raised about the publisher's contention that the tests are designed for administration by classroom teachers. Very few classroom teachers are going to understand the report. The saving factor in the situation is probably that they do not need to do so.

For reviews by Robert W. B. Jackson and Wilbur L. Layton of the complete battery, see 24.

[717]

*Stanford Achievement Test: Intermediate and Advanced Science Test. Grades 5–9; 1941–54, c1940–54; items identical to those in science sections of *Stanford Achievement Test;* IBM; Forms JM ('52), KM ('53), LM ('54); manual ('54); separate answer sheets must be used; $2.75 per 35 tests; $1.25 per 35 IBM answer sheets; 20¢ per machine scoring stencil; postage extra; 35¢ per specimen set, postpaid; 22(30) minutes; Truman L. Kelley, Richard Madden, Eric F. Gardner, Lewis M. Terman, and Giles M. Ruch; World Book Co. *

For reviews by Bertram Epstein and Paul E. Kambly of the previous edition, see 4:593. For a review by N. L. Gage of the complete battery, see 25; for reviews by Paul R. Hanna (with Claude E. Norcross) and Virgil E. Herrick of

*the previous edition, see 4:25; for reviews by
Walter W. Cook and Ralph C. Preston, see
3:18.*

BIOLOGY

[718]

★**Biological Science: Teacher Education Examination Program.** College seniors preparing to teach secondary school; 1957; for more complete information, see 543; IBM; 80(95) minutes; Educational Testing Service. *

For a review by Walter W. Cook of the entire series, see 543.

[719]

*****Biology: Achievement Examinations for Secondary Schools.** High school; 1951–53; Forms 1 ('51), 2 ('52), 3 ('53); no specific manual; no data on reliability; norms: Forms 1 ['52], 2 ['53], 3 ('53); 10¢ per test, postage extra; [60–90] minutes; B. R. Whitinger; Educational Test Bureau. *

[720]

*****Biology: Every Pupil Scholarship Test.** High school; 1926–58; new form usually issued each January and April; norms available following testing program; no data on reliability; 4¢ per test; 4¢ per scoring key; postpaid; 40(45) minutes; Bureau of Educational Measurements. *

[721]

*****Biology: Every Pupil Test.** High school; 1935–58; new form usually issued each December and April; norms available following testing program; no data on reliability; 3¢ per test; 1¢ per scoring key; cash orders postpaid; 40(45) minutes; Ohio Scholarship Tests. *

[722]

★**Biology: Midwest High School Achievement Examinations.** High school; 1955–57; Forms A ('55), B ('57); no specific manual; no data on reliability; norms: Forms [A, '55; B, '57]; 10¢ per test, postage extra; Form A: 60(65) minutes; Form B: 90[95] minutes; George H. Ramharter (A) and E. C. Halvorsen (B); Educational Test Bureau. *

[723]

*****College Entrance Examination Board Achievement Test in Biology.** Candidates for college entrance; 1915–58; for more complete information, see 599; IBM; 60(80) minutes; program administered by Educational Testing Service for the College Entrance Examination Board. *

REFERENCES

1. COLLEGE ENTRANCE EXAMINATION BOARD. *Science: A Description of the College Board Tests in Biology, Chemistry, and Physics.* Princeton, N.J.: the Board, September 1954. Pp. 39. (*PA* 29:2958)
2. EVENSON, A. B., AND SMITH, D. E. "A Study of Matriculation in Alberta." *Alberta J Ed Res* 4:67–83 Je '58. *

ELIZABETH HAGEN, *Assistant Professor of Education, Teachers College, Columbia University, New York, New York.* [Review of Form FAC.]

This test has been designed to provide a measure of the achievement of high school graduates in biology. Its scope and content were determined by the CEEB committee of examiners in biology in cooperation with the staff of the Educational Testing Service. There are 100 questions, 20 of which test content in reproduction, heredity, and evolution. The proportion of items on these topics seems out of line with the emphasis given them in a high school general biology course. On the other hand, the topics of human physiology and health seem to be under-represented. Since most of the CEEB applicants who take this test have had only one year of biology, it would seem more appropriate to have the test represent the content coverage of the general biology course than the specialized courses offered in a few high schools.

The construction of the individual items is adequate. Some of them have vague stems and some have unattractive foils, the result of the attempt to get at least five options for each item. The directions to Part C, which has a somewhat unusual answer pattern involving multiple answers, could be made clearer by the addition of a sample item. In spite of the unusual format, the items in Part C tend to be too factual in nature; they could be made more effective if they tested multiple causation or multiple effects. The items in Part D are based on two laboratory situations, but most of them could be answered if the situations were omitted.

The Kuder-Richardson reliability is reported as .92, with a standard error of 5.3. Since the test does not appear to be speeded, these data can be considered to compare favorably with data for other tests of biology. At the present time there is no evidence available on the value of the scores on the test for predicting course grades in college biology or in any other college course. The spread of difficulty in the items appears to be adequate, and there is evidence that science-oriented applicants score higher on the test than do nonscience-oriented applicants.

In summary, the *College Entrance Examination Board Achievement Test in Biology* is a satisfactory measure of the academic, somewhat traditional aspects of biology, except for too much emphasis on reproduction and heredity and too little emphasis on human physiology and health. In content coverage, processes measured, and item construction, however, it does not appear to be as good as the *Nelson Biology Test.*

For a review by Clark W. Horton of earlier forms, see 4:600.

[724]

★College Entrance Examination Board Advanced Placement Examination: Biology. High school seniors desiring credit for college level courses; 1956–57; for more complete information, see 600; IBM in part; 2 parts; 180(200) minutes; program administered by Educational Testing Service for the College Entrance Examination Board. *

CLARK W. HORTON, *Consultant in Educational Research, Dartmouth College, Hanover, New Hampshire.* [Review of Form FBP.]

The reader's knowledge of the purposes and general methods of the CEEB Advanced Placement Program is assumed. The 3-hour biology examination given in May 1958, Form FBP, consisted of Part 1, a 1-hour objective test of 80 five-choice items; and Part 2, a 2-hour essay test in which candidates wrote on four of six questions, the first two required, and each of the second two selected from two alternatives.

The test analysis data on Part 1 show it to be of suitable length, difficulty, and reliability for the 148 high school cases tested in 1958. About 85 per cent of the candidates finished, few scores fell in the chance score range at the bottom, and there was plenty of room at the top. The reported reliability coefficient is .88. The content appears to be a good sampling of biological knowledge. In general, the questions are well written and defensible, and require a precise and penetrating understanding. This part of the total examination seems to be a sound anchor to which the more questionable Part 2, the 2-hour essay test, can be tied.

The committees responsible for setting the questions of Part 2 and for grading it must face the slings and arrows that have been directed these many years at essay examinations. They appear to be trying conscientiously to set broad, representative questions that will elicit organized, exhaustive displays of the candidates' knowledge, and to use sound grading procedures; but in both areas they face difficult problems.

In Form FBP the two required questions were on surfaces in biological systems and ecological succession; and the others, from which two were to be answered, on aspects of evolution, reproduction, and adaptation to environment—all topics of book size if one had the background. When only four topics are used, their representativeness becomes crucial because a candidate can lose a large proportion of total score if he has not had the material. This year the required question on ecological succession, representing one sixth of final score, was "misinterpreted" by half of the candidates; that is, they did not know what it was about. What is important in biology and who says so is still a plaguing problem.

It is disturbing to find in the directive to the reading committees the following: "None of the questions....will be read by two readers, as in 1956. Instead, several readers will work on each examination, reading different questions. This method allows each reader to mark his question without worrying about how someone else is going to mark the same question." Such insouciance is not likely to be shared by persons trained in the methods of science, who *do* worry about the repeatability of observations, and about the soundness of conclusions drawn when such repeatability has not been established.

The above directive, a report from the Chief Reader in Biology, and the memorandum accompanying score reports to colleges give more detail on reading procedures than can be reported here. Briefly, each essay was scored on a 15-point scale, making a total possible score of 60 for Part 2. Subject matter was weighted about 80 per cent and organization, clarity of expression, spelling, and the like about 20 per cent. The Part 1 score was converted to the 15-point scale and then doubled to give it a weight of one third in the total score, which was then converted to the familiar 5-point scale: 5-high honors; 4-honors; 3-creditable; 2-pass; 1-fail. Papers of 49 college students tested at the end of the first year course were anonymously mixed with the 148 high school papers, and frequency distributions of Part 1 scores prepared, to permit comparison of the performance of the high school group with that of the college students. Sample papers were read and discussed "until there was general agreement on the basis for scoring." All readers worked together on one question at a time. The Chief Reader checked many papers at the start, and periodically thereafter, and answers were sometimes read aloud and discussed. No paper was scored entirely by one reader. Thus, a conscientious effort appears to have been made by the readers, working within the limitations of this examination method, to achieve sound grading practice. The practice of sending the scored essay test to the college with the candidate's score report serves in some measure to communicate to the college the grading standards used.

The goals of this program are eminently desirable. The secondary school should be encouraged to offer high level courses for able students, and the college to give advanced placement or credit to freshmen who know more biology than most sophomores. But why the directors of this project assume that these goals can be achieved best, or perhaps only, by turning time back 30 years on College Board history, and reliving and relearning the limitations and deficiencies of essay achievement examinations, is not clear to this writer. It is not a necessary condition for the success of the project; moreover, it is very expensive

Does the essay test do anything that could not be done more accurately, and much less expensively, by using the two hours for additional high quality objective testing? How reliable are the essay test scores? Since they correlate but .69 with scores on Part 1, which is the more valid measure? Beyond saying that high scoring candidates do well when given advanced placement, how valid are the scores reported to colleges? The observed agreement between the committee's grading of the 49 college students and the grades previously given them by their college instructors is substantial, but far from impressive. In cases of wide disagreement, which is the more valid estimate? More extensive application of the tests to college populations to get normative data and to make validity studies possible is needed. While impractical with an essay test, this could be done with an appropriate objective test. Whether the presumed virtues of the essay examination as a selling device in getting this project started outweigh its known limitations and deficiencies as a measuring device may be an open question. In the writer's opinion essay testing is not a necessary condition for the success of the advanced placement program in biology.

[725]

*Cooperative Biology Test: Educational Records Bureau Edition. High school; 1941–58; IBM; Forms ERB-RY ('57, revision of Form ERB-RX), ERB-SY ('58, revision of Form ERB-SX) ; no specific manual; general Cooperative manual ('51) ; no data on reliability; norms: Form ERB-RY ('57), Form ERB-SY ('58) ; 11.8¢ per test ; separate answer sheets may be used ; 4¢ per IBM answer sheet; 50¢ per specimen set; postage extra ; 40(45) minutes ; Committee on Biology Tests of the Educational Records Bureau; Educational Records Bureau. *

REFERENCES

1–2. See 4:602.
3. TRAXLER, ARTHUR E. "The 1957 ERB Edition of the Cooperative Biology, Chemistry, and Physics Tests, Form ERB-RY—Difficulty, Reliability, and Correlation With School Marks." Ed Rec B 70:65–70 Jl '57. *

[726]

General Biology Test: National Achievement Tests. High school; 1951; 4 scores: uses-processes-results, biologists, miscellaneous facts, total; Form A; no data on reliability; no norms for part scores; $3.50 per 25 tests; 50¢ per specimen set; postage extra; 35(40) minutes; Lester D. Crow and James G. Murray; Acorn Publishing Co. *

ELIZABETH HAGEN, *Assistant Professor of Education, Teachers College, Columbia University, New York, New York.*

Part 3 of the test is labeled "Miscellaneous Facts in Biology" and this is a good description of the total test. The items are entirely factual and completely neglect the important general principles and understandings of high school biology. A letter from the publisher states that the scope of the test was determined by "sampling biology texts used." The number or recency of texts used for the preceding purpose was not described, nor, for that matter, was there any indication of when this survey was undertaken. Unless this procedure was considerably better planned and carried out than the publisher's statement would indicate, it can scarcely be defended as a method of determining the coverage of the test.

There is no manual, and the only accompanying material is a combination directions and class record sheet which also gives a table of percentile norms based on 2,751 biology students. The characteristics of these students are not specified except that they come from "different sections of the United States, including village and city high schools." A letter from the publisher restates approximately this same information. No data on reliability are provided with the test. The publisher, in a letter to the reviewer, states that the split-half reliability is .95 but gives no information on the sample used to obtain this correlation. Since the test appears to be somewhat speeded, the split-half method of determining reliability would result in spuriously high reliability coefficients.

The data on reliability, validity, and norms are completely inadequate. There is really not much point in devoting space to a test which fails to meet even minimum standards for test construction. The opinion of this reviewer is that the *General Biology Test* should not be used by any school. Better achievement tests in biology can be found in any biology textbook and workbook.

CLARK W. HORTON, *Consultant in Educational Research, Dartmouth College, Hanover, New Hampshire.*

Most of the 120 selection type, 4-option items in this test are very short, the answers consisting of one word or a short completing phrase. The options are designated by letters, different letter series in different items, and the scoring key is a nine-letter word familiar to people in education. Correct answers are those whose letter is found in that word. Pupils answer by underlining their choice. Scoring involves leafing through the pages, identifying correct answers, marking, and counting. The lettering of the options, and the fact that item numbers begin anew in each part, both prevent use of a standard IBM answer sheet.

The division into parts is not meaningful, except that the 10 items of Part 2 all involve knowing the name of the biologist associated with the given idea: for example, that Mendel is known for his work with peas, not poultry, mice, or guinea pigs. The 50 items of Part 1, headed "Uses, Processes, Results," do not appear to differ in any important way from the 60 items of Part 3 headed "Miscellaneous Facts in Biology." In fact, the whole test might bear the latter title. Teachers who use the test with large groups might expedite scoring by mimeographing their own answer sheet, although this would affect the time limit. No data are given on speededness under the 35-minute limit. The test is clearly a commercial venture.

The disturbing thing about this test is the low level of biological understanding presumed by the items. The range of factual knowledge sampled is wide, but the depth or precision of understanding required is extremely shallow, consisting in most cases of nothing more than knowledge that two ideas are related: for example, that pollen is produced by the anther, not the pistil, ovary, or stigma; that rusts and smuts are fungi, not insects, viruses, or protozoa; that fossils are usually found in rocks, not in sand, sea water, or clay; that one of the concepts of Mendel's law is dominance of certain traits, not conservation of energy, survival

of the fittest, or inheritance of acquired characteristics.

Some deficiencies of understanding, or inaccuracies of expression, are evident in the items. The processes photosynthesis and respiration in plants are "the taking in, use, and giving off" of the gases involved. This is failure of the authors either to know or to say that plants don't "take in" or "give off" the gases; that the gases move into and out of intercellular spaces and across cell walls and membranes by diffusion; and that a proper definition of the chemical processes does not include the gaseous exchange. Certainly an understanding of diffusion is not too difficult for high school pupils. One learns from the test that the amoeba often "walks on" pseudopodia. Other items require more knowledge of specifics than this writer, formerly a botanist, can muster: for example, is the fish "used most extensively at present" the cod, salmon, halibut, or tuna?

The seriously disturbing thing about this test is the thought that it might accurately portray present objectives and practice in the teaching of high school biology. Is this achievement in biology, grades 9 to 12? Is this all high schools teach and expect from pupils? There is not in this test the slightest gesture in the direction of exploring the aspects of critical thinking, the methodology of the scientist's search for truth, the real understanding of how things work, the knowledge of casual relations and dependencies, that are presumed to be goals in the teaching of biology as a science. If the objectives and content of high school biology are now such that this test is an adequate measure of achievement in it, then the Russians are far, far ahead of us in this area, too, and something drastic ought to be done.

The test covers a wide range of superficial, associative information in biology; a person who knows much biology will make a higher score than one who knows substantially less. On the other hand, there can be no confidence that a person who gets a high score really understands much about the fundamentals of biology as a science, nor that he has made progress toward other important goals of instruction in science. Teachers who give a superficial course to not very able pupils may find use for it as one part of appraisal. But if the level of expectation set by a published test called an achievement test really does have an effect on teachers' concepts of what they ought to be doing and what they ought to expect from pupils, then the writer fervently hopes this one will not become a national achievement test in biology.

[727]

*The Graduate Record Examinations Advanced Tests: Biology. College seniors and graduate students; 1939–57; for more complete information, see 601; IBM; 180(200) minutes; Educational Testing Service. *

CLARK W. HORTON, *Consultant in Educational Research, Dartmouth College, Hanover, New Hampshire.* [Review of Form FGR.]

The Graduate Record Examinations program is widely accepted and respected. The tests are of high quality, and the program is characterized by intelligent concern for the needs of candidates, examiners, and the college and university officers who ultimately interpret and use the scores. The publications, which include a Score Interpretation Handbook for Deans and Advisers, a bulletin of Summary Statistics, and a compilation of uses in 377 colleges and universities, are excellent and help make the several aspects of this total program valuable tools in institutional appraisal, in the guidance of advanced undergraduates, and in the selection of candidates for graduate study.

The background information on the scaling of the tests, the tables of score equivalents as test forms and procedures have changed over the years, and the percentile norms reported, are satisfactory for general score interpretation. Institutions which use the program are urged to collect their own normative data, and presumably carry out their own validity studies. If there is any weakness in the published background material, it appears to be a lack of data on the long range predictive value of the scores.

The 3-hour advanced test in biology comprises 275 scorable items which for the most part require the selection of one from five optional answers, although in some kinds of problems the choice is made from three or four answers. The test is long enough to give very high reliability; a coefficient of .95 is reported. It is not speeded, and the timing seems about right for a power test. It is the writer's experience in administering the test to college seniors that all reach the last item in the three hours or sooner, although many quit reluctantly because they want to go back and rethink their work on some of the problems.

While no systematic analysis of content was made, it is the writer's impression that the questions represent a well balanced sampling of the subdisciplines in both botany and zoology: morphology, embryology, physiology, genetics, ecology, microbiology, et cetera. Many questions and problems cut across specialties and would be difficult to classify in the above sense. One of the strong features of the test are exercises in which all or almost all needed information is given, designed to explore the candidate's ability to draw sound inferences from data, to avoid unwarranted conclusions, to know what can and cannot validly be said at various points in the development of an experiment, and otherwise to demonstrate that he is equipped with the ability to think carefully, logically, critically, as it is hoped good biologists will. Also, in many questions where the selection of a correct answer seems to depend centrally on knowledge of underlying facts and principles, the phrasing of the options taps ability to weigh critically the fit of words to truth; to recognize the most precisely stated, or the most inclusive, or the otherwise most defensible, among answers which might appear to the less knowledgeable or less discriminating to be indistinguishable. The extent to which this test requires a high level of critical ability may well account for the fact that score on it correlates .74 with score on the verbal section and .64 with score on the quantitative section of the GRE Aptitude Test.

In spite of the very broad range of knowledge and the high level of critical thinking it requires, the test is not excessively specialized. The writer, who many years ago was a graduate student and instructor in botany, attempted to answer the questions and checked his answers against the key. Although clearly deficient in his knowledge of animal morphology and embryology and of more recent developments in physiology, he was pleasantly surprised at the large number of items he could answer with certainty. While deficiencies in some of the subdisciplines of biology will reduce score substantially below the perfect score level, a sound, penetrating grasp of basic principles and methods true 30 years ago, plus the ability to think straight about the problems presented, will still produce a good score.

This is an excellent test, eminently satisfactory for the level at which it is normally applied, and the writer unhesitatingly endorses it as the best high-level biology test in print. Incidentally, a 3-hour biology test of this type at a lower level, instead of the present one hour of objective and two hours of essay testing, would greatly improve the *College Entrance Examination Board Advanced Placement Test in Biology.*

For a review by Harold Seashore of the entire series, see 601.

[728]

Nelson Biology Test: Evaluation and Adjustment Series. Grades 9–13; 1951–54, c1950–51; IBM; Forms AM ('51), BM ('52); manual ('51); expectancy chart ['54]; separate answer sheets must be used; $4.15 per 35 tests; $1.40 per 35 IBM answer sheets; postage extra; 35¢ per specimen set, postpaid; 40(50) minutes; Clarence H. Nelson; World Book Co. *

For reviews by Clark W. Horton and Leland P. Johnson, see 4:605.

CHEMISTRY

[729]

★A.C.S.-N.S.T.A. Cooperative Examination in High School Chemistry. High school; 1957–58; IBM; Form N ('57, with minor revisions in second printing, '58); 2 parallel parts in 1 booklet, either or both of which may be administered; no specific manual; general A.C.S. directions ('57); no data on reliability; norms ['57]; separate answer sheets must be used; $4 per 25 tests; $1 per 25 IBM answer sheets; 25¢ per scoring stencil; 50¢ per specimen set; postage extra; 90(100) minutes; sponsored jointly with the National Science Teachers Association; Examinations Committee, Division of Chemical Education, American Chemical Society. *

EDWARD G. RIETZ, *Instructor in Chemistry, Wright Junior College, Chicago, Illinois.*

' This examination is the culmination of a rigorous selective process involving use of trial forms by various cooperating high schools. The scope and organization of the test reflect the competence and dedication that members of the development committees brought to their task. Essential concepts are stressed and sheer memorization of trivial detail is minimized. Among the essential concepts included are characteristics of metals and of the metallic state, the nature of chemical and physical changes, combustion, behaviors of gases, atomic structure, valence, atomic weight determinations, molecular and empirical formulas, redox reactions, generalizations from the periodic table, stoichiometry, balancing of equations, important industrial processes, chemical equilibrium, and the rudiments of organic chemistry.

The test consists of two parts, each containing 45 items of the 5-response multiple choice type. The questions are unambiguous and, with one exception, this reviewer could find no fault with the keyed answers. The lone dubious question concerned the volume of hydrogen obtainable in the decomposition of water. An argumentative student might maintain that either of two answers could be correct depending upon whether an active metal or electrolysis were employed in the decomposition.

Questions requiring numerical answers are considerably organized to permit calculation without laborious, time-consuming arithmetic and the answer choices are carefully selected to permit the discerning student to select the obvious choice with a minimum of effort. This reviewer was able to complete all necessary calculations by mental arithmetic and he is convinced that participants must share his conviction that this test unequivocally tests knowledge and aptitude without the annoyance of distractors and unnecessary handicaps.

The format is excellent and the test is easily administered and scored. Despite the variety of questions, time allotment is ample. In short, this reviewer enthusiastically endorses this examination.

WILLARD G. WARRINGTON, *Associate Professor, Office of Evaluation Services, Michigan State University, East Lansing, Michigan.*

Apparently this test is designed to provide a measure of basic knowledge gained from a high school chemistry course. Most of the items deal with very factual content, such as correctness of formulas, definitions of terms, valences of elements, and specific products of chemical reactions. Some computational tasks are presented, but even these make limited demands upon application of principles or generalization of knowledge to new situations. The test seems somewhat bookish and makes no attempt to relate the field of chemistry to more familiar aspects of everyday living.

All items are of the 5-response multiple choice type and, in general, are well written as to language usage and specificity of the problem. The format is adequate but larger print would make for a more readable presentation. Likewise, the directions to both the examiner and the student are almost lost due to the crowded appearance of the cover page of the booklet.

The two part arrangement is commendable since each 45-minute part can be given in the typical class period. However, no evidence is available to support the statement in the directions that the two parts are equally valid. While both parts represent a broad sampling of chemical knowledge, there is no reason to believe that the two parts should be considered as parallel forms since their contents are somewhat dissimilar. As a specific illustration, 6 of the 45 items of Part 1 deal with the periodic table while this important topic is not mentioned in Part 2. Also, the normative data provided with this test indicate that Part 1 is somewhat easier than Part 2. For example, in the norms for the "most typical" group, a raw score of 22 has a percentile rank of 55 for Part 1 but one of 65 for Part 2, even though both parts contain 45 items. Consequently, the reviewer would recommend that users be wary of comparing performances on the two separate parts of the test.

Due to the paucity of information provided with this test, it is very difficult to judge the adequacy of the normative data. Percentile ranks are shown for raw scores on the two parts and the total test for three different groups of high school students ranging from a "most typical" group to an "exceptional" group. While the list of schools from which the data were obtained is given, there is very little evidence to show just how typical the "typical" group is or how atypical the "exceptional" group is. It would probably be better to think in terms of developing local norms when using this test unless more adequate normative data become available.

In summary, then, if the user is interested in a test to measure the factual knowledge known by students at the end of a two-semester high school chemistry course, this 90-item test (Part 1 and Part 2 combined) should be a satisfactory instrument. However, other tests are available which will give more information as to the student's total knowledge of chemistry in an equal or a shorter period of time.

[730]
*A.C.S. Cooperative Chemistry Test in Qualitative Analysis. 1–2 semesters college; 1943–53; IBM; Forms H ('53), Y ('48); no specific manual; general A.C.S. directions ('57); no data on reliability; separate

answer sheets must be used; $6 per 25 tests; $1 per 25 IBM answer sheets; 25¢ per scoring stencil; 50¢ per specimen set; postage extra; Examinations Committee, Division of Chemical Education, American Chemical Society. *
a) FORM H. Part 1 is identical with Qualitative Analysis Supplement for General Chemistry; 3 scores: part 1 (second semester general chemistry), part 2, total; norms ['53]; 75(85) minutes.
b) FORM Y. 4 scores: descriptive information, problems and equations, chemical equilibrium, total; norms ['49]; 100(110) minutes; prepared with the assistance of Cooperative Test Division.

For a review by William Rieman III of Forms Y and Z, see 4:608; for reviews by William B. Meldrum and William Rieman III of an earlier form, see 3:562.

[731]
*A.C.S. Cooperative Examination in Biochemistry. 1–2 semesters college; 1947–54; 3 scores: first semester, second semester, total; IBM; Forms Z ('50, entitled A.C.S. Cooperative Biochemistry Test), K ('54, adaptation of Forms X and Z); no specific manual; general A.C.S. directions ('57); no data on reliability; norms: Forms Z ['50], K ['54]; separate answer sheets must be used; $6 per 25 tests; $1 per 25 IBM answer sheets; 25¢ per scoring stencil; 50¢ per specimen set; postage extra; 100(110) minutes; Form Z prepared with the assistance of Cooperative Test Division; Examinations Committee, Division of Chemical Education, American Chemical Society. *

[732]
*A.C.S. Cooperative Examination in General Chemistry. 1 year college; 1934–58; IBM; 3 booklets; no specific manual; general A.C.S. directions ('57); no data on reliability; separate answer sheets must be used; $1 per 25 IBM answer sheets; 25¢ per scoring stencil; 50¢ per specimen set; postage extra; Examinations Committee, Division of Chemical Education, American Chemical Society. *
a) [THREE PART FORMS.] 1954–56; 4 scores: information, application of principles, quantitative application of principles, total; Forms K ('54), M ('56), MS ('56, identical with Form M except for order of items and responses), 1958 ('58), 1958S ('58, identical with Form 1958 except for order of items and responses); norms: Forms K ['54], M ['56], 1958 ['58]; $6 per 25 tests; 105(110) minutes.
b) [SIX PART FORM.] 1934–53; 7 scores: information, application of principles, quantitative application of principles, scientific method, laboratory technique, total, organic chemistry (optional); Form G ('53); norms ['52]; no norms for optional subtest; $6 per 25 tests; 110(115) minutes.
c) [QUALITATIVE ANALYSIS SUPPLEMENT FOR GENERAL CHEMISTRY. 1953; identical with Part 1 of A.C.S. Cooperative Chemistry Test in Qualitative Analysis, Form H; Form J ['53]; $4 per 25 tests; 40(50) minutes.

REFERENCES

1–5. See 40:1593.
6–8. See 3:557.
9. See 4:610.
10. RICE, CECIL L., AND VINTON, KENNETH W. "An Experiment in Teaching Chemistry for Testing." Sch & Soc 52:43–5 Jl 20 '40. * (PA 14:5717)
11. NORTON, BAYES M. "College Admission With Advanced Standing: II, The Examinations in Chemistry, 1954–55." J Chem Ed 33:237–41 My '56. *

FRANK P. CASSARETTO, *Professor of Chemistry, Loyola University, Chicago, Illinois.*

The *A.C.S. Cooperative Examination in General Chemistry and the Qualitative Analysis Supplement* are excellent testing devices for the first year of college inorganic chemistry. The material covered is essentially basic, and representative of topics covered in freshman college chemistry. The questions reflect the judgment of experienced teachers as is evidenced by the names of the persons on the Examinations Committee and the General Chemistry Subcommittee of the American Chemical Society. The instructions are clear, and necessary diagrams and graphs are very good. The norms for the test are broken down to cover variations in freshman college chemistry courses from those offering no qualitative analysis to those placing emphasis on qualitative analysis in the second semester of the year's course. The *Qualitative Analysis Supplement* is particularly well done. It covers basic concepts of chemical equilibrium that a student should master in a freshman inorganic course.

The questions are numbered clearly and the choices are definitely marked. The distinction between choices is not obvious and requires careful logical reasoning for proper selection. A key for hand scoring can be followed easily and a key for machine scoring is supplied. The alternate forms (Forms 1958 and 1958S and Forms M and MS) are identical except for the sequence of questions and the order of responses; hence they may be used in conjunction with each other to insure security and minimize copying. With crowded college classrooms anticipated, this variant of the test will be an appreciated attribute.

Forms 1958 and 1958S contain 100 items organized in three parts. Part 1 covers general chemical information (30 items), Part 2, the application of principles (45 items), and Part 3, the application of principles in quantitative situations (25 items). Form G has 115 items broken down into six parts: General Knowledge and Information (25 items), Application of Principles (25 items), Quantitative Application of Principles (20 items), Scientific Method (20 items), Laboratory Technique (15 items), and Organic Chemistry (10 items). Part 6, Organic Chemistry, is optional. Separate norms are provided for each part score, as well as for the total score with and without Part 6.

These tests have been well prepared and serve their purpose well. They do, however, sacrifice giving the student the opportunity to organize his thoughts and express himself adequately in writing. If such a test is to be given at the end of a course as a means of evaluating general achievement and aptitude, an objective type, separate answer sheet test should be given prior to this test to condition the students to the multiple choice approach to chemistry.

PALMER O. JOHNSON, *Professor of Education, University of Minnesota, Minneapolis, Minnesota.*

Form G is described first since its structure differs somewhat from the other examinations in general chemistry. This test was prepared by the General Chemistry Subcommittee of the American Chemical Society and 15 members in collaboration with 23 professors of chemistry located in institutions throughout the United States. The test was designed for measuring achievement in elementary college chemistry covering the material of the entire freshman year. In terms of per cents, the 115 items are distributed among the objectives as follows: General Knowledge and Information (21.7), Application of Principles (21.7), Quantitative Application of Principles (17.4), Scientific Method (17.4), Laboratory Technique (13.0), and Organic Chemistry (8.7).

The remaining forms in general chemistry have been kept constant with respect to the coverage of objectives. The percentage distribution of the 105 items in each of these forms is as follows: Recall of Information (28.6), Application of Principles (42.8), and Quantitative Application of Principles (28.6). In these forms the scientific method section of Form G has been subsumed under Part 3, Quantitative Application of Principles, but the part on laboratory techniques has been abandoned.

The Qualitative Analysis Supplement is a test prepared by an analytic subcommittee of 10 members. It is presented in a separately printed booklet and consists of 45 items sampling the materials taught in many colleges in the second semester of general chemistry.

Form 1958 may be considered the first of a new series of tests in general chemistry. Over 60 teachers of college chemistry participated in the various aspects of its preparation. The 100 items were selected from some 400 originally submitted, after intensive criticism and pretesting of the most promising items at 31 "typical" institutions. The 5-choice multiple choice item is used throughout all forms and for all objectives. A detailed set of directions is provided. The test is scored by parts and a total obtained for the whole test. A correction for guessing formula is used.

Norms are provided for the entire group of students and for each of seven subgroups. The subgroups differ in various respects such as number of credit hours, length of course, and whether or not qualitative analysis was taken.

Since the norms are the only sources of objective data on which some estimate of the appropriateness of the tests for the students taking them can be based, these data were examined in some detail. For Form G, norms for the entire group are reported to be based on "a sample of 1,125 papers systematically drawn from a total population of 1,962 papers from 25 colleges." The subgroup picked for comparison is the qualitative analysis group—the group in which all students have had 10 or more weeks of qualitative analysis, including two to six lecture hours and three to six laboratory hours. The total raw scores for the entire group and for the qualitative analysis subgroup which fall at the 25th, 50th, and 75th percentiles are as follows: 37 and 42, 48 and 52, 61 and 63. Thus, the test was quite satisfactory for the qualitative analysis subgroup, but somewhat difficult for the entire group on the average. The distribution of scores was nearly symmetrical for the subgroup and somewhat skewed for the entire group.

The norms for Form K indicate that Part 3, Quantitative Application of Principles, is particularly difficult. For the qualitative subgroup the median score on this part is 9 while one half the total possible score is 15. For the entire group, the test as a whole is too difficult. These findings also apply to Form M. Again it is observed that all parts of the test are too difficult and that Part 3 is especially difficult, with a subgroup median of 8 when one half the total possible score is 12.5.

The above observations indicate a great need for analyzing the results from these tests. Studies are much needed on the difficulties of the test items for different levels of ability. There should be systematic pretesting of the test items to determine their properties. Information is needed on the speededness of the test and whether the time allotments for the

several parts of the test are valid. Study needs to be made especially of the items in Part 3 to note the difficulty levels of the problems with the view of selecting problems which the students should be able to solve if they have achieved the objectives of the course.

A big shortcoming of these tests is that no measures of reliability are provided either for the whole test or the several parts of the test.[1] Evidence of reliability would enable the critical user to determine whether scores on the tests are satisfactory for the recommended uses. Measures of relative and absolute variability should be provided. It would also be informative if the intercorrelations were given for scores on the several parts.

Information about the tests seems to be based chiefly on the assumption that the large number of cooperating instructors in chemistry pretty much guarantees a valid and reliable test. This cooperative effort very likely contributes to the content validity of the tests. However, it would be very useful if more information were given about the process of validation, such as information on the extent of agreement among the experts, the method of sampling and pretesting items, and the representativeness of the sample of institutions with respect to the whole populations of colleges for which the tests are intended.

The practice of giving norms for the various subgroups is an excellent one. It would be useful if more information were given about the procedures followed in the development of the norms. Random samples of clearly depicted groups would provide more valid results than the systematic method of selection now in use. The norms should be made available simultaneously with the release of the tests for operational use. It would also be very valuable if data could be provided on the equivalence between the new and old forms of the test.

These tests, constructed as they were by and under the auspices of such a powerful and important body as the American Chemical Society, will undoubtedly do much to shape the character and elevate the quality of chemistry instruction in the colleges of the United States. In this development, measurement will become more and more an integral part of instruction. Accordingly, it is increasingly important that every effort be made to improve the efficiency

1 Since the writing of this review, data on the reliability of Forms 1958 and 1958S have been made available. By Kuder-Richardson formula 21, these coefficients are: Part 1, .83; Part 2, .87; Part 3, .83; total, .94.

and quality of the tests developed. In this process, as in other scientific endeavors, it becomes tantamount to rely more and more on the facts in the case rather than on the impressions and dictates of authorities, no matter how much prestige they may have. As the A.C.S. continues to use for the improvement of the tests more and more of the information provided by the testing results, it is inevitable that both the efficiency of measurement and the effectiveness of instruction in chemistry will be continuously increased.

For a review by Kenneth E. Anderson of earlier forms, see 4:610; for reviews by Sidney J. French and Florence E. Hooper, see 3:557.

[733]

*[A.C.S. Cooperative Examinations in Organic Chemistry.] College; 1942–58; IBM; 4 nonparallel forms; no specific manual; general A.C.S. directions ('57); no data on reliability; separate answer sheets must be used; $6 per 25 tests; $1 per 25 IBM answer sheets; 25¢ per scoring stencil; 50¢ per specimen set; postage extra; 100(110) minutes; Examinations Committee, Division of Chemical Education, American Chemical Society. *

a) A.C.S. COOPERATIVE ORGANIC CHEMISTRY TEST. 2 semesters college; 1942–50; 9 scores: total, first semester total, second semester total, and the following subtests for each semester: general information, application of principles, problems; Form Y ('49); norms ['50]; no norms for subtest scores within semesters; prepared with the assistance of Cooperative Test Division.

b) A.C.S. COOPERATIVE EXAMINATION IN ORGANIC CHEMISTRY. 2 semesters college; 1953–58; 3 scores: first semester, second semester, total; Forms H ('53), 1958 ('58);

c) A.C.S. COOPERATIVE EXAMINATION FOR THE BRIEF COURSE IN ORGANIC CHEMISTRY. 1 semester college; 1956; Form MB; 2 parallel parts in 1 booklet, either or both of which may be administered; norms ['56].

For a review by Shailer Peterson of an earlier form, see 3:558.

[734]

*A.C.S. Cooperative Examination in Physical Chemistry. College; 1946–55; 4 scores: states of matter and solutions, thermodynamics-equilibrium-electrochemistry, structure of matter and kinetics; IBM; Form L ('55); no specific manual; general A.C.S. directions ('57); no data on reliability; norms ['55]; separate answer sheets must be used; $6 per 25 tests; $1 per 25 IBM answer sheets; 25¢ per scoring stencil; 50¢ per specimen set; postage extra; 110(120) minutes; Examinations Committee, Division of Chemical Education, American Chemical Society. *

For a review by Alfred S. Brown of an earlier form, see 3:559.

[735]

*A.C.S. Cooperative Examination in Quantitative Analysis. College; 1944–57; 3 scores: theory, problems, total; IBM; Forms Y ('50, entitled *A.C.S.*

Cooperative Chemistry Test in Quantitative Analysis), G ('52), N ('57); no specific manual; general A.C.S. directions ('57); no data on reliability; norms: Forms Y ('50), G ('52), N ('57); separate answer sheets must be used; $6 per 25 tests; $1 per 25 IBM answer sheets; 25¢ per scoring stencil; 50¢ per specimen set; postage extra; 110(120) minutes; Form Y prepared with the assistance of Cooperative Test Division; Examinations Committee, Division of Chemical Education, American Chemical Society. *

J Chem Ed 35:245 My '58. H. E. Wilcox. [Review of Form N.] This much needed new form of the quantitative analysis test follows closely the pattern set by the older Forms X, Y, and G. It is of the multiple-choice type, but the number of questions in the theory section has been reduced from 60 to 45, although the time allotted to this section remains unchanged. As in the past, thirty problems comprise the second part, including some which might be considered to be qualitative analysis types. Since the questions and problems are of approximately the same average difficulty as those in previous tests, the reduction in number of items should remove much of the time pressure. As might be expected, the questions and problems show a wide variation in difficulty from the simplest memory types to those which should challenge the reasoning ability of the best students. Still, it might have been desirable to have used "correct answer not given" as one of the five choices for at least some of the problems since all of the correct answers checked very closely by slide-rule calculations. In a shortened examination, however, one should certainly avoid redundancy, and this reviewer found some pairs of questions which impressed him as testing nearly identical areas of knowledge. Thus, while the coverage of material should be quite adequate for a one-semester course, there would probably be some incompletely tested areas if this test were used for students who had had a rigorous two-semester course in quantitative analysis in addition to qualitative analysis. Since this test will be used primarily as the final examination in one-quarter or one-semester courses, the above objection is not a serious one.

For reviews by William B. Meldrum and William Rieman III of an earlier form, see 3:563.

[736]

*A.C.S. Cooperative Organic Chemistry Test. College; 1942–50; 9 scores: total, first semester total, second semester total, and the following subtests for each semester: general information, application of principles, problems; IBM; Form Y ('49); no specific manual; general A.C.S. directions ['53]; no data on reliability; norms ['50]; no norms for subtest scores within semesters; separate answer sheets must be used; $4 per 25 tests; $1 per 25 IBM answer sheets; 25¢ per scoring stencil; 50¢ per specimen set; postage extra; 100(110) minutes; prepared with the assistance of Cooperative Test Division; Examinations Committee, Division of Chemical Education, American Chemical Society. *

For a review by Shailer Peterson of an earlier form, see 3:558.

[737]

*Anderson Chemistry Test: Evaluation and Adjustment Series. Grades 11–13; 1951–54, c1950–51; IBM; Forms AM ('51), BM ('52); manual ('51); expectancy chart ['54]; separate answer sheets must be used; $4.15 per 35 tests; $1.40 per 35 IBM answer sheets; postage extra; 35¢ per specimen set, postpaid; 40(50) minutes; Kenneth E. Anderson; World Book Co. *

THEO. A. ASHFORD, *Professor of Chemistry, Saint Louis University, Saint Louis, Missouri.*

This test is designed to measure achievement in chemistry in a "typical" high school. Each of the forms is made up of 80 items grouped into four parts. Part A, described as covering "understanding of functional facts and concepts," contains 38 items (47 per cent) testing mostly factual information, general knowledge, and terminology. Part B, concerned with "understanding and application of functional principles," is an interesting section made up of seven pairs of items (18 per cent); the first item in each pair calls for information and the second calls for the chemical principle that "explains" the answer to the first.

Part C, rather ambitiously described as measuring "understanding and application of the elements of the scientific method together with the associated attitudes in chemistry situations," contains 15 items (19 per cent) of three types. Six of the items call for the recognition of the class to which four of the five responses belong. Four items involve interpretation of a table of data and five are based on a drawing of an experimental setup. Part D, designed to test "ability to use the basic skills in chemistry," consists of 13 items (16 per cent) concerned with formula recognition, balancing equations, and problems.

From a technical and statistical standpoint, the test has a high degree of excellence. As related in the well written manual, a great deal of thought and work went into its construction. A large number of textbooks and courses of study were analyzed and used as guides in se-

lecting the subject matter areas and objectives. The items were pretested and analyzed; those selected for the final forms range in (inverse) difficulty from 20 per cent to 91 per cent, the average being 57 per cent. Great care was taken to balance the test as to subject matter and objectives, and to achieve equivalence between the two forms. The final forms were standardized in 76 schools. Reliability estimates of .90 and .93 (split-half) and .87 (alternate form) are reported. The manual gives a number of suggestions for the use of the tests. It is quite evident that the test was constructed under the guidance of experts in test theory.

This reviewer is not convinced that similar expert guidance was given on the selection of the *ideas* to be tested, as distinct from the *areas* of content. He is not impressed with the face validity of many items. About half of the items are excellent, and test simply and directly significant points; an additional 20 to 25 are fair or acceptable; the remainder are mediocre or poor. There are too many items that test mere terminology, factual information, or insignificant points. For example, the item on the proton tests that it is "a particle of positive electricity" and not "a planetary electron." Surely there are more significant things about the proton. Nor is the use of "because" always appropriate, as in the item "Sugar is a compound because it—has a definite composition." Sugar is not a compound *because* of that fact; rather, we *know that it is* a compound *from* that fact. A similar looseness in wording elsewhere appears to stem from lack of clarity of the ideas of chemistry and its methods, and results in needless ambiguity. In several items the decoys could be more imaginative, more plausible, and more searching.

In view of these misgivings, the reviewer cannot recommend the test without qualifications. To be sure, the large number of good items should confer on the test a fair amount of validity. However, the teachers should be aware of its limitations and under proper circumstances the students should be informed so that they will not get the impression that every question is significant or properly asked.

For a review by William Rieman III, see 4:613.

[738]

*Chemistry: Achievement Examinations for Secondary Schools. High school; 1951–53; Forms 1 ('51), 2 ('52), 3 ('53); no specific manual; no data on reliability; norms: Forms 1 ['52], 2 ['53], 3 ('53); Forms 1, 2: 10¢ per test; Form 3: $2.75 per 25 tests; 10¢ per specimen set; postage extra; [60–90] minutes; Clarence Boeck (1) and Robert Molkenbur (2, 3); Educational Test Bureau. *

[739]

*Chemistry: Every Pupil Scholarship Test. High school; 1928–58; new form usually issued each January and April; norms available following testing program; no data on reliability; 4¢ per test; 4¢ per scoring key; postage extra; 40(45) minutes; Bureau of Educational Measurements. *

[740]

*Chemistry: Every Pupil Test. High school; 1929–58; new form usually issued each December and April; norms available following testing program; no data on reliability; 3¢ per test; 1¢ per scoring key; cash orders postpaid; 40(45) minutes; Ohio Scholarship Tests. *

[741]

★Chemistry: Midwest High School Achievement Examinations. High school; 1955–57; Forms A ('55), B ('57); no specific manual; no data on reliability; norms: [A, '55; B, '57]; 10¢ per test, postage extra; Form A: 60(65) minutes; Form B: 90[95] minutes; Robert Molkenbur (A) and H. O. Bergee (B); Educational Test Bureau. *

EDWARD G. RIETZ, *Instructor in Chemistry, Wright Junior College, Chicago, Illinois.*

The avowed intent of the Midwest High School Achievement Examinations is "to motivate efforts of accomplishments by the students" and "to stimulate thinking ability based on mastery of contents resulting from efforts of work." The present examination is devoted to coverage of general information, chemical principles, laboratory procedures, and scientific method. Unfortunately, however, many questions are ambiguous, miskeyed, or unrealistic, or demand acceptance of obsolete concepts. Examples of specific objections follow:

a) The student is asked to determine the volume of hydrogen produced from a given weight of sodium under unspecified conditions of temperature and pressure. (The keyed answer assumes conditions to be standard.)

b) A keyed answer identifies an alkali metal as one of three elements least likely to react. (One of the elements is a rare gas, so the key is in error.)

c) The keyed answer to a question regarding the role of an inorganic salt in corrosion indicates that the salt undergoes ionization and that the ions react with the metal. The answer ignores the fact that most salts are highly ionized, even in the crystalline state, and does not recognize that corrosion is a voltaic phenomenon requiring electrolytic conduction (provided by the ionic material).

d) A question on stoichiometry involves calculation of the amount of carbon required for the reduction of 240 tons of iron ore containing 46 per cent Fe_2O_3. Inasmuch as an intelligent high school student would be conversant with the elementary metallurgy of iron, he would be confused by this question; for he would be obliged to determine whether the author logically expected an answer based upon blast furnace operation (in which case a 100 per cent efficient operation must be assumed), or whether the author illogically expected an answer based upon direct reduction of such a large quantity of low grade ore. The latter expectation requires a decision as to whether carbon monoxide or carbon dioxide is produced in the reduction. Reference to the keyed answer indicates that the author expected a direct reduction and that he assumed carbon dioxide to have been produced. The question is perplexing and unrealistic.

e) The format leaves much to be desired. The exercises are crowded and the numerical answers are not arranged in an ascending or descending order of magnitude as they should be for convenience of the student.

The publishers have provided a report of norms but these are restricted to the 25th percentile, the median, and the 75th percentile for high school students. No data are given concerning the high school students involved in establishing these norms and no data are provided with respect to reliability or validity.

In view of the test's numerous deficiencies, this reviewer regretfully must decline to recommend it.

[742]

*College Entrance Examination Board Achievement Test in Chemistry. Candidates for college entrance; 1901–58; for more complete information, see 599; IBM; 60(80) minutes; program administered by Educational Testing Service for the College Entrance Examination Board. *

REFERENCES

1–4. See 4:617.
5. COLLEGE ENTRANCE EXAMINATION BOARD. *Science: A Description of the College Board Tests in Biology, Chemistry, and Physics.* Princeton, N.J.: the Board, September 1954. Pp. 39. * (PA 29:2958)
6. EVENSON, A. B., AND SMITH, D. E. "A Study of Matriculation in Alberta." *Alberta J Ed Res* 4:67–83 Je '58. *

MAX D. ENGELHART, *Director, Division of Student Examinations, Chicago Public Schools, Chicago, Illinois.* [Review of Form FAC.]

This test was prepared by a committee of three teachers of elementary college chemistry and two secondary school teachers of chemistry, one from a public high school and one from a private school. The committee, appointed by the College Entrance Examination Board, was assisted by members of the professional staff of Educational Testing Service. Experiences of earlier committees aided in the making of decisions with respect to the nature of the test and of the types of exercises to be written. On the basis of these decisions, the committee members prepared new items which were reviewed individually and by the group and in relation to technical suggestions of staff members of the Educational Testing Service. The items were then pretested and the data thus obtained subjected to statistical analysis yielding information used by the committee members in revising items prior to final review of the test as a whole.

The content of this test is admirably distributed over the subject matter of high school chemistry. Basic concepts are emphasized rather than unimportant details. Numerous exercises require for their solution critical thinking in application of fundamental laws and principles. There are a number of exercises evaluating understanding of laboratory techniques and of phenomena observed in laboratory experimentation. A satisfying variety of quantitative problems are included. The chemical equations appearing in a number of the items are well chosen.

The first 20 items of the test are of the key list or classification type. Seven of these items are quantitative problems following five categories which are answers in round numbers— one, five, ten, twenty, and forty. The candidate must compute to ascertain which answer is nearest to his answer and thus best. This is a very ingenious series of items. One item, however, can be speculated upon. If one computes, as one should, the number of moles of oxygen necessary to obtain one mole of CO_2 on the basis of the equation for the reaction between a hydrocarbon and oxygen given at the start of the series of problems, the computed answer is 1.75 moles for which the nearest answer "one" is to be marked. If, however, one computes the number of moles of oxygen improperly from the equation $C+O_2 \rightarrow CO_2$, the exact answer "one" is obtained. The very low item-test correlation of this item may have resulted from such computation by less competent students while more able and conscientious students tended to omit the item on obtaining

the answer 1.75, so different from the answer to be marked. Listing answers in round numbers is an excellent device so long as improper solution of a problem does not yield the keyed answer, or nearly the keyed answer, and the directions more explicitly tell the student to select that listed answer which is exactly his computed answer, or nearest to his computed answer.

Forty-five of the 100 items are 5-response multiple choice exercises for which the candidate is to select the one best answer. In all but one of these exercises the problem of the exercise is in the item stem. This reviewer identified no obvious distractors. Only two of these exercises may be criticized. In Item 58, the equation is referred to as unbalanced when, in fact, it is already balanced. (Each coefficient should be one and their absence does not present an unbalanced equation.) In Item 63, the most difficult item in the test, the student, after being told that 5 moles of H_2SO_4 will produce 5 moles of hydrogen chloride, is asked to compute the "theoretical" number of moles of hydrogen chloride obtained from 29 grams of sodium chloride. The correct answer 0.50 seems to this reviewer more actual than theoretical. In 15 more multiple choice exercises a varying number of completions are correct though only one answer space is to be marked for each exercise: A if answers 1, 2, 3 are correct; B if 1 and 3 are correct; C if 2 and 4 are correct; D if only 4 is correct; and E if some other combination is correct. In general the exercises are excellent and require careful thinking. However, in three of these exercises the problem is not stated in the item stem. It seems to this reviewer, too, that answer E is too much to worry about where time is of the essence.

Ten items near the end of the test are "assertions" followed by "reasons." The student is expected to respond: A if the assertion is true and the reason is a correct explanation; B if both the assertion and the reason are true, but the reason is not a correct explanation; C if the assertion is true, but the reason is a false statement; D if the assertion is false, but the reason is a true statement; and E if both the assertion and the reason are false statements. It seems to this reviewer that these categories, though simply summarized for the candidates, are nevertheless too complex where time is at a premium. One possibility would be to use these four categories: A if the assertion is true and the reason explains why it is true; B if the assertion is true, but the reason does not explain why it is true; C if the assertion is false and the reason explains why it is false; D if the assertion is false, but the reason does not explain why it is false. The content of nine of the items is excellent, but the assertion that "silver chloride and silver bromide are widely used in making photographic film," though true with respect to silver bromide, is *not* true with respect to silver chloride.

The last 10 items of the test are equations. The candidate is to give the coefficient of one of the substances involved. The reviewer of an earlier form of this test stated with reference to such items: "The equations in Part IV are well selected, although it may be desirable to test the student's ability to balance separately from his ability to complete the equation. Moreover, requiring the student to give only one coefficient as evidence that he has completed the equation correctly would appear to leave too much to a lucky error." This reviewer disagrees. The correction for chance should take care of the "lucky error." If this assumption is correct, the determination of the correct answer on the basis of skill requires the student to balance the first 5 and to complete and balance the last 5 of the 10 equations, where the products are not given, before responding with his answers.

In the judgment of this reviewer, no secondary school teacher of chemistry should have reason to question the general fairness of this test in evaluating the achievement of his students who are candidates for college entrance.

The bulletin entitled *Test Analysis of College Entrance Examination Board March 1957 Achievement Examinations* states with respect to the chemistry and physics tests that "it is hard to say whether the scores reflect both power and speed or whether the apparent degree of speededness is really the result of candidates' unwillingness to respond to some of the items that may be quite unfamiliar to them." The hypothesis suggested by the last part of this statement should be investigated. Use of fewer than 100 items, or of a higher proportion of items requiring less time and hence less thought, would probably result in a test of lower reliability and validity. Worth considering, however, is modification of the multiple choice exercises with more than one completion correct and the assertions and reasons items in

the ways earlier suggested. It might also be desirable to tell candidates not to spend inordinate time on exercises with which they are quite unfamiliar, but to distribute their time over the test.

The bulletin mentioned above, the Technical Manual for Users of Test Analysis, the Supervisors Manual containing directions for administering the College Board Examinations, and the publication entitled *College Board Scores: Their Use and Interpretation* were all studied carefully in preparing this review. Such study leaves this reviewer greatly impressed with the efforts made to obtain adequate control of testing conditions, to accomplish the analyses contributing to the improvement of the examinations, and to provide information essential to college and university admissions officers in making wise use of College Board scores.

[743]
★College Entrance Examination Board Advanced Placement Examination: Chemistry. High school seniors desiring credit for college level courses; 1954-58; for more complete information, see 600; IBM in part; 180(200) minutes; program administered by Educational Testing Service for the College Entrance Examination Board. *

THEO. A. ASHFORD, *Professor of Chemistry, Saint Louis University, Saint Louis, Missouri.* [Review of Form FBP.]

This examination, constructed under the auspices of the Educational Testing Service by a committee of college and high school chemistry teachers, is designed to measure the achievement of high school students in a typical college chemistry course. Presumably, it is to be given to students who have had an "advanced placement course," though apparently the taking of such a course is not a formal requirement for taking the test.

The test consists of two sections. Section 1, containing 50 items of the 5-choice multiple response type, requires one hour of testing time. The items have a high face validity. They impress one as measuring the significant and important ideas of a good college chemistry course. They require understanding of the principles and theories of chemistry, and test factual information only incidentally. The items are good technically. They have been pretested in other examinations at the college level, or are modeled after very similar items. The balance of coverage is good. The reported reliability of this section is estimated as .87.

Section 2 is an essay test of four parts, requiring a total of two hours of testing time. In Part A the candidate chooses between two topics, each with several parts. The problems are straightforward, but require thorough and quantitative understanding of basic principles and ability to apply them. Part B offers a choice between two topics dealing with similar principles in other areas of chemistry. In Part C the candidate chooses one of three problems requiring the interpretation and presentation of broad concepts. Part D offers a choice among four problems requiring the interpretation or discussion of a more specific topic or principle.

The reliable scoring of Section 2 raises some misgivings, as is always the case with essay questions. However, this reviewer is impressed by the elaborate precautions taken to insure maximum reader reliability. The readers are selected from among college or high school teachers and are given extensive written and oral instructions in conferences preceding the scoring operation. The evaluation of typical items and the scores to be assigned to them are arrived at after group discussion. The grading is ultimately subjective, as it should be, depending upon the expert judgment of the reader, but every means is utilized to make it as free of individual bias as possible. Incidentally, this section cannot be read by clerks without judgment and competence in the field, however detailed the instructions. No reliability coefficients are given for the essay section, but the fairly high intercorrelations between the parts and between the two sections (.77) suggest good overall reliability.

The two scores in each section are transformed into standard scores, weighted in proportion to the testing time, 1:2, and added. The total score is reported to the college which the student plans to attend on a scale from 1 to 5. In addition to interpretive and normative tables, the papers for Section 2 are transmitted to the college for further interpretation by the school, which ultimately decides what credit or acceleration will be granted to the student.

In the opinion of this reviewer, the test is a well constructed instrument for the purpose. Every precaution has been taken to make the test scores meaningful, reliable, and valid. The reviewer would not hesitate to accept the results as measuring competence in chemistry, in so far as it can be measured by paper and pencil tests.

[744]
*Cooperative Chemistry Test. High school; 1933-50; IBM; Forms X ('47), Y ('48), Z ('50); no specific manual; general Cooperative manual ('51); norms ['37]; $2.95 per 25 tests; separate answer sheets may be used; $1 per 25 IBM answer sheets; 25¢ per scoring stencil; postage extra; 40(45) minutes; Paul J. Burke (X) and Joseph F. Castka (Y, Z); Cooperative Test Division, Educational Testing Service. *

FRANK P. CASSARETTO, *Professor of Chemistry, Loyola University, Chicago, Illinois.*

All three forms of this test were examined as to content and found to fulfill for chemistry the objective of the publisher for all of the Cooperative Achievement Tests as stated in the general manual: to construct and distribute professionally sound tests of scholastic aptitude and achievement which meet common educational and guidance needs.

Each of the forms is organized in two parts, the first part covering general information, and the second, laboratory technique, some application of chemical principles, and a few (too few) quantitative applications. The items are of the multiple choice type. In Form X the diagrams in Part 2 are so poorly drawn and so small that the student can be expected to have difficulty in interpreting them. In Form Y the diagrams are larger and better drawn but the diagram on page 7 is in error experimentally, and the graph on page 10 is crowded with so much data that it is an anathema. Both the diagram and the graph should be redrawn and the items based on the graph should be reworked. Form Z, with a larger and more representative editorial board, shows improvement over the other two forms.

A hand scoring fan key and a stencil for hand or machine scoring are provided. Most instructors will want to administer the test with answer sheets rather than in test booklets so that they will not have to use the fan type key. The norms for the test seem reliable enough so that the test results can be considered indicative of student capabilities.

This reviewer believes that these tests are good but that they are in need of revision to correct present imperfections and to bridge the gap in nomenclature and theory changes since 1950. The quantitative applications should be increased to emphasize basic reasoning with number concepts. More problems should be used and if necessary should be weighted accordingly to reward this ability.

WILLARD G. WARRINGTON, *Associate Professor, Office of Evaluation Services, Michigan State University, East Lansing, Michigan.*

These tests are designed as measures of achievement at the end of a one-year high school chemistry course. The three forms represent the latest revisions of a long series of tests in this area.

Each of the current forms contains a broad sampling of item content, with specific factual items and application items represented in about equal proportions. In several sections of each test data in the form of charts, graphs, or tables are presented and the student is asked questions involving the understanding and application of these data. Such items should provide a measure of knowledge beyond the rote memory level.

The format of the tests is good, directions to the students are satisfactory, and the diagrams of equipment and the charts and tables mentioned above should make the test interesting to take. The items, in general, are well written, the language is precise, and the specific problems are clearly stated.

The 40-minute test is timed in two parts, with 25 minutes allowed for Part 1 (52–54 items) and 15 minutes for Part 2 (27–29 items). Since the student would need to do two items a minute to complete the test, any total score will undoubtedly be to some degree a measure of speed, a factor which should certainly be taken into consideration in the interpretation of scores. However, the two-part timing and the direction to the student to answer the easier questions first should reduce the effects of the relatively short time limits.

The directions to the examiner and the general rationale for the development of the tests are somewhat inadequate because of the lack of a specific manual for this test. The general Cooperative manual provides sufficient information to insure a satisfactory testing situation, but a manual designed for this test in particular would be more valuable to most teachers in this area.

While the description of scoring procedures is generally satisfactory, the rather vague definition of scaled scores may result in some confusion when these scaled scores are converted to percentile ranks. On the fan key for each test, a scaled score of 50 is described as "the expected performance of the 'average' individual with 1 year of study of the subject tested at the end of the 12th grade." Yet in the normative data presented for the 7,000 twelfth grade students from 80 public high schools in the East, Middle West, and West with one year of chemistry, the scaled score of 50 has a percentile rank of 22. This apparent inconsistency should be explained as follows: The scaled score of 50 represents the average performance that would be expected of an unselected group of high school students if all high school students took chemistry. The percentile rank of 50 represents the average accomplishment of a sample of the highly selected group of high school students who actually do take chemistry. Consequently, users should be cautioned that these scaled scores as such, do not represent meaningful normative data in a selective course area such as chemistry.

Except for this weakness in presentation, the normative data provided appear to be adequate. Along with the scaled scores and percentile ranks some evidence is also shown as to the magnitude of the standard error for the scaled score. While the information in the manual describing this important concept is also somewhat vague, the mere mention is a welcome trend not seen in many test manuals.

In general, all three forms of the *Cooperative Chemistry Test* represent examples of measuring instruments that should be very useful in evaluating the outcome of most high school chemistry courses. The reviewer is somewhat concerned about the emphasis placed upon the speed factor but in view of the broad sampling covered by the tests and the high quality of the items, he would have no hesitancy in recommending their use.

For a review by John H. Daugherty of an earlier form, see 3:561; for reviews by Charles L. Bickel and Louis M. Heil, see 40:1592; for reviews by Edward E. Cureton and W. B. Meldrum, see 38:932.

[745]

*Cooperative Chemistry Test: Educational Records Bureau Edition. High school; 1941–58; IBM; Forms ERB-RY ('57, revision of Form ERB-RX), ERB-SY ('58, revision of Form ERB-SX) ; no specific manual; general Cooperative manual ('51) ; no data on reliability; norms; Form ERB-RY ('57), Form ERB-SY ('58) ; 11.8¢ per test; separate answer sheets may be used; 4¢ per IBM answer sheet; 50¢ per specimen set; postage extra; 80(85) minutes; Committee on Chemistry Tests of the Educational Records Bureau; Educational Records Bureau. *

REFERENCES
1–2. See 4:619.
3. TRAXLER, ARTHUR E. "The 1957 ERB Edition of the Cooperative Biology, Chemistry, and Physics Tests, Form ERB-
RY—Difficulty, Reliability, and Correlation With School
Marks." Ed Rec B 70:65–70 Jl '57. *

[746]
*The Graduate Record Examinations Advanced
Tests: Chemistry. College seniors and graduate stu-
dents; 1939–57; for more complete information, see
601; IBM; 180(200) minutes; Educational Testing
Service. *

*For a review by Harold Seashore of the en-
tire series, see 601.*

[747]
★A Junior Chemistry Test. 2 years secondary school;
1957; Forms A, B ['57]; 25s. per 25 tests; 1s. per
single copy; 1s. 6d. per manual ['57]; 3s. 6d. per specimen set; postpaid within Australia; 35(45) minutes;
C. M. Goldburg; University of Queensland Press. *

ROY W. STANHOPE, *Senior Lecturer in Science Education, Sydney Teachers' College,
University Grounds, Sydney, Australia.*

This test is intended chiefly as a measure of
attainment among pupils who have completed
the syllabus requirements prescribed in 1956
for the two-year introductory course in inorganic chemistry for Queensland secondary
schools. The test has also some applicability in
New South Wales and South Australia since
the subject matter covered also forms part of
the syllabus requirements in junior high school
chemistry in these states.

The primary emphasis in chemistry courses
and public (external) examinations at this level
in Australia and in most other parts of the
British Commonwealth is upon a dozen or so
gases—their preparation and properties, and
the equations for the reactions involved in such
preparations and property demonstrations.
More than half the test items in each form
call for factual information of this kind. The
remaining items reflect the secondary emphases.
They deal with the properties of a few metals
and nonmetals and of two or three compounds
of each; acids, bases, and salts; elementary
theory and general laws; and simple numerical
calculations.

The 60 items in each form are arranged in
five sections. Two are concerned with general
information, one containing 20 multiple choice
items and the other 10 completion type items.
A third section demands the reproduction of
15 equations, and a fourth the answers to five
numerical problems. The remaining section
comprises 10 items of the matching variety

concerned in Form A with gas properties, and
in Form B with common names and formulae.
This sectionalization of some aspects of the
field of chemistry permits the use of the test
for diagnosis of specific areas of weakness
amongst pupils.

After several preliminary trials, during
which item validation was effected by the acceptable upper-middle-lower thirds technique,
the two forms, with items paired for difficulty,
were administered one month before the Junior
Public Examination to 414 students constituting "a representative 10 per cent sample of all
the Junior chemistry candidates in Queensland." The manual reports a validity coefficient
of .77, as determined by rank order correlation
of pupils' scores on the test with teachers' estimates of their ability in chemistry, and a reliability coefficient of .91, obtained by the product-
moment correlation of scores on the two parallel forms. In the absence of details as to how
this validation was effected and how the parallel forms were administered, the reviewer is
unable to offer comments upon these statistical
measures. The split-half technique was used to
provide a further assessment of reliability. Presumably because these are timed tests, the author does not report reliability coefficients for
this analysis, noting only that differences in
scores on the odd and even numbered items
were found "to be not significant at the 5 per
cent level of confidence."

Percentile ranks at intervals of 10 are given
for either form and for combined scores on the
two forms. One would prefer, in addition, some
form of scaled scores of an equal-interval type.
A graph constructed by relating the scores of
the pupils in the selected sample to their marks
in the subsequent Junior Public Examination
affords a means of predicting the likely examination mark of a pupil. It is expected that
norms will be established at a later date for
children in the other states.

While the tests meet satisfactory standards
with regard to format, layout, spacing, type
size, and practice examples (on the back of
each test booklet), the instructions to pupils in
some sections are faulty. No instruction is
given, for instance, that dual responses are correct and required in Items 3 and 10 in Form A
and Item 15 in Form B. In the section on chemical equations, certain of the reactions will proceed only if the mixture is heated, but this necessary condition is omitted. No mention is

made of the fact that two equations are required in the case of "Burning magnesium in pure air" (Form B, Section D, Item 14).

The test booklets are not reusable since no separate response sheets are provided, nor are the tests machine scorable. The answer keys are deficient in that for a few items alternative and equally correct responses are not provided, and obscure and inconsistent in showing the dual responses previously noted. The provision of strip or fan keys would have been helpful. Since the time limit of 35 minutes restricts the subject matter coverage and the spread in scores for either form, it would be more satisfactory to total the pupils' scores on both forms. The two forms together would seem quite capable of measuring satisfactorily those aspects of elementary chemistry emphasized in the teaching and examining of Junior chemistry in Queensland. This test is the first in this field to be published in Australia since the longer and more comprehensive *Intermediate Chemistry Test* constructed by the reviewer in 1932–33.

MERVYN L. TURNER, *Research Assistant, Australian Council for Educational Research, Melbourne, Australia.*

This test was constructed for use as an achievement and diagnostic test in chemistry at the Junior Public Examination level in the state of Queensland. There are two forms, each containing 20 multiple choice, 10 matching, 10 completion, 15 equation, and 5 quantitative problem items.

Although the test handbook claims that the test "samples the whole field" of the Junior Public syllabus, classification of the items on a number of bases by the reviewer failed to substantiate the claim.

Analysis of items according to the content areas of the syllabus revealed a lack of representative sampling. About 100 of the 120 items in the two forms are based on the descriptive chemistry of the 17 elements included in the syllabus prescriptions, so that many important principles, generalizations, and theories also contained in the syllabus are not tested. Of these 100 items, 30 are concerned with nitrogen and its compounds. Seven elements account for 90 of the items. Even granting that different emphases should be given to different elements, this division appears unreasonable.

Analysis of the items against the background of the syllabus and contemporary Junior Public Examination papers indicates that the essential cognitive ability tested is that of recall of factual information. Many of the items test facts of doubtful importance in modern chemical curricula. For instance, is it important to test for knowledge of now seldom used "common" names of certain chemicals? The quantitative problem items are more likely to test knowledge of routine methods than abilities of analysis and application.

Item quality is not high and one could very reasonably hypothesize a large "item interpretation" factor in the test. Indeed, the item validities and test reliability (parallel forms, .91) may be due in large part to such a factor. Only one answer is accepted for each item. In many items, the reviewer feels that there are equally acceptable or more acceptable answers than those indicated as correct in the handbook.

Though balanced on difficulty, the two forms are not balanced on content. For instance, one form contains two separate items concerned with the reaction of sodium with water. One practice item appears in identical wording as an actual item in one form of the test.

The basic criticisms of the test are that it appears to have been constructed without specication and that content validity has been sacrificed for the sake of reliability. Validities of .77 (a rank order correlation of test scores with teachers' estimate of present status in chemistry) and .76 (test scores correlated with Junior Public Examination scores) have been obtained, but these are more censures of teachers, examiners, and curriculum makers in chemistry than a validation of the test. Teaching and testing in secondary education in all Australian states would benefit by more precise definition of objectives. This test will serve only to confirm the present limited and vague objectives.

GEOLOGY

[748]
*The Graduate Record Examinations Advanced Tests: Geology.** College seniors and graduate students; 1939-56; for more complete information, see 601; IBM; 180(200) minutes; Educational Testing Service. *

For a review by Harold Seashore of the entire series, see 601.

PHYSICS

[749]

***College Entrance Examination Board Achievement Test in Physics.** Candidates for college entrance; 1901–58; for more complete information, see 599; IBM; 60(80) minutes; program administered by Educational Testing Service for the College Entrance Examination Board. *

REFERENCES

1–3. See 4:633.
4. COLLEGE ENTRANCE EXAMINATION BOARD. *Science: A Description of the College Board Tests in Biology, Chemistry, and Physics.* Princeton, N.J.: the Board, September 1954. Pp. 39. * (PA 29:2958)
5. EVENSON, A. B., AND SMITH, D. E. "A Study of Matriculation in Alberta." *Alberta J Ed Res* 4:67–83 Je '58. *

THEODORE G. PHILLIPS, *Assistant Dean, Amundsen Branch, Chicago City Junior College, Chicago, Illinois.* [Review of Form FAC.]

This test is one of the options in the most recent battery of tests intended by the College Entrance Examination Board to provide colleges and universities with some evidence regarding achievement in physics of high school seniors who apply for admission. The tests are also designed to aid colleges and universities in predicting future performance of applicants with similar material at the college level.

The committee responsible for the construction of this test has done a thorough task of covering the various branches of physics. The test is in five parts and is entirely objective. Classification of the 98 items by the reviewer indicates 37 in mechanics, 18 in heat, 23 in electricity and magnetism, 14 in light, and 6 in sound. Perhaps the large number of items in mechanics should be reduced slightly in the next edition to allow for some elementary items in modern physics such as atomic structure, radioactivity, nuclear reactions, and atomic energy, all of which are conspicuously absent in the present form of the test. The inclusion of such items would reflect recent trends in the content of high school physics as well as the direction in which advances in physics are being made. Although all seven of the basic principles and concepts around which the American Association of Physics Teachers has recommended that introductory college physics courses be constructed are beyond the scope of high school physics, the conservation principles applicable to mass and energy, momentum, and charge could be effectively used in test items even at the high school level. In the present form of the test there are but two items on the principles of conservation—one on energy and the other on momentum.

In terms of the functions served by the questions, further categorizing of the items indicates that 14 are informational, 64 interpretive, and 20 problem solving. The emphasis on interpretive items is indeed properly placed at the high school level, with minimum emphasis on the memorization of factual material. Second in importance to interpretive material is problem solving, and this aspect is adequately covered in the 20 items devoted to it.

The fact that physics is an experimental science has not been overlooked by the committee. Two sets of ingenious exercises, totaling 16 items, to test the student's knowledge of laboratory technique and procedures are included.

There is some overlapping of material in a few items, such as those dealing with the determination of the electrochemical equivalent and electroplating, and the experimental determination of "g" and the frequency of a pendulum. It is further recommended that Item 3 be rephrased to state that the direction of force and the direction of the displacement are parallel. The choices for Items 6–10 are not coordinate, and the statement of Item 9 is not in the language of physics. In the directions to Items 21–25, the second sentence should be modified to read: "In geometry, for example...." Also, in Item 24, the resistance of a uniform wire should be modified to indicate "at constant temperature," or the directions changed to state that all other factors are to be assumed constant. In Part B, the instructions are too detailed and burdensome, particularly since they apply only to seven items, and this despite the efforts to simplify directions in a summary table. In Part B also, the five categories of choices could be reduced to four with equal effectiveness. Similarly, in Part E, the elimination of the fifth choice would not impair the value of this group of eight items.

In general, the test reflects the careful and objective work of the committee. Despite the minor limitations which have been pointed out, the test is a fair although difficult one. It should be emphasized that in identifying students of college caliber this instrument serves a higher function than that of an ordinary achievement test in high school physics given upon completion of the course.

For a review by Palmer O. Johnson of earlier forms, see 4:633.

[750]

★College Entrance Examination Board Advanced Placement Examination: Physics. High school seniors desiring credit for college level courses; 1954–58; for more complete information, see 600; IBM in part; 2 parts; 180(200) minutes; program administered by Educational Testing Service for the College Entrance Examination Board. *

LEO NEDELSKY, *Associate Professor of Physical Sciences, University of Chicago, Chicago, Illinois.* [Review of Form FBP.]

The test covers college level physics courses taught in secondary schools. It is administered in May, and grades of 5 (highest honors) to 1 (fail) are assigned to students by committees of the College Entrance Examination Board. At present 200 colleges grant to their entrants advanced placement, and in some instances also credit, in various courses on the basis of CEEB descriptions of the courses, schools' recommendations, test grades, and test booklets containing the students' work and answers. These materials reach the colleges in mid-July.

CONTENT OBJECTIVES. The test consists of two parts, a 1-hour objective test of 25 multiple choice items and a 2-hour essay test. Content sampled corresponds to a one-year college physics course. In part 2 the student may elect to show his knowledge of calculus. Content sampling in the form of the test being reviewed is somewhat biased; a student familiar with two fields only, mechanics and electricity, might get a high total score. Narrow as it is, however, such sampling may be adequate and fair if the physics courses given at various schools are very similar in content and emphasis, and if, within each school, the methods used for teaching all five major fields, mechanics, electricity, wave motion, heat, and atomic physics, are quite similar. Possible dissimilarities in the method may stem from unequal availability—among the five fields—of audio-visual aids, such as movie films and demonstration apparatus, and of laboratory facilities. It may well be that at present the two conditions are adequately satisfied. One may hope, however, that very soon physics courses in the colleges, and subsequently in secondary schools, will enter a period of radical experimentation and change recommended by the AAPT Conference on Improving the Quality and Effectiveness of Introductory Physics Courses, whose report is published in October

1957 issue of the *American Journal of Physics.* One may also hope that during this period CEEB tests will not act as brakes to progress, as standardized tests are only too prone to do.

BEHAVIORAL OBJECTIVES. The commonly accepted, if not always practiced, major behavioral objectives of introductory physics teaching are: (*a*) Knowledge of subject matter (The reviewer includes in this category the ability to solve problems and analyze situations similar to those treated in the textbook or in class.) (*b*) Ability to use methods of science (The situations which the student is asked to analyze must have considerable elements of novelty to him.) (*c*) Ability to understand scientific writing (Exercises should be at the level of passages from textbooks or semipopular articles that include graphs and tables.)

In the present test, the first objective is treated judiciously and well and the other two objectives inadequately. The booklet describing the Advanced Placement Program lists, among other objectives, an understanding of "restrictions or limitations" of physical concepts and principles and of "reasons for the acceptance of truth of statements." These objectives are not tested for. In general, behavioral objectives represented in the test fall short of what may be expected from a really good physics course, as judged by the standards that have found their way into print, but compare favorably with the objectives that determine grades in most college physics courses.

TECHNICAL POINTS. The test is validated against scores made on the test by college students. Statistical results show that time allowance for the test is about right. The reliability of the objective part, .68, is adequate. It would be desirable to know the reader reliability for the essay part. In a group of items no credit is given for an item unless the student identifies all of its right responses. Since the correct responses are not logically interconnected or only loosely so, giving the same score of zero to students who cannot pick out even one right response as to those who recognize some but not all of the responses is an inefficient use of the test and of students' time. It would be better to ask the student to mark each response as true or false. Doubling the length of the objective part, if the traffic could bear it, would be the easiest first step toward improved sampling. The extra hour of testing might be profitably devoted to an analysis of a short article or passage.

SUMMARY. The test under review is a carefully and competently prepared evaluative tool. On the basis of results on it and other data supplied by CEEB, colleges could grant physics credit to their entrants at least as confidently as they now do to transfer students from an average college.

[751]

Cooperative Physics Test. High school; 1932–50; IBM; Forms Y ('48), Z ('50, identical with test copyrighted in 1949) ; no specific manual; general Cooperative manual ('51) ; norms ['37] ; $2.95 per 25 tests; separate answer sheets may be used; $1 per 25 IBM answer sheets; 25¢ per scoring stencil; postage extra; 40(45) minutes; Paul J. Burke; Form Z prepared from materials developed by H. W. Farwell; Cooperative Test Division, Educational Testing Service. *

REFERENCES

1–2. See 3:581.
3. RANDALL, ROGERS E. "Performance of Twenty-two College Students on the Cooperative Physics Test, Revised Series Form X." *Sch Sci & Math* 56:708–10 D '56. *

THEODORE G. PHILLIPS, *Assistant Dean, Amundsen Branch, Chicago City Junior College, Chicago, Illinois.*

Each form of this test contains 77 items of the multiple choice type. Classification by the reviewer of the items according to the fields of physics gives for Forms Y and Z, respectively: mechanics, 24, 23 ; heat, 16, 16 ; electricity and magnetism, 22, 23 ; light, 8, 9 ; and sound, 7, 6. Categorizing the items of the test according to the function each serves gives for Forms Y and Z, respectively: informational, 26, 27 ; interpretive, 33, 30 ; and problem solving, 18, 20. Disparity between the two forms in the number of items on each subject is small indeed in view of the fact that there is some question regarding the grouping of items which cut across two fields, such as the classification of an item dealing with the equivalence of heat and work. Even the classification by function does not reveal marked differences between the two forms, although here the difference could influence the comparability of the test results, assuming, of course, that interpretive and problem solving items are considerably more difficult than items of the informative type. But again, it must be borne in mind that grouping items according to function served presents difficulties, for the lines of demarcation are not precise.

Regarding content, this reviewer finds little criticism other than that Form Z includes only one item on modern physics, and Form Y only

four such items, all included in the previous subject matter classification under electricity and magnetism. It is recommended that future editions of this instrument include some items of an elementary nature on atomic energy, radioactivity, atomic structure, and nuclear physics to bring the coverage more in line with what is generally recommended for high school physics courses.

In general, the items have been carefully written. A few inaccuracies appear here and there, however. In Part 1 of Form Y, Item 5 pertains to *rolling* the barrel up the plane, and Item 6 of Part 1 to *pushing* it up. Complications arising from the resulting rotation in Item 6 could be avoided by "pushing" or "sliding" *boxes* up the plane instead of "rolling" barrels. Item 7 of the same part should be rephrased to state the highest average speed of translation or straight-line motion for a gas. In Part 2, Item 34 should be rewritten since the hydrogen *ion*, a proton, is a subatomic particle. Similarly, with respect to Form Z, it is suggested that Item 17 in Part 1 should specify "at constant temperature."

Notwithstanding minor inaccuracies such as these in a few items, the test on the whole is a commendable piece of work. Many of the interpretive items are thought-provoking, and the problems require for their solution more than just the mere substitution of numbers into memorized equations.

For a review by G. P. Cahoon of earlier forms, see 3:581; for reviews by Andrew Longacre, Alvin W. Schindler, and Ralph K. Watkins, see 40:1608; for reviews by Ernest E. Bayles and A. W. Hurd, see 38:1088.

[752]

*Cooperative Physics Test: Educational Records Bureau Edition. High school; 1941–58; IBM; Forms ERB-RY ('57, revision of Form ERB-RX), ERB-SY ('58, revision of Form ERB-SX) ; no specific manual; general Cooperative manual ('51) ; no data on reliability; norms: Form ERB-RY ('57), Form ERB-SY ('58) ; 11.8¢ per test; separate answer sheets may be used; 4¢ per IBM answer sheet; 50¢ per specimen set; postage extra; 80(85) minutes; Committee on Physics Tests of the Educational Records Bureau; Educational Records Bureau. *

REFERENCES

1–2. See 4:635.
3. TRAXLER, ARTHUR E. "The 1957 ERB Edition of the Cooperative Biology, Chemistry, and Physics Tests, Form ERB-RY—Difficulty, Reliability, and Correlation With School Marks." *Ed Rec B* 70:65–70 Jl '57. *

[753]

*Dunning Physics Test: Evaluation and Adjustment Series. Grades 11–13; 1951–54, c1950–54; IBM;

Forms AM ('51), BM ('52); manual ('51); expectancy chart ['54]; separate answer sheets must be used; $4.15 per 35 tests; $1.40 per 35 IBM answer sheets; postage extra; 35¢ per specimen set, postpaid; 45(55) minutes; Gordon M. Dunning; World Book Co. *

ROBERT M. W. TRAVERS, *Professor of Educational Psychology and Head of the Department, University of Utah, Salt Lake City, Utah.*

The test shows evidence of having had some thoughtful planning which is an improvement over the typical test in science. Content coverage is well specified and includes mechanics, heat, sound, light, electricity, and modern physics. The topics included within each of these broad fields of knowledge are also well defined. The distribution of items within the test itself appears to correspond well to the outline of content provided. This, however, is the point where planning ends. It is true that the author states in the manual that certain well known references were consulted for the identification of suitable objectives to measure, but what these objectives were is left entirely to the imagination of the reader. A clear statement of the objectives which an achievement test is designed to measure should be found in the manual. It is difficult to envisage the planned use of a test without knowing what it is intended to measure, unless, of course, it is assumed that the objectives of the author can be deduced from an examination of the content.

In quality, the test is at least up to the average science test. The items appear to have been well edited, though some inadequacies will necessarily slip past even the best of editors. A few major errors were not caught by the editorial process. There are also some examples of the use of language lacking precision in a scientific sense though it is possible that in such cases the author considered that he was communicating with an audience that might have difficulty with a more precise and scientifically adequate mode of expression. A further comment should be made about the items themselves. While most of them are designed to determine the amount of information which the student has acquired, and while some also ask for the interpretation of simple situations, they cover only a very limited range of the possible objectives which such a test could cover. They include almost nothing which would assess the student's ability to interpret data, to read tables of physical constants, to interpret the results of simple experiments, to point out the flaws in simple experimental designs, or to develop experiments to test hypotheses. Objectives outside of the area of knowledge and understanding are not given any recognition, although the source materials supposedly used in the development of the test do recognize the importance of such broader goals in the teaching of science. One suspects that in the building of tests, as in the teaching of courses, the listing of objectives tends to be a ritual which has little influence on the process it is designed to direct.

A real effort has been made by the author and publisher to explore the statistical properties of the test. The two forms represent an attempt to build parallel forms by carefully matching the items for content. A check on this matching shows that it was done with considerable care and that a good match was achieved between the difficulty level of corresponding items. Furthermore, the raw scores on the one form correspond very closely, score by score with the raw scores on the other form. The correspondence is close enough that a teacher could well administer one form at the beginning of a course in physics and the other form at the end and could obtain a measure of progress simply by subtracting the raw scores. The reader does not have to be reminded that the interpretation of such difference scores is not the simple matter which it appears to be. The reliability of the test, based on a split half method of estimation, appears to be satisfactory. The norms are presented and discussed with commendable honesty. All in all, the statistical data provided are commendable. They have been thoughtfully prepared and leave one with the feeling that the author and publisher have placed all the cards on the table. It is a nice comfortable feeling.

The test impresses this reviewer as one which the typical classroom teacher will endorse. While it is related to only very limited objectives of teaching, the fact is that the objectives of most teachers of physics are also likely to be limited. It will probably be considered by teachers of physics as a respectable instrument and, it really is. There is, however, such a quality as dull respectability.

For a review by G. P. Cahoon, see 4:636.

[754]

*The Graduate Record Examinations Advanced Tests: Physics. College seniors and graduate students; 1939-57; for more complete information, see

601; IBM; 180(200) minutes; Educational Testing Service. *

Leo Nedelsky, *Associate Professor of Physical Sciences, University of Chicago, Chicago, Illinois.* [Review of Form FGR.]

The explanatory booklets state that the GRE tests are designed "to measure the students' achievement and ability to work in their major fields of concentration." The tests are most frequently given to second semester seniors. The scores have been used for admission to graduate schools or to candidacy, job placement, assessment of the student's achievement, counseling, and evaluating the efficacy of instructional programs.

The physics test consists of 117 multiple choice items which sample the subject matter taught in the usual introductory physics course for physics majors, except that it does not use calculus.

The objective or competence measured by the test is almost entirely what this reviewer calls knowledge: most situations and problems in the test, though chosen with wisdom and discretion, are hardly more than paraphrases of those explicitly treated in a conventional textbook. Even relative to this objective the test is not an adequate measure of the student's readiness for graduate work in physics. The knowledge of none of the following is adequately tested: calculus in physics; experimental evidence for major theories; realm of applicability of generalizations; role of experiment, theory, and definition. The student is not required to know any history or to have read a single original paper; in short, he need know little if anything of physics as a process of inquiry.

The other two major and commonly accepted objectives of physics teaching are the ability to use methods of science, which involves the ability to judge cogence of evidence, appropriateness of a hypothesis, or soundness of conclusions drawn from experiment; and the ability to read scientific writing. Both these objectives imply independent reasoning of the type that cannot be reliably tested in the context of stereotyped textbook situations that seem to be the mainstay of the test under review. This type of scientific reasoning—and it does not imply creativity or any great talent—is so vital a part of graduate scholarship that a student who has developed it in, say, chem-

istry or even biology, and who has only a mediocre knowledge of introductory textbook physics, may be a more promising candidate for a physics graduate school than the student who can only offer a higher, even a considerably higher, score on the test.

A test that does not measure *directly* major aspects of a student's competence is not an adequate basis for graduate school admission or, *a fortiori*, for evaluating instructional programs. The present test does, however, measure one of the major objectives of physics and therefore undoubtedly correlates positively with achievement in the other objectives. The degree of correlation is a function of the student's training, and the range of its values is not known. Nevertheless, a student who makes a very high score on the test—as judged by local or national standards—is likely to be a superior graduate student, and one who makes a very low score is not likely to do well. In the majority of cases, however, additional evidence is indispensable; the testmakers do realize, of course, the value of other evidence and recommend using it. The testmakers cannot be criticized for not sampling all the major objectives in a 3-hour test. It is a pity, however, that they concentrated on the competence that is most reliably measured by course grades and omitted those for which evidence is hard to get. Further, if it is agreed that major objectives are not measured by the test, this fact should be stated explicitly and forcefully, lest some departments be misled into believing that the test embodies an operational definition of proper undergraduate physics training.

Within its narrow compass of objectives, the test is technically very good. The language is concise yet very clear, and there is always a response that is unambiguously best. The standard error of measurement, 35, is low. (It is not negligible, of course, and test users should be urged to think of a student's score not as 400 but 400 ± 35.) A technical defect that can and should be removed is a "pairing" of the right response with one or two wrong ones. For example, if two out of five responses are similar, that is, they both contain the word acceleration, one of the two is much too often the right one. Students have learned to expect that. Another peculiarity of many items is the nondirectiveness of the stem and the nonhomogeneity of the responses. A directive stem is one that allows the student to formulate a tentative answer before he has read the prepared responses. The responses to the question "which of the following facts is the best evidence (for a specified theory)?" are homogeneous if they all are correctly stated facts of different relevance or cogency; they are not homogeneous if some are factually false and others are not facts but definitions. In the test under review, the student often cannot know what answer is expected of him until he has read all the responses, and the latter are so inhomogeneous that he must in effect make five separate and often disparate judgments, one for each response. Since the time allowance per item is only 90 seconds, the scales are tipped against those students who rely on reasoning from a few fundamental principles and in favor of those who have more detailed knowledge at their fingertips.

Most test users would probably welcome now unavailable data on the test's speededness and on correlation with the following: undergraduate grades, scores on the GRE Area Tests, graduate school grades, and other measures of success in advanced work or jobs. The predictive power of a prognostic test should be known.

The test under review gives a reliable measure of an important but narrow segment of the student's achievement: essentially, an understanding and recall of the subject matter and the ability to solve problems contained in standard textbooks used in the introductory physics courses for physics majors. No knowledge of calculus is required. The test does not measure the student's ability to read or write in the field of science, his understanding of physics as a process of inquiry, or his ability to reason beyond the familiar stereotypes of the textbook. This test alone cannot, therefore, provide an adequate measure of the student's readiness for graduate work in physics unless his score is unusually high or unusually low.

For a review by Harold Seashore of the entire series, see 601.

[755]

★A Junior Physics Test. 2 years secondary school; 1956; Forms A ['56], B ['56]; 25s. per 25 tests; 1s. per single copy; 1s. per manual ['56]; 3s. per specimen set; postpaid within Australia; 40(50) minutes; R. A. Squire; University of Queensland Press. *

Roy W. Stanhope, *Senior Lecturer in Science Education, Sydney Teachers' College, University Grounds, Sydney, Australia.*

This test has been prepared as an achievement test for pupils completing the two-year introductory course in physics in Queensland secondary schools. As well as affording a measure of total achievement in course content, the test may be used to diagnose strengths and weaknesses in the various branches of physics, since the 55 items in each of the two parallel forms are arranged in broad subject matter divisions. These divisions, and the number of items in each in Forms A and B respectively are: Measurement and Mechanics (12, 11); Properties of Matter (12, 13); Heat (14, 14); and Magnetism and Electricity (17, 17). This distribution is in fairly close agreement with the relative amounts of space given in the syllabus prescribed for the 1955 Junior Public Examination in Physics. Careful comparison of the subject matter in the test items with the syllabus prescriptions confirms the author's claim that the whole range of the course is covered, although electrostatics is rather overemphasized at the expense of current electricity.

The manual lists three "further" purposes of the test in addition to its use as a total measure of achievement in physics in the two-year course. These may be stated as: (*a*) to assess a pupil's knowledge and understanding of factual information; (*b*) to measure the ability of a student to recognise and apply basic principles; and (*c*) to determine a student's skill in solving numerical problems.

While the recognition of factual information receives undue emphasis, the 40 multiple choice items in each form, generally speaking, serve very well the first and second of these purposes. The third purpose is covered adequately in the remaining 15 items in each form. In each of these the required response is the number part only of the answer to a numerical calculation. In view of the importance attached to the names of units in quantitative statements, it would make for a better test if two credit points were allotted each of these items, the additional point being for the statement of the correct unit.

The procedures used in the construction and standardisation of this test were similar to those employed in the case of the companion *Junior Chemistry Test.* Correlation of pupils' test scores with teachers' estimates of capability in physics yielded a validity coefficient of .77, while the reliability figure of .84 was found on administration of both forms to the same pupils. A further assessment of reliability by the split-half technique showed, as with the chemistry test, that any differences in scores were not significant at the 5 per cent level. A table of percentile norms, based on a sample of Queensland children, is provided.

The reviewer's comments upon these statistical procedures and measures are much the same as those made with reference to the chemistry test and so are not here repeated. Attention should be drawn, however, to the use of the term "co-efficiency of correlation" in the section of the manual entitled "Reliability of the Test"; it is a term not known to the reviewer. "Co-efficiency" could, however, be another typographical error to be added to the few inconsequential ones noticed elsewhere in the manual.

In mechanical features and in the provision of practice examples, the tests are quite satisfactory. However, the test booklets are not reusable, nor are strip or fan keys provided.

Each form, as it stands, may be recommended to those seeking a means of assessing the attainment of students completing those courses in introductory physics which cover ground similar to that covered by the Queensland Junior physics course. If the suggestion made earlier that in the 15 numerical exercises credit be given for both the number part and the unit name be adopted, a greater spread in scores would probably be obtained and the test would afford a more satisfactory measure of total achievement in physics.

MERVYN L. TURNER, *Research Assistant, Australian Council for Educational Research, Melbourne, Australia.*

This test was constructed for use as an achievement test in physics at the Junior Public Examination level in the state of Queensland. The content of each subject of this examination is defined by a "standard of knowledge" prescribed by a board responsible to both the University of Queensland and the Queensland Minister for Education. These standards of knowledge are the prime determinants of the functions and functioning of secondary education for the whole state. Analogous systems operate in the other Australian states, where,

to different degrees, examinations set by authorities external to the school are used as the educational yardstick.

Lack of clearly defined objectives, other than such a standard, makes the task of achievement test construction difficult. The author of this test has defined the objectives that he is attempting to measure, and few would quarrel with them as a minimum, though it would be desirable that they be extended. The test aims to measure "(*a*) a student's knowledge and understanding of factual information related to physics; (*b*) the ability of a pupil to recognise and apply the basic principles of physics; (*c*) a student's skill in solving problems relating to physics."

Two forms, each containing 40 multiple choice and 15 quantitative problem items, have been developed. Each form has four sections (Measurement and Mechanics, Properties of Matter, Heat, and Magnetism and Electricity), the weightings of which appear to approximate closely the emphases given these areas in the Junior Public syllabus and examinations.

Item quality is generally good and item selection has produced two forms which closely match the "content" and "objective" specifications. Parallel form reliability is .84.

The test should be a good group achievement test for teachers of physics in Queensland schools and the use of both forms should make reasonable individual interpretations possible. It will be of much more limited use in other Australian states as syllabus content differs from state to state and in several states considerable revision of syllabuses is now occurring.

[756]
*Physics: Achievement Examinations for Secondary Schools.** High school; 1951–53; Forms 1 ('51), 2 ('52), 3 ('53); no specific manual; no data on reliability; norms: Forms 1 ['52], 2 ['53], 3 ('53); 10¢ per test, postage extra; [60–90] minutes; Clarence H. Boeck (1, 2) and Kenneth A. Berg (3); Educational Test Bureau. *

[757]
*Physics: Every Pupil Scholarship Test.** High school; 1926–58; new form usually issued each January and April; norms available following testing program; no data on reliability; 4¢ per test; 4¢ per scoring key; postage extra; 40(45) minutes; Bureau of Educational Measurements. *

[758]
*Physics: Every Pupil Test.** High school; 1929–58; new form usually issued each December and April; norms available following testing program; no data on reliability; 3¢ per test; 1¢ per scoring key; cash

orders postpaid; 40(45) minutes; Ohio Scholarship Tests. *

[759]

★Physics: Midwest High School Achievement Examinations. High school; 1955–57; Forms A ('55), B ('57); no specific manual; no data on reliability; norms [A, '55; B, '57]; 10¢ per test, postage extra; Form A: 60(65) minutes; Form B: 90[95] minutes; V. B. Rasmusen (A) and David M. Tibbetts (B); Educational Test Bureau. *

SENSORY–MOTOR

REVIEWS BY *Anna S. Espenschade and Magdalen D. Vernon.*

[760]

★Children's Perceptual Achievement Forms. Ages 6–8.5; 1955–58; test of visual development; 1 form (fifth edition, '58); teacher's manual (fifth edition, '58) which includes testing cards; procedure manual ['58]; $2 per set of testing cards; $2 per teacher's manual; $3 per procedure manual; $2 per 100 scoring sheets ['55]; $2 per supplementary manual ('56, see 1 below); cash orders postpaid; specimen set not available; (10) minutes; Eyesight Conservation Committee, Winter Haven Lions Club, Winter Haven, Fla. *

REFERENCE

1. LOWDER, ROBERT GLENN. *Perceptual Ability and School Achievement.* Doctor's thesis, Purdue University (Lafayette, Ind.), 1956.

[761]

*Harris Tests of Lateral Dominance. Ages 7 and over; 1947–58; 15 scores: knowledge of right and left, hand preferences, simultaneous writing, handwriting, tapping, dealing cards, strength of grip (optional), total hand dominance, monocular sighting, binocular sighting, visual acuity (optional), total eye dominance, kicking, stamping, total foot dominance; individual; 1 form ('55); manual, third edition ('58); the actual test materials, including the *A-B-C Vision Test for Ocular Dominance,* must be purchased or assembled separately; $3.15 per 50 record blanks ('55); 75¢ per manual; 90¢ per specimen set; postpaid; [10–15] minutes; Albert J. Harris; distributed by Psychological Corporation. *

REFERENCE

1. HARRIS, ALBERT J. "Lateral Dominance, Directional Confusion, and Reading Disability." *J Psychol* 44:283–94 O '57. *

For reviews by William G. Peacher and Miles A. Tinker of an earlier edition, see 4: 644; see 3:466 (1 excerpt).

HEARING

[762]

★ADC Audiometers. Grades kgn and over; 1957–58; range: –10 to +95 decibels in 5-db steps; individual; 2 models; no data on reliability; $1.15 per 100 audiogram cards ['54]; group testing accessories available: $19.50 per headset, $50 per coupling box for use with 10–30 receivers, $40 per junction box for use with each additional 10 receivers; postage extra; (10–15) minutes; Audiometer Sales Corporation. *

a) ADC CLINICAL DIAGNOSTIC AUDIOMETER. 1958; Model SC-3 ['58]; manual ['58]; $450 per set of test materials; $25 per hand type microphone.

b) ADC PORTABLE AUDIOMETER. 1957; Model SC-2 ['57]; manual ['57]; $333.50 per set of test materials.

[763]

★Maico Audiometers. Grades kgn and over; 1949–58; individual; no data on reliability; $1.15 per 100 audiogram cards ['49]; postpaid; (10–15) minutes; Maico Electronics, Inc.

a) AUTOMATIC AUDIOMETER. 1956; Model ARJ-3; range: –10 to +90 decibels; manual ['56]; $1,285 per set of testing materials.

b) PROFESSIONAL AUDIOMETER. 1950; Model H-1B; range: –10 to +100 decibels in 5-db steps; manual ['50]; $490 per set of testing materials.

c) PORTABLE AUDIOMETER. 1956; Model MA-2; range: –10 to +100 decibels in 5-db steps; manual ['56]; group testing accessories (for use in grades 3–12) available; $398 per set of testing materials.

d) OFFICE AUDIOMETER. 1958; Model MA-5; range: –10 to +100 decibels in 5-db steps; manual ['58]; $438 per set of testing materials.

e) POCKET AUDIOMETER. 1958; Model MA-6; battery operated; range: 0 to +90 decibels in 5-db steps; manual ['58]; $145 per set of testing materials.

REFERENCES

1. HENRY, SIBYL. "Children's Audiograms in Relation to Reading Attainment: I, Introduction to and Investigation of the Problem." *J Genetic Psychol* 70:211–31 Je '47. * (*PA* 22: 444)
2. HENRY, SIBYL. "Children's Audiograms in Relation to Reading Attainment: II, Analysis and Interpretation." *J Genetic Psychol* 71:3–48 S '47. * (*PA* 22:1848)
3. HEGARTY, INEZ E., AND MILLER, VIRGINIA R. "Audiometric Tests of Speech Defective College Students." *J Speech & Hearing Disorders* 13:361–5 D '48. * (*PA* 23:300)
4. YANKAUER, ALFRED; GEYER, MARGARET L.; AND CHASE, HELEN C. "Comparative Evaluation of Three Screening Methods for Detection of Hearing Loss in School Children." *Am J Pub Health* 44:77–82 Ja '54. * (*PA* 29:1420)

[764]

★Robbins Speech Sound Discrimination and Verbal Imagery Type Tests. Ages 4–8, 8 and over; 1948–58; individual; 1 form; 2 levels; revised manual ('58) contains all tests; no data on reliability; no norms; $1.50 per manual; postpaid; specimen set not available; Samuel D. Robbins and Rosa Seymour Robbins; Expression Co. *

a) VERBAL IMAGERY TYPE TEST FOR YOUNG CHILDREN. Ages 4–8; 1948–58; 1 form (revised edition, '58); 75¢ per 50 scoring sheets ['58]; (30) minutes.

b) PICTURE SPEECH SOUND DISCRIMINATION TEST FOR YOUNG CHILDREN. Ages 4–8; 1948–58; 1 form (revised edition, '58); 75¢ per 50 scoring sheets ['58]; (60) minutes in 2 sessions.

c) SPEECH SOUND DISCRIMINATION TESTS FOR OLDER CHILDREN. Ages 8 and over; 1948; 1 form ('48); 25¢ per scoring booklet ('48); 75¢ per 50 scoring sheets ['58]; (60) minutes.

[765]

*Sonotone Pure-Tone Audiometers. Ages 6 and over; 1941–57; individual; 1 form; 4 models; manual ['57]; no data on reliability; $1 per 50 record blanks ('41); postage extra; administration time not reported; Sonotone Corporation. *

a) MODEL 91M. 1957; for use by physicians; $295 per instrument.

b) MODEL 91B. 1957; same as Model 91M but without masking; $285 per instrument.

c) MODEL 91D. 1957; for schools and industry; same as Model 91M but without bone receiver and masking; $250 per instrument.

d) MODEL 91S. 1957; same as Model 91D but with a dummy receiver substituted for one of the "live" receivers; $242 per instrument.

MOTOR

[766]

Brace Scale of Motor Ability. Ages 8 and over; 1927; originally called Motor Ability Test; individual below grade 5; Forms A, B; David Kingsley Brace; instructions for administering and scoring are presented in the author's Measuring Motor Ability: A Scale of Motor Ability Tests (New York: A. S. Barnes & Co., 1927. Pp. xvii, 138. Out of print). *

REFERENCES

1. BRACE, DAVID KINGSLEY. Measuring Motor Ability: A Scale of Motor Ability Tests. New York: A. S. Barnes & Co., 1927. Pp. xvii, 138.
2. DIMOCK, HEDLEY S. "A Research in Adolescence: I, Pubescence and Physical Growth." Child Develop 6:177–95 S '35. * (PA 10:1233)
3. RUSSELL, TRENT SUMNER. An Evaluation of the Brace Test and Norms for Negroes. Master's thesis, New York University (New York, N.Y.), 1936.
4. ESPENSCHADE, ANNA. Motor Performance in Adolescence. Monographs of the Society for Research in Child Development, Vol. 5, No. 1, Serial No. 24. Washington, D.C.: the Society, National Research Council, 1940. Pp. viii, 126. *
5. BRACE, D. K. "Studies in the Rate of Learning Gross Bodily Motor Skills." Res Q 12:181–5 My '41.
6. ADOLPHSON, GUDRUN. The Relation of General Motor Ability to Personality Adjustment. Master's thesis, University of Colorado (Boulder, Colo.), 1942.
7. GIRE, EUGENIA, AND ESPENSCHADE, ANNA. "The Relationship Between Measures of Motor Educability and the Learning of Specific Motor Skills." Res Q 13:43–56 Mr '42. * (PA 16:3285)
8. HATLESTAD, S. LUCILLE. "Motor Educability Tests for Women College Students." Res Q 13:10–5 Mr '42. * (PA 16:3281)
9. VICKERS, VERNETTE S.; POYNTZ, LILLIAN; AND BAUM, MABEL POTTINGER. "The Brace Scale Used With Young Children." Res Q 13:299–308 O '42. *
10. ESPENSCHADE, ANNA. "Practice Effects in the Stunt Type Test." Res Q 16:37–41 Mr '45. * (PA 20:3559)
11. BRACE, D. K. "Studies in Motor Learning of Gross Bodily Motor Skills." Res Q 17:242–53 D '46. * (PA 21:2922)
12. ESPENSCHADE, ANNA. "A Note on the Comparative Motor Ability of Negro and White Tenth Grade Girls." Child Develop 17:245–8 D '46. * (PA 21:4526)
13. ANDERSON, THERESA, AND McCLOY, C. H. "The Measurement of Sports Ability in High School Girls." Res Q 18:2–11 Mr '47. *
14. ESPENSCHADE, ANNA. "Development of Motor Coordination in Boys and Girls." Res Q 18:30–43 Mr '47. * (PA 22:4860)
15. BRACE, D. K. "Motor Learning of Feeble-Minded Girls." Res Q 19:269–75 D '48. * (PA 23:5606)
16. ESPENSCHADE, ANNA; DABLE, ROBERT R.; AND SCHOENDUBE, ROBERT. "Dynamic Balance in Adolescent Boys." Res Q 24:270–5 O '53. * (PA 28:4103)
17. McCLOY, CHARLES HAROLD, AND YOUNG, NORMA DOROTHY. Tests and Measurements in Health and Physical Education, Third Edition. New York: Appleton-Century-Crofts, Inc., 1954. Pp. xxi, 497. *

ANNA S. ESPENSCHADE, Professor of Physical Education and Research Associate, Institute of Human Development, University of California, Berkeley, California.

This scale, first published in 1927, was designed to measure that ability which is "more or less general....more or less inherent, and which permits an individual to learn motor skills easily." It has been used extensively in physical education programs to classify students into homogeneous groupings for activity. Because it was designed to measure such aspects of motor ability as agility, balance, control, and flexibility and to minimize the importance of size and strength, it is more valuable in classifying students for individual activities rather than for team sports. It is especially applicable to programs emphasizing gymnastics, tumbling, dancing (modern and folk), diving, and games of low organization. It is the best screening device available in physical education for the identification of difficulties in gross motor coordination.

The scale consists of 20 stunts, all of which involve active manipulation of the entire body. Each stunt is clearly described by the instructions to the subject. No equipment and very little space is required. Scoring is in terms of success or failure. Specific statements of what constitutes failure are listed. The following examples of one very easy and one very difficult stunt will illustrate the nature of the test and the range of ability tested. It should be noted that the test is not sufficiently difficult to classify properly individuals who are especially outstanding performers.

Test 1. Walk in a straight line, placing the heel of one foot in front of and against the toe of the other foot. Start with the left foot. Take 10 steps in all, 5 with each foot. Eyes open.
Failure: (a) Losing the balance and stepping out of line. (b) Not walking in a straight line. (c) Not placing heel to toe.
Test 10. Hold the toes of either foot in the opposite hand. Jump up and jump the free foot over the foot that is held, without letting go.
Failure: (a) Letting go of the foot that is held. (b) Failure to jump through the loop made by holding the foot.

The test is appropriate for both sexes from elementary school through college. Children of the fifth grade or above may score each other in a group testing situation. A class of 40 can complete the test in about 45 minutes. It should be recognized, however, that results obtained in this way have obvious limitations. An inexperienced teacher or examiner should not attempt to test a large group.

A revision of the Brace scale, called the

Iowa Brace, was proposed by McCloy (*17*) in 1937. It is designed to minimize still further the importance of strength, power, maturity, and size but at the same time to show improvement with age. Separate batteries of 10 tests each are presented for elementary school boys and girls, junior high school boys and girls, and senior high school boys and girls.

The Brace and Iowa Brace correlate approximately .75 (*7, 8, 11, 13*). The latter is only half the length of the former and, as might be expected, is somewhat less reliable (*10*). The two tests are obviously similar, however, and if a quick rough measure in a practical situation is desired, the shorter Iowa Brace will be appropriate.

Norms for the Brace scale for boys and girls 11 to 16 years of age were published in the original Brace article. It has been shown quite clearly, however, that marked sex differences in performance should be expected after age 12. Mean scores by age and sex 10.5 to 17.5 years are reported by Espenschade (*14*). Scoring tables for the Iowa Brace batteries are given by McCloy (*17*).

The Brace scale administered individually or to small groups is a valuable research tool for the study of gross motor ability. Reliabilities are very high (.9 or above) when first trial results are correlated with second trial on the same day (*1, 3, 8*). Split-half and test-retest correlations are lower but acceptable (*8, 10, 16*). Retest correlations at intervals of six months were found to be .87 for children 5 to 9 years of age (*9*), and from .77 to .88 and .53 to .72 for secondary school girls and boys, respectively (*3*).

The scale was validated originally against judgment ratings of physical education teachers and against a battery of athletic events. Athletes score from one half to one standard deviation above the mean (*1, 3*). Recently, Anderson and McCloy (*13*) reported a correlation of .71 between the Brace test and detailed ratings of sports abilities of high school girls. It should be noted that both reliabilities and validities compare favorably with those of other measures of gross motor ability.

The Brace scale has been used effectively to study motor performance in 5-year-old children (*9*) and in adolescent boys and girls (*3*) and to analyze differential development of motor abilities of prepubescent, pubescent, and postpubescent boys (*2, 3*). The relationship between Brace scores and the learning of sport skills, stunts, rhythms, and tumbling (*5, 11, 13, 17*) has also been investigated. Correlations are higher with stunt type (.45 to .60) than with sport skill (.00 to .35) learning. These differences are attributed to the greater dependence of sports upon strength, power, and eye-hand coordination, qualities not emphasized in the Brace scale.

In summary, the Brace scale or revision has proven to be the best measure for use in physical education programs for the classification of boys or girls of junior high school age or above into homogeneous groups for activities dependent upon general bodily coordination, such as tumbling and stunts and modern dance. It is an excellent screening device for the rapid identification of difficulties in gross motor coordination. For these purposes it can be given as a group test. As a research tool, it is valuable for study of motor ability and related problems. For this purpose it should be used as an individual or small group test.

[767]

★The Lincoln-Oseretsky Motor Development Scale. Ages 6–14; 1955–56; the original *Oseretsky Test of Motor Proficiency* by N. Oseretsky was first published in Russian in 1923; a Portuguese adaptation by Maria Irene Leite da Costa was published in 1943; an English translation by Elizabeth Joan Fosa of the Portuguese adaptation was published in 1946; *Lincoln Adaptation of the Oseretsky Tests of Motor Proficiency* by William Sloan, based upon the Fosa translation, was published in 1948; individual; 1 form ['55]; manual ('55, see 8 below); tentative norms; $19 per set of test materials, 50 record blanks, and manual; $3 per set of 50 record blanks ['56]; $1.25 per manual; postage extra; (30–60) minutes; William Sloan; C. H. Stoelting Co. *

REFERENCES

1. FALLERS, J. *An Investigation of the Motor Ability of Thirty High Grade Mentally Defective Girls With the Oseretsky Tests of Motor Proficiency.* Master's thesis, MacMurray College (Jacksonville, Ill.), 1948.
2. SLOAN, WILLIAM. *The Lincoln Adaptation of the Oseretsky Tests: A Measure of Motor Proficiency.* Lincoln, Ill.: Lincoln State School and Colony, 1948. Pp. iv, 68. *
3. FRENCH, JOSEPH L. *A Pilot Study With the Manual Dynamic Coordination Section of the Oseretsky Test.* Master's thesis, Illinois State Normal University (Normal, Ill.), 1950.
4. GARNERO, JOSEPH. *A Pilot Study With the General Static Coordination Section of the Oseretsky Test.* Master's thesis, Illinois State Normal University (Normal, Ill.), 1950.
5. SLOAN, WILLIAM. *Motor Proficiency and Intelligence.* Doctor's thesis, Northwestern University (Evanston, Ill.), 1950.
6. SLOAN, WILLIAM. "Motor Proficiency and Intelligence." *Am J Mental Def* 55:394–406 Ja '51. * (*PA* 25:5420)
7. CAREY, ROBERT A. *A Comparison of the Lincoln Revision of the Oseretsky Test of Motor Proficiency With Selected Motor Ability Tests on Boys at the Elementary Level.* Doctor's thesis, Indiana University (Bloomington, Ind.), 1954.
8. SLOAN, WILLIAM. "The Lincoln-Oseretsky Motor Development Scale." *Genetic Psychol Monogr* 51:183–252 My '55. * (*PA* 30:4600)
9. THAMS, P. F. *A Factor Analysis of the Lincoln-Oseretsky Motor Development Scale.* Doctor's thesis, University of Michigan (Ann Arbor, Mich.), 1955. (*DA* 15:764)
10. RABIN, HERBERT M. "The Relationship of Age, Intelligence and Sex to Motor Proficiency in Mental Defectives." *Am J Mental Def* 62:507–16 N '57. *
See also references for 4:650.

ANNA S. ESPENSCHADE, *Professor of Physical Education, and Research Associate, Institute of Human Development, University of California, Berkeley, California.*

This scale is a complete revision of the original Oseretsky test. It now consists of 36 items arranged in order of difficulty. Descriptions of the items are clear and a number of helpful illustrations are given. Instructions to subjects are concise and scoring is specific. Little space is required for administration and the equipment is simple and inexpensive. The test is administered individually.

The manual includes a complete analysis of results obtained on 380 boys and 369 girls 6 to 14 years of age on each item retained in the present scale. Percentages passing each item at each age level, correlations of each item score with age (eta), and tentative percentile norms for the sexes, separately and combined, are given. Odd-even reliabilities for boys and for girls are reported.

About two thirds of the items consist of hand and arm movements measuring speed, dexterity, coordination, and rhythm. The remainder are gross motor items. Seven of these involve balance and four, jumping. Actually, the battery is more heavily weighted toward manual coordination than this count would indicate since a number of the manual items are scored for both right and left hands.

The author has validated the items solely in relation to changes with age. The question of just what is actually being measured has not been answered. Oseretsky claimed that his scale measured static coordination, dynamic coordination, and, in general, speed of movement and asynkinesia, but no statistical support of this analysis was ever published. In factor analysis of Lincoln-Oseretsky scores on 211 boys $7\frac{1}{2}$–$11\frac{1}{2}$ years of age, Thams (9) found only one common factor accounting for about 20 per cent of the variance. Age correlated with this factor .70. Thams concluded that the factor was one of motor development.

In a study on boys in grades 4–6, Carey (7) obtained a correlation of .68 with grade and .37 with age. With three tests of gross motor ability, he obtained correlations of .32, .24, and .37. Low positive correlations were also obtained with height, weight, and IQ.

The similarity of scores for boys and for girls reported by Sloan (8) and the low correlations with gross motor tests indicate that the Lincoln-Oseretsky does *not* measure strength or power. It can quite properly be called a scale of motor development, however, since the items sample a variety of motor performances and the scores improve with age.

Some questions should be raised concerning the scoring of test items. Although the maximum possible score on each test is 3 points, the only alternative score on 14 items is zero. Six items are scored 3-2-0 and the remaining 16, 3-2-1-0. There seems no logical reason for this variation. This inconsistency may result in unexpected weighting of some items in the total. Investigators using the test should be alert to this possibility.

The author himself has made excellent suggestions for further research in relation both to the scale itself and to its use in the study of child behavior. The scale in its present form should prove a valuable tool for the study of certain aspects of motor development of children, especially those between 6 and 12 years of age. No comparable scale exists at the present time.

For a review by Anna Espenschade of the Portuguese adaptation, see 4:650; for a related review, see 4:651; see 3:472 (1 excerpt).

VISION

[768]

*AO H-R-R Pseudoisochromatic Plates, Second Edition. Ages 4 and over; 1940–57; formerly called *Pseudo-Isochromatic Plates for Testing Color Vision;* 1 form ('57); manual ('57); record blank ('57); no data on reliability; no norms; $20 per set of test materials, postage extra; [1–3] minutes; LeGrand H. Hardy, Gertrude Rand, and M. Catherine Rittler; American Optical Co. *

REFERENCES

1–9. See 3:473.
10–17. See 4:661.
18. LOKEN, ROBERT D. "The Color-Meter: A Quantitative Color-Vision Test." *Am J Psychol* 55:583–8 O '42. * (PA 17:1481)
19. THOMAS, GARTH J. "Visual Sensitivity to Color: A Comparative Study of Four Tests." *Am J Psychol* 56:583–91 O '43. * (PA 18:422)
20. REED, J. D. "The Effect of Illumination in Changing the Stimuli in Pseudo-Isochromatic Plates." Abstract. *J Opt Soc Am* 34:350 Je '44. *
21. BOICE, MARY LOU. *The Relationship of Color Vision to Age in Members of the Academic Faculty of the University of Minnesota.* Master's thesis, University of Minnesota (Minneapolis, Minn.), 1947.
22. VAN DEN AKKER, J. A.; TODD, J. EDWARD; NOLAN, PHILIP; AND WINK, WILLMER A. "Use of a Monochromatic Colorimeter for the Study of Color Blindness." *J Opt Soc Am* 37:363–87 My '47. * (PA 21:2909)
23. BOICE, MARY L.; TINKER, MILES A.; AND PATERSON, DONALD G. "Color Vision and Age." *Am J Psychol* 61:520–6 O '48. * (PA 23:4053)
24. CHAPANIS, ALPHONSE. "A Comparative Study of Five Tests of Color Vision." *J Opt Soc Am* 38:626–49 Jl '48. * (PA 23:530)
25. CHAPANIS, ALPHONSE. "Relationships Between Age, Vis-

ual Acuity and Color Vision." *Human Biol* 22:1–33 F '50. * (*PA* 24:5045)

26. KEPHART, NEWELL C., AND TIESZEN, MELVIN J. "Ortho-Rater Color Vision Test Compared With the Ishihara and the Pseudo-Isochromatic Plates." *J Appl Psychol* 35:127–9 Ap '51. * (*PA* 25:7862)

27. HARDY, L. H.; RAND, G.; AND RITTLER, M. C. "H-R-R Polychromatic Plates." *J Opt Soc Am* 44:509–23 Jl '54. *

28. MAYER, JACK J., AND ZACCARIA, MICHAEL A. "The Evaluation of a Color-Naming Test for Color Blindness." *J Appl Psychol* 39:160–3 Je '55. * (*PA* 30:2168)

See 3:473 (1 excerpt).

[769]

★**AO School Vision Screening Test.** Grades kgn–12; 1955; modification of the *Massachusetts Vision Test;* individual; 1 form ['55]; manual ('55); no data on reliability; $195 per set of test materials, postage extra; administration time not reported; original test by Massachusetts Department of Public Health; manual by Hollis M. Leverett and Evelyn A. Backer; American Optical Co. *

REFERENCES

1. SHAFFER, THOMAS E. "Study of Vision Testing Procedures." *Am J Pub Health* 38:1141–6 Ag '48. * (*PA* 23:1127)

2. LEVERETT, HOLLIS M. "A School Vision Health Study in Danbury, Connecticut." *Am J Ophthal* 39:527–40 Ap '55. *

3. LEVERETT, HOLLIS M. "An Analysis of Referrals Based on School Vision Screening Tests." *Am J Optom* 33:580–93 N '56. *

4. RYAN, VERNON. "A Critical Study of Visual Screening." *Am J Optom* 33:227–57 My '56. * (*PA* 31:7147)

[770]

*AO Sight Screener. Adults; 1945–56; targets are available for both readers and non-readers of English letters and numbers; individual; Model 1235 ['45]; manual ('56); no data on reliability; no norms; leasing fees: $350 first year, $100 second year, $50 each year thereafter; sale price: $450 per set of test materials; $1 per 100 record blanks ('46); $1.25 per 100 record blanks for illiterates ('52); manual free; postpaid; [3–5] minutes; American Optical Co. *

REFERENCES

1–7. See 3:460.

8. WHERRY, ROBERT J. "A Factorial Study of Visual Acuity, Depth, and Phoria Measurements With Three Commercial Screening Devices." Abstract. *Am Psychol* 2:298 Ag '47. *

9. DEPARTMENT OF THE ARMY, THE ADJUTANT GENERAL'S OFFICE, PERSONNEL RESEARCH SECTION. *Studies in Visual Acuity.* PRS Report No. 742. Washington, D.C.: U.S. Government Printing Office, 1948. Pp. viii, 161. * (*PA* 23:2084)

10. STACK, HERBERT J. *Personal Characteristics of Traffic-Accident Repeaters.* Saugatuck, Conn.: Eno Foundation for Highway Traffic Control, 1948. Pp. 64. *

11. SULZMAN, J. H.; COOK, E. B.; AND BARTLETT, N. R. "The Validity and Reliability of Heterophoria Scores Yielded by Three Commercial Optical Devices." *J Appl Psychol* 32:56–62 F '48. * (*PA* 23:554)

12. CRANE, MARIAN M.; SCOBEE, RICHARD G.; FOOTE, FRANKLIN M.; AND GREEN, EARL L. "Study of Procedures Used for Screening Elementary School Children for Visual Defects: Referrals by Screening Procedures vs. Ophthalmological Findings." *J Sch Health* 23:1–9, 44–9 Ja, F '53. *

13. FOOTE, FRANKLIN M., AND CRANE, MARIAN M. "An Evaluation of Vision Screening." *Excep Child* 20:153–61+ Ja '54. * (*PA* 28:6975)

14. OLIVER, JOHN R., AND LAUER, A. R. "Correlation of Speed and Distance Judgment With Visual Acuity." *Am J Optom* 33:263–5 My '56. * (*PA* 31:7141)

15. RYAN, VERNON. "A Critical Study of Visual Screening." *Am J Optom* 33:227–57 My '56. * (*PA* 31:7147)

For reviews by Henry A. Imus and F. Nowell Jones, see 3:460.

[771]

★**Burnham-Clark-Munsell Color Memory Test.** Adults; 1955–56; also called *Test of Hue Memory;* individual; 1 form ('56); manual ('55, reprint of 1 below); $225 per set of test materials (color chips same as some in *The Farnsworth-Munsell 100-Hue Test for the Examination of Color Discrimination*),

100 scoring sheets, and manual; $4.50 per 100 scoring sheets ['56]; postpaid; (15–20) minutes; Robert W. Burnham and Joyce R. Clark; Munsell Color Co., Inc. *

REFERENCE

1. BURNHAM, ROBERT W., AND CLARK, JOYCE R. "A Test of Hue Memory." *J Appl Psychol* 39:164–72 Je '55. * (*PA* 30:2120)

[772]

★**The Color Aptitude Test.** Ages 16 and over; 1952; 1 form ['52]; manual ('52); score sheet ['52]; $35 per set of test materials, postage extra; (20) minutes; Walter A. Woods; Industrial Psychological Laboratory. *

[773]

*Dvorine Pseudo-Isochromatic Plates, Second Edition. Ages 3 and over; 1944–55; revision of *Dvorine Color Perception Testing Charts;* individual; 2 scores: nomenclature, color perception; 1 form ('53); $15 per set of test materials, 5% discount on cash orders; $5.50 per 100 record blanks ('55, available from Western Psychological Services); [3–5] minutes; Israel Dvorine; Scientific Publishers Co. *

REFERENCES

1–4. See 3:462.

5. DVORINE, ISRAEL. "Author's Comments Upon the Review of Color Perception Charts." *Am J Psychol* 58:397–9 Jl '45. * (*PA* 19:3273)

6. MURRAY, ELSIE. "A Reply to Dvorine's Comments." *Am J Psychol* 58:399–402 Jl '45. *

7. SLOAN, LOUISE L. "An Improved Screening Test for Red-Green Color Deficiency Composed of Available Pseudo-Isochromatic Plates." *J Opt Soc Am* 35:761–6 D '45. *

8. PRONKO, N. H.; BOWLES, J. W.; SNYDER, F. W.; AND SYNOLDS, D. L. "An Experiment in Pursuit of 'Color-Blindness.'" Comments by Israel Dvorine. *J Genetic Psychol* 74:125–42 Mr '49. * (*PA* 23:4706)

9. SYNOLDS, D. L., AND PRONKO, N. H. "An Exploratory Study of Color Discrimination of Children." *J Genetic Psychol* 74:17–21 Mr '49. * (*PA* 23:4712)

10. CHAPANIS, ALPHONSE. "Relationships Between Age, Visual Acuity and Color Vision." *Human Biol* 22:1–33 F '50. * (*PA* 24:5045)

11. CRAWFORD, AGNES. "The Dvorine Pseudo-Isochromatic Plates." *Brit J Psychol* 46:139–43 My '55. * (*PA* 30:303)

12. DVORINE, ISRAEL. "Preliminary Report on the Diagnostic Efficiency of the Second Edition of the Dvorine Pseudo-Isochromatic Plates." *Am J Optom* 32:259–61 My '55. * (*PA* 30:2133)

13. PETERS, GEORGE. "Color Blindness and Emotional Disorganization." *Am J Optom* 32:367–72 Jl '55. * (*PA* 30:4850)

14. PETERS, GEORGE A. "Color-Blindness Test for Use in Vocational Guidance." *Personnel & Guid J* 34:572–5 My '56. * (*PA* 31:4808)

15. GROSS, HERBERT, AND PETERS, GEORGE A. "Normative Data Information Exchange, No. 10-29." *Personnel Psychol* 10:363 au '57. *

16. PETERS, GEORGE A., JR. "Color Blindness." *Excep Child* 23:241–5 Mr '57. *

17. PETERS, GEORGE A., AND GROSS, HERBERT. "The Denial of Color-Blindness." *Am J Optom* 34:602–5 N '57. *

Am J Psychol 68:340–2 Je '55. Elsie Murray. Announced on the title page as a "second edition" but copyrighted (on an inner one) as a "revised edition" of the ponderous two-volume *Color Perception Testing and Training Charts* of 1944, this work is really a far cry from the earlier one, with only two or three of its 130 plates retained, and most of its unique and semi-heretical assumptions wisely jettisoned. * The training program of 1944 (probably generated by war pressures) has passed into the discard. The pairs of colors chosen are not haphazard combinations as formerly, but selected as genuinely pseudo-isochromatic for the red-green defective (for whom alone the test is planned). The designer, an optometrist, acknowledges helpful criticisms by Louise Sloan of the aptness or inutility of all but 11 of the combinations of the 1944 edition; suggestions also from Deane B. Judd relative to the 7 pairs of colors used in the new test. Section Two, designed for children, for illiterates, and for corroborative use, features the trail introduced by Ishihara, with one example each for the seven pairs of colors used in Section One, plus a red and blue demonstration-pattern. As to general makeup of the test, instruction, aim, and scoring, certain improvements over the 1944 schemata may be noted. As before, an identical patterning of dots on all the plates—a device now generally accepted both as economical and as minimizing the use by color-deficient cases of casual clues to identify a plate—is adopted. A loose-leaf binding now permits an altered order of the plates as a further deterrent to memorizing (rendered difficult also by the use of two-digit numbers). The *instructions for administering* the test are more precise, embodying cautions suggested by this writer in reviewing Dvorine's earlier work * As for *scoring,* no statistics or table of responses for the different plates are offered. We are asked to accept the designer's dictum that incorrect responses to 3 of the 14 plates indicate red-green deficiency. One to two errors may be due merely to a mysterious "predilection" (one surmises that *antipathy* is intended) for certain *colors in combination.* It will be recalled that in 1944 Dvorine insisted that most of the individuals classified as 'color blind' can see all colors *singly* with ease. Only when hues are juxtaposed does a kind of paralyzing psychosis set in, inducing figure-ground confusion—a handicap which he optimistically offered to remove by training. That unsupported and quite unscientific notion is here apparently revived to explain the occasional illegibility of a plate to the otherwise normal. There is no recognition of the existence of variants from typical sensitivity (on a presumably histological or physiological basis) such as Pickford's work indicates. There is no finesse in selecting color-pairs to test it (as in the forthcoming 4-degree Hardy-Rand-Rittler Polychromatic Plates), no codifying of errors on certain plates, no attempt to correlate the findings with the scores on other tests. The simple unsupported claim is made that the test

does not fail the normal or misclassify the defective. This reviewer, having made only limited laboratory observations with the plates, has at present no evidence to refute it. The colors paired, few of them highly saturated, appear genuinely pseudo-isochromatic for the average defective examined. On the debit side, there are numerous shortcomings that disqualify the test for clinical or for exact scientific use. For example, there is looseness or carelessness in language and terminology. "Similar" is used in reference to color-pairs where "identical" is intended; "dark tints and light tints," where saturated and desaturated are the truer designations (there are actually no "dark tints" in the plates). In the revolving nomenclature chart, with a 1-in. circular exposure-window showing in turn each of 8 saturated (or "dark tint") colors on one side, and on the other, tints of the same, the hue designated as "purple" (5P, it is true, on the unsatisfactory Munsell circle) is really a reddish violet, and is listed as *Vt* (or Violet) on the record-sheet for Plates 14, 15, and 23 (violet dots on a blue ground). In the duplex plates diagnostic of protanoid vs. deuteranoid, 6, 7, and 19 (the latter wrongly printed 23), a reddish purple is designated as *Ma* (for Magenta?) without explanation. There is no stabilization of terms, no recognition of the fact that *violet* is a spectral hue, and *purple* an off-spectrum mixture of red and violet. While there is no recurrence of the somewhat heterodox 1944 asseveration that there are three primary colors, red, blue, and yellow, three secondary colors obtained by mixture with brown (a mixture of all three primaries) and gray....there is little promise of the scientific usefulness of the test. No guarantee of the purity or constancy of the inks used is offered. One suggests that the sphere of the test is the high school course in physiology, or the optometry school, to illustrate the confusion-colors of the *average* defective—orange with olive-green, blue with violet, green with greenish yellow, light brown or buff with scarlet, purple with green or gray for the deuteranoid, red with dark gray for the protanoid —all readily explainable in terms of any good four-primary color system. With the Ishihara (or *AO*) plates, each of which commonly uses three to four hues, this simple demonstration of the "metamers" or pseudo-isochromatic hues, a practical understanding of which by the normal-visioned is highly desirable, is impossible.

Such a laboratory use should, of course, be under the direction of a competent instructor, able to caution against acceptance of the test-results as proof of normalcy or deficiency without further corroboration. A further use of the test is in demonstrating the need in scientific work of controlled conditions in distance, illumination, timing, and so forth. Munsell papers should be substituted for the inked colors used in the nomenclature disk. The plates, mounted on too-thin cardboard, tend to stick together, and should be equipped with 1-in. gummed gray tabs to be manipulated more readily, and since they are unnumbered, an identifying letter should be inscribed on the back of the tab. The loose-leaf rings would operate more easily if mounted on the lower, not the left-hand edge.

J Appl Psychol 39:142 Ap '55. Miles A. Tinker. In this revised edition of his plates for testing color vision, the author has profited by experience and constructive criticism. The number of colored plates has been reduced from 60 to 23. In 15 of these, the response is made by reading numbers; in 8, by tracing a path. As in the original, there is a series of colored discs for checking nomenclature of "dark tints" and "light tints." The present edition, now labeled "pseudo-isochromatic plates," is a big improvement over the original test. All the plates have been either validated by other researchers, evaluated by an expert in the field, or received extensive checking by the author. The 8 plates made up of pathways to be traced may be used to advantage for testing young children and illiterates, or to check results obtained on the first 15 plates. The test plates are assembled in a loose-leaf ring binder. It is in handy form for either individual or group testing. It is likely that the test will receive wide use in a variety of situations.

J Consult Psychol 18:154 Ap '54. Laurance F. Shaffer. The revised Dvorine test consists of the more discriminative plates from the longer series published in 1944. Although no adequate data are given with the test, a subjective appraisal suggests that the series compares favorably with other pseudo-isochromatic plates now in use. Pathway-tracing plates, a feature of the old Ishihara, are again made available for testing young children and illiterates. A color-naming test, with saturated colors and tints, helps to identify the color ignorant. Several

features are ingeniously designed to thwart malingerers.

For the original edition, see 3:462 (6 excerpts).

[774]

Eames Eye Test. Grades kgn–16 and adults; 1938–50; individual; 1 form ('38); revised manual ('50); no norms; $7 per set of test materials, postpaid; $1.15 per 35 individual record cards, postage extra; hand stereoscope essential for administration; [10] minutes; Thomas H. Eames; World Book Co. *

REFERENCES

1–5. See 3:463.
6. ROBINSON, HELEN M. "Visual Screening Tests for Schools." *El Sch J* 54:217–22 D '53. * (*PA* 28:7017)
7. ROBINSON, HELEN M., AND HUELSMAN, CHARLES B., JR. Chap. 2, "Visual Efficiency and Progress in Learning to Read," pp. 31–63. In *Clinical Studies in Reading, II*. Edited by Helen M. Robinson. University of Chicago, Supplementary Educational Monographs, No. 77. Chicago, Ill.: University of Chicago Press, 1953. Pp. x, 189. *

MAGDALEN D. VERNON, *Professor of Psychology, University of Reading, Reading, England.*

Although backwardness in school work is likely to be due to defective eyesight in only a minority of cases, it is desirable that all backward children be tested for defective eyesight in case it may be a contributory cause. In addition, the eyesight of children suffering from headaches, strained or painful eyes, or any of the other troubles listed in the manual should be tested also; for although eyesight may be tested as part of a routine school medical inspection, often only the Snellen chart is used. This in itself is not a very satisfactory instrument; and it does not measure defects other than shortsightedness and extreme astigmatism.

For testing visual acuity Eames includes a version of the Snellen chart, using capital letters and an E-shaped character in various positions. The child reads these at a distance of 20 feet, with and without lens. He also reads them with the card held in schoolbook position. The use of capital letters is unsatisfactory; young and backward children may be unable to read them, and they are not all equally legible anyway. The use of the "E" is reasonably satisfactory, though it might perhaps be worth considering whether the Landolt ring could not be used instead. In spite of these deficiencies, however, it is undoubtedly useful to have tests of both distant and near vision. The tests of binocular coordination and fusion are also useful. For these tests, testers must provide their own stereoscopes, but instructions and a test card are supplied for checking their adjustment.

The supplementary tests are perhaps less satisfactory. With the astigmatic test, the child might be asked: "Are all the lines equally black, or do some of them look blacker than others?" This should avoid the effect of suggestion possible when the child is asked only if all the lines are equally black. Finally, the test of eye dominance should be omitted. It is difficult to obtain any consistent measure of eye dominance, and the relationship of eye dominance to reading difficulty is so obscure that the measurement of it is best left to the expert.

The author reports that in an experimental study involving 100 children test results agreed closely with the findings obtained after complete eye examination by an eye physician, and agreement between test and retest results was high.

Although instructions for administering and scoring are admirably clear, any teacher not experienced in psychological testing should probably be trained in giving these tests, or at least should be given an opportunity to practise with them thoroughly before drawing any conclusions from their results. Subject to this proviso, and to the instructions given that any child who fails any one test should fail the whole test and then be referred to a doctor, the test can be strongly recommended.

[775]

*The Farnsworth-Munsell 100-Hue Test for the Examination of Color Discrimination. Mental ages 12 and over; 1942–57; formerly called *Farnsworth-Munsell 100-Hue Test for Anomalous Color Vision;* individual; 1 form ('42); revised manual ('57); $100 per set of test materials, 100 profiles, and manual; $4.50 per 100 profiles ['42]; 50¢ per manual; postpaid; (5–10) minutes; Dean Farnsworth; Munsell Color Co., Inc. *

REFERENCES

1–2. See 4:657.
3. MAYER, JACK J., AND ZACCARIA, MICHAEL A. "The Evaluation of a Color-Naming Test for Color Blindness." *J Appl Psychol* 39:160–3 Je '55. * (PA 30:2168)

For a review by Elsie Murray, see 4:657.

[776]

★Freeman Acuity-Tester. Ages 4 and over; 1954; instrument for testing vision to screen for professional eye examination; 1 form ['54]; no manual; no data on reliability; mimeographed key sheet; $125 per set of machine, key sheet, and carrying case, postage extra; (1) minute; Ellis Freeman; Freeman Technical Associates. *

[777]

★Freeman Protometer. Ages 6 and over; 1952; instrument for testing vision to screen for professional eye examination; 1 form ['52]; no manual; no data on reliability; $275 per set of apparatus, 500 record blanks, carrying case, and the complimentary *The Illuminant-Stable Color Vision Test;* postage extra; (2) minutes; Ellis Freeman; Freeman Technical Associates. *

[778]

*The Illuminant-Stable Color Vision Test, Second Edition. Ages 4 and over; 1949–54; 1 form ['54]; directions sheet ['54]; no data on reliability; $15 per set of test materials, postage extra; (1–5) minutes; Ellis Freeman; Freeman Technical Associates. *

REFERENCES

1–2. See 4:659.
3. DE NITTIS, GEORGE L. "Relative Effectiveness of Two Standard Color-Vision Tests." *J Appl Psychol* 39:437–41 D '55. * (PA 30:6717)
4. MAYER, JACK J., AND ZACCARIA, MICHAEL A. "The Evaluation of a Color-Naming Test for Color Blindness." *J Appl Psychol* 39:160–3 Je '55. * (PA 30:2168)

For a review by Elsie Murray of the original edition, see 4:659.

[779]

★Inter-Society Color Council Color Aptitude Test, 1953 Edition. Adults; 1944–53; 1 form ('53); directions sheet ('53); mimeographed directions sheet for examinees ['53]; record booklet ['53]; no data on reliability; $135 per set of test materials and 100 scoring sheets; $6.50 per 100 scoring sheets; postpaid; (60) minutes; Color Aptitude Test Committee, Inter-Society Color Council; Federation of Paint and Varnish Production Clubs. *

REFERENCES

1. DIMMICK, FORREST LEE. "The Inter-Society Color Council Color Aptitude Test." Abstract. *J Opt Soc Am* 32:745 D '42. *
2. THOMAS, GARTH J. "Visual Sensitivity to Color: A Comparative Study of Four Tests." *Am J Psychol* 56:583–91 O '43. * (PA 18:422)
3. DIMMICK, FORREST LEE. "A Color Aptitude Test, 1940 Experimental Edition." *J Appl Psychol* 30:10–22 F '46. * (PA 20:2223)
4. PARSONS, J. L., AND CROUP, A. H. "The Color Aptitude Test—1944 Experimental Edition." *Tech Assn Papers* 29:576–8 Je '46. *
5. DIMMICK, FORREST LEE. "Specifications and Calibration of the 1953 Edition of the Inter-Society Color Council Color Aptitude Test." *J Opt Soc Am* 46:389–93 Je '56. * (PA 31:4169)

[780]

*Keystone Visual Tests. Ages 5 and over; 1933–57; individual; 3 models; shipping and postage extra; Keystone View Co. *
a) KEYSTONE VISUAL SURVEY SERVICE FOR SCHOOLS AND COLLEGES. 1933–57; visual-survey telebinocular ['46]; 14 tests ['47]: simultaneous perception, vertical posture, lateral posture (2 tests), fusion (2 tests), usable vision (6 tests), depth perception, color perception; revised manual ('57); record form ('56); $261 per telebinocular and testing materials; (3–4) minutes.
b) KEYSTONE OCCUPATIONAL VISUAL SERVICE. 1935–52; occupational visual service telebinocular ['47]; 6 tests ['47]: eye coordination, usable vision, color vision, depth perception, clarity of vision, tunnel vision; manual ('51); record form ('52); $495 per telebinocular and testing materials; $58.50 per periometer attachment for testing lateral vision; $22 per set of rapid screening tests; (3–4) minutes.
c) KEYSTONE DRIVER VISION SERVICE. 1950; driver vision telebinocular ['50]; 6 tests ['50]: vertical balance, lateral balance, fusion, usable vision, depth perception, color perception; manual ('50); record form ('50); $220.50 per telebinocular and testing materials; $58.50 per periometer attachment for testing lateral vision; $7 per single card driver vision test; (2–3) minutes.

REFERENCES

1–43. See 3:467.
44. TIFFIN, JOSEPH, AND KUHN, HEDWIG S. "Color Discrimination in Industry." *Arch Ophthal* 28:851–9 N '42. * (PA 17:795)
45. WEYMOUTH, FRANK W., AND HIRSCH, MONROE J. "The Reliability of Certain Tests for Determining Distance Discrimination." *Am J Psychol* 58:379–90 Jl '45. * (PA 19:3294)

46. LINDZEY, GARDNER E. "Four Psychometric Techniques Useful in Vocational Guidance." *J Clin Psychol* 2:157-60 Ap '46. * (*PA* 20:3899)

47. "VISION TESTS." Editor's reply to query. *J Am Med Assn* 134:490 My 31 '47. *

48. BOICE, MARY LOU. *The Relationship of Color Vision to Age in Members of the Academic Faculty of the University of Minnesota.* Master's thesis, University of Minnesota (Minneapolis, Minn.), 1947.

49. WHERRY, ROBERT J. "A Factorial Study of Visual Acuity, Depth, and Phoria Measurements With Three Commercial Screening Devices." Abstract. *Am Psychol* 2:298 Ag '47. *

50. BOICE, MARY L.; TINKER, MILES A.; AND PATERSON, DONALD G. "Color Vision and Age." *Am J Psychol* 61:520-6 O '48. * (*PA* 23:4053)

51. DEPARTMENT OF THE ARMY, THE ADJUTANT GENERAL'S OFFICE, PERSONNEL RESEARCH SECTION. *Studies in Visual Acuity.* PRS Report No. 742. Washington, D.C.: U.S. Government Printing Office, 1948. Pp. viii, 161. * (*PA* 23:2084)

52. SHAFFER, THOMAS E. "Study of Vision Testing Procedures." *J Pub Health* 38:1141-6 Ag '48. * (*PA* 23:1127)

53. SULZMAN, J. H.; COOK, E. B.; AND BARTLETT, N. R. "The Validity and Reliability of Heterophoria Scores Yielded by Three Commercial Optical Devices." *J Appl Psychol* 32:56-62 F '48. * (*PA* 23:554)

54. CRANE, MARIAN M.; SCOBEE, RICHARD G.; FOOTE, FRANKLIN M.; AND GREEN, EARL L. "Study of Procedures Used for Screening Elementary School Children for Visual Defects: Referrals by Screening Procedures vs. Ophthalmological Findings." *J Sch Health* 23:1-9, 44-9 Ja, F '53. *

55. ROBINSON, HELEN M. "Visual Screening Tests for Schools." *El Sch J* 54:217-22 D '53. * (*PA* 28:7017)

56. ROBINSON, HELEN M., AND HUELSMAN, CHARLES B., JR. Chap. 2, "Visual Efficiency and Progress in Learning to Read," pp. 31-63. In *Clinical Studies in Reading, II.* Edited by Helen M. Robinson. University of Chicago, Supplementary Educational Monographs, No. 77. Chicago, Ill.: University of Chicago Press, January 1953. Pp. x, 189. *

57. BARNETTE, ZORA B. *The Effectiveness of the Keystone Telebinocular Visual Testing Device in the Westminster School.* Master's thesis, Clemson Agricultural College (Clemson, S.C.), 1955.

58. SMITH, WILLIAM. "Report of Vision Screening Tests in a Group of Ten Reading Problem Cases." *Am J Optom* 32:295-303 Je '55. * (*PA* 30:3395)

59. RYAN, VERNON. "A Critical Study of Visual Screening." *Am J Optom* 33:227-57 My '56. * (*PA* 31:7147)

60. STEINBAUM, MILTON, AND KURK, MITCHELL. "Relationship Between the Keystone Visual Skills Tests and the Snellen Chart." *Am J Optom* 34:491-9 S '57. *

61. STEINBAUM, MILTON, AND KURK, MITCHELL. "Relationship Between the Keystone Visual Skills Tests With Reading Achievement and Intelligence." *Am J Optom* 35:173-81 Ap '58. *

For a review by F. Nowell Jones, see 3:467 (1 excerpt).

[781]

*Massachusetts Vision Test. Grades kgn–16; 1942–54; individual; 1 form ['42]; for a modification, see *AO School Vision Screening Test;* manual ('54); no data on reliability; no norms; $140 per set of test materials, postage extra; [1–5] minutes; Massachusetts Department of Public Health; Welch Allyn, Inc. *

REFERENCES

1-5. See 3:468.

6. "VISION TESTS." Editor's reply to query. *J Am Med Assn* 134:490 My 31 '47. *

7. SHAFFER, THOMAS E. "Study of Vision Testing Procedures." *Am J Pub Health* 38:1141-6 Ag '48. * (*PA* 23:1127)

8. KELLEY, DOROTHY J. *The Validity of Using Children's Atypical School Achievements and Behaviors for Indicating the Presence of Ocular Defects.* Doctor's thesis, Northwestern University (Evanston, Ill.), 1949.

9. CRANE, MARIAN M.; SCOBEE, RICHARD G.; FOOTE, FRANKLIN M.; AND GREEN, EARL L. "Study of Procedures Used for Screening Elementary School Children for Visual Defects: Referrals by Screening Procedures vs. Ophthalmological Findings." *J Sch Health* 23:1-9, 44-9 Ja, F '53. *

10. ROBINSON, HELEN M. "Visual Screening Tests for Schools." *El Sch J* 54:217-22 D '53. * (*PA* 28:7017)

11. ROBINSON, HELEN M., AND HUELSMAN, CHARLES B., JR. Chap. 2, "Visual Efficiency and Progress in Learning to Read," pp. 31-63. In *Clinical Studies in Reading, II.* Edited by Helen M. Robinson. University of Chicago, Supplementary Educational Monographs, No. 77. Chicago, Ill.: University of Chicago Press, January 1953. Pp. x, 189. *

12. FOOTE, FRANKLIN M., AND CRANE, MARIAN M. "An Evaluation of Vision Screening." *Excep Child* 20:153-61+ Ja '54. * (*PA* 28:6975)

13. KELLEY, DOROTHY JONES. "Using Children's School Atyp-

icalities to Indicate Ocular Defects." *J Ed Res* 47:455-65 F '54. * (*PA* 28:7979)

14. LEVERETT, HOLLIS M. "A School Vision Health Study in Danbury, Connecticut." *Am J Ophthal* 39:527-40 Ap '55. *

15. GUTMAN, ELEANOR B. "School Vision Screening: A Comparison of Two Methods." *Sight-Saving R* 26:212-9 w '56. *

16. RYAN, VERNON. "A Critical Study of Visual Screening." *Am J Optom* 33:227-57 My '56. * (*PA* 31:7147)

17. DONABEDIAN, AVEDIS, AND ROSENFELD, LEONARD S. "Replicability of a Screening Test." *Sight-Saving R* 27:156-61 fall '57. *

18. ARNER, ROBERT S. "An Evaluation of the Massachusetts Vision Screening Test and Its Implication on the Genetic Theory of Myopia." *Am J Optom* 35:470-83 S '58. *

19. SULZMAN, JOHN H., AND DAVIS, C. JANE. "The New York School Vision Tester." *NY State J Med* 58:833-7 Mr 15 '58. *

See 3:468 (1 excerpt).

[782]

★New York School Vision Tester. Grades kgn and over; 1957; title on manual is *School Vision Tester;* 1 form; manual ['57]; $225 per set of test materials; copy of manual supplied free; postage extra; (2–5) minutes; Bausch & Lomb Optical Co. *

REFERENCE

1. SULZMAN, JOHN H., AND DAVIS, C. JANE. "The New York School Vision Tester." *NY State J Med* 58:833-7 Mr 15 '58. *

[783]

*Ortho-Rater. Ages 8 and over; 1942-58; 12 scores: binocular action of the eyes (4 tests), fineness of visual discrimination (6 tests), perception of depth, color discrimination; individual; 2 models; revised manual ['58]; profile ['52]; manual for perimeter attachment ['55]; $38 per perimeter attachment ['55]; $3 per 500 record blanks ['52]; postage extra; [2–5] minutes; Bausch & Lomb Optical Co. *

a) MASTER ORTHO-RATER. 1942-58; 1 form ['54]; $475 per set of instrument, test materials, and 500 record blanks.

b) MODIFIED ORTHO-RATER. 1952-58; 1 form ['57]; $250 per set of instrument, test materials, and 500 record blanks.

REFERENCES

1-30. See 3:471.

31. STUMP, N. FRANK. "Visual Functions as Related to Accident-Proneness." *Personnel* 21:50-6 Jl '44. *

32. TIFFIN, JOSEPH, AND WIRT, S. EDGAR. "The Importance of Visual Skills for Adequate Job Performance in Industry." *J Consult Psychol* 8:80-9 Mr-Ap '44. * (*PA* 18:2941)

33. GIESE, WILLIAM JAMES. *The Interrelationship of Visual Acuity at Different Distances.* Doctor's thesis, Purdue University (Lafayette, Ind.), 1945.

34. GIESE, WILLIAM JAMES. "The Interrelationship of Visual Acuity at Different Distances." *J Appl Psychol* 30:91-106 F '46. * (*PA* 20:2229)

35. IMUS, HENRY A. "Comparison of the Ortho-Rater With Clinical Ophthalmic Examinations." Abstract. *Am Psychol* 1:283-4 Jl '46. *

36. LINDZEY, GARDNER E. "Four Psychometric Techniques Useful in Vocational Guidance." *J Clin Psychol* 2:157-60 Ap '46. * (*PA* 20:3899)

37. TIFFIN, JOSEPH, AND KEPHART, N. C. "The Derivation and Validation of a Generalized Visual Skill Profile for Close Jobs." Abstract. *Am Psychol* 2:428 O '47. *

38. WHERRY, ROBERT J. "A Factorial Study of Visual Acuity, Depth, and Phoria Measurements With Three Commercial Screening Devices." Abstract. *Am Psychol* 2:298 Ag '47. *

39. WIRT, S. EDGAR; MORGAN, CLELLAN L.; AND FLOYD, WILLIAM. "Achievement of Grade School Pupils in Relation to Visual Performance," pp. 59-66. In *Claremont College Reading Conference, Twelfth Yearbook: Conference Theme, Types of Reading Material for a Functional Program of Instruction.* Claremont, Calif.: Claremont College Curriculum Laboratory, 1947. Pp. 158. *

40. CARR, E. R. *An Analysis of the Relationship of Phoria, Depth Perception and Color Discrimination to Job Performance.* Master's thesis, Purdue University (Lafayette, Ind.), 1948.

41. DEPARTMENT OF THE ARMY, THE ADJUTANT GENERAL'S OFFICE, PERSONNEL RESEARCH SECTION. *Studies in Visual Acuity.* PRS Report No. 742. Washington, D.C.: U.S. Government Printing Office, 1948. Pp. viii, 161. * (*PA* 23:2084)

42. JOBE, FRED W. "An Analysis of Visual Performance in Relation to Safety." *Am J Optom* 25:107-16 Mr '48. * (*PA* 22:3678)

43. KEPHART, N. C. "Visual Skills and Labor Turnover." *J Appl Psychol* 32:51-5 F '48. * (*PA* 23:969)

44. KERR, WILLARD A. "Vision Tests for Precision Workers at RCA." *Personnel Psychol* 1:63–6 sp '48. * (*PA* 22:4150)

45. KOETH, FREDERICK J. "Vision for the Job." *Bausch & Lomb Mag* 24:8–9+ [Ja '48]. *

46. MORGAN, W. GREGORY, AND STUMP, N. FRANK. "Important Uses of Industrial Vision Tests and the Medical Director." *Ind Med* 17:253–8 Jl '48. * (*PA* 23:3481)

47. SCOTT, JOHN, JR. "How Rocky Mount Mills Uses Visual Tests for Placement." *Ind Relations* 6:14–6 Ag '48. *

48. STUMP, N. FRANK. "Job Analysis as Related to Visual Skills." *Sight-Saving R* 18:190–202 w '48. * (*PA* 24:792)

49. SULZMAN, J. H.; COOK, E. B.; AND BARTLETT, N. R. "The Validity and Reliability of Heterophoria Scores Yielded by Three Commercial Optical Devices." *J Appl Psychol* 32:56–62 F '48. * (*PA* 23:554)

50. IMUS, HENRY A. "Comparison of Ortho-Rater With Clinical Ophthalmic Examinations." *J Aviat Med* 20:2–23 F '49. * (*PA* 23:4068)

51. McCORMICK, ERNEST J. *An Analysis of Visual Requirements in Industry.* Doctor's thesis, Purdue University (Lafayette, Ind.), 1949.

52. ROBINSON, HELEN M. Chap. 5, "Visual Efficiency and Reading," pp. 90–112. In *Clinical Studies in Reading*, I. University of Chicago, Supplementary Educational Monographs, No. 68. Chicago, Ill.: University of Chicago Press, June 1949. Pp. xiv, 173. *

53. TIFFIN, JOSEPH; PARKER, B. T.; AND HABERSAT, R. W. "Visual Performance and Accident Frequency." *J Appl Psychol* 33:499–502 O '49. * (*PA* 24:3465)

54. ZACHERT, VIRGINIA. *A Factor Analysis of Vision Tests.* Doctor's thesis, Purdue University (Lafayette, Ind.), 1949.

55. ELY, J. H.; KEPHART, N. C.; AND TIFFIN, JOSEPH. "Ortho-Rater Norms and Sex Differences." *J Appl Psychol* 34:232–6 Ag '50. * (*PA* 25:5961)

56. JONES, F. NOWELL, AND SMITH, CHARLOTTE JEAN. "Visual Skill and Performance in a Meat Packing Plant." *J Appl Psychol* 34:313–5 O '50. * (*PA* 26:554)

57. KEPHART, NEWELL C., AND MASON, JOSEPH M. "Acuity Differences Between the Two Eyes and Job Performance." *J Appl Psychol* 34:423–8 D '50. *

58. KEPHART, NEWELL C., AND WISSEL, JOSEPH W. "Variations in Visual Acuity of a Group Without Major Refractive Errors." *Am J Optom* 27:95–9 F '50. * (*PA* 24:6177)

59. McCORMICK, E. J. "An Analysis of Visual Requirements in Industry." *J Appl Psychol* 34:54–61 F '50. * (*PA* 24:6106)

60. KEPHART, NEWELL C., AND MAZZONI, HENRY A. "Changes in Visual Skills of School Children Following Summer Vacation." *Am J Optom* 28:30–5 Ja '51. * (*PA* 25:7256)

61. KEPHART, NEWELL C., AND PECSOK, JAMES D. "A Study of Tachistoscopic Vision." *J Appl Psychol* 35:130–2 Ap '51. * (*PA* 25:7861)

62. KEPHART, NEWELL C., AND TIESZEN, MELVIN J. "Ortho-Rater Color Vision Test Compared With the Ishihara and the Pseudo-Isochromatic Plates." *J Appl Psychol* 35:127–9 Ap '51. * (*PA* 25:7862)

63. ROBINSON, HELEN M. "Factors Related to Monocular and Binocular Reading Efficiency." *Am J Optom* 28:337–46 Jl '51. * (*PA* 26:2977)

64. SHERMAN, R. A. "An Approach to Personnel Problems Through Visual Performance Tests." *Am J Optom* 28:92–5 F '51. * (*PA* 25:7744)

65. ZACHERT, VIRGINIA. "A Factor Analysis of Vision Tests." *Am J Optom* 28:405–16 Ag '51. * (*PA* 26:2608)

66. BONDER, JOHN. *The Relationship Between Ortho-Rater Test Scores and Termination of Workers in a North Carolina Cotton Mill.* Master's thesis, North Carolina State College of Agriculture and Engineering (Raleigh, N.C.), 1952.

67. KEPHART, N. C., AND TIFFIN, JOSEPH. "Visual Skills Tests and Job Efficiency." Abstract. *Am Psychol* 7:360 Jl '52. *

68. KLEEMEIER, ROBERT W. "The Relationship Between Ortho-Rater Tests of Acuity and Color Vision in a Senescent Group." *J Appl Psychol* 36:114–6 Ap '52. * (*PA* 27:306)

69. BENTLEY, CHARLES S., JR., AND SPRINGER, DONALD A. "The Role of Certain Visual Phenomena in Adolescent Personality Adjustment." *Am J Optom* 30:227–43 My '53. * (*PA* 28:548)

70. CRANE, MARIAN M.; SCOBEE, RICHARD G.; FOOTE, FRANKLIN M.; AND GREEN, EARL L. "Study of Procedures Used for Screening Elementary School Children for Visual Defects: Referrals by Screening Procedures vs. Ophthalmological Findings." *J Sch Health* 23:1–9, 44–9 Ja, F '53. *

71. GERICK, STEVEN. *The Relationship of Ortho-Rater Depth Scores With Certain Personality Factors.* Master's thesis, North Carolina State College of Agriculture and Engineering (Raleigh, N.C.), 1953.

72. JENKINS, NORA CONGDON. "Visual Performance and Scholastic Success." *Sch R* 61:544–7 D '53. *

73. ROBINSON, HELEN M. "Visual Screening Tests for Schools." *El Sch J* 54:217–22 D '53. * (*PA* 28:7017)

74. ROBINSON, HELEN M., AND HUELSMAN, CHARLES B., Jr. Chap. 2, "Visual Efficiency and Progress in Learning to Read," pp. 31–63. In *Clinical Studies in Reading*, II. Edited by Helen M. Robinson. University of Chicago, Supplementary Educational

Monographs, No. 77. Chicago, Ill.: University of Chicago Press, January 1953. Pp. x, 189. *

75. STUMP, N. FRANKLIN. "Research in Occupational Seeing." *Am J Optom* 30:294–307 Je '53. * (*PA* 28:3427)

76. WALKER, WILLIAM B. "Vision and Production of Sewing Machine Operators." *Personnel Psychol* 6:291–5 au '53. * (*PA* 28:5015)

77. WILLARD, NORMAN, JR.; OLSON, HOWARD C.; AND ARNOLD, ROBERT D. "The Relationship Between Lateral Phoria and Some Tests of Real and Apparent Depth Perception." Abstract. *Am Psychol* 8:455 Ag '53. *

78. ZEIDNER, JOSEPH, AND GORDON, DONALD A. "A Comparison of Visual Acuity Measurements by Wall Charts and Ortho-Rater Tests." Abstract. *Am Psychol* 8:459 Ag '53. *

79. FOOTE, FRANKLIN M., AND CRANE, MARIAN M. "An Evaluation of Vision Screening." *Excep Child* 20:153–61+ Ja '54. * (*PA* 28:6975)

80. GORDON, D. A.; ZEIDNER, J.; ZAGORSKI, H. J.; AND UHLANER, J. E. "Visual Acuity Measurements by Wall Charts and Ortho-Rater Tests." *J Appl Psychol* 38:54–8 F '54. * (*PA* 29:264)

81. KEPHART, NEWELL C., AND DEUTSCH, STANLEY. "Effect of Illumination on Scores With Instrument Acuity Tests." *J Appl Psychol* 38:59–60 F '54. * (*PA* 29:273)

82. DAVIS, C. JANE, AND JOBE, FREDERICK W. "The Variation of Visual Characteristics in School Children as Measured by the Ortho-Rater." *Am J Optom* 32:251–8 My '55. * (*PA* 30:2132)

83. ALBRIGHT, LEWIS EDWIN. *The Development of a Selection Process for an Inspection Task.* Doctor's thesis, Purdue University (Lafayette, Ind.), 1956. (*DA* 16:2201)

84. ALBRIGHT, LEWIS E. "Validity Information Exchange, No. 9-44:D.O.T. Code 0-66.93, Seed Analyst." *Personnel Psychol* 9:522–3 w '56. *

85. MACRAE, DONALD S. "San Jose's Approach to Occupational Vision Testing." *Pub Personnel R* 17:129–31 Jl '56. * (*PA* 31:5530)

86. RYAN, VERNON. "A Critical Study of Visual Screening." *Am J Optom* 33:227–57 My '56. * (*PA* 31:7147)

87. DAVIS, C. JANE, AND JOBE, FREDERICK W. "Further Studies on the A.C.A. Ratio as Measured on the Ortho-Rater." *Am J Optom* 34:16–25 Ja '57. *

88. SPEER, GEORGE S. "Validity Information Exchange, No. 10-5:D.O.T. Code 5-00.933, (Relay Adjustors)." *Personnel Psychol* 10:80 sp '57. *

89. SCHWARTZ, IRA, AND DIMMICK, FORREST L. "Comparison of High Acuity Scores on Snellen and Ortho-Rater Tests." *Am J Optom* 35:309–13 Je '58. *

For reviews by Henry A. Imus and F. Nowell Jones, see 3:471.

[784]

*Spache Binocular Reading Test. Nonreaders and grade 1, grades 1.5–2, grades 3 and over; 1943–55; test of eye preference in reading; individual; 3 levels; manual ('55); record form ('55); no data on reliability for Test I; $12 per set of 4 stereographs, 50 record forms, and manual; $1 per 50 record forms; postage extra; administration time not reported; George D. Spache; Keystone View Co. *

a) TEST I. Nonreaders and grade 1; 1 form ('55).

b) TEST II, MY BIG RED CAR. Grades 1.5–2; 1 form ('55).

c) TEST III. Grades 3 and over; 1 form ('43).

REFERENCES

1–4. See 3:461.

5. SPACHE, GEORGE. "The Validity of the Binocular Reading Test." *J Ed Res* 41:461–6 F '48. * (*PA* 22:3647)

6. ROBINSON, HELEN M. Chap. 5, "Visual Efficiency and Reading," pp. 90–112. In *Clinical Studies in Reading*, I. University of Chicago, Supplementary Educational Monographs, No. 68. Chicago, Ill.: University of Chicago Press, June 1949. Pp. xiv, 173. *

7. ROBINSON, HELEN M. "Factors Related to Monocular and Binocular Reading Efficiency." *Am J Optom* 28:337–46 Jl '51. * (*PA* 26:2977)

8. ROBINSON, HELEN M., AND HUELSMAN, CHARLES B., JR. Chap. 2, "Visual Efficiency and Progress in Learning to Read," pp. 31–63. In *Clinical Studies in Reading*, II. Edited by Helen M. Robinson. University of Chicago, Supplementary Educational Monographs, No. 77. Chicago, Ill.: University of Chicago Press, January 1953. Pp. x, 189. *

For a review by Albert J. Harris of Test III, see 3:461.

SOCIAL STUDIES

Reviews by *Howard R. Anderson, Harry D. Berg, Donald T. Campbell, Robert H. Ferrell, James A. Field, Jr., Wayne A. Frederick, Richard E. Gross, John H. Haefner, David K. Heenan, David R. Krathwohl, Christine McGuire, John Manning, I. G. Meddleton, Raymond C. Norris, S. A. Rayner, Douglas E. Scates, Frederick H. Stutz, Ralph W. Tyler, and M. J. Wantman.*

[785]

*American History—Government—Problems of Democracy: Acorn Achievement Tests. Grades 9–16; 1942–53; 6 scores: growth of a national spirit, growth of democracy, the Constitution, foreign policy, problems of American democracy, total; Forms A ('53, identical with test copyrighted in 1942 except for minor changes), B ('44); directions sheets (A, '42; B, '44); teachers' guide ['44]; $3.50 per 25 tests; 50¢ per specimen set; postage extra; 40(45) minutes; Vincent McGarrett; Acorn Publishing Co. *

Richard E. Gross, *Associate Professor of Education, Stanford University, Stanford, California.*

The reviewer agrees with the remarks made by Howard R. Anderson in *The Third Yearbook* (see 3:590) and wishes to underscore and extend these. Time has made even more of the test items outdated.

While the Teachers' Guide claims that the test does *not* include current events items, many items, even in the history sections, reflect the fact that the test has never been seriously revised. Items which discuss the "ever-normal granary" concept and wartime priorities in the present tense are typical examples; one item refers to the Second World War, as follows, without any concluding date—(1939–   )!

All items are of the multiple choice type. Although this type of item can be used fruitfully to reveal depth of understanding of cause and effect relationships and ability to differentiate between lesser and more important events or long term and short term results and to assess problem-thinking, the great bulk of items in this test remain of a purely informational nature. In addition, a number of items are concerned with events of minor importance, such as one which attempts to ascertain the correct order in which the departments of the United States Cabinet were established and another which requires the testee to indicate whether it was Henry Morton, Edwin Booth, John Drew, or Otis Skinner who was not a star in the American theatre.

The reviewer tends to be most critical of the items lumped together in the problems of democracy section. Many of these are especially outdated, like the question which asks the testee to select from among Alben Barkley, Hamilton Fish, Martin Dies, and Carter Glass the member of Congress who has been chairman of an un-American activities committee. The same items are often concerned with relatively unimportant information, like the population of various American cities or states in terms of the 1940 census.

The tests contain the usual share of poor and ambiguous items, like the following:

15. Who of these favored free enterprise?
    a. Harry Truman
    n. Dwight Eisenhower
    c. Franklin Roosevelt
    r. Dean Atcheson [sic]
18. American policy since 1939
    d. has been consistently in agreement with Jefferson's foreign policy
    f. was opposed to the Monroe Doctrine
    s. reversed the attitude taken by the U.S. toward China after the close of the Boxer Rebellion
    b. has differed from Washington's foreign policy

Some items are so carelessly constructed as to penalize the able student. For example, the testee is given the names of Marion Anderson, Booker T. Washington, William C. Handy, and Dred Scott and asked which *is* a figure important in the field of Negro education. The word "is" might here lead a bright student who knows that the latter three are dead to select Marion Anderson as the correct answer. Finally, no test supposedly having gone through at least one revision should include spelling errors like "Gasden" in an item referring to the Gadsden Purchase.

The reviewer does not believe the test to be adequate for use in American history classes, and it is certainly not satisfactory for use in civics and problems of democracy classes.

Teachers will do far better to use up-to-date, separate, specific tests available in each of these areas, such as the *Crary American History Test* and the *Peltier-Durost Civics and Citizenship Test*.

For a review by Howard R. Anderson, see 3:590.

[786]

*College Entrance Examination Board Achievement Test in Social Studies. Candidates for college entrance; 1937–58; for more complete information, see 599; IBM; 60(80) minutes; program administered by Educational Testing Service for the College Entrance Examination Board. *

REFERENCES

1–6. See 4:662
7. BRAGDON, HENRY W. "College Entrance Board Social Studies Test." *Social Ed* 16:369–72 D '52. *
8. NEWMAN, SIDNEY H.; FRENCH, JOHN W.; AND BOBBITT, JOSEPH M. "Analysis of Criteria for the Validation of Selection Measures at the United States Coast Guard Academy." *Ed & Psychol Meas* 12:394–407 au '52. * (*PA* 27:6159)
9. COLLEGE ENTRANCE EXAMINATION BOARD. *Social Studies: A Description of the Social Studies Test of the College Entrance Examination Board.* Princeton, N.J.: the Board, 1953. Pp. 24. *

RALPH W. TYLER, *Director, Center for Advanced Study in the Behavioral Sciences, Stanford, California.* [Review of Form FAC.]

The test is one of 13 in the battery of achievement tests of the College Entrance Examination Board. As an achievement test it should measure the extent to which the high school student has attained the major objectives of the social studies. As part of the battery used for college admission purposes it should emphasize the most significant intellectual tasks of this field because of its influence upon teaching and learning of high school students. The test does avoid exercises which require only rote memorization but it falls far short of reflecting the best in the social studies.

In the first place it does not cover the social studies but deals only with history, primarily, but not solely, United States history. In the 100 items in the test, concepts, generalizations, and problems dealt with in the contemporary social sciences are not included as such, except for a group of six items on international trade and balance of payments. The effort of teachers of the social studies to help students to understand some of the major concepts useful in interpreting and analyzing important social problems, and to use valid generalizations in predicting possible consequences of courses of action employed to grapple with these problems is not reflected in the exercises. The test also fails to include items requiring the student to

identify or to use dependable sources of information about social phenomena.

Even as a history test it is not a well organized selection of exercises appropriate for appraising the extent to which high school students have attained the commonly recognized objectives of history. It samples three objectives but does not touch upon three other important ones. In this reviewer's opinion, the best exercises in reflecting the aims of history teaching are those requiring the student to explain the meaning and implications of certain important policies and movements, such as "dollar diplomacy," the British Labor Party, the TVA, and the Protestant Revolution. Twenty items are of this sort. Twenty items are also devoted to identifying major historic persons in terms of the policies they supported or viewpoints they held. Most of the remaining items sample the students' knowledge of historic events. Almost all the items in the test require the student to go beneath the label of doctrines, movements, or slogans to more significant knowledge of their content. This is commendable. However, the failure to test for understanding of the long-time development of major issues, policies, or practices and the omission of exercises dealing with the great debates of history are serious weaknesses. Even more serious in this reviewer's opinion is the lack of testing for elementary understanding of history as an intellectual discipline. A test which treats all historic matters as matters of fact without touching on the problems of "constructing" history is contributing to the intellectual confusion of our time.

The test is well edited and has good typography. The manual reports a reliability coefficient of .92. The time limit of 60 minutes is a bit short for the 100 items so that the high reliability may be partly due to the speed factor. The test is an improvement over history tests of earlier years but it is still inadequate for the needs of high school social studies.

For a review by Robert L. Thorndike of an earlier edition, see 4:662.

[787]

*Cooperative General Achievement Tests: Test I, Social Studies. Grade 12 and college entrants; 1937–56; manual uses the subtitle *A Test of General Proficiency in the Field of Social Studies;* 3 scores: terms and concepts, comprehension and interpretation, total; IBM; Forms XX ('53, revision of Form X), YZ ('51, revision of Forms Y and Z); no norms for

part scores; high school norms same as those published in 1938; separate answer sheets must be used; $2.95 per 25 tests; $1 per 25 IBM answer sheets; 25¢ per scoring stencil; 35¢ per battery manual ('56); $1 per specimen set; postage extra; 40(50) minutes; Jeanne M. Bradford (XX); Cooperative Test Division, Educational Testing Service. *

For a review by Harry D. Berg of earlier forms, see 3:596. For a review by Max D. Engelhart of the complete battery, see 6; for a review by Paul L. Dressel of earlier forms, see 4:5; for a review by John V. McQuitty, see 3:3.

[788]

★The Greig Social Studies Test. Grades 6–8; 1957; for Catholic schools; IBM; 1 form; $3.20 per 35 tests; separate answer sheets may be used; $1.40 per 35 IBM scorable answer sheets; 12¢ per scoring stencil; 50¢ per specimen set; postage extra; 40(50) minutes; Mary E. Greig; Scholastic Testing Service, Inc. *

DAVID R. KRATHWOHL, *Research Coordinator, Bureau of Educational Research, and Professor of Education, Michigan State University, East Lansing, Michigan.*

This test is intended "to measure the extent to which pupils in Catholic Elementary Schools have achieved the important objectives of courses in American History, Civics, and Geography offered at the sixth, seventh, and eight grade levels." The manual claims that both curriculum and test emphasize not only acquisition of factual knowledge, but also higher types of learning.

The development of an outline based on a review of test and curriculum materials from Catholic sources preceded the construction of a 125-item experimental test from which 100 four-choice items were selected for the final form. Selection of items was determined by the test outline, difficulty indices, and validity indices. According to the outline, approximately two thirds of the items might be expected to call for learning beyond the memorization of facts. This is very far in excess of the proportion of items the reviewer would so classify. Proper classification of the behaviors elicited by a test item requires a knowledge both of pupil background and of the nature of the item; judged solely by the latter criterion, however, very few of the items appear to test other than factual acquisition. For example, the statement on content says that "numerous items....are aimed at an interpretation of historical information and at reasoned inferences based on knowledge of the historical process," and the test outline indicates that 9 per cent of the items

can be classified as "reasoned inferences." The publisher graciously sent the reviewer a classification of the items. According to the classification, these items are examples of "reasoned inferences":

74. An agency set up by the federal government to give work in the forests to young men was
   a. the F.H.A.   c. the T.V.A.
   b. the W.P.A.   d. the C.C.C.
75. The main purpose of the Kefauver Committee was to investigate
   a. slums   c. housing
   b. excessive taxes   d. crime

It is difficult to understand on what bases these may be considered "reasoned inferences."

Split-half reliabilities are reported as follows: grade 6, .90; grade 7, .90; and grade 8, .93. Comparable Kuder-Richardson (formula 21) reliabilities are .92, .90, and .90, respectively. These estimates of reliability may be inflated by a speed factor at the sixth grade level. The standard errors of measurement are also given for each grade.

Norms are based on scores by 4,320 pupils in 20 schools in 7 well diversified states. A check of these norms against the results of 1,750 eighth graders from all the schools of a midwest diocese showed "substantial agreement" between the two. The norms tables give percentile equivalents for each raw score for each of grades 6–8. The norms show a marked progression in median raw score from grade to grade, successive medians for grades 6, 7, and 8 being 19.7, 30.8, and 48, respectively.

Since the test consists of 100 four-choice items and there is no correction for guessing, a chance score for a completed test is 25. The percentile equivalent for this score is 64 for grade 6, 31 for grade 7, and a reasonable 4 for grade 8. Thus, on the basis of the norms provided, about two thirds of the sixth graders who complete the test can be expected to score below chance. In view of the high reliability coefficients, it seems more likely the tests are speeded, at least for sixth graders. Introducing a speed factor into an achievement test of this type would be questioned by most teachers.

The test is printed in an acceptable format on strong paper. The directions for both administration and scoring appear to be clear and straightforward. The instructions for interpretation are written sensibly and in a manner understandable to the unsophisticated user. Only the total score is interpreted since the test is not diagnostic except as a teacher makes her own question by question analysis.

The authors are to be commended for developing a test manual along the lines of the standards for test users adopted by APA, AERA, and others. The test items are devoid of obvious flaws. But the test as a whole appears to be much more heavily oriented toward measurement of factual knowledge than higher mental skills despite the manual's claim to the contrary. Its use with the lower grades in its intended range appears questionable on the basis of the norms. Since only six out of the 100 items would be considered colloquial to the Roman Catholic curriculum, other social studies tests might fit the curriculum as well, or if the orientation is toward objectives other than memorization of information, better. The Catholic school teacher will do well to consider carefully alternative measures in this field.

[789]

*Introduction to Social Studies: Achievement Examinations for Secondary Schools.** High school; 1951–53; title on Form 1 is *Introduction to Social Science;* Forms 1 ('51), 3 ('53) ; no specific manual; no data on reliability; norms: Forms 1 ['52] ; 3 ('53) ; 10¢ per test, postage extra; (60–90) minutes; Kenneth D. Seeling (3) ; Educational Test Bureau. *

[790]

History and Civics Test: Municipal Tests: National Achievement Tests. Grades 3–6, 6–8; 1938–55; subtest of *Municipal Battery;* 3 scores: lessons of history, historical facts, total; 2 forms; 2 levels; directions sheets (A, '38; B, '39) ; no data on reliability; no norms for part scores; $1.75 per 25 tests; 50¢ per specimen set of either level; postage extra; 15(20) minutes; Robert K. Speer and Samuel Smith; Acorn Publishing Co. *
a) GRADES 3–6. Forms A ('48, identical with test copyrighted in 1938 except for minor changes), B ('49, identical with test copyrighted in 1939 except for minor changes).
b) GRADES 6–8. Forms A ('49, identical with test copyrighted in 1938 except for minor changes), B ('55, identical with test copyrighted in 1939 except for minor changes).

HOWARD R. ANDERSON, *Professor of Education, and Dean, University School of Liberal and Applied Studies, The University of Rochester, Rochester, New York.*

Each of the two forms for grades 3–6 includes 70 items—10 four-response multiple choice questions in Part 1, and 60 true-false questions in Part 2. The title "Lessons of History" seems pretentious for the shorter section. Consider these "lessons" tested for in Form A: Item 2, The Indians lost America because they "did not have a common government." Item 3,

From reading about wampum, we learn that "dollars and cents were not the first kinds of money." There must be other reasons why the Indians lost. And the reviewer doubts that any reasonably bright youngster, even though he had never heard about wampum, would believe that our monetary system was the first in the world.

The true-false statements are, for the most part, factual; for example, "Indian women were called 'braves' " and "The Pilgirms came to America from Russia." In Form A seven items mention Washington; five, Franklin; four, the Civil War; and three each, Lincoln, War of 1812, and Indians. Of course the item "In Franklin's time, most people travelled by steamboat" also calls for time judgment. About one half the items deal with the period before 1789, about one fourth with the period since 1865.

The two forms for grades 6–8 are similar to the tests just described. Part 2, however, has been given the more accurate title "Miscellaneous Facts." Whereas Part 2 in Form B contains 60 true-false items, there are only 48 such items in Form A. In Form B there are seven items on World War I, and about twice as many items for the period since 1917 as in Form A. About one fourth of the items deal with the period before 1789, and just over half with the period since 1865.

In Form A one might have difficulty discovering the "lesson of history" to be learned in Item 1. The stem reads, "From reading about Andrew Jackson we learn"; two of the responses are "he refused to enforce unpopular laws" and "he enforced laws he did not like." There is reason to think he did both. In this same form a true-false statement reads, "Misplaced persons in Europe were not admitted to the United States after World War Two." Another item in this form probably will give pupils more trouble: "To become a naturalized citizen, an illiterate alien must be at least 30 years old." Fortunate is the youngster who marks it false because the age restriction seems implausible, and who does not puzzle over immigration restrictions and whether an illiterate alien can qualify for citizenship.

Unless teachers actually teach the type of information tested for in this test, there is little reason why they should use it. Certainly there are superior tests, among them the social studies test included in the STEP program of the Educational Testing Service.

For a review by Harry D. Berg, see 4:664. For a review by J. Murray Lee of the complete battery, see 18; for a review by Ralph C. Preston, see 4:20; for reviews by A. M. Jordan and Hugh B. Wood of the complete battery for grades 6–8, see 40:1191.

[791]

*The Iowa Tests of Educational Development: Test 1, Understanding of Basic Social Concepts. Grades 9–13; 1942–58; IBM; Forms X-3S, Y-3S ('52); examiner's manual ('58); battery manual ('54); pupil profile leaflet, fourth edition ('58); profile card (no date); separate answer sheets must be used; $3 per 20 tests; $5 per 100 IBM answer sheets; 50¢ per scoring stencil; $3 per complete specimen set; postage extra; 55(65) or 40(50) minutes; prepared under the direction of E. F. Lindquist; Science Research Associates. *

For reviews by J. Murray Lee and Stephen Wiseman of the complete battery, see 17; for a review by Eric F. Gardner of earlier forms, see 4:17; for reviews by Henry Chauncey, Gustav J. Froehlich, and Lavone A. Hanna, see 3:12.

[792]

★Sequential Tests of Educational Progress: Social Studies. Grades 4–6, 7–9, 10–12, 13–14; 1956–57; IBM; Forms A, B ('57); 4 levels; manual ('57); battery directions ('57); battery technical report ('57); no data on reliability of Form B; separate answer sheets must be used; $3.95 per 20 tests; $1 per 20 IBM scorable answer sheets; 45¢ per scoring stencil; $1 per manual; $1 per battery technical report; $1.25 per specimen set of any one level; postage extra; 70(90–100) minutes; Cooperative Test Division, Educational Testing Service. *
a) LEVEL 4. Grades 4–6; Forms 4A, 4B.
b) LEVEL 3. Grades 7–9; Forms 3A, 3B.
c) LEVEL 2. Grades 10–12; Forms 2A, 2B.
d) LEVEL 1. Grades 13–14; Forms 1A, 1B.

RICHARD E. GROSS, *Associate Professor of Education, Stanford University, Stanford, California.*

These tests are not conventional instruments which attempt to measure the results of any separate subject matter course. While test items are drawn from the areas of history, geography, economics, government, and sociology, they tend to call for the application of one or more skills or of knowledge of the field rather than for the recall of information.

The geographically oriented map problems are particularly good; in some instances care is taken to avoid answers which depend only upon memory by providing maps of imaginary islands or areas where the testee must use his

knowledge and skills. The pictorial items are perhaps least satisfactory and, as is true of other items, assume a rich background on the part of the testee. In several, such as the picture at the top of page 13 of Form 2B, the important details (here, terracing) are so small as to make it difficult and time-consuming for even the bright and perceptive student to figure out the correct answers. Others query the testee about pictures which involve too much conjecture; in Part 1 of Form 3A, for example, Item 30 asks the testee to differentiate between the limitations in location of four factories depicted. Just because a river is shown adjacent to the buildings of factory 1 does not mean that that factory has to be near a flow of water; factory 4 might well be more dependent upon the huge power sources hinted by its belching chimneys. A more understandable picture could certainly have been selected to cover the questions on the 1930 depression in Part 2 of Form 2A; the right answers to these questions are debatable, to say the least. This part also presents a reproduction of a newspaper column showing the transactions of the New York Stock Exchange on a given day. Here no explanation is presented as to legends used in the table and a student unfamiliar with the terminology and abbreviations would be penalized in answering Items 21 and 23. The great bulk of items, however, is very well conceived, and with all the practical screening that the test items have had, the reviewer could find few with which to quibble. He feels that Item 24 in Part 2 of Form 2B, in which the organization of an army is described as similar to that of a business organization, is overdrawn. He also believes that a testee living in New York would have considerable advantage over a Floridian or a Nebraskan in answering Item 9 in Part 2 of Form 3A, which concerns the Erie Canal and travel time thereon. Aside from a few such points, the test items are far superior to those the reviewer has found in a number of other instruments that often have too many poorly constructed or ambiguous items and too many items that are limited primarily to informational assessment.

The reviewer feels strongly that many of the social science competencies necessary to do well on these tests are being neglected in too many schools across the country. In his opinion, if tests like these are used often enough in such situations, they may serve a significant purpose in upgrading instruction and promoting needed alterations in curricular emphasis. Therefore, in addition to their valuable evaluation role, these tests promise to make a real contribution towards improved and more functional social studies programs.

S. A. RAYNER, *Assistant Registrar, The University of Queensland, Brisbane, Australia.*

The *Sequential Tests of Educational Progress: Social Studies* represent the most commendable attempt known to this reviewer to apply modern doctrines of measurement in the preparation of social studies tests. The improvement over earlier tests in this field lies principally in the quality of the norms and in the comprehensive information in the manual and accompanying publications.

GOALS. The tests aim to measure development in seven skills and eight areas of understanding "which effective citizens should possess." As a check on whether such claims are justifiable, each item in Form 2B (intended for grades 10–12) was classified according to the principles in Bloom's *Taxonomy of Educational Objectives.* This analysis showed that at least three quarters of all items involve "translation," i.e., the ability required to explain a picture, a cartoon, a statistical table, a graph, and so on, or the ability to select a particular example of a general principle; the other items required the ability to interpret data. Very few items depended principally on knowledge or memory. However, although the STEP tests depend on both knowledge and skills, they do not primarily measure the higher mental processes.

Since the general goal of all the tests is to measure "the broad outcomes of general education rather than the relatively narrow results of any specific subject matter course," the tests draw on problems from many areas in history, geography, economics, government, and sociology; generally the questions involve an application to American affairs. Since each test contains only 70 items, it obviously cannot provide a reliable measure of any of these areas of knowledge.

FORMAT. Each test is attractively presented. The space in the test booklet is used economically but effectively. The uniformity of time limits, instructions, and answer sheets, which permits different forms of STEP to be administered to one group at the same time, is a practical advantage that will commend itself to the tester. One minor blemish is that the coloured dots which enable the marking stencil to be oriented rapidly on the answer sheet have not been placed correctly. This should be corrected in later printings.

NORMS. Improved sampling techniques are among the commendable features of the STEP norms. It has been realized that the adequacy of the standardization programme depends on the number of sampling units (in this case, school districts or colleges) rather than on the number of testees; for example, by selecting only two students per grade in 120 colleges and by stratifying the colleges by region and type, the sample of some two hundred students in each grade should provide more reliable norms than would a far larger sample of students drawn from a few colleges.

The norms draw attention to the importance of taking account of standard errors in the interpretation of scores. By showing that a given raw score indicates a relatively wide band on the percentile scale, the authors may discourage test users from regarding small differences in test scores as meaningful.

A third merit of the STEP norms is the attempt to convert scores on all tests to a common scale. However, there is no empirical evidence to show whether there is close agreement between the scale scores of students who have taken the tests at two levels.

RELIABILITY. The Kuder-Richardson estimates of internal consistency do not provide a satisfactory estimate of reliability for these tests. If the equation of scores between grades 4 and 13 implies a long term consistency in development, there is an obligation on the publishers to provide estimates of stability reliability.

VALIDITY. No evidence is provided on validity. The most satisfactory type of evidence would be agreement with the scores on another test prepared independently from the same specifications by experts of equal calibre. In lieu of this, each user must determine for himself how closely the test items appear likely to measure his own objectives. The publishers' promise to relate test scores to suitable criterion measures may be difficult to implement since the test itself may be the best available measure of such a criterion.

Correlations are reported between each form of STEP and the *Cooperative School and Col-*

lege Ability Tests (SCAT). The correlations range from .73 to .89, with a median of .80. Coefficients of this magnitude must raise the question of whether the STEP tests are measuring development in the social studies or whether they are virtually measures of general ability. The coefficient of .82 for Form 2B in grade 12 is, by Australian standards, incredibly high.

Form 2B was selected for an intensive check on the validity of individual items. In Part 1, the meaning of the first cartoon is not clear and there does not seem to be any particularly good answer to Item 2. To answer Item 14 correctly a student should have read the background statement carelessly, have been unfamiliar with Einstein's history, or have been ignorant of the geography of Europe; there is certainly no correct answer to the item as it stands. In Part 2 the analogy between an army and a modern business organization (Item 24) does not seem close enough to be worth making. The other items appear to cover a wide area and to provide a searching test.

OVERSEAS USERS. Few United States social studies tests would be suitable for use in Australian or English schools because of the many American references. If the tests were to be adapted for another country, most changes would be needed in the level 4 tests and fewest in the level 1 tests. Even at present, the level 1 tests appear to be within the range of an Australian undergraduate majoring in history.

EVALUATION. A specimen set of this series would be very suitable for use in a course in educational measurement since the tests and manual represent an admirable attempt to meet the specifications prescribed for attainment tests by leaders in the measurement field. The tests themselves contain minor blemishes which are probably due to the speed with which they were constructed. If they can be revised after use for a year or two and if additional information can be provided on them, they should become far superior to any social studies tests at present available.

RALPH W. TYLER, *Director, Center for Advanced Study in the Behavioral Sciences, Stanford, California.*

This series is constructed to provide samples of the student behavior defined as the objectives of social studies instruction by leading teachers in this field. By focussing on similar kinds of behavior throughout the four levels and by using overlapping scales, the tests furnish a means for assessing progress students are making in the development of these abilities and skills from the fourth grade through the sophomore year in college. They are a helpful attempt to meet a long standing and important need in the social studies.

They were planned to test the abilities involved in reading and interpreting social studies materials—maps, charts, graphs, cartoons, pictures, diagrams, and the printed word. The exercises require several kinds of behavior in interpreting these materials, such as to identify main points and central issues, to compare and contrast underlying assumptions, biases, and motives, to distinguish fact from opinion, to assess the adequacy and relevance of data, to apply appropriate outside information, and to use relevant concepts from the social sciences in analyzing, criticizing, and drawing conclusions. To lessen the influence of variations in specific content treated in different social studies courses, each exercise provides some necessary specific data and requires the student to recall and use some concepts and generalizations commonly treated in social studies courses throughout the country. Each test contains only 70 items so that it is not possible to get a reliable measure of each of these abilities and skills, but the total score is reliable enough (the reported coefficients of reliability range from .93 for level 4 to .84 for level 2) to give a useful measure of relative student achievement of the complex of abilities and skills which are common aims of the social studies. The provision of norms on a single scale for the four levels provides a beginning for measuring student progress. These norms are derived from cross-sectional samples rather than from repeated testing of the same students. Hence, they serve as approximations only to norms which may later be worked out on the longitudinal basis.

In the future development of these tests there are four steps to be taken to increase their validity. Exploration of new forms of items is needed to provide greater flexibility in testing more directly these abilities and skills. The more mature abilities required for problem solving, such as the ability to predict the probable consequences of social policies and courses of action, should be identified and become part of the specifications for test construction. A comprehensive list of the basic concepts useful in understanding social phenomena and analyzing social problems needs to be definitely identified so as to serve to specify the content for the tests. Finally, the senior high school and the college level tests should include exercises testing the students' understanding of the nature of the social sciences, the kinds of problems with which they deal, the kinds of methods they use, and the kinds of knowledge they produce. These developments are essential to provide tests appropriate for the sophisticated students in this field.

This reviewer has long urged the construction of tests which are built to appraise directly the students' attainment of objectives actually sought by good teachers and the more extended use of such tests to take the place of tests which are based only on an analysis of common content of textbooks and courses of study. This is necessary both to obtain a valid measure of student achievement and also to focus the attention of students and teachers upon important educational aims rather than upon memorization of course content. Tests exert a powerful influence on teaching and learning. Slowly testmakers are moving in this direction. The STEP tests are a fine contribution to this essential improvement in education.

For reviews by Robert W. B. Jackson and Wilbur L. Layton of the complete battery, see 24.

[793]
★Shearer Social Studies Test. Grades 7–9; 1952; Forms A, B; mimeographed manual; $1.20 per 25 tests, postage extra; 25¢ per specimen set, postpaid; 40(45) minutes; Lois Shearer; Bureau of Educational Measurements. *

REFERENCE
1. SHEARER, LOIS M. *The Construction and Standardization of a Social Studies Test.* Master's thesis, Kansas State Teachers College (Emporia, Kan.), 1952.

RAYMOND C. NORRIS, *Associate Professor of Psychology, George Peabody College for Teachers, Nashville, Tennessee.*

This test was developed to measure the understanding junior high school students have of material generally included in seventh, eighth, and ninth grade social studies. To assure more than local applicability, the author based her items on "leading text books of recommended or preferred lists in a number of states." Each form consists of 60 true-false, 40 matching, and 48 multiple choice items with the follow-

ing percentage distribution: history, 60; geography, 25; civics, 9; and citizenship, 6. Although prospective users should examine the test item by item to determine its relevance to their local curricula, it would have been helpful if the author had listed the texts or even the state lists used to assure content validity. It would have been helpful also if she had indicated the manner in which these materials were used to assure curricular validity.

Both split-half and parallel-forms reliability estimates appear high. For a group of 97 undescribed individuals the split-half coefficients for Forms A and B, respectively, were .91 and .89. For the same 97 subjects the correlation between scores on the two forms when administered within a week of each other was .86.

Percentile-within-grade norms are provided for the middle of the seventh, eighth, and ninth grades and for the end of the seventh and eighth grades. The normative sample is described only as consisting of the 1,553 pupils who participated in the Nation-wide Every Pupil Testing Programs of 1952.

Inspection of the test items and of the reliability data suggests that the test may be better than one might gather from the sketchy description of the method of development and of the norm groups.

[794]
★Social Studies: Every Pupil Scholarship Test. Grades 7–8; 1935–58; new form usually issued each January and April; norms available following testing program; no data on reliability; 4¢ per test; 4¢ per scoring key; postage extra; 30(35) minutes; Bureau of Educational Measurements. *

[795]
★Social Studies: Midwest High School Achievement Examinations. High school; 1955–57; title on Form B is *Social Science XII;* Forms A ('55), B ('57); no specific manual; no data on reliability; norms: [A, '55; B, '57]; 10¢ per test, postage extra; Form A: 60(65) minutes; Form B: 90(95) minutes; Lola Faye (A) and Kopple C. Friedman (B); Educational Test Bureau. *

[796]
*Social Studies: National Teacher Examinations. College seniors and teachers; 1940–58; for more complete information, see 538; IBM; 80(90) minutes; Educational Testing Service. *

For reviews by William A. Brownell, Walter W. Cook, and Lawrence G. Derthick of the entire series, see 538; for a review by Harry N. Rivlin of an earlier edition, see 4:802.

[797]

★**Social Studies: Teacher Education Examination Program.** College seniors preparing to teach secondary school; 1957; for more complete information, see 543; IBM; 80(95) minutes; Educational Testing Service. *

For a review by Walter W. Cook of the entire series, see 543.

[798]

*****Social Studies Test: National Achievement Tests.** Grades 4–6, 7–9; 1937–57; 2 forms; 2 levels; directions sheets ('45); no data on reliability; no norms for part scores; $2.75 per 25 tests; 50¢ per specimen set of either level; postage extra; 35(40) minutes; Robert K. Speer and Samuel Smith; Acorn Publishing Co. *
a) GRADES 4–6. 6 scores: human relations, life situations, social problems, products and peoples, meaning of events, total; Forms A, B ('55, identical with tests copyrighted in 1945 and 1939, respectively, except for minor changes).
b) GRADES 7–9. 7 scores: human relations, life situations, social interpretations, values of products, social ideas, miscellaneous facts, total; Forms A ('57), B ('45), identical with tests copyrighted in 1945 and 1939, respectively, except for minor changes).

For a review by Ray G. Wood, see 3:594.

[799]

*****Stanford Achievement Test: Intermediate and Advanced Social Studies Test.** Grades 5–9; 1940–54; same as the social studies sections of *Stanford Achievement Test;* IBM; Forms JM ('52), KM ('53), LM ('53); manual ('54); separate answer sheets must be used; $2.35 per 35 tests; $1.25 per 35 IBM answer sheets; 20¢ per machine scoring stencil; postage extra; 35¢ per specimen set, postpaid; 30(35) minutes; Truman L. Kelley, Richard Madden, Eric F. Gardner, Lewis M. Terman, and Giles M. Ruch; World Book Co. *

HARRY D. BERG, *Professor, Office of Evaluation Services, Michigan State University, East Lansing, Michigan.*

The present test is a separately published edition of that portion of the *Stanford Achievement Test* devoted to the measurement of social studies growth in grades 5 to 9. The general content of the items is divided quite equally over the areas commonly designated as history, geography, and civics or social problems. The specific item content and difficulty are based upon an extensive national survey of texts and courses of study used in the elementary school. In the latter connection, it may be significant to note the authors' comment that "despite frequent statements to the contrary there is, in fact, widespread agreement concerning much of the content of the elementary Social Studies curriculum." It is hoped that this is true, since the validity of a test using national norms is dependent in a large measure upon a considerable degree of uniformity in instruction.

Alternate forms of the test are available, each form containing about 100 brief multiple choice items. It is expected that all or nearly all pupils will be able to finish in the allotted time (30 minutes); thus the test is intended as one one of power rather than of speed.

All aspects of test making, administration, and interpretation have been handled in so adequate and professional a manner that this reviewer has only one issue to raise, but that is a rather fundamental one. It concerns the requirements of the items or the question of what constitutes social studies growth. The authors, who frankly state that "the items in the test measure primarily social studies content or information," are also "well aware of the many other objectives of social studies instruction in the grades." Factual information is important, measureable growth does occur with regard to it, and there is probably a high correlation between such growth and other objectives. But some prospective users may well wish a test which more directly measures growth in terms of understanding, critical thinking ability, and skills. A comparison might be made between the items on this test and those in social studies tests of the *Iowa Tests of Educational Development* and the recently published *Sequential Tests of Educational Progress.* These tests also attempt to measure social studies growth, but with different emphases.

However, assuming that he feels that the kind of growth measured in the Stanford test is significant, the user will have available to him a very excellent set of norms for measuring that growth. Three kinds of norms are provided: modal-age grade norms for the interpretation of individual scores, total-group grade norms for the interpretation of group averages, and within-grade percentile norms. An especially useful adjunct to the norms is the provision of standard errors of measurement. These factors and others make this examination, within the scope of its content, one of the finer products of the test builder's art.

For a review by Ray G. Wood of the previous edition, see 3:595. For a review by N. L. Gage of the complete battery, see 25; for reviews by Paul R. Hanna (with Claude E. Norcross) and Virgil E. Herrick of the previous edition, see 4:25; for reviews by Walter W. Cook and Ralph C. Preston, see 3:18.

ECONOMICS

[800]

***The Graduate Record Examinations Advanced Tests: Economics.** College seniors and graduate students; 1939–57; for more complete information, see 601; IBM; 180(200) minutes; Educational Testing Service. *

For a review by Harold Seashore of the entire series, see 601.

GEOGRAPHY

[801]

***Coordinated Scales of Attainment: Geography.** Grades 6, 7, 8; 1946–54; subtest of *Coordinated Scales of Attainment;* IBM; Forms A ('46), B ('49); 3 levels; directions for administering ['52]; battery manuals (A, '54; B, '49); separate answer sheets must be used; $1.90 per 25 tests; $1 per 25 IBM scorable answer sheets; 10¢ per scoring stencil; 50¢ per specimen set; postage extra; (20) minutes; Mendel E. Branom; Educational Test Bureau. *

For a review by Alvin W. Schindler of the complete battery, see 4:8; for reviews by Roland L. Beck, Lavone A. Hanna, Gordon N. Mackenzie (with Glen Hass), and C. C. Ross of batteries 4–8, see 3:6.

[802]

***Economic Geography: Achievement Examinations for Secondary Schools.** High school; 1951–53; Forms 1 ('51), 3 ('53); no specific manual; no data on reliability; norms: Forms 1 ['52], 3 ('53); 10¢ per test, postage extra; [60–90] minutes; Helen Haberman (3); Educational Test Bureau. *

[803]

★**Economic Geography: Midwest High School Achievement Examinations,** High school; 1952–55; Forms A ('55), B ('52, identical with Form 2 of *Economic Geography: Achievement Examinations for Secondary Schools*); no specific manual; no data on reliability; no norms; 10¢ per test, postage extra; 60(65) minutes; Helen Haberman (A); Educational Test Bureau. *

[804]

***Geography: Every Pupil Scholarship Test.** Grades 5–7; 1933–58; new form usually issued each January and April; norms available following testing program; no data on reliability; 4¢ per test; 4¢ per scoring key; postage extra; 30(35) minutes; Bureau of Educational Measurements. *

[805]

***Geography: Every Pupil Test.** Grades 4, 5, 6, 7; 1935–58; new form usually issued each December and April; 4 levels; norms available following testing program; no data on reliability; 3¢ per test; 1¢ per scoring key; cash orders postpaid; 40(45) minutes; Ohio Scholarship Tests. *

[806]

***Geography Test: Municipal Tests: National Achievement Tests.** Grades 3–6, 6–8; 1938–52; subtest of *Municipal Battery;* 3 scores: geographical ideas and comparisons, miscellaneous facts, total; 2 forms; 2 levels; no data on reliability; no norms for part scores; $1.75 per 25 tests; 50¢ per specimen set of either level; postage extra; 20(25) minutes; Robert K. Speer and Samuel Smith; Acorn Publishing Co. *
a) GRADES 3–6. 1938–52; Forms A ('52, identical with test copyrighted in 1938 except for minor changes), B ('49, identical with test copyrighted in 1939 except for minor changes); directions sheet ('38).
b) GRADES 6–8. 1938–51; Forms A ('50), B ('51, identical with test copyrighted in 1939 except for Item 8, Part 1); directions sheets (A, '50; B, '39).

For a review by Edwin H. Reeder, see 4:676. For a review by J. Murray Lee of the complete battery, see 18; for a review by Ralph C. Preston, see 4:20; for reviews by A. M. Jordan and Hugh B. Wood of the complete battery for grades 6–8, see 40:1191.

HISTORY

[807]

***American History: Achievement Examinations for Secondary Schools.** High school; 1951–53; Forms 1 ('51), 3 ('53); no specific manual; no data on reliability; norms: Forms 1 ['52], 3 ('53); 10¢ per test, postage extra; [60–90] minutes; M. J. Haggerty (3); Educational Test Bureau. *

[808]

***American History: Every Pupil Scholarship Test.** High school: 1926–58; 2 tests; norms available following testing program; no data on reliability; 4¢ per test; 4¢ per scoring key; postage extra; 40(45) minutes; Bureau of Educational Measurements. *
a) AMERICAN HISTORY TO 1865. New form usually issued each January.
b) AMERICAN HISTORY SINCE 1865. New form usually issued each April.

[809]

***American History: Every Pupil Test.** Grades 7–8, 11–12; 1931–58; 2 levels; norms available following testing program; no data on reliability; 3¢ per test; 1¢ per scoring key; cash orders postpaid; 40(45) minutes; Ohio Scholarship Tests. *
a) GRADES 7–8. 1935–58; new form usually issued each December; 2 tests: To 1840 A.D., 1840 and on.
b) GRADES 11–12. 1931–58; new form usually issued each December and April.

[810]

★**American History: Midwest High School Achievement Examinations.** High school; 1955–57; Forms A ('55), B ('57); no specific manual; no data on reliability; norms: [A, '55; B, '57]; 10¢ per test, postage extra; Form A: 60(65) minutes; Form B: 90(95) minutes; M. J. Haggerty (A) and Peter Otterness (B); Educational Test Bureau. *

HOWARD R. ANDERSON, *Professor of Education, and Dean, University School of Liberal and Applied Studies, The University of Rochester, Rochester, New York.*

The series manual states that the purposes of the examinations are "to motivate efforts of accomplishments by the students" and "to stimulate thinking ability based on mastery of contents resulting from efforts of work."

The American history test includes 150 items. There are 40 five-response, 65 four-response, and 15 three-response multiple choice items plus two matching exercises of 15 items each. Most of the questions deal with persons, events, dates, places, and things. For example, the pupil is expected to match "Cross of Gold," "Polar Bear Garden," "Swamp Fox," "The Fur Lord," and "The Raven" with Bryan, Seward, Marion, Astor, and Houston, respectively.

The only norms provided for this test are 25th percentile, median, 75th percentile, and perfect scores. The series manual contains the surprising statement that norms for all tests "are printed on one sheet to show variation of accomplishment from subject to subject." Surely there must be other reasons why the median on the 150-item American history test is 76 whereas the median on the 114–item world history test is 61.

The series manual states, "The scoring keys are as specific as possible." This statement does not guarantee accuracy. To illustrate: For Item 2, Renaissance is keyed as the name by which "the five centuries following the extinction of the Roman Empire" are known. For Item 39, Dag Hammarskjold is listed as the "U.N. general assembly president."

In some cases it is difficult or impossible to figure out how the author identifies the right answer in the responses provided. Thus, in Item 26 he gives Vicksburg, not Gettysburg, as the "high water mark of the Confederacy." In Item 62 he holds that sailboats had nothing to do with westward expansion although thousands went to California by clipper ship during the gold rush.

A few items in this test contain misleading or wrong information in the stem. For example, the stem of Item 3 states that the capture of Constantinople by the Turks closed "the connection between oriental and occidental trade routes." Items 31 states that the "Pan American Congress was inaugurated in 1889"; actually the first meeting was held on October 2, 1890.

This examination appears to have been hastily prepared and carelessly edited. It seems un-

likely that its use will "stimulate thinking ability" in American history. It would be unfortunate if teachers were misled into believing that the items included in this test identify the "contents" to be mastered by their pupils.

[811]

*American History Test: National Achievement Tests. Grades 7–8; 1937–56; 5 scores: lessons of history, time concepts, historical associations, miscellaneous problems, total; Forms A ('56, identical with 3 forms copyrighted in 1939, 1944, and 1949 except for minor changes), B ('45, identical with test copyrighted in 1938 except for minor changes); no data on reliability; no norms for part scores; directions sheets (A, '45; B, '38); $2.75 per 25 tests; 50¢ per specimen set; postage extra; 40(45) minutes; Robert K. Speer, Lester D. Crow, and Samuel Smith; Acorn Publishing Co. *

For reviews by Jacob S. Orleans and Wallace Taylor, see 40:1630.

[812]

★College Entrance Examination Board Advanced Placement Examination: American History. High school seniors desiring credit for college level courses; 1956–58; for more complete information, see 600; 3 scores: objective, essay, total; IBM in part; 2 parts; 180(200) minutes; program administered by Educational Testing Service for the College Entrance Examination Board. *

JAMES A. FIELD, JR., *Professor of History, Swarthmore College, Swarthmore, Pennsylvania.* [Review of Form FBP.]

This examination is designed to test advanced high school work in American history at a level described in the prospectus of the Advanced Placement Program as "equivalent to.... an introductory college course." It is made up of three parts: an objective section taking 45 minutes and counting 25 per cent of the total score, a discussion (for 20 minutes and 15 per cent) of an interpretation of an historical event, and two 50-minute essays amounting together to 60 per cent of the total. Fifteen minutes are given for review of the written work.

The objective section contains 75 multiple choice items of ingenious and demanding nature. Thirty-five consist of questions to be answered, incomplete statements to be completed, or statements to be placed in context; 17 present quotations for identification by name, meaning, or origin; there are 10 map questions; 13 questions involve the exegesis of three documents, one of which is a cartoon. Quite properly a number of the questions call for a fairly sophisticated discrimination, but only two or three seem to contain undesirable ambiguities.

For the essay on historical interpretation the student is offered a choice of one of four subjects ranging from the very general to the particular. By all odds the hardest was one concerning individual motivation; this was attempted by many of the better students (as judged by their scores on the objective section) with results, costly to them, which raise the question of how to avoid penalizing ambition and enterprise.

The booklet describing the Advanced Placement Program lists 16 topics (e.g., The Westward Movement, Divisive Forces in American History) as a guide to study. These are thoroughly covered in the 14 essay subjects offered in the examination, yet there are problems of emphasis. The favorite subjects of the examiners, as shown both here and in the objective section, lie in the areas where economics and politics interact, in the relations between farmer, labor, business, and the federal government. The period of the industrial revolution is sliced all ways for the essay writer, but there is no chance to discuss the antebellum South, slavery, territorial expansion, manifest destiny, or the causes of the Civil War. The student with an interest in the history of foreign relations would have some difficulty bringing his information to bear. Intellectual history is (perhaps properly) slighted.

This emphasis on the period of industrialization seems excessive. Complete ignorance of all that happened before 1860 would cost the candidate a mere 8 per cent of his possible score, and this only in the objective section where 20 of the 75 items concern the antebellum period. In comparison there are 35 items on the period from 1861 to 1919 and 15 on the years since the First World War; the three documents which form the basis for 13 questions all fall between 1875 and 1912. Although the short essay on interpretation offers a 50-50 choice, the long essays are weighted about two to one against the earlier time: 5 of the 14 topics call for postbellum information only, 3 permit and 5 require some antebellum information, and a single essay subject is restricted to the period before the election of Lincoln.

This disproportion appears to have been noted by the readers of the examinations, and may consequently be corrected in future editions of the test. In all other respects the examination seems generally of high quality.

CHRISTINE McGUIRE, *Assistant Professorial Lecturer in the Social Sciences, and Examiner, The University of Chicago, Chicago, Illinois.*

The Advanced Placement Program, as described in the booklet provided for prospective users, is an exceedingly interesting development, designed to encourage high schools to develop college level courses for superior students and to furnish colleges with reliable information on the basis of which they can consider for credit and advanced placement students who have taken such courses.

The description of the examination for the American history course makes clear that students will be expected to demonstrate "a thorough grounding in facts....[and understanding] of their contexts, their causes and results and their significance....[the ability] to read historical material analytically and critically, and.... to express themselves in good English." Illustrative items of both an objective and essay type are provided.

Unfortunately, the examination does not measure the student's achievement of these objectives. One fourth of the total test time is devoted to objective questions. These are excessively concrete, lack any consistent development of an idea or institutional form, and are usually very simple. In short, they test primarily the recall of often quite trivial information. For example, one question on a desegregation case merely refers to another case, but not to the principles of the recent decision, especially the introduction of modern psychological and sociolgical data as a basis for deciding public policy, nor to the role of equality as a value in modern America, nor to this value historically, nor to the processes by which values may be changed. In short, the item does not touch on the significance of the issue or of the decision. Again the "correct" answer to one question about Calhoun's "theory of concurrent majority" fails to address the major issue of popular government with which the theory was concerned and actually perverts the concept in its oversimplification. Similarly, the role of religion is dealt with by questions requiring the identification of the denomination of certain religious leaders rather than in terms of its or their significance historically, politically, or socially under the conformist pressures of an egalitarian society.

The conscientious teacher will try to shape his course so as to avoid placing his students at any serious disadvantage. Consequently, a test like this might very well lead to an excessive preoccupation with specifics at the sacrifice of abstract ideas and important skills.

The essay portion of the test does little to correct this tendency. Though some of the questions are excellent in requiring a thoughtful analysis or interpretation, the choice among a series of alternatives is so wide and the variation in quality is so great that narrow concentration in preparation in one or a few areas will certainly suffice. Nor are the standards employed in grading the essays reassuring in this connection. In the longer essays 25 per cent of the grade was based on mechanics of English and organization and another 25 per cent was determined by the accuracy, relevance, and sufficiency of the facts cited. Secondly, the passing standards even for these quite ordinary qualities seem to this reviewer to be exceedingly low.

The data supplied for the interpretation of test results are seriously inadequate. Though the usual data are reported for reliability, means, percentiles and the like, it is impossible to judge the significance of these data in the absence of information about the characteristics of the groups on which they were calculated. Further, it is not clear that the precautions to assure reliable grading of the essays were actually adequate in view of the rather large variations in the mean essay scores of students choosing to write on different questions and of the quite low intercorrelations of essay parts. Data on student performance on each item of the objective section are, necessarily, unavailable to teachers as a result of the agency's policy in not releasing specific items.

Though the program for which this test was designed is indeed a laudable one and certainly to be encouraged, the current form of the test is inadequate for judging whether or not students have achieved the stated objectives and hence is inadequate as a basis for granting college credit in American History. Unfortunately, no alternative tests are currently available for this specific type of collaboration between school and college.

[813]

★College Entrance Examination Board Advanced Placement Examination: European History. High school seniors desiring credit for college level courses; 1956–58; for more complete informa-

tion, see 600; 3 scores: objective, essay, total; IBM in part; 2 parts; 180(200) minutes; program administered by Educational Testing Service for the College Entrance Examination Board.

[814]

Cooperative World History Test. High school; 1934–49; IBM; Forms Y ('48), Z ('49); no specific manual; general Cooperative manual ('51); norms ['49]; $2.95 per 25 tests; separate answer sheets may be used; $1 per 25 IBM answer sheets; 25¢ per scoring stencil; postage extra; 40(45) minutes; Wallace Taylor (Y) and Frederick H. Stutz (Z); Cooperative Test Division, Educational Testing Service. *

DAVID K. HEENAN, *Assistant Professor, Office of Evaluation Services, and Examiner in the Humanities, Michigan State University, East Lansing, Michigan.*

The *Cooperative World History Test* is designed to furnish information about the capabilities, achievements, and competence of the student in the subject and to check the effectiveness of the materials, curriculum, and teaching methods used in a given class or school. The test contains 85 items covering the social, economic, political, and cultural aspects of world history from the prehistoric age to post-World War II. At best the items "spot check" the student's knowledge of details in a very broad field. At first inspection some of the items appear superficial and petty, but closer analysis reveals that a student who relies on rote memorization alone will not score well. Consequently, the tests should measure, at least by indirection, the extent to which the broad objectives of the world history course have been attained.

The manual supplied with the tests contains detailed instructions for administering and scoring the test and suggestions for recording and interpreting test results. Percentile norms based upon the results of 1,293 tenth grade and 281 eleventh grade students are provided separately.

Some parts of the test should be reviewed and revised. This is particularly true of the materials dealing with the United Nations and events during and immediately following World War II. Several items call for knowledge of specific facts which were receiving greater attention in the study of current events at the time the tests were written than they are at the present time: e.g., "Which of these agencies provided for in the United Nations Charter had no counterpart in the League of Nations organization? (Military Staff Committee)" and "Which of the following books was written as a result of the invention of the atomic bomb? (*One World or None*)" In the latter item the other foils are *The Power and the Glory, The Cornerstones of Peace, Mein Kampf,* and *One World,* all conceivably more familiar immediately after the war than they are now.

But the most striking weakness of the test (especially of Form Y) is the subject matter used in testing cultural history. One item reads: "The influence of ancient Egyptian architectural design may be seen in the (Washington Monument)." The fact that the Washington Monument is an obelisk does not necessarily mean that it was influenced by the Egyptian architectural style; more likely it was influenced by the Renaissance or Baroque designs. This is an example of some of the superficial questions on an important field. The item could be improved by asking for a comparison of the Greek style with a Greek revival building of 19th century America. Another item asks: "In which of the fine arts has there been *least* change since the Renaissance? (Sculpture)" This involves a judgment which most people are not equipped to make. The only way that one could answer this item is to accept the opinion of the writer of the textbook being used or conclude that all sculpture ended with the work of Auguste Rodin.

Other items involving judgment could be improved. One item, for example, asks, "Which of the following best explains the chief weakness of the political reform movement in western Europe around 1750? (Political power was not in the hands of the people.)" This type of item calls for the expected answer of a democratically oriented student and is not really a valid test of knowledge.

With some slight revisions this test would be a first-rate instrument for measuring the student's knowledge of world history. As it now stands, it is as good as any test the reviewer has seen in this field. Form Z, the more recent form, appears to contain fewer of the faults described above than does the older Form Y.

For a review by Kenneth E. Gell of an earlier form, see 40:1636; for a review by R. M. Tryon, see 38:1017.

[815]
Coordinated Scales of Attainment: History. Grades 4, 5, 6, 7, 8; 1946–54; subtest of *Coordinated*

Scales of Attainment; IBM; grades 4, 7: Forms A ('46), B ('49); grades 5–6, 8: Forms A, B ('49); 5 levels; directions for administering ['52]; battery manuals (A, '54; B, '49); separate answer sheets must be used; $1.90 per 25 tests; $1 per 25 IBM scorable answer sheets; 10¢ per scoring stencil; 50¢ per specimen set; postage extra; (20) minutes; Edgar B. Wesley; Educational Test Bureau. *

For a review by Alvin W. Schindler of the complete battery, see 4:8; for reviews by Roland L. Beck, Lavone A. Hanna, Gordon N. Mackenzie (with Glen Hass), and C. C. Ross of Batteries 4–8, see 3:6.

[816]
Crary American History Test: Evaluation and Adjustment Series. Grades 9–13; 1950–54; IBM; Forms AM ('51), BM ('52); manual ('51); expectancy chart ['54]; separate answer sheets must be used; $3.60 per 35 tests; $1.40 per 35 IBM answer sheets; postage extra; 35¢ per specimen set, postpaid; 40(50) minutes; Ryland W. Crary; World Book Co. *

REFERENCES
1. TOWNSEND, AGATHA. "A Review of the Crary American History Test." *Ed Rec B* 61:67–71 Jl '53. * (*PA* 28:4864)
2. COWNE, LESLIE. "Reliability of the Crary American History Test, Form Bm, and Correlation of Scores With School Marks." *Ed Rec B* 63:81–5 Jl '54. * (*PA* 29:4684)

FREDERICK H. STUTZ, *Professor of Education, Cornell University, Ithaca, New York.*

This test appears to be excellent in design and construction. The 90 items in each form have been selected to represent those aims of the study of American history which are accepted as standard by authoritative groups such as the National Council for the Social Studies. The test is designed to measure mastery of information, skills, understandings, and ability to interpret historical materials. There is a suitable emphasis on nearly all of the major aspects of the development of the American nation. There is an informative manual which explains the development of the test and its administration and uses, and which seems to be accurate and complete.

Though this is a good test, a teacher will want to use it as only one part of the evaluation process. For example, students will need to show power in answering essay questions as well as in handling the types of questions found in a test of this type. The test has two minor weaknesses. Though aspects of social and intellectual history are dealt with, little attention is given to developments in literature, the arts, and education. The map questions and certain of the matching questions may pose reading and identification problems of an unnecessary sort.

The test is a well designed and constructed

measure of the achievement of objectives in a course in American history. It should be a valuable instrument to be used with average or above average students in courses in the upper years of the high school.

For a review by Edgar B. Wesley, see 4:688.

[817]

*Cummings World History Test: Evaluation and Adjustment Series. Grades 9-13; 1950-54; IBM; Forms AM ('51), BM ('52); manual ('51); expectancy chart ['54]; separate answer sheets must be used; $4.15 per 35 tests; $1.40 per 35 IBM answer sheets; postage extra; 35¢ per specimen set, postpaid; 40(50) minutes; Howard H. Cummings; World Book Co. *

REFERENCE

1. TRAXLER, ARTHUR E., AND TOWNSEND, AGATHA. "Some Data on the Results of the Cummings World History Test Among Independent School Pupils." *Ed Rec B* 59:77-8 Jl '52. * (*PA* 27:2997)

For reviews by Dorothy C. Adkins and Howard R. Anderson, see 4:689.

[818]

*The Graduate Record Examinations Advanced Tests: History. College seniors and graduate students; 1939-56; for more complete information, see 601; IBM; 180(200) minutes; Educational Testing Service. *

ROBERT H. FERRELL, *Assistant Professor of History, Indiana University, Bloomington, Indiana.* [Review of Form EGR.]

This test requires both generalization and narrow factual knowledge, and the ingenious combination of these two requisites within one examination is a tribute to the skill of the Educational Testing Service. Especially well chosen are the quotations which students must read and interpret. Such intellectual exercises offer as acceptable a measurement of students' skills as do the usual essay examinations. The map questions seem difficult, and the choice of country on which they are based somewhat unfortunate—that country's history no longer has the importance it once had. And to pursue this matter of relevance, it does appear that the test is a little too traditional not merely in choice of the above mentioned country for map questions but also in its slighting of the history of a nation with which the United States presently is enjoying some serious relations. Too, there should be more questions on ancient history and modern European history before the 20th century. American history is given more attention than it should have, judging from the history curricula in most colleges today.

The chief comment of the reviewer, in an adverse sense, is that the test needs grammatical tightening. The language of some of the questions is unduly loose. For example, some questions contain a string of prepositional phrases, making it necessary for the student to read the question two or three times to find his way through the turgidity. There are bumbling expressions, one question inquiring about a "direct outgrowth"—whatever that is; another asking about something which "originally drew" the United States toward a course of action—seeming to mean that one can draw both originally and secondarily. An easy improvement in the style of the questions would be to eliminate passive verbs; there are entirely too many in these questions, and they require the student to turn a sentence upside down to get its sense.

Perhaps the reviewer should also enter a comment about some of the explanatory material which accompanies these tests: the Handbook for Deans and Examiners, the Supervisor's Manual, the Manual of Directions to Examiners. This material is mostly an elucidation of the obvious, or an impossible effort to answer every conceivable question—which may while away the time of a bored supervisor but will make little impression upon most individuals sincerely anxious to discover the mechanics of the testing. There is also a considerable amount of gratuitous advice in these manuals, such as: "Proctors should at all times give strict attention to their duties. *They should not read or engage in conversation while an examination is in progress.*" And again: "Your manner during the testing should be firm but pleasant." These remarks seem unnecessary when directed to a university audience.

Having said all this, the reviewer must repeat that taken as a whole the test is well done. Admittedly it is only one of several factors on which one can judge a student's promise; but, considered along with health, working habits, financial condition, and the like, it ought to assist greatly the graduate faculties in choosing for admission and scholarships the most attractive of each year's candidates.

For a review by Harold Seashore of the entire series, see 601.

[819]

*History: Every Pupil Scholarship Test. Grades 5-6, 7-8; 1933-58; new form usually issued each January and April; 2 levels; norms available following testing program; no data on reliability; 4¢ per test; 4¢ per scoring key; postage extra; 30(35) minutes; Bureau of Educational Measurements. *

[820]

★Kansas United States History Test. 1, 2 semesters in grades 7–8; 1957; IBM; Form A; 2 levels; $1.20 per 25 tests; separate answer sheets may be used; 85¢ per 25 IBM answer sheets; 30¢ per scoring stencil; postage extra; 25¢ per specimen set, postpaid; 30(35) minutes; Shirley Meares and M. W. Sanders; Bureau of Educational Measurements. *

WAYNE A. FREDERICK, *Social Studies Department, Isidore Newman School, New Orleans, Louisiana.*

The manual for this test states that the items cover "knowledge of facts, as well as the application of information and reasoning." Basically, the test measures only the retention of factual data. There are very few, if any, items which test the student's ability to reason from historical concepts, and none which measure his ability to apply historical concepts.

As a test of factual knowledge the items certainly cover the subject matter. All the important periods in United States history are covered. However, very little attention has been given to the significance of historical concepts. For example, the state in which Abraham Lincoln spent his boyhood years has relatively little significance as compared with the status granted California by the Compromise of 1850. Further, the significance of Lincoln's childhood does not rest on the fact that it was experienced in a certain frontier state, but that it was experienced in a frontier society of the Northwest Territory.

The manual indicates that the test may be used as a determinant of pupil achievement and as a check on the efficiency of instruction. Achievement should be measured not only in terms of identifying historical concepts, persons, and events, but also in terms of understanding historical relationships and of interpreting new historical data based on known concepts. In these two respects the test fails to measure pupil achievement and, consequently, the quality of instruction. The few items which test historical relationships do so only within a very narrow frame of reference. Test 2 includes more items of this type than does Test 1, but the items demand only a simple identification—recall ability, rather than the thinking abilities involved in seeing means-end and cause-effect relationships. No item in either test measures understanding of broad generaliza-

tions or the ability to interpret, analyze, or evaluate historical data.

A few minor points of criticism are as follows: (a) The type is much smaller in size than what seventh and eighth graders are accustomed to reading in their textbooks. (b) A few items are stated in terms of historical myths and not in terms of historical facts. (c) Several items have options which are neither pertinent to the concept nor parallel in construction.

Because the *Kansas United States History Test* measures only the student's ability to recall specific historical data in a direct and narrow frame of reference, it is not useful for the purposes for which it is intended.

JOHN MANNING, *Associate Professor, Department of Humanities, and Office of Evaluation Services, Michigan State University, East Lansing, Michigan.*

Each form consists of 65 four-option items of the multiple choice type. The items cover "knowledge of facts as well as the application of information and reasoning." They are said to survey "the most important subject matter commonly presented by a number of leading elementary textbooks and courses of study," and to be proportional to the amount of content and the emphasis given in these sources.

Coefficients of reliability for Test 1 are given as ranging from .71 to .86; for Test 2, from .70 to .80. Although the manual is reasonably complete in regard to statistical information, more information on reliability would be helpful. The manual would be improved further by giving a more adequate description of the normative population. Users of tests are entitled to have an accurate and detailed description of the group upon which a test is standardized.

It is to be regretted further, that only half a dozen or so items in Test 1 appear to measure reasoning ability, while the remaining items test knowledge of facts almost exclusively. About 18 items present choices of place names exclusively, and another 25 or more items involve choices from names of persons, etc. The proportions appear to be approximately the same in Test 2. Since the test constructors do not list the textbooks and courses of study which were used as source material, it is difficult to estimate whether more items involving cause and effect relationships, critical judgment, and cultural trends could have been validly included. In any event, more items of these latter types would be highly desirable.

The test itself shows evidence of care and technical skill in the construction of the items. For practical purposes, it appears to fulfill the purpose for which it was designed, that is, to test "the most important subject matter commonly presented by a number of leading elementary textbooks and courses of study."

Regrettably, it is probable that the sampling is a fairly accurate reflection of the amount of emphasis actually given to these factors in the average course in American history in grades 7 and 8.

[821]

*Modern World History: Achievement Examinations for Secondary Schools. High school; 1951–53; Forms 1 ('51), 3 ('53); no specific manual; no data on reliability; norms: Forms 1 ['52], 3 ('53); 10¢ per test, postage extra; (60–90) minutes; Lola Fay (3); Educational Test Bureau. *

[822]

★Modern World History: Midwest High School Achievement Examinations. High school; 1955–57; title on Form A is *World History*; Forms A ('55, revision of Form 2 of *World History: Achievement Examinations for Secondary Schools*), B ('57); no specific manual; no data on reliability; norms: [A, '55; B, '57]; 10¢ per test, postage extra; Form A: 60(65) minutes; Form B: 90(95) minutes; Lola Faye (A) and Don Estenson (B); Educational Test Bureau. *

[823]

*World History: Every Pupil Scholarship Test. High school; 1926–58; new form usually issued each January and April; norms available following testing program; no data on reliability; 4¢ per test; 4¢ per scoring key; postage extra; 40(45) minutes; Bureau of Educational Measurements. *

[824]

*World History: Every Pupil Test. High school; 1933–58; new form usually issued each December and April; norms available following testing program; no data on reliability; 3¢ per test; 1¢ per scoring key; cash orders postpaid; 40(45) minutes; Ohio Scholarship Tests. *

[825]

*World History Test: Acorn National Achievement Tests. High school and college; 1948–57; 6 scores: social studies terms, world geography, contributions of world peoples to civilization, political history, economic-social-cultural history, total; no norms for part scores; Form A ('48); directions sheet ('57, identical with sheet copyrighted in 1948); $3.50 per 25 tests; 50¢ per specimen set; postage extra; 40(45) minutes; Vincent McGarrett and Edward H. Merrill; Acorn Publishing Co. *

JOHN MANNING, *Associate Professor, Department of Humanities, and Office of Evaluation Services, Michigan State University, East Lansing, Michigan.*

The test is divided into five parts. The first part presents 10 four-option multiple choice items on terms commonly used in social studies. Some of these items appear to lack a certain amount of accuracy and discrimination. For example, the student is asked to define imperialism as a policy of "trying to add to the lands over which a nation rules," and plebiscite as a "vote of the people." The "gimmick" (used also in Parts 3, 4, and 5) of keying the items to and designating the options by the letters of a code word would seem to pose a definite problem in security and reliability.

The second part of the test consists of 15 assertive sentences to be matched with 15 geographic locations designated by letters of the alphabet scattered over an outline map of the world. The map itself is poorly drawn and the designated places are far from accurately located. A better testing situation could be secured by the use of heavy and clearly marked arrows running from the top of the page to each location and lettered in sequence across the top of the page. Technically, the items could then be improved by offering as options four or five letters for each of the items, instead of forcing the students to consider all 15 letters in connection with each of the sentences.

Part 3 consists of 25 items revolving around "contributions of world peoples to civilization." A number of these items, however, stress persons rather than contributions of peoples, such as "United States Senator Taft and Representative Hartley were co-sponsors of a law which was related to the same field as a bill sponsored by (Wagner-Connally)," and "Shadrach, Meshach and Abednego had reason to dislike (Nebuchadnezzar)." A number of items have either a stem that appears inaccurate (such as, "The democracy of the modern American town meeting is very much like that of....") or an answer that is not very carefully defined (such as, "As a bi-product [sic] of the development of the atomic bomb, scientists now have (a method of diagnosing diseases hidden within the body)"). In the latter item a word like "tracing" or "studying" would be preferable to "diagnosing."

Part 4 consists of 25 items designated as "political history," and Part 5 of 25 questions on what is termed "economic, social and cultural history." Several items in these sections are in need of improvement both technically and historically. Whether or not "The reference in the American Declaration of Independence to 'life, liberty, and the pursuit of happiness' stems from the writings of (Locke)," is an open question; it would be preferable to substitute "is similar to" for "stems." The item, "Jupiter held the same place among the gods of the Romans as the Greeks gave to (Zeus)," could be improved by substituting, "To which god did the Greeks allot a similar place as the Romans allotted to Jupiter?" One would be in a better position to appraise the validity of the content of the items if some indication were given of the text(s) or course(s) of study around which the items were constructed. Such an item as, "The contribution of Pindar to Greek literature was paralleled in Roman literature by the work of (Horace)" has little value *unless* the pupils have read some of the Greek or Roman literature involved. A question on the Bayeaux Tapestry is a little esoteric in a test designed for students in American high schools as well as those in college.

The sheet of directions gives a table of norms based on approximately 5,000 students "in schools in the East, Central, West and Southern sections of the United States," for grades 9 through 12, and for college. The sheet does not mention the stage in their college careers at which the college students took the test or the proportion of college to high school students. Neither does it say *when* the norms were established (In 1948, the original copyright date?).

The amount of attention given to geography and economic, social, and cultural history as well as political history is commendable. This test probably has served its purpose in the past, but it now needs technical revision. Up-to-date reliability and validity data should be added to (or clarified in) the directions sheet. Separate norms should be given for the separate parts of the test. Additional items involving judgment need to be added.

POLITICAL SCIENCE

[826]
*American Civics and Government Tests for High Schools and Colleges, Revised Edition. High school and college; 1930-54; Forms A, B ['54, same as forms copyrighted in 1949 except for minor changes]; directions sheet ['49]; reliability, validity, and normative data based on 1949 forms; $2 per 25 tests; 30¢ per specimen set; postpaid; high school:

40(50) minutes; college: 35(45) minutes; F. A. Magruder, R. J. Clinton, and M. M. Chambers; Public School Publishing Co. *

[827]
*American Government and Citizenship: Every Pupil Test. Grades 11-12; 1935-58; new form usually issued each April; norms available following testing programs; no data on reliability; 3¢ per test; 1¢ per scoring key; cash orders postpaid; 40(45) minutes; Ohio Scholarship Tests. *

For a review by Elizabeth C. Adams of an earlier form, see 4:699.

[828]
*American Government: Every Pupil Scholarship Test. High school; 1930-58; new form usually issued each April; norms available following testing program; no data on reliability; 4¢ per test; 4¢ per scoring key; postage extra; 40(45) minutes; Bureau of Educational Measurements. *

[829]
★Attitude Toward Politicians Scale. High school; 1954; 1 form; no data on validity; $2.20 per 35 tests, postpaid; specimen set not available; (5-10) minutes; Citizenship Education Project, Teachers College, Columbia University; distributed by C. A. Gregory Co. *

DONALD T. CAMPBELL, *Associate Professor of Psychology, Northwestern University, Evanston, Illinois.*

The supporting evidence for this test and the likelihood that the test will ever be used are both so small that reviewing it seems hardly justified. The test consists of 18 simply declarative statements, endorsed and scored in Likert fashion, of which the 10 most simply favorable and unfavorable are scored. The unscored items are the more interesting and indicate some of the multidimensionality which a full exploration of attitudes in this domain would involve. Of the scored items, five are positive and five negative, controlling response set. Test-retest reliability on 243 high school students is .76. No evidence of internal consistency or factorial structure is given. No evidence of validity or relationship to other measures is presented. Norms are provided based upon 6,342 high school students of unspecified selection or sex. The excessive size of the normative group represents a misuse of effort that might better have been placed elsewhere. The rule still holds for social attitude tests that the copyrighted tests are poorer than the uncopyrighted ones.

[830]
Civic Vocabulary Test. High school; 1951; 1 form ['51]; preliminary mimeographed manual ['51]; no norms; 5s. per 10 tests; 2s. per manual; 2s. 6d. per specimen set; postpaid within Australia; [10-30] min-

utes; S. A. Rayner; Australian Council for Educational Research. *

REFERENCE

1. RAYNER, S. A. *The Special Vocabulary of Civics.* A.C.E.R. Research Series, No. 65. Melbourne, Australia: Melbourne University Press, 1951. Pp. x, 105. *

I. G. MEDDLETON, *Deputy Head, Research Department, University of Queensland, Brisbane, Australia.*

This is a test of 36 items of the multiple choice type constructed to assess how well Australian pupils who are close to primary school leaving age understand the meaning of terms commonly used in current discussions of economic, political, and social affairs.

In establishing the validity of the test, the investigator has relied upon the careful selection (on a frequency basis) of the words used, the opinions of judges as to the value of each item for insertion in the test, and the discriminatory value of each test item when answered in a trial run using a slow learning group and an average or above group of children.

For a test compiled by an individual working with limited facilities, Rayner has done a good job. However, one feels that since the test is constructed for children "at the close of their primary schooling" and since the transfer age of primary school children in the states of Australia to secondary education varies from 12 to 14 years, the time has now arrived for the establishment of different norms in the various states based on representative samples of children and also for the calculation of more adequate estimates of reliability and validity based on the final form of the test.

[831]

*Constitution: Every Pupil Scholarship Test. High school; 1926–58; new form usually issued each January; norms available following testing program; no data on reliability; 4¢ per test; 4¢ per scoring key; postage extra; 40(45) minutes; Bureau of Educational Measurements. *

[832]

*Contemporary Problems. Grades 7–9, 10–12; 1951–54; 2 forms; 2 levels; manual ('54) separate answer sheets must be used; postpaid; specimen set not available; (20–40) minutes; Citizenship Education Project, Teachers College, Columbia University; distributed by C. A. Gregory Co. *
a) JUNIOR HIGH SCHOOL FORM. Grades 7–9; Form R ('54, identical with test copyrighted in 1951); $3.50 per 35 tests.
b) HIGH SCHOOL FORM. Grades 10–12; Forms C, D ('51); $2.65 per 35 tests.

HARRY D. BERG, *Professor, Office of Evaluation Services, Michigan State University, East Lansing, Michigan.*

The *Contemporary Problems Test* of the Citizenship Education Project is not concerned with intellectual outcomes, as such, but seeks to measure in the difficult and often controversial field of beliefs and attitudes. Specifically, an attempt is made to rate students according to their democratic or undemocratic tendencies. This is to be accomplished by presenting students with a series of realistic problems and asking them to select from alternative courses of action related to those problems, the course of action they think best in the situation. Some of these courses have been previously judged to be more "democratic" than others. Scoring is comparatively simple. It consists of adding together the weights assigned to the courses of action selected by any one student. Single scores secured in this manner can then be made meaningful by reference to a table of norms set up in terms of standard scores and percentiles.

The test was validated, to the extent that this kind of test can be validated, by submitting the problem situations and action alternatives to a distinguished panel of judges. The judges were asked to assign weights of one to five to the choices according to the democratic or undemocratic content of each course of action suggested. To assist them in the process, the judges were furnished with a set of points outlining the authors' concept of the democratic method. One such point was "acceptance of a spirit of fair play, open discussion, and respect for ideas." Another was "acceptance of public service and public duty as a primary obligation of life." The amount of agreement among judges was determined by computing Spearman coefficients for pairs of judges. It is significant that the agreement was considerably less than perfect. For the three forms, agreement ranged from a mean of .75 to a mean of .79, with some coefficients dropping as low as .43. By achievement test standards, the reliabilities were not high, either. The split halves method yielded coefficients of .76 for Form C, .81 for Form D, and .71 for Form R.

Leaving aside subjective judgments about the validity of the test, the statistical data available would indicate that the test results should be used with caution. Certainly not too much confidence should be placed in the score of a single pupil. To this reviewer, one of the most valuable uses of this test would not be for rating at all, but rather to provide the basis for a stimulating class discussion.

[833]

★Dimond-Pflieger Problems of Democracy Test: Evaluation and Adjustment Series. High school; 1952–54; IBM; Forms AM, BM ('52); manual ('53); expectancy chart ['54]; separate answer sheets must be used; $3.60 per 35 tests; $1.40 per 35 IBM answer sheets; postage extra; 35¢ per specimen set, postpaid; 40(50) minutes; Stanley E. Dimond and Elmer F. Pflieger; World Book Co. *

REFERENCE

1. LUNTZ, LESTER. "Some Reliability and Validity Data on the Dimond-Pflieger Problems of Democracy Test, Form Am." Ed Rec B 66:69–72 Jl '55. * (PA 30:5166)

JOHN H. HAEFNER, *Professor of Social Studies Education, State University of Iowa, Iowa City, Iowa.*

There are two forms of this test, each containing 80 items. The items, arranged in three parts, include 34 multiple choice items, 15 matching items, and 31 statements requiring the weighing of two or three possible answers. According to the classification of the authors, approximately 30 per cent of the items deal with government, 24 per cent with economics, 34 per cent with sociology, and 12 per cent with international affairs.

The technical construction of the items is, in general, acceptable, though the matching items in particular could be much improved. Directions to the students for some of the items in Part C, which are not typical multiple choice or "best answer" items, are not as clear as they might be. The parts of the test are so arranged that a single perforated stencil can be used for hand scoring and machine scoring both forms of the test. This is a convenient feature.

The standardization group consisted of 1,372 students attending 20 high schools in 15 states. This reviewer is not an expert on test standardization procedures; however, an analysis of the location of the 20 schools leads him to raise a question about the adequacy of the standardization population. In terms of the geographic areas and divisions employed by the U.S. Bureau of the Census, it appears that 8 of the 20 schools were in the Northeast Region and 11 in the North Central Region. Only one of the 20 schools was located in the Western Region, and none were from the Mountain Western, South Atlantic, East South Central, or West South Central states.

The manual states that "some knowledge of the more basic measurement concepts by the test user is presupposed, particularly those concepts pertaining to the general nature and purpose of standardized achievement tests, measures of central tendency and variability, the nature of interpretative scores, and measurement error." The nature of the subsequent paragraphs dealing with the interpretation of test results leads the reviewer to the conclusion that the test publishers are unduly optimistic in their presuppositions. Some portions of the suggestions for interpretation of the test are difficult to decipher and certainly presuppose specialized training in testing theory. Many teachers using the test have not had such training.

The manual also states that the test is not a diagnostic instrument nor does it furnish analytical measures of the individual student's mastery of various aspects of the subject. Instead, it is designed to measure the degree to which students have achieved "the important objectives of a high school course in problems of democracy." Unfortunately, no indication is given what these important objectives may be. An examination of the test items forces this reviewer to infer that the major objective of such a course is the memorization of factual material, much of it of questionable significance. The acquisition of certain mental abilities or skills, which are nowhere clearly defined, seems to be a second objective. There is little indication that the authors began their test building with a clearly formulated set of specific objectives. The content included in the 89 topics selected seems to have been the major point of departure, rather than the objectives of the problems course. The result is that the test as a whole seems to put a premium upon, and encourages, verbalistic learning.

The 34 multiple choice items in Part A of each form of the test illustrate this. With one or two exceptions, the content of these items is such that they should be cast in the true-false rather than the multiple choice form. They require no mental operation beyond that of recognizing the one correct fact and eliminating the four incorrect facts. Likewise, the matching items in Part B call for recognition (with no evidence that there is also understanding) of terms like gerrymandering, parity, and the like.

The 31 items in Part C of both forms are of a somewhat different nature. Some of these items represent an attempt to measure the ability to interpret materials in paragraph or chart form or to relate concepts with each other. Others measure the ability to arrange events in chronological order or to recognize when certain population trends emerged. In general, the items in this section do not reflect a high degree of expertness or ingenuity in constructing items of this kind. Some items in Form AM seem to be measuring skills and abilities quite different from those measured in Form BM. Thus, while the two forms may be comparable as regards validity and difficulty of items, they may not be measuring the same skills and abilities.

Measuring achievement over content as fluid as that contained in a problems of democracy course presents special difficulties. Many of these difficulties are represented in the Dimond-Pflieger test. Some of the items are obsolete or "dated." Some reflect a point of view commonly held at the time the test was constructed, but significantly modified since that time. Particularly in Part C, "correct" responses are often based quite largely on value judgments, for example, Items 14 and 61, Form BM. In other items, "correct" answers are based on unstated premises, for example, Items 66–70, Form AM.

The attempt to provide a standardized instrument to measure achievement in problems of democracy courses is a worthy one. It presents difficulties not encountered in other areas such as American or world history. The Dimond-Pflieger test impresses the reviewer as only a little better than the end of course examination which most teachers would build for themselves. Its chief limitation seems to be the failure to formulate clearly the objectives it is intended to measure (of which the knowledge of important factual details is certainly one). Techniques for measuring the subtler and more sophisticated mental abilities, such as the ability to draw inferences or the ability to compare and contrast points of view, are known and should be employed in a test of this kind. Properly revised, the Dimond-Pflieger test could be developed into a useful and much needed measuring instrument.

DOUGLAS E. SCATES, *Professor of Education, University of Florida, Gainesville, Florida.*

The manual states that this test "has been constructed to measure the extent to which students have achieved the important objectives of a high school course in problems of democracy." Under the names of the Director and the Evaluation Director of the 5-year Citizenship Education Study conducted in the Detroit Public Schools, this statement is nothing short of shocking. It may be that the authors of the test did not see copy for the manual; if not, whoever wrote the statement is, in the reviewer's mind, guilty of inexcusable carelessness or unethical procedure.

One quickly searches the manual in the hope of finding evidence that the opening statement, as quoted, is a misprint. He finds rather confirmation of the point of view: he reads that material was selected to "represent a balanced coverage of objectives." In a time when any employee of a major test publishing house would insist that he understood the meaning of the word "objectives," this statement becomes as misleading and indefensible as the first. On page 7 of the manual is the third unblushing statement that "the primary purpose of this test is to provide a valid, objective measure of achievement in problems of democracy for the individual student." The final paragraph of the manual attempts to atone: it is written in the spirit of someone who knew the truth and wanted to say what he knew but felt censored, either overtly or through his understanding that the publisher would not be made happy through allusions to possible limitations of the test.

Turning to the test itself, the reviewer's feeling is one of disappointment. The predominantly factual, relatively sterile group of items, most of which might be part of any routine course in modern history or formal civics, when set over against the outcomes that one might hope for in the area of "problems of democracy," stirs the reviewer's sense of professional integrity. For the authors of this test are the ones who wrote: "The quality of citizenship is directly related to the emotional development of the child." (This finding is apparently too basic to be considered among "the important objectives of a high school course.") "Civic lethargy is a disease that can destroy our way of life." (If it is a disease, it is obviously not an objective. But what about the alleviation of the disease?) "There is need....for participation in democratic activities." [1] (Ap-

1 DIMOND, STANLEY E. *Schools and the Development of Good Citizens,* pp. 2, 40, 209. Final Report of the Citizenship Education Study. Detroit, Mich.: Wayne University Press, 1953. Pp. 215.

parently this is of no concern for a course in problems of democratic living.) Our concern should be "not to give answers....but to supply students with technics for analyzing critically." [2] (Analysis in the sense of detecting problems or diagnosing them was not found in the test.) "Emotional adjustment leads to good citizenship." [3] (Not even knowledge of the importance of emotions is deemed worthy of a place in a test of problems of living.) "Keys to good citizenship" [4] include better emotional adjustment, clear thinking, engagement in civic action. (Yet these factors are negligible in a test of "the important objectives.")

Of course, the reviewer is confusing citizenship and the problems of democracy, something on the order of confusing members of the human race and people. Are we to assume that problems of democracy, when packed into the mold of a high school course, become mere intellectual statements—verbal pawns to be pushed at each other by teacher and pupil, with no more meaning for real life than a leaf blown across the lawn? No doubt the authors were told (or understood) that current practice and lofty (realistic?) conceptions are different things; that one cannot expect high school pupils to be enthusiastic over the large social problems of our day; that a test, to be successful (to sell), must be geared to the common practices of the average high school. Accordingly, with almost complete disregard for what the authors have contributed to our understanding of the essential ingredients in citizenship, a relatively commonplace group of facts from recent American history are described as representing "the important objectives of a high school course." The reviewer has an understanding of, and a genuine respect for, our American economic system; yet he must raise the question of how far it is necessary for publishers (and authors) to go, under the influence of competitive sales, in their distortions in a professional field of endeavor.

One need not take his departure from the published views of the authors; he may turn to his own expectations as an American citizen seriously interested in the public schools. A course in problems of democracy might, apart from any survey of widespread practice, be presumed (or hoped) to give our young people insights into the character of societal problems; to cultivate the ability to sense, analyze, and define problems and issues in the contemporary news of current publications; to heighten discernment in identifying the forces at work in the day-to-day and decade-by-decade problems of his own society in his own lifetime; to develop judgment concerning the direction of social trends and their possible consequences; to stimulate interest to the point of desire for some lifelong participation in the affairs of our larger social groups; to contribute an appreciation of the role of social skills, and the need for learning them, in any social enterprise. As American citizens, we desire a degree of critical mindedness, but not without appreciation based on the awareness that "many sincere, capable, and conscientious" persons have struggled to produce what we now have (Dimond, 1953, p. 10); we recognize the need for continued evaluation by every citizen, but not without understanding of the costs met by those who have built the present; we believe in the need for persons who are forward looking, who are to some extent dissatisfied, who feel and express the urge for better things—but not without historical grounding and philosophic perspective. And if we might have some tendency to hope that our schools would attempt substantial contributions in these directions, might we not also desire that the tests by which learning and teaching success are gaged—both in the public and in the professional eye— might lend their support to a major emphasis on such goals?

Those who know high school well may say that we should not expect so much from the limited opportunities of courses in school. The point is well taken. One cannot read the careful, scientifically oriented, refreshingly candid final report of Dimond (1953; cf. p. 202) without awareness of this fact. It is not, however, so much the degree as the character of the learning that represents the tremendous hiatus between carefully formulated goals and actual practice. It is the tendency to believe and proceed on the notion that learning must begin with facts and that, after some years, one may build on these facts. In virtually all areas of human behavior such a notion is highly fallacious, and in some areas it is about the worst

2 COLLINGS, MILLER R., AND DIMOND, STANLEY E. "Citizenship Education." *Nation's Sch* 46:42-4 N '50.
3 PFLIEGER, ELMER F., AND WESTON, GRACE L. "Emotional Adjustment Leads to Good Citzenship." *Nation's Sch* 46:61-2 D '50.
4 DIMOND, STANLEY E. "Keys to Good Citizenship." *Nat Parent-Teach* 49:19-21 F '55.

possible. It can be entertained only by those whose interest in the knowledge of facts is over and above their interest in practical competence. For facts are of value only to the person who is deciding and doing, and the barriers to human thought and action are greater and more serious than is the difficulty of becoming acquainted with relevant available facts. Let us therefore, as teachers, give major attention where the needs are major—such as the overcoming of complacency inertia; the breaking of the thought-action barrier; the identification of the self with the larger concern; easing through the fear of the unfamiliar—the transition from action in primary groups to action in secondary and tertiary groups; the steps necessary to avoid "going off half-cocked"— the need for punctilious care in *getting adequate relevant facts;* the importance of relating one's thoughts, attitudes, values, and plan of action to a larger context—lest one find oneself pulling in a direction embarrassing to one's other commitments; and the expectation that one will learn more as he works, and will make modifications in his ideas as he sees things partly in terms of the interests of others. (How different is such learning from that of the self-sufficient prig who knows everything in the textbook, blows the top off objective tests, gets the highest approbation of his school in terms of marks—and often knows nothing of life as it flows around and by him without making contact.) Objectives *are* important; they can be different.

It can be argued that a preponderant concern with the teaching (and learning) of facts is a serious detriment to priceless initiative, to the creative impulse, to the hope of desirable change. For one thing, the person (teacher or pupil) who starts with facts as his chief goal is likely never to separate himself from this goal. In any field, the accumulated mass is overwhelming, and new facts are produced daily at too rapid a rate for even the specialist to keep up with them. One therefore becomes ever more frantic in his lifelong squirrel-cage pursuit of what he conceives to be the mere foundation of an education. Teachers must somehow *from the start* give him an awareness that there are other things, other qualities, other learnings, other pursuits that make up the educated citizen.

Even more serious, however, than the misdirected life is the one that is stopped, bound, confined. We criticize civics texts and courses of the early part of this century because they offered young people a kind of learning about civic structure, civic processes, and civic attitudes that was akin to, let us say, learning in arithmetic. And the kind of attitude, the mental pattern, engendered in such factual teaching is what we might expect from saying day in and day out over the years, "Now young people, this is it; and if you don't do precisely as you are told you will be in trouble." For a still young and hopeful America there could be no greater trouble or danger than the stamping in of just such a mental pattern. So often in education we advertise goals of participation in constructive change, yet we teach "facts" ("This is the way it is.") in a matrix of inhibiting, fear-engendering reprisal for any hint of individuality in thought or behavior. It is difficult to say whether the social or the physical sciences are the greatest offenders. In any area such a position is a serious misconstruction. In the social sphere, we call attention to the danger of being a deviate; yet the facts are that there have been more changes in our culture in the past 50 years than in any other culture in any similar period. Do we dare teach (in problems in democracy) that our country was founded, largely peopled, and established by "deviates" of one kind or another—those who couldn't, or wouldn't knuckle down and conform to what the majority of Europeans would? In the physical sciences and mathematics, many persons regard the "facts" as inexorable, representing an ultra-human rightness that makes wrong anything one may wish to think that has not come down to him from the past. This despite the fact that mathematics during the past half century has had more *new* developments than in all its preceding history; or that physics in the past 50 years has added more to the power of mankind than it had in all its previous history. Those who think of "facts" as permanent verities must not have lived during the present century.

So the person who, in any field, is taught in such a way that he is permitted to get the impression that the world is "all set" and fixed, and that his business is to exist within the inherited confines of knowledge and propriety and to fight off any threat of change, has built into him habits of mind that ill fit him for participation in the swift currents of American cultural change, and that a long after-school life may never successfully alter. In an avowed democracy, should we not teach most of our courses (including problems of democracy) in such a way as to make the young person feel that he *has a place* in working out the changes that *are going to occur,* one way or the other, in his culture during his life? There are subtle but critical differences between the person who is taught primarily for the learning of facts and the person who is taught primarily to *function* as a member of his society, habitually taking the precaution to obtain the latest facts relating to his activity. The *ability to do* is not completely independent of hard facts; but creative ability so often places the "hard facts" in new perspectives, new relationships (such as 20th century mathematics has done) so that new ways of dealing with the facts are found and the old "facts to be faced" become merely relics of an obsolescent way of thinking. "Facts" can be so learned that they fit into schemes of use which are more important, more constructive, and more socially valuable than answering recall and discrimination questions at the end of a school course.

It may be felt that the reviewer is not writing from the background of current realities of the schoolroom, where problems of democracy is but one course among a number that the teacher must teach while the students, with nature on their side, exert every known form of resistance. Perhaps he is; perhaps he is making an appeal to textbook writers, testmakers, and those who prepare supplementary instructional materials not to handicap the stimulating teacher by concentrating on an inferior set of outcomes. It is difficult enough to accomplish results above the ordinary; it is cruel to have such efforts evaluated by an assessment scheme that omits them.

There are realities of many kinds—those in the classroom situation, those in our very dynamic contemporary culture, and those in curriculum and testmaking procedures. Perhaps we should be impressed when we read in the manual the serious (?) statement that the test was constructed by "(1) determining in the soundest manner possible the objectives to be measured; (2) determining the proper emphasis and weights to be assigned to the various objectives." But we are reminded of certain realities pointed out by Ralph Tyler 20 years ago: for test making purposes "each objective must be defined in terms which clarify the kind

of behavior that the course should help to develop among students." (Behavior includes all forms of reaction and doing.) "A definition of objectives in terms of expected student behavior differs from the analysis-of-content method * It does more than indicate the content to be covered. It defines the reactions which a student is expected to make to this content * With the same content it makes a great deal of difference." [5] (Tyler's statements were not meant to be coercive or restrictive; he was emphasizing that, for testing purposes, an objective needs to be stated in terms of *doing*—of which knowing is one form. But most course objectives fall outside this latter category.)

According to further statements in the manual, the "soundest manner possible" turns out to be that of analyzing textbooks and articles to find out what topics were dealt with. Topics! As though *topics* constituted the moving forces in the restless life of active youngsters sensing the dynamism of their elders in coping with a culture that surges with change. Ascertaining objectives merely by noting topics is a "sound" procedure only if one's thinking about methods of work consists essentially of a list of steps to be checked off after one has mechanically gone through certain motions. It is a far cry from topics to objectives; almost any topic lends itself to a very wide range of different objectives.

It is an interesting commentary on the technological age in which we live that professional judgment is virtually banned. In its place we have the respectability of "rigid standards" representing the imposition of relatively fixed (and often inappropriate) formalities, the spell cast by any sort of mumbo-jumbo reference to "the scientific method," the mesmerizing allure of a display of esoteric statistical terms, and, above all, the unquestioning belief in the miraculous revealing power of the modern pencil point wiggle.

The reviewer must, in fairness, note that the Dimond-Pflieger test has a number of qualities in which all persons concerned can take some satisfaction. Of the 80 items, nearly one third call for something other than recall and association: they require deduction, critical discrimination, inference, and general understand-

5 HAWKES, HERBERT E.; LINDQUIST, E. F.; AND MANN, C. R., EDITORS. *The Construction and Use of Achievement Examinations,* pp. 10–11. Boston, Mass.: Houghton Mifflin Co., 1936. Pp. x, 497.

ing (presumably untaught association). This is undoubtedly "better" than most teacher-made tests would do. The test has many earmarks of successful application of currently approved test-making procedures. The work has been done with technical sophistication. The test manual is commendably written, primarily to teachers. It is written simply, though at points carelessly or studiedly misleading, with no attempt to overawe the reader with technical flamboyancy. The test can be widely used with no more harm than centering the attention of students and teachers on the minor, relatively inconsequential outcomes of a subject area fundamentally important and potentially potent in the outlook and large social abilities of those who will soon inherit the real problems of our American democracy where we lay them down.

[834]
★General Knowledge Test of Local, State, and National Government. Grades 11–16; 1952; 8 scores: general, local, state, national executive, national legislative, national judiciary, national total, total; 1 form; norms ['52]; $3.95 per 25 tests; 40¢ per manual ['52]; 65¢ per specimen set; postpaid; 50(60) minutes; Mae Pullins Claytor; C. A. Gregory Co. *

WAYNE A. FREDERICK, *Social Studies Department, Isidore Newman School, New Orleans, Louisiana.*

This test is a comprehensive examination in local, state, and national government. Several sound features place the scope of the test beyond that of simple measurement of knowledge in terms of memorized factual data.

For one thing, although many items are designed to explore only the factual knowledge of the student, many more measure his ability to perceive relationships among basic concepts, and some call for an evaluation of perceived relationships. In this respect, Section 1, Government in General, is most carefully drawn.

For another, the items have been carefully selected to emphasize basic concepts in the several areas. Relatively few items concern themselves with trivia. The attention paid to pertinent historical concepts is to be commended.

Finally, the items have, in general, been well constructed. They are precise and cogent, with most of the options being parallel in construction and pertinent to the concept which the item is attempting to measure. Because of their weak construction a few items appear to be very easy. However, in no case does poor workmanship result in a confused or ambigu-

ous item. There are five true-false type items in Section 1 which cover concepts which could have been better tested by well made items of the multiple choice type. Also, in each of Sections 1 and 2 there is a set of sequential items carrying the same options. Most of these items test only factual knowledge, consequently weakening the test. Significant relationships concerning these same concepts could have been tested by some other device.

Basically this test appears to be what its author intended it to be—a sound comprehensive measure of the kind of knowledge that should be achieved by students in secondary schools and colleges. Since the items have been carefully drawn to measure concepts which are general in nature, the test can be used anywhere in the United States.

[835]
*The Graduate Record Examinations Advanced Tests: Government. College seniors and graduate students; 1939–56; for more complete information, see 601; IBM; 180(200) minutes; Educational Testing Service. *

CHRISTINE MCGUIRE, *Assistant Professorial Lecturer in the Social Sciences, and Examiner, The University of Chicago, Chicago, Illinois.* [Review of Form EGR.]

This examination, for college seniors majoring in political science, is designed primarily to test their competence in their field of concentration. Test results are used to evaluate the student's mastery of the materials as a part of a comprehensive departmental examination or to select among applicants for graduate study or special graduate appointments.

Descriptive material furnished with the examination does not specify the major objectives nor the particular areas of subject matter sampled in the test. However, copies of the examination are available to prospective users for inspection. Approximately half of the test consists of objective items sampling a miscellaneous array of discrete information. This reviewer could detect no skill required in answering items in this section of the test other than the rather simple recall of facts at various levels of detail. The balance of the test consists of objective questions based on quite interesting and often ingenious charts, diagrams, verbal descriptions of hypothetical situations, and passages representing a variety of points of view. In the questions related to these contextual statements the student is required to demonstrate the ability to read and understand the material in the form presented, to recall relevant information, and to apply general principles in interpreting the material and drawing conclusions or making predictions based on it. The questions in this section of the examination vary greatly with respect to clarity, freedom from ambiguity in the correct answer, and level of skill and understanding required of the student. The length of the test in itself (more than one item per minute, including time required for reading and studying the numerous charts and statements) precludes the inclusion of questions requiring any very complex form of analysis. Despite these deficiencies, this section of the test provides a very useful framework which it is hoped can be more successfully exploited to require the kinds of skills and understanding that might reasonably be expected of college graduates majoring in government.

In the absence of explicit criteria for determining the choice of subject matter and skills to be sampled, it is difficult to evaluate the coverage of the examination. However, in this reviewer's opinion some areas (for example, public administration) are given undue weight at the cost of neglecting or seriously undervaluing other equally important areas (for example, political theory, comparative government, international law and diplomacy, and analysis of the dynamics of public opinion formation and political behavior). Secondly, in the areas that are extensively represented, the particular questions asked suggest a more or less random (rather than a systematic) sampling of basic concepts and principles. Third, the test places too heavy a premium on the more simple skills of recall and comprehension and inadequate weight on the more analytical and integrative skills.

In addition to an individual score report for each student taking the test, the user is supplied with the usual data on reliability and correlations with aptitude tests, and with statistical tables relevant to the interpretation of the scaled scores in terms of which test results are reported. Two cautions should be observed in utilizing these data. First, the scale values were initially determined by a series of steps which require estimating, on the basis of the actual performance of a subgroup, the probable performance of a total group from "eleven colleges selected to be representative of colleges

using the Graduate Record Examinations." The *estimated* means and standard deviations may therefore be subject to certain errors, and the appropriateness of the scaling group for use as a reference group is exceedingly difficult to judge. The Score Interpretation Handbook for Deans and Advisers, November 1957, makes clear that for these and other reasons "a given college will probably find that norms collected at their own college or at a group of similar schools, will be more useful for their own purposes." Secondly, in the summary statistics provided for any given year, the only information about the group on which percentile rankings are based is a listing of the number of examinees from each participating institution. Under certain conditions the Educational Testing Service is willing to provide data on special groups that may be more appropriate for use as reference groups by a particular institution. However, in this reviewer's opinion, reports in the form of per cent of correct responses would generally be more useful to graduate schools to which a candidate is applying, and an analysis of responses to particular items would be more useful to departments from which groups of examinees are graduated.

In summary, this examination covers in considerable detail, but not necessarily in a manner that is systematically appropriate to any given department, several areas in the very broad field of government. It omits certain important areas and perhaps minimizes certain important skills in which majors in government should be able to demonstrate respectable achievement. The data supplied with test results are comprehensive but of limited usefulness in the absence of local norms.

For a review by Harold Seashore of the entire series, see 601.

[836]
★**The Kansas Constitution Test.** High school and college; 1957; Form A ['57]; mimeographed manual; no college norms; $1.20 per 25 tests, postage extra; 25¢ per specimen set, postpaid; 40(45) minutes; Louise Gardner and M. W. Sanders; Bureau of Educational Measurements. *

DAVID K. HEENAN, *Assistant Professor, Department of Humanities, and Office of Evaluation Services, Michigan State University, East Lansing, Michigan.*

This test consists of 125 items based on the formal structure and functions of the United

States Constitution. It covers vocabulary, history, and application of the Constitution. The items are drawn from the document itself or from textbooks which deal with the Constitution and related American history.

On the whole, the test is made up of incidental details which could be recalled only after an exhaustive study of the subject or memorization of the document. While the test adequately samples the factual information the student might have, it makes little effort to measure the student's *understanding* of these facts. Though a student might score well by being able to recall bits and parcels of information on the Constitution, rarely is he forced to compare or evaluate his accumulation of details.

Some of the items seem unnecessarily petty: "Closure is observed in the Senate to (stop a filibuster)." This is something that happens so rarely that it is hardly worth mentioning; certainly little time would be spent on this subject in class. Too many items call for "the number of this" or "the name of that," as in "The usual number of years given to a state to ratify an amendment is (seven)"; "The number of ways to become a citizen is (three)"; "The Elastic Clause of the Constitution is found in (Article I, Section 8)."

The test should be carefully checked by an authority on the subject of Constitutional history (this reviewer is not such an authority) to eliminate stem statements which lead to misunderstanding and confusion. For example, "If neither of the candidates for President receive a majority of all the electoral votes then the President is chosen by (the House of Representatives)." The word "none" should be substituted for "neither." "Neither" implies that there were only two candidates—in which case a majority of the electoral votes would be a mathematical certainty. Another item reads: "The framers of the Constitution were principally (lawyers)." Here perhaps there would be less chance of confusion if "delegates to the Constitutional Convention" were substituted for "framers" since some of the more active "framers" (Washington, Franklin, Jefferson, etc.) were not lawyers.

The test should be further checked for errors. In the item, "Congress created the Immigration and Nationalization Service which is regulated by the Department of (Justice)," "Naturalization" should be substituted for

"Nationalization." Again, in the item, "One of the first examples of the use of implied powers was the establishment of (the Federal bank)," "United States" should be substituted for "Federal."

It is unfortunate that in the few questions which require some exercise of judgment the testmaker has chosen subject matter on which there is strong disagreement. For example, "The method of choosing the President and Vice President provided for by the Constitution (has become obsolete and should be changed)." While this reviewer would also choose the expected answer, perhaps it is unfair to ask all students to concur in this judgment.

The test probably exemplifies the teaching approach used in most American secondary schools in dealing with the Constitution. The *details* of the Constitution become the object of emphasis at the expense of the philosophy of the document. Perhaps the best way to cut down on the trivial elements in the test is to shorten it. The whole test could stand editing and should be rewritten if it is to be a reliable instrument to measure students' knowledge and understanding.

[837]

★Newspaper Reading Survey: What Do You Read? High school; 1954; 4 interest scores: local, national, international politics, total; 1 form; $2.50 per 35 tests, postpaid; specimen set not available; (20–35) minutes; Citizenship Education Project, Teachers College, Columbia University; distributed by C. A. Gregory Co. *

FREDERICK H. STUTZ, *Professor of Education, Cornell University, Ithaca, New York.*

This test is designed to gauge the level of interest in political events relative to interest in other types of events. Students are expected to select from each of 10 groups of nine simulated newspaper headlines those three headlines which represent stories they would like most to read and the three which represent stories they would like least to read. Each group of nine headlines includes one each on local, national, and international political events.

Teachers of the social studies or citizenship education, especially those in junior high schools, will find this interest test to be worth using in an experimental fashion. By pretesting, they may discover something of the kinds of reading interests students have and be able to guide the development of interest in reading about political affairs. Post testing may help the teacher to determine shifts in reading interests as a result of instruction. The test is brief, well constructed technically, fairly easy to score, and accompanied by a useful set of instructions of admirable brevity.

The user should be fully aware of the limitations of a test of this sort. The scoring norms are derived from a limited administration of the test. Though validity has been sought by including headlines selected by groups with known special interests, it is by no means certain that the test will fully appraise relative levels of interest in political events. The headlines themselves, though they have been generalized by having names and dates removed, become rather quickly dated. Pupil choices of the nonpolitical headlines may be influenced by the fact that some of the political items are no longer of current interest.

The test represents a worthwhile effort to get at one of the neglected aspects of citizenship education, interest in politics. It should be used experimentally by teachers who are specially concerned with the teaching of citizenship ideas and practices. The test has limitations which should be fully recognized by users.

M. J. WANTMAN, *Visiting Director of Educational Measurement and Research, University of Malaya, Singapore.*

This test is designed "to enable teachers to evaluate the level of student interest in local, national, and international political events as compared with other interests." The student is presented with 10 groups of headlines which are similar to those found in newspapers. In each group there is a headline dealing with each of the following areas: music or art, religion, human interest, sports, science, economics, and local, national, and international political affairs. Thus, each group consists of nine headlines, three of which are political ones. The student is instructed to mark a plus sign next to three headlines for stories that he would MOST like to read, to mark a minus sign next to three headlines for stories that he would LEAST like to read, and to leave three headlines blank.

In the scoring of the test, a student is given 2 points for each political headline that he marked as "MOST liked to read," 1 point for each political headline left blank, and no points

for each political headline that he marked as "LEAST liked to read." Thus, a student marking all 30 political headlines, 10 local, 10 national, and 10 international, as "MOST like to read" would receive the maximum possible score of 60.

The norms for the test are based on 692 students in the 10th, 11th, and 12th grades in 20 high schools. The authors express the hope that "more complete norms may be included in future editions of this test." Four years after its initial publication, more complete norms are still not available.

Norms are presented in the form of percentiles, with separate values for the local, national, international, and total scores. The values recorded indicate that girls have a greater interest in political affairs than do boys. The authors make no comment on this result.

Test-retest (after three weeks) reliabilities are reported for 75 high school seniors as .89, .72, .81, and .78 for total, local, national, and international scores, respectively. Neither standard deviations nor standard errors of measurement are reported. Estimating the standard deviations from the table of norms, and using the reliability coefficients reported above, one can estimate the standard errors of measurement for the part scores to be in the neighborhood of 2 points, and for the total score to be in the neighborhood of 3 points. The low reliabilities with the accompanying relatively large standard errors of measurement are not surprising when one recalls that the test is in reality a 30-item test.

This instrument designed to measure interest in political affairs has the usual weaknesses of interest inventories. Fudging is possible in spite of the confident statement of the authors that the probability of the purpose of the instrument being detected by students is not great provided it is presented as a survey of reading interests. No evidence is presented for the validity of the instrument for its stated purpose. The method of choosing the items to be included in the inventory is described briefly. This description supposedly supports the contention of face validity for the classification of the headlines.

The *Newspaper Reading Survey* is not recommended by this writer to teachers who might wish "to evaluate the level of student interest in local, national, and international political events as compared with other interests."

[838]

★Patterson Test or Study Exercises on the Constitution of the United States. Grades 9–16 and adults; 1931–53; 1 form ('53, same as test copyrighted in 1937 except for minor changes); directions sheet ['53]; no data on reliability and validity; $2.25 per 25 tests; 35¢ per specimen set; postpaid; (40–50) minutes; Raymond G. Patterson; Public School Publishing Co. *

[839]

★Patterson Test or Study Exercises on the Declaration of Independence. Grades 9–16 and adults; 1931–52; 1 form ('52, combination of Forms A and B copyrighted in 1931 with minor changes); manual ('52); no data on reliability and validity; no norms; $2.25 per 10 tests; 35¢ per specimen set; postpaid; (40–50) minutes; Raymond G. Patterson; Public School Publishing Co. *

[840]

★Peltier-Durost Civics and Citizenship Test: Evaluation and Adjustment Series. High school; 1958; 2 scores: achievement, attitude; IBM; Forms AM, BM; $3.80 per 35 tests; separate answer sheets may be used; $1.40 per 35 IBM answers sheets; postage extra; 35¢ per specimen set, postpaid; 55(65) minutes; Charles L. Peltier and Walter N. Durost; World Book Co. *

[841]

★Principles of American Citizenship Test. Grades 11–12; 1952–53; formerly called *Premises of American Government Test*; Forms A, B ('52); manual ('53); $3.50 per 35 tests, postpaid; specimen set not available; 40(50) minutes; Citizenship Education Project, Teachers College, Columbia University; distributed by C. A. Gregory Co. *

REFERENCE

1. CITIZENSHIP EDUCATION PROJECT. *Premises of American Liberty, With Citation of Basic Documentation.* New York: Teachers College, Columbia University, 1952. Pp. 15.

HOWARD R. ANDERSON, *Professor of Education, and Dean, University School of Liberal and Applied Studies, The University of Rochester, Rochester, New York*

The manual for this test states that it was developed to measure the attainment of three objectives: "1. Knowledge of the documented accomplishments of liberty as these are revealed in history. 2. Knowledge of the principles and ideals upon which our democratic society is based and how these ideals apply to everyday life. 3. Knowledge of the problems and issues which beset our society to-day." Actually the test concerns itself chiefly with the second. No items specifically test knowledge of the historical evolution of liberty or its attainment in lands other than the United States. Nor does the test contain any item on unemployment, inflation, high taxes, the cold war, communism, or anti-Western feeling in former colonial areas, which surely are among "the problems and issues which beset our society."

The explanation that this test "measures the student's understanding of the United States citizen's rights and responsibilities and his ability to apply to specific situations the 'Premises of American Liberty' (formulated by the staff of the Citizenship Education Project)" is more accurate. But even this statement seems to exaggerate the function of such test items as "An individual nominated for public office is called (a candidate)," "A tax on money earned during the year is called (an income tax)," and "A unique power of the Senate....is....to (approve treaties)."

Undoubtedly this test includes items which measure knowledge commonly acquired in courses in civics, American history, and problems of American democracy. Some of the items go beyond direct recall to measure the pupil's understanding of how a democratic principle applies in a given situation. The 54 four-response multiple choice items included in each form of the test are almost always clearly phrased and free of technical imperfections. Two items in Form A may be dated, however. Item 37 gives as the "essential difference between a scientist in a democracy and a scientist in a totalitarian country" this statement: "[The latter] is under pressure to produce results in line with political beliefs." That may have been true in certain fields at one time but will hardly hold as a generalization. Item 40 calls for "made the public aware of its neglected responsibilities" as the correct response to "The greatest immediate value of the Senate investigation of organized crime (1951)." No high school youngster would remember this investigation nor would he be likely to have read about it. Doubtless he could, however, figure out the answer since the foils are: "eliminated most big-time gambling," "brought criminals to justice," and "taught the public how the Senate operates."

Percentile norms are provided for junior and senior high schools. These would not be too useful in evaluating achievement in a given grade. Social studies teachers naturally could not depend on this test alone to measure achievement in civics, American history, and problems of American democracy classes; but the test might well be used to supplement more traditional tests.

M. J. Wantman, *Visiting Director of Educational Measurement and Research, University of Malaya, Singapore.*

This test was originally designed to measure a student's mastery of the "Premises of American Liberty" compiled by the Citizenship Education Project of Teachers College, Columbia University. The subsequent change of the name of the, test to its present title is misleading since the test content is still restricted to the project's list of 90 premises.

The stated purposes of the test are so broad that one would hesitate to attempt to achieve them in a 54-item multiple choice test. There is no evidence presented that the authors even approached their goal.

The suggested uses of the results of the test include appraisal of class position as compared with that of other classes in the United States, appraisal of an individual's standing in a class, and teaching. Since separate norms are not presented for the various grades, comparison with other classes is impossible; the advice to teachers on the use of results to appraise an individual's standing in a class is couched in such words of caution that a teacher could not be expected to use the test for this purpose; there are no doubt better ways to teach the premises of American liberty than by means of this test.

The typography and format of the test are excellent. A single typographical error was noted—a misspelling in the correct option for Item 48 in Form A. The answer sheet is easily managed. The system for assigning letters to options is designed to minimize the student's mismarking his answer sheet.

The norms provided are based on 2,742 and 2,899 cases for Forms A and B, respectively. Since the cases for each form include both junior and senior high school students, the numbers on which the norms for each of these groups are based must be considered inadequate. In view of the limited number of cases, it is difficult to understand the authors' statement that the norms are "representative of the national high school population." They even indicate that "regional norms are available on request."

Separate norms are provided for Form A and Form B. The norms include only the nine deciles. Form A appears to be the easier of the two forms for junior high school students, while Form B is the easier one for senior high school students. No explanation is provided for this result.

The reliability of the two forms, computed by the split-half method, yielded values of .90 and .91 for Forms A and B, respectively. The number of cases on which these coefficients are based is not given.

There is no evidence presented that this test is valid for measuring the "student's understanding of the United States citizen's rights and responsibilities and his ability to apply to specific situations the 'Premises of American Liberty.'" The acceptance by a test user of the claims made for the test depends on the user's confidence in the judgment of the authors.

The *Principles of American Citizenship Test* should be used only in those situations where the "Premises of American Liberty" have been taught. Even then, as the authors warn, the results of individual students should be interpreted with caution. In view of the limitations of the test, the weaknesses of its norms, and its specificity for the "Premises of American Liberty," a classroom teacher would probably do well to devise his own test if he felt compelled to test for an understanding of the principles of American citizenship.

SOCIOLOGY

[842]
*The Graduate Record Examinations Advanced Tests: Sociology.** College seniors and graduate students; 1939–56; for more complete information, see 601; IBM; 180(200) minutes; Educational Testing Service. *

For a review by Harold Seashore of the entire series, see 601.

[843]
★Sare-Sanders Sociology Test.** High school and college; 1958; Form A; mimeographed manual; $1.20 per 25 tests, postage extra; 25¢ per specimen set, postpaid; 40(45) minutes; Harold Sare and Merritt W. Sanders; Bureau of Educational Measurements. *

[844]
★Sociology: Every Pupil Scholarship Test.** High school; 1943–58; new form issued each January; norms available following testing program; no data on reliability; 4¢ per test; 4¢ per scoring key; postage extra; 40(45) minutes; Bureau of Educational Measurements. *

VOCATIONS

REVIEWS BY *Brent Baxter, Edward S. Bordin, Arthur H. Brayfield, E. G. Chambers, J. F. Clark, Andrew L. Comrey, William C. Cottle, Jerome E. Doppelt, Henry S. Dyer, John W. French, Clifford P. Froehlich, Edward B. Greene, John W. Gustad, Lloyd G. Humphreys, John R. Jennings, A. Pemberton Johnson, Robert A. Jones, Clifford E. Jurgensen, Martin Katz, Raymond A. Katzell, Albert K. Kurtz, Wilbur L. Layton, John Liggett, D. W. McElwain, I. G. Meddleton, P. L. Mellenbruch, William J. Micheels, John B. Morris, Charles T. Myers, Mary Ellen Oliverio, John Pierce-Jones, Arthur B. Royce, William B. Schrader, Donald Spearritt, Donald E. Super, Erwin K. Taylor, Albert S. Thompson, Herbert A. Tonne, Arthur E. Traxler, S. Rains Wallace, Neil D. Warren, Alexander G. Wesman, Haydn S. Williams, and Alfred Yates.*

CLERICAL

[845]

★**A.C.E.R. Short Clerical Test.** Ages 13 and over; 1953–57; Forms A ('53), B ('56) ; no manual; mimeographed directions sheet ['57] ; no data on reliability and validity; no norms; distribution of Form A restricted; 6s. per 10 tests ; 1s. 6d. per set of directions and scoring key; 2s. per specimen set; postpaid within Australia; 10(15) minutes; Australian Council for Educational Research. *

[846]

*****A.C.E.R. Speed and Accuracy Tests.** Ages 13.6 and over; 1942–57; 1 form ['57] ; 2 tests: number checking, name checking; revised mimeographed manual ['53] ; no data on reliability; separate answer sheet must be used; 5s. per 10 tests ; 1s. 9d. per 10 answer sheets ; 2s. per manual ; 2s. 6d. per scoring key ; 5s. per specimen set; postpaid within Australia; 12(20) minutes; Australian Council for Educational Research. *

REFERENCES

1. HOHNE, H. H. *Success and Failure in Scientific Faculties of the University of Melbourne.* Melbourne, Australia: Australian Council for Educational Research, 1955. Pp. vii, 129. * (PA 31:3787)
2. BUCKLOW, MAXINE, AND DOUGHTY, PATRICIA. "The Use of Aptitude Tests in Clerical Employment: The Selection of Accounting Machinists." *Personnel Pract B* 13:35–44 S '57. *

For a review by D. W. McElwain of an earlier form, see 4:719.

[847]

*****Clerical Aptitude Test: Acorn National Aptitude Tests.** Grades 7–16 and adults; 1943–50; 4 scores: business practice, number checking, date-name-address checking, total ; 1 form ('50, identical with test copyrighted in 1943) ; manual ('50, identical with manual copyrighted in 1943) ; directions sheet ('50, identical with sheet copyrighted in 1943) ; no norms for part scores; $3 per 25 tests ; 25¢ per manual ; 50¢ per specimen set; postage extra; 40(45) minutes; Andrew Kobal, J. Wayne Wrightstone, and Karl R. Kunze; Acorn Publishing Co. *

REFERENCE

1. BAIR, JOHN THEODORE. *Factor Analysis of Tests Purporting to Measure Clerical Aptitudes.* Doctor's thesis, Ohio State University (Columbus, Ohio), 1949.

For reviews by Marion A. Bills, Donald G. Paterson, Henry Weitz, and E. F. Wonderlic, see 3:623.

[848]

★**Clerical Tests 1 and 2.** Ages 12–14.0; 1952–54; 1 form ; 2 tests; no data on reliability and validity; distribution restricted to directors of education; 4s. 6d. per 12 tests ; 5d. per single copy ; 1s. 6d. per manual ; postage extra; published for the National Foundation for Educational Research in England and Wales; Newnes Educational Publishing Co. Ltd. *
a) CLERICAL TEST 1. 1952–53; 1 form ['52] ; manual ['52] ; norms ['53] ; 40(60) minutes; M. K. B. Richards.
b) CLERICAL TEST 2. 1953–54; 1 form ['53] ; manual ['53] ; norms ['54] ; 43(75) minutes; G. A. V. Morgan.

[849]

*****[Hay Tests for Clerical Aptitude.]** Applicants for clerical positions; 1941–55; 4 tests; manual ('50) ; 75¢ per battery manual ('50) ; $1 per specimen set; postage extra; 13(28) minutes; Edward N. Hay; Aptitude Test Service. *
a) TEST 1: THE WARM UP. 1945–55; practice exercise to precede administration of battery; Form B ('50, revision of the 1945 form) ; directions sheet ('55) ; $1.25 per 25 tests ; 1(3) minutes.
b) NUMBER PERCEPTION TEST. 1947–50; Forms A ('47), B ('50, same as test copyrighted in 1947) ; $2 per 25 tests ; 4(7) minutes.
c) NUMBER SERIES COMPLETION TEST. 1941–55; Forms B ('50, same as test copyrighted in 1949), C ('55) ; no norms for Form C; $1.25 per 25 tests ; 4(7) minutes.
d) HAY NAME FINDING TEST. 1941–55; Forms C ('50, same as test copyrighted in 1949), D ('55) ; practice exercise, Form B ('49) ; $2 per 25 tests ; 4(11) minutes.

REFERENCES

1–8. See 4:725.
9. SEASHORE, HAROLD G. "Validation of Clerical Testing in Banks." *Personnel Psychol* 6:45–56 sp '53. * (PA 28:1670)
10. HAY, EDWARD N. "Comparative Validities in Clerical Testing." *J Appl Psychol* 38:299–301 O '54. * (PA 29:6351)

For reviews by Reign H. Bittner and Edward E. Cureton, see 4:725.

[850]

Minnesota Clerical Test. Grades 8–12 and adults; 1933–46; formerly called *Minnesota Vocational Test for Clerical Workers* (see 40:1664) ; 2 scores: number comparison, name comparison; 1 form ('33); revised manual ('46); $1.80 per 25 tests; 35¢ per specimen set; postpaid; 15(20) minutes; Dorothy M. Andrew, Donald G. Paterson, and Howard P. Longstaff; Psychological Corporation. *

REFERENCES

1–18. See 40:1664.
19–40. See 3:627.
41. HACKMAN, RAY CARTER. The Differential Prediction of Success in Two Contrasting Vocational Areas. Doctor's thesis, University of Minnesota (Minneapolis, Minn.), 1940.
42. STEAD, WILLIAM H.; SHARTLE, CARROLL L.; OTIS, JAY L.; WARD, RAYMOND S.; OSBORNE, HERBERT F.; ENDLER, O. L.; DVORAK, BEATRICE J.; COOPER, JOHN H.; BELLOWS, ROGER M.; AND KOLBE, LAVERNE E. Occupational Counseling Techniques: Their Development and Application. Published for the Technical Board of the Occupational Research Program, United States Employment Service. New York: American Book Co., 1940. Pp. ix, 273. *
43. CRISSEY, ORLO L. "Test Predictive of Success in Occupation of Job-Setter." Abstract. Psychol B 39:436 Jl '42. *
44. ACHARD, F. H., AND CLARKE, FLORENCE H. "You Can Measure the Probability of Success as a Supervisor." Personnel 21:353–73 My '45. *
45. COX, K. J. "Aptitude Testing in Industry." B Can Psychol Assn 5:99–102 D '45. * (PA 20:2035)
46. CARPENTER, EDWIN KENNETH. The Effect of Ego-Involved Attitudes on Aptitude Test Performance. Doctor's thesis, Clark University (Worcester, Mass.), 1947.
47. KENDALL, WILLIAM E., AND HAHN, MILTON E. "The Use of Tests in the Selection of Medical Students by the College of Medicine of Syracuse University." Abstract. Am Psychol 2:297 Ag '47. *
48. STRONG, EDWARD K., JR. "Norms for Graduate School Business Students on the Minnesota Vocational Test for Clerical Workers." J Appl Psychol 31:594–600 D '47. * (PA 22:2775)
49. BEAMER, GEORGE C.; EDMONSON, LAWRENCE D.; AND STROTHER, GEORGE B. "Improving the Selection of Linotype Trainees." J Appl Psychol 32:130–4 Ap '48. * (PA 23:965)
50. BAIR, JOHN THEODORE. Factor Analysis of Tests Purporting to Measure Clerical Aptitudes. Doctor's thesis, Ohio State University (Columbus, Ohio), 1949.
51. BLACK, MARGARET H. An Evaluation of the Differences Obtained by White and Negro Veterans on the Minnesota Clerical Test. Master's thesis, University of Delaware (Newark, Del.), 1949.
52. BLANCHARD, HOWARD L. A Comparison of Teachers' Marks With an Actual Battery of Aptitude Test Percentile Scores. Doctor's "Field Study No. 1," Colorado State College of Education (Greeley, Colo.), 1949.
53. CAPWELL, DORA F. Psychological Tests for Retail Store Personnel. Pittsburgh, Pa.: Research Bureau for Retail Training, University of Pittsburgh, 1949. Pp. 48. * (PA 25:3449)
54. CARTER, LAUNOR, AND NIXON, MARY. "Ability, Perceptual, Personality, and Interest Factors Associated With Different Criteria of Leadership." J Psychol 27:377–88 Ap '49. * (PA 23:4183)
55. JACKSON, JOSEPH. "An Analysis of the Minnesota Vocational Test for Clerical Workers in a High School Situation." J Social Psychol 30:149–53 Ag '49. * (PA 24:2652)
56. SUPER, DONALD E. Appraising Vocational Fitness by Means of Psychological Tests, pp. 164–83. New York: Harper & Brothers, 1949. Pp. xxiii, 727. * (PA 24:2130)
57. WIGHTWICK, BEATRICE. The Effect of Retesting on the Predictive Power of Aptitude Tests. Doctor's thesis, New York University (New York, N.Y.), 1949.
58. BERKSHIRE, ROGER, AND FLEET, DONALD. "College Junior Norms for 1947 A.C.E. and Minnesota Clerical Tests." Occupations 29:30–1 O '50. * (PA 25:3417)
59. BORG, WALTER R. "Does a Perceptual Factor Exist in Artistic Ability?" J Ed Res 44:47–53 S '50. * (PA 25:2921)
60. ENGELHARDT, OLGA E. DE CILLIS. "The Minnesota Clerical Test: Sex Differences and Norms for College Groups." J Appl Psychol 34:412–4 D '50. * (PA 25:4878)
61. HAY, EDWARD N. "Cross-Validation of Clerical Aptitude Tests." J Appl Psychol 34:153–8 Je '50. * (PA 25:3991)
62. JOHNSON, RALPH H., AND BOND, GUY L. "Reading Ease of Commonly Used Tests." J Appl Psychol 34:319–24 O '50. * (PA 26:299)
63. LEE, MARILYN C. Relationship of Masculinity-Femininity to Tests of Mechanical and Clerical Abilities. Master's thesis, University of Minnesota (Minneapolis, Minn.), 1950.
64. MILLER, RICHARD B. "Reducing the Time Required for Testing Clerical Applicants." Personnel J 28:364–6 Mr '50. * (PA 24:4872)
65. BAIR, JOHN T. "Factor Analysis of Clerical Aptitude Tests." J Appl Psychol 35:245–9 Ag '51. * (PA 26:3067)
66. BLAKEMORE, ARLINE. "Reducing Typing Costs With Aptitude Tests." Personnel J 30:20–4 My '51. * (PA 25:7749)
67. HAY, EDWARD N. "Mental Ability Tests in Clerical Selection." J Appl Psychol 35:250–1 Ag '51. * (PA 26:3071)
68. PETRIE, ASENATH, AND POWELL, MURIEL B. "The Selection of Nurses in England." J Appl Psychol 35:281–6 Ag '51. * (PA 26:3090)
69. PURDY, BENJAMIN FRANK. A Study of Certain Tests and Personal History Factors as Predictors of Job Success for a Group of Clerical Workers. Master's thesis, Southern Methodist University (Dallas, Tex.), 1951.
70. AMERICAN GAS ASSOCIATION, PERSONNEL COMMITTEE. Personnel Testing in the Gas Industry. New York: the Association, January 1952. Pp. 10. *
71. LEE, MARILYN C. "Relationship of Masculinity-Femininity to Tests of Mechanical and Clerical Abilities." J Appl Psychol 36:377–80 D '52. * (PA 27:6431)
72. ANDERSON, ROSE G. "Do Aptitudes Support Interests?" Personnel & Guid J 32:14–7 S '53. * (PA 28:4495)
73. BRAYFIELD, ARTHUR H. "Clerical Interest and Clerical Aptitude." Personnel & Guid J 31:304–6 F '53. * (PA 28:1616)
74. JENKINS, JAMES J. "Some Measured Characteristics of Air Force Weather Forecasters and Success in Forecasting." J Appl Psychol 37:440–4 D '53. * (PA 29:1642)
75. SEASHORE, HAROLD G. "Validation of Clerical Testing in Banks." Personnel Psychol 6:45–56 sp '53. * (PA 28:1670)
76. COYLE, FRANCIS P. The Effect of Perceptual Training Upon Minnesota Clerical Speed Test Performance. Master's thesis, Utah State Agricultural College (Logan, Utah), 1954.
77. GRAHAM, WARREN R. "Identification and Prediction of Two Training Criterion Factors." J Appl Psychol 38:96–9 Ap '54. * (PA 29:1798)
78. LEE, PHYLLIS JEANNE. The Effectiveness of a Test Battery in Predicting Chemistry Grades. Master's thesis, Alabama Polytechnic Institute (Auburn, Ala.), 1954.
79. LONGSTAFF, HOWARD P. "Practice Effects on the Minnesota Vocational Test for Clerical Workers." J Appl Psychol 38:18–20 F '54. * (PA 29:1645)
80. LOWE, LEWIS M. The Effects of Drill on the Numerical Aspects of the Minnesota Clerical Test. Master's thesis, Atlanta University (Atlanta, Ga.), 1954.
81. RUSMORE, JAY, AND MARTIN, FRED. "Validity Information Exchange, No. 7-053:D.O.T. Code 1-37.34, Clerk-Typist." Personnel Psychol 7:289 su '54. *
82. YOUNG, MARY B. The Predictive Value of the Wonderlic Personnel Test and the Minnesota Clerical Test in the Selection of Clerical and Telephone Sales Workers. Master's thesis, Boston University (Boston, Mass.), 1954.
83. FORSTER, CECIL R. The Relationship Between Test Achievement and Success in Training of a Selected Group of Tuberculosis Patients. Doctor's thesis, New York University (New York, N.Y.), 1955. (DA 15:1201)
84. KIRKPATRICK, DONALD L. "The Minnesota Clerical Test." Personnel Psychol 10:53–4 sp '57. *
85. SAWYER, JACK. "Validity Information Exchange, No. 10-12:D.O.T. Code 9-88.40, Order-Filler." Personnel Psychol 10:90 sp '57. *
86. LONGSTAFF, HOWARD P., AND BELDO, LESLIE A. "Practice Effect on the Minnesota Clerical Test When Alternate Forms Are Used." J Appl Psychol 42:109–11 Ap '58. *

DONALD E. SUPER, Professor of Education, Teachers College, Columbia University, New York, New York.

The Minnesota Clerical Test, first published in 1933, has become something of a fixture, almost an institution, among American test batteries. More thoroughly studied as a new test than are most such devices, supported by nearly a score of studies before it was much more than five years old, and with a manual which was revised according to contemporary ideas of what a manual should be immediately after World War II, this test was virtually a model test in a field surprisingly short of models. But now a dozen years have passed since the revised manual was published, and it is time to take another look at the test.

This reviewer examined seven studies published within the past 12 years. One (65) is a factor analysis of 18 clerical aptitude tests which isolated three factors, all of which are found to have heavy loadings in the MCT, making it one of the best in the group. The factors (perceptual analysis, speed, and comprehension of verbal relationships) are thus broken down further than they were in the earlier studies which used less refined batteries of tests. A second paper (*84*) reports a defect in the construction of the numbers test which seems not to have been noticed before. The others are minor normative studies, summaries of validities, and a study of the relationship between aptitude and interest.

Does the *Minnesota Clerical Test* need further studying, a new manual? Are validity, standards, and meaning permanent and immutable? Have new questions been raised? Are there any unanswered questions? It may be helpful to review the issues here. They fall under three headings: technical refinements, norms, and criteria.

TECHNICAL REFINEMENTS. Kirkpatrick has pointed out that, whereas in the names test the dissimilar elements in nonidentical pairs are evenly distributed throughout the names, in the numbers test 77 per cent of the differences are to be found in the last half of the numbers, 14 per cent in the first half, and 9 per cent in the middle. This means that an alert examinee can save time by reading each pair backwards, and that he and those who read backwards anyhow are favored in this subtest. Since the correlation between numbers and intelligence is negligible, not many alert persons can have noticed this fact, but the defect should be corrected.

NORMS. More significant than the ordering of the items is the matter of norms, for either these are old, based on very small numbers, and local in nature (Tables 4–5, 8–9), or, if more up to date, they are based on a single company in a single community (Tables 6–7) or on samples which are selected in undefined ways which make them not very meaningful (Tables 10–12). When these norms were first published, and even when the 1946 manual appeared, they were so much better than the norms available for most civilian vocational tests that they were widely welcomed. But what was good in 1946 is not good now, in the light of higher standards and of time in which to improve. Let me be specific.

The "Norms for Employed Clerical Workers" (Table 4) are presumably the crucial norms for a test of aptitude for clerical work when the aptitude has been shown not to be influenced by training or experience. Although it is not so stated, these appear to be norms

collected by the Minnesota Employment Stabilization Research Institute early in the 1930's, and, as stated, they include 284 women and 120 male clerical workers, presumably those used to provide the more specific occupational norms in Table 8. How adequate today are clerical norms based on 120 men in Minneapolis and St. Paul a quarter century ago? How representative now are the 17 bank tellers, 29 accountants and bookkeepers, 44 general clerical workers, and 30 routine clerical workers?

The educational norms can be criticized in the same way. The increase in scores with age and grade shown in Tables 10–11 may be due to selection, or it may be due to maturation. If the latter, then conversion tables are needed, based on age changes, so that adolescents may be compared with the adult occupational groups with which they will in due course compete. (Contrary to the statement made on page 6 of the manual, and by one of the reviewers in *The Third Yearbook,* one is not primarily interested in making age- or grade-group comparisons in vocational counseling; instead, one needs to compare the individual with those with whom he will compete, and his competitors are other entrants into the occupation he is considering, not his classmates.) The New England norms are not, as suggested, a "cross-section sampling of 6,262 pupils from 76 representative high schools from Maine to Rhode Island." Unless the reviewer was misinformed while working in that same area when those data were gathered, the boys and girls who took those tests were students in schools which *happened* to cooperate in Boston University's high school testing program, a program conducted more for public relations and recruiting purposes than for any other reason; furthermore, they were the boys and girls in those schools who wanted to take the Boston University tests. That hardly makes them a "cross-section sampling" from "representative high schools." We know how to do better than this now.

CRITERIA. The treatment of validity in the manual was, in 1946, unusually good. The results of studies are reported according to criterion type: ratings, grades in accounting, speed of typing, occupational differentiation, success (with training and work oddly confused), and other clerical tests. But reliance is, for today, too heavily on excellent original work, and, as one reviewer in *The Third*

Yearbook pointed out, the occupations have not been well enough defined. No use was made of studies cited by Ghiselli (*25*) and Copeland (*7, 12*), nor of the varied USES data reported by Stead and Shartle (*42*). Furthermore, we have learned a great deal about validation since World War II, so that during the ensuing decade many more studies should have been made of the criteria of success in various types of clerical jobs, and this test should have been validated against well defined criteria of success in specific clerical occupations. Hay's study (*31*) of success in machine bookkeeping is one such study that is cited in the manual: the criterion, number of entries per hour, was well studied and the job well defined, but the manual does not reveal this nor has any apparent effort been made to obtain more such data for other clerical jobs and to incorporate them in the manual.

In summary, the *Minnesota Clerical Test* is as good a test as it ever was, and still probably has no effective rival. But it has not kept up with the times, either in the studies which have been published concerning it or in the manual which guides its use by vocational counselors and personnel men. It is time for the authors and publishers to protect their investment in this test by investing in it again, to make a minor technical improvement, to collect current and representative age and occupational norms, and to validate it against well defined criteria of success in specific clerical occupations.

For reviews by Thelma Hunt, R. B. Selover, Erwin K. Taylor, and E. F. Wonderlic, see 3:627; for a review by W. D. Commins, see 40:1664.

[851]

*O'Rourke Clerical Aptitude Test, Junior Grade. Applicants for clerical positions; 1926–58; 2 parts; no manual; no data on reliability and validity; $1.95 per 50 copies of either part, postage extra; 25¢ per specimen set, postpaid; L. J. O'Rourke; Psychological Institute. *
a) CLERICAL PROBLEMS. 1926–35; Form 1 ('35); 25(30) minutes.
b) REASONING TEST. 1926–58; Form A ('58, essentially the same as Form A copyrighted in 1936 except for changes in a few items); 20(25) minutes.

REFERENCES

1–3. See 3:629.
4. BAIR, JOHN T. "Factor Analysis of Clerical Aptitude Tests." *J Appl Psychol* 35:245–9 Ag '51. * (PA 26:3067)

For a review by Raymond A. Katzell, see 3:629.

[852]

★Personnel Institute Clerical Tests. Applicants for office positions; 1957–58; manual ('58) for both batteries; no data on reliability and validity; $4.50 per 5 sets of tests of either battery; $3 per manual; $12 per kit of manual and 5 copies of each battery; postage extra; Personnel Institute, Inc. *
a) BATTERY A: FOR TYPIST-STENOGRAPHERS. 1957–58; 1 form ('57); 35.5(80) minutes.
1) *EM-AY Inventory.* Reprint under new title of *Otis Employment Tests,* Test 2, Form A ('22); intelligence; 20(30) minutes.
2) *Grammar Test.* 3(8) minutes.
3) *Spelling Test.* 2.5(7) minutes.
4) *Test of Typewriting Ability.* 10(20) minutes.
5) *Personal History Inventory.*
b) BATTERY B: FOR CLERICAL PERSONNEL. 1957–58; 1 form ('57); 26(75) minutes.
1) *EM-AY Inventory.* Same as *a*(1).
2) *Comparing Names Test.* 1.5(6) minutes.
3) *Copying Numbers Test.* 3(8) minutes.
4) *Arithmetic Test.* 1.5(6) minutes.
5) *Personal History Inventory.*

[853]

*Purdue Clerical Adaptability Test, Revised Edition: Purdue Personnel Tests. Applicants for clerical positions; 1949–56; 6 scores: spelling, computation, checking, word meaning, copying, reasoning; Form A ('56); manual ('56); $5 per 25 tests, postage extra; 50¢ per specimen test, postpaid; 47.5(60) minutes; C. H. Lawshe, Joseph Tiffin (test), and Herbert Moore (test); distributed by University Bookstore. *

REFERENCES

1. SINCLAIR, GORDON ROGERS. *Standardization of the Purdue Clerical Adaptability Test.* Master's thesis, Purdue University (Lafayette, Ind.), 1950.
2. LAWSHE, C. H., AND STEINBERG, MARTIN D. "Studies in Synthetic Validity: I, An Exploratory Investigation of Clerical Jobs." *Personnel Psychol* 8:291–301 au '55. * (PA 30:7381)

MARY ELLEN OLIVERIO, *Associate Professor of Education, Teachers College, Columbia University, New York, New York.*

The traditionally measured abilities of prospective clerical workers are included in the six subsections of this test.

Section 3, Checking, would have been more appropriately set up if the lines on the two pages matched. In this section, the subject should be instructed to mark the errors and then count them for recording the number in the blank at the end of the line. In the actual clerical situation, the worker marks copy where errors are to be corrected.

The manual contains a brief but clear description of the manner in which the test was constructed and of the reliability and validity measures used. The authors caution the test user as to the interpretations of the various measures used. The cautions are appropriate. For example, although norms are provided, the statement is made that the "safest and best way is for each user to develop his own norms." This caution is exceedingly important since the reader is given no information concerning the 3,970 applicants for clerical positions at Purdue University and the 650 applicants in eight companies whose scores were used for the establishment of the norms. Inasmuch as the test, during the experimental stages, was found to be far too difficult for girls just leaving high school and was revised, some question might be raised about the use of the norms given for large groups of young workers entering their first jobs. The user is not given the age, level of education, or previous experience of the groups used for the establishment of norms. It would be helpful to know if these 4,620 applicants are representative of the group entering clerical occupations each year.

This test should prove helpful to those organizations that must choose large numbers of clerical workers and that have clearly identified that the job skills needed are those measured in this test.

DONALD SPEARRITT, *Senior Research Assistant, Australian Council for Educational Research, Melbourne, Australia.*

Measurement of clerical aptitude appears to have reached the stage where the most useful item types are reasonably well established. As a result, most tests of clerical aptitude now exhibit a fairly common pattern, and the Purdue test is no exception. Clerical tasks differ among themselves, however, and it is satisfying to note that the authors of this test suggest that the results of a job analysis should guide the test user in deciding which subtest scores are worth using in his own situation.

The test itself leaves nothing to be desired in the way of layout or typography, but a number of criticisms can be made of the content and form of presentation of some subtests. Testees are warned against making "unnecessary" mistakes in two of the subtests. In the vocabulary test, "proper" is taken to mean the same as "propriety," while obscure words like ture, spodumene, naroud, and lyrate are included among the distractors.

The lowest one per cent of the norming sample made a score of 23 on the spelling test, so it appears that the number of items in this test could be greatly reduced, with a consequent saving in testing time. The procedure of counting as well as finding mistakes in the checking test does not seem to reflect the actual clerical task which usually requires only the identification of errors. Testees are given no indication of the approach they should adopt in working the copying test; a candidate who was under the impression that neatness or accuracy at all costs was the chief aim of this test would be penalised. For additional information on accuracy in a speeded task, the test user would do well to note the number of items attempted in the checking test, as the correlation between the speed test (checking) and the accuracy test (copying) is not high (.35).

In this revision of the test, the authors have incorporated the concepts of reliability and validity set out by the American Psychological Association in 1954. Although the difficulties involved in obtaining test-retest coefficients of reliability with applicant groups are formidable, it is essential to obtain such reliabilities for speed tests if no equivalent form of the test is available. High school groups in the last year of their course and with prospects of employment in sight should be sufficiently motivated to make a genuine attempt at the test early and late in the school year. The authors recognize that the split-half reliability coefficients are likely to be spuriously high for the speed tests. If the only reliability coefficients available for speed tests are split-half coefficients, it is debatable whether they should be presented at all. There is no mention of a standard error of measurement and no indication of the standard deviation of the scores of the group used for estimating reliabilities.

The brief note on content validity could be profitably expanded by making some analysis of common clerical tasks and showing how the subtest areas were related to these. The authors are right in emphasizing that the test user should build up his own evidence of predictive validity in his particular situation. Expectancy charts based on a very small number of cases suggest that the subtests have satisfactory predictive validity for later job performance. Extensive evidence of the test's concurrent validity for distinguishing between different types of clerical workers is presented in the form of group profiles. The concept of synthetic validity is also introduced. In requiring a more detailed statement of the operations involved in the criterion, it draws on the notion of content validity to some extent, but is mainly a variation of predictive validity. It would seem preferable to present validity data in terms of established concepts, rather than to introduce new concepts with which few test users would be familiar.

Despite the criticisms leveled at the test, the validity data suggest that it would be a useful aid in the selection and placement of clerical personnel. Its value could be better assessed if further evidence of predictive validity were collected, and if the characteristics of the norming sample were described in more detail. The inclusion of a reasoning subtest is likely to give it an advantage over tests such as the *Turse Clerical Aptitudes Test* for selecting higher level clerical personnel. But the extensive time required for its administration inevitably places it at a marked disadvantage with shorter tests such as the *Short Employment Tests*.

For reviews by Edward N. Hay, Joseph E. Moore, and Alec Rodger of the previous edition, see 4:731.

[854]
*The Short Employment Tests. Applicants for clerical positions; 1951–56; Forms 1 ('51), 2 ('51), 3 ('51), 4 ('51); 3 tests: CA ('51, clerical), N ('51, numerical), V ('51, verbal); revised manual ('56); distribution of Form 1 restricted to banks which are members of the American Bankers Association; Form 4 is restricted for special uses; $1.80 per 25 tests; 35¢ per specimen set; postpaid; 15(20) minutes; George K. Bennett and Marjorie Gelink; Psychological Corporation. *

REFERENCES
1. BENNETT, GEORGE K., AND GELINK, MARJORIE. "The Short Employment Tests." *Personnel Psychol* 6:151–7 su '53. * (PA 28:3339)
2. WILKINSON, BRYAN. "Validity of Short Employment Tests." *Personnel Psychol* 6:419–25 w '53. * (PA 28:8194)
3. RUSMORE, JAY, AND MARTIN, FRED. "Validity Information Exchange, No. 7-053:D.O.T. Code 1-37.34, Clerk-Typist." *Personnel Psychol* 7:289 su '54. *
4. WESTBERG, WILLIAM C.; FITZPATRICK, EUGENE D.; AND McCARTY, JOHN J. "Validity Information Exchange, No. 7-073: D.O.T. Code 1-37.32, Typist." *Personnel Psychol* 7:411–2 au '54. *
5. WESTBERG, WILLIAM C.; FITZPATRICK, EUGENE D.; AND McCARTY, JOHN J. "Validity Information Exchange, No. 7-074: D.O.T. Code 1-37.32, Typist." *Personnel Psychol* 7:413 au '54. *
6. WESTBERG, WILLIAM C.; FITZPATRICK, EUGENE D.; AND McCARTY, JOHN J. "Validity Information Exchange, No. 7-087: D.O.T. Code 1-37.32, Typist." *Personnel Psychol* 7:561–2 w '54. *
7. FITZPATRICK, EUGENE D., AND McCARTY, JOHN J. "Validity Information Exchange, No. 8-35:D.O.T. Code 9-00.91, Assembler VII (Electrical Equipment)." *Personnel Psychol* 8: 501–4 w '55. *
8. HUGHES, J. L., AND McNAMARA, W. J. "Relationship of Short Employment Tests and General Clerical Tests." *Personnel Psychol* 8:331–7 au '55. * (PA 30:7828)
9. BENNETT, GEORGE K., AND DOPPELT, JEROME E. "Item Difficulty and Speed of Response." *Ed & Psychol Meas* 16: 494–6 w '56. *
10. McCARTY, JOHN J., AND FITZPATRICK, EUGENE D. "Validity Information Exchange, No. 9-26:D.O.T. Code 5-92.621, (Foreman II)." *Personnel Psychol* 9:253 su '56. *
11. WALKER, FRANCIS C. "Normative Data Information Exchange, Nos. 5–6." *Personnel Psychol* 9:271–2 su '56. *
12. McCARTY, JOHN J. "Validity Information Exchange, No. 10-14:D.O.T. Code 1-33.01, Secretary." *Personnel Psychol* 10: 202–3 su '57. *
13. McCARTY, JOHN J. "Validity Information Exchange, No. 10-15:D.O.T. Code 1-33.01, Secretary." *Personnel Psychol* 10: 204–5 su '57. *
14. McCARTY, JOHN J. "Normative Data Information Exchange, Nos. 10-20, 10-21, 10-22." *Personnel Psychol* 10:242–4 su '57. *
15. McCARTY, JOHN J. "Normative Data Information Exchange, No. 10-30." *Personnel Psychol* 10:364 au '57. *
16. DUNNETTE, MARVIN D., AND KIRCHNER, WAYNE K. "Validation of Psychological Tests in Industry." *Personnel Adm* 21: 20–7 My–Je '58. *

P. L. MELLENBRUCH, *Professor of Psychology, University of Kentucky, Lexington, Kentucky.*

The *Short Employment Tests* were developed to supplement tests being used by member banks of the American Bankers Association for the selection of clerical workers. The Personnel Testing Committee of the ABA participated in the outlining of general specifications for the series, and recommends the SET as one of a group of tests suitable for use by member banks. The recommendation specifies that the tests are regarded as "suitable for use with candidates for clerical employment, but not for administrative trainees nor for maintenance employees." Further, it is suggested that banks administer all three tests—verbal, numerical, and clerical—to each such applicant, "rather than omitting a test which seems not to be closely related to the contemplated job."

The results of tests N and CA are said to be particularly important for general clerical jobs, while V score and the total score are to be stressed for stenographers and applicants for "positions involving much writing or oral communication." "Pending completion of local studies," the authors recommend cutoff scores corresponding to the 25th percentiles (for stenographers, the 50th percentile for the verbal score). No evidence is presented to show that these cutoff points were arrived at empirically.

The working time for each test is five minutes and the instructions are not too time-consuming, so the specification that the entire series not consume over 20 minutes has been met. A second specification was that test-retest reliabilities should exceed .80. Reliabilities seem fairly satisfactory for successive administrations of alternate forms. Reliabilities for V and N range from .83 to .91, and CA reliabilities range from .77 to .85. A third specification, that the directions and scoring be simple, is met easily for test N. Directions for V are clear though somewhat more complex than for N. Directions for CA are rather complex and probably quite foreboding to the type of person who will take the test. There is too much massed print in these directions and there are too many cases in the sample problem.

The final specification for the series was that "content should encompass verbal, numerical, and clerical skills." Herein lies the chief problem. Two of the three areas are not *encompassed*. There is a coverage of the various usual numerical operations involved in lower level clerical work; however, only one narrow segment or slice is measured in each of the verbal and clerical skills areas. Only word meaning is sampled in the V area and only classifying or filing is sampled in CA. If V and CA need no broader sampling than this, then perhaps N might well be made up of items involving but one single arithmetic operation, e.g., simple addition. No evidence is offered to show that the single ability sampled in V and in CA was arrived at empirically and that this sampling gives validity as good as or better than what would be given by a more *encompassing* array of items. As a matter of fact, if but a single kind of item is to be used, there is good reason to believe that a test composed of only the very best of the items which are provided would give as reliable and valid results as the total number employed in these tests, unless, of course, the test is also a test of fatigue and perhaps boredom.

Considerable attention has been given to the validation of this series. Nineteen studies, all based on female subjects, are reported in the manual. Generally speaking, the validity coefficients are not very impressive.

Of course, the reviewer is quite sure that the reported validity coefficients are spuriously low as is true for most reported test validities. First of all, the criteria are of questionable value. Supervisors' ratings, which were the chief criteria, are notoriously subjective. Furthermore, correlation rests upon an unsound principle with respect to most employment situations. This is true whether we use linear, biserial, or some other of the usual forms of correlation. The fallacy lies in the assumption that the higher the score on a particular test the greater the expectancy of success. For most jobs this is not true. Instead, for almost any job, there is an optimum range within the total span of scores for any differentiating trait which should serve as the most appropriate prediction of success. Scores outside the cutoff points used would indicate a greater probability of failure. Were cutoff points used, it would doubtless be possible to show that for various clerical jobs a particular candidate would most probably be a successful employee if his score fell within a predetermined range of scores on any one or more of the tests. Optimum cutoff points for each of these tests should, therefore, be established empirically for each class of clerical positions. If this were done, a satisfactory validity would be more probable.

Correlations with other tests as reported in the manual are about what might be expected. Each test shows a fair correlation with other tests which have face validity, but these figures are hardly sufficiently high to justify substituting one for the other.

Altogether, it might be more appropriate to identify the tests as V-vocabulary, N-numerical, and C-classifying, because there is no evidence that the verbal factor in office jobs can be satisfactorily measured by testing vocabulary only, or that CA (skills? aptitude?) can be adequately sampled by the single activity of classifying.

[855]

★**Turse Clerical Aptitudes Test.** Grades 8–12 and adults; 1955, c1953-55; 7 scores: verbal, number, written directions, learning ability, clerical speed, clerical aptitude, accuracy; 1 form ('55); manual ('55); no adult norms; no norms for accuracy; $3.35 per 35 tests, postage extra; 35¢ per specimen set, postpaid; 28(40) minutes; Paul L. Turse; World Book Co. *

REFERENCE

1. PRESCOTT, GEORGE A. "Prediction of Achievement in Commercial Subjects." *Ed & Psychol Meas* 15:491–2 w '55. * (PA 30:7772)

ROBERT A. JONES, *Assistant Director, Testing Bureau, University of Southern California, Los Angeles, California.*

This test consists of six subtests: Verbal Skills, Number Skills, Written Directions, Checking Speed, Classifying-Sorting, and Alphabetizing. Scores on the first three subtests are combined to give a measure of "learning ability," while the last three yield a clerical speed score and, optionally, a clerical accuracy score. All six in weighted combination yield the "general clerical aptitude" score.

The test booklets are not reusable. Since separate answer sheets cannot be used because the first three parts are, in general, made up of completion type items, the test must be hand scored. While care was exercised in designing the scoring keys to make scoring as simple as possible, scoring is not a rapid process. The method of scoring specified, i.e., no penalty for wrong answers even on the sections of 2-choice, highly speeded items, perhaps represents a compromise to shorten scoring time.

This seems rather undesirable to the reviewer. There is no objection to number right scoring on the first three parts.

The format of the test booklet, especially the cover page, seems a little cluttered. The practice items for Number Skills are not separated from the body of the subtest. Since the part is admitted to contain an element of speed, this seems to be inappropriate. Also, there are no practice items for Written Directions, which seems (to the reviewer) to need practice material. Perhaps practice material for Verbal Skills, Number Skills, and Written Directions could all be placed on a revised cover sheet.

The section of the manual covering instructions for test administration seems clear and explicit. The time required for test administration (less than the usual class period) seems reasonable for high school use, but the test probably requires too much time for business use as a pre-employment test.

The manual states that the general clerical aptitude score (the weighted total score) is a combination of twice the learning ability score plus the clerical speed score. In many clerical tasks accuracy is more important than speed. For this reason the author's decision to place emphasis on speed while making accuracy minor (optional) seems regrettable.

Except for norms for girls in a 12th grade commercial course and mean scores for boys and girls, separate norms by sex are not provided. Even though the author feels that such norms are not very useful in the high school, the differences between the total population norms and the norms for 12th grade girls and the mean scores by sex are large enough to be statistically significant. The test user should have available to him norms by sex in addition to those presently included. No adult norms are provided. Standard deviations are not presented so completely as means. More specific information about the composition of the norm group is needed.

Verbal Skills is more difficult than it should be for maximally efficient measurement for all groups included in the norms. The difficulty level may be acceptable for adults, but no data are presented for adults. While not intended to be the usual verbal measure, Verbal Skills includes, in addition to vocabulary items, items of spelling, word sense, and phonetic association. The subtest correlates highly (.68) with total scores on Form OM of the *Cooperative*

English Test. One type of item used sometimes seemed slightly obtuse to the reviewer. For example, a word written as it is pronounced (tox) is given and the examinee is to supply the correct spelling (talks).

In addition to test-retest values, corrected split-half reliabilities for the first three subtests (the least speeded parts) and the learning ability total are given. The manual states that these values for Written Directions differ appreciably. Standard errors of measurement are given for both test-retest and corrected split-half coefficients and, while notice is taken of the differences, those based on corrected split-half scores are not firmly disclaimed. The split-half correlation would better be left out entirely.

There are some other objections to the content of the manual. With regard to use of the test in making educational and vocational plans, the manual is a little expansive. The statement is made that "the student's profile of TCAT strengths and weaknesses will be helpful in determining the kind of clerical job that should be sought"; however, most of the facts needed for such counseling would have to be supplied by the user to supplement those in the manual. While, in general terms, the manual cautions the user in general about interpretation of test results, the possible relationship of response set to poor performance is not noted. No validation data on Written Directions are given.

In one study reported, the learning ability score correlated .72 with Terman-McNemar IQ's. Although the manual cautions that the learning ability score is a "rather restricted" measure of intelligence, the statement needs clarification in the absence of any other statistical evidence.

On the whole, the workmanship on this test is competent. While the existence of the test on the market is in no sense decried, the reviewer feels that the test does not meet uniquely any need which other tests do not fulfill just as well.

DONALD SPEARRITT, *Senior Research Assistant, Australian Council for Educational Research, Melbourne, Australia.*

The title of this test is sufficient to indicate its purpose to most test users. With the possible exception of the written directions test, the subtest item types are characteristic of those usually included in tests of clerical aptitudes. The test of verbal skills departs from the general practice in presenting phonetic association and word sense items in cyclic form with spelling and vocabulary items. A realistic coverage of the number skills involved in clerical work is attempted in the test of number skills, which covers cross-addition, cancellation, and negative balances, as well as the four basic arithmetic processes. These efforts to improve the content validity of the tests are commendable, but, at the same time, some comparison of their predictive validity for a given criterion with that of a single item type verbal or number test would have been desirable. The test of written directions takes the form of a test of attention; more realistic content, based on sets of instructions actually used in clerical situations, could have been devised. The three speed tests, which involve checking, classifying and sorting, and alphabetizing, all measure important aspects of clerical jobs. In selecting applicants for particular clerical positions, a personnel officer may find it necessary in some cases to look beyond the single clerical speed score obtained for these three tests.

The format and layout of the tests are adequate, and the folded strip and stencil scoring keys are simple and effective. The profile chart on the front page of the test enables the user to obtain a quick graphical picture of a candidate's performance and, equally important, some idea of the likely one standard error range for true scores on various subtests.

The manual contains most of the technical information that would normally be asked for by a test user. The provision in the general directions for the use of erasers seems to be unwise in the case of speed tests; blocking out wrongly marked answers would be preferable. Other minor faults in the manual concern the absence of information about the criterion used in the item analysis in the preliminary tryouts of the items and about the method or groups used to determine the weights for arriving at the general clerical aptitude score.

Correlations with various achievement measures are provided for all subtests except Written Directions. Most of these predictive validities attain a very satisfactory level. The amount of attention given to the collection of adequate validity data is praiseworthy, especially the preparation of work sample tests to assess the validity of the clerical speed tests. The discussion of validity could be improved, however, by the introduction of the concepts of content and construct validity. Reliability coefficients are satisfactory, except perhaps for Written Directions. The provision of test-retest reliability coefficients for all normed subscores and of standard errors of measurement based on these coefficients meets accepted technical standards for speed tests. The only criticisms that can be made in this connection concern the absence of clear data to indicate whether the standard errors of measurement differ at different points of the score range, and the need for additional interpretative material illustrating the actual use of the standard errors of the differences in subtest percentile ranks.

The problems involved in presenting both accuracy and speed scores in a meaningful way for the clerical speed tests may justify the author's decision not to present accuracy norms. But his statement that "it is necessary to determine the *number attempted* only if a Clerical Accuracy score is to be derived" does not seem appropriate to the use of the clerical speed tests in selection situations. It is often as important to know how many items a candidate marks wrongly in these tests as it is to know the number he marks correctly.

This test shows evidence of a highly competent and realistic approach to the task of measuring the important skills and abilities involved in clerical work. The technical information provided in the manual is of a high standard and indicates that the various subtests will give reliable predictions of success in relevant achievement and job performance areas. The test's most important deficiency is the absence of adult norms. For assessing aptitude for most clerical tasks, the test would seem to be superior to tests such as the *Purdue Clerical Adaptability Test* because of its higher content validity and shorter administration time.

INTERESTS

[856]

*Brainard Occupational Preference Inventory. Grades 8–12, adults; 1945–56; 6 scores: commercial, mechanical, professional, esthetic, scientific, personal service (girls), agriculture (boys); IBM; Form R ('45); revised manual ('56); no adult norms; separate answer sheets must be used; $3.25 per 25 tests; $1.90 per 50 IBM answer sheets; 25¢ per machine scoring stencil; 35¢ per specimen set; postpaid; (30) minutes; Paul P. Brainard and Ralph T. Brainard; Psychological Corporation. *

REFERENCES

1-4. See 40:1675.
5-6. See 3:634.
7. See 4:737.
8. TORR, DONALD V. "A Factor Analysis of Selected Interest Inventories." Abstract. *Am Psychol* 7:296 Jl '52. *
9. ANDERSON, ROSE G. "Do Aptitudes Support Interests?" *Personnel & Guid J* 32:14-7 S '53. * (*PA* 28:4495)

WILLIAM C. COTTLE, *Professor of Education, The University of Kansas, Lawrence, Kansas.*

This inventory covers six broad occupational fields, with 20 items each in commercial, mechanical, professional, esthetic, and scientific areas. For the sixth field, changes were made in the current revision to allow for sex differences, males now answering 20 items for an agricultural score, and females answering 20 items for a personal service score. Each field has four occupational sections with five items devoted to each section. For example, the 20 items in the commercial field have five items each devoted to accounting, clerical work, selling, and business management. One wonders how much validity and reliability can be attached to a score secured from only 20 items and what the effect of mixing four kinds of items within a field has had upon the reported reliabilities of each field.

Normative data have been developed on 9,695 pupils in 14 school systems. Means and standard deviations by grade for boys and for girls in grades 8-12 are also reported. Since not enough differences were found among grades, percentile norms reported are based on total groups by sex, undifferentiated by grade.

Correlations with the *Kuder Preference Record—Vocational* are reported. Although the manual points out that these correlations seem to indicate little relationship between the Brainard and Kuder interest inventories, the positive and negative relationships that one might logically expect between the scales of the two inventories are demonstrated. For example, the correlation between mechanical scales was .58 for boys and .51 for girls; that between scientific scales was .53 for boys and .58 for girls. The publishers claim that the Brainard has an advantage over the Kuder because it does not contain forced choice items. No other evidence of validity is reported and this is a major weakness at present. The counselor must develop validity in his local situation through experience in using the test and through local research.

The section on interpretation of scores points out that the raw scores show variations in an individual's interest among the six fields and the percentile ranks show strength of interest according to the norms groups. The user will need to verify any interpretations by personal experience.

The authors and publisher are to be commended for the improvements they have made in the test and in the new manual. Since the references above do not show as widespread use or as much research for this inventory as for the Strong or the Kuder, evidence of validity is quite limited. This means that the inventory must be used with considerable caution. However, with the addition of norms for grades 8-12, a simplified scoring procedure, and evidence of limited overlap with the Kuder, the Brainard inventory could possibly serve a useful function in high school counseling and placement.

For a review by Elmer D. Hinckley, see 4:737; for reviews by Edwin W. Davis and Herschel T. Manuel, see 3:634; for reviews by Jack W. Dunlap and M. R. Trabue of the original edition, see 40:1675; for a review by Everett B. Sackett, see 38:1176.

[857]

★**Devon Interest Test.** Ages 11-13; 1955; 2 scores: practical, academic; separate forms for boys and girls; 100 or more tests, 5d. each; 7d. per single copy; 2s. per manual ['55]; postage extra; administration time not reported; Stephen Wiseman and T. F. Fitzpatrick; Oliver & Boyd Ltd. *

REFERENCES

1. FITZPATRICK, T. F. "Summaries of Researches Reported in Degree Theses: The Construction of a Test of Practical Ability With Special Reference to Woodwork." *Brit J Ed Psychol* 23:133-5 Je '53. *
2. FITZPATRICK, T. F., AND WISEMAN, STEPHEN. "An Interest Test for Use in Selection for Technical Education." *Brit J Ed Psychol* 24:99-105 Je '54. * (*PA* 29:3038)
3. WISEMAN, STEPHEN. "The Use of an Interest Test in 11 Plus Selection." *Brit J Ed Psychol* 25:92-8 Je '55. * (*PA* 30:3469)

ARTHUR B. ROYSE, *Lecturer in Psychology, University of Hull, Hull, England.*

This new test is not a measure of general interests. It attempts only to determine whether, irrespective of strength of other interests, a child's practical interests are stronger or weaker than his academic interests. Devised to improve predictability of whether a child of 11 plus is better suited to a technical rather than an academic education, the test is intended to be used solely as an addition to customary selection procedures. In this very specific field it promises to be a useful addition if and when its predictive validity is established.

The child is required to indicate his like or

dislike for doing certain things by reacting to a series of statements, e.g., "learning history." The statements are grouped in 16 blocks, each block containing items reflecting practical, academic, social, and "distractor" activities. The child must also indicate which activity in each block he likes best and which he likes next best. Only practical and academic items chosen as best or next best liked are scored, thus yielding a practical (P) interest score and an academic (A) interest score.

Although the test can be given as a group test, some individual supervision is necessary to ensure that it is completed satisfactorily. Scoring is simple but its objectivity is a little marred by the authors' failure to give specific instructions for every possible scoring contingency. Illustrative norms are given but it is necessary for users to establish their own norms in relation to the number and type of school places available.

Reliability is good, split-half coefficients for the two scores varying from .85 to .91 on one 11 plus sample and two 13 plus samples. Self-consistency of P scores and A scores and their independence from the remaining items have been determined by an item analysis.

No predictive validity for the test has yet been established. The test has been published at this stage in the hope that follow-up experiments can be more widely based. The authors have tried to show from their available evidence, however, that follow-up studies now in progress can reasonably be expected to demonstrate some predictive validity, although whether this will be higher than that of existing selection procedures is by no means certain. This evidence (1-3) comprises demonstration of (a) very low correlations of P scores with intelligence, arithmetic, and English test results; (b) significant differences among the P scores and A scores of children at grammar, technical, and modern schools; (c) similar factor patterns between P scores and teacher estimates of practical interests and abilities; and (d) presence of an interest factor with loadings of .53 (P score) and −.92 (A score) which shows a higher variance than the k factor measured by those space tests customarily used for technical selection.

Although these results are only tentative, particularly the two factor analyses which are based on relatively few tests and children, the fact that the evidence is all in the same direction suggests that the hope that reasonably high predictive validity will be established is not unrealistic.

In short, the test shows some promise of becoming a useful addition to test batteries used for educational selection but whether this promise will be realised must await future experimentation.

ALFRED YATES, *Senior Research Officer, National Foundation for Educational Research, London, England.*

This test was designed for a strictly limited and utilitarian purpose—that of improving the methods of selection employed by education authorities in England and Wales. These authorities are required to allocate primary school leavers (children between 10 and 11 years of age) to courses of secondary education that are suited to their abilities and aptitudes. One important decision that has to be made is whether an able child shall proceed to an academic course or to a technical course. The aim of the *Devon Interest Test* is to furnish information that will improve the validity of this kind of discrimination.

The test is in the form of a questionnaire, requiring the testee to indicate his likes and dislikes from a wide area of activities and experiences. It yields two separate scores: a P-score (practical interest) and an A-score (academic interest). The authors outline a procedure, involving the use of this test along with tests of verbal intelligence, English, arithmetic, and spatial ability, whereby children may be assigned to a number of groups: those clearly suitable for an academic course, usually provided in grammar schools; those better fitted for a technical course; those between whose aptitudes it is not possible clearly to discriminate but who appear to be capable of succeeding in either type of course; those whose level of ability is such that they should be assigned to secondary modern schools, which, in most parts of England and Wales, cater to the least gifted pupils who lack the intellectual stamina to embark on courses that are designed to lead to further education in universities, technical colleges, and the like.

The procedure advocated by the authors has been tried out on a sample of 175 11-year-old boys and found to result in a positive classification in almost 60 per cent of the cases. Split-half reliabilities have been calculated for this sample and for a sample of 417 13-year-old boys and girls, the values ranging from .85 (A-score for boys of 11+) to .91 (P-score for boys of 13+). The authors emphasise that no predictive validity has yet been secured although there is research evidence to show that the inclusion of the test in a battery tends to improve the validity of selection for technical courses.

The authors make no claims for the usefulness of their test outside the limited context for which it was specifically prepared. Nevertheless, it could well be a useful instrument for other purposes and in other circumstances. It would accord well with the authors' intentions, however, if those who employ the test for purposes other than those for which it was designed do so on a strictly empirical basis. The authors warn that the norms supplied in the manual are tentative only.

[858]

★**G. C. Self-Scoring Interest Record, Second Experimental Edition.** Grades 9 and over; 1958; 12 scores: outdoor, managerial, social service, verbal, operative, skilled mechanical, scientific, persuasive, clerical, artistic, numerical, musical; Form 1 ('58); manual ['58]; tentative norms; $2.50 per 25 tests; 90¢ per 25 punch pins; 85¢ per 25 backing boards; 47¢ per 50 profiles ['58]; 30¢ per specimen set (must be purchased to obtain manual); postage extra; (30–40) minutes; H. M. Fowler and M. D. Parmenter; Guidance Centre. *

[859]

★**How Well Do You Know Your Interests.** Grades 13–16, adults; 1957; 54 scores: numerical, clerical, retail selling, outside selling, selling real estate, one-order selling, sales complaints, selling intangibles, buyer, labor management, production supervision, business management, machine operation, repair and construction, machine design, farm or ranch, gardening, hunting, adventure, social service, teaching service, medical service, nursing service, applied chemistry, basic chemical problems, basic biological problems, basic physical problems, basic psychological problems, philosophical, visual art appreciative, visual art productive, visual art decorative, amusement appreciative, amusement productive, amusement managerial, literary appreciative, literary productive, musical appreciative, musical performing, musical composing, sports appreciative, sports participative, domestic service, unskilled labor, disciplinary, power seeking, propaganda, self-aggrandizing, supervisory initiative, bargaining, arbitrative, persuasive, disputatious, masculinity-femininity; Form B-22; 2 editions (profiles only differ): college, personnel; $7.50 per 30 tests, postage extra; $2.74 per specimen set of any one level, postpaid; (20–30) minutes; Thomas N. Jenkins; Executive Analysis Corporation. *

JEROME E. DOPPELT, *Assistant Director, Test Division, The Psychological Corporation, New York, New York.*

This interest inventory consists of 120 statements of activities related to various kinds of occupations, use of leisure time, dealings with people, etc. The examinee indicates on a 6-point scale the extent to which he likes or dislikes each activity. The inventory booklet has been cleverly designed to permit the transcription of scores for 53 scales, and a score for either masculinity or femininity, directly on a profile sheet. The scales are grouped in interest domains such as "outdoor vocational interest domain" and "mechanical vocational interest domain."

It is rather startling to find that 53 scores are obtained from 120 items. Examination of the scoring templates reveals that each of 46 scales is based on two items and each of the remaining 7 scales contains four items. The scoring weights for an item range from 0 to 5, corresponding to the six possible responses. For a two-item scale, this gives possible scores of 0 to 10. For the scales containing four items, the scoring weights count only half and the range of possible scores remains 0 to 10. The manual points out that the raw score on a scale is meaningful in itself since scores below the neutral point of 5 indicate an overall negative attitude to the job functions, whereas scores above 5 tend to indicate positive interests. With two items in a scale it is, of course, possible to have a tremendous liking for one activity and an equally hearty dislike for the other activity. The corresponding responses would yield a score of 5 for the scale. It is difficult to think of such a score, obtained from two extreme feelings, as indicative of indifference or neutrality. Although one may not often encounter situations in which the subject gives such disparate responses, the user of the inventory should be aware of the possibility.

Percentile norms are available for composite groups of office and factory employees, college students, and a group of 200 young, unmarried men from 29 states. There is evidently recognition of the need for norms based on specific occupational, educational, and age groups since it is mentioned that such norms will be "published as they are completed."

The discussion of the factorial nature of the inventory does little to explain the structure of the instrument. It is emphasized that an objective in the development of the test was the selection of items which would yield pure and reliable measures of interest factors. What is meant by the purity of measurement is not made clear. The issue is further confused by the existence of higher order factors leading to "interest domains," a situation which would imply lack of purity among scales. The manual mentions that a considerable amount of research work was done in the process of developing the inventory but, unfortunately, no bibliography is given. Some issues might be clarified by reading the complete research reports. Conspicuously absent are data showing the relationships between this inventory and other measures of interest, information which would justify the titles and descriptions of the 53 scales, and evidence of validity in counseling or personnel selection.

The reviewer feels that the extraction of 53 scores from 120 items is an attempt to obtain an excessive amount of information from the specific activities listed in the inventory. The assumption that interest areas can be effectively measured or even identified by two items seems too hazardous to accept.

HENRY S. DYER, *Vice President in Charge of Research, Educational Testing Service, Princeton, New Jersey.*

The author of this interest inventory claims that it has five principal advantages over other similar instruments:

a) It is convenient to give and score. This is a valid claim. The directions and the wording of the items are so clear and simple that an average high school student should have little trouble doing the test under his own steam, though one may wonder whether such students are likely to have genuine familiarity with many of the activities to which they are expected to react. The format of the test itself and the ingenious hand scoring system make it possible to get the results much more quickly than is the case with other interest inventories known to this reviewer.

b) It is applicable to a wide variety of work and jobs. True. In the opinion of this reviewer, the test comes close to exhausting the vocational interest domain.

c) It gives information related to specific job tasks and duties. Also true. The test yields scores on 44 types of vocational activity and on 9 types of vocationally related behavioral tendencies, as well as on either masculinity or femininity depending on the sex of the examinee.

Each of the 55 rubrics is briefly and simply defined in the manual.

d) It utilizes a scoring method which permits a direct reading of an individual's dislikes or aversions as well as his interests. This claim rests not only on the scoring system but also on the type of response the examinee is required to make to each item. He has six options ranging from "like tremendously" to "dislike tremendously." The scoring system is such that a 10 automatically means extreme interest, a zero extreme aversion, and a 5 indifference. However, no evidence is given to show whether a given score, say 7, stands for the same *amount* of interest from scale to scale. An investigation is needed to determine to what extent the psychological distance between any two scale points is, as the scoring system implies, actually the same from scale to scale. Furthermore, the information on the test-retest reliability of the individual scales is insufficient to indicate how much of a difference between any two scale scores can be trusted.

e) The manual illustrates basic uses of different profiles of scores by means of a set of actual cases. Four actual cases of job applicants are analyzed in the manual. Four additional cases of students seeking vocational guidance are in preparation. In the opinion of this reviewer, these cases are well done and should be useful in showing personnel managers and guidance counselors how to make effective use of the scores.

The norms for this instrument are inadequate and not well defined. The fact that they are built into the profile chart seems to make the latter more confusing than helpful in the interpretation of the scores. A profile based on the raw scores only, with percentile norms furnished in separate tables as they accumulate, would make for easier, and probably safer, interpretation of the results.

Although the author reports "factorial validities" for the individual scales in terms of factor loadings which are comfortably high, he leaves this reviewer wondering just how valid the test is in terms of the degree to which it gives results which actually correspond to an individual's interests. The factorial validities are in a sense not much more than indicators of the internal consistency of each scale. Since most of the scales are based on only *two items each,* one can hardly escape the impression that the sampling of the subject's response to any one area of activity is too narrow to be representative. For each scale, the two—occasionally four—items were chosen on the basis of their factor loadings from an original set consisting of 7 to 12 items. In other words, the two (or four) were taken as most representative of the total set. From this it can be argued that the sampling in each scale is more representative than it seems on the surface; it means that the responses to the items selected are highly predictive of the responses to the items not selected. But no solid evidence is given on how well responses to the items selected predict responses to innumerable aspects of the actual job situation.

It should be obvious that this reviewer has some misgivings about resting the case on factorial validity alone. On the other hand, he gave the test to himself and was amazed at the accuracy with which the raw scores reflected his own interests and aversions. Perhaps there is more to this 120-item test than meets the eye. Perhaps in the hands of a wise clinician it will prove to be helpful.

[860]

*Interest Check List. Grades 9 and over; 1946–57; interviewing aid; 1 form ['57]; no data on reliability; no norms; $2.50 per 100 copies; 5¢ per single copy; 5¢ per directions sheet ['57]; postpaid; (20) minutes; prepared by United States Employment Service; United States Government Printing Office. *

For reviews by Milton L. Blum and Howard R. Taylor of the original edition, see 4:741.

[861]

*Inventory of Vocational Interests: Acorn National Aptitude Tests. Grades 7–16 and adults; 1943–57; interest in five areas: mechanical, academic, artistic, business and economic, farm-agricultural; 1 form ('43); manual ('57, identical with manual copyrighted in 1943); directions sheet ('56); no data on reliability; $2 per 25 tests; 25¢ per manual; 50¢ per specimen set; postage extra; (35) minutes; Andrew Kobal, J. Wayne Wrightstone, and Karl R. Kunze; Acorn Publishing Co. *

For reviews by Marion A. Bills, Edward S. Bordin, Harold D. Carter, and Patrick Slater, see 3:638.

[862]

★Kuder Preference Record—Occupational. Grades 9–16 and adults; 1956–58; 39 scores: verification, county agricultural agent, farmer, forester, minister, newspaper editor, physician [revised], clinical psychologist, industrial psychologist, YMCA secretary, school superintendent, accountant, meteorologist, personnel manager, department store salesman, psychology professor, mechanical engineer, counseling psychologist, journalist, architect ['57]; electrical engineer (revised), civil engineer, lawyer, retail clothier,

insurance agent, dentist, veterinarian, industrial engineer, pediatrician, psychiatrist, radio station manager, interior decorator, high school counselor, high school science teacher, high school mathematics teacher, chemist, mining and metallurgial engineer, druggist, job printer ['58]; IBM; Form D ('56); manual, second edition ('57); research handbook, second edition ('57); separate answer sheets must be used; $9.80 per 20 tests; $6.25 per 100 IBM answer sheets; $1 per scoring stencil for any one score; $2.50 per book of computational sheets ('56) for developing local occupational keys; $2.50 per research handbook; $2 per specimen set; postage extra; (25–35) minutes; G. Frederic Kuder; Science Research Associates. *

EDWARD S. BORDIN, *Professor of Psychology, University of Michigan, Ann Arbor, Michigan.*

The *Kuder Preference Record* is second only to Strong's *Vocational Interest Blank* in length of service as one of the leading interest inventories. This latest version, Form D (Occupational), is intended to give direct evidence of how closely a subject's responses typify each of 22 different occupational groups.

The format and contents follow the patterns laid down in the other forms (Vocational and Personal), in that the subject is asked to choose which one of three activities he would like the most and which one he would like the least. Many of the groups of items are drawn from previous forms.

One of the hallmarks of this test has always been ingenuity in the choice of items and soundness in the methods of item analysis utilized. This form is no exception. The manual and the Research Handbook, which are available for those who wish to construct additional scales, discuss and describe very thoroughly what considerations guided the accumulation of the pool of items and the statistical criteria applied for selecting the final set. The author proves in analytical terms his contention that it is more efficient to sacrifice internal consistency reliability for validity where one or more relatively independent variables are required to account for a criterion. Therefore, he argues, it is a matter of no great concern that the Kuder-Richardson reliabilities for the scales range from .42 to .82, with a median of .62. The median test-retest reliabilities are .79 and .86, respectively, for high school and college student populations. Unfortunately, we are not told the length of the time interval between testings.

This reviewer finds convincing Kuder's arguments regarding reliability as internal consistency, but contends that the equally important question of stability still remains. The user needs to know how much the interests tapped by this inventory may be expected to change with the passage of time for different age groups and what effects, if any, different types of intervening experiences may have. No evidence bearing on this question is presented. Nowhere, either in the manual or in the Research Handbook is this question ever discussed.

The occupational keys have been developed by selecting items which discriminate the selected occupational group from a norm group. The norm group, composed of 1,000 men selected among telephone subscribers in 138 cities and towns, defies identification. Approximately 70 per cent are from three major occupational classifications: professional and semiprofessional workers; proprietors, managers, and officials; and clerical, sales, and kindred workers. The test cannot be faulted on this because there is certainly no clear answer as to what is the most important base group to use for developing scales. However, the author and publisher are to be criticized for failing to offer any information about the expected distribution of scores among the relevant populations, e.g., high school or college students, the adult population at large. This lack is acknowledged and users are encouraged to develop their own norms.

Though its validity is to be the main index of its worth, there is remarkably sparse evidence offered. In fact, the only evidence is contained in tables that demonstrate that considerable success was attained in discriminating occupational groups from the norm group and that the degree of discrimination was fairly well maintained in cross validation samples. One may argue that not enough time has elapsed to permit the completion of the many other types of studies necessary to establish construct validity. Since interest inventories are rarely used to predict discrete behavioral criteria, e.g., level of academic achievement or job performance, the basis for their use rests most clearly on construct validity. Yet, such easily obtained basic information as the intercorrelation of the occupational scales is not made available. There is no sign or promise of the follow-up studies, lack of which has long been criticized in the vocational form. Perhaps it is assumed that data accumulated in connection with the vocational form can provide some

of this validational underpinning. Nowhere is this assumption explicitly stated; however, even if this assumption is made, then we need evidence that the relationship between the vocational and occupational forms is such as to make reasonable such a transfer of validity.

To summarize, this inventory is well developed and looks promising. However, at the present time it lacks most of the further data necessary for operational use.

John W. Gustad, *Professor of Psychology and Director, University Counseling Center, University of Maryland, College Park, Maryland.*

According to its author, this form of the *Kuder Preference Record* was produced to provide "a relatively short interest inventory suitable for use in the development of interest keys for specific occupations." It is to be used, Kuder indicates, by counselors trying to help vocationally undecided clients and by personnel directors in selection, placement, and classification. How successful it will be in these functions remains to be seen. On the whole, it looks promising.

Those familiar with the earlier vocational forms will recall that they contained 9 or 10 scales, each reflecting an area or cluster of activity such as mechanical, social service, or outdoor. These scales were developed by inbreeding items until a high degree of homogeneity was attained among the items of a scale. This method is in marked contrast to the approach taken by Strong in the development of his *Vocational Interest Blank*. Here, criterion groups of successfully employed men in a variety of occupations were compared with respect to their item responses to a presumably representative group of men in general. The aim was to develop keys—clusters of items—which would indicate whether the person taking the test resembled the successful men or not.

In this version of the Preference Record, Kuder has abandoned his earlier approach and taken the road blazed by Strong. In many ways, this revision resembles Strong's inventory more than it does earlier forms of the Preference Record. Although it is too early to tell whether it will be as useful as the Strong, the information provided in the manual suggests that it will receive much well deserved attention. The reviewer is inclined to feel that it will be used more in research than in practice, at least for some time. Considering the number of unanswered questions, this seems highly desirable.

The Kuder Occupational contains 100 triadic items very much like those used in earlier forms. Many items were, in fact, taken from the earlier forms, with some of them modified for clarity and readability. Items were selected by a modification of the criterion vector method which is described in some detail in the handbook accompanying the test. The reduction to 100 items reduces total testing time to about 30 minutes on the average, although there is no formal time limit applied in administration.

Of most interest in this form are the various occupational keys or scales. These were developed by locating a representative norm population, then contrasting their responses with those of certain occupational groups. The norm group contained a thousand cases, approximately 85 per cent of which came from professional through craft levels. It is thus a sample with considerable upward bias, but, as Kuder indicates, "The best reference group for any specific situation is ordinarily the group from which the subjects are to be distinguished."

Occupational groups were then selected in 22 fields or subfields. Item analysis methods were employed to identify items which differentiated the occupational group from the norm group. These item pools were then cross validated to see whether the differentiation held up. It seemed to do so quite well.

Only one kind of validity—concurrent—is dealt with. Using the approach indicated, concurrent validity is the kind which must be dealt with first. Concurrent validity is indicated by the extent to which the test corresponds to current criterion status. That is, it must be shown that the occupational keys do in fact yield different distributions for men in the occupations and for men in the norm group.

Concurrent validity is not enough, however. Predictive validity must be dealt with some time, and there is no evidence cited to show that the Kuder Occupational has predictive validity. Work of the sort done with the Strong must be done before the general utility of this form can be accepted for counseling or personnel work.

The reliability of the instrument appears to be satisfactory, at least with respect to its con-

current validity. Kuder-Richardson reliabilities range from .42 to .93. Test-retest reliabilities tend to be somewhat higher. The period between testings is not indicated, but it certainly does not approach the 18-year period discussed in Strong's latest book.

Interpretation of the scores is based on the differentiation ratio (DR). Percentiles of the norm and occupational groups are also available, but Kuder prefers the DR approach. This DR is the ratio of the proportion of the two groups, occupational and norm, exceeding a given score. The suggested meanings for these DR's lead one to many of the interpretive problems encountered in using the Strong.

Administration of the test appears to be at least as simple as with earlier forms. Scoring may be done by hand or on IBM machines. Raw scores are readily converted into DR's by means of tables printed on the scoring keys. A verification key, designed to assess the attitude and understanding of the test taker, is also included. The data cited seem to indicate that the test works well in screening out people who fail to understand the directions or who try to distort their answers.

In addition to the test and the manual, Kuder has developed a Research Handbook and a booklet of computation sheets. The first is of special interest since it contains detailed discussion of the theory and practice of interest inventory development and will enable even those without high level statistical skills to undertake the development of keys for special purposes. The Research Handbook is an intriguing and welcome addition to the test package.

This instrument is not ready yet for widespread use by counselors and personnel directors. It looks very promising for cautious experimental work by highly skilled and experienced psychologists. Until a great deal of research and clinical experience has been accumulated, however, it should not be considered on a par with the Strong or even with the earlier forms of Kuder's inventories. Its simplicity, the obvious care in its construction, its brief administration time, its easy scoring, and especially its potential as a source of new keys tailormade to specific situations makes it a very promising instrument, one which should receive a great deal of attention in the near future.

[863]

*Kuder Preference Record—Vocational. Grades 9–16 and adults; 1934–56; IBM; 2 forms; 2 editions; separate answer sheets or pads must be used; $9.80 per 20 tests; 75¢ per specimen set of any one edition; postage extra; (40–50) minutes; G. Frederic Kuder; Science Research Associates. *

a) FORM B [NINE SCALE]. 1934–46; 9 scores: mechanical, computational, scientific, persuasive, artistic, literary, musical, social service, clerical; masulinity-femininity score also obtainable; 1 form; 2 editions; revised manual ('46); 60¢ per 20 profile sheets for adults ('46) or for children ('44).

1) [Hand Scoring Edition.] Form BB ('42); $2.35 per 20 answer pads.
2) [Machine Scoring Edition.] IBM; Form BM ('42); $4.50 per 100 IBM answer sheets; $7.50 per set of scoring stencils.

b) FORM C [ELEVEN SCALE]. 1934–56; revision and expansion of Form B; 11 scores: same as for Form B plus outdoor, verification; 1 form; 2 editions; manual, sixth edition ('56); 60¢ per 20 profile sheets for adults ('51) or for children ('50); 90¢ per 20 profile leaflets for adults ('54) or for children ('53) for comparing vocational and personal (see 80) scores.

1) [Hand Scoring Edition.] Form CH ('48); $2.35 per 20 answer pads
2) [Machine Scoring Edition.] IBM; Form CM ('48); $4.50 per 100 IBM answer sheets; $7.50 per set of scoring stencils.

REFERENCES

1–2. See 40:1671.
3–62. See 3:640.
63–208. See 4:742.
209. HAHN, MILTON E. An Investigation of Measured Aspects of Social Intelligence in a Distributive Occupation. Doctor's thesis, University of Minnesota (Minneapolis, Minn.), 1942.
210. LESHNER, SAUL S. Interrelations Between the Vocational Interest Areas of the Gentry, Kuder and Thurstone Interest Inventories. Master's thesis, Temple University (Philadelphia, Pa.), 1942.
211. TRIGGS, FRANCES O. "Kuder Preference Record in the Counseling of Nurses." Am J Nursing 46:312–16 '46. *
212. BILLING, PATRICIA S. Voluntary Selection as Corroborated by the Kuder Preference Record: To Test the Value of Music as a Universal Outlet for Extracurricular Activity. Master's thesis, University of North Dakota (University, N.D.), 1948.
213. BURDETTE, WALTER E., JR. Norms for the Occupation of Industrial Arts Teachers in Conjunction With the Kuder Preference Record. Master's thesis, Kansas State Teachers College (Pittsburg, Kan.), 1948.
214. REDLENER, J. A Comparative Study of the Efficiency of the Kuder Preference Record and the Strong Vocational Interest Blank in the Prediction of Job Satisfaction. Master's thesis, University of Southern California (Los Angeles, Calif.), 1948.
215. WILSON, EARL H. Stability of Interest Patterns as Reflected in the Kuder Preference Record. Master's thesis, State College of Washington (Pullman, Wash.), 1948.
216. BATH, JOHN A. "Differential Interests of Agricultural College Students as Measured by the Kuder Preference Record." Proc Iowa Acad Sci 57:347–51 '50. *
217. CARSE, DOROTHY. A Study of the Relationships Between the Wechsler-Bellevue Intelligence Scale and the Kuder Preference Record-Personal. Master's thesis, North Texas State College (Denton, Tex.), 1950.
218. CASNER, DANIEL. Certain Factors Associated With Success and Failure in Personal-Adjustment Counseling. Doctor's thesis, New York University (New York, N.Y.), 1950.
219. CHASE, JOHN B., JR. An Analysis of the Change of Interest of One Hundred and Fifty Secondary School Pupils. Master's thesis, University of North Carolina (Chapel Hill, N.C.), 1950.
220. JOHNSON, RALPH H., AND BOND, GUY L. "Reading Ease of Commonly Used Tests." J Appl Psychol 34:319–24 O '50. * (PA 26:299)
221. NEUMANN, THOMAS M. A Study of the Relation of Occupational Interests to Certain Aspects of Personality. Master's thesis, Illinois State Normal University (Normal, Ill.), 1950.
222. VAUGHAN, GEORGE E., JR. Interest and Personality Patterns of Experienced Teachers. Master's thesis, North Texas State College (Denton, Tex.), 1950.
223. WEYNAND, ROBERT S. A Study of the Relationship Between Interest Preferences and Academic Success for 622 A. & M. College Students. Master's thesis, Agricultural and Mechanical College of Texas (College Station, Tex.), 1950.
224. WISDOM, JESSIE R. A Study of the Interest Patterns of Premedical Students as Revealed by the Kuder Preference Record and the Strong Vocational Interest Inventory. Master's thesis, North Texas State College (Denton, Tex.), 1950.
225. BROWN, MANUEL N. Clinical Status of Veteran Patients Related to Six Interest Variables. Doctor's thesis, University of Portland (Portland, Ore.), 1951.
226. DALY, JOAN M. A Comparison of the Relation of the Thurstone Interest Schedule to the Kuder Preference Record and to Self-Estimated Interests. Master's thesis, Fordham University (New York, N.Y.), 1951.
227. HILLMAN, CAROL. An Empirical Validation of a Sales Personnel Selection Program. Master's thesis, Vanderbilt University (Nashville, Tenn.), 1951.
228. HUFFMAN, WARREN J. Personality Variations Among Men Preparing to Teach Physical Education. Doctor's thesis, University of Illinois (Urbana, Ill.), 1951. (DA 12:28)
229. KERMEEN, BARBARA G. A Factor Analysis of the Differential Aptitude Tests and a Factor Analysis of the Kuder Preference Record, Vocational. Master's thesis, University of California (Berkeley, Calif.), 1951.
230. KUDER, G. FREDERIC, AND CRAWFORD, LURA E. Kuder Book List. Chicago, Ill.: Science Research Associates, Inc., 1951. Pp. 8. (Instructor's Guide, 1951. Pp. 4.) *
231. MANZANO, ILUMINADO B. The Relation of Personality Adjustment to Occupational Interests. Doctor's thesis, University of Southern California (Los Angeles, Calif.), 1951.
232. MARTIN, GLENN C. "Test Batteries for Trainees in Auto Mechanics and Apparel Design." J Appl Psychol 35:20–2 F '51. * (PA 25:7123)
233. PEMBERTON, CAROL L. "Personality Inventory Data Related to ACE Subscores." J Consult Psychol 15:160–2 Ap '51. * (PA 26:6569)
234. REID, JOHN W. "Stability of Measured Kuder Interests in Young Adults." J Ed Res 45:307–12 D '51. * (PA 26:6284)
235. SCHNEBLY, LOUIS M. A Comparison of the Scores Made by Teachers on the Kuder Preference Record and the California Test of Personality. Master's thesis, Montana State University (Missoula, Mont.), 1951.
236. SHERMAN, E. C. Relationship of Kuder Scores to Differential College Achievement. Master's thesis, Iowa State College (Ames, Iowa), 1951.
237. BARRETT, RUTH E. The Relation Between Strength of Kuder Preferences and Aptitude, Temperament, and Academic Achievement. Doctor's thesis, University of Pittsburgh (Pittsburgh, Pa.), 1952.
238. BOUTON, ARTHUR G. The Stability of Kuder Vocational Interest Patterns During Late Adolescence and Early Adult Life. Doctor's thesis, University of Pittsburgh (Pittsburgh, Pa.), 1952.
239. BUEGEL, HERMANN F., AND BILLING, PATRICIA STRATTE. "Inventoried Interests of Participants in Music Groups." J Ed Res 46:141–6 O '52. *
240. BURSCH, CHARLES W., II. "Certain Relationships Between the Kuder Preference Record and the Minnesota Multiphasic Personality Inventory." Calif J Ed Res 3:224–7+ N '52. * (PA 27:5144)
241. CARTER, GERALD C. "Measurement of Supervisory Ability." J Appl Psychol 36:393–5 D '52. * (PA 27:6801)
242. CASE, HARRY W. "The Relationship of Certain Tests to Grades Achieved in an Industrial Class in Aircraft Design." Ed & Psychol Meas 12:90–5 sp '52. * (PA 27:6106)
243. COCKRUM, LOGAN V. "Personality Traits and Interests of Theological Students." Relig Ed 47:28–32 Ja–F '52. * (PA 26:4229)
244. DRESSEL, PAUL L., AND MATTESON, ROSS W. "The Relationship Between Experience and Interest as Measured by the Kuder Preference Record." Ed & Psychol Meas 12:109–16 sp '52. * (PA 27:5957)
245. FRANDSEN, ARDEN N. "A Note on Wiener's Coding of Kuder Preference Record Profiles." Ed & Psychol Meas 12:137–9 sp '52. * (PA 27:5871)
246. FREEHILL, MAURICE F. "Student Self-Estimates as Guidance in Selecting Courses." Col & Univ 27:233–42 Ja '52. *
247. GUILFORD, J. P. "When Not to Factor Analyze." Psychol B 49:26–37 Ja '52. * (PA 27:33)
248. HALE, PETER PAUL. "A Comparison of Kuder Teachers' Interest Patterns With Those of Veteran Teacher Trainees." Ed Adm & Sup 38:412–20 N '52. * (PA 27:6172)
249. HARMON, LINDSEY R. Inter-Relations of Patterns on the Kuder Preference Record and the Minnesota Multiphasic Personality Inventory. Doctor's thesis, University of Minnesota (Minneapolis, Minn.), 1952. (DA 13:257)
250. ISAACSON, LEE E. "Predictors of Success for Cooperative Occupational Education Classes in Kansas City, Missouri, High Schools." Abstract. Am Psychol 7:379 Jl '52. *
251. KERNS, ROBERT DENEILLE. The Relation of Interests as Measured by the Kuder Preference Record to Level of Attainment in Engineering School. Master's thesis, University of Pittsburgh (Pittsburgh, Pa.), 1952.
252. KRUMM, RICHARD L. Inter-Relationships of Measured Interests and Personality Traits of Introductory Psychology Instructors and Their Students as Related to Student Achievement. Doctor's thesis, University of Pittsburgh (Pittsburgh, Pa.), 1952.
253. MAGILL, JOHN W. A Validation of the Kuder Preference Record Against Functional Criteria of Campus Activity.

Doctor's thesis, University of Pittsburgh (Pittsburgh, Pa.), 1952.

254. Mallinson, George Greisen, and Crumrine, William M. "An Investigation of the Stability of Interests of High School Students." *J Ed Res* 45:369–83 Ja '52. * (*PA* 27:2977)

255. Meleika, Louis K. *Intra-Individual Variability in Relation to Achievement, Interest, and Personality.* Doctor's thesis, Stanford University (Stanford, Calif.), 1952.

256. Moser, Wilbur E. "The Influence of Certain Cultural Factors Upon the Selection of Vocational Preferences by High School Students." *J Ed Res* 45:523–6 Mr '52. * (*PA* 27:2038)

257. Mugaas, Hendrik D., and Hester, Ruport. "The Development of an Equation for Identifying the Interests of Carpenters." *Ed & Psychol Meas* 12:408–14 au '52. * (*PA* 27:6184)

258. Renke, Wilferd W. *Discrimination of the Kuder Preference Record.* Doctor's thesis, University of North Dakota (Grand Forks, N.D.), 1952.

259. Rogge, Harold J. *A Statistical Study of Certain Personality Factors Among Pupils in a Selected High School.* Master's thesis, Ohio University (Athens, Ohio), 1952.

260. Rosenberg, Phyllis. *The Predictive Value of the Kuder Preference Record.* Master's thesis, Western Reserve University (Cleveland, Ohio), 1952.

261. Russell, Diana. *The Effect of Experience and Change of Occupational Choice on the Kuder Preference Record.* Master's thesis, University of Pittsburgh (Pittsburgh, Pa.), 1952.

262. Russell, Diana, and Herzberg, Frederick. "Kuder Occupational Interest Patterns in Vocational Counseling." Abstract. *Am Psychol* 7:383 Jl '52. *

263. Stanley, Julian C., and Waldrop, Robert S. "Intercorrelations of Study of Values and Kuder Preference Record Scores." *Ed & Psychol Meas* 12:707–19 w '52. * (*PA* 27:5906)

264. Steinberg, Arthur. "The Relation of Vocational Preference to Emotional Adjustment." *Ed & Psychol Meas* 12:96–104 sp '52. * (*PA* 27:5965)

265. Uecker, Albert E. *A Comparative Study of the Vocational Interests, Aspirations, and Achievements of Selected Groups of Veteran Psychiatric Patients.* Doctor's thesis, University of Minnesota (Minneapolis, Minn.), 1952. (*DA* 12:392)

266. Woodward, C. L. "A Critical Analysis of Certain Interest Tests." *Yearb Nat Council Meas Used Ed* 9:101–8 '52. *

267. Anderson, Rose G. "Do Aptitudes Support Interests?" *Personnel & Guid J* 32:14–7 S '53. * (*PA* 28:4495)

268. Ausubel, David P.; Schiff, Herbert M.; and Zeleny, Marjorie P. " 'Real-Life' Measures of Level of Academic and Vocational Aspiration in Adolescents: Relation to Laboratory Measures and to Adjustment." *Child Develop* 24:155–68 S–D '53. * (*PA* 29:3700)

269. Baer, Barbara S. *Interest Patterns for Four Occupations: Kuder Preference Record.* Master's thesis, Utah State Agricultural College (Logan, Utah), 1953

270. Beamer, George C.; Pender, Frances Russell; and Parton, Norma West. "Selection of Teachers of Homemaking." *J Home Econ* 45:98–100 F '53. * (*PA* 27:7412)

271. Beaver, Alma Perry. "Kuder Interest Patterns of Student Nurses." *J Appl Psychol* 37:370–3 O '53. * (*PA* 29:1483)

272. Bordin, Edward S., and Wilson, Earl H. "Change of Interest as a Function of Shift in Curricular Orientation." *Ed & Psychol Meas* 13:297–307 su '53. * (*PA* 28:4875)

273. Brayfield, Arthur H. "Clerical Interest and Clerical Aptitude." *Personnel & Guid J* 31:304–6 F '53. * (*PA* 28:1616)

274. Brogden, H. E.; Baier, D. E.; and Taylor, E. K. "Experimental Design: Utilization of an Unreliable and a Biased Criterion." *Ed & Psychol Meas* 13:27–33 sp '53. * (*PA* 28:112)

275. Canfield, A. A. "Administering Form BB of the Kuder Preference Record, Half Length." *J Appl Psychol* 37:197–200 Je '53. * (*PA* 28:3342)

276. Farrow, Edward G. *The Development of a Masculinity-Femininity Scale for the Kuder Preference Record-Personal.* Master's thesis, North Carolina State College of Agriculture and Engineering (Raleigh, N.C.), 1953.

277. Frandsen, Arden N., and Sessions, Alwyn D. "Interests and School Achievement." *Ed & Psychol Meas* 13:94–101 sp '53. * (*PA* 28:1560)

278. Freehill, Maurice F. "Interest Scores in Selection of Freshman Courses." *Col & Univ* 28:197–203 Ja '53. *

279. Givens, Paul R. "Kuder Patterns of Interest as Related to Achievement in College Science Courses." *J Ed Res* 46:627–30 Ap '53. * (*PA* 28:3234)

280. Haselkorn, Harry. *The Vocational Interests of a Group of Homosexuals.* Doctor's thesis, New York University (New York, N.Y.), 1953. (*DA* 13:582)

281. Healy, Irene, and Borg, Walter R. "The Vocational Interests of Nurses and Nursing Students." *J Ed Res* 46:347–52 Ja '53. * (*PA* 28:1679)

282. Herzberg, Frederick, and Russell, Diana. "The Effects of Experience and Change of Job Interest on the Kuder Preference Record." *J Appl Psychol* 37:478–81 D '53. * (*PA* 29:1615)

283. Holland, John L.; Krause, Allen H.; Nixon, M. Eloise; and Trembath, Mary F. "The Classification of Occupations by Means of Kuder Interest Profiles: I, The Development of Interest Groups." *J Appl Psychol* 37:263–9 Ag '53. * (*PA* 28:6172)

284. Kern, Donald W. *The Prediction of Academic Success*

of Freshmen in a Community College. Doctor's thesis, New York University (New York, N.Y.), 1953. (*DA* 15:85)

285. Livingston, Eugenia. *A Comparison of the Results of the Kuder Preference Record Given to One Hundred and Four Students as Freshmen and Again as Juniors in the Helena High School.* Master's thesis, Montana State University (Missoula, Mont.), 1953.

286. Long, Louis, and Perry, James D. "Academic Achievement in Engineering Related to Selection Procedures and Interests." *J Appl Psychol* 37:468–71 D '53. * (*PA* 29:1571)

287. Parker, James W., Jr. "Psychological and Personal History Data Related to Accident Records of Commercial Truck Drivers." *J Appl Psychol* 37:317–20 Ag '53. * (*PA* 28:6695)

288. Robb, George P. *Relationships Between Interests and Student Teaching Achievement.* Doctor's thesis, Indiana University (Bloomington, Ind.), 1953. (*DA* 14:1050)

289. Robbins, Arthur. *An Experimental Study of the Relationship Between Needs as Manifested on the Thematic Apperception Test and Kuder Preference Record Scales of Adolescent Boys.* Doctor's thesis, Columbia University (New York, N.Y.), 1953.

290. Rosenberg, Nathan. "Stability and Maturation of Kuder Interest Patterns During High School." *Ed & Psychol Meas* 13:449–58 au '53. * (*PA* 28:4891)

291. Shaffer, Robert H., and Kuder, G. Frederic. "Kuder Interest Patterns of Medical, Law, and Business School Alumni." *J Appl Psychol* 37:367–9 O '53. * (*PA* 29:1716)

292. Sternberg, Carl. "Differences in Measured Interest, Values, and Personality Among College Students Majoring in Nine Subject Areas." Abstract. *Am Psychol* 8:442–3 Ag '53. *

293. Sternberg, Carl. *The Relation of Interests, Values and Personality to the Major Field of Study in College.* Doctor's thesis, New York University (New York, N.Y.), 1953. (*DA* 13:1095)

294. Stoops, John A. "Stability of the Measured Interests of High School Pupils Between Grades Nine and Eleven." *Ed Outlook* 27:116–8 Mr '53. *

295. Tiffin, Joseph, and Phelan, R. F. "Use of the Kuder Preference Record to Predict Turnover in an Industrial Plant." *Personnel Psychol* 6:195–204 su '53. * (*PA* 28:3385)

296. Triggs, Frances Oralind. "Kuder Preference Record," pp. 782–8. (*PA* 27:7799) In *Contributions Toward Medical Psychology: Theory and Psychodiagnostic Methods, Vol. II.* Edited by Arthur Weider. New York: Ronald Press Co., 1953. Pp. xi, 459–885. *

297. Way, Harrison H. *The Relationship Between Forced Choice Scores and Differentiated Response Scores on the Kuder Preference Record-Vocational.* Doctor's thesis, Indiana University (Bloomington, Ind.), 1953. (*DA* 13:1097)

298. Bendig, A. W., and Hughes, J. B., III. "Student Attitude and Achievement in a Course in Introductory Statistics." *J Ed Psychol* 45:268–76 My '54. * (*PA* 29:2952)

299. Bernard, Jack. *Selection of Technical School Students: An Investigation of the Relationship Between Certain Personality Characteristics, Interests and Abilities, and Success in a Radio and Television Curriculum.* Doctor's thesis, New York University (New York, N.Y.), 1954. (*DA* 15:631)

300. Bourdo, Eric A., Jr. "The Interests of Forestry Students." *Ed & Psychol Meas* 14:680–6 w '54. * (*PA* 29:8150)

301. Brooks, Melvin S., and Weynand, Robert S. "Interest Preferences and Their Effect Upon Academic Success." *Social Forces* 32:281–5 Mr '54. *

302. Bruce, Martin M. "Validity Information Exchange, No. 7-079:D.O.T. Code 7-83.058, Electrical Appliance Serviceman." *Personnel Psychol* 7:425–6 au '54. *

303. Bryan, John L. *The Kuder Interest Test Patterns of the Students and the Graduates of the Fire Protection School at Oklahoma A. & M. College.* Doctor's thesis, Oklahoma Agricultural and Mechanical College (Stillwater, Okla.), 1954.

304. Bursch, Charles W. *Utility of the Kuder Preference Record in Selection of Students for Vocational Agriculture.* Doctor's thesis, Stanford University (Stanford, Calif.), 1954. (*DA* 14:2275)

305. Callis, Robert; Engram, William C.; and McGowan, John F. "Coding the Kuder Preference Record—Vocational." *J Appl Psychol* 38:359–63 O '54. * (*PA* 29:6347)

306. Carter, Gerald C. "Kuder Preference Record Scores and Success in Engineering College." *J Counsel Psychol* 1:196 fall '54. *

307. Conner, Harold T. *An Investigation of Certain Factors for the Selection and Guidance of Prospective Students Entering a School of Public Health.* Doctor's thesis, University of North Carolina (Chapel Hill, N.C.), 1954.

308. Curran, James P. *A Study of the Effectiveness of the Kuder Preference Record-Vocational in Private Secondary School for Girls.* Master's thesis, Catholic University of America (Washington, D.C.), 1954

309. Davis, Sandford S. *The Relationship Between School Superintendents' Ratings of Elementary Teachers and the Kuder Preference Record-Personal and Other Measured and Rated Teacher Characteristics.* Doctor's thesis, University of Colorado (Boulder, Colo.), 1954.

310. Durnall, Edward J., Jr. "Falsification of Interest Patterns on the Kuder Preference Record." *J Ed Psychol* 45:240–3 Ap '54. * (*PA* 29:3122)

311. Goche, L. N. *Relationship of Interests and Temperament Traits to Attrition and Survival of Engineering Students.* Master's thesis, Iowa State College (Ames, Iowa), 1954.

312. GOWAN, JOHN CURTIS. "The Interest Patterns of Student Leaders." *Ed & Psychol Meas* 14:151-5 sp '54. * (*PA* 28:8019)

313. GRANT, DONALD L. "Validity Information Exchange, No. 7-085:D.O.T. Code 1-01.05, Budget Clerk." *Personnel Psychol* 7:557-8 w '54. *

314. GRANT, DONALD L. "Validity Information Exchange, No. 7-086:D.O.T. Code 1-01.05, Budget Clerk." *Personnel Psychol* 7:559-60 w '54. *

315. GUAZZO, EUGENE J., JR. *Predicting Academic Success of Architecture Students.* Master's thesis, Alabama Polytechnic Institute (Auburn, Ala.), 1954.

316. GUILFORD, J. P.; CHRISTENSEN, PAUL R.; BOND, NICHOLAS, A., JR.; AND SUTTON, MARCELLA A. "A Factor Analysis Study of Human Interests." *Psychol Monogr* 68(4):1-38 '54. *

317. HAMMILL, DAMIEN. *An Analysis of the Interest Patterns of High School Seniors on Form CH of the Kuder Preference Record.* Master's thesis, Fordham University (New York, N.Y.), 1954.

318. HERZBERG, FREDERICK, AND BOUTON, ARTHUR. "A Further Study of the Stability of the Kuder Preference Record." *Ed & Psychol Meas* 14:326-31 su '54. * (*PA* 29:2605)

319. HERZBERG, FREDERICK; BOUTON, ARTHUR; AND STEINER, BETTY JO. "Studies of the Stability of the Kuder Preference Record." *Ed & Psychol Meas* 14:90-100 sp '54. * (*PA* 28:8114)

320. JACOBS, ROBERT, AND TRAXLER, ARTHUR E. "Use of the Kuder in Counseling With Regard to Accounting as a Career." *J Counsel Psychol* 1:153-8 fall '54. * (*PA* 29:5835)

321. KEGAN, ESTHER O. "Interests of Women Lawyers Shown on the Kuder Preference Record." *Personnel Psychol* 7:499-507 w '54. * (*PA* 29:8157)

322. KELLY, JAMES G. *Feelings of Dominance and Judgments of Humor as Measured by a Non-Projective Preference Scale and a Selected Population of Jokes.* Master's thesis, Bowling Green State University (Bowling Green, Ohio), 1954.

323. KRIEDT, PHILIP H., AND GADEL, MARGUERITE S. "Use of the Kuder Preference Record in Selecting Clerical Employees." Abstract. *Am Psychol* 9:409-10 Ag '54. *

324. LEACH, KENT W. "Intelligence Levels and Corresponding Interest Area Choices of Ninth Grade Pupils in Thirteen Michigan Schools." *J Exp Ed* 22:369-83 Je '54. * (*PA* 29:4651)

325. LEE, PHYLLIS J. *The Effectiveness of a Test Battery in Predicting Chemistry Grades.* Master's thesis, Alabama Polytechnic Institute (Auburn, Ala.), 1954.

326. LEVINE, PHYLLIS ROSENBERG, AND WALLEN, RICHARD. "Adolescent Vocational Interests and Later Occupation." *J Appl Psychol* 38:428-31 D '54. * (*PA* 29:5837)

327. LIPSETT, LAURENCE, AND WILSON, JAMES W. "Do 'Suitable' Interests and Mental Ability Lead to Job Satisfaction?" *Ed & Psychol Meas* 14:373-80 su '54. * (*PA* 29:2607)

328. McCARTY, JOHN J. "Validity Information Exchange, No. 7-077:D.O.T. Code 5-92.621, (Foreman II)." *Personnel Psychol* 7:420-1 au '54. *

329. McCARTY, JOHN J.; WESTBERG, WILLIAM C.; AND FITZPATRICK, EUGENE D. "Validity Information Exchange, No. 7-091:D.O.T. Code 5-92.621, (Foreman II)." *Personnel Psychol* 7:568-9 w '54. *

330. McCOY, RAYMOND A. *Stability and Change of Measured Vocational Interests of High School Students.* Doctor's thesis, University of Missouri (Columbia, Mo.), 1954. (*DA* 15:85)

331. McCULLY, CYRUS H. *The Validity of the Kuder Preference Record.* Doctor's thesis, George Washington University (Washington, D.C.), 1954

332. MEEK, CLINTON R. *The Effect of Knowledge of Aptitude Upon Interest Scores.* Doctor's thesis, George Peabody College for Teachers (Nashville, Tenn.), 1954.

333. PIERCE-JONES, JOHN. "The Readability of Certain Standard Tests." *Calif J Ed Res* 5:80-2 Mr '54. * (*PA* 28:8729)

334. PIERCE-JONES, JOHN, AND CARTER, H. D. "Vocational Interest Measurement Using a Photographic Inventory." *Ed & Psychol Meas* 14:671-9 w '54. * (*PA* 29:7438)

335. ROBERTS, S. OLIVER, AND GUNTER, LAURIE MARTIN. "An Evaluation of the Kuder Interest Patterns of Negro Nurses." Abstract. *Am Psychol* 9:456 Ag '54. *

336. ROSENBERG, NATHAN, AND IZARD, CARROLL E. "Vocational Interests of Naval Aviation Cadets." *J Appl Psychol* 38:354-8 O '54. * (*PA* 29:6363)

337. SHAW, CARL E. *An Investigation of the Validity of the Kuder Preference Record-Vocational for Educational Guidance.* Doctor's thesis, Purdue University (Lafayette, Ind.), 1954. (*DA* 14:1622)

338. SWEENEY, FRANCIS J. "Intelligence, Vocational Interests and Reading Speed of Senior Boys in Catholic High Schools of Los Angeles." *Calif J Ed Res* 5:159-65 S '54. * (*PA* 29:4656)

339. TAYLOR, ERWIN K., AND SCHNEIDER, DOROTHY E. "Validity Information Exchange, No. 7-023:D.O.T. Code 1-86.11, Salesman, Commercial Equipment and Supplies." *Personnel Psychol* 7:158 sp '54. *

340. TIEDEMAN, DAVID V., AND BRYAN, JOSEPH G. "Prediction of College Field of Concentration." *Harvard Ed R* 24:122-39 sp '54. * (*PA* 29:3058)

341. TRAXLER, ARTHUR E. "The Stability of Profiles on the Kuder Preference Records—Vocational and Personal—for Different Groups of Public Accountants." *Yearb Nat Council Meas Used Ed* 11:9-14+ '54. *

342. WESTBERG, WILLIAM C.; FITZPATRICK, EUGENE D.; AND McCARTY, JOHN J. "Validity Information Exchange, No. 7-073:

D.O.T. Code 1-37.32, Typist." *Personnel Psychol* 7:411-2 au '54. *

343. WESTBERG, WILLIAM C.; FITZPATRICK, EUGENE D.; AND McCARTY, JOHN J. "Validity Information Exchange, No. 7-087: D.O.T. Code 1-37.32, Typist." *Personnel Psychol* 7:561-2 w '54. *

344. WRIGHT, RUTH L. *Comparison of Mental Ability and Interest Preferences of a Group of High School Students as Measured by the Terman-McNemar Test of Mental Ability and the Kuder Preference Record.* Master's thesis, Southwest State Teachers College (San Marcos, Tex.), 1954.

345. ATKINSON, EDITH, AND BARON, SAMUEL. "Exploring Vocational Interests in the Ninth Year." *High Points* 37:46-8 Ja '55. *

346. COMREY, ANDREW L., AND HIGH, WALLACE S. "Validity of Some Ability and Interest Scores." *J Appl Psychol* 39:247-8 Ag '55. * (*PA* 30:5278)

347. COOPER, MATTHEW N. *To Determine the Nature and Significance, If Any, of Certain Differences in the Social and Personal Adjustment of Fifty-One Successful and Fifty-One Non-Successful College Students at Texas Southern University.* Doctor's thesis, New York University (New York, N.Y.), 1955. (*DA* 16:497)

348. FOLEY, A. W. "Adjustment Through Interest Changes." *J Counsel Psychol* 2:66-7 sp '55. *

349. FORCE, RONALD C., AND THOMAS, PAUL L. "Development of a Covert Test for the Detection of Alcohol Addiction by a Keying of the Kuder Preference Record." Abstract. *Am Psychol* 10:449 Ag '55. *

350. FORER, BERTRAM R. "The Stability of Kuder Scores in a Disabled Population." *Ed & Psychol Meas* 15:166-9 su '55. * (*PA* 30:3020)

351. FORSTER, CECIL R. *The Relationship Between Test Achievement and Success in Training of a Selected Group of Tuberculosis Patients.* Doctor's thesis, New York University (New York, N.Y.), 1955. (*DA* 15:1201)

352. KELLEY, ELVAN P. *An Investigation Into the Value of Selected Tests and Techniques for Guidance of Prospective Teachers Enrolled in Community Experiences Course.* Doctor's thesis, University of Houston (Houston, Tex.), 1955. (*DA* 15:1209)

353. KLUGMAN, SAMUEL F. "A Study of the Interest Profile of a Psychotic Group and Its Bearing on Interest-Personality Theory." Abstract. *Am Psychol* 10:366 Ag '55. *

354. McCULLY, C. HAROLD. "A Longitudinal Study of the Validity of the Kuder Preference Record." Abstract. *Am Psychol* 10:374 Ag '55. *

355. MAGILL, JOHN W. "Interest Profiles of College Activity Groups: Kuder Preference Record Validation." *J Appl Psychol* 39:53-6 F '55. * (*PA* 30:1564)

356. NEWMAN, JOSEPH. "The Kuder Preference Record and Personal Adjustment: A Study of Tuberculous Patients." *Ed & Psychol Meas* 15:274-80 au '55. * (*PA* 30:5059)

357. PATTERSON, CECIL H. *Test and Background Factors Related to Drop-Outs in an Industrial Institute.* Doctor's thesis, University of Minnesota (Minneapolis, Minn.), 1955. (*DA* 15:1024)

358. PERRINE, MERVYN WILLIAM. "The Selection of Drafting Trainees." *J Appl Psychol* 39:57-61 F '55. * (*PA* 30:1725)

359. SHOEMAKER, WILFRED L. *Rejection of Measured Vocational Interest Areas by High School Students.* Doctor's thesis, University of Missouri (Columbia, Mo.), 1955. (*DA* 16:499)

360. STERNBERG, CARL. "Personality Trait Patterns of College Students Majoring in Different Fields." *Psychol Monogr* 69(18):1-21 '55. * (*PA* 31:1705)

361. STEWART, LAWRENCE H., AND ROBERTS, JOSEPH P. "The Relationship of Kuder Profiles to Remaining in a Teachers' College and to Occupational Choice." *Ed & Psychol Meas* 15:416-21 w '55. * (*PA* 30:7792)

362. STOWE, EDWARD W. *The Relation of the Kuder Vocational Preference Record to Ammons' Apperception Test.* Master's thesis, Illinois State Normal University (Normal, Ill.), 1955.

363. TUTTON, MARIE E. "Stability of Adolescent Vocational Interest." *Voc Guid Q* 3:78-80 sp '55. *

364. ARBUCKLE, DUGALD S. "Client Perception of Counselor Personality." *J Counsel Psychol* 3:93-6 su '56. * (*PA* 31:4639)

365. BEAVER, ALMA P. "Psychometric Data and Survival in a College of Nursing." *Psychol Rep* 2:223-6 Je '56. * (*PA* 31:1738)

366. DOWNIE, N. M. "The Vocational Interest Patterns of Students Who Stay in Engineering Compared With Those Who Leave the Engineering Curriculum." Abstract. *Ind Acad Sci Proc* 66:324 '56. *

367. EWENS, WILLIAM PRICE. "Experience Patterns as Related to Vocational Preference." *Ed & Psychol Meas* 16:223-31 su '56. * (*PA* 31:4803)

368. GEHMAN, W. SCOTT, AND SOUTHERN, J. ALBERT. "The Kuder Electrical Engineering Scale for Counseling College Students." *J Counsel Psychol* 3:17-20 sp '56. * (*PA* 31:3749)

369. GOLDSTEIN, ARNOLD P. *The Fakability of the Kuder Preference Record and the Vocational Apperception Test.* Master's thesis, City College of New York (New York, N.Y.), 1956.

370. GOWAN, J. C. "Achievement and Personality Test Scores of Gifted College Students." *Calif J Ed Res* 7:105-9 My '56. * (*PA* 31:3783)

371. GUBA, E. G., AND GETZELS, J. W. "Interest and Value

Patterns of Air Force Officers." *Ed & Psychol Meas* 16:465–70 w '56. * *(PA* 32:977)

372. HALE, PETER P., AND LEONARD, REGIS J. "The Kuder Preference Record and the Professional Curriculum." *J Ed Res* 50:71–4 S '56. * *(PA* 31:6222)

373. HASELKORN, HARRY. "The Vocational Interests of a Group of Male Homosexuals." *J Counsel Psychol* 3:8–11 sp '56. * *(PA* 31:3211)

374. HENDERSON, ERWIN C. *The Kuder-Preference Record—Vocational in Appraising the Apparent Suitability of Vocational Choices of High School Students.* Master's thesis, Utah State Agricultural College (Logan, Utah), 1956.

375. HOLE, RICHARD M. *A Comparison of Students' Vocational Interests With Parental Judgments of Students' Interests.* Master's thesis, Ohio University (Athens, Ohio), 1956.

376. HOOVER, KENNETH H., AND MICKA, HELEN K. "Student-Parent Interest Comparisons in Counseling High School Students." *Personnel & Guid J* 34:292–4 Ja '56. * *(PA* 30:7735)

377. HYMAN, BERNARD. "The Relationship of Social Status and Vocational Interests." *J Counsel Psychol* 3:12–6 sp '56. * *(PA* 31:3212)

378. KINGSTON, ALBERT J.; GEORGE, CLAY E.; AND EWENS, W. PRICE. "Determining the Relationship Between Individual Interest Profiles and Occupational Forms." *J Ed Psychol* 47:310–6 My '56. * *(PA* 32:2043)

379. KLINE, MILTON V., AND CUMINGS, RUTH. "A Study of the Learning Characteristics of Public Health Nurses in Relation to Mental Health Education and Consultation: IV, Kuder Vocational Interest Patterns." *J Genetic Psychol* 88:37–59 Mr '56. * *(PA* 31:4805)

380. LANGE, HERBERT M. *An Analysis of the Kuder Preference Record Results at Hardin-Simmons University.* Master's thesis, Hardin-Simmons University (Abilene, Tex.), 1956.

381. LIVINGSTON, CHARLES D. *The Personality Correlates of High and Low Identification With the Father Figure.* Doctor's thesis, University of Houston (Houston, Tex.), 1956. *(DA* 16:2525)

382. SAMUELSON, CECIL O., AND PEARSON, DAVID T. "Interest Scores in Identifying the Potential Trade School Dropout." *J Appl Psychol* 40:386–8 D '56. * *(PA* 32:2126)

383. SHINN, EDMOND O. "Interest and Intelligence as Related to Achievement in Tenth Grade." *Calif J Ed Res* 7:217–20 N '56. * *(PA* 31:8844)

384. SINNETT, E. ROBERT. "Some Determinants of Agreement Between Measured and Expressed Interests." *Ed & Psychol Meas* 16:110–8 sp '56. * *(PA* 31:6226)

385. STERNBERG, CARL. "Interests and Tendencies Toward Maladjustment in a Normal Population." *Personnel & Guid J* 35:94–9 O '56. * *(PA* 31:7975)

386. THARPE, FRANK D. *Usefulness of the Kuder Preference Record for Predicting Shop Achievement of Senior High School Students in Industrial Arts.* Master's thesis, Iowa State College (Ames, Iowa), 1956.

387. VOPATEK, S. H. "Normative Data Information Exchange, No. 32." *Personnel Psychol* 9:544 w '56. *

388. ZENTI, RICO N. *A Comparison of the Results Obtained by the Mitchell and Kuder Interest Measures When Administered to Male Freshmen at the University of Michigan.* Doctor's thesis, University of Michigan (Ann Arbor, Mich.), 1956. *(DA* 17:1265)

389. ADAMS, FRANK J. *A Study of the Stability of Broad Vocational Interests at the High School Level.* Doctor's thesis, New York University (New York, N.Y.), 1957. *(DA* 19:270)

390. BEAMER, GEORGE C., AND LEDBETTER, ELAINE W. "The Relation Between Teacher Attitudes and the Social Service Interest." *J Ed Res* 50:655–66 My '57. *

391. BENDIG, A. W. "Validity of Kuder Differences Among Honors Majors." *Ed & Psychol Meas* 17:593–8 w '57. *

392. BONE, JOHN H. *A Statistical Analysis of Interest Patterns of High School Students and Their Relationship to Intelligence and Achievement.* Doctor's thesis, Pennsylvania State University (State College, Pa.), 1957. *(DA* 18:115)

393. BRAYFIELD, ARTHUR H., AND MARSH, MARY MARKLEY. "Aptitudes, Interests, and Personality Characteristics of Farmers." *J Appl Psychol* 41:98–103 Ap '57. *

394. BRODY, DAVID S. "Kuder Interest Patterns of Professional Forest Service Men." *Ed & Psychol Meas* 17:599–605 w '57. *

395. BRUCE, MARTIN M. "Normative Data Information Exchange, No. 10–42." *Personnel Psychol* 10:534–5 w '57. *

396. DAY, MERLE E. *Kuder Preference Record Responses of a Selected Group of Schizophrenics (Counseling Referrals) as a Function of Personality Traits.* Doctor's thesis, New York University (New York, N.Y.), 1957. *(DA* 18:654)

397. GOWAN, J. C. "Intelligence, Interests, and Reading Ability in Relation to Scholastic Achievement." *Psychol Newsl* 8:85–7 Mr–Ap '57. * *(PA* 32:3346)

398. GOWAN, J. C., AND SEAGOE, MAY. "The Relation Between Interest and Aptitude Tests in Art and Music." *Calif J Ed Res* 8:43–5 Ja '57. *

399. KLUGMAN, SAMUEL F. "A Study of the Interest Profile of a Psychotic Group and Its Bearing on Interest-Personality Theory." *Ed & Psychol Meas* 17:55–64 sp '57. *

400. KUDER, G. FREDERIC. "A Comparative Study of Some Methods of Developing Occupational Keys." *Ed & Psychol Meas* 17:105–14 sp '57. *

401. LAIRD, J. T. "A Note on the Scoring Rationale of the Kuder Preference Record." *Can J Psychol* 11:133–5 Je '57. *

402. MCCARTY, JOHN J. "Normative Data Information Exchange, No. 10–37." *Personnel Psychol* 10:527–8 w '57. *

403. MAIER, GLEN E. *The Contribution of Interest Test Scores to Differential Academic Prediction.* Doctor's thesis, University of Washington (Seattle, Wash.), 1957. *(DA* 18:150)

404. SHAH, SALEEM A. *An Investigation of Predictive Ability in Hospital Personnel and University Students.* Doctor's thesis, Pennsylvania State University (State College, Pa.), 1957. *(DA* 18:288)

405. STEWART, LAWRENCE H. "Does Knowledge of Performance on an Aptitude Test Change Scores on the Kuder?" *J Counsel Psychol* 4:161–4 su '57. *

406. STONE, SOLOMON. *The Contribution of Intelligence, Interests, Temperament and Certain Personality Variables to Academic Achievement in a Physical Science and Mathematics Curriculum.* Doctor's thesis, New York University (New York, N.Y.), 1957. *(DA* 18:669)

407. TOPETZES, NICK JOHN. "A Program for the Selection of Trainees in Physical Medicine." *J Exp Ed* 25:263–311 Je '57. *

408. ARNOLD, DWIGHT L. "Student Reaction to the Kuder." *Personnel & Guid J* 37:40–4 S '58. *

409. BARRETT, RICHARD S. "The Process of Predicting Job Performance." *Personnel Psychol* 11:39–57 sp '58. *

410. CRAVEN, ETHEL C. *Social Concomitants of Interest.* Doctor's thesis, Columbia University (New York, N.Y.), 1958. *(DA* 19:353)

411. FORCE, RONALD C. "Development of a Covert Test for the Detection of Alcoholism by a Keying of the Kuder Preference Record." *Q J Studies Alcohol* 19:72–8 Mr '58. *

412. FRENCH, JOSEPH L. "Interests of the Gifted." *Voc Guid Q* 7:14–6 au '58. *

413. GLAZER, STANFORD H. "Educational Attainment and Interest Patterns." *Voc Guid Q* 6:183–6 su '58. *

414. HILL, GEORGE E., AND HOLE, RICHARD M. "Comparison of the Vocational Interests of Tenth Grade Students With Their Parents' Judgments of These Interests." *Ed & Psychol Meas* 18:173–87 sp '58. *

415. HILL, GEORGE E., AND ROGGE, HAROLD. "The Relation of Kuder Preference Record Scores to Mental Maturity Scores in High School." *J Ed Res* 51:545–8 Mr '58. *

416. MOORE, CHARLES W. *Some Relationships Between Standardized Test Scores and Academic Performance in the College of Business Administration of the University of Houston.* Doctor's thesis, University of Houston (Houston, Tex.), 1958. *(DA* 19:356)

417. SAMUELSON, CECIL O. "Interest Scores in Predicting Success of Trade School Students." *Personnel & Guid J* 36:538–41 Ap '58. *

418. SMITH, D. D. "Abilities and Interests: I, A Factorial Study." *Can J Psychol* 12:191–201 S '58. *

419. WRIGHT, JOHN C., AND SCARBOROUGH, BARRON B. "Relationship of the Interests of College Freshmen to Their Interests as Sophomores and as Seniors." *Ed & Psychol Meas* 18:153–8 sp '58. *

CLIFFORD P. FROEHLICH, *Professor of Education, University of California, Berkeley, California.*

The principal differences between the earlier Form B (1942) and the later Form C (1948) are the addition of verification and outdoor scores and new normative data for adolescent and adult profiles. Since these changes represent substantial improvements in the instrument, this reviewer sees no reason for anyone to continue using the older Form B. Because that form is now obsolete no further reference will be made to it in these comments.

Form C follows the long established pattern of the *Kuder Preference Record* with claims for being "self-administering," and having "self-interpreting profiles." More accurate claims would be that the test is relatively easy to administer and that most persons are able to score it and prepare a profile of their scores. Interpreting the profile requires all the acumen a skillful counselor can bring to the task.

This reviewer's greatest dissatisfaction with

this instrument lies in the author's implication that the scores have *established* relevance to occupations. The latest manual (1956) again presents fragmentary percentile ranks of the median scores of a variety of occupations. Except in the instances where data were reported by other investigators, accurate descriptions of the occupational groups are lacking. What, for example, is the denominational affiliation of the 43 clergymen for whom median scores are reported? Or what positions are held by the 65 school administrators whose scores are reported?

Further lack of confidence in the occupational significance of the scores stems from the fact that many were contributed by test users. Whether these tests were administered to persons as a part of a counseling relationship or to persons seeking employment is unknown.

There is a need for the author to develop data which would facilitate the interpretation of the profile. The current manual suggests that scores above the 75th percentile indicate occupational areas which should be considered by the testee, and that those below the 25th percentile give clues to occupations which should be eliminated from consideration. Interpretation of the test in this manner neglects the pattern of scores. Work with the *Strong Vocational Interest Blank* indicates pattern analysis is a fruitful approach in understanding the meaning of an interest profile. This reviewer's opinion is that Kuder's halfhearted invitation for users to develop specific occupational keys by means of Fisher's discriminant function is no substitute for data which would assist the counselor in interpreting the profile as a whole.

The opinions expressed above should not be construed as meaning that this reviewer does not recommend this inventory. Among those available, it is his choice when the use of Strong's blank is inappropriate or not feasible. Perhaps his opinions are reinforced by impatience because the author and publisher have not made more data available for interpreting a test which has been so widely used and highly respected for almost 20 years.

John Pierce-Jones, *Associate Professor of Educational Psychology, The University of Texas, Austin, Texas.*

The Fourth Mental Measurements Yearbook presented three reviews of the *Kuder Prefer-ence Record—Vocational* (KPR-V) based mainly on the 1951 manual for Form C. Those discussions should be consulted by KPR-V users. This review considers the inventory in relation to various strengths and weaknesses pointed up in the earlier discussions.

The KPR-V is an attractive, popular inventory useful in vocational counseling with high school youth and many adults. It is easily administered and conveniently scored by hand or by machine. Appropriate answer sheets, scoring stencils, and profile sheets are available for Forms B and C. Examinees find the KPR-V an interesting inventory, although some have difficulty choosing among seemingly equally attractive, or unattractive, alternatives in the triadic forced choice items. It can still be said correctly that the KPR-V, among interest inventories, is a carefully planned, well constructed instrument approaching, without attaining, the standard of technical thoroughness set by the *Strong Vocational Interest Blank*.

In the past, an outstanding feature of the Kuder has been the conscientious provision by the author and the publisher of current interpretive data, research summaries, and improved norms. The 1956 manual is, however, essentially identical with the 1951 edition albeit 91 titles have been added to the list of references, and a slightly revised job chart (Table 1) appears. The published norms do not appear to have changed in five years. There seem to have been no additions to old reliability data; information concerning the temporal stability of scores is still missing. No important additional evidence regarding KPR-V validity has been summarized. Therefore, this reviewer thinks it important to sample some recent research bearing on these considerations.

Work with the SVIB has shown that its interest scores are remarkably stable over rather long periods. Does this hold also for the KPR-V? Certainly there is less evidence regarding the stability of Kuder scores, but what exists does point to relatively high stability. Rosenberg (*290*) examined high school pupils in ninth grade and, later, in twelfth grade obtaining test-retest correlations ranging between .47 and .75, a result corroborated by Herzberg and Bouton (*318*). Reid's (*234*) work with college level subjects resulted in a median retest correlation of .77 over a 15-month interval.

Validity, a complicated consideration in respect of any psychometric device, is an exceptionally complex matter in considering interest inventories. In the present KPR-V manual, as in earlier ones, mean profiles for small, not demonstrably representative occupational groups constitute the main evidence of validity. Meteorologists, for example, average high in scientific and low in persuasive interest. This is attractive but unconvincing material. The needed research using the KPR-V with specific criterion groups has appeared infrequently, but the present manual lags behind what exists. For example, Stewart and Roberts (*361*) have shown that female teacher trainees leaving a training college after two years had different profiles from those remaining to graduate. Kline and Cumings (*379*) found public health nurses different from other nurses, physicians, and laboratory technicians. Samuelson and Pearson (*382*) found no differences between successful trade school students and dropouts. Arbuckle (*364*) reported KPR-V differences between counselor trainees perceived by peers as those to whom clients would be most and least likely to go for help. Newman (*203*) and Forer (*350*) found evidence of relationships between Kuder scores and physical and emotional disabilities. Haselkorn (*373*) found differences between male homosexuals and matched controls. Klugman (*399*) reported that profiles for psychotics in remission do not differ significantly from Kuder's base groups. Pierce-Jones [1] has developed KPR-V scales which predicted an objective criterion of socio-economic status in cross validation groups. Still other recent research (*326, 334, 346, 372*) bears on the validity of this inventory.

In summary, a fair current appraisal of the KPR-V would seem to be that it is an excellent inventory for preliminary surveys of interests in counseling and in school guidance and occupational instruction. Immediate attention ought to be devoted to providing more representative occupational group norms and a more comprehensive edition of the manual including newer data on the stability of scores and on validity in terms of particular criteria. Perhaps, in view of the very extensive use that is made of the Kuder in clinical and educational settings, a volume dealing with the

KPR-V in the same way in which Strong treated the SVIB in *Vocational Interests of Men and Women* should be considered.

For reviews by Edward S. Bordin, Harold D. Carter, and H. M. Fowler, see 4:742; for reviews by Ralph F. Berdie, E. G. Chambers, and Donald E. Super of Forms BB and BM, see 3:640 (1 excerpt); for reviews by A. B. Crawford and Arthur E. Traxler of an earlier edition, see 40:1617.

[864]

*Occupational Interest Inventory, 1956 Revision. Grades 7–16 and adults, 9–16 and adults; 1943–56; 10 scores grouped in 3 categories: fields of interests (personal-social, natural, mechanical, business, the arts, the sciences), types of interests (verbal, manipulative, computational), level of interests; IBM; 1 form ('56); 2 levels: intermediate, advanced; intermediate manual ('56), advanced manual ('56); intermediate norms based upon norms for advanced form; $4.90 per 35 tests; separate answer sheets may be used; 4¢ per IBM answer sheet; 7¢ per Scoreze answer sheet; 60¢ per set of either hand or machine scoring stencils; postage extra; 50¢ per specimen set of either level, postpaid; (30–40) minutes; Edwin A. Lee and Louis P. Thorpe; California Test Bureau. *

REFERENCES

1–20. See 4:743.
21. BARKSDALE, ANNE. *Comparison of Achievement in Typewriting and Interest as Measured by an Occupational Interest Inventory.* Master's thesis, University of North Carolina (Chapel Hill, N.C.), 1947.
22. PRIDEAUX, GERALD G. *The Development of Diagnostic Aids for the Lee-Thorpe Occupational Interest Inventory.* Master's thesis, Kansas State Teachers College (Pittsburg, Kan.), 1949.
23. JOHNSON, RALPH H., AND BOND, GUY L. "Reading Ease of Commonly Used Tests." *J Appl Psychol* 34:319–24 O '50. * (PA 26:299)
24. BROWN, MANUEL N. *Clinical Status of Veteran Patients Related to Six Interest Variables.* Doctor's thesis, University of Portland (Portland, Ore.), 1951.
25. FERSON, REGIS F. *The Probabilities of Success in Trade Training as Estimated by Standardized Tests.* Doctor's thesis, University of Pittsburgh (Pittsburgh, Pa.), 1951.
26. VACCARO, JOSEPH J. *A Study of Psychological Factors That Contrast the Most and Least Efficient Psychiatric Aids in a Mental Hospital.* Doctor's thesis, Fordham University (New York, N.Y.), 1951.
27. LIEN, ARNOLD JUEL. "A Comparative-Predictive Study of Students in the Four Curricula of a Teacher Education Institution." *J Exp Ed* 21:81–219 D '52.
28. MACPHAIL, ANDREW H., AND THOMPSON, GEORGE R. "Interest Patterns for Certain Occupational Groups: Occupational Interest Inventory (Lee-Thorpe)." *Ed & Psychol Meas* 12:79–89 sp '52. * (PA 27:5960)
29. MASTEN, FRANK D. *The Personality Development and Occupational Interests of the Sixth, Seventh, and Eighth Grade Pupils at Father Flanagan's Boys' Home, Boys Town, Nebraska.* Doctor's field study, Colorado State College of Education (Greeley, Colo.), 1952.
30. TORR, DONALD V. "A Factor Analysis of Selected Interest Inventories." Abstract. *Am Psychol* 7:296 Jl '52. *
31. WOODWARD, C. L. "A Critical Analysis of Certain Interest Tests." *Yearb Nat Council Meas Used Ed* 9:101–8 '52. *
32. AUSUBEL, DAVID P.; SCHIFF, HERBERT M.; AND ZELENY, MARJORIE P. "'Real-Life' Measures of Level of Academic and Vocational Aspiration in Adolescents: Relation to Laboratory Measures and to Adjustment." *Child Develop* 24:155–68 S–D '53. * (PA 29:3700)
33. BRIDGE, LEOPOLD, AND MORSON, MEYER. "Item Validity of the Lee-Thorpe Occupational Interest Inventory." *J Appl Psychol* 37:380–3 O '53. * (PA 29:1042)
34. MACPHAIL, ANDREW H. "Interest Patterns for Certain Degree Groups on the Lee-Thorpe Occupational Interest Inventory." *J Appl Psychol* 38:164–6 Je '54. * (PA 29:4691)
35. SINGER, STANLEY L., AND STEFFLRE, BUFORD. "The Relationship of Job Values and Desires to Vocational Aspirations of Adolescents." *J Appl Psychol* 38:419–22 D '54. * (PA 29:5843)

1 PIERCE-JONES, JOHN. "Vocational Interest Correlates of Socio-Economic Status in Adolescence." *Ed & Psychol Meas,* in press.

36. GEORGE, CLAY E., AND KINGSTON, ALBERT J. "The Stability of Interest Scores of College Freshmen." *J Ed Psychol* 46: 243–6 Ap '55. * (*PA* 30:1557)
37. LINDGREN, HENRY CLAY, AND GILBERG, RICHARD L. "Interpreting Occupational Interest: The Relationships Between the Lee-Thorpe Occupational Interest Inventory and the Strong Vocational Interest Test for Men." *Calif J Ed Res* 6:15–21 Ja '55. * (*PA* 29:7430)
38. STEFFLRE, BUFORD. "Vocational Aspiration and Level of Interest Scores on the Lee-Thorpe Occupational Interest Inventory." *Personnel & Guid J* 33:385–8 Mr '55. * (*PA* 30:3031)
39. RAMEY, WALTER S. *Usefulness of the Lee-Thorpe Occupational Interest Inventory for Predicting Achievement and Choice of Core Areas in Des Moines Technical School.* Master's thesis, Iowa State College (Ames, Iowa), 1956.
40. CONGDON, ROBERT G., AND JERVIS, FREDERICK M. "A Different Approach to Interest Profiles." Comment by Paul Dressel. *J Counsel Psychol* 5:50–7 sp '58. *

MARTIN KATZ, *Assistant Director, Evaluation and Advisory Service, Educational Testing Service, Princeton, New Jersey.*

The manual for the *Occupational Interest Inventory* makes much of the fact that the scores for the six "fields of interests" are based on forced choices between paired statements. In discussing interpretation of scores, the manual recommends that after identification of the "one or two highest" interest fields, "the next step is a study of the 3 Types," which further refine the areas of major interest: "For example, a high score in the Personal-Social Field combined with a high score in the Manipulative Type would result in examination of a different group of occupations than would be the case if a high score in the Personal-Social Field were supported by a high score in the Computational or Verbal Types." This, on the face of it, might seem quite reasonable.

However, it should be noted that the type scores are not independently derived from forced choices between pairings of statements purporting to represent the different types. Instead, 90 of the 240 field statements are also designated as representing interest types (30 for each type). Thus, each tally for a type score rides in on the coattails of a forced choice for a field statement.

The manual recognizes that "several of these combinations [between field and type] are much more frequently found than are others," implying that such combinations reflect actual relationships which are significant for occupational focus. It neglects to point out that field-type score combinations are largely artifacts of the inventory. For example, of the 30 verbal type statements on the advanced inventory, 14 are designated also as personal-social field statements, 7 are business field, and 9 are arts field (on the intermediate inventory, the corresponding numbers are 13, 9, and 8).

Thus, it is not at all surprising to find in the intercorrelation matrices relatively high coefficients of correlation between verbal type and personal-social field scores (.64 to .74) and lower but still positive coefficients of correlation between verbal type and business field scores (.33 to .57) and verbal type and arts field scores (.19 to .40). Since not a single scientific field statement is classified as a verbal type statement, it is not surprising to find negative coefficients of correlation between verbal type and scientific field scores ($-.33$ to $-.49$). Thus, the inventory, *by the nature of its construction,* would tend to give a high verbal type score for people with high personal-social field scores but would rarely give a high verbal type score in conjunction with a high scientific field score.

To carry this demonstration further, on the intermediate inventory 15 of the 30 manipulative type statements are also arts field statements; only 2 of the 30 are mechanical field statements. Therefore, one must not be surprised to find on the intermediate battery correlation coefficients of .59 (for females) and .69 (for males) between manipulative type and arts field scores, along with correlation coefficients of $-.39$ and $-.24$ between manipulative type and mechanical field scores. However, in the advanced inventory only 8 of the 30 manipulative type statements are also arts field statements, while 7 of the 30 are mechanical field. Consequently, on the advanced inventory the correlation coefficients between manipulative type and arts field scores are $-.07$ and .06; but between manipulative type and mechanical field, .18 and .32.

Similarly, computational type statements are tied almost exclusively to business and scientific fields (respectively, 17 and 10 of 30 on the advanced inventory, 15 and 10 of 30 on the intermediate). Thus, the correlation coefficients between mechanical field and computational type scores range from $-.21$ to $-.47$, and a high mechanical field-computational type combination would tend to be rare.

It does not seem likely that the foregoing coefficients are offered as representative of hypothesized relationships between the various fields and types of interests. If so, some of them would be rather startling and provocative —for example, even allowing for idiosyncrasies of nomenclature, one would not ordinarily expect a negative relationship between categories labeled "Mechanical" and "Manipulative." On the other hand, to recognize the apparent relationships merely as artifacts of the inventory is to weaken seriously the publisher's case for interpretation of scores.

Unfortunately, this case is already quite weak. Normative and validity data presented in the manual are such that useful interpretation of scores must be, for the most part, arbitrary or intuitive. The previous edition of the inventory was soundly spanked (see 3:643 and 4:743) for two major deficiencies: failure to describe the composition of the norms group and lack of research on validity. It must be reported that the manual for the 1956 Revision still falls short of full disclosure. Here is the complete passage describing "The Normative Population" in the manual for the advanced inventory:

> The percentile norms presented in this Manual were obtained from over 25,000 Inventories given to high school and college students, veterans, and other adults. They are based on cases reported from New England, Tennessee, California, Utah, and Idaho. The norms are suitable not only for high school pupils and college students but also for the general adult population. This is particularly true because the instrument requires a comparison and choice between 120 pairs of activities in which the distribution of choices rather than a total score provides the significant data.
> Norms for the *Occupational Interest Inventory, Advanced* reflect the performance of examinees who are representative of the population nationally on interest inventory items which have been carefully selected and validated.

The glib array of nonsequiturs provided by the last three sentences is certainly no substitute for more specific information about the norms group. Lumping together these "over 25,000....high school and college students, veterans, and other adults" in unspecified proportions, with no hint of stratification, to provide omnibus or all-purpose norms, might be justified on the grounds that these subgroups were virtually indistinguishable from each other. Such a condition not only is contrary to logic; it is contrary to the few specific score summaries actually reported for different groups. Thus, the catch-as-catch-can "normative population" certainly cannot be said to provide an intrinsically meaningful comparison group for any individual's scores. There is no evidence that it is "representative of the population nationally," or that it is suitable for use with *any* of the groups mentioned (high school pupils, college students, general adult population), let alone all of them. In short, it is not

a norms group; it is merely an agglomeration of cases.

The manual for the intermediate inventory maintains that the intermediate norms are suitable "not only for junior high school pupils but also for the general adult population." In fact, the norms for the intermediate inventory were not independently derived, but were linked to the norms for the advanced inventory. Advanced and intermediate inventories were both administered to 118 male and 118 female 10th graders (no further characterization of this group is given):

> The two tests were equated on the basis of the raw scores. The raw scores of the Intermediate Inventory were then given the percentile rankings of the corresponding raw scores of the Advanced Inventory. The norms that resulted....were compared with norms based on cases reported for 5,470 male and 4,870 female students enrolled in grades seven to nine. The two sets of norms were encouragingly comparable.

In the absence of more precise data (and why so bashful about presenting "encouraging" data?), this reviewer cannot share the publisher's feeling of encouragement. He can derive no feeling of security from the knowledge that the intermediate norms are anchored in the amorphous jelly of the advanced norms. Even if the advanced norms were of firmer substance there would remain a need to state and reason about some of the assumptions involved in using this common anchorage.

Of course even well defined and coherent norms groups would not in themselves solve the many problems of meaningful interpretation of scores. They would, however, be more likely to lead to fruitful hypotheses and research on validity. At present, the manual stresses use of score patterns for guidance. But to what purpose should the counselor ascertain that Joe Smith, confronted with a series of forced choices, preferred more descriptive statements of a certain category than did 90 per cent—or 50 per cent—or 10 per cent—of an appropriate comparison group? First, he needs to know what, if any, significance Joe's relative preference for this and other categories of statements has for educational and occupational decisions. Thus, suppose Joe's scientific field score placed him at the 70th percentile of a normative population of 10th grade boys. What does this mean about his potential interest in a high school physics course? in a college engineering program? in medical studies? in the occupation of nuclear physicist? According to the manual, scores at the 70th percentile or higher in any category are to be regarded as significant for choices assumed to involve a substantial amount of activity corresponding to that interest category. Then, presumably, if Joe ranked at the 50th percentile in the mechanical field and at the 70th percentile in the scientific field, he would be described as having "more" interest in scientific than in mechanical fields and would probably be encouraged (ability data and other circumstances permitting) to consider educational and occupational choices characterized more heavily by "scientific" than by "mechanical" activities.

But even if we assumed the categories to be accurate and the norms unexceptionable, where is the evidence that preferences resulting in a 70th percentile on the scientific field are likely to lead to satisfaction or interest in high school physics, engineering college, medical school, or a career as a nuclear physicist? One might be equally justified in asserting that a 50th percentile in the mechanical field is more conducive to interest and satisfaction in a high school industrial arts course and the occupation of carpenter than a 70th percentile in the scientific field is to interest and satisfaction in a high school physics course and a career as a nuclear physicist. In the absence of the most elementary empirical validation, perhaps it is supererogatory to fuss about norms at all.

Certainly the validation of an interest inventory is a knotty problem. In the manual for the 1956 Revision of the *Occupational Interest Inventory* will be found no sword of Alexander to cut this Gordian knot. At best, there have been a few routine hacks at it with blunt scissors. Thus, phi coefficients for the statements in each category are furnished; correlation studies with *Kuder Preference Record* scales and with *Strong Vocational Interest Blank* scales are charted; there is some crowing about a factor analysis of six interest inventories including the *Occupational Interest Inventory*. (The manual does not name the other five inventories—among which, it turns out, was neither the Kuder nor the Strong. Analyses which have included these instruments have turned up factors less similar to the *Occupational Interest Inventory* rubrics.)

The correlation study with the Strong involved only 60 cases. Although the manual calls attention to the positive correlations which might have been expected a priori between some *Occupational Interest Inventory* fields and Strong scales, there is no attempt to account for the following correlation coefficients: between Strong physician scale and inventory personal-social field (which includes, as one of its subcategories, "Health and Medical Service"), $-.03$; between Strong policeman scale and inventory personal-social field (which includes "Law and Law Enforcement" as one of its subcategories), $-.16$; between inventory "level of interests" score and Strong scales for president (manufacturing concern), physician, mathematician, and physicist, $-.07$, $-.23$, $-.14$, and $-.03$, respectively.

Nevertheless, publication of such data is a step in the right direction. With more (and more ambitious) validity studies, the *Occupational Interest Inventory* may yet become useful. Meanwhile, it is a shame to have to describe it again, after the number of years in which it has been marketed and used, as a "promising instrument."

WILBUR L. LAYTON, *Professor of Psychology, and Assistant Director, Student Counseling Bureau, University of Minnesota, Minneapolis, Minnesota.*

It is very frustrating to this reviewer, in considering the possible impact of this review, to find that an inventory which received very unfavorable reviews in both the third and fourth *Mental Measurements Yearbooks* is still in existence, has been researched and revised so little, and is still being offered for sale as a valid instrument. The revision has consisted of the replacement of a few items and an increase in the number of items contributing to the type scores. In addition, some changes have been made in the manual. At present, the manual is written so that it breathes an air of respectability which close and critical scrutiny reveals is rather thin. Most of the research presented is based on the unrevised inventory, and attempts have been made to adjust these data to reflect changes in the inventory. There is no indication of how these adjustments were made or, for that matter, of the appropriateness of making such changes.

It is in the area of validity that the manual is perhaps most misleading. A great deal of weight is placed by the test authors on content validity, but, as the research of Strong has indicated, content validity is not a *sine qua non* to discriminating occupational groups on the basis of interest. There is little further evidence of validity, although the intercorrelation study by Torr (*30*) is presented as one demonstration of validity. In addition, correlations between the unrevised *Occupational Interest Inventory,* the *Strong Vocational Interest Blank,* and the *Kuder Preference Record* are presented as evidence of validity. Patterns of mean scores for several college and high school groups are also presented. These data are, however, very meager. The authors still have not collected data on occupational groups, although certainly this is most desirable. As the *Technical Recommendations for Psychological Tests and Diagnostic Techniques* points out, most interest inventories are used for prediction purposes. The interpretation of an interest inventory to a counseling client implies some predictive validity. Thus, it is particularly important that such inventories have evidence of predictive validity. Although the authors present the inventory as useful in counseling high school and college students, there has been no attempt to do a long-range longitudinal study which would provide meaningful data concerning the validity in predicting occupational criteria.

The only reliability data given are of the test-retest variety. There is no indication in the manual as to whether these data are based upon the revised or original form. It is to the credit of the authors that they present standard errors of measurement, but some of these are disturbingly large compared to the standard deviations listed. This means, of course, that the reliabilities for the scales involved are not good enough to justify their use in individual counseling. This conclusion is supported by the research of George and Kingston (*36*).

The norms are also inadequate; they are based on the unrevised advanced form. The authors state they are suitable, not only for high school pupils and college students, but also for the general adult population. But, there is no indication of the representativeness of these norms for any well defined population. The authors state the norms were adjusted to take into account the revision of the inventory. No details of this adjustment are given. The authors suggest that when the inventory is being used for selection and placement in business and industry the composite population norms should be used. This, of course, would obscure the relationship of sex

to score and, according to data presented, there is such a relationship. What justification the authors have for making this suggestion to business and industry is beyond this reviewer's comprehension.

On the basis of the limited amount of information available about the *Occupational Interest Inventory,* this reviewer recommends that it be considered an experimental inventory at best and that it be so labeled so that the unwary prospective user will not be led astray. He further recommends that it not be used in counseling individual students and that its use be restricted to experimental and research purposes until it has been properly standardized.

For reviews by Arthur H. Brayfield of the original edition, see 4:743; for reviews by Edward S. Bordin and Stanley G. Dulsky, see 3:643.

[865]
★Picture Interest Inventory. Grades 7 and over; 1958; 9 scores: interpersonal service, natural, mechanical, business, esthetic, scientific, verbal, computational, time perspective; IBM; 1 form; separate answer sheets must be used; $5.25 per 35 tests; 5¢ per IBM answer sheet; $1 per set of hand or machine scoring stencils; postage extra; 50¢ per specimen set, postpaid; scoring service available; (20–30) minutes; Kurt P. Weingarten; California Test Bureau. *

[866]
★Qualifications Record. Sales personnel; 1958; 45 interests in 7 areas: arts, biology, computation, literary, physical, social, technology; Form A; no data on reliability and validity: $23.75 per 100 tests; $1 per specimen set; $12.50 per individual job qualifications report; postpaid; (45) minutes; Keith Van Allyn; Bureau of Personnel Research, Inc. *

[867]
★Rothwell Interest Blank, Miller Revision. Ages 13 and over; 1958; Forms M, F ('58); manual ('58); 3s. per 10 blanks; 12s. 6d. per manual; postpaid within Australia; (20–30) minutes; Kenneth M. Miller and J. W. Rothwell; Australian Council for Educational Research. *

[868]
*Strong Vocational Interest Blank for Men, Revised. Ages 17 and over; 1927–59; 57 scoring scales (47 occupations, 6 occupational group scales, and 4 nonvocational scales): Group I: group scale ('38), artist ('38), psychologist ('28–49) by P. H. Kriedt, architect ('38), physician ('38–52), psychiatrist ('52), osteopath ('47), dentist ('38), veterinarian ('49) by T. E. Hannum; Group II: group scale ('39), physicist ('52), chemist ('38), mathematician ('38), engineer ('38); Group III: production manager ('38); Group IV: farmer ('38), carpenter ('38), printer ('38), mathematics-physical science teacher ('38), policeman ('38), forest service man ('38), army officer ('52), aviator ('40); Group V: group scale ('38), Y.M.C.A. physical director ('38), personnel manager ('38),

public administrator ('44), vocational counselor ('52) by Clements D. Brown, Y.M.C.A. secretary ('38), social science high school teacher ('38), city school superintendent ('38), minister ('38), social worker ('54); Group VI: music performer ('54), music teacher ('54); Group VII: C.P.A. owner ('38); Group VIII: group scale ('38), senior C.P.A. ('49), junior accountant ('38) [designation on scoring scale is accountant], office worker ('38), purchasing agent ('38), banker ('38), mortician ('46), pharmacist ('49) by Milton Schwebel; Group IX: group scale ('38), sales manager ('38), real estate salesman ('38), life insurance salesman ('38); Group X: group scale ('38), advertising man ('38), lawyer ('38), author-journalist ('38); Group XI: president of manufacturing concern ('38); nonvocational scales: occupational level ('39), masculinity-femininity ('38), specialization level ('52) by Milton G. Holmen, interest maturity ('41); IBM; Form M ('46); manual ('59); $4 per 25 tests; $1.15 per 25 individual report blanks ('59); 75¢ per 25 interest global charts ('43); hand scoring stencils: $1.25 per single scale, $10 per set of any 10 scales, $46 per complete set; separate answer sheets may be used; $2.25 per 50 IBM answer sheets; $2.25 per 50 Hankes' answer sheets ('47) for use with the scoring service of Testscor (see 529); machine scoring stencils: $2.50 per single scale, $20 per set of any 10 scales, $95 per complete set; postage extra; $1 per specimen set (does not include scoring stencils) of SVIB for men and for women, cash orders postpaid; (30–60) minutes; Edward K. Strong, Jr.; Consulting Psychologists Press. *

REFERENCES

1–71. See 40:1680.
72–175. See 3:647.
176–273. See 4:747.
274. HAHN, MILTON E. *An Investigation of Measured Aspects of Social Intelligence in a Distributive Occupation.* Doctor's thesis, University of Minnesota (Minneapolis, Minn.), 1942.
275. REDLENER, J. *A Comparative Study of the Efficiency of the Kuder Preference Record and the Strong Vocational Interest Blank in the Prediction of Job Satisfaction.* Master's thesis, University of Southern California (Los Angeles, Calif.), 1948.
276. DALEY, ROLLAND F. *A Determination of the Relationship Between Vocational Preference as Measured by the Method of Paired-Comparisons and the Strong Vocational Interest Test.* Master's thesis, Pennsylvania State College (State College, Pa.), 1950.
277. HANNUM, THOMAS E. "Response of Veterinarians to the Strong Vocational Interest Blank for Men." *Proc Iowa Acad Sci* 57:381–4 '50. *
278. JOHNSON, RALPH H., AND BOND, GUY L. "Reading Ease of Commonly Used Tests." *J Appl Psychol* 34:319–24 O '50. * (PA 26:299)
279. MITCHELL, WALTER M. *An Analysis of the Relationship Between Performance on the MF Scale of the Minnesota Multiphasic Personality Inventory and the Strong Vocational Interest Blank for Men.* Master's thesis, Montana State University (Missoula, Mont.), 1950.
280. WISDOM, JESSIE R. *A Study of the Interest Patterns of Premedical Students as Revealed by the Kuder Preference Record and the Strong Vocational Interest Inventory.* Master's thesis, North Texas State College (Denton, Tex.), 1950.
281. BROWN, MANUEL N. *Clinical Status of Veteran Patients Related to Six Interest Variables.* Doctor's thesis, University of Portland (Portland, Ore.), 1951.
282. GARRY, RALPH J. *Individual Differences in Ability to Fake Vocational Interests.* Doctor's thesis, Stanford University (Stanford, Calif.), 1951.
283. HILLIS, DONALD J. *Biographical Information Blank Responses as Related to Selected Areas of the Strong Vocational Interest Blank.* Master's thesis, Western Reserve University (Cleveland, Ohio), 1951.
284. MORGAN, HENRY H. *An Analysis of Certain Structured and Unstructured Test Results of Achieving and Nonachieving High Ability College Students.* Doctor's thesis, University of Minnesota (Minneapolis, Minn.), 1951. (DA 12:335)
285. PIERSON, ROWLAND R. *Vocational Interests of Agricultural Extension Workers as Related to Selected Aspects of Work Adjustment.* Doctor's thesis, Michigan State College (East Lansing, Mich.), 1951. (DA 12:274)
286. SIMES, FRANK J. *The Development of a Basis for the Selection of Resident Advisers at the Pennsylvania State College.* Doctor's thesis, Pennsylvania State College (State College, Pa.), 1951.
287. STRONG, EDWARD K., JR. "Vocational Interests and Occupation Twenty Years Later." Abstract. *Am Psychol* 6:497 S '51. *
288. TYLER, LEONA E. "The Differential Significance of 'Like' and 'Dislike' Responses on the Strong Vocational Interest Blank." Abstract. *Am Psychol* 6:497 S '51. *
289. ANDERSON, MARY R. *A Descriptive Study of Values and Interests of Four Groups of Graduate Women at the University of Minnesota.* Doctor's thesis, University of Minnesota (Minneapolis, Minn.), 1952. (DA 12:851)
290. BARNETT, GORDON J.; HANDELSMAN, IRVING; STEWART, LAWRENCE H.; AND SUPER, DONALD E. "The Occupational Level Scale as a Measure of Drive." *Psychol Monogr* 66(10):1–37 '52. * (PA 27:5778)
291. BILLS, MARION A. Chap. 8, "A Tool for Selection That Has Stood the Test of Time," pp. 131–7. In *Applications of Psychology: Essays to Honor Walter V. Bingham.* Edited by L. L. Thurstone. New York: Harper & Brothers, 1952. Pp. xi, 209. *
292. CLARK, PATRICIA N. *A Study of the Relationship Between the Interest Level on the Strong Vocational Interest Blank and Separation From College of a Selected Group of Students.* Master's thesis, Kansas State College of Agriculture and Applied Arts (Manhattan, Kan.), 1952.
293. ESTENSON, LYLE O. *An Investigation of the Relationship Between Personality as Measured by the Minnesota Multiphasic Personality Inventory and Occupational Interests as Measured by Strong's Vocational Interest Blanks.* Doctor's thesis, University of Minnesota (Minneapolis, Minn.), 1952.
294. FREDERIKSEN, NORMAN, AND MELVILLE, S. D. "Improving the Predictive Value of an Interest Test." Abstract. *Am Psychol* 7:285–6 Jl '52. *
295. GUILFORD, J. P. "When Not to Factor Analyze." *Psychol B* 49:26–37 Ja '52. * (PA 27:33)
296. GUSTAD, JOHN W. "Academic Achievement and Strong Occupational Level Scores." *J Appl Psychol* 36:75–8 Ap '52. * (PA 27:492)
297. HOLMEN, MILTON G. *Vocational Interest Patterns of Professional Specialists.* Doctor's thesis, Stanford University (Stanford, Calif.), 1952.
298. HOLT, ROBERT R., AND LUBORSKY, LESTER. "Research in the Selection of Psychiatrists: A Second Interim Report." *B Menninger Clinic* 16:125–35 Jl '52. *
299. KRIEDT, PHILIP H.; STONE, C. HAROLD; AND PATERSON, DONALD G. "Vocational Interests of Industrial Relations Personnel." *J Appl Psychol* 36:174–9 Je '52. *
300. LAWSHE, C. H., AND DEUTSCH, STANLEY. "The Interests of Industrial Psychology Students." *J Appl Psychol* 36:180–1 Je '52. *
301. LAYTON, WILBUR L. "Predicting Success of Students in Veterinary Medicine." *J Appl Psychol* 36:312–5 O '52. * (PA 27:5418)
302. MELVILLE, S. D., AND FREDERIKSEN, NORMAN. "Achievement of Freshman Engineering Students and the Strong Vocational Interest Blank." *J Appl Psychol* 36:169–73 Je '52. *
303. MOFFIE, DANNIE J., AND MILTON, CHARLES R. "The Relationship of Certain Psychological Test Scores to Academic Success in Chemical Engineering." Abstract. *Am Psychol* 7:379–80 Jl '52. *
304. MORGAN, HENRY H. "A Psychometric Comparison of Achieving and Nonachieving College Students of High Ability." *J Consult Psychol* 16:292–8 Ag '52. * (PA 27:4570)
305. NELSON, KENNETH G. *The Interests of Teachers of Vocational Agriculture as Related to Vocational Satisfaction.* Doctor's thesis, University of Minnesota (Minneapolis, Minn.), 1952. (DA 13:125)
306. POE, WESLEY A., AND BERG, IRWIN A. "Psychological Test Performance of Steel Industry Production Supervisors." *J Appl Psychol* 36:234–7 Ag '52. * (PA 27:3794)
307. STRONG, EDWARD K., JR. "Amount of Change in Occupational Choice of College Freshmen." *Ed & Psychol Meas* 12:677–91 w '52. * (PA 27:6760)
308. STRONG, EDWARD K., JR. "Interests of Negroes and Whites." *J Social Psychol* 35:139–50 My '52. * (PA 27:3479)
309. STRONG, EDWARD K., JR. "Nineteen-Year Followup of Engineer Interests." *J Appl Psychol* 36:65–74 Ap '52. * (PA 27:497)
310. STRONG, EDWARD K., JR. Chap. 7, "Twenty Year Follow-up of Medical Interests," pp. 111–30. In *Applications of Psychology: Essays to Honor Walter V. Bingham.* Edited by L. L. Thurstone. New York: Harper & Brothers, 1952. Pp. xi, 209. *
311. STRONG, EDWARD K., JR., AND TUCKER, ANTHONY C. "The Use of Vocational Interest Scales in Planning a Medical Center." *Psychol Monogr* 66(9):1–61 '52. * (PA 27:5483)
312. SUNDBERG, NORMAN D. *The Relationship of Psychotherapeutic Skill and Experience to Knowledge of Other People.* Doctor's thesis, University of Minnesota (Minneapolis, Minn.), 1952. (DA 12:390)
313. TORR, DONALD V. "A Factor Analysis of Selected Interest Inventories." Abstract. *Am Psychol* 7:296 Jl '52. *
314. TRAPHAGEN, ARTHUR L. "Interest Patterns and Retention and Rejection of Vocational Choice." *J Appl Psychol* 36:182–5 Je '52. *
315. TRUEBLOOD, GERALD E. *Predicting Achievement in Algebra From the Iowa Tests of Educational Development.* Master's thesis, Iowa State College (Ames, Iowa), 1952.

316. VERBURG, WALLACE A. "Vocational Interests of Retired YMCA Secretaries." *J Appl Psychol* 36:254–6 Ag '52. * (*PA* 27:3404)

317. WOODWARD, C. L. "A Critical Analysis of Certain Interest Tests." *Yearb Nat Council Meas Used Ed* 9:101–8 '52. *

318. BARNETT, GORDON J.; STEWART, LAWRENCE H.; AND SUPER, DONALD E. "Level of Occupational Interest: Deadweight or Dynamism?" *Ed & Psychol Meas* 13:193–208 su '53. * (*PA* 28:4496)

319. BERNSTEIN, ALVIN J. *Absence of Primary Interest Patterns in Adolescent Boys.* Doctor's thesis, Columbia University (New York, N.Y.), 1953. (*DA* 14:181)

320. BILLS, MARION A., AND TAYLOR, JEAN G. "Over and Under Achievement in a Sales School in Relation to Future Production." *J Appl Psychol* 37:21–3 F '53. * (*PA* 28:1664)

321. BURGESS, ELVA. *Personality Factors in Over- and Under-Achievers in Engineering.* Doctor's thesis, Pennsylvania State College (State College, Pa.), 1953.

322. COOPER, CHARLES E., JR. *Vocational Interests of Industrial Arts Teachers.* Doctor's thesis, University of Missouri (Columbia, Mo.), 1953. (*DA* 13:1099)

323. ERLANDSON, FORREST L. *Socio-Economic Factors Related to Vocational Interests as Measured by the Strong Vocational Interest Blank for Men.* Doctor's thesis, University of Minnesota (Minneapolis, Minn.), 1953. (*DA* 13:1256)

324. GARRY, RALPH. "Individual Differences in Ability to Fake Vocational Interests." *J Appl Psychol* 37:33–7 F '53. * (*PA* 28:1621)

325. HAGENAH, THEDA. *A Normative Study of the Revised Strong Vocational Interest Blank for Men.* Doctor's thesis, University of Minnesota (Minneapolis, Minn.), 1953. (*DA* 14:498)

326. HAMPTON, PETER JAN. "The Development of a Personality Questionnaire for Drinkers." *Genetic Psychol Monogr* 48: 55–115 Ag '53. * (*PA* 28:4571)

327. HASELKORN, HARRY. *The Vocational Interests of a Group of Homosexuals.* Doctor's thesis, New York University (New York, N.Y.), 1953. (*DA* 13:582)

328. HELPER, MALCOLM M., AND McQUITTY, LOUIS L. "Some Relations of Personality Integration to Occupational Interests." *J Social Psychol* 38:219–31 N '53. * (*PA* 28:6171)

329. HENDRIX, O. R. "Predicting Success in Elementary Accounting." *J Appl Psychol* 37:75–7 Ap '53. * (*PA* 28:1479)

330. LONG, LOUIS, AND PERRY, JAMES D. "Academic Achievement in Engineering Related to Selection Procedures and Interests." *J Appl Psychol* 37:468–71 D '53. * (*PA* 29:1571)

331. MACINTOSH, ARCHIBALD. *A Study of Factors Associated With the Stability of Vocational Goals in College Students.* Doctor's thesis, University of Pennsylvania (Philadelphia, Pa.), 1953. (*DA* 13:262)

332. NELSON, KENNETH G. "The Interests of Teachers of Vocational Agriculture as Related to Vocational Satisfaction." Abstract. *Am Psychol* 8:408–9 Ag '53. *

333. PERRY, DALLIS K. *Forced-Choice vs. L-I-D Response Items in Vocational Interest Measurement.* Doctor's thesis, University of Minnesota (Minneapolis, Minn.), 1953. (*DA* 14:552)

334. STORDAHL, KALMER E. *The Stability of Strong Vocational Interest Blank Patterns for Pre-College Males.* Doctor's thesis, University of Minnesota (Minneapolis, Minn.), 1953. (*DA* 13:1265)

335. STRONG, EDWARD K., JR. "Validity of Occupational Choice." *Ed & Psychol Meas* 13:110–21 sp '53. * (*PA* 28:1121)

336. STRONG, EDWARD K., JR. "Vocational Interest Test for Men and Women," pp. 789–96. In *Contributions Toward Medical Psychology: Theory and Psychodiagnostic Methods, Vol. II.* Edited by Arthur Weider. New York: Ronald Press Co., 1953. Pp. xi, 459–885. *

337. BRAASCH, WILLIAM F., JR. *Regional Differences in Occupational Interests.* Doctor's thesis, Columbia University (New York, N.Y.), 1954. (*DA* 14:1254)

338. BROWN, MANUEL N. "An Interest Inventory as a Measure of Personality." *J Counsel Psychol* 1:9–11 F '54. * (*PA* 28:7510)

339. CHILLE, RALPH A. *The Use of the OL Key of the Strong Vocational Interest Blank as a Predictor of Scholastic Success for Students in the School of Business at Niagara University.* Master's thesis, Niagara University (Niagara Falls, N.Y.), 1954.

340. CLARK, KENNETH E., AND GEE, HELEN H. "Selecting Items for Interest Inventory Keys." *J Appl Psychol* 38:12–7 F '54. * (*PA* 29:1044)

341. COLLISTER, E. GORDON. "A Comparison of Scoring the Strong Vocational Interest Blank for High School Senior Boys Using Group and Occupational Scoring Keys." Abstract. *Am Psychol* 9:350 Ag '54. *

342. COOPER, ALVA C. *A Study of the Group Scales of the Strong Vocational Interest Blank as Predictors of Academic Achievement and of the Relationship of the Group Scales to Primary Interest Patterns.* Doctor's thesis, Columbia University (New York, N.Y.), 1954. (*DA* 14:1176)

343. COTTLE, WILLIAM C. "Interest and Personality Inventories." *Personnel & Guid J* 33:162–7 N '54. * (*PA* 29:5695)

344. DuBois, PHILIP H., AND WATSON, ROBERT I. "Validity Information Exchange, No. 7-075:D.O.T. Code 2-66.23, Policeman." *Personnel Psychol* 7:414–7 au '54. *

345. FIELD, LEWIS W. *Personality Correlates of College Achievement and Major Areas of Study.* Doctor's thesis, University of Houston (Houston, Tex.), 1954. (*DA* 14:1344)

346. FREDERIKSEN, NORMAN, AND MELVILLE, S. DONALD.

"Differential Predictability in the Use of Test Scores." *Ed & Psychol Meas* 14:647–56 w '54. * (*PA* 29:7961)

347. GARMAN, GLEN D. *The Strong Vocational Interest Inventory as a Measure of Manifest Anxiety.* Doctor's thesis, University of Michigan (Ann Arbor, Mich.), 1954. (*DA* 14: 711)

348. GUSTAD, JOHN W. "Vocational Interests and Socio-Economic Status." *J Appl Psychol* 38:336–8 O '54. * (*PA* 29:6196)

349. HANNUM, T. E., AND THRALL, JOHN R. "Stability and Validity of the Strong Vocational Interest Blank in the Prediction of Success in Veterinary Medicine Curriculum." *Proc Iowa Acad Sci* 61:361–6 '54. * (*PA* 30:3461)

350. HEWER, VIVIAN H. *Vocational Interest-Achievement-Ability: Interrelationships at the College Level.* Doctor's thesis, University of Minnesota (Minneapolis, Minn.), 1954. (*DA* 14: 1257)

351. HOLMEN, MILTON G. "The Specialization Level Scale for the Strong Vocational Interest Blank." *J Appl Psychol* 38: 159–63 Je '54. * (*PA* 29:4752)

352. McARTHUR, CHARLES. "Long-Term Validity of the Strong Interest Test in Two Subcultures." *J Appl Psychol* 38: 346–53 O '54. * (*PA* 29:6355)

353. McCOLLUM, ERNEST L. *A Study of the Vocational Interest Profiles of USAF Personnel Officers With and Without Formal Personnel Training.* Doctor's thesis, University of Minnesota (Minneapolis, Minn.), 1954. (*DA* 14:2120)

354. McCORNACK, ROBERT L. *Sex Differences in the Vocational Interests of a Professional Group.* Doctor's thesis, University of Minnesota (Minneapolis, Minn.), 1954. (*DA* 14:1252)

355. MILAM, ALBERT T., AND SUMNER, F. C. "Spread and Intensity of Vocational Interests and Evaluative Attitudes in First-Year Negro Medical Students." *J Psychol* 37:31–8 Ja '54. * (*PA* 28:8027)

356. POWERS, MABEL K. *A Longitudinal Study of Vocational Interests During the Depression Years.* Doctor's thesis, University of Minnesota (Minneapolis, Minn.), 1954.

357. RUST, RALPH M., AND RYAN, F. J. "The Strong Vocational Interest Blank and College Achievement." *J Appl Psychol* 38:341–5 O '54. * (*PA* 29:6204)

358. STORDAHL, KALMER E. "Permanence of Interests and Interest Maturity." *J Appl Psychol* 38:339–40 O '54. * (*PA* 29: 5844)

359. STORDAHL, KALMER E. "Permanence of Strong Vocational Interest Blank Scores." *J Appl Psychol* 38:423–7 D '54. * (*PA* 29:5845)

360. STRONG, EDWARD K., JR. "Validity Versus Reliability." *J Appl Psychol* 38:103–4 Ap '54. * (*PA* 29:2618)

361. TRINKAUS, WILLIAM K. "The Permanence of Vocational Interests of College Freshmen." *Ed & Psychol Meas* 14:641–6 w '54. * (*PA* 29:7440)

362. WILKINSON, MARGARET A., AND JACOBS, ROBERT. "A Brief Study of the Relationships Between Personality Adjustment and Vocational Interests as Measured by the Multiple-Choice Rorschach and the Strong Vocational Interest Blank." *J Ed Res* 48:269–78 D '54. * (*PA* 29:7335)

363. BERDIE, RALPH F. "Aptitude, Achievement, Interest, and Personality Tests: A Longitudinal Comparison." *J Appl Psychol* 39:103–14 Ap '55. * (*PA* 30:1498)

364. COLLINS, CHARLES C. *The Relationship of Breadth of Academic Interest to Academic Achievement and Academic Aptitude.* Doctor's thesis, Stanford University (Stanford, Calif.), 1955. (*DA* 15:1782)

365. DARLEY, JOHN G., AND HAGENAH, THEDA. *Vocational Interest Measurement: Theory and Practice.* Minneapolis, Minn.: University of Minnesota Press, 1955. Pp. xvii, 279. * (*PA* 30: 4726)

366. ENRIGHT, JOHN B., AND PINNEAU, SAMUEL R. "Predictive Value of Subjective Choice of Occupation and of the Strong Vocational Interest Blank Over Fifteen Years." Abstract. *Am Psychol* 10:424–5 Ag '55. *

367. HANNUM, T. E., AND THRALL, JOHN B. "Use of the Strong Vocational Interest Blank for Prediction in Veterinary Medicine." *J Appl Psychol* 39:249–52 Ag '55. * (*PA* 30:5413)

368. HARRISON, ROSS; HUNT, WINSLOW; AND JACKSON, THEODORE A. "Profile of the Mechanical Engineer: II, Interests." *Personnel Psychol* 8:315–30 au '55. * (*PA* 30:7890)

369. JENSON, PAUL G. *A Normative Study of the Strong Vocational Interest Blank for Male Adult Workers.* Doctor's thesis, University of Minnesota (Minneapolis, Minn.), 1955. (*DA* 15: 2289)

370. KELLY, E. LOWELL. "Consistency of the Adult Personality." *Am Psychol* 10:659–81 N '55. * (*PA* 30:6915)

371. LAYTON, WILBUR L. "Theory and Research on the Strong Vocational Interest Blank: A Conference Report." *J Counsel Psychol* 2:10–2 sp '55. * (*PA* 30:1035)

372. LINDGREN, HENRY CLAY, AND GILBERG, RICHARD L. "Interpreting Occupational Interest: The Relationships Between the Lee-Thorpe Occupational Interest Inventory and the Strong Vocational Interest Test for Men." *Calif J Ed Res* 6:15–21 Ja '55. * (*PA* 29:7430)

373. McARTHUR, CHARLES. "Predictive Power of Pattern Analysis and of Job Scale Analysis of the Strong." *J Counsel Psychol* 2:205–6 fall '55. * (*PA* 30:4731)

374. McARTHUR, CHARLES, AND STEVENS, LUCIA BETH. "The Validation of Expressed Interests as Compared With Inventoried Interests: A Fourteen-Year Follow-Up." *J Appl Psychol* 39:184–9 Je '55. * (*PA* 30:3024)

375. MELTON, RICHARD S. "Differentiation of Successful and

Unsuccessful Premedical Students." *J Appl Psychol* 39:397–400 D '55. * (*PA* 30:7769)

376. PERRY, DALLIS K. "Validities of Three Vocational Interest Keys for U. S. Navy Yeomen." *J Appl Psychol* 39:134–8 Ap '55. * (*PA* 30:1726)

377. POWELL, FRANK V. *A Comparison Between the Vocational Interest Patterns of Students in Five Colleges of a State University.* Doctor's thesis, University of Wisconsin (Madison, Wis.), 1955. (*DA* 15:2471)

378. SCHULTZ, RAYMOND E., AND OHLSEN, MERLE M. "Interest Patterns of Best and Poorest Student Teachers." *J Ed Sociol* 29:108–12 N '55. * (*PA* 30:7790)

379. SEGAL, STANLEY J. "The Role of Personality Factors in Vocational Choice." Abstract. *Am Psychol* 10:365–6 Ag '55. *

380. STRONG, EDWARD K., JR. "Are Medical Specialist Interest Scales Applicable to Negroes?" *J Appl Psychol* 39:62–4 F '55. * (*PA* 30:892)

381. STRONG, EDWARD K., JR. "Predictive Validity of Interest Scores." Abstract. *Am Psychol* 10:375 Ag '55. *

382. STRONG, EDWARD K., JR. *Vocational Interests 18 Years After College.* Minneapolis, Minn.: University of Minnesota Press, 1955. Pp. xiv, 207. * (*PA* 30:4738)

383. THOMAS, ROSS R. "Permanence of Measured Interests of Women Over Fifteen Years." Abstract. *Am Psychol* 10:375 Ag '55. *

384. TUCKER, ANTHONY C. "Vocational Interests of Medical Administrative Officers." *US Armed Forces Med J* 6:685–90 My '55. * (*PA* 30:5310)

385. WOEHR, HARRY J. *The Relationship of Masculinity-Femininity Scores to Temperament and Interest Profiles.* Doctor's thesis, Temple University (Philadelphia, Pa.), 1955. (*DA* 16:388)

386. WOOLF, MAURICE D., AND WOOLF, JEANNE A. "Is Interest Maturity Related to Linguistic Development?" *J Appl Psychol* 39:413–5 D '55. * (*PA* 30:7711)

387. BARTHOL, RICHARD P., AND KIRK, BARBARA A. "The Selection of Graduate Students in Public Health Education." *J Appl Psychol* 40:159–63 Je '56. * (*PA* 31:6666)

388. BURGESS, ELVA. "Personality Factors of Over- and Under-Achievers in Engineering." *J Ed Psychol* 47:89–99 F '56. * (*PA* 31:8811)

389. DRAKE, JOHN D. *An Empirical Investigation of the Vocational Interest Blank for Men for Principles Governing the Construction of Valid Interest Inventory Items.* Doctor's thesis, Western Reserve University (Cleveland, Ohio), 1956.

390. DUNNETTE, MARVIN D., AND AYLWARD, MERRIAM S. "Validity Information Exchange, No. 9-21: D.O.T. Code, Design and Development Engineers." *Personnel Psychol* 9:245–7 su '56. *

391. ENGLAND, GEORGE W. *The Interest Factor in Undergraduate Engineering Achievement.* Doctor's thesis, University of Minnesota (Minneapolis, Minn.), 1956. (*DA* 17:902)

392. GOODLING, RICHARD A. ["Relationship Between the IM Scale of the SVIB and Scales of the Guilford-Zimmerman Temperament Survey."] *J Counsel Psychol* 3:146+ su '56. *

393. HASELKORN, HARRY. "The Vocational Interests of a Group of Male Homosexuals." *J Counsel Psychol* 3:8–11 sp '56. * (*PA* 31:3211)

394. HEWER, VIVIAN H. "A Comparison of Successful and Unsuccessful Students in the Medical School at the University of Minnesota." *J Appl Psychol* 40:164–8 Je '56. * (*PA* 31:6675)

395. KLOSTER, CLAIR G. *The Relation Between Measured Vocational Interests and Job Satisfaction.* Doctor's thesis, University of Minnesota (Minneapolis, Minn.), 1956. (*DA* 16:1104)

396. McCORNACK, ROBERT L. "Vocational Interests of Male and Female Social Workers." *J Appl Psychol* 40:11–3 F '56. * (*PA* 31:3216)

397. POWERS, MABEL K. "Permanence of Measured Vocational Interests of Adult Males." *J Appl Psychol* 40:69–72 Ap '56. * (*PA* 31:6225)

398. RHODES, GEORGE S. *An Investigation of Response Sets in the Strong Vocational Interest Blank for Men and Response Set Effects on Scores of Selected SVIB Scales.* Doctor's thesis, University of Kansas (Lawrence, Kan.), 1956.

399. SAUNDERS, DAVID R. "Moderator Variables in Prediction." *Ed & Psychol Meas* 16:209–22 su '56. * (*PA* 31:5101)

400. SINNETT, E. ROBERT. "Some Determinants of Agreement Between Measured and Expressed Interests." *Ed & Psychol Meas* 16:110–8 sp '56. * (*PA* 31:6226)

401. THOMPSON, JORGEN S. *A Study of the Relationships Between Certain Measured Psychological Variables and Achievement in the First Year of Theological Seminary Work.* Doctor's thesis, University of Minnesota (Minneapolis, Minn.), 1956. (*DA* 16:1846)

402. WITKIN, ARTHUR A. "Differential Interest Patterns in Salesmen." *J Appl Psychol* 40:338–40 O '56. * (*PA* 31:9058)

403. WITKIN, ARTHUR A. *The Prediction of Potentials for Effectiveness in Certain Occupations Within the Sales Field.* Doctor's thesis, New York University (New York, N.Y.), 1956. (*DA* 16:1718)

404. BRAMS, JEROME M. *The Relationship Between Personal Characteristics of Counseling Trainees and Effective Communication in Counseling.* Doctor's thesis, University of Missouri (Columbia, Mo.), 1957. (*DA* 17:1510)

405. DUNNETTE, MARVIN D. "Vocational Interest Differences Among Engineers Employed in Different Functions." *J Appl Psychol* 41:273–8 O '57. *

406. FREDERICK, MARVIN L. "Testing the Tests." *J Account* 103:42–7 Ap '57. *

407. GEHMAN, W. SCOTT. "A Study of Ability to Fake Scores on the Strong Vocational Interest Blank for Men." *Ed & Psychol Meas* 17:65–70 sp '57. *

408. GRAFF, FRANKLYN A. *Occupational Choice Factors in Normally Achieving and Underachieving Intellectually Superior Twelfth Grade Boys.* Doctor's thesis, University of Connecticut (Storrs, Conn.), 1957. (*DA* 17:2207)

409. HARKER, JOHN B. "A Comparison of Personality and Interest Patterns." Abstract. *Am Psychol* 12:408 Jl '57. *

410. HEWER, VIVIAN H. "Vocational Interest-Achievement-Ability Interrelationships at the College Level." *J Counsel Psychol* 4:234–8 fall '57. *

411. KING, LESLIE A. "Stability Measures of Strong Vocational Interest Blank Profiles." *J Appl Psychol* 41:143–7 Je '57. *

412. LYERLY, SAMUEL B. "'Chance' Scores on the Strong Vocational Interest Blank for Men." *J Appl Psychol* 41:141–2 Je '57. *

413. MAIER, GLEN E. *The Contribution of Interest Test Scores to Differential Academic Prediction.* Doctor's thesis, University of Washington (Seattle, Wash.), 1957. (*DA* 18:150)

414. STRONG, EDWARD K., JR. "Interests of Fathers and Sons." *J Appl Psychol* 41:284–92 O '57. *

415. COOPER, ALVA C. "The Strong Group Scales and Primary Interest Patterns." *Personnel & Guid J* 36:461–4 Mr '58. *

416. DUNNETTE, MARVIN D., AND KIRCHNER, WAYNE K. "Validation of Psychological Tests in Industry." *Personnel Adm* 21:20–7 My–Je '58. *

417. DUNNETTE, MARVIN D.; KIRCHNER, WAYNE K.; AND DeGIDIO, JoANNE. "Relations Among Scores on Edwards Personal Preference Schedule, California Psychological Inventory, and Strong Vocational Interest Blank for an Industrial Sample." *J Appl Psychol* 42:178–81 Je '58. *

418. ENGLAND, GEORGE W., AND PATERSON, DONALD G. "Relationship Between Measured Interest Patterns and Satisfactory Vocational Adjustment for Air Force Officers in the Comptroller and Personnel Fields." *J Appl Psychol* 42:85–8 Ap '58. *

419. GARMAN, GLEN D., AND UHR, LEONARD. "An Anxiety Scale for the Strong Vocational Interest Inventory: Development, Cross-Validation, and Subsequent Tests of Validity." *J Appl Psychol* 42:241–6 Ag '58. *

420. HUGHES, J. L., AND McNAMARA, W. J. "Limitations on the Use of Strong Scoring Keys for Selection and Counseling." *J Appl Psychol* 42:93–6 Ap '58. *

421. JENSON, PAUL G. "Relationship Between Stated and Measured Interests of Two Groups of United States Air Force Officers." *J Appl Psychol* 42:33–5 F '58. *

422. KING, LESLIE A. "Factors Associated With Vocational Interest Profile Stability." *J Appl Psychol* 42:261–3 Ag '58. *

423. LASCH, HENRY A. *A Comparison of the Results Obtained by the Mitchell and Strong Interest Measures When Administered to Male Freshmen at the University of Michigan.* Doctor's thesis, University of Michigan (Ann Arbor, Mich.), 1958. (*DA* 19:1286)

424. LAYTON, WILBUR L. *Counseling Use of the Strong Vocational Interest Blank.* Minnesota Studies in Student Personnel Work, No. 8. Minneapolis, Minn.: University of Minnesota Press, 1958. Pp. 40. *

425. RABINOWITZ, WILLIAM, AND ROSENBAUM, IRA. "A Failure in the Prediction of Pupil-Teacher Rapport." *J Ed Psychol* 49:93–8 Ap '58. *

426. WILLIAMS, RAYMOND E. *The Measurement and Prediction of Cooperating Teacher Effectiveness in Music Teacher Education.* Doctor's thesis, University of Illinois (Urbana, Ill.), 1958. (*DA* 19:1023)

For reviews by Edward S. Bordin and Elmer D. Hinckley, see 4:747; for reviews by Harold D. Carter, John G. Darley, and N. W. Morton, see 40:1680; for a review by John G. Darley of an earlier edition, see 38:1178; for related reviews, see B115, B414, 4:748, 3:648, 3:650, and 3:652.

[869]

*Strong Vocational Interest Blank for Women, Revised. Ages 17 and over; 1933–59; 29 scoring scales (28 occupational scales and 1 nonvocational scale): artist ('46), author ('46), librarian ('46), English teacher ('46), social worker ('46–54), psychologist ('46), social science teacher ('46), Y.W.C.A. secretary ('46), lawyer ('46), life insurance saleswoman ('46), buyer ('46), business education teacher ('48) by H. F. Koepke, office worker ('47), stenographer-secretary ('47), housewife ('46), elementary teacher ('46) by Ralph Bedell, music performer ('54), music teacher ('54), home economics teacher ('46), dietitian ('46), college physical education teacher ('55) by Rosena M. Wilson, high school physical education teacher ('46) by Patricia Collins, occupational therapist ('46), nurse ('46), mathematics-science teacher ('46), dentist ('46), laboratory technician ('46), physician ('46), femininity-masculinity ('47); IBM; Form W ('46); manual ('59); $4 per 25 tests; $1.15 per 25 individual report blanks ['59]; hand scoring stencils: $1.25 per single scale, $10 per set of any 10 scales, $25 per complete set; separate answer sheets may be used; $2.25 per 50 IBM answer sheets; $2.25 per 50 Hankes' answer sheets for use with the scoring service of Testscor (see 529); machine scoring stencils: $2.50 per single scale, $20 per set of any 10 scales, $48 per complete set; postage extra; $1 per specimen set (does not include scoring stencils) of SVIB for women and for men, cash orders postpaid; (30–60) minutes; Edward K. Strong, Jr.; Consulting Psychologists Press. *

REFERENCES

1–9. See 40:1681.
10–45. See 3:649.
46. PARSONS, RICHARD T. *The Home and School Backgrounds, Measured Vocational Interests, and Vocational Choices of 869 Students Who Entered the State Teachers Colleges of Pennsylvania in the Fall of 1940.* Doctor's thesis, Pennsylvania State College (State College, Pa.), 1942.
47. KUTNER, MILDRED. *The Prognosis of the Freshmen Achievement of Chemistry and Physics Students on the Basis of Interest Test Items.* Master's thesis, Pennsylvania State College (State College, Pa.), 1947. Pp. iv, 113.
48. MYDELLE, ELLA KLEIST. *A Vocational Interest Scale for Music Teachers.* Master's thesis, Stanford University (Stanford, Calif.), 1947.
49. ALLEN, CHARLES L. *The Development of a Battery of Psychological Tests for Determining Journalistic Interests and Aptitudes.* Doctor's thesis, Northwestern University (Evanston, Ill.), 1948.
50. DREFFIN, WILLIAM B., AND WRENN, C. GILBERT. "Spatial Relations Ability and Other Characteristics of Art Laboratory Students." *J Appl Psychol* 32:601–5 D '48. * (*PA* 23:3777)
51. ESPENSCHADE, ANNA. "Selection of Women Major Students in Physical Education." *Res Q* 19:70–6 My '48. * (*PA* 22:4635)
52. LINNICK, IDA. *Effect of Instructions and Resulting Vocational Classifications on a Vocational Interest Inventory as Related to Response Patterns of College Women.* Doctor's thesis, New York University (New York, N.Y.), 1948.
53. KLEIST, M.; RITTENHOUSE, C. H.; AND FARNSWORTH, P. R. "Strong Vocational Interest Scales for Music Teachers." *Occupations* 28:100–1 N '49. * (*PA* 24:2218)
54. MOREY, ELWYN A. "Vocational Interests and Personality Characteristics of Women Teachers." *Austral J Psychol* 1:26–37 Je '49. *
55. RITTENHOUSE, C. H. *Vocational Interests of Women Music Teachers.* Master's thesis, Stanford University (Stanford, Calif.), 1949.
56. SHEPLER, BERNARD F. "A Comparison of Masculinity-Femininity Measures." *J Consult Psychol* 15:484–6 D '51. * (*PA* 26:7011)
57. VERNSON, ELIZABETH E. *An Interpretation of the Housewife Scale of the Strong Vocational Interest Blank for Women as Applied to Women Who Have Expressed an Interest in Marriage.* Master's thesis, Pennsylvania State College (State College, Pa.), 1951.
58. ANDERSON, MARY R. *A Descriptive Study of Values and Interests of Four Groups of Graduate Women at the University of Minnesota.* Doctor's thesis, University of Minnesota (Minneapolis, Minn.), 1952. (*DA* 12:851)
59. MITZEL, HAROLD E. *Interest Factors Predictive of Teachers' Rapport With Pupils.* Doctor's thesis, University of Minnesota (Minneapolis, Minn.), 1952. (*DA* 12:712)
60. NAVRAN, LESLIE. "Validity of the Strong Vocational Interest Blank Nursing Key." *J Appl Psychol* 37:31–2 F '53. * (*PA* 28:1626)
61. TOMEDY, FRANCIS J. *The Relationship of Personality Characteristics to Measured Interests of Women Teachers of English, Social Science, Mathematics, and Physical Science in Certain Senior High Schools.* Doctor's thesis, New York University (New York, N.Y.), 1952. (*DA* 12:540)
62. SNYDER, DOROTHY F. *A Study of Relationships Between Certain Socio-Economic Factors and the Strong Vocational Interest Blank for Women.* Doctor's thesis, University of Minnesota (Minneapolis, Minn.), 1953. (*DA* 13:868)
63. GUNNELL, DOROTHY C., AND NUTTING, RUTH E. "Prediction of Achievement in Schools of Nursing." *Calif J Ed Res* 8:184–91 S '57. *
64. HOYT, DONALD P., AND KENNEDY, CARROLL E. "Interest and Personality Correlates of Career-Motivated and Homemaking-Motivated College Women." Comment by Charles McArthur. *J Counsel Psychol* 5:44–9 sp '58. *

For a review by Gwendolen Schneidler Dickson, see 3:649; for a review by Ruth Strang of an earlier edition, see 40:1681; for a review by John G. Darley, see 38:1179; for related reviews, see 3:650 and 3:652.

[870]

Vocational Interest Analyses: A Six-Fold Analytical Extension of the Occupational Interest Inventory. Grades 9–16 and adults; 1951; 6 scores in each of 6 areas; IBM; 1 form; 6 tests; tests administered only in those areas in which an examinee obtains high scores on the *Occupational Interest Inventory* (see 864); no data on reliability; no norms; $3.50 per 35 copies of any one test; separate answer sheets may be used; 6¢ per IBM answer sheet for use with any three tests; 60¢ per set of either hand or machine scoring stencils; postage extra; 75¢ per complete specimen set, postpaid; (25–35) minutes per test; Edward C. Roeber and Gerald G. Prideaux in collaboration with Edwin A. Lee and Louis P. Thorpe; California Test Bureau. *

a) PERSONAL-SOCIAL ANAYLSIS. 6 scores: domestic service, personal service, social service, teaching and related activities, law and law enforcement, health and medical service.

b) NATURAL ANALYSIS. 6 scores: general and crop farming, animal raising and care, garden and greenhouse care, fish-game-domestic fowl, lumbering and forestry, marine work.

c) MECHANICAL ANALYSIS. 6 scores: maintenance and repairing, machine operation and tending, construction, designing, bench work and bench crafts, processing.

d) BUSINESS ANALYSIS. 6 scores: clerical, shipping and distribution, bookkeeping and accounting, buying and selling, training and supervision, management and control.

e) THE ARTS ANALYSIS. 6 scores: art crafts, painting and drawing, decorating and landscaping, drama and radio, literary activities, music.

f) THE SCIENCES ANALYSIS. 6 scores: laboratory work, mineral-petroleum products, applied chemistry, chemical research, biological research, scientific engineering.

REFERENCE

1. MELTON, WILLIAM R., JR. "An Investigation of the Relationship Between Personality and Vocational Interest." *J Ed Psychol* 47:163–74 Mr '56. * (*PA* 31:8791)

WILBUR L. LAYTON, *Professor of Psychology and Assistant Director, Student Counseling Bureau, University of Minnesota, Minneapolis, Minnesota.*

Julian C. Stanley, in his review of the six *Vocational Interest Analyses* in the *Fourth Mental Measurements Yearbook* (see 4:747), stated, "Despite some indications of careful construction by Roeber and Prideaux, the Analyses seem to the reviewer severely limited in usefulness because they lack norms, internal consistency statistics, reliability coefficients, and evidence of empirical validity. In the reviewer's opinion, they were released prematurely. This becomes especially obvious when the two generally unfavorable reviews [see 3:643] of the parent instrument are considered in conjunction with the Analyses, which seem to have even more of the same flaws."

As far as the present reviewer can determine, only one research report has been published on the Analyses since Stanley's review, even though, in the 1951 manual, promises were made that reliability and validity data would be made available when the extensive studies, then in process, were completed. One can only conclude that these studies were never completed, or that they were completed and never published.

The authors also promised, in the 1951 manual, to investigate further the advisability of preparing percentile norms for the six Analyses. Evidently, this further investigation has resulted in the authors' conclusion not to provide percentile norms, although, to this reviewer, such norms would be highly desirable.

The approach to interest measurement offered by the combination of the *Occupational Interest Inventory* and the *Vocational Interest Analyses* is very seductive. One administers first an inventory to determine which of six broad areas incorporate the individual's interests. Then one administers the appropriate Analyses to subdivide the broad areas of interests into more specific interest areas. This approach is seductive because most counselors find it difficult to talk about specific occupations when faced with a high score in a broad interest area. The Analyses promise a solution to this problem. Of course, a more adequately standardized interest inventory, the *Strong Vocational Interest Blank,* has the solution to this problem built into the inventory. At any rate the authors have still presented no evidence that scores resulting from the Analyses provide for adequate further differentiation of individuals classified within a broad interest area.

This reviewer cannot recommend the *Vocational Interest Analyses* for counseling use. If the publisher wants to make these inventories available, they should be clearly labeled experimental and the prospective user should be warned against using them in individual counseling. It would be extremely desirable for the publisher to withdraw these Analyses from the market except for experimental use and present them for general sale again only after they have been adequately standardized.

For a review by Julian C. Stanley, see 4:746.

MANUAL DEXTERITY

[871]

*Crawford Small Parts Dexterity Test. High school and adults; 1946–56; individual; 2 scores: pins and collars, screws; 1 form; apparatus ('46); revised manual ('56); tentative timelimit norms; $29.50 per set of test materials, postpaid; worklimit (10–25) minutes or timelimit 8(15–20) minutes; John E. Crawford and Dorothea M. Crawford; Psychological Corporation. *

REFERENCES

1. BRUCE, MARTIN M. "Validity Information Exchange, No. 7-079: D.O.T. Code 7-83.058, Electrical Appliance Serviceman." *Personnel Psychol* 7:425–6 au '54. *
2. FITZPATRICK, EUGENE D., AND McCARTY, JOHN J. "Validity Information Exchange, No. 8-35: D.O.T. Code 9-00.91, Assembler VII (Electrical Equipment)." *Personnel Psychol* 8:501–4 w '55. *
3. BRUCE, MARTIN M. "Normative Data Information Exchange, Nos. 15, 33-5." *Personnel Psychol* 9:390–1, 545–50 au, w '56. *
4. BRUCE, MARTIN M. "Normative Data Information Exchange, No. 33." *Personnel Psychol* 9:545–6 w '56. *
5. OSBORNE, R. TRAVIS, AND SANDERS, WILMA B. "The Crawford Small Parts Dexterity Test as a Time-Limit Test." *Personnel Psychol* 9:177–80 su '56. * (PA 31:8973)
6. WALKER, FRANCIS C. "Normative Data Information Exchange, No. 9." *Personnel Psychol* 9:275 su '56. *
7. SPEER, GEORGE S. "Validity Information Exchange, No. 10-5: D.O.T. Code 5-00.933, (Relay Adjustors)." *Personnel Psychol* 10:80 sp '57. *
8. BAUMAN, MARY K. *A Manual of Norms for Tests Used in Counseling Blind Persons.* AFB Publications, Research Series, No. 6. New York: American Foundation for the Blind, 1958. Pp. 40. * (PA 32:1949)

NEIL D. WARREN, *Professor of Psychology and Head of the Department, University of Southern California, Los Angeles, California.*

This is a neat, well constructed test designed to measure "fine eye-hand coordination" of the sort involved in assembly and adjustment of such devices as electric clocks and hearing aids, and in manipulation of small hand tools.

All components of the test are contained in a 10-inch square board. There are three round wells for the parts to be manipulated, i.e., pins, collars, and screws; a metal plate containing 42 unthreaded and 42 threaded holes; two metal trays beneath the plate to receive the pins and screws; a tweezers; and a small screwdriver.

The test is administered in two separately scored parts. Part 1 requires the examinee to use the tweezers to pick up a pin, insert it in the small hole in the metal plate, and place a collar over it. The preferred hand is used. Part 2 requires him to pick up a screw, start it in a threaded hole with the fingers, and then screw it through the metal plate with the screwdriver. Both hands are used in the last operation. After 6 practice trials in each part, the remaining 36 holes constitute the test.

The test has been used mostly on a work limit basis, with the scores being the time required to complete the 36 operations in each part. The average time for Part 1 is approximately 5 minutes in addition to time for instructions and practice. The scores in various normative groups range from 3 to 10 minutes. The time for Part 2 averages about 10 minutes with a range of 4 to 18 minutes. It would appear that total testing time could be as much as 35 or 40 minutes in the case of very slow individuals.

The use of time limits of 3 minutes for Part 1 and 5 minutes for Part 2 is suggested by the manual. Timelimit norms are published for one group of 177 female applicants for assembly jobs. This procedure would reduce overall testing time and permit simultaneous testing of more than one examinee. There is no significant loss in reliability.

Split-half reliability coefficients for four samples range from .80 to .91 for Part 1 and from .90 to .95 for Part 2 using worklimit scores. Reliabilities for timelimit scores are reported as .90 and .89 for Parts 1 and 2, respectively.

The correlation between Parts 1 and 2 is relatively low, ranging from .10 to .50 for nine samples, with the median correlation being .42. This degree of independence is, of course, typical of dexterity tests. It is probable that correlations of about the same level would be found between either part of this test and such similar tests as the *Finger Dexterity Test,* the *Tweezer Dexterity Test,* and the *Purdue Pegboard.* No data concerning such relationships are given in the manuals, however. Correlations between the *Small Parts Dexterity Test* and various scores on the *Minnesota Rate of Manipulation Test* vary from .23 to .39 for one small sample. Correlations with measures of intelligence are low.

Considering the fact that this test was on the market for 10 years prior to the publication of the revised manual in 1956, the amount of validation data is disappointingly small. Four studies are reported, one of which involved six employees of an engraving firm, hired because they had exceeded critical scores on both parts of the test. The production of these employees is reported to have been "300% of former output." The reviewer agrees with the authors that, in such a study, "conclusions must be drawn with caution."

In a study of 56 female burlers and menders of woolen goods, the manual reports a tetrachoric correlation of .76 between "passing" or "failing" both parts of the test and high versus low piece rate earnings. A correlation of such magnitude needs confirmation from other studies. Moreover, one wonders what established "high" or "low" earnings since the group was not split at the median.

The other validation figures involved female electronic assembly workers. Two groups of 80 and 70 employees were used. Correlations between the test and supervisors' ratings varied from .17 to .49.

In general, it appears that the test stands most on face validity. Norms are provided for several groups, including students, job applicants, and employees. Differences in median scores of applicants and employees indicate a somewhat better test performance by employees. This, too, must be interpreted with caution since there are many unknown variables. The test could be used as part of a selection battery if validity correlations for specific jobs were determined and appropriate weights assigned to the test scores. Its use as an independent selection test or for vocational guidance purposes is not justified by the data provided in the manual.

The manual itself is attractive in format and clear in its instructions for using the test. It is unfortunate that it does not have more data on the test's usefulness.

For a review by Raymond A. Katzell, see 4:752; for a review by Joseph E. Moore, see 3:667.

[872]

*Moore Eye-Hand Coordination and Color-Matching Test. Ages 2–6, 7 and over; 1949–55; individual; 1 form; 2 levels; mimeographed supplementary data sheet ['55]; $1 per 100 score sheets ['49]; postpaid; Joseph E. Moore; Joseph E. Moore and Associates. *
a) THE MOORE EYE-HAND COORDINATION TEST: PRESCHOOL FORM. Ages 2–6; 1 form; 16-hole test apparatus ['55]; $10 per set of test materials; 50¢ per supplementary manual ['49]; (5–10) minutes.
b) MOORE EYE-HAND COORDINATION AND COLOR-MATCHING TEST. Ages 7 and over; 2 scores: eye-hand coordination, color matching; 1 form; 32-hole apparatus ['49]; $20 per set of test materials; 50¢ per manual ['49]; (10–15) minutes.

REFERENCES

1–6. See 4:750.
7. WILLIAMS, WILBUR ALLEN. *Relationship of Eye-Hand Coordination in Children to Total Development.* Doctor's thesis, University of Michigan (Ann Arbor, Mich.), 1952. (*DA* 12: 530)

For reviews by Norman Frederiksen and Jay L. Otis, see 4:750.

[873]
Purdue Pegboard. Grades 9–16 and adults; 1941–48;
5 scores: right hand, left hand, both hands, right plus
left plus both hands, assembly; 1 form ('41); $18.95
per testing apparatus; 95¢ per 20 profiles ('48); 25¢
per manual ('48); postage extra; 2.5(10) or 7.5(20)
minutes; Purdue Research Foundation under the direction of Joseph Tiffin; Science Research Associates. *

REFERENCES

1–3. See 3:666.
4–15. See 4:751.
16. COMREY, ANDREW L. "Group Performance in a Manual
Dexterity Task." *J Appl Psychol* 37:207–10 Je '53. * (*PA* 28:
3345)
17. RADLEY, SHIRLEY. *A Statistical Study Based on a Short
Experimental Music Test, Purdue Pegboard Scores, and General Intelligence.* Master's thesis, Syracuse University (Syracuse, N.Y.), 1953.
18. SOPER, MERWIN E. *The Value of the ACE Psychological
Examination and the Purdue Pegboard Test of Manual Dexterity in Predicting High School Typewriting Grades.* Master's
thesis, Drake University (Des Moines, Iowa), 1953.
19. BRUCE, MARTIN M. "Validity Information Exchange, No.
7-079: D.O.T. Code 7-83.058, Electrical Appliance Serviceman."
Personnel Psychol 7:425–6 au '54. *
20. COMREY, ANDREW L., AND DESKIN, GERALD. "Further Results on Group Manual Dexterity in Men." *J Appl Psychol* 38:
116–8 Ap '54. * (*PA* 29:2053)
21. COMREY, ANDREW L., AND DESKIN, GERALD. "Group Manual Dexterity in Women." *J Appl Psychol* 38:178–80 Je '54. *
(*PA* 29:3529)
22. FLEISHMAN, EDWIN A., AND HEMPEL, WALTER E. "A
Factor Analysis of Dexterity Tests." *Personnel Psychol* 7:15–
32 sp '54. * (*PA* 29:2061)
23. ALBRIGHT, LEWIS EDWIN. *The Development of a Selection Process for an Inspection Task.* Doctor's thesis, Purdue
University (Lafayette, Ind.), 1956. (*DA* 16:2201)
24. ALBRIGHT, LEWIS E. "Validity Information Exchange,
No. 9-44: D.O.T. Code 0-66.93, Seed Analyst." *Personnel Psychol* 9:522–3 w '56. *
25. SHIMOTA, HELEN EMMA. *The Relation of Psychomotor
Performance to Clinical Status and Improvement in Schizophrenic Patients.* Doctor's thesis, University of Minnesota (Minneapolis, Minn.), 1956. (*DA* 16:2530)
26. SIEGEL, MAX, AND HIRSCHHORN, BORIS. "Adolescent
Norms for the Purdue Pegboard Test." *Personnel & Guid J*
36:563–5 Ap '58. *

NEIL D. WARREN, *Professor of Psychology
and Head of the Department, University of
Southern California, Los Angeles, California.*

The purpose of this test is to aid in selecting
employees for industrial jobs requiring manipulative dexterity. It is intended to measure both
gross movements of arms, hands, and fingers,
and "tip of the finger" dexterity.

The pegboard is made of wood and contains
two rows of 25 holes into which pins are to
be inserted. At the top of the board are four
cups containing pins, washers, and collars to
be assembled. No tools are employed.

The test involves two types of operations.
One requires rapid placing of pins in the holes.
It is scored for each hand separately, for the
sum of right and left hand scores, and for
alternating right and left hand movements.
There is a time limit of 30 seconds for each
trial. The other operation requires assembly
of pins, washers, and collars using both hands.
The score is the number of components assembled in each 1-minute trial.

A profile sheet provides spaces for recording
scores and norms for converting scores to per-

centiles. Norms are given for male industrial
applicants and for a group of veterans and
college students. Norms for women are based
on combined groups of college students and industrial applicants except for the assembly task
where differences between the groups were
found. No information is given in the manual
concerning the composition of these groups as
relates to industry or job involved, age, or
other variable. Norms are available for one-
trial and for three-trial totals. The three-trial
norms are extrapolations from the one-trial figures. They were computed to take into account
the improvement resulting from practice. The
only data on such improvement are based on
performance of 484 college students. Whether
or not the same rate of improvement applies
to other groups should be determined and not
assumed.

The reliability data reported in the manual
indicates that test-retest correlations for the
one-trial administration range from .60 to .76
with a median of .68. The authors argue that
this is adequate in view of the relatively low
validity to be expected of such tests. This argument is not convincing. Stepping up the reliability coefficient to the three-trial length
raises the median to .86. In view of the low
reliability of the one-trial procedure there is
a serious question about the recommendation
of the manual that it be used for hiring purposes. Even at the three-trial level the reliability coefficient is about as low as usually considered acceptable.

The manual recommends that validation
studies be conducted on the population for
which the test is to be used. Essential as such
a procedure is, it would limit the test's usefulness to relatively large industrial organizations
and exclude it entirely from use for vocational
guidance. If the advice has been taken and
more validity studies have been done in industry, the data should be summarized in the manual for the guidance of the potential user. As
it is, he has little to go on except the face
validity.

All but one of the validity coefficients reported are based on various one-trial scores
and involve such small samples as to be virtually meaningless. If, as the manual reports,
the test has been experimentally administered
"in numerous plants which involved the testing
of several thousand employees in a wide variety of industrial jobs," validity coefficients

based on as few as 15 cases seem inexcusable. Moreover, the data are reported for four jobs only. For one sample of 233 radio tube mounters, given three trials of the assembly task, the correlation of scores with ratings was .64. It is not possible to determine how meaningful this criterion is, but if it has practical meaning, it is the kind of evidence which would justify use of the test as part of industrial selection batteries.

The manual points out the well known specificity of manipulative and dexterity tasks. However, no correlations are given with other frequently used tests in this area. Nor are there correlations among the scores on the various parts of the test.

In summary, the *Purdue Pegboard* is a widely used device measuring a variety of manual manipulations. The manual presents very limited evidence to justify its use as a selective device in industry or for vocational guidance. A more up-to-date manual containing more significant information is needed.

For reviews by Edwin E. Ghiselli, Thomas W. Harrell, and Albert Gibson Packard, see 3:666.

MECHANICAL ABILITY

[874]
*A.C.E.R. Mechanical Comprehension Test. Ages 13-6 and over; 1942-53; 1 form ['42]; revised mimeographed manual ['53]; no data on reliability; separate answer sheets must be used; 15s. per 10 tests; 1s. 6d. per 10 answer sheets; 2s. 6d. per manual; 6d. per scoring key; 4s. 6d. per specimen set; postpaid within Australia; 30(40) minutes; Australian Council for Educational Research. *

REFERENCES

1. OXLADE, M. "An Experiment in the Use of Psychological Tests in the Selection of Women Trainee Telephone Mechanics." *B Ind Psychol & Personnel Prac* 2:26–32 Mr '46. * (PA 20: 4838)
2. HOHNE, H. H. *Success and Failure in Scientific Faculties of the University of Melbourne.* Melbourne, Australia: Australian Council for Educational Research, 1955. Pp. vii, 129. * (PA 31:3787)

JOHN R. JENNINGS, *Research and Testing Officer, New Zealand Department of Education, Wellington, New Zealand.*

The test of 45 items has been in use since 1943. The standardization for children was carried out in Tasmania in 1947; the numbers tested are not given. Norms for adults, obtained in 1943, are based on 2,000 male recruits and 1,000 females. In addition, mean scores and standard deviations are reported for

715 first year students at Melbourne University, grouped according to faculty and sex. Similar data are reported for 277 male students in first, second, and third year classes at Melbourne College. Where separate norms for males and females are given, there are wide differences between them, with consistently superior performance being evident among the males. In the norming, an unfortunate complication was introduced by the use of two time limits, 30 and 40 minutes. The university group was given the longer time limit.

The diagrams in the test booklet are reasonably well reproduced. The mechanisms shown in the diagrams are not parts of standard machines, but have been specially drawn to illustrate various mechanical principles and mechanisms. Mechanisms illustrated include levers and pivots, wheels and connecting rods, pulleys and belts or cables, cog and gear wheels, cams and camrods, and the like.

Compared with Bennett's *Test of Mechanical Comprehension,* this test covers fewer theoretical principles and places more emphasis on mechanisms, some of them fairly complicated. The Bennett test includes questions on a wide range of topics not covered by this test, a good many of them outside what is usually understood as "mechanical," e.g., electricity, specific gravity, heat conduction, speed of sound and light, illumination.

The Bennett test, an excellent production, has been so widely used that it is useful to have an alternative test available. The *A.C. E.R. Mechanical Comprehension Test* is a reasonably satisfactory alternative. Though it does not tap nearly such a large range of theoretical knowledge, it does seem to give a reasonable measure of a subject's understanding of straight mechanical principles and of how mechanisms work. It may be regarded as particularly useful for the selection of apprentices to mechanical trades and for candidates for foremanship or junior management in positions where mechanical comprehension is required.

HAYDN S. WILLIAMS, *Assistant Superintendent of Technical Education, Education Department, Perth, Australia.*

This is a paper and pencil test of 45 items similar in kind to Bennett's *Test of Mechanical Comprehension,* but also reflecting the influence of the work of Cox in Great Britain in that the emphasis is on problems involving levers, gears, and pulleys. These are mainly connected in systems not likely to be familiar to persons taking the test. The test is attractively produced with good, clear diagrams. Separate answer sheets are used and marking is by means of a transparent sheet. The general format of the test and the adequate instructions and practice exercises suggest careful preparation.

The manual gives no information concerning the development of the test; it was, however, initially prepared for use in the Australian Armed Services during World War II. The aim, as given in the introductory section for test subjects, is "to see how well you understand mechanical ideas." In practice the test is widely used in vocational guidance organisations throughout the Commonwealth of Australia, and, in conjunction with a space form relation test of the *Minnesota Paper Form Board Test* variety, is used to predict success in practical type occupations mainly at the skilled trade and higher levels.

Although the manual does not report any direct occupational validity data, correlations of .36 and .51 are reported between scores on the test and average marks on woodwork, metalwork, and trade drawing for a group of industrial high school pupils. Evidence is also reported to suggest that, among university students, science and engineering students tend to score higher on the test than arts, law, and commerce students, and that there are higher mean scores produced by the more successful as compared with the less successful engineering students. It is understood that investigations of this test made by the services but not reported in the manual tend to support its value.

No reliability data are reported in the manual nor is any information provided on the test's factorial content, which is clearly complex. The form of the questions and the multiple choice answers suggests a considerable general verbal factor. A correlation of .39 is reported with the Higher Examination of the *Otis Self-Administering Tests of Mental Ability* for the group of high school boys previously referred to. Correlations of .5 between a derivative of this test and the Intermediate Examination of the Otis were obtained by the reviewer using representative samples of 13- and 14-year-old boys. As one might expect,

substantial correlations up to .47 are reported with the *Minnesota Paper Form Board Test*. It therefore appears likely that the test has also a substantial space factor component.

Norms in the form of percentile ranks and standard deviation units are provided for children aged 13.6 to 14.6 and male army recruits aged 18 to 19. The norming appears to have been carefully done on well defined and substantial populations.

To sum up, this test appears to be a well prepared one which warrants further investigation to establish its validity in a much wider range of situations. The manual could have given much more positive guidance to users as to the derivation of the test, its significance, and its uses, as well as the additional validity data which the manual suggests will be added as it becomes available. On the basis of the data so far presented, considerable caution needs to be exercised in the use of the test for individual prediction, where it should only be used as a supplement to other data. This limitation is apparently recognised by the publishers who will only supply copies of the test to persons who are graduates in psychology.

For a review by D. W. McElwain, see 4:756.

[875]
★A.C.E.R. Mechanical Reasoning Test. Ages 14-9 and over; 1951–54; abbreviated adaptation of *A.C.E.R. Mechanical Comprehension Test;* 1 form ['51]; mimeographed manual ['54]; separate answer sheets must be used; 7s. 6d. per 10 tests; 1s. 6d. per 10 answer sheets; 1s. per scoring stencil; 3s. per manual; 4s. 9d. per specimen set; postpaid within Australia; 20(30) minutes; manual by D. Spearritt; Research and Guidance Branch, Queensland Department of Public Instruction and the publisher; Australian Council for Educational Research. *

JOHN R. JENNINGS, *Research and Testing Officer, New Zealand Department of Education, Wellington, New Zealand.*

This test of 24 items is a shortened version of the *A.C.E.R. Mechanical Comprehension Test.* There are three new items, the remainder being reprinted, with some revision, from the parent test.

The question booklet is adequately produced, with diagrams that are larger and clearer than those in the longer test. The answer sheet and scoring key are neat and workmanlike. Mechanisms illustrated include levers and pivots, wheels and connecting rods, pulleys and belts or cables, cog and gear wheels, cams and camrods, and so on. Compared with Bennett's

Test of Mechanical Comprehension, this test covers fewer theoretical principles and places more emphasis on mechanisms.

So far as standard of production is concerned, this test is an improvement over the *A.C.E.R. Mechanical Comprehension Test.* However, it is difficult to be entirely happy about a test of this kind that contains only 24 items, particularly in the absence of any data on validity except the rather sketchy occupational norms. The longer test of 45 items seems well worth the extra 10 minutes of working time.

HAYDN S. WILLIAMS, *Assistant Superintendent of Technical Education, Education Department, Perth, Australia.*

This is a modified and shortened version of the *A.C.E.R. Mechanical Comprehension Test,* which is separately reviewed. It consists of 24 items in place of the original 45; three of the items are not in the parent test. There are five alternative answers to each question in place of four; there is some effort to reduce verbal content by replacing words with direction arrows; and more effective "three dimensional" diagrams are used for some items. Format and printing are clear and attractive. The manual which accompanies the test is an improvement over that for the parent test in format, printing, and content.

The test is "designed to assess a person's aptitude for solving problems involving the understanding of mechanical ideas." It is aimed at adolescents and is suitable for use with unselected male adults but is not sufficiently discriminating among university students and others taking technical courses at an advanced level. There is evidence of careful tryout of the items.

The only information which might be considered as validity data is a series of norms in deciles relating to six major occupational groups drawn from the army recruit population. From these it appears that fitters and mechanics of various kinds score higher on the test than constructional tradesmen, that clerks score nearly as high as constructional tradesmen, and that university students score higher than all other groups. The manual sounds a very proper note of warning concerning the tentative nature of these data in view of the small numbers involved, and the possi-

bility that they are not representative of the occupational groups concerned.

Reliability coefficients obtained by the split-half method and by the Kuder-Richardson formula 20 are of the order of .8, using a sample of 100 of the army recruits. A commendable feature is that this reliability is interpreted for the test user in terms of the probable error of measurement. The reliability is somewhat low compared with that normally considered as satisfactory for individual prediction. When this low reliability is taken into account with correlations of the order of .6 with a word knowledge test, verbal and nonverbal intelligence tests, and a spatial relations test, it appears that scores on the *A.C.E.R. Mechanical Reasoning Test* can be very largely accounted for by general verbal and spatial factors.

This is a carefully prepared test which deserves further tryout by qualified psychologists. The manual provides a satisfactory range of information concerning the test insofar as such information is available. However, the evidence at present available is not adequate enough to justify the use of the test for individual prediction at this stage. Since the test has been produced collaboratively by the A.C.E.R. and the Research and Guidance Branch of the Queensland Education Department, both of which are noted in Australia for sound scientific work in the field of test research, one can reasonably hope that further data on the test will be obtained and published.

[876]

★Chriswell Structural Dexterity Test. Grades 8–9; 1953–54; individual; Form B ('53, revision of unpublished Form A) hectographed manual ('53); $30 per set of test materials, 50 record blanks, and manual; $2.50 per 50 record blanks ['54]; $1 per manual; postage extra; 6.5(15) minutes; M. Irving Chriswell; C. H. Stoelting Co. *

REFERENCE

1. CHRISWELL, M. IRVING. "Validity of a Structural Dexterity Test." *J Appl Psychol* 37:13–5 F '53. * (*PA* 28:1618)

A. PEMBERTON JOHNSON, *Assistant Director, Counseling Center, Newark College of Engineering, Newark, New Jersey.*

The manual states that "structural dexterity may be defined as the ability to translate the visualization of structures into specific motor responses. It is probably closely related to the 'on-the-job' skill of interpreting blue prints through appropriate manual work on bench and machine."

This ingenious test will undoubtedly interest boys with the inclination to take machine shop courses. The product-moment correlation coefficient of .41 for 100 9th and 10th grade students between scores on this test and averaged ratings by two independent judges of layout, precision, and quality of work in making a small "c" clamp suggests a promising validity. Test-retest reliability is estimated at .86. Criterion reliability is estimated at .87 for ratings by two judges of the 100 students. A product-moment correlation coefficient of .51 between scores and the machine shop instructor's single rating is also promising ($r = .55$ with age partialled out).

The reference, "Validity of a Structural Dexterity Test" (*1*), gives evidence of careful experimental work on validity and on reliability, particularly the reliability of the criterion. Although reference to this article appears in the manual, the article presents the experimental results far more crisply and effectively than does the manual. The directions for administering the test could be improved. For example, in leading from the practice session into the beginning of Part 1, on which a 1-minute time limit is used, about 30 seconds of instructions appear after the wording "now you are ready to begin the test proper." A wording such as "now let me give you the instructions for the test proper" might result in more reliable scores. Test administration and scoring are time consuming.

Unfortunately, validity data for the *Revised Minnesota Paper Form Board* and the *MacQuarrie Test of Mechanical Ability* are not available on a comparative basis. One wonders whether one of these might not be as valid as the *Chriswell Structural Dexterity Test* in many technical and vocational high school situations and, at the same time, be far less costly to administer and score. (The manual appears to be overoptimistic in suggesting that as many as five examinees may be tested at one time by one examiner.) Perhaps other tests of ability to visualize and of dexterity might also be studied.

[877]

★Group Test 80A. Ages 15 and over; 1943–51; 1 form ['51]; no data on reliability and validity; mimeographed manual ['51]; separate answer sheets must be used; 27s. per 12 tests; 2s. 3d. per single copy; 1s. 6d. per 12 answer sheets; 2s. 3d. per manual; postage extra; 20(30) minutes; National Institute of Industrial Psychology. *

E. G. CHAMBERS, *Assistant Director of Research in Industrial Psychology, Psychological Laboratory, Cambridge, England.*

This test contains four subtests of spatial perception with practice examples for each. The first two subtests are called Turning Shapes Over; the third, Turning Shapes Round; and the fourth, Turning Shapes Over and Round. In each item a given shape has to be turned mentally and compared with four similar shapes, only one of which is the given shape turned over or round. Each subtest includes 20 items to be completed in 5 minutes, so that the overall time of the complete test is about 30 minutes. The score for the whole test is the number of correct answers less one third of the number of wrong answers to the nearest whole number. Norms from samples of unspecified size are given for boys in the general population for the ages 15-0 to 15-11 and 16+, and also for boys and girls of similar age in secondary grammar schools. No reliability or validation evidence is given.

The principle underlying the test is the recognition of shapes presented from different points of view, a principle common to most tests of spatial perception. The test is of moderate difficulty; the grading of difficulty in the subtests is obtained by making the four possible answers very similar in shape and size. This involves judgments of length of lines and size of angles which must be very close to the perceptual threshold in some instances since actual measurement is not allowed.

The test should be a useful one in the battery of the vocational adviser, but the reviewer feels that the rather arbitrary scoring system needs justification.

JOHN LIGGETT, *Lecturer in Applied Psychology, University of Durham, Newcastle, England.*

Group Test 80A consists of four sets of 20 spatial problems. In the first two tests, called Turning Shapes Over, the subject is required to select from four alternatives the shape which would be produced by laterally reversing the problem figures or, as the instructions say, by turning them over "sideways like a page of a book." The shapes employed range from simple parallelograms to complex irregular and overlapping figures. In the third test, Turning Shapes Round, the subject has to select from four alternatives the shape which represents an angular rotation in the same plane of the problem figure. Again a wide variety of shapes are employed, from triangles to irregular polygons. There appears to be no consistent principle underlying the selection of figures employed. The fourth set of problems, Turning Shapes Over and Round, requires the subject to imagine the problem figures both rotated and laterally reversed. The participation of the test administrator is limited to starting and timing the test and giving instructions to turn over pages at appropriate intervals. Detailed printed instructions are given to the subject on a separate printed page preceding each set of 20 problems and there are worked examples.

Norms issued with the test relate to (*a*) boys in the general population and (*b*) boys and girls from secondary grammar schools. Each group is subdivided into those above 16 years and those between 15 and 16 years. The manual gives no other information about the groups. The test publisher reports that the norms were obtained by giving a group both *Group Test 80A* and the *Form Relations Group Test*. Equivalent scores of the two tests were calculated from these data and norms for Test 80A were obtained from the *Form Relations Group Test* norms. The publisher indicates that Test 80A has been used mainly for industrial work, but that data from 1,738 school children have become available to check the norms.

The split-half reliability of the test, also reported by the publisher but not in the manual, is .86.

Though the aim and purpose of the test designer is nowhere stated, the main interest of the test presumably resides in its sensitivity to "spatial ability." The publisher, however, is unable to report any factorial or other studies which bear on this problem. The utility of the test as a cognitive measure is clearly limited by the scantiness of the normative data. It is possible, however, that the material may prove useful in original empirical studies (for example, in studies of brain damage), since the material is conveniently arranged and scoring is relatively simple. The investigator would no doubt want to consider very carefully the propriety, in relation to his special problem, of employing the verbal instructions as they stand. To use them would be to make serious assumptions about the verbal capacity of his subjects —assumptions which would render the test

much less a measure of "spatial ability" and much more a measure of other, including verbal, abilities.

[878]
*Mechanical Aptitude Test: Acorn National Aptitude Tests. Grades 7–16 and adults; 1943–52; 5 scores: comprehension of mechanical tasks, use of tools and materials (verbal), matching tools and operations, use of tools and materials (non-verbal), total; 1 form ('52, identical with test copyrighted in 1943); directions sheet ('43); no norms for part scores; $3 per 25 tests; 25¢ per manual ('45); 50¢ per specimen set; postage extra; 45(50) minutes; Andrew Kobal, J. Wayne Wrightstone, and Karl R. Kunze; Acorn Publishing Co. *

For reviews by Reign H. Bittner, James M. Porter, Jr., and Alec Rodger, see 3:669.

[879]
★Mellenbruch Mechanical Motivation Test. Grades 6–16 and adults; 1956–57; Forms A, B ('57); no norms for grades 14–16; $1.95 per 20 tests; $1 per specimen set (must be purchased to obtain manual) including 10 tests, manual ('56), and scoring key; postage extra; 35(40) minutes; P. L. Mellenbruch; Psychometric Affiliates. *

ARTHUR H. BRAYFIELD, *Professor of Psychology and Head of the Department, Pennsylvania State University, University Park, Pennsylvania.*

The antecedents of the present measure are to be found in the work of Rice, Toops, O'Rourke, and Stenquist who, almost 40 years ago, devised or developed picture recognition tests of mechanical information. Historically, such tests have had no clear rationale. They have been discussed by Fryer and Super in the context of interest measures; they also are components of tests labeled aptitude (Stenquist, O'Rourke). Actually, there has been so little empirical investigation of the nature of mechanical information tests of a picture recognition nature that it is difficult to appraise them with respect to a given rubric.

The brief manual for the *Mellenbruch Mechanical Motivation Test* explicitly states the fundamental assumption underlying the test: "Persons who are mechanically inclined are actively interested in all sorts of objects, machines and devices, and they are so definitely interested in these 'things' that they give attention to their uses, parts, and relationships. An adequate and proper sampling of one's 'recognition' of common objects and devices should therefore give us an index of one's mechanical inclination and hence his or her trainability." Apparently, the author attempted to measure a condition predictive of a person's ability to profit from training. It is clear that he was not interested in the conventional interest measure criterion of job satisfaction or continuance in an occupation.

The test consists of 84 pairs of items representing objects commonly seen and used (lamp, curling iron, skate key, bottle capper, hose coupling, etc.). The task is to match pairs of objects such as a faucet and its missing handle or an ice tong and an ice chopper. An item analysis of the responses of approximately 1,000 men and women was the basis for item selection. There are two forms available and the intercorrelation is given as .87, group unspecified. The test is easy to administer and score.

The print job is rather poor and the shading of some of the representations of objects affords cues for correct discriminations. Items which are not easily related on the basis of relative size or shape are included. This probably increases the difficulty level of a number of otherwise fairly obvious items.

Odd-even and alternate-form reliabilty coefficients are of the order of .87. The groups studied are not described and the existence of sex differences may have inflated these results if they are for combined groups. More data are needed.

Correlations with intelligence test scores are low but positive. Among a group of Air Force officers, the correlation with a test described only as "Stenquist (Rev.)" is .50. For a group of Air Force employees, the correlation with an Air Force mechanical information test is .61.

Among 57 women engineering drawing students, the test correlates .59 with a criterion described only as teacher estimates or teacher rank. The only other "validation" study reported is for 430 general population members whose test scores correlated .60 with "mechanical activities." This criterion appears to be an index (self-report) of the level of complexity of mechanical skill attained by the respondent through choice or necessity. Its significance as a criterion is problematical. Validation data for the test are inadequate.

There is an increase in mean scores by grade and therefore by age level among the groups sampled. Persons in selected mechanical pursuits (i.e., graduate mechanical engineers and aircraft shop men) make higher mean scores than does the general public. These findings are so inadequately reported that it is impossible to gain much information from them. There are significant (reviewer's estimate) sex differences.

Separate sex norms are available. The most extensive norms are by school grade groups. The general public norm groups are undescribed; there are norms for one male and two female occupational groups. The norms are inadequate.

This is an experimental edition (although not so labeled by the publisher) of a measure of one type of mechanical information about which very little useful data are reported in the limited one-sheet (printed on both sides) manual. There is little or no evidence stemming from the operations involved in developing the test which would justify its designation as a test of mechanical motivation. The test is sufficiently ingenious in conception and execution to merit inclusion in research projects concerned both with practical prediction problems and the theoretical problems involved in untangling the relationships among interest, aptitude, achievement, and satisfaction. Perhaps the test author's primary contribution has been to keep alive the historic *prospect* that interest *may* be appraised through the assessment of informational backgrounds.

John B. Morris, *Associate Professor of Psychology, and Director of Institutional Research, The University of Mississippi, University, Mississippi.*

The rationale for this test is that persons who are mechanically inclined are actively interested in all sorts of objects, machines, and devices and attend to their uses, parts, and relationships. The author believes that one's recognition of a sample of common objects and devices should yield an index of one's mechanical inclination and hence his mechanical trainability. The assumption that this technique measures motivation to the extent implied by the name given the test seems somewhat tenuous to this reviewer. In fact, the word "motivation" does not occur at any place in the manual except in the title, and the test is discussed in terms of its ability to measure "mechanical inclination" and "mechanical aptitude."

The task involved in the test consists of matching a mechanical object in the stimulus column with the object most closely related to it in an adjacent column. To reduce chance success, extra objects are included in each response group. The item quality appears to be good throughout the test, but the reproductions on tests furnished for review were, in many cases, of very poor quality.

There are 84 items on each form of the test, and they are so arranged that the same scoring key may be used on either form. The two forms are structurally similar and appear to be equivalent. A correlation of .87 is reported between the two forms, but no indication of the group used to obtain this figure is given.

In general, the test statistics reported leave something to be desired. For example, the odd-even reliability is reported as .88, but no indication is given as to whether this is a corrected figure or not. Moreover, there is some doubt as to the applicability of this technique for determining reliability anyway, inasmuch as the test is timed and no information is furnished to indicate the adequacy of the time allowed.

The validities reported for the test appear to be relatively high for specific cases. The correlation between test scores and teacher rank for women in engineering drawing classes was .59; between test scores and rank on a mechanical activities scale for the general public, .60. The test also correlated fairly well with other tests of mechanical aptitude; with tests of general intelligence the correlation was positive but low.

Percentile norms for several vocational groups, for men and women of the general public, and for boys and girls in grades 7 through 12 are supplied in the manual. In addition, mean scores are given for several selected groups. The manual states that these indicate that the test differentiates between the various groups. While there is a difference of about 4 points between the means of most groups, no indication of the amount of variability present in each group is given, making it difficult to assess the significance of the differences.

That this test has promise is evidenced by the relatively high validity coefficients reported. At the present time, however, some of the author's recommendations for use of it in employment and placement seem unjustified in the light of the scarcity of evidence. A more comprehensive and straightforward manual and a more descriptive title would do much to overcome some of this reviewer's objections.

[880]

★N.I.I.P. Squares Test. Grades 9 and over; 1944–51; formerly published by National Institute of Industrial Psychology; title on test is *Squares Test;* 1 form ['44]; mimeographed directions sheet ['51]; no data on reliability and validity; norms ['58] for first year university students only; 2s. 6d. per 10 tests; 6d. per scoring key; 6d. per directions and norms sheet; 1s. 3d. per specimen set; postpaid within Australia; 10(15) minutes; National Institute of Industrial Psychology; Australian Council for Educational Research. *

REFERENCES

1. HOLLIDAY, FRANK. "An Investigation Into the Selection of Apprentices for the Engineering Industry." *Occupational Psychol* 14:69–81 Ap '40. * (*PA* 14:3710)
2. SLATER, PATRICK. "Some Group Tests of Spatial Judgment or Practical Ability." *Occupational Psychol* 14:40–55 Ja '40. * (*PA* 14:2644)
3. HOLLIDAY, FRANK. "A Further Investigation Into the Selection of Apprentices for the Engineering Industry." *Occupational Psychol* 15:173–84 O '41. * (*PA* 16:732)
4. SLATER, PATRICK. "Tests for Selecting Secondary and Technical School Children." *Occupational Psychol* 15:10–25 Ja '41. * (*PA* 15:3177)
5. SHUTTLEWORTH, CLIFFORD W. "Tests of Technical Aptitude." *Occupational Psychol* 16:175–82 O '42. *
6. SLATER, PATRICK, AND BENNETT, ELIZABETH. "The Development of Spatial Judgment and Its Relation to Some Educational Problems." *Occupational Psychol* 17:139–55 Jl '43. *
7. LINGWOOD, JOAN. "Test Performances of ATS Recruits From Certain Civilian Occupations." *Occupational Psychol* 26:35–46 Ja '52. * (*PA* 26:6567)
8. HOHNE, H. H. *Success and Failure in Scientific Faculties of the University of Melbourne.* Melbourne, Australia: Australian Council for Educational Research, 1955. Pp. vii, 129. * (*PA* 31:3787)
9. KRATHWOHL, DAVID R., AND CRONBACH, LEE J. "Suggestions Regarding a Possible Measure of Personality: The Squares Test." *Ed & Psychol Meas* 16:305–16 au '56. *

J. F. CLARK, *Professor of Applied Psychology, New South Wales University of Technology, Kensington, New South Wales, Australia.*

This test was prepared as a spatial test by the National Institute of Industrial Psychology in London almost two decades ago. It has been reprinted without alteration by the Australian Council for Educational Research.

The test consists of 54 items of increasing difficulty, each of which is completed by drawing a straight line to divide an irregular two-dimensional figure into two smaller figures which when fitted together make a square. Thus it requires the person taking the test to be constructive, differing in this respect from those tests requiring simply a choice between a series of possible answers.

First impressions are that this is a promising test, but experience by psychologists using it over the years in Britain and Australia has shown that the test has only limited usefulness.

There are no norms, reliability, or validation data supplied by either of the distributors so the value of the test can be established only by using it. Those who have developed their own norms and validation data find that the test assists them only in a limited way for very specific purposes. It cannot, therefore, be recommended for general use.

[881]

★**Newcastle Spatial Test.** Ages 10-0 to 11-11; 1958-59; selection of students for technical schools or courses; 1 form ('58); mimeographed manual of instructions ['58]; provisional norms ['59]; no data on reliability and validity; 203s. 6d. per 100 tests; 3s. 6d. per manual; 3s. per single copy; postage extra; 39(60-70) minutes; I. Macfarlane Smith and J. S. Lawes; distributed by Department of Education, King's College, University of Durham, Newcastle upon Tyne, England. *

[882]

★**O'Rourke Mechanical Aptitude Test.** Adults; 1939-57; Forms A ('57), B ('39), C ('39); key-manual sheets (no dates); no data on reliability; $4.50 per 50 tests of Form A; $3.25 per 50 tests of Forms B or C; postage extra; 25¢ per specimen set, postpaid; 55(65) minutes; L. J. O'Rourke; Psychological Institute. *

[883]

★**Purdue Mechanical Performance Test.** Ages 17 and over; 1957; 4 scores: transfer boards, spatial relations, hub assemblies, total; individual; 1 form ['57]; manual ['57]; record sheet, Form A ['57]; $175 per set of test materials; postage extra; (20) minutes; Ernest J. McCormick and Robert L. Brown; Lafayette Instrument Co. *

REFERENCE

1. BROWN, ROBERT LEE. *The Development and Validation of a Mechanical Performance Test.* Doctor's thesis, Purdue University (Lafayette, Ind.), 1957. (*DA* 17:1583)

[884]

Revised Minnesota Paper Form Board Test. Grades 9-16 and adults; 1930-48; IBM; 2 forms, 2 editions; manual ('48); 35¢ per specimen set; postpaid; 20(25) minutes; original test by Donald G. Paterson, Richard M. Elliott, L. Dewey Anderson, Herbert A. Toops, and Edna Heidbreder; revision by Rensis Likert and William H. Quasha; Psychological Corporation. *

a) [HAND SCORING EDITION.] 1930-48; Forms AA ('41), BB ('41); $2.10 per 25 tests; French edition (Forms AA-FE, BB-FE, '55) available.

b) [MACHINE SCORING EDITION.] 1941-48; IBM; Forms MA ('41), MB ('41); $3 per 25 tests; $1.90 per 50 IBM answer sheets.

REFERENCES

1-9. See 40:1673.
10-57. See 3:677.
58-95. See 4:763.
96. EDWARDS, KARL D. *Work-Limit vs Time-Limit Scores on the Minnesota Paper Form Board Test.* Master's thesis, Kansas State College (Manhattan, Kan.), 1945.
97. FERSON, REGIS F. *The Probabilities of Success in Trade Training as Estimated by Standardized Tests.* Doctor's thesis, University of Pittsburgh (Pittsburgh, Pa.), 1951.
98. LITTLETON, ISAAC T. "Prediction in Auto Trade Courses." *J Appl Psychol* 36:15-9 F '52. * (*PA* 26:7256)
99. MOFFIE, DANNIE J., AND MILTON, CHARLES R. "The Relationship of Certain Psychological Test Scores to Academic Success in Chemical Engineering." Abstract. *Am Psychol* 7:379-80 Jl '52. *
100. NEWMAN, SIDNEY H.; FRENCH, JOHN W.; AND BOBBITT, JOSEPH M. "Analysis of Criteria for the Validation of Selection Measures at the United States Coast Guard Academy." *Ed & Psychol Meas* 12:394-407 au '52. * (*PA* 27:6159)
101. BODLEY, E. A. "Selection Tests for Women Packers." *B Ind Psychol & Personnel Prac* 9:24-32 Mr '53. *
102. COLEMAN, WILLIAM. "An Economical Test Battery for Predicting Freshman Engineering Course Grades." *J Appl Psychol* 37:465-7 D '53. * (*PA* 29:1562)
103. JENKINS, JAMES J. "Some Measured Characteristics of Air Force Weather Forecasters and Success in Forecasting." *J Appl Psychol* 37:440-4 D '53. * (*PA* 29:1642)
104. "Validity Information Exchange, No. 7-095: D.O.T. Code 7-94.112 and 7-94.100, Tool and Die and Machinist Apprentice." *Personnel Psychol* 7:573 w '54. *
105. BALINSKY, BENJAMIN, AND HUJSA, CHARLES. "Performance of College Students on a Mechanical Knowledge Test." *J Appl Psychol* 38:111-2 Ap '54. * (*PA* 29:3028)

106. DuBois, PHILLIP H., AND WATSON, ROBERT I. "Validity Information Exchange, No. 7-075: D.O.T. Code 2-66.23, Policeman." *Personnel Psychol* 7:414-7 au '54. *
107. GUAZZO, EUGENE J., JR. *Predicting Academic Success of Architecture Students.* Master's thesis, Alabama Polytechnic Institute (Auburn, Ala.), 1954.
108. HUEBER, JOANNE. "Validity Information Exchange, No. 7-089: D.O.T. Code 5-83.641, Maintenance Mechanic II." *Personnel Psychol* 7:565-6 w '54. *
109. SCHMITZ, ROY M., AND HOLMES, JOHN L. "Relationship of Certain Measured Abilities to Freshman Engineering Achievement," pp. 32-42. (*PA* 29:1584) In *Selection and Counseling of Students in Engineering.* Edited by Wilbur L. Layton. Minnesota Studies in Student Personnel Work, No. 4. Minneapolis, Minn.: University of Minnesota Press, 1954. Pp. iv, 89. *
110. CANTONI, LOUIS J. "High School Tests and Measurements as Predictors of Occupational Status." *J Appl Psychol* 39:253-5 Ag '55. * (*PA* 30:4722)
111. CUOMO, SYLVIA, AND MEYER, HERBERT H. "Validity Information Exchange, No. 8-19: D.O.T. Code 6-78.632, Floor Assembler." *Personnel Psychol* 8:270 su '55. *
112. HOHNE, H. H. *Success and Failure in Scientific Faculties of the University of Melbourne.* Melbourne, Australia: Australian Council for Educational Research, 1955. Pp. vii, 129. * (*PA* 31:3787)
113. MALLOY, JOHN P.; WYSOCKI, BOLESLAW; AND GRAHAM, LEO F. "Predicting Attrition-Survival in First Year Engineering." *J Ed Psychol* 46:217-21 Ap '55. * (*PA* 30:1624)
114. PATTERSON, CECIL H. *Test and Background Factors Related to Drop-Outs in an Industrial Institute.* Doctor's thesis, University of Minnesota (Minneapolis, Minn.), 1955. (*DA* 15:1024)
115. PERRINE, MERVYN WILLIAM. "The Selection of Drafting Trainees." *J Appl Psychol* 39:57-61 F '55. * (*PA* 30:1725)
116. POIDEVIN, B. "A Test Battery to Select Knitting Machine Operators." *Personnel Pract B* 11:22-6 Mr '55. * (*PA* 30:3577)
117. SMITH, OTTO B. *Predicting Grade Success of High School Students in Radio and Drafting.* Master's thesis, Alabama Polytechnic Institute (Auburn, Ala.), 1955.
118. BRUCE, MARTIN M. "Normative Data Information Exchange, No. 16." *Personnel Psychol* 9:392 au '56. *
119. OTTERNESS, WILLIAM B.; PATTERSON, C. H.; JOHNSON, R. H.; AND PETERSON, LENNIS R. "Trade School Norms for Some Commonly Used Tests." *J Appl Psychol* 40:57-60 F '56. * (*PA* 31:3803)
120. PATTERSON, C. H. "The Prediction of Attrition in Trade School Courses." *J Appl Psychol* 40:154-8 Je '56. * (*PA* 31:6680)
121. BRUCE, MARTIN M. "Normative Data Information Exchange, No. 10-5." *Personnel Psychol* 10:99-100 sp '57. *
122. BRUCE, MARTIN M. "Normative Data Information Exchange, No. 10-6." *Personnel Psychol* 10:101-2 sp '57. *
123. SPEER, GEORGE S. "Validity Information Exchange, No. 10-13: D.O.T. Code 0-88.31, Ship Pilot." *Personnel Psychol* 10:201 su '57. *
124. BARRETT, RICHARD S. "The Process of Predicting Job Performance." *Personnel Psychol* 11:39-57 sp '58. *

D. W. McELWAIN, *Professor of Psychology, The University of Queensland, Brisbane, Australia.*

The "form board" setting of problems was established in the earliest days of mental testing. Edouard Seguin developed what was probably the first set before 1850, and the use of such tests was well known before Binet began his work in Paris. The test was thought to be what we would now call a nonverbal measure of general cognitive capacity.

Spearman as early as 1905 conceived cognitive capacity to have a single underlying factor which he termed *g*. The first breakdown of this position came from the work of El Koussy, who showed that it was reasonable to posit a "space" factor to account for the intercorrelations of certain tests which could not be accounted for solely in terms of general capacity. The Minnesota researches of Paterson and others about 1930 into mechanical ability confirmed the existence of this special capacity to handle spatial relations. The *Minnesota Paper Form Board Test* arose from these studies. This test was later revised by Likert and Quasha to produce the present test.

The test has had many "pirate" forms, and although these may offend its originators, they are a tribute to the appeal of the test. The pirated forms are amazingly diverse in layout but maintain an extraordinary fidelity in the reproduction of the specific test items.

One of the most vexatious problems about the test has been the time provided. Some have preferred to emphasize the power function and to give a "long time" of 20 minutes or more. No one doubts that the late items in the test are difficult. Others have argued that there is no demonstrable increase in validity after 15 minutes' testing. The result has been a confused literature on the test. The authors plead for a fixed time of 20 minutes. A definitive investigation on the effects of time for testing on various validities would be welcomed.

There are many convincing studies on the usefulness of the test, especially where "spatial imagery" is a requirement, such as in engineering, architecture, military tactical exercises, drafting, fitting, and so forth. The predictions however are generally of the same order as are given by intelligence tests.

The factor loading of the test is not wholly clear, and in any case appears to alter with age and with sex.

The test appears to serve usefully even if regarded merely as a general test of cognitive capacity in a nonverbal medium.

Some recent investigations which have been undertaken with very primitive preliterates in the Territory of Papua and New Guinea show that the test if presented more concretely with moveable parts is a good predictor of "educable potential."

The five years since the *Mental Measurements Yearbook* last reviewed this test have provided no essentially new material but have confirmed that the test has a very useful place in the battery of the psychometrician.

For reviews by Clifford E. Jurgensen and Raymond A. Katzell, see 4:763; for a review by Dewey B. Stuit, see 3:677; for a review by Alec Rodger, see 40:1673.

[885]

*Spatial Tests I and II.** Ages 11-0 to 13-11, 10-7 to 13-11; 1950–56; 1 form; 2 tests; distribution is restricted to directors of education; 13s. 6d. per 12 tests; 1s. 3d. per single copy; 3s. 6d. per manual; postage extra; National Foundation for Educational Research in England and Wales. *

a) SPATIAL TEST I. Ages 11-0 to 13-11; 1950; 1 form ['50]; manual ['50]; 41(60) minutes; I. Macfarlane Smith.

b) SPATIAL TEST II. Ages 10-7 to 13-11; 1950–56; 1 form ['51]; manual ['51]; provisional norms ['56]; no data on reliability and validity; 26.5(45) minutes; A. F. Watts with the assistance of D. A. Pidgeon and M. K. B. Richards.

REFERENCE

1. SMITH, I. MACFARLANE. "Measuring Spatial Ability in School Pupils." *Occupational Psychol* 22:150–9 Jl '48. * (PA 23:1181)

E. G. CHAMBERS, *Assistant Director of Research in Industrial Psychology, Psychological Laboratory, Cambridge, England.*

Test I, designed for use in allocating children to technical courses, has six subtests: Fitting Shapes, Form Recognition, Pattern Recognition, Shape Recognition, Comparisons, and Form Reflections. These all deal with two-dimensional figures and patterns. According to the manual, the test has been shown to have a high loading in the spatial factor as well as in the general factor, and it "has been found to give high correlations with assessments in technical drawing."

Test II has five subtests: Match Box Corners, Shapes and Models, Square Completion, Paper Folding, and Block Building. All except the third of these involve three-dimensional representations.

These tests embody a number of principles involved in spatial perception, some of which are not commonly found in spatial tests. Although rather lengthy, the subtests are of sufficient variety to maintain interest and endeavour. They should be useful instruments in the hands of those responsible for allocating children to further training in technical disciplines, although no direct evidence of validation is given.

CHARLES T. MYERS, *Associate in Test Development, Educational Testing Service, Princeton, New Jersey.*

These tests have a very important advantage over most spatial tests in that they each use a variety of item types in separately timed parts. In general the directions for each type are clear and effective. The printing is good. The tests appear to be easy to administer. The item difficulty is well suited to the groups for which the tests are intended. The whole of the possible score range was effectively used by the norms sample. In these respects it would be hard to find a better spatial test. Unfortunately, the effect of these good qualities is mitigated by the serious lack of information in the manual about the reliability and validity of these tests and the norms for them.

Test I begins with Fitting Shapes, a test made up of items of the familiar paper formboard type. The next part, Form Recognition, is a multiple choice test of the Gottschaldt figures shown by Thurstone to be a measure of what he called the second closure factor. The other four item types, which are less familiar, call for matching or comparison of simple shapes. The total number of items is 100.

Test II, also a 100-item test, begins with Match Box Corners, a test which presumably measures Thurstone's first spatial factor. The second and fourth tests are Shapes and Models, which is a variety of surface development problem, and Paper Folding. Both of these tests are probably measures of Thurstone's second spatial factor, which has generally proved to be more valid than the first for most of the purposes for which spatial tests are used. Until more research has been done, however, it is probably wise to use somewhat heterogeneous measures to be on the safe side. It is too easy for a test taker to get off the track on a single spatial item type. The Shapes and Models item type has the same complication that seems to be present in the original *Minnesota Spatial Relations Test*—that a good deal of effort is required to find the figures you are looking for and that observation and memory have a large influence on test variance.

The selection of the item types used in these tests was in part based on research conducted in 1934 and reported in 1948 by I. Macfarlane Smith (*1*). Unfortunately, two of the six item types used in Test I and four of the five item types used in Test II were not included in this research and no information is given about these other item types. It may well be as ridiculous to assume that a test is a valid spatial test merely because it is presented pictorially as it would be to assume that a test is a valid vocabulary test merely because it is presented verbally. Tests of history, science, or music appreciation can be presented verbally. The United States Air Force research has demonstrated

that there are many different factors that can be measured by graphic tests. Even the above mentioned article demonstrated that several graphic item types failed to have any loadings on the spatial, or *k*, factor. All the item types used in these tests appear to be appropriate to the purpose of the test, but it would be sounder to have some better criterion than subjective judgment. Incidentally, several of the item types would probably be inappropriate for spatial testing at a higher level.

British and American psychologists generally have tended to disagree about the number and significance of the different factors that can be found in different graphic tests. The evidence on both sides of the argument still seems to be inconclusive, although, in general, the British point of view that there is only one spatial factor seems better borne out in studies of children and the American concept of several spatial factors is supported largely by studies of adults. One's judgment of the quality of these tests is, therefore, likely to depend in part on a judgment about this controversy.

Strangely enough in view of this, Test II has been designated "three dimensional." This reviewer is unaware of any research that shows a significant difference between so-called two-dimensional tests and three-dimensional tests. Further, a subjective examination of the item types used in Test II casts serious doubt about the fact that these item types are really three-dimensional. Three of the five item types do use drawings of three-dimensional objects, but the problems can always be solved in terms of successive two-dimensional steps. It is true that these item types can be distinguished from those in Test I in terms of complexity and this complexity seems in these three item types to be a by-product of the use of three-dimensional figures. In the reviewer's judgment, the complexity of the problems, the amount of inference required in their solution, the effect of time limits, and the degree of perceptual discrimination needed are all far more important than the number of dimensions in the objects represented in the drawings.

A further judgment, supported to some extent by United States Air Force research, is that the element of perceptual discrimination is likely to decrease the validity of a spatial test for most important criteria. Scales, dividers, and measuring tapes are easily bought and applied, thus minimizing the importance of perceptual discrimination, but the ability to solve spatial problems is not so easily obtained. A number of spatial tests, such as the famous *Revised Minnesota Paper Form Board Test,* seem to be measuring in part a trivial skill since in so many problems the difference between a right and a wrong answer is only a very small difference in the length of a line. Tests I and II have this characteristic to only a small extent, but in a number of problems it is difficult for the test taker to know how careful his discrimination must be. This unintended problem is likely to have the effect of distracting him from the problem that he is supposed to solve. This ambiguity also leads to some difficulty in scoring. Since there are so many possible ways of presenting spatial problems, it seems unfortunate that item types should be used where this is a problem. However, there seems to be no general consensus among testmakers, nor any clear statements, as to what type of mental activity they are trying to elicit with spatial tests and a testmaker may be justified in using his own judgment in this regard.

With tests that are intended for a purpose as abstruse as these, it would be well for the author to make a clear statement in the manual of what he thought his test would measure, taking more than a phrase to say whether it was spatial reasoning, visual imagery, ability to read drawings, adaptability to unfamiliar and nonverbal problems, mechanical intelligence, or something else. There are a number of less general comments that might be made about the tests and manuals. We would like to know how similar these tests are to the tests that were validated in Smith's study. We would also like more information about the sample on which the reliability estimate was based and about the conditions of the test-retest administrations. The norms sample should be more fully described in terms of age distribution, class in school, and sex. This reviewer would prefer norms based exclusively on boys since in most tasks in which this ability is pertinent a girl is likely to be competing mostly with boys. Some information should always be given about the speededness of tests. Although these tests do not appear to be speeded, this does not prove that speed of work is irrelevant. If used in America, the directions for administration would

need some slight revisions to clarify some British expressions for American children.

The norms of these tests are somewhat like IQ's since they have a mean of 100 and a standard deviation of 15. It is interesting to note that they have a smaller change with age than do intelligence quotients. Is this the result of some peculiarity of the norms sample or some lack of representativeness at each age level, or is it because this ability matures earlier and has nearly reached a peak by the age of 13?

In summary, then, these tests appear to have more good qualities than undesirable ones. Their variety of item types and their simple and effective directions particularly commend their use. They deserve further study and a more complete manual.

For a review by E. A. Peel of Spatial Test I, *see 4:753.*

[886]

*Survey of Mechanical Insight. Grades 9–16 and adults; 1945–55; IBM; 1 form ('55); manual ('55); no college norms; $4.20 per 35 tests; separate answer sheets may be used; 3¢ per IBM answer sheet; 20¢ per machine scoring stencil; 50¢ per specimen set; postage extra; 30(40) minutes; Daniel R. Miller; California Test Bureau. *

REFERENCES

1. MARTIN, GLENN C. "Test Batteries for Trainees in Auto Mechanics and Apparel Design." *J Appl Psychol* 35:20–2 F '51. * (*PA* 25:7123)
2. POE, WESLEY A., AND BERG, IRWIN A. "Psychological Test Performance of Steel Industry Production Supervisors." *J Appl Psychol* 36:234–7 Ag '52. * (*PA* 27:3794)
3. WORPELL, DONALD FREDERICK. *A Study of Selection Factors and the Development of Objective Criteria for Measuring Success in a Co-operative General Machine Shop Training Program.* Doctor's thesis, University of Michigan (Ann Arbor, Mich.), 1956. (*DA* 17:1270)

ARTHUR H. BRAYFIELD, *Professor of Psychology and Head of the Department, Pennsylvania State University, University Park, Pennsylvania.*

As stated in the manual, "the test is made up of thirty-five three-response multiple-choice items. Each item includes a drawing of a mechanical device. To the right of the drawing is a statement concerning some aspect of the machine's operation. Beneath this statement are three possible responses from which the examinee must choose the one that is most correct." The items appear to be based on general principles of mechanics.

This is a revision of the 1945 edition. According to the manual, "the figures in the test have been redrawn and the items have been arranged in order of difficulty." The directions for administration have been revised and the materials have been arranged in a new format.

The manual makes the claim that previous experience "operates minimally in this test, since the pictures do not depict machines that are currently being used." No data are presented to bolster this assertion.

Reliability data are inadequate. For a sample of 250 male and female trade and industrial personnel, the split-half corrected coefficient is .88; this probably is inflated due to sex differences. A second sample of 297 male applicants for laborer jobs with a large oil company gives a Kuder-Richardson formula 20 coefficient of .87.

Validity data are presented for four occupational groups. The test has been found to discriminate between "high" and "low" rated supervisors ($n = 33$) in a steel manufacturing plant. The publisher also presents data for 50 postage meter repairmen, 45 lathe operator trainees, and 45 auto mechanic trainees, using the criteria, respectively, of supervisor's merit ratings, instructor's ratings, and instructor's ratings of classroom work. The correlations are in the .40's. No reference is made to the nature of the ratings, their reliability, or the circumstances under which they were obtained.

The SMI has been correlated with scores on three other mechanical tests with r's generally in the .60's. The most informative is the correlation of .66 with Mechanical Reasoning of the *Differential Aptitude Tests* for 40 oil company construction department applicants. Apparently the same sample was used in an appraisal of the relationship between SMI scores and educational level; the correlation was .21. However, no grade distribution is given so that it is difficult to judge the results. The reviewer rank-ordered eight occupational norm groups on the basis of his judgment of general ability level requirements and correlated these rankings with the median SMI scores reported for the samples. The rank-order correlation was .9 which suggests that general ability *may* be significantly related to SMI scores. However, this is merely suggestive of further investigation of the relationship.

In short, there is some "loose" evidence for the validity of the test in predicting performance in a few mechanically related occupations, especially during the training period. However, the manual does not explicitly state that the validity data and the intertest correlations refer to the revised 1955 edition and, in fact, two of the validation studies almost surely were done with the original 1945 edition. The correlation between the two editions is not reported.

Nine additional norm groups are furnished in the revised manual for a total of 10. Obviously these samples were obtained on a fortuitous basis; seven are job applicant samples. The norms are not particularly helpful. Separate sex norms are not provided, although there is some evidence in one of the tables that, at least at the 10th grade level, there may be significant sex differences.

The publisher suggests that the per cent of items attempted be used for diagnostic purposes to classify four types of examinees. This is a dubious procedure and no evidence is given to back up the recommendation.

The manual itself is, in the reviewer's judgment, marked by ambiguity and a certain amount of indirection which amounts to overselling. For one example, there is overemphasis upon the use of a "short, single instrument" for selection purposes. This caters to an unfortunate trend in industrial testing which already is too prevalent.

In summary, the *Survey of Mechanical Insight* is a perhaps "promising" instrument for specific selection validation research although it should be "pitted" against other tests such as the Bennett *Test of Mechanical Comprehension*, which has a much more substantial history of test development. Its present utility for counseling is minimal. Research on the influence of previous experience and training is a very real need, particularly in view of "come on" statements in the manual.

For reviews by Reign H. Bittner, Jay L. Otis, and Shailer Peterson of the original edition, see 3:680.

[887]

*Survey of Object Visualization. Grades 9–16 and adults; 1945–55; IBM; 1 form ('55); manual ('55); $3.50 per 35 tests; separate answer sheets may be used; 3¢ per IBM answer sheet; 20¢ per scoring stencil; postage extra; 50¢ per specimen set, postpaid; Spanish edition available; 25(30) minutes; Daniel R. Miller; California Test Bureau. *

REFERENCES

1. WEISS, IRVING. "Prediction of Academic Success in Dental School." *J Appl Psychol* 36:11–4 F '52. * (PA 26:7296)
2. LAYTON, WILBUR L. "Predicting Success in Dental School." *J Appl Psychol* 37:251–5 Ag '53. * (PA 28:6712)
3. LYNCH, BENJAMIN L. *The Miller Object Visualization Test as a Prognostic Aid in Dental Education.* Master's thesis, Creighton University (Omaha, Neb.), 1953.
4. WEBB, SAM C. "The Prediction of Achievement for First Year Dental Students." *Ed & Psychol Meas* 16:543–8 w '56. * (PA 32:962)

5. WORPELL, DONALD FREDERICK. *A Study of Selection Factors and the Development of Objective Criteria for Measuring Success in a Co-operative General Machine Shop Training Program.* Doctor's thesis, University of Michigan (Ann Arbor, Mich.), 1956. (*DA* 17:1270)

WILLIAM J. MICHEELS, *Professor of Industrial Education and Chairman of the Department, University of Minnesota, Minneapolis, Minnesota.*

This test is designed "to measure aptitude for solving problems in perceptual recognition of an object's appearance in altered position or shape." The instrument is intended to be useful in identifying the ability to perceive spatial relationships.

Each of the 44 multiple choice problems consists of a flat pattern which, if folded on the dotted lines or rolled together correctly, would take the shape of one of the four objects pictured as options. To select the correct response, the examinee must be able to visualize the three-dimensional shape that the pattern would assume.

In the 1955 revision the items have been rearranged "in order of difficulty." Apparently this was done on the basis of an item analysis, although the technique is not mentioned. The major improvement of the new edition is in the test manual which now contains more validation and normative data. Directions for administration have been revised in order to insure more uniform administration of the test.

The 10 norm groups include a sample of 250 males and females in what is called the "general population"; worker groups in aircraft, petroleum refining, and drafting; and college students or applicants in dentistry (the largest group), engineering, clothing construction, and general college students. A catalog description of the survey states that it is appropriate for grade 9 through the adult level. The manual mentions young people and school students, but no meaningful data are included with respect to uses of the test at these lower levels. One wonders about the sampling adequacy in obtaining data for several of the norm groups. Most of the reported experiences in using the test refer to applicants for dental schools.

Reliability coefficients of .91 (split-half) and .92 (Kuder-Richardson formula 21) are reported for two different populations—a sample ($n = 266$) of male and female trade and industrial personnel and a sample ($n = 188$) of general helpers in the petroleum refining industry. Validity is indicated by a correlation coefficient of .44 between scores on the survey and freshmen technic grades in a dental school.

It would be interesting to see some data on survey test scores in relation to previous experiences with layout work or elementary drafting. The manual states that the test is "so designed that aptitude rather than experience is sampled." This is a moot question. More information is needed on the rationale and construction of the test.

The reviewer gave the test to an advanced graduate student with an engineering background. He reported that after working several items he stopped trying to visualize the total pattern and adopted a logical analysis approach wherein he identified the shape of a base, which usually eliminated one or two answer choices, and then counted sides or parts. With the aid of a few handy rules known to most persons familiar with layout work, it became rather easy to pick out the right selections without any conscious effort at visualizing the whole object. This is reported as an observation rather than a criticism since it may be that logical analysis is an important part of the visualization process. This leads the reviewer to suggest that the survey might serve a useful purpose as a pretest for courses in engineering graphics or mechanical drafting.

For those occupations that require this type of visualization ability, the test can serve a useful purpose. It can be quickly administered and easily scored. The new manual contains information on the several ways in which the test results might be used.

For reviews by Charles M. Harsh, Clifford E. Jurgensen, Shailer Peterson, and Patrick Slater of the original edition, see 3:681.

[888]

Survey of Space Relations Ability. Grades 9–16 and adults; 1944–49; IBM; Forms A ('44), B ('47); manual ('49); $4.20 per 35 tests; separate answer sheets may be used; 3¢ per IBM answer sheet; 20¢ per scoring stencil; postage extra; 25¢ per specimen set, postpaid; Spanish edition available; 15(20) minutes; Harry W. Case and Floyd Ruch; California Test Bureau. *

REFERENCES

1. CASE, HARRY W. "Selection of Aircraft Engineering Draftsmen and Designers." *J Appl Psychol* 31:583–8 D '47. * (*PA* 22:2769)
2. AMERICAN GAS ASSOCIATION, PERSONNEL COMMITTEE. *Personnel Testing in the Gas Industry.* New York: the Association, January 1952. Pp. 10. *
3. CASE, HARRY W. "The Relationship of Certain Tests to Grades Achieved in an Industrial Class in Aircraft Design." *Ed & Psychol Meas* 12:90–5 sp '52. * (*PA* 27:6106)

4. Poe, Wesley A., and Berg, Irwin A. "Psychological Test Performance of Steel Industry Production Supervisors." *J Appl Psychol* 36:234–7 Ag '52. * (*PA* 27:3794)

D. W. McElwain, *Professor of Psychology, University of Queensland, Brisbane, Australia.*

This is a so-called space relations test. It is clearly a derivative of the *Minnesota Paper Form Board Test* which in turn comes from El Koussy's studies under Spearman on the "space" group factor done about 1928. In the Minnesota test the testee is given some "parts" and asked which of 5 wholes could be made from the parts, but in this test he is given a whole and asked which parts from 10 given would make up the whole. The tests are otherwise similar—both being group, pencil and paper, two-dimensional, machine scorable tests scored with a correction for wrong answers.

The test has a "gimmick" in that the problems are presented in coarse white lines on a blue background, instead of fine black lines on a white background as in the Minnesota test. The blue printing is supposed to give the subject the impression that the test is fair and practical, since the test simulates blueprints. Since there are now better methods of reproduction of plans than blueprinting, the typography has no other virtue than novelty, or perhaps historical interest.

The standardization of the test is adequate. There are two parallel forms, though no direct data other than a bald assertion that they are alternate forms are presented concerning the equality of the forms. Relatively high reliability is reported.

The test has a practice section with but two items. Tests of this kind usually show large short-term practice effects which, unless diminished by longer fore-practice, decrease the validity of the test. This is particularly true if the subjects are nonacademic, as we might expect them to be if they are candidates for selection for training in skilled manual trades.

The format of the test is attractive. The directions for administering and scoring are clear. The scoring provides for what is in effect a rights minus wrongs formula (where the wrongs include omissions). It would be surprising if this formula rather than rights minus an empirically determined fraction of wrongs is optimal for validity.

The validity coefficients reported (correlations with supervisors' ratings and teachers' grades) are such as one would expect, gener-ally ranging from the .30's to the .60's. They are probably of the same order as would obtain for any group, cognitive capacity, pencil and paper, nonverbal test, using the criteria selected. This type of validity evidence is often useful, but one looks for any significant increase in predictive or selective capacity that a test of this kind can provide over and above that of the "ordinary" intelligence test. No such evidence is provided.

In short, the original features of this test (requiring the selection of parts to make a given whole and using white lines and blue background) are probably insignificant changes. The test is seemingly no better and probably no worse than the several dozen other available "space" tests of its kind.

For reviews by E. G. Chambers, Clifford E. Jurgensen, and James M. Porter, Jr., see 3:682.

[889]

*Test of Mechanical Comprehension. Grades 9 and over; 1940–54, c1940–57; IBM; 4 editions (labeled forms); separate answer sheets must be used; $4.25 per 25 tests; $1.90 per 50 IBM answer sheets; 35¢ per specimen set; postpaid; (25–45) minutes; George K. Bennett, Dinah E. Fry (BB, test only; WI), and William A. Owens (CC); Psychological Corporation. *
a) form AA. Grades 9 and over; 1940–54, c1940–55; 1 form ('40); manual ['47]; supplement ('54); French and Spanish editions available.
b) form BB. Men in grades 13 and over; 1941–51; 1 form ('41); revised manual ('51); Spanish edition available.
c) form CC. Men in engineering schools; 1949; 1 form; manual ['49].
d) form WI. Women in grades 9 and over; 1942–47; 1 form ('42); manual ['47].

REFERENCES

1–19. See 3:683.
20–47. See 4:766.
48. Johnson, Ralph H., and Bond, Guy L. "Reading Ease of Commonly Used Tests." *J Appl Psychol* 34:319–24 O '50. * (*PA* 26:299)
49. Lee, Marilyn C. *Relationship of Masculinity-Femininity to Tests of Mechanical and Clerical Abilities.* Master's thesis, University of Minnesota (Minneapolis, Minn.), 1950.
50. Ferson, Regis F. *The Probabilities of Success in Trade Training as Estimated by Standardized Tests.* Doctor's thesis, University of Pittsburgh (Pittsburgh, Pa.), 1951.
51. Miller, Gilbert E. "Some Components of Mechanical Composition." *Proc Iowa Acad Sci* 58:385–9 '51. *
52. Carter, Gerald C. "Measurement of Supervisory Ability." *J Appl Psychol* 36:393–5 D '52. * (*PA* 27:6801)
53. Case, Harry W. "The Relationship of Certain Tests to Grades Achieved in an Industrial Class in Aircraft Design." *Ed & Psychol Meas* 12:90–5 sp '52. * (*PA* 27:6106)
54. Gilbert, Harry B. "The Use of Tests and Other Objective Data in the Selection of Camp Counselors." Abstract. *Am Psychol* 7:369 Jl '52. *
55. Krathwohl, David R.; Ewing, T. N.; Gilbert, W. M.; and Cronbach, Lee J. "Prediction of Success in Architecture Courses." Abstract. *Am Psychol* 7:288–9 Jl '52. *
56. Lee, Marilyn C. "Relationship of Masculinity-Femininity to Tests of Mechanical and Clerical Abilities." *J Appl Psychol* 36:377–80 D '52. * (*PA* 27:6431)
57. Lingwood, Joan. "Test Performances of ATS Recruits From Certain Civilian Occupations." *Occupational Psychol* 26: 35–46 Ja '52. * (*PA* 26:6567)
58. Littleton, Isaac T. "Prediction in Auto Trade Courses." *J Appl Psychol* 36:15–9 F '52. * (*PA* 26:7256)
59. Poe, Wesley A., and Berg, Irwin A. "Psychological Test Performance of Steel Industry Production Supervisors." *J Appl Psychol* 36:234–7 Ag '52. * (*PA* 27:3794)

60. BRUCE, MARTIN M. "The Prediction of Effectiveness as a Factory Foreman." *Psychol Monogr* 67(12) 1–17 '53. * (*PA* 28: 5019)

61. COLEMAN, WILLIAM. "An Economical Test Battery for Predicting Freshman Engineering Course Grades." *J Appl Psychol* 37:465–7 D '53. * (*PA* 29:1562)

62. "Validity Information Exchange. No. 7-064: D.O.T. Code 5-92.411, Foreman I." *Personnel Psychol* 7:300 su '54. *

63. "Validity Information Exchange, No. 7-065: D.O.T. Code 5-92.411, Foreman II." *Personnel Psychol* 7:301 su '54. *

64. BRUCE, MARTIN M. "Validity Information Exchange, No. 7-076: D.O.T. Code 5-91.101, Foreman II." *Personnel Psychol* 7:418–9 au '54. *

65. BRUCE, MARTIN M. "Validity Information Exchange, No. 7-079: D.O.T. Code 7-83.058, Electrical Appliance Serviceman." *Personnel Psychol* 7:425–6 au '54. *

66. DuBOIS, PHILLIP H., AND WATSON, ROBERT I. "Validity Information Exchange, No. 7-075: D.O.T. Code 2-66.23, Policeman." *Personnel Psychol* 7:414–7 au '54. *

67. GROHSMEYER, FREDERICK A., JR. *Validation of Personnel Tests for a Paper Mill.* Doctor's thesis, Purdue University (Lafayette, Ind.), 1954. (*DA* 14:1796)

68. HUEBER, JOANNE. "Validity Information Exchange, No. 7-089: D.O.T. Code 5-83.641, Maintenance Mechanic II." *Personnel Psychol* 7:565–6 w '54. *

69. McCARTY, JOHN J. "Validity Information Exchange, No. 7-077: D.O.T. Code 5-92.621, (Foreman II)." *Personnel Psychol* 7:420–1 au '54. *

70. McCARTY, JOHN J.; WESTBERG, WILLIAM C.; AND FITZPATRICK, EUGENE D. "Validity Information Exchange, No. 7-091: D.O.T. Code 5-92.621, (Foreman II)." *Personnel Psychol* 7:568–9 w '54. *

71. SCHMITZ, ROY M., AND HOLMES, JOHN L. "Relationship of Certain Measured Abilities to Freshman Engineering Achievement," pp. 32–42. (*PA* 29:1584) In *Selection and Counseling of Students in Engineering.* Edited by Wilbur L. Layton. Minnesota Studies in Student Personnel Work, No. 4. Minneapolis, Minn.: University of Minnesota Press, 1954. Pp. iv, 89. *

72. CUOMO, SYLVIA. "Validity Information Exchange, No. 8-17: D.O.T. Code 5-92.601, Foreman II." *Personnel Psychol* 8: 268 su '55. *

73. CUOMO, SYLVIA, AND MEYER, HERBERT H. "Validity Information Exchange, No. 8-16: D.O.T. Code 5-92.601, Foreman II." *Personnel Psychol* 8:267 su '55. *

74. CUOMO, SYLVIA, AND MEYER, HERBERT H. "Validity Information Exchange, No. 8-19: D.O.T. Code 6-78.632, Floor Assembler." *Personnel Psychol* 8:270 su '55. *

75. FITZPATRICK, EUGENE D., AND McCARTY, JOHN J. "Validity Information Exchange, No. 8-35: D.O.T. Code 9-00.91, Assembler VII (Electrical Equipment)." *Personnel Psychol* 8: 501–4 w '55. *

76. FORSTER, CECIL R. *The Relationship Between Test Achievement and Success in Training of a Selected Group of Tuberculosis Patients.* Doctor's thesis, New York University (New York, N.Y.), 1955. (*DA* 15:1201)

77. HARRISON, ROSS; HUNT, WINSLOW; AND JACKSON, THEODORE A. "Profile of the Mechanical Engineer: 1, Ability." *Personnel Psychol* 8:219–34 su '55. * (*PA* 30:5414)

78. PATTERSON, CECIL H. *Test and Background Factors Related to Drop-Outs in an Industrial Institute.* Doctor's thesis, University of Minnesota (Minneapolis, Minn.), 1955. (*DA* 15: 1024)

79. SMITH, OTTO B. *Predicting Grade Success of High School Students in Radio and Drafting.* Master's thesis, Alabama Polytechnic Institute (Auburn, Ala.), 1955.

80. "Reducing Turnover in a Steel Company by Means of the Mechanical Comprehension Test." *Test Service B* (50):5 Je '56. *

81. BRUCE, MARTIN M. "Normative Data Information Exchange, No. 17." *Personnel Psychol* 9:393 au '56. *

82. BRUCE, MARTIN M. "Normative Data Information Exchange, Nos. 18, 37." *Personnel Psychol* 9:394, 552–3 au, w '56. *

83. McCARTY, JOHN J., AND FITZPATRICK, EUGENE D. "Validity Information Exchange, No. 9-26: D.O.T. Code 5-92.621, (Foreman II)." *Personnel Psychol* 9:523 su '56. *

84. OTTERNESS, WILLIAM B.; PATTERSON, C. H.; JOHNSON, R. H.; AND PETERSON, LENNIS R. "Trade School Norms for Some Commonly Used Tests." *J Appl Psychol* 40:57–60 F '56. * (*PA* 31:3803)

85. PATTERSON, C. H. "The Prediction of Attrition in Trade School Courses." *J Appl Psychol* 40:154–8 Je '56. * (*PA* 31: 6680)

86. WALKER, FRANCIS C. "Normative Data Information Exchange, No. 10." *Personnel Psychol* 9:276 su '56. *

87. McCARTY, JOHN J. "Normative Data Information Exchange, No. 10-31." *Personnel Psychol* 10:365 au '57. *

88. MOLLENKOPF, WILLIAM G. "An Easier 'Male' Mechanical Test for Use With Women." *J Appl Psychol* 41:340–3 O '57. *

89. SAUNDERS, WM. J., JR. "Normative Data Information Exchange, No. 10-32." *Personnel Psychol* 10:366 au '57. *

90. TOPETZES, NICK JOHN. "A Program for the Selection of Trainees in Physical Medicine." *J Exp Ed* 25:263–311 Je '57. *

91. BARRETT, RICHARD S. "The Process of Predicting Job Performance." *Personnel Psychol* 11:39–57 sp '58. *

92. DECKER, ROBERT L. "A Study of the Value of the Owens-Bennett Mechanical Comprehension Test (Form CC) as a Measure of the Qualities Contributing to Successful Performance as a Supervisor of Technical Operations in an Industrial Organization." *J Appl Psychol* 42:50–3 F '58. *

93. RILAND, LANE H., AND UPSHALL, CHARLES C. "Normative Data Information Exchange, No. 11-10." *Personnel Psychol* 11:275 su '58. *

For a review by N. W. Morton, see 4:766; for reviews by Charles M. Harsh, Lloyd G. Humphreys, and George A. Satter, see 3:683.

[890]

★**Tool Knowledge Test.** Ages 13 and over; 1951–54; 1 form ['51]; mimeographed manual ['54]; separate answer sheets must be used; 5s. per 10 tests; 1s. 6d. per 10 answer sheets; 9d. per scoring stencil; 2s. 6d. per manual; 3s. 9d. per specimen set; postpaid within Australia; 10(20) minutes; manual by D. Spearritt; Research and Guidance Branch, Queensland Department of Public Instruction; Australian Council for Educational Research. *

J. F. CLARK, *Professor of Applied Psychology, New South Wales University of Technology, Kensington, New South Wales, Australia.*

This test was devised to measure the interest in practical activities of 13-year-old boys faced with the problem of choosing between a technical and an academic course of further study. It is based on the hypothesis that tests of the tool information type are valid indicators of practical interest in boys who have had no formal experience with skilled trades work.

The test consists of a 4-page booklet containing 24 pictures of commonly used trade tools taken from an engineering catalogue. Each tool is accompanied by a question relating either to its name or its function or to the workman who would normally use it. The boys choose an answer from among five alternatives. Scores are interpreted in the light of a boy's home background and experience.

The test was prepared by the Research and Guidance Branch of the Queensland (Australia) Department of Public Instruction to assist guidance officers counseling youths at the time of choosing the nature of advanced secondary schooling. The manner in which the test was constructed appears to have been thorough. Pretesting and item analysis preceded the final selection of items and the determination of order of difficulty of the items in the final test. The test is well printed and the presentation of the photographs is clear.

The test has been used widely with school populations in Queensland, and norms are available for groups of average age 13-7 and 14-3. There are also norms on a Tasmanian population aged 14-9 to 15-3 and on a group of Victorian National Service trainees aged 18 years. From the Victorian group occupational norms have been computed for each of six general occupational classifications, viz., farmers, mechanics, carpenters, salesmen, clerks, and university students. In general, the level and spread of scores are satisfactory.

A split-half reliability of .72 and a Kuder-Richardson (formula 20) reliability of .82 have been obtained on each of 100 cases of Victorian National Service trainees.

For 783 trainees the test gave the following correlations with other tests: *A.C.E.R. Word Knowledge,* .39; Raven's *Progressive Matrices,* .45; Higher Examination of the *Otis Self-Administering Tests of Mental Ability,* .39; *A.C.E.R. Mechanical Reasoning Test,* .57; *Minnesota Paper Form Board,* .49. Thus, at least with older groups it seems to be testing abilities common to the so-called group intelligence and mechanical reasoning tests.

Apart from the so-called occupational norms which are based on broad occupational categories of 18-year-old youths, no data regarding predictive validity are presented. Tests of tool knowledge have been found useful in combination with mechanical appreciation, space form, and arithmetical tests for the prediction of success in engineering occupations. Whether this test, either alone or in combination with others, is useful for this purpose or valid in predicting future success in technical courses cannot be determined from the information presented in the manual. Until more information is available, this reviewer doubts its usefulness as a psychometric instrument but is willing to grant that it may be of some help when used as a counseling aid in the educational guidance of adolescent males.

I. G. MEDDLETON, *Deputy Head, Research Department, University of Queensland, Brisbane, Australia.*

The purpose of this test is to assess a boy's knowledge of trade tools—their names, their purposes, and by whom they are used. It acts as a measure of interest in rather than aptitude for practical activities. The manual cautions that scores are to be interpreted in the light of a boy's home background and experience.

The 24 items are based on pictures of commonly used tools, which the boy is required to identify by selecting the appropriate answer from among five alternatives. The pictures are excellent likenesses of the tools portrayed and the quality of the paper on which they are produced is good. Separate answer sheets are used. The time limit of 10 minutes is apparently ample, the manual showing that 96 per cent of an 18-year-old group of 100 servicemen completed the test within the time allowed.

The manual clearly sets out a description of the test, together with directions for administering and scoring it. The manual claims that the extent of a boy's interest in tools can best be assessed by comparing his score on the test with the scores of a group of boys living in similar environmental conditions. However, in assessing interest from test score, much is left to the examiner's interpretation and to experience gained by him in testing other boys.

Percentile norms are given in the manual for such groups as Queensland boys aged approximately 13-7 and 14-3, Tasmanian boys aged 14-9 and girls aged 15-3, and, despite the fact that the test was actually constructed for 13- and 14-year-old boys with little trade experience, for Victorian National Servicemen aged 18+ years. Further norms are given for male occupational groups within Australia, but the manual emphasises that these can be looked upon as a rough guide only. Unfortunately, the norms were obtained on an earlier printed version of the test. Since the present form has been slightly changed, it would appear that new norms are needed.

With 100 cases selected at random from among 783 trainees in the National Service group, a split-half coefficient of .79 was obtained for the earlier form of the test. For the same group, product-moment correlations of .45, .39, .57, and .49 were obtained between tool knowledge scores and scores on Raven's *Progressive Matrices,* the Higher Examination of the *Otis Self-Administering Tests of Mental Ability,* the *A.C.E.R. Mechanical Reasoning Test,* and the *Minnesota Paper Form Board Test,* respectively. The manual is not clear as to whether the earlier or the final form of the test was used in obtaining the product-moment coefficients.

In summary: the photo lithographics of the trade tools are excellently produced on paper of good quality. The directions and practice exercises are adequate. The norms are unsatisfactory; any extensive user of the test would do well to accumulate his own. Until further evidence is available regarding the prognostic value of the test, scores should be interpreted with caution.

MISCELLANEOUS

[891]

Aptitude Tests for Occupations. Grades 9–13 and adults; 1951; IBM; Form A; 6 tests; $14.35 per 35 sets of the 6 tests; separate answer sheets may be used; 4¢ per IBM answer sheet; 40¢ per either hand or machine scoring stencil; $1.05 per 35 profiles (free upon request with orders for all 6 tests); postage extra; 75¢ per complete specimen set, postpaid; 107 (135) minutes; Wesley S. Roeder and Herbert B. Graham; California Test Bureau. *

a) PERSONAL-SOCIAL APTITUDE. $2.80 per 35 tests; 20-(25) minutes.

b) MECHANICAL APTITUDE. $3.50 per 35 tests; 20(25) minutes.

c) GENERAL SALES APTITUDE. $2.80 per 35 tests; 20(25) minutes.

d) CLERICAL ROUTINE APTITUDE. $2.10 per 35 tests; 12(15) minutes.

e) COMPUTATIONAL APTITUDE. $2.10 per 35 tests; 15-(20) minutes.

f) SCIENTIFIC APTITUDE. $2.80 per 35 tests; 20(25) minutes.

LLOYD G. HUMPHREYS, *Professor of Psychology, University of Illinois, Urbana, Illinois.*

The *Aptitude Tests for Occupations*, six in number, have the following labels: Personal-Social, Mechanical, General Sales, Clerical Routine, Computational, and Scientific. There is ample precedent in the aptitude test literature for certain of the item types and names selected, e.g., Mechanical and Clerical Routine. For others, e.g., Personal-Social and General Sales, there is no adequate precedent, and the authors have not provided data in the manual to justify their selection. It is possible that interest measurement categories suggested these particular aptitude designations. A certain amount of parallelism between interest and aptitude tests might well promote the sales of both.

The battery is introduced as a differential aptitude battery early in the manual and in one way or another this theme recurs many times. The manual stresses the merits of the several tests for this purpose and neglects potential uses of separate tests for guidance or selection. The mechanical test, for example, has a promising selection of item types and might, with appropriate item difficulty levels and adequate timing, be quite useful.

The battery was adequately and fairly reviewed by Froehlich in *The Fourth Mental Measurements Yearbook*. He recommended that the publishers correct the errors in the manual, eliminate unsupported claims, and report sufficient data to provide a basis for judging the value of the tests. Also, since the date of publication of the tests, the test standards of the American Psychological Association have become available. Whereas Froehlich might have concluded in 1953 that the publisher had been careless and the authors uninformed concerning good psychometric practices, today one cannot be that generous. By offering these tests with the current manual for sale to the public in 1958 the authors and publisher flaunt their disregard for minimum technical standards for their product. "Careless" becomes "calculated" and "uninformed" becomes "contemptuous."

The bill of particulars is a lengthy one. Errors of commission or omission occur in every part. There are both known statistical errors and suspected errors of fact. The crystal ball is used generously. Since the reviewer's judgment is harsh, these errors are discussed in more than ordinary detail in the following paragraphs.

RELIABILITY. With the exception of one test-retest estimate on the acknowledged speed test of clerical routine, estimates of reliability are Kuder-Richardson coefficients. The claim is made that such estimates are conservative and that "true reliabilities are probably much higher than those indicated below." This statement would be undesirable under the best of circumstances, and present circumstances are hardly the best. Since the computational test is also described by the authors as a speed test, at least one of these Kuder-Richardson estimates is admittedly not applicable. The remaining tests are also somewhat speeded although the manual states otherwise. Experience with judgment items indicates that the 45 personal-social items covering most of seven pages cannot be answered by high school students in 20 minutes. As another example, the 60 generally complex mechanical items are also given a time limit of 20 minutes. The distribution of raw scores on the latter test is also very low. Even with moderate speeding, Kuder-Richardson reliability estimates are no longer conservative.

A second factor makes Kuder-Richardson estimates too high for several of these tests. Groups of sequentially dependent items are used rather frequently. This is particularly descriptive of the personal-social and scientific tests. This technique substantially increases the size of interitem correlations, but the increase is spurious from the standpoint of reliability estimation. A proper reliability estimate can be obtained by a split-half technique only if care is taken to place each homogeneous sequcy entirely in one half or the other.

The mistakes discussed in the preceding paragraphs are the merest of quibbles, relatively speaking, when the implications of this completely undocumented statement, which appears later in the same section, are grasped. "All coefficients have been corrected for range." What were the standard deviations in the samples used for reliability estimation? What were the assumed standard deviations to which correction was made? What was the basis for concluding that the latter would be more representative than the former of the distributions of examinees to whom the test would usually be given? These gaps in the discussion make the reliabilities reported meaningless.

As one looks into this matter further, there is some ground for believing that no such corrections were made after all! The reliability estimates in the grades 9–13 column of the summary table can be reproduced almost perfectly from the use of the average means and standard deviations given in adjoining columns. But these values are presumably based upon the formula scores and would erroneously inflate Kuder-Richardson estimates! The only thing certain is that the manual is seriously defective. There are several bases for inferring that the reliabilities are overestimates, but the amount of error cannot be guessed.

VALIDITY. The first validity data presented in the manual are the intercorrelations of the six tests. The manual suggests to the reader that these correlations be squared in order to estimate the amount of variance unaccounted for between pairs of tests. This practice is highly undesirable. It is significant that this is the only table of correlations in this section not corrected for attenuation. Even with the reliabilities presented in the manual, there would be a lot less unaccounted variance after taking errors of measurement into account. In several instances adequate reliabilities would leave very little indeed.

Next, correlations are presented between each of the *Aptitude Tests for Occupations* and various other tests. Unfortunately, this pairing is not systematic although adequate data must have been available. For example, the reader is informed concerning the correlation between the scientific score and the Q score of the *American Council on Education Psychological Examination,* but the correlation of the latter with the computational score is not reported. Systematic data here would provide a basis for judging the possibilities of differential prediction from the battery. The data actually reported are useless in judging the battery as a whole, and even for purposes of evaluating individual tests most of the *n*'s are inadequate (median = 47).

The predictive validity correlations are erroneously corrected for attenuation. Again only partial data are presented. Since selected tests were paired with grades in certain high school courses, information about differential prediction is therefore lacking. Would these predictions be just as good if some other test were used? Would they be even better if combinations of tests were used? Again the *n*'s are mostly so small (median = 54) that adequate answers to such questions could not be obtained.

The last tables presented in the validity section are inexplicable except as hocus-pocus. Certain of the aptitude tests are paired with other commonly used tests, five standard score points are selected (one assumes in a particular sample, but this is not clear), and the percentile ranks from the published norms of these standard score points are presented. In some cases the mean corresponds to the 50th percentile, in others it does not. For some of the paired tests the percentile ranks of the same standard scores are comparable, for others they are not. The first finding describes the extent to which a particular sample differs from published norms. The second finding describes the extent to which published norms for different tests correspond in a particular sample. These data could be useful if properly documented, but they are in no sense validation data.

OCCUPATIONAL PATTERNS. All too little is known about differential occupational patterns for standard aptitude batteries. Even less is known concerning some of the nonstandard tests used in the battery under discussion. The unsophisticated reader would not learn this from the manual. He is told that tests and occupations are related, but not that the relationship was determined from a cloudy crystal ball. Almost three pages of occupations are listed under each of the several tests and under combinations of the tests taken two at a time. There is a certain amount of hedging in this listing, since the same occupation frequently appears several times. Physicist, in one form or another, occurs four times and "research worker" is found in five categories. There are also some rather odd choices as seen in a different crystal ball. Mathematician is grouped under computational along with bookkeeper and accountant. College or university teacher is found under personal-social. An operator of statistical machines is placed under clerical routine. The specific grouping should not be overemphasized, however, since it is the encouragement to make use of a lot of chance differences between test scores that is most undesirable.

The emphasis here is clearly on differences. The section concludes as follows: "Regardless of where an individual's profile falls, the jobs of the occupational pattern list in which he has the highest aptitude should be considered." Rolling dice would be cheaper, and in an all too large proportion of the cases would be equally effective. The battery could, on the other hand, be used to detect across the board differences in profile level, and the importance of this is pointed out in the manual, but no standards for level are provided for any occupation.

DIRECTIONS FOR ADMINISTRATION. This section is generally straightforward. With a minor exception—the reviewer recommends that "time allotments" should not be modified by "suggested"—the directions are clearly written. The introductory statement to this section of the manual contains a curious statement, however. "This series is primarily diagnostic but it also yields percentile ranks and standard scores of examinees." One wonders how diagnostic information would be obtained from raw scores of tests of different lengths and unequal difficulties.

NORMS. At first glance the sampling design for obtaining norms looks good. Thus we find the following statements: "the United States was divided into eight regions for sampling purposes * Samples representative of large and small school districts and colleges were first drawn at random from each of these regions * the norms for the Aptitude Tests for Occupations have been based on a controlled (stratified) sampling." A closer look reveals that these fine words conceal something more aptly titled "catch as catch can" sampling. One clue is that California is listed as one of the eight

regions. Another is that so-called random sampling in New England and the deep South produced schools only in Maine and in Louisiana, respectively. It should also be noted that if school districts were sampled at random, the important *n* to be reported is the number of districts, not the number of students.

Other minor matters briefly noted are that the intelligence test used in stratifying is not named and that normalcy of the distributions was checked without giving the results. With respect to the first, intelligence tests are not sufficiently standardized in content or norming so that just any one could be used. With respect to the second, characteristics of the tables of percentile equivalents of raw scores indicate that some of the distributions may be normal, but others are certainly not. Normalcy is not really important in the raw score distribution, but the unsophisticated reader does not know this. The mention of normalcy in this context is apparently an attempt to propagandize the reader without imparting information.

CONCLUSION. Only one conclusion to a review of this sort is possible: it is recommended that the publisher remove the *Aptitude Tests for Occupations* from the test market. Test users should encourage the publisher in this course of action by refusing to buy the inadequate product.

For a review by Clifford P. Froehlich, see 4:710 (1 excerpt).

[892]

★[Biography Forms]: Application-Interview Series. Industry; 1948-56; 5 forms ('56): clerical, mechanical, sales, technical, supervisor; no specific manual; directions sheet ('56); 20¢ per single copy; postage extra; administration time not reported; Joseph E. King; Industrial Psychology, Inc. *

[893]

★Business Judgment Test. Adults; 1953-56; 1 form ('53); supplement ('56); norms ['56]; 15¢ per test; 25¢ per scoring key; 50¢ per manual ('53); 75¢ per specimen set; cash orders postpaid; (10-20) minutes; Martin M. Bruce; the Author. *

REFERENCES
1. BRUCE, MARTIN M. "Normative Data Information Exchange, No. 25." *Personnel Psychol* 9:404-5 au '56. *
2. BRUCE, MARTIN M., AND FRIESEN, EDWARD P. "Validity Information Exchange, No. 9-35: D.O.T. Code 1-55.10, Salesman, House-to-House." *Personnel Psychol* 9:380 au '56. *

EDWARD B. GREENE, *Supervisor of Personnel Research, Chrysler Corporation, Detroit, Michigan.*

Each of the 25 four-choice items consists of a short statement of a stress situation, followed by four actions which might be taken in the situation. The first person is used throughout. For instance, Item 16 reads:

> If I overheard a co-worker lie about his work to the supervisor, I would
> _____point out the error to my co-worker.
> _____explain the situation to the supervisor.
> _____overlook the matter altogether.
> _____tell the supervisor the truth in a letter.

Two keys are distributed with the test. On one, a single correct choice is indicated for each item and one point credit allowed for each item so marked. The other, marked "Revised Scoring Key," gives weighted credit to each choice, credit ranging from zero to three points. Although the weighted scoring system reflected in the revised key is intended to replace the original right-wrong approach, the author indicates that both keys are still distributed since some users prefer to continue using the original scoring method. There are, however, marked discrepancies between the two keys, particularly on Items 4, 7, 10, 13, 15, 16, and 19. On some of these items the preferred choice on the original key is either given little or no credit on the revised key or less credit than some other choice on the revised key. In the case of four items, the choice given three points credit on the revised key is given no credit on the original key. The two keys cannot be used interchangeably.

These discrepancies point to the problem of determining which choices are to be given credit in scoring. Two of the criteria used in selecting the test items were that men rated high in business judgment should tend to choose the designated "right" choices, and that men rated low should not select these choices. There is no indication as to what standards were used by the raters in assigning men to these high and low categories. It would be interesting to know whether the qualities or behaviors considered by the raters were the same as those which the test is intended to measure.

Since the author does not explain what he means by business judgment, the reviewer attempted to determine this through a subjective analysis of the response choices. It is possible to name, at least roughly, the attitude which could lead to making each choice. For instance, in Item 16 above, the first choice (given three points credit on the revised scoring key) seems to indicate an aggressive or dominating attitude. The second and fourth choices (for which no credit is allowed) might indicate willingness to help management and also some independence in willingness to tell on a co-worker. (These second and fourth choices would reflect good business judgment if the lie were serious or a lot of people were involved.) The third choice (given two points) seems to indicate withdrawal. If the foregoing analysis of motivating attitudes is correct, good business judgment depends, as far as this item is concerned, on attitudes either of domination or withdrawal but not on cooperating with the management if it involves tattling. Similar subjective analysis of the remaining 44 choices which are assigned some credit on the revised key shows 19 choices which could indicate withdrawal and 14 an initiating or dominating attitude.

To ascertain the fakability of the test, the reviewer asked three men and three women to mark it so as to please an employer who wanted aggressive employees. The average score (weighted scoring key) for the dominating choices was 30.4 and for the submissive choices, 4.6. Another group of office clerks was asked to mark the test to imitate people who are meek and mind their own business. The average scores were 12.2 for dominating choices and 27.0 for submissive choices. Similar results were obtained with a third group of factory employees. It appears that this test can be faked by unsophisticated employees to a very significant degree.

The test title is misleading, since, to many businessmen, business judgment refers to familiarity and wisdom in merchandising, finance procedures, and related fields. The test is primarily concerned with attitudes about tact, initiative, submission, and getting facts in a variety of situations, some of which are not business situations. There is considerable evidence that many people behave somewhat differently in nonbusiness situations than in work-stress situations.

In view of the probability of persons obtaining the same score with very different attitudes, the fakability, the lack of analysis of what is being measured, and the inadequacy of validation data reported, this test is NOT recommended.

[894]

Cancellation Test. Adults; 1946; perceptual speed; Form J; no data on reliability and validity; $1.10 per 25 tests, postage extra; 10¢ per specimen set, postpaid; 10(15) minutes; John R. Roberts; Educational Test Bureau. *

HERBERT A. TONNE, *Professor of Education, New York University, New York, New York.*

This test consists of a jumbled sequence of letters in which every "A" and every "B" are to be crossed out. The raw score is simply the number of letters correctly marked. Raw scores are converted to standard scores, the nature of the scores not specified. The only normative data are means and standard deviations based on the scores of 79 factory workers, distributed in six different job classifications.

The directions say: "This test seems to measure speed in the visual perception of minute details * It may be useful in the selection of visual inspectors, proofreaders, and the like." The caution is very much justified for the likelihood of meaningful validity seems slight. Visual inspectors are so varied in their work that almost nothing can be said about their specific assignment except that they use their eyes. Proofreaders have numerous elements to look for in their tasks, among which the correction of misplaced letters seems to be quite a minor activity. An automobile driver's test which limited itself to a check on whether the prospective driver knew how to use the brake when the car was not running would probably be worse than no test at all because it would give some the notion that successful completion was evidence of the ability to drive. That seems to be the status of this test.

The test seems useless. If a proofreader is to be hired, why not give him a job of proofreading? If a parts inspector is to be hired, why not give him a trial in inspecting a typical segment of the parts he is to inspect?

For a review by Joseph E. King, see 3:684.

[895]

*[Employee Rating and Development Forms.] Executive, industrial, office, and sales personnel; 1950–58; $2 per manual ('50) for *a*(2–3); postage extra; (5–30) minutes; Robert N. McMurry and associates; Dartnell Corporation. *
a) [PATTERNED MERIT REVIEW FORMS.] 1950–56.
  1) *Patterned Merit Review—Executive.* Form No. MR-407 ('55) ; 15¢ per copy.
  2) *Patterned Merit Review Form—Plant and Office.* Form No. MR-405 ('50) ; 15¢ per copy.
  3) *Patterned Merit Review—Sales.* 1950–55; Form No. MR-406R ('55) ; 10¢ per copy.
  4) *Patterned Merit Review—Technical Office, Special Skills.* Form No. MR-408 ('56) ; 10¢ per copy.
b) PATTERNED EXIT INTERVIEW. Form No. EX-501 ('53) ; 10¢ per copy; $2 per manual ('53).
c) PERSONAL HISTORY REVIEW FORM. 1 form ['57] ; 10¢ per copy.
d) PHYSICAL RECORD. Form No. PX-701 ('58) ; 15¢ per copy.

For reviews by Harry W. Karn and Floyd L. Ruch of a(2–3), see 4:781.

[896]

*[Executive, Industrial, and Sales Personnel Forms.] Applicants for executive, office, industrial, or sales positions; 1949–56; interviewing aids for personnel selection; postage extra; Robert N. McMurry and associates; Dartnell Corporation. *
a) [EXECUTIVE PERSONNEL FORMS.]
  1) *Application for Executive Position.* 1949–53; Form No. EA-301 ('53) ; 10¢ per copy.
  2) *Patterned Interview Form—Executive Position.* Applicants for management positions; 1949–53; Form No. EP-302 ('53) ; 30¢ per copy.
  3) *Patterned Interview Form.* Applicants for positions of supervisor, foreman, engineer; 1955; Form No. EP-312; 15¢ per copy.
  4) *Telephone Check on Executive Applicant.* 1950–53; Form No. ET-303 ('53) ; 7¢ per copy.
  5) *Selection and Evaluation Summary.* 1950–55; Form No. ES-404R ('55) ; 6¢ per copy.
  6) *Position Analysis.* 1956; Form No. JA-601; 7¢ per copy.
b) [INDUSTRIAL PERSONNEL FORMS.]
  1) *Application for Position.* 1950–52; Form No. OA-201 ('52) ; 7¢ per copy.
  2) *Application for Employment.* 1950–53; Form No. OC-200 ('53) ; 6¢ per copy.
  3) *Application for Office Position.* 1953; Form No. OA-205; 7¢ per copy.
  4) *Patterned Interview (Short Form).* 1949–53; Form No. OP-202 ('53) ; 10¢ per copy.
  5) *Patterned Interview Form.* Same as *a*(3) above.
  6) *Telephone Check [With Previous Employers.]* 1949–53; Form No. OT-203 ('53) ; 6¢ per copy.
  7) *Telephone Check With Schools.* 1949–53; Form No. OS-204 ('53) ; 7¢ per copy.
  8) *Selection and Evaluation Summary.* Same as *a*(5) above.
  9) *Position Analysis.* Same as *a*(6) above.
c) [SALES PERSONNEL FORMS.]
  1) *Application for Sales Position.* 1950–53; Form No. SA-101 ('53) ; 10¢ per copy.
  2) *Patterned Interview Form—Sales Position.* 1950–52; Form No. SP-102 ('52) ; 15¢ per copy.
  3) *Telephone Check on Sales Applicant.* 1949–53; Form No. ST-103 ('53) ; 7¢ per copy.
  4) *Sales Application Verification.* 1953; Form No. SV-104; 6¢ per copy.
  5) *Home Interview Report Form.* 1954–55; Form No. SH-114R ('55) ; 7¢ per copy.
  6) *Selection and Evaluation Summary.* Same as *a*(5) above.
  7) *Position Analysis.* Same as *a*(6) above.

For a review by Floyd L. Ruch, see 4:773.

[897]

★The Fiesenheiser Test of Ability to Read Drawings. Trade school and adults; 1955; 1 form; hectographed manual; $4 per 50 tests; $1 per specimen set (must be purchased to obtain manual) ; postage extra; 30(35) minutes; Elmer I. Fiesenheiser; Psychometric Affiliates. *

[898]

★Hiring Summary Worksheet. Industry; 1956; forms for summarizing scores obtained on tests and biographical forms published or distributed by the publisher relevant to each of 24 positions; 1 form; 24 worksheets; no specific manual; 10¢ per single copy, postage extra; directions sheet by Joseph E. King; Industrial Psychology, Inc. *

[899]

*Identical Forms. College and adults; 1958, c1947; perceptual speed; Research Form IF47; mimeographed directions sheet ['58]; no data on reliability and validity; tentative norms; $1.30 per 20 tests; 15¢ per specimen set; postage extra; 3(10) or 5(10) minutes; L. L. Thurstone; Science Research Associates. *

[900]

*Merit Rating Series. Industry; 1948–57; formerly called *Employee Evaluation Series;* 1 form; 5 scales; 20¢ per scale; 20¢ per normal curve summary ('53); $3 per complete specimen set; postage extra; (10–20) minutes; Joseph E. King and Judith W. Wingert (*b, c, d, e,* and descriptive material); Industrial Psychology, Inc. *

a) PERFORMANCE: CLERICAL. 1957.
b) PERFORMANCE: MECHANICAL. 1953.
c) PERFORMANCE: SALES. 1953.
d) PERFORMANCE: TECHNICAL. 1957.
e) PERFORMANCE: SUPERVISOR. 1953.

For a review by Brent Baxter of the original series, see 4:770.

[901]

★Per-Flu-Dex Tests. College and industry; 1955; 7 tests: symbol number substitution, letter perception and counting, number counting and perception, word completion and verbal fluency, arithmetic computation, manual speed of movement, aiming accuracy and speed; 1 form; $2 per 50 tests; $2 per 50 profiles; $1 per specimen set (must be purchased to obtain manual); postage extra; 7(25) minutes, 1(5) minutes for any one test; Frank J. Holmes; Psychometric Affiliates. *

a) PER-SYMB TEST.
b) PER-VERB TEST.
c) PER-NUMB TEST.
d) FLU-VERB TEST.
e) FLU-NUMB TEST.
f) THE DEX-MAN SCALE.
g) DEX-AIM TEST.

ANDREW L. COMREY, *Associate Professor of Psychology, University of California, Los Angeles, California.*

These seven 1-minute tests require the following activities: (*a*) labeling figures with numbers according to a code given at the top of the test page; (*b*) counting the number of K's in rows of interspersed letters K and H; (*c*) counting the number of 6's in rows of interspersed numbers 6 and 8; (*d*) adding letters to make words; (*e*) performing simple addition, subtraction, multiplication, and division; (*f*) marking X's in small squares on a zigzagging line of small squares; and (*g*) marking X's in large squares in several rows of squares.

There is a discrepancy between the standardization sample sizes given in the manual and those alluded to on the norm tables provided with each test key. In fact, the manual does not describe any norms sample as such, referring to sample sizes only in connection with various investigations concerning reliability and validity. Since the norm tables refer to sample sizes (150 college students and a business and industrial group of 38 for some tests and 74 for others) having no corresponding numbers in the manual, one may infer that standardization data other than those mentioned in the manual were used in preparing the norms. No mention of any "business" group could be found in the manual despite the fact that "business-industrial" norms are presented. Test-retest reliabilities based on only 95 students range from .71 to .95. Test intercorrelations based upon combined college student and assembly worker groups range from zero to .56.

Various bits of data are put forth as evidence of validity. Median scores on each test are compared for 12 female assembly workers rated high on job performance by their foremen and for 12 rated low. Four of the tests are said to reveal significant differences, although no variability data are reported. Median scores on each test for the top 25 and bottom 75 per cent of students in a college general psychology class are reported. Six of the tests are said to give significant differences. Unaccountably, the numbers of cases for these two groups are given as 25 and 83, respectively. Median scores for 10 students rated by deans as "leaders" and 30 rated as "non-leaders" are listed. No significance data are given. Finally, median scores for students pursuing different major fields are compared. Where given, the numbers of cases for these groups range from 11 to 23. No significance data are given.

The *Per-Flu-Dex Tests* are not recommended by this reviewer for the following reasons: (*a*) The rationale, if it exists, is not sufficiently elaborated in the sketchy manual. (*b*) The standardization samples are unrepresentative, too small, and inadequately described. (*c*) Virtually no evidence is given to show what these tests are measuring. No factorial investigations are reported relating these tests to one another or to other tests. No evidence is offered to show in what way these tests actually supplement other standardized tests, as they are supposed to do. (*d*) The validity data reported are based upon insufficient numbers of cases and fail to provide information upon test score variability in the groups compared. (*e*) Carelessness is evident in the preparation of the tests and the test manual. The manual is dittoed from stencils which contain visible strike-over typing errors, crossed out words, and poorly aligned columns. Numbers and kinds of cases fail to agree between the manual and test norms. Percentages and numbers of cases lack consistency at one point. (*f*) Lastly, although the reliabilities reported are high for 1-minute tests, in several instances they are not adequate for careful psychometric work.

JOHN W. FRENCH, *Research Associate, Educational Testing Service, Princeton, New Jersey.*

One-minute tests of this kind are quite feasible. The reviewer has found many to have reliabilities at least as high as the range of .71 to .85 reported for these. As suggested in the manual, their usefulness will be in supplementing batteries of intelligence, clerical, or mechanical ability tests. Despite their possible usefulness, it is not easy to find anything to commend in the way these tests have been selected, set up, or described in the manual.

The manual says that the testing literature indicated these seven different measures of perception, fluency, and dexterity to be suitable for administration in groups. The tests selected are suggestive, but only suggestive, of the factors established by the United States Employment Service in the course of the thorough studies leading to the development of the *General Aptitude Test Battery.*

Examination of the probable factorial content of the seven tests indicates that there is some unnecessary overlapping and confusion of what is being measured. Per-Symb, Per-Verb, and Per-Numb all seem to test a perceptual speed factor that may be called speed of symbol discrimination. In addition to this factor, Per-Symb probably measures speed in making associations between symbols and numbers, an ability of possible use, but one tested here only in an indirect way. Per-Verb and Per-Numb are more direct measures but may suffer from the distraction produced by the counting requirement. The other perceptual speed factor found useful in measuring clerical competence, that best exemplified by tests requiring the rapid comparison of such things as numbers or addresses, is not tested here.

Flu-Verb probably measures what Thurstone called "word fluency," a semantic habit not as yet having any proven validity. Flu-

Numb seems to be a quite reasonable test of number facility. Dex-Man is much the same as other standard paper and pencil manual or motor dexterity tests. Dex-Aim probably measures much the same thing as Dex-Man. To measure factors of aiming or eye-hand coordination, the drawing of an X should not be required, and the degree of precision should be increased by making the squares on the response sheet smaller.

In general, the tests and manual are set up in a manner that is acceptable for practical purposes. However, some sloppy typing and freehand supplements to the typing are not conducive to whetting a reviewer's admiration. Art work on a test should, perhaps, be considered irrelevant, but that displayed here deserves special notice for its unspeakable ugliness.

The directions in the manual for administering the tests, the directions appearing on the test copies, and the scoring directions printed on the keys are all adequate. The manual's overall attitude of caution and suggestion that the tests be used only as supplementary instruments are commendable. However, the tables of figures shown, particularly those concerned with validity, are misleading. Appropriate discrimination by some of these tests between levels of excellence in clerical and mechanical jobs may be expected, but the large relationships found with academic work in various fields and with campus leadership seem only to reveal biased or lucky samples. The very small number of cases for many of the groups may have led to the astonishing relationships reported. Judging from the behavior of similar tests in other academic and industrial situations, the reviewer has no alternative but to disbelieve that the figures can be generalized.

[902]
★The Performance Record. Industry; 1955; form for recording behavior incidents; 1 form; 3 editions: hourly employees, nonsupervisory salaried employees, foremen and supervisors; $3 per 20 record booklets of any one edition; 35¢ per administrator's manual; $3.45 per 20 employee handbooks; 50¢ per supervisor's handbook for any one edition; postage extra; John C. Flanagan and Robert B. Miller; Science Research Associates. *

REFERENCE
1. FLANAGAN, JOHN C., AND BURNS, ROBERT K. "The Employee Performance Record: A New Appraisal and Development Tool." *Harvard Bus R* 33:95-102 S-O '55. *

ALBERT K. KURTZ, *Professor of Psychology, University of Florida, Gainesville, Florida.*

The *Performance Record* is not a test. It is not a criterion either, although it might have been if its authors had desired to make it so. Rather, it is a procedure for classifying and recording critical incidents, for conferring with employees concerning their progress, and, in short, for doing most of the other things commonly associated with merit rating.

From the viewpoint of the worker, the *Performance Record* is a sheet on which his foreman or supervisor records good (blue) and bad (red) things that he does. From the viewpoint of the supervisor, it is a procedure for recording and evaluating the actions of his men. From the viewpoint of the administrator, it is "a standardized personnel program for getting and using the facts of job performance." From the viewpoint of its authors, it is "a procedure for collecting the significant *facts* about employe performance * It is not simply a new form, but *a new approach.*" (Italics as in original.) From the viewpoint of this reviewer, it is a method of classifying items of good or bad behavior under 10 to 16 headings, adding these up under each heading (but never getting a grand total), and then using these 20 to 32 subtotals along with the blank in talking to the employee and in making personnel decisions.

There are different record forms for hourly employees, nonsupervisory salaried employees, and foremen and supervisors. There are three corresponding handbooks for the foremen, supervisors, and superintendents who keep and use the three types of records designed for these three types of employees.

The *Performance Record* form for hourly employees, for instance, contains 16 topics:

Physical and Mental Qualifications
  1. Physical Condition
  2. Coordination
  3. Checking and Inspecting
  4. Arithmetic Computations
  5. Learning and Remembering Procedures and Instructions
  6. Judgment and Comprehension
  7. Understanding and Repairing Mechanical Devices
  8. Improving Equipment and Showing Inventiveness
Work Habits and Attitudes
  9. Productivity
  10. Dependability
  11. Accepting Supervision and Organizational Procedures
  12. Accuracy of Reporting
  13. Response to Departmental Needs
  14. Getting Along with Others
  15. Initiative
  16. Responsibility

Each of these topics is divided into two parts with from 2 to 10 subdivisions for classifying good or bad critical incidents. When an incident occurs, the supervisor classifies it (e.g., 14 A blue = getting along with others—remained calm under stress—good) and enters at the appropriate place on the form the date, the designation of the subdivision, and two or three key words to help him remember it later. It is said that it took less than 5 minutes a day to record all critical incidents in a department of 30 people when records were kept daily. (Even if it should take twice this long, it is still fast.)

All the printed materials are written for production people. Hence, it is difficult and perhaps unfair to evaluate them in terms of the standards usually applied in this *Yearbook.* Even so, it is a bit distressing to note the cavalier fashion in which "old-fashioned merit rating" is dismissed as being "necessarily biased and unfair" and requiring nearly impossible tasks, while the *Performance Record* "is based on established fact." No figures are cited to back up such claims as "The 'halo effect' is eliminated" or "A single outstanding characteristic cannot bias his [the supervisor's] judgment."

Supervisors are told to get red and blue totals, which are counts of the numbers of critical incidents under each of the 2 by 16 headings, but they are told not to regard these totals as scores and not to add them together to get a single overall score or rating. This, of course, means that there can be no possible quantitative comparison of this procedure with any (other) merit rating. For people who like to look at a configuration of subtotals and individual incidents, this is fine; for those who like to have an objective procedure that can be evaluated quantitatively, it leaves much to be desired. This is reminiscent of the perennial arguments between advocates of projective techniques and advocates of objective tests.

The reviewer has attempted to evaluate the *Performance Record* in terms of some relatively common objective standards, realizing that there may be intangible values not readily susceptible to measurement: *reliability,* unknown—no data; *validity or relevance,* unknown—no data; *face validity,* high; *objectivity,* dubious—"what you might consider a 'blue' incident of effective performance could actually be a 'red' incident of ineffective performance in another department"; *practicality,* high; and *norms or other standards,* none.

To summarize: The *Performance Record* may well be a good method of evaluating employees; it probably is, but it is unfortunate that its very nature makes it well nigh impossible to ascertain objectively whether or not this is so. It is even more difficult to find out how it stacks up against competing procedures.

ALBERT S. THOMPSON, *Professor of Education, Teachers College, Columbia University, New York, New York.*

The *Performance Record,* a standardized personnel program for getting and using facts of job performance, is based on research and development in a variety of military and civilian situations. This research utilized the critical incident technique to derive a series of behavior descriptions symptomatic of successful or unsuccessful job performance. The *Performance Record* for nonsupervisory salaried employees, for example, includes 15 sections with headings such as Carrying Out Instructions, Accuracy, Productivity, and Response to Need for Extra Effort. Under each section are specific behaviors representing desirable or undesirable job performance. Record forms have been developed for three broad categories of jobs: hourly employees, nonsupervisory salaried employees, and foremen and supervisors.

The *Performance Record* is not a rating scale or measuring instrument per se. It is a *program,* consisting of record forms and procedures designed to help supervisors analyze and evaluate the performance of their employees. The "incident sheet" helps supervisors to direct their observations, to record critical incidents accurately and systematically, to classify behaviors, and to review employee performance (with the employee) from time to time.

As a personnel form, the *Performance Record* is admirably suited to practical use. The form is attractively printed with red and blue sections to identify unsatisfactory and satisfactory behavior. For each form, there is a handbook for use by the person filling out the form. This contains clear explanations of the rationale underlying the procedure, guides for its use, and sample exercises to develop familiarity with its content and procedures. If used conscientiously and systematically, there is little doubt that personnel evaluations will be fairer,

personnel decisions will be based more on facts, and supervisors will be more alert to careful observation and evaluation of their supervisees' behavior.

In a review for a measurements yearbook, one is tempted to evaluate it as a measuring device. This cannot be done, at least from the information made available by the publisher, since the usual data on reliability, validity, norms, etc. are not provided. They are not provided presumably because they are irrelevant; the *Performance Record* is a program for recording and analyzing behaviors, not a scale for measuring human characteristics. As the manual states, "Supervisors are not asked to rate the people with whom they are in intimate daily contact. They merely record the facts of what employees do or fail to do. Individual differences show up in the recorded facts."

There is an implicit assumption, of course, that the critical behaviors included on this form will be similarly critical in a wide variety of settings. The items were initially derived from research and have high logical and face validity, but whether they will really separate the sheep from the goats on a particular job in a particular company is a matter for local research by the user. It is hoped that the publisher will provide help in such research as well as in the installation of *Performance Record* programs.

[903]

*Personal Data Blank. Counselees of ages 15 and over; 1934–52; 1 form ('52); $3.50 per 25 sets of record blanks and summary sheets; 25¢ per manual ('52); 50¢ per specimen set; cash orders postpaid; J. Gustav White; Consulting Psychologists Press. *

ARTHUR E. TRAXLER, *Executive Director, Educational Records Bureau, New York, New York.*

This instrument is not a test but a blank for obtaining detailed information from counselees. The blank was first prepared more than 20 years ago, but the present version was copyrighted in 1952, the same year that a 16-page manual for the blank was issued.

The blank includes 93 items, most of which are open-end questions, grouped under the following headings: (*a*) personal history, (*b*) your problems, (*c*) your interests and traits, (*d*) your education, and (*e*) your occupation. There is a sixth section called "Your Story," in which the counselee is asked to write anything about his life that he feels is important.

The blank can be used with anyone from the age of 15 on, but it appears to be best suited to vocational counseling with college students and young adults.

After filling out most of the questions in the blank, the present reviewer estimates that an hour or more would be required for doing the blank completely, including the free writing section, "Your Story." This amount of time may seem excessive to some counselees, but the information obtained should be of considerable help in counseling interviews.

Three items on the first page having to do with race, religion, and church affiliation may be objectionable to some counselees, and it would be contrary to law to ask these questions in certain states. The author frankly recognizes these possible objections and comments upon them in the manual. This reviewer agrees with the author's position that information on these items is useful in counseling, but it may be preferable to infer these kinds of information from observations made during interviews rather than to run the risk of antagonizing some counselees by asking for this information directly in the blank. The other questions in the blank seem well designed to obtain the cooperation of the counselee in supplying the needed data.

The last page of the blank provides for a summary and discussion of the counseling data followed by general recommendations. A facsimile of this page is printed on a separate sheet so that it may be filled out in duplicate and one copy turned over to the counselee, if desired.

In the upper portion of the summary page, a table for use in summarizing the results of the tests is printed. The results are to be entered on a graphic percentile or letter grade scale. This reviewer does not find that table very satisfactory, and he would not be inclined to use it. The general areas of measurement provided for in the table are mental classification, aptitudes, personality, and vocational interests. The printed designations under these general headings seem too restricted. No provision is made for recording results on achievement tests, and only one space is allowed for a score on a personality inventory. Space is provided for the recording of six areas of vocational interests in order of preference; a profile allowing for the showing of contrasts in interests would be likely to be more useful in counseling than the listing of the more pronounced

interests with percentile ratings. In fairness to the author, however, it should be stated that he indicates that additional special reports on the test results should be carefully noted.

A column headed "Norm" in the table for test results is ambiguous. There is no indication as to whether the kind of norm group, such as public school grade 10 or independent school grade 9, should be entered in the column or whether the mean or average score, which is sometimes referred to as a norm, should be shown there.

In the manual the author explains the purpose and structure of the blank, gives directions for administering and suggestions for interpreting, reviews general counseling tools, and provides a list of references. The manual is addressed directly to the counselor; everyday language rather than technical terminology is used; and the style is simple and clear.

This reviewer's assessment of the *Personal Data Blank* and the accompanying manual is generally favorable, but he suggests that another revision designed to correct several weaknesses, particularly in the summary page, would be desirable.

For reviews by Edward S. Jones and Donald G. Paterson of an earlier edition, see 40:1669.

[904]

★**Personnel Institute Hiring Kit.** Business and industry (applicants for sales positions); 1954–57; individual in part; manual ('56); no data on reliability and validity; $10 per kit of manual and 10 copies each of *a–d*; postage extra; scoring service available; $15 per applicant when *e* is used, $30 per applicant when *f* is used; fee includes scoring, interpretation, and report of results; Personnel Institute, Inc. *

a) PRELIMINARY SCREENING INTERVIEW. 1 form ('57); individual; $1 per 10 copies; 10 minutes.

b) PERSONAL HISTORY INVENTORY. 1 form ('57); $1.50 per 10 copies; 30(45) minutes.

c) DIAGNOSTIC INTERVIEWER'S GUIDE. 1 form ('56); individual; $2 per 10 copies; 30 minutes.

d) WORK REFERENCE INVESTIGATION. 1 form ('57); individual; $1 per 10 copies; 10 minutes.

e) SELECTOR TEST BATTERY. Applicants for routine selling jobs; 1955–56; directions sheet ('56); scoring by publisher only; (85–100) minutes.

1) *EM-AY Inventory.* Reprint under new title of *Otis Employment Tests,* Test 2, Form A ('22); test of mental alertness; 30(35) minutes.

2) *ESS-AY Inventory.* 1 form ('55); test of sales aptitude; (40–45) minutes.

3) *The Personality Inventory.* 1 form ('35); (15–20) minutes.

f) COMPREHENSIVE TEST BATTERY. Applicants for complex selling jobs; 1955–57; directions sheet ('57); scoring by publisher only; (195–220) minutes.

1) Same as *e*(1) above.

2) Same as *e*(2) above.

3) Same as *e*(3) above.
4) *Vocabulary Inventory.* 1 form ('56); (30) minutes.
5) *Social Intelligence Test.* 1 form; 3 scores: tact and diplomacy, understanding of human nature, total; (40) minutes.
6) *B-B-ESS Inventory.* 1 form ('56); test of business skills; 8 scores: comparing, computation, reading, spelling, vocabulary, arithmetical reasoning, English, total; 40(50) minutes.

[905]

★SRA Employee Inventory. Employees; 1951–58; attitudes toward job; 1 form; 2 editions; manual, third edition ('52); directions for administering, second edition ('52); profiles and report forms ['51–52]; preliminary norms ('52); typed norms supplement ['58]; (10–25) minutes; Robert K. Burns, L. L. Thurstone, David G. Moore, and Melany E. Baehr; Science Research Associates. *

a) REGULAR EDITION. Form A ('51); separate answer pads must be used; 85¢ per test; $3 per 20 answer pads; 75¢ per manual; 25¢ per directions for administering; $1 per specimen set; postage extra.
b) GOVERNMENT EDITION. Form GX ('51); test materials rented only; details may be obtained from publisher.

REFERENCES

1. ASH, PHILIP. "The SRA Employee Inventory—A Statistical Analysis." *Personnel Psychol* 7:337–64 au '54. * (*PA* 29:4762)
2. BAEHR, MELANY E. "A Factorial Study of the SRA Employee Inventory." *Personnel Psychol* 7:319–36 au '54. * (*PA* 29:4763)
3. WHERRY, ROBERT J. "An Orthogonal Re-Rotation of the Baehr and Ash Studies of the SRA Employee Inventory." *Personnel Psychol* 7:365–80 au '54. * (*PA* 29:4788)
4. DABAS, ZILE SINGH. *The Dimensions of Morale: An Item Factorization of the SRA Employee Inventory.* Doctor's thesis, Ohio State University (Columbus, Ohio), 1955. (*DA* 16:798)
5. MOORE, DAVID G., AND RENCK, RICHARD. "The Professional Employee in Industry." *J Bus* 28:58–66 Ja '55. *
6. BAEHR, MELANY E. "A Reply to Robert J. Wherry Concerning 'An Orthogonal Re-Rotation of the Baehr and Ash Studies of the SRA Employee Inventory.'" *Personnel Psychol* 9: 81–91 sp '56. * (*PA* 31:4017)
7. WHERRY, ROBERT J. "A Rejoinder to Baehr's Reply on Rotation of the SRA Employee Inventory Studies." *Personnel Psychol* 9:93–9 sp '56. * (*PA* 31:4017)
8. BRAYFIELD, ARTHUR H.; WELLS, RICHARD V.; AND STRATE, MARVIN W. "Interrelationships Among Measures of Job Satisfaction and General Satisfaction." *J Appl Psychol* 41:201–5 Ag '57. *
9. BRUCE, MARTIN M. "Normative Data Information Exchange, No. 10-35." *Personnel Psychol* 10:370 au '57. *
10. DABAS, ZILE S. "The Dimensions of Morale: An Item Factorization of the SRA Inventory." *Personnel Psychol* 11: 217–34 su '58. *

ERWIN K. TAYLOR, *President, Personnel Research and Development Corporation, Cleveland, Ohio.*

Broadly viewed, there are three major approaches to the measurement of employee attitudes: (*a*) the polling approach, in which the percentages of responses to alternatives of individual questions are tabulated; (*b*) the clinical approach, usually based on "depth" interviews which are interpreted in the light of the interviewer's background; and (*c*) the mental test approach, in which attitudinal domains are empirically identified and groups of items measuring each incorporated in an objective instrument.

Most employee attitude surveys are of the political poll type. In smaller surveys the clinical approach is often used. The *SRA Employee Inventory* is, to the best of this reviewer's knowledge, the first attempt to apply the mental test approach to attitude measurement on a commercial scale. The inventory consists of 78 short statements such as "The people I work with are very friendly." Subjects respond to each statement by indicating one of the following three alternatives: (1) agree, (2)?, (3) disagree. The test booklet is reusable, answers being marked on a snapout carbon form which is prekeyed on the back for easy scoring.

The inventory purports to measure 15 a priori attitudinal areas with from two to seven items in each. Factor analyses of the scales (omitting the total) by Ash (*1*) and Baehr (*2, 6*) and the integration of these by Wherry (*3, 7*) strongly indicate that the areas suggested by the publisher have no independent reality. This is reinforced by the factor analysis for the 78 items in the scale reported by Dabas (*10*). On the basis of these findings, it would seem that the original areas should now be abandoned and new scoring keys developed on the basis of the factor analysis results.

From a study of the General Manual and Directions for Administering and Scoring the SRA Employee Inventory, it would appear that this instrument was developed primarily for use by amateurs whose knowledge of the appropriateness of conducting an attitude survey and of how to interpret and use the results effectively is questionable. This reviewer is concerned with the availability of psychological devices to individuals not adequately trained to evaluate the appropriateness of their application in a given situation, their limitations, or the proper interpretation of results. The *SRA Employee Inventory* appears to have been intentionally designed to appeal to the untrained "do-it-yourself" market. Recent advertising by the publisher claims that "high morale almost invariably means: high productivity, low absenteeism and turnover, confidence in management, a harmonious and creative atmosphere." No research of which the reviewer is aware justifies so broad a generalization.

The manual makes no mention of norms as such. These are taken care of by plotting raw scores on the profile sheet. It is implied that the 1952 norms were based on "approximately 25,000 inventories." The fourth edition of the Report of Survey Results (February 1953) shows some substantial differences (particularly at the low end of the scales) from the second (January 1952) edition. The first percentile for the "inventory as a whole" was 33.70 in 1952 and 27.00 in 1953. The median for this scale changed from 49.40 to 50.75 and the 99th percentile from 65.22 to 69.00. Whether this is a function of changing times or of the broader sample of the normative population, we do not know. In any event, the user should be certain to be consistent in his use of the forms or he may find shifts taking place that are purely a function of the edition of the report form used.

A January 1958 norms supplement not generally distributed gives a population breakdown of the general norms based on 35,000 cases and compares it with the Department of Commerce percentages for the total work force. In May 1958, the publisher announced (but did not supply) separate norms for four industries and production workers and supervisors. Separation of male and female norms groups has evidently not been made.

In summary, the *SRA Employee Inventory* appears to be the first attempt by a commercial test publisher to employ the test construction approach in attitude measurement. Its a priori scoring has been demonstrated to be unsound, and available norms are somewhat questionable. It has been too highly touted as supplying pat answers to involved questions and as being effectively usable on a "do-it-yourself" basis. Nevertheless, it is probably a better device than the average, homemade questionnaire. Scored in accordance with the factor analysis findings, separately standardized by sex, occupation, and level, and used by professionals qualified to interpret its results in a psychologically meaningful manner, the *SRA Employee Inventory* would constitute a valuable psychological tool.

ALBERT S. THOMPSON, *Professor of Education, Teachers College, Columbia University, New York, New York.*

An "ideal" instrument to determine the attitudes of employees toward their work has to meet a variety of requirements. It should be short and easily read and answered. It should be easily scored and yield a measure of overall level of morale as well as of attitudes toward specific aspects of the work situation. It should be reliable and should stimulate a desire to answer truthfully and completely. It should permit comparisons of individuals with groups, subgroups with each other, and local groups with national groups. It should permit study of factors peculiar to the specific setting.

The *SRA Employee Inventory* meets most of these requirements. Its 78 items can be answered in 10 to 20 minutes and are phrased in language understandable to employees with fourth grade education or better (according to the manual). It yields a total inventory score and 14 profile category scores, such as Job Demands, Pay, Confidence in Management, Adequacy of Communication, etc. To the 78 standard items printed in the published form can be added up to 12 tailor-made items. A special edition adapted for use with employees of government agencies has been devised. Test-retest reliability coefficients from several studies range in the .60's and .70's for category scores of individuals and in the high .90's when used as a group instrument.

It is designed to be answered anonymously, but it has space to record desired group identifications, such as department, length of service, etc. The printed answer sheet has space for free comments.

The instrument was originally prepared at the Industrial Relations Center of the University of Chicago and resulted from careful construction and pretesting of the items. The publisher has further developed it, particularly with respect to format, administration, and profiling of results. A confidential test used by the consulting division of SRA, it is made available to clients for attitude surveys of their employees. In addition to purchasing arrangements, SRA provides the materials, scoring and analysis of group results at a charge (as of April 1958) of $1.65 per employee surveyed.

So far, so good. As a device to elicit responses to the 78 job related statements listed, it is certainly better than the potpourri of items frequently thrown together by hurried personnel workers faced with an order from above to make an attitude survey. The procedures for administering, scoring, and analyzing the results are well worked out and designed to yield quickly information of value to management.

On the matter of its value as a scientific measure of employee morale or as a systematic survey of the basic attitudes of employees, however, one must reserve judgment until more data are available. There is little or no information as to the relationship between the category scores and criterion measures of these categories. Factor analysis studies were used in the original grouping of items into the 14 categories, but subsequent studies have yielded fewer factors and one investigator has questioned the factor method used and presented evidence of a large general factor.

The manual and catalog descriptions refer to national norms based on over 1,000 companies with industrial and occupational breakdowns, but the latest manual, dated 1952, does not present or describe these norms.

In summary, as a device for obtaining employee attitudes toward the 78 items involved, the *SRA Employee Inventory* and the related consulting services of the publisher should provide a useful personnel tool. Considered as an instrument to measure morale and its basic components, it needs further research and development, a comment which can be made about most attitude survey questionnaires.

[906]

★**A Self-Rating Scale for Leadership Qualifications.** Adults; 1942–48; 1 form ('48); profile ('48); no manual; no data on reliability and validity, no norms; 25¢ per single copy, postage extra; administration time not reported; E. J. Benge; National Foremen's Institute, Inc. *

SPECIFIC VOCATIONS

[907]

★**Accounting Orientation Test: High School Level.** Grades 11–12; 1953–56; 4 scores: vocabulary, arithmetic reasoning, accounting problems, total; IBM; Forms S, T ('53); manual ('56); preliminary norms; $2.50 per 25 tests; separate answer sheets may be used; 2¢ per IBM answer sheet; postage extra; 25¢ per specimen set, postpaid; 40(50) minutes; Committee on Personnel Testing, American Institute of Certified Public Accountants. *

REFERENCES

1. JACOBS, ROBERT, AND TRAXLER, ARTHUR E. "A Professional Aptitude Test for High School." *Clearing House* 28:266–8 Ja '54. *
2. MORICI, ANTHONY R. "Relation Between the Scores on the A.I.A. Orientation Test With the A.I.A. Elementary, Advanced Accounting Tests and Accounting Grades." *J Ed Res* 51:549–52 Mr '58. *

[908]

★**Achievement Tests in Nursing.** Nurses; 1952–58; IBM; 1 form; 12 tests; directions sheet ['57]; norms ['58] for each test; no charge to schools requiring Entrance Examinations for Schools of Practical Nursing; 35¢ per test per student for other schools, postpaid; (40) minutes per test; Psychological Corporation. *
a) ANATOMY AND PHYSIOLOGY. 1953–58; 1 form ['53].
b) CHEMISTRY. 1954–58; 1 form ['54].
c) COMMUNICABLE DISEASES. 1953–58; 1 form ['53].
d) MEDICAL NURSING. 1952–58; 1 form ['52].
e) MICROBIOLOGY. 1952–58; 1 form ['58].

f) NUTRITION AND DIET THERAPY. 1952–58; 1 form ('57).
g) OBSTETRICAL NURSING. 1952–58; 1 form ['52].
h) PEDIATRIC NURSING. 1952–58; 1 form ['52].
i) PHARMACOLOGY. 1952–58; 1 form ('57).
j) PSYCHIATRIC NURSING. 1952–58; 1 form ('57).
k) PSYCHOLOGY AND SOCIOLOGY. 1958; 1 form ['58]; no data on reliability; no norms.
l) SURGICAL NURSING. 1952–58; 1 form ('57).

[909]

★**Achievement Tests in Practical Nursing.** Practical nursing students; 1957; 2 scores: medical and surgical nursing, nutrition-pediatric-obstetrical nursing; IBM; 1 form; 2 parts; directions sheet ['57]; no charge to schools requiring Entrance Examinations for Schools of Practical Nursing; 35¢ per student for other schools, postpaid; (100) minutes; Psychological Corporation. *

[910]

★**Admission Test for Graduate Study in Business.** Business graduate students; 1954–58; test administered 4 times annually (November, February, April, July) at centers established by the publisher; 3 scores: quantitative, verbal, total; IBM; examination fee, $10; fee includes reporting of scores to any 3 schools designated at time of application; $1 per additional report; 200(230) or 205(235) minutes; Educational Testing Service. *

[911]

*★American Institute of Certified Public Accountants Testing Programs.** Grades 13–16 and accountants; 1946–57; IBM; 2 programs; $2.50 for 1 to 12 transcripts; American Institute of Certified Public Accountants. *
a) COLLEGE ACCOUNTING TESTING PROGRAM. Grades 13–16; 1946–57; tests available 3 times annually (fall, midyear, spring); manual ['57]; postage extra.
   1) *Orientation Test.* Grades 13–16; 1946–49; 3 scores: verbal, quantitative, total; Forms A ('46), B ('46), C ('49); 50¢ per student; 50(70) minutes.
   2) *Achievement Test: Level 1.* Grades 13–15; 1946–57; 3 long forms: Forms A ('57), B ('47), C ('51), 120(140) minutes; 3 short forms: Forms A-S ('55), B-S ('56), C-S ('57), 50(70) minutes; 50¢ per student.
   3) *Achievement Test: Level 2.* Grade 16; 1946–51; 2 long forms: Forms A ('47), B ('49), 240(260) minutes; 2 short forms: Forms C ('51), D ('50), 120(140) minutes; 50¢ per student.
   4) *Strong Vocational Interest Blank for Men, Revised.* See 868; grades 13–16; 1927–50; Form M ('38); blank scored for 27 scales and plotted on an accountant's profile ['50]; 1–24 students, $1.80 each; tests not distributed for local scoring; (40) minutes.
b) PROFESSIONAL ACCOUNTING TESTING PROGRAM. Accountants; 1947–57; tests available to accounting employers at any time; tests also administered at regional testing centers throughout the year; 4 tests; revised manual ('51); norms ('54); $2.50 per examinee if test is scored locally; $5 per examinee if test is scored by publisher; 3 transcripts available free; postpaid.
   1) *Orientation Test.* 1946; Form A; same as *a*(1) above.
   2) *Achievement Test: Level 1.* 1946–57; Form A ('57); same as *a*(2) above.
   3) *Achievement Test: Level 2.* 1946–51; Forms A ('47), C ('51); same as *a*(3) above.
   4) *Strong Vocational Interest Blank For Men, Revised.* Same as *a*(4) above; tests not distributed for local scoring; $2 per examinee.

REFERENCES

1-15. See 4:787.
16. HENDRIX, O. R. "Predicting Success in Elementary Accounting." *J Appl Psychol* 37:75-7 Ap '53. * (*PA* 28:1479)
17. HENDRIX, O. R. "'A Note' Acknowledged." *J Appl Psychol* 38:9 F '54. * (*PA* 29:1451)
18. JACOBS, ROBERT. "A Note on 'Predicting Success in Elementary Accounting.'" *J Appl Psychol* 38:7-8 F '54. * (*PA* 29:1456)
19. FREDERICK, MARVIN L. "Testing the Tests." *J Account* 103:42-7 Ap '57. *
20. MORICI, ANTHONY R. "Relation Between the Scores on the A.I.A. Orientation Test With the A.I.A. Elementary, Advanced Accounting Tests and Accounting Grades." *J Ed Res* 51:549-52 Mr '58. *
21. NORTH, ROBERT D. "Tests for the Accounting Profession." *Ed & Psychol Meas* 18:691-713 w '58. *

[912]

*[American Transit Association Tests.] Transit operating personnel; 1941-51; 4 tests; $3.50 per battery manual ('46); postpaid; Glen U. Cleeton, Merwyn A. Kraft, and Robert F. Royster; American Transit Association. *

a) STANDARD EXAMINATION FOR TRANSIT EMPLOYEES. 1941-46; intelligence; Forms A ('41), AA ('43) for street car operators; Forms B ('41), BB ('43) for bus operators; manual ('46); $7.50 per 100 tests; 20(30) or 30(40) minutes.

b) PERSONAL REACTION TEST FOR TRANSIT EMPLOYEES. 1943-46; personality; Series A ('46); manual ('46); no data on reliability; $10 per 100 tests; (30) minutes.

c) THE PLACEMENT INTERVIEW FOR TRANSIT EMPLOYEES. 1946; 9 ratings (moral character, mental ability, motor ability, health, motivation, stability, maturity, sociability, manner and appearance) in 3 areas (work experience, schooling and childhood, personal history) ; 1 form; $5 per 100 interview forms.

d) A STANDARDIZED ROAD TEST FOR BUS OPERATORS. 1951; 1 form; $2 per 100 checklists; 50¢ per manual.

For reviews by Harold G. Seashore, Morris S. Viteles, and J. V. Waits, see 3:696.

[913]

*Aptitude Index. Prospective male life insurance agents; 1938-56; 1 score combining an evaluation of personal background, interests, and attitudes; Forms 5 ['54], 6 ['56]; forms differ in experimental items only; manual ['54]; separate scoring keys for United States and Canada; no data on reliability; separate answer booklets must be used; distribution restricted to home offices of member life insurance companies; details may be obtained from publisher; cash orders postpaid; French edition available; (60) minutes; Life Insurance Agency Management Association. *

REFERENCES

1-5. See 40:1646.
6-19. See 4:825.
20. BILLS, MARION A., AND TAYLOR, JEAN G. "Over and Under Achievement in a Sales School in Relation to Future Production." *J Appl Psychol* 37:21-3 F '53. * (*PA* 28:1664)

For reviews by Donald G. Paterson and Albert S. Thompson of an earlier form, see 4: 825.

[914]

*Aptitude Associates Test of Sales Aptitude: A Test for Measuring Knowledge of Basic Principles of Selling. Sales applicants; 1947-58; Form A ('47); hectographed manual, 16th edition ('58); 15¢ per test; 25¢ per scoring key; 75¢ per manual; $1 per specimen set; cash orders postpaid; (20-30) minutes; Martin M. Bruce; the Author. *

For reviews by Milton E. Hahn and Donald G. Paterson, see 4:824.

[915]

★A Chart For the Rating of a Foreman. Ratings of foremen by supervisors; 1941-48; 1 form ('48); no data on reliability; no norms; 50¢ per single copy, postage extra; administration time not reported; R. D. Bundy; National Foremen's Institute, Inc. *

[916]

*Dental Aptitude Testing Program. Dental school applicants; 1946-58; tests administered 3 times annually (January, April, October) at centers established by the publisher; IBM except *a*; 5 tests; examination fee, $15; fee includes reporting of scores to any 5 schools designated at time of application; $1 per additional report; postpaid; scores not reported to examinees; 323(415) minutes in 2 sessions; Division of Educational Measurements, Council on Dental Education, American Dental Association. *

a) CARVING DEXTERITY TEST. 1946-58; 90(110) minutes; Committee on Aptitude Testing.

b) AMERICAN COUNCIL ON EDUCATION PSYCHOLOGICAL EXAMINATION FOR COLLEGE FRESHMEN. See 308; 1924-54; 3 scores: linguistic, quantitative, total; IBM; 1954 Edition; 38(75) minutes.

c) READING COMPREHENSION IN THE NATURAL SCIENCES. 1953-55; IBM; Forms 54 ('53), 55 ('54); 80(85) minutes; Committee on Aptitude Testing.

d) SPACE RELATIONS TEST. See 605; 1947; IBM; Forms A, B ('47); 40(45) minutes.

e) SURVEY OF THE NATURAL SCIENCES. 1951-58; 5 scores: biology, chemistry, factual, application, total; IBM; 1 form ('58); 75(80) minutes; Committee on Aptitude Testing.

REFERENCES

1-2. See 4:788.
3. MARLES, LESLIE. *A Study of the Relationship of Academic Achievement to Aptitude Scores of the American Dental Association's Experimental Testing Program.* Master's thesis, Temple University (Philadelphia, Pa.), 1948.
4. PETERSON, SHAILER. "Validation of Professional Aptitude Batteries: Tests for Dentistry," pp. 35-45. (*PA* 26:595) In *Proceedings of the 1950 Invitational Conference on Testing Problems, October 28, 1950.* Princeton, N.J.: Educational Testing Service, 1951. Pp. 117. *
5. ANDERSON, ADOLPH V., AND FRIEDMAN, SIDNEY. "Prediction of Performance in a Navy Dental Prosthetic Technician Training Course." Abstract. *Am Psychol* 7:288 Jl '52. *
6. WEISS, IRVING. "Prediction of Academic Success in Dental School." *J Appl Psychol* 36:11-4 F '52. * (*PA* 26:7296)
7. LAYTON, WILBUR L. "Predicting Success in Dental School." *J Appl Psychol* 37:251-5 Ag '53. * (*PA* 28:6712)
8. WEBB, SAM C. "The Prediction of Achievement for First Year Dental Students." *Ed & Psychol Meas* 16:543-8 w '56. *

[917]

★Dental Hygiene Aptitude Testing Program. Dental hygiene school applicants; 1947-57; tests administered 3 times annually (October, February, May) at centers established by the American Dental Hygienists' Association; IBM; 1 form; 4 tests; manual ['57]; examination fee, $9; fee includes reporting of scores to 3 schools designated at time of application; $1 per additional report; scores not reported to examinees; postpaid; 98(175) minutes; Psychological Corporation. *

a) STUDY-READING TEST. 1955; Form S; 20(25) minutes.

b) DENTAL HYGIENE APTITUDE TESTING PROGRAM, PARTS 1 AND 2. 1947-57; IBM; 1 form ['57]; 48(55) minutes.

c) COLLEGE QUALIFICATION TEST, TEST 1. See 320; 1955-56; IBM; Form A ('56); 30(35) minutes.

d) THE PERSONAL PREFERENCE SCHEDULE. 1953-55; adaptation of *Edwards Personal Preference Schedule* (see 47); 1 form ('55); (40-60) minutes.

[918]

*[Driver Selection Forms and Tests.] Truck drivers; 1943–55; part of White Motor Co.'s *Continuing Control System of Truck Management;* individual in part; manual out of print; 25¢ per specimen set; postage extra; Dartnell Corporation. *

a) [DRIVER SELECTION FORMS.] 1946–55.

  1) *Employment Application.* 1946; Form Nos. 111 (city delivery drivers), 211 (over-the-road drivers), 311 (long distance drivers); 7¢ per copy.

  2) *Telephone Check.* 1946–53; Form No. OT-203 ('53); 6¢ per copy.

  3) *Driver Interview.* 1946; Form No. 13 ['46]; 10¢ per copy.

  4) *Physical Examination Record.* 1946–54; Form No. 19 ('54); 5¢ per copy.

  5) *Selection and Evaluation Summary.* 1950–55; Form No. ES-404R ('55); 6¢ per copy.

b) [DRIVER SELECTION AND TRAINING TESTS.] 1943–54.

  1) *Traffic and Driving Knowledge.* 1946–54; Form No. 16 ('46); no manual; no data on reliability; 6¢ per test; 6¢ per directions sheet-scoring key ('54, Form No. 17); administration time not reported; Amos E. Neyhart and Helen L. Neyhart; also distributed by Institute of Public Safety, Pennsylvania State University.

  2) *Road Test in Traffic.* 1943–46; 3 scores: specific driving skills, general driving habits and attitudes, total; individual; 1 form ['45]; instruction sheet ('45); score sheet ('46, Form No. 18); 5¢ per copy; (30–60) minutes; Amos E. Neyhart; also distributed by American Automobile Association and Institute of Public Safety, Pennsylvania State University.

For a review by S. Rains Wallace, Jr., see 4:789.

[919]

★Engineering Aide Test 50-A. Engineering aides; 1957; Form 50-A; preliminary mimeographed manual; no norms; separate answer sheets must be used; PPA member agency: 10–49 tests, 96¢ each; others, $1.20 each; $2 per specimen set; postpaid; 90(100) minutes; Public Personnel Association. *

[920]

★Entrance Examinations for Schools of Practical Nursing. Practical nursing school applicants; 1942–57; tests administered at regional testing centers established by the publisher; IBM; 1 form; 3 tests; manual ['57]; examination fee, $6; fee includes reporting of scores to one school designated at time of application; $2 per additional report; scores not reported to examinees; postpaid; 95(210) minutes; Psychological Corporation. *

a) ENTRANCE EXAMINATION FOR SCHOOLS OF PRACTICAL NURSING. 1957; 5 scores: verbal ability, numerical ability, academic ability, household information, arithmetic; Form A ('57); 65(75) minutes.

b) TEST OF MECHANICAL COMPREHENSION. See 889; 1942; Form W1 ('42); 30(35) minutes.

c) THE PERSONAL PREFERENCE SCHEDULE FOR STUDENT NURSES. 1953–55; adaptation of *Edwards Personal Preference Schedule* (see 47); 6 scores: achievement, orderliness, persistence, congeniality, altruism, respectfulness; 1 form; (45) minutes.

[921]

★Firefighter Test. Firemen; 1954–58; title on Form 20-A is *Test for Firefighter;* IBM; Forms 20-A ('54), 20-B ('57); revised mimeographed manual ('57); norms ('58); no data on reliability and validity; separate answer sheets must be used; PPA member agency:

10–49 tests, $1.20 each; others, $1.60 each; $2 per specimen set; postpaid; 105(115) minutes; Public Personnel Association. *

[922]

★General Test on Traffic and Driving Knowledge. Drivers; 1949–50; 1 form (50); directions sheet ('49); no data on reliability; no norms; 47¢ per 25 tests, postage extra; specimen set free; administration time not reported; Traffic Engineering and Safety Department, American Automobile Association; published jointly by American Automobile Association and Institute of Public Safety, Pennsylvania State University. *

[923]

*The Graduate Record Examinations Advanced Tests: Engineering. College seniors and graduate students; 1939–57; for more complete information, see 601; IBM; 180(200) minutes; Educational Testing Service. *

For a review by Harold Seashore of the entire series, see 601.

[924]

★Hall Salespower Inventory. Salesmen; 1946–57; title on test is *Salespower Inventory;* 10 scores: background, intelligence, aggressiveness, dominance, sales temperament, sales interest, introversion-extroversion, motivation, emotional, total; Form A ('46); no data on reliability and validity; norms ('53); distribution restricted to industries; 1–10 tests, $2.50 each; $5 per set of scoring keys and manual ('57); postpaid; (60) minutes; Clifton W. Hall and Richard M. Page; Hall & Liles. *

[925]

★Hanes Sales Selection Inventory, Revised Edition. Insurance and printing salesmen; 1954–55; 3 scores: verbal, personality, drive; 1 form ('55); manual ('55); no data on reliability and validity of drive score; $3 per 20 tests; $1 per specimen set (must be purchased to obtain manual); postage extra; (30–40) minutes; Bernard Hanes; Psychometric Affiliates. *

[926]

How Supervise? Supervisors; 1943–48; Forms A ('43), B ('43), M ('48, consists of items from Forms A and B); revised manual ('48); $2.45 per 25 tests; 35¢ per specimen set; postpaid; administration time not reported; Quentin W. File and H. H. Remmers (manual); Psychological Corporation. *

REFERENCES

1–5. See 3:687.
6–13. See 4:774.
14. HOLMES, FRANK J. "Validity of Tests for Insurance Office Personnel." *Personnel Psychol* 3:57–69 sp '50. * (PA 24:5490)
15. MILLER, FRANK G., AND REMMERS, H. H. "Studies in Industrial Empathy: II, Managements' Attitudes Toward Industrial Supervision and Their Estimates of Labor Attitudes." *Personnel Psychol* 3:33–40 sp '50. * (PA 24:5504)
16. CARTER, GERALD C. "Measurement of Supervisory Ability." *J Appl Psychol* 36:393–5 D '52. * (PA 27:6801)
17. MALONEY, PAUL W. "Reading Ease Scores for File's *How Supervise?*" *J Appl Psychol* 36:225–7 Ag '52. * (PA 27:3804)
18. MILLARD, KENNETH A. "Is *How Supervise?* an Intelligence Test?" *J Appl Psychol* 36:221–4 Ag '52. * (PA 27:3805)
19. WICKERT, FREDERIC R. "*How Supervise?* Scores Before and After Courses in Psychology." *J Appl Psychol* 36:388–92 D '52. * (PA 26:6822)
20. WICKERT, FREDERIC R. "Relation Between *How Supervise?*, Intelligence and Education for a Group of Supervisory Candidates in Industry." *J Appl Psychol* 36:301–3 O '52. * (PA 27:5453)
21. WEITZ, JOSEPH, AND NUCKOLS, ROBERT C. "A Validation Study of 'How Supervise?'" *J Appl Psychol* 37:7–8 F '53. * (PA 28:1672)
22. "Validity Information Exchange, No. 7-065: D.O.T. Code 5-92.411, Foreman II." *Personnel Psychol* 7:301 su '54. *

23. JOHNSON, ROSSALL J. "Validity Information Exchange, No. 7-090: D.O.T. Code 5-91, Foreman II." *Personnel Psychol* 7:567 w '54. *
24. PATTON, WENDELL M., JR. "Studies in Industrial Empathy: III, A Study of Supervisory Empathy in the Textile Industry." *J Appl Psychol* 38:285–8 O '54. * (PA 29:6378)
25. BARTHOL, RICHARD P., AND ZEIGLER, MARTIN. "Evaluation of a Supervisory Training Program With *How Supervise?*" *J Appl Psychol* 40:403–5 D '56. * (PA 32:2189)
26. DECKER, ROBERT L. "An Item Analysis of *How Supervise?* Using Both Internal and External Criteria." *J Appl Psychol* 40:406–11 D '56. * (PA 32:2190)
27. McCORMICK, ERNEST J., AND MIDDAUGH, RICHARD W. "The Development of a Tailor-Made Scoring Key for the How Supervise? Test." *Personnel Psychol* 9:27–37 sp '56. * (PA 31:5203)
28. FARBRO, PATRICK C., AND COOK, JOHN M. "Normative Data Information Exchange, No. 10-7." *Personnel Psychol* 10:103 sp '57. *
29. MOWRY, HARLEY W. "A Measure of Supervisory Quality." *J Appl Psychol* 41:405–8 D '57. *
30. SAUNDERS, WM. J., JR. "Normative Data Information Exchange, No. 10-33." *Personnel Psychol* 10:367–8 au '57. *
31. DUNNETTE, MARVIN D., AND KIRCHNER, WAYNE K. "Validation of Psychological Tests in Industry." *Personnel Adm* 21:20–7 My–Je '58. *

For a review by Milton M. Mandell, see 4:774; for reviews by D. Welty Lefever, Charles I. Mosier, and C. H. Ruedisili, see 3:687.

[927]
★**Information Index.** Life insurance agents; 1951–58; Forms A, B ('57); manual ('57); directions sheet ['57]; norms supplement ['58]; separate answer sheets must be used; distribution restricted to home offices of member life insurance companies; details may be obtained from publisher; cash orders postpaid; Canadian edition available; 60(70) minutes; Life Insurance Agency Management Association. *

REFERENCES
1. GUEST, THEODORE A. *The Construction and Analysis of a Test of Life Insurance Information.* Master's thesis, Trinity College (Hartford, Conn.), 1952.
2. BAIER, DONALD E., AND DUGAN, ROBERT D. "Tests and Performance in a Sales Organization." *Personnel Psychol* 9:17–26 sp '56. * (PA 31:5169)
3. BAIER, DONALD E., AND DUGAN, ROBERT D. "Factors in Sales Success." *J Appl Psychol* 41:37–40 F '57. *

[928]
*Law School Admission Test. Law school entrants; 1948–58; test administered 4 times annually (November, February, April, August) at centers established by the publisher; IBM; examination fee, $10; fee includes reporting of score to any 3 law schools designated at time of application; $1 per additional report; 215(245) minutes; Educational Testing Service. *

REFERENCES
1–6. See 4:815.
7. JOHNSON, A. PEMBERTON, AND OLSEN, MARJORIE A. "Comparative Three-Year and One-Year Validities of the Law School Admission Test at Two Law Schools." Abstract. *Am Psychol* 7:288 Jl '52. *
8. OLSEN, MARJORIE A., AND SCHRADER, WILLIAM B. "An Empirical Comparison of Five Methods of Shortening a Test." Abstract. *Am Psychol* 7:286–7 Jl '52. *
9. BUCKTON, LaVERNE, AND DOPPELT, JEROME E. "Freshman Tests as Predictors of Scores on Graduate and Professional School Examinations." *J Counsel Psychol* 2:146–9 su '55. * (PA 30:3453)
10. JOHNSON, A. PEMBERTON. "The Development of Shorter and More Useful Selection Tests." *J Ed Psychol* 46:402–7 N '55. * (PA 31:3790)
11. JOHNSON, A. PEMBERTON; OLSEN, MARJORIE A.; AND WINTERBOTTOM, JOHN A. *The Law School Admission Test and Suggestions for Its Use: A Handbook for Law School Deans and Admission Officers.* Princeton, N.J.: Educational Testing Service, April 1955. Pp. 148. * (PA 31:6677)
12. OLSEN, MARJORIE. *The Law School Admission Test as a Predictor of Law School Grades, 1948–53.* Statistical Report SR-55-9. Princeton, N.J.: Educational Testing Service, March 1955. Pp. i, 17. *
13. BRESLOW, EVELYN. "The Predictive Efficiency of the Law School Admission Test at the New York University School of Law." *Psychol Newsl* 9:13–22 S–O '57. * (PA 32:4586)

For a review by Alexander G. Wesman of Form YLS2, see 4:815.

[929]
★**LIAMA Inventory of Job Attitudes.** Life insurance agents; 1956; job satisfaction scores in 17 areas; 1 form ['56]; no data on reliability; no norms; distribution restricted to home offices of member life insurance companies; details may be obtained from publisher; cash orders postpaid; [20–30] minutes; Life Insurance Agency Management Association. *

[930]
★**Managerial Scale for Enterprise Improvement.** Supervisors; 1955; job satisfaction; 1 form; hectographed manual; $3 per 50 tests; $1 per specimen set (must be purchased to obtain manual) including 10 tests, manual, and scoring key; postage extra; (12) minutes; Herbert A. Kaufman, Jr.; Psychometric Affiliates. *

BRENT BAXTER, *Director of Agencies Research, Prudential Insurance Company, Newark, New Jersey.*

This scale is a list of 34 conditions which might affect morale in a business enterprise. The respondents, supposedly only management personnel, indicate where they perceive the current status of each condition in the range from "very good" to "very poor." The total score is supposed to reveal "management morale."

The manual reports a corrected odd-even reliability of .89 for 213 management people, presumably from one company's department heads, supervisors, and foremen. For this same group a tetrachoric correlation of .47 between score and length of management experience is reported, the author claiming that this reveals validity. Percentile norms for the group are given.

The only unusual feature about this instrument is that the respondent is oriented toward evaluating conditions in the company that need improvement. This may be contrasted to the more direct morale survey approach which frankly asks the respondent to tell how he feels about his job. There is no evidence to suggest that this new approach is superior to the direct approach.

This instrument is not likely to find widespread use. The list of job conditions is not unique, but is drawn from conventional sources. Evidence demonstrating validity is not convincing. The directions for administration are incomplete. The norms are limited and inadequately described. This is not an instrument especially adapted to management personnel. A homemade instrument would probably be preferred since it could be adapted to local terminology and problems.

EDWARD B. GREENE, *Supervisor of Personnel Research, Chrysler Corporation, Detroit, Michigan.*

This is a 34-item rating sheet to be filled out anonymously by supervisors. Each item is a short statement such as, "Fair allocation of work force." The statements are printed in a column on the left side of a sheet. On the right hand side are five blank columns with the words "very good," "good," "average," "poor," and "very poor" printed across the column tops. Over the column of statements is boldly printed the one word "REQUIREMENTS." The significance of this word is not explained, nor is it clear to the reviewer.

Although no specific instructions are given, one is cautioned in the manual *not* to tell the respondent that the scale is a measure of morale, but rather to indicate that it is for the purpose of enterprise improvement.

Although most of the items seem fairly clear, some are not. For instance the statements "Administrative encouragement of fundamental supervisory achievement" and "Effectiveness of supervisory voice in policy making" seem ambiguous. No analysis is given of the areas covered by the form.

The form requests the respondent to indicate whether he is a department manager, a supervisor, or a foreman. This also need clarification because, in many offices and plants, the word supervisor is a general term which includes both department managers and foremen.

To score the form one simply adds the checks in each column and allows 5 points for "very good," 4 for "good," 3 for "average," and so on. Omitted items are all scored 3. The percentile norms indicate a 50th percentile of 106 points for 213 supervisors. On the assumption that managers with more than 90 days experience were "more successful in meeting the goals which make for managerial satisfaction" than managers with less than 90 days experience, the author computed a tetrachoric correlation between performances of the two groups. He found this to be .47 and concluded that this indicated the tendency for "individuals with greater experience to have higher management morale." An odd-even reliability coefficient of .89 (stepped up by the Spearman-Brown formula) is reported.

The reviewer is *not* happily impressed with this form because of its appearance, its vagueness, and the lack of analysis of what it covers.

[931]

★**Measure of Consociative Tendency.** Applicants for sales and supervisory positions; 1951; personal history blank; 1 form; mimeographed directions sheet; $2.50 per 100 blanks, postage extra; specimen set not available; (10–20) minutes; Doncaster G. Humm and Kathryn A. Humm; Humm Personnel Consultants. *

[932]

＊**Medical College Admission Test.** Medical school entrants; 1946–56; 4 scores: verbal, quantitative, modern society, science; test administered 2 times annually (May, October) at centers established by the publisher; IBM; examination fee, $10; fee includes reporting of scores to any 3 schools designated at time of application; $1 per additional report; scores not reported to examinees; 245(275) minutes; Educational Testing Service. *

REFERENCES

1–11. See 4:817.
12. RALPH, RAY B., AND TAYLOR, CALVIN W. "The Role of Tests in the Medical Selection Program." *J Appl Psychol* 36: 107–11 Ap '52. * (*PA* 27:674)
13. STALNAKER, JOHN M. "Medical College Admission Test," pp. 797–805. (*PA* 27:8040) In *Contributions Toward Medical Psychology: Theory and Psychodiagnostic Methods, Vol. II.* Edited by Arthur Weider. New York: Ronald Press Co., 1953. Pp. xi, 459–885. *
14. BUCKTON, LaVERNE, AND DOPPELT, JEROME E. "Freshman Tests as Predictors of Scores on Graduate and Professional School Examinations." *J Counsel Psychol* 2:146–9 su '55. * (*PA* 30:3453)
15. DAVIS, JOHN ROBERT. *Predicting Students' Performance in a General Medical Clinic.* Doctor's thesis, University of Colorado (Boulder, Colo.), 1955. (*DA* 16:1182)

ALEXANDER G. WESMAN, *Associate Director, Test Division, The Psychological Corporation, New York, New York.*

In *The Fourth Mental Measurements Yearbook,* the *Medical College Admission Test* was reviewed by Morey Wantman. The reader would do well to acquaint himself with that review. Most of the statements in the earlier review, both favorable and critical, apply as fully to the succeeding Forms CMC1, CMC2, DMC, and EMC as they did to the 1950 form discussed by Wantman. The high standards of test construction, the clear writing of the bulletin of information sent to applicants, and the well organized, complete directions to examiners are again very much in evidence. The format of the booklets remains excellent. The Educational Testing Service is to be commended for maintaining this quality.

Unfortunately, too little attention has been paid to the adverse criticisms directed at the instrument and accompanying materials. The applicant is better informed concerning the profitability of guessing; but he is still being misled with regard to the desirability of intensive review of science and social studies materials. In the absence of evidence to the contrary, one must assume that with the kind of content in the test, intensive review may quite likely prove a good investment. Similarly, the reassurance of the applicant that "there is no reason to become disturbed if you....are unable to finish" is still unwarranted; the examinee should be informed of the advantages of finishing the test. (The publisher reports that the forthcoming bulletin of information will correct these impressions.)

The reliability coefficients reported for the new forms are not as high as those for the 1950 form; for the verbal and science sections the decrease is negligible—from .93 and .91, respectively, in the older form, to .91 and .89 in the succeeding editions. The quantitative and understanding world affairs sections do not fare as well. The former drops from .89 to .82 in Form EMC; the latter drops from .94 to .84 in Form CMC2. Partly because the coefficients are computed by the Kuder-Richardson technique, which may be overestimating reliability because of the speededness of the tests, Wantman said, "The reliability data reported for the 1950 tests cannot be judged to be more than 'satisfactory.'" The lower coefficients reported for later forms offer less reason for satisfaction.

Coefficients of intercorrelation among the tests are a little lower, and therefore better, for all the later forms. They average about .60; this is probably as low as one may expect in view of the verbal saturation of three of the tests.

The tests are obviously shorter than those of the 1950 edition. Working time for the four tests is approximately three hours; another 30 to 60 minutes is devoted to pretesting experimental material for which no score is reported. The total administration is accomplished in a testing session of approximately four and a half hours—a single sitting, but a long one.

The earlier review of MCAT took issue with the policy of withholding scores from applicants. The present reviewer agrees with the policy, rather than with his predecessor. A rejected student who knew his score was higher than that of an accepted student might draw a number of unpleasant, and probably unwarranted, conclusions about admission practices of a particular institution. The potential harm of revealing scores to students outweighs the probable benefits.

The crucial question concerning any test or battery is that of validity. In the case of the MCAT, one may expect two broad goals to be sought: the prediction of success in medical school, and the selection of those applicants who will be the kind of people the medical schools believe the profession wants or needs. There is evidence that the AAMC has been preoccupied with the latter criterion and that the content of the test battery (e.g., inclusion of the section on understanding modern society) has been at least partly determined by these considerations. Whether or not the tests do actually select the kind of people the profession wants is a matter of subjective judgment—no data are available, so far as the reviewer is aware.

Data are becoming available (at long last) with respect to success in medical school. The reviewer has been permitted to see coefficients of correlation between MCAT test scores and rank in class, scores on tests of the National Board of Medical Examiners, and grades in courses. The data were prepared separately for each of 16 medical schools.

Since only admitted students are included in the research populations, the prediction is probably better than the validity coefficients seem to indicate. Nevertheless, the reviewer finds the results of the studies disappointing. For example, in half the institutions, the highest coefficient between any of the four parts of MCAT and freshman rank is below .40; when senior rank is the criterion, the best coefficient in 14 of the 16 institutions is below .30. The prediction of scores on the Medical Board tests is somewhat better, as one might expect.

The overall picture of validity provokes one to question whether the individual medical schools are (or should be) satisfied with the program. If, as is possible, the schools accept indifferent validity in the tests because of believed defects in the grades, perhaps further research efforts might better be devoted to improving those grades rather than to experimenting with more esoteric item types. In any event, if medical schools are willing to settle for validity of the order thus far demonstrated, the applicant might well be spared at least half the time and money he now expends; a shorter, more efficient test is very likely to do as well. The reviewer's hope is that the Association of American Medical Colleges, which sponsors the MCAT program, will somehow persuade medical schools to reappraise their grading methods with a view to clarifying the criterion, and will instruct the test constructors to concern themselves with efficient measurement of the improved criteria. The selection of students who will be the kind of people the schools think the profession wants or needs might well be left to the subjective judgment of admissions committees.

For a review by Morey J. Wantman, see 4:817.

[933]

★**Minnesota Engineering Analogies Test.** Candidates for graduate school and industry; 1954–55; Forms E, F ('54); preliminary manual ('55); distribution restricted to specified licensed testing centers; details may be obtained from the publisher; (45–60) minutes; Marvin D. Dunnette; Psychological Corporation. *

REFERENCES

1. DUNNETTE, MARVIN D. "The Minnesota Engineering Analogies Test." *J Appl Psychol* 37:170–5 Je '53. * (*PA* 28:1847)
2. DUNNETTE, MARVIN D. "The Minnesota Engineering Analogies Test—A New Measure of Engineering Ability." *J Personnel Adm & Ind Rel* 1:1–10 Ja '54. * (*PA* 29:3224)
3. DUNNETTE, MARVIN DALE. *A Special Analogies Test for the Evaluation of Graduate Engineers.* Doctor's thesis, University of Minnesota (Minneapolis, Minn.), 1954. (*DA* 14:1250)
4. DUNNETTE, MARVIN D. "Tests for Guidance and Counseling." *J Eng Ed* 46:434–40 Ja '56. *
5. DUNNETTE, MARVIN D., AND AYLWARD, MERRIAM S. "Validity Information Exchange, No. 9-21: D.O.T. Code, Design and Development Engineers." *Personnel Psychol* 9:245–7 su '56. *
6. OWEN, MARJORIE L. "Validation of a Test Battery for Engineers." Abstract. *Am Psychol* 12:450 Jl '57. *

A. PEMBERTON JOHNSON, *Assistant Director, Counseling Center, Newark College of Engineering, Newark, New Jersey.*

The items in this test, like those in the *Miller Analogies Test,* are concisely stated analogies with, however, a heavy mathematical and scientific content. In this test, familiarly known as the MEAT, the conceptual analogies may be wholly verbal, wholly mathematical, or mixed verbal and mathematical. They frequently cross subject matter boundaries. The concepts of the 50 items in each form are taken largely from the first two years of "core" courses for all engineering students, in inorganic chemistry and physics (about 37 per cent), mathematics through integral calculus (about 37 per cent), mechanics—including statics, dynamics, and hydraulics—and strength of materials (19 per cent), and thermodynamics and basic electrical engineering (7 per cent).

Estimates of reliability indicate that although use of a single form is probably adequate for group survey comparisons (where Hoyt reliability coefficients of .75 to .87 were obtained for groups of 44 to 488 cases), average or summed scores for both forms are preferred in evaluating individuals.

Content validity, which one would infer from the manual to be reasonably high, is most difficult to insure with 50 items in any one form. This is true also because engineering curricula are undergoing critical reevaluation and change in many parts of the United States. The severe restriction of the item type precludes use of items which evaluate functional understanding of many important basic principles and laws. The author has, however, largely avoided items which require the memorization of minutiae. All any test in this field can do is to sample some basic areas. The manual does not mention the setting of content objectives or the review of content by an expert committee.

Information on concurrent validity consists of correlations of MEAT scores with undergraduate and graduate grades. One study (6) reports a low predictive validity ($r = .30$) against salary for 156 development engineers. Some construct validity is indicated by higher mean scores for research engineers than for supervisory, production, and design engineers; and median scores 3 to 6 points higher for engineers with the doctor's degree than for holders of bachelor's degrees.

Normative data are inadequate for employed engineers 0–2 years after graduation and particularly for graduate students. Apparently several companies have begun to accumulate data for sizeable groups which, it is hoped, can soon be made available.

The MEAT is a potentially useful measure of that limited aspect of engineering ability to reason by analogy using one's knowledge of basic science and mathematics. It does not purport to measure knowledge of the scientific method, creativity, managerial ability, practical know-how, cost mindedness, ability to use experimental data, ability to report findings in simple, effective language, or other important traits of engineering graduates. Engineers in many of the special fields of engineering will, by the very nature of the design of this test, find little of especial interest to them.

The average score of both forms should be used in ranking individuals. For work placement of engineering graduates the test should only be used along with interview data, interest and personality test data, and preferably at least brief experience with the functional types of engineering work involved.

In general, the separate items are excellently fashioned although the same concepts underlie parts of several different items in the same form. Unpublished data at one company for a group of about 130 young engineers show the dual verbal-mathematical content of the test: there is a .67 correlation coefficient between MEAT scores and scores on the highly verbal *Miller Analogies Test,* and a .71 correlation coefficient between MEAT scores and *Doppelt Mathematical Reasoning Test* scores.

Better normative data for engineering graduates, either those newly employed in industry or those applying for graduate work, are needed if the test is to have wider use. Further validity studies involving larger clearly specified groups are also needed. It is hoped that somehow the publishers of the MEAT and of the *Graduate Record Examinations Advanced Tests: Engineering* might cooperatively seek, from appropriate employed and graduate student populations, comparative normative, validity, and reliability data on these two tests.

WILLIAM B. SCHRADER, *Director, Statistical Analysis, Educational Testing Service, Princeton, New Jersey.*

This is a relatively brief, easily administered, power test designed to measure abstract reasoning and engineering achievement at a difficulty level appropriate to graduate engineers. Presumably, its most frequent use would be in predicting success in graduate study or in engineering work. The items are set in the form of analogies, but they draw heavily on information and concepts learned during the first two years of study in an engineering college. About two fifths of the items are mathematical. The test yields a single overall score.

The mechanics of the testing process have been competently handled. Instructions are explicit, brief, and complete. The booklet is a convenient 8½ by 11 inch size and is well printed, except that exponents, especially fractional exponents (Item 37 of Form E and Item 19 of Form F) are printed in such small type as to place unnecessary demands on visual discrimination. Adequate space for scratch work is provided on the answer sheet. The preliminary manual is well written and attractively printed. The interpretive materials provide some information on virtually all the points which the user needs to know.

A serious weakness is the inadequate description of test development procedures. The manual says nothing about the item analysis work

which was done. Moreover, no evidence is given that qualified persons, other than the author, participated in writing or reviewing the items or in establishing content specifications. It is true that an effort was made to distribute the emphasis by areas of instruction to correspond to the proportion of time given to these basic areas in a typical engineering curriculum, and the author has succeeded well enough in avoiding trivial or esoteric items. Nevertheless, a test which is as clearly concerned with achievement as this one is should draw on the experience of a number of teachers if a balanced instrument is desired. In the reviewer's opinion, there is an undue emphasis on terminology, factual matters, and relatively simple skills, and too little emphasis on problem solving of a relatively complex kind, on application of knowledge, and on reading comprehension. This underemphasis probably resulted in part from the decision to use analogies items only.

The reliability of either of the two forms of this test is somewhat below customary standards. Indeed, for engineering school seniors, the reliability coefficients, as determined by the Hoyt method, are about .75. For graduate students, they are less than .80. These results lend weight to the author's suggestion that both forms be administered where higher reliability is needed. A reliability higher than .75 would surely be needed if appreciable importance is to be given to scores in making decisions about individuals. Hoyt coefficients for employed engineers were about .85. Alternate-forms reliability coefficients for five small groups of employed engineers ranged from .71 to .88.

With respect to norms, the author properly stresses their tentative character and urges the development of local norms. The norms given are broken down according to academic level for engineering students and according to years of experience for employed engineers. It may be noted that the data presented indicate that the test was appropriate in difficulty for the available norms groups. Unfortunately, no useful description of the norms groups is provided with respect to such matters as the universities and companies from which the sample was drawn, the relative proportion of different types of engineers included, and the motivating conditions under which the examinees took the test. Moreover, there is no indication that a systematic norms program which would go beyond data submitted by users is under way.

A number of validity coefficients are reported. All of the empirical studies described in the manual are concerned with concurrent validity, a fact which complicates the interpretation of the results. The test shows reasonably high correlation coefficients with success in graduate school, but the findings regarding relationships with ratings of employed engineers must be regarded as inconclusive.

The test is based on a reasonable approach to obtaining an overall measure of promise in graduate study or engineering work. In spite of certain limitations in the test and in the interpretive materials provided, it should provide useful and pertinent information about the ability level of students who have completed an engineering program.

[934]

***NLN Achievement Tests for Basic Professional Nursing Program.** Students in state-approved schools of professional nursing; 1943–58; IBM; 1 form; 16 tests; manual ['58]; interpretive manual ('58, see *1* below); norms ['58]; *a–n:* 75¢ per test per student; *o–p:* $1 per test per student; $1.25 per interpretive manual; postpaid one way; (90–120) minutes per test; National League for Nursing, Inc.

a) ANATOMY AND PHYSIOLOGY. 1943–55; Form 155 ('55).
b) CHEMISTRY. 1943–55; Form 155 ('55).
c) MICROBIOLOGY. 1943–55; Form 155 ('55).
d) NUTRITION AND DIET THERAPY. 1946–57; Form 757 ('57).
e) PHARMACOLOGY AND THERAPEUTICS. 1944–55; Form 155 ('55).
f) MEDICAL NURSING. 1944–49; Form 149 ('49).
g) SURGICAL NURSING. 1944–49; Form 149 ('49).
h) NURSING OF CHILDREN. 1945–55; Form 155 ('55).
i) COMMUNICABLE DISEASE NURSING. 1946–55; Form 155 ('55).
j) PSYCHIATRIC NURSING. 1945–55; Form 155 ('55).
k) SOCIAL SCIENCES IN NURSING. 1956; Form 156 ('56).
l) MEDICAL-SURGICAL NURSING. 1956; Form 156 ('56).
m) OBSTETRIC NURSING. 1945–56; Form 156 ('56).
n) PUBLIC HEALTH NURSING. 1956; Form 956 ('56).
o) NATURAL SCIENCES IN NURSING. 1957; Form 957 ('57); 3 scores: facts and principles (knowledge, application), total.
p) MATERNAL AND CHILD HEALTH NURSING. 1958; Form 658 ('58): 3 scores: psychological aspects, non-psychological aspects, total.

REFERENCE

1. NATIONAL LEAGUE FOR NURSING. *The NLN Achievement Test, Second Edition.* The Use of Tests in Schools of Nursing Pamphlet No. 2. New York: National League for Nursing, Inc., 1958. Pp. iii, 44. *

[935]

***NLN Graduate Nurse Qualifying Examination.** Registered professional nurses; 1945–56; tests administered throughout the year at centers established by NLN; IBM; 1 form; 3 tests; norms ('57); manual ['54]; interpretive manual ('54, see *1* below); Plan A, all tests: examination fee, $10; Plan B, *Clinical Test* and one other: examination fee, $9; Plan C, *Clinical Test* only: examination fee, $8; fees include reporting scores to one college and examiner's fee if taken with group of 10 or more; less than 10,

applicant or college assumes administration costs; $2 per additional report; $1.25 per interpretive manual; postpaid one way; National League for Nursing, Inc.
a) AMERICAN COUNCIL ON EDUCATION PSYCHOLOGICAL EXAMINATION FOR COLLEGE FRESHMEN. See 308; 3 scores: quantitative, linguistic, total; 1954 Edition; 38(65) minutes.
b) READING COMPREHENSION: COOPERATIVE ENGLISH TEST: HIGHER LEVEL, TEST C2. See 179; 2 scores: speed, level; Form Z ('53); 25(35) minutes.
c) CLINICAL TEST. 4 scores: medical-surgical nursing, maternal and child health nursing, psychiatric nursing, total; Form 1253 ('53); 3 booklets; 295(325) minutes.

REFERENCE

1. NATIONAL LEAGUE OF NURSING. *The NLN Graduate Nurse Qualifying Examination.* The Use of Tests in Schools of Nursing Pamphlet No. 3. New York: National League of Nursing, Inc., 1954. Pp. v, 39. *

[936]

***NLN Practical Nurse Achievement Tests.** Students in approved schools of practical nursing; 1950–58; IBM; 1 form; 2 tests; no manual; mimeographed norms ('58); postpaid one way; National League for Nursing, Inc.
a) PRACTICAL NURSE BASIC ACHIEVEMENT TEST. 1957–58; 4 scores: body structure and function, basic nursing procedures, nutrition and diet therapy, total; Form 857 ('57); mimeographed directions sheet ('58); examination fee, $1; (90) minutes.
b) PRACTICAL NURSE ACHIEVEMENT TEST. 1950–56; Form 856 ('56); mimeographed directions ['57]; examination fee, 75¢; (120) minutes.

[937]

***NLN Pre-Admission and Classification Examination.** Practical nursing school entrants; 1950–58; IBM; 1 form ('50); 2 tests; directions booklet ['54]; norms ['58]; examination fee, $3 per student; fee includes scoring service and reporting scores to any one school of practical nursing; National League for Nursing, Inc.
a) GENERAL INFORMATION AND JUDGMENT EXAMINATION. 3 scores: information and judgment, arithmetic, total; Form 650 ('50); 75(85) minutes.
b) VOCABULARY EXAMINATION. Form 650 ('50); 30 (35) minutes.

[938]

***NLN Pre-Nursing and Guidance Examination.** Applicants for admission to state-approved schools of professional nursing; 1941–57; tests administered throughout the year at centers established by the NLN; 1 form; 5 tests; manual ['57]; interpretive manual ('57, see *2* below); examination fee, $10 if taken with group of 10 or more; less than 10, applicant or college assumes administration costs; fee includes reporting scores to one school of nursing; $2 per additional report; $1.25 per interpretive manual; postpaid one way; 168(230) minutes in 2 sessions; National League for Nursing, Inc.
a) AMERICAN COUNCIL ON EDUCATION PSYCHOLOGICAL EXAMINATION FOR COLLEGE FRESHMEN. See 308; 3 scores: quantitative, linguistic, total; 1954 Edition; 38(65) minutes.
b) READING COMPREHENSION: COOPERATIVE ENGLISH TEST: HIGHER LEVEL, TEST C2. See 179; 2 scores: speed, level; Form Z ('53); 25(35) minutes.
c) MATHEMATICS. Adaptation of *Cooperative Mathematics Test for Grades 7, 8, and 9* (see 421); Form Q ('40); 35(40) minutes.
d) COOPERATIVE GENERAL ACHIEVEMENT TESTS: TEST II, NATURAL SCIENCE. See 703; Form T ('42); 40(50) minutes.

e) COOPERATIVE GENERAL CULTURE TEST, PART II, HISTORY AND SOCIAL STUDIES. See 7; Form XX ('51); 30 (40) minutes.

REFERENCES

1. SHAYCOFT, MARION F. "A Validation Study of the Pre-Nursing and Guidance Test Battery." *Am J Nursing* 51:201–5 Mr '51. *
2. NATIONAL LEAGUE FOR NURSING. *The NLN Pre-Nursing and Guidance Examination, Second Edition.* The Use of Tests in Schools of Nursing Pamphlet No. 1. New York: National League for Nursing, Inc., 1957. Pp. v, 42. *

[939]

★Personnel Service Rating Report. Library personnel; 1948; 1 form ['48]; no manual; no data on reliability; no norms; $1.25 per 25 scales, postage extra; specimen set not available; administration time not reported; Subcommittee on Service Ratings of the ALA Board on Personnel Administration; American Library Association. *

[940]

★Policeman Test. Policemen; 1953–57; Forms 10-A ('53), 10-B ('56); revised mimeographed manual ('57); norms ('56); no data on reliability and validity; separate answer sheets must be used; PPA member agency: 10–49 tests, $1.20 each; others, $1.60 each; $2 per specimen set; postpaid; 95(105) minutes; Public Personnel Association. *

[941]

★Punched Card Machine Operator Aptitude Test. Prospective IBM punched card equipment operators; 1952–55; 1 form ('52); revised manual ('55); separate answer sheets must be used; no charge; 32(40) minutes; Walter J. McNamara; distributed by International Business Machines Corporation. *

[942]

★Purdue Trade Information Test for Sheetmetal Workers: Purdue Personnel Tests. Sheetmetal workers; 1958; 1 form; preliminary manual; reliability data based on preliminary form; $4 per 25 tests, postage extra; 50¢ per specimen set, postpaid; (30–45) minutes; Joseph Tiffin, B. R. Modisette, and Warren B. Griffin; distributed by University Book Store. *

[943]

★Purdue Trade Information Test in Carpentry: Purdue Personnel Tests. Vocational school and adults; 1952; 1 form; preliminary manual; $4 per 25 tests, postage extra; 50¢ per specimen set, postpaid; (35–50) minutes; Joseph Tiffin and Robert F. Mengelkoch; distributed by University Book Store. *

REFERENCE

1. MENGELKOCH, ROBERT F. *A Trade Information Test for Carpenters.* Master's thesis, Purdue University (Lafayette, Ind.), 1953.

P. L. MELLENBRUCH, *Professor of Psychology, University of Kentucky, Lexington, Kentucky.*

This carpenter's test represents another instance in which a test is put on sale before it is ready. Information about the test is limited and the evidence as to its value is meager.

The authors state in the preliminary manual that the test is designed "to aid industry and vocational schools in determining the amount of information in this field that is possessed by applicants or students. The test is particularly useful as an aid in the selection of new carpen-

ters from applicants who claim to have had training and/or experience in this trade." The test is also suggested as a "terminal achievement examination" for vocational schools.

No data are presented to indicate whether the test actually is suitable for carpenters who are applying for jobs. In fact, there is no evidence that the test has ever been tried out on carpenters presently employed as such, and, consequently, no attempt has been made to obtain cutoff scores or norms for those who are now doing carpentry work. It would seem better under the circumstances to make no reference to the use of this test for selection purposes.

The test was developed apparently in a Smith-Hughes trade school atmosphere and all of the testing of the test confined to such vocational school students. The original items were "submitted to an expert [one?] tradesman" to be checked for "aptness of the subject matter, plausibility of the incorrect answers, and correctness of the right answer."

The reviewer attempted to get some additional information respecting the test by administering it to members of the carpenters' union at Lexington, Kentucky. Out of a group of some 60 persons attending the union meeting he succeeded in getting 22 to complete the test. Some half dozen or so who had volunteered turned in their booklets when they saw the length of the test. The general reaction was that it might be a good test for home construction carpenters but it had little in it related to commercial carpentering.

Though the number of cases is small, three very broad concluding observations might be made: (*a*) Amount of schooling seemingly does not affect one's score appreciably. (*b*) There are too few difficult items. (*c*) This test represents an excellent problem on the MA degree level but was published prematurely.

[944]

★Purdue Trade Information Test in Engine Lathe Operation: Purdue Personnel Tests. Vocational school and adults; 1955; 1 form; preliminary manual; $4 per 25 tests, postage extra; 50¢ per specimen set, postpaid; (50–65) minutes; Robert Cochran and Joseph Tiffin; distributed by University Book Store. *

WILLIAM J. MICHEELS, *Professor of Industrial Education and Chairman of the Department, University of Minnesota, Minneapolis, Minnesota.*

This test is intended to "aid industry and vocational schools in determining the amount of information....possessed by applicants or students" on engine lathe operation.

It is a test of what a person knows about engine lathe operation rather than what the person can do on an engine lathe. The 74 items measure primarily a knowledge of specifics. There are very few questions that call for application of knowledge or problem solving abilities related to engine lathe operation. A large majority of the items are of a highly factual nature.

If this test is to have wide use, considerably more attention must be given to preparing a more informative manual. The test can serve a useful purpose in quickly screening out people who have had little or no experience with engine lathe operation. It is doubtful, however, whether the test should be used alone as "a terminal achievement examination."

[945]

★**Purdue Trade Information Test in Welding, Revised Edition: Purdue Personnel Tests.** Vocational school and adults; 1951–52; 1 form ('52); preliminary manual; $4 per 25 tests, postage extra; 50¢ per specimen set, postpaid; (65–80) minutes; Joseph Tiffin and Warren B. Griffin; distributed by University Book Store. *

[946]

★**Road Test Check List for Testing, Selecting, Rating, and Training Coach Operators.** Coach operators; 1958; 1 form; no data on reliability; 48¢ per set of 25 score sheets and manual, postage extra; specimen set free; driving jerk recorder essential for administration; Amos E. Neyhart; published jointly by American Automobile Association and Institute of Public Safety, Pennsylvania State University. *

[947]

*****Sales Comprehension Test.** Sales applicants; 1953–57; revision of *Aptitudes Associates Test of Sales Aptitude;* Form M ('53); supplement ('57); 20¢ per test; 25¢ per scoring key; 75¢ per manual ('53); $1 per specimen set; cash orders postpaid; (15–20) minutes; Martin M. Bruce; the Author. *

REFERENCES

1. BRUCE, MARTIN M. "A Sales Comprehension Test." *J Appl Psychol* 38:302–4 O '54. * (PA 29:6346)
2. BRUCE, MARTIN M. "Normative Data Information Exchange, Nos. 19–22." *Personnel Psychol* 9:395–9 au '56. *
3. BRUCE, MARTIN M. "Validity Information Exchange, No. 9-45: D.O.T. Code 0-97.61, Manager, Sales." *Personnel Psychol* 9:524 w '56. *
4. BRUCE, MARTIN M., AND FRIESEN, EDWARD P. "Validity Information Exchange, No. 9-35: D.O.T. Code 1-55.10, Salesman, House-to-House." *Personnel Psychol* 9:380 au '56. *
5. BRUCE, MARTIN M. "Normative Data Information Exchange, No. 10-23." *Personnel Psychol* 10:245 su '57. *
6. HECHT, ROBERT, AND BRUCE, MARTIN M. "Normative Data Information Exchange, No. 10-43." *Personnel Psychol* 10:536 w '57. *
7. MURRAY, L. E., AND BRUCE, MARTIN E. "Normative Data Information Exchange, No. 10-9." *Personnel Psychol* 10:105–6 sp '57. *
8. ALBRIGHT, LEWIS E.; GLENNON, J. R.; AND SMITH, WALLACE J. "Normative Data Information Exchange, No. 11-12." *Personnel Psychol* 11:277 su '58. *
9. BRUCE, MARTIN M. "Normative Data Information Exchange, No. 11-4." *Personnel Psychol* 11:133–4 sp '58. *
10. SMITH, WALLACE J.; ALBRIGHT, LEWIS E.; AND GLEN-
NON, J. R. "Normative Data Information Exchange, No. 11-11." *Personnel Psychol* 11:276 su '58. *

RAYMOND A. KATZELL, *Professor of Psychology and Management Engineering, New York University, New York, New York.*

The present revision consists of 30 items drawn, on the basis of item analysis, from the 50 constituting the earlier form of the test. The selected items were those which continued to discriminate between salesmen and nonsalesmen, and which showed some degree of consistency in distributions of responses in three successive item analysis samples. New scoring weights have been computed for the selected items, proportional to their power in differentiating between salesmen and nonsalesmen.

This abbreviation, while having the obvious virtue of reduced administration time, seems to have done the test no harm. In one study where scores were obtained by both keys, the two had nearly equal validity, exhibiting correlations of about .3 with performance ratings of sales personnel ($n = 86$). Test-retest reliability was also approximately the same for both editions, being in the .70's. A correlation coefficient of .65 was obtained between the scores yielded by the old keys and the new keys in a large heterogeneous sample.

VALIDITY. By way of cross validating the scoring key for the revised edition, the mean score of 334 salesmen was compared with that of 661 nonsalesmen. Both samples appear to have been rather heterogeneous with respect to employing agency and geographical distribution, but no data are provided regarding their comparability with respect to age, education, test variance, or other pertinent factors. In any event, the difference between their means was significant at beyond the 1 per cent level of confidence (presumably the mean for the sales group was higher, although this is not stated). Several validation studies have recently been reported in the Validity Information Exchange of *Personnel Psychology* (2-10). The *Sales Comprehension Test* exhibited statistically significant validity (concurrent) in three of these studies, in which the samples comprised, respectively, house to house salesmen, wholesale steel warehouse salesmen, and a group consisting mainly of wholesale salesmen. The test clearly lacked validity in one study utilizing six samples of salesmen of foodstuffs; on the other hand, it fared no worse than did a variety of 14 other psychometric scales which were used. In a fifth study, based on 82 sales managers in the cosmetics industry, the t-ratio between the test means of "good" and "poor" criterion groups turned out to be 1.9, which falls slightly short of the 5 per cent level of confidence.

RELIABILITY. Test-retest reliability was .71 in a sample of 103 college students. The interval between tests is not reported, although this would be useful in interpreting the result. Using this *r*, the reliability of the test was estimated for a heterogeneous sample comprising salesmen, nonsalesmen, and women. The resulting estimate was .79. The more restricted range of scores that would probably characterize the applicants of a given company would lead one to guess that the unaugmented figure of .71 is closer to what would obtain for such samples.

NORMS. Percentile equivalents are provided in the manual for a sample of 397 miscellaneous salesmen, heterogeneous samples of 872 men and 132 women, 55 supply salesmen, 86 electronics salesmen, 360 college students of salesmanship, plus a few additional small samples of special sales groups. In addition, the author has been conscientiously reporting supplementary tables in the Normative Data Information Exchange of *Personnel Psychology*.

OTHER CORRELATIONS. The *Sales Comprehension Test* appears to measure something other than tested intelligence. Its correlation with the total score of *SRA Primary Mental Abilities* is essentially zero, and that with the *Otis Self-Administering Tests of Mental Ability* is slightly negative. There is a significantly positive correlation (.39) with the persuasive score of the *Kuder Preference Record*.

GENERAL COMMENTS. The test's content, together with its correlations with other tests, support the author's contention that it is a measure of "understanding and appreciation of basic principles of selling." That such a measure may be of use in selecting sales personnel is supported by the positive results of several validation studies. That this utility is not universal is indicated by other studies, employing either the revised or original edition.

It is one of the hopes of the editor and reviewers of *The Mental Measurements Yearbooks* that their efforts may lead to the improvement of tests. Without inferring direct cause and effect, this reviewer was gratified to find ameliorations in the revised edition of this test that correspond to several of those recommended in the reviews of the original edition.

Among them are the retitling of the test as a comprehension rather than an aptitude test, the compilation of additional norms for specific sales groups, and the accumulation of more studies of the test's correlation with sales performance. It is hoped that further progress in this last regard will result in better understanding of the situations in which this type of measure is likely to be valid or not; studies of predictive validity would be particularly welcome. Also desirable would be information on how test performance is related to such background factors as education and job experience. In the meantime, the test merits experimental use for purposes of sales personnel selection.

For reviews by Milton E. Hahn and Donald G. Paterson of the original edition, see 4:824.

[948]

★**Sales Motivation Inventory.** Sales applicants; 1953; Form A; 20¢ per test; 25¢ per scoring key; 50¢ per manual; $1 per specimen set; cash orders postpaid; (25-30) minutes; Martin M. Bruce; the Author. *

REFERENCES
1. BRUCE, MARTIN M. "Normative Data Information Exchange, Nos. 23-4." *Personnel Psychol* 9:400-3 au '56. *
2. MURRAY, L. E., AND BRUCE, MARTIN M. "Normative Data Information Exchange, No. 10-10." *Personnel Psychol* 10:107-9 sp '57. *

S. RAINS WALLACE, *Director of Research, Life Insurance Agency Management Association, Hartford, Connecticut.*

This test is "designed to aid in the appraisal of interest in or motivation for sales work." Sales work is defined as a type of job for which compensation takes the form of commissions or bonuses based on amount of sales. The test score is claimed to provide an objective measure of one aspect of sales aptitude for the use of the tester in industry as well as the vocational counselor.

There are 75 items, each consisting of a group of four activities from which the subject picks one. The format is simple and clear, although the instructions seem somewhat inadequate. The scoring procedure and stencil appear to lend themselves to considerable error.

The test was "validated" by showing a statistically significant differentiation between 210 salesmen (type unspecified) and 521 nonsalesmen (334 men and 187 women). No cross validation data are provided in the Examiner's Manual but subsequent publications in the Normative Data Information Exchange of *Personnel Psychology* tend to support the conclusions obtained from the original study. Norms are presented for the various groups and show acceptable consistency. The odd-even reliability is estimated from the original sample as .90. No test-retest reliabilities are available.

While the test is a workmanlike job and supporting data have been carefully obtained, there are three negative features. The absence of any predictive validity for actual sales performance leaves the test in an experimental status so far as the tester in industry is concerned. For the vocational counselor, the assumption of a general sales aptitude is troublesome. Validities for similar predictors against performance in different sales fields indicate that the assumption is subject to considerable doubt.[1] Furthermore, the high correlations between this test and the three sales keys of the *Strong Vocational Interest Blank* (.71 to .83) might lead the counselor to prefer the older test for which predictive validity in some fields has been demonstrated.

Finally, as is true with most self-report tests, the possibility of faking seems great.

[949]

★**Sales Personnel Description Form.** Salesmen; 1953–55; forced-choice rating scale; 1 form ('53); mimeographed manual ['55]; no data on reliability and validity; no norms; 50¢ per form including scoring service; 25¢ per specimen set; cash orders postpaid; [10] minutes; Personnel Research Institute. *

[950]

★**Steward Life Insurance Knowledge Test.** Applicants for life insurance agent or supervisory positions; 1956; 5 scores: arithmetic, vocabulary, principles, functions, total; 1 form ('56); manual ('56); no data on reliability and validity; tentative norms for total score only; $1.50 per 5 tests; $1.50 per manual; postage extra; specimen set not available; administration time not reported; Verne Steward; Verne Steward & Associates. *

[951]

★**Steward Occupational Objectives Inventory.** Applicants for supervisory positions in life insurance companies or agencies; 1956–57; ratings in 8 areas: caliber level, life insurance knowledge, selling skills, leadership ability, supervisory skills, personal adjustment, survival on job, supplementary items; 1 form ('57); $3.75 per 5 tests; $3 per manual ('57); postage extra; specimen set not available; (90–105) minutes; Verne Steward; Verne Steward & Associates. *

[952]

★**Steward Personal Background Inventory.** Salesman applicants; 1949–57; ratings in 7 areas: health, education, experience, financial status, activities, family status, miscellaneous; 1 form ('57); manual ('57); $2 per 5 tests; $2.25 per manual; postage extra; specimen set not available; (60–70) minutes; Verne Steward; Verne Steward & Associates. *

1 HUGHES, J. L., AND MCNAMARA, W. J. "Limitations on the Use of Strong Sales Keys for Selection and Counseling." *J Appl Psychol* 42:93–6 Ap '58. *

[953]

★**Steward Sales Aptitude Inventory.** Applicants for sales positions; 1957–58; 5 scores: business knowledge, arithmetic skill, selling aptitude, vocational interest in selling, freedom from personal handicaps; 1 form ('58); $2 per 5 tests; $1.25 per manual ('58); postage extra; specimen set not available; (60–80) minutes; Verne Steward; Verne Steward & Associates. *

[954]

★**The Store Personnel Test.** Food store employees; 1946–51; 2 scores: checking, problems; Form FS ('46); manual ('51); tentative norms ('50); distribution restricted to food stores; $11 per 100 tests; specimen set available upon request; postpaid; 20(25) minutes; Harold G. Seashore and Charles E. Orbach; Psychological Corporation. *

REFERENCE

1. DOPPELT, JEROME E., AND BENNETT, GEORGE K. "Reducing the Cost of Training Satisfactory Workers by Using Tests." *Personnel Psychol* 6:1–8 sp '53. * (PA 28:1601)

RAYMOND A. KATZELL, *Professor of Psychology and Management Engineering, New York University, New York, New York.*

As stated in the manual, the *Store Personnel Test* "was developed to meet the need for a single test measuring mental alertness and speed and accuracy" and having face validity for food store personnel. These objectives were achieved by constructing a test comprising a 3-minute checking subtest and a 20-minute "mental ability" subtest. The latter consists of reasoning, vocabulary, information, and computation items, in cycle omnibus arrangement. Most items in both subtests are couched in terms manifestly related to the food industry. The format is such that the test answers must be marked on the booklet and scored by hand; a slotted key is provided.

VALIDITY. Correlation coefficients are reported between each subtest and ratings of initiative, adaptability, and performance on the job, plus the sum of the three ratings. In a sample of 215 male produce workers, the correlations of the checking and mental ability subtests with the sum ratings were, respectively, .21 and .42. The comparable correlations in a sample of 109 male checkers were .16 and .36; in a sample of 248 female checkers they were .37 and .35. Commendably, all the foregoing coefficients represent predictive, rather than merely concurrent, validity. In one organization, a sample of 50 managers was divided into upper and lower halves on the basis of overall job success; statistically significant mean differences were found between the groups on both subtests. The direction of these differences is not indicated, but we hope for the best.

RELIABILITY. Test-retest reliability coefficients were .82 and .87, respectively, for the two parts of the test in a sample of high school students. The corrected odd-even reliability coefficient for the mental ability part was .92 for the sample of students, and .94 for a sample of employees.

NORMS. Percentile equivalents are given for scores on each part of the test for each of the following normative samples: 93 male managers and supervisors in a single food chain; 469 applicants (male and female combined) who were hired by a single chain; 162 male checkers, 261 female checkers, and 229 male produce department employees, tested at the time of application and hired by another single chain; 101 commercial students (both male and female) in a single high school. The manual points out the bias introduced in the norms by the representation of hired applicants only. Another limitation is that the norms are by now at least seven or eight years old.

OTHER CORRELATIONS. The correlation of the two parts is fairly high (about .6) suggesting that performance on the checking part may more heavily reflect its verbal than its numerical content. The mental ability part was found to correlate .67 with the *Wonderlic Personnel Test,* in a sample of 328 employed workers; the latter test seems to have had a rather restricted range, suggesting that the former may have a more appropriate distribution of difficulty for this type of population.

GENERAL COMMENTS. The *Store Personnel Test* has adequate reliability, and shows moderate validity for the selection of food store clerks. While the test probably measures essentially what would be measured by any standard checking test and low-level test of mental ability, its face validity may be of some advantage for use with food store personnel. The manual is complete and explicit. Indeed, a deliberate effort has been made to pitch the presentation at such a level that the test can be applied and interpreted by nonpsychologists. But there remain technical problems that transcend a simplified procedure and lucid manual. For what classes of personnel is the test appropriate? (The manual mentions not only store clerks, but also supervisors and managers; one doubts that the test is ideal for the latter group, but would the central office of a food chain know this?) What are the effects of time, and a changing labor market, on the test's norms and validity? Should not age differences enter into interpretation of the test results? Is it sufficient to set selection standards on the basis of norms, or should there not be some effort to ascertain functional critical scores? And so forth. It would seem that the use of competent psychological consultation or supervision, even in such a program, is not only a matter of saving "time and money," as the manual advises, but more crucially a question of sound practice. Should not the "do-it-yourself" movement be stopped short of professional psychology?

JOHN B. MORRIS, *Associate Professor of Psychology, and Director of Institutional Research, The University of Mississippi, University, Mississippi.*

The authors of this test state that it was developed "to meet the need for a single test measuring mental alertness and speed and accuracy" for retail food stores. The test is a good example of an instrument developed for a specific industry, a practice that was not so popular when this test was issued in 1951, but that seems to be growing at the present time.

The specifications for this test were suggested by advisers from the retail food industry. The advisers stipulated that the test must have "face validity" and that it must be simple enough to administer, score, and interpret that company personnel could be trained to use it efficiently. The copy of the test submitted for review, Form FS, represents a good effort at meeting the foregoing criteria.

Part 1, Checking, is a 3-minute test of speed and accuracy in inspecting two lists of food store merchandise. The task consists of inspecting successive pairs of items to determine if each member of the pair under the "merchandise billed" heading is identical to that in the "merchandise delivered" column. The testee records his response by making a check if the items are in agreement and a cross if they are dissimilar. This section of the test consists of 75 items.

Part 2, Problems, is a 17-minute mental ability test that is similar in content to several popular tests of this type that are currently on the market. It contains 80 reasoning, vocabulary, information, and simple numerical computation items.

The entire test is scored for the number of correct responses by use of a single scoring key. In order to use the key, some maneuvering on the part of the scorer is necessary, but, in the opinion of this reviewer, this difficulty is outweighed by the convenience of having a single template.

The test is attractively arranged, and item quality appears good throughout the test. Only one item appeared to be ambiguous to the reviewer.

The manual is attractive, well written, and should be understood easily, even by personnel managers who are not well versed in test statistics. While test technicians might wish for information that is not included, it is doubtful that those for whom the manual was prepared (it is restricted in sale to food store organizations) will find it deficient. The general quality of the technical data supplied is good if somewhat sparse. The authors recognize some of the deficiencies and urge that companies using the test conduct experimentation before attempting to set definite cutoff points for employment. They cite an example of what was done by one company as a possible guide.

The only estimate of reliability available for Part 1 is based upon two administrations of the test to 101 commercial department students in the 10th, 11th, and 12th grades. The coefficient of correlation between the tests, repeated after an interval of one week, was .82. The same technique and students yielded a reliability of .87 for Part 2.

Further evidence of reliability for Part 2 is reported from a study based upon a random sample of 100 cases drawn from a population of newly hired employees of a food store chain in Texas. The corrected odd-even coefficient was .94. The odd-even technique could not be used appropriately for Part 1 as it is a highly speeded test.

Correlations between Part 1 and Part 2 are given for three separate samples. The values reported for these studies are .55, .61, and .56. The authors state that these values are "quite typical of correlations generally found between checking tests and intelligence tests."

The test was validated against criteria selected by food store personnel. Each worker who took the test and was subsequently employed was rated on initiative, adaptability, and performance by his supervisors. The ratings were accomplished independently of knowledge of test performance. The validity coefficients obtained varied with the position held, the factor rated, and the part of the test used. For male produce workers and female checkers the tests were reasonably predictive. For males rated as checkers the tests had lower predictability. In general, judicious use of the different parts of the test in selecting workers for various positions should make use of the tests advantageous in the selection of successful workers.

In summary, this is a test for a specific purpose that quite frankly recognizes regional differences in norms and refuses to generalize from a small sample in one geographic region to an industry that is national in scope. The fact that its usefulness to an organization is partially dependent upon the ability of someone in that organization to run further studies of reliability and validity and to construct local norms may account in part for an apparent lack of acceptance by the food distribution industry. It may be that industry still wants test constructors to supply them with *the* reliability and *the* validity of a test whether or not they are appropriate for the local situation.

[955]

★Supervisory Practices Test. Supervisors; 1957; 1 form; 20¢ per test; 25¢ per scoring key; 75¢ per manual; $1 per specimen set; cash orders postpaid; (20-30) minutes; Martin M. Bruce; the Author. *

REFERENCE
1. BRUCE, MARTIN M., AND LEARNER, DAVID B. "A Supervisory Practices Test." *Personnel Psychol* 11:207–16 su '58. *

CLIFFORD E. JURGENSEN, *Assistant Vice President in Charge of Personnel, Minneapolis Gas Company, Minneapolis, Minnesota.*

This test consists of 50 completion type items dealing with attitudes and opinions toward supervisory actions involving people. Its purpose is to aid in appraising supervisory ability and potential.

The test is self-administering, has no time limit, and is scored with a strip key. Percentile norms, mean, standard deviation, and standard error of measurement are reported for each of three groups: 52 executives, 239 managers, and 598 nonsupervisors. The test correlates .27 with total score on the *SRA Primary Mental Abilities* and .56 with Form M of *How Supervise?*

Two status validity studies showed a significant difference between means of supervisors and nonsupervisors at the 1 per cent level. Two studies are reported on concurrent validity: a rank correlation of .81 was found between SPT scores and the ratings of 15 foremen; a product-moment r of .38 was found between SPT scores of 16 foremen and the mean attitude scores on the *SRA Employee Inventory* of the employees under their supervision. Two testimonial cases are cited: a manufacturing manager who scored within the top 5 per cent of supervisors was rated by subordinates as the best supervisor they had had in 14 years, and a vice president who scored at the 12th percentile before being hired was fired at the end of six months for inability to gain acceptance and cooperation from his department heads.

Item weights were determined by the ability of the item to differentiate between nonsupervisors and supervisors, and the degree to which supervisory as well as nonsupervisory personnel agree. The second of these criteria is based on the rationale that the perspective of the majority, whether supervisors or nonsupervisors, is important. This emphasis on communality will be disputed by some persons and in some companies.

The manual is more complete than usual; it was prepared using the recommendations of the APA Committee on Test Standards and of the Committee on Ethical Standards on Psychology. It fairly and wisely points out that "the responses given by a person in an artificial or test situation are no guarantee of the person's acting in that fashion when he is faced with the actual situation," and that the person using this test in a business or industry should be oriented to the organization because "the generalizations concerning desirable supervisory practices may not always be applicable in a specific organization." The author is to be commended for mentioning these points which decrease test validity for selection purposes.

A test-retest correlation of .77 is reported for 112 supervisors. Split-half biserial reliability for 177 supervisors and nonsupervisors is .82. The manual states that "this appears sufficiently high for group situations to warrant confidence in its consistency of measurement." The word *group* in the previous sentence is important. The author does not claim that the test is sufficiently reliable to warrant confidence in the score of an individual.

Reliability is probably reduced because item stems do not (and cannot) always give all relevant and necessary information. The "best" answer sometimes depends on factors not mentioned. If the respondent makes the same assumptions as the test author, he is likely to get a higher score than if he makes other assumptions. In some tests, of course, such differences

in assumptions account for test validity, but this does not seem to be the case here. Low reliability is not surprising if item weights are analyzed in relation to norms. A change in response to a single item—whether resulting from carelessness, absence of relevant data, item ambiguity, or what have you—can change the raw score as much as 10 points and the percentile rank on executive norms as much as 37 points.

Because of the unreliability of scores for individual predictions, differing "best" answers in various companies, and absence of information necessary to determine the best answer in some items, this reviewer recommends the test not be used in situations where total scores are obtained. Nevertheless, there is one type of situation where the test is recommended. This is in supervisory training conferences and classes. Thoughtful and profitable discussion can result if members of the group fill in the test and then discuss answers to each item. The weaknesses of the test for selection purposes become strong points when the test is used for training. Discussion brings out differing viewpoints, approaches, and assumptions. These differences can be used to emphasize the importance of looking at supervisory problems thoroughly and from all angles rather than jumping to conclusions without considering all relevant factors.

MARY ELLEN OLIVERIO, *Associate Professor of Education, Teachers College, Columbia University, New York, New York.*

This test claims to provide a measure of only one aspect of supervisory ability: the ability to function effectively in situations which require decisions involving people. The test consists of 50 items written in the first person. The subject is to assume that he is the supervisor faced with the problems identified in the items. He is asked to choose the solution he feels is the best in each instance.

The test is simple to administer and can be taken individually as well as in a group. Some question might be raised about the test's being untimed. Deliberation on the items might well lead to more frequent selection of the BEST solution, since the best solution tends to become more obvious with rereading. There would be some merit in getting the immediate response of the subject.

The procedure used in developing the items,

analyzing them, weighting them, and checking the validity and reliability of the final form of the test appears to be generally sound. The author states that predictive validity is suggested by several case histories, but only two are cited. It is not clear whether or not these cited are representative of the case histories.

Norms are based on the scores of 52 executives, 239 managers, and 598 nonsupervisors. No information is given concerning the source of the samples or their representativeness of the total groups. The executives appear more homogeneous than the nonsupervisors, for example. This difference could reflect the fact that executives are more alike than are nonsupervisors in the variable under study. At the same time, there is no way of knowing what a larger sample of executives would reveal.

This test might have value in those situations where the evaluator has had no opportunity to learn how a prospective supervisor makes decisions involving people. Many such situations occur when people in a company are being considered for promotions.

[956]

★**Truck Driver Test 60-A.** Drivers of light and medium trucks; 1957–58; 1 form ('57); preliminary mimeographed manual ('58); general PPA mimeographed directions ['57]; no norms; separate answer sheets must be used; PPA member agency: 10–49 tests, 80¢ each; others, $1 each; $2 per specimen set; postpaid; 90(100) minutes; Public Personnel Association. *

[957]

★**Veterinary Aptitude Testing Program.** Veterinary school applicants; 1951; tests administered at centers established by the publisher; 4 scores: reading comprehension, science information, verbal memory, total; IBM; 1 form; 4 tests; manual ['51]; examination fee, $6; fee includes reporting of scores to any 2 schools designated at time of application; $1 per additional report; postpaid; scores not reported to examinees; 145(180) minutes; Loyal C. Payne and William A. Owens; Psychological Corporation. *
a) VETERINARY APTITUDE TEST, PARTS 1, 3, 4. 1 form ['51]; 105(115) minutes.
b) VETERINARY ACHIEVEMENT TEST, PART 2. 1 form ['51]; 40(50) minutes.

REFERENCES

1. OWENS, WILLIAM A. "Development of a Test of Aptitude for Veterinary Medicine." *Proc Iowa Acad Sci* 57:417–23 '50. *
2. LAYTON, WILBUR L. "Predicting Success of Students in Veterinary Medicine." *J Appl Psychol* 36:312–5 O '52. * (*PA* 27:5418)
3. PAYNE, LOYAL C. *Development and Validation of a Veterinary Medical Aptitude Test.* Doctor's thesis, Iowa State College (Ames, Iowa), 1954.

Books and Reviews

* * * * *

The following roughly classified index has been prepared to assist readers to locate books on a particular subject. In addition to using this index, readers are urged to skim over titles and excerpts in search of works which otherwise may be overlooked.

GENERAL

Bibliographies and reviews, B82–4, B106, B311–2
Growth, B404, B412
Guidance, B64, B88, B135–6, B148, B151, B162, B183, B198, B217, B244, B252, B260, B264, B329, B364, B366, B417
Miscellaneous, B8, B11, B13–4, B124, B133, B141, B150–4, B211, B258, B378–9, B437–8, B469, B481–2
Proceedings, B220–6, B292, B304–10, B324, B470–6
Selection, B6, B12, B113, B119, B142, B230, B271, B334, B397, B401, B447, B457, B459–60, B478, B484
Testing programs: CITY, B10; COLLEGE, B94, B125–7, B235, B292, B302, B324, B328, B334, B377, B400, B450, B457; STATE, B64, B427; SECONDARY, B95–101, B112, B275
Textbooks and handbooks: EDUCATION, B20, B24, B56, B74–5, B81, B113, B181–2, B238, B269, B283, B321, B350–1, B361, B374, B376, B422, B424, B429, B432–3, B445, B454, B477, B483; PSYCHOLOGY, B33, B42, B90, B158, B179, B189, B393, B425; WORKBOOKS, B110, B180, B263, B362, B453

ACHIEVEMENT

General, B59, B62, B166, B172, B212, B269, B325–6, B426
Miscellaneous, B38, B72, B132, B242, B436
Subjects: AGRICULTURE, B381; BUSINESS EDUCATION, B54, B194, B382; ENGLISH, B97, B129, B317, B371, B383; FOREIGN LANGUAGES, B98, B373, B386, B388, B443; HOME ECONOMICS, B49; INDUSTRIAL ARTS, B391; MATHEMATICS, B87, B99, B122, B139, B319, B387, B458, B468; MUSIC, B156, B255, B389; PHYSICAL EDUCATION, B57, B85, B218, B278, B288, B416, B464; READING, B19, B102–3, B114, B193, B354, B406; SCIENCE, B100, B130–1, B318, B390; SOCIAL STUDIES, B45–6, B101, B128, B384–5; STUDY SKILLS, 301

INTELLIGENCE

Group testing, B6, B96, B120, B219, B240–1, B357
Individual testing, B149, B184, B249, B332, B342–3, B440–1, B463

Miscellaneous, B23, B65–6, B68, B107, B140, B163, B202, B256, B276, B279, B293, B355, B367, B396

MISCELLANEOUS

Blind, B16, B58, B201, B289
Civil service, B16, B439
Delinquency, B53, B200
Factor analysis, B17, B21, B23, B25–7, B89, B105, B164, B205, B423
Grading, B195, B363, B413
Item analysis, B145, B365
Military, B1, B30, B81, B219, B436
Miscellaneous, B18, B155, B339, B341, B344, B356
Observational methods, B93
Oral tests, B287
Preparation for examinations, B5, B9, B77, B207–8, B214, B228–9, B262, B268, B285, B335, B442, B461
Psychiatry and medicine, B197, B210
Report and record forms, B4, B392, B410, B451
Scaling, B104, B134, B138, B352, B430, B462
Socio-economic status, B61, B196
Student teaching, B28, B291, B435
Test theory, B43, B48, B111, B185, B188, B215–6, B243, B272, B297
Vision, B3, B7, B109

PERSONALITY

Attitudes, B349
General, B35, B91, B143–4, B147, B171, B173, B303, B409, B446
Graphology, B286, B290, B360, B398–9, B405, B411, B421, B448
Group morale and leadership, B157, B169, B203, B267
Miscellaneous, B29, B51–2, B76, B117, B121, B137, B146, B160–1, B165, B167–8, B187, B209, B232, B236–7, B250, B253, B261, B270, B273, B277, B282, B295–6, B403, B408, B420, B434, B449, B480
Nonprojective, B159, B178; MMPI, B108, B199–200, B467
Projective, B31, B44, B192, B265, B274, B298, B327, B338, B347–8, B368, B375, B395, B418, B428; DRAWING, B50, B67, B86, B175, B191, B234, B246, B251,

VOCATIONS

[B1]

★Army Personnel Tests and Measurement. Department of the Army Technical Manual TM 12-260. Washington, D.C.: United States Government Printing Office, April 1953. Pp. v, 125. Paper. $0.55. *

J Appl Psychol 38:280 Ag '54. Harold E. Burtt. This is a good little summary of the use of tests and rating procedures in the Army. It reads much like a standard text on employment psychology condensed and written down to the level of readers without a psychology background. For psychologists in the Army it might serve as a useful refresher and almost approximates a manual. For other Army personnel needing some familiarity with the field, it would be very helpful if read carefully and, preferably, with an elementary statistics text on the side. * The work has a number of commendable features. It is concise and there is not a word wasted. Effective use is made of graphic materials—some of them quite ingenious. There is interesting adaptation of military terminology to conventional psychological presentation. For instance, reliability and validity are interpreted in terms of "calculated risks." The treatment is down to earth and practical, but entirely scientific withal. There is always the problem of how to handle statistics in a work like this. The present authors employ conventional statistical terminology, but do not indicate how anything is computed. There is a frequent suggestion that "any statistics book" covers some particular item. The authors do about as well as could be done under the circumstances with brief explanations of some statistical notions and graphic materials to clarify the explanation. According to an insert the major responsibility of the work appears to have been carried by Baier, Bayroff, and Rundquist. They are to be congratulated on having done an interesting and useful minor piece of work.

Personnel Psychol 7:431-3 au '54. W. S. Paul. * a real contribution to the general field of personnel psychology * Even though the manual is intended for two audiences, it seems that the second audience (those interested in improved technical understanding) is given preference throughout. However, it should be stated that the first audience (users or instructors) is given a wealth of material in easily readable form which in turn can be used for practicable purposes. Even though an effort has been made to simplify the technical content of this manual there are many Army readers and users who would have to spend a considerable amount of study and thought in order for the information to be fully digested or comprehended. * The use of illustrations, pictures, diagrams, and charts adds to the usefulness of this manual. The chapters on the development of personnel measuring instruments; criteria; the meaning of scores; and the practical value of scores contain a vast amount of technical content which is slanted toward usefulness in terms of military personnel problems. Even so, it is doubtful whether either of the intended audiences will spend the required amount of time in digesting the technical content contained therein. * the information given in Chapter 1, Section I, "The effective utilization of manpower," provides an excellent framework in which to place the succeeding technical considerations. Summaries at the end of each chapter provide the reader with an excellent preview of the material contained in that particular chapter. *

Personnel Psychol 7:433-5 au '54. Edwin E. Ghiselli. * my first attempt to read this manual was not wholly successful. It contains many page-long paragraphs that are simply not conducive to maintaining interest. * the organization of the material and the explanations are excellent. The reader is nicely eased into the more difficult technical topics. Many of the more difficult concepts are readily understood through the use of excellent pictographs that are generously scattered throughout the manual. A reader without any background in psychological measurement will readily add to his vocabulary such terms as reliability, validity, and criteria. Furthermore, he will attain a pretty good concept of the meanings of such terms and of their implications. This would be accomplished, of course, only providing the reader is willing to continue through seemingly endless connected chains of sentences. As far as coverage of topics and factual information is concerned, the manual is excellent. It covers all of the areas of personnel placement procedures, test development, validation, rating, interviewing, and administration of tests, that are necessary to provide a general understanding of the field. The newer methods, such as forced-choice procedures, are sufficiently described. It took a great deal of courage on the part of the authors of an elementary manual to deal with such complex topics as personnel classification, the selection ratio, and standard scores. It is apparent that a great deal of thought went into the preparation of explanations, and as a consequence it is unlikely that the reader will fail to achieve a fairly high level of understanding of problems and procedures. Similarly, the reader will be well educated with respect to his attitudes toward systematically developed placement procedures. Many discussions of personnel procedures either overestimate or underestimate their importance. But this manual presents a nice balance in points of view. Systematically developed placement procedures are neither oversold nor undersold. The reader will be convinced with respect to the positive value of tests and allied devices, and yet he will not expect too much from them. In this connection the manual is very convincing on the need for developmental work and the reader will become well aware of the need for and the value of continuing research. In this reviewer's opinion, the manual is not one that he would distribute to management with the intent of developing a sympathy for a systematic personnel placement program. It is doubtful whether anyone in top management would or could take the time to read through the entire manual. It is something that needs study and restudy. However, if a member of top management did read all the way through the manual it is very likely that he would become enthusiastic, and both he and the psychologist would be rewarded. The situation is quite different for students of industrial

psychology. They expect to have to work their way through endless pages of material. They do not expect to grasp an entire field in one reading. As reference or outside reading, the manual should serve well.

Personnel Psychol 7:435–7 au '54. Lee J. Cronbach. * The limitation of the manual to 124 pages is a grievous one. The writers must had many troubles in staying within the limits, and they have done as well as possible in such a space. The style of writing is controlled for readability and brevity. The treatment is in consequence unfortunately dull. The authors could have presented fascinating descriptions of tests or procedures to illustrate particular points. Instead, they refer to everything abstractly. "The man is high on Aptitude Area II" or "particular traits which made up cryptography aptitude" are typical phrases. We would welcome psychological meat on these bones: What are these aptitude areas? What traits related to mapmaking? As a manual for use in the Service, this should do very well. No important topic is omitted. Any officer giving ratings or having personnel workers under his command should be aided by this background. The report sometimes tries to give technical instruction to classification workers, specifically on how to compute standard deviations and how to operate scoring machines. This material is too sporadic to fulfill such functions. Since the report describes a program which has always had good technical leadership and a consistent philosophy, it is basically sound and internally consistent. Imperfect statements can be found, but even in these cases the authors probably intended to say what brevity prevented. Item-test correlations are discussed with exceptional caution, but the authors then say that the procedure is useful only for "pure" tests; not so, if the predominant factors are more important than the others. Recent research shows that in multiple-choice items the ideal percentage passing an item is higher than the percentage to be passed by the test; the manual says the percentages should be equal. Morale effects of item difficulty are given no consideration. The treatment of norms does not make clear whether standard scores are based on a recruit population or on the group tested, which in some instances is a selected school population; shifts in norm groups are confusing to test users, and should be discussed. The usual error in discussing sampling statistics is made : sample values are said to distribute normally about the value observed in the sample at hand. The statement (p. 26) that if no combat criterion is available one should validate a test against whatever criterion is available is likely to give a seriously wrong impression. The treatment of face validity is less satisfactory than Mosier's well-known article ; the writers spread the term over content validity, validity postulated from past testing experience, and validity based on job descriptions. The concepts are, however, properly distinguished from empirical validity. These faults are minor, in the context of the whole. The fact that the report is limited to concerns of the Personnel Research Branch means that tests are considered only from the point of view of mass testing, primarily for predictive purposes. Thus while the interview is properly dismissed as a "measuring" device, the reasons given do not reflect the many acceptable reasons for using interviews in personnel classification. The treatment of achievement tests is sound, but scarcely adequate for the purpose of an instructor who wishes to make better use of tests. The manual may have values for undergraduate students who wish to know about personnel testing programs. Brief as it is, the manual covers some matters better than any other elementary source. Notable are the discussions of differential testing, use of suppressor keys and forced-choice methods in self-report tests, and the improvement of ratings. These are matters where PRB has pioneered, and it is good to have a straightforward review of their thinking. The manual cannot serve by itself as a text for the general student. The viewpoint of PRB is limited by its mission. The definition of tests as necessarily having questions with right and wrong answers, for instance, rules out of court all evaluation and assessment procedures where the subject is led to try to give the right answer but where the examiner is looking at his process of performance and there may be no "right answer." The manual does not cite data to support opinions advanced. Thus we are told that proficiency is usually correlated with job knowledge. For students, we need to know how large the correlation is, and in what field this generalization holds. Insufficient background is given to permit students to evaluate critically the recommendation favoring multiple regression over multiple screens, or objective tests over essay tests, or the implication that nor-

mal distribution derives more from the nature of man than from the nature of tests. The examples of forced-choice rating scales, together with the claims made, remind us that published research on the technique is quite inadequate for its evaluation. This is a standing responsibility of investigators in and out of PRB. The preceding reviewers were asked to consider the book in terms of those functions for which it may be best suited. The reviewer who is asked to judge the book technically must be more adverse, chiefly because of the brevity of the report rather than the soundness of the thinking behind it. The manual will serve a useful purpose, and its faults will not interfere with the major function of enlightening non-psychologists about classification testing.

[B2]

★Dr. Hermann Rorschach Psychodiagnostics Bibliography: The Most Important Publications About the Rorschach Test (Until 1954). New York: Grune & Stratton, Inc., 1955. Pp. 64. Paper. $1.50. *

[B3]

★A Guide for Vision Screening of School Children in the Public Schools of California. Sacramento, Calif.: California State Department of Education, 1953. Pp. viii, 27. Paper. *

[B4]

★Handbook on California Cumulative Records. Bulletin of the California State Department of Education, Vol. 25, No. 5. Sacramento, Calif.: the Department, 1956. Pp. x, 30.

[B5]

★High School Entrance and Scholarship Examination Preparation Book. New York: Youth Education Systems, Inc., 1958. Pp. 47. Paper, mimeographed. $1.98. *

[B6]

★Intelligence Testing: Its Use in Selection for Secondary Education. Special articles from the *Times Educational Supplement* with two leading articles by P. E. Vernon and letters to the editor. London: Times Publishing Co. Ltd., 1952. Pp. 31. Paper. 1s. *

Brit J Ed Psychol 23:72 F '53. C. W. Valentine. This is a report out of two important articles by Professor Vernon which were published in *The Times Educational Supplement,* and of the letters and leaders to which they gave rise. The attention of readers was apparently concentrated too much on one aspect of Professor Vernon's articles, namely the report of a research by one of his students, as to the large increase in scores in group Intelligence Tests, as the result of special coaching ; whereas Professor Vernon himself points out that one or two hours' coaching is enough to produce almost the maximum possible effect. In at least one centre, such coaching of all the candidates in the junior school has been practised for a number of years. One or two of the correspondents rightly emphasize the much greater evil of premature and constant special coaching in Arithmetic and English for the 11+ examination in the junior and even infants schools, as well as further cramming in some homes; and it is to be hoped that those who have jumped to the conclusion that it "has been shown that intelligence tests are no good" (not too strong a phrase to describe some letters not published in this booklet) will note the last sentence of Vernon's final letter, which states that intelligence tests and objective attainment tests still provide the most reliable means of selection, without extraordinary precautions as to teachers' assessments, which are usually impracticable. Professor Vernon is good enough to say that "Professor Valentine's Quota scheme would be a real step forward." "But," he adds, "I find it difficult to envisage its application in areas containing a number of very small primary schools." The difficulty is felt, I imagine, because a number of such very small schools would have to be told that, as the result of the Intelligence Tests, not even one place in the grammar schools could be allocated to them. But would that be as bad as what happens now, namely, many small schools labouring hard and forcing on their pupils, for the 11+ examination to gain a grammar school place, and year after year failing to do so? In such cases disappointed parents will usually attribute it to poor teaching in the school. Whereas, under the Quota scheme, the parents would be told that the local education authority had not awarded any grammar school place to the school, on the basis of intelligence tests, the results of which did not depend on the school teaching. It is to be hoped that there will be a fuller report of Mr. Navathe's research, so that it can be compared in detail with other findings. In the meantime, any teachers or members of the press, or irate parents, who imagine (and state in letters or leaders) that psychologists have, up till recently, been assuming that intelligence tests are infallible and unaffected by coaching, might turn up the fore-runner of this Journal, *The Forum of Education*, Vol. 3, 1924, where was published an article by a colleague in my University Department, Mr. H. E. Chapman, who claimed to show very large percentage improvements in tests through coaching. That was nearly thirty years ago!

[B7]

*Manual of Ocular Tests and Requirements, Third Edition.** Minneapolis, Minn.: Council of Education and Professional Guidance, American Optometric Association, Inc., 1953. Pp. 79. Paper. $3.50. *

[B8]

★**Mental Testing Number.** *Education and Psychology,* Vol. 1, Nos. 4–5. Delhi, India: Education and Psychology, 1954. Pp. ii, 180. Paper. Rs. 4. *

Brit J Psychol 46:323 N '56. *Boris Semeonoff.* It is difficult to assess the purpose underlying the publication of this special number. Side by side with accounts of the standardization of group tests in various Indian languages are several vehement and unoriginal denunciations of mental testing, including a particularly irresponsible example emanating from an English university ("....intelligence tests have been widely used to 'prove' the mental superiority of the white over the coloured peoples...."). Also included are personal contributions by each of the joint editors, of which one, a review of a book on the same general theme, contains this remarkable *volte-face:* "We are in agreement with [the author's] fundamental objections to the theory and practice of intelligence testing. But we see no reason why [he] objects to its use if they help us in proper educational guidance." The scientific papers are uneven in quality, but fairly wide in scope (e.g. R. G. Chatterjee presents "An Evaluation of Reaction Time, Time Sense and Cutaneous Sensitivity in Three Pick-pockets"), and the writers show an earnest desire to make use of and apply the methods and findings of Western research.

[B9]

★**Queensway Intelligence Tests.** London: Evans Brothers Ltd., 1955. Pp. 96. Paper. 2s. 6d. *

[B10]

*The School Testing Program: A Guide to the Selection and Use of Standardized Tests, Revised Edition.** University of the State of New York Bulletin, No. 1454, July 1958. Albany, N.Y.: New York State Education Department, 1959. Pp. 26. Paper. *

[B11]

★**Standardized Testing—An Adventure in Educational Publishing.** Yonkers, N.Y.: World Book Co., [1955?]. Pp. 16. Paper. Gratis. *

[B12]

★**Studies in Selection Techniques for Admission to Grammar Schools.** University of Bristol, Institute of Education, Publication No. 3. London: University of London Press Ltd., 1952. Pp. 68. Paper. 2s. 6d. *

B Int Bur Ed 27:77 2nd q '53. A useful contribution to the debate on the best methods for selection of pupils for secondary schools, based on four-years' experience of the University of Bristol Institute of Education acting as the examining board for the schools in Wiltshire, and on the subsequent research work which lasted for another year. The tentative conclusions reached indicate the inadvisability of relying too much on marking schemes, the important function of the essay or "free writing" in the written examination, and the desirability of having some form of a final assessment in terms of an actual child, correlating all available evidence.

[B13]

★**Technical Recommendations for Achievement Tests.** Prepared by the Committees on Test Standards of the American Educational Research Association and the National Council on Measurements Used in Education. Washington, D.C.: American Educational Research Association, National Education Association, 1955. Pp. 36. Paper. $1.00. *

[B14]

★**Technical Recommendations for Psychological Tests and Diagnostic Techniques.** Prepared by a joint committee of the American Psychological Association, American Educational Research Association, and National Council on Measurements Used in Education. Supplement to the *Psychological Bulletin*, Vol. 51, No. 2, Part 2, March 1954. Washington, D.C.: American Psychological Association, Inc., March 1954. Pp. ii, 38. Paper. $1.00. * (*PA* 28:8692)

[B15]

★**Testing as Applied to Office Workers.** New York: Office Executives Association of New York, Inc., May 1953. Pp. 15. Paper. $2.00. *

[B16]

★**Tests for Blind Competitors for Trades and Industrial Jobs in the Federal Civil Service.** Washington, D.C.: Test Development and Occupational Research Section, United States Civil Service Commission, June 1956. Pp. vi, 72. Paper. Gratis. *

[B17]

★**Uppsala Symposium on Psychological Factor Analysis, 17–19 March 1953.** Nordisk Psykologi's Monograph Series 3. Stockholm, Sweden: Almqvist & Wiksell, 1953. Pp. 91. Paper. 10 kr.

Brit J Psychol 45:223–4 Ag '54. Godfrey Thomson. * It was a very important move in the development of factor analysis to bring some British statisticians who have shown interest in factor analysis into fertilizing contact with the famous Swedish School. * Peel's paper was a readable and illuminating review of past and present, not in the main mathemati-

cal. He suggested recommendations for the future, and the Symposium report ends with a valuable list of ten such, decided upon after general discussion. Bartlett's paper was a very clear account of the mathematical history of factor analysis, and in his last three pages he adds another original contribution to the many he has made, namely a discussion of an attempt to transcend the hypothesis of linearity in the fundamental equation of factor analysis. * The quite important papers of Rasch on simultaneous factor analysis in different populations, and of Lund on a ball and wire model, nevertheless stood somewhat apart from the main issue, which was on the papers by Lawley and Whittle. Whittle's paper presents I think the most novel idea. He succeeded in estimating in one stage both the loadings of the factors in the tests, and the factor values possessed by the people tested. He does it by fitting, not the matrix of covariances or correlations, but the matrix of scores, an oblong matrix. He makes no assumption about the distribution of factor values in the population, but only about the ratios of the residual variances in each test. Lawley assumes, in addition, the factor values to be normally distributed. Their results are very similar but differ by a factor, which each confessed he was as yet unable to explain. * The Uppsala Symposium is a milestone in the progress of factor analysis. What I would like to happen next is an elementary seminar with explanations as simple as possible of the points discussed at such a high level at Uppsala. The members would have to be given prerequisite reading, and examined on it!

[B18]

★**A Welsh Linguistic Background Scale.** University College of Wales, Faculty of Education, Pamphlet No. 2. Aberystwyth, Wales: the College, [1954]. Pp. ii, 9. Paper. 6d. *

[B19]

★ADAM, R. S. **The Construction and Standardization of English Reading Tests for Schools in Fiji.** Educational Research Institute for Fiji and Western Pacific Territories, FIER/3. Suva, Fiji: Government Press, 1953. Pp. xiv, 74. 2s. 6d. *

[B20]

★ADAMS, GEORGIA SACHS, AND TORGERSON, THEODORE L. **Measurement and Evaluation for the Secondary-School Teacher: With Implications for Corrective Procedures.** New York: Dryden Press, Inc., 1956. Pp. xiii, 658. $5.75. * (*PA* 31:3766)

Cath Ed R 55:63–4 Ja '57. Robert B. Nordberg. Here is a thorough book—almost too thorough! It probes into more nooks and crannies of mental measurement than any other single volume of which the reviewer is aware. Its aim throughout is to enable the teacher to deal more effectively with individual differences in every phase of behavior. * The development of each topic is very good, if the frame of reference provided by current eclectic psychology is accepted. The ideas on measurement of achievement tend to be behavioristic; psycho-analytic theory influences the chapter on evaluation of personal-social adjustment; while Gestalt views are visible in the frequent admonitions to take a global, student-centered approach. This absence of any consistent point of departure probably reflects more upon the condition of contemporary psychology than upon this book. The difficulty is nonetheless serious in this case, because the writers make frequent forays into psychological territory to justify the procedures they recommend. As textbooks on mental measurement and evaluation go, though, this one is unquestionably "the best I've seen."

Cont Psychol 2:169 Je '57. Walter F. Johnson. * the book is a noteworthy contribution to the field of measurement and evaluation * It is an excellent reference for on-the-job use (especially Part 2, *The Study of Individuals,* and Part 3, *The Improvement of Instruction*). It will be a satisfactory text for course instruction, if the instructor provides additional theoretical and technical background material. The coverage given to the more informal techniques of evaluation is particularly good. Some users may prefer to follow a different pattern of organization of the subject-matter; others may feel that the book is encyclopedic; but, generally speaking, the book should meet with favor among instructors and students, teachers, and counselors.

Ed Res B 36:242–3 O 9 '57. R. Roderick Palmer. * Reading this book will evoke lively, stimulating thought and discussion. It is encouraging that finally we have a book on measurement and evaluation which presents techniques that can be used to appraise all-round growth. * Ample coverage is given to the techniques of evaluating the academic as well as the emotional and social phases. What is really different about modern evaluation can be understood only when we see evaluation as a phase of education instead of something outside education that is used to measure how effective education is. One reads the book with enthusiasm: here is an approach to this difficult prob-

lem which is practical, reasonable, and scientific. The reviewer is of the opinion that experienced teachers, educational-guidance workers, and student teachers will find the material unusually worth while. Instructors who use the book as a textbook will be pleased with the helpful reading lists, diagnostic aids, workable techniques, and suggested tests of all kinds. It is richly illustrated with references to many recent studies from which the most pertinent data have been extracted. Many figures and tables are used to illustrate the content. The reader will also find innumerable case studies which describe teen-age boys and girls and their problems of adjusting themselves to the task of growing up. He must dig deep, however, to absorb and utilize the wealth of technical data. The book has been organized so that great flexibility in use is possible. Evaluated in terms of the authors' stated purposes, the book measures up unusually well. It is a volume which cannot be ignored, for it has been published at a strategic and appropriate time when there is growing concern regarding reappraisal of measurement and evaluation on the secondary-school level.

Personnel & Guid J 35:472–3 Mr '57. Wm. C. Cottle. * Part II dealing with the study of the individual and Part III centering about the improvement of instruction are spotty and need to be read carefully to detect errors of omission and commission. For example, Chapter 8 does a good job of presenting theoretical aspects of personal-social adjustment, yet minor distractors like the term "unadjusted students" (p. 136) are included. (There is no student without some kind of adjustment.) Except for these, the sections dealing with the nature of personal-social adjustment are excellent. The poorest parts of the book are those dealing with measured vocational interest and personality inventories. These parts are somewhat naive and relatively unsophisticated. The Strong Vocational Interest Blank for Men is discussed as contrasting the interests of occupational groups versus "men-in-general" (p. 112). Changing this to read "professional men-in-general" would be more accurate * An actual error occurs in the discussion of the Kuder-Vocational and the California Occupational Interest Inventory. The text says, "Both inventories have separate *forms* for men and women students" (p. 113). The purpose of using personality inventories to get at how a person feels about himself is confused with trying to get at "facts" by such an instrument. This is illustrated in the discussion of items using the word "frequently" (p. 148). Frankness of response is stressed instead of involuntary bias in discussing the validity of these inventories. No discussion of criterion groups is given in the discussion of validity of the inventories. There is a good section dealing with sociometrics included in Chapter 9. However, no general warning is given that the sociometric choices apply only to the original purpose for which they are made. * No reference is made to Pauline Pepinsky's excellent article on sociometrics or to Mary Northway's *Primer of Sociometry*. Part III dealing with the improvement of instruction covers classroom and standardized tests. The chapters on diagnosis and test construction are best in this section with an excellent statement about the values of combining essay and objective tests (p. 234). All the subject fields are covered adequately * Each chapter has a good summary which does a better job than the table of contents in showing what the chapter covers. * In conclusion, this reviewer would recommend the book as a supplementary text for beginning classes in guidance and as a possible text in measurement courses. However, specific inadequacies would need to be pointed out by the instructor when the text is used in this fashion.

[B21]

★Adcock, C. J. **Factorial Analysis for Non-Mathematicians.** Melbourne, Australia: Melbourne University Press, 1954. Pp. 88. (London and New York: Cambridge University Press, 1954; 1955. 17s. 6d.; $3.00.) * (PA 29:4896)

Brit J Psychol 46:158 My '55. Arthur Summerfield. * Criticisms from the point of view of factor analysis are that the basis of factorial methods is not said to be measurements but correlations, that no account is given of how product-moment correlation comes logically to be involved, that use of the tetrachoric coefficient is even made to appear better, and that the mistaken procedure of inserting new communalities for the calculation of each successive centroid factor is advocated. The statistician can also point to the isolation of the discussion from any general consideration of statistical methods and their requirements. The main commentary is contained in chapters on the logic of factor analysis, rotation, interpretation of factors and the role of factor analysis.

Here the arguments advanced can be held to suffer from their brevity and may be found persuasive rather than logically compelling. With qualifications, therefore, the book has much to recommend it as a teaching device, and it is of interest for its straightforward presentation and comparisons of the principal methods of group factor analysis.

Ed & Psychol Meas 15:520–1 w '55. Anne Anastasi. * Adcock's....aim is to present the fundamental logic and methodology of factor analysis in as nearly non-mathematical terms as possible. No previous knowledge of statistics is assumed and mathematical symbols are scrupulously avoided. The major ideas of factor analysis are expressed in a direct, conversational style and illustrated with simple numerical examples. * The author states that Chapter V should be omitted by readers who are not concerned with the use of factor analysis, although such advice certainly applies as well to the two following chapters. * It is doubtful whether a reader could learn enough about the techniques of factor analysis from this book alone to apply such techniques in actual practice. Moreover, some of the procedures described in Chapters V, VI, and VII may not be comprehensible to the uninitiated reader without supplementary explanations. Apart from these limitations, there are a few minor weaknesses which could easily be remedied in a revised edition. The illustrative interpretation of factors in Chapter VIII could be made more meaningful by the addition of brief descriptions of the variables which were factor analyzed. The reader is now left quite in the dark by a discussion of variables which bear such names as "checking," "obsessional," "poets," and "70/23." The book would also gain from the inclusion of a glossary. For example, such terms as "matrix," "vector," "inverse," and "transpose" are not defined when first used in the text and are never very clearly explained. The practice of printing only the upper half or correlation tables also appears to be a dubious economy, since a number of processes involving column sums would be easier for the beginner to follow if the entire table were visibly before him. The merits of the book, however, far outweigh its possible shortcomings. One of its outstanding features is to be found in the ingenious demonstrations and schematic examples which are used, especially in the early part of the book. Another desirable characteristic is the inclusion of both American and British techniques of factor analysis, unlike other books which deal predominantly with one or the other approach. This book is undoubtedly an excellent introduction for persons who wish merely to understand the major concepts of factor analysis. It should also prove helpful as collateral reading, to clarify and render more vivid the content of the more advanced texts. Similarly, it may be used for review purposes, its very brevity tending to focus attention upon an over-all view of the subject.

Occupational Psychol 29:201 Jl '55. David Duncan. * sets out to cover the essential processes of factor analysis in such a way as to make clear the underlying logic in simple language * The aim of the book is laudable, and it may well succeed in reducing for some the cost, in effort, of acquiring an understanding of factor analysis. It is clearly written and short enough to skim through at a sitting. Even working through it with a pencil and paper, as one must do to understand fully a book of this type, should not be too onerous a task. However, it will not bring applause from all factor analysts, and the reader should be warned of its main shortcoming. One would have liked to see in this book some recognition and a more balanced assessment of the fundamental and important work done by Spearman in this field. * Such scant treatment for the inventor of factor analysis does no credit to the science. * As a sort of powder for those who are upset by this book, the reviewer would recommend as supplementary reading Chapter VIII, pp. 158–170, of Professor Vernon's book *The Measurement of Abilities* (University of London Press, 1940), where a more objective general account of factor analysis may be found. * Where many reliable tests can be given to many people, factor analysis can be a powerful tool. But in the industrial world such tests and samples are the exception rather than the rule, and the possibilities of factor analysis are limited. Of more timely service to the statistician in industry would be a method of intercorrelating observations over time, such as indices of production, labour stability, turnover, absence, and quality of work, and extracting the principal factors from them.

[B22]

★Adcock, C. J. **Intelligence and High Level Achievement.** Victoria University College, Publica-

tions in Psychology, No. 1. Wellington, New Zealand: Department of Psychology, Victoria University College, 1952. Pp. 27. Paper, mimeographed. Out of print. * (*PA* 28:9034)

Brit J Ed Psychol 24:126–7 Je '54. P. E. Vernon. Psychologists in New Zealand work under considerable difficulties because of their isolation, and in particular, they lack outlets for publications. Thus one welcomes the appearance of a new series of short monographs from Wellington, which has the largest Department in the country. Considering, though, that the contents are duplicated, not printed, it seems a pity that room could not be made for the Appendix giving the detailed tables, to which several references are made in the text. Dr. Adcock is interested in studying the structure of abilities among intelligent adults, such as psychology and education students. Though the work reported here is technically skilled, its appearance is perhaps a little premature. The application of very miscellaneous batteries of tests to groups of about fifty students at a time, and their inter-correlation by the tetrachoric technique, could only be expected to yield highly irregular factorial results which are almost impossible to interpret with any degree of objectivity. However, if the researches provide a basis for the construction of several tests for each of the alleged factors, which can then be explored more thoroughly, a useful contribution may have been made which might link up with work in this country on student selection, and with the large-scale investigations of high-level abilities that Guilford is carrying out in America.

[B23]

★Adkins, Dorothy C., and Lyerly, Samuel B; with the assistance of Goldie Demb and Daniel W. Campbell. **Factor Analysis of Reasoning Tests.** Chapel Hill, N.C.: University of North Carolina Press, 1952. Pp. iv, 122. Paper, mimeographed. $2.00. (London: Oxford University Press. 16s.) * (*PA* 26:4652)

J Ed Psychol 44:189–91 Mr '53. Edward E. Cureton. * This study shows a remarkable number of points of disagreement with previous factor analyses. Since it is the first major study aimed specifically at determining the nature of the factors in the reasoning domain, some disagreement with the results of previous work is to be expected. However, the points of difference are so numerous and serious that to the present reviewer the substantive findings (the factors) must still be considered tentative, and their interpretations hypothetical. It is possible that a re-analysis of these data might result in a large improvement in the interpretability of the results. The authors indicate that their subjects also took all tests of the Army Classification battery, and that the intercorrelations among the ten tests of that battery, as well as their cross-correlations with the sixty-six variables of the present study, were computed. The use of some at least of these additional test scores would undoubtedly improve the definition of some of the reasoning factors, and especially of some of the reference factors. It is also probable that in the case of these data a recomputation by principal axes or maximum likelihood would yield a sharp cut-off of common factor variance after the fourteenth or perhaps some earlier factor. A new rotation might then provide a much clearer picture. It is very much to be hoped that such a re-analysis will be made. The reviewer is impressed by the effort and ingenuity that have gone into this study, but disappointed by the inconclusiveness of the results. His own evaluation suggests that this inconclusiveness may possibly not be intrinsic to the data.

Psychometrika 18:182–4 Je '53. Lyle V. Jones. * The interpretations which appear in the book, in general, are convincing. They depend not only upon the characteristics of tests exhibiting high factor loadings, but also upon the nature of tests not exhibiting high factor loadings—it is often of critical importance to discover "Why not?" There is apparently a tacit recognition of the provisional character necessarily imposed, by inherent limitations of factor analysis, upon interpretations of rotated factors. The frequent references to earlier studies are of considerable aid to the reader in establishing similarities between factors here reported and those identified in previous investigations of mental abilities. Differences, too, are reported, particularly with respect to the Air Force studies. There is discovered no correspondence between the characteristics of the several reasoning factors discussed in the Air Force Report No. 5 and those of the reasoning factors isolated here. To the reviewer the interpretations of the present study seem to provide a more satisfactory picture of reasoning abilities and the interpretations make good sense, psychologically. However, further investigation of the discrepancies certainly is warranted. In most respects, this book is ex-

tremely comprehensive. Each test is described succinctly in terms of content, time limits, scoring formula, etc., and both raw score and normalized score frequency distributions are exhibited. Complete tables of test intercorrelations and of 16th-factor residuals are presented, in addition to tables of centroid and oblique factor loadings, the transformation matrix, and the matrix of cosines of reference vectors. Useful information which might have been presented, but is not, includes the distribution of number of items completed on each test (from which it would be possible to obtain an estimate of the level of chance performance) and graphical representation of pairs of reasoning factors (to supply pictorial guidance for the assessment of interrelations among these factors). This work provides considerable advance toward the goal of organizing our knowledge of reasoning abilities. The study supplies a framework of hypotheses, the confirmation or revision of which might be expected to lead directly to stable primary abilities of reasoning. In addition to serving as a guide valuable to both theoreticians and practitioners interested in the measurement of intellective functions, the study serves as an example of one of the most fruitful applications of factor analysis methods.

[B24]

★Ahmann, J. Stanley, and Glock, Marvin D. **Evaluating Pupil Growth.** Boston, Mass.: Allyn & Bacon, Inc., 1959. Pp. xiii, 605. *

[B25]

★Ahmavaara, Yrjö. **On the Unified Factor Theory of Mind.** Annals of the Finnish Academy of Science and Letters, Series B, No. 106. Helsinki, Finland: Suomalainen Tiedeakatemia, Academia Scientiarum Fennica, 1957. Pp. 176. Paper. 750 mk. *

[B26]

★Ahmavaara, Yrjö. **Transformation Analysis of Factorial Data and Other New Analytical Methods of Differential Psychology With Their Application to Thurstone's Basic Studies.** Annals of the Finnish Academy of Science and Letters, Series B, No. 88, Part 2. Helsinki, Finland: Suomalainen Tiedeakatemia, Academia Scientiarum Fennica, 1954. Pp. 150. Paper. * (*PA* 29:8182)

Am J Psychol 69:332–4 Je '56. Henry F. Kaiser and William B. Michael. * To summarize, Ahmavaara has in Part I presented his fundamental contribution, the transformation method. This method is probably the best extant for scientifically adjudicating the most important psychological question in factor analysis: are factors true, invariant psychological entities, or are they merely convenient descriptive variables? Chapter III applies the method in a straight-forward manner to the classic PMA studies. It is regrettable that the last four chapters appear with the first three, for they only dilute the impact of the earlier, very significant contributions. In a sense this book is a study in contradiction. The last half, in which Ahmavaara often engages in wild flights of speculation, contains just the sort of material which Ahmavaara's transformation method seeks to put out of business. [See original review for additional critical comments not excerpted.]

Cont Psychol 1:50–1 F '56. Joseph R. Royce. One of the most important methodological issues in factor analysis today has to do with the problems of factorial invariance. What happens to a factor, we ask, when tests are added to a test battery or subtracted from it, or when older or younger subjects are used as the experimental population? * The major portion of this monograph is concerned with providing a methodological answer to this problem. In Part I of the monograph Dr. Ahmavaara develops the mathematics and the theory for the "transformation method." * In the application of the "transformation method" to Thurstone's Primary Mental Abilities in Part II of the monograph, Dr. Ahmavaara's invariance coefficients indicate that factors V, W, and S are invariant, but that factors N, R, and P are not. At this point we come up against a weakness in an otherwise flawless procedure. Now that we have the invariance coefficients, how shall we interpret them? How large do the values of the normalized transformation matrix have to be in order to indicate invariance? For example, in Table 16 Dr. Ahmavaara lists seven invariance coefficients for seven factors as follows: $N = .744$, $W = .979$, $S = .968$, $V = .967$, $M = .929$, $R = .848$, $P = .689$. From these data, he concludes that "the result shown in Table 16 is clear enough: among the actual intellective factors the factors W, S, and V turn out to be highly invariant with their invariance coefficients well over .960, whereas the invariance coefficient of all the other intellective factors are conspicuously low." A value of .848 does not seem to be much below the value of .967. Furthermore, he seems to beg the issue regarding the intermediate case of factor M with an invariance coefficient of .929. Lacking a standard-error formula or other criteria as a basis

for drawing the line as to whether a given coefficient reveals "invariance," it must be admitted that the "relative" basis used by Ahmavaara is the only procedure open to him at present. It would appear to be premature, however, to make firm decisions regarding invariance on such a statistically inadequate basis. Several other less important methodological and theoretical concepts are taken up in the third and final portion of the monograph. The most important of these is the "method of residual spectra." This monograph contributes unification to the factorial literature, and the reviewer finds it exciting. There seems little doubt that in the future, in addition to "factoring" and "rotating," factor analysts will be computing "transformations," thereby linking factors in the study at hand with other factor studies pertaining to the same domain.

[B27]

★AHMAVAARA, YRJÖ, AND MARKKANEN, TOUKO. **The Unified Factor Model: Its Position in Psychometric Theory and Application to Sociological Study.** Finnish Foundation for Alcohol Studies, Alcohol Research in the Northern Countries, Vol. 7. Stockholm, Sweden: Almqvist & Wiksell, 1958. Pp. 188. Paper. Sw. kr. 18. *

[B28]

★AIKMAN, LOUIS P., AND OSTREICHER, LEONARD M. **Development of an Inventory for Measuring Satisfaction With Student Teaching.** College of the City of New York, Division of Teacher Education, Office of Research and Evaluation, Publication No. 22. New York: Office of Research and Evaluation, the Division, July 1954. Pp. iii, 22. Paper, mimeographed. $0.75. * (*PA* 29:7979)

[B29]

★AINSWORTH, MARY D., AND AINSWORTH, LEONARD H. **Measuring Security in Personal Adjustment.** Toronto, Canada: University of Toronto Press, 1958. Pp. xiii, 98. $2.95. (London: Oxford University Press. 24s.) * (*PA* 32:5224)

[B30]

*AIR UNIVERSITY, AIR COMMAND AND STAFF SCHOOL. **Evaluation in Air Force Instruction, Revised Edition: Academic Instructor Course, Vol. II.** Maxwell Air Force Base, Ala.: Air University, November 1953. Pp. vi, 90. Paper. *

Ed Res B 32:163 S 16 '53. Robert E. Hubbard. * most of the text is concerned with the practical aspects of test construction, scoring, and analysis. One chapter presents a brief discussion of problems of marking. * the booklet would be of most value to the novice in the field of testing. The two chapters concerned with construction of test items follow a pattern of presenting a "poor" item and then an "improved" version of the same item. The principles of good test construction are made quite clear through this procedure. In general, the entire publication is written in a clear and direct style *

[B31]

★ALEXANDER, THERON. The Adult-Child Interaction Test: A Projective Test for Use in Research. Monographs of the Society for Research in Child Development, Vol. 27, No. 2, Serial No. 55. Lafayette, Ind.: Child Development Publications, Inc., 1955. Pp. v, 40, plus 8 cards. Paper. Out of print. (PA 29:7252)

Brit J Psychol 46:320 N '55. H. Phillipson. "This test is planned to give information primarily about perceptive experience of adults in reference to children and children's perception of adults." As such the test contains the germ of a valuable idea for a projective approach. But the method here developed is disappointing. The rationale offered neglects the more important questions concerning perception and personality, nor does it give any framework within which to think about motivations in terms of interpersonal relations. In the few pages devoted to the theoretical basis of the test we find vague generalizations which gloss over these important issues. * With such a general basis and with only the most slender references to any clinical appraisal of behaviour, it is not surprising that the selection of picture situations shows no originality, that the method of analysis provides little of insight into personality dynamics and that the conclusions seem naïve and superficial.

[B32]

★ALLEN, ROBERT M. Elements of Rorschach Interpretation: With an Extended Bibliography. New York: International Universities Press, Inc., 1954. Pp. 242. $4.00. * (PA 29:2424)

Am J Mental Def 59:698-9 Ap '55. William M. Cruickshank. The most valuable portion of this book is the extended bibliography of references pertinent to Rorschach interpretation included by the author. It is difficult indeed to determine the use to which this work may be put. The author states that "the purpose of this volume is to introduce the beginner to the complexities of evaluating and interpreting the various components of the Rorschach protocol." It escapes this reviewer to ascertain the contribution which the author makes in this regard as opposed to the much more basic, thoughtful, comprehensive, and accurate previous works of Klopfer, Beck, Halpern, or Piotrowski. In general the volume is character-

ized by lightness and superficiality. The offhand approach of the author is neither pertinent nor appropriate, and serves to disturb the thoughtful reader. The author warns the reader that his book will result in "raised eyebrows, quizzical expressions, and vehement verbalizations—pro and con." He has succeeded in producing each of these responses in this reviewer, save one—verbalizations "pro." The Rorschach Test is founded in a specific psychoanalytic frame of reference. This fact has been overlooked by the author. He has presented information encompassing the various points of departure of several of the leading authorities on the Rorschach Test. In his attempt to approach the problem from an eclectic point of view he has achieved confusion and has produced a mass of data, some conflicting, which is inappropriate for a "beginner." The Rorschach Test is an important, complicated, delicate psychological instrument. It is a tool which requires that the examiner be well oriented in psychology, abnormal psychology, and psychopathology. For a beginner who has the background of professional preparation and clinical experience required, the text is essentially naive. For one who does not have the background, the volume would be confusing and inappropriate. This reviewer does not want to leave the impression that the data included in the text is inaccurate. The data which has been included in the volume is accurate. The limited presentation of a complicated problem and the superficiality of treatment of almost every aspect of the problems of interpretation included within the book render the accuracy of the data ineffectual.

J Consult Psychol 19:235 Je '55. J. R. Wittenborn. Although....presented at a rather elementary level, it can scarcely be claimed that the elements of Rorschach interpretation receive a comprehensive treatment. * In general, his discussions are rich in claims for the significance of Rorschach responses, but poor in rational and empirical justification for these claims. To a conspicuous degree, the textbook is a recital of the point of view, opinions, insights, and practices of the author. It does not appear to be an impersonal presentation of commonly accepted elemental bases for Rorschach interpretations.

J Proj Tech 20:88 Mr '56. Fred J. Goldstein. * To all intents and purposes, this book offers nothing new, and doesn't do as well as some of the recent revisions of Beck and Klopfer, or the new texts by Sarason, and Schafer. * The author prefers an oversimplified, additive approach for the beginning student on pedagogical grounds, while the present reviewer would incline more towards approaches that stimulate and challenge the student rather than baby him. However, telling the student that sequential analysis is to appear in the next installment, and then leaning heavily on just such techniques in the case examples might confuse the beginner. Also the introduction of auxiliary data (not presented to the reader) in the test write-ups might prove equally confusing. On pragmatic grounds, too, the present reviewer would question the desirability of deliberate omission of other clinical data, language cues, and nosological types that would be part of one's daily experience in any clinic setting. Since Dr. Allen is an active contributor to Rorschach experimental literature, it was hoped to find a fairly critical treatment of the role of color, the nature of the evidence for various determinants, etc. Unfortunately in this text, the author abandons the critical role, choosing instead to rely on the clinical impression of usefulness of the Rorschach rather than on experimental data. In his theoretical discussions he was most disappointing for the present reviewer. His definition of perception is perhaps the clearest example of what the reviewer objects to. "Normal perception is a function of anxiety threat inherent in the field stimuli as he (the subject) sees them." (p. 18). The implication that the New Look in perception has dethroned the physical world, the role of light and the visual threshold or at least that such aspects become less important is strongly implied. Even in current psychoanalytic discussions one finds the admission of a conflict-free sphere of perceptual functioning. The perceptual styles suggested by the Klein group, for example, emerge when the role of physical characteristics such as lighting, time of exposure (or formal definiteness) have been minimized. The philosophical, non-objective implications of Stern's statement that has so impressed Dr. Allen, "Keine Gestalt, ohne Gestalter" need not concern us here. Despite these various objections, the book is easy to read, has a very valuable bibliography, and should readily acquaint the beginning student with some of the procedures of the clinical psychologist. For the more advanced student,

this text is not a match for some of those currently available.

[B33]

★ALLEN, ROBERT M. **Guide to Psychological Tests and Measurements.** Coral Gables, Fla.: University of Miami Press, 1954. Pp. iv, 116 (half the pages are blank). $1.25. * (PA 29:4897)

Ed & Psychol Meas 16:167–9 sp '56. *William Coleman.* * more of an outline than a complete book * a number of statements....need to be expanded for greater clarity or documented more fully if they are to be accepted * In summation, it does not seem to the reviewer that many instructors will find the present edition of "Guide to Psychological Tests and Measurements" as useful as the books by Anastasi, Cronbach, Freeman, Goodenough, or Remmers and Gage.

[B34]

★ALLEN, ROBERT M. **Introduction to the Rorschach Technique: Manual of Administration and Scoring.** New York: International Universities Press, Inc., 1953. Pp. ii, 126. Paper. $3.00. * (London: Bailey Bros. & Swinfen, Ltd. 24s.) (PA 28:2607)

J Proj Tech 18:252–3 Je '54. *Mortimer M. Meyer.* * the paper is of good quality; the print, even in footnotes, is highly readable; and the general format well planned * specifically planned for the beginner * The author points out the wisdom of having the subject sit in a position so that the examiner can observe all facial reactions. However, with the position indicated in the drawing, it is difficult to see how such observation can be made. The Second section goes into a simple explanation of scoring and includes many illustrations of the various scorings. Such illustrations are valuable additions to any beginner's text. On the whole, the author follows Klopfer's modifications of Rorschach except for the use of Rorschach's F plus and F minus. In a footnote (pg. 44) the author comments, "Neutral F is also used by some Rorschach workers in those instances where there is ambivalence between F plus and F minus. This should be kept to a minimum since it solves nothing. To this reviewer it seems as though the author is missing the basic concept in the so-called neutral F since, as in all other normally distributed scores, it provides a category for the usual response and thus actually sharpens the meaning of F plus and F minus scores and avoids the arbitrary forcing of responses into two categories. With the two category plan there is no indication from the F minus score whether the minus quality is a negligible one or a serious deviation from the usual response whereas with the three categories the plus or minus following an F is an immediate indication of variance from the usual. In the section on scoring, two minor errors were noted. One is page 39 where the "dx" score is attributed to Klopfer. It should be attributed to Beck. The second is on page 50 where the author reports Klopfer as scoring imposed expressions such as grinning masks as Fm. Actually Klopfer scores an F with an additional m. Where an actual face is seen with such expression the score is M. A more important misinterpretation, on page 68, results from the acceptance of a quotation from Buhler which states, "Scores are listed as main and additional in order of appearance, with the exception of certain signs which have preference over others, e.g. M scores precede all other signs, bright color scores (not C') rank second, FM third, Fc scores fourth. The other signs follow without discrimination. This rule corresponds to Klopfer's present technique." This is a distortion of Klopfer's statement that when two determinants within the same response seem to be of equal stimulus value, use the above as a rule of thumb. To follow the rule as rigidly as stated must cause distortions. For example, in a response such as two roosters fighting and they have red combs, the color is only an accessory, yet to follow the rule, the color score would come first. Similarly with a well described vista response if a small or tiny detail suggesting a human in movement is included the M would have to be scored first, if the rule is followed. The third section deals with inquiry, testing the limits, and computations. The author makes an important point in the opening of this section. He points out that "The temptation to pass over commonly produced and popular responses without inquiry may lead to a serious error in scoring and interpretation in addition to poor testing habits." (pg. 81). He then proceeds to suggest techniques for eliciting additional information to round out the examination. In a footnote on page 96 he states that, "the inquiry and Testing the Limits assume an intimate knowledge of the test itself, otherwise the kind of information sought will represent trial-and-error fumbling rather than directed and purposeful questioning." The reviewer agrees with this whole-heartedly but must raise a fundamental

question at this point about the many presentations, including the one being reviewed, in which scoring is taught as a blind technique instead of teaching it in integration with basic interpretation. Since inquiry and testing of limits can have little meaning without a knowledge of the meaning of the Rorschach technique in its entirety, the teaching of scoring as a separate item results in the tendency for students to worship scoring as an entity in itself rather than as a shorthand method of recording the responses. It also results in the inefficient process of requiring the student to learn scoring and then to have to re-learn it in association with its meaning. In general, the book fulfills the author's stated purpose of being a highly simplified presentation, helpful to the beginner when the Manual is used as an adjunct to the teaching situation.

Psychiatric Q Sup 27:318 pt 2 '53. * In general, it is well written, but it would seem that in places the material is rather advanced for the beginning student. The book should also be of value as a laboratory source and reference work in scoring of this test. It can be criticized on the grounds that it is too concise in discussing some of the important determinant areas, and also in that it does not give sufficient examples of borderline type responses—something which would be of value to the student in scoring.

Q R Biol 29:299–300 S '54. Myrtle Astrachan. * largely a repetition of what is available in several standard texts on the Rorschach test.

[B35]

★Allen, Robert M. **Personality Assessment Procedures: Psychometric, Projective, and Other Approaches.** New York: Harper & Brothers, 1958. Pp. xi, 541. $6.00. *

[B36]

★American Association of Examiners and Administrators of Educational Personnel. **Principles and Procedures of Teacher Selection: A Monograph.** Philadelphia, Pa.: the Association (c/o W. C. Hopkins, Board of Education), 1952. Pp. viii, 146. Paper, lithotyped. $5.00. *

J Teach Ed 4:322 D '53. Harrison F. Heath. This report is the outcome of more than ten years of collective thinking, discussion, investigating, and concluding by this Association. It is intended to serve as a reference to be used by superintendents, examiners, educational personnel workers, and members of boards of education. It aims to help in placing teacher selection on a high professional level, as independent as possible of political considerations. According to this monograph, the appointment of every teacher results from an examination of some sort, ranging from a superficial inspection of a set of credentials to a most extensive and exacting battery of tests. It is gratifying to note that modern principles of testing are suggested for every sort of examining procedure, insofar as applicable. All evidence acquired should be valid, *i.e.,* pertinent to the task; it should be reliable, which is to say coherent and consistent; it should be as objective as possible in situations where subjective humans are appraising other humans; and it should be comparable with similar evidence collected about other candidates. Although pointedly suggesting the Educational Testing Service's annual, nine-hour National Teacher Examinations as excellent and growing in reputation and use, the report recognizes that many local examining boards devise written tests of their own, covering not only subject matter of instruction but also a knowledge of educational principles and procedures, general cultural background, reasoning ability and other aspects of intellectual fitness. The section on the improvement of test construction is excellent, even if brief. There is even a section on improving essay tests, the crux of the advice being to ask more questions with shorter discussion of each, and to develop scoring keys that are at least semi-objective. Non-written examinations, including interviews, evaluation of transcripts and credentials, observation of the candidate's teaching or other project work, and the like, are lower in reliability than written tests, but they may well be, and often are, more valid and useful. The report is very sane and helpful in the treatment of these techniques. The process of teacher selection is closely related to recruitment, and the various techniques of appraisal should be applied throughout the whole period of preparation. Even in these days of critical shortages of teachers, employers are entitled to feel that teacher training institutions have made careful, objective, unbiased evaluation of their graduating candidates, and are frank and honest in reporting the results. In the college where I work, I am sure this monograph will prove to be a valuable handbook for members of our teacher selection committee, and a useful reference in our courses in educational measurement.

[B37]

★AMERICAN BANKERS ASSOCIATION, CUSTOMER AND PERSONNEL RELATIONS DEPARTMENT. **Clerical Testing in Banks.** New York: the Association, 1952. Pp. v, 65. Paper, spiral binding. $3.00. * (*PA 27*:2228)

Personnel J 3:69 Je '52. * report of a study conducted over a period of more than two years by the American Bankers Association * 126 banks cooperated in the program and test scores were obtained from more than 30,000 job applicants. The report outlines the role of tests in selection and placement; it discusses the qualities of a good test; describes the requirements for administration of a test program; and then describes the methods used in this program. Much space is devoted to two tables of norms and to describing those tests which were found useful. One chapter is devoted to a description of validation studies which were carried out in a number of banks. Actual results are reported, indicating that a number of different test batteries were found efficient in predicting success among clerical applicants. The report will repay careful study by anyone interested in the problem of test selection and placement, since much of the work done by bank clerks is like clerical work everywhere. The success of this impressive study is due to the vision and persistence of Mr. Powers who has succeeded in proving to many banks that the proper use of tests will improve clerical selection and save money for the employer.

[B38]

★AMERICAN COUNCIL ON EDUCATION, COMMITTEE ON THE EVALUATION OF THE TYLER FACT-FINDING STUDY OF THE AMERICAN COUNCIL ON EDUCATION. **Conclusions and Recommendations on a Study of the General Educational Development Testing Program.** Washington, D.C.: the Council, 1956. Pp. xv, 72. Paper. $1.00. *

[B39]

★AMERICAN GAS ASSOCIATION, PERSONNEL COMMITTEE. **Personnel Testing in the Gas Industry.** New York: the Association, January 1952. Pp. 10. Paper. *

[B40]

★AMES, LOUISE BATES; LEARNED, JANET; MÉTRAUX, RUTH W.; AND WALKER, RICHARD N. **Child Rorschach Responses: Developmental Trends From Two to Ten Years.** New York: Paul B. Hoeber, Inc., 1952. Pp. xv, 310. $7.50. * (London: Hamish Hamilton Ltd., 52s. 6d.) (*PA 27*:7066)

Am J Psychother 6:582–4 Jl '52. M. L. Aronson. * contains the most comprehensive and satisfactory normative data on children's Rorschach responses yet approached * One of the most striking results of this study is the fact that many Rorschach responses which would be considered pathological in adult records, may occur with considerable frequency in the records of children who appear to be reasonably well-adjusted both on other tests and on clinical observation. Thus, for example, "contaminations" (two entirely incompatible interpretations simultaneously given to the same area of the inkblot) are found quite commonly in the records of normal children from 4½ to 5½ years of age: most authorities would consider such responses to be at least highly suggestive of schizophrenia if they occurred in an adult record. Not only individual responses but also the overall configuration of the average child's Rorschach, at certain age levels, may closely resemble the pattern seen in the records of seriously disturbed adults. * Probably the most important theoretical finding of this study is the fact that the personality picture revealed by the Rorschach at any given age level has unique and distinctive qualities which set it quite apart from the pattern of every other age level. Or, as the authors put it, "each age level has its own essence and characteristicness." * Unfortunately, the authors make no attempt to relate their results to postulates of the psychoanalytic theory of psychosexual development. It is recognized that it would be extremely difficult, in practice, to translate the usual Rorschach scoring indices into psychoanalytic terms. Nevertheless, the task does not appear to be an impossible one, and it is to be hoped, it will be attempted in the future. Certainly, the results would be of considerable theoretical interest. In summary, this book can be recommended as an important contribution to the Rorschach literature on child development. It will, undoubtedly, prove of great practical use to those who use the Rorschach as a technique for understanding the behavior of children. The mere accumulation of group norms, of course, will not in itself enable the inexperienced Rorschach worker to arrive at a rich and clinically meaningful description of the individual child,—just as it would not suffice in the interpretation of an adult record. Nevertheless, the results of a study of this type can appreciably shorten the tedious process of building up a personal frame of reference, and what is more important, it can help to correct

the distortions which inevitably color "subjective norms." Since much of this book is rather technical and assumes some familiarity with the mechanics of the Rorschach, it will probably not be of much interest to the general reader. However, to those who are interested in theoretical aspects of child development, it is recommended that at least the non-technical conclusions of the study be consulted. These conclusions suggest many fascinating hypotheses and they should lead to further, much needed research.

[B41]

★AMES, LOUISE BATES; LEARNED, JANET; MÉTRAUX, RUTH W.; AND WALKER, RICHARD N. **Rorschach Responses in Old Age.** New York: Paul B. Hoeber, Inc., 1954. Pp. xv, 229. $6.75. * (PA 29:637)

Am J Psychother 8:771–2 O '54. Warner L. Lowe. * Despite some limitations,....[this volume] is an insightful and workmanlike piece of research * Only with the accumulation of longitudinal data can scientific understanding and prediction of behavior be envisaged. The author's own contribution in this respect is limited to data concerning eight subjects between the ages of seventy-two and ninety-nine who were given a second Rorschach two years after the first. Furthermore, the study cannot be considered as statistically representative, and the analysis of the responses is carried out without attempts at validation by means of additional clinical, historical or other test data. In the absence of information about dynamic processes in subjects throughout the years, categorized Rorschach records of aged people give the impression of snapshots sorted on the basis of an arbitrary number of known characteristics with which individuals of more or less similar features are henceforth to be compared. *

J Proj Tech 19:78–9 Mr '55. Mortimer M. Meyer. * deals with the much needed area of norms in the Rorschach technique * In the normal group half were institutionalized and half non-institutionalized but in the two other groups more than two-thirds were in institutions. Some of the comparative measures given might be open to question. However, the presentation of the collection of this much needed material, even if only for use of the non-comparative data, is a most worthwhile and useful work. The book is neatly organized so that its use as a reference text is most convenient. There are sections on statistical presentation of results, attempts to structure the collective personality as represented by the Rorschach responses, and sample records with extremely brief interpretations. This reviewer has much question about the suitability of using the mean or presentation of the determinants as organized at the beginning of each classification, a procedure used in the previous publication also. To indicate that .1 C or .3 FC is typical for a group is suggestive of slavish adherence to statistics without recognition for the fact that these results have no real meaning. It may be that for some groups it is not possible to present some findings but certainly it would be more meaningful to state simply as is done in Table 10 that 52% of the group use M's or perhaps that 75% of the group use 1 M and 25% 2 M's and so on. A second question which this reviewer would raise is the basis for the decision to use a European form of scoring. The investigators mention their awareness that this is a form of scoring unfamiliar to the majority of American workers but nevertheless follow it. The use of a foreign scoring method in an American publication not only means the introduction of another scoring scheme to the American scene but it means a reduction in the usefulness of their data in this country. Without the original data even those hardy souls who would attempt the translation, are unable to do so. In the analysis of the data, the authors present a number of guides for distinguishing the normal, the pre-senile, and the senile. They indicate that there is not only a difference in frequency of certain signs but a gestalt difference as well. A cross-validation would seem a most desirable step at this point to insure the accuracy of the conclusions especially in view of the possible biased sampling. All taken into account, this series of publications needs to be studied thoroughly by every serious Rorschach worker. It is to be hoped that the authors' investigations will not stop with this series but will proceed to the next and vital step of examining the relationship between these findings and prediction, since even within this presentation, interpretations are made as if the psychological significance of the findings had been as carefully evaluated as are the normative data presented.

[B42]

★ANASTASI, ANNE. **Psychological Testing.** New York: Macmillan Co., 1954. Pp. xiii, 682. $6.75. * (London: Macmillan & Co. Ltd. 47s.) (PA 29:901)

Brit J Med Psychol 28:86–7 pt 1 '55. R. W. Pickford. * a very thorough and complete survey of the whole field of mental testing * a description of the tests, will be a valuable addition to the library of the clinical psychologist and every other person interested in mental measurement and the study of personality *

Brit J Psychol 45:311 N '54. G. A. Foulds. * The book is written in a style very much more familiar to British readers than is customary in American publications on Psychology. Such readers may, however, be somewhat disturbed at finding no reference to Burt, Thomson or Vernon in the discussion on Factor Analysis and only about three or four references to British tests. Readers in other European countries may be similarly dismayed. If the Monroe Doctrine is to apply to Psychology, Professor Anastasi's book would lose nothing by being re-named *Psychological Testing in America.* In spite of this ruffling of European pride, it is unlikely that serious students of psychological testing will find this book other than skilful in presentation, balanced in judgement and generally much too good to miss.

Brit J Stat Psychol 7:125 N '54. Florence Mitchell. * As the book is designed for practical workers, the author rightly decided that, instead of the usual "statistical chapter," it would be better to introduce statistical concepts as they are needed, explaining each in an appropriate context. British readers may at times be tempted to criticize the context chosen. Writers in this country seem usually to start off with the results of factor analysis, as indicating the chief distinguishable aspects of human personality which the psychologist is called upon to test. In the present volume factor analysis is not mentioned until we reach Part III (the differential testing of special abilities). Consequently, the evidence for accepting the concept of a "general cognitive ability," distinct from "special or group factors," is omitted. Dr. Anastasi, however, explains that "intelligence tests are now more properly described as general classification tests." Even so, however, if a *general* classification is to claim validity, that surely can only be done by demonstrating the presence of a *general* factor. No doubt factorial analyses by themselves can do no more than confirm such a hypothesis; but its advocates usually contend that it is supported by experimental, neurological, and biological evidence as well. Some critics too will also question the historical account of early British work. We are told that the factorial method was "initiated by Charles Spearman," and that later "American investigators, such as Kelley and Thurstone, proposed a number of group factors, rather than a single *g* factor." Spearman, however, claimed, not to initiate, but merely to correct and simplify the earlier multifactor techniques developed by Pearson and his followers. And the distinction between "general ability" and "special abilities" was due not to Spearman but to Galton. These, however, are minor points; and every reader will readily acknowledge the clear and scholarly way in which the author has discussed both problems and procedures.

J Consult Psychol 18:472 D '54. Ann Margaret Garner. * a carefully planned and integrated volume, which begins with a consideration of the principles of psychological testing, proceeds to employ carefully selected examples of tests of general classification, aptitude, and achievement, and ends with measures of personality characteristics ranging from inventories through projective techniques and situational tests. In every instance, the instruments selected for illustration are representative, and their advantages and shortcomings are handled critically. Although the book is primarily a college text, it cannot fail to attract the attention of practicing psychometricians and clinicians. Particularly important for both students and practitioners are the sections on the ethics of control of tests, on test validity, on the limitations of infant and preschool tests, and on the peculiar characteristics of projective techniques and situational tests.

J Ed Res 49:70–1 S '55. B. Fruchter. * a competent, encyclopedic treatment of modern psychological testing * A useful list of references is given at the end of each chapter. The book is profusely illustrated with specimen test pages and other materials that will provide useful aids in teaching. The broad up-to-date coverage of this book and its emphasis on principles should make it an excellent introduction to the field of psychological testing as well as a useful guide to the professional worker. It will need supplementation, however, in courses where the emphasis is on educational testing.

Occupational Psychol 29:269 O '55. Alec Rodger. Professor Anastasi's aim has been "to provide an introduction to the principles of psychological testing....to acquaint the reader

with the major types of test in current use.... (and) to prepare the reader for the proper evaluation of psychological tests and interpretation of test results." In this she has succeeded very well. Perhaps she is just a little unsatisfactory on factor analysis, homogeneity and percentiles, and has a bee in her bonnet about differential aptitude tests; but it is clear that she is a real expert at her job and at teaching it to others. The reviewer does not know any other book on testing which he would recommend more confidently than this *

Personnel & Guid J 34:244 D '55. Merle M. Ohlsen. * The author's....excellent analysis of current tests, testing problems, and the basic principles of testing should be useful to the personnel specialist as well as to the general psychology student. * The theoretical orientation to tests and their use and the treatment of individual differences are all done exceptionally well. Another outstanding feature of the book is the interpretation of the American Psychological Association's code of ethics with reference to use of tests. Furthermore, the author presents a consistent philosophy of testing throughout the book; she makes a strong case for the factor view of intelligence and differential testing of abilities. * most persons who have not had at least an elementary course in statistics will have difficulty in reading the chapters on test reliability, test validity, item analysis, test norms, and factor analysis * Perhaps in the future editions, she could correct the difficulty by including one or two chapters on the basic statistical concepts * the general psychology student can obtain an exceptionally good orientation to psychological tests, an excellent analysis of tests and their use, and glean many good ideas from the more difficult sections of the book on testing theory and test construction. School counselors, school psychologists, and personnel workers in business and industry should find this book to be a very useful reference—one which they will want in their professional libraries.

Personnel Pract B 11:67–8 Mr '55. R. J. Thomson. * The quality throughout the book is fairly even. However, the explanations of the basic concepts introduced in Part 1 are sometimes too compressed and leave too much to be inferred by the reader, and the section on the Rorschach, in Part 4, appears to state certain criticisms which are not made sufficiently explicit. Anastasi also criticises rather extensively imperfections in the construction and standardisation of the Wechsler-Bellevue, while similar imperfections in the Stanford-Binet are glossed over. To sum up, this is a book for the field worker rather than the research worker, but both should find in it not only material which is new to them, but also a competent exposition and analysis of many features of such basic concepts as reliability, validity, standardisation, item analysis, etc., which too often either have to be accepted on faith by the reader or are treated only at a superficial level by the authors of books about psychological tests.

Psychol B 52:97–8 Ja '55. J. P. Guilford. This book is naturally to be compared within the frame of reference provided by similar works written by Super, Cronbach, Goodenough, and Greene. In this context, Anastasi's book will definitely hold its own. It is scholarly, thoughtful, and thorough. Its coverage is broad, yet there has necessarily been selection. The selection has been generally good and the emphases well placed. As an example of textbook organization and writing, this volume may well serve as a model. In spite of good writing, however, the reading will not be found easy except by the better students. Many well-selected illustrations are incorporated and effectively used. Documentation is quite adequate. * Her evaluations are forthright and unafraid and rarely overlook significant points that can be made. I doubt that anyone can properly charge her with being unfair. She brings into high relief the great amount of floundering that has occurred in connection with attempts to measure deterioration, with projective techniques, and with situational tests. * Like most authors who write about tests, she thinks of them entirely as measures of individual differences. It is time that we broaden this conception and recognize that "occasional differences" are also measured by means of tests and that the experimental psychologist is perpetually using tests for this purpose. In only one important place does the author seem uncritical: when she accepts the "projective line" that projective tests take the "global approach." "Global" is a good-sounding word, but few writers clearly define it or think through the implications of it. While the objective of a "global approach" may be to obtain a greater coverage of an individual's personality and to view intraindividual relationships, a necessary

step is to describe him in terms of trait names. The same objective can also be achieved through other than projective tests. It is difficult to find flaws in this book, technical or otherwise. One or two may be suggested, though some are admittedly debatable. The heading "General Classification Tests" of Part II will be misleading to some readers. As used, it refers to classification in educational and social groups, not classification in job assignments. In discussing the factors in the Stanford-Binet tests, the author, for some reason, bases her conclusions on the abortive analyses of McNemar rather than on the more complete analyses of Jones. Even the Jones analyses probably fail to do justice to the number of factors represented—through no fault of his. It would require additional reference tests to do the job right. A debatable point, which Anastasi recognizes, is the false dichotomy that has persisted between aptitude tests and personality tests. Surely an individual's abilities are a part of his personality. Perhaps we need a contest and a prize for a good term embracing the non-aptitude aspects of personality.

[B43]

★ANDERSON, CHARLES C. **Function Fluctuation.** British Journal of Psychology Monograph Supplements, No. 30. London and New York: Cambridge University Press, 1958. Pp. vii, 104. Paper. 21s.; $4.00. *

[B44]

ANDERSON, HAROLD H., AND ANDERSON, GLADYS L. **An Introduction to Projective Techniques and Other Devices for Understanding the Dynamics of Human Behavior.** New York: Prentice-Hall, Inc., 1951. Pp. xxv, 720. $7.25. *

Am J Psychiatry 109:76–7 Jl '52. Robert I. Watson. * A section of interest to the psychiatrist, quite apart from the major intent of the volume to serve as the introduction to projective techniques, is the last section of the book devoted to projective techniques in therapy. * In meeting the major intent, to serve as an introduction to projective techniques, the editors and authors are eminently successful at the level of specific instruments. For this purpose the volume can be enthusiastically recommended. However, this reviewer must admit to a slight disappointment. In the Preface the editors speak of "a consistent conceptual structure or theory of personality and behavior," and go on to point out that this is an essential element in the training and skill in the use of such techniques. Discussion of this matter, although mentioned by the various authorities in connection with specific techniques or in terms of a particular point of view, is nowhere brought into proper common focus. This necessary introductory or closing summary and integration is conspicuously lacking. The Foreword by Henry A. Murray comes nearest to serving this function but of necessity is far too short to do justice either to his conception of the matter or to the topic itself.

Am J Psychol 66:672–3 O '53. Leslie Phillips. * a thorough, almost encyclopedic, coverage of the field of projective techniques * The treatment is in general thorough and realistic, although the chapters show the uneven quality inevitably associated with separate authorship. There are differences not only in style, quality, and depth, but in the clinical and research emphases underlying the presentation of each technique. Since each author is a leading proponent of the technique he describes, these differences in emphasis undoubtedly reflect the current status of work in the field. *

J Abn & Social Psychol 48:318–20 Ap '53. William Schofield. * In the opening chapter, there is recognition by one of the editors (H.H.A.) that the term *projection* has come to mean many things to many people, but he sees the classical definition a la Freud as a point of orientation for "most of the contributors to this book." That the editing of the book has erred on the side of liberality is suggested by the observation of H. A. Murray in the foreword: "Of projection, according to Freud, I have seen in this collection of papers, practically no evidence." * in view of the several meanings of projection as applied to instruments for personality study and of the heterogeneity of the meanings and techniques subscribed to by the writers appearing in this volume, there is need for a chapter devoted to delineation of the various facets of projection and concerned with a logical ordering of the multitude of procedures which have come to be labeled (or mislabeled) as "projective" techniques. There is such a chapter, by R. B. Cattell, but one may be disturbed to find that it is the third chapter of the book, that it follows rather than precedes an excellent discussion of validation problems (Chapter II by Jean Walker Macfarlane and Read D. Tuddenham) and that the exposition of "Design Principles in Projective Techniques" seems somewhat subservient to an account of the construction,

reliability, and validity of some of Cattell's paper-and-pencil "dynaception tests." Nevertheless, Cattell should be thanked for providing the only systematic development of the psychology of projection in relation to the design of techniques in general, and the editors must be complimented for courage to fly in the face of prevailing cultural winds by including in a volume on projectives a chapter that proposes to measure dynamisms with what superficially appear to be those most unpopular of devices, so-called "structured" tests. What one would ordinarily expect to be the introductory chapter, Chapter One, presents only a fleeting reference to the definitional problem and then develops a theoretical discussion of personality growth. This discussion is pertinent, of course, to projective techniques, as any account of personality development would be. However, the discussion is a general one and not clearly tied to the problems presented by projective theory and devices. In this sense it seems almost detached from the major content of the book and does not properly or adequately serve an introductory function. The lack of an orientational chapter concerned with the definition of terms, a statement of fundamental psychological principles, and a general review of current status might well have been offset by a summary chapter but such a summary is also lacking. More positively, it may be said that the three chapters which constitute Part I, those by H. H. Anderson, Macfarlane and Tuddenham, and Cattell, constitute a more thorough and more critical, albeit somewhat disjointed, introduction to the subject of projective techniques than has been provided in other surveys. * Something of the unevenness of scholarship is attested by the fact that of the three writers who trace the origin of "projection" to Freud, the sources cited in each instance are different and bear the dates 1894, 1933, and 1938 respectively! It is interesting that R. R. Holt in developing the rationale of the TAT does not concern himself with the origins of projection as a recognized dynamism but does draw parallels between Freud's analysis of the "alchemy" of dreams and the process of theme formation. Twenty-three of the twenty-four chapters have reference lists the average length of which is 30 items. In view of the mountain of publications on projectives, this volume obviously was not intended, or at least will not serve adequately, as a reference work. For example, the chapter by Rabin, which is supposed to review validating and experimental studies with the Rorschach, cites only 37 references. Holt's chapter on the Thematic Apperception Test carries but 43 references. Clearly there has been selection, and from the general tenor of these and similar chapters clearly the selection has been pro-projective. This is not entirely inappropriate in a book of this nature and one assumes that the limited citations given by the various authors are at least partly reflective of editorial limitations on space. Inasmuch as scholarly, exhaustive examination of all pertinent literature was prohibited by general space limitations and similar considerations, the editors might have sought a degree of impartial reporting by selecting as their writers on the various devices individuals having no prominent identification with them and hence no likely proclivity for axe-grinding. This was not done, and most of the techniques are reported by workers having marked investments, e.g., Beck on the Rorschach, van Lennep on the Four-Picture Test, Machover on the Draw-a-Human technique, Mayman, Rapaport, and Schafer on the Wechsler, Wolff on graphology, and Moreno on psychodrama. Again, this is not necessarily inappropriate or undesirable, but the professional reader or student should be aware of these selectivities so as not to assume that he is being served the "whole truth and nothing but the truth." On the other hand, this reviewer did not detect the general aura of extravagance which has characterized so much of the polemics of projectivists. There is very little evidence from any of the authors of an attitude of *"This* is the technique nonpareil." One wonders if this sweet reasonableness results primarily from editorial policy which discouraged exhortation, or if it reflects the current attitudes of projectivists who may recognize the precarious status of projective devices which are most secure in terms of universality of popular use and most insecure in terms of convincing evidence of usefulness. In this regard, the general rationale argued for the "tests of expression" presented in this book gives them all of the inherent validity and all of the actual predictive usefulness of an assertion, "All men will die." * The goal of this book is to survey the field of projective techniques. It is, by title, an *introduction*. The goal has been well achieved, and the title is accurate. The editors are to be complimented for their

selection of the techniques which are represented, a selection process made difficult by the amoeba-like birth rate of projectives. The book will serve well for introductory survey courses. It is of limited value for practicum courses, inadequate as a text for advanced graduate students, and does not provide a comprehensive reference work. It does a good job of what its editors intended it to do. It is hardly a criticism of the editors that they have not given us what is most sorely needed in this field at this time, namely, a thorough critique of the psychology of projection and an exhaustive analysis of the current *scientific* status of projective devices.

J Proj Tech 17:104–6 Mr '53. Arthur Burton.
* attempts to be encyclopedic in its coverage of projective tests and almost succeeds in its quest * the volume does not restrict itself to narrowly defined projective techniques, so that even the projective elements of the Wechsler-Bellevue and Stanford-Binet come in for treatment along with play, puppetry, graphology, fingerpainting, psychodrama, and other techniques. To achieve this psychiatrists as well as psychologists are called upon. The editors indicate that the purpose of the book is a "general survey of the field of projective techniques," and it seems to this reviewer well-suited to its task. * while the book will probably have its best application in a first course in projective techniques, several of the chapters are pitched at the second or third course level, or are even applicable to the fully qualified practitioner. The intent is didactic: to describe the nature of each projective technique and its application to clinical problems on an introductory level. Most of the chapters do this well, and some extremely well. Some fall short. One wishes in this regard that the procedure of introducing test protocols and interpretative case material could have been made uniform for every chapter. At any rate some element of unevenness is inherent in all symposia and no great defection is involved here. * the Make-A-Picture Story Test might well have received chapter status and, as Murray has pointed out, the Tri-dimensional Test of Twitchell-Allen seems worthy of inclusion somewhere. If we disregard for the moment the content of the book which either frankly or implicitly attempts to instruct in the use of one or another of the projective techniques, then the contributions dealing with design and validity become most

important. Of the several excellent contributions in this area, that of Macfarlane and Tuddenham, and Robert R. Holt, were outstanding in the reviewer's opinion. Macfarlane and Tuddenham in a systematic and brilliant way analyze the discrepancy between the contemporary clinical application of projective tests and our fundamental knowledge of what the tests measure. They conclude that present day research has neither made a case for nor against projective tests but that such tests should be employed until something better comes along. * These two chapters summarize the state of projective testing today according to the methods of science. The picture is not an encouraging one. One sees no easy solution to the dilemma of the clinical psychologist who has an inner perception that he is contributing in a unique way to the understanding of the patient but knows that research often finds that his clinical statements from projective data may be suspect. The fact that the State of California, for example, is spending over a hundred thousand dollars for twenty additional psychologists for the 1952–53 fiscal year, largely to give projective tests, confirms his evaluation of himself as providing valid and meaningful services to patients. It appears that now that the status problems of psychologists are further along the way toward solution psychologists should face up to the realities of their liabilities and assets. We have oversold projective tests—and are fearful of admitting it—and have undersold the clinical psychologist as a professional person with a contribution to make. Just as long as we are dependent upon mysterious and possibly specious tests for our security as members of the psychiatric team, so long will our scientific foundation remain nebulous and our feelings anxious. It is significant that no member of the symposium has advocated a moratorium on projective tests until sufficient objective evidence has accumulated as to their value. Can it be that despite projective tests the psychologist has been found to contribute to the welfare of the patient? Too much emphasis has been placed upon the test and too little upon the test-observer equation, or the observer himself. Attempts to find an inherent validity in a projective test divorced from the dynamics and personality orientation of the observer are doomed to sterility. There is no absolute analysis of a dream as there is no absolute analysis of a

TAT protocol. An observer handling dream material in a unique and personally meaningful way may be able to manipulate a patient in a therapeutically advantageous way. But a second observer may arrive at an identical goal by using diverse dream elements or varying procedures. So it is at present with projective tests—and the non-standardized variable seems to be the observer. Greater research effort expended upon him, we feel, will pay increased dividends. This book will certainly be an aid in the training of numerous clinical psychologists in projective techniques. As part of an introductory course, it will find a very much needed place.

Personnel & Guid J 31:136 N '52. Walter L. Wilkins. * concern about validity is notable in this volume * Most of the authors of this volume are properly conservative where validation is as yet unavailable. Morris calls the eight techniques he reviews promising methods and Rabin calls attention to the paucity of evidence on the Szondi. Even Rosenzweig's picture-frustration test, according to Clarke, has undemonstrated validity, because of the difficulty in nearly all research on personality—the criterion against which to demonstrate discriminative power. Yet clinicians make wide use of these techniques and on an empirical basis find them worthy of confidence in hospital and clinic. The ordinary pencil-and-paper personality tests so long used by counselors in school and industry are now in rather poor repute because of repeated demonstrations of poor validity, unless they be standardized on the particular population they are used on. It is harder to demonstrate the invalidity of projective techniques, which are resistant to counting and categorization. But eventually the projective devices will have to demonstrate their validity scientifically as well as clinically. In the meantime, the insight given in many individual cases by such techniques will keep clinicians using them. The present volume is commendable therefore, not only because of its sound discussion of most of the techniques in general clinical use, but also because of its constant emphasis on aspects of validity.

[B45]

*ANDERSON, HOWARD R., AND LINDQUIST, E. F.; REVISED BY HARRIET STULL. **Selected Test Items in American History, Fourth Edition.** National Council for the Social Studies, Bulletin No. 6, Fourth Edition. Washington, D.C.: the Council, National Education Association, October 1957. Pp. iii, 124. Paper. $1.25. * For reviews of earlier editions, see 3:734-5 and 40:B827.

[B46]

*ANDERSON, HOWARD R., AND LINDQUIST, E. F.; RE-VISED BY HARRY D. BERG. **Selected Test Items in American Government, Revised Edition.** National Council for the Social Studies, Bulletin No. 13, Revised Edition. Washington, D.C.: the Council, National Education Association, April 1950. Pp. v, 90. Paper. $1.00. *

[B47]

★ARBOUS, A. G. **Selection for Industrial Leadership.** London and New York: Oxford University Press, 1953. Pp. xiv, 179. 30s.; $4.80. *

Brit J Psychol 45:225 Ag '54. P. E. Vernon. * The value of the book lies less in the psychological results that we have outlined than in its review of the literature of group methods, and its contributions to the statistical methodology of selection. The former provides an excellent and critical survey of WOSB, CSSB and OSS work, though exception must be taken to one quite crucial point—namely the applicability of the formula for indirect selectivity. Arbous argues that in CSSB selection, for example, the follow-up group was selected on a subjective and unspecifiable combination of variables. True, the Final Selection Board mark was derived from such a complex combination, but the selection—so far as the statistician is concerned—was based exclusively on the FSB mark, and therefore satisfies the conditions for applying this supremely useful technique. Nearly half the volume deals with the interpretation of validity coefficients which, as Arbous makes clear, have little meaning apart from the practical conditions of application of the selection procedure. Everything depends on the proportion of candidates it is proposed to select, and on the training wastage and wastage of wrongly rejected candidates that can be permitted. Techniques, and specimen graphs, are given so that employers can determine the precise effects of putting the procedure into practice (but though the description is lucid, an employer would need a good deal of statistical training to follow it). The reviewer is not entirely convinced of the value of such techniques, since validity coefficients (particularly multiple ones) vary so much from one sample to another. Moreover, the very common situation where the selector expects an improvement in the quality of selectees by raising the passmark (e.g. all educational selection) is not covered. Nevertheless, Arbous's approach is un-doubtedly stimulating, and any psychologist concerned with selection problems would profit from studying his contributions.

Human Relations 7:393-4 Ag '54. Geoffrey Hutton. * It is a little difficult to decide whether the book is mainly a description of the selection programme and its validity, or an account of the possibilities of a shorter battery drawn from it. Perhaps the book would have been better balanced had the author devoted a few more pages to describing the origin of the project, the relations between the Institute and the Corporation and the actual administration of the tests. Many of the tests and rating methods are attractive, and the material is presented in great detail in appendices, but it is not clear, for instance, what principles were used in the interview and in interpreting the projective test responses, nor how the final decision on the candidates was reached. The information which is available on the results of the programme as a whole might fruitfully have received separate treatment. At present the book seems to over-emphasize the meaning of the validity coefficient which was based upon only a part of the candidate population, some of the tests, and criteria of limited interest. Mr. Arbous clearly does not ignore the danger of assuming that the tests used in the validation study, if separated from the rest of the procedure and transferred to another situation, would necessarily produce the same result. This point is, however, sufficiently important to warrant greater stress than is accorded to it in a few paragraphs at the end of the book.

Personnel Psychol 8:150-1 sp '55. Charles E. Scholl, Jr. * The discussion in most sections is geared to the research worker who is interested in selection and test validation studies. Consequently, the merits of the book will be lost on administrative personnel who are concerned with the broad problem of industrial leadership. *

[B48]

★ARBOUS, A. G. **Tables for Aptitude Testers: The Operating Characteristics of Aptitude Test Batteries.** Johannesburg, Union of South Africa: National Institute for Personnel Research, South African Council for Scientific and Industrial Research, 1952. Pp. iii, 86. 50s. (Toronto, Canada: Oxford University Press. $6.75.) *

Appl Stat 3:134 Je '54. E. Elliott. * It is difficult to recommend the tables to people who are concerned with practical selection problems. In the first place, the simple form of selection for which they are appropriate is uncommon. Secondly, it is notorious that suitable criteria for such exercises are difficult to find. Thirdly, in cases where suitable criteria might be found and where simple selection is appropriate, the technical resources needed for initial validation, for securing adequate sampling, and for other procedures, which Arbous insists are necessary, are not to be found in many organisations. In other words, few personnel officers will find a use for these tables in day-to-day work. Research workers will certainly be interested in the basic concepts which Arbous discusses; but they will want to examine Sichel's original work first, and their practical requirements probably would be met by much abbreviated tests or even by a few graphs. Indeed, the cost of producing tables as elaborate as these should have suggested economies; for instance, some columns, which merely perform an addition for the user, could be omitted; and all entries, which are worked to at least five decimal places, would have been adequate if given to three places. While it has been necessary to deny a practical utility, which any set of tables should serve, it must be admitted that Arbous's—or rather Sichel's—method is an attractive way of presenting a class of information about tests. But surely publishing these tables is not the best way of introducing the subject; what is needed to catch people's interest is a simply written paper in some widely read journal.

Occupational Psychol 28:123 Ap '54. Olgierd Porebski. These tables ought to be welcomed by every serious worker in the field of personnel selection. They are extremely well produced; they have a complete explanatory text on their use; and they contain more information than any other probability tables of the same kind that have appeared hitherto. * Since the tables are symmetrical, space is economised by using the same table for the positive and negative value of a particular cutting score on the criterion. It is confusing, however, to find that the scale of test scores presented in the first column goes together with the sign presented in the last column, while the scale presented in the last column goes together with the sign presented in the first column. This, however, is only a small inconvenience which can easily be avoided by the reader who studies carefully the instructions or checks the obtained values by common sense. A word of

warning should be issued to the less sophisticated reader against a too literal acceptance of all the implications that can be derived from the tables. Under certain conditions, for instance, the reader may find that his test battery with perfect validity coefficient may have an extremely small index of efficiency as defined by these tables. This will arise when the cutting score on the criterion is very high and the cutting score on the test very low. In such a case the selector does not necessarily need to lose confidence in his test battery or in his coefficient of validity or in the practical value of his selection procedure. He may very often find greater satisfaction in reflecting on the arbitrary way in which the cutting score on the criterion was chosen. This may lead him to doubt the reality of the corresponding index of efficiency which to a great extent depends on the cutting score. Nevertheless, provided the selector knows what he is doing, these tables may be very useful in economising the time of computation, and thus facilitating the quantification of the selection procedure. To that extent they are definitely worth having. The reviewer recommends that they should be added to the stock of manuals in the possession of every selector, unless, of course, the selector happens to be a person who knows all the answers without any statistics.

Personnel Pract B 11:67 Mr '55. N. F. Holt. * a valuable contribution because of the high quality of the experimental battery of tests developed, and because it has brought together and refined previous work in the field of testing for leadership qualities. The technical reader will be particularly interested in the demonstration of the power of the statistical techniques used in the analysis of the data. * From the point of view of the non-technical reader, the difficulty of the material limits its usefulness. However, executives and personnel workers could profitably read the introductory chapters which summarise the present position on group selection methods and the selection of industrial leaders, and the chapters describing the tests and other experimental measures that were used in the study. In addition, the industrial reader who examines the book will have the opportunity to assess the possible value of the scientific approach to selection in a field where intuitive judgment is still dominant.

Personnel Psychol 7:582–3 w '54. Robert L. Thorndike. * When a normal distribution seems reasonable, the....charts....should prove illuminating in showing what may be expected to result from various sorts of manipulation of the cutting score on the predictor or the minimum success level on the criterion, and from shifts in the validity of the predictor. * his tables should help personnel psychologists to translate their correlation coefficients into a form which will have more meaning—not only for the layman in management but also to the statistician himself.

[B49]

★ARNY, CLARA BROWN. **Evaluation in Home Economics.** New York: Appleton-Century-Crofts, Inc., 1953. Pp. xiii, 378. $4.00. *

[B50]

★ATHERTON, SARAH. **Projective Techniques in the Public School Curriculum, 1940–1954: The Analysis of Line Drawings in the Orientation of Eighth Grades.** Rowayton, Conn.: the Author (98 Highland Ave.), 1953. Pp. 59. Paper. $1.00. *

[B51]

★AULD, FRANK, JR. **The Influence of Social Class on Tests of Personality.** Drew University Bulletin, Vol. 40, No. 4; Drew University Studies No. 5. Madison, N.J.: Drew University, 1952. Pp. 18. Paper. Gratis. * (*PA* 27:7185)

Brit J Psychol 44:271–2 Ag '53. The author shows that lower-class and middle-class children differ considerably in their responses to an inventory intended to assess degrees of maladjustment, and he gives reasons for thinking that the different scores reflect class-induced habits and attitudes rather than differences in personal adjustment. He questions, therefore, the interpretation of some of the class differences found in Rorschach scores, and he rightly emphasizes the importance of keeping social status constant in assessing the influence on test responses of some other variable differentiating two groups. Although slight in itself this short paper raises a problem of major importance.

[B52]

★BAIRD, CLYDE RAY. **The Autobiography: A Technique for the Counseling Interview and the Classroom.** *The Educational Leader,* Vol. 17, No. 2, October 1, 1953. Pittsburg, Kan.: Office of Publications, Kansas State Teachers College, October 1953. Pp. 3–23. Paper. *

[B53]

★BALOGH, JOSEPH K., AND RUMAGE, CHARLES J. **Juvenile Delinquency Proneness: A Study of the Kvaraceus Scale.** Washington, D.C.: Public Affairs Press, 1956. Pp. iv, 35. Paper. $1.00. * (*PA* 31:3398)

[B54]

★BALSLEY, TROL WHITMORE. **A Study of the Validity of Some Methods of Measuring Straight-Copy Typing Skill.** Ruston, La.: Department of Business and Economic Research, School of Business Administration, Louisiana Polytechnic Institute, November 1956. Pp. 59. Paper. Gratis. *

[B55]

★BARNETT, GORDON J.; HANDELSMAN, IRVING; STEWART, LAWRENCE H.; AND SUPER, DONALD E. **The Occupational Level Scale as a Measure of Drive.** American Psychological Association, Psychological Monographs, Vol. 66, No. 10, Whole No. 342. Washington, D.C.: the Association, Inc., 1952. Pp. iii, 37. $1.50. Paper. * (*PA* 27:5778)

[B56]

★BARON, DENIS, AND BERNARD, HAROLD W. **Evaluation Techniques for Classroom Teachers.** New York: McGraw-Hill Book Co., Inc., 1958. Pp. xi, 297. $5.50. (London: McGraw-Hill Publishing Co., Ltd. 43s.) *

Ed & Psychol Meas 18:646–7 au '58. Max D. Engelhart. * While in general the book is well written and should serve the purpose for which it is intended, it seems to this reviewer that in certain efforts to be non-technical in explaining necessarily technical matters, the treatment is confusing rather than clarifying. This seems especially true of pages 53–63 where an effort is made to explain the differences between percentile ranks and standard scores. With respect to standard scores the authors state: "These equal units of measurement throughout the scale result from the weighting of scores at the extremes to compensate for lower frequencies at these levels." Certainly the size of a standard deviation is most influenced by measures at the extremes of a distribution, but how this is related to the *equality* of the units of standard scores is something this reviewer does not comprehend. * this reviewer regrets the failure to mention the effects of heterogeneity on test reliability * Furthermore, the appendix would not have become too technical if it had included a simple means of obtaining percentile ranks rather than percentiles, the computation of the standard deviation and of standard scores, and a simple means of computing a coefficient of correlation from paired scores. A simple method of item analysis might also have been explained. * Use of the term "split-half" in describing the process of obtaining equivalent forms of a test may confuse students who learn about "split-half" coefficients of reliability. The statement that "tests usually include only enough items to minimize the chance factor, for additional items do not seem to add to the accuracy of the test" is simply not true. Consider in this connection the Spearman-Brown formula for the reliability of a test when lengthened. * much more could have been included on the construction of teacher-made tests, both essay and objective. This reviewer knows of no other means as effective as experience in writing exercises designed to evaluate different types of instructional objectives in increasing teacher understanding of objectives and of exercise writing. While a few paragraphs deal with exercise writing in relation to objectives, little is said that will cause teachers to write objective exercises useful in evaluating anything other than recall of factual information. It is possible that this text will be useful to instructors of classes in educational measurement where only a very elementary text can be justified. It should be evident from what has been said above that the instructor will need to supplement the text to promote clearer understanding of elementary statistics and certain misconceptions with respect to testing.

Personnel & Guid J 37:156–7 O '58. Dugald S. Arbuckle. The aim of this book....is to present the basic features of tests and testing in terms understandable to classroom teachers. Their guideposts, the authors state, are brevity, the intent to direct material to classroom applications, and the attempt to keep the book in such a form as to provide for flexible use. The reviewer feels that the authors have achieved their aim and held to their guideposts. * In reading through the book one may sometimes feel, "Did they have to explain this obvious point in such detail?" Yet, as one considers the purpose of the book, its simplicity is doubtless deliberate and necessary. The *Mental Measurements Yearbook* is frequently quoted as the Bible, which it probably is, but the usefulness of the [Baron-Bernard] book might have been enhanced if the authors had named more tests and indicated just where these tests are available. Many of the readers....will never have heard of Buros and will not likely take the time or the trouble to check with Buros to see where they might procure a test that might possibly be useful for them. One of the most serious criticisms the reviewer could make of the book is that parts of it give the impression of having been written some time ago. No book is written overnight, and every author has the problem of trying to determine how his first chapter, which may have been written originally three years before his last chapter, can be kept up to date. Numerous chapters in this book, however, have no reference to any research or writing in the past five years. * The chapter on "Appraising Personality" gives valid cautions on what not to do, but it does not help the teacher too much on the question of what to do. Rightly or wrongly, one of the functions of the teacher is the appraisal of personality, and this fact is not recognized enough by the authors although they do have a chapter on this topic. More stress might have been placed on how what is now being done poorly could be done better. In a book on testing, too, it might have been that more than three pages could be given over to the discussion of projective techniques. On page 253, the statement "the cautious use of projective techniques and sociometry may offer the teacher some help in handling personality problems" would seem to imply that sociometry and projective techniques are somewhat similar regarding the difficulty of their use. It would seem that most teachers who could use sociometric techniques fairly safely should not be using the vastly more complicated and dangerous projective devices. There could possibly have been more reference, too, to the more pragmatic measures of an individual—what he does, what he thinks of himself, what teachers think about him, what his fellows think about him, what he appears to know, and so on. The fact that a child hits other children, calls them names, and is sarcastic toward teachers might be a better indication of hostility than the results on a personality inventory. To this reviewer, the chapter on "Evaluating Classroom Social Relationships" was very good and quite unique (although the figure showing a sociogram has one unexplained line). Almost equally useful was the chapter on "Constructing and Using Teacher-made Tests," the one on "Improving Appraisal Practices," and the Appendix. This is not an easy book to review, since it is primarily a simple, how-to-do-it book, with little in the way of theory, or philosophy, or concepts, or ideas. This, however, is the way the authors intended it, and it should fill a real need in giving teachers, at least, a book on measurements that they have some hope of understanding.

[B57]

★Barrow, Harold M. **Motor Ability Testing for College Men.** Minneapolis, Minn.: Burgess Publishing Co., 1957. Pp. ii, 24. Paper, lithotyped. $1.00. *

[B58]

★Bauman, Mary K. **A Manual of Norms for Tests Used in Counseling Blind Persons.** AFB Publications, Research Series, No. 6. New York: American Foundation for the Blind, 1958. Pp. 40. Paper. $0.65. * (PA 32:1949)

New Outlook for Blind 46:146–7 May '52. K. M. * a timely, practical, refreshingly brief guide to the psychologist in his contacts with blind clients. There is nothing "deep" about it. The authors have not permitted themselves to be sidetracked into theoretical discussions of any kind. * it is specifically a service publication which will make an important contribution through bringing to the clinician a feeling of ease in the presence of someone who cannot react to visual cues; sufficient understanding of the interrelationships between the blind client and his everyday environment so that he can be appreciated as an individual in his own right, unavoidably subjected to an extra array of daily tensions and strains, possessed of genuine assets and equally genuine limitations, rather than as a physical and mental defective possessed chiefly of limitations; information regarding tests which have thus far been adapted or evolved for use with the adult blind; a bibliography of source material through which more detailed information may be had on tests, testing, and test interpretation; suggestions on how to set up, and what to include in, psychological evaluations which are to be used by vocational counselors under the federal-state rehabilitation program. Although all five contributions are important, probably the first holds the greatest value because of its uniquely insightful introduction of the blind person to the clinician whose past experience with the visually handicapped may be limited. Nothing is more vital in the construction of an accurate, usable psychological evaluation of a blind person than the initial establishment of good rapport between counselor and client and between tester and client. This good rapport cannot be had unless the counselor and tester themselves have achieved a feeling of ease in the presence of someone who cannot move about freely in a new environment, who cannot react to nods of the head or to visually geared directions. A careful study of the first half of the Manual should go far in helping the psychologist and

his tester to achieve the necessary personal orientation. Although the authors do not make a distinction between psychologist and tester it seems worthy of emphasis here because of the increasing frequency with which the actual testing is done by psychometrists, or by graduate students who may need the help of a manual such as this even more than does the more highly experienced, full-fledged psychologist. Unless the tests are given and reported by individuals who can handle the test situation with insight, and even with ingenuity based on such insight, the psychologist's final evaluation is likely to be skewed no matter how emphatic he, himself, may be. * an excellent article by Dr. DiMichael has been reprinted in full from the *Journal of Consulting Psychology* on "Characteristics of a Desirable Psychological Report to the Vocational Counselor" * The Manual contains a really good discussion of degrees of blindness and varieties of visual handicap. Probably as much attention is given to secondary handicaps as is advisable in a publication of this sort, although one cannot help wishing that something had been said about the blind who are spastic but who may be employable. The Bauman-Hayes Manual should be available to every psychologist, every tester, every vocational counselor of the blind and should be well studied. It should prove of especial value to the clinician who has had limited previous experience with this particular group of the handicapped. To quote from the authors, "Remember that when a blind and a seeing person do not have good rapport, the situation is usually caused, not by blindness, but by the seeing person's obvious feeling of discomfort, fear or patronage."

[B59]

★Bean, Kenneth L. **Construction of Educational and Personnel Tests.** New York: McGraw-Hill Book Co., Inc., 1953. Pp. viii, 231. $4.50. (London: McGraw-Hill Publishing Co., Ltd. 36s.) * (PA 28:5205)

Clearing House 28:246 D '53. Philip Rothman. A good handbook of test construction for the use of secondary and college teachers would undoubtedly be very useful. There is little question that one of the weakest areas of present-day high school and college teaching is that of constructing useful classroom tests. Unfortunately this book, while it has much merit, does not satisfy the need. The author gives evidence of much experience in the field of test construction; and when he deals with the specific phases of test construction, such as over-all planning, writing of test items, choice of test form, and tryouts and reviews, he gives a thorough, readable, and useful presentation. However, the author's experience seems to have been mostly in personnel work, and the approach of the book as a whole is probably much more applicable to the personnel field than to teaching. Thus in the treatment of goals and objectives the author fails to pay sufficient attention to the broader and more important aspects of the goals of modern education. Throughout the book there are very few examples or illustrations which would be meaningful or useful to the teacher. The book is written in simple but precise language, is very readable, and deals with material of much importance. While it falls short of satisfying the need of teachers for a thorough but usable handbook, the interested reader will get much benefit from it and probably would be able to improve the caliber of his tests.

Ed & Psychol Meas 16:169–70 sp '56. Wayne S. Zimmerman. * Bean describes his work as an attempt to bring together widely scattered research studies so that they can be applied to meet practical needs. In this reviewer's opinion he has done a very good job of presenting the material in as practical a fashion as possible. The book is filled with practical examples and is rich in outlines and lists of techniques, methods, and materials. Although there is obviously much material that has been reviewed, there are few quotations or direct references. Bean states that "to include many details would probably be out of line with the practical aims of this somewhat brief manual." There are necessarily thereby a number of undocumented statements which the serious reader is likely to want to pursue. The general style of writing and grammatical construction should probably be rated adequate or good. Yet if this reviewer were to allow himself freedom to be hypercritical he would have to say that, in his opinion at least, ease of reading could be facilitated somewhat by improved clarity of expression, especially in certain portions of the book where the grammatical construction seems a bit awkward. Bean has prepared an exceedingly worthwhile and practical manual for the use of anyone interested in the immediate problem of constructing a test. The book probably should not be recommended for use as a class-

room text unless it were to be used for a very elementary and practically oriented course, or in conjunction with a more scholarly and complete text and/or other references.

[B60]

★BECK, SAMUEL J. Rorschach's Test: III, Advances in Interpretation. New York: Grune & Stratton, Inc., 1952. Pp. x, 301. $6.00. * (PA 28:926)

Am J Orthopsychiatry 23:848–9 O '53. William Healy. The voice of authority, albeit modestly, speaks in this book, for assuredly Dr. Beck is a leading investigator of many phases of the theoretical and clinical aspects of the Rorschach test. * Lengthy details of four case studies—a young boy, an adolescent youth, and two adult males—form the bulk of this volume as test interpretations are confronted with the clinical records. This makes lively and interesting reading for any psychotherapist. But concerning deep appreciations of Beck's acute assays of the structure and dynamics of each personality as related to the test findings, this book is not for anyone who lacks training in the use of the test. For the latter, and perhaps indeed for those not far enough along to have some expertness, it seems as if zest to the text might have been added by indicating what the liberally used alphabetical symbols stand for. It is perfectly clear that the main purpose of the book, skillfully oriented from the standpoint of teaching values, is to further the adeptness of Rorschach testers who are already well trained. It would be a preciously valuable experience for such a psychologist to take the various response records and under the given headings of mood, ego functioning, fantasy life, treatment assets, etc., see how nearly Beck's rich evaluations can be approached—and still better to repeat this after assimilating the chapter on advanced interpretations. If there are any evidences of overestimation of the value of the test, such as might with some probability be expected from one who has been so immersed in it, they are not readily apparent. As for criticisms of Beck's interpretations of individual test responses, that can only be undertaken by other experts. But any reader can discern the remarkable agreements between the clinical notes and Beck's prior perceptions with regard to the personality make-up and the nature of behavior reactions. Not that there are no disagreements: Witness in one case "the test logic" (a term that Beck allows himself to use repeatedly) shows the father to be the probable source of the boy's conflicts or moods, while clinically it is the mother who appears as the cause. And in another instance there is a similar difference in assigning the parental source of trouble. Beck makes it clear that for the treatment process the main usefulness of the Rorschach is that it can shorten the therapist's labor of elucidating the personality components and reactive tendencies so that he can more speedily and surely get ahead with his job. The type and the thoroughness of treatment indicated are often apparent from the diagnostic and etiologic interpretations. Some predictions are offered for the cases given; e.g., C. is "suffering from a probably never-ending neurosis"; he will get relief, but "the outlook is that he will be periodically returning for treatment." But elsewhere it is stated that "the findings are never an absolute prediction" though for a given type of person they do imply behavior latencies. * Picturesque wording characterizes the book and the author's ready associations bring forth many apt literary allusions. This makes good writing which together with the subtle humanistic interpretations in the four cases leads the reviewer to sense that there are two Samuel J. Becks—the scientist and the artist.

Am J Psychiatry 110:319–20 O '53. Herbert Dörken, Jr. It becomes obvious on reading this book that the author is presenting not isolated facts but an intimate understanding of human behavior and an exposition of the extent to which it can be evaluated by the Rorschach test. Personality is complex and the text avoids oversimplification. In a time when condensations, abstracts, and introductions seem the order of the day, it is a real asset to have a publication addressed not to the beginner or the "interested," but to the serious student. Beck places proper emphasis on the evaluation of the personality structure *per se* and its psychodynamics, and only secondarily does he offer implications for diagnosis, prognosis, and therapy. The text is so written—and this is a distinct advantage—that it does not lend itself for use as a "cook-book" for test diagnosis. * Perhaps the only disappointment is that Chapter II, "Advances in Interpretation," is only 49 pages in length. The case studies that follow, however, serve as "a statement of where the Rorschach test, as I use it, is at the present time."

B Menninger Clinic 18:38 Ja '54. Helen D. Sargent. In Beck's hands, the Rorschach is more than a test. It is a theory of personality. As usual, he compliments the reader by believing that theoretical formulations need no spelling out, creating an effect which is frustrating but stimulating. It is regrettable that scoring factors introduced since his second volume (1945) are not fully discussed (affective ratio, lambda index, T), but Beck's skillful handling of Rorschach interpretation in the records presented leaves no doubt that he achieves what he states is still only partially possible: "application of the test to the whole personality conceived as a universe of interacting forces."

Brit J Psychol, Gen Sect 44:76 F '53. B. M. Spinley. * While primarily of interest to those immediately and practically engaged in diagnosis and treatment, the book will interest all seriously concerned with the problems of Rorschach research, particularly problems of validation. Dr Beck is one of the great exponents of the test, and he impresses with his caution. Throughout he notes those rules of interpretation which have been statistically validated, those which he believes sufficiently supported by clinical observation, and those which are merely possible leads. It would be more convenient if the norms to which he frequently refers were published again with the text. The interpretations excite admiration, but in a busy clinic the time for similar detailed use of the test is seldom available. Perhaps the most satisfying feature of the work is the echewing of special Rorschach terminology and the use of the more familar language of psychology. This is not an easy book to read. It is written in a rapid, machine-gun style, with a misleading effect of dogmatism; ugly words and phrases are frequent, e.g. "concretistic," "synthesizing at expectancy." Most certainly it is not matter for beginners. For the experienced Rorschach student it is in places wonderfully illuminating, at times very controversial (especially if the student has been educated along Klopferian lines). It is stimulating throughout.

J Ed Psychol 44:378–80 O '53. David Wechsler. * Beck continues his exhaustive analysis of the Rorschach Test and its ever widening compass. Like the first two volumes, it is characterized by a scholarship and a literary flavor that has come to be associated with Beck's writings; even more than the first two, it will serve the experienced Rorschacher rather than the beginner. * Beck rejects in particular Allport's principle of independent traits and the view that the continuity of the individual is historic rather than functional. This uncompromising holism is not implicit in Rorschach's original approach (Beck would disagree), but it is necessary to support Beck's conviction that the entire personality is describable by the symbols of the Rorschach Test and its quantitative ratios. This may represent the experience of psychologists whose test armamentarium is restricted to the Rorschach, but the claim would be widely questioned by clinicians using other instruments along with the Rorschach in evaluating personality. There is no test so good but that another one may be more revealing at different times or for different individuals. Human personality is too complex to project itself in its totality on a single surface. The second section, entitled "Advances in Interpretation," comprises not so much new material as further exploration and reinterpretation of the conventional Rorschach symbols. Of particular interest is Beck's discussion of the Rorschach elements which are claimed to reveal ego-strength, ego-insufficiencies, and ego-defenses. The items particularly emphasized are the F+%, the amount of W and Z, the sequence and approach, and interestingly enough, the P%—the determinants which Beck associates with intellectual productivity in contrast to those which deal with manifestations of emotion (C, Y, V, M). He regards P as a special and most concentrated form of the F+ response. According to Beck, a subject's P per cent indicates not only closeness of identification with the norm setting group but reflects further the degree of the subject's ability to integrate successfully. * this chapter will be found to be very provocative but, although reference is made to studies either in progress or about to be published, few factual data are presented. In the third, and by far the longest section, Beck devotes over two hundred pages to detailed analyses of seven Rorschach protocols obtained from four patients, three of whom were tested before and again after therapy of varying duration. In these analyses Beck gives renewed evidence as to why he is estimated by many as one of the leading, if not the leading, Rorschacher in the country. To be able to write forty pages on a single protocol involving some thirty responses is in itself *tour de force;* to be able to do so and be convincing would be a

greater achievement. In this respect Beck is only partially successful. The reports are much too long for even an initiated Rorschacher to follow. They are made additionally difficult by Beck's penchant for metaphor and analogy. The net result is that what he has to say is very interesting at any given point but far from clear when taken as a whole; nor do the summaries at the end of each case help much to clarify the total picture. As always, Beck's case presentations are profitable reading, but one hopes that in his next publication he will be a little less literary and more succinct.

J Proj Tech 17:361-2 S '53. Mortimer M. Meyer. * The second section, the new addition in the series and a welcome one, is titled "Advances in Interpretation." The organization of the sub-sections is a most provocative one for the clinician because the titles outline areas with which the clinician is constantly faced. Samples are, "The insufficient ego," "The defenses," "Anxiety." Unfortunately, it falls short of its potential because of the highly discursive style. The wealth of his material is evident but the difficulty of getting it is great and much seems lost in the process. The potentiality is particularly evident in a short passage on page 42 and 43 where there is an attempt at an organized comparison of "anxiety-shock" and "color-shock." The third section is the presentation of a detailed analysis of four records. These records are used as a framework for the presentation of the author's mode of approach and analysis rather than being representative of any category, diagnostic or otherwise. This presentation includes analysis of retests and therapeutic prediction. Pertinent case material is included. In this section also, the style presents a problem. Although free association is far more appropriate here than in the previous section, there is still some question in this reviewer's mind whether the wealth of association does not become a distraction rather than an asset. Nevertheless, the opportunity to see the detailed thinking process which goes on as the author analyses a record is certainly a contribution of importance. The fourth and last section is titled, "Synopsis and Comment—Critical and Speculative." * This section dealing with a most difficult and vital area is the most clearcut and well organized. Again, it makes this reviewer nostalgic for the "what might have been." Despite the limitations of style, every experienced user of the Rorschach should be acquainted with this volume.

Psychiatric Q Sup 26:287 pt 2 '52. This book is the long-awaited Volume III by Dr. Beck on the Rorschach Test. * Because of the considerable research done on the Rorschach in recent years, the present volume has been eagerly awaited by clinical psychologists. * Chapter II is an important chapter, "Advances in Interpretation." The rest—and this is the main body of the book—is devoted to discussions of four cases, including Rorschach results, and discussion of therapy including notes of the therapeutic sessions. Thus Volume III presents fewer cases but more detailed discussions of them than were given in Volume II. *

Psychol B 50:221-3 My '53. Lee J. Cronbach. Dr. Beck has high standing among those who study the Rorschach in America, because of his steady interest in improving the technique and his desire to communicate clearly his procedures and theories. His new book presents his method of interpretation more completely than before. Those who are using the test or training others in it will find great use for the clear and intelligent discussions of theory and of four case analyses. * The "advances" in Beck's statements do not represent a marked change in viewpoint. As always, he insists upon regarding the examination as an opportunity to sample behavior and thought production, not as a device for generating scores. He makes this clear by commenting that Tredgold, with the Mare and Foal Test, could make the same type of dynamic interpretation. This point of view might seem to cut the ground from under most of the talk about interpretation of Rorschach per se; as would also the recent report that in interpreting the adjustment shown in protocols, a qualified psychologist who knew nothing about Rorschach could agree with trained Rorschachers as well as they could agree with themselves. Beck, however, considers the Rorschach performance an unusually good source of revealing cues, and this book is an attempt to make those cues explicit for other testers. The cues now employed differ little from those discussed in his earlier books. He elaborates more clearly than before and distinguishes, for instance, between the significance of a cue in patients and the interpretation of the same cue in superior non-patients. Beck has explored many new leads, such as the Levy-Zubin analysis of movement.

He points out nuances in each type of response which should qualify the interpretation of the main scores. He does not reverse any earlier interpretations. This in itself should suggest that the book is disappointing. We have now had thousands of research studies, some well conducted, which have failed to establish validity of many interpretations commonly made. One would expect such evidence to be used in revising the interpretative scheme, or that positive evidence would be advanced to demonstrate the validity of Beck's statements as to the equivalence of test behavior and personality structure. Beck does suggest that this might be a later step, but many readers would prefer to find a psychological proposition accompanied by, or preceded by, the reason for affirming it. Beck discusses in a few pages current research on the test. He criticizes some studies for trying scoring innovations instead of validating Rorschach's Rorschach test. These innovations have, I think, rarely been sufficient to obscure the significance of positive or negative findings. His second criticism is more substantial, that attempts to validate single signs or scores do not take into account the interactions between cues that an interpreter might use. It is apparent, however, that Beck in this book makes many statements about the significance of single scores, i.e., about main effects. While these interpretations would be qualified by added facts from other scores or qualitative features, such additions are embellishments to a main interpretation that he implies would be true more often than false in persons generally. We find Beck turning his back on research evidence in the way that is too common in the literature and in the conversation of clinicians, by saying, in effect, "Evidence or no evidence, these propositions have clinical validity" (p. 43). In view of Beck's desire to make his *operations* public so that the Rorschach test will be a part of psychology rather than a cult, it is regrettable that he does not make his *validation* public. He does not see that so-called clinical validity is a type of private, or subjective, validity and hence not acceptable save as a source of questions to be tested by research. The matter of color shock will serve to document this criticism. The literature now contains several studies which make it doubtful that color shock is truly color shock, or that it has the correlates claimed for it. Beck however treats color shock in the traditional manner, going further to regard color shock as evidence of anxiety regarding present temptation, while shading expresses guilt regarding past misdeeds. A rather attractive rationalization for this position is offered. Beck then dismisses the negative findings of objective research on color shock by citing Siipola and others as if their work negated the other studies and supported his position. An examination of the original will disclose that their findings do not substantiate conventional procedures for measuring color shock. Before the Rorschach can hold an established position among those who are deficient in the "wish to believe," the interpretative statements such as Beck presents must be accompanied by explicit evidence. Such evidence would not say (to quote at random), "This inability to react to color is the mark of the person insensitive to the world's exhilarating values" (p. 45). It would say, "Persons who show no responses scored *C*, *CF*, or *FC* are judged to be emotionally unresponsive by such-and-such criteria *in x cases out of one hundred.*" Here is the crucial problem. Beck and others word statements as if generally true, although the context makes it clear that the interpretations are not true in 100 cases out of 100. Hence the propositions are not to be accepted as stated. This approach to the Rorschach does not leave us with testable claims. The Rorschach enthusiast can say that the truth is contained only in his many qualifications. But this too easily becomes an evasion of responsibility. If one tries to take all the qualifications into account, he arrives at a unique pattern of scores and cues for each record. One cannot find a reasonable number of cases with this pattern, and therefore cannot make the required assessment of the statement's *degree* of correspondence to reality. To verify a proposition we must know its probability of being true. As the propositions become more complex, they become unverifiable. If the main effects are indeed assumed in interpretation, it is *their* degree of validity which must be reported. So much stress on what Beck's book lacks reflects my sense of proportion, not Beck's. He gives almost no space to these issues, compared to the extensive discussion of cases. Those discussions can be evaluated, perhaps, by some other clinician who would report whether they agree with his private experience. There are few persons who can match Beck in experience, or in the care with which he traces his own conscious thoughts.

A reader might choose to test the statements in terms of plausibility. On this ground, Beck stands high. He gives a long train of argument to support each interpretation, rather than issuing it as from an oracle. He is painstakingly self-critical in specifics, while not being so critical of his major premises. Judged from the viewpoint of interest and the quality of Beck's thinking about personality, the book is admirable. The book is frequently poetic. It is written with far more style than most of its contemporaries, and many passages are quotable. In criticizing Lewin's disinclination to the genetic approach, for instance: "Lewin's deficit for this kind of construct was that he was not clinically trained. He can think in two dimensions. But his anxiety as experimentalist blocks his moving into the third" (p. 11). Throughout, Beck does a good job of expressing in hundreds of illustrations the concept of personality as an interaction of many forces and perceptions within the person. Whether the Rorschach is a dependable tool or not, a book like this affords an excellent basis for thinking about the extreme complexity of personality. It is a powerful antidote for an oversimple view of personality as described by a few common traits or factors. The book will perform this service, even for many Rorschachers, by debunking naive interpretations of the psychogram or the single numerical score. In summary, the book appears to be a fine one for Rorschach users or students who plan to continue with the test. Beck has rich experience to report, and the fact that it is subjective does not prevent its being useful to other interpreters. The book will not change the opinion of those who presently regard most claims for the Rorschach as rationalizations or statements of faith. The book will be of little assistance to the minority who regard the validity of the test as an open question which must be settled by determining which interpretations hold up in what proportion of cases. Beck has an extensive research program in process, and it may be that his reports from them will belatedly give us reason to have confidence in the present book.

[B61]

★BELCHER, JOHN C., AND SHARP, EMMIT F. **A Short Scale for Measuring Farm Family Level of Living: A Modification of Sewell's Socio-Economic Scale.** Oklahoma Agricultural and Mechanical College, Oklahoma Agricultural Experiment Station, Technical Bulletin No. T-46. Stillwater, Okla.: the Station, September 1952. Pp. 22. Paper. Gratis. *

[B62]

★BELL, C. R. V. **Examination Time: A Book for Teachers Who Have to Set and Mark Examinations.** London: Longmans, Green & Co., Ltd., 1957. Pp. 55. Paper. 2s. 3d. *

[B63]

★BELLAK, LEOPOLD. **The Thematic Apperception Test and the Children's Apperception Test in Clinical Use.** New York: Grune & Stratton, Inc., 1954. Pp. x, 282. $7.50. * (PA 29:4032)

Am J Psychiatry 112:399 N '55. *Douglas M. Kelley.* The catchy title on this book is bound to fascinate any visitor who spots it on your shelf and it should prove a good conversation piece, if nothing else. To the more sophisticated, the discussions concerning the thematic apperception tests and children's apperception test will prove most useful. The author, who is well known for his writings in projective technique areas, has taken material from his many publications, added much new data and come up with a well-organized discussion of these useful diagnostic devices. * chapters include excellent literature surveys, coupled with the author's own approach * The same approach is applied to the Children's Apperception Test, although here the material is not as voluminous, since this technique is of much more recent development. Interpretive approaches are given in considerable detail and this section of the book represents the only really well done available manual on this test. Interpretive material and typical responses make this section most practical. The Thematic Apperception Test has long been established as a worthwhile projective device and this book can be considered an excellent introduction to the method. The material on the Children's Apperception Test is especially useful to beginning workers and the whole volume is well worthwhile to novices. Experts will of course find it especially profitable as a splendid example of comparative experience.

Am J Psychother 9:737–9 O '55. *Frank L. Catalano.* * Those sections....in which Bellak demonstrates his approach in analyzing TAT and CAT records are particularly commendable. * Bellak points out that test data may demonstrate fantasies and psychodynamics which even a skilled therapist will not anticipate or suspect after many months of psychoanalysis. This is a crucial point deserving of more attention from psychotherapists. The ultimate value of any projective test, however reliable and valid the test may be, will depend upon its ability to reveal those aspects of personality which are not more readily assessed by other means.

Austral J Psychol 8:88 Je '56. *J. G. Lyle.* * Useful chapters are provided on elementary theory of projective testing, largely within a psychoanalytic framework. Only Bellak's own psychoanalytic method of interpretation is dealt with and this far too sketchily. One would like to have been shown many more analyses of records, with the interpretations related to case history material. Bellak's method sometimes permits of quite profound interpretation, though the experienced clinician may feel that, followed too rigidly, it becomes somewhat mechanical. For example, surely *every* story about a boy wanting to learn to play the violin can't be interpreted as "wanting to fiddle like father." The author does not sufficiently analyse the verbal elaborations of the thema, nor adequately explore the possibilities of *sequence analysis.* In fact, there are many *nuances* of interpretation which are not mentioned. But Bellak's concise reports are very well structured and very revealing of the patients' conflicts, relationships and psychic structure; and clinicians in this country would do well to use them as models. The "methodologic bluenoses (who often mistake obsessive doubt for a scientific attitude, and their intellectual sterility for caution and eclecticism)" will not be impressed by this book. Clinical psychologists will regard it as a useful introductory text for teaching thematic apperception techniques. But they will be disappointed that this noted clinician did not produce a more integrated theory of T.A.T. interpretation, and a more instructive way of illustrating his methods.

Brit J Psychol 46:156–7 My '55. *Boris Semeonoff.* * Bellak's major contribution in the earlier (and slightly longer) portion of the book, which deals with TAT proper, is the presentation of his own system of analysis, which, in so far as it is based on the use of a number of "scoring categories" concerned more with content than with form, most closely resembles Wyatt's system (1947, *J. Psychol.* XXIV, 319–30), and stands in contrast to Rapaport's and to some extent to Murray's own, although something rather like need-press analysis is to be found in Bellak's listing of the "main needs of the hero," together with "conception of environment," "parental (and other) figures," "significant conflicts," "nature of anxieties," etc. All this accurately reflects the author's clinical purpose; a more rigorous methodological innovation, reminiscent of Tomkins's approach, is his recommendation that the "Main Theme" be progressively restated on various levels (up to five) of generalization or abstraction. Scrutiny of the data thus assembled, it is claimed, usually enables one to recognize a repetitive pattern in the subject's responses, and to proceed thence to a final report, which may or may not offer a diagnosis. Since he does not regard TAT as primarily a diagnostic instrument, Bellak recommends the use of some such formula as "The data represented in the TAT are consistent with a diagnosis of...." Such diagnosis, he says, should never be made on test evidence alone, without additional information provided by a clinical interview. * Bellak makes out a fairly convincing case for the substitution of animal for human figures. The age range recommended is three to ten, and the material is claimed to be relatively culture-free. This latter seems to this reviewer to be rather a questionable assumption: not only the humanized animals but some of the family-life situations are unmistakably American. Accordingly, it comes as rather a surprise to read in the Appendix on "Publications and Work in Progress," that extensive work on the CAT is going on in India, France, the French colonies and elsewhere. One also gets the impression that too close a preoccupation with some of the stock "psychoanalytic" and allied themes (e.g., primal scene, castration fantasy, the body-image, etc.) has been allowed to divert attention from the possibly more superficial but nevertheless pressing problems which form the staple of child guidance work, at least in this country. It has been necessary in this review to concentrate on the descriptive side of Bellak's work, but the book also contains a good deal of valuable and thought-provoking general discussion of projective theory and practice. It is eminently a readable book, the author's style being both succinct and at times pleasantly colloquial.

J Consult Psychol 19:75 F '55. Laurance F. Shaffer. * References to completed research are minimal, but there is a short chapter outlining needed studies. Because the informal richness of the picture-story method is best revealed by studying many examples analyzed from varying viewpoints, this manual will be instructive for clinicians and students. It is probably not, in

itself, a sufficient textbook in projective methods.

J Ed Psychol 47:317–8 My '56. A. S. Edwards. * The greatest value of the book probably lies in the detailed discussions of clinical uses, interpretations and special problems in relation to a large number of cases. * The entire work is the result of thorough preparation and training and long experience in one of the best clinical settings. One cannot go through the details of this volume without becoming well acquainted with much that is being done with the tests. * It is a question as to whether some of the broad generalizations can be accepted. The experimentally oriented psychologist may look with some wonder at the statement that "The main efforts in American Psychology are directed toward making projective methods the tools of nomothetic science...." Whether or not they can agree with this, it does not detract from the mass of clinical material that is of great value for the student of projective testing. This is a valuable contribution in a special field and in the efforts at progress in the stream of American psychology.

J Proj Tech 19:196–8 Je '55. Edwin S. Shneidman. * a refreshing and lively book which may irritate some of the more advanced TAT workers with its dogmatism and its superficiality, but which may stimulate and thrill some of the TAT beginners with its commonsense, and clinical feel, and practical approach. Its usefulness for the beginner, however, far outweighs its shortcomings. The book is unusual, perhaps the more useful for being so. It is a *clinical* book—"meant primarily to be of practical use to the student and practitioner" —and is not intended, to quote Bellak, for the "methodologic bluenoses (who often mistake obsessive doubt for a scientific attitude and their intellectual sterility for caution and eclecticism)...." The practical aspect of the book, with its emphasis on interpretation and case illustrations is good enough, but that stuff about obsessive, sterile bluenoses, wow! * The book is informative, easy to read, often chatty, at times an amazingly personal document. More than any recent textbook, it reminds one of a stimulating conversation with a knowledgeable person. The book sounds as though it were dictated, or taken from transcriptions of lectures. There is much first person in the book; the Preface is entirely a short biography (of a rather remarkable man), and consistent with this friendly style there occurs in the first chapter a footnote which is without precedent for its candor and disarming charm: "I am aware of the fact that some formulations in this chapter are still rather loose. A more lengthy (sic) statement is being prepared." It is obvious that this reviewer implies that length alone will not turn the trick. The task of synthesizing the concepts inherent in TAT use with those in personality is truly a Herculean task—and it is no disgrace to Bellak that his efforts to date have not completely succeeded. The interested reader is referred to a previous review, one by Dr. Julian Rotter. This review....on Bellak's theoretical chapter, which appeared in different form in Abt and Bellak's *Projective Psychology,* expresses an opinion with which the present writer concurs: "For all its shortcomings, this attempt to clarify the assumptions of projective testing is a step in the right direction and is worth reading." As for Bellak's system of thematic analysis, it appears to be a valuable and usable combination of the atomistic and the global elements in test protocol, and is certainly one of the possible systems to be recommended for mastery. The story-by-story analysis of three TAT protocols is presented in detail and constitutes a worthwhile contribution. The section on diagnostic groups (Chapter V) is filled with disappointments and rewards. Some of the material is so brief as to be cryptic. * The last 120 pages of the book constitute a manual for the CAT. It is a fair job as a manual. It is inferior, for example, to the manual for the recent Michigan Picture Test; it does not include as many of the "Essential" features—as outlined by the 1952 APA Report of the Committee on Test Standards—as one would hope for. On closer inspection, one finds that the section on the CAT is really not a manual at all, but a series of case illustrations. The section on "Norms" (pp. 233–236) for the CAT-S is inadequate; no norms for the CAT are given, and the frequencies of themes are based on forty children of someone's B.A. thesis. Bellak's own concluding line in this section of norms is (like Card No. 5 of his CAT-S) rather lame: "At any rate, even without norms, a clinician would have considered this story as indicative of special problems of aggression and fear and compliance." The possibility of being called a "bluenose" notwithstanding, one must state that the section on the CAT—having, as it does, nothing on validity or

reliability, and consisting of seven cases, four of them quite brief—is disappointing and inadequate. In 1950, Robert R. Holt, in reviewing the CAT....said: "Taken as a whole, the test (and particularly the manual....) shows signs of being put out in a little too much of a hurry...." Somehow, five years later, the same indictment can still be made. But all in all, Bellak has written one of the best books on the clinical application of the TAT for the beginner—it is more complete than Stein's, it is more practical than Tomkins', it is more understandable than Aron's, it is more elementary than Rapaport's, and it is more focussed on one method of analysis than Shneidman's. On the other hand, it does not replace Stein's compact manual, Tomkins' logical tour de force, Aron's scholarly work, Rapaport's monumental study, or Shneidman's collection of sixteen different methods of thematic analysis. In spite of all the negative comments one can make, it is no contradiction to state that the book is very worthwhile, if only to share the thoughts of an intuitive and enthusiastic clinician. Thus, in summary, the book is interesting for the TAT professional, useful for the TAT journeyman, and important for the TAT novice.

Psychol B 52:370–1 Jl '55. Max L. Hutt. More than anything else this book gives evidence of the extensivity and maturity of Bellak's clinical experience. Both in the expository sections of the volume....as well as in the case illustration sections....there is a richness in clinical wisdom and an erudition in psychoanalytic personality theory. However, there are shortcomings of the book as a *manual* for TAT and CAT interpretation, unless one wishes to accept Bellak's interpretive procedure "lock, stock, and barrel." * one may question the value of Bellak's schema on several counts, not necessarily of equal significance: (*a*) There is no necessary relationship between his projective theory and his method of analysis. The bridge is a tenuous one. (*b*) No evidence is presented concerning the scoring reliability for the suggested "scoring categories." Many of these apparently require considerable clinical skill, and may, presumably, be evaluated differently by different examiners. (*c*) One may be fascinated by the nature of the scoring categories but one may also wonder what the relationship of each of them is to the observed or latent personality characteristics of the examinee. Bellak has frequent recourse to the phrase "in my experience," but this type of evidence may not be convincing to other clinicians. (*d*) There are no clear bases for judging the "adequacy" of such factors as "severity of superego" and "integration of the ego." In a sense, each examiner is forced to define these phrases operationally in terms of test protocols and hope that they mean the same things in TAT material as they do in dreams, therapeutic sessions, etc. (*e*) While reference is made to experimental and clinical studies of TAT by other authors, these findings seem to have no observable impact on the question of the validity of Bellak's "system." In all of the above, I am not presuming that results achieved with Bellak's methodology lack validity. I only mean to point out that the evidence for any judgment in this regard is almost entirely lacking. It seems to this reviewer that there should be a clear distinction made between theoretical constructs, admirable as they may be, and the *validity* of evaluative methods for describing or predicting specified aspects of behavior on the basis of thematic protocols, which are developed *in relation to* such constructs. It is conceivable that the first pillar may be essentially sound and that the second, inferred and operational, pillar may be of questionable soundness.

[B64]

★BERDIE, RALPH L.; LAYTON, WILBUR L.; AND HAGENAH, THEDA. **Using Tests in Counseling: A Manual for the State-Wide Testing Programs of Minnesota.** Minneapolis, Minn.: University of Minnesota Press, 1953. Pp. vii, 86. Paper. $1.00. *

[B65]

★BERGER, R. M.; GUILFORD, J. P.; AND CHRISTENSEN, P. R. **A Factor-Analytic Study of Planning Abilities.** American Psychological Association, Psychological Monographs: General and Applied, Vol. 71, No. 6, Whole No. 435. Washington, D.C.: the Association, Inc., 1957. Pp. 31. Paper. $1.00. *

[B66]

★BHATIA, C. M. **Performance Tests of Intelligence Under Indian Conditions.** Bombay, London, and New York: Oxford University Press, 1955. Pp. xi, 144. Rs. 10; 17s. 6d.; $2.65. * (*PA* 31:598)

Brit J Ed Psychol 26:82 F '56. W. H. K. The writer has performed a useful service in explaining in simple terms the formation of performance tests of intelligence for an Indian population in order to "open up a field so far completely closed to the Indian education psychologist." The battery of tests includes part of Kohs' Block Design test, Alexander's Passalong test, a new Pattern drawing test, an immediate Memory test and a Picture Construc-

tion test. Difficulties encountered in giving the tests to literate and illiterate groups of boys (ages 11 to 16) are described in some detail and obviously great care was taken to base norms on a representative sample. An account is given of the factorial analysis of the results and the standardisation that was carried out for illiterates and literates. This very efficient handbook ends with conversion tables which give performance quotients corresponding to half-yearly intervals from 11 to 16 years for literates and illiterates.

Brit J Psychol 48:80 F '57. A. E. G. Pilliner. * a straightforward account of the construction and standardization of a battery of individual performance tests suitable for use with Indian children. * There is an interesting, though brief, account of the special measures taken by the testers to establish good relations in the villages visited, a prime necessity in obtaining a suitable atmosphere for testing, much of which seems to have been carried out in the open with an audience. A more detailed account of the difficulties met with in testing might have helped to augment the Western reader's insight into the Indian scene. Not unexpectedly, the mean performance of literates is found to be superior to that of illiterates on every test. * The chapter on "The Nature of Intelligence" is sketchy and might well be expanded.

[B67]

★BIELIAUSKAS, VYTAUTAS J. **The H-T-P Bibliography.** Los Angeles, Calif.: Western Psychological Services, July 1957. Pp. 10. Paper, mimeographed. $1.50. *

[B68]

★BISCHOFF, L. J. **Intelligence: Statistical Conceptions of Its Nature.** Doubleday Papers in Psychology, [No.] 5. New York: Doubleday & Co., Inc., 1954. Pp. vi, 33. Paper. $0.85. * (*PA* 29:905)

[B69]

★BJERSTEDT, ÅKE. **Interpretations of Sociometric Choice Status: Studies of Workmate Choices in the School Class and Selected Correlates With Special Emphasis on the Methodology of Preferential Sociometry.** Studia Psychologica et Paedagogica, Series Altera, Investigationes 8. Lund, Sweden: C W K Gleerups, 1956. Pp. 408. Paper. Sw. kr. 40. * (*PA* 30:7030)

Am Sociol R 22:117–8 F '57. Leslie D. Zeleny. * of substantial merit. It includes a "discussion of general principles for collection and analysis of socio-preferential data" followed by the report of two experiments * exceptionally careful methodological study * [a model] of social psychological-sociometric research. Experimentation was started only after a careful study of previous research and of current hypotheses. Modern refined statistical methods of analyzing findings were used: and, conclusions were in the form of new hypotheses to be tested. It is upon a foundation of studies like....[this] that social *science* can be built.

Brit J Ed Psychol 26:226–7 N '56. D. M. Edwards Penfold. The author is to be congratulated on producing a most scholarly volume. The first part is an attempt to systematize the terminology, definitions and methodology of sociometry * In the second part a large-scale investigation in Swedish schools is reported * The scale of the experiment was large enough to give some reliable results, and will probably provide the starting point for much future research. The statistical inferences are drawn very carefully and competently. Thus, the book has much to recommend it for inclusion in the collections of all who work in the field of sociometric research. The object of combining the theoretical and experimental parts into a single volume is not altogether clear, as there is comparatively little direct connection between the two. * the printing and presentation are agreeable, and....the English is faultless. Nowhere does one receive an impression that the writer was writing in a foreign language, and it adds greatly to the interest of the book that quotations from the writings and sayings of Swedish children read in translation in the manner and vernacular of our own.

Brit J Psychol 47:318–9 N '56. A. R. MacKinnon. * Throughout....there is ample evidence of a vigorous scientific inquiry. The work of most sociometric researchers is given a careful examination and the results are compared with the author's work. A continual attempt is made to effect a synthesis or to improve on the techniques. Such an approach points out many areas that require further—and often immediate—attention. Those using sociometric techniques will find many valuable suggestions in the book. For those who have not used sociometric methods and are attracted towards their use, this book should be required reading, for, as few other more general works on sociometry have done, there is illustrated here the essential "frontier" character of sociometric research, the still unfinished state of the techniques, the dangers of over-simplification and naïve interpretation, and the tentative character of most results. The author's concluding remark is that "there is still much to be done."

This would seem true not only for the methodology of sociometry but for all that is purposed by using the techniques.

[B70]

★Bjerstedt, Åke. **The Methodology of Preferential Sociometry: Selected Trends and Some Contributions.** Sociometry Monographs, No. 37. Beacon, N.Y.: Beacon House Inc., 1956. Pp. 156. Paper. $3.50. * (*PA* 31:7643)

Am J Sociol 63:430–1 Ja '58. Renato Tagiuri. Sociometric devices are among the most commonly encountered empirical methods used by social scientists. Yet there has not been available an impartial treatment of the history, complexity, and subtlety of the many variations of this seemingly simple methodology. Bjerstedt's elegant work fulfils this need. In fact, the reviewer cannot think of a better source for the advanced student who wishes to gain a good perspective of this area. * A most impressive and eclectic bibliography rounds out the work. This is a scholarly, advanced book, written with a broad perspective in sociology and psychology as well as in the general area of formal scientific methodology. It is undoubtedly the most systematic treatment of the material, with original and useful formulations and terminological innovations.

Cont Psychol 2:130 My '57. Edgar F. Borgatta. This monograph should be gratifying for the American reader. It reflects a sensitivity and responsiveness to empirical research not often enough associated with our European colleagues in the area of *social* psychology. Especially, however, it constitutes a thoughtful and careful attempt to organize the concepts and the literature of "sociometry." Bjerstedt.... places Moreno and others in a reasonable and sane perspective. His scholarship is quickly located not only by his ability to handle outlandish claims of discoveries, but also by his ability to find parallels for work which is often ignored by persons who work in or in response to the cultish interest that sociometry has so often represented. Of particular importance is the attention that he gives to earlier foreign publications. Bjerstedt's approach is a cross between a review of the literature, a poll of the experts, and an attempt to compromise differences of opinion. * A substantial contribution in this volume is Bjerstedt's orderly review of the published data on different methods of asking preference questions. Among unlimited choice, *k* choice, total ranking, total rating, and pair comparisons, the k-choice method is indicated as questionable on the empirical basis of low correlation to the others. In this general connection, he discusses in a useful manner both the logical and the empirical problems, including those of the number and meaning of criteria utilized and the levels of reality involved. On the other hand, one must note that there is an inherent limitation in considering "sociometric measures" as something special, rather than as a class within a broader framework of personality measures. For example, the closely related work in the ratings of persons on their characteristics by their peers, which has become an important area of sociometrics, is omitted. The name of Rosalind Dymond (Cartwright), which is important in the area of interpersonal perception, does not even appear in the bibliography, and this omission is symptomatic of the bias. Nevertheless the bibliography of 550 items, within its defined limit, is well chosen. Bjerstedt gives a good proportion of space to a contribution of his own in the mapping of social relations, and also to the question of developing a shorthand for indicating relationships. His handling of this subject is sophisticated, and this section of the monograph will be particularly rewarding to clinical as well as social psychologists.

[B71]

★BLADE, MARY F., AND WATSON, WALTER S. **Increase in Spatial Visualization Test Scores During Engineering Study.** American Psychological Association, Psychological Monographs: General and Applied, Vol. 69, No. 12, Whole No. 397. Washington, D.C.: the Association, Inc., 1955. Pp. 13. Paper. $1.00. * (PA 30: 5226)

[B72]

★BLOOM, BENJAMIN S.; ENGELHART, MAX D.; FURST, EDWARD J.; HILL, WALKER H.; AND KRATHWOHL, DAVID R. **Taxonomy of Educational Objectives: The Classification of Educational Goals: Handbook I, Cognitive Domain.** New York and London: Longmans, Green & Co., Inc., 1956. Pp. xiii, 207. Paper. $1.50; 10s. 6d. *

Brit J Ed Psychol 28:84–5 F '58. American educationists spend far more time than British (too much time, perhaps) discussing their educational "objectives," and planning their curricula, teaching methods, and examinations to cover these. Professor Bloom and an imposing committee of educational leaders and psychologists have attempted, with considerable success, to produce a systematic and impartial classification of objectives in the cognitive field—that is, omitting, for the time being, attitudes and values, interests and personality qualities, which

schools may try to develop. The book contains an interesting discussion of the rationale of the classification, together with sets of specimen essay and new-type questions, designed to sample each of the categories. There is no doubt that school and university examiners in this country might improve their examining by considering the questions they set, and how they mark them, in the light of this discussion. *

Ed & Psychol Meas 16:401–5 au '56. William E. Coffman. No single reading of this volume, however intensive, can result in an adequate appraisal of its usefulness for the field of education or even for the practicing specialist in test construction. It constitutes an attempt to provide for the cognitive domain of educational objectives a taxonomy which will "be of general help to all teachers, administrators, professional specialists, and research workers who deal with curricular and evaluation problems." (p. 1) A full evaluation of the effort must rest on its acceptance and use by workers in the field as they deal with their problems. This is a book to be digested and tested over time rather than one to be sketched and laid aside. There seems, however, little doubt that it will stimulate thought about fundamental issues and that it is a step toward a clarification of the nature of educational goals. The volume is the first in a series designed to produce a complete taxonomy of educational objectives in three major areas—the cognitive, the affective, and the psychomotor. It is the work of an informal association of college and university examiners who were interested in developing a theoretical framework which could be used to facilitate communication among examiners. As discussion continued, it became evident that the taxonomy might have wider implications. It is offered as a tool to help educational workers discuss curricular and evaluation problems with greater precision; to set forth for the curriculum builder a range of possible educational goals; to provide a relatively concise model for the analysis of educational outcomes in the cognitive area of remembering, thinking, and problem solving; to provide suggestions for measuring the different classes of objectives; and to provide research workers with a framework for viewing the educational process and analyzing its workings. * It is with respect to the particular items chosen to illustrate the categories that the reader may find himself in most disagreement with the authors. In view of the claims that the taxonomy is applicable throughout the educational system, it is unfortunate that most of the illustrative items have been drawn from the college level. * In spite of deficiencies in some of the items as illustrations of the several categories, the overall effect of the illustrative material is to set forth in a striking manner the kinds of cognitive behavior which are intended. Furthermore, the test specialist finds here a wealth of ideas for the construction of test items. If the volume did no more than to provide these model items, it would be a valuable addition to the worker's library. * The handbook....represents a pioneer attempt to provide a framework for the analysis of educational problems. It makes clear the organic relationship between evaluation and the teaching and learning process. A new way of looking at relationships among the several organized fields of knowledge has been set forth in a challenging way. The effort merits the close attention of all who are concerned with the behavioral goals of schools and colleges.

Ed & Psychol Meas 17:631–4 w '57. Julian C. Stanley and Dale L. Bolton. * The *Taxonomy of Educational Objectives* probably has great value for classifying and clarifying educational objectives. There also seems to be enough agreement among graduate students independently classifying test items to warrant the regular analysis of teacher-made and standardized tests. If each publisher of achievement tests would note carefully the levels of the items being devised for a new test and insure that they match the levels of the objectives set up in specifying the content and operations of the test, we might eventually get away from having the majority of the items testing "mere" knowledge.

J Ed Res 51:392–3 Ja '58. Henry J. Ehlers. * Many who study the *Taxonomy* may feel that Bloom's stratification of the cognitive domain into six neat, hierarchical levels—not to mention the various sub-classifications—is somewhat arbitrary, and even a priori. * This reviewer rejoices that the Bloom *Taxonomy* is in an inexpensive paper-covered edition. For whether the readers agree or differ with the precise nature of the classification, all surely will agree that testing (and teaching) in the cognitive domain should aim toward something better than mere tid-bits of factual information.

J Higher Ed 28:290–2 My '57. Anthony Nemetz. This volume effectively demonstrates that education as a discipline is maturing. As a philosopher I can only applaud what seems to me a radical advance in the level of discussion about educational problems. Gone are the watchwords, the slogans, the *cliches* and shibboleths; instead, this volume initiates a discussion organized by principles with a consequent emphasis on research rather than on persuasive skills. * Unfortunately there is a real danger present in this volume, one which will rigidify thinking. Briefly stated, the danger consists in tacitly accepting the supposed dichotomy between fact and value. * In sum, the authors contend that in their presentation they are striving for neutrality toward values and objectivity in presenting values and goals as facts. The issue is whether this is at all possible. I think not * I confess that I am more than a little puzzled by what seems to be a paradoxical result of the structured taxonomy. In the first place, evaluation as an educational objective is regarded as the most complex of all educational behavior and is given the top spot in the hierarchy of objectives. Yet the authors state that "formal education in a democracy has generally been extremely cautious in dealing with problems of evaluating" (page 188). One of the reasons given for the chariness is fear that the school may be doing special pleading. If the authors are serious when they say that the goals being classified are those given by society, how can we account for the fact that the schools are not carrying out the social mandate? Moreover, if facts and values can be separated and if one can be neutral with respect to the facts, is there any justification possible for the supposed fear? If the cognitive domain is in fact separable from other domains, should there not be an endless pleading within for evaluation? However, there is no excuse for only dwelling on the problems which the book raises, for the volume has merit. Apart from the intrinsic accomplishments of the book, I think its real contribution consists in setting a tone of educational discussion which will force the large academic community to join in solving a problem which belongs to all.

[B73]

★BLUM, LUCILLE HOLLANDER; DAVIDSON, HELEN H.; AND FIELDSTEEL, NINA D.; WITH THE ASSISTANCE OF LOUIS GETOFF. **A Rorschach Workbook.** New York: International Universities Press, Inc., 1954. Pp. iv,

169. Paper. $2.00. * (London: Bailey Bros. & Swinfen, Ltd. 16s.) (*PA* 29:4034)

J Consult Psychol 19:318 Ag '55. E. Lowell Kelly. * introduces the student to each of Klopfer's major scoring determinants and provides an extensive series of scoring exercises for each. The "correct" answers are provided in an Appendix. * Neither the text nor the exercises are concerned with interpretation, which in the authors' opinion should follow the development of skill in scoring. The "basic bibliography on scoring" has seven titles.

J Proj Tech 19:345 S '55. Leonard B. Olinger. * [merits] a rating of high acceptability. Well organized, lucidly presented, and sensibly graded for increasing difficulty and complexity, it takes the beginning student by the hand, figuratively speaking, and leads him progressively into the thickest parts of the inkblot forest. In the process, one gets the feeling that no attempt is made to circumvent some of the underbrush merely because the task is tortuous. Rather, it is as if every pitfall that could be anticipated is sought out and successfully negotiated, the emphasis being on facilitation and practice rather than on spurious oversimplification. * the workbook is, in a limited way, also a manual—one that follows, in general, the procedures of administration and interpretation suggested by Klopfer and elaborated by Salter and others. There are three appendices presenting the keys to the self-testing exercises, sample records with keys, and a comparative table of location and determinant scores. These appendices should prove very helpful to the student, as is the basic bibliography on scoring which is listed on the last page of the book. There are experienced Rorschach workers who declare that scoring is meaningless and wasteful. The authors make a rather convincing case in support of scoring procedures, pointing to the advantages of ordering the mass of otherwise unwieldy—and, to the beginner, bewildering—material. The essence of the scoring system, which is not limited to the Klopfer method, is clearly communicated with detailed diagrams and explanations. This approach seems to reflect wide experience in teaching Rorschach technique and a sympathetic understanding of the problems of the beginning Rorschach student. The foreword.... states....that "....a workbook should lighten the arduous task of the instructor and reduce the frustrating insecurity of the beginner who cannot yet see the forest for the trees." * this workbook goes a long way toward meeting both of these objectives.

Psychiatric Q Sup 29:332 pt 2 '55. * This small workbook should prove of considerable value to the student lost in the intricacies of Rorschach language.

[B74]

★Bowyer, Ruth. **Mental Measurement.** University of Bristol, Institute of Education, Publication No. 4. London: University of London Press Ltd., 1953. Pp. 32. Paper. 2s. *

[B75]

★Bradfield, James M., and Moredock, H. Stewart. **Measurement and Evaluation in Education: An Introduction to Its Theory and Practice at Both the Elementary and Secondary School Levels.** New York: Macmillan Co., 1957. Pp. xiv, 509. $5.50. (London: Macmillan New York. 28s. 6d.) * (*PA* 32: 936)

Ed & Psychol Meas 18:418–20 su '58. Edith Jay. * The first section is the happy result of a mathematician writing in collaboration with an educator. It is up to date in theoretical issues as well as formula presentations, and is enriched by numerous illustrations which are simple and clear. Many of these illustrations are drawn from diverse fields and show the related problems other professions have in measurement. Technical terminology is carefully explained and all formulas are outlined in a cookbook fashion so desired by those students who are less facile in algebra than in words. However, the vocabulary level throughout is relatively high and sometimes the authors introduce additional terms of their own, leading to a vocabulary load well beyond considerable numbers of college students. * The second section, which begins after 215 pages of basic principles, is carefully planned and rigidly systematic in its organization. Almost equal chapter lengths are devoted to Language Arts, Social Studies, Science and Mathematics, Performances-Activity Areas, Intelligence and Personality and Character. The result is a somewhat uneven distribution of effective coverage of present literature in the fields. The field of reading, for example, probably has more test materials in wider variety than all the other achievement areas combined. Seven pages are devoted to this topic * The authors have not tried to review a representative sample of contemporary tests. They have instead endeavored to set up evaluation standards for each subject and often for activities within a subject field, then use tests when they illustrate a method for evaluation according to these standards. * This is an original and worthwhile approach in the reviewer's estimation. However, the pedantic method of using the same outline for each chapter provides organization and system, but sacrifices some of the appeal which other texts have. Probably the most stimulating aspect of the book is this consistent emphasis on evaluative standards. The distinction between evaluation and measurement as explained in Chapter IX, might well serve as required reading by students in other classes. The authors apply pragmatic as well as scientific standards in their discussion, and, though they differ somewhat from Bloom's taxonomy, achieve much the same result in structuring qualitative as well as quantitative information on a similar scale. The final chapter on school-wide testing programs includes discussion of cumulative records, ability grouping and other topics, but unfortunately fails to apply any evaluative standards to their content or use. A few do's and don't's are specified, but this chapter seems to lack the obvious final touch—of evaluating the child's progress on a long term basis as well as intermittent appraisal, and evaluating the school's total achievement of its objectives. Each chapter is concluded with a good bibliography, and an extensive glossary of terms is provided in Appendix A. *

J Ed Res 51:553 Mr '58. Philip Himelstein. * The reviewer would like to recommend.... that....this book be given strong consideration. The authors....have done an excellent job in introducing the student to the first course in educational statistics. * The text is an excellent one for introductory courses in measurement. The book is written in clear and readable language that will appeal to most students. More important, the text offers the student an opportunity to obtain more than a vague notion of meaningless statistical procedures. The book is written so that the reader will think about and comprehend problems of measurement as they affect the teaching process.

[B76]

★BROGDEN, HUBERT E. **The Primary Personal Values Measured by the Allport-Vernon Test, "A Study of Values."** American Psychological Association, Psychological Monographs: General and Applied, Vol. 66, No. 16, Whole No. 348. Washington, D.C.: the Association, Inc., 1952. Pp. 31. Paper. $1.00. * (*PA* 27:7191)

[B77]

★BROWNSTEIN, SAMUEL C., AND WEINER, MITCHEL. **How to Prepare for College Entrance Examinations, Revised Edition.** Great Neck, N.Y.: Barron's Educational Series, Inc., 1958. Pp. v, 295. Paper, $1.98; cloth, $3.95. *

[B78]

★BRUCE, MARTIN M. **The Prediction of Effectiveness as a Factory Foreman.** American Psychological Association, Psychological Monographs: General and Applied, Vol. 67, No. 12, Whole No. 362. Washington, D.C.: the Association, Inc., 1953. Pp. 17. Paper. $1.00. * (*PA* 28:5019)

[B79]

★BUHLER, CHARLOTTE; LEFEVER, D. WELTY; KALLSTEDT, FRANCIS E.; AND PEAK, HORACE M. **Development of the Basic Rorschach Score: Supplementary Monograph.** Los Angeles, Calif.: Rorschach Standardization Study, 1952. Pp. iv, 71. $2.50. * (*PA* 26:5602)

B Menninger Clinic 17:155 Jl '53. Walter Kass. Scoring weights of 99 signs comprising the Basic Rorschach Score, reported in the authors' *Rorschach Standardization Study I,* are cross-validated on a new sample of 397 psychiatric cases. The finding of "a highly satisfactory degree of similarity between the scoring weights derived from two essentially independent samplings of clinically defined cases" meets the main methodological and statistical deficiency of the earlier study. This is a noteworthy successful quantification of intricately interrelated Rorschach variables. Unique in its attempt to span the gap between personality theory and Rorschach rationale, it delineates four levels in the integration-disintegration continuum: "adequacy," "conflict," "defect," and "reality loss." *

J Consult Psychol 16:412–3 O '52. Ann Magaret. * All four studies represent significant contributions to the task of Rorschach standardization.

[B80]

★BULLOCK, ROBERT P. **Social Factors Related to Job Satisfaction: A Technique for the Measurement of Job Satisfaction.** Ohio State University, Bureau of Business Research, Research Monograph No. 70; Ohio Studies in Personnel. Columbus, Ohio: the Bureau, 1952. Pp. xii, 105. Paper. $2.00. * (*PA* 28:5020)

Personnel Psychol 7:195–6 sp '54. L. Lawrence Schultz. * The sampling used....is a trifle weak in so much as the pre-test group of university upperclassmen is a far cry from the typical industrial workers. Readers must bear in mind the situations surrounding the final conclusions. Perhaps a knowledge of which social factors are positive motivating elements could be used in selection, but it is questionable if industry can have a deep interest about factors over which they have little or no control once the worker is on the job. The bibliography indicates subject matter written during the era of acceptance of job-satisfaction's relation to productivity, but in more recent days industry is taking a second look at the relative value of measuring job-satisfaction.

[B81]

★BUREAU OF NAVAL PERSONNEL, RESEARCH DIVISION. **Constructing and Using Achievement Tests: A Guide for Naval Instructors.** NAVPERS 16808-A. Washington, D.C.: United States Government Printing Office, 1949. Pp. iv, 94. Paper. * (Reprinted with minor corrections in 1952.)

[B82]

★BUROS, OSCAR KRISEN, EDITOR. **Classified Index of Tests and Reviews in The Fourth Mental Measurements Yearbook.** Highland Park, N.J.: Gryphon Press, 1953. Pp. 60. Paper. $0.25. * (*PA* 27:3886)

Occupational Psychol 27:225 O '53. H. F. Lock. This booklet constitutes a preliminary advertisement for the Fourth Mental Measurements Yearbook, which will no doubt be reviewed in due course. It is not without interest or value in itself, however. * The Index distinguishes between new tests and tests which appear, not because they originated during the period but because further work, of one kind or another, has been done upon them. A total of 793 tests are listed; this reviewer has not attempted to count the new ones, but by inspection they are certainly more numerous in the index than are the old ones. It is a staggering thought that over 100 new tests have been published each year for at least the last four years. Essentially, the booklet now noticed is nothing more than an expanded table of contents for the Year Book. It is, however, quite definitely useful in itself as indicating the fields in which test development has been and is proceeding; the tests are classified by the purpose of the test, so that it is readily possible to refer to any particular group. It is news to at least one reader that there are no less than four tests of etiquette.

[B83]

BUROS, OSCAR KRISEN, EDITOR. **The Third Mental Measurements Yearbook.** New Brunswick, N.J.: Rutgers University Press, 1949. Pp. xv, 1047. $12.50. * (*PA* 23:3523) For reviews, see 4:B71.

[B84]

★BUROS, OSCAR KRISEN, EDITOR. **The Fourth Mental Measurements Yearbook.** Highland Park, N.J.: Gryphon Press, 1953. Pp. xxv, 1163. $18.00. * (*PA* 27:6280)

Am J Psychiatry 111:78–9 Jl '54. Leola E. Neal. * All test users will find the Yearbook valuable. The detailed and accurate information on construction, validation, and the uses and limitations of specific tests will enable them to select tests more wisely. The same information or the absence of it should re-emphasize some of the dangers involved in uncritical acceptance of tests even though they have been prepared by well-known authorities.

Brit J Ed Psychol 24:54 F '54. * The volume provides a most valuable and indeed unique work of reference, which should be in any University or other library which claims to cater for research students in psychology or education.

Brit J Psychol 45:154–5 My '54. Peter McKellar. * Buros has again provided psychologists, educationalists and other test users with a most valuable reference book. He has, moreover, performed an additional service that becomes apparent immediately one starts to use this book or its predecessor. In the detailed instructions given to the contributing test reviewers....Buros states his aim: "to stimulate progress towards higher professional standards in the construction and use of tests, by commending good work, by censuring poor work, and by suggesting improvements." This editorial policy, supported by more than three hundred special reviewers, makes the book valuable not only as a work of reference but also as a very thorough piece of "reality testing" of one of psychology's most important tools. Good, well-standardized tests are given the credit due to them, but no reader can long remain unaware of just how many tests of unknown reliability or uninvestigated validity are in widespread use. The reviewers have not failed in the task assigned to them of making their criticisms specific, of mentioning alternative better-standardized tests when available, and of indicating weaknesses or omissions of fundamental kinds in test construction and standardization. The book is, as a whole, rather depressing in that it indicates just how widespread faults of this kind are; it also serves to make this fact unmistakably plain to the world of professional psychologists. Those who consult it must inevitably come to sympathize with its editor and his contributors in their efforts "to impel test authors and publishers to present more detailed information on the construction, validation, uses and misuses of their tests." *

Future volumes....might perhaps develop a stage further to include a separate list of approved, properly standardized tests. The residue of the book could comprise tests of dubious value, together with those at the quite legitimate stages of research development; this residue would form the main body of the book. It is unfortunate that both this and the earlier *Yearbook* are so bulky; this limits their usefulness, since it is a laborious task for each reader to evaluate the better tests for himself. A place on such a "white list"—one hesitates to suggest a "black list"—might in the course of time come to be eagerly sought. This would greatly hasten the achievement of the wholly admirable aim of the book's editor and contributors. Separate publication of the section on books as opposed to tests would also diminish size and costs. Again the present system of test classification is not wholly satisfactory; larger printed numbers would assist quicker location of test entries; the Universal Decimal System of numbering merits consideration; and tabulation might be used to shorten the test reviews. Yet it would be ungrateful to press minor criticisms of a major contribution towards the more rigorously scientific developments of psychology. Despite its cost this is a book which no responsible institution concerned with psychological testing can afford to do without.

Calif J Ed Res 4:190–1 S '53. Like its predecessors, *The Fourth Mental Measurements Yearbook* is another milestone in the field of tests and measurements. Again, this encyclopedia and buying guide is a "must" for test users. * The reviews are, in general, evaluative in nature—sometimes brutally so! Psychologists and counselors will welcome the initial reviews of such widely used instruments as the *Leiter International Performance Scale,* the *Wechsler Intelligence Scale for Children,* the *Blacky Pictures,* the *Symonds Picture Story Test* and the *General Aptitude Test Battery.* Equally valuable are the reviews of other recently published tests. In addition to thoroughly listing and reviewing tests, Buros performs a similar valuable service with the 429 books on tests and measurements appearing since his previous yearbook. As with Buros' previous works, the yearbook is unusually well indexed. * In summary: It is difficult to refrain from becoming statistical in reviewing this book; one tends to cite numbers of pages, journals, books, reviews, reviewers, excerpts, references and so

forth. Briefly, *The Fourth Mental Measurements Yearbook* is as essential to test users as a phone book is to one who uses a telephone!

Calif J Sec Ed 29:177 Mr '54. Arthur P. Coladarci. * The stature of the *Yearbooks* among test users in education and psychology has increased with each edition to the point where only the ill-advised will deny their indispensability to the serious members of these professions. The *Fourth Yearbook* consists entirely of new material covering the years 1948 through 1951 and, continuing past policy, supplements rather than supplants the previous yearbooks. A few statistics may reveal the monumental nature of the book. The section "Tests and Reviews" contains descriptions of 793 commercially available tests published as separates in English-speaking countries, 596 original test reviews by 308 reviewers, 53 excerpts from test reviews in 15 journals, and 4,417 references on the construction, validity, and use of specific tests. The section "Books and Reviews" lists 429 books on measurement and 758 excerpts from book reviews in 121 journals. A reviewer of one of the earlier volumes referred to it as "the mental test Baedeker"; in view of the foregoing description, the label surely can apply to the present volume without running the risk of an unnecessary hyperbole! This yearbook and its predecessors deserve a place in the professional libraries of all schools. The constant availability of such a competent and frank reference will contribute much to the reduction of unsystematic and uncritical selection, acceptance, and use of tests in educational practice.

Ed Adm & Sup 41:126–7 F '55. Jack A. Holmes. The administrator, turning to *The Fourth Yearbook,* will find a series of searching analyses by qualified reviewers on all personality-, achievement-, intelligence-, and vocational-tests published in all English-speaking countries during the period from 1948 through 1951. * So succinctly, yet so comprehensively, has been the coverage that, without undue overlap, 793 tests have been critically evaluated in some 649 original reviews and excerpts from reviews. * The volume has been organized so that one may gain the maximum utility by simply acquainting oneself with a set of systematic key-classification devices, such as, table of contents, classified index, cross references, catchwords, as well as indexes of titles, authors' names, publishers, and periodicals. * The traditional courage of the Editor of these yearbooks is again to be commended. The determination of each reviewer to be intellectually honest has resulted in a positive and substantially potent force which, when fully recognized by school people (the largest single consumer), will finally impel test authors and test publishers to publish in test manuals the really important and detailed information regarding the construction, validity, reliability, norms, uses and misuses of their instruments when they are placed on the market. In other words, this reviewer thinks that tests which are used to classify, diagnose, or depth-probe children and/or to evaluate teaching must be selected with regard to the honest merits of the instruments and not on the particular appeal of an especially catchy advertising campaign!

H Sch J 37:259–60 My '54. Jacob T. Hunt. * the seventh volume of a distinguished series on tests initiated in 1935 by Professor Buros, director of the Institute of Mental Measurements, Rutgers University * The very size of the volume may be disturbing to those unfamiliar with the other yearbooks or to the casual administrator or teacher looking for "the best test to use." The few minutes necessary for reading the section in the preface, "How To Use This Yearbook," will be rewarding in more efficient use. In addition to the Table of Contents are directories or indexes of periodicals, publishers, test titles, and names. With so many contributors it was inevitable that the reviews would vary in length, quality, and degree of critical orientation. Although concise reviews (300–500 words) were requested by the editor, some will run to considerable length, in a few cases exceeding 5,000 words. Most of the discussions read (the reviewer admits readily to a sampling rather than to a complete reading) are properly concerned with the construction and characteristics of the tests, although a few reviewers described rather than appraised. Both weaknesses and strengths are usually pointed out candidly. Highly capable and experienced persons were selected to do the reviews. In general, this Yearbook, which reflects an enormous amount of time and effort and careful editing, is an excellent reference; to the student of measurements and to the serious user of tests, it is an indispensable one.

J Consult Psychol 17:465 D '53. Anne Roe. * includes the staggering total of 793 tests, 130 more than the *Third Yearbook.* Many more personality tests have been included, together with a number of tests which are available only as a part of restricted testing programs. * This volume, as have been the preceding ones, is magnificently organized, indexed, and cross-indexed. The complete bibliographies for each test are invaluable. Some criticisms of previous volumes have been well heeded, as the listed instructions to the test reviewers, and their performance, indicate. The level of the test reviews is generally high, and for the most part judicious. A few reviews are possibly excessively bitter. Most possibly controversial tests have two or more reviewers, and a comparison of the reviews serves to control the problem of possible personal bias of the reviewer; study of the reviews of several different tests by one reviewer may also be very illuminating here. Any prospective test user can certainly learn quickly, authoritatively, and painlessly what tests there are for any purpose, and what he needs to know about any test, so far as the knowledge is available anywhere. Would-be test constructors are urged to read and reconsider—maybe their brain child should be aborted. But if it must be brought to term, what should and should not be done is amply exemplified here. Read and heed!

J Ed (London) 85:536 N '53. Cyril Burt. * With an amazing energy and power of organization,....Buros and his associates have drawn up lists of all publications on mental testing, extracted or summarized reviews from the standard periodicals, and supplemented them by brief descriptions and criticisms written specially for this volume. In this way they hope "to persuade authors and publishers to place fewer and better tests on the market, to inculcate upon test-users a keener awareness of the values and dangers accompanying the employment of such tests, and to impress upon them the desirability of suspecting all tests unaccompanied by detailed data as to their construction, validation, use, and limitations." Tests published in this country receive their full share of attention; and nearly every well-known British psychologist who works in the field of mental testing has contributed critical notices. The whole forms an encyclopaedic work of reference, which should be on the shelves of every library for psychologists and teachers, and will undoubtedly prove invaluable for everyone who uses such tests, whether for practical or for theoretical purposes. It is admirably arranged, indexed, and produced; and the venture deserves all the support it can possibly receive. *

J Ed Psychol 45:314–7 My '54. Lee J. Cronbach. Every testing specialist has learned to rely on the Buros Yearbooks as desk companions. Every teacher or counselor using published tests should study MMY as a whole, and consult it frequently. MMY is a bibliographer's dream: references to all tests, to all recent studies on each, and to books on testing. The organization and printing are magnificent. The heart of the book is its critical reviews of tests. In the new Yearbook, these are invariably thoughtful. Except in the area of classroom achievement tests, reviewers have frequently tried out the tests and many reviewers report minor research performed to gather new data for the review. Criteria for judgment are much the same as in former yearbooks. The reviews give less weight than formerly to picayune errors, more to the function of a test in instruction and clinical interaction. A long honor roll could be prepared of superior reviews. The following have exceptional general interest: a spectacular review of Shimberg of *Health Inventories* (ETS); Anastasi on "primary abilities" tests; Westby on *Progressive Matrices;* Courtis on the *Thorndike Handwriting Scale* (some notable history); Fowler on *Henmon-Nelson;* and Kaulfers on *CEEB French Reading.* The yearbook draws attention to new tests which might otherwise be overlooked. Judging from the reviews, the person interested in tests should become acquainted with these: *1947 Progressive Matrices, California Cumulative Guidance Record* (Elem.), *Differential Abilities Test, SRA Self Scorer, IPAT Culture-Free Intelligence, GRE Aptitude, Diagnostic Reading Tests, Wing Musical Intelligence, Children's Apperception Test, Functional Evaluation in Mathematics.* While important, the *General Aptitude Tests of USES* and the *Weschler Scale for Children* were disappointing to reviewers. There are a good many negative reviews. Only three major publishers— World Book, Psychological Corporation, and ETS—are generally producing tests which the reviewers regard as adequately developed, and even these houses fail to maintain high standards consistently. Some other large publishers are accused of serious violations of judgment and even of ethics. Over and over, reviewers say that tests have been released prematurely, that they are acceptable for research use but because of insufficient validation or standardization are not suitable for practical use. This points up a major policy issue. Should we encourage the release of a test incorporating new ideas, even though the fundamental test development is incomplete? We need innovations, and yet we know that even the shiniest ideas may not survive careful research. Should research on a test precede general distribution, or follow it? Who should do it—the inventor or the customer? The reviewers demonstrate that we have gone too far in the direction of releasing tests prior to the required fundamental research. The majority of newer tests are at present suitable for use only by those who will conduct research on the tests in their own setting, but they are usually distributed without such limitation. A favorable sign is the report that many manuals have been revised to meet criticism from the last MMY. Older tests, however, have generally continued in print with neither revision nor continued research. Their authors would do well to withdraw some of them. Buros has now perfected his yearbook technique. It is regrettably necessary to question the program and basic conception he holds, even though the series is marvellous if it can be sustained. The price of the volume is $18, and this does not cover all costs. MMY is priced out of its market. If it cannot sell in volume, some new plan is needed. Changes can be made which will reduce the yearbook's value far less than they will reduce costs. An editor might consider these alterations. (1) Eliminate four hundred and fifty pages of reprinted book review excerpts, a costly feature not much used. (2) Eliminate reviews of foreign tests unlikely to be suitable for the American market. This is a provincial suggestion, but it would be better at this point to disseminate MMY more widely in this country than to pursue comprehensiveness. (3) Remove the exhaustive and expensive bibliographies on tests. (4) Eliminate analytic reviews of obsolete tests. A balanced review of (for example) the Zyve test is not needed. One sentence stating that this test should not be used for such and such purposes, signed if necessary by a group of adequate authorities, tells the student all he needs to know. Buros has this year made an effort to resurvey old tests, to such lengths as seven pages on variants of Army Alpha. Some retrospective reviews are of current value, but most could be reduced to much more blunt statements that a test is obsolete, or that, while originally "experimental," in twenty years it has not been improved to the point of usefulness. (5) Possibly more radical suggestions would be worth considering. Suppose the test-by-test reviews in the vocational interest field, for example, were replaced by a single summary of the field, signed by Super, Bordin, Carter and Bennett. This could provide perspective, balance, and guidance far beyond that allowed by the present organization, however perfect MMY is by librarianship standards. Few individuals have made so singular a contribution to the profession as Buros. Devotion, self-sacrifice, clarity of purpose, and editorial talent are evidenced in every page of Buros' series. It is gratifying that the leading measurement organizations have recently adopted a testimonial resolution recognizing this. Criticism can say only that the world is perhaps not yet ready to support a project of this elegance, and that Buros can compromise with his editorial ideals without seriously compromising his professional contribution.

J Nat Inst Personnel Res 6:121–2 Mr '56. L. E. Cortis. * The service supplied here grew steadily since 1935, and seems to have improved in quality and competence. * The fact that every yearbook is intended to supplement rather than supplant earlier publications has certain drawbacks. To obtain the fullest benefit from this volume, previous ones should be available. Inconvenient as this may be, it seems unavoidable. The system of reference which Buros has established is extensive, and only permits duplication to a very limited extent. * The point to note is that the service which Buros provides is in many ways unique and should call for the greatest support from all psychologists and psychological organizations. * Some of [the test] criticisms are very severe, and seem so well justified, that one wonders whether the tests in question will receive enough support to warrant their publication. One notes therefore that in addition to supplying factual information about tests, Buros' yearbooks serve an extremely important function of weeding out bad tests, and improving the quality of existing tests. All test entries are accompanied by adequate descriptive information, e.g. the groups for which the test is intended, the time taken to administer it, the author, the publisher, the cost, etc. The reader may feel the lack in some instances of data on the standardization and validation of the tests. While this is available for the majority of the tests, indication is given in the other instances whether such information is to be found in the test manuals. A very welcome innovation is the list of contributing test reviewers found at the beginning to this yearbook. Most of them come from the United States, less than 10% coming from other English-speaking countries. * A general criticism that may be raised against this publication is that it has a strong American bias. One misses, for instance, the noteworthy contributions made by Scandinavian and South African psychologists, published in English. It is hoped that Buros will rectify this in future issues of his very valuable and unique publication.

Med Times 82:303 Ap '54. Frederick L. Patry. This monumental publication is a vade mecum to the clinical psychologist and all those concerned with the application of psychological tests and measurements in education, industry, psychiatry, psychology, et cetera. * Like previous volumes it has proved its practical value in assisting psychometrists to locate and evaluate tests and find pertinent references in the literature. * This volume is the "Bible" of all those working in the ever growing science of psychological tests and measurements. It represents a striking growth since the first two publications in this series of noncritical bibliographies of tests published in 1935 and 1936. It augurs well for the steady and future growth of this specialized field of applied psychology.

Mental Hygiene 39:136 Ja '55. Frank K. Shuttleworth. Those who use educational, vocational, or psychological tests will find this book an indispensable tool. * The heart of the matter is the 596 reviews especially prepared for this volume by some 306 individuals, each chosen for his competence. Uniformly, these reviews are clear and evaluative. Often they are highly critical. They are condensed, but long enough to be adequate. They will prove rewarding reading even for the experts. It is clear that reviews of previous yearbooks and of the present one have exerted and will continue to exert a powerful influence on test authors and publishers to improve their products. The volume is a most important contribution.

Occupational Psychol 27:226–7 O '53. D. F. Vincent. To that section of the psychological world whose work is intimately connected with tests and the literature of tests, "Buros" needs no introduction. To most test users it is as much a household word as Whitaker, Hansard or Baedecker. They will welcome the appearance of a new edition and their chief interest will be in how much new material has been added. * English readers will be pleased to note that of the new tests added a large number are English. Eight tests issued by the National Institute of Industrial Psychology are among the additions. Fifty-four per cent. of the tests described have been reviewed, and about twenty per cent. have been reviewed by more than one authority. The reviewing is really more extensive than this fact suggests, as the practice of giving references to reviews contained in earlier editions has been continued. Judging from the references quoted for the National Institute's tests it seems that the bibliographies given beneath the descriptions of each of the tests are fairly complete. Test users are sure to be pleased with the new "Buros." Probably because the Mental Measurements Yearbook is necessarily rather expensive and has to be purchased with dollars, it is not as well known to psychologists not intimately concerned with testing as it deserves to be. * It is perhaps a pity that all the tests could not be reviewed by more than one reviewer, for in the field of testing, as everywhere else, individual opinions vary considerably. Of the reviews of tests that the writer knows intimately, some have appeared to him to be decidedly generous and others extremely critical. Two reviews of every test is, however, not practicable; the book is large enough as it is, and if its size were increased any more it would need to be produced in more than one volume, with consequent increase in cost. * In addition to the usual tables of contents the Fourth Mental Measurements Yearbook has two very useful indexes. One of the names of tests, and one of the names of persons, which includes, as well as the names of authors, reviewers and institutions, any names that are mentioned in the reviews. No reference book as comprehensive as "Buros" could be easy to use, but the indexing and page headings make it as easy to use as is possible.

Personnel Adm 16:34 Jl '53. O. Glenn Stahl. This task is like reviewing an unabridged dictionary. There is simply nothing to compare with the object of the review. * monumental reference book * Indexes to periodicals and

publishers, as well as to titles and names referred to, adds to the utility of this yearbook as a manual. A minor flaw to some users is the placing of the number of the first item on a page (each test listed is numbered for easy reference) at the top of that page, thus making the use of page numbers, also at the top of each page, confusing. The use of bold-face type for the item numbers in the running text would appear adequate for quick finding by item number, without the page-top reference. It goes without saying that this most comprehensive reference work has become an almost indispensable tool to all concerned with psychometrics—whether psychologist, educator, vocational counselor, personnel man, or subject matter specialist. The *Fourth Yearbook* is a credit to a splendid, well-conceived series. I repeat—there is nothing to match it.

Personnel & Guid J 32:118-9 O '53. Robert L. Ebel. * No conscientious test author or publisher and no discriminating user of mental tests can afford to be without this volume, which is the latest and best in a distinguished series. * While there is duplication between this and previous volumes in some of the tests and a few of the books listed, there is no duplication in the reviews printed. Adequate indexes and cross references....have been generously and expertly supplied. * If essential accessory materials such as a manual, tables of norms, or reliability coefficients are missing, specific mention is made of the deficiency. This is intended to emphasize the importance of such information, and to spur test authors and publishers to provide it. * In general the reviews are of high quality, written by competent critics who have obviously studied the tests carefully and expressed their judgment honestly. Many of the reviews make very interesting reading. They reflect the insights and biases of the particular reviewer as well as the merits and defects of the test under review. It would no doubt be possible to use excerpts from these reviews to compile a comprehensive and stimulating set of readings on the theory and techniques of mental measurement. No reader is likely to accept all that he finds in these reviews as true, relevant and important. The wise provision for multiple reviews of many tests tends to limit the damage which a single biased review might do. Further, any reader of a single critical review ought to know that he is dealing with the observations and judgments of only one person. The evaluation of tests is not so precise and formal that perfect agreement is to be expected, even between thoroughly competent and perfectly fair critics. Oscar Buros has undertaken to produce a volume which will be both a useful guide to mental tests and a positive force for their improvement. He has succeeded in both aims. This is not to say that test publishers will immediately accept all of the soundly based criticisms and suggestions of the reviewers. But it is evident that they are aware of the book's existence and sensitive to its praise or blame. They may be forgiven for lagging somewhat behind their critics if only they will maintain standards higher than those demanded by typical test users. This leads to the almost self-evident observation that *The Fourth Mental Measurements Yearbook* will best serve its intended purposes in the hands of educators, personnel workers, and others who buy and use tests. If they follow the guidance of this book, they are certain to become progressively better informed and more discriminating test users. It is fervently to be wished that enough of them will buy the book to justify continuance of an essential service.

Psychol B 51:297–9 My '54. Irving Lorge. * the seventh in a series of publications intended to make available to practitioners in psychology, education, and related disciplines the rich resources of tests and measurements. The series began modestly with the little pamphlet "Educational, Psychological, and Personality Tests of 1933 and 1934" (issued in 1935) * The current volume is a beautifully printed and well-organized tome of more than 1,100 pages. In no way can it be compared with the first little pamphlet. The earliest three publications were primarily test bibliographies. The shape of things to come was first evident in the 1938 publication. For in that volume, Buros undertook the prodigious tasks of getting cooperative reviews of tests (issued as separates in the English-speaking countries) and of compiling significant excerpts from published reviews of books and monographs related to tests and measurements. In 1940, he made this task his by tradition; in the present volume, he has dignified the tradition by an opulently produced book. * the current volume....lists, for the first time, restricted tests together with reviews of a few of them. Indeed, Buros, as well as the test organizations, is to be congratulated for removing some of the so-called secrecy from the instruments utilized by agencies like the College Entrance Examination Board, the Educational Testing Service, and the National League for Nursing Education. * In a sense, Buros' publications represent a compromise. In the early thirties he intended to develop a test-consumers' research organization. Failing to realize such an accomplishment, he devoted himself to the lesser, but very important, goal of supplying to all, particularly to test consumers, "frankly critical reviews." Such a limitation, of course, meant that he had to become dependent on outside reviewers rather than upon members of his own research staff. During the years, Buros has had the cooperation of the leading specialists in test construction and test utilization. Nor has Buros left the task to them alone; he has supplied the bibliography of published research related to each listed test. Such cumulation of related material has been, and should continue to be, a valuable resource for the student and the scholar. For example, the cross-references for the Wechsler-Bellevue Intelligence Scale now goes to 312; and for Rorschach to 1,219. As for books about measurement, the review excerpts that he has edited and compiled make another basic contribution toward appreciating the growing sophistication of test constructors. An editor who conceives his function to be the improvement of test making and hence the improvement of test using deserves well of all who make and use tests. Indeed it is fitting that the Division on Evaluation and Measurement of the American Psychological Association and the Psychometric Society jointly expressed their appreciation for his enterprise over the past 20 years. The fact that these two organizations memorialized Buros indicates the value and significance of the work. Indeed, the volume's deficiencies seem entirely attributable to Buros' limited financial resources rather than to any administrative or intellectual constraints. The volume, in so far as it is not cumulative, makes it necessary for the interested user to manipulate several volumes, for test reviews are to be found in the four volumes for 1938, 1940, 1949, and 1953. Perhaps the time has now come when test listing and test reviewing can be done best through the medium of an official magazine sponsored by the American Psychological Association. Such a publication would give greater currency to the newer tests faster. With the expanding test field, it seems too long to have to wait four or five years for Buros' next volume. Indeed, if subscribers are willing to pay $18 every four or five years, there may be even more who can afford $4 or $5 every year for more current material. Buros, in his attempt to be fair to every test maker, has "leaned over backwards." At one time, he forwarded the critical reviews to the test authors and/or publishers to make certain that the critiques were related to the facts. This apparently was so formidable a task that he abandoned it in favor of trying to achieve at least three reviews of each test by different analysts. Fair as that may be, it seems not nearly as valuable an objective as getting at least *one* review of every listed test. In a random sample of 20 entries, four were not tests at all (a manual on aphasia, a book on Rorschach, a manual for driver selection, a series of forms for employee selection); seven were of new tests not previously listed, but which remained *without* review; three were for new tests not previously listed with a review; four were for reviews of a revised or supplemented test; and two were reviews for tests which had been previously listed and reviewed. Perhaps editorial energies could have been expended to get all the new entries reviewed at least once. It is not difficult, however, to recognize that the reviewers themselves frequently add their personal prejudices to their test appraisals. Sometimes these biases are minor ones, such as criticizing the directions, sometimes they are major ones, such as questioning the use of primary batteries of standardized achievement tests. For one reasonably familiar with the proclivities of the individual reviewers, it is quite a confirming reaction to be able to designate the reviewer just from the review. In a field as diverse as testing, various specialists have developed special attitudes: e.g., criticism of objective scoring as restricting the scope of testing, or the impossibility of getting truly representative national norms, or the overclaims on diagnostic profiles. As is inevitable, the reviews are uneven because of the very specialization of the reviewers. In one sense, the user of the volume should have available specifications of "all the players." Nevertheless, most of the advice is significant and cogent. * Future editions of the volume will profit from attempts to classify the *relevant* information by validity, reliability, sampling for normative data, character of norms, relevance for specified objectives of appraisal or of instruction. It is the lack of a comprehensive plan for coverage that makes for the primary difficulty with the reviews: they tend to be so prolix and discursive as to omit much information that a consumer should have for his decisions. Certainly, the bulk of the reviews fails significantly to meet Buros' requisite: "Reviews should be written primarily for the rank and file of test users." Too often, the reviews seem to be prepared for the reviewer's peers. The current reviews, however, occasionally give evidence that earlier reviews have led the authors to make improvements in subsequent revisions of their tests; unfortunately, in too many instances, the reviews give contrary evidence that the test authors were immune to such analyses. Over the 20 years, however, Buros has raised the standards for the technical aspects of test making. It is hoped that a magazine may continue these important reviews to make them more up to date and available at a price that will allow the rank and file to use them more freely. I know of no one as capable as Buros to be its editor.

Sch R 61:517–8 D '53. Maurice L. Hartung. Editorial. Fortunately for progress, there are a few men in every generation who see a vision and are so inexorably persistent that they bring it to reality. Professor Oscar Krisen Buros of Rutgers University, editor of *The Fourth Mental Measurements Yearbook,* is one of these men. Fifteen years ago there was no comprehensive source to which to turn for critical reviews of tests and other evaluation instruments. Professor Buros thought there ought to be one and in 1938 published the first book of this kind. The most recent volume in the series, covering the period 1948 through 1951, supplements rather than supplants the earlier numbers of the series. In his Preface Professor Buros says the book is "designed to assist test users in education, industry, psychiatry, and psychology to locate and to evaluate tests and books on testing." It is, in fact, an almost indispensable reference for many workers in these fields. The editorial staff of the *School Review* customarily relies on it for checking data on tests mentioned in the articles published. This editorial writer regularly requires his students in courses on methods of teaching to use the volume in connection with their examination of tests in their fields. Graduate students use it to survey available materials as they plan research projects. The book ought to be in the professional library of every school system for the use of teachers and others who have responsibility for selecting published tests. Valuable as the book is as a tool, Professor Buros from the beginning has had in mind another value. He hoped that authors and publishers of tests would be stimulated to improve their product, and the several *Mental Measurements Yearbooks* that have been published have undoubtedly been a force in that direction. In general, recently published tests are superior to earlier ones, but it would be difficult to isolate the effects of the critical reviews encouraged by Buros from the effects of other books and developments in the field of educational and psychological measurement.

Teachers Col Rec 55:107 N '53. Frederick B. Davis. * tremendous volume * an immensely valuable bibliographical guide. In addition, it is an exceedingly rich source of evaluative information about tests, since the 308 experts in measurements presumably gave a good deal of thought and labor to writing the original reviews presented. Every serious worker in educational and psychological measurement will want to make use of the yearbook; any library that serves students in these fields should have a copy on the reference shelves. The writer sampled the original reviews and found them to be interesting and generally accurate, to the best of his knowledge. Quite naturally, they vary in quality and scope. The excerpts from the reviews of books that are presented in the second part of the yearbook bring together a good deal of critical evaluation of more-or-less current publications, but the writer cannot help wondering whether this merit justifies their reprinting. Even if it does, he would like to urge consideration of the alternative of printing them in a less expensive format and binding them separately from the *Mental Measurements Yearbook*. It seems doubtful that most book reviews are worthy of expensive reprinting, especially when they are rather widely available in their original form. In conclusion, it seems appropriate to pay tribute to the editor of the *Fourth Mental Measurements Yearbook*, Oscar K. Buros, for his industry and pertinacity in gathering and compiling data.

For reviews of earlier volumes in this series, see 4:B70, 3:788, 40:B856–8, 38:B325–6, and 36:B45–6.

[B85]
★CALIFORNIA STATE DEPARTMENT OF EDUCATION, BUREAU OF HEALTH EDUCATION, PHYSICAL EDUCATION, AND RECREATION. **California Physical Performance Test.** Sacramento, Calif.: California State Department of Education, 1958. Pp. ix, 29. Paper. $0.25. *

[B86]
★CALIGOR, LEOPOLD. **A New Approach to Figure Drawing: Based Upon an Interrelated Series of Drawings.** Springfield, Ill.: Charles C Thomas, Publisher, 1957. Pp. xii, 149. $4.50. (Oxford, England: Blackwell Scientific Publications, Ltd. 34s.) * (*PA* 31:7902) For reviews, see 131.

[B87]
★CAMPBELL, DONALD F. **Factorial Comparison of Arithmetic Performance of Boys in Sixth and Seventh Grade.** Washington, D.C.: Catholic University of America Press, Inc., 1956. Pp. vi, 39. Paper. $0.75. *

[B88]
★CAREY, ROBERT E. **Testing for Guidance Purposes.** American Guidance Monographs, No. 10. Boston, Mass.: Research Publishing Co., Inc., 1953. Pp. 24. Paper, mimeographed. $1.00. *

[B89]
★CATTELL, RAYMOND B. **Factor Analysis: An Introduction and Manual for the Psychologist and Social Scientist.** New York: Harper & Brothers, 1952. Pp. xiii, 462. $6.00. (London: Hamish Hamilton Ltd. 48s.) * (*PA* 26:6649)

Am Sociol R 17:657–8 O '52. Roy G. Francis. The author attempts two things in this volume: First, to prove the scientific *necessity* for factor analysis, and second, to demonstrate workable techniques for accomplishing factor analysis. With respect to the latter, he certainly goes into fine detail— at times quite schematic—describing various necessary operations. The acceptability of these techniques depends largely on the acceptability of the argument for this type of analysis. In turn, the incompleteness of the prior argument seems to reduce the significance of the operations as presented. The text seems to offer good coverage of the factor analysis techniques, and for those who already agree to its basic logic, has much to offer. This reviewer was gratified to note Cattell's argument for oblique rotation in those instances where the traditional orthogonal rotation seems "forced onto the data." The author's "P-technique"—in which a single individual is given a series of tests to determine any clusterings of items in respect to him—seems worthy of continued use, though with less enthusiasm than the author exhibits. But the book is not simply a restatement of factor analysis; nor is it simply an argument within that field. It includes a defense of the technique, an attempt to "sell" factor analysis to the psychological and social sciences in general. While one can agree that factor analysis has something to offer these sciences, the structure of Cattell's argument requires closer scrutiny. For the sake of brevity, we will limit our comments to two basic operations which have not, in this text at least, been sufficiently generalized to warrant Cattell's belief that the social sciences ought now to take over factor analysis. The operations to be discussed are "reflection" of the correlation ratios, necessary to subsequent inferences about "factors," and drawing inferences from the factors which have been isolated * The process of reflection involves the assumption that by reversing the algebraic sign of any correlation, we can make inferences about the converse of a variable. When reflected, "sociability" becomes "unsociability" and, presumably, "love" becomes "hate." It remains theoretically possible that such variables are not merely polar opposites of the same dimension but represent different dimensions. Failure to be theoretically careful in redefining the reflected variables leads to the danger of assuming data which are not actually present in the materials dealt with....This leads to further confusion in drawing inferences from the "factors" which have been isolated by the technique. That is, when certain items cluster sufficiently to warrant the inference that a factor has been isolated, what does the factor imply? When the number of sunspots, the number of immigrants, the size of the army, and other similar items lead to the inference that a particular factor measures "Expansive living vs. Restricting hard times," the difference between reading into one's data and reading out of them is virtually destroyed. The text offers no justification either for analyzing a particular set of items, or for the inference that is drawn from them. Until such a system, logically defensible, is derived, the general utility of factor analysis remains questionable. This reviewer feels that if greater care were paid to the development of the logical assumptions of factor analysis, and the problems which flow from those assumptions, this technique would gain more adherents. At present, this particular book fails in that respect, however polemic Part I may be. It is doubtful that this particular presentation of factor analysis will convert many from other systems of analysis. The difficulties of drawing inferences from the various factors have not been removed, nor are they clarified in this volume.

Brit J Psychol, Gen Sect 44:78 F '53. Philip E. Vernon. Few psychologists can have carried out as many large-scale factorial analyses as Prof. Cattell, and he must certainly hold the record for rotating to oblique Simple Structure. Thus a book which sets out the fruits of his practical experience, and his broader speculations on the nature and use of factorization, could not fail to be of value. It is indeed a fine piece of work—clearly and very objectively written, and packed with interesting ideas and helpful illustrations. Parts of it, however, are very heavy-going and the book hardly succeeds in providing the working manual which any Ph.D. student could follow, for which there is a great need. The first Part does present a fairly simple survey of the whole topic of centroid analysis, which should be useful to many Honours students; nevertheless, the reviewer would still be inclined to recommend Sir Godfrey Thomson's book in preference. It is the more complex second Part (dealing with working methods and particularly with the art of rotation), and the third Part (on general principles and problems), which add most to the standard text-books by Burt, Thomson, Thurstone and Holzinger. * Cattell....makes ambitious claims, and presents strong arguments, for its wider use in general psychological research, and its combination with classical experimental, or with modern Fisherian, techniques. The psychologist or statistician who is suspicious of the whole topic should certainly study Parts I and III with care. A number of doubts, nevertheless, still remain in the reviewer's mind. Apparently any really adequate analysis involves giving some sixty tests to a few hundred subjects, extracting a dozen factors, and spending about six months full-time on computation and rotation (even with machine aids). But scarcely one in a hundred professional psychologists could undertake research on such a scale; indeed scarcely one in a hundred is likely to be able to learn how to carry out blind rotation to oblique Simple Structure. Either then we must be allowed to carry on with simpler researches involving less than twenty variables and half a dozen factors, with orthogonal rotation or no rotation at all, or else factor analysis looks like becoming an even more esoteric and specialized approach, even more divorced from the main stream of psychology, than at present. Finally, if factorization is so fundamental to any advance in psychology, why is there still so little agreement regarding the basic components of intellect and personality which it is supposed to reveal? These are some of the questions which Prof. Cattell has not answered; though it is a little unfair to raise them in view of the vast number of points—not mentioned in this review—which he does cover.

J Ed Psychol 44:254–6 Ap '53 *W. J. E. Crissy.* The author states that the book has been written to meet three major requirements. "First, it sets out to meet the need of the general student in science to gain some idea of what factor analysis is about and to understand how it integrates with scientific methods and concepts generally." * "Second, it is intended as a textbook for statistics courses which deal with factor analysis for the first time, either as an appreciable part or as the whole of the semester course." * "The third objective of this work is to supply a handbook for the research worker, the student, and the statistical clerk which will be a practical guide with respect to carrying out the processes most frequently in use." * Cattell has met these requirements which he has set for himself. The resulting text is highly readable, even entertaining. The multiplicity of diagrams, charts and examples plus the questions and exercises at the end of each chapter make the book teachable at the advanced undergraduate level and above. The author has kept the almost inevitable complex mathematical formulations and proofs to the barest minimum, though he furnishes pertinent references for the interested reader. The student new to the jargon of factor analysis, will make frequent use of the well-prepared glossary. The author, as has been his wont in other writing, occasionally stops the reader dead in his tracks with neologisms and relatively unusual words. This Cattellian quirk will probably stimulate most persons though it may irritate a few. The latter group are reminded that a little frustration can do no harm and it may facilitate learning! With respect to the whole field of factor analysis, the book is neither comprehensive nor eclectic. It couldn't be and fulfill the stated requirements within the confines of a work of usual textbook size. The following instances are cited more as illustrations of the previous statement than as criticisms: A better case can be made for orthogonal, as contrasted with oblique, rotation than is done in the text. Cattell presents a strong argument for obliqueness and conjectures that only rarely will the best fit to

psychological data be an orthogonal one. He treats only indirectly and summarily the orthogonalist's argument of the case of conceptualizing factors which are uncorrelated. He would seem to make computational ease the fundamental argument pro orthogonal factors. Many factor analysts, however, would insist on going beyond orthogonal factors to uncorrelated factor scores using partialling techniques to insure the latter. The author gives little attention to the metheod of principal components and the advantages which inhere in this mode of analysis for some purposes. In an early chapter the author includes a brief summary of various non-factorial statistical methods. However, he fails to mention canonical correlation and this method probably relates more closely to factor analysis than any of the others, yielding, as it were, a general factor common to both predictor and criterion measures. The work has two unique features in terms of content which combine to make the book an indispensable addition to the professional library of everyone concerned in any way with factor analysis. First, throughout the book fundamental importance is attached to appropriate experimental designs. Cattell presents a model relating the various factor analysis designs to various experimental hypotheses. Also, he has devoted much of the third part of the book to a lucid explanation of how to incorporate computation, reliability, and validation checks in the design of various kinds of experiments employing factorial procedures. Second, he presents an exposition, with illustrative data, of his much discussed P and O analyses. He also proposes two new factor designs, S and T. * The format and typography are excellent. *Errata* are seemingly few. The reviewer caught only one which can have serious consequences for the unwary reader. There are two miscalculations in Table 17, p. 163, which cause an accumulation of error in the table and lead to the reflection of signs on the wrong variables. An appendix is provided containing instructions for doing matrix multiplication by using electronic calculators, a feature useful to those fortunate researchers who can get access to such equipment. Anyone interested in factor analysis should add this work to his professional library. Instructors of factor analysis whose students have sparse mathematical background will welcome this text. Cattell has made another major contribution to the psychological literature.

J Ed Res 47:78–9 S '53. Dorothy M. Knoell.
* Two of the main sections....are devoted to an elaborate and thought-provoking discussion of concepts and principles relating to factor analysis. * The larger contribution....is probably in the ideas presented rather than in the working techniques. * Q-technique is regrettably treated with less sympathy than the other variations of R with little attention paid to its possible uses. The development of the concept of the "specification equation," in predicting behavior of individuals and groups in various situations is generally useful, being presented in more detail than the usual discussion of factor scores. Chapters....on manipulation in the "classical factor analytic experiment" and on factor analysis with controlled experiment present material....should stimulate thinking among users of factor techniques. The main criticism of the book stems from its planned appeal to the reader with little mathematical background. No attempt is made to tie in factor analysis with mathematical theory in general; in fact, mathematicians are chided for insisting upon some of the "niceties" in factor solutions. This is especially true in the presentation of the centroid method where use of some of the procedures outlined will not give a set of factors which is a true centroid solution. For example, the author suggests in his discussion of reflection procedures that it is not always desirable to maximize the sum of the matrix when the first centroid factors are being extracted. It is hoped that the casual reader will not attempt to follow the centroid method outlined in an early chapter not realizing that a more adequate presentation is made later in the book. Group methods of factoring are treated in some detail but several available computational checks are not mentioned. Detailed numerical examples would have been a useful part of the outline of steps for diagonal factoring and for computing inverses. * Existing techniques for direct rotation to primary structure are ignored completely. His dismissal of positive manifold (a criterion in rotation) as purely a myth implies some misunderstanding, i.e., that the criterion should be applied to all solutions, indiscriminately, rather than to solutions for matrices that are essentially positive at the outset. Persons already familiar with factor analysis will probably object to the notation used, particularly V for variable and F for primary factor, since V and F have already taken on other meanings in the Thurstone school of factor analysis. Also, use of the terms "projection" and "loading" may be criticized although a proper distinction is made between "loading" and "correlation." While not winning friends among psychologists who already reject factor analysis as lacking mathematical respectability, Cattell's *Factor Analysis* should find an enthusiastic audience among readers looking for ideas about the technique and among novices who are frightened by equations.

J Genetic Psychol 83:185–94 S '53. A. S. C. Ehrenberg. * Cattell's *Factor Analysis* is intended as an introduction and manual, and rather than consider the merits of the general factor analytic principles, we have tried in this review to examine what some of those practical procedures for handling data which are given in the book have been shown to do. In the centroid analysis, for example, it would appear that fundamental steps like "reflecting" and "choosing communalities" have not only not been said to satisfy any important general principles, but that no such principles have in fact been set up. In the absence also of any *a posteriori* deductions, the centroid solution presented might therefore be judged rather meaningless, and inadequate for inclusion in a laboratory manual. Centroid factors apparently have to be "rotated" by applying the principle of "simple structure." However, the only proven property of the computational solution put forward is that is does not actually satisfy the principle of simple structure. As far as the "factors" are concerned, it does not therefore seem to differ from any other possible solution in any material effect. Any factors, once obtained, must be interpreted. In multiple factor analysis with non-unity communalities no way of finding appropriate factor scores is known, and the only generally used criterion of interpretation is to consider the variables most highly loaded in the factor in question. Nothing much seems to be known about this procedure, except that even factors with identical patterns of saturation can be completely orthogonal, i. e., not the same. Whilst therefore Cattell may have succeeded in his aim to produce a simpler account of factor analysis, his subject matter appears to be largely compounded of unverified speculation and rather unsuccessful guess work, and this he has not made sufficiently explicit. [See original review for additional critical comments not excerpted.]

J Social Psychol 40:339–45 N '54. *Charles Wrigley.* * The earlier accounts of factor analysis have been revised, but Cattell's is the first completely new account in a decade. Let us consider, then, how Cattell handles these new features of factor analysis in his textbook. First we may note that the book is avowedly written for the psychologist rather than the statistician. * The book should be well suited to the audience for which it is designed. There is no one who has used factor analysis more extensively than Cattell or who is more familiar with its practical problems and manipulations. The account will be within reach of the graduate student without extended mathematical training. There is a pleasant style of writing, and diagrams and numerical examples are freely given. All in all, Cattell has written probably the simplest account of factor analysis to date, and for that reason alone his text represents a very welcome addition to the psychological literature. It is hardly surprising to find that Cattell stresses the computational side, since no one has done more than Cattell and his co-workers (notably Saunders and Haverland) to show how efficiently punched-card equipment can be used for calculating correlations and factor loadings. * the student is insufficiently warned of the somewhat arbitrary nature of many rotational decisions. Nor does Cattell appear to provide any systematic defense in this book of his claim that a simple structure solution is more nearly invariant and more meaningful scientifically than any other. A similar point might be made with respect to Cattell's treatment of communalities; we find in Cattell's book (as is true to some extent of all other textbooks in factor analysis) that there is an implicit acceptance of the need for communalities. No evidence is provided that the present methods for estimating communalities succeed in reducing the correlation matrix to minimal rank. Nor is it shown that the factor loadings are appreciably altered and the interpretation of factors changed as a result of inserting communalities rather than unities in the principal diagonal of the correlation matrix. The graduate student might be pardoned for getting the impression that the factor-analyst subscribes to communalities and to simple structure as articles of faith. Cattell gives useful and fair-minded discussions of alternative precedures which have been suggested for estimating communalities and for rotating to simple structure, but fails to make

any detailed examination of his reasons for adopting these key concepts. Cattell recognizes that a major weakness—perhaps the major weakness—of contemporary factor analysis is its dependence upon subjective judgments. He points out that "it is to some extent possible to manipulate the number of factors (by communality assessments) and their nature (by rotation) to fit quite a range of hypotheses" (p. 124). He advocates "blind rotation" (p. 90) in an effort to avoid this. Yet even in this "blind rotation" there is no assurance that two investigators starting with the same correlation matrix will reach the same results. The skillful and experienced factor-analyst seems to be as much an artist as a scientist. It might be held that the most urgent challenge to factor-analysts in the nineteen-fifties lies in the development of objective techniques. We need exact procedures for deciding upon the number of factors to be extracted, for calculating rotated factor loadings, and for the matching of factors. Mathematical help will almost certainly be required in the solution of these problems. * Cattell's own contributions to factor analysis, such as the applications of the covariation chart techniques, parallel proportional profiles, and the use of marker variables in a matching formula, are considered in some detail. For the person already versed in factor analysis, this may well prove to be the most useful section, providing a view of the current development of Cattell's own thinking. In Chapter 20 Cattell urges that factor analysis be used along with controlled experimentation. He has some intriguing suggestions as to ways in which experimental conditions may be systematically varied and the results handled by factor analysis. For example, in his method of "condition-organism factorization," his plan is to vary stimulus conditions in a controlled way from subject to subject. His design will have been structured in such a way that these variations in stimuli appear as factors in a factor analysis of the responses of the subjects if the responses have indeed been affected by these changes in experimental conditions. In effect, he is seeking to combine characteristics of the analysis of variance and of factor analysis into a single experimental design. This indicates a greatly widened view of the rôle of factor analysis in psychological research. Classical experimentalists and mathematical statisticians alike have generally argued that factor analysis is appropriate only in those situations where hypotheses are not readily formulated. Its function is merely to supply a broad overview of the relations in the field. On this view factor analysis is a "last resort" technique to be used only when there is no other available way of analyzing the data, and to be replaced by analysis of variance and other statistical techniques once psychologists are able to express their hypotheses more exactly. Cattell, then, is seeking to extend the area of usefulness of factor analysis. The onus appears to be upon him and his co-workers to design experiments which show that his proposals are valid. This seems to imply a logical task as well as an empirical one, viz., an intensive examination of the relationship of factor analysis and the analysis of variance. These two techniques have mostly been developed independently of each other, and each provides a statistical technique for handling data with multiple sources of variation. * Cattell....seems to suggest that....factor analysis will often meet the demands of the psychologist more adequately than analysis of variance, "in requiring no supposition as to which are dependent and independent variables, and in revealing whether the independent variables as assumed in the analysis of variance are in fact mutually independent and the really important independent influences in the field" (p. 10). The further development of Cattell's views and the course of his experimentation promise to be of the greatest interest. It seems clear that we have by no means exhausted the possibilities in factor analysis of novel designs, and there is no one who has displayed greater ingenuity than Cattell in the planning of factor analyses in very diversified fields. If he can effectively use factor analysis for the designing and analysis of experiments in the way he proposes, he will have made a major contribution to method in psychology. Before factor analysis can hope to fill this rôle, more needs to be known about the extent to which factors vary from one experiment to another. * To summarize, Cattell has written the simplest account we possess of the theory and practice of factor analysis, including a detailed consideration of the rotational problem and a rather full account of computational methods. Mathematical discussions are kept to a minimum. His book will be very useful not only to the graduate student but also to the "practitioner." His account of the use of factor analysis in classic experimental situations is of the greatest theoretical interest. My main criticism—and this is perhaps more a criticism of contemporary factor analysis than of Cattell's book—is that factor analysis is presented largely as a subjective technique, which is dependent upon the exercise of judgment. Skill in factor analysis is acquired only from long experience. After 50 years, it is evident that we have not yet an objective and rigorously developed statistical procedure.

Occupational Psychol 27:49–50 Ja '53. Edward Elliott. * A prefatory quotation clearly indicates that Cattell sees his book as a distillation of the well-known texts by Burt, Holzinger and Harman, Thomson, and Thurstone. Thus we have an ambitious book which, if it achieves just one or two of its aims, must prove extremely valuable. * it is disappointing to find that Cattell's attempt at simple exposition is not very successful. His style is clear and pleasant; but his temperament is that of an eager research worker, and he rushes from simple and basic matters into the more esoteric departments of his subject. He never can resist an aside which will show up an intriguing line of future research; and, although he generally eschews direct statistical discussions, his text abounds in references to statistical niceties which will be incomprehensible to newcomers to his subject. At the beginning of Chapter 2 he even admits this tendency, saying that "the full implications of the previous chapter's discussion of the methodological role of factor analysis cannot be clear until factor analytic processes are understood in some detail." To take no pains to make an opening chapter of a section designed for beginners as lucid as possible is asking for failure; and Cattell does fail to produce a good introduction to factor analysis. The more advanced reader, who, from the outset, can follow the arguments, understand asides or know when to ignore them, and distinguish between what is well established now and what may be well established in ten years' time, will be much better suited; and on this level we have a stimulating and most welcome synthesis of hitherto scattered information. Features which are likely to be particularly appreciated are, first, Cattell's emphasis throughout the book on the design of factor studies, and secondly, his chapters on working methods. The former should go some way to persuade factorists that applying their techniques to any handy set of data is the least economical and productive form of research. We might hope too that Cattell's treatment of the almost universally applied R-technique (factorization of tests) as merely one of six possible techniques may stimulate more interest in the less used techniques. Occupational psychologists, who often must deal with small numbers of people, should be aware of the potentialities of these techniques, which do not depend always on having large samples of persons. The whole of Part II is devoted to working methods. Here there are numerous hints and, in a chapter on the "basic art of rotation by graphs," some very ingenious mechanical contrivances for getting work done systematically and economically. The final chapter of Part III is on "strategy and tactics of economy in computing"; and we meet the idea of design again, on this occasion to reduce computational labours. None of this finds a place in the usual run of lectures and books, and, if it does not entirely save students from the labour of finding their own methods, it should be invaluable as a guide to the general possibilities of economy in computation. The book ends characteristically with an appendix on "essential steps in matrix multiplication by electronic digital calculators."

Psychol B 50:227-9 My '53. Henry E. Garrett. * this book has been written to meet the needs of (1) the general student who wishes to learn what factor analysis is about, (2) the instructor who wants a textbook in factor analysis as part of a course in statistics, and (3) the research worker in this field. * Considerable attention is given to the need for oblique factors in Part II, and methods are provided for the extraction of orthogonal and oblique factors by the centroid method. Cattell does not overlook other factor methods, but he places the main emphasis upon the centroid as being the most flexible and generally useful. In this judgment the reviewer concurs. * Cattell has met his third objective, namely, that of preparing a handbook for research workers, better than his first two. The difficulty level of the book is not adapted to the non-mathematically trained student. It is doubtful whether the beginner can read profitably beyond the first two chapters, and most graduate students in psychology will understand very little of Part II unless it is preceded by a review of analytical geometry and matrix algebra. The problem of rotation as presented in Chapter 12 is unnecessarily discursive; and the student is

not likely to get from Chapter 13 a clear idea of the real need for and value of oblique factors. While Cattell has clarified the distinction between references axes and factors, his treatment is hampered by a confusing terminology. Rules laid down for carrying out a technique are not sufficiently well illustrated to make the rules readily applicable. As an example, the procedures to be followed in making a multiple group centroid analysis (pp. 178-184) are set down without illustration in 11 steps and 8 supplementary notes. This book is a real contribution to the literature of factor analysis and should be read by everyone seriously interested in research in this field. The final chapter on shortcut procedures will be especially valuable to the research worker. A feature of the book is its sprightly style, occasionally refreshed with a touch of humor.

Psychometrika 20:166-8 Je '55. William B. Michael. * Cattell has done well in explaining at a readily-grasped intuitive level the basic principles underlying factor analysis and in stating the numerous uses to which the factor analytic techniques can be put. One of the strongest features of the text is the thorough and penetrating discussion of the place of factor analysis in the design of experiments. * As a manual numerous shortcomings are apparent: (1) It would appear that an attempt has been made to explain too many methods of centroid extraction, communality estimation, and factor extraction relative to the limited space devoted to those topics. A somewhat more extensive explanation of a fewer number of techniques might have been desirable. (2) The steps involved in the various clustering methods do not seem to be easy for the beginner to grasp, since the illustrative examples are not clearly related to the procedures described. For example, the explanation of the group method of factoring (pp. 174-8) seems to be unnecessarily confusing and ambiguous. The origin of the entries appearing in the table at the top of page 176 remains a mystery to the reviewer. (3) The format of the computational explanations is such that one cannot grasp in a readily-apparent fashion the objectives toward which the writer is trying to lead the reader. Paragraph captions or headings would be particularly helpful. In short, each of the steps involved in the calculations is simply not clearly set forth for the reader to perceive. Each rule or procedural item should be directly related to a specific numerical operation. (4) The explanation concerning the rotation process through use of graphs is substantially inadequate if the text is to serve as a manual. What is seriously needed is a set of graphs to illustrate in a step-by-step fashion the solution of a representative problem involving between 10 and 20 test variables. In addition, a paragraph or two in which an explanation is given as to why each rotation was undertaken would be most helpful to the beginning student. Both orthogonal and oblique rotations should be considered at much greater length. Although mastery of the art of rotation requires extensive experience, a list of guiding principles that are related to illustrative plots would constitute an important teaching aid. (5) The presence of numerous errors is particularly annoying and confusing to both the beginner and the experienced worker [see original review for a partial listing] * (6) Much needed is a summary in one location of the matrix equations that are frequently employed in factor-analysis studies—a set of 12 or 15 equations that show various interrelationships among the primary-factor, reference-factor, arbitrary-orthogonal-factor loadings, the intercorrelations of the factors (both types), and the relationship of correlation coefficients to various types of factor loadings. Such a summary would serve to unify much of the illustrative material. * the third requirement has not been realized. Since the book as a manual is somewhat limited in the clarity of its exposition with respect to the use of numerical procedures, the second requirement concerning its function as a textbook has not been met to an adequate degree. * One of the most pleasing features of the book is Cattell's style of writing, which is informal and conversational in its tone. His ample use of cleverly devised figures of speech such as similes, personifications, and metaphors offers many an opportunity for a smile as well as a refreshing change of perspective in the reader's orientation to the field of abstractions that pour forth page after page. * In its current form the book is an excellent source for the person interested in the general principles of factor analysis, in the place of factor analysis in experimental design, and in types of problems in the social sciences for which factor analysis may be useful. However, as a guide or manual to be employed in the actual performance of a factor analysis the book is of doubtful value. Despite the limitations as a manual, it would be useful

as a supplementary text in beginning courses in factor analysis.

Q R Biol 28:104 Mr '53. James Deese. * This book is meant....as an introduction to factor analysis * At best, the author only partially achieves his aim. I am not very sure that the complete novice would find this book understandable, without considerable guidance. A good deal of statistical sophistication is assumed (by and large, implicitly), and examples are few and far between. Most of the examples come from Cattell's own research and are likely to be a bit esoteric to the outsider. The book would have profited much from the addition of frequent, tailor-made examples of the sort one finds in introductory statistics books. Despite these difficulties, the careful and persistent reader will be able to achieve a fair understanding of the method of factor analysis with a minimum of mathematics. Since there is considerable enthusiasm among the factor analysts for the application of their method, research workers outside of psychology ought to become more acquainted with it. At this point, however, another criticism of Cattell's book needs to be mentioned. Cattell himself is apparently convinced of the almost universal applicability of factor analysis. This conviction gets enough in his way that he glosses over or does not mention the many inherent difficulties and limitations of the method. Undoubtedly this book will find use as an elementary textbook in factor analysis, and if the author's enthusiasm is justified, the book will become more important with the passing of the next few years.

[B90]

*CATTELL, RAYMOND B. **A Guide to Mental Testing: For Psychological Clinics, Schools, and Industrial Psychologists, Third Edition.** London: University of London Press Ltd., 1953. Pp. xv, 446. 35s. * (Champaign, Ill.: Institute for Personality and Ability Testing. $6.00.) (PA 28:1846)

Brit J Ed Psychol 23:214 N '53. * Perhaps it may be regretted that Professor Cattell still omits discussion of individual tests of the Binet type; but no doubt the inclusion of those would expand unduly the size of the volume which, as it stands, is certainly a very useful reference book.

Brit J Psychol 45:153-4 My '54. A. Richardson. * The present enlarged and revised version contains a number of minor changes and a few major ones. Anachronisms which remained in the last edition have been removed.

For example, the reference to "Cox's recent research" into tests of manual dexterity has been amended to read, "Cox's basic research." The chapter on the Measurement of Intelligence now contains new and more conveniently presented norms on the Cattell Intelligence Scales. The major changes occur in the chapters on Tests of Temperament and Disposition, and Measures of Character Factors and Probes of Emotional Adjustment. In the first of these a Brief Selective-Answer Misperceptive Test of Personality Factors has been included. It has been constructed to measure, "five of the more important and firmly established primary personality factors." Two other new tests of personality have also been included. One is a humour test and the other a musical preference test. Both are reported to distinguish normal from abnormal populations. In the second of the chapters mentioned above Cattell discusses his Sixteen Personality Factor Questionnaire and includes the items from the shortened form of this test. This is apparently intended to replace the Questionnaire for Personality Factors which was published as Appendix II in the last edition. Among the tests that users of this guide might wish to see mentioned is likely to be the Wechsler Intelligence Scale for Children. Although this test is becoming increasingly popular no reference is made to it. It is perhaps unfortunate that the theoretical limitations that the author imposes upon himself are passed on to the practising psychologist in this way. However, if these limitations are accepted, *A Guide to Mental Testing* provides a convenient reference to a wide range of useful tests.

J Ed (London) 85:536 N '53. Cyril Burt. * the greater part of his book consists of ingenious tests (many devised by himself) for the study of personality and character. These, as he points out, cannot claim the high reliability or accuracy of the older tests of intelligence or scholastic knowledge; but, when cautiously and critically applied, may be useful and suggestive in individual cases. The present edition is nearly half as large again as the original. The Introduction and the theoretical discussions have been thoroughly revised. * New sections on the measurement of "Vocational Interests and Attitudes" and of "Intra-familial Attitudes" have been added; and the chapters on "Temperament and Disposition" and "The Measurement of Character Factors and Emo-

tional Adjustment" have been largely rewritten. The result is an instructive and up-to-date handbook which will be of great practical service to teachers, school medical officers, and clinical psychologists.

For reviews of earlier editions, see 4:B84, 40:B860, 38:B329, and 36:B48.

[B91]

★CATTELL, RAYMOND B. **Personality and Motivation Structure and Measurement.** Yonkers, N.Y.: World Book Co., 1957. Pp. xxv, 948. $9.25. * (London: George G. Harrap & Co. Ltd. 55s.)

Brit J Ed Psychol 28:294–5 N '58. John Beloff. This is the latest and perhaps most ambitious of the three big volumes which the author has brought out over the past decade and which taken together represent a high water mark in psychological taxonomy. When one learns of the taxonomic troubles which to-day beset even the botanist, one can imagine the magnitude of the task which confronts any would-be Linnaeus of human behavior. Yet nothing less, surely, is the role for which Cattell has cast himself. The result is formidable. In his latest proposal for a universal factor index, he lists some eighteen factors derived from the use of ratings, a further twenty in the questionnaire medium and no fewer than sixty-two, if we include abilities, drives, interests, etc., from objective test data. Nor is this the end. He points out that he has listed only the better established factors which have emerged from more than one study and adds "nearly twice as many factors, on a good experimental basis, could be found by the diligent searcher." Now, since one would suppose, the justification for a taxonomy is that it reduces the number of basic concepts required in a given field, one cannot help wondering at what point in this multiplication of entities does the process begin to defeat its own ends? At least, after reading this book, one can sympathize with the Maudsley School when they decide to concentrate on just a few, possibly second-order, factors whose natural history can be plotted with more assurance. What then can the practical psychologist do confronted by this profusion? The future of the system may depend on the success of what Cattell calls the "specification equation" that is the formula which allows one to predict an individual's performance in a given situation from a knowledge of his factor-scores plus the situational indices. In this volume, a promising start is made in this direction by giving the factor profiles of a variety of special groups both occupational and psychiatric. Much of the book is devoted to the measurement of motivation, and the author believes that a revolution in clinical practice would result from a widespread acceptance of the methods he advocates. Let us hope so. It is high time the clinical psychologist was cured of his addiction to projective techniques and supplied with tests of known reliability and validity. There is also much here to interest the educationist in particular when it comes to guiding pupils of equal ability along different vocational paths. The most vulnerable spot in a factor analysis is, inevitably, in the interpretation of the factors. In default of unequivocal validation descriptive titles are liable to be more misleading than helpful. Letters of the alphabet make safer labels but are too austere to be popular. For these reasons the reviewer welcomes an attractive new crop of neologisms (Parmia, Prensia, Praxernia, etc.) with their vaguely floral flavour, though the glossary might have been enlivened by giving us their Greek etymology. No brief review, however, could possibly do justice to the wealth of information which the book contains nor to the unflagging resourcefulness of its author in devising means for testing every facet of personality from the age of four years onwards. It should become an indispensable handbook for the psychometrist and a useful reference for all who wish to profit from the latest advances in psychometric techniques.

Ed & Psychol Meas 18:648–9 au '58. Edgar M. Haverland. This survey of research in personality from the point of view of factor theory is no mere collation of studies but rather a vista of the future. The studies surveyed are presented with confidence that justifies the broad and optimistic view set out. * In the discussions in this book, nothing is sacred. The theories and practices of clinicians and experimentalists alike are scored; the one for a lack of systematic observation and measurement, the other for too narrow and inadequate formulations. The author particularly scorns the paper-and-pencil bound school of psychological measurement, deriding it as "itemetrics"! One point at which a critical reader is likely to encounter difficulty is that at which the author discusses whether a variable (test) *causes* a factor or vice-versa (pp. 301–302). A factor is clearly an abstraction from observed events, but it is not clear whether the term variable in this discussion refers to concrete behavioral events or to some abstraction from a class of such events, and the notion of causality is not at all clear. The book is intended for use as a text, hopefully at the advanced undergraduate level, and exercises are provided at the end of each chapter. But its most important use is likely to be for intensive graduate study and as a summary of factor research on personality. Beyond this, many new, unsettled methodological and theoretical issues are discussed. It will probably be many years before these issues are properly evaluated and the advances in research and practice advocated in this book are accomplished and consolidated. For those readers who expect a tightly organized and disciplined treatment of the subject material which conveys an impression of neatness, completeness, and finality, this book is likely to be disappointing and confusing. But for those who will immerse themselves in the stream of the author's thoughts, following the ramifications spun out in many directions from the material at hand, the reading of this book can be an interesting and stimulating experience. For here we see something of the process as well as the results of the activity of a sensitive and fertile mind at work upon the problems of a vast and complex area of investigation. There is little limitation of the material to be dealt with; the author's discussions range across wide areas including both clinical and experimental approaches to personality study; the whole gamut of personality manifestations from physiology and perception through intelligence and motor behavior, to emotion, interest, and imagination; and a wider array of possible applications of and developments from factor analytic methodology than can be found in any other source. There is little anonymity of the author; the distinctively adventurous and uninhibited quality of Cattell's thought shines through everywhere.

J Clin Psychol 14:102–3 Ja '58. * Cattell and his....staff have accomplished a truly stupendous amount of work in personality study using factorial methods. The development of his theory, research program and practical test design has progressed so rapidly as to require frequent extensive reviews of their theoretical and practical implications. The fact that Dr. Cattell is one of the most prolific and original thinkers on the current psychological scene renders it very difficult to write an authoritative review of all the concepts and data included in this compendious work which covers such a wide range of topics that not many contemporary psychologists are competent to comprehend the technical details of all that is presented. Indeed, the whole field of factor analysis is so new and with so many unsettled problems, that the ultimate validity of much that Cattell has done must await the time when there can accumulate sufficient data and cross-validation experiments so that general agreements on basic issues can be reached. Cattell's sweep is so broad that his enthusiasm frequently leads him into relatively uncharted areas where speculations reach far beyond what has been actually validated. It will require patient checking in independent laboratories to determine whether Cattell's results can be replicated and cross-validated. * Cattell's work has not received the attention it deserves in American psychology, partly because its scope is beyond the comprehension of many of his critics and partly because Cattell's enthusiasm to pioneer new areas has sometimes led him into premature conclusions which have been unfairly cited as characterizing his whole work. We suggest in all seriousness that the American Psychological Association would do well to organize symposia and study groups to bring the best minds in the profession to bear on Cattell's work in order to arrive at a better understanding of its ultimate validity. In the meantime, this advanced text is heartily recommended to those serious readers who have the patience and the background to encompass all that is presented.

[B92]

★CHAMBERS, E. G. **Psychological Tests for Accident Proneness and Industrial Proficiency.** Privy Council, Medical Research Council Memorandum No. 31. London: Her Majesty's Stationery Office, 1955. Pp. iii, 30. Paper. 2s. *

Brit J Psychol 46:321 N '55. Boris Semeonoff. This Memorandum summarizes five I.H.R.B. reports by E. Farmer and the author, published between 1926 and 1940, and all now out of print. It contains no new material nor fresh treatment of the data. Over 4000 industrial and transport workers, including Services personnel, were subjected to a wide variety of psychological tests, and accident records for many more were examined. Two main conclu-

sions emerged: that accident proneness was a relatively stable personality characteristic, and that a selective process that increased industrial proficiency would at the same time tend to decrease accident rate.

[B93]

★COHEN, DOROTHY H., AND STERN, VIRGINIA. **Observing and Recording the Behavior of Young Children.** Practical Suggestions for Teaching No. 18. New York: Bureau of Publications, Teachers College, Columbia University, 1958. Pp. ix, 86. Paper. $1.00. *

[B94]

★COLLEGE ENTRANCE EXAMINATION BOARD. **Advanced Placement Program.** New York: the Board, 1956. Pp. 136. * (PA 30:7756)

[B95]

★COLLEGE ENTRANCE EXAMINATION BOARD. **A Description of the College Board Achievement Tests.** Princeton, N.J.: Educational Testing Service, 1956. Pp. 133. Paper. $0.50. * (PA 31:1744)

[B96]

★COLLEGE ENTRANCE EXAMINATION BOARD. **A Description of the College Board Scholastic Aptitude Test.** Princeton, N.J.: Educational Testing Service, 1956. Pp. 64. Paper. $0.50. * (PA 31:1745)

[B97]

★COLLEGE ENTRANCE EXAMINATION BOARD. **English Composition: A Description of the English Composition Test of the College Entrance Examination Board.** Princeton, N.J.: the Board, June 1954. Pp. 35. Paper. $0.50. * (PA 29:1443)

[B98]

★COLLEGE ENTRANCE EXAMINATION BOARD. **Foreign Languages: A Description of the College Board Tests in French, German, Latin, and Spanish.** Princeton, N.J.: the Board, April 1954. Pp. 31. Paper. $0.50. * (PA 29:1444)

[B99]

★COLLEGE ENTRANCE EXAMINATION BOARD. **Mathematics: A Description of the College Board Tests in Intermediate and Advanced Mathematics.** Princeton, N.J.: the Board, September 1954. Pp. 27. Paper. $0.50. * (PA 29:2957)

[B100]

★COLLEGE ENTRANCE EXAMINATION BOARD. **Science: A Description of the College Board Tests in Biology, Chemistry, and Physics.** Princeton, N.J.: the Board, September 1954. Pp. 39. Paper. $0.50. * (PA 29:2958)

[B101]

★COLLEGE ENTRANCE EXAMINATION BOARD. **Social Studies: A Description of the Social Studies Test of the College Entrance Examination Board.** Princeton, N.J.: the Board, 1953. Pp. 24. Paper. $0.35. *

[B102]

★COMMITTEE ON DIAGNOSTIC READING TESTS, INC. **Diagnostic Reading Tests: A History of Their Construction and Validation.** New York: the Committee, Inc., 1952. Pp. 56. Paper, lithotyped. $1.00. * (PA 27:6738)

[B103]

★COMMITTEE ON DIAGNOSTIC READING TESTS, INC. **Diagnostic Reading Tests: Their Interpretation and Use in the Teaching of Reading.** New York: the Committee, Inc., 1952. Pp. 44. Paper. $2.00. * (*PA* 27:6739)

[B104]

★COOMBS, CLYDE H. **A Theory of Psychological Scaling.** University of Michigan, Engineering Research Institute, Bulletin No. 34. Ann Arbor, Mich.: University of Michigan Press, May 1952. Pp. vi, 94. Paper, lithotyped. $1.75. * (*PA* 27:3879)

J Appl Psychol 38:66–7 F '54. *Marvin D. Dunnette.* If you've had a hard day measuring attitudes, don't expect this small monograph to provide an evening's relaxation. It's packed from cover to cover with non-superfluous material. It is to the author's credit that he has said so much in so short a space; nevertheless, persons lacking expertness in scaling theory will not digest the contents properly. On the other hand, scaling theorists will accept this tidbit as a juicy morsel and will soon be looking for more. * The author openly states that the theory is not in final form. By implication, it is his hope that this publication will initiate interest resulting in a wider range of development for the theory in both its abstract and real aspects. To this end, the monograph represents a good start.

Personnel Psychol 6:496–501 w '53. *Ardie Lubin.* Can a personal experience have a unit of measurement common to different persons? How does one tell whether a psychological attribute observed in one individual is the same attribute in another individual? These and other basic problems of psychological measurement are explored in this closely-reasoned, highly technical monograph by Professor C. H. Coombs. The primary question to which he devotes himself is a rather elaborate one. Suppose a psychological attribute exists on which individuals or stimuli can be represented as if they were points on a straight line. Further suppose that a test (in the form of a questionnaire, or a set of paired comparisons, or a set of stimuli to be ranked, etc.) of this psychological attribute were administered to such a group of subjects. Would the observed responses form a scale? If so, what kind of scale would result? * an ambitious attempt to set down a formal theory of psychological scaling in the hope that it can be extended to cover all known situations in which measurement of psychological attributes plays a part * Coombs has decided views on the place of measurement in psychol-

ogy. He rightly points out that most theorists have tried to *construct* scales, to fit a mathematical model to the data regardless of whether the data fit the model, whereas the real problem is to see whether or not the scale "exists"— to test the fit of the model to the observed behavior. "Scales should be *sought,* not made" (p. 76). It is Coombs' conviction that data collected with present techniques will not satisfy the postulates necessary for a common unit of measurement. So he solves the problem by eliminating it—"i.e., avoiding assumptions which lead to a common and universal unit of measurement" (p. 7). In consequence, although an underlying quantitative continuous scale is assumed, we are left with only discontinuous scales and non-numerical scale values. In Coombs' system there is no hope of ever getting back from the observations to the "true" scale values. This position is seemingly caused by Coombs' assumption that a model such as Thurstone's necessarily imposes an unidimensional, quantitative scale on the data even when the observed behavior simply does not follow the model. However, why not devise parametric (and non-parametric) tests of significance to see if Thurstone's model fits the data? Surely this is a more logical extension of Coombs' basic hypothesis-testing viewpoint about scales than an a priori denial that such models will fit human behavior. As a matter of fact, Thurstone has always insisted that Thurstone scales should be tested by seeing if the obtained scale values reproduced the proportions in the paired comparisons table. If a chi-square goodness-of-fit statistic were devised for the observed discrepancies, this would seem to be an adequate test. Difficulties with such a suggested statistical hypothesis-testing approach would arise immediately for Coombs because of one basic characteristic of his models—they are non-probabilistic. If, in comparing stimuli A, B, and C, a subject prefers A to B, B to C, and C to A, then by Coombs' reasoning, a rank order scale of A, B, and C does not exist (with certain exceptions). There are no such things as probabilities of preferring A to B, and there are no errors of measurement, although he allows subjects to vary with time. All variation is "true" variation. Consequently, Coombs never (well, hardly ever!) finds that the data are scalable. "....experience has shown that a single joint scale....satisfying *all* the responses....of a group of individuals to a group of stimuli rarely, if ever, occurs." (p. 76) From this point of view, to describe data that do not fit the systematic part of your model as "error" is to make one or more of three assumptions: (1) Different individuals are replications of each other for the stimulus; (2) Different stimuli are replications of each other for the same individual; (3) Data incompatible with the measurement model constitute error. (If theory and observations conflict, the observations must be wrong!) Some such assumptions may be necessary for certain purposes, such as making decisions to give scholarships to certain subjects and not to others. But why should these unwarranted assumptions be foisted upon a theory of measurement? Many of the interesting new scales developed by Coombs are not used on either the genotypic or phenotypic level because of the restriction of psychological attributes to a genotypic scale which is an interval scale of the usual quantitative continuous nature. After showing us how easily different kinds of scales can be constructed to match the most intricate psychological situations, Coombs defines a psychological attribute as *necessarily* being an interval scale. This restriction was imposed on the theory at present partly to reduce the task to manageable proportions and partly because this kind of scale is what many people mean when they talk about "measurement." Coombs' monograph is, in the reviewer's opinion, an important work which foreshadows a real flowering of the field of psychological scaling. His attempt to supply an axiomatic basis for psychological measurement has led to certain deductions that can be checked experimentally. For example, the theory says that a Law of Comparative Judgment solution to paired comparison judgments of preference would be what Coombs calls a "folded J scale." In the monograph several experiments are summarized which he feels confirms this deduction. The theory has also led to the Unfolding Technique, which has already proved useful. A great deal can be learned from a theory which gives rise to testable deductions and useful procedures. Unfortunately, the monograph is so written as to be unintelligible to most psychologists. There are not enough verbal materials and examples to make the main points clear to those who must read in between the algebra. The writing style is tortuous, and the terminology new and difficult. This is inevitable since Coombs has attempted to use concepts

for which no terms existed. Were it not for the aid of a former student of Professor Coombs, the reviewer would have been completely baffled. The mathematical material presented is difficult enough so that the reviewer can claim no technical competence in judging whether the conclusions really do follow from the assumptions. At least one of the postulates appears to contain a self-contradiction (the definition of a monotone stimulus on p. 13). There is a notable lack of actual algebraic models for each type of proposed scale; which is pointed out by Coombs himself. Quite obviously this monograph should be viewed as the start of a very large project rather than as the finished product. Much mathematical and statistical work remains to be done, but it seems that this monograph has greatly broadened a field which may have considerable consequences for social psychology. *

Psychometrika 19:89–91 Mr '54. Allen L. Edwards. * In Chapter 3, Coombs gives his definitions and postulates. Here we find the distinction made between Task A and Task B. Task A is concerned with the preference judgments of stimuli with the individual as point of reference. Task B is concerned with judgments of stimuli with respect to some attribute. For Task B, the individual's own position on the continuum under investigation is irrelevant, i.e., the judgments made are assumed to be independent of the location of the judge on the continuum. This is Thurstone's contention, stated in 1939, that judgments of the degree of favorableness and unfavorableness of attitude items are independent of the attitudes of the subjects doing the judging. * An over-all judgment of Coombs' contribution would be an exceedingly difficult task, regardless of whether the judgment is made from the point of view of Task A or Task B. Without concern for the nature of the scale involved, the Task B judgment of the reviewer is that in some respects Coombs falls somewhere near Lazarsfeld, in that both, for example, are interested in genotypic or latent systems. In some respects he also falls near Guttman, for both are interested in the discovery rather than the construction of scales. In terms of techniques used for the collection of data, such as the method of paired comparisons, Coombs might be placed near Thurstone. Again without concern for the nature of the scale involved, from a Task A point of view, the judgment is easier. From a preference point of view, this reviewer belongs at that point on a continuum where fall those who like strong postulational systems, the consequent operations of arithmetic, and the applications of error theory and random variation. Coombs, by choice, has scaled himself at the point where those who prefer weak postulational systems fall. Consequently, if a single continuum is involved, Coombs is at one end and the reviewer is at the other.

[B105]

★COOMBS, C. H., AND KAO, R. C. **Nonmetric Factor Analysis.** University of Michigan, Engineering Research Institute, Engineering Research Bulletin No. 38. Ann Arbor, Mich.: University of Michigan Press, 1955. Pp. vii, 63. Paper, lithotyped. * (*PA* 32:2288)

[B106]

*CORNELL UNIVERSITY, UNIVERSITY TESTING AND SERVICE BUREAU. **Cornell University Test List, 1956 Revision.** Ithaca, N.Y.: the Bureau, 1956. Pp. ii, 64. Paper, mimeographed. $1.00. *

[B107]

★CORTER, HAROLD M. **Factor Analysis of Some Reasoning Tests.** American Psychological Association, Psychological Monographs: General and Applied, Vol. 66, No. 8, Whole No. 340. Washington, D.C.: the Association, Inc., 1952. Pp. iv, 31. Paper. $1.00. * (*PA* 27:4995)

[B108]

★COTTLE, WM. C. **The MMPI: A Review.** Kansas Studies in Education, Vol. 3, No. 2. Lawrence, Kan.: University of Kansas Press, March 1953. Pp. vi, 82. Paper. Out of print. *

[B109]

★CRANE, MARIAN M.; FOOTE, FRANKLIN M.; SCOBEE, RICHARD G.; GREEN, EARL L.; AND PRICE, BRONSON. **Screening School Children for Visual Defects: Report of a Study Conducted in St. Louis, Missouri, 1948–49.** United States Department of Health, Education, and Welfare, Children's Bureau Publication No. 345, Washington, D.C.: United States Government Printing Office, 1954. Pp. iii, 92. Paper. $0.35. *

Sight-Saving R 25:64 sp '55. * Six hundred and nine sixth-grade students and 606 first-grade students in the public schools were given a thorough ophthalmological examination and tested with certain commonly used vision screening procedures. The report deals with the subjects, methods and findings of the study and includes a discussion of such factors as improving test construction and more effective use of present tests. Of all the procedures evaluated the simple Snellen test for distance acuity and the Massachusetts Vision Test gave the highest correlations with the ophthalmological examination. With the binocular testing instruments 50 to 71 per cent of the students were referred, an unmanageably high proportion for most schools. Teachers were apparently

able to administer the Snellen test about as efficiently as the technician and nurses. *

[B110]

★CRAWFORD, CLAUDE C., AND RILEY, THOMAS M., EDITORS. **Evaluation Syllabus: Appraisal Techniques for Functional Teaching and Learning.** Los Angeles, Calif.: C. C. Crawford, 1949. Pp. vii, 116. Paper, mimeographed. $2.00. *

[B111]

★CRONBACH, LEE J., AND GLESER, GOLDINE C. **Psychological Tests and Personnel Decisions.** Urbana, Ill.: University of Illinois Press, 1957. Pp. x, 165. $3.50. *

Austral J Psychol 9:194 D '57. J. A. Radcliffe. * Many of their conclusions are more systematic restatements of familiar principles, but some are new—notably that, contrary to previous studies, utility is a linear function of validity at *all* selection ratios with "fixed treatment selection" based on a single test or battery, but a curvilinear function with "adaptive treatment selection." Their assumptions differ, however, from those of previous studies. They stress that this confirms that the "index of forecasting efficiency" and similar statistics may well be inappropriate values for test evaluation. Their conclusions do not necessarily have immediate practical implications because some limiting assumptions are made, e.g. that all relationships are linear and that both an employee's value to the institution and the cost of testing may be expressed in the same units. But the monograph should achieve its aim "to stir up the reader's thoughts." Particularly might those in vocational guidance see the possibilities of using a "strategy matrix" to evaluate and improve their decisions; those in educational psychology be stimulated by the suggestion that general ability tests have been overrated; and clinicians be both heartened and cautioned on the possible implications of decision theory for projective techniques. The mathematical analysis is intended to be simple but it requires careful reading, particularly to understand some of the assumptions (e.g. normal distribution of "pay-off function" on p. 33). The diagrams are excellent but the print could be larger. There is a typographical error in Formula (9). The general theme of the monograph is that test utility is a function both of validity and the decision situation and "since the topics include efficient design of tests, construction of selection batteries, interpretation of validity coefficients, and use of tests for individual assessment....the results will concern a large and diverse audience of test users." For these psychologists it will repay careful reading.

Brit J Psychol 48:312–3 N '57. H. C. Baker. Using the concepts and techniques of Decision Theory the authors tackle the problem of selection and placement with the most interesting results. The term selection covers not only ability tests but also interviews and personality tests; placement refers to educational, industrial, and psychiatric placement. * By using pay-off functions the authors show how it is possible to compare the utility of training programmes over the whole range of a given ability when the conventional methods only give the best programme without any information on the usefulness of the programmes for different levels of ability. For developing training schemes such detailed knowledge would be invaluable in making policy decisions on the relative advantages of grouping people in terms of ability. Perhaps the most important contribution this new approach makes is to query the adequacy of the present methods of validating tests. The coefficient of determination is found to apply only under certain conditions and the coefficient of forecasting efficiency is suggested as having no relevance whatsoever. The present methods of validating tests do not take into account what the authors call the *a priori* strategy, i.e. knowledge such as academic records which could be used as a means for selection and placement without reverting to tests. They maintain that it is in relation to this that a test should be validated. * This stimulating book has brought much needed cohesion to the subject and has overcome some of the problems that have faced conventional test theory. Whether the solutions it advocates will be accepted by its readers will depend not upon the rigour of the mathematics, which cannot be faulted, but upon the assumptions from which the mathematical arguments are developed. The generality of the new approach will appeal to the mathematically inclined psychologist but the consequences of it are important to all applied psychologists. The empirical work entailed in the development of tests in accordance with the theory will be more exacting but at the same time more rewarding than that for conventional theory. Decision Theory is potentially a powerful tool for exploring new areas of psychology. To apply it, however, requires mathematical competence and a sound knowledge of the subject-matter to be explored; both qualities are shown by the authors. For applied psychologists this book is an absolute must because it deals with classification problems pertinent to their work. It can be recommended to all psychologists as being amongst the studies extending psychological theory into new and important fields. Whilst at times non-mathematical readers will find the arguments a little difficult to follow they need not be abashed by the book since the authors put the minimum of formulae in the text, preferring to give the mathematical development of the theory in appendices. Before reading this book most readers will find it helpful to read *Design for Decision* by I. D. J. Bross (New York: Macmillan Co., 1953) which gives a good popular introduction to Decision Theory. There are two misprints in Appendix 3, p. 142; they concern formulae (3.3) and (3.4).

Brit J Stat Psychol 10:64 My '57. W. R. Norton. * an admirable account of the construction and use of mental tests from this highly practical standpoint. It should be in the hands of all who work in the fields of educational psychology or personnel selection.

J Counsel Psychol 5:156–7 su '58. Jerome E. Doppelt. * The monograph raises a number of provocative issues in the field of personnel decisions and makes a convincing argument for the rule of decision theory in a modern test theory. Many readers will find the first three and the last two chapters very worth while for their lucidly-presented view of decision theory in relation to testing and decision-making. A much smaller number of readers, principally those who have done previous reading in this field, will be interested in the solutions of specific problems discussed in chapters 4–9. More widespread use of decision theory in testing is unfortunately hindered by the complexity of the theory. As Cronbach and Gleser note, "As compared with the algebra of measurement theory or the discriminant function, the mathematics of decision theory is involved and laborious."

Personnel Psychol 11:137–9 sp '58. Richard H. Gaylord. This small book is certain to be one of the most important publications in the field of test theory to appear in this decade. This is despite many deficiencies * Its importance stems from its focus upon the decisions and the utility of decisions that are based upon psychological instruments. For many of us this is not a new emphasis, having been the guiding principle of our research, but like many basics, it is difficult to present and as far as this reviewer knows, has not been the sole subject of even a journal article, let alone a book. This is not to say that nothing new is offered. Decision theory and its consonant disciplines, the theory of games and information theory, has contributed many concepts whose transposition into test theory give new insights of considerable heuristic value. Their application in the text yields new research designs and test application strategies of potentially great importance. The book is divided into 11 chapters, the first and last of which consist of commentaries on decision theory. The reader should not look to these as a source of information concerning decision theory *per se*. The first chapter is an attempt to delimit the contribution of decision theory to the book. The last attempts to evaluate the contribution of the book. Boh are disappointing, the first because it appears to be an apology where none is necessary; the last because it departs from the rigor recommended in the body of the text to present a number of gratuitous generalizations that could only be reached through extensive research. This chapter does a real disservice since among other things it suggests that one might defend the use of projective devices, seldom shown to be valid bases for any decisions, as "wide-band" devices that might be a little bit valid as bases for a great many decisions. Too many catch words of this type have already been used to defend instruments of doubtful utility. Chapter Two, "Types of Personnel Decisions," and Chapter Three, "Characteristics of Decision Problems," set the stage for the remainder of the discussion. Here we find a penetrating analysis of personnel decisions and their utility. Both chapters are very thought-provoking and should clarify thought in research design. Of these, Chapter Three is the most indispensable, displaying a method of analysis that should always precede research. The remaining seven chapters, consider each of a number of testing problems. Five are concerned with standard subjects: selection, placement, classification, efficiency of testing, and evaluation of outcomes (the criterion). Two deal with new topics: "Two-Stage Sequential Selection" and "The Band-width-Fidelity Dilemma." All deal with testing problems from

the point of view of a new mathematical approach and new constructs from decision theory. Each is well worth considerable study. Although thought provoking in every chapter, the reader is to be warned that no chapter can be considered a definitive treatment of its subject. Although apparently well documented, serious gaps appear. To illustrate, the discussion of differential classification is cited in Chapter Nine. It is here implied that a useful solution does not exist for the general case of differential classification involving partial rejection, multiple treatments, and differential quotas. Actually, a solution to this problem was published by Brogden as early as 1946 [1] and the reader is referred to Brogden's 1954 paper [2] for a simple presentation and bibliography. If the reviewer has seemed harsh, let it be understood that this is not to decry the potential contribution of the book. It has been rather an attempt to warn the reader of certain difficulties lest he accept too little or too much. All of us will find our understanding of tests sharpened by this volume.

Psychometrika 23:179–80 Je '58. Bert F. Green, Jr. * The book is well organized and has many pertinent figures. Ample references are made to the relevant literature. Most of the mathematical development has been placed in a series of appendices, while the main text states the problems and discusses the results. Nevertheless it is a book for specialists, assuming knowledge of psychometrics and personnel psychology, and requiring some mathematical sophistication. * the small type and the soporific style combine to dull the stimulating effect of the new ideas. It is clear that the authors view their book as more than a stirring rod—indeed they hope that it is the harbinger of a new test theory. Conventional test theory has focused attention on the test score. Most of the chapters in Gulliksen's *Theory of Mental Tests* are concerned with the properties, meaning, and interpretation of test scores. Cronbach and Gleser have focused attention on outcomes. Their extensive analysis of personnel problems is from a view point that may be characterized as "Validity for What?" Their success in dealing with a wide variety of problems in a single framework is impressive. Decision theory lends coherence to a diverse testing literature focused

1 BROGDEN, HUBERT E. "An Approach to the Problem of Differential Prediction." *Psychometrika* 11:139–54 S '46.
2 BROGDEN, HUBERT E. "A Simple Proof of a Personnel Classification Theorem." *Psychometrika* 19:205–8 S '54. *

on outcomes. If enough professional testers manage to read the book, there is a good chance that the authors' hopes for a new test theory will be realized.

[B112]

★CUMMINGS, HOWARD H.; GAUMNITZ, WALTER H.; HULL, J. DAN; LUDINGTON, JOHN R.; AND TOMPKINS, ELLSWORTH. **Pupil Appraisal Practices in Second-ary Schools: Report of the Fifth National Con-ference Sponsored by the Office of Education and the Commission on Life Adjustment Educa-tion for Youth, Washington, D.C., October 6–8, 1952.** Office of Education, Circular No. 363. Washing-ton, D.C.: United States Government Printing Office, 1953. Pp. vi, 111. Paper, lithotyped. $0.50. *

[B113]

★DALE, R. R. **From School to University: A Study With Special Reference to University Entrance.** London: Routledge & Kegan Paul Ltd., 1954. Pp. xi, 258. 16s. (New York: Grove Press. $4.50.) *

Austral J Psychol 6:97–8 Je '54. C. Sanders. * a synthesis extending from the facts of uni-versity entrance examinations, including their bearing on pupils and schools, to the results of research into selection for universities and into the prediction of academic success. The cover-age of the subject is generous and the arrival of the book timely. For some years there has been a need to integrate psychological, socio-logical and educational results from Britain, the United States and elsewhere. This has now been done most successfully by Mr Dale al-though he makes clear that there is a good dis-tance still to be travelled before we arrive at an acceptable solution of the university selection problem. Those who study Mr Dale's book will, however, have a much clearer conception of the relative worth of "examinations," "inter-views" and "objective tests" as selection meas-ures. And while they will gain an impression of weaknesses and pitfalls in our estimates of human potential, there is an occasional flash of optimism. The book does more than review wartime and post-war selection methods and relate them to subsequent success in university examinations. It discusses not only British practices and procedures, including the relevant research literature, but also American and Aus-tralian. It also deals at some length with the problem of failure. From this view point alone it should commend itself to those interested in educational psychology as well as to members of academic staffs. * Dale's major contribution ....is to the psychology and sociology of his sub-ject. There is a human as well as a rational approach to the problem he presents. The book

therefore, is much more than a treatise on tests and examinations. It represents a contribution to the fascinating and elusive task of human assessment. Its appeal, therefore, is to the edu-cator and to the research worker as well as to the historian and the administrator.

Brit J Ed Psychol 24:125 Je '54. P. E. Ver-non. The appearance of this book is timely. * He believes that a less mechanical considera-tion of the secondary school career, of head master's and class teachers' reports, and of these other relevant circumstances, would much improve the accuracy of selection. But the dan-gers of relying on interview judgments of per-sonality (as distinct from weighing of facts in an interview) are stressed. This is a point which seems, to the reviewer, to require ex-perimental demonstration. War-time work in personnel selection suggested that subjective synthesis of case-history material is often dis-appointing, being less predictive than the re-sults of a few objective measures. Perhaps Mr. Dale would himself collect and review the evi-dence on a batch of entering students and see how well his predictions are fulfilled. A strong case is made for guidance by careers teachers (assisting the secondary school head master in his traditional role), and for guidance at the university on choice of courses, study methods, use of the library, etc., as well as on personal problems. * the book largely covers familiar ground; it contributes little which will be new to educational psychologists. Nevertheless, it is full of interesting suggestions which merit the serious consideration of university, school and local authorities. It draws on a wide range of publications and researches, presents them impartially and, on the whole, coherently. Oc-casionally, it may put off the nonpsychologist reader by its lists of correlations and other technicalities, and occasionally it goes beyond the research evidence * But these are minor blemishes in what should be regarded as a major contribution to university education in Britain.

Brit J Ed Studies 3:80–2 N '54. James Hen-derson. * Dale has assembled the results of many recent inquiries made in the United States, Australia and New Zealand and this country on the predictive value of various ad-mission procedures. These results are clearly stated, but with due warning of the limits within which deductions can be made, and how far the calculations of correlations may be trusted in this matter. As he says, researchers using the method of correlations "have a strong tendency to spend most of their time on the mathematical computations and far too little on the interpretation of the correlations." * An arresting chapter on examination failures at the end of the first year in the University by a case-study approach provides useful information; but generally the reasons for failure are familiar to University teachers already. * Dale goes on to discuss the use of psychological tests. As a basis of selecting students for admission to a large university their application seems likely to be very limited; and it appears that logically a different set of tests would be required for the Engineer, the Doctor, the Economist, and so on. * Dale has provided in this book a valuable review of the problems of students in their advance from the schools to the universities.

[B114]

★DANIELS, J. C., AND DIACK, HUNTER. **The Standard Reading Tests.** London: Chatto & Windus Ltd., 1958. Pp. 215. 21*s*. *

[B115]

★DARLEY, JOHN G., AND HAGENAH, THEDA. **Vocational Interest Measurement: Theory and Practice.** Minneapolis, Minn.: University of Minnesota Press, 1955. Pp. xvii, 279. $5.00. (London: Oxford University Press, 1956. 40*s*.) * (*PA* 30:4726)

Am J Psychol 70:325–7 Je '57. *T. A. Ryan.* * a thoughtful volume upon interest-measurement and its implications which should be of interest to psychologists at large even though it is intended primarily for the counsellor. They deal with (*1*) procedures and results of standardizing and validating the Strong Vocational Interest Blank, and procedures for interpreting the scores, (*2*) empirical studies of the relationships among interest-scores and various other measures of personality, and (*3*) theories concerning the origin and development of interests, and of their relationship to variables of motivation, learning, and socialization. * The treatment of this first topic is highly successful and leaves the reader with a sense of the practical value of interest-measurement in college counselling. The research available upon the other two topics is summarized as clearly and carefully as the first, but there are serious limitations in the material itself which make the research difficult to evaluate. The authors have chosen to present the results at their face value, however, without looking critically at the underlying methodological or conceptual prob-

lems. This orientation is understandable since their book seems to be directed primarily at the practical user of interest scales. What follows is to be regarded, therefore, not as a criticism of Darley and Hagenah, but as a statement of certain deficiencies in the present state of the field which they are summarizing. These deficiencies need to be stated in order to characterize the status of theory in the field. An impressive amount of research is summarized in the chapter dealing with the relation of interest-scores to other measures of personality. This reviewer was left, however, with an uncomfortable impression that the interpretations and conclusions move dangerously far from the raw data and from the concrete behavior, beliefs, and perceptions of the subjects. Interest-scores are themselves derived in complex ways from answers to a questionnaire. The personality variables with which they are being correlated also are derived from answers to questionnaires. Overlooking the fact that there is overlapping in the content of the questionnaires themselves, there is still the possibility that the correlations may be a function of the way in which questionnaires are answered, rather than representing relationships which could be observed in interests and traits measured in some other way. The interpretation of the interrelationships is further complicated by the fact that each study involves the working out of a large number of correlations on a single group of subjects, and that the answers to the same questions on the Strong Blank are used repeatedly in working out the various scores. The use of a common sample of subjects for studying a number of interrelationships is a feature of a large number of fields of research, and seems to be generally overlooked in applying significance tests to the results. The use of a common set of questions for getting a number of different scores is a less widespread but also commonly ignored problem. To take a single very crude example, it is not at all surprising that the "occupational level" scores correlate with various scores for specific occupations, if we look at the way in which scores for occupational level are developed. To describe these relationships as though they represented relationships between independently measured characteristics of the subjects is certainly misleading. On the other hand, to investigate these relationships is not redundant, since they cannot be predicted completely from the standardization procedure. It might turn out, for example, that the items which differentiate occupational levels are of relatively low weight in determining specific occupational scores. Thus such investigations have a definite use, but we suggest that they should be treated as studies on a quite different level from those in which different methods of measurement, based upon non-overlapping information, are used. In fact, there is a need here for a careful theoretical analysis of the methods of interpreting this kind of information. The theoretical portion of the book is concerned with very broad questions, rather than with the kind of technical problem which we have mentioned above. * The authors admit that there is a large gap between the empirical results which they have summarized and the theoretical discussions of these broad problems. Perhaps no one is now capable of closing the gap. At any rate, Darley and Hagenah have adopted the more modest aim of pointing out the problems "that others may succeed where we have failed." This reviewer believes that more progress could be made if there were more attention paid to problems of definition. The question of whether interests are related to value-systems, needs, motivations, is meaningless unless these terms are explicitly defined. They can be defined in such a way that they are related *by definition* and no empirical studies are needed. A more fruitful approach would be to define different terms by means of different kinds of behavior, or behavior as observed in different ways. Then the problem of interrelation becomes an empirical one. Without definition, however, we cannot collect meaningful facts and interrelationships, or even define our problem. In Darley and Hagenah's discussions we are left to choose our own definitions of terms, and it is therefore difficult to decide exactly what issue is in question at any given point. For the general psychologist, Darley and Hagenah's book makes clear that interest-measurement raises many issues about fundamental psychological problems—motivation, learning, personality development, and the like. It also shows that the interest-scale is a useful tool for research upon these problems as evidenced by the number of studies which the book summarizes. Some may also agree with this reader that the nature of this tool as a means of research must be more critically scrutinized.

Cont Psychol 1:277 S '56. Lawrence H. Stewart. * The authors have attained their objectives fairly well. In so doing they have written a monograph which will be both challenging and frustrating. It will be challenging to the research-oriented worker because of the many research ideas included, but it will be frustrating to the practitioner who is looking for pat answers. One cannot read the monograph without becoming painfully aware of the large gaps in our knowledge of vocational interests. The reviewer believes that counselors or personnel technicians will find here much that will be of interest to them. The case materials in Chapter VI are most valuable. Also the counselor will be able to use the Strong Blank much more effectively after he becomes acquainted with the theoretical contents of this book. The authors draw on research from many different fields and attempt to relate to the measurement of interests the research on such topics as needs, job satisfaction, occupational choice, and identification. Their efforts serve to point up the fragmentary nature of the data which tie these concepts together. Yet when the data are seen in perspective, the suggested relationships make a lot of sense. * The book has two major limitations. In the first place, it is difficult to read. Terms such as *interests* and *occupational choice* sometimes appear to be used interchangeably, a use that tends to result in confusion. * Secondly, the monograph deals almost exclusively with research related to the Strong Blank. There is a growing body of research data on other measures of interest such as the Kuder Preference Record, and these data need to be analyzed in relation to research studies on the Strong Blank. The net result, however, is a book that will take its place among the most significant in the field of interest measurement. The ideas expressed were not all original and credit has been freely given where due; but the authors, out of their keen insight and the broad background of experience, have written a volume which will be cited in research studies for many years to come.

J Counsel Psychol 3:309 w '56. Barbara A. Kirk. * The authors have done a masterly job in condensing and summarizing a mass of research data, extending over a period of 25 years. Chapter II....organizes the wealth of technical information on interest test construction, reliability, validity, and applicability. This chapter lends itself particularly well as a teaching tool * Chapter V....is an exceptional presentation of the history of this theory, with critical evaluation and clarification. * A very welcome addition to the superlative handling of this enormous amount of research and speculation is the chapter entitled "Analysis of Interest Patterns—A Normative Study." * the weakest division of the book is that which attempts to present individual cases. These are preceded by some excellent principles of test interpretation in the counseling interview, with particular attention to the Strong *Vocational Interest Blank*. The cases, however, perhaps because of an attempt to over-simplify their presentation, fail to adhere in practice to the theoretical position taken by the authors. As has been indicated, excerpting the cases for this purpose has probably caused them to lose a good deal. The attention to interests and interest measurement appears to be at the expense of demonstrating the relationship of interests and their measurement and development to total personality, nor is the counseling process itself well represented. Overall, this is a volume which, as a reference work and as a historical survey, is indispensable for the library of the counseling psychologist. It is probably of less interest and value to the practicing counselor.

Personnel & Guid J 35:261 D '56. Wm. C. Cottle. This concise, incisive treatment of theory and practice in the field of interest measurement is described....as a revision of Darley's 1941 monograph. It appears to be considerably more than that. * Of particular pleasure to this writer were the comments of Darley about Fryer's book on interest measurement. He says, "Fryer appears in all bibliographies with credit for having 'reviewed the literature' up to 1931; he is occasionally selectively and briefly quoted; but he seems to have achieved the status of a rather widely unread classic" (p. 139). In reference to the book by Ginzberg, Ginsburg, Axelrad and Herma, Darley and Hagenah say, "In the tradition of the great Dorothy Parker, one is tempted to suggest that their approach substantially missed the green. Their disregard for the research literature is equalled only by the inadequacies of their own sampling and the dubious value of their own experimental methods" (p. 161). * These and other critical comments of a positive as well as negative nature combine to make the reader glad that Darley has written again. * minor points of disagree-

ment do not detract from the total picture of a logical well-substantiated discussion of the structure of interest measurement, the position of interests in a theory of personality development and the origin and development of interest measurement. Such discussion is pertinent for the experienced counselor as well as the neophyte. The chapter devoted to analysis of interest patterns revives Fryer's concept of interest as "acceptance-rejection reactions" and considers the meaning and influence of patterns of rejection upon the overall interpretation of the profile, as well as a presentation of frequency of occurrence of high *and low* patterns. This has been too long a neglected area in interest measurement. Chapter VI is devoted to a consideration of individual Strong profiles along with a brief selected case history of each individual. Most of the common problems of interpreting interest scores are illustrated here. This reviewer agreed with interpretation in all but two of the cases. In the case of Karl Brooks (p. 219 ff.) the counselor might have found clues pointing toward music and music education in the pronounced Mf score of Multiphasic and the combination of Musician and non-occupational scales of the Strong. The case of Charles Brandig (p. 233 ff.), in addition to illustrating "meaningful results at age fifteen" of SVIB scores, also illustrates the importance of the three non-occupational scales in such an interpretation. Emphasis in the case discussion is given to Group II scores whereas, in the opinion of this reviewer, the non-occupational scales on both profiles (pp. 235 and 236) are more like those found with Group I scores, particularly with physicians. This book should be a useful text in a course in vocational interest measurement but will certainly need to be supplemented by research on interest inventories other than Strong.

Personnel Psychol 9:409–13 au '56. Donald E. Super. * Their discussion of intrinsic-extrinsic interests is particularly worthwhile, and should stimulate further research in the development of extrinsic interest scales which would be useful at the lower occupational levels * The relationship between personality and interest has been explored in a splendid review of the literature, and further data on the relationship between social adjustment and occupational interest are reported: Darley's thesis now appears to be rather well documented. At the same time, the authors appear inconsistent in their evaluation of the role of aptitude in the development of interest: on page 187 they assign it "no major place," and on page 190 they see it as the means of attaining interest goals. While the facts do indicate that interests often persist despite lack of ability in adulthood, this does not necessarily mean that they have no role in childhood. It is true that personality factors seem prepotent. The cases with which the book concludes illustrate well the role of the *Vocational Interest Blank* in vocational counseling: several of them have excellent instructional value. But it is somewhat disturbing to note that, if the family group is omitted, four of the nine cases needed psychotherapeutic counseling (as the authors recognize) but were not helped to get it. The uncomfortable feeling pervades these case notes, that since they came only for vocational counseling this was all they could be given.

[B116]

★DECKER, ROBERT LEE. **A Study of Three Specific Problems in the Measurement and Interpretation of Employee Attitudes.** American Psychological Association, Psychological Monographs: General and Applied, Vol. 69, No. 16, Whole No. 401. Washington, D.C.: the Association, Inc., 1955. Pp. 11. Paper. $1.00. * (PA 31:1849)

[B117]

★DEGAN, JAMES W. **Dimensions of Functional Psychosis.** Psychometric Monograph, No. 6. Princeton, N.J.: Psychometric Society (P.O. Box 572), 1952. Pp. v, 41. Paper. Out of print. *

[B118]

★DELAY, J.; PICHOT, P.; LEMPÉRIÈRE, J.; AND PERSE, J. **The Rorschach and the Epileptic Personality.** New York: Logos Press, Inc., 1958. Pp. xx, 265. $6.00. *

[B119]

★DEMPSTER, J. J. B. **Selection for Secondary Education: A Survey.** London: Methuen & Co. Ltd., 1954. Pp. vii, 128. 8s. 6d. *

Brit J Ed Psychol 24:190-1 N '54. *Stephen Wiseman.* This survey of methods of selection will be of value to many psychologists and teachers. Dr. Dempster, in fourteen short chapters, gives a picture of methods and techniques appropriate for use in this field, and brings together a good deal of information which hitherto has been scattered in theses and technical journals. The book does not pretend to offer any "best" method. Its aim is rather to describe methods which are in use, and to point out the basic requirements of an adequate selection programme. Indeed, in some instances, one might wish that Dr. Dempster had been

rather more critical: for example, in discussing borderline techniques, or in the combination of broad grades for selection purposes. But it would be churlish to cavil at matters of emphasis in a book which manages to cover so many points of detail in a mere 100 pages or so. There are one or two points of criticism which perhaps need to be made. In Chapter III, Dr. Dempster dismisses too easily the claims of the "creative" answer item as opposed to the multiple choice. It is true that objectivity of marking becomes more difficult, but many may feel (as the reviewer does) that the advantages to be gained from this type of item more than offset the greater labour of construction. In Chapter IV there is not a clear enough distinction drawn between the IQ as derived from age-norm tests such as the Binet, and the standardised score derived from tests (like Moray House) applied to single age-groups. This is followed in Chapter VIII by an error in two diagrams, which show normal and skewed distributions. Surely, these should be distributions of raw scores, and not of standardised scores or "quotients"? Again, one would have been happier if Dr. Dempster had referred his readers to more accurate methods of standardising scores and of calculating age-allowances. It is, of course, right and proper that the simple graphical methods should be described, but a reference to Lawley's Method, for example, would have been valuable to many of his readers. Such criticisms are, however, minor when put beside the book as a whole. The author reveals a sane and balanced approach to the many problems of selection which is at once refreshing and salutary. The needs of the child and the importance of the school are constantly emphasised. Dr. Dempster's own enquiries in Southampton (e.g., into the effects of speeded tests—which he deplores—and the reasons for premature leaving in the grammar school) find their appropriate place, as well as the results from recent (and often unpublished) researches from many sources. The book can be confidently recommended, not only to the administrator whose job it is to select children for appropriate secondary schools, but also to the teacher and the teacher-in-training for the balanced picture it gives of the aims, methods and limitations of psychological and educational techniques of selection. Dr. Dempster insists that "selection is a servant of the educational system rather than a master"; this is not always true, but this book is likely to play a useful part in making it so.

J Ed (London) 86:350 Jl '54. A. F. Watts. * a useful survey * an interesting account of the problems that face those who are responsible for examining candidates for grammar school entrance. His book illustrates very clearly the trend of thought which is active among the more progressive of our administrators. He represents the questioning attitude of those who are moving away from the selection of grammar school entrants by means of marks gained in a one-day examination and yet are unwilling to accept every alternative that is offered them. For this reason Dr. Dempster's book is a timely contribution to an important subject. * Dempster's *speed* experiment can scarcely be accepted as a satisfactory one. He first of all gave a Moray House Arithmetic test, with the usual time-limit, to large numbers of children and then gave it again to the same children without a time-limit. The attribution of the different orders of merit, which were secured on the second occasion, to the elimination of the *speed* element is much too simple to be accepted. * The author will no doubt wish to make a good many corrections in a second edition. * I look forward to reading a second edition of the book with greatly increased satisfaction.

[B120]

★DESAI, KRISHNAKANT G. **The Construction and Standardisation of a Battery of Group Tests of Intelligence in Gujarati for the Age-Group 12 to 18 (and 18+) Studying in Standards VII to XI of Secondary Schools.** Ahmedabad, India: Bharat Prakasham, 1954. Pp. 320. Rs. 7. *

[B121]

★DOLL, EDGAR A. **The Measurement of Social Competence: A Manual for the Vineland Social Maturity Scale.** Minneapolis, Minn.: Educational Test Bureau, 1953. Pp. xviii, 664. $7.75. * (*PA* 28:4347)

Am J Psychol 67:754 D '54. Ira Iscoe. The Vineland Scale, first published in 1936, represents a unique attempt to measure social maturity in terms of data elicited from an informant well acquainted with the everyday behavior of the person to be evaluated. The volume at hand—crammed with a mass of detailed material on the rationale, construction, validation, administration, scoring, and use of the scale—replaces the brief and inadequate manual which was, up to the present time, the only available guide. The impression is gained of a careful, competent piece of work which makes a significant contribution to the evaluation of the physi-

cally handicapped, the illiterate, and the mentally retarded. It is recommended to those counsellors who routinely base their judgments on scores derived from intelligence tests alone.

Excep Child 20:360+ My '54. Oliver P. Kolstoe. The painstaking labor begun even before 1935 culminates in this 1953 edition, a scholarly, readable, witty volume * Although designed to be of help to people of varying degrees of psychometric sophistication, the scale is in reality a clinical interview tool to be used by persons who have pretty firm clinical psychology background training. Even to be used at a superficial level, the scale administrator would need to be well aware of his own limitations. It would seem, therefore, that in terms of difficulty to use, the scale would be somewhere between the Binet and projective devices. In short, even more skill is necessary for the interpretation and use of the Vineland Social Maturity Scale than for the administration and interpretation of the Stanford revision of the Binet test of individual intelligence. To complicate the problem still more, the standardization population is restricted to a selected group of children (10 male and 10 female at each age level) from the environs of Vineland, N.J. This well described group may or may not be representative of other populations, but the evidence at hand is insufficient to allow a judgment to be made. For the time being, it would seem to be quite profitable for users of the scale to attempt a determination of the degree to which the standardization group is representative of the general population. Likewise, the "feebleminded" population was a select group from the Vineland institution. One could wish for more experimental results from less select population as confirmation data for generalizing the results. Certainly the above is not an indictment of the work done thus far. It is to say, however, that the job of standardizing the scale is not finished, and that the extent to which the "normal" and "feebleminded" groups represent the general "normal" and "feebleminded" populations is yet to be determined by other investigations. For both the research investigator and the classroom teacher, this scale may prove to be as important a clinical tool as the Binet. For here is a device which can be used to yield either a total evaluation of the social developmental level of a child or can be used for an analysis of the social strengths or weakness for capitalization or remediation. Furthermore the device may be used without the presence of the person being evaluated. This in itself should help make it popular. Of special strength is the section of the book dealing with research in which the scale was involved. This may prove to be a fruitful source for suggesting master's and doctor's studies for many years to come.

Excep Child 20:362–3 My '54. Wm. M. Cruickshank. * doubt is cast on how representative the sample is of the country in general * the test user should confine his generalization to the range of variables evaluated and consider the proposed standardization as tentative rather than final. The statisical method of scaling that was adopted is applicable only through item 101, out of a total of 117, or to a life age of 20 years. Beyond item 101, the norms have to be approximated. Further, the limited number of subjects in the item validation sample (240 feebleminded subjects) does not permit an evaluation of validity of items beyond item 89 or a life age of 15 years. It would appear then that the scale is statistically valid, considering the limitations of the size and character of the sample, for those items up to a life age of 15 years. Caution should be exercised by the examiner when evaluating performance beyond this age level. * In general, the statistical work with the scale included in this volume suggests that it is "reasonably adequate" for practical purposes. It remains for future investigators to increase the confidence in the applicability of the scale by making the necessary extensions of sampling size and representativeness. In its present state, "heed should be paid to the tentative status of both the principle and procedures (including population sampling) inherent in the construction and standardization of the scale." Any person concerned with the evaluation of human behavior will find this book to be an invaluable aid. Psychologists, sociologists, educators, and social workers will find it a reasonably well-standardized and validated research and clinical tool for the measurement of social competence.

J Consult Psychol 18:74 F '54. Laurance F. Shaffer. * is an unusual psychological instrument, not a test but a method for quantifying observations of social maturation. It is one of the few devices that can be applied reliably and usefully in the absence of the examinee from the reports of persons who have observed his developmental achievements. The Scale....is now provided with a comprehensive manual which

enhances its usefulness. * Most of the evidence supports the value of the Scale: its good repeat reliability, its effective scaling of items, and its applicability to many practical and research problems. It is something of a shock, however, to find that the present standardization is based on only 20 cases, 10 male and 10 female, at each age from 0-1 to 30. The paucity of cases is offset by the unusual care exercised in selecting the normative subjects and by the supporting data from consecutive ages. The manual, like the Scale, has many merits and a few clear shortcomings. The completeness of the data presented, and the cautiousness of the interpretations, may serve as models for other test authors. On the negative side, the manual, while attractive in appearance, is organized so as to make essential data hard to find; the index seems to provide frustration as often as help. The diligent searcher, however, is ultimately rewarded. The Social Maturity Scale has now come to its own maturity, and should become as essential as a clinical tool as the intelligence test.

J Consult Psychol 20:408–9 O '56. Morris Krugman. * For the first time in thirty years, the rationale, the details of the standardization process, scoring samples, methods of interpretation, and other pertinent data usually supplied when psychological instruments are first presented for general use, are made available for the *Vineland Social Maturity Scale.* Although the brief 1947 manual mentions the care with which the standardization process was carried out, any real idea of the meticulousness of this process can be gained only from the voluminous 1953 manual. Each of the 117 items of the scale is described in minute detail with possible variations, normative curves are presented for each item, and means, medians, *SD*s and *CR*s supplied. Line drawings illustrating typical behavior are added. One wonders whether the treatment of data was overelaborated, since the norms are based on ten males and ten females at each age level from 0-1 to 30, a total of 620 subjects. The scale is too well known to require detailed description here. Briefly, it consists of 117 items, scaled in order of difficulty and arranged by years from 0 to 30. The items are distributed among six categories: self-help (general, eating, and dressing), self-direction, occupation, communication, locomotion, and socialization. "Each item is conceived as representing a general growth in social responsibility which is expressed in some detailed performance as an overt expresion of that responsibility. Consequently, the value of the detailed items is to be determined principally by the extent to which they reflect this personal independence in personal activities, in respect to which the detailed performances are otherwise relatively unimportant." The items "reflect progressive freedom from need of assistance, direction, or supervision on the part of others." Although direct rating by the examiner is not ruled out if opportunity for observing or knowing the subject is available, the usual method of use is by interviewing an informant who is thoroughly familiar with the behavior of the subject. The fact that the subject being examined and rated need not be present or observed is both an advantage and a disadvantage. The obvious advantage is the case of applying the scale by questioning a generally mature, competent adult about an immature, incompetent, or handicapped individual. The disadvantage lies in the possibility of gross distortion and incorrect rating. The reviewer has always experienced a feeling of greater confidence about ratings when the subject was seen even briefly after the usual rating by means of an informer, and when a few items of the scale have been spot checked. Usually, the publication of basic data about a clinical instrument serves to clarify issues and strengthen the use of the instrument. This is not the case with the *Vineland Social Maturity Scale.* That the scale is a very useful clinical adjunct with many different types of subjects it attested to by the almost uniformly favorable literature over the past twenty years. This reviewer has used it for many years and has tremendous respect for it. But this respect is not increased by careful reading of the new manual. The small number of cases at each level has been mentioned and indeed was known from the earlier manual, but the elaborate statistical and graphic treatment of each item is not convincing, since, in spite of the fact that continued appraisal of each item was made statistically, experimentally, and clinically, not one of the 117 items has been shifted up or down, nor have items been replaced or modified. Equally questionable is the upper end of the scale, intended for normal and superior adolescents and adults. Although based on normative data, this part of the scale could well be an extrapolation of the lower end of the scale, and it hardly makes sense. An ingenious method of

measuring defects in social maturation of children and adults, and indicating the level of social development of children who are not necessarily retarded in development, the Vineland Scale is artificial when applied to normal or superior adolescents or adults. Most users of the scale simply ignore the upper levels. The *Vineland Social Maturity Scale* has its greatest usefulness in distinguishing between real and pseudo-feeblemindedness, in providing a measure of social development in studies of child growth and development, and in appraising levels of social function among handicapped individuals of many kinds and in many types of pathology, particularly in cases of arrested development or deterioration. It has made a permanent place for itself in clinic and laboratory, and newer approaches to the appraisal of social maturity have not succeeded in replacing it. The fact that it has not been found necesary to modify or "improve" the scale over these many years can be accepted as evidence of the carefulness with which it was originally constructed, and the keen clinical insight that obviously determined the original construction and standardization.

J Consul Psychol 20:409–10 O '56. Edwin S. Shneidman. * Although Doll says that *"The scale is not a rating scale and scores are not to be based on mere opinions"* (italics his), nevertheless the scale would seem to be in the same tradition and of the same genre as the Gesell *Development Schedules,* the Malamud and Sands *Psychological Rating Scale,* the Ferguson-McReynolds *Hospital Rating Scale,* etc. * The items at the upper end of the scale (ages 20 up) such as "Uses money providently," "Contributes to social welfare," "Systematizes his own work," "Inspires confidence," "Promotes civic progress," "Advances the general welfare," etc. seem extremely hard to evaluate. * Certainly the careful use of the scale to distinguish those subjects who do deviate from the norms of "social maturity," so that further study of those individuals can be made, would be a useful and rewarding application of this instrument. However—and this is the burden of this review—the *Vineland Social Maturity Scale* lends itself easily to other interpretations. Ordinarily, when one uses an intelligence test in order to obtain an IQ, the main purpose of such an effort is to ascertain what the IQ is, although the implicit assumption may be that the higher the IQ, the better. This implicit assumption operates in a much more subtle and in a more questionable way in the case of the *Vineland Social Maturity Scale*. Specifically, the assumption is that social behavior (including social motivation) is desirable as it approaches social conformity. Further, the implicit assumption is that optimal behavior lies in adjustment to a standardized society and conformity to the "normal." Without becoming embroiled in the intricacies of the late Robert Lindner's concepts of rebellion and salutary nonconformity, it still remains that the *Vineland Social Maturity Scale* de-emphasizes the individual's fealty to his own image, his strength to be himself, his positive (that is creative or effective) idiosyncrasies, his areas of adaptation which may bring him pleasure, or the application of his resources (within his total personality organization) toward creativity or self-actualization. The recent work of Jean Macfarlane at Berkeley and Lois Murphy at Sarah Lawrence would seem to indicate that the conforming person is not necessarily the best adjusted person. One is reminded of a section of D. B. Klein's book *Mental Hygiene* entitled, "In Defense of the Shy Child" (who does not necessarily become schizophrenic) and one wonders if a section should be added in defense of the nonconforming child (who need not necessarily become maladjusted, psychopathic, or feebleminded). The point of all the above statements is that the *uncritical* use of the *Vineland Social Maturity Scale* may imply an unwarranted assumption of the merits of conformity and standardization and permit a confusion between aberrant or pathological nonconformity (schizophrenia, for example, at one extreme). To make these assumptions would be to gainsay the infinite variety and the rich diversification of talents and gifts of human subjects. As a clinical psychologist—and as a father of four—I am not sure that I know what the "best" age for toilet training, for example, really *is*. I would also ask whether the *child* has a problem if he isn't toilet trained by "that" age or rather cannot the parent create problems by imparting parental and societal anxieties and concerns—*his* problems—to the child. *

Training Sch B 50:203–6 Ja '54. John E. Anderson. * this Scale can add greatly to the assessment of children who deviate downward or away from the normal developmental course. Even with all the refinements of scaling and

standardization that modern knowledge of methods and statistical procedures give, such an instrument cannot be expected to give as precise measurement as is available with many other instruments in the psychologist's repertoire. But it does give a broad look at the developmental process in terms of a series of standardized life situations. It is a measure of achievement rather than of potentiality. While, because of its positive correlation with intelligence, it may offer some possibilities for predicting outcome, measures of intelligence are generally better for prediction. A professional examiner is aware of these limitations. * Professional workers and clinicians who have used the Scale and college and university instructors who present it to their classes will welcome the full analysis, exposition and critique of an instrument that has been available and used for almost twenty years.

[B122]

★DONOHUE, JAMES C. **Factorial Comparison of Arithmetic Problem-Solving Ability of Boys and Girls in Seventh Grade.** Washington, D.C.: Catholic University of America Press, Inc., 1957. Pp. viii, 39. Paper. $1.00. *

[B123]

★DOWNIE, N. M. **Fundamentals of Measurement: Techniques and Practices.** New York and London: Oxford University Press, 1958. Pp. xi, 413. $6.00; 48s. *

[B124]

★DOYLE, ANDREW M. **Some Aspects of Ability and Achievement in High School Girls.** Catholic University of America, Educational Research Monographs, Vol. 17, No. 2. Washington, D.C.: Catholic University of America Press, Inc., 1952. Pp. viii, 27. Paper. $0.75. * (*PA* 27:8037)

[B125]

★DRESSEL, PAUL L., EDITOR. **Evaluation in General Education.** Dubuque, Iowa: Wm. C. Brown Co., 1954. Pp. viii, 333. Paper. $4.00. * (*PA* 29:3033)

Jun Col J 25:544–6 My '55. B. Lamar Johnson. * the reader who is looking for suggestive ideas for evaluating and improving his teaching and the program of his college will be rewarded by the study of this book *

[B126]

★DRESSEL, PAUL L., EDITOR. **Evaluation in the Basic College at Michigan State University.** New York: Harper & Brothers, 1958. Pp. viii, 248. $4.00. *

[B127]

★DRESSEL, PAUL L., AND MAYHEW, LEWIS B. **General Education: Explorations in Evaluation: The Final Report of the Cooperative Study of Evaluation in General Education of the American Council on Education.** Washington, D.C.: American Council on Education, 1954. Pp. xxiii, 302. $3.50. *

Ed & Psychol Meas 16:153–60 sp '56. Henry S. Dyer. The focus of this study, as originally conceived, was fairly narrow. The main purpose was not to assess the outcomes of general education, but to see whether dependable means for doing so could be contrived. This was a study of evaluation *in* education, not *of* it. Furthermore, as the title of the report suggests, it purported to be no more than an exploratory study. The instruments and devices produced are not offered as definitive means for testing the effectiveness of general education programs; they are only attempts to see what can be done in this direction. The authors are cautious in their claims; they take as much trouble to describe their failures as their successes. Perhaps one of the chief values of the study is its reminder that educational evaluation is a slippery business, still full of problems not easily solved. * Although the Study has scarcely produced instruments which can be relied upon blindly to assess the effects of general education, it has opened up a number of new possibilities which any college seriously interested in the evaluation problem should consider worth trying. Further attempts to appraise the educational process must take account of the results of this study, not only because of the promising leads it may suggest, but also because of the blind alleys it has marked for avoidance. [See original review for critical comments too lengthy to excerpt.]

Personnel & Guid J 37:78–9 S '58. Edmund G. Williamson. * summarizes the experiences of 19 colleges and universities over a period of four years. Four academic disciplines were selected for intensive evaluation—social sciences, communications, science and humanities. A special study was made of two pervasive objectives—critical thinking and attitudes. As a result of this study, 18 tests or evaluation instruments were developed, new instructional materials were assembled, and data were collected concerning gains on specially constructed instruments. The project was oriented favorably to the motivation of students learning through self evaluation * The authors report step-by-step procedures which committees and workshops used to find agreement on objectives of courses; identification of "critical abilities"; analysis of topics; criteria for the selection of instructional materials; and test items for common examinations. Since common knowledge of facts did not seem essential in the humanities

course, evaluative criteria were defined in terms of changes in attitudes, interest, and in actual participation in creative and other related humanistic activities. * Since there was no standardization of subject matter content in the various institutions, the tests assumed the form of comprehensive examinations. Consequently, comparison of gains pre- and post-testing from one campus to another are difficult to interpret. The authors do point to institutional patterns of gains, but we do not know what differentiates institutions with respect to instructional methods, content of courses, and similar variables. It may well be that variations in content and emphasis from one campus to another would preclude improvement or changes in a general comprehensive examination, either subject matter or all pervasive objectives such as critical thinking. Since the institutions were not described in terms of relevant differences, gains on the tests are difficult to interpret. With respect to the second pervasive objective, changes in attitudes, this study reports appraisal in a very complex and difficult endeavor. Desirable and desired attitudes resulting from general educational experiences were carefully defined, and the final form of the inventory consisted of 120 statements distributed among these four categories: ideas and institutions; social groups; individuals; interpersonal relations and self (page 220). To this reviewer, an expectation that any course of instruction, general education or otherwise, would radically change even an impressionable freshman in such a comprehensive philosophic orientation is to expect too much. These ambitious expectations were not realized except in a few instances. On pages 249–253 the authors state an interesting hypothesis of the effect upon intercorrelations among tests of general educational objectives as a result of instruction. Such a program of instructions, they conclude, should result in an individual who performs more consistently over a wide range of tests, and these tests should be more highly correlated as a result of instruction. It is as though the authors were saying that (some) intra-individual differences will decrease as a result of general educational instruction. This is an interesting hypothesis to be tested, but it recalls the dictum that instruction increases individual differences rather than decreases them. The authors, beginning with page 263, re-examine critically the role of objectives in general education. Since this cooperative program was essentially one of refining objectives and developing effective means of realizing and testing these objectives, this discussion serves as a summary evaluation of the project itself. When evaluated in terms of clarifying faculty thinking about general education and the supporting programs of instruction and experiences, this research project clearly justifies itself. Four years of critical examinations of objectives and content of instructional courses serves the end of critical appraisal of general instruction.

[B128]

★DRESSEL, PAUL L., AND MAYHEW, LEWIS B., EDITORS. **Critical Thinking in Social Science.** Dubuque, Iowa: Wm. C. Brown Co., 1954. Pp. viii, 36. Paper. $1.35.

Jun Col J 25:546 My '55. James M. Wood, Jr. * A total of eight tests are set up as guides in evaluating evidence. These include the ability to recognize stereotypes and cliches, to recognize bias and emotional factors, to distinguish between verifiable and unverifiable data, to distinguish between the relevant and irrelevant, to distinguish between the essential and non-essential, to recognize the adequacy of data, to determine whether the facts support a generalization, and to check consistency. Educators who feel that only one mode of evaluation is of merit will find little to support their views in this work. Chapter II deals exclusively with objective methods of evaluation, showing practical means of testing thinking ability rather than factual material. Chapter III applies the same ideas to written essay and oral methods of evaluation. Unlike many educators today, the editors point out that even though essay examinations have beeen subject to much criticism, they can be of real value, both in teaching and in evaluating student achievement. * not intended to be a complete work on the subject, but a mere beginning. It does an excellent and challenging job of providing this original core of material.

[B129]

★DRESSEL, PAUL L., AND MAYHEW, LEWIS B., EDITORS. **Handbook for Theme Analysis.** Dubuque, Iowa: Wm. C. Brown Co., 1954. Pp. v, 78. Paper. $1.65.

Jun Col J 25:547–8 My '55. Hobart Burnett. Here are 15 writing assignments, each followed by a student's paper and an analysis of the paper by the members of the Communications Committee of the Cooperative Study of Evaluation in General Education. The assignments are provocative (representing a wide range of type and subject), and the themes are real (with gradations from feeble to excellent). The first evaluation is a general comment "which attempts to summarize the principal flaws and shortcomings, as well as the major excellences of the paper" (p. 3). The theme is then presented again and paralleled by a detailed running commentary. The response of most teachers to any dissertation on evaluation is, "I do not have the time." On page 7 are some excellent suggestions for using the *Handbook* in the classroom to interrelate teaching and evaluation, and save time. The writers of themes have little understanding of how their papers are evaluated, and certainly the readers of themes —whether of little or long experience—feel the need to redefine their criteria for evaluation. This book is useful for individual study, for staff discussions, and as a teaching-learning device in the classroom. * a helpful book

[B130]

★DRESSEL, PAUL L., AND MAYHEW, LEWIS B., EDITORS. **Science Reasoning and Understanding.** Dubuque, Iowa: Wm. C. Brown Co., 1954. Pp. viii, 223. Paper. $3.75.

Jun Col J 25:546–7 My '55. Jeremy P. Ward. * The complexity of evaluation problems and procedures presented in this report may limit its usefulness for some college teachers of science. The report represents, however, another constructive approach to the improvement of evaluation in general education, notable particularly because it describes specific teaching and testing procedures as these are related to the often stated objectives of science in general education.

[B131]

★DRESSEL, PAUL L., AND NELSON, CLARENCE H., EDITORS. **Questions and Problems in Science: Test Item Folio No. 1.** Princeton, N.J.: Cooperative Test Division, Educational Testing Service, 1956. Pp. xvi, 805. Loose-leaf binder. $27.50. *

J Ed Res 51:392–3 Ja '58. Henry J. Ehlers. * a "must" for natural science teachers * the items....represent the labor of thousands of teachers during the past generations. This reviewer regrets that the Dressel-Nelson volume is so huge and expensive; but any science division can purchase the $27.50 volume and then split it up between the several departments. *

[B132]

DRESSEL, PAUL L., AND SCHMID, JOHN. **An Evaluation of the Tests of General Educational Devel-**

opment. Washington, D.C.: American Council on Education, 1951. Pp. x, 57. Paper. Out of print. *

J Higher Ed 23:283–4 My '52. H. T. Morse.
* It is surprising to read that responses of colleges seemed to indicate that the reception of the college program was much less wholehearted than was the case with the high-school program, and that credit-seeking by G.E.D. test performance was not widely encouraged. Undoubtedly the unfortunate experience of too much credit allowance for military service after the First World War made the colleges wary of repeating similar mistakes. In the survey of the rather considerable research available on the tests and in the special research projects, the authors give careful consideration, among other things, to the questions of their reliability and validity. They conclude that all available data indicate that the G.E.D. tests compare very favorably in reliability with other such tests. Validity is more difficult to determine, but by various criteria it seems to be reasonably well established, with the significant qualification which "suggests that general educational development as measured by these tests cannot be clearly separated into the four or five content areas" (page 40). The other comments and conclusions in the final chapter will also be of particular interest to educators. The authors have done their job well, and it was one which very much needed to be done. The undoubted extension of educational privileges to veterans of the Korean War, and perhaps to other service personnel as well, and the increasing use of these tests by other than educational agencies make such careful appraisal highly desirable. It is significant that the Veterans' Testing Service is currently constructing two new forms of the college-level G.E.D. tests for use in the Army education program, a commendable undertaking, since the original forms were constructed as far back as 1943. The topic with which this monograph deals, therefore, makes it considerably more significant, especially to educational institutions, than its limited size would imply.

[B133]

★DRISCOLL, JUSTIN A. **Factors in Intelligence and Achievement: A Study of the Factor Pattern Resulting From Analysis of the Scores of Boys in Junior Year of High School on Intelligence and Achievement Tests.** Catholic University of America, Educational Research Monographs, Vol. 16, No. 7. Washington, D.C.: Catholic University of America Press, Inc., June 15, 1952. Pp. viii, 56. Paper. $1.00. * (*PA* 27:3330)

[B134]

★DU MAS, FRANK M. **Manifest Structure Analysis.** Montana State University Studies, Vol. 3. Missoula, Mont.: Montana State University Press, 1956. Pp. ix, 193. $6.00. * (*PA* 31:75)

Am Sociol R 21:793–4 D '56. Karl F. Schuessler. The author of this volume, a psychologist, feels that the possibility of utilizing qualitative information to predict a quantitative variable has been neglected (Chapters 1–3). In response to this neglect, he has assembled a "new scale theory" which consists of three ways in which attributes may be related to a variable quantity. Although his charge of neglect may be true, his claim for a "new scale theory" is, if not false, something of an exaggeration. Persons familiar with correlational analysis, particularly as expounded by Yule and Kendall, and Guttman, will observe immediately the correspondence between du Mas' models and certain types of statistical association. (1) The segmental model (Chapters 6 and 7) requires that a given attribute be associated with a given quantity and conversely that a given quantity be linked with only one attribute. In other words, it calls for two-way association. Its conditions would be fulfilled, for example, if every man weighed exactly 200 pounds and every woman 100 pounds, for then it would be possible to give everyone's weight from knowledge of their sex. (2) The intensive model (Chapters 8 and 9) is less restrictive than the segmental, since it permits a given quantity to be predicted from a combination of attributes. However, combinations must be cumulative in that every larger combination must include the elements of every smaller. This model then requires that the joint frequency distribution between a set of attributes and a variable be triangular. It is identical with Guttman's perfect scale. It would be realized, for instance, if all persons who were short, fat, and blond had an IQ of 150, all persons who were short and fat but not blond had an IQ of 100, and all persons who were short but not fat and blond had an IQ of 50. Given these circumstances, from a short, fat, blond individual, it would be possible to predict with no error an IQ of 150, and so on. (3) The clustery model (Chapters 10 and 11) is least limiting in that any combination of attributes, whether cumulative or not, may be used to predict the variable. It fits whenever certain combinations, however composed, are uniquely associated with certain intervals along the continuum. Although the clustery model is regarded by the author as general and the other two as special, it would be possible to view the segmental as general, since any combination of attributes may be reduced to a single attribute. This point of view is implicit in the author's suggestion that combinations be numerically weighted so that the resulting scores be perfectly related to the outside variable. Manifest structure analysis, as the name suggests, falls into the same field of endeavor as scale analysis and latent structure analysis. It differs from scale analysis in that the variable is not derived from the distribution of attributes, and in that it predicts from attributes to the variable, rather than the reverse (as in scale analysis). It resembles latent structure analysis in that it presumes to handle patterns which in their original form are neither perfectly linear nor triangular; it differs in that it hypothesizes no latent factors to account for the manifest relations. It most nearly resembles a multiple regression technique in which a team of attributes are used to estimate a variable quantity. There is nothing in the writing to indicate that the author sees manifest structure analysis as being tied to a particular theoretical orientation or field of research. Apparently, its use, as is true of all statistical routines, would depend on the nature of the problem and the nature of the data. In view of its generality, any researcher, including sociologists, who for one reason or another have occasion to examine the connection between a variable and a set of attributes, would probably secure some benefits, direct or fringe, from a reading of this monograph.

Ed & Psychol Meas 17:634–6 w '57. David G. Hays. Manifest structure analysis....is a theory of measurement which is said to be applicable when two chief conditions are fulfilled: (i) There is a continuous (or at least multivalued) variable which is empirically measurable (manifest). This is the criterion variable. (ii) There are several dichotomous variables (items or categories) from which the criterion variable is to be predicted. The first of these conditions actually sets MSA outside the whole field of scale analysis. The manifest criterion variable cannot well be compared with the latent variable of latent structure analysis. Neither can it be compared with total score on a test composed of dichotomous items, since du Mas makes it clear that the criterion variable is measured independently of the items or cate-

gories which are used to predict it. Finally, the manifest variable must be distinguished from the item values derived from judges' placements, as used by Thurstone, for two reasons. First, Thurstone's judges deal only with the items, while du Mas assumes a direct measurement of each subject. Second, very difficult problems arise when error of measurement of the criterion variable is introduced; the difference between "clear" and "subjective" criteria enters du Mas' discursive argument, but not his technical development. "Scaling" is a term traditionally applied to techniques which rely on criteria of internal consistency for test analysis. MSA, with its assumption of a measured criterion variable, need not rely on internal consistency. The problem, in fact, is simply one of multiple regression: the regression of a continuous variable on a number of dichotomous variables. The method of minimizing error of estimate seems applicable, but du Mas does not introduce it. du Mas argues that traditional methods of item analysis are not always applicable, inasmuch as they depend on assumptions which fail for large classes of empirical data. This argument is sound, and has been voiced before; he cites several critics. He notes phenomena which are analogous to non-linearity of regression on continuous variables; he also observes that the multiple correlation of a criterion with a set of predictors may be large, even though its simple correlation with each predictor is zero. From this argument it would seem to follow that some method analogous to multiple non-linear regression is required. Instead, du Mas introduces rule-of-thumb techniques which depend on the internal consistency of the dichotomous data. His methods appear closely related to Guttman's method of image analysis, not to multiple regression at all. The availability of criterion measurements does not appear critical to the method, although it is the focus of du Mas' discursive arguments. A second confusion appears in manifest structure analysis, between two directions of prediction: Is the continuous variable to be predicted from the patterns of response to the dichotomous items, or are the patterns of response to be predicted from the continuous variable? On page 154, du Mas asserts that his aim is to predict the continuous variable. On page 150 he gives an example of a "perfect clustery catescale" in which the criterion predicts the response patterns perfectly, while the response patterns do not predict the criterion variable at all. Unfortunately this confusion appears to permeate the whole book. These two confusions—between efficiency of prediction and internal consistency; between the two possible directions of prediction—are not trivial. It is much to be regretted that clarification was not achieved prior to publication of the book.

Percept & Motor Skills 6:152 Je '56. R. B. Ammons. From time to time a book is published which abounds in new and significant concepts. This is such a book. Early in it the author demonstrates his unique approach to the solution of certain problems. From a philosophical background he generates a scale theory and from a scientific background he develops several new concepts, the most important being the *catinuum,* the *catemension,* and the *catescale.* He continues his new development with discussion of paradoxical scales, nonparametric test methods, and the substitution of the single term, probability, for the notions of reliability and validity. His chapter entitled "Models and Their Empirical Analogues" is a lucid explication of the relationships of conceptual models to empirical data. This chapter could well be read by all beginning graduate students. The basic idea contained in the book is that categories, stages, levels, or classes may be uniquely ordered along a dimension. Quantitative criteria are made from patterns of quantitative and qualitative properties. This book is not all abstraction. The author's pragmatic objective is to attain a way of analyzing any kind of data whatsoever, such as that typically contained in interview forms, application blanks, and case histories. He develops three models which permit such batches of data to be analyzed efficiently. Step-by-step computational examples are given which can easily be followed by an intelligent undergraduate. The final chapter entitled "Speculations" presents a radically new conceptual model for science, which attempts to relate simultaneously both quantitative and qualitative aspects of phenomena. This book has its share of shortcomings. It would be far more palatable to most psychologists if it contained more actual empirical data. Of the three models presented the "clustery model" is quite unusual and this reviewer doubts that empirical data can be found which will fit this model. Proofs of the theorems for the intensive model are not as rigorous as one could hope for, since they depend essentially upon a kind of

mathematical induction. In the introductory chapter, the author's survey of important concepts in scale theory omits some of the most important names in the history of psychometrics. For example, there is no mention of Coombs or Spearman. Regardless of whether one does or does not agree with the author's occasional flights into scientific fantasy, one has to admit that he writes lucidly and makes a strong case for his point of view. This book may well become both a classic in the field of psychological theory and a cookbook of recipes for dishing out fast, practical research results.

[B135]
★DYER, HENRY S. **College Board Scores: Their Use and Interpretation.** New York: College Entrance Examination Board, [1953]. Pp. xxiii, 70. Paper. (*PA* 28:4936) For revised edition, see B136.

[B136]
★DYER, HENRY S., AND KING, RICHARD G. **College Board Scores: Their Use and Interpretation, No. 2.** New York: College Entrance Examination Board, 1955. Pp. viii, 192. Paper. $1.50. * (*PA* 30:1616) For supplement, see B148.

J Higher Ed 27:405–6 O '56. Hubert S. Shaw. * provides review material for trained users and a primer for the uninitiated * An interesting chapter, "The Hidden Human Factor," has been added; and, references to "practice and growth," "coaching," and "fatigue" serve to emphasize the individual and the caution with which his test records should be evaluated. * For the admissions officer especially, "Technical Information" holds many valuable data. The tables provide norms for practically any comparative study that is desired. * a useful book that answers many questions about test scores and the part they can play in counseling and admissions. The problem of having as clear a description as possible of a candidate's abilities will always be present, and the resources suggested by the authors in this and future books should be welcomed by school and college personnel.

[B137]
★EDWARDS, ALLEN L. **The Social Desirability Variable in Personality Assessment and Research.** New York: Dryden Press, Inc., 1957. Pp. xv, 108. $2.75. * (*PA* 32:464)

[B138]
★EDWARDS, ALLEN L. **Techniques of Attitude Scale Construction.** New York: Appleton-Century-Crofts, Inc., 1957. Pp. xvi, 256. $4.00. * (*PA* 31:2741)

Cont Psychol 2:237–8 S '57. Leonard W. Ferguson. * How....can attitude researchers be so completely oblivious to the problem of validation? With one minor exception and, in a section which rightly demonstrates that no complete one-to-one relationship between behavior and verbal (or other symbolic) expression of attitude can be expected, Edwards nowhere gives more than passing mention to the basic problem of the validation of attitude scales. True, he does describe and with commendable clarity many, if in fact not all, of the techniques for attitude scale construction now in common use. * Certainly any student desiring to know something about the techniques by which attitude researchers construct their various measuring devices will find Edwards' book a most helpful summary. He discusses each method clearly and succinctly and points up, significantly, many of the problems which each method involves: problems such as reliability, internal consistency, scalability, reproducibility, ambiguity, scale value, irrelevance, discriminal dispersion, universe of content, scale and nonscale type, marginals, cutting points, response-pattern stability. But, after all is said and done, every one of these problems pertains only to some phase or other of internal consistency—consistency from one response to another, from item-response to total score or vice versa; from one scale to another; or from one judge, person, or subject to another. Not a single one—and this is indeed the puzzlement—touches upon the predictive value of the scales, nor upon methods of showing that resultant scores, no matter how derived, are useful in the sense of enabling us to predict behavior, whether symbolic or nonsymbolic, when the event to be predicted is extrinsic to the content of the scale. It may very well be that scales which meet the criteria which Edwards sets forth as desirable are more valid than scales which do not meet these criteria. On this point, however, our author gives us no data. So we remain in the dark as to what effect, if any, the meeting of any of the various criteria of internal consistency may have on a scale's practical utility. * attitude researchers have concerned themselves, as Edwards' book amply demonstrates, much too much with the trivia of scale construction—and much too little with the psychological significance of any results which, by the use of attitude scales, they have been able to secure. Now that we have in Edwards' book an excellent summary of the techniques, let us see if we cannot, in the next

decade or so, devote a greater proportion of our effort to the psychologically significant problems of attitude-scale validation and prediction therefrom.

Ed & Psychol Meas 18:417-8 su '58. Samuel Messick. * The topics discussed include: Thurstone's methods of paired comparison, equal-appearing intervals, and successive intervals; Likert's method of summated ratings; Guttman's scalogram analysis: and the Edwards-Kilpatrick scale-discrimination technique. Because of their recent origin and limited application, Edwards understandably but nevertheless lamentably omitted Coombs' unfolding technique, Lazarsfeld's latent structure analysis, and multi-dimensional scaling. Only limited aspects of these new developments were mentioned.* The book's main emphasis is on computational procedures and methodology. Its orientation away from scaling in general toward attitude measurement in particular is carried primarily by a widespread use of attitude data in the numerical examples and an introductory chapter which briefly stresses some advantages of attitude scales over direct questioning and direct observation. From a psychometric point of view, the text suffers from the absence of measurement theory, even in terms of the usual ordinal-interval-ratio hierarchy. From a social psychological viewpoint, there is little integration of measurement methods with attitude theory; those aspects of scaling models, such as latent structure analysis and Guttman's theory of components, which, right or wrong, have potential contributions for the psychology of attitudes were not mentioned. As an elementary description of scaling techniques, the treatment is simple, well-organized, and helpfully extensive if brief. * Emphasis is placed upon the equal variance cases of paired comparisons and successive intervals; some coverage is allotted to the computation of unequal discriminal dispersions, although the simultaneous solutions for the scale values, dispersions, and category boundaries of successive intervals are not treated. Thus, at least the possibility of unequal dispersions is considered—a flexibility in the Thurstone models which has been largely overlooked in practice, especially in psychophysics. Although not necessarily a criticism in a work not intended as an extensive treatise, the descriptions of underlying models, while simple, also seem casual and vague, particularly with respect to successive intervals. In addition to the elementary recipes for scaling, the book has several distinct assets to recommend it. While not a comprehensive review of the literature, it summarizes and evaluates many pertinent research findings on the applications and comparisons of scaling methods and can serve as a convenient, limited secondary source. Edwards wisely orients the validation problem away from correlations between scales and overt behavior, of which attitude is only one of many interrelating various attitudes or correlating attitude scales with measures of ability and personality. The book also contains informal criteria for writing and selecting items, for constructing rating or judging procedures, and hints for obtaining adequate scales, including some recommended controls for often ignored response set effects.

Personnel & Guid J 36:57 S '57. H. H. Remmers. * a useful introduction to the currently known technical aspects of attitude scale construction, and he has done it with his usual lucidity as exemplified in his previously published books on statistics and experimental design. His knack of clear and simple presentation without sacrifice of rigorous treatment is to be commended to all writers of textbooks. * The book is not, and does not purport to be, an exhaustive treatise of psychological scaling methods. Advanced students may wish that the author had included the substance of the seminal unfolding technique developed by Coombs, the latent structure conceptualization of Lazarsfeld, the developments in multidimensional scaling. The author states, however, quite correctly, that the recency of these models has precluded their application to attitude scaling to any great extent. Perhaps a somewhat more accurately descriptive title for the book might thus have been An Introduction to Techniques of Attitude Scale Construction. By avoiding the more recent and complex model, the author has provided a test suitable for upper division undergraduates as well as for graduate students, since the mathematics involved is in general elementary algebra only. The author envisages the use of the book both as a text and a laboratory manual—the latter by means of the problems and questions at the end of each chapter. This is psychologically sound, especially in view of the appositeness of the end-of-chapter exercises. The book will be a welcome addition to a rapidly growing scientific literature.

[B139]

★EDWARDS, ROBERTA MILLER. **Factorial Comparison of Arithmetic Performance of Girls and Boys in the Sixth Grade.** Washington, D.C.: Catholic University of America Press, Inc., 1957. Pp. viii, 45. $1.00. *

[B140]

★EELLS, KENNETH; DAVIS, ALLISON; HAVIGHURST, ROBERT J.; HERRICK, VERGIL E.; AND TYLER, RALPH W. **Intelligence and Cultural Differences: A Study of Cultural Learning and Problem-Solving.** Chicago, Ill.: University of Chicago Press, 1951. Pp. xii, 388. $5.00. * (PA 27 :5738)

Am J Sociol 58:209–10 S '52. S. Stansfeld Sargent. This very important study will be of great interest to psychologists as well as social scientists, particularly to those concerned with constructing and giving tests. Actually, it is but another step, though a large one, in the environmental direction already much traveled by psychologists. * psychologists should welcome this first major effort to study the effects of American social status upon intelligence * In general the authors favor tests of developmental intelligence having a "common-culture" approach—i.e., utilizing types of problems equally common and prominent in the cultures involved. * the authors realize that this "common-culture" approach "might necessitate limiting the test to such a narrow range of experiences that it could not possibly be representative of the most important kinds of problem-solving ability in either high-status or low-status culture." Or, again, the instrument might be a battery of tests, each measuring problem-solving ability in some one cultural or status area. * However disappointing the authors' indecisiveness may be as to concrete suggestions for improving intelligence tests, it speaks well for their scientific integrity. For their research has added further doubts as to the validity of intelligence tests, and there simply are no easy answers to the questions they have raised. Continuing collaboration between psychologists, sociologists, and other social scientists is necessary. These researchers' findings as to status differences in I.Q.'s are clear cut. They deserve great credit for not attributing such intelligence differentials exclusively to cultural influences; for, after all, they have no conclusive evidence that a genetic factor is not operating—i.e., that persons of greater inherent ability may be more socially mobile and advance into the higher-status groups. Certain minor criticisms can be made. The authors might have described and evaluated attempts by psychologists to devise "culture-free" intelligence tests (e.g., Brigham's and Cattell's). Now and then they imply that pictorial and geometric tests are better measures of intelligence than verbal tests because status differences are smaller in the former area. But "general intelligence" must involve a fairly wide range of performance; if only one or two types of material are used, the test comes close to being one of special aptitude or ability. The authors might have discussed somewhat more the use of tests to reveal individual differences as compared with group differences. Many psychologists might feel that a test which is too culture-bound to indicate valid group differences (which are usually of small magnitude) may yet have value in depicting individual differences, which are often of such great magnitude that they could hardly be due to cultural differentials. (Why hasn't someone suggested working a status-characteristics ingredient into the I.Q. formula, so that, of two childern performing equally well on a given test, the one from the poorer cultural background would get the higher index of ability?) This is a very important study and an excellent example of collaboration among members of various disciplines. It is to be hoped that they and their colleagues will continue with related research problems. Perhaps the greatest danger is that psychological testers may not pay sufficient attention to *Intelligence and Cultural Differences*.

Am Sociol R 18:219–21 Ap '53. William H. Sewell. * This review will be confined to the actual research reported in Parts II and III. * From this and other research it is apparent that differences in the measured intelligence of children from different status groups are due in part to culture-biased items in existing intelligence tests. To the extent that this is true, these tests are inadequate for measuring either the genetic or the developmental intelligence of children from these groups. Consequently, those who have used results produced by existing group intelligence tests to prove that lower status children have lower genetic or developmental intelligence than higher status children probably have overstated the case. It has long been recognized by researchers that tests standardized in one culture should not be used in other cultures, and some have argued against the use of existing tests for members of subcultures within a society; however, this is the most ambitious and satisfactory study yet made showing the influence of cultural bias on intelligence tests. It is a well designed and well executed study, and the results are clearly stated. The statement of factors contributing to status differences in intelligence and the suggestion made about the development of new tests of developmental intelligence seem quite insightful and reasonable but are not products in any direct sense of the research. The case made for the construction of new tests of developmental intelligence is a good one. The admonition that a test of developmental intelligence should exclude culture-biased items and those subjected to cultural differences in test motivation but should not exclude those cultural or status influences which are reflected in true differences of present ability, is hardly a sufficient chart for anyone who wishes to construct such a test. On this and many other difficult methodological problems, few, if any, procedural suggestions are made. Also, it should be emphasized that there are many legitimate uses for existing intelligence tests. To the extent that our dominant culture is a middle-class culture and success is achieved by solving problems that are middle class oriented, the most functional estimate of intelligence for many purposes may be that provided by present tests which seem to be culture-biased in favor of middle-class backgrounds.

J Negro Ed 21:180–1 sp '52. Rachel T. Weddington. The current volume is of special importance to teachers and examiners of children of minority groups—which children because of the restrictions placed upon their participation in the greater culture are generally considered to have had experiences inferior to the norm. *Intelligence and Cultural Differences* is a challenging consideration of the extent to which intelligence as measured is a reflection of assumptions, underlying tests, which do not give adequate consideration to the full possibilities of such cultural influences. As such, it merits becoming "required reading" for every active and potential user or interpreter of intelligence test scores. * This challenging analysis confirms the belief of this reviewer that the existent so-called intelligence tests might better be labelled tests of academic aptitude.

Psychol B 49:370–1 Jl '52. Quinn McNemar. First a word about the multiple authorship of this volume, 90 per cent of which was written by Eells. Herrick's name appears because of a six-page inadequate review of the literature.

Both Davis and Tyler get in by rehashing previously published articles, and Havighurst's contribution is six pages. Thus future bibliographers are burdened unnecessarily with four extra names. * The unique part of this research is the extensive item analysis, which is concerned mainly with the performance of a high-status group (top 10 per cent of the status index distribution) compared with that of a low-status group (bottom 15 per cent of distribution). * The chief finding is that the verbal type items, in general, yield the larger differences. * Two long and tedious chapters are devoted to a comparison of high- and low-status groups as regards correct and incorrect responses to certain items. Here one finds after-the-fact rationalizations in terms of differences in cultural backgrounds, but no explanation is found for a "rather substantial number of items" showing large status differences. There seems to be some dismay that certain supposedly culturally biased items did not yield status differences. The study, though rather well executed and reported, is not free of questionable points. Pertinent differences in test *SD's* are not considered (pp. 146–147; 155). The correlational term is ignored in computing certain standard errors of differences (pp. 114–117; 136–139). Subgroups are compared statistically with total groups without necessary allowance for lack of independence (p. 191). Inflated *N's* are encountered (pp. 201–204). Eells, perhaps in tune with his mentors, concludes that "variations in opportunity for familiarity with specific cultural words, objects, or processes required for answering the test items seem....to be the most adequate general explanation for most of the findings." He favors the construction of a common-culture test as a means of securing scores not subject to cultural bias. There are those who will say that Eells has not yet performed the crucial experiment since possible (and likely) genetic factors were uncontrolled.

[B141]

★ELMGREN, JOHN. **School and Psychology: A Report on the Research Work of the 1946 School Commission, 1948:27.** Göteborg, Sweden: Institute of Psychotechnics, University of Göteborg, 1952. Pp. 342. Paper. *

B Int Bur Ed 27:30 1st q '53. A detailed and clear account of the battery of tests, its manner of application, and the results, comprised in the research work of the Swedish 1946 School Commission. The investigation covered practical and theoretical aptitude, knowledge, factorial maturity, linguistic maturity and also the problem of differentiation.

[B142]

★EMMETT, W. G. **The Use of Intelligence Tests in the 11+ Transfer Examination.** London: University of London Press Ltd., 1952. Pp. 8. Paper. 1s. *

J Ed (London) 84:541–2 N '52. C. Birchenough. Mr. Emmett's pamphlet should do something to bring about a sense of proportion in the controversy that rages around the use of standardized tests, and especially intelligence tests. As a result of experiments carried out with Moray House tests, Mr. Emmett is satisfied that ordinary coaching has not the dire effects that are sometimes supposed. The children who are affected are naturally the borderline children. Under the worst conditions some 10 per cent. of children entering grammar schools would be affected, but whether they would displace others more worthy is a moot point. Universal coaching is indefensible on any ground. It is bad educationally and it would accentuate the effect of differences in the quality of teaching that intelligence tests endeavour to minimize. The solution is to get teachers as a body to set their faces against coaching for such tests. At the same time authorities should provide a variety of types of secondary education and arrange for the transfer at 13 years of age of selected children.

[B143]

★EYSENCK, H. J. **The Scientific Study of Personality.** London: Routledge & Kegan Paul Ltd., 1952. Pp. xiii, 320. 30s. (New York: Macmillan Co. $4.50.) * (*PA* 27:5745)

Brit J Delinquency 4:63–5 Jl '53. Cyril Burt. * There is....one respect in which Dr. Eysenck's approach differs from that of most practical workers in this country. British psychologists have nearly always held that factor analysis is merely one convenient device for securing a more rigorous verification of plausible hypotheses advanced on more concrete grounds: and they have generally insisted that it is essential to combine statistical studies with clinical case-studies—the two lines of attack supplementing and supporting one another. Dr. Eysenck, however, has become highly sceptical of the clinical methods adopted in psychiatry. So far as available evidence goes, he believes we are still "in a position where any belief in psycho-therapy depends on faith, not on scientifically demonstrated fact." Accordingly, he prefers to confine himself solely to the measurements obtained from "objective tests of personality," and to base his conclusions on these. Nevertheless, for the numerous patients whom he and his fellow-workers have so assiduously tested a vast amount of psychiatric and psychoanalytic material must have been available; and most readers will feel a little disappointed to find all this parallel work ignored as destitute of scientific interest or value. *

Brit J Ed Psychol 22:220–1 N '52. Cyril Burt. * Eysenck, it will be observed, shows a youthful fondness for emphatic statement. But in point of fact I fancy the differences between us remain much smaller than he supposes. We both still agree that "factors are principles of classification"; and we both believe the interpretation of every factor must be checked by reference to external as well as internal criteria. As regards the three main factors—those accounting for the greater portion of the individual variance—namely, "general intelligence" (questioned by most American writers), "general emotional instability," and "extraversion-versus-introversion," as well as the main factors underlying body-build, we seem in almost entire accord. We differ over the relative value of simple laboratory tests for personality. But on those issues which are of greatest interest to teachers and educationists, there seems to be very little divergence. And, if he now treats my views a little severely, an older writer should be ready to hear with tolerance, and even to welcome, the criticisms of a former student, who continues to accumulate fresh data from similar fields. Beyond all question, the ingenuity displayed in devising laboratory tests, the industry that has been expended in accumulating and analysing large masses of figures, and the lucid and provocative way in which Dr. Eysenck states his conclusions, deserve high praise. Those who remain unconvinced by the choice of experimental methods or by the mode of argument adopted should feel stimulated to repeat or supplement the inquiries by researches of their own. Teachers, educational psychologists, and others who are interested in the investigation of the individual mind may profit richly by a study of Dr. Eysenck's book, and, let us hope, may themselves attempt, by taking up these problems at the earlier and simpler stages of mental growth, to throw further light on the issues at stake.

Brit J Psychol 44:72–4 F '53. James Drever. Dr Eysenck has a laborious and peremptory way with him which will repel many psychiatrists and some clinical psychologists. Nevertheless, they should all read this book. If they disagree with Dr Eysenck's methods and conclusions then they should give their reasons as clearly as he has done, and suggest alternatives. Otherwise their case may go by default. It is no use mobilizing resistances or brushing up alibis. The whole argument is central to the clinical field. It may conveniently be divided into three stages. First of all Dr Eysenck states certain implications of our traditional scientific logic relative to the psychology of personality; then he puts forward statistical procedures worked out in the light of these implications; and finally he shows how in fact these procedures have given rise to new knowledge of a scientific kind in the fields in which they have been used. The researches referred to include his own earlier work, and that of his collaborators as well as a good deal of recent American work along similar lines. The first step of the argument embodies two claims; that science should use the hypothetico-deductive method, and that measurement is necessary for the verification of its deductions with a known degree of probability. Stated thus Dr Eysenck's position seems a strong one. The scientist must be able to specify the data relevant to his generalizations, and, in current jargon, he must have some system of feedback to let him know whether these generalizations fit. Otherwise he is not so much groping in the dark as gesticulating in a vacuum. At the same time we must keep in mind the proviso that scientists, particularly successful ones, often seem to break the rules that the logicians lay down for them. It is when he comes to particularize that Dr Eysenck begins to leave an occasional loophole. Consider his attacks upon holistic theories and their allied techniques. He is right in pointing out that all psychologists "atomize" or break down the total personality whether or not they may claim to treat it as a whole. He fails to make it clear, however, that this breaking down can follow very different lines. He instances the Freudians and their "Oedipus complexes and super egos, regressions and transferences, cathexes and libidos, fixations, symbolisms, compensations, catharsis, Narcissisms, and many other strange entities jostling each other, all of them attempts to analyse what is elsewhere declared to be 'unanalysable.'" This list is in itself rather an unfair hotch-potch, but that is not the point. What Dr Eysenck appears to imply is that its contents can be compared with descriptive traits such as neuroticism or extraversion as though they were the same sort of thing but not nearly so "scientific." This is just misleading. To take a parallel case: One may describe a car in terms of its cylinders, its pistons, its ignition and its transmission, deriving these, if you like, as constructs from its "behaviour." One may also describe it in terms of its horse-power, its weight, its mechanical efficiency, and so on. In terms of these two descriptions one may "explain" the motion of the car in two ways: either in terms of what happens inside it or in terms, say, of its horse-power/weight ratio. There are other possibilities both in psychology and engineering. They are complementary and may be equally valid. In this case the former approach may seem the more useful of the two, but the question of usefulness is not really relevant here. If someone were to say "I have a car. Its horse-power is x and its weight y. It won't go. What shall I do?" Dr Eysenck could fairly reply "Sir, I am a physicist not a garage mechanic." There is the further point of course that in the case of Freudian theory, whatever one may feel about its possible usefulness, there has, as Dr Eysenck points out, been rather a dearth of the sort of empirical studies that would enable us to choose between sparking plugs and gremlins. Nor is Freudian theory alone in this. All the applied psychological enterprises stand in need of more formal validation than has in general been accepted so far. A good deal of work in this field is already going on, though perhaps with a less explicit theoretical framework than Dr Eysenck would like. The second stage in Dr Eysenck's argument has to do with the problem of measurement in the psychology of personality. "If science depends on measurement," he says, "then we must know what to measure," and this requires the establishment of operationally defined dimensions. These dimensions can be—indeed must be—in a sense arbitrary or conventional, and personality may be measured in terms of different sets of dimensions so long as some technique of translation from one to the other is available. Dr Eysenck himself feels, however, that the experimental

facts will gradually prune the alternatives that inventive psychologists might think up or derive from their correlational matrices. This means that, although they are in one sense conventional, in another the dimensions of personality derived from this kind of study are real and objective. This process of pruning is clearly crucial, and to consider it one must turn to the logic of the statistical techniques which Dr Eysenck proposes. Starting with an exposition of classical factor analysis he traces the reasons which led Thurstone to modify the orthogonal pattern of factor axes and to allow intercorrelation between factors. He then goes on to point out why "simple structure" is not likely to reveal itself in such a new and complex field as that of personality testing. Finally he puts forward criterion analysis as a method which may be used to determine the position of oblique axes in a manner conforming to the general hypothetico-deductive method of science. The procedure is most ingenious. If we regard a factor as a sort of average then we can give it meaning by determining through our choice of tests what is in fact being averaged. This calls for some prior knowledge of what constitutes, say, neurotic behaviour or extraverted behaviour. We can then use our tests on groups classified normal-neurotic or introverted-extraverted as the case may be. By correlating each test with this dichotomous criterion we can add a "criterion column" to our matrix, and show the correlation with it of our factor saturations. By moving our axis slightly we can then bring this last correlation to a maximum thus making our factor more or less invariant. Having done this we can turn back upon our tests and set about improving them as measures of the factor with which we are concerned, and so in turn we can improve our criterion until the whole procedure reaches a high degree of efficiency. The obvious criticism, and Dr Eysenck deals with it at some length, is that we are arguing in a circle. At one end we use some general psychiatric views as to what constitutes neurotic behaviour, and at the other we use a psychiatric diagnosis to obtain our two criterion classes. Dr Eysenck's claim is that such apparent circularity derives from the necessarily conventional nature of measuring. He points out that a procedure very like his own is used by physicists to establish measures of length or temperature. Here rough and ready techniques lead to a first generalization in terms of which the techniques can be improved, thus making possible an increase in the scope and precision of the generalizations. The analogy appears to hold with the exception that in the physical fields there seems possible at the outset a basic pointing operation to something given as dimensional. A similar operation may be possible for intelligence but neuroticism seems more doubtful. The operation by which Dr Eysenck places normals and neurotics on a continuum is not one of pointing. The clinician might have an answer here if he could understand what he was being asked. As it is, while one cannot say that Dr Eysenck has smuggled in the rabbit which he later produces, there does remain a suspicion that at some stage in the proceedings he has left his hat lying about in a rabbit warren. These theoretical considerations, however, comprise only a small part of the book, and its author would no doubt claim that it should be judged primarily by its factual contribution. Here the material presented and referred to is impressive. Dr Eysenck and his associates during the post-war years have carried out a co-ordinated series of researches which achieves much and promises more. The scope of the work may be limited but the limitation is deliberate. At least it is explicit both in its methods and its findings so that anyone may repeat the investigations and confirm or modify the results so far obtained. In the book under review the factual matter consists first of all in an analysis of existing research on neuroticism from which is derived an operational definition of the neurotic dimension. Then follows an account of the various techniques of measurement and the results to which they have given rise. Some readers may feel that the assortment of tests, inventories and apparently trivial antics which is used cannot possibly measure a single variable. Objections along this line are not valid, or at least could only be validated by further experiment. Having defined and used his measuring instrument, Dr Eysenck returns again to the question of the "reality" of the neurotic dimension. One would say that he shares, in an open-minded and self-critical way, the suspicions expressed about the provenance of his rabbit. What he tries to do is to break out of the circle, if circle it be, and show that what he is measuring varies in terms of some quite independent factor, in this case a genetic one. Is there a difference in terms of neuroticism

between fraternal and identical twins? The hypothesis that such a difference does exist is provisionally verified and whatever is being measured—neuroticism, emotional instability and lack of integration are equivalent verbal forms—thus acquires a biological as well as a clinical anchor. Further investigations here are clearly of great practical as well as theoretical importance. Dr Eysenck next turns to the psychotic dimension, using Kretschmer's later work as his starting-point. The dimensional approach does seem to tidy up the diagnostic situation here. If a psychiatrist is only entitled to use one label on a patient whose condition varies in a number of dimensions then clearly he has an impossible task, which can only be attempted in a qualitative unsystematic verbal way. Other applications of this method are given in a chapter which deals with its employment in the educational and industrial fields as well as its more familiar clinical use. Finally, a return is made to general topics in a comparison between the organismic and analytic ways of studying personality. Dr Eysenck attacks, in particular, the claim that so many complexly related factors operate in the determination of behaviour that only a skilled clinician can make the necessary assessment and integration. If the factors can be identified, he says, their most effective integration can be mathematically determined. The clinician cannot hope to do better and he may not do as well. There seems a way out in that the mathematical integration holds for a group in general, whereas intuitive variations might produce more satisfactory diagnosis or selection in the case of individuals. Unfortunately, recent work shows that clinicians and selectors do not improve upon tests, and may even impair their value, by using interview procedures. It is a pity that we should simultaneously have to cope with evidence suggesting, on the one hand, that tests are our most reliable diagnostic tools and, on the other, that the most reliable kinds of tests are not very reliable. The apparent sensitivity of tests to all sorts of environmental factors makes the repetition of this work by other investgators in other centres an urgent task. Any attentive reader will find himself asking questions; for instance, are hysterics really less suggestible than the average? Even to look at the pictures raises the query, how much variance is due to the charm and efficiency of the testers and how much to the tests. Postgraduate students would

be far better checking points like this than thinking up some bright irrelevance of a Ph.D. subject. Devising new projective techniques is almost an occupational disease among them just now. It was suggested at the outset that all psychiatrists and clinical psychologists should read this book. Most of them will be well advised to read it at least twice.
Brit J Psychol 44:164–8 My '53. R. C. Albino. "Some Criticism of the Application of Factor Analysis to the Study of Personality." [See original article for critical comments too lengthy to excerpt.]
Brit J Psychol 44:169–72 My '53. H. J. Eysenck. "The Application of Factor Analysis to the Study of Personality: A Reply." [See original reply for critical comments too lengthy to excerpt.]
J Consult Psychol 17:154–5 Ap '53. Laurance F. Shaffer. * Eysenck's....use of objective tests in the appraisal of personality, in contrast to questionnaires and projective methods, deserves wider attention in the United States. The studies lead to one main proposition, of the existence of three dimensions of personality which are relatively independent: introversion-extroversion, neuroticism, and psychoticism. In this frame of reference "....the question: 'Is this person psychotic or neurotic?' becomes as unreasonable as the question: 'Is this person intelligent or tall?' " (p. 285). The experiments which support these hypotheses are, in the main, neatly designed and analyzed, and yield sharp tests of propositions deduced from theory. Some of them, however, seem to suffer from the lack of cross validation on independent groups. Such a statically cross-sectional approach, however ably applied, leads almost inevitably to a hereditarian position. Eysenck espouses "constitution" as the cause of individual differences in personality, and generally belittles psychogenic hypotheses based on clinical evidence. One may hope that someday he will undertake the experimental investigation of learning, and apply his considerable talents to the study of change as well as to the study of status.
Occupational Psychol 27:109–10 Ap '53. Boris Semeonoff. * Eysenck at least partially fulfils expectations by a more detailed description of method, and by an even more than usually outspoken and polemical statement of his position as an elementalist in the field of personality description, and indeed in psychology

in general. * Eysenck's positive contribution, and whether it be viewed as the statement of a standpoint, or as an account of carefully controlled experimental work, its value is considerable. Where it may rouse antagonism, on the other hand, is in the directness or ruthlessness —even brutality is not too strong a word—of the author's attack on points of view and techniques with which he is not in sympathy. Particularly is this so in the case of projective techniques. Possibly Dr Eysenck weakens his case by persistently referring to these as "tests," and by quoting results of investigations in which findings are reported (often surprisingly) in the form of "scores." Dealing with Kretschmer's system (to which he seems to be considerably attracted), Dr Eysenck writes:

We have attempted to state Kretschmer's hypotheses in such a way that a statistical and experimental test of them becomes possible; while we believe that in stating them in this fashion we have not misrepresented him in any way,....it should be borne in mind that in thus reducing a complex and difficult system to two brief fundamentals we may have done violence to this system.

Such a concession is never made in his dealings with projective methods, and while group forms of Rorschach (such as Dr Eysenck himself uses) are admittedly often "scored" in terms of simple indices, *etc.,* this is not so in the case of the Thematic Apperception Test. When, therefore, Dr Eysenck, almost in his opening pages, makes much of an apparently random distribution of correlations between T.A.T. "scores" and teachers' ratings, he is clearly dealing with an atypical approach which may itself be said to "do violence" to the technique in question. Rather similar is the author's treatment of the "unreliability" of the unstructured interview as an instrument of personality assessment. Psychoanalytic concepts, again, are dismissed almost out-of-hand, or with open contempt. That there is much in the book, then, that will arouse controversy, disapproval, anger—and even anxiety—is undoubted, and one finds oneself picking almost with satisfaction on a number of typographical slips (including some in tables) which one would have overlooked had not the author made characteristic reference to "the inability of some writers to make their column figures agree with their totals, or to calculate percentages accurately." Other minor criticisms are easy to advance; thus, certain chapters bear all too clearly the marks of having been assembled from journal articles without sufficient care to avoid repetition or even, occasionally, obscurity. Certain portions of the text, again, are somewhat disfigured by excessive detailed quotation of factor saturations, *etc.*, which, while adding weight to the argument by their evidence, detract from readability. On the other hand, the skilful choice of photographic illustrations has in many cases obviated the need for lengthy descriptions of experimental procedures. Finally, the book, like its predecessor, stands out as an admirable if not unique example of large-scale team research on a unified project. The importance of Dr Eysenck's work as a contribution to scientific enquiry is unquestionable. Whether it will recruit many converts from the ranks of "dynamic" psychologists (a term Eysenck always writes in quotation marks) is another matter. Yet many will no doubt agree with the author to the extent that "clearly the onus of proof is now with the organismicists."

Personnel Psychol 7:189–92 sp '54. Samuel S. Dubin. * Eysenck....relies primarily on "objective behavior tests" and comments that "questionnaires, projective tests and ratings on psychiatric interviews are of doubtful value." Questionnaires are rejected "because of their known lack of validity"; projective tests because of the "absence of proof that they measure anything" and ratings because of "their known unreliability." This reviewer feels that this is a harsh appraisal. Improved validity studies on personality questionnaires were obtained with military personnel during the Second World War and higher validities are usually obtained when personality tests are administered individually. * this volume is a significant contribution to the area of personality measurement and is strongly recommended to the professional reader * The test designs are novel and provocative. *

Psychol B 51:284–7 My '54. Dan L. Adler. * provocative and....provoking * combines the virtue of sophisticated deduction and the vice of blatant bias. Although occasionally it carps and quibbles, the unfolding of its theme tantalizes to the very end. * In Chapter 4, Eysenck reports the first full-scale use of this method. Employing an axis rotation which maximizes the correlation between factor saturation and criterion indices, he makes an attempt to identify the factor of neuroticism and its subcategories. It is here that one begins to raise questions about the author's presentation. (1) Hav-

ing administered a battery of 76 tests, he selects 28 for factorial analysis. The basis of this choice is not made clear. Presumably, the number of subjects involved does not determine the choice since in three tests $N = 38$, and in the remainder $N = 96$. Nor does the choice seem to depend on the significance of the correlation ratios (pp. 127–150). One wonders what principle of elimination was used. (2) The selection of criterion groups is based upon psychiatric ratings with which Eysenck repeatedly finds fault until a positive attitude is useful to his argument. Thus "....psychiatric diagnosis is of doubtful validity and low reliability" (p. 33). Later, after a discussion of inconsistent inductee rejections on neuropsychiatric grounds, he says: "We are left with the unreliability of psychiatric assessment as the most probable cause" (p. 91). But, he then maintains, "....as we have shown in the preceding section, the validity of psychiatric ratings for future breakdown has been established; it would seem to follow that methods correlating highly with psychiatric assessment would also show a certain degree of validity" (p. 99). Practically all of the experiments which bolster his arguments for a neuroticism factor depend upon psychiatric diagnoses or ratings of severity of neurotic disorders (e.g., pp. 106 f.). (3) A similar tendency on the part of the author to favor expedient interpretations is exemplified by his variable interpretation of correlation coefficients. Thus, a correlation of $-.21$ between intelligence and neurotic tendencies is considered to be a "very small one" (p. 116) and it is interpreted as indicating no close relationship (p. 149). Nevertheless, a series of correlations between level of aspiration tests and examination scores "gave results in the expected direction," albeit they are $-.20$ and $-.11$ in one case, and $-.15$ and $-.10$ in another (p. 266). There is little doubt that psychologists will follow Eysenck's logical reasoning about neuroticism, despite the lapses indicated. But the step which follows will separate the environmentalist sheep from the hereditarian goats. Employing Holzinger's h^2 as an estimate of the contribution of heredity to total variance, Eysenck concludes that neuroticism as a factor is a biological unit which is inherited as a whole (p. 187). The crux of his argument lies in the differences between identical and fraternal twins on tests which Eysenck employs to differentiate normals from neurotics. Although mean test scores are the same for the two types of twins, pairs of identical twins are characterized by higher intracorrelations, and the group of identicals as a whole is characterized by greater variance. * Eysenck rejects the notion, attributed to Freud, that psychoticism is a part of a normal-neurotic-psychotic continuum. Although by criterion analysis he distinguishes between "psychopath" and "hysteria-anxiety" types of neuroticism, he finds little difference between manic-depressive and schizophrenic types of psychoticism. The reader may be inclined to wonder if the basic premises of criterion analysis are sound. Quite apart from Eysenck's conclusions, it is probably no more difficult to distinguish psychotic subtypes than it is neurotic subtypes. On a priori grounds one would expect psychiatric judgments to be at least equally valid in making these distinctions. Yet having employed the distinctions to create criterion groups, we are required to believe that the differences we "see" are not valid because test behaviors of the groups do not satisfy a statistical notion. In this instance, at least, we might conclude that criterion analysis is better used to discover what is not known than to corroborate what is. Eysenck's book is an important one because of its generally convincing logic and its freshness of approach. These virtues may well operate to make it a new choice point in psychological history. Such importance makes it imperative to evaluate this factorial method in the light of our developmental frame of reference. Apart from the specific criticisms already made, two major points should be emphasized: (1) Criterion analysis presumably has the advantages of being a hypothetico-deductive process. Careful examination indicates, however, that the hypotheses are mainly validated internally, i.e., within the confines of the method itself. (See particularly the first full-scale application of the method described in Chapter 4.) The few exceptions in Chapter 7 notwithstanding, it fails to comply with the rigorous requirement of independent external validations. (2) Criterion analysis is admittedly elementaristic, and its sponsor is openly opposed to organismic interpretations of behavior or personality (pp. 277–285). Citing hand-picked experiments, he refutes the meaningfulness of gestalt qualities and substitutes for them scalar values on orthogonal dimensions. Nowhere is it clear how this index description of personality can help determine the dynamics

—the causes of change—of behavior. Nowhere is it clear how measured body sway—a reliable index of "neuroticism"—will predict today's equanimity and tomorrow's moodiness. Eysenck himself cites the difficulties inherent in standardizing his factor-loaded tests: "....whether the tester is a pretty young girl, a domineering male, or a mature, sympathetic woman—all these influences may, and in some cases do, affect a person's scores. They are difficult to control, particularly as the same stimulus—a pretty young girl as tester, for instance—may mean quite different things and arouse quite different emotions, in subjects differing in age, sex, and marital happiness" (p. 294). He might well have added here that the same stimulus may be perceived differently by the same subject from day to day or minute to minute. Not only the test, but the whole theoretical structure is thereby placed in jeopardy.

[B144]

★Eysenck, H. J. The Structure of Human Personality. London: Methuen & Co. Ltd., 1953. Pp. xix, 348. 37s. 6d. (New York: John Wiley & Sons, Inc. $5.75.) *

Am J Orthopsychiatry 24:648–50 Jl '54. Richard L. Jenkins. * The volume is unique as a systematic review of factor analysis studies of personality. * Eysenck's greatest interest seems to be in what he apparently regards as the two most important dimensions of personality. On the basis of his own work he apparently has developed a conviction that these are what he calls "neuroticism" and what he calls "introversion." * "Neuroticism" he identifies with a factor found by Webb in 1915 and described by him as "consistency of action resulting from deliberate volition or will." This "consistency of action" and "neuroticism" are the names given to the two extremes of a single continuum. * "neuroticism," as used by Eysenck, is a term far wider in its meaning than the presence of tendencies characteristic of psychoneurosis * The reviewer does not like the factor label "neuroticism," for the label "maladaptation" seems more appropriate. Moreover, it would appear that the label leads Dr. Eysenck sometimes to identify this broad maladaptation factor specifically with the psychoneuroses—which, after all, are only one group of maladaptations. Whether through having his attention diverted by the name he has assigned or not, he seems to overlook the significance of the *psychotic break*. * The second factor Eysenck identifies widely he calls introversion-extraversion and, again, the reviewer is not very happy about the name. * In his factor analysis of Ackerson's material from a child guidance clinic, what Eysenck calls introversion seems perhaps better described as inhibition, for if we contrast the extremes they are the staff diagnosis of psychoneurosis at one extreme with the accompanying traits of sensitiveness, daydreaming, absent-mindedness, seclusiveness, and depressed or discouraged attitudes at one end and stealing, truancy from home, and truancy from school at the other end. It seems to the reviewer that the latter end of this factor is not well described merely as extraversion. One of the more fascinating chapters deals with analysis of interests and attitudes. Two well-defined factors come out in a number of studies. One is radicalism versus conservatism. The other is called tough-mindedness versus tender-mindedness. To the reviewer, it appears better described as respect for the individual or the lack of it. * This is a most valuable and interesting volume which, marking as it does the gradual accumulation of systematic and quantified study of personality, is a milestone of at least incipient scientific advance. It is worth the attention of all serious students of personality structure.

Am J Psychiatry 111:795–6 Ap '55. Hiram K. Johnson. In *The Structure of Human Personality*, Eysenck, the great Maudsley psychologist, continues his courageous rear guard action in defense of scientific psychology. Probably not many psychiatrists will read through this formidable work which a future generation may well look upon as a classic. For factor analysis is made of stern stuff. A complete understanding of it requires a ready facility with higher mathematics. * Factor analysis has been bitterly criticized. The factors themselves have been called by some, statistical fictions, by others, mathematical artifacts. Despite such criticism, the clinician will discover an exciting correspondence to diagnostic concepts. This reviewer, in particular, was struck by the close correspondence between Cattell's factors (p. 63) and the various subgroups of The Personality Trait and Personality Pattern Disturbances in the new A. P. A. classification. Other factors lead to very interesting nosological speculation. Eysenck's coverage of his specialty is extraordinarily complete, and nothing important is left

out. His book thus covers his own not insignificant contribution to factor analysis, so that like Caesar, we find Eysenck commenting on Eysenck, always with the winning simplicity of the truly great mind. * Eysenck has a hatred of humbug. For wooziness in thinking, he has nothing but scorn, the acidulous and at times testy scorn of the pure scientist. Thus of his critics he can say, "....let us follow psychoanalytic practice and lay it down that criticism of factor analysis should be confined to those who have themselves been factor analysed." It is exciting—and at times a little uncomfortable to watch what he does with the "holistic," or "organismic" approach (Harvard's "Assessment of Men," p. 80), Sheldon's typology (p. 71), and Murray's famous missing chapter on the intercorrelation of variables (p. 73). *The Structure of Human Personality* is a work of utter integrity. Insofar as such stubborn material permits, it is an exciting book. Continuously we are in the presence of a taut mind; brilliant, courageous, and ruthlessly scientific.

Austral J Psychol 7:95–6 Je '55. J. A. Radcliffe. * His first chapter is on "Theories of Personality Organization." He attempts a definition to incorporate both "behavioural acts" and "dynamic concepts," but with indifferent success, and his section on generality vs. specificity adds nothing new. But his treatment of trait vs. type theories is refreshing. He cogently argues that many (especially in America) have misrepresented most type theories and provides a valuable review of the theories of Jordan, Gross, Jung, Kretschmer, Pfahler and Jaensch, and their interrelations. This section well illustrates his close acquaintance with continental literature, especially with recent developments not elsewhere readily available. * Many will not see....as much support for his hierarchical theory as does Eysenck. Some will consider him too wedded to his "neuroticism," "psychoticism" and "introversion-extraversion" dimensions and will, for example, be dubious about his equation of factors from ratings, questionnaires, objective tests, and physiological measures with the one "neuroticism" factor. They may also wonder whether his criticism of Thurstone's identification of "nationalism" may not be equally directed at his own 1947 identification of "neuroticism." But, in all, here is a valuable book for those interested in personality study—valuable for reference, especially to some of the less well-known work, for sound criticisms and for research suggestions. It is highly factual and not easy reading, but is well worth the effort, even by clinicians, because even though the reader may not always agree with his factorial emphasis and his interpretations, he must agree that here is an important "store of facts....which any theory....(of) personality must account for."

Brit J Ed Psychol 24:51 F '54. P. E. Vernon. * Whether we agree with this position or not, we must be grateful to Dr. Eysenck for bringing together, and giving a clear and organized account of, the vast number of factorial investigations which have been carried out in the field of temperament, personality and character. Clinical psychologists and other opponents of psychometric work on personality are unlikely to be convinced by the book; but most readers will find it a moderate and relatively non-controversial survey of an impressive body of research, and will probably accept the following main conclusions: (*a*) that much more research is needed with "mixed" measures, i.e., not merely with ratings, or questionnaires, or behaviour tests; and that such research can best be carried out by co-operation between teams of investigators; (*b*) that factorial research requires to be better planned to test definite psychological hypotheses; (*c*) that hand-in-hand there should be intensive experimental studies of the psychological characteristics of particular tests or other techniques. Somewhat more disputable is the view that the hierarchical organization of personality can best be revealed by following Thurstone's methods of oblique and second-order factors. The author has not attempted such analyses himself so-far, and there is little evidence that it has produced fruitful results in other laboratories. Again he insists so strongly that the second-order factors of neuroticism, extraversion-introversion and psychoticism are well-established, that he is apt to distort other writer's results to fit into this mould. To the reviewer it seems very dubious whether external ratings (like Webb's), questionnaires (like Guilford's), tests (like Eysenck's) and physiological measures (like Wenger's) can be regarded as measuring one and the same neuroticism or emotionality or "w" factor, although there is certainly some overlapping. The other two dimensions are still less satisfactory, having shown very small variance in any researches that have been conducted so-far with "mixed" measures. In other words, Dr. Eysenck is perhaps rather too optimistic regarding the progress that has already been made. However, the book contains so many sensible criticisms of the poorer researches, and stimulating interpretations of the better ones, that it will be of considerable value to lecturers, students, and future investigators. It is only unfortunate that, due to the amount of tabular and graphical material, the price is so high. In conclusion, Dr. Eysenck does not try to deal directly with educational applications such as the improvement of cumulative record cards, nor the assessment of perseverance among secondary school candidates. But psychologists who are interested in such problems cannot afford to neglect the basic psychometric researches in personality which he does describe.

Brit J Med Psychol 27:260-2 pt 4 '54. J. D. Uytman. * The difference between Eysenck and the medical psychologists is illustrated by his use of terms like "organization," "adjustment," "system," "configuration," and, for that matter, "structure," and his easy dissection of *behaviour* into "conative," "affective," "cognitive" in the style of the older academic psychology. Eysenck's attitude to personality is perhaps illustrated appositely by interest scores which he quotes, in another connexion, from Thurstone (p. 217). There "Psychology....has a loading of 0.77 in science, of 0.47 in language, *of* −0.04 *in people,* and of −0.28 in business." (Reviewer's italics.) * A good deal of his book, however, is devoted to the amendment of the conclusions of other workers who, it would seem, have been less skilful in devising scientific and objective techniques or in interpreting their results. Sometimes the statistical work is imperfect, but even when this is not the case it would appear that the science and objectivity introduced in the techniques of testing and of statistical analysis may leak out again in the interpretation. Eysenck quotes Thurstone— "this matter of naming the factors is entirely extraneous to the statistical analysis. The statistical work may be correct, while considerable argument might conceivably be made about the naming of the factors.... When multiple-factor analysis is undertaken there is absolutely no guarantee that the resulting factor loadings will so arrange themselves that they can be readily named." This would not matter too much if the whole thing were an exercise in algebra, but when we are endeavouring to decide what at-

tributes are to be ascribed to actual people, healthy or sick, it becomes a matter of some importance. The worst feature of all this is that one can analyse one's data and interpret one's results, and interpret them wrongly, without ever seeing the subject, the patient, the person, at all. Why it is more scientific to have a fallible skill in dealing with statistics than to have a fallible skill in dealing with one's fellow-humans is not quite clear. One is supposed not to be swayed by subjective influences (though surely that is just the problem described by Thurstone), but among the subjective influences that are now prohibited are those of insight and sympathy and empathy. * "neuroticism"....is a concept which Dr Eysenck defends with a zeal which he insists is scientifically and not emotionally motivated, and he shows very considerable ingenuity in demonstrating that other workers really agree with him even when at first sight they do not appear to do so. In due course he is so sure that he has succeeded in this demonstration that he is found referring confidently to "truly significant psychological variables, such as neuroticism." No doubt this variable is statistically significant, but we have seen above that there are possible difficulties in interpreting the significance (in the ordinary sense of the term) of statistical results. It is, for instance, difficult to tell, from the many definitions quoted by Dr Eysenck, whether "neuroticism" is regarded as a potentiality or an actual characteristic. If the latter, it might as well be called "neurosis" and would apparently indicate only that some people can be more ill than others psychologically as well as physically. If "neuroticism" is a potentiality it would seem to measure the tendency to neurotic breakdown quantitatively, but without any qualitative information. Admittedly, if we accept Dr Eysenck's hysteria-extraversion and "dysthymia"-introversion linkages, we have some kind of qualitative indication; that is, either the subject is liable to hysteria or he is liable to one or all of the other neurotic clinical syndromes. This would not seem immensely useful. * This book, then, while providing a most comprehensive survey of related work, and while no doubt furnishing excellent pabulum for the factor analyst, does not sustain its title's promise for the medical psychologist and other subjects with a low statisticism index. *
Brit J Psychol 45:300 N '54. D. Graham. * a thorough and sometimes sharply critical ac-

count * One would not deny that factorial methods can be of considerable value in enabling us to clarify and improve our classificatory categories. Many, however, would not agree with Dr Eysenck that the value of typologies or systems of classification can be established only by factorial methods. Dr Eysenck lays stress on the use of the "hypothetico-deductive method." But his use of the term "hypothesis" appears to the reviewer somewhat doubtful. For example, he claims to test "Jung's hypothesis that the conduct of extraverts is more determined by objects and relations in the external world, while the actions of introverts are more determined by their inner subjective states" (p. 29). He uses the "level of aspiration" technique, and finds that introverts (represented by dysthymics) aspire higher than they perform, and perform better than they estimate, while the reverse is true of extraverts (represented by hysterics). This is taken as supporting the hypothesis. Now, assuming that one accepts Dr Eysenck's selection of his two groups, the question is whether the hypothesis is a genuine hypothesis in the sense that it could be disproved conclusively by experimental procedure. One might legitimately argue that any experimental procedure such as Dr Eysenck's is not unambiguously relevant to the hypothesis, so that a critical experiment would not be possible. To put it in another way, all that one could conclude from a negative result would be that the behaviour referred to by the terms "introvert" and "extravert" does not include the behaviour in the experimental situation. This is the same kind of point as that made by Albino in his recent article in this Journal. It does not, of course, imply that it is not interesting and valuable to endeavour to define or extend the range of classificatory categories. A few other points might be made. For example, one would like to know how it comes about that rating of obsessional tendencies has a zero-loading on a factor of "neuroticism" in one study (p. 55), while in another study involving subjects classified as cases of psychopathy, obsession, hysteria, anxiety state or post-traumatic personality change, "the first component (severity of neurosis) ranks the groups in order from normal to obsessional and psychopathic" (p. 57). Such questions, however, should not be allowed to detract from the principal merits of the book, which should be read by all interested in the assessment of personality.

J Consult Psychol 18:75 F '54. Laurance F. Shaffer. Eysenck's most recent contribution to the study of personality is a survey of research. But it is more than a survey; it is a critical and creative integration which brings order to a diversity of quantitative studies. Eysenck espouses factor analysis as the prime technique for revealing the organization of personality. * Many studies are reinterpreted, sometimes with new analyses of their data, so as to bring a semblance of agreement to results previously considered contradictory. Eysenck does not indulge in the petty virtue of impartiality but the blows he gives his opponents, while often severe, are fair and well aimed. The book will appeal to psychologists and students who prefer theory buttressed by research to vague professions of faith. They may not agree with every word but they will learn and be stimulated.

Psychol B 51:287–8 My '54. Dan L. Adler. * useful primarily as a source book for those who would examine personality by the criterion of factor analysis. As such, it contains excellent summaries of factorial studies * For those who have read The Scientific Study of Personality, it goes without saying that the critique is made through no ordinary orthogonal eyes, but through maximally rotated Eysenckian ones. In this regard, it is regrettable that Eysenck does not maintain throughout the sense of humor which shows up so well in the Preface: "....it might be wise to follow psychoanalytic practice and lay it down that criticism of factor analysis should be confined to those who had themselves been factor analysed!" (p. xiv). We are treated, instead, to a steady display of the argumentative ingenuity and the perspicacity that are so characteristic of the author. Although the book is intended in part "to bring together in one volume some of the major theories of personality organization...." (p. xiii), very little use is made of theories or experimental devices which do not imply either a factorial approach or a trait-type interpretation. Such organismic or "specificity" studies as do appear are employed mainly as foils for a dimensional point of view. The preliminary anticipation—and the concluding assertion—made by Eysenck is that an examination of the seemingly contradictory data in factorial explorations of personality actually demonstrates a

basic agreement. The evidence for many different personality dimensions is traceable mainly to semantic disagreements, inadequacies of the factor techniques employed, and the differences in aims of respective investigators. That these differences are peripheral is made clear by reference to a hierarchical structure of personality organization—from specific responses, through habitual response and trait levels, to a type level. At this highest organizational (type) level, he believes that three orthogonally related dimensions are implicitly agreed upon—Neuroticism, Extraversion-Introversion, and Psychoticism. Eysenck does not imply that these are the only higher-order noncognitive factors. In fact, he states: "Nor can it be maintained that these are the only higher-order factors which may be discovered; nothing can be said yet about the total number of such factors required" (p. 319). Yet, curiously, in discussing second-order factors involved in social attitudes, he strongly denies the likelihood of their being more than the R (conservative-radical) and T (tough-tender minded or practical-theoretical) factors already determined (p. 244). Such assurance seems out of keeping with the scientific spirit so readily invoked elsewhere by the author. *

[B145]

★FAN, CHUNG-TEH. Item Analysis Table: A Table of Item-Difficulty and Item-Discrimination Indices for Given Proportions of Success in the Highest 27 Per Cent and the Lowest 27 Per Cent of a Normal Bivariate Population. Princeton, N.J.: Educational Testing Service, 1953. Pp. 32. Paper, lithotyped, spiral binding. $1.00. *

[B146]

★FELDMAN, MARVIN J. A Prognostic Scale for Shock Therapy. American Psychological Association, Psychological Monographs: General and Applied, Vol. 65, No. 10, Whole No. 327. Washington, D.C.: the Association, Inc., 1951. Pp. v, 27. Paper. $1.00. * (PA 26:7028)

[B147]

★FERGUSON, LEONARD W. Personality Measurement. New York: McGraw-Hill Book Co., Inc., 1952. Pp. xv, 457. $6.00. * (London: McGraw-Hill Publishing Co., Ltd. 51s.) (PA 27:5868)

Am J Psychol 67:195–6 Mr '54. J. P. Guilford. * a book directed to the description of tests and other devices for the assessment of personality, their development, and their applications. The descriptions are the competent work of one who has had first-hand experience with that concerning which he writes. The content is long on descriptions of techniques but short on basic theory either of personality or of measurement. The subject has been treated at a relatively superficial level, presumably with the intention of bringing it within the reach of the student who probably is not prepared to use wisely the information he is given.

Am Sociol R 18:440–1 Ag '53. Harrison G. Gough. Most sociologists and psychologists who read this book will probably find it very difficult to get beyond the first chapter, which contains some of the most banal and naive observations and writing which this reviewer has seen in recent years in a textbook. For example, as an illustration of "the effect of group on individual," a Kinsey finding of a linear relationship among rural boys between amount of education and frequency of sexual contact with animals is cited. Correlations of .23 and .33 between diameter of areola (pigmented ring around the nipple) and interviewer's rating of degree of "maternal feeling" are advanced as illustrations of "constitutional determinants" of personality; and as an example of the "effect of the individual on the group," Marriott's *Maria, The Potter of San Idlefonso* is recommended "....as a must for anyone interested in the effects which the personality of one individual can have upon the characteristics and way of life of a cultural group." Yet, if the reader can find the courage to persevere beyond this flapdoodle, he will find good payment for his efforts. The very next chapter (Chapter 2), in fact, gives an exemplary discussion of the Strong Vocational Interest Test. The strong points of this book are what one would expect from a successful applied and industrial psychologist—practicality, and a realistic evaluation of tests and assessment devices. The weaknesses, outside of the near-fatal first chapter, have to do mostly with matters of structure and with editorial aspects. The tables, for example, are overly complicated and difficult to interpret, with the necessary information for headings, captions, etc., usually missing. Names are constantly mentioned in the text without reference citations, and a goodly number are presented without any listing in the bibliography at all. The writing, too, is often awkward and cumbersome and imposes a strain on the reader. What this book needs, in the present reviewer's opinion, is a re-write and thorough overhauling under expert editorial guidance. It has many of the elements of a good book—broad coverage, careful scholarship, and critical thinking—but the writing, organization, and general pres-

entation is unlikely to attract the audience which the book's essential merit deserves.

Brit J Psychol 44:271 Ag '53. J. D. Handyside. * a concise and lucid critical evaluation of a wide range of measurement techniques. His touchstones are reliability, validity, objectivity of scoring, feasibility of the method and usefulness of results. A particularly valuable feature of his approach is his use of the historical method in showing how early and unsatisfactory techniques were refined and improved by the rigorous application of statistical procedures, but he does not fail to note cases of tests which have remained unsatisfactory because the statistical procedures used in their refinement were based on bogus logic. * Ferguson does not pull his punches and is not afraid to attack what he regards as big myths. The Rorschach cult is hammered for its "crude and shallow analogies"—"If the Rorschach test has merit, very little of this merit has been demonstrated....because most Rorschachers back away from a rigid validation procedure." The O.S.S. Assessment Staff's work is held up as an example of shocking bungling. Murray's T.A.T. is rejected as both dubious in its results and excessively inconvenient in its application. Amongst tests which receive approval are the Strong Interest Test, the M.M.P.I., the Insurance Selling Aptitude Index, Thurstone's Attitude scales and Eysenck's experimental approaches. These facts seem to the reviewer to be sufficient evidence of the book's acceptably high level of reliability, validity and objectivity.

J Consult Psychol 16:475 D '52. Laurance F. Shaffer. * The book is deceptively simple. Its language structure gives a first impression of being almost too much in "words of one syllable," and statistical complexities are omitted. Beneath the apparent simplicity, however, the author comes to grips with many really complicated issues of technique, but communicates them with remarkable clarity. Elementary students can use the book, and quite advanced students will still find much of profit in it.

J Social Psychol 38:303–8 N '53. H. J. Eysenck. * The discussion is throughout factual, extremely well documented, unprejudiced by any of the current "isms," and it is apparent that the author is familiar, through personal experience, with the field he is discussing. * There are two main criticisms, however, which may justifiably be made of this book. The first of these relates to the omission of what are important and valuable areas; the second relates to the lack of stress on theory, which is evident throughout the book. To take the former point first, Ferguson has omitted completely two areas of personality measurement which are attracting a great deal of attention at the moment, and about which the student would rightly demand to obtain information. The first of these is the field of psychophysical relations. The recent work by Wenger, Freeman, Jost, Theron, Malmo, and Shagass, and many others, has raised high hopes that entirely objective physiological measures of autonomic lability, homeostatic recovery, ease of conditioning, and so forth, may prove to be very highly correlated with behaviour patterns which are easily recognizable in everyday life. None of these studies is mentioned, and the whole field is passed over. Much the same is true of the constitutional field and the relationship between body build and personality. The recent interest in Sheldon's adaptation of European contributions to the subject may, to the rigid experimentalist, appear something of a fad, and the experimental and statistical inadequacies of his contribution may make an account of it less inviting than it might otherwise have been; nevertheless, evidence in favour of the Rorschach or the Thematic Apperception Test is no better than evidence in favour of constitutional indices as measures of personality, and one might have expected at least a brief account of this important field. However, this difficulty of omission could easily be remedied in a second edition, which will undoubtedly be called for in a short time. The main fault of the book, however, would be very much more difficult to remedy. We have already noticed that in his first chapter, Ferguson lays great stress on the importance of theory and theoretical formulation; yet when it comes to dealing with a large body of empirical data and of organizing these into some kind of system, theory is almost entirely excluded. * Ferguson has written a book which in many ways is an excellent introduction to the field he has surveyed....it may be recommended as a textbook for courses in personality measurement. A proviso must be added, however, that if it is so used, the instructor himself would have to provide the theoretical background and the integration of the various studies recorded; he will have little help from the book itself. [See original review for additional criticisms not excerpted.]

Mental Hygiene 39:130–1 Ja '55. Frank K. Shuttleworth. The nearly forty tests of personality selected for examination....constitute a good representation of the best tests, of the variety of tests, and of some of the more recent developments in ratings and performance tests. The details of test construction, item selection, scoring, standardization, reliabilities, intercorrelations, and validities are presented quite clearly. The selected tests are categorized under seven types, each of which involves two contrasted approaches. Separate chapters are devoted to each type and each approach, as follows: vocational-interest tests, empirical and rational approaches; attitude tests, *a priori* and *a posteriori* approaches; personality tests, unidimensional and multidimensional approaches; adjustment tests, diagnostic and prognostic approaches; ratings, nonanalytical and analytical approaches; projective techniques, perceptual and imaginal approaches; and performance tests, observational and experimental approaches. However ingenious these categories may be, they are often based on superficialities. They will surely confuse many students. Except for the vocational-interest tests, there is little discussion of applications or pitfalls in the interpretation of individual test scores. Indeed, the client, with all of his idiosyncrasies, seems to be nonexistent. The text seems to presume an introductory course in tests and measurements, because there is no discussion of the general theory and fundamentals of test construction. It does not seem suitable, however, as an advanced text for majors in clinical, vocational, or business psychology because each of these groups needs a broader and more intensive study of materials especially relevant to their special problems. It may perhaps best serve as a text where advanced courses in these specializations are not offered.

Psychol B 50:317–8 Jl '53. Ross Stagner. A volume devoted to the special problems of personality measurement has been needed for a long time, but Ferguson fills only a portion of this gap. A definition of personality is lacking, which would serve as a focal point for the measurement material. Many problems in the logic of measurement are sidestepped, such as the extent to which the addition of item-responses on interest inventories, questionnaires, and projective devices gives us scalable material. Ferguson's book, therefore, must be thought of primarily as a collection of interesting and useful facts about the reliabilities and validities of numerous instruments intended to be measures of aspects of personality. The first chapter of the book is well calculated to stir the reader's enthusiasm. A case of a college student suicide suggests that we may get interesting clinical studies on validity; a discussion of group differences in personality (national, racial, etc.) hints of measurement problems in cross-cultural comparisons; and three pages on morale whet an appetite for a critical analysis of morale measures. Unfortunately, most of these expectations are unfulfilled; cultural group differences in personality are not mentioned again, and morale studies are given only casual attention. There is a good deal to be said in favor of Ferguson's arrangement, starting with problems of interest and attitude measurement, which makes it possible to deal with simple concrete materials before getting into some of the more complex devices. It is questionable, however, whether these two topics merit 116 pages (or 25 per cent of the volume) compared to the treatment given to projective devices in 35 pages (or 8 per cent of the book). The suggested imbalance in Ferguson's presentation is further illustrated in the treatment of the projective tests. The chapter on the Rorschach test gives a protocol of a fairly interesting case, and discusses some of the mechanical aspects of scoring. However, at no point is the interpretation quoted; that is, the description of the total personality, which is presumably the main diagnostic claim of the Rorschach approach. Even on the level treated by Ferguson (the statistical analysis of specific response determinants), the work of such investigators as Wittenborn and Cronbach has been ignored. And just why the study of sales managers by Kurtz should be considered evidence on the validity of the Rorschach is hard to see. The sections on objective, questionnaire-type devices are the best in the book. They summarize data on an enormous number of different inventories, from the Woodworth Personal Data Sheet to the Minnesota Multiphasic Personality Inventory. And information on method of development, reliability, group norms, and validity studies is offered for each of these tests. There is lacking, however, a discussion of such logical problems as what kind of scale results when we simply add the number of "diagnostic" answers. What one also misses is an incisive discussion of just what would constitute substantial validation. This is a difficult assignment, but it cannot be evaded legitimately in a volume on personality measurement. This book should be useful as a text for a graduate course in personality measurement, if it is liberally supplemented by journal articles or other sources, and if the instructor provides some balance to the over-emphasis on empirical findings and on questionnaire-type tests. The treatment is clear and straightforward; the style is readable without being overpopularized. It will certainly help to give students a model of organization for data on development, reliability, and validity of any test device. They should also learn a good deal about appropriate applications of statistics to defined measurement problems.

[B148]
★FISHMAN, JOSHUA A. **1957 Supplement to College Board Scores No. 2.** New York: College Entrance Examination Board, 1957. Pp. vi, 206. Paper. $1.50. *

[B149]
★FITT, A. B. **The Stanford-Binet Scale: Its Suitability for New Zealand.** New Zealand Council for Educational Research, Studies in Education Series No. 14. Christchurch, New Zealand: Whitcombe & Tombs Ltd., 1953. Pp. 32. Paper. 3s. 6d. (London: Oxford University Press. 3s. 6d.) *

J Ed (London) 86:574 D '54. C. M. Fleming. * presents a neat summary of evidence as to results obtained from the systematic testing of 719 children at six age levels with comparative studies of 733 children who had been tested for other reasons. Full details of the findings are presented and suggestions are made as to the placing of certain items and as to desirable change in wording. While the number of cases is not great, the scale as a whole seems to have secured in New Zealand responses very similar to those obtained in surveys in the United States and in Scotland. *

[B150]
★FLECK, HENRIETTA. **How to Evaluate Students.** Bloomington, Ill.: McKnight & McKnight Publishing Co., 1953. Pp. 85. Paper. $1.00. * (PA 28:3289)

Clearing House 28:118-9 O '53. Bernard Rabin. * a commendable effort to interpret for home-economics teachers the broad concept of evaluation and to show how a teacher can actually attack evaluating the growth of students. A generally sound broad concept of evaluation is examined briefly and is followed by discussion of ways and means of evaluating the following aspects of growth of home-economics students: attitudes and beliefs, values, personal and social adjustment, critical thinking, needs and problems, interests, social sensitivity, functional information, experiences, appreciation, and human relations. The examination of existing devices for gaining information about students and for assessing their growth in the above areas is specific enough to be practical in nature for a teacher. Though written specifically for home-economics teachers, much of the booklet is directly applicable to every area of the curriculum and to every level of educative effort.

J Teach Ed 4:324 D '53. * a well-written pamphlet exploring the wider ranges of evaluation, particularly in the field of home economics * The material should be stimulating to any teacher able to substitute his own subject field for that of home economics.

Personnel & Guid J 32:308–9 Ja '54. Lysle W. Croft. * It is rather doubtful if this book is of interest to the professional counselor or student personnel worker as the contents are basically those of good counseling, but it is good material for any teacher desirous of improving his method of understanding the individual student better.

[B151]
★FLEMING, W. G. **Aptitude and Achievement Scores Related to Immediate Educational and Occupational Choices of Ontario Grade 13 Students.** Atkinson Study of Utilization of Student Resources, Report No. 3. Toronto, Canada: Department of Educational Research, Ontario College of Education, 1958. Pp. xix, 380. Paper, lithotyped. $5.00. *

[B152]
★FLEMING, W. G. **Background and Personality Factors Associated with Educational and Occupational Plans and Careers of Ontario Grade 13 Students.** Atkinson Study of Utilization of Student Resources, Report No. 1. Toronto, Canada: Department of Educational Research, Ontario College of Education, 1957. Pp. xii, 158. Paper, lithotyped. $2.50. *

[B153]
★FLEMING, W. G. **Ontario Grade 13 Students: Their Aptitude, Achievement, and Immediate Destination.** Atkinson Study of Utilization of Student Resources, Report No. 4. Toronto, Canada: Department of Educational Research, Ontario College of Education, 1958. Pp. ix, 55. Paper. $1.00. *

[B154]
★FLEMING, W. G. **Ontario Grade 13 Students: Who Are They and What Happens to Them?** Atkinson Study of Utilization of Student Resources, Report No. 2. Toronto, Canada: Department of Educational Research, Ontario College of Education, 1957. Pp. 59. Paper. $1.00. *

[B155]
★FORLANO, GEORGE, AND O'CONNOR, RICHARD J. **A Summary of the Evaluation of the Aetna Road-**

ometer Performance Test. Board of Education of the City of New York, Bureau of Educational Research, Division of Tests and Measurements, Divisional Bulletin No. 2. New York: Board of Education, August 1951. Pp. iv, 12. Paper. Gratis. * (*PA* 26:5882)

[B156]
★FRANKLIN, ERIK. **Tonality as a Basis for the Study of Musical Talent.** Göteborg, Sweden: Gumperts Förlag, 1956. Pp. 193. $3.50. * (*PA* 31:636)

Cont Psychol 2:24 Ja '57. Carroll C. Pratt. * Franklin....has presented....an impressive challenge to all psychologists and musicians interested in the testing of musical talent. He is convinced that most tests in this field, patterned as they are after the pioneer studies of Seashore, do not get at the heart of the problem. Good discriminations of pitch, time, rhythm, intensity, changes in tonal sequence, and even tonal intervals, consonance and dissonance, and the like, may be among the necessary conditions for success in music, but they are not sufficient. * Music in our Western culture has developed during the last few centuries around a more or less steady feeling for tonality—*Tonalitätsgefühl*—and it is this dominant characteristic of music that Franklin has tried to make use of in his study of musical talent. He is not bothered by the fact that many contemporary composers are running away in all directions from *Tonalitätsgefühl,* for he thinks it will be many decades before the habits of centuries will have been undone. * One of the most salient characteristics of *Tonalitätsgefühl* is the manner in which a melody comes to an end. It was this feeling for cadence that Franklin decided to use in the construction of his tests. He made up a large number of melodies and tried them on small groups of subjects in order to pretest for degrees of difficulty. The melodies were played through to the next to last note, and the task of the subject was then to hum or whistle the last note, which after a long series of trials Franklin decided must always be the tonic. * The author gives an excellent review of almost every test devised for the study of musical talent. He is fully appreciative of those psychologists who have tried to transcend the limitations of atomistic tests—Schoen, Lowery, Semeonoff, and especially Wing—and regards his own work only as a small step forward in the baffling area of the analysis of musical talent. In the last chapter Franklin reports the results of a factor-analysis of hodgepodge of tests: atomistic tests of auditory discrimination, tests of form (the Gottschaldt figures), various tests of intelligence, his own tests, and those of Wing. Someone must have misled him into believing that throwing such material into a statistical hopper would yield evidence more valuable than his own original data, which are good enough in themselves. To his credit it must be said that he regards the results not too seriously. They tend to confirm his own hypothesis. The loadings for "musical talent" are much lower at the atomistic level than at the levels of form-discrimination and of cognition. Franklin's manuscript was first written in Swedish, and then translated by his brother into English. The translation is incredibly bad: misspellings and grammatical blunders occur on almost every page. Citations are wrong, authors are misquoted sometimes to the point of nonsense (e.g., Riggs, p. 121), and the bibliography, although useful because of the large number of references to works not generally known in America, is made difficult by the use of unfamiliar abbreviations. The author also commits, for a scholarly work, the unforgivable sin of furnishing no index at the back of the book. Yet in spite of the many mistakes in composition, the meaning and importance of what Franklin tries to say are for the most part clear enough.

[B157]

★FREDERIKSEN, NORMAN; SAUNDERS, D. R.; AND WAND, BARBARA. **The In-Basket Test.** American Psychological Association, Psychological Monographs: General and Applied, Vol. 71, No. 9, Whole No. 438. Washington, D.C.: the Association, Inc., 1957. Pp. 28. Paper. $1.00. *

[B158]

*FREEMAN, FRANK S. **Theory and Practice of Psychological Testing, Revised Edition.** New York: Henry Holt & Co., Inc., 1955. Pp. xvi, 609. $5.25. * (PA 29:7275)

Cont Psychol 1:17–8 Ja '56. H. Glenn Ludlow. Psychologists and related professional personnel who have been pleased with the first edition of this book will find the revised edition an even more useful and complete volume. Critics of the 1950 publication will note several important modifications which should result in greater popularity of the present text. * the treatment of projective techniques has been extended so as to be more useful to students not specializing in clinical psychology. These chapters appear to be especially well written for consumers of the results of projective analyses. * the new edition gives more attention to the psychological analysis of the functions be-

ing tested by each of the several types of measuring devices. In this connection, Chapter 3, "Definitions and Analyses of Intelligence," is as good as the reviewer has ever read. * Approximately one-half (11 chapters) of the content is concerned with the measurement of intelligence. * Although Freeman is objective, fair, and scientific in his writing, he does not hesitate to take a stand. * Tests and principles are evaluated and criticized in a lucid way. The question and discussion technique employed in the sections dealing with the Stanford-Binet and Wechsler tests are fine examples of good professional writing. One of the best contributions is the account of the historical background of the Binet scales. * [the revision] would have been further improved by a little more attention to the criterion of teachability. Surely problems and exercises inserted at appropriate places would assist student readers materially in the reflective process as well as ease the burden of instructors. Also brief, well-selected, and annotated chapter reading lists would be a welcome addition. Another question of less importance occurs in connection with the loss of the lists of tables and figures available in the first edition. Students of education will be disappointed at the scant treatment given to achievement testing. * Some readers will consider the omission of the chapter on statistics a distinct loss. In general one may ask: How long will psychologists continue to ignore the results of their own experimental evidence on retention? All in all, this publication represents a real addition to the field of psychological testing. It is an attractive, thoroughly readable, sound treatment of the subject. Dr. Freeman is to be complimented for actually revising a "revised text."

Ed & Psychol Meas 15:516–8 w '55. Wimburn L. Wallace. * begins with two excellent chapters covering general principles of psychometrics. They provide a clear and concise description of such topics as reliability, validity, standardization, methods of expressing scores, and trait sampling. For the student with some understanding of elementary statistics, these explanations provide a solid foundation for the main body of the text which describes a number of tests and techniques that have been or are currently available and in use. The clarity which characterizes the introductory chapters permanently disappears thereafter. Chapter 3 deals with definitions of intelligence and analyses of mental abilities. This is a topic of fundamental importance, which, to say the least, is not an easy one for the student to understand. It is unlikely, however, that Freeman's discussion of it will provide clarification for many readers. The extensive reference to factor analysis included in the chapter seems to be somewhat abortive and does not ameliorate the impression of reconditeness. Of the next four chapters, three are devoted to the Binet scales and one to the Wechsler. It is now that the reader is impressed with the too-easily-overlooked warning in the Preface to the effect that the emphasis in this book "....is on individual and clinical interpretation of test findings." (p. x). This statement could validly have been extended to say that the emphasis is on individually administered instruments used in the clinical milieu. Chapters 8 and 9 continue with individual tests, covering performance and preschool scales, respectively, in a prosaic fashion. * The relative emphasis on different types of group tests and the basis for describing some instruments while excluding others are nowhere explained, nor are they self-evident. Freeman seems to use popularity among psychologists and widespread use as criteria of the importance of an instrument in some instances, but then he relegates interest inventories to a most cursory and inadequate treatment. Incidentally, it is in this brief discussion of interest measures that he comes closest to leading the student astray in a generally cautious text; the erroneous implication is to the effect that the Kuder and the Strong (the only inventories mentioned) measure just about the same things in the same way and have had the same type of validation. Clerical tests receive similarly brief attention and are exemplified by only three of the older instruments in this area. It is suggested that their application may be to a pupil's "....guidance in the selection of a high-school course...." (p. 328), while no mention is made of their use in employment screening and placement. In fact, the personnel man or industrial psychologist would seek in vain in this book for adequate information about most of the tests he might appropriately consider using. It is indeed difficult to understand why such topics as rating scales, play, psychodrama, and the O.S.S. situational assessment techniques are afforded so much attention in this text at the sacrifice of thorough reviews of many of the well-established psychological tests. Such inclu-

sions tend to belie the implications of the title and preface of the book. If these techniques belong in the contents, why not also the diagnostic interview and psychoanalysis? The classification of a number of the tests that are included is mystifying. * At the end of the review of each type of instrument there is a section labeled as the "Evaluation" of the tests covered. This is a good procedure, but it can easily imply to the reader that the author's opinions are confined to this section. In this book, however, the descriptions of the tests are themselves replete with value judgments. Finally, the up-to-dateness of information about different instruments varies greatly. In one instance a 1955 revision is described, while in others, important revisions of manuals and improvements in data published as much as three years earlier are ignored. Similarly, some fairly new tests are mentioned while others appearing about the same time and making at least as much original contribution to the field are omitted. This book can be recommended as a class text to instructors whose particular preference for emphases in the presentation of elementary tests and measurement happens to coincide with those in the book. There should not be many. For anyone else there is a choice among several other works in the area which are superior to this one.

J Ed Res 49:239-40 N '55. A. W. Tamminen. * The format, subtitling, and arrangement are very much improved giving this edition a readability which should make it more attractive to students. * His discussion of "operational" and "functional" validity may mislead the reader for whom the term "operational" has a somewhat different connotation. He uses the terms to distinguish between mediating and more ultimate criteria of validity. It is vital to recognize that a test may be valid for measuring finger dexterity (operational validity), yet be invalid for predicting success in watchmaking (functional validity); but to couch this problem in novel terms serves no real purpose especially since he never uses the terms again in his discussion of tests. This reviewer would have liked to see more detailed emphasis on empirical bases for validity and especially on cross-validation, which so incisively cuts spurious validity coefficients down to size. * On the whole, Freeman handles the stupendous task of reviewing psychological tests with very creditable success and in a scholarly and painstaking manner. He is most thorough in his coverage of mental ability tests and most individual in his emphasis upon the importance of the clinician, his art, skill, and experience, in test interpretation. This book and Anastasi's *Psychological Testing* (1954) could well be used to supplement each other; what one misses, the other covers. The two approaches and the individual flavor of differing viewpoints, taken together, give the reader something of a "3-D" perspective on the entire field of psychological testing.

Personnel & Guid J 34:117–8 O '55. Leona E. Tyler. * The book seems to be intended more for would-be clinical psychologists than for counselors, personnel workers, or researchers. Its defects are of three main varieties. The first fault seems to arise from the fact that the earlier edition has not been thoroughly worked over in producing this revision. Much important new material shows up in footnotes rather than in the body of the text. There is an overemphasis on early tests, and some like Army Beta which are practically obsolete are still included. The second flaw is in the treatment of general test theory. There are many inaccuracies and ambiguities in the explanation of principles of test construction. For example, instead of the clear and authoritative ideas on validity that could have been taken from the American Psychological Association manual on technical recommendations published in 1954, the author sets up a distinction between what he calls *operational* and *functional* validity, concepts that are not used by other psychologists in evaluating tests. Factor analysis is covered very inadequately in Chapter 3. From then on its contributions are largely ignored and a kind of intuitive psychological analysis is used in explaining what various specific tests measure. One gets the impression that the approach to reliability, validity, and standardization is essentially an old-fashioned one, and that the attempt to graft in the newer ideas that have come to dominate the testing field since World War II has not been successful. The third defect is a matter of emphasis and organization. Even if the book were solely for clinical students, it seems hard to justify the allocation of about one-fourth of the total amount of space to Binet and Wechsler, Rorschach and TAT, when these are the very topics that constitute the subject-matter of advanced courses which clinical students will be required to take. It

seems very doubtful whether a beginning text should include details about the scoring procedure for the Rorschach. On the other hand, thirty pages devoted to tests of dexterity, mechanical aptitude, and clerical aptitude would seem to be far too few, since clinical students will probably never encounter these topics formally again. For trainees in counseling and school psychology programs this imbalance is even more serious. A number of less serious criticisms of the organization could also be made. It would have been better to have placed the systematic discussion of performance and non-verbal scales *before* rather than after the chapter on the Wechsler. Interest tests like the Strong and the Kuder would fall more naturally into the section on personality testing than into the chapter entitled "Aptitude Tests: Fine Arts and Professions." The practice of giving brief descriptions of several tests and then evaluating them as a group works well in some areas—*e.g.,* infant tests—but not in others— *e.g.,* personality inventories. Important distinctions, such as that between inventories with empirical scoring keys like the MMPI and inventories with "a priori" keys like the California, are covered up by this procedure. In spite of these weaknesses there is a large amount of useful material in this volume. There are good chapters on infant scales, miscellaneous projective methods, the use of intelligence tests as clinical instruments, tests of mental impairment, and situational tests. A good teacher who could fill in the gaps and supplement the treatment of test construction would find this a very satisfactory text. It is readable and rich in illustrative material. Students should react favorably to it.

For reviews of the first edition, see 4:B155.

[B159]

★FREEMAN, M. J. **The Development of a Test for the Measurement of Anxiety: A Study of Its Reliability and Validity.** American Psychological Association, Psychological Monographs: General and Applied, Vol. 67, No. 3, Whole No. 353. Washington, D.C.: the Association, Inc., 1953. Pp. 19. Paper. $1.00. * (*PA* 28:2903)

[B160]

FRENCH, JOHN W. **The Description of Aptitude and Achievement Tests in Terms of Rotated Factors.** Psychometric Monograph No. 5. Chicago, Ill.: University of Chicago Press, 1951. Pp. x, 278. Paper. $4.00. *

J Ed Psychol 44:249–51 Ap '53. Lee J. Cronbach. * This monograph contains a summary of each investigation, with a description of tests and subjects and rotated factor loadings. Then there is a tabulation by factors, indicating what tests are loaded with each. Finally, we have a test index, name index, and factor index. The whole is prefaced by thirteen pages of text. There are eight-hundred test descriptions, which in itself constitutes no minor piece of labor. Having all this material assembled under one cover will benefit those concerned with factor analysis. The book will be of use to the general student if he does not take the material too seriously. This reviewer cannot escape the impression that French does worship factor analysis unduly, and that his work is peculiarly biased. Whenever his work touches on any unsettled issue, he appears to accept as final whatever position has been tentatively favored by Thurstone. French looks forward to the day when the test-constructor has a file of tests, each measuring one factor of the mind, which imputes to factors a status in nature rather than looking on them as a convenient way of establishing a frame of reference. As in many other reports based on the centroid method, no attention is given to unique factors. Another evidence of possible bias is found where it is implied (page 6) that a study which does not arrive at simple structure is "unsuccessful." French limits his summary to studies using rotation to simple structure, and says with scarcely an apology, "To many groups of workers in this field it may appear unfortunate not to include any of the analyses of Spearman, T. L. Kelley, Brigham, Holzinger, Swineford, Hotelling, and Thomson, or of workers using their methods." It may indeed! The summaries might have been improved if all studies had been rerotated in terms of some common criterion. This would have allowed use of data from studies not aimed toward finding simple structure. The author interprets tests in terms of ability when another psychologist might see the tests as influenced by set or motivation. Thus he prefers to see others' "Plodding" and "Carefulness" factors as abilities. French's report on the Age factor is surely open to criticism on this score. The factor is represented in several tests of an analysis by Harrell. Harrell's report but not this summary makes clear that the loadings reflected differences in attitudes of younger and older workers in the particular cotton mill studies. That is to say, the tests do not measure anything inherent in Age.

In general, French speaks of factors as inherent in tests, not as functions of test and sample of persons. The introductory pages contain some theorizing which is of interest but needs further thought. Such a statement as "genetic factors are best measured by aptitude tests and experiential factors by achievement tests" is either circular or naïve. This summary will find its greatest service as a compendium of research by the Thurstone school of factor analysis.

Psychol B 50:387-9 S '53. Wayne S. Zimmerman. "A Note on the Recognition and Interpretation of Composite Factors." [See original article for critical comments.]

Psychol B 50:391 S '53. John W. French. "A Rejoinder to Zimmerman's Note." [See original reply for critical comments.]

[B161]

★FRENCH, JOHN W., EDITOR. **Conference on Factorial Studies of Aptitude and Personality Measures at Educational Testing Service, Princeton, N. J., November 5-7, 1951.** Princeton, N. J.: Educational Testing Service, April 1952. Pp. 33. Paper, lithotyped. * (*PA* 28:7116)

[B162]

★FROEHLICH, CLIFFORD P., AND DARLEY, JOHN G. **Studying Students: Guidance Methods of Individual Analysis.** Chicago, Ill.: Science Research Associates, 1952. Pp. xviii, 411. $4.25. * (*PA* 27:2983)

Ed Res B 32:192-3 O 14 '53. Frank M. Fletcher, Jr. * the most complete treatment yet written on individual analysis of students. The basic concepts of individual analysis are dealt with in a straightforward manner. The teacher without special training in the area can profit greatly from this book. Statistical methods—a sound understanding of which is absolutely prerequisite to satisfactory individual analysis —are explained clearly. The book covers all major aspects of individual analysis within the practical range of use by the guidance worker. The sections on making and recording observations, the interview, record forms, and the autobiography are excellent. The greatest emphasis in the book is given to the testing program. All types of tests are discussed and evaluated in terms that can be understood by all educators if they have studied the preceding sections of the book. Appraisal of personal adjustment receives rather brief treatment, but this is such a complicated subject it was not feasible for the writers to deal with it fully in this book. In general, this is a book that should be in every high-school library. It is a "must" for all schools which are developing a guidance and testing program.

J Ed Res 46:631–2 Ap '53. J. David O'Dea. This book is a welcome departure from the great majority of texts in the guidance field in that the authors diligently attempt to avoid "rehashing" what has been repeatedly published. * The book, a combined evidence of the authors' technical competence, presents writing skill, documentation, suggested readings, and new material in a style which will meet the highest requirements of counselor trainers. *Studying Students* presents a unified approach to the area of objective and subjective methods of measuring and evaluating students. * an excellent aid for school staffs who may be searching for an in-service training volume * Considerable emphasis is devoted to the interview as a fact-finding device. This presentation is an example of the colorful writing skill of the authors. * This book, when compared with earlier texts in the field of guidance, offers a magnificent example of the rapid growth and development of a specialized area of educational psychology. *Studying Students* is, indeed, an important teaching tool for counselor trainers seeking a comprehensive approach to the problems of individual analysis.

J Teach Ed 4:82–3 Mr '53. J. T. Hunt. * Although experienced teachers and counselors will be disappointed by the introductory nature of this book, they are sure to find something of interest. They will be encouraged by the authors' awareness of and realistic approach to the practical school situation as it typically exists rather than as we would like it to be. * A particularly helpful feature of the book is its inclusion of these nontest methods in individual guidance. The chapters on interviewing and sociometric techniques are among the best. The inexperienced counselor will appreciate the selectivity of the writers in the area of testing. Only the better known tests which they have liked and found to be most helpful are discussed. * Unfortunately the student is given little help in interpreting or applying these results in a guidance situation for an individual. Written in a simple, readable style, the book has a minimum of professional terms and can be readily understood by the undergraduate student or the inexperienced teacher or counselor. It will doubtless find wide use in the

beginning portions of the counselor-trainer programs.

For reviews of the first edition, see 3:828.

[B163]

★FROMM, ERIKA, AND HARTMAN, LENORE DUMAS. **Intelligence: A Dynamic Approach.** Garden City, N.Y.: Doubleday & Co., Inc., 1955. Pp. ix, 52. Paper. $0.85. * (*PA* 30:6901)

[B164]

★FRUCHTER, BENJAMIN. **Introduction to Factor Analysis.** New York: D. Van Nostrand Co., Inc., 1954. Pp. xii, 280. $5.00. * (London: Macmillan & Co. Ltd. 37s. 6d.) *

Am J Psychol 68:164–6 Mr '55. William B. Michael. At long last a textbook has been written that can be used successfully in a beginning graduate course in factor analysis. In writing *Introduction to Factor Analysis,* Fruchter has provided enough material in eleven chapters covering slightly more than 200 pages for a one-semester course of three hours credit. Following Thurstone's point of view, the author has achieved a balanced exposition of the field in the development of the general principles of factor analysis, in the explanation of several methods of factor-extraction and axis-rotation, and in the description of carefully chosen experimental studies that illustrate the numerous potential applications of the techniques. The arrangement of the chapters is sound both from a logical and from a pedagogical standpoint. The exposition is particularly well suited to the needs of the beginner who wishes to have a manual at his finger tips. In step-by-step fashion, a given procedure is outlined and usually illustrated with numerical data, and at the end of nearly every chapter, there are illustrative problems and answers. * In Chapter 3, the essential background in mathematics is succinctly and clearly presented in terms of the minimum requirements of matrix-algebra and matrix-geometry. * In Chapter 6, multiple-group and principal-axis methods of factoring are described, and applications of these methods of analysis to given data are clearly demonstrated. * One of the high spots of the book is the thorough, step-by-step description of orthogonal rotation of the five axes of a centroid matrix consisting of eleven test-variables. Accompanying each of the eleven rotations is an explanation of the reasons underlying the execution of the particular rotation in question. The only major suggestion that the reviewer would make at this point is that a summary list of guiding principles might have been included to which the reader could refer—a list in which cautions as to what not to do might be summarized in addition to positive statements regarding courses of action to be taken. A minor suggestion regarding the calculation of the transformation matrix might also be in order. It would seem advisable to point out that the entries in each of the successive Λ matrices actually constitute cosines of the angles of rotation between corresponding pairs of axes. In a recent seminar on factor analysis, students with a fair amount of mathematical background considered the finding of direction numbers and normalizing the vectors to be a waste of time when actually one had only to measure the angle between two positions of an axis with a protractor and to look up the cosine of the angular separation in a table. It would appear that a justification of the procedure followed, and mention of the fact that it does lead to the realization of the cosines of the angles between corresponding pairs of axes, would further the reader's understanding of the value of the transformation matrix and of the value of the normalizing process. * Particularly helpful to the beginner in the interpretation of the results of factor analysis is the material in Chapter 10. The findings of a variety of studies from various content-areas of psychology are reported and discussed in considerable detail. Actually this chapter can be assigned to advantage after study of Chapter 4 or Chapter 7. In Chapter 11, "Some General Considerations," numerous problems are briefly treated. Although Fruchter ably distinguishes between simple axes (normals to hyperplanes) and primary axes, more might have been said concerning the differences between *structure* and *pattern*. In particular, interrelationships could have been pointed out between both perpendicular and parallelogram-type projections of a test-vector upon the two types of axis. Simultaneously, twelve or fifteen matrix equations could have been written to represent the numerous possible interrelationships occurring among various combinations of the following parameters: factor loadings (two types), correlations of tests with factors, correlations between factors, and intercorrelations of tests. Amplification of the existing geometric figures could have been effected to make such interrelationships apparent at a visual level. * A useful section on

the "Calculation of the Estimated Factor Loadings of a Variable not Included in the Original Analysis" is included in the *Appendix*. A bibliography of material written primarily since 1940 is another helpful feature. In all, Fruchter's *Introduction to Factor Analysis* is a valuable contribution to the field of psychometrics. As a teaching aid for a beginning course, it is without peer. In a six-week summer course in factor analysis at the University of California the book worked out exceedingly well. As a manual which the research worker with limited mathematical training can use in the diversified content-areas of the social sciences, the book also will serve a valuable purpose. Every student of factor analysis and every research worker who has occasion to employ factor-analytical techniques should have a copy.

Ed & Psychol Meas 15:92–6 sp '55. D. R. Saunders. * The detailed development of the topics of factor analysis leaves much that this reviewer was looking for still to be desired. Consider, for example, the topic of communality: On page 8, we encounter the symbol h^2 in a table illustrating Spearman's Theory of Two Factors. It looks like a misprint because its values are precisely g^2 and, never having studied factor analysis before, we wonder about it. On page 9 we read that "this value is known as the communality of the test,....and indicates the proportion of the total variance of the test which is held in common with *the general factor.*" (Reviewer's italics.) On Page 10 we find another table with a column for h^2; again the values are correctly computed, but they *do not fit* the definition just given! This situation remains confused until we encounter a new approximation to a definition of communality on page 47—"The communality of variable j is the sum of its independent common *variances* and is represented by the symbol h^2_j" (Reviewer's italics). A correct statement finally appears incidentally on page 51—"The communality (h^2) of variable j....is that proportion of the total variance of a variable which is correlated with other variables." Why not say this, or something equivalent, the first time? This example is unusual only in the sense that at least one correct definition of communality was found. Here are some other brief quotations that cannot be taken as literally true (again with reviewer's italics): "Factor loadings represent correlation and must be squared to be converted to *variance* (page 9)"; they merely become proportional to variance. "A vector is a straight line with a given *starting point*, length, and direction (page 31)"; vectors do not have starting points. "Variance is an index of the extent to which a test *discriminates* individual differences (page 45)"; validity would be an appropriate index of test discrimination. "There are no exact criteria for stopping extraction of factors (page 77)"; compare what is said on page 104, "Lawley's maximum-likelihood method....has the added considerable virtue of providing a chi-square test for the number of significant factors." An essential aspect of simple structure is "that each variable contains a different combination of factors (page 110)"; this simply is not so; a major goal of many factor analysts is to construct a test battery with several tests for each factor, and each test pure in its factor. When an estimated communality exceeds the estimated reliability, "this would *not* be expected from theoretical considerations (page 153)." "If some of the entries in the inverse matrix are greater than 1.0, the indication is that the factors are *linearly dependent* (page 166)"; they are merely not orthogonal. There are scores of places where Fruchter trips over details; one that he trips over particularly often is caused by overlooking the existence of common factor variance caused by sampling errors of measurement. Most of these troublesome details are important. Every one of them will cause either immediate confusion or later retroactive inhibition on the part of students. We are led to ask just what permanent effect Fruchter seeks in his students? This book seems mainly to cater to the dogmatic, fragmented, true-false brand of presentation and examination that characterizes a lot, indeed, too much, of present-day undergraduate teaching; the book could be recommended strongly for this purpose if it did not contain so many misstatements and inconsistencies. Apparently Fruchter is also interested in generating an interest in factor analysis in his students, and an ability to read the literature intelligently. This is evidenced by his inclusion of "abstracts" of ten different studies employing factor analysis. Even to this reviewer, these are a very interest-provoking group of studies, and this unusual feature of Fruchter's book is a good one. If he had taken the liberty of evaluating the strengths and weaknesses of these studies in even a rudimentary way, it would probably be very much more

beneficial to the critical ability of his students. Most of the studies seem to be chosen solely for their exotic flavor, and do not represent first-class factor-analytic workmanship. Some of them, by virtue of their negative or ambiguous results, leave the impression that factor analysis was and is not of much value. Even if this is a true impression, it is hardly one to be fostered by an introductory text. It seems highly unlikely that Fruchter hopes to turn out students who are ready to contribute to the literature of factor theory, although he evidently does expect them to be able to apply factor analysis to their own field of special interest. It seems highly unlikely to the reviewer that good studies will result, unless a good teacher is used to clarify, supplement and supplant the text at appropriate points. For example, nowhere does Fruchter discuss the influence of sample size, or of selection of variables. Van Nostrand has done a good, but not excellent job of producing this book. The typography, paper and binding are heavy and attractive. About a dozen typographical errors, or notational inconsistencies, were noted—most of them in the tables. There is an index conveniently combining subject and author references in one listing, in addition to an almost complete bibliography for the period 1940–1952. The latter actually occupies one-sixth of the entire book, and contains 786 references. In summary, this book achieves mediocre success when measured against an absolute standard of excellence. Nevertheless, for its stated purpose, it may well be the best book available. Teachers of factor analysis may wish to use it despite its difficulties, but not without knowledge of its difficulties. More advanced students may want to use it to practice their own critical faculties. Workers in the field will be interested in Fruchter's procedure for finding the inverse of *any* matrix (pp. 28, 145), and in the bibliography. The book has a few other good features, too, which are unfortunately outnumbered.

Personnel Psychol 7:577–81 w '54. Ardie Lubin. * Much of the text is a well-illustrated manual for computing a Thurstone-type of factor analysis. The step-by-step demonstrations are clear and easy to follow. Verbal explanations, diagrams, and summation algebra are used freely—the corresponding matrix algebra formulas are usually given in footnote form. (This is true even in the chapter on matrix algebra—the basic rules for multiplication of matrices, addition of matrices, etc. are given in a footnote.) However, it is not a cookbook that can be handled on a purely clerical level, for the step-by-step directions are often given in terms of matrix algebra. * These, then, are the two horns of the dilemma: cookbook or mathematical treatise? Fruchter has taken a compromise course by writing a simplified manual of Thurstonian factor analysis which requires matrix algebra in order to follow it. The fundamental matrix algebra formulas are carefully tucked away in footnotes so that the beginner can read the text without confusion. Obviously, this approach has many merits, but what kind of difficulties does the novice encounter? One serious consequence of the compromise approach is the lack of proofs. Examples are very welcome devices for illustrating methods, but cannot be considered adequate substitutes for the full matrix algebra statements and proofs. Another serious consequence is the set of incorrect inferences the student is likely to draw from the verbal explanation, if he does not follow the matrix algebra formulations in the footnotes. * After all, the gist of factor analysis does not lie in verbal explanations or clear-cut examples, helpful as these are—it is contained in a handful of matrix algebra formulas. It is unlikely that the student can deduce these formulas and their relationships by himself. What conclusions will the student draw when he turns to the answers Fruchter has provided for the exercises, and finds the caveat, "Since there are no unique answers to most factor analysis problems, these values are to be regarded as suggested solutions"? Some will think that factor analysis is really not part of applied mathematics since the solutions can be neither proved nor disproved. They may, in fact, conceive of factor analysis as a kind of "clinical" psychometrics. One sets out with a problem, does long and laborious juggling of numbers, and comes up with an "answer" which depends upon the intuition of the factor analyst. It follows that one answer is as good as another except for the verbal rationalizations which accompany them. No answer can be proved to be wrong. Now, it is certainly true that there are always vast areas of science where uncertainty reigns. But, can you imagine say, an "Introduction to Physics" where the exercises dealt only with unsolved problems? Surely one job of an elementary

text is to convey to the student, as simply as possible, the questions that *can* be answered, the answers that *have* been found. In the case of factor analysis, I think that this can be done in exactly the way that Fruchter suggests it can be done—by the rigorous use of matrix algebra, both to phrase the questions and to give the answers. * There are many statistical problems in factor analysis. (Indeed, factor analysis itself is most profitably regarded as just another multivariate statistical technique.) One of the most important is the criterion for the number of factors. Fruchter states (p. 77) "There are no exact criteria for stopping extraction of factors." Not so. This *is* one of the statistical problems that has been solved. In 1940, D. N. Lawley published a maximum likelihood method of estimating factor loading and gave a significance test for the number of factors so estimated. ("The estimation of factor loadings by the method of maximum likelihood." *Proc. Roy. Soc. Edin.,* 60, 64–82). * None of this detracts in any way from the virtues of Fruchter's text. As a condensation and simplification of Thurstone's techniques it is eminently satisfactory. The danger lies in the possibility that this text may increase the number of mathematical illiterates who wish to erect a mystic numerology on the basis of the simple linear factor analysis model. Perhaps we should imitate Plato and post a warning: "Let no man ignorant of matrix algebra enter here." Or is it too much to demand that a student should be able to understand a technique as well as apply it?

Psychometrika 20:259–60 S '55. Charles Wrigley. * Fruchter's statement of factor analysis differs in two main ways from the books already familiar to the readers of *Psychometrika.* First, his account is briefer and probably simpler than that of any of his predecessors; secondly, it has a better claim to be a textbook, less claim to be a personal statement. * Fruchter stresses (a) the practical applications of factor analysis, and (b) the computations. Ten examples of the use of factor analysis are given in the chapter entitled "Applications in the Literature." These are of an interesting diversity, ranging from investigations of conditioned responses and rat maze learning to prepsychotic personality traits and Supreme Court voting records. *Q-* and *P-*technique are represented as well as *R-*technique. The chapter should be useful in reminding the psychological student that in studying factor analysis he must remain a psychologist. The computations in factor analysis are presented in detail in chapters 5 through 8. The various steps are itemized, and the instructions are for the most part clear and straightforward, so that the student who works diligently through the presentation should be able to calculate a factor analysis in a research of his own. The more experienced factor-analyst will probably be glad to have these step-by-step descriptions both for his own reference and for supplying to the student who seeks his aid. A price is paid, naturally enough, for this emphasis upon learning by doing. For the most part the controversial issues of theory are eschewed. Key concepts are frequently introduced with so little discussion that the student may have trouble in seeing why the factor-analyst has adopted the particular procedure. For example, the account of communalities is brief and in my own view very unsatisfying. The use of communalities is probably the factor-analytic procedure which has been most criticized by statisticians. The student whose knowledge is derived from this book will hardly be able to reply to any criticism. The distinction between common and specific variance is initially made (p. 45) without any mathematical or logical reason being supplied for its adoption, and the brief discussions on pp. 46–47 and pp. 51–52 might well serve to confuse rather than clarify issues for the student. For one thing, Fruchter points out that communalities enable one to reproduce the correlations, and unities enable one to reproduce the original test scores; however, Fruchter provides no reason for preferring the former to the latter. For another, the information that specific variance is potentially common variance needs further development. As written at present, the distinction between the two types of variance is made to appear an entirely arbitrary one depending upon the particular selection of tests made by the investigator. The discussion of orthogonal and oblique rotation is no more satisfactory. The distinction between simple axes and primary axes (i.e., factor structure and factor pattern) is deferred until the final chapter, which is a pot-pourri of theoretical issues set aside earlier. Yet it is doubtful whether the student will get any real understanding of the techniques of oblique rotation presented in an earlier chapter without knowledge of this distinction. Secondly, the controversy between those who favor orthogonal and those who favor oblique rotation is also held over to the final chapter. Even then the arguments for both sides are summarized very briefly, with Fruchter making no attempt to adjudicate upon the issues. * For the already settled issues, Fruchter's avoidance of controversy is probably a strength. Factor analysis may have had overmuch of polemics in the past. It is in respect to the currently unsolved problems that Fruchter's approach seems to me a less happy one. The critical student who asks: "Is simple structure invariant?" or "Do the present tests of significance work?" or "How can we be sure that the rank of the matrix is reduced by the present means for estimating communalities?" does not get answers from Fruchter's text. Probably Fruchter cannot be expected to have answers to all of these, but at least they might have been indicated to be unsolved questions. The student who reads Fruchter alone can hardly know how many issues remain unsettled. To summarize, Fruchter has set himself a limited objective. He has dealt very lightly with the mathematics and with the more theoretical issues of factor analysis. His emphasis is upon the calculations. Within these limits, Fruchter has done a good job. His survey is well balanced and impartial. For the student who needs to become familiar with the computations, the book will be very helpful. For the person who desires an understanding of factor analysis beyond that required for routine calculation, the book will not in itself be a sufficient guide.

[B165]

★FRUMKIN, ROBERT M. **Measurement of Marriage Adjustment.** Washington, D.C.: Public Affairs Press, 1954. Pp. ii, 13. Paper. $1.00. * (PA 29:2358)

Psychiatric Q Sup 29:338 pt 2 '55. Sociologists have been trying to develop "marriage adjustment scales" with foreseeable negative results—foreseeable to the dynamic psychiatrists, that is. Sociologists themselves still argue about the advantages of the "direct" vs. "indirect" test. Frumkin is more in favor of the "indirect" test, with only very tangential insight that all these tests do not even approach tangentially the real state of unconscious affairs.

[B166]

★FURST, EDWARD J. **Constructing Evaluation Instruments.** New York: Longmans, Green & Co., Inc., 1958. Pp. xv, 334. $4.75. * (London: Longmans, Green & Co., Ltd. 35s.) (PA 32:3343)

[B167]

★GAGE, N. L. **Judging Interests From Expressive Behavior.** American Psychological Association, Psychological Monographs: General and Applied, Vol. 66, No. 18, Whole No. 350. Washington, D.C.: the Association, Inc., 1952. Pp. 20. Paper. $1.00. * (*PA* 27:7135)

[B168]

★GAGE, N. L.; LEAVITT, GEORGE S.; AND STONE, GEORGE C. **Teachers' Understanding of Their Pupils and Pupils' Ratings of Their Teachers.** American Psychological Association, Psychological Monographs: General and Applied, Vol. 69, No. 21, Whole No. 406. Washington, D.C.: the Association, Inc., 1955. Pp. 37. Paper. $1.00. * (*PA* 30:7781)

[B169]

★GARDNER, ERIC F., AND THOMPSON, GEORGE G. **Social Relations and Morale in Small Groups.** New York: Appleton-Century-Crofts, Inc., 1956. Pp. xi, 312. $6.00. * (*PA* 30:8184)

Cont Psychol 2:107–8 Ap '57. Walter H. Crockett. * The authors feel [that they] have overcome the shortcomings of traditional sociometric techniques by providing a measure of interpersonal relations which (*a*) insures an interval scale, (*b*) makes possible comparisons between different groups, and (*c*) is grounded in the psychology of human needs. This approach springs from their interest in the gratifications that persons receive from belonging to groups. Thus, in a given group, the relationships between every pair of group members is examined to determine the degree to which participation in the group satisfies certain specified needs for each member. For example, in the study of fraternities reported here, members rate each other's capacity for reducing the needs for affiliation, "playmirth," succorance, and achievement-recognition. In other groups the ratings are relative to other needs. The measuring instrument first requires that the respondent consider some large group of his male acquaintances as goal objects capable of reducing in varying degree each of the needs described above. For each need a continuum, ranging from least satisfying to most satisfying, is established, and the respondent provides the names of five persons from this large population, who, in his opinion, divide that continuum into four segments of equal length. Using these names as benchmarks, he then identifies the position on the continuum of every member of the smaller group under investigation. On the assumptions that the reference population is common for all respondents, that the intervals of each respondent's scale are of equal length, and that all members of a given group use the

same scale of judgment, the ratings received and given by group members are averaged, and several indices of within-group variance are computed. By adding the further assumption that the judgments are independent of group membership, various "social relations indices" obtained from different groups are compared. These are powerful assumptions. Considering the extraordinary difficulty of finding even an ordinal scale in judgments of the simplest social-psychological phenomena, the tenability of the present ones seems highly questionable. In fact, the one test made of the assumption of equal intervals shows significant differences between intervals at different segments of the continuum, significant differences between interval sizes for different groups, and a significant interaction between interval size and group membership. There are two ways of reacting to such a result: (*a*) one may ignore it, or (*b*) one may utilize a method of analysis which does not require the questionable assumptions. The authors choose the former alternative on the grounds that the differences "are sufficiently small to warrant....the assumption of equal interval sizes" (p. 140). An examination of the data, however, indicates that the differences are small because the interval sizes themselves are small (Table 15, p. 134); the data do not satisfy the assumption of equal intervals. The authors expected that respondents whose social needs were satisfied within a given group would be highly attracted to that group and would work diligently to help achieve the group's goals. Nine fraternities at Syracuse University participated in a study testing this hypothesis. Social-relationship indices obtained for the fraternities were correlated with a number of measures of group morale and group effectiveness. Many of the measures of morale and effectiveness were interestingly constructed, and there were a goodly number of respectably large correlations between these measures and the indices of social relationship. They present, however, no theoretical rationale to account for the pattern of positive and negative correlations. Furthermore, the reader is left to ferret out for himself the profile of correlations between any one index of social relations that may interest him and the various measures of morale and effectiveness used. Further research is likely to produce a new version of this technique, one based upon less restrictive assumptions. Such a technique, however, will supple-

ment, rather than supplant, traditional sociometric methods; for, while conventional sociometric techniques and modifications thereof
may not provide comparative information about
the need-reducing properties of groups, they do
permit—as the method described here does not
—an analysis of the connections between individuals and subgroups that reveals the regular
patterns of interaction, the structure, of the
group. In fine, we may note that this book provides a series of contrasts. The long section on
scaling theory is poor and the assumptions required by the measurement technique appear to
be untenable, but the basic conceptions underlying the methods of analysis are both novel
and provocative. The interpretations of statistical tests are sometimes questionable, yet
the empirical relationships are often extremely
interesting. The style of writing is highly redundant and laden with unnecessary jargon;
nevertheless it is evident that much thought,
time, and careful analysis have gone into this
work. All in all the authors have provided us
with a number of stimulating and thought-provoking ideas.

J Counsel Psychol 4:78–9 *sp* '57. *Leon Gorlow.* Gardner and Thompson have produced a
volume which will have considerable influence
upon the efforts of research workers who are
concerned with providing objective accountings
of group structure and group effectiveness. I
foresee their work as provoking a vigorous and
fruitful line of research into the social relations of all kind of groups. Their book is a report of four years of research with an improved
sociometric device. * Readers may be troubled
by an assumption which is basic to the entire
argument and development. It is the assumption that "if each person in a group specifies
the person he would *least like* (among all the
males he knows) and the one he would *most
like* (among all the males he knows), the positions on a scale occupied by these lowest (and
highest) ratings are comparable from individual to individual in a psychological sense." This
assumption is basic, necessary and, as the authors indicate, not open to test. Here rests the
only significant reservation with respect to the
entire proposal. The authors acknowledge the
problem. In sum, Gardner and Thompson have
provided us with a valuable orientation toward
social structure analysis in small groups. Group
research workers will want to read it. It is a
clear and straightforward statement. And it

will, I believe, provide a way for increasing the
predictable variance in the behaviors of all
kinds of small groups.

[B170]

★GEE, HELEN HOFER, AND COWLES, JOHN T., EDITORS.
**The Appraisal of Applicants to Medical Schools:
Report of the Fourth Teaching Institute, Associ-
ation of American Medical Colleges, Colorado
Springs, Colorado, November 7-10, 1956.** Evan-
ston, Ill.: Association of American Medical Colleges,
1957. Pp. xix, 228. Paper, $2.00; cloth, $3.00. *
(*PA* 32:3345)

[B171]

★GEHLMANN, FREDERICK; FERGUSON, LEONARD; AND
SCOTT, JOHN F. **Personality Tests—Uses and Limitations.** Civil Service Assembly Personnel Report No.
561. Chicago, Ill.: Public Personnel Association, 1956.
Pp. v, 23. Paper. $2.00. * (*PA* 30:7195)

[B172]

★GERBERICH, J. RAYMOND. **Specimen Objective
Test Items: A Guide to Achievement Test Construction.** New York: Longmans, Green & Co., Inc.,
1956. Pp. xi, 436. $4.75. * (*PA* 31:1752)

El Sch J 57:459–60 *My* '57. *John R. Ginther.*
* This volume should....inform teachers of the
variety of types of test items available. If this
particular mission is accomplished by the book,
the author will have achieved a major triumph.
The volume may also raise with teachers the
possibility that there are educational outcomes
other than "knowledge." * The selected bibliographies at the ends of the chapters will save any
student in the field of testing untold hours of
library work. The Glossary will be of some
value to neophytes in the field of testing. * fails
to make clear distinctions among various kinds
of behavioral outcomes in education * the author does not attempt to present a "skill" as a
type of behavior which is generalizable and can
be sought for in similar fashion in a number of
areas of learning. In this regard he beclouds an
issue which was beginning to be clarified by
Tyler and by Bloom and his associates. Furthermore, his insistence on talking about "tangi-
bility of outcomes" of education is confusing
to the reviewer. In view of the fact that understandings, concepts, knowledges, and appreciations, among others, are no more sharply defined than are skills, the designation of particular test items as measurements of one or the
other of these behaviors is not, in the reviewer's
opinion, necessarily accurate. Nevertheless, as
mentioned earlier, this volume will tend to make
teachers aware of a variety of types of items
and of a variety of types of educational outcomes. The reviewer intends to use the book as
a reference in his classes in evaluation. He will,

however, continue to use other sources in developing clearer definitions of the behaviors which he wishes to have stand as possible outcomes of the process of education.

Psychometrika 22:297–8 S '57. Robert L. Ebel. This book presents a new approach to the problem of helping class-room teachers and other test constructors improve their tests. It concentrates primarily on item writing, and seeks to aid prospective item writers by providing models—a wide selection of forms, types, and varieties of objective test items drawn from tests in all subject matter fields, and at all educational levels. This basic emphasis on the importance of item writing, and this procedure of presenting a variety of examples are both admirable. Many teachers, unfortunately, resort to testing for trivia whenever they use objective test items. The primary function of this book is to guide them in the development of items which measure some of the more important outcomes of education. * A striking and valuable feature of the book is the extensive and well-organized lists of references, which occupy approximately 80 pages and include over 1,000 references to journal articles and books. * Gerberich has wisely chosen to emphasize major learning outcomes as the primary basis for classifying these sample items. But some of the terms used to identify these outcomes, terms which teachers use frequently with apparent understanding, seem to mean quite different things to different people. To deal with this problem the author begins each chapter on a particular learning outcome by citing one or more authoritative definitions of that outcome. While these definitions shed some light on the meaning of the term, they seldom *define* it in the sense of setting up precise limits to its meaning. They seldom provide criteria which can be used to classify a given test item definitely as measuring one particular learning outcome rather than some other. The net result is that one finds items which seem almost identical in the task they present to the examinee classified under entirely different learning outcomes. * The difficulty here seems to lie chiefly with the vagueness of the category concepts. Perhaps it would be fruitful to try building a system for organizing sample test items, not on the basis of these conventional labels for supposed learning outcomes, but rather on the basis of the tasks they present to the examinee. One might then arrive at a set of categories

bearing descriptive labels like "interpretation of symbols," "knowledge of word meanings," "recall of factual information," "ability to solve numerical problems," and "ability to make correct decisions in practical problem situations." These might provide a scheme for a somewhat more clearly determinate classification of test items. * if the reviewer had written this book he would have written it somewhat differently. This is true. But the aim and method of the book would have been essentially the same. * It is a good book, one we have needed very much. I commend it to the class-room teachers for whom it was primarily written, and also to test specialists. They too will find it a valuable reference.

[B173]

★GETZELS, J. W., AND WALSH, J. J. **The Method of Paired Direct and Projective Questionnaires in the Study of Attitude Structure and Socialization.** American Psychological Association, Psychological Monographs, Vol. 72, No. 1, Whole No. 454. Washington, D.C.: the Association, Inc., 1958. Pp. 34. $1.50. *

[B174]

★GHISELLI, EDWIN E. **The Measurement of Occupational Aptitude.** University of California Publications in Psychology, Vol. 8, No. 2. Berkeley, Calif.: University of California Press, 1955. Pp. ii, 101–216. Paper. $1.50. * (*PA* 30:7824)

Cont Psychol 1:298–9 O '56. Donald E. Super. In this little booklet Ghiselli has attempted to report a distillation of the results of all published studies of the validity of tests for occupational prediction. The literature covered is American, which may be a wise limitation in view of possible cultural differences in occupations, although that limitation is not explicitly made. Ghiselli's method differs from that of Buros in the *Mental Measurements Yearbooks* in that he makes no mention of specific tests, but focuses on types of tests and types of jobs, attempting a synthesis. It differs from the present reviewer's, in that Ghiselli covers all tests and disregards questions of the adequacy of the studies which provided the validity coefficients. The results of this novel approach, essentially the statistical combination of correlation coefficients by type of test and type of job, are most helpful to the constructors of tests and the vocational appraisers. The figures point up clearly the occupational significance of each type of test, giving the developer of a test battery and the selector of tests for personnel evaluation or for vocational counseling more than vague generalizations to go on. Interesting findings include a lack of relationship between success in training and success in most jobs, and a lack of correspondence between existing occupational classifications and an empirical classification based on aptitude patterns. The latter finding is more damaging to the empirical finding than to the existing classifications.

Personnel Psychol 9:413–5 au '56. Donald L. Grant. * The summary of validity information presented in this monograph represents a major undertaking. Much useful data are made available in relatively few pages. The monograph should prove a useful addition to the reference library of the personnel psychologist, vocational counselor, and employment manager.

[B175]

★GOBETZ, WALLACE. **A Quantification, Standardization, and Validation of the Bender-Gestalt Test on the Normal and Neurotic Adults.** American Psychological Association, Psychological Monographs: General and Applied, Vol. 67, No. 6, Whole No. 356. Washington, D.C.: the Association, Inc., 1953. Pp. 28. Paper. $1.00. * (*PA* 28 :4354)

[B176]

★GOLDWAG, ELLIOTT M. **A Survey on the Use of Psychological Tests in Selecting Salesmen.** New York: National Sales Executives, Inc., 1956. Pp. 64. Paper. $5.00. *

Personnel Psychol 10:126–7 sp '57. S. Rains Wallace. The author states two main objectives of the study reported in this monograph. (1) To ascertain whether there are significant differences between companies using psychological tests for selecting salesmen and those that do not use tests. (2) To determine some of the differences in the application of tests by companies now using them. It is also stated that "....this report provides basic data which might be useful in weighing the merits of such tests." The main objectives are fairly well achieved. The additional statement is not justified since no real evidence is presented either in terms of the classical type of validation studies or controlled studies of the effect of testing programs on turnover or performance level. In short, the study tells the sales executive what the other guys are doing. The question of whether he should remain in the parade, or join it, or do something different finds no answer here. The study is based on the questionnaire returns of 890 companies out of 24,541 members of the National Sales Executives. * The questionnaire seems adequate except that the definition of "psychological test" sounds somewhat over the heads of lay respondents. The dangers in combining data on different kinds of industries, products, and salesmen are not discussed. There are some findings of academic interest and some that stimulate conjecture. To choose a few— the median length of testing time for those firms which use tests is 3 hours. The 36.9% of the firms currently using tests differ from the others in that they are older, have larger sales forces, more often use newspapers and employment agencies as recruiting sources, have a lower selection ratio, are more likely to have an over-all turnover rate (ratio of number terminated in a calendar year to total sales force) of less than 20% but less likely to have a turnover of 0. The users employ a wide variety of tests but intelligence, interest, and personality tests predominate. Sales executives rank sales volume, sales volume against quota, number of calls made, and personality in that order, as the most important criteria for evaluating the success of salesmen(?). More than half of the users reported better than 70% rate of success with men hired through testing (whatever this means). Twenty-five of them stated that their tests proved 100% accurate! Unfortunately, the author could not content himself with reporting his results and interpreting them. He gives the reader his advice and expert opinion often irrelevant to his data and certainly open to dispute. We are told that, "The fact that periodic opportunities are afforded a salesman to discuss his problems....contributes greatly toward reduced turnover and helps to develop successful, productive salesmen." "The value of a psychological testing lies not only in its use as a selective device, but also, if properly implemented, as an effective means of guiding future development...." "Enormous sums of money may be saved by companies observing the necessary procedures in the scientific selection of men." If the author has real evidence for these statements he should write a different book.

[B177]

★GRANT, MARGUERITE Q.; IVES, VIRGINIA; AND RANZONI, JANE H. **Reliability and Validity of Judge's Ratings of Adjustment on the Rorschach.** American Psychological Association, Psychological Monographs: General and Applied, Vol. 66, No. 2, Whole No. 334. Washington, D.C.: the Association, Inc., 1952. Pp. ii, 20. Paper. $1.00. * (*PA* 27 :2724)

[B178]

★GRASSI, JOSEPH R. **The Grassi Block Substitution Test for Measuring Organic Brain Pathology.** Springfield, Ill.: Charles C Thomas, Publisher,

1953. Pp. ix, 75. $3.00. (Oxford, England: Blackwell Scientific Publications, Ltd. 21s. 6d.) * (PA 28:105) For reviews, see 60.

[B179]

*GREENE, EDWARD B. **Measurements of Human Behavior, Revised Edition.** New York: Odyssey Press, 1952. Pp. xxxi, 790. $4.75. * (PA 27:6847)

J Consult Psychol 16:413 O '52. Laurance F. Shaffer. Like its earlier edition of 1941, this revision consists mainly of a compilation of descriptions of tests, most of them extracted uncritically from test manuals. It is up to date only in mentioning many recently published tests. The data about the older tests tend to be unchanged from the first edition, even when relevant critical studies exist which should be cited. Two new chapters, on military tests and on personality theory, add little to the usefulness of the book.

J Genetic Psychol 82:319–21 Je '53. Robert M. Allen. This book....has found general acceptance either as the main or supplementary text for courses in Tests and Measurements. This reviewer has considered Greene's volume as a less expensive substitute for Buros' *Mental Measurements Yearbook.* The 1952 revision is a more complete presentation of the techniques for measuring all aspects of human behavior. * The content changes are many. * This volume is surpassed only by the *Yearbook* as a catalogue and source of vital information on various paper and pencil, performance, and individual psychological tests. This alone would justify its inclusion in the applied psychologist's and educational tester's book shelf. * The presentation of the statistical concepts is quite palatable to students in view of the emphasis on the applications * This portion could have been strengthened if the author had differentiated the rôles of descriptive and sampling statistics as related to the problems of test construction. The chapter on Factor Analyses is too simplified and might leave the naïve reader with the impression that factor analysis is a pure statistical process. It is this reviewer's opinion that students should be made aware of the compulsion of factor analysts to divide an orange into its component parts—orange peel, orange pulp, and orange juice—three constituents which separately could not possibly be mistaken for the whole, colored, edible citrus fruit. The third part of this book, Dynamic Patterns, is most valuable since it represents the most significant improvement over the original edition.

It is a cursory survey of personality theories and related methods of appraisal. This attempt to cover a wide field of study falls far short of what the student might be expected to learn in this area. In the 22 pages of Chapter XV, Personality: Dynamic Theory and Structure, there are discussions of physical growth, learning, physical bases for personality appraisal, psychoanalytical theory, and several other topics. If the purpose is to create curiosity, whet the appetite, and stimulate further study, it is adequately accomplished for the serious student. On the other hand, it may give a smattering of ignorance to the student who is willing to less than half-learn, especially Freudian psychology. The rôle of the projective method enjoys a much wider and intensive treatment in this revision. * While the theoretical rationale is kept to a minimum, there is a surprising amount of material on each of these instruments of personality appraisal (supported by a wide sampling of research reports) which imparts excellent ideas regarding the areas of application for these tests. At best, the coverage is survey in nature; it could not be otherwise in a book such as this one. * The revision suffers somewhat from the omission of the earlier section on the persistent problems of the measurement of human behavior. Some of this material is more appropriately placed in other portions, but the student should be sensitized to the problems of practice effect, scaling of units of measurement, and the issues related to the appraisal of physical and psychological growth of the organism. * An overall view of the revised edition reveals a decided improvement of this popular and standard textbook. It is recommended for continued use in undergraduate courses in Tests and Measurements.

Personnel Psychol 6:388–91 au '53. Roger T. Lennon. * In content, scope, organization, and size the revised edition is substantially similar to the original. The major changes consist of a greatly expanded coverage of personality measures in the new volume, and the omission of the section on "Persistent Problems" (scaling, measurement of growth, etc.) which appeared in the first edition. * The six chapters on particular classes of tests are essentially descriptive, though there are frequent references to the need for additional research either in connection with an entire category of tests, or a specific test. Greene cites liberally from research findings for various tests, but more often by way of illustrating some practical application or use of the test than for the bearing such findings may have on evaluation of the test. The classification of tests in some instances seems at variance with conventional use: e.g., clerical aptitude and professional aptitude tests are treated as educational achievement measures rather than as special aptitude or group tests of ability, and tests of literary information and style are treated under "Stories and Fantasies" in the section on personality measurement. Some minor peculiarities of organization of materials in this Part may be noted : the prediction of academic achievement, for example, is discussed both in the chapter on measures of achievement and in the one on group tests of ability. Part Two is a 66-page treatment of elementary statistics. * The treatment is extremely condensed and, perhaps as a consequence, difficult, if not actually misleading, in spots. One may ask, for example, whether it is possible to discuss meaningfully tests of significance, or sampling errors, without introducing the concept of a random sample ; this is illustrative of the types of problems to which the abbreviated treatment gives rise. * The extensive treatment of projective methods is a chief point of difference between this revised edition and the earlier book. As in Part One, these chapters tend to be descriptive rather than critical and there is, it seemed to the reviewer, insufficient alerting of the reader to the very large gaps in our knowledge about the validity of measures in this area. The chapters on interests and attitudes are longer and more comprehensive than the other chapters in this part, and evince a more critical point of view than does the treatment of other types of instruments. One must admire Greene's effort to produce a comprehensive work on psychological measurement, and recognize the wealth of information that he has brought together in this volume. It is hard, however, to escape the conclusion that this comprehensiveness has been bought at the price of adequacy of coverage of many issues and that the very mass of detail may hinder rather than aid the beginning student in the education of principles and development of understanding. Reviewers of the original edition expressed a fear that that volume attempted to cover too much ground, but Greene has elected to make no change in this respect in the new edition. As a general survey of the contributions that psychological measurement can make in a variety of fields, of the types of tests available, and of many specific titles in the various categories, this volume deserves careful consideration. Where the objective is rather the development of understanding of basic issues in measurement and of an ability to evaluate critically various types of instruments for measuring human attributes, it seems to the reviewer that other volumes, such as Cronbach's *Essentials of Psychological Testing,* might be more suitable. A list of publishers of tests, a classified list of tests and inventories, and a helpful bibliography of almost 600 references (of which about a third have appeared since 1941) add to the usefulness of the book. The glossary of measurement terms, which many found useful in the earlier edition, does not appear in the new volume. There is a profusion of illustrations, though in some instances (*e.g.* pages 177, 184, 377) it is noted that the illustrations are of editions of tests which have since been superseded. Study guide questions, which are given at the end of each chapter, in general call merely for information specifically given in the chapter.

Psychol B 51:193–4 Mr '54. Evelyn Raskin. Readers familiar with the first edition....will be disappointed, however, in their expectations of a more tightly integrated book with a clearer and more precise exposition of basic principles and concepts of psychological measurement. The fault may lie in the nature of the task the author set for himself. What was difficult in 1941 has become virtually impossible a decade later. Measurement and evaluation devices have proliferated rapidly in all areas of psychology and the development of their systematic rationale has not kept pace with empirical applications. Any book which attempts to encompass practically all the techniques (and little of the underlying theory) which have been or are employed in quantifying and assessing human behavior must suffer from some superficiality and lack of coherence. And the range covered in this one is formidable : from psychophysical methods to the Szondi test, from Thurstone's attitude scaling to OSS evaluation procedures and Kinsey's interviewing methods. Unfortunately, the book is also exasperatingly crammed with minutiae, often irrelevant. Even the subjects who posed for the photographs of test administrations are graciously identified by name. The introductory chapters provide only a weak foundation for supporting this mass of material. * it is regrettable that the chapters in the earlier edition on "persistent problems" were deleted * The chapters on attitude-, interest-, and personality-measurement have been greatly expanded. They are preceded by a distressing introduction to dynamic theory and structure of personality. The need for such a chapter is clear since many projective tests are discussed. But the oversimplified and, in places, muddled account points up the unrealistic design of the book. * Some errors of fact and naiveté are understandable in a survey text of this scope. Still, inaccuracies like the following are too frequent: "the word trait....is used to refer to any physical aspect of a person....or to any mental aspect such as speed of reading...."; "the sum of the verbal test scores [on the W-B] yields a verbal MA...."; "this [the standard deviation] provides a method of scaling scores ....comparable with the best physical scales...."; "the K score [on the MMPI] is the number of answers omitted because the client cannot say or will not choose." The breadth of content combined with the unsystematic approach limits the audience for the book. It can probably best serve as a reference text for advanced students who wish to become acquainted with a wider variety of tests than the standard laboratory and practicum courses are able to cover. The profusion of visual illustrations, the research bibliographies, and the fairly complete classified lists of available tests and inventories should be particularly helpful for this purpose.

For reviews of the first edition, see 3:912.

[B180]

*GREENE, HARRY A., AND CRAWFORD, JOHN R. **Workbook in Educational Measurements and Evaluation.** New York: Longmans, Green & Co., Inc., 1954. Pp. 141. Paper. $2.00. * (PA 29:3041)

[B181]

*GREENE, HARRY A.; JORGENSEN, ALBERT N.; AND GERBERICH, J. RAYMOND. **Measurement and Evaluation in the Elementary School, Second Edition.** New York: Longmans, Green & Co., Inc., 1953. Pp. xxi, 617. $5.25. (London: Longmans, Green & Co., Ltd., 1954. 35s.) * (PA 28:3291)

Ed & Psychol Meas 17:444–6 au '57. Jack C. Merwin. * This book covers the same material as the 1942 edition but in a somewhat reorganized and basically rewritten presentation. The over-all general organization remains the same. * This is a book which emphasizes *what* to do and *how* to do it in contrast with *why* do it. This is best illustrated by the presentation

of helpful step by step procedures for manipulating data. The authors see the purpose of this book as twofold: "(1) to interest the student of education in the possibilities of measurement and evaluation in education, and (2) to stimulate the teacher and supervisor to more effective use of tests and other evaluative devices as integral parts of enlightened teaching practice." They may succeed in interesting and stimulating teachers and students but, in addition, may very well cause a good deal of consternation for these people as they attempt to use the techniques described in situations not specifically described in the book. The basic weaknesses of this book are its lack of "why do" and lack of clarity and consistency of terminology. The students meeting situations not specifically covered in this book, taking further courses in this area, or reading other books and research reports that use the same terminology are apt to find confusion. * The students will find many authors using some of the terms in the glossary when the meaning is clearly not the glossary definition. * Instructors who found the 1942 edition to their liking will welcome this latest edition. This reviewer, however, would like to call to the attention of any instructor using the book the desirability of (1) tying up the terminology in this book with that generally found in other writings in this area, and (2) pointing out qualifications and limitations of many of the generalities made and implied in this book.

J Ed (London) 86:348–9 Jl '54. Cyril Burt. * The new edition has been thoroughly revised; and much fresh material has been incorporated, especially in the chapters on performance tests and methods of studying personality. In spite of the vogue which picture tests, ink-blot tests, and so-called "lie-detectors" of every sort have recently enjoyed, the authors rightly insist that all such methods of testing personality are at best still in the experimental stage, and that the teacher will be well advised to rely chiefly on first-hand observation of actual behaviour, and for the rest seek trustworthy reports from the best-informed sources that are open to him. The writers have kept almost exclusively in view the special conditions obtaining in the United States, and, even in their historical chapters, make little or no use of work done in this country. Indeed, the few references to British writers seem to be more often erroneous than correct. Thus the distinction between general ability and special aptitudes is attributed to Spearman, whereas in point of fact, as he expressly states, he himself borrowed it from Francis Galton. On the other hand, the practical chapters, which form after all the major and more important part of the book, are excellent. The suggestions for diagnosing the causes of backwardness in particular school subjects and for adapting coaching and corrective treatment to the individual case should prove most helpful to the teacher in the classroom. *

Personnel & Guid J 33:236–8 D '54. Harold F. Cottingham. * Outstanding among the desirable features of the book are its generally sound organization throughout, objective and clear style of writing, practical approach through examples, and proven choice of topics in terms of needs of elementary teachers. Such devices as facsimile illustrations, schematic diagrams for presenting concepts, and wise use of topic headings add to the readability of the book. Especially valuable is a glossary which, though not exhaustive, may render a real service to the reader. * It is in the over-all approach to evaluation, supported by methodology for appraising attainment of outcomes that the book fails to measure up to its title and purpose, "....to introduce the student....to the newest and best evaluative techniques that have thus far appeared" * although chapter nine examines the meaning and tools of evaluation, no set of general principles or guiding procedures are set forth. The reader, seeking a commentary on how to establish outcomes for non-academic performance and ways of measuring accomplishment toward such ends, is given only a brief discussion on this vital problem. * Even the space devoted to pupil profile charts, progress charts, cumulative records, report cards, and class analysis charts is short and fails to stress the need for the integration of these with other evaluation tools to give an over-all basis for the study of pupil growth toward objectives. A particularly glaring weakness is the absence of recent bibliographical or footnote references to the journals and other literature treating evaluation. In several of the chapters devoted to the use of tests, particularly in the field of personality, attitude and interest measurement, the authors suggest tools for use without justifying their choices. For example, the Kuder Preference Record and the Lee-Thorpe test (if applicable to the elementary level) are omitted

while the Strong Vocational Interest Blank is mentioned. One might question why the Strong is listed when admittedly it is not recommended for use in elementary schools. * one is surprised to find no mention of such other pupil-contributed evaluation media as the Blacky pictures, finger painting, work samples, or the autobiography as well as other similar subjective evidences of behavior. Recent developments in projective techniques are hardly touched upon (three paragraphs) while such topics as "the nature of personality" (p. 279) are covered in a few pages with five footnotes out of nine dated prior to 1937. In conclusion, this volume appears to have considerable value as a guide book in measurement particularly with reference to subject-matter areas in the elementary school. Its chief limitation seems to be a woefully inadequate treatment of the theory and practice of evaluation.

For reviews of the first edition, see 3:914.

[B182]

Greene, Harry A.; Jorgensen, Albert N.; and Gerberich, J. Raymond. **Measurement and Evaluation in the Secondary School, Second Edition.** New York: Longmans, Green & Co., Inc., 1954. Pp. xxii, 690. $5.00. (London: Longmans, Green & Co., Ltd., 1955. 35s.) * (PA 28:8078)

Personnel & Guid J 34:124–5 O '55. Walter M. Lifton. * The authors have certainly achieved their objective of constructing a book for laymen which will be understandable and comprehensive. Each chapter is complete in itself and well-outlined at the beginning to help the student prepare for the material to be covered. The very inclusiveness of each chapter tends to make for some repetitious use of catch phrases. * In the light of their emphasis on the problems of the measurement of intelligence it is indeed rather odd, however, that no reference is made to the Wechsler Intelligence Scale for children. For many institutions this instrument, especially at the secondary school level, has replaced the Stanford Binet. The major criticism of this text, for this reviewer, lies in the authors' apparent naiveness in relating the use of tests to the guidance process. They make statements like these, page 109, "Furthermore, it is charged that little or no attempt is made to direct children away from fields in which they apparently have little aptitude," and on page 233, "The interview deserves only brief attention here, for the teacher is not directly concerned with it in its formal sense. The interview may, however, be informal and it may deal only with the areas of the child's interests, needs, and background about which the teacher needs information." Intentionally or not, the writers have succeeded in conveying the idea that tests are primarily for the use of the teacher to evaluate, direct or organize a child's goals and school activities. The role tests can play in the counseling process and their possible effect upon a client's self concept, is barely mentioned. It is hoped that readers seeking help in the area of measurement and evaluation in the secondary school will make use of this text. Let us also hope, however, that our teachers in the high school will show equal concern over the way they can learn to help students measure and evaluate themselves.

For a review of the first edition, see 3:915.

[B183]

★GREER, EDITH S., AND ROTTER, GEORGE E. **Learning to Know Your Pupils.** Lincoln, Neb.: University Publishing Co., 1951. Pp. 96. Paper. $0.80. *

[B184]

★GRIFFITHS, RUTH. **The Abilities of Babies: A Study in Mental Measurement.** London: University of London Press Ltd., 1954. Pp. x, 229. 20s. * (New York: McGraw-Hill Book Co., Inc. $6.50.) (*PA 29:76*)

Brit J Ed Psychol 25:63 F '55. C. W. Valentine. * Gesell classified his items and tests into four groups—Motor, Language, Adaptive and Personal-Social. Dr. Griffiths, dissatisfied especially with Gesell's placing of some items under "Adaptive behaviour," has grouped her items under five categories, viz.: Locomotion, Personal-Social, Hearing and Speed, Hand and Eye, Performance. * A great amount of work has gone to the preparation of these scales and Dr. Griffiths must be commended for her patient industry. She rightly stresses the advantage of having the same tester for all ages and all lists. I welcome warmly also Dr. Griffiths's recognition that at these early ages no single testing can be relied on: indeed, in view of the great variability of mood and momentary interest of a child of under two or three, three or four sessions would be the minimum even after the child has become quite accustomed to the tester. Dr. Griffiths's assignment of a given item to a specific month is hazardous as the average number of babies of a given month was only twenty-five; and indeed for one month there were only sixteen, and Dr. Grif-

fiths states that some of the children included in the results for the second year were already included in the first year, though there was no retesting in less than six months. The various socio-economic levels also might not have been fairly represented for each month. The chapters on standardisation and frequency curves show similar results to averages and scatters gained with recognised Intelligence Tests at later ages; but as to "validity" Dr. Griffiths only offers some results gained by retesting a group of infants with her own series. Her scales, however, do provide a valuable basis for follow-up studies; and it is to be hoped that she will be able to retest a substantial number of her infants with recognised standard tests at say 5 and 10 years. Such a research might lead to the selection of certain of her present many items in each scale, as being of much greater prognostic value than others, and the elimination of many as of little use. Special mention should be made of the value of the arrangement of the scales for children with various forms of handicaps, e.g., for deaf, blind or spastic babies.

Brit J Psychol 45:236–7 Ag '54. Margaret Martin. * the scale consists of five subscales lettered *A* to *E* and all very nearly equal in difficulty. Each subscale covers one vital aspect of infant development namely: *A,* locomotor development; *B,* personal-social adjustment; *C,* hearing and speech; *D,* eye and hand co-ordination; and *E,* performance. From a summation of the scores from these five subscales Dr Griffiths gives a means of obtaining a G.Q.— General Intelligence Quotient. Apart from this G.Q. it is also possible to calculate QA, QB, QC, QD and QE, each representing respectively a quotient indicative of the child's ability in each of the five subscales. Since these five scales are very nearly equal in difficulty it is possible to show the total mental level attained by a subject at the time of testing. This has been done by the profile method, which from the diagnostic point of view should prove most valuable in that it depicts general or specific disabilities or the presence of exceptional ability in one or more of the basic developmental processes. The inclusion in the book of developmental profiles of particular cases, and of excellent photographs of the responses of babies to different situations, adds to the clarity of the exposition. There is an excellent bibliography. Methods of scoring the tests and assessing results are assembled with admirable economy and clarity in Appendix I. *The Abilities of Babies* will be of interest and of value to all concerned with the health and well-being of children, and particularly to the psychiatrist and the psychologist working in the field of child psychology. It offers a new approach to assessment and to diagnosis. It suggests many new avenues for further research. This scholarly work commands respect for its clear exposition of each step in procedure, its integrity of observation and report, and its wealth of detail which illumines the text without tedium. Young research workers will find research procedures fully mapped out. Dr Griffiths intends to "continue the work on the new scale beyond the second year and this will then make differential diagnosis as outlined in this book available for testing children over two years of age." We look forward to the completion of this further research. Such a scale carried to years five or seven would prove invaluable, particularly in the field of the handicapped child.

Mental Health 14:37 au '54. V. Franks. * Griffiths' work is probably one of the most comprehensive efforts to date in the field of infant testing. * the scale she has devised contributes an original approach to the problem in that it enables the tester to secure a profile of the baby's abilities in 5 different areas * Her testing scale is....carefully constructed and her chapter on "Approach to the Infant in the Testing Situation" contains much valuable information for the psychologist interested in obtaining an accurate assessment. She makes an attempt to investigate the validity of her test by retesting the babies. However as the distance in time between the test and the retest varied from 7 weeks to 70 weeks with an average interval of 30 weeks, it is obvious, that though her results showed consistency it cannot be truly assumed that the test will give a true prediction of the child's future abilities. If the test is used by a skilful examiner it can yield useful information about the baby's present level of functioning, but it should not be used by an inexperienced person or by an anxious parent as a device to determine whether or not a child will grow up to be grammar school material or perhaps mentally deficient. What these scales measure may be quite different from intelligence scales used later on with an older child. Even the so-called "speech scale" here may be measuring a different quality if intelligence is

ultimately defined as an abstract reasoning ability. Thus the fact that a child may be able to identify objects at an early age may rest more on a memory feat and it is possible that this same child may later have difficulty in grasping abstract concepts. It is too early to assess the ultimate contribution of this book. It is certainly a valuable addition to the psychologists' addendum but, judging from Dr. Griffiths' own comments, she would be the last person to recommend her scale as a mechanical device for predicting a baby's future abilities.

Q R Biol 30:198–9 Je '55. J. H. Conn. * a new, carefully standardized series of intelligence tests for infants. The author deserves praise for a very difficult piece of research which has been brought to a successful conclusion. The book is to be highly recommended.

[B185]

*GUILFORD, J. P. Psychometric Methods, Second Edition. New York: McGraw-Hill Book Co., Inc., 1954. Pp. ix, 597. $8.50. (London: McGraw-Hill Publishing Co., Ltd. 61s.) * (PA 29:102)

Brit J Psychol 46:145–6 My '55. Roland Harper. * A lengthy chapter (11) is devoted to the Rating Scale as a psychological instrument. Whereas this forms an excellent summary of available facts, little seems to be added to what was already known and compiled. A most important chapter (12) is devoted to Principles of Judgement. In this Guilford summarizes the main factors influencing human judgement, and in doing so collects together for the first time the results of many recent psychophysical studies. Some of these were first published as late as 1952. From the point of view of the interested specialist this chapter will be one of the high-lights of the present volume. * The last chapter presents an admirable exposition of the theory and practice of Factor Analysis with emphasis on the American point of view. It is no mean accomplishment to have stated so much with clarity in so short a space. One may not agree with current American practice in Factor Analysis, but since it represents one important thread in contemporary psychology it is desirable for a concise yet effective statement of the procedures in use to be available. This chapter provides such a review, including worked examples. The typography and layout of this volume are excellent, and remarkably few errors have been detected. * The student who wishes to obtain guidance on how to carry out one of the many specific techniques dealt with in this volume may consult it to his advantage. However, the more sophisticated reader will often retain mental reservations concerning the assumptions which have to be made in order to proceed with the more elaborate techniques. In a volume this size more space might profitably have been devoted to the qualitative implications of the assumptions which particular techniques force upon the investigator, and of the precise meaning of their end-products. It is quite clear from short interpolated paragraphs that Prof. Guilford is well aware of the necessity of stating clearly what assumptions can legitimately be made. However, he repeatedly throws upon the reader the responsibility for a decision on this point in applying the techniques outlined to practical problems. The beginner, for whom the mathematical introduction is intended, will not be in a position to decide such questions for himself. Furthermore, the sections on psychological scaling, on the psychometrics of mental testing and on Factor Analysis seem to be more advanced than the non-mathematical reader can approach in an intelligent and critical manner. Readers in the United Kingdom may regret the scanty reference to relevant work originating in this country. However, much of this work could not have been taken into account without reducing the reference to American work which is perhaps less accessible to many readers. It might well be argued that we have here not one but the makings of more than one volume. Although one might just agree on the relevance of Factor Analysis to the main theme the three chapters on psychometric problems of test development seem to belong to a different "dimension" from the rest of the book. Individual sections will be of value to the general reader, and will certainly stimulate the expert in the field concerned. *Psychometric Methods* is probably best regarded as a reference book which should be included on the shelves of the psychological section of all libraries. Indeed the present reviewer had sufficient confidence in the importance of what Prof. Guilford writes to recommend that this new edition be purchased without having first scrutinized it in detail. This action has been fully justified by the book itself, even if one does not share all opinions expressed or the assumptions made.

Ed & Psychol Meas 15:87–92 sp '55. Allen L. Edwards. * The new edition will serve as both a text and a reference book for the serious student of quantitative methods. * In addition to being written at a higher level of mathematical sophistication, the new edition is longer than the old. * drastic changes have been made in both content and organization * The chapter [on factor analysis] in the new edition is much longer. The treatment of rotations is much more complete. In the old edition Guilford was doubtful, or at least undecided, about the desirability of oblique axes in factor analytic methods. In the present edition, the emphasis and detail given to oblique solutions indicates that he believes the "more extensive experience with factor methods" required for resolving his doubts is now at hand. * It is good to find C. I. Bliss's table for the transformation of percentages reprinted. * On the value of indicating paired comparisons by "pair comparison," I have doubts that only time and the adoption of Guilford's usage will be able to dispel. Again, I would prefer the term "successive intervals" —as originally introduced by Thurstone—to Guilford's use of "successive categories" for this scaling method. The method of successive categories does not imply the necessary ordering and continuity that the method of successive intervals does. And successive intervals, like paired comparisons, is a concept that has already been given widespread usage in current psychological literature. * answers to all problems are provided * Throughout the book checks on computations are stressed. This is also a valuable aid to the student. Very good and concise summaries of general principles on a given topic appear frequently. * Guilford's scholarly approach to his subject matter is reflected in the reference lists to be found at the end of each chapter. The literature published in the interim between the old and new editions has been covered thoroughly and has influenced the treatment of topics in the new edition. In a very real sense, the second edition of *Psychometric Methods* is not a second edition at all. There is not too much in common between the two editions other than the quantitative spirit that influenced the writing of both. It is perhaps more accurate to describe the second edition as a new and modern book dealing with psychometric methods—and a very good one it is, indeed. That it may be regarded as a new book is a tribute to Guilford, Thurstone, Helson, and others, too numerous to mention, who have contributed so much to the development and use of quantitative methods in psychology during the past 20 years.

Psychometrika 20:163–5 Je '55. Bert F. Green. * the new edition includes some major changes * The book begins with a lucid account of the logical basis of psychological measurement, and a discussion of nominal, ordinal, interval, and ratio scales. * It is not possible to encompass all of present-day psychometrics in a single volume. However, Guilford has managed to include most of the popular techniques, and has provided extensive references for those who want supplementary information. In the areas of psychophysics and scaling, where references are scattered and reviews are few, Guilford's treatment is more thorough than in the areas of testing and factor analysis, where other good summaries are available. There was obviously not space enough to include all of the new techniques and ideas. The up-and-down method, probit analysis, and Coombs' general approach to scaling all deserve more extended treatment than they receive. In general, though, Guilford's coverage is excellent. Guilford's treatment of the method of successive categories is the weakest section in the book. In contrast to the usual clarity of exposition, this section is fuzzy and very difficult to follow. (There are some printing errors to add to the confusion). Some of the details are right, others are wrong, or at least dubious. His method for estimating category boundaries—or limens—is standard, but then he suggests locating the stimuli by finding the interpolated medians of the judgment distributions on this scale of limens. According to him, means are harder to find, and in either case, trouble arises when judgment distributions are truncated, i.e., when many judgments are in an extreme category. Actually, when appropriate procedures are used, the stimulus means are easy to determine, and the method is indifferent to truncation. The basic difficulty with the presentation is that the successive categories model is never stated explicitly. In fact, Guilford seems to reject the model when he argues that the categories themselves should somehow be scaled rather than the boundaries between categories. His procedure for scaling the categories makes no sense to this reviewer. Since the method of successive categories has great utility, this section of the book is especially disappointing. Guilford's exposition is usually very clear, and his style is straightforward. The clarity is

slightly compromised by the fact that Σ never appears with an index of summation or limits. This is sometimes confusing, although seldom ambiguous. The text includes many examples that help the reader to follow the development. However, it would have been better strategy to draw more psychophysical examples from sensory psychology. Emphasis on problems like discrimination, masking, and target detection in vision and audition, rather than on lifted weights might interest students who now find psychophysics dull. In a book of this sort, it is sometimes necessary to introduce formulas magically, either because there is not space to derive the formulas, or because the development would be beyond the mathematical abilities of most students. In *Psychometric Methods* magic is used quite frequently. There are several places where a few words of explanation would reveal the trick and allow the student to understand the development or at least to get an intuitive grasp of the idea. * The book has its share of errors. Most of these are in the numerical examples, the table headings, and in the formulas. * The appendix contains a fine collection of useful tables. Table *C,* which gives normal deviates and ordinates for various values of the area, is especially valuable and can be found almost nowhere else. The major changes in *Psychometric Methods* are in scope and organization. The reader's evaluation of the second edition can be predicted accurately from his estimate of its predecessor.

For reviews of the first edition, see 36:B124.

[B186]

★GUILFORD, J. P.; CHRISTENSEN, PAUL R.; BOND, NICHOLAS A., JR.; AND SUTTON, MARCELLA A. **A Factor Analysis Study of Human Interests.** American Psychological Association, Psychological Monographs: General and Applied, Vol. 68, No. 4, Whole No. 375. Washington, D.C.: the Association, Inc., 1954. Pp. 38. Paper. $1.50. *

[B187]

★GUILFORD, J. P., AND ZIMMERMAN, WAYNE S. **Fourteen Dimensions of Temperament.** American Psychological Association, Psychological Monographs: General and Applied, Vol. 70, No. 10, Whole No. 417. Washington, D.C.: the Association, Inc., 1956. Pp. 26. Paper. $1.00. * (*PA* 31 :5789)

[B188]

GULLIKSEN, HAROLD. **Theory of Mental Tests.** New York: John Wiley & Sons, Inc., 1950. Pp. xix, 486. $7.50. * (London: Chapman & Hall, Ltd., 1951. 48*s.*) (*PA* 25 :4998)

J Ed Psychol 43:181–5 Mr '52. John B. Carroll. * Gulliksen's book admirably answers the need for a basic text in the theory of mental tests; in fact, it bids fair to become the standard work in the field for a number of years to come. Not only does it present in an ingeniously organized form the fundamental theorems on reliability, validity and errors of measurement developed many years ago by Spearman and Kelley, but it also reviews in a balanced way the work of the last ten or twenty years, and presents in detail a number of the most recently developed methods. As if these virtues were not enough, the book is designed as a good textbook. In general, the textual matter and the mathematical development reach high standards of clarity. * The instructor will be grateful for appendices which give sample examination questions in test theory and statistics. Finally, the book includes an excellent bibliography. * all the usual equations for the reliability of tests, the standard error of measurement, the reliability of lengthened tests, and the relations between the observed, true and error variances [are derived]. This material could have been presented much more compactly; most of the equations could have been derived first in their most general forms, with easy transitions to the various special cases. Gulliksen prefers, however, to present the simpler cases and then to generalize a procedure which will probably ease the work of the student. Chapters 2 and 3 present an interesting contrast—in the former, the fundamental equations are derived along the lines of a conceptual model in which it is assumed we know true scores and error scores, while in the latter, the same equations are derived as limits of expressions for K parallel tests as K approaches infinity. Chapter 4 has the merit of clearly distinguishing between four ways of expressing test error; after reading this chapter, nobody will have any excuse to use the standard error of measurement in a situation where he ought to be using the standard error of substitution. * Chapters 6 to 8 should give pause to those who still speculate on the "validity" of the Spearman-Brown equations. * Chapter 10 presents the extremely interesting work of Mollenkopf on the relation of the skewness and kurtosis of the score distribution to the magnitude of the standard error of measurement, and Chapter 13 gives the most complete account of the effects of multivariate selection now available. Incidentally, this reviewer would urge caution in applying Mollenkopf's formulation to tests where there is a large guessing component, since such a test might not very well fulfill some of the assumptions made in his derivation, in particular that specified by equation (52). Further investigation of the generality of Mollenkopf's derivations is needed. Test theorists should be grateful to Gulliksen for suggesting to his colleague Wilks the problem of discovering a statistical criterion for parallel tests. This is one of a great many special statistical problems which arise in test theory, and which in many cases are unique to that field. He presents a clearly written treatment of Wilks' results, as well as those obtained by Votaw for the problem of "compound symmetry," the problem of whether tests are parallel with respect to their correlations with a criterion. It occurs to this reviewer to speculate whether the methods are applicable to testing the equivalence of items as well as tests, for in the case of equivalent items the means are functionally related to the variances—a condition not specified in Wilks' development. Chapter 15....presents a good discussion of the advantages and disadvantages of the conventional methods of determining reliability (test-retest, alternate forms, split-half, etc.). In addition, it discusses a highly promising technique of constructing random subtests by matching items on difficulty and validity, and gives a neat formulation of the problem of reader reliability. Chapter 16, "Reliability Estimated from Item Homogeneity," is disappointingly short; in essence it presents the rationale for Kuder-Richardson formulas 20 and 21. * Many will disagree....with Gulliksen's definition of a pure "speed test" as one "composed of items so easy that the subjects never give the wrong answer to any of them." This definition makes the speededness of a test dependent upon the sample being tested; furthermore, it ignores the possible factorial composition of tests in terms of speed and level components. Gulliksen fails to mention the almost classical problems of the correlation of speed and level, though perhaps this is a psychological rather than a statistical problem. Test constructors will find a number of interesting suggestions in Chapter 18, which concerns "Methods of Scoring Tests," but it is evident that numerous problems still remain in this area. Chapter 19 takes up "Methods of Standardizing and Equating Scores"; much of this material is an elaboration of what can be found in any good text in educational statistics, but the presentation of some of Thurstone's scaling methods and a method for equating forms of a test given to different groups makes the chapter valuable. Chapter 20 is a thorough but difficult essay on problems of weighting scores in a composite, with some reference to the problem of differential prediction. Of particular technical interest is the proof that the crucial characteristics of a set of weights, insofar as its effect on the correlation of composites is concerned, is the ratio of its standard deviation to its mean. * Perhaps because of the undisciplined growth of the field, Gulliksen apparently found it hard to decide what was to be covered in the book. The treatment is uneven in difficulty level: some of the material is almost laboriously elementary, while other parts will challenge even the best-prepared student. * On the other hand, a number of topics are passed over as "beyond the scope of an elementary treatment": for example, analysis of variance methods of assessing sources of unreliability in a test (p. 221), scoring methods for determining "level reached," and certain absolute scaling methods (p. 245). The book is not a comprehensive review of all the significant work that has been done in test theory; many important items in the bibliography are not even alluded to in the text. To have provided full discussion of these would have lengthened the manuscript considerably, of course. Nevertheless some space might have been saved for fuller discussion of recent advances by condensing some of the earlier chapters. Perhaps the most disappointing feature of this book, despite its over-all excellence, is that little attention is paid to relations between conventional test theory and (a) the technique of factor analysis in isolating the trait dimensions measured by tests, and (b) psychophysical theory. Such omissions can hardly be traced to any fault of the author, however, for little work has been done along these lines in any case. The omissions merely serve to point up the fact that test "theory" does not yet have a rigorous theoretical foundation; instead, it is a collection of formulas based on a very small number of assumptions concerning true scores, error scores, and the like. Except in a few instances, problems of statistical inference regarding population parameters have not been worked out. Furthermore, most of the formulations deal with tests whose items are scored "right" or "wrong,"

and few persons have ventured to consider the more general problems raised by other types of test situations, or by tests designed to measure personality traits, interests, or attitudes. It is this reviewer's belief that a rigorous theory of tests can be developed only by considering the characteristics of various types of psychometric scales and the properties of various stimulus-response situations in relation to those scales. It is to be hoped that Gulliksen's work will stimulate new efforts in these directions. *Psychometrika 18:123–30 Je '53. Louis Guttman.* * Our basic criticisms of the book can be summarized in seven major points: (a) The theory of reliability is based on the notion of "parallel" tests. This notion does not lead to a unique definition of the reliability of any given test and hence cannot serve as the basis for a universal theory of reliability. (b) No distinction is made between the algebraic consequences of different concepts of reliability. This creates inconsistencies between and within the concepts and the algebra presented. (c) Retest theory defines the most universal kind of error, and all other theories introduce *additional,* variously specialized, notions of deviation. Hence retest coefficients are upper bounds to all other types of reliability coefficients. The book perpetrates the interpretation that retest coefficients are "spuriously" large, instead of pointing out that this larger size must *theoretically hold* if all hypotheses are satisfied. (d) Only one full-fledged excursion is made into modern statistical theory—in connection with Wilks' statistical test of parallelism of alternate forms. There is an incomplete excursion with respect to analysis of variance in Chapter 5; otherwise, old algebraic formulations are retained, with resulting inconsistencies in formulas. Most of the practical sampling problems of reliability and validity are not mentioned. (e) In general, reliability and validity are discussed in terms of test length. This implies that only a single universe of content is being studied and one which has a certain kind of structure. But most prediction problems in testing involve several universes of content and more complex structures. (f) Whereas an exact multivariate analysis is presented for the parameters of multivariate selection, only bivariate techniques are advocated for item analysis for weighting problems that equally require a multivariate treatment. (g) The basic data of most mental tests are qualitative; yet no treatment is given of the theory of such qualitative data. Instead, an attempt is made to adapt to qualitative items least-squares theory appropriate to quantitative items. [See original review for additional critical comments not excerpted.]

Psychometrika 18:131–3 Je '53. Harold Gulliksen. [A reply to the above review by Louis Guttman.] Dr. Guttman's review of *Theory of Mental Tests* is essentially an attempt to indicate the main avenues along which he would like to see contributions made to test theory. My aim in writing *Theory of Mental Tests* was to summarize the major areas of the literature in the field, to indicate some of the major areas for needed work, and to make some progress toward a unified theory. Guttman's review indicates both that these objectives were fulfilled and that much still remains to be done. * [See original reply for critical comments not excerpted.]

For additional reviews, see 4:B183.

[B189]

Gurvitz, Milton S. **The Dynamics of Psychological Testing: A Formulation and Guide to Independent Clinical Practice.** New York: Grune & Stratton, Inc., 1951. Pp. xvi, 396. $6.75. * (*PA* 26:4007)

Am J Psychiatry 109:319 O '52. Robert I. Watson. In keeping with the aim to present precisely how the psychologist uses tests, this volume is organized in a novel fashion. Most of the book is devoted to the presentation of all 17 cases that the psychologist tested during a single month. They had been referred to the author by the therapists because they were diagnostic problems. The psychological reports he supplied to the therapist were prepared independent of knowledge of the case histories. The introductory statement concerning the psychologic procedures, specifically how the Wechsler-Bellevue, Rorschach, and Draw-A-Person are used and interpreted by this psychologist, is useful only for this purpose. It is too short a presentation to be useful independent of the rest of the book. * The case presentations are done with considerable clinical acumen, although the inevitable disagreements that other psychologists would have with the interpretations offered are also to be found. The interpretations show that the author is an experienced clinical psychologist working in a psychoanalytic tradition. For a description of how one such psychologist works this book

may be recommended. * The most disconcerting implication of this volume to this reviewer is that the psychologist's findings apparently are to be judged almost exclusively by the extent to which they agree with the therapist's already formed, independent interpretations. This method of evaluation is inherent in the organization of the case presentations. Each psychological report is interspersed with statements by the therapist, which he inserted upon reading them. In other words, after each major statement of the psychologist, the therapist would make a short comment. The great majority of these comments consist of nothing more than the two words, "I agree." Hardly ever is there anything in the therapist's comments to show that some new conception, some novel way of viewing the patient has been brought about by the psychologist's efforts. New vitality, different vistas, and added perspectives as results of the psychological report would appear to be a better criterion than the extent of agreement with the therapist. That these cases were seen after they had been under treatment for some time reduced the chance of new and different conceptualizations of dynamics, but the nature of the comments lead to the impression that the psychological reports were rather empty of any meaning that led to action on behalf of the patients.

B Menninger Clinic 17:40 Ja '53. Martin Mayman. The author describes this book as a "public post-mortem" of seventeen diagnostic test reports made during one (presumably atypical) calendar month at Hillside Hospital, a private, psychoanalytically-oriented sanitarium in New York. * Its chief merit lies in its conception rather than its execution of a research method. I agree with the author that it is time for a critical examination of the validity of statements made in a psychological test report, but I believe it should be done more systematically than was done here and should be based on a more intensive, more searching correlation of test and clinical interview material.

Can J Psychol 6:149–50 S '52. Bruce Quarrington. * The book has considerable instructional value for student and practising clinical psychologist. Personal participation of the reader is particularly invited by the full presentation of test data. The breakdown of report material certainly aids the reader in following the author's inferences and in checking these against clinical impressions. One danger in this method of presentation is of reducing to a common level the significance that the various sorts of assertions have for the understanding and treatment of the patient under consideration. A tendency to reduce the whole matter of psychological evaluation to a game emphasizing the number of correct answers may well be encouraged. To some extent, this is encouraged by the reports made by the author which concern themselves in detail with the nature of intellectual functioning and psychodynamics but which include only one point as recommendation. As a presentation of the method and status of clinical testing to-day this book does an excellent job. The achievements and shortcomings of the book are not peculiar to it but characterize the field.

J Ed Psychol 44:185–7 Mr '53. Lee J. Cronbach. * a thorough demonstration of one style of clinical interpretation * It is a mistake for Dr. Joseph Miller, who writes the foreword, to refer to this as research. It is essentially a report of clinical experience and opinion. There is no guarantee that Gurvitz did not select cases where his diagnostic procedures worked well, and so this provides no solid evidence of the validity of the specific procedures. The reports do show that tests can contribute greatly to the understanding of patients. Gurvitz is an able interpreter of behavior. He studies his patient as a person, making as much note of his over-all behavior as of the test responses. He has a wise viewpoint regarding his tests, making excellent critical comments on some of the proposals of Rapaport, Wechsler, and the Rorschach sign systems. The book as a whole shows high level psychological skill in action. Gurvitz makes especially good use of the Wechsler and figure drawing data. Too often, Gurvitz writes statements which, read by themselves, would encourage mechanical and unintelligent use of tests. Once in a while he seems to say that a diagnosis is decided by some single response of the patient. He seems, despite his disclaimers, to use signs himself in diagnosis. For intance, on the subject of W:M in Rorschach, he says (p. 21): "If M predominates, then we have a surfeit of ability and creativeness but insufficient drive to project it out into the world." Gurvitz relies heavily on a Freudian terminology and way of thinking which does not seem to be an integral part of his diagnostic skill. His dogmatic and atomistic statements about particular indicators will blind

some readers to the fact that his actual diagnosis is based on a thorough integration which allows each fact about the patient to add to the significance of each other. The Rorschach interpretation suffers greatly from an incautious attitude. Gurvitz seems to accept almost every idea of Klopfer without reëxamination. The literature contains enough validation research by this time to suggest that many items in this interpretive system are questionable. The statement quoted about W:M ignores questions of unreliability. It does not admit that the relation between personality and action is so complex that not even the most valid statement will be true of all cases. It does not acknowledge that the current literature contains almost as many conflicting theories of the meaning of M as there are writers. It does not warn the reader that a test indicator which goes with some defect in a hospital population will also appear among any normal group tested, with no corresponding defect. Gurvitz probably makes a more flexible use of the Rorschach, and a more cautious use, than his generalizations will suggest to the reader. It is perhaps too much to hope that writers like Gurvitz will follow each suggested interpretation with a statement of the percentage of cases for which the interpretation is valid, out of all those where the indicator appears. Until they do make statements in those terms, they can expect that non-clinicians will continue to regard clinical psychology as dogmatic and unsound. This book can be used profitably with advanced students in clinical diagnosis by two types of instructor. The ones who wish students to be skeptical of over-enthusiastic and fine-drawn interpretations will find here examples worthy of critical attention. These reports are neither illogical nor lacking in insight. The reasoning is careful and the psychology insightful; criticism must therefore focus on the premises underlying the interpretation. The instructors who want to teach students to squeeze test protocols for all they are worth, without too much fretting about lack of validation, should also use this book. If students are to learn this brand of clinical psychology, they should be taught from a model as skilled as Gurvitz. While Gurvitz' writing does not do justice to his acumen, his thinking about tests is in many ways sounder than that of some other clinicians and of those who look to a test for a score and nothing but a score. *

Occupational Psychol 27:175 Jl '53. Stephen Griew. * The detailed testing records may be of interest to clinical psychologists, but the experiment described in the book is not really an experiment at all. The small number of cases involved, and the very questionable evaluation of the results, allow no valid conclusions to be drawn. No attempt is made to establish a valid criterion of successful investigation and diagnosis by way of a legitimate follow-up: the author's agreement with the psychiatrist is regarded as a valid criterion. The cases investigated are not, the author tells us, typical, and the tests employed in individual cases vary, and yet the final conclusion is in terms of "the battery of tests" and "the type of patient encountered." Dr Gurvitz emphasises that testing depends largely upon the approach of the tester, and that test results are meaningful only in relation to personal histories, but he makes no attempt to reduce the number of possible errors due to the tester's approach, and his purpose is to manage without personal histories. There are similar inconsistencies which, together with its pretentious and not always meaningful language, make this a difficult book to understand.

Psychol B 49:372 Jl '52. William A. Hunt. This is a disappointing book. Its purpose is excellent: to present and analyze seventeen unselected cases which represent the routine work during one month of a clinical psychologist in a mental hospital. For each case we are given the diagnostic problem presented, complete protocols of all tests (including reproductions of figure drawings), analysis of the protocols, the psychologist's report (written before the case history was seen), the psychiatric therapist's comment on the validity of the statements in the psychologist's report, case history, and a final summary critique. There is an opening statement on the clinical use of tests which this reviewer found admirable and stimulating. The author then presents the discussion of the tests used. His comments on the Wechsler-Bellevue are adequate, but one often wishes that the field offered him more experimental data to back up some of the statements made. The sections on the Rorschach are disappointing. They are written much too briefly, on a level which will not be intelligible to the beginner, and do not offer enough discussion and elaboration for the experienced worker. The chapter on diagnostic formulations is sketchy and inadequate. The case records are complete and

interesting and will make excellent teaching material. The comments of the psychiatrist on the psychologist's report are interesting, but again sketchy. The flat acceptance of a single psychiatrist's statement of agreement or disagreement as an adequate criterion for the validity of the psychologist's interpretations is of dubious objective value. When these agreements and disagreements are counted and the chi-square formula is then applied, the result is an impression of statistical pretentiousness completely unwarranted by the inadequacies of the data. Scattered throughout are many pithy statements and illuminating comments, but the book as a whole suffers from loose organization. The publishers might well have supplemented the excellent format they have given the book by a tighter editorial rein on the author.

[B190]
★HALPERN, FLORENCE. **A Clinical Approach to Children's Rorschachs.** New York: Grune & Stratton, Inc., 1953. Pp. xv, 270. $7.00. * (*PA* 28:2635)

Am J Psychother 9:350-1 Ap '55. Lily Gondor. * one of the best that have been written for the clinician who wishes to avail himself of all the sources of information the test can furnish * This book is of great importance not only to the psychologist who works with children, but to every clinician. * The book is a most valuable contribution to the field of clinical psychology and can be highly recommended.

Austral J Psychol 6:200 D '54. J. Lyle. * The author apologises from the beginning for the lack of reliability and validity studies with this technique, saying that what is offered works and has proved of clinical use, and that the validation studies will have to come later. Without a doubt she is correct in this view; but one would have liked to see age norms for the various Rorschach categories, and some sort of validation figures for her unusual symbolic approach to interpretation. For example, she states that Card IV seems to be a "Father" card, and Card VII a "Mother" card, and bases a good deal of her interpretation upon these assumptions. Structural aspects of the profile are largely disregarded. Examples of well adjusted and maladjusted records are provided under several age groups. These should be of considerable use to those inexperienced in working with children. Special sections on Schizophrenia, Organic Disorders and Mental Retardation are also included, but these are disappointing in that in a number of the examples offered the tests results do not seem to be diagnostically conclusive, and the author takes little trouble to explain how the differential diagnosis is made. Personally I distrust some of the diagnoses, and suspect that the author's interpretations are sometimes inadvertently based on known case history details rather than on the test data. Chapters on Test Administration and Scoring are useful but the theoretical bases of interpretation are not as clearly stated as they might have been. In all, the book represents a sincere effort to convey the problems and "feel" of the Rorschach with young children; and it should help the inexperienced Rorschach worker. But Halpern's extremely intuitive, symbolic approach is not likely to find favour with clinicians in this country.

B Menninger Clinic 20:52 J '56. Dorothy S. Fuller. * Most valuable book yet published on the interpretation of Children's Rorschachs * One questions the rather broad generalizations about the interpretive significance attached to certain blots, for example, that Card IV represents the father figure.

Psychiatric Q Sup 28:329 pt 2 '54. * a significant contribution to Rorschach literature since it represents some of the results of much-needed validation of children's (ages two and one-half to 10) records * Some excellent material on the general interpretive problems of the Rorschach is offered.

[B191]
★HAMMER, EMANUEL F. **The H-T-P Clinical Research Manual.** Beverly Hills, Calif.: Western Psychological Services, 1955. Pp. iii, 58. Paper, mimeographed. $3.00. *

[B192]
★HAMMER, EMANUEL F., EDITOR. **The Clinical Application of Projective Drawings.** Springfield, Ill.: Charles C Thomas, 1958. Pp. xxii, 663. $13.50. (Oxford, England: Blackwell Scientific Publications, Ltd. 102s. 6d.) *

[B193]
★HAMMETT, J. F. **A Study of Various Methods of Appraising Rate of Reading.** University of Toronto, Ontario College of Education, Department of Educational Research, Educational Research Series No. 22. Toronto, Canada: the Department, 1950. Pp. i, 19. Paper, mimeographed. $0.25. *

[B194]
*HARDAWAY, MATHILDE, AND MAIER, THOMAS B. **Tests and Measurements in Business Education, Second Edition.** Cincinnati, Ohio: South-Western Publishing Co., 1952. Pp. x, 434. $3.00. * For reviews of the first edition, see 3:933.

[B195]
★HARRIS, FRED E. **Three Persistent Educational Problems: Grading, Promoting, and Reporting**

to Parents. University of Kentucky, College of Education, Bureau of School Service Bulletin, Vol. 26, No. 1. Lexington, Ky.: the Bureau, 1953. Pp. 92. Paper. $1.00. (*PA* 28:9040)

[B196]
★HARRIS, MARY JORDAN. **Review of Methods of Scale and Item Analysis and Their Application to a Level of Living Scale in North Carolina.** North Carolina Agricultural Experiment Station, Progress Report RS-13. Raleigh, N.C.: the Station, 1951. Pp. 31. Paper, mimeographed. *

Rural Sociol 17:93-5 Mr '52. Paul J. Jehlik. * The author made an analysis of a level-of-living scale, its items, its differentiating ability, and other attributes that had been developed by John Paul Leagans and used in his doctoral dissertation * The development of the level-of-living scale was incidental to the objectives of Leagan's study, but, since the sample and the data collected were considered adequate and representative, the author proceeded to try to refine and further standardize the scale for use in the housing study. This attempt is one of a growing number of efforts being made to develop level-of-living scales with sufficient sensitivity and discriminating ability to differentiate living levels among farm families within regions, states, or smaller areas. * Much scale construction and item analysis have been done on attitude scales and educational tests. The author took the unique approach of determining the application of some of these methods to the study of a level-of-living scale for North Carolina. Among them were: Thurstone's method of Equal-Appearing Intervals, Guttman's Cornell Technique of Scale Analysis, and Likert's Method of Summated Ratings. * Of the original 30 items, those that ranked highest by all the methods were then chosen to make up the level-of-living scale for the state. These included: (1) sink in the kitchen; (2) running water; (3) tub or shower bath; (4) power washing machine; (5) mechanical refrigerator; (6) screens; (7) tractor power; (8) daily newspaper; (9) separate living room; (10) electric lights; (11) separate dining room; and (12) farm magazine. * For purposes of this study nonmaterial items, such as education, tenure, and cropland operated, were omitted from consideration. * The author concludes that, in the construction of a scale for measuring a well-defined quantity, the use of the critical-ratio test, *phi* coefficient, or point-biserial correlation is adequate for choosing best items from a number of items. Experience in this study lends encouragement to those who may be struggling with the problem of techniques or methods for selecting a group of items that will adequately measure level of living. Similar types of experimentation carried out in other states would serve to validate and implement the North Carolina experience and to add appreciably to the progress in refinement of level-of-living scales. Whether or not the components of level-of-living scales should be limited to material factors is a moot question. To increase the sociological significance of such scales, inclusion of nonmaterial factors and their testing for significance would appear to be an imperative. On this point the North Carolina study cannot be criticized, since the analysis was confined to data already collected.

[B197]

★HARROWER, MOLLY. **Appraising Personality: The Use of Psychological Tests in the Practice of Medicine.** New York: W. W. Norton & Co., Inc., 1952. Pp. xvii, 197. $4.00. * (London: Routledge & Kegan Paul Ltd., 1953. 18s.) (PA 27:6532)

Am J Orthopsychiatry 24:433-4 Ap '54. James M. Cunningham. * The conversational method of presentation makes for easy reading. * Harrower has great facility with language. She writes simply and with clarity. She has something to say and says it beautifully. As she states in her concluding remarks, "Interdisciplinary, interprofessional communication, we believe, is the direction in which the clinical psychologist can make an important contribution at the present time." This she has ably illustrated in the present volume. It will pay the student of psychology to study this book from the point of view of how to present psychological findings and conclusions so that they are meaningful and useful to the physician. It will also help other professional workers whose job it is to deal with people to gain an understanding of the tools of the psychologist and of their usefulness in helping in the understanding of the client.

Brit J Psychol 45:155 My '54. * There is a suggestion that the projective responses are regularly striking and impressive, the psychologist always right and the outcome invariably successful: this is perhaps but the result of the attempt to write a popular book on a notably tricky subject. Something of the difficulties and limitations as well as the conspicuous successes of the techniques would have given a more realistic picture and, probably, added to the reader's confidence in the methods discussed. However,

the author's handling of the projective material is shrewd and clearly rests on sound experience.

J Proj Tech 18:253-4 Je '54. Lawrence S. Rogers. * well written * the theme is built up with considerable skill * the reviewer was surprised to find the T.A.T. mentioned only on a list of tests and the M.M.P.I. mentioned not at all. Essentially, the purpose of the book is to describe the tests to those groups who would be using the services of the clinical psychologist. However, the entire emphasis is placed on the interplay between the psychologist and the medical practitioner. All illustrative cases are cases referred by the physician. It appears to the reviewer that an opportunity was lost to demonstrate how the clinical psychologist could be of service to "social workers, personnel workers, child guidance workers and educators" to mention the groups to whom this book is purportedly addressed. While the presentation of material is very well done, the author does include some points of view that might not be typical for clinical psychologists. For example, Dr. Harrower implies that the function of the clinical psychologist is to do testing only on referral by physician (except under most unusual conditions) and also implies that treatment should be left to the psychiatrist. * While the author takes a realistic approach concerning the limitations of psychologists, she only pays lip service to questioning the validity of the tests themselves. The only test where validity is considered is the Szondi and even this consideration is minimal. The statement is made, "There is still controversy among psychologists as to its (Szondi test) validity" (p. 115), but later on one reads "persons who dislike the manic faces are, without exception, unhappy and pessimistic in their outlook" (p. 128). The uncritical reader would certainly believe the tests were well-nigh infallible. The author has her physician raise practically all the usual questions concerning projective techniques (except those referring to validity) put to clinical psychologists. In the reviewer's opinion, she answers these questions skillfully and meaningfully. This is an excellent explanation of and introduction to projective techniques for any professional worker who wants to understand what the clinical psychologist does. It is also well worth reading by any clinical psychologist who is called upon to explain projective techniques to his non-psychologist colleagues.

Psychol B 51:293-4 My '54. Dan L. Adler.
* The method of presenting these devices is an
unusual one—a not very Socratic dialogue between a physician and a clinical psychologist.
The physician is no ordinary general practitioner, being much too well primed. He asks
about the Szondi pictures, "What are these
strange looking faces?" and later, "In what way
may I be legitimately paranoid? What does it
show if I like the paranoid faces?" The psychologist replies with characteristic clarity,
"You would accept consciously the need to be
emotionally driven beyond yourself, to become
involved in or involved with other things or persons and by so doing extend your own frontiers
and boundaries" (p. 126). It is unfortunate that
instances of this type of dialogue occur all too
frequently, the psychologist speaking with equal
assurance on each such occasion. It is possible
to summarize his confidence (Harrower identifies with a male psychologist in this book) on
the basis of the statement "...by and large, psychological tests have the same margin of error
as do those concerned with somatic phenomena." She is referring specifically to the 10 per
cent of false positives on the Wassermann test,
which was taken as a sample of somatic diagnostic techniques. It would seem that Harrower's interpretation of validation studies is at
great variance with that of Vernon, Eysenck,
and most American psychologists. While all
might place credence in the ability of these devices to mirror some extremes of personality,
their present determinable accuracy for an unselected group would certainly be less than 90
or even 50 per cent. Harrower does present one
area with more restraint, viz., her interpretation
of "scatter" on the Wechsler-Bellevue. Especially good is her review of responses to single
test items, particularly with respect to the clinician's opportunity to make judgments by observing the patient in action. It seems quite
likely that much more of the diagnostic success
of these techniques is attributable to such observation than to the test indices and scores
themselves. * Psychologists of logical bent
know that somewhere they must *hold* the line,
theoretically speaking. This book, although cer-
certainly written from honest convictions, is apt
to designate where they will *draw* the line, instead.

Sci 117:433-4 Ap 17 '53. Arthur L. Benton.
* Written in an engaging, rather breezy manner, the presentation is quite effective. One
gains a clear impression of what a clinical psychologist is, what he tries to do when he sets up
in private practice, what his procedures purport
to measure, how he goes about interpreting performance, and how the interpretation helps in
the individual case. Although the picture is
clear enough, it is not, in the reviewer's opinion,
an altogether well-rounded one. As is perhaps
natural in a book by a medical psychologist addressed to physicians, the field of clinical psychology is presented as a sort of laboratory
adjunct to medicine, providing formal psychodiagnostic services to the physician. This is a
formulation which the majority of clinical psychologists would hold to be much too restricted.
As conceived by its practitioners, clinical psychology consists not only of formal diagnostic
functions (the "method of tests") but also of
more comprehensive behavioral evaluation and
of techniques for the modification of behavior,
such as counseling, re-education, and psychotherapy. Psychological test methods are introduced by way of the timeworn (and thoroughly
unsound) "X-ray analogy," wherein they are
conceived as being able somehow to penetrate
to the basic personality structure and the fundamental dynamics *behind* behavior. Although
this metaphor may have had some utility in the
past, it is surely time that test methods be presented for exactly what they are—namely,
measurements of selected behavioral samples
with actual or assumed predictive significance.
In this regard, it must be said that a good deal
of psychodiagnostic work, particularly with
projective techniques, rests upon assumptions
which either still lack empirical validation or
have been demonstrated to be probably invalid.
It is in this area of critical evaluation of the
procedures themselves that the book shows a
decided weakness. Interpretations of details of
performance on the Rorschach and drawing
tests are rather glibly presented as having a
solid foundation in controlled clinical experience which they do not in fact possess. The use
in clinical practice of the Szondi test, a procedure that has not met empirical tests of validity,
is defended on the ground that "nonetheless, it
works and can be extraordinarily helpful at
times." But, of course, whether the test "works"
is precisely the question which systematic validational study has attempted to answer. Here,
an analogy is drawn with the Wassermann test
as a procedure, the exact nature of which is
unknown, but which nevertheless "works." The

analogy is inappropriate. Regardless of what is known or not known about the basic biochemistry of the Wasserman, it does show sufficiently consistent relationships with other events to provide a basis for sound diagnostic inference. In short, it is a valid test. This is not true of the Szondi. Yet, despite the uncritical nature of the exposition, the book has merit as an introduction to current formal psychodiagnostic practice. It is quite readable and should at least, as Alan Gregg states in the introduction, "remove the burrs of misunderstanding and ignorance." Once these burrs are removed, some medical scientists can be depended upon to raise pertinent questions about the validity of specific procedures.

[B198]

★HARVARD COLLEGE, HARVARD OFFICE OF TESTS. **The Proper Use of Objective Test Scores: A Handbook for Harvard Advisers.** Cambridge, Mass.: Office of Tests, Harvard College, [1951]. Pp. iii, 42. Paper. *

[B199]

HATHAWAY, STARKE R., AND MEEHL, PAUL E. **An Atlas for the Clinical Use of the MMPI.** Minneapolis, Minn.: University of Minnesota Press, 1951. Pp. xliv, 799. $9.75. * (London: Oxford University Press. 78s.) (PA 25:7468)

J Abn & Social Psychol 47:130–1 Ja '52. Clare Wright Thompson. * an impressive collection of 968 case histories, 8 figures, 23 tables, 259 bibliographical references, and 8 indices * Throughout the 21 introductory pages, the authors repeatedly emphasize that the material they present is descriptive rather than interpretative. Let it be emphasized, as well, that this review is descriptive, not evaluative. For this is a book to be referred to and consulted, not read. The proof of the pudding, then, lies in how appropriate and useful is the information one obtains from these referrings and consultings. An adequate appraisal would be based upon at least a year's use in a situation involving many questions about MMPI profiles. If this volume is found to be useful, it will be as a substitute for, or as a complement to, clinical experience. It gives the raw material by which the inexperienced clinician, faced with an MMPI profile, can do what the experienced clinician does regularly with more or with less formality. He can look at the record in his hand and review the people who have previously given similar records. For most profiles of psychiatric patients, he will find here sufficient case histories for an adequate sample of similar

findings on patients the same sex and age, from which to make some kind of generalizations. * to browse in the volume enough to be really aware of what it contains and what uses it might serve is decidedly worth while. Doing this one learns many diversified but useful facts, among them the following. The published standard scores for L and F are not optimal. A hospitalized psychiatric patient who gives a normal profile is "very likely to be basically paranoid but with enough self-control and contact with the environment to be able to hide the fact." Referring to the "Diagnostic Index" for verification of this, we find that two-fifths of all patients included, whose primary diagnosis is Psychosis, Paranoid, gave no scale with a score above 70. From the figures we learn that, of a sample of almost 2,000 each, 25 per cent of ninth-grade boys and 29 per cent of ninth-grade girls have a "high point" at Psychopathic Deviate. For many of these, the standard score is above 70. For both men and women university students, on the other hand, Hypomania is the preferred "high point" and is given by two to three times as many subjects as is Psychopathic Deviate. Of the Atlas profiles given by "organic types," 17 per cent have the Hypochondriasis scale as highest or second highest, and 15 per cent have the Hysteria scale in one of these positions. Of the 11 Atlas patients where "Psychosis, Toxic" is the primary diagnosis, almost none has a psychotic MMPI profile. A thorough combing of the book would yield limitless information of this sort, information which would certainly enable one to make more meaningful statements about MMPI profiles. Essentially, this book seems one which must rise or fall according to how adequately it provides a substitute for clinical experience, and how useful it is in a learning or teaching situation. It seems unlikely that a clinician who has already developed his own method of analyzing MMPI profiles will find himself routinely looking up every record in this volume. There is a certain tediousness to the process of coding a profile, finding similar records from the index, reading the case histories and making notations from them. This done, there remains the task of making some sort of psychological sense from the data thus obtained. The impression from admittedly insufficient use of the Atlas is that for most profiles it is as easy and as profitable for the experienced clinician to try to make sense from the profile itself by whatever means he is best versed in, without the intervening steps.

J Appl Psychol 36:279 Ag '52. George S. Welsh. Despite the title, the *Atlas* does not deal with clinical uses of the MMPI. It consists of ....case histories * Each of the 968 cases is headed by one or more MMPI profiles and related diagnostic and descriptive data. The profiles have been reduced to a code which summarizes the form or shape and gives some information about the intensity or elevation. The cases are arranged according to this code and are extensively indexed and cross-indexed. This enables the user to look up cases on the basis of the MMPI pattern and provides material on all the usual profile configurations and many atypical ones. However, the reader will have to have had considerable experience with the MMPI before he can profitably use the *Atlas.* The discussion prerequisite to an informed and sophisticated use of the instrument is not provided in the book. * Of particular interest are other tables giving two-digit codes for fifteen common diagnostic groups contrasting their relative frequencies with those obtained in a normal population and in a general clinical sample. There are a great many relationships inherent in the tabular and textual material which the authors have not made explicit. It may be expected that other workers will carry out researches on the contents of this volume much as governmental and census statistical reports are often utilized. This would require evidence for the accuracy and representativeness of the samples and case material presented; such evidence is, unfortunately, at present not available for evaluating the book from this standpoint. The coding employed in the *Atlas* has two major disadvantages: first, scales with T-scores from 46 to 55 are not coded; second, "low" scales with scores below 46 are coded from lowest to highest—just the opposite of the "high" scales. This reversal led to awkwardness if there is more than one low scale. The first deficiency causes variability in code length if any scales lie in the uncoded range. Also it may be impossible to tell which is the lowest (or in some cases the highest) scale if more than one scale is uncoded. This difficulty is exemplified by Table I, page xxvii where 50.4% of 710 male psychiatric patients have their low points uncoded; there is no way of determining whether these low points are distributed in the same proportions as those

with coded low points. The utility of all the tables and figures is reduced because of this shortcoming. The *Atlas* should encourage clinical workers to utilize the profile patterning and configural approach to the MMPI and should discourage the unprofitable adherence to the diagnostic terminology of the individual scales. It will then be possible to determine empirically and without psychiatric bias the personality correlates—both normal and abnormal—of the various profile patterns.

For additional reviews, see 4:72.

[B200]

★HATHAWAY, STARKE R., AND MONACHESI, ELIO D., EDITORS. **Analyzing and Predicting Juvenile Delinquency With the MMPI.** Minneapolis, Minn.: University of Minnesota Press, 1953. Pp. viii, 153. $3.50. (London: Oxford University Press. 28s.) * (PA 28:2970)

Am J Sociol 60:321–2 N '54. Karl F. Schuessler. * The central theme, never expressed dogmatically, is that delinquency is symptomatic of personality disturbance and that the treatment of the personality is the most practical, and perhaps the best, method of controlling delinquency. The articles present in great detail the score differences between selected groups but intentionally neglect the important theoretical question of how flaws in personality are translated into delinquent behavior. Surprisingly, in view of the title, the studies as a whole contain relatively little material on actuarial prediction. * any interpretation, narrow or otherwise, must be regarded as quite tentative until certain methodological problems are solved. First, the use of the MMPI with adolescents is questionable, especially in view of the finding that most adolescents are below average in personality. One wonders whether the MMPI score differences between delinquents and nondelinquents would be similar in size and direction if test norms had been based on adolescent rather than adult populations. The editors defend the application of adult norms to young people on the ground that the "adjustment of the norms would obscure the very real fact that there is a significant, almost universal, quality in young people that makes them prone to socially unacceptable behavior. We want our scales to show behavior differences that are significant to society even if the implied personalities are 'normal' for the age level" (p. 25). But to do so is, apparently, to shift ground, since the MMPI was not applied to measure social conformity but rather to measure deviant personality factors. Second, the consistent differences yielded by scale 4, *psychopathic deviate,* must be construed in light of the fact that this scale was derived from persons who were "often young and delinquent" (p. 17). This scale is to a certain extent, then, a "delinquency scale" in the sense that it measures aspects of delinquency itself. Measurements from such a scale cannot be used to explain delinquency, since they are not independent of the object to be explained. Third, the term "delinquency" had no constant meaning throughout this series of studies. The results are therefore not additive in a strict sense. As an aggregate they can only be given a loose interpretation. Fourth, score differences may have been due in part to the fact that delinquents and controls were not always carefully matched on relevant variables. Differences were observed between urban and rural subjects (p. 50) and between high- and low-income groups (p. 105), suggesting that these and similar factors should be held constant in comparing delinquents and controls. Two of the studies were devoted to prediction. In one study, fifty MMPI score profiles were used to predict thirty-three cases of successful post-institutional adjustment and seventeen failures. No experience table was constructed, but rather the fifty profiles were submitted to five persons "moderately skilled in the interpretation of MMPI data." They were given the task of separating the profiles into thirty-three successes and seventeen failures. Three raters made sixteen errors apiece, and two raters made eighteen errors apiece. If every case had been predicted a success, seventeen errors would have resulted. Prediction from the MMPI codes was therefore no better than prediction from the over-all success rate. In the other study delinquency rates were computed according to one hundred "primary codes" for a population of approximately four thousand boys and girls in which the over-all delinquency rate was about 22 per cent. Only one of these one hundred classifications required that the prediction of nondelinquency based on the over-all rate be changed to a prediction of delinquency, and this change did not reduce the prediction errors based on the over-all rate. In view of these results, the conclusion that "MMPI categories yield practical actuarial data" (p. 136) hardly seems justified. A final word on the conception of delinquency as a

symptom rather than a social habit. Such a view ignores the distinction, generally regarded by sociologists as valid and useful, between the idiosyncratic delinquent and the cultural delinquent. The hypothesis that delinquency is a social habit, acquired within a deviant cultural setting, is at present just as tenable as the notion that delinquency is a consequence of deviant personality. Its tenability is heightened by the finding that delinquents and controls give very similar replies to the MMPI questionnaire.

Am Sociol R 19:490–1 Ag '54. Clarence Schrag. * Several of the studies have previously been reported in scientific journals. However, enough new material is provided to make the book a valuable contribution to social science, particularly criminology. The editors begin with a discussion of the MMPI, its relevance to the study of delinquency and other behavior disorders, its validity as a diagnostic device, its component scales, and the personality profiles which can be constructed by comparing a person's scale scores with the norms that have been established for adults. Among published descriptions of the MMPI, this is one of the briefest, clearest, and most informative. The reader, whether pro or con in his attitude toward personality scales and inventories, will be impressed by the generally cautious and unpresumptuous tone of the argument. Careful study of the first twenty-eight pages is a prerequisite for any understanding of the research reported in the remainder of this book. * The authors maintain that "personality variables are more closely and usefully related to delinquency than are the environmental variables acting on the individual" (p. 12). While this assumption has apparently been growing in popularity among researchers in the field of delinquency (note, for example, the recent work of the Gluecks), the book under review fails to provide convincing evidence of its validity. MMPI responses of delinquents differ too little from those of nondelinquents to afford a sound basis for prediction or reliable diagnosis. In addition, MMPI scores vary with age (p. 40), sex (pp. 97, 108), place of residence (pp. 50, 101–104), education (p. 101), socio-economic status (pp. 105–107), and probably many other factors, both genetic and environmental. Some of these factors are highly associated with delinquency. Their predictive efficiency was not compared with that of the

MMPI. Consequently, the predictive and diagnostic superiority of the MMPI is not established by the consistent and sometimes statistically significant association between scale scores and delinquent behavior. * Personality profiles of delinquents were compared with those of nondelinquents in the total test population. * Unfortunately, the number of cases was frequently too low for adequate estimates of profile reliability. Nevertheless, the profile data are among the most challenging, and possibly the most important, reported in the book. Readers will look forward to further applications of the MMPI in delinquency research.

Fed Probation 18:62–3 S '54. Helen L. Witmer. * the test proved to be of more value for predicting who would not become delinquent than who would * The most interesting of the studies reported....is a 2-year followup of all ninth-grade students in Minneapolis to discover which of them had police or court records. * The authors are modest in discussing the significance of the findings. They caution that these are only probability figures, which apply to groups and not to individuals, and then only under conditions that are similar to those under which the study was conducted. They think—and this reviewer agrees—that the chief usefulness of the findings lies in the identification of two particular types of delinquents that need clinical treatment, and in the discovery that many children of specified personality makeup are very unlikely to become delinquent.

J Ed Psychol 47:63–4 Ja '56. H. Meltzer. * In the light of all the clinical and social knowledge that has been coming in, it is doubtful whether this kind of an instrument will be the desirable one to use for the general study and treatment of delinquency. But if by the use of it some basic knowledge can be discovered, studies with the use of this instrument can make a contribution to knowledge in the field. * A contention of the editors is that the objective personality test approach is, with all of its limitations, superior to present practices in evaluating need and effectiveness of treatment. This conclusion can be questioned from the point of view of situations as they develop and people as they can be helped. However, it is safe to say that all students interested in the objective approach will find in this volume useful information.

Social Service R 28:112–3 Mr '54. Howard F. Hunt. * This reviewer believes the data warrant the editors' summarizing conclusion that the MMPI seems to provide a useful basis for categorizing adolescents into high- and low-risk groups with regard to probability of delinquency. The editors make the very important point that such a categorization permits society to allocate its limited prophylactic facilities where they are needed most—to the persons in the high-risk categories. The social value of an inexpensive, objective method which will aid us in arriving at such decisions is so obvious that it requires no further comment. Though an introductory chapter provides, in condensed form, the information on the MMPI one needs to follow the argument, persons unfamiliar with the test, its lore, and the vocabulary which has grown up around it may find the book a bit difficult. Similarly, those unused to statistical tables as a source of information may miss some of the most important implications of the research, particularly in the case of the last study. The actuarial table there, covering four pages, really is the *pièce de résistance* of the entire book, but time and effort are required to digest it. Unfortunately, because of the sort of data the MMPI produces, there seems to be no other economical way of presenting all this information in summarized form. Nevertheless, this book deserves and will repay the careful attention of serious students in the area. The actuarial material presented in it has some immediate and practical value, if properly understood and used. In addition, the book presents empirical support for the argument that the comparatively inexpensive and straightforward personality inventory can contribute to the understanding and prediction of human behavior.

[B201]

★HAYES, SAMUEL P., EDITOR. **First Regional Conference on Mental Measurements of the Blind.** Perkins Publications, No. 15. Watertown, Mass.: Perkins Institution and Massachusetts School for the Blind, February 1952. Pp. 32. Paper. $0.25. *

[B202]

★HEIM, A. W. **The Appraisal of Intelligence.** London: Methuen & Co. Ltd., 1954. Pp. vii, 171. 12s. 6d. * (PA 29:922)

Ann Eug 19:250 F '55. L. S. Hearnshaw. Dr Alice Heim....Cambridge, is well known in this country for her work on tests of high-level intelligence. There is unfortunately very little reference to her own work in the present book, which is a mainly critical account of the assumption underlying the measurement of intelligence by means of psychological tests. Dr Heim's chief criticisms are that "psychometrists" have attempted to employ a quite spurious exactitude and objectivity in a process which ought to be regarded as vague and qualitative, and which is more appropriately termed "appraisal" than "measurement," and that they have abstracted intelligence from mental activity as a whole, and have ignored "the whole child in the total test situation." She wants us, therefore, to go back to the clinical approach of Binet, who, she thinks, was almost the only psychologist to study "the individual as a living person!" Dr Heim concludes with a number of constructive suggestions, some of which are interesting but some of which, however, are much less novel than she seems to imagine, and a profession of faith, which seems strangely unsupported by anything that has been previously said in the book, that intelligence tests are "the best single means of estimating intelligence in a short time." The need for a scholarly and careful re-examination of the whole problem of the nature and assessment of intelligence is at the moment a very urgent one. Dr Heim has clearly seen the need for this, and a number of her criticisms of current tendencies are pertinent. She has fallen far short, however, of giving us the book we are looking for. It is hard not to feel that she is in fact out of touch with a great deal of psychological work and practice in the field of intelligence testing; for example, she seems totally unaware of the work of the clinical psychologists on tests other than projection tests, and of the selection board procedures used in the armed and civil services during and since the war. Her criticisms, therefore, are constantly missing the mark. The book also shows a rather imperfect acquaintance with what has already been written on the theory and practice of intelligence testing. The positive standpoint to which she adheres—a vague wholism which decries analysis or precision—has often been advocated before, particularly by German writers, and has stood up badly to practical examination. The chapter which might have proved of some direct interest to readers of this journal—the chapter on "Intelligence and Environment"— is both short and superficial.

Brit J Ed Psychol 25:60–1 F '55. *Cyril Burt.*
* this book....begins with a criticism of the term intelligence, as psychologists are supposed to use it, and endeavours to show how they have gone astray. Dr. Heim examines the conflicting descriptions offered by contributors to an American symposium some 33 years ago: she overlooks the fact that many of the difficulties have since been cleared up by later research. She brings the matter up to date with a further chapter on "current definitions"; but this is confined to two—Mr. Raven's and her own. She herself maintains that psychologists should abandon any formula that "masquerades as an exact and measurable concept," and "give the word a meaning which is comfortably compatible with that of the layman." This, she believes, was the real intention of Binet. But, unfortunately, she only quotes him at second hand. A reference to his article will show that Binet, who of course was mainly thinking of the classification of educationally subnormal school children, makes three important distinctions. First, he distinguishes those who are lacking in intellectual capacity from those who are lacking in moral or emotional stability. Secondly, he distinguishes the lack of "natural" capacity from the lack of acquired knowledge or "instruction." Thirdly, he distinguishes between what he calls "partial aptitudes" (memory, mechanical ability, verbal ability, and the like) and the "fundamental faculty" assumed to be common to *all* cognitive processes, from sensation up to reason—a distinction which is as old as Aristotle. We thus reach a concept defined in three ways, namely, an innate, general, cognitive capacity. For such a concept it is convenient to have a short and simple name: Binet and his followers adopted the term "intelligence." The word was originally coined by Cicero to translate Aristotle's Greek label for the generic cognitive faculty; and from his day to that of Hamilton and Spencer, it was regularly used by psychological writers with this technical meaning. Like many of our older technical terms (gas, energy, soda, for example) it strayed long ago into popular parlance, and got blurred as a result. But why is the scientist now required to conform to the loose usage of the layman rather than to that of the specialist who has studied these intricate problems? The remaining chapters are intended to present a critical review of "objective techniques" for measuring intelligence and test-efficiency. They

deal with the usual topics—I.Q., reliability and validity of tests, distribution of intelligence, and "the approach of the factor analyst." In the main, the author's criticisms are directed against a group of people generically termed "psychometrists." In spite of their claim to objective exactitude, we are told, their assessments and conclusions are constantly vitiated by "subjective bias," "verbal imprecision," and "publicly discredited presuppositions." These indictments are rarely supported by references to specific writers or specific publications; and it is difficult to think of any competent investigators who have committed the faults that are laid at their door. No authoritative writer has ever regarded the mental age or the intelligence quotient as a really "scientific unit," as Dr. Heim implies. Nor do psychometrists simply "assume" that intelligence is normally distributed: by actual investigation they have proved that the distribution is *not* strictly normal, but follows a hypergeometric curve, slightly skewed for well-known reasons. They have not "ignored" the possibility that the standard deviation may vary appreciably with age: from the earliest L.C.C. surveys to those of Dr. Fraser Roberts and his colleagues, they have repeatedly shown that it does so, and devised a suitable correction. Long ago they examined the alternative procedures that Dr. Heim now puts forward—such as validating intelligence by chronological age and measuring it by percentiles—and have demonstrated the defects of each of them. They have never used "item analysis" to measure "reliability": Dr. Heim has probably confused "item analysis" with "analysing the variance of items." And it is quite the reverse of the actual facts to suggest that "factor analysts" *in general* assume "the existence in the mind of separate faculties and a God-like insight as to what these are." No doubt a few young investigators, who might perhaps be classed as "psychometrists" or "factor analysts," have been guilty of these and other careless practices; and many of the fallacies Dr. Heim has pilloried could be found in these submitted by research-students or even in reports presented by teachers. Hence her vigorous warnings may have a welcome and beneficial effect. Certainly, in spite of—and perhaps because of—her own manifest slips and misconceptions, her book is well worth the attention of all who think of embarking on an investigation with mental or educational tests.

She writes with a lively and provocative pen; and even those who disagree with her contentions will find much that is stimulating and suggestive.

Brit J Med Psychol 28:84–5 pt 1 '55. *R. M. Mowbray.* * Heim tackles intelligence-testing by swift, pertinent and sometimes epigrammatic discussion of the concepts and faiths we cling to in what might be called classical intelligence testing and theory. She is relentless in her search for theoretical flaws and develops her case, not merely on the kinds of defects she discloses, but on their vast numbers. The first eleven of her thirteen chapters contain her destructive criticisms and are of value as a survey of problems in intelligence-testing. Her style sometimes leads her to inaccuracies in emphasis on particular topics, but her breadth of survey is sound enough to stimulate reflexion on the contemporary philosophy of intelligence-testing. The final two constructive chapters start from a reconsideration of the concept of flexibility, reaffirm the indivisibility of mental life and lead to ideas and suggestions about qualitative appraisal of intelligent activity. (It is surprising that Wechsler's non-cognitive factors in intelligence are not discussed here.) This clinical attitude is attractive and those of us for whom intelligence-tests are tools rather than end-products will share the author's belief that the germs of temperament should be allowed to seep into the emotionally aseptic atmosphere of intelligence-testing. To share beliefs, speculations and suppositions is not enough though. Dr Heim's last two chapters have too much "psychologizing" in them and not enough observation to help us towards "appraisal" rather than measurement of intelligence.

Brit J Psychol 45:311–2 N '54. *Stephen Wiseman.* * The sins of the psychometrist, the applied psychologist and the factor analyst are described with exhaustive fluency and no quarter is given. The only psychologist to emerge from the fray with credit is Binet—indeed, the author appears at times to lean over backwards in her desire to give full credit to his genius. It is inevitable that in the heady intoxication of combat Miss Heim is occasionally led to the setting up of papier-maché ogres just for the joy of laying them low, and that in a number of places the writing becomes tendentious and perhaps a little querulous. Yet this is a book which was well worth writing, and one which is strongly recommended for students as well as psychometrists. There are not enough books of this kind available: attacks on intelligence tests and testers are too often written by those who do not know their subject and who are incapable of appreciating the technicalities behind the methods they attack. The chapters dealing with the nature of intelligence and the concepts of mental age and I.Q. will be of considerable value to students, as will those covering reliability and unreliability. These chapters, perhaps, could be expanded a little in any future edition —the consideration of the standard error of score, for example, would be a useful addition. As one might expect from Miss Heim's own research work, the section on speed versus power is of considerable interest. Much of what Miss Heim has to say about validation and its difficulties is excellent, but one feels that the omission of any reference to follow-up studies as a validating technique makes the discussion less valuable. For the educational psychologist, the "validity" of an intelligence test is often to be found in its predictive power. Perhaps Miss Heim would find this an inadmissible use of "validity"—if so, she ought to argue the case. The final two chapters make more constructive suggestions after the largely destructive criticism of the previous eleven, and here many pertinent and suggestive points are made for future research. It is interesting to note that many of these points—e.g. difficulty of items, speed, the use of creative instead of choice responses—are those which in the educational sphere have recently begun to receive more attention. Miss Heim's suggestion for new methods of appraisal of intelligence will appeal particularly to the clinically-orientated psychologist working with adults. Most of these suggestions need working out more fully, with a particular eye on a number of the criticisms made by Miss Heim herself in earlier chapters. May we hope that these suggestions are an indication of future lines of research by the author?

[B203]

★HEMPHILL, JOHN K. **Group Dimensions: A Manual for Their Measurement.** Ohio State University, Bureau of Business Research, Research Monograph No. 87. Columbus, Ohio: the Bureau, 1956. Pp. xi, 66. Paper. $2.00. * (*PA* 31 :7657)

Personnel Psychol 10:383–5 au '57. Jay M. Jackson. * As part of the Ohio State Leadership Studies, and his research on the situational determinants of leadership, Hemphill developed a set of scales to describe 13 different dimen-

sions of groups. He now has written a little technical manual providing instructions for administering this *Group Dimensions Descriptions* questionnaire, a convenient scoring method, norms for comparison with a standard population, and the available evidence on reliability and validity of the measures. For one who would like to discover how the members of a "group" —defined broadly as any social unit regardless of its size, geographical distribution or internal organization—perceive its "Autonomy," "Homogeneity," degree of "Intimacy," amount of "Participation," "Stratification," "Stability," and other interesting characteristics, this questionnaire lies ready to be used. The presentation is straightforward, clear, and complete; with the exception of a brief section on factor analysis, it is ideally suited for the non-technical reader. Yet one wonders whether the practicing personnel man or progressive administrator, convinced that groups are important to successful administration, will be able to utilize this carefully devised instrument as a management tool without more extensive and definitive basic research. The *Group Dimensions Descriptions* questionnaire was first published in 1950, and has been used in a number of Ohio State projects, among them studies of an insurance company office, the departments of a liberal arts college, religious organizations, public school staffs, and some small laboratory groups. From this wide variety of groups, properly not represented to be a sample from any particular population of groups, norms have been constructed and findings are presented regarding reliability, validity, and "relationships with other variables." Estimates of reliability from three studies are certainly adequate, although these measures of internal consistency may be somewhat inflated, since all the items from a given scale are grouped together within the questionnaire and respondents do not like to contradict themselves. The discussion of validity raises a number of perplexing questions that are much broader than the scope of this compact monograph. When the members of a group disagree markedly about the attributes of a group, as they often do, does this mean their perceptions are *invalid?* When they all describe the group the same way, which is rare in Hemphill's data except on a few dimensions, is this evidence of *validity?* Why should relationships between the group dimensions scores and other variables be expected, and why should they be considered evidence of *validity?* Social scientists' efforts to discover attributes of groups or organizations that predict consistently to management objectives, without adequately considering the mediating factors present in both the situations being studied and those in which the knowledge is being applied, have been marked by considerable frustration and failure. Hemphill and his colleagues are not alone. The group dimensions scores have as yet demonstrated little ability to predict to productivity, turnover, or administrative reputation. The substantial relationships between a number of scales and job satisfaction are potentially exciting, but they may result from emotional loading of some of the items. (It is found, for example, that people are less satisfied with their job when they report in their groups the presence of "hostility," "bickering," "lack of respect," "conniving," "petty quarrels and animosity," and "undercurrent of feeling"; and are more satisfied when they report that "personal dissatisfaction" is small, and that members do not "continually grumble about the work." The practical application of knowledge about groups is a social engineering activity that demands diagnostic and action skills. Yet it must derive from scientific understanding of the formation, structure and dynamics of groups. The investigator in pursuit of such systematic knowledge will welcome these scales and the technically sound development research described in this manual. In combination with a theoretical rationale for using them, such as undoubtedly exists in the larger program of research activity from which they are drawn, they will constitute a useful contribution to the implements of social research.

[B204]

★HENRY, WILLIAM E. **The Analysis of Fantasy: The Thematic Apperception Technique in the Study of Personality.** New York: John Wiley & Sons, Inc., 1956. Pp. xiii, 305. $6.00. (London: Chapman & Hall, Ltd. 48s.) * (*PA* 30:8292)

Am J Orthopsychiatry 27:837 O '57. *Frederick A. Zehrer.* * includes an excellent, extensive dichotomized bibliography of the TAT consisting of 548 titles of published materials. The bibliography alone is worth the price of the book. The breakdown into topics makes it a most convenient reference source. * a clearly written book, well organized, and consistent in manner of presentation. It is refreshing to find interpretations so close to the data available:

this is a pattern which will assist in the effort to make projective techniques more scientific. The author's use of "normal" personality information throughout adds much to his contribution. Such material, well illustrated, is useful in preventive aspects of mental health as well as offering more valid criteria in assaying clinical data, inferences concerning possible dynamics, and the role of fantasy as an adaptive mechanism. * a real contribution in the area of personality study * a valuable item not only in the university library and classroom but also for reference for those interested in mental health research and practice.

Am J Psychol 70:158–9 Mr '57. *Theodore R. Sarbin.* The title of this well-written treatise is somewhat of a misnomer, since the author concerns himself primarily with the products of imagination as elicited by Murray's TAT (in some cases modified for use with Indian Ss). Conspicuously lacking is a treatment of the structure and function of fantasy as one of the "higher mental processes." The subtitle [is] more apt. * Early in the book, the author—unlike most writers in this field—explicitly states the major dimensions of his theory of personality. In an exposition remarkably free from the hoopla often encountered in writings on projective tests, Henry sketches a theory of personality organization which does not neglect social and cultural features. * To the reviewer, Chapter 6, which provides "a conceptual framework for individual case analysis," is a high point in the book. Every psychologist who employs clinical instruments does, of course, develop his own framework. This one, however, has much in its favor. If it had been developed and widely adopted ten years ago, then today, instead of hodge-podge, we might have accumulated a body of data which would have permitted systematic and comparative studies of persons and of groups. In this brief review, suffice it to say that the framework is comprehensive, realistic, and readily communicable. The illustrative analyses are convincingly impressive. * Applicable to the general field of projective testing as well as to *The Analysis of Fantasy* are two related criticisms: (1) the assumption of validity of interpretations and (2) the failure to slant the interpretations toward the prediction of events. Henry acknowledges that a systematic treatment of validity is lacking. In this connection, one might assert that rigorous studies of validity can be planned and prosecuted now that an easily communicable set of concepts is available. For the prediction of specific behavior, the TAT must be used with extreme caution, warns Henry. "To describe the personality of a subject is an easier task than describing the projection of that personality into behavior in its social context" (p. 36). The emphasis on personality-description over behavior-prediction is a shortcoming that should be noted. Although not a manual in the usual sense, the interested reader will find many tips, hints, and suggestions that will be helpful in interesting TAT stories. *The Analysis of Fantasy* should be regarded as required reading by all students who intend to use the TAT or similar methods in personality research or in clinical practice. Forthright, clear, and modest in its claims, this book is the best introduction to thematic apperception now available.

Austral J Psychol 9:190–1 D '57. F. N. Cox. This book is not just a description of yet another way of analysing TAT stories. While it does contain the author's method of dissecting fantasy products, it also covers more general topics which should interest both practising clinicians and those of us who are concerned about general theoretical problems in the field of personality. * most of the merit of the book lies in Part 1. Henry's first chapter, in particular, is a lucid and thoughtful analysis of the social and psychological nature of interpretation. Further, this chapter contains some interesting speculations about the parameters of adjustment, the learning of social skills, and the development of individuality. Much of the material in this chapter could have been expanded, but what is there certainly stimulates both thought and discussion. The remaining chapters in Part 1 deal with the more technical aspects of interpreting TAT stories, but the author continues to raise wider issues and, unlike so many clinical writers, he does not relapse into verbose and idiosyncratic jargon. One of the questions which Henry raises is that rather unfashionable, one might almost say disreputable, concept of the "self." His discussion centres around Erik Erickson's notion of "ego identity," but Henry emphasises environmental factors rather more than Erickson. The same emphasis is evident in the author's discussion of interpretation in general * Another interesting point which Henry makes in passing is that we don't *have* to try to interpret all projective test data—rather, our task should be to attempt

to use as little or as much TAT (or Rorschach) evidence as we need to explain and predict behaviour. He makes the related point that the nature of one's interpretation of projective test data depends, more than anything else, upon one's purposes—that is, Henry rejects the naïve, but surprisingly common, idea that there is one "correct" interpretation of fantasy products. * While most of....[the book] is unsuitable for undergraduate courses on projective techniques, selected chapters could certainly be studied profitably by beginners in this field. The whole book is eminently suitable for postgraduate clinical study: indeed, Parts 1 and 3 contain the most concise and thoughtful description of the TAT which this reviewer has read.

Cont Psychol 2:109–11 Ap '57. Bert R. Sappenfield. * The theoretical portion....is not easy to read. Whether this difficulty is attributable to the psychologist's unfamiliarity with sociologically derived concepts or due simply to ponderous writing is, in itself, a difficult question; but the reviewer's untested hypothesis is that the author does not feel so secure in dealing with theoretical material as he feels when attacking the analysis of a set of TAT stories. So, in passing from the theoretical to the strictly technical portion of the book, the reader senses a change not unlike that of driving from a section of road under construction onto a finished superhighway. The reader who is conversant with psychodynamic concepts and partial to them is likely to gain a mixed impression of Henry's two chapters of theoretical discussion. On the one hand, he will recognize in the author's formulations something he has known all along; but, on the other, he will sense a foreign quality in them. Thus there is the expected acceptance of "psychic determinism" and the customary emphasis on the consistency and uniqueness of personalities (with due regard to the personality features common to a given cultural milieu); there is sufficient recognition of motivation and anxiety as central concepts in personality dynamics; and there is some discussion of introjection, projection, and impulse denial as important features of adjustive behavior. Yet there is also a sociological or interpersonal emphasis in the formulations, one that is disturbing to the intellectual balance of the psychologist who is accustomed to locate behavioral determinants within the behaving organism. This complication is the outcome of theory construction within a sociological frame of reference, incorporating concepts of Lewin, or Freud, and of Sullivan. This comment is not meant to suggest that there is any critical fault to be found in the theoretical formulations which Henry has provided, though it does at least raise a question as to whether it is logically necessary (even though defensible) to introduce interpersonal concepts in order to give an adequate account of behavior. The reviewer, at least, remains unconvinced that it is necessary to look outside the individual for the determinants of behavior, whether it be in response to TAT pictures or in response to other kinds of "reality stimuli." In justice to the author, it should be noted that he explicitly denies himself the privilege of formulating a complete theoretical substructure for thematic test analysis. "The task of summing the knowledge relevant to interpretation is not only beyond the skill of the author but out of place in this volume." And, while he maintains that "any theory justly described as psychodynamic will provide the flexibility necessary to interpret fantasy material," and while he does not explicitly espouse Freudian psychodynamics, there is ample evidence in his technically oriented chapters that, like many other TAT interpreters, he relies heavily on Freudian principles for his contentual interpretations. In the remaining chapters....the author has provided what is perhaps the best of the existing manuals for TAT interpretation. One is impressed, first of all, with Henry's exhaustive analysis of variables for the description of behavior in response to the TAT. Not only does he differentiate the many variables relating to the content of stories, but he also differentiates a number of variables relating to their structure or form. He makes explicit here, as he has done elsewhere....that many Rorschach-derived concepts are applicable to TAT analysis. * Henry can....be credited with being the first to suggest "Rorschaching the TAT." Although Henry is not distinguishable from other TAT interpreters in respect of his reliance on yet-to-be-validated intuitions, and although he devotes little effort to going outside the TAT stories for purposes of external validation, nonetheless he displays an awareness of this general deficiency in work with "projective" instruments. * One of the major contributions of the present work is the author's refreshing emphasis on the significance of "normal and ordinary" responses to TAT pictures, for it is in such responses that an interpreter

can discover the control functions or the assets of a personality. Previous discussions have tended too strongly to imply that meaningful personality data are to be derived only from unique responses, which show evidence of idiosyncratic perceptual distortions and which lend themselves to psychopathological interpretations. Five of the twelve chapters deal with "illustrative analyses," in which the reader is given an opportunity to observe the author in action as a TAT interpreter. These chapters provide a richer exhibition of the author's approach to interpretation than is customarily to be found in such manuals. * Henry's interpretations are highly credible and reflect exceptional sensitivity and skill. Although this book is not the first to present a treatment of "the stimulus properties of the pictures," the reviewer doubts that any other set of descriptions is as adequate. Since an accurate understanding of the "demands" made by the TAT stimuli has for TAT interpretation an importance comparable to that of norms for the interpretation of psychometric tests, it must be said that Henry has made a significant contribution through his publication of these descriptions. In summary, then, it is the reviewer's opinion that, in spite of the fact that its theoretical introduction is spotty and in some respects gratuitous, and in spite of the author's pervasive modesty regarding his own work, this book is probably the best of the existing technical contributions to thematic test analysis. The student who is acquiring his first knowledge of TAT interpretation can learn much from it, and probably all clinical psychologists will be able to find in it some valuable additions to their present understanding.

J Proj Tech 20:456 D '56. *Mortimer M. Meyer.* * the author indicates his purposes and plans. I quote one because it is of universal importance and one which he achieves so well: "....to be able to formulate their practices and principles in ways sufficiently clear to permit both systematic investigation and a transmittal of these principles to their colleagues and students." Essentially his other purposes are to show in simple fashion how the Murray Thematic Apperception Test can be used to infer psychodynamics whether it be specifically for clinical purposes or for a variety of research. * In considering the criteria for selection of the pictures he recommends that "It further seems advisable to make the initial selection of pictures along the lines of basic interpersonal relations rather than primarily along the lines of selected emotions" or "situations." This recommendation is particularly important in planning the battery of tests where the examiner should consider the rationale for his choice of tests. Often, in the eyes of this reviewer, the Rorschach is over-extended to interpret attitudes towards object relationships instead of making use of a more pertinent approach such as the T.A.T. Although there is no attempt to plumb the depths, this book is an excellent presentation and because of the clarity of style and organization may appear deceptively simple to some readers. The book certainly can be highly recommended as a text for courses dealing with the use of the T.A.T.

[B205]

★HENRYSSON, STEN. **Applicability of Factor Analysis in the Behavioral Sciences: A Methodological Study.** Stockholm Studies in Educational Psychology, No. 1. Stockholm, Sweden: Almqvist & Wiksell, 1957. Pp. 156. Sw. kr. 15.00. * (*PA* 31:6916)

[B206]

*HERTZ, MARGUERITE R. **Frequency Tables for Scoring Responses to the Rorschach Inkblot Test, Third Edition.** Cleveland, Ohio: Western Reserve University Press, 1951. Pp. iv, 240. Paper, lithotyped. $4.00. * (*PA* 26:7001)

[B207]

★HESTON, JOSEPH C. **How to Take a Test.** Chicago, Ill.: Science Research Associates, 1953. Pp. i, 48. Paper. $0.40. * (*PA* 28:4944)

[B208]

★HESTON, JOSEPH C. **Learning About Tests.** Chicago, Ill.: Science Research Associates, 1955. Pp. 40. Paper. $0.50. *

[B209]

★HILDEN, ARNOLD H. **Manual for Q-Sort and Random Sets of Personal Concepts.** Webster Groves, Mo.: the Author (628 Clark Ave.), 1954. Pp. i, 20, plus 16 sheets. Paper, mimeographed. $3.00. *

[B210]

HOCH, PAUL H., AND ZUBIN, JOSEPH, EDITORS. **Relation of Psychological Tests to Psychiatry.** The Proceedings of the Fortieth Annual Meeting of the American Psychopathological Association, Held in New York City, June 1950. New York: Grune & Stratton, Inc., 1951. Pp. viii, 301. $5.50. *

Am J Psychiatry 109:876-7 My '53. B. H. McNeel. * the book can be divided into certain general problems, several of which run through almost all papers, and an assortment of specific investigations that are reported in the latter chapters of the book. The general problems are frequently implied rather than clearly stated but are pretty well shopworn, *e.g.,* the value and place of the clinical psychologist, the compara-

tive value of tests versus clinical experience. In spite of the staleness of the subject, some, but not all, of the discussion is fresh and stimulating. Intelligence tests, which are frequently belittled, have their champions and are shown to be at least valid and rather specific. Projective tests, which have been so glamorized, are seriously questioned as to validity and reliability, but are shown to be versatile and of great value as clinical stimuli. Rather marked differences of opinion are voiced regarding various tests, but the ones that were of particular interest to the reviewer were the high evaluation of the M.M.P.I. (by one author) and the low evaluation of the various tests for deterioration, including the Wechsler Bellevue scale. The only general conclusion that one can reach is that tests are only the tools of the clinician and that the real measuring instrument is the competent psychologist rather than the test. The inevitable comparison of the clinical interview versus psychological tests comes up again. In one paper, the clinical interview suffers by comparison chiefly because of the very inadequate type of interview rather than the superiority of the Rorschach method. One practical point, which comes out regarding the function of the clinical psychologist, is the opinion expressed by more than one author that a full day or more is necessary for adequate psychological evaluation of the patient. The practical and experimental papers in the latter part of the book, which include 2 papers on the conditioned reflex, are interesting and provocative. This book will be disappointing to the reader looking for technical information. It is concerned rather with an evaluation of psychological procedures, and more particularly of psychological tests.

Am J Psychol 66:517 Jl '53. Wayne H. Holtzman. * The main papers are loosely organized under four headings: (1) the historical bases for psychological tests, (2) the diagnostic use of tests, (3) the influence of exogenous factors on testing procedures, and (4) the influence of the "psyche" on test-performance. As one might expect from the heterogeneity of the intended audience and the wide variety of participants, the quality of the individual contributions varies considerably. Although there are several reports of original research which are worthy of note, the collection is too omnibus in nature to be of great value to most psychologists.

Psychiatric Q 26:695–6 O '52. * The content is interesting, in that it concerns the touchy problem of the entire relationship of clinical psychology to psychiatry. Outstanding men contribute to this volume, representing both disciplines, and the material is presented in a give-and-take manner that adds interest to consideration of the present problems of relationship between the professions. * The book brings one fairly up to date but adds nothing new regarding the role of the clinical psychologist in his professional relationship.

[B211]

★HOHNE, H. H. **Success and Failure in Scientific Faculties of the University of Melbourne.** Melbourne, Australia: Australian Council for Educational Research, 1955. Pp. vii, 129. Paper, mimeographed. * (*PA* 31:3787)

Brit J Ed Psychol 26:229–30 N '56. D. M. Lee. * covers the evaluation of entry qualifications and test scores for two successive intakes of students in the years 1943 and 1944, follow-up studies of these students during their courses, and subsequent evaluation of the original predictors against success in first-year and final examinations * the progress of each student was followed until his course was completed or abandoned, and this sometimes extended over a period of eleven years. An interesting attempt is made to evaluate entry qualifications by means of an "entrance score" based on academic competence as well as relevant standards of attainment. The initial battery of tests included verbal and non-verbal types and some personality assessments. * Hohne's work gives much food for thought to those who teach in universities and secondary schools, and to psychologists in general. Many of his findings concur with those made in R. R. Dale's book, *From School to University,* and of these many people are aware. This broad illustration of the complexity of university prediction adds greatly to the likelihood of a solution in measurable time.

[B212]

★HOLMQUIST, A. M., EDITOR. **Manual of Examinations, Second Edition.** Northfield, Minn.: St. Olaf College Press, 1950. Pp. iii, 41. Paper, mimeographed. $1.00. *

[B213]

★HOLSOPPLE, JAMES QUINTER, AND MIALE, FLORENCE R. **Sentence Completion: A Projective Method for the Study of Personality.** Springfield, Ill.: Charles C Thomas, 1954. Pp. xiii, 179. $5.50. * (Oxford, England: Blackwell Scientific Publications, Ltd.) (*PA* 29:4061)

Brit J Psychol 46:157 My '55. Boris Semeonoff. Subtitled "A Projective method for study of personality" this book presents a collection of 73 "openings," from which, it is claimed, the clinician may hope "to obtain material from which [to] draw valid inferences concerning unconscious and semiconscious desires, motives, conflicts and systems of personality organization." How this may be done is described almost exclusively by reference to illustrative records, which occupy about three-quarters of the book. Only one case, however, is interpreted at all fully; this subject's Rorschach record is appended, verbatim, but entirely without comment, except to call attention to "the clear consistency which may be found when sentence completion and Rorschach materials are compared." Lists of "characteristic completions" are provided, but again without comment, and there is no statement of rationale, no mention of any definable technique of interpretation other than intuitive empathy, nor any data relating to standardization or to validity, which is assumed. Only passing reference is made to earlier work (e.g. Tendler, Rhode) in the same field. The book is attractively produced, but 40s. seems rather much to pay for so fragmentary a presentation of what is not, after all, an original idea.

J Consult Psychol 19:154 Ap '55. Edward Joseph Shoben, Jr. This little book has many charms. First, it is packed with illustrative protocols of sentence completions by persons described in sufficiently relevant detail for the reader either to check his own interpretations, or to determine for himself whether or not the responses really have the flavor of genuine clinical utility. Second, it contains an extensive case interpretation that is a model of teaching by example. Third, the book is thoroughly free from both clinical jargon and extravagant claims. Holsopple and Miale overtly deny that the sentence completion method is a "test," constructed on the model of a yardstick or a clock, and argue that the task involved in using sentence completions is that of sensitive interpretation, not of scoring. This appropriate frankness leads them to emphasize the point that the clinician is actually part of the instrument in the sentence completion technique, as in virtually all projective devices. It leads them away from any attempt to quantify, beyond a voluminous listing of the most frequent completions to their particular stems. As a result, they implicitly raise the two central issues of what attributes characterize a competent clinician and to what extent clinical psychology may accept Thorndike's dictum about the measurability of all things. That Holsopple and Miale do not deal directly with these problems is hardly to their discredit. They have faced them in a context that is instructive, reflective of an intimate and sympathetic knowledge of the clinician's job, and fruitfully suggestive for all clinical psychologists who take their obligations seriously.

J Proj Tech 19:347–8 S '55. Leonard B. Olinger. * The authors have made a useful contribution to the needs of the student in publishing protocols on representative cases. A large number of the openings used in the protocols appear in the literature for the first time, and seem to offer especially good opportunities for subjects to reveal themselves in responding to these items which are of varying degrees of structure and cover a number of areas of personality functioning. The item-by-item analysis of the case presented in Chapter IV may be particularly helpful to students interested in learning how to use one interpretative method. Unfortunately, however, the book falls disappointingly short of its stated purposes. There is little in it that is likely to catch the fancy of the experimental or social psychologist, as the authors anticipate. Apart from the new items introduced, it is doubtful that the skilled and experienced clinical psychologist will find anything novel in the material and its treatment. The prudent caution against too-hasty interpretation which is made seems to be offset by frequently inadequate and occasionally unwarranted interpretations of the patient's test productions. The latter results in a situation such that an apparently appropriate response given by a subject is dismissed as "coincidence," seemingly because it is at odds with what is expected from a person with known pathology. One would feel that a word about ego-strengths inferred from such a response might be useful to the student. The kind of evaluation made in the sample case unwittingly gears the interpreter to look under the patient's bed for pathology with the damned-if-you-do and damned-if-you-don't philosophy imparted. In short, the reader is not furnished with reliable and trustworthy guideposts to help him to discriminate accurately between pathological and non-pathological responses. The absence of a bibliography which might place this book in relation to other re-

views and studies of the sentence completion test is regrettable, in that the authors thus seem to ignore the worthwhile contributions which a number of investigators have made. This, and the failure to provide more detailed data extracted from the 1,700 protocols reportedly collected in the development of the test items (including crucial normative information), seem to this reviewer to place further limitations on the value of the volume. So widely used and so potentially helpful an instrument as the sentence completion test would appear to merit more exhaustive treatment and a more rigorous approach than this book accords, and which the apparently considerable investigatory efforts of the authors held promise of yielding.

Psychosom Med 17:335 Jl–Ag '55. George A. Talland. Although purporting to form part of a series of psychological monographs, this small book cannot be read as anything but a parody aimed at those tender-minded souls who, possessing very little or no training in the discipline, none the less claim recognition as psychologists. Their claim is usually based precisely on the fact that, unfretted by formal training or concern about such considerations as objectivity of approach and validity and reliability of observations and findings, they can bring sympathy and intuition directly to their interpretation of personality. However, even those who are avowedly unwilling or unfit to make the modest efforts required for the practice of the more familiar projective techniques need some magic instrument. "The sharp and powerful tool" offered here is sentence completion, harmless enough and simple, and recommended by the authors for being a compromise between two other techniques, both of which are described with mild sarcasm in terms of their shortcomings only, without a suggestion that they possess any virtue. With nothing worth leaning upon, it is perhaps not unreasonable that the authors say: "Our group of incomplete sentences was developed through a most informal trial and error procedure. It was not systematically designed to conform with the structure of any established psychological theory, nor were criteria for construction, inclusion, exclusion, and modification of sentence openings firmly fixed in our minds." Indeed, they admit with disarming charm that "for many items, the only criterion of selection which can now be identified is that they seemed to be a good idea at the time, and we suspect that some of them remained in the series because we liked them." There are, of course, the many portentous statements based neither on empirical evidence nor, surprisingly enough, on partisan authority (the book does not contain a single reference, not even to the innumerable previous sentence completion tests), and also there are the insightful case studies. At times the jest gets out of hand, as for instance in the comment attached to a rather witty sentence completion taken from the record of a case presented on the true intuitionist grounds, for "it is hard to recapture the exact reason for our selection....it is neither dramatic nor wholly commonplace." With a gentle sense of humor the subject rounded off the stimulus, "To be a good liar one must....," with the single word "practice." Whereupon the Aunt Sally of a psychologist remarks with pious disapproval: "This is a dull, unimaginative response which fails to differentiate between lying and any other skill, playing the piano, for instance." Illustration of the technique occupies 161 of the 177 pages. Instead of summary there is a brief postscript which contains this gem of irony: "Valid interpretation of the sentence completion is easily demonstrable by sympathetic, emphatic, experienced clinicians with a minimum of technical training." There are more ways than one to combat the forces which, under the banner of projection, assault not only the use of scientific method (objectivity and the demand for validation) but also mere insistence on logic and meaning in psychology. Possibly this caricature may succeed where serious criticism has had no effect.

[B214]

★Hook, J. N. **How to Take Examinations in College.** College Outline Series, No. 106. New York: Barnes & Noble, Inc., 1958. Pp. viii, 180. Paper. $1.25. *

[B215]

★Horst, Paul. **A Technique for the Development of a Differential Prediction Battery.** American Psychological Association, Psychological Monographs: General and Applied, Vol. 68, No. 9, Whole No. 380. Washington, D.C.: the Association, Inc., 1954. Pp. 31. Paper. $1.00. * (*PA* 29:4924)

[B216]

★Horst, Paul. **Technique for the Development of a Multiple Absolute Prediction Battery.** American Psychological Association, Psychological Monogaphs: General and Applied, Vol. 69, No. 5, Whole No. 390. Washington, D.C.: the Association, Inc., 1955. Pp. 22. Paper. $1.00. *

[B217]

★Hotchkiss, Kenneth H. **Analyzing the Individual.** American Guidance Monographs, No. 13. Boston,

Mass.: Research Publishing Co., Inc., 1953. Pp. 27. paper, mimeographed. $1.00. *

[B218]

★Hunsicker, Paul A., and Montoye, Henry J. **Applied Tests and Measurements in Physical Education.** New York: Prentice-Hall, Inc., 1953. Pp. x, 149. Paper, lithotyped. Text edition, $2.50; trade edition, $3.35. (London: Bailey Bros. & Swinfen, Ltd., 1955. *27s.*)

[B219]

Husén, Torsten, and Henricson, Sven-Eric. **Some Principles of Construction of Group Intelligence Tests for Adults: A Report on the Construction and Standardization of the Swedish Induction Test (The I-Test).** Stockholm, Sweden: Almqvist & Wiksell, 1951. Pp. 100. Paper. 5 Sw. kr. * (*PA* 26:3134)

Q J Exp Psychol 4:90 My '52. A. D. H. When the first large scale trial of mental tests was undertaken in World War I, there was already considerable experience, some of it experimental and some clinical, awaiting wider application. There was also a theory of what mental tests were for, which, if modest by later standards, was fully adequate to the practice of the time. At the beginning of World War II there was no comparable reserve of unapplied knowledge; the theoretical structure had scarcely altered inessentials since 1914, and there seemed little prospect that psychologists could do more than demonstrate once again the value of tests in the somewhat crude classification of large populations. The interval between the wars had been mainly devoted to the standardization and refinement of methods, to controversy over technical detail, and to the seemingly endless attempt to keep one step ahead of those who were to take the tests. Moreover, it was becoming evident that mental testing had run into a period of diminishing returns. Each modification in the construction, administration or scoring of tests required a labour of computation and analysis steadily more disproportionate to the gain in predictive power. In these circumstances tribute must be paid to the work done by service psychologists, continuously under fire for leaving undone what they had never claimed to do or, alternatively, for doing what they had never done and never wished to do. Just how much work was involved in producing and standardizing tests for the Armed Forces has already been made clear by British and American publications. Dr. Husén and Hr. Henricson provide yet another careful record of the results in this field. The Swedish Induction Test (I-Test) was prepared in a new version in 1948. (Induction, it should be recalled, like Intelligence, has a different and more concrete significance in military affairs.) It was designed to supersede the Classification and Induction Test used in 1944-1947, and was based on two years' research during which 406 intercorrelations were computed, each of them by two different methods. Coefficients of reliability and validity (against officers' ratings) were found for each component of the test, and extensive factor analyses were carried out; finally, a new and presumably better test emerged. Dr. Husén and Hr. Henricson place great emphasis—too much for the reviewer's taste—on the "innards" of the test, its reliability and factorial structure, while they deal summarily with validation. The Spearman-Brown Prophecy formula and Spearman's correction for attenuation make an unwelcome appearance, and the surprising claim is made that "factor analysis liberated test construction, to a certain extent, from depending upon subjective estimates of various test types." Factor analysis, surely, is just as dependent on "subjective estimates" as any other method. Those factors which are identified with the greatest regularity are those which had been distinguished before factorial methods were used. Indeed it is difficult to see how any truly novel factor could be identified: it is usual, if a factor is found which will not fit into any of the traditional categories, to dismiss it as "psychologically meaningless." Apart from a few reservations of this kind, the book is a useful and mercifully direct guide to current practice in test construction. That it contains little of theoretical novelty is the fault of the times, not that of the authors.

[B220]

★INVITATIONAL CONFERENCE ON TESTING PROBLEMS. **Proceedings of the 1951 Invitational Conference on Testing Problems, November 3, 1951.** Henry S. Dyer, Chairman. Princeton, N.J.: Educational Testing Service, 1952. Pp. 119. Paper. $1.00. *

[B221]

★INVITATIONAL CONFERENCE ON TESTING PROBLEMS. **Proceedings of the 1952 Invitational Conference on Testing Problems, November 1, 1952.** George K. Bennett, Chairman. Princeton, N.J.: Educational Testing Service, 1953. Pp. 138. Paper. $1.00. *

[B222]

★INVITATIONAL CONFERENCE ON TESTING PROBLEMS. **Proceedings of the 1953 Invitational Conference on Testing Problems, October 31, 1953.** Walter N. Durost, Chairman. Princeton, N.J.: Educational Testing Service, 1954. Pp. xi, 179. Paper. $1.00. *

[B223]

★INVITATIONAL CONFERENCE ON TESTING PROBLEMS. **Proceedings of the 1954 Invitational Conference on Testing Problems, October 30, 1954.** Edward E. Cureton, Chairman. Princeton, N.J.: Educational Testing Service, 1955. Pp. 135. Paper. $1.00. *

[B224]

★INVITATIONAL CONFERENCE ON TESTING PROBLEMS. **Proceedings of the 1955 Invitational Conference on Testing Problems, October 29, 1955.** Ralph F. Berdie, Chairman. Princeton, N.J.: Educational Testing Service, 1956. Pp. 152. Paper. $1.00. *

[B225]

★INVITATIONAL CONFERENCE ON TESTING PROBLEMS. **Proceedings of the 1956 Invitational Conference on Testing Problems, November 3, 1956.** Irving Lorge, Chairman. Princeton, N.J.: Educational Testing Service, 1957. Pp. 125. Paper. $1.00. *

[B226]

★INVITATIONAL CONFERENCE ON TESTING PROBLEMS. **Proceedings of the 1957 Invitational Conference on Testing Problems, November 2, 1957.** Arthur E. Traxler, Chairman. Princeton, N.J.: Educational Testing Service, 1958. Pp. 127. Paper. $1.00. *

[B227]

★JACKSON, PATRICIA LEE. **Employee Testing for Retail Stores.** New York: Personnel Group, National Dry Goods Association, 1951. Pp. iv, 84. Paper, lithotyped. $3.00 to members; $10.00 to nonmembers. *

[B228]

★JAMES, W. S. **Practice and Coaching Exercises for Intelligence Tests.** Exeter, England: A. Wheaton & Co. Ltd., 1952. Pp. 16. 9d. * Key edition, 1s. 6d. *

[B229]

★JAMES, W. S. **Tests of Practical Ability: Space Tests.** Exeter, England: A. Wheaton & Co. Ltd., [1952]. Pp. 32. 1s. * Key, 2s. 6d.

[B230]

★JEFFERY, G. B., EDITOR. **External Examinations in Secondary Schools: Their Place and Function.** London: George G. Harrap & Co. Ltd., 1958. Pp. 128. 7s. 6d. *

[B231]

*JENNINGS, HELEN HALL. **Sociometry in Group Relations: A Manual for Teachers, Second Edition.** Washington, D.C.: American Council on Education, 1959. Pp. xi, 105. Paper. $1.50. * For reviews of the first edition, see 4:B217.

[B232]

★JENSEN, ARTHUR R. **Aggression in Fantasy and Overt Behavior.** American Psychological Association, Psychological Monographs: General and Applied, Vol. 71, No. 16, Whole No. 445. Washington, D.C.: the Association, Inc., 1957. Pp. 13. Paper. $1.00. *

[B233]

★JOHNSON, A. PEMBERTON; OLSEN, MARJORIE A.; AND WINTERBOTTOM, JOHN A. **The Law School Admission Test and Suggestions for Its Use: A Handbook for Law School Deans and Admission Officers.** Princeton, N.J.: Educational Testing Service, April 1955. Pp. 148. Paper, plastic binding, lithotyped. Gratis. * (PA 31:6677)

[B234]

★JOLLES, ISAAC. **A Catalogue for the Qualitative Interpretation of the H-T-P.** Beverly Hills, Calif.: Western Psychological Services, 1952. Pp. 97. Paper. $2.50. *

J Consult Psychol 16:476 D '52. *Laurance F. Shaffer.* This is a cookbook if there ever was one. The *Catalogue* consists of an alphabetical list of aspects of House-Person-Tree drawings with the psychological interpretation of each. A sample is: *"Clouds—Generalized anxiety referred to situation represented by whole with which drawn."* Such an inventory would be justified only if each item were accompanied by a reference to a research demonstrating the validity of the inference. No such studies are cited, nor do they exist for the greater part of the proposed interpretations. In its present form this *Catalogue* represents a real danger to scientific progress in clinical psychology.

J Proj Tech 17:365–6 S '53. *Wilson H. Guertin.* The title for the book seems to have been carefully chosen. It does not pretend to be more or less than a *catalogue* for *qualitative* interpretation. These two descriptive designations raise questions of a methodological nature which could carry us far outside the scope of this review. Like similar catalogues, this book sanctions to some extent the "sign approach." Jolles is clearly aware of deficiencies in such an approach and urges in heavy print, "....all of them (diagnostic hypotheses) must be interpreted in the light of all the factors in the test and in the case history and general clinical picture." The word "qualitative" seems to imply a lack of sufficient published studies demonstrating validity. Jolles clearly acknowledges this deficiency in the H-T-P technique by stating, "Actually, however, many of these interpretations are still in the hypothetical stage...." One quickly gets the feeling of intellectual integrity on the part of the author by reading his preface. The material he presents is taken from two published guides to interpretation (Richmond proceedings and original manual). Nothing much has been added, according to the author, but a reorganization and integration has been effected. Jolles has felt that a catalogue would be useful since, "Very early in the writer's experience with the H-T-P technique it was observed that considerable time was spent searching through the manual for the probable meaning of certain aspects of the drawings."

Thus, he would seem to desire to assist the neophyte in developing facility with this technique. Buck, the originator of the technique, recommends this book to the novitiate. Still Jolles expresses reluctance over putting such a catalogue in the hands of a beginner by stating, "One who is not well acquainted with the general, fundamental concepts of the qualitative interpretation of the H-T-P would find little value in this catalogue." Indeed, he proceeds to employ terminology that often is clear only to one who has read previous interpretation guides. After considering the catalogue itself, some conclusions as to its application can be made more readily. In general, the format of the catalogue is good. The size is such that it can be placed in a coat pocket and handled conveniently. The type and paper combine to make excellent readability. Ease in locating items is facilitated by the author's avoidance of excessive detail under each of them. The author's successful employment of phrases instead of cumbersome sentences is in the same vein. Large item headings with indented material play no small part in contributing to the ease of locating items. Occasionally the item heading is continued on the second line, which led to little confusion on the reviewer's part. Typographical errors are few, for the most part. The leaves of the book are printed on only one side even though each side is numbered, thus permitting the user to make his own supplementary entries or elaborations on catalogued items. To evaluate this catalogue on its own merits it would seem unfair to criticize the H-T-P technique in its present stage of development. Rather, it seemed desirable to see how valuable the catalogue would be in actual application. Through some limited contact with this technique and its proponents over a period of years this reviewer has attained sufficient technical knowledge to employ the catalogue. Two cases were selected from the reviewer's file, and the more significant features of each of these drawings listed. Reference to the catalogue should have then revealed directions for hypothesizing about each of these features. Without question the application of the catalogue was profitable in terms of indicating hypotheses or directions of thinking about the case, with fairly good interconsistency and agreement with the clinical material. Some of the features noted for these H-T-P's could not be found in the book. For example, the sig-

nificance of a porch or the types of leaves on
the tree did not seem to be indicated specifically.
However, these were only a few exceptions as
compared with the relatively good information
on the other features. It would appear that exceedingly rare features are not generally covered in this catalogue, but then, one would not
expect to find such a necessarily large number
of items covered by this guide. Nevertheless,
the reviewer was pleasantly surprised to find
listed some of the features that would seem to
be rare in occurrence. At this point it would
be well to mention the absence of a cross-
reference index. Perhaps the indoctrinated
H-T-P'er can apply the catalogue efficiently but
the rest of us will have to leaf through the section of the book on the house to find that what
we call a path is called a walkway in the catalogue. While a cross-reference index would not
appear essential to this reviewer, the value of
the catalogue to the beginner would have been
enhanced thereby. Having considered the catalogue for what it is, let us return to the original
question of whether it is for the beginning or
the advanced H-T-P'er. The book seems to employ too technical a vocabulary for the uninitiated and it might encourage excessive dependence upon signs. Further, since the system of
interpretation with its specific hypotheses is all
too tentative, many people may feel that, like
giving a loaded gun to a baby, prefatory cautions are not enough. This reviewer agrees
with the author that the book is not for independent beginners. New students of the technique, who have developed a mature approach
from working in the clinical field, will find the
book quite worthwhile. Advanced students will
find the material too brief and oversimplified
to encourage their use of the catalogue. Such
advanced H-T-P'ers, who are flexible in their
thinking about a case, probably already have the
essential material well digested and available
for intuitive clinical application. Probably the
greatest contribution of the catalogue will be
to the advanced clinician who is taking a serious interest in learning the technique. Such a
book should prove a great asset in H-T-P
workshops in the future.

[B235]

★JONES, EDWARD S., AND ORTNER, GLORIA K. **College
Credit by Examination: An Evaluation of the
University of Buffalo Program.** University of Buffalo Studies, Vol. 21, No. 3. Buffalo, N. Y.: the University, 1954. Pp. 119–201. Paper. $0.50. *

[B236]

★JONES, MARSHALL B. **The Pensacola Z Survey: A
Study in the Measurement of Authoritarian
Tendency.** American Psychological Association, Psy-
chological Monographs: General and Applied, Vol. 71,
No. 23, Whole No. 452. Washington, D.C.: the Asso-
ciation, Inc., 1958. Pp. 19. Paper. $1.00. *

[B237]

★JONSSON, CARL-OTTO. **Questionnaires and Interviews: Experimental Studies Concerning Concurrent Validity on Well-Motivated Subjects.**
Swedish Council for Personnel Administration Report
No. 12. Stockholm, Sweden: the Council, 1957. Pp
185. Paper. Sw. kr. 22.50. * (*PA* 32:375)

[B238]

★JORDAN, A. M. **Measurement in Education: An
Introduction.** New York: McGraw-Hill Book Co.,
Inc., 1953. Pp. xi, 533. $5.25. * (London: McGraw-Hill
Publishing Co., Ltd. 45s.) (*PA* 27:6154)

Calif J Ed Res 4:94 Mr '53. * presents....a
clear definition of the place of measuring instruments in the whole educative process in
terms of three major areas: the definition of
objectives, learning, and evaluation and appraisal * In addition to describing the usual
tests, the book calls attention to tests of fine
arts and music, mechanical and clerical attitudes,
and physical education. Recent advances in
measuring for understanding achievement, critical consideration of personality inventories, and
evaluation of tests by authorities in the *Third
Mental Measurements Yearbook* are covered. It
considers newer tests, and the adaptation of
social science concepts to measurement. The
book is well-written, well documented and illustrated. It should prove to be an excellent
source book for teachers, and prospective teachers.

Cath Ed R 51:643 N '53. *Mary A. Lanigan.*
This is a new and comprehensive introduction
to measurement in education. It is likely to be
popular with teachers, due to its clarity and
specific information. * College teachers will find
the questions at the end of each chapter real
helps in directing students' thinking. Internal
chapter organization lends itself well to ease in
study. This book is recommended not only as
a college text but also as a basic reference for
elementary and secondary teachers.

[B239]

★KAHN, SAMUEL. **Rorschach Resume: Rorschach
Ink Blot Personality Testing.** Ossining, N.Y.: Dy-
namic Psychological Society Press, 1956. Pp. vii, 63.
Paper. $1.50. * (*PA* 30:5988)

[B240]

*KAMAT, V. V. **Measuring Intelligence of Indian
Children, Second Edition.** Bombay, India: Oxford

University Press, 1951. Pp. xvi, 243. For latest edition, see 241.

Brit J Psychol 44:191 My '53. George Westby. * a clear account of a conscientious and intelligent adaptation by Dr Kamat of the Binet-Simon Tests and Stanford Revision for Indian use in the Kanarese and Marathi languages, originally published in 1940 without the two appendices on "Sex Differences among Indian children in the Binet-Simon Tests" and on "Heredity and Environment." Readers of this *Journal* may wish to know whether any striking conclusions on these two latter problems emerge: the answer is no. Sex differences are in favour of boys as against those found by Burt in favour of girls, but the difference is insignificant in populations of 638 boys and 436 girls. Heredity is a factor, environment is a factor, in the intelligence test performances of Indian children.

For reviews of the first edition, see 3:964.

[B241]

*KAMAT, V. V. **Measuring Intelligence of Indian Children, Third Edition.** Bombay, India: Oxford University Press, 1958. Pp. 284. 17s. 6d. For reviews of the earlier editions, see B240 and 3:964.

[B242]

★KATZ, MARTIN R. **Selecting an Achievement Test: Principles and Procedures.** Evaluation and Advisory Service Series No. 3. Princeton, N.J.: Educational Testing Service, 1958. Pp. 32. Paper. Gratis. *

[B243]

★KEATS, J. A. **A Statistical Theory of Objective Test Scores.** Melbourne, Australia: Australian Council for Educational Research, October 1951. Pp. viii, 48. Paper, mimeographed. 7s. 6d. * (*PA* 27:3882)

[B244]

★KENNEDY, E. G., EDITOR. **Problems in Individual Analysis (Emphasizing Standardized Tests and Measurements): Report of a Conference of Teachers, Counselors, Directors of Guidance, and School Administrators Held at Kansas State Teachers College, Pittsburg, Kansas, June 14–15, 1951.** Kansas State Teachers College Bulletin, Vol. 48, No. 7. Pittsburg, Kan.: the College, 1952. Pp. 86. Paper. Gratis. *

[B245]

★KING, JOSEPH E. **Selecting and Using Practical Personnel Tests.** California Personnel Management Association, Management Report No. 140. Berkeley, Calif.: the Association, 1952. Pp. 15. Paper, lithotyped. $1.00. *

[B246]

★KINGET, G. MARIAN. **The Drawing-Completion Test: A Projective Technique for the Investigation of Personality Based on the Wartegg Test Blank.** New York: Grune & Stratton, Inc., 1952. Pp. xv, 238. $7.50. * (*PA* 27:430) For reviews, see 130.

[B247]

★KLOPFER, BRUNO; AINSWORTH, MARY D.; KLOPFER, WALTER G.; AND HOLT, ROBERT R. **Developments in the Rorschach Technique: Vol. I, Technique and Theory.** Yonkers, N.Y.: World Book Co., 1954. Pp. x, 726. $6.50. * (London: George G. Harrap & Co. Ltd. 42s.) (*PA* 28:7533)

Austral J Psychol 7:197–8 D '55. J. G. Lyle. * This new manual differs from the old in a number of important respects. Firstly, there is more emphasis on the *enquiry,* though in the reviewer's opinion this is still not adequately amplified. The very considerable skill involved in Rorschach administration lies largely in the ability to conduct a sensitive and penetrating enquiry. One feels that this aspect has not received its due weighting. Secondly, there are minor differences in *scoring.* Changes have been made in the *Fm* category, the *M* and *FM* categories having thereby been affected. The basis of the *Fm* concept has now become "parts of humans, animals which are seen as frightening, threatening or evil; or abstract forces operating upon persons." This represents a more limited use of this category since it earlier comprised all expressive descriptions. * whilst *sinister* looks, a *frightening* mask, a *horrible* monster, are scored *Fm,* faces *scowling,* faces with *mournful* eyes, cat's face looking *mad,* are scored *M* or *FM.* Many Rorschach workers will be reluctant to make this fine distinction on the grounds that all of these examples represent projections of feelings. The failure to mention the connection of this type of response to paranoidal reactions (projections of guilt), and phobic reactions (projections of fear) is surprising. Many will also object to the over-frequent scoring of *M* and *FM* and will prefer to follow the stricter criteria of Beck and Rorschach. Thus, "fingers pointing," "women sleeping," "dogs standing proudly," "upper half of bullfrog croaking," "toads squatting," are all scored *M* or *FM.* "Carved figureheads with thrust-out chests" is scored as a *M* tendency. The third important difference is the greater emphasis and the elaboration of Form Rating Scale. The computation of ratings is very clearly explained, but little clarification is made of the use which can be made of them. The lack of norms limits their usefulness; but used as ratings of reality testing and in conjunction with intelligence tests, important statements about the patient's functioning level (as distinct from his capacity level) can obviously be made. The interpretative significance of the various categories is very well presented as unvalidated hypotheses. But the most important change in this text (exemplified in the Illustrative Case Study) is the low weighting given to percentages and ratios, and the high weighting given to a qualitative appraisal by means of *sequence analysis* and symbolic interpretation within a psychoanalytical framework. This Illustrative Case Study should be read by every Rorschach worker. (The advanced student may find two or three important points relating to sexual difficulties and family tensions which have been overlooked by the authors.) It should also be read by those who would try to test the validity of the Rorschach piecemeal by correlating the so-called "scores" with outside criteria. Problems of validation, and the formulations of such theorists as Allport, Lewin, Freud, Murray, Jung and Angyal are well covered in separate sections. The latter section could be profitably read by all students of psychology. In general, this book will remain a standard manual in Rorschach technique for many years to come. Those who are disappointed at the small number of illustrative examples of interpretation will eagerly await Volume II.

Brit J Psychol 46:72–3 F '55. Boris Semeonoff. * the present volume....is nearly twice the size of the familiar "Klopfer and Kelley" of 1942. This comparison not only indicates the immense amount of Rorschach research that has been carried out in these twelve years; it also reflects the increased care and clarity with which most of the basic concepts are set out, and the much fuller theoretical discussion now provided * Of probably greater value still is the series of explicitly stated "interpretative hypotheses" introduced at the outset of the discussion of each scoring category or relationship among factors. The effect, for the beginner, is to make the interpretative significance of the various types of response both clearer and more convincing; for the experienced Rorschach worker it affords an opportunity of re-examining the theoretical bases of the technique, which he might otherwise have been liable to take for granted. Certain changes in practice, foreshadowed in the 1946 *Supplement,* are now fully developed. Chief among these is the discarding of the $F+$ category in favour of "Form-level rating," a device which now assumes major importance, but which to the present reviewer has always appeared clumsy and irrational, especially when the ratings,

which are made on a scale which is discontinuous, are averaged. The whole question of quantification in Rorschach is one which still requires to be thrashed out; thus, percentages and "normal limits" are frequently quoted, but almost inevitably with the proviso that below a certain minimum (e.g. of total length of record) these findings cannot be applied, a safeguard which cannot but cast doubt on the validity of the relevant interpretation *within* the permitted limits. Other innovations in method include the introduction of "Sequence analysis," and of an "Analogy period" (between the Inquiry and the Testing-the-Limits procedure). The former is almost self-explanatory in its intention, and strikes one as a valuable tool but one difficult to apply without undue expenditure of time. The conduct and function of the latter are, unfortunately, poorly defined. Additional contents include a very fully reported case-study (nearly 80 pages), and a description of a "Prognostic Rating Scale" designed to predict a patient's response to psychotherapy. It is perhaps a pity that the new book could not have been so written as entirely to supersede the earlier work. Much of the exposition (particularly in the first chapter of all, on "Administration") is couched in language (not to say jargon) which presupposes familiarity with Rorschach concepts, and certain examples and other material previously cited are not repeated. That being so, one is tempted to look for redundancies, but in practically every case one cares to test the new is an improvement on the old. Consequently, the present work becomes one's vade-mecum, with Klopfer and Kelley retaining its place on the shelf, for reference.

J Ed Psychol 46:121–3 F '55. Lee J. Cronbach. No book has had more influence on American Rorschach technique—and therefore on clinical diagnostic practice—than the Klopfer-Kelley book of 1942. The present volume is a successor to it in part. A Volume II, on application, is promised. * We have first a handbook for administration and scoring. The didactic chapters are clear, with numerous well-chosen examples. There is a good brief chapter on report writing. Undoubtedly, these chapters fulfill their teaching function. A critic might differ from the authors in some scoring decisions, but in the absence of validation any system for scoring is arbitrary. This manual makes explicit how the Klopfer system is intended to be applied, but of course cannot provide evidence that this set of rules is superior to any alternative. Throughout the book, a second level is continually evident. These authors are speaking over the heads of students to their professional colleagues, arguing basic issues regarding the Rorschach test. This is especially notable in chapters on interpretation of scores, ratios, sequence, content, and so on. * Holt's chapter on personality theories covers briefly the writings of Allport, Rapaport, Angyal, and others, discussing how their theories relate to Rorschach interpretation. Holt succeeds in demonstrating that personality theory makes little contact with Rorschach theory, and the reasons he offers for this are plausible. It was perhaps unwise for him to omit general behavior or perceptual theory, including the works of Miller, Postman, and many others; the relatively mundane and observable constructs of experimental psychology are currently providing an astringent flavor in personality research which Holt's chapter lacks. But this chapter is undoubtedly a fair assessment of the extent to which Rorschach elaborations lack grounding in explicit and logical theory. Klopfer seeks to provide theoretical roots by relating Rorschach method to a Jungian ego psychology. The constructs of this chapter float unanchored, far out of reach of any potentially damaging rocks of observable fact. When the authors take up interpretation and validation, they show a healthy awareness of the criticism heaped on the head of the Rorschacher. Interpretations are no longer advanced as unquestionable truth; instead, each major statement about behavioral correlates of Rorschach scores is labelled a "hypothesis." The authors give serious thought to the negative evidence on such matters as the M-creativity relation, and color shock. Moreover, care has gone into the wording of the hypotheses to reduce ambiguity. The favorable impression is extended by the theoretical aspects of Ainsworth's chapter on validation. As an essay on problems of Rorschach validation, it is magnificent. The point of view is inclusive and informed; no previous writing has shown such penetration into the great scientific dilemmas posed by Rorschach hypotheses. The book's presentations regarding the evidence for Rorschach interpretations are completely unsatisfactory. Nowhere is the paramount question of validity faced head-on. Ainsworth, in treat-

ing methods of validation, brings in numerous examples, but she does not provide a systematic review of findings. Her oblique examination of validity leads her to express conclusions regarding validity *en passant*. These casual statements are not an adequate way to deal with the necessary critical questions. Moreover, the chapter gives some impression of special pleading. Studies which have advanced negative evidence are thoroughly criticized. These criticisms are just, and do explain away the evidence in these instances. But Ainsworth cites positive results without comparable criticism, and does not cite studies yielding negative evidence based on sound procedures and logic. The other place where the authors take a position on validity is the chapter on interpretation. Here, a "hypothesis" is usually stated with no accompanying evidence. Only fourteen studies are cited in the entire chapter on quantitative determiners. Usually no comment is made as to the degree of support available for an "hypothesis." While the authors are in general careful to word their claims regarding validity modestly, the failure to provide a frank and explicit statement about the presumed validity of each proposed interpretation is most unfortunate. The authors recognize that negative evidence should be taken seriously, and that it may often be used as a guide in modifying or sharpening a hypothesis. This is true. But the trouble is that neither Ainsworth nor her colleagues considers for a moment abandoning a hypothesis. In twelve years, no element of Klopfer's system has been eliminated. If a study proves that some score does not measure what was claimed for it, the score is retained, and the interpretation is rephrased so that the negative data no longer apply. No one goes to the trouble of testing the modified hypothesis before announcing it. To respond to negative evidence by bringing forth new hypotheses which people are expected to use daily in clinical practice, and for which there is no weight of public evidence, is inexcusable. While a systematic review of evidence would be required to form a solid judgment, it is the reviewer's impression that a large number of the Rorschach hypotheses are speculative or definitely wrong. This book, by failing to support its hypotheses, strengthens that belief. It would accord well with scientific ethics to abandon the Rorschach test, save in research studies, until such time as the true and the false hypotheses are much better distinguished. It is pleasant to see in such books as these the dawn of a scientific conscience in Rorschach writing. The book as a whole cannot be regarded as a realistic appraisal of the Rorschach, however useful it may be as a *vade mecum* for acolytes.

J Consult Psychol 18:230 Je '54. Edward Joseph Shoben, Jr. * Probably the great majority of clinical psychologists will find something of interest and value here, a situation which attests at once to the book's comprehensiveness and to the depths to which the Rorschach has penetrated the clinical culture. * In its role of manual, *Technique and Theory* represents a considerable advance over the older Klopfer, and Kelley. * This part of the book is informative, teachable, and most welcome. The three chapters comprising the "theoretical monograph" are stimulating, if a bit uneven. Holt's chapter on the implications of contemporary personality theories for a Rorschach rationale is exceptionally able and constitutes the most serious and sophisticated effort to date to relate the test to broad and potentially testable issues in theoretical psychology. One senses a degree of defensiveness in Dr. Ainsworth's discussion of validation problems, but she has done a fair, intelligent, and thorough evaluation of the voluminous literature, and her chapter will be invaluable as a source of information. Bruno Klopfer's concern with Rorschach hypotheses and ego psychology is essentially speculative and given to too certain interpretative assertions. ("The earliest communicated response to shading shows a mixture of *cF* and *Fc*. This represents a considerably differentiated need for affection and belongingness" p. 590.) But read with an eye both to clinically useful insights and to the formation of hypotheses about Rorschach and about personality functioning, this vigorous chapter is challenging and evocative. There can be no gainsaying the importance of the book at this particular stage of clinical psychology's development. The judgment of history will depend on the quality and outcome of the research that it should stimulate.

J Proj Tech 18:256–8 Je '54. Albert Ellis. * Klopfer's *The Rorschach Technique*, originally issued in 1942....was a remarkable book. With a directness, compactness, and lucidity rare among psychological texts, it covered the history, administration, scoring, and interpretation of the Rorschach method so adequately

that many Rorschachists have not only used it for a bible during the last decade but have found it to be virtually a self-sufficient text. * *Developments in the Rorschach Technique,* which is the successor....to the old Klopfer and Kelley manual, is an even more remarkable work than its remarkable predecessor. It is an excellent job. Part One....is concerned with administration and scoring. * A new content category, AH, representing figures that are part human and part animal, is employed. Otherwise, the original Klopfer contributions to Rorschach scoring are left pretty much intact. Whether many oldtime Rorschachists will choose to accept the new form-level ratings, which are far more precise than the F+ and F− ratings widely used by Beck and others but which are also far more cumbersome to ascertain, is questionable. For research purposes, however, they would appear to have a real usefulness. And the concepts behind form-level ratings should furnish some useful insights to many busy clinicians who may not actually employ such ratings in a rigorous manner. One may always quibble with a scoring system, and certainly that of Dr. Klopfer and his associates is not perfect. Its pertinence and practicality are, as they have always been, noteworthy. Its most vulnerable point is still, perhaps, its rather rigid concepts of popular responses: which in this edition are still rigorously restricted to the same ten as before, and for which no particular statistical supporting evidence is given. Part Two....is devoted to interpretation. * An unusual contribution to the chapters on interpretation is the presentation of the analyses in the form of hypotheses rather than statements of dogma. It may unfortunately be predicted that many of the users of this text will, after awhile, quite neglect the hypothetical forms in which the interpretations are consistently stated and come to view them as indubitable statements of fact. The authors themselves tend to do this from time to time, as when they remark, on page 578, that "the hypothesis that FM indicates impulses for immediate need gratification makes it clear that FM is closely associated with the handling of 'stress tolerance.' " A hypothesis, of course, can hardly make anything clear until it is firmly factually validated; and, as yet, the hypothesis that FM indicates impulses for immediate need gratification is hardly in this class. In spite of such lapses as this, the attempt of Dr. Klopfer and his associates to lean over backwards to state their interpretative hypotheses as hypotheses rather than facts is a most healthy sign, and is an immense improvement on many of the more dogmatic formulations of the original text. Part Three, on theory, is an especially worthwhile section * Robert R. Holt's chapter, "Implications of Some Contemporary Personality Theories for Rorschach Rationale," is easily the best discussion on this topic which has ever appeared in the literature and should be required reading for all clinical psychologists. Bruno Klopfer's chapter on Rorschach hypotheses and ego psychology adds to the usual Freudian interpretative frame of reference for the Rorschach some highly provocative Jungian modifications of ego psychology. The present reviewer, who heartily agrees with Dr. Holt that much Rorschach interpretative terminology lacks any clear and unambiguous referent in clinical observation, and who has for many years been biased against the thoroughly muddled ego-superego-id terminology of the Freudians, can see only still greater psychological confusion resulting from the addition of the Jungian Self, which is said to be less conscious and less differentiated than the ego. A more operational statement of all the Rorschach hypotheses included in this work, and especially those in Dr. Klopfer's chapter on the Rorschach and ego psychology, might well help clarify considerable semantic-personological confusion. The final part....consists of a chapter on the principles of report writing by Walter Klopfer which is exceptionally incisive and important; a beautifully illustrated case study by Mary Ainsworth; and a potentially useful Rorschach prognostic rating scale devised and exposited by Bruno Klopfer. This final section will be particularly helpful for Rorschach beginners. All told, this new Rorschach manual is an essentially conservative document that keeps the original Klopfer system of scoring and interpretation fairly intact, but makes some interesting and important additions to it. If anything, it remains a little too diehard and never, except in Dr. Holt's chapter, faces squarely up to the problem of clinical validation although it seriously considers this problem at many points. What it does do is present in an unusually well-organized well-delineated, and well-printed manner, the Rorschach-Klopfer system that has always had, and definitely still has, few peers and no superi-

ors. Volume I on *Technique and Theory* may not be the best Rorschach manual that will ever be written, but it will probably be a long time before it is superseded by a better one—except, perhaps, by a later revision of itself. If ever there was a *must* for the personal library of every Rorschacher, this certainly is it.

Psychol B 52:360–1 Jl '55. George W. Albee. There is something for everyone in this....volume. * The sections on administration and scoring are written clearly and numerous examples are provided to clarify scoring problems. * The sections on interpretation are well written and will stir little controversy among experienced users of the technique. Some readers are certain, however, to criticize the failure of the authors to support their statements with data in the literature. The authors, anticipating this objection, present their interpretations as "hypotheses" and indicate that the usefulness of these hypotheses has been established in clinical practice and that they may be used "pending the conclusion of the extensive investigations that will be necessary to evaluate their relative validity." Apparently existing validation studies do not fit their criteria. Certainly clinical use has resulted in few changes in interpretation. The authors also indicate, wisely, that "the integration of the findings into some sort of meaningful dynamic picture depends largely upon the examiner's basic understanding of human personality." Again, there is much in the literature which could be used to document this hypothesis. The section on validation problems makes a case for the point of view that "there is no sharp dividing line between validation research and the clinical use of the Rorschach technique....indeed, the technique itself is continually changing through the validation process." A test of this latter hypothesis through a comparison of scoring and interpretation procedures by the same authors over the years, and by an examination of possible gradual rapprochement between different schools, would possibly raise some doubts here. The section on validation concludes with the statement that "validation research should be planned and the results discussed by those who have more than a superficial understanding of the basic concepts involved in Rorschach interpretative hypothesis...." Few will disagree, though the statement leaves a nice opening for a rejoinder by the statisticians! To single out these statements does not give an accurate picture of the generally excellent discussion of the problems of validation and of existing approaches to these problems. Also included is a brief, though stimulating chapter on implications of contemporary personality theories, a somewhat more esoteric chapter on ego psychology, a long case study, and a Rorschach Prognostic Rating Scale (experimental) designed to predict a patient's response to psychotherapy. This latter *may* be just what Eysenck has been looking for, though again it may not. It would be interesting to hear him discuss it with the authors at a symposium. * There is little doubt that the present work will find a wide audience and deservingly so.

[B248]

★Klopfer, Bruno; with contributions by Mary D. Ainsworth, Dorothy V. Anderson, Gertrude Baker, Hedda Bolgar, Jack Fox, A. Irving Hallowell, Eileen Higham, Samuel Kellman, Walter G. Klopfer, Gertrude Meili-Dworetzki, Edwin S. Shneidman, Robert F. Snowden, Marvin Spiegelman, Marie D. Stein, Evelyn Troup, and Gertha Williams. **Developments in Rorschach Technique: Vol. II, Fields of Application.** Yonkers, N.Y.: World Book Co., 1956. Pp. xx, 828. $6.50. (London: George G. Harrap & Co. Ltd. 50s.) * (PA 30: 7202)

Brit J Med Psychol 30:122–3 Je '57. Theodora Alcock. * an excellent classified bibliography and index. The genetic section....contains a scholarly chapter by G. Meili Dworetzki on the development of visual perception in childhood, reflecting the influence of Piaget, but specifically related to the developmental processes evidenced in Rorschach records of young children. Another chapter relating clinical material produced in the test and in psychotherapy shows close correspondence in this way, but is less satisfying in its failure to recognize unconscious dynamics involved in both situations, especially those relating to transference phenomena. However, relationships between the latent and manifest content of a Rorschach record, with the apparent mechanisms of ego affect and ego defence, are well described by Bruno Klopfer and Marvin Spiegelman in that part of the book concerned with the differential diagnosis of adult patients. Dr Klopfer's case studies, especially the third, are illuminating, though even here one could wish that space had allowed him to demonstrate his great skill more adequately. Two long chapters by Gertrude Baker, devoted to diagnosis and case studies of patients with organic brain damage, make a valuably significant contribution to the lit-

erature on this subject. In the social psychology section there is an admirably clear and thorough description by Irving Hallowell of personality and culture studies, and by others some interesting notes on the potential use of the Rorschach technique in the field of industry. To summarize, Dr Bruno Klopfer has "done it again" by producing a book which all serious users of the Rorschach method should study with profit. Some more factual evidence of norms, as of frequencies in diagnostic syndromes, would have been welcome, but perhaps one may look forward to the inclusion of these in Volume III.

Brit J Psychol 48:150–1 My '57. B. Semeonoff. Because of the high level of one's expectation, it was perhaps almost inevitable that vol. II of "the new Klopfer" should prove something of a disappointment. Unlike its predecessor....the present volume follows very closely the current fashion for publication in symposium form. Consequently, while there is a quite remarkable unity of theoretical orientation, the diversity of treatment is at times disconcerting, particularly in the case of contributions which bear signs, as some do, of having been prepared for use in some other context. Further, not all the contributing authors write equally well, and the reader who is sensitive to language may find himself wincing from time to time. In his Foreword, Bruno Klopfer concedes the point regarding diversity; he also admits that he and his co-authors are "just beginning to pile up convincing evidence for the statements made." Edwin Shneidman, again, in his chapter "Some relationships between the Rorschach technique and other psychodiagnostic tests," opens with the remark that "the exact relationships among psychological tests are almost entirely a matter for future research." The cynic will no doubt say that the truth of both statements is all too evident, and suggest that the present publication might well have been postponed. If one looks to the book for "all the answers" one may be tempted to agree with our hypothetical critic. Nevertheless, its four parts, each devoted to a broadly defined "field of application"....contain much that is of value, not only in terms of Rorschach practice, but also in relation to the general study of personality in its varying aspects. Particularly interesting, from both points of view, are Gertrude Baker's chapters on "Diagnosis of organic brain damage in the adult," and Gertrude Meili-Dworetzki's on "The development of perception in the Rorschach." This latter is essentially a research report with normative data, which, while simply presented and conservatively interpreted, are adequate and convincing. A third disclaimer, amounting almost to a main theme of the book, is summarized (by Hedda Bolgar) in the concluding sentence of the last chapter: "....we do not know too clearly what the boundaries are between the stimulus effect of the test material and the stimulus effect of the examiner...." This recogntion of the test situation as a social or even therapeutic relationship represents a considerable advance in projective practice, and forestalls a good deal of criticism impugning dubious reliability and validity. In this connexion the reader is referred to Shneidman's chapter, already mentioned. Contrary to beliefs entertained in some quarters, Rorschach practice does seem to be moving in the direction of behavioural analysis and away from arbitrary systems of interpretation from "signs." *

Cont Psychol 2:253–5 O '57. Samuel J. Beck. The volume here under review is the second of two which continue the exposition of an orientation first published as The Rorschach Technique, by Klopfer and Kelley, in 1942. Their "technique" has imposed extensive and radical changes on the test as Rorschach published it in his Psychodiagnostik (in 1921; all references to his monograph, in this review, will be to the 1932 German edition), and as it is being used, with a few modifications, by those trained in his principles. Depending on which procedure is used, significant consequences follow as to the validity of the findings. Also, a confusion of these two methods which differ fundamentally—a difference screened by (a) their common use of Rorschach's original ten inkblot stimuli and (b) their general similarity in "scoring" notations—has in many circles put the test in a false perspective. The present book with its companion Volume I are explicit in formulating the basis on which the technique rests. This review provides, therefore, the opportunity to clear up the distinction and confusions between the technique and the test. The book, let it be said at once, is invaluable for the many psychologists whose Rorschach foundations are set in the technique. It ranges over a broad area, including fields in which much has been written but which have not hitherto been synoptically surveyed. It ex-

emplifies practice and expounds theory. It does all this consistently with the central thesis of the volume as high lighted in the title—the Rorschach technique. What then is the technique? A nuclear point of departure in its procedure is—form level. In establishing form level, the examiner follows certain steps. First, he judges the "fit or match of concept to blot area" (I, p. 207). In this way he decides on the "accuracy" of the "concept" (i.e., of the association). Each examiner decides, further, whether "the concept would refer to a class of objects that have a certain specified shape as a common feature." The second step is called "specifications," and the examiner decides whether these are "constructive" or "irrelevant" (I, pp. 211 ff.). The third is the organizing of parts of the blot (I, pp. 218 f.) into larger meaningful wholes (concerning which, more presently). Having made these judgments—and every examiner does so as he sees the fit or match—he then assigns certain numerical credits to his evaluations (I, pp. 219–223). Or he subtracts credits, when, e.g., "specifications weaken the form level" (I, p. 216). The algebraic sum of these values as thus decided upon is the patient's form level. The psychologist then comes out with a number. And numbers are science! In casting out normative data, statistically derived, the authors have the courage of their convictions. They explicitly reject statistics. "A number of Rorschach researchers hold the view that many dimensions of the Rorschach are to be defined by statistical means. * We do not hold this view," (II, p. 4). Rather, "all dimensions of the Rorschach have attached to them a conceptually defined meaning." This position is restated with reference to the selected details of the blot stimuli. They are "the result of the phenomenological analysis of the blot properties....and are, therefore, conceptually defined dimensions rather than statistically defined categories" (II, p. 5) and "the dimension of the usual details is not primarily defined by the frequency of its occurrence....On the other hand, unusual detail is defined as an arbitrary, idiosyncratic subdivision of the card, without regard to the card's natural organization. Again, there is no reference to the statistics of its occurrence; the definition is conceptual" (italics as in the text). In the pages following the authors reaffirm the principle with regard to form level, and also in discussing the Popular and the Original associations: "The examiner can solve this problem by relying on his apperceptive mass. While this seems very subjective, it is also very practical" (II, p. 9). Form level in the technique apparently replaces Rorschach's $F+$, $F-$ concept. Concerning $F+$, Rorschach's language is: "In order to exclude subjective judgments as far as possible, we could proceed only by statistical method" (*Psychodiagnostik*, p. 23). He was well aware of the difficulties in establishing a normative set of $F+$ responses; and he did not deceive himself concerning the play he must allow for subjective judgment. Similarly, what is a major detail can be established "by statistical method, somewhat like the good forms" (p. 41). Although Rorschach found this "unnecessary," since experience early identifies them, still there are "certain smaller details which, on basis of statistical frequency, must be classed as normal details." His "original" response is one which "in about 100 experiments in normals appears *once*" (p. 54; Rorschach's italics). His Popular percept (*Vulgär*) is one given "by approximately every third normal person" (p. 196). In this context, too—the most detailed interpretation of a test record which he has left us—he is even more emphatic about "the plus sign....The decision as to the quality of the form perceived, may not and must not (*soll und darf aber nicht*) be made on subjective opinion (*Schätzung*) but from statistical frequency." Rorschach himself is thus one Rorschach researcher who held that many dimensions of the Rorschach test are to be defined statistically. Also here are at least three kinds of Rorschach data —form perception, selected detail, originality— for which the boundaries can be established by the basic procedure of counting. We can thus have empirical data in the test. What each kind of datum means generally is a problem for general and experimental psychology and must be established by nomothetic method. What the interactions between these data in any one record mean in portraying a unit individual, in his surface behavior and in depth, belongs to the field of idiographic statistics. The two kinds of attack are indispensable in a problem of organized complexity (Warren Weaver's term) such as is the human personality, and no idiographic procedure can be better than the nomothetically derived norms on which it rests. Rorschach's statistical thinking was perhaps naïve (yet possibly not for 1921?). What is

important is that he created a new, experimental universe, free of conventional binding, one made up of objective stimuli and yielding data that can be manipulated statistically. $F+$, e.g., tells, in the language of this universe, whether the patient's accuracy or reality perception agrees with that empirically found in the normative group. Insofar as the Rorschach data can be translated into general psychological, or even conventional language, and validated by tests other than the Rorschach, we have the psychologist's bridgehead into that as yet uncharted land: the scientific study of the whole human personality. To acquaint himself with the rationale of the technique's appeal to phenomenology, the reader will be well advised in reading Chapter 9, especially pp. 275–280. Here is the heart of the technique's premised position—one which it is of course entirely free to elect. But, having so elected, the technique is bound by the rules which these premises and their related principles set up. Nevertheless findings by the technique are being constantly treated as though they were behavioral. Chapter 9 makes reference to Snygg and Combs and to Husserl. Snygg has, however, written another paper to which the authors do not refer, one in which he acutely points out the fallacy of crossing over from the phenomenological to the behavioral disciplines, or going in the contrary direction. Now most American psychologists have been trained in behavioral principles. What happens, therefore, when they use the technique is that they practice phenomenology and statisticize behavioristically. Hence the confusion about Rorschach "results" that are out of focus from the point of view of both the test and the technique, and with inconsistencies and discrepancies that have driven some other psychologists to tear their hair—Dollard, for instance, as well as Zubin. They need not, however. This pain is suffered mainly in vain. It is unnecessary, if (*a*) the logical error in crossing of disciplines is avoided and (*b*) statistical method, appropriate to the unit personality, is applied. With regard to logical fallacies, we must note that the form-level concept begs the question in all its procedures, especially in including among its criteria the organizing of details into larger meaningful wholes. The concept of organization is a sound one, but organizations of any quality can be found with any quality of form perception. I can cite examples endlessly. Here is an arbitrary mixing up of psychological variables. The technique errs on more than one count with respect to M, the movement response, that most original and exciting of Rorschach's discoveries. Rorschach saw it as an instrument penetrating deep into the unconscious, evoking dream material out of our waking patient. He devotes many pages of his monograph to a laborious validation of his M-concept on the basis of sound clinical logic. How compulsively deep this validation was I myself learned only when I watched Oberholzer (Rorschach's closest co-worker) in Zurich. In fact *every* test scoring was for Oberholzer a hard-won datum, confirmed by reference to the clinical data of his psychoanalytic practice. The authors of the technique write: "Movement responses include those where the subject has read into the static ink blots some kind of action, movement, expression, posture, or life" (I, p. 100). They beg the question in this definition. The examples which they include would, on the basis of Rorschach's interpretive principles, tell that the respective patients had, either in fantasy or in dream, experienced being, for example, a croaking bullfrog, a spinning top, a billowing cloud, a crawling spider, or a stream of water. By the technique's definition of movement, and from a study of its samples, the presence of a verb or a verb-form in the association is a dictate for scoring some nuance of M (M, FM, or m). This rule substitutes a grammatical criterion for a psychological one. It looks like a nice example of Von Doramus' paralogic (identity of predicate): all movement responses have verbs in them; this response has a verb in it; this response is movement. The contributions of four authors (there are sixteen besides Klopfer) stand out. They include the sections of Meili-Dworetzki on perception and some experimental problems incident to what goes on in associating to the Rorschach inkblots and Baker's excellent expository chapter on the test in patients with brain pathology. Best of all, by this reviewer's lights, is Hallowell on anthropological research. It gives one a lift as a scholarly achievement, broad in coverage, balanced in judgment, bespeaking a Socratic devotion to intellectual integrity. Bolgar discusses theory incident to objective method in handling the data of the "private world" (her term) as evoked by projective tests. Her survey omits some important discussions, both American and European (less excusable in a polylingual student like Bolgar). The bibliography, by Marie D. Stein, is the best I have seen anywhere (although there is an omission here, Verschuer on the test in twins), and it will be a valuable reference source for many years. There are other omissions. Baker makes no bibliographic reference to Oberholzer's basic paper and none at all to Rorschach himself. In fact, the only times Rorschach's name appears in any chapter bibliography is in Hallowell's chapter and in the chapter by Williams and Kellman (Industrial Psychology). Are writers on the Rorschach technique not reading Rorschach any more? For clinical groupings, only the young child, the brain-damaged, and the aged are exemplified in full test records. The clinical investigator will miss samples from the neuroses, the schizophrenias, and the depressions. Sporadically throughout the book, there are numerous high spots, sound diagnostic reasonings, good clinical logic, excellent ideas for experiment, but too frequently the interpretations seem not to be warranted by the Rorschach test-data, and at times they are extravagant. They often have the flavor of being rationalizations of clinical information, superimposed on the data of the technique. So used, the material is neither test nor technique, but self-deception. Surprising too are some pontifications concerning the "blind" diagnosis (II, pp. 215–216). Here is an obfuscation of an issue and it takes Hallowell (II, pp. 512–516) to bring it into accurate focus and help dissipate the clouding. The point at issue here is the same as the central one in this review: whether the Rorschach test can be a test in the strict sense of the word—an experiment with operations that are public and repeatable, whether it can follow the rules we learn in our first courses in undergraduate psychology. Rorschach put his own self-anchoring into the words: "Every test starts by being an experiment." So this reviewer believes that every administration of the ten inkblot stimuli is a laboratory experiment, one to be validated by agreement with the life's data for the person tested, and by its potential for predicting the course he will take.

J Proj Tech 22:248–50 Je '58. Bernard I. Murstein. * a well coordinated combination of experimental and empirical data relating to the use of the Rorschach * if it were only for the bibliography itself, the book would be invaluable for the Rorschach researcher. In addition to individual bibliographies for each chapter, Marie Stein has compiled an alphabetical bibliography of 786 items relating to the Rorschach up to the year 1945. A valuable classified bibliography covering 1945–1955 includes 1899 entries. Further, Ainsworth's indexes for Volumes I and II seem quite thorough. In addition to the many good qualities of the book, however, there are rather serious drawbacks. The very homogeneity of the contributors' viewpoints gives the book a narrow theoretical and methodological range, though the content coverage is broad. The gods of "statistics" and "quantity" are brutally waylaid as seducers of the "qualitative approach." Scarcely an author refrains from dipping his lance in the blood of the "witch of multiple signs" while strange to say, genuflecting to her cousin, the fair damsel of "configuration." Many of the authors do not grasp the utility of statistical application to the Rorschach technique. * The assumptions made throughout the book are often not based on empirical findings. * The psychoanalytic frame of reference of some of the authors often lead to paper-thin, airy assumptions. * It is regrettable that....so little space is devoted to a coverage of projective theory. * In an earlier review, Beck has brought Klopfer to task for his deviation in the use of the Rorschach from the procedure used by its founder, Herman Rorschach. This criticism is unjustified. We should no more criticize Klopfer for improving on Rorschach than we might object to the innovations of missileman Von Braun on the aerodynamic concepts of the Wright brothers. Time brings into play ever new and more valuable insights. Klopfer's addition, among other contributions, of the determinants *FM* and *m* are welcome extensions to the conceptual armamentarium of the clinical psychologist. One can recommend the reading of this book to the graduate student for the valuable clinical observations and descriptive case analyses. Only, let the student steer clear of the book's philosophy with its anti-quantitative edicts and anti-statistical accents. Such ukases appear to the reviewer as antediluvian.

[B249]
★KNOBLOCH, HILDA, AND PASAMANICK, BENJAMIN. **A Developmental Questionnaire for Infants Forty Weeks of Age: An Evaluation.** Monographs of the Society for Research in Child Development, Vol. 20, No. 2, Serial No. 61. Lafayette, Ind.: Child Develop-

ment Publications, Inc., 1956. Pp. 112. Paper. $2.50. * (*PA* 31:673)

[B250]
★KNUTSON, ANDIE L. **Personal Security as Related to Station in Life.** American Psychological Association, Psychological Monographs: General and Applied, Vol. 66, No. 4, Whole No. 336. Washington, D.C.: the Association, Inc., 1952. Pp. iii, 31. Paper. $1.00. * (*PA* 27:4261)

[B251]
★KOCH, CHARLES. **The Tree Test: The Tree-Drawing Test as an Aid in Psychodiagnosis.** Berne, Switzerland: Hans Huber, 1952. Pp. 87. (New York: Grune & Stratton, Inc., 1952. $4.50.) * (*PA* 27:3137)

J Ed Psychol 45:186–7 Mr '54. *Goldine C. Gleser.* In this book are presented the interpretations which the author has found applicable to elements of the form, location, and graphological features of drawings of trees, used as a projective technique. For this purpose the subject is requested "to draw a fruit tree." The author further suggests that the subject draw additional trees "if one has the impression that the first drawing obtained does not correspond with the person tested or that the drawing differentiates too little." He claims that such successive productions tap different layers of the psyche. The introduction, which comprises the first half of the book, consists of a lyrical and imaginative treatise on the symbolism of the tree followed by several illustrative analyses of test subjects. With regard to the validity of his interpretations the author states only that they have been proved correct "(1) by the nature of the recorded expression, (2) by comparative investigations, by direct observations, by testing and by judgements of independent persons." The test has been employed mainly in the vocational guidance of adolescents and adults, and the author points out with proper caution that additional samples would be needed to extend the interpretation of tree drawings to special groups such as the mentally deficient or the mentally ill. He also suggests that the test be used in conjunction with other tests for diagnosis and counseling so that the findings may check and augment each other. It is unfortunate that the author does not see fit to extend the same cautious and critical attitude toward the interpretations themselves. The only objective data contained in the book are tables presenting the developmental trends for various tree-drawing characteristics in the age range from five to sixteen years, and a comparison between two groups of the same age but different mental endowment. Unfortunately, all statistics are presented as percentages with no indication of the sizes of the samples studied. The second half of the book contains clear and detailed illustrations of possible variations in the drawings of root, trunk, and crown together with lists of interpretations for each detail. The many different interpretations suggested for any one drawing characteristic should give the psychodiagnostician ample leeway for employing his imagination in producing a rich character portrayal of the subject. However, being a skeptic with regard to the principles of graphological interpretation and the "scientific analysis of forms of expression," this reviewer is inclined to wish for less fantasy and more fact. This book may have some value for those who are particularly interested in drawing as a projective technique. It would be quite interesting to compare the interpretations given here with those offered for the tree drawings on the HTP test. It might also be of interest to determine whether the same developmental trends obtain in this country as those found by the author for Swiss children.

J Proj Tech 18:258–9 Je '54. *Bertram R. Forer.* This is one of those clinical books whose publication is, fortunately, becoming increasingly rare. While Koch may be a sagacious and perceptive clinician and his style of communication adequate to his task, his book represents to this reviewer so much dead wood. Koch refers to a few European students who have worked diagnostically with tree-drawing, calls upon graphologic data for supporting evidence, and launches into 40 pages of drawing characteristics which he has found diagnostic. There is no reference to American work such as the H-T-P, human figure drawing, or experimental findings in drawing or expressive movement. The sole condescensions to statistics are two trivial tables showing age changes of a few drawing features, expressed in percentages without indications of either the sizes or natures of the samples. No other normative data are presented. However, he promises some in a future publication. While there are a few sample interpretations, they are presented with no evidence of validity, congruent or otherwise. The Rorschach protocols with which the drawings are compared and case history material are both lacking. While the book may prove to be a useful source of hypotheses to those who wish to do research with the H-T-P, as a contribution to the theory of projective methods or the

science of clinical psychology, the book has little to offer.

[B252]

★Kough, Jack, and DeHaan, Robert F. **Teacher's Guidance Handbook: Part 1, Identifying Children Who Need Help, Elementary and Junior High Edition.** Chicago, Ill.: Science Research Associates, 1955. Pp. 149. Loose-leaf. $2.75. * (*PA* 30: 6323)

[B253]

★Kreinheder, Albert. **Objective Measurement of Reality-Contact Weakness.** American Psychological Association, Psychological Monographs: General and Applied, Vol. 66, No. 11, Whole No. 343. Washington, D.C.: the Association, Inc., 1952. Pp. ii, 23. Paper. $1.00. * (*PA* 27 :5882)

[B254]

★Kutash, Samuel B., and Gehl, Raymond H. **The Graphomotor Projection Technique: Clinical Use and Standardization.** Springfield, Ill.: Charles C Thomas, 1954. Pp. xi, 133. $3.75. * (Oxford, England: Blackwell Scientific Publications, Ltd. 27s. 6d.) (*PA* 29 :1768) For reviews, see 137.

[B255]

★Kwalwasser, Jacob. **Exploring the Musical Mind.** New York: Coleman-Ross Co., Inc., 1955. Pp. x, 189. $4.50. * (*PA* 30 :4221)

Cont Psychol 1 :206–7 Jl '56. *John T. Cowles.* * This attractive little volume....presents the abstracted results of about seventy-five descriptive studies of musical talent. The majority of these are from unpublished master's theses, prepared by students of the author during the past twenty-five years, but principally during 1941–1952. These theses were concerned primarily with the obtaining of normative measurements on large groups of school children with the Kwalwasser-Dykema Music Tests, the Kwalwasser-Ruch Musical Accomplishment Test, and certain laboratory-type tests of motor performance. The remainder of the studies are drawn from the work of others in the same general field, but of earlier vintage, about 1920–1940. * Rather casually Kwalwasser introduces his test batteries, which provide the real core of this book, but strangely he omits the expected description of the rationale, development, content, and internal statistics of the tests. * The more novel contributions of this book lie in the last few chapters, wherein are reported some relatively recent and ingenious measures of body equilibrium, finger-tapping rate, tongue-agility, vocal intonation, and music reading, as well as the relations of certain of these measures to scores on the Kwalwasser-Dykema Music Tests. Supplementary measures were not obtained, however, to determine to what extent the generally greater motility of the musically higher-scoring children is due to selection on favorable physical factors, to emotional instabilities, or to practice effects. * Students of educational measurement will doubtless share this reviewer's disappointment with the author's disregard of present-day standards for presenting test results. He not only fails to report essential statistics on the nature of the tests themselves but does not cite the published studies of others on the validity, or interrelations of his tests. A "talent profile" of the pupil is suggested as valuable to the teacher or counselor, but one wonders if the several subtests have sufficient reliability or independence to warrant profiling of scores. Buros' *The Third Mental Measurements Yearbook*....for example, cites 29 references to studies of these tests, of which Kwalwasser cites only four. In fact, it is even more disturbing to discover that only 43 of the 189 titles in Kwalwasser's *Bibliography of Works Cited* are actually cited in his text. Mean scores are plentifully given, but standard deviations or Ns are not always included, and the statistical significance of innumerable differences which are discussed is rarely indicated. The author is careless in many of his statements accompanying correlation coefficients, such as when he misinterprets the index of forecasting efficiency by saying: "there is only a 6% accuracy in a correlation coefficient of $+.33$" (p. 55), or again, an r of $+.34$ "contains a prediction error rate of 94%" (p. 57). And there are other errors and inaccuracies as well as minor editorial slips: (*Ballast-on-Spa, New York* for *Ballston Spa*, etc.). Thus the book deserves a reading, a cautious one, by all who are interested in musical talent and its measurement—for its historical significance in summarizing a series of related studies, and for the ideas it suggests for future studies, but not as a source of well-presented, conclusive data on the nature of musical talent.

Ed & Psychol Meas 16:409–10 au '56. Paul R. Farnsworth. The test philosophy of this little book by Kwalwasser is very similar to that to be found in his 1927 *Tests and Measurements in Music*. Both books accept hereditarianism and the idea that certain groups are inherently superior. Kwalwasser still believes that all of the famous "Seashore Measures of Musical Talents" and more of the members of his own "Kwalwasser-Dykema Music Tests" uncover native talent, a potentiality which train-

ing can never alter. Kwalwasser's new book contains a bibliography of 189 titles. Yet one cannot find in this list references to the studies which show beyond reason of doubt that with proper procedures music test scores can be markedly improved. These later studies, e.g., those of Ruth Wyatt, use, it should be noted, far better measures of sensitivity than the KD test series. * In 1953 Kwalwasser put on the market a ten minute "Music Talent Test." Unfortunately, his publishers supply no supporting reliability data. It was, therefore, the reviewer's hope that proper normative values would be offered in the present book. However, a fairly careful reading failed to uncover any such evaluative materials. As a matter of fact this "quickie" test receives only very brief mention. * *Exploring the Musical Mind* expands considerable space on family line analyses; "racial" and national differences in music test scores; and age, sex, IQ, and training differences. Much of this material is anything but definitive and takes one little beyond the knowledge level of the earlier Kwalwasser tome. But a few of the present volume's later chapters, particularly those on motor measurement, tongue-agility, and stroboscopic measurement have buried in them notes on heretofore unpublished minor studies done by Kwalwasser's students. These alone probably justify the publication of a book which otherwise belongs pretty much to the earlier days of mental measurement.

[B256]
★LAFITTE, PAUL. **Melbourne Test 90.** Australian Journal of Psychology, Monograph Supplement No. 1. Melbourne, Australia: Melbourne University Press, May 1954. Pp. 107. Paper. 12s. 6d. * (*PA* 29:4690)

[B257]
★LA FON, FRED E. **Behavior on the Rorschach Test and a Measure of Self-Acceptance.** American Psychological Association, Psychological Monographs: General and Applied, Vol. 68, No. 10, Whole No. 381. Washington, D.C.: the Association, Inc., 1954. Pp. 14. Paper. $1.00. * (*PA* 29:5713)

[B258]
★LALJANI, M. R. **Evaluation in Basic Schools.** Institute of Rural Education, Studies in Basic Education, No. 1. New Delhi, India: Institute of Rural Education, 1955. Pp. viii, 80, xxv. Rs. 3. *

[B259]
★LAUGHLIN, FRANCES. **The Peer Status of Sixth and Seventh Grade Children.** New York: Bureau of Publications, Teachers College, Columbia University, 1954. Pp. x, 85. $2.75. * (*PA* 29:3729)

[B260]
★LAYTON, WILBUR L. **Counseling Use of the Strong Vocational Interest Blank.** Minnesota Studies in

Student Personnel Work, No. 8. Minneapolis, Minn.: University of Minnesota Press, 1958. Pp. 40. Paper. $1.25. *

[B261]

★LEARY, TIMOTHY. **Interpersonal Diagnosis of Personality: A Functional Theory and Methodology for Personality Evaluation.** New York: Ronald Press Co., 1957. Pp. xix, 518. $12.00. * (PA 31: 2556)

Am J Sociol 63:244–5 S '57. Jeanne Watson. * There is ambiguity throughout the book as to whether the system rests on a distinction between sixteen themes, eight themes, or two dimensions. * Perhaps the most interesting aspect of the book for sociologists and social psychologists is that personality is defined as an interpersonal phenomenon. Each of the sixteen basic themes is stated in terms of a readiness to act in certain specified ways toward others and simultaneously to provoke or "pull" specified behavior from them. Such terminology gives operational meaning to the concept of "interpersonal system." Leary proposes that the same thematic terms be used to describe both normal and pathological behavior, with differences in intensity indicating the degree of rigidity or pathology. Actually, most of the work reported in this book was done in a clinical setting, and the results are correspondingly limited. Interpersonal behavior is viewed exclusively as an attempt to avoid anxiety. The major situation about which predictions are made is the interaction of a patient with his therapist. The one attempt to use the system to analyze a "normal" (top-level management) group served only to high-light "misperceptions and rigid destructive symbiotic interactions." The assumption that this system will be useful in analyzing healthy or creative interpersonal relationships is intriguing but as yet unproved. One other difficulty arises from the very complexity of the system, with its sixteen themes, four degrees of intensity, five levels of personality, and simultaneously scoring of self and other, distinctions which, although conceptually illuminating and valuable, in practice are unmanageable. Leary meets this problem with mechanical rather than theoretical simplification, proceeding to combine categories, compute averages, and ignore large segments of information. In doing this, he introduces distortion as well as simplification. Despite its limitations, this system must be recognized as a major advance in the treatment of the interpersonal dimension of personality. It offers both a systematic classification of interpersonal tendencies and some careful thinking about the structure of personality.

B Menninger Clinic 21:269 N '57. Helen D. Sargent. In the "cookbook" era of psychological research, fortunately or unfortunately, in its ascendant phase, this book is an important event. An ambitious system is offered for rating personality data in terms of sixteen interpersonal variables at five "levels of communication." Conversion into code descriptions and discrepancy indices permits an infinite number of correlations and measures of change. In the search for "objective" methods applicable to psychotherapy research, uses beyond interpersonal theory, as such, will be stimulated. In spite of its mathematical sophistication, the contribution is, essentially, to classification. Linneaus was not Darwin, and Leary is not Freud. There is, however, a place for systematic hierarchical ordering in psychology as in any natural science. The system's contribution to process research in psychotherapy depends upon whether that process can be captured by a molecular approach.

Cont Psychol 2:227–9 S '57. William C. Schutz. * In sum, despite the reviewer's negative comments, this book has real merit. As a contribution to clinical diagnosis it is outstanding. As a contribution to personality theory and methodology it presents many provocative, sound, and clever ideas, many of which I have been unable to mention. Compared to most other attempts to objectify "depth" personality concepts, this work represents a great advance both in the substantive progress and in the optimism implied in undertaking such a project. With such work and a few other projects like those at Minnesota and Michigan, it will be more difficult for future psychological trend-analyzers to maintain that clinical concepts are outside the realm of experimental techniques. Most of my negative comments have referred to the content, not the form of the research, for the form merits emulation, and the content consideration and constructive criticism. [See original review for critical comments not excerpted.]

Ed & Psychol Meas 17:639–40 w '57. Louis P. Thorpe. * The objective of the investigation described in the present volume was that of developing a multilevel model of personality and of offering techniques for measuring interpersonal expressions at the previously mentioned different levels of behavior. This approach was likened to a *dynamic behaviorism* possessing the two attributes: (1) the impact that one person has or makes in dealing with others and (2) the interaction of psychological pressures among the various levels of personality. * Of special interest is the sociometric technique used in ascertaining a given patient's self-rating, as well as a rating of every other patient in his group, on a diagnostic grid featuring such dimensions of personality as (1) managerial—autocratic, (2) competitive—narcissistic, (3) aggressive—sadistic, (4) rebellious—distrustful, (5) self-effacing—masochistic, (6) docile—dependent, (7) cooperative—overconventional, and (8) responsible—hypernormal. A variety of other techniques of measurement of multilevel patterns of personality will be of interest to students of the subject. The same may be said of applications to clinical, managerial, and group dynamics situations. On the positive side it can be said that author Leary and his associates have presented a unique, though complicated, picture of the organization of personality as it involves interpersonal behavior principally in a clinical setting. If there is a negative aspect to this fairly monumental research project and its theoretical considerations, it would seem to be that certain of its categories of behavior, e.g., adjustment mechanisms and multilevel diagnosis, as well as certain of the measures of interpersonal behavior, have been more or less arbitrarily selected and presented as though they presumably would meet with widespread approval. However, although critics of the system as presented may object to certain of its subjective and intangible aspects, they would no doubt be hard put to come up with one which is freer of such deviations from strictly operational or empirical procedures.

J Counsel Psychol 4:168–9 su '57. *Laurence Siegel.* * In summary, Leary has described a method of personality evaluation with a firm foundation in a theory of personality. The major advantages of the System are derived from the fact that it requires integration of isolated measures at different levels and is functional, allowing predictions of behavior in specified interpersonal situations (particularly in psychotherapy). The potential user of the System will find that it is complex, that the Manual is at times unclear and that certain of his questions are not satisfactorily dealt with

in the Manual. In spite of these factors, however, the System is clearly beyond the experimental stage and is ready for operational application.

J Counsel Psychol 4:259–60 f '57. *Leon Gorlow.* * The project is a grand effort in a difficult field, and those of us who are interested in personality assessment will have to read Leary's exploration with considerable care. This is not an easy book, but the reader will be repaid for his efforts by a specification and elaboration of dimensions which Sullivan had insisted upon in the course of his professional career. There are some general considerations which are worth recording for the purpose of critical review. The present effort, *as measurement,* does not solve the problem of adding or combining the units of response into scores which have known scale properties. In this way, there is no more success here than that which has already been achieved by researchers working with psychotherapy protocols. * The reader will also note that there are literally thousands of possible combinations and permutations among variables and levels. The fruitfulness and practicality of such a system of multilevel diagnosis will have to be demonstrated before other individuals will be persuaded to adopt the system. A final word needs to be added with respect to possible factor-analytic explorations. In these days of statistical analyses and accountings, it is appropriate to wonder about the independence and the relative purity of the variables utilized in the course of Leary's researches. Factor analysis, too, would seem to hold promise for simplifying and reducing the complex structure without appreciable loss.

[B262]

★LEECH, D. COLLINS. **Twenty Weeks Entrance Examination Tests.** Exeter, England: A. Wheaton & Co. Ltd., 1957. Pp. 103. Paper. 3s. *

[B263]

★LEFEVER, D. WELTY, AND CARNES, EARL F. **A Workbook in Measurement and Evaluation.** Los Angeles, Calif.: College Book Store, 1956. Pp. ix, 128. Paper, spiral binding, lithotyped. $2.50. *

Ed & Psychol Meas 17:153–5 sp '57. *Max D. Engelhart.* This workbook is well worth calling to the attention of teachers of tests and measurements. It can be employed effectively with any one of the recent widely used texts in the field. * Following a listing of various types of measuring devices are forms to be used by the student in evaluating tests of different kinds. These would seem to the reviewer to be an excellent means of directing students in their study of examples of each type of test or measuring instrument. * Especially commendable is the assignment dealing with item analysis as a means of group diagnosis. * this workbook should provide the basis for an excellent introductory course in testing. As the authors suggest, an instructor may disagree with some of their points of view regarding measurement and evaluation as expressed in responses to certain items; yet "these answers can serve as the basis for class discussion thus permitting the underlying issues to be clarified." The students who complete a substantial proportion of the exercises in the various assignments should acquire the kind of understanding which contributes to effective applications of their knowledge in testing situations.

[B264]

★LEFEVER, D. WELTY; NASLUND, ROBERT A.; AND THORPE, LOUIS P. **Measuring Pupil Achievement: A Handbook for Teachers, Counselors, and Administrators in Junior and Senior High Schools.** Chicago, Ill.: Science Research Associates, 1957. Pp. 47. Paper. $1.00. *

[B265]

★LEONHARD, DIETZ L. **Consumer Research With Projective Techniques: A Case Report of Theory and Successful Experimentations in Market and Marketing Research.** Shenandoah, Iowa: Ajax Corporation, 1955. Pp. ii, 151. Paper. $2.00. *

Personnel Psychol 10:129–31 sp '57. Melvin S. Hattwick. This is an exciting *little* book with a *big* impact. Its 151 pages contain the report of one business man's efforts to bring certain motivation research techniques out of the clinical laboratory and apply them to everyday business problems. The results—although they sometimes reflect a lack of laboratory control some would prefer—make for exciting reading. And they should make sense to applied psychologists, personnel men, and management people. Any book on this subject must, I suppose, do first of all what Mr. Leonhard does first: discuss some of the merits and limitations of conventional who-buys-what-when-where-how-much type of research. What this author, based on training and experience, says and documents about the questionnaire, the interviewer, and the respondent, will jolt many a market researcher from the complacency with which some of us view these topics. To make one quote from the author, "If market research is to fulfill its function as an aid to modern man-

agement, it must try to study and to use discipline other than economics, statistics, and analysis. It must learn to replace with new principles that nose counting survey, whose results may be definite (including the sampling error) but also often times tired and meaningless." Have you ever asked yourself, "Why doesn't someone put down in less technical language what these T.A.T. and other projective techniques are, how they may be used, and not used?" If you *have* asked such a question the author will give you some answers which are enlightening. Certainly he is more positive and provocative than most social scientists would be. His statements are at times more inclusive than perhaps is warranted, but certainly none can quarrel with his objective, which is to throw more light and less heat on this subject of "Application of Theory to Practical Experimentation in Business Research." The final section will provide the real "meat" of this book to many who read it. It includes four case studies of projective techniques in action. The problem, the method, the responses, and some results are given. In a time when most of us are talking theory and revealing few results, the case histories presented here are a major contribution. Mr. Leonhard has found time in a busy schedule to provide some meat on which many of us can chew for some time to come. You may not always like the taste of it, and you may, perhaps, find the chewing a bit tough. But certainly, he provides a great deal of food for thought. Leonhard's monograph won the 1955 Honor Award of the Chicago Chapter of the American Marketing Association, an award well deserved in the reviewer's judgment.

[B266]

★LESSA, WILLIAM A., AND SPIEGELMAN, MARVIN. **Ulithian Personality as Seen Through Ethnological Materials and Thematic Test Analysis.** University of California Publications in Culture and Society, Vol. 2, No. 5. Berkeley, Calif.: University of California Press, 1954. Pp. iii, 243–301. Paper. $0.75. * (PA 29:757)

[B267]

★LIBO, LESTER M. **Measuring Group Cohesiveness.** University of Michigan, Institute for Social Research, Research Center for Group Dynamics, No. 3. Ann Arbor, Mich.: University of Michigan Press, 1953. Pp. ix, 111. * (PA 28:8654)

Am Sociol R 19:785–6 D '54. Chris Argyris. * "Attraction-to-group" or the resultant force acting on a member to remain in his group is hypothesized to be a function of the degree to which membership in the group is actually or potentially need-satisfying. One must keep in mind that Libo is focusing only on those sources of attraction which stem from the valent characteristics of the group itself. The present formulation of the concept is based on the assumption, therefore, that the forces toward membership are driving (i.e., people need to remain in the group), not restraining, forces and that it is the valent group in a natural situation, rather than other coercive or external factors, which is to arouse an individual's need to belong to the group. Consequently, the results, Libo points out, are not relevant to groups where pressure to remain is due to (a) a sense of obligation or duty, (b) prohibitions against leaving the group, and (c) fear of exclusion or rejection from the group. For the "field-oriented" researcher studying already existing groups, these are interesting limitations. One may ask, how many "actual" groups exist without any of these characteristics? It is to Libo's credit that he makes explicit the limitations of his research. * Libo describes research conducted on two methodological problems: (a) perfecting a behavioral criterion which can be used to validate either experimental manipulations of group attractiveness or measures of attraction-to-group, and (b) constructing a measure of attraction-to-group which was less obvious in its intent than a questionnaire. To accomplish the first aim, a "locomotion measure" was developed. To accomplish the second aim, a projective technique called The Group-Picture-Impression (G.P.I.) test was developed. * The G.P.I. test was found capable of discriminating (1) between subjects assigned in the high experimental conditions and those in the low, (2) between subjects who stayed in their groups and those who did not. However, it is interesting to note that Libo also administered a questionnaire to each subject which also tapped the individual's "attraction-to-group." The questionnaire was found to be, in some areas, a better predictor of behavior than the more elaborate projective technique. Such results help confirm the hypotheses that projective techniques may not be necessary when we are dealing with those needs that relatively normal people manifest and which they are not defensive about. It may be that a projective technique is more necessary for abnormal people whose personality structure is "loaded" with defense mechanisms. *

J Proj Tech 19:80–2 Mr '55. *Ruth Tolman.*
* A neat experiment is described, and the presentation is orderly and systematic. It suggests many practical implications and raises provocative questions. * This investigation....undertakes to manipulate experimentally in a laboratory situation some of the variables which make for high and low group "attractiveness" and then to measure the results by three methods: a behavioral criterion called the "locomotion measure," a projective device called the Group Picture Impression (or G-P-I) technique, and a brief paper-and-pencil questionnaire. * The Group Picture Impression (GPI) technique will be of special interest to readers of this journal and two of the four chapters in the book are devoted to a description of it and to a Manual for its interpretation. It is regarded by the author as an extension or enlargement of the potential measurement applications of projective approaches. It is an attempt to capitalize on the "sensitivity" of the projective instrument to social factors in the test administration situation. Group-administered, it is a three-picture technique, eliciting short stories which can be coded and scored with high reliability and which yield a score for each member of the participating group. The score is reported in two parts: (a) the total score, and (b) the number of stories with a score, the latter representing presumably the subject's degree of involvement with the story-writing task and thus serving as a kind of screening device to indicate the validity (or invalidity) of the total score. In the appendix the author himself raises the question which must necessarily bedevil the reader: what of the validity of the assumption that the story is a direct reflection of the subject's attraction to membership in the group of which he is now a member? How would the individual respond in isolation from any group? Are the stories tapping permanent and basic attitudes toward group relationships rather than reactions toward the immediate group situation? The type of investigation necessary to answer these questions has not yet been attempted with G-P-I, but it badly needs doing. Furthermore, although re-test reliability of the G-P-I is low, a study of the relation of changes in an individual's score to changes in group conditions has not been attempted. There is something rather arbitrary, and sometimes questionable, about the determination of the code-able unit in scoring the GPI stories. But

this is a minor detail. More important is the fact that this approach is a novel and promising one in the investigation of group behavior and should lend itself, with some modifications, to the study of many other group situations, particularly of group therapy processes.

[B268]

★LIEBERS, ARTHUR. **How to Take Tests and Pass Them.** New York: Arco Publishing Co., Inc., 1958. Pp. 184. $2.00. (London: Arco Publications, Ltd. 15s.)

[B269]

LINDQUIST, E. F., EDITOR. **Educational Measurement.** Washington, D.C.: American Council on Education, 1951. Pp. xix, 819. $6.00. *

Am J Psychol 65:141–2 Ja '52. Lloyd G. *Humphreys.* * The first part, in four chapters, provides a basic philosophy for the use of measurement in the schools. Outstanding in this section is the first chapter which sets forth a realistic and useful position with regard to individual differences and their measurement in the learning situation. It is unfortunate that the discussion of educational placement in the fourth chapter is limited almost entirely to the college level, although this emphasis is understandable in view of background of the authors. * The last chapter, particularly the portion which compares different methods of interpreting test-scores and profiles, should be required reading for all students of clinical psychology and vocational guidance. * The quality of the work is uniformly high, reflecting both careful editing and a good choice of authors, and the reviewer found little with which to disagree. In several of the chapters there was a disturbing tendency to veer unpredictably from discussion of achievement tests to discussion of predictive tests. While many of the problems involved in the construction of the two types of test are the same, others, such as those involved in planning and validation, may be quite different. Three minor difficulties in connection with the chapter on validity might be noted. First, formula 25, one of those used to correct for restriction of range, is presented without an explicit statement of its major assumption, namely, that the restriction is in the second variable while the variances of the first are known. Secondly, while the assumptions underlying the use of correction formulae do not make them applicable to biserial validity coefficients, the error involved in their use is small, particularly if the amount of restric-

tion is moderate and the dichotomy is not extreme. Furthermore, the error is in the direction of underestimation rather than overestimation of validity in the unrestricted range. Finally, an objection may be voiced to the use of the term "ultimate" in speaking about criteria. There are probably no ultimate criteria as defined, all criteria being either working criteria or intermediate criteria. The term should, therefore, not be used, even for purposes of exposition. The volume, which varies considerably in difficulty (from the undergraduate level in most of the chapters in the first and second parts to the graduate level in the third), should be useful both in psychology and education. Students of education are more likely than students of psychology to be familiar with the uses of measurement in the schools, but less likely to be familiar with the statistical material presented in the third part. Students of psychology will find much new material in the first part. The material in the third part may be somewhat familiar, but much of it goes beyond that which is covered in the usual courses on statistics. In general, the volume will serve as a textbook for courses in the construction of tests and as a reference work for courses in statistics, measurement, guidance, and evaluation.

Harvard Ed R 22:58–9 w '52. Julian C. *Stanley.* * should serve splendidly as a textbook for advanced graduate students as well as a handbook for professional workers. It is curiously uneven in difficulty. Some of the material can be comprehended easily by intelligent college sophomores while a few portions will tax bright doctoral candidates. * a rich mine of achievement-testing lore * despite the genuine excellence of Lorge's chapter concerning "The Fundamental Nature of Measurement," one might suppose that it would have been even better had S. S. Stevens, a psychologist keenly interested in the theory of scales of measurement, served as its co-author. Though fifty-one collaborators assisted the authors, some of them to considerable extents, similar comments could be made about several other chapters. * The third part.... presupposes background equivalent to about twelve quarter hours (eight semester hours) of statistics though much of the material can be comprehended reasonably well with less training. The present writer prefers to offer Part 3 during the third quarter after his graduate students have completed Cronbach's text and the first two parts of *Educational Measurement*. By this time, they have also had eight quarter hours of statistics and may be enrolled for four more. So much of the content of this book was sheer "word of mouth" knowledge before it appeared in print that the educator interested in measurement who does not read Parts 1 and 2 will be lacking erudition not acquirable elsewhere. Though practically all the chapters make distinct contributions, in Part 2 three of these stand out as of paramount importance for educators who use or construct tests: Lindquist's "Preliminary considerations in objective test construction," Ebel's "Writing the test item," and Stalnaker's "The essay type of examination." Davis' "Item selection techniques" is valuable for measurement workers but far more difficult for the statistically uninitiated. *

J Higher Ed 23:165 Mr '52. Cyril Burt. * collated and edited, with admirable skill * an excellent survey by F. B. Davis of the principles of item analysis and the techniques available for item selection. A new and particularly helpful feature consists in detailed chapters on "the art of test construction." Designing tests, writing test-items, trying out test-materials, scoring and interpreting the results —all the "tricks of the trade," in fact, are explained in practical detail. The last section deals with the theory of mental measurement. This includes some of the most valuable chapters in the book. * The scattered literature has been thoroughly sifted and studied, and every chapter ends with a selected list of useful references. It will be plain to the careful reader that not all the collaborators are agreed on each of the main issues; but such minor inconsistencies are to be welcomed as a sign of an impartial treatment, and as a reminder that finality is as yet by no means attained. To aim at an eclectic presentation rather than at a unified theory is a far wiser policy in a rapidly growing field. This is unquestionably not only a useful handbook for senior students of educational psychology, but an indispensable work of reference for investigators who are embarking on research in this or allied subjects.

Psychol B 49:194–6 Mr '52. Robert M. W. Travers. * It is extremely difficult to review a work so encyclopedic in character and so heterogeneous in authorship—because of the varying quality of different parts of the work, and because different authors have different audiences in mind and hence write at different levels of difficulty. The difficulty is enhanced in the present volume, where chapters vary from the platitudinous to the profound. Of course, what is a platitude to one still may be a profundity to another. The part of the volume which seems to come closest to the stated purposes is Part 3 on "Measurement Theory." The five authors of this section reflect in their writing a level of scholarship far above that found in most of the rest of the volume. * The remainder of the volume presents a much less happy picture. To the authors of the first four chapters on "The Functions of Measurement in Education" must inevitably fall the lot of saying what has been said many times before. They discuss the usual generalities about the functions of measurement in a commonplace way. Often the discussion is vague and general. * Part 2 of the book is devoted to a presentation of techniques used in the construction of achievement tests * The most notable contribution of this part.... is a chapter by Frederick B. Davis on "Item Selection Techniques." This chapter is commensurate in scholarship with those in the final part of the volume. Particularly inadequate is the chapter on "Planning the Objective Test." In this chapter there is practically no discussion of the difficult but important problem of defining a domain of behavior within which measurement is to take place and yet this is a fundamental step in the handling of achievement tests. The omission of a proper discussion of how to specify what a test is to measure is not rectified by an adequate discussion of the topic in the chapter on "Writing the Test Item." The latter chapter is devoted almost entirely to the discussion of the form of test items rather than of their function. For example, there is an excellent discussion on suggested rules for writing multiple-choice items and yet one cannot find out the kinds of purposes for which multiple-choice items might be used. The paragraph on the applicability of multiple-choice questions begins with a statement, "The multiple-choice form is widely applicable," and nothing more is said concerning the kinds of achievements which they may be used to measure. Of what avail is a multiple-choice item which illustrates all the suggested rules of good item writing if it measures an achievement which is trivial or irrelevant? * The function of a test item must be a determiner of its form, and yet in this volume the various forms of test items are discussed without relating them to the functions they may serve. Finally, there is one major criticism of the book as a whole which cannot be omitted. The work seems to imply that educational measurement consists mainly of the measurement of academic achievement of the type which has been stressed in traditional schools. It is to be hoped that advanced courses in the measurement for which the book is designed will cover some of the broader aspects of the measurement of growth. Educational measurement cannot be preoccupied only with intellectual development in an age when so much stress is being placed on the nonintellectual aspects of growth. Much has been done already to assess the development of interests, values, attitudes, and other aspects of personality and these must surely be given some place in an advanced course in measurement. Unless this is done such courses will be geared to an educational philosophy which is no longer too widely accepted.

For additional reviews, see 4:B247.

[B270]

★LIVERANT, SHEPHARD. **The Use of Rotter's Social Learning Theory in Developing a Personality Inventory.** American Psychological Association, Psychological Monographs: General and Applied, Vol. 72, No. 2, Whole No. 455. Washington, D.C.: the Association, Inc., 1958. Pp. 23. Paper. $1.00. *

[B271]

★LOCK, H. F. **The Use of Tests in Selection Procedures.** London: British Institute of Management, 1956. Pp. 26. 5s. *

Occupational Psychol 31:57 Ja '57. Denis McMahon. It is good to read something by an author who knows what he talking about. Into this 26-page booklet....Lock and his colleagues have packed a remarkable amount of information and good sense. Short but crystal-clear paragraphs on validity, reliability, standardisation and item analysis prepare the way for brief descriptions of the main types of tests. These are models of modesty and caution. The best section of the booklet is on the place of testing in selection procedure. The whole thing is rounded off with a two-page account of group techniques and a reading list. The Appendix gives suggested programmes

and timetables for four different kinds of selection procedure. The Appendix alone is worth five shillings to personnel and line managers who want a quick but reliable briefing.

[B272]

★LORD, FREDERIC. **A Theory of Test Scores.** Psychometric Monographs, No. 7. Princeton, N.J.: Psychometric Society (P.O. Box 572). Pp. x, 84. Paper. Out of print. (*PA* 28:1886)

[B273]

★LORR, MAURICE. **Multidimensional Scale for Rating Psychiatric Patients, Hospital Form.** Veterans Administration Technical Bulletin, TB 10–507. Washington, D.C.: Veterans Administration, November 16, 1953. Pp. 44. Paper. *

[B274]

★LOWENFELD, MARGARET. **The Lowenfeld Mosaic Test.** London: Newman Neame Ltd., 1954. Pp. 360. 50s. *

Brit J Med Psychol 28:199–200 Je '55. Lydia Jackson. This is a long-awaited manual for use with the author's well-known Mosaic Test. It embodies almost a quarter of a century of experimentation, and includes chapters on the classification of patterns, on the use of the test in the study of child development, of normal personality, subnormal intelligence, neurosis, mental disorder and of cultural problems. * The field covered is a very wide one, and Dr Lowenfeld is the first to stress the point that the material obtained so far from some of the groups studied can only be used as a guiding line for further research. She takes similar care to emphasize that the designs obtained from subjects do not lend themselves to facile interpretation, or to "blind" diagnosis, and that a thorough training in the use of the test, and probably a special talent as well, are required to get meaningful and reliable results. The account of its use in making the differential diagnosis of diseases of the brain from mental diseases is impressive. In the same chapter (9) some striking examples of patterns made by schizophrenic patients are discussed. In another context Dr Lowenfeld herself refers to the—not unexpected—difficulty in distinguishing these from patterns made by the severely neurotic, or the very dull. She also mentions the paradox of mental defectives who occasionally produce an excellent design! The book abounds in such tantalizing vistas of regions to be explored. Not the least fascinating prospect lies in the field of cultural differences. The contrast between the Am- and the Eu- patterns revealed by this test may be taken as an awful warning against applying hypotheses based on the material obtained from one culture to the products of another, unless it were with the aim of verifying them. The main virtue of the Lowenfeld Mosaic Test, in the opinion of this reviewer, is that it occupies an intermediate position between the unstructured interview and a more rigidly constructed test, thus combining the advantages of both. Yet the very freedom the subject enjoys in using his creative potentialities increases the difficulties of interpretation. The Test, however, does not appear to be offered as a single exhaustive means for investigating personality, but as an additional tool to be used in uncovering some of its aspects, not easily accessible by other means. Its use in following the changes in personality during treatment seems especially promising.

Brit J Psychol 46:155–6 My '55. M. Collins. * Some of the interpretations are extraordinarily interesting such as those of two sisters whose designs show striking similarity. The chapter on children's designs, tabulating the changes in the form of the design with age, is of value from the point of view of children's development. * The different facets of the test seem unlimited, and if one can judge from the contents of the book, the test is being extensively tried out in different fields, and used in different countries. One considerable disadvantage from which it suffers is the difficulty of making a permanent record of the results. Apart from colour photography, white paper has to be placed on the tray beforehand, a tracing made before the pieces are removed, and finally the design has to be coloured—a time-consuming process. A second disadvantage of the test, as it appears to the reviewer, is that the interpretation of the designs still seems to be largely subjective. As is stated in the book, to classify and to interpret the designs is like learning a new language, and the only reliable method of learning is said to be personal experience and direct personal teaching. "It must also be granted that for the full use of the test and an appreciation of its subtler aspects, a certain special quality is needed in the investigator, one akin to the quality in the musician that makes elements of form and rhythm obvious to him that, to the unmusical, are imperceptible" (p. 48). If this is so, then the use of the test is certainly

limited, and this unfortunately is the impression one receives from perusal of the text. While the book makes interesting reading, one would have liked the contents of some of the chapters to have been arranged more systematically.

J Consult Psychol 19:154–5 Ap '55. Laurance F. Shaffer. * The standard directions for administration, and especially the definitions and illustrations of the terms used to describe the designs, are useful to both clinical and research workers. At last they now will have a uniform method for communicating about the Mosaic. The 144 color plates make concepts clear that are hard to describe in words or even in uncolored illustrations. In its clinical sections, the book displays honest confusion. Numerous case studies give, by implication more than direct assertion, the "typical" designs produced by patients with many syndromes, children of various developmental stages, and people of several cultures. In discussing generalities, the author sometimes makes glowing claims—"....the L. M. T. often makes it possible to make a rapid and certain diagnosis in cases of doubt...." (p. 246)—and sometimes shows awareness of the limitations of her method—"....differential diagnosis between a severe degree of neurosis, a low level of inherent intelligence, and severe schizophrenia, is one of extreme difficulty, since in all three cases subjects are apt to...." (p. 146). A striking omission, all too familiar in books on new clinical techniques, is even the simplest evidence on validity, other than anecdotes. Is it too much to ask that authors at least count and report the percentages of hits and misses made by the test when predicting certain verifiable diagnoses or other events?

J Mental Sci 101:414 Ap '55. M. Bassett. * There are 360 pages in....[the book], yet it is difficult for me to say much or to report on what is its hard core, for I feel much as if confronted by the grin of a Cheshire cat. The book abounds in contradictions of theory with practice, in promises of explanation which remain unfulfilled, and in exasperating statements * One may wonder how the test can be interpreted, since on the one hand the author explicitly states that neither verbal nor statistical methods of evaluation are practicable while on the other hand she eschews publishing psychoanalytic interpretations, subjective evaluations and other scoring methods. The fact is that the Lowenfeld Mosaic is not an established Test but a technique which has yet to be validated. As a projective method it may be worth exploring, and Dr. Lowenfeld's originality in developing the project must be warmly acknowledged. Whether or not her theories underlying the technique are valid could quite easily be tested rigorously. Up to the present, it seems that Himmelweit and Eysenck are the only two workers who have attempted serious validation of the technique (*Br. J. Med. Psychol.,* 1944, 20, 203). Though their tests were not extensive they found that an experienced user of the technique could write personality sketches from mosaics with better than chance success when these were matched against psychiatrists' reports. *

Psychol B 52:369-70 Jl '55. Morris Krugman. * This book will probably do for the Mosaic Test what the English translation of the "Psychodiagnostik" did for the Rorschach; it will transform it from an esoteric technique into a popular clinical instrument. And, as in the case of the Rorschach, some psychologists will not be too happy about this. * Diagnostic procedures are presented tentatively throughout, and the reader is frequently cautioned to use this test experimentally rather than as a finished instrument. * In spite of the cautions constantly presented, the impact of the "typical" cases and the large number of case descriptions leaves the impression that the test can be used with a reasonable degree of assurance as a diagnostic clinical instrument. The chapters dealing with the description of the test convey the impression that the designs produced by subjects can be readily classified into stated categories which lead to almost automatic diagnosis. On the other hand, the parts of the book which concern themselves with the use of the test bring the reader back to reality with a jolt. Warnings about the difficulties in classification experienced with live cases, examples of borderline and ambiguous designs, samples of overlapping diagnostic possibilities for similar designs, instances of subjective interpretation, and conflicting reports by different workers abound in the many case samples presented, and serve to disabuse the reader of any hopes for a reasonably simple and useful technique for personality appraisal, in the event that he had entertained such hopes. In spite of twenty-five years of experimentation and clinical use, this test is still in its beginning

stages. It is now ready for validation. There is no doubt about the fact that competent clinical psychologists will find this a useful projective technique—an important addition to the clinical battery—if they are not already using it. But then, competent clinical psychologists can find almost any series of samples of human behavior useful for diagnostic purposes, particularly one that has had considerable use, and therefore presents some basis for comparison of results. Those who insist on "respectable" methods of objectification, and on standard approaches to reliability and validity will, no doubt, be as violent in opposition to this test as they are toward other projective methods. The 144 separate plates, beautifully printed in color, constitute, in effect, approximations to norms for the Mosaic test, although this is disclaimed by the author. They add a great deal to the usefulness of the volume.

[B275]

★McAbee, Harold V. **An Economically Administered Testing Program for Secondary Schools.** Curriculum Bulletin, No. 136. Eugene, Ore.: School of Education, University of Oregon, March 9, 1954. Pp. 14. Paper, mimeographed. $0.20. *

[B276]

★McCall, John R. **Sex Differences in Intelligence: A Comparative Factor Study.** Catholic University of America, Studies in Psychology and Psychiatry, Vol. 9, No. 3. Washington, D.C.: Catholic University of America Press, Inc., 1955. Pp. viii, 65. Paper, lithotyped. $1.00. * (*PA* 30:4171)

[B277]

★McCarthy, Mary Viterbo. **An Empirical Study of the Personality Profiles Characterizing Differential Quantitative and Linguistic Ability.** Catholic University of America, Studies in Psychology and Psychiatry, Vol. 8, No. 4. Washington, D.C.: Catholic University of America Press, Inc., 1953. Pp. viii, 45. Paper. $1.00. * (*PA* 28:4043)

[B278]

★McCloy, Charles Harold, and Young, Norma Dorothy. **Tests and Measurements in Health and Physical Education, Third Edition.** New York: Appleton-Century-Crofts, Inc., 1954. Pp. xxi, 497. $6.75. *

J Sch Health 24:200 Je '54. Charles H. Keene. * The thorough revision of the older material and inclusion of some fifteen chapters that are practically new, has made this text a real leader in tests and measurements, and also in the field of scientific teacher training in this specialty. It is a necessity for all teachers and for mature minded students in health and physical education.

For reviews of the first edition, see 40:B1003.

[B279]

★McCormick, William Pauline. **Factors of Intelligence in High and Low Cognitive Ability Groups.** Catholic University of America, Educational Research Monographs, Vol. 18, No. 2. Washington, D.C.: Catholic University of America Press, Inc., 1954. Pp. viii, 70. Paper. $1.00. *

[B280]

★MacMillen, John W.; Moore, Harriet Bruce; and Bellows, Roger M. **Effective Testing Developments.** Personnel Report Series, No. 522. Chicago, Ill.: Civil Service Assembly, [1952]. Pp. iii, 23. Paper, lithotyped. $2.00. *

[B281]

★McMurry, Robert N.; Arnold, James S.; Browne, Robert F.; Hamstra, R. Hollis; Miller, Katherine S.; Shaeffer, Robert E.; and Shaeffer, Ruth J. **Tested Techniques of Personnel Selection.** Chicago, Ill.: Dartnell Corporation, 1955. Pages not numbered. Looseleaf. $20.00. * (PA 30:7833)

Personnel 33:198–9 S '56. Milton M. Mandell. This manual summarizes in outstanding fashion the knowledge that has been gained in the area of personnel selection during the past 20 years. Dr. McMurry properly points out that the systematic methods he describes aid not only in better initial selection but also in proper placement and in the utilization of marginal workers. While these methods would be beyond the grasp of a personnel clerk and at too low a level for a trained psychologist, the manual offers valuable material for employment specialists between these two extremes. Though much of the material is not new, the systematic organization and completeness of presentation are unique. As could be expected from the author's previous writings, he places most emphasis on the patterned interview and the checking of references by telephone as evaluation methods. Nevertheless, his approach is comprehensive, and the need for adequate job specifications, adequate recruiting, and adequate testing is properly stressed. The form used for "man" specifications is unusually inclusive and recognizes, as do other sections of the manual, findings from clinical and social psychology. Especially valuable are the complete case records— of which the manual provides several examples. These can be used to train employment specialists in the analysis of information—though it should not be overlooked that similar practice is needed in the equally important and complementary phase of obtaining the information itself.

Personnel Psychol 10:123–5 sp '57. Edwin R. Henry. * This reviewer can sum up his reactions to this manual in two statements: (1)

After all the glowing promises in the introduction, he felt let-down, disappointed, even cheated, by the rest of the volume. Instead of the most recent, the most up-to-date, revolutionary, new principles and techniques, he was served the same old stuff and not even well prepared. (2) As a do-it-yourself project, the program leaves him cold. A professional with the background and competence of a McMurry might apply it successfully. In the hands of a less sophisticated "ordinary personnel executive," the experience of doing-it-yourself may either be completely frustrating, or even worse, lead to a feeling of security and expertness not justified by the facts.

[B282]

★McQuitty, Louis L. **Theories and Methods in Some Objective Assessments of Psychological Well-Being.** American Psychological Association, Psychological Monographs: General and Applied, Vol. 68, No. 14, Whole No. 385. Washington, D.C.: the Association, Inc., 1954. Pp. 28. Paper. $1.50. * (PA 29:7243)

[B283]

★Magnuson, Henry W.; Larson, Carl A.; and Shellhammer, Thomas A. **Evaluating Pupil Progress.** California State Department of Education Bulletin, Vol. 21, No. 6. Sacramento, Calif.: the Department, April 1952. Pp. 184. Paper. $0.75. *

Calif J Ed Res 3:189 S '52. * this monograph emphasizes the instructional values to be derived from an all-inclusive program of evaluation. Its major purpose is to assist teachers in gathering and interpreting evidences of growth in the skills, knowledges, attitudes, and understandings that receive emphasis in the modern program of education. Over 150 supervisors and directors of instruction, superintendents, teachers, college deans, and representatives of lay groups reviewed, criticized, and supplemented the original manuscript. Some of the topics discussed in the monograph are: (1) the role of evaluation in education; (2) testing in an evaluation program; (3) appraising capacity for learning; (4) appraising personality development; (5) evaluating attitudes; (6) defining and observing pupil behavior; (7) techniques to appraise pupil behavior; (8) reporting pupil progress, etc.

Ed Res B 32:193–4 O 14 '53. Guy W. Buddemeyer. * Although no one of the topics discussed is dealt with exhaustively, it provides in a manageable volume a great many practical suggestions, and in general includes the basic principles applicable to the evaluation of pupil progress. * The guide offers evidence of an interesting trend in evaluation concepts that has developed in recent years—the emphasis on observation. * Although there might be some question regarding certain details such as the use of the phrase "appraising capacity for learning" (pages 39–48) and the chapter title "Techniques to Appraise Character Traits— the Rating Scale" (pages 97–124), this compact volume would serve any teacher as a valuable source book on evaluation of student progress. Other features of the handbook include an extensive bibliography, numerous illustrations and examples, and an appendix in which questions frequently asked by teachers are answered on the basis of current practice and recent literature in evaluation.

[B284]

★MANDELL, MILTON M. **A Company Guide to the Selection of Salesmen.** Research Report No. 24. New York: American Management Association, 1955. Pp. 161. $4.75. * (*PA* 30:1719)

[B285]

★MANUEL, HERSCHEL T. **Taking a Test: How to Do Your Best.** Yonkers, N. Y.: World Book Co., 1956. Pp. ii, 77. Paper. $0.96. *

Ed Res B 36:27–8 Ja 9 '57. Marie A. Flesher. * The book has several desirable features: it is short, is written in a clear and readily understandable manner, contains a number of novel illustrations, is applicable to the problems which concern most of the persons reading it, and provides immediate practice on many of the suggestions presented. The individual who studies this book independently may wish that a key had been provided for the exercises which are included in the book. However, it seems likely that the person taking a test will gain in skill and confidence if he follows the advice of the author.

[B286]

★MARCUSE, IRENE. **The Key to Handwriting Analysis.** New York: McBride Co., Inc., 1955. Pp. 144. $3.50. *

[B287]

★MASLOW, ALBERT P. **Oral Tests: A Survey of Current Practice.** Personnel Report Series, No. 521. Chicago, Ill.: Civil Service Assembly, [1952]. Pp. ii, 26. Paper, lithotyped. $2.00. *

[B288]

★MATHEWS, DONALD K. **Measurement in Physical Education.** Philadelphia, Pa. and London: W. B. Saunders Co., 1958. Pp. x, 359. $5.25; 37s. *

[B289]

★MAXFIELD, KATHRYN E., AND KENYON, EUNICE L. **A Guide to the Use of the Maxfield-Fjeld Tentative Adaptation of the Vineland Social Maturity Scale for Use With Visually Handicapped Preschool Children.** New York: American Foundation for the Blind, 1953. Pp. ii, 30. Paper, lithotyped. * (*PA* 29: 1406)

[B290]

★MEYER, JEROME S. **The Handwriting Analyzer.** New York: Simon & Schuster, Inc., 1953. Pp. iii, 103. $2.95. * (London: Dennis Dobson, 1954. Pp. 101. 10s. 6d.)

Psychiatric Q Sup 28:167 pt 1 '54. This book pretends to be somewhat more than what it is. According to the publishers "it provides many hours of entertainment as well as interesting information about old friends and new. *The Handwriting Analyzer* is so accurate that it can be recommended for personnel work in business." The author is not a professional psychologist, and there is no evidence that any careful research studies substantiate the validity of the character analyses given. Whereas no objection can be leveled at its use as a game for parlor entertainment, the book should not be used for serious purposes.

[B291]

★MICHAELIS, JOHN U. **The Prediction of Success in Student Teaching From Personality and Attitude Inventories.** University of California Publications in Education, Vol. 11, No. 6. Berkeley, Calif.: University of California Press, 1954. Pp. iii, 415–84. Paper. * (*PA* 30:1657)

[B292]

★MILLER, ROBERT D., EDITOR. **Program and Proceedings of the Conference on Evaluation in Higher Education, February 12–13, 1954, The Florida State University, Tallahassee, Florida.** Tallahassee, Fla.: Florida State University, 1954. Pp. iv, 88. Paper. *

[B293]

★MINER, JOHN B. **Intelligence in the United States: A Survey—With Conclusions for Manpower Utilization in Education and Employment.** New York: Springer Publishing Co., Inc., 1957. Pp. xii, 180. $4.25. (London: Interscience Publishers, Ltd. 32s.) * (*PA* 32:1344)

Brit J Ed Psychol 28:93 F '58. Dr. Miner's study is of interest because, with the aid of Gallup Polls, he was able to collect a very highly representative sample of the total U.S. population aged 1 upwards. These 1,500 individuals were given a 20-item vocabulary test by the interviewers, and the results are here analysed by age, sex, race, religion, geographical area, education and occupation. The introductory and the concluding chapters have less to offer. The former presents the arguments for a general factor in intelligence, much along British lines, whose essential functions are reasoning and grasping relations; but they fail to show why— in that case—a pure vocabulary test was used as a measure of intelligence. The later sections discuss the utilization of the nation's intellectual potential, and are based on the common fallacy that, because most college students score above a particular vocabulary level, therefore, everybody with equally high scores should go, or should have gone, to college.

Brit J Psychol 48:317 N '57. A. W. Heim. This book is a strange mixture of over- and under-statements. The author claims that he has made a survey of a cross-section of the U.S. population "with conclusions for manpower utilization in education and employment." This would appear to be overstating the case since the book is based simply on the results of testing 1500 subjects (1347 whites and 153 Negroes, ranging in age from 10 years to 75+) on one 20-word, multiple-choice vocabulary test, and comparing their scores with their occupations ($n = 316$), race ($n = 2$), religion ($n = 4$), social class as self-estimated ($n = 4$) and sex ($n = 2$). The other variables considered include education, place of residence, marital status, and age. On the basis of his subjects' scores on the vocabulary test and their position on these other variables, Dr Miner estimates what proportions of people in the U.S.A. are over- and under-employed, over- and under-educated. He expounds, in percentages correct to one—sometimes two—decimal place, how many should be "promoted" and how many "demoted." It is among these conclusions especially that understating of a kind occurs. For example, having ascertained "the degree of manpower wastage as indicated by tests of verbal learning" and specified the numbers at every level who should be promoted, he adds with apparent light-heartedness: "In order to determine the extent to which our present occupational placement system produces a deviation from one *based entirely on a verbal ability criterion,* all that is necessary is to compare an individual's vocabulary score with the ranges that have been established and then determine whether it would be necessary to promote or demote him to ensure his employment at a level consistent with his *intelligence.* The degree of deviation can then be specified in terms of the percentage of the working population who would have to be promoted to a higher occupational level to attain a perfect intelligence-occupation correlation. An equal number will, of course, have to be demoted in order to keep the number of people working at each level

constant" (reviewer's italics). The last sentence (which ends the section) strikes the reviewer as a masterly understatement of difficulties—leaving aside any question as to the defensibility and value of Dr Miner's plan. Dr Miner is interested above all in avoiding wastage. Towards the beginning of his chapter on "The utilization of intellectual resources in the educational system" he says: "The data, to be presented in this and the following chapter, on educational and occupational manpower wastage are unique." The reader, pursuing page after page of what can only be called autistic thinking, becomes inclined to agree. Dr Miner's conclusions rest on two assumptions. The first is the infallibility of the 20-word vocabulary test at all levels and for all purposes. The second is the fact—rather than assumption—that 90% of any given group score above the 10th percentile! * Towards the beginning of the book the reader has difficulty in deciding just where the author is going. By the end of the book, he has decided that it would have been better not to travel at all than to travel hopefully.

Ed Res B 36:243-4 O 9 '57. Howard A. Moss. * The innovations that the author proposes constitute a highly ambitious and lofty undertaking. Many of his ideas and suggestions deserve further exploration and study. However, it seems that the use of a 20-word vocabulary test as a predictor of reasoning ability and productivity is inadequate and the author over-interprets in arriving at the conclusions that he does from his data. This test lacks sufficient generality and does not adequately take into account chance errors of measurement to warrant the generalizations that are made. Nevertheless, the author should be commended for calling attention to the need for a more effective utilization of human resources.

J Higher Ed 28:288-9 My '57. John B. Carroll. * Two introductory chapters offer what to this reviewer is the most interesting material in the book, for here the author presents his theory of intelligence. Performance is viewed as a function of native potential, the learning sets (in Harlow's sense) acquired by the individual in his environment, and motivation. But the development of verbal abilities is paramount in determining the degree of success in the social system, and hence "through the techniques of correlation and item analysis we have developed tests that mirror the society as a whole" (page 32). Abilities other than verbal, such as numerical, spatial, and musical, simply represent special clusters of learning sets. This general theory makes much sense and accords with contemporary findings in factor analysis. Nevertheless, possibly Miner underestimates the role of constitutional factors in special abilities. * The implications for education and manpower utilization, presented in the final chapters, are open to considerable debate. Miner attempts to show that a large portion of our children are "underplaced" in school; by playing a sort of grand game of musical chairs he would promote some and demote others to confront each student with material of suitable difficulty, meanwhile making the curriculum more challenging. Somewhat similar proposals are made with respect to man-power utilization. This is all very well, but many will believe that Mr. Miner is overimpressed with the single variable of intelligence as a determinant of the individual's educability and ability to contribute to society. Nevertheless, the arresting quality of his proposals will tend to add to the value of the book, which, incidentally, is scholarly and well documented.

Personnel & Guid J 36:504 Mr '58. Harold Goldstein. This book attempts to present a cross-section of the intelligence of the population of the United States and draw conclusions for education, employment, and manpower utilization. * what is unique in this study is the elaborate analysis based on an instrument that is basically so oversimple, one-dimensional, and lacking in discrimination. To cite one example, the unskilled laborers averaged 9.6 words correctly identified, the skilled craftsmen 10.6, with standard deviations of over 3 in each case. Does an instrument which finds no significant difference in intelligence between these two groups adequately and sensitively measure intelligence for any useful purpose? The author goes on to draw implications from his material for education. The implications are staggering. On the basis of students' performance on this 20-word vocabulary test, it was determined that 27 per cent of the grammar school students over nine years of age should be shifted to the 10th to 13th grades, and "only 3.9 per cent" should be put in college, while 22 per cent of the college students should be demoted to the 9th grade or below. Having put the educational system in order, the author wheels up his 20-word vocabulary test and trains it on the utilization of workers in industry. When he is fin-

ished, the same kind of reshuffling has taken place as in the educational system: 4 per cent of the unskilled workers have been promoted to professional jobs, and 13 per cent to skilled jobs, while 59 per cent of the professional and 42 per cent of the skilled workers have been demoted. In short, in pursuing a broadly conceived plan, feeble resources have been stretched far beyond the breaking point. It is unfortunate that the significant task undertaken in this book fails in its execution. There is still need for a thorough and penetrating study of this subject.

[B294]

★MITZEL, HAROLD E.; OSTREICHER, LEONARD M.; AND REITER, SIDNEY R. **Development of Attitudinal Dimensions From Teachers' Drawings.** College of the City of New York, Division of Teacher Education, Office of Research and Evaluation, Publication No. 24. New York: Office of Research and Evaluation, the Division, October 1954. Pp. vi, 49. Paper, mimeographed. $1.50. * (*PA* 29:7999)

[B295]

★MITZEL, HAROLD E., AND RABINOWITZ, WILLIAM. **Assessing Social-Emotional Climate in the Classroom by Withall's Technique.** American Psychological Association, Psychological Monographs: General and Applied, Vol. 67, No. 18, Whole No. 368. Washington, D.C.: the Association, Inc., 1953. Pp. 19. Paper. $1.00.* (*PA* 29:1596)

[B296]

★MITZEL, HAROLD E., AND RABINOWITZ, WILLIAM. **Reliability of Teachers' Verbal Behavior: A Study of Withall's Technique for Assessing Social-Emotional Climate in the Classroom.** College of the City of New York, Division of Teacher Education, Office of Research and Evaluation, Publication No. 15. New York: Office of Research and Evaluation, the Division, June 1953. Pp. v, 30. Paper, mimeographed. $0.50. * (*PA* 28:3311)

[B297]

★MITZEL, HAROLD E.; RABINOWITZ, WILLIAM; AND OSTREICHER, LEONARD M. **Effect of Certain Response Sets on Valid Test Variance.** College of the City of New York, Division of Teacher Education, Office of Research and Evaluation, Publication No. 26. New York: Office of Research and Evaluation, the Division, February 1955. Pp. ii, 23. Paper, mimeographed. $0.75. * (*PA* 30:118)

[B298]

★MORAN, MAURICE J. **An Experimental Study of Certain Aspects of Paranoid Schizophrenic Mosaic Field Organization and Their Interrelationships.** Washington, D.C.: Catholic University of America Press, 1954. Pp. 55. Paper, lithotyped. $0.75. * (*PA* 29:2814)

[B299]

*MORENO, J. L. **Who Shall Survive? Foundations of Sociometry, Group Psychotherapy, and Sociodrama,** [Revised Edition]. Beacon, N.Y.: Beacon House Inc., 1953. Pp. cxiv, 763. $12.50. * (*PA* 28:4178)

Am J Psychiatry 111:157–8 Ag '54. Earl A. Loomis, Jr. * The book....has an excellent bibliography, a glossary, and indices; and the format is good. Unfortunately, it is too long to read as a whole, but if one can treat it as a collection of volumes and read each separately, it is well worthwhile having them all, since they are interrelated and present together the composite necessary to understand the parts. * One could criticize much of the style, with its repetitiousness (valuable as it may be to the newcomer, for didactic reasons), polemics, apparently gratuitous digs at Kurt Lewin and at psychoanalysis, to which Moreno does not always acknowledge *his* indebtedness. Nevertheless there is a refreshing quality to his zealous, exuberant, and optimistic manner of thought which can well serve to counteract an excessive moroseness, sobriety, and "realism" of some of our scientists. Most psychiatrists would have appreciated more detailed instructions in the handling of patients in groups and in group psychotherapy and psychodrama—*i.e.,* how to put all this theory to work in the hospital and clinic. These will have to follow in a later volume or be found in other books and in group psychotherapy journals. Analysts will resent the couch and office being relegated to areas of the abstract opposite of "action techniques," since most would admit the importance of appropriate active testing in life as the patient advances in therapy. They will cringe at transference being seen as *only* a pathological phenomenon, a bastard form of *"tele."* Others will wonder whether and why the author *must* use so many new words and whether they are all as necessary and as different in meaning from our familiar jargon as the author asserts or implies. *Who Shall Survive?* has come a long way since 1934 and so have its author and his movement. The adoption of action techniques by psychoanalysts using group therapy (such as Serge Lebovici in Paris) may bring it closer to psychoanalysis. Perhaps someone adept in the philosophy, techniques, and verbiage of both fields can show how much closer together they really are than either knows. This book is certainly a potential milestone and guidepost along the pathway toward that goal.

Am Sociol R 19:358–9 Je '54. Edgar F. Borgatta. The revised edition of the now classic *Who Shall Survive?* has been greatly enlarged, and is in many ways a new book. * A good part of the new book (about 95 pages) is devoted to the "Preludes of the Sociometric Movement," an autobiographical account of Moreno's position in social science and psychiatry. This account may hurt the sensitivities of those who feel that an author's personality should be kept out of a book, especially if the author does not tend to modesty. It will hurt the sensitivities of some even more when they find that Moreno is quite facile and candid in naming friends and enemies, and in producing withering (though often humorous) criticism of positions he feels incompatible to his own. On the other hand, some may find his openness quite refreshing in this age of subtlety and practiced professional politeness. Whatever the response, if these things should discourage the reader, it will have been the reader's loss. * The style of writing used by Moreno is clear and simple, save for the use of words he has coined which are as yet unfamiliar (tele, sociosis, bioatry, axiodrama, etc.). * This book does not make easy reading. This may be due to the fact that Moreno presents enough ideas to fill several volumes but frequently does not follow through with their analysis, and, further, because he encompasses problems in parallel at different levels, switching back and forth. These difficulties are minor, however, in comparison to the benefit which can be derived from this unique book, and no serious student of sociology, psychology, or psychiatry can afford not to read it.

Can J Psychol 8:173–4 S '54. Mary L. Northway. It is unusual for a man to write two books with the same title. Moreno has done so. *Who Shall Survive? A New Approach to the Problem of Human Interrelations,* published by the Nervous and Mental Disease Publishing Company in 1934, was a monograph describing the use of sociometric techniques in a girls' training school. It marked the birth of sociometry in America. The 1953 book, which is not indicated as a second edition, is a systematic summary of the accomplishments of sociometry, group psychotherapy, and sociodrama as these are viewed by the mind of Moreno. He discusses sociometry not merely as a technique but as a theoretical basis for the clinical developments of sociodrama and group therapy. He also considers it the essential foundation for understanding the structure of society. The book includes findings from most of the important studies of the past twenty years. Although direct reference to the specific investigators is rarely given, an intensive bibliography shows the great number of scientists who have been involved. This book will be an essential encyclopaedia for all future workers in this area. Moreno includes a section called "Preludes" (114 pages) in his new book. This is partly an autobiography and partly the biography of the sociometric movement. This may clarify the current confusion between sociometry as science and sociometry as doctrine, at least by revealing its sources. Moreno's statements, such as "An idea book like *Who Shall Survive* cannot be conceived in collaboration," and "I have written two bibles, an old testament and a new testament," indicate why sociometry has had difficulty being accepted among the scientific brethren; they also reveal why, in spite of the fact that within its own ranks there have been so many dissenters, the orthodox sociometry army has succeeded in militantly marching on, saluting the banners of the Leader.

J Abn & Social Psychol 49:478–80 Jl '54. Eugene L. Hartley. * an important volume which has much to contribute to improving our understanding of the social nature of man and the nature of man's social behavior * retains the same central research material that was presented in the 1934 original. However, the context is very different. The development of the sociometric movement during the intervening 20 years is reviewed in "Preludes," which includes also additional material on the pre-1933 background. It is this section of about 100 pages that departs most from traditional scientific writing. However, this is Moreno's statement of the history of "his" approach. The pages are given Roman numerals, and even if unusually long, are completely in the character of prefaces to which we are more accustomed. There are in the Moreno personal statement such items as characterization of the book as a bible ("The Words of the Father," the old testament; "Who Shall Survive?" the new, p. lxvii); an insistence on sole authorship of the book, emphasizing that "An idea book like Who Shall Survive? cannot be conceived 'in collaboration'" (p. lxxxvii) (yet in the 1934 edition, Helen H. Jennings is described as a collaborator); the description of an imaginary correspondence with H. A. Murray in which "he sends me letters which he never actually wrote and I send him letters, often in the middle of the night, which he receives promptly and without benefit of mail carriers" (p. xc); and an attack upon the integrity of some of the leaders of the current group dynamics move-

ment (p. cii ff.). However future historians may accept or "correct" the version Moreno gives, these Preludes are important documentation for a history of the social science, and valuable for a study of the process of writing history. Moreno recognizes that there is far more controversy about his person than there is about his theories. He concludes this presentation with the statement: "I have tried to explain why an individual of my type was particularly suited to produce them. I hope that I succeeded some and that everyone, friends and enemies, will enjoy them, because they are autobiography 'unadulterated.' Now I fear only that many will read the Preludes and not the book" (p. cviii). Your reviewer shares these fears and has dwelt on this section of the book to make explicit what is likely to prove the major drawback for many readers. Other readers, however, will appreciate the insights this kind of statement will give them into the nature of the originator of one of the most productive approaches currently available to students of social processes. The body of the book remains much as in the original. * The final section, however, "Who Shall Survive?" is greatly elaborated. * the first edition contained only 41 items on a one-page bibliography, while the new volume claims over 1,300 references in a 31-page bibliography. This single quantitative index may serve as a clue to the impact of Moreno's ideas during the 20-year period, and the difference between the original and the second edition of the book. *

J Consult Psychol 17:466 D '53. Fred McKinney. In his 114-page "preludes of the sociometric movement," Moreno presents a professional autobiography and concludes it with this apparently cogent insight: "There is no controversy about my ideas; they are universally accepted. I am the controversy." There is no statement as to how this large volume differs from the 1934 edition, to which he refers here as a "bible of human relations" (p. lxvi). Comparison of the two indicates that this is an expansion of the basic outline with slightly more discussion of sociodrama, group psychotherapy, and psychodrama, although much less than one might expect from the subtitle and extensive bibliographies devoted to them. More attention is given in this book than in its predecessor to the broader implications of sociometry and sociometric and spontaneity theory. The original book presented the theoretical bases for sociometry and the use of sociometric techniques with various groups. Despite the fact that the bibliography is greatly expanded (1,300 titles as compared to 41 in the first edition) there is no attempt to integrate systematically this wealth of material into the text proper. The book is an unabashed exposition of Moreno's ideas and is limited largely to a consideration of their influences. Certainly Dr. Moreno has made a great and widely recognized contribution to the study and effective use of the group. However, the reviewer feels that these important ideas could have been presented with greater effect in fewer pages and would have been enriched by integrating them with the outstanding work of others which has appeared since the date of the first edition.

Mental Health 13:130–1 su '54. R. B. Morton. * Moreno is completely carried away by his exuberance and becomes positively euphoric over the great disclosures he makes, frequently to the detriment of other workers in the same field and showing a biased critical analysis of their work as a whole. Even if one allows oneself to become fired by his enthusiasm, it is another matter to practice what he preaches without his attribute of self-display. * There can be no doubt that this authoritative work is not in the same category as the general medical textbooks; at the same time it is the best comprehensive treatment of Group methods that I have yet read. It is not too easily read, and there is a lot of wading through a marshy conglomeration of explanation in which one is liable to get bogged down before one comes on solid ground. If there is one good factor alone which emerges and stands out, it is the technique he has created of *measurement.* "Every science refers to a constellation of facts and the means of their measurement." Group techniques, if they are to become accepted and recognised methods of treatment, must be capable of assessment in the good that they do. The sociogram has been evolved as the test method, measuring the amount of organisation by social groups. This by itself makes the work valuable and acceptable, even if it does provoke, as Moreno has himself suggested, "a lot of personal controversy."

Occupational Psychol 28:183–4 Jl '54. Thelma Veness. * What has been added to increase the first edition of xvi + 437 pages to the cxiv + 763 of the second? * Useful additional material is difficult to find. There are new and elaborate tables and charts, for the most part re-presentations of old data (in one case, different results from apparently the same study); there is surprisingly little fresh empirical data. * The expansions in the text....[are of a] dream-like character, disjointed, wildly speculative, grandiose and critical of other theorists in the social sphere. With the possible exception of a half-page account of the sociometric test and the sociometric questionnaire on p. lxxi of the Preludes, no straightforward account of what sociometry does occurs until p. 81 (*i.e.,* after any reader with the habit of reading straight through a book has read 180 pages). A reader with little previous knowledge of sociometry will by this time be thoroughly bewildered. Having been dragged through a fantastic maze of strange speculations, he will be in danger of having built up an expectation of blind alleys only, just as he reaches the point, which is roughly where the first edition began. In fact, the great advantage that the first edition has over the second is that its presentation does allow one to appreciate Moreno's achievements, whereas the second chiefly demonstrates how far short they fall of his aspiration, which appears to be nothing less than the re-creation of the universe. It is a long step from the study of girls living in cottages with housemothers to the following claim: "The simultaneous applications of revolutionary sociometric methods in the United States as well as in Soviet Russia might bring about a rapprochement between the two types of government. The revolutions of the socialistic-marxistic type are outmoded; they failed to meet with the sociodynamics of the world situation. The next social revolution will be of the 'sociometric' type." The next American evangelist for Harringay? But Moreno assures that he has no illusions as to his own importance: "I am fully aware that sociometry might have come into existence without me, just like sociology would have come into existence in France without Comte, and Marxism in Germany and Russia without Marx."

Psychol B 51:322–3 My '54. Leon Festinger. * In the long preface the author tells us that: (1) Sociometry is a religion as well as a science (e.g., page xv): "I tried to do through sociometry what religion without science has failed to accomplish in the past...." (2) The author is a genius (e.g., page xxxvii): "All my books (nine) published between 1919 and 1925, were anonymous. The natural state of genius is anonymity....*The Words of the Father* I wrote with red ink on the walls of an Austrian castle." (3) Sociometry is the final development (e.g., page lxvii) : "Actually, I have written two bibles, an old testament and a new testament, *The Words of the Father* and *Who Shall Survive?*" (4) Psychoanalysis is finished (e.g., page liv) : "....the psychoanalytic system was stillborn to start with....The psychoanalytic couch has become a piece of furniture in the sociodynamic field of the psychodramatic stage." (5) Group therapy, group dynamics, and, it seems, all work on small groups and large groups are developments of, or secessions from, the sociometric movement (pages lxix, lxx, and xcvii to cviii). The body of the text is devoted to an exposition of the theory, methods, and accomplishments of sociometry. While it is difficult to give a brief review of over 700 pages, I will try to list the major points which are made. (1) The most important concepts of the sociometric system are spontaneity, creativity, Tele, the social atom, and underlying social networks. There is considerable discussion which conveys to the reader a vague feeling concerning the meaning of these terms. There are no very specific or rigorous definitions. (2) The basic techniques of sociometry are psychodrama, sociodrama, role-playing, group psychotherapy, and the sociometric test. Only the discussion of the last of these is at all elaborated in detail. There is little more than brief mention of the others. The only empirical data presented concern the sociometric test, the essence of which is asking people with whom they want to associate. (3) A major portion is devoted to detailed description of two studies using this sociometric test. Data are presented to show that the distribution of choices is different from chance, the pattern of choices changes with age, attractions among persons are not always in accordance with formal or existing associations, and that if groups are made up in accordance with the desires of the members, these groups hold the members' interest better. To this reviewer it seems that there are many pages devoted to stating how important sociometry is. There is, however, little space devoted to any convincing empirical demonstration that these claims are valid.

For reviews of the first edition, see 40: B1022.

[B300]

★MORENO, J. L., EDITOR. **Sociometry and the Science of Man.** New York: Beacon House Inc., 1956. Pp. viii, 474. $7.50. * [Same as *Sociometry*, Vol. 18, No. 4.]

Cont Psychol 2:159–60 Je '57. Ben Willerman. * papers by [Moreno] discuss the role of sociometry in the development of social science and his theory of spontaneity and creativity. He regards these phenomena as *the* problems of psychology. Some aspects of this theory are so speculative as to be untestable, and thus the empirical findings which he cites seem to bear little relation to the theory. Moreno's position seems to be that the creativity which accompanies or characterizes a response in interpersonal relations is not different from that which is present in solving other kinds of problems. If this is so, Moreno's theory could have profited by contact with the technical literature in such areas as motivation, set, and problem-solving. * It is a good book for learning about the sociometric movement and its recent developments. There are in it also some valuable suggestions for the use of sociometric techniques in practice and research. The contributions on sociometric indices and the probability models for evaluating the distribution of choices stand out as among the best in the book. The sociological contributions are relevant in only a strained fashion. Surely sociometry has affected sociology more than these papers would indicate. One difficulty in assessing sociometry is in deciding just what it is. Moreno wants the term to refer to practically all of group psychology (and sometimes to all of social science), not only for semantic reasons but also for reasons of theoretical and methodological priority and influence. No consensual validation for this position is, however, to be elicited from the majority of persons who do research on group behavior. * As to the claims of priority, many students, including the reviewer, are more than willing to grant the productive Moreno his deserved position in the Hall of Fame for originating or promulgating a variety of diagnostic and therapeutic techniques, such as the sociometric test, sociogram, role-playing, sociodrama and psychodrama, and certain concepts and indices of group structure. Nehnevajsa's thorough, well-organized, and only slightly partisan historical summary of these contributions leaves little room for doubt on this score. According to Moreno, however, this already impressive list of innovations is incomplete. Despite his admission that recent developments in the social sciences "have demonstrated 'collective' originality," at times he indirectly suggests that history may credit him with the innovation of systematic small-group research. In reality, without making an intensive search of the literature, one finds that Terman's *experimental* study of leadership in 1904 (which, by the way, any current small-group researcher would be proud to have on his list of publications) included controlled observations of behavior and sociometric-type questions, such as "What one of your schoolmates would you rather be like if you were not yourself?" From other fields, Thrasher's classic study of gangs in 1927 and the Hawthorne research which demonstrated the importance of the work group in setting output standards (Mayo, 1933) may also be cited as occurring at least concurrently with Moreno's scientific studies. Moreno has affected group psychology, but he overestimates the extent of his influence. Much of small group research stems from the long line of studies by such psychologists as Terman, F. H. Allport (1920), Whittemore (1924), South (1927) and so on through Sherif (1936). Lewin and Lippitt's 1940 pioneer study, in which they manipulated leadership style so as to study its effect on group behavior, included sociometric tests as a tool for equating the interpersonal relations of the members of the compared groups. But here is where its resemblance to any of the studies reported in *Who Shall Survive* (1934) ends. The systematic and systematically analyzed observations, the rich but close conceptual analysis of cause and effect, the testing of deduction from theory, the incorporation of theories of motivation and action—all characterizing the Lewin-Lippitt study—are only partially present in Moreno's work. It is just not possible to take him seriously when he says (p. 17), "Looking backward, it seems natural that even within the sociometric movement itself, separate cliques should have emerged, trying to identify themselves by different terms like group dynamics in the middle forties, small group research in the early fifties." Surely, Moreno was, however, one of the first to combine a profound appreciation of the fact that the arrangement of persons in a community could markedly affect them as individuals and

the community as a whole with a research program that not only had therapeutic but also scientific aims. Certainly the exaggerated claims and the mystical and religious overtones which at times characterize Moreno's writings should not affect the appreciation of his pre-scientific and scientific contributions.

[B301]

*MORSE, HORACE T., AND McCUNE, GEORGE H. **Selected Items for the Testing of Study Skills and Critical Thinking, Third Edition.** National Council for the Social Studies, Bulletin No. 15, Third Edition. Washington, D.C.: the Council, National Education Association, 1957. Pp. vii, 80. Paper. $1.25. * For reviews of earlier editions, see 4:B280 and 3:1039.

[B302]

★MUKERJI, NIROD. **An Inquiry About Examination (Calcutta University).** Calcutta, India: Das Gupta & Co., Ltd., 1954. Pp. viii, 67. Paper. *

[B303]

★MURPHY, LOIS BARCLAY; WITH THE COLLABORATION OF EVELYN BEYER, ANNA HARTOCH, EUGENE LERNER, L. JOSEPH STONE, AND TRUDE SCHMIDL-WAEHNER. **Personality in Young Children: Vol. I, Methods for the Study of Personality in Young Children.** New York: Basic Books, Inc., 1956. Pp. xx, 424. $6.00. * (PA 31:2656)

Cont Psychol 2:69–70 Mr '57. Frank Barron. * tells of the origin and development of a distinctive method of psychological observation which, in the hands of these researchers, is organically united with a special area of valued concern. Their special concern is with the maintenance of psychological health in normal children; their way of working is one in which a trained observer is brought into contact with children in a fashion designed to minimize artificiality and to maximize freedom of response in a relatively unconstrained and unstructured situation (as they say). The situation is that of natural, if somewhat uncommon, play: with a variety of toys, including "Miniature Life Toys," a sort of small-fry copy of the big world, and "Sensory Toys," offering the fairly exotic sensory experiences obtainable from such substances as excelsior, acetate black "hair," and wax dust, and such unlikely objects as a kaleidoscope, a strip of fur, a copper-mesh ball, a tapping bell, and a humming top; group games either requiring leadership or presenting special opportunities for it; games in which there is an implied invitation to break various highly breakable things, such as balloons; and play with dough and cold cream (very unstructured). * The kind of crude quantification which psychology has achieved is unhappily often at the expense of a careful scrutiny of process. Particularly in the study of children is it evident that our study must be of dynamics; in rapidly growing organisms the fact of change is the preeminent fact, and change, especially change of patterns, is precisely what is least representable by our current quantitative techniques. It is much to the credit of Lois Murphy and her associates....that they attended with sensitivity and patience to the changing patterns of growth of the nursery-school children who were at once subjects and benefactors of this study, which has extended in time from the childhood of the first subjects into their psychologically healthy maturity. There is, nevertheless, a tantalizing quality about this research, because its fascinating techniques and often brilliant speculations are not always accompanied by sufficient self-criticism concerning evidence and the grounds for belief. At the risk of seeming ungrateful while sitting down to a feast, one could wish for more abstraction at the observational level and more low-level but more surely confirmed generalizations. The book is, on the one hand, a riot of concreteness, for a great many play sessions are reported in rich detail, but, on the other hand, a compendium of high-level generalizations which may be true but which are unsupported by controlled observation. Still, when one gets through, he has the feeling of having had a lot of fun and stimulation playing with ideas (in a relatively unstructured cognitive situation), and surely that is nothing to complain about.

[B304]

★National Council on Measurements Used in Education. **The Ninth Yearbook of the National Council on Measurements Used in Education, 1951–52.** New York: the Council, [1952]. Pp. v, 119, xxxii. Paper, lithotyped. *

[B305]

★National Council on Measurements Used in Education. **The Tenth Yearbook of the National Council on Measurements Used in Education, 1952–53.** New York: the Council, [1953]. Pp. iii, 90, 19. Paper, mimeographed.

[B306]

★National Council on Measurements Used in Education. **The Eleventh Yearbook of the National Council on Measurements Used in Education, 1953–54.** New York: the Council, [1954]. Pp. iv, 108, xviii. Paper, lithotyped. *

[B307]

★National Council on Measurements Used in Education. **The Twelfth Yearbook of the National Council on Measurements Used in Education,**

1955, Parts 1 and 2. New York: the Council, [1955]. Pp. v, 105; iii, 91. Paper, mimeographed. *

[B308]

★National Council on Measurements Used in Education. **The Thirteenth Yearbook of the National Council on Measurements Used in Education, 1956.** New York: the Council, [1956]. Pp. v, 178. Paper, lithotyped. *

[B309]

★National Council on Measurements Used in Education. **The Fourteenth Yearbook of the National Council on Measurements Used in Education, 1957.** New York: the Council, [1957]. Pp. v, 147. Paper, lithotyped. $3.00. *

[B310]

★National Council on Measurements Used in Education. **The Fifteenth Yearbook of the National Council on Measurements Used in Education, 1958.** Edited by Edith M. Huddleston. New York: the Council, 1958. Pp. v, 175. Paper, lithotyped. $3.00. *

[B311]

★National Education Association, American Educational Research Association, Committee on Educational and Psychological Testing, Frederick B. Davis, Chairman. **Educational and Psychological Testing.** Review of Educational Research, Vol. 23, No. 1. Washington, D.C.: American Educational Research Association, February 1953. Pp. 110. Paper. $1.50. *

[B312]

★National Education Association, American Educational Research Association, Committee on Educational and Psychological Testing, Max D. Engelhart, Chairman. **Educational and Psychological Testing.** Review of Educational Research, Vol. 26, No. 1. Washington, D.C.: American Educational Research Association, February 1956. Pp. 110. Paper. $1.50. *

[B313]

★National League for Nursing. **The Construction and Use of Teacher-Made Tests.** Use of Tests in Schools of Nursing Pamphlet No. 5. New York: the League, Inc., 1957. Pp. vi, 102. $2.50. * (PA 32:3350)

Personnel & Guid J 36:363 Ja '58. Thomas M. Magoon. This rather detailed cookbook.... is quite readable, well illustrated with many nursing-related examples and written to specific points. The two largest sections of the pamphlet cover construction of all of the common forms of test items, and analysis and interpretation of test data. The pamphlet is designed to assist instructors in schools of nursing in building and using tests which will measure student achievement of certain objectives of the nursing training program. Particularly since this effort is geared to such a specific group, it is the reviewer's hope that some effort will be made to assess the impact of this handbook on measurement in nursing education.

[B314]

★NATIONAL LEAGUE FOR NURSING. **The NLN Achievement Test, Second Edition.** The Use of Tests in Schools of Nursing Pamphlet No. 2. New York: the League, Inc., 1958. Pp. iii, 44. Paper. $1.25. *

[B315]

★NATIONAL LEAGUE OF NURSING. **The NLN Graduate Nurse Qualifying Examination.** The Use of Tests in Schools of Nursing Pamphlet No. 3. New York: the League, Inc., 1954. Pp. v, 39. $1.25. *

[B316]

★NATIONAL LEAGUE FOR NURSING. **The NLN Pre-Nursing and Guidance Examination, Second Edition.** The Use of Tests in Schools of Nursing Pamphlet No. 1. New York: the League, Inc., 1957. Pp. v, 42. Paper. $1.25. *

[B317]

★NEW YORK STATE EDUCATION DEPARTMENT, BUREAU OF EXAMINATIONS AND TESTING, TEST ADVISORY SERVICE. **Sourcebook of Test Items for Teachers of English, Grades 7–9.** Albany, N.Y.: the Department, 1957. Pp. 48. Paper. *

[B318]

★NEW YORK STATE EDUCATION DEPARTMENT, BUREAU OF EXAMINATIONS AND TESTING, TEST ADVISORY SERVICE. **Sourcebook of Test Items for Teachers of General Science, Grades 7–9.** Albany, N.Y.: the Department, 1956. Pp. 47. Paper. *

[B319]

★NEW YORK STATE EDUCATION DEPARTMENT, BUREAU OF EXAMINATIONS AND TESTING, TEST ADVISORY SERVICE. **Sourcebook of Test Items for Teachers of Mathematics, Grades 7–9.** Albany, N.Y.: the Department, 1956. Pp. 51. Paper. *

[B320]

★NEWMAN, SIDNEY H.; HOWELL, MARGARET A.; AND HARRIS, FRANK J. **Forced Choice and Other Methods for Evaluating Professional Health Personnel.** American Psychological Association, Psychological Monographs: General and Applied, Vol. 71, No. 10, Whole No. 439. Washington, D.C.: the Association, Inc., 1957. Pp. 27. Paper. $1.00. *

[B321]

★NOLL, VICTOR H. **Introduction to Educational Measurement.** Boston, Mass.: Houghton Mifflin Co., 1957. Pp. xxi, 437. $5.75. *

Ed & Psychol Meas 18:644–6 au '58. Samuel T. Mayo. * This book is very readable, both from the usual standpoint of clarity and on the basis of its excellent typography. The material is well organized and titled. The tables and figures are concise and lucid. Numerous realistic examples are given in order to illustrate the concepts and principles presented. Also, a good job of relating the measurement and instructional processes has been done. The reviewer was pleased to note that on page 105 the author had encouraged teachers to be experimentally-minded, when he suggested that "teachers and prospective teachers should use or experiment with all current methods of measurement."

Also, it is gratifying to see in this text for the introductory course in measurement that three kinds of validity—"curricular," "logical," and "empirical"—have been clearly differentiated. * In the reviewer's opinion, too much specific detail was devoted to the selected standardized tests and not nearly enough to sources of information about tests. In view of the prospect that many of our current tests may be replaced in a decade or so with new tests, it would seem well to emphasize more the orientation of the prospective teacher toward ways of keeping up to date on new tests. Also, there would seem to be some merit in de-emphasizing the coverage of standardized tests in favor of more extended coverage of teacher-made test construction for the introductory course. For example, more varied test item types might have been described for teacher-made tests. * the minor criticisms made here are more than compensated for by the many excellent features of this textbook. The wonder is that there seem to be so few needed revisions in a first edition. It is to be hoped, however, that an instructor's manual will be published at an early date, so that this book may better compete with some current texts which do have such manuals. This is a book with which every instructor of introductory tests and measurements courses should be familiar.

[B322]

★NORTHWAY, MARY L. **A Primer of Sociometry.** Toronto, Canada: University of Toronto Press, 1952. Pp. vii, 48. Paper, $1.50; cloth, $2.25. * (*PA* 27:5083)

Can J Psychol 8:172–3 S '54. Mary J. Wright. This book is modestly called a primer because "it introduces the student to the basic principles and practices of sociometry and guides him gently into the intricacies of the literature in the field," but it does much more than this, and merits the attention of the experienced worker as well as the novice. Its significance lies not only in its value as a practical handbook and theoretical treatise, but in its contribution as a summary of what has been accomplished, and as a preview of what must yet be done. It is research-oriented. The reader is given new theoretical insights, and is constantly reminded of unsolved problems and of hypotheses to be investigated. * Although statistical techniques are not emphasized, reference is made to the various methods which have been devised for handling these types of data. Specific references are provided throughout.

This material should help the beginning student to avoid the errors in procedure which have invalidated the findings of a number of previous investigators. *

Psychol B 51:101 Ja '54. Helen Hall Jennings. * The book orients the beginner to the nature and role of sociometry and provides the advanced worker with perspective of what has been accomplished and what lies ahead as untouched territory for investigation. It achieves these ends in 48 pages of refreshing, clear, and compact writing. The need for such a publication is widely felt and this one bids fair to become a classic of its kind in the midst of a literature which over the last 25 years contains about as many unreliable as dependable reports. Well-balanced and critical discussion is directed upon the merits and limitations of sociometric method, analysis, and evaluation of results. To this reviewer, the only unimportant or irrelevant discussion for the purposes of the presentation appears to be the brief use of comparisons with other methods. * the author gives profoundly suggestive treatment to elements which appear likely to remain universally important to choice reactions between people. Study directed toward them may be fruitful for many generations. Hence, *A Primer of Sociometry* can be seen as a practically useful and theoretically significant research guide to students of social, emotional, and group processes.

Sociometry 15:400 Ag–N '52. Helen Hall Jennings. It is a typical British understatement to entitle this book *A Primer of Sociometry*: it is a primer only if the term is defined as a basic contribution having such uncompromising clarity that any reader can understand and learn from it, whether or not he is familiar with the topic. This book is certain to hold the attention of many people who have never studied or worked in this area of investigation of social patterns as well as all who have. It clarifies by subtle distinctions which makes the difference between confusion and comprehension for the reader. *A Primer of Sociometry* is profound, lucid, succinct: it provides penetrating analyses of masses of findings, sifting out what is crucial to understand social structure and personality and organizing well-substantiated interpretation in such fashion as to clear and chart the ground for new work. The treatment of sociometric theory, practice, and applications in research design will im-

mensely aid faculties of schools and universities to help their students to enter gateways which may lead to important contributions. Moreover, by campactly presenting the interplay of impressive varieties of Canadian work with that done in France and the United States, *A Primer of Sociometry* provides an essential text for research teams among many countries, the most important of which would be comprised of elementary school teachers to whom health of child personality is of primary concern, side by side with social workers, psychiatrists and psychologists.

[B323]

★Northway, Mary L., and Weld, Lindsay. **Sociometric Testing: A Guide for Teachers.** Toronto, Canada: University of Toronto Press, 1957. Pp. vii, 72. $1.95. * (London: Oxford University Press. 16s.) (PA 32:379)

[B324]

★O'Connor, James P., Editor. **College Counseling and Testing: Proceedings of the Workshop on College Counseling and Testing Conducted at the Catholic University of America, June 14 to June 25, 1957.** Washington, D.C.: Catholic University of America Press, Inc., 1957. Pp. ix, 244. Paper. $3.75. *

[B325]

★Odell, C. W. **How to Improve Classroom Testing.** Dubuque, Iowa: Wm. C. Brown Co., 1953. Pp. vi, 156. Paper, spiral binding, lithotyped. * (PA 28: 8087) For latest edition, see B326.

Cath Ed R 53:64 Ja '55. Robert B. Nordberg. This volume will provide valuable assistance to those whose subject-matter is amenable to additive measurement, but is likely to be regarded less kindly by those who are chiefly interested in the organization and communication of knowledge. * The types of tests proposed are excellent to measure informational objectives, but largely inadequate for others. * The treatment of thought questions is much weaker. * That Professor Odell does not consistently carry through any gestalt approach to essay examinations is evidenced in the fact that he would grade them additively. In a volume devoted so basically to the additive viewpoint, it is a little surprising that certain vexing problems were not explicitly developed: (1) homogeneity of items, (2) the relativity of "zero," (3) the essential nature of units in psychological measurement. This work is, however, mainly consistent with its own premises. Chapter xiv on statistical methods of improving tests should be quite helpful.

J Ed Psychol 44:320 My '53. Chester W. Harris. * Students of education will be pleased to find that he sets the problem of measuring achievement in the context of curriculum development by taking the objectives of education as the definitions of the achievements that are desired. * a good source of ideas for test item types, and as such it should be of value to teachers * The chief contribution of the manual is its rather extensive and practical advice on how to develop and use informal tests.

[B326]

★ODELL, C. W. **How to Improve Classroom Testing, Revised Edition.** Dubuque, Iowa: Wm. C. Brown Co., 1958. Pp. vii, 213. Paper, spiral binding. $4.00.

[B327]

★OKARSKI, JOSEPH F. **Consistency of Projective Movement Responses.** American Psychological Association, Psychological Monographs: General and Applied, Vol. 72, No. 6, Whole No. 459. Washington, D.C.: the Association, Inc., 1958. Pp. 26. Paper. $1.00. *

[B328]

★OSBORNE, R. TRAVIS, EDITOR. **A Review of Educational and Psychological Tests and Their Uses: A Survey of Test Use Research in the University System of Georgia From January 1, 1933, to August 31, 1951.** Athens, Ga.: the University, 1952. Pp. viii, 192. Paper, mimeographed. Out of print. *

[B329]

★PALMERTON, L. R. **Testing Coordination in the Total Program.** American Guidance Program Monographs, No. 11. Boston, Mass.: Research Publishing Co., Inc., 1951. Pp. 24. Paper, lithotyped. $1.50. *

[B330]

PASCAL, GERALD R, AND SUTTELL, BARBARA J. **The Bender-Gestalt Test: Quantification and Validity for Adults.** New York: Grune & Stratton, Inc., 1951. Pp. xiii, 274. $6.50. * (PA 25:8106)

Am J Orthopsychiatry 22:655–7 Jl '52. Adolf G. Woltmann. * very detailed and richly illustrated scoring manual * Pascal and Suttell state on several occasions that this scoring method will not yield a psychiatric diagnosis. It is intended to differentiate between so-called normal persons and those "who are the patients of a psychiatrist." If this scoring does not yield a psychiatric diagnosis, or if it fails in the diagnostic refinement, what does it attempt to measure? Pascal and Suttell suggest that the scores and the deviations on which they are based "are measuring some aspect of ego strength, a term for which we have no adequate definition except to say that, among other things, it seems to lie along some continuum with the extent to which reality is distorted, as do our scores." More exactly, they are concerned with "interpretative factors which obtrude between perception and execution."

These factors which attest to the capacity of the organism to respond adequately to stimuli in the environment are "sometimes referred to as a function of the ego." What is the value of this book? How does it help the clinician to gain a better understanding of human dynamics? One finds in this book a gold mine of pictorially presented possible deviations that might occur in the copying of the Gestalt figures. Any clinician will welcome this extended knowledge. Unfortunately the book does not say what to do with this knowledge. The reasons for assigning numerical values to these deviations are not clear and sound a bit arbitrary. No specific reason is given why Figure A is excluded from the scoring system. The greatest shortcoming seems to lie in the fact that with all this wealth of knowledge very little is gained in terms of diagnostic refinement. What does it mean when a catatonic schizophrenic makes a score of 50 (p. 212) and a psychoneurotic with anxiety compulsion gets a score of 49 (p. 213)? Psychological testing started with statistical concepts and hypothetical norms. We still are so deeply rooted in these concepts that we apply them even when new approaches are based on a different psychological rationale. The ultimate answer does not seem to lie in the numerical summation of deviations from the norm. We need more of an understanding of human dynamics. Why do deviations occur? How do they differ in various disease entities? What diagnostic clues do these deviations contain? How do they help us to understand the personality in its so-called normal and abnormal states? The book is recommended for its impressive pictorial material on possible deviations from the test figures. It is not helpful for clinical-diagnostic refinement.

Austral J Psychol 7:91–2 Je '55. J. G. Lyle. * The authors suggest—not very convincingly —a theory centring around "ego-strength" or reality testing to explain how the test works. This may be adequate to explain the pathological deviations of psychotic patients, but hardly to explain the minor errors (tremor, wavy lines, reworking of designs, inexact correspondence, etc.) which go to make up most scores. These, it seems, could be best explained as functions of anxiety, uncertainty, over-conscientiousness and carelessness, which it is agreed, should occur with greater frequency in a maladjusted than a well-adjusted group.

But none of these signs (except perhaps tremor) justifies a diagnosis of neurosis in any particular case. Moreover, the authors seem to be unaware of the importance of the instruction: *Subject is given a sharp pointed pencil with an eraser.* The eraser gets no further mention except incidentally in the Appendix; but it appears that if the subject completely erases his error it is not scored. It is clear that in many cases a neurotic score will depend not upon "ego-strength" but upon whether the subject is observant enough to notice the eraser on the end of his pencil, or tidy enough to use it. To provide the subject with a separate eraser would presumably invalidate the test, since his attention would be drawn more to it. The test is very short (about ten minutes), easily administered to a group and not too difficult to score once practice has been gained. It would be worth while trying out this test in a battery for screening out maladjusted persons.

Brit J Med Psychol 26:79–81 pt 1 '53. J. L. Boreham. * Pascal and Suttell have attempted a standardization and clinical validation of Bender's test, and they have devised a quick scoring system by means of which one arrives at a single numerical score for the whole test. Whether or not quantification to this extent offers meaningful information about the patient will depend on the degree of one's understanding of what it is that the test is measuring, but beyond the empirical observation that a person's score on the test relates to the severity of psychological illness, the authors have little to offer in answer to this question. * During the last few years clinical psychologists have become increasingly interested in the interdependence of personality dynamics and perceptual processes, and one wishes that the authors had paid more regard to this current interest. It would have been fruitful to have assumed that similar dynamic factors are at work in the distortion of reproductive execution in the Bender test as have been demonstrated to operate in perception, e.g. that in perceiving the stimulus figures the patient brings an unconscious expectancy to the task which will operate as a partial determinant of his perception, and that in his reproduction of the figures the quality of the resultant deviations from the stimuli will relate to this expectancy. Further, one might suppose that if one could bring sufficient clinical sensitivity to bear one should be able to reach some understanding of those distortions in terms of the way the patient is expressing and seeking resolution of his inner tension systems in his performance of the task. It may seem that this is asking too much of the Bender test, and that the material does not lend itself to an analysis of this kind, but such a protest is at the same time an indictment of the test as the "valuable clinical tool" that the present authors claim it to be. Psychological illness appears to be essentially related to the individual's pattern of conscious and unconscious relationships with people, and if a psychodiagnostic test is to be of real clinical value it must enable the patient to express his human relationship problems, hereby also providing a means of increasing the examiner's sensitivity to the live transference relationship existing between the patient and himself. It is not justified to criticize a test for failing to do something that its author has never claimed it to do, but I mention these theoretical issues because Pascal and Suttell make explicit claims about the clinical value of the test. The Bender test material of arbitrary designs, and the over-general theoretical formulations that the present authors submit are too far removed from the complex subject-matter of mental illness to provide meaningful clinical insights into the nature of a patient's emotional disturbance. The test, in the form that Pascal and Suttell present it, is an empirical procedure of low sensitivity, and by virtue of this is of limited value in clinical practice. Within the framework of this limitation the authors have presented a very competent statement of their findings. The administration and scoring of the test are discussed, and some provisional data on reliability and validity are presented. Their American standardization population of "normal" subjects is highly selective, so that the value of their quantitative findings, especially for British users of the test, is conjectural. The Scoring Manual, which comprises over half the book is, however, written with clarity and precision. The scorable deviations for each design are clearly defined in the text, examples being given, and forty-five actual records are reproduced which the reader may score, subsequently comparing his scoring with that of the authors. It is claimed that a scorer reliability coefficient of 0.90 is achieved by such self-tuition from the manual. In a lengthy chapter on the records of patients with intracranial damage the authors conclude that the test can only indicate the presence of cortical damage when that damage is of a serious nature. Of much greater value in this chapter is the discussion of the records of normal children between ages 6 and 9, although the educational psychologist would be well advised to refer to Bender's original monograph for a fuller understanding of children's records. Pascal and Suttell also devote a chapter to the psychogenic disorders but, as in the case of organic impairment, their findings are unspectacular. * The test is....of limited value in clinical psychological practice, adding nothing to the diagnostic information that can be obtained more reliably by means of other tests whose theoretical frameworks are more fully understood, and even as a screening device it would appear to be too crude and unreliable an instrument as yet to be of much value. Pascal and Suttell's book will appeal most to those interested in the fundamental research possibilities of the test, particularly in the understanding of the disturbance of perception and execution in organic and psychotic conditions, and it is as a good introductory manual to the Bender-Gestalt test as a research method, rather than as a clinical tool, that this book is to be recommended.

For reviews of the first edition, see 4:B303.

[B331]

*PATERSON, DONALD G.; GERKEN, C. D'A.; AND HAHN, MILTON E. **Revised Minnesota Occupational Rating Scales.** Minnesota Studies in Student Personnel Work, No. 2. Minneapolis, Minn.: University of Minnesota Press, 1953. Pp. ix, 85. Paper. $2.00. * (PA 28:9074)

J Consult Psychol 18:230–1 Je '54. Anne Roe. * The scales consist of ratings, based on the pooled judgment of vocational psychologists, for seven abilities or aptitudes as these are required for each of 432 occupations. The abilities, each rated at four levels, are academic ability, mechanical ability, social intelligence, clerical ability, musical talent, artistic ability, and physical agility (new in this revision). The variation in the ratings from scale to scale yields an occupational pattern, e.g., ratings for eminent lawyer are A D A B D D D. These ratings are presented in a table in which jobs are arranged alphabetically, each preceded by an identifying number, and followed by the D.O.T. code number for jobs at every level of each ability, and a pattern classification that makes easy a consideration of occupational al-

ternatives. Uses of the scales and the Individual Counseling Record are explained. By this system, both the counselee and the job are rated in the same terms.

For a review of the first edition, see 3:689.

[B332]

★PATERSON, C. H. **The Wechsler-Bellevue Scales: A Guide for Counselors.** Springfield, Ill.: Charles C Thomas, Publisher, 1953. Pp. viii, 146. $3.75. (London: Blackwell Scientific Publications, Ltd. 27s. 6d.) * (PA 28:2664)

Am J Psychotherapy 8:330–1 Ap '54. Robert K. Robison. This book is designed to acquaint vocational counselors with the "potentialities and limitations of the Wechsler scales in counseling." Insofar as these potentialities—exclusive of a qualitative approach—exist they are adequately reported. The scales (Form I only) are treated according to: their objective and subjective nature (a la Rapaport); their reliability and validity; administration; clinical use, including diagnostic potentialities, measurement of mental deterioration and aptitude; lastly, according to the validity of their abbreviated forms. The author handles all of this material with caution, clarity, and ease. He has an appreciation for the background of his readers, keeping technical discussions to a minimum, though never skimping. I regret to report that in spite of its virtues this book is rather misleading: it promises to be a guide for vocational counselors, yet a large part is devoted to a sedulous examination of research demonstrating that the Wechsler offers little assistance to the counselor. Only about five pages are concerned with an over-all application of the tests to counseling. All too frequently one comes across summaries like: "Diagnosis of psychopathic personality on the basis of Wechsler patterns thus appears to be impossible at the present time." It is indeed disheartening to be confronted with the fact that the Wechsler has remained largely impervious to research assaults formulated to illuminate neurotic and psychotic symptomatology. This, of course, is no reflection on the author's work, but indicates that the use of this manual is much more limited than its title implies. In view of this fact, the price seems excessive. However, if one is interested in studying the research done on the Wechsler this book with its 250-item bibliography provides an excellent reference. There are only two things I would like to add: that Jastak's un-published work on the Wechsler and similar scales has gone considerably further than what Patterson has been able to present here, but for which he cannot be held accountable; that some of the flagrant discrepancies appearing on the Object Assembly test may well result from the fact that the original set was made of wood, while subsequent sets were pressed from card-board. Try the two sets and observe the dif-ference.

J Consult Psychol 17:319 Ag '53. Laurance F. Shaffer. * a thorough and competent review of the research literature about the Wechsler-Bellevue, with a bibliography of 250 entries. The presentation is well organized, and each major section ends with an integrative sum-mary of the conclusions justified by the evi-dence. It is indeed a "guide for counselors" in the sense of displaying the values of the test and also its limitations.

[B333]

★Peek, Roland M., and Quast, Wentworth. **A Scoring System for the Bender-Gestalt Test.** Hastings, Minn.: Roland M. Peek (Box 292), 1951. Pp. iii, 72. Paper, mimeographed. * (*PA 27*:1183)

[B334]

★Petch, James A. **Fifty Years of Examining: The Joint Matriculation Board, 1903–1953.** London: George G. Harrap & Co. Ltd., 1953. Pp. 226. 15s. *

Brit J Ed Studies 2:169 My '54. A. C. F. Beales. * A history of an examining body might well have been dull. But on the contrary this survey, for all its wealth of detail in the day-to-day story, is lively and at times more than lively.

[B335]

*Peters, Alison. **How to Pass College Entrance Tests, Third Edition.** New York: Arco Publishing Co., Inc., 1956. Pp. 185. Paper, $2.00; cloth, $3.50. For a review of the first edition, see 4:B310.

[B336]

★Peterson, Shailer. **Manual on the Preparation of Examinations in the Feld of Dentistry, Second Revision.** Chicago, Ill.: American Dental Associa-tion, 1952. Pp. 63. Paper. *

[B337]

★Phillips, Leslie, and Smith, Joseph G. **Rorschach Interpretation: Advanced Technique.** New York: Grune & Stratton, Inc., 1953. Pp. xiii, 385. $8.75. * (*PA 28*:2666)

Am J Psychiatry 112:236 S '55. Douglas M. Kelley. The Foreword frankly states that this book is "composed largely of statements about relationships between Rorschach performance and other behavior," and that "most of these

relationships represent guessed-at laws....best employed with equal parts of faith and skepti-cism." Considered in this light and not as a definitive source of diagnostic specifics, the text is a useful contribution to the Rorschach literature, representing the extensive experi-ence and impressions of the authors. It is es-sential to emphasize this point, since the title "Advanced Technique" may indicate to some readers that here is the last word. That it is not the last word can be demonstrated by state-ments like: "The underproduction of M rep-resents the absence of empathic responsivity and may be a function either of a) fixation at or regression to a genetically low level of per-ception or b) a restriction of function in re-sponse to interpersonal difficulties." This is sometimes true, but in many hundreds of cases of apparently normal persons who seem to be getting by, records will be given in which there are no human movement responses and yet no clinical evidence of any type of restrictive or regressive variant of psychopathy can be shown. Probably the best approach to this book, therefore, is simply to accept the fact that it represents a viewpoint and that the authors' statements, especially in terms of clinical meaning, may be true in some cases and not in others. On the positive side, the authors have done a great deal of good work in analyzing the literature, particularly in discussing form levels, movement responses, and especially the use of color. Here they have not only reviewed other authorities, but have interwoven their in-formation with their own experience and pro-duced some really useful material. The section on Content Analysis is also handy, since it represents alphabetical classification of fre-quent responses which can be easily looked up. The hazard here in adapting from the text a meaning for an individual response is higher than in any other section, since what may be significant to one person may be coincidental to another. Generally, such "dream book" inter-pretations are risky and this section of the book should be approached with greatest cau-tion. The latter part of the text presents an in-triguing discussion on general attitudes and role playing as restricted to Rorschach responses, and is a useful contribution. The section on Shock tends to suffer from over-emphasis on timing, but otherwise is good. Sequence Analy-sis is reasonably well demonstrated, and the final long Case Analysis is well done. The authors have included some tables of form levels which will actually be more helpful to the beginner than the expert, and there is a good Index. In general, the merits of the book, outweigh the potential hazards—hazards which the authors of course cannot prevent, since they are inherent in students who tend to accept as gospel, any written word. If the title were changed to read "Rorschach Speculations—Our Method," it could be highly recommended.

Am J Psychother 8:564–7 Jl '54. Ruth A. Neu. This stimulating book has much more to offer to the reader than the modest title implies. "Advanced Technique" covers considerable wealth of new ideas as to the possible inferences to be drawn from a Rorschach protocol, and a full consideration of the many unsolved problems and sources of error in clinical practice. This is a courageous book in its frank criticism of some commonly accepted practices in Rorschach interpretation. It makes a positive contribution to the field, especially by suggesting new techniques for the objective appraisal of non-scorable utterances produced in the test situation. * This reviewer found the chapter on "Attitudes, Role Playing and Life Thema" the most stimulating and original one. * Whether or not one agrees with the authors in all their statements, one will find here an immensely interesting and thought-provoking book. Many aspects of Rorschach interpretation are shown in a new light and possibilities for new studies are opened. So far, in this field, too many criteria have been considered objective only because they were numerical, and too much material has been neglected because it was not scorable. The main contribution of this book seems to lie in the demonstration that a statistical and an intuitive approach may be combined in the objective evaluation of Rorschach data.

J Ed Psychol 45:125–7 F '54. Lee J. Cronbach. Principles and procedures for Rorschach interpretation are nowhere more carefully explained than in this book. The authors set forth in detail many procedures clinical interpreters have otherwise had to pick up by observation and imitation. The procedure is not thereby oversimplified or stereotyped. The authors firmly believe that every fact must be related to every other, and they carry their suggestions to the utmost frontier of Rorschach interpretation. No cue is too faint, no relationship too

speculative, to be included as a suggestion. A unique feature of the book is that the authors are aware that their interpretations may be invalid. Their first paragraph is refreshing: "This book is intended primarily as a practical clinical reference. It is composed largely of statements about relationships between Rorschach performance and other behavior. Unfortunately, few of the relationships which are asserted have been corroborated; most represent guessed-at-laws. They are perhaps best employed with equal parts of faith and skepticism." The writers warn that one proceeds by successive refinements, setting up tentative inferences on Card I which constitute predictions about subsequent cards; they can therefore be confirmed or modified (p. 261). Of course the hypothesis that results after ten cards then requires *its* "cross validation" from further data. It is in not stressing this need for testing the Rorschach interpretation that writers on the test err. Despite their sophistication and their excellent section on errors, Phillips and Smith do not succeed in maintaining their rigorous or skeptical attitude throughout the book. Wherever the writers do reëxamine current doctrine, they make contributions. They often explain why interpretations are proposed. They develop much improved criteria for scoring location and form level. They describe the interpretation of "style" or nonscored behavior most helpfully. They present new developmental norms derived from theses by Hemmendinger, Siegel, and Friedman. The reviewer does not feel that their genetic approach to interpretation is always helpful. To say that an adult has a score common among children is not explained by describing this as a "genetically early level," or describing him as fixated at or regressed to this level. The significant point is that he has now acquired a positive way of behaving with his present organic potential, presumably because this way of behaving is relatively rewarding. Wherever analysis in genetic terms appears, it seems to crowd out discussion of learning processes or dynamics generally. Recognizing the good features of the book, one still is startled by much of its content. "Shock on Card I is evidence for an unresolved and intense relation with a mother figure....Shock on Card II is characteristic of....uncontrolled destructive impulses." Remarks like "any time limits are characteristic of persons with obsessive-compulsive character features," "The concept 'teeth'.... appears to be associated with masturbation and/or sibling rivalry as a reaction to frustrated dependency needs." Such comments are generally expanded in a way which gives them plausibility, yet the fact that the cables of evidence anchoring them to reality have all the tensile strength of moonbeams, and the authors' introductory warning that what they say may be either true or false, cause one to question just how such writings can have a place in a science. If this book were read by a man from some "ivory tower" who happened not to know that the Rorschach is currently taken seriously, it would sound to him like *Ralph 1245C+* sounded to its first readers. Good science fiction is written with logic, any known facts, and imagination; at its best, its plausibilities foreshadow some things that science later establishes. Perhaps it is fairer to say that Rorschach interpretations are to the science of psychology as historical novels are to history. The writer seeks internal consistency and plausibility, with due regard for established fact. Where there is a gap in fact, the scholarly historian acknowledges the gap, but the fiction writer fills it with what might reasonably have happened, i.e., with an artistic creation. The argument between scientist and clinician disappears if we see that clinical interpretation is an art at the present time. In the early days of testing it was a technology, wrong at times but never seeking to be creative or intuitive. Now, instead, the clinician is first of all a portraitist who abhors unfilled areas on the canvas. This occurs because there is a practical demand for answers about people, not for uncertainties. Society has rewarded this new species of artist; we can scarcely criticize him for satisfying the demand. New entrants in the field want to be successful artists, and books like the present one which tell how to complete an attractive and convincing portrait are wanted. When authors like Phillips and Smith can also help keep portraits closer to reality than they would otherwise be, that is so much gained. Once we grant that the clinician is going to provide descriptions which go beyond proven fact, we should welcome any book which contributes to making him a good non-scientist. The scientist cannot complain if the portrait is used as a guide to further inquiry about the patient or about personality in general. Both science fiction and historical fiction

have suggested leads to serious investigations of their fields. This emphatically demands that the clinician's suggested interpretations should send further study in promising directions, not up "blind alleys." There is good reason to think that the Rorschach or other clinical interviewing methods can do this often enough to be useful, even though, according to the evidence, their suggestions on any case are not correct enough to be trusted without further support. The scientist should object when he is told that he or the practitioner who receives a Rorschach analysis should believe it. Among all the books yet written on the Rorschach, the book under review comes closest to filling a practical demand for training clinicians to be artistic portraitists, without making unacceptable claims that such portraits are dependable.

Psychiatric Q Sup 27:309 pt 2 '53. * should prove very useful as a clinical manual for practising clinical psychologists as well as a supplementary test for instructors of advanced courses on the Rorschach. It will do little to advance the Rorschach as a scientific instrument, however, since it is based mainly on empirical clinical practice and does not purport to be a validation study. Thus, the scientific worker will find little here beyond speculation and empirical deductions based on clinical practice. At times, this speculation becomes difficult to take, particularly in the chapter on "Attitudes, Role Playing and Life Thema," where the authors attempt to infer a testee's role concepts mainly from the side remarks and comments which he makes. This reaches rather ludicrous proportions in such highly speculative inferences as the following: " 'O.K.' implies that the subject has mastered the situation and is able to participate actively in it, but only within the limits established by the examiner. 'Now' and 'o.k.' when they initiate a response, represent a methodical ordering of his response pattern by the subject and so imply obsessive features. Both emphasize the tasklike character of the situation for the subject. 'Now,' alone of these delaying remarks, implies intellectual vigor and mastery." It seems to this reviewer that the authors could well have omitted such dubious speculation, since actually the important thing, as far as the psychologist is concerned, is the interpretation of the test protocol itself, i.e., *what* the subject sees. The chief assets of the book for this reviewer are the chapter on content analysis which fills a real need since little has been published in this area; the generally good documentation throughout so that the book serves a real purpose as a reference source with concrete data for the practising clinician; the generally clear exposition throughout; and the liberal references to the works of leading authorities on the Rorschach. Although there are detailed sections on interpretation including sequence analysis, some of this material seems unwieldy in being too detailed, and in trying to tease too much out of dubious side remarks, etc. * This book can be recommended as a useful, up-to-date clinical source reference on the Rorschach Test. As indicated in the title, it is not for beginners, but should prove useful to advanced students and to workers in the field.

[B338]

★PHILLIPSON, HERBERT. **The Object Relations Technique.** London: Tavistock Publications, Ltd. 1955. Pp. x, 224. 21s.; with test cards, 63s. (Glencoe, Ill.: Free Press, 1956. $6.00; with test cards, $10.00.) * (PA 30:5441) For additional reviews, see 151.

Brit J Ed Psychol 26:231–2 N '56. G. Keir. Mr. Phillipson is to be congratulated, not only on producing a test the usefulness of which is at once apparent, but also on having had the sense of exactitude and the patience not to publish it until now, when it is accompanied by a text containing a wealth of information on its administration and interpretation. Too many tests are put upon the market before they are really ripe for it. Mr. Phillipson's test is not one of these. * The test, consisting of thirteen cards, is an ingenious combination of certain principles of a Thematic Apperception Test and the Rorschach Test. It is less structured than the first and more structured than the second. The rationale is based upon the psychoanalytic theories of Klein and Fairbairn. * Phillipson devotes the major part of the text to problems of interpretation. One case record is presented in very great detail and is a most useful source of reference. As the author himself says, however, not all psychologists would wish to adopt the same procedure in interpretation, and method may also vary with the purpose of the investigation and with the individual way in which a subject may reveal himself. Hence, Mr. Phillipson presents six further records, each one described and analysed in a slightly different fashion, though each, of course, embodies the major concepts underlying any method of thematic apperception analysis. This is one of

the most important sections of the book for the psychologist who may not want to accept all the psycho-analytic formulations on which the technique as a whole is based. He will find most helpful guidance in these sets of analyses. Finally, there is included in the text a set of norms for the frequency of responses. It is true, as Mr. Phillipson admits that the samples are small in number and rather selected. He hopes, when the test is in general use (which it undoubtedly will be), to accumulate more information, which will enable him to compile an enlarged set of norms with more general application, thereby widening their usefulness. In the meantime, let us be content with what information we have on this technique, which is much, and of which it is certain that wide use will be made.

Brit J Med Psychol 29:173–4 pt 2 '56. Ralph Hetherington. This new test offers no competition, either to the T.A.T. or to the Rorschach. It stands in its own right as an excellent technique for eliciting projective data of a kind not easily obtained by means of other projective tests. Nevertheless, it borrows something from the methods of both Rorschach and T.A.T. From the former it borrows stimulation arising from texture, chiaroscuro and colour, from the latter the situation where a story has to be constructed to fit a picture. * The author has been most fortunate in his two illustrators, Miss Carlisle and Madame Dormondie, who have produced pictures which are pleasant, stimulating and at times challenging. The reviewer has had an opportunity of trying the test out with some twenty mental hospital patients and even with this small number, he is convinced that the technique produces new and valuable material not obtained as easily in any other way. * The book includes one very long case study (57 pages) and several shorter ones. The long case study consists of a minute examination of the stories given by a patient to the thirteen cards, in which the author allows himself a degree of speculation about the significance of the material which many people would consider unjustified. The shorter case studies are, in the reviewer's opinion, more satisfactory illustrations of the value of the technique. The normative data given consist of a clinic sample of fifty patients and a research sample of forty adolescent girls. In both cases responses to each picture are analysed in terms of human content, reality content and reality context. These data are interesting, but, as the author himself says, are not yet adequate for standardization purposes. This test will be widely used by clinical psychologists, whether familiar with object-relations theory or not, as it undoubtedly produces projective material the value of which is by no means dependent on psychoanalytical interpretation.

Brit J Psychol 47:73 F '56. *Boris Semeonoff*. At first sight Mr Phillipson's contribution to the published range of projective techniques would appear to be little more than yet another variant of T.A.T. It has, however—in contrast to both T.A.T. and Rorschach, which are somewhat loosely based on an eclectic depth psychology—the distinguishing feature that it has been designed and developed as an adjunct to therapy carried out within the framework of a single theory of the development of personality—the object-relations theory of which Klein and Fairbairn are the best-known proponents. * There are three series of pictures, distinguished by the style of drawing: *A,* in light charcoal shading, misty in quality; *B,* in heavy shading approaching a silhouette technique; *C,* with colour introduced, and more definite detail. * The *A* series, it is claimed, "will stimulate primitive dependent needs and the consequent anxieties"; in the *B* series "the emphasis (is) on phantasy relation with threatening and uncompromising objects"; the *C* series is intended "to present a world rich in opportunity and challenge." How far this attempt to systematize stimulus material has been successful is not clear from the normative data provided. * the extreme ambiguity of, particularly, the *A* pictures may produce a Rorschach-type attitude (puzzling over detail etc.) which tends to inhibit both the production of a "story" and the identification phenomenon stressed by Henry Murray. In view of the underlying theory this may not be important in the clinical situation proper, but if, as the flap description suggests, the material may also be used "outside the clinical field, in social research and in personnel selection in industry and elsewhere" it may be that avoidance of structuration has been carried to excess. One will await with interest further reports of the use of the technique (as promised, e.g. in articles listed as "In Preparation"). Perhaps it will not be regarded as too uncharitable also to hope eventually for a clearer account of its "quantitative possibilities" to which Dr J. D. Sutherland

refers in his Foreword. The author must, however, be congratulated on the degree of success he has achieved in his main purpose—the linking of the projective hypothesis with current thought in perception theory, and the application of both to a coherent system of personality dynamics.

Ed & Psychol Meas 17:160–2 sp '57. *S. B. Sells.* * The strategy of this test, as seen in the design of the pictures and the analyses of responses presented, is quite impressive in providing data for the types of dynamic interpretation set forth. The interpretations provided by the author in the illustrative cases are effectively presented and reflect his skill and experience as a clinician in relating psychoanalytic dynamic concepts to the responses of the patients. The basic questions of validity, however, are left unanswered, and as in the case of the related projective technics, the nature of the O-R Technique itself interposes several major obstacles to productive research on the problem. First, there is no specified interpretive system, but rather, extensive reliance on the experience, skill, wisdom and intuitive processes of the clinician. As a result, reliability of scoring is an unresolved issue, but more damaging is the seeming impossibility of differentiating between inferences attributable to the test per se and those which arise principally from the general acumen of the clinician. Second, the theoretical constructs from which the rationale of the O-R approach derives are not formulated in terms of testable hypotheses. Most of these comments apply to projective technics and psychoanalytic theory generally, as well as to the O-R method specifically. Thus, the contribution appears to consist of an attractive set of new projective stimuli and some clinically attractive hypotheses related to their use in personality assessment which have been developed and tested against clinical experience. It is expected that this Technique will be admired by clinicians who accept the TAT and Rorschach for interpretation of unconscious dynamics, particularly those with greater experience in psychoanalytic studies. However, its wider acceptance may be limited by lack of scoring guides or conventions and cookbook type suggestions for interpretation. Tests or adaptations of tests which incorporate such "advantages" are more likely to be adopted in graduate training courses, research projects and clinics. Substantial quantitative research using this Technique is not at present indicated for reasons set forth above.

J Consult Psychol 20:237–8 Je '56. Laurance F. Shaffer. * Normative information is given for 50 clinic outpatients and for a sample of 40 normal adolescent girls. Although such data may seem scanty if judged by standards appropriate to mass testing, they exceed the material usually offered with a new projective method and are unquestionably useful. The pictures are sensitively conceived, and their systematic plan commends them both for clinical use and for research. This instrument deserves a thorough exploration by American psychologists and may well prove to be a major development in projective methods.

J Proj Tech 22:250–2 Je '58. Mortimer M. Meyer. * The addition of shading and color is an interesting variation. Unfortunately, the author provides no rationale for this combination. * it is difficult to evaluate why the shading and color were added and how it is anticipated that they may be interpreted within the context of this approach. The very detailed analysis of one case illustrates clearly the mode of interpretation intended by the author and the emphasis on inter-personal relationships. However, it is markedly evident in the author's approach, that it is not the technique itself which provides the rich information. It is the author's psychoanalytic knowledge which he applies to the subject's fantasies. With minor reservations, his approach can be used with other stimuli which provide fantasies about interpersonal reactions. This comment is meant not to detract from what the author offers but as a warning that there is no magic in the stimulus alone and it will provide rich results only if the examiner can bring a wealth of background to it. This can be contrasted with the MAPS and the TAT which because of their increased structure and more obvious figures, permit more direct interpretations when the examiner feels unable or disinclined to make interpretations on the more unconscious level. In the TAT and MAPS the stimuli are more controlled so that fantasies about more specific relationships are evoked. From the other point of view—its uniqueness of contribution, a very important question can be raised. What does the technique offer that the MAPS, TAT, Rorschach, and the like do not offer. The author implies that the ORT is based on a rationale more effectively than other approaches.

This implication does not seem sustained. The discussion of the concept of object relations and the presentation of a series of cards with human figures are not a unique combination. What the author has done is to present an illustration of how the psychoanalytic concept of object relations can be applied to fantasies evoked by a stimulus. He has in no way demonstrated that the same concept cannot be applied equally well to the TAT or the MAPS. The manual for the TAT published by Stein ten years ago presents a detailed case analysis that is on the same level and with the same detail as that offered by Phillipson. If the cards he uses offer something different, he has certainly not demonstrated it. He has certainly failed to demonstrate the advantage of including shading and color. In addition, there is a question whether the publication of this technique with its poverty of normative data is justified. For example, in some of the interpretations the author says, "this is unusual," "this is frequent." These interpretations are based on a total of ninety patients, fifty outpatient adults, 38 of whom were men and only 18 women, and forty normal adolescents. To talk of typical and atypical on such a sampling seems somewhat presumptuous. At this date, the need for projective techniques is not so great that another technique should be released with so little preparation. In summary it may be said that the author refers to a theory of projective methods but does not incorporate it in the ORT. Since he offers no organized mode of interpretation, the ORT cannot be considered a technique. Thus the only offering it makes is that of another set of stimuli. There is little creativeness in the ORT. It is a slightly modified combination of already existing techniques. This combination may be useful in some unique way but this has not been demonstrated. The use of ambiguous figures is certainly a fruitful approach but the degree of advantage of this ambiguity over existing stimuli has not been demonstrated. The normative data are so limited that it cannot be said that the ORT has any particular advantage in terms of norms. This reviewer is forced to conclude that here is an approach which has possibilities but must be judged as either arriving on the field too late or too early. Too late because the ideas are not new and too early because not enough work has been done on it by the author prior to publication. Even a dissertation, something done by a novice in research, would not be accepted with such an absence of attempts at validation.

Occupational Psychol 31:57–8 Ja '57. Denis McMahon. * First, the theoretical basis: Phillipson (following Freud and others) believes that our attitudes to people and our relationships with them are largely determined by the relationships we have established in our early years and of which we may not be conscious. Furthermore, he believes (following Klein and Fairbairn) that the infant's confusion of himself with the not-self leaves a deposit of *internalised* object relations, some perceived as "good" and some perceived as "bad," and that frustrations and tensions arising out of the search for the "good" and the rejection of the "bad" objects may, if unresolved, profoundly influence our perception of situations and people. The relevance of recent work by Bruner and Postman is touched on. It is important to note that "object relations" refer not so much to early relationships with simple objects like tables and feeding bottles as to people and social situations. * A reviewer's interest in the theoretical basis can be limited to the question of how far the test material and the account of its use seem to tie up with the theory. In any event, this reviewer has neither the space nor the competence to embark on a thorough-going critique of the basic theory from which the test material derives. * the case studies....show how the story provided by a patient is analysed in accordance with the theory, although one feels that the material could have been interpreted in terms of quite different theories, with equal consistency and conviction. It is for this reason that one turns with keen anticipation to the last chapter, headed "Normative Data," hoping that here evidence will emerge that the object relations technique is a valuable instrument of personality assessment in hands other than those of Phillipson and his colleagues. But this chapter is disappointing: it comprises abstracts of types of responses of 50 out-patients of the Tavistock Clinic and, separately, of 40 normal girls. As the samples cannot be equated, for age, socioeconomic status and the like, comparisons are of little value, and, indeed, are not attempted.

Personnel & Guid J 35:539–40 Ap '57. Samuel B. Kutash. * The publishers state that the pictures used in this technique are particularly suitable for the use of "experienced psychologists working outside the clinical field, in social research and in *personnel selection in industry and elsewhere.*" This opinion is based on the author's experience with the test over a period of five years. Unfortunately, the data presented while highly interesting and pertinent for the clinical worker does not bear on the possibilities in the fields of personnel selection and guidance. This is not to say that there may not be potentialities in that direction. The strength of the *Object Relations Technique* lies in the fact that it was constructed to conform to a carefully stated theoretical rationale of a rather precise nature. Since this rationale is essentially a psychoanalytic one—the *psychoanalytic theory of unconscious object relations*—it offers the possibility, like the Blacky Test, of another means of verifying or testing out psychoanalytical concepts. Research along such lines as, for example, the prediction of transference phenomena for individuals, and of interpersonal relationships, could well utilize these pictures. Whether they would, however, be any more useful in the fields of personnel selection and guidance than other projective techniques must await further research and accumulation of data with this method in suitable contexts.

Personnel Psychol 10:133–5 sp '57. Edwin C. Nevis. * What is most valuable in Phillipson's approach and represents a decided contribution is the care and thought which went into the development of the pictures which make up the technique. * The Object Relations Technique as it now stands will probably be of little value in personnel assessment work. However, those of us who would seek means of making projective techniques more valuable in this area can learn much from the approach to the stimulus materials. To this reviewer it appears quite possible to start out along the lines of this technique and develop a series of pictures designed to measure variables immediately applicable to performance in various jobs.

[B339]

★PINSENT, A. **The Construction and Use of Standardised Tests of Intelligence and Attainment: With Special Reference to the Problems of a Mixed Language Area.** University College of Wales, Faculty of Education, Pamphlet No. 3. Aberystwyth, Wales: the College, [1954]. Pp. 52. Paper. *1s. 6d.* *

[B340]

★PIOTROWSKI, ZYGMUNT A. **Perceptanalysis: A Fundamentally Reworked, Expanded, and Systematized Rorschach Method.** New York: Macmillan Co., 1957. Pp. xix, 505. $6.75. (London: Macmillan New York. 47*s.*) * (*PA* 32:501)

Brit J Psychol 49:172–3 My '58. B. Semeonoff.
* Lacking experience of testing Piotrowski's rationale, one has to rely on impression which suggests that, while on occasion he shows quite brilliant clinical insight, the work is far below that of the Klopfer group as regards scientific approach. There are numerous cases of *non sequitur,* circular reasoning, and the like, and—as is unfortunately all too common in Rorschach literature—statements are often made quite dogmatically without supporting evidence. One of the few places where detailed figures are quoted is in a discussion of the ranking of plates in terms of initial reaction time; here the issue is confused by the figures being mean ranks whereas the discussion refers to mean reaction times. The interpretation seems to be at variance with the figures, but there is no way of telling whether this is indeed the case. It is difficult to get an all-over picture of Piotrowski's scoring system, since he gives no summary list of symbols, ratios calculated, etc. Two important innovations, however, stand out. First, his admission of an *MC* response, i.e. one that contributes equally to the human movement and the colour scores, and an extension of this principle to other combinations of two or even three determinant categories. This allows him to abolish the necessity to recognize "precedence" of one determinant over another, and the often meaningless distinction between "main" and "additional" scores of the Klopfer method. Secondly, his treatment of shading responses is entirely original, in that he uses two basic symbols only: *c* for "light grey and variegated shading" and *c'* for "dark-shading." Each of these is also made the subject of a weighted score analogous to "colour sum." While this treatment obviates many scoring problems, it fails to recognize the interpretative significance of the texture response which many Rorschach workers finds particularly illuminating * A comparable innovation, on the interpretative level, is the recognition of specific "shock" elements associated with each plate. In the reviewer's experience, plate IX frequently produces disturbances in response which appear to be due to difficulties in form interpretation rather than to the colour content. To describe such a disturbance simply as "Plate IX shock" (for which, of course, the author has a rationale) would appear to be an advance on the assumption—which one sometimes suspects has been made—that because stimulus variables are pres-

ent they are necessarily operative. Notwithstanding some of the foregoing criticisms, a fair summing-up would be that this is a stimulating book, with many original and controversial features to assure its welcome. Particularly interesting is the information regarding the background and early history of the technique, including frequent references back to Rorschach's own writings. Only the out-and-out sceptic will deny that it throws fresh light on the many problems of personality dynamics.

J Clin Psychol 14:441 O '58. * Piotrowski's approach....is still in terms of deductive-inductive logic, supported by clinical impressions and the as-yet sparse experimental literature in the field. We look in vain for the attempt to integrate the findings of perceptanalysis with the rapidly growing base of core personality variables which have been demonstrated by factorial methods. At a time when methods are available to establish the *factorial* validity of personality concepts used in clinical work, it seems less than adequate to fall back upon *logical* validity and *face* validity as do so many workers with projective methods. Projective psychology will continue to be an isolated realm until its coordinates are integrated by experimental-statistical findings with the charted areas of psychological space. Piotrowski advances some imaginative new interpretive methods and conclusions which still must be recognized as speculative until such time as validating evidence is forthcoming.

J Proj Tech 22:110–1 Mr '58. Mortimer M. Meyer. * The title "Perceptanalysis" represents the author's wish to emphasize the attention he feels should be given to the analysis of the perceptual aspects of responses to the blot in contrast to the content. * the question must be raised here as with most other texts on Rorschach. What about the incorporation of the vast research on the Rorschach? Although some research is cited, this book is much more of a dialectic presentation of the author's views, beliefs, and experiences. Sarason's book is the one attempt to incorporate research extensively in the presentation. Piotrowski does not at any point refer to the over-all research in the field. In the introduction he does state, "Of course no assumption is made that the mere statement of a view proves its validity." Although there may be good reason to present a whole scheme of things in such detail without research evidence, it seems desirable that the author at least present some rationale for taking this approach. He states, also in the introduction, "One of my main goals was to contribute to the process of tidying up and tightening perceptanalysis as a scientific procedure." This reviewer will agree that the presentation is a fairly tidy one but sees no evidence "tightening perceptanalysis as a scientific procedure." Rather it appears to be an accumulation of the author's working hunches—possibly very good ones—but neatness and uniformity of interpretation are not necessarily the same as scientific procedure. There are some disturbing moments in the early sections of the book as the author discusses perceptanalysis in which he seems to imply that he alone after Rorschach is the true prophet. He spends twenty seven pages discussing perceptanalysis as a science and in this elaborate discussion tends to become defensive rather than explanatory. There is a brief interesting historic summary of developments with inkblots prior to Rorschach. On the whole, this is quite clearly a book which is stimulating to read, reflects a sincere and very carefully considered approach, and can serve as an excellent text for an elementary course in the Rorschach as part of organized graduate training.

[B341]

★PISULA, DOROTHY HELEN. **A Study of Mental Maturity and Personality Structure at the Eight Year Level.** Washington, D.C.: Catholic University of America Press, Inc., 1954. Pp. vi, 33. Paper. $0.50. *

[B342]

★PORTEUS, S. D. **The Porteus Maze Test Manual.** London: George G. Harrap & Co. Ltd., 1952. Pp. 64. 6s. * [Reprinted in part from *The Porteus Maze Test and Intelligence.*]

Brit J Delinquency 4:144 O '53. T. G. It is amazing that a test devised in 1914 should be gaining in popularity in 1953. Although originally intended as a measure of general intelligence the Maze has been little used for this purpose: its reliability was too low to make it practical as a clinical instrument, and it did not correlate highly enough with other accepted measures of intellectual functions. But exactly its relatively low correlations with other tests have been the source of the Maze's revival. It is suggested that the Maze measures some aspects of mental apparatus not covered by other techniques. Whether they are essentially related to social adjustment (as the author believes) is open to question, but it is clear that the test uncovers an element of in-

telligent behaviour which *is* impaired in many delinquents and which becomes impaired in most cases of "successful" neuro-surgery. The test has been recently used in many leucotomy researches. Its use with delinquents has been relatively neglected and there is much to be said for its inclusion in future researches.

Brit J Ed Psychol 24:56 F '54. This is a welcome booklet by the originator of the Porteus Maze Tests. It includes not only a detailed guide to the use of the tests but a very interesting chapter on the validity and history of the tests, and the results of recent applications.

[B343]

★PORTEUS, STANLEY D. **The Maze Test: Recent Advances.** Palo Alto, Calif.: Pacific Books, 1955. Pp. 71. Paper. $2.00. * (*PA* 30:1051)

J Consult Psychol 19:405 O '55. *Laurance F. Shaffer.* This monograph, valuable to any user of the Porteus Mazes, summarizes recent research on the test and describes the development and standardization of the Maze Extension Series, an alternate form. The second form for retesting is a welcome supplement to the Maze Test which, after forty years, is surely one of the most durable of psychological instruments.

[B344]

★POSTMAN, LEO, AND RAU, LUCY. **Retention as a Function of the Method of Measurement.** California University Publications in Psychology, Vol. 8, No. 3. Berkeley, Calif.: University of California Press, 1957. Pp. ii, 217-70. Paper. $1.00. *

[B345]

★QUARRINGTON, BRUCE. **The Statistical Basis of Sociometry.** University of Toronto, Institute of Child Study, Research Pamphlet No. 5. Toronto, Canada: the Institute, 1952. Pp. 9. Paper, mimeographed. $0.25. *

[B346]

★RAINIO, KULLERVO. **Leadership Qualities: A Theoretical Inquiry and an Experimental Study on Foremen.** Annals of the Finnish Academy of Science and Letters, Series B, No. 95, Part 1. Helsinki, Finland: Suomalainen Tiedeakatemia, Academia Scientiarum Fennica, 1955. Pp. 211. Paper. 750 mk. *

[B347]

★RAVEN, J. C. **Controlled Projection for Children, Second Edition.** London: H. K. Lewis & Co. Ltd., 1951. Pp. 176. 25s. * For reviews, see 127; for reviews of the first edition, see 3:29.

[B348]

★REISSENWEBER, MARION. **The Use of Modified Block Designs in the Evaluation and Training of the Brain-Injured.** American Psychological Association, Psychological Monographs: General and Applied, Vol. 67, No. 21, Whole No. 371. Washington, D.C.: the Association, Inc., 1953. Pp. 28. Paper. $1.00. * (*PA* 29:2467)

[B349]
★REMMERS, H. H. Introduction to Opinion and
Attitude Measurement. New York: Harper &
Brothers, 1954. Pp. viii, 437. $5.00. * (PA 28:8655)

Am J Psychol 68:694–5 D '55. *Ralph R.
Canter.* * There is plenty of room left for the
instructor—on several counts. Very few references date after 1948 * Many of the studies
described are summarized so succinctly that
their purpose is unclear: "Is this work included to illustrate a method or to present
findings?" was a question which arose frequently during reading. The reviewer would
have appreciated more examples of actual materials used in studies; the instructor will have
to collect them himself. In describing methods,
Remmers gives about 6 pages to Thurstone,
3 pages to Likert, 32 pages to Guttman and
scale analysis (an excellent summary), and
about 4 pages on the scale discrimination technique of Edwards and Kilpatrick. The approaches of Lazarsfeld and Coombs are not
discussed. Another point for the instructor to
consider is that the student must have a basic
grounding in psychological statistics to understand a good deal of the material presented.
Perhaps what is missed most in the book is
some treatment of basic attitude-measurement
theory. Statistical testing of hypotheses is
briefly described, but there is practically nothing on the purpose of measurement, on what
is being measured, on the framing of hypotheses, on the development of specific questions used to obtain responses suitable for testing, and so forth. It must be understood that
the book contains a very large amount of information, readably presented and accurately
discussed. Many instructors will find it quite
suited to an introductory course in attitude
measurement, for which (to the reviewer's
knowledge) there is nothing comparable on
the market.

Cont Psychol 1:52–3 F '56. *Robert P. Abel-
son.* * one looks to Remmers' book to mark
the integration and maturity of the emergent
discipline of attitude measurement. Unfortunately the book falls short of this expectation
in style, clarity, organization, and precision.
Both beginning and advanced students are apt
to be dissatisfied with it. For instance, the
beginner is frequently tripped up by the questions at the ends of chapters, questions that
demand considerable sophistication in psychology. In addition, concepts are very often in-

troduced before they are explained, if they
ever are. Examples are: *normal distribution,
stratified sampling, zero-order correlation,* and
multivariate distribution. Furthermore, some
confusing topics (viz., Guttman scaling with
polychotomous items) are dwelt upon without
adequate illustrative examples, and many discursive passages make garbled reading. The
advanced student may also feel perplexed by
the book, for many passages are conceptually
and theoretically banal or meaningless or both
(e.g., "Hero worship is an extreme....form of
attitude [toward the hero] acting as a motive," and "the functional psychoses have their
origin in the attitude patterns of the individual") and occasional clinkers are to be found
in the statistical treatment (like the confusion
between tests of significance and confidence
limits and the definition of *all* cumulative frequency distributions as "ogives"). This reviewer is less displeased by the content coverage of the book. In it seven chapters are devoted to techniques of attitude measurement;
they cover opinion sampling, elementary statistics, item construction, the Thurstone, Likert, and Guttman scales, personality inventories, and indirect measures of attitude. Five
chapters deal with applications: to business,
government, industry, community interrelations, and education. There is no chapter on
applications to theoretical research. If the
reader makes allowance for the omission of
advanced or specialized topics, such as the
method of successive intervals, content analysis, experimental design, latent structure analysis, and factor analysis (the book does not
profess, after all, to be more than introductory), and if he recognizes that only seven
references dated later than 1951 appear in the
bibliography, then he finds the range of topics
and the fund of examples and references actually quite rich. The coverage is perhaps even
too inclusive, for attitude is defined very
broadly by the author. Remmers' emphasis
upon applications of attitude measurement is
designed to convince the student that much
can be done with objective methods in applied social psychology. His book is apt for
this purpose. This reviewer, however, would
not recommend the book as an aid in teaching the details of the content matter.

J Appl Psychol 38:377–8 O '54. *Sidney S.
Goldish.* * fairly comprehensive, succinct—in
the main—a readable presentation * The chap-

ter on scaling techniques contains an able exposition of the Thurstone and Likert contributions * Unhappily, the book appears to lack freshness. Some of the material is obviously "dated"; one gains the impression that the author, except in a few instances, stopped collecting data along about 1947 or 1948, though much that is worth while has appeared in the literature since then. * The implication conveyed by the word "Introduction" in the title, that this is a textbook for beginners, may be somewhat misleading; it quickly becomes apparent that the college student will find himself in deep water unless he has been forearmed with preliminary work in statistics and psychology. Notwithstanding, the volume is a scholarly and well-planned treatise. In writing it, Dr. Remmers has made a substantial contribution toward effecting the kind of "popular understanding of the importance and implications" of the findings of the social scientists which he, at the outset, urges. *

J Counsel Psychol 2:160 su '55. Donald E. Super. * essentially the content of a course in that subject taught by Remmers, a broad treatment of that topic. Although it does not include content analysis, "less amenable to measurement" (p. vii), it does include the Szondi, "the ease of administration and evaluation should make it an instrument of great utility" (p. 205). What strange judgments are these? Perhaps they result from attempting to treat too much within the covers of one book. The incomplete sentences technique, for example, gets less than half a page (p. 199), with references only to Payne and to a second article in the *International Journal of Opinion and Attitude Research.* Remmers would have done better to have omitted the whole of Chapter VII on less direct methods, and done more justice to the topics which are typically treated under his general heading. Such texts tend to misinform undergraduates, and they fail to provide graduate students and researchers with the specific and detailed knowledge they need ....But enough—I started this paragraph thinking I would make some passing criticisms and would end up with a plug for the book, surprised myself by discovering, while writing, that my specific and general disappointment in it far exceeds my pleasure with certain parts!

Personnel Pract B 11:73 D '55. G. D. Bradshaw. * Part I....is concerned with the tech-

nical problems involved in attitude measurement, and to follow the material in this part the reader needs to have a reasonable knowledge of statistical method. For university students, however, it provides a satisfactory if somewhat uncritical survey of the techniques available. A more detailed discussion including the nature of attitudes and their relationships to other variables would have been desirable in such an introductory textbook. In addition it tends to be rather inconsistent in emphasising the importance of unidimensionality while giving favourable treatment to a variety of "summated questionnaires." But this inconsistency reflects fairly accurately the present position in the field of attitude measurement. Part II of the volume provides a very readable non-technical treatment of the applications of attitude measurement to a variety of activities. * Part II can be read without first reading Part I.

[B350]

*REMMERS, H. H., AND GAGE, N. L. **Educational Measurement and Evaluation, Revised Edition.** New York: Harper & Brothers, 1955. Pp. xv, 651. $5.50. * (PA 29:7969)

Ed & Psychol Meas 15:515-6 w '55. William Coleman. * a thorough revision * much of the material has been rewritten, and many recent studies and developments in measurement are quoted * To facilitate a student's learning the important and essential material in the book, an instructor using it will need to eliminate several of the chapters and sections of others * Comprehensive discussions of the findings of research studies with such instruments as the SRA Youth Inventory are interesting, but not pertinent in a book devoted to *methods* of evaluation and measurement. * books should be written to communicate to the reader important concepts and principles in a given area. To facilitate such communication, writers need to be selective rather than catholic in the material they include. Providing an "abstract" at the beginning of each chapter is an important aid. Readers will need to refer back to these abstracts after going through the discursive discourse that characterizes many of the chapters. The chapters on administering the evaluation programs, interpreting test scores, and evaluating school personnel are perhaps outstanding in providing helpful information for school personnel. On the other hand, the introductory chapter on "Why Evaluate?" might have been strengthened by referring to some of the concepts presented in the first three chapters of *Educational Measurement* edited by Lindquist. A chapter on problems and issues in grading and promoting would have been heartily welcomed by teachers who are confronted with this aspect of evaluation in their classrooms. Though the reviewer agrees with most of the concepts and points of view expressed by the writers, he would question seriously the following statements or concepts: (1) *"Evaluation is to validity as measurement is to reliability."* (p. 29, italics in original) (2) In essay examinations, no choice should be permitted among questions to preserve equality of difficulty. (p. 184) (3) "We must distinguish between special *abilities* and all other aspects of pupils that are predictive of vocational success. In one sense, every aspect treated in this book may be considered an aptitude insofar as it is related to vocational success." (p. 255) This may not represent a point of disagreement, but the present wording of this statement makes it difficult to determine just what the authors are trying to say. (4) Tests measuring special abilities in Chapter 10 are discussed without emphasizing repeatedly that comparatively few good validity studies have been made with these tests. No mention is made of the USES functional classification study of jobs which is utilizing GATB scores in developing occupational profiles. (5) Emphasis is placed on the value of personality inventories in schools in Chapter 12. Inventories such as the SRA Youth Inventory may help identify some of the problems that students feel they have and are willing to reveal, but in a text for teachers stress should be placed on the inadequacy of such devices for measuring personal adjustment. Critical reviews in Buros and well-conducted research studies do not support the optimism over personality inventories expressed by Remmers & Gage. (6) In describing personality factors, the authors might have made use of the 1953 E.T.S. publication describing the more commonly derived factors from a large number of factor analysis studies involving personality inventories. In their efforts to make this book useful to classroom teachers, counselors, (and students of attitude measurement) Remmers & Gage have probably covered too much territory. By being se-

lective, however, instructors preparing students in these areas will find this book useful.

For reviews of the first edition, see 3:1112.

[B351]

★RICHARDSON, C. A. **An Introduction to Mental Measurement and Its Applications.** London: Longmans, Green & Co., Ltd., 1955. Pp. vii, 102. 8s. 6d. (New York: Longmans, Green & Co., Inc. $1.65.) *

Brit J Ed Psychol 25:212 N '55. L. B. Birch. * The first half deals with such concepts as standard deviation, percentile, significance, correlation coefficient and regression, using only the simplest arithmetic to illustrate them. It is very clearly written and a student who is undergoing a course in elementary statistics will find much here which will clarify his thought. It is doubtful, however, whether many readers with no statistical background will be able to understand these (to him) novel concepts without the experience of them in numerous contexts; this will be specially true of the chapters dealing with correlation and factors of the mind. The second half of the book is a clear, modest statement of the uses and limitations of tests in schools for classification purposes, for comparing standards and for detecting the underfunctioning child. There is a sound chapter on allocation to secondary schools and a cautious survey of the present position in the use of tests for vocational guidance. The book will probably find its main use in the hands of teachers and others who, having some background knowledge, wish to bring their knowledge up to date.

Occupational Psychol 29:200–2 Jl '55. P. E. Vernon. * a brief and quite elementary introduction to mental testing and statistics * it is, perhaps, most suited to education students and teachers who have difficulties in "getting the hang" of standard scores, reliability, factor analysis, etc. from the ordinary statistical textbooks. But its very brevity involves a good deal of condensation and a somewhat abstract treatment. One doubts, for example, whether many of those for whom the book is intended can really be expected to understand rotation of axes. The statistical chapters are followed by several short, but very sensible chapters on the nature of intelligence, the use of tests for classification of children, secondary school selection, and other applications. Four pages on vocational guidance hardly seem sufficient to be worth-while, though they do manage to bring out the limitations of tests in this field. There is an interesting point in the chapter on educational selection, namely that one reason for its causing so much heart-burning is that it really acts as an instrument of vocational selection. If employers were more willing to accept leavers from the upper streams of modern schools (who are often as able as the lower streams of grammar schools) many of the problems might disappear. *

[B352]

★RILEY, MATILDA WHITE; RILEY, JOHN W., JR.; AND TOBY, JACKSON; IN ASSOCIATION WITH MARCIA L. TOBY, RICHARD COHN, HARRY C. BREDEMEIER, MARY MOORE, AND PAUL FINE; WITH CONTRIBUTIONS BY URIEL G. FOA, ROBERT N. FORD, LOUIS GUTTMAN, AND SAMUEL A. STOUFFER AND ASSOCIATES. **Sociological Studies in Scale Analysis: Applications, Theory, Procedures.** New Brunswick, N.J.: Rutgers University Press, 1954. Pp. xii, 433. $6.00. * (*PA* 29:737, 840)

Am J Psychol 68:168–9 Mr '55. *H. J. Eysenck.* * It is doubtful to the reviewer if it should really be called a book at all in the ordinary sense of the term. It is a collection of articles, notes, and theoretical discussions, many mere reprints of published papers thrown together in a rather haphazard fashion and without any very definite plan. Thus, for instance, after 272 pages of frequently very complex argument and sophisticated statistical discussion dealing with the application of Guttman's scales to sociometric problems, the reader is suddenly treated to a very simplified, told-to-the-children kind of introduction to the Guttman scaling techniques. There seems to be no reason for this odd placement, except that this introduction happened to occur in a published paper which, for other reasons, was thought to be more relevant to a later part of the book than to an earlier one. Unless the reader, therefore, is relatively knowledgeable and sophisticated to begin with, he will almost certainly be completely puzzled by the contents of this volume in their present arrangement. The expert will undoubtedly find a number of interesting leads, methods of analysis, and new areas of application; he may also be grateful to have reprinted in easily accessible form a number of important papers which might otherwise not be readily obtainable. Even so, he might have preferred a book of the more usual kind, *i.e.* one written with a clear plan and purpose, with a beginning, a middle, and an end, and with an arrangement both logical and sensible. Another

difficulty which the psychological reader may find with this book is the terrible prolixity which seems to afflict the writers, particularly in connection with theoretical subjects. An attempt seems to be made to relate sociological theory to scaling, but this attempt is very largely on a semantic level, which is perhaps not surprising since sociological theories, particularly those connected with Parsons and Shils, are not usually of a kind which lend themselves to verification or disproof. An illustration of the perfunctory way in which the task is performed may be found in a footnote on page 39. The authors are talking about an analysis of the rôles of individual players and their structure, or interrelationship. They go on to refer to "the distinction between *action* patterns and *plurality* patterns in Leopold von Wiese and Howard Becker, *Systematic Sociology,* John Wiley and Sons, 1932. Although the present empirical effort, by contrast, focuses only upon limited aspects of patterned acts, on the one hand, and structured rôles, on the other, there may well be an element of theoretical continuity in the two frames of reference. Nor is this proposal unrelated to such important distinctions as are made in the theoretical works of Pitirim Sorokin and Florian Znanieki." Such phrases as "there may well be" and "nor is this proposal unrelated" indicate that the integration between theory and what is done in this book is of a very loose and woolly kind. The example quoted illustrates a tendency which the reader will find throughout the whole book. A further point which will occur to the critical reader is this : Technical procedures in scale analysis are discussed in great detail, and working methods set out sufficiently well to enable anyone to follow them easily. What seems to be lacking, however, is the much more important discussion of fundamental points of criticism. The reader of this volume will in vain seek enlightenment as to the grounds on which these scaling techniques have been attacked, and equally vainly will he seek for a refutation of these criticisms. Altogether then, this appears to be a hastily put together compendium dealing with a large number of loosely related points in the general field of scale analysis, touching in a very non-rigorous fashion on a great variety of sociological theories of the more speculative and semantic type. It has much of interest and importance to say to the expert, but would prove a very purgatory for the beginner trying to find out about scale analysis. The book is enlivened by a number of empirical studies which appear to be essentially of a trivial nature, and are not designed to answer any very obvious psychological questions.

Am Sociol R 20:127–8 F '55. David Gold. * What will perhaps be novel and extremely suggestive to many, especially to those not too well acquainted with the analysis of sociometric data, is the distinction made between subject and object scales. The same body of data can be analyzed both in terms of the actors (subject) and in terms of the recipients of action (object). What distinguishes such analysis from the usual sociometric analysis is the use of multiple items as well as multiple individuals to classify each individual. The variables of the scales are status, consensus, and reputation. Some may disagree with the way these variables have been conceptualized (theory), but their operational translation is clear (method). And this is the great merit of the approach of these investigators; you know precisely how they know what status or consensus is. * For those unfamiliar with Guttman scale analysis, Parts Two and Three may well seem somewhat incomprehensible. Unfortunately, prior reading of Part Four may not help, for it does not contain a good simple introduction to the operations of scale analysis. The chapter by Robert N. Ford, which is presumably intended to fulfill this function, rapidly moves from the too general to the too technical. For those whose familiarity with Guttman scale analysis is based upon experience, Parts Two and Three should prove stimulating, both in terms of the novel applications and the methodological questions that are suggested. The whole volume may be characterized more as a manual of procedure than a methodological treatise, for little consideration is given to crucial general questions of methodology in scaling, though they are mentioned or implied from time to time. For example, what effect does the number of items used have on scalability? How many subjects does one need for an adequate test of scalability? Upon what are Guttman's edicts in these matters based? How large a difference must be observed between the coefficient of reproducibility and chance reproducibility in order to be considered significant? There is the matter of possible over-capitalization on chance in the successive combination of response categories that is always necessary to achieve an "accept-able" scale when dealing with items which originally have more than two response categories. The new techniques presented for "improving" cumulative scales and Guttman's "image analysis" make this possibility an even more pressing matter to be investigated. In almost all cases a set of multiple-choice items must be treated as dichotomous in order to achieve a scale. Yet there is evidence that respondents do not in fact make the choices on the dichotomous items that they would be expected to make on the basis of their earlier responses to the same items with multiple-choices. Some researchers are getting a bit suspicious about the fact that hardly ever, if at all, do they *not* get a Guttman scale through successive combinations when they start with twelve or fifteen multiple-choice items. The use of the fold-over technique to get information on consensus (taken to be the second component of the object content scale) needs more clarification than that provided by Richard Cohn in his mathematical note. If the fold-over technique is used, nothing but a U-shaped curve can result when consensus (intensity, as Guttman has used this second component) is plotted against content. The relationship then becomes an artifact of the mathematical analysis and needs demonstration of its validity before it can be accepted. The whole matter of higher components of Guttman scales and their interpretation needs elucidation. At this point most of us can hardly be content with a statement such as that by Uriel G. Foa. "The closure curve (third component) has two bending points which separate high from low intensities. The far-reaching psychological and methodological implications of this discovery hardly need to be stressed." We would like to have had these implications spelled out. This volume does provide a useful and fresh exposition of the uses to which scale analysis may be put. Its emphasis upon the derivation of clean sociological variables and the determination of the relevancy of the group as a research unit makes this work a most valuable contribution to all sociology.

[B353]

★Robbertse, P. M. **Personality Structure of Socially Adjusted and Socially Maladjusted Children According to the Rorschach Test.** American Psychological Association, Psychological Monographs: General and Applied, Vol. 69, No. 19, Whole No. 404. Washington, D.C.: the Association, Inc., 1955. Pp. 20. Paper. $1.00. * (*PA* 30:6983)

[B354]

★Robinson, Helen M., Editor. **Evaluation of Reading: Proceedings of the Annual Conference on Reading Held at the University of Chicago, 1958.** Supplementary Educational Monographs, Vol. 20, No. 88. Chicago, Ill.: University of Chicago Press, 1958. Pp. vii, 208. *

[B355]

★Roesslein, Charles G. **Differential Patterns of Intelligence Traits Between High Achieving and Low Achieving High School Boys.** Catholic University of America, Educational Research Monographs, Vol. 17, No. 5. Washington, D.C.: Catholic University of America Press, Inc., 1953. Pp. vii, 64. Paper. $1.00. * (PA 29:1472)

[B356]

★Roff, Merrill. **A Factorial Study of Tests in the Perceptual Area.** Psychometric Monograph No. 8. Princeton, N.J.: Psychometrics Society (P.O. Box 572), 1953. Pp. v, 41. Out of print. (PA 28:3735)

[B357]

★Rogers, Carl A. **Measuring Intelligence in New Zealand: A Re-standardisation of Thurstone's Primary Mental Abilities (or Intermediate Test) for Ages 11 to 17 Years.** Auckland University College, Monograph Series No. 2. Auckland, New Zealand: Pilgrim Press, 1956. Pp. 127. 17s. 6d. * (PA 32:2658)

[B358]

★Rohde, Amanda R. **The Sentence Completion Method: Its Diagnosis and Clinical Application to Mental Disorders.** New York: Ronald Press Co., 1957. Pp. xii, 301. $7.50. * (PA 31:6123)

Personnel & Guid J 37:77–8 S '58. Margaret Ives. The sentence completion method of investigating personality is a valuable addition to the repertoire of projective tests, and Dr. Rohde has done as much as anyone to bring it to its present state of usefulness and general acceptance. * Rohde believes that this method will prove useful not only to experienced clinicians but also "to social workers, vocational guidance counsellors, teachers, and others who deal with problems of interpersonal relations." Even though they may not have developed skill in psychological testing nor have a background in abnormal psychology, they may be able to reach "important and valid deductions" without making elaborate formal analysis of the results. It should be pointed out here that they may also reach faulty conclusions and most certainly will miss a great deal which is of importance. To be sure, Rohde points out that the most penetrating results are obtained by experts who "systematically interpret the responses in accordance with a comprehensive set of behavior variables." She gives explicit directions for scoring and interpreting which should be easily comprehensible to anyone familiar with Murray's conceptual scheme of

personality variables: needs, presses, etc. Standardization of the test was carried out on junior high school students from a variety of locations and on veterans now supposedly well adjusted in the community and ranging in age from 24–45 years. A wide variety of occupational and educational levels was tapped. The results were compared with completions done by persons with various kinds of personality disorders, by psychoneurotics including a special group with speech deviations, and by schizophrenics from two widely separated Veterans Administration hospitals. All results were analyzed by Murray's system. The findings justify the claim of the Sentence Completion Test to be a valuable member of the group of projective devices investigating personality. It provides penetrating insight into the thinking and the problems of the person being tested, which are probably more often limited by lack of skill on the part of the examiner than by weaknesses of the test. Also, it lends itself easily to group testing and therefore can be time saving in schools or as a screening device even when used alone. Nevertheless, it seems to this reviewer that the test is best used as part of a battery in combination with an intelligence test and other projectives, such as the Rorschach, Draw a Person Test, or Bender Gestalt. While all of these reveal, for example, the presence of anxiety, the Sentence Completions show in a different fashion the specific attitudes lying back of the anxious feelings and give clues to situations or areas of experience which may be responsible. The Sentence Completions more nearly parallel the Thematic Apperception Test in primarily disclosing content rather than structure and provide a shorter, more easily administered examination. Thus a carefully chosen combination of tests for each subject will often include this test and present to the skillful clinician the best evaluation of the individual personality.

[B359]

★Rohrer, J. H.; Hoffman, E. L.; Bagby, J. W., Jr.; Herrmann, Robert S.; and Wilkins, W. L. **The Group-Administered Rorschach as a Research Instrument: Reliability and Norms.** American Psychological Association, Psychological Monographs: General and Applied, Vol. 69, No. 8, Whole No. 393. Washington, D.C.: the Association, Inc., 1955. Pp. 13. Paper. $1.00. * (PA 30:1056)

[B360]

Roman, Klara G. **Handwriting: A Key to Personality.** New York: Pantheon Books, Inc., 1952. Pp. xi, 382. $6.50. * (PA 27:5135)

Am J Psychother 6:599–600 Jl '52. Deso A. Weiss. This book helps to redeem graphology from the blame of charlatanism and constitutes a healthy sign of the coming of age of this valuable but treacherously subtle technique. It reads as a colorful course of introductory lectures, and the profuse illustrations—among them the handwritings of many world-wide known artistic, scientific and political personalities—make it a fascinating study. The points are well taken but rather illustrated than proven in detail. The literary quotations are well chosen and representative. The writer takes care to repudiate the often used "impressionistic" techniques, the mysticism and the occasional dishonesty of earlier graphological dreamers or quacks, but leaves the door open for some intuitive approach. Her main concern is with the enhancing of the scientific reliability of this oldest of the "projective techniques." Work-sheets and sample analyses help to introduce the beginner to the laboratory of the scientific graphologist. The book is well edited and the illustrations are as good as can be expected from the offset technique. This reviewer would have liked at least an occasional reproduction of good photo copies in order to obtain the full flavor of the originals. * The chapter about the change of handwriting in puberty and adolescence and its endocrinological implications is particularly impressive. * The chapter dealing with the close interrelations of speech and writing, especially in cases of stuttering and stammering, is very convincing. Here the writer has done considerable pioneering work. * Mrs. Roman's work is a valuable introduction for the beginner but it also brings ample material for the advanced student of graphology. It can be highly recommended.

J Proj Tech 17:234–6 Je '53. Rose Wolfson. * a very readable, interesting and informative book but if a distinction between information and instruction is valid, this book falls short of the claims for a "well organized, clear, simply worded survey of the methods and techniques used in handwriting analysis" made for it by the publishers. Indeed, the most conspicuous weakness of the book is its loose organization, which may derive from the practical attempt to produce a book that would be both inviting to the lay reader and scientifically acceptable to the professional. Nominally, the book is divided into two parts, "Developmental Stages of Handwriting" and "Analysis and Interpreta-

tion," but much of the material within the chapters and subdivisions, especially the early ones, is frequently so premature, discrete or digressive as to interfere seriously with continuity of subject. An understanding of Part I, for example, depends so much on material found in Part II that the beginner, at least, would be better advised to follow a reverse plan of reading and start with Part II. In addition, Roman skips down many attractive sidepaths, which, while interesting, are also distractive from the main course of the book. Once Roman gets into her subject proper, graphology, she often achieves unquestionable excellence, particularly when dealing with topics closely associated with her experimental interests and experiences. Here beginner and advanced student alike are likely to derive much. Of special note are her sections on graphic indices of speed, factors affecting speed, handedness, pressure, and tension and release. In contrast, and regrettably, there is only suggestive reference to speech pathology and handwriting expression, another area of research in which Roman has specialized. Her theory of expressive movement seems somewhat over simplified, implying a one to one relationship between handwriting and speech, speech and gait, handwriting and gesture, etc. If we have learned anything about human behavior it is that *consistency* and *similarity* are not necessarily the same. Allport hurdled this difficulty by referring to "congruence" for characteristics that seemed to contradict the integrity of the personality. This tendency towards oversimplification runs throughout the book, with varying degrees of benefit to the beginner. It is all to the good when applied to her method of analysis, which employs a worksheet as a mechanical aid. By and large, most reputable graphologists consider the same indices for interpretation even though they shift them under different headings or descriptive terms. Roman places indices under three primary components: *movement, form* and *arrangement,* in an earnest effort both to objectify and simplify the analytical procedure. Points of overlap on the worksheet, as with *expansion of movement* subsumed under *movement* then considered as *zonal proportion* under *arrangement,* suggests that the simplicity is more apparent than real, but as a "skeletal model," so recognized by Roman herself, it should help discipline subjective judgment. Although Roman takes a dim view of

Klages' theories and speculations, her theory of tension and release, directly or indirectly, like that of many another graphologist, draws blood from this main German artery of thought which laid the foundations for the psychology of expressive movement. An active point of departure, however, not only from Klages but also from Saudek, Lewinson and others who follow him in this special practice, is the use of the school model as her standard instead of an aesthetically "superior" form. In this reviewer's opinion, there is much in research to confirm the essential logic of Roman's "norm." The symbolism underlying Roman's orientation follows the traditional tri-division of space into above, center, below, animated by Pulver's psychoanalytic insights and elaborations. Generally, interpretations tend to follow those of other seasoned and expert graphologists although there are occasional differences as with *line direction* and *endings of words*. But there are also new observations and assumptions, one of the more interesting referring to signatures. Contrary to the thinking of many other graphologists who believe signatures to be of only negligible usefulness for analysis because they are stereotyped through continual practice, Roman believes that because the signature is mastered earlier than the rest of writing, it tends to reflect, more truly, repressed or rationalized infantilism. Similarly, it more readily mirrors creative or imaginative powers, and thus can tell us much concerning the dreams, realized or otherwise, of the writer. Roman correctly cautions against independent analysis of the signature, Wolff's encouragement to the contrary notwithstanding. The basic meaning of a signature cannot be determined without study of a longer text by the same hand. * the main purpose of the book, graphological instruction, was only partially achieved because of the many incidental objectives followed. The book consequently is more definitive than pedagogical, and as such is of greater usefulness to students of comparative graphology than to beginners in this field.

Psychosom Med 15:636–7 N–D '53. Elizabeth C. Anderson. * Miss Roman's book is not only a useful and welcome textbook for a student of graphology but also offers information and stimulation to the advanced worker in that field. The author has gained great experience from her research work with various groups of normal and disturbed people. This gives her authority to judge writing disturbances against the background of normal development. Of special interest are her chapters on developmental disturbances, speech defects, and left- and right-handedness. Her work touches on various problems of clinical and experimental psychology. Personality disturbances such as psychosomatic manifestations, homosexuality, alcoholism, and criminal tendencies are discussed and the practical help is pointed out that graphology can give in the diagnosis and treatment of such cases. The physiology of handwriting movement is clarified by an interesting experimental method, the so-called graphodyne, which records the expended and unexpended energy of the writer and thus gives a measure of this tension. Miss Roman's book clearly shows the significance of handwriting analysis as a diagnostic tool which compares well with other projective techniques of psychological diagnosis. An extensive bibliography and index will prove of value to the reader.

[B361]

*ROSS, CLAY C.; REVISED BY JULIAN C. STANLEY. **Measurement in Today's Schools, Third Edition.** New York: Prentice-Hall, Inc., 1954. Pp. xvii, 485. Text edition, $5.00; trade edition, $6.65. * (London: Bailey Bros. & Swinfen, Ltd., 1956. 53s. 6d.) (PA 29: 1580)

Ed Res B 34:162–3 S 14 '55. Chester O. Mathews. * The chapter on guidance has been reduced to six pages....a very inadequate treatment. * One of the principal omissions....is an adequate treatment of techniques and procedures for appraising a great many of the objectives of the educational program. One looks in vain for suggestions, devices, and specific procedures for the appraisal of intelligence, attitudes, human relationships, skills, personality adjustments, and the like. The text deals so largely with generalized principles that it may not meet very adequately the needs of teachers and administrators for specific help in appraising their objectives. The chapters which deal with "objective" and "essay" tests of information and understanding will give fairly good guidance in developing teacher tests on intellectual objectives. These comments are not primarily a criticism of Stanley's revision but rather of the original organization and scope of this text. Stanley has introduced many new references and ideas which have grown out of recent research; he has brought chapters up to date in respect to the content which they earlier contained; he has introduced a new final chapter dealing with some present trends which forms a fitting conclusion to the text and to a course in measurements. *

J Ed Psychol 46:319–20 My '55. Lee J. Cronbach. * No major changes in the pattern of the book or the point of view have been made since the first edition. * Students have liked the Ross text for its definiteness. It gives specific procedures for item preparation, and covers many topics of interest to administrators and supervisors. On the other hand, the text seemed conservative even at its first appearance, and the revisions have preserved this character. The student is told many things which must seem to him purely academic in interest, and some chapters seem so to the reviewer also. The style is one of old-fashioned scholarship, with long and uninspired quotations, numerous tables, and footnotes by the dozen. On the positive side, Ross' treatment was sound, in the light of the knowledge of the 1930's. Stanley has clearly undertaken to change the book as little as possible. He has added new footnote references, has greatly modernized the chapter reading lists, and has added paragraphs at a few points. Several illustrative tables have been replaced with better examples. He has judiciously removed paragraphs by Ross, but has never rewritten material even where Ross' view is questionable. One change in the text increases an unfortunate overemphasis on item analysis as a way of determining test content. The interpretation of correlation is damaged by introducing a chart in which the Fisher z is taken as showing "the amount of relationship represented" by a given r, and by omitting Ross' reference to Taylor and Russell. To compensate for the absence of new ideas in the main chapters, Stanley has added one chapter on present trends. This material is too cursory to be significant; one simply cannot deal intelligently with factor analysis in five sentences, no matter how well chosen. This chapter does provide reassurance, lacking elsewhere in the book, that the testing field has not stagnated in recent years. The chief fault in Ross' book is one which could not be remedied by retouching. The book is oriented around the superficies of measurement, such as scoring of rearrangement items and using legible record forms, rather than around behavior and learn-

ing. This is made obvious by the fact that the objectives of instruction and their relation to testing are discussed only in one three-page section. Curricular validity is dismissed with the trivial and incredible comment that this idea has "shifted the center of gravity from the curriculum to the child." Those instructors who have been satisfied with the Ross text will be grateful for a revision such as might have been expected from Ross himself. The revision will not, however, appeal to any new audience.

For reviews of earlier editions, see 4:B325 and 3:1131.

[B362]

*Ross, C.; revised by Julian C. Stanley. **Workbook to Accompany** *Measurement in Today's Schools*, **Third Edition.** New York: Prentice-Hall, Inc., 1954. Pp. vi, 80. Paper, lithotyped. $1.50. *

[B363]

★Rothney, John W. M. **Evaluating and Reporting Pupil Progress.** What Research Says to the Teacher, [No.] 7. Washington, D.C.: National Education Association, March 1955. Pp. 32. Paper. $0.25. *

[B364]

★Rothney, John W. M.; Danielson, Paul J.; and Heimann, Robert A. **Measurement for Guidance.** New York: Harper & Brothers, 1959. Pp. xii, 378. $5.00. *

[B365]

★Rummel, J. Francis. **The Computation and Use of Item-Analysis Data in the Improvement of Teacher-Made Examinations.** Curriculum Bulletin No. 103. Eugene, Ore.: School of Education, University of Oregon, 1952. Pp. 11. Paper, mimeographed. $0.20. *

[B366]

★Rummel, J. Francis. **Know Your Pupils.** Prepared for the Oregon State Department of Education, under the editorial direction of the Improvement of Instruction Committee of the Oregon Education Association. Eugene, Ore.: Oregon State Department of Education, 1951. Pp. 37. Paper. *

[B367]

★Ruszel, Humphrey. **Test Patterns in Intelligence: Comparative Factor Analyses for High School Boys and Girls.** Catholic University of America, Educational Research Monographs, Vol. 16, No. 5. Washington, D.C.: Catholic University of America Press, Inc., 1952. Pp. viii, 70. Paper. $1.00.

[B368]

★Samuels, Henry. **The Validity of Personality-Trait Ratings Based on Projective Techniques.** American Psychological Association, Psychological Monographs: General and Applied, Vol. 66, No. 5, Whole No. 337. Washington, D.C.: the Association, Inc., 1952. Pp. ii, 21. Paper. $1.00. * (*PA* 27:5161)

[B369]

★Sarason, Seymour B. **The Clinical Interaction: With Special Reference to Rorschach.** New York:

Harper & Brothers, 1954. Pp. xi, 425. $5.00. * (PA 29:896)

Am J Mental Def 60:199 Jl '55. Henry C. Schumacher. * Part II, the Rorschach, is an unexcelled introduction to that test. No other text known to the reviewer makes such extensive use of research findings both to support its claims and to buttress its doubts and negative findings. * this book should be prescribed study for the many who today are making unwarranted deductions, interpretations, and reports based on inadequate theory and failure to freely consider the variables in the clinical interaction.

Am J Psychol 68:166–8 Mr '55. H. J. Eysenck. This book may be evaluated from two different points of view, and one's final decision must be determined very largely by one's decision as to the proper frame of reference. On the one hand, we may accept it as a contribution to the Rorschach literature, in respect to which we agree to take a large number of things for granted (such as the validity of the Rorschach Test as a whole, the diagnostic usefulness of psychotherapy, the truth of certain psychoanalytic doctrines, and so forth). On the other hand, we may ask ourselves questions regarding the contribution of this book to the science of psychology, using the term in a reasonably rigorous sense. The fact that these two universes of discourse exist and require separate consideration is in itself an interesting comment on the state of modern psychology. Judging the book then in the first place as a contribution to the Rorschach literature, we should say that it is clear, well written, knowledgeable, critical, and altogether superior to the great majority of books in this field. * With much of what the author says it would be difficult to disagree. There is stress on experimental verification throughout. * Sarason's critical survey of the literature suggests to him a certain minimal number of statements which may usefully and validly be made about the Rorschach. These statements and this discussion certainly are much more down to earth and realistic than the type of material one has been used to in connection with the Rorschach Test. In spite of these good points, the book appears less valuable than it might otherwise have been because the author fails to take into account sufficiently the second of the two universes of discourse mentioned at the beginning of this review. He seems to be aware of this omission because he points out to "the reader who is not a clinician...that the clinician is expected to give some kind of answer to the problems which are presented to him, and he cannot avoid answering the problems because of uncertainties about the assumptions upon which he operates" (p. 295). To what extent this social pressure should lead the clinician to make use of unvalidated tests, inspired guess work, and the like, this is not the place to discuss. From the point of view of the science of psychology, it must be pointed out, however, that a contribution has to satisfy much higher standards before it can be regarded as acceptable. Sarason himself draws attention to the fact that different authors use different instructions and different procedures, different scoring systems, and different principles of interpretation; he reports investigations showing that the personality of *E,* as well as the setting, the social class of *S,* and many other variables, affect the outcome of the test. Nevertheless, he spends a good deal of the time comparing different researches, which differ in all these respects, and it is difficult to see just what the point of such a procedure can be. Surely, before any results can be compared, the effects of variation in procedure and other matters must be known and discounted. This is only one example of a split which seems to go through the book. Criticism of individual experiments and comparison of their results is carried out with insight and in terms which would seem reassuring to the scientifically trained investigator, yet throughout there is a failure to face the fact that major requirements for the comparison of individual studies, such as those outlined above, are lacking. The critical reader, who follows all the experimental documentation regarding the many uncontrolled factors determining Rorschach responses, may end up by asking whether knowledge regarding this test has really reached a point where anything positive whatsoever can be said regarding it. He may also wonder why this test was chosen in preference to other methods of investigating personality which are less subject to such damaging criticism. There are a few minor points of criticism which should be mentioned. It is not always clear why the author quotes certain studies rather than others; thus, he relies heavily on Wittenborn's factorial analysis of the Rorschach Test, but gives no reference to the analyses by Sen, Cox, and others, which would superficially seem to be even more relevant. There is some evidence of poor proofreading. Thus, the reviewer found his name (incorrectly spelled) in the author index; looking up the page given there, he found no mention of his work until two pages later, where his name occurred, again incorrectly spelled. A rapid survey disclosed that all references to the bibliography were misplaced by two pages, an error which might be very annoying to the unwary reader.

Brit J Med Psychol 29:174 '56. R. M. Mowbray. * The major part of the book is....a technical discussion of the Rorschach test, ending with some illustrative protocols and interpretations. By itself this is a valuable commentary on, and review of, Rorschach procedure, but it adds very little to the thesis. The author seems to have forgotten that this section was intended to illustrate aspects of clinical interaction and not to provide a Rorschach compendium. As it stands, this makes for a badly balanced presentation. It is unfortunate that Dr Sarason has swamped his arguments so unnecessarily, for he has much to contribute, both in his thinking and experiments, to a systematic understanding of variables in the two-person clinical situation.

J Consult Psychol 18:474 D '54. Laurance F. Shaffer. * a unique volume and a most stimulating one * much more than a Rorschach book * Extensive use is made of research findings; no other work on the Rorschach supports its doubts and claims with so much data. The negative nature of much of the evidence is faced frankly. * The volume quite evidently leaves its author conflicted— a feeling that will be shared by many readers. When we remove from the Rorschach all of the beliefs controverted by evidence, the remaining substance is thin. Instructors who like their students to think, instead of to be indoctrinated in a ritual, may well consider this book seriously.

J Proj Tech 19:201–2 Je '55. Mortimer M. Meyer. * Part one, Situational Variables, deals with "the major variables operative in an interpersonal interaction." * The style of writing is generally a very effective one although at times the degree of detail becomes more pedantic than seems necessary. Nevertheless, on the whole, the material is valuable and well presented especially for those new to the concept of examiner-subject interaction. Part II, the Rorschach, presents the basic aspects of scoring and interpretation essentially as organized by Klopfer. For each of the categories, he presents the underlying hypotheses and presents the most pertinent research with a critique. For most classrooms in which the elementary aspects of the Rorschach is taught, this portion of the book lacks seriously the detail and scope necessary for a basic text. There is inadequate presentation of explanations and samples in scoring and what is there is so imbedded in the research discussion as to confuse the beginner. On the other hand, for the reader who is already familiar with the technique, interspersing the instructional material in the presentation of the research interrupts the flow and becomes a distraction. This section could have gained considerably by sub-dividing it into a section on instructional material with more detail and a section on the research organized around the hypotheses. Despite these criticisms, this section is a valuable supplement to the more usual texts in the field which, on the whole, tend to ignore the research findings. Part III, Individual Interpretation, is best discussed in two sections. The first section uses case history and therapeutic material to point out some major formulation of psychodynamics. This is the least useful and meaningful portion of the book. The second section presents the author's analysis of six protocols. These are very useful, yet disappointing. After the lengthy evaluation of the research dealing with the formal characteristics of cards, the author's interpretation fails to use these and leans heavily on content interpretation so that although the interpretations are instructive and point up somewhat the interaction element, they essentially ignore a major portion of the book rather than illustrating it. As a total, this book is probably the most stimulating of the recent books dealing with the Rorschach. It certainly is essential reading for any serious course on the Rorschach and certainly will also be useful to any psychologist working with the Rorschach who wishes to obtain a global picture of pertinent research findings.

Psychol B 52:168–9 Mr '55. Leonard D. Goodstein. Clinical psychologists who use the Rorschach technique have been sorely criticized by their more experimentally oriented colleagues for failing to take into account the numerous Rorschach research studies. The use of the Rorschach as a psychodiagnostic instrument still seems to be based upon the original, pre-experimental statements of Rorschach and some of his disciples, with little or no attention paid to those investigations that have attempted to validate such statements. Sarason's effort to handle this problem of integrating research findings with the clinical use of the Rorschach will help answer these criticisms and will bring the Rorschach closer to the main body of contemporary empirical psychology. The present volume is not, however, a research compendium, but is rather a detailed presentation of several carefully selected studies, including some unpublished investigations from the Yale laboratories, as well as the implications of these studies for Rorschach interpretation. Of the multitude of Rorschach studies, the author has selected fewer than one hundred for mention or discussion. One fortunate outcome of this selection is that many studies with equivocal results, inadequate design, etc. are excluded. On the other hand, many readers will search in vain for studies that they regard as especially relevant or significant to the problem under discussion. * The final section of the volume begins with a rather uneven discussion of psychic determinism, the purposiveness of behavior and the defense mechanisms. The graduate students and professional clinical psychologists for whom this volume seems intended will find much of this section quite elementary. The last chapter presents six complete Rorschach protocols together with Sarason's response-by-response, card-by-card interpretation. This is done in an attempt to spell out the interpretive process and represents a courageous beginning to our understanding of the psychology of the *Rorschacher*. The author's pro-Rorschach bias occasionally leads him to conclusions that others might find unacceptable. This bias is clearly seen in the treatment of the Rorschach indices of performance under stress (pp. 149–155); Meyer Williams' original investigation is presented here as evidence of the Rorschach's capacity to predict such performance. While the several unsuccessful attempts to cross-validate Williams' findings are also discussed, the reader comes away with the impression that Sarason is rather unimpressed with these failures, and Williams' results are substantially

unchallenged. One less favorably disposed toward the Rorschach certainly might come to an entirely different conclusion. Despite the above criticisms, the present volume represents a significant contribution to the literature of the Rorschach and general clinical psychology. The psychologist who would like to have a more solid empirical basis for his clinical use of the Rorschach ought to regard this book as required reading.

[B370]

★SARGENT, HELEN D. The Insight Test: A Verbal Projective Test for Personality Study. The Menninger Clinic Monograph Series No. 10. New York: Grune & Stratton, Inc., 1953. Pp. xii, 276. $7.50. * (PA 28:2672) For additional reviews, see 143.

Am J Orthopsychiatry 25:433–5 Ap '55. Herman B. Molish. The primary purpose of this erudite volume is the introduction of a new projective technique, the Insight Test. The thoroughness of Dr. Sargent's evaluation of this new test within the framework of theoretical aspects of projective techniques and the intricate application of the test to the many facets of psychopathology and personality structure can be regarded as an outstanding contribution of equal importance with the introduction of this new technique. * Sargent demonstrates a critical approach which reflects the skill and appreciation of an experienced clinician. The trained clinician and student alike will find Chapter 1, "Orientation," of great value in its discussion of problems concerning diagnosis, nosology, and theory of personality. Of special import is a proposed schema for "Diagnostic Inference, Reasoning, and Abstraction" to be applied to the interpretation of projective techniques and the exploration of problems in diagnostic research. * The stimulus material of this test is composed of a series of problem situations outlined briefly to which the subject is asked to respond by relating what the leading character did, and why, and how he felt about it. * Certainly this new projective test will be an excellent adjunct to other projective techniques, since it introduces a social situation into which the subject projects himself. Perhaps through the Insight Test more knowledge about an individual's social personality may be obtained. * this excellent text should be included in the reading list of any course given on projective techniques. The experienced clinician will not only sharpen his thinking as to the theoretical aspects of projective techniques by reading this text, but new avenues for needed research will be stimulated. The beginning student will gain a sound respect for the skill and experience required by one before he attains a reasonable level of proficiency in interpreting projective test material.

Am J Psychother 11:159 Ja '57. Frank L. Catalano. * As the author acknowledges, the scoring system is likely to appear cumbersome and arbitrary. Moreover, when the data regarding norms, reliability, and validity are carefully evaluated, the test still must be considered in the experimental stage. Unfortunately, the standardization data presented in this book offer no significant improvements over the originally published material. Nevertheless, the test does have definite advantages over the more highly "structured" paper and pencil tests and would appear to warrant further exploration.

J Ed Psychol 47:190–1 Mr '56. Henry H. Morgan. * should be of interest to clinical psychologists who wish....one more weapon for attacking the ego structure of their clients. However, the book and test will be of little value to psychologists or educators who are not already thoroughly familiar with dynamic psychology and the theory and practice of projective techniques. * The author claims that ....the scoring system....can be easily learned and need not take more than thirty or forty-five minutes per record, as a rule. Even so, this represents an expenditure of time and effort that the busy clinician may be reluctant to spend on a new and still frankly experimental test, especially when he is told that the Insight Test is best used as a supplement to such time-consumers as the Rorschach and T.A.T. * To a clinician who is sympathetic to projective testing and who is willing to do a good deal of work and experimentation himself, Sargent's book will prove to be worthwhile reading. To the psychologist who is concerned largely with normal or non-pathological behavior or who has reservations regarding projective psychology, the book will be read, if at all, with skepticism. What is needed now is more research evaluating the predictive usefulness of the Insight Test in diagnosis and therapy.

J Proj Tech 18:521–4 D '54. Jules D. Holzberg. * The test....is one to measure the ability of the individual to perceive other people's motives, behavior and feelings. This reviewer was misled by the title given the test, since he approached it with the expectation that it was designed to elicit information concerning a subject's self-awareness. While the author of the test is aware of this possibility of misinterpretation, she has apparently not felt any need to offer a more descriptive title. The Insight Test is a verbal projective technique which can be taken orally or in writing. Inasmuch as the test stimuli can be read to the subject, it may be especially useful for subjects with visual handicaps. * The first chapter in the volume is concerned with the author's schema for projective test interpretation which she describes as a four-step process, beginning with the raw data elicited by the test and finally emerging in the diagnostic solution to the problem. Her discussion, although brief, seems to this reviewer to be a real contribution that may be extended to other projective techniques in that it is an attempt to make explicit the logical processes by which the psychologist interprets projective technique material. To be sure, the technique of interpretation will require much finer analysis than the author offers but it is at least one step in the direction of clarifying the interpretative process which is clearly the most significant aspect in the utilization of projective tests. The test consists of items which are called armatures, a term the author has selected from the fields of art and architecture. An armature is "....a flexible frame on which an artist constructs his model," and the author feels that this description of her test items is most appropriate in that each item serves as the standard frame upon which the subject models the image of his personality. While making for a more precise semantic description, this reviewer feels that it may add some confusion in communication between psychologists and between psychologists and other professionals. It is already clear that even objective test items, such as are found in intelligence tests, can be interpreted projectively so that any test item can be conceived of as an "armature." * The author....does not indicate on what basis the alternate forms were established so that it is difficult to judge their equivalence. * The author estimates that it takes approximately an hour to administer the long form and thirty to forty minutes to score the items. This is a fairly lengthy procedure and raises the question as to the circumstances under which one would wish to utilize this test in the usual clinical situation where time demands are such that the test could not be readily added to a battery without displacing some of the other more commonly used tests like the Rorschach and TAT. * The scoring system devised by the author seems rather complicated, although probably necessary in the early stages of demonstrating the reliability and validity of a new technique. The author reports no attempts at systematic cross-validation of her data. * Apparently, the author has not been interested at the present time in establishing gross normative data but more in validating the test clinically, i.e., studying and comparing the protocols of patients in different nosological groups. * There is some indication that the test does have a reasonable degree of reliability, consistent with that found with most projective techniques where scoring is similarly as subjective. The author attempts to justify the absence of a large normal population among her data on the grounds that it is difficult to distinguish between normality and abnormality since they both exist on the same continuum. However, if the test is to be used as a diagnostic tool in nosological classification, data on a normal population, carefully screened, must be procured to establish the limits of normal response patterns. The Insight Test is a carefully devised test that seems to have potential usefulness in clinical and research work. While the use of the long form seems a costly procedure in terms of time, the availability of the short form may make for its finding a place among the more frequently used clinic procedures. While the scoring procedure seems complicated, the data elicited by the test can be dealt with in terms of content as one does with the Thematic Apperception Test. For research purposes, the present scoring system may be very helpful. One would hope that further cross-validation research with the test will be attempted, and that the normative populations will consist of reasonably adequate samples. The reviewer must compliment the author for the very restrained manner in which she has described the test and its applicability. One feels that in her hands the test will develop into a responsible member of the projective technique armamentarium.

Psychiatric Q Sup 28:337 pt 2 '54. * Sargent should be commended for eliminating the static sign-approach from her technique and, instead, employing a dynamic viewpoint which freely utilizes psychoanalytic theories in evaluating the individual—in terms of defenses, ego-organization, habitual modes of adaptation, etc. However, the many disadvantages of this technique—the lack of suitable norms and adequate standardization, the doubtful reliability of the parallel sets of armatures, and the rather complicated scoring system—do not as yet recommend this test for employment independently in the clinic with any level of confidence. Indeed, Sargent is quite cognizant of her test's shortcomings, and wisely delimits the use of this manual as "primarily for the clinician and the clinical research worker, in the expectation that he will take creative liberties with the stimulus material, the method of analysis, the technique of administration, or with any other aspects of the test by which it may be made more effective for special purposes."

[B371]

★SAVAGE, H. W. **An Evaluation of the Cooperative English Test of Effectiveness of Expression for Use in Ontario.** Atkinson Study of Utilization of Student Resources, Supplementary Report No. 1. Toronto, Canada: Department of Educational Research, Ontario College of Education, 1958. Pp. vi, 39. Paper. $1.00. *

[B372]

★SCHAFER, ROY. **Psychoanalytic Interpretation in Rorschach Testing: Theory and Application.** Austen Riggs Foundation Monograph Series, No. 3. New York: Grune & Stratton, Inc., 1954. Pp. xiv, 446. $8.75. * (PA 29:2472)

Am J Psychiatry 112:575–6 Ja '56. S. J. Beck. * Schafer....provides valuable discussion of the effects of interpersonal relations between the examiner and patient on the test results. * One can read only with pleasure the "postscript" (pp. 138–139) regarding the scientific problems involved in getting at the meaning of Rorschach test content. Similarly the 6 criteria which the author sets up for judging one's test report are valuable to have in print and will serve good purpose in instruction. Most important and most needed at present are chapters 6–10 * My reaction to the book as a whole is that, in his absorption with content, Schafer is seriously neglecting formal personality structure. Rorschach's unique contribution to personality testing was in designing an instrument making possible the structuring of the psychologic forces composing the personality, the impersonal forces. The present emphasis on content certainly adds to the usefulness of the instrument; however, in focusing on it to the exclusion of structure, psychologists are reverting to the pre-Rorschach period when approaches to personality (as in the word-association experiment) were bound to content. The great progress in penetrating personality by psychological tools, with fruitful contributions in clinical diagnosis as well as in personality theory, and in the more general field of perception, can trace its origin to the publishing of Rorschach's *Psychodiagnostik*. To jettison the formal personality structure is itself a regression. A second major criticism bears on the theory within which Schafer works. This is especially explicit in his criticism of Phillips and Smith (pp. 33 and 143). He calls them to task (p. 33) for an approach which "runs the risk of leading to what may be called a Rorschach theory of personality—an intra-test, closed system of inferences that presumes to encompass the total personality." On this point the issue must be squarely jointed. It is this reviewer's position that the Rorschach, or any other psychological instrument is such only if it is adequate by its own assumptions and produces results which are thus logical. It must of course have validity. That is, it must be accurate as checked by criteria outside itself—results obtained on the same patients by other methods. Psychoanalytic findings provide the best outside criteria for testing the Rorschach, but they can not be applied until after the test results have been completed exclusively by the principles with which it presumes to operate. Unless so, the findings are likely to be not those of the test, but from outside sources, and by psychoanalysis in particular. Some of Schafer's interpretations do in fact appear to be just that: psychoanalytic findings rather than those from the test record. Thus (p. 198), what evidence is there in the test protocol, that to this woman patient, the "orchid" has "passive-receptive connotation"? or (p. 198) that "the seven dwarfs in Snow White" is "fantasy or hope of being the lovely, innocent, virginal (sexually repressed) little girl who is waited on hand and foot by gallant, sexless and somewhat foolish, depreciated beaux"? The limits of a review do not permit more examples. If the quoted interpretations do have these meanings to the patient, Schafer knows them from his knowledge of psychoanalysis. In interpreting as if from the test, he is committing the fallacy against which he wisely warns throughout his book, that of overinterpreting beyond the test data. The neglect of structure is only too obvious in his case interpretations. The author does, to be sure, in his general exposition, constantly refer to formal structure, but he uses it very little. Thus in his illustrative case material, he seriously fails to exploit each record's potential for uncovering the dynamics in the individual producing it. One aspect of this inadequacy appears in Schafer's total discarding of important technique, *e.g.* sequence. One investigator (Skalweit) looks on sequence as next to pathognomic for schizophrenia. Schafer makes a valuable suggestion for the "extended F+" against Rorschach's original "basic F+." This reviewer, as happens, did, in 1931, spend some months in experimenting with the extended F+ as described by Schafer and tried it out against Rorschach's basic F+. Validating by the clinical records (in the Boston Psychopathic Hospital) he found that Rorschach's F+ consistently gave more valid results. However, an investigation of the two methods is in order. A very serious error in test administration is that of obtaining the inquiry after each test card rather than at the close of the test as a whole (p. 76). Rorschach is explicit on this point: "Nur darf man die Versuchsperson niemals während des Versuchs selbst darüber befragen, sondern immer erst nach Erledigung des ganzen Versuchs" (*Psychodiagnostik*, p. 26). He is here writing about M only. But at another point he makes it clear how concerned he is, with an experimentalist's caution: "Hauptsache ist, dass das Experiment möglichst frei von allem Zwange durchgeführt werde" (*ibid.*, p. 16). Questioning concerning one test figure before the next one has been presented can not help but set up interpersonal relations, such as Schafer describes, affecting the patient, and hence distorting the results. Returning to the book's merits, in his exposition of the defenses, Schafer has made ingress into an uncharted and difficult terrain in Rorschach test study. His penetration here is illuminating, at times exciting. These chapters are bound to be a stimulus for fruitful labor in a sector where it is now most needed. Close in importance is the stimulus which the book will give to the decidedly needed research on interpretation of content, but within a strictly Rorschach sphere of reference. This will sharpen the test for clinical diagnosis as well as in personality investigation generally. However, content or personal dynamics has meaning only in relation to psychologic structure of the personality: how strong or how weak a character has the patient, how bright or dull is he, how emotional or placid, how imaginative or torpid? These, as structures, are the skeleton and vital organs of the personality. These must be understood, and to do so requires disciplined effort. For those persons who have subjected themselves to such discipline, and are set solidly on such foundations, Schafer's book will be a new point of departure and a long-time reference source in broadening their interpretive understanding.

Austral J Psychol 8:90–1 Je '56. J. G. Lyle. * Schafer capably describes the interpersonal dynamics of the test situation, dealing with the motives and defences of the tester as well as of the testee. In another excellent theoretical chapter he explains perceptual responses to the Rorschach as representing various levels of psychic functioning on a "dream-percept" (irreality-reality) continuum involving different degrees and kinds of regression. But some illustrations of reality-oriented "concrete" thinking, and of the compulsive reality-testing of incipient psychotic patients would have been a worthwhile inclusion at this point. Illustration of the application of theory to the Rorschach is however, most generous. * Schafer is magnificent when interpreting the symbolic content of Rorschach responses, but occasionally one is disappointed at his interpretation of the *determinant* and *location* categories, to which he too often tries to attribute motives (e.g. too frequent use of W does not always signify grandiose fantasies. It may also signify fear of analysing the blot, or an inability to do so, or uncritical reality testing). In general, this is an essential handbook and the only one I have seen which would further the understanding of an experienced clinician. The level is strictly postgraduate, and too difficult for the beginner. Some of the symbolic interpretations would however serve admirably as illustrations of defence mechanisms and indirect expressions of conflict for undergraduate classes.

Brit J Psychol 46:319–20 N '55. Theodora Alcock. In 1923, with the posthumous publication of the case-study entitled "The Application of the Interpretation of Form to Psy-choanalysis," the marriage of the Rorschach method with psychoanalysis was announced by its founder. Dr Roy Schafer cements this fruitful alliance in his valuable book, which to a notable extent co-ordinates and enlarges the work of other writers in the field, adding much that is original with a refreshing clarity of reasoning and economy of words. As is stated in the preface, this is not an easy book to read, for to profit by it adequately there is required not only a thorough grounding in Rorschach principles and technique but also considerable familiarity with psychoanalytic literature and methods. This warning, however, should not deter any serious Rorschach worker, since at every point hypotheses are clearly stated before any conclusion is drawn, so that the reader is gently educated as he goes. * All those using projective tests, especially those who tend to jump to conclusions when interpreting Rorschach material, will profit by studying Dr Schafer's criteria for judging the adequacy of interpretations. These provide a salutary check upon intuitive and get-there-quick methods with over-facile deductions. The long section on the interpretation of defences, which comprises two-thirds of the book, is of outstanding value. Others with psychoanalytic orientation have taught that analysis of the mechanisms of ego-defence is essential for full understanding of Rorschach data, but here there is published for the first time a well-documented and expanded study of the subject with a wealth of illustration to clarify its points. From an admirable summary of the psychoanalytic concept of defence the reader is led to consider defensive operations in the Rorschach response process. In his introduction to this section and in the subsequent chapters the author uses all that he and the Rorschach method have got and the result is impressive. * The level of this publication is so high that one is led to wish for expansion in some respects, as, for example, a more sensitive scoring of shading that would illuminate the tactile responses as associated with early feelings in the mother-child relationship. More about depression might also have been welcome, but it is unfair to ask for everything, and the reader can certainly give thanks for what he has received, with respectful congratulations to the writer.

J Proj Tech 19:349–51 S '55. Mortimer M. Meyer. * The book as a whole is an excellent exposition of the interpretation of the Rorschach responses within the framework of psychoanalytic theory. The presentation is very lucid, but, as the author indicates, may be difficult for those who do not come to the book with a fairly good knowledge of psychoanalytic theory. This comment is not a criticism of the author but rather a reviewer's remark to the potential reader who is looking for six easy lessons on "deep interpretation." Those who are highly critical of psychoanalytic theory will be similarly critical of the book. More pertinent criticism will come from those who, because there is still only a small body of established evidence for psychoanalytic theory, find no attempt at supporting evidence for the point of view and approach espoused in the book. Nevertheless this book is a must for every psychologist who uses the Rorschach seriously in clinical situations. Whether the reader accepts the author's technique or not, the stimulation of the author's thinking as represented by his approach will force the reader to do more thinking about his own approach. [See review for other critical comments not excerpted.]

Mental Health 14:116–7 su '55. Cyril M. Franks. * To those clinical psychologists who believe implicitly in the dogma of Rorschach and psychoanalytical theory, this book will be very welcome and an invaluable aid to diagnosis. To those psychologists who believe that psychology should be a science, based only upon validated concepts, this book will be of little practical use since the major part of both Rorschach and psychoanalytic theory fails to meet the basic requirements of scientifically-minded psychologists. Dr. Schafer makes almost no attempt to discuss how the many unvalidated concepts of either Rorschach or psychoanalytical theory could be validated experimentally; in general he ignores such experimental studies as do exist. He writes as if the common assumptions of these two doctrines are established facts rather than a series of, as yet, unvalidated beliefs which have gradually accumulated over the years and which have become, by virtue of time and a devout following, to be regarded as proven facts. The superabundance of esoteric jargon in both these disciplines have added to the confusion and made it even more difficult to separate fact from fancy. This book has a limited appeal in that it is of little use to social workers and people in allied professions and even among psychologists it will only be of use

to Rorschach workers who have a marked psychoanalytic inclination. In the opinion of this reviewer the great need at the present stage of Rorschach usage is not for new books which complicate Rorschach theory by introducing even more unvalidated and ill-defined concepts but for a critical and experimental evaluation of existing "knowledge" in the hope that a precise tool will one day emerge.

Psychol B 52:271–2 My '55. Roy M. Hamlin. Skinner teaches an alert pigeon to peck a bulls-eye in five minutes, by first reinforcing any approximate success. Struggling with a much more challenging puzzle, the book reviewed here is no bulls-eye, but may be hailed with cautious enthusiasm as the most encouraging near miss of its kind yet published. The author presents a detailed attempt to establish feedback between painstaking observation of complex individual behavior and general "laws." The fact that some of the laws are tentative or dubious need not be emphasized with undue distress. The attempt itself hits at the core of the projective problem. The Rorschach was never a test in the Binet tradition, simplified by design to point up specifically what should be counted. The inkblots call forth behavior which retains a high degree of uniquely individual complexity. To look at such behavior and start counting (M, H, D), or testing fruitless hypotheses, is easy. To tease out a pattern, theme or process that constitutes a meaningful unit is a problem that has baffled both clinicians and statisticians. Those clinicians who seem to have the art have had little success in writing the method. Statisticians like R. B. Cattell disdain the "inventive" response of the projective method, throw up their hands, and say: What we want is a traditional model test of dynamisms! Schafer's approach involves chiefly three elements: (a) a vocabulary or classificatory system taken from the psychoanalytic terminology for ego defenses; (b) the use of judgment in teasing out units, with this judgment based on a background of empirical observation, experimental evidence, and thoughtful speculation; and (c) a rough check back of these broads units against other empirical evidence (descriptive case material). This still crude approach is not new, but Schafer's formulated approximation represents a step forward in specificity and scope. The author's bias or biases need not be approved with equal enthusiasm. Specific biases that mar some chapters and some elements throughout the book can be mentioned only with an important reservation: as started here they represent 90 per cent the reviewer's projections and only 10 per cent the author's attitudinal style. Bluntly, however, on some pages the author does seem to feel that (*a*) the well-adjusted (analyzed) psychologist in a medical setting should accept the healthy masochistic role of a second-class citizen; (*b*) an expert is more someone with wide and approved experience than someone who should be asked to produce expert evidence; (*c*) psychoanalytic theory may not be the ultimate final word, but it is the current final word as far as party line handed down to second-rate citizens is concerned; and (*d*) usually anything the Rorschach reveals is best understood if labeled with a derogatory word (infantile, sadistic, compulsive). Actually the author struggles consistently against such biases: lauding solid evidence, rejecting Rorschach's fascinating notes on the inkblots as the final word in this area, and recognizing that there is something "fundamentally neurotic" about reporting all observations in terms of derogatory value judgments. Yet his own problems of professional and scientific identity peek through. He nevertheless succeeds in setting forth the general outline of a process of clinical judgment, or "intuition," that makes sense. Successful judgments may involve the cancelling out of many details based on false assumptions, self-deception, and initially loose speculation. The relaxed acceptance of all elements, good and bad, checked then with critical rigor against general guide lines which Schafer calls theory, may be important. The general feel for such a process is conveyed by Schafer's book. The further analysis of such judgment processes is important to psychology, as a field of study and as a research tool. The pattern of this approach may lead to more fruitful progress than a pattern based from the beginning on an unimaginative reading of the APA's *Technical Recommendations for Psychological Tests*.

[B373]

★SCHENCK, ETHEL A. **Studies of Testing and Teaching in Modern Foreign Languages: Based on Materials Gathered at the University of Wisconsin by the Late Professor Frederic D. Cheydleur.** Madison, Wis.: Dembar Publications, Inc., 1952. Pp. vi, 72. Paper. *

Mod Lang J 38:210 Ap '54. Theodore Huebener. * should be of interest to every teacher of modern languages. It is really a compact summary of the work of Frederic D. Cheydleur * Of particular significance was his work in the placement and attainment examinations programs, the rating of teaching efficiency and the standardized testing done in basic language courses. Profesor Cheydleur originated and developed the Wisconsin plan for placement and attainment examinations in foreign languages, now used in about 100 colleges and universities. The bulletin describes the placement tests, attainment examinations and the evaluation of teaching. * This bulletin gives a good idea of some of Professor Cheydleur's valuable contributions to language teaching. It is an excellent example of *multum in parvo*.

[B374]

*SCHONELL, FRED, AND SCHONELL, F. ELEANOR. **Diagnostic and Attainment Testing: Including a Manual of Tests, Their Nature, Use, Recording, and Interpretation, Second Edition.** Edinburgh, Scotland: Oliver & Boyd Ltd., 1952. Pp. viii, 174. 18s. 6d. (Toronto, Canada: Clarke, Irwin & Co. Ltd. $3.70.) *

[B375]

★SCHUTZ, WILLIAM C. **FIRO: A Three-Dimensional Theory of Interpersonal Behavior.** New York, N.Y.: Rinehart & Co., Inc., 1958. Pp. xiii, 267. $6.50. *

[B376]

★SCHWARTZ, ALFRED, AND TIEDEMAN, STUART C.; WITH THE ASSISTANCE OF DONALD G. WALLACE. **Evaluating Student Progress in the Secondary School.** New York: Longmans, Green & Co., 1957. Pp. xiii, 434. $4.75. (London: Longmans, Green & Co., Ltd. 35s.) * (*PA* 31:6683)

Brit J Ed Psychol 28:196 Je '58. W. H. King. The title of this book is misleading. In addition to a detailed summary of information required for student guidance in the American secondary schools, the authors deal at great length with the construction of various tests, rating scales, questionnaires, interviews and sociometric ratings. Standardised tests and their interpretation, together with a useful list of American tests suitable for different grades and school subjects, occupy a considerable section of the book. Essentially, this is a reference book and as such is presumably a report of current practice in the United States. Research workers in psychometry will find nothing new; teachers will not have the time to digest and employ the evaluation methods suggested; if they did, it would be difficult to find time for teaching. This book is only one of many from the United States that deals with "evaluation," and it is difficult to believe that it is an improvement on any of the others. It may be useful in American Schools but it does not appear to be superior to *Measurement and Evaluation in the Secondary School,* by Greene, Jorgensen and Gerberich.

Ed Res B 37:52 F '58. Paul Klohr. This book, the authors report, was written to help classroom teachers who continuously face the task of appraising outcomes of the teaching-learning process in which they are involved with students. * the book used in this way can be a very helpful resource. Especially noteworthy is the importance the authors attach to purpose in the evaluative process. * Also significant is their assertion that highly effective learning requires an involvement of students in the selection and organization of curricular content and in the analysis of behavior to be achieved. * In view of increasing evidence to support the proposition that a teacher must develop an adequate self-concept if he is to function most effectively, one wishes that the authors had explained what this means in the total evaluative process. Until a teacher senses clearly what kinds of operations are involved here, there is a strong probability that this crucial dimension of the process will continue to be short circuited.

[B377]

★SCIENCE RESEARCH ASSOCIATES. **Using the Iowa Tests of Educational Development for College Planning, Second Edition.** Chicago, Ill.: Science Research Associates, 1957. Pp. 64. Paper. $3.00. *

[B378]

SCOTT BLAIR, G. W. **Measurements of Mind and Matter.** London: Dennis Dobson, 1950. Pp. 116. 10s. 6d. (New York: Philosophical Library, 1956. $4.50.) * (PA 27:25, 31:38)

Am Sociol R 22:128 F '57. Orville G. Brim, Jr. * The first few chapters provide a brief and non-technical discussion of elementary principles of measurement and of the concept of dimension. The primary dimensional characteristics used as examples are physical, e.g., time, length. While the untutored may well profit from this very introductory treatment, it lacks sharp organization and as an introduction to the area is not as good as that available in several other books. The consideration of measurement in psychology deals almost solely with two topics: psychophysical concepts and factor analysis as a method of establishing useful dimensions. It is in this area that the discussion suffers from an unexplained publishing fact, namely, that the manuscript was completed and in proof in 1949, but published only now. Thus

developments during the past decade in scaling and measurement theory (by Hempel, Coombs, Lazarsfeld, Guttman, etc.) are conspicuously absent. The author's discussion, brief and excellent as it is, is clearly dated and serves to emphasize how remarkable the growth in this area has been in the past ten years. The author informally presents his solution for combining dimensions, which is referred to as the Principle of Intermediacy. The solution, which seems to share certain assumptions with a factor analytic approach, is difficult to grasp clearly, perhaps in part because of the informality of its treatment. While the student of measurement theory may wish to examine in particular this latter contribution of the author, in the reviewer's opinion there is little about the book as a whole which demands the attention of the professional sociologist.

Cont Psychol 2:161–2 Je '57. George H. Collier. Some have limited the domain of science to those areas in which "exact" measurements can be made. This book questions this view and defends modes of "measurement" which are not "exact," such as one finds, for example, in the author's own area, rheology, and in psychology. * This book may be made difficult for psychologists by the fact that it was written for an audience of doubting physicists (perhaps imaginary), and that it assumes a familiarity with controversies and techniques, particularly dimensional analysis, which are typically not in the psychologists' repertoire. That difficulty is further increased by the book's brevity, which makes many of the arguments enthymematic, and also by the author's tendency to introduce considerations which are irrelevant to the main theme. * the author's analysis of psychological measurement gets bogged down in the philosophical morass of the mind-body problem surrounding psychology, as, for example, in his discussion of the measurement of sensations. Many, if not most, of the problems he discusses would disappear if the principle, which he seems to advocate for physical measurement, were accepted, i.e., that the measuring operations have to meet the axioms of order, not the things that we construct out of them.

For additional reviews, see 4:B52.

[B379]

★SCOTTISH COUNCIL FOR RESEARCH IN EDUCATION. **Educational and Other Aspects of the 1947 Scottish Mental Survey.** Publications of the Scottish

Council for Research in Education [No.] 41. London:
University of London Press Ltd., 1958. Pp. xvii, 150.
15s. *

Brit J Ed Psychol 28:299–300 N '58. * Since
the survey measured verbal I.Q. only, the
strictly educational implications are somewhat
meagre, though a certain amount of information on school progress is provided in terms of
the classes reached by the pupils in their primary
schools. The sizes of the schools and of school
classes seem to yield little of interest. However,
the variations in mean score by ten major areas
of the country, ranging over 6.8 score points
(roughly equivalent to I.Q. points) are noteworthy * An attempt is made to estimate the
effects of previous testing on scores and it is
concluded—admittedly on rather shaky grounds
—that only about 0.5 points of the 2.0 points of
increase between 1932 and 1947 can be attributed to test-sophistication. More than two-
thirds of the book consists of tables and appendices; thus, we may regard as its main
object, the publication of the basic data of a
monumental investigation, rather than the presentation of new findings.

[B380]

★Scottish Council for Research in Education.
**Social Implications of the 1947 Scottish Mental
Survey.** Publications of the Scottish Council for Re-
search in Education No. 35. London: University of
London Press, Ltd., 1953. Pp. xxiii, 356. 10s. 6d. *

*Brit J Psychol 45:238 Ag '54. Alexander
Laing.* * Maxwell makes a careful and thorough analysis of the sociological data collected
about a random sample of 7380 children *
Maxwell frankly admits that the Survey "raises
more problems than it solves." It offers, for
instance, no further light on the problem of the
relative contributions of heredity and environment or of the different factors within the environment to the better (on the average) performance of the "upper class" child from a
good home on an intelligence test, but it is
"fairly definite" in its conclusion that "intelligence, as measured by the test, does vary with
environmental circumstances to a considerable
degree." Included in the volume is an analysis
of the test scores of 947 twins from the *total*
survey group. This confirms the observation of
other investigators that twins are on average
four or five points of I.Q. below non-twins, but
throws no further light on the reasons for this
difference.

J Ed (London) 86:84+ F '54. Cyril Burt. *
In the intelligence tests the average obtained
by the children in the professional classes was
54.3 marks out of a possible 70, and that of
children of unskilled manual workers only 31.1.
Nevertheless, every social class contains "high
scorers" (children scoring over fifty marks);
and "intelligent pupils are found in the most
adverse social circumstances." On the other
hand, "there are no low scorers in the highest
occupational class." This last result is somewhat
surprising: congenital defectives and dullards
are, of course, to be found both in the professional classes and among the well-to-do; and
it would have been interesting to hear how they
managed to escape the surveyors' net. Possibly
the non-cooperative attitude of many of the
private schools, to which the earlier publication alludes, provides the real explanation. With
this exception the conclusions reached are thus
in full agreement with those reported in earlier
surveys carried out in London and elsewhere.
To the educationist and teacher it will be of
special interest to learn that the "socio-psychological patterns" found in one part of Britain
reappear in quite a different geographical area.
The chief value of the inquiry, however, lies in
the unprecedented amount of detailed information that has been collected, and in the thorough
and systematic analysis to which the material
has been subjected.

*Occupational Psychol 28:123–4 Ap '54. P. E.
Vernon.* * As one would expect of Moray
House publications, it is comprehensive, clearly
presented, and cautious. Over half of it consists
of detailed tables, graphs and scatters. Now it
is seldom that survey material, as distinct from
specially planned experiments, can provide definite answers to important problems, since the
relevant factors interact in too complex a fashion (this should be particularly obvious to industrial psychologists). Mr Maxwell has teased
out the factors as well as anyone could; but it
would be difficult to claim that the results are
very enlightening psychologically. * A further
volume on the educational implications of the
survey will be awaited with considerable interest.

[B381]

★Scottish Education Department. **Scottish Leav-
ing Certificate Examination: Memorandum for
the Guidance of Teachers on the Setting and
Marking of School Tests and Examinations:
Agriculture.** Edinburgh, Scotland: Her Majesty's
Stationery Office, 1955. Pp. 5. Paper. 9d. *

[B382]

★SCOTTISH EDUCATION DEPARTMENT. **Scottish Leaving Certificate Examination: Memorandum for the Guidance of Teachers on the Setting and Marking of School Tests and Examinations: Commercial Subjects.** Edinburgh, Scotland: Her Majesty's Stationery Office, 1955. Pp. 12. Paper. 9*d.* *

[B383]

★SCOTTISH EDUCATION DEPARTMENT. **Scottish Leaving Certificate Examination: Memorandum for the Guidance of Teachers on the Setting and Marking of School Tests and Examinations: English.** Edinburgh, Scotland: Her Majesty's Stationery Office, 1955. Pp. 24. Paper. 1*s.* 3*d.* *

[B384]

★SCOTTISH EDUCATION DEPARTMENT. **Scottish Leaving Certificate Examination: Memorandum for the Guidance of Teachers on the Setting and Marking of School Tests and Examinations: Geography.** Edinburgh, Scotland: Her Majesty's Stationery Office, 1956. Pp. 23. Paper. 1*s.* 9*d.* *

[B385]

★SCOTTISH EDUCATION DEPARTMENT. **Scottish Leaving Certificate Examination: Memorandum for the Guidance of Teachers on the Setting and Marking of School Tests and Examinations: History.** Edinburgh, Scotland: Her Majesty's Stationery Office, 1955. Pp. 16. Paper. 1*s.* *

[B386]

★SCOTTISH EDUCATION DEPARTMENT. **Scottish Leaving Certificate Examination: Memorandum for the Guidance of Teachers on the Setting and Marking of School Tests and Examinations: Latin and Greek.** Edinburgh, Scotland: Her Majesty's Stationery Office, 1956. Pp. 20. Paper. 1*s.* *

[B387]

★SCOTTISH EDUCATION DEPARTMENT. **Scottish Leaving Certificate Examination: Memorandum for the Guidance of Teachers on the Setting and Marking of School Tests and Examinations: Mathematics.** Edinburgh, Scotland: Her Majesty's Stationery Office, 1955. Pp. 14. Paper. 1*s.* *

[B388]

★SCOTTISH EDUCATION DEPARTMENT. **Scottish Leaving Certificate Examination: Memorandum for the Guidance of Teachers on the Setting and Marking of School Tests and Examinations: Modern Languages.** Edinburgh, Scotland: Her Majesty's Stationery Office, 1956. Pp. 38. Paper. 2*s.* *

[B389]

★SCOTTISH EDUCATION DEPARTMENT. **Scottish Leaving Certificate Examination: Memorandum for the Guidance of Teachers on the Setting and Marking of School Tests and Examinations: Music.** Edinburgh, Scotland: Her Majesty's Stationery Office, 1955. Pp. 7. Paper. 9*d.* *

[B390]

★SCOTTISH EDUCATION DEPARTMENT. **Scottish Leaving Certificate Examination: Memorandum for the Guidance of Teachers on the Setting and Marking of School Tests and Examinations: Science.** Edinburgh, Scotland: Her Majesty's Stationery Office, 1955. Pp. 20. Paper. 1*s.* *

[B391]

★SCOTTISH EDUCATION DEPARTMENT. **Scottish Leaving Certificate Examination: Memorandum for**

the Guidance of Teachers on the Setting and Marking of School Tests and Examinations. **Technical Subjects.** Edinburgh, Scotland: Her Majesty's Stationery Office, 1955. Pp. 12. Paper. 9*d.* *

[B392]

★SEGEL, DAVID. **Measurement and Cumulative Record Index.** Miscellaneous 3405. Washington, D.C.: United States Office of Education, 1952. Pp. i, 25. Paper, lithotyped. Gratis. *

[B393]

★SEMEONOFF, BORIS, AND TRIST, ERIC. **Diagnostic Performance Tests: A Manual for Use With Adults.** London: Tavistock Publications Ltd., 1958. Pp. xvi, 176. 32*s.* *

[B394]

★SHEA, JOSEPH AUGUSTINE. **Predictive Value of Various Combinations of Standardized Tests and Subtests for Prognosis of Teaching Efficiency.** Catholic University of America, Educational Research Monograph, Vol. 19, No. 6. Washington, D.C.: Catholic University of America Press, Inc., June 1, 1955. Pp. xi, 44. Paper. $1.00. *

[B395]

★SHNEIDMAN, EDWIN S. **Manual for the Make A Picture Story Method.** Projective Techniques Monograph No. 2. New York: Society for Projective Techniques and Rorschach Institute, Inc., 1952. Pp. iv, 92. Paper. $2.50. * (*PA* 27:6542)

Am J Orthopsychiatry 23:215-7 Ja '53. *Hedda Bolgar.* This is above all a courageous book. It is also an ambitious one. * [The] clear and uncompromising statements of purpose are representative of the excellent planning and organization of the entire volume. The design is simple—it is a comprehensive one-case study. * The richness of the material, the range and variety of clinical approaches, and the coverage of many schools of personality theory may be overwhelming for the novice or the stranger to the field of projective methods but they are a delight to the experienced clinical psychologist and a rich fund of information for both teachers and students. Compared with the satisfactions which the practicing clinical psychologist derives from this volume, the rewards are somewhat disappointing for the reader whose major interest lies in its scientific contribution. The promise of a "psychological autopsy" is tempting indeed, but if it has been fulfilled by the authors I have failed to find it in the pages of this book. Dr. Shneidman in his introduction states that "the postmortem is performed not on the patient but on the test interpretations. This is made possible by the availability of the clinical and psychiatric data...." However, in the same introduction he also states that "these behavioral data are not presented as validating criteria for the psychological tests, but rather as another set of observations on the same person." The discrepancy in these two statements is both confusing and frustrating; how, one wonders, are the authors going to reconcile them? Will the predictions made by the experts be compared for significant agreement with the behavioral data? No, they are not presented as validating data. With commendable frankness it is stated that "all that was done was what any reader of this volume can do; i.e. we read all the material and came to some general conclusions." This seems to leave us pretty much where we have been for so many years, with considerable confidence in the usefulness of our projective methods and the general soundness of our clinical judgments but without the knowledge that our confidence can stand up under scientific scrutiny. Fortunately, the authors have recognized their responsibility "for rigorous statistical inquiry" and plan a separate publication of the statistical treatment of these data using primarily W. S. Stephenson's Q-technique. While it would have perhaps been wise to delay the publication of this book until the statistical analysis could be included, even its publication in the future will go a long way to remedy the one major weakness of this otherwise so very generous cooperative effort.

Am J Psychiatry 109:158 Ag '52. E. L. Schott. * Most of the book deals with the analysis and interpretation, by different "experts," of one patient's responses to the Thematic Apperception Test (TAT) and the Make A Picture Story Test (MAPS). Practically every published method for such test analysis is tried on material from a single clinical case and presented by its own authors in a separate chapter. These authors knew nothing of the case except age, sex, and marital status before they presented their analyses of John Doe's verbatim test responses. * learn very early in the book.... that "the editors' own contributions are not presented in this volume, but have been withheld for a sequel." Stating it differently, the reviewer considers it very disappointing that what he regards as one of the most significant excuses for such a book, the statistical analysis of the results, is planned for a separate publication! The editors' purposes, however, are quite clearly put, in 7 statements (beginning on p. 3) and a discussion of "limitations and delimitations" (on pages 4 and 5). Briefly stated, the "project was done within the framework of the desire to contribute to psychology and psy-

chodiagnostics as *predictive* sciences." But if one gets any such contribution from this volume, he must figure it out for himself. Unfortunately such cogitations by different readers may lead to some widely different conclusions that the editors would not care to emphasize. A few simple tabulations that the reviewer has made, or that anyone could make for himself from the material scattered through the book, show significant and interesting findings. These items include test interpretations, impressions as to diagnosis and prognosis, and suggestions relative to therapeutic methods best suited to the case under consideration. In these we find some positive statements and genuine agreement between 4 or 5 of the 25 special authors, but also considerable disagreement, expected and otherwise, among others, with some dubious interpretations and evasions. By these authors, John Doe is classified in many categories ranging from "a normal person" to "a paranoid dementia praecox." The latter is also the final diagnosis from the clinical picture at the time of psychiatric follow-up 28 months later. Meanwhile, as mentioned by the editors in their summary (p. 307), we must content ourselves with the profound observation that.... "undeniably there is something to the clinical interpretation of projective test results." Just what that "something" is, however, they admit is for the future to tell. Without further comment all we can do is join in the hackneyed chorus, "more research is needed" (also given in the editors' summary!), and then await the next publication.

J Abn & Social Psychol 50:277 Mr '55. Charles McArthur. * Both during his analysis of the data and in a supplementary chapter, each psychologist introspects about what he is doing, at times offering interesting vignettes of the "feel" of the process of clinical inference. This is especially valuable, since most major contributors to TAT methods are represented, though in one notable instance we do not hear from the master but only from his eminent pupils. To "go on record" this way required moral courage that did credit to the statures of the contributors as scientists. One feels poetic justice in the circumstance that nearly all the blind interpretations were "along the right track." Relative validity was, perhaps because the test record being analysed had been collected from a psychotic, proportional to boldness of inference. The fifteen analyses together constitute evidence that the embarrassing variety of approaches to the TAT in use today is no proof of the invalidity of the test nor even of its interobserver unreliability. The limitation, of course, is that this is an experiment where $N = 1$. The editor asks the further question, "Valid for what?" As handled by these fifteen interpreters, the TAT and MAPS gave most light upon diagnostic category, motives, and patterned structure of motives, least light upon values and attitudes. Behavior was predicted by inferences two steps removed from the test data or else not predicted at all. In short, thematic test material is depth material. Perhaps for that reason, "clinical" methods of analysis turned out to be more valid than analyses by check list. It might also be said, though it is not, that those methods nearer to the historically original use of the TAT turn out distinctly better than recent innovations. It would be very nice to see a study patterned after Shneidman's, in which a whole case was analysed under blind conditions by proponents of various methods or even several proponents of one method, like psychoanalysis. The outcome might be similar, all roads leading to insight, if only the psychologist remained clinical as opposed to mechanical. The TAT does seem to be a neat miniature of this larger problem. Shneidman's book would therefore be an excellent teaching device to introduce graduate students to the art of "personality diagnosis." In such use, special attention might be called to the fact that Shneidman can analyse out parts of the "intuitive" process. He notices that for most workers the first step is Charcot's: to look and look and look at the data. The second is regularly "semiorganized notes" on repetitive or logically coherent patterns. Generalization in terms of theory may come next, though the best usage seems to be an extensive application of the criterion of internal consistency for refining trial hypotheses about the structure of the testee's motives. In the end, some theory, if only a nosology, does seem to get applied. * Introduction and syntheses by the editor hold the book together, though so much discussion from so many views is, in its nature, disjunctive. The editorial conclusions offered are well taken, if understandably tactful. One can find no ground for criticizing an editor who began his book with such an interesting plan and carried out his plan with so much care for every detail.

J Consult Psychol 16:317 Ag '52. Laurance F. Shaffer. Research on the single case is often discussed but rarely achieved. In this remarkable volume, fifteen well-qualified contributors give their blind interpretations of the TAT and MAPS protocols of "John Doe" * The first impression of a psychological reader is of the richly revealing nature of the thematic materials, sensed in the raw protocols and amplified in the interpretations. The varied qualities of the analyses used by the contributors, which range widely from quantitative to intuitive, also stand out; on the whole, the intuitive approaches seem to come out best. As a textbook in thematic analysis, the volume can offer much to students. Yet the enthusiasm for the study must be tempered by some cautious reservations. In spite of the authors' circumspect intentions to the contrary, the presentation tends to seduce the reader to a greater faith in thematic tests than the coldly considered facts should permit. "John Doe" is a complex character, blending anxiety, obsessive-compulsive, depressed, homosexual, schizoid, paranoid, and not a few other features. The hospital and clinic could not really decide whether he was psychoneurotic or schizophrenic; neither could the thematic test analysts. Such a case provided a maximum of clinical "richness" and a minimum of critically regarded certainty. A full evaluation of a clinical technique still awaits the evolution of research methods that will bridge the present dilemma between scope and precision.

J Ed Psychol 43:369–70 O '52. Lee J. Cronbach. * a file of raw material of great interest to the investigator who wishes suggestions for dealing with protocols, and to the advanced student of projective methods and abnormal psychology. * The range from objectivity to impressionism is fairly represented, and the writers of the separate chapters make clearer than does Shneidman that the different systems are intended to answer rather different questions. There is an inevitable tendency to compare the writers in terms of the adequacy of their guesses vis-à-vis the case history. To conclude that X's method did not lead to comprehensive insights into the patient is manifestly unfair, if X's system of analysis is intended for a specific research use. The interpreters who tried to describe the full dynamics of the case seem to have been rather successful. The record selected includes a great deal of frankly paranoid material, and generous verbalization—but is not an unreasonably easy one to interpret. The negative criticisms that can be made, granting the intent of the book, are few. The inclusion of the MAPS test is understandable, but of seemingly minor value. Most of the interpreters made some gestures toward MAPS interpretation, but in most cases the treatment is perfunctory and adds little to the TAT. Whether MAPS could add more if scored by those accustomed to it is an open question; but this book would be tighter knit and equally useful without MAPS. The interpretations of supplementary tests are of varying value. Rorschach is thoroughly and coherently treated by Klopfer. The Wechsler and MMPI materials are routine. The analyses of Bender-Gestalt by Hutt and of Draw-a-Person by Machover must be characterized as astonishing. The Bender calls for drawing simple geometric figures from memory. Hutt tiptoes step by step over some very tenuous analysis to the judgment that the root difficulty is a dominant mother figure toward whom the patient is very attracted sexually. That this fact is verified by the case history makes the reasoning process no less remarkable. Machover is equally free to elaborate on the smallest of indicators, and again her interpretations would be dismissed as pure fancy were it not for the correspondence with the case history. It would surely be dangerous to suggest to students that they can interpret projective tests as freely as these experts do; but it is well to have this cleanly gathered material at hand as an example of the ideal of the diagnostician. Under negative remarks, we note also the bad printing of some pages. The final value of this book will depend on the ingenuity with which it is used. Despite Shneidman to the contrary, it is not "a research." He promises some later statistical analyses, but it seems unlikely that formal analysis will elicit any worth-while generalizations. (To ask which method works best, for example, is not feasible in a study where $N = 1$.) The material is first and last food for thought. One can envision some fine seminars where this book will be used with students who can be both imaginative and critical. The book lends solid support to present enthusiasm for thematic techniques. But what ideas one takes away from the book will depend on how one reads it, for the book has no central message.

J Proj Tech 16:507–9 D '52. Samuel B. Kutash. * there is considerable variability in the methods of analyzing and interpreting projective test results and in the skill with which personality interpretations based on projective studies are arrived at and communicated. Some rare and gifted clinicians are able, through what might seem to the less experienced to be an intuitive clinical sixth sense, to ferret out with unusual accuracy and detail, the major truths about a particular patient's personality without having available the social history of the individual under study. An important question is whether such superior clinical artistry is derived from a superior method and rationale of interpretation of the projective material or whether it is an attribute of the psychologist or psychiatrist as the major clinical instrument. Certainly a book such as *Thematic Test Analysis* throws light on this important question. * The most startling and major finding is that most of the contributors, regardless of the method or conceptual scheme for thematic test analysis used or the particular test or projective device used, came remarkably close to agreement with each other and to the clinical picture, information about which was withheld. This clearly implies that clinical acumen is something lodged in the background, training, skill, etc., of the clinician and that the method used is important but secondary. Thus, the best clinical instrument would appear to be the clinician himself. He manages to find the method, conceptual scheme and techniques which work best for him. * The mere fact that over 30 different methods or conceptual schemes for working with thematic test material have been devised and published emphasizes further that perhaps each expert clinician finds or devises a method that works best for him just as certain equally proficient musicians or creative artists prefer certain media and instruments that suit them best. The book under review will enable the young clinician to look over the shoulder of sixteen experts and see how they work with thematic tests, how they treat the data and arrive at clinical inferences and interpretations. He can select and try out different methods until he finds one that seems most fruitful for him. He will find a succinct, well prepared resumé in each chapter of the sixteen modes of thematic test analysis and an example of how it was applied by its originator. He can compare and contrast the methods, check their results with the other test data and interpretations as well as the history material. He can decide for himself whether the predictions made were in agreement with or were borne out in the subsequent history of the patient. In one chapter he will find well-integrated syntheses of the TAT and MAPS test comparisons made by the various contributors as well as synthesis of the thematic approaches by Walther Joel. The book is well-planned and edited and is perhaps the most intensive "psychological autopsy" on a single case ever published. Its conception is unique, exciting, and bold. Few could have had the daring to suggest to so many clinicians of standing that they make public "blind analyses" of TAT and MAPS stories, especially perpetuating them in a book in which they are published together and all interpreting the same anonymous case! Yet the challenge was accepted * The author, better than any reviewer, points out the limitations and delimitations of the study. It is a systematic organized project but not a controlled research study. * The book does not solve the problem that plagues thematic test users—when does a trend in the story represent what is likely to be the behavior of the subject in reality and when does it represent wish fulfillment, compensatory fantasies, or latent possibilities? This is still a matter of individual artistry rather than something which one method can do better than another. This book is of current practical interest. It does not represent basic research of a definitive nature but satisfies the natural curiosity of clinicians and provides material of teaching and training value. It should and does furnish hypotheses for much needed researches into the nature of clinical artistry or skill, the comparative values and usefulness of various conceptual approaches to personality, and the validity of inferences about personality from thematic test stories.

Psychol B 51:97–100 Ja '54. Thelma G. Alper. * Shneidman concludes with two "rather striking impressions" (p. 307): (1) The various clinicians show "remarkable" agreement with each other (p. 307), and "they correlate quite well with the behavioral data" (p. 303). (2) There is a commendable spirit of objective inquiry and personal humility prevailing among clinicians; they are willing "to take a position, right or wrong and to run the risk of public scrutiny" (p. 307). Neither of these conclusions will satisfy the scientifically oriented reader.

To correlate "quite well" is statistically meaningless, especially in the absence of quantification. "To run the risk of public scrutiny" is nothing new to the scientist. * For the student who wishes to become proficient in a given scoring system, not enough details are given by most of the analysts. Some score all of the stories, others only one or two. Moreover, many of the schemes depend so heavily on the intuition and background knowledge of the analyst that very little can be gained from the sketchy working notes which have been included. What we have here would be better termed a brief survey of scoring schemes, not a manual. A more basic problem for evaluation centers on Shneidman's own methodology. Here the toughminded experimentalist will find much to trouble him. He could fairly object to the lack of scientific rigor in the research plan and to the plan itself. Just what, he could ask, is being examined here? Is the ultimate object of the research to test the relative usefulness of two different sets of projective materials, TAT and MAPS, for the blind diagnosis of one John Doe; or are the relative merits of the several different scoring schemes per se the major concern? Neither purpose is adequately served by the data assembled for analysis. The data, stories told by a 25-year-old unmarried male patient to eleven TAT pictures and seven MAPS settings, were not obtained under comparable conditions. * Another serious shortcoming is that individual scoring schemes were devised for the TAT, but not for the MAPS test. * The problem of quantifying the results of the analyses is further complicated by the nature of the individual analyses since the schemes vary from fairly precise scores based on checklists (e.g., Fine) and rating scales (e.g., Eron, Hartmann, Klebanoff) to intuitive, impressionistic interpretations (e.g., Bellack, Rotter and Jessor). * And what of the "supplementary tests" and the psychiatric data which are included presumably for prediction checks? Three of the tests were given before insulin therapy, two after it. Moreover, how are these tests really to be used? If they are to serve as validation data to evaluate the relative merits of the TAT and MAPS are we ready to accept the Rorschach or the Draw-A-Person, for example, as a validating instrument for the TAT or MAPS in the same way that we accept the Wechsler-Bellevue IQ as a measure against which to test estimates of John Doe's intellectual capacities as revealed by the TAT? These are questions which clinicians cannot answer without very precise experimental study. On the other hand, if the psychiatric material is to be used as the validation data, here, too, Shneidman's material is poor. Five different psychiatrically trained workers interviewed John Doe from time to time. Some were social workers, others were medical men. The psychotherapy undertaken with John Doe was apparently sporadic. He seems to be one of those patients who wander in and out of hospitals and outpatient clinics, who are seen by many people for longer or shorter periods of time, and for whom no systematic treatment plan evolves. How seriously do these methodological factors limit the usefulness of these materials? Shneidman acknowledges that they do constitute "a limitation upon the possible conclusions" (p. 4). "This investigation," he continues, "is a research but not an experiment; it employed systematic observation, not controlled experiment." This admission hardly excuses the lack of scientific rigor. * The mere availability of case material, however, does not in itself justify its extensive manipulation for publication. One final approach to this material remains for consideration: What does it reveal about the present state of thematic tests? Taking these fifteen scoring techniques as representative of the manner in which the TAT is now being used, it is clear that much has been added to the original need-press scoring scheme of Murray and Sanford even by those who retain some of the basic structure (e.g., Aron and Holt). Yet the fundamental problem of the meaning of "projection" has not been resolved. What level of personality do these tests tap? How much effect does the stimulus (TAT picture, MAPS setting, inkblot) have on what is revealed? Are these tests primarily useful as diagnostic tools or are they better for revealing underlying dynamics? The experts do not yet agree. Most of the analysts end up with the diagnosis of schizophrenia for John Doe. Some are of the opinion that the MAPS test shows a healthier pattern than does the TAT (Klebanoff, p. 131), others find even clearer evidence of pathology in the MAPS test (Arnold, p. 36; Korchin, p. 142). Some regard the MAPS test as better for diagnostic purposes, the TAT for the dynamics. Some stress the absence of guilt (White, p. 198), others find striking evidence of guilt (Bellak, p. 51).

Since all of the analysts have had considerable experience as clinicians, the differences between them stem, presumably, from differences in scoring rationale. To resolve these differences research is indeed needed. Given the present materials the reader could choose between these schemes largely in terms of personal preference for the normative vs. the intuitive approach, for example, or for present ego-functioning vs. an approach which emphasizes reconstruction of the past. He could not choose in terms of which is the most valid technique.

[B396]

★SHUEY, AUDREY M. **The Testing of Negro Intelligence.** Lynchburg, Va.: J. P. Bell Co., Inc., 1958. Pp. xv, 351. $4.00. *

Sci 128:297 Ag 8 '58. Anne Anastasi. Representing the most exhaustive literature survey of the intelligence-test performance of American Negroes yet attempted, this book covers over 300 references that appeared between 1913 and 1957. * Research results are presented in the form of summary tables and text discussion, one chapter being devoted to each of the following: young children (primarily in nursery schools and kindergartens), school children, high-school and college students, the armed forces, deviates (including gifted and retarded), delinquents and criminals, racial hybrids, and selective migration. All varieties of intelligence tests are covered, including group, individual, verbal, nonverbal, performance, and "culture-fair." * Despite the meticulous care with which minutiae were ferreted out, the treatment of certain studies may be such as to create misleading impressions. For example, in discussing D'Angelo's study (pp. 12, 16, 22), in which no significant Negro-white difference in Draw-a-Man IQ was found, Shuey concludes that the results are uninterpretable because the subjects were selected by nursery directors and did not comprise all cases meeting the age and language specifications. In actual fact, *all* children who met these two requirements were tested, the nursery directors merely providing the names of those who fulfilled these specifications. It is also difficult to understand why reference is made to D'Angelo's unpublished dissertation but not to the later article, by Anastasi and D'Angelo in the *Journal of Genetic Psychology* (1952), which covered more cases and provided more refined statistical analyses. Similarly, in discussing a study by

Boger (pp. 68, 77, 110, 122–3), Shuey fails to mention that intelligence-test scores of Negro children improved more than those of whites as a result of perceptual training. Only the performance of both groups prior to training is reported. On the whole, Shuey's survey serves only to document the old familiar finding that whites usually excel Negroes in mean intelligence-test scores, although overlapping is extensive and all levels of test performance can be found in both groups. With these purely descriptive facts few psychologists have ever taken issue. The major differences have centered around interpretation. Although Shuey concludes that the data "point to the presence of some native differences between Negroes and whites as determined by intelligence tests" (p. 318), few of the studies shed even a glimmer of light on causal factors, and their results are at least equally consistent with an environmental interpretation of group differences.

[B397]
★SIMON, BRIAN. **Intelligence Testing and the Comprehensive School.** London: Lawrence & Wishart Ltd., 1953. Pp. 112. Paper, 6s.; cloth, 8s. 6d. *

Brit J Psychol 45:146–7 My '54. P. E. Vernon. This is an intelligent and persuasive exposition of the familiar left-wing criticisms of intelligence tests and secondary school selection. It is worth the careful attention of psychologists, since many have in the past been too prone to believe that their tests do measure inborn and unalterable ability. But the author neglects to mention the more widely accepted current view that any hereditary potential depends for its realization on a suitable environment; that measured intelligence is therefore the product of genetic and environmental factors, and that comparisons of groups or individuals brought up in widely different environments (e.g. civilized against primitive) are illegitimate. Although this implies that the I.Q. is to some extent inconstant and affected by social class, intelligence tests do nevertheless possess useful reliability and validity as selection instruments; moreover, social class differences are themselves partly genetic. The irrefutable scientific evidence for these statements is ignored, since is would of course contradict the party line. Mr Simon's complaint that the psychologist's concepts, such as intelligence, are conditioned by his cultural ideology, is also quite sound—in the light of contempo-

rary field theory. Indeed there is much to be said for discarding the term "intelligence" tests, especially at the 10–11 year examination, and substituting tests of "educational aptitude." But his account of the controversies over the definition of intelligence, and of the solution provided by factor analysis, is muddled and misleading. Far from the various definitions being "mutually exclusive," it is because they—or at least the tests devised to measure them—overlap so much that it is possible to isolate g, and progressively to analyse out the verbal, spatial and other content factors and such formal factors as speed, facility with new-type items, etc., which often enter into our alleged tests of intelligence. Much is made, too, of the circularity that is sometimes involved in arguments about the normal distribution of abilities; for the extreme socialist cannot stomach the idea that only a limited proportion of the population has sufficiently high capacity to be able to tackle advanced secondary school courses. While it may well be true that present methods of streaming in primary and secondary schools do not give the more backward as good a chance to make up as more individual and flexible classroom organization, there was plenty of evidence of ineradicable intellectual differences in the days before intelligence tests or streaming in state schools had ever been thought of. And the claim that in Russia and Poland all children can be brought on at a relatively equal rate and achieve a much more equal level of educational attainment is so dubious that it can presumably never have been put to the test. Many of the author's criticisms of the present system of secondary school organization and selection are justifiable. Its bad effects on primary school teaching are deplored by thoughtful educationists and psychologists. They would agree that there is no perfect method of selection for grammar schools, especially at such an early age as 10, and that numerous pupils relegated to modern schools (particularly in areas with low grammar school provision) might with a better education surpass some of those admitted. But to ascribe all these ills to the wicked psychologist and his class-conditioned concept of intelligence is ridiculous. Mr Simon nowhere attacks the parents whose class prejudices in favour of a grammar school education are largely responsible for the examination becoming so highly competitive. And he ignores the extremely complex historical factors and the political considerations which underly the present differentiation of our various types of secondary schools. It is probable that few of the people concerned with educational selection or guidance have so little influence on educational policy as the psychologist. Nevertheless, in the present writer's view, the time is ripe for psychologists to get together and attempt to decide how far their instruments are doing harm, and how they could be better employed. This is one reason why a rather slight book, which might be regarded by many as mere political propaganda, has been accorded a fairly lengthy review. Mr Simon has taken the trouble to study the technicalities of his subject far more thoroughly than most propagandists (though it is a pity that he relied so heavily on a book written by the reviewer 15 years ago) ; and his distortions of fact are remarkably few. He has made a serious case, and deserves a serious answer.

J Ed 86:134+ Mr '54. A. F. Watts. Mr. Simon would like to see all children taught in unstreamed comprehensive schools. He thinks it nonsense to talk about the desirability of suiting the curriculum to the varying abilities and aptitudes of children before they begin to be interested in their vocational future, *i.e.* at about the age of 14 or 15. * This separation of working-class children from their peers is being effected at present, apparently not unwittingly, by means of "intelligence" tests, administered at the primary school leaving age for the purpose of selecting those children deemed fit to enter grammar schools. * Mr. Simon goes on to say that "it is impossible to advocate a common secondary education with any real hope of success until we are clear about the question of inherited intelligence" (p. 30). Mr. Simon is quite clear about both the question and the answer: ability differences are due to the differences in opportunity. * This point having been cleared up to Mr. Simon's satisfaction, he is forced to believe that there is "something phoney about intelligence tests." He is quick to spot some of their minor deficiencies. Their greatest weakness in the eyes of our author is not so much that they are crude and unreliable instruments as that they do an uncommonly good job in separating the working-class child from the middle-class child. I find this point difficult to grasp. Today it is a well-established principle in test-construction that questions which favour one type of child against

another are rigorously excluded. * Mr. Simon's knowledge of "intelligence" tests is admittedly second-hand, so that one does not know whether the errors in his criticisms are due to himself or to his mentor. * He tells us that "the normal junior school, therefore, is almost inevitably organized, not so much with the aim of providing the best possible education for all the children, as with that of obtaining the greatest number of 'scholarships' or passes in the selection examination at ten" (p. 17). The evidence offered in support of this charge is (*a*) that Mr. R. Morley, M.P., has said that *some* headmasters have organized their schools in this manner, and (*b*) that the chief education officer for the West Riding of Yorkshire, Mr. A. B. Clegg, has expressed the view that *certain* head teachers can always be relied upon to do so whatever form the transfer examination may take. Mr. Simon gives his reader just as misleading an idea of the techniques of selection as of the junior school and the "intelligence" test. He would have us believe that selection is practically everywhere a mechanical process limited to the adding together of examination marks and drawing a line somewhere across the list. Only a small minority of education authorities would seem to do otherwise. He is not above sowing the seed of suspicion in the mind of the uninformed reader that calculated unfairness sometimes creeps in. "A class criterion of intelligence has by now become inseparable from the whole practice of testing" (p. 64). * The reader will by now have gathered that Mr. Simon is a hot-gospeller for his thesis and is unable or unwilling to see the world except in terms of black and white. It is a pity that he should choose to bring educational discussion down to the tub-thumping level of back-bench party politics. Unfortunately, we have no instances of a Simonized comprehensive school in this country that can serve as a model for our study. It may well be that such schools could be organized and run with success. Teachers and administrators are not, however, going to remodel the existing system and introduce unstreamed comprehensive schools because, as Mr. Simon reports, "the experience of eastern European countries, and in particular of the U.S.S.R., shows that this is a practical objective." Have we not had reports lately that all is not well with the education of Russian children? What is more likely in this country is that we shall continue to employ the English method of making progress by trying to remove admited weaknesses and abuses where they can be shown to require removal, aware all the time that radical change hurriedly undertaken is pretty certain to bring in its own train of unforeseeable anomalies and disadvantages.

[B398]

★SINGER, ERIC. **A Handwriting Quiz Book: Graphological Exercises.** London: Gerald Duckworth & Co. Ltd., 1953. Pp. 60. 6s. *

[B399]

★SINGER, ERIC. **Personality in Handwriting: The Guiding Image in Graphology.** London: Gerald Duckworth & Co. Ltd., 1954. Pp. 120. 10s. 10d. * (Westport, Conn.: Associated Booksellers, 1956. Pp. 120. $2.50.)

Brit J Psychol 46:157–8 My '55. Lorna M. Simpson. * The approach to the subject is dogmatic and unscientific, and the book should appeal only to the uninquiring layman. *

Mental Health 14:84 sp '55. I. M. Stirling. This book is the work of an experienced and serious graphologist, but it falls between two stools, in that it is too complicated for the average reader and has very little new material to offer to the serious student of this fascinating subject. Nor are the reproductions of the samples of handwriting satisfactory. The idea of the "guiding image" of which Dr. Singer makes much, seems unnecessarily elaborate and even suggests that by thinking, one can alter one's handwriting, whereas this can only take place if the character of the writer changes. There is a good deal of over simplification. No one factor of handwriting can mean anything by itself, as it is intimately affected by many others. (H. J. Jacoby in his lucid "Analysis of Handwriting" gives nineteen factors whose combinations are endless.)

[B400]

★SKARD, ØYVIND; AURSAND, INGER MARIE; AND BRAATEN, LEIF J. **Development and Application of Tests for University Students in Norway: A Report on Parts of a Research Project.** American Psychological Association, Psychological Monographs: General and Applied, Vol. 68, No. 12, Whole No. 383. Washington, D.C.: the Association, Inc., 1954. Pp. 24. Paper. $1.00. * (PA 29:7971)

[B401]

★SKEET, D. V. **The Child of Eleven: A Brief Survey of Transfer Tests Between Primary and Secondary Schooling.** London: University of London Press Ltd., 1957. Pp. 176. 10s. 6d. *

A.M.A. 52:237 O '57. * a most lucid explanation of the tests used in the 11 plus examination. It is written without bias and without abuse. He explains the manufacture and aims of intelligence tests, standardised tests in English and arithmetic. Where he should be critical, he is critical. Mr. Skeet gives one of the best studies that I have so far read of the case for and against the comprehensive school. Even here, he sees no escape from some form of test for allocating and guiding boys and girls to suitable courses. If we were starting *de novo,* we might well come down in favour of universal comprehensive schools. "But it happens that we already possess large numbers of schools, and it is manifestly out of the question that they shall all now be scratched." Quite rightly, Mr. Skeet says that the real need today is the blurring of border lines between types of school. "The schools should severally aim at providing an education suitable to their pupils' ability." I have no hesitation in recommending this new book.

[B402]

★SMALL, LEONARD. **Rorschach Location and Scoring Manual.** New York and London: Grune & Stratton, Inc., 1956. Pp. ix, 214. $6.50; 46s. * (PA 30:7226)

Am J Psychother 10:801–2 O '56. Zanvel A. Liff. * a valuable short-cut to the time-consuming process of locating and scoring test responses. This manual fulfills a long-time need in its attempt to combine the scoring experiences of many leading Rorschach workers. The author has alphabetically categorized over 6,000 responses and has scored each percept for area, determinant and content, as well as the degree of form accuracy. All Rorschach workers should welcome this important reference book.

J Proj Tech 21:217 Je '57. Gertrude Baker. * It is stated in the Introduction that there are "more than 6000 responses scored by Beck and 17 other Rorschach workers." Actually, as explained later, all scoring has been converted to the Beck system; and the scoring of the seventeen other Rorschach workers has been omitted. Offered as a "manual....designed to expedite Rorschach scoring," the claim is made that the "6000 responses are scored for area, determinant and content" (Introduction). However, the "responses" in themselves consist in most instances of very few words indicating the *content* of the response (e.g. "Bear," "Head, beaver's"), and in most instances not enough information is given for any confident scoring of determinants. Very few responses contain the information that is usually obtained by adequate inquiry. Furthermore, while the name of the author originally publishing the response is indicated by an abbreviation system in each case, the reference is not given, rendering it difficult, if not impossible, to seek more information from the original source. Scoring for location and content, both of which are satisfactorily taken care of in this manual, usually give the Rorschach student little trouble. On the other hand, scoring for determinants and the technique of obtaining adequate information through proper inquiry in order to score are among the most difficult tasks the student faces. Thus, not only does this manual fail to accomplish what it claims to do, but also it fails in some of the most necessary and complicated aspects of training in the Rorschach technique. In the Introduction the student is "cautioned against using this manual to score responses in a mechanical and rigid manner." This is a well-taken warning, and yet the scoring of responses which contain as little information as many of these do is likely to encourage the rigid, mechanical approach that the author warns against. Perhaps the author has left it to the course instructor to guard against the misuse of this manual; however, any good manual should have built into it as many as possible of the proper precautions for use of its contents and not depend upon the good judgment or conscience of others to supply the necessary safeguards. The locations for the responses are delineated on the charts in solid black, making them easily seen; but the reader is left to guess at how the subject actually saw the concept. That is, parts of a concept—such as head, arms, legs and so on—are not indicated; and an inexperienced student could thus fall into the error of assuming that all subjects giving the same content to a certain blot area perceive the content in the same way—or as the student himself perceives it. The importance of determining just how the response is perceived is thus neglected in this manual. The vast number of responses listed in this volume have been sorted according to card and location only, and no information about the subjects giving the responses is offered. Neither has any attempt been made to separate responses according to sex, age, intelligence, diagnosis or any other category. While such information is not necessary for scoring, such a use of the kind of ma-

terial contained in this book might have been of far greater value than its present designated purpose of a scoring manual. From the standpoint of format, this is a handsome volume. The contents are well-arranged, and it is thumb-indexed for easy access to the material about the different blots. Any real usefulness for the book other than to satisfy curiosity about diversity of content of responses to specific blot locations escapes this reviewer. The limitations referred to above, particularly in respect to adequacy of specification of responses, reference sources and information regarding the subjects who gave them, greatly attenuate its value in doing what a good Rorschach scoring manual needs to do.

[B403]

★SMITH, LOUIS M. **The Concurrent Validity of Six Personality and Adjustment Tests for Children.** American Psychological Association, Psychological Monographs: General and Applied, Vol. 72, No. 4, Whole No. 457. Washington, D.C.: the Association, Inc., 1958. Pp. 30. Paper. $1.00. *

[B404]

★SONTAG, LESTER W.; BAKER, CHARLES T.; AND NELSON, VIRGINIA. **Mental Growth and Personality Development: A Longitudinal Study.** Monographs of the Society for Research in Child Development, Vol. 23, No. 2, Serial No. 68. Lafayette, Ind.: Child Development Publications, Inc., 1958. Pp. 143. Paper. *

[B405]

*SPIER, JULIUS. **The Hands of Children: An Introduction to Psycho-Chirology, Second Edition.** London: Routledge & Kegan Paul Ltd., 1955. Pp. xvi, 199. 28s.

Brit J Psychol 46:240 Ag '55. R. W. Pickford. * The new edition contains a second appendix by Herta Levi on the hands of the mentally diseased, with 46 plates to illustrate it * To the empirical and experimental psychologist a book of this kind offers many problems and little help. It has developed out of traditional chirology and uses its language. Like graphology, it has adopted Jung's psychology as its theoretical background, and claims to be the intuitively established basis of a scientific approach to the psychology of personality. Exactly how much of it would survive strictly scientific and experimental tests, if they could be applied, remains problematic, though it contains numerous significant observations. Herta Levi shrewdly points out in the preface to the second edition that, as a scientific method, chirology is still in its infancy and requires a good deal of body-building nourishment in the shape of factual data and statistics, but adds that very few of us have the great intuitive powers of a Julius Spier, and therefore have to rely more on scientific methods and exchange of information!

[B406]

★STARR, JOHN W., 3RD. **Analysis of Reading Readiness Tests.** Curriculum Bulletin No. 180. Eugene, Ore.: School of Education, University of Oregon, 1957. Pp. 10. Paper, mimeographed. $0.50. *

[B407]

*STEIN, MORRIS I. **Thematic Apperception Test: An Introductory Manual for Its Clinical Use With Adults, Second Edition.** Cambridge, Mass.: Addison-Wesley Publishing Co., Inc., 1955. Pp. xviii, 365. $7.50. * (PA 29:7324) For reviews of the first edition, see 4:140.

[B408]

★STEPHENSON, WILLIAM. **The Study of Behavior: Q-Technique and Its Methodology.** Chicago, Ill.: University of Chicago Press, 1953. Pp. ix, 376. $7.50. (London: Cambridge University Press, 1954. 56s. 6d.) * (PA 28:6810)

Am J Psychiatry 111:479–80 D '54. Bernard Glueck. * Ever since 1913, when I was engaged as a medical officer of the United States Public Health Service, in the mental examination of immigrants at the Port of New York, I have been hoping that someone would come along and put some sense into the protean array of "intelligence tests." * Having accepted for a long time now the principle of the "universality of uniqueness," first enunciated, I believe, by the late H. G. Wells, I never could get myself to take these tests seriously, at any rate not until the arrival of the various projective methods upon the scene. I think the Q method, which this book deals with, furnishes the long-awaited stable and dependable frame of reference for dealing with this entire subject, even though I readily acknowledge that some parts of this book are beyond my depth. * Psychiatrists, indeed all clinical workers, will readily go along with Stephenson as regards his avowedly "holistic" point of departure. * the differences between any two human beings, no matter how slight these may be, is of very great importance for the destiny of a human life. A technique, therefore, which offers an unlimited array, for all practical purposes, of approaches to the understanding of a specific individual human being should be highly welcome to the clinician, both as investigator and therapist.

Brit J Stat Pschol 7:62–3 My '54. Charlotte Banks. The aim of Dr. Stephenson's book is to describe what he believes to be a "new methodology." * Stern had drawn a clear distinc-

tion between correlating traits and correlating persons—between *inter-individuelle* and *intra-individuelle Korrelation,* as he called it, and expounded (with the aid of diagrams like those of Cattell) the various kinds of problems to which each is more appropriate. Strange to say, Stephenson nowhere mentions Stern's discussion, though it provided a useful terminology adopted by later writers, including Stephenson himself. Burt, he says, like Spearman, Thurstone, Holzinger, and the rest, is still preoccupied with "inter-individual differences": Q-technique is concerned with "intra-individual significance." Burt only correlates persons when the factors could just as well be obtained by correlating traits. As evidence, he quotes a long passage from what he says is "a statement by Burt. " But, as a matter of fact, the statement was not written by Burt at all: it comes (as the reference shows) from Babington-Smith's attempt to "make Stephenson's position clearer." If Stephenson will refer to Margaret Davies's historical review of previous work on "Correlating Persons" (*Brit. J. Psychol.,* XXIX, 1939, pp. 404–21), he will find numerous early analyses which are certainly "intra-individual," some even relating to changes within a single person only. Take, for example, the experiments on artistic appreciation carried out in collaboration with Margaret Bulley, Heather Dewar, Violet Pelling, and others, in which one or more persons ranked 50 pictures: does Dr. Stephenson suppose that these could have been factorized just as well by R-technique? * The second part of the book deals with "practical applications." It is not so much a review of results already achieved as an illustrated programme of experiments which might prove fruitful. Here we are told how "Q-methodology" should throw light on clinical, social, type- and self-psychology, and how it may be applied to data obtained with projective tests or questionnaires. These chapters indeed form the most interesting portions of the whole volume. Throughout his book Dr. Stephenson is full of new and original ideas. He is not always clear or convincing; but he has a lively and entertaining style. And those interested in novel possibilities for factorial work will find his many suggestions well worth study and reflection.

J Ed Psychol 45:374–6 O '54. H. J. Eysenck. * Of the two innovations which Stephenson claims to have introduced, it may be said that the Q-sort presents a somewhat novel and, under certain circumstances, a probably useful technique of self-rating. The subject is given a large number of statements similar to those appearing in orthodox questionnaires; he is then asked to rank these in order of applicability to himself, putting the one that characterizes him best at the top, and the one least like him at the bottom. The relationship between a Q-sort and an ordinary 'Yes'-'No' type of questionnaire appears to be essentially the same as that between a product-moment correlation and a tetrachoric correlation; though both do pretty much the same sort of thing, under certain circumstances the one may be preferable to the other. Stephenson never discusses in detail why he considers a Q-sort to be preferable to an ordinary questionnaire, and this reviewer, at least, found it difficult to see why claims made for the Q-sort should not be applied in equal measure to the despised questionnaire. On the evidence supplied by Stephenson, then, we can only conclude that the Q-sort, while ingenious, is unlikely to support the elaborate super-structure erected on it by Stephenson. With regard to the technique of correlating persons, we find ourselves in the midst of a very stormy controversy. Most orthodox psychologists have pointed out that the techniques used by Stephenson are not new, that many of the detailed applications are subject to damaging statistical criticism, and that the results in cases where the method can legitimately be applied are no different from those which would have been reached by the more orthodox technique of correlating tests or questionnaire items. A good deal of Stephenson's book is taken up with attempts to answer these criticisms, and the reader is liable to get lost in these somewhat heated exchanges. By and large, this reviewer has come to the conclusion, after examining the evidence carefully, that the critics are right and that anyone wishing to use this technique would be well advised to discuss the methodological principles involved with someone expert in this field. Stephenson does not help his case by showing a somewhat disingenuous tendency to change the meaning of the term Q-technique over the years, whilst pretending that what he now means by it is what he has meant by it all along. Simple examination of his earlier papers and the examples quoted therein is sufficient to show that his views have changed considerably. There is no harm, of course, in changing one's

views, but it does make controversy exceedingly difficult to follow when, quite justifiable, criticisms of earlier work are rebutted by referring to later and quite different definitions and interpretations. Stephenson has, from the beginning, illustrated his discussions by means of small-scale experiments, not, presumably, meant to be taken very seriously and serving only illustrative purposes. In the present book, one might have hoped for a somewhat longer, detailed, and worked-out example of his technique, demonstrating precisely how it could be useful in advancing psychological theory and knowledge. Stephenson has not taken this opportunity, however, but has relied again on a large number of very small and often exceedingly trivial examples. It is difficult to judge a method in the absence of even a single instance where it has been applied to its best advantage. However, on its present showing it seems difficult to take very seriously the somewhat extravagant claims which Stephenson makes for it. The reviewer is willing to reverse his judgment if a convincing example could be given to demonstrate the usefulness of Q-technique. In view of the failure over a period of twenty years to provide such an example, however, it seems unlikely that this judgment will be reversed. One last feature of the book calls for comment; namely, its style. A great deal of the argument is difficult to follow because of Stephenson's somewhat explosive and disjointed manner of writing. There is little in the way of sustained argument, but a constant switching of discussion from statistical detail to philosophical speculation, to attack on critics, to illustrative example, and back again to statistical detail. Distrusting his own reaction to this, the reviewer handed the book to several statisticians who confirmed his opinion that, from the statistical point of view at least, it was impossible to find any concise, consecutive, and properly documented demonstration of Stephenson's main claims. In summary, there is much that is ingenious, interesting, and suggestive in this book, but it cannot be recommended to anyone not thoroughly familiar with the field and able to discount the more unorthodox and less acceptable parts of the argument.

Occupational Psychol 29:58 Ja '55. Cyril Burt. The analysis of human behaviour presents a far more complicated problem than is generally realised. Every measurement which the psychologist obtains is by its very nature liable to vary in three respects. As Stern put it forty years ago, a mental measurement is a measurement for (1) a particular quality or *trait* of (2) a particular *person* (3) obtained on a particular *occasion*. Hence in any statistical research the traits may differ; the persons may differ; and the occasions may differ. To keep the issues as simple as possible the psychologist usually holds one of the three variables constant, and then averages out the variations in one of the other two by means of a product-sum formula. In this way he is able to secure a set of correlations between variables of one type only—between different traits (T-technique), between different persons (P-technique), or between different times or occasions (O-technique). However, each kind of correlation can be calculated in two distinct ways. Thus, if we confine ourselves to measurements obtained on a single occasion, we may either average the persons and correlate the traits, or average the traits and correlate the persons. And similarly with the others. In all therefore there are six methods of obtaining correlations, and six ways of planning a factorial research. Dr. Stephenson's book is concerned chiefly with the first two procedures—those in which the data are obtained on a single occasion only. From time to time he refers to the others; but he does not, I think, make it clear that in doing so he is passing to another kind of technique, which involves all the difficulties of correlating time-series. The method most commonly employed is the correlation of traits, called R-technique by Dr. Stephenson. But the others have been in occasional use from the beginning of factorial research. To overcome what he considers to be the defects of the older forms of "P-technique," Dr. Stephenson has developed certain devices of his own. These changes, he believes, provide us with an entirely new statistical procedure, which he has christened Q-technique. He rightly complains that the recent custom of using "Q-technique" as a label for every kind of factorial research that starts by correlating persons is not only confusing to the reader but unfair to himself and to his predecessors. And the first part of his book consists in an endeavour to compare the relative merits of the different techniques, and more particularly to defend his own proposals against the objections which Professor Cattell and other factorists have raised. The second part is concerned with "practical applications." Its purpose is, not so

much to survey results already achieved by using Q-technique, as to present a comprehensive programme of experiments with instructive illustrations of each type. Throughout Dr. Stephenson writes with a lively and amusing pen. His style is perhaps not always as lucid or as logical as the reader could wish; and at times the reader may detect signs of carelessness or haste. Thus, when examining my own earlier efforts at factorizing correlations between persons, he quotes several paragraphs which he describes as "a statement by Burt"; in point of fact, however, the statement was written, not by me, but by Mr. Babington Smith, who was not referring to my views, but (as he says) "attempting to make Dr Stephenson's position clearer." There are, too, several slips in the arithmetic and algebra. But these are minor defects. Whether or not the industrial psychologist will be able to follow or accept the arguments set out in the theoretical chapters, he can certainly study with profit the original and ingenious suggestions put forward in the second half of the book. Much of the discussion has a direct and obvious bearing on problems of vocational guidance and selection; and the experimental schemes proposed well deserve trying out on a more extensive scale.

Psychol B 51:527-8 S '54. Quinn McNemar.
If Stephenson had set forth his purposes in writing this book, which carries the subtitle "Q-technique and its methodology," the reviewer's task would be easier. Our inference is that his aims were the following: (*a*) to challenge much of current methodology in psychology, (*b*) to explain Q-methodology and (*c*) to show by illustration how it can put psychology's "house in scientific order," and (*d*) to demonstrate that theory testing and scientific conclusions are possible on the basis of a single case. Perhaps when the author speaks of the "platform upon which we are to campaign," he is telling us that his sole aim is to promote Q-methodology. We shall not attempt to list here all of the concepts and all of the people against which and whom Stephenson arrays himself for battle. He does not have any faith in ordinary factor analysis (R-methodology), in measurement, in norms, in large samples, or in any so-called generalizations springing therefrom. He admits that he alone is "in step and all others out" (p. 348), but this does not keep him from citing whatever supporting fragments he can find, whether these be found in the writ-

ings of J. R. Kantor or of J. M. Keynes or of some very obscure person. His sallies, courageously set forth, will be found either interesting or irritating, according to the proclivity of the reader. With regard to purpose *b,* one would expect that an author who complains because such intellects as Godfrey Thomson and Cyril Burt have misunderstood his writing would make a special effort at clear and concise exposition. Instead, we find a poorly organized, piecemeal presentation, more confusing than enlightening. Thus, we can anticipate continuing misunderstanding, and consequent misuse of Q-methodology. The second half of the book is devoted mainly to applications of Q-methodology in the areas of type psychology, questionnaire analysis, social psychology, self-psychology, personality, projective tests, and clinical psychology (a chapter to each area). We are told that "Q-technique has its applications in almost every nook and cranny of psychology in its research aspects" (p. 338) and "in every branch of psychology where *behavior* is at issue" (p. 343). If we are to judge from the given illustrative applications, the quoted claims represent wishful thinking. Clinicians and others who, by necessity or by choice, deal with a single case will find comforting reassurance and be motivated to read further by "We are to work, instead, with a single person, at the call of a theory. Yet we shall reach valid, scientific conclusions" (p. 5). The continuous stress on the merits of the single case leads ultimately to "In principle, one may work scientifically for a lifetime with a single case" (p. 343). Unfortunately, by the time one has spent a lifetime developing a set of principles for predicting (or explaining) every fragment of behavior of a single case, the subject will have ceased to behave. Or another logical conclusion to this sort of thing is that psychologists must develop two and a half billion "sciences" to explain the behavior of the two and a half billion human inhabitants on this planet! What of the task of animal psychologists? The fact that our comments have been restricted to general reactions should not be misconstrued as indicating that the margins of the reviewer's copy of the book are free of specific questions. Far from it.

Psychometrika 19:327–30 D '54. Lee J. Cronbach and Goldine C. Gleser. * In summary.... we find that Stephenson's proposals are not ready for adoption except by sophisticated investigators who can trace his reasoning and

evaluate the specific methodologies for themselves. *It is imperative to discourage students of personality and social psychology from copying Stephenson's designs as he presents them.* Many research investigators have run into difficulty—usually unrecognized by them—which made it impossible to establish the intended conclusions. We fear that Stephenson's book may misdirect much research effort. Our own tentative evaluation of Stephenson's ingenious schemes, subject to re-examination when the necessary technical studies are made, is as follows: The method of gathering data includes real advances. Recording evaluations of others on structured questionnaires is likely to be a fine tool for validation of assessments and studies of social perception. Obtaining repeated responses from the same person with changing sets will be useful in studying change during therapy, change in role from situation to situation, etc. It is possible that the organization of questionnaires to measure interactions between traits by means of a structured design is an important lead. Among the methods of treating data, analysis of variance is potentially advantageous *if* the forced distribution is abandoned, and if the sampling problems described above can be overcome. There may be some value also in the card-sorting technique, provided forcing is omitted. On the other hand, we would discard the Q correlation as a general technique to measure profile similarity. Factor analysis of Q correlations or other measures of profile similarity appears to have little value. Stephenson's writing is showy, and lacks the care and explicitness that must be demanded in methodological writing. Readers may overlook the tiny sentences where Stephenson mentions the limitations of his methods. A loose style is especially unfortunate in a book advertised as "a treatise on the sociopsychological study of human behavior....(which) offers experimental foundations for almost all general psychology (and) for the direct operational study of self-psychology and psychoanalysis." Specialists in psychometrics will be dissatisfied with Stephenson's style, manner, and lack of clarity, but if they have the patience to disentangle his arguments, they are likely to pick up several ideas worthy of more rigorous thought than they have yet received. [See original review for additional critical comments not excerpted.]

Psychometrika 19:331–3 D '54. William Stephenson. [A reply to the above review by

Lee J. Cronbach and Goldine C. Gleser.] * In a general way I take little exception to the review. * My reviewers, however, have perhaps read the book from too concrete a standpoint, and thus fail to notice that it requires a rather more abstract treatment. * The details of technique, and my illustrations, have to be regarded as indications rather than definitive instructions. * as to many matters of statistical detail and nicety I have no quarrel with the reviewers: non-forced distributions, and new non-parametric devices of various kinds will no doubt be useful in particular circumstances. However, the forced-choice procedure is still of paramount significance: but it is not because standardization "is often undesirable" that one uses it—for subjective operations no other rationale seems possible. And this, if I might say so, remains a source of considerable confusion for my reviewers. The trouble, however, is not any lack of clarity on my part, but an unwillingness on the part of my reviewers to argue from the right premises. *Non sequitur* arguments indeed characterize the more critical sections of the review. Granted the reviewers' premises, their conclusions of course follow. The real point is, however, whether the premises can stick. * I must suggest, indeed, that deep-seated proto-postulatory matters separate the reviewers and myself, and that from these many of the apparent difficulties of my style and their frustrations stem. In their case it stems from an impossible search for "constant" conditions. In my case a certain perversity, no doubt, can be discerned, which, however, I enjoy. My own treatment of Q is linked, of course, to the classical psychophysical methods, especially to the *constant* methods and to that of *single stimuli* in particular. But I learned long ago to stop looking for "constant" conditions. My reviewers still have to take this plunge. * What I mind most, however, is that I should be regarded as lacking in clarity. For any real lack that remains after honest effort is made to follow my arguments, I humbly apologize. But I deny that there is really much substance to this criticism: new ideas are perhaps worth pondering over, by readers and author alike. And if my critics persist in arguing from premises I not only do not make but am at great pains to deny, then I think I know where the charge of lack of care and explicitness has at least some of its beginnings. I would repeat, however, that I appreciate much of the review, and that I

echo its words of caution, without, however, agreeing that any inroads have been made by the review into the really substantial matters of the book. A word is due, finally, about factor analysis. The reviewers again, if I may say so, are on unhappy grounds here. Far from factor analysis of Q correlations appearing to have little value, the situation is otherwise. Again, however, it depends upon one's purposes. Mine are at least clear to me: they are to the effect that I use factor methods in complex situations, to help me to understand theoretical matters, for example, theoretical matters in psychoanalysis or in self-theory. Quite rough and ready procedures are adequate for this purpose, since one's real interest is in the psychology, and not in any search for strict parameters or the like of sophisticated statisticians. Again I would ask for caution about these procedures, but not from my reviewers, because they are likely to be quite other than bees in anyone's bonnet. [See original reply for additional critical comments not excerpted.]

[B409]

★STERN, GEORGE G.; STEIN, MORRIS I.; AND BLOOM, BENJAMIN S. **Methods in Personality Assessment: Human Behavior in Complex Social Situations.** Glencoe, Ill.: Free Press, 1956. Pp. 271. $6.00. * (*PA* 30:6922)

Brit J Ed Psychol 26:233–4 N '56. F. W. Warburton. This book makes an original approach to the methodology of personality assessment. Written largely from the point of view of Murray's theory of personality, it breaks new ground by elaborating four complex methods of evaluating students. * In the first experiment, three "ideal" and three "undesirable" students were studied. The analytic method led to a correct identification of the two types of students, despite the fact that the Wechsler-Bellevue and estimates of emotional stability provided no clear indication of these groups. This procedure is time consuming, extending over days. No control group was set up to see whether the same result could have been obtained in five minutes by reading the students' application forms for entry to the course. * The clinician may feel that he is asked to take too much for granted in this work. Few of the original data are made available to the reader; no psychograms are provided for the Rorschach or T.A.T. tests, and no reference is made to norms for Americans of the age group studied. Some of the new tests, scales and inventories have surprisingly high validities, particularly Drawing (of a teacher in a classroom) and Relevant Thinking, an index of the proportion of relevant thoughts a subject reports on hearing a record played back of a previous class discussion. The follow-up data are sketchy; multiple regression is not used; the techniques of validation are as various as the methods of diagnosis, and the results are nowhere adequately summarised; empiricists are in for a great deal of page turning. Samples are small (6, 10, 63 and 162); postdiction is sometimes used instead of prediction, with the attendant danger of the unconscious transmission of information; the subjects are often extreme deviates, good and bad students, stereopaths and non-stereopaths, high and low achievers, plus and minus one sigma men instead of complete populations. A more rigorous statistical comparison of the predictive efficiency of the four methods would seem an essential preliminary to piecemeal investigation of the more interesting results. Readers interested in psychodynamics will enjoy the material on new techniques, rôle formation and the interaction between different types of assessors; but the findings, although of considerable methodological interest, are inconclusive from the statistical point of view. The bibliography contains very few references to British work and the book is written in broad A.P.A. dialect. We learn, for example, that "behaviour represents an ongoing field process. It is the resultant of the transaction between the individual and other structural units in the behavioural field." There is no doubt that the chapters on methodology would repay translation into English.

Cont Psychol 1:333–4 N '56. *Kenneth R. Hammond.* * this book should have an important effect on what psychologists do, as well as on what they say. The authors make a competent and valuable effort to dynamite the rock upon which previous assessment programs have foundered—the criterion problem. The steady self-confidence of their attack on this problem is refreshing after recent gloomy pronouncements. ("Assessment in the OSS style has now been proved a failure," said Cronbach, in the 1956 *Annual Review of Psychology*.) Moreover, the results reported in the illustrative research projects are excellent. The authors put the criterion problem first and resolve it partially by some theoretical discussion of the environment (Murray's *press*), but principally

by the arduous procedure of studying the persons doing the ultimate evaluating of the assessees. As they state, "It is the evaluation which is being predicted, rather than the performance." Therefore performance has meaning only "as some evaluative judgment has been placed upon it." This point of view is so sound that the occasional omission of details in its exposition may be overlooked. With the criterion problem as a pivot, four assessment methods are presented. (1) The *analytic* method requires the staff to make a situational analysis and develop a criterion in terms of functional roles described in the terminology (mainly Murray's) of personality theory. Tests are then selected, conferences held, and predictions made. Unhappily, "it is almost an impossible task to state the principles by which the staff actually sets about predicting how the subject will perceive and react to the press." (2) The *empirical* method involves no new techniques. (3) The *synthetic* method requires the staff to "synthesize" a hypothetical personality type and predict the consequences when such a type inhabits the criterion environment. The synthetic method allows prediction only when the environment is known to the assessors, but it does not require the intensive study of evaluators as does the *analytic* method, nor does the *synthetic* method require one to make a prediction for every assessee. (4) The *configurational* method consists of transposed (inverse) factor analysis by means of which are discovered personality "models" which provide test specifications for new subjects. The book has two faults. Better copy editing would have prevented one. The second fault lies in an Olympian attitude toward tradition and related research. For example, in naming the four methods the authors overlook the traditional methodological distinction between *analytic* and *synthetic*, and the parallelism between *synthetic* and *empirical*. Their distinction among the four methods, though not altogether new (cf. Cronbach, 1949) is valuable, and it is to be hoped lasting; therefore the need for more suitable terminology is urgent. Another example lies in the absence of recognition of other attempts to cope with the criterion problem (e.g., Flanagan's critical incidents, and Thorndike's threefold criterion classification) and of attempts like Edwards' to control test faking. More detailed cognizance of the troubles encountered by others would have enhanced the caliber of the book. For example, current doubts about the value of projective tests seem never to have disturbed these writers. (Why all the research, if we ignore it?) Furthermore, the sporadic, casual references to transactionalism serve no purpose. These criticisms, however, are but slight dispraise of an important and significant contribution to the methodology of personality assessment.

J Counsel Psychol 4:77–8 sp '57. Charles F. Warnath. This is a disturbing and exciting book. Disturbing because it challenges the adequacy of old methods; exciting because it points the way to new. It is a book about criteria, perhaps the most important single problem for the counselor. * Stern, Stein, and Bloom have presented a fresh insight into the problems of diagnosis and prediction. They have moved beyond actuarial evaluation of skills as a predictor of general success or failure to the assessment of specific personalities in specific situations. Though this book is about research, it is amazingly unencumbered by the polysyllables, newly coined words, and Greek symbols which social scientists are tempted to parade as a sign of erudition, but which often serve only to frighten off all but the most dedicated. The authors have proved that one can write significant scientific material while retaining an interesting and readable style. This book should be stimulating for those who are primarily engaged in research but, at the same time, those who are devoting most of their time to counseling can discover much to discuss in their staff meetings. It should be on every counselor's "must" list— even if only for scanning.

Personnel Psychol 9:581–4 w '56. Barbara J. Suttell. * The authors' approach to, and discussion of, the criterion problem is....the major contribution of the book. It is emphasized that in initiating a research study the immediate efforts should be directed to criterion development rather than to the development of predictors, with the criterion as an afterthought. Moreover, these authors confine their criterion development to the specific situation. They formulate the demands of the particular situation, the kinds of persons who have met those demands successfully, and the system of values of the judges who will make the ratings which will serve as criterion measures. This method goes beyond the traditional concept of job

analysis in recognizing explicitly the interpersonal and social aspects of the job, and also the standards of those who will make the criterion ratings of job performance. The authors make a nice point—one not adequately recognized in most discussions of the criterion problem—of the differentiation between a *standard of performance* and a *true psychological criterion.* The assessor in their opinion fails unless he takes into account the different psychological requirements involved in two job situations which on the surface may appear to be the same. * The authors have made no significant strides in research methodology per se. Rather, their contribution has been to clarify and illustrate four assessment methodologies which underlie current assessment practices and to examine these methodologies, for the reader, in the light of a consistent transactional theoretical orientation. The authors have demonstrated that assessment problems can be approached systematically. Perhaps most important, they have emphasized the primary importance of the realistic total criterion. The subject matter of this book is of current and vital concern to psychologists concerned with the problems of personnel selection and diagnostic testing. Certainly this book is recommended reading for the conscientious researcher or personnel administrator planning a program of assessment. The book is clearly written, well organized, and at least partially fills the need for clear and explicit analysis of the relationship between assessment theory and current practice.

[B410]

★STESSIN, LAWRENCE. **Source Book of Personnel Forms: A Manual for Improving Personnel Administration.** Deep River, Conn.: National Foremen's Institute, Inc., 1948. Pp. 188. Loose-leaf binder. $7.50. *

[B411]

★STOGDILL, RALPH M., AND COONS, ALVIN E., EDITORS. **Leader Behavior: Its Description and Measurement.** Ohio State University, Bureau of Business Research, Research Monograph No. 88. Columbus, Ohio: the Bureau, 1957. Pp. xv, 168. Paper. $2.00. * (*PA* 32:1466)

Personnel Psychol 11:289–92 su '58. Robert Fitzpatrick. * describes....the development of the Leader Behavior Description Questionnaire (LBDQ). * The LBDQ started out like many another questionnaire. The research staff and their students thought up a large number of items, which were then gradually narrowed down to a manageable number through rational and statistical means. But then they tried factor analysis. And up came the now famous pair of factors: Consideration and Initiating Structure. Several factor analyses were tried in different situations and other factors appeared, but always these two or something like them. The Consideration factor seems to measure good human relations betwen the leader and his group. Initiating Structure activities occur when the leader defines the status of the group members, organizes the work, schedules work, and maintains standards. * the leader who scores high on Initiating Structure is likely also to rate high with his superiors. The high Consideration leader looks good to his subordinates. But there are several lines of evidence (not all of them presented in this book) to indicate that the best leaders of all are those who score high on both. This is indeed an encouraging finding. * Surely this is enough excitement to lure an avalanche of book orders to Ohio State * The....book can scarcely have been edited at all. Many of the articles (with the notable exceptions of those by Fleishman) appear to have been written without any knowledge that the others would be printed with them. There is repetition and there are gaps. The writing styles are uniform only in their dullness. * The....writers frequently fail to specify just which of the several versions of the LBDQ they are talking about. And omitted from this book (though available elsewhere) are many of the most interesting studies, such as that of Fleishman on International Harvester foreman training. * The extent to which LBDQ provides a measure of leader behavior, as distinct from some types of generalized "halo," is questioned by some of the Ohio State researchers themselves. A simplified questionnaire has many advantages in a research program. Chiefly, it makes readily possible the amassing of many cases. But often these advantages are gained at the cost of superficiality. That [this research program] rose above superficiality is a tribute to the technical competence of the researchers. Nevertheless, one cannot help but wonder how much further [it] might have gone with a more behavioral approach. *

[B412]

★Stott, Leland H. **The Longitudinal Study of Individual Development: Techniques for Appraising Developmental Status and Progress.** Detroit,

Mich.: Merrill-Palmer School, 1955. Pp. x, 113. Paper, spiral binding. $2.75. * (*PA 32:321*)

Brit J Ed Psychol 27:73–4 F '57. C. B. H. * Stott's short guide....is based on the methods of individual case study....used at the Merrill-Palmer School, Detroit, where each student makes a detailed study of one child. * There can be little doubt that a student using the methods described would learn a great deal about assessing growth and development, and would gain a useful insight into the life of the child he studied. * At the back of the book is a large and interesting collection of curves, profiles and charts for displaying graphically the information obtained, but the author is under no illusion that all the relevant information can be charted, and draws attention to the importance of writing notes of observations, and impressions. In regard to the family, a useful list of qualities for rating includes the adequacy with which mother and father fulfil their respective roles; the emotional climate of the home; and the kind of parental guidance exercised. Many of these ratings, as the author confesses, are of necessity made on the basis of rather sketchy evidence, and the reliability and validity of some of the scales are not mentioned. * A major criticism....is that there is no reference to the subjective aspects of development: the child's phantasies, play themes, modes of thought, his perceptions of his family and his surroundings, or of his purposes and values. This remains the weakness of a great deal of American work on child development, and though difficult to accomplish, one would like to see some attempt to treat of such matters in a guide of this kind.

Cont Psychol 1:311–2 O '56. Lois Meek Stolz. * designed to serve as a background and guide to the study of an individual child where developmental records are available and child and family are accessible for firsthand observation. Nevertheless, the material it contains will also be useful in the teaching of child development and in observational study of a child, even when longitudinal records are not available. The section (Part II) which discusses various aspects of development is well organized in a concise form. There is perhaps too great a dependence upon sources from Merrill-Palmer School and at times upon secondary sources rather than original research. Normative data are given on a variety of developmental behaviors which have been assembled at Merrill-Palmer over the years and which have not been available before. It is to be regretted that most of the tables present only means without measures of variability, in spite of the fact that the author emphasizes the importance of individual variation. One of the most useful sections contains the figures, at the back of the book, which show how to present in various graphic forms data concerning an individual child.

[B413]
★STRANG, RUTH. **How to Report Pupil Progress.** Chicago, Ill.: Science Research Associates, 1955. Pp. 47. Paper. $1.00. *

[B414]
★STRONG, EDWARD K., JR. **Vocational Interests 18 Years After College.** Minneapolis, Minn.: University of Minnesota Press, 1955. Pp. xiv, 207. $3.75. (London: Oxford University Press, 1956. 30s.) * (PA 30:4738)

J Counsel Psychol 3:74 sp '56. *John C. Flanagan.* * As pointed out by the author, the fact that approximately half the sample is composed of graduate students somewhat limits the generalization of the findings of this study to the usual guidance testing situation. It is not known what per cent of the students were in training at the time of original testing for the occupation in which they were found to be engaged "18 years" later. Some evidence that this group had made at least a tentative selection of occupation is indicated by the fact that all but 6 of the 181 business students went into some business occupation and only 6 of the 145 graduate students entered a business occupation. However, the fact that the scores for the freshmen are only about 1.5 points lower for the subsequent occupation engaged in "18 years" later than those of the remaining group, suggests that it is quite possible that the findings may not be very different from what might be obtained from a similar group composed entirely of college freshmen. * In summary it appears that the *Vocational Interest Blank* scores have definite predictive value with respect to which occupation the individual will be engaged in "18 years" later. Over this same interval there is a substantial degree of consistency in the pattern of interests indicated on the blank. On the other hand, the extent to which the scores will predict self-ratings of *satisfaction* in an occupation "18 years" later is very much smaller.

As the author points out, this may be at least partially due to the complex nature of occupational satisfaction and the difficulties of measuring it. * a definite contribution to knowledge regarding the measurement of interests and will be welcomed by both counselors and technicians.

Personnel Adm 19:45–6 Jl–Ag '56. *Allen O. Gamble.* * Strong concludes that the scores of students while in college predict future occupations "86 per cent as well as can be expected." This apparently ambiguous statement is due to the complicated method used in comparing the student groups with the professional groups on which the tests were originally standardized, and to the method of scoring the test itself. One of the difficulties of this book is that the standard statistical terminology of reliability and validity is not used, and perhaps cannot be, at many points where the reader would desire it. * This book invites the attention of the personnel technician, particularly if he is also interested in vocational guidance.

Personnel & Guid J 34:383–4 F '56. *E. Gordon Collister.* Dr. Strong has done it again! Ever since the publication in 1943 of his *Vocational Interests of Men and Women,* that volume has been the indispensable reference for persons concerned with the measurement of vocational interest. The current volume will take its place beside its predecessor, but will not replace it. * Our professional literature would be much improved if all authors would adhere to their plans as succinctly as Strong has done. * His discussions of criteria, job classification, satisfaction, the MF and OL scales, revision of scales and the relationship between abilities and interests are thorough and challenging. * The reviewer was disappointed with this volume in only two respects. The first concerns the use of group scales. In *Vocational Interests of Men and Women* (p. 169) Strong presents a fascinating hypothesis concerning the use of group scales in early stages of educational planning. In the present volume the author comments "The writer's greatest disappointment in all his research is the failure to develop effective group scales.... But it is still true that better prediction is obtained by any combination of scores on related occupational or group scales." The reviewer's disappointment stems from the fact that no data are presented on this issue. The second disappointment concerns the lack of data concerning the use of the women's SVIB. Obviously, it is difficult to obtain such data from studying samples of men and in this respect the disappointment is invalid for this volume—but the disappointment is still felt. Perhaps in his next major publication Dr. Strong can enlighten us on these counts. This volume is indispensable for anyone who considers himself professionally competent in the fields of counseling or interest measurement. The book will have to be studied; it cannot be given the "once over lightly" treatment. We all owe Dr. Strong a vote of thanks for making a vast amount of information so conveniently available.

Personnel Psychol 9:409–13 au '56. Donald E. Super. * The criterion problem is handled in a way which leaves this reviewer dissatisfied, despite a good chapter on satisfaction. Strong reports that while many factors affect satisfaction, "freedom from interference" is possibly the one most important factor in men from the higher occupational levels. "Liking one's work means continuing in it; disliking means changing one's situation, if possible." Interest correlates with job satisfaction, but not as highly as Strong would apparently have liked (*r*'s range from .23 to .30), though he recognizes that most dissatisfied men had probably made their changes by the time these data were collected. The point of this reviewer's dissatisfaction has to do with the cavalier treatment of success as a criterion—or at least it seems cavalier as reported in this monograph. "It is doubtful if it (the success criterion) is as good as it seems. Fifty per cent of the people must always be less successful than the average. Counseling evaluated on such a basis must always appear rather ineffective." But by the same token intelligence tests should be useless, for 50 per cent of the people will always be less intelligent than the average— and the same argument applies to satisfaction or any other continuum! Similarly, "continuation in an occupation" is dismissed after less than a page of discussion and the reporting of no data: surely an 18-year follow-up deserves more thorough consideration and reporting of these possible criteria. Interests proved to be extraordinarily stable, as we already know, and even more extraordinarily predictive, which many have been reluctant to believe in the case of an instrument which violates one of the cardinal principles of test construction.

[B415]

★STRONG, EDWARD K., JR., AND TUCKER, ANTHONY C. **The Use of Vocational Interest Scales in Planning a Medical Center.** American Psychological Association, Psychological Monographs: General and Applied, Vol. 66, No. 9, Whole No. 341. Washington, D.C.: the Association, Inc., 1952. Pp. vi, 61. Paper. $2.00. * (*PA* 27 :5483)

[B416]

★STROUP, FRANCIS. **Measurement in Physical Education: An Introduction to Its Use.** New York: Ronald Press Co., 1957. Pp. xiii, 192. $3.50. *

J Ed Res 51:558 Mr '58. L. Joseph Lins. Stroup treats, in a very elementary way, basic statistical concepts as applicable to evaluation in physical education. It would seem that this book would be very inadequate with a great deal of supplementation for a graduate course and would hardly meet the requirements for an undergraduate course; the book might be used to cover part of a course in tests and measurements.

[B417]

★SUPER, DONALD E., COMMENTATOR. **The Use of Multifactor Tests in Guidance: A Reprint Series From the *Personnel and Guidance Journal.*** Washington, D.C.: American Personnel and Guidance Association, [1958]. Pp. ii, 91. Paper. $1.00. *

[B418]

★SZONDI, L. **Experimental Diagnostics of Drives.** New York: Grune & Stratton, Inc., 1952. Pp. x, 254. $13.50. * (*PA* 27 :5910)

Am J Psychiatry 110:399 N '53. Irwin J. Knopf. * Szondi boldly makes a variety of claims for the instrument, such as his assertion that "This experimental device serves to differentiate diagnostically between the neuroses, the prepsychotic states and the fullblown manifest psychoses" (p. 23). However, convincing empirical data to support these claims are not included in this volume. There are many assumptions inherent in Szondi's theory with little in the way of adequate experimental evidence to support them. This is not to say that the usefulness and validity of the test *per se* necessarily rises or falls with the adequacy of its rationale. However, the negative results of research to date, both here and abroad, do not add to our confidence in its validity.

J Proj Tech 17:369–72 S '53. Henry P. David. The much heralded and long awaited English language translation of Szondi's *Experimentelle Triebdiagnostik* has at last materialized, nearly six years after publication of the original version. Szondi is frustratingly difficult to comprehend in German and it is not surprising that several earlier attempts to translate his work floundered amidst his picturesque synonyms, symbolisms, and involved sentence structure. Dr. Gertrude Aull, who modestly fails to mention her own excellent training both in Europe and in this country, deserves empathy and praise for her heroic effort to make Szondi readable. For those seriously interested in Szondi's work, however, the *Experimental Diagnostics of Drives* will come as a disappointing anti-climax, hardly worth the prohibitive cost of $13.50. It seems to this reviewer that the volume's major shortcoming does not lie in the text per se, but rather in the publisher's assumption that Szondi in translation would take to the English language habitat and prevailing scientific philosophy as he did to his native European *Seelenkunde*. It is unfortunate that the usual Translator's Preface was omitted and that there was no attempt to place the *Experimental Diagnostics of Drives* in its proper perspective relative to the development and continuing growth of Szondi theory and research. Thus there is no mention that Szondi's latest volume, the *Triebpathologie* (1952), introduces considerable changes in Szondi test administration and interpretation which render the current text at least partially obsolete. The Szondi test is an integral part of Szondi theory and should not be considered a thing apart, as has unfortunately been the custom in this country. Szondi considers himself primarily the originator of a genetically oriented theory of personality, not the advocate of a new psychological test. * The volume is a typically Szondiesque mixture of theoretical statements and empirical data complete with formulae, categories, and diagnostic signs and syndromes, all of it offered without any evidence of statistical significance. Not infrequently, Szondi spices this mixture with his own remarkably unfettered and picturesque intuition, which in one case is productive of a treatise on ego development. He presents the hypothetical ego constellation at birth, assuredly not based on test data, describes the various "ego vicissitudes" of adolescence and adult life, all of which merge into the ego pattern of old age, which in turn, bears a striking resemblance to that of the baby. Szondi may be indulging in the kind of *Seelenkunde* so dear to European intuitive thinkers,

but the very limited evidence available (David, 1954) does lend some general support to his theory of ego development. There are some important differences between the *Experimental Diagnostics of Drives* and Deri's introductory volume (1949). It might have been noted in a Translator's Preface that some factorial constellations which Szondi originally scored ambivalent were considered positive or negative choice reactions by Deri (4:2 or 2:4). This in itself would make for some differences in test interpretation. Deri elaborates what Szondi termed the "free or intuitive" method of interpretation, whereas the major portion of *Experimental Diagnostics of Drives* is devoted to Szondi's "systematic or restricted" approach of formal test analysis, a technique which Deri describes in her text (1949, p. 47–64), but does not recommend. It is noteworthy that in his latest volume, the *Triebpathologie* (1952, p. 159), Szondi comments that most clinicians are not blessed with the rare kind of intuition required by the free method but that an approach based solely on vectors, factors, ego patterns, and diagnostic tables is also inappropriate unless the individual is carefully considered as a totality in Szondi theory. He repeatedly stresses that his test loses its meaning outside its theoretical setting, a notion cavalierly rejected by Deri in the *Third Mental Measurements Yearbook* with "actually one can very well work with the test without accepting this 'gene-theory'" (1949, p. 100). *The Experimental Diagnostics of Drives* contains a great deal more than the title implies. Szondi's subtitle, untranslated in the English language edition, "depth psychological diagnostics in the service of psychopathology, criminal psychology, vocational guidance, personality, and education," gives some inkling of the wide scope of his thinking and the varied personality descriptions throughout the text. It's all summarized in 27 grandiose psychodiagnostic tables, which remain untranslated, but, the reader is told, have been appended "reproduced unchanged from the original German because of their importance as source material." A few comments about the translation itself appear to be in order. Dr. Aull's noble aim to render Szondi readable is only partially successful. Most sorely missed is a Translator's Preface which might have imparted some of the information which a personal inquiry elicited from Dr. Aull. Thus, "Schicksalsanalyse" is not translated as "Fate Analysis," the term used by Szondi in his only other English language publication (1937), but as "Analysis of Vicissitudes." This new term is attributed to Mrs. Deri and was selected because vicissitudes, rather than "passively suffered fate or destiny," suggested "critical and significant life experience" with an emphasis on the development and active participation of the individual in the formulation of his life story. Vicissitude may be technically correct in terms of Szondi theory but it sounds stilted and not particularly suited for classroom or clinical communication. Aside from the already noted failure to translate subtitle and diagnostic tables, which may not be attributable to Dr. Aull, there are such minor errors as translating a chapter heading one way in Szondi's Author's Preface and differently in the text, although Szondi used the identical words. Unfortunately, Dr. Aull also falls into that old trap of German translators, confusing "charakter" with "character," when the proper meaning refers to "personality." Perhaps such "vicissitudes" are forgivable, however, when faced with "translating" Szondi. In the final analysis, many clinicians will continue to be perplexed by Szondi's mixture of heredobiological concepts and depth psychology. They may be disturbed by the absence of pertinent statistical data. They will find it difficult to incorporate such concepts as "drive tendencies" and "ego vicissitudes" into the professional climate currently prevailing in this country. Yet, they will also recognize that purely psychological rationales are not always completely explantory. Thus, when Deri talks of needs system and valences, she acknowledges that "what this original intensity and quality of needs depends on, we probably do not know. That is the point in our casual thinking where we have to resort to explantory concepts such as 'constitution' or 'genes' " (1949, p. 28). As long as researchers appear unwilling to accept the Szondi test within the framework of the rationale that fathered it, it seems unfair to urge further purely test-oriented research, and more appropriate to accept Szondi's postscript to his *Triebpathologie* (1952, p. 511), "A test and a tester without an adequate psychology are far more dangerous than a psychology and a psychologist without a test."

Psychol B 51:198–9 Mr '54. Victor C. Raimy. For two reasons the English translation of this volume, first published in German in 1946, is something of an anticlimax. Most psychologists in this country are now generally familiar with Szondi's tests and unusual theories through the work of his student and co-worker, Susan Deri. Furthermore, research results on the Szondi Test appearing in recent years are generally unfavorable. There is little need to touch on the test itself in this review despite the fact that the book contains the basic manual and, presumably, the validating evidence for the test as a psychodiagnostic instrument. Borstelmann and W. Klopfer's excellent review and critical evaluation of the research on the test appeared in the March 1953 issue of this journal. Although Susan Deri claims that the test is not dependent upon the genetic theories of its author, Szondi apparently believes that data obtained from the test results verify his theories. In *Experimental Diagnostics of Drives* Szondi presents a highly speculative theory of personality which, he states, is derived from a union of genetics and depth psychology (psychoanalysis) validated by the results of "more than 4000 experiments." The several thousand experiments evidently refer to that many individual administrations of the Szondi Test to an unreported number of subjects from an unspecified sample of the "general population," and to undescribed criterion groups of abnormal subjects. His preferred technique for citing evidence consists in anecdotal descriptions of single cases whose test profiles always seem to coincide exactly with the principle under discussion. The text also contains a number of percentage tables, but two of these are labeled "relative frequencies (assumed)," and the others are related in some undisclosed fashion to the "4000 experiments." Sample *N*'s, means, and dispersions are not given. This book is definitely not concerned with research on motivation, at least as we know it. The inclusion of the word "experimental" in the title and in many chapter headings is misleading. Thus the reader is forced to assess the personality theory on the basis of its reasonableness and internal consistency. To the American psychologist, the theory's reasonableness is immediately suspect from Szondi's preface which declaims that this "new approach serves as an independent means of psychodiagnosis in the service of psychopathology, vocational psychology, psychology of delinquency, pedagogy and characterology * According to the working hypothesis repressed latent genes in the lineal (inherited) unconscious determine the choice in love, friendship, profession, sickness and death (*sic*)." The role of dominant manifest genes in this psychology of predestination is not mentioned. Motivation, he claims, is based on eight specific drive needs (factors) derived as arbitrary polarities from four independent hereditary syndromes. He implies that the syndromes are accepted by geneticists interested in mental disorder. As there is no qualitative difference in motivation between the normal and the abnormal, the drive needs must be universals. The book *may* contain some intuitive, basic insights into human personality, but as far as can be judged, Szondi's insights are largely Freudian constructions translated to a new and less reasonable framework.

[B419]

TABA, HILDA; BRADY, ELIZABETH HALL; ROBINSON, JOHN T.; AND VICKERY, WILLIAM E. **Diagnosing Human Relation Needs.** Washington, D.C.: American Council on Education, 1951. Pp. xi, 155. Paper. $1.75. *

El Sch J 52:487 Ap '52. Joe McPherson. * describes six devices for use in diagnosing needs * student diaries, parent interviews, schedules for assessing the activity participation of students, sociometric procedures, open questions (questions requiring students to write answers), and teacher logs of class procedures. * Each technique is described in a separate chapter with sufficient detail to permit ready use. The authors provide ample discussion on the rationale for using such instruments and give specific instructions for gathering, analyzing, and interpreting the data. The devices themselves are not unusual, but the suggestions for tabulating and summarizing the results should be very helpful. The authors seem aware of the shortcomings of such devices and the importance of appropriate attitudes on the part of the teacher who gathers and interprets data as intimate as diary material. * As the authors point out, the analysis of student needs by the use of these instruments will be realistic and useful in program-planning to the extent that the teacher understands American culture and the pupil's relation to its varied pattern. This point should be amplified. The maximum usefulness of the data gathered with the aid of these devices will depend upon the background of the teacher, how aware he is of the developmental tasks of children, the

value differences of certain social classes, the roles that students play in the classroom, and so forth. This book is aimed primarily at the practitioner. More rigorous analyses of the results would be needed if the devices are to be used as major research tools. A fine addition to the publication would have been a case study showing how data from these six devices could be integrated to develop a picture of a class and its community. The book is one that teachers who wish to make systematic study of the needs of pupils will certainly find helpful.

Personnel & Guid J 31:136–7 N '52. Douglas D. Blocksma. Again Hilda Taba has rung the bell with a practical book which helps the teacher produce both socio-emotional and academic gains for adolescents. The authors are group dynamics and intergroup experts. They have made a sound contribution to school guidance by involving the teacher in the classroom in a mental hygiene approach utilizing especially the group forces which form the adolescent culture. Their work takes the mystery out of variations we all see in classroom atmosphere. Many practical instructional and guidance procedures evolve from the diagnostic data gleaned by the classroom teacher regarding pupil attitudes, group values, degrees of belongingness, roles played in the group, peer relationships, family relationships, cultural backgrounds. * The contribution of Dr. Taba and her staff is to arm the teacher with useful procedures which make the classroom contribute significantly to the life-adjustment of the pupil without shelving academic instruction. A teacher who uses these group techniques will know his pupils better, his pupils will know him and one another better, roles will be distributed, learning experiences and teacher methods will be analyzed, new relationships will be established with pupils and parents. Supervisory and school policies should also improve. This book can be placed in the hands of teachers who, with supervision, can do much for adolescents through study and use of these procedures and ideas. It is the first of a series of experimental studies in intergroup education. This series in applied social psychology should do much (1) to balance the emphasis of the past 30 years on psychometry with sociometry; (2) to implement the recent findings on effects of social class on learning; (3) to take diagnostic studies out of central files and into use in the management of everyday youth problems in their ongoing groups; (4) to include situational group forces as well as individual factors in studying and guiding children's growth; (5) to objectify inter- and intragroup processes in such a way that teachers can use their classrooms to improve the adjustment of youth.

[B420]

★TAKALA, MARTTI. **Studies of Psychomotor Personality Tests I.** Annals of the Finnish Academy of Science and Letters, Series B, No. 81, Part 2. Helsinki, Finland: Suomalainen Tiedeakatemia, Academia Scientiarum Fennica, 1953. Pp. 130. 400 mk. *

Brit J Psychol 45:312 N '54. Peter Venables. The work....which is reported in this monograph, falls into four parts. The first, concerned with the establishment of factors of motor performance common to different tests, reports results obtained from the factor analysis of variables derived from psychomotor tests given to a group of student subjects. Of the five factors resulting from the analysis, three seem to be of importance. These are identifiable as being concerned with (1) speed, (2) smoothness *v.* disturbance, and (3) suddenness *v.* sluggishness, of psychomotor reaction. The second factor is thought to be related to a general neuroticism factor, whilst the third, it is tentatively suggested, may be analogous to an overactivity-inertia type factor. The second part of the work is concerned with a very thorough analysis of the Mira test, the results of which should be of value to anyone intending to employ this technique. An attempt is made in part three to relate Mira test variables to the three factors outlined in the first part. Results indicated that some wider interpretation of these factors may be necessary. The relation of the psychomotor to other personality tests is treated in part four. This yields some additional information, but on the whole correlation coefficients are not higher than usual in this type of work; a state of affairs which the author rightly says should lead to further development of research methods with attempts to improve the reliability and validity of the tests. The assessment of the work reported is made more difficult than necessary by the use of non-standard scoring methods for tests for which data are available in this country. It is also to be regretted that the work was not carried out within the framework of some general hypotheses, which would have permitted a clearer evaluation of this otherwise careful work.

[B421]

★THEWLIS, MALFORD W., AND SWEZY, ISABELLE CLARK. **Handwriting and the Emotions.** New York: American Graphological Society, Inc., 1954. Pp. ix, 264. Lithotyped. $8.00. *

[B422]

★THOMAS, R. MURRAY. **Judging Student Progress.** New York: Longmans, Green & Co., Inc., 1954. Pp. xiii, 421. $4.50. (London: Longmans, Green & Co., Ltd., 1955. 30s.) * Accompanying *Instructor's Manual.* Pp. 31. Paper, lithotyped. Gratis. (*PA* 28:8090)

El Sch J 55:177–8 N '54. J. Thomas Hastings. * This is one of the first evaluation books which appears to have been written for teachers and about teachers. The incidents in each chapter sound authentic. The language is direct and comparatively nontechnical. For the elementary school, particularly the intermediate and upper levels, this book does what few books or articles do: it puts the emphasis on techniques and uses of evaluation (with "tests" playing a significant but small role) and does it in the setting of the classroom rather than the laboratory. * The *Instructor's Manual* presents examples of evaluation techniques and suggestions for their use in teaching. The suggestions are good but should be unnecessary for the college teacher who knows the field. The author chose his audience and his purpose and stuck to both. The elementary teacher in training or the practicing elementary-school teacher who wishes to learn about evaluation will do well to study this book. If he attempts to apply the material in the classroom, he will be far ahead in knowing his students and knowing how the class is progressing toward objectives. His reporting practices and his conferences with parents will have more meaning. Those who want to emphasize that the student should have a part in the total evaluation process may feel that the author's incidents and examples leave far too much to the teacher and staff committee. This appears to be a matter of relative emphasis. Certainly the principles set forth could easily be exemplified in pupil-initiated evaluation. Although the examples used concern "Central Elementary School," the material in the book and the style of presentation should be of help to teachers at all levels. This is a useful addition to the available textbooks for in-service programs and college classes.

[B423]
★THOMSON, GODFREY H. **The Geometry of Mental Measurement.** London: University of London Press Ltd., 1954. Pp. 60. 6s. 6d. * (*PA* 29:3308)

Brit J Ed Psychol 25:63–4 F '55. E. A. Peel. * The material is clearly and precisely presented, which by its nature could give difficulty to students having "only a very meagre mathematical equipment." Godfrey Thomson, however, has demonstrated again how lucidly he can expound this material. He uses the geometrical model of factor analysis and this is the one which occurs most readily to the beginner. For such a person, the present volume could act as an intermediary between the accounts of the arithmetical processes of factor analysis set out in the body of the earlier *Factorial Analysis,* and the concise matrix treatment provided in the arithmetical appendix of the same volume. In fact, a good exercise for the earnest research student would be to translate the contents of *The Geometry of Mental Measurement* into the terms of the mathematical appendix of the earlier volume. Thomson deals with all the important problems of the geometrical interpretation of factors and introduces the reader to the field of prediction and estimation. He would do a further service to this branch of psychometrics if he were to do the same for problems of maximum prediction of multiple criteria. In all, this clear little book should be read by *every* student of psychometrics and studied with great care by those writing theses on factorial research.

Brit J Psychol 45:225–6 Ag '54. M. A. Creasy. * Any psychologist who has a slight mathematical background and is "willing to think spatially" should certainly read it, for the author's lucid style and omission of any irrelevant details will help many readers to appreciate in a new way the significance of techniques with which they are already familiar. * The author does not concern himself here with sampling problems, calculations, rotation of axes, or the psychological interpretation of the relationships discussed; his treatment is essentially abstract and, for the geometrically inclined, it is very refreshing.

Brit J Stat Psychol 7:125 N '54. Arthur Summerfield. * The clarity of the exposition is greatly aided by simple pictorial examples in which the reader is invited to visualize dimensions in terms of rooms and table-tops. Most of the diagrams are excellent * The book will

be found instructive by advanced students as well as by beginners. In the closing sections the consequences of using communalities are examined from a geometrical standpoint, and the result is highly illuminating. Unfortunately the discussion is so phrased as to suggest that uncorrelated factor estimates can invariably be realized as actual numerical quantities. It is true that this is qualified by the statement that "we cannot allot these estimates to individual men, so they are not of practical use"; but the implications might be found misleading. In the same section the reader learns that another writer (Kestelman, this *Journal,* V, pp. 1–6) has shown "how the values of the uncorrelated factor-estimates can be *calculated*" (my italics) when communalities are used. Kestelman, however, merely proved that such estimates, *must exist;* he did not give a process for their calculation. In spite of these minor defects the book can be heartily recommended to those whose acquaintance with factor analysis is restricted to its arithmetical techniques or to an algebraic approach. A page or two giving references for further reading and an index of subjects would probably be welcomed by the novice who makes this book his primer.

J Ed Res 49:398 Ja '56. L. Joseph Lins. The most unusual aspect of this volume....is the commencing of each chapter except the last with a school or classroom incident. This technique of introducing the problem....makes the evaluation techniques more meaningful and...."breaks the ice" for the teacher who has a mental block toward statistical manipulations. All too frequently evaluation techniques are discussed in isolation of actual use.

[B424]
★THORNDIKE, ROBERT L., AND HAGEN, ELIZABETH. **Measurement and Evaluation in Psychology and Education.** New York: John Wiley & Sons, Inc., 1955. Pp. viii, 575. $5.75. (London: Chapman & Hall, Ltd. 44s.) * (*PA* 30:129)

Austral J Psychol 8:186–7 D '56. J. Lumsden. * The book is....superior to any others in the field for this object. Lacking the critical depth of Goodenough's book and the wide coverage of Anastasi's it appears more suitable for test-users because the organization of topics and the sturdy practicality....are calculated to give the naive reader a feeling of confidence as he goes from topic to topic. * All chapters are distinguished by a crisp, logical exposition which shows familiarity with the kind of problems which bother students when they are first introduced to psychometrics. Despite the simplicity of the presentation there was very little that could be criticized for technical inaccuracy. * Chapter 6....deals with validity, reliability and practicality. The exposition....is excellent and the authors have succeeded in cutting through technical difficulties without obscuring the problems. It is pleasing to see emphasis given to the value of the standard error of measurement in the interpretation of a score but it is unfortunate that an invalid inverse probability interpretation of the standard error of measurement is given on p. 134. One other possible criticism....is that the authors' enthusiasm for parallel-form estimates of reliability may lead students to underrate the importance of other methods of defining and estimating reliability. Chapter 7 entitled "Norms and Units for Measurement" maintains the high standard of exposition of Chapter 6. * One inaccuracy is the assertion (p. 166) that non-normalized standard scores have the same meaning from one test to another. This is, of course, not true unless the tests have score distributions of the same shape. Insufficient space seems to be given to discussion of normalized standard scores which are probably the most widely used of all. Considering the emphasis placed on validity throughout the book it is strange that this chapter makes no reference to the use of raw score expectancy tables which are far more useful for practical guidance purposes than the usual norms. Chapter 8 entitled "Where to Find Information about Specific Tests" is a welcome innovation and it is hoped that in the future many more books on elementary psychometrics will include a similar feature. The only important omission from Thorndike and Hagen's book is a section on using test manuals. Some reference to the sort of information likely to be found in a test manual is found in Chapters 6 and 8 but a much more thorough treatment would be desirable for an avowedly practical book. It is only fair to say, however, that no other book known to the reviewer gives adequate space to the use of test manuals. This book can be recommended for a first course in either psychology or education and will be particularly useful for teachers, administrators, etc. who wish to obtain an adequate understanding of the fundamentals of testing by independent study.

Brit J Ed Psychol 26:152 Je '56. D. A. P. * Its approach....is essentially American, and the very great difference in attitude towards the use of tests in this country and the U.S.A. is made clear to the British reader. Two chapters, for example, are devoted to "teacher made" tests, and although the advice given is both sound and thorough there are few teachers in this country, I imagine, who would be prepared to go to the lengths described to prepare their end of term examination papers. * undoubtedly a first-class book * while the orientation of the book is towards the practical needs of the test user, discussion is based upon a sound analysis of the underlying logical and methodological issues involved, so that few who are interested in this field of study would fail to learn something from it.

Cont Psychol 1:197–8 Jl '56. Walter N. Durost. This is a good book; it has many technical excellences and few things which can be considered errors, either of fact or of judgment. In spite of this, in the writer's opinion the book is too comprehensive in its coverage for a single beginning course, too uneven in the level of ability, background knowledge, and skill which it assumes of its readers, and finally, too inclined to the "easy generalization" which leaves the student with a recommendation but without the recipe to put the recommendation into effect. The organization of the book is logical but not inspiring. * The book is not easy to read. To be sure, its style is clear and direct, and it avoids much of the overwordiness that sometimes characterizes books in this area. The student needs, however, to possess a substantial background of knowledge in order to read the book intelligently and to comprehend fully the principles and generalizations presented. It is inconceivable to the reviewer that this book could serve adequately as a basic text for the average class in measurement in an average teacher-training institution, like a typical state teachers college. The book would be useful primarily in the larger institutions that offer graduate work, where the process of selection is rather rigid and only the ablest students get to the point of taking the basic course in measurement. The authors....include a chapter on basic statistical concepts. * the subsequent development of the text assumes not only a mastery of the statistical concepts presented in the book but much more. Formulas are given and references are made to statistical concepts that are not treated in the book. To a vast majority of students without previous training in statistics or an excellent background in mathematics, these references must be quite unintelligible. * the book is too advanced even for those responsible for the major part of the professional instruction in the field. One of its most useful potential markets might be for reference and "brushing up" by the teacher of courses in tests and measurements who is not himself a specialist in this area. The authors....seem to assume that their students will be becoming personnel psychologists, school psychologists, guidance workers, clinical psychologists, and counselors and teachers. The result is that their generalizations are too often made without supporting information and their recommendations too often given for practices unilluminated by specific illustration and discussion.

J Ed Res 50:77–8 S '56. Paul L. Dressel. * The book is well written. Among its strong points are the following: (1) Suggested additional readings at the end of each chapter, (2) discussion questions at the end of each chapter which focus attention on practical situations involving ideas presented in the chapter, (3) attention to the role of objectives in test development, (4) a lucid discussion of the various types of validity, (5) an excellent chapter, 17, on the problems of marking wherein all nonsense about the relevance of the normal curve to grade assignment is eliminated, and (6) tables summarizing in concise form information of considerable complexity * Chapter 10, "The Measurement of Special Aptitudes," attempts to cover in 23 pages tests of mechanical, clerical, musical, and artistic aptitude as well as aptitude test batteries. This leads to such absurdities as two-thirds of a page devoted to a discussion of professional school aptitude batteries without reference by name to any specific test program or recent work on such selection programs. This chapter contains perhaps the worst but not the only examples of superficiality imposed by expansive coverage in limited space. One cannot refrain from wondering whether inclusion of all topics treated is really necessary even in a course catering to diverse groups. * Considered from the viewpoint of the classroom teacher who desires to construct his own tests, the relevant chapters are well done, but in the reviewer's experience, teachers in the various fields gain most when they can focus on the specific problems of testing in their own field. * Some of the preceding critical comments reflect an opinion as to what the authors should have done instead of what they did do. If educational and psychological testing are to treated in a single book, it is difficult to criticize what has been done here. Certainly, the text is a worthy and highly usable addition to the field.

Personnel & Guid J 34:302–3 Ja '56. Ralph F. Berdie. Of the several excellent introductory volumes on testing published during the past years, this undoubtedly will be the best text for most teaching purposes. It is comprehensive, scholarly, based on sound psychometric theory, and well written. Throughout are kept in mind the needs and interests of prospective teachers, personnel workers, and clinicians who will, for the most part, be the readers. The authors' philosophy concerning the role of tests is one that most of us will heartily agree with and endorse. * contains more relevant information on evaluation than do most such texts. The effects of preselection upon test validity, the combination of test and nontest data, the relative efficiency of clinical and actuarial judgments, the functions of a marking system, reporting school appraisals to parents, factors affecting rater's ability to rate accurately, situational tests—these are but some of the many important topics usually omitted from such works. About the only broad problem concerning modern psychometrics that the authors fail to discuss is the problem of profile similarity. * throughout, the discussion is based upon scholarly treatment of test research and theory. In spite of this sound theoretical basis, the presentation is not abstract and most points are well illustrated with examples familiar to teachers and other test users. The chapters on test construction present in much detail the entire process of making a test, from defining the course objectives through discussing tests with students. A word of warning might have been appropriate to reassure readers that many test makers and users, particularly classroom teachers, are unable to follow the statistical and psychometric rigors prescribed. The presentation of statistics is particularly good. * The authors' careful survey of the literature apparently failed to reveal to them one important study relevant for this discussion on the validity of personality inventories. In light of the Hathaway-Monachasie study which revealed the effectiveness of the Minnesota Multiphasic Personality Inventory in predicting delinquency, a statement that "inventory scores have generally failed to predict anything much about the future success of the individual either in school, on the job, or in his personal living" needs qualification. The book is unusual also because of the attention given to projective tests and the detailed presentation of nominating techniques, forced choice methods, and the validity of observational methods. Although this would adequately serve as a text in almost any beginning course in evaluation, it is outstandingly suitable for teaching a course for prospective teachers; for this group, no better text can be found. The person who wishes a readable introduction to test theory and practice, or the person who wishes to quickly review testing methods and learn of new tests, and to become acquainted with newer psychometric theory and methods also will find he can do no better than make use of this book.

Psychometrika 21:94–5 Mr '56. John E. Milholland. This book...."undertakes to provide the foundations that....workers in different branches of education and psychology will need in order to use and interpret tests, move ahead into more specialized testing courses, and go ahead independently to study their own practical testing problem." (Preface, p. v). It seems admirably suited to these purposes; it should also be an excellent handbook for the school administrator who is not an expert on testing to peruse and to have available for reference. * a sound evaluation of tests in terms of what they can and cannot contribute to the making of decisions, principally in education. * The discussion of the correlation coefficient and its interpretation is particularly good for the level of sophistication the authors have chosen. * The discussion of reliability is especially good, but the treatment of validity differs from that of the recent APA Technical Recommendations, without any particular gain, it seems to me. Furthermore, the term "construct validity" is used with a meaning different from that of the APA committee. The four common types of norms—age, grade, percentile, and standard-score—are next described and evaluated. In the discussion of standard scores the authors seem to go completely off

the track, and are actually perpetuating the prevalent fallacy that there is some magic in the process of substracting the mean and dividing by the standard deviation. * an excellent discussion of profile interpretation, emphasizing the necessity for taking into account the reliabilities of difference scores. * In the chapter on Marking and Reporting, Thorndike and Hagen take the position that course marks can be only a relative appraisal, with respect to some reference group. They ignore the alternative of assigning marks based on the extent to which the students have achieved the operationally defined objectives of instruction. Sufficient progress has been made in this direction, certainly, to make it a functional alternative, and, for me at least, a preferable one. *

[B425]

★THORNE, FREDERICK C. **Principles of Psychological Examining: A Systematic Textbook.** Brandon, Vt.: Journal of Clinical Psychology, 1955. Pp. vii, 494. $7.50. * (PA 29:8625)

B Menninger Clinic 21:121–2 My '57. Paul W. Pruyser. It is not necessary to agree with Thorne's preference for eclecticism, basic science and factor analysis to describe this as a thorough, systematic and broad textbook. It is singularly unphilosophical in its treatment of many thorny problems, but even this can be refreshing at times. It deserves a place on desk or shelf as a corrective for many partisan or just very original books, but in turn, needs the greater inspiration often found in the latter.

Cont Psychol 1:215–6 Jl '56. J. Richard Wittenborn. * Thorne has given us an extraordinary vista of human behavior, unmatched in breadth and rich in detail. * The reader may not accept the necessity for the eclectic quality of Thorne's integrative approach but he will find the author's summaries of the content of human behavior thorough and of such breadth as to be provided only by an intent student of broad psychological training and long clinical experience. Since no theory of behavior is sufficient to the author's requirements, he must in many places extend the integrative quality of his discussion by referring to the contributions of factor analysis. (This is not a quantitatively oriented book and most of the material from factor analysis has been drawn from the summaries of Cattell and French.) It is not necessary, however, to suppose that the organization of behavior as indicated by a factor analysis has any general validity or a transcending descriptive merit. Whether factors describe basic regularities in behavior or incidental regularities among present data is an unanswered question. Even if the results of factor analysis were to provide bench marks of great descriptive value, such simple descriptions are not likely to afford either an understanding of the conditions under which the individual arrived at his present behavior state or an anticipation of the conditions under which his behavior may be modified. Dr. Thorne meets this difficulty by placing reliance on the principle of self-consistency and upon the broad predictive implications that may be inferred from a study of the style of life as conceived by his former teacher, Dr. Adler. Despite his willingness to use the results of factor analysis, he perceives that life in all of its manifestations is a process and that all current arrangements of behavior have potentials for future function. Because of its breadth, eclectic balance, and clinical context, this book should be required reading for most students of clinical psychology, psychiatry, and social work. Despite its diversity of content, the text is sound, though it may not always satisfy the scholar's need for depth and detail. Nevertheless, appropriately supplemented with readings in theory and technique, this book could become a desirable basic text in clinical psychology.

J Counsel Psychol 2:311–3 w '55. David V. Tiedeman. * an eclectic book * The sweep of this book through the areas of neurology, medicine, comparative psychology, instinct theory, associationism, introspectionism, behaviorism, Gestalt psychology, field theory, psychoanalysis, psychometry, sociology, social psychology, and anthropology is truly magnificent. Such a scope makes understandable Dr. Thorne's comment in the preface that 15 years of his spare time have been given over to consideration of the problems of relating psychotherapy to diagnosis. The results of this effort are commendable. Students of the applied fields of psychology for many years to come will benefit from this effort at integration of so much which previously they have had to integrate alone. * this reviewer was irritated by the brevity of the treatment of the problems of the assessment of ability (Chapter 14), attitudes, sentiments, interests, and aversions (Chapter 19), and the style of life

(Chapter 21). We know much more about these problems than Thorne has chosen to include. * Personality is defined as organization of behavior at a particular time and place. Hence over time an individual does not have personality; *he has personalities*. This position is achieved by postulating hierarchical levels of personality organization in which lower levels of organization may take precedence over higher levels of organization, and by postulating prepotent factors which serve to organize personality within any level. In the reviewer's opinion this model of personality on which Thorne's whole book is really based is inconsistent with the model of factor analysis to which Thorne attributes the status of censor (pp. 49, 477) of the work of the clinician. Thorne has probably been the victim of semantics in taking this position. It is true that the words, "hierarchy," "general factor," and "specific factor" are in the vocabulary of factor analysis, just as they are in the vocabulary of Thorne's system of personality. However, factor analysis is essentially a linear mathematical model which does *not* suspend operation of all but one variable when that variable is prepotent. Factor analysis is also a system which in its most common use postulates stability of personality and largely seeks to reduce the number of variables necessary for explanation of the multiple sets of observations on a group of people. In reality Thorne has almost entirely capitalized on only the latter aspect of factor analysis. Consequently, the contents of the volume suffer little from this misunderstanding of the ultimate inconsistency of the two models. In attempting to be eclectic, however, one must still be consistent. * Although Thorne's book is laden with suggestions for avenues of inquiry which are intriguing, the book does *not* contain directions for the *particular* associations of observations which can lead to *specific* diagnoses.

[B426]

★TINKELMAN, SHERMAN N. **Improving the Classroom Test: A Manual of Test Construction Procedures for the Classroom Teacher.** Albany, N.Y.: New York State Education Department, 1957. Pp. 56. Paper. *

[B427]

★TINKELMAN, SHERMAN N. **Regents Examinations.** University of the State of New York, Bulletin No. 1424. Albany, N.Y.: New York State Education Department, 1953. Pp. 21. Paper. Gratis. *

[B428]

★TOMKINS, SILVAN S., AND MINER, JOHN B. **The Tomkins-Horn Picture Arrangement Test.** New York: Springer Publishing Co., Inc., 1957. Pp. xvi, 383. $10.00. * (*PA* 32:2926) For reviews, see 167.

[B429]

★TORGERSON, THEODORE L., AND ADAMS, GEORGIA SACHS. **Measurement and Evaluation for the Elementary-School Teacher: With Implications for Corrective Procedures.** New York: Dryden Press, Inc., 1954. Pp. xiii, 489. $4.90. *

Ed & Psychol Meas 15:319–21 au '55. Robert A. Jones. * characterized throughout by a thorough emphasis upon understanding the individual child and the individualization of instruction. This is a strong point of the book. The point of view seems to be consistent with the recent thinking in this respect. Each chapter concludes with a summary. The summaries are well-done and should be valuable for instructional purposes. While the text is called measurement and evaluation, which would seem to imply a certain emphasis on measurement, measurement is certainly not accorded as extensive treatment as might be desired. Evaluation, however, is very well treated. The list of standardized tests which is included in the appendix seems to be quite adequate as a reference list for the student teacher. A somewhat disproportionate use in the text of California Test Bureau materials as illustrative examples is evident. * When the editor of the book states that statistical concepts are kept to a minimum, he somewhat understates the case. A little broader statistical approach would help. Concepts such as the standard error of measurement and the mode are not included while the average deviation and the semi-interquartile range are accorded a page and a half. In a volume where so much emphasis is placed on individualized instruction it would seem worthwhile to stress the importance of the standard error of measurement. In some places the statistical accuracy is a little loose. * On the whole the authors have written a most readable textbook. Except for a slight reservation about the underemphasis on measurement, the text is to be commended. With its emphasis on a functional approach this book should be well received.

El Sch J 55:305–6 Ja '55. Althea Beery. * unique in its emphasis on understanding the individual child * written in a clear, readable style, intelligible to a classroom teacher without previous work in statistics or measure-

ment. Its point of view is consistent with present thinking in education concerning the importance of individualized instruction and a comprehensive study of individuals; yet the complexity of the classroom situation and the need to give instruction to children in groups are not ignored. The treatment of measurement is less exhaustive and comprehensive and less well documented than in some other books, but this volume is deserving of serious consideration as a textbook for undergraduates in teacher education or as an introductory textbook for teachers in service.

[B430]

★TORGERSON, THEODORE L.; ADAMS, GEORGIA S.; AND WOOD, ERNEST R. **Students Workbook: Measurement and Evaluation for the Elementary-School Teacher.** New York: Dryden Press, Inc., 1955. Pp. 192, unnumbered. Paper. $2.00. *

[B431]

★TORGERSON, WARREN S. **Theory and Methods of Scaling.** New York: John Wiley & Sons, Inc., 1958. Pp. xiii, 460. $9.50. (London: Chapman & Hall, Ltd., 76s.) *

[B432]

★TRAVERS, ROBERT W. M. **Educational Measurement.** New York: Macmillan Co., 1955. Pp. xix, 420. $4.75. (London: Macmillan & Co. Ltd. 33s.) *

Brit J Ed Studies 4:23 N '55 C. M. Fleming. * The book is deliberately too abbreviated to appeal to senior research workers but its inclusion of examples of test material of many kinds and the obvious educational significance of the topics it discusses combine to make it one to be commended to any general reader in the field of education.

Ed & Psychol Meas 15:315–7 au '55. Edwin Wandt. According to the preface, this book was written "....to present an account of the appropriate uses of measurement procedures within a framework of modern education." The author has attempted to emphasize "....the psychological and educational theory underlying the use of particular types of instruments" rather than "....to familiarize the student of education with an array of techniques and devices which he is expected to be able to use at his own discretion." * Travers largely has been successful in achieving his objectives, particularly in Part I. Background for Educational Measurement, which is the strongest section of the book. Any person reading this section cannot fail to have a clear understanding of the place of evaluation and measurement in the educative process. There are some specific weaknesses which detract from the book's overall quality. Since the book is intended to be used as a textbook for an introductory course in educational measurement, it would seem natural that there would be a liberal supply of references to other sources in the field. In spite of the numerous references in some chapters....there is a lack of references in some areas. * Some of the information in the chapter on attitude measurement is misleading. Approximately eight pages are devoted to the Thurstone-Chave method of attitude-scale construction. The reader is told that "The Thurstone and Chave method seems to be the one which the teacher can best apply, since it calls for little specialized mathematical knowledge. Other methods require substantially greater knowledge of statistics." The Likert-type scale is mentioned only briefly, and is dismissed with the following comment: "However, since the teacher will probably not be sufficiently familiar with the statistical techniques needed for developing a Likert-type scale, it will not be further elaborated upon here." This comparison between the Thurstone-Chave method of attitude scale construction and the Likert method of construction is completely misleading. In fact, the Likert method is the simpler method, and was developed to reduce the labor involved in the Thurstone-Chave method, which it does with no loss in reliability. The experimental evidence is clear on this point. The section on Disguised Methods of Measuring Attitudes in the same chapter is deficient in its coverage. The only indirect method included is that of projective devices. Other indirect methods, such as those summarized by Campbell, are not even mentioned. Another example of limited and somewhat misleading coverage is the section on art aptitude tests. These tests are covered in two paragraphs. The following excerpts indicate the nature of the coverage "....the field has been dominated by a single test developed by Norman C. Meier." and "The difficulty of producing tests of artistic judgment probably accounts for the fact that Meier's test has had over the years only one major competitor (sic)—The McAdory Art Test. The latter test has also been studied over a period of nearly two decades and there is some relatively recent evidence to show that it measures a somewhat different aspect of art aptitude than is measured by the Meier test." The fact that there is a second basic approach

to testing artistic aptitude—that of attempting to get at the productive as opposed to the judgmental aspect of art, is not mentioned in the book, and no reference is made to tests (e.g. Horn, Knauber, Lewerenz) which are based on this principle. In spite of the preceding shortcomings, and some others which have not been mentioned, there is no question that Travers has made a significant contribution to the literature of educational measurement. Readers who feel that most books on educational measurement make rather "dry" reading will be pleased by the readability of this book. Contributing to this readability is the inclusion of interesting and important material drawn from the research and development in the field of educational measurement during the past sixty years.

J Ed Res 49:636–7 Ap '56. Robert A. Davis. * The most practical part....is Part II, "Measuring Intellectual Outcomes." * The material of Part III, "Personality Development," will be welcomed theoretically but rejected practically. Many teachers give a great deal of lip service to the point of view that the important outcomes of instruction are to be found among the intangibles of education such as attitudes, interests, appreciations and social development. But in practice they continue to place maximum stress upon measuring intellectual outcomes. * The....book provides a sound basis for an introductory course in measurement and evaluation. * easy to read. Technical problems involving statistical manipulation and difficult concepts are held to a minimum. Measurement and evaluation are not limited to the intellectual aspects of the learner's development but are extended to interests, attitudes, and values. There is a desirable balance between teacher-made and standardized tests.

Personnel & Guid J 34:177–9 N '55. Leo R. Kennedy. * a major objective of this text is to help the instructor to achieve in his students the goal of professional, as opposed to mere technical, competency in educational measurement. Generally Travers has been successful in this respect. But at times....he has over-extended himself, particularly in view of the fact that the only stated prerequisite for the course is introductory educational psychology. * in Chapters 1, 2, and 4....Travers has made a good contribution to a more meaningful approach to measurement and evaluation. These chapters are among the best in the text and should raise the sights of the student from the how-to-do-it to the why-we-do-it level. His discussion, in Chapter 3 of validity is well done, but his presentation of additional statistical concepts definitely assumes the student achieved a good mastery of the fundamentals of descriptive statistics in educational psychology. This reviewer believes Travers has presumed too much here. Chapters 5, 6, and 7 relate to the measurement of thinking, study, communication, and work skills as the basic products of general education. The viewpoint is good. But the considerable doubt he casts upon the meaningfulness of diagnostic reading tests may be rejected by some readers, if for no other reason than that his most recent reference, with the exception of a test, is 1944. * the material is very readable and should be useful to the student * Part Three....is interested in the assessment of personality, interests, social development, and the measurement of attitudes. There is nothing unusual in his presentation, with the exception of a brief, but useful, treatment of sociometric techniques in the assessment of social development. Generally, in part three he seems to fall short of his standard of writing up to the student's abilities. One wonders, too, (p. 229) why the K Scale was omitted in discussing the M.M.P.I. * Section Four....relates to predicting pupil progress. * A sound presentation of the values of intelligence and aptitude tests is made; all this with special relation to problems in prediction. Section Four is very well done. * The reviewer is somewhat disturbed by the characteristic absence, in the chapter bibliographies, of recent studies in the field. This is the more distressing since the author set out to write a text that would challenge the student's presumed abilities. This text definitely cannot be classified among the "do-it-yourself" type. Nor was it so designed. Most students will have to burn some midnight oil. This book requires a well prepared teacher and good teaching. All of which, of course, is on the plus side of the ledger.

[B433]

★Traxler, Arthur E.; Jacobs, Robert; Selover, Margaret; and Townsend, Agatha. **Introduction to Testing and the Use of Test Results in Public Schools.** New York: Harper & Brothers, 1953. Pp. xi, 113. $2.50. * (PA 28:1580)

Cath Ed R 53:67–8 Ja '55. Robert B. Nordberg. * The writers assert the superiority of the essay test for measuring objectives such as "ability to organize and evaluate broad subject matter areas," but most of the work is slanted toward standardized tests and objective classroom examination. Here we have another instance of an abstract acceptance of the proposition that educational wholes are not the sums of their parts, coupled with a concrete tendency to proceed as if the proposition were false. Within limits implied above, this book can be recommended as having an unusually balanced and non-technical approach to a field long characterized more by technical advances than by perspective.

Clearing House 28:374 F '54. Harry D. Loveless. * The book is very readable and has many illustrative charts and graphs which provide useful suggestions for teachers and counselors working with test results. * provides the assistance which is needed by so many teachers and counselors in securing the most from the testing program of the school. The importance of tests in the program of guidance services is very clearly stated. * This book would be a very valuable addition to the professional library of any public school.

J Ed Psychol 44:381–2 O '53. Dora E. Damrin. * written in a way that any teacher....can readily grasp the basic concepts which are presented and which are a fair sample of those prerequisite to any intelligent use of current measuring devices in the classroom. The book is intensely practical in its orientation, and it seems apparent that the authors have had first-hand experience with classroom teachers of many types. The principles of selecting, administering, scoring, analyzing, recording and using test results which are presented are undoubtedly sound, and the brevity, clarity, and conciseness with which they are presented will appeal to the busy educator already overloaded with a full teaching or administrative schedule. The final chapter in the book particularly will find hearty acceptance even among teachers who are generally familiar with the contents of the preceding nine chapters. Here is presented the case history of an incoming student along with a detailed account of what tests were given him and when, why these particular tests were selected, how the scores were interpreted and used, and what the end-result of the program was upon his graduation. This reviewer, however, believes that the naïve reader should be made aware of the fact that the book represnts a somewhat narrow philosophy of educational measurement. Tests are conceived of as tools which the teacher can employ as aids to guide the learning experiences of students. Practically no reference is made to the fact that tests can serve other equally worthy purposes. The use of measurement as an active rather than a passive agent in the learning process receives no emphasis. The use of measurement as a powerful method for inducing and directing curriculum change is barely touched upon. The notion that students, as well as teachers, might profitably have some hand in the selection of the tests which are to be used for their own guidance, is entirely absent. Although such criticisms may seem of relatively minor importance, there is some danger that users will fail to realize the fact that the book presents only one of the important points of view about educational tests and their uses. For this particular point of view, the book is quite good and will undoubtedly find wide acceptance among persons not intimately acquainted with tests.

J Ed Res 47:710–1 My '54. Carl H. Waller. * The material covers the subject comprehensively, yet in concise manner deals with various pertinent and practical problems confronted by school people from the time group evaluation begins until final test results are used to assist individual pupils. * this book was prepared by people who understand the major problems teachers and administrators meet in using tests * Some attention to the specific limitations of tests is presented in timely and emphatic fashion as a guard against the enthusiasm, perhaps too frequently found in some school situations, where test results alone are used out of proper perspective in making generalizations about pupils. The philosophy that teachers should have an active part in planning the testing program, in selecting tests, and in administering and using test results is a practical and sensible point of view. This discussion gives in "sugar coated" form information which teachers need in order to function in the area of psychometrics. This information, when presented in such understandable fashion, meets a great need in public schools as, in the past, many teachers have lacked the theoretical and practical understandings essential to use tests in optimum ways. A particular strength of this volume is the final chapter in which a particular case is used to illustrate how the results of many tests, along with other data the school accumulates, may assist teachers to help a

given boy make good use of his school experience. * easily read * well illustrated with graphs and tables * Although the volume will probably find its greatest use as a basic text in teacher training....it should meet a recognized need of many school counselors and administrators for a practical reference.

[B434]

★TUDDENHAM, READ D. **Studies in Reputation: I, Sex and Grade Differences in School Children's Evaluation of Their Peers; II, The Diagnosis of Social Adjustment.** American Psychological Association, Psychological Monographs: General and Applied, Vol. 66, No. 1, Whole No. 333. Washington, D.C.: the Association, Inc., 1952. Pp. v, 58. Paper. $1.50. * (*PA* 27:2980)

[B435]

★TYLER, FRED T. **The Prediction of Student-Teaching Success From Personality Inventories.** University of California, Publications in Education, Vol. 11, No. 4. Berkeley, Calif.: University of California Press, 1954. Pp. 233–313. Paper. $1.25. * (*PA* 29:4709)

Occupational Psychol 29:202 Jl '55. P. E. Vernon. * the investigation is considerably more polished statistically than most of its predecessors, and it provides an interesting comparison of multiple regression, descriminant function, and multiple cutting score techniques. (The last of these—which is far the simplest—seemed the most effective.) The monograph also contains a valuable critique of the defects of earlier studies. One point apparently not mentioned is that teaching success is, in all probability, a far from homogeneous or unidimensional variable. It seems extremely likely that all sorts of different personalities are capable of becoming good teachers (or bad ones). Hence psychologists should not expect to make much progress in measuring an ideal type of teaching personality. The situation is not dissimilar to that in Army officer selection. There too no combination of linear variables appears to have any worth-while validity. But the more flexible, even if more subjective, approach based on group observation has at least provided something more valid than the interview. If, in the future, the supply of teaching candidates begins to exceed the demand, an extension of WOSB methods (along the lines that are being tried out at Manchester) seems the most hopeful means of selecting better teachers.

[B436]

★TYLER, RALPH W. **The Fact-Finding Study of the Testing Program.** Madison, Wis.: United States Armed Forces Institute, 1954. Pp. v, 304, 35. Paper, mimeographed. *

[B437]

*ULETT, GEORGE. **Rorschach Introductory Manual: A Primer for the Clinical Psychiatric Worker: With Interpretive Diagram to Permit Clinical Use While Learning the Ink-Blot Technique, Second Edition.** Beverly Hills, Calif.: Western Psychological Services, 1955. Pp. 49. Paper, spiral binding. $4.00. * For reviews of the first edition, see 4:128.

[B438]

★ULLAH, SALAMAT. **Examinations in India: Their Defects and Remedies.** Calcutta, India: Orient Longmans Ltd., 1951. Pp. vii, 123. *

[B439]

*UNITED STATES CIVIL SERVICE COMMISSION. **Specimen Questions From U.S. Civil Service Examinations.** United States Civil Service Commission Pamphlet 11. Washington, D.C.: United States Government Printing Office, 1952. Pp. 35. Paper. $0.20. *

[B440]

*VALENTINE, C. W. **Intelligence Tests for Children, Fifth Edition.** London: Methuen & Co. Ltd., 1953. Pp. xiii, 84. * For latest edition, see B441.

[B441]

*VALENTINE, C. W. **Intelligence Tests for Children, Sixth Edition.** London: Methuen & Co. Ltd., 1958. Pp. xiii, 87. 8s. 6d. * For reviews, see 405; for reviews of earlier editions, see 4:344–5 and 3:283.

[B442]

★VAN TREESE, LARRY, AND TARR, HARRY A. **How to Pass National Merit Scholarship Tests.** New York: Arco Publishing Co., Inc., 1956. Pp. 300. Paper. $3.00. *

[B443]

★VEON, DOROTHY HELENE. **The Relationship of Learning Factors Found in Certain Modern Foreign-Language Aptitude Tests to the Prediction of Shorthand Achievement in College.** Stillwater, Okla.: College of Business, Oklahoma Agricultural and Mechanical College, 1950. Pp. 74. Paper. $0.85. *

[B444]

★VERNIER, CLAIRE MYERS. **Projective Test Productions: I, Projective Drawings.** New York: Grune & Stratton, Inc., 1952. Pp. viii, 168. Spiral binding. $6.00. *

B Menninger Clinic 17:111 My '53. Leonard Horowitz. * While there is a definite need for this type of book, it is felt that the author fell short of her goal. The author's comments on the drawings could have been more detailed and complete. Frequently inferences are suggested rather than explicitly stated resulting in undue vagueness. In spite of these shortcomings it should serve as a useful volume for clinicians interested in furthering their skill in the use of drawings.

Can J Psychol 7:93 Je '53. A. Jean Brown. * a useful handbook for those working in the field of psychology. We are rightly warned in the introductory chapter that the projective drawing test should as yet be used only as one of a battery of tests in the hands of an experienced clinician. * There is a brief and clear description of the main features of the syndrome illustrated by case material and figure drawings for each of the cases listed. This ready-made clinical material serves to increase the knowledge of the beginner: it is material which would take the clinician considerable time to accumulate. Actually, the need now with respect to the Projective Drawing Test is for validation of the clues set out in this book.

J Consult Psychol 16:414 O '52. Morris Krugman. * a very attractive, spiral-bound publication built around perhaps a hundred full-page reproductions of human figure drawings * In spite of frequent warnings by the author about the tentative nature of the analyses of the drawings, it is quite likely that this publication will be used as a manual for the clinical interpretation of drawings, since the material is concisely presented. This would be a misuse of the publication. It is by no means a research report; it is an attempt to present impressions gained from drawings of clinically diagnosed cases. Some of the impressions are clear and some are vague and overlapping. The "normal" group is the most confusing of all, since it presents many of the elements characteristic of disturbed groups. This report is a brave beginning, but only a beginning. Experienced psychologists will find it valuable. Others should handle the material gingerly.

Psychol B 50:318 Jl '53. Irene R. Pierce. This is a well-organized collection of drawings made by persons of a variety of clinical diagnostic groups (the psychoses, neuroses, and brain-damaged) and includes the productions of normal subjects as well. The author offers this book primarily as a teaching tool in courses on projective techniques, and for this end it should be most valuable. * In surveying these productions it is certainly evident that the "Draw-A-Man" test can be valuable in capturing graphically some personality characteristics. What is also strikingly evident, however, is the tremendous overlap of so-called clinical signs from one diagnostic group to another, especially into the normal group. This should allow for considerable humility and care in the use and interpretation of the test until a more standardizing system of dealing with the data can be developed. Vernier's data may present a significant step in this direction. It is important to recognize, however, that most of the observations made about the drawings by the author are ex post facto, which sometimes get her into trouble. In one instance drawings made by a paranoid patient (Figure 2), in which the figures both had small heads, were intrepeted as follows: "minimal head emphasis is of interest in view of the patient's lack of either intellectual aspirations or control mechanisms" (p. 6). However, in a drawing made by another paranoid schizophrenic (Figure 4) there is also a small head which is not mentioned; instead, the midline emphasis or double belt line is considered to be a reflection of the patient's emphasis on intellectual controls. There are a large number of similar examples. In general, however, this book should be of considerable value for the teacher of projective techniques, for the practicing clinician, and in suggesting further research with this test.

[B445]

*VERNON, PHILIP E. **The Measurement of Abilities, Second Edition.** London: University of London Press Ltd., 1956. Pp. xii, 276. 20s. *

Brit J Ed Psychol 26:235 N '56. D. M. Lee. Research workers in many fields will welcome this new edition of Professor Vernon's classic book. Readers will find additional material on new tests, the nature of intelligence, coaching and practice in intelligence tests, school records and teachers' estimates in selection, and recent results in factor analysis. Some statistical sections have also been expanded. Once again a succinct and up-to-date account of the psychological and statistical theory of mental testing is readily available. Students, teachers and research workers in the Human Sciences have here a handbook which will clarify and broaden their present knowledge. In the wider field of Applied Statistics, students of methodology will find here much food for thought, for some difficult statistical problems are generated within the framework of Educational Statistics. This new edition fills an important place on the shelves of every reference library.

Brit J Ed Studies 6:92 N '57. A. C. F. Beales. * this new edition altogether supersedes its predecessor, and is indispensable for all serious students.

Brit J Psychol 48:75–6 F '57. Boris Semeonoff. * The work....retains its unique character as a comprehensive survey of all aspects of testing and measurement in education, including traditional examinations, and its genuine

comprehensibility to the non-mathematician has not been attained at the cost of misleading oversimplification. The invaluable classified list of tests available in this country, now completely reconstructed, is exemplary for the clarity of its layout.

Occupational Psychol 31:60 Ja '57. John D. Handyside. * distinguished text book * Are the changes sufficient to justify the possessor of a 1940 edition buying a copy of the new one? In your reviewer's opinion he would be wise to do so if he teaches psychology students or student teachers, or if he wants a convenient and up-to-date catalogue of commercially available tests. Others should see that their reference libraries have the new edition. To the undergraduate psychology student who has not yet read either edition—what are you waiting for?

For reviews of the first edition, see 3:1219 and 40:B1115.

[B446]

★VERNON, PHILIP E. **Personality Tests and Assessments.** London: Methuen & Co. Ltd., 1953. Pp. xi, 220. 18s. * (New York: Henry Holt & Co., Inc., 1954. $3.75.) (*PA* 28:2684)

Brit J Ed Psychol 23:200–2 N '53. Cyril Burt. * Hitherto practical workers in this country have had to rely almost entirely on American textbooks, like those of Symonds, Rapaport, or Bell, which naturally have in mind the assessment of American personality rather than of English, and, not unnaturally, seldom refer to investigations carried out in this country. As a result, the younger generation among teachers, school medical officers, and psychiatrists are apt to suppose that tests of personality are a recent importation from the United States. Professor Vernon's book is, therefore, doubly welcome; it deals more specifically with the problems that confront the British student and seeks more particularly to cover the work of British contributors. Many readers will be astonished to discover how many of the various techniques which have recently been championed as American novelties are developments of devices invented by Galton, McDougall, and their followers nearly fifty years ago. Professor Vernon reminds us that what was "not only the first projection test, but also one of the earliest methods for exploring such differences" —the test of free association—was "developed by Galton in 1879." He does not, however, note that the earliest systematic investigation of such tests was carried out by a London Head Mistress—in her day one of the most famous of British educationists—Dr. Sophie Bryant. She applied several "tests of character" not only to her own school pupils but also to eminent psychologists like Stout and J. M. Cattell. It was McDougall who first aroused the active interest of psychologists and teachers in emotional and social characteristics; and the earliest attempt to compare various types of test—free association, apperception of inkblots and pictures, unconscious motor reactions, the psychogalvanic reaction, and various laboratory tests of pulse, breathing, and the like—on the basis of empirical correlations, was prompted by his suggestions, and eventually reported in the forerunner of this journal (*Journ. of Exp. Pedagogy and Training College Record*, I, 1912, pp. 279f.). * All who are concerned with the study of individual personality—teachers as well as educational psychologists—will find every page of his book well worth the closest examination and reflection. The discussion is both lucid and terse, the survey comprehensive and impartial; and few books on psychology have succeeded in packing so much information into so little space.

Brit J Med Psychol 28:84–5 pt 1 '55. R. M. *Mowbray.* * Vernon....presents a comprehensive survey of the approaches and methods of personality assessment by scholarly, canny and constant reference to the appropriate investigations. * Prof. Vernon's honesty might well be mistaken for pessimism. However, his conclusion that "even the application of the highest psychological skill and technical accomplishment cannot be expected to bring about rapid success" contains at least "cold comfort" for the clinician in his search for the relevant variables of personality. The psychometric approach to the assessment of personality has not yet shown enough supremacy to woo the busy psychiatrist away from his intuitions and judgements about personality.

Brit J Psychol 44:387–8 N '53. Florence Macneill. This book was badly needed from a British author. One would expect an objective and informative account of personality tests from Prof Vernon. * Throughout the book much research evidence is reviewed in evaluating the tests which have been selected for discussion. In the main the author is concerned with the descriptive rather than the explanatory approach. The general impression of the book,

however, is that it is another contribution to "trait" psychology. The author emphasizes that he is concerned to show which of the tests (very few) are actually usable in applied psychology. He believes, too, that even if it is considered to be a narrow approach, the difficulties arising out of the lack of a generally accepted framework for personality description can only be surmounted in the meantime by making use of a small number of operationally defined composite variables. One might criticize the author's general approach from the point of view that he seems over-concerned with regarding personality "tests" as potentially analogous to tests of intelligence and other abilities; one might question the existence of those many well validated tests of "other abilities." * Within its scope this book contains a great deal of information, and very good references.

J Consult Psychol 18:153 Ap '54. Laurance F. Shaffer. * a compact but impressively comprehensive survey of all methods used for the appraisal of personality: interviews, physical signs, expressive movements, tests, ratings, questionnaires, and projective techniques. His discussion is based mainly on research findings; almost every page cites relevant evidence to support his conclusions. American research studies are sampled wisely and references are made to numerous useful British studies which probably are less well known to American readers. Personality theory is given a subordinate role, represented only by an able but limited introductory chapter. Emphasis is placed on the use of assessments for educational and vocational selection in which criteria are available to permit the determination of validities. Measurement for clinical description is regarded as a "most intractable problem" because of the absence of appropriate external criteria. With its merits of thoroughness and unprejudiced objectivity, Vernon's book should find wide use as a text. Our students should be acquainted with it.

Occupational Psychol 28:121–2 Ap '54. Alec Rodger. Here is yet another remarkable display of Professor Vernon's erudition, and of his talent for presenting his facts and opinions with exceptional verbal economy. * the greater part of the material is quite new, and the whole is thoroughly documented with references to literature published only a few months before the book itself. The introduction gives a survey of relevant theory, with special comments on factor-analysis and type-psychologies. The reader who tackles it seriously will have to do a good deal of further study, if he is to derive full benefit from Dr Vernon's pithy summaries and comments; but that is what he is meant to do, and he will find the task a rewarding one. In the next chapter the author discusses interviewing, and although it may be questioned whether he is wise to talk and generalise about the validity and reliability of something called "the interview," it is clear that all the material gathered together in the chapter is very important. Then comes a chapter on physical signs of personality, inevitably thinner than the first two, and rather of the nature of a rest-pause, much needed before the three that follow, on expressive movements, simple behaviour and cognitive tests, and miniature and real-life situations. Next are chapters on ratings and judgments of personality, self-ratings and personality questionnaires, and the measurement of attitudes and interests, followed by a lively chapter on projection techniques. In his final chapter, called Conclusions and Future Developments, Dr Vernon flings out research topics in rich miscellany. As he truly remarks, "There is scarcely a method either praised or condemned in this book which could not be clarified by further investigation. Results are so variable in the personality field that the repetition, extension, and interlocking of previous researches would be more useful than the continued construction of more or less novel tests." It is probably true to say that no book published in this country in recent years shows more convincingly than his the need for planned advance along these lines.

Psychol B 51:288–9 My '54. Dan L. Adler. * Vernon reports and interprets data in a calm and studied manner. Because of its brief but unhurried digestion of assessment devices and its cogent but dignified criticism, this book is recommended to the students and scholars alike who desire an unbiased orientation to the field of personality testing. It brings no solace to those who seek vindication of one or another technique, but treats all techniques as legitimately adventurous early steps in the learning-to-walk period of valid assessment. * His eight-page concluding chapter, "Conclusions and Future Developments," is a masterpiece of fulsome brevity. It conveys neither the extent to which his summaries cut cleanly to the heart

of the evaluation, nor the number of research programs implicitly designed. Its three sections deal with the situations in which personality assessments are principally required: selection, experimentation, and diagnosis or guidance. The use of personality tests in selection procedures is the most successful, Vernon feels, because theoretical problems of personality are at a minimum, and external validation criteria are readily available. From the standpoint of diagnosis, guidance, treatment, and control, however, the reverse is true. Theoretical problems are maximal, and criteria—both internal and external—are generally lacking. For those who are familiar with Vernon as a protagonist of factorial and trait-composite research, his recognition that they are cross sectional, and not dynamic, may come as some surprise. Even more unexpected, perhaps, is his hope "that a more fruitful system will eventually replace [trait psychology]" (p. 205). His final plea is expressed as a need for the direct recording of behavior. This, he feels, will reconcile trait psychology with field theory, with the study of social groups and processes, and with longitudinal studies of personality development. Nowhere, perhaps, will the American psychologist be brought face to face with one of his own problems more clearly than in this book. His English colleagues have observed and have often pointed out the limitations of clinical techniques, such as interviews, Rorschachs, and ratings, when used as everyday diagnostic tools. Although the critical studies most often cited have been made in this country, they have had less influence here than abroad in actually changing practice. It appears to be difficult for at least two English psychologists of repute—Eysenck and Vernon—to understand how we can, at the same time, be scientifically self-critical and clinically self-indulgent. This trait composite has yet to be explored by the culture-oriented psychologist.

[B447]

★VERNON, P. E., EDITOR. **Secondary School Selection: A British Psychological Society Inquiry.** London: Methuen & Co. Ltd., 1957. Pp. 216. 15s. *

Brit J Psychol 48:307–9 N '57. F. W. Warburton. * the first of what, it is hoped, will be several volumes on topics of public interest, published under the auspices of the British Psychological Society * It is a chock-a-block with facts, arguments and theories, in which the influence of Prof. Vernon, who has edited the text, is clearly to be seen. Few psychologists will agree with all the findings put forward, but no one familiar with the problem could fail to appreciate the thoroughness and objectivity with which this task has been carried out, and it has certainly succeeded in showing how large a contribution psychology has made to this problem of national importance. This book should go a long way to dispel the notion that the eleven plus examination is strongly supported by all psychologists, most of whom, it asserts, dislike the system, and look to alternative types of school organization based on the concepts of allocation (blessed word) and guidance rather than competitive selection * The report errs perhaps in giving a rather piecemeal emphasis to clinical experience concerning the effect of the examination on the four-fifths of the population who fail it, even if the emotional effects on the children are probably less than the ill-feeling caused among the parents. * Educational administrators will find advice on numerous topics, including scaling techniques, the use of subjective data, age allowances, the expected number of grammar school misfits, the marking of essays, school records, teachers' estimates, the selection of children attending small schools, the delimitation of the border zone (50th to the 95th percentiles), various borderline procedures, individual and panel interviews, an account of the extremely thorough method used in the city of Lincoln, and the West Riding scheme for scaling against the junior schools' results in previous years, or retrospectively against the pupils' performance on tests given when they reach the secondary schools. The appendices might reasonably have included some material from the main text, as the discussion of such technicalities as multiple criteria and correction for attenuation and homogeneity are of little general interest, although everyone would be well advised to look at the appendices, if only to gain some insight into the complexities involved in selection. * The report emphasizes the very convincing evidence found in nearly every investigation of the superiority of the intelligence test as an overall predictor of later success, but fails to bring out clearly enough the additional advantage that fluctuations in I.Q., although larger than originally suspected, will usually be less than those in Arithmetic, English, or any other selection variable. The

important point is made that intelligence tests act much more as a class leveller than as a class perpetuator and that it would be more logical for left wing critics to welcome them than to decry them, since on both theoretical and experimental grounds it seems likely that in areas where the intelligence test has been abandoned fewer working-class children will gain grammar school places than in those areas where they still constitute part of the examination. Authorities who abolish intelligence tests are probably making a decision to withhold educational opportunity from working-class children. Teachers will be interested to know that, in an important investigation, the scaled teachers' estimates gave correlations of the same order as those of the external examinations, and higher than those of the objective attainment tests, although the likely error of a teacher's unscaled estimate of the average ability of his class is twice that of the error of an estimate based on a mediocre intelligence test. "Old type" examinations, when constructed by persons with experience of psychometric technique, can reach the same efficiency as the objective attainments test; and the essay, despite the unreliability inherent in its marking, does add appreciably to the validity of prediction, although no weight should be attached to a single marking of a single composition. The advice given about coaching is rather ambiguous. It is considered that coaching should be discouraged, but that if it cannot be controlled, adequate previous practice and explanation in all schools should be authorized. It is also admitted that the abilities of individual children are more variable than was earlier supposed, and that rigid streaming may have harmful educational and social consequences, although these are often exaggerated. * The report will also serve as a text-book for students, and as a guide to lecturers in educational psychology. It includes sections dealing with the history of intelligence testing, theories of the nature of intelligence, the work of Hebb, the effects of environment and heredity on test scores, and the normality of I.Q. distributions. The excellent suggestion is made that the term "general educability" should be substituted for "general intelligence," on the ground that this term makes no claim that psychologists are measuring purely innate ability. * Nor does this section on "How Far Do Intelligence Tests Measure Inborn Ability?" refer to the extensive work of Burt in this field, which also points to the predominance of genetic factors. Research strongly suggests that in our present system differences in I.Q. scores are mainly determined by heredity. * until contrary experimental results rather than hypotheses are advanced it would be more scientific to emphasize the innate component in intelligence test scores. Everyone would agree with the working party that psychologists should frankly acknowledge that a completely accurate classification is impossible at eleven years, but they should also add that perfect prediction of complex human behaviour at any age is impossible, and that psychological principles can no more be applied unerringly to individual children than the principles of physics can afford predictions of the exact path of a slate that falls off a roof. The important point is made that the best vindication for a system of selection is that it admits of fewer errors than would occur with any other method, and that we are now near the limits of predictive efficiency, which is a considerable technical achievement. Yet the claim on the dust cover that the procedure is accurate for some 90% of children may be disputed, since it assumes that the correlation of an imperfectly reliable selection procedure with a perfectly reliable scholastic criterion is close to plus 0.90. In fact, scholastic criteria are by no means perfectly reliable, and the effect of this correction for attenuation is to give a somewhat optimistic estimate of the efficiency of selection procedures, although the discrepancy is not very great. It must be remembered that (as stated in the text) a quarter of those selected, on present standards, do not deserve their place. And is it fair to state that in view of the high validities achieved we can hardly expect that "tinkering with" selection procedure, e.g. including essays as well as subjective English tests or additional personality assessments, would produce any marked improvement? The addition of essays and personality estimates are scarcely "tinkering," since they raise the reliability, mitigate backwash effects on the school curriculum, and may eventually replace the original tests without lowering the overall validity. Statistical psychologists will enjoy the appendices. * A question raised in everyone's mind is whether this report is not bolting the stable door after the horse has gone, since secondary school selection seems likely to be dropped by several authorities. However,

educational provision in this country is such that any immediate wholesale change seems improbable, and, in any case, the authors of this report believe that, if comprehensive schools become general, psychology will have at least as much to contribute to the techniques of diagnosis and guidance within such schools as it has to the more restricted aim of accurate selection.

[B448]

★VICTOR, FRANK. **Handwriting: A Personality Projection.** Springfield, Ill.: Charles C Thomas, Publisher, 1952. Pp. xii, 149. $3.75. (Oxford, England: Blackwell Scientific Publications, Ltd. 27s. 6d.) * (PA 26:6986)

J Consult Psychol 16:317 Ag '52. Laurance F. Shaffer. Victor's theory of graphology has a number of features that seem to commend it to psychologists: handwriting is regarded dynamically as expressive movement; the major concepts of release, tension, and energy are harmonious with all important systems of psychological theory. Other aspects are not so attractive: for example, the symbolic values of *above* (high, ideal) and *below* (low, imperfect) are applied arbitrarily to movements above and below the base line of handwriting. The validity of the system is supported only by arguments, cases, and appeals to "the collective experience of three generations of graphologists." A concluding note specifically rejects the experimental validation of graphology as "futile," leaving the critical reader with the impression that, as a verifiable and dependable technique, graphology is futile, too.

J Proj Tech 17:236-7 Je '53. Gerald S. Blum. "The changing slant often found in children's handwritings indicates that they cannot decide whether to turn to their father or mother for advice or warmth." This statement by Dr. Victor admittedly gives us a new "slant" on the age-old and sometimes very humorous problem of not knowing which way to turn. Unfortunately, though, the quotation, along with many similar pronouncements, also leaves the reviewer with a rather squirmy feeling in trying to evaluate the book. Assumptions which localize the Mother at the left side of a sheet of paper and the Father at the right are sufficiently intriguing to warrant some independent evidence. Instead the author, following the tradition of earlier works on handwriting, implicitly asks us to accept on faith what may be remarkable revelations. This will be difficult for some readers to do. The reviewer felt especially let down because the early pages of the book are liberally sprinkled with comments concerning the need to make graphology "scientific," the fallacy of applying pat interpretations, the desirability of training psychologists in the analysis of handwriting, and so on. The method which Victor advocates to accomplish such noble objectives is called "Basic Graphology." The latter system emphasizes the point that handwriting is a symbolic utilization of movement in space. Fundamental are the concepts of release, tension, and depth. Instead of trying to answer "What does this loop or hook mean?" Victor prefers to pose the question "How did this loop or hook originate?" In the author's words, the system "coordinates all the details of handwriting by recognizing in them a common basis for interpretation—movement." Besides organizing and unifying the content of handwriting analysis, Basic Graphology also neatly solves the problem of how to interpret handwriting psychologically. This *tour de force* is achieved with startling simplicity, merely by separating Basic from Applied Graphology. The former "deals only with the dynamic elements of handwriting and leaves the interpretation of these elements to Applied Graphology...." Thus Basic Graphology stands aloof from specific psychological theories, which are relegated to the applied realm. In fact the author amply demonstrates the versatility of his Applied Graphology by interpreting the same handwriting sample according to the theories of Jung, Kretschmer, Sheldon, and Horney! This solution to the problem of handwriting interpretation struck the present reviewer as ingenious but confusing. Logically it appears to beg the question. Granted the importance of techniques to analyze handwriting, the essence of graphology nevertheless must lie in psychological interpretation. Any separation of the two seems highly artificial. The book is clearly written and relatively easy to follow, except for some minor difficulty in trying to locate the appropriate illustrative figures. One may question the author's decision to concentrate on a few rather than a broad range of illustrative materials, but again this is not a serious objection. A noticeable omission in the bibliography, however, is Sonnemann's *Handwriting Analysis,* which has been widely read. In summary, Victor's monograph represents a sound contribution to methodology in hand-

writing study, but falls short of its mark with respect to the alignment of graphology with science.

Psychol B 50:163-4 Mr '53. Werner Wolff. * For the first time Victor makes the important point that basic psychological observation, which he calls "basic graphology," is a science of objective observation and can be independent of all graphological theories which, though interesting for any theory of personality, belong to what he calls "applied psychology." * the author would have better used the term "applied graphology" instead of "basic graphology," and "theoretical graphology" instead of "applied graphology." Victor calls handwriting a personality projection, considering the letters as somewhat similar to an inkblot. Although, as the present reviewer observed, letters may become a screen for even a projection of images, handwriting seems to him an expression rather than a projection. As a direct expression of inner motions in outer motions, handwriting is a graphogram, more similar to an electroencephalogram than to a Rorschach inkblot. Handwriting is the recording of inner psychological movements, of which Victor considers as the basic ones release, tension and output of energy. He compares in a suggestive way these different forms of rhythm with rhythmical forms in poetry. On one hand, the author makes the point that handwriting as a dynamic movement does not allow any fixed correlation between graphic forms and personality traits. On the other hand, he tries to establish a correlation between handwriting and constitutional types according to Sheldon. The author should have elaborated upon this double aspect. Handwriting is both form and expression, frozen gesture and flowing motion, and it is from the relationship of both that the personal equation results. Victor's book presents a good condensation of graphological concepts. However, it does not present any new observations and does not emphasize enough the need for graphological experiments and for a systematic correlation between elements of graphic expression and definable temperamental, clinical, and professional entities. The author's justified call for a basic graphology can be solved only if basic graphological elements can be correlated with basic mental and emotional patterns to be formulated by a scoring system. This, ultimately, will make graphology the most important psychodiagnostic instrument because the diagnosis by handwriting is the only tool which does not require the client's, or patient's, presence, and the diagnosis deals with the direct personality record itself, without using any foreign material such as inkblots or picture cards. With the proper technique it will take the least effort for a major output.

Psychol B 50:164–6 Mr '53. Julian B. Rotter. Most serious students of projective methods of personality measurement would at least concede that if factors of handedness, conditions of sampling, and special training are controlled, better than chance relationship may be found between some aspects of handwriting and similar aspects of other motor tasks. They might also agree that handwriting may reveal at a better than chance level such characteristics as the educational attainment or experience of the subject. In some cases markedly individualistic writing may allow for the "diagnosis" of some generalized and significant personality characteristics. Speaking generally, however, American psychologists have refused to accept the thesis that handwriting may be confidently used as an efficient, reliable, or valid method of predicting significant personality variables. * Since the author does not feel that it would be profitable to come to grips with the American tendency to insist upon objectivity, quantification and experimental tests, it is the reviewer's impression that this book will fail in its goal of obtaining wide acceptance of handwritting analysis in this country. It should be said in all fairness to the author, however, that the reviewer's handwriting reveals a veritable bonanza of pathologies and produces considerable aggression in his secretary. For the reviewer, the typewriter was a wonderful invention.

[B449]
★VÜTAMÄKI, R. OLAVI. **Personality Traits Between Puberty and Adolescence: Their Relationships, Development and Constancy With Reference to Their Relation to School Achievement.** Annals of the Finnish Academy of Science and Letters, Series B, No. 104. Helsinki, Finland: Suomalainen Tiedeakatemia, Academia Scientiarum Fennica, 1956. Pp. 183. Paper. 700 mk. *

[B450]
★WAGNER, MAZIE E. **Anticipatory Examinations for College Credit: Twenty Years Experience at the University of Buffalo.** University of Buffalo Studies, Vol. 20, No. 3. Buffalo, N.Y.: the University, 1952. Pp. 105–33. $0.50. * (*PA 27:8041*)

[B451]
★WALKER, ALICE S. **Pupils' School Records: A Survey of the Nature and Use of Cumulative**

School Records in England and Wales. National Foundation for Educational Research in England and Wales, Publication No. 8. London: published for the Foundation by Newnes Educational Publishing Co., Ltd., 1954. Pp. xviii, 199. 21s. *

Brit J Ed Psychol 26:236 N '56. * it is extremely valuable to have this comprehensive survey....to show us where we have got to and what are the essential difficulties and problems * Certainly, it will be our standard reference work on the subject for a long time to come. Miss Walker is, indeed, so thorough and fair in her presentation of all the arguments for and against every controversial point, that one almost regrets that she does not make more attempt herself to clear up the mess, and that she leaves so many points of policy for the reader to decide. For example, she is probably the first commentator to face up properly to the difficulties of making personality assessments, and to bring out the theoretical and practical impossibilities of covering personality by a series of allegedly normally distributed traits. Her own analysis of sets of ratings of eight hundred 11 year children's N.F.E.R. cards shows that 70 per cent of the variance of all the assessments (including I.Q., E.Q. and A.Q.) is accounted for by a single factor, presumably representing general educational adjustment; and that teachers in general do not consistently differentiate special abilities or personality traits to any useful extent. She does describe the attempts of certain L.E.As. to substitute other forms of personality description, but is unable to provide much in the way of positive recommendations. However, if this is a fault, it is in the right direction. More irritating is the extraordinary way in which the book is put together, with chapters, appendices and summaries mixed up higgledy-piggledy, and with no index; she even introduces totally new material into the final Summary and Conclusions. Though admittedly the topic is a complex one, there seems to be no reason why it should not be treated as a consecutive whole, nor why the administrator should be allowed to get away with the notion that he can understand the essential issues without reading the (slightly more technical) appendices. Actually, she writes so clearly that the educationist with a minimum of psychological and statistical training should find little difficulty in following her. However, it would be unfair for this review to leave the impression that Miss Walker and the National Foundation do not know their own minds. Far from it, the book embodies a very broad conception of the functions of record cards and, if one searches for it, one can find full discussions of, and much wise advice on every aspect of their use.

Brit J Ed Studies 4:83–5 N '55. R. R. Dale. "Pupils' School Records" is a very necessary but rather dull subject. That this book is not dull is therefore a tribute to the author's able organization of material and to her clear style. The description is competent and informative, criticism constructive and judgment notably well balanced. Teaching is an art which increasingly utilizes scientific aids. Intelligence tests, attainment tests, diagnostic tests, record cards, are all valuable tools in the hands of the skilled teacher, and the art of teaching consists in part in knowing when to use them. But this enquiry shows that many teachers are somewhat uncertain about their use and particularly uncertain about the best methods of recording the various types of examination results. * The National Foundation of Educational Research is to be congratulated on adding another useful and thoroughly sound publication to its list. This is a book which should be in the hands of every local education authority and in the library of every school.

[B452]

★WALLACE, ANTHONY F. C. **The Modal Personality of the Tuscarora Indians as Revealed by the Rorschach Test.** Smithsonian Institution, Bureau of American Ethnology, Bulletin 150. Washington, D.C.: United States Government Printing Office, 1952. Pp. viii, 120. Paper. $0.60. * (*PA* 27:6505)

[B453]

★WALTON, LEWIS E. **Methods of Pupil Appraisal.** Guidance Workbook Series, No. 3. Coral Gables, Fla.: University of Miami Bookstore, 1951. Pp. iv, 39. Paper, mimeographed. $1.00. *

[B454]

★WANDT, EDWIN, AND BROWN, GERALD W. **Essentials of Educational Evaluation.** New York: Henry Holt & Co., Inc., 1957. Pp. 125. Paper. $1.40. *

Ed & Psychol Meas 18:420–1 su '58. Edith Jay. In approximately 100 pages, this inexpensive little book introduces the prospective teacher to some of the measurement and evaluation problems involved in classroom teaching. Whenever a course in measurement is not a curriculum requirement in teacher training this text fills a definite need for a unit on this important subject. * The authors have done a surprisingly good job of keeping the material

coherent and scientifically sound in spite of its simplicity. * Appendix B is a short discussion of reliability and validity. Illustrations are well chosen and diverse in content. * As a unit within some more general course, it appears to have considerable value. As a textbook for a course in measurement it would be far too brief. The style is straightforward, concise and clear. Impossible standards of perfection are not presented. The writer feels that a teacher may show even greater ingenuity after this introduction than after studying a more ponderous and mathematical treatise. While no very high level of sophistication is reached, at least the student may be encouraged to continue to study in the field * This reviewer recommends the book for use in any introductory course where a self contained unit of this sort is needed. If the exercises are conscientiously done, the volume can contribute greatly to the elementary school teacher's handling of evaluation tasks, from report card making to the daily quiz. If, in addition, the suggested additional readings are suitably assigned, the unit may lead to a greater breadth of understanding than is gained in more technical courses. However, secondary teachers probably would need some supplementation of the unit in the several subject fields, which are included in the text.

[B455]

★WANDT, EDWIN, AND OSTREICHER, LEONARD M. **Validity of Samples of Classroom Behavior for the Measurement of Social-Emotional Climate.** American Psychological Association, Psychological Monographs: General and Applied, Vol. 68, No. 5, Whole No. 376. Washington, D.C.: the Association, Inc., 1954. Pp. 12. Paper. $1.00. * (*PA* 29:4622)

[B456]

★WANDT, EDWIN, AND OSTREICHER, LEONARD M. **Variability in Observed Classroom Behaviors of Junior High School Teachers and Classes.** College of the City of New York, Division of Teacher Education, Office of Research and Evaluation, Publication No. 16. New York: the Division, 1953. Pp. iv, 31. Paper, mimeographed. * (*PA* 28:4975)

[B457]

★WARBURTON, F. W. **The Selection of University Students.** Publications of the University of Manchester School of Education, No. 1. Manchester, England: University of Manchester Press, 1952. Pp. vii, 46. 4s. 6d. *

Brit J Ed Psychol 22:221 N '52. This is a very useful survey of methods of selection of University students, including an examination of evidence as to the value of the Higher School Certificate results, Headmaster's Reports, Interviews, Intelligence and Aptitude Tests. The exposition is clear and admirably concise, and the general attitude critical and well balanced. The booklet is the first research publication of Manchester University School of Education, and provides a very promising start.

Occupational Psychol 28:58 Ja '54. A. H. D. Tozer. * an admirably clear non-technical account of the problems involved in the selection of university students and a survey of research work on the subject done and still going on in Great Britain, including some investigations in several departments of Manchester University which do not appear to have been published * A useful bibliography sensibly distinguishes between British work in this field and that carried out in the USA where conditions are very different. *

[B458]
★WATTERS, LORAS J. **Factors in Achievement in Mathematics: A Study of the Factor Patterns Resulting From Analyses of the Scores of Boys and Girls in Junior Year of High School on One Mathematics Test.** Catholic University of America, Educational Research Monographs, Vol. 18, No. 3. Washington, D.C.: Catholic University of America Press, Inc., 1954. Pp. 62. Paper. $1.00. *

[B459]
★WATTS, A. F. **Can We Measure Ability?** London: University of London Press Ltd., 1953. Pp. 80. Paper 3s. *

Brit J Ed Psychol 24:127 Je '54. * The clear and easy approach in the early chapters would make a very good introduction to the subject for teachers and others who are sceptical about the value of intelligence tests and largely ignorant of what they have been proved to do. * In discussing the problem of the late developer, Dr. Watts gives evidence of fluctuations in the orders of children in intelligence test scores at the ages of 8, 11, 13 and 16. But such records fail to give due weight to the different nature of the tests necessarily used at such different ages, and to the fact that several tests about the same time are necessary to give a reliable estimate of a child's general intelligence at that time. A few marked fluctuations may occur in a large group of children even with a very similar test given only a week or so later. Still, the booklet is a sensible and clear exposition for beginners.

[B460]
★WATTS, A. F.; PIDGEON, D. A.; AND YATES, A. **Secondary School Entrance Examinations: A Study of Some of the Factors Influencing Scores in**

Objective Tests With Particular Reference to Coaching and Practice: Second Interim Report on the Allocation of Primary School Leavers to Courses of Secondary Education. National Foundation for Educational Research in England and Wales, Publication No. 6. London: Newnes Educational Publishing Co. Ltd., 1952. Pp. 77. 6s 6d. *

A.M.A. 48:96-7 F '53. After studying the full N.F.E.R. Report—everyone should do so —I feel that the investigators have sometimes overestimated the range and validity of their results. They have sometimes relied on numbers far too small for statistical safety. Even in the London experiment, complete results were obtained only for 1,214 children, which probably means that less than 50 teachers were involved; and, since the children were divided into eight groups, it may well be that no more than six teachers were concerned with the coaching of any particular group. Now the teacher is all-important; there are just as many ways of coaching for intelligence tests as for anything else; and every teacher is either unique or incompetent. I must, therefore, assume that a multitude of complicating factors are imperfectly represented, or unrepresented, in the results. One such factor, recognised in the pilot Twickenham experiment, appears to have been ignored in the larger London one. In the former, among secondary modern pupils, it was found that slackening of interest which affected the results could be remedied by the offer of money prizes. Now the lure of admission to a grammar school is a potent stimulus also. The London pupils, who had already been allocated to secondary schools at the time of the experiment, seem to have lacked such stimuli. Under the circumstances, it is not surprising that those coached for six hours got bored. The fact that those coached for nine hours did better than those coached for six, and as well as those coached for three, probably indicates that good teaching will ultimately triumph over the most boring syllabus. In this connection, I note that, in the pilot Twickenham Experiment, a majority of the (stimulated) children reached their peak of achievement only at the eighth, ninth, or tenth of ten tests; in other words, most of them were still improving after ten tests. Now, in many junior schools, coaching is given not in large doses over a relatively short period, but in small daily doses continued for a year or more. The effect of such coaching has not yet been investigated, I think; it is probably very great indeed. However that may be, it is clear that to stop practice after "at least two," or after any small number of tests, is to favour a minority at the expense of the majority. One important complication, recognised by the investigators, is ignored in their summary. Boys profit from coaching more than girls, girls from practice more than boys. Thus, it may be especially profitable to coach boys. There is the further fact, recognised by everyone, that individual children vary in their response to coaching and practice. We may see coachers developing a technique of giving a bit of coaching to all, selecting those who profit much from it, and then giving to those a bit more.... and so on. Unfair?....I don't think it wise to call coaching unfair. Every good teacher is tempted to do his best for his pupils. Many cannot resist the temptation. It is very dangerous to impress a contrary principle on the others. If, then, I condemn the idea of universal coaching, it is for reasons other than those of the investigators. To me, universal coaching would be a bad way of bolstering a bad test. * On the question of transfer after 11+, the investigators again confirm the results of our own experience. Why is it that candidates from secondary modern schools generally do worse in the Allocation Examination than they did a year earlier? Can it be that in the secondary modern school they miss their little daily dose of coaching?

Brit J Psychol 45:147 My '54. A. H. D. T. * Its content is accurately indicated by the subtitle "a study of some of the factors influencing scores in objective tests with particular reference to coaching and practice." The authors survey a number of recent investigations into the effects of coaching and practice and describe some experiments of their own designed to answer certain definite questions about their influence. There remain some inconsistencies between the findings of different investigators which are not cleared up, and there are some puzzling results which are difficult to interpret. It is hard to see, for example, why both three hours and nine hours of coaching should consistently be more effective than six hours. * The authors disapprove of universal coaching for the intelligence test which has been recommended in some quarters and see no need for it. They advise sufficient practice to swamp the effects of differences in preparation—not a great deal is necessary. They have also a number of sensible comments and recommendations on the general problem of secondary school allocation and indicate where further research is especially needed.

[B461]

★WAVERLEY, MARTIN. **Preparation for the Working of Intelligence Tests.** London: George G. Harrap & Co. Ltd., 1953. Pp. 43. 5s. *

[B462]

★WEBB, SAM C. **Studies of Scale and Ambiguity Values Obtained by the Method of Equal-Appearing Intervals.** American Psychological Association, Psychological Monographs: General and Applied, Vol. 69, No. 3, Whole No. 388. Washington, D.C.: the Association, Inc., 1955. Pp. 20. Paper. $1.00. * (*PA* 30:133)

[B463]

*WECHSLER, DAVID. **The Measurement and Appraisal of Adult Intelligence, Fourth Edition.** Baltimore, Md.: Williams & Wilkins Co., 1958. Pp. ix, 296. $5.00. * (London: Baillière, Tindall & Cox, Ltd. 40s.) For reviews of earlier editions, see 3:299–301, and 40:B1121; for related reviews, see 414–5, 4:361, 3:298, and 40:1429.

[B464]

★WEISS, RAYMOND A., AND PHILLIPS, MARJORIE. **Administration of Tests in Physical Education.** St. Louis, Mo.: C. V. Mosby Co., 1954. Pp. 278. Paper, lithotyped. $4.50. *

[B465]

★WELCH, JOSEPHINE S., AND STONE, C. HAROLD. **How to Build a Merchandise Knowledge Test.** University of Minnesota, Industrial Relations Center, Research and Technical Report 8. Dubuque, Iowa: Wm. C. Brown Co., 1952. Pp. vi, 21. Paper, lithotyped. $1.00. * (*PA* 27:734)

J Appl Psychol 37:64 F '53. Edwin E. Ghiselli. This excellent monograph concisely presents the methods for the development of job knowledge tests. * the procedures are general and can be applied to any type of job. The authors do not claim that they are describing any new methods. What they have done is to bring together for trade tests the procedures for item development, item validation, test validation, cross validation, and the setting of critical scores, in a most clear and logical fashion. The rationale for each step is well outlined. The monograph is liberally documented with judiciously chosen illustrations, so that each step is readily understandable. The monograph will not only serve as a technical manual for those concerned with selection problems, but should be an invaluable piece of outside reading for a course in test construction or in psychological measurement. The only shortcoming is in the discussion of the types of items that might be used in job information tests. While a reader unfamiliar with the field will ultimately obtain some notion concerning the scope of possible items, in no single section is this aspect well developed.

[B466]
★WELCH, JOSEPHINE; STONE, C. HAROLD; AND PATERSON, DONALD G. **How to Develop a Weighted Application Blank.** University of Minnesota, Industrial Relations Center, Research and Technical Report 11. Dubuque, Iowa: Wm. C. Brown Co., 1952. Pp. vi, 19. Paper, lithotyped. $1.00. * (*PA 27* :8066)

[B467]
★WELSH, GEORGE SCHLAGER, AND DAHLSTROM, W GRANT, EDITORS. **Basic Readings on the MMPI in Psychology and Medicine.** Minneapolis, Minn.: University of Minnesota Press, 1956. Pp. xvii, 656. $8.75. (London: Oxford University Press. 70s.) * (*PA 31*: 1080)

Am J Orthopsychiatry 27:841–2 O '57. Frederick A. Zehrer. * The editors have done a good job of selecting materials * One who has not been exposed to the University of Minnesota clinical psychology training program may not find it easy to comprehend the devotion and attendant emphasis given the MMPI as a diagnostic instrument. The 689 titles listed in the bibliography include 27 Ph.D. dissertations written by University of Minnesota graduate students (including both editors, in 1949) and 37 Ph.D. dissertations produced by students in other universities. In addition, 34 Master's degree theses are listed. * For anyone using the MMPI, or interested in adding to evaluative procedures in a clinical or research setting, the book should prove to be a useful library addition. It contains much to stimulate critical discussion which should assist in the development of a concept among beginners wherein the MMPI can be accepted as one of several useful evaluative instruments.

Can J Psychol 12:55–6 Mr '58. Richard H. Walters. * The editors present brief and generally somewhat superficial introductions to the sections, each of which is followed by a footnote indicating the sources of the material for the section being introduced. A survey of these footnotes indicates that there is, in fact, much less original material in this volume than the authors' foreword might lead us to expect. Undoubtedly, it is convenient to have so much pertinent material on the MMPI presented together in a single volume. In view of the inadequacy of the manual which accompanies the test, the bringing together of information about the construction of the scales is especially valuable. However, if the reader already has doubts about the value of psychological an-

thologies, this publication will almost certainly serve to strengthen them. In the first place, no attempt has been made to indicate the extent to which individual articles have been subjected to the editorial axe. Secondly, the introductory sections provide little in the way of critical appraisal of the material which is presented. The editors' time might have been spent more profitably in providing psychologists with an account, both descriptive and evaluative, of the development of the MMPI and of the extent to which its subsequent employment in research and practice has revealed its potentialities and weaknesses. A sufficiently stimulating account might also have served, more than the present book, to direct the reader's attention to the original articles. These weaknesses detract from the value of this text as a systematic contribution. However, as a source book for the busy clinician, it is a convenient and well-organized reference.

Cont Psychol 2:80–1 Mr '57. Irwin A. Berg. * the scope of research interest in the MMPI is a phenomenon without close parallel in the history of professional psychology. The present book is, in part, a recognition by editors Welsh and Dahlstrom that Johnny-come-latelies to the MMPI scene simply cannot cover the available literature. So, in consultation with Starke Hathaway, one of the MMPI authors, they selected 66 articles (including some unpublished materials) with the goal of providing a representative ten-percent sample. They were successful in achieving their goal. A comparison of several of the original articles with the edited version shows some pruning and snipping, but this literary surgery was so skillfully executed that the abbreviated articles represent an improvement in each instance. As in all many-authored volumes, the style, of course, varies widely from author to author. There is sparkling, incisive prose by Paul Meehl, straightforward declarative sentences from L. E. Drake, and determined, clumping phrases by Welsh. Yet, for all that, the book gets its content across rather effectively. This is not to assert that *Basic Readings* in the MMPI is without flaw. At times, for example, the editors work overtime in striving to avoid the slightest shadow's being cast upon the MMPI. Their handling of the *Mf* scale is a case in point. This particular scale is really not capable of a reasonably valid identification of individual homosexuals as it was intended to be, apparently because homosexuals can usually obtain "normal" scores if they so choose. In this connection, when Cottle in a 1953 review of the MMPI literature summarized a study by Benton, he noted, "When Benton retested nine homosexuals with instructions to fake normal, six were able to secure normal scores." But when the editors refer to the Benton study in an introduction to the section on psychiatric problems, they note (p. 375), "Of the ten cases of homosexuality, four were not able to reduce their scale 5 (*Mf*) scores." The increase from nine to ten cases apparently came from some unpublished data supplied by Benton. There is probably nothing wrong with digging up an extra case nor with reversing the original author's negative statement to a positive form, since the article itself is reprinted later in the book; yet the fact remains that two-thirds of a small group of confessed homosexuals were able to fake normal *Mf* scores. Further, non-homosexual college students who take the MMPI under standard administration procedures often obtain significantly high *Mf* ratings. Glossing over or ignoring such data is unnecessary, even misleading, and serves to weaken somewhat an otherwise excellent book. The MMPI is a splendid clinical instrument and needs no verbal pirouettes to distract attention from an occasional shortcoming in a few of the scales. * The psychologist who studies Welsh and Dahlstrom's selections will understand the significance of the MMPI as a carefully conceived and painstakingly validated schedule. He will know the theory behind the test, how the test was constructed, and he will grasp the meaning of the various scales as well as their diagnostic significance. The mysteries of coding test profiles will be unravelled as thoroughly as it is possible to accomplish this end in print, and the reasons why the MMPI is far more than just a super *Bernreuter Personality Inventory* will also be apparent. Further, the reader will obtain a fair picture of how the test works out in clinical settings and as a general personality measure. All in all, the editors have done a good job.

J Counsel Psychol 4:78 sp '57. Charles McArthur. * The book is a source book. Its editors deserve praise for selecting with judgment, grouping with clarity, and cutting with intelligence a vast, technical, and unreadable literature. * Unnecessary duplications, like parallel "reviews of the literature," have been cut out of these versions of the journal articles and some editorial matter has been added to aid the continuity of what is, after all, an anthology. If one reads rapidly from cover to cover, one unreels the story of the MMPI's development. At the same time any single article repays close perusal. Bibliographies contain 689 and 181 items. Psychometric methodology underlying the MMPI is scrupulously reported. The chapters on each scoring scale are most welcome. Some have not appeared in print before. The reader is glad to know just how each scale was derived. He may occasionally register shock, as at discovering that only nine items in one scale are nonoverlapping with two or more other scales, or that another scale was validated against a group not in the diagnostic category for which one would assume the scale to be named. The provincial origins of the samples on which these scales were "validated" may startle a sociologically-minded reader. Some comfort appears later in the book, however, when it turns out that the scales almost always cross-validate on quite different samples of the American population. * In summary, the book does contain, as its title claims, "basic readings." They will remain basic so long as the MMPI and the new look in psychometrics that seems to be growing out of MMPI thinking retain their importance in psychology. The usefulness of the test itself seems beyond question. The chief criticism one must level against the test—at least as it is represented in this volume—is its lack of systematic rationale. Much of the science offered is low-level generalization, mere psychometric methodology or patchwork insight into human dynamics. At moments one is fascinated by the insight, as when it is shown how even "expert" judges misjudge the verbal behavior that will be shown in neurosis, but at moments one is struck by the lack of awareness of the rest of psychology, as when the first two factors in the MMPI turn out to be very familiar factors in the Rorschach, or even the humble Brownfain, and no writer seems aware of the duplication. As a case history in how psychology goes nowadays, this volume is without peer. Instrument-bound thinking seems to be pretty widespread in our profession. If MMPI enthusiasts get bound up in the clerical game of "coding" their test, one must be aware that Rorschach enthusiasts spend a lot of energy devising multiple systems for "scoring" theirs. It is to be hoped that both specialists may soon come to see that they are proving the same laws of human nature, e.g., that being worried about oneself vs. unthinking acting-out is a major polarity, or that the American core culture produces slightly psychopathic, hypomanic, CF, D males who do well in the business world, "selling" themselves and their product. May this reviewer dare hope that one day it will be agreed that commonalities in findings are worth more emphasis than differences in method?

Psychometrika 23:385–6 D '58. Lee J. Cronbach. A collection of 66 papers and a 698-item bibliography provide a systematic compilation of representative information on the most prominent of all personality inventories. The collection is an excellent representation of papers interesting to the clinician, covering the basic validations of the instrument, the principal papers on fringe scales for dominance, ego-strength, and so on, and naturalistic reports on patient groups whose diagnoses range from alcoholism to cancer. The articles are skillfully edited to avoid duplication, and new papers written specially for the volume fill critical gaps. The reports of the scale development present a fascinating example of the research process in the hands of flexible investigators who can be honest with themselves. The first papers (ca. 1940) optimistically embarked on developing quantitative discriminant scales for psychiatric diagnosis. As the validities proved disappointing, trial and error was used in the hope of improvement. One hopeful attack introduced suppressor items, and later (1946) the K scale to correct for test-taking attitudes. Even the corrected scales were not very much in agreement with diagnoses, and from this date forward the papers increasingly deny that prediction of such criteria is or should be the function of the test. The most meaningful subsequent research is directed to connecting scales and patterns with general descriptive constructs. Considering the prominence the *MMPI* attained by virtue of its timely appearance, just as the war thrust new demands upon clinical psychology, it is incredible that its foundations are so shaky. The authors, though painstaking, established weights for items on tiny clinical samples. The sample N's for original item selection were as

follows: *HS,* 50; *D,* 50; *PT,* 20; *Hy,* several samples; *Ma,* 24; *PD,* 100 plus a second sample of unstated *N;* etc. The fact that *MMPI* scales have worked at all on cross-validation conflicts sharply with the opinion of many authorities that samples for establishing item weights should be 500 or larger. The authors freely criticized their own scales, repeatedly using such words as "disappointing" and "weak." Three of the main scales, indeed, were released with the intention of replacing them later. Hindsight indicates that the inventory was designed quite inefficiently. The *T-F-?* pattern invites maximal distortion by response sets; the indiscriminate mixing of obvious and subtle items prevents the interpreter from capitalizing on the virtues of either type; the weighting of items which differentiate patient groups from normals may leave wholly out of consideration items which differentiate patient groups from each other, and leads to undesirably high scale intercorrelations. [In a patient sample, eight intercorrelations out of 36 are between .60 and .86 (p. 259)]. Moreover, the generally very low intercorrelations between *MMPI* scales and the *CPI* scales derived by Gough from essentially the same items indicate that the basic *MMPI* scores extract only a small fraction of the information in the responses. The papers presented show consistent but weak relations between *MMPI* and behavior. The research reports are too little integrated to indicate just how much confidence can be placed in any particular interpretation. A number of studies suggest that clinicians assign patients to categories with about 70 per cent success, in experiments where chance success would be 50 per cent. None of the studies in this volume bear on the more pertinent question of success when realistic base rates are taken into account. This volume is not a collection of model studies. Few studies contain gross errors, but many of them reflect designs and conceptualizations which have become outmoded in the last decade. The investigations which seem most meritorious in terms of their soundness and informativeness are those by Black on college girls (p. 151), Peterson on predicting hospitalization of outpatients (p. 407), Schiele and Brozek on experimental starvation (p. 461), and Barron on ego-strength (p. 579). Two of the four are written for this volume. Some older studies show several faults in addition to neglect of base rates and use of small samples. In studies of group differences the significance tests outnumber the subjects as much as 20 to 1; under these conditions, probability values are meaningless. "Signs" are generally cross-validated in a suitable manner, but in one instance (p. 311) the signs are revised on the second sample and significance is then tested on the same cases for the revised signs. Elsewhere (p. 330) signs are claimed to give a significant χ^2 for selection of teachers, but correct application of a 2 x 2 table would show nonsignificance. Outside of two papers by Gough, insufficient recognition is given to facade or "hello-goodbye" effects. In this book, as in other *MMPI* literature, great emphasis is placed on "patterns." This term is applied indiscriminately, and the experimental designs rarely bear on the conclusions drawn. Conclusions of the form *"Pt* is higher than *Sc* in group X" should be tested by showing what proportion of group X has $(Pt - Sc) > 0$. The majority of studies make such interpretations from inspection of the mean difference, and compute significance by showing that one or both scores taken separately differ from the normal—a finding irrelevant to the conclusion. As in this example the so-called "patterns" are often no more than simple difference scores. The writer would advocate reserving the terms "pattern" and "configuration" for conjunctive, nonlinear formulas. Where nonlinear formulas are offered (for example in Welsh's internalization ratio), the claim for configural validity ought to be supported by showing that this statistically awkward form is actually more valid than a suitable linear composite. The study by Little and Shneidman (p. 332), the most truly configural in the book, requires special criticism. A *Q*-sort of a single case was made by *MMPI* judges and *Q*-correlated with the sort made on the basis of the clinical case record. The average validity is said to be .67. Such an index is meaningless by itself, since selection of statements could swing the validity in either direction by almost any amount. In this case it reflects chiefly an impression of bad adjustment (four *T*-scores are over 90!) rather than a "personality pattern." The *Q*-sort for *any other patient* with manifest extreme disturbance would surely correlate highly with the criterion for this man. As a minimum, the authors should show how the correlation for

A's *MMPI* sort with *A*'s criterion sort compares to correlations of *MMPI* sorts for patients *B, C,* and *D* with *A*'s criterion sort. One can only commend the compilers for providing so adequate a picture of *MMPI* history. A reader is left with respect for the progress we have made, particularly in discarding over-optimistic expectations. He should also be dismayed that so much conscientious effort on our most carefully planned personality inventory leaves us in our present state. Interpretation of *MMPI* profiles rests far more on the interpreter's "experience" than on validated principles. Within any typical intake group in a clinic or a student body, it seems quite doubtful that one can consistently make dependable inferences about an individual's degree of disturbance or personality structure. It is fortunate that so many of these papers urge that the test be used only tentatively, as a supplement to other means of investigating the individual.

Psychosom Med 19:263–4 My–Je '57. George A. Talland. A characteristic feature of contemporary psychology is diffuse experimentation with a few popular instruments and techniques, often in relation to problems far removed from those for which these instruments were originally designed. This kind of experimentalism is evidently rewarding to its practitioner, and may indeed produce findings of wider significance every so often. Whether the best corrective of its defects is the publication of readings is more open to doubt, but then readings, too, are in fashion. Conceivably, the most valuable service a dedicated student might have rendered to the Minnesota Multiphasic Personality Inventory would be a systematic presentation of the theory on which this test was designed, an evaluation of its services in clinical diagnosis, and a critical account of the various attempts to extend its use. The material for all this is certainly incorporated in this huge volume, but the arduous task of sifting the wheat from the chaff has been left entirely to the reader who may question the worth of the effort. No doubt, the editors are well qualified to do this for him, or else they would not have undertaken the project which has materialized in this book, but their brief introductory chapters are unlikely to help the reader, no matter how little or how much he knows about this test or of psychological work in general; and their selection of the 66 articles suggests a catholic reverence for the technique rather than a thoughtful appraisal of its achievements. The book is offered with a utilitarian justification; i.e. to make available conveniently in one volume a selection of articles dispersed in many journals, for the clinician, research worker, and teacher. Few of these are likely to be satisfied with the work of selection or abstraction done for them. Having registered a protest against the uneconomic presentation of the material, the reviewer must acknowledge that many interesting observations and results are scattered over the pages, and several chapters, particularly those contributed by Meehl, would make instructive reading for the clinical psychologist or psychometrician. It is evident that the MMPI has not adequately solved the problems of diagnostic testing, but has achieved a certain success toward this goal, and has been used more thoughtfully by some than most other personality tests. Much care and ingenuity has been spent on validating the test, and on isolating its component scales. It is therefore disappointing to discover that, even though applied as a configural test, the MMPI has no characteristic normal pattern, that its most common profile is typical of only 4.3 per cent of the population sampled, and that "masculinity" is the most common peak for women as well as for men. No harm will be done as long as the exponents of this technique adhere to their avowed operationism. The methodological restraints of the founders, however, do not seem to have passed on to all the others who have borrowed the instrument, and conclusions of several chapters bristle with the meaningless platitudes at the depth level, so familiar from the literature of clinical psychology. Plausible conjectures are presented as findings, rather than as hypotheses to be tested, as in the last of one author's three widely separated chapters on his "ego-strength" scale. The same chapters also illustrate how this psychometric method can be exploited for personality theory. In sum, quite a number of useful lessons can be drawn from this book, and clinicians or research workers who prefer to use selected readings for their source of information will find it informative on questions relating to the MMPI.

[B468]
★WERDELIN, INGVAR. **The Mathematical Ability: Experimental and Factorial Studies**. Studia Psy-

chologica et Paedagogica Series Altera, Investigationes 9. Lund, Sweden: C W K Gleerups, 1958. Pp. 356. Paper. Sw. kr. 25. *

[B469]
★WERNICK, ROBERT. **They've Got Your Number**. New York: W. W. Norton & Co., Inc., 1956. Pp. 124. $2.95. *

Col & Univ 33:66 f '57. H. J. Sheffield. This book, written for sale to the general reading public, has a racy, breezy style, parallels its text in part with cartoons, and dedicates itself to debunking tests and testers. The psychometrician, the psychologist, and the personnel specialist see themselves stripped of much of their glamour and one of their crutches. * Persons who are subjected to tests are urged to use physical violence, cheat, or take every test in sight so as to become "test sophisticated." In order to answer most test questions correctly, the person being tested is urged to try to put himself in the place of a stupid psychologist making up a test. When called upon to take a test in applying for a position, "The general rule is this: get a clear idea of what kind of position you are aiming at, concentrate on some particular person you know who is filling that position successfully, and then answer the questions as if you were that person." * The book doesn't live up to its colorful jacket with its promise that it is "All about the mind measures, the psychological testers, and the plans they have for you." Members of the general public who read the book won't know whether or not to believe it. Those who read it with a background in tests and testing will range in their reactions from mild anger and rejection, to condescension with an occasional faint chuckle of superior mirth at the author, at the psychologist, and at themselves.

Psychiatric Q Sup 30:144 pt 1 '56. The author of this broad lampoon on psychological tests and psychological testers does not identify himself, but he could be a disillusioned professional on a mildly hypomanic holiday, or he could be a disgruntled student doing some heavy projecting. At any rate, *They've Got Your Number* is a lively custard-pie comedy with psychology and psychologists as the targets. The material covered is considerable, if superficial; and, if the author is not in the field himself, he seems to have had the benefit of expert advice on points and procedures vulnerable to criticism. *They've Got*

Your Number appears to have been published as general humor, perhaps with an idea of Christmas sales. Fortunately, it is a little esoteric for enthusiastic public purchasing; for the unsophisticated reader, if he managed to understand it, might conclude that psychology is a racket and its practitioners pretty poor specimens indeed. How the informed reader will react may depend on the state of his sense of humor and on his ability to applaud custard pie in the face of the just as well as of the unjust. This reviewer thinks that all of us in the field—not simply the psychologists—may sometimes overdo the testing business and overlook the limitations of test procedures. Wernick's lampoon of this test-happy state of mind may serve a useful end; and some not-too-sensitive folk will be immoderately amused by it besides.

[B470]

★WESTERN REGIONAL CONFERENCE ON TESTING. **First Annual Western Regional Conference on Testing Problems, April 4, 1952.** Francis L. Bacon, Chairman. Princeton, N.J.: Educational Testing Service, [1952]. Pp. ii, 59. Paper, plastic binding, lithotyped. Out of print. *

[B471]

★WESTERN REGIONAL CONFERENCE ON TESTING. **Second Annual Western Regional Conference on Testing Problems, 1953.** Clifford P. Froehlich, Chairman. Princeton, N.J.: Educational Testing Service, [1953]. Pp. iv, 41. Paper, plastic binding, lithotyped. Out of print.

[B472]

★WESTERN REGIONAL CONFERENCE ON TESTING PROBLEMS. **Third Annual Western Regional Conference on Testing Problems, March 12, 1954.** H. B. McDaniel, Chairman. Princeton, N.J.: Educational Testing Service, [1954]. Pp. iv, 64. Paper, plastic binding, lithotyped. $1.00. *

[B473]

★WESTERN REGIONAL CONFERENCE ON TESTING PROBLEMS. **Fourth Annual Western Regional Conference on Testing Problems, March 4, 1955.** D. Welty Lefever, Chairman. Princeton, N.J.: Educational Testing Service, [1955]. Pp. iv, 87. Paper, plastic binding, lithotyped. $1.00. * (*PA* 30:1617)

[B474]

★WESTERN REGIONAL CONFERENCE ON TESTING PROBLEMS. **Fifth Annual Western Regional Conference on Testing Problems, April 13, 1956.** Harry Smallenburg, Chairman. Princeton, N.J.: Educational Testing Service, [1956]. Pp. iii, 78. Paper, plastic binding, lithotyped. $1.00. * (*PA* 31:8486)

[B475]

★WESTERN REGIONAL CONFERENCE ON TESTING PROBLEMS. **The Sixth Annual Western Regional Conference on Testing Problems, March 8, 1957.** Quinn McNemar, Chairman. Princeton, N.J.: Educational Testing Service, [1957]. Pp. ii, 59. Paper, plastic binding, lithotyped. $1.00. *

[B476]

★WESTERN REGIONAL CONFERENCE ON TESTING PROBLEMS. **The Seventh Annual Conference on Testing Problems: Testing for the Discovery and Development of Human Talent, March 14, 1958.** William B. Michael, Chairman. Princeton, N.J.: Educational Testing Service, [1958]. Pp. ii, 76. Paper, plastic binding, lithotyped. $1.00. *

[B477]

★WHILDE, NOEL E. **The Application of Psychological Tests in Schools.** London: Blackie & Son Ltd., 1955. Pp. xi, 179. 9s. *

Brit J Ed Psychol 25:211–2 N '55. *Stephen Wiseman.* This is an elementary book, designed for teachers. It covers intelligence and attainment testing in some detail, and looks briefly at performance tests, personality tests, rating scales, etc. Many of the staff-room criticisms of tests are considered and met, and the advice on the use of tests is, on the whole, sound and helpful. The author's experience and interests (in child guidance) are to some extent reflected in the relative emphasis laid on different topics. For example, "reliability" receives a most cursory treatment, although a fuller development of this, leading to a discussion of standard error of score, would have illuminated the section on "constancy of the I.Q." and helped to prevent the not uncommon belief in the accuracy of quotients to within one point. The author quite rightly says, in his preface: "Tests suffer from those who claim too much for them as well as from those who are prejudiced against them." It is probable that, for books at this level, it is more important to prevent an increase in numbers in the former category than to attempt to reform those already in the latter. For this reason alone, it is unfortunate that the list of test material available contains such things as the Lowenfeld Mosaic and Kaleidobloc tests and Burt's Questionnaire on Neurotic Symptoms. In any case, a long list of intelligence and attainment tests such as this does little to help the teacher to choose the test which really suits his purpose. Even the time-lengths are given for only a few of them. A shorter list, with fuller informative (and critical) notes, would be more useful. Probably this book would be most effectively used in teachers' courses, to supplement other reading such as Vernon's *Measurement of Abilities,* Dempster's *Selection for Secondary Education,* and Richardson's *Mental Measurement.*

Times Ed Sup 2082:319 Mr 25 '55. Among the numerous books that have been published on intelligence and attainments tests, this stands out because of its intimate understanding of the ordinary school teacher's problems and of the objections that he or she often raises to tests. It covers familiar ground—objects of testing, available tests of different types, hints on application, interpretation of test results, and such elementary statistical notions as the normal curve, the standard deviation of I.Q.s, and percentiles. But it does manage to show how these are important in relation to the school class and to the individual backward pupil. It is thus primarily concerned with the educational guidance of pupils at any age, rather than with the narrow application of tests for selection at 11 plus. While it should be really useful to any teacher willing to study it carefully, it should be particularly suitable as reading matter in a refresher course for practising teachers on mental testing or backwardness. Two or three minor weaknesses may be noted. Mr. Whilde adheres rather uncritically to the dogma that intelligence tests really measure inborn ability. He also seems to find a good deal more value in Jung's sensation, intuition, and other mental types than do most psychologists. A more serious point is his omission to warn the reader of the inadequacies of present-day educational test norms. This arises partly as a result of the decline in standards during the war, partly because tests like Burt's and Ballard's are nearly 40 years old, and partly because of the difficulties of securing really representative samples for standardization purposes. Finally, it is a pity that he cannot make up his mind how to spell F. M. Earle's name.

[B478]
★WIGFORSS, FRITS. **The Entrance Examination in View of Later School Performances.** International Institute Examinations Inquiry. Publications of the Swedish Society for a Psychological Pedagogical Institute, [No.] 1. Stockholm, Sweden: P. A. Norstedt & Söners, 1937. Pp. 131. Paper. * (*PA* 13:2738)

[B479]
★WOLF, WILLIAM B. **Merit Rating as a Managerial Tool: A Simplified Approach to Merit Rating.** Seattle, Wash.: Bureau of Business Research, College of Business Administration, University of Washington, 1958. Pp. ix, 91. Paper, lithotyped. $1.75. *

[B480]
WOLFF, CHARLOTTE. **The Hand in Psychological Diagnosis.** London: Methuen & Co. Ltd., 1951. Pp. xv, 218. 32s. 6d. *

B Menninger Clinic 17:112 My '53. P. H. C. Tibout. In the introduction to another book,

The Hands of Children by Julius Spier, C. G. Jung says: "After two hundred years of intensive scientific progress, we can risk resurrecting the almost forgotten (medieval) arts (of chirology, etc.) testing them in the light of modern knowledge for possible truths." That the knowledge of the form and even of the creases of the hands could contribute to our knowledge of personality is thinkable; but to test this hypothesis scientifically, one would need all of the data—anatomical, physiological, and psychological (statical and dynamic)—that modern constitutional research requires. Charlotte Wolff's book by no means meets these requirements. Although often one is struck by interesting remarks, the unclearness and inaccuracy (especially of the parts supposed to give psychiatric and biological explanations) is such that one is inclined to see the book more as a challenge than as a contribution to science. As the technique of making hand-prints is simple, this might be included in the examination, for instance, of certain groups of children for research purposes.

Brit J Med Psychol 26:175 pt 2 '53. F. K. Taylor. * not intended to be a text-book of hand diagnosis, which, as is repeatedly emphasized, cannot be learned from book study alone, and should be practised only by medically and psychologically trained persons. In spite of these statements a large part of the book is, however, addressed to the lay reader, for whose benefit psychological concepts are described in language which is often so loose and inadequate as to convey no meaning. Perhaps the worst example of these pseudodidactic efforts is the following definition: "Paraphrenia means a mind that is beside itself or gone astray." A number of the early chapters in the book are marred by the author's diffuse style and vague usage of scientific terms. Chapter II, however, contains some interesting descriptions of the hands of patients with endocrine disorders, and chapter V gives a good account of the author's classification of hands into six fundamental types, and of her method of hand interpretation. In the second part of the book some clinical studies of the hands of mentally ill and defective patients are reported. In two of these investigations the findings in a control group of normal persons are also given. These data are fully presented in several tables which will be of great interest to the serious student of the subject. The author evaluates her data in detail, though in an impressionistic rather than statistically exact manner. It appears that the diagnostically most significant abnormalities occur in the hands of schizophrenic and mentally defective persons, whereas the hands of manic-depressive and epileptic patients provide insufficient clues for clinical diagnosis. The main thesis of the book is that the study of hands is a useful method in assessing personality traits, especially temperament and intelligence, and can be of value in psychiatric diagnosis. To what extent the author has succeeded in proving this thesis is doubtful. Some rather extravagant claims are made; for instance, that hand diagnosis may be a more reliable criterion of intelligence than the psychological tests in common use. It is true that the clinical studies reported indicate that there is an association between hand abnormalities and the degree of mental deficiency, but the magnitude of this association remains unknown and is not likely to be large enough to allow a reliable diagnosis in individual patients. The same criticism may be levelled against the association of hand features and temperamental traits. These objections may, however, fail to give due credit to the intuitive skill acquired by the author in years of specialized endeavours. *

Brit J Psychol, Gen Sect 43:240-1 Ag '52. B. S. * a sequel to the author's earlier work *The Human Hand,* and embodies the results of more recent research, on the basis of which she has found it necessary to modify some of the opinions previously expressed. Nevertheless, one is still referred to the earlier book for a full exposition of the author's "Method of Hand Interpretation." Dr Wolff's approach has much in common with that of Sheldon, from whose work she seems to have received considerable inspiration. Although the book.... is partly addressed to "every intelligent educated person," it is rather weighed down by technical language, particularly from the field of endocrinology. Very full research data are quoted in support of the interpretation method, and these, in the absence of first-hand experience, cannot fail to impress the reader. In contrast, the underlying psychological assumptions are less convincing. Thus, Dr Wolff writes: "The radial portion of the right hand is the most important tool of conscious ac-

tivity and it is understandable from this that the quality of the intelligence has a special correlation with this part of the hand. The whole left hand as well as the ulnar part of the right have a different significance. The left is the passive side and not only in regard to the hand but to the whole body....One can assume that the whole left side of the body and the left hand in particular, are linked with the emotional and imaginative side of the personality and therefore with the subconscious mind. The ulnar part of the left hand ought to be especially significant in this respect as it is the least used for action. The same holds good to a minor degree for the ulnar zone of the right hand." It is in the impossibility of validation of this type of functional symbolism that the inherent weakness of work such as Dr Wolff's lies, and this irrespective of the statistical evidence for differences between groups formed on some principle deriving from such assumptions. To this reviewer, at least, even the more rarefied graphological "signs" carry more conviction.

Psychol B 50:162 Mr '53. William A. Hunt. The clinician who approaches this work with the anticipation that he will find a careful, objective analysis of diagnostic indicators and a scientific evaluation of their predictive limits will be disappointed. Nor will he find its theoretical treatment particularly stimulating since it is based on a vague and outmoded "faculty" psychology. A brief quotation may illustrate: "This use of the forefinger transmits the human faculty of discrimination, which is an essential quality of intelligence." The book unfortunately is "clinical" in the outdated, derogatory sense of the term.

[B481]

★WOOD, HUGH B. **Improving Pupil Evaluation.** Curriculum Bulletin, No. 118. Eugene, Ore.: School of Education, University of Oregon, November 15, 1952. Pp. 47. Paper, mimeographed. $0.70. *

[B482]

★WRIGHTSTONE, J. WAYNE. **What Tests Can Tell Us About Children.** Chicago, Ill.: Science Research Associates, 1954. Pp. 48. Paper. $0.50.*

[B483]

★WRIGHTSTONE, J. WAYNE; JUSTMAN, JOSEPH; AND ROBBINS, IRVING. **Evaluation in Modern Education.** New York: American Book Co., 1956. Pp. xiii, 481. $5.00. * (*PA* 30:7778)

Ed & Psychol Meas 16:405-7 au '56. James C. Reed. Flexibility seems to be the keynote for this book. "The textbook is designed for flexible use" (p. v). When an evaluation technique is clinical or pseudo-clinical, "flexible objectivity is especially desirable" (p. 52). Certainly, there is need for flexibility in a book which is intended to appeal to (a) graduate and undergraduate students in college or university classes; (b) guidance counselors, psychologists and research personnel who face day-by-day problems in evaluating all aspects of growth and development of pupils; (c) school administrators and supervisors; and (d) teachers-in-service who wish to have a handbook. In attempting to present to such a wide audience a comprehensive view of major evaluation techniques and methods of evaluating major educational objectives, there is a danger that the goal may be achieved at the expense of rigor and precision. The authors did not escape the danger. Throughout the three principal divisions there are inconsistencies, dogmatic statements with no source of evidence indicated, moralistic and value judgments, and citations and referrals to not too recent books and articles. * the references and suggested reading are not particularly up to date * The discussions on sociometric methods and projective techniques are highly repetitive. In addition, a great deal of space is devoted to sheer listing of the tests that are available in different curricular areas. Organizing elements are lacking in this section. It is never mentioned that the problem of evaluating appreciations and social adaptability is fundamentally the same as assessing growth in word-recognition skills. This section could have profited from an editing by one grounded in philosophy of science and by one acquainted with the rules of evidence. Instead of resorting to dictionary definitions of attitudes and values, instead of raising questions as to whether aptitudes are innate or acquired, instead of speculating as to whether they are unitary or pluralistic, use might have been made of operationalism. It might have been pointed out that the essential problem is to identify those behaviors subsumed under the particular construct, whether it be skill in long division, interest in the American novel or appreciation of the cultural heritage, and then to sample randomly from that universe of behaviors. After all, these are ramifications of the authors' concept that educational objectives must be stated in terms of measurable human behaviors. The reviewer feels that the book does not present basic and primary issues in evaluation. There is no discussion on the nature and underlying assumptions of measurement. The uses of operationalism and of what constitutes acceptable evidence are omitted. The student is not introduced to the problems of stating educational objectives in terms of behavior and the difficulties in constructing situations which permit relatively easy and objective identification of these behaviors. Rigorous experimental design and its place in evaluation are not considered. Perhaps the authors had no such intention. Perhaps these topics do not come under their definition of "comprehensive." If so, there is a limit to the amount they may be criticized for not writing a different book.

[B484]

★YATES, ALFRED, AND PIDGEON, D. A. **Admission to Grammar Schools: Third Interim Report on the Allocation of Primary School Leavers to Courses of Secondary Education.** National Foundation for Educational Research in England and Wales, Publication No. 10. London: Newnes Educational Publishing Co., Ltd., 1957. Pp. xv, 260. 25s. *

[B485]

★ZULLIGER, HANS. **Behn-Rorschach Test: Text.** Bern, Switzerland: Hans Huber, 1956. Pp. 200. (New York: Grune & Stratton, Inc., 1956. $7.50.) *

Periodical Directory and Index

* * * * *

References are to test and book entry numbers under which review excerpts from the given journal will be found, not to page numbers. Book entry numbers begin with the letter B. The name and address of the editor and the review editor are given for each journal. Test references are not indexed.

A.M.A.—THE A.M.A. Journal of the Incorporated Association of Assistant Masters in Secondary Schools. 8 issues (Ja, F, Mr, My, Je, S, O, N); vol. 54 started Ja '59; 1s. per issue; M. C. Constable, editor, 6 Grayland Close, Birmingham 27, England: B401, B460

Am J Mental Def—American Journal of Mental Deficiency. Published by the American Association on Mental Deficiency. 6 issues; vol. 63 started Jl '58; $14 per year; $3 per issue; Richard H. Hungerford, editor, Harry C. Storrs, review editor, Laconia State School, Laconia, N.H.: 52, B32, B369

Am J Orthopsychiatry—American Journal of Orthopsychiatry: A Journal of Human Behavior. Published by the American Orthopsychiatric Association, Inc. 4 issues; vol. 29 started Ja '59; $10 per year; $2.75 per issue; George E. Gardner, editor, 295 Longwood Ave., Boston 15, Mass.: B60, B144, B197, B204, B330, B370, B395, B467

Am J Psychiatry—The American Journal of Psychiatry. Official journal of the American Psychiatric Association. 12 issues; vol. 115 started Jl '58; $12 per year; $1.25 per issue; Clarence B. Farrar, editor, 216 St. Clair Ave., West, Toronto 5, Ont., Canada: 137, B44, B60, B63, B84, B144, B189, B210, B299, B337, B372, B395, B408, B418

Am J Psychol—The American Journal of Psychology. 4 issues; vol. 71 started Mr '58; $7 per year; $1.85 per issue; Karl M. Dallenbach, editor, University of Texas, Austin 12, Tex.; G. L. Kreezer, review editor, Washington University, St. Louis 5, Mo.: 130, 773, B26, B44, B115, B121, B147, B164, B204, B210, B269, B349, B352, B369

Am J Psychother—American Journal of Psychotherapy. Official organ of the Association for the Advancement of Psychotherapy. 4 issues; vol. 13 started Ja '59; $12 per year; $3.50 per issue; Emil A. Gutheil, editor, 16 West 77th St., New York 24, N.Y.: B40-1, B63, B190, B332, B337, B360, B370, B402

Am J Sociol—The American Journal of Sociology. 6 issues; vol. 64 started Jl '58; $6 per year; $1.75 per issue; Everett C. Hughes, editor, 1126 East 59th St., Chicago 37, Ill.: B70, B140, B200, B261

Am Sociol R—American Sociological Review. Official journal of the American Sociological Society. 6 issues; vol. 24 started F '59; $8 per year; $2 per issue; Charles H. Page, editor, Michael S. Olmsted, review editor, 4 Tyler Annex, Smith College, Northampton, Mass.: B69, B89, B134, B147, B200, B267, B299, B352, B378

Ann Eug—Annals of Eugenics. Title changed to *Annals of Human Eugenics (q.v.)* beginning with vol. 19, part 1, Jl '54.

Ann Human Eug—Annals of Human Eugenics: A Journal of Human Genetics. Title was *Annals of Eugenics·* through vol. 18. A publication of the Galton Laboratory, University College, London. Issued irregularly, usually one four-part volume per year; vol. 23 started N '58; 100s. per volume; 30s. per issue; L. S. Penrose, editor, Bentley House, London N.W.1, England: B202

Appl Stat—Applied Statistics: A Journal of the Royal Statistical Society. 3 issues; vol. 7 started Mr '58; 30s. per year; 12s. 6d. per issue; Donald G. Beech, editor, 76 Thistley Hough, Penkhull, Stoke-on-Trent, England: B48

Austral J Psychol—Australian Journal of Psychology. Published by the Australian Branch of thte British Psychological Society. 2 or 3 issues; vol. 10 started Je '58; 20s. per year; 10s. per issue; D. W. McElwain, editor, University of Queensland, St. Lucia, Queensland, Australia; W. M. O'Neil, review editor, University of Sydney, Sydney, New South Wales, Australia: B63, B111, B113, B144, B190, B204, B247, B330, B372, B424

B INT BUR ED—Bulletin of the International Bureau of Education. 4 issues; year 33 started 1st quarter '59 (no. 130); 10 Swiss francs per year; 2.5 Swiss francs per issue; International Bureau of Education, Geneva, Switzerland: B12, B141

B Menninger Clinic—Bulletin of the Menninger Clinic. 6 issues; vol. 23 started Ja '59; $4 per year; 75¢ per issue; Jeanetta Lyle Menninger, chairman, editorial board, The Menninger Foundation, Topeka, Kan.: 39, 130, B60, B79, B189-90, B261, B425, B444, B480

Brit J Delinquency—The British Journal of Delinquency. The official organ of the Institute for the Study and Treatment of Delinquency. 4 issues; vol. 9 started Jl '58; 30s. per year; 10s. per copy; the Institute, 8 Bourdon St., Davies St., London W.1, England: B143, B342

Brit J Ed Psychol—The British Journal of Educational Psychology. Issued by the British Psychological Society and the Association of Teachers in Colleges and Departments of Education. 3 issues (F, Je, N); vol. 29 started F '59; 30s. per year; 15s. per issue; P. E. Vernon, editor, Institute of Education, Malet St., London W.C.1, England: 127, B6, B22, B66, B69, B72, B84, B90-1, B113, B119, B143-4, B184, B202, B211, B293, B338, B342, B351, B376, B379, B409, B412, B423-4, B445-6, B451, B457, B459, B477

Brit J Ed Stud—British Journal of Educational Studies. 2 issues; vol. 7 started N '58; 16s. 8d. per year; 10s. per issue; A. C. F. Beales, executive editor, King's College, Strand, London W.C.2, England: B113, B334, B432, B445, B451

Brit J Med Psychol—The British Journal of Medical Psychology. A publication of the British Psychological Society. 4 issues; vol. 31 started '58; 60s. per volume; 20s. per issue; T. F. Main and Joseph Sandler, editors, 96 Portland Place, London W.1, England: B42, B144, B202, B248, B274, B330, B338, B369, B446, B480

Brit J Psychol—The British Journal of Psychology. A publication of the British Psychological Society. 4 issues; vol. 50 started '59; 60s. per year; 20s. per issue; Boris Semeonoff, editor, University of Edinburgh, Edinburgh, Scotland: 127, 131, 137, B8, B17, B21, B31, B42, B47, B51, B60, B63, B66, B69, B84, B89-90, B92, B111, B143-4, B147, B184-5, B197, B202, B213, B240, B247-8, B274, B293, B338, B340, B372, B380, B397, B399, B405, B420, B423, B445-7, B460, B480

Brit J Stat Psychol—The British Journal of Statistical Psychology. A publication of the British Psychological Society. 3 issues; vol. 11 started My '58; 30s. per year; editors: Cyril Burt, 9 Elsworthy Road, London N.W.3, England; and John Whitfield, University College, Gower St., London W.C.1, England: B42, B111, B408, B423

CALIF J ED RES—California Journal of Educational Research. Published by the California Teachers Association for the California Advisory Council on Educational Research. 5 issues (Ja, Mr, My, S, N); vol. 10 started Ja '59; $6 per year; $1.50 per issue; Garford G. Gordon, editor, California Teachers Association, 1705 Murchison Drive, Burlingame, Calif.: B84, B238, B283

Calif J Sec Ed—California Journal of Secondary Education. Published by the California Association of Secondary School Administrators. 8 issues (omitting Je, Jl, Ag, S); vol. 34 started Ja '59; $4 per year; 60¢ per issue; 2220 Bancroft Way, Berkeley 4, Calif.: B84

Can J Psychol—Canadian Journal of Psychology. A publication of the Canadian Psychological Association. 4 issues; vol. 12 started Mr '58; $4 per year; $1 per issue; J. D. Ketchum, editor, 100 St. George St., Toronto 5, Ont., Canada: 60, B189, B299, B322, B444, B467

Cath Ed R—The Catholic Educational Review. A publication of the Department of Education, the Catholic University of America. 9 issues (omitting Je, Jl, Ag); vol. 57 started Ja '59; $5 per year; 60¢ per issue; Joseph A. Gorham, editor-in-chief, 302 Administration Building, the Catholic University

of America, Washington 17, D.C.: B20, B238, B325, B433

Clearing House—The Clearing House: A Faculty Journal for Modern Junior and Senior High Schools. 9 issues (omitting Je, Jl, Ag); vol. 33 started S '58; $4.50 per year; 60¢ per issue; Joseph Green, managing editor, Forrest A. Irwin, review editor, Fairleigh Dickinson University, Teaneck, N.J.: B59, B150, B433

Col & Univ—College and University: The Journal of the American Association of Collegiate Registrars and Admissions Officers. 4 issues; vol. 34 started fall '58; $3 per year; $1 per issue; S. A. Nock, editor, Cedar Crest College, Allentown, Pa.; Wm. Glasgow Bowling, review editor, Washington University, St. Louis 5, Mo.: B469

Cont Psychol—Contemporary Psychology: A Journal of Reviews. Published by the American Psychological Association, Inc. 12 issues; vol. 3 started Ja '58; $8 per year; $1 per issue; Edwin G. Boring, editor, Memorial Hall, Harvard University, Cambridge 38, Mass.: B20, B26, B70, B115, B138, B150, B158, B169, B174, B204, B248, B255, B261, B300, B303, B349, B378, B409, B412, B424-5, B467

ED ADM & SUP—Educational Administration and Supervision. 6 issues; vol. 44 started Ja '58; $5.50 per year; $1.10 per issue; Warwick & York, Inc., 10 East Centre St., Baltimore 2, Md.: B84

Ed & Psychol Meas—Educational and Psychological Measurement: A Quarterly Journal Devoted to the Development and Application of Measures of Individual Differences. 4 issues; vol. 18 started spring '58; $8 per year; $2 per issue; G. Frederic Kuder, editor, Box 6907, College Station, Durham, N.C.; William B. Michael, review editor, University of Southern California, Los Angeles 7, Calif.: B21, B33, B56, B59, B72, B75, B91, B127, B134, B138, B158, B164, B181, B185, B255, B261, B263, B321, B338, B350, B429, B432, B454, B483

Ed Res B—Educational Research Bulletin. Published by the Bureau of Educational Research, Ohio State University. 9 issues (omitting Je, Jl, Ag); vol. 38 started Ja 8 '59; $1 per year; 25¢ per issue; R. H. Eckelberry, editor, Ohio State University, Columbus 10, Ohio: B20, B30, B162, B283, B285, B293, B361, B376

El Sch J—The Elementary School Journal. A publication of the Department of Education, University of Chicago. 8 issues (omitting Je, Jl, Ag, S); vol. 59 started O '58; $4.50 per year; $1 per issue; Kenneth J. Rehage, editor, University of Chicago, 5835 Kimbark Ave., Chicago 37, Ill.: B172, B419, B422, B429

Excep Child—Exceptional Children. Journal of the Council for Exceptional Children, National Education Association. 9 issues (omitting Je, Jl, Ag); vol. 25 started S '58; $4 per year; 50¢ per issue; John McCormick, editor, 1201 16th St., N.W., Washington 6, D.C.: B121

FED PROBATION—Federal Probation: A Journal of Correctional Philosophy and Practice. Published by the Administrative Office of the United States Courts in cooperation with the Bureau of Prisons of the Department of Justice. 4 issues; vol. 22 started Mr '58; Victor H. Evjen, editor, Supreme Court Building, Washington 25, D.C.: B200

H SCH J—The High School Journal. A publication of the School of Education, University of North Carolina. 8 issues (omitting Je, Jl, Ag, S); vol. 41 started O '57; $2 per year; 40¢ per issue; Samuel

M. Holton, editor, Box 810, Chapel Hill, N.C.: B84

Harvard Ed R—Harvard Educational Review. Published by the Graduate School of Education, Harvard University. 4 issues; vol. 28 started winter '58; $4 per year; $1.10 per issue; Theodore R. Sizer, chairman, editorial board, Wells Hively II and Wade M. Robinson, review editors, Lawrence Hall, Kirkland St., Cambridge 38, Mass.: B269

Human Relations—Human Relations: A Quarterly Journal of Studies Towards the Integration of the Social Sciences. 4 issues; vol. 11 started '58; 42s. per year; 12s. per issue; John Harvard-Watts, editor, Tavistock Publications Ltd., 2 Beaumont St., London W.1, England: B47

J ABN & SOCIAL PSYCHOL—The Journal of Abnormal and Social Psychology. Published by the American Psychological Association, Inc. 6 issues in 2 volumes; vol. 57 started Jl '58; vol. 58 started Ja '59; $16 per year; $3 per issue; M. Brewster Smith, editor, Department of Psychology, University of California, Berkeley 4, Calif.: B44, B199, B299, B395

J Appl Psychol—Journal of Applied Psychology. Published by the American Psychological Association, Inc. 6 issues; vol. 42 started F '58; $8 per year; $1.50 per issue; John G. Darley, editor, 408 Johnston Hall, University of Minnesota, Minneapolis 14, Minn.: 773, B1, B104, B199, B349, B465

J Chem Ed—Journal of Chemical Education. Published by the Division of Chemical Education, American Chemical Society. 12 issues; vol. 36 started Ja '59; $4 per year; 60¢ per issue; William F. Kieffer, editor, College of Wooster, Wooster, Ohio: 735

J Clin Psychol—Journal of Clinical Psychology. 4 issues; vol. 15 started Ja '59; $8.50 per year; $2.50 per issue; Frederick C. Thorne, editor, 5 Pearl St., Brandon, Vt.: 60, B91, B340

J Consult Psychol—Journal of Consulting Psychology. Published by the American Psychological Association, Inc. 6 issues; vol. 23 started F '59; $8 per year; $1.50 per issue; Edward S. Bordin, editor, Department of Psychology, University of Michigan, Ann Arbor, Mich.: 32, 37, 39, 47, 52, 58-9, 70, 85, 94, 100, 104, 122-3, 125, 133, 145, 150, 153, 342, 773, B32, B42, B63, B73, B79, B84, B121, B143-4, B147, B179, B213, B234, B247, B274, B299, B331-2, B338, B343, B369, B395, B444, B446, B448

J Counsel Psychol—Journal of Counseling Psychology: A Quarterly Journal of Counseling Theory and Research for Psychologists and Personnel Workers Concerned With the Counseling of Clients, Students, and Employees. 5 issues; vol. 6 started spring '59; $6 per year; $1.75 per issue; C. Gilbert Wrenn, editor, University of Minnesota, Minneapolis 14, Minn.: 16, 24, 58, 104, 135, B111, B115, B169, B261, B349, B409, B414, B425, B467

J Ed (London)—The Journal of Education: A Monthly Record and Review With Which Is Incorporated *The School World.* Discontinued with vol. 90, no. 1064, Mr '58; E. Salter Davies, editor, Amen House, Warwick Square, London E.C.4, England: B84, B90, B119, B142, B149, B380

J Ed Psychol—The Journal of Educational Psychology. Published by the American Psychological Association, Inc. 6 issues; vol. 49 started F '58; $8 per year; $1.50 per issue; Raymond G. Kuhlen, editor, Department of Psychology, Syracuse University, 123 College Place, Syracuse 10, N.Y.: 130, B23, B60, B63, B84, B89, B160, B188-9, B200, B247, B251, B325, B337, B361, B370, B395, B408, B433

J Ed Res—Journal of Educational Research. 9 issues (omitting Je, Jl, Ag); vol. 52 started S '58; $6 per year; 60¢ per issue; A. S. Barr, chairman, editorial

board, University of Wisconsin, Madison 6, Wis.: B42, B72, B75, B89, B131, B158, B162, B181, B416, B422, B424, B432-3

J Genetic Psychol—The Pedagogical Seminary and Journal of Genetic Psychology: Child Behavior, Animal Behavior, and Comparative Psychology. 4 issues in 2 volumes; vol. 92 started Mr '58; vol. 93 started S '58; $14 per year; $5 per issue; Carl Murchison, editor, 2 Commercial St., Provincetown, Mass.: B89, B179

J Higher Ed—The Journal of Higher Education. 9 issues (omitting Jl, Ag, S); vol. 30 started Ja '59; $6 per year; 75¢ per issue; R. H. Eckelberry, editor, Ohio State University, Columbus 10, Ohio: B72, B132, B136, B269, B293

J Mental Sci—The Journal of Mental Science: The British Journal of Psychiatry. A publication of the Royal Medico-Psychological Association. 4 issues; vol. 104 started Ja '58 (no. 434); 60s. per year; 15s. per issue; G. W. T. H. Fleming, editor-in-chief, Barnwood House, Gloucester, England: B274

J Nat Inst Personnel Res—Journal of the National Institute for Personnel Research. A publication of the South African Council for Scientific and Industrial Research. 2 or 3 issues per year; vol. 7 started O '57; S. Biesheuvel, editor-in-chief, P.O. Box 10319, Johannesburg, South Africa: B84

J Negro Ed—The Journal of Negro Education: A Quarterly Review of Problems Incident to the Education of Negroes. A publication of the Bureau of Educational Research, Howard University. 4 issues; vol. 28 started winter '59; $4 per year; Chas. H. Thompson, editor-in-chief, Howard University, Washington 1, D.C.: B140

J Proj Tech—Journal of Projective Techniques. Published by the Society for Projective Techniques and Rorschach Institute, Inc. 4 issues; vol. 22 started Mr '58; $8 per year; $2 per issue; Bruno Klopfer, editor, Bertram R. Forer, executive editor, 2170 Live Oak Drive, East, Los Angeles 28, Calif.: 130, 141, 150, 152, B32, B34, B41, B44, B60, B63, B73, B197, B204, B213, B234, B247-8, B251, B267, B340, B360, B369-70, B372, B395, B402, B418, B448

J Sch Health—The Journal of School Health. A publication of the American School Health Association. 10 issues (omitting Jl, Ag); vol. 29 started Ja '59; $4 per year; 50¢ per issue; Marie A. Hinrichs, editor-in-chief, 344 East Quincy St., Riverside, Ill.: B278

J Social Psychol—The Journal of Social Psychology. 4 issues in 2 volumes; vol. 48 started Ag '58; vol. 49 started F '59; $14 per year; $5 per issue; Carl Murchison, editor, 2 Commercial St., Provincetown, Mass.: B89, B147

J Teach Ed—The Journal of Teacher Education. Published by the National Commission on Teacher Education and Professional Standards. 4 issues; vol. 10 started Mr '59; $3 per year; $1 per issue; T. M. Stinnett, editor, Wilbur A. Yauch, review editor, National Education Association, 1201 Sixteenth St., N.W., Washington 6, D.C.: B36, B150, B162

Jun Col J—Junior College Journal. Official organ of the American Association of Junior Colleges. 9 issues (omitting Je, Jl, Ag); vol. 29 started S '58; $4 per year; 50¢ per issue; James W. Reynolds, editor, College of Education, University of Texas, P.O. Box 7998, Austin 12, Tex.: B125, B128-30

MED TIMES—Medical Times: Journal for the Family Physician. 12 issues; vol. 87 started Ja '59; $15 per year; Perrin H. Long, editor-in-chief, 1447 Northern Blvd., Manhasset, L.I., N.Y.: B84

Mental Health—Mental Health. Published by the National Association for Mental Health. 4 issues; vol.

18 started spring '59; 7s. 6d. per year; 2s. 6d. per issue; R. F. Tredgold, editor, Maurice Craig House, 39 Queen Anne St., London W.1, England: B184, B299, B372, B399

Mental Hyg—Mental Hygiene. Quarterly Journal of the National Association for Mental Health, Inc. 4 issues; vol. 43 started Ja '59; $6 per year; $1.50 per issue; George S. Stevenson, editor, 10 Columbus Circle, New York 19, N.Y.: B84, B147

Mod Lang J—The Modern Language Journal. Published by the National Federation of Modern Language Teachers Associations. 8 issues (omitting Je, Jl, Ag, S); $4 per year; 50¢ per issue; J. Alan Pfeffer, University of Buffalo, Buffalo 14, N.Y.: B373

NEW OUTLOOK FOR BLIND—The New Outlook for the Blind. A publication of the American Foundation for the Blind, Inc. 6 issues; vol. 47 started Je '56; $2 per year; issue price varies; Editor, 15 West 16th St., New York 11, N.Y.: B58

OCCUPATIONAL PSYCHOL—Occupational Psychology. Published by the National Institute of Industrial Psychology. 4 issues; vol. 32 started '58; 40s. per year; Alec Rodger, editor, 14 Welbeck St., London W.1, England: B21, B42, B48, B82, B84, B89, B143, B189, B271, B299, B338, B351, B380, B408, B435, B445-6, B457

PERCEPT & MOTOR SKILLS—Perceptual and Motor Skills. 4 issues; vol. 9 started Mr '59; $10 per year; $3.50 per issue; R. B. Ammons and C. H. Ammons, editors, Box 1441, Missoula, Mont.: B134

Personnel—Personnel. Published by the American Management Association, Inc. 6 issues; vol. 36 started Ja-F '59; $10 per year; $1.75 per issue; Juliet M. Halford, editor, American Management Association, Inc., 1515 Broadway, New York 36, N.Y.: B281

Personnel Adm—Personnel Administration. Published by the Society for Personnel Administration. 6 issues; vol. 22 started Ja-F '59; $5 per year; $1 per issue; Cecil E. Goode, editor, 3 Waggaman St., McLean, Va.; Lionel V. Murphy, review editor, 5406 Carolina Place, N.W., Washington 16, D.C.: B84, B414

Personnel & Guid J—The Personnel and Guidance Journal. Published by the American Personnel and Guidance Association, Inc. 9 issues (omitting Je, Jl, Ag); vol. 37 started S '58; $7 per year; 80¢ per issue; Joseph Samler, editor, 1605 New Hampshire Ave., N.W., Washington 9, D.C.: 167, B20, B42, B44, B56, B84, B115, B127, B138, B150, B158, B181-2, B293, B313, B338, B358, B414, B419, B424, B432

Personnel J—Personnel Journal: The Magazine of Labor Relations and Personnel Practices. 11 issues (Jl-Ag combined in one); vol. 38 started My '59; $6 per year; 75¢ per issue; Harrison M. Terrell, managing editor, P.O. Box 239, Swarthmore, Pa.: B37

Personnel Pract B—Personnel Practice Bulletin. 4 issues; vol. 14 started Mr '58; 12s. 6d. per year; 3s. 6d. per issue; Personnel Practice Section, Commonwealth Department of Labour and National Service, Melbourne, Australia: B42, B48, B349

Personnel Psychol—Personnel Psychology: A Journal of Applied Research. 4 issues; vol. 11 started spring '58; $8 per year; $2.50 per issue; G. Frederic Kuder, editor, P.O. Box 6965, College Station, Durham, N.C.; Theodore Kunin, review editor, Psychological Consultants to Industry, 210 Grant St., Pittsburgh 19, Pa.: B1, B47-8, B80, B104, B111,

B115, B143, B164, B174, B176, B179, B203, B265, B281, B338, B409, B411, B414

Psychiatric Q—The Psychiatric Quarterly. Official scientific organ of the New York State Department of Mental Hygiene. 4 issues; vol. 32 started '58; $8 per year; $2.25 per issue; Newton Bigelow, editor, Utica State Hospital, Utica 2, N.Y.: B210

Psychiatric Q Sup—The Psychiatric Quarterly Supplement. Official scientific organ of the New York State Department of Mental Hygiene. 4 issues; vol. 31 started '57; $4 per year; $2.25 per issue; Newton Bigelow, editor, Utica State Hospital, Utica 2, N.Y.: B34, B60, B73, B165, B190, B290, B337, B370, B469

Psychoanalytic Q—Psychoanalytic Quarterly. 4 issues; vol. 27 started '58; $8 per year; Raymond Gosselin, editor, 57 West 57th St., New York 19, N.Y.: 127

Psychol B—Psychological Bulletin. Published by the American Psychological Association, Inc. 6 issues; vol. 56 started Ja '59; $8 per year; $1.50 per issue; Harry Helson, editor, Department of Psychology, University of Texas, Austin 12, Tex.: B42, B60, B63, B84, B89, B140, B143-4, B147, B160, B179, B189, B197, B247, B269, B274, B299, B322, B369, B372, B395, B408, B418, B444, B446, B448, B480

Psychometrika—Psychometrika: A Journal Devoted to the Development of Psychology as a Quantitative Rational Science. Official journal of the Psychometric Society. 4 issues; vol. 23 started Mr '58; $14 per year (including a second complete set for binding at end of year if requested); $3.50 per issue; Lyle V. Jones, managing editor, Psychometric Laboratory, University of North Carolina, Chapel Hill, N.C.; John B. Carroll, review editor, 7 Kirkland St., Cambridge 38, Mass.: B23, B89, B104, B111, B164, B172, B185, B188, B408, B424, B467

Psychosom Med—Psychosomatic Medicine: Journal of the American Psychosomatic Society. 6 issues; vol. 21 started Ja-F '59; $8.50 per year; $1.75 per issue; Carl Binger, editor-in-chief, 265 Nassau Road, Roosevelt, N.Y.: B213, B360, B467

Q R BIOL—Quarterly Review of Biology. 4 issues; vol. 34 started Mr '59; $10 per year; $2.75 per issue; Bentley Glass, editor, Department of Biology, Johns Hopkins University, Baltimore 18, Md.: B34, B89, B184

RURAL SOCIOL—Rural Sociology. Official journal of the Rural Sociological Society. 4 issues; vol. 24 started Mr '59; $7 per year; $2 per issue; J. Allan Beegle, editor, Michigan State University, East Lansing, Mich.; Walter C. McKain, Jr., review editor, University of Connecticut, Storrs, Conn.: B196

SCH R—The School Review. A publication of the Department of Education, University of Chicago. 4 issues; vol. 67 started spring '59; $5 per year; $2 per issue; Maurice L. Hartung, chairman, editorial board, 5835 Kimbark Ave., Chicago 37, Ill.: B84

Sci—Science. A publication of the American Association for the Advancement of Science. 52 issues in 2 volumes; vol. 128 started Jl 4 '58; vol. 129 started Ja 2 '59; $8.50 per year; 35¢ per issue; Graham DuShane, editor, 1515 Massachusetts Ave., N.W., Washington 5, D.C.: B197, B396

Sight-Saving R—The Sight-Saving Review. Official quarterly of the National Society for the Prevention of Blindness, Inc. 4 issues; vol. 28 started '58; $2.50 per year; 65¢ per issue; Franklin M. Foote, editor-in-chief, 1790 Broadway, New York 19, N.Y.: B109

Social Service R—The Social Service Review: A Quarterly Devoted to the Scientific and Professional Interests of Social Work. A publication of the School of Social Service Administration, University of Chicago. 4 issues; vol. 32 started Mr '58; $6 per year; $2.25 per issue; Rachel B. Marks, editor, University of Chicago, Chicago 37, Ill.: B200

Sociometry—Sociometry: A Journal of Research in Social Psychology. A publication of the American Sociological Society. 4 issues; vol. 22 started Mr '59; $9 per year; $2.50 per issue; Leonard S. Cottrell, Jr., editor, Russell Sage Foundation, 505 Park Ave., New York 22, N.Y.: B322

TEACH COL REC—Teachers College Record. A publication of Teachers College, Columbia University. 8 issues (omitting Je, Jl, Ag, S) ; $4 per year; 75¢ per issue; vol. 60 started O '58; Max R. Brunstetter, editor, 525 West 120 St., New York 27, N.Y.: B84

Times Ed Sup—The Times Educational Supplement. 52 issues; vol. 23 started Ja 4 '57 (no. 2172) ; The Times Publishing Co. Ltd., Printing House Square, London E.C.4, England: B477

Training Sch B—The Training School Bulletin. 4 issues; vol. 55 started My '58; $2 per year; 50¢ per issue; Editor, The Training School, Vineland, N.J.: B121

Publishers Directory and Index

*   *   *   *   *

References are to test and book entry numbers, not to page numbers. Stars indicate test publishers which issue catalogs devoted entirely or in large part to tests; asterisks indicate other publishers of one or more tests listed in this volume. Book entry numbers begin with the letter B.

★ACORN Publishing Co., Inc., Rockville Centre, Long Island, N.Y.: 18–9, 26, 178, 190–1, 219, 230, 241, 303–4, 429, 463–4, 555, 557–8, 560, 634, 642, 646–8, 695, 707, 712, 726, 785, 790, 798, 806, 811, 825, 847, 861, 878

*Addison-Wesley Publishing Co., Inc., Reading, Mass.: 77, B407

*Administrative Research Associates, P.O. Box 1160, Chicago 90, Ill.: 541, 546

Air University, Maxwell Air Force Base, Ala.: B30

Ajax Corporation, P.O. Box 469, Shenandoah, Iowa: B265

Allyn & Bacon, Inc., 41 Mount Vernon St., Boston 8, Mass.: B24

Almqvist & Wiksell, 26 Gamla Brogatan, Stockholm C, Sweden: B17, B27, B205, B219

American Association of Examiners and Administrators of Educational Personnel, Parkway at 21st St., Philadelphia 3, Pa.: B36

*American Automobile Association, Pennsylvania Ave. at 17th St., Washington 6, D.C.: 594, 922, 946

American Bankers Association, Customer and Personnel Relations Department, 12 East 36th St., New York 16, N.Y.: B37

American Book Co., 55 Fifth Ave., New York 3, N.Y.: B483

American Chemical Society. See Examinations Committee.

American Council on Education, 1785 Massachusetts Ave., N.W., Washington 6, D.C.: B38, B127, B132, B231, B269, B419. See also Veterans' Testing Service.

*American Dental Association, 222 East Superior St., Chicago 11, Ill.: 916, B336

American Educational Research Association, 1201 16th St., N.W., Washington 6, D.C.: B13, B311–12, B363

*American Film Registry, 1018 South Wabash, Chicago 5, Ill.: 579

American Foundation for the Blind, Inc., 15 West 16th St., New York 11, N.Y.: B58, B289

American Gas Association, 420 Lexington Ave., New York 17, N.Y.: B39

American Graphological Society, Inc., 200 West 34th St., New York 1, N.Y.: B421

*American Guidance Service, Inc., 720 Washington Ave., S.E., Minneapolis 14, Minn.: 349, 444

*American Institute of Certified Public Accountants, 21 Audubon Ave., New York 32, N.Y.: 907, 911

*American Library Association, 50 East Huron St., Chicago 11, Ill.: 939

American Management Association, Inc., 1515 Broadway, New York 36, N.Y.: B284

*American Optical Co., Buffalo 15, N.Y.: 768–70

*American Orthopsychiatric Association, Inc., 1790 Broadway, New York 19, N.Y.: 172

American Personnel & Guidance Association, Inc., 1605 New Hampshire Ave., N.W., Washington 9, D.C.: B417

American Psychological Association, Inc., 1333 16th St., N.W., Washington 6, D.C.: B14, B55, B65, B71, B76, B78, B107, B116, B146, B157, B159, B167–8, B173, B175, B177, B186–7, B215–6, B232, B236, B250, B253, B257, B270, B282, B295, B320, B327, B348, B353, B359, B368, B400, B403, B415, B434, B455, B462

*American Transit Association, 292 Madison Ave., New York 17, N.Y.: 912

Appleton-Century-Crofts, Inc., 35 West 32nd St., New York 1, N.Y.: B49, B138, B169, B278

*Aptitude Associates, Inc., Merrifield, Va.: 56, 198, 395, 437, 466

*Aptitude Test Service, Swarthmore, Pa.: 311, 523, 849

Arco Publishing Co., Inc., 480 Lexington Ave., New York 17, N.Y.: B268, B335, B442; Arco Publications, Ltd., 10 Fitzroy St., London W.1, England: B268

Associated Booksellers, 2106 Post Road, Westport, Conn.: B399

*Associated Personnel Technicians, 118 South Main St., Wichita 2, Kan.: 302

Association of American Medical Colleges, 2530 Ridge Ave., Evanston, Ill.: B170

*Association Press, 291 Broadway, New York 7, N.Y.: 117

Hoeber (Paul B.), Inc., 49 East 33rd St., New York 16, N.Y.: B40–1

Holt (Henry) & Co., Inc., New York, N.Y.: B20, B137, B158, B429–30, B446, B454

*Holtzman (Wayne H.), University of Texas, Austin 12, Tex.: 140

★Houghton Mifflin Co., 2 Park St., Boston 7, Mass.: 16, 28, 100, 114, 199, 342, 350, 411, 413, 665, 677, B321

*Huber (Hans), Marktgasse 9, Berne, Switzerland: 154, 162, 170, B251, B485

*Humm Personnel Consultants, 1219 West 12th St., Los Angeles 15, Calif.: 69, 931

*INDUSTRIAL Psychological Laboratory, Box 718, Sparta, N.J.: 772

*Industrial Psychology, Inc., 35 East Wacker Drive, Chicago 1, Ill.: 71, 74, 602, 892, 898, 900

*Institut pedagogique Saint-Georges, Mont-de-La-Salle, Montreal 9, Canada: 115

★Institute for Personality and Ability Testing, 1602 Coronado Drive, Champaign, Ill.: 70–4, 90, 112, 343, B90

Institute of Child Study, University of Toronto, Toronto 4, Canada: B345

Institute of Psychotechnics, University of Göteborg, Göteborg, Sweden: B141

*Institute of Public Safety, Pennsylvania State University, University Park, Pa.: 594, 922, 946

Institute of Rural Education, Jamia Millia Islamia, Jamia Nager, New Delhi, India: B258

*International Business Machines Corporation, 590 Madison Ave., New York 22, N.Y.: 530, 941

International Universities Press, Inc., 227 West 13th St., New York 11, N.Y.: B32, B34, B73

Interscience Publishers, Ltd., 88–90 Chancery Lane, London W.C.2, England: B293

*Iowa State College Press, Ames, Iowa: 570, 593, 595

*JEWISH Education Committee of New York, Inc., 1776 Broadway, New York 19, N.Y.: 278

*Journal of Clinical Psychology, 5 Pearl St., Brandon, Vt.: 141, B425

*Jurgensen (Clifford E.), 6101 Oliver Ave., South, Minneapolis 19, Minn.: 513

KANSAS State Teachers College (Emporia). See Bureau of Educational Measurements.

Kansas State Teachers College (Pittsburg), Pittsburg, Kan.: B52, B244

*Keystone View Co., Meadville, Pa.: 780, 784

*Krout (Maurice H.), 1938 Cleveland Ave., Evanston, Ill.: 93

*LAFAYETTE Instrument Co., North 26th St. and 52 By-Pass, Lafayette, Ind.: 883

Lawrence & Wishart Ltd., 81 Chancery Lane, London W.C.2, England: B397

*Leonard (Hal) Music, Inc., 64 East Second St., Winona, Minn.: 253

*Lewis (H. K.) & Co. Ltd., 136 Gower St., London W.C.1, England: 127, 370, B347

*Life Insurance Agency Management Association, 170 Sigourney St., Hartford 5, Conn.: 913, 927, 929

*Livingstone (E. & S.) Ltd., 15–17 Teviot Place, Edinburgh 1, Scotland: 587

Logos Press, Inc., 491 Avenue of the Americas, New York 11, N.Y.: B118

Longmans, Green & Co., Inc., 119 West 40th St., New York 18, N.Y.: B72, B166, B172, B180–2, B351, B376, B422; Longmans, Green & Co., Ltd., 6–7 Clifford St., London W.1, England: B62, B72, B166, B181–2, B351, B376, B422

Louisiana Polytechnic Institute. See Department of Business and Economic Research.

*Loyola University Press, 3441 North Ashland Ave., Chicago 13, Ill.: 589, 591–2

*Lyons & Carnahan, 2500 Prairie Ave., Chicago 16, Ill.: 626, 669

MCBRIDE Co., Inc., 200 East 37th St., New York 16, N.Y.: B286

McGraw-Hill Book Co., Inc., 330 West 42nd St., New York 18, N.Y.: B56, B59, B147, B184–5, B238; McGraw-Hill Publishing Co., Ltd., 95 Farringdon St., London E.C.4, England: B56, B59, B146–7, B185

*McKnight & McKnight Publishing Co., Bloomington, Ill.: 549, B150

Macmillan Co., 60 Fifth Ave., New York 11, N.Y.: B42, B342, B432; Macmillan & Co. Ltd., 10 St. Martin's St., London W.C.2, England: B42, B432; Macmillan New York, 10 South Audley St., London W.1, England: B340

*Maico Electronics, Inc., 21 North Third St., Minneapolis 1, Minn.: 763

Melbourne University Press, Carlton N.3, Victoria, Australia: B21, B256

Merrill-Palmer School, 71 East Ferry Ave., Detroit 2, Mich.: B412

*Methuen & Co. Ltd., 36 Essex St., Strand, London W.C.2, England: 163, 360, 405, B119, B144, B202, B440–1, B446–7, B480

*Mills Music, Inc., 1619 Broadway, New York 19, N.Y.: 244, 248

Montana State University Press, Missoula, Mont.: B134

*Moore (Joseph E.) and Associates, 4406 Jett Road, N.W., Atlanta 5, Ga.: 872

*Morningside College, Sioux City, Iowa: 539

Mosby (C. V.) Co., 3207 Washington Blvd., St. Louis 3, Mo.: B464

*Munsell Color Co., Inc., 10 East Franklin St., Baltimore 2, Md.: 771, 775

*NATIONAL Bureau of Educational and Social Research, Department of Education, Arts and Science, Pretoria, Union of South Africa: 31, 355, 479, 604, 654

National Council for the Social Studies, 1201 16th St., N.W., Washington 6, D.C.: B45–6, B301

National Council on Measurements Used in Education, 21 Audubon Ave., New York 32, N.Y.: B304–10

National Dry Goods Association. See Personnel Group.

National Education Association. See American Educational Research Association; National Council for the Social Studies; and United Business Education Association.

*National Foremen's Institute, Inc., 100 Garfield Ave., New Haven, Conn.: 906, 915, B410

★National Foundation for Educational Research in England and Wales, 79 Wimpole St., London W.1, England: 132, 187, 189, 192–3, 254, 334, 356–7, 367, 369, 390, 393, 396–7, 435–6, 461, 465, 489, 606, 652, 848, 885

National Institute for Personnel Research, South African Council for Scientific and Industrial Research, P.O. Box 10319, Johannesburg, Union of South Africa: B48

*National Institute of Industrial Psychology, 14 Welbeck St., London W.1, England: 338–40, 877

*National League for Nursing, Inc., 2 Park Ave., New York 16, N.Y.: 934–8, B313–16

National Sales Executives, Inc., 136 East 57th St., New York, N.Y.: B176

★Scholastic Testing Service, Inc., 3774 West Devon Ave., Chicago 45, Ill.: 15, 23, 201, 380, 484, 627, 650, 681, 788

School of Education, University of Oregon, Eugene, Ore.: B365, B406, B481

*Schubert (Herman J. P.), 500 Klein Road, Route 2, Buffalo 21, N.Y.: 129, 382

★Science Research Associates, Inc., 57 West Grand Ave., Chicago 10, Ill.: 17, 20–2, 34, 80, 92, 102, 104–5, 116, 118, 122, 128, 150, 197, 200, 217, 235, 245, 305, 310, 319, 353, 359, 372, 376–8, 391, 428, 483, 518, 540, 608, 614, 649, 668, 685–6, 692, 696, 713, 791, 862–3, 873, 899, 902, 905, B162, B207–8, B252, B264, B377, B413, B482

*Scientific Publishing Co., 2328 Eutaw Place, Baltimore 17, Md.: 773

★Sheridan Supply Co., P.O. Box 837, Beverly Hills, Calif.: 45, 63–5, 78, 383, 694

*Shipley (William U.), P.O. Box 39, Yale Station, New Haven, Conn.: 111

Simon & Schuster, Inc., 630 Fifth Ave., New York 20, N.Y.: B290

Society for Projective Techniques and Rorschach Institute, Inc., 210 East Wilson St., Glendale 6, Calif.: B395

Society for Research in Child Development. See Child Development Publications.

*Sonotone Corporation, Elmsford, N.Y.: 765

South-Western Publishing Co., Inc., 5101 Madison Road, Cincinnati 27, Ohio: B194

*Spache (George), Reading Laboratory and Clinic, University of Florida, Gainesville, Fla.: 142, 228

*Specialty Case Manufacturing Co., 1701 North Eighth St., Philadelphia 22, Pa.: 609

*Springer Publishing Co., Inc., 44 East 23rd St., New York 10, N.Y.: 167, B293, B428

*Stanford University Press, Stanford, Calif.: 559; see also Consulting Psychologists Press, Inc. for tests formerly published by Stanford University Press.

*State High School Testing Service for Indiana, Purdue University, Lafayette, Ind.: 643

State University of Iowa. See Department of Physical Education for Women.

*Steck Co., Austin 1, Tex.: 11, 14, 389, 458, 544, 680, 699

*Steward (Verne) & Associates, 14828 Mar Vista St., Whittier, Calif.: 950–3

★Stoelting (C. H.) Co., 424 North Homan Ave., Chicago 24, Ill.: 137, 160, 171, 242, 406–8, 412, 767, 876

Suomalainen Tiedeakatemia, Academia Scientiarum Fennica, Snellmaninkatu 9–11, Helsinki, Finland: B25–6, B347, B420, B449

Swedish Council for Personnel Administration, Hantverkargatan 78, Stockholm, Sweden: B237

*TAVISTOCK Publications Ltd., 2 Beaumont St., London W.1, England: 151, B338, B393

Test Development and Occupational Research Section, United States Civil Service Commission, Washington 25, D.C.: B16

*Testscor, 1554 Nicollet Ave., Minneapolis 3, Minn.: 529

*Thomas (Charles C), 327 East Lawrence Ave., Springfield, Ill.: 148, B86, B178, B192, B213, B254, B332, B448

Times Publishing Co., Ltd., Printing House Square, London E.C.4, England: B6

*UNITED Business Education Association, 1201 16th St., N.W., Washington 6, D.C.: 506, 508, 511, 514–5, 522, 526–7

United States Armed Forces Institute, Madison, Wis.: B436

United States Civil Service Commission. See Test Development and Occupational Research Section.

*United States Employment Service, Washington 25, D.C.: 609

United States Government Printing Office, Washington 25, D.C.: 609, 860, B1, B81, B109, B439, B452

United States Office of Education, Washington 25, D.C.: B392

*University Book Store, 360 State St., West Lafayette, Ind.: 237, 644, 853, 942–5

University College of Wales, Aberystwyth, Wales: B18, B339

University of Buffalo, Buffalo 14, N.Y.: B235, B450

University of California Press, Berkeley 4, Calif.: B174, B266, B291, B344, B435

University of Chicago Press, 5750 Ellis Ave., Chicago 37, Ill.: B140, B160, B354, B408

*University of Denver Bookstores, 1445 Cleveland Place, Denver 2, Colo.: 109

University of Durham. See Department of Education.

University of Göteborg. See Institute of Psychotechnics.

University of Illinois Press, Urbana, Ill.: B111

University of Kansas Press, Lawrence, Kan.: B108

University of Kentucky. See Bureau of School Service.

★University of London Press Ltd., Little Paul's House, Warwick Square, London E.C.4, England: 35, 325, 337, 351, 392, 398, 476, B12, B74, B90, B142, B184, B379–80, B401, B423, B445, B459

University of Manchester Press, Manchester, England: B457

University of Maryland. See Department of Psychiatry.

University of Miami Bookstore, Coral Gables 46, Fla.: B453

University of Miami Press, Coral Gables 46, Fla.: B33

University of Michigan. See Department of Psychology.

University of Michigan Press, 311 Maynard St., Ann Arbor, Mich.: B104–5, B267

*University of Minnesota Press, Minneapolis 14, Minn.: 88, 113, 243, 571–2, 598, 687, B64, B115, B199–200, B260, B331, B414, B467

*University of Natal Press, P.O. Box 375, Pietermaritzburg, Union of South Africa: 165

*University of Nebraska Press, 1125 R, Lincoln 8, Neb.: 83, 533

University of North Carolina Press, Chapel Hill, N.C.: B23

University of Oregon. See Curriculum Bulletin; and School of Education.

*University of Queensland Press, George St., Brisbane, Australia: 747, 755

University of Toronto. See Department of Educational Research; Guidance Centre; and Institute for Child Study.

University of Toronto Press, Toronto 5, Canada: B29, B322–3

University of Washington. See Bureau of Business Research, College of Business Administration, University of Washington.

University Publishing Co., 1126 Q St., Lincoln 1, Neb.: B183

University System of Georgia, Athens, Ga.: B328

University Testing and Service Bureau, Cornell University, Ithaca, N.Y.: B106

VAN NOSTRAND (D.) Co., Inc., 120 Alexander St., Princeton, N.J.: B164

Veterans Administration, Washington 25, D.C.: B273

*Veterans' Testing Service, American Council on Education, 6018 Ingleside Ave., Chicago 37, Ill.: 27, 181, 216, 426, 683–4

Victoria University College. See Department of Psychology.

*WAHR (George) Publishing Co., 316 South State St., Ann Arbor, Mich.: 257, 260–2

*Wahr's Book Store. See Wahr (George) Publishing Co.

*Warwick Products Co., 1572 Riverbed Road, Cleveland 13, Ohio: 609

*Washington Publications, 3915 Military Road, N.W., Washington 15, D.C.: 258–9

*Webster Publishing Co., 1808 Washington Ave., St. Louis 3, Mo.: 682

*Welch Allyn, Inc., Skaneateles Falls, N.Y.: 781

★Western Psychological Services, 10655 Santa Monica Blvd., Los Angeles 25, Calif.: 39–40, 60–1, 82, 94, 110, 124, 133–5, 139, 153–4, 158, 490, B67, B191, B234, B437

Western Reserve University. See Personnel Research Institute.

Western Reserve University Press, Cleveland 6, Ohio: B206; see also Personnel Research Institute.

Wheaton (A.) & Co., Ltd., 143 Fore St., Exeter, England: B228–9, B262

Whitcombe & Tombs Ltd., Box 954, Christchurch C.1, New Zealand: B149

Wiley (John) & Sons, Inc., 440 Fourth Ave., New York 16, N.Y.: B144, B188, B204, B424, B431

Williams & Wilkins Co., Mt. Royal and Guilford Aves., Baltimore 2, Md.: B463

Winter Haven Lions Club. See Eyesight Conservation Committee.

*Witkin (Herman A.), Psychological Laboratory, State University College of Medicine, Downstate Medical Center, 450 Clarkson Ave., Brooklyn 3, N.Y.: 49

*Wolters (J. B.), Groningen, Holland: 410

*Wonderlic Personnel Test Co., P.O. Box 7, Northfield, Ill.: 400

★World Book Co., Yonkers, N.Y.: 25, 58–9, 66, 79, 154, 164, 176, 195, 210, 233, 326, 335, 361–3, 368, 402, 422, 439, 443, 451–2, 478, 480, 487, 497–8, 562, 577, 582, 585, 597, 610, 636, 656, 660–1, 671, 679, 697–8, 700, 715, 717, 728, 737, 753, 774, 799, 816–7, 833, 840, 855, B11, B91, B247–8, B285

YOUTH Education Systems, Inc., 2612 Grand Central Terminal Bldg., New York 17, N.Y.: B5

*ZANER-BLOSER Co., 612 North Park St., Columbus 8, Ohio: 551

Index of Titles

* * * * *

References are to test and book entry numbers, not to page numbers. The entry numbers for facing pages are given in the running heads of the text next to the outside margins. Entry numbers for book titles begin with the letter B. Test references are not indexed.

Index of Names

* * * * *

Bluett, Charles G.: *ref,* 375(17)

Blum, Gerald S.: *test,* 125; *exc,* B448; *ref,* 125(11-3, 16, 33-4), 154(1315), 164(321)

Blum, Lucille H.: *test,* 402, 585; *bk,* B73; *ref,* 154(1666), 585(1)

Blum, Milton L.: *cross ref,* 609, 860

Blum, Richard H.: *ref,* 148(26), 172(69)

Blumberg, Albert I.: *ref,* 125(35)

Blumberg, Eugene M.: *ref,* 86(394)

Blyth, David D.: *ref,* 154(1305)

Blyth, M. Isobel: *test,* 443

Bobbitt, Joseph M.: *ref,* 30(128), 204(7), 308(296, 302), 318(24), 786(8), 884(100)

Bodily, Gerald P.: *test,* 394

Bodley, E. A.: *ref,* 884(101)

Boeck, Clarence: *test,* 738, 756

Bogartz, W.: *ref,* 154(2275), 416 (131)

Boger, Jack H.: *ref,* 314(44), 362 (20)

Boice, Mary L.: *ref,* 768(21, 23), 780(48, 50)

Bolander, W. G.: *ref,* 86(284)

Bolgar, Hedda: *bk,* B248; *exc,* B395; *ref,* 154(1667, 2063), 168 (7)

Bolin, B. J.: *ref,* 139(69), 308 (374), 362(29), 370(83)

Boling, Lenore: *ref,* 154(2112)

Bolinger, Russell W.: *ref,* 145(15, 18)

Bollenbacher, Joan: *rev,* 675, 679

Bolton, Dale L.: *exc,* B72

Bolton, Euri B.: *ref,* 179(110), 308 (292, 343), 645(43)

Bolton, Floyd B.: *ref,* 370(84)

Bond, Guy L.: *test,* 626, 669; *ref,* 30(124), 86(292), 114(87), 310 (30), 342(27), 348(51), 359(54), 363(96), 614(143), 661(7), 850 (62), 863(220), 864(23), 868 (278), 889(48); *cross ref,* 660

Bond, Nicholas A., Jr.: *test,* 45; *bk,* B186; *ref,* 114(112), 863 (316)

Bonder, John: *ref,* 783(66)

Bone, John H.: *ref,* 863(392)

Boneau, C. A.: *ref,* 400(59)

Bonk, Edward C.: *ref,* 86(546), 363(113)

Bonner, Leon W.: *ref,* 199(14)

Bonney, Merl E.: *test,* 33

Bonsall, Marcella Ryser. See Sea, Marcella Ryser.

Booker, Ivan A.: *cross ref,* 2, 622, 657

Booth, E. G., Jr.: *ref,* 86(733)

Bordin, Edward S.: *rev,* 862; *ref,* 863(272); *cross ref,* 861, 863-4, 868

Boreham, J. L.: *exc,* B330; *ref,* 154(1668)

Borenstein, Betty A.: *ref,* 164(470)

Borg, Walter R.: *ref,* 63(30, 47), 64(32, 46), 78(33, 47), 850(59), 863(281)

Borgatta, Edgar F.: *exc,* B70, B299; *ref,* 77(6, 10-11, 13), 154 (1852, 1869); *other,* 77(10)

Borghi, Eugene: *ref,* 86(613)

Borislow, Bernard: *ref,* 47(36)

Borko, Harold: *ref,* 86(321), 172 (53)

Bornstein, Harry: *ref,* 155(84)

Bornston, Frieda L.: *ref,* 155(159)

Borstelmann, L. J.: *ref,* 162(90)

Boruszak, Ruby J.: *ref,* 413(548), 416(66)

Bosquet, Kennison T.: *ref,* 154 (2017)

Bossom, J.: *ref,* 172(70)

Boston, Mary: *ref,* 126(3), 154 (1295)

Botel, Morton: *ref,* 318(25)

Botwinick, Jack: *ref,* 86(299), 415 (392, 462)

Bouise, Louise M.: *ref,* 46(1)

Boulger, John R.: *ref,* 609(38, 46)

Bourdo, Eric A., Jr.: *ref,* 863(300)

Bourguignon, Erika E.: *ref,* 154 (1853)

Bousfield, W. A.: *ref,* 114(117)

Bouton, Arthur: *ref,* 863(238, 318-9)

Bova, Louis W., Jr.: *ref,* 147(30)

Bowen, Barbara: *ref,* 147(17-8, 37)

Bowers, Scott T.: *ref,* 38(30)

Bowland, John A.: *ref,* 172(116)

Bowles, J. W.: *ref,* 773(8)

Bowley, Agatha H.: *test,* 587

Bowman, Howard A.: *ref,* 17(7)

Bowyer, Ruth: *bk,* B74

Boyd, C. E.: *ref,* 123(9)

Boyd, Foster: *ref,* 57(30)

Boyd, Herbert F.: *ref,* 314(62), 408(37), 413(588)

Boyd, Joseph D.: *ref,* 179(117), 318(33), 359(69)

Boyd, Robert W.: *ref,* 154(1245)

Boydston, Donald N.: *ref,* 558(3)

Boyer, Lee E.: *ref,* 308(402), 359 (75)

Boyer, Roscoe A.: *ref,* 308(403)

Boykin, Leander L.: *ref,* 30(145), 645(46)

Boynton, Paul L.: *ref,* 117(3)

Braasch, William F., Jr.: *ref,* 868 (337)

Braaten, Leif J.: *bk,* B400; *ref,* 308(366), 400(43), 615(10)

Brace, D. K.: *test,* 766; *ref,* 766(1, 5, 11, 15)

Brackbill, Glen A.: *ref,* 86(481, 673), 154(2018, 2152), 415(592)

Bradburn, Wendy M.: *ref,* 49(9), 154(2253)

Bradfield, James M.: *bk,* B74

Bradford, E. J. G.: *cross ref,* 161

Bradford, Jeanne M.: *test,* 6, 179, 645, 787

Bradford, William: *cross ref,* 111

Bradley, Mary O.: *ref,* 164(566)

Bradley, Philip H.: *ref,* 530(50)

Bradshaw, G. D.: *exc,* B349

Bradt, Kenneth H.: *ref,* 164(307), 359(58)

Bradway, Katherine: *ref,* 154 (1493), 415(529)

Brady, Elizabeth H.: *bk,* B419

Bragdon, Henry W.: *ref,* 786(7)

Bragg, Emma W.: *ref,* 308(404), 645(50)

Brainard, Paul P.: *test,* 856

Brainard, Ralph T.: *test,* 856

Bramlette, Carl A., Jr.: *ref,* 164 (380)

Brams, Jerome M.: *ref,* 86(677), 352(36), 868(404)

Branom, Mendel E.: *test,* 801

Branston, W. T.: *ref,* 154(1494)

Brayfield, Arthur H.: *rev,* 879, 886; *ref,* 86(678), 605(69), 850(73), 863(273, 393), 905(8); *cross ref,* 864

Brazier, Mary A. B.: *ref,* 76(11)

Brecher, Sylvia: *ref,* 154(1854, 2019)

Bredemeier, Harry C.: *bk,* B352

Bregman, Martin: *ref,* 86(681), 308(418), 688(9)

Bregoli, Elmo J.: *ref,* 313(6)

Breiger, Boris: *ref,* 154(2077), 415 (566)

Brembeck, Winston L.: *ref,* 700 (4-5)

Bremner, Elizabeth A.: *other,* 154 (1551)

Brenner, Anton: *ref,* 335(89)

Bresee, Clyde W.: *ref,* 59(8), 107 (7), 155(160), 597(8), 645(51)

Breslow, Evelyn: *ref,* 928(13)

Bressler, Mildred B.: *ref,* 415(530)

Brewington, Ann: *cross ref,* 519, 522

Brice, Barbara C.: *ref,* 164(304)

Brice, Marshall M.: *ref,* 308(417), 363(114)

Bridge, Leopold: *ref,* 864(33)

Bridges, A. Frank: *test,* 558; *ref,* 558(2)

Bridgman, C. S.: *ref,* 400(66)

Briggs, Dennie L.: *ref,* 43(46), 164(431)

Briggs, Peter F.: *ref,* 86(697, 734)

Bright, H. F.: *ref,* 530(49)

Bright, Howard A.: *ref,* 416(86)

Brim, Orville G., Jr.: *exc,* B378

Brimer, M. A.: *rev,* 174, 182-3; *test,* 187, 193, 397, 465; *cross ref,* 1

Bristol, Marjorie: *ref,* 154(2086)

Bristow, William H.: *test,* 19

Britton, Joseph H.: *ref,* 335(67, 80)

Brockway, Ann Lawler: *ref,* 154 (1669)

Brodman, Keeve: *test,* 43, 552; *ref,* 44(1-2)

Brodsly, William J.: *ref,* 145(6)

Brody, Claire M. H.: *ref,* 147(44), 154(1855)

Brody, David S.: *ref,* 863(394)

Brody, Gertrude G.: *ref,* 154(1495)

Brody, Janice R.: *ref,* 154(2072), 164(546)

Brogden, H. E.: *bk,* B76; *ref,* 114 (93), 863(274); *cross ref,* 63, 78, 400

Broida, Daniel C.: *ref,* 86(482), 154(1670-1), 164(432)

Bromley, D. B.: *ref,* 370(69)

Brooks, Marjorie: *ref,* 154(2166, 2255)

Brooks, Melvin S.: *ref,* 863(301)

Brooks, Nelson: *rev,* 255, 266; *test,* 265

Brotman, Sanford: *ref,* 86(547)

Freeman, Kenneth H.: *ref*, 363(86)

Freeman, M. J.: *test*, 55; *bk*, B159; *ref*, 55(1-2)

Freeman, Robert A.: *ref*, 86(335)

French, Elizabeth G.: *ref*, 47(40)

French, John W.: *rev*, 45, 901; *bk*, B160-1; *exc*, B160; *ref*, 30 (128), 204(7, 20), 308(296, 302), 318(24, 34, 41), 786(8), 884 (100); *cross ref*, 87; *f*, 112

French, Joseph L.: *ref*, 767(3), 863(412)

French, Sidney J.: *cross ref*, 732

Freud, Sheldon L.: *ref*, 86(639), 414(23)

Frick, J. W.: *ref*, 86(427, 560), 308(406)

Fricke, Benno G.: *rev*, 20, 58-9, 560; *ref*, 86(627-8, 693-4), 179 (133), 645(55)

Friedhoff, Walter H.: *ref*, 597(7)

Friedman, Bert: *ref*, 155(185), 162(137)

Friedman, Howard: *ref*, 154(1343, 1522)

Friedman, Ira: *ref*, 154(2261), 164(573)

Friedman, Kopple C.: *test*, 795

Friedman, Pearl: *ref*, 598(6)

Friedman, Sidney: *ref*, 916(5)

Fries, Margaret E.: *ref*, 154(2262)

Friesen, Edward P.: *ref*, 893(2), 947(4)

Fritz, Martin F.: *test*, 98; *ref*, 98(1, 3, 6-9), 308(349)

Froehlich, Clifford P.: *rev*, 609, 863; *bk*, B162; *ref*, 605(50); *cross ref*, 891

Froehlich, Gustav J.: *rev*, 319-20; *exc*, 17; *cross ref*, 27, 181, 197, 216-7, 235, 428, 684-7, 692, 713, 791

Fromm, Erika: *bk*, B163; *ref*, 413 (605)

Fruchter, Benjamin: *rev*, 610, 613; *bk*, B164; *exc*, B42; *ref*, 11(5), 310(33), 362(21), 605(35)

Frumkin, Robert M.: *bk*, B165; *ref*, 84(3, 7-8)

Fry, Dinah E.: *test*, 889

Fry, Franklyn D.: *ref*, 86(336-7), 155(102), 164(330, 390-1)

Fry, Lois M.: *ref*, 415(572)

Frye, U. Cassian: *ref*, 415(573), 614(152)

Fujita, Ben: *ref*, 47(8, 21)

Fulk, Byron E.: *ref*, 310(34)

Fulkerson, Samuel C.: *ref*, 415 (565)

Fuller, Dorothy S.: *exc*, B190

Furfey, Paul H.: *cross ref*, 120

Furneaux, W. D.: *test*, 357; *ref*, 357(2)

Furst, Edward J.: *bk*, B72, B166; *f*, 716

Furuya, Kenji: *ref*, 126(16)

G., T.: *exc*, B342

Gabriel, K. R.: *ref*, 370(78)

Gadel, Marguerite S.: *ref*, 863(323)

Gage, N. L.: *rev*, 25, 114; *bk*, B167-8, B350; *cross ref*, 487, 656, 698, 717, 799

Gaier, Eugene L.: *rev*, 83, 371; *ref*, 86(474), 95(285)

Gainer, William L.: *ref*, 415(422)

Galanter, Eugene H.: *ref*, 139(38)

Galinsky, M. David: *ref*, 49(9), 154 (2253)

Gallagher, James J.: *ref*, 86(302, 428-9, 495), 89(33, 46), 154 (1250, 1698), 314(62), 408(37), 413(588)

Gallese, Arthur J., Jr.: *ref*, 148 (27), 164(439)

Gamble, Allen O.: *exc*, B414

Ganung, G. R.: *ref*, 86(430, 660)

Garcia, Dolores: *ref*, 688(14)

Gardner, Bruce: *ref*, 117(16-8)

Gardner, Burleigh B.: *ref*, 164(301)

Gardner, Eric F.: *rev*, 427, 653; *test*, 25, 487, 656, 698, 717, 799; *bk*, B169; *exc*, 17; *cross ref*, 24, 197, 217, 235, 428, 686-7, 692, 713, 791

Gardner, R.: *ref*, 53(4)

Garfield, Reed L.: *ref*, 86(676)

Garfield, Sol L.: *ref*, 111(30, 39), 164(331)

Garman, Glen D.: *ref*, 868(347, 419)

Garner, Ann Magaret: *exc*, B42, B79; *ref*, 111(28, 31), 154(1389), 164(335)

Garnero, Joseph: *ref*, 767(4)

Garrett, Henry E.: *rev*, 349, 381; *exc*, B89; *cross ref*, 314, 348

Garrison, Karl C.: *ref*, 89(38), 363(78)

Garry, Ralph J.: *ref*, 868(282, 324)

Gaskill, P.: *ref*, 370(104), 415 (599)

Gaston, Charles O.: *ref*, 86(629), 154(2123, 2132)

Gaston, E. Thayer: *test*, 252

Gates, Arthur I.: *test*, 630-3, 662; *ref*, 630(1), 633(1); *f*, 174, 222

Gates, Helen D.: *ref*, 38(81)

Gatto, Frank: *test*, 455

Gault, Una: *ref*, 416(70)

Gaumnitz, Walter H.: *bk*, B112

Gaver, Mary V.: *test*, 693

Gawkoski, R. Stephen: *test*, 15, 23, 201, 484, 627, 650

Gaylord, Richard H.: *exc*, B111

Gebhart, G. Gary: *ref*, 47(41)

Gee, Helen H.: *bk*, B170; *ref*, 868 (340)

Geers, John B.: *ref*, 162(65)

Geertsma, Robert: *ref*, 352(32), 415(555)

Gehl, Raymond H.: *test*, 137; *bk*, B254; *ref*, 137(1-3, 7)

Gehlmann, Frederick: *bk*, B171

Gehman, Ila H.: *ref*, 413(589), 416(109)

Gehman, W. Scott, Jr.: *ref*, 95 (267, 290), 863(368), 868(407)

Geist, Harold: *ref*, 86(338), 95 (275), 326(8)

Gelbmann, Frederick: *ref*, 147(21)

Gelfand, Leonard: *ref*, 154(1699)

Gelink, Marjorie: *test*, 854; *ref*, 854(1)

Gell, Kenneth E.: *cross ref*, 814

Gengerelli, J. A.: *ref*, 154(1863)

George, C. E.: *ref*, 154(1523, 1797, 1878), 863(378), 864(36)

Gerard, Donald L.: *ref*, 154(1734)

Gerber, Vernon R.: *ref*, 609(47)

Gerberich, J. Raymond: *rev*, 1, 175; *bk*, B172, B181-2; *ref*, 530 (44); *cross ref*, 4, 174, 194, 456, 620

Gerboth, Renate: *ref*, 415(421)

Gerick, Steven: *ref*, 783(71)

Gerken, C. d'A.: *bk*, B331; *ref*, 308(309), 399(5)

Germain, George L.: *ref*, 415(423)

Gerson, Elaine: *ref*, 147(36)

Gerstein, Alvin I.: *ref*, 415(619)

Gertz, Boris: *ref*, 67(5)

Getoff, Louis: *bk*, B73; *ref*, 154 (1666)

Getzels, J. W.: *bk*, B173; *ref*, 114 (125), 863(371)

Geyer, Margaret L.: *ref*, 763(4)

Ghiselli, Edwin E.: *bk*, B174; *exc*, B1, B465; *cross ref*, 873

Gibb, Cecil A.: *rev*, 76-7, 138

Gibbens, T. C. N.: *ref*, 412(84)

Gibby, Robert G.: *ref*, 154(1344-5, 1524-6, 1539, 1700-3, 1879)

Gibson, Frederick J.: *ref*, 413 (536), 415(470)

Gibson, James J.: *ref*, 154(2042)

Gibson, Norma L. B.: *ref*, 38(68)

Gibson, Q. H.: *ref*, 343(3), 370 (57)

Gibson, Robert L.: *ref*, 117(8), 154 (1564)

Giedt, F. Harold: *ref*, 154(1552)

Giedt, Helen Moore: *ref*, 415(424)

Giese, William J.: *ref*, 305(7), 513 (2), 783(33-4)

Gilberg, Richard L.: *ref*, 864(37), 868(372)

Gilberstadt, Harold: *ref*, 86(339, 531)

Gilbert, Harry B.: *ref*, 87(22, 24), 399(4), 889(54)

Gilbert, W. M.: *ref*, 6(16), 308 (300), 889(55)

Gilchrist, A. A.: *ref*, 164(579, 595)

Giles, H. H.: *cross ref*, 219

Gilgash, Curtis A.: *ref*, 415(600)

Gilhooly, Francis M.: *ref*, 154 (1346), 164(332)

Gill, Ethan M.: *test*, 554

Gill, Marie R.: *ref*, 370(94), 413 (581)

Gilliland, A. R.: *test*, 411; *ref*, 69 (59-61), 86(342)

Gilman, Samuel F.: *ref*, 37(9)

Gilmore, John V.: *test*, 671; *ref*, 671(1)

Gingles, Ruby H.: *ref*, 66(13)

Ginsparg, Harold T.: *ref*, 126(17)

Ginther, John R.: *exc*, B172

Gire, Eugenia: *ref*, 766(7)

Gittinger, John W.: *rev*, 167

Givens, Paul R.: *ref*, 863(279)

Gjernes, Oscar: *ref*, 609(112)

Glad, Donald D.: *ref*, 154(1408), 164(343)

Gladstein, Gerald A.: *ref*, 326(4)

Gladstone, Roy: *ref*, 154(1347)

Gladwin, Thomas: *ref*, 154(1527), 164(392)

Meyer, Bill T.: *ref*, 154(1575)
Meyer, George: *ref*, 154(1398, 1576)
Meyer, Herbert H.: *ref*, 400(29, 50), 884(111), 889(73-4)
Meyer, Jerome S.: *bk*, B290
Meyer, Mortimer M.: *exc*, B34, B41, B60, B204, B338, B340, B369, B372; *ref*, 134(4), 154 (1338, 2137), 164(502-3)
Meyers, Charles E.: *test*, 122
Miale, Florence R.: *bk*, B213
Michael, Carmen Miller: *ref*, 172 (134)
Michael, William B.: *rev*, 308-9, 377; *exc*, B26, B89, B164
Michaelis, John U.: *bk*, B291; *ref*, 86(469-70)
Michal-Smith, Harold: *ref*, 139 (39)
Micheels, William J.: *rev*, 887, 944
Micheli, Gene S.: *ref*, 614(114)
Micka, Helen K.: *ref*, 863(376)
Middaugh, Richard W.: *ref*, 926 (27)
Midkiff, Katherine L.: *ref*, 335 (87), 370(91)
Milam, Albert T.: *ref*, 114(113), 868(355)
Milam, James R.: *ref*, 164(453)
Milam, Otis H.: *ref*, 308(329)
Milburn, Braxton: *ref*, 147(51)
Miles, T. R.: *rev*, 52, 337, 393
Milholland, John E.: *rev*, 314, 350; *exc*, B424
Mill, Cyril R.: *ref*, 86(447), 154 (1577), 164(408), 402(3), 614 (145)
Millar, Mary A.: *ref*, 126(4)
Millard, Kenneth A.: *ref*, 926(18)
Miller, Carmen: *ref*, 154(1399, 1928), 172(118)
Miller, Christine: *ref*, 86(515, 772)
Miller, Daniel R.: *test*, 886-7; *ref*, 125(13), 154(1315, 1345, 1525-6, 1539, 1578, 1702-3), 164(321)
Miller, Elsa: *ref*, 402(2)
Miller, Frank G.: *ref*, 926(15)
Miller, Gilbert E.: *ref*, 889(51)
Miller, Jerome S.: *ref*, 164(454, 504)
Miller, Joseph S. A.: *ref*, 154 (1352), 415(428)
Miller, Katherine S.: *bk*, B281
Miller, Lawrence W.: *test*, 109
Miller, Lyle L.: *ref*, 329(7)
Miller, Minnie M.: *test*, 266, 271, 291
Miller, Peter M.: *ref*, 204(12)
Miller, Richard B.: *ref*, 400(24), 850(64)
Miller, Robert B.: *test*, 902
Miller, Robert D.: *bk*, B292
Miller, Robert S.: *ref*, 65(22, 29), 86(516, 583, 706)
Miller, Velma J.: *ref*, 16(3), 413 (558), 630(2), 661(5)
Miller, Virginia R.: *ref*, 763(3)
Miller, W. S.: *test*, 306, 352
Millett, Ruth: *test*, 549
Mills, Eugene S.: *ref*, 154(1929)
Mills, William W.: *ref*, 86(517)
Milne, G. G.: *ref*, 415(579)

Milstein, Victor: *ref*, 415(475, 515), 416(57, 75)
Milton, Alexander: *ref*, 86(764)
Milton, Charles R.: *ref*, 95(279), 363(103), 868(303), 884(99)
Mindess, Harvey: *ref*, 154(1400, 1579, 1930, 2203), 415(606)
Miner, John B.: *test*, 167; *bk*, B293, B428; *ref*, 164(550), 167(4-5)
Minkler, F. W.: *test*, 13
Minnesota State Employment Service: *ref*, 609(55-6)
Minski, Louis: *ref*, 154(1931), 155(153), 412(73)
Mintz, Elizabeth E.: *ref*, 154(2086)
Mires, Katherine C.: *ref*, 422(2)
Mirin, Bernard: *ref*, 154(1932)
Mirmow, Esther L.: *ref*, 155(107-8)
Misbach, Lorenz: *cross ref*, 69
Misch, Robert C.: *ref*, 154(1754)
Mitchell, Blythe C.: *ref*, 610(1)
Mitchell, Claude: *test*, 312
Mitchell, Dorothy P.: *ref*, 164(303)
Mitchell, Florence: *exc*, B42
Mitchell, J. H.: *ref*, 339(3)
Mitchell, James V., Jr.: *ref*, 38 (115), 313(12), 342(38), 362 (30), 614(153)
Mitchell, Mary Alice: *test*, 666
Mitchell, Mildred B.: *ref*, 154 (1401)
Mitchell, Walter M.: *ref*, 86(294), 868(279)
Mittlemann, Bela: *test*, 43-4; *ref*, 44(1-2, 11)
Mitzel, Harold E.: *bk*, B294-7; *ref*, 869(59)
Moeller, George: *ref*, 164(518)
Moffie, Dannie J.: *ref*, 95(279), 363(103), 868(303), 884(99)
Moffitt, J. Weldon: *ref*, 93(2)
Moldawsky, Patricia C.: *ref*, 415 (441)
Moldawsky, Stanley: *ref*, 415(441)
Molish, Ellen Elste: *ref*, 154(1236)
Molish, Herman B.: *exc*, B370; *ref*, 43(46), 154(1236, 2004, 2087-8, 2277); *f*, 154
Molkenbur, Robert: *test*, 738, 741
Mollenkopf, William G.: *ref*, 889 (88); *cross ref*, 444
Monachesi, Elio D.: *bk*, B200; *ref*, 86(346, 438, 502, 646); *other*, 86(405, 418, 439, 444)
Monahan, Francis X.: *ref*, 27(50)
Money, Lester, Jr.: *ref*, 164(424)
Money-Kyrle, R. E.: *f*, 151
Monroe, Harold J.: *ref*, 111(44), 154(2204)
Monroe, Jack J.: *ref*, 415(442)
Monroe, Marion. See Cox, Marion Monroe.
Mons, W. E. R.: *ref*, 154(1755, 1933)
Montalto, Fannie D.: *ref*, 154 (1402)
Montoye, Henry J.: *bk*, B218
Montross, Harold Wesley: *ref*, 112(17), 118(3)
Moody, Caesar B., Jr.: *ref*, 614 (115)
Mooney, Ross L.: *test*, 89

Moore, B. G. R.: *ref*, 315(13)
Moore, Charles W.: *ref*, 179(142), 308(435), 863(416)
Moore, Clark H.: *ref*, 86(707)
Moore, David G.: *test*, 905; *ref*, 905(5)
Moore, Harriet Bruce: *bk*, B280
Moore, Herbert: *test*, 853
Moore, Jacqueline A.: *ref*, 155(89)
Moore, Joseph E.: *test*, 872; *ref*, 63(35), 375(19); *cross ref*, 11, 853, 871
Moore, Mary: *bk*, B352
Moran, F. A.: *ref*, 415(443-4)
Moran, L. J.: *ref*, 57(47), 164 (551), 415(443-4)
Moran, Maurice J.: *bk*, B298; *ref*, 147(42)
More, Douglas M.: *ref*, 164(562)
Moredock, H. Stewart: *bk*, B75
Moreno, J. L.: *bk*, B299-300
Morey, Elwyn A.: *ref*, 869(54)
Morgan, Antonia Bell: *test*, 198, 395, 466
Morgan, Carl Elwood: *ref*, 86(295)
Morgan, Clellan L.: *ref*, 783(39)
Morgan, G. A. V.: *rev*, 16, 405; *test*, 189, 192-3, 461, 465, 489, 848
Morgan, Henry H.: *exc*, B370; *ref*, 86(312, 363), 164(312, 355), 868(284, 304)
Morgan, Joseph P.: *ref*, 609(51)
Morgan, Marcellus: *ref*, 609(36)
Morgan, W. Gregory: *ref*, 783(46)
Morgan, William J.: *test*, 395, 437, 466
Morici, Anthony R.: *ref*, 907(2), 911(20)
Morrice, J. K. W.: *ref*, 86(708)
Morris, Charles: *ref*, 118(6)
Morris, Charles M.: *ref*, 36(10)
Morris, Donald: *ref*, 605(66)
Morris, John B.: *rev*, 879, 954
Morris, John R., Jr.: *ref*, 162(133)
Morris, Robert P.: *ref*, 37(27), 107(8)
Morrisby, J. R.: *test*, 606
Morrison, Edward J.: *ref*, 155(90)
Morrison, R. L.: *ref*, 154(2089)
Morrow, Robert S.: *ref*, 172(107)
Morse, H. T.: *bk*, B301; *exc*, B132; *cross ref*, 7
Morse, Nancy C.: *ref*, 335(89)
Morson, Meyer: *ref*, 864(33)
Mortenson, Rodney H.: *ref*, 172 (124)
Morton, N. W.: *test*, 375; *exc*, 138; *ref*, 375(11); *cross ref*, 868, 889
Morton, R. L.: *cross ref*, 464
Morton, R. B.: *exc*, B299; *ref*, 47 (20), 164(551, 571-2)
Morton, Sheldon I.: *ref*, 86(364)
Mortvedt, Audrey R.: *ref*, 179 (104), 308(330)
Mosbo, Alvin O.: *ref*, 677(1)
Mosel, James N.: *ref*, 27(62), 29(1)
Moser, Harold E.: *rev*, 455, 472
Moser, Ulrich: *ref*, 162(109)
Moser, W. E.: *ref*, 605(50), 863 (256)
Moses, Peggy Lou: *test*, 680
Mosier, Charles I.: *cross ref*, 95, 926

Poull, Louise E.: *ref,* 354(4)

Pounders, C. J.: *ref,* 371(3)

Pounds, Ralph L.: *ref,* 179(125), 308(391)

Powell, Elizabeth K.: *ref,* 125(39)

Powell, Frank V.: *ref,* 868(377)

Powell, Joan A.: *ref,* 413(507), 415 (401)

Powell, Muriel B.: *ref,* 850(68)

Powers, Clair A.: *ref,* 148(20)

Powers, Mable K.: *ref,* 868(356, 397)

Powers, William T.: *ref,* 154(1948, 2265, 2283)

Poyntz, Lillian: *ref,* 766(9)

Praag, Jules V.: *ref,* 86(650), 154 (2106)

Pratt, Carolyn: *ref,* 154(1416-7)

Pratt, Carroll C.: *exc,* B156

Pratt, Martha A.: *ref,* 30(130)

Pratt, Willis E.: *test,* 1, 174, 455-6, 620-1, 675; *ref,* 675(1-2)

Preble, Elizabeth: *ref,* 17(9)

Pred, Gordon D.: *ref,* 305(5)

Prescott, Daniel A.: *cross ref,* 69

Prescott, George A.: *ref,* 855(1)

Preston, Ralph C.: *ref,* 318(25); *cross ref,* 1, 18, 25, 174, 190, 456, 463, 487, 620, 648, 656, 717, 790, 799, 806

Price, Arthur C.: *ref,* 154(1590), 413(500, 607), 416(24, 115)

Price, Bronson: *bk,* B109

Price, H. Vernon: *rev,* 467, 496; *test,* 421

Price, John R.: *ref,* 415(558), 416 (101)

Price, Ray G.: *cross ref,* 506

Prickett, Frances S.: *ref,* 117(13)

Prideaux, Gerald G.: *test,* 870; *ref,* 864(22)

Pringle, M. L. Kellmer: *rev,* 327, 367, 387; *ref,* 632(9), 651(7); *cross ref,* 651

Pronko, N. H.: *ref,* 773(8-9)

P.othro, E. Terry: *ref,* 343(9), 370(89)

Proud, Ann P.: *ref,* 149(33)

Providencia, M.: *test,* 591

Pruitt, Ray C.: *ref,* 50(7), 59(6), 156(12), 400(35)

Pruyser, Paul W.: *exc,* B425; *ref,* 154(1949)

Psychological Corporation: *test,* 908-9, 917, 920

Ptacek, James E.: *ref,* 60(3), 415 (520)

Public Personnel Association: *test,* 317, 516, 919, 921, 940, 956

Publicover, Phyllis R.: *ref,* 577(6)

Pugh, Derek S.: *ref,* 154(1765)

Pummell, M. F.: *test,* 13

Pumroy, Donald K.: *ref,* 86(765)

Pumroy, Shirley S.: *ref,* 123(11)

Purcell, Claire Kepler: *ref,* 86 (373), 154(1591), 415(446)

Purcell, Kenneth: *ref,* 154(2284), 164(553, 600), 412(78), 415(584)

Purdue Research Foundation: *test,* 873

Purdue University. See Personnel Evaluation Research Service.

Purdy, Benjamin F.: *ref,* 362(19), 850(69)

Pustell, Thomas E.: *ref,* 86(766)

Putman, Phil H.: *ref,* 27(39)

QUALTERE, Thomas: *ref,* 164 (395), 370(108)

Quarrington, Bruce: *bk,* B345; *exc,* B189; *ref,* 154(1699), 155 (124)

Quasha, William H.: *test,* 884

Quast, Wentworth: *bk,* B333; *ref,* 172(46, 140)

Quay, Herbert: *ref,* 86(463, 525, 586-7), 155(136)

Queensland Department of Public Instruction: *test,* 520, 875, 890

Quinn, Stanley Brittain: *ref,* 86 (712)

Quirk, Eve-Lyn: *ref,* 139(64)

Quirk, D.: *ref,* 154(1950)

RABIN, Albert I.: *rev,* 126, 416; *ref,* 125(45), 154(1766-8, 1898, 2213), 162(79, 84), 415(559, 575); *cross ref,* 149, 162

Rabin, Bernard: *exc,* B150

Rabin, Herbert M.: *ref,* 767(10)

Rabinovitch, M. S.: *ref,* 154(1592, 1769, 1951)

Rabinovitch, Vivian: *ref,* 104(2)

Rabinowitz, William: *bk,* B295-7; *ref,* 162(73, 91), 597(10), 868 (425)

Rachiele, Leo D.: *ref,* 416(59)

Racusen, Frances Rhea: *ref,* 154 (1418, 1593), 164(360)

Radcliffe, J. A.: *rev,* 58-9, 68; *exc,* B111, B144

Rader, Gordon E.: *ref,* 154(2214)

Radford, E.: *ref,* 154(2107)

Radley, Shirley: *ref,* 873(17)

Rafferty, Janet E.: *test,* 156; *ref,* 156(11, 13)

Raifman, Irving: *ref,* 154(2215)

Raimy, Victor: *exc,* B418; *ref,* 162 (74); *other,* 86(544)

Raine, Lois Margaret: *ref,* 415 (378)

Rainio, Kullervo: *bk,* B346; *ref.* 154(1952)

Rainwater, Lee: *ref,* 162(127)

Rakusin, John M.: *ref,* 154(1273)

Raleigh, William H.: *ref,* 313(4), 413(524), 416(40)

Ralph, Ray B.: *ref,* 609(42), 932 (12)

Ralph, Sally: *ref,* 6(12)

Ramey, Walter S.: *ref,* 864(39)

Ramharter, George H.: *test,* 722

Ramsay, Rose. See Mariani, Rose Ramsay.

Rand, Gertrude: *test,* 768; *ref,* 768 (27)

Randall, Rogers E.: *ref,* 342(34), 751(3)

Randolph, John F.: *cross ref,* 6, 420

Rankin, Richard: *ref,* 308(371)

Ransom, Dorothy: *ref,* 154(1953)

Ranson, Frances C.: *test,* 642

Ranzoni, Jane H.: *bk,* B177; *ref,* 154(1349, 1541)

Rapaport, Irene: *ref,* 413(508)

Rappaport, Sheldon R.: *ref,* 57 (38), 413(541), 415(489)

Rappaport, Sidney M.: *ref,* 154 (1770)

Raskin, Evelyn: *test,* 613; *exc,* B179

Rasmusen, V. B.: *test,* 759

Rasmussen, Elmer M.: *ref,* 308 (304)

Rasmussen, Otho M.: *test,* 501

Rasor, Floyd: *ref,* 38(34)

Ratzeburg, Fred: *ref,* 86(411)

Rau, Lucy: *bk,* B344

Raven, John C.: *test,* 127, 370; *bk,* B347; *ref,* 127(2, 5), 154(2108), 370(59, 109)

Rawn, Moss L.: *ref,* 70(2)

Ray, Charles D.: *ref,* 154(1474)

Ray, J. B.: *ref,* 154(1954), 162 (94), 413(497)

Ray, Thomas S.: *ref,* 162(135)

Raymaker, Henry, Jr.: *ref,* 86 (651)

Rayner, S. A.: *rev,* 673-4, 792; *test,* 830; *ref,* 830(1); *cross ref,* 24

Read, John G.: *test,* 715; *ref,* 715 (1)

Reckless, Walter C.: *ref,* 37(25)

Redlener, J.: *ref,* 863(214), 868 (275)

Redlo, Miriam: *ref,* 86(314, 370-1), 154(1406)

Reeb, Mildred: *ref,* 162(71)

Reed, Charles F.: *ref,* 37(24)

Reed, J. D.: *ref,* 768(20)

Reed, James C.: *exc,* B483

Reed, Max R.: *ref,* 86(713), 136 (5), 148(46)

Reed, Virginia M.: *test,* 496

Reed, Woodrow W.: *ref,* 125(31)

Reeder, Edwin H.: *cross ref,* 806

Rees, Robert E.: *ref,* 622(1)

Rees, W. Linford: *ref,* 154(1274)

Reese, D. G.: *ref,* 154(1506)

Reeves, Margaret Pegram: *ref,* 164(457)

Regal, Jacob: *ref,* 86(448, 526)

Regelin, Clinton: *ref,* 69(56)

Reich, H.: *ref,* 415(402)

Reichard, Suzanne: *ref,* 154(2109)

Reichart, Robert R.: *ref,* 308 (293)

Reichenberg-Hackett, Wally: *ref,* 335(77)

Reid, Alice R.: *ref,* 86(588)

Reid, J. William: *ref,* 156(15)

Reid, John W.: *ref,* 863(234)

Reid, Melvin P.: *ref,* 154(1771)

Reid, T. James: *ref,* 177(1)

Reidy, Mary E.: *ref,* 416(41)

Reile, Patricia J.: *ref,* 120(87)

Reilly, William J.: *ref,* 308(392)

Reiman, M. Gertrude: *other,* 147 (36)

Reindl, Mary O.: *ref,* 28(45), 59 (14)

Reiser, Morton F.: *ref,* 154(2236)

Reisner, Martin: *ref,* 65(38)

Reissenweber, Marion: *bk,* B348

Reitan, Ralph M.: *ref,* 86(589, 591), 154(1594-5, 1772-3, 1955-7, 1962)

Reiter, Sidney R.: *bk,* B294

Remmers, H. H.: *rev,* 16, 612; *test,* 101, 104-5, 199, 596, 643, 926; *bk,* B349-50; *exc,* B138;

Rosenzweig, Saul: *test*, 155; *ref*, 155(110, 125, 169), 363(89)

Rosevear, William H.: *ref*, 154 (1792)

Rosner, Benjamin: *rev*, 625; *ref*, 350(1)

Ross, Alexander T.: *ref*, 86(591), 154(1962)

Ross, C.: *bk*, B362

Ross, C. C.: *cross ref*, 9, 11, 23, 180, 223, 469, 639, 704, 801, 815

Ross, Charles S.: *rev*, 480, 484; *cross ref*, 458, 463

Ross, Clay C.: *bk*, B361

Ross, Donald: *ref*, 154(1308, 1782), 164(376)

Ross, Grace: *ref*, 120(88), 409(9)

Ross, Harvey L.: *ref*, 154(1781)

Ross, Laurence W.: *ref*, 375(12, 19)

Rossi, Asconia M.: *ref*, 86(676)

Rossi, Philip D.: *ref*, 415(450)

Rosskopf, Myron F.: *rev*, 429, 443

Rosvold, H. Enger: *ref*, 154(1782)

Roswell, Florence G.: *test*, 667

Roth, Martin: *ref*, 370(70, 75), 415(473, 490)

Rothe, Harold F.: *cross ref*, 519

Rothman, Philip: *exc*, B59

Rothney, John W. M.: *rev*, 79, 122; *bk*, B363-4; *ref*, 614(140) ; *cross ref*, 120, 413

Rothstein, Harvey J.: *ref*, 415 (491)

Rothwell, J. W.: *test*, 867

Rotter, George E.: *bk*, B183

Rotter, Julian B.: *test*, 156; *exc*, B448; *ref*, 154(2050), 156(11, 13) ; *cross ref*, 86, 164

Roulette, Thomas G.: *ref*, 154 (1276)

Rousey, C. L.: *ref*, 415(601)

Rowan, Thomas: *ref*, 155(163)

Rowell, John T.: *ref*, 86(587)

Royal, E. Ann: *ref*, 139(76)

Royce, Joseph R.: *exc*, B26

Royer, J. Everett: *ref*, 179(126), 308(393)

Royse, Arthur B.: *rev*, 386, 857

Royster, Robert F.: *test*, 912

Rubin, Eli Z.: *ref*, 154(2193)

Rubin, Harold: *ref*, 86(529), 139 (40, 50), 154(1603), 415(492)

Rubin, Stanley B.: *ref*, 86(315)

Rubin-Rabson, Grace: *ref*, 415 (586)

Ruch, F. L.: *test*, 607, 888; *cross ref*, 895-6

Ruch, Giles M.: *test*, 24, 487, 656, 698, 717, 799; *cross ref*, 421

Rudoff, Alvin: *ref*, 37(23)

Ruedisili, C. H.: *cross ref*, 926

Ruess, Aubrey L.: *ref*, 154(2287), 164(601), 326(35)

Ruff, William H.: *ref*, 530(45)

Rugen, Mable E.: *cross ref*, 557

Rule, Evelyn T.: *ref*, 154(1783)

Rumage, Charles J.: *bk*, B53; *ref*, 79(4)

Rummel, J. Francis: *bk*, B365-6

Rushing, John R.: *test*, 452

Rusmore, Jay: *ref*, 59(11), 400 (42), 850(81), 854(3)

Russell, David H.: *cross ref*, 675, 678

Russell, Diana: *ref*, 863(261-2, 282)

Russell, George E.: *ref*, 415(522)

Russell, Ivan L.: *ref*, 172(110), 326(24)

Russell, Trent S.: *ref*, 766(3)

Russon, Allien R.: *ref*, 6(18), 179 (105)

Rust, Ralph M.: *ref*, 154(1604), 868(357)

Ruszel, Humphrey: *bk*, B367

Rutledge, John A.: *ref*, 86(596)

Ryan, F. J.: *ref*, 154(1604), 868 (357)

Ryan, Loretta C.: *test*, 555

Ryan, T. A.: *exc*, B115

Ryan, Teresa M.: *test*, 175-6

Ryan, Vernon: *ref*, 769(4), 770 (15), 880(59), 781(16), 783(86)

Ryan, William: *ref*, 154(2112)

Ryans, David G.: *cross ref*, 118

Ryden, Einar R.: *test*, 695

S., B.: *exc*, B480

Sackett, Everett B.: *cross ref*, 856

Sackman, Harold: *ref*, 154(1605, 1784)

Sacks, Elinor L.: *ref*, 413(527)

Sacks, James: *ref*, 172(62)

Sacks, Joseph M.: *ref*, 154(2113, 2219), 412(79)

Sadnavitch, Joseph M.: *ref*, 413 (616)

Saetveit, Joseph G.: *test*, 251

Sager, Clifford J.: *ref*, 154(1998)

St. Clair, Norman E.: *ref*, 597(9)

Sakheim, George A.: *ref*, 154(1785, 1963)

Salcines, Ramon A.: *ref*, 86(779), 154(2297)

Sale, William M., Jr.: *f*, 206

Sales, Robert C.: *ref*, 695(2)

Salfield, D. J.: *ref*, 154(1277)

Salk, Lee: *ref*, 154(1964)

Salter, Mary D.: *ref*, 154(1428)

Salyers, Martha Hopkins: *ref*, 38 (71)

Samborski, Gloria: *ref*, 114(117)

Samenfeld, Herbert W.: *ref*, 308 (331), 359(62)

Samuels, Henry: *bk*, B368; *ref*, 154(1429), 164(363), 172(63)

Samuelson, Cecil O.: *ref*, 609(143), 863(382, 417)

Sandercock, Marian G.: *ref*, 413 (528), 416(42)

Sanders, C.: *rev*, 296-7, 307; *exc*, B113

Sanders, M. W.: *test*, 175, 820, 843

Sanders, Richard: *ref*, 154(1606)

Sanders, Wilma B.: *ref*, 30(129), 86(647), 601(33), 871(5)

Sanderson, Herbert: *ref*, 154(1430)

Sanderson, J. Wesley: *ref*, 86(381, 452)

Sandler, J.: *ref*, 154(1607, 1965)

Sandra, M. Elaine: *ref*, 30(137), 155(137)

Sanford, Nevitt: *ref*, 86(559, 625)

Sangren, Paul V.: *ref*, 354(5)

Sangster, C. H.: *ref*, 177(2)

Santiccioli, A.: *ref*, 123(9)

Sappenfield, Bert R.: *rev*, 133, 155; *exc*, B204

Sarason, Barbara R.: *ref*, 164(602)

Sarason, Irwin G.: *ref*, 86(654), 164(602, 608)

Sarason, Seymour B.: *bk*, B369; *ref*, 36(18), 154(1527, 1608, 1678, 1786, 2288), 164(392, 415), 415(437)

Sarbin, Anne: *ref*, 154(2114), 164 (555)

Sarbin, Theodore R.: *exc*, B204; *ref*, 154(1431) ; *cross ref*, 30

Sare, Harold: *test*, 843

Sargent, Helen D.: *test*, 143; *bk*, B370; *exc*, B60, B261; *ref*, 143 (2, 4) ; *cross ref*, 154; *other*, 154(1486)

Sargent, S. Stansfeld: *exc*, B140

Saslow, George: *ref*, 44(7), 76 (19-25), 154(2276)

Saslow, Harry L.: *ref*, 154(2220)

Sassenrath, Julius: *ref*, 308(371)

Satlow, I. David: *rev*, 389, 504

Satter, George: *ref*, 2(19), 57(42), 120(89, 91-2), 139(51), 172(92), 370(82, 92), 412(71, 75), 413 (561, 577), 415(523, 560), 614 (147) ; *cross ref*, 889

Satterlee, Robert L.: *ref*, 117(14)

Satz, Martin A.: *ref*, 179(106), 308(332)

Saugstad, Randolf G.: *ref*, 39(1)

Saum, James A.: *ref*, 336(3)

Saunders, David R.: *rev*, 65, 106; *test*, 90, 112; *bk*, B157; *exc*, B164; *ref*, 73(2), 868(399)

Saunders, Roger: *ref*, 162(67, 118)

Saunders, Wm. J., Jr.: *ref*, 363 (120-1), 889(89), 926(30)

Saunders, William W.: *ref*, 162 (95, 110)

Saupe, Ethel: *test*, 495

Savage, H. W.: *bk*, B371

Sawrey, James M.: *ref*, 326(17), 415(583)

Sawyer, Clifford R.: *ref*, 329(3)

Sawyer, George W., Jr.: *ref*, 155 (92)

Sawyer, Jack: *ref*, 237(2), 850 (85)

Saxe, Carl H.: *ref*, 164(300)

Sayons, K.: *ref*, 154(1609)

Sayons, Z.: *ref*, 154(1609)

Scagnelli, D. P.: *ref*, 123(9)

Scales, Margaret Beron: *ref*, 154 (1966)

Scandrette, Onas C.: *ref*, 38(94)

Scarborough, Barron B.: *ref*, 66 (12), 415(587), 863(419)

Scarr, Elizabeth H.: *ref*, 413(542)

Scates, Douglas E.: *rev*, 11, 833; *cross ref*, 699

Schaefer, Earl S.: *ref*, 154(1278)

Schaefer, Willis C.: *ref*, 530(46)

Schafer, Roy: *bk*, B372; *ref*, 154 (1316, 1432, 1610, 1787, 2115), 164(603)

Schaie, K. Warner: *ref*, 47(6), 614 (124, 148)

Schanberger, William J.: *ref*, 147 (27)

Schapero, Max: *ref*, 65(15)

Schaw, Louise C.: *ref*, 164(556)

Stein, Harry: *rev,* 462, 619; *ref,* 154(1980, 2129)
Stein, M.: *test,* 107; *ref,* 107(3)
Stein, Marie D.: *bk,* B248; *ref,* 154(2063)
Stein, Marvin: *ref,* 76(22)
Stein, Morris I.: *bk,* B407, B409; *ref,* 164(512), 352(31-2), 415(554-5); *f,* 135, 142
Stein, Seymour P.: *test,* 316
Steinbaum, Milton: *ref,* 780(60-1)
Steinberg, Arthur: *ref,* 162(97), 863(264)
Steinberg, Martin D.: *ref,* 853(2)
Steiner, Betty Jo: *ref,* 863(319)
Steiner, M. E.: *test,* 154
Steiner, Meta: *ref,* 154(1625)
Steisel, Ira M.: *ref,* 154(1284, 1447)
Stempel, Ellen F.: *ref,* 416(61), 614(126)
Stenger, Charles A.: *ref,* 415(502, 564)
Stennett, R. G.: *ref,* 172(156)
Stenquist, John L.: *ref,* 326(7)
Stepat, Dorothy L.: *ref,* 87(17)
Stephenson, Margaret: *test,* 549
Stephenson, William: *rev,* 74, 103; *test,* 388; *bk,* B408; *exc,* B408; *ref,* 154(1626, 1800), 164(464); *cross ref,* 65, 114
Stern, George G.: *bk,* B409
Stern, John A.: *ref,* 154(1904)
Stern, Virginia: *bk,* B93
Sternberg, Carl: *ref,* 86(461, 597, 659), 114(109-10, 122), 863(292-3, 360, 385)
Sternberg, Thomas H.: *ref,* 154(1269, 1294), 415(399)
Sterne, David M.: *ref,* 414(30)
Sterne, Spencer B.: *ref,* 154(1812)
Stessin, Lawrence: *bk,* B410
Stevens, Lucia B.: *ref,* 868(374)
Stevens, Phyllis Wolfe: *ref,* 154(1801)
Stevenson, Frank: *ref,* 53(6)
Steward, Verne: *test,* 950-3
Stewart, Barbara M.: *ref,* 86(549, 598)
Stewart, G. Kinsey: *ref,* 154(1802)
Stewart, Horace: *ref,* 172(143, 157)
Stewart, Lawrence H.: *bk,* B55; *exc,* B115; *ref,* 605(71), 863(361, 405), 868(290, 318)
Stewart, Naomi: *rev,* 122, 332; *ref,* 6(13); *cross ref,* 148, 335
Stewart, Ursula: *ref,* 147(29, 46, 54)
Stice, Glen F.: *ref,* 90(6), 112(13, 15)
Stiel, Agnes: *ref,* 154(1554)
Stiff, Margaret P.: *ref,* 154(1297, 1475)
Still, Dana S.: *ref,* 577(9)
Stillwell, Lois: *ref,* 326(36)
Stilson, Donald W.: *ref,* 67(5)
Stinson, Pairlee J.: *ref,* 605(39)
Stirling, I. M.: *exc,* B399
Stogdill, Ralph M.: *bk,* B411
Stolper, Rhoda: *ref,* 50(13)
Stoltz, Robert E.: *ref,* 47(48)
Stolz, Lois Meek: *exc,* B412
Stone, C. Harold: *bk,* B465-6
Stone, Calvin P.: *other,* 154(1389)

Stone, Clarence R.: *test,* 682
Stone, David R.: *ref,* 86(660-1), 124(1)
Stone, George: *bk,* B168
Stone, Harold: *ref,* 154(1627), 164(420, 560)
Stone, John T.: *ref,* 154(1890)
Stone, Joics B.: *test,* 159; *ref,* 7(29), 308(368)
Stone, L. Joseph: *rev,* 168; *bk,* B303; *ref,* 154(2037); *cross ref,* 126
Stone, Solomon: *ref,* 87(31), 118(11), 308(429), 863(406)
Stoops, John A.: *ref,* 863(294)
Stopol, Murray S.: *ref,* 154(1285, 1803)
Stordahl, Kalmer E.: *ref,* 868(334, 358-9)
Storm, Thomas: *ref,* 164(524)
Storment, Charlyne Townsend: *ref,* 154(1286, 1628)
Storms, Lowell H.: *ref,* 86(648), 172(154)
Storrs, Sibyll V.: *ref,* 415(453), 609(43-4)
Stotsky, Bernard A.: *ref,* 154(1448, 1524, 1526, 1539, 1700-3, 1879, 1981-2, 2233), 375(22), 412(79), 415(454)
Stott, D. H.: *test,* 35
Stott, Leland H.: *bk,* B412
Stott, Sterling S.: *ref,* 114(115)
Stott, Warren W.: *ref,* 154(1629)
Stouffer, Samuel A.: *bk,* B352
Stoughton, Robert W.: *ref,* 605(61)
Stowe, Edward W.: *ref,* 863(362)
Straight, Glenn H.: *ref,* 86(662), 95(296)
Strang, Ruth: *rev,* 696, 698; *test,* 666; *bk,* B413; *cross ref,* 21, 25, 869
Strange, Frank B.: *ref,* 415(495)
Strange, Jack R.: *ref,* 154(1335)
Strate, Marvin W.: *ref,* 905(8)
Strauss, F. H.: *ref,* 164(465)
Streit, L. Robert: *ref,* 352(19)
Strickland, Ruth: *rev,* 196, 201; *cross ref,* 23
Strieter, Edith: *ref,* 147(54)
Stromberg, Eleroy L.: *ref,* 305(6)
Stromer, Walter F.: *ref,* 413(529)
Strong, Edward K., Jr.: *test,* 868-9; *bk,* B414-5; *ref,* 850(48), 868(287, 307-11, 335-6, 360, 380-2, 414)
Strother, Charles R.: *rev,* 109, 141; *ref,* 47(6), 402(1), 614(148); *cross ref,* 52, 57, 149, 158
Strother, George B.: *ref,* 850(49)
Stroud, J. B.: *test,* 665, 677; *ref,* 416(122-3); *cross ref,* 179, 645
Stroup, Attlee L.: *ref,* 84(2)
Stroup, Francis: *bk,* B416
Strowig, Ronald W.: *ref,* 352(22)
Struening, E. L.: *ref,* 38(113), 78(54), 86(658)
Struhs, Isabel: *ref,* 370(102), 413(598)
Stuart, Joan E.: *test,* 367
Stucky, Philip: *test,* 452
Stuit, Dewey B.: *cross ref,* 884
Stull, Harriet: *bk,* B45

Stump, N. F.: *ref,* 783(31, 46, 48, 75)
Sturm, Norman H.: *ref,* 63(35)
Sturrock, George W.: *rev,* 470, 489
Stutz, Frederick H.: *rev,* 816, 837; *test,* 814
Suburban School Study Council, Educational Service Bureau, School of Education, University of Pennsylvania: *test,* 100
Suczek, Robert F.: *test,* 144; *ref,* 144(4), 172(65)
Sugarman, Daniel A.: *ref,* 154(1972)
Suhr, Virtus W.: *ref,* 112(14)
Sullivan, Arthur: *ref,* 370(110), 415(610)
Sullivan, Daniel F.: *ref,* 86(743)
Sullivan, Elizabeth T.: *test,* 313-4; *f,* 314
Sullivan, Ellen B.: *ref,* 154(1294), 415(399)
Sullivan, Helen B.: *test,* 661
Sullivan, Patrick L.: *ref,* 86(386, 772)
Sultan, Florence: *ref,* 154(2155), 164(477)
Sulzman, J. H.: *ref,* 770(11), 780(53), 781(19), 783(49)
Sumerwell, Harriet C.: *ref,* 164(608)
Summerfield, Arthur: *exc,* B21, B423
Sumner, Earl D.: *ref,* 47(49), 114(143)
Sumner, F. C.: *ref,* 114(113), 868(355)
Sumner, W. L.: *cross ref,* 471
Sundberg, Norman D.: *rev,* 413; *ref,* 86(387, 663-4), 868(312)
Supeau, Gerald A.: *ref,* 308(396)
Super, Donald E.: *rev,* 606, 850; *bk,* B55, B417; *exc,* B115, B174, B349, B414; *ref,* 363(94), 609(142), 614(159), 850(56), 868(290, 318); *cross ref,* 863; *other,* 605(65)
Surko, Elsie F.: *ref,* 416(110)
Surratt, Carolyn: *ref,* 326(1)
Sutcliffe, J. P.: *rev,* 39; *ref,* 154(2130), 155(156, 181)
Sutherland, John: *rev,* 461, 473, 485
Sutherland, LaVerne D.: *ref,* 169(4)
Sutker, Alvin R.: *ref,* 156(19)
Suttell, Barbara J.: *bk,* B172, B330; *exc,* B409; *ref,* 172(47, 66)
Sutter, Everett L.: *ref,* 164(368, 421)
Sutter, Nancy A.: *ref,* 27(44)
Sutton, Marcella A.: *bk,* B186; *ref,* 114(112), 863(316)
Sutton, Mary L.: *ref,* 86(388)
Swan, Robert J.: *ref,* 86(462, 718)
Swanson, Edward O.: *ref,* 605(73)
Swartz, Melvin B.: *ref,* 154(1630, 2234)
Sweeney, Francis J.: *ref,* 314(52), 863(338)
Sweetland, Anders: *ref,* 86(463, 525), 107(6), 155(136)

Classified Index of Tests

* * * * *

This index serves as an expanded table of contents for the section "Tests and Reviews" by presenting a complete list of the tests and reviewers. Numbers preceding titles indicate the entry numbers to be consulted for full bibliographic entries, test references, and reviews. Stars indicate new tests not previously listed in this series; asterisks indicate tests which have been revised in some way or have been issued in new form since they were last listed.

34. ★*A Book About Me.* Review by Florence M. Teagarden.
35. ★*Bristol Social-Adjustment Guides.*
36. *Brown Personality Inventory for Children.*
37. ★*California Psychological Inventory.* Reviews by Lee J. Cronbach and Robert L. Thorndike; and an excerpt from a review.
38. *California Test of Personality, 1953 Revision.* Review by Verner M. Sims.
39. ★*The Cassel Group Level of Aspiration Test, 1957 Revision.* Reviews by W. Grant Dahlstrom, Harrison G. Gough, and J. P. Sutcliffe; and excerpts from two reviews.
40. ★*The Cassel Psychotherapy Progress Record.*
41. ★*Child Personality Scale.* Reviews by Robe.t H. Bauernfeind and Dale B. Harris.
42. ★*Community Improvement Scale.* Review by Wimburn L. Wallace.
43. *Cornell Index.*
44. ★*Cornell Word Form 2.*
45. ★*DF Opinion Survey.* Reviews by Andrew R. Baggaley, John W. French, and Arthur W. Meadows.
46. *Detroit Adjustment Inventory.* Review by Laurance F. Shaffer.
47. ★*Edwards Personnel Preference Schedule.* Reviews by Frank Barron, Åke Bjerstedt, and Donald W. Fiske; and excerpts from two reviews.
48. ★*The Ego Strength Q-Sort Test.*
49. ★*Embedded Figures Test.*
50. *The Empathy Test.* Review by Robert L. Thorndike.
51. ★*Evaluation Modality Test.* Review by Wilson H. Guertin.
52. *Examining for Aphasia: A Manual for the Examination of Aphasia and Related Disturbances, Revised Edition.* Review by T. R. Miles; and excerpts from two reviews.
53. ★*Family Adjustment Test.* Review by Albert Ellis.
54. ★*Fatigue Scales Kit.*
55. ★*The Freeman Anxiety Neurosis and Psychosomatic Test.*
56. ★*Friend-Critic Statement.*
57. *Goldstein-Scheerer Tests of Abstract and Concrete Thinking.*
58. ★*Gordon Personal Inventory.* Reviews by Benno G. Fricke and John A. Radcliffe; and excerpts from two reviews.
59. ★*Gordon Personal Profile.* Reviews by Benno G. Fricke and John A. Radcliffe; and an excerpt from a review.
60. ★*The Grassi Block Substitution Test: For Measuring Organic Brain Pathology.* Excerpts from two reviews.
61. ★*The Grayson Perceptualization Test.* Reviews by D. Russell Davis and William Schofield.
62. ★*Group Cohesiveness: A Study of Group Morale.*
63. *The Guilford-Martin Inventory of Factors GAMIN, Abridged Edition.*
64. *The Guilford-Martin Personnel Inventory.*
65. *The Guilford-Zimmerman Temperament Survey.* Review by David R. Saunders.
66. *Heston Personal Adjustment Inventory.*
67. ★*Hospital Adjustment Scale.* Review by Maurice Lorr.
68. ★*Human Relations Inventory.* Reviews by Raymond C. Norris and John A. Radcliffe.
69. *The Humm-Wadsworth Temperament Scale.*
70. ★*The IPAT Anxiety Scale.* Reviews by J. P. Guilford and E. Lowell Kelly; and an excerpt from a review.
71. ★*IPAT Contact Personality Factor Test.* Reviews by Cecil D. Johnson and S. B. Sells.

72. ★*IPAT High School Personality Questionnaire.*
73. ★*IPAT Music Preference Test of Personality.* Review by Neil J. Van Steenberg.
74. ★*IPAT Neurotic Personality Factor Test.* Reviews by S. B. Sells and William Stephenson.
75. ★*Institute of Child Study Security Test.* Review by Laurance F. Shaffer
76. *Interaction Chronograph.* Review by Cecil A. Gibb.
77. *Interaction Process Analysis.* Review by Cecil A. Gibb.
78. *An Inventory of Factors STDCR.*
79. *KD Proneness Scale and Check List.* Review by John W. M. Rothney.
80. *Kuder Preference Record—Personal.* Review by Dwight L. Arnold.
81. ★*Life Experience Inventory.* Reviews by Dan L. Adler and Douglas T. Kenny.
82. ★*The MACC Behavioral Adjustment Scale: An Objective Approach to the Evaluation of Behavioral Adjustment of Psychiatric Patients.* Review by Maurice Lorr.
83. ★*McCleery Scale of Adolescent Development.* Reviews by Eugene L. Gaier and John E. Horrocks.
84. ★*A Marriage Prediction Schedule.*
85. *Minnesota Counseling Inventory.* Excerpt from a review.
86. *Minnesota Multiphasic Personality Inventory, Revised Edition.* Reviews by Albert Ellis and Warren T. Norman.
87. *Minnesota Personality Scale.*
88. *Minnesota Rating Scale for Personal Qualities and Abilities, [Fourth Revision].* Review by Dorothy M. Clendenen.
89. *Mooney Problem Check List, 1950 Revision.*
90. ★*Objective-Analytic Personality Test Batteries.* Review by H. J. Eysenck.
91. ★*Personal Adaptability Test.* Review by Harold Webster.
92. ★*The Personal and Social Development Program.* Reviews by Edward Landy and C. Gilbert Wrenn (with Roy D. Lewis).
93. ★*The Personal Preference Scale.*
94. ★*The Personality Evaluation Form: A Technique for the Organization and Interpretation of Personality Data.* Review by Dorothy H. Eichorn; and an excerpt from a review.
95. *The Personality Inventory.*
96. ★*Pictorial Study of Values: Pictorial Allport-Vernon.* Reviews by Andrew R. Baggaley and Harrison G. Gough.
97. ★*The Power of Influence Test.*
98. ★*Practical Policy Test.*
99. ★*Primary Empathic Abilities.* Review by Robert L. Thorndike.
100. ★*Pupil Adjustment Inventory.* Reviews by Robert H. Bauernfeind and John Pierce-Jones; and an excerpt from a review.
101. *The Purdue Rating Scale for Administrators and Executives.* Reviews by John P. Foley, Jr. and Herbert A. Tonne.
102. ★*Rating Scale for Pupil Adjustment.* Reviews by William E. Henry and Morris Krugman.
103. ★*SAQS Chicago Q Sort.* Reviews by William Stephenson and Clifford H. Swensen, Jr.
104. *SRA Junior Inventory.* Review by Warren R. Baller; and excerpts from two reviews.
105. *SRA Youth Inventory.*
106. ★*The Science Research Temperament Scale.* Reviews by John D. Black and David R. Saunders.
107. *Security-Insecurity Inventory.* Reviews by Nelson G. Hanawalt and Harold Webster.
108. *Self Analysis Inventory.* Reviews by Warren R. Baller and John W. Gustad.

109. ★*Self-Perception Inventory: An Adjustment Survey With Special Reference to the Speech Situation.* Review by C. R. Strother.

110. ★*The Sherman Mental Impairment Test.* Reviews by D. Russell Davis and William Schofield.

111. *Shipley-Institute of Living Scale for Measuring Intellectual Impairment.*

112. **Sixteen Personality Factor Questionnaire.* Review by C. J. Adcock.

113. **Social Participation Scale, 1952 Edition.*

114. *Study of Values: A Scale for Measuring the Dominant Interests in Personality, Revised Edition.* Review by N. L. Gage.

115. ★*Temperament and Character Test.*

116. ★*Survey of Attitudes and Beliefs.* Reviews by Donald T. Campbell and C. Robert Pace.

117. *Test of Personality Adjustment.* Reviews by Dan L. Adler and Harrison G. Gough.

118. *Thurstone Temperament Schedule.* Review by Neil J. Van Steenberg.

119. ★*Tulane Factors of Liberalism-Conservatism.* Reviews by Donald T. Campbell and C. Robert Pace.

120. **Vineland Social Maturity Scale.*

121. ★*A Weighted-Score Likability Rating Scale.*

122. ★*What I Like to Do: An Inventory of Children's Interests.* Reviews by John W. M. Rothney and Naomi Stewart; and an excerpt from a review.

123. ★*Wittenborn Psychiatric Rating Scales.* Reviews by H. J. Eysenck and Maurice Lorr; and an excerpt from a review.

PROJECTIVE

124. ★*The Auditory Apperception Test.* Reviews by Kenneth L. Bean and Clifford H. Swensen, Jr.

125. *The Blacky Pictures: A Technique for the Exploration of Personality Dynamics.* Review by Kenneth R. Newton; and an excerpt from a review.

126. **Children's Apperception Test.* Reviews by Douglas T. Kenny and Albert I. Rabin.

127. **Controlled Projection for Children, Second Edition.* Excerpts from three reviews.

128. ★*Curtis Completion Form.* Review by Alfred B. Heilbrun, Jr.

129. ★*Draw-A-Person Quality Scale.* Review by Philip L. Harriman.

130. ★*The Drawing-Completion Test: A Projective Technique for the Investigation of Personality.* Excerpts from four reviews.

131. ★*The Eight Card Redrawing Test (8CRT).* Reviews by Cherry Ann Clark and Philip L. Harriman; and an excerpt from a review.

132. ★*Family Relations Test: An Objective Technique for Exploring Emotional Attitudes in Children.* Reviews by John E. Bell, Dale B. Harris, and Arthur R. Jensen.

133. ★*The Five Task Test: A Performance and Projective Test of Emotionality, Motor Skill and Organic Brain Damage.* Reviews by Dorothy H. Eichorn and Bert R. Sappenfield; and an excerpt from a review.

134. ★*The Forer Structured Sentence Completion Test.* Reviews by Charles N. Cofer and Percival M. Symonds.

135. ★*The Forer Vocational Survey.* Reviews by Benjamin Balinsky and Charles N. Cofer; and an excerpt from a review.

136. ★*Franck Drawing Completion Test.* Review by Arthur W. Meadows.

137. ★*The Graphomotor Projection Technique.* Review by Philip L. Harriman; and excerpts from two reviews.

138. *Group Projection Sketches for the Study of Small Groups.* Review by Cecil A. Gibb.

139. **H-T-P: House-Tree-Person Projective Technique.* Review by Philip L. Harriman.

140. ★*The Holtzman Inkblot Test.*

141. ★*The Howard Ink Blot Test.* Review by C. R. Strother; and an excerpt from a review.

142. ★*An Incomplete Sentence Test for Industrial Use.* Review by Benjamin Balinsky.

143. ★*The Insight Test: A Verbal Projective Test for Personality Study.* Review by Richard Jessor.

144. ★*Interpersonal Diagnosis of Personality.*

145. **Kahn Test of Symbol Arrangement.* Reviews by Cherry Ann Clark and Richard Jessor; and an excerpt from a review.

146. ★*The Lowenfeld Kaleidoblocs.*

147. **Lowenfeld Mosaic Test.* Review by C. J. Adcock.

148. *Machover Draw-A-Person Test.*

149. **Make A Picture Story.*

150. ★*The Michigan Picture Test.* Reviews by William E. Henry and Morris Krugman; and excerpts from two reviews.

151. ★*The Object Relations Technique.* Review by George Westby.

152. ★*The Picture Impressions: A Projective Technique for Investigating the Patient-Therapist Relationship.* Excerpt from a review.

153. ★*The Picture World Test.* Review by Walter Kass; and an excerpt from a review.

154. **Rorschach.* Reviews by Samuel J. Beck, H. J. Eysenck, Raymond J. McCall, and Laurance F. Shaffer.

155. *Rosenzweig Picture-Frustration Study.* Reviews by Richard H. Dana and Bert R. Sappenfield.

156. *The Rotter Incomplete Sentences Blank.*

157. ★*Self Valuation Test.*

158. **Sentence Completions Test.*

159. ★*Structured-Objective Rorschach Test: Preliminary Edition.*

160. ★*Symbol Elaboration Test.* Review by Richard H. Dana.

161. *Symonds Picture-Story Test.* Reviews by Walter Kass and Kenneth R. Newton.

162. **Szondi Test.*

163. ★*A Test of Family Attitudes.* Review by John E. Bell.

164. *Thematic Apperception Test.* Reviews by Leonard D. Eron and Arthur R. Jensen.

165. ★*Thematic Apperception Test for African Subjects.* Review by Mary D. Ainsworth.

166. *Thematic Apperception Test: Thompson Modification.* Review by Mary D. Ainsworth.

167. ★*The Tomkins-Horn Picture Arrangement Test.* Reviews by Donald W. Fiske, John W. Gittinger, and Wayne H. Holtzman; and an excerpt from a review.

168. **The Toy World Test.* Review by L. Joseph Stone.

169. **The Travis Projective Pictures.* Review by Edwin S. Shneidman.

170. ★*The Tree Test.*

171. **Twitchell-Allen Three-Dimensional Personality Test.*

172. *Visual Motor Gestalt Test.*

ENGLISH

173. *A.C.E.R. English Usage Tests.* Review by J. A. Richardson.

174. **American School Achievement Tests, Part 3, Language and Spelling.* Reviews by M. A. Brimer and Clarence Derrick.

175. **Barrett-Ryan English Test.* Review by J. Raymond Gerberich.

176. **Barrett-Ryan-Schrammel English Test, New*

Edition. Reviews by Leonard S. Feldt and Cleveland A. Thomas.

177. **California Language Test, 1957 Edition.* Reviews by Constance M. McCullough and Winifred L. Post.

178. *College English Test: National Achievement Tests.* Review by Osmond E. Palmer.

179. **Cooperative English Test: Lower and Higher Levels.*

180. **Coordinated Scales of Attainment: English.*

181. **Correctness and Effectiveness of Expression.*

182. *★Cotswold Junior English Ability Test.* Reviews by M. A. Brimer and John C. Daniels.

183. **Cotswold Measurement of Ability: English.* Reviews by M. A. Brimer and S. C. Richardson.

184. **English: Every Pupil Scholarship Test.*

185. **English IX–XII: Achievement Examinations for Secondary Schools.*

186. *★English IX–XII: Midwest High School Achievement Examinations.* Review by Roger A. Richards.

187. *★English Progress Tests A–F.* Reviews by Neil Gourlay and Stanley Nisbet.

188. **English Survey Test: Ohio Scholarship Tests: Ohio Senior Survey Tests.*

189. *★English Test (Adv.).*

190. **English Test: Municipal Tests: National Achievement Tests.*

191. **English Test: National Achievement Tests.*

192. *★English Test 2.* Reviews by Reginald Edwards, S. C. Richardson, and Cleveland A. Thomas.

193. *★English Tests 1, 3–8.*

194. **English Usage: Every Pupil Test.*

195. *★Greene-Stapp Language Abilities Test: Evaluation and Adjustment Series.* Reviews by Richard A. Meade and Osmond E. Palmer.

196. *★Hoyum-Schrammel English Essentials Tests.* Reviews by Worth R. Jones and Ruth Strickland.

197. **The Iowa Tests of Educational Development: Test 3, Correctness and Effectiveness of Expression.*

198. *Modern English Usage Test.* Review by Holland Roberts.

199. *★The New Purdue Placement Test in English.* Reviews by Gerald V. Lannholm and M. J. Wantman.

200. *★SRA Achievement Series: Language Arts.* Reviews by Constance M. McCullough and Winifred L. Post.

201. *★Scholastic Achievement Series: English-Spelling.* Reviews by Geraldine Spaulding and Ruth Strickland.

202. *★Survey Tests of English Usage.*

203. **Tressler English Minimum Essentials Tests, Revised Edition.*

COMPOSITION

204. **College Entrance Examination Board Achievement Test in English Composition.*

205. *★College Entrance Examination Board Advanced Placement Examination: English Composition.* Review by Robert C. Pooley.

206. *★Sequential Tests of Educational Progress: Essay Test.* Reviews by John S. Diekhoff, John M. Stalnaker, and Louis C. Zahner.

207. *★Sequential Tests of Educational Progress: Writing.* Reviews by Charlotte Croon Davis, John M. Stalnaker, and Louis C. Zahner.

LITERATURE

208. *★American Literature: Every Pupil Scholarship Test.*

209. **American Literature: Every Pupil Test.*

210. *★Center-Durost Literature Acquaintance Test:*

Evaluation and Adjustment Series. Review by Holland Roberts.

211. *★College Entrance Examination Board Advanced Placement Examination: Literature.* Review by John S. Diekhoff.

212. *★English Language and Literature: National Teacher Examinations.*

213. *★English Language and Literature: Teacher Education Examination Program.*

214. **English Literature: Every Pupil Test.*

215. **The Graduate Record Examinations Advanced Tests: Literature.* Review by Robert C. Pooley.

216. **Interpretation of Literary Materials.*

217. **The Iowa Tests of Educational Development: Test 7, Ability to Interpret Literary Materials.*

218. **Literature: Every Pupil Scholarship Test.*

219. **Literature Test: National Achievement Tests.*

SPEECH

220. *★The Graduate Record Examinations Advanced Tests: Speech.*

221. *★Weidner-Fensch Speech Screening Test.* Review by Louise B. Scott (with Robert S. Cathcart).

SPELLING

222. *★A.C.E.R. Spelling Test (Form C).* Reviews by J. A. Richardson and D. K. Wheeler.

223. **Coordinated Scales of Attainment: Spelling.*

224. **Graded Word Spelling Test.* Review by John Nisbet.

225. **Lincoln Diagnostic Spelling Tests.*

226. *★Phonovisual Diagnostic Spelling Test: A Test for All Consonant Sounds and the 17 Fundamental Vowel Sounds.*

227. **Spelling and Vocabulary: Every Pupil Test.*

228. *★Spelling Errors Test.*

229. **Spelling: Every Pupil Scholarship Test.*

230. **Spelling Test: National Achievement Tests.* Review by James A. Fitzgerald.

231. **Traxler High School Spelling Test.*

232. **Wellesley Spelling Scale.* Review by Janet G. Afflerbach.

VOCABULARY

233. *★Durost-Center Word Mastery Test: Evaluation and Adjustment Series.* Review by A. N. Hieronymus.

234. **The Inglis Tests of English Vocabulary.*

235. **The Iowa Tests of Educational Development: Test 8, General Vocabulary.*

236. *★New Standard Vocabulary Test.* Reviews by Richard A. Meade and Osmond E. Palmer.

237. *★Purdue Industrial Supervisors Word-Meaning Test: Purdue Personnel Test.* Reviews by Jerome E. Doppelt and Bernadine Meyer.

238. *★Quick-Scoring Vocabulary Test: Dominion Tests.*

239. **Survey Test of Vocabulary.*

240. **Vocabulary: Every Pupil Scholarship Test.*

241. **Vocabulary Test: National Achievement Tests.*

FINE ARTS

ART

242. **Horn Art Aptitude Inventory.* Review by Orville Palmer.

MUSIC

243. **Aliferis Music Achievement Test: College Entrance Level.* Review by Herbert D. Wing.

244. *Conrad Instrument-Talent Test.* Review by Herbert D. Wing.
245. ★*Drake Musical Aptitude Tests.* Reviews by Robert W. Lundin and James Mainwaring.
246. ★*The Farnum Music Notation Test.* Reviews by Kenneth L. Bean and William S. Larson.
247. *The Graduate Record Examinations Advanced Tests: Music.* Review by William S. Larson.
248. ★*Kwalwasser Music Talent Test.* Reviews by Paul R. Farnsworth and Kate Hevner Mueller.
249. ★*Music Education: National Teacher Examinations.*
250. *Musical Aptitude Test: Series A.* Review by Robert W. Lundin.
251. *Seashore Measures of Musical Talents, Revised Edition.*
252. ★*Test of Musicality, Fourth Edition.* Reviews by Paul R. Farnsworth and Kate Hevner Mueller
253. ★*Watkins-Farnum Performance Scale: A Standardized Achievement Test for All Band Instruments.* Review by Herbert D. Wing.
254. *Wing Standardized Tests of Musical Intelligence, [Revised Edition].*

FOREIGN LANGUAGES

ENGLISH

255. ★*Diagnostic Test for Students of English as a Second Language.* Reviews by Nelson Brooks and Herschel T. Manuel.
256. *English Examinations for Foreign Students.* Reviews by Ralph Bedell, John A. Cox, Jr., and Charles R. Langmuir.
257. *English Language Test for Foreign Students.* Review by John A. Cox, Jr.
258. ★*An English Reading Test for Students of English as a Foreign Language.* Reviews by Ralph Bedell and John A. Cox, Jr.
259. ★*English Usage Test for Non-Native Speakers of English.*
260. ★*Examination in Structure (English as a Foreign Language).*
261. *Test of Aural Comprehension.* Reviews by Herschel T. Manuel and Clarence E. Turner.
262. ★*Test of Aural Perception in English for Latin-American Students.*

FRENCH

263. *College Entrance Examination Board Achievement Test in French.*
264. ★*College Entrance Examination Board Advanced Placement Examination: French.*
265. ★*Cooperative French Listening Comprehension Test.* Reviews by Walter V. Kaulfers and Kathleen N. Perret.
266. ★*First Year French Test.* Reviews by Nelson Brooks and Mary E. Turnbull.
267. *French I and II: Achievement Examinations for Secondary Schools.*
268. ★*French I and II: Midwest High School Achievement Examinations.* Review by Mary E. Turnbull.
269. ★*French: Teacher Education Examination Program.*
270. *The Graduate Record Examinations Advanced Tests: French.* Review by Walter V. Kaulfers.
271. ★*Second Year French Test.* Reviews by Geraldine Spaulding and Clarence E. Turner.

GERMAN

272. *College Entrance Examination Board Achievement Test in German.* Review by Harold B. Dunkel.

273. ★*College Entrance Examination Board Advanced Placement Examination: German.* Review by Herbert Schueler.
274. *First Year German Test.* Review by Herbert Schueler.
275. *German I and II: Achievement Examinations for Secondary Schools.*
276. ★*German I and II: Midwest High School Achievement Examinations.* Review by Harold B. Dunkel.

GREEK

277. *College Entrance Examination Board Achievement Test in Greek.* Review by Konrad Gries.

HEBREW

278. ★*Uniform Achievement Tests.*

ITALIAN

279. *College Entrance Examination Board Achievement Test in Italian.*

LATIN

280. *College Entrance Examination Board Achievement Test in Latin.* Review by Konrad Gries.
281. ★*College Entrance Examination Board Advanced Placement Examination: Latin.*
282. *First Year Latin: Every Pupil Scholarship Test.*
283. ★*Kansas First Year Latin Test.*
284. *Latin I and II: Achievement Examinations for Secondary Schools.*
285. *Latin I and II: Every Pupil Test.*
286. ★*Latin I and II: Midwest High School Achievement Examinations.*

SPANISH

287. *College Entrance Examination Board Achievement Test in Spanish.*
288. ★*College Entrance Examination Board Advanced Placement Examination: Spanish.*
289. *The Graduate Record Examinations Advanced Tests: Spanish.*
290. ★*Kansas Second Year Spanish Test.*
291. ★*Spanish and Latin American Life and Culture.* Review by Kathleen N. Perret.
292. *Spanish I and II: Achievement Examinations for Secondary Schools.*
293. ★*Spanish I and II: Midwest High School Achievement Examinations.*
294. ★*Spanish: Teacher Education Examination Program.*

INTELLIGENCE

GROUP

295. ★*A.C.E.R. Advanced Tests AL and AQ.* Review by Duncan Howie.
296. *A.C.E.R. Advanced Test B40.* Review by C. Sanders.
297. *A.C.E.R. Higher Test M.* Review by C. Sanders.
298. ★*A.C.E.R. Intermediate Tests C and D.* Review by James Lumsden.
299. *A.C.E.R. Junior A Test.* Review by R. Winterbourn.
300. ★*A.C.E.R. Junior B Test.* Review by R. Winterbourn.
301. ★*A.C.E.R. Junior Non-Verbal Test.* Review by D. A. Pidgeon.

302. ★*APT Performance Test.*
303. *Academic Aptitude Test: Non-Verbal Intelligence: Acorn National Aptitude Tests.*
304. *Academic Aptitude Test: Verbal Intelligence: Acorn National Aptitude Tests.*
305. *Adaptability Test.* Review by John M. Willits.
306. ★*Advanced Personnel Test.*
307. ★*Advanced Test N.* Reviews by A. E. G. Pilliner and C. Sanders.
308. *American Council on Education Psychological Examination for College Freshmen.* Reviews by Hanford M. Fowler and William B. Michael.
309. *American Council on Education Psychological Examination for High School Students.* Review by William B. Michael.
310. *Army General Classification Test, First Civilian Edition.*
311. ★*The Business Test.* Reviews by Louis C. Nanassy and James H. Ricks, Jr.
312. ★*California Analogies and Reasoning Test.*
313. *California Short-Form Test of Mental Maturity.* Review by Cyril Burt.
314. *California Test of Mental Maturity, 1957 Edition.* Reviews by Frank S. Freeman and John E. Milholland.
315. *Cattell Intelligence Tests.* Review by I. Macfarlane Smith.
316. *Chicago Non-Verbal Examination.* Review by Raleigh M. Drake.
317. ★*Classification Test 40-A.*
318. *College Entrance Examination Board Scholastic Aptitude Test.* Review by John T. Dailey.
319. ★*College Placement Test.* Reviews by Gustav J. Froehlich and David V. Tiedeman.
320. ★*College Qualification Tests.* Reviews by Gustav J. Froehlich, A. E. G. Pilliner, and David V. Tiedeman.
321. ★*Concept Mastery Test.* Reviews by J. A. Keats and Calvin W. Taylor.
322. ★*Cooperative School and College Ability Tests.* Reviews by Frederick B. Davis, Hanford M. Fowler, and Julian C. Stanley.
323. ★*Cotswold Junior Ability Tests.*
324. *Cotswold Measurement of Mental Ability.* Review by A. W. Heim.
325. ★*Daneshill Intelligence Test.* Reviews by A. W. Heim and F. W. Warburton.
326. ★*Davis-Eells Test of General Intelligence or Problem-Solving Ability.* Reviews by Cyril Burt, Raleigh M. Drake, and J. P. Guilford.
327. ★*Deeside Picture Puzzles.* Reviews by Charlotte E. K. Banks and M. L. Kellmer Pringle.
328. ★*Detroit General Intelligence Examination.*
329. *[Detroit Intelligence Tests.]*
330. ★*The Dominion Group Test of Intelligence.*
331. ★*Doppelt Mathematical Reasoning Test.*
332. ★*Easel Age Scale.* Reviews by Naomi Stewart and Florence M. Teagarden.
333. *The Essential Intelligence Test.* Review by R. Winterbourn.
334. ★*General Verbal Practice Test G1.*
335. *Goodenough Intelligence Test.*
336. *The Graduate Record Examinations Aptitude Test.* Review by John T. Dailey.
337. ★*Group Selective Test No. 1.* Review by T. R. Miles.
338. ★*Group Test 75.*
339. *Group Tests 33 and 33B.*
340. *Group Test 90A.* Review by John Liggett.
341. *Group Test of Learning Capacity: Dominion Tests.*
342. *The Henmon-Nelson Tests of Mental Ability, Revised Edition.* Reviews by D. Welty Lefever and Leona E. Tyler; and an excerpt from a review.

343. *IPAT Culture Free Intelligence Test.* Review by I. Macfarlane Smith.
344. *Jenkins Non-Verbal Test.*
345. *Junior Scholastic Aptitude Test, Revised Edition.*
346. ★*Kelvin Measurement of Ability in Infant Classes.*
347. ★*The Kingston Test of Intelligence.* Review by A. W. Heim.
348. *Kuhlmann-Anderson Intelligence Tests, Sixth Edition.*
349. ★*Kuhlmann-Finch Tests.* Reviews by Walter N. Durost, Henry E. Garrett, and Charles O. Neidt.
350. ★*The Lorge-Thorndike Intelligence Tests.* Reviews by Frank S. Freeman, John E. Milholland, and D. A. Pidgeon.
351. ★*Manchester General Ability Test (Senior) 1.* Review by A. E. G. Pilliner.
352. *Miller Analogies Test.* Review by John T. Dailey.
353. *Moray House Intelligence Tests.*
354. *New Rhode Island Intelligence Test.* Review by Raymond C. Norris.
355. ★*New South African Group Test.*
356. *Non-Verbal Tests.* Review by Cyril A. Rogers.
357. ★*Nufferno Tests of Speed and Level.* Reviews by John Liggett and E. A. Peel.
358. ★*The Ohio Penal Classification Test.* Review by Norman Eagle.
359. *Ohio State University Psychological Test.* Review by Cyril J. Hoyt (with W. Wesley Tennyson).
360. ★*An Orally Presented Group Test of Intelligence for Juniors.* Review by Elizabeth D. Fraser.
361. *Otis Quick-Scoring Mental Ability Tests.*
362. *Otis Quick-Scoring Mental Ability Tests, New Edition.* Reviews by D. Welty Lefever and Alfred Yates.
363. *Otis Self-Administering Tests of Mental Ability.*
364. *Personnel Research Institute Classification Test.*
365. ★*Personnel Research Institute Factory Series Test.*
366. ★*Personnel Tests for Industry.* Review by Erwin K. Taylor.
367. ★*Picture Intelligence Test 1.* Reviews by Charlotte E. K. Banks and M. L. Kellmer Pringle.
368. *Pintner General Ability Tests: Verbal Series.*
369. ★*Primary School Verbal Intelligence Test 1.* Reviews by John Nisbet and F. W. Warburton.
370. *Progressive Matrices.*
371. ★*Proverbs Test.* Reviews by Eugene L. Gaier and Alfred B. Heilbrun, Jr.
372. ★*Purdue Non-Language Test.*
373. *Quick-Scoring Test of Learning Capacity: Dominion Tests.*
374. ★*Reasoning Tests for Higher Levels of Intelligence.* Review by Reginald R. Dale.
375. *Revised Beta Examination.*
376. ★*SRA College Classification Tests.*
377. ★*SRA Tests of Educational Ability.* Reviews by Joshua A. Fishman, William B. Michael, and E. A. Peel.
378. *SRA Verbal Form.*
379. ★*The Scholarship Qualifying Test.* Reviews by Lee J. Cronbach and Roger T. Lennon.
380. ★*Scholastic Mental Ability Tests.* Reviews by Walter N. Durost and Alexander G. Wesman.
381. ★*Schrammel General Ability Test.* Review by Henry E. Garrett.
382. ★*Schubert General Ability Battery.* Review by William B. Schrader.
383. ★*Ship Destination Test.* Review by C. J. Adcock.

Arithmetic. Reviews by Joseph Justman and J. Fred Weaver.

457. ★*Analytical Survey Test in Computational Arithmetic.* Review by Emma Spaney.

458. **Arithmetic Essentials Test.* Review by J. Wayne Wrightstone.

459. **Arithmetic: Every Pupil Scholarship Test.*

460. **Arithmetic: Every Pupil Test.*

461. ★*Arithmetic Progress Test.* Reviews by William Curr and John Sutherland.

462. **Arithmetic Test: Fundamental Operations: Dominion Tests.* Review by Harry L. Stein.

463. **Arithmetic Test (Fundamentals and Reasoning): Municipal Tests: National Achievement Tests.*

464. **Arithmetic Test: National Achievement Tests.*

465. ★*Arithmetic Tests 1–2, 4–7, 7E.*

466. ★*Basic Number Skills Test for Employee Selection.* Reviews by Dorothy C. Adkins and Marion F. Shaycoft.

467. **A Brief Survey of Arithmetic Skills, Revised Edition.* Review by H. Vernon Price.

468. **California Arithmetic Test, 1957 Edition.* Review by Robert D. North.

469. **Coordinated Scales of Attainment: Arithmetic.*

470. ★*Cotswold Junior Arithmetic Ability Test.* Reviews by William Curr and George W. Sturrock.

471. **Cotswold Measurement of Ability: Arithmetic.*

472. ★*Diagnostic Tests and Self-Helps in Arithmetic.* Review by Harold E. Moser.

473. **Diagnostic Tests in Arithmetic Fundamentals: The Dominion Tests, Revised Edition.* Review by John Sutherland.

474–5. ★*Diagnostic Tests in Vulgar Fractions, Decimal Fractions and Percentages.* Review by Reginald Edwards.

476. *Graded Arithmetic-Mathematics Test.* Review by Stanley Nisbet.

477. ★*Group Test of Speed and Accuracy in Arithmetic Computation: Dominion Tests.* Reviews by Frances E. Crook and William Harrison Lucow.

478. ★*Madden-Peak Arithmetic Computation Test: Evaluation and Adjustment Series.* Reviews by Theodore E. Kellogg and Albert E. Meder, Jr.

479. ★*Milne Arithmetic Test.*

480. ★*New York Test of Arithmetical Meanings.* Review by Charles S. Ross.

481. **Primary Arithmetic: Every Pupil Scholarship Test.*

482. **Revised Southend Attainment Test in Mechanical Arithmetic.*

483. ★*SRA Achievement Series: Arithmetic.* Reviews by Robert D. North and J. Fred Weaver.

484. ★*Scholastic Achievement Series: Arithmetic.* Reviews by Joseph Justman and Charles S. Ross.

485. **Schonell Diagnostic Arithmetic Tests.* Review by John Sutherland.

486. **The Staffordshire Arithmetic Test.*

487. **Stanford Achievement Test: Arithmetic.*

488. ★*Survey Test of Arithmetic Fundamentals: Dominion Tests.* Review by Frances E. Crook.

489. **Tests of Mechanical Arithmetic.* Reviews by George W. Sturrock and Jack Wrigley.

490. ★*The Tiedeman Arithmetical Knowledge and Information Test.* Review by James H. Ricks, Jr.

GEOMETRY

491. ★*Chicago Plane Geometry Test.* Review by Lynnette B. Plumlee.

492. **Geometry: Every Pupil Test.*

493. **Plane Geometry: Achievement Examinations for Secondary Schools.*

494. **Plane Geometry: Every Pupil Scholarship Test.*

495. ★*Plane Geometry: Midwest High School Achievement Examinations.* Review by Harold P. Fawcett.

496. *Schrammel-Reed Solid Geometry Test.* Review by H. Vernon Price.

497. **Seattle Plane Geometry Test: Evaluation and Adjustment Series.* Review by Harold P. Fawcett.

498. **Shaycoft Plane Geometry Test: Evaluation and Adjustment Series.*

499. **Solid Geometry: Achievement Examinations for Secondary Schools.*

500. ★*Solid Geometry: Midwest High School Achievement Examinations.*

TRIGONOMETRY

501. *Rasmussen Trigonometry Test.* Review by Lynnette B. Plumlee.

MISCELLANEOUS

BUSINESS EDUCATION

502. **Bookkeeping: Achievement Examinations for Secondary Schools.*

503. **Bookkeeping: Every Pupil Scholarship Test.*

504. ★*Bookkeeping: Midwest High School Achievement Examinations.* Review by I. David Satlow.

505. **Bookkeeping 1: Every Pupil Test.*

506. **Bookkeeping Test: National Business Entrance Tests.*

507. ★*Business Education: National Teacher Examinations.*

508. **Business Fundamentals and General Information Test: National Business Entrance Tests.*

509. **Business Relations and Occupations: Achievement Examinations for Secondary Schools.*

510. ★*Business Relations and Occupations: Midwest High School Achievement Examinations.*

511. **General Office Clerical Test (Including Filing): National Business Entrance Tests.*

512. *Hiett Simplified Shorthand Test (Gregg).* Review by Gale W. Clark.

513. *Kimberly-Clark Typing Ability Analysis.*

514. **Machine Calculation Test: National Business Entrance Tests.* Review by Dorothy C. Adkins.

515. **National Business Entrance Tests.* Reviews by Edward N. Hay, Jacob S. Orleans, and Wimburn L. Wallace.

516. ★*Office Worker Test 30-A.*

517. ★*Personnel Research Institute Test of Shorthand Skills.*

518. ★*SRA Typing Adaptability Test.* Reviews by Gale W. Clark and Edward B. Greene.

519. **The Seashore-Bennett Stenographic Proficiency Tests: A Standard Recorded Stenographic Worksample.*

520. ★*Shorthand Aptitude Test.* Review by James Lumsden.

521. **Shorthand 1: Every Pupil Test.*

522. **Stenographic Test: National Business Entrance Tests.* Review by Edward B. Greene.

523. ★*Test for Typing Skill.* Review by Bernadine Meyer.

524. ★*Typewriting 1 and 11: Every Pupil Scholarship Test.*

525. **Typewriting 1: Every Pupil Test.*

526. **Typewriting Test: National Business Entrance Tests.* Review by Clifford E. Jurgensen.

527. ★*United Students Typewriting Tests, Volume 14.*

COMPUTATIONAL AND SCORING DEVICES

528. ★*The Bowman I.Q. Kalculator.*
529. *Hankes' Answer Sheets.*
530. *IBM Test Scoring Machine.*

EDUCATION

531. ★*Academic Freedom Survey.*
532. ★*Attitude Toward Student Ratings of Instruction.*
533. *The Case of Mickey Murphy: A Case-Study Instrument in Evaluation, [Third Edition].* Review by Dwight L. Arnold.
534. *Diagnostic Teacher-Rating Scale.* Review by Dorothy M. Clendenen.
535. ★*Educational Interest Inventory.*
536. ★*Faculty Morale Scale for Institutional Improvement.*
537. *The Graduate Record Examinations Advanced Tests: Education.* Review by Harry N. Rivlin.
538. *National Teacher Examinations.* Reviews by William A. Brownell, Walter W. Cook, and Lawrence G. Derthick.
539. ★*A Pupil's Rating Scale of an Instructor.*
540. ★*SRA Educators Opinion Inventory.*
541. ★*A Self Appraisal Scale for Teachers.*
542. ★*The Teaching Evaluation Record.*
543. ★*Teacher Education Examination Program.* Review by Walter W. Cook.
544. ★*A Test on Adult Attitudes Toward Children.*
545. ★*What Would You Do? Perplexing Incidents in Human Relations.*
546. *The Wilson Teacher-Appraisal Scale.*

ETIQUETTE

547. ★*The New Century Social Conduct Test.*
548. ★*Parsons Social Comprehension Test.*
549. *Test on Social Usage.*

HANDWRITING

550. *Ayres Measuring Scale for Handwriting.*
551. ★*Evaluation Scales for Guiding Growth in Handwriting.*

HEALTH

552. *Cornell Medical Index—Health Questionnaire.*
553. ★*Elementary Health: Every Pupil Scholarship Test.*
554. *Gill-Schrammel Physiology Test.* Review by Clarence H. Nelson.
555. *Health and Safety Education Test: National Achievement Tests.* Review by Clarence H. Nelson.
556. *Health Education and Hygiene: Every Pupil Test.*
557. *Health Education Test: Knowledge and Application: Acorn National Achievement Tests, Revised Edition.*
558. ★*Health Knowledge Test for College Freshmen: National Achievement Tests.* Review by James E. Bryan.
559. *Health Practice Inventory.* Review by James E. Bryan.
560. *Health Test: National Achievement Tests.* Review by Benno G. Fricke.
561. ★*High School Health: Every Pupil Scholarship Test.*

562. *Kilander Health Knowledge Test: Evaluation and Adjustment Series.*
563. ★*Physical Education: National Teacher Examinations.*
564. ★*Physical Education: Teacher Education Examination Program.*
565. ★*Physical Education Tests.*
566. *Sex Knowledge Inventory, Experimental Edition.*
567. ★[*Winsberg Tests: Examinations for Physical Education Major Students.*]

HOME ECONOMICS

568. *Clothing: Every Pupil Scholarship Test.*
569. *Foods: Every Pupil Scholarship Test.*
570. ★*Johnson Home Economics Interest Inventory.* Reviews by John D. Black and Leona E. Tyler.
571. *Minnesota Check List for Food Preparation and Serving, Third Edition.*
572. ★*Scales for Appraising High School Homemaking Programs.*

INDUSTRIAL ARTS

573. ★*Garage Mechanic Test.*
574. ★*Industrial Arts Education: National Teacher Examinations.*
575. *Industrial Arts: Every Pupil Scholarship Test.*
576. ★*Industrial Arts: Teacher Education Examination Program.*

LISTENING COMPREHENSION

577. ★*Brown-Carlsen Listening Comprehension Test: Evaluation and Adjustment Series.* Review by E. F. Lindquist and Irving Lorge.
578. ★*Sequential Tests of Educational Progress: Listening.* Review by E. F. Lindquist and Irving Lorge.

MISCELLANEOUS

579. ★*How Well Can You Read Lips?*
580. ★*What Do You Know About Photography?*

PHILOSOPHY

581. *The Graduate Record Examinations Advanced Tests: Philosophy.*

PSYCHOLOGY

582. ★*Engle Psychology Test: Evaluation and Adjustment Series.* Review by Harold Seashore.
583. *The Graduate Record Examinations Advanced Tests: Psychology.* Review by Harold Seashore.
584. *Hogan Psychology Test.* Review by Harold Seashore.

RECORD AND REPORT FORMS

585. ★*Blum-Fieldsteel Development Charts.*
586. ★[*The Cassel Developmental Record.* Review by William E. Henry.
587. ★*A Pre-School Record Form.*

RELIGIOUS EDUCATION

588. ★*Attitude Inventory.*
589. ★*Bible History Tests.*
590. *Peters Biblical Knowledge Test.* Review by Janet G. Afflerbach.
591. ★*Religion Test for Grades Two and Three.*
592. ★*Religion Test for High Schools.*

SAFETY EDUCATION

593. ★*Lauer Driver Reaction Inventory.*
594. ★*Road Test Check List for Passenger Car Drivers.*
595. ★*Rogers-Lauer Driver Rating Inventory.*

SOCIOECONOMIC STATUS

596. *The American Home Scale.*
597. ★*Sims SCI Occupational Rating Scale.* Review by Henry Weitz.
598. *The Social Status Scale, 1952 Revision.*

TESTING PROGRAMS

599. *College Entrance Examination Board Admissions Testing Program.*
600. ★*College Entrance Examination Board Advanced Placement Examinations.*
601. *The Graduate Record Examinations.* Review by Harold Seashore.

MULTI-APTITUDE BATTERIES

602. *[Aptitude-Intelligence Tests.]* Review by Harold P. Bechtoldt.
603. *Detroit General Aptitudes Examination.*
604. ★*Differential Ability Tests.*
605. *Differential Aptitude Tests.* Reviews by John B. Carroll and Norman Frederiksen.
606. ★*Differential Test Battery.* Reviews by E. A. Peel, Donald E. Super, and Philip E. Vernon.
607. ★*Employee Aptitude Survey.* Reviews by Dorothy C. Adkins and S. Rains Wallace.
608. *Flanagan Aptitude Classification Tests.* Reviews by Harold P. Bechtoldt, Ralph F. Berdie, and John B. Carroll.
609. *General Aptitude Test Battery.* Reviews by Andrew L. Comrey, Clifford P. Froehlich, and Lloyd G. Humphreys.
610. ★*Holzinger-Crowder Uni-Factor Tests.* Reviews by Anne Anastasi, Benjamin Fruchter, and Philip E. Vernon.
611. ★*The Jastak Test of Potential Ability and Behavior Stability.*
612. ★*The Multi-Aptitude Test.* Review by H. H. Remmers.
613. ★*Multiple Aptitude Tests.* Review by Ralph F. Berdie.
614. *SRA Primary Mental Abilities.* Reviews by Norman Frederiksen and Albert K. Kurtz.
615. *Yale Educational Aptitude Test Battery.* Reviews by Anne Anastasi and Ruth Churchill.

READING

616. *A.C.E.R. Silent Reading Tests.* Review by Fred J. Schonell.
617. *A.C.E.R. Silent Reading Test, Form C.* Reviews by Fred J. Schonell and D. K. Wheeler.
618. *A.C.E.R. Silent Reading Tests: Standardized for Use in New Zealand.*
619. *Achievement Test in Silent Reading: Dominion Tests.* Reviews by Harry L. Stein and Magdalen D. Vernon.
620. *American School Achievement Tests, Part 1, Reading.* Reviews by Russell G. Stauffer and Agatha Townsend.
621. ★*American School Reading Tests.* Reviews by Henry S. Dyer and Donald E. P. Smith.
622. *California Reading Test, 1957 Edition.*
623. ★*Chapman Reading Comprehension Test.* Review by Russell P. Kropp.

624. ★*Commerce Reading Comprehension Test.*
625. ★*Davis Reading Test.* Review by Benjamin Rosner.
626. ★*Developmental Reading Tests.*
627. ★*Diagnostic Reading Test: Pupil Progress Series.*
628. ★*Elementary Reading: Every Pupil Scholarship Test.*
629. *Elementary Reading: Every Pupil Test.*
630. *Gates Advanced Primary Reading Tests.*
631. *Gates Basic Reading Tests.* Review by S. S. Dunn.
632. *Gates Primary Reading Tests.*
633. *Gates Reading Survey.*
634. *High School Reading Test: National Achievement Tests.* Review by Victor H. Noll.
635. *Holborn Reading Scale.* Review by Stanley Nisbet.
636. ★*Kelley-Greene Reading Comprehension Test: Evaluation and Adjustment Series.* Reviews by Russell P. Kropp and Magdalen D. Vernon.
637. *The Kingston Test of Silent Reading.* Reviews by Neil Gourlay and Magdalen D. Vernon.
638. *Lee-Clark Reading Test, 1958 Revision.*
639. ★*Nelson-Lohmann Reading Test: Coordinated Scales of Attainment.*
640. *Primary Reading: Every Pupil Scholarship Test.*
641. *Primary Reading: Every Pupil Test.*
642. *Primary Reading Test: Acorn Achievement Tests.*
643. *The Purdue Reading Test.*
644. ★*Purdue Reading Test for Industrial Supervisors: Purdue Personnel Tests.* Reviews by Jerome E. Doppelt and Louis C. Nanassy.
645. *Reading Comprehension: Cooperative English Test: Lower and Higher Levels, C1 and C2.*
646. *Reading Comprehension Test: National Achievement Tests [Speer and Smith].*
647. *Reading Comprehension Test: National Achievement Tests [Crow, Kuhlmann, and Crow].*
648. *Reading Test (Comprehension and Speed): Municipal Tests: National Achievement Tests.*
649. ★*SRA Achievement Series: Reading.* Reviews by N. Dale Bryant and Clarence Derrick.
650. ★*Scholastic Diagnostic Reading Test.* Reviews by Russell G. Stauffer and Arthur E. Traxler.
651. *The Schonell Reading Tests.* Review by R. W. McCulloch.
652. ★*Sentence Reading Test 1.* Reviews by Reginald R. Dale and Stephen Wiseman.
653. ★*Sequential Tests of Educational Progress: Reading.* Reviews by Eric F. Gardner, James R. Hobson, and Stephen Wiseman.
654. ★*Silent Reading Test.*
655. *The Standard Reading Tests.*
656. *Stanford Achievement Test: Reading.* Reviews by Helen M. Robinson and Agatha Townsend.
657. *Techniques in Reading Comprehension for Junior-Senior High School: Every Pupil Test.*
658. *Williams Primary Reading Test.*

MISCELLANEOUS

659. ★*Doren Diagnostic Reading Test of Word Recognition Skills.* Reviews by B. H. Van Roekel and Verna L. Vickery.
660. *Durrell Analysis of Reading Difficulty, New Edition.* Reviews by James Maxwell and George D. Spache.
661. *Durrell-Sullivan Reading Capacity and Achievement Tests.* Review by James Maxwell.
662. *Gates Reading Diagnostic Tests.* Review by George D. Spache.

663. *Individual Reading Test.* Review by R. W. McCulloch.

664. ★*McGuffey Diagnostic Reading Test.*

665. ★*Primary Reading Profiles, [Revised Edition].* Reviews by James R. Hobson and Verna L. Vickery.

666. *Reading Diagnostic Record for High School and College Students.* Reviews by Marvin D. Glock and Donald E. P. Smith.

667. ★*Roswell-Chall Diagnostic Reading Test of Word Analysis Skills.* Review by B. H. Van Roekel.

668. ★*SRA Achievement Series: Language Perception.*

669. ★*Silent Reading Diagnostic Tests: The Developmental Reading Tests, Experimental Form.*

670. ★*Stanford Diagnostic Phonics Survey, Research Edition.*

ORAL

671. ★*Gilmore Oral Reading Test.* Reviews by Lydia A. Duggins and Maynard C. Reynolds.

672. ★*Leavell Analytical Oral Reading Test.* Reviews by Lydia A. Duggins and Maynard C. Reynolds.

673. *Oral Diagnostic Test of Word-Analysis Skills, Primary: Dominion Tests.* Review by S. A. Rayner.

674. ★*Oral Word Reading Test.* Reviews by S. A. Rayner and D. K. Wheeler.

READINESS

675. *American School Reading Readiness Test.* Reviews by Joan Bollenbacher and Helen M. Robinson.

676. *Group Test of Reading Readiness: The Dominion Tests.* Review by N. Dale Bryant.

677. *The Harrison-Stroud Reading Readiness Profiles.* Review by S. S. Dunn.

678. *Lee-Clark Reading Readiness Test, 1951 Revision.* Review by James R. Hobson.

679. *Murphy-Durrell Diagnostic Reading Readiness Test.* Reviews by Joan Bollenbacher and S. S. Dunn.

680. ★*Reading Readiness Test.*

681. ★*Scholastic Reading Readiness Test.*

682. ★*Webster Reading-Readiness Test.*

SPECIAL FIELDS

683. *Interpretation of Reading Materials in the Natural Sciences.*

684. *Interpretation of Reading Materials in the Social Studies.*

685. *The Iowa Tests of Educational Development: Test 5, Ability to Interpret Reading Materials in the Social Studies.*

686. *The Iowa Tests of Educational Development: Test 6, Ability to Interpret Reading Materials in the Natural Sciences.*

SPEED

687. ★*Tinker Speed of Reading Test.* Review by Leonard S. Feldt.

STUDY SKILLS

688. ★*Brown-Holtzman Survey of Study Habits and Attitudes.* Reviews by James Deese and C. Gilbert Wrenn (with Roy D. Lewis).

689. ★*California Study Methods Survey.*

690. *Cooperative Dictionary Test.* Review by A. N. Hieronymus.

691. ★*Evaluation Aptitude Test.* Reviews by J. Thomas Hastings and Walker H. Hill.

692. *The Iowa Tests of Educational Development: Test 9, Use of Sources of Information.*

693. ★*A Library Orientation Test for College Fresh-*

men, *1955 Edition.* Reviews by Janet G. Afflerbach (with Lois Grimes Afflerbach) and J. Wayne Wrightstone.

694. ★*Logical Reasoning.* Reviews by Duncan Howie and Charles R. Langmuir.

695. ★*Pictographic Self Rating Scale.*

696. *SRA Achievement Series: Work-Study Skills.* Reviews by Robert L. Ebel and Ruth M. Strang.

697. ★*Spitzer Study Skills Test: Evaluation and Adjustment Series.* Review by James Deese.

698. ★*Stanford Achievement Test: Study Skills.* Reviews by Robert L. Ebel and Ruth M. Strang.

699. *A Test of Study Skills.* Review by Marvin D. Glock.

700. *Watson-Glaser Critical Thinking Appraisal.* Reviews by Walker H. Hill and Carl I. Hovland.

SCIENCE

701. ★*Biology and General Science: National Teacher Examinations.*

702. ★*Chemistry, Physics, and General Science: National Teacher Examinations.*

703. *Cooperative General Achievement Tests: Test II, Natural Science.*

704. *Coordinated Scales of Attainment: Science.*

705. *Elementary Science and Health: Every Pupil Test.*

706. ★*Elementary Science: Every Pupil Scholarship Test.*

707. *Elementary Science Test: National Achievement Tests.* Review by William Harrison Lucow.

708. *General Science: Every Pupil Scholarship Test.*

709. *General Science: Every Pupil Test.*

710. ★*General Science: Midwest High School Achievement Examinations.*

711. *General Science III: Achievement Examinations for Secondary Schools.*

712. *General Science Test: National Achievement Tests.* Review by Robert M. W. Travers.

713. *The Iowa Tests of Educational Development: Test 2, General Background in the Natural Sciences.*

714. ★*Physical Science: Teacher Education Examination Program.*

715. *Read General Science Test: Evaluation and Adjustment Series.*

716. ★*Sequential Tests of Educational Progress: Science.* Reviews by Palmer O. Johnson, Julian C. Stanley (with M. Jacinta Mann), and Robert M. W. Travers.

717. *Stanford Achievement Test: Intermediate and Advanced Science Test.*

BIOLOGY

718. ★*Biological Science: Teacher Education Examination Program.*

719. *Biology: Achievement Examinations for Secondary Schools.*

720. *Biology: Every Pupil Scholarship Test.*

721. *Biology: Every Pupil Test.*

722. ★*Biology: Midwest High School Achievement Examinations.*

723. *College Entrance Examination Board Achievement Test in Biology.* Review by Elizabeth Hagen.

724. ★*College Entrance Examination Board Advanced Placement Examination: Biology.* Review by Clark W. Horton.

725. *Cooperative Biology Test: Educational Records Bureau Edition.*

726. *General Biology Test: National Achievement*

Tests. Reviews by Elizabeth Hagen and Clark W. Horton.

727. *The Graduate Record Examinations Advanced Tests: Biology.* Review by Clark W. Horton.

728. *Nelson Biology Test: Evaluation and Adjustment Series.*

CHEMISTRY

729. ★*A.C.S.-N.S.T.A. Cooperative Examination in High School Chemistry.* Reviews by Edward G. Rietz and Willard G. Warrington.

730. *A.C.S. Cooperative Chemistry Test in Qualitative Analysis.*

731. *A.C.S. Cooperative Examination in Biochemistry.*

732. *A.C.S. Cooperative Examination in General Chemistry.* Reviews by Frank P. Cassaretto and Palmer O. Johnson.

733. *[A.C.S. Cooperative Examinations in Organic Chemistry.]*

734. *A.C.S. Cooperative Examination in Physical Chemistry.*

735. *A.C.S. Cooperative Examination in Quantitative Analysis.* Excerpt from a review.

736. *A.C.S. Cooperative Organic Chemistry Test.*

737. *Anderson Chemistry Test: Evaluation and Adjustment Series.* Review by Theo. A. Ashford.

738. *Chemistry: Achievement Examinations for Secondary Schools.*

739. *Chemistry: Every Pupil Scholarship Test.*

740. *Chemistry: Every Pupil Test.*

741. ★*Chemistry: Midwest High School Achievement Examination.* Review by Edward G. Rietz.

742. *College Entrance Examination Board Achievement Test in Chemistry.* Review by Max D. Engelhart.

743. ★*College Entrance Examination Board Advanced Placement Examination: Chemistry.* Review by Theo. A. Ashford.

744. *Cooperative Chemistry Test.* Reviews by Frank P. Cassaretto and Willard G. Warrington.

745. *Cooperative Chemistry Test: Educational Records Bureau Edition.*

746. *The Graduate Record Examinations Advanced Tests: Chemistry.*

747. ★*A Junior Chemistry Test.* Reviews by Roy W. Stanhope and Mervyn L. Turner.

GEOLOGY

748. *The Graduate Record Examinations Advanced Tests: Geology.*

PHYSICS

749. *College Entrance Examination Board Achievement Test in Physics.* Review by Theodore G. Phillips.

750. ★*College Entrance Examination Board Advanced Placement Examination: Physics.* Review by Leo Nedelsky.

751. *Cooperative Physics Test.* Review by Theodore G. Phillips.

752. *Cooperative Physics Test: Educational Records Bureau Edition.*

753. *Dunning Physics Test: Evaluation and Adjustment Series.* Review by Robert M. W. Travers.

754. *The Graduate Record Examinations Advanced Tests: Physics.* Review by Leo Nedelsky.

755. ★*A Junior Physics Test.* Reviews by Roy W. Stanhope and Mervyn L. Turner.

756. *Physics: Achievement Examinations for Secondary Schools.*

757. *Physics: Every Pupil Scholarship Test.*

758. *Physics: Every Pupil Test.*

759. ★*Physics: Midwest High School Achievement Examinations.*

SENSORY-MOTOR

760. ★*Children's Perceptual Achievement Forms.*

761. *Harris Tests of Lateral Dominance.*

HEARING

762. ★*ADC Audiometers.*

763. ★*Maico Audiometers.*

764. ★*Robbins Speech Sound Discrimination and Verbal Imagery Type Tests.*

765. *Sonotone Pure-Tone Audiometers.*

MOTOR

766. *Brace Scale of Motor Ability.* Review by Anna S. Espenschade.

767. ★*The Lincoln-Oseretsky Motor Development Scale.* Review by Anna S. Espenschade.

VISION

768. *AO H-R-R Pseudoisochromatic Plates, Second Edition.*

769. ★*AO School Vision Screening Test.*

770. *AO Sight Screener.*

771. ★*Burnham-Clark-Munsell Color Memory Test.*

772. ★*The Color Aptitude Test.*

773. *Dvorine Pseudo-Isochromatic Plates, Second Edition.* Excerpts from three reviews.

774. *Eames Eye Test.* Review by Magdalen D. Vernon.

775. *The Farnsworth-Munsell 100-Hue Test for the Examination of Color Discrimination.*

776. ★*Freeman Acuity-Tester.*

777. ★*Freeman Protometer.*

778. *The Illuminant-Stable Color Vision Test, Second Edition.*

779. ★*Inter-Society Color Council Color Aptitude Test, 1953 Edition.*

780. *Keystone Visual Tests.*

781. *Massachusetts Vision Test.*

782. ★*New York School Vision Tester.*

783. *Ortho-Rater.*

784. *Spache Binocular Reading Test.*

SOCIAL STUDIES

785. *American History—Government—Problems of Democracy: Acorn Achievement Tests.* Review by Richard E. Gross.

786. *College Entrance Examination Board Achievement Test in Social Studies.* Review by Ralph W. Tyler.

787. *Cooperative General Achievement Tests: Test I, Social Studies.*

788. ★*The Greig Social Studies Test.* Review by David R. Krathwohl.

789. *Introduction to Social Studies: Achievement Examinations for Secondary Schools.*

790. *History and Civics Test: Municipal Tests: National Achievement Tests.* Review by Howard R. Anderson.

791. *The Iowa Tests of Educational Development: Test 1, Understanding of Basic Social Concepts.*

792. ★*Sequential Tests of Educational Progress: Social Studies.* Reviews by Richard E. Gross, S. A. Rayner, and Ralph W. Tyler.

793. ★*Shearer Social Studies Test.* Review by Raymond C. Norris.

794. ★*Social Studies: Every Pupil Scholarship Test.*
795. ★*Social Studies: Midwest High School Achievement Examinations.*
796. *Social Studies: National Teacher Examinations.*
797. ★*Social Studies: Teacher Education Examination Program.*
798. *Social Studies Test: National Achievement Tests.*
799. *Stanford Achievement Test: Intermediate and Advanced Social Studies Test.* Review by Harry D. Berg.

ECONOMICS

800. *The Graduate Record Examinations Advanced Tests: Economics.*

GEOGRAPHY

801. *Coordinated Scales of Attainment: Geography.*
802. *Economic Geography: Achievement Examinations for Secondary Schools.*
803. ★*Economic Geography: Midwest High School Achievement Examinations.*
804. *Geography: Every Pupil Scholarship Test.*
805. *Geography: Every Pupil Test.*
806. *Geography Test: Municipal Tests: National Achievement Tests.*

HISTORY

807. *American History: Achievement Examinations for Secondary Schools.*
808. *American History: Every Pupil Scholarship Test.*
809. *American History: Every Pupil Test.*
810. ★*American History: Midwest High School Achievement Examinations.* Review by Howard R. Anderson.
811. *American History Test: National Achievement Tests.*
812. ★*College Entrance Examination Board Advanced Placement Examination: American History.* Reviews by James A. Field, Jr. and Christine McGuire.
813. ★*College Entrance Examination Board Advanced Placement Examination: European History.*
814. *Cooperative World History Test.* Review by David K. Heenan.
815. *Coordinated Scales of Attainment: History.*
816. *Crary American History Test: Evaluation and Adjustment Series.* Review by Frederick H. Stutz.
817. *Cummings World History Test: Evaluation and Adjustment Series.*
818. *The Graduate Record Examinations Advanced Tests: History.* Review by Robert H. Ferrell.
819. *History: Every Pupil Scholarship Test.*
820. ★*Kansas United States History Test.* Reviews by Wayne A. Frederick and John Manning.
821. *Modern World History: Achievement Examinations for Secondary Schools.*
822. ★*Modern World History: Midwest High School Achievement Examinations.*
823. *World History: Every Pupil Scholarship Test.*
824. *World History: Every Pupil Test.*
825. *World History Test: Acorn National Achievement Tests.* Review by John Manning.
826. *American Civics and Government Tests for High Schools and Colleges, Revised Edition.*
827. *American Government and Citizenship: Every Pupil Test.*
828. *American Government: Every Pupil Scholarship Test.*

829. ★*Attitude Toward Politicians Scale.* Review by Donald T. Campbell.
830. *Civic Vocabulary Test.* Review by I. G. Meddleton.
831. *Constitution: Every Pupil Scholarship Test.*
832. *Contemporary Problems.* Review by Harry D. Berg.
833. ★*Dimond-Pflieger Problems of Democracy Test: Evaluation and Adjustment Series.* Reviews by John H. Haefner and Douglas E. Scates.
834. ★*General Knowledge Test of Local, State, and National Government.* Review by Wayne A. Frederick.
835. *The Graduate Record Examinations Advanced Tests: Government.* Review by Christine McGuire.
836. ★*The Kansas Constitution Test.* Review by David K. Heenan.
837. ★*Newspaper Reading Survey: What Do You Read?* Reviews by Frederick H. Stutz and M. J. Wantman.
838. ★*Patterson Test or Study Exercises on the Constitution of the United States.*
839. ★*Patterson Test or Study Exercises on the Declaration of Independence.*
840. ★*Peltier-Durost Civics and Citizenship Test: Evaluation and Adjustment Series.*
841. ★*Principles of American Citizenship Test.* Reviews by Howard R. Anderson and M. J. Wantman.

SOCIOLOGY

842. *The Graduate Record Examinations Advanced Tests: Sociology.*
843. ★*Sare-Sanders Sociology Test.*
844. ★*Sociology: Every Pupil Scholarship Test.*

VOCATIONS

CLERICAL

845. ★*A.C.E.R. Short Clerical Test.*
846. *A.C.E.R. Speed and Accuracy Tests.*
847. *Clerical Aptitude Test: Acorn National Aptitude Tests.*
848. ★*Clerical Tests 1 and 2.*
849. *[Hay Tests for Clerical Aptitude.]*
850. *Minnesota Clerical Test.* Review by Donald E. Super.
851. *O'Rourke Clerical Aptitude Test, Junior Grade.*
852. ★*Personnel Institute Clerical Tests.*
853. *Purdue Clerical Adaptability Test, Revised Edition: Purdue Personnel Tests.* Reviews by Mary Ellen Oliverio and Donald Spearritt.
854. *The Short Employment Tests.* Review by P. L. Mellenbruch.
855. ★*Turse Clerical Aptitudes Test.* Reviews by Robert A. Jones and Donald Spearritt.

INTERESTS

856. *Brainard Occupational Preference Inventory.* Review by William C. Cottle.
857. ★*Devon Interest Test.* Reviews by Arthur B. Royse and Alfred Yates.
858. ★*G. C. Self-Scoring Interest Record, Second Experimental Edition.*
859. ★*How Well Do You Know Your Interests.* Reviews by Jerome E. Doppelt and Henry S. Dyer.
860. *Interest Check List.*
861. *Inventory of Vocational Interests: Acorn National Aptitude Tests.*
862. ★*Kuder Preference Record—Occupational.* Reviews by Edward S. Bordin and John W. Gustad.

863. *Kuder Preference Record—Vocational.* Reviews by Clifford P. Froehlich and John Pierce-Jones.

864. *Occupational Interest Inventory, 1956 Revision.* Reviews by Martin Katz and Wilbur L. Layton.

865. ★*Picture Interest Inventory.*

866. ★*Qualifications Record.*

867. ★*Rothwell Interest Blank, Miller Revision.*

868. *Strong Vocational Interest Blank for Men, Revised.*

869. *Strong Vocational Interest Blank for Women, Revised.*

870. *Vocational Interest Analyses: A Six-Fold Analytical Extension of the Occupational Interest Inventory.* Review by Wilbur L. Layton.

MANUAL DEXTERITY

871. *Crawford Small Parts Dexterity Test.* Review by Neil D. Warren.

872. *Moore Eye-Hand Coordination and Color-Matching Test.*

873. *Purdue Pegboard.* Review by Neil D. Warren.

MECHANICAL ABILITY

874. *A.C.E.R. Mechanical Comprehension Test.* Reviews by John R. Jennings and Haydn S. Williams.

875. ★*A.C.E.R. Mechanical Reasoning Test.* Reviews by John R. Jennings and Haydn S. Williams.

876. ★*Chriswell Structural Dexterity Test.* Review by A. Pemberton Johnson.

877. ★*Group Test 80A.* Reviews by E. G. Chambers and John Liggett.

878. *Mechanical Aptitude Test: Acorn National Aptitude Tests.*

879. ★*Mellenbruch Mechanical Motivation Test.* Reviews by Arthur H. Brayfield and John B. Morris.

880. ★*N.I.I.P. Squares Test.* Review by J. F. Clark.

881. ★*Newcastle Spatial Test.*

882. ★*O'Rourke Mechanical Aptitude Test.*

883. ★*Purdue Mechanical Performance Test.*

884. *Revised Minnesota Paper Form Board Test.* Review by D. W. McElwain.

885. *Spatial Tests I and II.* Reviews by E. G. Chambers and Charles T. Myers.

886. *Survey of Mechanical Insight.* Review by Arthur H. Brayfield.

887. *Survey of Object Visualization.* Review by William J. Micheels.

888. *Survey of Space Relations Ability.* Review by D. W. McElwain.

889. *Test of Mechanical Comprehension.*

890. ★*Tool Knowledge Test.* Reviews by J. F. Clark and I. G. Meddleton.

MISCELLANEOUS

891. *Aptitude Tests for Occupations.* Review by Lloyd G. Humphreys.

892. ★*[Biography Forms]: Application-Interview Series.*

893. ★*Business Judgment Test.* Review by Edward B. Greene.

894. *Cancellation Test.* Review by Herbert A. Tonne.

895. *[Employee Rating and Development Forms.]*

896. *[Executive, Industrial, and Sales Personnel Forms.]*

897. ★*The Fiesenheiser Test of Ability to Read Drawings.*

898. ★*Hiring Summary Worksheet.*

899. *Identical Forms.*

900. *Merit Rating Series.*

901. *Per-Flu-Dex Tests.* Reviews by Andrew L. Comrey and John W. French.

902. ★*The Performance Record.* Reviews by Albert S. Thompson and Albert K. Kurtz.

903. *Personal Data Blank.* Review by Arthur E. Traxler.

904. ★*Personnel Institute Hiring Kit.*

905. ★*SRA Employee Inventory.* Reviews by Erwin K. Taylor and Albert S. Thompson.

906. ★*A Self-Rating Scale for Leadership Qualifications.*

SPECIFIC VOCATIONS

907. ★*Accounting Orientation Test: High School Level.*

908. ★*Achievement Tests in Nursing.*

909. ★*Achievement Tests in Practical Nursing.*

910. ★*Admission Test for Graduate Study in Business.*

911. *American Institute of Certified Public Accountants Testing Programs.*

912. *[American Transit Association Tests.]*

913. *Aptitude Index.*

914. *Aptitude Associates Test of Sales Aptitude: A Test for Measuring Knowledge of Basic Principles of Selling.*

915. ★*A Chart for the Rating of a Foreman.*

916. *Dental Aptitude Testing Program.*

917. ★*Dental Hygiene Aptitude Testing Program.*

918. *[Driver Selection Forms and Tests.]*

919. ★*Engineering Aide Test 50-A.*

920. ★*Entrance Examinations for Schools of Practical Nursing.*

921. ★*Firefighter Test.*

922. ★*General Test on Traffic and Driving Knowledge.*

923. *The Graduate Record Examinations Advanced Tests: Engineering.*

924. ★*Hall Salespower Inventory.*

925. ★*Hanes Sales Selection Inventory, Revised Edition.*

926. *How Supervise?*

927. ★*Information Index.*

928. *Law School Admission Test.*

929. ★*LIAMA Inventory of Job Attitudes.*

930. ★*Managerial Scale for Enterprise Improvement.* Reviews by Brent Baxter and Edward B. Greene.

931. ★*Measure of Consociative Tendency.*

932. *Medical College Admission Test.* Review by Alexander G. Wesman.

933. ★*Minnesota Engineering Analogies Test.* Reviews by A. Pemberton Johnson and William B. Schrader.

934. *NLN Achievement Tests for Basic Professional Nursing Program.*

935. *NLN Graduate Nurse Qualifying Examination.*

936. *NLN Practical Nurse Achievement Tests.*

937. *NLN Pre-Admission and Classification Examination.*

938. *NLN Pre-Nursing and Guidance Examination.*

939. ★*Personnel Service Rating Report.*

940. ★*Policeman Test.*

941. ★*Punched Card Machine Operator Aptitude Test.*

942. ★*Purdue Trade Information Test for Sheetmetal Workers: Purdue Personnel Tests.*

943. ★*Purdue Trade Information Test in Carpentry: Purdue Personnel Tests.* Review by P. L. Mellenbruch.

944. ★*Purdue Trade Information Test in Engine Lathe Operation: Purdue Personnel Tests.* Review by William J. Micheels.

945. ★*Purdue Trade Information Test in Welding, Revised Edition: Purdue Personnel Tests.*

946. ★*Road Test Check List for Testing, Selecting, Rating, and Training Coach Operators.*

947. **Sales Comprehension Test.* Review by Raymond A. Katzell.

948. ★*Sales Motivation Inventory.* Review by S. Rains Wallace.

949. ★*Sales Personnel Description Form.*

950. ★*Steward Life Insurance Knowledge Test.*

951. ★*Steward Occupational Objectives Inventory.*

952. ★*Steward Personal Background Inventory.*

953. ★*Steward Sales Aptitude Inventory.*

954. ★*The Store Personnel Test.* Reviews by Raymond A. Katzell and John B. Morris.

955. ★*Supervisory Practices Test.* Reviews by Clifford E. Jurgensen and Mary Ellen Oliverio.

956. ★*Truck Driver Test 60-A.*

957. ★*Veterinary Aptitude Testing Program.*